ISBN 978-0-260-21025-8
PIBN 11172107

INDEX TO VOLUME VII.

A

ABATTOıR question, 76, 550
Abbey: Fountains, 237; St. Albans, 582; West-
minster, 59, 189, 500
Air: engine, 418; syphon, 487, 499,—leader on,
577
Almshouses: Brick's (misnamed Still's), 510, 533;
Duppa's, 259; Pawnbrokers', 305; Printers',
271
Amphitheatre at Arles, 238
Ancient: remains at Fountains Abbey, 155; of
priory at Bury, 453; sculpture, 513
Ant-plague, 550, 580
Antiquarian: gleanings, 297, 561; Society, Here-
ford, 80,—Newcastle, 82
Antiquities: of Chester, 361; corporation, London,
241, 260, 271, 281; Indian, 490; of Jerusalem,
65, 86, 99, 116, 126
Aqueduct: Boston, 6; Croton, 621
Arch: ceiling, hollow brick, 183, 198; marble, 29,
135, 274, 322, 382, 583, 620; pointed, 290, 303
Archæological: Association, British, 237, 521, 545,
571, 607,—Cambrian, 394, 442; diggings at
Bury, 500,—Chester, 322, 334,—Chesterford,
81,—Cirencester, 442, 451, 466, 514, 525,—
Ickleton, 81,—Mountsorrel, 418,—Winchester,
238; Institute, 238,—at Salisbury, 355, 364; So-
ciety, Bedfordshire, 310, 237,—Liverpool, 6, 297,
—Norfolk, 35,—Northampton, 237,—Norwich
and West Suffolk, 478,—Somerset, 250, 453,
475,—Sussex, 394,—Warwickshire, 33
Arch-ery, Irish, 388
Arches: laminated timber, 371; see also under
"Railway"
Architect, value of in Hastings, 441
Architects: and architecture in Jamaica, 377, 548;
Benevolent Fund, 101; charges, 380; diplomas,
545, 559; employment of, 454
Architects, Institute of, 16, 65, 101, 130, 145;
at night at, 241; medals, 182; movement in,
218, 337; Earl De Grey at—words to council, 337; appeal from, 435; amendment of, 509;
opening—Lord de Grey's address—Dr. Whewell
on styles, 529; on Artesian wells at, 553; enlargement of—its scope, 580; 603.
Architects: one order of, 619; position of, 97;
Queen's College of, Birmingham, 129; raising
profession of, 559; remuneration, 457, 474, 524;
rights and responsibilities, 50, 111,—in France,
507, 518; standing, 616; stupid, 73; troubles,
596; works, interference with, 332.
Architectural: advantages and deficiencies of London, 220; and archæological meeting, 237,—
Society, Bedfordshire, 310, 569,—Liverpool 6,
297,—topography reviewed, 561
Architectural: Association, 109, 477, 485, 494, 562,
598; character of age, 526; competitions, 332,
341, 435,—See also under "Competition;" copyrights, 441; criticism and taste, 351, 368; effect,
291, 314; exhibition, 70, 109, 145, 457; knowledge, 331; lectures, 465; libraries, 17, 251,
409; 574; mathematicians, 320; propositions,
590; Publication Society, 133, 329; scrap book,
297; societies, union of, 592; society, Bedford,
173, 214,—Bristol and West, 550, 610,—Chester, 286,—East Anglian, 274,—Exeter, 454,—
Lincolnshire, 238,—Liverpool, 585, 610,—Oxford, 321, 533, 609, 622,—St.. Albans, 550,—
Yorkshire, 33, 190, 237, 347; Soirée at Liverpool, 163; teachers, ill taught, 49
Architecture: ancient of Scotland, 603; and Royal
Academy, 100,—see also under "Royal Academy;" and civil engineering, lecture on, 470,
482; bank, 608; church, 269; class prizes for,

334; definition of term, 382; ecclesiastical, history of, 110, 147, 405; Egyptian, 52; Gothic,
see "Gothic;" Grecian Doric, 86; in Oxford,
23; Italian, 63; lectures on, Professor Cockerell's, 16, 28, 52, 62, 86, 124; monumental, 4,
14; national, 356; on public, 349; position of,
337,—and prospects, 530, 578; Roman, 62, 253,
266; rudimentary, 409; school, 133; street,
115, 172; styles in, 148; "The Seven Lamps
of," 229, 246; value of, 247
Area, shape in respect to, 94, 130
Art: abroad, 181; Early Christian, 249; education, 459, 424; gossip in leader, 181; industrial,
525; make knowledge of general, 490; means of
progression in, 494; National Gallery, finish,
189; principles, 122, 133; progress of, 1; Society, Arundel, 69
Art-Union: London, and Board of Trade, 22,—
council report, with prizeholders, 193-5,—exhibition, 145, 394,—paintings bought, 260, 346;
"The Smile" and "The Frown," 437
Art-Unions in America, 593
Art-workmanship, mediæval and modern, 561
Art-works, sale of at Rome, 226
Artistical matters, leader on, 145
Artists: caution to, 238; conversazione, 58; General Benevolent Fund, 162; Society of British,
145
Artisans: "Home," Spicer-street, efforts to im-
prove condition of people, 589, 609; present
condition of—able men among them—endurance
—emigration, 37
Arts: Society of, 68, 116, 201, 236, 298, 550, 573,
621
Awards: arbiters', errors in, 346; see also under
"Buildings Act"

B

BANK: Architecture, 608,—at Liverpool, 43,—
Manchester, 18.
Basilicas of Christian Rome, 424
Baths and Washhouses: 298, 365, 454, 622; Bir-
mingham, 537; Manchester, 405; Marylebone,
597; Metropolitan, 88; Newcastle, 164; Ox-
ford, 502; St. Luke's, Old-street, 478; West-
minster, 106; Whitechapel, 106
Baths, public and private, 584
Beams: strength of, 355, 490
Beauty in Towns and Villages, 175
Bells: abroad, 166; rhymes of ringers of, 488
Bim, Bay of, 218
Birmingham, 445, 226, 596, 314, 554, 237; see
also under "Competition," "Exhibition," &c.
Blind: Builders, 17, 34, 67, 82, 94, 118, 130, 156,
166,, 214, 310, 352, 371,. 394, 405, 453, 453,
465, 562, 622; drain pipe-makers, 459; dredgers,
233; gas-fitters, 316; surveyors, 549
Books: 22, 25, 105, 129, 133, 142, 154, 169, 213,
225, 229, 260, (leaders on, 265,,277), 297 (349,
a budget of), 400, 405, (leader on; 409), 429;
439, 452, 465, 513, 523, 529, 561, (leader on,
565), 586: See more particularly under "Re-
view of Books," &c.
Books, preservation of,.58
Boston Athenæum, U.S., 404
Brass and other alloys of zinc, 55
Brasses of notaries, 496
Breakwaters, 81, 284, 342, 367
Brick: arches, ancient, 183; duties, 68, 161, 197,
226, 416, 449, 526
Bricklayers' taskwork, 519
Bricklaying legislator, 274
Brickmakers, caution to, 508

Bricks: colouring, 621; drain, 68; hollow, 183,
198, 199, 212; ventilating, 359
Bridge: girder, see " Girder;" high level, on
Tyne, 286; Pesth suspension, 58, 219, 419;
suspension, at Chester, 370,—over the Dneiper,
430; Westminster, 512, 532; whinstone, 34,
63, 101
Bridges: Chinese, 214; suspension, rolling bars
for, 273; tubular, 137, 310, 322, 381, 406, 416,
417, 441, 445, 502,—personal question as to,
362,—Switzerland, covered, and, 391
Bridgewater House, altered plan of, 484
Brighton, 497, 549
Bristol, 501, 281, 394, 596, 397, 489, 584, 466,
379, 178: see also "Church," "Competition,"
&c.
British: Association at Birmingham, 445; Museum, 94, 188, 198, 350, 418
Britton Testimonial and Club, 172, 594
Bronze in monuments, 488
Builders: architects v., 149; and building, 106;
Benevolent Institution, 10, 20, 148, 268, 339,
370, 586, 610; blind, see " Blind;" caution to
10 :" Counsel" to, 158; Foremen, Institution of,
35, 53, 70, 347, 597; rights and follies, 224;
rights and responsibilities of, in France, 507,
518; society, 80.
Building: Artificers' Provident Society (leader on,
433), 464, 509, 550, 554, 597; materials, 450,—
in Paris and Seine Valley, 177, 307,—novel,
466; perfection in, 206; societies, 388, 554,
571, 602
Buildings Act, Liverpool.—letter a. spirit 352
Buildings Act, metropolitan: amendment of, 268,
285, 370,—leader on—registrar v. referee, 385.
Buildings Act, metropolitan: Awards: cellars, 490;
cornices, 43; district surveyors' fees, 43,—duties,
436; eaves, 43; party-walls, 257, 259; shop
fronts, 153,—blinds, 172; stairs, 437; warehouses, 257
Buildings Act, metropolitan: district surveyors' fees,
262; greenhouses, 367; overseers' expenses, 188
Buildings: fireproof, 116; in Italy and Sicily,
chronology of, 243, 256, 318; national, meddling
with, 397; supervision of, in Vienna, 177
Burial: ground, parish, 460, 478, see also "Churchyard," "Cemetery," and "Graveyard;" in
towns, 13, 129, 166, 176 (222, a blow at), 242,
355, 379, 393, 413, 422, 477, 513
Byzantine capitals, 486

C

CAEN stone, qualities of, 26, 38, 67, 514
Calculating machine, 178
California and gold "diggings," 69
Campanile of Giotto, Florence, 274
Carpenters: Company, history of, 121; ball, 477;
hours, 572; Society, 156, 472
Casement, details of French, 562
Castle: Conway, 403; Flint, 403
Cathedral: Andersach, 439; Antigua, 595, 605;
Canterbury, 205, 347; Chester, 375; Cologne,
182; Ely, 151, 418; Lincoln, 261, 318; Salis-
bury, 364; St. David's, 197; St. Patrick's, 46;
Spanish Town, Jamaica, 377, 548
Ceilings: hollow brick arched, 183; wirework, 317
Cements used in Paris, 208
Cemeteries, 124, 453, 489: see also " Burial"
Chapel: Alcock's, 151; Congregational, Reading,
164; Jesus College, Cambridge, 562; Osmaston,
472; polygonal, 464; Roman Catholic; Farm-
street, 258; Roslin, jaunt to, 205; Wesleyan,
Liverpool-road, 608

Chapels, Elizabethan, 526
Chelsea, 94, 125
Chester, 361, 375
Chimney: church, 55; enormous, 537; flues, 57; piece, Mr. Hope's house, 534
Chimneys: smoky, 489, 526, 573
Chinese: builders in California, 598; bridges, 214
Chisels and gouges, improvement in, 214
Chronological account of buildings in Italy and Sicily, see under "Buildings"
Chryselephantine statues, 112
Church: Barrow, 57; Beverley, 105; Byzantine at Wilton, 373; Christ, Battersea, 382; Floating, 118; Fownhope, 80; Great Yarmouth, 442; Greek, London-wall, 422; Greenstead, wooden, 22, 45, 115; Holy Trinity, Cork, dry rot in, 321; Kingsdown new, fall of, 495; Normanton, 343; "Our Lady Star of the Sea" at Greenwich, 390; Pantheon formed, at Musta, 565; Presbyterian, Manchester, 451; Redcliffe, north porch of, and "Nil Desperandum," 1,—at Caoynge Society, 367; Romsey Abbey, 397; St. Andrew's, Trent, 321; St. Dunstan's-East, 506; St. George's, Canterbury, discoveries in 9; St. Jude's, Bristol, 489, 584; St. Martin's, Birmingham, 314; St. Mary's, Guildford, 558; St. Mary-at-Hill, Thames-street, 244; St. Mary's, West Brompton, 283, 370; St. Michael's, Cambridge, liability to repair, 581; St. Michael's, Chester, 17; St. Nicholas's, Hamburgh, 520; St. Paul's, Derby, 307; St. Peter's, Belmont, 574; St. Peter's Chester, 620; St. Peter's, Croydon, 454; St. Peter's, Everton, 128; St. Saviour's, Southwark, 118; St. Stephen's, Wallbrook, 160, 561, 584; St. Thomas's, Coventry, 442; Sarawak, Borneo, 550; Saxon, at Stowe, 165; Stoke Gregory, Somerset, 306; Stowe Bardolph, 591; Thornbury, 269; Treyford St. Peter, 559; Unitarian, Hope-street, Liverpool, 8; Upleadon, 389; Wavendon, 449
Church: architecture, 269; building news, 439, 449, 512, 521, 580, 607;—see also "Notes in the Provinces;" how one should be built, 365; ──────, 466; ──────; ──────, 449, 478,── St. Mary's, Ware, 426,—Sherborne, 562; spire, St. James's, Clerkenwell, 512; steeple, Halstead, 82; tower, Redcliffe—example to "betters," 113,—St. Mary's, Taunton, 473
Churches: access to, 29; in Liverpool, 8, 9; insurance of, 155; middle age, 465; new at Westminster, 557; one sided, 377; parish, 169; Spanish, 454
Churchyard: monuments, 443; St. Margaret's, Westminster, 46; St. Paul's, 16
Churchyards, country, 393
Cisterns: flow from, 514; sediment in, 488, 496
Clay, calcined granite, 142
Club-house: Crockford's, 125; Military, Naval, and County Service, 225; professional, 501; working-class, 485
Coal Exchange, 462, 521, 538, 573
Coins, old, how to cleanse, 403
Cold harbour, 82, 202
College: buildings, Oxford, 562; St. Barnabas's, Pimlico, 162
Colonnades are out, 550
Colour: in architecture, 247,—decoration, 374, 389,—painting, Linton on, 412
Compensation cases, 405, 418, 537, see also under "Railway"
Competition: architectural, 392; Aylesbury assize lodgings, 106, 162; Bedford corn market, 106; Blind institution, Birmingham, 502; Birmingham workhouse, 46, 50, 68, 73, 94, 196, 202, 327,—second, 406, 411, 425, 434, 446, 459, 474, 502; Bracknall Church, 286, 238; Bradford workhouse, 502, 521, 598; Bridgewater Church, 214, 226, 237, 250; Brigg corn exchange, 454; Bristol bridge improvements, 286, 394; Bucks lunatic asylum, 490; Cardiff drainage, 419; Cheltenham Church, 298, 310, 332, 341, 365, 598; Chichester training school, 10, 22, 28; Chippenham drainage, 607; drainage of St. Thomas Apostle, Devon, 561, 607; Dundee Royal arch, 130, 151, 237, 260, 261; Essex

lunatic asylum, 310; Guildford drainage, 55, 130, 226; church at Hawes, 514; Heptonstall Church, 82; Hull corn exchange, 538; Independent College, St. John's-wood, 370, 382; Leicester union enlargement, 584, 561; Lewes free school, 73; London: drainage, 481—see also under "Drainage" and "Sewers' Commission"—Fever hospital, 111,—National school, St. Martin's-in-the-Fields, 178,—St. Luke's workhouse, Chelsea, 310,—Small-pox hospital, 94, 139, 155,—union workhouse, 379; Newark corn exchange, 126; St. Thomas's, Newport, 550, 617; Northampton corn exchange, 118, 283, 399, 411, 429; Northfleet church restoration, 417, 430; Scarborough Independent Chapel, 608; Sandford Church, Cheltenham, 353; Stockton union, 583, 607; Walsall gas works, 140; Warwick drainage and water supply, 514, 607; Wesleyan Chapel, York, 573, 583
Competitions: architectural, 427, 435, 451, 452, 461, 531, 583, 607; engineering—drainage of Guildford, 55
Concrete piers, 430
Construction, improvements in, 137
Contract: cheap, 595; law, 333, 340; system—ruinous, 512
Contract-tenders: Chelmsford union, 370; Chester, St. Peter's, 224; Devonport prisons, 393; Hampstead workhouse, 177; city prison, Holloway, 188; Lowton church, 224; see also end of almost every weekly number
Contract-tenders, correct, 572
Contractors, important to, 166
Contracts: French, 519; low, 106
Cookery Bookery, 439
Copyism, age of, 133
Corn Exchange: Edinburgh, 586; Hertford, 538; Hull, Newark, Northampton, &c., see under "Competition"
Cornices, mould for mitres of, 272
"Cosmos," or Right Study of Nature, 154
Cottages: floors of, 6, 20, 29, 81; for 10l. a-piece, 21; labourers, 286, 298, 517
Crickets, to destroy, 598
Crystal curtain, 608
Cube, multiplication of, 284, 356
Cyclorama, Royal, 165
Cylinders, metal, cast without cores, 466

D

DAGUERREOTYPE, 68
Damp in buildings, 85, 620
Dead, what to do with, 547
Death in sewers, 497, 505, 525, 537, 544, 549
Decoration: cast zinc in, 389; colour in, 389; ecclesiastical, 169; house, 134; in Paris, 309; permanent, for rooms, 356
Decorations: church, 285; exhibition of, 116; from abroad, 151, 196, 223
Decorative art: ancient, colours in, 374; in glass, 542; Grecian, Periclean age of, 112; Roman period of Greek, 160; Society, 8, 566
Design: in art and manufacture, 429, 548; in calico printing, 580; in metalwork, 236; ornamental, 569
Design, School of: 181, 202, 212, 219, 238; Birmingham, 310; central, good moment in, 94; mutual instruction at, 113; Dublin, 250; Edinburgh, 68; Irish, 591; Leicester, 45; Manchester, 212; Newcastle, 490; Sheffield, 440; Parliamentary committee on, 391; report on, 417
Design: study of, from vegetable growth, 8; works of, destruction of—Mr. Hope's house, Piccadilly, 572, 583
Designers, importance of art-principles to, 122, 133
Designs, theory of registered, 166
Diorama, 213
Dilapidations, on, 40, 130, 188, 238, 409, 537,—ecclesiastical, 571
Disc engine, 309
Dispensary, plan of, 160
Dock: Great Grimsby, 208; Keyham, 214
Dockyard: expenditure, 142; reductions, 178
Door: bolts, 549; knobs, 369
Drainage: 565; bad, 549; converging, 347; Guild-

ford, 55, 130, 226; Hertford Gaol, 560; house, 8, 466; Hull, 82; iron pipe, 382; Kensington, 464; metropolitan, 368, 399, 452, 458, 476, 481, 512,—see also under "Sewers' Commission;" New Houses of Parliament, 31, 41, 58; town, 549, 453; Westminster, 428, 464
Drains: cost of, 165; flushing, 620; small, 232, 479; trapping, 233, 272
Drawings: chalk and crayon, to fix, 261; commencing, 344
Drying-closets, 177, 209, 219, 245, 273, 333
Dry-rot, extraordinary, 321
Dwelling-houses, word to wise on, 411
Dwellings: erection of, parish, 561; for rich and poor in union, 176; improvement of, 13, 21, 34, 261, 325, 436, 451, 478, 518, 537, 561, 566, 589,—in France, 574, 615

E

ECCLESIASTICAL: and architectural topography, 213, 561; architecture, 110, 147, 405; decoration, interior, 169
Ecclesiological: Society, 250,—Irish, 610
Edinburgh, 297, 298, 379, 406, 489, 538, 586
Editor's addresses, opening, 1, closing, 613
Egyptian: architecture, 52, 241, 293; monuments, 10
Electric light, 156, 430
Electro-telegraphic progress, 20, 34, 81, 127, 141, 164, 190, (208, Company's charges) 225, 236, 247, 272, 322, 340, 394, 405, 466, 489, 514, 526, 574, 622
Electrotype, 621
Engineer: French honour to English—Mr. R. Stephenson, 610; Tom Steele an, 59
Engineering: lecture on, 470, 482; remuneration, 531
Engineers: Civil, Institution of, 23, 34, 76, 98, 135, 142, 155, 188, 202, 226, 238, 250, 273, 284, 310, 358, 549, 562, 585, 598, 609,—Queen's College of, Birmingham, 129; Mechanical, Institution of, 226, 237
Engines, carbonic acid gas, 274; disc, 309; hydraulic, 418; hydroelectric, 453; rotary, 442, 452
Estimating, curiosities of, 137; see also under "Contract-tenders"
Euston station, 234, 246
Etruria, the walls of, 34
Etty's Works—an honour to the nation, 280
Exchange: see "Coal;" Wolverhampton, 513
Exhibition: architectural, 70, 109, 145, 457; at Society of Arts, 116; at Paris, 213, 268, 298; at Birmingham, 64, 429, 447, 610; British Institution, 75; French industrial, Hyde-park, 261, 569; industrial, of Nations, 440, 502, 574, 586, 611; of inventions, 94, 137, 166; of machinery at Ghent, 214; Royal Academy, 217, 230, 255; free, 145, 412

F

FARM buildings, 142, 517
Fever stills, 413, 422, 434, 453
Filter, cheap, 489
Fire: annihilator, 166; escape, 526, 574; preservation of life from, 538; proof buildings, 116,—flooring and roofing, 155, 466; security against in theatres, &c., 91; suppression of in coal mines, 225
Fires: from shoring, 10; in noblemen's mansions, 562
Fixtures: law of, 409, 448
Flaxman's works, 9
Floors: arched brick, 212; barn, 94; desiccated, 490; fire-proof, 155, 466; for cottages, 6, 20, 29, 81; iron, 103; pottery and iron, 350
Flues, chimney, 57
Flushing and flashing, 46, 428
Foley's "Ino and Infant Bacchus, 322
Forge, Lancefield, 418
Freemasons of the Church, 32, 106, 142, 226, 501
Fuel: block, 490; pitch, 190

G

GAOL: Boston, 207; cost of City and Surrey, 93; estimates, 571; see also "Prison"

Gardens: Cremorne, 430; Farnesian, 294; Kensington, 62; Rosherville, 405
Gas: at Lincoln, 532; at Ware, 485; camphine, 394; companies, rating, 343; engineers' institute, 250; explosions, 572, 610; generater, 394; holder, destruction of, 59; jet, colliery, 419; lighting, 561,—Leslie's burners, 91,—liquid hydro-carbon for, 188; in churches, 586; profits, 476; monitor, 165, 177; movement, 43, 58, 64, 171, 333, 595, 621; pipes, 97, 382; ventilation, 577; works, Walsall, 262
Geographical Society, origin of, 258
Geometrical proportion, 118
Girder: bridge, Barnes, 165,—hollow, 320, 512; iron, 82, 446
Glass: Albion Company, 118; breakage, 406; colour in, 211; decorative art in, 542; foreign window, 166, 375; manufacture, 388, 448; mosaic, 454; pipes on great scale, 81; rough plate, what is? 541, 562, 603; silver, 237; soluble, 271; trade, 190
Glaziers, important to, 585
Glazing in Paris, 309
Gloucester, 129, 142
Godwin, George, F.R.S., passim
Gothic: exemplars (leader on), 264; see also "Architecture," "Ornament," "Pointed," &c.
Graveyards: Clerkenwell, 393, 413, 429, 441: see also "Burial"
Greenhouses, construction of, 367
Groynes, at Sunderland Docks, 155
Gutta percha, 178; wonders of, 190, 237, 259, 322, 365, 502; tubing in churches—laying it on, 406; use of in repairs, 580

H

HALL: Bowood, 474; British Museum, 198; Euston station, 234; old, at Gainsborough, 488; St. George's, Liverpool, 153, 183, 198; Pembroke College, 65
Harbour of refuge, Dover, 9
Health: Act, proceedings under, 10, 13, 46 (leader on, 61), 103, 226, 289; association, 182; bill, engineering remuneration under, 531; question, 62, 352, 436
Heating dwellings, 44
Heraldry, 6, 22
Hierophantine fragments, 231
Hollow brick arched ceilings, see "Bricks"
Hope, Mr., M.P., house of, in Piccadilly, 493, 534, 572, 583
Hospital: Cheltenham general, 235; Greenwich, 22, 53; Manchester lunatic, 598; Middlesex, 10, 22; Small-pox, cost of, 94; see also under "Competition"
House: agents, to, 226; drainage, 8; of Francis I. at Paris, 175; of Mr. Hope, Piccadilly, 493, 534, 572, 583
Houses: backs of, 474; for very poor, 615; iron, 221, 382, 417, 487
Hoxton ragged schools, 598
Hull, 82,—sanitary, 103
Hydrostatic pressure regulator, 46

I

IMPROVEMENT: of dwellings—see "Dwellings;" of Poole, 235; of open spaces, 58; of south side of Thames, 404; of structures at Hamburg, 62; see also under "Metropolitan"
Ink, colourless, 137
Ionic volute, production of, 295
Iron: 550; as used in Paris buildings, 309; beams, corrugated, 45, 53; business, 526; casting, 58; enamel, 441; see "Floor;" galvanized, rot in, 81, 113, 157: see "Girder," and "Houses;" imports and exports, 451; nature and properties of, 197, 396; pipes, 382, 458, 513, 536; with lead, 82; railings, corrosion of, 274; roof, 454, 543; sewer, 417; soldering, cast with wrought, 250; steamers, 236; trade, 34, 82, 98, 166, 214, 250, 274, 286, 319, 346, 298, 485, 586, 598; windows, 33; working in England, 488
Italy: see "Buildings;" terra cotta of, 415; travelling in by architect, 2, 217

J

JERUSALEM, see "Antiquities"
Joiners' machine for mortising, &c., 502
Joints, vulcanized india-rubber, 298

K

KENNINGTON Common, 44

L

LAMBETH, City lands in, 70
Landlords and Tenants, 226, 249, 380, 557, 585
Landscape gardening, 349
Lead: 309; effect of, on water, 22; shot towers, 609
Leasehold, enfranchisement of, 5, 23, 39, 46, 87, 377
Leicester-square, 22, 556, 617
Libraries: public, committee on, 69,—report of, 469; railway, 128
Life assurance, 249, 429
Lighthouses, 177
Lightning conductors, 291
Limes: Paris, 308; see also "Mortar"
Liverpool, 56, 79, 128, 149, 153, 163, 183, 198, 237, 250, 314, 425, 454, 579
Lock, reliance detector, 322
London: architectural advantages and deficiencies of, 220; antiquities, 241, 260, 271, 281; City, improvements, 555,—see also "Metropolitan;" City prison, 463; City union, 400; extension of, 572; graveyards—cholera, 379,—see also "Burial," "Graveyards," &c.; levels of, 466; wonderful, leader on, 302; see also under "Coal Exchange," "Competition," "Drainage," "Fever Stills," "Sewers," "Water Supply," &c.
Louvre, The, 58, 218

M

MAHOGANY, artificial, 286
Manchester, 103, 190, 212, 454, 502, 586, 598
Maps, pictorial, 329, 585, 622
Market: Islington, 93, 129; Smithfield, 273, 343, 397
Masons' Provident Institution, 118, 466
Mechanics' Institute: Leeds, 550; London, 511; midland, 526; Steyning, 490; suggested, 489; Yorkshire, 283
Metallic lava, 393, 430
Metals: 296; artistic design in, 236; corrosion of, 94; exports of, 514; improvement in shaping, 146; liquid for cleansing, 491; nature and properties of, 55, 197, 386
Metropolitan: houses, 443; improvements, 118,—Chelsea, 94,—Holborn, 156, 245,—Islington, 68, 93, 105,—Leicester-square, 556,—Longacre, 196,—south side of Thames, 404, 584; parks, 459; see also "London"
Model: dwellings, see under "Dwellings,"—at Bath, 34,—Glasgow, 261; lodging-houses, and Society, 325; of Cologne Cathedral, 182,—of Lancashire and Yorkshire, 88; town houses, middle class, 566; towns, 400, 429
Modelling, plan, 88
Models, card board, colouring, 141
Monument: Culloden, 370; Sir Hans Sloane's, 70, 82, 94; Mr. P. Nicholson's, 85; Picton's, 58; Yarborough, 112
Monumental: architecture, 4, 14; inscriptions, to colour, 142
Monuments: bronze in, 488; in cemeteries, 124, 443; Egyptian, 10; for Madras Cathedral, 437; maintenance of ancient, 294
Mortar, ancient, 593, 608; see also "Limes"
Mosaics: glass, 454; Pompeii, 3
Mosque: of Omar, 65; Turkish, contribution to, 610
Mosques and Moorish palaces, 328
Moulds, 272,—elastic, 69

N

NAIL making, 274,—machines, 598
Necessaries, public, 160
Nelson Column, 478, 488, 586, 596

New York, 274, 544
Newspaper folders, 598
Nicholson, Peter, recollections of, 615
Nineveh: 297, 586
Notes in provinces, see each weekly number.

O

OAK, to restore, 105
Obituary: Mr. Austin, 205; Sir Marc Isambard Brunel, 609; Mr. Harvey Eginton, 101; Mr. William Etty, 562; Mr. Alderman Johnson, 9; Sir R. Morrison, 557; Mr. Robert Sibley, 160; Mr. David Smith, of Leith, 202; Mr. Vernon, 250; Mr. John Woolley, 451
Opera-house, Covent Garden, 92, 97, 105, 137,—scenery in, 233, 370
Ordnance survey: civil surveyors' 178; also see under "Sewers Commission"
Ornament: from Bologna and Ferrara, 415; Gothic, 25; from Venice, 532; works on, 565
Ornamental: art, Gothic era of, 495; design, errors in, 569
Ornamentation, new style of, 25
Ovens, improvement of, 65

P

PÆSTUM, 218
Painters: brushes (house), 129; in Water Colours, New Society of, 200, 209
Painting: art of, new works on, 277; and glazing in Paris, 309; colours used in, 412; mural, 369,—at Barnstaple, 502,—Columpton Church, 322
Palace: Buckingham, 583; Hampton Court, 327; John O'Gaunt's, 189; Westminster, see under "Parliament"
Panorama: "four mile," 189; of Nile, 297, 352, 441, 574
Paper-hangings, flower pattern, 358
Paris, 93, 130, 175, 178, 213, 268, 277, 298, 307, 457, 523, 568, 570
Parks, 44, 130, 140, 329, 459, 497, 586
Parliament, new Houses of, 31, 41, 58, 93, 98, 341, 457, 520
Parsonages, 560
Patent: caters, 262; laws, 57, 155, 596, 622
Pavilion, Brighton, 370, 549
Peat: charcoal, to sweeten metropolis, 370, 389, 502; Irish, extracts from, 370
Perspective, vanishing lines in, 256
Photography, 68
Piccadilly, past and present, 493, 534
Piers, yielding, 81; concrete, 430
Pile-driving process, pneumatic, 9
Pipes, cost of, 165; glass, 81; iron, 382, 458, 536; playing on, 538: see also "Steam"
Plans, right to copy, 92, 105
Plasterers, our, 513
Pointed: arch, 290, 303; architecture, Saxon, 110; style, 316
Polytechnic Institution, Regent-street, 416
Pompeii, 2
Porch, see "Redcliffe"
Portrait gallery, Drayton Manor, 440
Portraits, a leash of, 140
Prison: accommodation, cost of, 526; construction, 63, 100; reform, Howard and, 523: see also "Gaol"
Projected works: see each weekly number
Pulpits, stone, Early English, 450
Pump, centrifugal, 429

R

RAILWAY: accidents and prevention, 56, 77, 430, 572, 583; arches for destitute, 9, 21, 118,—Samaritan Society, 549; arches, fall of, 57; assessment, 9; balloon, 101; bars, oxidation of, 500; bridges, how we build, 538, see also "Bridge;" buffers and springs, india-rubber, 465; carriers' question, 212, 320, 572; company, honour of, 435; compensation, 56, 77, 358, 394, 491, 526; Eastern Counties, moveable time table, 544; economy v. extravagance, 547; libraries, 128; locomotives, 202, 209, 226,—England's light, 499; opening, 274; rates, 70,

214, 525, 550; return ticket question, 213; sheds, 20; signals, 128; stations, 9, 79, 135, 234, 246, 425, 523, 560; statistics, 189, 236, 344, 512; transit, movement during, 369; works, 443, 526,—failure of, 57, 128, 271, 382, 533, 536, 561, 569, 585; world, present state of, 253, 322.

Railways, English and American, 430

Rates: poor, exemption from, 82, 94, 286, 297, 310; in Bethnal-green, 466; gas companies, 343; on public buildings in Ireland, 442; St. Mary's, Whitechapel, 545

Record office, public, 35, 261

Redcliffe, St. Mary's, north porch of, see under "Church"

Resistance of posts to flexure, 473

Review of Books, &c.: Architectural Society's Illustrations, 133; Art of Landscape Painting, 586; Art-Workmanship, 561; Barnard's School - Architecture, 133; Barr's Strixton Church, 133; Bloxam's Gothic Architecture, 405; Bowman and Crowther's Middle-Age Churches, 465; Brandon's Parish Churches, 169; Brandon's Open Roofs, 265; Buckingham's Model Towns, 400; Burke's Historic Lands, 225; Burt's Life Assurance, 429; Bury's Rudimentary Architecture, 409; Butler and Hodge's Scrap-book, 297; Clark's Heraldry, 22; Coggin's Short-hand, 465; Colling's Gothic Ornaments, 25; Dempsey's Drainage, 565; Denison's Wanderings, 565; Dixon's Howard, 525; Dollman's Ancient Pulpits, 265; Downing's Landscape Gardening, 349; Dwyer and Laugher's Freehand Studies, 566; Frank's Glazing Quarries, 265; Fergusson on British Museum, 350; Gibbon's Dilapidations, 409; Grady's Law of Fixtures, 409; Gray's Tables, 513; Halliwell's Rhymes, 261; Hobbes's Collector's Manual, 277; Holland's Tables, 465; Humboldt's Cosmos, 154; Ince's Outlines, 213; Jones's Holy Matrimony, 556; Jopling on the Volute, 409; Kennedy and Hackwood's Tables, 526; Lea's Tables, 142; Marshall's Index Ready Reckoner, 105; Merrifield's Art of Painting, 277; Morris's Tables, 465; Museum Disnaeum, 25; Rickman's Topography amplified, 213, 561; Robson's Decorative Art, 566; Ruskin's Seven Lamps of Architecture, 299; Ryan's Manuring, 452; Scott's Antiquarian Gleanings, 297, 561; Shaw's Tenant Right, 261; Smart's Logic, 260; Smith's Tide-table, 586; Soyer's Modern Housewife, 439; Tate's Calculus, 429; Tate's Euclid, 513; Transactions of Society of Arts, 349; Turner's Copyright, 429; Twining's Philosophy of Art, 277; Wakeman's Archæologia Hibernica, 105; Weale's Rudimentary Treatises,—Electricity, 129, Geology, 129, List of Terms, 565, Mechanics, 129, Well-digging, Boring, and Pump-work, 129; Whittaker on Ornamentation, 25; Wright's Ireland, 297; Timb's Year-book, 105.

Rigging, new, 156; springs—india-rubber, 202

Roads, 273, 461, 535

Roman: arch, 266; architecture, 253; remains, see "Archæological;" pavements, 596

Romanesque: art, 328; style, 410

Roofs and roofing, 155, 173, 284, 320, 340, 377, 404, 423, 454, 543

Rot, dry, 321

Rotary engine, new, 442, 452

Royal Academy: 200, 213, 217, 230, 244, 247, 255, 256, 413, 592, 605; see also under "Architectural," "Architecture," "Exhibition," &c.

Royal Society, 49, 200, 298

S

SALISBURY, notes in, 373; see also "Archæological" and "Cathedral"

Saloon, bowling, 118, 213

Sand, sea, 10

Sanitary: inquiries, see "Health Act;" measures and window tax, 524'; movement, 10, 13, 14, 33

Saracenic art, 328

Saw filing and setting machine, 155

Saxon work, Iver church, 496

Scaffolding, suggestion for, 502

Scenery: theatrical, 82; see also "Opera" and "Theatre"

Scenes behind New Oxford-street, 334

Schools, 103, 261, 294, 383, 437, 449, 451, 452, 454, 538, 598

Screens, public, or penalties inevitable, 344

Sculpture, 22, 65, 123, 129, 442, 513

Sepulchres, 4, 8, 14; see also "Burial"

Serpentine river, state of, 34, 62

Sewage: 190, 201, 284, 598; manure company, 69, 105, 118, 213

Sewer: deep tunnel, 313, 369; explosion, 477, 478; iron, 417; Kenilworth-street, Pimlico, see "Death in Sewers"

Sewers: Act, 285, 377; city, commission of, 200, 334,—condition of, 81; Chester, cost of, 269; cholera and, 13; collection from, and clearing river, 152

Sewers Commission, new Metropolitan, see almost every weekly number; but see also :—letter to, on house drainage, 8; Mr. Barry and, 31, 41; a word in season to, 49; closed door business of, 105, 117, 129, 141, 154, 165; protest against Committees, 154, 165; Ordnance survey and, 154, 165, 225, 249; retirement of commissioner from, 202; stir in, and drainage of Goulston-street and Whitechapel, 305; position of—retirement of officers—deep tunnel sewer, 313; extraordinary proceedings of, 404; the obstructive question at, 417; leader on, 421; reorganization of, 441, 481; new new, opening of, 501

Sewers: form of, 14; Kensington, 135, 164, 225; Newcastle and Gateshead, 437; ventilation of, 233, 501, 525, 549

Shakespeare, face of, 393; house of, 202

Sheffield, 142, 163, 440, 550

Sicily, buildings in, chronological account of, 243, 256, 318

Smoke of towns, 233, 273

Socialism, Owen and, 429

Society Season, leader on, 529

Specification, precision in—what is rough plate glass? 541

Spitting Bank notes, 69

Stables, ventilation of, 392

Staircases, arrangement of, 490

Statue: Jephson, 274; Rutland, 491, 514; Shakespeare, 81; Wellington, at Edinburgh, 82, —interference with architects' works, 332

Statues: Chryselephantine, 112; in lead, 238; public, 500, 622

Steam: boiler, explosion, 59, 307, 562,—horse power packet, 10, 32; cutters for frozen seas, 214; engines, portable, 165; husbandry, 370; pipes, 4

Stench trap, 610,—grid, 584

Stone: Bath, use of, 8, 46; building, at Paris, 278; Caen, qualities of, 26, 38, 67, 514; drill, steam, 155; facing, patent, 152; indurated, 463; whin, see under "Bridge"

Stonehenge, 373

Stove-grate, pyro-pneumatic, 106

Street: architecture, 115, 172, 246; cleansing, 69; crossings, 353; waterer, 297

Streets, 201, 314, 466

Strikes and unions, 45

Style, system in, 160; see also "Gothic," &c.

Styles: in architecture, 148,—growth of, 529, 558

Submarine telegraphs, 34, 127

Supervision of buildings in Vienna, 177,—of places of public resort, 97

Surveyors' Association (Land), 214

Synagogue, West London, 307

Syphon, air, see "Air Syphon"

Syro-Egyptian Society, 297, 441

T

TABLES: for curves, 526; useful, 465

Taormina and Mola, 537

Task-work, 475; among bricklayers, 593

Tempering edge tools, American mode of, 417

Temples: lighting of Greek, 19; one sided—leasehold, 377

Tenders, see "Contract-tenders"

Terra Cotta, 441, 415

Thames: clearing, of sewage, 152; tunnel, 173

Theatre: Adelphi, 238, 500; Drury-lane, 524, 608; her Majesty's, 141, 188, 269, 359; Lyceum, 129, 173, 514, 620; Olympic, 189, 601, 619; Prince's, Royal, Glasgow, 74

Theatres: safety in, 157; scenic anachronisms in, 233; stairs and accesses to, supervision of, 20, 97

Thorwaldsen's works, sale of, 514

Tidal: observations on Thames, 458; survey, 586

Tomb: altar, 55; Bonzi's, 556; Napoleon's, 130

Tombs, 4, 8, 14, 80

Tower: La Martorana, 427; leaning, 156; porcelain, 262; St. Mary's, Taunton, 475

Town: at Llandudno, 429; Flint, 403

Towns: beauty in, 175; drainage of, 453; model, 400, 429; water to, 514

Tread-wheeled coach, 286

Trossachs Inn and Chapel, 257

Trusses, arched, of bent timber, 297

Tubes, india-rubber, for closets, 584; earthenware, 430; gutta percha, 322

Tunneling, improvements in, 603

U

UNIVERSITY of Catania, 436

V

VASE, Etruscan patterned, 70

Vatican, stealing from, 610

Ventilation: see "Air Syphon;" domestic, 466; gas, 577; new mode of, 441; stable, 392; sewer, see "Sewers;" warming and, 44, 262

Vernon: club, 538; testimonial, 34

Villages, beauty in, 175

W

WALL: Westminster Palace, 93; paintings, see "Paintings"

Walls: new, crystallisation on, 250; damp, 620; facing, 137; of Etruria, 34; pise and cob, 211; wire-worked, 317

Water: cheap filter for, 489; effect of lead on, 22; for tower, 478; iron pipes for, 382, 458, 513, 536; power in air-tight pipes, 142; pure, 496; softening and purifying, 250; supply, 178, 463,—to Amsterdam, 139,—Buckingham palace, 466,—city, 63,—Constantinople, 201, 236, 273,—London, 63, 81, 439, 511—schemes for, 553, 622,—New York, 621,—Southampton, 620,—Windsor Castle, 383,—town, 514

Water Colour Societies, see "Painters"

Weale's rudimentary works, review of, 129, 565

Weevil, cure for, 244

Wells, Artesian, 81, 93, 553

Westminster: abbey, see under "Abbey;" improvements, 473, 512, 514, 532, 598; new churches in, 557

Whitewash, American, 418

Window: French, description of, 543; gardens, 525; glazing, 103; monumental, 418; sashes, 453; stained, 382; tax, 178, 524

Windows, ornamental iron, 33; patent, 139

"Wonders in locomotion"—new power, 209

Wood, preservation of, 70, 466, 526.

Woods and Forests, charges against, 98, 118, 590

Woods used in Paris, &c., 308

Workhouse: London City, 400; for St. Margaret's parish, 115

Workhouses, cost of, 452; see also "Competition"

Working-class: club-house, 485; hall for, 586; news and reading-rooms, 506; condition of, 146, 157; elevation of, 231; books for, 487; masters and, 548, 558, 572; mode of discharging, 524; note to, 185, 211; want of ambition among, 178; welfare of, 223, 250

Works: public, 556,—in France, 422; money for, 393, 490; 619

Wrought-iron pipes, see under "Iron pipes"

Z

ZINC: alloys of, 55; cast, decorative, 353; imports, 302; paint, 430, 507.

LIST OF ILLUSTRATIONS.

A

ABBEY Church, Romsey, twelfth century, 402
Alcock's Chapel, Ely Cathedral, date 1488, 150
Almshouses, Bishop Duppa's, Richmond : A.D. 1661—view and sketch of entrance to, 259
Almshouses, Bishop Still's, Wells : sixteenth century, 510 ; details of same, 511
Almshouses, Printers', Wood Green, Tottenham, 270
Altar screen, St. Alban's Abbey, Herts, 582
Altar tomb in Exeter Cathedral (Early English) : four sketches, 54
Ancient art, examples of : four engravings, 27 ; ironwork, 380
Andernach Cathedral, on the Rhine, 438
Antigua, church of St. John's, 594
Architecture in Catania : two sketches, 436
Ashlesteel-bridge (Whinstone), 63
Art, ancient, examples of : four engravings, 27
Aurelian gate at Rome, 114

B

BANK of England, (branch) at Liverpool : Mr. Cockerell, R.A., architect, 42 ; cornice, &c., of same enlarged, 43
Bank, Sir Benjamin Heywood's, Manchester : Mr. J. E. Grogan, architect, 18
Bishop Alcock's Chapel, Ely Cathedral : date 1488, 150
Bishop Still's Almshouses, Wells, 510 ; details of same, 511
Bench-ends, carved : four sketches, 280
Bonzi family's tomb at Rome, 556
Book cover from Stowe, carved, 91
Boston Gaol, ground plan of, 207
Bowood Hall, 474
Brick's Almshouses, Wells, 510, 511 (misnamed Still's—see p. 533)
Bridge, Ashlesteel (Whinstone), 63
Bridgewater House, present plan of, 484
British Museum, entrance front of : Sir Robert Smirke, R.A., architect, 187 ; hall and staircase of same, 198 ; museum of old time, 199
Byzantine Capitals : nine sketches, 486

C

CANOPY, stone, in Presbytery of Winchester Cathedral ; Decorated period, 30 ; details of same, 31
Capitals, Byzantine : nine sketches, 486
Carved : bench-ends : four sketches, 280 ; book-cover from Stowe, 91 ; chimney-piece, Mr. Hope's house, Piccadilly : Messrs. Dusillion and Donaldson, architects, 534 ; stall, Sta. Salute, Venice, 506 ; stalls from Fiezole, Tuscany : 16th century, 258 ; stalls, Perugia, Italy, 351
Casement, French, details of : six sketches, 543
Cathedral of Andernach, on the Rhine, 438
Cathedral, Chester, chapter-house of, 366
Cathedral, Lincoln, east end of : 13th century, 318
Cathedral porch, Salisbury (north), 354
Cavendish-street Schools, Manchester : Mr. E. Walters, architect, 102
Cemetery, parochial, data for, 460
Chancel, Stowe Bardolph Church, south wall of, 591
Chapel, Alcock's, Ely Cathedral : date 1488, 150

Chapel in St. Mary's Church, Guildford, 558 ; detail of same, 559.
Chapel, Osmaston, Derbyshire, 472
Chapel, Roman Catholic, Farm-street Mews, Grosvenor-square : Mr. J. J. Scoles, architect, 258
Chapel, Roslin, Scotland, 210
Chapter-house of Chester Cathedral, 366
Cheney Church doorway (Belgium), 619
Chester Cathedral, Chapter-house, 366
Chester, old house at, 361
Chimney, Aslackby Church, Lincolnshire, 55
Chimney-piece, carved, Mr. Hope's house, Piccadilly, 534
Chimney-piece, Villa Madama, Rome, 232
Church, Abbey, Romsey, 402
Church doorway, Cheney, in Belgium, 619
Church, Greensted, restored, 115
Church of St. John, Antigua : Mr. Thomas Fuller, architect, 594
Church of St. Dunstan's-in-the-East, London, 507
Church, St. Mary's, West Brompton, Middlesex, Mr. George Godwin, F.R.S., architect, 282
Church, St. Paul's, Derby : Messrs. Barry and Brown, architects, 307
Church, Stoke Gregory, view of, 306
Church tower, St. Mary's, Taunton, 475
City of London Union Workhouse : Mr. R. Tress, architect, 378 ; general block plan of same, 400
Coal Exchange, London : Mr. Bunning, F.S.A., architect, 463
College Hall, Pembroke, Oxford, 66
College, St. Barnabas's, Pimlico, 160
Cornice : from entrance to University of Catania, 436 ; of Branch Bank of England, at Liverpool, 43 ; of Colonna Palace, Rome, 172 ; of house at Rome, 172 ; of Palazzo Borghese, Rome, 172 ; mould to run mitres of, two sketches, 272
Crypt of Bow Church—a London fever still, 414
Custom-house, Rouen : M. Ed. Isabelle, architect, 546
Cyclometer, 603

D

DECORATED window, Ware Church, Herts, 426
Decoration, the hop in, 247
Decorations from abroad, two sketches, 151 ; four sketches, 196 and 319
Design for the Small-pox Hospital (Mr. S. A. Matthews, architect), to which the second premium was awarded, 138
Designs for knockers : two sketches, 223
Diagrams : to article on Vanishing Lines in Perspective, 256 ; to article on Multiplication of the Cube, 284, 356 ; to article on A Cyclometer, 603
Dispensary, Cleveland-place, Bath, plan of, 160
Door-handle and key-hole, Halle aux Laines, Bruges, 244
Doorway of Cheney Church, Belgium, 619
Doorway, Renaissance, St. Andrew's, Joigny, France, 487
Doorway, Villa Borghese, Fracati, 580
Doric portal of Palazzo, Sciarra Colonna, Rome : A.D. 1603, 220
Duppa's Almshouses, Richmond : A.D. 1661—view and sketch of entrance, 259

E

ENTRANCE front of British Museum, 187

Entrance to Montacute House, Wiltshire, 330 ; details of same, 331
Entrance to University of Catania, 436
Euston station, great hall, 234 ; general meeting-room, 246 : Mr. P. C. Hardwick, architect
Examples of ancient art : four engravings, 27

F.

FACING with stone, patent method of, 136
Farnesian Gardens, Rome : Vignola and Michael-angelo, architects,—plan, section, and entrance gateway, 295
Fever-still, London, crypt of Bow Church, 414
Forms for window-glazing, 103 ; four sketches, 127
Free schools, Yarmouth : Messrs. Brown and Kerr, architects, 294
French casement, details of : six sketches, 543
Frets of eighth century, 196

G

GAOL, Boston, U. S., ground plan of, 207
Gardens, Farnesian, Rome, plan and section, and entrance gateway, 295
Gate, Janiculan at Rome, 114
Gatehouse, Walsingham priory, 447
General meeting-room, Euston station, 246
Girders, four sketches to article on, and on malleable iron floor, 104
Gravestone at Islay, 80
Great hall at the Euston station, 234
Greek temples, lighting of, four sketches, 19
Greensted church, Essex, restored, 115
Grill, iron, Sta. Maria Novella, Florence, 375

H

HALL and staircase of New British Museum, 198
Hall at Bowood, 474
Hall, great, at Euston station, 234
Hall, new, Pembroke college, Oxford : Mr. John Hayward, architect, 66
Hall, St. George's, Liverpool, plan of, and section of great arch, 186
Heywood's bank, Manchester, 18
Hospital, Small-pox, design for (second premium), 138
House of Francis I., Champs Elysées, Paris, 174 ; details of same, two sketches, 175
House of Mr. Hope, M.P., in Piccadilly, 498 ; iron railing to same, 499
House, old, at Chester, 361
Houses for the very poor, elevation and general plan, 514
Houses, model, in town, for middle classes : view and plan, 567
Hurwood's patent for moving windows, 139

I

IRON grill, Sta. Maria Novella, Florence, 375
Iron railing to Mr. Hope's mansion in Piccadilly, 499
Ironwork, ancient, 380
Ironwork of fourteenth century, 196
Iron (wrought) water-pipes : five figures, 536
Italian ornamentation from Palace Vendramini Calerghi, Venice, 532

J

JAMICULAN Gate at Rome, 114
Jerusalem, ancient and modern, plan of: J. J. Scoles, architect, Menst., 90

K

KNOCKERS, designs for: two sketches, 223

L

LA MARTORANA, tower of, at Palermo, 427
Lecterns from bas relief, Canterbury Cathedral, 535
Lighting of Greek temples: four sketches, 19
Lime-street station of North-Western Railway, Liverpool: Mr. Tite, F.R.S., architect, 78; plan of same, 79
Lincoln Cathedral—east end, 318
Liverpool Branch Bank of England, 42; cornice, &c. of same, 43; St. George's Hall, plan of, with section of great arch, 186
Lodge, Manor Park, Streatham: Mr. Roumieu, architect, 163
London City Union Workhouse, 378; general block plan of same, 400
London Coal Exchange, Thames-street, 463
London fever-still: crypt of Bow Church, 414

M

MANCHESTER: Cavendish-street schools, 102; Heywood's Bank, 18
Mansion of H. T. Hope, Esq., M.P., Piccadilly: Messrs. Dusillion and Donaldson, architects, 498
Marble panel, San Marco, Rome, 223
Middle-class model town-houses: view and plan, 567
Minster, Southwell, 410
Model-houses for families, Streatham-street, Bloomsbury: Mr. H. Roberts, honorary architect,—view and plan, 326; plan of tenements of same, 327
Model lodging-house, Hatton Garden, plans of, 325
Model town-houses for middle classes: view and plan, 567
Montacute-house, Somersetshire (not Wiltshire, as printed), entrance to, 330; details of same, 331
Mosaics from Pompeii, six sketches, 3
Mould to run mitres of cornices: three sketches, 272

N

NORTH porch of Redcliffe Church, Bristol, restored, 7
North porch, Salisbury Cathedral, 354

O

OLD house at Chester, 361
Olympic Theatre: Mr. F. W. Bushill, architect, 606; plan of same, 603; longitudinal section of, 618
Open roof, Ware Priory, 342
Ornamentation from Palace Vendramini Calergbi, Venice, 532
Osmaston Chapel, Derbyshire, 472
"Our Lady Star of the Sea," Roman Catholic Church at Greenwich: Mr. W. W. Wardell, architect, 390; plan of same, 391

P

PALACE at Pisa, ground floor window of, 144

Palais des Beaux Arts, Paris: Chateau Gaillon—a variety of sketches, 570
Palazzo Rezzonico, Venice, 126
Palazzo Della Consulta, at Rome, angle of, 114
Palazzo Sciarra Colonna, Rome, Doric portal of, A.D. 1603, 222
Panel from frescoes at Caprarola, circular, 151
Panel from tomb of Cardinal Sforza, Rome, 151
Panel, marble, San Marco, Rome, 223
Paris: house of Francis I., Champs Elysées, 174; details of same—two sketches, 175; Palais des Beaux Arts at, elevation, plan, and details, 570; Strasbourg railway station, 522; block plan of same, 523
Parthenon, section of, 19
Pavement, Caprarola, 303
Pembroke College, Oxford, new hall at, 66
Plan of Jerusalem, ancient and modern, 90
Pompeii, mosaics from: six sketches, 3
Porch, north, of Redcliffe Church, Bristol, restored: Mr. George Godwin, architect, 7
Porch, north, Salisbury Cathedral, 354
Porta St. Pancrazio at Rome, plan and elevation of, 114
Portal, Doric, of Palazzo Sciarra Colonna, Rome—A.D. 1603, 222
Portraits (two) of members of City Carpenters' Company in seventeenth century, 122
Printers' Almshouses, Wood-green, Tottenham: Mr. W. Webb, architect, 270
Prior's room, Bradenstoke Priory, Wilts, 387
Priory Gatehouse, Walsingham, 447
Pulpit steps, Pisa Cathedral, 343
Pulpit, stone, Early English, 450

Q

QUOIN, entrance to Catania University, 436

R

RAILING, iron, at Mr. Hope's house, Piccadilly, 499
Railway station (Strasbourg) at Paris, 522; block plan of same, 523
Redcliffe Church, north porch of, restored, 7
Renaissance doorway, St. Andrew's, Joigny, France, 487
Roman Catholic Chapel, Farm-street Mews, Grosvenor-square, 259
Roman Catholic Church, "Our Lady Star of the Sea," at Greenwich, 391; plan of same, 391
Romsey Abbey Church, 402
Roof, French Riding Schools, 423
Roof, open, Ware Priory, 342
Roslin Chapel, Scotland, 210
Rouen Custom-house, 546

S

SAINT BARNABAS'S College, Pimlico: Messrs. Cundy, architects, 162
St. Dunstan's in the East, London, 507
St. George's Hall, Liverpool, plan of and section of great arch, 186
St. John's Cathedral, Antigua, 594
St. Mary's Church tower, Taunton, 475
St. Mary's Church, West Brompton, Middlesex, 282
St. Paul's Church, Derby, 307
Salisbury Cathedral porch, north, 354
Schools, Cavendish-street, Manchester, 102

Schools, free, Yarmouth, 294
Schools, Northern, St. Martin's-in-the-Fields, London: Mr. James Wild, architect, 451
Screen (altar), St. Alban's Abbey, Herts, 583
Sewage reservoir, proposed, sketch of, 153
Shrine of St. Thomas, at Canterbury, 447
Small-pox hospital, design for, which obtained second premium, 138
South wall of chancel, Stowe Bardolph Church, 591
Southwell Minster, 410
Staircase and Hall of New British Museum, 198
Stall, carved, Sta. Salute, Venice, 507
Stalls, carved, from Fiezole, Tuscany, 268
Stalls, carved, Perugia, Italy, 351
Station, Lime-street, Liverpool, North-Western Railway, 78; plan of same, 79
Station, Strasbourg Railway, Paris, 522; block plan of same, 523
Stench trap grid, sketch illustrative of, 585
Steps to pulpit, Pisa Cathedral, 343
Still's Almshouses, Wells, see "Brick's"
Stoke Gregory Church, view of, 306
Stone canopy, in Winchester Cathedral, 30, details of same, 31
Stone facing, patent mode of, 136
Stone pulpit, Early English: circa 1270, 450
Strasbourg railway station, Paris, 522; block plan, 523
Streatham lodge, 163
Street-architecture, suggestions for: nine engravings, 114, 172

T

TAUNTON Church tower (St. Mary's), 475
Temple at Eleusis, section of, 19
Temple of Jupiter at Agrigentum, with plan of same, 19
Temples, lighting of Greek: four sketches, 19
Terra cotta works in Italy—details from Bologna and Ferrara: three sketches, 415
Theatre, Olympic, London, 606; longitudinal section of, 618; plan, 603
Tile pavement, Caprarola, 303
Tomb, altar, in Exeter Cathedral, Early English: four sketches, 54
Tomb of Bonzi family, Rome, 556
Tower of La Martorana, Palermo, 427
Tower of St. Mary's Church, Taunton: 15th century, 475
Town-houses (model) for middle classes, view and plan, 567

V

VENICE, Palazzo Rezzonico at, 126
Ventilator at Prince's Theatre Royal, Glasgow, section of, 74
Ventilation, sketch illustrative of a simple plan of, 496

W

WINDOW, decorated, Ware Church, Herts, 426
Window from Florence, 317
Window glazing, forms for, four sketches, 103, four additional sketches, 127
Window of Palace at Pisa, 114
Windows, Hurwood's patent for moving, two sketches, 139
Workhouse, London city, 378; general block plan of same, 400

Y

YARMOUTH free schools, 294.

The Builder

| NUMBER 309. | VOLUME FOR 1849. | SATURDAY, JAN. 6. |

BEGINNING THE YEAR.

E ended our last volume with thanks for favours received, and with a claim on the confidence and kind consideration of our readers. We begin the new one with promises of continued endeavours to improve the character of our journal in all its departments, and so to merit increased support on the part of the public.

Our field is a large one, and, well tilled, cannot fail to yield abundant good. We have pressed into the service fresh labourers, shall avail ourselves of all new discoveries and appliances, and, labouring earnestly and continuously ourselves, shall look with confidence to the time of harvest.

The present would seem to be a turning point in the progress of art amongst us. The cry of " forward," uttered at first by timid voices and with the fear of powerful opponents before their eyes, is now heard loudly in more quarters than one, and begins to have echoes. We have been stationary too long, if not going *backwards*, say they; our arts are a disgrace to us, and the apathy and ignorance in respect of them, which exist even in the upper classes, deplorable and degrading. See what our forefathers did in architecture: look at the beautiful parish churches and noble cathedrals thickly spread over the country. And shall we, far, far advanced before them as we are in knowledge, and in science which is systematized knowledge, with powers and means within our control of which they never dreamt, pronounce ourselves inferior to them, insist on imitation, and forbid even the attempt to advance? Is art never again to have vitality, and shall we not ourselves strike one blow for progress?

To aid this movement will be our province and our pleasure. Precedent should be an aid, not a trammel,—our servant, not our gaoler; nor shall we relax in our efforts to obtain improved and extended education in art, and to obtain for art that better appreciation which, as a mighty *teacher*, it would have were it so understood.

The improvement of dwellings; sanitary arrangements; construction; decoration; the literature of art and science; architectural jurisprudence; will receive constant attention; nor shall we cease to afford our readers the earliest intelligence on all matters likely to interest them, looking, as heretofore, into all parts of the United Kingdom for information and instruction. Our country friends may make this part of our work very complete by brief communications from their separate localities.

We have in preparation illustrations of various buildings now in progress, and shall be glad to have our attention directed to others.

THE NORTH PORCH OF THE REDCLIFFE CHURCH, AND "NIL DESPERANDUM."

EVERY one has heard of the " Red cliffe " Church at Bristol, St. Mary's; and most of our readers, probably, have seen it. Piety, science, art, literature, and mystery, have jointly and severally put their mark upon this beautiful structure, and made it an object of interest to so many classes of minds, that there are few buildings in this country which have a fame so world-wide.

Founded by one Bristol merchant, completed by another, and re-edified by a third, the Christian (even if careless of material beauty) may view it, beside its holy purpose, as a noble monument of the stint-less devotion of men in those times,—of men who thought not of the " nicely calculated less or more," and considered no expenditure short of the extreme of their power, no personal efforts and sacrifice, sufficient offering in the cause of the Great Good;—a spirit, let us say in passing, not extinct in our days, and often guided by higher considerations, perhaps, than actuated some at the period of which we are speaking.

The antiquary, the architect, the man of taste, find in it an exhibition of skill and inventive power of the highest character, producing, as a result, extraordinary beauty: it is to them also an invaluable autograph—the autograph of a past time, speaking loudly, and not uninstructively, to the present. Further, there are models for the draughtsman, an involved history to engage the attention of the archæologist, and a peculiarity in the joining together of the work of different periods at the west end, which increases the difficulty of the disentanglement.

Then, for the poet, the student of our literature, the investigator of mind in all its strange and startling phases, the biographer, the philanthropist, the lover of romance, its connection with the wondrous boy who perished in his pride—the unhappy Chatterton, who, wanting so little, lost so much, an imperishable and pure renown—has made it a shrine demanding a pilgrimage.

Circumstances have thus concurred to increase the interest, as we have already said, attaching to Redcliffe Church, and it would seem that the list is to be lengthened. A mystery in our prosaic days,—in days when *everything* can be explained to meanest capacities, whether it be the cause of an earthquake, the ruin of a nation, or the advent of bad weather, is a rarity: yet, lo! another mystery arises to throw its attractive mist around St. Mary's: a mist which, by exciting attention and awakening curiosity, makes obvious while it shrouds.

We need not now tell our readers of the miserable and much to be deplored condition of the fabric in question, for we have done so before; or that a certain amount of restoration has been effected at the east end; that there is an energetic restoration committee; the chairman of which, Mr. Proctor, has devoted himself hand and mind to the object in view; or that a " Canynge Society " has been established to aid in the good work, with the present (and three times before) mayor of Bristol, Mr. John Kerle Haberfield, at its head.

On the 22nd of June Mr. Proctor received a letter, signed " Nil Desperandum," following out a suggestion which had been made that the restoration of the church might be effected by inducing individuals to undertake distinct portions, and inquiring if the committee would obtain drawings from their architect for the restoration of the north porch, and estimated from three respectable contractors in Bristol, for the execution of the work, to enable the writer to judge whether or not it would be in his power to provide sufficient funds to carry it out. The letter pointed out the mode of correspondence to be adopted, made secrecy an express condition of his contribution, stipulated that no effort should be made to discover him (his letters were to be seen by none but the chairman), and enclosed 20l. as an evidence of his sincerity. The committee of course gladly fell into his views, and the required tenders were obtained. The amount of the lowest was 2,500l.—a large sum when the size of the structure is considered,—indeed, larger than it should have been, resulting probably from the difficulty of estimating rightly the cost of the carving; and when " Nil Desperandum" was informed of it, he at once replied, that it so far exceeded his anticipation that he could not engage to proceed under it. He offered, however, to furnish a certain sum of money, and to make a further contribution in the course of a year, and more afterwards, if the committee would undertake to expend it in the shape of Caen stone and labour, under the direction of their architect.

Almost at the same time the committee found another coadjutor, where perhaps they would scarcely have looked for it. Mr. Richard Rowe, a liberal dissenter, addressed a letter to the chairman, offering,—as an evidence of his belief that the recent changes by which Bristol is made a free port will tend to restore the trade of the city, and at the same time to shew his appreciation of the zeal of the Redcliffe committee, and of the voluntary principle adopted,—to bring, at his own cost, in a vessel belonging to him, 100 tons of stone from Caen freight free! Without going further into details, suffice it to say that the money came, a cargo of stone was bought in Caen, and was freighted by Mr. Rowe; an able foreman, with others, well used to Gothic work, was engaged, and, quietly under cover, they are now proceeding vigorously, carving corbels and canopies, and storing them up ready for spring weather, when they will begin to set.

Annexed we give an engraving of the porch restored, as seen from the north-east, and

* See page 7.

showing a portion of the nave on one side and of the tower above. The body of the church, some of our readers will remember, is in the Perpendicular style throughout, with some of the details, especially in the transepts, little removed from the decorated. The porch in question is pure decorated, and this is most curiously connected with the church by an inner porch of beautiful Early English character.

To affix precise dates to the parts is not easy, nor have we here set ourselves that task. We shall content ourselves with saying, that though MSS. state that "a church was built [commenced] to our Lady of Redcliffe, by Sir Simon de Burton, in the year 1292," it is certain that a church was here previously. The inner porch is usually considered a remaining part of Burton's work, but might very well belong to a somewhat earlier period. Part of the tower is also ascribed to him. William Canynge, the elder, according to the received accounts, completed Burton's church by 1376, or soon after.

In 1442 or 1445, the spire was struck by lightning,* and, in falling, greatly ruined the body of the church so as to render re-edification necessary. This was done by William Canynge, the younger, to such an extent as to acquire for him the title of its founder.

Neither the builder of the north porch nor its exact date appears to be known. We should be disposed to attribute it to De Burton, who was Mayor as late as 1305, rather than to the elder Canynge, especially if, as seems likely, the body of the church was built by the latter much as we now see it, the re-edification by the younger Canynge being strictly a restoration. The upper part of the porch may have been injured when the spire fell.

The beauties of this work, the surprising variety of surface where "light and shade repose," which it presents, and the vigour and feeling exhibited in the carving, can be but feebly conveyed by any drawing. In shape the porch is a hexagon, 25 feet in diameter outside the walls, but being attached, only four of the sides and part of the fifth (next the tower) are exposed below: above, however, where it clears the inner porch, the whole of the hexagon is seen.† At each angle is a hexagonal buttress, of which four sides are seen, terminating above in one of square form, set angularly, on which was originally a large crocketed pinnacle, with four smaller pinnacles at the foot of it, as shewn in the view. Towards the south on the east side is a stairs' turret. This adjoins the inner porch, but belongs to the composition of the outer porch. A series of admirably designed canopies fill the lower part of a window in each face of the structure, and there are similar niches in the faces of the buttresses in continuation of this series, as well as in the lower story of them. When these were filled with sculptured figures (" cum ymaginibus regum operatis subtiliter in opere de frestone," as William Wyrcestre says), if these displayed the same skill as the figures in the corbels which supported them do, the effect must have been extremely striking. The whole is now a black decaying mass, but sufficient remains of the latter to prove their great merits.

The sculpture around the north (or principal) doorway, is unique in design, rich, and beauti-

* " St. Marr's Church has stood the test
    Of many a raging storms ;
    And though the lightning struck her crest,
    It stopt ashamed, and spared the rest,
    As if unwilling to repair
    A pile so holy and so fair."

† The height of the porch from the ground to the coping is 54 feet.

ful, but we want space for description. In the side next the turret there is a second doorway, very elegantly adorned with sculpture, and, strange to say, in the parallel face to this, or that immediately to the west of the principal entrance, there was a precisely similar doorway, now blocked up, but having the enrichments remaining.

Within there are several, curious points which would well repay discussion, but we must content ourselves at this moment with alluding to the singular luxuriance of fancy which the carving displays. Every boss in the groined vaulting,* every patera, every corbel, is different,—some of them of very remarkable design. The whole appears to have been elaborately painted and gilt, though now totally obscured, carrying whitewash a quarter of an inch thick.

Dallaway, in his curious work " William Wyrcestre Redivivus," says,—" To propose that this portico should be restored to its pristine beauty, would be to indulge in a dream : because, although I am confident that ingenious masons might be found, competent to the undertaking, the funds of the trustees of the church do not equal the resources of Parliament. Besides, in a few years, the mischief would renew; and it would be as easy a task to remove Vesuvius, and to set it in the sea, as these pyramids [the neighbouring glass-houses], which, not like other volcanos—have a certain cessation, but continue to throw out volumes of dense smoke, both by day and night."

The dream, however, seems now more than likely to become a reality. The reason which the worthy gentleman gave for not attempting the restoration, reminds us of Billy Black, in the farce, who couldn't see the good of washing his face, since it would be dirty again to-morrow.

The circumstances attending the restoration of this part of the church have naturally excited much interest in the neighbourhood. On one day, Nov. 25, four of the Bristol papers, Felix Farley's Journal, the Mercury, the Mirror, and the Times, contained able leading articles on the subject; and, since then, some very cleverly written " conjectures" have appeared in the last-named paper, shadowing out individual inhabitants of the city as the probable benefactor. For our own part, we make no attempt to solve the mystery—

" A worthy act declares a worthy wight ;"
and we trust that the good example which he has set may be followed by others, to the extent of their ability.†

The motto of all now concerned in the church—and we commend it to other restoration - committees engaged throughout the country—is, with strong faith in it—

    Nil Desperandum.

               GEORGE GODWIN.

* Above the vaulting is an apartment, known as the " Muniment-room," lighted by a series of openings seen in the view, wherein were (and are) the chests whence Chatterton, as he asserted, took the once-disputed MSS.

† Hear Rowle. " One one's Ladies Chyrche."
    " As one a bylle one eve sittynge,
    At oufte Ladie's Chyrche mouche wonderynge,
    The counynge handieworke so fyne,
    Han well nighe dazeled mine eyne ;
    Quod I ; some counynge fairie bande
    Yreer'd this chapelle in this lande ;
    Pulle well I wote so fine a syghte
    Was ne yreer'd of mortall wighte.
    Quod Trouthe; thou hackest knowleachynge ;
    Thou forsoth ne wotteth of the thynge.
    A Rev'rend Padre, William Canynge hight,
    Yreered uppe this chapelle brighte ;
    And eke another In the Towne.
    Where glassie bubblynge Trymme doth roun.
    Quod I ; no doubte for all he's given
    His soule will certes goe to heaven.
    Yea, quod Trouth ; than gee thou home,
    And see thou doe as hee hath donne.
    Quod I ; doubte, that can ne bee ;
    I have ne gotten mackes thre.
    Quod Trouthe ; as thou hast got, give almes-dedes soe ;
    Canynges and Gaunts culde doe ne moe."

TRAVELLING NOTES IN ITALY.

BY AN ARCHITECT.

POMPEII.

THE position of the city is superb,—unsurpassed by any in Italy,—worthy even of Greece. On one side Vesuvius, sweeping up out of the rich plain, with its long heaving wave-like outline, and sending forth its cloud of smoke by day and vomiting out flame at night; to the south the delicious Bay of Naples, with its headlands and islands; and to the east the remoter Apennines. Looking from the FORUM, the files of Doric columns, broken, yet still erect, fall into magnificent combinations with the distant mountains mellowed into the softest aerial purple. All that the picture requires is vastness in the architectural foreground. How superior this to any scene amid the ruins of imperial Rome ! There the columns are few and scattered, blackened, half-buried, or built up, and never viewed in combination with a fine mountain distance. Before the great eruption which destroyed the city, the sea is thought to have washed the walls, though now some miles distant.

I had been so impressed at a former visit with the diminutiveness of every thing at Pompeii, that I was now surprised to find objects so large. The streets, if they fall short of our ideas of ancient magnificence, are as wide as most of those . of modern Rome ; usually straight and intersecting at right angles. They are paved with the massive polygonal blocks of basalt, commonly found on such fragments of the old Roman ways as still exist in Italy. The traces of cart and chariot wheels are very distinct, and sometimes worn deep into the stone. Unlike the streets of modern Italy, these are furnished with a raised footway, and in the secondary streets, blocks, placed two or three in a row, enabled pedestrians to pass more conveniently . from one footway to another ; an arrangement more important, when, after heavy rains, the narrow roadway became a mere torrent of water. Occasionally you may see a perforation in the curb-stone, supposed to be intended for securing a horse while the rider might be within the adjacent house. Some of the footways are paved with a kind of concreted mosaic, like that now known in Italy as the " Opera Venesiana." At one house, opposite the entrance, the word " HAVE " (for " AVE "), inscribed in large letters on the pavement, welcomed the approaching visiter to the mansion.

The profuse display of mosaic, frescoes, arabesques, and ornamental bronze utensils, all found within the third part of a provincial town, is very remarkable, and gives a high idea of the wealth and luxury, and devotion to art that once existed in these cities of the Campagna. How different would be the result were a modern town, even in this land of art and artists, to be hereafter disinterred ! The entire towns of Portici and Castellamare, should they be buried under some future eruption of the still smoking crater, would not furnish forth so many objects of artistic curiosity as one of the secondary streets of Pompeii.

We are also struck, on examining the larger houses, with the fondness for gardens, fountains, flowers, and the life " al fresco" which distinguished the epicurean inhabitants of these doomed cities ; a taste which Greek colonists probably brought with them from the East, and which is proved by the paintings still existing in the ancient tombs of Egypt to have been equally prevalent among the Egyptians.† A patrician's mansion, instead of the long suite of saloons which you find in a modern Italian palazzo, presented a series of colonnaded courts, uncovered halls, and little architectural gardens, all opening upon, or

* In some of the broader streets of Naples, a light bridge thwarts the central part of the way for the same purpose.

† " The ancient plans of gardens show that the Egyptians were not less fond than our ancestors of mathematical figures, straight walks, architectural decorations, and vegetable avenues; and that we thoroughly entered into the idea of seclusion and safety suggested by inclosures within inclosures. It has been remarked that in some old English places that were almost as many walled compartments within, as our apartments within doors : the same may be said of Egyptian country-houses. This principle of seclusion, and an excessive love of uniform arrangement, are remarkably displayed in the plan of a large square garden, which is engraved in Rosellini's work. Here

    " Grove nods at grove, each alley has a brother,
    And half the platform just reflects the other."

Wathen's Arts and Antiquities of Ancient Egypt.

MOSAICS FROM POMPEII.

visible from each other. Such was the "house of Sallust," in its original state (for it seems to have undergone successive alterations by its owner); as you stood in the central court you had a small garden before you, and another on each side. Some examples occur of a stone channel for flowers round the lip of a reservoir or tank; an idea which might be happily introduced into modern gardening. In one garden there were four parterres round a central fountain, each presenting a regular pattern, formed by similar channels made with tiles. The fountains were often attached to the wall, and incrusted with rustic work, or coloured mosaic, or with shells, the several architectural members being marked by the use of different shells. Fountains consisting of a simple stone water-spout were also common in the streets.

The general arrangement of the houses reminds the eastern traveller of the dwellings of Damascus, and of the mosques of Cairo, an arrangement which was introduced with their architecture by the Moors into Spain. Instead of rooms lighted by windows, the Pompeian house consisted of large recesses, or *ulcoves*, (the very word has been borrowed from the Saracens), open to the central court ; — one always opposite the entrance, and others on each side, the fountain sparkling in the sunshine, being in the centre, and the deep cerulean sky forming the roof. Such a mansion in such a delicious climate, would be equally well adapted to the dreamy inactivity—the *dolce far niente* life of the Asiatic, and to the gay conviviality of the more mercurial Greek.

The shops are small, and open towards the street. A counter extends along the front, leaving a narrow entrance. Those for the sale of oil are recognised by the immense oil jars imbedded in the solid counter. The *sills* of the shop fronts are of stone, and the groove for the shutters is still seen. Doors turned on bronze pivots, inserted in the pavement and the doorhead. The lintels of openings were of wood : the original ones having been burnt into charcoal during the catastrophe, they have been replaced by the excavators with new.

The fronts of the principal houses are of stone, but brick and stucco were the ordinary materials employed in the city. Stone columns were even occasionally stuccoed. The lower third of the column was painted red or yellow, those in one atrium or court being dissimilar to those in another. Painted capitals are rare. There is one instance of a mode of construction like our *brick-nogging.* F. ingeniously conjectured that this was adopted in repairing the damage caused by the earthquake which preceded the fatal eruption, in order to avert future injury from such a cause. The mode of constructing the semi-hypaethral roof of the atrium is shown in the paintings on the walls. There was a large central opening in the roof over the square basin or *impluvium* in the middle of the pavement. The margin or curb of this opening was formed by the main timbers crossing each other at right angles, and these supported the ends of the joists which carried the roof.

In the suburban house of Diomed we have, perhaps, an example of the ordinary Pompeian villa. Here a large garden court is inclosed by a corridor of piers and square interspaces. Painted chambers, or rather recesses, open upon one side of this court. These are the apartments which Bulwer, in his "Last Days of Pompeii," gives to the wealthy Diomed's daughter Julia. This house had three stories. Under the corridor runs a suite of cellars, lighted by loops from above. Here, resting against the wall, still stand the *amphorae* as the owner left them. The fact that these *amphorae* were filled with ashes may give some idea of the insinuating, irresistible nature of the showers of volcanic matter which entombed this devoted city. In the courtyard above were found two or three of the few skeletons that have come to light during the excavation. A key was found near one of them, but it had no wards, and may have been merely an emblem of office.

The BATHS, though diminutive in comparison with the immense *thermae* of Caracalla and Diocletian at Rome, are, from their completeness, far more interesting to the antiquary than

those ruined piles. If the HOUSES of Pompeii remind us of those of Oriental cities, so do the BATHS recall the elaborate system of bathing which has prevailed in the east from time immemorial. In both we find the same gradation of temperature as you proceed from the *frigidarium* to the inner chamber, containing the hot bath. This system, if originally invented in Italy, was probably first transplanted into Egypt after its conquest by the Romans, and there it must have come into universal use, since we hear that when the Saracens, under Amrou, took Alexandria, there were no fewer than 4,000 baths there. In one chamber stands a bronze brazier for charcoal, as large as a bedstead.

The mode of heating the *Caldarium* is obvious on a glance at the construction, and is very well contrived. The walls and pavement are lined with tiles, leaving a narrow interval or flue all round the chamber, through which permeated the hot air or vapour from the hypocaust. Saloons were sometimes warmed in the same manner.

The plan of the Temple of Isis was borrowed with her worship from Egypt. Instead of standing out to public gaze on the Forum, the temple and its bald priests were shut up within a small court, where they enjoyed all that seclusion and privacy so necessary in celebrating the obscene orgies of the Isiac mystery.

The designs and patterns of the painted walls and tesselated pavements are very varied and admirable. Black and white tesselation is common. One curious mosaic, in colour, represents Theseus slaying the Minotaur,—and this occupies the centre of a labyrinth of lines very much like a plan of the Labyrinth at Hampton Court, which was, no doubt, borrowed from Italy. In footways, a cheap kind of mosaic was much in vogue, consisting of a kind of "Opera Veneziana," with a simple pattern traced out by means of small diamonds of white inserted in the ground.*

Outside the city gate were the tombs bordering the highway, as at Rome. One of the

* Sketches of a few of these are annexed.

largest consisted of a circular mass with attached columns, raised upon a square basement. One tomb still retains its marble dwarf door, secured by irons. Near the gate are circular alcoves with stone benches, where pedestrians and loungers might repose and exchange the gossip of the day. The city walls, though low, are very massive, slightly receding inwards externally as they ascend, by means of offsets. Within the portal are arched lateral recesses.

I visited a house then in progress of excavation, and observed, in section, the several layers of ashes as they had fallen in succession. The paintings on the lower part of the wall had been concealed, but not injured, by a bed of small white ashes, but above this, a layer of black ash, which had probably fallen hot, had changed the deep vermillion into a dull Indian red. Here you might better conceive the brilliant effect of the Pompeian mode of decorating walls when in its pristine beauty. The designs and patterns were rich and uncommon; the colours, which were still fresh and vivid, had been laid on with a free and vigorous pencil. The house had probably been decorated by an artist of repute, for the owner appears to have cut away some of the paintings from the walls after the destruction of the city.

"Is it not rather surprising that rooms so mean in their dimensions should have contained works of such elegance?—that friezes scarcely a foot high should embrace such a world of fancy? Every extravagance that Vitruvius condemns in the grotesque enters here. The human and the brute forms are blended fantastically; the decorations remind us of the ancient elephants dancing on the tight rope; the landscapes are but the caperings of a sportive genius, and the architecture runs as mad as the Chinese."—*Forsyth.*

Nearly all the utensils in use at Pompeii appear to have been of bronze, as they were in ancient Egypt. A large collection of them, found in course of excavation, are now in the Museum at Naples. One of the most curious objects there is a little portable cooking apparatus, beautifully wrought in bronze, having its grate surrounded by a boiler after the most approved modern mode,—the whole scarcely larger than a folio volume. This elegant toy may perhaps once have formed the ornament of some rich lady's boudoir.

Pompeii was buried under falling ashes; Herculaneum, being nearer the crater, was submerged by a flood of running lava, which, of course, when cool, hardened into solid rock. Hence, to disinter the former, you have merely to remove the superincumbent ashes; while, to reach the ruins of Herculaneum, you must mine through the lava rock. As the excavations at Pompeii could thus be carried on with far greater facility and less cost than those at Herculaneum, the latter was soon abandoned, and the staff of Government explorers confined their operations to Pompeii. You descend into the theatre of Herculaneum by a shaft, and as you pass round its silent shadowy galleries, lighted by your torch, with the lava rock above, below, and around, you can better realise the awful catastrophe which entombed the city. In other respects, Herculaneum offers little of fresh interest to one who has already examined Pompeii.

ACCIDENT IN A CHURCH FROM STEAM PIPES.—At St. Ann's Church, Manchester, on Sunday morning last, about 35 minutes after 10 o'clock, and soon after the commencement of Divine service, an accident of an alarming character occurred. The sacred edifice is heated by means of pipes containing hot water, and one of these, from some cause, burst with a report so loud and startling that many people rushed from their seats much alarmed. The report was followed of course by the emission of a great quantity of steam, and two Sunday school boys, sitting near to the pipe, were scalded about the face. The remedy for these explosions is one of those points on which scientific men have not made up their minds, and "when doctors disagree, who shall decide?" It is to be hoped, however, that in public buildings, where this mode of warming is adopted, while the danger exists care will be taken not to let the apparatus get out of order. —*Manchester Examiner and Times.*

ON MONUMENTAL ARCHITECTURE.*

THE sentence to which the fables of mythology have doomed the unburied in this world, to wander restless on the Stygian banks for a century, ere the ruthless Charon would ferry them across the flood to their future abodes in the regions of Elysium, is but the poetical realization of feelings which are natural to mankind in every stage of society.

A reverence for the dead, and an affection for their memory, have ever caused the rites of sepulture to be held as a sacred duty, and intuitively suggest some means to mark the place of burial, in order to preserve it from unwitting sacrilege, to rescue from oblivion, and to cherish in the minds of surviving friends the memory of the deceased.

A pillar of stone, afterwards rudely carved, or a raised mound of earth, sufficed for these purposes, and as the most simple and natural means, have been the types for sepulchral structures in all early stages of civilization. We find their remains even now abounding in most countries, having outlived many a more ambitious monument of later times.

Coeval, and almost as extensive, was the custom of depositing with the dead their arms, ornaments, or utensils, on the supposition that they would require them in their future state of existence, and it has been continued down almost to modern times, long after the idea which gave it birth had completely vanished.

The striking resemblance, however, that the relics of the northern Celtic nations of Europe bear to those found on the borders of the Mediterranean, hardly discovering the difference that might be expected from their distinct national peculiarities, may perhaps be traced to some such means of communication as the commerce of the roving Syrian or Phœnician traders might afford. True it is that in the more opulent south, at times, these monuments attained an importance from their size, that the ruder cairns and barrows of the north never reached. Herodotus, for instance, mentions one raised to the memory of Alyattes, king of Lydia, which was three-quarters of a mile in circumference; and they were often surmounted by a pillar, or planted with trees, to increase their effect.

As yet art lent not its aid to add to the impressions which men sought to convey by size alone, and they vainly strove to rival in magnitude the lofty mountains that surrounded them. But when civilization advanced, and architecture, uniting character to utility, with its sister arts, painting and sculpture, afforded a medium for the expression of thought, and disclosed its capability of creation, other means of impression then opened to their view —proportion and symmetry were found to possess elements of grandeur and beauty beyond what mere vastness could produce; and in *monumental architecture*, deeply rooted as was its origin in the universal feelings and affections of man, this new language, as it were, soon discovered its influence, and was preserved, by the very solemnity of its purpose, from all affectation and meretricious display. Perhaps more than in any other branch of art, it reveals, simply and earnestly, the thoughts, actions, manners, national characteristics, the religion, superstitions, and mythologies of the people, with their progress in refinement and art, their costumes, implements, and weapons, link after link in the chain of the universal history of man, which else had perished with the lost records, or been mingled in hopeless confusion among the contradictory traditions of successive generations.

The Egyptians, who made the first advances in this march of civilization, have left many wondrous examples of their monumental architecture, impressed with the solemn and mysterious character of the superstitions under which their priestcraft ruled them, and characterised by the extreme solicitude with which every access to them was concealed; while, nevertheless, the utmost magnificence was lavished on the interiors, although intended not for mortal inspection. In the valley of Bibau El Molook, each king, from the commencement of his reign, carved for himself his royal sepulchre,—whose rude portal once passed, gallery after gallery led to chambers now stretching onwards in the rock, now branching out on either side; the whole adorned with paintings and hieroglyphics; the roof sustained by colossal pillars; till at last the golden hall, with its vaulted ceiling, displayed the costly sarcophagus, in which lay enshrined the monarch, with his exploits emblazoned on the walls around him.

Asia-Minor, in many places, as at Myra and Petra, presents numerous instances of a similar class of sepulchre, excavated in the precipitous sides of the bold hills, but differing in that the decoration was reserved for the exterior,—the substance of the stone being carved into architectural façades, with attached orders, porticoes, pediments, sculptured groups, and inscriptions, or with square mullions and panelled fronts, presenting the Greek type of a wooden construction. At times, a huge block, that may have rolled into the valleys, has been fashioned into shape for the same purpose. These monuments have a peculiar and striking effect, harmonising well with the scenery around. Similar façades, but with the orders of their own fanciful architecture, are to be found among the Hindoos.

The most general modes of burial among the ancients being those of embalming the body and depositing it in a sarcophagus, or burning it and collecting the ashes in cinerary urns,—where no rocks afforded the opportunity for excavation, tombs were constructed of sufficient size to contain a chamber in which ceremonies might be performed, and which were often ornamented with mosaics or paintings, and the front of the sarcophagus usually displayed some bas-relief or inscription. An idea of the magnificence of some of these structures may be gathered from the description of the tomb of Mausolus, by Pliny:—It was 411 feet in circumference; 140 feet in height; surrounded by thirty columns, above which rose a pyramid with a marble chariot on the summit. The sculptures, brought to England from Bodroum, are supposed to have belonged to it.

At Palmyra there are some peculiar sepulchral towers, of considerable height, divided into stages with bas-reliefs in semicircular recesses, representing the parents reclining, with their children standing around them. These, rising above the desert, have an imposing appearance.

In Greece and Italy the tombs were usually ranged along the sides of the streets approaching the cities (within which burial was not permitted); thus affording a ready access to the mourning trains which annually repaired to hold a feast to the memory of the dead, in the enclosure which, for this purpose, surrounded each monument, and also impressing the stranger with due reverence for their departed great men. The Via Appia, in its course through the solitude of the vast campagna, displays on either side the ruins of those monuments that once graced its approach to the imperial city, which now, picturesquely covered with rank herbage and festoons of luxuriant creepers, and spoiled of their treasures to enrich the museums and galleries of Europe, still attest to what magnificence they attained in those days, when the wealth of conquered provinces swelled the luxury of Rome. Some were the sepulchres of a family, with all its retainers and slaves; and the spacious chamber requisite for such a purpose, with the small niches for each cinerary urn, obtained them the name of Columbaria. The mausoleum of Hadrian, shorn of its columns and statues and converted into a fortress, having withstood the effects of violence and siege for ages, still stands like a watch-tower guarding over the city. The tapering pyramid of Caius Cestius, once covered with marble, gleamed brightly in the sunlight, and now, at its feet, nestles the more humble Protestant cemetery. The tomb of Cecilia Metella is also an imposing and beautiful monument: its sarcophagus, an exquisite work, is in the court of the Farnese palace. In general, the objects contained within the tombs merit attention. The sepulchral Cippi urns, inscriptions as well as the sarcophagi, display works of sculpture, sometimes of great beauty of execution, representing the fables of mythology, historical events and traditions; the exploits and battles of the deceased, busts, bas-reliefs, portraits, &c. The sarcophagus

* Read before the Architectural Association, by Mr. Seddons.

taken from Scipio's tomb—a chaste and exquisite adaptation of the Doric order—adorns the gallery of the Vatican.

But these monuments, beautiful though they be, and expressive of their purpose, and from which many a lesson of simplicity and solemnity of character may be gathered, still speak of the superstition under which the age laboured—their emblems are mournful, they speak of death as a deprivation of the joys of life, and a bereavement to their friends; they tell of the history of the past, but of no hope in the future; all beyond the grave was shrouded from their view by the mists of uncertainty and superstition. The reversed torch, skulls, and implements of the charnel-house, and idle fables of mythology, but ill befit the sacred character of the tomb. But when Christianity dawned on the world, and at first the new faith was professed amid persecution and derision, they yet hopefully laid the martyr to his rest in the simple catacomb, and carved above the cheerful emblems of their religion, and death was to them a welcome guest. Hence sprung another class of monumental architecture, which, if it lacked the material beauty of refined Greece, or the magnificence of Rome, spoke more to the heart and less to the sense; and when at length Christianity triumphed over Paganism, and the clouds of superstition were dispelled, the church gathered its members around and within it, the dead as well as the living, and there lay the crowned monarch, the mitred bishop, and mailed warrior, their hands lifted in prayer, reposing calmly as if but in sleep. The cross, the emblem of their faith, the palm branch and olive, the signs of victory, carved upon the tomb, all pointing to the more hopeful character of their religion. This spirit of Christianity among the chivalrous Teutonic nations of northern Europe, and in the hands of the masonic fraternity of artists, was embodied in their conception of ecclesiastical architecture, which, as the visible church on earth, in its perfect unity of design, soared to heaven in imitation of its prototype. The monumental architecture likewise partook of the same impulse, and they both advanced together to their full development, mutually enhanced by the connection; for the simple headstone and slab of bold design, in the same style as the details of the cathedral, extended its architectural character beyond the immediate walls; and within, the panelled altar tombs, with their rich canopies, added to the effect of the interior, increasing the playful distribution of light and shade, breaking the flatness of the walls, and by the colour and gilding with which they were often decorated, sparkling like gems amidst the grey columned aisles, whose clustered shafts needed but the reflected tints that streamed from the painted windows upon them, and thus was the richness harmoniously distributed throughout the whole.

In England but few of the mediæval monuments of a date anterior to the twelfth century remain, and those are of a simple character, often as it were but the covers to the stone coffins, narrowing gradually from the head to the feet, and sometimes ridge-shaped, with crosses carved upon them. Their proportions are generally good, and the mouldings rich and bold. In the early part of the twelfth century effigies of ecclesiastics, and, in the latter part, of knights in armour, appear, as yet, on very low tombs; still in general the covers of the coffins sunk beneath the pavement. In the thirteenth century they were often placed under arched recesses in the wall, which at first were plain and obtusely pointed, and later equilateral and richly foliated, surmounted by finials, with pinnacled buttresses carried up at the angles: they harmonise well with the architecture of the church, even more so, perhaps, than those which were afterwards placed between the piers of the nave. The monument of Sir James Douglas, in Douglas Church, is a fine and characteristic example.

In the fourteenth century, the altar or table tombs, with their cumbent effigies, placed in an isolated position in the church, became the type of the monuments in all those countries where the Gothic architecture flourished. Their simple appropriate character, chaste and elegant design, with the abundant variety and tasteful application of the ornament with which they were decorated, devoid of the exuberance and profusion of minute detail, which prevailed at a later period, with the sculptured figures upon them, reposing as it were from the turmoil of their earthly life, with a calm and cheerful countenance, the hands raised in a suppliant attitude, and sometimes the husband and wife lying side by side, not to be separated even by death; clad in the ecclesiastical robes, or the armour and costume of the period, with angels often supporting the head, and the feet resting on the heraldic animal of their armorial bearings,—all mark them as the most beautiful and perfect of sepulchral monuments, whether viewed in themselves or in their relation to the edifice they adorn. Their material is often of the richest quality, and the brilliant colouring of the enameling on the trappings and shields and inlaid bronze bands of black letter inscriptions within the mouldings, contrast finely with the grey tone of the marble monument, and shew the judicious application of these effective enrichments.

The tombs of Sir Oliver Iugam and Sir Roger and Margaret de Boys, in Ingam Church, Norfolk, of King John in Worcester Cathedral, and of John Beaufort, Duke of Somerset, and his duchess, in Wimborne Minster, which is of marble, and the effigies of alabaster, relieved with gold, are good and bold examples; as also that of the Black Prince in Canterbury Cathedral, whose effigy is of copper gilt, burnished, and enamelled with the utmost delicacy, on a rich tomb of grey marble, with a broad brass inscription plate let into the surbase mouldings; and in each panel round the sides of the tomb is a shield of enamelled brass, bearing the royal arms of France and England.

The canopies, which were often erected over these tombs, form a most picturesque and beautiful accessory, affording an opportunity for the display of that delicate lacework of tracery in which the Gothic architects took such delight; they were of various forms, some horizontal and attached to the pillars of the church; pyramidal or ogee shaped, such as the exquisite Percy shrine at Beverley; and in others rising in clustering pinnacles, with all the lightness of metal work, as from the graceful elliptic arch of Archbishop Bowet's shrine, York, and the monument of Sir Hugh de Spencer, Tewkesbury Church.

These canopies, at a later period, were extended, as it were, into Chantry chapels, surrounding the tombs with a protecting veil of gossamer tracery, numberless pendants hanging from the groined ceiling in intricate confusion. The Cathedral of Winchester is remarkably rich in these beautiful works, particularly those of the Bishops Fox, Wykeham, Waynefleet, and Beaufort. That to Isabel, Countess of Warwick, Tewkesbury Church, is a fine instance: they were formerly much more numerous than at present, having been destroyed by the Iconoclasts, and the only trace remaining being the small piscina in the wall. To royal or noble families Mortuary Chapels were often erected, in connection with the church, to contain their monuments, which cluster round the choir, like the rich jewels in a casket, elaborate in ornament to a degree unsuited to the more important structure. In the centre stands the tomb, enhanced by the richness of its enclosure, the banners of the family suspended above, and their armorial bearings forming a repeated theme for the sculptor's chisel and for the painted glass, which, throwing its mellowed light over the whole, completes the richness of effect. Of these, Henry the VII.'s Chapel, with its delicate panelling and fan-groined ceiling, is a magnificent specimen, as also Wolsey's tomb-house, St. George's Chapel, Windsor, and the Beauchamp Chapel, Warwick.

Sculpture, however, being an art which depends on the individual feeling of the artist for its expression, and not to be confined by the rules to which architecture was with advantage subjected by the freemasons, without detriment, although the general sentiments of the Gothic type are conveyed by these effigies, a certain stiffness of manner generally prevails in their attitudes and a want of individuality of character. In some instances, however, much grace and dignity, with a freedom in the disposition of the draperies, are to be found in English works of Gothic art, and a beneficial influence is attributable to the sculptors from Italy, who visited England at various times. The statue of Eleanor, Queen of Edward the First, in Westminster Abbey, is a work of great beauty, and even ideality of conception and delicacy of execution. Her expression is youthful and sweet, the hair flows down to her shoulders, the hands are disposed with ease, and the drapery falls in long and graceful folds, covering the feet.

The monument of Aymer de Valence unites the excellencies of sculpture with those of architecture. The effigy, with the beautiful kneeling angels at its head, the figures in the niches surrounding the tomb, together with the foliage of the canopy, are exquisite. The tombs of Henry the Seventh, and the brass effigy of the Countess of Richmond, his mother, by Torregiano, an Italian, are very fine. And the monument of Sir Francis de Vere, over whom four knights support his armour, on a tablet, is grand in conception and picturesque in effect.

In the vaults of S. Denis, near Paris, which contain the monuments of a long line of the monarchs of France, there are some beautiful examples of recumbent statues, which possess peculiar sweetness and grace.*

SHORT LEASES A SOCIAL EVIL.

THE importance of this subject, recently treated of in THE BUILDER,—"The Enfranchisement of Leasehold Tenures" over twenty years, has struck the attention of many who never before considered the evils inflicted on society at large by that pernicious custom of short leases.

Seeing that it is impossible to obtain building leases in or near the metropolis for longer periods than 80, 70, or 60 years, builders are compelled to accept them, and that, too, on the terms of the few great landlords, or to stop business and speculation; and in the valuable trading localities, or fashionable quarters, it is not unusual to make costly erections on 50, 40, and even 30 years' terms.

It is manifest that houses raised on such foundations cannot be built with the same solidity as if the duration of the lease were longer—and that rents must be higher in proportion as the annuity is curtailed.

But the evil is worse as regards tenants on half-elapsed leases, which may have, say 20 or 30 years to run. In such cases, renewal being next to impossible, unless at a premium amounting to a fee-simple purchase, the occupier, if he be a man of business, and prosperous, scruples not to disburse on his shop or country-house large sums, the produce of his thrift; or if a gentleman of fortune, and his mansion occupies an eligible position—this latter thinks nothing of laying out thousands in order to secure a fitting town mansion. But as prosperity in commerce is fluctuating, and the position of the wealthiest not free from the chances of reverse, what was expended by the father to improve his convenience, or gratify his taste, may to the son in adversity be an object of great importance.

The sums, however, thus lavished are for ever gone from the tenant, and become the property of the more deeply-calculating lessor. A preference may be given of preoccupation or lease to the outgoing tenant, on expiration of his lease—but it is only a preference at rack rent, or the amount which the premises might fetch in the market.

Few indeed are the holdings on long lease, upon which large sums have not been expended by the occupiers; and yet fewer are the houses in London which are held on freehold tenure—there is hardly such a thing to be had.

For years past the corporations of London have been adding to their estates such properties, and thus extending the evil of short leases. This is not done overtly, indeed, for John Smith, or some other indifferent person, is deputed to attend the sale (lest the biddings should be swelled as against a public body), and to add the item to the colossal estate of the Vintners', or Merchant Tailors', or some other guild.

Such, too, is the practice of great proprietors, who are adding to already inflated rentals every thing attainable within the limits of our Babylon.

This was not always so; but within the

* To be continued.

ast century, the capital of a few noblemen has grown into leasehold principalities, and so well has the leasing practice told, that the body of moneyed oligarchs, compacted on a system, have engrossed pretty well all the *fixed capital* of the community so far as London is concerned.

The means of the multitude have been expended in fabrics, only to flow, through the lapse of two, or at most three generations, into the ocean (I fear not the Pacific one) of aristocratic abundance.

Surely this is not a beneficial result, that the few should be enriched and the multitude impoverished.

The greatest good for the greatest number is a modern maxim, but so rooted is the principle we are speaking of, and so systematized, that the people have no power to redress it. If one man object to three or five guineas a-foot, for building plots, besides paying largely for the old structure, another will be found to outlay his principal on the alluring site, and the landlord has the legal right to reserve or forestall. It is a LEAGUE (the league of wealth and power) against the nation, and nothing but an enactment of the Legislature can correct or redress it.

As your article of the 15th stated, Parliament found no difficulty in passing a law to enfranchise copyholds, because that grievous description of tenure affected the landed estates of the legislators. Copyholds were as much a private right of property as leaseholds, and there can be no just reason for continuing the widely injurious tenure on leases, any more than the now antiquated custom of exacting fines and heriots on the alienation of lands, or on the death of their proprietors.

As the enfranchisement of a copyhold tenure may be fairly estimated and requited in a money payment, so may the interest in a lease be estimated. by a valuation jury, or by any other equitable mode of purchase.

To the tenant in most instances the purchase would be an object of the deepest interest, while the lessor could not complain, as he too should have his equivalent in money to invest at large; and although perhaps not over one fourth part of the leaseholders would purchase the freehold of their occupations; still the practice of leasing out plots anew for building, on an extensive scale, would, by this plan, be effectually checked.

Of all the advantages, however, that must ensue from such an enfranchisement, the greatest would be the diffusion of fixed capital, the next the estoppal of the frightful *concentration of property* in a *few noble families*, who must in one more generation *clutch within their grasp the heritage* of the dispossessed families of London!

It must be apparent that the desired enfranchisement of leases will have the happiest influence on architecture—that substantiality will supersede economy, haste, and insecurity —that an Englisman may truly call his house his castle, and that the arts will be encouraged and exhibited in embellishment.

QUONDAM.

LIVERPOOL ARCHITECTURAL AND ARCHÆOLOGICAL SOCIETY.—A meeting of this society was held on the 20th December, Mr. J. A. Picton, vice-president, in the chair, when a paper was read by Mr. Hornblower on "Constructive Carpentry." The chairman observed, in pointing to various drawings and models, that lessons could be drawn from the defects as well as from the excellencies of the designs presented. Pointing to the roof of St. Paul's, Covent Garden, by Inigo Jones, he said that its construction was very poor indeed, and proved that Jones was no carpenter. He then called attention to the scientific principles upon which the old roofs were constructed, and observed the peculiarity that there was scarcely ever any iron used. Mr. Hay explained the causes of the failure of the roof of St. Peter's Church, at Rock Ferry. Mr. Reed explained the method of raising the Egyptian obelisks, as shown in Rossellini's plates of the tombs, and as actually executed in Hindostan 80 or 90 years since, witnessed and recorded by Major Russell.

LECTURE ON HERALDRY.

MR. W. PARTRIDGE has recently delivered some lectures on heraldry at various institutions, with the view chiefly of shewing that a knowledge of armorial ensigns is not solely the province of the antiquary or archæologist, but is important as a branch of general knowledge, and has a direct bearing on accuracy of taste in many of the arts and manufactures.

After noticing the discordant opinions respecting the origin of heraldry, some seeing the origin of it in the Phonetic alphabets of ancient India, others in the old Mexican sculptures, or in the double shields of Egypt, while others allow it to be not older than the Crusades, he traced it to the necessity for modes of distinction in the early stages of society, for the sake of order and discipline. He then took the two prominent features of heraldry, viz., shields and banners; the shield from its first and simplest construction among the early Greeks, its various shapes, sizes, and materials, from the fabulous, but magnificent shield of Achilles, by Homer,

> "The immense and solid shield,
> Rich, various artifice emblazed the field,"

down through the historic periods of Greece and Rome to the middle ages, showing the subject to be closely blended with the state of the arts and manufactures in all these ages and countries, and alluding to the superb shield made recently as a present from the King of Prussia to the Prince of Wales.

The banners of various ages, Pagan and Christian, the several abbeys, the crusades, rival roses, tournaments, chivalry, and the important uses of heraldry in war, in property, as a key to architecture, history, and poetry, are intimately mixed up with the progress of every age, shewing the importance of accuracy in all works, and the want of such knowledge in some glaring instances in architecture and painting. In some of the latter, the period of history intended was falsified, and in the former the effect of the edifice often injured by the heraldic devices being both ill designed and incorrect in themselves; making the importance of the subject even to practical men apparent.

LIME-ASH FLOORS FOR LABOURERS' COTTAGES.

THE following letter from Sir Shafto Adair to Mr. Henry Roberts, the honorary architect of the Society for the Improvement of the Condition of the Labouring Classes, contains a detailed statement of the mode adopted in Somersetshire, of forming lime and sand floors for farm-houses and cottages in agricultural districts:—

"I have received the particulars of the mode of forming the stucco floors for farm-houses and cottages, employed in Somersetshire, and supposing it may form an useful addition to your valuable suggestions for building labourers' cottages, I take the liberty of transmitting it to you. My informant is Mr. John Easton, an intelligent farmer, residing in the parish of Bradford, near Taunton.

Directions for making.—Take good washed sand, free from all earth, and the ashes of lime, as taken from the lime-kiln, in the following proportions, viz.—Two-thirds sand, and one-third lime-ashes. Mix them well together and let them remain in a body for three days, then temper the mortar, and form the floor with it, three inches thick; let this remain so formed three days, when it will bear treading by men: their shoes *must be without nails*. After it is well and equally trodden, beat it with a flat wood mallet every day for two weeks, until it is become hard, then use a little water on the surface, and smooth it with a trowel; after this keep the floor free of dirt or dust, sweeping it with a brush till it is quite hard and solid. I have known our best floors last for forty years. The price we pay is 5d. per square yard (9 feet) for labour, and 8d. per yard for materials; altogether, 1s. 1d." *

* A correspondent suggests that if a portion of pounded coke were used with the lime-ashes, it would render the floor exceedingly hard and durable.—ED.

THE BOSTON AQUEDUCT.

ON 25th October last, the extensive works for the conveyance of water from lake Cochituate (or Koo-chee-awa, an aboriginal term for "clear, beautiful, water"), to Boston, a distance of nearly 20 miles by the usual route, were so nearly completed that the water was formally let on with great ceremonial, through an ornamental fountain at Boston common, when it immediately sprung to a height of nearly 80 feet, amidst the gratulations of an immense multitude, assembled from all parts of the state of Massachusetts, and even of new England throughout. The day was one of jubilee, opening with the sound of bells and cannon, followed by military reviews, and civilian processions through triumphal arches, and closing with the spectacle of fireworks and illuminated fountains.

The undertaking was begun only two years and two months before, and was deemed one of peculiar difficulty. Indeed, it was only by the unintermitted labours of 3,500 men, chiefly Irish,—labourers, bricklayers, masons, blacksmiths, &c., inclusive,—most of whom carried on their labours, by turns of eight hours, night and day, that the difficulties were overcome and the work accomplished. One of the chief obstacles consisted of a long extent of quicksands, in the valley of the Snake brook, where five steam-engines, capable of raising 12,000,000 gallons 10 feet high in twenty-four hours, have been in constant employment. Another heavy labour in the same section of the contract consisted in the hardness of the porphyritic rock, which was estimated to have required seven times the usual quantity of powder and of labour in rock excavation. A work of still greater difficulty consisted of tunnel-excavation through two hills of equally hard rock, with water perpetually flowing through its seams and rents. The two tunnels measure 3,500 feet in length, and were excavated in eighteen months, through shafts seventy to seventy-five feet in depth, and by help of steam power.

The culvert is a brick oval in hydraulic cement, 6 feet 4 inches in height, and nearly 15 miles in length, extending only from the lake gate-house, which is of granite, to Brookline, where it ends in a reservoir of granite, whence the water is carried through cast-iron pipes to the town reservoirs. The other works in masonry are chiefly in granite, plain, but substantial. At Charles River, the aqueduct descends and re-ascends in form of two inverted syphons, connected with gate-houses on each height, and with a waste weir at the low level. Both culverts and pipes are principally under ground. The fall, throughout, is only about 3 inches to the mile; and the flow about 1¾ mile an hour. For further particulars as to the works extending from the culvert at Brookline to Boston, including the reservoirs at the termination, some of which stand at an elevation nearly as high as that of the lake itself, and whence the water will be forced by its own pressure through the highest building in the city,—we must refer to THE BUILDER, vol. v. p. 618. One of the reservoirs will contain two weeks' supply for the whole city, while the aqueduct is capable of discharging more than ten millions of gallons a day.

The small pipes which are to be run into each house at the public expense, and of which about 100,000 feet were laid at the opening, are of lead; and as the water is said to be of remarkable purity, it is to be hoped that the prudence of thus using a metal so apt to be acted on by water in the direct ratio of its purity has been well tested.

About three millions of dollars have been expended on these works, and about half a million more will be requisite to complete the reservoirs and distribute the water at South Boston. The town lands, it is said, will redeem the whole expense in a few years, independent of the rate charged to individuals, which is to be a very low one, till altogether withdrawn, as it is intended ultimately to be, if not deemed requisite as a source of increased income to the city.

The chief engineer of the main division of the works, namely, between the lake and Brookline, was Mr. E. S. Chesbrough, of Newton: resident engineer, Mr. McKean.

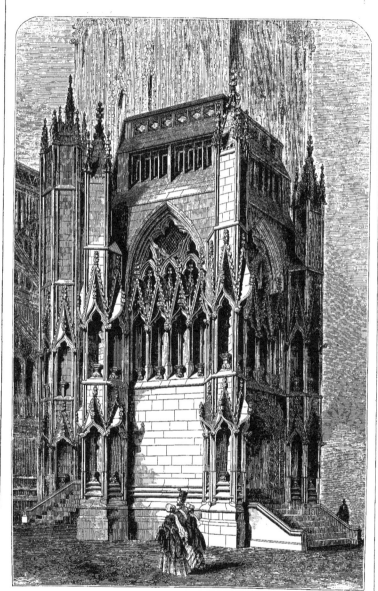

THE NORTH PORCH OF REDCLIFFE CHURCH, BRISTOL, RESTORED.

GEORGE GODWIN, F.R.S., ARCHITECT.

ON THE STUDY OF DESIGN FROM VEGETAL GROWTH.

DECORATIVE ART SOCIETY.

AT a late meeting of this society a paper was read by Mr. Laugher, "On the Study of Design from Vegetal Growth," illustrated by large sketches recently made in the Royal Botanic Gardens at Kew, by members of the society. This paper originated from a visit to Kew by some members of the society, who were influenced by a desire to trace the relation which form and colour, as applied in the decorative arts, hear to prototypes of vegetal growth, and also, by a wish to render practically evident, a mode by which simple and beautiful designs may readily be derived for the purposes of the industrial arts. The writer stated that an effort of this kind conveyed an assurance, that the members were fearlessly seeking an acquaintance with the beautiful in nature,—being self-dependent, without any other guides than their own reasoning faculties to enlighten their path. We may read often, and it was generally admitted, it was said, that whatever is excellent in art, is simply so from its harmonizing with natural results, more or less common to human experience. The conceptions and expressions of grand works in painting, sculpture, and the other arts, it was observed, derive their value from such an embodiment of scene, or action, or object, as shall have the harmonizing *probability* of a natural aspect rationally sustained throughout. It would be found, that it is this kind of probability which at once excites our sympathy, and induces those associative suggestions which are most impressive on the mind, whilst the reflective faculty, comparison—guided as it always is, and always must be, by human experience—constitutes the test-tube, in which refinement in art can properly be estimated.

It was said that, in an endeavour to recognise and develope the beautiful in sketches from vegetal leaves and stems, it is accordingly necessary to perceive and set forth, in the first place, a general probability of resemblance, and that comparison would afterwards enable us, individually, to trace the limits of application and value of purpose in each sketch. Under such restrictions and considerations, it was contended, that a broad and free translation of effect upon the sketch, rather than the actual minutiæ of microscopic imitation, should be attempted, for-as-much-as poetic ideality can only be developed under the boldest and simplest aspects of *probability*, so thereby art becomes more congenial with, more readily suited to, and more self-sufficient for, the grasp of the human intellect.

A reference was made to the improbabilities in art, as evinced in the romantic phantasies, the exuberant caprices, of Raffaelle's grotesques, on the one hand; and in the inane and meaningless incongruities, so unredeemingly applied, in our day, as decorations for manufactures, on the other. It was asked,—How much of probability can be discovered in the myriads of acanthusian nonentities in the *femoral* scroll, or "thigh-bone nausea" of the French school, with which every description of manufacture has of late years been infested? None, it was said; and that such should therefore be laid aside, as of a degraded class of conventionalities, being without sympathetic appeal to, or influence on, the mind,—in short, as being without art.

After these remarks, the writer observed that it becomes necessary to divest the mind of the spurious elaborations with which the patterns of our manufactures abound, so as to prepare the intellect for detecting and tracing the ever-varying lines of beautiful form, and the endless gradations, contrasts, and harmonies of colour, which pervade all Productions of vegetal growth. He said, it was also to be borne in mind that, in thus looking for the beautiful, no two persons are competent to discern it with equal readiness and intensity; practice, and educational training, being necessary to an expert and keen discrimination in such a matter, and more especially so when it becomes the business of life to translate it for the reading of others,—when, as in literature, it would be found that the poetic rendering proves more prepossessing and interesting, as art, to the million, than all the matter-of-fact, dry, and prosy details of merely exact imitation.

USE OF BATH STONE IN LIVERPOOL.

WITH reference to your observations on the Unitarian Church, now in course of erection in Liverpool under our superintendence, we beg to say a few words as to the introduction of Bath stone, which you appear to think undesirable.

You are mistaken or misinformed in supposing that a desirable stone is easily obtained in this locality, at a price *nearly* approaching that of Bath stone, when the comparative amount of labour is considered. It is also difficult, even at an increased price, to obtain *any* stone which so well contrasts with our Upholland (not Rochdale) wall stone. Previously to our obtaining tenders for this church, we made a careful examination of the several descriptions of stone which were calculated to suit the building, and reported thereon to the committee. They were as follows:—Darley Dale stone (Derbyshire), Glasgow stone, Caen stone (which we chiefly wished to introduce), Longridge and Haughton Moor stone (in this neighbourhood), Bath stone, and, as a last resource, Stourton (Cheshire) stone. From motives of economy, all, except the two last-mentioned descriptions of stone, were rejected, as involving an expenditure beyond the available funds, and the question was between Bath and Stourton. It may be as well to mention that the Stourton stone, though much used in this neighbourhood, is very generally condemned, owing to its loose and clayey veins and its great liability to chip from atmospheric action: it is also coarse in grain; and these causes render it especially unsuitable for Gothic work, where sharp arrises, delicate carving, and deep undercutting abound. Now, Bath stone is admirably adapted for these mouldings, and for the most elaborate carvings and tracery, and we have here obtained it at a cost of 5 per cent. beyond the price of Stourton.

We have been the first to introduce Bath stone into Liverpool; and when we look at the churches and public buildings in and about London, and throughout the southern, western, and midland counties in England, in which Bath stone has been adopted, we do not think that we have taken a singular or an unadvised step in using it here, where good stone is so difficult to be had at a fair price. Besides, we have yet to learn that Bath stone is of that perishable nature, of late (and only of late) so much attributed to it.

Nine-tenths of the failures imputed to this stone have occurred through the ignorance or inattention of workmen, or superintendents, in neglecting to work the stones so as to lay on their natural beds, which has laid the pores of the stone open to the effects of rain and frost. Yet, although there have been failures (and we think we are justified in saying that they have only been *partial* failures, and chiefly, if not entirely, owing to the neglect alluded to), there have been many successful specimens of Bath stonework, which may be seen in London, Oxford, Bath, Bristol, &c.

We know an instance on the borders of the Bristol Channel, where an extension of a church was effected some twelve years since, in which, although singularly exposed to saline action, no symptoms of decay have manifested themselves, although the walls were cased throughout with Bath ashlar.

We have troubled you with this letter, not so much for the purpose of explaining as to the material we have used, as in the hope that it will lead to some practical remarks, which may elucidate more clearly how far Bath stone is or is not suitable for the buildings of this country. BARRY AND BROWN.

CURIOUS DISCOVERY IN ROME.—The following interesting announcement forms part of a letter dated "English College, Rome, Sept. 28, 1848."—"In a vineyard belonging to the chapter of St. John Lateran, some curious sepulchral remains have been discovered, but the series will not be altogether excavated before November. One piece represents a doorway to a temple in the forum, and even this remnant, in consequence of the name and site being inscribed on the cornice, threatens to disturb some portions of our Roman topography. As yet no one is allowed to sketch the fragments.

HOUSE DRAINAGE.

In a letter on this subject, addressed by Mr. Montagu Marriott to the Metropolitan Commissioners of Sewers, the writer gives evidence, founded on personal experience, in favour of small drains. Discovering "that no brick drain of ordinary construction would keep clean for any length of time," the supply of water being insufficient to prevent the solid matters from accumulating in the drains, and eventually stopping them, "although they have varied in sectional area from 113 to 16 square inches," he says he found an effectual remedy, which he then proceeds to describe,—

"I commenced by using 9-inch pipe drains, which, although much better than those of brick, were subject to some of the same inconveniences, the chief of which was their too great size. I then tried 6-inch, 4-inch, and eventually 3-inch, which size I now use, and find them sufficient for all purposes, and much more easily kept clean than any others.

One of the greatest evils of the old system of drainage was the obligation enforced by the Commissioners of Sewers of carrying every drain through the house to the front, frequently a length of 60 feet, although a much better course might be found at the rear of the premises, within one-fourth of the distance, and which would avoid the injury to health and great part of the expense consequent upon the above regulation. On these considerations alone a back drainage, wherever practicable, should be adopted; but there is another of great importance, viz., that there is much less chance of a deposit being formed if the whole sewage and waste water of a range of houses be carried along one channel than if it were divided into twenty driblets through as many separate drains.

The plan I now adopt, and which I find very effectual with houses not having water-closets, is to run a 3-inch pipe drain of glazed stone-ware from the privy along the backs of the houses, when practicable, to the nearest sewer, keeping it down as low as possible, but allowing a fall of from one to two inches in ten feet, according to circumstances: the cesspool is then emptied and filled up with rubbish, and the drain brought up with an elbow to receive a common glazed stoneware closet-basin, the neck of which ought to be contracted to two inches to prevent any larger substance from passing through. The next step is to provide a supply of water, and although the quantity furnished by the companies at enormous prices is notoriously deficient, and in most cases only supplied three times per week, it may nevertheless, by carefully attending to the rule laid down above of keeping the drain as low as possible, be made to answer the purpose of thoroughly cleansing it. The ball tap should be entirely removed from the supply-pipe,* and a waste-pipe 1¼ inches internal diameter fastened into the water-butt within about two or three inches of the top: this waste-pipe should then lead to and be connected with the orifice left in the water-closet pan for that purpose, care being taken to make a syphon-bend in the lower part to prevent any possibility of the water becoming contaminated. Branches from the rain-water pipe and sink are connected with the drain by means of proper junctions made for that purpose in the earthenware drain pipes: by these means the drain is thoroughly washed down three times per week, or as often as water is supplied to the houses, and all deposit prevented. The tenants in the houses where this plan has been tried speak of it in the highest terms, as rendering the lower rooms both habitable and healthy.

* * * * *

With houses of a superior class where water-closets are already in use, a similar method should be adopted, with some slight variations. The old brick drain should be removed or stopped up, the former if possible, and replaced by a new tube-drain, and the water-closet traps carefully looked to and altered to the ∽ or syphon form, if not acting well. I do not consider it perfectly safe to remove the ball tap from the cisterns, as, from their being generally attached to the houses, the consequences of an accident, from frost or other causes, would be serious; but the waste-pipe should be cut two or three inches shorter than usual, and the mouth enlarged, so as to allow the water to pass rapidly off as soon as it rises to a certain height, and the ball tap would still act as a perfect safeguard against overflowing in case of a stoppage of the waste-pipe.

The proper size of pipe drains is a question much discussed and not yet decided. The only necessary point to observe, in order to determine a minimum diameter, is the quantity of storm water they may by any possibility be required to carry off. Now, the greatest quantity I believe, with only one exception, registered during the last forty years, amounted to two inches per hour, which is the utmost it is necessary to provide for; and if we take

* What do the water companies say to this?—ED.

the average surface of a third-rate house and outbuildings at 650 superficial feet, this will give about 108 cubic feet, and suppose the garden or yard to afford half as much, this would give a total of 162 feet (or 1,012½ gallons) per hour: now it has been found by experiments lately made at the Sewers'-office, Soho-square, that this quantity of water will pass through fifty feet (the average length of a house drain) of four-inch pipes, laid at a dead level and without any head of water, in about 24 minutes; and although the relative capacity of the three-inch pipes is, compared with the four-inch, only as nine to sixteen, yet being laid with a fall of five inches in fifty feet and with a head of water of from one to three feet, they would carry off quite as much water as four-inch pipes laid on a dead level, and be amply sufficient to take the heaviest fall of storm water from two third-rate or three smaller houses, or the ordinary drainage from three times those numbers."

APPROPRIATION OF RAILWAY ARCHES.

IT is a melancholy, but a certain truth, that in this immense metropolis a great amount of human suffering exists, for want of shelter during the inclement nights of winter. The police reports have shewn that several persons have even made a resting place of the dry trench in Hyde-park, and only a few days since an unfortunate man who was crippled by a railway accident, appeared in custody of the police, before a magistrate, for making a noise at the door of Lambeth workhouse, on being refused a night's lodging, having slept on the preceding evening on a heap of stones.

The parish of Lambeth spans a great part of the southern bank of the Thames, and contains a vast portion of the humble and miserable abodes of the indigent classes. At one period before the new Poor-law was exacted, there were five thousand out-door poor persons receiving weekly relief. In this very parish the recent extension of the South-Western Railway to the Waterloo-road, has occasioned the erection of two hundred and sixty-four dry arches. With the exception of the few appropriated to roadways, here are then the greater number of them of no apparent utility, merely openings to receive refuse filth, engender damp, and to create cutting drafts of air during the wintry blasts.

If these arches were floored, and boarded on the sides, they would form a refuge for the houseless to sufficient extent that no unfortunate person in London would want a dry covering in the inclement season. A merely raised flooring on each side, like those in the military guard-rooms, would afford the worn and weary a better repose than a heap of stones, or dry trenches in the parks. Other details would be readily suggested by the philanthropic; but even for baths and wash-houses for the poor, as well as soup-kitchens, these arches are well adapted. For the latter purpose, an enormous and constant supply of hot water could be obtained from the wasted heat of the extensive coke-ovens at Nine Elms, if boilers were erected there, from whence it could be conveyed in pipes,—and the heated pipes, by passing through those arches fitted up as receptacles for night refuge, would keep them healthily dry, and give genial warmth to the emaciated and distressed denizens.

If the pauperised parish of Lambeth cannot afford the cost of establishing a nightly home for their houseless poor, surely the various societies, who usually during the winter season display their humane care for fellow beings, might find the central position of these unemployed arches worthy of being permanently turned to some such purpose. Sufficient means would soon be found by a subscription, and the railway authorities would doubtless be glad to let the arches for this intention, upon easy terms.

IDLER IN LONDON.

ASSESSMENT OF RAILWAYS.—A correspondent informs us, that at the Rugby sessions just held, the London and North-Western company appealed successfully against a poor-rate in the parish of Church Lawford, levied at 1,800*l.* per mile per annum. It was argued by the company, and confirmed by the bench, that 750*l.* per mile per annum should be the sum assessed in future, and in other portions of the parish the rate was reduced from 1,500*l.* per mile, to 500*l.*

NOTES IN THE PROVINCES.

THE new church of All Saints, in Great Nelson-street, Liverpool, was consecrated on Friday week. It was founded in March last, on a plan by Mr. A. H. Holme, who superintended the erection. It is a plain structure, of red stone, in the Early English style, with accommodation for about 1,050 persons, 600 sittings free, and cost, it is said, about 4,000*l.* The front to Great Nelson-street comprises a tower, with spire about 120 feet high, and four entrance-doors, the two central with porches. In the centre of the elevation is a lofty gable, with lancet and circular windows. The pitch of the roof is said to be great, with large sky-lights visible from Great Homer-street; but interiorly it has been arranged to present the appearance of a clerestory and is regarded as a novelty. The gallery is supported by bronzed spiral pillars. The free benches have sloping backs and foot-boards and other conveniences. The brickwork was executed by Messrs. Duckworth; the masonry by Messrs. Nuttall and Hargraves; the woodwork by Mr. Burroughs; and the plumbing by Mr. Crellin. ——At Ancoates, says a Manchester paper, the mansion of Messrs. Kennedy, adjoining their mills, has been converted to the use of the women and young children, who, by the new Factories' Act, are excluded the mills at certain hours, during which they have generally been obliged to take their meals in the streets. The building has been well ventilated, and fitted up with benches, tables, large fires, gas-burners, washing and dressing places, &c.,—a worthy example to hundreds of those whose wealth is based on the like foundation.——The Christ Church schools at Hull were opened on Wednesday week. The style is Gothic, and ventilation and space have been considered. The rooms will accomodate 640 children. The architect was Mr. C. Brodrick. Ground and building cost about 1,400*l.*—— The church at Edithweston, says a Lincolnshire paper, has been restored internally at the cost of Mr. and Mrs. Lucas, Sir Gilbert Heathcote, and others, with new open seating on a raised floor, walls stripped of whitewash, &c. A painting in fresco, 7 feet high, was uncovered between the clerestory windows. The restoration was executed by Mr. Collins, of Stamford.——A school of design is about to be formed at Leicester.——Plans and estimates for a lock-up, &c., at Solihull, have been made out, and a memorial for its erection presented to the magistrates at quarter sessions. ——The church at Kemp-town, says a Brighton paper, is now finished, and will be shortly consecrated. It has been erected by the Marquis of Bristol.

Miscellanea.

DISCOVERIES IN ST. GEORGE'S CHURCH, CANTERBURY.—In this ancient edifice, which has lately been cleared out, for the purpose of re-pewing, some curious relics of early times have been brought to light. In the south wall, near the east end, were discovered three elaborately ornamented sedilia, or stone seats. One of these has apparently been used, since the Reformation, as a window, opening into the street, on which side of the wall is a square stone casement. The ancient iron hooks and the latchet hook of this window are as perfect as if only just placed there, so that they could not have been much used after they were fixed. Upon the east wall, and near to these seats was found, immediately concealed beneath a coating of lime, a piscina.

DOVER HARBOUR OF REFUGE.—According to the *Dover Chronicle*, the works here are conducted with industry. The timber framework of this great sea barrier has been carried out upwards of 260 feet from the point of shore at the old Cheeseman's-head; and by the aid of several diving-bells, helmets, &c., and an arrangement of travelling cranes, the ponderous stonework has been securely bedded in the chalk rock to a similar distance, and brought up almost to the level of high water, within eight months. This compact body of masonry is said to contain no less than 150,000 cubic feet of stone of large dimensions. There is a steam-engine, driving several sets of mortar and cement mills, and a crane for unloading vessels.

THE CENTRAL RAILWAY STATION, NEWCASTLE.—If we may judge from an account of this station, in the *Civil Engineer's Journal*, it is an important work. The following are some of the particulars that are given:—The façade, or principal front, is 600 feet in length. The style of the building is Roman; and the most striking feature in the design is the portico in the centre, 200 feet in length by 70 feet in width, flanked on each side by an arcade, the same length by 35 feet in width, allowing sufficient room for carriages to drive in at the end of each arcade, to turn, and go out at each end of the projecting part of the portico. The exterior front of the portico is composed of seven arches, each 14 feet in width by 32 feet in height, divided by coupled insulated Doric columns, 29' feet in height, elevated on a basement of 7½ feet, and supporting a broken entablature and attic of the same style. The arcades on each side are formed of arches, of the same width as the portico, divided by double inserted columns. These columns, with the key-stones of the arches, support a continued unbroken entablature, without an attic. The ends of the arcade terminate in front in a niche, having coupled insulated columns on each side, supporting an entablature and low attic. The entrance to the end of each arcade is by an arch 25 feet in width; and the arcades will be covered with groined ceilings of stone, with a circular light at each intersection. The front of the station-house facing the platform is concave, forming the segment of a circle of 800 feet radius. This form was rendered necessary by the junction of the various lines of railway at this point; and the elevation is of rubble-stone, from Prudhoe quarry, of a plain Roman character, the doors and windows having arched heads, with moulded imposts and archivolts. The shed is 236 yards long and 61 yards wide, covering an area of 14,426 yards, or about three acres. The roof is composed of iron, divided into three compartments, and supported by columns 33 feet apart, and 23 feet high from the platform to the springing of the roof. It is wholly of stone, and is from the designs of Mr. Dobson.

DEATH OF MR. ALDERMAN JOHNSON.—On Saturday morning Mr. Alderman Johnson expired at his residence, Millbank. The deceased alderman, who, in conjunction with his brother, succeeded to his father's business, was in early life extensively engaged as a paviour, and both also inherited a large fortune from their father, who made a fortunate speculation in a quarry in Devonshire, since known as the "Haytor Granite." He undertook the contract for the breakwater at Plymouth: this and other fortunate speculations tended to place the deceased alderman at the head of the stone trade. In 1845 he was elected to fill the civic chair, and during the year of his mayoralty distinguished it by a princely entertainment to scientific, literary, and artistical celebrities.

FLAXMAN'S WORKS.—Our readers know that a series of casts, from the works of Flaxman, have been presented to University College, Gower-street, by his niece Miss Denman. According to the *Athenæum*, the library just erected will be approached through a vestibule which, with its dome, forms so conspicuous a feature in the front view of the edifice. In this vestibule will be placed the casts in question. The well-known group of the Archangel Michael overcoming Satan (the first work executed in bronze for the Art-Union of London), will form the leading feature—standing immediately under the centre of the dome.

THE PNEUMATIC PILE-DRIVING PROCESS. —A hollow iron cylinder, 24 feet in length and 4½ in diameter, was lately sunk, for mining purposes, into dry sand on the sea shore, at Wheal Ramorth Mine, Perranzabuloe, Cornwall, by Dr. Potts's pneumatic pile-driving process. The sinking, on the occasion first recorded, went on at the rate of 24 inches in 50 minutes; but the process was suspended to allow scientific men to witness its further progress on a day appointed, when the descent was continued "at the rate of 3 inches a minute, accomplishing a descent of 2 feet 9 inches in 8 minutes, when it was feared that it would disappear altogether, and the work was abruptly suspended."

PROJECTED WORKS.—Advertisements have been issued for tenders, by dates not specified, for building an inn at the Gretna station of the Caledonian Railway; and for constructing a sewer at Southampton.

A HORSE-POWER POCKET-BOILER.—At a recent meeting of the Academy of Sciences, at Paris, as already noticed by the *Literary Gazette*, M. Boutigny announced that M. Beauregard (a young engineer), had at length succeeded in forming a steam-engine, which was moved by the vapour or gases of water, generated on red hot plates, and known as water in the spheroidal state. The tremendous and explosive power of such vapour in a common boiler is but too well known; but it is doubtless quite possible to put even a power such as this—so dangerous when neither looked for nor wanted—into safety harness. From a mere globule or spheroid of water thus managed in a miniature boiler, an immense power is generated, which would appear to require decomposition of its elementary gases to explain; and if it be true that a drop of dew contains electric power enough to get up a good thunder-storm, a drop of water in a boiler like a snuff-box, may well yield the power of a single horse. It is a singular fact, too, that the drop or spheroid of water in such circumstances does not at once exhaust itself, or altogether evaporate in yielding such a power. It rolls about on the red hot surface, slowly yielding immensely elastic vapours or gases, and never rising in temperature itself beyond 190 degrees, and this we should think not so difficult to account for as may be imagined. The red heat or the salient electricity excited by the heat, is no doubt capable of decomposing a film of the water in contact with the surface, and this in its immense expansion absorbs, and for the moment exhausts, so great a quantity of the elastic salient forces that the remainder of the globule is kept, if not frozen, cool, and rolling about, till another film be expanded as before, with the like reactive cooling effect. The law of *constitutional or latent* heat and electricity, rightly understood, thus readily explains all. A 400-horse-power engine on this principle is about to be made in this country. It is stated by a correspondent of the *Times*, however, that some years since a British steamer was navigated to Lisbon and back with boilers acting on a like principle, but that to prevent "the immense oxidation of the plates" mercury was used between two series of them while the water was injected on the upper one; and the mercury escaped so as to injure the health of the stokers.

CAUTION TO BUILDERS.—In the course of an inquiry into the cause of a fire on premises, Clement's-court, Wood-street, Cheapside, Mr. Braidwood said, upon examining the place where the fire originated, he found that some workmen had lighted a fire on a hearth-stone of a newly-erected fireplace, there being no stove fixed. He attributed the fire to the ignition of a timber shoring, which was only divided from the fireplace by about four inches of brickwork. Out of 700 fires occurring annually for the last twelve years, the great majority had been occasioned by the fact of timber existing in the brickwork of old buildings. He would suggest the necessity of builders boring the party walls of old buildings prior to constructing fireplaces, and then they would soon discover any of the old wood, well known to form a portion of the old houses in the city. The jury returned the following verdict:—"That the fire, which was accidental, originated in the ignition of certain portions of timber in an old party wall, against which had been recently erected a fireplace: and the jury recommend that, in addition to the usual precautions adopted in such constructions, builders should adopt the most stringent regulations in all such cases, for the better protection of life and property."

THE CHICHESTER COMPETITION.—"A Sufferer" (who forwards his address), says, I paid the carriage of my drawings down to Chichester. I have had them returned with one shilling to pay, no cord round the case, three of the drawings burst (though they were mounted on strainers), and not a line accompanying them either of thanks, apology, or even acknowledging in any way their ever having seen them!

IMPROVEMENTS IN MIDDLESEX HOSPITAL.—The improvements which have been going on here for some time past, mainly in consequence of the munificent bequest of Lady Murray, are now nearly completed. The ward windows are cleverly arranged to open so that the current of air is upwards. The sinks have been so altered that effluvium is carried away into the external air. The inconvenience of incrustation in boilers and pipes from hot water is sought to be avoided by carrying the steam from a boiler in the basement, after supplying the laboratory, vapour baths, surgeons' rooms, washhouse and laundry, &c., through a coil of iron pipe in a cold tank, which holds 1,000 gallons of water. The steam is there condensed, the earthy deposit takes place on the exterior of the heating surface, and by feeding the boiler with the condensed steam instead of fresh water, incrustation is prevented. The floors are covered with desiccated wood, and the walls with a non-absorbent plaster, to lessen the chance of propagating any epidemic. Messrs. Wyatt and Brandon are the architects engaged. If it be true as stated that 20,000*l*. have been spent in these improvements, the wisdom of the course adopted by the Government becomes questionable.

EGYPTIAN MONUMENTS.—At a meeting of the Syro-Egyptian Society, on the 12th December, the original drawings of Egyptian architectural remains, by Mr. Roberts, R.A., were arranged round the room in chronological order. Mr. Roberts pointed out the most interesting points connected with each sketch, and called attention to the evidences of the action of fire which were visible in many of the interiors. Messrs. Sharpe and Bonomi pointed out the architectural varieties of style observable in the works of the Greek and Roman periods, as compared with those of the Pharaohs; and commented on the remarkable fact, that both Greeks and Romans in Egypt adhered to the Egyptian style of architecture, and though well acquainted with the use of the arch, did not employ it in their constructions. Mr. Roberts having stated an opinion entertained by Professor Cockerell, that the palace of the Pharaohs had been erected upon the roofs of the temples—an opinion founded on the presence of holes in the roofs, apparently for receiving posts for the support of some superstructure, and of spouts for carrying off water from the roof, in a country where rain falls so unfrequently,—a discussion was raised upon that point. The view taken by Professor Cockerell was opposed by Mr. Scoles, Mr. Nash, and others; who considered that the holes in the roof, which are usually about 4 inches in diameter, were for the insertion of flag-staves, similar to those known from ancient Egyptian drawings to have been placed in front of the propylæa.—Mr. Johnston, however, observed that the Abyssinian sovereigns of the present day reside in tents, and that the holes in the roof alluded to might have supported canvas coverings.

SEA-SAND.—Speaking of the conversation at the last meeting of the Institute of Architects, and of those who thought that sea-sand, when well *blown*, might be used for mortar, the editor of the *Literary Gazette* says,—"We advise the use of any sand in preference to sea-sand, blown or unblown, for those who wish to have their apartments to continue unstained with picturesque drippings, or papered without tatters hanging grotesquely down. We had a cottage wall *between* the kitchen and dining-room fire-places once built with sea-sand; but no fire nor heat could prevent its droppings!"

ENGRAVED PORTRAITS.—Mr. G. R. Ward, whose portraits in mezzotint we have had occasion to mention before, has recently completed two others—Mr. George Hudson, M.P., after a painting by F. Grant, R.A., and Mr. W. Astell, M.P., late Chairman of the East-India Company, from a painting by Mr. F. R. Say. These are good specimens of Mr. Ward's skill in his art, the head of Mr. Astell in particular, which is luminous and life-like. The accessories in the full length of Mr. Hudson are better than the figure. The right hand of the honourable member wants a little more work on it. It is at present a blot. A portrait of Mr. Maunder, engraved by Mr. E. Finden from a picture by Mr. Waugh, is the representation of a laborious, clear-headed, and painstaking writer, to whom the rising generation are much indebted.

AN ARCHITECT'S CARD.—Sir: As the enclosed is a bit of a curiosity in its way, it may prove amusing to your readers. I assure you geniuses of this grade are by no means uncommon, which, taking into consideration the extent of talent required to master five or six professions and trades, is rather surprising: still this is the first instance I have ever witnessed of one of these universal architectural geniuses having had the boldness to publish such a card as this:—"—— ——, Land Surveyor, Architect, Builder, Deal and Timber Merchant, &c. &c. &c., M——. Parishes, estates, manors, and townships, surveyed and mapped, maps and plans of estates, buildings, &c., drawn, or copies of the same to any scale required. Levelling for railways, drainage, &c. Designs for cottages, villas, farm-houses and outbuildings. Also specifications and estimates prepared with accuracy and dispatch. —— begs to inform the trade and the building public in general, that he intends to manufacture sashes, frames, shop fronts, doors, and all other kind of joiner's work, on the lowest possible scale of prices. A price for any of the above may be had on application. An assortment of deals, timber, &c., always on band, also cut stuff, on the lowest possible terms for cash. Roman Cement—being connected with, &c. &c. Enamelled Slate—this beautiful material has been introduced &c. &c. &c. &c."—"S.," Fleetwood.

HEALTH ACT IN UXBRIDGE.—On Monday, December 18, Mr. Ranger, one of the inspectors appointed by the General Board of Health, opened a court of inquiry at Uxbridge. A number of witnesses gave testimony of the necessity for the introduction of sanitary measures. The commissioner, attended by Mr. W. Rayner, surgeon, and several others, made a personal inspection of most of the localities. According to our informant, many of the courts were found very deficient in drainage. Gas is supplied to the public at 10s. per 1,000 feet by a company who promised a great reduction, but who have not yet made it.—The south side of the church has lately been rebuilt, with flint and Bath-stone dressings, under the direction of Mr. C. J. Shoppee, architect.

THE PHILHARMONIC CONCERT-HALL, LIVERPOOL.—With reference to a letter dated from Liverpool, and signed "John Cunningham," on which we commented in a recent article, we have received another communication from Liverpool, also signed "John Cunningham," stating that the first letter was written by one of his "*good friends*" there, and requesting us to insert his "flat denial of its authorship." We are obliged to take for granted that the second letter is correct, and the first not, although upon the face of them there is nothing to make us doubt one more than the other. We sincerely hope that Mr. Cunningham has not many such "good friends;" and that he will succeed in punishing the author of what would seem to be nothing less than a forgery.

BUILDERS' BENEVOLENT INSTITUTION.—The arrangements for the ball in aid of the funds of this institution, which, as already mentioned, is to take place on the 9th, are progressing satisfactorily. Lord Dudley Stuart has promised to attend if in town, a good band has been engaged, and 300 out of the 400 tickets are already disposed of.

THE PEDESTAL TO THE STATUE OF CHARLES I. AT CHARING GUOSS.—"A Subscriber" writes,—I think it is much to be regretted that some effectual step is not taken to restore the beautiful pedestal of Charles the First's statue at Charing Cross, before the ornaments and mouldings have entirely perished, to preclude the possibility of tracing either the one or the other.

MEETINGS OF SCIENTIFIC BODIES

Held during the ensuing week.

MONDAY, JAN. 8.—Institute of British Architects, 8 P.M. (Paper on Caen Stone).

TUESDAY, 9.—Institution of Civil Engineers, 8 P.M. (Opening meeting).

WEDNESDAY, 10.—Graphic Society, 8 P.M.

THURSDAY, 11.—Royal Society, 8½ P.M.; Society of Antiquaries, 8 P.M.

FRIDAY, 12.—Archæological Association, 8½ P.M.

TENDERS

Delivered for the two new Small-pox and Vaccination Hospital, Highgate.

Pritchard and Son	£19,930
Smith and Appleford	19,440
Young	18,540
Lee and Son	18,300
Holland	17,699
Paffick	17,420
Grimsdell	17,085
Kelk	16,953
Cubitt and Co.	16,900
Locke and Nesham	16,500
Myers	16,431
Piper and Sons	16,936

TO CORRESPONDENTS.

"*Mouldiness from Damp.*"—"Sir : I have laid down a wood floor, and ways, in a cave, and afterwards gave it two coats of linseed oil. Now the damp penetrates through the pores of the wood, and causes it to mould greatly, which gives it an ill effect. Perhaps some of the readers of THE BUILDER will inform me of some chemical preparation that will destroy the mould without injuring the effect of the floor."

"*Ants in Dwellings.*"—We have been frequently asked for a remedy, and must just again refer to pp. 302 and 514 of vol. IV. Cajeput oil, or julap with sugar, are the recommended : see also p. 371, vol. VI.

Received.—"J. P.," "Old Subscriber" (Hull), "M.P.," "S. S. T.," "Mr. T.," "Mr. H. B. P." (statement alluded to has not reached us), "W. C." (try warm water, or Condy's Ventilating Stove), "W. F. G." (thanks), "W. G. C.," "J. A. B.," "Mr. P." "Y." (inquire of the secretary at the school, Somerset House), "Mr. B.," "J. M. L.," "C. R.," "W. M." (We should say, yes), "Hyal" (The College of Chemistry is in Hanover-square, north-west corner : analyses can be made there or at the Polytechnic Institution, Regent-street), "One of the Committee," "J. D." Newark (We do not know the plaster named), "Quondam," "J. B.," "S. L.," "A Subscriber," "J. B. L.," "J. A. N.," "The Gloucester Book of the British Archæological Association" (Bohn, York-street, London) : Weale's "Prentices" "Geology," by Col. Pottlock, and "Well-digging," &c., by J. G. Swindell ; "Supply of Water to London by Henley Works :" "The History of Ireland," by Thomas Wright, M.A. (Tallis) ; "Materials for a New Style of Ornamentation, consisting of Subjects drawn from Nature," by Henry Whitaker (the Author, 79, Newman-street, and Weale) ; "The Practical Cabinet-maker's Treasury of Designs," by H. Whitaker (Fisher and Son), parts 16 to 38 ; "Harbours of Refuge," by W. H. Smith (Longman) ; "Tait's Magazine" for January ; "Con. Cregan," No. 1 (Orr and Co., London).

"*Books, Prices, and Addresses.*"—We have not time to point out books or find addresses.

ADVERTISEMENTS.

No. CCCX.

SATURDAY, JANUARY 13, 1849.

OME recent disastrous events can scarcely fail to re-awaken public attention to the importance of well constructed dwellings, to the evils of inefficient drainage, want of ventilation, and crowded graveyards in the midst of towns, and otherwise to quicken the sanitary movement, which had begun to lag. When the Registrar-General makes a report that while the annual deaths in the town districts of Manchester, for example, are 37 to 1,000 males living, in the extra-metropolitan parts of Surrey they are but 19,—in other words, that though the population of Surrey exceeded that of Manchester, yet in seven years 16,000 persons died in the latter place over and above the deaths in Surrey, and that these fell a sacrifice to known causes,—" Here in the most advanced nation in Europe—in one of the largest towns of England—in the midst of a population unmatched for its energy, industry, manufacturing skill—in Manchester, the centre of a victorious agitation for commercial freedom—aspiring to literary culture —where Percival wrote and Dalton lived,"— the public mind is roused to the necessity of proper measures, and for a time the subject appears to make good progress. Speedily, however, the fact is forgotten; and the enemy being hidden, they fall back into the more comfortable belief that they have been frightened at shadows, and that none exist.

Recent events, however, as we have said,— the circumstances under which the more serious outbreaks of cholera amongst us have occurred, a consideration of the localities wherein it is and is not found, will speak trumpet-tongued, and will materially aid in hastening the admission as axioms of those truths at which individuals long since arrived by painful and lengthened investigations, but which have been until recently wholly disregarded by the multitude. And these once universally admitted, the succeeding steps are easier.

When we find the first cases occurring near the mouth of a sewer; when we hear a jury summoned to inquire into the cause of death in the case of those persons who died recently in Rosemary-lane, Whitechapel, bringing in as their verdict—"That the deceased persons died natural (?) deaths from Asiatic cholera, caused by the fœtid and abominable condition of the habitations situate in the courts and alleys in which they resided;" that at the Establishment for Pauper Children at Tooting, where there has been such a fearful loss of life, stagnant ditches, filled with decomposing vegetable and animal matter, abound, and that in a prison where the disease has begun to rage violently, those who are able to judge ascribe it in great part to defective ventilation,—the necessity of steps to remove these causes of loss, suffering, and deprivation, becomes obvious to all.

What has been already gradually achieved by improvements made without the full appreciation of their paramount worth, should further encourage to persevering efforts. The term of human life has been lengthened over

the whole kingdom,—unnecessarily shortened, fearfully sacrificed, as it still is. "The year 1685," says Mr. Macaulay, in his philosophical and admirable history of England (the perusal of which has afforded us more enjoyment than we can well express), " was not accounted sickly; yet in the year 1685 more than one in 23 of the inhabitants of the capital died. At present only one inhabitant of the capital in 40 dies annually. The difference in salubrity between the London of the nineteenth century, and the London of the seventeenth century, is very far greater than the difference between London in an ordinary season, and London in the cholera."* And yet how much does it still need improvement; how greatly might life still be lengthened; how obvious, in many cases, are the means which offer themselves! Let us all strive to aid in the great work.

The superintending inspectors appointed by the Board of Health have been actively engaged in taking evidence in various towns, and the reports in some cases are, we believe, nearly ready. From these we shall be able to judge of the advantages which are likely to follow the inquiry. From Gloucester, amongst others, where numerous defilements exist, we have received intimation that the inspector, Mr. Cresy's, inquiry has been very elaborate and careful, which, knowing what we do of Mr. Cresy, is nothing more than we anticipated. Letters from another town, as to temper and prejudice exhibited by the inspector sent down there, are less satisfactory; we forbear, however, from any definite statements on the subject just now. It is stated that nearly one hundred towns and places have petitioned the Board to send down an officer to make public inquiry, with a view to the application of the Health Act: and, in consequence, the Board have appointed two additional inspectors, namely, Mr. T. W. Rammell, and Mr. W. Lee, of the firm of Flockton, Lee, and Flockton, of Sheffield, of which town he was surveyor of highways.

At Chelmsford, where the inquiry has just commenced, the inhabitants are entering warmly into it,—anxiously affording all the assistance in their power. We are glad to find foremost in the official announcement of the subjects to be inquired into, "The State of the Burial Grounds," and sincerely hope that no pains will be spared to obtain accurate information on this head. That the burial grounds are most fruitful sources of disease, there can be no doubt on the minds of unprejudiced men who have inquired into the matter.

In the course of the investigation under the Act, which is now going on in Worcester, Mr. Orwin, a surgeon, brought the matter very prominently forward, giving a startling picture of the condition of the graveyards in that city. We extract two or three paragraphs from his evidence:—

" ST. MARTIN'S.—The present sexton has lived in a house adjoining the churchyard about six years. When he first resided there, he frequently

experienced a very unpleasant smell, which affected his health very much, but he has now become more accustomed to it, and does not find the evil so serious. This ground is so full that they cannot tell where to make a grave without first boring the ground. The sexton has known the gravedigger take up a coffin, in mistake, containing a corpse in a state of putrefaction, which he has been obliged to put into the ground again and close the grave, and make one elsewhere.

SAINT NICHOLAS.—This churchyard has been closed for some time, owing to its being so over-crowded with the dead. There is a crypt beneath this church, in which corpses are buried in wooden coffins. The exhalations, which issue through the apertures on each side of the crypt, have caused great annoyance to the rector, who lives close to the church.

ST. HELEN'S.—This churchyard is so full that it has been closed. A respectable inhabitant, who lives near, has been frequently very much annoyed by the offensive stench. Interments have taken place in the church in wooden coffins; and the sexton informed me that, when a vault has been opened, he has known the smell to be almost intolerable, and has been obliged to throw the church windows open, and leave them so for some time.

ALL SAINT's.—This churchyard is very full, although interments still take place there. A very great annoyance used to be experienced by some of the inmates of the houses adjoining the churchyard, which have been recently pulled down. These houses were partly below the level of the yard, and in close contact with the soil. It was stated to me by some of the occupants that the putrid matters actually oozed through the wall, rendering it damp and discoloured, and causing a most offensive smell. The health of all the members of the family was more or less affected.

ST. ANDREW'S.—Coffins are frequently exposed in digging graves. Many coffins have been placed in this ground with not more than 17 inches of earth above them.

ST. ALBAN'S.—The smell arising from interments here is frequently of a very obnoxious kind. There is also a plot of burial-ground banked up against the back of the church, and enclosed from a populous street by a high wall, through which the rain may percolate and carry impurities from decomposed bodies into the street on the one hand, and underneath the church on the other."

Some extraordinary facts, proving the death-dealing power of the gases given off by decomposing bodies on opening the ground, even long after interment, and where no smell was perceptible, will presently be made public. It is a mistake to suppose that when there is no smell there is no danger. On this point Mr. G. A. Walker says, in a recent letter to the Times,— " Though the nose is not merely an ornamental appendage to the face, but the registrar of odours; and though the "sentinel" may be constantly on guard, he cannot persist in the recognition of even the most disgusting effluvia beyond a certain period of time. Yet what does this prove? Why, that by the sense of smell we recognise the presence or absence of an odorous compound—that is all. Let not people, therefore, deceive themselves, or deceive others. Life has, in myriads of instances, been destroyed without any smell being perceptible. If it were not so, how comes it that the fathers and mothers of the generations that are past, have never smelt the miasms that impaired the health or destroyed the lives of their offspring by the various diseases to which childhood is more especially liable—as measles, scarletina, &c., &c.? Or why was it that, about this time last year, when the mortality in London alone exceeded by thousands the ordinary two-weeks' average—why was it, I say, that no man smelt anything peculiar; whilst this year, when cholera (an exaggerated form of typhus) is the destroying angel, have the victims seen, or have they recognised by the nose, the peculiar principles that have poisoned their blood, and ' knawed' them out of their lives ?"

In this same letter, speaking of Clement's-lane, Strand, and its graveyard, he says,— " That in this lane, in which the living breathe on all sides an atmosphere impregnated with the odour of the dead, the proportion of

* The following quotation from the same work will be found not impertinent. "Of the blessings which civilisation and philosophy bring with them, a large proportion is common to all ranks, and would, if withdrawn, be missed as painfully by the labourer as by the peer. The market place which the rustic can now reach with his cart in an hour was a hundred and sixty years ago a day's journey from him. The street which now affords to the artisan, during the whole night, a secure, a convenient, and a brilliantly lighted walk, was, abandoned and sixty years ago, so dark after sunset that he would not have been able to see his hand, so ill-paved that he would have run constant risk of breaking his neck, and so ill-watched that he would have been in imminent danger of being knocked down and plundered of his small earnings. Every bricklayer who falls from a scaffold, every sweeper of a crossing who is run over by a carriage, may now have his wounds dressed and his limbs set with a skill such as a hundred and sixty years ago, all the wealth of a great lord like Ormond, or of a merchant prince like Clayton, could not have purchased. Some frightful diseases have been extirpated by science, and some have been banished by police."

deaths on the eastern, the graveyard side of it, are at the rate of one in each house. That is, there are thirty-seven houses on that side, and thirty-seven dead bodies are taken out of these thirty-seven houses during the year."*

Our recent statement in respect of St. Margaret's Churchyard, Westminster, is even further borne out by fresh correspondents, with offers of evidence if required.

Passing to another and most important branch of sanitary inquiry,—the new Metropolitan Sewers' Commission has at length been issued and opened. A notice of the proceedings at the first meeting will be found in another place, including an admirable address by the Earl of Carlisle that will be read with interest.† It would not be amiss if one of their first acts were to direct their officers to set themselves right with the public to the extent that they have been damaged by the report of Messrs. Walker, Cubitt, and Brunel, on the city of London sewers, which by inference seems to question, in the politest manner it is true, something *more* than the judgment even of these officers.

Apart from any special statements, it must be distressing to such of the public as are anxious to arrive at the truth, to find an entire difference of opinion between men standing so high in estimation as the three engineers named, and those to whose direction the metropolitan sewers (without the city), are confided. While the latter attach considerable importance to the form of sewer, and condemn the flat bottomed, the former says:—"Although in strict theory the velocity of a given quantity of water running in the bottom of a sewer of the same height, width, and elevation, will be greater in the narrow-bottomed or egg-shaped than in the circular, it does not follow as a necessary consequence that this greater velocity or greater depth of water will more effectually carry with it the grit and sand that collect in the bottom. Practically the wear of the flatter sewer will be more uniform, and, as we have observed, experience has proved that the shape but little affects the deposit, while in other respects the flatter shape has advantages. So much are we impressed with this opinion, that in place of advising an invert more pointed and contracted than the semicircle, we should recommend the trial of a *flat bottom* of stone, or other hard material, 14 in. broad, for a sewer of 3 ft. in width at the springing of the arch, and 5 ft. high, as more likely to keep itself clear, less subject to unequal wear, and certainly very much more convenient for being cleansed."

This, and other wide differences as to the size and efficiency of existing sewers are most important questions, and ought to be set at rest forthwith.‡

The "water question" can scarcely fail to occupy public attention, being one of the utmost importance. We have several pamphlets on the subject before us, but must seek another opportunity to refer to them. The reform of our cattle markets, and the removal of Smithfield, too, belong to the movement, and are brought to notice at this moment by the reopening of the Islington cattle market, which took place on the 9th.

Mr. R. B. Grantham, civil engineer, saying, with Shakspeare—

"Away with me, all you whose souls abhor
Th' uncleanly savour of a slaughter-house,
For I am stifled with the smell,"—

has put together some valuable information on the abattoirs of Paris, and has considered, in an unprejudiced and able manner, the advantages to be gained by the introduction of similar establishments into England. Those who are investigating the question will do well to consult his treatise.*

We would again urge the paramount importance of the general question of sanitary improvement on our readers and the public, earnestly bidding them remember, that the great objects in view are,—

To SAVE MONEY,
To LESSEN SUFFERING, AND
To LENGTHEN LIFE:

and, moreover, that these grand results may all be obtained with certainty.

ON MONUMENTAL ARCHITECTURE.†

IN Germany, the sculptors of the different schools—those of Cologne and Nuremburg, in particular—attained considerable perfection in their art, and a greater energy and variety of character may be found in their works in consequence. Of their altar tombs, those of Louis IV., Landegrave of Thuringia and Hesse, at Rheinhardsbrunn, of the thirteenth century, of the Landegraves Conrad and des Eisemen, with his wife, at Marburg, are fine specimens. On that of the Archbishop Peter of Aspett, in the Cathedral of Mayence, he is represented with three youths, on two of whom he lays his hand to bless them. Some effigies are also to be found placed upright against the wall.

In the bronze tomb of the Emperor Maximilian, at Inspruck, the work of Tyrolese artists, the whole spirit of Feudal chivalry seems embodied. He is represented kneeling on his sarcophagus, and around him stand in solemn order the effigies of twenty-eight vassal sovereigns, dressed in their full costumes and armour, as if guarding the remains of their imperial lord. The execution is vigorous and bold, and in character with the grand conception of the whole.

The Gothic of northern Europe found no congenial resting-place in Italy. The hand of classic influence and fame, of civil freedom and contesting republics, had but little sympathy with Teutonic feudalism. The style of ecclesiastical architecture introduced from Germany was completely modified,—it flourished only as an exotic, and as it were on sufferance, the native principle of horizontalism, which had descended as an heirloom from antiquity, continually battled against the aspiring tendency of the other. Still more powerfully was this influence exerted upon the monumental art. Surrounded by the classic models, the Italian sculptors drank deeply of the well thus invitingly offered to them; and their art depending for its progress on the exertions of the different masters of the various schools, in whom the profession of architecture and even of painting were generally combined, a greater individuality of character and energy of action supplanted the calmer repose of the Gothic monuments, which seem rather the reflex of the feelings of their nation and age, than the language of the individual thoughts of their authors. The simple piety and purity of mind of these early artists prevented their feeling any sympathy with the uperstitious and pagan imagery of their models, from which they gathered only the principles of their art, the attitude and expression of the figures, composition, and arrangement of the draperies. Their spirit was as yet completely Christian, and it was from sacred subjects, and the traditions of the church, that they selected the themes for their chisel. In this progress Pisa took the lead; her school gave the type of the early Italian monumental architecture; she adopted the sarcophagus in opposition to the altar tomb; a lofty canopy with pointed arch overshadowed it; two angels, drawing aside a curtain, revealed the effigy of the deceased in slumber or in death, while sometimes the figure was repeated above, seated or in action, dressed in the royal or sacerdotal robes, or in armour, or even mounted on a war horse. At times, the lower figure is represented naked, or in the habit of a monk, to mark by the contrast the vanity of earthly grandeur. Of these, the tombs of Gregory X. at Arezzo, by Margaritone, and Pope Benedict XI. in S. Domenico, Perugia, by Giovanni Pisano, are good examples. That of Urbertino, in the Bardi Chapel, S. Croce, by Maso, represents him in a fresco within the arch, instead of the usual marble figure, rising from the sarcophagus in full armour at the summons of the last trumpet.

At Naples there are some magnificent sepulchral monuments, possessing more of the chivalrous spirit of northern Europe. Those of King Robert, and his son Charles, Duke of Calabria, in the church of S. Chiara, by Masaccio, are exceedingly rich; their figures are easy and dignified, represented both in life and in death. The king is seated on his throne, and beneath, lying on his sarcophagus, in the habit of the Franciscans. In the church of S. Giovanni, at Carbonara, is the tomb of Ladislaus, King of Hungary, by Ciccione. The equestrian statue of the monarch surmounts the arched canopy, which is supported by four caryatides.

But when Brunelleschi recurred to the circular arch, and, abandoning every Gothic tendency, struck out a fresh path in architecture, and Michelangelo's genius in sculpture authorised the study and adaptation of the antique, the cinque cento revival burst every barrier to its progress, and, like a mighty torrent, swept onwards, overwhelming the pure spirit of Christian art, and having firmly established its rule throughout Italy, gradually spread over the whole of Europe. The spiritual and universal character of monumental art expired: henceforth we look only for the creations of the master minds of the epoch. The new style had no feelings of its own, no religious enthusiasm; it thrived on the mythology of the past, which at best combines but ill with the sacred character of a Christian tomb. For instance, see the heterogeneous combination of heathen gods and goddesses, sirens, angels, and saints, with Roman warriors and emperors, that adorn the tomb of the Doge Vendramini at Venice, which is otherwise a fine work of art. It is by their richness, elegance, and delicacy of execution that the best monuments of this period claim our attention. But though the pulsations of this change beat to the very extremities of civilised Europe, the genius which atoned for it at its source was more sluggish in its circulation. England in particular had but little reason to be thankful for the innovation. In exchange for the glorious monuments of her Gothic architecture a cumbrous, heavy, tasteless, and corrupt style in general prevailed, till they sank at last into the most barbarous, mindless copyisms, whose numbing influence, with a reaction as complete and as general as was the change wrought by the cinque cento in the first instance, flowed back through the veins it had traversed till it froze the very life-blood at the heart itself.

To Italy, however, this was the age of her maturity in the arts: popes and princes rivalled each other in the patronage they extended to them, and many and noble are the names of the great architects, painters, and sculptors who have immortalized themselves by the works which they have left to us. Thankfully do we acknowledge the grandeur of their conceptions, the exuberance of their fancy and powers of invention, with the richness and delicacy of their execution, and yet, particularly in the

* It appears from the last quarterly report of King's College Hospital that there is every prospect of this burial-ground being shortly closed.

† Subjoined are the names of the commissioners:—The Earl of Carlisle, Lord Ashley, M.P., Viscount Ebrington, M.P., Hon. Frederick Byng, Sir James Clark, Bart., Sir Edward North Buxton, Bart., Sir John Burgoyne, R.E., Sir Henry De la Beche, Very Rev. Dr. Buckland, Dr. Arnott, Dr. Southwood Smith, Mr. Joseph Hume, M.P., Mr. R. A. Slaney, M.P., Mr. John Walter, M.P., Mr. G. Biddell Airey, Mr. E. Chadwick, C.B., Mr. John Leslie, Mr. W. John Broderip, Mr. R. Hutton, Mr. R. L. Jones, Mr. John Buller, Mr. John Bidwell, Mr. J. Hodgson, Captain James Veitch, Captain Robert K. Dawson, Mr. W. R. Groves, F.R.S., Mr. T. Banfield, Mr. E. Lawes, Mr. A. Bain, Mr. Thomas Hawes, Mr. Cuthbert Johnson, Rev. William Stone, M.A., Rev. Morgan Cowie, M.A., Rev. E. Murray, M.A.: Lewis C. Hertslet, Clerk.

‡ Amongst other inventions connected with drainage, which have been lately brought before us, is "Ashe's self-acting drain and sewer cleanser,"—an arrangement to catch and hold all available waste water until it amounts to about fourteen gallons, when it suddenly overbalances and throws the water with velocity into the soil-trap, and so through the drain.

* "A Treatise on Public Slaughter Houses, considered in connection with the Sanitary Question," with plans. By R. B. Grantham. London: Weale. Renshaw. Another pamphlet, called "An Inquiry into the present state of Smithfield Cattle Market," by John Bull (Ridgway), gives a strong picture of this abomination.

† See page 4 *ante*.

subject before us, we cannot but deplore the loss of that simplicity and earnestness which animated the early masters, now superseded by a restless spirit of display, with the revived imagery and mythologies of paganism, which suited not as well as the monumental architecture of Christianity.

The general type is but little changed,—the body rests on the sarcophagus as before, the pointed arch of the canopy is become semicircular, classic columns and panelled pilasters, filled with graceful arabesques supported it, and they were adorned with statues and bas-reliefs representing the heathen deities, fawns, satyrs, griffins, and other fabulous creatures mingled with the personages of sacred and profane history, and the traditions of the Church. This was the prevailing tendency of the age, yet, from the vigorous hands of those masters whose genius shone with a splendour like that of the evening stars—their very brilliancy deepening, by the contrast, the shades, which, when they were gone, obscured the arts, we have many fine works impressed with their individual originality of character.

Michelangelo, the leader of this revolution, has bequeathed to us, of the mighty creations of his impetuous imagination, the majestic figure of Moses and the four caryatides, designed for the mausoleum of Julius II., and the monuments of Giuliano and Lorenzo de Medici, with their celebrated figures of Night, Morning, Noon, and Evening; and above them, in their separate niches, the stern armed statues of the two heroes themselves, of whom thus speaks Rogers in his "Italy:"—

"There, from age to age,
Two ghosts are sitting on their sepulchres.
That is the Duke Lorenzo: mark him well.
He meditates—his head upon his hand.
What from beneath his helm-like bonnet scowls?
Is it a face, or but an eyeless skull?
'Tis lost in shade, yet, like the basilisk,
It fascinates, and is intolerable.
His mien is noble, most majestical!
Then most so when the distant choir is heard
At morn or eve.—Nor fail thou to attend
On that thrice hallowed day, when all are there—
When all, propitiating with solemn songs,
Visit the dead. Then wilt thou feel his power."

The adaptation of the church of S. Francis de Rimini, by Alberti, to the purpose of a mausoleum for Sigismond Malatesta, who desired that his marshals, with whom his fortune in this world had been cast, should be associated with him in death, is a noble conception. A simple arcade, of fine proportions, adorns the flank wall, under each recess of which, in their solemn order, stands one sarcophagus, and on the adjoining pier a tablet records the name of its inmate.

Well suited to the condition of society and character of the nation in France, with the gay and voluptuous Francis I. and his pleasure-seeking Court at their head, the spirit of the revival—introduced from Italy by Jean Joconde, the pupil of Brunelleschi, Demigiano, and Paul Pouce Trebati—soon became naturalised there; and in the hands of the sculptor architects of the time, its career was brilliant. Exuberant in richness and invention, graceful in execution, and delighting in the charms of beautiful females, whose naked forms every where meet the eye in their works of sculpture, painting, or jewellery,—we may wonder that, in some of their sepulchral monuments, a deep and serious feeling, and even a dignified propriety of character may be found, as in the tomb of Louis XII. and Anne de Bretagne in the Church of S. Denis, the design of which was by Jean Just, and the sculpture by Paul Pouce. Naked and stiff in all the fearful reality of death, their bodies are laid out on a rich sarcophagus, an arcade of light and elegant proportions surrounds them, in each opening of which is seated an apostle bearing his respective insignia: panelled pilasters, sculptured with arabesques of inconceivable delicacy and grace, support the entablature, which is broken over each, giving a playful effect: above are the kneeling statues of the king and queen in prayer. The whole stands on a basement of black marble, with panels of bronze, representing the victories of Louis.

Of similar arrangement is that of Henry II., by Germain Pilou, also in S. Denis, but deficient in the chaste and severe sentiment which characterizes the other. Even by the naked body of the king, three Pagan graces are represented holding the vase which contains his heart.

The reclining figure of Phillip Chabot, admiral of France, by Jean Cousin, is a fine work by that vigorous and powerful artist.

The tomb of Louis de Breze, in Rouen Cathedral, is an effective monument, of black and white marble. His body lies on a fluted sarcophagus. The projecting wings are each supported by two columns, on the lower stage, and by caryatides above: under an arch in the centre compartment of the upper stage, is the equestrian statue of Louis, armed *cap à pié*, and very spirited in execution. Also in this cathedral is the tomb of Cardinal Amboise, by Roullant Le Roux, a *chef d'œuvre* of the Renaissance, displaying all the characteristic elegance, richness, picturesque variety of details, and delicate execution, of the style, but wanting in the appropriate character of a sepulchral monument.

Gradually, however, these last gleams of the borrowed light of classic Paganism died out, after having irretrievably destroyed the purer spirit of mediæval Christian art. A mist of thick darkness then crept over the monumental architecture; for, awed by the superior excellence of the great artists of the revival, and in despair of ever equalling them, their successors dwindled into insufferable copyists: the mantle of Michælangelo had not fallen upon his unworthy imitators, and never did genius exercise so disastrous an influence on posterity, as in this instance. Then were all the stores that were previously undisturbed, ransacked for ideas. Copies, like portraits taken from the clay cold corpse, utterly without regard to propriety: unintelligible, abstruse allusions; quotations from a dead language, were palmed upon a credulous age, under the specious authority of antiquity. Pyramids, obelisks, and urns, with scraps from Greek and Roman models, and every style that had ever existed, were now reproduced in barbarous confusion, and as if the numbing influence of inability blighted every thing they touched: all the grace, the elegance and beauty of proportion of the originals had vanished, and they deserve not even the credit of faithful copyists. In the mediæval ages, men worked for the honour of God and for the rest of the souls of the departed; and, mistaken though they were in the latter motive, it was yet with them a labour of love and devotion. But now the pomp and pride of heraldry had usurped their place; the attempt to impose, and the vain, selfish spirit of display, obtrude themselves in all the works of the time, marring every effort, like the corroding influence of rust. The architecture became cumbrous and disproportionate, orders were piled above orders, with broken pediments and entablatures, surmounted by escutcheons and scrolls, lavishly adorned with gaudy colour and gilding, and with long pompous inscriptions. The effigies are stiff and coarse in execution, and represented leaning on one arm, kneeling, sitting, or standing; the husband and wife at times facing each other with a faldstool between them, and often their children in succession between them, or in a panel below, the males on one side (the eldest of whom usually was alone clad in armour), and the females on the opposite side; while Cupids and Griffins support the shields with the coats of arms or heavy wreaths and draperies.

Towards the seventeenth century, however, a change appears to have taken place, the predominant architectural character of the monuments declined, and gave place to the composition and grouping of the sculpture, with an increased energy of action and expression in the figures. They are consequently more dramatic than contemplative, and are thus opposed to the abstracted imaginative symbolism, and calmer repose of the works of the infancy of Christian art,—a necessary result of the comparative conditions of society, and not indeed to be regretted had the same simple, earnest spirit still animated them as formerly, for those were but as the budding blossoms of an expectant, trustful spring, which had now passed into the more mature and full blaze of an autumnal sun, under the influence of which, the fruits, of which they only saw the promise, were enjoyed. But unfortunately this position had its perils as well as its advantages, both in the restless, undirected wanderings of mediocrity, and in the still more fatal lapses of overweening selfishness, affectation, and impiety, which have induced a general want of purpose and character in these monuments, with overstrained attitudes and far-fetched allegories.

But in some better hands they have fared differently, and we have many works of modern times, which even more than answer our expectations, and shew that degree of excellence which we have a right to demand from the age. For, standing on a high vantage ground above the heathen of antiquity, groping in superstition, and over the mediæval Christians, not only in the comparative purity of faith, and freedom from error, but also in the advance of science and knowledge, of civilization and liberty, we have a place in the universal history of art, which it is our duty to occupy;—a path of progress, and not retrogression, which we ought to tread.

The aim, then, of modern monuments being the representation of the ideal and the expression of action, they claim to be judged of by the general canons of art, according to their individual merits.

Rysbrack, Roubiliac, Banks, Bacon, Flaxman, Chantrey, Canova, and Westmacott are among the chief of those sculptors whose monumental works are to be found principally in St. Paul's and Westminster Abbey, and a few scattered in other cathedrals and churches.

In St. Paul's they appear to the best advantage, combining well with the architecture, and imparting a life to its otherwise dreary untenanted space, and, although considered separately, most of them are unsuited to a Christian church, yet in their general effect such blemishes are lost.

In Westminster Abbey and the Gothic cathedrals they seem utterly out of harmony with the building, in one place blocking up a mullioned window, at another cutting into the panel work or hiding the piers, and by the violent contrasts of colour and even by the introduction of classic mouldings and details, can only be considered as hurtful to the general effect.

Considered individually, however, the greater part will not bear too close an examination. The hero often bears but a subordinate part in the composition, perched up on a column, perhaps merely a bust or medallion of him which some condescending angel is putting in its place, or crowning with a wreath, while the accompaniments have little of a sepulchral character, weeping genii and cherubs, with perhaps Hercules or Mercury attended by tame lions, or sitting composedly on the hulk of a ship, with a canopy of sail cloth suspended above, the affinity of all which, to a Christian monument, it might be difficult to discover.

The monument to Mrs. Nightingale, by Roubiliac, in Westminster Abbey, from the lower part of which death, as a skeleton, lifts his dart to strike her, whom the husband is endeavouring to shield, is very original and of consummate execution, but displays all the terror that death can inspire, without the consolation that the religion (to which the edifice that contains it is consecrated) might be supposed to afford. Chantrey's Bishop Heber, who is blessing two children, is appropriate; and, taken by itself, the monument to Sir Ralph Abercrombie is effective, and well grouped; the repose of the sphinx on either side contrasts finely with the more violent action of the centre, where a soldier supports the hero as he falls from his horse. The monument to Mrs. Warren in the Abbey is, however, a better work, by Sir R. Westmacott. In the works of Flaxman we find a proper sentiment and deep feeling, with high technical merit, general composition, grace, and management of drapery; his monument to Lord Mansfield is a noble work; those to Nelson and Earl Howe are good. But it is chiefly from his basreliefs the studies and casts of which have been lately given to University College, London, that a due estimate of his excellence can be gained; they are truly a rich store, from which many a useful hint may be gleaned, even with respect to the architectural composition of monuments.

Among the eccentricities of genius, I would allude to a tomb which defies classification, but stands alone, remote from every thing which has been, is, or ever will be conceived —Sir John Soane's monument to the memory of his wife, in the burying ground of St. Giles-in-the-fields, St. Pancras: it is as capricious as his own museum, and nearly as deserving a pilgrimage.

These works, however, are confined to a few places, beyond which they seem to have had but little influence. In the general mural monuments of our churches, and in the cemeteries, in which we possess a magnificent arena for the display of art, and where the imagination need not to be so restrained as in a church, we have indeed nothing as yet to leave to posterity, to mark our national character, religion, feelings, or tastes,—no trace of any originality of sentiment can be found. Ancient emblems of immortality, sometimes rendered in cement, as if in mockery, dwarf and triangular obelisks, broken columns, with urns and jars of every conceivable inelegant form, as if the custom of burning the dead still existed; and all the mournful, cheerless, emblems of paganism and mortality in disgusting profusion, yet none that the rich stores of the catacombs of Rome or the Gothic tombs would supply.

In all monumental works, simplicity is essential, yet not the false simplicity of the cemeteries, which places one huge slab on four square blocks, to resemble a seat as much as a tomb, and which causes so many of our monuments to have no other interest than may be attached to polished specimens of granite or marble, mere empty concessions to inability;—but that arising from terse language with fulness of thought, suggesting more than is expressed, disdaining all gaudy fritter and affectation, but not forbidding richness and magnificence where there is much to be told.

Also a solemnity of treatment, remembering their purpose, and withal a cheerfulness of character, in that the faith of a Christian should look beyond the terror of the grave. Mournful despair should have no part therein.

Then a due regard should be had to its propriety with the situation it is intended for. If to be in a building it should harmonize with the architecture, of which it should, as it were, form a part and an ornament.

If the building be a church, which indeed is an appropriate place for the memorials of her children, the character of the monument should be in accordance. No Pagan heroes or mythological allusions can there be tolerated. The dead lie there as members of the Christian church, and that which would have been indecorous for him when alive to have done, should not appear on his tomb, neither the orator on his rostrum, the soldier in the breach, nor the trumpetings of fame, can be permitted on her monuments.

Yet again, if the building be a senate-house or a walhalla, the case would be altered, nor would there be any impropriety in such representations. There, worldly glory should receive its meed of posthumous renown, and the love and gratitude of their fellows may fitly vie in appropriate panegyrics. Man's, is there the presiding genius of the place, but not so in the temple of God. JOHN P. SEDDON.

PROFESSOR COCKERELL'S LECTURES ON ARCHITECTURE.

THE annual course of lectures on architecture at the Royal Academy commenced on Thursday the 4th instant. The professor said that the object of these lectures was to place before the students those essential theoretical points which do not present themselves prominently in professional practice. At the outset, the student flattered himself that his time was to be spent in the study of design, and the cultivation of the attractive graces of the art; but in the urgency of his office duties, he soon found that little time was left for these delights. Technical details demanded his attention, and what ought to be first became last. He became appalled at the extent of the demands upon his powers. He soon came to regard the fine art as a thing secondary in importance, whilst he learnt the truth that the urgency of office business is indeed the urgency of daily bread, finding, too, after all, his noble aspirations regarded by the vulgar as vain enthusiasm.

Another contingency which would befal the student, was the special preference which the master under whom he studied might have for a particular style. This the student followed, and to all else became a bigot. Were the style mediæval, he felt no excellence but in copying; if Greek, all else was barbarism. He found, too, that he was subject to fashions in architecture, which he must follow, as he might those of dress, and unhesitatingly, almost enthusiastically. The adoption of the Egyptian style, and of the Greek were such instances. In the case of the latter, the taste was signalized by complete misappropriation, and every house was built to make-believe a hexastyle Doric temple. The art had long wanted some learned champion, who should take up the cudgels of sound criticism, and battle for the right.

Upon such rocks as these, then, the professor said, the student might suffer shipwreck, and therefore what should be his means of safety? How should we emancipate ourselves? It was plain that if fashion were to be the arbiter, a doubt would arise in the student's mind as to the true dignity of his art. He might ask,—Is taste but a fashion?—How should he aspire, then, to think, originally? The answer should be found in these and similar institutions.

The professor then referred to the increased advantages now within the reach of the student, the different lectures and classes affording the means of acquiring every branch of knowledge; and although, as he showed, they were not so fortunate in this respect as the students in France, yet as these were advantages which our predecessors never had, present time ought to spare something for the art. He also adverted to other requisite qualifications, saying that the architect should be a good workman, and distinguished by *dexterity* of hand as well as of mind, and cited Anaxagoras, who attributed the supremacy of man as much to the powers of the hand, as of the head. He also related an anecdote of Rennie, who having repaired the wheel of a stage coach, in which he and an aristocratic fellow-traveller had previously been on colloquial terms, found himself, as a workman, treated with great reserve and *hauteur*, and described the amusing discomfiture of the same traveller, on finding next day that the most honoured guest of the noble lord with whom he had to dine, was his companion, the workman, who now treated *him* with corresponding distance.

The professor then made observations of a similar tendency to some in a previous course, on the influence which was to be attributed to painters, condemning, in the words of Philibert de l'Orme, the "pretty drawings" in which aerial effects, and efforts foreign to the art of architecture, were discernible. He said that the picturesque had been a characteristic of all the arts of "the revival;" but in all cases, whichever art was prominent, the others were drawn towards it. For example, Greek art was sculpturesque, Egyptian art architectonic. This we should do well to bear in mind; and the greatest conceptions of our art had unquestionably been when architectonic art was paramount, and of opposite character, when following the treatment of painting and sculpture. In speaking of drawing, the professor conveyed the impression, that he did not esteem it of the engrossing importance sometimes claimed for it. Wren spoke of perspective, but it did not appear that he was a great draughtsman; but on his works might be inscribed, *numero, pondere, mensura*. Amongst the French architects, who had devoted much time to delineation, and amongst them great skill was to be found, the higher qualities of design he believed were impaired, whilst he had noticed that the architect of the Hotel de Ville, was inferior as a draughtsman. In the present day, we found the great number of our resources was being continually augmented, and calling for fresh adaptation of means to an end; but the art in its principles was ever unchangeable.

Finally,—in words which we must give verbatim, the professor said,—I congratulate you on the choice of a profession so entirely that of a gentleman; for as my German friends truly say, "no man can be a thorough gentleman unless he has something of the artist in him; and no man can be a thorough artist unless he is (in mind and character at least) a thorough gentleman."

I congratulate you because in this art and science, are comprehended all the supremacy and all the faculties of our nature, and all the privileges of the lord of the creation; for all intellectual rank and authority are accorded to him, and all the conquests of the artificer man are his enjoyments,—the whole field of science, exact and natural, are open to his investigation, and explained and tested by him. As a thinker and as a workman, he finds the fullest enjoyment, and an ever fresh pursuit,—he is incapable of tedium, languor, or ennui. His associations are amongst the gifted, the virtuous, and the diligent; with them and from them he is ever learning "wisdom and understanding and knowledge," like Bezaleel or Hiram. He stands before princes, as their counsellor and confidential friend, and holds their purse-strings; and he takes by the hand the humblest artificer. As entrusted and endowed with so many talents and privileges, he is their appointed arbiter, and establishes justice and judgment and equity between the little and the great; and thus discharging them with fidelity and modesty and skill, he becomes the key-stone of the social arch, and binds all the speculative and industrial classes together in a mutual support.

THE ROYAL INSTITUTE OF BRITISH ARCHITECTS.

AT a meeting of the Institute, held on Monday the 8th, Mr. Sydney Smirke, vice-president, in the chair, Mr. C. H. Smith read a paper, "On the various Qualities of Caen Stone," which was written expressly for our pages, in continuation of the inquiry therein commenced, and will appear in due course. The paper will be found very valuable, comprising analyses of the stone, and experiments on the ability of the different beds to resist compression, and on their powers of absorbtion.

Mr. Smith, in the course of reading the paper, made some additional remarks. As to Henry VII.'s chapel, he said, a general impression existed that it was originally built of Caen stone, and the miserable state into which it had fallen previous to its restoration had tended to destroy confidence in that stone. He could not find any record bearing on the subject, and it was his firm belief, after a long and careful inquiry, that it was *not* built of that stone. Speaking of the fact, that where the stones of a building in a smoky town are seen of their natural colour, decay is generally going on,—he said that temperature materially affected stone;—those sides of a building which received the rays of the sun decayed soonest.

The Chairman said nothing was more important to the architect than the proper choice of materials; he was like the painter in this respect, but was worse off, because cost must always be considered. This question of cost had aided the introduction of Caen stone. In one building erected under his own direction, the use of Caen stone instead of Portland involved a saving of 1,200*l*. or 1,400*l*.

Mr. Godwin being requested, made some observations on a table of experiments on the resistance of Caen stone to pressure exhibited by him,—to which we shall refer hereafter.

Mr. Bellamy and others also spoke.

SOMETHING ABOUT ST. PAUL'S CHURCHYARD, LONDON.

To begin at the beginning—as every city, town, or village presents the productions of the builder's art, in contra-distinction to the glorious works of nature on the broad expanse of hill and dale, so do these works of the human hand, where man delighteth to dwell, become pre-eminently distinguished above the rest when the architect has lavished on them the resources of genius in fine art conception and decoration. These enduring monuments record to after ages the degree of civilization and mental acquirements of the epoch; they form the history of a people typified in marble or in stone. The Tower of London, Westminster Abbey, and St. Paul's Cathedral are the three great landmarks of this vast metropolis,—the first, by its antiquity, indicating the advent of the Norman race to English rule; the second pourtraying the chivalric age of the Edwards and Henrys, entombed within its walls; and St. Paul's standing the most glorious of all the sacred edifices ever raised solely for Protestant Christian worship.

Lord Byron describes London as—

"A motley mass of brick, and smoke, and shipping
Dirty and dusky, but as wide as eye
Could reach, with here and there a sail just skipping
In sight, then amidst the forestry
Of masts, a wilderness of steeples peeping
On tip-toe, through their sea-coal canopy;
A huge, dun cupola, like a foolscap crown
On a fool's head,—and there is London town."

In the poet's imagination, the huge dome is the sole distinguishing feature of the City, and what painter could idealize the capital without its crowning crest? Thus, every visiter and traveller, either native or foreign, wends the way, on his arrival, to contemplate the fabric of Christopher Wren's master mind. After toiling tortuously up Ludgate-hill, with an occasional glimpse of a slice of the principal front, steering amidst a throng of persons, all of whom appear to be a minute too late, the lover of architecture arrives at the corner of the churchyard, as the area around the cathedral is called. Here he finds the pathway and roadway, which encircle the edifice, narrowed by a heavy and supremely ugly iron railway, erected on a dwarf wall. The concourse of pedestrians, porters, cabs, omnibuses, coaches, carts, and waggons, are constantly choking the way, to the infinite profit of a numerous progeny of pickpockets, who readily detect a stranger, by his gaze on the architectural glories before him, the price of permission to view them being the abstraction of a handkerchief, a snuff-box, a purse, or a pocket-book. The Mansion-house police reports constantly register the active performances of this peculiar race of small depredators. The visiter may look wistfully to escape from the wire-drawing of the moving population in the confined circuit, by hoping to indulge his reveries within the three gates of the enclosure, but that they are rarely opened is proclaimed by their dirty condition, and the abundant stains of pollution. The passage on the northern side could not permit the transit of vehicles from its extreme narrowness, without danger; every one thrusts through the crowd here in a hurry—a crowd much augmented by the shewy shops of a bazaar of silk-mercers, haberdashers, milliners, and ladies' cap-makers, attracting the gaze of the fair sex. Here, with their countenances rivetted on the pretty things seen through the plate-glass windows, they present an obstruction of bustles and flounces, while the City men, to save apologizing for accidental concussions of Crinoline (compliments are not profuse among wholesale traders), dart along almost in the longitudinal kennel which runs parallel with the church-yard enclosure. In this channel of stagnant and peripatetic vitality, the true Londoner may be detected with Cuvier-like perspicacity by his earnest walk and unshifting eye, as he wriggles through the current. A business man who has for 20 years run this gauntlet twice a-day at least, felt surprised and doubted the fact, when he was informed that a large portion of the enclosure at the north-east corner was a burial-ground, filled with tombs and grave-stones; he had never ventured to let a look wander so far. The City blades have made it a standing subject of wagers whether or not there is a tree growing within St. Paul's church-yard, so little was the locality ever made a subject of contemplation or remark.

Having already described a kennel running close by the wall of the enclosure, on the northern side, there will be found no fewer than seventeen tributary open east-iron gutters leading from the habitations across the pavement, discharging their contents into the main stream. These transverse gutters are very suspicious of soap suds or dish washings—as some of them were streaming to the main channel during the intensely frosty days; the longitudinal grand gutter did not consequently get a holiday through the low temperature, but was active in conducting the specious fluid into the large gratings of the sewer which are studded at intervals. The open jaws of these cavernous deposits may not emit the sweetest of breaths, at least no violets bloom on their brinks. To increase olfactory attractions, a bevy of omnibuses have made a terminus of one portion, where the continued presence of horses adds to the aforesaid kennel a tolerable volume of stable droppings, which a troop of live fowls are incessantly occupied in tossing about. Further on, and opposite the official abode of some of the church dignitaries, a stand is erected for porters to rest their loads thereon, and the wall is here largely desecrated in the same manner that defiles the gates of the area in front of the edifice. The graveyard at the north-east corner completes the condition of the northern side: of such an adjunct the voice of reprobation has already spoken with trumpet tongue. A cab-stand occupies part of the southern side, and another on the eastern side, both obstructive to locomotive circulation.

It has always been regretted that London's greatest architectural ornament should be so barred from an adequate view. The enormous value of house property here has hitherto rendered any expansion of space a serious question of expenditure. The house of Messrs. Butler, at the north-east corner, and that of Messrs. Goodyear, the corner of Watling-street, appear built purposely to create impediments. An angular slice from the fronts of Messrs. Hitchcock and Allanson, on the north side, would restore much of an evenness of line there, and these removals would be of comparatively small cost. But how much greater would be the advantages of display, if the ugly iron railing were demolished, and the entire area paved and made open, like Trafalgar-square, or the space opposite the Royal Exchange. The ruinous condition of the wall on which the cumbrous railing is fixed, will eventually throw it down, unless the influence of good sense should add an embellishment to the city of London, instead of perpetuating an obstruction, until time shall make the dwarf wall a heap of ruins, crushed by the massive weight it bears. Ample room would be obtained for the traffic, by enlarging the roadway on the south side, and the two cab-stands would become no inconvenience if provided for on the south-eastern space. The majestic portico would rise into due consequence, as well as the beautiful semi-circular ones of the transepts. Between the steps of the northern portico and the railing, twenty feet more of width would be added to the thoroughfare. What is now redolent of many evils, would become a great improvement and ornament of the metropolis, a source of enjoyment to the cultivated class of inhabitants and visiters, as well as causing the abolition of a constricted circulation in its present impure and nasty state. The open areas recently added at Trafalgar-square and the Royal Exchange, afford delightful breathing room to enjoy the scenes around, a kind of refuge from the sweeping torrent of the multitude in the incessant pursuit of mundane matters. There is no apprehension of the steps of the portico being infested by improper persons, as may be already evidenced at St. Martin's Church and the Royal Exchange. The presence of a single policeman would always ensure due propriety and decency.

AN IDLER IN LONDON.

ARCHITECTURAL LIBRARIES.—Sir: I was much pleased with the remarks of B. in your last as to the Architectural Association, and as I conceive it to be the duty of all members of the profession to put forth any suggestion that shall tend to strengthen the hands of that association, I would submit a proposition for the promotion of a society in connection therewith, for enabling each person becoming a member within a certain period to see all, and be in possession of some, architectural books of his own selection. This I conceive might be done by every member subscribing a certain sum per month, having a right from time to time, as the funds of the society permit, first of drawing numbers on the list, and then in virtue of being one of certain numbers selecting a work of not more than a certain price (unless they pay the difference); parties having paid their subscriptions to be entitled to draw, but those who have not paid up to within a certain period, or who have not subscribed a certain sum by the drawing day, to be disqualified for that time. Or something might be done in the way of an ordinary book club; the work purchased, after having been circulated, being put up to auction amongst the members. C.

ST. MICHAEL'S CHURCH, CHESTER.

WE are happy to learn that the spirit of restoration is stirring in Chester. A subscription is being raised for the purpose of renovating St. Michael's Church, and a design has been decided upon for repairing the tower (which is now in a very dilapidated and dangerous state) by competition, the successful party being Mr. James Harrison, of that city. The other architects that competed were Messrs. Hodkinson, Welch, and Park. The expense of the work will probably be about 600*l*. The present structure is of the Early English style of architecture, plain in character. The chancel was added to it in 1494, and enlarged in 1678. The present tower was built in 1610, and (like most of the other ecclesiastical edifices of that city) of the soft perishable red sand-stone of the district; and the consequent decomposed and weather-beaten aspect of the exterior gives it an appearance of greater antiquity. "This circumstance," says an historian, "seems to have caught the attention of Dean Swift. When this wit was once on his way from London to Dublin, he stopped for some time at the Yacht Inn, in Watergate-street; and being alone, sent an invitation to several clergymen in the city to dine and spend the evening with him. Not one of them, however made his appearance, upon which the Dean vented his spleen in the following epigrammatic philippic:—

"The church and clergy of this city
Are very near akin;
They're weather beaten all without,
And *empty* all within."

It is intended to restore the tower of the church in the same style of architecture, but of a more ornamental character (?) to strengthen the pillars that support it, and to add buttresses at the angles. It is proposed to case the whole of the exterior of the tower with *red sand-stone* varying from 18 inches to 10 inches in thickness, and, it is said, of same quality of stone that has given so many proofs of its inapplicability for work of this character. It was proposed to cover this tower with Portland cement, but the building committee have prudently abandoned that intention.

BLIND BUILDERS, OXFORD.

As you are ready at all times to expose the present injurious system of competition, which the building business is subject to, I beg you will accept of the subjoined list of tenders delivered on the 17th ultimo, for refitting the parish church at Hooknorton, Oxon. The drawings were made by Mr. Underwood, architect, of this city, and the most explicit information given, yet a dozen builders are found whose opinions vary in such an extraordinary degree upon so small a work.

So long as builders continue to rush blindly into competition at all hazards of sacrificing not only their time but their capital also, so long will the *London Gazette* teem, as of late, with the names of those engaged in this department of commerce—and so long will private individuals and committees cling to a system which in itself both tends to the ruin of the respectable tradesman, and to result in the abominable practice of executing the work by employing improper craftsmen, and bad and unseasoned materials, which cannot fail to end in the mortification of those with whom the direction and the choice are placed:—

Lockwood, London	£895	0	0
Symms, Oxford	798	14	0
Cowley, Oxford	754	15	0
Davis, Banbury	743	17	6
Long, Witney	729	15	0
Franklin, Deddington	720	0	0
Plowman and Hack, Oxford	697	0	0
Wyatt, Oxford	657	0	0
Strong, Stow-in-the-Wold (accepted)	585	0	0
Herbert, Chipping Norton	575	0	0
Claridge, Banbury	546	2	0
Mackröy, Great Milton	499	10	0

Amongst other lists recently forwarded to us is one of tenders for a new shop-front in Pall-mall East. The highest of five is 620*l*. (a highly respectable London firm); the lowest 340*l*.

SIR BENJAMIN HEYWOOD'S BANK, MANCHESTER.

MR. J. E. GREGAN, ARCHITECT.

SIR BENJAMIN HEYWOOD'S NEW BANK, MANCHESTER.

IN the course of a recent article on Manchester we made a few remarks on a bank then only partly up, which was being erected in St. Ann's-square, for Sir Benjamin Heywood and Co., under the direction of Mr. J. E. Gregan, architect.

Annexed we now give an engraving of the entrance front. The main building contains, on the ground floor, the public office of the bank, with the safes beneath—all of fire-proof construction, as already mentioned; and in the upper stories the principal rooms of a residence for one of the head officers of the establishment: this part of the building is faced externally with Halifax stone. Those who are concerned in the erection say that, "with the exception of the small columns and architraves of window-dressings, every stone is placed upon its natural bed; being laid in the work exactly as it lay in the quarry. This precaution has been taken in order to preven the premature decay which occurs too frequently in our stone buildings, and which is almost invariably to be seen on those stones standing on edge, that is, with their natural bed outwards, and consequently exposed to the corroding influence of the atmosphere."*

* The miserable condition of St. Ann's Church immediately opposite this bank (and a comparatively modern work), is ascribed by the Manchester people to this oversight. It was here that the accident with the steam pipes happened the other day.

THE LIGHTING OF GREEK TEMPLES.

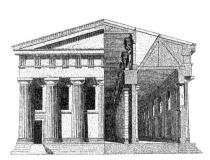

Fig. 1.—TEMPLE OF JUPITER AT AGRIGENTUM.

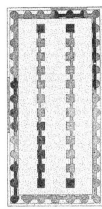

Fig. 2.—PLAN OF TEMPLE OF JUPITER AT AGRIGENTUM.

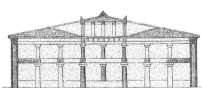

Fig. 3.—SECTION OF TEMPLE AT ELEUSIS.

Fig. 4.—SECTION OF PARTHENON.

The lower building adjoining contains the domestic offices of the residence, and other rooms not immediately connected with the business of the bank, and is externally constructed with stock brickwork and stone dressings. In other respects the drawing explains itself.

The works are not being done by contract, but by measure, and schedules of prices already agreed upon.

THE LIGHTING OF GREEK TEMPLES.
MR. FERGUSSON'S "INQUIRY INTO THE PRINCIPLES OF BEAUTY IN ART."

We have already given our readers some idea of the opinions on matters of art in England entertained by Mr. Fergusson, and of the bold and fearless manner in which he has attacked some errors and prejudices. What we have said has, we hope, led many of our readers to study his book themselves and to enjoy the pleasure the perusal of it affords.

As yet, however, led away by the more salient points, we have not referred to any of the architectural questions which Mr. Fergusson has sought to solve, and this omission we desire now to rectify.

There is nothing connected with the disposition of Greek temples which has given rise to more discussion than—the *mode of lighting them.* " Many authors, who have been shocked at the clumsiness with which modern architects restore the hypæthron, which is always done by merely removing the roof off the cell, and exposing the latter to the weather as an open court, have denied its existence altogether." Our author, with justice, will neither believe

that the light of day was altogether shut out from the temples, nor that they were without roofs. Referring to the sculptured frieze round the cell of the Temple of Apollo Epicurius, at Phigalia (now in the British Museum), he urges that no artificial means would have lighted this as it should be, and that the Greeks never would have placed such a work where it must remain in the dark.

" The architects," he observes, "who restored this temple for Stewart's 'Athens,' as well as M. Blouet, felt this, and, to avoid the difficulty, omitted the roof over the cell altogether, making it merely an open court—a sham temple, in short, a peristyle and dead wall surrounding nothing : such ideas, I know, occur quite naturally to architects now-a-days, but never were executed anywhere except by them ; so that this, certainly, is not the solution of the problem."

Our author then points out what he considers was the mode of lighting adopted, and this will be better conveyed by the annexed woodcuts than by words.

The annexed plan of the temple of Jupiter, at Agrigentum, which first led the writer to this view of the question, " shews an immense cell, at least 230 feet long by 50 wide and 70 high, which no one will, I am sure, contend was ever lighted by lamps. Mr. Cockerell,[*] from whom the plan is taken, has, in his restoration, admitted the light correctly enough into the side aisles (except that in a Doric building the jambs could not have been sloping), but how he could help seeing that the centre was lighted by windows between the Talamones I cannot understand. To me it appears so easy to effect this, and so self-evident that this was

[*] Stewart's " Athens," vol. v.

the mode by which light was introduced into the cell, that I am content to refer the proof to the annexed woodcut (fig. 1), which, without pretending to minute accuracy, or to being an ornamental restoration, at least explains how it could be done, and with a little pains it would not be difficult to shew how it could be done ornamentally."

The " Section of Temple at Eleusis" shews how he would restore the roofs of that structure, and he translates the word *opaion* in Plutarch's notice of this temple, in his life of Pericles, " clerestory."

Fig. 4. shews the same system applied to the Parthenon ; and this ingenious theory is strongly corroborated by the fact, that the Egyptians used this mode of lighting in their great halls and some of their temples.

PROJECTED WORKS.—Advertisements have been issued for tenders, by 17th February, for the erection of a new church at Rusthall, near Tonbridge Wells, to be executed in stone ; by 25th inst., for the erection of a parsonage-house at Exbury, with offices, chaise-house, &c.; by 1st March, for deepening, widening, &c., 100 miles of drain within the Middle Level, Norfolk, &c., with erection of bridges, sluices, tunnels, &c.; by 15th inst., for alterations and additions to Cleobury Mortimer Union Workhouse ; by 16th inst., for the formation of a public sewer at Newcastle ; by 17th inst., for laying down water-pipes at Southampton ; and by a date not specified, for a gas-holder and cast-iron tank, for the United General Gas Company, with six tons of tank plates, and 500 yards of 10-inch, and 400 yards of 6-inch gas mains.

FLOORS FOR COTTAGES.

A PRACTICAL plasterer writes as follows:—I have tried most materials for floors, and, as a composition, I think the best and most economical mode for ground floors is to lay, on a hard bottom, clean gravel, sand, lime, and tar, to form a concrete, and to prevent damp from rising: then lay down an inch and half thickness of good cement,—either Blashfield's No. 1 and three of coarse sand, or Atkinson's cement and three of sand, or patent Portland cement and four of clean coarse sand, doated in by a rule on screeds; care being taken to prevent as much as possible the joints from setting, so that it may be one sheet. If the cement set slow, while soft trowel it down, but not when it is setting or it will injure the face. If it set too quick for that, leave it with a rough key, and cover it an eighth thick with fine mortar, and trowel it down gently before it begins to set. If the floor is not likely to be damp, instead of the gravel, &c., pave it with clean hard brickbats, half an inch apart, and cover it an inch thick only of good cement; this will make a very durable, hard, cheap floor, that will not harbour dirt, wet, nor vermin: when done, it must not be trod on for a few days. As to lime-ash floors,—any lime compositions harden slowly, and don't set hard at once, so that they would not be fit to tread on for a long time; but lias lime and metallic sand trowelled a thin coat on a rough coat of good cement, makes a lighter colour and very good floor; or where time is not an object, coarse metallic sand, in proportion of three to one of lias lime, finished with fine stuff, and well trowelled, makes an excellent floor.

When I saw in THE BUILDER, the desire of "a correspondent" to know how the "lime ash" floors are made, I sent no reply, because I hoped to see a communication from one who had seen them adopted in different counties (which I have not), and could thus compare their repective merits. The directions printed in your last are very clear, but there are two or three matters I would like to add whilst the subject is open. The first is that the sand should be fine, free from small stones, which would be loosened if in the surface of the floor, and, eventually, would quit their resting place. Secondly, in Devonshire (whence I obtained my knowledge of these floors), they mix the lime ash and sand in *equal proportions*, instead of "two-thirds sand and one-third lime ashes," and I have found it answer admirably. The third observation I will make differs from your correspondent, who states that the mixture is to remain "in a body, for *three days*." It should rather remain a *fortnight* (more rather than less), in order that the lime may be thoroughly slaked; for, otherwise the floor "*bubbles*," and the holes, thus formed, are enlarged in an incredibly short time through moving the various articles of furniture. When once the surface is broken, it crumbles annoyingly; this renders repairs difficult and unsatisfactory, yet it is scarcely worth consideration, except to guard against its necessity, when we reflect that they last without it for so long a period. I have seen floors that have lain for nearly forty years, and they are now without symptoms of decay. We must bear one thing in mind; that the success of the work is almost entirely dependent on the care bestowed in preparing it.

WM. BOUTCHER.

Another correspondent says:—As, in a late number, you invite remarks on the formation of cottage floors, I can recommend to those gentlemen who have plenty of rough timber, and a common circular saw mill on their estates, in cutting their fire-wood, to reserve for *wood bricks*, of the same width and depth as common bricks, and in longer or shorter lengths, the offal pieces of timber, which might otherwise be thrown into the fuel basket.

They should be properly laid upon a sound foundation of lime, or coal ashes, are cheap, and more comfortable than brick or stone floors, and particularly adapted for children's feet in parish or other schools.

The objection to wood is, its retention of damp after washing.

VALUE OF EXEMPTION FROM SUPERVISION.

RAILWAY SHEDS—THEATRE STAIRS.

THE Caledonian Railway Company have lost property to the extent of several thousands of pounds by a fire at the station in Lothian-road, Edinburgh. A spark from the engine (probably) set fire to a truck full of goods, which did the same bad office for the rest of the train. It then communicated to the goods' shed, which was wholly of wood, then to the northward passenger shed, which was of the same material, and then to the southward passenger shed, and this being mainly of iron the destruction was here stopped.

When the recent fatal accident at the Victoria Theatre, London, occurred, it was at first attributed to part of the gallery staircase having given way. We avoided referring to it, however, because this did not seem to be certain, and it would appear from the verdict of the jury (though the statements were any thing but clear) that this was not the case. The jury recommended greater attention to ventilation in similar approaches where large numbers of people may congregate.

Now, whatever may have been the cause of this particular accident, it ought to lead attention to the condition and arrangement of the staircases, lobbies, and modes of exit in several of our theatres, and reconcile parties to the clause in the Buildings Act, giving to the referees control over staircases and passages in public buildings. This clause only applies to new buildings or alterations, and it is really a question whether it ought not to be made to apply to existing structures, and extend to obtaining for the public the means of ready egress. Were it not for the possibility of causing an excitement and perhaps injuring the property of individuals, we could point to some places of amusement and for public meetings where the public assemble under circumstances of the greatest danger.

RAILWAY JOTTINGS.

The *Morning Post* announces that the Railway Commissioners "have approved of one amongst a multitude of plans for ensuring the safety of passengers in railway travelling," namely, the formation of "a series of footboards and holdfasts along the extent of a train, and by means of which, in the event of accident, the guards may communicate with either engine-drivers or passengers." In so long and so pertinaciously thrusting this desideratum on the notice of all and sundry interested in the public safety, we were encouraged in a series of efforts seconded by none (except through more or less prominent quotations from THE BUILDER itself), by the well grounded assurance that to this result at last it must and would come; and if the recommendation of the Railway Commissioners be now seconded by the companies as it ought to be, we shall find the free transit of the guards to and fro along a train to be a most variously useful and successful means of ensuring one of the great objects for which the press has so long contended, namely, the safety and confidence of the public during railway transit. Then, too, will be the fitting time and opportunity for experiments with those much more varied than original details of plans for summoning the guards to particular carriages,—calls to which then only can they properly respond,—and then too will the name of "guard' itself be for the first time no misnomer.——In the United States a patent has been taken out for an improved mode of warming passenger trains by a combination of flues, connected by elastic and flexible hose with openings and registers in the bottom of the carriages.——Another of those desperate endeavours by which some companies have been striving of late 'to make both ends meet' was lately complained of in the *Times*, by one of the North-Western clerks. The directors, it seems, intend to reimburse themselves for any defalcations of which the dishonest amongst those comparatively few clerks who finger the company's funds may plunder them, by themselves adopting a system of indiscriminate plunder out of the poor little salary fund of the honest clerks, as it passes through their own directorial fingers. Two-pence to four-pence a pound per annum off each, or 1,000*l.* to 2,000*l.* in all, is to be the amount of the mulct, whatever be the limit of the defalcation,—only, should there be no defalcation, the directors have generously determined to—withdraw their fingers from the honest clerks' pockets? Oh no! Once there, at any rate, they are not to be at that trouble for nothing; the honest clerks must then pay the penalty exigible for the *want* of defalcations and dishonest clerks, "by making up the deficiency" out of an incidental penny a pound, which is still to stick to the tarry fingers! Is it credible?—"We pause for a reply." Meantime, however, we may also ask—What has become of that still more noble and hopeful scheme of "the whole railway interest" under which careful "railway servants" were to be mulcted "to the extent of one-fifth of their annual salary," in order to "mitigate the losses" of "sufferers" by accidents arising not even so much from the faults of those careless servants whom the directorial "sufferers" wished to engage on such *reasonable* security, as from their own.——The second tube at Conway was finally tested, prior to its being opened for traffic, on Wednesday week. The tube in use will be closed for a time, so as to substitute sleepers of iron for the present ones of wood. The entire structures will then consist of 2,600 tons of iron, slung over a span of 400 feet.——Over nearly half an acre, the extensive erections at the Edinburgh station of the Caledonian line have been ravaged by the fire. Twenty carriages, and a great quantity of goods, have been destroyed, as well as the sheds, &c., on the ground.——A project for uniting all the railways round Paris, by a line forming a circle to go from station to station, is mentioned in the French papers. The several companies interested have, it is said, already asked the Government to obtain the assent of the National Assembly to a grant of the necessary aid for the employment of the working classes around the metropolis.

ELECTRO-TELEGRAPIC PROGRESS.

The United States men are far a-head of us. President Polk's cumbrous message, says the *New York Express*, a message containing upwards of 50,000 words (!) was dashed all the way from Baltimore to St. Louis in twenty-four hours, and this, too, with the minutest punctuation marked in the document. Copies were also dropped on the way at York, Harrisburg, Carlisle, Chambersburg, Bedford, and Pittsburgh, in Pennsylvania; Massillon, Cleveland, Zanesville, Columbus, Dayton, and Cincinnati, in Ohio; Madison and Evansville, in Indiana; Louisville, in Kentucky; and Saline, in Illinois. The gentlemen who accomplished this wonderful mental, mechanical, and electrical feat are Messrs. O'Reilly, of the Atlantic and Lake Telegraph Company, and H. J. Rogers, of the American Telegraph Company, who wished to prove beyond all cavil that the lightning line can be made available for the transmission of large documents as well as for short messages.——The various telegraph offices along the line from Cincinnati to Pittsburg, says the *Cincinnati Times*, were thrown into some excitement last evening by an incessant and uniform ticking, which occurred in their various registers. It appears that Professors Walker and Locke have connected an astronomical clock with the line in such a manner that its beats were conveyed to Pittsburg for determining longitude. That a clock going in Cincinnati should tick so loud as to be heard in Pittsburg or Philadelphia, and along the intermediate line, at one and the same moment, is an item of "natural magic" which a few years ago could scarcely have been predicted.——It has been found at Hull, that, notwithstanding the admission and pressure of sea water which has obtained access to the pipes (once water pipes) used, in crossing under one of the docks there, for enclosing the waterproof cased wires of the telegraph, not the slightest deflection of the needle has been discovered in experiments instituted with a 72-plate battery.

BUILDERS' BENEVOLENT INSTITUTION.—The ball given in aid of the funds of this institution on the 9th, passed off very satisfactorily, much to the credit of the acting members. We were sorry not to see more of the leading builders present.

COTTAGES AT £10 A-PIECE.

A WRITER in the Chelmsford paper has been shewing how agriculturists may provide cottages for his labourers, on their own land, at 10*l*. a-piece, by using *clay lumps*. We think with the editor of the paper in question that our labourers are entitled to a house something better than 10*l*. will rear; still the suggestion is not without use. The writer says,—"The best material for cottage building, both for health and comfort, is the dried clay lump; the plan of construction should be a cross, by which means the dwelling room may be lengthened at the expense of the scullery. The walls should be placed 8 feet apart, leaving two rooms 16 feet long by 8 wide; the dwelling room may then be 24 feet by 8, and the scullery 8 feet by 8. Any labourer can prepare the clay (which should have short straw well trodden in by a horse), and cast the lumps in a mould, 20 inches long by 10 wide and 7 deep, at 3s. 6d. per hundred. When thoroughly dry the lumps should be placed in the same material as they are made with, and raised on the walls about three courses a day; the cost of laying is 2s. per hundred. The walls being only 8 feet apart, the rafters for thatching may be made of slight poles nailed on another pole embedded on the wall; the window-frames are built in the walls, and the windows open on a pivot."

His estimate, very close cut, is as follows:—

Thirteen hundred lumps, at 3s. 6d.; ditto, laying at 2s. 6d.	£3	18	0
Deal boards for five doors and seven windows, carpenter's work, &c., with glass for windows	2	10	0
Thatching (exclusive of straw, supposed to be on the farm)	1	10	0
Two bushels of lime	0	1	0
Small poles for rafters, &c.	0	15	0
One hundred bricks for hearth	0	3	6
Piece of wood over fire-place	0	4	0
Plastering the walls and ceiling, &c.	0	15	0
	£9	16	6

NOTES IN THE PROVINCES.

IN Ely Cathedral the introduction of stained glass windows is rapidly going on. The large north-east window under the lantern—"the especial glory of the church"—has just been fitted by Wailes, as far as the funds raised by the undergraduates of Cambridge would allow. The principal figures represent King Edward, who was educated at Ely, and his Queen. In addition to the five stained windows provided by the munificence of the Rev. E. B. Sparke, four others, it is said, are in hand, to be presented by the Dean of Ely and others.——The keeper of the Lincoln Cathedral 'shew' lately met with a salutary lesson while rudely turning out an individual caught in the sacrilegious act of coming up through the aisle without coming down with the dust. The gentleman so 'caught' and pertinaciously expelled, turned out to be 'a tartar' in the shape of the new sub-dean, on whom it is to be hoped that this incidental perspective of the *a posteriori* visage of Janus will produce an equally salutary impression, not to be obliterated by the 'amiable countenance' that may meet his eye in future visits to his venerable Alma Mater.——A 'Penitent Females' Home' is to be erected at Lincoln, from plans prepared by Mr. Pearson Bellamy, a local architect. Contracts, according to the *Lincolnshire Times*, are to be speedily called for.——A disputed point with respect to work performed at the Springfield Gaol above the estimate and contract has arisen between the county magistrates and Messrs. Curtis, who threaten equity proceedings. The work, it is said, though not provided for in the contract deed, was done by order of the county surveyor; but there appears to be, nevertheless, a desire on the part of both magistrates and surveyor to stand by 'the bond.'——The sum of 8,500*l*. has been ordered by the Essex county magistrates to be raised on loan, to pay for the site at Brentwood for the County Lunatic Asylum, and certain architects have been selected to furnish plans for a substantial building, without unnecessary ornament, to accommodate 200 males and 200 females, and capable of extension: plans to be sent in before 29th March, with estimates of all costs. The premiums to be awarded are 150*l*., or the usual commission, for the best, 100*l*. for the second, and 50*l*. for the third.——In cleaning out and sinking the water-course called Stream Ditch, at Faringdon, Berks, an extensive workshop, belonging to a Mr. J. Fidel, and full of timber, deals, and tools, has been undermined and entirely destroyed. —— The following estimates were sent in for the erection of the Corn Exchange at Stourbridge:—

Mr. Edward Smith	£465	10	0
,, Thomas Nash	430	0	0
,, William Smith	380	0	0
,, Thomas Ostins	303	0	0

The commissioners voted by a majority for "Mr. Smith's estimate"—so says our authority—but which Mr. Smith does not appear; though, from preceding remarks as to the engagement of Mr. Edward Smith to "have the building completed in six weeks from the commencement of operations," it rather appears that his is the chosen estimate.——Nearly the whole of the new Lunatic Asylum at Birmingham is roofed, except the central building. Plans and specifications for a supply of water are being obtained, and the boundary wall and other works contracted for are in rapid progress.——The old butter cross at Doncaster is being carefully taken down, to be re-erected elsewhere. The bell-turret came down with a crash while letting it through the roof with ropes.——The foundation-stone of a new 'British school' has been laid at Mexborough.——The warerooms of the Hull Glass Works lately took fire, and insured property valued at between 1,000*l*. and 2,000*l*. was destroyed.

OPENING OF THE NEW CONSOLIDATED COMMISSION OF SEWERS.

THE long-delayed commission, under the new Sewers Act, was issued on Saturday last; and the members chosen to carry its operations into effect, by her Majesty, met for the first time on Wednesday, at the office, Greek-street, Soho-square. The names of the commissioners we have already given. The following were present:—The Earl of Carlisle, viscount Ebrington, M.P., Hon. Frederick Byng, Very Rev. Dr. Buckland, Dr. Southwood Smith, Mr. Joseph Hume, Mr. Edwin Chadwick, Mr. John Leslie, Mr. William J. Broderip, Mr. Robert Hutton, Mr. R. Lambert Jones, Mr. John Bullar, Mr. John Bidwell, Mr. Joseph Hodgson, Captain Robt. Kearsley Dawson, Mr. W. R. Grove, Mr. Thomas Banfield, Mr. Edward Lawes, Mr. Alexander Bain, Mr. Thomas Hawes, Mr. Cuthbert Johnson, Rev. W. Stone, Rev. Morgan Cowie, and Rev. Edward Murray.

The Earl of Carlisle having been called to the chair, the clerk formally opened the business by reading the Queen's commission by which they had been summoned, and the subjects given to them in charge for the benefit of the public.

The Earl of Carlisle then rose and spoke as follows:—I have much satisfaction in opening the new consolidated Metropolitan Commission of Sewers. It has indeed been a subject of regret to me that, in consequence of legal and technical hindrances, this has not taken place sooner. We ought only the more steadily to resolve, by increased diligence and exertion, to make up for any time that has been inevitably lost. It would be hardly becoming among ourselves that we should dwell upon the composition of the commission. I think any one who attentively scrutinizes it, will perceive that the selection has been guided by a wish to comprise, within a manageable number, persons qualified by special experience, by high acquirements, by successful exertions in the general cause of sanitary reform, and over whose unemployed leisure the Government might be presumed to have some fair claims. However, the best indication of the selection will be the character of the services performed, the work we turn out. Let us remember that we enter upon our labours at no ordinary time—under no common circumstances. If this metropolis has as yet been but lightly visited by the hateful cholera, we cannot be sure that its destructive energies may not be now bound by the strong chain of winter, and that it may not, when loosened by the mild breath of spring, sweep afresh upon us with a hundred-fold power. Much may be feared, much may be learned from what has taken place so near as the village—suburban, shall I call it—of Tooting; and the state of our workhouses and hospitals cannot be too watchfully examined. Viewed thus in connection with the dangers of the time, in connection with the public attention which has been given to the whole subject of sanitary progress, in connection with the enlightened exertions which are being made in a variety of quarters, the business and aims of the commission must assume a different and a higher character than belonged to any of its predecessors. You are aware that the legislature has recently constituted a Board of Health, whose labours the Government contemplate with unceasing anxiety, and I think it will be wise both in this commission and in that board, to establish an interchange and reciprocity of assistance and services with each other. For this reason I look upon it as very desirable that at least one of the superior officers should have a mutual communication with both bodies. Although the number of this commission, as compared with former bodies of the kind, is most materially reduced, I think it plain that much which requires minute detail, and constant superintendence, can only be efficiently performed by committees and sub-committees, and it will be one of the most essential foundations we can lay this day for our future operations, to effect some organisation of these committees. The very extent and variety of the acquirements, and reputations which are comprised in the list of the commission, must render inevitable occasional discrepancy of views and conflict of opinions. Let me earnestly, most earnestly enjoin upon all a spirit of candour and modesty, of allowance and forbearance for each other, of patient inquiry, and searching after truth, with a determination to find out the truth, and nothing but the truth. Let me recommend that we should combine a strict attention to the pecuniary interests of those for whom we act, with a fair and liberal consideration for the officers, and that above all we should bear in mind, that where there is so much matter controverted, unsettled, and still to be learned and established, our proceedings are bound to be cautious, tentative, gradual,—taking nothing for granted, and proving all as we go along. With these observations, which I feel that I owe some apology for having offered, I will only add one word of reference to the only source of wisdom and help, that He may guide our way and bless our work. (Loud and continued cheering.)

On the motion of Mr. Bullar, the rates made by the late commissions were re-enacted by the new commission.

On the motion of Lord Ebrington, it was agreed that the ordinary courts should be held on the first Thursday in every month, at ten in the morning.

The Earl of Carlisle said that before they met, it had been recommended that in consequence of Mr. Stable's advanced age, he should not be continued in office as clerk to the Commission, but that his case should be referred to a committee for consideration. This suggestion was agreed to. It was also ordered that Mr. Stable's accounts should be handed over to Mr. Hatton, who should take charge of them provisionally.

A recommendation from the General Purposes Committee was read, that in consequence of the greatly increased services of Mr. Hertslet, clerk, and Messrs. Roe and Phillips, surveyors, they receive an advance of salary of 250*l*. to Messrs. Hertslet and Roe, and 200*l*. to Mr. Phillips. In the case of Mr. Hertslet, it appeared that he has performed the duties of clerk to Westminster and Middlesex Commission, to Holborn and Finsbury, Tower Hamlets, Poplar and Blackwall, St. Katherine's, Surrey and Kent, and Greenwich Commissions, without any addition to the salary received as clerk to Westminster Commission alone.

Mr. Hume wished to know whether any report had been received recommending this advance of salaries?

The Earl of Carlisle replied in the affirmative, and the resolution was carried.

It was next proposed and carried that Mr. Roe be the consulting surveyor, at a salary of 400*l*. per annum, with liberty to retire at any time, on giving three months' notice, at 200*l*., provided he takes no other salaried office.

It was agreed that the solicitors should deliver a retainer to Mr. John Henderson, as standing counsel to this commission.

That the offices in Greek-street, Hatton-garden, Bethnal-green, and Borough-road, be continued as the district offices of this commission.

That complaint books be kept at each office, in which every ratepayer having any complaint to make should enter the same.

In reference to the last resolution, Mr. Hume wished to know whether the books would be open to all persons, or only to ratepayers.

The Earl of Carlisle was of opinion that no objection would be offered to an inspection by the public generally.

Mr. Bullar said that the complaint books were open to every person making a complaint, so that they might see whether they had been attended to.

Adjourned to Tuesday next.

APPROPRIATION OF RAILWAY ARCHES.—We are glad to find that our suggested appropriation of railway arches as refuges for the poor, is likely to be carried into practice, benevolent individuals having been led by the remark to exert themselves to effect this.

Books.

An Introduction to Heraldry: containing the Origin and Use of Arms; Rules for Blazoning; Dictionary of Terms, &c., &c. By HUGH CLARK. Fourteenth edition. London: Washbourne, New Bridge-street, Blackfriars.

A BOOK which has passed through fourteen editions scarcely needs a recommendation: but having been asked by some correspondents to name a concise introduction to the science of heraldry,* and this edition (published 1845) coming before us, we point it out to them as well calculated to supply their want.

A chapter on heraldry in conjunction with architecture, which has been added in this issue, gives it a further claim to notice.

The editor of the book cites the large shields on the side walls of the nave of Westminster Abbey, erected during the reign of Henry III., A.D. 1249, as one of the early introductions of heraldry as an adjunct to architecture; and to Henry VII.'s Chapel at Westminster as a building wherein it was the most largely applied.

A paragraph on this same subject will be found on another page.

Miscellanea.

NECESSITY FOR APPLICATION AND INDUSTRY.—"This age," says Mr. Lyon Playfair, in an interesting address to the students at Putney College, 'On the importance of studying abstract science,' "is an age of action, and if you are to succeed in future life, you must now brace and prepare yourself for the struggle. If you fall asleep while you are young, in vigour, and able to prepare yourself for future life, the world will not know you when you awake, and it will be a long and a sad struggle for you to overtake those who were active when you were passive. Recollect, that it is only by study, downright hard study now, that you can acquire that mental strength and vigour that will enable you to overcome the increasing difficulties of progress in life. The hopes that I have held out are hopes certain to be realised by him who employs his youth well in acquiring a fundamental and accurate knowledge of the applied sciences, but they are hopes equally certain of frustration to him who has misspent his period of study in idleness and neglect." Again,—"If you resort to the story of the human race from the earliest periods till now, if you view them in their aggregate as nations or in their individualities, as exhibited by the great men of a particular period, you will find the same result in all, that the habits and studies of the young determined the character of an epoch, of a nation, or of an individual. No man in any profession ever rose to fame or station without in youth having exhibited habits of application and industry. If you do not show in youth that you have vigour and strength to hold your own in the stream of life, and skill to steer your bark amidst its shoals and perils, depend upon it, in age your bark will be pushed aside by those who have devoted their time to acquire a knowledge of how to manage their own vessels, while you will be constantly in trouble, hazard, and dismay, running against shoals, tossed on the banks, and shipwrecked in your dearest hopes. Be assured, that in these days, the carving out of your fortunes is entirely in your own hands. In this busy community of your own, the bees do not make honey for the drones. But the hive is still large enough to contain and cherish all those who enter in with habits of industry and skill in applying it."

IMPROVEMENTS AT MIDDLESEX HOSPITAL.—With regard to a paragraph on this subject, Mr. Wyatt asks us to say:—1st. The recent alterations in no way originated from, or were dependent upon, "the munificent bequest of Lady Murray." It was not until *after* a special general court of the governors had sanctioned the works, at an outlay of 12,000*l.*, that they were informed of this handsome gift. 2ndly. The alterations have not cost 20,000*l.*, as reported, and will probably not involve a greater outlay than *half* his original estimate for a *new hospital.*

* A sort of question which, as a general rule, we are compelled to decline answering.

THE WOODEN CHURCH, GREENSTED, ESSEX.—We have already alluded to a paper by Mr. Burkitt on this subject, read at a meeting of the British Archæological Association. In this church was enshrined the body of Edmund the Martyr. According to the paper, Mr. Letheuillier, in 1728, drew up an account of this wooden church, which was published in the *Vetusta Monumenta*, at which time there existed nearly entire the series of split trees which formed the four walls of the nave, since which a considerable portion of the old edifice has been removed. The east end opening into the chancel was pulled down to connect the two parts, as well as a large portion of the west end connecting it with the tower, which is used as the vestry; the south side has also been broken into, to form the modern entrance, leaving the north side the only fair specimen of the original building. The entire length of the shrine was 29 feet 9 inches, the breadth 14 feet. The sill rested on a low wall of brick, which formed the groundwork; the upper part of the frame consisted of rough-hewn timber, with a groove cut in the under part, and the uprights forming the walls, being cut in the form of a wedge at the top, by being inserted into the groove, were made fast by wooden pins. The series of the outer timbers were segments of the tree, with a board about 2 inches thick, taken from the middle, these boards probably serving for the interior lining of the shrine. On examining the state of the timber, during its recent demolition, it was too evident that neglect alone has been the cause of the serious inroads made on the otherwise sound timber, by the *Ptinus Pectinicoinis*, an insect well known to antiquaries, from its destructive powers on wood carvings, old books, &c., the larger sort attacking the stoutest timbers, and in a very short time reducing them to powder. It is this insect which has, in a very short time, rendered it absolutely necessary to remove the wooden portion of Greensted Church, and although efforts have been made to replace some of the old material, the portions rendered useless have been very considerable. Mr. Burkitt urged the necessity of using means, by washing the timber with some liquid obnoxious to the insect, that the present age should be guiltless of the charge of neglecting one of the most interesting memorials of past times.

GREENWICH HOSPITAL: SCULPTURE.—A subscriber writes thus:—"I recently had occasion to visit Greenwich Hospital, and in going into the Painted Hall it at once struck me how imposing and grand it might be rendered by the introduction of statues of the several naval commanders, placed on each side up the centre of the room. It is an opportunity that seldom occurs, of rendering it one of the most imposing rooms in the country by the introduction of statues of the several great commanders whose valour and prowess is depicted on the walls in the several pictures. In a country like our own, where every Englishman feels proud in hearing the names of its great commanders extolled, both by sea and land, statues of such men create additional interest in the minds of the people. These things are not lost sight of on the continent, then why in this country? It has a parsimonious appearance which ought not to exist, it is a want of proper pride. If you cast your eye on Trafalgar-square or Waterloo-bridge, what an opportunity again offers itself by the introduction of such ornaments, more especially on the latter—one of the most splendid bridges in the world; and what could render it a more imposing object still than by being surmounted by statues of generals, with a grand composition of an arch leading from the Strand, more especially as it has now become one of the leading thoroughfares of the great metropolis. It is to be regretted that these opportunities are so long lost sight of."

THE CHICHESTER TRAINING SCHOOL COMPETITION.—We strongly suspected that things were not going quite correctly here, and said so. Our suspicions would seem to be thoroughly borne out by an extraordinary statement received just before going to press, from Mr. John Elliott, who speaks more fearlessly than architects are in the habit of doing. We will not risk weakening its force by a too hasty digest of it, and therefore defer it till our next.

IMPROVEMENT OF LEICESTER-SQUARE.—The renewed suggestion in our pages to throw open the area of Leicester-square, has again been largely echoed and approved,—to such an extent, indeed, as ought to lead to its adoption. The *Literary Gazette* and *Athenæum* both call it an excellent suggestion, which they would be glad to see carried into execution. The *Athenæum* remarks,—"Green trees in the heart of a city 'are and ever were most commendable,'—but the Dryads have evinced an insuperable objection to live in Leicester-square. Nature has no chance in that locality against art; Flora has been dead beat in that arena by Miss Linwood and Madame Wharton. One can conceive of any kind of singing in Leicester-square but the singing of birds. It is useless for the householders to cling to the fond belief of an Arcadia before their upper-floor windows. Grass wont grow even in the untrodden part of that crowded but melancholy-looking thoroughfare. 'It is on evidence,' says the correspondent of THE BUILDER, 'that no person ever walks in the inclosure; the walks are mud,—and the trees that should be green are black.' Traffic is here so much the engrossing object of life that 'nursery maids and children idling or taking exercise, as they do in the more aristocratic squares, would seem quite out of character.'—To reclaim this waste from its aspect of vegetable desolation by the scheme in question would certainly give an air of cheerfulness to the site by which both the passer through the square and the sojourner therein would be gainers:—and we recommend the hint to those commissioned generally with the improvement of the architectural appearance of the metropolis, and to those particularly whom the subject more directly concerns."

THE BOARD OF TRADE AND THE LONDON ART-UNION.—By a letter from Sir Denis Le Marchant to the hon. secretary, dated the 3rd instant, the Board of Trade have withdrawn all their proposed alterations, being reluctant "to urge their views against the strongly expressed and deliberate sentiments of the committee of the London Art-Union, with whom they have been all along most anxious to co-operate." Having made a great mistake, the wisest course their lordships could adopt was to retrace their steps, and this, we are glad to find, they have done with a good grace. It is to be hoped they will never again, by uncalled for interference, risk the prosperity of this most important institution.

THE POLLUTION OF WATER BY POISONOUS SALTS OF LEAD AND COPPER,—a subject, to the great importance of which THE BUILDER was the first popular medium through which the public attention was excited, now attracts particular attention. Facts and circumstances of more or less recent occurrence have been stated in the *Times*, *Morning Herald*, &c., by competent authorities (in the latter throughout a long and most interesting communication from Stratford-on-Avon, by Dr. Thomas Thomson), confirmatory of every thing stated or suggested in THE BUILDER. The evil, Dr. Thomson believes, is a far more general and more deadly one (though probably not within the bounds of the metropolis), than is even yet conceived; and in allusion to the discovery at Claremont, seeing that even royal palaces have not been exempted, the painful suspicion is excited that the health and strength of one who was much beloved by the nation at large in bye-gone years were thus undermined while resident there. It is found to be in the precise ratio of its purity, as we long since noticed, that water becomes impregnated with the poison; for when it contains various neutral salts, especially sulphates, a protective crust is formed on the surface of the cistern, &c., which it is now recommended, as already in THE BUILDER, to preserve rather than cleanse away. Besides the more serious symptoms of paralysis, colic, &c., a frequent index to the action of such poison is a dark blue line along the translucent edge of the gums. Sulphuric acid, diluted largely, in doses of 10 to 12 drops at a time, has been recommended as a remedy, but determined *prevention* is better than cure; and to that end, wherever water tends to take up lead or copper, earthenware pipes, glass pumps, and perhaps zinc cisterns—all cheap articles—are advisable.

INSTITUTION OF CIVIL ENGINEERS.—At the opening meeting, January 9, Mr. Joshua Field, president, in the chair, the paper read was "A Description of the improved Form of Water-wheels," by Mr. William Fairbairn. After noticing the opportunity for improvement afforded by the substitution of cast and wrought iron for timber, in the construction of hydraulic machines, the author pointed out the disadvantages and loss of power attending the principle and the form of the old water-wheels, which disadvantages had induced him to adopt the construction described in the paper, and which he termed "The Ventilating Water-Wheel." The general object of these modifications was to prevent the condensation of the air, and to permit its escape during the filling of the bucket with water, as also its re-admission during the discharge of the water into the lower mill-race. These wheels were described to possess advantages beyond the overshot, the undershot, or the common breast wheels, and were best adapted for falls not exceeding eighteen or twenty feet, and where at times there was a considerable depth of back water. The wheel had a close sole, the tail ends of the buckets were turned up at a distance of two inches from the back of the sole plate, and running parallel with it, terminated within about two inches of the bend of the bucket, immediately above it. The water, in entering the bucket, drove the air out by the aperture into the space behind, and thence into the bucket above, and so on in succession. The converse occurred when the buckets were emptied, as the air was enabled to flow in as fast as the wheel arrived at such a position as to permit the water to escape.

ARCHITECTURE IN OXFORD.—The *Oxford Herald* mentions various architectural improvements with which the liberality of the university, of particular colleges, or of individuals, as well by the restoration of ancient buildings as by the erection of new ones, has lately adorned Alma Mater. One is the restoration of St. Mary's the Virgin, under the directions of Mr. Blore, at an expense which they think cannot be short of 3,000l. In the cathedral church, from the nave two cumbrous pews have been ousted, and their places supplied by low and massive oaken benches, the carving on their standards designed to harmonise with the massive Romanesque architecture of that portion of the cathedral. The principal and fellows of "the King's Hall and College of Brasenose" have caused no small portion of the old walls, built originally of the crumbling Headington stone, to be renovated and repaired, that they may hand down their college buildings to their successors in a more perfect state. The new hall of Pembroke-college quadrangle is third pointed, with a tower at the end, and is well spoken of; there are new cemetery chapels, situate respectively in Jericho, Osney, and Holywell. The first of these is "Romanesque," while the two others are of the pointed styles.

SHORT LEASES AND THE LEGACY DUTY. —I am glad to see that, amongst other misconceptions of even the present day, the law of building on leases is likely to be discussed calmly, and, I will venture to say, amended in consequence at no very distant period. What can be a greater injustice than the following:—Society requires healthful places of residences. The lord of a piece of land where such residence is not alone necessary but imperative, lets his land on building leases, not *at its value*, but at a hundred times *its value yearly*,—a building is erected on it, worth, say 1,000l., it is to be the property of the erector for 61 years, taking the city leases for their suburb lands. In 20 years the owner dies and leaves it to a relative, the descendant of his grandfather; as it respects him it is personal property, and he must pay a legacy duty of 6 per cent.—60l. In 20 years more he dies, and leaves it also to a relation more distant, and again a legacy duty must be paid of 104l.; a further period of 21 years elapses, and in comes the landlord and takes all, stock and block, and the owner may thank his stars if he be not called upon to pay for some dilapidations which the indulgent landlord finds out can be charged according to law. Now, Sir, if a great railway company have a *penchant* for my house or lands, they can take it at such value as a British jury of twelve men on their oaths say it is reasonably worth, although it may be my ruin. Why, then, should not land wanted for building in suitable places not be subject to the like regulations—the well-being and health of people congregated together must surely be of equal moment. The landlord has all along had more than his due: and at length the descendants of the man who has spent 1,000l. in building on such freehold land, having paid legacy duty over and over again, find the landlord's descendant in possession of all, and not liable to legacy duty at all, because it is freehold! Can such things be, and overcome us like a summer cloud without our special wonder? Is there any man alive bold enough to take this bull by the horns.—L.

MEETINGS OF SCIENTIFIC BODIES
Held during the ensuing week.

TUESDAY, JAN. 16.—Institution of Civil Engineers, 8 P.M. (anniversary.)
WEDNESDAY, 17.—Society of Arts, 8 P.M.
THURSDAY, 18.—Royal Society, 8½ P.M.; Society of Antiquaries, 8 P.M.

TO CORRESPONDENTS.

Received.—"XX.," "D.J.," "C.C.," "M.A." Oxford (we shall use the drawings : they shall be returned when done with), "J.C." (Kilburn), "Lady C.V." "J.H.P.," "G.G." (Charing-cross), "G.T." (Banks), "Quendam" (unavoidably postponed), "H.P.," "A.S.S.," "E.G.O." (thanks), "H.F.S.," "W.H.," "J.B.," "P.C.W.," "E.W." (Manchester), "G.M.," "J.G." Hanwell (we will endeavour to obtain the address). "The Architectural Scrap Book," by J. Butler and H. Hodge (15, Beaufort-buildings) ; "Hints on Cottage Architecture," by Henry Weaver, architect (H. Pope, Budge-row, London) ; "Report to the Town Council of Chester on the Sewerage and other Works," by the Borough Surveyor, Mr. Baylis.

ADVERTISEMENTS.

ROYAL POLYTECHNIC INSTITUTION.—Lectures on the Cultivation of the Vine, and on the Art of Singing, by G. Clifford, Esq., with various illustrations...

TO ARCHITECTS—COMPETITION AND OTHER DRAWINGS.
MR. THOMAS S. BOYS, Member of "The Picturesque Architecture of Paris, Ghent, Rouen, &c."...

TO ARCHITECTS AND ENGINEERS.
MR. EDWARD is desirous of meeting Gentlemen who require Coloured Architectural Designs...

COON having discovered a New Method of LITHOGRAPHING PLANS of every description...

GRUEBER & Co.'s PATENT ASPHALTE ROOFING FELT, one penny per square foot: DRY HAIR FELT for covering Boilers, Steam Pipes, &c., and SHEATHING FELT.—Agent, HENRY AMERY, 26, Bucklersbury, London.

FIRE BRICKS.—A parcel of the best Newcastle Bricks to be SOLD at a low price in small lots.—Apply to WARD and COMPANY, Agents for ditto, Honduras wharf, Bankside, and Jamaica Cottage House, Guilford...

BUILDERS AND CONTRACTORS.
TARPAULINS for COVERING ROOFS during Repairs. SCAFFOLD CORD and every description of ROPE used by Builders upon the lowest terms...

PHANTASMAGORIA for CHRISTMAS.—AMUSEMENT and INSTRUCTION by means of CARPENTER and WESTLEY'S improved PHANTASMAGORIA LANTERNS, with the CHROMATROPE and DISSOLVING VIEWS...

CLEANLINESS is necessarily at all times conducive to health, and thus as well as economy, is greatly promoted by substituting for the tedious process of painting with oil and white lead, STEPHENS'S DYES for STAINING WOOD, as a SUBSTITUTE for PAINT...

Right column

A CATALOGUE, with Engravings, Prices, and ample Particulars of COMMUNION LINENS, ALTAR-CLOTHS, SURPLICES, ROBES, ECCLESIASTICAL CARPETS, &c. &c. Forwarded free by Post to ARCHITECTS, CLERGYMEN, and CHURCHWARDENS, on application to the Manufacturer, GILBERT J. FRENCH, BOLTON, LANCASHIRE.

IRON FOUNDRY, 9, Brick-lane, Old-street. St. Luke's.—J. J. JONES having made great additions to his STOCK OF PATTERNS, begs to inform the Trade, that he can now supply them with Plain and Ornamental Iron Castings, Girders, Railings, Gates, Iron Coping, Balconies, Window Guards, Verandahs, Ornamental Staircase Panels, Iron Staircases, Tomb Enclosures, Trellis Panelling, Lamp and other Brackets, Cauldrons, Newel Rails, Water Closet Works, Area Gratings, Fly and other Wheels, Wheel Plates, &c. BAKERS OVEN WORK. Forge Backs and Tuyeres, Rain Water Pipes and Gutters, Sash Weights, Furnace Bars, Stoves, Ranges, &c., always in stock.

PATENT SUSPENSION STOVES.—As a precaution against cholera, the Board of Health strongly recommend "warmth and ventilation." For the attainment of this all-important object, the PATENT PORTABLE VENTILATING SUSPENSION STOVES were expressly invented...

WARMING by means of the circulation of WARM AIR.—BURBIDGE and HEALY beg respectfully to inform the public, that they are prepared to undertake the warming of structures, hot houses, &c. with a new apparatus of the most simple and durable construction, which they can warrant to keep in order any length of time, and which is capable of effectually warming buildings of any magnitude in a most economical manner.—BURBIDGE and HEALY, 130, Fleet-street.

HOT-WATER APPARATUS.—The attention of architects, builders, and others is respectfully requested to BENJAMIN FOWLER'S superior method of heating churches and chapels, halls, staircases, conservatories, forcing and greenhouses, manufactories and warehouses, kitchen ranges for drying timber, &c., and every variety of purpose for which artificial heat is required...—BENJAMIN FOWLER, 63, Dorset-street, Fleet-street.

IRON FOUNDRY, 169, DRURY-LANE, and CHARLES-STREET, DRURY-LANE.
JOSEPH GLOVER, Solicits the attention of the Trade to his extensive Stock of PATTERNS for CASTINGS of EVERY DESCRIPTION, comprising columns, railways, bar work, gutters, &c., and every variety of ornamental Wheel Pinion and Engine Palsettes; Range Stoves and Hot Plate Metal. A stock of Rain-Water Pipes, Plain and O G Guttering, Air Bricks, Sash Weights, &c., &c. A very superior description of Soot Door, particularly suitable for internal work, being perfectly secure, and not easily lifted. ESTIMATES given for IRON ROOFING and every description of Ironwork...—GLOVER'S FOUNDRY, 169, DRURY-LANE, and CHARLES-STREET.

TO BUILDERS and CARPENTERS.—Ellipic Stoves, double hooks, 5d. per inch. Register, 6½d, 7d, &c. per inch. Cottage Ranges, with Ovens and Boilers, 3 ft. 3 in. 40s.; 3 ft. 6 in. 45s.; 3 ft. 9 in. 44s. Self-acting Ranges, with Circular Oven and Back Boiler...

TO BUILDERS, CARPENTERS, AND OTHERS.
BENJAMIN WALMSLEY, Wholesale Ironmonger. Brass-founder, Stove-grate, and Kitchen-range Manufacturer, at the Padlock, 157, London-road, Southwark. Self-acting Ranges, with oven and boiler and revolving shelves complete...

TO ARCHITECTS, BUILDERS, &c.
HAYWARD, BROTHERS, late H. HENLY and Co., WHOLESALE IRONMONGERS, and Manufacturers of KITCHEN-RANGES, STOVES, &c., 187, Blackfriars-road, and 117, Union-street, Borough. Strong Self-acting Kitchen Ranges, with Back Boiler and Oven, and Wrought Bars...

No. CCCXI.

SATURDAY, JANUARY 20, 1849.

F making books, there is no
end:" nor do we desire there
should be. If there *were* an
end, what should we poor
critics do? many of our contemporaries would say. To "book some new
thing," is not an easy or often-occurring matter: new ideas and great thoughts are less
plentiful than gold,—at all events, in California,—and some real *thing* yet unsaid is
found with difficulty. To diversify the surface of knowledge, however; to put it in a
fresh light, especially if a stronger; to gather
together scattered fragments, and form there-
out a whole; to lure some minds to what they
had before disregarded, or provide instructive amusement for others, is of no trifling
consequence: and long, therefore, may the
world be able to exclaim, " of making books
there is no end." What should we do without books,—what should we *be* without books?
They preserve for us the best part of the best
men; give us pure joys, and alleviate our
sorrows: they take us back into the past, and
aid us in preparing for the future.

With books such as those to which we are
now particularly alluding, we have not edito-
rially much to do, but they are our recreation
and delight,—the medicine which " physics
pain," and increases enjoyment,—and we speak
in thankfulness.

In graver strain, and all the quieter for the
foregoing spasm, let us make known to our
readers the contents and character of two or
three books now before us, which belong to
our province, and have a certain sort of connection. First, then, of the

"MUSEUM DISNEIANUM."

The number of specimens of ancient art,
real and forged, to be found treasured up in
museums, and scattered about all over
Europe, is quite extraordinary, and if it could
be correctly stated, would scarcely be believed.
In England alone these collections are enormous, and in many cases are little known.
Available records of them, it need scarcely be
said, are very valuable; while unknown beyond
their owner's immediate circle, they are comparatively useless to investigators, and it is
therefore most desirable that their possessors
should be led to print catalogues and descriptions of them.

Amongst the finest of these collections is
that belonging to Mr. Disney, F.R.S., at the
Hyde, near Ingatestone, and, under the title
we have just now quoted,* Mr. Disney has
recently published two elegant volumes of
descriptions, illustrated by numerous woodcuts and lithographs. The first part was exclusively dedicated to marbles. The second
part, now issued, is confined to bronzes, some
Anglo-Roman pottery, and three cinerary urns.

During a residence in Italy from 1795 to
1798, a relative of the collector was enabled to
acquire many specimens taken at the time
from Herculaneum and Pompeii, at much less
cost and trouble than they can be procured
for now. In those days the state of the
country was such, and the indolence of the

* *Museum Disneianum,* being a description of a collection
of various specimens of ancient art in the possession of John
Disney, Esq., F.R.S." London: Rodwell. Bond-street.

court of Naples in these matters so great, as
almost to amount to indifference, and consequently the people had more facilities of
selling objects which they found there. Greater
care is at present taken of these relics; they
are deposited in the *Museo Borbonico ;* and the
site of Pompeii, as all recent travellers know
to their cost, is watched and guarded; so
much so, indeed, that of many things even
sketches cannot be obtained without putting
a piece of silver on the eyelids of eager functionaries, to prevent them temporarily from
seeing.

Of each object in Mr. Disney's collection an
engraving is given, all executed by Mr. George
Measom, and they are apparently very truthful. A few of them will doubtless be acceptable to our readers.

Fig. 1* is a tripod found at Pompeii in 1790.
This was probably used (says Mr. Disney) to
hold the frankincense and verbena upon the
altar, and thence called a *thuribulum.* The
interior (fig. 2) is highly wrought with leaves
and the, so-called, honeysuckle, in a circle: in
the centre is a head of Medusa.

Fig. 3 is a lamp found at Herculaneum about
1795, and ascribed to the best time of the
Greek republics. It is 9 inches in diameter,
and has ten lights, each terminating in a bull's
head, so contrived that the flame would issue
out from between the horns. Several other
lamps are given in the work.

Fig. 4 is a vase handle, with two heart-shaped
ears, highly ornamented, by which it seems to
have been attached to the bowl. It is 5½ inches
wide and 6 inches high.

While one class of minds are discovering,
collecting, and arranging the works of classic
times,—and truly wonderful works these are,
produced for the most part before the
Christian era commenced,—others are working in the mediæval mine, and are multiplying
for present use, and saving for posterity, by
means of an accurate pencil and printer's ink,
the forms of works which are scarcely likely to
endure so long as those last mentioned. Mr.
J. K. Colling has just now completed the first
volume of

"GOTHIC ORNAMENTS DRAWN FROM
EXISTING AUTHORITIES,"

and a very nice volume it is, containing 104
plates, 19 of which are enriched by gold and
colour.† Well may the author say in his
preface that he " has often paused in his
labours to gaze, with wonder and admiration,
at the never-ending variety and glorious genius
displayed by our forefathers in the various
portions of their works." The variety *is* never-
ending; and yet how few were the principles
on which these men worked! how simple the
course of their proceeding!

Our author continues,—" How great is the
regret which arises in the mind when it is observed that, in our modern ecclesiastical
structures, ornament is too often either altogether banished, on account of its expense, or
left to the untutored hands of a common
workman!

Of late, however, a better spirit has arisen,
and there are edifices erecting in different parts
of the country which would do credit to our
masons of old. Should the present work be
found to conduce ever so slightly to the general promotion of this spirit, and assist the
artist in his progress, the labours of the author
will be amply repaid, and his utmost object
realised."

* See p. 27.
† " Gothic Ornaments; being a series of Examples of
Enriched Details and Accessories of the Architecture of
Great Britain." Drawn from existing Authorities, by Jas.
K. Colling, Architect. London: Geo. Bell.

Viewed rightly as materials for study, as
evidence of the mode adopted by the mediæval
workmen in ornamentation, and as a collection of beautiful forms and arrangements for
re-combination, it will assist the artist in his
progress; but if it be used only as a collection of patterns, to be blindly and slavishly
copied, it will only tend, in common with
similar works, to perpetuate the reproach
which attaches to us as a race of feeble imitators.

The examples are all classed, as Early
English, Decorated, and Perpendicular; and
a good notion of the peculiarities of ornamentation belonging to each style may be
gained by an examination of the volume.
Some of the coloured plates are very excellent; and it is satisfactory to observe
a gradual improvement in the plates from
first to last, because it leads to the anticipation that the second volume will be even
better than the first, and ought to induce
many who may have hesitated about subscribing till the work was finished, at once to
send in their names, and so to encourage the
artist in what must be a costly undertaking.

The book is particularly rich in examples
of the decorated period. One of these we
have engraved for our pages, as well because
it is a beautiful specimen, and shews the
application to nature made by the mediæval
ornamentalist, as well as an evidence of the
character of the book. It represents a stone
canopy, from an arcade in the presbytery of
Winchester Cathedral, on a scale of 1½ inch to
a foot.*

Throughout the book this resort to natural
types, especially during the best period of
mediæval art, is made evident, and has been
fully felt by the author.

Having so often dwelt on the advantage
which would follow a return to this study of
natural forms for ornamental purposes, we
have received with considerable satisfaction
Mr. Whitaker's

"MATERIALS FOR A NEW STYLE OF
ORNAMENTATION,"

which consists of fruits and flowers drawn
from nature in outline.† Amongst them we
need scarcely say will be found the type of
many a familiar object of ancient and mediæval
art:—

" The sunpurge presents the type of many
a Gothic roset; the horny gentian, Solomon's seal, and red misletoe are almost
well-known Grecian borders; in the convol-
volus, the left hand flower is precisely the
same as one on an Etruscan vase in the British
Museum; the camelia, with the globe, having
in the centre only a plain hollow, which follows the loss of the inner petals, they falling
off a short time after the flower has blown, is a
striking ancient type; about the honeysuckle, it
is superfluous to say any thing; the iris must
have given the idea of the Gothic finial; and
the light-foot has the leaf most prevalent in the
same style: the flowers in the drawings which
agree with the ancient centres of architectural
capitals is useless to point out, as they all so
palpably shew the derivation of those sculptured ornaments."

The great point is to teach the student
how natural objects should be represented to
render them consistent with architectural
design. There is always a point of sight
which is most advantageous, and this requires
to be determined with judgment.

We have before this ventured on the asser-

* See p. 30.
† " Materials for a New Style of Ornamentation, consist-
ing of Botanical Subjects and Compositions, Drawn from
Nature." By H. Whitaker. 1849. London: Weale.

tion that natural forms, *geometrically* arranged, should be resorted to for ornamentation. Mr. Whitaker takes the same view, using, indeed, almost our words. Speaking of such an application of flowers in their natural form as is sometimes seen, without any connection with architectural features, he says,—"There has hitherto been a conventional blindness to the absurdity of their adoption in this way, which is a mode totally different from the one I am propounding, which proposes in the first instance to give by means of a geometrical representation an architectural character, and then to connect them with architectural designs on the most approved principle revealed in antique and mediæval art."

The book contains fifty plates, nicely lithographed, and will be found of important service, not merely to architects and decorators, but to muslin and calico designers, bookbinders, plasterers' modellers, paper-stainers, and all connected with ornamental design. We are firmly of opinion that Mr. Whitaker has done service by the production and publication of this book, and we hope it will find the good sale it deserves.

"Life is short and Art is long." Those who smooth the way deserve well of their fellows.

ON THE VARIOUS QUALITIES OF CAEN STONE.

IN all well-regulated concerns of an extensive kind, a judicious division of labour is indispensable: an architect would require his life and faculties to be prolonged to the extent of the patriarchs of old were he to attempt, by his own personal observations, to gain a thorough knowledge of the numerous materials employed in an extensive edifice. The practical part of his profession alone, if scientifically studied, is far too extensive for the brevity of one man's life; it must be the result of accumulated knowledge, the collective labour of many observant individuals; such a mass of information can, therefore, only be acquired collaterally, through the medium of books, and oral communications.

It is a duty incumbent on every member of society to use his best endeavours, however insignificant, to facilitate the advancement of knowledge, and to make his fellow creatures as much wiser and as much better informed as lies in his power. Under these impressions, I venture to shew my zeal in the cause, by offering some observations on the nature and properties of stone from the quarries at Caen and its neighbourhood.

The stone in most general use for ornamental architecture, in the south of England, is obtained chiefly from that extensive tract of country usually denominated the "Oolitic district," which passes from Yorkshire through the various counties until it reaches the coast of Dorsetshire. The same kind of stone again appears in Normandy, and its characteristic features prevail in the celebrated quarries around the city of Caen: diverging into several branches or ranges of hills, it traverses France, forms the great mass of the Jura Mountains, and constitutes part of the chain of the Alps. The Oolitic rocks of Normandy present a close analogy in their general, and even in some of their minor divisions, to those of southern England: commencing in the vicinity of Havre de Grace, and extending our observations to the neighbourhood of Caen and Falaise, we find a series of beds corresponding with those of the Oolite in our own country. It would thus appear, that throughout a considerable portion of France and England, the causes which produced the Oolitic rocks did not differ materially; shewing, that at the time of their production, similar general causes were in action over a particular portion of the two countries, probably long before the sinking of the land which produced the English Channel.

The entire country from the sea to some distance beyond Falaise, and from Bayeux to a considerable distance east of Caen, is composed of the same mineralogical description of strata; remarkably horizontal, and in all probability continuous, or without interruptions. The comparative insignificance of elevations or depressions, merely of a few yards, up or down, is unimportant when considered on the principle of a general level. It rarely happens that a district, of 30 or 40 miles in area, presents so tame and unpicturesque a scene, so apparently undisturbed by any geological phenomena, as is to be found in the neighbourhood of Caen. All these various beds of Oolitic limestone are of marine origin—consequently they must have been deposited at the bottom of an ancient sea, and then upheaved to their present position, where they appear to have remained undisturbed since the period of their consolidation, affording a striking example of long continued tranquillity; and remarkably contrasting with the violent distortions, depressions, fractures, and denudations, so conspicuous on the opposite coast, from the Isle of Wight to the extremity of Dorsetshire. The only instance of a geological disturbance in the district appeared to me to be in the line of the river Orne, and the variation of level about the entrances to the principal quarries, which seems to have been caused by a *fault*, either of elevation or subsidence; and I am inclined to believe that the very same strata, which have been so long worked for architectural purposes, might be found beneath the meadows, on the low side of the river. Such a disruption of rocky masses is at first startling to the imagination of a common observer, but extremely insignificant to the geologist. Whether such change took place by upheaving or sinking, it must have been uniform over a considerable area, for there is hardly an instance in which the strata are bent or contorted from the level.

On approaching the coast of Normandy, from the English Channel, and for some distance up the river Orne, on the eastern bank, rocky masses of a hard calcareous nature are abundantly sprinkled near the coast, and scarcely to be seen above water, which renders the navigation so far dangerous, that vessels are compelled to take a pilot to enter the Orne. This same stratum of limestone, being very nearly level, continues also inland to the eastward, where there are quarries at Cagny and at Bonneville; but the most extensive quarries of this material are situated at Ranville, close to the eastern bank of the Orne, about halfway between the sea and the city of Caen. This stone is composed almost entirely of broken shells, occasionally rather oolitic, and containing fragments of very small fossil corals: the whole slightly and irregularly laminated, is united into a mass with a strong calcareous and highly crystalline cement. In geological position this limestone rests upon the Caen freestone. It resembles in general structure and composition several varieties of similar material to be found in our own country, such as the Hamhill stone near Yeovil, the Taynton near Burford, that of Weldon-in-the Wood, Northamptonshire, and a few more, all of which are well known to be extremely durable, although they are usually rather too coarse grained to be used for minute ornaments, but no doubt admirably adapted for bold architectural or engineering works.*

Before particularising the stone of any precise spot, it may be well to state that the city of Caen, together with its entire environs, rest immediately upon the rocks of freestone. The bare strata may be observed on the surface of the ground, all round the foundations of some of the principal buildings of the city and villages in the neighbourhood. Although the beds in general appear to be perfectly level, nevertheless, upon a more attentive examination, through a distance of 10 or 12 miles, an evident depression may be observed from inland towards the sea, of probably about 100 feet, or an angle of something like 1 in height to 500 in length; for this reason the beds of Caen freestone are not to be found on the coast, where, if they are continuous, they are buried beneath the Ranville rocks, and probably form the bed of the sea.

From the general flatness of the country it is rather difficult to distinguish the precise localities where older rocks have risen from beneath to the surface through the freestone beds; and in the immediate neighbourhood of Caen such features appear to be of rare occurrence. It is pretty certain that the same calcareous strata may be traced in continuity round the city as far as St. Croix and Tourville on the west; also to Fontenay; and on the road from Caen to Falaise, with one or two slight interruptions, similar stone may be found throughout nearly the whole distance of 20 miles, for I am disposed to consider the quarries of St. Pierre and Aubigny merely as modifications of the same rock.

Leaving the consideration of subjects which may appear remote and hypothetical, I now proceed to the main object of inquiry, which is to describe the different qualities of Caen stone. As I have already stated, there are many places in the neighbourhood from whence building stone is at this time procured; and there are others where the name and inequality of surface would lead us to suppose that, in by-gone times, quarrying operations had been practised to a considerable extent, although long since discontinued. Even close to the walls of the citadel, and midway between two of the largest buildings in the city, namely, the churches of St. Stephen and the Holy Trinity, there are places still retaining the names of the "Old Quarries," the "New Quarries," and the "Little Quarries:" of these I shall have occasion to offer some remarks hereafter. But the principal quarries from whence Caen stone is procured, which, from their number and extent, we may infer have been in work during several centuries, are situated from 1½ mile to 2 miles' distance, on the south-west of the city, near to the village of Haute Allemagne. The surface of the country, especially that part over the quarries, is nearly level, having a very slight inclination towards the north-east, so as to drain into the river which divides the high from the low land. The river above the city is very narrow and shallow, little more than a brook or rivulet, and has never been used for the conveyance of stone, although it runs close by the entrances to the principal quarries. The quarries, to the number of about 30 or 40, are all subterranean, and are entered from a road along the side of the hill, or escarpment. A few shafts have been sunk from the surface perpendicularly, up which the blocks of stone are hoisted. The shaft quarries are situated at a considerable distance from those which are entered from the side of the hill, and have therefore no communication from one to the other. In one or two cases, these shaft quarries have been deserted, on account of the water finding its way from the surface into them.

The surface soil in the vicinity of Caen, as is usual in stone countries, is made up of little stones, partly disintegrated rock, and a small quantity of mould, or decomposed vegetable matter. Beneath this, from 20 to 50 feet deep, according to situation, as it may be near to, or distant from, the river, are numerous strata of hard coarse rubbly limestone, of various thicknesses, from a few inches to 3 or 4 feet, with, occasionally, layers of small cherty nodules between the beds, a few inches thick. This entire mass of useless matter forms what is termed the head of the quarry. The actual number of beds is uncertain, for only six have been selected as marketable, or most fit for architectural purposes: beneath these, the stone is not extracted. These six beds, which rest upon each other without interposition, vary in thickness from about 2 feet to 5 feet or more. The estimated aggregate thickness of them all, may be taken at about 17 feet, although in some places the total depth may probably amount to 22 feet. The natural vertical joints being square to each other, and wide apart, blocks of large and varied size can be obtained, even to the extent of 15 feet in length, by 5 feet or more square, but such dimensions are never extracted or required, on account of the many practical difficulties in removal and transport. The names, dimensions, and certain distinctive characters of these workable beds, have been so ably described by Mr. Donaldson and have so recently appeared in THE BUILDER, from the pen of Mr. Godwin, that I need not attempt a repetition.*

Such then is a general outline of the geology of the Caen stone district. The next part of

* I am informed that Ranville stone is being supplied for some part of the sea-wall of the Harbour at Dover.

* See Vol. VI., p. 481 and p. 493.

EXAMPLES OF ANCIENT ART.——(Sᴇᴇ Pᴀɢᴇ 25.)

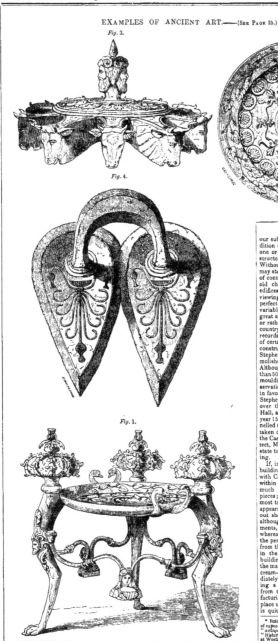

Fig. 3.

Fig. 2.

Fig. 4.

Fig. 1.

our subject will be to notice the present condition of buildings in the city of Caen, and
one or two in this country, which are constructed, beyond doubt, with similar material.
Without mentioning any particular building, I
may state in general terms, and with little fear
of contradiction, that all the richly decorated
old churches and other highly ornamented
edifices, of early date, in the city of Caen are,
viewing them collectively, in a comparatively
perfect state ; the stonework being almost invariably in good condition, considering the
great age of some of the structures. There is,
or rather was, one building of celebrity in this
country, to which I may allude, because the
records of the time state particulars and cost
of certain quantities of Caen stone used in its
construction.* I mean the chapel of St.
Stephen, at Westminster, very recently demolished, except the crypt or under chapel.
Although this building could not have been less
than 500 years old, yet the carved ornaments and
mouldings were in a most excellent state of preservation. I will mention one more circumstance
in favour of Caen stone. The cloisters of St.
Stephen's Chapel and ornamental Gothic work
over them, on the east side of Westminster
Hall, are said to have been erected about the
year 1530. The greater portion of the richly panelled tracery above these cloisters has just been
taken down to make certain alterations, and
the Caen stonework is considered by the architect, Mr. Barry, to be in a sufficiently perfect
state to be reconstructed without fresh working.

If, in the same manner, we examine modern
buildings, or such as have been constructed
with Caen stone, either in France or England,
within the last twenty or thirty years, we find
much variety in the durability of different
pieces ; some appear effectually to resist the
most trying atmospheric influences, and, to all
appearance, will remain for many years without shewing the slightest symptom of decay,
although wrought into the most delicate ornaments, and placed in very exposed situations ;
whereas other stones, immediately adjoining
the perfect ones, begin to moulder and perish
from the first day after they have been placed
in the building. In some few instances of
buildings of recent date, the entire surface of
the masonry retains very nearly the same clean,
cream-coloured appearance which it had immediately after completion. Beware of so flatter-
ing a prospect. In an atmosphere remote
from the metropolis, or from a smoky manufacturing town, such circumstances may take
place unattended by premature decay ; and it
is quite possible that an architect, in his de-

* Rolls of the time of Edward III., containing accounts
of expenses relating to the erection of this chapel.—Smith's
"Antiquities of Westminster."—Brayley and Britton's
"History of the Ancient Palace and Houses of Parliament
at Westminster," 1836.

clining years, may look with pleasure upon the ornaments which he had designed while yet a youthful aspirant to professional honours, without the annoyance of seeing them in a mouldering condition, or else half obscured by soot. But in London, whenever I see an elevation, after ten or a dozen years' completion, with a clean surface, and presenting the natural colour of the stone, I always expect to find symptoms of slow, gradual, and certain disintegration from the surface of the stone. Such process of decay may be unobserved in months or seasons, but an insignificant cause will produce a very surprising effect when continued for ages.

It may appear difficult to explain the reason of so much difference in the durability of materials procured from the same locality; but such variety is not peculiar to the Caen stone district alone; it is so with Portland stone, it is so with Bath, with Anston, and I believe it to be the same with all other stones. The numerous old and new buildings in this great metropolis alone, without mentioning any in the provinces, will abundantly prove my assertion.* C. H. SMITH.

* To be continued.

PROFESSOR COCKERELL'S LECTURES ON ARCHITECTURE.

THE second lecture of the course on architecture, at the Royal Academy, was delivered on Thursday, the 11th inst. Having in his former lecture endeavoured to reply to any scepticism in reference to the existence of true theoretical principles of architecture, the professor further urged the necessity of inquiring into their nature. The successful pursuit of every art and science required, first, innate feeling; and second, the acquirement of sound theory. He argued that, without the first, as it was hopeless to attempt to teach music to one who had never whistled a tune, so it was to expect that education and labour would, to the requisite extent, supply the want of a natural aptitude for the art of architecture. He mentioned the case of Sir John Leech, who had commenced the study of architecture, but relinquished a pursuit for which be found himself unfitted, for the profession of which he became one of the brightest ornaments.—But, however fortunate the student might be in natural qualifications, he had still much to derive from theory. It might, therefore, be expected that these principles should be attempted to be established by writers, but it was somewhat disappointing to find their perspicuous development lost in metaphysical speculation, of which we might almost say—as had been sometimes said of the philosophy of Kant,—that it was doubtful whether the writer himself understood what he was attempting to enunciate. Criticism might assist the student in gaining the correct views he was in want of, were it dictated by any settled principles. But the critic dealt his blows right and left; we found sounding terms, but what these were he failed to tell us. Certainly we were entitled to expect some clear doctrines in the place of all such demonstration; but, after the indulgence of much ill blood, we were left to ask—in plain *parlance*—is there a theory of architecture, and what is it?

The professor argued that the existence of such a theory was as undeniable as the existence of fixed laws in the works of the great Architect of the Universe; and he proceeded to indicate the way in which that theory might be discovered.—The objects in nature and art were the same; beauty of form and colour were the ends contemplated by both. Regularity was the pervading principle of the works of nature, in which every thing was dictated by the purest taste and the most refined geometry. This was instanced by the beautiful process of crystallization. Peculiar uses became peculiar ornaments—the ornament was co-existent with, and arising out of the use.

We were, perhaps, in the habit of taking many things as mere appendages, without sufficient inquiry into their origin. For example, in the case of the horns of animals—as of the bull and stag. In southern countries, where means of defence were most required in the animal, we found the long horns of oxen, whilst nearer home short horns were common; and so, in inquiring into the development of all the works of nature, we should first trace an object of utility, and afterwards that the forms were those which conduced to ornament. The architect raised the arch and vault, and counteracted the thrust by buttresses, and the casual observer believed these beautiful features were so placed for ornament alone. But if the architect employed a roof with tie beams, and consequently avoided thrust, he dispensed with buttresses, and could substitute columns, and a character accordant with the altered construction. If he had to design a building for a southern latitude, where it was desirable to make the windows small, his design was not discordant with that object, but effect was gained by breadth, and the character given by the piers. But in a northern latitude, where the admission of the sun's rays was to be courted, he imparted character to the *windows*, and followed what was called the "fenestral" order of composition. And thus the skilful architect turned every circumstance of climate or purpose into a source of beauty. For it was only the pedantic architect who applied to all countries, and on all occasions, the same features, and who thus lost the lesson which nature gave. Of this our own empire furnished most striking instances. Instead of applying in particular climates such styles as had originated in similar climates, the lesson of nature, and all previous art, taught nothing to the modern architect. The stoa, or portico, which might be desirable in a southern climate, might, in a northern, be a nuisance, unless glazed, as were the cloisters. The Grecian Doric order, on the Acropolis, seemed to grow out of the rockwork itself; but when placed in our modern streets, and combined with vertical lines, it appeared out of place, like an elephant in a cage. So, place upon a lofty pedestal an elaborate Gothic building with pinnacles and statues, and the effect would be equally inappropriate.

Thus, the professor said, structure was seen to be an important element in art, and out of it arose numerous and surprising results. No fabric could equal the most ordinary one of nature, and if Sir Joshua Reynolds had said that painting was the art of seeing nature, we might say that architecture was the art of understanding it. In proof of the immediate advantage which was to be gained by a study of nature, the professor cited the instance he had given,* on former occasions, of the derivation of the construction of the dome of the cathedral at Florence from the structure of the human skull,—the great difference between this example and that at the Pantheon, in the openings, and particularly in the size of piers, the construction of which he could not be altogether aware of, rendering it necessary that Brunelleschi should devise some method which should combine strength with great lightness. The professor illustrated this part of the subject by a sketch on the board, shewing in section the two thicknesses of the skull, and he also shewed that all the bones, on the same principle, combined strength with lightness. He also gave the other instance, in the derivation of the steeple of St. Bride's Church, with its spiral staircase and central pillar or newel, from a common form of spiral shell having a similar *columella*.† In St. Paul's we might not discover the same direct adaptation, as in Wren's other work just mentioned, but the professor shewed that it was not less the work of a child of nature. He also contrasted the methods practised in the domes, and for the support of the lanterns in St. Paul's, and in the Pantheon at Paris, by Soufflot, and said he could not conceive why the French architect had neglected the simple model of the baptistry at Pisa, which Wren was doubtless well acquainted with, as he was with everything else, and why he should have used the three domes, and why the middle dome, when the other method appeared to be equally convenient in the section. It could only have arisen from the mere bravado of doing something different. The professor, also, alluding to the foresight of Wren, mentioned the stability of the foundation of St. Paul's, and said that openings to the casements were provided only on that side of the building where the cold and damp air would not be likely to find admittance.—We have not space to do justice to all the instances which were given of the analogy between architecture and nature, seen even in the structure of shells, in which was noticed the principle which had been applied in one of the latest improvements of ship building, nor to do more than mention the beautiful passage in a work of Sir Charles Bell, in which the most striking instances of mechanical skill were shown to be infinitely surpassed in the structure of the human form, evidencing as these did, the creative power which the persecuted Galileo saw even in the straw on the floor of his dungeon. The professor reserved for future notice many instances of this analogy in more minute details, as in the parallel cases of the right lines of architecture, and the line of the horizon at sea, and in the similarity of the forms of waves, and the outlines of sinuous mouldings. He cited such instances to show the uniformity which must exist in all styles, and that the great principles of taste must be always the same. He had shown that there was a theory in art as in nature, that we spoke of "the great Architect of the Universe," that there was one great school of architecture, and that there was no other school, or "taste," or prophet under heaven, which could be compared with it; that it was not the knowledge of various styles, and not the going to Greece or Rome, which made the true architect, but that the flowers of the field offered better models than could be found in the works of man, and that if a national style was ever to be established, nature presented the true road to the grand in architecture.

* *Vide* THE BUILDER, vol. 4, p. 63.
† *Vide* vol. 4, p. 63.

THE CHICHESTER SCHOOL COMPETITION.

Mr. John Elliott has published some correspondence on this matter, involving two or three curious points. It seems that the money was provided by subscription for a memorial of Bishop Otter, and that a school being determined on as the form of the memorial, a competition took place several years ago, and a plan submitted by Mr. Elliott being considered the best, he was elected the architect. The matter remained dormant for a time, but his design, he states, was retained on the understanding that he was to be employed when the work was commenced.

On the appearance of the recent advertisement requesting plans for a school to be sent in competition, Mr. Elliott put forth his claim to the appointment, and as it seems to us (knowing nothing more of the circumstances than what appears in print), with great right. He had spent money on a chance in a lottery, and had drawn the prize, such as it was: it seems rather too bad to tell him afterwards there was no prize.

The reply by the Rev. Mr. Parrington to his application was, that the "Otter memorial committee had handed over their whole powers and trust to the committee of the Chichester Training School," and that they knew nothing of his appointment: knew nothing of his plans.

But, says Mr. Elliott,—"The 'handing over of powers and trust' from one committee to another, surely implies the handing over also of obligations and liabilities. I will take the case that the present committee select a design from those to be sent in; they promise the architect that he shall be employed, but circumstances prevent the intention so formed and announced from being carried into immediate effect; in the mean time, some of the members of this committee are changed, a change in the extent of the plan is deemed necessary, not in its purpose,—would either or both these changes afford the shadow of a pretence for disregarding the claim of the architect who had devoted his time and his talent on the chance of being so elected, and who, being successful, had a moral right to the fruits of his labour? And in what respect, permit me to ask, does my case differ from this imaginary one? I devoted my time to preparing designs and estimates in a similar competition, and I was successful: for several years the matter has been in abeyance, but considering that I was in the hands of honourable men, who would, when the time arrived, fulfil what had been promised to me, I made no application whatever for remuneration of any kind." He further offered, without extra charge, to make as many designs as they required till one was obtained to meet their views.

The sub-committee, however, had made up their minds, and all Mr. Elliott could get was a recommendation to compete again. His original plans being "discovered," were returned to him. The fresh competition he declined; and in a long letter asserted that he has been exposed to persecution and loss of practice by certain clergymen, and can only conclude that they are acting in the spirit of a policy "openly advocated by clergymen of the new school, to exclude from employment all architects objecting to go freely in certain papistical bye ways, miscalled the 'old paths.'" And he asserts that "those architects who will not zealously further such views, are regularly hunted down by their organ, libelled without mercy, or the slightest regard to truth, and refused redress on the plea that it was all done *pour l'amour de Dieu*."

Mr. Elliott goes on to shew how it was attempted, in another case, to put him aside, "in favour of Mr. Butler, the builder employed by the chapter;" and says,—"It was this same Mr. Butler, one of the very last men I should have to fear as a competitor in my profession (in which he is an interloper), whom the 'cathedral party' and the chapter agents have for some time past been so unfairly attempting to force into my practice, with whom I had to compete on the occasion when the committee chose my design for the Training School. It was not considered expedient to appoint him at once after such a result, so it was resolved to have another competition, of which no intimation was conveyed to me. A very ingenious advertisement was drawn up, and an equally ingenious reply framed, for those architects who might be foolish enough to waste their time in competing, and write for particulars,—the substance of it being that, if they required information other than the advertisement afforded, they must find it out for themselves. These things savoured so strongly of an intended wrong, that they excited the suspicion and drew forth the comments of the editor of THE BUILDER. The competition over, the seventy or eighty unlucky architects are informed by another ingenious advertisement in THE BUILDER, that the committee have decided on the design marked "December, 1848;" and that the other parties may receive back their plans on application: of course the competitors must all be satisfied at this—the committee do not even yet know the name of the party who has got the prize: by the most extraordinary chance in the world, however, it turns out that "December, 1848," is *Mr. Joseph Butler*, the chapter's own man, the very party whom every one knowing any thing of the circumstances connected with the affair, knew it was intended should have it, by book or by crook." We give the pith of this not uninstructive story just as it comes to us, and leave our readers to draw their own inferences.

ACCESS TO CHURCHES.

DURING my late rambles in the provinces, as often as I came to a large town and wished to explore its ecclesiological remains, so often had I to utter the invariable cry,—"Where are the church keys?" With hardly a single exception, I found the church locked up, the clergyman living at a distance, the clerks engaged in their secular occupation, and even the sextoness sometimes gone "a-washing." In a few places a board is stuck up, stating that the sextoness lives in such-or-such a place; but when the tired stranger has reached that locality, and inquired for this indescribable female, he is generally informed that she has changed her abode—perhaps to some distance. He then goes there, and finds she is "a-washing" at Mrs. Thompson's, or on some such woman's errand. On one occasion, having repaired to the advertised residence of a sextoness in a dark alley, I found her abode changed for one at some distance, where, having tracked her out with much difficulty, and mounted to some four-pair back, I found the poor female alone, ill in bed, the keys of the sacred edifice being entrusted to her sole care!

When recently in Bristol, on my applying to a sexton for admittance to a church, I was coolly informed by him that, being engaged in his secular occupation, "he could not attend to me, and without him no one might visit the church, lest a Prayer-book should be stolen!!" I urged my plea that, as a stranger, I might not again have an opportunity of visiting the edifice, but to no effect; and, at a great inconvenience, had again to wait on him at the hour he named.

But, Sir, should this be so? If this utilitarian age consider it sufficient to worship God collectively once a-week, is it right, is it decent, that our churches should be sealed up as hermetically as a prison—admittance hardly to be obtained—the keys found only after great delay—and when a hasty glance has been cast at the building, to be greeted, as I have been in a parochial church at Glastonbury, with the show-like expression, "We charges a shullin a head, zur!" If strangers found everywhere the courtesy displayed at St. Mary's Redcliffe, there would then be no need of complaint.

In making these observations, I have not urged, as I could have done, the obstacles daily thrown in the way of members of the architectural profession, when endeavouring to obtain some memorial of past art. That these impediments are numerous, no one can deny; that none is more unnecessarily vexatious than this hiding of church keys, every one will admit; and it is in the hope that your columns will be open to deprecate so unjustifiable a system, I have now ventured to address you.

F. C. W.

THE MARBLE ARCH IN ST. JAMES'S PARK.

THE danger is imminent; the palace advances to completion; soon the hoard will be removed, and the arch, the costly monument of George the Fourth, is doomed to demolition. Perhaps this structure is not very remarkable for beauty of design, or for any elaborate finish; it stands, however, a solitary instance of regal magnificence, being the only evidence in marble of an architectural portal in London, and with its bronze gates, which are good specimens of their kind, is not an unworthy memento of a monarch whose refinement of taste conduced not a little to the embellishment of the metropolis and the encouragement of art.

Is this *Arc de Triomphe* to be abated, and to be lost to the nation whose liberality furnished 70,000*l.* to its edification? For the sake of the capital which boasts but two arches we hope not.

By the way, says my boy who stands beside me, and to whom I refer sometimes as a mentor (for juvenile ideas have their value, albeit he is occasionally a tor-mentor), "Sir, you are mistaken, for there is Highgate Archway, and also the Bar where the arch civic authority receives majesty, and tenders the keys of the city,—Temple Bar."

Well, it is true we do possess these monuments: but still we hope that some site may be found whereon to reconstruct that which, if sold for its intrinsic worth, may not realize 2,000*l.*

Our city has a goodly range, and its locale is happily chosen. Piazzas and largos we have not, save the national fountains; yet there is no deficiency of positions where the restored marble arch might perpetuate the taste of its royal founder.

Could not some public contribution be got up to effect works of great public utility? We do know that St. Peter's was accomplished by such means, and that Peter's pence were collected for the object throughout all Christian Europe. We know that Mr. Cobden and Mr. Hudson had testimonials—colossal ones; and that now a monumental tribute is being collected for a mausoleum to Lord George Bentinck. Then why not, in this wealthy community, collect a fund to illustrate the greatest city of earth,—London? This might be done in shape of a poundage tax, to be levied within the range of the City and Liberties of London and Westminster.

The noble esplanade extending from St. Martin's Church through Pall Mall, now become the street of palaces,—what a glorious approach would that make to Hyde-park, if continued through Cleveland-row, and in a straight line to Buckingham Garden! At one end the spire and portico, at the other the open park: this access breaking out half way between the palace and the Triumphal Arch (from which it might be distant about 200 yards) would present the finest central avenue in Europe, and afford an approach, without a hill, to Hyde-park.

It would be necessary to purchase the corner house of St. James's-street, and six other houses in Cleveland-row, and also the insulated mansion facing the Green-park; this would open the space between Lord Ellesmere's new ball, the Duke of Sutherland's, and St. James's Palace; for the rest, the *débris* of the houses would form the road (about a quarter of a mile) over the flat park, and would effect a truly royal approach to Buckingham Palace.

At the point of junction I would place the marble arch. By this alteration, the noble mansions and palace would be worthy of this emporium of the world, and the gorgeous clubs of Pall Mall would add dignity to the central Boulevard, thus made light and ventilated by vital air.

At the same time, for the embellishment of the new palace and the St. James's-park, the old Mall behind St. James's might be broken up and clothed in shrub and verdure, only reserving the width between two ranges of the trees, now trampled and hardly vegetating there: that is, maintaining the present road through one alley (there are now four) for royal use, and for the privileged classes, between the new palace and the Admiralty.

This would greatly enhance the beauty of St. James's-park, and form a noble vista from the Portal Royal; for there is a space of at least twelve acres of russet gravel at present wasted in road.

In the days of James and Charles this was the Mall, and, therefore, had its uses; but now the promenaders frequent Hyde-park: and the lugubrious trees of the old Mall give melancholy shade to only a few stragglers; for the wandering valetudinarian, nurses and children, range the pleasant sward and water-side within the rails; the external *parterre* is any thing but pleasing, and is avoided, as would be a desert in an Oasis.

QUONDAM.

LIME-ASH FLOORS FOR COTTAGES.

TWENTY years ago the almost universal cottage floor in Devonshire was produced by doating down an admixture of pounded lime (used tolerably fresh), smiths' ashes, and clean drift sand, in equal proportions; this was "run down" on a substratum of coarse gravel, brick bats, and lime core, about 6 inches in thickness, well saturated, then beaten to a level surface.

The lime door should be 3 inches thick and well floated, and then "ironed down" (the more labour the better), and beginning at the further corner of the room, the man should gradually "work himself out" at the door, so as not to walk upon the new work. In a week it will become hard and durable. It is easily repaired when requisite.

If smiths' ashes cannot be got in sufficient quantities, one-half of brick dust may be mixed with them before they are finally chaffed up with the lime and sand.

JOHN BURGES WATSON.

Another correspondent says, that—In Somersetshire, artificial stone floors are constructed in the following manner:—The ground is prepared to receive the material; a concrete is then laid on, about two inches thick, consisting of one part lime to four of sand, well mixed together, taking care not to make it too wet. It is then well rammed with a flat punner, until it becomes sufficiently consolidated to receive the second coat; another layer is then laid on, the same thickness as before, and well rammed: care must be taken to keep the surface level. After a short period it will be sufficiently hardened for use. It is then rubbed over with common oil, which gives it the appearance of stone instead of sand. "Cupola" ashes are used to give the floor a dark appearance. I have seen floors made of this material in imitation of tesselated pavement,—the ashes and lime making the dark portions, and the sand and lime the light parts. This description of flooring costs there about 11d. per square yard.

STONE CANOPY IN THE PRESBYTERY, WINCHESTER CATHEDRAL.

(THE DECORATED PERIOD.)

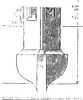

J.K.COLLING

PLAN AT C

O.D.LAING Sc

Scale 1½ inch to a foot.

[See page 25.

DETAILS OF STONE CANOPY.

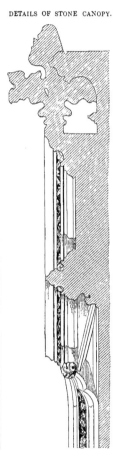

SECTION OF MOULDINGS AT B
¼ FULL SIZE.

PROJECTED WORKS.—Advertisements have been issued for tenders, by 31st inst., for alterations and additions to Wharton Church, Cheshire; by 8th February, for the erection of prisoners' cells, infirmary, kitchen, &c., at County Gaol, Huntingdon; and by 25th inst. for the erection of a Parsonage House, at Exbury.

MR. BARRY AND THE SEWERS' COMMISSIONERS.

DRAINAGE OF THE NEW HOUSES OF PARLIAMENT.

A VERY curious document, comprising the report of Mr. Austin (on the part of the commission) on the drainage of the new Houses, Mr. Barry's reply, and Mr. Austin's observations thereon, has been printed, and is about to be issued for the use of the commissioners.

The matter can scarcely remain where it is, and is likely to excite much interest.

Circumstances having rendered an examination of the sewers at the building in question desirable, Mr. Austin was directed to make it, and to report to the board. From this report we learn (omitting other particulars) that a private sewer, 5 feet 6 inches high and 3 feet wide, traverses the whole length of the new buildings, joining the public sewer in Abingdon-street, at the southern end, and going directly (although not originally so) to the outfall into the river at Westminster-bridge, at the northern end. "On examination," says the report, "it is found that the portion of the sewer running through the buildings is constructed above the level of the floor of the vaults. On looking through one of the flapped communications which enter just above the invert, the sewer appeared to be at that point nearly its entire height above the ground level. On reaching the centre of the buildings, however, we discovered an opening about 2 feet square broken through the arch of the sewer, apparently for some temporary purpose. On clambering through this opening we found ourselves in the very vaults of the new buildings."

The report continues—"The condition of this main sewer throughout its entire length must be regarded as extremely dangerous to the health of those who reside in, and frequent these buildings. It is nothing but a continuous cesspool from one end to the other, emitting most noxious effluvia; and being blocked up at each end with heavy flaps, the only source of ventilation is into the buildings themselves, or into the court-yards into which these buildings look.

Dr. Reid has been at great pains, and considerable cost, in the construction of an air shaft, to avoid taking air for ventilation from near a sewer, while all the time a sewer of the first class is pouring forth into the buildings, from one end to the other, malaria, evaporating from a surface of foul matter of between 2,000 and 3,000 square feet in extent.

The foul matter throughout its whole extent is nearly equal to the full width of the sewer, and presents an evaporative surface for the exhalation of noxious effluvia equal to 150 ordinary cesspools."

Of the various communications from the buildings which open into the sewer, a most singular description, illustrated by sketches, is given. "Some of them," it is said, "are brick barrel drains, of 9, 12, 15, and 20 inches in diameter, wretchedly constructed. The outlet into the sewer of one 20-inch drain is about a fourth part of the drain itself.

Some of the communications are half-tile drains covered with brick flat, with square openings broken through into the sewer. Several are stone-ware pipes; some of them projecting into the sewer several inches, others stopping several inches short; some broken right away at the mouth by being driven forcibly in. Some are obstructed at the outlet by bricks and lumps of cement."

It proceeds:—"So much has recently been said on the extravagant size of sewers which generally prevails, that it will be unnecessary to enlarge upon this part of the subject; but it may be urged as a reason for such large constructions in this immediate district, that a certain amount of reservoir is required for the storage of storm waters during high tides, when the outlets of the sewers are closed; but these reservoirs, where indispensable, should never form the receptacles of the general refuse drainage. In the buildings in question, where every facility exists for the immediate discharge of all surface water into the river, this consideration should never have weighed at all; and in the new plans contemplated for the neighbourhood, it would indeed be extremely injudicious to admit into the general system the surface waters from buildings occupying an area of between six and seven

acres, from which no decomposing matter would be conveyed by the rain, and from which any amount of storm water may at all times be immediately discharged into the Thames.

Two fifteen-inch pipes falling each way and discharging north and south, with the inclination and pressure that would be obtained, would carry off the waters of the greatest storm upon record from nearly double the surface, or twelve acres of covered ground."

"The main sewer through the building Mr. Barry has it in contemplation to alter, by cutting off its junction with the Abingdon-street sewer, and directing the inclination all in one direction, from the south end of the buildings to the outlet at Westminster-bridge; but if the proposed separation and immediate discharge of the surface waters were to be effected, a construction of these large dimensions would be totally unnecessary, inasmuch as it would be upwards of thirty times greater than the utmost provision that should be made; and as, while it is allowed to continue, the buildings can never be maintained in a healthy condition, I would strongly advise its entire removal.

The cost of the alteration would be comparatively most trifling; but even if it were considerable, it would be folly to be spending many thousands upon ventilation, and an attempt to provide fresh air, while this fruitful and extensive source of malaria is permitted to exist.

A nine-inch pipe, with a fall each way of an inch in ten feet, which can be obtained along the present line of sewer, would discharge 72,000 gallons of water per hour; a supply many times beyond what the requirements of the buildings can ever furnish."

Mr. Barry is, of course, somewhat angry with this, and complaining that "its highly-wrought descriptions and numerous mis-statements likely to be prejudicial to his professional character, have got into print," earnestly requests the Commissioners to assist him in giving the same publicity to his replies, as the allegations have had. Mr. Barry commences with the following remarks on the system of drainage adopted :—

"That it was devised and commenced in accordance with the rules and regulations of the late Commission of Sewers for Westminster, and that the lowest available depth of drainage was adopted of which the data furnished by that Commission would admit.

That the system was arranged at a time when the present vaults of the building were not in contemplation.

That the system is as yet only partially carried out, in consequence of the unfinished state of the building; and that many of the existing arrangements connected with the drainage are either unfinished, or are of a temporary nature.

That during ten hours upon an average in every tide, the outfalls of the public and palace main sewers are closed by the rise of the tide in the river, and all drainage from the New Palace is consequently stopped for that time periodically.

Under these circumstances, no other system than that which was adopted was found to be practicable; but it has been long the intention of the architect to recommend the adoption of an exclusive system for the New Palace, by which its drains should be entirely cut off from the public sewers."

Omitting his replies to those parts of the report not mentioned by us, we pass to this,—"The main sewer is not, as stated, constructed above the floor of the vaults; the latter were not even projected when the sewer was formed. It is not the fact that it is even now in the vaults of the building; on the contrary, it passes nearly throughout its entire length under the courts and open gateways of the building. Under the courts it is imbedded in the earth, and under the gateways it occupies a space which is not a vault, and where it is intended to be imbedded in solid concrete. The only portion of it which passes under the building is for about 36 feet in length at the north end of it, where it is entirely below the vault-floor level, and imbedded in the earth. At no part of its length is the main sewer, as stated, 'nearly its entire height above the ground level,' or, as doubtless Mr. Austin means, the vault-floor level."

Mr. Barry complains of a sketch which Mr. Austin gives in his report to shew the appearance of the sewer in the vaults, as conveying an exaggerated idea of the latter, which he says are not vaults, but "arched spaces under an open gateway," "intended ultimately to be filled in around the sewer with concrete." He thinks that, "Owing to the levels of the outfalls of the public sewers into the river, the lower portion of the palace main sewer cannot be otherwise than a reservoir (termed by Mr. Austin, a continuous cesspool) for ten hours in every tide; but no inconvenience or nuisance can possibly arise from this circumstance, when every drain connected with the main sewer is properly trapped, which is proposed to be done as they are successively connected with it.

The condition of this sewer, ventilated temporarily as it has hitherto been from the man-holes at the two extremities of the building, cannot even in its present unfinished state be considered, as reported, 'dangerous to health;' not the slightest escape of noxious effluvia has ever been noticed either before or since the publication of Mr. Austin's Report during repeated and careful examinations made by the architect and his assistants, some of whom have remained in the sewer itself for three hours continuously without experiencing the slightest inconvenience.

Upon a very careful examination, the surface of the foul matter within the sewer, instead of being, as stated, 'between 2,000 and 3,000 feet in extent,' has been found not to exceed 1,350 square feet, and this deposit has been principally occasioned by the bricks and rubbish which have unavoidably fallen into the sewer in making the numerous communications with it that have at various times been required, and which, of course, will be entirely removed from time to time as the building approaches completion."

Mr. Austin says the currents of air through openings communicating with the sewer set *outwards* (showing that the foul air was passing into the buildings); Mr. Barry says they have been found invariably to set *inwards*.

"All communications with the main sewer, which are intended to be permanent, are properly and fairly constructed; the reported 'singular collection' consist of temporary, but, for their present purpose, effective communications with that sewer which have from time to time been required during the progress of the works, and will either be removed or made perfect when necessary.

The brick barrel drains are not, as alleged, 'wretchedly constructed.' On the contrary, it is impossible that such drains can be more perfectly constructed."

He thinks "the two 15-inch pipes recommended, considered, as they must be, as reservoirs for the storage of storm water during the time when the outfalls are closed by the tide, are utterly insufficient; they would not, for instance, contain 1-40th of the quantity of water which fell in three hours upon the area mentioned in the storm in the month of August of the present year (1848).

The dimensions of the main sewer are considered by the architect to be no greater than are absolutely necessary for the reception of the waters which at times must enter and be retained in it. The escape of noxious effluvia from it when the drainage is completed will be impossible (?)

The cost of its removal, instead of being trifling, as alleged, would be very considerable. The system of drainage now adopted, especially if rendered, as already mentioned, independent of the public sewers, will, in the opinion of the architect, be effective and free from all objections.

The 9-inch pipes here recommended for the ordinary drainage of the New Palace would, for the reasons stated in respect of the 15-inch pipes, be utterly inadequate."

Upon this Mr. Austin rejoins, alluding darkly to a "very serious oversight of another kind in connection with the sewerage," mention of which was kept out of the printed report, and carries his attack even farther than before. He denies that the Westminster Commission, "whatever blame they may have to bear," had anything to do with the faults of drainage of the new Houses. As to the "vaults," he says,—

"It would appear to matter little by what term these portions of the basement of the building should be called; the fact being that there exists a perfect communication throughout the building by their means; that the whole of these works, whether of 'vaults' or 'arched spaces,' appears to be of precisely similar construction, and have, I am informed, always been known and spoken of before committees, and on the works, without distinction, as 'vaults;' and that although open gateways may exist immediately above this part, the exposed sewer itself passes within about 12 yards from the basement of the grand central saloon connecting the Houses of Lords and Commons, with the vaults or arched spaces of which there is perfectly open communication, and through which I have myself passed more than once to the sewer."

Mr. Austin then re-asserts his statements; shews that in 1846 Mr. Phillips, in reply to complaints from Mr. Barry as to the public sewer with which the sewer in question communicates, had pointed out that the latter was simply "an elongated cesspool, the great evil of which must eventually be very obnoxious and injurious," and that the main drainage should be entirely re-arranged;* and he further urges that, by certain works done since his report, closing man-holes, &c., the sewer has been reduced to a more dangerous condition.

"Cut off from all possibility of ventilation, with constant foul deposit therein, the whole length of this sewer must shortly become nothing better than a vast retort, capable of holding some 15,000 cubic feet, in which the foulest gases will be perpetually generating and escaping in a concentrated form into the buildings.

It is a fallacy to suppose that flaps, placed at the mouths of the drains, communicating with the sewer, will at all times prevent the escape of this dangerous miasma. Even supposing that the contact of the surfaces could at all times be perfectly preserved, every time that a discharge takes place, and the flap is raised, an opening is formed through which the foul and pent-up gases will rise and escape into the building."

We cannot, however, give space for more of the report than this one statement, viz., that "The defects of this construction and the bad consequences which must arise from it are manifold, and of that serious nature, that nothing short of the *entire removal* of so faulty a work can cure the evil. It will admit of no real and practicable improvement, and after the attention which has been brought to bear upon the subject of improved drainage, and the sounder doctrines which have recently been promulgated, the precedent cannot surely be allowed of a drainage work, full of defects, and devoid of all correct principle, remaining in connection with the most costly building of the country."

That the drainage in question is utterly bad seems to us clear, and we are sorry that Mr. Barry should have been betrayed, by what he may consider the too *tranchant* character of the report, into attempting to defend what is really indefensible, and what, if the report speaks truly, he himself considers so. We do not care about the minor points in the report, we will not ask if the report be exaggerated or not, nor even think it necessary to inquire if the sewer be above ground in "vaults," or "arched spaces." We dwell on the simple fact that there is beneath the building this enormous reservoir for the generation and retention of deleterious gases, and which, it would seem, cannot be kept cleansed but by constant flashing. To prevent these gases, by means of traps, from discharging themselves into the buildings, seems to us impossible.

In conclusion, we would not have it inferred that we desire to attach blame to Mr. Barry. The sewer, it should be remembered, was built in 1837, when the received views in respect of sewerage were very different from what they are now; and as to the mode in which the communications with the drains are made, the clerks of works and the builders are responsible.

ARTISTS' CONVERSAZIONE.—The first of these *Conversazioni* will be given on the 27th inst.

* Reported in THE BUILDER at the time.

FREEMASONS OF THE CHURCH.

THE first meeting of the above society, for the present year, was held on January 9th, Mr. G. R. French in the chair. After the usual business, Mr. Jarman exhibited an Oriental casket of carved ivory mounted in steel. The chairman observed the singular likeness exhibited in this work, in its ornamentation, to many European productions of the thirteenth century. Mr. W. Harry Rogers exhibited a rubbing he had taken from an elaborate carved sandal-wood casket of the close of the fifteenth century, in the collection of the late Sir S. Meyrick. This interesting relic is decorated with a profusion of knot-work, executed in relief, with the addition of roses, hearts, and the initials M. R. Mr. George Isaacs also exhibited an ancient jewel casket, of perpendicular taste, remarkable as being unusually architectural in its features. The corners of the lid are supported by four twisted columns, and the spaces between them are enriched with empanelled work of delicate finish. A short discussion having been entered into respecting the purpose and origin of these caskets, of which the middle ages produced an abundant supply in various materials, Mr. J. W. Archer read a paper by Mr. D. Wilson, secretary of the Royal Scottish Society of Antiquaries, "On some peculiarities in Scottish ecclesiastical architecture, with special reference to the Collegiate Church of the Holy Trinity at Edinburgh, demolished A.D. 1848." After detailing the wanton destruction of this venerable fabric, which was founded in 1462 by Mary of Gueldres, the widowed queen of James the Second of Scotland, and levelled with the ground in 1848, for the purpose of enlarging the area of a railway terminus, Mr. Wilson proceeded to the narration of some facts on the comparative dates of the successive styles of Gothic architecture in England and Scotland, particularly urging the very early introduction of decorated work in Scotland before even a symptom of its approach had been manifested south of the Tweed.

The chairman then announced the next paper, to be read February 13th, "On the importance of a knowledge and observance of the principles of art by designers," by Mr. W. Smith Williams.

THE HORSE-POWER POCKET-BOILER.

Your paper of the 6th instant contains a notice of a new steam-engine by Mr. Beauregard, in which it is stated, "a correspondent of the *Times* asserts that a steamer was navigated to Lisbon, some years back, on a similar principle," &c.

The fact, that the principle sought to be obtained in this steamer, was the very reverse of that stated to be employed by M. Beauregard, renders it desirable that it may be generally known, in order that your readers may not be led away by chimerical accounts of results that never can be realised.

The vessel alluded to was the *Comet*, a Government steamer of 80-horse power, which was filled with Mr. Thos. Howard's vaporizers, by Messrs. Penn, the engineers. The heating surface of these vaporizers containing but 6,298 in., being equal to 78·7 in. per horse-power, may well challenge a comparison with M. Beauregard's "horse-power pocket-boiler," and further, from dry plates being used in both cases. But here all comparison must end. It was Mr. Howard's object to inject the water in an extreme state of divisibility, upon plates, maintained at from 350° to 450° Fahrenheit, it being found, and confirmed by experiment, that the vaporization of water goes on much more quickly than at higher temperature. The maintenance of the "spheroidal state," as it is termed by M. Beauregard, was that sought to be avoided. This state occurs when water is thrown on plates at very high temperatures, and arises from its being kept from actual contact by a film of steam forming beneath it, and holding it in suspension, thereby causing its spheroidal form, and preventing its speedy evaporation.

I will not here enter into the system of surcharging the steam, &c., employed by Mr. Howard. Suffice it to say, that the practical difficulties of employing heating surfaces at temperatures of 400° to 500°, were found to be insuperable, and his plan, which was excellent in theory, was given up on account of them.

How perfectly insurmountable these difficulties will become when "red-hot plates are employed," is known to every engineer; and in heartily wishing M. Beauregard every success from his invention, I must recommend him to seek it from water in other forms than its "spheroidal state," and produced by other than "red-hot" surfaces.

WM. JEAKES, JUN.

SANITARY PROGRESS.

IT appears evident from the medical inspector, Mr. Grainger's reports to the Board of Health, that the open ditches and other abominations in the neighbourhood of Mr. Drouet's establishment for pauper children, at Lower Tooting, together with the crowding of nearly 1,400 children into an improperly planned, ill ventilated, and incommodious establishment, were predisposing causes, which, together with the epidemic condition of the atmosphere, produced so many cases of cholera among the children. Doubtless, too, pauper fare was an additional predisposing cause, otherwise the evil might have affected others in the same unwholesome vicinity, where moats of foul black putrefaction show an open surface of between 40,000 and 50,000 square feet to the face of day. Shortly previous to the outbreak, one of the foul ditches near the premises was emptied, and the filthy mud spread upon the banks in contravention of the regulations of the Board of Health, a circumstance quite sufficient of itself to explain the predisposition of these children, in particular, to such an attack in such a neighbourhood.——A superintendent inspector is to be forthwith sent to Birmingham, at the request of the town, to make public inquiry as to the sewerage, water, burial grounds, &c. ——The Smoke Nuisance Committee of the Birmingham Street Commissioners have reported favourably of its suppression throughout the town. Thirty-one steam engines are under periodical inspection. Some of the worst chimneys at Newhall-hill have been rendered smokeless. —— Mr. Smith, of Deanston, has been engaged in sanitary inquiry at Lancaster, where the rate of mortality is above the average, and where Government have, therefore, sent Mr. Smith, without any petition from the inhabitants, who seem to be reckless of their bad pre-eminence in the provincial 'bills of mortality.'——An instalment of the complete and thorough sewerage of the borough of Newcastle has been announced, in the shape of an advertisement for tenders for the construction of two great sewers, one along Pilgrim-street and Northumberland-street, from the Royal Arcade to St. Mary's-place; and the other from Union-street, by Newgate-street, to Green-court.—— The Glasgow magistrates are ordering the discontinuance of burials in various over-crowded burying grounds within the city bounds as nuisances. The details are just a repetition of those awful and sickening desecrations of the sacred remains of humanity with which the public are already but too familiar in reports of the state of intramural grave-yards.

RAILWAY JOTTINGS.

THE calls for January amount to 2,587,225*l*. about a million and a quarter more than for last month.——On the London and North-Western the following persons are employed, including those occupied in the collection and delivery of goods:—2 secretaries, 1 manager, 2 superintendents, 966 clerks, 3,054 porters, 701 police constables, 738 engine and firemen, 3,347 artificers, 1,452 labourers: total number, 10,263. The number of horses employed is 612, ditto vans, &c., 253. This great company has virtually abandoned the unworthy design of clipping their clerks' salaries of a per centage, under the pretence of a "mutual" assurance fund scheme against defalcations. A per centage of 2d. a-pound, however, was first exacted, with a circular threat of dismissal against all grumblers, though "the full concurrence of the parties affected," is now alleged to have been a proviso of this notable scheme. The London and North-Western have succeeded in reducing their rates in the Warwickshire district from 1,500*l*. to 500*l*. per mile, and in another from 800*l*. to 400*l*.—— The recorder of Canterbury has respited the rating case of the South-Eastern in Canterbury, the company to pay half the amount of future rates, till a decision of appeals, and the parish to allow the company any sums that may be paid in excess.——Nearly 30,000 gallons of milk are now sent weekly to the metropolis along the different lines of railway. ——The Edinburgh and Northern have compromised the suit brought against them on behalf of the children of Mr. Wilson, dentist, Edinburgh, who was killed by falling into a cellar at the station, in October, 1847, for 1,100*l*., each party paying their own expenses. ——"It is said," says *Herepath*, referring to the Dover, "that, among other things, a large sum, about 40,000*l*. (not 4,000*l*., as erroneously printed in our last) has been used of the Company's money for other purposes. The financial statement which has been expected, it is understood, will not be presented before the meeting."——An immense mass of chalk and earth, it is said, has again fallen in within a short distance of the spots where two previous falls took place, under St. Catherine's Hill, about half a mile from Guildford, and three and a half from Godalming.——A Shropshire paper also states that the Oakengates tunnel, near the Holyhead road, has again given way, and caused some of the road to sink in.——The embankment and sea-wall of that portion of the South Wales line which extends across the sands between Llanelly harbour and Burry-port, contracted for by Mr. Joseph Douglas and others, has been almost entirely washed away by the tide. It is not ascertained whether the loss will fall upon the contractor or the company, as the work was stopped by order of the directors.——"We were the first," says the *Manchester Examiner*, "to use the electric telegraph for the purpose of reporting, on the occasion of Mr. Cobden's election for the West Riding of Yorkshire; and we learn that on the meeting in the Free-trade Hall, the office succeeded in transmitting a column and a quarter of that meeting to London, giving a summary of the proceedings, for the London papers, in three hours. The telegraph is beginning to be more appreciated as a means of communication."

METROPOLITAN COMMISSION OF SEWERS.

A SPECIAL court was held on Tuesday, at the Sewers' Office, Greek-street; the Earl of Carlisle in the chair.

A letter was read from Mr. Roe, one of the surveyors, stating that in consequence of age and imperfect eyesight, he should accept the offer of a retiring allowance of 200*l*. per annum; but should nevertheless be at all times ready to render any service to the commission in his power.

The Late Cases of Cholera at the Asylum at Tooting.—A report by Mr. Lovick on the state of Tooting, presented to the General Board of Health, was read by Mr. Hertslet to the court.

Mr. Chadwick rose and said,—The considerations arising from the reading of that report as to the effects of the effluvia from the sewers and receptacles described, upon the unfortunate occupants of the one over-crowded establishment, or the effects which might be produced upon the occupants of other establishments, whose sites are washed by the sewers, need not be dwelt upon before the court. Serious duties devolved upon the commissioners, who would have been moved to execute them at once, but that the place was not at the time the report was made within the jurisdiction of the commission. Since the new commission had been issued, Tooting had been brought under that jurisdiction, which was now called upon to exercise it. As against a summary exercise of power, it was objected that the works in question were private property. Now, in respect to the works for damming up the sewer water for productive purposes, he must allege that it was an invasion of the public property. By custom, by the usual course of legislation, and on all the principles which govern the application of such refuse, it belongs to the public, and he (Mr. Chadwick) submitted that steps should be taken to repress this invasion, and to prevent the like invasions at the expense of the lives, the health, and the convenience of the population. It appeared to him to be a case which came within the duty which devolved under the old statute of sewers, to amend and prostrate public encroachments. There could be no doubt that the remedial principles of the old law were too commonly overlooked, and that fitting occasions to recur to them were furnished, by such cases as the present. He took the liberty of reading the text of the old law, as laid down by Blackstone:—"Every man may abate a common nuisance. The nuisance may be abated, that is, taken away or removed by the aggrieved thereby, so as he commits no riot in doing it." "And the reason," says Blackstone, "why the law allows this private and summary method of doing one's self justice is because injuries of this kind, which obstruct or annoy such things as are of daily convenience and use, require an immediate remedy, and cannot wait for the slow progress of the ordinary forms of justice." And the annotator adds, "That security of the lives and property may sometimes require so speedy a remedy as not to allow time to call on the person on whose property the mischief has arisen to remedy it." He concluded by moving "That a Committee should be appointed, to view the encroachments, and if they saw fit, to order them to be abated."

Mr. Broderip seconded the resolution, which was put by the Chairman, and unanimously adopted. It was next agreed "That this operation be assigned to a district to be called the 'Wandle district,' and the expense debited thereto."

It was ultimately agreed that Capt. Veitch, and Messrs. Hutton, Hawes, Johnson, and R. L. Jones, be the members of such committee.

New Palace at Westminster.—Reports were then read on the drainage of the New Palace at Westminster, to which reference will be found in another page. The reading of them excited much interest.

They were ordered to be printed and circulated among the commissioners.

A deputation attended the court from the meeting, held in Westminster last week, on the subject of "street orderlies," requesting the assistance of this court to carry out their philanthropic objects.

The Earl of Carlisle said the application should receive every attention.

Mr. Cochrane (who headed the deputation), thanked his lordship for the courtesy with which they had been received.

Miscellanea.

YORKSHIRE ARCHITECTURAL SOCIETY.—The quarterly committee meeting of this society was held on January 4th. It was stated by Mr. R. H. Sharp, that in consequence of a grant made at a former meeting towards the restoration of the tower windows of St. Saviour's Church, a very liberal sum had been allowed by the feoffees and churchwardens of that church, in furtherance of this desirable object. A grant of 40*l*. was made in aid of a fund for filling the west window of St. Mary's Church, Beverley, with stained glass, the design of which was submitted to the society and approved. Other grants were also made for restorations at Thorp Arch and Howden Churches.

WARWICKSHIRE ARCHÆOLOGICAL SOCIETY.—The quarterly meeting of the Warwickshire National History and Archæological Society was held at the Museum in Thursday last week, and was well attended. The chief feature was a lecture on "The Religious Architecture of the Middle Ages, more particularly in reference to the Monuments of Egypt," by Mr. J. G. Jackson, of Leamington.

AN EXTENSIVE UNDERTAKING.—The Chapel-hill pits, belonging to the British Iron Company, are at length freed from the enormous quantities of water—the accumulation of years—which have so long flooded them, and coal has at last been found. The water, two years ago, when operations were first commenced, was 84 yards deep, and the expense attending its draining is estimated at no less a sum than 10,000*l*. This includes the erection of engines, stacks, and whimseys, and the losses occasioned by breakages, &c.—*Worcester Chronicle*.

IRISH MANUFACTURES—ORNAMENTAL CAST-IRON WINDOWS.—The Messrs. M'Adam, of Soho Foundry, Belfast, have recently completed a number of ornamental windows for the new palace of the Pacha of Egypt: they are of cast-iron, and of very large dimensions, being 20 feet high and 8 feet wide—each window weighing 5 tons. They are to be bronzed and gilt after being erected. The same firm have also erected on the banks of the Nile, for the Egyptian Government, a number of very large steam pumping-engines, to raise the water of the river for the purpose of irrigation. These facts are interesting.

General Meeting of Institution of Civil Engineers.—On the 16th of January, Mr. Field, President, in the chair, the annual general meeting of this institution was held, when the following gentlemen were elected to form the council for the ensuing year:—J. Field, President; W. Cubitt, J. M. Rendel, J. Simpson, and R. Stephenson, M.P., Vice-Presidents; J. F. Bateman, G. P. Bidder, I. K. Brunel, J. Cubitt, T. Fowler, C. H. Gregory, J. Locke, M.P., I. R. McLean, C. May, and J. Miller, Members; and W. Harding and T. Piper, Associates of Council. The report of the Council was read, and with reference to the pressure of the times, held out cheering hopes for the future, for, as it observed, "in a country like Great Britain, whose distinguishing characteristic is energetic and indomitable courage in circumstances of difficulty, it is not probable that any foreign political excitement can long continue to exercise a prejudicial effect: already the horizon is brightening, and a little reflection will demonstrate that, in proportion to the injury arising from the late stagnation, must be the activity on the resumption of the works; and it appears to be acknowledged that the forced economy which has been practised during the past year, has caused such a necessity for supplies of working stock, and for the improvement of works, that the engineering profession must be generally benefited on the return of confidence in financial affairs." Satisfactory reasons were given for the annual delay in the publication of the minutes of proceedings, and a plan was detailed for paying off the debt incurred for the alterations of the house of the institution. Telford medals were presented to the Right Hon. the Earl of Lovelace, Messrs. Harrison, Mitchell, and Ransome; council premiums of books to Messrs. Harrison and Jackson, and Telford premiums of books to Messrs. Redman, Green, and Rankine; and memoirs were then read of deceased members.

The Walls of Etruria.—Nothing, says Mr. Dennis, (in his work "The Cities and Cemeteries of Etruria,") gives a more exalted idea of the power and grandeur of this ancient people than the walls of their cities. These enormous piles of masonry, uncemented, yet so solid as to have withstood for three thousand years the destroying hand of man, the tempests, the earthquakes, the invisible yet more destructive power of atmospheric action, seem destined to endure to the end of time, yet often show a beauty, a perfection of workmanship that has never been surpassed. The style of masonry differs in the two great divisions of the land, and is determined in part by the nature of the local materials. In the northern district the walls are composed of huge blocks, rectangular in general, but of various sizes and irregular arrangement, according as the masses of rock were hewn or split from the quarry; and in some instances small pieces are inserted in the interstices of the larger blocks. There are, also, a few instances of the irregular, polygonal style,—as in the Cyclopean cities of central Italy. In the southern district the masonry is less massive and very regular.

A New Line of Railway Research.—According to an amusing railway article in the *Quarterly Review*, attributed to Sir Francis Head, it appears from the books that the annual consumption at the Wolverton refreshment rooms averages—

182,500 Banbury cakes.	5,110 lbs. of moist sugar.
56,940 Queen's cakes.	16,425 quarts of milk.
29,200 parés.	1,095 ,, cream.
36,500 lbs. of flour.	17,520 bott. of lemonade.
13,140 ,, butter.	35,040 ,, soda water.
2,920 ,, coffee.	70,030 ,, stout.
43,800 ,, meat.	35,040 ,, ale.
6,110 ,, currants.	17,520 ,, ginger beer.
1,277 ,, tea.	730 ,, port.
5,840 ,, loaf sugar.	3,650 ,, sherry.

And, we regret to add,

730 bottles of gin.
731 ,, rum.
3,660 ,, brandy.

To the eatables are to be added, or driven, thirty-five pigs, who, after having been from their birth most kindly treated and most luxuriously fed, are impartially promoted, by seniority, one after another, into an infinite number of pork pies.

Ashiesteel Bridge. — Whinstone Rubble Construction. — We mentioned some time since that a notice of this piece of construction, by Messrs. J. and T. Smith, of Darnick, was read at the Institute of Architects. The bridge has excited much interest in the neighbourhood, and we take the following particulars of it from the *Border Advertiser*:—The arch is elliptical, commencing from the abutments on each side with a short curve drawn to a radius of 24 feet, with a chord line of about 15 feet. This is surmounted by a curve drawn to a radius of 110 feet. The arch springs exactly from the summer level of the river, and its height is 26 feet, with a span of 131½ feet. The breadth of the arch at the abutments is nearly 19 feet, and converges by regular curve lines on each side to 16 feet at the crown. The thickness of the arch, from the abutments to within 24 feet of the keystone, is 2½ feet, backed by four ribs, each 2½ by 2½ feet, and the depth of the arch from there to the keystone is 4 feet. The spandril walls in the haunches rest upon the ribs already mentioned, and are so managed as to be an exact counterpoise to the crown of the arch. The plan of the bridge is simple and plain: and with the exception of the cornice and coping of the parapet walls, there is not a hewn stone in the whole building. The whole of the arch is of common whinstone rubble, built with lime, with here and there a little levelling of the beds with Roman cement. There has been much talk among engineers and architects, as well as others, as to the probable issue of the experiment, and many have been the prognostications of its failure. It is supposed to be the boldest arch ever executed of the same material. The estimate, we understand, was only about 1,200*l*. Ashiesteel is the place where Sir Walter Scott lived so long at, before sitting down at Abbotsford. It is some miles up Tweed.

Submarine Telegraphs.—Mr. Faraday having pointed attention to the highly insulating power of gutta percha, the very obvious application of it in covering the wires of the electric telegraph was forthwith suggested, as in a notice some time ago in The Builder. The fact of its mere capability of doing so scarcely required a formal trial. What is of much more importance is to test its permanency, especially in sea-water, for marine telegraphs. A formal trial, however, of the mere fact of its waterproof and insulating properties was lately made at Folkstone, when, notwithstanding the stupid and absurd management alluded to by the *Literary Gazette*, it was of course found that messages conveyed from a steamer through coils laid through the harbour (they might as well have been laid in the Thames or in a bucket at the London station of the South-Eastern, and thus have saved the trouble of sending reporters all the way to Folkstone) were safely delivered in London, and met with a prompt response—all now mere child's play. The serious question is, whether gutta percha be a prudent coating under sea water, and accordingly it has been suggested that the potent halogens chlorine, bromine, and iodine, which pervade the ocean, as well as sulphuric and other acids also prevailing in marine combinations, may speedily macerate and alter, if not destroy, a vegetable substance such as it is. But there is even a still more imminent peril, that no one seems to have thought of. Gutta percha may be a perfect tit-bit to myriads of the heterogeneous and indescribable living creatures which teem in the ocean, and bore their way through sand, and wood, and rock, consuming all that is not mineral. Time only, with experiments on a comparatively small scale, should be the test of such destructive agencies, and then the "bites of large fishes," the "dragging of anchors," and other probable or dreaded agencies, may be dared on the large scale.

The Model Lodging-House at Bath has been opened in Westgate-buildings, for forty persons, with separate beds, washing-stands, cupboards and boxes with locks and keys for all, a coffee-room, sick-room, gas throughout, &c., all, with cooking and attendance, for 1s. 9d. a week, and yet self-supporting: testimonials as to character are very properly demanded from candidates for so much comparative comfort at so little expense.

Testimonial to Mr. Vernon. — The proposal to raise by subscription sufficient funds to pay for the preparation of dies, and to present annually a gold medal, to be called the Vernon medal, for the encouragement of painting and sculpture, and in commemoration of Mr. Vernon's gift to the nation, appears to have found favour with all parties. A committee has been formed, containing many excellent names, and will shortly put the plan before the public. The medal will be confided to the Royal Academy.

Large Scythe Factory in America.—The scythe manufacturing establishment of Reuben B. Dunn, Esq., at North Wane, in Maine, is the largest of the kind in the world. The establishment consists, besides warehouses, furnishing shops, &c., of three principal buildings for manufacturing, two of which are 144 feet in length. In these, and in departments connected with the establishment, are employed about 100 men, many of whom have families settled at the place. A flourishing village has grown up within a few years, and is rapidly increasing. 12,000 dozen scythes are annually manufactured, to produce which are required 450,000 lbs. of iron, 75,600 lbs. of steel, 1,200 tons of hard coal, 10,000 bushels of charcoal, 100 tons of grindstones, and half a ton of borax. This last article is used in the process of welding. Mr. Dunn is erecting additional works in the vicinity, which will be soon completed, when he will be enabled to turn out 17,000 dozen scythes annually. This establishment is now more than double the extent of any other in the world—none even in England being found to compete with it.—*New York Farmer and Mechanic.*

The Iron Trade.—At the quarterly meetings just held, the masters again failed to raise prices, even as usual nominally, though, according to their out and out supporters, there was not only an improved demand, but a slight tendency to an advance. It must ever be remembered, however, that at these meetings of the masters, there is always 'a slight tendency to an advance.' Our steady refusal to quote their fictitious quarterly price-nominal, has at length been homologated by the example of one of their own respectable Birmingham supporters, the *Journal*, who says, "We will not attempt to give precise figures, inasmuch as prices, in some slight degree, must vary according to the situation of the works and the condition of the firms, &c.," all of which is quite true, if '&c.,' only comprehended the great desire of the quarterly meeters even for the nominal shadow of 'an advance,' failing the substance. For purchasers, the market is still of course in a very favourable position.

The State of the Serpentine River, Hyde-park.—Finding that no steps have yet been taken towards cleansing the Serpentine, a public meeting of the inhabitants of the neighbourhood was held at the Literary Institution, in Sloane-street, on Tuesday last, when Dr. Jas. Copland took the chair; and Mr. Lilwall, Mr. Goolden, Dr. Wilson, Mr. Geo. Wooley, and others, addressed the meeting, and shewed the necessity for improvement. The chairman said,—The Serpentine River had now become as certain a source of disease as the waters in the rivers of Africa. Indeed, he should say, from his own practical experience and observation, that the water in these rivers were not so foul or pestilential as that which constituted the Serpentine, the latter only requiring an equally high state of temperature to develope those diseases which appear in tropical climates.—The sum of 35,000*l*. was stated to be required for effecting the improvement. Surely the evil might be effectually remedied for a much less amount than this. If the mud be removed it must be done with great caution.

Blind Builders.—The following is a list of tenders for the brewery, &c. at Camberwell-green, for Mr. Fleming, Mr. Robt. Brown, architect, opened on the 9th inst.:—

Myers	£2,867	0	0
Crawley	2,512	0	0
Wells	2,490	0	0
Hill	2,296	0	0
Tombs	2,048	0	0
Willson	1,983	0	0
Brown	1,975	10	7
Thompson	1,885	0	0

NORFOLK ARCHÆOLOGICAL SOCIETY.—
The Bishop of Norwich attended the annual
meeting of the Norfolk Archæological Society,
which was held on Thursday week. He said
he had to congratulate the meeting on two
points. The first being that the present was
the best exhibition since the commencement
of the society, and he hoped it would increase
the interests of its proceedings. In the next
place he had great pleasure in referring to a
fact which would appear from the report that,
unlike all the others in the city and county,
this institution was in a flourishing state. The
subscriptions were increasing, and this would
be a source of great satisfaction to them all.

INSTITUTION OF BUILDERS' FOREMEN.
—It will be seen by an advertisement, that the
anniversary dinner of this Association will
take place on the 31st. We shall be glad to
find it well attended.

OUR RECORDS.—The occurrence of the
late disastrous fire in Lincoln's-Inn affords
an opportunity which should not be lost,
of again forcing upon the public mind
the importance of fire-proof buildings becoming more generally adopted, particularly
when used as the repositories of valuable
deeds and documents, the loss of which,
as in the above instance, no amount of
insurance can replace. Our national records
too are liable to the like contingency ; surely it
is time they were better cared for. Let the
columns of THE BUILDER again send forth
the voice of warning ere it be too late, and let
this reproach to England be erased, that she
has no proper edifice in which to deposit her
records, but that they are stowed away in
un-come-at-able places, and liable to be destroyed at any time by the merest accident.
　　　　　　　　　　　E. S.

MEETINGS OF SCIENTIFIC BODIES

Held during the ensuing week.

MONDAY, JAN. 22.—Institute of Architects, 8 P.M.
WEDNESDAY, 24.—Society of Arts, 8 P.M.
THURSDAY, 25.—Royal Society, 8½ P.M. ; Society of Anti-
quaries, 8 P.M.
FRIDAY, 26.—Archæological Association, 1 P.M.
SATURDAY, 27.—Institute of Fine Arts, 8 P.M.

TO CORRESPONDENTS.

Received.—"J. J. L.," "H. J.," "J. R. M.," "W. M."
(We cannot give the addresses of manufacturers), "R. C."
(Ditto), "A Subscriber" from 1844 " (ditto), "R. G. C.,"
"Would-be-Architect," "E. F." (Thanks), "G. M.,"
"E. S.," "J. B.," "J. T." (You cannot go on the
premises without authority. Ask your solicitor), "W. F."
Blockport (Covers for binding may be obtained at the office),
"J. C." (We do not know), "J. A.," " Bibliotheca,"
"J. L." (Difficult), " F. D." (The secretary at any of
the institutions will give information required. Plans of the
Russell Institution will be found in Britton's " Public
Buildings of London "), " E. P.," " W. W.," " J. S.,"
" Landscape Gardener," " Sir T. D.," " Mr. W.," " R.
J. E." (Appears to have been overlooked. Declined with
thanks), " J. B. S." (Many thanks for a most acceptable
plan).

" *Books, Prices, and Addresses*—We have not time to
point out books or find addresses.

No. CCCXII.

SATURDAY, JANUARY 27, 1849.

MONGST the artisans of England are a large number of singularly intelligent, shrewd, and sensible men,—much larger than is supposed by the majority of those who, by their position, are removed from contact with them: men worthy of respect, and deserving the greatest consideration. Many of the multitudinous essays by working men, On the Sabbath, which were called forth not long ago by offered premiums, astonished those who were appointed to decide on their relative merits, by the closeness of reasoning, ability, and wisdom which they displayed.

Within a recent period there have been in our own pages more than one communication penned by hands made heavy and intractable by the mallet, yet full of sound sense, and shewing enlarged and comprehensive views. These are not men to be classed with the vulgar and uncared for. "These are not vulgar people," says Dante, "merely because they live in small cottages, lowly places: but those are vulgar who, by their thoughts and deeds, strive to shut out any view of beauty." There are vulgar rich men as well as vulgar poor men. Being poor is not of itself a disqualification for being a gentleman. To be a gentleman is to be elevated above others in sentiment rather than situation. And the poor man with an enlarged and pure mind may be happier, too, than his richer neighbour without this elevation. Let the former only look at nature with an enlightened mind,— "a mind which can see and adore the Creator in his works, can consider them as demonstrations of his power, his wisdom, his goodness, and his truth; this man is greater, as well as happier, in his poverty, than the other in his riches. The one is but little higher than the beast, the other but a little lower than an angel."[*]

Our simple object, however, is to say, in plain words, that the honest, upright, intelligent artisan deserves the consideration of all who have it in their power to improve or ameliorate his condition. And we are impelled to this by the recent receipt of several saddening letters from men of this class, overcome by hope deferred. These are records of suffering; can we wonder that they are interspersed with complaints and repinings? We may say to the writers of them, with Feltham, that "We do not wisely when we vent complaint and censure. Human nature is more sensible of smart in suffering than of pleasure in rejoicing, and the present endurances easily take up our thoughts. We cry out for a little pain, when we do but smile for a great deal of contentment."

But their complaints are too serious,—the grounds for them too apparent, for the reproach conveyed in this to apply. They have laboured all their lives; they are willing still to labour, but they can find no employer.

The story of some amongst them who *have* work is sad enough: take the following, and let it not provoke derision, but desire to aid :—

* Jones of Nayland.

"I am a journeyman carpenter," says one, "thirty-eight years of age, and it is my firm conviction that I have worked physically upwards of ten hours on an average every day of my life since I was twelve years old, and worked hard too. From twelve to fifteen years I laboured for an existence with a donkey and water-butt on a carriage, and after a while with a horse-butt, loading and drawing water from the river Lea, hawking it about the streets in a suburban village, and selling of it for a penny a turn,—a turn being the quantity of four common pails, which I used to carry in large ones with a pair of yokes, and empty into the butt or vessel of those that bought it. At fifteen I went to the trade; at eighteen my master broke. I turned journeyman at twenty, married ["There's the rub!"], and three months afterwards fell out of work, and was out six months. I have been the father of ten children, five alive and five dead. I have been obliged to work (or leave the employ) Sundays, Good Fridays, and Christmas days, whilst my employers have taken their carriage and gone to church, and all day and the major part of the night for weeks consecutively. As I lived upwards of two miles from the place, I have slept as I walked home, and once ran against a wall in my sleep. I so deranged the system by excessive labour, that it produced a deception of the vision, so that all manner of hideous figures would appear to dance or walk before me, and have appeared to be so close to me sometimes, that I have put my hand out to touch them. It has left a speck in each eye up to the present time, as a mark of the effect of excessive labour on the organ of vision. I have never been abstemious in the necessaries of life, and never indulged in the luxuries; yet with all my working and abstemiousness I am still miserably poor, and I am not an exception to my class."

Truly, as one of the same said in a letter to the *Times* a few days ago,—

"If the possessors of wealth could see beneath the surface of a poor man's life, or obtain a secret view of his home, they would do their utmost to alleviate the condition of respectable but poor mechanics."

Words to men in want may be called wind; nevertheless, there may be comfort in the reminder that there is still good in their struggles. Hear what the benevolent Channing says :—

"I have faith in labour, and I see the goodness of God in placing us in a world where labour alone can keep us alive. I would not change, if I could, our subjection to physical laws, our exposure to hunger and cold, and the necessity of constant conflicts with the material world. I would not, if I could, so temper the elements that they should infuse into us only grateful sensations, that they should make vegetation so exuberant as to anticipate every want, and the mineral so ductile as to offer no resistance to our strength and skill. Such a world would make a contemptible race. *Man owes his growth, his energy, chiefly to that striving of the will, that conflict with difficulty, which we call effort.* Easy, pleasant work does not make robust minds, does not give men such a consciousness of their powers, does not train to *endurance*, to perseverance, to steady force of will, that force without which all other acquisitions avail nothing."

And then listen to what Charles Mackay, the poet of the people, sings of this same endurance :—

"Were the lonely acorn never bound
In the rude, cold grasp of the rotting ground;
Did the frigid frost never harden up
The mould above its bursting cup:
Were it never soaked in the rain and hail,
Or chilled by the breath of the wintry gale,
It would not sprout in the sunshine free,
Or give the promise of a tree;
      *   *   *
Or stand in the woods among its peers,
Fed by the dews of a thousand years.
      *   *   *
So thou, O man of a noble soul,
Starting in view of a glorious goal,
Wert thou never exposed to the blasts forlorn—
The storms of sorrow—the sleets of scorn?
Wert thou never refined in pitiless fire,
From the dross of thy sloth and mean desire;
Wert thou never taught to feel and know
That the truest love has its roots in woe,
Thou would'st never unriddle the complex plan,
Or reach half way to the perfect man;
Thou would'st never attain the tranquil height
Where wisdom purifies the sight,
And God unfolds to the humblest gaze
The bliss and beauty of His ways."

One of the correspondents to whom we are addressing these few recollections of what others have said rather than thoughts of our own, inquires as to the advisability of *emigrating to Australia*, no prospect opening to him here. We would say, obtain proper advice and guidance, and go by all means. If you are able and willing to labour, you will not fail to find there a fair field for your exertions.[*] Emigration generally we regard as a cure for many of our social evils. Admit that under better arrangements England could maintain in comfort a much larger number of persons than is now the case, still it is certain that the alterations necessary must be the work of time, and those who find it impossible to obtain remunerative employment here will do well not to wait, but turn their attention to other quarters, and seek "fresh lands and pastures new."

"Pent in wynds and closes narrow,
   Breathing pestilential air,
Crush'd beneath oppression's barrow,
   Faint with famine, bowed with care,—
Gaunt affliction's sons and daughters!
   Why so slow to hear the call
Which The Voice upon the waters
   Preaches solemnly to all?

Hark! old Ocean's tongue of thunder
   Hoarsely calling bids you speed
To the shores he held asunder
   Only for these times of need;
Now, upon his friendly surges
   Ever roaring, Come,
All the sons of hope he urges
   To a new, a richer Home!

England and her seagirt sisters
   Pine for want in seeming wealth;
Though the gaudy surface glisters,
   This is not the hue of health;
O! the honest labour crying
   Vainly here to earn its bread,—
O! the willing workers dying,
   Unemployed, untaught, unfed!
     *   *   *   *

* Dr. Laing gives the following as an example of what may be done by a labouring man in Australia. John M'Millan, a native of Skipness, in the highlands of Scotland, had, previous to the year 1840 (when he obtained a free passage for himself and family, as bounty emigrants to Port Philip) been for five or six years a common porter on the streets of Greenock. He had only from five to ten shillings altogether when he arrived at Melbourne, and that sum he had received for some petty services on board; but his wife was a stout active Highland woman, and he had nine sons and one daughter, of various ages, from infancy to twenty years. He had no trade or handicraft, but as labour of all kind was in great demand at the time, he obtained 9l. a-week as a stonemason's labourer, and those of his sons who were fit for service of any kind were hired out under various masters. With the first savings of the family he bought a cow, which cost 15l.; and another and another were added from time to time, till his herd amounted—increase and purchases included—to 400 head. In the meantime he had purchased, from the earnings of the family (from a gentleman who had bought 5,900 acres of land, at 1l. per acre, which he selected within a few miles of Melbourne, in the hope of making a fortune from its rise in value), forty-two acres of ground, at 7l. an acre, at a place called Brighton, on the sea-coast, within the gulf, about 6 miles from the town. The whole of this land he had cleared, divided into paddocks with rail fences, and brought into a high state of cultivation; and as land of the same description immediately adjoining had cost 45l. an acre for clearing—for it was heavily timbered—the real price of it may be considered as having been 12l. an acre. The soil appeared to be light and sandy, but it bore crops of wheat from thirty to forty bushels an acre. M'Millan had rented a small farm adjoining his own during the year 1845, and from both he had reaped from 700 to 800 bushels of wheat, and collected sixty tons of oaten hay; and he considered himself worth altogether 1,100l.

England's frank and sturdy bearing,
  Scotland's judgment, true and tried,
Erin's energetic daring,
  And the Welchman's honest pride,—
Send these forth, and tame the savage,
  Sow his realm with British homes,
Where till now wild monsters ravage,
  Or the wilder Bushman roams!

Let, as erst in Magna Græcia,
  Nobles, sages, join the ranks;
And for vacant Austral-Asia
  Leave for good these swarming banks;
Not as Exiled,—but with honour!
  Told in tale, and sung in song,—
With the Queen,—GOD's blessing on her!
  Speeding this good work along!

* * * *

Haste, then, all ye better natures,
  Help in what must bless the World!
See, those cellar-crowded creatures
  To despair's own dungeon hurl'd,—
Send—or lead them o'er the waters
  To the genial shores, that give
Britain's sacred sons and daughters
  Man's great privilege—to Live.

There,—for grudged and scanty wages,
  Grinding rent and parish tax,—
In the wood, unheard for ages,
  Rings the cheerful freeman's axe;
Whilst in yonder cozy clearing,
  Home, sweet Home, rejoices life,
Full of thoughts and things endearing,
  Merry babes and rosy wife!

There,—instead of festering alleys,
  Noisome dirt, and gnawing dearth,—
Sunny hills and smiling valleys
  Wait to yield the wealth of Earth!
All She asks is—human labour,
  Healthy in the open air;
All She gives is—every neighbour
  Wealthy, hale, and happy There!*

With *energy* and determination much may be done, let a man's position be what it may; without these, nothing. The possession or want of energy makes much of the difference between the weak and the powerful. Let some of our friends think over this: have a fixed purpose, and pursue it steadily.

And to those of our readers who have the direction of extensive works, to the Government especially, and important corporations, we would say with great earnestness, Pause before you determine on discontinuing operations: if money must be saved, save it in other quarters, but do not add to the enormous amount of distress already existing, by discharging workmen.

If what we have here written prove of little value, it has, at least, a good intention and a pure purpose, which must serve as our excuse.

GEORGE GODWIN.

ON THE VARIOUS QUALITIES OF CAEN STONE.†

IT seems to be the general opinion of the proprietors of quarries and their quarrymen, as well as of the masons and builders at Caen, that the most durable stone is obtained from the uppermost of the six workable beds, or from those beds which are nearest to the top, and freest from the little pebbly concretions which abound in the ceiling bed; and also that the lowest beds are softer, and thereby more readily disintegrated by exposure to the weather. I feel disposed to pay attention to this statement, because it corresponds with practical observations and opinions entertained by most people who are well acquainted with quarrying and working stone of a similar mineralogical character in our own country. The top beds of Portland, Bath, Ketton, and other oolitic limestones, are all the most durable; whereas the undermost strata in the same quarries are well known to moulder away, if exposed to moisture and the usual atmospheric influences.

It is with all the varieties of Caen stone as with most other stones, that the goodness or power to resist decay depends chiefly upon the quantity and quality of the cementing substance by which the component grains adhere to each other. The cement that unites the grains, the ova, or other loose particles, into a mass, is formed of the same elements as the grains themselves, but more crystalline; it is, in fact, the decomposition of some of the superincumbent mass, saturating and crystallizing throughout the beds beneath. Water, even in its simplest state, may be considered to act as a solvent to most things; but when it contains acid, its power of dissolving calcareous substances is considerably augmented. Many waters are impregnated with carbonic acid, obtained partly from the atmosphere and frequently from subterranean sources. If they contain a superabundance of carbonic acid, they will rapidly decompose limestone, and carry the atoms thus sustained in solution until a certain quantity of the acid, in a gaseous state, has evaporated, when the atoms of limestone will again solidify in crystals, and perhaps assume a totally different character. If this ingenious process of nature be carried on for a great length of time, over a considerable thickness of loose calcareous matter, the probability is, that the water thus charged with lime and carbonic acid will saturate the more porous parts, and thus ultimately form a well-cemented and compact limestone, of what was originally a congeries of loose ova, or grains.

Under these, or similar circumstances, it is but reasonable to suppose that in the deep recesses of the earth, where the extreme changes of surface-temperature, and vegetation, and the influences which produce organization and life, cease to act,—there, even there, a creative power still pursues its never-ending task of giving new forms to matter, and that, the longer a slightly-connected or porous limestone remains buried beneath a certain quantity of calcareous material, the more solid and indurated it will become. And if this stone be ultimately extracted, and used for ornamental architecture, it will be more durable than that which is of recent formation.

Exactly the converse of this process takes place after a stone is removed from its natural position in the quarry, and exposed to the numerous vicissitudes of climate, temperature, moisture, and other atmospheric changes which are constantly in operation. From the moment of its removal, destruction commences, and continues incessantly. In some instances, the action is far more rapid than in others; but whether the ruin be effected in ten years, or ten thousand, is only a question of time,—the same influence is for ever at work to bring about the disintegration, decay, and final dissolution of all things.

Of all the causes of decay in stone, none is more destructive than variations of temperature: the vicissitudes of heat and cold, dryness and moisture, frequently alternating, are more ruinous to the carved parts of a building than either of these extremes constantly operating. However slight the additional heat may be to which a body is subjected, it will expand under its influence, and contract when the temperature is lowered. The thermometer will probably vary 100 degrees from the severe frost of a winter night to the direct rays of an afternoon summer sun, which never shines upon the north or north east sides of a building, except very obliquely at rising and setting; but the south and west fronts have the same degree of cold as the north and east during the night, with the additional warmth of meridian splendour daily. Such extremes must tend to loosen the component parts, and thereby separate many small fragments from the surface of stones, especially if the mass is made up of different substances, in which case some will expand and contract more, in proportion to their size and density, than others. The test of time proves this to be correct, for in all cases the greatest amount of disintegration has taken place, where the inequalities of temperature are greatest.

It is pretty evident, from both theory and practice, that there is a considerable difference between the upper and lower beds. The next question is, did the architects and builders of the numerous old edifices in Caen and its neighbourhood generally, use only the top beds in the construction of their elaborate architectural works; or did they frequently, if not on all occasions, apply the stone from one particular quarry or district, to the exterior of their buildings; and a softer, or more expeditiously working material to the interior, in situations protected from the weather.

If we examine the granulated texture of a fresh-broken fracture, from an old building, appearances are certainly in favour of the stone having been procured from some of the uppermost beds; or more probably, from a totally different quarry, for the stone is much harder, and of a lighter colour, than is to be found in any of the Allemagne quarries. But as there is no very evident distinction, no fossils or organic remains, peculiar to one bed more than another, no certain conclusion can be arrived at, from the most attentive examination in this manner. After the lapse of several centuries, the only mode of procedure is to draw an inference from circumstantial evidenee.

The road which passes along the entrances to most of the quarries (about 35 in number), is on a level above the lower beds, or in other words, the road is formed upon those beds which are considered unfit for external works; consequently, whenever any of these subterranean quarries were opened or began to be worked, the stone first procured from them must have been taken from those beds which are now considered to be most durable; and as there is a regular descent, of a very slight inclination, from the road to the interior, nearly approaching to the extreme end of the quarries, it is quite certain that an enormous quantity of stone, of the best quality to be obtained in that particular district, must have been extracted, probably during several centuries, before they got far enough in, and deep enough down, to make use of the lower beds.

In all countries, during feudal times, the hills or protuberances were generally occupied by the barons, either for the beauty of the prospect, or more probably on account of their commanding situation: thus, we find the castle at Caen, originally a fortress of considerable strength, surrounded by strong, lofty walls, and elevated on a rock considerably higher than any other ground in the neighbourhood. The inspection of these fortifications, and the rock on which they are built, leads us to presume that the same stone which had been removed to form a moat was applied to construct the wall,—thus answering two purposes, and thereby rendering the approach of a hostile party more difficult. Buildings for protection against an enemy, generally precede those for the service of religion; and by finding a superabundance of stone, in constructing a fort upon the crown of a rock, they would naturally be induced to open a quarry, close at hand, to supply materials for the erection of churches and other public edifices,—and accordingly we find the remains of many extensive quarries in different places near the ancient castle.

If we observe the distance of the Allemagne quarries, and the proximity of those by the castle, to many of the old buildings, including the churches of St. Etienne and the Holy Trinity, it will require no great stretch of imagination to suppose that the architects or builders of these venerable structures availed themselves of good materials within a short distance, in preference to fetching stone of a doubtful quality from three or four times the distance; and this opinion is strengthened by carefully examining specimens taken from the exterior of some of the celebrated churches at Caen. According to tradition in the neighbourhood, no stone has been extracted from these ancient quarries for several hundred years: it is supposed they were deserted soon after those at Allemagne were discovered and became in more general use,—perhaps from fear of the town being endangered by undermining, or because the more recent quarries were found to produce a softer and more easily-working material.

Between the beds of Caen stone, we sometimes find a thin stratum of highly ferruginous loam, especially between the lower beds; and this clayey oxide of iron may be traced, to a slight extent, throughout the stone of all the beds, particularly in that of the Franc Banc, giving to it a deeper colour, somewhat of a rusty tint: this circumstance may very likely be one of the causes why that bed is more perishable than the upper ones.

It is quite surprising to notice the great difference of hardness in the same specimen of Caen stone when thoroughly saturated with

* We are indebted for these lines to Mr. Martin Tupper, the author of "Proverbial Philosophy," whose pen has before this enriched our pages.

† See page 26 ante.

water, and when perfectly dry. In one case it may be almost abraded with the naked finger, and the nail will readily make an indent on the surface; whereas the very same piece of stone, when completely dried, is comparatively so indurated, that it cannot be effaced without a sharp instrument, or some more violent effort. Independent of the gradual decomposition produced by the solvent power of water, a stone so absorbent and so softened by moisture, as it must frequently be, in a climate where wind and rain continue for days and weeks without ceasing,—such stone must be liable to be damaged by mechanical violence in a thousand ways that would have no effect upon a harder material.

Much stress is generally laid upon Caen stone being "well seasoned:" although this caution is important to a certain extent, it is usually overrated. All kinds of stone while in the rock, or when recently quarried, are more thoroughly saturated with moisture than can ever be accomplished after they have been once allowed to get dry. If the stone be remarkably soft, it is advisable not to let it dry too fast, after it has been taken from the quarry, for fear of its cracking, in consequence of the moisture being removed from the outside before that in the interior of the block can have had time to evaporate; hence, while the central part remains of its original size, and extremely damp, the surface will dry and shrink, thereby causing many unobserved cracks, the effect of which will be evident in the following winter. The Caen stone merchants take no other care of the blocks after they are exposed for sale, or shipment, on the quay, than to cover them with matting during frosty weather. In addition to this, I would recommend placing them under an open shed, where they might have a free current of air, protection from rain, and be shaded from the sun, which might otherwise cause them to dry too rapidly on the surface.

The cost of Caen stone buildings, compared with works constructed of materials produced in this country, will, in a great degree, depend upon locality and other circumstances. At this time, Caen stone may be delivered on a wharf in London for about two-thirds the price of Portland; and, for labour alone, the expense is certainly not more than half that upon Portland stone, or of that which is now being used at the New Houses of Parliament. Although elaborate architectural works may be constructed in that beautiful material, for a comparatively small sum, I wish it to be clearly understood that the material now generally known in the markets as Caen stone differs, in many essential particulars, from the stone which forms the exterior of the venerable edifices which have adorned the city of Caen from the period of William the Conqueror until this time. Therefore it is too much to expect that the palace of our Sovereign, the mansions of the wealthy, and the palatial looking club-houses, which have recently been constructed with Caen stone in the metropolis of England, should endure for seven or eight centuries, with as little appearance of decay as is at this time observable on the sacred structures in the vicinity of the quarries. However, if good judgment be exercised in selection, it is probable that the buildings now erecting with Caen stone in this country may continue in a fair state of preservation for at least one or two centuries.

In all cases, before commencing a work of magnitude or importance, I strongly recommend a visit to the quarries, and an attentive examination of old buildings in the vicinity, and, if possible, an interview with the proprietor or principal quarryman.

Before I describe and comment upon the tables and experiments,* I will briefly say a few words on the mode of investigating or searching after these unknown truths.

To examine the granular aggregation of a stone, with a view to its fitness for exposure to the sun, air, moisture, &c., it should be washed thoroughly clean, to get rid of all dust or foreign matter from the surface; and observations should particularly be made on surfaces as large as possible, for they will present more palpable and more numerous distinguishing characteristics than minute ones. All experiments made with little bits of stone, however accurately they may be watched, are but vague approximations, the best of which are likely to lead to erroneous results, owing to the variable nature of the stones upon which the experiments are performed. For example, if you observe the party-coloured appearance of some stones, and the tint of one entire slab compared with another, each slab representing a vertical section of one block of Caen stone, you will perceive by the colour, when half dry, the different qualities of hard and soft stone, each of which will, no doubt, vary considerably in duration.

C. H. SMITH.

* To be given next week.

ENFRANCHISEMENT OF LEASEHOLDS.

THE articles on this subject published in THE BUILDER, appear to have attracted considerable attention, and perhaps some remarks as to the utopian objects of the promulgator. The lords of wide urban domains, whose interests (or at least the interests of whose sons, grandsons, or successors in tail) are the subject of revision and change, may cry aloud, "The plan is one of spoliation—it is a socialist doctrine, designed to enrich the many, by confiscating the estates of the few;" whilst a great portion of the community, fearful of approaching any theory which hath the savour of an invasion on property, perhaps recoil from a measure that seems to have that tendency.

But in truth nothing can be more illusory than the prejudice of either party in the present consideration; for its prominent characteristic is, that the enfranchisement of leasehold tenures, carried out on an equitable basis, cannot injure nor reduce the rentals of great proprietors; nor can it fail to benefit society at large by the creation of an extensive class of freeholders in houses, and at the same time put a stop to that concentration of fixed capital in oligarchic families, which prejudices the freedom of the electoral voice, harasses the relations of the civic family of mankind, bereaves the heirs of local residents of their houses and stations, and hath for its inevitable issue, the building up of auriferous principalities in the heart of England.

It is far from our design to interfere with or reduce the *head* rents reserved in original leases; or to abate from the independence of families possessing *thousands of houses*; but as in every question of national policy, the scruples of the few must cede to the manifest welfare of the many,—so perhaps in this scheme, the abstract notions of vested interests of the oligarchy of wealth, must ultimately be made to have some regard to the common weal.

The feu rights of lords of manors to copyhold levies of fines, heriots, &c. &c., were equally legitimate privileges, before the legislature thought fit to abrogate these seigniorial dues; the rights of freeholders in the tenure of freehold lands, were as indefeasible, until the national Parliament enacted that in all cases where a line of railway should intersect private property, individual benefit should give way to that of the public, and that such sections of property as fell into the plan of the proposed lines should be valued by sworn juries; and that the amount adjudged as the value thereof should be paid to the possessors on the transfer of such properties to the public company for such purposes.

In framing this Act of Parliament, however, a very discreet reservation was carefully guarded, on behalf of the proprietors of parks (the legislators themselves being ordinarily the tenors), that no park, lawn, &c. &c., should be understood as coming under the provisions of the Act! This was a salvo for the wealthy,—for the veto lay with *them* in all cases of converting private domain lands; and wherever such have been needed to carry out the plans of a railroad company, the most extortionate prices have been exacted and paid to propitiate the repugnance of the resident lord,—in many cases amounts equal to twenty times the fee simple value of the segment appropriated! Here the farmer, the modest yeoman, or town burgess, have to submit to the statutory enactment, whilst the magnate of the park could only be brought out at *his own valuation*.

These are but examples to prove the acknowledgment of the Legislature that private right must cede to public utility and convenience, the right being duly compensated for.

In the matter of enfranchising leasehold tenures, the whole resident community is deeply concerned. If in the metropolis there are 300,000 houses and householders, we may safely infer that 100,000 must be deeply interested in any measure which would tend to the assurance of perpetuity in their abodes—in the houses of their sites and progenitors—in the security that the habitation (in which, in many instances, the independence of their condition has been amassed, and upon which large sums have been disbursed) shall not be forfeited, but transmitted to their children. On the other hand, these 100,000 houses belong to comparatively but few in number of the renter class. Several of the leviathan lords are lessors and proprietors of above *one thousand houses!* and some of five times that number; and the longest lease known on such estates is *ninety-nine*,—but latterly *seventy* and *sixty-one* years have become the usual term on building estates. One estate in the most valuable part of the town has above 2,000 first and second-class houses, 2,000 third-class, and building sites for as many more. One-half of this estate is of new creation, and has seventy years to run, at ground rents averaging two guineas a foot, or 50*l.* a house! On every house of this city of palaces at least 1,000*l.* has been expended by the adventuring builder; so that, on the lapse of seventy years, supposing that no greater sums are disbursed in embellishments or improvements, the startling sum (in fixed property) of 8,000,000*l.* will fall into the hands and disposition of one sole potentate in rents! and this to the exclusion of the short-sighted outlayers of private capital. But this is not half,—turn we to the other moiety of the estate,—of the other 2,000 houses. One-third part were leased ninety years back, one-third sixty, and one-third twenty, at the ground-rents incident to the value of these periods. For the lapsed portion, that is relet at rack rents (generally giving the preference on lease to the lessee or occupier), therefore one-third part has sixty years to run, and the last third portion has thirty years to run.

These statements are in general terms, but not far from the truth. Now for the tenants' interest on these holdings. The rule on this estate is, that no lease shall be renewed until within twenty years of its lapse or expiration. At this period the valuation is made, not by the tenant, nor by a valuation jury, but by the landlord; he estimates the value to the tenant, and lays it on accordingly. The original rent in first-rate tenements may average 50*l.* a-year, the improved rental on a renewed lease, from 250*l.* to 300*l.* a-year. The more money the predecessor or ancestor of the lessee has laid out on the premises, the greater will be the value thereof; and, therefore, the tenant, whose father or grandsire has converted a shop into a mansion, or a mansion into a palace, has to pay over again the improved value, if he wish to retain his ancestral dome.

It is thus, that in the lapse of sixty years, the whole extent of this great town and its suburbs will be divided amongst a few, and remain to be dealt with at their discretion; and of these the westward division will present the paramount feudalisms of Grosvenor and Belgrave, Portland, Portman, Bedford, Fitz-Hardinge, Southampton, Northampton, Arundel, or Norfolk, Sutton, and some other hospodars, pachalics, and principalities; so that the second generation issuing from the present and existent one, inhabiting one half of the metropolis, will be under the proprietory dominion of some dozen Archons or Crœsuses, who, knit together by a community of feelings and interests, must form a fearful *imperium in regno*,—as dangerous to state policy as to civil polity.

To simplify the proposition which, although perhaps novel, has nothing of spoliation, violence, or injustice in it, the following development will sufficiently suffice.

Suppose a tenant of a building plot, 30 feet frontage, in any new locality, held on lease of 80 years at a ground-rent of 20s. a foot, or 30*l.* a year;—if disposed to purchase the perpetuity before he builds, let him serve notices to that effect on the landlord or his agent, and on the surveyor of the district. Within one month after the service of such notice (according to the desiderated law), a jury should be summoned to assess the amount of increased value for such perpetuity, either at an increased ground-rent, or in amount of purchase-money : at the option of the tenant so proposing. As no building has been erected on the plot, and as the term of surrender to the lord is so remote, a very trifling yearly increased rent would be surcharged on the original rent.

Or, suppose a case where the house and premises had been erected and the interest sold to an occupying tenant, and that ten years had elapsed (the vicinage being generally covered and occupied), then a comparatively larger, but still moderate, though increased amount of rental or purchase would be required.

Next take, for example, a house which may have been built forty years on an original lease of 80 years, which may have changed hands from purchaser to purchaser, and suppose the lease thereof has 40 years to run, at a ground rent of 50l. a-year (this is an ordinary case, as many mansions in the first situations have been leased at about 10s. a-foot, or say 50l. rental).

The same formalities of notice and valuations will follow. As the period of resumption by the landlord is more proximate, and the value of the buildings and locality are more considerable, then a larger award of compensation will be made by the jury ; such as perhaps 500l. to purchase, or 25l. a-year to rent, added to the original head rent of 50l. a-year in perpetuity, if the tenant in occupation should be willing to take it at a rental.

In the same manner, the remaining unexpired terms of long leases at head-rents may be calculated, on the principles of justice and equity to both landlord and tenant ; but in no case is it contemplated to affect or interfere with leases of houses let at rack-rent for 7, 14, or 21 years (reserving to the tenants the option of surrender at the determination of any seven years) ; nor would this be of general advantage to the class of occupiers who take houses with a view to short residence, either as standings for business or private residence : nor does equity seem to require in these cases any new modification, as such occupiers seldom outlay their capital on improvements.

The new law of enfranchisement would of course provide for the payment of the jurors (who should be professional men) and of the district surveyor, the charges for whom should be borne by the tenant or person issuing such notices.

The proceedings in this respect might be advantageously assimilated to those of valuations under railroad enactments, which appear to work well, and to give as little dissatisfaction as is possible between, on the one side, extortionate requirements, and parsimony or niggardliness on the other.

As matters now stand, the holders of outrunning leases in valuable localities have no certitude of renewal at any price. The family residence held for 70 years at a rental fair at the time of its origination, and upon which 5 or 10,000l. has been sunk, may be denied to the occupier and given to another, or the owner may wish to play the same game over again,—not to accept a premium, but to impose a rack-rent of, say, 300l. (an ordinary advance), and the still more onerous imposition of a compulsory clause to rebuild, and to expend 10,000l. more, for the benefit of the succeeding heritors on the lapse of 60 years more.

The predicament of an occupier and lessee in some cases is still harder ;—having a lease of some 20 years to run at the original head-rent renewed 60 years back ; his house has fallen into decay, and is antiquated ; requiring to be rebuilt, he proposes for a renewal, but is refused ; such proposal is referred to the landlord's own committee of arbitration ; but no, the lord has other views as to the house in question.

This is no imaginary case ; it is matter of fact. So the unfortunate heritor or occupant of a favourite house is forced to abide in discomfort, if not slow torture and even imminent danger, or to throw up his term into the lap of the leviathan lord !

His tenement is crazy, he must prop it ; the dry rot eats on its career, he must abide the issue ; or if he be like the foolish builder (more foolish than he of the Scripture, for the certain mulct and forfeiture are before him),

then he must lose his outlay—for even in case of an ultimate renewal, the sum expended will lay a reduplicated valuation at his door.

Although this thesis does not contemplate the complete purchase of all head rents, that object is far from being unattainable ; for an Act of the Legislature might with perfect equity compass such an enfranchisement also, varying the purchase on a scale of unexpired years, from thirty-three years' purchase (the highest price of funds) down to fifteen years, graduated according to the extent of unexpired term. The purchase of the head rent would be as equitable as that of the term in perpetuity, saving the head rent.

Instead of increasing in house property, which may be called the only *fixed property* of the capital, the landlord class would, in the event of large conversion of their rents into money, become great capitalists, and the multitude renting houses must, on the other hand, become freeholders, with fixed local interests ; and there can be no question as to the effect of such a change on the population ; or that the subdivision of house ownership must have the best influence, whether with respect to their domestic comforts, their fiscal importance, or to the character of the buildings, that must in such case supplant the structures raised to endure but for a season.

The arts, chiefly architecture, have important concern in this subject ; the municipal rights of every citizen are wound up in it, as are the interests of the present generation, but most of all, their heirs in the generation to come.

QUONDAM.

ON DILAPIDATIONS.

THIS subject is [one that has never received proper consideration from the hands of a large class who are interested and affected by it— "tenants." Men who are daily imposing upon themselves heavy responsibilities, the extent, or the peculiar obligations, and the ultimate result of which they are totally unacquainted with.

Few persons on taking a lease think of raising objections to covenants which are, they are informed, of the usual character ; or, it prudent enough to pledge themselves to an agreement of but three years, they fearlessly, and without hesitation, affix their signatures to a clause promising to "uphold, maintain, and sustain," &c., or that which really may turn out an impossibility ; for some houses, so to speak, have the elements of destruction and disease upon them from their infancy. Bad brickwork, causing by its humidity damp walls, rots everything : unseasoned timber, that shrinks and twists in all directions, throwing floors out of their level, and making settlements from top to bottom, through which the doors and windows have to be constantly eased and rehung ; faulty and imperfect drainage, which becomes constantly choked ; the roof acting like a sieve : and this list of ills that modern houses are heir to is no exaggeration ; yet many a man, and he, too, who may be esteemed in his own business a prudent man, is induced, from a want of consideration, readily to promise to do and perform all needful and necessary repairs, or at least to leave the house in tenantable repair. It is not a little amusing to observe the tenant's surprise at the end of his tenancy on receiving a notice of dilapidations. What ! he exclaims, and leave the house 100 per cent. better than when I took it ? This and the various sums of money paid to jobbing tradesmen, all the accounts of whom he can enumerate by heart, constitute the anchor of hope to the poor tenant, when informed, in spite of all the benefits the house has derived from him during his tenancy, that still such and such are dilapidations, and as such he is answerable for their being reinstated. In the present age, remarkable for the number of scantily-constructed houses, with so nice and clean, yet deceitful, an exterior, invitingly waiting for tenants on lease or agreement, it cannot fail to be useful to consider the nature of the obligation that exists between landlord and tenant upon the hire of house property ; for as mistakes will happen in the best regulated families, so do the friendship and good understanding that may have existed between landlord and tenant suddenly cease with the termination of the lease. Covenants to repair, when once entered into,

are irrevocable ; it is, therefore, most important that each party should clearly understand what constitutes repairs or dilapidations; and as to all defects, whether they arise from accident, neglect, or decay, and by which party they are to be made good.

A landlord, on making a claim from his tenant for dilapidations, must shew that they are such as were stipulated for ; in the lease, as the obligation on the part of the tenant to make good varies, in nearly every case, according to the different covenants of the lease, by which the tenants are bound by more or less stringent clauses, involving greater or less responsibilities.

Mr. Gibbons, in an excellent treatise on this subject, defines dilapidations as the act or default of a person having to use a tenement, to the injury of another having a right to the same tenement, or a tenant's obligation may be considered as depending on the old maxim—"You must not injure another's property, but use it as your own."

It is an imperative act of justice to himself for the future tenant to make a stipulation that, previous to the commencement of his tenancy, the premises shall be surveyed ; so that, if then there can be considered any thing unsound or defective on the premises, it may be made good before the agreement is concluded, otherwise the tenant will find that he must make good all, whatever was the state of repair when he took possession of the premises.

Houses held on lease.—In the case of premises being let on lease, a tenant should not be compelled to supply and make good defects that may arise from time and use, because, as the tenant bargained for use, and gives to the owner an equivalent rent, the landlord has a claim only for a restoration of the tenement as injured by the tenant, but has no right to make a claim for the wear to be made good ; but then, as the tenant agrees to keep the house in tenantable repair, he is bound to supply all occasional and accidental defects which may expose the premises to premature decay. Accidents happening during his tenancy, if not inevitable, must be made good by the tenant, for it is fair to presume, that had he adopted proper precautions, the accident might have been prevented ; therefore, there exists an obligation not to suffer dilapidations, and it is evident that the tenant is equally bound not to do any act that will cause an injury to the tenement.

Voluntary waste means an alteration in the tenement, it being held in law that a lessee cannot change the nature of the thing demised : the act of alteration exceeds the right to use, and infringes on the condition that the landlord shall receive back the premises in the same state and condition as when the lease was granted. It is, therefore, essential that a tenant contemplating an alteration or improvement should receive proper permission and authority from the landlord.

Permissive waste consists of a neglect on the part of a tenant to supply the repairs required by time and use, and also a neglect to make good occasional and accidental dilapidations. Houses and outbuildings are the principal subject of dilapidations, but the law extends to trees, land, changing the course of industry, &c. ; but the chief subject is buildings. These, though subject to decay in the progress of time, are capable of having the defective or decayed parts made good, and are therefore subject to both permissive and voluntary waste.

A tenant hiring premises on lease is bound to perform tenantable repairs, which may be divided into three heads—the ornamental, which includes the trades of painter and paperhanger ; the substantial, which includes the trades of bricklayer and carpenter : the third includes all works which tend to preserve the fabric from decay—as stopping out wind and weather, which includes the trades of the joiner, plasterer, and glazier.

Dilapidations caused by accident are very serious upon a tenant, as not only is the accident considered as a dilapidation, but all injuries arising therefrom, of which the following is an illustration from Mr. Gibbons :—"If a building be covered with weather boarding, and such boarding decay from age, so long as it forms an entire and complete covering, it is no dilapidation, but if, owing to any neglect, any of the internal woodwork become injured, that is a dilapidation. If the main timbers decay, they are not chargeable as a dilapidation so long as they are an efficient support; but, if they give way, the tenant is bound not only to replace the timbers, but all damage done by their fall. Accident, shown to be inevitable, such as resulting from tempests, does not fall upon the tenant, as in the case of a house being prostrated, the tenant need not rebuild, but if the roof be blown off the tenant must replace it. A tenant generally speaking is *not* answerable for dilapidations resulting from natural decay, or the result of time, or fair ordinary wear and tear, but *is* answerable for all extraordinary decay. For instance, as to decay caused by the premises being exposed to the weather, as if the roof be suffered to go in bad repair, the tenant must make good the rafters and other timbers, if they are injured. Lord Chief Justice Tindal defined a tenant's obligation to repair thus:—"Where an old building is let, and the tenant enters into a covenant to repair, it is not meant that the old building is to be restored in a renewed form at the expiration of his tenancy, or that the premises shall be of greater value than it was at the commencement. What the natural operation of time flowing on effects, and all that the elements bring about in diminishing the value, which so for, as it results from time and nature, constitutes a loss, falls upon the landlord. But then the tenant must be careful that the tenement do not suffer more than time and nature would effect. He is bound to keep the premises in nearly the same state of repair as when demised."

An annual tenant's obligation has been thus laid down by Lord Kenyon. "A tenant from year to year, is bound to commit no waste, and to make from time to time fair and tenantable repairs, such as windows and doors that be injured during the tenancy." Lord Tenterden decided that an annual tenant was bound to keep the premises wind and water tight.

It seems but justice, that under any mode of letting or hiring of house property, a tenant should be bound to use all ordinary precautions to preserve the building from decay; therefore there exists an obligation to keep the outside and the roof sound, perfect, and water tight; and if the internal woodwork decay sooner than it otherwise would do for want of paint, &c., the tenant is bound to restore it. Glass, if cracked or broken, becomes dilapidation, it being an outside covering.

A tenant with no agreement as to duration of his tenancy, cannot be bound to perform any repairs, the nature of his tenancy being so weak that he cannot be expected to do any repairs, as his landlord might immediately determine his tenancy, and reap the advantage to be derived from the outlay: besides, if the house require any repairs being done, the landlord can enter and take any necessary steps for its preservation; but not so with premises let for a definite time,—then, the landlord having granted the use for a certain period, has not right to enter upon the premises until the expiration of the tenancy. A tenant under this mode of letting, is however bound neither to commit nor permit waste. This kind of tenancy may be considered rather as a "deposit than as a letting on hire," and the tenant's obligation may be defined as "to use the house with care."

FRANCIS CROSS.

HOUSE PROPERTY.—A friend informs us that the St. Paul's Head freehold public-house, in Crispin-street, Spitalfields, was sold by auction at the Mart, on Thursday, in last week, to Messrs. Taylor, the brewers, for 1,160 guineas. The rent receivable for the next thirteen years is only 42*l.* per annum. Property in Chippenham, Wilts, must be materially depreciated in value, for we learn from a local paper that property mortgaged some years since for 600*l.*, and yielding a rental of 40*l.* per annum, will not realize in the market 300*l.*; another property, let at 23*l.* per annum, and for which 400*l.* was refused eight years since, has been sold during the last week for 250*l.*

MR. BARRY AND THE METROPOLITAN SEWERS COMMISSIONERS.

DRAINAGE OF THE NEW PALACE AT WESTMINSTER.

SIR,—In the last number of THE BUILDER you have, as it seems to me, been betrayed into making unfavourable remarks upon the drainage of the New Palace at Westminster, from not being fully acquainted with all the circumstances relating to it. I think I cannot, therefore, do better, in order to disabuse your mind on the subject, than to send to you the enclosed copy of a letter which I have this day forwarded to the Metropolitan Commissioners of Sewers, relative to Mr. Austin's rejoinder to my remarks upon his report on the drainage of the New Palace, to which, as well as to the documents therein referred to, I have to request of you to bestow an attentive perusal.

I am, Sir, yours faithfully,

CHARLES BARRY.

Westminster, January 23, 1849.

This we have done, and we think we shall best discharge our duty to all parties by letting Mr. Barry speak for himself. We, therefore, give the principal part of his reply even where it refers to charges which we did not print. The letter is dated January 22nd. At the commencement Mr. Barry repeats his assertion that the only information which the commissioners' engineer ever received from him relative to the drainage of the New Palace "was, as he well knows, afforded to him for a far different purpose than that of enabling him to understand the system of it in detail, or to form any competent judgment upon its merits as a whole." He repeats, that the system adopted was carried out in accordance with the rules and regulations of the Westminster Commission and the data and assistance furnished by their officers.

"That with respect to the outfalls of the New Palace sewer, it was impossible, under the circumstances, that they could be placed otherwise than in connection with the public sewers.

That, agreeing with Mr. Austin, in thinking it immaterial whether the main sewer of the palace passes through 'vaults,' or 'arched spaces,' I have to observe that the term 'arched spaces' was made use of by me, to correct, in some degree, the false impression created by the exaggerated description and pictorial illustrations of those contained in his report; from which, it might be inferred, that the main sewer had been constructed in spacious vaults under the entire building, instead of passing, as it does, through comparatively small and insignificant spaces, at intervals, and under open gateways, intended to be filled up solid with concrete. It matters not, therefore, under such circumstances, whether the sewer passes, as he states, within 'about 12 yards from the basement of the grand saloon connecting the Houses of Lords and Commons, or immediately under it.'

The hole in the sewer alluded to, by which the engineer passed more than once into the vaults, was of course for temporary convenience. Mr. Barry understands one passage in the rejoinder as again referring to this hole, but this is not the case.

"That the whole of the statements in my remarks upon Mr. Austin's report, as to the levels of the main sewer, and the dimensions of the arched spaces through which it passes are correct, although attempted to be falsified by Mr. Austin, and that the inference which he deduces from one of them, as to the position of the summit level, is not warranted."

"That no part of the sewer was to my knowledge constructed at variance with the plans prepared for it, namely, with a current in the wrong direction; but that if this be the case, either from neglect or subsidence of the soil, the consequences are immaterial, and the remedy is simple and inexpensive.

"That the cause of a want of free drainage from the New Palace Sewer, has constantly been owing to the foul condition of the public sewers connected with it."

"That Mr. Phillips's offer of assistance in improving the drainage of the building was not solicited, and was not accepted, as I did not consider any re-arrangement of it to be necessary.

"That the 'safety flap,' which is sneeringly alluded to by Mr. Austin (but the omission of the mention of which in his report is not accounted for), is so named, for a very different reason than that which he supposes, or chooses to infer; but that it did really protect the New Palace from the stench of the public sewer, at the time of his examination, I have no doubt.

"That Mr. Austin has unfairly assumed what he is pleased to state I ought to have said as to the ventilation of the sewer, and has erroneously stated that I have acknowledged that foul air has escaped into the buildings and courts."

"That no inconvenience or nuisance *can by any possibility arise* from the main sewer of the palace being at times a reservoir for the retention and discharge of the drainage at every tide, such reservoir being perfectly ventilated by an up shaft, and every branch drain communicating with it being properly trapped, which Mr. Austin might have ascertained to be a part of the system, if he had thought proper to have duly examined or inquired into this matter.

"That the works recently executed in the sewer in furtherance of its completion, so far from reducing it to a dangerous condition, have, in fact, improved it.

"That it is not cut off, as stated, from all possibility of ventilation, being, as alleged, 'no better than a vast retort of 15,000 cubic feet, in which the foulest gases will be perpetually generating and escaping in a concentrated form into the buildings.' On the contrary, it is perfectly ventilated, and whatever gases may be generated cannot, in any form or degree, escape into the buildings,—a fact which I am prepared to prove to the commissioners, if they are disposed to accompany me in a personal inspection of the sewer, and of which fact Mr. Austin might have been convinced, if he had applied to me for explanation as to the completion of the system adopted."

This ventilation of the sewer by artificial means is an important feature, which did not appear in the report or reply.

"That the flaps to the branch drains are not fixed for the purpose of preventing the escape of foul air into the building, as Mr. Austin seems to suppose, although they may contribute to that object; but that other and perfectly effective means are provided for that purpose, of which he appears to be ignorant. All Mr. Austin's reasoning, therefore, upon these flaps, and the admission of foul air into the building, falls to the ground."

Mr. Barry denies the foul state of the sewer, and invites the commissioners to accompany him in a personal inspection.

He thinks it is utterly impossible that any serious effects can be apprehended from the foul matter that may collect in the main sewer, and that the inference of Mr. Austin to the contrary is altogether false, and calculated only to create unfounded alarms and unfavourable impressions.

That there are no defects of a serious nature, as stated, in the drainage of the New Palace, to justify the removal of the work connected with it, as recommended by Mr. Austin; and that, if the remedy the latter recommends were attempted, the consequence might be most serious, and the expense to be incurred, which he thinks must necessarily be very great, would be a most wanton waste of public money.

Mr. Barry considers that the provision of a reservoir for storage water and sullage is neither a great mistake, nor is it mischievous, and that the proposed 15-inch and 9-inch pipes would, under the circumstances, be insufficient and inefficient to meet the unusual and extraordinary contingencies of the site.

Mr. Barry, remarking that he is in a condition to prove the truth of any assertion which he has made, and is "ready to do so before any competent, impartial, and unprejudiced tribunal," thus concludes:—

"With respect to Mr. Austin's assertion, that I have myself admitted to a member of the Sewers Commission in his (Mr. Austin's) own hearing, since the issue of his report, that 'the drainage of the New Palace was as bad as it could be,' I have to state, that to my knowledge I have never seen Mr. Austin since he made his report, and that I could not have made such an admission to any member of the Sewers Commission, inasmuch as I firmly believe, and ever have believed, that the drainage of the building is as perfect as it can be, all local and other circumstances being duly considered. If there is an impression on the mind of any commissioner that I have delivered a contrary opinion, such an impression must have arisen from misapprehension."

"CEMENTED BRICKS."—We read in the *Oxford Chronicle* that the first annual ball of the "Oxford Cemented Bricks" was held on Friday, the 5th inst. Who these bricks are, or what is the purpose of their being cemented into a society, we are not informed. We sincerely hope it is for something better than "moistening their clay."

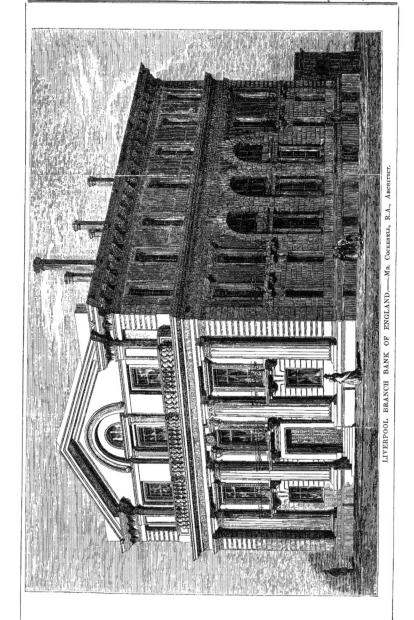

LIVERPOOL BRANCH BANK OF ENGLAND.——Mr. COCKERELL, R.A., ARCHITECT.

BRANCH BANK OF ENGLAND, LIVERPOOL.

CORNICE, &c., ENLARGED.

SCALE OF FEET

BRANCH BANK OF ENGLAND, LIVERPOOL.

WE have already alluded to the building erected in Liverpool for the Bank of England, as one of Mr. Cockerell's most successful works, and we now give a perspective view of it, and an enlarged outline of part of the front.

It stands in Castle-street, at the corner of Cork-street; the frontage next the former is 60 feet, and next the latter 117 feet. The height to the top of the blocking is about 62 feet, and to the apex of the pediment 72 feet. The columns in front are 4 feet 2 inches in diameter, and about 31 feet high. Both fronts are executed in Darley Dale stone: the plinth is granite. The entrance has a moulded red granite door-case, polished; each jamb is in one stone, 12 feet 3 inches high, 2 feet 3 inches deep, and 1 foot 3 inches face for architrave.

The central portion of the banking office (the whole area of which is 47 feet by 50 feet), is 31 feet high, and occupies two stories in height — namely, the ground and one-pair stories. The ground and basement stories are fire-proof.

Messrs. Holmes are the contractors for the bank, at the sum of 23,135l.

The flank elevation, although plain, is exceedingly effective in execution.

Mr. Cockerell has just commenced another building for the bank of nearly equal dimensions, but not so lofty, eastward of the new bank. This consists of fire-proof chambers for merchants, and has a stone exterior.

AWARDS OF OFFICIAL REFEREES.

DISTRICT SURVEYORS' FEES.

WITH regard to the premises No. 2 and 3, Cushion-court, Old Broad-street, in the district of the northern division of the City of London, the referees received a requisition from Messrs. Sabine, which recited "that the said premises, or house or houses, are united by means of openings in the third and fourth stories, being the two topmost stories; and that the said premises taken as two distinct buildings are each of the second rate of the first class, but, taken together, constitute one building of the extra first rate, and that the district surveyor claimed that in respect of any services performed by him as district surveyor in respect of any part of the said premises, such services are to be considered as services performed in respect of the whole, that is, in respect of one extra first-rate dwelling-house." Messrs. Sabine, however, contended that any service or work performed in respect of part of the said premises would be a service performed in respect of such part only, that is, in respect of, or to one second-rate dwelling-house; and they requested the referees, the district surveyor concurring in the application, to determine whether the said premises, by reason of their being united, were to be deemed for the purposes of the Act, one building only as claimed by the said district surveyor, or two distinct buildings, as claimed by the said William Sabine and Son.

The question had relation to the fee chargeable by the district surveyor for inspecting and reporting to the official referees upon party walls, and the district surveyor stated at the hearing that he grounded his claim upon the rule in Part 1 of schedule C. of the Metropolitan Buildings Act, headed "Rule for ascertaining area," and contended that the premises constitute one building of the extra first rate, the whole of the one pair or third story being united by openings in the party structure, and the whole of the said premises being in one occupation; to which Mr. Sabine replied that the premises had two separate entrances and staircases, and that the rates had been paid on the premises as for two houses.

The referees determined that the premises were to be deemed for the purposes of the Metropolitan Buildings Act, as to the matter in question, to be two distinct buildings, and that the fee payable to the surveyor was the fee for a building of the second rate. The costs to be paid jointly.

CONSTRUCTION OF EAVES AND CORNICES.

In the case of two third-rate dwelling-houses in Studley-road, Clapham-road, in the district of the southern division of Lambeth, the district surveyor lodged an information to the effect that Mr. Robert Cox had commenced the works requisite for the completion of the said two houses, without any notice of the same to the district surveyor, as directed in section 13 of the said Act, and had constructed overhanging eaves of timber, and covered the facia and soffit with galvanized iron or zinc, contrary to schedule E of the said Act.

At the hearing it appeared that the roofs of the houses are separated by a party wall, but that the eaves are not so separated, that the two houses stand at a distance of about 7 feet from the next adjoining buildings in other occupation, and of about 3 feet 6 inches from ground in other occupation, and that the houses stand on one side of a wide road, and are consequently far removed from the opposite houses.

The referees directed that such parts of the cornices as abut upon other buildings or ground not in the same occupation with the buildings, whereof the said cornices form a part, should be amended, by taking down the metal casings which have been fixed upon the ends of the rafters, and replacing the same with iron laths and lime-and-hair plastering, such laths being laid into the brickwork at the least 4 inches, and bent up to form a base for the plastering of the facia, and so as to cover the ends of the rafters and the edge of the eaves board; and, as respects the cornices on the fronts of the said houses, that the same should be amended, by separating them in the line of the party wall by a corbel of brick or stone of the full width of the party wall, and carried at the least 2½ inches above the roof, and 1 inch at the least below the soffit, and 1 inch at the least beyond the outside of every part of such cornices, such corbel being built or fixed, as the case may be, to the satisfaction of the surveyor of the district.

THE GAS MOVEMENT.

MISCELLANEOUS NOTES.

EVERY ward or other district within the city bounds has of late been rising, one after another, into an energetic resolve to have an abundant supply of cheap and good gas. At one of the most recent of these manifestations, in the ward of Farringdon Without, attention was drawn to another of those indirect means by which we have exposed some of the most cherished secrets of the gas-house,—the report of a public establishment as to the expense of providing its own gas. The report referred to was that of the Pentonville Prison, from which it appeared that, in the consumption of gas and the expense of manufacturing it for that establishment, a very considerable saving had been effected, as shown by the following statement :—

	£	s.	d.
Sum expended in coals	488	17	7
„ in wages, &c.	140	19	11
„ in retorts, &c.	122	2	10
Total	£752	0	4

The sum produced by the sale of coke was 398l. 6s. 3d., leaving the net cost of gas 353l. 14s. 1d. The quantity of gas consumed in the prison was 2,693,000 cubic feet, which was at the rate of 2s. 7½d. per thousand, but which previously they had paid the company 7s. 6d. for, and which would have cost 942l. instead of 353l. Deduct the cost of manufacturing, &c., and there was a net saving of 538*l.* 17s. by manufacturing their own gas. This report, therefore, fully justifies our exposal of "the average cost of gas" from the records of an extensive establishment at Leicester obtained for the purpose. The meeting passed resolutions expressive of their determination, and advised the appointment of gas inspectors by the City authorities, and the stamping and adjustment of meters, as of all other measures and weights. A continued 'pressure from without' upon the authorities was also resolved on.——A hybrid between a consumers' company and one of the old stock has been announced as "The Surrey Consumers' Gas-light and Coke Association," for the supply of gas at 5s. per 1,000 cubic feet, with a bonus to the consumer of one-fourth of the profits, the other three-fourths being reserved to the proprietors, who are also to sell superior screened coals at a reduced price, using the small for coke. The general want of faith in meters is proposed to be obviated by a return, where desired, to the contract system, at charges per burner ranging from 2*l.* to 4*l.* per annum—surely far too high, as the 5s. per 1,000 also is, in these economical and reforming times, and especially with profits on coal, &c.——In an unsuccessful attempt of the Bedford County magistrates lately to get the price of gas supplied to the prison reduced, the gas company confessed that "the practice of making a difference in the charges between public bodies and private individuals was unjust." The price charged is 7s. 6d.—not a fair price, as the county surveyor maintained. Six shillings were offered, but refused by the company, and the surveyor stated, when the subject of making their own gas was under consideration, that while 75*l.* per annum was payable to the company for lighting the prison, works would cost in all only 600*l.*, expense of making the gas nothing, and saving on whole at least 3s. per 1,000 feet. Parties had undertaken to supply both gaol and town at a moderate rate. The Bedford Company, we perceive, by the way, sell their coke at 25s. per ton—'*reduced* price'—a fact that may hereafter be of use.——At Lynn the price of gas has been reduced to the still rather too respectable price of 7s. per 1,000 feet. ——At Cambridge, lately, while the authorities had the subject of gas under discussion, and on a statement being made that the profits of the company did not amount to 10 per cent., an exposure was made by Mr. Foster of the but too general falsity of such statements. By this company's act a capital at least double what is called for or necessary, or in fact used, is authorised, and on the whole of this the goodly interest or profit of nearly 10 per cent. is thus being reaped. "After a careful examination," added Mr. Foster, "I am prepared to prove that the cost price of gas ranges below 2s. 6d. per 1,000 cubic feet, taking every thing into consideration. That would bear a profit of 1s. 6d. at a price of 4s. I trust the company will read, mark, learn, and inwardly digest these things. Taking the necessary capital at 15,000*l.*, the per centage is thus at once raised to 18 per cent."——A correspondent of the *Liverpool Albion* complains, that since the amalgamation of the companies there, he can scarcely distinguish the three FS,—fish, flesh, and fowl, at his dinner table, by the light they supply him with.—— While Liverpool is thus retrograding into the darkness, some of those few primitive localities, which have never till now come out of it, are at length rejoicing in the light. Such, with the new year's advent, is the new state of things at Soham.——An ingenious pitman at Garesfield colliery, near Gateshead, according to the local *Observer*, has of late been fitting up miniature gas works, for single establishments, at about 25*l.* each. A Mr. Thomas Waugh, of Berry Edge, Gateshead, a publican, is amongst those already supplied.

"THE INDEX."—Under this title the spirited manager of the Western Literary Institution has commenced "a weekly Repertory of the Results of Modern Progress." It was the first to give an abstract of Mr. Staite's patent, enrolled on the 12th. We do not find anything in this specification, by the way, which removes our fear as to the cost of producing the light.

A DEMONSTRATION ON KENNINGTON COMMON.

THE open spaces, known as squares, which peculiarly distinguished London from other metropolitan cities, have always been a theme of gratulation for healthful purpose, notwithstanding access to the enclosures is available only to a privileged few, and the external boundaries are not always kept in the neatest trim. The portion of the metropolis on the Surrey side, embracing so great an extent, is singularly deficient in this leading feature, with but one available exception. This is Kennington Common, an open area covering an exposure of seventeen acres. This ample space would make amends for the absence of lesser sanitary valves, if it were put into a condition for leisurable enjoyment and rational recreation. As this common and a great portion of the adjacent neighbourhood forming the manor of Kennington, an appendage of the Duchy of Cornwall, it exhibits a sad neglect of the administration of this property that such visible neglect should exist. The want of funds can never be pleaded for an excuse, as only within a short period the sum of 75,000*l.* has been paid as a fine on renewal of the lease of the manor. This sum was exacted on account of the improvement of the value of the property, and surely it would be augmented in a great proportion beyond the outlay, if a small part of the above fine were applied to rescuing this seventeen-acre common from its present degraded and dilapidated state.

In its present condition it is fenced with a low wooden rail, much of which disappeared at the Chartist meeting of April 10th last year, and a bar or a rail vanishes so frequently since that it may soon become an open waste, liable to all kinds of pollution. The ground is a flat, lying below the level of the surrounding roads, worked into numerous hollows, with some pathway tracks crossing it as innocent of a layer of fresh gravel, as the trails of wanderers over the endless prairies of the far west. The stunted herbage is trodden and soiled by a troop of cows belonging to a neighbouring milkman. A kind of pond near one corner, and a deep ditch opposite South-place, are the cemeteries of all the dead puppies and kittens of the vicinity. Their decaying carcases may be seen floating on the surface of their watery graves, in all the green and purple tints of putrefaction, and smelt too, if the nose is not too strongly tickled by the fumes of the adjacent vitriol works. A diagonal trackway from Newington-place to the Brixton and Camberwell roads, is a great saving of distance to the tired, but after nightfall the pedestrian is exposed to annoyance, and when the weather proves continuously wet, the transit resembles the intricate navigation of an archipelago.

In the day time the common is the resort of idle youths occupied in low gambling, and towards the afternoon of summer days, numerous parties playing at cricket obstruct the paths in all directions, and render any desire of tranquil respiration liable to the penalty of having an eye knocked out or a nose broken, which have happened on occasions. The respectable persons who sometimes use it as a cricket ground need not complain of any privation of their amusement, as not more than a hundred yards from the common, the enclosure of the Oval offers, at a very insignificant cost, ample accommodation, without causing annoyance or creating danger.

The extensive vitriol works on the eastern side emit a constant stream of sulphuric vapour exceedingly annoying to the nostrils. Whether the inhaling of it is beneficial or injurious to the lungs, is a question that ought to be answered by the sanitary oracles, but at any rate, they are so offensive to respiration that one is always glad to escape from their range. There can be no mistake though of the impurity of the ditches around and about the vitriol works: a very long one leading towards Camberwell, skirted by a foot-path, presents an accumulation of black offensive muddy liquid, receiving constant contributions from numerous unmentionable conveniences attached to a line of low cottage erections. The drainage of this locality being remarkably difficult, the foul matter of these ditches can only be absorbed by atmospheric action, instead of being conveyed to the "cloaca maxima," or universal cesspool, called the Thames.

Kennington Common, seventeen acres in extent, would at some outlay by able hands, become a great ornament to the southern half of the metropolis, if it were planted and laid out on a similar principle to the enclosure in St. James's-park. A broad walk should intersect it from Newington-place to the Brixton-road. Raised, gravelled, and lighted, it would become a public convenience, and it might be fenced off slightly, with occasional openings to be shut after dark. The entire circuit should be enclosed with a handsome railing, and gates at the required entrances. Opposite the Horns Tavern, a lodge, with a portico, might be introduced, in which some of the Quadrant cast-off columns would assist to construct an architectural ornament, in addition to an erection of utility.

About a mile beyond this, another smaller open space is in a worse condition of filth and neglect. Camberwell-green has been suffered to be converted into a vast deposit of slush and mud of all descriptions. Carts are constantly emptying their contents into it; and it is now so loaded with soft wet stuff, that any attempt to penetrate otherwise than by the narrow beaten track, would inevitably plunge the daring adventurer knee deep. A solitary ancient tree in the centre wears the weeds of witherhood, and a few dwarf lime trees on one of the sides seem ashamed to bear any leaves. Camberwell-green will soon be a misnomer.

IDLER IN LONDON.

VENTILATION: WARMING.

THE subject of ventilation is not confined to the dwelling-house alone, but extends to the air of cities and towns. It is scarcely necessary to allude to the innumerable sources of deleterious vapours, exhalations, odours, and gases that are constantly generated in cities where there is a deficiency in sewers, pavements, water, and general habits of order and cleanliness. This subject fortunately has attracted much attention, and is beginning to be pretty generally known.

History informs us that pestilence, the scourge of society, has prevailed frequently and virulently in ages, countries, and even special districts, in which cleanliness and the proper ventilation of houses have been little considered. Without entering on the various theories respecting the exciting causes of pestilential disease, a little research will afford sufficient proof that want of cleanliness has been a principal cause of their aggravation and rapid diffusion. If we read the account of our own metropolis during the last calamitous visitation of the plague in 1665, and compare it with its present state, we may convince ourselves, that our present exemption from the recurrence of such an evil is secured to us on better grounds than those of precautionary laws of quarantine. At that period, in the history of that vast city, the streets were narrow, the houses projected in the upper story, and the spaces between them crowded with large signs hung across, thus checking the free circulation of air, essentially necessary for the health of the inhabitants.

To the miasma constantly engendered and rising from open drains and neglected sewers, were added those caused by the fermentation of heaps of rubbish ejected from every house, and which the indolent inhabitants could scarcely be compelled to remove. Nature has provided means of carrying off impure air and replacing it with such as is suited to animal respiration; but here its intentions were defeated both by the construction of the buildings and the habits of the people. Drainage as well as ventilation of the buildings, was at one time totally disregarded, and the result was, a perpetual recurrence of fevers.

G. J. R.

Another correspondent, S. S. T., calls attention to the common practice of planning and running up buildings, without first arranging the mode of warming and ventilating them. He says,—It often happens that, from want of this previous arrangement, the kind of apparatus best adapted to the purpose cannot be used; or the walls have to be cut into, disturbing their solidity; or something unsightly or inconvenient has to be introduced into the apartments; to say nothing of the risk of fire, which is often incurred. Now, every one who understands warming buildings could arrange his plans, and give his estimate of them, quite as well from the architect's drawings as from the building itself. If architects would prepare for what was to be done beforehand, we might have better apparatus arranged, in a more convenient manner, at less expense.

Once a fortnight we are coolly asked to describe the various methods which might be used for warming this staircase or that house, and to point out the best. We have on various occasions treated the general question of heating and ventilating (may do so again), and never omit to mention fresh suggestions or inventions bearing upon it. The treatment of special cases we cannot enter upon: we recommend application to (ourselves professionally, if they please) properly qualified parties, who will advise with reference to the particular circumstances.

PORTER'S PATENT CORRUGATED IRON BEAMS.

Mr. Porter, of the Iron-roofing Works, Southwark, who has used *corrugated iron* largely in the construction of portable houses for exportation, has taken out a patent for the employment of it in the construction of beams, believing that the corrugations so far strengthen the iron as to obtain for beams so formed, great power of resistance with small weight of metal.

The following is an account of an experiment recently tried upon two beams made on this plan, of the extreme length of 22 ft. The span between supports was 20 ft. 6 in.; depth of beam, 18 in.; weight of beam, $8\frac{1}{2}$ cwts.; the top and bottom frames were of 4 in. × 4 in. T-iron, and the base $\frac{5}{8}$ in. thick; the plates of corrugated iron forming the beam being of No. 16 gauge, and the bands $1\frac{1}{2}$ in. × $\frac{1}{8}$ in. thick. The two beams were placed 9 ft. apart, and across these were laid two large oak blocks, weighing 1 ton 3 cwts., and supporting the further load. These blocks, or bearers (the one 19 in. and the other 24 in. wide), were 4 ft. 3 in. apart from centre to centre, and equidistant from their centres to the centre of the beam, $25\frac{1}{2}$ in.; upon these were laid cast-iron blocks, weighing 6 tons 17 cwts. This weight was put on on Saturday and remained till Tuesday, without causing any deflection. On Tuesday, in the course of an hour-and-a-half, an additional load was applied of 121 bundles plate-iron, weighing 7 tons 3 cwts. 0 qr. 16 lbs., producing a deflection of $\frac{9}{16}$ in. This load was allowed to remain from 1 p.m. on Tuesday until 10 a.m. on Wednesday, in course of which time the deflection had increased $\frac{1}{16}$ in. Fifty-one bundles of plate-iron, weighing 3 tons 9 cwts. 1 qr. 2 lbs., were now added, which caused a total deflection of 1 in. bare; rested a quarter of an hour, when 32 bundles of plate-iron, weighing 1 ton 18 cwts. 0 qr. 12 lbs. were added, which increased the deflection to $1\frac{3}{8}$ in. and $1\frac{5}{16}$ in. respectively; the difference being evidently occasioned by the settling down of the piers, giving a greater load to one beam. A further load, weighing 2 tons 8 cwts. 3 qrs., brought the deflections to $1\frac{5}{8}$ in. and $1\frac{3}{4}$ in. This loading was proceeded with gradually during three hours, when the load was left for an hour. In the meantime a slight noise called attention to a partial dividing of the bottom flange of T-iron, in the beam which hitherto appeared the least strained: upon examination, it was found to have originated in a flaw near a "shut" in the T-iron, distant 6 ft. 3 in. from the point of support,—this caused a further deflection of $\frac{1}{16}$ in., but the fracture did not appear to increase during half-an-hour. The deflection of the beams increased to 2 in. and $1\frac{5}{8}$ in., with an additional load of 2 tons 6 cwts. 2 qrs. 22 lbs. load applied gradually during three-quarters of an hour. After a further lapse of 10 minutes, a further load of 7 cwts. caused a rapid deflection in the already-weakened beam, the corrugated iron giving way at the same time to the strain of the rivets longitudinally. The beams were now blocked up to prevent any accident from the sudden falling of the load. The corrugated iron of the other beam was also found to have yielded in several places to the longitudinal strain of the rivets, principally in the lower part of the beam.

The breaking weight is, therefore, considered to be about 25 tons, exclusive of the weight of the beams.

The inventor considers that his beams will not weigh more than one half, or 5-8ths, of the weight of cast-iron beams to carry the same load, and that they may be made for 21*l.* per ton.

A SCHOOL OF DESIGN FOR LEICESTER.

An influential and respectable meeting lately took place at Leicester, to memorialise Government for aid in their endeavours to establish a School of Design there. The mayor presided, and a series of addresses followed. Mr. Alfred Burgess impressed on the attention of the assembly the importance of an idea of our own, that the young should be taught to express or describe their ideas by drawing, or in forms, just as they are taught to express them by writing, or in words; and the allusions of others to the same idea, as well as the responses of the meeting itself, were evidence that it was appreciated. Mr. Hollings remarked that the pursuit of the fine arts might be shewn to be necessary to society at large, as materially involving the diversion of labour into various channels. Want of a greater variety of employment was one of the great causes of existing distress. Let it not be said, either, that the advantages of the fine arts were to be seen merely in the production of luxuries. What was the luxury of one age, became a necessary in the next. How much occupation was now afforded even there by the employments of carving, gilding, painting, inlaying, designing of furniture, marbling, engraving on copper and wood, &c. Yet how serious would be the effect, if those engaged in their production were suddenly withdrawn from this field of labour, and thrown into that of the staple manufacture of the town! Moreover, the fine arts were so essentially connected, that the study and practice of one almost invariably called forth or involved that of others; and then, too, how much indirect advantage they further afforded, as involving numerous other occupations in themselves not purely artistic. Take, for instance, the manufacture of an ordinary porcelain vase—to be found on the mantelpiece of most of the middle classes in the town. How many branches of industry were connected with it, with which the genius of the designer had nothing to do. There was the collection and preparation of the crude material by the various processes of breaking, sifting, and working—the manufacture of the metallic oxydes to be used by the artist—the subsequent processes of glazing and firing; all distinct branches these, to be carried on both before and after the impression of the design upon the ornament—the only process upon which art was directly though essentially concerned. In short, the more we multiplied the influence and operations of art in connection with the production of luxuries, the more we should multiply profitable occupation and employment for the people. For, in this case, the usual maxim of political economy was reversed; instead of the demand creating the supply, the supply created the demand. As an illustration, just let them look at the improvement in the form and material of common earthenware within the last hundred years,—a change entirely owing to the residence of a few cheap Italian modellers in England. It was for the above and similar reasons that he should like to see a School of Design established in Leicester. The importance of design and variety of pattern and style, even in the staple manufacture of embroidered gloves, fancy hosiery, &c., themselves, was afterwards also pointed out by others ere the meeting closed.

COMBINATIONS AND STRIKES.

We have received several letters on the subject of recent differences between operatives and their employers, but do not think it desirable to prolong the agitation by publishing them. The majority of them are from working men, deprecating, to the credit of the writers be it said, any thing like intimidation. Some of them display much good sense. The following is part of one from "An Old Mason."

"Combinations and strikes are decidedly injurious, diminishing trade on the one hand, increasing immorality on the other; and are one of the great causes of our present distress, for an increase of crime will cause an increase of poverty. Crime, and that which leads to it, are the most expensive of all evils; witness, for instance, our prisons, hospitals, poor-houses, police force, and a multiplicity of other officers to put in force the laws of the country. These are some of the natural consequences and expenses attendant on crime; and unless there be a decrease of crime, we may look in vain for better times.

We are as a nation conscious of labouring under great difficulties, and many and loud are the complaints against those who sit at the helm of affairs. But one truth is evident, that while such large sums of money are necessary for the punishment of crime, the expenditure must greatly diminish the means for promoting the moral welfare of the people. It is also obvious to any strict observer, that many of those who are loudest with their complaints, and are crying out for reform, are most effectually impoverishing their country. Even under present circumstances, the industrious and frugal mechanic can usually maintain himself respectably; and if we make a fair calculation, two-thirds of the poverty and distress experienced among the working classes are brought on themselves by bad habits. There is too much ocular demonstration in this city for the fact to be denied. We want better times, is the common cry; we want wages raised and taxes diminished. Let us suppose we could obtain them both. A few that are economical would make more rapid progress to independence; the many who are careless and prodigal would descend in the scale. But still the desired object may be obtained, and obtained fairly. A decrease of crime will naturally cause a decrease in the taxes. Peace between employers and employed, the government and the people, will promote the prosperity of trade. Plenty of labour will of itself ensure a fair remuneration. A proper improvement of wages will keep poverty at a distance, and secure to us peace and plenty. It is evident, therefore, that crime, poverty, disease, and distress go hand in hand, whilst peace, industry, and frugality lead to happiness and independence. Reader, choose for yourself, but remember, the man who is punished for his crimes at his country's expense is increasing the burthen of the honest and industrious."

THE ANCIENT CHURCH AT GREENSTEAD.

Sir,—I infer, from a paragraph in The Builder, that a wrong impression has gone forth as regards the wooden church at Greenstead, namely, that it has been destroyed, or at least partially so. Now, Sir, that is not the fact, and if any person, having seen the outside of the timbers six months ago, could see them at the present time, they would scarcely be able to say, from their appearance, whether they had been removed or not. It was also stated that it was owing to the ravages of insects that it had become necessary to take it down. This in some measure is correct, as the lower ends of the timbers were in many instances perforated, but not to any great extent. The principal cause of its being taken down was this: the oak cills having been laid on the earth, with merely some rough flint put under them at intervals, had become so rotten as to let the upright timbers drop through, and had not the ends of the wall plates rested on the brickwork of the chancel, a great part of the nave must have fallen. It has been the particular wish of the rector, the Rev. Philip Ray, by whom the expense of the rebuilding the church is principally defrayed, and also of Mr. Wyatt, the architect, that every part of the old timbers should be preserved, and I have been careful to carry out those wishes: the only parts lost are about 6 inches cut from the lower ends; the timbers have been fresh tenoned and inserted in oak cills laid on brickwork, 12 inches from the ground, so that there is every reason to presume they will last as long as they have already stood, for the planks, when cut, were so hard as almost to defy the saw. A new roof, open, and stained oak has been put on, having dormer windows, with stained glass, inserted. The whole of the plastering having been taken off, the planks are now seen inside. The pews are taken away and new seating fixed. The church will be open for divine service about the middle of February next, when any who feel a veneration for the relics of bygone days, will be able to see that this ancient structure has been preserved to the fullest extent possible. James Barlow, Builder.

Chipping Ongar, Essex.

FLUSHING AND FLASHING.

SIR,—I see that you have used the word "dashing" (BUILDER, vol. 7, p. 32, col. 2) with reference to the cleansing of sewers by water. Will you permit me to make a friendly protest against the substitution of "flashing" for "flushing?" "Flush" appears to be derived from the German FLUSS, a flood,—and to be generally used with reference to fulness or bulk, as well as rapidity or violence. The idea involved appears to be that of a flood, or rushing body of water. "Flash" appears to be derived from φλοξ, or the Anglo-Saxon *Fliccerian*, and to be generally used with reference to brilliancy and extension. The idea involved appears to be that of a flame or sparkling appearance. I would submit that the rush of a bulk of water through a sewer may properly be termed a "flush," and the splashing of a sheet of water over a street might as properly be termed a "flash." If this distinction should be adopted, the advocates for each of the words would have, it may be hoped, plenty of opportunities for using both without confusion; for if it be good that our sewers should be cleansed, it will not be denied that it would certainly be beneficial to the public, to have a little better scavengering above them than prevails at present; and the water which had "flashed" the streets from hose or water-cart, might be dammed up, under ground, until it had head enough to "flush" the sewers. N. R.

Miscellanea.

ST. PATRICK'S CATHEDRAL.—The 4,000*l.* some time since subscribed for the restoration of much that was dilapidated and out of order, have not only been exhausted, but the Dean, the Hon. H. Pakenham, who began the work at his own expense, has become responsible himself for one-half of an equal sum, namely, 2,000*l.*, and has paid the interest on it till now that he has subscribed a second time 1,000*l.* to aid in making up the deficiency and further advancing the good work, which is by no means complete, though twelve arches which had been blocked up have been disencumbered, and other works accomplished. The lady chapel still lies uncovered, and the choir itself is in a most unfinished state. Subscriptions, therefore, are again solicited.

BIRMINGHAM WORKHOUSE COMPETITION.—Fifty-three sets of plans have been sent in. One would suppose, says the *Birmingham Journal*, that architects had been doing nothing else for the last month or two but making workhouses on paper, and erecting little models for the accommodation of the midland counties. The same paper doubts, with great reason, that the best design will be chosen, and thinks a proposition which was made, to "toss up for it," not so absurd as it seems.

ST. MARGARET'S CHURCHYARD AGAIN.—Sir: Perhaps there is greater danger in opening the ground here for interment than in any other churchyard in or near the metropolis. The soil is a loose sand, like the sand of an hour glass, and such is its tendency to run back that when opening a grave it is necessary to support the sides from top to bottom: it does not absorb the defunct remains, but they lie a dreadful compound, engendering malaria of direful effect. After rains, in hot weather, the evaporation is charged with effluvia as unbearable as a death chamber; add to which, the church is entirely lined with woollen cloth, and when the doors and windows are open, of necessity gets charged with this deleterious vapour. Although there may be some doubt of its affecting the stones of the abbey, there can be none that the numerous inhabitants of the abbey precincts must suffer incessantly from the bad atmosphere it creates. I know a lady injured in her health, which her physician attributed to her passing through the place, and gentlemen, whose avocations call them that way, avoid passing through. No time should be lost in covering over this pestiferous ground. It is a plague spot, that the most valuable lives in the empire, during the sitting of Parliament, are exposed to: besides, it is surrounded by a large population and overlooked by an hospital for the sick and maimed. —NO IDLER IN LONDON.

GOVERNMENT INQUIRY AT CHELMSFORD.—On Tuesday week Mr. Cresy's inquiry was opened. Mr. Fenton presented a laborious map, said to show the exact state of the drainage in every house, and which is to be published (for behoof of sensible tenants, we presume, and as a hint to landlords, and an example to other towns). The drainage is exceedingly defective. Nuisances of a foul character were discovered lurking in back drains and ditches, and the sewerage also was found to be generally imperfect. In one spot 100 recently built houses are drained into one totally inadequate cesspool. Mr. Gresy suggested the formation of a system of sewerage into tanks for agricultural purposes (the sewage in which, Mr. Baker observed, could be precipitated by mere ordinary whitewash and the inodorous water drained off). The inspector also pointed out that housedrains, in place of passing below the apartments to a front or street sewer, might be centered in a sewer along the backs of the houses, and much more out of the way of pollution to the inhabitants. The supply of water from the Burgess well, ten or twelve Artesian wells, and otherwise, was examined, and the means of increasing and raising the supply to the second floors of houses considered. A diminution of late years was attributed to leakage and artesian wells. The crowded state of the principal church-yard was complained of, and four others considered, and it appeared but too probable that even the water was contaminated. The inclusion of Springfield with Chelmsford, and the universal dissatisfaction with the operation of the present Act, were the other chief subjects brought under the inspector's notice.

EVILS OF SHORT LEASES.—Sir: I am delighted to find you holding up to light the evils of short leases. I have lived in France, America, Canada, and all the Channel Islands: in all these countries leases, if leases they can be called, are without limit; and in all these places the leaseholder has the right to buy off the charge or give some other property for rent, and make his own free for ever. I went once with a friend in Paris to buy a large piece of land, near the Triumphal Arch. The owner told my friend that the purchase-money was 57 francs per toise, but he only required one house to be built, that all the purchase-money should lie at 5 per cent. until the purchaser pleased to pay it off. My friend agreed, built one house, and then sold the residue at a good profit. In consequence of the good title of all building land in France, and every other country I know but England, house property, being freehold, *ranks first in the list of securities for capital.* It is quite the reverse in London: *too* true is this baneful story told. Look at the many mouldering carcases, fit for nothing but to pull down, standing on the Crown and City lands, New Oxford-street, Holborn, &c. &c., taxed with a ground-rent of ruinous extent, and a lease so short that no honest or calculating man would have anything to do with them.—J. C.

USE OF BATH STONE.—We have received several letters in favour of Bath stone, but no end would be answered by inserting them. The mere assertions of parties (however respectable), unknown beyond their own circle, will not weigh against recorded facts, and the published opinions of impartial men known to have studied the matter. Fresh facts and experiments establishing facts we will gladly insert and give attention to. One correspondent from Bradford, Wilts, who says he has used many thousand feet of it, writes thus:—The principal failure in Bath stone is attributed to inappropriation, and the remedy for this as advised, is to lay the stone as in its native bed. This system holds good in plain faces, but in cornices or other projecting parts which are more exposed, it does not: the stone should be used *joint headed*, and so of copings. There are many difficulties in the selection of stone, from whatever quarries it may be brought, particularly in Bath stone, which is dug in a range of hills extending many miles, each hill producing stone of a different relative value; and these are not to be selected by any inexperienced person, as it often happens that the best in appearance is the worst for use and durability, and it is even so that in the same block we may find one portion more durable than the other.

PROJECTED WORKS.—Advertisements have been issued for tenders, by 10th February, for erecting prisoners' cells, kitchen offices, infirmary, boundary wall, &c., at the county jail, Huntingdon; by 26th February, for the masons' and paviors' works, supply of Guernsey granite chippings and Yorkshire paving for one year, for the parish of St. George's, Hanover-square; and by same date for the supply for one year of workmen's tools and hammers for stone breaking and repairs of same, as also for iron lamp posts and gas fittings.

NOT BORN TO BE DROWNED.—A lad named Gilder, an embryo mason, was descending a ladder near Liverpool, when a round broke, and he fell to the ground upon his feet. Rebounding, he next came down into a deep well, whence he was drawn unhurt. Such escapes should be no encouragement to carelessness. A fall of as many inches another time may be his death. We remember seeing a carpenter some years ago fall from the top of a high building to the bottom, passing two floors of naked joists in his way (going through his work neatly, if we may so speak) and getting up unhurt; while on the same day an acquaintance coming down stairs, and fancying he was at the bottom of the flight when there was in reality yet one step to descend, broke his leg in the fall that ensued.

HYDROSTATIC PRESSURE REGULATOR.—A simple apparatus has lately been invented and registered by Mr. Bryce, plumber, Glasgow, for the reduction and regulation of the hydrostatic pressure in supply-pipes connected with street water-mains. It is said, by its means, whatever the initial head pressure may be, the supply may be taken off for domestic purposes at any desired pressure less than such head pressure, with the view of avoiding the inconveniences resulting from an inordinate height of column, extreme rush of the water, the wear and leakage of cocks, &c.

CHURCHWARDENISMS.—A correspondent says,—"About six or seven weeks ago, I was surprised at finding that the pinnacles which crowned the buttresses of St. Peter's Church, Dorchester (the oldest one in this borough), were removed, for what purpose I could not then discover. However, I have since found out that it was in consequence of the churchwardens imagining that they *might* fall on some unlucky passer-by! although they had remained so many years immovable, and were at a distance of at least ten feet from the pavement, which was separated from the church by an iron railing. I hear, also, that there is no intention of their ever being replaced." Not knowing their condition, it is impossible for us to say whether or not the act is blameable. We trust, however, that the removal will lead to restoration.—"The churchwardens of Moulton" ("THE BUILDER should be upon their bones," remarks the *Gateshead Observer*), are said to have "removed the mullions and stone tracery from almost all the windows" of the beautiful parish church "to allow the passage of more light into the interior." It is comparatively seldom, we are happy to say, that we have to record such acts now. Surely there are some persons in Moulton who will vindicate architectural propriety. Had it been in Moultan instead of Moulton they could not have done any thing more barbarous.

PRESERVATION OF BOOKS.—A correspondent wishes to be informed the most desirable way of preserving books from the effects of mildew and damp, whether cases with glass doors, or frames without, and which is the most desirable wood for their construction.

SALE OF CAST-IRON.—Messrs. Hutchison and Dixon, auctioneers, Glasgow, sold at Troon, by auction, about 1,203 tons cast-iron. Mr. Dixon explained that the metal consisted of tram rails, and chairs, which had been used on the Kilmarnock and Troon Railway. The whole was divided into eight parcels, and sold at from 38s. to 41s. per ton. The malleable iron scraps brought 63s. 6d. The attendance of founders and dealers (the former of whom were the buyers) from all parts of the country was numerous. The sale was a quick and most spirited affair,—the biddings at the outset being near the prices realised. In addition to the price, there falls to be paid 3s. 9d. per ton of carriage to Glasgow, which brings the old iron nearly to the figure at which certain brands of pig are selling here.—*North British Daily Mail.*

TENDERS

For erecting infirmary wards at Poplar Union:—

King	£680
Brigg	661
Jeffery	606
Mitchael	600
Slade	597
Church	596
Hedges	595
Taylor	589
Wood	589
Heath	587
Walker and Soper	585
Bilson	578
Curtis	574
Howlett	568
Lister	558
Pilbeam	556
Catlin	553
Reader	553
Masted and Harris	548
Blackburn	546
Tomlis	538
Wicks	531
Carder and Hack	499

For a house at Streatham, for Mr. W. N. Coupland. Mr. J. Cole, architect:—

Ward	£2,580
Germen	2,325
Lawrence and Son	2,290
Plumber	2,252
Dean	2,253
Hicks	2,120
Higgs and Son	2,045
Taylor	1,980

MEETINGS OF SCIENTIFIC BODIES

Held *during the ensuing week*.

WEDNESDAY, JAN. 31.—Society of Arts, 8 P.M.

THURSDAY, FEB. 1.—Royal Society, 8½ P.M.; Society of Antiquaries, 8 P.M.

FRIDAY, 2.—Archæological Institute, 4 P.M.

TO CORRESPONDENTS.

"*Purification of Rain Water*."—Some correspondents ask further particulars concerning the filtering tanks proposed for Norwich.

Received.—"T. H. H." ("Flues" shall appear), "J. and T. S.," "E. W." (Manchester), "A Friend" (at least he says so), "J. R." "T. H.,", "J. E.," "Y.Z." (next week), "O. H." (Hyde-park), "E. S." (has been anticipated), "Young Builder," "J. W." (Glasgow), "R. S. F." (glue was advertised January 13th), "J. H. M. (the lead must surely be defective. Such dripping can scarcely be caused by condensation. Consult the architect), "S. J. C. (declined, with thanks), "F. P." (we shall be glad to see tracing), "A. W. R." (we believe no recommendation is necessary), "T. J. P.," "J. A. (write to 9, St. James's-square, Bristol), "J. G. G.," "J. M. L." (if the inquiry relates to a proposed architects' club, nothing is yet determined on), "Constant subscriber," (if within the operation of the Buildings Act, and the due notice be given of intention to raise wall, A. may, on expiration of the notice, go on to B.'s premises for the purpose. Otherwise it would be a trespass).

Several articles are unavoidably postponed.

"*Books, Prices, and Addresses*."—We have not time to point out books or find addresses.

ADVERTISEMENTS.

CAST-IRON PIPES, IRON WORK FOR OVENS, &c.

RAIN PIPES, &c.—F. A. TIDDEMAN, Purfleet Wharf, Earl-street, City, near Blackfriars-bridge, keeps a large stock of Rain Pipes, Heads, Shoes, Elbows, &c., half round and O. G. Gutters, Socket Pipes for Water or Gas, Flanch Pipes, Sash Weights, and other Castings; Iron Work for Baker's Ovens of every description, fitted complete, to be had in sets or in parts.—Prices equal to all competition. Contracts taken to any extent.

LIGHTERAGE.—To Contractors, Builders, Stone, Timber, and Slate Merchants, or others requiring Lighterage.—CHARLES STRUTTON, Lighterman and Timber Rafter, having a large number of craft of all sizes, is ready to undertake large or small CONTRACTS at prices particularly advantageous to his employers.—31, Commercial-road, Lambeth (near Waterloo bridge), and Trinity-street, Rotherhithe (near the Commercial Docks).—BARGES LET on HIRE.

J. and J. WRIGHT, VARNISH, JAPAN, and FRENCH POLISH MANUFACTURERS, respectfully inform their friends and the public that they have REMOVED their business from Hammersmith to more central and convenient premises, No. 134, HIGH HOLBORN (nine doors east of New Oxford-street), from whence all orders in future will be executed. Varnishes adapted to every description of decorative art of first-rate quality and durability at very reasonable prices. To those who pay cash is given the full advantage of so purchasing.

TO ARCHITECTS, ENGINEERS, BUILDERS, &c.

GEORGE JENNINGS, Patentee of the SHOP SHUTTER SHOE and FASTENER.
INDIA-RUBBER TUBE COCK.
IMPROVED WATER-CLOSET, without PAN or VALVE.
JOINTS for CONNECTING LEAD or other PIPES without SOLDER.
IMPROVED CLOSET VALVES.

29, Great Charlotte-street, Blackfriars-road.
For drawings and testimonials see "The Builder," January 6.

PAINTING WITHOUT SMELL; a fact accomplished by the use of the newly discovered SWEET OIL of TURPENTINE, instead of the deadly abomination called oil or spirits of turpentine. Paint mixed with it is free from smell, is improved in brilliancy of colour, and the baneful properties of the lead being neutralized, does not emit those noxious exhalations which have hitherto been so universally associated with painting. By this really valuable discovery house painting is now converted into a sanitary operation, that may be effected at any season of the year, being productive of health and comfort, without causing the slightest derangement to the domestic economy. Sold by the gallon, cwt., or ton, by every respectable oilman in the kingdom, and at the depot, 1, Bream's-buildings, Chancery-lane, where may be seen, and copies had of, the original certificate of Dr. Serny, a senior member of the College of Chemistry. Sold also in sample bottles, 2s. each, bottles included.

TERRA-COTTA, or VITRIFIED STONE WORKS, King Edward-street, Westminster-road, London.—M. H. BLANCHARD, from late Coade's Original Works, Belvedere-road, Lambeth, begs to inform the Nobility, Gentry, Architects, and Builders, that he has re-established the manufacture of that invaluable material, which has been successfully adopted by our eminent Architects and others, in the adornment of our noblest buildings, nearly 100 years has proved the imperishable nature of the material, the specimens of those times now exhibiting all their primitive sharpness.

Groups, statues, friezes, capitals, pannelling, pinnacles, finials, terminals, Tudor, and other chimney shafts, balustrading, fountains, fonts, tazzas, vases, coats of arms, devices, and every description of architectural ornament, at prices in many instances nearly half the cost of stone.

Specimens of the material to be seen at the Office of "The Builder," 2, York-street, Covent Garden, and at the Works.

TO STONE MERCHANTS AND PAVIORS.

A CARGO of CORNISH GRANITE KERB, just arrived in the River, 12 by 8 and 12 by 6, with some Circular ditto; also some Foot Paving.—Apply to R. WARNER, Scovell's Wharf, Tooley-street.

YORK STONE.—Buy your York Paving Slabs and Landings, your Bramley Fall, Portland, Park Spring, and Harehill Block Stones, at the VICTORIA STONE WHARF, ISLE OF DOGS, opposite the Greenwich Hospital.

THE CHEAPEST WHARF IN LONDON FOR CASH.

Stone delivered to any wharf in the river in large or small quantities.

PAVING, 2s. 9d. PER SQUARE YARD, Basements, Foot-walks, Malt-houses, Corn Stores, Floors of Warehouses, and every description of Pavement laid down at the above low price, and the work guaranteed.—Apply to JOHN PILKINGTON, POLONCEAU'S BITUMEN PAVEMENT OFFICE, 18, WHARF-ROAD, CITY-ROAD.—N.B. Country Agents and Railway Engineers and Contractors supplied with the best bitumen for covering bridges and arches.

ANSTONE STONE WHARF, STANGATE.—Mr. GRISSELL has the honour to inform Architects and Builders that he has made arrangements for the SUPPLY of the ANSTONE STONE for all building purposes, and which can now be seen at the above wharf by application to Mr. W. G. WARDLE, of whom every necessary information can be obtained.

N.B. The stone used in the erection of the New Houses of Parliament was supplied *exclusively* from these quarries.

August 30, 1848.

ANSTON STONE, used for Building the New Houses of Parliament.—W. WRIGHT and Co. beg to inform Architects, Engineers, Builders, and others, the Anston Stone can be supplied in any quantity on the shortest notice. This valuable stone, so celebrated for its durability, colour, and texture, is well known, having been selected in preference to all others, by the Commissioners of Woods and Forests, for building the New Houses of Parliament. It is very superior for Monuments, Tombs, &c. &c.

W. Wright and Co. have made arrangements to have a stock always on hand at Brine's Marble and Stone Wharf, Horsfall-basin, Maidenlane, King's-cross.—Any further information can be obtained on application to W. WRIGHT and Co., Anston, near Sheffield; or to T. SHARP, their Sole Agent in London, 27 Burton-crescent.

LUARD, BEEDHAM, and CO., extensive Proprietors of CAEN STONE QUARRIES, Allemagne, Calvados Department, beg to solicit inspection of their Caen Stone for external and internal works. They continue their importations of the first quality, carefully selected at the quarries.

L., B. and Co. have on hand a large stock of the best-quarried stone, at their Depôt, Caen Sufferance Wharf, Rotherhithe, where samples and information may be obtained.—Shipments made direct from Caen to any part of the United Kingdom.

AUBIGNY STONE QUARRIES.—LUARD, BEEDHAM, and Co., beg to inform the Architectural and Building Profession generally, they are importing the above stone from Aubigny, near Falaise, Normandy; and from its general adoption (where known), are assured of its great utility.

Aubigny resembles Portland in colour and texture, but free from shell, flint, and other obstructions in working. Its durability may be known from its appropriation to lighthouses, dock and quay walling, and the Royal Chateau, Normandy.

L. B. and Co., have a large and seasoned stock at their Depot, Caen Sufferance Wharf, Rotherhithe, near the Lavender Dock Pier.—Orders executed with dispatch to any part of the United Kingdom.

CAEN STONE.—Original Sufferance Depôt, Norway Wharf, Greenwich.—W TUCKWELL, Caen Stone Quarry Proprietor and Importer, begs to invite the attention of Architects, Surveyors, Builders, and others to the Stock of DRY SEASONED CAEN STONE on his Wharf, comprising 90,000 feet cube, which has been selected with judicious care, and is fit for immediate use. Shipments made to any port direct from his quarries at Caen.

N.B. Orders received at the wharf as above; also at the offices of Mr. R. A. WITHALL, Surveyor, 80, Cheapside, where further information and samples may be obtained.

STIRLING'S BELVEDERE SLATE WORKS, Belvedere-road, Lambeth.—A reduced list of prices of the best WELCH SLATE SLABS, planed both faces, will be sent on application (post paid) being made, and inclosing a postage stamp. The prices are under those advertised for inferior slates.

SAMUEL CUNDY, Mason and Builder, PIMLICO MARBLE and STONE WORKS, Belgrave Wharf, Pimlico, begs to inform ARCHITECTS and the PUBLIC that he has availed himself of improvements in his MACHINERY, by means of which he is enabled to produce GOTHIC WINDOWS, MOULDINGS, PANNELS, &c. &c., at a very cheap rate, out of a superior stone from the west of England, as durable as any soft stone, and particularly sound.

S. C. has an economical method of dressing the above stone over, which produces, by the action of the atmosphere, a surface of crystalline hardness, and improves the colour.

FONTS from 5l. upwards. Specimens on view of the various styles.

First-rate ARTISTS retained for SCULPTURED and CARVED Works.

Vein Marble Chimney-pieces, of the best quality of material and workmanship, by improved machinery	40s.
Stone ditto, from	8s.

A variety on view in stock.

MEMORIAL CROSSES, MONUMENTS, TOMBS, HEADSTONES, &c., in great variety of design.

RESTORATION of CHURCHES. SAMUEL CUNDY having had much practice in this branch, is desirous of Estimating for Restorations.

CLERKS of WORKS have their particular attention called to the above establishment. Coats of Arms, Decorated Pannels, and other enriched works, promptly executed.

Every description of Stone or Granite work prepared, ready for fixing.—Delivered at the various Railways, and carefully packed in trucks.—Pimlico Marble and Stone Works, Belgrave Wharf, Pimlico.

ENAMELLED SLATE.—CAUTION!—Some discarded workmen of Mr. Magnus's, having pirated his invention of marbling slate, and palmed upon the public trashy imitations, which unfortunately are frequently confounded with MAGNUS'S ENAMELLED SLATE, until a few months' wear has shown them in their true light, Mr. MAGNUS, who has expended a fortune in perfecting and introducing his enamelled slate articles (which articles have won for him the patronage of the highest personages in the realm, the approbation and support of the first architects, and the medal of the Royal Society of Arts), deems it incumbent upon him for his own protection, and that of the public, and for the just fame of his invention, to caution the inexperienced against these imitations. The public are, therefore, requested to observe that the address is MAGNUS, PIMLICO SLATE WORKS, and in future all articles of his manufacture will be so marked.

Patronised by her Majesty, Prince Albert, the Duke of Wellington, the Duchess of Sutherland, the Duchess of Grafton, the Marquis of Westminster, the Marquis of Londonderry, the Earl of Denbigh, the Earl of Dartmouth, the Earl of Bandon, the Earl of Waldegrave, the Countess Wilton, Viscount Combermere, Lord Robert Grosvenor, the Bishop of London, the Bishop of Bath and Wells, the Hon. Col. Douglas Pennant, Mr. Assheton Smith, Col. Challoner, Sir J. Easthope, Sir Francis Lawley, Sir Ralph Howard, the Hon. Capt. Duncombe, Sir W. Gordon, the Hon. C. Shaw Lefevre, and numerous others of the nobility and gentry of this and other countries; by the most eminent architects and surveyors, the engineers and directors of the principal lines of railway, the Board of Public Works, and by the public generally.

SLATE SLABS.—Mr. MAGNUS having machinery in Wales capable of sawing and planing some thousands of tons annually, is enabled to supply the public at a much lower rate than any other house not possessing the same facilities. Parties ordering large quantities will be allowed a considerable discount off the recently reduced price list.—Address, MAGNUS, Pimlico Slate Works.

CHAS. WM. WATERLOW,

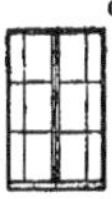

MANUFACTURER of Sashes and Frames, and Joiner to the Trade, 121, Bunhill-row, Finsbury-square.—Well-seasoned materials, superior workmanship, lowest prices.—Upwards of 400 DOORS, and a large variety of Sashes and Frames, always on sale. Glazed goods securely packed for the country. Steam-struck Mouldings in any quantity.—N.B. This Establishment is worth the notice of all engaged in building.

CHEAP ORNAMENTAL GLASS.—I beg to inform my friends and the public, that I have now completed a new ENGINE, and, owing to the facility with which I can execute orders, I am enabled to reduce my former prices considerably. The prices are now from ONE SHILLING PER FOOT SUP., and borders from SIXPENCE PER FOOT RUN. A large quantity of the cheapest patterns always in stock. Embossing and painted work on the most moderate terms.—CHARLES LUNG, No. 1, King-street, Baker-street, Portman-square.—Cash only.

PATENT PLATE GLASS.—HETLEY and CO. beg to inform Architects, Builders, and the Trade generally, that their new Tariff of PRICES for the above is now ready, and will be forwarded on application. A REDUCTION of about 40 per cent. has been made on the usual Glazing sizes.—Sheet, Crown, and Ornamental Window-Glass Warehouse, 35, Soho-square, London.—ROUGH PLATE GLASS.

E. and W. H. JACKSON beg to call the attention of Builders and the trade to the reduced prices of their PATENT PLATE GLASS, which, from its cheapness, is now superseding crown in all respectable dwelling-houses. BRITISH and ROUGH PLATE, CROWN, SHEET, STAINED, and ORNAMENTAL GLASS, supplied of the best manufacture, and at the lowest terms. List of prices, estimates, and every information can be had on application at their warehouse, 315, Oxford-street.

PATENT PLATE GLASS.—CLAUDET and BOUGHTON beg to remind Architects, Builders, and the Trade of the very low price at which they are now selling PATENT PLATE GLASS, the effect of which is to supersede the use of Crown Glass in the principal windows of all the better class of dwelling-houses.—PLATE, SHEET, CROWN, COLOURED, and ORNAMENTAL WINDOW GLASS Warehouse, 89, High Holborn.

*** Lists of the reduced prices forwarded free on application.

PAINTED and STAINED GLASS and ORNAMENTAL GLASS of every kind, for Windows.—CLAUDET and BOUGHTON, 89, High Holborn, execute every description of Ornamental Glass for Windows, in ancient or modern style, at the lowest prices consistent with superior workmanship, either in plain colour, ornamental in white, embossed, engraved, or richly painted.—Patterns and specimens may be seen at their Warehouse, 89, High Holborn.

THE UNION PLATE GLASS COMPANY beg to call the attention of architects, surveyors, builders, large consumers, and the trade generally, to the quality, colour, and substance of their highly-finished glass, and as the discounts vary according to size, they prefer giving a special estimate for each quantity required. To encourage the use of Plate Glass for glazing purposes, the price is considerably reduced, which will, for its durability and appearance, insure the preference to any other description.

ROUGH PLATE GLASS supplied for skylights, warehouses, workshops, and flooring, 3-8ths, ½, ¾, and 1 inch thick.

London Warehouse, 99, Hatton-garden, Holborn.

H. CHRISTIE, Agent.

WINDOW GLASS.—THOMAS MILLINGTON solicits an inspection of the different GLASSES he has now in stock, the qualities of which will be found to be very superior.—87, Bishopsgate-street, Without.

NEW TARIFF.—Sheet in various large dimensions delivered free in London.

Common in	100 foot cases		20s. 0d.
Do.	200	do.	38s. 0d.
Thirds	200	do.	42s. 6d.
Seconds	200	do.	66s. 8d.
Best (very superior)		do.	100s. 0d.

ROUGH PLATE GLASS for WINDOWS, SKYLIGHTS, and FLOORS in sizes not exceeding 5 feet superficial.

¼ thick	1s. 0d.	¾ inch	2s. 0d.
3-8th inch	1s. 2d.	1 inch	3s. 0d. per foot.
½ inch	1s. 6d.		

PATENT ROUGH PLATE TILES.

¼ thick	0s. 11d.	3-8th inch	1s. 7d.
½ inch	1s. 3d.	¾ inch	2s. 0d. each.

GLASS DOMES for SKYLIGHTS, from 18 to 50 inches in diameter. These are well worth notice.

C C C Crown per crate 18 tables		£1	16	0
C C do.	do.	2	0	0
Fourths do.	do.	2	7	0
Thirds do.	do.	3	2	6

Large Crown Squares in 100 foot boxes ...... 2½d. per foot.
8 by 6 — 10 by 8 do ...... 2d. do.

Very superior Plate for Pictures and Windows, averaging 26oz. from 1s. 6d. per foot upwards.

STAINED GLASS WINDOWS and LEAD LIGHTS, for Cathedrals, Churches, Chapels, &c., in Patent Rolled Glass, white and coloured, 26oz. to the foot, or 1-8th of an inch thick.

Plain glazing, in white quarries	1s.	3d.	per foot super.
" " and coloured border	1	6	"
" In tinted quarries (yellow or green)	1	6	"
" And coloured border	1	9	"
Ornamental quarry lights, in white or tinted glass	3	6	"
" " In white or tinted glass	5	0	"
Ornamental quarry lights, in a superior style, in white or tinted glass	7	6	"
Windows of geometrical design, in plain colours	7		"
Mosaic and diaper windows, without figures	10	6	"
" " With one figure	15	0	"
Mosaic and Gothic windows, elaborately designed and of the highest description of art, with letters and figures	20	0	"
Headings for Gothic windows .... from	15	0	"
" " .... to	20	0	"

Ornamental Borders, from 1s. 6d. to 5s. per foot run.

N.B. The foregoing are the prices at which windows will be delivered all complete, in any part of the kingdom.

REMARKS.—Being the only manufacturers of the Patent Rolled Glass, we are enabled to execute Windows at our manufactory much cheaper, and having the command of every variety of tint, in the harmonious blending of which everything depends, we possess greater facilities than any other house.

The introduction of this glass in cathedrals and churches furnishes a new era in the history of stained glass; for, since the time of the ancients, there has not been discovered, till now, any glass that equals theirs in richness or brilliancy.

A great drawback to the more general use of stained glass has hitherto existed in the uncertainty as to its actual cost. In the foregoing tariff this is entirely removed, for by it any architect or clergyman, by getting the measurement of the openings, can arrive at the precise cost of any description of window; and, it will be observed, there are no after incidental charges or expenses further than the mere placing in the building.

Attention is particularly directed to the prices of plain glazing, viz., white glass, 1s. 3d.; tinted glass, 1s. 6d. per foot complete, which are cheaper than has been charged for the common crown or sheet glass.

Patent rolled glass is peculiarly adapted for the glazing of all kinds of ecclesiastical edifices; it is more in character with the building, for being translucent and at the same time not transparent, a subdued but not obscured light is admitted, and, without darkening the interior, the glare of the sun is excluded. Its extreme strength, one-eighth of an inch thick, is also in favour of its general adoption.

*** A book of designs to select from will be forwarded on application, or parties may furnish their own designs, and be charged according to the foregoing tariff.

JAMES HARTLEY and Co. Glass Manufacturers, Sunderland.

No. CCCXIII.

SATURDAY, FEBRUARY 3, 1849.

HERE are three or four matters that have come before us during the week, on which we desire to say a few words to our readers ; and not having left ourselves space or time to treat each of them separately, we must string them together, as we have done on some other occasions, although in truth they have not much immediate connection.

On Thursday in last week, after listening to a paper on pointed architecture, at the Society of Antiquaries, written by the veteran architect, Mr. John Adey Repton (how much a veteran was shewn by the fact, that this was the continuation of a paper commenced by him forty years ago), we looked in at the adjoining pleasant room, where the Royal Society hold their meetings, to know what was going on there. We say a pleasant room, but to our minds it is the most pleasant room in London; its old sconces and wax lights, the quiet that prevails there, the portraits which cover every inch of the walls, including at all events one great architect, the men who are occasionally to be found there dozing with dignity amidst the hum of a paper, and the mace on the table, which, before Mr. Weld scandalously destroyed the belief, by proving that Charles the Second not merely bought but paid for it, we were able to point out to a country visiter as the veritable "bauble" which Cromwell bade his soldiers "take away,"—all concur to make it so.

There were very few members present—perhaps not forty—and Sir Robert Harry Inglis, bland and unctuous, with that bit of the beautiful in his button-hole in the shape of a flower, which seems as much part of his dress as his coat (and we like him for it), had by the hand a venerable looking, though not old man, and was admitting him, in the name of the Royal Society, "a fellow thereof;" and then he added a few happily chosen words, to mark his consideration of the new member—Sumner, Archbishop of Canterbury, and Primate of all England. Another neophyte approached, whom Sir Robert admitted as Lord John Russell, and to whom he said, in more and better words than we can remember, that he should not meet the views of the fellows if he did not add to his official duty, an earnest expression of their hope that all his lordship's efforts, as the Prime Minister of England, for the advantage of the country, might be crowned with success. The fellows regarded with no ordinary pleasure, he said, the accession of one who, he was satisfied, felt with him, that no earthly pursuit had stronger claims on the attention of all than the pursuits of science.

Our old friend the new secretary, Professor Bell, who has quite settled down into his seat, then began to read some statements of the average fall of rain during certain showers, which will doubtless be very useful when printed, but as we did not desire to have cold water thrown on the feelings which what we had seen had induced, we straightway departed, determined that our readers should have a note of it.

And surely, taken in connection with what is passing around us, and the state of other countries, this was a remarkable and significant scene, not without interest to any. While the infallible head of another church is a fugitive and an exile, and the ministers of other countries can scarce preserve the land from anarchy and spoliation,—here were the head of our church, and the prime minister of our country, quietly giving their adhesion to the cause of science, and taking their seats amongst its representatives.

On the previous evening we attended a meeting of a different character, from which we came away less satisfied. A placard on a wall in Westminster, setting forth that a lecture would be delivered to the Young Men's Missionary Association, on the 24th of January, by the Rev. John Aldis; subject—"The Connection of Idolatry and Architecture," took us to the Baptist Mission House in Moorgate-street. The library, a good room, adorned with the prize pictures of "The Baptism of Christ," concerning which much was said at the time of the competition, was filled with persons; and the reverend lecturer spoke eloquently and fluently, though we cannot say well ; for his eloquence was sadly thrown away on a futile idea, and his audience must have left with their notions on the subject of architecture curiously mystified and perverted. The dogmas which he specially wished to inculcate were these : that architecture was purely idolatrous; that while Paganism had produced an architecture, Christianity had done nothing for it (our glorious cathedrals were quite forgotten), and—chief point of all, that columns in Druid, Egyptian, Greek, and Roman architecture were simply symbols of gods or their attendants ! In Greek buildings, for example, he said, the columns were wholly useless, and were not put up with the view of beauty of use ; they were the beginning and the end of the building, representatives of gods to awe the worshippers. His main proof (good luck !) he rested on this, that all the *parts* of an order were symbolical, and that surely, therefore, the leading idea, the column, was so too. Thus, he said the triglyphs were suggestions of Apollo's harp ! and the flutings of the columns were to represent the folds of a robe. The Doric order, he continued, had no *pediment*, the robe was supposed to be so large as to hide it. In the Ionic the robe was less (the column, therefore, smaller), and the *pediment* was visible. For a time we could not understand what the reverend gentleman meant by saying the Doric had no *pediment*, but as he went on we came to the conclusion that he meant " pedestal," and ought to have said " base." As to the constant use of columns in absurd situations by ourselves, which he condemned (he was not quite so wrong here), we had, like many other imitators, taken up an absurdity, although we would not have originated it ; but he repeated, in classical architecture columns were simply representatives of gods, and purely idolatrous.

The rev. gentleman appeared to possess the ear and entire confidence of the meeting as one of their pastors ; and making all his statements not as being in any degree matters of doubt, but as received truths, they were doubtless so considered by the majority of his audience.

With a protest against such blind teaching, let us leave the speculative, however, and turn to the practical.

It is pretty evident, from the proceedings at a late Court of Sewers, reported in our present number, that the Barry-Austin controversy is one which may lead to considerable inconvenience. Now let us, by way of friendly warning, recommend the commissioners to keep themselves as much as possible out of hot water. They have clean and dirty water questions enough already on their hands, and they have a vast amount of serious business to get through, all of which will require the exercise of cool brains, and the assistance of a friendly public opinion. We have had too many occasions of late for regretting the evident infusion of a mixture of acerbity, acidity, and acridity, into certain sanitary compositions, and what appeared to us a frequent diverging from the straightforward path of business for the sake of giving an unexpected kick at some real or imaginary opponent. There is much to be objected to in the tone of Mr. Austin's report on the drainage of the new Houses of Parliament, and to some of the circumstances attending it. If he had put forward a plain statement of facts in very temperate language, he would have laid a good ground for a temperate discussion. As the matter now stands, there is too much feeling involved in it, too much making of a case, and striving for victory, for us to hope that the controversy will end very pleasantly or profitably. The new views that have been recently taken on the subject of town drainage may be wholly or partially right or wrong. It is very important to the public that their accuracy or inaccuracy should be distinctly ascertained, and that we should have the full benefit of a calm, unprejudiced investigation of the whole subject of town drainage by impartial and practical men of science, of whom there are several in the commission. If, however, the officers of the commission should be allowed to indulge in any thing approaching personalities, or should so shape their reports as to hurt in any avoidable manner the feelings of others, the consequence would be the excitement of something like party feeling, occasioning heated instead of temperate discussion, in the turmoil of which poor TRUTH might find herself flashed, or flushed, if our readers like it better, into a bottomless cesspool. Moreover, opposition to the views of the commission would be excited in numerous quarters where otherwise good will and aid might have been looked for. And though we have put the matter hypothetically, the truth is, this feeling *is* being excited, and an opposition *is* growing, and, therefore, we do most earnestly advise the commissioners to check any disposition to gladiatorial exhibition which may shew itself amongst them.

We have carefully endeavoured to steer an unbiassed course; our views, long ago and often expressed, are mainly those of the commission,—we " have done the state some service, and they know it ;" but we have not the less painfully felt the injustice, as well as the impropriety in a political and in a mere gentlemanly point of view, of the apparent endeavour to cast a slur on men of standing and experience in their departments, which has been evinced by several recent publications, and which seems to have no other exciting cause than the fact, that the practice of these gentlemen and the new views are not altogether in accord. An obstinate adherence to antiquated notions clearly proved to be wrong, might justify a condemnation, which no man could be fairly required to suffer in silence, merely because he is told without proof that all his theory and practice have been based on error ; but such a condemnation is doubly exasperating when it is pronounced with an assumption of infallibility on points obviously still unsettled.

Let us hope, then, that the Metropolitan Commissioners of Sewers, whom we cordially wish well through their arduous labours, will establish an additional claim to the confidence of the public, by carefully preventing the publication of any report which is not couched in the most temperate terms. If they do not, they may find the task of *deodorizing* more difficult than they think for.

We are not fond of finding fault, or even of exposing misdoings; we would rather praise than blame; still, when occasion arises, we never shrink from the task, and unfortunately this is too often the case, especially in architectural competitions. The ink of our notice of very suspicious proceedings at Chichester was scarcely dry before we were called on to refer to others equally so at Birmingham.

To expect a just decision, excepting through chance, in a competition where a board of guardians, unaided, are to make the selection, even if they have the best intentions, and earnestly desire to do right, is simply ridiculous. In the case now under discussion, to which we referred last week, there would seem to be influences at work, apart from this actual impossibility, which will prevent the likelihood of justice being done to the competitors,—at least, if the statements forwarded to us, and others publicly made, be true.

We have before us the names of fifty-two competitors, and the initials of two. How these came to be public we do not know; but supposing that the competitors understood that it was to be so, we do not object to this. Twenty-eight of these, according to the list, are from London and its suburbs, including some respectable names, and five are from Birmingham. In two meetings, or at most three, forty-seven of the designs were got rid of, seven being selected as the best. Of these seven, how many will our readers say were of the twenty-eight from London, and how many from the Birmingham list? Supposing the talent equal in both places, and making some allowance for superior facilities for obtaining local information possessed by the architects of the town, the calculation is not difficult. We will wager a new case of instruments, however, with the best arithmetician who reads us, that the result of his sums will not coincide with the fact. *The committee's list includes all five of the Birmingham competitors* (at least so goes our information) *and not one of the London men.*[*]

The *Birmingham Journal* of Saturday last has a sensible leading article on the subject, pointing out the injustice that is being done to the competitors. In speaking of the selection the writer says, after remarking that of the two meetings in which the work had been done, considerable part of one was occupied in discussing merely the mode of determining the best,—" It may be as well to remind our readers that not one in ten of the guardians in committee assembled had the slightest practical knowledge of the subject before them. Few unprofessional men are able to 'read,' as it is termed, an architectural plan so as to understand even its general features, and we do not libel the guardians in saying that they are quite as competent to read a Greek poem, or a Sanscrit MS., as they are to analyse, still less to generalise, the necessarily elaborate and complicated details before them. If this be so, we are at a loss to determine on what principle they judged of, and threw overboard, the

forty-six plans referred to. Look also at the express speed with which they got through their work. Admitting that several of the plans were ineligible on the score of expense, or, for some cause not connected with their architectural arrangements, did not require examination, there was still a number sufficient to occupy the time of a competent tribunal for a week. Consider the facts already stated; the time the mere arrangement of the plans occupied, the numerous details demanding separate consideration with reference to themselves and to the building as a whole, the cost of producing these plans, and the professional character of the architects in some measure involved in the decision, then estimate the competency of the judges, and the attention bestowed on the plans at the two meetings with these considerations, and it must be admitted that the tribunal was as incompetent as the trial was hurried and unfair."

The writer, in conclusion, urges the guardians to retrace their steps; to appoint three architects of character who are not interested in the competition, and request them to examine and report upon the plans for the guidance of the Board.

One of the guardians has attempted, in a letter to *Aris's Gazette*, to reply to the *Journal*, but says nothing more so far as relates to the real question at issue than that the board had three meetings instead of two.

One of the competitors has, in a praiseworthy manner, exerted himself to obtain a reconsideration of the designs. A meeting of competitors was fixed to take place at Birmingham on Tuesday (it being understood that the board would make their final selection on Wednesday), but the notice was so short that we doubt if many were able to attend.[*] Several members of the board themselves feel that an injustice (if only through want of knowledge) is being committed, and have offered, we are told, to co-operate in bringing the matter fairly before the public, and giving the competitors a chance of redress.

And so, having discoursed of Prime Ministers and Baptist Missionaries, Commissioners of Sewers and Board of Guardians, wandering without apology from London to Birmingham, we commend the matter of our paper to the consideration of the various parties whom it may concern, considering they will not find it wholly uninstructive.

THE RIGHTS AND RESPONSIBILITIES OF ARCHITECTS.

THE mutual positions of ARCHITECTS[†] and their EMPLOYERS, differ in no material respect from the ordinary relations as by law established between principals and their agents. The most prominent peculiarity attaching to the intercourse between them arises from the nature of their association,—which is neither honorary, as in the case of barristers and physicians in respect of their clients or patients, nor yet subject to any fixed and certain claims for services, as are the attendances of attorneys and solicitors. Hence it follows, that in all engagements made with architects, unless controlled by an express agreement, the amount of compensation due to them for their 'professional assistance is estimated on the *quantum meruit* principle, and therefore must depend mainly upon the evidence adduced in each particular transaction, in support of the amount of skill and labour entitled to remuneration. A contract will be implied as having been entered into by the one party

to pay a fair and reasonable compensation to the other, in consideration of the duties and responsibilities which he assumes, and of the labour and services which he performs. This, in the absence of an express contract, is the extent of the implied agreement. The only question that can possibly arise out of this state of things goes to the value of the services actually rendered.

An architect's engagement or retainer is not, as has been frequently erroneously supposed, necessarily co-extensive with the completion of his original design, nor continuing to the entire execution of the works primarily entrusted to his charge. The employer may at any time discharge one architect and engage another. In such a case, the architect discharged must seek his remedy on *quantum meruit*. Nor would his claim be limited to the works then actually performed or in progress; he would also be entitled to a remuneration commensurate with the prospective advantage accruing to his employer from the adoption of that design which he is denied the privilege of perfecting.

An architect is bound to exercise due care and skill in execution of the trusts committed to his charge. Nor will any thing short of a personal investigation into all the details of every matter delegated to him be sufficient to exonerate him from the imputation of neglect. In case of the occurrence of any unforeseen disaster, it will be no valid plea for him, in answer to the charge of negligence, to show that the particulars on which his calculations have been erroneously grounded were furnished to him by his employer. It is his duty to inspect, to test, and verify all data which may be supplied to him, if on the correctness of those data the success or failure of his work depend. Hence, an architect, having been employed by a committee to erect a bridge, it was held that he was bound to ascertain for himself *by personal experiment* the nature of the soil; although a person previously appointed by the committee for that purpose communicated to him, by their express desire, the result of his inquiries.[*]

Nor can an architect establish any claim in respect of his services, when, either through neglect or ignorance, his calculations have been proved erroneous, and his estimates deceptive. Indeed, it is a general and most equitable rule that no agent can demand remuneration as for work and labour done, unless the principal derives some benefit from his assistance.[†] Common sense will accord its approval to that dictum of the law which declares want of competence or want of candour to be equally unworthy. Hence an architect, who, by means of a grossly incorrect estimate, induces his employer to undertake work which cannot be completed otherwise than at a much greater expense than was originally contemplated, is not entitled to recover any thing for his trouble, either in the making of such estimate—or for the execution of the works performed thereunder—or for any services connected therewith.[‡] In such a case—that is to say, when the estimate is utterly erroneous and deceptive, no remedy is given to the architect in action upon *quantum meruit*; since the defendant may, without notice, and under plea of the general issue,[§] reduce the damages " by showing that the work was improperly done; and may entitle himself to a verdict by establishing its total inefficiency."[‖]

The words of Mr. Justice Le Blanc applied to an analogous case,[¶] may be quoted as forming a very appropriate summary of the points involving the necessity for the exercise of a fair degree of skill and care by an architect, for, as he observes, " the plaintiff must be prepared to show that his work was properly done. If a man contracted with another to build him a house for a certain sum, it surely would not be sufficient for the plaintiff to show that he had put together such a quantity of bricks and timber in the shape of a house,

---

[*] The names of the selected are (without reference to the order of merit), Coe and Goodwin, Lewisham; Bodrick, Hull; and Whatley, Druly and Bateman, Newey, Hemming, and [we believe] but this is not quite clear in our list] Empson, all of Birmingham.

[*] We were requested to co-operate by giving intimation of the meeting to the London competitors, and presiding at the meeting, but did not receive the letter until too late.

[†] It is almost unnecessary to state that the rights and responsibilities of ARCHITECTS and SURVEYORS are here treated as identical.

[*] *Moneypenny* v. *Hartland*, 1 C. and P., 382; 2 id. 378 S. C. on second trial.
[†] See *Stewart* v. *Kayte*, 3 Stark, 161; *Hamond* v. *Holiday*, 1 C. and P., 384.
[‡] *Moneypenny* v. *Hartland.* Ante.
[§] *Chitty on Cont.*, 569; *Denew* v. *Deverel*, 3 Camp, C., 451; and *Farnsworth* v. *Garrand*, 1 Camp. 38.
[‖] *Bullile* v. *Kell*, 4 Bing. N. C., 638.
[¶] *Basten* v. *Butter*, 7 East—479 and 484.

if it could be shown that it fell down the next day; but it ought to be shown that he had done the work according to his contract; and it is open to the defendant to prove that it was executed in such a manner as to be of no value to him."

The contract thus implied by the law to be incumbent on architects in common with all other professional men, being that they will exercise a reasonable amount of skill and care in the performance of their duties, any dereliction from these implied obligations will incapacitate them from recovering the remuneration otherwise usually accorded to their services.

Nor is an architect liable only for his own personal default. Being individually and personally trusted by his client, he is responsible also for those whom he employs in situations of a subordinate character; and therefore for his clerk of the works. No employment requiring skill or discretion can be legally delegated to another.* Nor would the fact of the employer undertaking to pay such clerk of the works discharge the architect from his liability. The subordinate is still regarded as the mere deputy or representative of his superior, who would be bound for his competency, and answerable for his conduct, on the principle of the ancient maxim *qui facit per alium, facit per se*. The architect receives remuneration for his superintendence of the works, nor would his delegation of that duty to another person, nor his neglect to keep a strict watch over that person's proceedings be covered even by the proof that such an arrangement had been well known to, or approved of, by his (the architect's) employer. Such an appointment would be purely vicarial. The clerk is a mere agent of the architect, who ought to be, and hence impliedly becomes, the accredited judge of and guarantee for his proficiency.

Our course of reading has not furnished us with any judicial decision, especially applicable to this particular point. The dictum here by analogy laid down may, however, be received with confidence.† The practice of the profession is such as to show that it admits the responsibility. Of the many cases that might be cited in support of this view, one of the most remarkable as well as more recent may suffice.

An architect superintended the erection of a chapel from his own designs, and in due course received his commission-charge upon completion of the works.

Some few years had elapsed when some material defect manifested itself in the subsidence of the roof. On examination, it appeared that the original construction of the roof, as designed by the architect, had been varied by the builder, either with the consent, or through the carelessness of the clerk of the works, and that the default now becoming apparent, had been occasioned by these variations in its construction. The architect, at once acknowledging his liability, defrayed the costs of reinstatement.

When the architect's certificate is made a conditional precedent to the payment of a builder's bill, the latter cannot recover in an action without producing it; and this will be the rule whether such action be brought upon a contract or on an *ad valorem* charge. It is the usual practice to make the architect's certificate a condition precedent to payment in every builder's agreement; and in such a case, an account, the items of which are merely checked by the architect, and by him forwarded to his employer, will not amount to a certificate sufficient to satisfy such a condition, and to give the builder right of action.‡ The certificate must state decidedly and unequivocally that the builder is entitled to a certain sum of money.

But although the architect's certificate is thus, in the great majority of cases, rendered necessary to the builder before he can recover his demand, he is not utterly without remedy when that certificate has been unfairly withheld or unreasonably refused. It seems certainly very doubtful whether any

* *Ess* v. *Truscott*, 2 M. and W.—385.

† On this subject see also "Story on Agency," pp. 12-14.

‡ *Morgan* v. *Birnie*, 3 M. and Sc. 76—9; Bing. 672. See also *Worsley* v. *Wood*, 6 T. R., 710; and *Bradley* v. *Milnes*, Bing. N. C., 644; 1 Scott, 626—697.

action at law could be sustained against an architect to compel the granting of a certificate. But a bill in chancery might be filed to enforce the special performance of that portion of his duty; and unless he could then show satisfactorily that his refusal was justifiable under the peculiar circumstances of the case, he would undoubtedly be desired to grant it. Until, however, it has been procured by some means, and is produced, it is quite clear that no action can be maintained, unless it can be shown that the defendant himself prevents the plaintiff from complying with the condition; or that the condition itself has become impossible of fulfilment, as in the case of the death of the architect.* The hardship entailed upon the plaintiff, by making the doing of an Act by a third party essential to complete his right of action, forms no just ground for complaint, since he himself voluntarily assented to the contract upon these terms; and having once agreed to such a stipulation, he will not be allowed afterwards to repudiate it, simply because it has become inconvenient.

The remuneration of an architect has long been a *vexata quæstio*. Nor has the law laid down any fixed principles by which it may be generally estimated. The profession have endeavoured to establish a customary scale of charges by commission on the outlay, amounting in the aggregate to five per cent.,† generally subdivided thus,—

Plans............	1¼ per cent.
Estimate	1¼ „
Specification......	1¼ „
Superintendance ..	1¼ „

This scale, however, has never been recognised in our courts. Indeed, it is questionable whether it should be so recognised, at least in its details, which, although promulgated by those who rightly ought to be the fittest judges and protectors of their own interests, are manifestly unequal and unjust. Surely the study, thought, and time bestowed upon the preparation of a plan worthy to be adopted, and fit to be exactly carried out, is worthy of a higher reward than the per centage here accorded it. Again, the specification is a work of labour, to which the estimate is merely supplementary. Least of all is the superintendence entitled to the same remuneration.

The courts have long and pertinaciously endeavoured to avoid a recognition of this per-centage principle; and even its most strenuous supporters must allow that some objections to it stand upon a broad and stable basis. In such a standard of remuneration (say its opponents), the architect engaged to guard the interests of his employer finds a direct incentive to neglect, if not to treachery. His profit is proportionate to the expenditure, not to the saving. His wits are exercised in daily contravention of his own interests. All his experience is directed to his own detriment. His honesty can be rewarded only by a correspondent diminution in its recompense. Perpetual self-denial only entails continual self-sacrifice; whilst the temptation is at once certain in its realisation, and secure of its enjoyment.

To these most matter-of-fact and plausible objections, it is but an indifferent reply to urge that every architect acquires reputation, and its consequent advantages by the economy which he exercises in the execution of his designs. This is a proposition which experience has failed to prove. Even were such success the certain and unfailing consequence of uniform adherence to the strict path of duty, many would still be found more anxious to secure immediate advantage, than to live on in faith of fame deferred. The world must change its ways much before honesty becomes the rule, and want of it, the exception.

Faulty, however, as we all must acknowledge the per-centage principle to be, and determined as has been the opposition of the legal authorities to its establishment; it finds general favour with the public, and is practically adopted by all juries. Lord Denman, in a recent case,‡ in vain inculcated his anti-

* See *Holkam* v. *The East-India Company*, 1 F. R., 638; *Davis* v. *Mure and Others*, cited id. 642; and *Jones* v. *Berkeley Douglas*, 665.

† The fire-offices pay their surveyors 5 per cent. on all works executed, and 2½ per cent. on all works estimated, but not executed; the examination of premises, &c., being covered by a salary.

‡ *Mayor* v. *Ward*. 10 *Jur.*, 796.

commission doctrines upon the jury, who, nevertheless, gave the prescribed commission on a *quantum meruit* count; and on a subsequent motion for a new trial, the court refused to nullify the verdict. So, in a similar case* before Lord Ellenborough, that eminent judge left it to the jury to say whether the mode of charging by commission was vicious or unreasonable, and if they thought it so, to deduct from the damages accordingly. But, although he hinted his own disapprobation of the principle, the jury sanctioned it by giving the plaintiff a verdict for the full amount of his claim. Lord Kenyon held that a commission-charge was not recoverable as such.

Amongst the various suggestions which have been lately put forward as actually tested by successful practice, is that of a direct establishment of a contract between the parties, by the delivery of a card of terms at the time of engagement. This remedy, however, seems worse than the disease. No professional man would wish to commence an acquaintance with a collision so immediately in view—whilst such an intimation of suspicion must be equally distasteful to his employer. It might, perhaps, place architects on higher ground with their employers, and certainly it would be more just to themselves, if the per centage were attached to the estimated, instead of the actual cost. Such an arrangement could in no manner prejudice the client, whilst the architect would feel a double pride in exercising his disposition for economy, when certain of its full appreciation, and many bickerings would be removed from both. In default, however, of the substitution of some better and more equitable scheme for that which now exists, architects must rest content with the per-centage system; nor will they generally be disappointed in submitting their fair claims under that customary compensation to the decision of a jury.†

The architect's right to remuneration accrues, in case of an express contract, only upon completion of his duties. Such remuneration being contingent on benefit to be derived by the employer from services rendered, no reward will be due until the employer has actually obtained some definite advantage.‡ Where, however, the contract is only implied and not expressed, the architect will be justified, after the expiration of a reasonable time, in refusing to continue his labours unless he be paid a sum on account proportionate to the work already performed.§ He may, moreover, on refusal, throw up his engagement, and recover to the extent of such work, on *quantum meruit*.‖

The practice of competition having of late been much extended, it may be well here to observe that there does not appear to be any copyright in architectural designs.¶ Nor can any remuneration as for work and labour done, be recovered from any committee or individual who may have advertised for plans and estimates to be sent in upon the usual terms of competition. Architects thus invited to submit designs for any particular object, and complying with such invitation, are altogether without remedy in respect of compensation for the time and labour bestowed upon them. And this, even although the amount of reward may be specified, and the particulars and requisitions of the parties advertised strictly adhered to. Nor is it incumbent on the advertisers to select any one design, to justify their exclusion or rejection of the others; since the parties soliciting the competition have impliedly constituted themselves

* *Chapman* v. *De Tastet*, 2 Stark, 291.

† In fact, the remedy rests with those whose interests are said to suffer most under the existing state of things. When the Society of Auctioneers found their proceedings hampered by the difficulty of establishing a general and satisfactory scale of charges, the most influential men amongst them met together, and having drawn up such a scale as they considered fair, put it forth for the adoption of their brethren, as the scale which they would invariably adopt, and which they were ready and willing to support by their evidence as fair and reasonable. Why should not the architects adopt a similar course?

‡ *Hughes* v. *Lenny*, 5 Mee. and W., 188—and *Rees* v. *Lines*, 8 C. and P., 126. Coleridge.

§ Architects engaged on large undertakings are usually paid 5 per cent. on the amount of the builder's bills, certified by them in the progress of the works.

‖ *Roberts* v. *Havelock*, 3 B. and Ad., 404.

¶ It does not appear that any copyright is reserved to *pictures*. Strange as the omission may seem, the invention is left unprotected, whilst the publication of the invention (by means of an engraving) vests a right in either publisher or author, under the 7 Geo. III., c. 38.

sole judges whether any remuneration has been merited or not.*

A striking case of this kind recently occurred. A committee having advertised for competition plans, to be designed in accordance with certain detailed particulars, received several. Of more than twenty which were offered, one design only was in strict accordance with the instructions issued; and the committee chose one which was utterly and altogether in direct contravention of their own prescribed rules. The architect who had conformed to the instructions consulted counsel on the merits of his case, and was advised that he had no apparent remedy, since he was altogether dependent upon the good faith of the committee, who might vary their rules at pleasure, and, in default of any express contract, might make their own selection, however unjustly, without incurring any responsibility in respect of other parties. G. Tattersall.

PROFESSOR COCKERELL'S LECTURES ON ARCHITECTURE.

The third lecture of the course at the Royal Academy was given on Thursday, the 18th ult. On the previous occasion the professor had shown that, in regard to fitness and conception, nature was ever the great mistress of our art, and, by instances from the practice of Brunelleschi and of Wren, the advantage of copying from the original, rather than from copies, as we were so apt to do. The analogies he had then given were mainly in reference to structure, but were equally to be discovered in what related to beauty, and he proceeded to show this analogy in the cases of straight and curved lines.

In arriving at this part of his subject, he spoke of the conceit shown in admiring the work of art, simply from its being such, and neglecting to appreciate the beauty of a corresponding production of nature. For example, in some kinds of stone was a fossil of beautiful spiral outline, called the *cornu ammonis*. Discovered on the face of some one of the stones of a garden wall, it would attract little attention. But, if this beautiful spiral were known to be a work of art, great would be the interest excited by it. There would be much discussion as to its origin, and much speculation as to the mode of generating the curve, and we might be certain that afterwards, no other form of volute would be used but this. Whilst in the wall, the simple gardener would almost ask pardon for presuming to admire any thing so ordinary; but considered as a work of art, it would be rated beyond all price. As ascribed to nature, it was a matter of course,—to art, a matter of wonder.

The professor also noticed the beauty of form and structure in the common *echinus*, or sea urchin, and showed how suggestions might be taken from it, for the form and decoration of domes. If compared with any existing domes—for example, such as had any surface decoration, as in that of the Invalides at Paris—how vastly superior was the work of nature.

Thus, in some of the most pleasing works of art, we discovered the delightful freshness of nature. If we drew from the Grecian honeysuckle, we felt that it was an adaptation from nature. In the cornice of the nave of York Cathedral, we found an ornament which was, in fact, the common savoy-cabbage without disguise. In the capitals and other carvings we discovered the foliage of hedge-rows. Everywhere we had the evidence of the presence of nature, and eulogised the work as "just like nature." Now, if thus we were always so reminded of nature, we could not but regard the labours of those who added to the knowledge of her as useful to our art. It was not to be wondered at, that a notion had prevailed that the old schools had been consulted *usque ad nauseam*, and been worked out, whence aspirations after dangerous novelty, and the idea that the powers of science exceeded those of art, now shown to be erroneous views. As Pope said,—

"Learn hence for ancient rules a just esteem,—
To copy nature is to copy them."

The professor then proceeded to give instances of the universality of the influence, found in the different fashions of architecture,

* *Taylor v. Brewer*, 1 M. and Selw. 210.

in contradistinction to the structural part of architecture, which altered with the progress of science. Amongst these instances were noticed right lines, angles, curves of mouldings, scrolls, spirals, and volutes, and the conic sections.—In illustration of the effect produced by a simple line, he sketched the line of the horizon on the ocean, contrasted with the rocky scenery of the coast. It was, he said, from the tranquil sublimity of this line, breaking in extended length on the view of the Grecian soldiers, in a foreign land, which made them exclaim θαλασσα, θαλασσα, as much as because they there beheld the road by which they might reach their native country. It was the maritime situation of Greece which made the horizontal line so delightful to her people, and the contrast of the low long line of the Grecian temple with rocky scenery excited our admiration in the architecture of Athens, as also in Agrigentum, where the energy of the long lines of the architecture would be confessed by every one. The too frequent breaks, often found in later styles, were apt to give feebleness, and what he might call collapse, to architecture so broken up. The works of the Adams might be instanced as indicative of this effect, which was seen in Stratford-place, Oxford-street. The best works of the Italian architects were remarkable for their length of line, as in the Library of St. Mark, at Venice, and the Farnese Palace. A change to a broken effect, however, took place, and the altitude affected in the thirteenth century no doubt influenced the departure from the horizontal. It was seen in the works of Michelangelo, and also in those of Sir Christopher Wren. It would seem as though the horizontal and vertical systems had gained prevalence by turns.

When a building was seen in oblique perspective, there was no doubt, the professor said, that the horizontal principle was the important one to be observed, and the Library of St. Mark was so circumstanced. But, in parallel perspective, as when a building formed the termination of a street, the vertical principle was desirable, and it was therefore correctly employed in the triumphal arches; and, in the case of the façade of Guildhall, any other than the vertical character would have been inappropriate.—The same contrast and variety which proved the charm of the low building in elevated districts, dictated the choice of lofty outline and vertical character in flat countries, and it was merely the natural impulse for the Assyrians to exclaim—"Let us build a city and a tower, whose top may reach unto the heavens." The recollection of such objects and emotions would explain much that would otherwise be perplexing in the history of architecture.

In continuing the subject of contrast of lines, he alluded to that afforded by lines placed at angles, and made some interesting remarks on the value of the pediment in design. He referred to the absence of this feature in Egyptian architecture, as supplied by the pyramid, and by pyramidal inclination in certain portions of the buildings, noticed the use of pediment amongst the Greeks, and thence passed to the use of sculpture in pediments, and the general treatment of this branch of the art in Greece. It was the aim of the architects here, he said, constantly to carry out this same principle of contrast, as evidenced by the general tendency of the lines of the groups in the pediments, and of the figures of the metopes, contrasted with the lines which enclosed them. The professor illustrated this part of his lecture by some clever sketches on the board, and amongst other remarks, he attributed the introduction of sculpture in the metopes, and the general tendency of the lines in the groups, to the desire to get rid of the square form of these spaces. He remarked that lines at right angles were avoided by the engraver, and instanced the effect of masonry set in cubes, to shew the deformity which there was danger of, in an art in which construction naturally led to the effect produced by right angles, and which was avoided in the entablature of the Doric order, by the introduction of sculpture; and he referred to what has been called "decorative masonry," carefully attended to by Palladio and others, as intended to obviate the defect of lines.

The professor then passed to the consideration of circular and curved lines. He compared the beautiful form of the rainbow with the appearance of the arch in passing under a bridge, and noticed the constant use of circular forms amongst the ancients, as seen in the apse, so often found in the Roman baths, and in the basilica of Trajan—a building of a size so vast that it would have enclosed the whole section of Westminster Hall, buttresses included. In the buildings of Paris, he remarked that there were several instances of the successful use of circular forms: in this country, their beauty had been scarcely attended to as it might have been, but he instanced Inigo Jones's projected Persian court at Whitehall. and the plan of the tower of St. Vedast's Church, Foster-lane. In the square tower, and other portions of buildings, we had a constant use of angular forms, but it could hardly be doubted that at some time to come the tendency would be again in favour of the circular styles. Amongst the ancients, he instanced the constant recognition of the beauty of these forms, as in the tholus of the Greeks, in the dome of the Pantheon, and in the form of the column, especially when in contrast with the pilaster. In mouldings—as in the torus and cavetto—nothing could be admitted as so essential, for all the beauty of mouldings lay in the beauty of contrast; and it was the contrast of the curves and hollows with the straight lines, and the contrast of size in the different features, which made the beauty of the human profile. In the contrasted size of the ovolo and bead under it, we had the charm produced by proportion and quantity. When, as a youth, he first saw a certain combination, which he delineated, of a plain fascia with a crowning and bed moulding, he was at once struck with the beauty which was produced, by consideration of quantities. If these combinations struck the young mind, they must be beautiful, for *it* came nearer to nature than the old mind, oppressed with business, or wrought with care.—He also instanced the use of large with small columns, and the defect in one part of the 13th century, where the mouldings were all resembling each other. He then alluded to the other circular forms,—as the cyma, or line of beauty, and the scroll,—remarking upon the subject of ornaments, that these should always take the form of the moulding which they were intended to decorate.—In speaking of the value of the conic sections, he showed that the cone gave us the lesson of the pyramidal form, applied in the spire and pyramid. Gradation in form was as essential as in colour. Diminution in objects was a natural desire, and was made to take place *from* the eye, as in the spire of a church, and the leg of a table. It had been lately certified, that the axes of the columns in Grecian temples inclined towards the cella. He also compared the treatment of the curves of mouldings by the Greeks and by the Romans. Venus was held to have two natures, to one of which there was no corporeal resemblance. She was worshipped under the form of a cone, the type of beauty. Finally, the professor said, he did not broach any new doctrine, but he recommended the recurrence to nature on all occasions, by which, in proportion to its attention to such system, each school had been successful, and he might say, in the words of Pope,—

"First follow nature, and your judgment frame
By her just standard, which is still the same:
Unerring nature, still divinely bright,
One clear, unchanged, and universal light,
Life, force, and beauty, must to all impart,
At once the source, and end, and test of art."

* * * * *

"Those rules of old discover'd, not devised,
Are nature still, but nature methodized:
Nature, like liberty, is but restrain'd
By the same laws which first herself ordain'd.
Hear how learn'd Greece her useful rules indites,
When to repress, and when indulge our flights:
High on Parnassus' top her sons she show'd,
And pointed out those arduous paths they trod;
Held from afar, aloft, the immortal prize,
And urged the rest by equal steps to rise.
Just precepts thus from great examples given,
She drew from them what they derived from Heaven.
The generous critic fann'd the poet's fire,
And taught the world with reason to admire."

* * * * *

"When first young Maro, in his boundless mind
A work to outlast immortal Rome design'd,
Perhaps he seem'd above the critic's law,

And but from nature's fountains scorn'd to draw:
But when to examine every part he came,
Nature and Homer were, he found, the same.
Convinced, amazed, he checks the bold design,
And rules as strict his labour'd work confine,
As if the Stagyrite o'erlook'd each line.
Learn hence for ancient rules a just esteem,—
To copy nature is to copy them."

GREENWICH HOSPITAL—IRON BEAMS.

ROYAL INSTITUTE OF ARCHITECTS.

AT a meeting held on Monday, the 22nd ult., Mr. Bellamy in the chair, a number of donations were announced, including Mr. Warrington's new volume on stained glass, from the author, a handsome present, and a number of the original drawings for Greenwich Hospital, with Hawksmoor's signature upon them.* The latter were presented by Mr. Francis Dollman, and were justly considered by the members a valuable addition to the folio. One of the drawings is very interesting, as shewing a plan for the completion of the centre.

Mr. Bailey, honorary secretary, said, that knowing these drawings were to be presented, he had looked at Evelyn's "Diary," amongst other books on the subject of Greenwich Hospital, where he found some memoranda, which seemed to him interesting. He then read the following extracts from that work:—

May 5, 1695. I came to Deptford from Wotton in order to attend the first meeting of the commissioners for endowing an hospital for seamen at Greenwich. It was at the Guildhall, London. Present — The Archbishop of Canterbury, Lord Keeper, Lord Privy Seal, Lord Godolphin, Duke of Shrewsbury, Duke of Leeds, Earls of Dorset and Monmouth, Commissioner of the Admiralty and Navy, Sir Robert Clayton, Sir Christopher Wren, and several more.

May 17. Second meeting, and a committee appointed to go to Greenwich to survey the place, I being one of them.

May 21. We went to survey Greenwich, Sir Robert Clayton, Sir C. Wren, Mr. Travers, the King's surveyor, Capt. Sanders, and myself.

24. We made a report of the state of Greenwich House, and how the standing part might be made serviceable at present for 6,000*l*., and what ground would be requisite for the whole design. My Lord Keeper ordered me to prepare a book for subscriptions, and a preamble to it.

31. Met again. Mr. Vanbrugh was made secretary to the commission by my nomination of him to the Lords, which was all done that day.

June 7. The commissioners met at Guildhall, when there were scruples and contests of the Lord Mayor, who would not meet, not being named as one of the quorum, so that a new commission was required, though the Lord Keeper and the rest thought it too nice a punctilio.

14. Met at Guildhall, but could do nothing for want of a quorum.

July 5. Met at Guildhall; account of subscriptions about 7,000*l*. or 8,000*l*.

June 30, 1696. I went with a select committee of the commissioners for Greenwich Hospital, and with Sir C. Wren, *where with him I laid the first stone of the intended foundation, precisely at 5 o'clock in the evening*, after we had dined together,—Mr. Flamstead, the King's astronomical professor, observing the punctual time by instrument.

July 4. Note. That my Lord Godolphin was the first of the subscribers, who paid any money to this noble fabric.

The subscription list given by Evelyn amounts to 9,046*l*. 13s. 4d.

Amongst the subscribers are, the King, 2,000*l*.; Archbishop of Canterbury, 500*l*.: Lord Keeper Somners, 500*l*.; Lord Godolphin, 200*l*.; Sir Stephen Fox, the Paymaster of the Forces, 200*l*.; Lord Chief Baron Wood, 66*l*. 13s. 4d.

Nov. 4, 1696. Expense of the work already done was 5,000*l*. and upwards, towards which the treasurer had not received above 800*l*., "so that they must be obliged to stop the work unless there can be a supply of money both from the several noblemen and gentlemen."

It was announced that a folio work, in twenty-one volumes, illustrating buildings, paintings, masques, &c., had been purchased by the honorary secretary for the Institute, at the sale of the Stowe library. From the transient glance we had at one of the volumes, this seems to be a valuable acquisition. We shall make acquaintance with it,—for the advantage of our readers.

Mr. Olinthus Donaldson, in the absence his father, then read "A Description of the Malleable Iron Beam-bridge, constructed in 1839, over the Polloc and Govan Railway, on the Carmunnock-road, near Glasgow, by Mr. Andrew Thomson, engineer."

The chairman, with reference to girders constructed of boiler plate, said a difficulty presented itself to his mind in the general use of rivets rendered necessary by the shortness of the lengths of iron, inasmuch as they were liable to be loosened, and when so loosened formed the germ of destruction. Information on the subject of iron girders was much to be desired, and would, he hoped, be contributed by members.——Mr. Pocock wanted to know how such girders were to be repaired when they became dilapidated?

Mr. Fowler observed that it was worth mention that the official referees, in reporting on buildings wherein cast-iron girders were used, always thought it necessary to warn parties against their uncertainty.——Mr. Jennings said that, on examining an iron aqueduct which had failed, he found the defect was in the masonry and brickwork rather than in the ironwork, and that this had probably been caused by the contraction and expansion of the metal.

Mr. Papworth said it was a curious fact that in Southwark-bridge, which was one of our most important iron bridges, no preparation had been made at first to admit of the expansion and contraction of the ironwork, and that it became necessary, in consequence, to cut through the granite at the abutments afterwards, at a greatly increased cost. He understood that the iron of this bridge flaked off in pieces of considerable size.

Mr. Godwin thought it scarcely necessary to mention that, for large spans, cast-iron girders were out of the question; and that even as regarded small spans, the fact that firemen were more fearful in entering a building when on fire, where the walls were carried on cast-iron, than they were in a building where the girders were of wood, showed that consideration was necessary in their use. He described Mr. Porter's corrugated iron beams (mentioned in our last number), thought them deserving of investigation by those who needed iron beams, and re-urged the suggestion made by Mr. Thomas Cubitt, in the report on the mill at Oldham, that Government should offer premiums for machinery for producing large wrought-iron girders.

Mr. Barry, jun., described an invention recently patented, and on which he had seen experiments, wherein the whole floor formed a single beam, so to speak; there was boiler plate, top and bottom, connected by a web of the same material, if we understood rightly, and filled in solid with concrete. The concrete, though its weight was objectionable, had the advantage of making the floor fire-proof.*

Mr. G. Jennings, by permission of the meeting, afterwards explained the construction of his new water-closet.

NEW COAL FIELD.—We are informed it is intended to open coal fields in the neighbourhood of Bristol.

DINNER OF THE INSTITUTION OF BUILDERS' FOREMEN.

THE anniversary dinner of this institution took place on Wednesday, 31st ult., at the Bay-Tree Tavern, St. Swithin's-lane, City. Mr. G. Godwin, architect, presided, and Mr. Crosse, in the absence of Mr. Thomas Allom, through illness, was in the vice chair. The attendance was very numerous, and included several of the master builders of the metropolis. Letters were read from Professor Cockerell, expressive of his interest in the institution; Mr. Moseley, architect (with donation of one guinea), Mr. Biers, Mr. Allom, with donation;* and other donations were announced from Mr. Bunning, architect, Mr. Piper, Messrs. Locke and Nesham, Mr. T. Patrick, and others. The Patent Dessicating Company sent the very handsome sum of 5*l*. towards the provident fund.

We are anxious to aid what seems to us a very useful institution, and in giving the gist of the chairman's remarks, when proposing the principal toast of the evening, it may be taken as the expression of our own opinions. He congratulated the meeting on the receipt of the letters already mentioned, as indicating that the objects of the Institution were becoming better understood, and that the feeling of distrust was gradually disappearing. The objects of the Institution were two-fold, benevolent and social,—to provide against illness and misfortune (to purchase or erect an asylum hereafter), and to obtain for foremen and clerks of the works, whose position is necessarily somewhat isolated, the advantage of intercourse with men of their own occupation, and the opportunity of discussing points of construction and gaining information. The Directors repudiated any interference between master and man, any attempt to coerce wages: they desired but to aid themselves, and hurt no one else. An anecdote occurred to him which might not be considered irrelevant. It was said that when the Emperor Augustus was passing through the baths at Rome on one occasion, he saw a veteran who had fought with him rubbing himself, after bathing, against one of the columns. The emperor inquired why he had not a boy to do this? and being told that he was too poor, ordered him the means of paying one. On his next visit he saw at every column an old man rubbing himself; and on making the same inquiry he received the same reply. His rejoinder, however, was not what they expected; for he said,—Well, gentlemen, as there are so many of you, I should advise you to *rub one another*. Augustus here taught them sound wisdom; he taught them not to depend on the caprice of a patron, but to help one another. And this, the speaker continued, was what the members of the association were trying to do; and when compelled by illness or distress to receive aid, they might regard it as simply a return for money invested by themselves when the sun shone. The working men of England, by their conduct in the late crisis, when the working men of other countries had been levelling others instead of trying to raise themselves, had entitled themselves to the respect of the upper classes; the men had wisely seen that the interests of the employer and the employed were the same, and that injuring their masters was not the way to benefit themselves. That the good feeling which now prevailed might increase; that knowledge might spread; and that every man might find employment, was his earnest wish. He thought the masters would do well to aid this institution more than they had done; and then the general public, when they saw this, would give their aid too. In the name of the committee he asked the public for this assistance; and he invited those present to drink with hearty expression of good will,—

"*Success to the Provident Institution of Builders' Foremen.*"

* The following is from Walpole's "Anecdotes of Painting:"—NICHOLAS HAWKSMOOR (born 1666), at 18 became the scholar of Wren, under whom during his lifetime, and on his own account after his master's death, he was concerned in erecting many public edifices. He assisted in conducting the works at St. Paul's to their conclusion. He was deputy surveyor at the building of Chelsea College, and clerk of the works at Greenwich Hospital. He designed several of the new churches in the reign of Queen Anne, viz:—St. Mary Woolnoth, in Lombard-street; Christ Church, Spitalfields; St. George, Middlesex; St. Anne, Limehouse; St. George, Bloomsbury. He also built part of All Souls' College, Oxford; a mansion at Easton Neston, Northamptonshire: and assisted Vanbrugh at Blenheim and Castle Howard. He died March 25th, 1736, aged 70.

* The recent destructive fires should aid in leading to the adoption of fire-proof constructions. 26,000*l*. is spoken of as the amount of the loss by the fire in New-square, Lincoln's-Inn, and numerous deeds, court rolls, &c., were burnt which cannot be replaced. The fire at Irongate wharf destroyed a large amount of property. The buildings burnt down were 90 feet by 60 feet, and contained machinery of great cost.

* Mr. Allom said,—"That while all connected with the business of building must acknowledge the extreme value of the class for whose benefit this meeting takes place, it will be of the utmost importance to the future success of the institution, that it should endeavour in every possible way, to exercise a moral influence over all its members; and that master builders, instead of dreading combination against their interests, may feel that in each member of the Institution, they may depend on a trustworthy, efficient, and honourable assistant. That, from the intimate connection existing between each individual foreman, and the best interests of the builder, the architect, and the employer, such qualities cannot be over-rated, and will require that the institution should be only more fully known to ensure its unequivocal and complete success."

ALTAR TOMB IN EXETER CATHEDRAL.
(EARLY ENGLISH.)

FIG. 1

FIG. 2

FIG. 5

ALTAR TOMB IN EXETER CATHEDRAL.

THIS very beautiful specimen of early English work (supposed to be the tomb of Bishop Marischall, who died in 1206), is placed under one of the arches separating the north aisle and choir: it appears to be of more ancient date than that part of the cathedral in which it stands, said to have been begun by Bishop Quivil, between 1281 and 1291.

The tomb, constructed of Purbeck marble, is much decayed; it is surmounted by a quaint and stiffly-carved effigy of the bishop, in a kind of trefoil headed niche; one hand holds a crozier, the other is raised in the act of blessing. The figure is very flat, as usual on monuments of the period.

Fig. 1 of the accompanying illustrations represents the north side of the tomb, and Fig. 2 the south side. Fig. 3 is a spandril ornament, between two quatre-foils, each containing sculpture in the west end, and Fig. 4 a section at A A.

The present east end is a plain slab, but is probably not the original : Fig. 5. a compartment of foliage from the north side : Fig. 6. section at B, Fig. 7. section at C, Fig. 8. section at D.

The details are drawn one-fourth the actual size.   E. S.

DRAINAGE OF GUILDFORD.
ENGINEERING COMPETITIONS.

As the drainage of towns is becoming an important subject, perhaps on account of what is doing here may be interesting as well as instructive. The borough of Guildford comprises St. Mary's, Holy Trinity, parts of Stoke, Shalford, and St. Nicholas' parishes, that is the new borough,—the old borough, previously to its enlargement, consisted of the whole of St. Mary's, part of the Holy Trinity, and part of St. Nicholas' parishes. In 1812 an Act was obtained for paving, cleansing, improving, &c., which is now in existence, and its provisions are carried out by a board of paving commissioners, having power to raise certain sums for that purpose not exceeding in the whole 5,300l. Recently a committee of the commissioners has been appointed to inspect and obtain the removal of nuisances; and with a view to keep out of the operations of the Health of Towns' Bill, the committee advertised in THE BUILDER and in the Times, about the middle of December last, "That engineers be requested to furnish the best plan for draining the town of Guildford," as to surface drainage, and that also "engineers be requested to specify the best mode of disposing of the refuse contents of the sewage, whether into tanks," &c., &c.; for an effectual system of drainage for the town, and that "plans, specifications, and estimates be prepared by them in accordance," &c., &c.; the successful engineer to carry out the works, and obtain tenders within his own estimate, with the usual allowance of 5 per cent., and the committee not binding themselves to accept any one of the plans. Such an advertisement was calculated to bring forward men of ability and standing in the profession to compete; and on the 15th of January (the day appointed), nineteen plans, specifications, and estimates were sent in ; but the committee had not the candour to allude at all to their limited Act of Parliament ; they did not say to these gentlemen, that although we put forth that advertisement, we have no power beyond the old borough ; neither did they say (which is the most important part) that they only had power to raise 5,300l., and that they were already in debt more than half that sum. Nineteen respectable engineers came forward, relying on the honour of the committee, and that they really meant what they said, that the competition would be fair, plans having to be sent in with a number or motto; and after great trouble, expense, and loss of time, have the mortification to find the committee have not the means to pay or power to raise a sum much over 2,000l., they having required engineers to furnish estimates, &c., for works amounting at least to from 6,000l. to 15,000l. Surely these nineteen gentlemen have been ill-used, and might claim remuneration for what they have suffered in pocket and in time.   Y. Z.

CHIMNEY——ASLACKBY CHURCH, LINCOLNSHIRE.

W.D.C.   LAING SC

A CHURCH CHIMNEY.

IN a late number there is a letter from Mr. Orford, about ecclesiastical chimneys : I inclose a sketch of one from Aslackby Church, Lincolnshire, which you may think interesting enough to publish. It is on the north side of the tower. The label seen in the sketch belongs to an arch now stopped up with a perpendicular facing ; it is about 20 feet from the ground. The jointing of the chimney, though it has been complained of, is, I believe, correct.   THOS. M. RICKMAN.

Birmingham.

ON THE NATURE AND PROPERTIES OF THE METALS USED IN THE BUILDING TRADES.
BRASS AND OTHER ALLOYS OF ZINC, &c.

ALMOST all the metals combine with zinc, and some of its alloys are of great importance. The most ancient and universal of them all, however, is brass, which, strange to say, was made and known for centuries by those who knew not that zinc, one of its two sole constituents, had even an existence,—that is, as a metal ; although, as already remarked, the Chinese and Hindoos were an enlightened exception.

Brass has been most usually and easily made from copper and calamine, the latter an ore of zinc in which the metal is corroded and invisible, hence the ancient popular ignorance just noted. Strata or layers alternately of plate copper and of a mixture of calamine and charcoal,—the latter to absorb the corroding oxygen of the former ; or a mixture of granulated copper and the same ingredients, exposed till red heated, enables the metallic zinc to volatilise, or rise in vapour, and penetrate, or unite with, the copper, so as at once to form, according to the relative proportions of the materials, either some one of the varieties of brass, or other of its kindred alloys, such as pinchbeck, prince's metal, tombac. Or these varieties may readily be formed, or brass modified, by afterwards uniting the alloy, once got, with additional proportions either of copper or zinc. The metallic zinc, however, may also be at once united with copper by fusion, but the operation is critical.

The authorities whom we have consulted differ greatly as to the actual or best proportions of zinc and copper for making brass. English brass, according to Parkes, consists of one particle or atom of zinc and one of copper ; Dutch brass of one-zinc, two-copper. In the "Encyclopædia Britannica," however (supplement to latest edition) two of zinc to one of copper are stated as the best proportions. The heavier brass is, the more copper it contains, the lighter, the more zinc, as might be expected, zinc being the lighter metal. The specific gravity of brass, however, is greater than that of its separate metals. In Knight's "Cyclopædia" the process of formation, and the proportions of calamine, &c., are stated as follows—The copper is poured into water, and converted into shot copper, the metal being thus granulated into pieces from the size of small shot to that of a bean. Of this 45lb., to 60 lbs. of powdered calamine, and an equal quantity of charcoal, are put into earthen crucibles, and fire applied for seven or eight hours. By pouring the molten metal into shallow granite moulds, it is made to form plates of brass, which are afterwards rolled into thin sheets called latten. For bars, cast-iron moulds are also used.

Brass is more fusible than copper, and hence more easily cast. It is also much less liable to tarnish as well as considerably malleable and ductile, and may therefore be beat out into very thin leaves, and drawn into fine wire. The thin leaves called Dutch gold, or Dutch metal, are just brass beaten out into an imitation of gold-leaf. The 'yellow metal,' patented by Mr. Muntz, of Birmingham, and made into sheets thick enough for sheathing ships, in place of copper, is a composition of zinc (chiefly Belgian, we believe) and copper. Zinc itself, by the way, is now extensively used on the continent, and is even being introduced into this country, for a similar purpose.

Iron and zinc were, till lately, regarded as metals not easily united, on account of the volatility of the latter and the infusibility of the former. Dr. Graham, however, gave a different opinion : and, at all events, when plates of hot iron were dipped into a bath of melted zinc, it was found that an appearance of tin plate was acquired, and the iron thus prevented from rusting. This is the process whereby "galvanized iron" is said to be prepared. And it is a curious fact, that when zinc is even merely kept in contact with iron, it will protect the iron from rust, and thus iron nails may be used with zinc sheeting, though nails of zinc itself are best of all, inasmuch as all galvanic action is thus prevented, whereas even with iron, though the iron, as the less electro-positive or more electro-negative metal, will be protected by an exaltation of the negative, it must, or at least would be, at some small expense of zinc, from an equivalent increase of its tendency to oxidize, were it not that the first slight scurf of grey oxide on its surface forms a firm, resistive, and complete coat of mail, protecting itself from all further injury by oxidation from ordinary causes. Zinc, in fact, is thus a most singular and anomalous mass of contradictory properties. Chemically speaking, it so greedily devours oxygen, that it will strip even iron of it, yet we see how completely it can protect its own substance from this very tendency to oxidize, and this, too, from its very strength of affinity for oxygen. Chemically speaking it is so combustible, that it may be made to burn and blaze; and yet from its practical power to cover itself with a firm though thin shell or crust of stony or glassy oxide, and from the much stronger heat required to melt it, we have no doubt that it will constitute (though not a fire-*proof* material like iron or stone), a safer covering for roofs than lead at least; for though, where the ordinary inflammables have already originated a conflagration, it will much rather promote than retard the blaze, yet certainly it will protect the woodwork of roofs from sparks, and burning embers, &c., contributed by adjoining conflagrations, both by its surficial incrustation, and by its solidity in circumstances where lead would melt and disappear, exposing the timber beneath to the burning embers.*

Bronze is another of those alloys into the composition of which zinc essentially enters. Bronze is a composition of copper, zinc, and tin, and, like brass, is of ancient origin. Bronze vessels have been found at Nineveh and also at Herculaneum. With tin alone, too, zinc forms a useful alloy. In China and India various utensils and ornaments are made of zinc, inlaid with other metals. The 'white copper' of the Chinese is a composition of zinc, copper, and nickel, the zinc 7-16ths of the whole, and the remaining 9-16ths, of copper and nickel to each other as 5 to 13. The amalgam of zinc, or its alloy with mercury, is made by trituration in a mortar. This is the metaline substance which is spread over the rubber of the electrical

apparatus for creating electricity by friction. The use of zinc, also, in the galvanic circuit in connection with copper, has been already noted; but we may here remark that cast-iron, which contains the electro-negative carbon, was some time ago discovered to constitute for the negative or copper-plate in the galvanic circuit. With other artificial associations of zinc with metals we have still less to do than even with some of the preceding; but we may remark, in conclusion, that while 1-20th part of platinum destroys the malleability of zinc, the mere presence of molten iron in a crucible, side by side with molten gold, will render the gold quite brittle.

The metals with which zinc is naturally associated, and which also tend, as well as sulphur, to injure or destroy its malleability, are iron, lead, and arsenic. Probably the curious and anomalous fact, that impure, commercial, brittle, zinc, if heated to a certain temperature, will become malleable, and afterwards remain so even while cool, is attributable to arsenic or sulphur, which the heat may separate, these being both more volatile than zinc. A writer, however, remarks, that "a small per centage of iron is what renders most of the spelter, particularly English, unfit to roll."

NOTES IN THE PROVINCES.

The curious and interesting process, but seldom resorted to, of drawing sloping walls back to the perpendicular by means of iron rods heated and thus lengthened, and then screwed up to the outer side of the wall, cooled again, and thus shortened, pulling the declining wall back to the perpendicular, has just been carried out on the walls of Barrow Church, which were more than a foot out of the perpendicular. They were also underpinned with what was regarded as a firm foundation. Other restorations and improvements have been effected, both externally and internally, including a new open timber chancel roof of high pitch, with grey tiles, and new gables, above, and a solid body of concrete thrown in around the building below. Carved stalls, encaustic tiles, painted window glass, and other ornamental work have also been partially made use of in the restorations, which do not yet include the nave and other parts of this edifice.—Attempts to procure the erection of a corn exchange at Bedford have been renewed, 2,000l. being to be raised in 10l. shares for the purpose.—Roxton Church has been repaired at an expense of about 1,200l.—The Southampton Water Works Company have received the tenders called for for laying 1,050 yards lineal of cast-iron water- ipes. They were from Mr. Butler, 46l. 5s., and 9 d. per yard; Mr. Eyre, 75l. 10s., and 1s. per yard; Mr. Emmett, 49l. 15s. 6d., and 9d. per yard; Messrs. Gale and Coombs, 47l. 10s., and 10d. per yard; Mr. Weston, 39l. 14s., and 8d. per yard. The tender of Mr. T. Weston, of East-street, was of course accepted.—It has been resolved to erect a church at the village of Hucclecote, near Gloucester, from designs by Mr. John Jacques, architect.—Mr. Strong, builder, of Stow-on-the-Wold, has undertaken to refit the parish church at Hooknorton, Oxon, for 585l. Twelve firms, says the *Gloucester Chronicle*, competed; the highest offer was 895l.; the lowest 499l. 10s.—The parish church at Runcorn, re-erected at a cost of 10,000l., was consecrated on Thursday week before last.—An obituary stained glass window has been put up in the south aisle of the choir of Chester Cathedral, at a cost of 100l., by the dean of Chester.—Besides the district churches already built and projected at Sheffield, subscriptions have been opened for one at Moorfields. The Pitsmoor one is to be begun early in the spring. Two church-sites, one in Fenton-street and another in Coal-pit-lane, have been applied for to the town trustees. A sum has been offered towards the erection of a tower to the new church in Eldon-street.—The following is a return, by Mr. Rushton, the building-surveyor, of houses and warehouses erected, or in course of erection, within the borough of Liverpool, from 1st January to 31st December, 1848 :—74, under 12l. per annum; 506, from 12l. to 25l.; 48,

from 25l. to 35l.; 28, from 35l. and upwards; total, 656 houses, together with 6 warehouses. The houses erected since 1838 are as follows :—in 1835, 1,052; 1839, 997; 1840, 1,676; 1841, 1,761; 1842, 2,027; 1843, 1,390; 1,844, 2,450; 1845, 3,728; 1846, 3,460; 1847, 1,220; 1848, 656; total, 20,317.—The first stone of a bridge across the Don, at Sprotbro', near Doncaster, was laid by Lady Charlotte Copley, on Monday week. It will consist of seven arches, one of 100 feet span. Messrs. Waring, of Swinton, are the contractors.—The melodious voice of the great Peter Bell—not of Wordsworthian memory, but of York Cathedral tower—whose tongue has long lolled uselessly out of his capacious mouth, is now about to be made to tell the hours for behoof of all within hearing, by help of a weighty hammer, with clock-work power sufficient to strike him on the mouth with. The tenor in the other tower, in former use, is cracked.—On the Lancashire coast great damage has been done to property, particularly sea walls in Morecambe bay, by late strong gales and inundations of the sea. Even through the rise of the tide in the river Lune, the river overflowed, and inundated many houses and cellars, the promenade, and part of the North-Western Railway.—A water company in Sunderland supplies 400 poor families, *gratis*, with service pipes and water-taps in their houses, and with an unlimited supply of water at the rate of one penny per week. A model water company, indeed!—The workmen employed by the Derwent iron Company, says the *Gateshead Observer*, have subscribed 50l. towards the erection of the new district church at Shotley-bridge.—Since the opening of the Newcastle Baths and Washhouses, in September, warm baths have been taken by 3,000 males and 260 females; plunge bath by 2,246. The washhouses have been attended by 1,341 persons.—A new hospital for children is about to be erected at Edinburgh, with money bequeathed by a Mr. Daniel Stewart, and now amounting to 90,000l. How many more?

RAILWAY JOTTINGS.

A correspondent, "A. S. S., Railway Inspector, Knaresborough," suggests that, for the protection of the boxes for facing points, from dust, rain, snow, &c., a cover with a short slip for the handle, over the long one in which it works, should be locked upon it, unless when worked, in which case it might he so adjusted as to be readily pushed back, to allow the free working of the handle till again drawn over the open slip, and locked as before.—Under Lord Campbell's Act regarding compensation in railway accidents an important case has just been settled by jury at Dundee, in which a Mrs. Cargill laid damages at 5,000l. for the loss of her husband, a farmer. The Company (the Dundee and Perth) compromised the case by settling 75l. a year on the widow for life.—"A case," says the *Cambridge Chronicle*, "was lately decided in one of the courts by which it is now ruled that husbands who lose their wives by railway accidents can only claim, in compensation, the amount of any income which may have been cut short by their death. Thus, 'virtuous accidents,' who were only crowns to their husbands,' will be valued, according to the tombstone cutter's rule, at five shillings. It has been suggested that at railway stations, beside the 'ladies' refreshment room,' there should be a 'ladies' valuation room,' with a proper officer in attendance. As the ladies pass, scenes of the following tenor, it is supposed, would pass also. 'What sort of a wife are you, ma'am?' — 'Sir?' 'Of what value are you to your husband?' — 'Your question is very impertinent, Sir. I believe, although I did not bring my husband a shilling, he would be filled with deep sorrow were he to lose me.' 'O, we have nothing to do with that, ma'am—sorrow does not enter into railway calculations. You may pass.' Another enters — 'Pray, ma'am, how does your husband estimate you?' 'You are as great a brute as my husband, I believe, and that is saying a great deal. I bring him ten thousand a year, which goes back to my relations if I die, as we have no children, and yet the wretch uses me worse than ——.' 'Station-master! quick, quick! Get a special train instantly for this lady, and let a pilot engine go before, and a guardian angel behind!'"——The South-Eastern trains now run right into the harbour terminus at Folkestone, to the steam-boat station, greatly to the discontent of some, though to the equal convenience of others. A great swing bridge has been thrown across the quay constructed for this purpose. The Company are about to enlarge their station accommodation there, with a view of making Folkestone their great water terminus.——The great North-Western is about to be converted into a huge circulating library, provided with all sorts of mental provender, 'to be consumed on the premises,' in transitu or rather in circuitu. Mr. Huish, the manager, it is said, is entitled to the merit of the suggestion, and at same time, in order to effect a circulation not only of books but of cash, the whole of the stations on the line are to be 'undertaken'—for a very considerable consideration doubtless—by one party, namely, Messrs. Smith and Son, of the Strand. The passenger will have no more to do than merely to select his book at a station-stall, paying the price of it in the meantime—and, after travelling any time or distance on the line, will receive back his cash, less a trifle for perusal, on returning his book at either the same or any other stall. The idea is really a good one, and useful to the public; and when it is considered that six millions of passengers travel annually over the 500 miles of the North-Western, assuredly it ought to be a profitable one, both to the Company and their librarians.——The dividend of the North-Western, to be declared at next meeting, says *Herepath*, will be, we hear, at the rate of 7 per cent., leaving a surplus of 80,000*l*. The dividend of the Lancashire and Yorkshire will be 6 per cent.; that of Berwick 7 per cent., with a surplus of nearly 100,000*l*.; the York and North Midland 7; the Eastern Counties is variously reported, from 5s. upwards.——Mr. Andrews, Q.C., has awarded 148*l*. to one farmer and 145*l*. to another, for damage done to buildings and corn-stacks adjoining the Eastern Counties at Needingworth, fired by burning coke from the tunnel of the engine of the mail train.——The railway-station at the village of Hatfield Peveril, on the Eastern Counties line, about three miles from Witham, has been destroyed by fire. Being small, and built of wood, it was speedily reduced to ashes, together, it is said, with books, tickets, and everything belonging to it, the brick chimney only being left standing. How the fire originated remains a mystery. But the *Ipswich Express* suggests that a cinder from the mail-train may have been the cause, though not likely, from the fact that it passes on the line farthest from the station. It is rather remarkable, adds the same authority, that the company had desired to take down this station altogether, and that considerable hostility had very naturally been shown by the inhabitants of Hatfield at the risk of being subjected to such inconvenience.——On the Liverpool and Bury line recent heavy rains are to blame for considerable damage to works. In many places the embankments have been injured by large portions of earth being washed from the slopes; but more serious mischief has resulted from the same cause, particularly at Wigan, in the partial destruction of an arch over the river Douglas. It is supposed that the headlong current of the Douglas undermined the foundations, and produced this disaster. A breakwater has now been formed in the middle of the river, to destroy the force with which, during heavy rain, it rushes through the arch. Some other bridges have been slightly impaired, and are being strengthened and renewed. A similar arch to the one over the Douglas has since given way at Weethoughton, according to the *Wigan Herald*.——The affairs of the Waterford and Kilkenny Company are now in a condition verging on bankruptcy, with receipts for the last eighteen weeks of only 700*l*., whilst the expenditure amounts to 1,700*l*. This company has raised and expended 250,000*l*., and also a loan of 30,000*l*. obtained from Government.——The first section of the Demerara Railway has just been opened, and the planters are availing themselves largely of the facilities it affords for the transmission of sugar, &c., from their estates.——An electric telegraph is about to be erected between Berlin, Cologne, and Frankfort-on-the-Maine.

FALL OF RAILWAY ARCHES AT MANCHESTER.

On Saturday week one of the brick arches of the North-Western's "Manchester, South Junction, and Altrincham" line of railway, adjoining Gloucester-street, Oxford-road, Manchester, gave way, and on the ensuing Thursday was followed by two more. The first fell while the centering was in course of removal, but the two latter had not had their centering at all loosened. By the fall of the first, three bricklayer's labourers were killed, and an inquest was therefore held on the bodies, at which it appeared in evidence that the arches which fell were to adjoin a central iron arch in widening the station works over Gloucester-street, and from a turn in the line at that point they were built somewhat askew. The dimensions of the first that fell were 40 feet span in the widest part, with a spring of 8 feet, the thickness of the brickwork being 2 ft. 9 in. It had been built about a month, and was supported by a centering of 12 ribs. Four of these had been removed, when a portion of the arch about 18 feet long at one end, and 7 feet at the other, suddenly gave way.

Mr. George Shoreland, the corporation surveyor, gave it as his opinion that the arch had buckled up just above the spandrils on one side. He had no doubt the centres of the arch were correct before the brickwork was laid. The work had been grouted in the usual way with thin mortar, which would render the work more substantial. The fall, he conceived, was entirely accidental.

Mr. G. C. Pauling, civil engineer and railway contractor, said: From a very careful examination of the work and materials, I think they are as good as could be put together. In my opinion, the mortar was composed of one-and-a-half part sand to one part of lime in the arch, and of two-and-a-half parts sand to one of lime in the spandril, but it is difficult to speak with accuracy after the action of the air upon the mortar for a month or six weeks. I believe the cause of the falling of the arch was the recent wet weather. On taking out the outside ribs they would throw a greater weight on the narrow side of the arch, from the backing of the wide end being much heavier. This caused the end to buckle and fall in a mass in Gloucester-street. My opinion is strengthened by the fact that a fracture has taken place in a parallel line with the ribs of the centre.

Mr. William Edwards, joiner, builder, and contractor, said that, taking into consideration the recent wet weather, three weeks were long enough for the centres to be under the arch. I have examined the mortar, which seems to be good, and sufficient for the purpose. I consider it is fully as good as is usually made, and that more care has been taken of it than usual, after having gone through a certain process. Each brick would absorb about a pound of water, and the weight of the moisture, no doubt, pressed the bricks down, and caused the arch to give way.

The jury returned the following verdict:—"That the men were accidentally killed when removing the centres from underneath an arch by the falling in of a portion of the arch, rendered insecure by the recent wet weather."

The contractors for this portion of the works are Messrs. David Bellhouse and Son, who are said to have hitherto escaped all fatal or considerable accident in the progress of their contract.

PATENT RIGHTS—CHIMNEY FLUES.

For the encouragement of arts, and the security of inventors of original discovery, or the application to useful purposes of what may not be even novel in itself, those privileges granted by the Crown are supposed to afford ample protection to the patentee; on looking, however, a little below the surface, we may easily discover the fact that the originator of an useful theory in science or invention in art is frequently thrown out of his justly acquired merits, and debarred from its reward by others, who either boldly pirate or adapt his conceptions to a slightly modified arrangement.

About eight years back, the writer of this article took out a patent for building in the solid walls circular flues of iron-stone-ware, or terra-cotta; he applied them in structures, and found them to answer the purposes of a perfect draught for the smoke and the obviation of concreted soot in chimneys: the material being hard, solid, and extremely durable, resisting the action of both fire and water, he also applied the same tubes for sewers.

The heat acquired and generated in the chimney accelerated the draught, whilst the smooth surface gave a free flow to the sullage, and the circular form admitted of no deposit.

Having incurred the expense of 120*l*. for the patent, &c., and 500*l*. more for a quantity of the material, which he had conveyed from Burslem, in Staffordshire, to a wharf at Belgrave Basin, London, he then published a pamphlet, and dispersed it widely amongst the architects and builders of the kingdom; from whom some orders and large acknowledgments and admissions of utility were received.

It should be here mentioned that a circular tube of 7 inches in diameter, for conveying the ashes from every stage of a building to a pit in the basement, formed part of the patented application (for a tube can hardly be called an invention). Well, for three years, the wharf was kept open for the sale of the materials, at only 10 per cent. profit on the cost price; a clerk was paid for that period, and yet not more than half of the supply on hand (only 500*l*. worth) was consumed or bought.

It may be supposed that the patented invention was not brought into use—but such was not the fact—for in her Majesty's Palace (Buckingham) they were applied, as they were also in all Mr. Cubitt's, Mr. Seth Smith's, and other wholesale builders' cities of mansions; and they are now applied, or being used, in all the clubs, mansions, Houses of Parliament, or palaces that we see springing up, and assuming the most ornate exteriors that art and expense can accomplish.

Complainant saw all this, and did complain; but he was told to seek an injunction in chancery.

After expending 1,000*l*. on the adventure, he was in no humour to embroil himself further; having been already seven years in that court, and sunk in its morasses 10,000*l*. and upwards in costs only.

At length, however, he submitted to the Commissioners of Sewers samples of his ware, as admirably adapted to sewage: his views were adopted, and suggestions approved—and the honourable Commissioners gave him 100*l*. for the residue of the flues (9 inches in diameter), which had cost him twice that sum. The office of Sewers has since adopted the plan, finding it eminently effective, but have discovered some other market for the commodity—having never given, nor offered, a contract to their slighted illuminator.

As the natural patron of arts, artists, science, and practical utility, The Builder is appealed to for publicity to these wrongs, if not for aid in their redress. "*Sic vos non vobis*" was the plaint of the poet long before copyrights or patents were thought of; edificates *apes* (which you may pronounce as you like) might be added by your correspondent, Quondam.

I would send you a specimen of my patent flues, but they are now patent in every street in London where sewers are being repaired, and in every large house in progress of construction.

METROPOLITAN COMMISSION OF SEWERS.

A special court was held on the 23rd ult., at the house, Greek-street; the Hon. Frederick Byng in the chair.

The late Cases of Cholera at Tooting.—In pursuance of a resolution passed at the last court, the committee, consisting of Capt. Veitch, R.E., Capt. Dawson, R.E., Mr. Johnson, Mr. Hutton, and Mr. Hawes, inspected the whole of the drainage of Tooting, on Friday last, and this day presented their report to the court. The conclusion arrived at by the committee was, that it would be inexpedient to remove the penstocks altogether, as exposing the sullage and fœtid matter to atmospheric exhalation would increase rather than diminish the evil. The committee recommended some temporary measures of relief till the adoption of some general and uniform system of drainage. The report being received,

Mr. C. Johnson said that, as one of the committee, he wished to state in open court, that the committee were struck with the carelessness—if not the recklessness—of any public body, in the choice of such a place as they saw for the alms-houses of St. Clement Danes, which appeared to have been purchased at an expense of 400*l*. per acre, with an offensive open ditch close by the property. This work, commenced in error, was defended on the ground that the parish of St. George, Southwark, were in treaty for the adjoining field for a similar purpose. He deprecated this carelessness—he would not call it by a stronger name—in this total disregard of public health, and he had felt it his duty to bring the matter before the court, as a caution to other bodies in their choice of sites for building.

Dr. Southwood Smith, in an able speech, called the attention of the court to a particular case, as an exemplar of a class of cases which appeared to him to require the immediate and earnest attention of the commission. The General Board of Health have directed one of their medical superintending inspectors, Mr. Grainger, together with Dr. Arthur Farre, to examine the present condition of the workhouses of the metropolis, and more especially the state of the various establishments for pauper children, such as that at Tooting. The very first report made by these gentlemen on the establishments for pauper children, contains a representation as to the Norwood House of Industry for children in connection with the parish of Lambeth, showing, amongst other points, the existence of an open ditch in the neighbourhood, formed by the drains of the establishment: that immediately after a severe storm, in August, 1846, when the drains were overflowed, 120 of the children were seized with opthalmia in the course of three days, and that since improvements were made in the privies, opthalmia, previously a prominent and prevailing disease among the children, had nearly disappeared. The time may be short (said Dr. Smith) that is left us to labour at the work of prevention, and one of the most obvious means of prevention is the immediate removal from the close neighbourhood of dwelling houses of such nuisances as that in question. I therefore move, "that the surveyor inspect the open ditch near the Norwood House of Industry, and report to the Committee of Works thereon." I earnestly hope (he continued) that we may be spared any further visitation of cholera; but we cannot conceal from ourselves that it is hovering over us, and that it may swoop down upon us at any instant.

Mr. Broderip seconded the motion, and it was ultimately carried.

Resolutions were passed that two additional assistant surveyors be appointed at salaries of 250*l.* per annum; and that all future appointments be for one year only, at the expiration of which time they are to be re-considered.

The Drainage of the New Palace at Westminster.—The clerk read a document from Mr. Barry, on the subject of the drainage of the new Houses of Parliament, the pith of which has already appeared in our pages.

Mr. Bullar said this question reminded him of a controversy that took place in France, commencing in pamphlets, and ending in volumes, and he wished to know where this controversy was to end.—Mr. Broderip said, where two gentlemen were at issue so much, a lawyer would say let a jury come at once.—The Rev. W. Stone said it was most important the principles contained in the two systems should be properly ascertained.

Mr. Leslie thought any money spent on this subject well bestowed, to show the value of the two systems, and moved, "That at the request of Mr. Barry, and for the advantage of the public, the charges made by Mr. Austin, with Mr. Barry's reply, be printed in juxtaposition, together with the subsequent rejoinders of both these gentlemen."—Motion put and agreed to.

Miscellanea.

"Artists' Conversazione."—The first, for the present session, of the series of conversazioni, given annually under this title at the Freemasons' Tavern, was held on the 27th ult. Amongst the works of art exhibited were a charming drawing of "Fox-Gloves," by Mrs. Withers; a nice little picture, in Topham's style, by Mr. J. H. Mole; and a portfolio of sketches by the same artist; a clever miniature by Miss Cole; and a drawing in the Temple Church, by her sister Miss E. Cole. Mr. E. A. Goodall exhibited an interior, more like some recent works of his brother than his paintings are usually, and a portfolio of sketches. There were also a set of sketches in Tasmania, by Mr. Skinner Prout; illustrations of the Collegiate Church of the Holy Trinity, at Edinburgh, by Mr. D. Wilson; and other interesting matters. This association has now been in existence about twenty years, and is the root whence sprung "The Graphic,"—but it has pursued the even tenour of its useful way so quietly that it is less known than many bodies of more recent establishment. The want of a more distinctive title, too, has perhaps had something to do with this.

Monument to Picton.—The monument erected at Carmarthen to the memory of Picton is at last completed. According to the *Cambrian*, which terms it a monument of bad management, it is a clumsy disproportioned pyramid, manifesting by the rapid tapering of the shaft that the cash of the managers was exhausted, or that the builder was tired of his job. At the base run out four promontories, from each of which a large cannon, with feeble carriage, frowns on passengers as they approach what they may mistake for the chimney of a manufactory.

Suspension Bridge at Pesth.—The bridge which is erected over the Danube at Pesth, was commenced in 1840, according to the designs and under the direction of William Tierney Clark, civil engineer, and has just been completed at a cost of 650,000*l.* This bridge has a clear waterway of 1250 feet, the centre span or opening being 670 feet. The height of the suspension towers from the foundation is 200 feet, being founded in 50 feet of water. The sectional area of the suspending chains is 520 square inches of wrought iron, and the total weight of the same 1,300 tons.

Preservation of Books.—About 25 years ago I was annoyed by finding the backs of several rows of books, some in a bookcase having glazed doors, which were kept locked, and others on adjoining open shelves, frequently mildewed. Wiping them carefully cleaned them only for a time, for fresh crops of mildew speedily disfigured them again. Remembering to have seen my father, who always made his own ink, finish off by pouring a small glass of spirits of wine into the ink jar, in order to prevent its becoming mouldy, I lightly washed over the backs and covers of the books with spirits of wine, using, as a brush, the feather of a goose-quill. I frequently saw the books during the next five years, and I have occasionally seen them since, and there has not, so far as I am aware, been a single spot of mildew on them since the spirits of wine were applied. I have used spirits of wine to prevent mildew with equally good effect in other cases. N. R.

The Louvre.—The Minister of Public Works, M. Vivien, has prepared an elaborate report of the present condition of the Louvre, for necessary repairs and embellishments, as well as opening other saloons. The sum required for the present year is 200,000 francs, and 1,800,000 for the following one. The report is at considerable length; the principal features being—1st, The entire reconstruction of the roof of the grand gallery, to admit the light from the top, and to close the side windows. 2nd, To redecorate and alter the disposition of the *Grand Salon*, and the *Salon des Sept Cheminées*. 3rd, The entire reparation of the Gallery of Apollo. In the budget for the present year, the first item is calculated to cause an expenditure of 160,000 francs. The redecoration of the *Grand Salon* is estimated at 600,000 francs; the *Salon des Sept Cheminées* is set down at 400,000 francs; and finally, the expenses calculated to restore the Gallery of Apollo at 1,000,000 francs. In consequence of this report, a commission was nominated to consider the proposition, and on its meeting, in the Hall of the Institute, most of the distinguished artists of Paris were present. The plan given by M. Dubau, the architect, was the subject of a very learned discussion. The style of ornamentation especially was investigated. M. Ingres proposed a red ground, with very rich decorative details; his opinion was strongly enforced by Messieurs Drolling and Horace Vernet. M. Delacroix suggested a more sober colour as the ground, with very slight ornament. It was remarked that good colourists had always preferred a ground that would lower the lustre of tints, and render their brilliancy more harmonious by opposition with a positive vivid colour; while, on the other hand, it was agreed that where colour was not the characteristic of artistic works, a more unobtrusive ground would give them due advantage. The proposition of Messieurs Ingres and Horace Vernet obtained the suffrages of the commission, and was finally adopted.—*Art Journal.**

* The new number of the *Art-Journal*, with two fine engravings from the Vernon Gallery, and a profusion of other illustrations, is quite a marvel in periodical literature.

Projected Works.—Advertisements have been issued for tenders, by 18th February, for building a new savings' bank and a new market-hall and corn-exchange, at Lichfield; by 20th, for the erection of a house at Harbledown; by 8th, for erecting prisoners' cells, kitchen offices, infirmary, boundary wall, &c., at the county jail, Huntingdon; by 21st, for the various works to be done in the erection of the poor's hospital new buildings and offices at Paisley; by 6th, for the erection of a parsonage-house and offices at Ripon; and by 6th, for a survey of the town of Abingdon, Berks, and a report of the expense of draining the same by proper and efficient sewerage.

Gas: Reductions in the Price, &c.—In consequence of past reductions at Doncaster, the consumption has so much increased that the Company have declared their intention, on that special ground, to repeat the experiment, by a further reduction to 4s. 7d. per 1,000 cubic feet.——The Cambridge shareholders appear to have now also as hopeful a prospect before their eyes in determining to carry out the like principle. They have just announced a reduction from 7s. to 6s., and the chairman "also stated that the committee of management had reason to hope that ultimately no town in the kingdom, of comparative size and population, would be lighted by gas at a less expense than Cambridge."——At Fareham, on the contrary, the company have the stupidity to refuse to reduce their price *to* 7s. 6d., while the consumers have not only determined not to pay more, but have been offered a supply at 5s. 6d.——The company at Brigg have reduced their price from 10s. to 8s. 4d., with the "hope that there will be an increase of private consumers," which there doubtless will be, though only to an extent equivalent to the smallness of the reduction, or rather to the largeness of the remainder. They had already supplied the railway station at 5s., exclusive of pipes and fittings.——It is proposed to light the shire hall at Chelmsford from gas jets outside the windows, a principle which we learn has been adopted in other court houses with excellent effect, both in brilliancy and comfort.——A petition to the Commons is in progress at Birmingham, according to the *Journal*, praying them to enact that all gas meters shall be properly proved and inspected, as measures generally are, and that the irresponsibility of companies, or of those by whom meters are supplied, as well as the liability of meters to register incorrectly, may be thus or otherwise properly checked. Mr. N. Scholfield, M.P., is to introduce a bill in the forthcoming session to remedy this evil.

Improvement of Open Spaces.—With reference to the suggestions for laying out Kennington-common, and the improvement of Camberwell-green, in your last number, allow me to suggest for further comment, that many wide spaces and thoroughfares round London are easily susceptible of similar improvement: Whitechapel-road, Islington, Blackfriars-road, and the various so called greens might be planted and systematically laid out, so as to present a pleasing aspect and healthy promenade, and that at comparatively trifling expense. In many of the narrowest roads, the small gardens in front of the houses should be purchased for the widening of the thoroughfares before the value is enhanced by their being converted into shops,—a process which is rapidly taking place in all the roads leading to the metropolis. In short, a public inspector ought to be appointed for the better regulation of such matters; it would not fail ultimately to save the public from great inconvenience as well as expense. For while we are going to great expense in widening some thoroughfares, we are suffering others to be as fast closed up.—Footpad.

Large Casting.—A cylinder, 95 inches in diameter and 10 feet stroke, was cast yesterday afternoon, at the Novelty Works, in presence of a large number of persons, who had been invited to witness the operation. No less than 25,000 lbs. of molten iron were used for the casting, which, when finished, will be about 20,000 lbs. This is, probably, the largest and heaviest casting of the kind ever made; and is for the first of Collins's line of sea-steamers, which are now in a great state of forwardness, two of which, we learn, will be launched early in January.—*American Paper.*

DESTRUCTION OF A LARGE GASHOLDER.
—At the Edinburgh Gas Company's Works,
on Thursday week, a new telescopic gasholder
tilted over by the breaking of a guide rod, and
by the friction, or otherwise, exploded, or at least
set fire to, the gas, of which it contained nearly
300,000 cubic feet, being the largest gasholder
in Scotland—40 feet in depth and 100 feet in
diameter. Both gas and gasholder were
destroyed, and the loss is estimated at about
2,000l. The adjoining houses, windows, &c.,
were considerably injured.

**STEAM-BOILER EXPLOSIONS IN THE
UNITED STATES.**—A report has just been
presented to Congress, upon the subject of
explosions in American steam-boilers. The
report includes the number of accidents of
this character from 1816 to 1848, and shows
a total of 233 explosions, calculated from
the average of the given cases.—Pecuniary
loss—233 cases, at 13,302 dollars each,
3,099,366 dollars.—Loss of life—11 each,
2,563.—Wounded—9 each, 2,097=total killed
and wounded, 4,660.

CURIOUS INVENTION.—Mr. Coupland, of
Skellingthorpe, near Lincoln, has just produced a very curious invention, for the purpose
of preventing the strong glare of the sun's
light being cast upon windows which front the
south.

MEDIÆVAL REMAINS.—The original floor
of the ancient refectory at Durham has been
discovered. About a foot and a half below
the joists was an uniform surface of rubbish,
on removing a portion of which, to the depth
of about 3 feet, the workmen struck upon the
floor of the ancient refectory. It is composed
of plain red encaustic tiles, about 10 inches
square, and of much rougher composition
than is now deemed requisite.—*Sunderland
Herald.*

WESTMINSTER ABBEY.—The following
extract from the *Northampton Mercury*, of
more than a hundred years since, will interest
some of our readers:—" London, February
23, 1722-3.— The rebuilding of Solomon's
porch and the rest of the north front of
Westminster Abbey is now finish'd, according
to the model of the old building of the Gothick
order; and the workmanship, in the opinion of
competent judges, is reckon'd very beautiful
and curious, in which the moderns have not
only equal'd, but even exceeded the ancients
in their own manner of architecture. The
great window of 32 foot square in the front
is likewise glazed with glass curiously painted
after the Antique fashion, by Mr. Price, who
is reckon'd the only artist in England capable
of doing it; so that that ornamental art is not
so entirely lost as some have alleg'd."

" TOM STEELE " AN ENGINEER.—Tom
Steele, the devoted follower of O'Connell,
whose melancholy end a short time since our
readers will remember, was an associate of the
Institute of Civil Engineers. In a memoir of
him which was given at the general meeting of
the Institution, mentioned last week, it was
said that his attention being directed to the
bad state of the navigation of the river Shannon,
he determined to make a personal survey of
the bed of the river, which he did in the most
complete manner, employing sometimes very
original means; such, for instance, as stopping
along the line of a reef or shoal, supporting
himself with one hand upon the stern of a
boat, whilst he measured and recorded all the
inequalities of the surface, and ascertained the
nature of the rock or ground. An account of
this survey was published by him; and no
greater proof of its utility can be given than
the fact of the greater portion of his suggestions having been followed in the works that
have been since executed. His attention being
thus directed to the diving hell, he devised
several alterations in its construction and application; particularly a method of lighting the
divers during their submarine labours. All
these, with many similar subjects, were published in the current periodicals of the day,
and some of them were communicated to the
Institution. At a later period, a favourite
theme upon which he repeatedly addressed the
Institution was the purchase of the birth-place
of Sir Isaac Newton, and its preservation to
the scientific world, in the same manner that
Shakspeare's house has since been obtained by
the exertions of literary and dramatic men.

MEETINGS OF SCIENTIFIC BODIES

Held during the ensuing week.

MONDAY, Feb. 5.—Institute of Architects, 8 P.M.
TUESDAY, 6.—Institution of Civil Engineers, 8 P.M.
WEDNESDAY, 7.—Society of Arts, 8 P.M.
THURSDAY, 8.—Royal Society, 8½ P.M.; Society of Anti-
quaries, 8 P.M.
FRIDAY, 9.—Archæological Association 8½ P.M.

TO CORRESPONDENTS.

Received.—" C. N.," " Antiquity," " J. H.," " Fair
Play," " Tartan" (yes), " A. R.," " H. P.," " An Old
Mason," " An Old Subscriber," " T. B. L.," " J. G.,"
" C. F." (next week), " W. F.," " Trader" (that appear),
" G. W." (next week), " Looked-on," " G. M. T.,"
" R. G.," " J J.," " W. H. S.," " H. M'C." (yes), " E.
T. B.," " J. C." (a filter so formed above ground would
doubtless answer. We are promised a relief from Norwich),
" Young Plasterer" (we do not understand his question),
" An Architect," " F. V. C." (copy shall be sent), " A Sub-
scriber," " H. W. B." (we cannot advise our correspondents
to take the step he speaks of: architectural modellers find
little employment), " End of Amateur" (thanks for the
suggestion and friendly tone), " J. G." (Manton), " Mr.
W.," " E. S." (thanks—next week), " An Architect"
(make out a bill for the business actually, estimating time,
&c., employed). " The Gold Seeker's Manual," by David
Ansted, M.A. (Van Voorst, Lond. 1849); " Con. Cregan,"
No. II.; " The Family Friend," I. and II.

ADVERTISEMENTS.

No. CCCXIV.

'ATURDAY, FEBRUARY 10, 1849.

HE Superintending Inspectors appointed by the Board of Health are actively proceeding in their inquiries, shifting from town to town, receiving evidence, and making general examinations of the cality. We have before us a pile of the ridence offered in different quarters, several ommunications on the subject, and not a few iquests that we should let the London public now what is going on in this respect. The umber and extent of the inquiries (though in ome cases, we may say in parenthesis, not by ny means extensive enough, being conducted a what may be called the "touch and go" ystem), would prevent us from doing so at ny length, even if we were certain that the najority of our readers would be pleased by uch a course. We will refer, however, to ome of the principal points elicited during wo or three of the more recent inquiries.

The bad condition of *Lancaster* in respect of .ealth has been known for some time. Professor)wen, in his startling report on this place, .ublished in the " Second Report of the Commissioners for inquiring into the state of large owns,"* put a mark upon it, which rendered ny further proof that remedies are required here unnecessary. Mr. Smith, of Deanston, /as the inspector appointed to attend there, nd he opened the inquiry at the end of last 1onth. The present mayor of Lancaster is 1r. Edmund Sharpe, architect, who is .nown to many of our readers by his fine book, Architectural Parallels," on the merits of 'hich we spoke at some length not very long go, and this gentleman went very fully into the .ubject, and gave a large amount of evidence, ot merely in his capacity of mayor, but as .presentative of a local committee of health.

Hear, however, first, what Mr. Grant, the iperintendant registrar of the district, said, as the rate of mortality there. Omitting the .natic asylum and workhouse, so far as ncerns paupers not belonging to Lancaster, makes the deaths 28·96 per annum in ery thousand, or one in every 37. " The aths in the rural parts of the district are out 17 per annum per thousand, showing an :cess of deaths in Lancaster of 130 per num." He found some time since that the erage age at death in Lancaster was about *enty-eight years*, while in the other part of the strict it is about *thirty-five years*. As regards e infantile mortality of the working class, he und that about 15 per cent. of the deaths of at class are under six months old, about 44 ider five years, and nearly 50 per cent. under 1 years.

Mr. Sharpe drew the inspector's attention to r. Owen's report, already alluded to, and)ecially to a diagram in it, representing the eam of life in three columns, which it is possible not to view, in connection with the .te of things, without the deepest regret that little has been done to improve the health the town, and particularly the health of the orer classes. This diagram, as the witness

* 8vo. edition, vol. ii., p. 71.

pointed out, represents the duration of life in three classes of the inhabitants of Lancaster respectively,—the gentry, the tradesmen, and the operatives,—and it appears from these returns that of every hundred that are born among the gentry, eighty-five live, on the average, to the age of ten years. In other words, it takes ten years to kill off fifteen individuals. How long does it take to kill off the same number among the working classes? According to the same return, only six months! Again, how many of the hundred survive to the age of thirty? Amongst the gentry, 72; amongst the operatives, 36, or one-half the former! Making due allowance for the many other causes that depress the state of health of the young of the poorer classes, it is impossible for us to close our eyes to the probability that the state of the atmosphere in which they live is one of the most important and fatal of those causes. This report was published in 1845, and two years and upwards passed over, continued the witness, without a remedial step of any kind having been taken to abate the shocking state of things so circumstantially described by him. He did not desire to impute blame, but nothing had been done, and eight weeks ago the town was in the same state that it was five years ago. One main point dwelt upon by the witness,— referring both to the sewers and wells of Lancaster, and which will scarcely be credited, even by those accustomed to hear of extraordinary things in matters of this nature,—was, that the whole of the substratum upon which the town of Lancaster stands is strongly impregnated with the sewage of the town. "This is a startling assertion, but the fact is as I say. It is the common practice of builders in Lancaster to carry down the cesspools from water-closets and privies until they reach the gravel; and having done so, to provide no overflow, the whole of the sewage being drained off by the gravel. It frequently happens, that persons opening their cesspools after the lapse of several years, and expecting to find them full, have found them, to their great surprise, entirely empty. The whole contents have gone into the gravelly substratum in which the wells of the whole town are situated. The water in Lancaster is believed by many to be good. There may be isolated instances of good water, under peculiar circumstances of protection to the well, but no analysis that has ever yet been made, gives other than most unsatisfactory results. What has been here said of cesspools applies equally to sewers, public and private, many of which are built with dry walling at the sides, and none of which are water-tight." He then handed in analyses of the water from various wells, made by proper parties, as the foundation of his assertions. Other witnesses corroborated the statement.

Mr. Johnson, a medical man of the town, said that much of what the mayor had stated was fallacious ; but afterwards, when giving connected evidence, he said nothing but what was confirmatory of the general statements of the miserable condition of the town in a sanitary point of view.

Evidence was given of the positive occurrence of fever through the stoppage of drains, and of its cessation when the stoppage was removed ; of the evils of the window-tax, and the mischief caused by damp paths and roads with a decomposing surface.

We do not find, however, that any material inquiry into the state of the burial-grounds took place,—a circumstance much to be regretted. It does seem most strange that, in

spite of the overwhelming amount of evidence which exists proving the death-dealing character of over-crowded burial-grounds in towns, this most important matter is constantly shuffled out of sight by those in power. The victim cannot point to the spot and say, " Here I took the poison;" circumstantial evidence is disregarded, and deaths are looked upon as part of an inevitable course of events, which ought not to have occurred for years, and would not but, for our suicidal disregard of undeniable facts.

At *Whitehaven*, Mr. Rawlinson has been conducting the inquiry; and there Dr. Falcon gave evidence relative to the crowded state of St. Nicholas's, or the old church-yard. He had lived opposite it twenty years, and during that period his family, he said, had suffered greatly from sickness, which he principally attributed to the noxious air which emanated from the church-yard.

The great want complained of here and elsewhere, was an adequate supply of pure water. Mr. Clarke, surgeon, agreeing in this, said something might nevertheless be done by making drains and sewers. The importance of proper sewers might be shown by a case which had come within his own practice as a surgeon. He had been called to attend a case of dysentery, which had arisen from the imperfect state of a drain in George-street, which ran under the lobby of the house of his patient, and was covered only with thin boards. The effluvia arising from the sewer had made the whole of the inhabitants—four persons—exceedingly ill. Two of the cases terminated in death ; and, subsequently, he had been called in to attend the other two with fever!

At *Leicester*, Mr. Ranger was the inspector engaged, and much anxiety seems to have been shewn on the part of the inhabitants to give information, and obtain a satisfactory result. The inspector referred, in his opening address, to the comparative average duration of life at Leicester and Billesdon at the last census, from which he said it appeared that the total average loss of life to every individual in Leicester, as compared with the inhabitants of Billesdon, was 12½ years ; and taking the population into account, with the average of wages at 7s. per week, the total loss in labour had been to this town no less than 90,000*l.* since that time. It was shewn by witnesses that the houses in which the women were engaged in stocking-making were ill-ventilated—in some cases back to back without through air; that the cesspools were often dug down to the springs, to avoid necessity for cleansing out, by which means the water was poisoned ; and that the drainage, even in the best parts of the town, was most defective.

As to the supply of water, which will be insisted on by the Central Board here and elsewhere, the inspector said he would at once state that it is intended, in the sanitary regulations to be made, to have a full and constant supply of water, and perfect drainage : there is to be no *intermission* of the supplies of water—it will be constantly laid on to each house, and the sewerage will not be allowed to remain in a quiescent state. Indeed, he thought there could be no effectual drainage without an unceasing supply of water ; it would be folly to attempt it without. The proper supply of water is, therefore, a matter determined upon.

At Leeds the town council have absurdly determined, by a majority of one, to postpone the consideration of the sewerage of the town for *six months*. If it can be proved hereafter that death has occurred through want of efficient drainage, the council ought to be indicted for manslaughter.——At *Gateshead*, Mr. Dobson, architect, has been called in to advise as to the best mode of sewering the main thoroughfare.——And at *Lincoln*, Mr. Giles, engineer, is preparing plans, by direction of the corporation, for a system of underground sewers.*

A striking evidence of the effect of locality, and improved structural arrangements, on the health of the inhabitants of towns, has just appeared in the shape of a report from Hamburgh, by Mr. Grainger.† The fire of 1842 led to the re-arrangement of the greater part of the town, and under the direction of Mr. Lindley, engineer, the water supply, drainage, laying out of the streets, &c., have been carefully attended to. The result is said to be a diminution of disease to a considerable extent, and an exemption from cholera particularly, during the visitation of the present year, as remarkable as it is important.

The facts given in this report afford an additional confirmation of the great principle established by former researches—"that amidst the town populations the cholera visits with most severity the same class of persons and the same places, and is governed by similar circumstances, as typhus." "The firm establishment of this position is of infinite moment, inasmuch as by bringing cholera into the same category as low fever, no one accustomed to these inquiries would doubt that as certainly as the per-centage of typhus decreases with improved drainage, paving, and ventilation, so also will epidemic cholera. The proof of this has been afforded on a grand scale at Hamburgh. The ravages of the disease have received a marked check, in the present outbreak, by the *substitution of wide, open, and well-drained streets, for narrow, filthy, and damp thoroughfares*; by the removal of high mounds of earth, blocking up the streets and overshadowing the houses, and *by guarding a large evaporating surface of water from contamination*."

The influence of these improvements will not cease with the present year, but will be perpetuated for ages to come; they will benefit not merely the existing race, but distant generations of inhabitants; and the immediate expense incurred in effecting them will be found to be a vast ultimate economy, even in money, irrespective of the result—which is beyond price—the gain in improved health and lengthened life.

The Serpentine and Kensington Gardens.—The commissioners of her Majesty's Woods, &c., are now draining the Serpentine, prior to the measures they are about to adopt to remedy the stagnant state of the water. Would not this be a good opportunity to remove the *dumb waiter* at the end of the ornamental water in Kensington Gardens, and substitute a fountain of some architectural pretensions? A very small outlay would effect this, and I am sure, even those who have the most extreme views of retrenchment, would not object to see something there that *we* should not be ashamed of (as we all are at present). The two floating islands also, for the ornamental water fowls, *alias* common ducks, if necessary, might likewise be improved.—O.H.

* Amongst the publications before us is a very comprehensive "Report to the Town Council of Chester, on the Sewerage and other Works under the Improvement Act," by Mr. Baylis, the borough surveyor.—Mr. Whichcord, Jun., architect, has just now published (Wickham, Maidstone; Longman, London), "Observations on the Sanitary Condition of Maidstone, with a view to the introduction of the Act for Promoting the Public Health," which appears to be a sensible production.

† In the official circular (No. 4) issued by the Board of Health.

PROFESSOR COCKERELL'S LECTURES ON ARCHITECTURE.

The fourth lecture of the course, at the Royal Academy, delivered on Thursday, the 25th ult., to which the limits of our usual summary hardly allow us to do proper justice, was a very able exposition of what the professor described as the two cardinal principles in design, namely, first, precedent or authority, and second, invention exercised by means of new combinations, or sometimes new elements. With regard to the first, he said that it was the great duty of institutions like the academy to direct attention to the models of antiquity, and to indicate the authors who were to be consulted. It was its office to stand, in the full conservative spirit, in opposition to all depreciation of tried experience. In a proper understanding of these models depended the true value of precedent. The love of it must not, however, be allowed to hold entire possession of the architect, or it would easily degenerate into superstition. Two states of the mind, therefore, were necessary, the one retrospective, the other prospective, and we were to dispense with neither one nor the other: each had claims—each defects.

We might reflect that the intellectual man was compounded of knowledge, stored up in his early days. The appetite was suited to the age. The time came when he repented of every idle hour, and when he had to employ the knowledge he might possess. He would become deeply sensible of the value of information, and would be impressed with a wholesome reverence for precedent, but feeling these, he must guard against the danger of superstition and pedantry, which might tend to the dogmatic belief in no other model than the particular one he set up for himself, or no other master than the one from whom he gained his assumed precepts. Some in the love of novelty might depreciate former things; but it was hardly possible for an artist of sensibility to contemplate, without emotion, the monuments of former art, such as so powerfully impressed the mind of Brunelleschi in the grand monuments of ancient Rome. But we must guard against the misconception alluded to by the poet, who said,—

> "To observations which ourselves we make,
> We grow more partial for the observer's sake:"

We must enter into the considerations of structure in our buildings, and turn peculiar requirements into peculiar advantages. In so doing, we should find—

> "Spontaneous beauties all around advance,
> Start e'en from difficulty, strike from chance."

We must impress our works with a character peculiarly their own, and not afford the opportunity of a contrast, such as that between the truth and beauty of the portraits of the old masters, and the portraits of our grandfathers.

On the other hand, the professor continued, we had to deal with the innovators in art, and these were of two kinds. We had those who professed to have discovered some entirely new principle, or made some new invention, and who argued with a certain show of reason. Such theories might, or might not, be correct, but we were not able to get ourselves to understand and assent to them. The injustice to the authors of such theories could not be avoided, and they must be content, if able, to rank themselves with Socrates, and others who were before their age, and whose opinions sooner or later might prevail. Others there were who laboured to show the defects in the present practice of the art, and what ought to have been avoided in this work or the other. But these gave us nothing in the place of what they condemned,—no stable principles,—but confessed that they must be left to time to unfold. It must of course be recollected that there were two parties to all inventions, namely, those who originated, and those who received the invention, that was to say, the public. The elements of our art, indeed, were few, but were capable of a multitude of combinations. From the seven notes in music were produced a great number of beautiful melodies; from the twenty-six letters of the alphabet was compounded all that Shakspeare had written. In these cases how small in number were the elements, but, how to accomplish a similar number of beautiful combinations, there was "the rub."

Away, then, said the professor, with those ideas of absolute novelty which presented themselves to some persons. Those who knocked down, must erect something instead. Our neighbours knocked down a monarchy, and they erected a republic.—He recommended the critical examination of buildings, as calculated to improve the mental qualifications for the practice of design, but impressed upon his hearers the propriety of accompanying criticism with moderation of temper. He suggested that they should strive to find out in what parts of a composition æsthetical character was attained, and where it was deficient, and whether the proportion was right or wrong, and why. Criticism, he urged, was one thing, and abuse or diatribe another; and he pointed out by which spirit we should most contribute to what was accordant with morality. He, the professor, had shewn that there was a theory of taste and beauty, as surely as there was a theory of beauty and geometry, in nature,—that nature was

> "At once the source, and end, and test of art,"—

and that the great artists were those who best understood nature; and he intended also to shew, by a review of the history of the art, how minute were the changes which took place, and in answer to some who urged the desirableness of an entire alteration in present systems, with a view to novelty, how gradually the inventions of the old masters had been fostered. Comparing great things with small, that was to say, the laws of nature with those of art, we were struck by the occurrence of the same features in all animals, modified by a law of gradation. The snout of one animal became in another a proboscis, or, in opposite terms, the features which were expanded in one animal, in another were hardly recognizable. The arcuated and trabeated systems pervaded the whole of architecture, and yet invention had long consisted merely in the recombination of these elementary principles, at least not in the attainment of absolute novelty.

The professor then, to illustrate the subject further, glanced at the progress of invention, as seen in some of the most important examples of architecture. Commencing with the trabeated, or post-and-beam system, he showed that this, whether amongst the Egyptians, the Greeks, the Druids, or other nations, continued for a long period to hold possession of the art. Variations of character were effected by variations of size, or by other means, as for example, sculptured decoration, and the arch known to the early Egyptians, and used at an early period by the Romans in works of utility, did not for centuries create any change in the decorative character of buildings. Instances of the importance of the arch in Roman architecture, were shewn in the sections of one of the temples at Baalbec, and in that of Venus at Rome. In the latter, the vault which formed the ceiling was 70 feet in span. Before alluding to the use of the arch in the Roman *thermæ*, he described the corresponding buildings of Greece, or *gymnasia*. He said, we must still hope for further enlightenment on the arrangement of these buildings, which, existing at such places as Hierapolis, and Alexandria Troas, it would be extremely interesting to find contemporary with the age of Alexander. He gave a striking instance of the importance attached to *gymnasia*, and of their magnitude, in shewing that the gymnasium at Ephesus was one of three which existed in that city, and, by one of his clever comparative plans, that the building would cover a square space extending from the back of the Horse Guards up to the enclosure of the park. He also showed how Mr. Wilkins, who was the first to clear up the difficulties of the other commentators of Vitruvius, developed the plan of the building in accordance with the description of the author. Passing on to the *thermæ*, he showed the vast extent of the baths of Caracalla, which would cover a space equal to that enclosed by Pall-mall, St. James's-street, Piccadilly, and Regent-street. He pointed out the beautiful forms, and the variety in the plans of the different apartments, and the effective introduction of apsidal and circular forms, and showed the immense size of the *cella solaris*, the dome of which was second only to that of the Pantheon. He also spoke of the ingenuity in providing the necessary

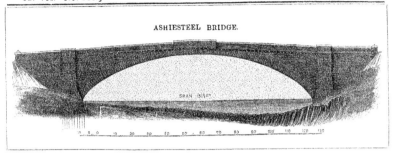

ASHIESTEEL BRIDGE.

SPAN 131½·

abutments for those vast vaults, by disposition of the walls of the different apartments.

As Brunelleschi—when questioned by the pope as to his celebrated boast, replied, "Yes, give me a fulcrum and I can move the world;" so, in the next step in the progress of the arch, the architect of the Church of Sta. Sophia might have said, "Give me an abutment, and I can suspend a dome in the air." The professor gave a clear explanation of the manner in which this was effected, by means of "pendentives:" he then alluded to the night of darkness in which Europe existed subsequently, and the use of the Byzantine style, and showed how the pointed arch—the next step—might have originated by omitting the crown of the lofty vault of the hall of the baths, and prolonging the lines of the haunches, which would then meet in a point. He also showed how naturally the column placed against a pier, in the same apartment, and supporting the portion of the vaulting here concentrated upon it, might have led to the clustered columns and shaft supporting the groining in Gothic buildings. So, said the professor, here we saw instances how, from one link to another, the gradual chain of architectural progress was carried forward.

After describing the plan of Ely Cathedral, he passed to the condition of the art in Italy. In the earlier period of Italian architecture, we found that each house was a kind of fortress, and whatever decoration was practised was reserved for the internal courts. But when, with the revival of learning in Italy, a state of comparative quiet accompanied it, then a new field was open for the inventions of architects. Bramante, for instance, adopted a double order; and this, perhaps suggested by previous works, was certainly not found in the antique. Vignola employed cantilevers in an entablature, as afterwards practised by Sir Christopher Wren. Vignola might have gained some idea of this method from ancient paintings, but certainly not from the temple at Baalbec, where a similar method is found, for Vignola had never heard of that place. Another feature, the window, underwent important modifications. Previously small, and shuttered below;—in the palace at Florence it was ornamented with a pediment, and other decorations. At first, so great an innovation seemed as if it would occasion nothing but ridicule, but this method of treating the window had endured ever since. These features, therefore, and others like these, had never previously been seen in architecture: this, then, was truly invention, and this the only description of novelty which could be successful.

These instances, the professor concluded, he had cited to show that, by attention to points arising out of structure, in our buildings, we might best attain excellence; but we must, at the same time, impress the character of the nineteenth century upon our works, and whilst recognising the value of precedent and authority, not shut our eyes to every other important consideration.

SUPPLY OF WATER TO THE CITY. — It is stated that the New River Company have agreed to furnish water to the whole of the courts and alleys in the city twice a day, *gratis*, for sanitary purposes.

ASHIESTEEL BRIDGE — WHINSTONE CONSTRUCTIONS.

SIR,—In the number of THE BUILDER for December, 1848, page 617, we observe a short notice of a bridge which we built last year at Ashiesteel, given in a report of a meeting of the Institute of British Architects,* in which Mr. Burn expressed his disapprobation of the *material* of which the bridge was built, by cautioning the junior members against the impression that this was a *good* material for construction.

What a strange conclusion he comes to! An arch has been built of 131½ ft. span to a radius of 110 feet, all of whinstone rubble, and yet Mr. Burn cautions the junior members against the impression that this is a good material. Why, Mr. Burn (unintentionally, we believe) does us much more honour than we think we are entitled to, as we differ from him so far as to hold that the material is good, more particularly for arches, and we beg to observe that it is a material far too much underrated by most of the architects and engineers of the present day. In many situations in Scotland and elsewhere, a saving from the use of it might be had, from three to four hundred per cent., in place of hewn stone or granite. A good whinstone arch is equal, if not superior, to hewn stone, the one being much more durable than the other. We never heard of a whinstone arch falling from age, and there are some in this country many hundred years old.

With this we beg to hand you a small sketch of our bridge, which we hope you may think worthy a place in THE BUILDER.

JOHN AND THOS. SMITH.

Darnick.

ON THE CONSTRUCTION OF PRISONS.

THERE is no department in architecture which should call forth more of the study and attention of the architect than that of "prison-building," and being aware of many of the deficiencies which are apparent in the edifices already erected, the writer ventures to offer the following remarks to the public, trusting they may meet with a favourable reception, and be productive of beneficial results. Having for some time made this subject my particular study, and having taken every care to investigate, as far as possible, those defects to which I allude, I am inclined to hope that, in calling attention to it, I may not be considered as having entered the field unprepared. In this enlightened age, when art and science are making rapid strides to perfection, I consider it the duty of every man to contribute as much as may lie in his power to the advancement of those principles which are calculated to aid society in its moral and refined improvement. As there is no class of persons on whom more labour should be bestowed, in endeavouring to effect their reclamation, than the inhabitants of a prison, so should it be the utmost desire of every wellwisher to society, to neglect no opportunity of assisting in this praiseworthy object. Before immediately entering into a detail of the construction, I shall make a few preliminary remarks as to the advantages which

* It was further described in our last number but one, p. 34, *ante.*

one species of discipline appears to possess over another, which cannot be deemed inconsistent, as the plan of a prison will materially depend on the system which it is intended to carry into effect.

Punishment is the reward of crime; but though it is indispensably necessary for its suppression, and for the protection of the community against the assaults and malicious intents of the wicked, yet this alone is not the only point we are to consider;—there is another and a more exalted one, which should receive our strict attention — namely, the "reclamation of offenders." Since prevention is better than the cure, let us rather study the best possible means for the suppression of vice, than the most severe and painful mode of punishing those who have fallen victims to it. How often are we afforded examples of punishment strengthening crime: the greater the chastisement received by a man hardened in villany, the more determined he becomes to resist the arm of the law. What benefit, then, does society receive, if the individual sentenced to undergo a certain term of confinement within the walls of a prison—that time having expired—comes forth again upon the world unimproved, and contemplating the commission of more wickedness? It does not follow, because a man may fall a victim to passions which induce him to commit a crime, and for which the law sentences him to be incarcerated, that he may not be possessed of qualities which, if properly developed, would not only enable him to occupy a respectable position in society, but would also tend to the suppression of those evil propensities to which human nature is subject. In *what* does the line of demarcation consist, which is so widely drawn between the wild untutored savage and the educated man? In *what?* but in the cultivation of the mental faculties and understanding which man, in his most primitive state, is endowed with. Then it is the duty of those who are invested with authority to exercise their power both humanely and judicially; not only to reward the good, and punish the wicked, but, by a careful education of the uncultivated faculties of the latter, to try and restore to society those who, perhaps from want of instruction alone, are looked upon as useless members. This is the grand desideratum to be obtained, and punishment alone will not effect it. Let the understanding and feelings of the prisoner be appealed to; let him be instructed in those principles which tend to the exaltation of the mind; let his habits be well regulated; and, above all, let him have sufficient time and opportunity for meditation and reflection. In the temptations and allurements of a sinful world, intoxicated by pleasure or hardened by misfortune—contaminated by bad examples or driven to desperation by the artful cunning or malicious advice of depraved associates,—many a man, possessing innately good and honest principles, may be prematurely hurried into sin, which, if a little time were afforded for reflection, never would have been committed.

When I enumerate the many beneficial influences which reflection has upon the mind, I wish it also to be understood that a certain regimen of discipline is necessary to be observed, which may aid in the furtherance of the objects for which it is intended.

That which I consider to be an indispensable accompaniment to the provision of time and opportunity for reflection, is "a complete seclusion from all those characters who, by precept or example, might interfere in each other's reformation." It is, then, for *us* to find out *that* species of discipline which will embrace the objects I have enumerated, and which will combine not only the punishment of the offender, but also assist in every possible manner in his ultimate, if not his immediate, reformation. It is unnecessary to dwell, at any considerable length, upon the pernicious results arising from evil company and bad example; and as man, in his intercourse through life, is continually exposed to temptation, let his sojourn in a prison be calculated to enable him to resist the allurements of vice when his term for confinement shall have elapsed, and let him return to the world a better man than when first he entered his cell. It is against reason to expect that a man who has been tempted, or, perhaps, in a great measure forced, to sin, by dissolute companions, will, while under the influence of their precepts, make the slightest advances towards a reformation; and therefore it is absolutely necessary that a species of discipline be adopted, which will prevent the possibility of such communication taking place.

It is almost unnecessary for me to say (as it can be easily concluded from the preceding observations), that I am a strict advocate for the maintenance of the *separate system;* and though prejudices have been cast upon the public mind as to its influences, by the erroneous opinions of authors, who have either taken an unfair view of them, or have not given themselves the trouble to inquire into the results produced by its observance, but have taken particular care to point out defects which existed onlyin their own imagination,—it has been advanced that, on first viewing the principles of the separate system, humanity becomes affected by the means employed in carrying them out; but it is only in consequence of the mind being uninitiated in the beneficial results arising from their practice, and never for a moment taking those into consideration, but solely depending and giving its opinion on the effect produced upon its own nature, that this hasty conclusion is come to. There are many who consider that one of the principal advantages to be derived from the *silent system* (as opposed to the separate system), is, that the prisoners have the consolation of seeing each other. Now, I have already said sufficient, with respect to the detriment which arises from bad company, to render any furthercomment unnecessary; but those who admit that such communication is advantageous, in my opinion, advocate a doctrine which is contrary to all reason and common sense. Another defect which is very manifest in this system is, the opportunities which are offered prisoners of committing breaches of discipline. I have heard it said that the great vigilance of the officers who enforce the observance of this system, prevents the chance of any intercourse taking place between the prisoners; but it is my firm conviction that, no matter how great the watch that may be kept upon them, or however efficient the officers may be to discharge their duty, they will, notwithstanding, find means to explain to one another their sentiments. A look, a gesture, a motion of the hand, will frequently convey feelings which the tongue dares not utter. It must, then, follow as a matter of course, that detection and punishment are the immediate results of a violation of the prison laws. Now, how much better would it be to prevent all possibility of such being the case, than to throw a man in the way of temptation, and punish him for indulging in it. It would appear to me that, to carry out this system to any proper extent, the workshops of the prison should be constructed on the same principle as a *whispering gallery*, so as to reverberate the least sound distinctly; for it is impossible that any human ear, without artificial aid, could detect the whispers among a number of prisoners in a large room. I could enumerate many other deficiencies which are obvious in this system, but as too minute an examination into its principles might be considered irrelevant to the purposes of my essay, I shall merely content myself with making such remarks as are necessary for my subject.

Let us now take a glance at the principles on which the separate system is conducted; and having compared the one with the other, I shall then leave the subject to my readers' discrimination, to draw their own conclusions. The prisoner inhabits an airy, well-ventilated cell, he is supplied with whatever machines and implements are suitable to his trade,—or, if he has never applied himself to any, he is taught one; he is permitted to have pens, ink, paper, and books (particularly those which are calculated to improve his mind and inspire within him a sorrow for the past, a solace for the present, and resolutions of amendment for the future. He is visited daily by the governor or his deputy; he receives comfort from the spiritual advice of the chaplain, he is permitted to have free communication and opportunities of intercourse with the officers of the prison, occasionally his friends are admitted to see him, he is allowed a sufficient quantity of air and exercise, recompensed for the amount of his labour,—and, in a word, he is provided with everything necessary for existence. It is only by contrast we can judge impartially, and I cannot understand how any man, giving the subject proper consideration, can declare himself to be an enemy to a system which is based on principles that are the very foundation of everything that is calculated to bring a man to a proper sense of his duty, both spiritually and temporally.

The prison in Philadelphia is constructed for the observance of the separate system, but there is one very manifest defect in it, which I cannot but notice. On the principal story, small narrow yards are attached to the cells—of course intended for the recreation of the prisoners. Now, for two reasons this should be objected to. In the first place, it prevents his inspection by the officers; and, in the second, it must prove detrimental to his health, as it is necessary to be observed that they should be detached from the main building, and constructed so as to admit a thorough current of air to pass through them: and I also find that, on the other stories, in order to compensate for the want of the yard, two cells are allowed to each prisoner. However pernicious the first defect may be to which I have referred, *this*, I do not hesitate for a moment to say, is doubly so.

There are no structures which require more precautions to be taken for the preservation of the health of the inmates, than "prisons," and there is a great responsibility thrown upon the architect to make such provision as will enable the governor and his officers to carry out the system, without affecting the health of those under their charge. As the mental faculties of every human being are more or less influenced by the state of his health, it is of very important consequence that the physical, as well as the moral benefit of the prisoner, should be attended to. The first advance towards this object should be in the selection of a site whereon to erect the building, and to this point too much consideration cannot be given. We are frequently afforded examples of malignant distempers breaking out and spreading to a fearful extent in prisons, and hurrying immense numbers of the unfortunate inmates to a premature grave; and these results have been too often found to arise from a previous inattention to healthful principles, in constructing the buildings in low, damp situations, exposed to the injurious effects of fogs, or in the neighbourhood of stagnant water. However destructive such inattention may be in the erection of other structures, it is doubly so in a prison, when we take into consideration that its inhabitants must perpetually suffer from its influences, and are denied the possibility of refreshing themselves by inhaling the pure atmosphere beyond its walls.* J. J. L.

Dublin.

Exposition of Manufactures in Birmingham.—A committee has been appointed to arrange an exposition of local manufactures, on the occasion of the visit of the British Association to this town in September next. We trust the endeavour will meet with the earnest co-operation of the manufacturers.

* To be continued.

THE GAS MOVEMENT.

METROPOLITAN AND PROVINCIAL.

While of late recording the wondrous alacrity and zeal with which (on the eve of certain city elections, we believe) the majority of the City Sewers Commissioners were advocating the city gas-consumers' interests, and determining, with the aid of half a million of money, to extinguish all monopoly of gas within the city bounds for ever,—by a slight misgiving as to the somewhat suspicious intensity of that zeal, and even while giving, as in courtesy bound, to those who displayed so much of it, all due credit (more, it now appears, than all the credit really due), for its sincerity, we were induced just gently to hint, that "the city gas-consumers seemed to be somewhat suspicious of the permanence of the good intentions of the authorities." Now, it only remains for us, as in equal courtesy bound, to compliment "the city gas-consumers" on the perspicacity of their suspicions, and the depth of their sagacity. They were clearly far too old and experienced "birds of a feather" either to be caught with chaff, or entrapped by those "good intentions" with which Guildhall was at that time paved; and they hence resolved not to leave their good and hopeful cause entirely in the hands of such ticklish paviours. The City Sewers Commission has, in fact, eaten in its own wordy vapouring "bill," without even choaking on the tail of it. By a majority of 19 to 7, all its determinations and protestations have suddenly vanished in the cool *resolution*, "that no further proceedings be taken in prosecuting this bill." The few staunch and consistent supporters of previous resolutions, now in the minority, "were extremely indignant," as well they might, "after the infinite pains taken by the corporation to accomplish a reduction in the exorbitant price of so necessary an article." A trick such as this may be played but once, and may be played moreover at rather too high a stake. As to those, however, who can scarcely be said to have been betrayed,since theynever really trusted, we doubt not they will go on with energy and resolution, increased, in place of diminished, by an act of self-stultification so complete.——A "Plain Statement" was lately addressed to these commissioners, by a "Director of one of the Metropolitan Gas Companies,"—doubtless a city one, reciting a few of the fusty old fallacious arguments in favour of monopoly and high prices, arguments which might have been urged, with equal ineptitude, years since, while prices were double what they even already are. But "One of the Commissioners of Sewers for the City" (of course, one of the staunch seven), has thought it advisable to publish "An Examination of the 'Plain Statement,'" in which he good-humouredly, but efficiently, knocks the director off his wooden pegs. It is needless for us, however, 'at this time of day,' to enter further into either 'Statement' or 'Examination.' Nor shall we deign even to fence with another 'Statement' which the alarmed monopolists have profusely showered over all the walls, in at least one extensive district of the metropolis. All we need do is to refer to The Builder's "Indices," under head of "Gas Movement," &c., for the last few years. ——On the 12th of February last, under head of "Gas in Guernsey," we made an assault on the stronghold of gas monopoly there, and endeavoured to point out to the gas proprietor (a resident in the metropolis by the way), the impracticability of such a price as 12s. per 1,000 cubic feet, and the folly, therefore, of persisting in the attempt to profit by sustaining it. The *Guernsey Sun* had also called the attention of the Guernsey gas consumers—or would-be gas consumers rather—to our disinterested efforts in the cause of cheap, good, and abundant gas-light. The subject, it appears, continued thereafter to ferment, until the proprietor has at length been induced to promise a reduction of 2s. per 1,000 feet; but, foolishly for himself, postpones the reduction till a time when the consumers altogether cease from using their expensive gas for six months longer. Doubtless the proprietor calculates on thus diminishing the chance of competition (threatened at a further reduction of 3s. per 1,000) in the mistaken idea that he is putting off an *evil* day, while he is only tampering with his own best interests;

though, indeed, he need not expect *much* benefit from so small a reduction on so large a price. As it is, he has actually prevented his shop-keeping customers, by mere exorbitance of charge, from lighting their shops with gas, except on a Saturday night; and has kept the streets of a town parish population of 16,000 to 17,000, without even the expensive luxury of a gas light, "Saturday or Sunday." ——The Wirksworth Gas Company have reduced their price, at one step, from 12s. to 8s. 4d. ——The Hull corporation have resolved to allow the pipes of a new company to be laid through the streets of the town, the inhabitants having failed to induce the present lessee to lower his rate of charge from 6s. 8d. to 5s., as both lessee and shareholders have to reap their separate profits off it. They will probably *now* come to a mutual understanding. —— Stockport and Belfast are to be lighted, it is said, with the hydrocarbon gas prepared from tar and water. It is to be hoped the authorities are awake to the fact that failures abroad have already occurred with gas prepared on a like principle, and to the necessity therefore of being well-assured that the causes of previous failures have been overcome. Gas is thus prepared, it is said, at 1s. per 1,000 cubic feet.

ROYAL INSTITUTE OF ARCHITECTS.

At a meeting held on the 5th inst., Mr. Poynter in the chair, a donation of great interest and value from Mr. Henry Gatling, Fellow, was announced, namely, 20 folio volumes, including an early edition of Palladio (1570); Hamilton's Vases; Original Designs, by Lewis; Chambers' Civil Architecture, 3rd edition, with autograph of the author; W. Addam's designs (of Edinburgh); Gibb's works; and Rondelet's *Traité Théorique et Pratique de l'Art de Bâtir*. The chairman very properly commented on the excellence of the quality as well as the number of the works thus liberally presented by Mr. Garling.

The library of the institute is now becoming very extensive and excellent, and will, it is to be hoped, be made good use of by the students. Mr. John Edward Gregan, of Manchester, was elected a Fellow.

Mr. Scoles then read a paper "On the Topography and Antiquities of the City of Jerusalem," the principal portions of which we shall give *in extenso* hereafter. In the course of it, the writer alluded to Mr. Fergusson's published theory as to the Mosque of Omar and the Church of the Holy Sepulchre, and that gentleman being present, an interesting discussion ensued. Mr. David Roberts, R.A, (some of whose capital sketches were amongst the illustrations of the paper), joined in questioning Mr. Fergusson, who stood gallantly and good-naturedly a cross fire of objections.

Mr. Fergusson's views, as we gathered, may be briefly stated thus: namely, that the building known as the Mosque of Omar is, in truth, the Church of the Holy Sepulchre, and that what is called the Church of the Holy Sepulchre, and was burnt in 1808, was a building not earlier than the 12th century. His principal reasons for the first part of this belief are, that the so-called Mosque of Omar is unquestionably a circular Christian building of the time of Constantine, and is built over a rock standing up 15 feet from the floor, with a cave in it; further, that it could not have been a mosque, its shape and arrangements being contrary to the requirements of the religion. In reply to the question, at what period was the truth lost sight of and the title of Church of the Holy Sepulchre given to the edifice which now bears it, Mr. Fergusson said about 150 years before the Crusades.—Mr. Scoles did not believe that the (so called) mosque of Omar *was* of the age of Constantine; the main arches were slightly *pointed*. He had never seen a pointed arch as old as Constantine. He considered that the columns used were from a more ancient building, but the structure itself was of a comparatively recent period.—Mr. Fergusson contended that the arches being pointed in no way weakened his opinion; he had elsewhere shown that the pointed arch, from 800 years B.C., had been the arch of that country—that is, the horizontal arch bracketted inwards to a point.

The Dean of Westminster, with reference to a specimen of the stone of which the walls of Jerusalem are built, remarked that the stone in some of the most ancient buildings was not from beds of ancient formation, but from those which were actually in course of formation at the time, and which were taken from the quarry while ductile, and indurated afterwards. The temples at Pœstum, known as antiquities by the ancients themselves, were of limestone, the formation of which is still going on,—an imperishable material.

IMPROVEMENT OF OVENS.

I have long been anxious to turn the attention of practical men to a most important improvement in the construction of bakers' ovens. In a word, in place of the close unwholesome oven now in use, I propose to substitute a *ventilating* one, securing at once the health of the journeymen, and saving a large quantity of a very valuable product, alcohol, to wit. The recent discovery by M. Violette, of the carbonization of wood, by means of heated steam, is greatly calculated to further this desirable innovation. By means of steam heated to 480 degrees Fahrenheit, it has been ascertained that the dough is converted into a light, fragrant, well-baked, and well-tasted loaf. There is no risk attendant on the process, as the steam, after coming in contact with the bread, is suffered to escape, loaded with all the impurities emitted by the bread, not into, but beyond the precincts of the bakehouse. The steam is generated by a helix, or spiral iron tube, placed in a common furnace, which would further serve to heat the oven, and economise the steam. The other important economical applications of M. Violette's discovery, in roasting coffee, cooking, in the seasoning of timber, in the pharmaceutical and other arts, I do not here propose to enlarge on. Henry M'Cormac, M.D.

SCULPTURE IN RELATION TO MODERN MEANS AND REQUIREMENTS.

At a *conversazione* held in the Royal Institution, Manchester, last week, Mr. George Wallis delivered an address on the subject, and urged that our artists should use English instead of Greek eyes. He thought the artist should go to nature, but if so, it was essential he should read nature for himself: that he should not do it without availing himself of the tests and aids which those who had preceded him were able to give him was true, but to bind himself down to the forms of expression produced before him was wrong. If he did so, he thought in a groove which he could not get out of, for he found himself pressed ou by the standard set up for him, and he could not give vent to his genius for the realisation of the works he proposed to accomplish. He must look to the productions of antiquity as the standard by which he was to work in the spirit of his own time. Hence it was that the artist should seek objects from his own times, from his own religion, and for his own times, and endeavour to realise them: he said this of painting as of sculpture. We heard an outcry for originality in art, but they who joined in it forgot that when a new work was produced, it was criticised and judged of by an antique standard, for which we went back to the past.

Speaking of modern architecture he said,—Beauty had not been considered to any extent, and where originality had been studied it had run into absurdity rather than beauty. One great cause of this want of beauty was that we were trammelled by fiscal restrictions, and until we could mould bricks into forms and shapes, with which we could produce beauty in a building, we must be content to go on with square bricks made according to an exciseman's notion. In speaking of sculpture he was not alluding to mere marble statuary, but to all works in any material capable of carrying fixity of shape. Within the last century the mechanical arts had progressed to an extraordinary degree; new materials had been discovered, in which works of art could be produced, and of which the ancients had never dreamt. We had means of production which, fifty years ago, would not have been conceived, and, with them, means of adapting forms of beauty to objects of utility. By getting our sculptors to pay more attention to the generalization of their art, and the diffusion of that beauty which they had been too apt to consider as merely applicable to one department of it, we should produce such an effect on the public taste, as would educate the people to appreciate its higher developments. But to suppose that no man was a sculptor unless he was a carver of marble, was to use the term in a confined sense.

In the course of a discussion which ensued, Mr. Wallis, remarking that we could not expect the public to give reward unless their minds were educated, said,—Our institutions were not fulfilling the purposes for which they were established; our schools of design were only drawing schools, and far from inculcating originality of conception or thought in the student, simply taught the mechanics of the art and nothing more.

THE NEW HALL, &c., PEMBROKE COLLEGE, OXFORD.

Various additions have lately been completed in Pembroke College, Oxford. Our engraving is a view of the new hall, which forms the western side of the new court there. This is a room 74 feet 8 inches by 27 feet, and 42 feet high from the floor to the ridge of the roof. The hall is divided into six bays, one of which, at the extreme end, where the dais is placed, is a trifle wider than the others. The main ribs of the roof spring from stone corbels, ornamented with roses, the badge of the college; the spaces between the ribs are filled with tracery, and the wall plate is carved with shields and roses alternately. The roof is surmounted with a lantern, constructed with a view to obtain ventilation. The hall is lighted by four four-light windows on each side, two lights in height, and also by a large bay window on the dais, of eighteen lights. All these windows are to be filled with stained glass, which is to be executed by Messrs. Chance, of Smethwick, near Birmingham. The dais window has a stone groined ceiling on the inside.

The hall is warmed by a fire-place on the west side, with a carved chimney-piece of Painswick stone, containing the arms of the college; and likewise by an apparatus in the basement, from which a constant stream of temperated air is passed into the body of the hall. The northern end is divided off by an oak screen, surmounted by a gallery, and the whole room is lined with wainscot panelling 8 feet in height. The entrance is by the tower at the north-east angle, forming an open porch, groined with stone, the external doorway of which is at a right angle, by which direct draughts of air are avoided.

In the centre of the ante-hall, behind the screen, is the buttery hatch, and further on the service-door for the kitchen, which, with the other offices, is placed in the basement, under the hall. The access to the tower archway is by a flight of steps, seen in the view. The range work of the hall is of Bladon stone, and the dressings of Bath stone, from Combe Down.

The northern side of the new quadrangle, of which a part is seen in the view, consists of entirely new buildings, containing a bursary, common-room, lecture-rooms, and lodgings for fellows, and sixteen sets of rooms for undergraduates. The latter are less ornamental in character than the former, and separated from them by a slightly recessed building. The whole forms a pile 160 feet long.

The doorway to the fellows' rooms stands between two large bay windows, two stories in height, containing carved tracery, panelling, and shields. This building is parapeted, but that containing the undergraduates' rooms has ornamental eaves gutters of galvanized iron. The eastern side of the new court consists wholly of old buildings, which have been made to accord with the court of which they form a part.

The architect is Mr. John Hayward, of Exeter. Mr. M. Arding, of London, has erected the hall and restored the east side of the court. Praise is due to Dr. Jeune, the master, and the fellows of the college, for their efforts to improve the college committed to their care.

THE NEW HALL, PEMBROKE COLLEGE, OXFORD.——Mr. John Hayward, Architect.

EXPERIMENTS, &c., ON CAEN STONE.*

TABLE A.—*Chemical Analysis.†*

	Gros Banc.	Banc de 4 Pieds.	Franc Banc.	Outside of St. Stephen's Chapel, Westminster.
Carbonate of lime	86·5	86·9	82·5	97·3
Silica	10·5	10·5	13·6	} 2·0
Alumina	3.0	2·2	3·2	
Oxide of iron	A trace.	0·4	0·7	0·7
Magnesia...................	A trace.	A trace.	....	A very slight trace.

R. PHILLIPS, F.R.S.

TABLE B.—*Weight of 6-inch Cubes.*

	Ordinary state.			Thoroughly wet.			Thoroughly dry.			Weight absorbed		
	lbs.	oz.	dr.	lbs.	oz.	dr.	lbs.	oz.	dr.	lbs.	oz.	dr.
Gros Banc	15	4	1	16	14	9	15	2	10	1	11	7
Pierre Franche	15	8	6	17	2	5	15	7	0	1	11	5
Banc de 4 Pieds...........	14	12	1	16	7	14	14	10	1	1	13	13
Pierre de 30 pouces.........	16	0	10	17	10	7	15	15	7	1	11	0
Franc Banc................	14	8	4	16	5	14	14	5	12	2	0	2
Ranville	17	12	12	18	10	5	17	12	5	0	14	0
Aubigny	18	12	13	19	7	12	18	12	14	0	10	14

C. H. SMITH.

TABLE C.

Experiments upon Cubes of 2-inch Sides, on power to resist crushing.‡

Name of Quarry or Bed.	Pressure on bed.	Pressure on edge.
	Tons.	Tons.
Gros Banc .. Top of block	3·25	....
,, .. Middle do........	....	8·05
,, .. Do. do........	5·97	....
,, .. Bottom do........	2·97	....
Pierre Franche	7·18	....
,, ...	....	6·63
Banc de 4 pieds	2·57	....
,, ...	....	2·38
Pierre de 30 pouces	3·35	....
,, ...	....	2·07
Franc Banc....................	2·10	....
,, ...	....	2 25
Ranville	6·2	....
,, ...	5·43	....
,, ...	....	5·79
Aubigny	7·41	....
,, ...	10·78	....
,, ...	....	9 78

GEORGE GODWIN, F.R.S.

THE accompanying tables shew the physical and chemical properties of Caen stone. The specimens experimented upon were obtained direct from the quarries for this especial purpose, and may be considered fair average samples of the stone which the beds respectively produce. Of the five beds from the Allemagne quarries, three have been subjected to analysis by Mr. Richard Phillips, F.R.S.—namely, the gros banc, the banc de 4 pieds, and the franc banc. It will be observed from table (A) that, as regards chemical composition, these three beds appear to be almost identical; and there is no reason to suppose that in this respect either of the other beds differs from them. The analysis of one specimen of old Caen stone, taken from the exterior of St. Stephen's Chapel, at Westminster, is placed in the table for comparison, because, in general appearance, this stone resembles that employed outside the oldest buildings at Caen. It has been exposed to the usual atmospheric influences for several centuries, and presents scarcely any symptoms of decay, therefore it will be interesting to see in what respects an old stone, well known to be durable, differs from the three samples obtained from the Allemagne quarries. In this instance we learn that a durable stone is composed almost entirely of carbonate of lime, with very small portions of other ingredients; whereas the franc banc, usually considered to be a perishable stone, contains a smaller quantity of carbonate of lime, and a larger amount of silica, than either of the other specimens.

Table (B) exhibits the avoirdupois weights of 6-inch cubes (one eighth of a cubic foot)—

first, the weights of the specimens in the state in which the stones are usually employed for building purposes, having only been squared, and placed under an open shed, exposed to the atmosphere for several weeks.

The second column indicates the weights of the same cubes, after having been immersed in water forty-eight hours, so as to become completely saturated, such weights having been ascertained immediately after the cubes were taken out of the water, and wiped with a dry cloth.

The third column contains the weights of the same specimens, after having been perfectly dried, in a hot-air chamber, for several days; in the meantime, being frequently weighed, until ultimately they ceased to decrease in weight.

The fourth column shows the difference of weight between the same specimens, in their dried and in their saturated state; and indicates, therefore, the quantity (by weight) of water absorbed by each stone.

Table (C) shows the results of experiments relating to the cohesive strength of the stones, or their resistance to pressure, made with a hydrostatic press, under the eye of Mr. Godwin, upon cubes of 2-inch sides, in duplicate: the figures represent tons and decimals of a ton. The chief value of this table is to determine, if possible, whether any difference exists in the cohesive strength, if crushed with the pressing surfaces parallel to the horizon, as the stone lay in the quarry, or if the pressure be applied edgewise. It has long been the custom to attribute all failures of perishable stone to inattention in not placing them in the building on their natural bed. In a recent number of THE BUILDER (309, January 6th), a correspondent, advocating the use of Bath stone for a church at Liverpool, states that, " Nine-tenths of the failures imputed to this stone have occurred through the ignorance or inattention of workmen or superintendents in neglecting to work the stones, so as to lay on their natural beds, which has laid the pores of the stone open to the effects of rain and frost." From my childhood this has been the universal theme of those who are half-learned in such matters. It is easy to determine the bed-way of sandstones; but with reference to limestones and oolites, in the absence of fossil remains—and such things are of extremely rare occurrence in either Bath or Caen stone—I cannot discover any means of detecting the slightest symptom of lamination, or, when once a block of Caen stone has been disturbed, of saying which way it lay in the rock. I have frequently heard this question discussed, during the last 30 years, by many

intelligent practical masons, and others conversant with the subject, who have professed their ability to determine, to a certainty, which is the bed way of a specimen of Bath or Caen stone. But, although I have grown grey in the service, I candidly confess that I am still ignorant upon the subject; and must either be extremely dull of comprehension or they are deficient in the means of communicating this learning to a " brother chip." The importance of such precaution is generally very considerably overrated; I do not think it signifies which way a stone is fixed unless it presents a decidedly laminated structure, which scarcely ever occurs amongst the oolites. A stone of an open, powdery, and slightly cemented texture will, if exposed to the weather, decompose in a comparatively short space of time, in whatever direction it may be fixed, or whichever surface may be parallel to the horizon.

Throughout the whole of these investigations and experiments, the utmost care has been taken to attend to the marks, indicating the uppermost side of the stones, with reference to their position in the quarry; thereby to insure the greatest accuracy, especially as regards cohesive strength. The table of experiments now under consideration, will do little or nothing towards proving that there is an appreciable difference in crushing the stones flatwise, or edgewise, of the bed. According to theory, we might expect that they would bear a greater pressure, if applied parallel to the bed, than if edgewise; in the table before us, there is very little difference, and in two cases out of the seven, namely, the gros banc and the franc banc, the specimens bore a greater force edgewise than on their bed.

Were it possible to determine this question to a certainty, so that the mason would have no difficulty in ascertaining the bed, or in working the stones for a building, so as to lay them all on their natural bed, the cost of masonry would then be greater, because he would frequently have to cut the blocks to a great disadvantage.

C. H. SMITH.

BLIND BUILDERS.—For building a farm house, farm buildings, and two cottages; Messrs. Morris and Hebson, architects:

Watkins	£3,449
York...................	3,090
Clements	2,960
Higgs	2,838
Bent ,,,,,,,,,,,,,,,,,,	2,500

The quantities were supplied.

* See p. 38, *ante.*

† This, so far as we know, is the first analysis of the Caen stone which has been made. Considering that an analysis would be useful to the public, we solicited this from the Museum of Economic Geology, for which the public pay. The director of this establishment, however, considering perhaps that it was rather to benefit ourselves than the public that the application was made, declined to comply with it. We do not quarrel with the decision, but we venture nevertheless to remark that a contrary course would have been more gracious, and, we cannot help thinking, nothing more than the public and ourselves might expect. However, this being the case, we obtained the professional assistance of a gentleman (connected, too, with the Museum), in whom our readers will place confidence, Professor R. Phillips, and, though probably the half-dozen lines, the result of his investigation, will not lead to the sale of as many additional copies of THE BUILDER as their cost guineas to obtain, the occurrence will, we trust, serve to show our anxiety to place the subject before our readers in as perfect a form as possible.—ED.

‡ These experiments were made at Thames Bank (by the kind permission of Mr. Cubitt), with the assistance of Mr. Dines and an excellent hydrostatic press. The singular and striking difference in the results of the experiments on the *gros banc* is attributable to the varying strength of different parts of the stone, even in cubes of 2 inches adjoining each other in the block. This fact makes the table of comparatively little value towards determining the strength lost or gained by placing the blocks in a building the same way as in the bed.—ED.

BIRMINGHAM WORKHOUSE COMPETITION.

The voting in committee on the seven selected plans terminated thus:—Mr. Hemming (Birmingham), 17; Messrs. Drury and Bateman (Birmingham), 16; the rest no where. The greatest dissatisfaction prevails, and has caused a shower of letters on us, containing charges against various parties. Both the plans on which the question ultimately turned are by ex-members of the board, whose places are positively not yet filled up.

It remains to be seen if the Board will ratify the decision of the Committee without further investigation,—we hope not. The selected plans may, for aught we know, be the best submitted, but unquestionably the circumstances attending the selection are most disreputable.

The following is suggested by a correspondent as a course to be taken:—

1st. That a requisition, signed by all the competing architects, be addressed to the Board of Guardians, requesting them to appoint three architects of reputation, from a list to be submitted, with instructions

2nd. To examine and report upon the several designs for the proposed new workhouse.

3rd. To select three such designs as may best provide for the accommodation of 1,550 inmates,—having due regard to convenience of arrangement and classification; ready access between the various classes and their dining-hall and chapel; economy of labour in the working and household departments, supervision, ventilation, and drainage; ample, but not unnecessary extent of buildings; cheerfulness of aspect; sound, but not extravagant, construction, combined with a sufficiently ornate style consistent with the object of the buildings.

4th. To make especial remarks as to the respective merits or demerits of the three designs so selected.

5th. That the authors of the three so selected be requested to furnish such further explanations as the objections urged against their respective designs may render necessary.

6th. That the Board of Guardians, being in possession of such evidence, proceed to select such design as shall best fulfil the several conditions.

7th. That when the final selection shall have been made, the opinions of the three examining architects be printed, and the whole of the designs sent in competition be exhibited to the public.

ENCROACHMENT ON THE NEW-ROAD, ISLINGTON.

METROPOLITAN IMPROVEMENTS.

Whilst contemplating with satisfaction the progress of opening new lines of street, widening others, and removing obstructions, it may excite some surprise to have our attention called to a movement in the opposite direction, which demands the attention, if not the interference, of the public.

The most important thoroughfare along the north side of the metropolis is the New-road, and in proportion as its importance has increased from the vast extension of buildings beyond it, which has rendered it now more an internal street than an external road, so it has been gradually encroached upon, and is likely to become, in a few years, in its central portion, more like an ordinary street than the fine open avenue that it was originally. The fact is, that from the corner of Osnaburg-street to the top of the hill at Pentonville, the ground in front of the houses, originally appropriated as gardens or open courts, has, in numerous instances, been built upon, to form shops and places for business, close out to the foot-path, particularly between the first-mentioned point and the Hampstead-road; and a large group of shops has very recently been erected near the corner of Osnaburg-street. Thus, the view and free air are obstructed, and the openness which characterized this leading thoroughfare is becoming gradually extinguished. For many years past I had observed the increase of this evil, and lamented it as one that could not be remedied or prevented, conceiving that the parties had a right so to deal with their premises, and that the public view of the matter, if it ever occurred to them, was not for a moment weighed against the commercial or pecuniary advantages to be gained by this mode of occupying their frontage ground. Under these circumstances I was agreeably surprised to learn that these erections are actually *illegal*, and in contravention of a law specifically framed for the prevention of all such obstructions; it is, therefore, not a little astonishing that the law should not have been enforced, and that it should so long have remained inoperative.

The Act of the 7th Geo. IV., for the consolidation of the metropolitan roads, provides that no building shall be placed within 50 feet of the New-road, or within 40 feet of the City-road, on any new foundations; and gives summary power to remove any such buildings as nuisances; but the powers of this Act were transferred by the 10th Geo. IV., to the respective parishes on which the roads are situated; and the result shows how inefficient are such powers when so distributed, as compared with a central body of commissioners. Where private interests are involved, and legal proceedings are necessary to carry out a public object, it is hopeless to expect the interference of a parochial vestry, unless they can be urged forward by the force of public opinion, and this certainly is a case in which that potent lever might and ought to be employed. I hope, therefore that the powerful aid of The Builder will not be wanting on this occasion. Whilst so many thousands are being spent in widening and disencumbering our streets and thoroughfares, it would be a great reproach to allow one of the principal lines to be narrowed, and probably occasion hereafter a large outlay of public money to remedy an evil which the legislature had wisely provided against, but the proper authorities had foolishly and culpably neglected.

Viator.

SOCIETY OF ARTS.

On the 31st of January (Mr. W. Tooke, F.R.S., in the chair), a paper by Mr. A. Claudet was read, "On the Photographometer, for measuring the intensity of the chemical action of the rays of light on all photographic preparations, and for affording a means of comparing the sensitiveness of the same." The art of photography, observed the author, is founded on the property with which light is endowed, namely, that of producing a photographic effect when it strikes upon certain chemical compounds. The effect being in proportion to the intensity of the light during a given space of time, it is necessary, for the success of the operation, to be able to ascertain the exact power of the light at any particular moment; and the only means of so doing hitherto possessed by the photographer is the effect it produces on the eye. A few only of the rays which emanate from the sun are capable of producing on the chemically-prepared surface an effect which is the cause of the photographic picture; and if it were possible to admit into a room only the rays which are endowed with the power of affecting the photogenic preparation, the objects in the room would not be visible to the eye, as the room would appear to be plunged in darkness, while the objects in it would reflect some invisible rays which are capable of producing the photographic image. The property of absorption possessed by red, orange, yellow, and green glass being known to photographers, and the power of admitting through blue glass nearly all the photogenic rays which are not luminous, combined with the improvements which have taken place since the discovery of the art by Daguerre, enable the photographist of the present time to employ a very soft light, and to place the sitter in the shade. As the result of the photographic operation depends on the intensity of the actinic rays, and also upon the degree of the sensitiveness of the chemical preparation, Mr. Claudet has constructed an apparatus which is not only capable of measuring the photogenic light, but of testing the sensitiveness of the chemical preparation of the Daguerrotype plate. This instrument is constructed so that a plate being placed upon an inclined plane will always fall with the same rapidity for each operation. The plate has seven vertical slits or openings cut in it; these are placed parallel to each other, —the first being 1 millometre wide, the second 2 millometres, the third 4, the fourth 8, the fifth 16, the sixth 32, and the seventh 64 millometres. The photographic surface is placed at nearly the bottom of the inclined plane, under a metallic plate pierced with seven circular holes corresponding with the openings of the moveable plate containing the proportionate apertures. When the moveable plate passes before the photogenic surface covered with the seven circular holes, the light strikes upon the spaces left open by the circular holes in various intensities. The space lighted by the opening of 64 millometres will be affected by an intensity double that which is lighted by 32 millometres, quadruple that of the next under the opening of 16, and so on until the last opening, which, being only 1 millometre, will have received 64 times less light than the first; so that after the operation, seven round figures, or less, according to the intensity of light, are represented on the photographic plate. The photographer is thus enabled to ascertain how long it will be necessary to submit the plate to the action of the light on the camera, by the length of time required to develop the seven round figures.

DRAIN BRICKS AND THE DUTY.

An application for a new trial, in the case "The Attorney-General *v.* Walker," on the ground of misdirection on the part of the Chief Baron, having been made, wherein the question is, whether bricks marked "Drain," and exempted by 2nd & 3rd of Victoria, cap. 24, sect. 18, from duty, might be used in *bridges over drains?* the judges in the Court of Exchequer have given their opinion and pronounced for a new trial. Mr. Baron Rolfe thought that no bricks were exempt which were not immediately necessary for the drainage, and that it was not enough that the necessity for the works should arise collaterally from those authorised or required for the purpose of draining land. Necessary works must be taken to mean "physically necessary," and such as were reasonably used with reference to the physical necessity. If the bridges and parapets were not necessary to the drain, the bricks used ought to pay duty; and it did seem that these works, though convenient and desirable, did not fall within the exemption as physically necessary.—Mr. Baron Alderson said it was clear that these bridges did not assist the drainage; on the contrary, they might impede the water in times of flood, and it was difficult to see how such works could be necessary to the drain.—Mr. Baron Parke was of the same opinion.—Sir F. Pollock, Chief Baron, was sorry to differ from the rest of the Court. His opinion was, that bricks were exempt from duty which were used on works either legally or physically necessary for the purpose of drainage. "Necessary" meant "reasonably" necessary, in his view of the Act. If a large open drain were to be made, it would be legally necessary that it should be walled in for the protection of the public, or arched over, and the arch or wall would be essential to the drain. It was the wish of the Legislature to confine the exemption to *bonâ fide* works executed for drainage, and to exclude all which were merely collateral, and were not physically and legally necessary by reason of some legal obligations which entailed their construction on the architect in connection with the drainage. Here the works are executed under a public Act by commissioners. The object of the Act 2nd & 3rd Victoria was to encourage such works, and its provisions ought to receive a liberal construction; and he could not think that the Legislature meant to confine its operations to works which were merely physically necessary, and to exclude those which were legally necessary, but that it was to be extended to such works as bridges and parapets as well as to the mere watercourse of the drain under them.

Edinburgh School of Design.—The competition drawings, &c., at the school under charge of the Board of Manufactures, were exhibited on Friday week, in the galleries of the Royal Institution, and the prizes awarded by the Duke of Buccleuch. A marked improvement is said to have been displayed in the various branches of study.

METROPOLITAN COMMISSION OF SEWERS.

A GENERAL court was held on Thursday, 1st inst., at the Sewers Court, Greek-street, Soho-square. Lord Ebrington, M.P., in the chair.

The Metropolitan Sewage Manure Company.—In answer to an application made by Dr. Guy, and a deputation, on behalf of the Metropolitan Sewage Manure Company, a resolution was passed to the effect that, as soon as arrangements were completed, the company would be permitted to take the sewage water from the Counters Creek sewer for agricultural purposes, for a certain specific time.

A recommendation was received from the general committee, that it would be desirable to continue Mr. Roe as the consulting surveyor of this commission, at a salary of 200*l*. per annum, such amount at the end of the first year to be further considered. Mr. Hale was also appointed assistant surveyor at a salary of 200*l*.

Regulation of Business of the Commission.—A paper of suggestions, drawn up by Mr. Chadwick and Mr. Bullar, for the regulation of the business of the Consolidated Commission, was laid before the court, but no decision upon it was come to. Among the matters of most immediately pressing importance, the following works are recommended:—

1. The scale and details of the survey map.
2. Street cleansing.
3. The manufacture of pipes, and provision of materials.
4. The house drainage report and plan.
5. The Westminster general drainage reports and plans.
6. The land drainage report and plans.

Street Cleansing by Hose and Jet.—A report by the assistant surveyor, on the subject of a variety of experiments in street cleansing by the use of hose and jet, set forth that many of the streets and courts in which these experiments were performed, were, before cleansing, in a most filthy and insalubrious condition, the surface coated with mud, and strewn with offal and refuse of the most disgusting nature; in the interstices between the paving, and in the hollows formed by its partial settlement, stagnant fœtid liquids had collected, charging the atmosphere with their offensive exhalations. The calculation made for the Strand is, that the whole of the carriage and footways should be daily cleansed thoroughly for 4½d. per house per week, including the courts adjacent thereto; and for the borough of Southwark, at 3½d. per house per week. According to this plan, taking the number of houses in London at 270,000, and the carriage-way to each house at 27.7 square yards, equal to a total of 7,500,000 square yards; assuming this to be a paved surface, the cost of its application daily (carriage-way and foot-way), would be 93,414*l*. per annum; while under the present process of merely sweeping, the cost would be 171,804*l*. per annum.

Miscellanea.

THE ARUNDEL SOCIETY.—Under this title a "Society for promoting the Knowledge of Art," has been established for the publication, to annual subscribers of one guinea, of translations of foreign works, or original essays, illustrating the principles or the history of art, and engravings from important examples of architecture, painting, &c. The prospectus says,—"The machinery which has proved so effective in the cultivation of literature, science, and archæology, has hitherto been employed only to a limited extent in promoting the knowledge of art. The productions, indeed, of ancient Greece and her colonies, their edifices and their sculpture, have been illustrated by the labours of the Dilettanti Society; and recently much light has been thrown upon mediæval architecture through means of the numerous institutions devoted exclusively to its elucidation. But no such body has hitherto attempted the systematic study of the monuments of painting, nor of the various ornamental arts in which the middle ages were so eminently successful; nor has any undertaken the investigation of the theoretic principles common to all branches of art, by which its efforts should ever be guided, and its achievements judged." The council includes some good names, but will need an infusion of working men.

LEAMINGTON CHURCH CLOCK.—A clock has been placed in the tower of the parish church: the dials, 7 feet diameter, of masonry coated with mastic, are painted purple, and have the surface "smalted," as it is termed, that is, strewn with pulverised or fragmentary glass. The figures, 15 inches in height, are gilt.

CALIFORNIA AND THE GOLD DIGGINGS.—We have purposely avoided reference to the gold finders till now, having a natural suspicion that the extraordinary statements on the subject which have been flying over the country, were exaggerations that succeeding accounts would correct. Nothing, however, has yet occurred to confirm the misgiving, and we must be contented to believe and wonder. Mr. Wyld has published a map of the gold regions, and some "Geographical and Mineralogical Notes" to accompany it. Baily, Brothers, have issued all the information they could rake together, under the title of "The Gold Regions of California;" and now even so staid and steady a writer as Professor Ansted is carried off by the prevailing current, and has published "The Gold Seeker's Manual,"* which even those who do not propose to give up kid gloves and take in "washing" at California may peruse with advantage. Mr. Ansted does not think that the quantity of the precious metals will be sufficiently great to alter permanently their value. — A stimulus will be given to industry, new markets will be opened, and, unless we are deceived, England will be more benefitted in the long run by this discovery than America. The *Liverpool Albion* says that Messrs. Starkey, requiring a place to store goods in now going to California, arranged to send one out. A contract was consequently made with Messrs. Vernon for one to be built of iron, under the directions of Mr. Grantham, civil engineer. The warehouse is of iron, and the roof is similar to those used at railway stations. The sides and roof are thin, covered with galvanized corrugated iron plates. There are large folding-doors in the centre, and windows in the roof. The order was given on the 5th ult., and the men were fairly at work on the 9th; and on Saturday, the 3rd inst., it was entirely erected and ready to be taken down, having been constructed in the short space of twenty-three working days.

ELASTIC MOULDS.—At the Sheffield School of Design, last week, Mr. Young Mitchell, the master, gave a lecture, illustrated by experiments, on the art of making elastic moulds. These seem to have great advantages over the old plan. The moulds may be made at small cost, and with great rapidity. That which would occupy five or six days in the modelling, may be furnished by this process in half that number of hours. The principal material used for the elastic moulds is glue or gelatine. The best fish glue will answer as well as gelatine, and is much cheaper. The material is dissolved like glue, in a vessel placed over the fire in a pot of hot water, stirring it during the process. To each pound of the gelatine it is necessary to add three quarters of a pint of water and half an ounce of bees' wax. It is ready for use when about the thickness of syrup. The model must be oiled carefully with sweet oil, and the composition must be poured upon it while warm, but not boiling. Having set, it may be taken off the model. When the model is small it should be placed in a shoe or case, which gives facility for shaking the mould well when the plaster is poured in, so as to drive it well into the crevices. The plaster should be fine, and in order that it may harden and set quickly, about half an ounce of alum should be added to each pint of water, used in mixing it. Before using the mould it should be carefully oiled. Great care is required in mixing the plaster, and watching it when in the mould, for if it be allowed to remain long enough to heat, the mould is destroyed.

HINT TO DUNDEE.—Sir: Having remarked, in your valuable periodical, advertisements for designs for a memorial to be erected on the quay of Dundee, to celebrate the landing of her Majesty *there*, I beg to suggest to the respected inhabitants of that flourishing town that it would be much more to their convenience, much more to their health, and much more to their credit, were they, in lieu thereof, to employ their spare cash in draining their town (an operation which is very much required), and erecting certain conveniences in a more decent manner, especially as the amount they propose to spend is but a tithe of what would be required to erect a monument of the magnitude proposed, or of the style which the occasion deserves.—ONE WHO HAS USED HIS OLFACTORIES.

* Van Voorst, Paternoster-row.

RAILWAY JOTTINGS.—A new, and it is thought, improved patent express locomotive engine has recently been manufactured by Messrs. R. Stephenson and Co., and placed on the York, Newcastle, and Berwick Railway. Its driving-wheels are 6 feet 6 inches in diameter. A single stroke covers nearly seven yards in length, and the rate of speed has been found to be nearly a mile a minute.——In the formation of a locomotive, there are 5,416 pieces to be put together and adjusted as accurately as the works of a watch.——A 'pit lad' at Killingworth colliery, ambitious, no doubt, to sustain the renown of that nursery of a Stephenson's genius, has invented an apparatus for working railway breaks and preventing collisions, which the *Gateshead Observer*, who patronises the meritorious object of the inventor in providing for the public safety, describes as a substitute for the screw and lever either on tenders or on carriages. By this apparatus, each carriage being provided with a piece of cord the length of itself, having a hook at one end and a loop at the other, a whole train can be placed at the command of the engine-driver as well as of the guard, and if on the tender, it would also work the break of the engine. Every wheel could thus be locked in a moment if necessary, the apparatus exerting a retarding power six times greater than that of the ordinary break, although costing but a trifle more.——The last annual report of the Railway Mechanics' Institution, at Rugby, states that there are seventy-six members, that the library contains 260 volumes of useful works, besides 100 more to be added, and that twelve lectures are delivered half-yearly, on instructive and mechanical subjects.——The Great Western works, from Slough to Windsor, are in rapid progress.——"There seems a fatality," says the *Railway Record*, "attending the endeavours of the Great Western contractors under Mr. Brunel, to obtain an adjustment of their transactions with the railway companies. Mr. Nixon, in respect of his 'contract' works, and other or 'extra' works, for the Taff Vale Company, many years since, claiming a balance of 9,000*l*., has just been told by the Court of Chancery, that his remedy is at law, and not in equity; but this decision has been delayed so long, as to deprive him of that *legal* remedy. Mr. M'Intosh's executors, after five years' litigation at law and in equity, have lately resorted to a court of equity to take the accounts of works in respect of which half a million is claimed against the Great Western. Mr. Ranger resorted to the same tribunal, eleven years ago, against the same company, and has not yet learnt where his accounts are to be taken. The London and North-Western sent *their* account with Mr. Burton to an accountant last year; and the result is, that the whole has been adjusted! The Manchester and Southampton sent their engineering accounts with Mr. Freebody to a referee, *not a lawyer*, and the result was equally favourable."

PUBLIC LIBRARIES.—We are glad to see that Mr. Ewart is about to move for a select committee upon the public libraries of Great Britain and Ireland, with the view of securing means for their improvement and extension.

SPLITTING BANK NOTES.—Mr. Editor: Knowing you to be a firm friend to the working class, induces me to trouble you with this statement, that the process of splitting a bank note, or any other piece of paper, is the invention of a person, a print-mounter, who was induced to try the experiment to obtain the engraving from one of the illustrated papers without the letter-press showing through from the other side. The experiment of splitting a note was first tried at the house of Mr. Anderson, the George Tavern, Lambeth-walk (or at least for him): my motive for troubling you with this is, that the world may know that a working man is the originator of the above invention, which is the result of ten years' study.—A WORKING MAN.

A contemporary gives the following mode for splitting paper:—Procure two rollers or cylinders of glass, or amber resin, or metallic amalgam; strongly excite them by the well-known means, so as to produce the attraction of cohesion, and then with pressure pass the paper between the rollers. One half will adhere to the under roller, and the other to the upper roller, and the split will be perfect. Cease the excitation and remove each part.

THE CITY LANDS IN LAMBETH.—Sir: The notice in your paper of 23rd December last has brought down the ire of the officers, who have visited the principal tenant with a distress-warrant for rent only due at Christmas, scarcely asked for, and that before the usual time, as a terror to other complainers about drainage. Here, at Lambeth, is land forming at one time part of the Marsh overflowed by the tide (built on under leases by those who foolishly thought sixty-one years could never arrive), which is covered with property placed on it by others, and yielding to the landlord—the city of London—thousands a-year, and yet they are so narrow-minded as to refuse draining any of the houses into the common sewers at their expense; and those tenants who endeavour to point out to them the propriety and necessity of it are visited with the revengeful spirit above described. It is said the city has been a great obstacle to the salutary measures required for health, and this instance would seem to prove that it is truly said; for here is a case of the direst necessity treated with the meanest harshness, because it is brought under their notice. I inclose my card.—ANOTHER SUFFERER.

BUILDERS' FOREMEN'S INSTITUTION.—In reference to the report of the annual dinner of the Provident Institution for Builders' Foremen, which appeared in your last publication, I beg you will add the following handsome donations:—Mr. Cooper, 2*l.* 2*s.*; Mr. Stirling, 2*l.* 2*s.*; Mr. W. Trego, 2*l.* 2*s.*; Messrs. Luard and Beedham, 2*l.* 2*s.*; Mr. Lee, 2*l.* 2*s.*; Mr. Taylor, 2*l.* 2*s.*; Patent Lava Metallic Company, 2*l.* 2*s.*; Mr. Husler, 2*l.* 2*s.*; Mr. Dowell, 2*l.* 2*s.*; The Chairman, 1*l.* 1*s.*; Mr. Withall, 1*l.* 1*s.*; Mr. T. Eden, 1*l.* 1*s.*; Mr. Edw. Eyre, 1*l.* 1*s.*; Mr. C. Haynes, 1*l.* 1*s.*; Mr. Brown, 1*l.* 1*s.*; Mr. Rose, 1*l.* 1*s.*; Mr. Manuche, 1*l.* 1*s.* Several of the donors gave in their names as contributors of one guinea per annum to the provident fund. The stewards are anxious publicly to return their sincere thanks to the numerous donors and friends who responded to their invitation, and beg to assure them they close their labours with a deep sense of gratitude for the honour conferred on them by so respectable and numerous an attendance; and also for the very great assistance contributed to the Provident Fund for the Benefit of Aged and Decayed Builders' Foremen.—W. ALLARD, Secretary.

ELABORATE SILVER VASE IN THE ETRUSCAN FASHION.—A German workman (Antoine Vechte) in the employment of Messrs. Hunt and Roskell, has lately completed an alto-relievo richly wrought or embossed silver vase, the result of three years' labour, and mainly representing, in anatomical and other forms, the destruction of the Titans by Jupiter. The shape is Etruscan, of elegant contour. It is about 32 inches in height, with a cover and two handles, and measures from handle to handle 13½ inches. Round the body of the vase are numerous groups of giants, climbing, falling, &c., while the handle or knob of the cover is in the form of Jupiter Tonans. Every portion of the surface is wrought in different grades of high and low relief. The article was commissioned by the artist's employers, and is on sale for 2,000*l.*

TOWN HALL FOR CORK.—A town hall is about to be erected in Cork, but there seems to be some difficulty in finding an appropriate site. A laudable anxiety is manifested in the city that the building should be worthy the age, and well placed.

DECORATION OF THE QUEEN'S ROBING ROOM.—The eighth report of the Commission on the Fine Arts, which has just been published, informs us, that the commission is ready to enter into an agreement with Mr. W. Dyce, R.A., for the decoration of her Majesty's robing-room in the palace at Westminster, with fresco illustrations of the legend of King Arthur. Mr. Dyce undertakes to complete certain stipulated works within a period of six years, for which he is to be remunerated (as proposed) at the rate of 800*l.* a-year.

PLAN OF CLAPHAM, SURREY.—Messrs. A. and R. Bland, Charlton, Kent, have just now completed an engraved plan of the parish of Clapham, in the county of Surrey, on a large scale.* It shews every house, gives a section, and is altogether a nice thing.

* Published by Batten, Clapham Common.

PROPOSAL FOR A STATUE FOR JENNY LIND.—A correspondent, "W. Tomlinson," of Norwich, proposes that the inhabitants of that city should testify their gratitude to this lady (not more distinguished by her vocal power than by her benevolence and goodness), by erecting a statue to her, and he offers a subscription of 5*l.* towards it. A proposition at present current in Norwich, to place a picture of Miss Lind in St. Andrew's Hall, he does not think a sufficient return for the immense assistance to the local charities afforded by her. If not a statue, he suggests a commemorative window in the cathedral.

ARCHITECTURAL EXHIBITION.—The exhibition of architectural works determined on by "The Architectural Association," is fixed to take place in March next, at the gallery of the new Society of Painters in Water Colours, in Pall Mall. The committee will be prepared to receive, during the latter part of the present month, drawings of works contemplated or in progress; designs submitted in competition during the year; studies and delineations of existing buildings and antiquities, and architectural models. The drawings should be either in frames or upon strainers. Considering the elevation of their art, by the diffusion of taste amongst the public, to be no less an object than the direct advantage of the profession, the society have determined to constitute the exhibition *free*, with the exception of Saturdays. We hope they will receive the cordial co-operation of the profession.

RATING OF RAILWAY PROPERTY.—Endeavours are being made by the principal railway companies to obtain a remission of local taxation; they complain greatly of the present system of assessments. A deputation of the chairmen of some of the companies had an interview lately with the chief Poor-law Commissioners on the subject. According to *Herapath*, the ten principal railways pay, on the average, the following sums per acre per annum for parochial taxes:—London and North-Western, 13*l.* 6*s.*; Great Western, 9*l.* 16*s.*; Lancashire and Yorkshire, 14*l.* 10*s.*; Midland, 7*l.* 6*s.*; York and North Midland, 5*l.* 14*s.*; York, Newcastle, and Berwick, 4*l.*; Eastern Counties, 4*l.* 12*s.*; South-Western, 7*l.* 16*s.*; Brighton, 10*l.* 14*s.*; Dover, 14*l.* 6*s.*

RAILWAY COMPENSATION.—LANCASTER AND CARLISLE RAILWAY.—According to the local paper, a trial took place, January 23, at Carlisle, before a special jury, to assess the value of six acres of land belonging to the Maryport and Carlisle Railway Company (now in the possession of Mr. Hudson), but which were required by the Lancaster and Carlisle Railway Company. Mr. Hudson, on behalf of the Maryport Company, first demanded 100,000*l.*; he then called about a dozen witnesses, who valued it at sums varying from 75,000*l.* to 79,800*l.* The Lancaster and Carlisle Company had previously offered 7,005*l.* for the land. The jury, after two days' investigation, gave a verdict for 7,171*l.* Can this be *correct?* We run no risk of being in error when we answer, no.

PRESERVATION OF TIMBERS.—A contemporary says,—that in taking down, a few years ago, in France, some portion of the ancient chateau of the Roque d'Ondres, it was found that the extremities of the oak girders, lodged in the walls, were perfectly preserved, although these timbers were supposed to have been in their places for upwards of 600 years. The whole of these extremities buried in the walls were completely wrapped round with plates of cork. When demolishing an ancient Benedictine church at Bayonne, it was found that the whole of the fir girders were entirely worm-eaten and rotten, with the exception, however, of the bearings, which, as in the case above mentioned, were also completely wrapped round with plates of cork. These facts deserve to be inquired into.

PIN-HOLES IN IRON.—A correspondent from Sheffield says,—Can any of your scientific correspondents inform me what will prevent metal castings ½ of an inch thick from the cupola, from being, when ground and got up bright, full of small pin-holes? Pig-metal from nearly all the blast furnaces in the three kingdoms, has been tried and variously mixed, but none appears free from them. If any composition or material can be named to prevent it, it will confer a lasting benefit on iron-founders.

PROJECTED WORKS.—Advertisements have been issued for tenders, by 26th inst., for building a new grammar school at Lichfield; by 20th, for the repair and restoration of the chancel and chancel aisles of the Collegiate Church of Wimborne Minster, Dorset; by 12th, for the erection of offices and workshops for the Liverpool United Gas Company; by 18th, for the whole works in building a new market-hall and corn-exchange at Lichfield; by same date, for the whole works in building a new savings' bank at Lichfield; by 23rd, for the maintenance of the permanent way of the Chester and Holyhead Railway; by 15th, for the execution of a viaduct in St. Pancras Parish; by 1st March, for the supply of 20 cattle waggons of East-India teak for the Great Northern Railway; by 3rd May, for supplying the Government dock-yards with cast-iron articles for twelve months' certain; and by a date not specified, for a condensing engine of 12 to 16-horse power, and one of 6 to 8-horse power, 30 tons of rails, and 160 feet of 9-inch pumps, at Leeds.

ELECTION OF THE CITY COMMISSIONERS TO THE METROPOLITAN COURT OF SEWERS.—On Thursday a Court of Common Council was held, when the subject of the appointment of four commissioners to the Metropolitan Court of Sewers, to represent the interests of the City of London, was resumed. On behalf of the Court of Aldermen, the names of Alderman Lawrence and Alderman Humphrey were proposed, but the former was elected by a large majority. Various gentlemen being proposed *seriatim* to fill the offices as members of the Court of Common Council, a very decided show of hands was in favour of Mr. Deputy Harrison and Mr. Deputy Peacock, but the Lord Mayor said the show was so nearly equal between Mr. Norris and Mr. H. L. Taylor, that he was unable to state on whom the choice had fallen. A second show was then taken, which his lordship declared to be in favour of Mr. Norris; therefore the new commissioners are Mr. Alderman Lawrence, Mr. Harrison, Mr. Peacock, and Mr. Norris.

SIR HANS SLOANE'S MONUMENT.—Happening to pass the old Chelsea church, which stands at the end of Cheyne Walk, Chelsea, where rest the remains of Sir Hans Sloane, I stopped to read the inscription on the monument, which occupies a prominent position in the churchyard, close by the roadside; but, alas, it was with difficulty I could do so; the letters are all but obliterated. The monument itself is simple and imposing, and the inscription appeared to be equally so. Would it not be desirable to call attention to its state in your valuable journal, in order that some of the more public-spirited of the inhabitants of that *locale* may be induced to subscribe a few shillings to have the letters re-cut deep into the stone before it is too late to decipher them?—ANTIQUARY.

DURHAM COLLEGE LIBRARY AND MUSEUM.—For architectural or other remains, a room nearly 200 feet long and of suitable breadth and height, is to be added to the library of the dean and chapter, by the appropriation of some of the old conventual apartments adjoining, vacant by the death of Dr. Wellesley, one of the prebends.

TENDERS

For building of a new Wesleyan Chapel, in Jewin-street City, on the site of the present chapel:—

Wilkinson	£2,534
Ward	2,520
Ashby	2,368
Smith	2,298
Lawrence	2,285
Jeffrey	2,167
Wood	2,145
Curtis (accepted)	2,044

For the Exbury Parsonage:—

White, Hythe	£1,202	6	5
Emmett, Southampton	1,185	10	0
Roe, ditto	1,177	0	0
T. Burton, London	1,143	0	0
Wheeler, Cowes	1,140	0	0
Mansill	1,097	0	0
Gover and Son, Winchester	1,092	0	0
Brown, Southton	1,088	0	0

For two houses, Endell-street, St. Giles's. Mr. Harry Oliver, Architect.

I'Anson	£2,319
Piper	2,222
G. Mansfield	2,195
Hayward and Nixon	2,180
Curtis	2,142
Ashby	2,138
Brass and Son	2,098
Locke and Nesham	2,060
Holland (accepted)	2,005

Quantities supplied.

L MEETINGS OF SCIENTIFIC BODIES
Held during the ensuing week.

TUESDAY, FEB. 13. — Institution of Civil Engineers, 8 P.M.
WEDNESDAY, 14.—Society of Arts, 8 P.M.; Graphic Society, 8 P.M.
THURSDAY, 15.—Royal Society, 8½ P.M.; Society of Antiquaries, 8 P.M.
SATURDAY, 17.—Institute of Fine Arts, 8 P.M.

TO CORRESPONDENTS.

" *Antiquity.*"—Our correspondent will find in vol. iv. p. 99, some particulars as to Old St. Pancras Church.

" *The City and Suffrey Gaols.*"—Several comments on the recent tenders, &c., have been received, and shall have attention.

" *Colouring Card Models.*"—A " Tyro" asks what should be used for colouring card-board architectural models to represent red brick, Caen stone, and slate? The most obvious reply is—Venetian red for red brick, yellow ochre for Caen stone, and Prussian blue with indian ink for slate.

Received.—" W. M.," " W. and A. H.," " Constant Reader" (the " Encyclopædia of the Buildings Act" published at THE BUILDER Office), " D." (may be quite satisfied), " W. D.," " C. and Co." (the specimen shall be mentioned), " An Old Subscriber" (we know of no lending library. The library of the Institute is open to members; Mr. C. J. Richardson's works will be found very useful); " E. J. N. S.," " J. Guardian" (Birmingham), " C. R. S." (shall be looked to), " Jack-Plane," " W. T." (Banks), " T. G." (there is much information on the subject in Hope's " History of Architecture"), " John Coupland" (we have received a letter thus signed, but can only regard it as a hoax), " J. C." (we are not disposed to recommend), " Auld Lang Syne" (we are surprised that our correspondent should discover any " flippant" allusion to (Roman) Catholicism, or an unfavourable comparison with Pope Pius, in the article in question. We simply mentioned a political fact,—a subject of congratulation for one country and regret for another); " F. P." (we do not understand it, and therefore cannot repay), " T. S. (we have a view of the church in preparation), " G.," " Constant Reader," " J. S.," " R. R. J." (out of our province), " J. D." (we are sorry that we cannot advise), " A. S.," " S. Moorgate-street," " F. Le C.," " A. A.," " A Commissioner."—Marshall's " Index Ready Reckoner" (Longman); " School Architecture, or Contributions to the Improvement of School-houses in the United States," by Henry Barnard, 2nd edition (New York, Barnes and Co.); " Elevations, Sections, &c., of Stretton Church, Northamptonshire," by H. E. Barr (J. H. Parker, Oxford and London); Wood's edition of the " Songs of Scotland," Parts 23 and 24, edited by W. and F. Graham (Novello, Dean-street, London), a cheap and excellent work; " Lecture on Colonization," by Mr. W. H. G. Kingston (Trelawney Saunders, Charing Cross).

" *Books, Prices, and Addresses.*"—We have not time to point out books or their addresses.

TO PROVINCIAL READERS.—In reply to complaints of the irregular delivery of THE BUILDER in provincial towns, we beg leave to state that it is invariably published by seven o'clock on Friday morning; and that the irregularity complained of rests entirely with the parties through whom it is obtained.

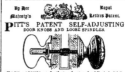

The Builder.

No. CCCXV.

SATURDAY, FEBRUARY 17, 1849.

POOR Architects! Or perhaps we should be nearer right if we said, stupid architects! for the indignities to which they are now constantly subjected, have been mainly led to by their own proceedings. The workhouse plot at Birmingham thickens. Private interest fighting against private interest led to disclosures at a meeting of the guardians, on the 6th, which otherwise, probably, would not have come out. The opposition to the selection made by the Committee appears, on the part of some of the guardians, to be no evidence of a desire to do justice to all the competitors, and discharge their duties conscientiously, but would seem to proceed simply from a desire to serve their own particular friend. Thus one of the committee stated at the meeting, that the sole reason why another member of the Board opposed plan No. 1, was, that *his son was in the office of the architects of No.* 2. It is to be hoped, however, that a majority of independent men will be found to look at the question in its proper light, and act irrespectively of private feelings and connections, so as to remove, if possible, the stigma which has been cast upon their body.

It would seem that the fraud practised on the stranger-architects, who responded to their invitation, was systematic, and intended from the beginning. One of our correspondents shows that, even in the matter of time, the leaning to their local friends was evident. He says, as to depositing the plans.—"It was stated in the instructions that all plans must be sent in on or before the 1st of January, at twelve o'clock; and further, that all plans received after that time would not be looked at, but put on one side till applied for by their respective owners. Now this, one of the most important conditions (for a day is of infinite value in finishing such elaborate drawings as they must necessarily be for a building of this magnitude), was violated, and altogether set on one side by keeping the office open till eleven P.M.; and no notice of this was given to the competitors (excepting, of course, the Birmingham men, all of whom were fully aware of it), unless something like the following, which I received the day after my plans were deposited:—Requiring some explanation respecting the site, I wrote to the person appointed to furnish architects with particulars: I received an answer on the 2nd, with the necessary information, and also informing me of the extension of time to eleven P.M. I am sure no non-resident availed himself of this desirable extension,—for, upon depositing my plans, which I did some time before 12 on the 1st, I was told they were the forty-seventh. The above answer to my letter, coming on the 2nd of January, was certainly an Irishism, but whether wittingly or not I cannot say.*"

* The same writer, who forwards his name, says,—"One thing more I would allude to, viz., the manner in which the committee came in possess on of the names of the competitors. The instructions stated that each design was to be accompanied by a sealed letter, containing estimate, &c. Now I understood from this, and I am sure many others did the same, that the designs were to be sent in under a motto; but it appears that the Birmingham men, fearful lest their friends in committee should mistake, sent in their plans with their names written in full. This will account for the committee so easily selecting their friends."

Even the strict prohibition from canvassing the guardians, which was published, must have been for the purpose of deterring the strangers only from endeavouring to make interest, for the canvassing on the part of the local architects, and of members of the Board for them, is not denied.

This view of the matter was fully borne out by one of the speakers at the meeting alluded to (Mr. Allday), who pointed out, at considerable length, the injustice which had been done to architects at a distance from Birmingham. "Those architects," he said, "were called on to prepare and send in plans; they were led to believe that there was no limitation as to the expense of their buildings, while it was a fact that the Birmingham architects well knew that it was an understanding in the committee that the estimate should not exceed 30,000*l*. Was that fair? And yet he could shew that it was not an accidental thing; that the omission of such a fact was *intentional*. It was moved in the committee that the printed instructions should set forth that the estimate should not exceed 30,000*l*., but that motion could not be entertained. That was not doing justice to architects at a distance. If they had known this fact, as the local architects knew it to be a fact, did any one think that the architects in London and other places would have sent in plans varying in cost from 80,000*l*. to 30,000*l*.? He could state it to be a fact, that the majority of the plans sent in were estimated at more than 30,000*l*., and some of them, of the most perfect and beautiful description, were rejected because they did not come within that sum. He left that fact before them; and, in his opinion, it gave ground for the charges made in the *Birmingham Journal* and THE BUILDER, that the majority of the architects had not had fair play."

"Comment," says the *Journal*, with reference to this striking new feature in the case, "would spoil the effect of this revelation. We had formed and expressed a very strong opinion on the *mala fides* of the proceedings, but no such deliberate trick as the above entered into our imagination. The knowledge of it should be sufficiently condemnatory of the whole transactions of the Committee from first to last; for it is quite evident that the omission was designed to lead competitors into error."

After much discussion, Mr. Edmonds, one of the guardians, moved—"That with a view to obtain further information, and more certainly limiting the cost of the new workhouse within the reasonable expectations of the ratepayers, the report be referred back to the Committee, who for that purpose shall be authorised to procure the written opinions of architects or builders of reputation, as to the relative merits of such of the plans as are not excluded from competition by the printed instructions, together with the grounds on which such opinions are based; that on the receipt of the opinions so obtained, the committee proceed to report to this Board their opinion of the plan which ought to be ultimately selected; and that the opinions of the architects and builders be published in our local newspapers, for the information of the ratepayers." This was discussed at considerable length, and ultimately the meeting was adjourned to Tuesday, the 13th, but what was then done we do not yet know.

It appears that no less than 264 architects applied for copies of the printed instructions to competitors.

According to the report of the committee the estimated cost of the plan recommended is 27,700*l*., or at the rate of 16*l*. 15s. per head for 1,664 inmates. The accommodation is for 258 male, and 351 female adults; for 227 boys, 289 girls, and 143 infants. In the infirmary, provision is made for 159 males and 159 females. There is also accommodation for 26 male, and 26 female tramps, and for 22 married aged couples. There is a chapel, two separate dining halls, three separate schoolrooms, with two class rooms attached to each. The style was said by the committee to be *Italian*, but this some of the speakers denied, saying it was *Elizabethan*, and that this assertion was itself sufficient to prove the inefficiency of the tribunal by whom the plans had been judged. Alas! poor architects and poor architecture!*

But abuse is thrown away, and pity is thrown away. See what the committee for restoring the Lewes Free Grammar School have the impertinence to make public. We were about to say the *courage* to make public, but it needs no courage. Architects have lost all proper spirit and self-esteem. The advertisement is directed—"To the Architects and Builders of Sussex," and stands thus,—"The architects and builders of Sussex are invited to furnish plans and estimates for rebuilding the Lewes Free Grammar School at an expense not to exceed 2,000*l*., to be prepared according to instructions from a sub-committee already organized for that purpose, which instructions may be had on application at the office of Messrs. 'Gull and Co.,' to whom such plans and estimates are requested to be delivered on or before the 27th of February next. The architect or builder whose plan and estimate shall be finally adopted, will be entitled to a *remuneration not exceeding ten pounds ten shillings*, at the discretion of the committee."

A remuneration! mark that, ye rising Wykehams and little Wrens. "Remuneration" means, according to the dictionary, reward, requital, recompense, but what does it mean according to these gentlemen of Sussex, on whose "discretion" architects are to depend? Why, it means, the remote *chance* of getting, for the work done, not one-fifth of what ought to be received for it without any risk at all. It marks the *status* the profession enjoys: it shows the contempt in which architects are held. A thing is worth what it will fetch, they say. If your talent is to

* One correspondent, to select from a dozen on the general subject of competitions, says,—"What in the name of all that is extraordinary is the real and unsophisticated meaning of the word 'competition?' In the present day it seems to have undergone a complete change, and is now only to be interpreted by sets of churchwardens and committees, each in their peculiar way, striving to make it synonymous with the word 'jobbing.' From the numerous iniquitous cases, where this has been done, which you have from time to time so justly exposed and commented on, more especially from the recent disclosures in the Chichester affair, the wonder is that any architect can be fool enough to waste his time on such utterly fruitless labour, as joining in one of these unintelligible enigmas. For my own part, experience has taught me to desist altogether, having frequently nibbled at the attractive bait held out in the advertisements, and, as a matter of course, as frequently been 'taken in.' With respect to the competition for Edmonton Church, which appeared in your paper some months ago, I could a tale unfold that would not be over creditable to the committee of that affair, but forbear saying more than that it is fully entitled to a high rank under the head 'job.' With a view to lessen the evil, I propose to form a society, to be called the 'Anti-competition or Jobbing Society,' each member of which should be required to take an oath, that he will never send in for a competition unless he have a written statement from the parties advertising, that he is to have the job, no matter who else or how many are applied to for drawings; that he shall read this statement before a general meeting of the members, in order that they may communicate the same to their friends, and thus relieve them from the necessity of making tools of themselves by wasting their time and talents on useless pursuits. Some such movement made by the rising generation might, I think, be productive of much good, and open the eyes of the juvenile members of the architectural profession a little wider than they are wont to be." And another correspondent says—"Our friends, in *Punch*, often take a leaf from your book: might I suggest for once that we should follow their example, and as they criticise the use and abuse of the Queen's English in the advertisement to the world at large, do you, Sir, bestow five minutes of your editorial time in submitting to the rules of Lindley Murray, of venerated memory, the specification issued by the worthies of Birmingham for this workhouse." For our own parts, however, we will not question their grammar, if they will but mind their manners.

be estimated by what it fetches at Lewes, it is small indeed. We are too much out of humour to discuss the matter further, and will only say to those who may be tempted by this "remuneration" to make plans and estimates for rebuilding Lewes Free School, what we exclaimed at the commencement,—stupid architects!

It has been suggested to us at various times that some of the best architectural subjects given in THE BUILDER, if printed in a superior manner on good paper, with the accompanying descriptions, plans, &c., and issued periodically, would form a work that would be acceptable not only to those who are not buyers of THE BUILDER, but to many who are,—the current engravings being often creased by the news vendors or otherwise injured. We are disposed to try the experiment, and to publish, in a neat wrapper, under an appropriate title, about eight plates, with eight pages of letter-press, folio size, every second month, price half-a-crown. The first part would consist of Osborne House, with plan; Bridgewater House, plan and details; Church of St. Isaac, Petersburgh; Kensington Union Workhouse; Pembroke College, Oxford; the Liverpool Branch Bank; and the north porch of St. Mary Redcliffe, Bristol. Before determining upon the scheme, however, we should be glad to receive the names of such gentlemen as would be willing to become subscribers to the work.

THE NEW "PRINCE'S THEATRE ROYAL," GLASGOW.

In case they may happen to contain some points of practical interest to readers of THE BUILDER, I have thrown together the few following particulars of the construction of this theatre; and which may, perhaps, serve to elicit further information on the general subject from those who have had occasion to direct their attention to it.

The premises which have just been converted, were erected, under my direction, about two years ago, for the exhibition of certain dioramic pictures by the brothers Daguerre. In building the original structure, I recommended to the proprietor, in regard to its stability and permanency, that instead of limiting it to the probable existence of the diorama exhibition, it should be made capable of being finished interiorly in an architectural manner, and adapted to the purposes of a public hall, in which I considered the locality stood in need.

Accordingly, the mode of construction adopted consisted as follows:—Two-feet coursed-rubble stone walls were erected to the height to receive the floor, which is 13 feet above the ground line, leaving the entire area underneath clear, excepting the posts and pillars carrying the floor beams, and to be appropriated to another purpose. Upon these walls was set a massive framing of timber, consisting of a cill plate, 12 inches by 9 inches; angle and intermediate posts averaging about 12 feet apart, and measuring 12 inches by 12 inches; and a head plate 12 inches by 6 inches, the posts being tenoned at top and bottom into the plates, and braced up with struts 9 inches by 6 inches where they occurred over openings in the stone walls beneath, in each of which cases the cill was sustained by the post above with a strong bolt, in the same manner as the tie-beam of a roof. The spaces in the framing were filled in with 9-inch brickwork, the connection of which with the posts was insured by the insertion, midway in its thickness, of tongues of wrought iron, about 10 inches by 5 inches, and ¾ inch thick, having a long spike at one end for driving into the posts, into which they were inserted at short intervals, of course edgeways. The roof, in order to its being of a lightness suited to the walls, I formed something like the deck of a great ship, namely, a platform, with an external camber of—say 10 inches; in construction it consisted of trussed timber beams spanning the width of the building, placed coincident with the posts in the

side walls, and carrying joists 9 by 2, about 4 feet from centre to centre, these in their turn carrying inch floor boarding, the joints grooved and tongued in the lower, and caulked with oakum in the upper part, then covered with strips of zinc, put on with zinced tacks, and the entire surface being over with tar, lime, and sand, and finished with a coat of white, in order to its reflecting the sun's rays. The space thus enclosed measured 90 feet by 63 feet, and 33 feet high from floor line to top of wall framing.

The truss beams were as follows: each consisted of two 12 by 5 flitches in the width, and these in two equal pieces in the length, well scarved and keyed together. These were set two inches apart, making the beam 12 inches square; and they rested, at the scarves, upon a cast-iron bearing-plate, 30 by 12, having a central bearing upright tongue, a few inches high, occupying the space between them. On either side of the plate was a square stub for preventing its moving longitudinally, and along the centre below was a semicircular groove for containing the tension rod, which was of two-inch round iron, and passed under it. This compound beam was, at its extreme ends, inserted into a cast-iron box, having flanges below, outside and inside the head plate of the wall framing, and a strong cylindrical sloping part on the top, at the back of which the tension-rod, which was passed through it, with screwed ends, was secured with a nut at least 4 inches long: at intervals between the end boxes and central bearing-plate, were introduced between the flitches circular blockings 6 inches diameter, and 4 inches thick, sunk an inch into the timber on either side, through which the flitches were bolted together: in the boxes they were kept apart by a piece of 2-inch board. Where the upper edge of the boxes would have bit deeply into the wood, upon the tightening of the tension rods, a piece of boiler-plate (malleable iron), was introduced; and where the end grains at the scarves would have penetrated each other from the same cause, that is, in the under joints, pieces of sheet-iron were inserted. On the other hand, the upper joints of the scarves, the tendency of which was to open, were strengthened with plate-iron and bolts; the beams were tied down to the wall framing, by bolts passing diagonally through both: for a few feet at both ends, the tension-rods were increased in diameter, so as to preserve the solid part of the screw the full 2 inches.

In the screwing up of these beams, I had an opportunity of observing an effect of which those trussing cast-iron beams of similar construction might remain in ignorance, namely, a decided tendency to turn up at the ends, caused by the tension-rod proceeding in a downward inclination from a point above the beam, and which, accompanied with the camber over the centre bearing-plate, produces something of a wavy form. In the present case, the distance of that point above the beam, and consequently the derangement produced, was very trifling; but in trussed-girder railway bridges which I have seen, with fins at their ends, and at the joints—the former for the very purpose of elevating the points of

suspension, the strain thus produced must in some instances be dangerous. Shortly after the completion of the building, in order to allay the anxiety of the timid, who looked with some dread at the wide expanse of flat roof, and having sufficient space, I put in struts at either end, with straining-pieces between their heads, and another tye-rod at their feet. It seems strange that, notwithstanding its having been years ago ascertained that tension-trussing, with a central point of support, is much stronger than with two points, inasmuch as the centre is necessarily the weakest point, engineers do yet continue the latter practice, when they could, where the span required it, employ the central supported point of their beams as a point of suspension by aid of which to truss the two halves.

The foregoing description explains the general form of the building; but it remains to be mentioned that the diorama picture, which was selected as the first to be exhibited, was of such a size as to require that the end where it was hung should have a sinking in the floor of 4 feet in depth by 8 in width, as well as that the truss-beam there should be omitted, and a span-roof, with collar-tie, be thrown over the wide bay thus left in the main roof. By adopting this as the stage end, what with the elevation of the stage, its rise backwards (¼-inch in the foot), and the depression in the floor, a range of dressing-rooms were obtained. The picture referred to required also an extension, on one side, of the width of the building, which has added to the commodiousness of the stage; and, to increase the vista in forest and other scenes, the central portion has been carried some distance backward, in the form of a wing to the main building. At the side of this is a building containing the green-room, property-room, wardrobe, sundry dressing-rooms, &c.

I now proceed to give some particulars of the construction and fitting-up of the theatre.

The box and gallery tiers are carried on beams, curved by forming them in thicknesses set edgeways: these beams are 9 inches square, having eight 1¼th inch boards in their breadth. The mode of constructing them was as follows, taking the inner circle or horse-shoe, for example:—the figure being described full-size on the floor, a quantity of right-angled triangular brackets, about 15 inches by 9 inches, were set on edge on the floor, radiating inward from the inner line, and against these the first board was nailed; the other thicknesses were then nailed on the outside successively, breaking joint carefully, until the required thickness was completed, when the whole was further secured together by bolting it through at short intervals, suited especially to the situations of the external cross joints. By this plan, an exceedingly tough beam was obtained, having this advantage over a built one, that the grain of the wood was much less broken, and, in a manner, run round from end to end. Having such beams as these in front, and corresponding ones at the back, the joisting followed naturally · in a radiating fashion. The back beams were well secured to the walls, to counteract any tendency to travel in the direction of the stage.

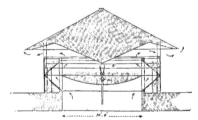

The above is a section of the ventilator over the pit, in which A is a shield of sheet iron, 9 feet 11 inches in diameter, on which the heat from the lights suspended below it strikes, and thus accelerates the upward current; B is a beam, with a pair of

whorls in the middle, over which ropes pass from a small windlass at one side, and allow the gas-pendant to be lowered, when unscrewed at the coupling, for the purpose of the globes being cleaned, &c.

Lighting.—Credit is due to the firm of

Laidlaw and Son, of Glasgow and Edinburgh, for the manner in which they have executed the gas-fittings, a branch requiring, in a theatre, more skill and ingenuity than is brought into requisition in any other description of building. Two 1½ inch pipes extend round the edge of the stage, with Argand burners, chimneys, and shades to each: the burners in each pipe are 6 inches apart, but those in one row placed alternately, in relation to those in the other: the lights on the outer pipe have green glass chimneys, for moonlight scenes; those on the inner one, colourless chimneys for ordinary use: for melo-dramatic effects, wherein the pyrotechnists' art is commonly brought into play, I suppose red chimneys would, according to this mode, suffice. The 'gas-battens,' which light up the wings and borders, are a quarter-circle in their section, about a foot in width, and their lengths suited to the height and width of the stage openings; they are lined with galvanized sheet-iron, and hooped across in the open part, to prevent any combustible material which might flap against them coming in contact with the jets of gas, the pipe being placed in the hollow of the quarter-circle. At the prompter's place, where the arrangements are made for the raising and lowering of the lights in the stage and audience departments, the risk of the gas being turned off altogether, is obviated by having, at the stop-cock on each large pipe, small parallel pipes extending, so as to connect the large one in its two portions on either side, the small pipe being also provided with a stop-cock, should occasion require it. While the curtain is down, the house is kept brilliantly lit up; but during performance, the light is reduced, in order to enhance the effect of the *tableau*.

Seeing.—As regards the form of the house, it was greatly regulated in its proportions by those of the original structure; and these happily favoured the wide rather than the long form, which has the disadvantage, that the audience have a difficulty in seeing past each other, and are placed in an uncomfortable, constrained attitude, looking, as it were, *askance* at the stage. In taking up the subject, and considering the pitch of the different tiers, increasing, as they do, in steepness, as seen, say in the longitudinal section, it becomes obvious that the longer the central space is as compared with its width, the more must the pitch of any one tier increase in steepness in the direction from the centre round on either side towards the proscenium; for then the audience are looking more and more, as it were, into a well. This increase is usually, and most conveniently obtained by keeping the passages at the back about level, and lowering the inner beams as they approach the stage-end: by this means, the advantage is gained to the audience of seeing comfortably over each other, when looking towards the stage, as well as when looking at the lower tiers opposite them. The view from the back rows, to be perfect, ought of course to embrace the whole proscenium; this, however, it appears, involves a degree of comfort which it is not customary to attempt obtaining; the consideration being rather how little of the height of the proscenium will suffice, so as to reduce the entire height or get in the greatest number of tiers of which it is capable.

Hearing.—The material of the ceiling is canvas, dense in quality, and rendered more so by the operations of the artist. Writers on acoustics affirm that sonorous vibrations will be propagated in a speaking-trumpet lined with cloth, with equal effect as if it were formed of a metallic substance; and we have Dr. Arnott's interesting relation of the ringing of the bells in the city of St. Salvador, on the Brazilian coast, having been distinctly heard on board-ship 100 miles at sea, the sound being wafted by a gentle wind over smooth water, and interrupted in its progress, and concentrated to a focus, by the concave sail of the vessel; thus much for canvas: a dense body of vapour, even, it is allowed, may cause the reverberation of sound; and hence we have reasons to justify the use of so pliant a substance as canvas for a surface to reflect sound where a wooden sounding-board is not conveniently available. But woollen cloth, I have reason to believe, is a great absorbent of sound: at this theatre I have had an opportunity of comparing the singing in the rehearsals with the same in the public performance; when I was struck with the loss that was occasioned evidently by the presence of the audience, and which I mainly attribute to the amount of broad cloth present, though partially to the interruption caused to the rays of sound in passing towards the various reverberating surfaces; at the same time, not to forget the reverberable power of vapour, some slight share of said loss might possibly be chargeable to the diminished purity of the atmosphere (not to confess, for all that, that our ventilator was inefficient). We know that the more carbonic-acid gas is generated in an assembly the more dense the atmosphere becomes, the density of that gas being half as much again as pure air; the thick imperfect tones of the speaker in a church or ball crowded to suffocation, compared to the ringing sonorousness of his voice when he happens not to be quite so attractive, are very perceptible, and may be referred to the causes I have mentioned.

Means of communication all round the house have been preserved in the various tiers, as well as ample means of egress. In such places the latter is of much importance, as well as that the doors that are kept shut during performance should open outwards; it is also desirable to have the entrances to the various parts nearest those *places* which are least advisable: for experience proves that if they are at the best places, these will get first filled, and thus form a barrier to reaching the others.

Besides the precautions taken with the gas-battens against fire, arrangements are in progress for laying on a supply of water, at high pressure, in a standing-main behind pit, boxes, and gallery, with a short hose and nozzle to each; also a cistern on each wing-platform, with hose descending for the supply of a portable fire-engine on the stage: the partition which separates the audience and stage departments on either side of the proscenium-opening is also of brick; and the small circular staircases which communicate with all the private-boxes and with the wing-platforms are of the same material.

In Glasgow, buildings are not regulated by any Buildings Act, but there is a board, called the Dean-of-Guild Court, before which parties intending to build are required to appear, in order to their plans having its sanction, after affording to the owners of properties abutting upon the one in question, an opportunity for bringing forward objections. It takes cognizance, also, on the part of the lieges, of all cases, in respect to buildings, wherein danger may threaten, or accident have occurred. This court, for the satisfaction of the public, the gentleman for whom the theatre has been fitted up, memorialised, at my recommendation, for an inspection to be made by efficient persons as to the security of the structure. A readiness, in this manner, to consult the feelings and allay the fears of the uninitiated portion of the public, should ever be evinced; and I am disposed to think that, in many cases, public buildings ought not to be opened for use without the concurrent testimony of experienced professional men being first obtained: in the present case, sundry things were required, and being reasonable, were of course readily conceded.

The decorations are in *carton-pierre*, and were furnished by Messrs. Jackson, of Rathbone-place:* they are in high relief, and comprise festoons of fruit and flowers, medallions, and panels, containing groups of children; a mimic orchestra of these are perched in the box-front, on brackets in the line of the pillars; while over them, in the gallery-front, are termini, with brackets bearing crystal gas-lustres. The enrichments are white, picked out in gold, with pale blue back-grounds in panels, and the fronts of the tiers rose-colour.

The scenes are chiefly what, in theatrical phraseology, are termed flats; the act-drop is, however, an exception, and it is due to the able young artist, Mr. Bough, who painted it, to state, that it is a work which foretokens distinction to him as a painter.

The whole arrangements evince the good taste of the manager, Mr. Edmund Glover, son of Mrs. Glover, of the Theatre Royal, Haymarket; and the style in which the house-furnishings, the stage properties and dresses, and all other appointments have been prepared, show that he has spared neither pains nor expense. The performances are opera, vaudeville, and ballet, — the operatic corps being led by the able *bâton* of Mr. Howard Glover. The theatre was opened (notwithstanding the ill-instigated statement of a London contemporary, that it could not be), on Monday, January 15th, with the opera of "Giselle, or the Night Dancers," and the vaudeville of the "Imperial Guard."

The theatre is calculated, when it is "a full house," to accommodate 1,400 persons comfortably.

JAMES WYLSON.

* We had the pleasure of recommending these manufacturers to Mr. Glover, for this work; induced to do so by the able manner in which they had carried out Mr. Bradwell's views at the Lyceum Theatre, Strand.—ED.

EXHIBITION OF THE BRITISH INSTITUTION, PALL-MALL.

THE earliest of the annual displays of modern art was opened to the public on Monday last, in the rooms of this association, and it may be pronounced as a very tolerable, if not absolutely a good collection. About 400 pictures are annually offered on its walls for sale, chiefly painted by artists to whom the disposal of their performances is of vast object. They are offered at a season when there is no competition of the greater gatherings, and the society being composed of the highest and most intellectual amateurs of modern art—individually its greatest patrons — at once brings the rising artist into prominent contact with their very best friends, on the most solid basis to promote future success. These are surely sufficient grounds for the public to recognise with approbation the labours of the association called the British Institution for the promotion of the fine arts of the country, and cause regret when its affairs are not well administered. An accusation has been founded on a demand to enlarge the premises where the exhibition is held, and no doubt such an addition is very desirable. Reference thereon has been made to the fortunes of the governors and directors, and some inuendoes of apathy on this point have occasionally been promulgated. This is scarcely just, for the directors have made many efforts to obtain property in the rear for the purpose; and, although the property sought for was not of vast value, yet the impurity or vice of its application rendered it lucrative to the possessors,—consequently they have been met by the most outrageous and extravagant demands, such as could be viewed only as a gross attempt at extortion.

We are not going to enter into a discussion of the usual range of critical remarks, nor dwell with feminine rapture on works being replete with sweetness, or delicious colour, or delightful bits, or charming softness; for art-criticism demands other phrases, and certain fundamental acquirements upon which the capacity of judging can alone, with safety, be formed. It is not founded on vague perception, arises from no concatenation of ideas, is not taught by school learning. The sublime and beautiful in all objects of ocular investigation, influence the intelligent observer and the unlearned spectator, upon notions diametrically opposite. To arrive at a pure knowledge of a work of art, requires an acquaintance with its inflexible principles of invention, the artistic construction, the difficulties of execution to be surmounted, and the degree of success with which any production has been completed. The scholar may arrive at a just understanding of the ideal and the inventive portion; although the fine arts form no branch of university education. But let him once wander into the technical, and then we hear similar absurdities promulgated, as when a late writer on Spanish art, talks of *transparent* greys and ultra-marine with warm white glazings. And also Dr. Waagen, of Berlin, whose name is almost authoritative, does not scruple to praise the French school as a school of colour, thus running from the stony pallid hues of German art, to the opposite excess of tinsel gaudy glare. There are besides many who pretend to be connoisseurs, and employ their pen on the subject, whose sole attainment arises from a comparison of what they have seen; omitting all reference to other existing examples, and not even taking the pains to be informed by reading what has been written by the most accredited writers on the subject. On the other hand artists may be imagined to possess the most competent knowledge, but they are disposed to narrow their views to the single class of artistic works they have adopted for their own practice; and it is much to be regretted, however painfully true, that a number of our living painters are disqualified by the absence of sufficient general education to undertake the task. There are, nevertheless, great exceptions, but unfortunately they are much too chary of their labour for the public to profit by their instruction. The writings of Barry and Haydon are sound in principle, although imbued with more than a tinge of acerbity; nor can any maxims, more perfectly just and gracefully enunciated, exist, than are found in the writings of Sir Joshua Reynolds.

The difficulty of combining literary attainments with the routine of the atelier, and the theoretic attainments of anatomy, perspective, and other sciences, ought to damp the ardour of the ordinary critics upon pictorial art. In rendering an account of the present exhibition, we propose therefore to advance rather a *résumé* of its contents, and invite amateurs to investigate narrowly for themselves the exhibited works, upon the principles of composition, drawing, expression, colour, light and shade, with aerial and linear perspective. These qualities once achieved, the eye may then seek its pleasure in the choice of subject.

The catalogue contains 518 numbers, 504 of which are attached to pictures, and fourteen to sculpture. As the elder sister, the sculptors' performances claim the precedence of notice over painting. The most consequential work is the life-size recumbent group in marble of "Ino and the infant Bacchus," by J. H. Foley, executed for the Earl of Ellesmere, in whose mansion it will form a becoming ornament. A marble statue of a satyr, and a bust personifying innocence, by W. Calder Marshall, A.R.A., as well as a small marble figure of Musidora, by T. Earle, comprise the amount of noticeable works.

In painting, only one of the royal academicians (W. Lee) exhibits, and only five of the associates are in the same category.

The historical, or figure subjects, are not in great strength. The Chevalier Bezzuoli, President of the Florentine Academy, displays a picture taken from the life of Giotto, of considerable merit: the figures are well drawn, and the folds of the draperies broad and well cast. Still, if it is to be taken as a specimen of the condition of historical art in modern Italy, it will not rank very high; it possesses a good deal of the ancient Italian technicalities, but depicts the defunct body, from which the soul has departed. R. T. Bott (to us a new name), has a composition of many figures, illustrating Victor Hugo's tale of the death of the banished lord. A good deal of clever arrangement of the subject on the surface is manifested, and some well-disposed lines. One of the most important of figure compositions, being a group of nymphs and infants, with the inviting title of "Dolce far niente," conceals the painter's name under the initials of G. F. W., to which a very professional address is appended in the catalogue. The picture is worth examining for many good qualities. A small picture of a sitting figure, nude, called "A Naiad," by W. E. Frost, A.R.A., placed on the screen of the secretary's desk, is an elegant personation of the female figure, painted in rich tones, with admirable chiaro-scuro. It may be called a gem.

In the lower department of figure pictures, either conversational or amatory, there are many of considerable merit, nor is there a small affluence of the domestic pathetic, intended to excite the sighs and sympathies of the fair sex. In pictures that may be termed dramatic, stands first, a work of high imaginative power by F. Danby, A.R.A., representing a mountain chieftain's funeral in the olden times. This picture has rarely been equalled for a mysterious depth of tone; the faint moonlight that beams o'er the towering mountains is treated with all the mastery of art; the entire scene is conceived with great grandeur of chiaro-scuro, and developed with true poetic feeling. Probably it will not please the multitude, because, as they will say, "it is so dark." On the opposite wall is placed one of John Martin's inspirations of biblical miracles; although a veteran in fame, he appears in all the vigour and freshness of his earliest powers. It is a representation of Joshua commanding the sun to stand still. There is an awful sublimity in the lighting up of the distant mountains, and the vast architectural edifice crested on the rock is pregnant with noble ideas, which will delight the student in this art. The sky is a problem not readily solved by an ordinary observer of the phenomena of nature. It will make an admirable engraving.

Among the interiors or exteriors of buildings more particularly interesting to this journal, is a picture upwards of 13 feet long by 4½ feet high, representing the interior of the picture gallery at Stafford-house, St. James's, painted by J. D. Wingfield. This apartment, the most gorgeous of any in the palatial abodes of the metropolis, is here made public to the hundreds who have sighed in vain to see the original. The portion represented is that where, encased in the walls, are the two wondrous Murillos. The mural decorations, with the massive chandeliers and candelabra, are painted in their minutest details. The enrichments of the fireplace in the centre have such a fac-simile of relief in the mouldings and ornaments, that we felt a desire to ascertain by the finger if they did not really project; but were deterred by reflecting that we should descend to the level of the birds which pecked at the imitative cherries of the ancient Greek painter.

Landscape is the branch of art in which the school of England wields the sceptre of supremacy over all the European schools, and in the present exhibition is the dominant feature. "The Deserted," by C. Branwhite, takes a first place in the ideal. The scene is a continuous lake, environed by forest scenery terminated only by the horizon, and seen from the ruins of a terrace: the sun is sinking below the horizontal line, and steeps in its evening gilding every part of the solitary glen. The picture depends on a single thought,—a very felicitous one, rendered magnificent by the scale of colour, although bordering on Germanism in scale. The opposite excess of purely natural transcript is contributed by R. Redgrave, A.R.A., called "Strawberry Gatherers in Norbury Woods." The Professor of Botany in the Government School of Design has justified his appointment by the elaborate study of wild plants and perfection of foliage. The picture is of the highest order in its class; and a significant warning to the noviciate, that the road to success is the unflinching study of natural objects, and that in landscape painting it is the foreground which marks the degree of excellence in rural scenes. Thomas Danby has two views in Wales. This painter came out with remarkable strength last year; but his present pictures do not quite equal the past. There is an unnatural blackness and want of atmosphere in the group of trees that intervenes between the stream and the distance of his principal work. The brother, James Danby, has a view of Scarborough, well lighted and very transparent, C. Marshall has a lake scene with mountains called "Lynn Grafnant, Caernarvonshire," which no one can mistake to have been painted on the spot, so fully is it invested with the natural charms of sunny light and atmosphere.

There are many other excellent landscapes worthy of examination. The most pretentious are two by F. R. Lee, R.A., with groups of cattle, by S. Cooper, A.R.A. Enough has been already written on these talented artists to render remark superfluous. In animal subjects, R. Ansdell worthily supplies the absence of E. Landseer. He has three pictures, all admirable. The department of still life is supremely maintained by G. Lance, in five pictures. There is a good sprinkling of marine subjects and coast scenes, none betraying novelty, or wandering beyond the ordinary routine, although they are generally pleasing.

"On the Gulf of Spezzia," by G. E. Hering; "A Scene in Epping Forest," by W. Linton; "Prayer before the Mid-day Alms," by A. C. Hayter, jun.; "The Harvest Field," by H. Jutsum; "The Murder of Thomas à Becket," by J. Gilbert; "Burns and Capt. Grose," by R. S. Lauder; "The Trial of Laud," by Alex. Johnston, all deserve notice.

LINCOLN'S-INN FIELDS POPULARIZED.

London increases so rapidly in extent that every inch of open and available space within its present boundary should be carefully preserved, and improved for the healthful exercise and recreation of its inhabitants. Among places especially adapted to this purpose, the enclosed areas of the numerous public squares demand particular notice. It not unfrequently occurs that those who live in the surrounding houses are far too exclusive and aristocratic, or too much occupied to expose themselves to the observation of their neighbours by adopting them as places of promenade, while at the same time numbers of residents in the immediate vicinity, of equal respectability, are strictly precluded the privilege. At the West-end of the town, where the parks afford so much facility of air and exercise, this is, perhaps, of no great moment. There are, however, other localities where it is a matter of considerable importance. To those who are unacquainted with the topography of the metropolis east of Tottenham-court-road, it may be a subject of curious information to learn that there is such a region as Lincoln's-Inn Fields; that the houses which surround it form one of the noblest quadrangles in Europe, the site of which, if appropriated to public buildings, would afford a better opportunity for architectural display than ever did the Forum of old Rome.

Within this imposing quadrangle, and enclosed in its entire circuit by a strong iron fence, there appears a well-wooded and fertile area, of great, if not unknown, extent. The few who are chartered to enter its umbrageous paths seem never to avail themselves of the advantage; and it is even supposed by some that, saving the solitary woodsman or occasional cultivator, it has never yet been trodden by human foot: whether its coverts and thickets harbour animals of the chase or wild beasts of prey, is also a question of curious speculation and conjecture. Can it be that the laws of William the Norman, as relating to the New Forest, are still in force in this and several similarly favoured spots, which now stretch in a northerly direction from this locality towards Camden-town?

If this should prove to be the case, some effort should be made towards having them relaxed on behalf of all respectable persons, at least at certain times and seasons, as has been done at the Temple Gardens. Footpad.

THE ABATTOIR QUESTION.

INSTITUTION OF CIVIL ENGINEERS.

At a meeting on February 6, Mr. Joshua Field, President, in the chair, the paper read was a "Description of the Abatoirs of Paris," by Mr. R. B. Grantham. It appeared from the account that, previous to the opening of the Paris abattoirs, in 1818, slaughter-houses existed in the crowded districts of the city; and that (as at present in London) the passage of the cattle through the streets, and the consequent nuisances, were found to be intolerable. The five abattoirs were designed with great care; they were erected within the barriers, at an average distance of a mile and three quarters from the centre of the city.

It appeared that the revenue (derived from tolls, charged upon all the meat killed, at per killogramme,) amounted, during one year, to 47,608*l*. 16s.; that the total expenses were 4,958*l*. 12s.; leaving a profit to the city of Paris of 42,650*l*. 4s., or about 6¼ per cent. upon 680,000*l*., the original cost of all these establishments. The paper argued that, if this revenue was obtained from the tolls, &c., for slaughtering meat for a population not exceeding 1,000,000 souls, who did not consume anything like the amount of animal food that Englishmen habitually indulge in, how much greater would be the profit of such establishments for London, where there was a population nearly approaching 3,000,000 of souls!

In the discussion which ensued, and in which Mr. E. Chadwick, Professor Owen, Mr. Leslie, and others, took part, very interesting statistical facts were given in connection with the present state of the Smithfield market, which, it was said, appeared to be upheld merely as a question of revenue to the city, for which the public not only paid heavily, but suffered severely, by common annoyance, and by the deleterious effects on public health.

BIRMINGHAM BRASS-WORK.

IN connection with the projected exposition of manufactures at that place, the *Birmingham Journal* has commenced a series of articles on its importance, wherein the various manufactures of the town are reviewed. We take from one of them the following remarks on the brass-work:—The history and progress of brassfounding in Birmingham has yet to be written, and we trust it will be done in brass on the stalls of the Exposition: in no town in England has the art been followed to greater advantage, as far as regards extensive production; how far successful as regards elegance and purity of design, we will not pretend to say—let the specimens sent for inspection show. At a period when the blind led the blind, much could not be expected; the spirit of active improvement has not broken in upon the dull calm routine of every-day life. Content to copy the common-place models of their predecessors, it is not to be wondered at there was for a very long period a reign of mediocrity, if not something worse. Then came an impression that something must be done; what to do, and how to do it, ended in the adoption of a bastard style of ornament, a wretched compound of shell and scroll. These, multiplied *ad infinitum*, clung like limpets to our bell-pulls, disfigured our curtain-pins, and perpetuated the sum of deformities. An impression got abroad, somehow or other, that the Grecian style was the only legitimate one; then honeysuckle and acanthus leaf, wretched approximations to the beautiful creations of Greek art, spread their unsightly shapes over all things of brass, useful or ornamental. A rage for animalism then took the place of the other two styles; our door-knockers were transformed into fearful-looking lions' heads, which grinned horribly at us; our tables were supported on their paws, while solemn-looking sphinxes reclined, watching over the mysteries of the drawing-room. The inapplicability of these various styles of ornamentation for their different purposes, was only equalled by the inferior mechanism or tame execution of the articles adorned; the substitution of the bell lever for the meagre looking cord, and the curtain band for the pin, was an era; it became necessary that a superior style of ornament should be introduced, and give an impetus to the trade generally. Minute and trifling as many of the details are which make up a cabinet brassfounder's trade, there are none, saving those embracing the precious metals, in which greater taste may be shown, or more mechanical ingenuity applied. He who calls to mind the purchases made by the School of Design from the Parisian Exposition, will remember the richly foliated ornaments which covered not a few of the bronze articles containing each a lesson in themselves. But these days of false economy have wrought foul wrong to the trade whose progress we are attempting to describe: the stamp has been exchanged for the casting box,—as a consequence, tinselly and gaudy ornament has taken the place of the quiet and rich leafage, which looked so substantial and natural when finished. That this is not confined to our own country, is most true. Our market has been deluged with the multitudinous drapery adornments of "Marsaux." Compelled in self-defence to fight against such fearful odds, it is not to be wondered at that we have, to a certain extent, been obliged to follow, or compete—how unsuccessfully will best be shown by the mention of the disadvantages we labour under: first, that in the knowledge of design we are yet much behind. (In France it is not the fault of the workman himself if he is not instructed in this department of his trade.) With us, until of late years, it was impossible to acquire this important branch of education. And secondly, most people are aware that the French mechanic can subsist on a pittance upon which our own countrymen would starve. We, however, are of opinion that the evil already mentioned will soon work its own cure, and that a better and more substantial class of articles must speedily take place of the flimsy productions of the day; such are in truth the butterflies of a craft which the first touch of the winter of a severer taste, and the acknowledgment that all is not really substantial which seems so, will speedily dissipate: we trust our exposition specimens will help to prove this in a satisfactory manner. It may not be improper to remark, that these observations have been made in consequence of the deteriorating influence which the production of brass goods from plates of sheet metal and by pressure, exert upon the progress of legitimate ornament. The process of stamping effectually precludes the possibility of the shelving or undercutting being introduced, which gives relief to the prominent parts, and is the foundation of all effect and true artistic beauty. It must not, however, be supposed that we are retrograding; far from it, there is a sensible improvement; there seems to be a better understanding abroad as to what is right or wrong, and the ornamentation is more applicable to the purposes or use of the object so ornamented: this recognition is an advance, and indicates a step in the right direction.

NOTES IN THE PROVINCES.

THE Braintree Union guardians have resolved, by a majority of one, "that a competent architect be employed to examine the union-house, and report to the board what can be done in the way of enlargement, and the expense thereof."——There are now three established churches and eleven dissenting in the parish of West Ham. Of the new church for the district of Stratford Marsh, named Christ Church, two lithographic views, an exterior and interior, have been prepared, for subscribers of one guinea and upwards towards the building fund.——At a public meeting in the Council Chamber, Salisbury, to decide as to the erection of a new workhouse wing, at a cost of 5,000*l.*, or alterations of the old, at a cost of 2,200*l.*, it was stated by a member of council, who succeeded in postponing the decision for six months, that there was reason to believe the Government designed "to amalgamate seven or eight unions so far as regarded the juveniles, where they could be educated and brought up to industry."——Cullumpton Church is to be reseated and repaired, one gallery removed, and another reduced in scale, with other alterations, all under the superintendence of Mr. Ashworth, of Exeter, architect.——The restoration of Christchurch Priory Church is advancing. The rood screen is finished, and works are in progress in the south aisle.——The new church at Leverstock Green, near Hemel Hempstead, will be ready for consecration in a few months.——A Gothic chapel is proposed to be erected in Heaton Norris, Stockport, from a design by Mr. E. Walters, of Manchester, architect, and under the name of Wycliffe Chapel. The cost will be about 2,200*l.*, and the dimension 65 feet in length by 40 feet in width.——All the larger rooms of the new Athenæum at Sheffield are nearly completed, and the opening of the new institution has been announced.——The dock works at Grimsby are in rapid progress, and it is reported that H.R.H. Prince Albert intends visiting them on 11th April, to lay the chief stone.——A Yorkshire genius, an innkeeper at Sowerby, according to a Leeds contemporary, has invented a steam machine to blow the bellows of Sowerby Church organ, to ring the church bells, and to keep the sitters 'warm without' while inwardly occupied with those more spiritual comforts, which themselves, too, have already been proposed to be administered wholesale by the electro-telegraphic machinery.——At Uplentham Hall, the Earl of Zetland's seat in Yorkshire, 900 feet of glass pipes have been laid down.——The Darlington Gas Company, with a view to supplying the town with water, have had the Tees water analyzed, and find it to be remarkably pure.——Upwards of one-half of the 2,000*l.* to be realized for the commencement of the new Congregational Church at Scarborough has been subscribed.——Captain Washington, of the harbour and railway department of the Admiralty, has been at North Shields investigating the merits of a proposal to erect new quays, wharfs, and landings there.——At the lead mines near Alston, and elsewhere, the miners are paid 10s. a-week as 'subsistence money,' and the balance (if any) of the sum for which they may have worked, as 'pay,' at the year's end,—a sum which, it is said, occasionally amounts to 100*l.* for one man. At a late reckoning at Nenthead, the 'pay' exceeded, by 1,000*l.*, the amount divided in any year within the last quarter of a century.——The carpenters at Messrs. Ritson and Co.'s yard, at Maryport, are standing out, it is said: 18s. a-week have been offered, with a prospect of constant employment for a lengthened period.——Tenders for the Workington Lock-up having been lodged, Messrs. Thomas Bromley and William Brown, builders, both of Workington, have been declared the contractors.——The ancient stone bridge at Inverness has been destroyed by an overflow of water from Lochness. The west side of the town has been much flooded.

RAILWAY JOTTINGS.

ONE of the new order of light branch-traffic steam-carriages was tried on the Eastern Counties, and worked satisfactorily till it 'broke down' at express speed 'from an over-straining,' as was said, 'of the delicate machinery.'——An American paper mentions a new casualty in railway travelling. One night, the water in the engine of the afternoon train from Lawrence to Salem was frozen in Middleton Woods; and the passengers, about fourteen in number, were obliged to occupy the cars all night.——The gates on the Grimsby line, facing the Midland station, are now opened and shut by machinery.——A float for trains in crossing the Forth, similar, we presume, to that for crossing the Tay, so amusingly described by *Punch*, was lately launched at Glasgow into the Clyde. It is 170 feet in length, 34 feet in width between the paddles, and 10 feet in depth; and from the limited breadth of the river, it was launched broadside, falling safely 2½ feet into the water. An engine of 56-inch cylinder and 3 feet 6 inches stroke, with a chimney, has been shipped at each paddle. The whole float is of iron, ribbed with ½-inch plates on the bottom.—By a mail-train accident on the Caledonian line, near Carlisle, five passengers (all labourers) have been killed. A second-class carriage, of improper gauge, belonging to the North-Western, is blamed.——Another casuality, but happily without loss of life, has occurred on the Edinburgh and Glasgow, by the breaking, it is said, of a driving-wheel tire only eight days in use.——Lord Brougham, in the House of Lords, has been advocating, by implication, the necessity of realizing our Austrian idea of rendering railway authorities responsible to a jury, in cases of neglect in the adoption of the best possible means of preventing accidents. In allusion to some experiments before the Privy Council on the strength of axles, in which the superiority of Hardy's patent axle was alleged to have been satisfactorily exhibited, his lordship said,—Some hundred weight was placed on the axle, and a shock of the most startling magnitude was given to the carriage. That patent axle was bent into a completely circular shape, without a single fracture being visible in it. Indeed, it was as good an axle, in point of solidity, after the accident as before it. Out of fifty other common axles which were submitted to the same shock, only two were able to stand it. He complained that the directors of railways did not substitute these patent axles, which were 30 per cent. cheaper than the common axles, for those axles, until they were either broken up or worn out. He took this opportunity of letting this fact be known to the Directors; for, if death should ensue hereafter from the breaking of an axle, he knew well what the verdict of a jury would be.——A railway ring, it is said, has just been carried completely round that whirling circle of magical revolutions, Paris.——The communication by rail is now either complete, or will soon be, *viâ* Calais, right through the heart of Europe, including Paris, Brussels, Cologne, Antwerp, the Rhine, Berlin, Warsaw, Leipsic, Vienna, Switzerland, and Venice. Arrangements are already in progress for a grand continuous tour, or route, through most of the places here named. Paris itself will thus be approximated to London by a time distance of only eleven hours, or a run actually shorter than that to either of its own provincial capitals, Edinburgh or Dublin.

ROYAL ACADEMY.—Mr. Richard Westmacott has been elected a Royal Academician.

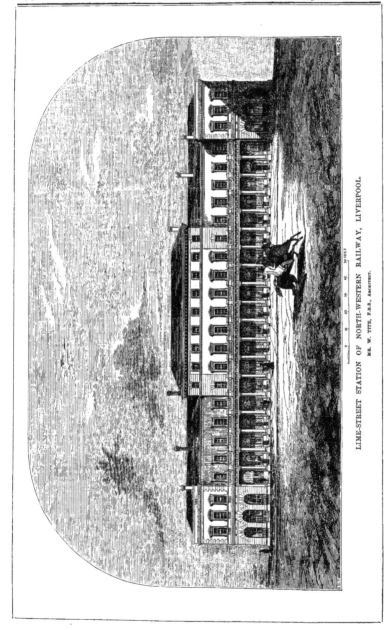

LIME-STREET STATION OF NORTH-WESTERN RAILWAY, LIVERPOOL.

MR. W. TITE, F.R.S., ARCHITECT.

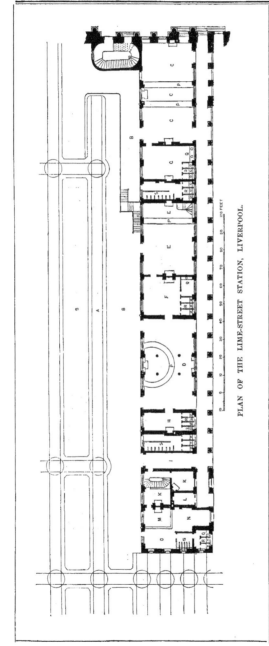

PLAN OF THE LIME-STREET STATION, LIVERPOOL.

THE LIME-STREET STATION OF THE NORTH-WESTERN RAILWAY, LIVERPOOL.

THE Lime-street station, to which we have already briefly alluded, was originally built by Mr. Cunningham, of Liverpool. The façade, however, towards Lime-street, was erected from a design by Mr. Forster, the architect to the corporation, who received from the Company the necessary funds for that purpose. The station having become much too small for the greatly-increased traffic of the line, it was determined by the Directors, in 1846, to remodel and re-arrange it. To this end, the tunnel front has been cut back, and a very large area obtained by purchasing houses and premises to a great extent in Hotham-street, Gloucester-street, and Sydney-street. Hotham-street is now crossed by a bridge, which allows the continuance of the platforms under that bridge up to the face of the tunnel, and by this means platforms, 500 feet in length, have been obtained.

This bridge is a level beam bridge, of cast-iron, carried on Tuscan columns of very good proportion. It was designed and executed by Mr. Edward Wood, the resident engineer.

The general arrangements of the stations are from the designs of Mr. J. Locke, M.P., the engineer-in-chief of the railway. The design of the offices, of which we engrave the elevation and plan, was entrusted to the care of Mr. W. Tite, F.R.S., architect, of London.

The principal entrance is from the street called Lord Nelson-street; and the offices are all arranged lengthways on the platform. The one-pair floor is appropriated to the accommodation of the Board, the secretary, treasurer, &c., and the second, or upper floor to the ticket department.

The contractor is Mr. John Jay, of London-wall; the amount of the contract about 30,000*l.*

The material used is principally brick; the colonnade and dressings being the mill-stone grit quarried at Darley-dale, in Derbyshire, the same stone as is used at St. George's Hall. The plinths of the columns and of the buildings generally are Devonshire granite.

From the difficulty of erecting the new buildings without interfering with the large and active business carried on, it has been necessary to proceed very slowly with the work and to build it in two detached portions.

The part constructed now consists of a centre and the left wing, and to adapt this for temporary purposes the refreshment rooms are "for the nonce" used for the booking offices of the Northern trade. In the basement, are extensive offices, kitchens, third-class refreshment rooms, guards' and porters' rooms, and the other various requirements of a railway station.

The great shed is, at present, temporary. Mr. Turner, of Dublin, has contracted for an iron roof, in one elliptical span, the conjugate diameter being 150 feet. The first experiments on the principals of roof, made in Dublin in the autumn of last year, were unsatisfactory, the ribs having given way. He is now, however, as we understand, making another attempt with ribs of a different form.

References to Plan.

A   Great shed.
B   Departure platforms.
C   Booking-office for Manchester, Bolton, and Preston.
D   Booking-office for London and Birmingham.
E   Refreshment-room.
F   Ladies' first-class waiting-room.
G   Ladies' waiting-room.
H   Ladies' second-class waiting-room.
I   Entrance gateway.
K   Superintendent's rooms.
L   Bullion-office.
M   Left cloaks, umbrellas, &c.
N   Porters'-room.
O   Lamps.
P   Counters.
Q   Wash.
R   Water-closets.
S   Urinals.

CONDITION OF THE BRITISH MUSEUM. —Part of the evidence taken by the commissioners, appointed to inquire into the constitution and management of the British Museum, is about to be laid before the House of Commons. The commissioners seem to be moving very slowly: another commission must be appointed presently to inquire into *their* condition.

GRAVESTONE AT ISLAY.

GRAVESTONE AT iSLAY.

THE accompanying sketch is taken from a simple slab in the old burying ground in the island of islay, Argyleshire. There is no inscription, or any characters upon the stone, and the device itself is very rudely sculptured. it is a curious arrangement of four hearts, four rings (query, wedding?), a cross, and two circles, all blended one in the other, without confusion.

POWNHOPE CHURCH, HEREFORDSHiRE.
HEREFORD ANTIQUARIAN SOCIETY.

AT a recent soirée given by this society, Dr. Strong, of Ross, read a paper on Fownhope Church. In the course of it the writer said,—Many hundred years has this temple mouldered and decayed in neglect and contempt, but the day has at length dawned when the taste and intelligence, the munificence and the skill, the piety or the pride, that presided over its erection and added roof to roof for its rural worshippers, shall be again understood and appreciated, and even emulated. The size of the fabric is sufficiently considerable to arrest attention, being no less than 110 feet long in the clear, and how a pile so large and so irregular came to be erected we have no written record, but there are stones about the edifice which, rightly interpreted, will throw a clear light upon its history. The most ancient, or at least the most authentically striking piece in the whole building, is the scriptural tympanum in the western wall, of which a cast was taken by the very Rev. the Dean of Hereford, and exhibited at the first soirée for the present season.

There can be no question but this stone once filled up the semi-circular part of a Norman portal—a peculiarity of this style, the origin of which is unknown. Some have supposed that the early architects, not having as yet had much experience of the principle and resistance of the arch, thought it prudent to strengthen their work by imposing a stone between the door-jambs: hence this support is commonly called the "impost-stone." it thus became a sort of compromise between the Greek and the Roman doorway. Considerable pains have recently been taken to preserve this relic of the Norman era, but no trace of the arch or of the side-jambs remains either here or in any other part of the walls. And this is one of several reasons for concluding that the present church has been rebuilt. The early erection may even have been standing here prior to the conquest, like Bridstowe Church, which is in the same style, and which, upon the authority of the Liber Llandavensis, was consecrated two years before the battle of Hastings.

There appears to have been a custom prevailing among the architects who succeeded the Normans of preserving the doorways of those churches they rebuilt or altered, for doorways such as this in the Anglo-Norman style still exist in many churches, the other portions of which were erected at a much later period. The reason for this may have proceeded from a laudable wish to retain some visible remembrance of the piety of the founder, by whom the original work was designed. Some impaired bases and capitals of Norman pillars, of a size corresponding with the doorway, were, upon the authority of an antiquary who has long resided near the locality, to be seen some years since, as well as some fragments of very early Norman work under the singing-gallery. The two capitals are now preserved and used as flower-pots at the Vicarage-house door.

An investigation of this unpretending fabric will reveal no less than five styles of architecture, marking as many equivalent epochs in our history, and lighting up in an unexpected manner, and from an unpromising quarter, some of the proceedings of the so-called dark ages. The Norman and semi-Norman styles are very decided; the succeeding styles, viz., the early English, the Decorated, and the Perpendicular, no less so, though not so highly prized by the antiquary.

The style then of the impost-stone, or tympanum, leads to the conclusion that it formed part of the door-way to a small Norman chapel of the size of those at Kilpeck or Shobdon, which stood upon the site of the present chancel. it might have been in existence about a century when the addition to the fabric of the present tower was made: this is 25 feet square, and exhibits particularly well the state of transition from the circular or Norman to the pointed or early English style. Thus, in the second story of the tower may be observed a lancet-headed couplet included in a pointed arch; while in the story immediately above is a circular window divided into two lights by a central pillar with regular bases and capitals, flanked by columns wrought in the jambs with corresponding mouldings, presenting a valuable specimen of early Norman workmanship. The intermixture of the Norman and early English styles in this fine tower, satisfactorily establishes the date of its erection; for this semi-Norman style originated about 1150, and is known to have continued in vogue until near the close of the century, when the round arch was finally abandoned. The tower, therefore, was undoubtedly built between 1250 and 1200; and as the noble family of Berkeley had these lands assigned to them soon after the Conquest, we may very reasonably conclude that it was erected at their expense. The two handsome towers of Exeter Cathedral, which in the twelfth century constituted the western entrance, but now form the transepts, exhibit precisely the same transition or semi-Norman style; and there are documents extant to show that they were constructed within the half cen_{t,u}y above named.

The present spire, we may be sure, was

never contemplated by the Norman architec It is framed of timber, and seems to be covere by shingles, which, from the peculiar way i which they are split (along the veins of the wood), are found to be much better adapted t resist the weather than ordinary-sawn plank. It may be of the same date, or earlier than th Court-house already mentioned. The Norma work finishes with the characteristic zig-za ornament along the parapet, and the entir edifice, as it looked in the year 1000, must hav been a very fine specimen of its class.

In the thirteenth century the Fownhop estates passed by marriage from the Berkeley to the Chandos family, in the reign of Henr the Third, and the event would almost seem t be commemorated by the very liberal addition to the fabric, of the present nave. That it was constructed in this century we conclude from the graceful early English entrance on the north side, whose slender banded pillars form a striking contrast to the massiveness of such parts of the structure as are of more remote date.

ST. JAMES'S CHURCH, CONGLETON.

THIS church was consecrated last week. We take the following particulars from the Chester Courant. The church, which consists of a nave, aisles, and chancel, is built of stone from the quarries of Congleton Edge. The pillars and arches, internally, are formed of the white stone from the quarries of Ollington, near Uttoxeter. The roofs of the church and chancel are high pitched, and are covered with green Westmoreland slate. The chancel has a triple lancet window at the eastern end, and single lancets at the side. On the north side of the nave there is a porch. The nave and aisles are 77 feet long by 50 wide; the chancel 30 feet long by 17 wide. Mr. Samuel Faram, of Odd Rode, was the principal contractor, and Mr. Edward Massey, of Lawton, executed the wood work. There is a bell gable at the west end of the nave. internally, the roof of the nave is open, shewing the timbers which support it. At the east end of the chancel is a stained-glass window, by Mr. Wailes, of Newcastle. The working people of St. James's district first commenced a subscription for this window, and what they were not able to raise was bountifully made up by a committee of ladies in Congleton and the neighbourhood, to whose exertions the church owes many of its many costly decorations. The window contains ten scenes from our Saviour's life. Within the chancel is a spacious pavement of encaustic tiles, a considerable portion of which are the gift of Mr. Minton. The pulpit is of carved oak, and an ancient one. it was purchased at a sale in Staffordshire, some time ago by the ladies' committee. In shape it is a hexagon. The panels are all finely carved. Two coronas suspended by rods of blue and gold from the roof of the nave light the church for evening service. They are of light iron and brass work, of Gothic tracery and design, in character with the church, and are painted partly blue, partly scarlet, with some gilding. The seats are all open, and will accommodate 700 persons. Mr. James Trubshaw was the architect.

BUILDERS' SOCIETY.—We had the pleasure of attending the fifteenth anniversary dinner of this society, on the 8th inst., held at the Freemasons' Tavern, when Mr. Thomas Piper presided, and Mr. W. Cubitt, Mr. Field (President of Institution of Civil Engineers), Mr. W. Herbert (who, although he has given up building, has not given up the builders), Mr. Haward, Alderman Lawrence, Mr. Henry Lee (president of the society), and others, made observations well deserving note, and would have it, too, did we not feel that the meeting was considered to be rather for the encouragement of friendly feelings than for public expression of opinions. Mr. Piper discharged his duty admirably,—as we should have said even if he had not, in the name of the society, also alluded to THE BUILDER in terms which, in conjunction with what was said recently by the Foremen's institution, show a consideration for us, on the part of both masters and men, that is peculiarly gratifying.

Miscellanea.

CONDITION OF THE CITY SEWERS.—Mr. W. Hayward, the surveyor to the City Sewers Commission, has made a report on the present state of the sewers within their jurisdiction, setting forth that they have been rendered "throughout the whole of the city, entirely free from all deposit which, by its retention and decomposition, might generate injurious vapours. All such inorganic matter, as by its situation or extent might have proved an obstruction to the general flow of the sullage, has also been removed, but there is still much ballast in the sewers, more especially in those lines connecting with the county, it being for the most part the *detritus* from the Macadamized roads, which is constantly coming down during times of rain. I will here state that which, perhaps, is not generally known, viz., that the whole of the gullies in the public streets within the city of London are *trapped*, so that the escape of vitiated air is as much as possible prevented, by the side of the footways, or near to the houses. Most of these gullies have been trapped for many years, although the raps, it is true, are not so perfect in their ction as those which modern science has proluced. These it will be advisable to replace, as quickly as circumstances will permit, with hose of the more approved construction. To your honourable court is due the credit of the ntroduction of the system of trapping the street gullies, they having been first used by he city fifteen years since, by your then surveyor, Mr. Kelsey. The requisite ventilation of the sewers is still obtained by shafts, which rising from the crowns of the sewers, terminate with open gratings in the centre of the carriage-ways. This mode of ventilation must be admitted to be defective, and bad in principle; in truth, the ventilation of sewers, without great expense, appears to be a difficult problem, which should have the earliest consideration; the existing mode, however (bad as it is), is, I believe, the only one which has been attempted any where within the metropolis; and this much may be said of it, that t allows the escape of the vitiated air as far removed from the line of foot traffic and houses is possible, and in that situation where, obaining the most uninterrupted current of air, t is most quickly diluted by the atmosphere, nd its noxious qualities to that extent negaived. This mode of ventilation was first levised by your former surveyor, Mr. Kelsey, nd applied to your sewers about thirteen ears ago."

METROPOLITAN STATUE OF SHAKSPEARE. —A correspondent points our attention to an dvertisement calling for designs for a metropolitan statue to Shakspeare, to be erected at he west-end of London. He remarks that,— "To all lovers of the works of this great poet, uch a tribute would afford gratification, but t is earnestly to be desired that it will not rove a second Nelsonian affair, and that the udges, or those on whom the selection of the est design may devolve, will not be led away y the brilliant colouring and elaborate finishng of any of these productions,—many of which vill, no doubt, lay claim to this accomplishment. very good and highly-finished drawing may nake a 'very pretty picture,' but in this case ntellect in design should rule the choice, that uch a monument may be erected as will be vorthy of the great poet, and a lasting honour o the nation." All we can say is, that we now nothing of the matter; but, as a general emark, if artists submit designs without nowing who the parties are that ask for them, nd how the tribunal will be composed which s to decide upon their merits, they deserve vhat they will probably get, namely, their rouble for their pains.

MARYLEBONE SAVINGS' BANK.—At the 9th annual general meeting, held on the 9th nst., it appeared that 2,070 new deposits had een made in the last year. 19,019 deposit ccounts remained open on the 20th November last, of which 14,455 held balances veraging less than 3*l*. 3s. 1d. each. Upwards f 291,386*l*. was then invested with the commisioners for the reduction of the national debt. This amount has since risen to 295,886*l*. The ontinued evidence thus afforded of the disposition of the working classes to provide against he casualties of life will prove a source of ratification to all reflecting minds.

YIELDING PIERS AND BREAKWATERS.— Mr. W. H. Smith, C.E., has published a description of an invention, the result, as he says, of seven years' study, by means of which he hopes to overcome various obstacles, and ensure the establishment and continuance of available harbours of refuge, piers, breakwaters, &c., on all coasts and in all circumstances. The structure is of timber, supported from the top and the sheeting separately, by yielding braces, so arranged and moored to mooring-blocks, and balanced by counterbalance weights, that pressure in either direction gradually strikes the strain on either the blocks or the weights downwards into or upon the ground, while it also, in reaction, produces a similar strain downwards on the whole structure, which, moreover, is so connected and separated, so jointed and pivoted, as to admit of a horizontal and spiral freedom of motion throughout. All shocks are thus to be either eluded directly or thrown downward on the solid floor of the sea. Yet the power of resistance is said to be sufficient to overcome a momentum on the counter-balance weights and moorings equal to 2,000 tons. Mr. Smith calculates that a harbour, which, on existing principles, would cost 50,000*l*., will thus be made, by contractors of responsibility, for half as many hundreds.

GALVANIZED IRON.—TODD *v.* GELL.— This was an action tried last week, in the Court of Queen's Bench, in which the declaration alleged that the defendant, by representing to the plaintiff that the defendant had manufactured certain galvanized tin-iron, which was impervious to rain, and would effectually protect the roofs of houses from the effects of wet, had induced the plaintiff to employ the defendant to cover a house of the plaintiff's with that material, and the plaintiff alleged that it had not sufficiently protected the house, and that thereby the wet had got to the roof, and injured the same. The facts appeared to be, that the plaintiff, who had built several houses in the neighbourhood of St. John's Wood, had employed the defendant to roof some of them with this material, that the roof of one of them had sustained injury from the wet, and after many small repairings had taken place, the galvanized metal was obliged to be removed, and one of zinc substituted. The plaintiff's witnesses, on cross-examination, expressed their opinion that there was something defective in the roofing itself, or in the way in which the slates had been put on, so that the water came through holes and underneath the galvanized metal. The counsel for the defendant, under these circumstances submitted that the declaration was not supported. Lord Denman being of that opinion, the plaintiff was nonsuited.

SUPPLY OF WATER TO THE PARISH OF ST. MARTIN-IN-THE-FIELDS.—The committee appointed by this parish to inquire concerning the means of obtaining a cheaper, better, and more abundant supply of water, have published a report, wherein they state that by means of Artesian wells, "for the sum of 4,068*l*., (about half the sum now paid by the parishes for the present intermittent, scarce, and impure supply) the two parishes could be provided with an abundance of pure water, laid on at high pressure daily, and throughout the day: the quantity would be unlimited, and would be served by small pipes laid on to the main; it would not be contaminated by standing in cisterns, which constantly require cleansing, but would be as pure as when raised from the bowels of the earth."* They say truly, at the conclusion of their report, "There is no subject fraught with more annoyance to individuals—indeed, to the public generally—than the present ill-contrived and obnoxious method of water-supply to the metropolis. Fairly speaking, water should not be an article of traffic: like air, it should be untaxed, save for machinery necessary to adapt it for public use."

* "At Hanwell Lunatic Asylum, the Artesian well is 290 feet deep; it penetrates into the stratum of flint, and at the surface discharges 100 gallons per minute, and rises with sufficient force, in a tube, to discharge, at 26 feet above the ground, 23 gallons per minute. In Orange-street, the Artesian well descends to 383 feet, and the contract with Government stipulates that, if necessary, 350 gallons per minute shall be supplied to the Palaces of Westminster and Pimlico and the public offices." A correspondent from Hadham says, "An attempt has been made to make an Artesian well in that neighbourhood, which has failed, the water only flowing within 178 feet of the surface. Will it be practicable or possible to fix a lift-pump in this bore hole, which is only six inches in diameter? Some of your readers will, perhaps, favour us with a few observations upon this."

PROJECTED WORKS.—Advertisements have been issued for tenders, by 3rd March, for the erection of a new chapel near Bolton; by 1st, for erecting a school-house and dwelling-house near Penrith; by 12th, for heating the new asylum at Prestwich; by 20th February, for supplying and fixing gas piping and fittings at the Borough Gaol, Manchester; by a date not specified, for lighting part of Hammersmith parish; and by 7th March, for the valuation of all the rateable property in Tunbridge Wells.

COMPETITION.—A premium of 20*l*. is offered for the best plans for renewing and otherwise improving the interior of the parish church of Bridgewater.

ELECTRO-TELEGRAPHIC. — The gutta-percha wire coating, we suggested, might be a perfect tit-bit to some of the fishy tribes, even if the wires themselves defied the sharks. We now observe that it is in the meantime likely to be an acceptable morsel in Chancery, where it has gone in a suit between Mr. Wharton—whose patent for its use dates from 1846—and the Electric Telegraph Company, who, we suppose, have no patent right to use it at all.—— Whatever be the insulating merits of gutta percha, however, or whoever may be best entitled to the exclusive benefit of Faraday's experimental genius and discovery, our imperial insular triunity is about to be more closely connected in the mutual bonds of telegraphic fellowship, by the casting of a submarine electric rope across the Irish Channel, from Holyhead to Dublin, whereby that drifting, reckless, weaker vessel of State, poor Ireland, is to be taken a little closer in tow, as a *tender*—we can scarcely call her a *jolly*-boat—along side the Britannia. The Treasury and the Admiralty, it seems, have granted to Mr. C. J. Blunt, C.E., the privilege of laying down this line of telegraph, and a Company is in course of formation for its accomplishment.

COTTAGE FLOORS.—Sir: In several of your late numbers I have noticed some remarks on floors for cottages. Allow me to say I have had the floors of barns laid with a concrete, formed of six parts of clean gravel to one of ground Lias lime, which has answered the purpose well, showing a smooth surface, and being impervious to damp, with the advantage of preventing the approach of vermin, as neither rats or mice can penetrate this material, especially if carried up six or eight inches as skirting. The floor would be sufficient for all purposes in a cottage, if three or four inches thick, which would not take more than half a bushel of lime (value 6d. in London), to the square yard superficial, and where gravel or ballast is cheap, the cost would be very trifling.—T.

GLASS PIPES ON A GREAT SCALE.—New York, it is said, is about to be supplied with the Saratoga water by a company with a capital of 300,000 dollars, who mean to carry it from the springs to the city, as the *Courier and Inquirer* informs us, through a series of glass pipes passing under ground through grooved bricks, the space between the grooves and the bricks to be filled with cement. The expense is estimated at 1,000 dollars per mile, or 180,000 dollars for the entire distance.

THE DISCOVERIES AT ICKLETON AND CHESTERFORD.—The current number of the journal of the British Archæological Association contains an interesting account, by Mr. C. R. Smith, of the foundations of villas, &c., opened at Ickleton and Chesterford, on the borders of Essex and Cambridgeshire, which seem, as the writer shews, to have all the characteristics of Roman work. The remains of the hypocausts are to be seen, painted mural decorations, and fictile vessels in great variety.* According to a report of the proceedings of the Cambridge Antiquarian Society, given in the current number of the *Gentleman's Magazine*, it appears that the Cambridge antiquaries believe these remains belong to a later time. On what ground they arrive at this opinion, we cannot tell: judging simply from the statements and engravings before us, there would seem to be not the slightest doubt that they are correctly described as Roman work.

* The same number of the journal contains "Observations on the practice of embalming among the ancient Egyptians," by Mr. Pettigrew; "On the charge in heraldry called a 'rest,' or 'clarion,'" by Mr. Planché; "On the sepulchral character of cromlechs in the Channel Islands," by Mr. F. C. Lukis; &c., &c.

HALSTED OLD CHURCH STEEPLE.—From the force of a rough squall of wind, lately, the vane of the steeple, which was fixed in a wooden socket, rotten from age and neglect, became alarmingly displaced while the church was occupied, and the congregation being hastily and imprudently warned, rushed towards the doors like a flock of sheep and jammed up the way, so that had the whole mass been about to fall through the rotten roof, they adopted the very course likely to lead to their own destruction. As it was, they escaped with much less harm than in too many similar instances. The church authorities, in place of repairing the spire or otherwise replacing it, demolished the vane and razed half the steeple, leaving nothing but the stump, while they sold the lead and other materials to pay the expenses. Their design, however, may have been thus to appeal to the sympathies and purses, as well as the pride, of their fellow townsmen, in default of funds of their own. A document inclosed in a tin case, and dated in 1792-3 and 1803, was found in course of the demolition, from which it appears that a somewhat less prodigal measure than that of selling the materials to pay for the piecemeal demolition of the fabric had been then adopted, in the renewal and repair of certain portions of the same appendages, when "a bean-feast was given to the workmen on the top scaffold, the ball being under the senter of the table, whereupon eight men dined in the presence of a great number of spectators below." This record of bye-gone days and deeds was "wrote by Jos. Hayward, jun., whitesmith, of Halstead," whose name also appears in the list of workmen, employed by "Jos. Hayward," senior, we presume, and "Edward Argent."

STOCK OF IRON.—It is said that the immense increase in the make of iron both in Wales and Scotland has called forth an expression of some apprehension on the part of many conversant with the trade. "The stock of pig iron in the latter country at the beginning of the present year was supposed to be about 110,000 tons, and the probable make is calculated at 650,000 more, while the whole quantity disposed of during the year 1848 was only 550,000 tons, and that much exceeded the consumption of 1847; so that a large increase of stock is feared during the present year."——Pig iron in Staffordshire is in considerable request, and the best qualities command rather higher figures.

NEWCASTLE SOCIETY OF ANTIQUARIES.—On the 5th inst., the members held their annual meeting in the Castle Keep. The senior secretary read the report, which was favourable on the whole, and recommended an appeal to the public for pecuniary assistance towards fitting up the castle. A vote of thanks was given to Mr. Dobson, the architect, for his services in partially restoring the castle.

DRAINAGE OF HULL.—According to the local papers, the Superintending-Inspector (Mr. Smith), who has been holding an inquiry at Hull, said that although in most of the towns he had seen the drainage was bad, in no case had he met with it so bad as in Hull.

A RARE BIRD KNOWN TO BRICKLAYERS.—An amateur naturalist has offered a reward to the man who will furnish him a live specimen of the "brick *bat*." This must surely be the same individual who was inquiring the other day about the new fish recently discovered, and which turned out to be the gutta percha *sole*.

BLIND BUILDERS.—Sir: Pray don't let the provincial blindnesses escape notice. The following tenders were opened on the 8th inst., for erecting some new agricultural buildings near Wainfleet, Lincolnshire. Mr. W. A. Nicholson, architect.

Corby, Lincoln	£2,650
Johnson, Hull	2,440
Dunckley, Hagg	2,350
Tinker, Lincoln	2,250
Foreman and Frow, Hull	2,220
Hutchinson and Son, Hull	2,145
C. Ward, Lincoln	2,105
B. Andrew, Stickford	2,051
Wallace and Chapman, Market Rasen	2,030
Johnson, Laceby	1,978
Kirk and Son, Lincoln	1,950
Carter, Horncastle	1,885
J. Andrew, Wainfleet; tender accepted. Precise amount not known; something less; certainly not more than	1,800

ORIGIN OF THE TERM "COLD HARBOUR."—The constant occurrence of this title throughout the country will be remembered by many of our readers. A few weeks ago a discussion as to its origin took place at the Society of Antiquaries, and this elicited a letter to the *Literary Gazette* from Mr. H. Fox Talbot. Mr. Talbot says, "As I think I have given the true origin of the curious name 'Cold Harbour' in my 'English Etymologies,' I beg to submit it to your judgment, and that of the learned society in question. The following is my account of the matter:—*Cold Harbour*. It has been suggested in the proceedings of the Philological Society, on the authority of a passage in Pepys, that this name signified a place where *coals* were deposited. It may be conceded that such was the meaning in the instance referred to, and perhaps in some others; but was it the custom to have *depôts* of coal (that is, *charcoal*) all over the kingdom in ancient times? *Cold Harbour* means '*shelter from the cold*,' a good name enough for a small inn or public house, in a bleak and solitary situation. Or, more literally, it meant 'the *Cold Inn*.' Not an inviting name, certainly; but in old times people were not so particular, when journeys were always sure to be full of hardships. Nor are inns always to be judged of by their titles, since one of the best inns in Savoy is named *Maltaverne*. But if any one doubts, notwithstanding, our interpretation of 'the *Cold Inn*,' we can produce good proof that such is the meaning. For, the name of Cold Harbour is found in Germany as well as in England. The name in German is *Kalten Herberg*; the meaning of which is evidently *Cold Harbour*. Such an inn is encountered by the traveller on the road from Basie to Freiburg, &c. &c. *Herberg* (French *Auberge*) is the English *Harbour*; whence we say 'to *harbour* a person' (receive him, give him lodging, entertainment, &c.), to *harbour* a criminal (shelter him, hide, &c.), to *harbour* a thought (entertain it)."

SCENERY.—In Buckstone's clever drama, "The Green Bushes," now playing again at the Adelphi, there is some very clever landscape scenery. We would particularly notice "A log cabin on the banks of the Missisippi" and "The Missisippi by sunset." They tell of this piece and the singularly long time during which it has been running, how that a sailor having seen it one night left for America, and, having accomplished his journey and returned, went again to the Adelphi and found the Green Bushes still on the bills; moreover, that afterwards going to India, he again found, on his return, the same company playing it at the Haymarket.——At the *Lyceum*, the continued success of Mr. Planché's capital piece of fun and splendour, "The King of the Peacocks," prevents us from having any fresh matter to chronicle.

SIR HANS SLOANE'S MONUMENT.—Your correspondent "Antiquary," recommends the lettering on Sir Hans Sloane's monument to be "recut deep into the stone," as it is nearly obliterated. If this be done I would beg to suggest, after they are so cut, that instead of merely blacking the letters inside, they should be filled up with a cement, flush with the surface; and this, if adopted, would insure more durability to all stone lettering. L.

THE DUKE'S NEW EDINBURGH STATUE, AND ITS SITE.—This further addition to the hundred-and-one Wellington memorials is, we learn, to be placed on its site in front of the Register House, on 18th June next. The Lord Provost and magistrates are being petitioned in the meantime by numerous parties on the propriety of throwing back the screen in front of the building, so as to obtain a wider and more spacious communication between Leith-street and Princes-street.

COMPETITION FOR CHURCH AT HEPTONSTALL.—A correspondent says, Messrs. Mallinson and Healy, of Bradford, obtained the first premium; Mr. Crowther, of Manchester, the second; and Mr. Shellard, of Manchester, the third.

"A SECOND DANIEL."—A correspondent mentions that one of the old oaks in Donnington-park, the seat of the Marquis of Hastings, measures in girth (14 feet from the ground, where the branches expand), 36 feet! It is known in the neighbourhood as "Daniel Lambert."

EXEMPTION OF LITERARY INSTITUTIO[NS] FROM POOR-RATE.—In the case of "Th[e] Birmingham New Library," touching th[e] power of enforcing a poor-rate assess[ment] upon it, Lord Denman said, "In ord[er] to bring the society within the exem[p]tion provided by the statute, it was nece[s]sary that it should be established for th[e] promotion of literature and science, or th[e] fine arts, exclusively; it must be support[ed] wholly or in part by voluntary contribution[s] and must be prohibited by its laws fro[m] making any distribution of its property amon[g] its members. Upon the first point there coul[d] be no question that the Birmingham New Library was a literary society within the mean[]ing of the Act. There was some difficulty i[n] ascertaining what was meant by a society sup[]ported by voluntary contributions, but th[e] court was of opinion that the subscription[s] might be considered as voluntary if they wer[e] commenced at the parties' own choice, an[d] could be continued or discontinued withou[t] subjecting the subscribers to any action or los[s] other than that of the privilege of membership. According to this construction of the word[s] 'voluntary subscriptions,' the society in ques[]tion was entitled to the exemption claimed. As to the third point, the society at an annua[l] general meeting, held in the year 1845, passe[d] a resolution against the division of its propert[y] expressly in the words of the Act. But it wa[s] contended that by another rule, in contraven[]tion of this, a profit might be made by a mem[]ber in transferring his share, and that this de[]prived the society of the statutable exemption. The court, however, was of opinion that i[t] would not, especially as there was no limit t[o] the number of the members of the society. Then it was said, that the society at a genera[l] meeting might dissolve itself, and make a divi[]sion of the common stock; but the 6th rule which defined the power of general meetings seemed to exclude their power to dissolve th[e] society. A better answer to the objection was that the statute must have a reasonable con[]struction, and be taken as applying to a con[]tinuing body, and not as intending to deprive a society of the exemption which it conferre[d] merely because the property of the society, in case of its dissolution, might, by the rules, become divisible among the members. Upon all these grounds, the court was of opinion that the society was entitled to the exemption claimed." This expression of the opinion of the court is important.

IRON GIRDERS.—A correspondent, with reference to cast-iron girders, suggests for consideration the advisability of inserting a piece of *flat wrought iron* within the substance of the bottom flanches of girders, which may easily be done in the casting; he says,—it adds very much to the strength of the short beams, as I have proved by experiment. It appears to me to be simply carrying out more fully the principle laid down by Professor Hodgkinson in his "Treatise on Cast-iron."

EFFECT OF SECURING IRON WITH LEAD.—In the course of a paper by Mr. Highton, on improvements in Electric Telegraphs, read at the Society of Arts on the 7th inst., the writer alluded to the rapid oxidation of the iron railings in the squares of London, and showed, as noted by others also, that the effect was due to a galvanization arising from the use of lead for connecting the iron with the stone walls.

THE MURDER NEAR BRIGHTON.—Mr. George Stonhouse Griffith, who was murdered on the 6th instant, near Brighton, was the late estimable assistant secretary to the committee for promoting the establishment of baths and washhouses for the labouring classes. The share which he had in examining the competition plans for the model establishment, and his polite attention to us when looking over them, call for this notice of him in our obituary.

THE OLD WATER-COLOUR SOCIETY.—Mr. Branwhite and Mr. Jenkins were elected members of the Old Water-Colour Society on Monday last.

MEETINGS OF SCIENTIFIC BODIES

Held during the ensuing week.

MONDAY, FEB. 19.—Institute of Architects, 8 P.M.
TUESDAY, 20.—Institution of Civil Engineers, 8 P.M.
WEDNESDAY, 21.—Society of Arts, 8 P.M.
THURSDAY, 22.—Royal Society, 8½ P.M.; Society of Antiquaries, 8 P.M.
FRIDAY, 23.—Archæological Association, 8½ P.M.

TENDERS

For the erection of St. Augustine's Roman Catholic Church, Liverpool. Messrs. Baffy and Brown, Architects. (Quantities supplied.)

Weannys and Carnefon	£2,654	0	0
Paffell and Griffiths	2,540	0	0
Thomas Mackarell	2,497	0	0
William Luef	2,341	0	0
Furness and Kilpen	2,325	0	0
Murty Flynn	2,916	0	0
Mulloy and Latham	2,199	15	0
Thomas Yates	2,146	16	0
Maher and Brian	1,996	0	0
John Blullin	1,995	0	0
Samuel M'Afhall	1,960	0	0
John Mackarell	1,935	0	0
Clarkson and Waistell	1,923	0	0
Hugh Yates (accepted)	1,860	0	0

For the erection of St. Paul's Church, Derby. Messrs. Baffy and Brown, Liverpool, Architects. (Quantities supplied.)

Winstanley, Derby	£2,391	0	0
Yates, Liverpool	2,270	0	0
Jarron, Leicester	2,224	0	0
Moody, Derby	1,960	0	0
Lee, Derby	1,899	5	0
Thompson, Derby	1,877	0	0
Watts and Nadin, Derby	1,845	10	0
Woods, Derby (accepted)	1,750	0	0

For two villas at Canonbury-park, for Mr. Samuel Atkinson.

Walker and Soper	£1,475	0	0
Underhill	1,143	0	0
Smith	1,398	0	0
Donnally	1,346	0	0
When	1,266	5	10
W. and A. Howlett	1,176	0	0

TO CORRESPONDENTS.

Received.—" J. C.," Gloucester (declined with thanks); " J. B.," Dlverton (we shall be glad to receive the description); " V. H." (drawing is lying at publisher's: we feel obliged, although not disposed to avail ourselves of it; " R. D." (such chimneys are often formed); " C. E.," " W. S. Jun.," " Silverpen" (next week), " J. B." Temp. (thanks), " R. W.," " R. B." (next week), " W. P." (we have seen the above), " F. V. C." (rightly inferred), " D. W. R." (shall appear), " A. B." (the Town Hall of Manchester is Ionic), " R. S." (thanks), " W. T." (we shall be thankful for the notes), " Herefordshire Rector" (next week), " Sir R. S." (we do not remember the receipt, but will refer), " G. M.," " H. B." " Sir B. M."

Books.—We are in affect with our notices, but will presently bring up with a wet salt. *Received:* " Architectural Scrap Book," No. 2; " Taylor's Price Book," for 1849; " Public Health Act," with Notes (Taylor, Wellington-street, Strand); " Railway Compensation Practice," a letter by Mr. Rice Hopkins (Rigg, Parliament-street); " Year Book of Facts," 1849, by John Timbs (Bogue, Fleet-street); " Plan for removing Smoke and Ventilating Sewers," by W. Prockton (Hamilton and Co., London).

" *Books, Prices, and Addresses.*"—We have not time to point out books or find addresses.

ADVERTISEMENTS.

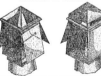

PIERCE'S NEWLY-INVENTED
PATENT PYRO-PNEUMATIC PURE WARM AIR SELF-ACTING AND VENTILATING STOVE-GRATE,

SPECIALLY ADAPTED FOR

CHURCHES, CHAPELS, INFANT AND OTHER SCHOOLS, PUBLIC BUILDINGS OR PRIVATE DWELLINGS, BANKING HOUSES, RAILWAY OFFICES
PICTURE GALLERIES, ENTRANCE HALLS, LECTURE ROOMS, INVALIDS' APARTMENTS, &c. &c.

Sketch of the Pyro-Pneumatic Stove-Grate.

Notices of the Public Press upon Pierce's Patent Pyro-Pneumatic Stove-Grate.

No. CCCXVI.

SATURDAY, FEBRUARY 24, 1849.

O pray tell me exactly how to make our house dry." "How shall we prevent the damp destroying the wood linings where there are any against our church walls, and producing ugly stains where there are none?" "Be so kind as to explain to us clearly how we may prevent our drawing-room chimney from smoking and spoiling the decorations for which we have just now paid a hundred and fifty pounds." "Please give me in few words, and not technically, a comprehensive system of ventilation for my residence."——Such, literally, are some of the requests which are forwarded to us week after week, and week after week again. Within these last six days we have received no less than four to the effect of the first of them alone.

There are usually no particulars,—without which even an approximate answer could not be given; and we are expected, empirically, to provide a cure applicable to any sort of case. Even if particulars are given, however, we are compelled to decline complying with such requests, for reasons which ought to be obvious. The general questions involved in such inquiries, as we recently had occasion to say with regard to heating, we have often discussed, and we shall, of course, continue to pursue the same system, but their application to special cases must be left to those who are enabled to examine the premises and weigh the various existing circumstances.

The endeavour to gain a cure for a damp or smoky house is not to be wondered at, the evils of either are so great and so obstinate. To obtain a perfectly dry house is no trifling achievement, and is seldom done. Consideration should more often be given to this, when building, than is now the case, especially in putting in the foundations and carrying up the underground work. When soft spongy bricks, or even good bricks or masonry, are placed on damp soil, forming a dry area, between the side of a wall and ground which may be against it, is of little use, because the damp will be absorbed from the bottom and rise, brick by brick (by capillary attraction), up the wall, until it reach a point where it is carried off by the external atmosphere or other influences. A layer of concrete under all the walls of a building (an excellent step in many other respects), will be found of great use in preventing the rise of damp. The bricks for the footings—if bricks are used—should be sound and dense, as slightly absorbent as they can be had; and the employment of cement, instead of mortar, in this position, is very desirable, and would make a scarcely appreciable difference in the cost of the structure. And, indeed, it may be said of good and bad work generally, that the expense of the former over the latter, considered as a per-centage on the whole cost of the building, would be in most cases trifling, and not to be weighed in any against the advantages which attend the former.

The ground, then, being kept off the external face of the wall by an area (formed, say, by a 4½-inch wall placed 4 inches from the face in question, and arranged so as to admit

of the circulation of air), and the internal face freed from the soil, or protected from it, much would have been done towards preventing the evil so far as the bottom is concerned.

In many cases it is desirable to take out the ground from the area enclosed by the building, and substitute a rough sort of concrete, or dry brick rubbish grouted in situ, to keep down damp vapours; and in others to provide an additional precaution in the shape of a layer of impermeable matter in all the walls above the level of the soil. A layer of slates in cement is often used for this purpose. In some cases the horizontal surface of the wall is covered with a thin sheet of lead, but the duration of this for any length of time could not always be depended on.

In the case of a public building in Hull, where zinc, bedded in loam, and having the course of bricks immediately above it bedded in the same material, was thus employed, the zinc was found, when examined nine months after, at the time of introducing hot-water pipes, full of holes, and in a rapid state of oxidation. In many churches the earth lies against the walls to a higher level even than the floor of the church; as a matter of course, the walls are saturated with moisture,—the air within the church is affected by it; the woodwork in contact with the walls is rotted. Clearing away the earth so as to admit the sun and air to the walls, and forming a paved channel close against them, all round, so as to take away the surface-water, would often do much towards a cure.

There appears to be strong evidence in favour of the use of asphalte for the above purpose. A writer in M. Daly's *Revue Générale de l'Architecture*, quoted in the appendix to the second report of the Commissioners on the Fine Arts, says,—" In 1839 I superintended the construction of a house of three stories on the Lac d'Enghien. The foundation of the building is constantly in water, about 19½ inches below the level of the ground-floor. The entire horizontal surface of the external and internal walls was covered, at the level of the internal ground-floor, with a layer of Seyssel asphalte, less than half an inch thick, over which coarse sand was spread. Since the above date no trace of damp has shown itself round the walls of the lower story, which are for the most part painted in oil of a grey stone colour. It is well known that the least moisture produces round spots, darker or lighter, on walls so painted. Yet the pavement of the floor, resting on the soil itself, is only about 2½ inches above the external surface of the soil, and only 19½ inches at the utmost above that of the sheet of water."

In a lodge which the same writer built on a higher level, less exposed to moisture, the asphalte was not used, and there, he says, the walls are spotted with damp. And of another house built at the same period, he says,—" The area of the ground-floor of this second house is 2 feet 1½ inch above the level of the garden, and rests on sleeper-joists separated from the soil by an empty space of above 2 feet 7 inches in height, which is ventilated by numerous air-holes. Before this floor was laid, the horizontal surface of the foundation walls had been covered with a layer of Roman cement, about an inch thick. Notwithstanding all these precautions the damp has ascended the walls as high as 3 feet and some inches above the level of the flooring.*"

To prevent a partial slip of the materials in

the event of an unequal settlement of the foundations, where the layer of asphalte was used, rows of flints were incrusted midway in the thickness of the masonry (and covered by the asphalte), to form a sort of key.

Various compositions have been proposed at different times in our pages for preventing damp from penetrating enclosing walls. Amongst the prescriptions is one which some of our querists, who were not then amongst our subscribers, may be glad to have. It came from a practical man, and is as follows:—

"Boil two quarts of tar with two ounces of kitchen grease, for a quarter of an hour, in an iron pot; add some of this tar to a mixture of slaked lime and powdered glass which have passed through a flour sieve and been dried completely over the fire in an iron pot, in the proportion of two parts of lime and one of glass, till the mixture becomes of the consistence of thin plaster. This cement must be used immediately after being mixed. It is not well to mix more at a time than will coat one square foot of wall, as it quickly becomes too hard for use, and continues to increase its hardness for three weeks. Great care must be taken to prevent any moisture from mixing with the cement. For a wall which is merely damp it will be sufficient to lay on one coating of cement about one-eighth of an inch thick, but should the wall be more than damp or wet, it will be necessary to coat it a second time. Plaster made of lime, hair, and plaster of Paris, may be afterwards laid on the cement. This cement when put in water will suffer neither an increase nor diminution in its weight."

The great point is, however, in all cases to take the evil at its source, and prevent the access of wet to the wall.

When dampness proceeds from deliquescence, nitrate of soda, &c., being present in the mortar,—washing the wall with a strong solution of alum has been tried with success.

In the report of the Fine Arts' Commissioners, to which we have already alluded, an account is given of the means of excluding damp from the internal surface of walls, not protected above the foundation in the way we have mentioned, by two French chemists, MM. D'Arcet and Thénard. To prepare the cupola of the Pantheon, Paris, for painting on, the face of the stones composing it was heated bit by bit, and a composition applied consisting of one part wax and three parts of oil, boiled with one-tenth of its weight of litharge. The absorption took place readily by means of heat, and the liquid penetrated the stone from a quarter to half-an-inch. The composition acquired solidity as it cooled, and became hard in six weeks or two months.

For ordinary purposes resin might be substituted for wax: the ingredients then are, one part of lithargized oil to two or three parts of resin. This composition has been employed with effect, with the aid of heat, to protect internal walls from damp. A remarkable instance of its successful application, related in the same memoir, is here added. "Two rooms on the basement story at the Sorbonne happen to be several feet lower, on the east and south sides, than the ground-level of the neighbouring houses. The walls of the two rooms on these sides are impregnated with saltpetre. Some years since it was thought advisable to coat them with stucco, in the hope of driving the saltpetre to the outside; but it penetrated the stucco, and re-appeared on its surface, producing so much damp that the plaster began to be decomposed, and the place became

* A similar instance of the inefficacy of cement for the purpose in question is recorded in the "Transactions of the Institute of British Architects," vol. i., p. 59.

uninhabitable even in summer. Our method was tried in these rooms in the following manner:—A mastic was composed, consisting of one part linseed oil, boiled with one-tenth of its weight of litharge, and two parts of resin. The latter was melted in the lithargized oil in a cast-iron vessel, the fire being duly regulated. The substances tumefied considerably at first, but, the fusion once completed, this effect ceased: the composition was suffered to cool, to be again heated for use. The tumefaction which takes place requires that the resin should be dissolved in the oil by degrees, otherwise it will overflow. The walls being very damp, it was necessary to dry them by means of a portable furnace."

The plaster was first thoroughly dried, then heated piece by piece, to enable the mastic to penetrate it: the mastic was applied without intermission till the plaster ceased to absorb.

A similar way of rendering pavements dry is also described. Vitruvius recommends a mixture of oil and lime as a cement well calculated to exclude damp from pavements.

This subject, which can scarcely be called a *dry* one, deserves further consideration.

PROFESSOR COCKERELL'S LECTURES ON ARCHITECTURE.

The fifth lecture of this course was delivered on Thursday, the 1st instant. The professor began by expressing a hope that, in speculating on the subject of classical art, he had not disseminated an idea that no other school was worthy of our regard. Each system had its proper application. He believed that the supremacy of classical art was as incontrovertible as was our superiority in mental and moral philosophy, and every discovery tended to the establishment of this fact. The Greeks ever would be our masters in art, and those who followed them, as the Romans and the artists of the Revival, had their proportionate measure of our regard.

He remarked, that if we looked to the commentators on Vitruvius, we were struck with their comparative ignorance of things with which we had become well acquainted. In his own time, great advances had been made, down to the discovery of the *scamilli impares* in Athenian buildings, by Mr. Penrose, and he inferred that we were only on the threshold of accurate knowledge of the principles of all that we now so empirically admired. In *proportion*, especially, we had much to learn, and he considered that there was room for glory to our own country, by a new edition of Vitruvius.

The progress of investigation, from time to time demanded fresh examination of all subjects. In the history of Greece and Rome, all early histories were now as waste paper; in mediæval architecture, the statements of the earlier writers, since the labours of Professor Willis, would have to be re-cast. It was to the abuse, and not the use, of classical architecture that certain of his strictures had been directed. He recommended a latitudinarian spirit, rather than one of bigotry, in regard to style. Each peculiarity of architecture had its application to time and place. Nature was eminently latitudinarian, but nevertheless was governed by principles. He had therefore recommended the study of nature, and it was better to become pupils of her than of Ictinus, Phidias, or Inigo Jones.

Quoting a passage from Alberti, to the effect that beauty was never distinct from utility, he remarked that utility was the characteristic of the Roman works, which were those of engineering, and the same might be said in England, for though he had never found any objection expressed to beauty in a design, he had certainly never found it enjoined as a necessity.

On the subject of proportion, the professor remarked that each master had a theory of his own. In some measure we all judged by a natural instinct, and we flattered ourselves that we had an eye for proportion. But, whilst, as Vitruvius said, other men than the artist could discover the good and the bad, the difference between the artist and the workman was, that one could foresee, and the other could not. He urged the importance of the study of proportion, in order to avoid those lamentable failures of which there were such frequent instances. The architect of a building often found too late, that with more modesty, and with good advice, and repeated study in drawing, and above all by models, he might have better attained the effect which he sought to impress upon the child of his hopes. Yet the architect should not consult too much his friend, nor too much his enemy, but rather endeavour to avoid the prejudices of each. He impressed upon his hearers the importance of recollecting the wonderful power of proportion. By it, not only character, but magnitude was given to a building; it could make the small look large, and the large look small. In illustration of the former characteristic, he quoted a passage from an author, descriptive of a small figure of Hercules, which, though it might be held in the hand, as you looked at it seemed to expand into a colossus; and of the latter, he instanced the interior of St. Peter's, at Rome, which was so ill devised that it actually appeared smaller than it was, a great error, and in expense extravagant in proportion to the result. Why were these opposite effects?

Proportion, he defined to be of three kinds:—1st. Proportion of elements, expressed in the orders; 2nd. Proportion of cubes and solids, which would govern that of halls and apartments; and 3rd. The proportion of areas, courts, and squares. In the orders we found expressed, in the most perfect manner, the charm of quantities. The best masters had constantly devoted their attention to these features of architecture; so much so, that Wren complained, that architects attended to them as though they were the whole matter of the art. In considering the question of magnitude, it was to be remarked, how in the early Doric there were larger capitals and rapidly diminishing shafts, as compared with the late Doric, in which we noticed a gradual tendency to the vertical and pyramidal. Greek architecture was characterised by a certain finality, and it resulted from that characteristic, that where applied as a lower story it was bad, as we saw it in Buckingham Palace. He inferred that it was bad to diminish greatly the Doric in street architecture, and that it was from this application of it by the Romans that the altered diminution resulted. He inferred, too, that the large capital was found incompatible with the altered position, and that it was intended to give magnitude by being diminished.

The Grecian Doric order, when alone, would never look large; whilst the Roman columns, as that of Trajan, shewed the perfect consideration for this object of proportion. In the Corinthian order, varying the height of the capital altered the appearance of length in the columns; a lofty capital made the column look short; whilst by diminishing the capital, magnitude was attained. Similar means were apparent in all three of the orders. The system was found in the Parthenon especially. He found from Vitruvius, that the ancients recognised that the proportion should alter with the magnitude. In the temple of the Giants at Agrigentum, the columns of which had a diameter of 13 feet, we found base mouldings,—an entirely new feature in the Grecian Doric. At Pæstum, instead of the ordinary number, the columns had each twenty-four flutes. But at Sunium, where they were small, and where breadth of effect in the temple, viewed from the sea, was desirable, they had sixteen flutes. I am not, said the architect, raising a toy or a model, but a building in which I must take into consideration all circumstances of size and position. He thought, therefore, that had he large columns to deal with, he should increase the number of the flutes, and diminish the capitals, whilst in small columns he might have sixteen or twelve flutes. As we found in nature, the youthful face had smooth outlines; but with the new dignity of strength and manhood, the features became more marked. The oak, as a young sapling, differed in like manner from the full grown tree, with its arms set at right angles, and the corrugated surface of its bark. To give magnitude, therefore, multitude of parts was necessary. Comparing the front of St. Peter's at Rome with that of the Parthenon, how inferior was the former. The four columns in the front were of immense size, yet the façade was one which would have been better suited to a parish church than to so vast a cathedral. It was to give magnitude that the new Parthenon had eight columns, instead of six, the number in the former building.

The professor then alluded to a theory which he had broached in former lectures, and which will be found referred to in our reports—viz., that beauty of proportion arose from inequalities. He illustrated this by diagrams, comparing the unequal disposition of parts in the man, with the opposite mode of distribution in the monkey. In like manner the horse was contrasted with the ass. The principle was shewn to be of similar value in proportioning the heights of stories in houses. This, he said, was the Ευρυθμια of Vitruvius.

Vitruvius had given directions for observing the different "styles" or dispositions of columns, as 1½ diameters apart for the pycnostyle, and so on. These directions were very important; but there was another practical point to be considered along with this—viz., varieties of height, according to the character of the building, whether tall or short. Now, this had never been sufficiently well attended to, for the commentators had drawn their illustrations to all scales, or according to the size of the paper. To render this as clear as requisite, the different "styles" should have been drawn to the same scale. Taking the pycnostyle and aræostyle as the two extremes, it would then be apparent there were certain characters; as in the latter instance, the low and compressed, and in the former, the tall—the other "styles" ranging between these extremes. Each of these distinct orders of disposition, no doubt, had its appropriate application. Now, instead of observing such a system as that here shadowed forth, each of us had a type by which we measured all things. One artist invariably made his figures tall, another short—but this was not nature. An architect, wanting a door, would go to an example, or to Sir William Chambers, and, without reflecting, would apply any proportion or size of aperture indifferently to a broad or tall disposition of columns. The professor shewed that in the aræostyle the door should be large in proportion to the order; whilst, in the pycnostyle, the opposite method should be practised; and so, he said, every aperture, and indeed every stone, should have a general harmony with the design and character of the particular building. But, in opposition to this, one master was for the broad, another for the narrow gauge.

The professor vindicated the authority of Vitruvius from the aspersions cast upon it, through ignorance of its true value, as shown in the instance he had given, by modern writers, who were certainly not artists. He quoted the lines from the Iliad, in which Helen describes the figures of Agamemnon, Ulysses, and Ajax, and said that these were no doubt designed by the poet to express what we found in the works of Albert Durer, Titian, and sometimes Raffaelle, viz., *character*. Each of the characters we might affect had its own proper modulus or type, and by applying each in its place, we obtained that contrast and beauty which was the charm of architecture. He instanced the guard-house at Cologne, by Schinkel, as admirably suited to its position. He also mentioned Nottingham Castle, said to be a work of Inigo Jones, which contained some singularities, but had an admirable effect at a distance. Another building was the Loggia of the merchants, at Venice, by Sansovino. It was only 30 feet high, and in any case, to give dignity to a building which was at the foot of a tower 300 feet in height, was not easy. The professor pointed out how this was effected, and said that the result was a low compressed character, which was in complete contrast with the tower above. Sansovino, on other occasions, had shown how he could feel like an artist, when he had opposite circumstances to deal with, when he adopted the tall character: his art was not that of a bigot; he suited the character to the place. In giving examples of successful attention to these principles, the church of St. Paul, Covent Garden, could not be forgotten, as an instance of the fine effect of the low broad character.

It would be recollected, the professor said, in

considering subjects of this kind with the aid of books, that illustrations were not drawn to the same scale. He said that considerations of this sort were much neglected in buildings. For example, we found the eustyle in relief, which made all the difference, and windows imprisoned as it were between the columns. He instanced the front of Lord Spencer's house, in the Green-park, as an example of the successful treatment of an engaged order with windows, the columns being there placed diastyle, and consequently there was complete space for the windows, and all dressings. In our copies of Greek temples on the contrary, we had generally fallen into the error which the architect of that beautiful building had avoided. We had, indeed, been Greek mad, but not from too much learning, but from too little. He believed that, some day, a type of proportion would be discovered, applicable to every building. Wren had an eye to this. The interior of St. James's Church, Piccadilly, had a certain proportion of height, and magnitude was gained by that proportion. He instanced Sir Robert Taylor's garden-front of the Bank, as an instance of successful proportion. Sanmichele was a great master in this; his gate in the front of the Lido had a rusticated Doric order, managed with the hand of a giant. In civic buildings he said, where frequent piers could not be avoided, character might be given by decorating the alternate windows.

The principle of a certain modulus of proportion, applied to interiors. St. Peter's, at Rome, ought to have had the bridge-like expanse, rather than, with a more vast dimension, the ordinary proportion of a church. In mediæval architecture, the height was governed by the point of an equilateral triangle, and Wren was so true a mason, that he followed the same method. He concluded by remarking, that although there were many things which could hardly be taught, it behoved us still to reflect, and to acquire all the skill which we could possess, by learning on every side, in preference to depending upon the inspiration of genius.

ENFRANCHISEMENT OF LEASEHOLDS.

As no question of a novel nature can have a more beneficial influence upon the arts and architecture, nor a greater claim to the attention of the resident population of the metropolis, than this, no apology is needed for a few additional remarks upon it.

Having before shown that the proprietary, or landlord class, can make no objection to enfranchisement on the score of inequitable adjustment, and that full compensation can be meted out to them by valuation juries,—now it only remains to prove,—

That changes more direct, not to say more arbitrary and violent, have been made by enactments of the legislative Parliament, in all sorts of property, whether lay or ecclesiastical, corporate or private.

That where the interests of the many, urged by the public voice, or the expediency of an altered system of law (led on by *retired judges*) required a sweeping charge in our social or relative positions as to property, no respect for private privileges interposed to stop the invasion of rights thitherto considered sacred.

If rights in law were immutable, and the "*nolumus leges Angliæ mutari*" of Magna Charta, were still to coerce the advances of science and arts, and to conserve the usages of black letter jurisprudence, what a standstill generation should we be! What was suited to the state of society in the days of King John, became prejudicial in those of Henry the Eighth; and the expanding mind of a great nation in the latter reigns—discovering that, in progression of time and prosperity, the shackles of old institutions were unsuited to the giant growth of a matured power—emancipated itself from the trammels of prejudice, and scrupled not to reform or abrogate those laws which repressed its luctant energies. It was in this spirit that the Act of Limitation was passed which abolished, totally abolished, all claims, grounded in the 21st James II., to debt, on which legal process had not been entered up for a period of six years. If any one act of the Legislature could be stigmatized as an act of *spoliation*, it was that which deprived the creditor, who was too lenient, or perhaps who had slept upon his right, of all suit or demand against his debtor, who had eluded or avoided the demand of his debt for that period. It would be curious to ascertain what might have been the sum total of immunity from payment consequent upon that act; of how many millions, or hundreds of millions the tradesmen and merchant have been debarred, and what portion of that immunity fell into the lap of the Lords and Commons, their relatives, and adherents. In this case the right of the honest tradesman was lost, and totally confiscated, no valuation having here interposed to give him a *pro tanto* annuity over time, as a requital; and yet we heard little complaint, certainly of no public demonstration against the passing of that law, for it was manifest to all that much litigation was saved, and the greater good achieved by that act of extinction. Another very recent interference with vested rights, took place on the enactment of 3+ William IV., chapter 27. By that statute the fact of possession for twenty years conferred on the holder or tenant of fixed property, the absolute freehold title as indefeasible against all claimants. Here was an utter annihilation and defeasance of all heritable claims on property, so circumstanced, how clear soever might be its deduction, and although the family of the rightful claimant might have been in possession up to twenty-one years antecedent, or his ancestors from the days of Harold in lineal succession.

We will not inquire what were the operations of this statute, nor what complications of interests were set at rest by it, but only adduce these examples to prove that legislative wisdom hath abrogated and wholly annulled usages which hitherto admitted claims (rightful claims) to fixed property, and that, too, without contemplating any equivalent.

The remarks which have been made by powerful parties who are opposed to the enfranchisement of leasehold property, induce me to offer these examples in addition to those already instanced, of "the enfranchisement of copyhold tenures," and the "valuation, freehold, leasehold, copyhold, &c., Act, empowering railway companies to purchase."

However, in the proposed enfranchisement, or rather, the continuation in perpetuity of existing leases (originally above twenty-one years) to the tenants in possession, the rents now payable must also be continued in perpetuity; and as in the great majority of cases, householders wishing to renew or perpetuate their tenures, would take that perpetuity at an increased rental, rather than on purchase: so the immediate yearly income of the great landlords should be vastly increased; as, for instance, a house in Belgrave-square having 60 years to run, at 100*l*. a-year ground-rent, but now worth in the market 500*l*. a-year, might, by the payment (or valuation), be subjected to an additional 50*l*. a-year; a sum which, by accumulation on compound interest, must, in 60 years, exceed the value of the mansion at the end of the lease.

In the valuation of shorter terms, unlapsed, the increased rent would be proportionately larger; as for example, a house in Grosvenor-square having but 20 years of lease to expire, and subject to 50*l*. a-year, the present value being 500*l*. a-year; in this case 150*l*. a-year additional rent for the perpetuity might not be considered excessive; but however it might appear to others, the occupant would, in nine cases out of ten, rather pay it than suffer his term to lapse; and the more especially so, as on the renewed lease he might modernize, improve, and consolidate his mansion; whereas, if he were to suffer the lease to lapse, he must continue to occupy a dingy dwelling, falling into decadence, unsuited to his requirements, and to the improving taste of the day.

Hence it is clear that the head proprietor can in no case get less than his original rent, with a sum of money equivalent to the improved value of the premises leased in perpetuity; and that by such arrangements as should give an increased rental, instead of purchase, the present actual rental of the landlord must be trebled.

On one estate only, the estimate of increase (rough though it be) is not far from the mark. It stands thus: Of 200,000*l*. a-year, one-half would be perpetuated on an increased rental adding at once 200,000*l*. a-year! one-fourth would be purchased at the present estimated rental, or 50,000*l*. a-year, being the reduplicated amount of rent, and this, at twenty years' purchase, would produce one million in money, which would be, in round numbers, (at medium fund price) 30,000*l*. a year—leaving still the head rent undisturbed; and the other fourth part would probably be allowed to run out of lease.

This estate then, now producing 200,000*l*. a-year, by such regulation would return 330,000*l*. a-year until the lapse of the remaining fourth part, and of that portion the returns would be trebled on reletting, realizing a total income of 480,000*l*. a-year.

In estates which are strictly entailed, provision should be made by the Legislature for entailing in the funds of the country the amount of purchase money paid on enfranchisement,—these funds being subject to the same limitations as the houses converted into money. On the estate before referred to, no less a sum than one million would probably be invested,—this on only one estate. The total sum so invested must be in the event enormous; and the fixed capitalization of such amounts would obviously tend to the stability of Consols, from the value of which, at the time of enfranchisement, the equivalent, or price, would be calculated.

No one can argue that this is a confiscation; in truth there are but very few great proprietors in London and the environs—I should say but twenty at the most, possessing colossal incomes; and taking these twenty at an average of 2,000 houses each, there are of consequence 40,000 householders who would be benefited by the proposed enfranchisement, who, being tenants at a rent certain (that rent not being immoderate), would expend large sums in the consolidation and improvement, as well as the embellishment of their holdings. What a stimulus would this apply to the languishing tradesman—the bricklayer, mason, carpenter, and all the artists who follow in their train!

But let the present system of terminable leases go on for fifty years more, and then see the state of society,—all the habitations of the great towns will be at the disposal of twenty proprietors, who may expel, evict, dispossess, and disperse the whole population, as seems best to their lordly wisdom or caprice. Go thou there—rest thou here—this square shall be the abode of lords, that of commoners; this street shall be allotted to the squirearchy, and that to the professions!

One incident may explain more forcibly the tendency of the present practice of *leasing* than all that has preceded:—a certain tract of fields on the leviathan estate near Vauxhall, was let out lately to a great building firm, on a lease for ninety years, on condition of building 5,000 houses; and this at a rental of 5,000*l*. a year,—these houses were to be of a class to assure the expenditure of 1,000*l*. or 1,500*l*. a house. It requires no complex arithmetic to prove that at the end of the term, or on the lapse of three generations, the enormous sum of five millions, disbursed by the public, must, at the expiration of that term, fall into the possession of the lessor lord, or of his posterity; and that the rental of those houses so erected by the community, if averaged at only 100*l*. a year, must make the enormous addition of 500,000*l*. to the rental of the already too-rich landlord. Is this for the advantage of the community? that one family should command whole districts of habitations, and that all mankind should be ousted? The reverse conclusion is so obvious that it needs no elucidation; for better is it that 5,000 householders, with an interest in the tenements, should enjoy their privileges, municipal and other, than that all should fall into only one heritage. But at the end of the ninety-nine years, not only these 5,000 houses, but also, in half that period, 5,000 more of the old town (now the fashionable part), must fall to the same proprietor, unless the wisdom of our Legislature stop this frightful accumulation and forestalling of all fixed property in tenements. The forecast which provideth for a family should provide for a nation; and if the legislature hath the power to interpose a safeguard for the people, there can be no reason why they should not be protected, seeing that an equitable recompense can be made to all superior interests. The enfranchisement of leaseholds may be a new theory, but it is facile as it is just. The interests of humanity require it; and the consummation of such an act will reflect credit on the member who may carry such a measure as this suggested by

Quondam.

SURFACE DELINEATION AND PLAN-MODELLING.

CARRINGTON'S MODEL OF YORKSHIRE AND LANCASHIRE.

At the present moment, while sanitary improvements and the general drainage of land occupy so much of the public attention, it is a matter of importance that the most judicious and economical mode of showing the undulating surface of ground, so as to devise the best method of draining it and effecting improvements at the least possible cost, should be known.

The present system of sections and contour lines gives but a partial knowledge of the character of ground, inasmuch as the undulations can only be shown where the traverse is made with the level. Beyond this (on either side of the line traversed), no information is supplied; so that, to arrive at any thing like a knowledge of the surface of a country, many sections and cross-sections are requisite. In like manner, contours following out lines of equal altitude show the form of the ground only where the level passes. Moreover, the expense of contouring a piece of country is more costly than most persons are aware of. To contour ground for practical purposes, so as to enable parties when on the ground to find the line traversed, it is requisite to have the contour line staked out: the distance between the stakes averages about one chain.

For towns, a series of sections taken through the streets is unquestionably the best method of obtaining the different altitudes.

It is surprising to hear so many persons praise the system of contouring towns. Are they aware that, to a great extent, it is fiction? It may look very pretty on paper, and persons may fancy they have a knowledge of the ground from such a mode. Test its accuracy! It will be found void of truth. You cannot follow out a contour line in a town, where its direction would be intercepted by buildings and offsets and obstructions innumerable. Contouring of towns, and of precipitous and rocky grounds, has never yet been accomplished.

Valuable and indispensable as sections are, they fail to give that which is most desirable in designing and carrying out any great work, a comprehensive and detailed whole.

This defect then existing, it seems a matter of regret to find that a beautiful and economical method of delineating ground has been passed over. This method (the horizontal delineation of ground, and which is so little known) was introduced into the Ordnance Department by Mr. Dawson. So valuable and important was this particular study considered, that his Grace the Duke of Wellington, when Master-General of the Ordnance, ordered a limited number of young gentlemen to specifically study that art, in addition to every other branch of surveying.

Mr. Frederic A. Carrington, a gentleman who held an appointment from the Master-General and Board of Ordnance, and who was specially instructed in the above studies, after having delineated large tracts of country, and made finished topographical "hill" drawings for the Ordnance, of more than 8,000 square miles of country, has for the last three years particularly devoted his attention to the delineation of ground, and to modelling for practical purposes.

This system of horizontal delineation (correctly done), combined with a judicious mode of levels, imparts a thorough knowledge of the surface of a country. Minute features, as well as rocky and contorted ground, are clearly expressed; and in designing the improvements and drainage of towns and estates, it is very valuable.

Were London, Liverpool, or any of our great towns surveyed in this manner, not only might the rise and fall of every street be exhibited, but the continuity of the fall. The height in feet at the intersection of the streets, and every other remarkable point, could be added.

Then, as regards estates, take the case of our great landed proprietors, anxious to improve their property in laying out new roads and draining the land.

Supposing they were desirous of carrying out the work progressively, or from year to year, by having the estate delineated in the manner proposed, all improvements, as well as the thorough drainage of the property, could at once be projected; and, if required, laid out with the greatest nicety and economy.

Models of towns, estates, and districts of country, executed in this manner, can be multiplied at a comparatively small cost. They can be produced in a composition resembling ivory, gutta percha, papier maché, &c., impervious to water. Among those we have seen are Blyth and Serlby Hall, in Nottinghamshire (to show its applicability to estates), on a scale of four chains to an inch; that of part of the town of Dundee, on a scale of 100 feet to an inch, for towns and boroughs generally; and, lastly, that which may be called the chief work, in illustration of a tract of country, on a scale of one inch to the mile. The portion chosen for this purpose is, perhaps, among the most difficult and interesting in the kingdom, "the great manufacturing districts of Yorkshire and Lancashire." There is much for contemplation in the district thus embraced, extending from Lincoln westwards some 70 miles, to Congleton, in Cheshire; from Congleton northwards, by Manchester to Burnley (say 45); from Burnley, east, by Bradford and Leeds to South Cave on the Humber; and from the Humber, south to Lincoln,—it forms a parallelogram including a surface of about 3,000 square miles. The site of six and forty cities and towns, villages innumerable, parks, woods, roads, railroads, and canals, are all shown in relief. The sources and windings of all the rivers and streams, among the hills and through the plains; the Trent and the Mersey, the Derwent and the Don, the Calder and the Dane, the Irwell and the Rother, may be seen at a glance.

The physical peculiarities are, if anything, still more interesting. At once it may be seen why geologists call the country near Manchester, the "Manchester basin"; the term is most apt, for the hills form a perfect crescent around it, of which it is as nearly as possible the centre. The great mountain ridge that divides Lancashire and Yorkshire, running in a north-west and south-east direction, is, to the north-east of Manchester, broken in a most remarkable manner, forming at this point the celebrated pass of Todmorden, which, circuitous and narrow, has been taken advantage of for turnpike, canal, and railroad, as affording, in the first instance, the easiest and best transit between the counties.

The summit ridge previously named, formed of millstone grit, varying from 1,500 to 2,000 feet above the sea (with the Lancashire and Yorkshire coal fields on its west and east side), is divided in two at the Peak of Derby, to make way for the upheaved mass of mountain limestone, of which the greater part of that county is composed. The next great feature on the Yorkshire side is what may be called the magnesian limestone ridge, from 200 to nearly 600 feet high, gradually dying off in the soft features of the new red sandstone, till lost in the valley of the Trent, and the great flats near the Isle of Axholme, when it is again relieved by the lesser, but well-marked, oolite ridge, on which Lincoln stands, and along which the great line of the Roman road is taken direct to the Humber.

Where the canals were first constructed to aid the transit between the counties, the railroads have followed in nearly a parallel line, with the exception of that great work, the Manchester and Sheffield line. We see in a moment where and to what extent, from the neighbouring hills, the Lancashire towns can be supplied with water for domestic, manufacturing, and sanitary purposes. The same in reference to Yorkshire, and far distant as they are, the whole produce of the sources of the Derwent and the Dove, could be brought to the metropolis, should it so be willed. As it is necessary to impound and store the water in the hill districts for use; so in the plains, an important object is gained if we can regulate the upland drainage, or find means for its being more rapidly carried off from these low lands, in order to bring what are now marshes into cultivation, to turn what is waste to profit, to make what is now a source of disease healthy and valuable.

Again, in a military point of view (for the use of an officer in command), nothing else can at all approach a work of this kind. To the Government such a work (always of course supposing it correct) is invaluable.

What do we know of our exposed southern coast and harbours? If such be the case at home, what must it be in reference to our possessions in the east and elsewhere? Who knows India? What is Sidney like? What are the features of the Cape Colonies and Port Natal?

Impressed with the obvious advantage of this mode of surface-delineation, we are anxious that Mr. Carrington's system should have a fair investigation, and if found to fulfil all that it promises, a liberal encouragement.

PUBLIC BATHS AND WASHHOUSES.

For a special purpose, we are asked for some relative information concerning the baths and washhouses of the metropolis. The baths at George-street are a long strip of a building, irregular, and taking parts of two sides of a square. A general description of it has appeared in our pages.

Those at Glasshouse-yard are merely half a dozen baths fitted up in different parts of the large refuge for the houseless poor. There are also scattered washing tubs and troughs.

The building at Goulston-square ("The Model Establishment,") described in The Builder more than once, covers a piece of ground, not quite rectangular, about 90 feet by 120 feet. It has a basement containing tank, coal cellars, boiler-room, engine-room, towel washing-room, &c., and a ground-floor nearly equally divided into two parts, one the bathhouse and the other the washhouse.

The St. Martin's "baths and laundries," cover a piece of land about 80 feet by 40 feet. The basement has the boiler-room, &c., the ground-floor, the baths, and the first story the washhouse. The model establishment will probably not cost less than 22,000*l.*: it has ninety four baths, each in a separate apartment 6 feet square, and ninety-six washing places, each with its separate drying closet.

St. Martin's will probably cost 15,000. About sixty-four baths and fifty-six washing places, each with its separate drying closet. Cheaper plans are needed. At Goulston-square they have had and still have to go through the cost and disappointment of experiments. The plans have not been published.

The success at St. Martin's is said to be considerable. With only about thirty baths completed for use, the bathers during the first nineteen days have been 6,701, and the receipt 94*l.* 13s. 2d.

Baths and washhouses are about to be erected in Macclesfield.

ON THE TOPOGRAPHY AND ANTIQUITIES OF THE CITY OF JERUSALEM.*

The following paper relates first to the topography of the city of Jerusalem, and afterwards to the existing antiquities. To illustrate the topography, I annex a plan taken by me in the year 1825. It was measured under circumstances of considerable difficulty, for at the period of my visit Jerusalem was in the possession of the Arab natives, who had some time before expelled their Turkish governor and his garrison; and during my sojourn there, we were in expectation of a combined attack from the armies of the pashas of Damascus and Acre.

Since then, circumstances have been more favourable for research in the East. From the exhibition of Mr. Catherwood's panorama and the publications of various travellers, the subject of the topography and antiquity of Jerusalem has engaged the attention of the biblical antiquary, and has given rise to much controversy and to many wild theories. My object in this paper is not so much criticism as to give some information on a subject interesting alike to the architect and the archæologist, and to direct the attention of the members and othe

* Read at the ordinary ... stitute of British Architec

architects who may contemplate a journey abroad, to the fact that a visit to Jerusalem will afford much interest, and if they will give their attention to the investigation of the doubtful points, they will themselves derive much valuable information from the research, and contribute greatly to elucidate biblical antiquity. It requires not only the *accuracy* but the *eye* of the *travelled* architect, who has been accustomed to antiquarian research, to decide on the disputed points; the doubts arise principally from the discoveries and descriptions being by those whose attention had not been previously directed to architectural detail.

The published works of Mr. Williams, Mr. Bartlett, and Dr. Robinson, and the notes by Mr. Tipping to Dr. Trail's new edition of Josephus, with others, will direct the attention of those who may contemplate what is now only a summer's excursion (a visit to the Holy Land) to the debateable ground, and I will take this opportunity to state, that I shall not only be willing, but even feel obliged, by being consulted, as I have many questions to ask and much information to obtain on a subject which has at intervals occupied a portion of my thought.

Jerusalem stands on the southern extremity of an elongated plain of a range of limestone mountains, elevated about 2,000 feet above the Mediterranean Sea. The city is bounded on the east by the valley of Jehosaphat, in which runs the brook Kedron, on the south by the valley of Ben Hinnom, on the west by the valley of Gihon, and on the north by the plain alluded to. The general appearance of the country around is dreary, desolate, and barren; the valleys and ravines, however, are fertile, and the olive tree flourishes on the sides of the hills and ravines. Jerusalem occupied the site of four hills: Zion, or the upper city, on the south-west; Moriah (on which the temple was built), on the east; Bezetha, the new town, on the north; and Acra, the lower city, in the middle, and to the north of Zion. Zion was the highest of the four hills: it is computed about 250 feet above the valley of Jehosophat. A deep valley, called Millo, separated Acra from Moriah, which was in part filled up by the Asmonæan race, in order to join the lower city to the temple. The continuation of the valley is called by Josephus the Tyropoeon, and separates Zion from Acra as well as from Moriah. Zion was probably the first of the hills occupied, and on it stood the city or strong place of the Jebusites, which was finally taken by David A.M. 2957, who made it his capital, instead of Hebron, and called it the City of David. "He built round about from Millo inward," and Hiram, King of Tyre, sent cedars, and carpenters, and masons, and built him (David) a house on Zion. Mount Moriah, at this period, was the threshing-floor of Ornan, the Jebusite, of whom David purchased it, as a site for the house of the Lord, which Solomon began to build 32 years after the defeat of the Jebusites (A.M. 2992).* This mount is also the spot where Abraham had raised an altar to make the offering of his son Isaac as a sacrifice. The building the house of the Lord (Solomon's temple), as described in Kings and Chronicles, has given rise to many ingenious designs, learned dissertations, and curious theories. Solomon† having selected 70,000 men to bear burdens, 80,000 more to hew in the mountains, and 3,600 to oversee them, sent to Hiram, King of Tyre, to send him "a man cunning to work in gold, and in silver, and in brass, and in iron, and in purple, and crimson, and that can skill to grave with the cunning men that are with me in Judah and Jerusalem," whom David his father had provided. And Hiram sent him a cunning man (endued with understanding). From the description by the sacred penman which follows, Wilkins has designed a Greek Doric temple, supposing from the situation of Tyre on the coast that the architecture of Greece at that period was adopted in Syria. I must own I at one time inclined to this view, that is, as regards the style of the architecture of the temple; but after exploring the coast of Syria, and after an examination of the remains of the Egyptian buildings, I have thought it likely that the architecture of the temple resembled more the architecture of Egypt than that of Greece. We know there was much communication between Egypt and Syria. Solomon had horses and linen from there, and married a daughter of Pharaoh; and by a monument cut in the work (of Egyptian design, and of the period assigned to Sesostris), at the Nahr al Kelb, near Beirout, on the coast, a cast of which was brought to this country by Mr. Bonomi, and placed in the British Museum, we see that the architecture of Egypt was used in Syria at a spot more remote from the parent country than even Jerusalem, and a similar monument has been since found in Cyprus, whereas I am not aware that any example exists of Greek architecture of the age of Solomon in Jerusalem, or even Syria.

* 2 Chron., iii., iv., v.

† 2 Chron., ii. 18; v. 2—7.

The two pillars, "Jachin and Boaz," erected before the temple, and "the porch before the house,"* remind me of the Egyptian obelisk and the great propylons, whilst the "chambers round about the house," the "flat ceilings and roofs," resemble much more the temples of Egypt than those of Greece, besides the total absence of any indication of a pediment and slanting roof, in the description of Solomon's temple,—features so prominent in the Greek temples. However, there is little hope of a satisfactory solution of this problem,—the successive destruction and rebuilding of the temple, I fear, has obliterated all traces of its original style.

After the first destruction of the temple by Nebuchadnezar, it was rebuilt and dedicated in the fifth year of the reign of Darius, A.M. 3416. The second temple—of which, I believe, there is no description on record—was rebuilt by Herod about four years before the birth of Christ, after having stood, like the former, about 500 years.

This building of Herod is the temple of the New Testament, and was the scene of many of the events of our Saviour's life. The description of it by Josephus, though perhaps much exaggerated as regards its beauty and dimensions, proves that it was a building of greater magnificence than any of the preceding ones. When more favourable times than the present will allow of excavation and further research on its site, it is probable that many fragments will be brought to light, and a restoration of its main features may be accomplished with some degree of certainty. (Some of the existing antiquities, which I shall hereafter describe, are probably of this period.)

During the great siege of Jerusalem by Titus, A.D. 70 or 72, the destruction of this work of Herod was so complete as to verify the prophecy that "one stone should not be left on another."

Since then the site of the temple has been occupied by various buildings, Christian and Saracenic,—and finally the present mosque of Omar was built, partly of ancient fragments, —a spot so sacred to the Mahommedan that none others are allowed to enter even into the outer enclosure, much less to explore the building, and only a few other individuals by stratagem have succeeded in obtaining a casual inspection of this mosque. M. Bonomi, accompanied by Messrs. Catherwood and Arundale, were however, some few years since, allowed to examine, measure, and make drawings of every part, under a misapprehension of the authorities that they had been deputed by Ibrahim, Pasha of Egypt, to report on the alleged dilapidated state of the mosque.

To proceed with the topography of Jerusalem. It seems probable that Acra was occupied in the time of Solomon, and was always, as it is now, the most populous part of the city. Bezetha was a suburb occupied by the increasing population until the time of Agrippa, who enclosed it with a wall *a few years after* the crucifixion. (It is necessary to bear this fact in mind, as my plan of the restoration of the city walls, according to Josephus, has relation to *this* circumstance.)

At the *present day* Jerusalem is surrounded by an embattled wall of imposing appearance, built by the Sultan Soleyman A.D. 1542, partly on old foundations; they are about 2½ miles in circuit, built of small squared stones, decorated at intervals by plain patnas, with fragments of older materials, columns, &c., worked in; and in many parts the ancient walls are standing to a considerable extent, both in length and height (which we shall hereafter allude to more particularly). Of the five gates now open, those called Zion and Damascus are the most ornamented, and the latter is a fair specimen of the style of the period. The wall runs in a north-east direction to the Damascus gate, and continues eastward to the north-east boundary of the city, abutting on the valley of Jehosaphat. The wall from thence runs southward, forming the eastern side above the same valley, the greater portion of it being also the enclosure of the temple area, in which is seen an ancient gateway, walled up, known as the Golden Gate. A portion of the south wall of the enclosure of the temple forms likewise the city boundary, from whence there is a considerable jutting out of the wall southward, on a portion of the rock of Moriah, called Ophel. The south wall passing westward across the Tyropoean valley, passes over the upper part of Mount Zion, half of which is now without the walls. At the summit the wall turns off at right angles to the north, where it unites with the citadel, now called David's Castle. This being the entrance from Jaffa and Bethlehem, the gate here is called not only by those names, but also the "Pilgrims' Gate," who generally arrive in the Holy Land by way of Jaffa. The wall diverges to the north-west (and completes the western boundary), where it joins the angle at which I commenced the circuit.

* 2 Chron. iii. 15.

Of the objects of most note within the walls, commencing at the north-western corner, are the Latin Convent, where travellers usually take up their abode;—the Church of the Holy Sepulchre, situate in the western part of the city, a description of which was given us two sessions since by Professor Willis, containing, among other assigned sacred localities, the site of the Crucifixion and the Sepulchre of our Lord, and the cave where St. Helena discovered the cross;—the "Via Dolorosa," or the way by which our Saviour carried the cross from Pilate's house (on the site of which is the present governor's house) to Calvary, passing under by the Gate of Judgment, and the arch of "Ecce homo," which is probably one of the ancient gates. On the site of Pilate's house, the "Scala Santa" (by which Christ ascended), now at Rome, was taken. A large excavation called the Pool of Bethesda, is seen in front of the north wall of the Temple, enclosing probably part of the deep ditch in front of the famous fortress of Antonia. Another pool near to the tower of David, perhaps that formed by Ezekief, and near the same tower, is the spot where the Protestant Church is being built. The convent of the Armenians is a large building, said to be on the site of the martyrdom of St. James; and, lastly, the mosque of Omar, which is by far the grandest object existing at Jerusalem at this time. Without the walls are some excavated tombs on the north and north-west, and in the Valley of Jehosaphat: those called the pillar of Absalom and the tomb of Zachariah, I described in a paper read here some few years since.

Passing by the garden of Gethsemani, from the valley of Jehosaphat, where exist some olive trees of great antiquity, a road leads to the summit of the Mount of Olives, which commands a fine view of Jerusalem. A hill, called Mount Offence, the traditional site of Solomon's idolatry, and the Hill of Evil Counsel, the supposed site of the house of Caiaphas, where the priests and elders took counsel to destroy Christ, are conspicuous features in the scenery around Jerusalem.

Opposite the village of Siloam is a fountain called of "The Virgin," from whence is a subterranean communication for the water to the Pool of Siloam, by a channel cut in the rock through the ridge called "Ophel." The pool is reached by a descent of time-worn steps: the clear refreshing waters, which ebb and flow, and the beauty of the vegetation around on the walls of this pool, impart a peculiar charm to the spot. This, and the cultivated spot below, at the intersection of the valleys by the Well of Nehemiah, form a sort of oasis in this desolate region.

Near here is a remarkable white mulberry tree, the scene of the martyrdom of Isaiah the prophet.

The sides of Zion, without the walls, contain a mosque on the site of the tomb of David; and the places of the sepulchres of the kings of Judah (probably formed in the rock) may be found buried under the accumulation of ages, and the ruins of the ancient palaces and buildings which once embellished this now half-

given amount of light, because it does not follow that, irrespective of modes of combustion, the same amount of gas consumed will furnish the same amount of light. You may burn a limited quantity of gas and have a very splendid light with one arrangement, while with another a prodigious consumption may be going on and but little light obtained. It is then important to ascertain under what circumstances a maximum amount of light is obtained. The arrangement which I have placed on the table this evening, and which I think brings the true principles of economizing gas into application, is the very beautiful "tube burner" of Mr. Leslie, which is most probably well known to many of you. I am sorry my time will not permit me to go into the details of the consumption of gas, but, perhaps, it is scarcely necessary; but there are some points about this flame which may be made obvious on the instant, and without long calculations. See the beautiful, clear, steady, white flame as it stands almost motionless in the glass "combustion-chamber." Now let me remove this glass and replace it by one of the common old cylindrical kind; the quantity of gas burnt is just the same as before, but every one sees that the light has lost all its best qualities. I have admitted too much air by so doing, and therefore get less light; the deposit of carbon goes on as before, but it now goes on too rapidly, and we have a smoke. To get the same amount of light with this glass we must burn twice the quantity of gas which was required with Mr. Leslie's burner.

Having expressed a very favourable opinion of Mr. Leslie's burner and his glass "combustion-chamber" on theoretic grounds, and since then tried them practically with much satisfaction, we are glad to find ourselves strengthened by such an opinion as that we have given above.

The burner and glass are making their way into use steadily. The exterior of the Ordnance office, Pall Mall, affords a good specimen of their value for street lighting. The London Gas Company have put on eight of these burners from Scotland-yard to the corner of Whitehall. This company, we may mention, has the contract with the Woods and Forests for the whole of Regent-street, from the palace at Westminster right through to Regent's-park.

At the General Post-office, St. Martin's-le-Grand, the burners have been in use three months, and if we are rightly informed the saving of gas over the corresponding thirteen weeks before is about eight hundred thousand cubic feet. The Thames Tunnel, also, is now lighted by them.

RIGHT OF ARBITRATORS TO COPY PLANS ENTRUSTED TO THEM.

ROYAL ITALIAN OPERA-HOUSE, COVENT GARDEN.

SIR,—Under a deep sense of the duty I owe to the profession at large, as well as to myself, I feel bound, however reluctantly, to expose the following facts, which, if tacitly sanctioned, I consider would be derogatory to my professional character and highly prejudicial to the ends of justice, and I hope to meet at your hands the candour and support that my case deserves, and which it is well known you never withhold.

The lessees of the Royal Italian Opera House chose, about a year after its completion, to contest two-thirds of my bill of 2,300*l.* for superintending the erection of it, &c., obliging me to institute legal proceedings to recover the balance of it, when, after paying into court 825*l.* more than they had offered me just before going to the jury, they begged a reference (which I had originally offered and they refused). To this I acceded, and Mr. T. L. Donaldson and Mr. T. Bellamy were appointed referees, and by them Mr. Samuel Angell was named as umpire, and, as the referees could not agree, Mr. S. Angell became the sole arbitrator and the depository of all my original designs and documents necessary to substantiate my claim.

On Mr. Angell's award being delivered, (of which, as you have, perhaps properly, refused to admit any comments on it, I must say nothing, whatever I may think), I applied at his office for my papers, and found to my astonishment that the most complete of my designs, working drawings, and papers, were missing from the portfolios and tin boxes, and that many had been copied in Mr. Angell's office by two of his assistants, one of whom, being found by me in the act, was obliged to admit that it was by Mr. Angell's order that he had done so. Such proceedings seemed to demand an explanation, and I wrote to him that after the solemn assurance he had given to me in the presence of Mr. Donaldson, Mr. Smith, and others, as to the safety of my papers when delivered into his hands, I could not but regard his conduct as wholly unjustifiable, inasmuch as he was acting as umpire in the performance of a professional and judicial duty, and I requested him to deliver to me the other documents in his possession, and to render to me the most explicit explanation on the subject. Mr. Angell's reply was that the documents I claimed of him remained in his strong closet during his absence from town, but he admitted that my drawings and extracts of my papers had been copied in his office by his authority, and that he considered he had a perfect right to have any copies or extracts made from any documents or drawings put in by me as evidence in support of my claim, in order that his memoranda might be complete, should there be hereafter any occasion to refer to it; and he went on to assure me that I need be under no apprehension whatever, and that he was quite prepared at any time to show the tracing made from my drawings to Mr. Donaldson, or to Mr. W. Cotterill (my solicitor), in expectation of satisfying them as to his mode of acting.

These explanations cannot be regarded as offering anything like satisfaction, and as to his giving explanations to Mr. Cotterill, or Mr. Donaldson, I have only to refer to these gentlemen's letters, in which Mr. Donaldson says, that "the award has caused great surprise and disappointment to him, particularly as regards Julian's salary, and that after much thought he could not understand why copies of my drawings were taken by Mr. Angell, they not being necessary to substantiate any point in the award, and that in so doing he had erred in judgment in this case altogether;" while Mr. Cotterill, the other gentleman referred to, wrote to me that "he had read over my correspondence with Mr. Angell, but did not see any use in examining the copies he had taken from my drawings. Certainly," Mr. Cotterill, says, "I cannot see any possible use in Mr. Angell's copying any of them for any purpose of the arbitration."

To these opinions of the gentlemen to whom he appealed, and of a great many more professional men to whom I have mentioned the circumstances, it is necessary to add, that one of the copies made from my designs, and on which his assistant was discovered, is marked No. 52, the title of which runs thus—"Longitudinal section of the new theatre, saloons, stage, &c., from the foundations to the roofs, complete as executed." On this copy Mr. Angell's assistant has written "Copies of this and some other drawings of Mr. Albano's works of Covent Garden by Mr. Angell's order were taken by me and Mr. Wood, and are in Mr. Angell's possession. September 27, 1848, G. Judge, jun."

The law affording me no redress at this stage, I am obliged to state now what otherwise I would under no other circumstances bring forward. I have been a member of the profession of civil engineers for a quarter of a century in this my adopted country, and have been engaged upon various works, which I presume have sufficiently established my claim to some ability; if not I would willingly allow my reputation to be estimated by what I have done at Covent Garden Theatre, the manner in which it has been accomplished, the very short period in which it was effected, and the smallness of the expenses attending it, considering that it required fifty-four original and elaborate designs, and above a hundred working drawings, specifications, &c. &c. (all put in evidence), besides daily and nightly attendance to the extent of from sixteen to twenty hours a-day, directing and superintending from the very foundations the construction and decoration of the new theatre, her Majesty's apartments, and the improvement of the whole establishment; converting at the same time the whole of the old materials; on which were daily engaged from 1,000 to 1,600 workmen of all trades, as well as the attendance of six of my assistants and a clerk of the works, all their expenses and salary being defrayed by me during above six months up to the opening of the theatre and for about eight months afterward the expenses of myself and two assistants. I can confidently appeal to Mr. Hosking, who, in his official capacity as official referee, inspected most minutely all my designs, and in his evidence declared that he saw the whole of the works and foundations, and that, to the best of his judgment, they were executed in an admirable manner, and displayed great ability without extravagance, and that he should not have allowed the theatre to be opened unless it had been properly done. I could also appeal to the evidence of Mr. Allason, Mr. Braithwaite, Mr. Godwin, Mr. C. H. Gregory, Mr. W. Laxton, and Sir John Rennie, who had often visited the works during their progress, and unanimously declared it to be a very creditable work, and considering its great intricacy and the short time allowed, it was executed in a scientific, workman-like, and economical manner, and as a work of art carried on with great skill and success: and they all spoke very particularly as to my indefatigability and the fairness of the amount of my charges for a work unequalled for the great sacrifice and exertion it demanded, and which had been admired by all impartial Judges, to whom, as well as for the favourable unanimous opinion expressed by the public press, I owe a deep debt of gratitude.

I consider myself in duty called upon, on public as well as on private grounds, to appeal to the judgment of my profession, either as engineers or architects, to the members of which I look with confidence, satisfied that their high character and honourable feelings will induce them to form a right estimate of these proceedings, and will not allow my professional rights to be trampled on with impunity. I contend that Mr. Angell had neither right nor pretext whatever to take copies of my designs; his duty in the office to which he was appointed was to determine on the remuneration, which, in equity, I was entitled to upon my claim, without having any further duty to perform; and certainly nothing which could render it necessary or proper for him to retain copies of my drawings; and I leave it to the profession and to the public to form their opinion, both as to his conduct and the motive which may have influenced him on this occasion to copy my papers, which he still retains in his possession, conduct which I contend is wholly unprofessional and indefensible, and I refer it to the profession and to the public, on whose well-known love of impartial justice and hatred of oppression I can confidently rely.

I am, Sir, &c., B. ALBANO.

Office, 22, King William-street, Strand,
February, 1849.

NOTES IN THE PROVINCES.

THE church of St. Nicholas, Ipswich, has been considerably altered and enlarged. The old pewing has been replaced by seating in form of benches, but with separate sittings. In a part added to the north aisle a window partly filled with stained glass has been put up, the stained glass the work and gift of Mr. R. B. King. The alterations in all have cost between 500*l.* and 600*l.*, of which the incumbent, Rev. M. G. Edgar, contributed 100*l.* and oak of equal value. Some curious carved figures, said to be of Saxon origin (?) have been discovered, and inserted in the north wall.——At the Ely sessions the propriety of taking down the old court-house at Wisbech, said to be in a dangerous state, and of erecting a new one next the gaol, was lately taken into consideration. It was stated that the old materials were worth 1,600*l.* to 1,800*l.*, a sum sufficient, it was said, to build the new one.——The foundation-stone of the Philanthropic Society's farm-school and chapel will be laid by H.R.H. Prince Albert on 30th April, near the Redhill and Reigate station of the Brighton Railway.——The re-building of Holy Rhood Church, Southampton, proceeds with quickness, and the style and dimensions of the arches, and the proportions of the chancel, are now rendered clear, but the roof of the building closely behind the east window is much complained of in the local papers.——The vicinity of Portsmouth has been much improved, it is said, by the conversion of South-sea common into an agreeable park, by Lord F. Fitzclarence, and others, with the Clarence esplanade crowning the beach, and now a favourite promenade. ——Two new veins of coal, between 5 and 6 feet thick, have been discovered in the parish of Radstock, on the Countess of Waldegrave's property, by Mr. Charles Ashman, the engineer and manager of her ladyship's other mines. The poor people in the parish are in joyful anticipation of employment, and general rejoicing has been manifested by the ringing of bells, &c.——A Liverpool paper says, with reference to the Birkenhead Docks, "It is now certain that these works must go on. The contract has been 'signed, sealed, and delivered,' and on Thursday the dock trustees held meetings for the purpose of arranging the details of the works."——The guardians of the Wincanton Union have accepted the tender of Messrs. Miles and Golding, of Shaftesbury, for the enlargement of their workhouse. There were five tenders given in for the work, and the difference between the highest and lowest was 316l.; the one accepted being 530l., and the highest from a builder at Frome), 846l.——Mr. Walker, engineer, and Mr. May, the resident engineer, have surveyed the whole line of the Caledonian Canal from end to end. Every part of the canal, from the summit level westward, is said to have been in good order.——The Glasgow Harbour works at Springfield have been rather seriously interfered with by a heavy flooding in the Clyde, which filled the excavations. The new line of quay, however, is in an advanced state of progress.

METROPOLITAN COMMISSION OF SEWERS.

A GENERAL court was held on Thursday last, the 15th, at the Sewers Court, Greek-street, Soho-square; Lord Ebrington, M.P., in the chair. On the recommendation of the finance committee, several payments were ordered, and amongst the rest, a cheque was directed to be placed in the hands of Mr. Groom, the official assignee in bankruptcy, for the amount due to Mr. Starkie, the contractor for the Grosvenor-square sewer, from the late Commissioners of Sewers, prior to his bankruptcy. This long-litigated affair will now be brought to a close on the solicitors of this court receiving a satisfactory acknowledgment of the same. All the real business of the commission seems now to be done snugly and quietly in committee, a system against which, when in the old Westminster commission, one at all events of the present commissioners was in the habit of protesting pretty constantly and loudly,—whether rightly or wrongly we do not stop now to inquire. The new Sewers Act appears to be very defective in several points, and is felt to be so by the Commissioners. Those who drew it up don't exactly understand the operation of some parts of it; so, unless we are wrongly informed, other opinions have been sought.

ENCROACHMENT ON THE NEW ROAD, ISLINGTON.

METROPOLITAN IMPROVEMENTS.

REGRETTING equally with your correspondent "Viator," that the line of this road is being constantly trenched upon by the erection of buildings upon the fore-courts of the houses, I am sure he cannot be aware of the various attempts that have been made from time to time to prevent this great evil, or he would have thrown his sarcasm upon the parties who have really caused an Act of Parliament, intended for the protection of this line of road, to become totally inoperative, rather than have censured the parochial vestries, who have neither foolishly nor culpably neglected their duties, but have endeavoured to enforce the law, though without avail, the magistrates refusing to convict. Further, the very parties who should have supported them have been the first to infringe its regulations, as may be seen in the instances of the Park-crescent, York-place, &c., which were advanced beyond the prescribed limit by the Commissioners of Woods, &c.; and latterly the official referees defined the line of frontage of two public buildings as being 50 feet back from the footway, while a few months

subsequently these gentlemen came to a resolution to allow these erections on the fore-courts one story in height in roads 60 feet in width,—and, consequently, a few hundred yards off, two private buildings are now in course of erection at the western end, adjoining the Edgeware-road, as well as those referred to by your correspondent near Osnaberg-street. So much for the protection of the public interests to be derived from central commissioners, whom your correspondent is so enamoured of, who to-day undo that which they have given effect to on the previous one. I am quite satisfied the parochial vestries of this metropolis have public spirit enough to place themselves above private interests, and only require the aid of the administrators of the law to maintain inviolate the powers vested in them, but which, unfortunately, is rarely given where the public interests are concerned, thereby aiding the designs of those whose interests it is to advance centralization, to the prejudice of the great fundamental law of this country,—local self-government.　　　C. E.

THE COST OF THE CITY AND SURREY GAOLS.

IF we were to print some of the comments we have received on this matter generally, they would displease more persons than one, and so far as we can see would do no good. Considerable surprise is expressed as to the difference of cost between the two prisons. The Surrey prison, to be built on Wandsworth-common, is to contain, as we understand, 790 cells, including chapel, laundry, boundary walls, and airing-grounds. The city prison, to be built at Holloway, is to contain 500 cells, chapel, laundry, and boundary walls. The Surrey prison is to cost 130l. per cell, and the city of London 184l. per cell. How is this difference made? say some. Some part of it is to be attributed to the introduction of masonry in the city prison; and it may be that more fittings are included in one than the other.

The difference between the highest and the lowest tenders, 17,410l. in one, and 11,720l. in the other, sounds large, especially as it was made wholly in the pricing,—the quantities being supplied: but looked at as a per centage on the amount, it is not so great as is often the case. The lowest tender for the city may be called 16 per cent. less than the highest, and that for the Surrey prison rather more than 10 per cent. One of our correspondents says that the charge made by the surveyors for taking out the quantities for the city prisons, including lithographing the bills, was 2,824l. The 2½ per cent. pays better than the 5.

THE RIVER-WALL OF THE HOUSES OF PARLIAMENT.

A FEW days since, in passing over Westminster Bridge, my attention was drawn to the works now in progress for the purpose of removing the dam in front of the new palace. I was not a little surprised to observe that the piles forming the dam were being drawn. On a closer inspection I observed that these piles were a distance of at least 16 feet in the ground. Now it struck me as being a most ill-advised plan to draw these timbers at all, inasmuch as the operation amounts to cutting a trench, or rather two trenches, there being two rows of piles, the whole length of the river frontage, and 16 feet deep, which I am disposed to think, with that unfortunate spectacle Westminster Bridge before one's eyes, is, to say the least, running an unnecessary risk. Moreover, as there is no good end served, I cannot conceive what can have been the motive for drawing the piles instead of cutting them off level with the proposed ground line, which every practical man knows could have been done at an expense of certainly not more than 500l. or 600l. over the present method, and there would then have been scarcely a possibility of the river frontage ever being injured, inasmuch as the timber left in the ground would have afforded an additional security in the event of the present bridge being removed, and another erected in all probability on a fresh site, which is as likely to cause an alteration in the set of the tide, and thereby to

deepen the river bed, as did the removal of the old London Bridge.

I repeat, that without any end served, it is a matter of astonishment that the present course should have been pursued. I am aware that there is a line of piles at the foot of the river wall intended as a protection, but still the fact of disturbing a mass of ground to such a depth (to the bottom of the sheet piling) within a few feet of the wall, is most unadvisable. True, no immediate injury may result, but look at the bridge. I have no doubt, that when that structure was completed, it was deemed a substantial erection; but what has time proved it to be? And it may fairly be said, that a little foresight would have prevented its present deplorable appearance and a large outlay of money. Gain experience from the past: a motto which in this instance is deserving particular attention.　　　T.

Miscellanea.

ISLINGTON MARKET.—This market was built by the late Mr. John Perkins, about fifteen years since, having obtained an Act of Parliament, which gives the power of holding the market, of slaughtering cattle, melting the fat for tallow, manufacturing the offal, &c. The area within the walls is 15 acres, and for the sake of comparison, to enable any one to judge of its extent, we will quote Russell-square, which contains 11 A. 1 R. to the walls of the houses, and Lincoln's-inn Fields contains 10 A. 1 R. 29 P. There is accommodation for 8,000 head of cattle and 50,000 sheep, besides layers having 3,280 feet in length of roof, or nearly 2 acres. The extent of freehold property, upon which there are thirty houses, is 7 acres, exclusive of the market, and 7 acres leasehold, upon which it is intended to erect abattoirs and a dead-meat market. A main public sewer passes within 300 feet of the eastern entrance, and it is 18 feet lower than the surface of the market. The East and West India Dock Railway passes to within 400 yards of the market.

ARTESIAN WELL AT HADHAM.—I observe in the last number of THE BUILDER, that a correspondent wishes to know if it be practicable to fix a lifting pump in an Artesian bore of 6 inches diameter, the water level of the spring being 178 feet from the surface: [such an operation is possible; it is obvious the rod should be arranged and steadied inside the rising main. The bucket and clacks require periodical examination; means of access to them should therefore be provided; indeed, facilities should be given for removing the whole pump, combined with perfect steadiness when fixed: it is almost needless to remark the pump must on no account choke up the bore. These matters require care in detail, and should be directed by a professional man. —JOHN G. SWINDELL, 3, Kilburn Priory.

IMPROVEMENTS IN PARIS.—For completing the Louvre the estimates are—for the ground required for completing the Louvre, 6,379,250f.; for the buildings and other works, 23,000,000f.; and for the continuation of the Rue de Rivoli, 3,119,630f. The Municipal Council have come to the resolution that the city should contribute the 3,119,630f. towards the continuation of the Rue de Rivoli. The plans for the new buildings comprise the establishment of the National Library, in the wing to be constructed towards the Rue de Rivoli, special galleries for the annual exhibition of the works of modern painters and sculptors, and for the periodical exhibition of the products of the useful arts, next the gallery of the Museum; and the formation of an intermediate quadrangle, with a colossal fountain in the centre, surrounded by four quincunxes, ornamented with statues.

ORSI AND ARMANI'S METALLIC LAVA.— Of this material for paving we have already spoken briefly without offering any opinion on its merits, time being necessary to decide these. It would really seem, however, well deserving examination and to have many advantages, especially in places where the surface of other floorings would be made moist and mouldy by rising damp. Messrs. Orsi and Armani have produced from our pages, in their black and white lava, some of the mosaics from Pompeii, which we gave in a recent number (page 3).

PROJECTED WORKS.—Advertisements have been issued for tenders, by 1st May, for repewing, &c., Bridgewater Church (with plans and drawings); by March 5th, for an addition, alteration, &c., at a shop in Caistor, Lincolnshire; also for a shop front with mahogany sashes and plate glass; by 24th, for the erection of a new aisle, &c., for Chiselhurst Church, Kent; by 12th, for the erection of the new workhouse for the Fulham Union; by 1st, for the erection of certain almshouses at Hereford; by 28th inst., for rebuilding the parish church at Birch, Essex; and by 2nd March, for lighting the public lamps in the Grosvenor-place district with gas for five years or more.

LITERARY INSTITUTIONS AND TAXES.—The claim of the Greenwich Scientific Society to have their building exempted from taxes has been rejected by Baron Alderson, Anti-corn-law and other meetings having been held in it.

CHELSEA IMPROVEMENT ACT.—RATING.—Mr. Bult, of Chelsea, having declined to pay the Chelsea Improvement rate, was summoned before Mr. Burrell, at Westminster. Mr. Bult argued that he was not bound to pay, because the 174th section of the Chelsea Improvement Act stated, "that it shall be lawful for them (the commissioners) to make a rate upon the occupiers of all messuages, &c., which *at the time of passing this Act* were by law liable to be rated to the repairs of the highways within the said limits," and neither his house nor any part of the street in which he resided was built at the time of the passing of the Act. He had come forward to oppose the claim from a sense of right, and complained that there were no gutters or gulley-holes in his street to carry off the rain, that there was no road formed, that it was in a most filthy and unwholesome state, that his own and family's health had been much affected by exhalations from filthy matter, and that his three children had but recently recovered from fever, caused by the nuisances produced by the filthy condition of the street.—Mr. Bodkin, on the part of the commissioners, said that the construction put upon the section was monstrous. The section clearly intended to mean, not the identical buildings at that time in existence, but all that description of property which should subsequently be erected. The magistrate took the same view of it, and declared Mr. Bult liable to the rating.

SIR HANS SLOANE'S MONUMENT.—With reference to the recent remarks in THE BUILDER, on the monument to the memory of Sir Hans Sloane, which stands at the east corner of the old churchyard, Cheyne-walk, Chelsea, this monument, as well as the inscription in its present dilapidated condition, demands the attention and aid of the public, in order that it may be restored and saved from the ravages of time, so that the memento, erected with so much liberality to the memory of the scientific attainments, devoted to the use and benefit of the public, of so celebrated a character, may be handed down to posterity. At a time when other improvements were being effected in this neighbourhood, the churchwardens wrote to the family of the late Sir Hans Sloane, calling their attention to the dilapidated state of the monument, in the hope that they would cause the same to be repaired. The answer they received to his communication was, I believe, that the property had been dispersed, and that no funds remained in the hands of the trustees or executors, applicable thereto. The churchwardens, not having any funds which they can legally lay out in its repair, and the inhabitants also having already expended much upon the improvements, there remains but little probability that anything can be done to rescue it from decay and ultimate ruin, unless, by being brought before the public through the medium of your widely circulated journal, there may be found among the various scientific bodies of our country, and public spirited individuals, a sufficient number who may feel sufficiently interested in the matter so as to aid by a small subscription, the repairing and restoring the monument. J. PERRY.

Chelsea.

N.B. The Worshipful Company of Apothecaries are the trustees for the public of the collection, at Chelsea, of Sir Hans Sloane's botanical specimens.

LAVATORIES FOR THE BRITISH MUSEUM.—Now that the "commissioners" have instructions to improve the arrangements of the Museum, it will be well for them to bear in mind the necessity of providing greater conveniences for those who frequent the library. A lavatory is rather a necessity, if only for the protection of valuable works from being soiled, than a luxury. The present arrangement of the conveniences for the gentlemen is very unsatisfactory, and in any alteration the ladies should be consulted.

BIRMINGHAM WORKHOUSE COMPETITION.—The guardians resolved that the report of the committee should not be received, but that the six selected plans should be submitted to the test of ballot. On the 21st the votes were taken, and the result was a majority of 10 for Mr. Hemming; the numbers being—Hemming, 36; Drury and Bateman, 26. The whole affair is very discreditable to the Board.

PREVENTION OF CORROSION.—According to the *Chemical Times*, the best means of preventing the corrosion of metals is to dip the articles first into very dilute nitric acid, to immerse them afterwards in linseed oil, and to allow the excess of oil to drain off. By this process metals are effectively preserved from rust or oxidation.

NORMAN TOWER, BURY ST. EDMUNDS.—The committee have reported to the subscribers that the restoration of the tower is completed. 3,100*l*. have been disbursed, and about 300*l*. remain to be paid.

VERY BLIND BUILDERS.—I beg to inclose, says one correspondent, and seven others have done so in other words,—a specimen of estimating as exhibited on the 15th inst. at the offices of Mr. Lambert, for finishing fourteen 8-roomed houses, now in carcass, building outhouses, &c. There is evidently something very wrong in the system of contracting now followed by some men. One would think they were entirely ignorant of what they were doing, or grossly dishonest; one or the other is quite apparent.

H. Search	£5,420
R. Newport	5,026
T. Howard	4,982
Thos. Burton	4,951
J. Rivett	4,712
W. Higgs	4,647
R. and E. Curtis	4,484
W. Norris	4,397
J. Foot	4,340
W. Perry	4,289
A. Cripps	4,190
W. Blenkham	4,179
D. Bodger	4,094
J. Mullins	4,018
W. Loynes	4,000
E. Mares	3,985
J. T. Taylor	3,960
Walker and Soper	3,947
J. J. Billson	3,875
J. Raycrup	3,750
G. Bugg	3,500
J. Sutton	3,430
W. Pillbeam	3,298
D. Catlin	3,290
J. Greenwood	3,000
C. Lloyd	2,920
J. K. Vote	2,656
J. Vaughan	2,548
J. Pooley	2,175
J. Richards	1,999

COST OF THE SMALL-POX HOSPITAL.—Sir: It seems very desirable for the sake of competitors, that you should print the tenders for the Small-pox Hospital: Mr. Daukes, architect:—

Pritchard	£19,930
Smith	19,410
G. A. Young	18,549
Lee and Son	18,300
Holland	17,699
Patrick	17,430
Grimsdell	17,085
Keik	16,953
W. Cubitt and Co.	16,900
J. Locke and Co.	16,600
Myers	16,431
Messrs. Piper	15,938

These amounts are exclusive of the foundations and drains, which have been put in at an expense of 2,800*l*.—AN ARCHITECT WHO TRIES TO BE HONEST.

*** We have received some letters commenting in strong terms on the conduct of both committee and architect, but are not disposed to insert them, except with the writers' names attached.

A GOOD MOVEMENT IN THE SCHOOL OF DESIGN.—At Somerset House an association of the students has just been formed, for the purpose of mutual improvement, the first meeting of which was held on Saturday, the 10th, in the large room at Somerset House, the use of which has been granted by the council. An introductory paper was read by Mr. D. W. Raimbach, the substance of which we shall give.

EXPOSITION OF INVENTIONS. — It is thought, with reason, that a free exposition of patented and registered inventions would be an advantage to the public, and at the same time, facilitate the object which manufacturers have in view, viz., making their inventions generally known, and it is intended to open an exposition of the kind at the Baker-street Bazaar. A manager and assistants will be appointed, for the purpose of explaining the use and advantage of each invention, and to effect sales.

SHAPE IN RESPECT OF AREA.—Having seen, some time since, in THE BUILDER, some questions as to the squaring of numbers, it occurred to me that it would be interesting to mention a fact relating to the areas of squares for buildings. A figure which has all its four sides equal, contains the greatest area within the same length of wall, viz.:—

Feet.	Feet.	Feet.	
80^2 =	6400	and 320	length of walls.
60 × 100 =	6000	and 320	,,
70 × 90 =	6300	and 320	,,
50 × 110 =	5500	and 320	,,

This may be useful to those concerned in building warehouses, &c., which case first called your obedient servant's attention to the fact.—R. B. GRANTHAM.

WOODEN BARN FLOORS AND RATS.—Barn floors may be made impervious to rats by the following cheap method:—Dig around the building that has its foundations in the ground (in contradistinction to those supported on stone or brick piers), a dry area, say 14 inches wide by 9 inches deep, pave the bottom with brick flats, the side farthest from the building to have two courses of 4½-inch work, whilst the other has a course of plain tiles or slates, nailed to the outside surface of the building: as this is finished, fill in the area with the earth dug out. The rats will endeavour to make their entrance by burrowing, but they will invariably work themselves out at the surface, as they cannot effect their object, try how or where they will, and cunning as they are, they never commence burrowing away from the building, but close around it. This plan has never failed: rid yourself of the inside members and no outsiders can enter. The doorways may be similarly secured by carrying up a dwarf wall along the opening.—JOHN B. WATSON.

IMPROVEMENT IN SCOTLAND.—The writer of a paragraph relative to Dundee, which appeared in your paper of last week, under the signature of "*One who has used his Olfactories,*" is entitled to the thanks of every well-wisher of Scotland. Aware of the high estimation in which THE BUILDER is held in Scotland, would you permit an admirer of that country to suggest, not only to the inhabitants of Dundee but to those of Scotland generally, that probably the most delicate and esteemed compliment they could pay to the Queen and Prince Albert, would be for the upper and middle classes in every parish throughout the country, by their example, advice, and assistance, to endeavour to effect an improvement as regards cleanliness in the habits of the lower classes. If each parish had a distinct society formed for the purpose of carrying out such improvements, great, doubtless, would be the benefits derived therefrom; and it would ere long become a brand and a disgrace to build houses without having the usual *conveniences* attached.—R. B.

BREATHING ROOM FOR THE TOWER HAMLETS.—Some eight years since I proposed (through the medium of the press), the removal of that disgusting, and very unwholesome nuisance, the Tower ditch or moat, and at the same time suggested that its site might, advantageously, be converted into a public garden or promenade. Shortly after I had the gratification of seeing my proposition partly acceded to. The ditch was drained, but instead of completing the above arrangement, the bed was merely levelled (and not raised as I intended), and is now used once or twice a-month, as an exercise ground, for the soldiers stationed within the garrison. Now, Sir, I appeal to you, as the acknowledged champion of metropolitan improvement, and ask your aid, in behalf of this densely peopled locality, in urging the Government to grant at once this highly desirable alteration, for no part of London is so destitute of " breathing " places as the Tower Hamlets. I had intended speaking also of the enclosure in Trinity-square, Tower-hill, admission to which can only be obtained by paying " to some one" a fee of two guineas per annum, but will reserve that for a future occasion.—N.

MEETINGS OF SCIENTIFIC BODIES

Held during the ensuing week.

Tuesday, Feb. 27.—Institution of Civil Engineers, 8 P.M.
Wednesday, 28.—Society of Arts, 8 P.M.
Thursday, March 1.—Royal Society, 8½ P.M. ; Society of Antiquaries, 8 P.M.
Friday, 2—Archæological Association, 4 P.M.

TO CORRESPONDENTS.

Received.—" Z. Z. Z." (ask a merchant), " J. N. C.," " T. C.," " W. J.," " C. B., jun.," " C. H. W." (thanks), " D. T." (Hull), " G. P.," " F. A.," " R. S.," " W. W.," Derby (thanks : such an arrangement does not deserve re-cord), " W. H.," " A. R. H." (we should say, as in heraldry, that the *south wing* of Buckingham Palace is the " right "), " Constant Reader," " H. Lee " (we are unable to advise), " J. C." (we should use the Caen), " F. E. K.," " W. D." (already mentioned), " J. G." (the suggestion has been made before), " An Architect " (Birmingham), " J. L." (Chester), " J. S.," " W. S.," " W. M.," " Old Subscriber " (we have several times stated what we know as to destroying ants, and cannot repeat ourselves), " J. C." " Humboldt's Cosmos," translated, with author's sanction, under direction of Colonel Sabine, 2 vols. (London, Longman and Co. ; John Murray.—1849) ; " The Public Health with National Gain," pamph. (Ridgway—1849) ; " Tenant Right," digest of the evidence before Committee of House of Commons (London, Ridgway.—1849) ; " Rail-way Taxation," by S. Laing, Esq., pamph. (London, Vacher.—1849) ; " Rudimentary Mechanics," by Charles Tomlinson (Weale's Series).

" *Books, Prices, and Addresses.*"—We have not time to point out books or find addresses.

NOTICE.— All communications respecting *advertisements* should be addressed to the " Publisher," and not to the " Editor :" all other communications should be addressed to the Editor, and *not* to the publisher.

The Builder.

No. CCCXVII.

SATURDAY, MARCH 3, 1849.

MANY matters press upon us for consideration. Amongst them the late fearful calamity in the Theatre Royal at Glasgow, where nearly 70 persons lost their lives in the crush produced by an alarm of fire, must not be passed by without comment. Several questions of great importance, and often discussed in our pages, are involved,—namely, the defective arrangement of the stairs and accesses in many of our theatres, the importance of obtaining a cheap and efficient mode of fire-proof construction, and the necessity, or, otherwise, for Government supervision.

At the beginning of the year, on the occurrence of a serious accident at the Victoria Theatre, we drew attention to the condition and arrangement of the stairs, lobbies, and modes of exit in several of our theatres, and said it should reconcile parties to the control over staircases and passages given to the official referees by the Buildings Act; and that, as the clause only applied to new and altered buildings, it was a question whether it ought not to be made to apply to existing structures, and extend to obtaining for the public the means of ready egress.

With ourselves this is no longer a question; some step, with the same end in view, is imperatively demanded, and we suggest that the Government should, as a first move, name three or more competent persons (the referees, if their time be not too much occupied), to examine and report on the metropolitan theatres, concert-rooms, and other places of public resort, with reference to the means afforded in them for safe and rapid egress.

To managers themselves, and the proprietors of these structures, we would say, do not wait for this, but set yourselves to work to render the approaches fire-proof, so far as possible, and the means of egress safe, ample, and commodious. Let it be well understood by the public, that this has been done, and the chance of panic, and of tumultuous rushing to escape on the slightest alarm, by which the mischief is always brought about, will be materially lessened.

The sense of security felt when it is known, as in the Royal Italian Opera House, Covent Garden, constructed under the provisions of the Act, that the staircases from the highest part of the building, and the accesses, are indestructible, can scarcely be overlooked. We mention the Covent Garden Opera House, not as being the *only* house where a certain degree of security in this respect may be enjoyed, but as a result of the compulsory clause in the Buildings Act.*

Were a fire to occur in some of our theatres, or even an alarm to be given sufficient to lead the audience to endeavour, panic stricken, to escape, the result would be fearful.

"We will venture to say," remarks the *Examiner*, taking our view of the subject, "that there is not a theatre in London which at this moment would hear inspection, with a view to the safety of all its avenues, passages, and staircases. There is not one in which, in the event of fire or the false alarm of it, in some one quarter, or more than one, there would not be a jam of crushed and smothered bodies like that of Glasgow, but probably on a greater scale of destruction. But the Legislation which so sagely and carefully levels the powers of the law against penny theatres and unlicensed performances, takes no precautions to guard against this frightful mischief. There is an authority to prevent the performance of a play in which a word offensive to morals or decorum may be found, but there is none to prevent performances in a theatre so defectively constructed, that the false alarm of any drunkard, fool, or pickpocket may cause the destruction of masses of people inextricably jammed and pounded together, and perishing more cruelly than the sufferers in the black hole at Calcutta."

Irrespective of the materials composing the stairs and accesses, a careful revision should be made of the barriers and other obstructions on the stairs and in the passages. The doors, if not made to swing both ways, should all open outwards.

We have received from Glasgow a plan of the staircase wherein the disaster occurred. The stairs vary in width from 4 feet to about 4 feet 4 inches. One half the staircase forms a right angle with the other, and at the junction, where there are winders, there was a barrier, 5½ feet high, and 2 feet 3 inches wide, opening outwards, but held in its place by an iron bar attached to the wall, and hooking into a staple in the door, so as to narrow the passage to 23 inches. Lower down, and nearer to the entrance from the street, was a pair of folding doors, each 21 inches wide. The one to the right (going down stairs) opened outwards, the other half opened the reverse way, and this was kept closed by a strong bar hooking into a staple in the door, so as to prevent any large number of persons from passing through at one time. Judging from the statements before us, it seems it was at these barriers that the mischief was done, and persons on the spot think the same thing. "On looking at the matter coolly," says the *North British Mail*, "at this distance of time, and after a careful examination of the premises, there can be no doubt that, to the obstructions offered by the two fixed doors in the stair, the awful catastrophe may be attributed. Of course, had there been no panic, the narrow passages left open past the doors would have been sufficient to permit the leisurely and regular exit of the whole audience. But the possibility of a panic should always be provided for in such buildings, and the arrangements of the manager framed with a view of obviating such an occurrence should it happen."

There should be no *fixed* obstructions in the stairs or passages of a theatre.

Most of our readers have doubtless learnt from the daily papers the very trivial cause of the panic, but we will nevertheless repeat it in few words for a purpose.

Round the front of the upper gallery are several large crystal globes, with a gas light in the centre of each. The lights on each side are supplied with gas through a block-tin tube of about half-an-inch in diameter, connected with an iron gas-pipe at the end of the gallery —that is, the globes on each side of the gallery are supplied from separate pipes. Had this not been fortunately so, the flame would have extended each way and over double the distance. In this half-inch pipe a leak took place, the escaped gas found its way into the space formed by the framing, and a piece of lighted paper thrown down by a boy who had used it to light a pipe, ignited the escaping gas. The result was that the flame soon heated the pipe to the melting point, and the aperture gradually enlarged, until, in a few seconds, a portion of the *pipe was entirely melted away*, when the inflamed gas would issue with the full volume and force of a pipe of that diameter. The pipe continued thus to melt away gradually, and the ascending flame struck against the boarding forming the front of the gallery. A carpenter extinguished the flame by squeezing up the pipe with his blue bonnet, and all danger was thought over, when, from some unexplained cause, the panic occurred and the disaster followed.

Now, it was a curious coincidence that, on the morning of the day on which the accident occurred, a letter appeared in the *Glasgow Citizen*, from our correspondent Mr. Wylson, on various defects in construction which increase the chances of conflagrations,* which contained the following paragraph:—"One more fire-raiser, and I have done: namely, *composition and block-tin gas-tubing*,—which I hope 1850 will see an end of. The relative costs of composition tube (*i.e.* old lead, with a few old solder joints), block-tin tube, and wrought-iron tube, are about as 2, 3, and 4; hence the inducement to adhere to the two former; but the first is worthless for horizontal work, being soft and liable to sag between its bearings, and hold water; and both melt readily; and here is the danger. When a flame reaches the tube, it melts—the gas is ignited—and away it travels, burning and melting, behind lathing, up hollow partitions, over ceilings, through roofs, and only ceasing when its metal is exhausted, leaving the gas flaring at its source—the main."

It might really be thought that this was written after the occurrence, instead of before it, and should serve as a proof to Mr. Wylson's fellow citizens of his correctness and foresight.

It is a mercy that we have not to record a

* Some few alterations are being made in the Italian Opera House ready for the coming season, with a view to afford additional accommodation to visiters. The lower gallery, known as the box stalls, has been formed into boxes, and the corridor, heretofore cut off on this floor, continued all round the house. The amphitheatre has been increased by forming two rows of seats on both sides of the house in lieu of the top tier of boxes. Not content with having one of the best houses in London for seeing and hearing in, the proprietors have thought desirable to increase for its visiters the facility of *being* seen; and have accordingly cut down the fronts of all the boxes to the extent of several inches; the same ornaments are replaced, and are thus necessarily brought closer together. What effect the alteration will have on the general appearance of the house remains to be seen.

* "If we cannot put an end to all fire insurance, by adopting those principles of construction which render buildings completely incombustible, there are yet improvements on ordinary practice which may be effected at little extra cost, and the omission of which I would fain see building proprietors entirely set their faces against. For example, there is an item in carpenters' accounts in Glasgow, 'safe lintles' by name—mark it well—which are wooden lintles laid over the inner portion of window and door openings, and carrying rubble masonry upon them; there is also a universal practice of inserting the ends of every tier of joists into the walls, resting on a thin board half through their thickness. Now, it is palpable that the walls of a building erected of stone or brick, when a fire does occur in it, and its combustible contents are consumed, ought to be found after about as good as they were before the fire, it being only necessary to reinstate the floors, roof, and finishings; yet, by the use of 'safe lintles,' and by catacombing, and nearly cutting the walls across at every floor level, the necessary consequence of a thorough *gutting* by fire is, that the very walls themselves are reduced to ruins, and the loss thus increased far beyond what might have been the limit; whereas, by the use of proper stone arches, and laying the joists longitudinally instead of transversely, carried by beams which have cilled and lintled openings provided for them, or by inserting an iron socket for every joist laid in the ordinary way, such extra loss might have been prevented; the latter mode, however, has still the objection that the burning joists act with a powerful leverage in falling, and strain and shatter the walls accordingly." * * * *

"Another source of conflagrations is the practice of inserting into the masonry of chimney-breasts the wooden plugs to which the lath-strapping is affixed. The holes for these "dooks," as they are called by workmen, frequently penetrate to the flue, and the plug then offers itself as a conductor of fire from the chimney to the lathing and straps inside. It is a very laudable custom to give the wall at that part a coat of plaster between the straps, to prevent fire coming through the beds and joints of the masonry, which are narrow there; but this is not sufficient; the dooks should disappear, and iron hold-fasts take their place. Could hollow partitions, and hollow spaces behind lathing on walls, be done away with, the spreading of fires would be greatly retarded."

loss of life in London similar to that in Glasgow of which we have been speaking. On Sunday last St. John's Chapel, Bedford-row, was fired by means, it is said, of the iron smoke pipes from the furnaces, used to warm the building. The heat being intense, had ignited the bond timbers, and the flames from them extended to the roof. A rush was made into the street by the congregation, but fortunately there were few people present, and no check-taker's barriers in the way, so that all escaped unhurt.

We were present at a meeting of the Institution of Civil Engineers on Tuesday evening last, when the general question of fire-proof constructions was discussed at some length. A paper by Mr. Braidwood was read, to which we shall refer hereafter, and an interesting discussion followed, wherein Professor Hosking, Mr. Farey, Mr. Cottam, Mr. Thomas Piper, Mr. Dines, and others, took part.

Apropos of warming, we must mention that poor Mr. Barry has again got into Dr. Reid's hot water. A petition from the doctor was presented to the House of Commons a few evenings since, complaining that obstructions were thrown in the way of carrying out his plans in the New Houses, and praying that a committee might be appointed to investigate the matter, and to call himself and the architect before it.

It is much to be regretted that Mr. Barry ever permitted any right of interference with his plans and arrangements to be given to another. He owes it to himself and the profession to make a stand and maintain his right position as architect. The architect is "the chief of the works," "first workman," and whatever is done should be subject to his approval and in accordance with his views. There cannot be two firsts in one series.

It is time that architects bestirred themselves; the prospect for them does not seem very brilliant. A new garrison chapel, which has been erected in Dublin, has led to some correspondence in the papers. The style is Norman, with transition to early English, and according to the designer's own statement, was taken from a church lately built in the west of England. The estimate was 3,000*l.*, and the cost about 2*l.* per sitting. The building was executed by contract, after public competition, by a builder who lost by the bargain. The accommodation afforded is for 1,560 adults and 224 children. A colonel in the Royal Engineers was the architect : and this is why we mention it.

If matters go on as they have begun, there will soon be little occupation for the professional architect. Clergymen are found to be the best qualified to design and erect churches and schools; soldiers to construct barracks, gateways, and castles; sailor officers, docks and bridges; actors, theatres ; and Manchester mill-owners, warehouses and dwellings. Othello's own occupation being gone, the only course remaining for him is to try another. There are some architects who would make uncommonly good manufacturers, and two or three who, if they would take to the stage, could play the "Jetemy Diddler" line of parts with considerable advantage to—themselves, a result which they seem usually to keep in view. There are many others, however, who would supply what the stage has often wanted,— well-bred and accomplished gentlemen, and for the sake of these, and for the sake of the art, we see with pain and regret how architects are being shouldered on all sides. Going to California would, perhaps, be thought *infra dig* (pronounce it how you like, if in the

humour for a pun), but unless architects begin to look about them, they will soon have little chance of picking up gold or reputation anywhere else.

Some of our contemporaries, during the week, have been commenting on two of the craft, who, in former times, did manage to pick up the first part of these very desirable things somewhere in the neighbourhood of the Regent's Park.

The appendix to a Parliamentary report on the management of the Woods and Forests, just now published, has supplied materials for an attack on the proceedings of this office in former times, of no ordinary force. It appears that parties possessing influence have received leases of land at ridiculously small rents, to the disadvantage, of course, of the national income. In some of the cases quoted it is not improbable that an explanation of the circumstances in connection with the "take," would put the matter in a different light ; as, for example, in respect of Nash, the architect, to whom, it appears, that for fifty-three houses out of sixty in Augustus-street, Regent's-park, his representatives pay only 1*l.* *per annum* ground-rent ; or in the case of James Burton, to whom the land on which is built Chester-terrace, Regent's-park, was leased in such a way that, for each of thirty-one of these houses, a ground-rent of 6*l.* per annum only is paid.

We all know that owners are quite willing to let to one speculator a large piece of land at the commencement of operations, and, when there is a certain amount of risk attaching, for a much smaller sum than could be realised by letting for single houses at a later day, when the matter is fairly afloat; and further, that the speculator is often permitted so to divide the sum paid by him (within certain limits), that some of the houses would have but a nominal ground-rent : indeed, it is by this arrangement that the speculators in building-land look for their profits, the sale of the improved ground-rents, subject to which the houses thus circumstanced can be disposed of, being certain.

We allude to these facts simply as showing that it is not unlikely that the discrepancy between the real value of the plots of land alluded to, and the rents agreed to be paid for them by these two "lucky architects" as they are termed, would be found less than it appears, if all the circumstances were known.

An explanation of this sort, however, could scarcely be looked for in the bulk of the cases quoted, as they mainly refer to members of the aristocracy, to whom plots of land have been let for their private purpose at singularly incommensurate rents. Thus, it is stated that George Fulke, Lord Lyttelton, had "a piece of ground, part of Greenwich Park," assigned to him in 1802, for 61 years, at 1*l.* per annum; nor does it appear that any fine or premium in respect of this grant was paid.

"The beauty of the Green-park," says the *Observer*, "is celebrated in history and song. On the one hand it has the park of St. James's and its ornithology, with the Palace of Buckingham and the gardens thereto attached ; on the other it has Piccadilly, with the triumphal arch, the statue of Wellington ; below is greensward, and around are the mansions of the great and the titled ; in the centre was Rosamond's-pond, but it has been filled up, and at one side is the reservoir of some rich water company. Who knows not the Green-park? But those who think they know it best, know very little of the private history connected with certain portions of it. For

instance, is there one man in a million aware of the fact that the Most Noble the Marquis of Salisbury—the successor of him who shook his head so significantly—the great Lord Burleigh—holds a piece of ground in this park, for 99 years from April 5, 1796, at an annual rent—nominal rent would be a more accurate description—of 10*l.* 7*s.* 7*d.*, and that he has never paid a penny as fine for the same. Most lucky as well as "most noble" Marquis of Salisbury ! But he is not the only Adam in this fiscal Eden before the fall. There is Lord Vernon, who has another "piece of ground" adjacent, at 8*l.* per annum; Lord Yarborough a third, at 7*l.* 9*s.* 5*d.* per annum ; Sir John Hoste a fourth, at 4*l.* 14*s.* per annum; Viscount Gage a fifth, at 8*l.* 18*s.* 6*d.* per annum ; Lord Romney a sixth, at 5*l.* 4*s.* per annum : Lord Dundas a seventh, at 13*l.* per annum ; the Earl of Cork an eighth, at 9*l.* 2*s.* per annum ; and the Earl of Moira a ninth, at 7*l.* 16*s.* 3*d.* per annum,—all without prejudice in the shape of fine."

" Contrast this," says the journal we have quoted, " with the condition of certain tradesmen in the Strand, who have also the fortune to hold leases under the Crown. The house No. 2, Lowther-arcade, which is combined with No. 11 in the Strand, pays 60*l.* a-year ground-rent to the Woods, Forests, and Land Revenue Board. No. 5, in the Arcade, which is a single house, consisting perhaps of four rooms, pays 24*l.* per annum. No. 8, which is in the same predicament, pays 35*l.* ; while Nos. 9 to 11, all similarly circumstanced, pay each 50*l.* a-year to the Crown—nearly as much as the Earl of Ellesmere pays for Bridgewater House, and ten times more than is paid by the Lord Romney. Contrast it also with the sum paid by the Duke of Buccleuch for his house and grounds in Privy Gardens—stretching from Whitehall to the Thames, a miniature park before, a French pleasure garden behind —viz., 70*l.* 16*s.* ; or with the sum paid by Lord Prudhoe, 72*l.*, for his mansion in the same place ; or with the sums in fact paid as ground-rent by any nobleman to the Crown ; and then ask yourself whether or not one law for the rich and another law for the poor has not been the practical rule in this country? The Marquis of Hertford pays for the grounds on which his villa stands, in the Regent's-park, occupying perhaps one-tenth of the superficial area of that place of public recreation, only 66*l.* per annum; while a tailor or a grocer, a hatter or a hosier, in Regent-street, pays from 60*l.* to 155*l.* a-year for the scanty plot upon which stands his frail tenement— pays it to the Crown in the same manner as the most noble the Marquis of Hertford. Instances *ad infinitum* might be multiplied, but these will suffice for the present."

We are disposed to think that explanation would put a different face on some of these transactions, which certainly, as they now stand, look glaringly unjust.

THE IRON TRADE.—We hope that our hint, some short time since, to purchasers, as to the then favourable state of the market, was appreciated, as there appears to be now some little probability that the tide may turn. Indeed, an advance of 20*s.* on the nominal quarterly price has been already declared, and although little dependence need be placed on such an announcement, there are other slight symptoms of a start. The increased demand, however, exclusively arises, no doubt, from the mere fact that the market has lately been in so favourable a state for purchasers ; there being no additional outlet for the article, nor any great call for its production.

ON THE TOPOGRAPHY AND ANTIQUITIES OF THE CITY OF JERUSALEM.*

HAVING in the previous paper described the principal localities connected with the present city, I will now as briefly as possible refer to the topographical description by Josephus before I call attention to the existing antiquities.

Josephus describes the city of Jerusalem as being fortified with three walls. The oldest walls, he says, began on the north, at the Tower Hippicus, and extended to a place called the Xistus, ending at the western porch of the temple. It passed on the other side, reckoning from the same place, by Bethso to the Essene Gate, and to the southward by the Fountain of Siloam, where it struck off to the eastward towards the Pool of Solomon (Fountain of the Virgin), and thence by Ophlas to the east porch of the temple. The second wall began at Genath, a gate belonging to the former wall, and so runs by the north side of the city to the fort Antonia.

The third wall began at the tower Hippicus, and ran to that of Psephinos, which is described as being on the north-west angle, over against the sepulchre of Helena and by the royal caverns, from the tower at the corner of the monument of the Fuller, whence it came up to the old wall, in the valley of Kedron. The foundation of this wall was the work of Agrippa, A.D. about 40, for the security of that part of the town he had built, as the city by this time had become so populous, that its space was too circumscribed; and the inhabitants had crept into a kind of suburb on the north side of the temple, next the hill called Bethesda, which is further alluded to as fronting Fort Antonia. The stones of this wall are described as being 20 cubits long, 10 broad, and very hard (probably of the native rock, as Mr. Roberts has possession of a fragment of the ancient walls, a compact limestone, similar to the rocks around); this wall had ninety towers, the middle or second wall fourteen, and the old wall sixty.

The circumference of the walls was thus 33 stadia. The tower of Ptephinos is described as a most exquisite piece of workmanship, octangular in form, and the summit afforded a prospect of Arabia, the sea, and the utmost confines of the Hebrews.

Herod built three towers on the old walls, called Hippicus, Phasael, and Mariamne, adjoining which, on the inside (therefore on Zion), was his palace, magnificent beyond description.

Herod also built the Fort Antonia, on an angle looking west and north, raised on a rock 50 cubits high, which was faced with thin scales of marble from the bottom to the top, both for ornament and security; it was so slippery there was no possibility of ascending or descending it. It commanded the whole temple, and joined the galleries of the temple with passages for the soldiers to go down to the temple.

The description of the Temple, its courts, galleries, porticoes, &c., as built by Herod and described by Josephus, is no doubt familiar to all, and its restoration has engaged the attention of many students.

The dimensions and description given by Josephus must be regarded with caution; he evidently amplifies when he is on the subject of the magnificence of his city, and as he wrote his work at a distance from the scene of the events, and after a lapse of some years, the particulars and measurements of his buildings and walls were most probably given from memory.

After the destruction of the temple by fire, in the siege and the taking of the city, in the second year of Vespasian, by Titus, he gave orders for laying the city and temple level with the ground, and to leave nothing standing but the three famous towers Phasaelus, Hippicus, and Mariamne, and, for the purpose of keeping a garrison, so much of the wall as enclosed the city on the left, which, as the attacks had been from the north side, would be either the west wall of the temple area, which formed the eastern boundary of Acra and Zion, or the east wall of the same Acra, which formed the extreme boundary of the whole of Jerusalem, both of which walls are, to a considerable extent, now standing.

To return again to the subject of the walls, it appears that, A.D. 136, Adrian rebuilt the walls, and called the city Ælia, and included in it several places which formerly were without the gates. This addition, I imagine, was on the north side, as traces of wall in that direction have been discovered by Dr. Robinson and others beyond the present walls, but which are generally ascribed as the remains of the third wall built by Agrippa; but, in my opinion, the remains are of the wall built by Adrian.

From the period of the restoration of the city by Adrian, the buildings erected by Constantine and Justinian belong to comparatively modern times, and now, what remains of the earlier periods of this once magnificent city, of the splendour of Solomon, or of the magnificence of Herod, and of its later Roman conquerors—of its walls, stately towers, royal sepulchres, kystus, bridge, palaces, and fortresses? Nothing but some courses of ancient masonry of a doubtful period, some tombs of small dimensions and of questionable taste, and some vaults, cisterns, and reservoirs; but nothing that can be called a building, or that will even lead to the restoration of any edifice, has hitherto been discovered. The remains in the citadel (supposed to be the tower Hippicus) consist of the lower part of a quadrangular building, about 70 feet by 56 feet, and 50 feet high, built of stones varying from 10 feet to 12 in length, and 3 feet in height. Hitherto no entrance has been found to the tower; but it is not probable that it is a solid mass of masonry 70 feet by 56 feet. At the joints of the stones the face is accurately sunk or channelled, as we term it, horizontally as well as vertically, but the face is left rough.

The springing stones of a large arch (probably of the bridge or viaduct over the Tyropeon alluded to by Josephus as connecting Zion with the temple) are worthy of notice. Three courses of the arch remain, abutting on and connected with the ancient wall of the temple enclosure, near the south-west angle, extending lengthways 51 feet, and by calculation would give the arch a span of 60 feet, and as the distance to the precipitous natural rock on Zion is about 300 feet, it is conjectured there were five arches in the whole. The stones are above 20 feet in length, and one is 5 feet 4 inches thick; at the joints are similar sinkings to those of the tower of Hippicus; but in this remain the extreme surface of the stone is worked perfectly smooth. I think the masonry of both these remains are of the same age—perhaps that of Herod. I cannot assign it to any period anterior to the Roman, certainly not to Solomon, as some authors imagine.

A similar style of masonry and construction is seen on the lower part of the city walls, and those which surround the temple area. On the south, east, and west sides of the latter, particularly at a spot on the west side, called the Jews' Wailing Place (where they, the Jews, have purchased permission to approach the boundary of the temple, to wail over the desolation of Judah, and implore the mercy and forgiveness of their God), are considerable remains. In the eastern wall are seen the remains of an arched double gateway, walled up with Saracenic masonry, called the Golden Gate. The ornamental details of this arch are shown in a very careful sketch by Mr. Roberts, which leads me to suppose that it is a work of the period of Constantine, and not of Adrian, as some supposed. The interior of this gateway was first explored by Mr. Bonomi and his companions; and from the sketches made by him I think the style of architecture of the interior fully fixes on this remain as a work of Constantine.

The wall that now encloses the tower on the north side I always conceived to be on the site of the Agrippa's or the third, wall. I am confirmed in this opinion by the published report of Mr. Tipping, who has recently visited Jerusalem for the purpose of illustrating a new edition of Josephus, who has described this wall as exhibiting remains of the ancient masonry to a considerable extent at the eastern angle, and as built of stones 24 feet long by 5 feet 8 inches broad and 3 feet 2 inches deep on the return angle, and likewise at the inner parts of the Damascus Gate; and, if I remember rightly, I saw some ancient masonry at the northern angle of this same wall. As it appears that the same style of masonry exists at these several spots, some of which we know the date of (Agrippa's wall for instance), we cannot, I think, ascribe one part to the age of Solomon without ascribing the whole to that king. I should have mentioned that the arch called "Ecce homo" being, I think, of ancient masonry, corroborates my view that the second wall passed in that direction according to the description of Josephus.

Among other existing remains is an arched chamber or reservoir of ancient Roman masonry, and a conduit for water, hewn out of the rock at a depth of 23 feet below the present surface, discovered by Mr. Johns, the architect, in digging for the foundation of the Protestant church near the citadel or town of Hippicus. Besides this discovery of Mr. Johns, a fragment of a Corinthian capital and a Doric capital (similar to that of the tomb of Zachariah) were dug up on this site.

The researches of Mr. Catherwood on Mount Moriah, led to the discovery of very extensive substructure under the mosque of El Aksa, and adjoining the east wall, consisting of piers of squared stones, with arches from one to the other, and the spaces between vaulted, through which the roots of the trees growing on the ground around the mosque had penetrated and taken root again on the ground of the vaults beneath. I am not able to give any decisive opinion on the age of these substructures; the vaulting may be of a later date than the piers, probably of Justinian's time. Mr. Tipping has since then discovered some more arched chambers, with columns, piers, and arches, and a gateway leading to the south side of the temple area, but the engravings from his views are not sufficiently clear to enable me to form a proper opinion of the age of these great works.

These substructures require a careful examination, and it is probable that the whole area of the temple platform may consist of similar constructions. I shall not attempt any description of the mosque of Omar, as my object is to describe the antiquities, and not the modern buildings. Even had I attempted I could only have done it from the dictation of Mr. Bonomi, who I hope will give some account of that beautiful and singular building.

In conclusion, I will allude to some of the points that have given rise to recent controversies. From the situation of the Holy Sepulchre, within the precincts of the present city, doubts have arisen as to the authenticity of the site. If the second wall ran, as I suppose it to have done, and the third wall, built after our Saviour's death, by Agrippa, was where the present north wall stands, the topographical difficulty at once ceases. As regards traditionary evidence, there can be no doubt, I think, of the correctness of the site. Many of the Christians who returned to Jerusalem after the seige of Titus, must have been alive at the period of the Crucifixion, and the author of "Epitome Bellorum Sacrorum," asserts that forty-six years after the desecration of the city by Titus, the Christians obtained permission of Adrian to rebuild a church over the tomb of our Saviour, and to enclose in the new city the other places venerated by Christians. From this time to Constantine and downwards, we have successive attestations of the correctness of the site of Calvary. Another important argument in favour of the present site is, that tradition has never assigned any other locality for this sacred spot, and those who have rejected the present site have not been able to point out another site, excepting one writer (Mr. Fergusson), who has made a most startling suggestion, viz.—if I rightly understand him—that the church of the Resurrection was on Mount Moriah, north of the temple of Solomon.

The situation of Zion has only been, I believe, disputed by two writers. Dr. Clarke supposed the City of David to be on the Hill of Evil Counsel, and what we called Zion to be Acra,—an assumption that has never been supported by any writer. It is manifestly untenable, from the fact of its making Zion a mile from Mount Moriah, to which we know it was contiguous, and joined by a bridge.

Mr. Fergusson, whom I have just alluded to, has supposed Mount Moriah to be also Zion, in consequence of a passage in Maccabees, wherein it is mentioned that the destruction of the altar of the Lord was witnessed from Zion, and that they "fortified Zion with high walls and strong towers, lest

* See p. 88, *ante*.

the Gentiles should come and destroy it again." Whereas I conceive the word "Zion," as here used, merely means the *City of Jerusalem*.

J. J. Scoles.

ON THE CONSTRUCTION OF PRISONS.*

Resuming the consideration of this subject, another important object to be obtained is a perfect sewerage, and a complete and speedy removal of all substances and fluids which, exhaling noxious effluvia, must prove most destructive to health. This, together with a wholesome system of ventilation (of which I shall speak more fully hereafter), are points which too often receive but very indifferent attention, and yet are those on which much depends. It will of course be a considerable advantage obtained to keep, under the rules of the system, a large number of prisoners with as few officers as possible; but I have found, in many instances, that too strict an observance of this principle has rendered the discipline exceedingly defective, and much devolves upon the architect to make such provisions for officers as he thinks will be suitable in proportion to the number of prisoners. The entire front of the building should, in my opinion, be devoted to the accommodation of persons connected with the superintendence of the prison; with suitable residences for the governor and chaplain equidistant from the centre. Those portions should project from the main building, and be supplied with private entrances so as to afford seclusion to themselves and families from the rest of the apartments appointed for the minor officers of the prison; but care should be also taken that means be afforded of immediate communication with the rest of the building when desirable. Although I am a great advocate for the buildings being constructed on a principle of "radiation," as proposed and effected by the model plans on the Pentonville system, and which have been considered as the *ne plus ultra* of perfection, yet I must say that when it is intended to accommodate male and female prisoners, I think that its principles are still open to suggestions for improvement. So many instances have occurred of communication taking place in consequence of inattention to proper discipline, but more particularly on account of a mal-arrangement in the plan, that this is a very material point to be considered. In order to carry out the discipline fully, the male officers should be separated from the females, in the same manner as the prisoners, and in fact the plan should be so designed as to construct two prisons in one building, and, though in immediate connection, so arranged as that the inhabitants of one may no more interfere with the other than if they never existed. This cannot be effected by the plan above alluded to, and as the male and female prisons radiate from the same central point or inspection hall, the consequence must be, that opportunities of communication are afforded, which by some consideration could be prevented. The method by which I propose to obviate this difficulty, without interfering with the principles of radiation, is, by having separate halls for the reception of male and female prisoners placed at each side of the centre building, appropriated as officers' apartments, leading by corridors to inspection halls, from which the buildings designed for the males, and those for the females, respectively radiate. By this means the object will be completely gained, and no intercourse of any kind whatsoever can take place between the officers of the different sides of the prison. I could, from my own personal knowledge, enumerate many instances of communication of the most disgraceful description occurring in prisons where this defect exists, but I trust that the mere reference to its destructive principles will be sufficient to aid in guarding against them, without requiring me to enter into a minute catalogue of those which have come under my own immediate observance. It is also the fact that in some prisons where the silent system is carried out (or rather attempted), female nurses attend sick male patients in the hospital wards, and sleep in rooms immediately contiguous to them. This is a point so glaringly defective, that it requires but very little comment, and by some foresight on the part of the architect, many of those deficiencies, and the bad results arising therefrom, could be easily prevented. Each corridor should be under the care of at least one officer, who, by his humane and affable disposition, would be suited for the discharge of the responsible duties which are imposed upon him. Suitable provision should therefore be made for one at an extremity of each corridor. So much depends upon the prudence and generosity which the officers exhibit to those under their charge, that a great deal of care should be taken in the selection of sober, steady, and intelligent persons to fill these situations. I would suggest that at another extremity of each corridor a wash room should be provided, not for ordinary purposes, but that the prisoners may occasionally have the opportunity of bathing themselves, and effecting a thorough cleansing of their persons. This will be found most conducive to health. As an occasional change of wearing apparel is absolutely necessary, fumigating apartments with steaming apparatus complete should be fitted up in the basement story, for the purpose of removing vermin and all infectious tendencies which the clothes may have acquired. It would be desirable in large prisons to supply such accommodation as is necessary for religious distinctions. In almost all the buildings which I have inspected, I remarked that there is a great inattention paid to this point, and that it is too often looked upon as a minor one, while it is in fact very material and deserving of much consideration. Great inconveniences must arise from the celebration of the ceremonies of different persuasions in the same apartment, not to speak of the infringement of moral principles which this arrangement causes, and I think that there should be separate accommodation provided for the followers of each persuasion. I do not of course mean that there should be a distinct place of worship for the disciples of every sect which is likely to exist in a prison, but I wish to show that suitable distinction should be made between those which require apartments differently constructed and fitted up for the practice of their respective ceremonies. A church and chapel will effect the required objects. The seats would be so arranged in each as to prevent prisoners from seeing each other, at the same time affording them an opportunity of having a perfect view of the officiating clergymen.

Infirmaries should be constructed at each side of the building for the accommodation of both sexes, consisting of sick wards, surgical ward, operation room, and convalescent ward, together with a bath room and nurse's apartments. Independent of these it would be well to construct apartments (with all necessary appendages) for patients suffering from fever and all other contagious diseases, in order to prevent their spreading to the rest of the inmates. Spacious airing grounds should be in immediate connection with each infirmary, and all the arrangements planned to afford facilities for carrying out the system.

To the juvenile departments of the prison school-rooms should be attached for instruction, fitted up with seats similar to the chapel, and supplied with a pulpit, from which the teachers have full inspection of their pupils; and adjoining these rooms there ought to be apartments provided for the accommodation of the master and mistress.

The kitchen, culinary offices, &c., should be so arranged as to prevent the intercourse above alluded to, and to admit of the discipline being carried out as fully in *this* as well as *other* portions of the building. I think it would be advisable to place at each side of the prison such offices as are best suited to each sex; for instance, the laundry and all necessary accommodation at the female side; and the bakehouse, with the requisite stores, at the male side: by this plan each class may mutually assist the other in those departments which are best suited for the respective sexes. These buildings must be so designed as to admit of free access, and be situated within the space enclosed by boundary wall: apartments for officers should be judiciously distributed throughout, in order to afford them a perfect surveillance of the prisoners in fulfilling their different avocations.

Airing yards, on a radiating principle, with an inspecting officer's station in the centre, should be constructed at each side of the prison, with open railings at each end, and of such dimensions as will supply sufficient space for the recreation and exercise of the prisoners.

The space between the boundary wall and the main building should be at least 30 feet, and extend around the entire prison, that free communication may be afforded to all parts. The outer wall must be 20 feet high, in order to prevent the possibility of escape. In many instances space enclosed (if any) by the boundary wall, is so narrow, and the wall itself so low, that it frustrates the intention of preventing the escape of prisoners, and by its construction frequently affords them facilities for so doing. The depth of its foundations should also be attended to, as examples have been known of their having been undermined in a very short time.

The corridors should be sufficiently spacious to prevent the prisoners communicating with each other from opposite cells—say 10 feet in width. The cells (particularly when the separate system is intended to be carried out) should be large enough to admit of the prisoners moving about, and exercising themselves therein: 13 feet by 8 feet are considered good dimensions, and on no account should they be less than 12 feet by 7 feet, and 10 feet high. This proportion is best adapted for inspection. There should be a total absence of wooden floors and ceiling joists; in the first place, for the purpose of preventing communication and the spread of fire. The cells should be floored with substantial flagging, and have ceilings arched with brick. A window must be supplied to each cell, which will admit a proper amount of light, placed at sufficient height from the ground to prevent the prisoner from looking out. All necessary apparatus for the convenience and comfort of the prisoner should be fitted up in each apartment, and furnished with the means necessary for the preservation of his health. The doors ought to be formed of strong oak, sheeted with iron on both sides, with apertures for inspection and for the supply of provisions formed in each.

All the buildings should be constructed on a fire-proof principle.

The only point which now remains for me to draw attention to, is "the system of ventilation and warming to be observed throughout." Up to the present time so many improvements have been made in this department, that it is difficult to know which of the different systems most to approve of; but I have selected that which I consider the simplest and most economical, and which experience has shown to be efficacious. As the principle of ventilation may be reduced to two heads, namely, "the supply of fresh or heated air (as occasion may require), and a withdrawal of foul air," I shall explain how these may be effected. An apparatus is generally placed in the basement story of each side of the building, fitted with all necessary tubes, pipes, &c., with which there is in immediate connection a large cold air flue, supplied by a shaft out of doors. The air by this means introduced may either be warmed or left at its natural temperature, and passes hence into a flue constructed under the corridor floor, from which small flues branch off, and pass up the inner wall, terminating immediately under the ceiling of the cells, through which the fresh or tempered air is diffused by means of an iron grating. The foul air is extracted by a grating placed near the floor of each cell diagonally opposite to where the fresh air is introduced: this is the opening of a lateral flue which passes down the outer wall, and communicates with a main foul air flue, placed under the floor of basement. All the corridors are similarly ventilated. In order to effect a proper circulation, the main foul air flues are placed in the perpendicular ventilating shaft, on each side of the smoke flue of the apparatus, which is built up between them to about 15 feet of the top. It will be found desirable to construct the smoke flue of iron instead of brick, as the former is much better adapted for the propagation of heat. A damper (which will be under the command of a superintending officer) should be placed in the extracting flue, close to the outer doors of the cells, and so constructed as to leave sufficient room to effect a proper circulation. It would be well to observe that all chance of communication by means of the ventilating flues, should be strictly guarded against by the

* See page 63, *ante*.

architect. In conclusion, I cannot but observe that there is a very great carelessness and indifference manifest in want of attention to some most essential points in constructing prisons; and I trust that these few notes may prove advantageous.

Dublin. J. J. L.

ROYAL INSTITUTE OF ARCHITECTS.

ARCHITECTS' PROPOSED BENEVOLENT FUND.

On the 12th ultimo, a general meeting of the Institute was held, to receive a report from the Committee appointed to inquire into the above matter.

It appears that the objects of the charter do not comprise the establishment of a benevolent fund, and the solicitor thinks that the Institute have not legally the power of establishing and administering such a fund. The committee, therefore, had confined themselves to the consideration of the proposed distribution of the fund through the medium of the Artists' General Benevolent Institution. From a letter addressed by the memorialists to the Council of the Institute, it appeared that such proposed arrangement was by no means satisfactory to the general body of the memorialists,—the committee therefore suggested, "that a communication be made by the council to the memorialists, to the effect that it regrets the insuperable difficulties arising from the terms of their charter, which prevent the Institute from undertaking the formation and distribution of the proposed benevolent fund, but offering, at the same time, to afford such support and encouragement for the establishment and maintenance of such a fund as the constitution of their charter will admit, and as the council of the Institute may from time to time consider expedient."

The report was received and adopted, so that the memorialists are just where they were at starting; and the profession, irrespective of the Institute, must take the matter into their own hands if they wish the fund established.

On Monday, the 19th ult., Mr. Sydney Smirke in the chair, Mr. James Fergusson (author of "An Inquiry into the Principle of Beauty in Art") and Mr. H. Oliver were elected associates.

Specimens of moulded bricks from the estate of the Earl of Leicester, Holkham-park, were exhibited, including labels, copings, mullions, paving tiles, chimneys, &c. made of an excellent material. The price of a handsome Tudor chimney-top, 8 feet high, thus formed, was stated to be 4*l*. 10*s*.

Whinstone.—Mr. Burn said he wished, before proceeding to the business of the evening, to withdraw an observation he had made on a recent occasion, to the effect that Whinstone was a very absorbent material. He had been misled by adopting a general opinion. Experiment, to which he had been led by what was then said, had shewn him that Whinstone was but very slightly absorbent, and he wished to set himself right.

Mr. Charles Barry, Jun., then gave an account of a mode of constructing malleable iron fire-proof flooring, recently patented by Mr. Beardmore, the substance of which we give elsewhere. A variety of objections to the invention raised by members were ably replied to by Mr. Barry; and Mr. Donaldson, in moving, and Mr. Poynter, in seconding, a vote of thanks, congratulated the profession on the *début* of the son of their esteemed colleague.

Mr. T. H. Wyatt made some remarks upon the church of St. Andrew, at Greensted, in Essex, mainly in reply to published assertions that the ancient church had been demolished. We shall give a view of the church as restored, and append to it some few of Mr. Wyatt's notes.

Exhibition of the Scottish Academy.—The present exhibition in Edinburgh is well spoken of, and attracts large numbers of persons. A taste for the fine arts is certainly increasing amongst the Scotch generally. Amongst the principal works are enumerated pictures by the late Sir D. Wilkie, the late W. Collins, and the late W. Simson; Roberts, Sir W. Allan, Maculloch, Noel Paton, and Watson Gordon.

THE LATE MR. HARVEY EGINTON.

Mr. Harvey Eginton was the son of Mr. Raphael Eginton, a glass painter of some note, under whom he commenced his architectural career. His chief opportunity for acquiring a knowledge of architecture was limited to the resources afforded by studying in the cathedral of the city (Worcester) in which he resided; but this, with the information his father was able to render him, soon qualified him (being of a very persevering disposition) to assume the profession in which he afterwards made rapid progress. Having executed a few works of minor importance, he obtained the countenance of Mr. H. G. G. Ludlow, a magistrate of the county of Wilts, under whom he executed a work of magnitude, and whose friendship he retained up to the time of his decease, having lately completed a church built and endowed by that gentleman. Soon after this he was appointed (through the recommendation of Mr. Britton) architect for carrying out the restoration of the parish church of Stratford-on-Avon. About this time, too, he was engaged in the restoration of St. Lawrence Church, Evesham. One of his last and best works was the restoration of the parish church of Kidderminster. At the time of his decease he held three public appointments, that of county surveyor, architect to the Incorporated Society for Building Churches and Chapels for the Worcester District, and Architect to the Worcester Diocesan Church Building Society. The following are the principal edifices upon which he was engaged. The erection of Broseley Church, Shropshire; Dawley Church, Shropshire; St. Luke's Church, Birmingham; St. Michael's, Worcester; Westbury Church, Wilts; Malvern Link Church; Headley Cross Church; Trimpley Church; North Hill Church, Malvern; St. Paul's Church, Worcester. The restoration of Paulers Pury Church, Northamptonshire; Bredon Church, Worcestershire; Pershore Abbey Church; Walton Church, Warwickshire; Clifton-on-Seine Church, Worcestershire; Stoke Prior Church; Honeybourn Church; Powick Church; Grimley Church. The erection of Tenbury Vicarage; twelve police stations; a mansion at Malvern; a mansion at Yelverton; Martley schools; Spetchley schools; St. Nicholas schools, Worcester; Westbury schools; steward's house, Spetchley; glebe houses, Malvern; extension of Worcester County Prison; restoration of Sudeley Castle and of Astley Hall. Mr. Eginton died on Ash Wednesday, at the early age of 40.

THE "BURIAL OF HAROLD."

A CURIOUS CASE.

Sir,—On the north side of Leicester-square, beneath the entrance to the premises known as Miss Linwood's Gallery, and subsequently as the Walhalla, you descend a few steps, where, on a very unpretending entrance, is inscribed "Wine Shades." It consists of two spacious saloons, laid out for refreshments in the usual style. Within these few days, whispers and rumours have led many of the curious, the inquisitive, and the most eminent in art, to make a visit to this subterranean abode of the juicy divinity; and it must be openly avowed that a problem is here elicited which must be satisfactorily solved, or the integrity and reputation of an artist will be injured.

We all recollect that Mr. F. R. Pickersgill, A.R.A., painted a picture representing the "Burial of Harold," which was rewarded by a first-class premium, in the exhibition at Westminster Hall, in 1847. This picture was subsequently purchased by Government, at the recommendation of the Royal Commission for promoting the Fine Arts, to be placed in the New Palace at Westminster. What will be the astonishment created when it is stated that, in one of the saloons of this "Wine Shades," on the right-hand side in entering, there is hung a picture of this same composition, of small size, exactly the same in the arrangement of all the figures, with the single exception that one of them, in the middle distance, bears a shield. The straining-frame and canvas on which this phenomenon is painted bear the impress of at least half a century of manufacture, on examining the back. The execution of the picture is extremely wretched, and would at first glance impart the notion of being the production of a feeble hand copying a better work.

There can be no hesitation in asserting that the entire affair must be fully explained, and it behoves Mr. Pickersgill to take the initiative in the matter. If it prove to be, as we hope, a rascally daub got up upon an old canvas to ruin the character of a talented artist, no reprobation would be too strong for the transaction. As there is no restraining the extensive circulation of verbal calumny until the public ear becomes thoroughly poisoned, it is better that the circumstance should be investigated without delay. One of the attendants in the room where the picture is hung said, 100*l*. had been offered for the picture since its new-born notoriety. If true, by whom?

M.

*** We have not inserted this without consideration and inquiry. We gave Mr. Pickersgill intimation of this picture, and his reply is, that he "has never seen the picture in question, nor is he aware of the existence of *any work* resembling the 'Harold,' either in subject or arrangement." The identity is unquestionable, and the paint has a settled and old look, which does not appear, under the recent coat of varnish, to be deception. The possession of the picture has been traced for five years.

BALLOON RAILWAY.

A Mechanician in Great Portland-street has been taxing his invention, with the view of forwarding the quiet design of the Yankee Government to attract all sorts of 'lads of metal' to the great, but probably still more greatly exaggerated, Californian magnet, where they press and rub against each other much more like files than filings, loose particles though they be, much more than integral and useful members of those communities whence they are attracted. For the facilitation of this useful process, it is proposed to supersede the mission of the iron horse altogether, even while following his railway track, or laying it down rather, right across the continent of America, up hill and down dale, and clear of all tunnelling, even through the Rocky Mountains. And the grand succedaneum to 'hell in harness' is the locomotive influence of that 'power of the air,' a fair wind, operative on an aerial, or really winged Pegasus, in the form of a manageable balloon—that hitherto impracticable phenomenon, which it is now proposed to accomplish by help of a straight line of wooden rail with a saddle of iron (though without the horse), and with wheels to run underneath the saddle in place of on the rail, and to guide the flighty Pegasus and its gold hunting riders, with a fair wind direct, from Washington to the gold-washing fields of California, at the goodly rate of 50 miles an hour. And even though the wind should not be quite fair, the running train is to act as a rudder, the rail as a keel, and the balloon, we presume, as a sail, so that the 'land lubber' may cut along even by a side wind. Should the wind turn right in its teeth, or the ship-shape machinery chance to be becalmed, the 'angelic train' might come down from above, "by means of ropes, in a car." But what they might then do, especially in the midst of a boundless horizon of prairie-ocean, or a rushing and irresistible buffalo-tide, is prudently left to the pre-occupied fancies of the gold-hunting emigrants themselves.—— The same really ingenious patentee has invented a wheel-rigged ship, or a whirligig-ship, we are not sure which, wherein the lame, the halt, and the blind, not likely to run away on arrival, may be made to work their way out of the old world into the new, *vid* California, *and back again*,—the latter a difficulty which, though only now somewhat singularly realised, at one time, by anticipation, very much pre-occupied the minds of unbelievers in the transatlantic land-seeking mission of that Noah's Dove, Columbus, ere he took wing on the ocean waste in search of the golden land.

Sheffield Ware.—The proprietors of the *Sheffield Times* have offered a prize of 10*l*. for the best essay on the present condition and future prospects of the staple trades of Sheffield.

THE CAVENDISH-STREET SCHOOLS, MANCHESTER.——MR. EDWARD WALTERS, ARCHITECT.

THE CAVENDISH-STREET SCHOOLS, MANCHESTER.

In the course of our notes in Manchester at the end of last year,* we mentioned an extensive school-house, then building, in Cavendish-street, behind Dr. Halley's Independent Chapel.' The annexed engraving is a representation of the schools, and shews also a part of the chapel.

The building covers an area 127 ft. by 44 ft., containing boys', girls', and infants' schools on the ground floor. A spacious centre staircase leads to the grand centre hall, or Sunday school, on the upper door, 80 ft. by 40 ft., with library and lecture room at either end, 44 ft. by 20 ft., separated from the hall by an enriched screen (glazed), affording a view of the entire range of building.

The height of the hall is 38 feet, divided into seven bays, with open principals filled in with tracery. The hall is lighted by seven three-light windows on each side. Galleries carried on projecting brackets from the screens on three sides of the hall, afford communication to ten class-rooms over library and lecture rooms, these rooms being only 14 ft. in height. The schools on the ground floor are 18 ft. 6 in. high. In the basement are kitchens, and on the ground floor, in addition to what has been mentioned, are accommodations for parties residing on the premises.

The cost of the building was 4,700l. without fittings, these, namely forms and desks, will probably cost 500l. more.

The building was erected under the superintendence of Mr. Edward Walters, architect.

PROCEEDINGS AT BIRMINGHAM, MANCHESTER, AND HULL.

SANITARY inquiries have been going on at Birmingham and Hull; and one of the aldermen of Manchester has been lecturing his colleagues and constituents there on the sanitary, business, and other general improvement of that busy city.

The Government Inspector at Birmingham was Mr. R. Rawlinson, appointed by the Board of Health in compliance with the request of one-tenth of the ratepayers of the borough.

From the evidence adduced before him, it appears that the sewerage, so far as it has been carried out, is deemed unobjectionable; indeed, the inspector complimented the town surveyor, Mr. P. Smith, on the fact that, "unlike many other towns, Birmingham would not be required to undo anything of what they had done with regard to the sewerage." But the great evil there to provide against was the want of sufficient power to compel parties to lay in their drains. Throughout 4½ miles 71 yards of the new sewerage of 1845, only about seventy-five private drains had been laid in. Whereas privies, water-closets, and open cesspools, without such issue, not only abounded, but were on the increase. In note than one of the more aristocratic parts of the town, the water-closet refuse was regularly emptied into the street gutters! The town surveyor considered that the Commissioners for whom he acted should have power to form the drains as well as the sewers.

The defective supply of water,—the unwholesome state of some of the grave-yards, the clerical proprietors of the worst of which had refused to abate the nuisance,—the unhealthy state of courts and lodging-houses,—the prevalence of local nuisances, in shape of foul ditches, slaughter-houses, &c. &c., were also all discussed. It appeared, however, that as far as possible an effective system of street cleansing by machines and otherwise was adopted, and that Birmingham had by no means a bad pre-eminence as to fever or general mortality compared with Manchester, Sheffield, &c.

The Hull inspector was Mr. Smith, of Deanston. Great complaint was made of the prevalence of pulmonary diseases in this district, an evil more particularly attributed to the saturation of the soil with undrained moisture. But the general mortality is greatly more than the lowest estimate at which the Board of Health think it right to interfere.

* See vol. vi., p. 577.

Dr. Daly declared that house drainage in Hull had virtually no existence. Even the chief place of business is not half drained, and yet the inhabitants themselves appear to be ostentatiously anxious to promote the salubrity of their respective neighbourhoods, or at all events their own individual reputation for cleanliness, as Mr. Smith remarked that "in many streets which were in a very defective condition, the inhabitants paid particular attention to the cleanliness of the flags in front of their doors." Some of the graveyards appear to be in a bad condition. St. Mary's, in Lowgate, had no drainage whatever, and rises 6 feet above the old level of the street from the mere accumulations of human remains. The wells near it are polluted, and a heavy odour prevails all round it. Many of the inhabitants make most piteous complaints about the dirty, stinking, brackish, hard, Hull water with which they are, medically speaking, still cleared out. Others stoutly uphold its salubrity, even while admitting that it is impregnated with all the sewerage of Beverley and Hull. The supply too is not sufficient.

The Manchester alderman, Mr. Hopkins, in course of a comprehensive and able disquisition, in the Royal Institution, on the various requisites to the healthfulness, comfort, and business convenience of the city—a disquisition which we cannot venture to broach—alluded to the water-works now in course of construction by the corporation to the east of the town. These, he remarked, "will, at an early period, furnish a supply of twenty millions of gallons of water each day, and, if it should be required, thirty millions. As the quantity furnished at present is only about three millions, it is evident there will not only be sufficient to supply the inhabitants, flush the sewers, and wash the streets, but also to use for any other public purpose that may be thought desirable, such as watering the streets, supplying fountains, &c. &c. This water is intended to be conveyed to every dwelling in the borough; and, as it will always be on—by night as well as by day—no want of it will be experienced by the poorest inhabitant."

FORMS FOR WINDOW GLAZING.

Nº I

Nº II

Nº III

Nº IV

FORMS FOR WINDOW GLAZING.

WE give the annexed specimens of glazing from buildings on the continent, as suggestions. Nos. 1 and 4 are from the Church of St. Denis, St. Omer; No. 2 from the Church of St. Etienne, Beauvais; and No. 3 from the Church at Aire, in Flanders. Each pattern is about 2 feet square. We have others to follow.

ON A NEW FORM OF MALLEABLE IRON FLOOR,

LATELY PATENTED BY MR. NATHANIEL BEARDMORE, CIVIL ENGINEER.

The paper on this subject, read by Mr. Barry, jun., at the Institute of Architects, as already mentioned, commenced by remarks upon the want of toughness in cast-iron, and its dangerous nature when highly heated, with a review of the comparative strength of cast and wrought-iron, as shown in the following table :—

Table of Comparative Qualities of Cast and Wrought-iron.

	Power to resist Tension.	Power to resist Compression.	Safe limits of Tensile Strength.	Price.
	Per square inch.	Per square inch.	Per square inch.	Per ton.
Cast-iron	7 tons.	56 tons.	4 tons.	9l.
Wrought-iron	24 tons.	Maximum by Hodgkinson, 25 tons. Rondelet, 31.5 tons. Buchanan, 27 tons.	16 tons.	27l. for plate girders, as boiler work.

From this it will be seen that, while the tensile strength of wrought with respect to cast iron may be computed at 4 to 1, their prices are in an inverse ratio, viz. as 3 to 1. It should, however, be remarked that in the case of cast iron, 4-7ths of ultimate strength cannot be safely exceeded, while in the case of wrought-iron, although 2-3rds of the ultimate strength is the load to be assumed for practice, a much higher proportion can be borne by it as a passing load, from its non-liability, as is the case with the former material, to fail at once, frequently from internal and unseen imperfections.

The many great failures in cast-iron girders in the manufacturing districts, and the experiments to ascertain the best form for the Holyhead tubular bridges, induced Mr. Fairbairn of Manchester to consider this subject, and in 1845 he patented a beam formed with two webs connected by upper and lower flanges, riveted in each direction, the whole being in the form of fig. 1; the tendency of the webs to bulge or collapse being counteracted by short transverse pieces of tubing, through which pass rivet bolts. The experiments, however, of Mr. Fairbairn and Mr. Hodgkinson, showed that there was a limit to the reduction of weight in wrought-iron beams, when used in thin and light forms: thus the compressibility of cast-iron is probably never less than 50 tons per square inch, while, in their experiments on rectangular wrought-iron tubes, formed of plate ½ inch, ¼ inch, and ⅛ of an inch thick respectively, the resistance to compression per square inch was only 19¼, 14½, and 7¾ tons. This great reduction in strength by the use of thin metal was caused, not by want of resistive strength, but from want of stability. The result of the experiments above referred to, is the very general introduction of tubular wrought-iron girders for railway bridges, but the price (from 28*l.* to 32*l.* per ton) must render them, without some modification, too expensive for ordinary use in buildings. It occurred then to the author of the floor which is described in this paper, that if some form could be adopted where advantage was taken of the full tensile strength of wrought-iron, while at the same time by insuring its stability power to resist compression were given, then it might be used very economically. No stronger construction was then known than the combination of square cells used for the floor of the Conway tubular bridge—a form of construction, however, far too expensive for ordinary floors, from the cost of riveting the top sheet of iron, especially on a small scale. After some consideration, experiments were made to determine the effect of a combination of iron for tensile and some other material for compressive strength, and several beams were made of the form fig. 2, where *a* is a T beam of sheet-iron stiffened by brickwork, as shown at *b*; but it was found on loading these that the bricks cracked and slipped off, in the manner indicated in the figure, showing that the mere resistance of brickwork to longitudinal pressure would not practically be of any value.

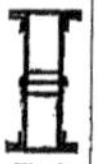

Fig. 1.

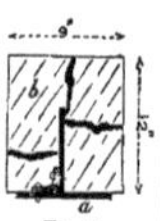

Fig. 2.

A rectangular tube was then selected, after one in Mr. Hodgkinson's experiments, formed of malleable iron 1-16th of an inch thick, 6 inches deep, 4 inches wide, and 7 feet 6 inches bearing; the top plate was omitted, but tie-bolts were placed at intervals, connecting the sides, and the whole was filled in with concrete; the weight to break this down, when hung in the centre, was 7,206 lbs., the same tube empty, but with a top plate, was, by Mr. Hodgkinson's report, crushed with 3,156 lbs.

In the above experiment the failure was by the sides of the tube bulging outwards at the centre, and it suggested itself, that if there had been concrete outside as well as inside, the bulging would not have occurred. A model was therefore constructed of sheet and angle iron of the dimensions shewn in Fig. 3, the part lightly shaded being filled in with concrete; the bearing was 12 feet, and the breaking weight in the centre 5 tons 14 cwt., the bottom of the beam having been torn asunder without the slightest buckling of the vertical plates.

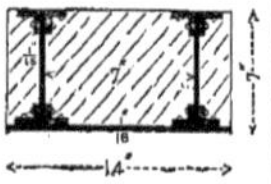

Fig. 3.

A beam of similar construction 23 feet bearing, and 13 inches deep, was made of sheet iron, 1-12th inch thick; the weight of iron altogether in this beam was 656lbs., and it carried 12 tons equally distributed (including the weight of concrete), for several weeks, with a deflection of 1¼ inch, 1 inch of which recovered itself on removing the weight, a large portion of the remaining ¼ inch being due to a defective scarf. The weight of a cast-iron beam capable of supporting this load would be 1,800lbs. These experiments and numerous others seemed to shew that the uniform pressure of concrete against the whole surface of the web, and under the top flanges of the beam, would produce the effect of a continuous strut, and thus enable comparatively thin plates to assume the true character of a beam or girder.

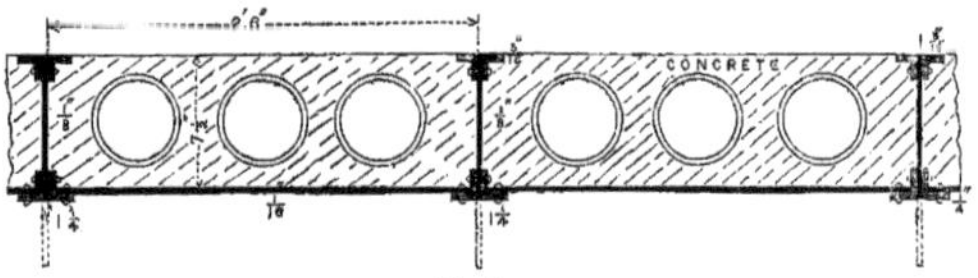

Fig. 4.

Fig. 4 shews the form of construction proposed by Mr. Beardmore, as evolved from the above and other experiments, for floors up to 18 feet span: it is constructed of vertical plates of sheet iron, with angle iron rivetted through. These light beams are then placed on the walls at the proper distances, and plates are rivetted to the bottom angle irons, and the whole filled in with concrete. Lightness may be obtained by introducing earthenware pipes, or this object may be effected by lengthening the vertical webs (as shown by dotted lines), when the floor may have a less thickness of concrete. The bottom plates, when liable to corrode, may be either of galvanised iron,* or iron coated with the peroxide paint patented by Mr. Welch.

The weight of the above floor, contrasted with one formed with cast-iron girders and half-brick arches, is shown in the following table:—

	Per square.	Per foot.	Span.	Depth of floor.
Floor formed with cast-iron beams and half-brick arches:—	lbs.	lbs.	feet.	inches.
Cast iron	1,008	10.1	15 to 18	14
Brick, &c.	5,824	58.2		
	6,832	68.3		
Fig. 3, as described above:—				
Wrought iron..........	600	6.0	15 to 18	7½
Concrete, with earthenware pipes	4,972	49.7		
	5,572	55.7		

The concrete used in all these experiments was formed of White's Portland cement and shingle, in proportions of from 1 and 6 to 1 and 9. The cost of such is less than good brickwork, and is remarkable from its setting properties and strength to resist compression.

The following is the inventor's summary of the apparent advantages of the proposed mode of construction:—

1. The necessity of the floor being fire-proof from its mode of construction.

2. The non-liability to disintegrate when exposed to fierce flame, as brick arches are known to do, in flakes.

3. That being of malleable iron, its cohesion could not be destroyed by sudden cooling when heated.

4. The small depth of this floor when contrasted with one of cast-iron of equal strength.

5. The absence of all lateral pressure on walls, and consequent necessity for tie bolts: and,

Lastly, that whereas in cast-iron constructions it is necessary to calculate the beams to bear not only the weight of the expected traffic on the floor, but also the weight of the brick arches themselves; in the proposed mode the concrete is not a weight independent of the floor which it is required to sustain, but a necessary element of the floor itself, thus rendering it nearly impossible to accumulate a great weight on any one spot, the floor being as it were one continuous beam, while with cast-iron girders the weight in the entire floor is necessarily thrown on them alone, which are consequently strained beyond the average strength required.

* We have received several serious statements relative to galvanised iron, to which we shall give attention.

NOTES IN THE PROVINCES.

THE prior's tomb, in the chancel of the church of St. Nicholas, Yarmouth, was opened on Monday week, and found to contain, in a white Purbeck marble coffin, a skeleton in good preservation, but evidently disturbed during a previous opening, it is supposed in 1650. No chalice, pastoral staff, &c., were found, though other traces of high ecclesiastical rank are said to have been noted.——"A house-agent in this town," says a Leicester paper, "has threatened to turn out every tenant of dwelling houses of which he has the management, who calls the attention of the inspectors of nuisances to any nuisance on the premises they occupy." We know, too, of instances in which tenants themselves refrain from complaint of nuisances from the mere anticipation of disagreeable contact with their landlords. It is to be hoped, however, that a little moral courage on the one hand, and a little forbearance on the other, will gradually work out much sanitary benefit. We can readily conceive that landlords may be much annoyed with complaints and expense without great reason, but where a wholesale threat like the above is uttered *in terrorem*, as a gag to tenants suffering from nuisances, it is also to be hoped, and indeed it is highly probable, that every house so tabooed from all cleansing process will become a "noted house" in its neighbourhood, into which tenants will be as afraid to enter as if it were haunted, or the scene of some recent slaughter; so that its landlord or agent may be at length induced to adopt as effectual means for turning *in* a tenant as those now threatened may, to his chagrin, *really* prove to be in turning him *out*.——Gloucester Cathedral lately stood in imminent peril, from fire in the college school-room over the chapter-room. One of the stoves is supposed to have set fire to the floor, which was much burnt, while books in flames fell into the chapter-room below.——The Mariners' Chapel at Gloucester was opened on Sunday week. The *Journal* describes it as a simple and appropriate structure. Mr. Jacques, of Gloucester, was the architect, and Mr. William Wingate, also of the same city, was the builder.——The Macclesfield committee for erection of baths and washhouse have selected the plan for a building at an estimated cost of about 1,200*l.*——St. John's Church, Hurst, was consecrated on Monday week. It is in the Early English style of 13th century. Internally it is about 69 feet long by about 43 feet wide, and divided into a nave and side aisles. It is without clerestory. The chancel is about 18 by 19 feet, with a vestry on the north side. In the west gable are two lofty lancet windows, with a quatrefoil light, surmounted by a plain bell turret, rising upwards of 50 feet from the ground. Near the south-west corner, on the south side, is a porch with high gabled roof. The nave pillars are of polished stone, the pews are low, and the roofs are open timbered stained in oak. There is a small gallery. Sittings in all 750. Mr. E. H. Shellard, of Manchester, was the architect, and Messrs. Eaton and Hallas, stone-masons, were the contractors.——Styd Church, Ribchester, is to be renovated.——The Bradford council have formally discussed the smoke nuisance, and appointed a smoke committee.——The works connected with the new Mechanics' Institute, in the city of Durham, have been commenced; and the building will be finished, it is thought, in October next.——The large hospital to be erected at Calside, Paisley, by the Abbey Board, has been contracted for, says the *Reformer's Gazette*, by the following tradesmen:—The mason-work by Mr. William Bowes, Paisley; joiner do., J. Lamb and Son, Greenock; slater do., Mr. Wm. Gillespie, Paisley; plumber do., Mr. J. Gilmour, Paisley; plaster do., Mr. Andrew Mitchell. Architect, Mr. J. Lamb.

RIGHT OF ARBITRATORS TO COPY DRAWINGS.

ROYAL ITALIAN OPERA-HOUSE, COVENT-GARDEN.

SIR,—In a personal matter I should best consult my own feelings in abstaining from asking for a space in your valuable columns, which you might otherwise fill with some subject of greater interest to your readers, but as an imputation has been made against my professional character in a charge brought against me by Mr. Albano, in your last week's journal, I have to request the favour of your insertion of a few words in reply.

Upon the matter of reference of Mr. Albano's accounts, in which I acted as umpire, it is impossible for me to say one word, but with regard to that part of Mr. Albano's letter complaining of my having, in his opinion, improperly caused traced copies of some of his drawings to be made, I beg to say that I am not disposed to enter on the discussion of the abstract right of an umpire to copy drawings produced in the course of any reference. In this case I acted under legal advice; and in the steps I have thought proper to take I have done nothing whatever derogatory to my character as an architect or a gentleman.—I am, Sir, &c.,   SAM. ANGELL.

18, Gower-street, Feb. 28, 1849.

WORKS AT BEVERLEY.

THE great window and the west end of the church of St. Mary being in an unsafe condition, it was resolved to have it restored. The cost of the restoration of the window, west front, doorway, and turrets, was estimated at about 1,000*l.*, and this the churchwardens hoped to effect by the funds of the church in two years, at the rate of 500*l.* a-year. To restore the window with common glass would have cost about 50*l.*; but Mr. Pugin proposed to put in superior stained glass for 300*l.*, and furnished a design, which was approved of by the parishioners and also by the Architectural Society. The necessary sum has been subscribed, and it is expected that the window will be restored and the painted glass put in during the present year. The subject of the design is our Saviour and the twelve apostles, with the patron saint of the church, filling the fourteen compartments of the window. One or more of the nave windows, it is expected, will be restored and decorated in a similar way.

The church of St. Mary, Beverley, as remarked by the correspondent to whom we are indebted for the above particulars "is well worth the attention of every one who admires or appreciates beautiful design and execution, and it is lamentable, here as elsewhere, to observe how little the decay of centuries has been arrested, and how dilapidated the structure has become. Here, however, there has been no daubing or defacing, and although there is much to restore there is little to pull down."

A site has been secured in the centre of the town for a national school, for the united parishes of St. Mary and St. Nicholas, and a design has been prepared by Mr. Pearson, of London, architect. Subscriptions are in progress to defray the cost, which is estimated at 571*l.* 10s., exclusive of site 455*l.* Of the whole sum, about 300*l.* only remains to be made up by contributions, in aid of which a bazaar is about to be held. The design is satisfactory.

To RESTORE OAK.—A few weeks since a correspondent asked for something that would restore oak to its original whiteness. I have often used, with success, 2 oz. oxalic acid dissolved by friction in one quart of cold water. If the oak has been varnished it must be scraped clean before using the acid.—G. C.

ENCROACHMENT ON THE NEW ROAD.

SIR,—On looking into the current number of THE BUILDER, I was greatly surprised to find your correspondent, "C. E.," attacking the official referees on the ground, if I understand him rightly, that they, in common with the magistrates, were lending their aid to infringements of the Act of Parliament, 7 Geo. 3, to the extent of authorising buildings to be brought forward, so as to reduce the New Road to a less width than that statute prescribes and requires that it should be. A serious charge this: but your correspondent must surely be in error, as from all I know of the proceedings of this body, they have been found—to the sore discomfiture of many—to be strict conservators of the metropolitan streets and roads, be such streets and roads ever so wide; and I cannot help thinking that if the charge were to be inquired into, it would be found that when the Central Board "*defined*" (found ?) the line of frontage of two public buildings as being 50 feet back from the footway," they were doing their best to revive and uphold the Act of Parliament above mentioned, and that it would be further found that they have not, and moreover could not—if they had the will to do so—have given any decision or performed any other official act that could in any way lessen or abridge the provisions of that Act, and I should incline to the supposition that any *resolution* which they have come to (if they have come to any such resolution as "C. E." describes), must have reference to localities to which no statutory restrictions that would have the effect of imposing prohibitions against the erection of any inclosed projections before a house, other than the shop front of ordinary projection, do apply or ought to be applied: and it would appear strange, if the "two private buildings" referred to by "C. E." are being erected in the New Road in consequence of any such resolution, that similar erections, long ago devoutly wished, are not being consummated in the various other roads over which the Act, 7 Geo. 3, *has no control*, and which, as I had supposed, were lying under the ban of the official referees.   SUUM CUIQUE.

Books.

The Year-Book of Facts in Science and Art, exhibiting the most important discoveries and improvements of the past Year. By JOHN TIMBS, Editor of "The Arcana of Science and Art." London. Bogue.

"THE industrious ants of science," said Lord Northampton, at a meeting of the British Association, "laboriously bring to her granaries their numerous though small additions; and, in truth, accumulate facts destined for materials for the greater minds, that reason and systematize." For many years has Mr. Timbs, who quotes this on his title-page, quietly played the ant, for the advantage of the public, when he might, if he had pleased, have taken a more assuming part; and much is due to him for the good he has done in that capacity. As the original editor of the "Mirror," he is perhaps best known to many of our readers, and now in connection with the widely-circulated "Illustrated News," the public have weekly the advantage of his intelligence and ability without knowing it.

The present "Year-Book," which consists of valuable facts extracted from the periodicals of the day, not forgetting our own, which furnishes its full share, is illustrated with a portrait of Sir David Brewster, and forms an excellent present-book for the young of either sex, which they cannot open without picking up something useful.

Archæologia Hibernica. A Hand-Book of Irish Antiquities, Pagan and Christian: especially of such as are easy of access from the Irish Metropolis. By W. F. WAKEMAN. Dublin, M'Glashan; London, Orr and Co.

EVERY person interested in architectural antiquities, who visits Ireland, should possess himself of this little hand-book, which is nicely illustrated, and very sensibly put together. Nor is its value confined to those who are about to visit the green island; those who are not able to go there will find in it much to interest them. Ireland contains an extraordinary series of monuments, commencing from a very ancient date, which are much less known than they deserve to be.

Marshall's Index Ready Reckoner, for the Calculation of Wages. London: LONGMAN and Co.

THIS little work is especially adapted to the use of railway contractors and other parties employing a number of hands, and who require expedition in calculating the amount due to each. The calculations advance by quarters of a day, from one quarter to thirty days, at rates from one shilling to five shillings. A marginal index shows at once the page to be turned to, and adds much to the value of the work.

Taylor's Builders' Price-Book, corrected to the Year 1849. Edited by EDWARD CRESY, Architect. London: Taylor, Wellington-street.

THE new edition of this long-established pricebook, edited by Mr. Gresy, contains, in addition to its ordinary information, the Public Health Act, in full; notes upon it, and a number of new tables of considerable value.

Mr. Taylor has published the Health Act separately in a convenient form.

Miscellanea.

THE SEWAGE MANURE COMPANY.—The secretary of this company wishes it to be stated that the resolution in their favour actually passed by the Commissioners of Sewers, is as follows:—"Resolved, that saving all the jurisdiction and rights of the Metropolitan Commission of Sewers, facilities be given to the Metropolitan Sewage Manure Company, for carrying out their experiments completely, by allowing them to take sewer water of a stronger quality than that chosen, viz., the Counters Creek Sewer." The secretary thinks that our report of the resolution come to by the Court of Sewers (p. 69 *ante*), is calculated to damage the company, and though we are disposed to think he greatly overrates the difference, we willingly give the company all the advantage which the words of the resolution may be to them. We shall be glad to find this company seriously at work. Anxious as we are to further every effort to prevent the future defilement of the Thames, and to turn the sewage of the metropolis to its proper use, we have never found ourselves able to advocate warmly the interests of this company. They have never appeared to see their way, and we very much doubt if they do so yet. We shall be glad to be undeceived.

THE CLOSED-DOOR BUSINESS OF THE METROPOLITAN COMMISSION OF SEWERS.—Sir: I am happy to find that the "hole and corner" proceedings of the new commission have attracted attention, and drawn forth the remarks contained in your last number. It certainly does appear strange that a body professing the most unbounded regard for the public interests, and having in their hands so large a sum of the public money, should so closely imitate the worst features of some of the former Commissions of Sewers, by transacting nearly the whole of their business, involving the outlay of several thousands of pounds, with closed doors. It is true, that the amount is mentioned in the open court required for certain works,—not for the sake of information, but merely to give it a formal legality, and this is done in so brief and hurried a manner, as to appear to the commissioners almost "like a thrice-told tale." No reason for it is given, no information is conveyed as to its necessity; but merely this or that "committee" recommend it. A late member of the House of Commons once remarked,—" If I wish a snug job to be done, give me a select committee." That this remark may not apply to the present Metropolitan Commission of Sewers is the earnest hope and desire of—

ONE AMONGST THEM.

* A long debate on this subject took place at a meeting of the commissioners on the 1st instant, but we are forced to postpone report of it.

PROJECTED WORKS.—Advertisements have been issued for tenders, by 7th inst., for the erection of the Printers' Almshouses; by 6th, for the erection of a farmery for 700 acres of land at Eldo House, Rougham, near Bury St. Edmund's; by a date not specified, for finishing a few third-rate houses near Mornington-crescent; also for the formation of a new road, 70 feet wide, from the Royal-crescent, Notting-hill, to Warwick-square, Kensington; by 28th inst., with plans, specifications, &c., for the erection of lodgings, and accommodation for the judges of assize, at Aylesbury; by April 7th, with plans, specifications, &c., for erection of gas-works, &c., at Aylsham, Norfolk; by 12th inst., for the erection and completion of the two chapels, cloisters, catacombs, &c., at the Leicester Cemetery; by 12th, for the erection of a workhouse at Fulham; by 13th, for executing the masonry, brickwork, and other works, and also the remainder of ironwork requisite for extending the Liverpool and Bury Railway to Tithebarn-street, Liverpool; by 19th, for the execution of the works required for the completion of the Knottingley branch of the York and North Midland Railway, a length of about three and a-quarter miles; by 19th, for the execution of the whole works necessary for the completion of the Bishop Auckland branch of the York, Newcastle, and Berwick Railway, and of the branch of same from Pensher to Sunderland, the former in two contracts of about 7½ miles each, and the latter in one contract of 7 miles in length; by 19th, for a supply of 30 fifteen-feet and 30 twelve-feet turntables for the same line; by 8th, for 200 goods trucks for the Eastern Counties; by 19th, for the supply of the various cisterns, pipes, taps, and apparatus for distributing water through the Birmingham Lunatic Asylum for paupers, and for the works connected with fitting and fixing the same; by a date not specified, for an iron tank, about 30 feet by 30 feet, and 4 or 6 feet deep, for St. John's Wood; by 10th April, for ironmongery,—by 20th inst., for crown and sheet glass and window lead,—and by same date, for iron-plate-workers' wares, all for the navy.

COMPETITIONS.—Plans, specifications, and estimates are wanted, from "architects and others," for lodgings and suitable accommodation for her Majesty's judges of assize at Aylesbury.——Twenty pounds and ten pounds are offered for the two best designs for a corn-market at Bedford.

MASTER AND MAN.—On the 13th, at the Town-hall, Nottingham, the following case was heard before the mayor and two other magistrates. Mr. Lonsdale, plasterer, having employed a man 50 miles from Nottingham, to whitewash some ceilings at stations upon the Sheffield and Lincoln railway, refused to pay him his charge without the certificate of the foreman of the works (George Clark). This the foreman refused to give, because the man had charged for twelve days' work during two weeks, whereas he had only worked eight days. A summons being granted against Mr. Lonsdale, the foreman attended the court, to prove to the magistrates the time that the man had worked, by book, showing the number of hours each day that he had worked. The magistrates arrived at the following decision:—that when the man had been at his work any part of a day, he was entitled to a full day's wages: two days the man admitted that he was not within 20 miles of his work, these were struck out of his account,—the bench allowing him ten days, instead of twelve days, which he had summoned his master for. Mr. Lonsdale to pay the costs (1*l*. 19s. 6d.).

ENGLAND IN AN AMERICAN'S EYES.—Mr. Ralph Emerson, in a lecture on England at Boston, after his recent visit, referred to the elements of that power which the English now hold, and have held for centuries. After looking at her manufactories, scattered all over the land, her commerce, her agriculture, her arts, and witnessing the stupendous results which have been wrought out, one is convinced, said he, that if he would see the best development of common sense (the standard sense), he must go to England to witness it. The land, in every part so like a garden, shews the triumph of labour; the fields look as if finished with the pencil, and not the plough. Every arable spot has been cultivated, and everything turned to the best possible use. England, he continued, is a huge mill, a grand hotel, where everything is provided to one's mind. On the railroads we ride twice as fast, and with one-half the shaking, that we do upon our roads. All England is a machine—everbody moves on a railway—no Englishman ever touches the ground. England has the best working climate in the world; it is never hot nor cold; their winter days are like our November days in the early part of the month. One of the few drawbacks which Mr. Emerson mentioned was the dark, dense smoke of many of the manufacturing towns, pervading and completely enveloping at times every surrounding object.

BUILDERS AND BUILDING IN LONDON.—Our forefathers built houses singly; we build whole neighbourhoods. Belgravia, together with the new Bromptonian territories; Tiburnia, and a new district recently discovered by northern travellers, east of Camden Town, sprung up at once. All this has not happened and is not going on without hands, hence the Directory tells us of 406 architects, 779 builders, 431 bricklayers, 672 carpenters, 167 stone and marble masons, 66 plasterers, 400 plumbers, and 315 painters and glaziers. For the wholesale handy work of these artificers we beg to put in a plea against an imputation cast upon them by the author of "The Town," who says,—"In Elizabeth's time the London houses were still mostly of wood. We see remains of them in the Strand and Fleet-street, and in various parts of the city. They are like houses built of cards, one story projecting over the other; but unless there is something in the art of building, which may in future dispense with solidity, the modern houses will hardly be as lasting. People in the old ones could at least dance and make merry. Builders in former times did not spare their materials, nor introduce clauses in their leases against a jig. We fancy Elizabeth hearing of a builder who should introduce such a proviso against the health and merriment of her buxom subjects, and sending to him with a good round oath, to take a little less care of his purse, and more of his own neck." We have heard of such clauses, but believe they appertain to houses "run up" about the beginning of the present century, when the art of building was not so well understood as now. Although we do not deny that even some of the suburban contract-job villas are not built for eternity; nor, indeed, for perfect integrity after a severe equinox; yet the scientific researches of architects and builders into the relative ratios of the strength to the bulk of materials, and the frequent substitution of iron for wood, have enabled them to build most of the modern houses with equal stability, but with infinitely less clumsiness than their predecessors.—*Daily News.*

PYRO-PNEUMATIC STOVE GRATE.—We have several times said that the great *desideratum* in heating and ventilating is to get a constant supply of pure air admitted to the apartment at a proper temperature. Under the above title, Mr. Pierce, of Jermyn-street, has patented a stove-grate which proposes to supply this want. It has an open fire-place, and is lined with fire-lumps. Within these lumps are tubular air-ways, made to communicate with the external atmosphere, which, in thus passing into the apartment, is warmed without coming into contact with heated metal. The fire-clay lining makes it economical also: metallic linings are very wasteful.

PROPOSED BATHS AND WASH-HOUSES FOR THE PARISHES OF ST. MARGARET'S AND ST. JOHN'S, WESTMINSTER.—A meeting of the vestrymen of the above parishes was held on Saturday, in the vestry-room of St. Margaret's Church, for the purpose of considering the propriety of erecting baths and wash-houses. Mr. Trollope occupied the chair. The Hon. C. J. Talbot moved the appointment of commissioners under the Act 9 and 10 Vict., for encouraging baths and wash-houses. The question was opposed by Mr. Sawyer and Mr. Sugg, and warmly supported by Mr. George Wilson, Mr. Whateley, Q.C., and Mr. Freeman, and carried by a majority of ten—there being nineteen for and nine against the motion. The following gentlemen were then appointed as the commissioners for the carrying out the Act in these parishes:—The Hon. J. C. Talbot, Lieut.-Colonel Short, Rev. J. Jennings (Rector of St. John's), Mr. George Wilson, Mr. Hawes, Mr. Trollope, and Mr. Burridge.

FREEMASONS OF THE CHURCH.—A meeting of this society was held at 49, Great Marlborough-street, on February 13th, the Rev. George Pocock, LL.B., in the chair. Mr. Brown exhibited a chart illustrating the first principles of perspective, intended as a first step in perspective. It was the object in this drawing to place at one view the meaning of the terms used in this art, illustrated by such familiar examples as will render them easily understood by the young student, and place in a more simple light the mathematical rules which will afterwards be required. Mr. Pell, of Southwark, attended for the purpose of placing before the chapter a series of ornamental glass windows, manufactured by him on a patent principle, for halls, passages, and conservatories. Mr. Wilmshurst, upon this subject, offered some remarks, explaining the effect frequently obtained in windows by a very moderate use of colours, strengthening his observations by reference to examples in many continental cathedrals, and especially in that of Seville. Mr. William Smith Williams then read a paper on "The Importance of a Knowledge and Observance of the Principles of Art by Designers," to which we shall recur.

VALUE OF ESTATES.—A short time ago the estates of Lord Suffield, at Middleton and Thornham, about 5 miles from Manchester on the one side, and equally distant from Rochdale on the other, were brought to the hammer at the Palatine Hotel, Manchester. The auctioneer described the capabilities and qualities of the property; after which some bids were made, the first of which was for 100,000*l*., by Mr. Robert Ashton, cotton manufacturer, at Hyde. Ultimately, Mr. Fisher said that there was a reserve bid of 200,000*l*. on the property, and any advance on that of 1,000*l*. would be received, but otherwise the property would be withdrawn. The required offer not being made, the sale was abandoned, and it is understood the property will be offered in small lots. The estates are freehold, comprising about 3,000 acres, including plots suitable for building purposes at Middleton, and containing also some valuable seams of coal. The property also includes the valuable advowson of the rectory of Middleton, and the manorial rights. The present average rental has been about 10,000*l*. per annum, the average rental of the land being about 34s. 6d. per acre.—*Cheltenham Journal.*

HOW LOW CONTRACTS ARE CARRIED OUT.—Sir: I have frequently been much edified by the information which you have afforded under the head "Blind Builders," and beg to offer for your use the following particulars of a job which was to have been executed for the Corporation of this city (Manchester). The work consisted of the excavation of about 9,000 yards of earthwork, the fair cost of which might probably be some 400*l*. There were about a dozen estimates tendered, varying from 115*l*. to 1,020*l*. The lowest was accepted, as is the custom in this neighbourhood. Some few "navvies" made their appearance, and slinked about as though they were arranging to begin in good earnest. This, however, proved to be a mere *ruse* to obtain a few weeks' credit at the beershops at which they located themselves. In order to support appearances, a few waggons were sent on the ground, but these, with the "navvies," mysteriously vanished before daybreak one fine morning, when it was found no further credit could be obtained, and neither have since been heard of. The job remains *in statu quo*.—O.

TO OUR READERS.

IT has been suggested to us at various times that some of the best architectural subjects given in THE BUILDER, if printed in a superior manner on good paper, with the accompanying descriptions, plans, &c., and issued periodically, would form a work that would be acceptable not only to those who are not buyers of THE BUILDER, but to many who are,—the current engravings being often creased by the newsvendors, or otherwise injured. We are disposed to try the experiment, and to publish, in a neat wrapper, under the title, "BUILDINGS AND MONUMENTS, MODERN AND MEDIÆVAL," about Eight Plates, with eight pages of letter-press, folio size, every second month, price half-a-crown. The first part would consist of Osborne House, with plan; Bridgewater House, plan and details; Church of St. Isaac, Petersburgh; Kensington Union Workhouse; Pembroke College, Oxford; the Liverpool Branch Bank; and the north porch of St. Mary Redcliffe, Bristol. Before determining upon the scheme, however, we should be glad to receive the names of such gentlemen as would be willing to become subscribers to the work.

MEETINGS OF SCIENTIFIC BODIES

Held during the ensuing week.

MONDAY, March 5.—Institute of Architects, 8 P.M.
TUESDAY, 6.—Institution of Civil Engineers, 8 P.M.
WEDNESDAY, 7.—Society of Arts, 8 P.M.
THURSDAY, 8.—Royal Society, 8½ P.M.; Society of Antiquaries, 8 P.M.
FRIDAY, 9.—Archæological Association (Anniversary).

TO CORRESPONDENTS.

"*Young Joiner.*"—"*Quadrant*" is the quarter of a circle. "A bottom step with quadrant end" means that the end, instead of forming an angle, is rounded to a quarter circle, and is a correct expression.

"*An Old Subscriber*" may apply to Mr. Geyelin, No. 12, Manchester-buildings, Westminster.

Foolproof.—" Review of Mr. Poole's book," " Chelsea Hospital," " Parks and Approaches," Mr. Wornum's Lecture, &c.

ReceNed.—" A Subscriber" (Millo), " J. C.," " D. Y." (we see no advantage in opening the question), " Anti-Iconoclast" (thanks; we will look), " W. J., jun.," " R. P." (Temple), " C. E.," " Foolpad," " Anti-Peckensill" (cannot prevent his employer from publishing the designs as his own, and, as it seems to us, ought not if he could. We may perhaps say a few words soon on the principle involved), " W. S. J.," " E. W. E. P.," " T. M.," " F. C. W.," " J. R. R.," " E. S." (Lewes), " C. H.," Essex (the burners are quite suitable: 59, Conduit-street, Regent-street), " E. B. J.," " B. H. S." (shall hear from us), " C. A. J.," " X. Y. Z.," " G. D.," " E. F. B.," " Antiquary," " W. C." (we do not consider ourselves bound to verify the correctness of every advertisement. On receipt of sufficient evidence, however, we would refuse admittance to the advertisement in question).—" The Principles of the Differential and Integral Calculus Simplified," by Thomas Tate (London, Longman and Co.), Dolman, Blackwood, &c., 1849; " Con Cregan," No. 3 (Orr), a spirited and well-written story.

NOTICE.—All communications respecting advertisements should be addressed to the " Publisher," and not to the " Editor;" all other communications should be addressed to the EDITOR, and not to the publisher.

No. CCCXVIII.

SATURDAY, MARCH 10, 1849.

 HE endeavour of the Architectural Association to establish an annual exhibition of architectural art, free to the public, deserves the thanks of the profession generally, and should have commanded more assistance beyond its own walls than has yet been given to it. Composed as the association is, for the most part, of quite young men, students, this endeavour, which necessarily entails a considerable expense likely to fall on themselves, shows a degree of enthusiasm, energy, and *pluck*, if we may use a vulgar but expressive term, that commands our sympathy and praise. We suggest that a small subscription should be made by parties interested in the progress of our art, to meet the expenses of the gallery and attendants, so that the cost of a praiseworthy endeavour may not fall on the young society, or the subscribers individually. Members of the profession who would willingly have forwarded designs for exhibition, had their occupations spared them time to arrange them, and there were several in this position, may thus still lend their aid to the movement : we gladly do so ourselves.

It gives us much pleasure to find that the association is in a prosperous state, and comprises nearly 140 members. Many very good papers have been read (some afterwards appeared in our pages), and the class of design has been well attended. Our readers will remember that the Architectural Association grew out of the " Association of Architectural Draughtsmen." The inauguration meeting of the new society was held in October, 1847, and Mr. Kerr, the first president (by whom the remodelling of the society had been induced), thus stated the object it had in view :—

" The Institution of the Architectural Association is an endeavour towards an improved system of architectural study—an endeavour on the part of the students themselves. The fundamental position that architectural education—the present system of training the architect, is defective and insufficient, if it has not been frequently agitated and loudly proclaimed, has not been the less continually felt by every thinking mind, and earnestly lamented by every aspirer after progress. And there may be nothing of novelty in a serious attempt to improve upon the system—an energetic endeavour for progression. If architecture is ' the only branch of human ingenuity, which is an exception to this century in its intellectual advancement,'—if the profession of the architect has been a strange anomaly among professions, so unsettled in the principles of its subject and so uncared for in investigation and teaching, it has not been so without many an earnest mind having been aroused to complain, and many an energetic scheme having been perseveringly urged. But in the present project there is certainly a novelty of nature. Whether it may succeed or not may scarcely yet be predicted ; but as a scheme aiming at the association together on the largest scale, of the entire body of our professional youth, for the end of *self-education*, and with the *good trust* of simple *self-reliance*, it possesses a novelty which ought to

be attractive enough to ensure an indulgent trial, and a straightforward earnestness of good purpose which deserves of every old man favour, of every young man help." We thought so too, and willingly assisted in making it known and extending its influence ; but we said then and we say now, that we could see no reason why this work should not be done *in connection with the Institute,*— why this body of young and rising men should not be enabled to do exactly what they were about to do, in the rooms of the Institute, so as to avoid the payment of *rent*, which keeps down the efforts of all societies, and be aided by the use of the now excellent library of the Institute and the co-operation of the elder members of the profession, its members.

It seems to us most desirable for all parties that this junction should take place, and if any change be necessary in the rules of the institute to admit of it, the change should be made. The Institute must open its arms wider, increase the number of its allies, objurgate narrownesses, and maintain its position, not by keeping back others, but by advancing itself.

We are being led away, however, from the exhibition, which was privately viewed on Wednesday, and is now open to the public free every day, except Saturday, when a shilling will be charged—an arrangement which it is supposed will enable that portion of the public who are interested in the progress of art, and can afford to assist the experiment to the extent of twelve pence, the opportunity of doing so, but which in practice, we fear, will have the effect of keeping the gallery empty one day out of the six.

Of this disinclination to pay, we will not too much complain, if we see the rooms well frequented on the other days. As the association say in their preface, " whether the public will appreciate an exhibition exclusively devoted to architectural art, is a question never yet practically tested." We trust that the reply will be satisfactory, and agree with them in saying, that " whatever may be the deficiencies of that now offered to their notice—viewed as the initiative—we hope for it a candid judgment and liberal reception ; and that ere long it will receive that full co-operation of the profession, which shall render it not unworthy of a position among those galleries of art that are annually thrown open to the public." We shall hope especially to see the various artisans of the metropolis availing themselves of the opportunity of inspecting the drawings which is thus gratuitously afforded to them.

The gallery contains 171 drawings and 9 models. The most noticeable of them have been exhibited before, and have been mentioned in our pages. Thus Mr. G. G. Scott sends his design for the Army and Navy Club House (No. 7), and Newfoundland Cathedral (No. 68) ; Mr. Allom his fine drawing of the banks of the Thames (No. 38), and in conjunction with his partner, Mr. Crosse, a design for Chichester Training Schools (No. 31), the New Kensington Workhouse (No. 92), design for Army and Navy Club (No. 145), and others. Mr. E. B. Lamb is a good contributor : Shooting Residence at Loch Tulla (No. 40), Wadhurst Castle, Sussex, shewing alterations (No. 102), charming little drawings ; Church and Schools at Prestwood (No. 118), are amongst the works he has sent. Mr. Papworth exhibits his design for a façade to St. Maria del Fiore, at Florence (No. 21), a Metropolitan Music Hall (No. 169), and a National Record Office (No. 170), all

old friends : and his brother, Mr. Wyatt Papworth, has sent with other things, his design for a library, exhibited last year. Mr. Leeds has several of his suggestions for street architecture, thoughtful and original usually, but owing little to the colouring by which they are set forth, which indeed does not do justice to the ideas. Mr. Donaldson has sent his design for the mansion of the late Lord Hallyburton, in Angusshire (No. 115), Mr. R. W. Billings, the Gothic screen, executed for Great Malvern Church (No. 103), Mr. Roumien, drawings of some villas now being erected, and a view of Old St. Pancras Church recently restored, and Mr. Raphael Brandon, some designs for churches (the Holy Trinity Church, Leverstock-green, Herts, now being erected, No. 150, and others), which shew us he has not studied the village churches of old England uselessly.

The designs for churches are numerous, and mostly show an adherence to ancient models, and a congruity, whatever want or avoidance of invention may be observable. No. 5 is a design for a church at Tunbridge, by Mr. Ewan Christian, (geometrical, with tower on south side of chancel). No. 9, Design for a Church, by Mr. Colling, (Early English, founded on the Temple Church, London). No. 33, New Church, &c., now building at Newton, by Mr. J. Colson (Early English, nave and chancel). No. 76, Design for a Parish Church, by Mr. C. Geoghan (Early English). No. 90, Design for the Consecrated Chapel at Leicester Cemetery, by Mr. J. Johnson (Tuscan in style) ; and No. 117, by the same architect, New Church, Heptonstall, Halifax (Early decorated, with massive square tower).

Nos. 1, 2, and 3 give the elevations and section of Wren's original Design for St. Paul's, by Mr. E. C. Sayer, very nicely drawn, though the coloured decorations shown in the section are more suited to a drawing-room than a cathedral. No. 8 is a design for the Brighton Dispensary, by Mr. G. S. Clarke, to which the second premium was awarded : the style is Tudor, and the design has a turret at the angle.

No. 56, Entrance front of Villa designed for Alderman Moon, by Mr. Owen Jones, is founded on the Alhambra ; clever, but, as it seems to us, unsuitable. No. 73 is a very clever Design for Carriage Gates, by Mr. J. P. Seddon. In No. 48, by the same, the arrangement of the lines is similar, but there is a mixture of styles which makes it less satisfactory.

No. 67, Design for Galleries or Arcade over the roadway and footpaths fronting the National Gallery, by Mr. G. A. Elliott, is a curiously wild notion, effectively set forth. No. 93 gives a series of clever pen-and-ink sketches of Northamptonshire Churches, by Mr J. D. Wyatt. No. 135, Font and Cover, Manchester Cathedral, by Mr. Truefitt, will enable our readers to judge if our commendation of the work some time since was deserved.

Mr. Leonard Collman, besides a view of the British Museum Hall as decorated by him, has a design for a sideboard (No. 137), which is one of the most masterly drawings in the room.

We can only add, that there are other designs by Messrs. Jayne, Horace Jones, Charles Baily, C. Lee, C. Tinkler, G. P. Boyce, Butler and Hodge, C. W. Young, &c. &c. ; and that Mr. C. Fripp exhibits a model entitled, " Study for a Façade," which, if we mistake not, is the design he submitted for the Army and Navy Club.

THE HISTORY OF ECCLESIASTICAL ARCHITECTURE IN ENGLAND.*

THE INFLUENCE OF THE SAXON PERIOD UPON POINTED ARCHITECTURE.

IN the interesting account of his laborious researches, which Mr. Layard gives in his recent book on ancient Nineveh, and in the examination of the works of a people of whose history and manners all other evidence has passed away,—in Pompeii—aptly termed a fossil remain of ancient life and manners,—in the rock-cut temples of India, or the pyramids of Egypt,—in the old world or the new,—wherever the growth of intelligence in man can claim a record in history, there the architect points to the value of *his* art as the mirror and impression of the past. As the silent deposits of the ocean, and the great convulsions of the land, have enabled the geologist to pourtray the structure and habits of animate beings in ages past in the *earth's* history—to which the thousands of years which date from the fall of Nineveh, are an insignificant fraction of time—so the mounds of the desert and the ashes of the volcano enshrined the existence of other generations, for the discovery and wonder of the present.

The Assyrian passed away, and the empire which extended from beyond the Tigris to the Mediterranean, was lost to the historian, the very name of Nineveh was forgotten, and another race built upon its site, and, like its predecessor, perished in the night of time, and its works were covered with the sand; but the accumulations of ages only preserved the enduring record of architecture to be exposed in our own time. Shall, then, the architect not claim as a great art, that which has this high power of contributing to so vast a field of human inquiry? or shall the world think lightly of the enthusiasm which is aroused by the arts of Greece, or the relics of mediæval art in our own country?

A modern generation, boastful of ingenuity in research, and power to accomplish great undertakings, may well marvel at the vast power of conception and the tasteful execution in the works of the mediæval architects in Europe. The untiring energy which was brought to bear on the erection of structures, which still, even in their state of comparative poverty and dilapidation, so powerfully impress the beholder, and the deep religious feeling of which it was the expression, are occasionally forgotten by some, who see only the superstition and priestcraft which did too often accompany it. We, however, can find such evidence of the beautiful in art, and the good in Christian effort and example in these relics, that we are not altogether surprised, that some should now almost identify themselves with the whole spirit of the middle ages; and they are not without words to answer those who venerate other schools of art, less Christian in purpose and character. Looking, however, from an age essentially practical, upon the works of "the masters of a great art in its highest application," with an anxiety to aid every effort to place before us, as Mr. Poole says, "a more vivid, as well as a more just perception of the merits of their works," hailing, indeed, every work that helps to complete the chain of that great history of human progress, of which—as we before said—architecture is the expression, we cannot but often wish that a different use were made of these works by some non-professional writers—as we so often wish a different application of their architectural features by architects. We therefore regret that Mr. Poole, in the laborious compilation which is very usefully included in the scheme of his history, has not, as it appears to us—notwithstanding the disclaimer in his preface—sufficiently distinguished in the text, between the opinions and feelings of the monkish historians—"left to speak for themselves on such subjects as miracles, doctrines, and counsels of perfection," and his own treatment of the subject. It is true we read that—"We neither do nor can think, believe, and feel with them ourselves, and we should deprecate nothing more seriously than a use of their works which should lead others to an indiscriminate reception of their facts, or of their theology;" and *we* also are disposed to consider that "the opinions which they express, the feelings which they avow, even the stories which they relate, whether they be or be not real and true in themselves, or in our judgment, are clearly so in the philosophy of the history of art;" but a practised writer might have been expected continually to provide against the possibility of misconception in this particular, as well elsewhere as in a preface, and we the more regret this peculiarity of our author's style, as he displays in many places, a judicious critical discrimination between the characteristics of the art. Thus in speaking of polychromy for example, where he says, "we do not now think colour an additional beauty to really good imagery and carving," he is favourably contrasted in our mind, with some who seem to "plead in excuse of the excessive use of colour in the ecclesiastical decorations of the middle ages."

The author has endeavoured to combine, in his volume, "a general history of the greater English ecclesiastical architects of the middle ages with an equally general review of their works, and of the characters which distinguish the buildings of their respective ages;" and the work may therefore be taken to be a history of the church, as illustrated by the progress of pointed architecture, rather than a mere notice of peculiarities of styles, to which branch of the subject other writers had more particularly devoted themselves. Mr. Poole seems to have addressed himself to the general public, less than to those who may possess other works on the subject, since his book has the peculiarity—in these days of elaborate illustration—of being entirely destitute of plates and woodcuts. A knowledge of the characteristics of the different styles, consequently, can perhaps better be gained by a novice, from other works, the author here seeming to enter rather into the *rationale* of a change, than to depict every imaginable variation in its occurrence.

But if, for a tolerable idea of the great skill, and the beauty of design and workmanship, displayed in the details of Gothic edifices, we must look elsewhere, Mr. Poole has given us evidence of the abilities and zeal of the men who erected the ecclesiastical edifices. The immense influence of this zeal, it is indeed difficult to convey an adequate impression of. Taking up the map of any country, wherever we find a church indicated, we shall make few mistakes in attributing it to the period which preceded the Reformation. Not that churches were *never* erected in the reigns of Charles II. and Queen Anne, or that the last few years have been idle in the work of building, but the number of such structures is insignificant, compared with the multitude of those, of which the thickly set villages of the country can each furnish an interesting example. In the year 1268, Branescombe, bishop of Exeter, is said to have consecrated no less than forty churches in his diocese, whilst we are told that now Devonport in the same diocese, "with a population of 26,000, has not a single church."

But this holy ardour in the erection of ecclesiastical edifices, is by no means peculiarly remarkable in the period subsequent to the Conquest, but is apparent during the Saxon period. If, indeed, it may be doubted whether Sprott in his "Chronicle," has accurately stated the number of churches, at the time of the Conquest, at 45,011, there is very little reason to doubt Mr. Poole's accuracy in inferring that it amounted to four thousand, or about one-third of the present number.

But these remarkable ancestors of those whom something more than national pride now characterizes as a remarkable race, were not distinguished merely by their zeal in spreading the influence of religion, nor by the number only of their contributions to its exercise. The architect accustomed to the rude masonry of such of the churches as are ascribed to the Saxons, might perhaps pass over as unimportant, the inventions of a people who may not have had the ability to conceive the beautiful models of their successors. But, even omitting the evidence of ancient manuscripts and illuminations to the skill of Saxon artists,—which, however, is most important in the history of art, when its several branches were more united than they are at present,—we find a great amount of skill in many branches of ecclesiastical art, in which, as it would be impossible to deny magnificence of effect, it might be equally easy to recognise the element of taste. Indeed, whilst Italy passed through centuries of time, in which it is difficult to discover any evidence of the influence of art, the churchmen of England were devoted to the service of religion through its agency. Accomplished in all the learning of Glastonbury, and possessed of remarkable energy and devotion to all that could advance the influence of the church and the priesthood, Dunstan, as he was the most celebrated man of that day, so is he no unfit type of the learning of his class. His future greatness shadowed forth in childhood,—according to one of the characteristic stories of the period,—by the vision of an angel, who stretched a surveyor's measuring-line over the area of a church ("Mensoris funiculum per plana atrii extendens"), becoming "learned beyond all his fellows in philosophy, he was also wonderfully skilled in manual operations. He was a painter and a scribe, and we have still proofs remaining of his proficiency in these arts." But it is still more important to find the remark, that he was "a diligent and skilful artificer in gold, silver, brass, and iron, and used the more delicate graver's tools as well as the hammer and the tongs." And it is not unnecessary to notice, that he was acquainted with both the science and practice of music, and that he was able to make organs, nor that he could design patterns for embroidery. And we cannot read of the profuse application of the precious metals to the purposes of architecture, and the constant use of painting and sculpture, without inferring a very different state of the art during the Saxon period than the mere evidence of such churches as Brixworth or Earl's Barton now afford.

Though materials are found for the history of ecclesiastical architecture in a period even preceding that of the Saxons—commencing with the wooden building at Glastonbury, of the year of our Lord 63, unanimously allowed to have been the oldest Christian church, and shown by Mr. Petrie to have been most important in its influence over the churches of Ireland,—and although we find the name of King Lucius, in the second century, associated with the names of some which were afterwards important buildings—Westminster Abbey amongst the number; although we have mention of a church at St. Albans "of most beautiful workmanship," and containing a shrine decorated "with gold and jewels," and although it has not been omitted to remark upon the indirect influence of the Roman sway, which taught the workmen of Britain the use of mortar, and made them famous, and in which the use and disposition of bricks—often actually worked up into succeeding buildings—greatly influenced the decoration of the Saxon and Norman architects,—although in the pages of Geoffry of Monmouth, and the story of Merlin, we might find evidence of the skill in the arts of construction which afterwards led to such great results, and we have notices of cathedrals and monasteries *rebuilt* by King Arthur—who dwelt in palaces adorned with gilded roofs—as well as the direct statement that during that time "Britain had arrived at such a pitch of grandeur that, in abundance of riches, luxury of ornaments, and politeness of inhabitants, it far surpassed other kingdoms;" it is to our *Saxon* ancestors that we must more particularly look for influences upon the characteristic features of pointed architecture.

The influence of the Saxons is generally dated from the conversion of Ethelbert by Augustine, about the year 597, and, in the history of the venerable Bede, we soon find records of the building and reparation of churches, and of the conversion of heathen temples to the service of Christianity; we also find that sacred vessels, vestments, books, and relics were furnished from Rome, and the future state of architecture in England is thus early shadowed forth in the institution of monasteries, and the erection of churches at Canterbury, Rochester, London, and York, and oratories in various parts of the island. Then too, Iona, a barren rock in a tempestuous sea, became a school of knowledge, so that, though in a later style of architecture, it has to this day "memorials of its past importance not to be surpassed in historic interest by the mighty piles of York and Durham, or the halls of Oxford or of Cambridge." So important a seat of learning was not without influence in

* A History of Ecclesiastical Architecture in England," by George Ayliffe Poole, M.A., Vicar of Welford. London, Masters. 8vo.

places far from its remote locality. We find records of oratories and cathedrals raised by consecrated missionaries from the island of S. Columba; and though timber was the material often employed on a kind of building described as that of the Scots, of split wood with reed thatch,* stone appears to have been equally common, and lead for a covering was even brought into use. Glass was introduced from Gaul in 671, by Benedict Biscop, at which time we find mention of the importation of pictures, and images, and relics from Rome, and of the use of masonry in the "Roman manner." These particulars we need not allude to the importance of, in the history of architecture, and the influence of Benedict Biscop is scarcely to be overrated.

With Mr. Poole, we feel the difficulty of coming to a satisfactory conclusion in respect to the masonry of the "Roman manner," as it seems clear that, as regards mere masonry, there must have been many examples of Roman work in England. Our author suggests that the difference might be, at least partly, one of ritual, and "altogether, *rather of degree than of kind.*" Thus the arch may have been more freely employed, consequent upon an adaptation of the aisles of the Roman basilica, along with the apse, and generally a more extensive character of building. He might, however, have noticed the use of the baluster in Saxon buildings, as showing a remarkable coincidence with so important a feature of the Italian architecture of later date; and it might afford curious matter for discussion, whether its presence does not argue in favour of the existence of the baluster in the architecture of Rome, previous to the time of Brunelleschi, a mode of reasoning by induction which we do not remember has ever been brought to bear upon the interesting question of the origin of the use of the baluster by Italian architects. But, perhaps the most significant fact in the history of this period, was the introduction of the practice of burying in churches,—a practice of the most important influence on the forms of churches, and one which has retained its hold more completely than any other custom of the middle ages, destructive as it has been to many of our finest works of architecture, as well as to health.

These important features having been introduced, it soon followed that works like those of men who had been to Rome,—as of Wilfrid at Hexham, York, and Ripon,—should be remarkable for their porticoes and polished pillars, marvellous length and height of walls, winding passages and spiral stairs, crypts and oratories, and sculptured and polychromatic decorations, as well as for their gold, silver, and precious stones, and purple and silk hangings. Wilfrid seems also to have introduced the use of whitewash. It is, however, most interesting, to find mentioned in the church at Hexham three distinct stories, showing that the triforium must have been in use in the middle of the seventh century. During this century, also, an influence scarcely less important than the introduction of burials in churches was introduced, resulting from the division of the country into parishes. It is remarked by Mr. Poole, that the effect of this would be that, whilst without the parochial system there were many distinct oratories, after the change took place, these would be united with, and become decorations of an existing fabric; and churches, though perhaps lessened in number, would become more important in regard to size and decoration, by combined resources of several parishes.

As it is in the monastic system that we discover the origin of the principal works of architecture in England, so this influence was greatly forwarded by the introduction of the Benedictine order in the tenth century, by Dunstan, who early commenced the quarrels between the monks and the secular clergy, which are often thought to have had so important an influence upon the sculpture of ecclesiastical edifices. King Edgar is said to have erected, or restored, forty-eight monasteries.

In the building of the abbey in the Isle of Ramsey, in Huntingdonshire, we find that pile-driving and concrete for foundations were employed; and if we recollect that the church at Brixworth,—the most important Saxon church now remaining,—must have been only a second or third-rate building, we shall be able to agree with Mr. Poole, that the arches there are evidence of the existence of much larger arches in more important buildings, and that in the accounts to which we have referred, and in remains generally, we have evidence of great constructive skill, whether in vaulting or other portions of buildings. Many more important structural characteristics of mediæval architecture, too, were thus early apparent. The use of a division into nave and aisles, of the chancel, with apsidal termination, of the plan of the cross with a central tower, of the ordinary bell-tower, and—in one instance at least—of two towers, one in each of these positions; the important feature of the clerestory, the use of glass for windows; of lead, and even of copper, and of tiles, sometimes gilded, for roofs; the constant use of bells, and the provision requisite for organs and church music, along with other elements, some of them peculiar to England, even at this early period, contributed to the peculiar characteristics of Pointed architecture. The importance of these elements is well illustrated by Mr. Poole, as follows:—

"This notice of bells and clocks is not disproportioned to the influence which their introduction has had on ecclesiastical architecture. It is to the use of church-bells that we are indebted for the most prominent feature of almost every ecclesiastical fabric, and that which serves most to harmonise all the parts of a whole, sometimes so vast, and almost always so various, as a Gothic church. From the low central tower of a Norman abbey, but just rising above the roof, at the intersection of the cross, to the lofty towers or spires of Boston, Gloucester, Salisbury, Coventry, Louth, or Whittlesea, in whatever part of the church it may be placed, the steeple still gives an inexpressible grace and dignity to the whole outline, correcting immoderate length, reducing all minor parts to proportion, giving variety to sameness, and harmony to the most licentious irregularity. The judicious use of the tower or spire is a great part of the secret of the characteristic boldness in minor details of the mediæval architects. The little excrescences of such a building as York Minster, which are now lost in the grand whole, would at once become deformities if the towers were removed. The cathedral of Milan is in some respects one of the most splendid buildings in the world; but, for want of a steeple of proportionate elevation, it is but a gigantic grove of pinnacles, in which statues seem to have lost their way, and to be wandering without aim and without end. If, as is most probable, the central tower of Fountains had perished before the present northern tower was erected, what a heavy mass of irregularities must that splendid pile have seemed. The tower reduces all to proportion, and makes it once again a whole. Bolton Abbey had also suffered the loss of its tower, and that at the west end was never raised above the level of the nave; and though it is far smaller and less irregular than Fountains, what a long unrelieved length it presents to the eye. What is it which gives such vastness and importance to the cathedral, such grace and beauty to the parish church, at a distance, but the tower or spire? Nay, what is it but the bell-gable which in mere outline often distinguishes the retired chapel from some neighbouring barn? And for all this we are indebted to the introduction of bells; or if not for the existence of these, or the like additions to the beauty of outline in our churches, yet at least for what is a part of their beauty,—their having a use, and being exactly adapted to their use."

We do well, then, to attend to any important element of this nature. But it was not in structural peculiarities alone, that the architecture of the Saxon period originated features of most extensive development in succeeding periods. The Saxon masonry, known as "long and short work," analagous to the binding courses of brick in Roman masonry, differs from it in this remarkable manner—viz., that it is vertical; and looking at the engaged shaft rising to the gable of the highly conical roof in the tower of Sompting Church, we cannot but suppose that these were perhaps the first germs "of that verticality in Gothic art which at last expanded into the spires of Salisbury and Coventry," and of that feature of panelling which was so marked a characteristic of the style of the fifteenth century. With the accession of Edward the Confessor the Norman variety of Romanesque was introduced into England; but to this period, and that of Pointed architecture, we must devote another paper.

* Possibly the church at Greensted, noticed in our pages, may have been a church of this description.

THE LONDON FEVER HOSPITAL COMPETITION.

ARCHITECTS' RIGHTS.

SIR,—I beg to hand you a memorandum of the Council of the Institute of British Architects, relative to the new Fever Hospital competition, which I introduced to your notice by letter on the 26th of August, 1848, when I stated I should lay the case before the council of that body for its deliberation and decision.

In the letter above named I admitted the right of the committee to use my design in these words:—"The plans and working-drawings were paid for and delivered to the committee, and the claims for the design abandoned." In another paragraph I added:—"A legal right may exist with the committee, (in the use of the design), but there is an evident want of moral feeling; but this has arisen from the influence of the president, Lord Devon. But what, Sir, is to be said of a member of the profession, one of reputed high standing, who can attach his name to the ideas and almost the design of another competitor?"

It is on this latter point that I insisted, as involving the interests of the profession, and I leave it to your readers to form their own opinion upon the report of the Council, and the admission made by Mr. Fowler.

I did not solicit the intervention of the Institute on personal grounds, and am, therefore, glad to find that the record of the opinion of the Council embraces the rules of practice which should have been followed in this case as in the establishment of a general principle, which is urged upon each and every individual of the profession. D. MOCATTA.

Old Broad-street, March 6, 1849.

"Royal Institute of British Architects, Incorporated 7th William IV.

16, Lower Grosvenor-street.

Extract from the Minutes of Council, dated 26th of February, 1849.

Memorandum.—A reference to the Council of the Institute having been made by Mr. David Mocatta, Fellow, and by Mr. Charles Fowler, Fellow, relative to certain proceedings connected with the recent competition in which they were engaged for the new building for the London Fever Hospital:—The Council having taken into consideration the statement of the case received from Mr. Mocatta, bearing date 9th November, 1848, and a communication in reply thereto from Mr. Fowler, bearing date 22nd January, 1849, and having likewise examined the various documents and drawings for the building, are of opinion—

That the building now in progress under the direction of Mr. Fowler resembles strongly, more especially in the application of double wards, the design submitted in competition by Mr. Mocatta, and selected by the Building Committee, and for which he subsequently accepted a certain remuneration.

That it does not appear that Mr. Fowler, in the design submitted in the competition, contemplated the introduction of double wards; the Council therefore consider that, although the trustees purchased Mr. Mocatta's drawings, and had a right to adopt any portions of the design they might see fit: yet that an acknowledgment of such application is due from Mr. Fowler to Mr. Mocatta, as expressed in Mr. Fowler's letter to the Council of the 22nd January, wherein he says—'It may be proper to state that the trustees paid Mr. Mocatta for his plans, &c., therefore they had an undoubted right to make every and full use of them; at the same time, it must be admitted that so far as their architect has done so, he is bound to acknowledge it, and this I am most willing to do.'

The Council record their opinion as a general principle to be acted upon, to ensure full justice to the most deserving competitor, that the author of an original idea, if it be adopted, should be engaged to carry out his own conception, and that every member of the profession should individually do his utmost to establish this principle.

Extracted from Minutes of Council, 1st March, 1849.

GEORGE BAILEY, } Honorary
J. J. SCOLES, } Secretaries.

Resolved,—That a copy of the memorandum of the Council relative to the London Fever Hospital be forwarded to Mr. Mocatta and Mr. Fowler."

THE PERICLEAN AGE OF GRECIAN DECORATIVE ART.

THE CHRYS-ELEPHANTINE WORKS, &c.

A SERIES of lectures on the Periclean and Alexandrian ages of Greek art is in course of delivery by Mr. Ralph N. Wornum, at the Government School of Design, to a crowded and miscellaneous audience—of the people, properly so called, all of whom, young and old, female and male, high and low, seem to listen throughout to the details of art with the closest attention. Such at least was the case on the evening of Friday, the 2nd, at the lecture whence the following notes were taken.

From the time of Pericles to Alexander the Great, rather more than a century, ornamental design in Greece itself was constantly progressing in richness and variety, perpetually exhibiting new and beautiful combinations, although, in Greece, the decorative arts never at any time attained that florid development which so conspicuously distinguishes the great works of Rome, in the beginning of the empire. In these, however, notwithstanding the beauty of the individual members, the whole effect was materially injured by the superabundance of detail, by the overloading of ornament, carried to such an excess in some monuments as scarcely to leave a single portion of plain surface. There is no repose for the eye in such works, and the effect becomes merely general. This is a want of judgment, and calls to mind the memorable reproof of Apelles to one of his pupils, who had painted a picture of Helen of Troy, and loaded her with ornaments:—"So! said Apelles, because you could not paint her beautiful, you have made her rich!" However much the Romans merit such a rebuke, certainly the Greeks do not. In their art nothing was overloaded, some of the most beautiful being remarkable for the comparatively moderate application of ornament, at least till about the Roman Conquest, when the Greek artists probably themselves followed out their art in the Roman capital, and to the Roman taste.

Reviewing the development of ornamental art among the Greeks (as the lecturer had previously been doing with illustrated reference to the spiral, acanthus, guilloche, &c.), we find the first great efforts at Samos, then at Ephesus, Ægina, Athens, and Delphi, Pæstum, and Sicily. Athens finally triumphed through the fostering care of Pericles, and the great school which arose out of his efforts reached its utmost perfection in the time of Alexander. This is true not only of ornamental art, but of all other arts dependant on form and colour. The grand essential qualities of art developed in the works of Polygnotus and Phidias received their last refinements under the hands of Lysippus and Apelles, and their contemporaries.

Some idea was then given of the progress of the rivalry between the Doric in the west and the Ionic in the east; of the decorations of those temples in which both orders were combined—the Propylæa of Athens and Eleusis for example; of the finer monuments of both orders grouped together on the Acropolis, or citadel of Athens, and particularly of the Doric Parthenon, and the Ionic Erectheium. The probable general style of the polychromic embellishments of the Parthenon was illustrated by the restoration of Dr. Kugler of Berlin. The sanctuary, continued the lecturer, contained the goddess's statue, of gold and ivory, of most colossal proportions, the work of Phidias, and one of the greatest of those surprising and costly productions of the Greeks called chrys-elephantine, that is of gold and ivory, and of which Phidias alone executed six.

The Chrys-elephantine statue of Minerva, in the Parthenon, was about 40 feet high. The flesh was entirely of ivory, the costume of gold, and the ornaments of gold, colour, and precious stones. There have been many speculations as to how these ivory figures were constructed, and the eminent French antiquary, M. Quatremère de Quincy, has devoted an elaborate essay to this subject. Though ivory was much more abundant in ancient times than it is now, it is not to be for a moment supposed that these Chrys-elephantine figures were built entirely of ivory, even though hollow. The ivory was a mere outer casing, fixed in small pieces upon a core of wood, or perhaps some other material, skilfully prepared to receive it; and it was probably laid on in uniform thicknesses—not a very difficult process, when we consider that the Greeks were in possession of a method of softening their ivory. Plutarch mentions the softeners of ivory as one of the distinct classes of artists employed by Pericles, and these were the men probably employed to fix the ivory upon the core. Pausanias also mentions that the Greeks flattened the round pieces of elephants' tusks by first rendering them soft by heat—perhaps by steaming; and being then allowed to cool under pressure they might assume the required shape. When thus fixed the sculptor could fashion the various parts to his taste.

The great triumph of this species of art was the colossal sitting statue of Jupiter, in his temple at Olympia, in Elis, a cluster of temples in the plain where the great periodical games of the Greeks took place. This incomparable work was the masterpiece of Phidias, and, like the Temple of Diana at Ephesus, one of the seven wonders of the world. The lecturer then described this celebrated statue in the words of Pausanias, which, for the sake of some of our own readers, who may not be familiar with, or may wish to recall, the idea of this wonder of the ancient world, we may here also note down from the lecturer's description. The god was represented seated on his throne, under the covering of the temple, and the whole height of the statue, exclusive of the pedestal, is said to have been something more than 40 feet, an almost incredible magnitude, when we consider the material and the manner of its workmanship. It occupied Phidias and his assistants about four years, during the 80th Olympiad, or from 437 to 433 B.C., inclusive, and immediately after the completion of the Minerva of the Parthenon.

"The god," says Pausanias, "is seated on a throne made of ivory and gold. He wears a crown of olive branch on his head. In his right hand is the figure of Victory, also of gold and ivory, with a crown on her head, and holding a fillet. In his left hand he holds a beautiful sceptre set with all kinds of precious stones. The bird on the top of it is an eagle. His sandals are also of gold, and his mantle likewise, which is ornamented with figures of animals and lilies. The throne itself is variegated with gold, stones, ivory, and ebony, and is decorated with painted reliefs. It is adorned, also, with statues. At each foot or leg of the throne are four dancing victories, and two others on the pedestal of each foot. On (above?) the two front feet are Theban youths carried away by sphinxes, and below the sphinxes are Apollo and Diana destroying the children of Niobe."

The charge of this statue, which remained at Olympia undisturbed for about 800 years, was given, in perpetuity, to the descendants of Phidias. Their duty was to keep it clean, and to rub it constantly with oil, to preserve the ivory from suffering any injury from the marshy atmosphere of the grove in which the temple stood. They were called Phaidruntæ, which means, literally, polishers or cleaners. They had still the care of it in the time of Pausanias, who visited Olympia 500 years after the death of Phidias. This great sculptor died in the year 432 B.C., not many months after the completion of this master-piece.

There seems to have been considerable difficulty in keeping these chrys-elephantine works in order, the great difficulty being the climate, though, in Greece, at Olympia, it was too damp, at Athens too dry. While the Olympian Jupiter required to be frequently anointed with oil, the Minerva of the Parthenon, on the lofty dry Acropolis of Athens, required to be constantly sprinkled with water. A work, however, of this class, also by Phidias, wholly free from these objections, was the statue of Esculapius at Epidaurus, which was placed immediately over a well, the evaporations from which maintained a constant degree of moisture in the atmosphere, and thus preserved the statue—a remedy as simple as efficacious.

The Olympian Jupiter is said, though not upon very authentic sources, to have been carried to Constantinople, by the orders of Theodosius the Great, and there to have perished, about a century afterwards, in the fire which consumed the Lauseion, in which it was placed, in the year 475.

After a cursory allusion to the still more gigantic bronze statue of Minerva Promachos, in the Acropolis at Athens, made from the spoils of Marathon, and forming the greatest of all the works of Phidias, the lecturer proceeded to explain, in detail, the various ornamental and other portions of Greek architecture previously alluded to, and especially with reference to the Erectheum, the distinction between the Attic and Ionic column and base, and other decorative contrasts and comparisons, in which the Ionic temple of Ephesus, and various other examples, were illustrated, the elements of the voluted and Corinthian orders of architecture at large described, and the progress of the Periclean age of decorative Greek art traced through its increasing tendency to richness and abundance of ornament, rather than chastity of principles, till the conquest of Asia introduced a taste for even oriental display, which steadily progressed till the time of Nero, when mere vermillion and gilding were preferred to the tasteful polychromy of the Parthenon, and carved scrolls or griffins, or other monstrous combinations, were substituted for the noble decorations of Phidias. A disquisition on dolphins, tritons, satyrs, fauns, and 'chimeras dire' then followed, with an account of the lavish expenditure of the Greeks on mural and other household decorations in the time of Alexander, who, according to Pliny, paid Apelles 50,000*l.* for a single picture of himself, as Jupiter Tonans. Then it was that artists had their golden age, even though at times compelled by threats and imprisonment, no less than by bribes and honour, to undertake their prized productions.

Where the artist was so much in request as in Greece, whether painter, sculptor, or architect, he took his social position accordingly, and many of the Greek artists assumed an extraordinary degree of consequence, being most sumptuous in their habits, indulging in a costliness of costume worthy of a Sybarite. Zeuxis and his rival Parrhasius, were notorious for ostentation and magnificence of dress. Zeuxis, latterly, even gave away his pictures, declaring that they were beyond all price, and he appeared in public with his name embroidered in letters of gold around the hem of his mantle. Parrhasius also always appeared in public with a golden head-dress and a purple robe. His sandals were bound by golden straps, and he carried a golden-headed staff otherwise richly decorated. Such was the appearance of a Greek painter in the time of Socrates; and though Parrhasius may have been somewhat extreme in his love of display—his dress rather according with our notions of regal costume than that of an artist—a man of such taste and eminence in art would never have made himself *ridiculous* by his costume; and doubtless, therefore, the splendour of his attire was quite justified by the fashions of his times.

When considered together with what we read of the gorgeous dress of the Sybarites, this shows us that the love of art, when once developed, spreads itself in all directions, impressing every object with its beneficial influence, not less those of use than those of luxury. The costly and gorgeous structures of the Greeks were not mere works of luxurious extravagance. Though the contrast between the palace of the prince and the cottage of the artificer may be great, we must recollect that whole villages of cottages have sometimes owed their very existence to the erection of one of these palaces. The prince cannot indulge in the gratification of his taste for splendour without at the same time, either directly or indirectly, gladdening the hearts of thousands of poor artificers; and we should look upon the greatest buildings not as monuments of the extravagance of luxury, but rather of the skill and industry of the artist.

THE YARBOROUGH MONUMENT, at Bembridge-down, east end of Isle of Wight, had its capping-stone placed on Monday week. The structure, which is an obelisk, is of Penryn granite, 75 feet high, 14 feet at the base, and 28 feet at the lower step. A lightning conductor passes through the centre. The panels for an inscription to the late Earl and Yacht-commodore, have not yet been filled up. The building, according to the *Hampshire Advertiser*, is to serve as a sea-mark, the site having been carefully selected to that end. Mr. Peter Rolt was the builder.

MUTUAL INSTRUCTION AT THE SCHOOL OF DESIGN.

THE following is the substance of the address read by Mr. Raimbach at the meeting of students mentioned in our last:—

Fellow Students,—You are aware that this school was established for the twofold purpose of educating a class of designers who should be able successfully to compete with the foreign ornamentist; and a sufficient number of skilled draughtsmen and pattern drawers to assist in carrying out the works of the first-mentioned. It is generally allowed that the latter object has been successful, and that not only this school, but the branch schools also, have produced first-rate draughtsmen in every department. But there is still the impression, among all who are interested in the subject, that the schools have altogether failed as schools of design. It is still asked, where are the designers the schools were established to supply—who were to drive French and German patterns out of the British market—who were to raise the commercial value of our manufactures, by introducing beauty of design even in the meanest article of use or ornament, and to elevate the people by familiarising them with that elegance of form, harmony of colour, and fitness for use combined, which are only found among the productions of a refined age and nation?

Although the school has been established above ten years, it is yet, perhaps, too much to expect so desirable an effect. But are we nearer our object than ten years ago? The patterns, as well of textile fabrics as of such articles as paper-hangings, furniture, and pottery, are as ordinary, not to say as ugly, as ever,—and, as regards the latter, a substitute for the "willow pattern" is yet to be devised. If it be impossible to walk through any of our great thoroughfares without being struck with the great improvement displayed in every kind of silk, satin, shawl, or muslin; who will say that the revision of the tariff has not had more effect in producing that improvement than the schools of design? Who will deny that, where the manufacture is native, the pattern is foreign? And when we hear of any nobleman's or gentleman's mansion being decorated with more than ordinary splendour, it is sure to have been done under the superintendence of some Herr Von Homberg, assisted by foreign artists and workmen, brought over from the continent at an enormous expense. The same practice is applied to club-houses, play-houses, palaces, and exchanges: our churches we adorn ourselves,—with whitewash.

And here let me remind you that I do not dispute the superiority of the foreign ornamentists (though I think the preference for their works is supported rather by fashion than by judgment), but I will maintain that there is no reason that this superiority should continue. It does not exist in *fine art*, why should it in art applied to manufactures? That many difficulties have interposed to prevent the attainment of the chief object for which the school was established, I am well aware. The greatest obstacle is, doubtless, the very general ignorance of the students as to the manufacturing processes to which their designs must, more or less in every case, be adapted. This circumstance renders the designs produced in the school so usually unfitted for manufacture, as to make them practically useless. It matters little enough that a design possesses every artistic excellence, if it be incapable of adaptation to a manufactured article; and while our manufacturers, by importing French patterns (in Manchester alone to the amount of above 20,000*l.* per annum), can obtain exactly what is suited to their purpose, it is not to be expected they will purchase what is not. This deficiency in the course of instruction was at one time attempted to be supplied. In 1843 a course of practical lectures on manufactures was delivered by Mr. Cowper, of King's College. But although regularly and numerously attended, they were discontinued. They comprised calico, silk, and letter-press printing; hand, power, plain, and figured weaving; pottery and porcelain, engraving and sculpture by machinery, type and stereotype-founding and the framing of machinery,—some of them rather foreign to the purpose for which they were intended.

The annual report for 1845 still alludes to the great want of practical and technical knowledge, and proceeds to say, "It is remarked generally of all the schools, that instances continually occur of students who possess superior natural endowments, with competent knowledge of art and power of execution, but who from deficiency of that technical knowledge which can only be effectually learned by actual experience in the factory and workshop, cannot procure from manufacturers the employment they seek; while others who have found means to add this requisite information to their artistic knowledge readily obtain engagements."

I differ in opinion from this report, in so far that I think *much* practical knowledge may be obtained without attending the factory or working at the loom. A good lecture, with proper diagrams, can often explain a process which is quite unintelligible in actual operation; and a man might stew himself a long time in an engine-room before he got so clear a knowledge of the principles of action in the steam-engine as may be derived from a careful perusal of Dr. Lardner's book; and it is my firm belief and conviction that this difficulty can be best overcome by the students themselves, and that the formation of this association supplies a means not only for accomplishing this, but for the removal of other difficulties which have impeded the operations of the school ever since its commencement.

Our association has been formed under circumstances peculiarly favourable, and at a time when public attention, fatigued with the excitement of foreign revolutions and rebellions, and relieved from the fear of domestic disturbances, is returning to the contemplation of our own progress as a nation, the revision of our laws, the improvement of our manufactures, the advancement of our arts. The commendatory letter received from Mr. Deverell, on the part of the council of the school, and the interest taken in its welfare by the masters, are circumstances on which we may well congratulate ourselves. The free use of this noble room, in which to hold our weekly meetings; the fact of being surrounded by examples of the highest class in every department of ornamental art of every age and from all countries; the power of reference to a valuable collection of books of prints and specimens, and the extended access to the lending library which has been accorded to such of our members who, in the preparation of papers or essays, wish to consult works on similar subjects, are further evidences of the favour with which we are viewed by the council and authorities. It is, therefore, incumbent on us to exert ourselves for our own advancement, and that we are both able and willing to do so is proved by the list of papers in preparation, which has been posted on the door of this room, among which are several on practical manufacturing subjects.

But our association has further objects in view; there is the management of the specimens of art belonging to the school, and the formation of a catalogue: the collection of materials under a uniform system will be a suitable employment for our younger members. The want of such a catalogue has long been felt, not only by the students but by others. The school being open to the public, strangers may occasionally be seen, who, on entering, stare vacantly around, at a loss where to begin, apparently confused by the very heterogeneous arrangement of objects before them, and who, after a very short visit, depart neither improved nor gratified; whereas, with a proper arrangement and a cheap descriptive catalogue, an afternoon might be both profitably and amusingly passed by the artisan, tradesman, manufacturer, or artist.

The formation of a museum of ornamental art and other projects are so dependent on the extension of the accommodation provided by Government, that it would be premature to speak particularly of them; but that the attainment of them will be much accelerated by the exertions of this association is unquestionable. Only let each member do his best, let each freely impart the knowledge he possesses (and remember that there is nothing we learn so thoroughly as that we teach to others), and we shall see our association gaining strength and power, extending branches to the provincial schools, and rendering this school, as it should be, the best market for the manufacturer in want of designs—the shortest road to a knowledge of ornamental art in all its provinces, and a means of placing our nation above all others in art applied to manufactures, as it is now in every other branch of civilization.

AN EXAMPLE FOR THEIR "BETTERS."

REDCLIFFE CHURCH TOWER.

FOR some time past St. Mary Redcliffe Church, Bristol, has been kept open for visiters the whole day, free of any fee. A box is placed in a convenient position to receive donations towards the restoration from such as are disposed to aid a good work. There is also a book in which the donor may register the gift. A few weeks ago, three working men, wayfarers, examined the building in all its parts with evident delight, and on quitting left this entry in the subscription-book—"From three journeymen carpenters, on their way from London to Cork, seven shillings and six pence."

All honour to them for the good and right feeling which prompted the act, and may it serve as a stimulus to others!

The following report, which has appeared in the various Bristol papers, tells its own story:—

"To the Vicar, Churchwardens, and Vestry of the Parish of St. Mary Redcliff, Bristol.

"Gentlemen,—By direction of your churchwarden, I beg leave to report to you that my attention being directed to the condition of the spiret, or pinnacle, as it is more commonly called, of the south-east turret on the tower of the parish church, I carefully examined the same on Monday last, and found it to be in an imminently insecure and dangerous state.

"This applies not only to the spiret, with its finial, but to the upper part of the turret itself: the stones composing it are eroded and crushed, it is rent in various places, and appears to have settled over slightly towards the body of the church, while the finial and top of the spiret have fallen towards the spire.

The whole is in such a condition that, although it might remain as it now stands for some time, a high wind, the slightest discharge of the electric fluid, or the further failure of some of the stones, which might happen at any moment, could scarcely fail to precipitate it, for the most part on to the roof of the nave, and probably cause most serious damage to the inside of the church, and to the organ immediately below.

"It is with much reluctance that I recommend any step that will make more evident the ruin which is rapidly falling on this tower—a tower with scarcely its equal for beauty in the kingdom. The threatening state of the turret, however, forbids hesitation, and makes it my duty to advise that the upper portion of the spiret should be taken down, and the lower parts, at the foot, pinned up with cement, so as to render apparent any further movement.

"The other turrets are in a miserable state of disruption and decay, but do not seem to threaten immediate danger.—I have the honour to subscribe myself, gentlemen, your obedient servant,

"GEORGE GODWIN, Architect.

"Brompton, Middlesex, Feb. 14, 1849."

Part of the turret has since been taken down.

GALVANIZED IRON.

WE have before us a specimen of galvanized iron taken from a cistern which has been erected but two years. It is full of holes and utterly destroyed. We received, sometime since, from another quarter, a similar example of failure, but forbore from mentioning it. Remembering the high opinion of this material expressed by Professor Brande and others, and that it is now being very extensively used in lieu of lead and copper, it is desirable that the public should have the means of judging between that which will last and that which will not. One Company has addressed a letter to us, asserting that in their process no admixture of *tin* is used, and leading to the inference that it is where this second material is used that the result is unsatisfactory. What is wanted, however, is the guaranteed actual experience of disinterested parties, and this we shall be glad to receive.

SUGGESTIONS FOR STREET-ARCHITECTURE.

PLAN AND ELEVATION OF PORTA ST. PANCRAZIO, AT ROME, ALSO CALLED THE AURELIAN AND JANICULAN GATE.

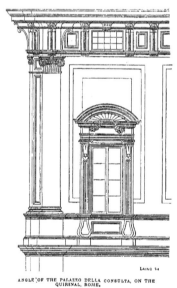

ANGLE OF THE PALAZZO DELLA CONSULTA, ON THE
QUIRINAL, ROME.

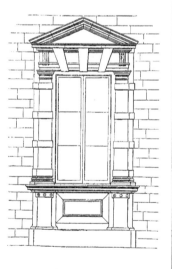

GROUND-FLOOR WINDOW OF A PALACE ON THE LUNGO
L'ARORO, AT PISA.

GREENSTED CHURCH, ESSEX, RESTORED.

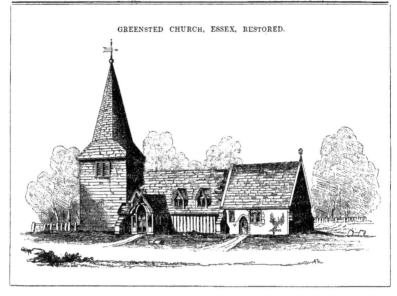

SUGGESTIONS FOR STREET-ARCHITECTURE.

PLAN AND ELEVATION OF PORTA ST. PAN-GRAZIO, AT ROME, ALSO CALLED THE AURELIAN AND JAMICULAN GATE.

This gate was built on the site of an older one, by Antonio de Rosái, about the middle of the seventeenth century.

ANGLE OF THE PALAZZO DELLA CON-SULTA, ON THE QUIRINAL, ROME.

This palace was built for Clement XIIth, by Fuga, about the year 1730. It stands on the most elevated ground in Rome, and forms one side of the square of Monte Cavallo. It is used for different public offices.

GROUND-FLOOR WINDOW OF A PALACE ON THE LUNGO L'ARCRO, AT PISA.

This palace was built by Michelangelo Buonarotti, and is also interesting as having been Lord Byron's residence during his stay in Pisa.

WOODEN CHURCH AT GREENSTED, ESSEX.

THE interest due to this little building arises from the material of which it is constructed, from its undoubted antiquity, and from the strong evidence that exists of its having been originally built as a place for the reception of the corpse of St. Edmund, which, on its return from London to Bury St. Edmund's, in the year 1013, was, as Lydgate, a monk of that monastery (St. Edmund's) informs us, conveyed in a chest or feretory.

St. Edmund began to reign in "East Anglia," A.D. 855. He was crowned the following year at Bury. He is supposed to have been killed in battle fifteen years afterwards.

Of the application of timber to the construction of sacred buildings, we have, in these early days, abundant evidence in many of the northern countries, as well as in England. "One very remarkable building of this kind is yet in existence in Norway; it is the church of Hitterdall, in Tellemark, erected about the twelfth century. It is reared of balks of fir, now hardened and blackened by time, and decorated with carvings of scales and lozenges." And with us, "There was a time," says the Venerable Bede, "when

there was not a stone church in all the land, but the custom was to build them all of wood." At York, the earliest cathedral was constructed of wood. The abbey church of Athelingey, built by the great Alfred, was built only of wood. And later still we find, "previously to the foundation of the present cathedral at Salisbury, in the thirteenth century, the first business of the monks was to erect and consecrate a wooden chapel for temporary use."

It is not then to be wondered at, that in a retired spot, for a purely temporary purpose, and in a county devoid of stone, wood should have been adopted as the material for a small structure, even of a very sacred kind. The inclosing walls of this building are apparently of oak, and not of chesnut, as has been supposed by some. They are about 6 feet high, including the cill and plate, and are formed of rough half trees, averaging about 12 inches by 6 inches (the greatest length on the base line being 18 inches by 9 inches, and the least 8 inches by 6 inches). Mr. Suckling does not believe them to have been "half trees," but that "they had a portion of the centre, or heart, cut out, probably to furnish beams for the construction of the roof and cills; the outsides or slabs thus left being placed on the cills." We see no evidence of this, for the timbers were evidently left rough, and the dimensions prove them to have been, as nearly as may be, "half trees." These uprights were laid on an oak cill, 8 inches by 8 inches, and tenoned into a groove 1½-inch deep, and secured with oak pins. The cill on the south side was laid on the actual earth; that on the north side had, in two places, some rough flints, without any mortar driven under. The roof plates averaged 7 inches by 7 inches, and had a groove corresponding with the cill, into which the uprights were tenoned and pinned. The plates were also of oak, but they and the cills were very roughly hewn, in some parts being 10 inches by 10 inches, and in others 6 inches by 6 inches or 7 inches.

There were twenty-five planks or uprights on the north side, and twenty-one on the south side. The uprights in the north side were the least decayed. Those on the south side required an average of 5 inches of rotten wood to be removed, those on the north about 1 inch only, and the heights of the uprights, as now

refixed, measuring between plate and cill, are, on the north side, 4 feet 8 inches, on the south side, 4 feet 4 inches, the cills being bedded on a few courses of brickwork in cement to keep them clear of damp. The uprights were tongued together at the junction with oak strips, and a most effectual means it proved of keeping out the wet; for although the interior was plastered, there was no evidence, in any part, of wet having driven in at the feather edge junction of the uprights,—a strange contrast to many of our modern churches, where, with all the adjuncts of stone and mortar, it is found no easy matter to keep out the driving weather from the south-west.

The roof was heavy, and without any particular character; it consisted of a tie-beam, at less than 6 feet from the floor, with struts. The covering was tile. The inside of the timbers were plastered, so that internally the character and interest of the construction was lost.

The seats were of all sorts of height and form, and, for so small a church, afforded some good specimens of the "cattle pen."

The church derived light from three dormer windows of most "domestic" appearance; and an open wooden porch, without any style or beauty, gave access to the church on the south side by means of a very low door.

The restoration, as our readers are aware, has been effected under the direction of Messrs. Wyatt and Brandon.

PROPOSED NEW WORKHOUSE FOR ST. MARGARET'S PARISH.—The Commissioners for Westminster Improvements have given notice to the parochial authorities of St. Margaret, Westminster, that in six months hence they shall require a wing of the present workhouse for the new Victoria-street, and the whole of it cleared away in two years. The question has, therefore, been raised, as to where the new workhouse shall be built, as it will be necessary to set about it immediately, to have it ready for the reception of the poor by the expiration of the period named. The estimated cost of a new workhouse is 20,000l. This parish is governed by a close vestry, and the course which will be adopted for obtaining the best design is looked for with some interest.

ON FIRE-PROOF BUILDINGS.

Mr. BRAIDWOOD, in his paper "On Fire-proof Buildings," read at the Institution of Civil Engineers, on the 27th ult., demonstrated, by a collection of specimens of metal from buildings that had been destroyed by fire, that occasionally the temperature in the conflagration of large buildings rose almost to the melting point of cast-iron, and that, even in a small fire, beams and columns of cast-iron would be so affected by the heat and the jets of water upon them, that they would probably be destroyed, and sometimes cause a fearful loss of life, as in many of the so-called fire-proof warehouses of the city: a number of persons employed on the premises slept in the upper floors, and, if the lower beams gave way, the whole would be dragged down suddenly; whereas timber beams resisted fire some time, and allowed time for the inmates to escape.

Another point which the author considered had not been sufficiently insisted on, was the derangement of the brickwork by the expansion of the iron beams at high temperature, and its sudden contraction on the application of cold water; and, also, from the mortar becoming pulverized by the excessive heat—instances of which have been known to occur.

The following were the principles on which Mr. Fairbairn had proposed to construct fire-proof buildings:—

1. The whole of the building to be composed of incombustible materials, such as iron, stone, or brick.

2. That every opening or crevice communicating with the external atmosphere be kept closed.

3. An isolated stone or iron staircase to be attached to every story, and to be furnished with a line of water-pipes communicating with the mains in the street.

4. The different warehouses to be divided by strong partition walls, and no more openings to be made than are absolutely necessary.

5. That the iron columns, beams, and brick arches be of a strength sufficient not only to support a continuous dead pressure, but also to resist the force of impact to which they are subject.

Lastly. That in order to prevent the columns from being melted, a current of cold air be introduced into the hollow of the columns from an arched tunnel under the floors.

Mr. Braidwood submitted that large buildings containing considerable quantities of combustible goods, and constructed on the usual system, were not practically fire-proof; and that the only construction which would render such buildings safe, would be groined brick arches, supported by pillars of the same material laid in cement. The author was also of opinion, that the loss by fire would be much reduced if warehouses were built of a more moderate size, and completely separated from each other by strong party-walls, instead of being constructed in immense ranges, into which, when fire had once penetrated, it set at defiance all efforts to extinguish it.

In the discussion which ensued, it was generally acknowledged that the principles upon which many buildings, particularly dwellings, were constructed, were very erroneous. It was argued, that even with the ordinary materials, if attention was paid to filling-in the partitions and ceilings, as practised in France, and mentioned in Professor Hosking's book on the regulation of buildings; using slate or stone for the stairs, as from its present cheapness might be done, taking care to support the steps properly, a fire would spread very slowly, and would allow ample time for the escape of the inhabitants.*

At the following meeting (Tuesday, March 6) the discussion was renewed, and extended to such a length as to preclude the reading of any paper.

It was remarked, that the consideration of what was the actual loss of strength of cast-iron, under different degrees of elevation of temperature, was of vital importance. It appeared, from the evidence of Fairbairn's and Hodgkinson's experiments, that there was very little difference of strength between iron, at a temperature below freezing point, and when raised to nearly 600 degrees Fahrenheit. When, however, cast-iron columns and beams were practically subjected to the draught, or current of air, of a tremendous fire, in an extensive warehouse filled with combustible goods, and at the same time receiving large quantities of water from the engines, they must fail, either by melting or crushing.

It appeared, that all the means of arresting fires generally failed, when there was a large area on fire, and that the only effective means of prevention would be, to have smaller and detached warehouses, or separating walls within the larger storehouses; but, inasmuch as this was a very expensive mode of building, and the land where warehouses were required was very costly, it became entirely a mercantile question, whether it was better to lay out a large capital in making a building perfectly fireproof, and providing such means as were in use in a mill at Oldham, for deluging the rooms, on an alarm of fire, or pay an insurance and incur a certain amount of risk.

It was shown, that the system of constructing mills containing machinery, with iron beams and brick arches, was as much for the purpose of avoiding the tremulous movement imparted by wooden beams and floors, as for avoiding the risk of fire; for such were the precautions and care in the mills, that very few were destroyed by fire. It was suggested, that bricks might be made expressly of the proper form to surround the slight iron columns used in buildings, and thus completely protect them from any injury from fire.

* We are surprised to find Mr. Hosking's book so much less known than it deserves to be.

MANUFACTURES AND DECORATIONS AT THE SOCIETY OF ARTS.

A LARGE number of persons assembled in the Society's rooms on Wednesday evening at the opening of the third annual exhibition of specimens of recent British manufacture and decorative art. Sir John Boileau took the chair, in the absence of the Duke of Buccleugh, who was expected, while the energetic secretary of the society, Mr. Scott Russell, read a report, congratulating the members on the important character of the present collection, and the progress of the society (it now numbers 569 subscribers), and entering into some particulars as to the award of prizes.

The exhibition is particularly rich in works in gold and silver, to which her Majesty, amongst others, has contributed.

At the suggestion of Prince Albert, prizes were offered for wood-carvings, executed by artisans who were not professional wood carvers, with the view of encouraging a home occupation. The result appears satisfactory as a commencement: the first prize was awarded to G. Cook, son of the gate-keeper, at Hyde-park-corner.

There is a collection of paper-hangings at which we may look when the room is less crowded.*

* We have received the following from a correspondent:—"At the exhibition of recent British manufactures and decorative art, at the house of the Society of Arts, there is a copy of the famous shield modelled by Pitts, and the catalogue states that a prize has been awarded to Messrs. Hunt and Roskill for the exhibition of this shield of Æneas. It would be interesting to the public to know on what ground this prize is awarded: is it for the excellence of the electro-type deposit, or simply for the exhibition of the work of another? I presume the latter,—as numerous wealthy manufacturers and dealers figure prominently in the list as exhibitors, while little is said or known of the artists whose works they parade. The wording of the catalogue with regard to this shield is so ambiguous, that many persons may suppose Pitts never completed the same; and it is desirable that the public should know that he did so. Pitts, after modelling this shield, executed a cast, finely finished, in plaster of Paris, and this cast was seen by many of the Royal Academicians and most members of the Graphic Society,—and, if my memory do not fail me, it was exhibited at Somerset House. After the completion of the plaster shield, he commenced the execution of a copy in silver, after the old manner of working silver—viz., by taking a cast, in pitch and resin, of one of the compartments of the shield, and laying over it a sheet of silver, and by pressure and hammering bringing the silver to the form of the pitchy model. The work was then finished by the punch and the graver, and such tools as are employed in silver-chasing. He had completed several of these plates, when, in a fit of bodily and mental anguish and despair, aggravated by poverty staring him in the face, he terminated his existence. He left behind him, besides this shield, another, called by him the shield of Hercules; and it would be curious to know what sum his poor widow and children received for these models; also what went with his beautiful group—the Pleiades adorning Night—and some other of his works. The shield of Æneas is the finest composition in the present exhibition: and it is melancholy to think that wealthy exhibitors are receiving a testimonial for the work, while the poor artist, whose poetical genius entered into the spirit of Virgil, and gave form to this grand work, lies forgotten in his grave." Δ.

ART-UNION OF LONDON.

IT will be remembered that the council o the Art-Union of London offered the sum o 100*l*. for an original bas-relief in plaster, on base of 24 inches by 8 inches high, to b afterwards engraved by the any-glyptograp process, for general distribution, to the sub scribers of the current year, in addition to th "Sabrina."

In reply to this advertisement, twenty-five bas-reliefs were sent in on the 1st inst., bearing the following titles:—

1. Slaughter of the Innocents.
2. The Entry into Jerusalem.
3. The Death of Juturna.
4. Greatheart's Conquest over Giant Maul.
5. A Grecian Harvest Festival.
6. Pilgrims to Jerusalem.
7. The Entrance of Richard II. and Bolingbroke into London.
8. Reception of Henry VIII. and Emperor Charles V. by Cardinal Wolsey.
9. The Death of Boadicea.
10. Hermione.
11. Comus offering the Cup to the Lady.
12. Suffer little Children to come unto me.
13. Christ entering Jerusalem riding on the Ass.
14. Orpheus.
15. The Lady rescued by her Brothers.
16. A Triumphal Procession.
17. Jubal.
18. The Fall of Satan.
19. St. Paul preaching.
20. Hope the alluring.
21. The Brothers rush in with drawn Swords (Comus).
22. The Beggar died, and was carried by the Angels into Abraham's Bosom.
23. Acteon.
24. Britannia Triumphant: and
25. (Unfinished) Train up a Child in the way he should go.

After examination, the council resolved that the prize of 100*l*. be adjudged to No. 13, as best adapted for the purpose advertised,—and opening the letter sent in with the device marked on No. 13, it was found to contain the name of John Hancock, 4, Brecknock Crescent, and 101, Stanhope-street, Mornington Crescent.

They afterwards decided that, in consequence of the merit of the bas-relief No. 9, overtures should be made to the artist for the purpose of purchasing it for the use of the society. This was found to be by Henry Hugh Armstead, of 37, Liquorpond-street.

The subscription-lists will close on the 31st.

TOPOGRAPHY OF JERUSALEM.

WHAT WAS MILLO?

IN the interesting description of Jerusalem given in your pages, the writer states that a "*deep valley, called Millo*, separated Acra from Moriah." This, I venture to observe, is a mistake, there being no authority whatever for the supposition that there was a *valley* or district of any kind within the walls of Jerusalem called by that name. Several old writers have entertained the opinion that the *causeway* formed in the valley between Mount Zion and Mount Moriah was the Millo in question, but the weight of authority, based on the evidence of Scripture, is in favour of another view of the subject.

The "House of Millo" is referred to (Judges ix. 6, 20; 2 Kings xii. 20). "He (Hezekiah) built up all the wall that was broken, and raised it up to the towers, and *repaired Millo in the city of David*, and made darts and shields in abundance," (2 Chronicles xxxii. 5). "So David dwelt in the fort, and called it the city of David, and David built round about from Millo and inward," (2 Samuel v. 9). "Solomon built Millo, and repaired the breaches of the city of David his father," (1 Kings ix. 24). These numerous instances in which Millo is referred to, and the express terms used in several of the passages to denote its locality, place it beyond doubt, first, that Millo was a *building*—one of distinction both as to position and destination, and secondly, that it stood within or in close proximity to, the bulwarks of the city of David. The expression, that David "built round about from Millo and inward," favours the supposition that the "house of Millo" was a building of note, that the work per formed was extensive, and that a great distance lay between the house of Millo and other distinguished buildings of the city, and that they were united by king David, as described in the foregoing text. * *

NOTES IN THE PROVINCES.

It is proposed to have St. Martin's Church, Salisbury, wholly repaired, at an estimated cost of 1,000*l*., of which nearly 600*l*. have been secured.——It is also proposed to restore the Poultry Cross at Salisbury.——The first stone of Cookley New Church, near Kidderminster, was recently laid by Mrs. William Hancocks, who means to present the chancel window. Mr. E. Smith, of Oldswinford, near Stourbridge, builder, is the contractor for the building, a design for which he also furnished. There is to be accommodation for 400, 147 of which will be free sittings.——The committee of the Welsh Educational Institution are about to erect a new college at Llandovery, from a design by Messrs. Fuller and Gingell, of Bristol. Tenders for the works will be called for shortly.——On the Birkenhead Dock-works, 160 men were lately set to work, and it was intended shortly to increase the corps to 500 or 600.——A project has been started for the erection of a temperance hall in Leicester. According to the *Journal*, it is to have two tiers of galleries, with seat-room for 1,665 persons, and a large reading-room, library, club-room, committee-rooms, kitchen, &c. The design, it is added, is in the hands of Mr. Flint, who estimates the cost at 300 guineas. ——On Tuesday week the foundation-stone of a church was laid at Shelf, between Halifax and Bradford. Messrs. Mallinson and Healey are the architects. Mr. John Hardy has given 500*l*. towards the building, and 2,500*l*. towards the endowment. The church will consist of a nave with aisles and a chancel. At the west end of the nave will be a bell-gable. The design is decorated, and similar to that now erecting at Bank Foot, also by the munificent aid of Mr. Hardy. The accommodation will be about 490, nearly all free. Cost of erection, including repair fund, about 1,800*l*.—— The Lords of Treasury have consented to the sale of a piece of corporation land at Doncaster to the Cemetery Company there for the new cemetery. The area is 7 a. 2 r. 13 p., and costs 500*l*., to be applied in payment of corporation debts.——The town council of Newcastle have resolved on the erection of a new street from Neville-street and Westgate-street to the Bigg-market, on condition that 10,500*l*. be sufficient to realize the project. ——Two rows of workmen's houses, ten in a row, with a foreman's 'mansion' as a terminus between them, all under the somewhat ambitious title of 'New Gateshead,' have been erected behind the ironworks of Messrs. Hawks, Crawshay, and Sons, of Gateshead, as residences for some of those in their employment. The lot, however, merits notice, according to the *Gateshead Observer*, who, speaking of the unity of the design, as a cross-breed between the Elizabethan and the Swiss, declares that the whole has quite a collegiate aspect.—May such classical precincts never be defiled by 'puddle,' 'pig,' or 'donkey,'—irony or not irony, all the same. Moreover, may they be illuminated with a never-ceasing shower of "sparks from the anvil," ever and anon elicited by some choice collegiate, with 'head and harigals' as clear as may their precincts ever then be.—The plan, when completed, will comprise half-a-dozen such erections, each apart from the rest, but all facing inwards on a verdant square. The architects are Messrs. J. and B. Green, of Newcastle, and the contractor (at least of the section already erected) is Mr. C. J. Pearson, of Gateshead. The whole design, so far as regards the improvement of the physical condition of their workmen, is, says our authority, quite characteristic of the firm at whose desire and expense it is being carried out; and we cordially re-echo the aspiration—Would it were characteristic of every other!——A correspondent, says the same paper, calls our attention to the accidents —frequently serious, sometimes fatal—which occur at the Sunderland docks, now in progress of construction, and suggests that some better provision is needed 'for such emergencies. The infirmary, says he, is nearly a mile distant from the dock, and an hour must elapse before surgical aid is rendered—perhaps 'too late.' A levy is made on the workmen by the contractors, to which, I believe, they contribute themselves; and all that is required is the provision of a properly furnished room at the docks, in which, if need be, a surgeon may render immediate assistance. Some better mode of conveyance to the infirmary might also be adopted. We are sure that the contractors will give a ready ear to such suggestions.——The town council of Edinburgh have agreed to apply to Government for leave to throw back the screen in front of the Register House, for 10 or more feet, so as to widen the carriage-way at the head of Leith-street, long a subject of complaint by the citizens.——Four sites, extending in all to about 150 acres, have been selected at different points adjacent to Glasgow, where it is proposed to form pleasure-grounds for the people, with bowling-greens, curling and skating ponds, archery grounds, promenades, garden-lots, &c., and also with buildings for in-door amusement and instruction.

METROPOLITAN COMMISSION OF SEWERS.

IMPORTANT QUESTION.

A GENERAL court was held on Thursday, the 1st instant, at the Sewers'-office, Greek-street; the Right Hon. the Earl of Carlisle in the chair.

A decree was received from the Lord Mayor of London, setting forth that, in compliance with the Act 11 & 12 Vict., four commissioners to represent the interests of the city of London at this court had been appointed—viz., Alderman Lawrence, Mr. Deputy Harrison, Mr. Deputy Peacock, and Mr. Norris.

The Closed-door Business of the Commission.—The Hon. F. Byng moved that the minutes of the general committee of the 22nd Feb. be read. These set forth that a motion had been made in that committee by Mr. Leslie, seconded by Mr. Byng, that it be recommended to the Court of Sewers not to adopt the report of the Bye-laws Committee, dated Feb. 9, on the ground of the illegality of the recommendations contained therein, as no authority to delegate the powers of the commission to committees is to be found in the commission itself, or in the general statutes on sewers; but that every facility was given in the 11 & 12 Vict. to the commission, as a court of record, to carry out most advantageously for the public (by making the public fully acquainted with all its proceedings) the objects for which the commission issued. That the proceedings of this court could be reviewed by the Court of Queen's Bench; that the appointment of committees was in violation of the statute, and that the time of the officers, which ought to be occupied in the various works in progress, was taken up in almost daily attendance upon some one or other of the special or sub-committees. This motion in the committee was negatived by a large majority.

The Earl of Carlisle wished to offer a few words on a point that occurred to his mind, without expressing any opinion on the main question involved in the resolutions that had been read, as to the manner of carrying on the business of this court. Whatever might be the expediency of that course, it was a question so material to the constitution and working of that court, he thought, if any doubt were entertained, that such doubt should be immediately cleared up; and therefore he suggested that a special case should be drawn up and submitted to the highest law officers of the crown.

Mr. Byng said the adoption of that course would not prevent him protesting against the illegality of what had been done already. He had before submitted a motion on the illegality of their proceedings, but how was that resolution met? Why, by the members of the Works' Committee passing certain resolutions; and therefore the attendance of himself and other commissioners was useless. Every proceeding of that commission should be made public, for, unless they carried the public with them, the public would be unrepresented, and their entire acts would be looked upon with suspicion; and, after all, what had these committees done? The time had been wasted, for they had done little or nothing, but employed the officers of the court to the neglect of their ordinary duties. He had no wish unnecessarily to detain the court, his former motion having been negatived, but he contended that all courts and committees should be open. Now, as to the constitution of the Works' Committee, it was most essential that it should comprise gentlemen of the greatest practical experience, several of whom were not to be found on this committee. There was, he believed, no authority whatever for standing committees. There might be special inquiries for special works—special committees and adjourned committees,—but the court, and the court alone, were qualified to judge of their necessity. There was no difficulty in the court carrying out great works, as they had been carried out by the court before. It was his opinion that all standing committees were illegal, especially constituted as they were of persons having no special knowledge of the work they had to superintend; and, as an instance, he might mention that he himself, without his knowledge or consent, had been placed on the finance committee, although he knew nothing of figures. As a member of the late Westminster commission, he had worked, and with Mr. Leslie, succeeded, in bringing it into that contempt it eventually received; but as a commissioner of the present, he was by no means satisfied to act under any other board, not even the Board of Health. He hoped he should receive credit for having given every degree of force in his power to that board, but he would not give up his powers as a commissioner to make a branch of that board, or to pay the expenses of it. He hoped to see this court well carried out for the benefit of the public, but he objected to any proceedings or works that were not known to the public, who might well become suspicious of a small body—and that body, too, appointed by the Crown—with immense powers to rate property to the amount of seven millions. If their deeds were good they ought to carry the full approbation of the public with them. He could not omit to notice that on an hon. commissioner opposite being spoken to on this subject (Mr. Chadwick), that gentleman thought that if he (Mr. Byng) was dissatisfied with the course adopted, the most gentlemanly way would be to retire from the commission, and a threat was implied that if commissioners obstructed—that is to say—if they created discussion, they would be superseded from the commission, and the names of other persons substituted; and the paid assistant secretary to the Board of Health, who was also a sewers' commissioner, was at the same time personally rude to him. During fifteen years he had been a commissioner, and during stormy times, yet he had never received such an affront in that room before. He again denounced these committees as an evasion of the law, and feeling the duty he owed to the public, he would not be implicated in their acts, or attend there to register the proceedings of a committee which he firmly believed to be illegal. The hon. gentleman concluded by moving that all courts and committees should be open.

Mr. Chadwick said there was a very great difference between the new and old commissions, when courts were held at long intervals, and the works were brought forward in a mob, and in a state that rendered it impossible that they could be properly considered; and proofs of it might be found in the works of the old commissioners, which were admitted to be a waste of the public money, even by the gentlemen opposite. He justified the subdivision of labour by committees, and this was proved by the operation of the Ordnance Survey Committee. A member of the House of Commons well acquainted with map-making, had said that the survey could not be executed and carried out in less than six years, and at an expense of 300,000*l*. However, notwithstanding the obstructions unnecessarily thrown in the way by members of the old commission now in the new commission, he believed the work would be got through in one year; and that works that would formerly have cost 10,000*l*. to 20,000*l*. would now be done better and more completely for 3,000*l*. or 4,000*l*. There was no doubt that the necessities of the public now required different means of improvement to those carried on by the hon. gentleman and his colleagues in the old commission, and had it not been for the violent obstruction to the subject of house drainage by members of the old commission—

The Earl of Carlisle objected to the use of the word "obstruction;" every commissioner had a right to express his opinion.

Mr. Chadwick resumed, and justified the subdivision of labour, for by it the wants of three districts would be met by the same expense that gentlemen opposite did not, three years ago, think out of the way for one. He was opposed to open committees, as it would be impracticable to carry on the business of experiment if every body was allowed to be present. He then reviewed the works of improvement, and the saving effected in the works performed, and maintained it was in open vestries and open courts that "jobs" were more easily perpetrated.

Mr. Leslie said he knew nothing of old or new commissioners. He was there as a commissioner under the Act 11 and 12 Vict., as a trustee for the public, and to do his best for the public interest, and that he would do; and he could not let the present opportunity pass without one or two observations on what had fallen from the commissioner opposite (Mr. Chadwick), which should be of the most friendly character. Mr. Chadwick thought the business of the commission best done by committees, and upon this point he (Mr. Leslie) took issue after thirteen years' experience. When he entered the Westminster commission he found enormous sized sewers, and he took great trouble to get the adoption of the egg-shaped sewers, and obtained the opinion of Sir Charles Pasley and other scientific as well as practical men concurring in his opinion, and they were ultimately adopted. The hon. commissioner had spoken of the great difficulty experienced through the opposition to house drainage. Why, the report had been about thirteen months, and they had never had a discussion. The report was full of error, and wrong in principle. He then referred to various points in it, which were all debatable questions, and ought to be brought into the court and discussed. He thought the public ought to be made acquainted with every thing that took place. The time of the officers, too, was completely taken up by these committees, instead of their being out and engaged in works of drainage; and at the last Finance Committee Mr. Lovick had stated that it was quite impossible that he could attend to his duties, for every day in the week he was in attendance on committees. He found eighty-five pages taken up with the minutes of these committees for a week. What were the commissioners to know of this "mob" of business, some of which involved engagements with a company which was not authorised by law, and involved a principle never discussed in that court? If the law officers of the Crown gave their opinion that under the 23rd section they could appoint committees, special committees, and sub-committees, there would be an end of the matter; but although they had lost their motion, yet in fact they had carried it, for the committee had passed a resolution to suspend their works, and that all commissioners might be present at committees.

A Commissioner said they might be present, but were not allowed to speak or vote.

Mr. Leslie—At any rate we have got the wedge in. He concluded by supporting Mr. Byng's resolution.

After a few words from Lord Ebrington, Sir H. de la Beche, and Mr. Lawes, the noble Chairman's suggestion was adopted, that the solicitor to the Court do prepare a special case, to be submitted to the law officers of the Crown, for their opinion as to the legality of transacting the business of the commission by committees.

The Metropolitan Sewage Manure Company.—A long discussion ensued on the following resolution:—"Resolved—Pursuant to the recommendation of the Works Committee, the court do allow 1,500 feet of pipe to be put down to connect the sewer at Walham-green with the sewer at Stamford Villas, Fulham-road, at an estimated expense of 437*l*., the Metropolitan Sewage Manure Company being allowed to divert the sewage to their works for one year, the company paying rent of 8 per cent. thereon for the year."

Mr. Leslie opposed the motion as illegal, and this view was taken by some of the shareholders themselves, and a protest has been liberally circulated as to the illegality of the proceedings of the company.

The motion, however, was eventually agreed to. Several orders for works were agreed to, and the court adjourned.

Miscellanea.

THE ATTACK ON THE OFFICE OF WOODS.—The suppositions that we offered last week, in reply to the attacks made by contemporaries on the office of Woods, prove to be correct, especially as regards the two "lucky architects," Nash and Burton. At the moment that our last number, shewing what was *probably* the real state of the case, was at press, Lord Carlisle, in the House of Peers, was stating *positively* that our explanation was correct. The small rent, too, paid by certain members of the aristocracy for land in the Green-park is stated to be not for the land on which their houses stand, but for certain small pieces of pleasure-ground adjoining.

THE ALBION PLATE GLASS COMPAY.—A meeting of the shareholders of this incipient incorporation was held at the offices, Railway-place, Fenchurch-street, City, on 27th ult., when office-bearers were elected, and a resolution to hasten the complete establishment of the company unanimously passed, on the ground that a great necessity exists for a further extension of the manufacture of plate glass. The manager, Mr. H. Howard, is said to have made considerable improvements for cheapening the manufacture, about to be patented. In the report read to the meeting, a comparison of British and foreign tenders for certain specific quantities of plate glass was made, and the amounts quoted as follows:—

	Foreign houses.	English houses.
For glazing purposes..	£277 19 2	£190 0 0
For silvering purposes	119 19 8	108 15 10

These prices of the English manufacturer, it was said, afford a large profit—averaging about 1s. per foot, so that it was believed foreign competition is now virtually excluded from the English market.

PROJECTED WORKS.—Advertisements have been issued for tenders, by 21st inst., for the erection of a new church at Mansfield, Nottingham; by 27th, for alterations and additions to Hampstead workhouse; by April 2nd, for rebuilding a house and offices (chiefly with old materials) at Petham, near Canterbury; by 3rd, for the erection of a borough prison at Devonport; by 12th inst., for the construction of a pipe sewer of glazed stoneware, from the sewer at Walham-green to the sewer at Stamford Villas, Fulham; by 13th, for the construction of sewers in Tudor-street, Dorset-street, Primrose-hill, and elsewhere; by 26th, for the erection of the National, Industrial, and Infant Schools at Henley-on-Thames, Oxon; by 21st, for the erection of St. Edmund's Church, Northampton; by 17th, for finishing four houses in Richmond-road, Westbourne-grove, Paddington; by 14th, (extension of time) for the erection of the Printers' Almshouses; by 13th, for the erection of a school-house at Montpelier; by 15th, for the necessary works in the erection and completion of butchers' and fish markets at Worcester; by 24th, for the erection of a police station and strong rooms at Witham; by a date not specified, for the erection of a stone bridge near Airdrie, and for making a road there; also for constructing a road at Birmingham-heath; by 13th, for repairing, paving, &c., footways and carriageways at Cambridge (separate contracts); by 20th, for 4,000 tons of railway chairs, for the Great Northern Railway; by 12th, for laying nine miles of water-pipes at Boston; and by 26th, for laying 25 miles of lead-jointed iron pipes for Derby water-works.

COMPETITION.—Plans are required for the erection of a corn exchange and other buildings in the town of Northampton, at an outlay not exceeding 8,000*l*.

A FLOATING CHURCH.—The *English Churchman* gives a description, accompanied by an engraving, of an ecclesiastical edifice which is, as yet, we believe, without a parallel,—a real church afloat, a new Gothic structure with tower and spire, belfry and bell, and capahle of accommodating 550 worshippers. Its seats are all free. Built, of course, of wood, it is painted to represent brown stone: from the deck to the ball on the spire is 80 feet in height—its dimensions are 86 feet by 34 feet, with a passage all round it. The whole rests on two boats of 90 tons burden. It was constructed at New Jersey, for the Churchmen's Missionary Association, and is to be moored at a wharf in Philadelphia, for the especial use of sailors and boatmen.

MASONS' PROVIDENT INSTITUTION.—The third annual meeting of the above institution was held on Tuesday evening, March 6, at the City of Westminster Literary Institution; Mr. William Freeman, Treasurer, in the chair. The report of the committee and auditors for the past year shewed the balance in the hands of the institution to be 244*l*. 19s. 2d., including the purchase of stock 3 per cent. consols to the amount of 250*l*. 4s. 9d.; and although not so gratifying as might have been anticipated, in consequence of the great depression of trade, congratulated the members upon the steady progress of the society. A resolution upon the choice of a president, in the room of the late Mr. Alderman John Johnson, will be found in our advertising columns.

LONDON IMPROVEMENTS.—Do, pray, direct public attention to the necessity of opening up Picket-place into Lincoln's-Inn-square, and pulling down all the houses which are now in the courts and alleys near it. The whole of that part north of the Strand is perfectly disgusting, and inhabited by people of the worst description. If a handsome street were built as a continuation of the present Picket-place to Lincoln's-Inn-square, the houses would let at high rents as chambers, and the ground floors might be occupied as shops.—R. P.

APPROPRIATION OF RAILWAY ARCHES.—We peceive that the suggestion made in THE BUILDER, for the conversion of railway arches for the houseless poor, is proposed to be carried out by an association under the title of "The Samaritan Society of England," but in their prospectus we do not see any reference whatever to the quarter whence the suggestion originated on which the scheme of benevolence is founded.

ST. SAVIOUR'S, SOUTHWARK.—A correspondent says, relative to a *restoration* here "The south transept has a pinnacle at each corner surmounting the buttress, one of which it had become necessary to repair; this feat has been accomplished by about one-third being sliced off, and a flat stone with projecting edge being placed on it, giving it the appearance of a jelly glass turned topsy-turvy, or a flat-bottomed extinguisher." On examination, we find the statement correct, but can scarcely suppose that the step in question is any thing more than a temporary measure. The condition of this church, in other respects, is a sad disgrace to the parish.

GEOMETRICAL PROPORTION.—At the conversational meeting of the York Philosophical Society, on the 26th February, Mr. Fowler Jones, architect, read a paper on the geometrical proportion of Gothic architecture, as introduced by Mr. Griffith in his work on that subject; and showed by examples in proof of alternating squares, triangles, and hexagon, being the framework on which the plans and sections were constructed, that there was no doubt of the application of the system in the plan of York Minster, St. Mary's Abbey, York, the chancel of Howden Church, Selby ditto, Skelton, and various others.

THE SMITHFIELD NUISANCE.—An attempt of Mr. J. T. Norris, in the City Court of Common Council, to have a special committee appointed to provide a more suitable site for the market, was met by "the previous question," and by a deal of speechifying, *con.* much more than *pro*, on the delivery of which the question was put, and the motion negatived without a division.

A BOWLING SALOON, on the American principle, has been recently got up at Liverpool, in a very showy style, it appears, and with five bowling alleys, and, of course, 'a commodious bar,' and suitable lounges and refreshment-rooms, &c. "The entrance," says a Liverpool paper, "consists of a vestibule, enriched with windows of stained glass, and profusely decorated with ornaments in white and gold, and communicates with the interior by handsome folding-doors. The internal appearance on entering is extremely handsome and striking, the walls being divided into compartments, in each of which is a landscape, drawn in a masterly style, by an artist of celebrity, and ornaments of *papier mâché* and gutta percha gilded are introduced in abundance, and with great skill and effect. The bowling-alleys have circular projections at the ends surmounted by statues. The saloon is fitted up in the richest style of splendour." The whole concern was designed and executed by Messrs. Furness and Kilpin.

BLIND BUILDERS.—EWELL CHURCH.—The following tenders, says a correspondent, were delivered for works required to be done in pulling down the old parish church at Ewell, and for alterations and additions to the tower, to form the same into a burial chapel, and for building boundary walls round the new churchyard: Mr. Hy. Clutton, architect.

Haynes, Ewell............	£329 15 1
Stone, ditto	277 18 0
Hards, ditto	122 4 6

Old materials remaining to be the property of the contractor.

TO OUR READERS.

IT has been suggested to us at various times that some of the best architectural subjects given in THE BUILDER, if printed in a superior manner on good paper, with the accompanying descriptions, plans, &c., and issued periodically, would form a work that would be acceptable not only to those who are not buyers of THE BUILDER, but to many who are,—the current engravings being often creased by the newsvendors, or otherwise injured. We are disposed to try the experiment, and to publish, in a neat wrapper, under the title, "BUILDINGS AND MONUMENTS, MODERN AND MEDIÆVAL," about Eight Plates, with eight pages of letter-press, folio size, every second month, price half-a-crown. The first part would consist of Osborne House, with plan; Bridgewater House, plan and details; Church of St. Isaac, Petersburgh; Kensington Union Workhouse; Pembroke College, Oxford; the Liverpool Branch Bank; and the north porch of St. Mary Redcliffe, Bristol. Before determining upon the scheme, however, we should be glad to receive the names of such gentlemen as would be willing to become subscribers to the work.

TENDERS

For alterations at 17, Cheapside; Mr. J. Tillott, architect.

Piper	£5,776
Locke and Nesham	5,592
Lindsey	5,496
Ashby	5,311
Lawrence	5,257
Haward and Nixon	5,147
Hicks	5,051
T. Burton	4,973
Brass and Son	4,820
Grimsdell	4,681

MEETINGS OF SCIENTIFIC BODIES

Held during the ensuing week.

TUESDAY, March 13.—Instit. of Civil Engineers, 8 P.M.

WEDNESDAY, 14.—Society of Arts, 8 P.M.; Graphic Society, 8 P.M.

THURSDAY, 15.—Royal Society, 8½ P.M.; Society of Antiquaries, 8 P.M.

SATURDAY, 17th.—Institute of Fine Arts, 8 P.M.

TO CORRESPONDENTS.

Received.—"T. N., jun.," "Messrs. R. and Co.," "O. H.," "C. F. D." (thanks and good wishes), "J. J. P.," "Tartan," "W. H.," "J. G.," "C. H. S." (next week), "J. M.," "G. E. S." (the application will be attended to), "G. F. J.," "R. S.," "W. T.," "W. B.," "R. S. W." (we will inquire as to numbers), "Subscriber," Guildford (the inconvenience cannot be avoided), "H. W." (the Editor is waiting to visit the spot), "A. G.," "J. K." (sugar is scarcely within our range), "Amicus" (the work in question has been favourably noticed by us), "J. T.," "J. L. S." (Nos. 252, 253, 254, 255, and 259 may be had; 256 is out of print). "A Competitor," "E. W.," "C. J. G.," "W. H.," "S. H.," "Cockney," "J. K.," "Messrs. S. and S.," "J. O.," "H. B.," "Plumb Bob" (the building in question is *not* "insulated"), "Constant Reader" (few architects would refuse to give the particulars; the *power* to refuse depends on wording of the contract). "Drainage of Lands, and the Sewerage of Towns: a Paper on Relief Mapping," by J. Bailey Denton (London, Weale—1849); "The Weekly and Monthly Orthodox," Part II. (Andrews, Little Britain); "Parish Churches, accompanied by Plans drawn to uniform Scale," by R. and J. A. Brandon, Architects (London, G. Bell).

"*Books, Prices, and Addresses.*"—We have not time to point out books or find addresses.

NOTICE.—All communications respecting *advertisements* should be addressed to the "Publisher," and not to the "Editor:" all other communications should be addressed to the EDITOR, and *not* to the publisher.

ADVERTISEMENTS.

MARKET WHARF, REGENT'S-PARK BASIN.—Messrs. MARTIN and WOOD (late Scoles and Martin) solicit the attention of Builders, Masons, and others, to their stock of Portland, York, and Derby Stone; also Bangor Slates, Lime, Cement, Plaster, Bricks, Tiles, Laths, Fire-goods, Firestone, &c., sold at the lowest possible prices for Cash. Portland Headstones, Ledgers, Steps, Landings, &c., cut to order on the shortest notice. Tarpaulings let on hire. A Stock of Northen's Drain Pipes, Syphons, &c., always on hand. Mortar, Lime and Hair, Fine Stuff, &c.

WHITE SUFFOLK and RED FACING BRICKS, of superior quality. Moulded Bricks to any pattern.—Apply to Mr. BENJAMIN GOUGH, 37, Newington-crescent, Newington-butts.

N.B. Cowley and Kent Bricks of every description, and Kentish Rag Stone direct from the Quarries.

BRICK MANUFACTURERS desirous of obtaining, by the ensuing season (the desideratum), MACHINES for making cheap and perfect BRICKS, are invited to the inspection of a recently patented PORTABLE BRICK MACHINE, to be seen in action daily, between the hours of Ten and Four, at 41, Bermondsey-square, Grange-road, Southwark.

BRICKS.—Superior White and Red Facing Bricks, Hard Stable, Paviours, &c. &c., may be had at W. and S. WRIGHT'S Brick and Tile Works, Hanwell, Middlesex. Moulded Bricks and Tiles to any pattern on liberal terms. The above works adjoin the Grand Junction Canal and Great Western Railway, from whence goods may be conveyed to town and country at a trifling expense. Where large quantities are wanted for public works, mansions, &c., W. and S. W. will contract to make them on the spot.

FIRE BRICKS.—To Builders, Gas Companies, Engineers, &c. &c. WARD and CO., Honduras Wharf, Bankside, have now on hand an extensive and well-selected Stock of every description of Fire Bricks, Lumps, Tiles, Clays, &c., used in Gas Works, Coke Ovens, Furnaces, Kilns, &c., which they are offering on very liberal terms to consumers, and the trade in general; also, Malm Paviors, Stock Bricks, Patent Malting Tiles, Pan, Plain and Ridge Do., Windsor and other Oven Tiles, Sand, Gravel, Lime, Cement, Windsor and other Loams, Red and White House Sand, Dutch Clinkers, Sanitary Pipes, and every article connected with general Building. Goods made to pattern on the shortest notice. Country buyers and consumers will find this the best and cheapest market.

MOUNTED DRAWING PAPER.—HENRY POPE has in stock Drawing Paper, which has been mounted on Linen for TWO YEARS and UPWARDS, in various lengths, of 4 ft. 9 in., 3 ft. 3 in., and 1 ft. 4 in. wide. Tracing Papers, Drawing and Writing ditto, Envelopes, and every description of Stationery at wholesale prices. Publisher of Weaver's "Hints on Cottage Architecture," with Plans, Elevations, and Estimates, imperial 4to., cloth, 25s.—22, Budge-row, Watling-street.

JORDAN'S PATENT MACHINE CARVING and MOULDING WORKS for WOOD and STONE, Belvedere-road, Lambeth, and 154, Strand.—TAYLOR, WILLIAMS, and JORDAN beg to call the attention of the building community to a new feature of their establishment, and, at the same time, to thank their numerous patrons and friends for the very liberal support they have lately experienced, which, they assure them and the public, it will be their constant endeavour to deserve, by giving their customers an increasing share of the advantages arising from the constant improvements in the machinery which they have just succeeded in applying to the production of the most intricate carving in Caen and other freestones, and in statuary marble.

T., W., and J. particularly solicit the attention of architects and builders to the fact that, by the use of this machinery, a very large saving, both of time and money, is effected,—so great, indeed, that in many cases they can deliver a well-finished article in Caen stone for less money than it can be obtained in cement, while their wood-carving will, in some cases, be found to come into close competition with the best kinds of composition ornament.—For prices and estimates apply at 154, Strand.

TESTIMONIAL FROM CHARLES BARRY, ESQ.

"Westminster, May 16th, 1848.

"Gentlemen,—In reply to your letter requesting my opinion of your Patent Carving Machinery, I have much pleasure in stating, from an experience of more than two years, in its application to the production of the wood carvings of the House of Peers, and other apartments of the New Palace, at Westminster, that I am enabled to make the most favourable report concerning it, and to add that it has more than justified the favourable terms in which I recommended it in 1845 to her Majesty's Commissioners of Woods and Works for adoption.—I remain, Gentlemen, yours faithfully,

"CHARLES BARRY."

"Messrs. Taylor, Williams, and Jordan."

REDUCED PRICES.—WILLIAM CLEAVE, of Wilton-road, Pimlico Basin, begs to acquaint Builders and the Trade that he has now on hand, at his Manufactory (the first of its kind ever established), a very large Assortment of Dry and Well-seasoned OAK AND DEAL PREPARED FLOORING BOARDS and MATCH BOARDING of all sorts, from 1 inch to 1½ inch thick, planed to a parallel width and thickness, and at greatly Reduced Prices. Also, Timber, Deals, Oak Planks, Scantlings, Sash Sills, Mouldings prepared by Machinery, Laths, &c.

Apply at W. CLEAVE'S Flooring Manufactory and Timber Yard, Wilton-road, Pimlico Basin, late C. MOORE and SON.

A REDUCTION in the PRICE of FLOOR BOARDS.—ALFRED ROSLING begs to inform the Trade and Consumers generally, that he has REDUCED the PRICE, and keeps constantly in stock a large and very general assortment of Prepared Floor Boards and Matched Boarding, planed to a parallel breadth and thickness, and fit for immediate use; also a variety of machine-prepared Mouldings, which are finished with great accuracy and attention to quality of workmanship.—Southwark Bridge Wharf, Bankside, and Old Barge Wharf, Upper Ground-street, Blackfriars.

GREAT REDUCTION IN THE PRICE OF FLOOR BOARDS AND MATCH BOARDING.—THOMAS ADAMS (late S. Darel), Mahogany and Timber Merchant, Bermondsey New-road, Southwark, near the Bricklayers' Arms, begs to inform his friends and the trade generally, that he has in stock a large assortment of the above goods, fit for immediate use, at prices which only require a trial to prove their decided cheapness. Also mouldings prepared by machinery from the very best material, and in a superior manner; cut deals and scantling of every dimension; mahogany, cedar, rosewood, wainscot, elm, beech, oak, &c., in planks, boards, veneers, and logs; pantile, oak, and fir laths; wheelwrights' goods. All sawn and prepared goods (except timber) delivered free of expense; sawing charged at mill prices. Very extensive drying sheds.

MUIR'S PATENT PLANING MACHINE.

SAW MILLS, GILLINGHAM-STREET, PIMLICO.

TIMBER of any size, PLANK, DEALS, and BATTENS, &c., Sawn on the most approved principle. Boards, &c., Prepared, Matched, and Grooved, by Muir's Patent Machinery. The Mills have all the advantages of navigation and water-carriage, being connected with the Thames by the Grosvenor Canal. Goods fetched from the docks and carted home free of charge.

Address to HENRY SOUTHAM,
Saw Mills, Gillingham-street, Pimlico.

N.B. Estimates given for Sawing and Planing.

GENERAL WOOD-CUTTING COMPANY.—SAWING, PLANING, AND MOULDING MILLS, Belvedere-road, Lambeth, between the Suspension and Waterloo Bridges. SAWING and PLANING in all their branches executed with the greatest despatch and punctuality. A large Stock of seasoned and beautifully WORKED MOULDINGS, consisting of upwards of 100 different patterns kept constantly on hand; also an extensive assortment of dry prepared FLOORING BOARDS, of all qualities and at reasonable rates.

MARBLE and WOOD SAWING MILLS, Commercial-road, Pimlico, London.—DRY RIGA WAINSCOT.—Buyers of well-seasoned Wainscot have the choice of selecting from the largest stock in London, cut from three to four years, in thicknesses from ½-inch and upwards. FLOOR BOARDS: all kinds in general use, of the same age. A large stock of MARBLE and STONE, in block and slab, for Shops, Head-stones, Balcony-landings, Chimney-pieces, &c. Country consumers will find this Wharf equal to any in London, for quantity, quality, and price.—Apply on the Premises, to J. HOLME, Agent.

WOOD THOROUGHLY SEASONED in DAYS instead of YEARS, by DAVISON and SYMINGTON'S PATENTED PROCESS, at the Patent Desiccating Company's Establishment (for Seasoning, Sawing, and Planing Wood), at the Grand Surrey Mills, immediately adjoining the Commercial and East Country Docks, Rotherhithe. The new process ensures the entire removal of moisture, hardens the gums, prevents further shrinkage, and strengthens the fibre.—For scale of prices, or license to work the patent, or any further information, address, post-paid, or apply to

ANGUS JENNINGS, Secretary.

The Patent Desiccating Company's Offices are REMOVED from 28, New Broad-street to No. 40, GRACECHURCH-STREET, CITY.

The Company's Agents are—Mr. WM. LANE, Irwell-buildings, Manchester; Mr. THOS. MILLIE, Kirkaldy; Messrs. RANDOLPH, ELLIOT, and Co., Glasgow; Messrs. CLIFFORD and BROWN, Hull.

By Her Majesty's Royal Letters Patent.

PITT'S PATENT SELF-ADJUSTING DOOR KNOBS AND LOOSE SPINDLES.

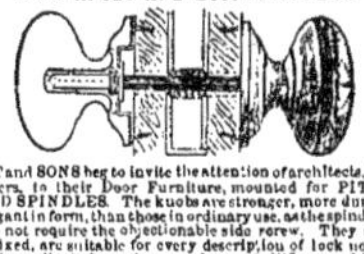

HART and SONS beg to invite the attention of architects, builders, and others, to their Door Furniture, mounted for PITT'S PATENTED SPINDLES. The knobs are stronger, more durable, and more elegant in form, than those in ordinary use, as the spindles, being loose, do not require the objectionable side screw. They are more readily fixed, are suitable for every description of lock now in use, and, as they adjust themselves to doors of different thicknesses, without alteration, are particularly adapted for the country or for exportation. They are made (to suit every style of decoration) in China, crystal, amber, and opal glass, buffalo, horn, ivory, ebony, brass, &c., en suite with finger-plates, bell-pulls, levers, &c.—May be obtained of all Ironmongers; or of the proprietors and sole manufacturers, HART and SONS, Wholesale Ironmongers, 53, 54, and 55, Wych-street, Strand, London.

N.B. PITT'S PATENTED SPINDLE, being the only one that does not require a screw in the side of the knob or mounting, the use of any lock furniture without such side screws would be an infringement of the patent.

PATENT CORRUGATED GIRDERS, ROOFS, DOORS, &c., either Galvanized or Painted.—WALKERS and HOLLAND (late Richard Walker), the patentees of the above, having noticed in some publication the announcement of a patent having been obtained for Wrought-iron Girders, Fire-proof Ceilings and Columns, distinctly assert that they have manufactured and erected the above articles some years past, and are therefore prepared to execute any kind of work where corrugated iron may be introduced, and at such prices as will insure the continued patronage of all parties concerned.—Plans and every information may be had on application at 121, Leadenhall-street, and the Works, Grange-road, Bermondsey.

IRON FOUNDRY, 80, Coswell-street (late of Brick-lane, St. Luke's).—J. J. JONES having made great additions to his STOCK of PATTERNS, begs to inform the Trade, that he can now supply them with Plain and Ornamental Iron Columns, Girders, Railings, Gates, Iron Coping, Balconies, Window Guards, Verandahs, Ornamental Staircase Panels, Iron Staircases, Tomb Enclosures, Trellis Panelling, Lamp and other Brackets, Cantilevers, Newel Bars, Water Closet Work, Area Gratings, Fly and other Wheels, Wheel Plates, &c.

BAKER'S OVEN WORK, Forge Backs and Troughs, Rain Water Pipes and Gutters, Sash Weights, Furnace Bars, Stoves, Ranges, &c., always in stock.

GAS-FITTINGS, LAMPS, and CHANDELIERS.—THOMAS LEDGER, 173, Aldersgate-street, London (two doors from Little Britain), Brass-founder, Gas-fitter, and Manufacturer of Chandeliers, Lamps, and every description of Gas-fittings. Estimates furnished, and experienced workmen sent to any part of town or country. Builders and the Trade supplied.—Warehouse and Show-rooms, 173, Aldersgate-street; Workshops and Foundry, 152, Aldersgate-street.

BUILDERS and CARPENTERS' IRONMONGERY WAREHOUSE, 18, Blandford-street, Manchester-square, leading out of Baker-street, Portman-square. Lists of prices may be obtained on pre-paid application.

JOHN and EDWIN YOUNG, Proprietors.

TO THE OWNERS OF SAW MILLS, PLANTATIONS and Collieries; to Builders, Millwrights, Engineers, &c.

IMPROVED CIRCULAR SAWS, Upright Saws, for timber and deal frames; Patent Tempered Machine Plane Irons, saw files, improved engineers' files; Patent Tempered Machine Knives, and cutters of all descriptions, made on the most scientific and economical principles, with dispatch, by BLAKE and PARKIN, the Meadow Steel Works, Sheffield.

LAP WELDED IRON TUBES.—W. H. RICHARDSON, Jun., and Co., MANUFACTURERS of every description of WROUGHT IRON TUBES for Locomotive and Marine Boilers, Gas, Steam, and other purposes.

PATENT TUBE WORKS, DARLASTON, STAFFORDSHIRE.

HOT-WATER APPARATUS.—The attention of architects, builders, and others is respectfully requested to BENJAMIN FOWLER'S superior method of heating churches and chapels, halls, staircases, conservatories, forcing and greenhouses, manufactories and warehouses, kilns, rooms for drying timber, &c. and every variety of purpose for which artificial heat is required. Within the last twenty years some hundreds of buildings have been heated upon this plan, and the parties for whom they were executed are constantly expressing their satisfaction, also their willingness to vouch for their efficiency. An improved wrought-iron boiler, which requires no brickwork, may be seen in action upon the premises.—BENJAMIN FOWLER, 63, Dorset-street, Fleet-street.

TO ARCHITECTS, BUILDERS, &c.

HAYWARD, BROTHERS, late R. HENLY and Co., WHOLESALE IRONMONGERS, and Manufacturers of KITCHEN-RANGES, STOVES, &c., 196, Blackfriars-road, and 117, Union-street, Borough.

Strong Self-acting Kitchen Ranges, with Back Boiler and Oven and Wrought Bars:—

3 ft.	3 ft. 3 in.	3 ft. 6 in.	3 ft. 9 in.	4 ft.
£3.	£3. 10s.	£3. 10s.	£4.	£4. 10s.

Henly's Patent Improved, with back Boiler and Wrought Iron Oven:—

3 ft.	3 ft. 3 in.	3 ft. 6 in.	3 ft. 9 in.	4 ft.
£5.	£5. 15s.	£6. 5s.	£6. 10s.	£7.

Best Register Stoves, at 7d., 8d., and 9d. per inch.
Do. Elliptic do., at 3½d. and 4d. do.

Manufacturer of WOLFASTON'S PATENT REGISTER STOVES, a certain cure for SMOKY CHIMNEYS, and effecting a great saving in fuel. To be seen in use daily.

Orders from the Country, accompanied with a remittance or reference, will meet with prompt attention.

TO BUILDERS and CARPENTERS.—Elliptic Stoves, double backs, 3d. per inch. Registers, 6½d. 7d., 8d. per inch.

Cottage Ranges, with Ovens and Boilers, 3 ft. 2 in. 40s.; 3 ft. 4 in. 42s.; 3 ft. 6 in., 44s.

Self-acting Ranges, with Circular Oven and Back Boiler, best Wrought Bars and Bright Fittings,
3 ft., £2. 18s. 3 ft. 6, £3. 7s. 4 ft., £3. 16s.

Best Patent Cut Clasp.

5d.	6d.	8d.	11d.	1s. 4d.	1s. 10d. per 1,000
3d.	4d.	6d.	8d.	10d.	20d.

Best Sheet Floor Brads 13s. 6d. per cwt.
Best Town Glue 38s. Do. Scotch, 52s. per cwt.

Best Patent Sash Line.

4s. 3d.	5s.	5s. 6d.	7s. 6d.	10s.	12s. per gross.
1	2	3	4	5	8

At F. R. WILLIAMSON'S IRONMONGERY and STOVE WAREHOUSE, 35, Chiswell-street, Finsbury-square.

Lists of Prices had on application at the Warehouse, or by letter pre-paid, inclosing postage stamp.—Warehouse closes at 7 o'clock.

CHUBBS' LOCKS, FIRE-PROOF SAFES, AND CASH BOXES.

CHUBBS' PATENT DETECTOR LOCKS give perfect security from false keys and picklocks, and also detect any attempt to open them. They are made of all sizes, and for every purpose to which locks are applied, and are strong, secure, simple, and durable.

CHUBBS' PATENT LATCH, for front doors, counting-house doors, &c., is simple in construction, low in price, and quite secure. The keys are particularly neat and portable.

CHUBBS' PATENT FIRE-PROOF SAFES, BOOKCASES, CHESTS, &c., made entirely of strong wrought-iron, so as effectually to resist the falling of brick-work, timber, &c., in case of fire, and are also perfectly secure from the attacks of the most skilful burglars.

CHUBBS' CASH and DEED BOXES, fitted with the Detector Locks.

CHUBB and SON, 57, St. Paul's Churchyard, London.

UNSUCCESSFUL ATTEMPT to OPEN A CHUBB'S FIREPROOF SAFE.

From the "Stamford Mercury," 19th January, 1849.

"BURGLARY.—On Friday night last, the offices of Mr. Wilkinson, solicitor, in Peterborough, were entered by thieves, who picked the lock of the door, and so obtained an entrance. They appeared to have first forced open a drawer of the table in Mr. W.'s office, whence they abstracted a few halfpence, and several keys belonging to the clerk's desks, with which they opened various boxes and cupboards. From one clerk's desk about 5s. in silver was taken, and a quantity of receipts belonging to the Phœnix Fire-office, most likely mistaken for other papers. Returning to Mr. W.'s office, the thieves ransacked the drawers, cupboards, tin boxes, and two portable desks, the contents of which they strewed over the floor. The chief point seems to have been a large iron chest in Mr. W.'s office: this at the time contained a considerable amount in cash, notes, gold and silver, which had been omitted to be paid into the bank during the day. The chest was one of Chubb's celebrated make; in this the burglars broke their picklocks, which were abstracted by means of a magnet the following morning. Having failed with the lock, they next tried to force open the lid; but here again they were foiled; the metal was too tough to break, and too solid to be wrenched or cut, and the thieves were baulked of their expected prize."

C. CHUBB and SON have received a letter from Mr. Wilkinson confirming the above statement, and expressing his gratification at the result.

57, St. Paul's Churchyard, London.

LEADBEATER, FIRE-PROOF SAFE AND DETECTOR LOCK MANUFACTURER TO HER MAJESTY'S BOARD OF ORDNANCE.

CAUTION to Purchasers of FIRE-PROOF DOORS for Strong Rooms, Safes, Chests, and Detector Locks, &c. &c. LEADBEATER, many years manufacturer for Chubb.

LEADBEATER begs most respectfully to inform Architects, Surveyors, Builders, &c., that he can supply them with IMPROVED DETECTOR LOCKS for universal purposes, STRONG WROUGHT IRON FIRE-PROOF DOORS, SAFES, and CHESTS, &c., on the most improved principles of security against FIRE and THIEVES, without the aid of "expensive machinery," which is employed by some inexperienced makers, but must be paid for; at prices 25 per cent. under any other house in London.

LEADBEATER offers ONE HUNDRED POUNDS reward to any person who can pick his improved detector locks or latches. Some thousands of Leadbeater's strong-room doors and safes have now been put up without a SINGLE COMPLAINT, and fifteen years' practical experience, during which he has adapted every possible improvement to real security, enables him to challenge competition with any house in London. A large assortment of all sizes on sale and made to order. A pair of extra strong wrought-iron fire-proof folding-doors with ventilating gates, made expressly for a banker's strong room, may be viewed at his manufactory. Strong wrought-iron doors for party walls, with wrought-iron rabitted frames, and secured by the BEST DETECTOR LOCKS in ENGLAND, 6 feet high by 2 feet 2 inches wide and upwards, price 10l. each, always on hand at LEADBEATER'S MANUFACTORY, 56, ALDERSGATE-STREET, LONDON.

No. CCCXIX.

SATURDAY, MARCH 17, 1849.

HE records of the London trade-guilds, fraternities, mysteries, crafts, or, as they are now called, Companies, contain much interesting and useful matter, which would serve to throw light on the state of society in early times, to illustrate history, and to show, amongst other things, the progress of building and the growth of the metropolis. Indisposition on the part of the companies to permit access to these documents is probably the reason why little use has been made of them. We have a general history of the twelve principal companies, but there is a wide and promising field of research here yet open for the historian and archæologist.

In 1846, when describing the decorative paintings discovered in Carpenters' Hall, London-wall,* we suggested that the charters and records of the Carpenters' Company, which company formerly exercised great power over the trade, would probably afford much interesting information, and we expressed a hope that we might soon be able to avail ourselves of them. Since then, and led to it by the inquiries and remarks made at that time, Mr. Edward B. Jupp, the clerk of the company, has diligently examined all their records, and has now published a historical account of the company, chiefly compiled from these, which will be read with considerable interest by many, and will, we hope, serve as an inducement to others to follow the example.†

The formation of guilds in our own country dates from an early period in our history; they played an important part in the development of society, enabling the trading classes to resist the tyranny of the nobles, and lessening the distance between the two. Reigning monarchs saw what powerful checks these combinations were on the aristocracy, and, willingly granted them charters of incorporation and important privileges.

The earliest charter possessed by the Carpenters' Company is dated 7th July, 1477 (the 17th of Edward IV.), but it is not by any means certain that this was the first; the common seal of the company and grant of arms are dated 1466, and there is a distinct notice of a guild of carpentry in 1421-2. Going still further back, the city records shew that at least as early as 1271, two master carpenters, and the same number of master masons, were sworn as officers, to perform certain duties with reference to buildings and walls, of much the same nature as those which were confided to the same number of members of these two companies, under the title of city viewers, until within little more than a century ago. Chaucer, too, in his "Canterbury Tales," written probably in the reign of Richard II., introduces five individuals of different trades, whom he describes as clothed in the livery of "a grete fraternitie," and of these, one is a carpenter,—

"A haberdasher and a *carpenter*,
  A webbe, a deyer, and a tapiser,
' Were all y' clothed in o livere,
  Of a solempne and grete fraternite."

* See vol. IV., p. 87.
† "A Historical Account of the Worshipful Company of Carpenters of the City of London, compiled chiefly from records in their possession, by Edward Basil Jupp, Clerk of the Company." London, Pickering.

The earliest entry in the Company's books is dated 1438, and is headed (abandoning the spelling of the time, which Mr. Jupp has carefully preserved), "Jesu and his mother dear have mercy on Croffton the carpenter. He gave you this book to all the company."

The preamble of the first charter, already alluded to, sets forth, on the part of King Edward, that understanding "that divers workmanships, or works in the mystery of carpentry, have oftentimes heretofore been made, and daily are made, insufficiently, which thing, if it should be suffered to be so done it would redound not only to our prejudice but also to the manifest deceit of our liege people and subjects, and that for want of government, correction, and oversight, to be had in the said mystery, we, willing to meet with such prejudice and deceit as we are bounden for the bettering of our lieges and subjects aforesaid," give license for the establishment of the guild, &c.

In this charter, full power and authority is given to the master and wardens "to oversee, search, rule, and govern the said commonalty and mystery, and all men occupying the same, their servants, stuffs, works, and merchandise whatsoever" appertaining to the mystery within the city, suburbs, and precincts, and to punish and correct at their discretion.

Various entries in the books show the course taken by the company under these powers: they granted licenses for the erection of buildings, and punished by fine or imprisonment where license had not been taken or the work badly done. We must content ourselves with two or three specimens :—

Thus, in 1474,—" Item; paid to serjeants by diverse times for arresting of stuff" (seizing defective timber) 6s."

1500. " Item; received of Gyffte to have the good-will of the fellowship to set up a house in Bridge-street, 10s."

1503. " Received of a foreign carpenter to have license to set up a house within Serjeant's Inn, Chancery-lane, 20d." (w' in the Serleant in, in Chauncelor-lane.)

1567. " Received of Thomas Huat for that his boards did not bear measure, 2s. 6d." And then in 1572, " John Curtis was committed to ward at the master's commandment, for the work which he did in St. Paul's Churchyard, without license of the master and wardens."

Matters in dispute were usually either decided by the court or referred to arbitrators, who in an early order-book of the company are styled "daysmen," an old term for umpire;* and it is seen that members of the company were sometimes made answerable for the "yll words" of their wives. Thus, in 1556, " Received of Frank Steleerag a fyne for ill-words that his wife gave to John Dorant, 2s." The ladies of the company are much better behaved now-a-days.

In the same year, John Griffin was fined 6d. for coming to the hall in his coat and leather apron; and Master Abbot to the same extent, because he "helde not his peess before the master bade knockyd with the *sylence* 3 times."

The opposition offered by the company to foreigners (a term which applied also to non-freemen) was very determined and continuous.

* The term daysman is employed, says Mr. Jupp, in rendering that fine passage in the book of Job—' For is he not a man as I am, that ' I should answer' him, and we should come together in judgment; neither 'is there any *daysman* betwixt us, that might'lay his hand upon us both." Spenser, also, in the " Faery Queene, says :—
" For what art thou
That mak'st thyself his *daysman* to prolong
The Vengeance prest ? "
—Vol. 11., canto viii., v. 28.

The entries of payments for their arrest are numerous.

In 1607 the jurisdiction of the Carpenters' Company was extended by charter of King James I. to the compass of two miles round the city. By this charter the oversight, search, correction, government, and reformation of all works and things concerning the art of carpentry, and of their measures, were granted to the company, also the control of all reparations and buildings. Power was given to a certain number of members of the company to enter into the premises of any one following the trade of a carpenter, to see if the works were skilfully done, to seize and dispose of all improper stuffs, punishing the offenders; and, upon application of any party grieved, to reform and correct the buildings, works, or reparations.

In the same year a set of stringent bye-laws were framed for the regulation of the company. By these no person of the fellowship is to meddle with other branches of the building trade, under penalty of 20s., more or less at the discretion of the master and wardens. And in order to discountenance masons, bricklayers, and others, who "oftentimes do take upon them in a bargain by great, not only to deal for such things as appertain to their own art, craft, or mystery, but also to finish diverse parts, and many times the whole buildings," "whereby the king's majesty's subjects, being owners of the buildings, are very much and often deceived of true and substantial stuff and workmanship,"—no carpenter was allowed to work for any mason, bricklayer, or other so acting, "by bargain in great" (in the lump), but only for wages by the day, under a penalty not exceeding 3l.

Another bye-law provides that the master and wardens shall search for timber, boards, joists, quarters, &c., belonging to the carpentry, to be sold, to see that the same contain the just length, measure, &c., according to a schedule which is given at length.

By a charter of Charles I., in 1640, the company's jurisdiction was further extended to a compass of four miles round the city of London, and their former powers were confirmed, with the exception of that of reforming and correcting buildings, "in lieu of which they were empowered to retard and delay all insufficient buildings, works, and workmanship until the Commissioners of the Crown in the cities of London and Westminster, and the neighbouring places, or any two or more of them, should have notice from the master and wardens, and should provide a fit remedy."

In connection with the powers of search, some of the entries are curious, showing that it was exercised very resolutely. In these searches the King's "master carpenter" was permitted to accompany the wardens if he pleased. Of those who held this appointment Mr. Jupp gives some particulars, as he does also of those who held the office of surveyor of the King's works. On our next page is a portrait of Portington, who held the former office many years, engraved from a picture in Carpenters' Hall : the second engraving is from a painting also in the hall.

The books of the company contain many entries connected with the impressment of workmen for the service of the crown. Amongst the latest instances is this :—" 1668; 22nd July—Spent with Sir John Denham, the King's surveyor, and others, about the twelve carpenters charged to be impressed for the King's work at Whitehall, 35s. 6d."

At the beginning of the seventeenth century,

Wᵐ Portington Esqʳ, Mʳ Carpenter in yᵉ office of his Maᵗⁱᵉ buildings, who served in yᵗ place 40 yeeres & departed this life yᵉ 28 of March 1628, being aged 84 yeeres. who was a well wisher in this Societie, this being yᵗ gift of Mathew Bankes who served him 14 yeeres, & is at this present Mʳ of the said Co'pany Aug. 19. 1637.

This Picture of John Scott Esqʳ, Carpenter and Carrage Maker to the Offic of Ordnance In the Reigne of King Charles the 2d Was Placed Here By his Apptentic Matthew Bancks Esqʳ, Master Carpenter to his Majᵗⁱᵉ and Master of This Company this present yeare : 1698.

differences occurred between the Carpenters' Company and the Joiners' Company, and articles were drawn up by a committee describing minutely the several branches of trade to be pursued by each. At the end of that century the feud was renewed, but the companies nevertheless united to prevent the incorporation of the sawyers, and succeeded in their opposition. In 1654, the company, by direction of the Court of Aldermen, reported on the means of preventing the firing of buildings, wherein timber was laid too near the fire in chimneys; and in 1655 they gave the Lord Mayor recommendations for reducing the wages of labourers and workmen. These were as follows :—

1. That labourers take for wages 16d. a-day only.

2. That sawyers take only for sawing of timber as followeth. For oak by the hundred 2s. 8d., for elme by the hundred 2s. 6d., for fir by the hundred 2s. 4d., and for sawing of deal boards, 2s. 4d. a dozen only.

3. That "sufficient" carpenters take but 2s. 6d. a-day for wages at the most.

Soon after the great fire of 1666, Parliament passed an "Act for Rebuilding the City of London," in which it was enacted that the outsides of all buildings in and about the city should be made of brick or stone.

Surveyors were to be appointed by the city to carry the Act into execution, and severe penalties were imposed on persons building contrary to it,—thus superseding the Carpenters' Company in more ways than one. The Act also gave permission for carpenters and others not freemen of the city to enjoy the privileges of working as if they had been apprenticed for seven years; and all who should actually work in rebuilding the city for seven years had liberty to work at their trades for the rest of their lives as freemen. The company strove against this, but ineffectually ; and although they still claimed right of search, their power was in reality gone. The natural course of events led to the abandonment of pageantry and pomp, and they found their only remaining but very important duty was, to cultivate social and kindly feelings, and to supply the wants of their poorer brethren.

·Mr. Jupp has performed his self-imposed task with care and ability, and has added a very interesting volume to the library of the antiquary and the historical student.

ON THE IMPORTANCE OF A KNOWLEDGE AND OBSERVANCE OF THE PRINCIPLES OF ART BY DESIGNERS.

The importance to designers of a knowledge of the ruling principles of the arts of design is so obvious, that it may appear almost superfluous to urge the necessity of understanding and observing them. Never, certainly, in this country, has so much attention been paid to the study of *style* as at the present time. In architecture, the principles of construction and adornment of Pagan and Christian temples have been investigated by both professional and amateur students ; and if some architects of eminence in our own day are apt to regard the ' letter ' of detail more than the ' spirit ' of the *ensemble*, in their imitation of the classic and Gothic styles, such solecisms as Inigo Jones committed, when he stuck up a Corinthian portico before the old cathedral of St. Paul,—and Wren, when he reared the western towers of Westminster Abbey, would not now be tolerated. Yet there still remains much to be done in developing, defining, and enforcing the fundamental principles which should regulate every branch of design, as well as every style of art,—principles of taste, rationally deduced from scientific data, and regulated by the refined perception of fitness and congruity,—of utility and beauty.

An accurate imitation of style is often mistaken for observance of the principles of art ; but style is only a special part of a general comprehensive whole. By studying the principles of Greek or Christian architecture and ornament, one may imitate these styles to admiration ; but something more is required in order to invent. It then becomes necessary to investigate, understand, and act upon those broad fundamental principles which form the basis of all art, and apply equally to every style, past, present, or to come ; for without such observance of principles, ingenuity becomes perverted, invention runs wild, and then the types of past ages must be moulds in which alone the ever active mind of genius can pour forth its ideas with the certainty of their assuming shapes of beauty and dignity.

Two distinct movements, in opposite directions, are now observable in the world of art : the one is retrograde, the other progressive. The retrograde movement, however, is a far greater stride in point of science and taste, because it has the lights of the antique world and the miscalled " dark ages " to guide it ; while the progressive movement, having no chart of principles to direct its onward course, is devious as that of a traveller on a trackless desert without a guide, or a ship at sea without rudder or compass.

No wonder that those who reverence the monuments of antiquity that time has spared, and who have refined their taste by the study of those noble works of art, should be reluctant to leave " standing on the ancient ways," when they see the puerile absurdities and extravagant incongruities perpetrated by adventurous spirits in search of novelty.

But art cannot stand still : it must move either backward in the old tracks, or forward in new. The vitality and strength of genius consists in its originating faculty. Our greatest poet, Shakspeare, whose fecundity of invention is equal to the truth and vitality of his creations, is an instance of a writer forming a new style of the drama : his departures from prescribed forms caused his crabbed contemporary, Ben Jonson, to say that Shakspeare wanted art ; but we have come to discover, by the test of experience, that he was as great in the knowledge of his art as in the exercise of his imagination. So of the latest grand style of architecture, the Pointed English, or as it was nicknamed by the copyists of the debased classic style, the Gothic ; and which even Wren called " crinkle-crankle," we have but recently come to appreciate the scientific daring shown in its construction, the infinite variety and beauty of its forms and ornaments, and its picturesque effects of light and shadow. This style was the growth of the English mind, elevated by the Christian faith, and it is in every point truly national : suited to the nature of our climate, to the forms of worship and habits of the period, and to the varied requisitions of domestic life as well as conventual, characterized by utility and fitness in plan and elevation, its adaptability is no less remarkable than the majestic grandeur of its masses, the sublime elevation of its spires, and the infinite richness and elegance of its details.

Yet neither Shakspearian drama nor pointed architecture, both English as they are, and alike admirable for the union of grandeur with beauty, of elegance with variety, should confine our poets and architects to the imitation of these glorious forms. The spirit of every age should impress the products of that age ; and it is the privilege of genius alone to stamp the image of greatness and a character of originality upon the art of a period. But genius cannot adequately fulfil its mission unless it be unfettered by prescription and precedent ; it must be free to strike out its own course, neither restricted to a prescribed track, nor oked to the chariot of antiquity. Let me not e misunderstood, however. In advocating ae freedom of genius from restraints of preedent, I am not asserting its superiority to, r independence of, principles; what the laws f nature are to human existence, the true priniples of art are to the efforts of genius. The rtist of original powers may strike out a new ath, but if he want to reach the goal of uccess he must know the bearings of his ourse and his object in taking it. Genius nay overstep minute rules with advantage, ut can never violate great principles with mpunity.

What, then, are these fundamental princiiles of art, is the natural question. To enuniate them fully and definitely would require iot only more space than is allowed me, but, will frankly avow, more exact and extensive nowledge than I can lay claim to. I only ssume to enforce the importance of ascerаining and observing these principles. It nay be reasonably expected of me, however, o indicate and exemplify them, and this I will ndeavour to do.

The province of the arts of design—the ormative arts, or the fine arts, whichever they nay be called—is to enrich, enliven, and eleate the mind by means of new and suggestive deas of beauty and grandeur, of gaiety and race, through the medium of representations f natural objects or fanciful inventions deived from the forms and colours of nature.

From this definition I would deduce three undamental, or governing principles, which like apply to all the formative arts:—

1st. That all art is only a medium for the xpression of ideas tending to delight and urify the mind.

2nd. That art, being the silent utterance of deas of beauty and grace, of grandeur or aiety, in visible shapes, whatever is ugly withut being enlivening, or repulsive without eing sublime, is alien to it.

3rd. That art, being only a medium for the xpression of ideas, deceptive imitation is oreign to its purpose, because in illusion the ttention is necessarily diverted from the ideas hat ought to be conveyed to the trick of leception.

To the author of that eloquent and oriinal work on "Modern Painters," the graluate of Oxford, we are indebted for the nunciation and enforcement of these princiiles. The distinction between imitation and epresentation has been too often lost sight of. The notion yet prevails very extensively that painting and sculpture are merely imitative rts; but to prove that they are not so would ccupy too much time. I will only observe, hat if they be merely imitative, then wax-work s superior to either, and the models of Madame Tussaud are greater works of art than the culptures of Michelangelo, or the paintings of Titian. The nearer the imitation of the subtance and surface of living realities in shape, olour, and texture, the more strongly is felt he absence of those essential attributes of life —breath and motion. Hence the ghastly effect f wax models; the deception first shocks the ense, and then becomes ludicrous. Besides eing amenable to these general principles, ach branch of art also has its peculiar limiations and functions,—consequently its paricular governing principles. Their observance, o far from being a restraint to genius, is a neans of strengthening its powers.

In architecture, the science of construction nters so largely into consideration, that the rt of design forms but a part, though a conpicuous and essential part, of the architect's tudies. And when it is considered that a reat building lasts for ages, and is not easily emoved or remodelled; that an ugly edifice is perpetual eye-sore, and a handsome one a ontinual delight,—the elevation of a structure ecomes a matter of public concern. Even he fragment of a noble design is a beautiful bject; and the façade of the Banquetingouse, Whitehall, is one of the finest of the ew fine works of art in the metropolis. Leigh Hunt has felicitously characterized it as 'a piece of the very music of Inigo's art— he harmony of proportion." What the city f London owes to Wren, none know so vell as those who have to pass their days vithin its dingy precincts; and since this has ecome my own lot, I have learnt to venerate the name of Wren, and feel grateful for the relief which the dome of St. Paul's, and the spires of the churches in Cheapside and Cornhill, afford to the dreary monotony of the street perspective.

Justness of proportion is so universally acknowledged to be the main feature of beauty in architecture, that however rarely it may be attained, it is not in much danger of being neglected. The necessity of designing a building so as that the elevation may convey an idea of its uses, and that the exterior may accord with the character of the interior, does not appear to be so generally recognized. Where utility is the basis of elegance, as in architectural and ornamental design, fitness is obviously an important element of beauty; but when we have a museum with the façade of a mausoleum, and a picture gallery and a college fashioned according to the same recipe, with useless porticoes and superfluous cupolas, it becomes needful to call attention to this principle. The importance of projection, both in plan and details, is also paramount, when it is considered that on this depends the effect of the sky outline, and those effects of light and shadow which are the painting of architecture. The buildings in the metropolis, from the commonest street to the last new palace, look as if they had been pared down by the abhorred shears of some demon of bad taste. The Gothic style, which not only admits of, but requires strong projections and deep recesses to give due effect to its picturesque capabilities, is too often reduced to tame, thin, colourless monotony, with walls seemingly thin as pasteboard, and ornaments as flat as filagree. The defect of that superb and costly structure, the Palace of Parliament, is its flat and monotonous façade.

The discussion of styles of architecture involves too many considerations to be entered into here; but it may be well to observe, that in the choice of style, the site, as well as the use of the building, should be taken into account, and that the imitation of any building, however grand or beautiful, is unworthy of a great architect, and a solecism in taste. The attempt to emulate the majestic simplicity and beauty of Grecian temples, where the vast masses of polished marble rise in lustrous purity against brilliant blue skies, in edifices of brick and stucco, of sandstone or iron, soon to be blackened by the coal smoke and moisture of our dense atmosphere, is so futile, that had due regard been paid to the first principles of art, and the very rudiments of taste, such flagrant absurdities would never have been perpetrated. The colossal and costly folly that disfigures the grandest and most picturesque city in the kingdom, and makes Edinburgh a very modern Athens indeed, is an *argumentum ad absurdum* on this point. We may excuse tasteful churchwardens, who degrade an Athenian choragic monument to the office of a parish pump, with the additions of a spout like the snout of a rhinoceros, and a handle like a pigtail; but when we see Grecian pediments and Corinthian columns crowned with red chimney-pots, intermingled with zinc smoke-funnels in hideous variety, the reproach and ridicule must fall upon those from whom better things might have been expected. If the Greeks had been a fire-side people, their chimney-stacks would have been so elegant in design, that we should probably have converted them to colonnades, and perhaps have lined Regent-street or façaded the Museum with attic chimneys instead of Doric columns.

Our architecture is as yet imitative, not original; and when ancient styles are adapted to modern uses, it is rarely in the spirit of the ancients. The Greeks rendered use subservient to ornament; the flower of beauty blossomed from the stem of utility. So it should ever be. True, the Greeks imitated some of the forms and characteristics of wooden structures in marble edifices; but they did this with such consummate skill and grand effect, that it is impossible to object to the result; though, like the painting and gilding of statues, it was a relic of barbarism. The Greeks erred magnificently; but do not let us moderns perpetuate their errors, or caricature their beauties. Principle before precedent always.

We use a new material for building,—iron, which ought to have given a distinct character to the design of our architecture, as it has done in part to its construction. Yet we see marble columns and stone arches imitated in cast iron, instead of displaying light shafts of slender columns supporting parabolic arches of wide span. Iron roofs can now be suspended over a vast area, almost as simply as the awnings which covered the amphitheatres of old, yet this does not visibly affect our edifices. We erect Gothic spires in iron, 'tis true, but it is only imitative of stonework; and carving, admirable in stone, becomes mere mechanical work when cast in metal. An ingenious inventor lately devised a scheme of metallurgic architecture, in which new effects of light and shade externally, and of interior ornament, were to be produced, and some material improvements in construction were suggested. This was a bold step in the right direction, though, as yet, nothing has been done to test the value of it.

In sculpture, the due observance of right principles is of the greatest importance. The sculptor's aim is to represent life in rigid and monotonous substances—marble, metal, wood, or plaster. To imitate the appearances of living flesh and blood is impossible; though the effect of animation on the aspect of living men and animals can be represented vividly, by means of forms carved in relief. But in aiming at imitation of the colours of life, by painting a statue, the result is a gigantic toy; indeed, there are one or two equestrian statues in this metropolis which exemplify the toyman's craft without the aid of paint, as may be seen in Cockspur-street and at Hyde-park-corner. The main points on which the sculptor has to rely being the outline of the mass —which in a detached group or figure varies with every change of the point of view—and the effect of light and shadow on the surface, the importance of a well-studied design, in which the effect of the whole shall be considered on every side, becomes evident; the *ensemble* should be expressive of character and suggestive of life, whether viewed near or from a distance. The Wellington statue, seen from Cumberland-gate, certainly conveys no idea whatever of heroic grandeur and dignity; it is more suggestive of a peasant on his mule or a costermonger on his donkey, than the hero of a hundred fights on his charger. Nor is it expressive of life on a nearer view; the horse appears a hollow thing of metal, the legs look like tubes, the cloak seems not to cover a human figure, and the cocked hat, with its plume of clinging feathers, is an extinguisher of any life there may have been in the head. Colossal in actual size, it does not seem grand, because the eye is distracted by paltry details; it is a huge heap of lifeless littleness. Chantrey's statue of Pitt, in Hanover-square, is one of the best examples of character in physiognomy strikingly expressed in sculpturesque style. No sculptor of modern times has equalled Chantrey in the happy art of giving living intelligence to the eye, and in expressing physiognomical characteristics with delicacy and dignity: his busts seem to think. And this is attributable to the skill with which he observed the principles of his art in the modelling of his forms as well as in the design of the mass: he cast the strongest and sharpest shadows of the face from the brow, but so as that the play of light and shade should give intelligence and vivacity to the eyes. We never find in his busts blank, sightless eyeballs, nor is our attention diverted from the brow to the lower parts of the face by the strong shadows of dilated nostrils or parted lips, as is often the case in sculpture; and the fleshy character of his modelling is inimitable. His statues of Horner and Watt, in Westminster Abbey, are fine examples of the excellence of Chantrey as a sculptor.

The statue of Voltaire, by Houdon, in the vestibule of the Theatre Français, at Paris, might be cited as a wonderful example of the representation of mobility of feature and vivacity of expression. That of Newton, by Roubiliac, in the chapel of Trinity College, Cambridge, is remarkable for its animated air; though there is too much flutter of drapery, and the *pose* of the figure is better suited to a professor of legerdemain than a philosopher. Roubiliac himself recognised the prevalent defect of littleness and want of mass in his figures, when, after revisiting Italy and seeing the antique sculptures there, he exclaimed, when viewing his own works in Westminster Abbey,—"They look like tobacco pipes:" a sentence that might be passed on other sculptures besides those of Roubiliac.

W. SMITH WILLIAMS.

PROFESSOR COCKERELL'S CONCLUDING LECTURE ON ARCHITECTURE.

THE sixth and concluding lecture of the course at the Royal Academy, which was delivered on Thursday, the 8th ultimo, was very numerously attended by the leading members of the profession. In the ordinary progress of the subject, the professor said, that ornament would be the next point to which he ought to call their attention, did not matters of a more practical nature claim further consideration. Having previously gone into the theoretical principles of classical architecture, he now proposed to offer remarks upon their practical application, upon certain conventional licenses, and upon the proper method of carrying on our studies in early life. He therefore proceeded to consider what might be the opinion of foreigners upon peculiarities in our national practice, remarking upon the value of the hint of a friend, or the sarcasm of an enemy, towards removing the tendency to self-gratulation in our own practice, and the works of our own country. He urged the danger of restricting ourselves to ideas derived from our own school, and the limited circle in which an artist moved. Although we ought to know how much animadversion to ascribe to pure malice, he said that the prevailing vice of the artist's mind was self-gratulation.

A foreigner visiting this country would remark, that whilst we had adopted Greek architecture, we had abjured too often the principles which belonged to other styles, as in the case of the arch. We had to a great extent made use of the Palladian style, yet we had not sufficiently valued some of the most important characteristics of Palladio's works, especially in omitting his practice of weaving a minor order with a major, which gave proportion by comparison. In the same manner, we had neglected to give expression to our roofs, a point much attended to by Palladio, in his villas especially. It might be said, that in England the roof formed no part of our study. It was an anomaly in design: we neither made it altogether terrace fashion, with a balustrade, nor yet altogether projecting, with a cornice. Vignola was always good in this part of the design, whilst Palladio, though attentive to the effect of the roof in his villas, was negligent in his town houses. But in England, where, for example, we might expect a terrace, we had a bit of roof just peeping over a parapet. The sky-line in our buildings—coincidently with this kind of defect—was unattended to, and any effect which might be produced by the gable, was unthought of in England now, although our streets during the middle ages gave sufficient evidence of the recognition of this feature. He instanced the Foundling Hospital, as a building in which a good effect was given by the disposition of the roofs.

He said there was less reason for omitting to make use of the roof as an integral part of the composition, because we were untrammelled—compared with other countries—in the structural arrangement of that part of the building. We were not confined to a high pitch, for we had little snow, and the best slates in the world. He believed that the great masters always considered the roof at the outset. Now, a foreigner would say,—if we are obliged to have heavy roofs, we treat them boldly; but you, in England, would have nothing to prevent your making them graceful, if you knew how. Many a fine building was spoilt by the roof, which we were so much afraid of making heavy. In the same manner, we had neglected chimney shafts. Somerset House was spoiled by its chimneys; but Vanbrugh displayed a consummate knowledge of effect in these features, as shown in Blenheim, and at King's Weston, near Bristol, where they were connected by arches, so as to group into a sort of tower.

A foreigner might continue to say,—You have turned your court-yards into squares and streets, which are of such extent that they are admirably suited to your foggy climate; but your excessive use of columnar architecture, adopted in every building, whether prison or palace, or in the use of columns of the Jupiter-Stator order over a shop front, would imply that such materials were your all in all. Your streets are characteristic enough of a nation of shopkeepers, everything being sacrificed to shop windows; but the same objects might have been better attained, without the deformity, by raising the bressummer to the second-floor window-sills, as actually done in some instances.

In continuing the subject of columnar architecture, the professor urged the advantage of using pedestals to columns in interiors. If columns were placed on the floor, they lost much of their dignity, if only from being partly concealed by furniture; and Raffaelle and other great architects always employed pedestals: it might, too, be ascertained that it was the Greek system to use them in interiors. In the treatment of windows, broad lights and narrow piers were justifiable in many cases; but, as before stated, opportunity had not been taken to decorate the alternate windows.—He noticed, in like manner, similar instances of inattention, particularly in buildings in the country, where, he said, our love of Palladio had amounted to positive insanity. Sufficient advantage had not been taken in the arrangement of interiors, of the opportunity of heightening principal rooms by throwing the ceiling into the upper floor. In another particular, too, a great mistake had been common,—that of stowing away all the offices in a separate building at the side of the main one, which building was intended to be hid by a plantation, which, however, was never done,—whilst in the works of architects like John Thorpe, offices and principal rooms were combined in one grand design.

But our affectation of a feudal character of architecture would create still more astonishment. The foreigner might see towers and battlements, approach by a drawbridge, and raise a ponderous knocker, and be ushered in, not by a dwarf or a giant, but by servants in new liveries, to modern drawing-rooms, furnished with articles of Gillow's latest patterns,—all this expressing that we lived in peace and security in our homes, whilst we tried to make believe the contrary; and yet such anomalies we were hardly aware of, till they were pointed out.—But, in reference to church architecture, although during the last thirty years 1,500 churches had been erected for the established religion alone, what would be the impression produced on the foreigner? It might naturally have been expected, that the arrangement of churches for the Protestant religion would have become settled after the accumulated experience of previous years, yet in almost every fifth year we had had a change of style. The commissioners had complained that they could get no suggestions from architects, but they had actually sealed up all the documents of the commission of the reign of Queen Anne, which was composed chiefly of architects. The present commission had been formed in distrust of architects.—The last change had been to the Roman Catholic arrangement, suited to other times, and to another ritual. He (the professor) had at one time given great offence to a certain society, by saying that the proper form of the Protestant church was that of the *auditorium*. Gothic architecture for churches better suited the old England of the rural districts than the new England of the towns. We were, indeed, afflicted with the Pointed style, and with forms in total disunion with the neighbouring architecture; and an affectation of monastic structures in the present day was as ridiculous as it would be to see the Duke of Wellington ride to the House crowned with laurel, and clad in the Roman toga.—The professor then reviewed the question of proportions of interiors, alluding to the greater length required in the mediæval church; and he examined the general outline of the village church, particularly remarking upon the want of balance between the tower and the chancel, which a skilful master would have united in one composition. He considered that the Greek cross was the best form for our church, with the requisite elevation given by the lantern.—However, he pointed out the marked difference between the classical and the mediæval systems, the former embodying the carnal mind, the latter the spiritual mind; the one the body, the other the soul; the one the intellectual or the sumptuous, the other, heavenly aspiration. The mediæval edifice was full of sentiment, and the professor gave some instances of those details which have a symbolic meaning. Any misuse of the characteristics of the opposite styles, as to put large doors in the Gothic church, only betokened the ignorant mind, from which might God preserve us.

Continuing, in a similar manner, his notices of modern practice, he passed to the architectural characteristics of our public buildings. Who would suppose, he said, that in the dark courts of the India House was carried on the government of a vast empire, or that from the Horse Guards the thunders of British power were heard over the whole world? The law sent forth its edicts from holes and corners, such as Rhadamanthus occupied in the infernal regions; and the goddesses Themis and Nemesis, certainly worshipped in England, had not such temples as that at Rhamnus. How would our public buildings compare with those of the little state of Bavaria?

In concluding the present course, the professor expressed the pleasure which the lectures had always afforded him, and said he frankly confessed, that *he* had learnt as much from preparing them, as he had been able to impart to his hearers, and more than by all the travels and the labours of his life. "*Docendo docitur*," he said. Whether he had been able to impart as much to them, remained to be proved by their future works. Schools might produce good scholars, but we could never become good masters without we avoided the practice of begging and borrowing from everything indiscriminately. It must be regretted that opportunities of instruction were not so great in London as might be wished; but still we had colleges in which the whole subject of architecture was explained by the most eminent professors, and the architects of London might challenge the world. He recommended travel, as likely to give independence of thought, but it should not be according to the ordinary rule of travel, not the rushing down to Italy and Greece, and losing ourselves in sentimentalities; but certainly we ought first to see every part of our own country, full of objects of interest, and next, rather the north of Europe than the south, and climates analogous to our own; and, *lastly*, Italy and Greece. Some of the best architects had never travelled at all,—and of these Wren was a striking instance. Architecture was an art which required thought as much as observation, and more might be done within four walls than in galloping over the world. It was possible to have seen everything, and yet have learnt nothing. When we had built up the fabric of our education, it became us to devote ourselves to the strict fulfilment of our duties; and impressing the importance of these upon his hearers, the professor wished them health, industry, and success, until he next met them, concluding a most interesting course of lectures amidst the hearty applause of his audience.

MONUMENTS IN CEMETERIES.

THE cause of the inscription upon Sir Hans Sloane's monument, at Chelsea, being almost illegible, arises not so much from the dilapidated state of the entire monument, as from the unfitness of the material of which the tablet alone is composed. The epitaph is inscribed upon a Carrara marble slab, let into solid Portland stone: a method of every day occurrence, as may be seen in the cemeteries around the metropolis. The delicate nature of white marble renders it extremely difficult to colour the letters with a durable paint, without staining the surface of the tablet. Whether the letters are to be black, or any other colour, is immaterial; the question is, what vehicle the pigment shall be mixed with: if oil is used, no matter how small the quantity, the colour will remain in the letters many years, but there will be a permanent dirty-brown stain, half an inch round every letter. To avoid such stain, some kind of spirit varnish is used, which, during the process of drying and hardening, shrinks, loses its adhesive quality, and, therefore, in many cases, separates from the marble without leaving the slightest trace in the cavity of the letters. At present, I know of no remedy for these defects, if marble is introduced in situations exposed to the weather.

Within a few years, it has become the practice amongst the wealthy to have sepulchral monuments constructed entirely of marble, either to gratify the vanity of surpassing a humble neighbour, or under the impression of it being the most durable substance. Although marble, when fresh from the workman's hand, is a more beautiful material than common stone, yet it has disadvantages which ought to preclude it from ever being applied to external decorations. When Carrara marble has been exposed to the weather, and to variations of temperature, for thirty or forty years, the crystals no longer adhere firmly to each other; the external appearance as yet remains unaltered, but the decomposing influence of atmosphere continues to penetrate deeply into the mass; the cohesion of the particles is imperceptibly destroyed, and, after the lapse of a century, it entirely falls into a kind of sparkling sand. The group of Queen Anne, &c., in front of St. Paul's Cathedral, executed in Carrara marble by Francis Bird, the beginning of the last century, has long since been painted, in order to preserve it a little longer from total ruin. The statue of George the Third, executed in marble by J. Wilton, R.A., and placed in one of the niches at the old Royal Exchange, was taken down to be repaired, about twenty-five years since, and was found to be too much decomposed to be put up again: it has since actually crumbled to dust. A mural monument, in the utmost state of decay, still exists at the external end, facing the east, of the church of St. Giles's-in-the-Fields. The church itself, built with the best kind of Portland stone, is in a remarkably perfect condition, whereas the monument, made of Carrara marble some years after the completion of the church, is now in such a mouldering state, that it must very shortly fall completely to atoms. Numerous other instances might be named, but it is hoped the above are sufficient to show the unfitness of that description of marble for such purposes.

Many sculptors and masons entertain a high opinion of the durability of Ravaccioni marble, erroneously called Sicilian, of which the arch now in front of Buckingham Palace may be named as a specimen.* There certainly is reason to believe it to be a material likely to resist the action of an English atmosphere longer than Italian veined, or white Carrara marble; but, on attentive examination, it will be found that its chemical and mineralogical character scarcely differs from them, except in weight, hardness, and containing a little more carbonaceous matter. These qualities are by no means sufficient to warrant an idea that the Ravaccioni marble will last considerably longer than such as have heretofore been in general use.

The question may be asked, "why have the Elgin marbles, and other antique sculptures, resisted the mouldering touch of time for more than twenty centuries?" A long and highly interesting article might be written upon this subject; but for the present, suffice it to say that the same elements uniting in the same proportions do not necessarily generate the same body. Common chalk, Carrara marble, and many of the oolitic limestones scarcely present a trace of difference in their chemical composition. To all appearance, the marble of Pentelicus, in the neighbourhood of Athens, is an aqueous deposit, similar to the stalagmites, travertines, and other calcareous formations, constantly operating in the fresh-water currents of Italy; most of which are extremely durable when applied to architectural purposes. Taking many circumstances into consideration, besides observing the progress of decay in Carrara marble, and comparing them with a long series of experiments, undertaken some years back by Sir James Hall, to verify a principle previously assumed by Dr. Hutton, in his "Theory of the Earth," we are induced to believe that Carrara marble, has been materially modified in its crystalline structure, by volcanic agency, acting under an excessive pressure of superincumbent earth, and excluded from the atmosphere. The same elements are consolidated in one case through the agency of water; and in the other, by the influence of fire; therefore we must expect, that the produce will vary considerably in duration, if subjected to the same atmospheric influences: and the instances already mentioned are quite sufficient to show that Carrara marble is a material wholly unfit to be placed in situations exposed to the weather in this country.

C. H. Smith.

* The Italian Veined, white statuary, dove-coloured, and Ravaccioni marbles, mineralogically considered, are but slight variations of the same substance: they are all procured from quarries in the immediate neighbourhood of the town or Village of Carrara in Tuscany.

CHELSEA HOSPITAL GARDENS AND THE RIVER BANKS.

The instruction and healthful recreation of the dense mass of human beings living in this overgrown metropolis, has been recognised to be one of the duties of national government. The principle has been acted upon to a considerable extent during a few past years, but many of its great capabilities still remain untouched. A good deal of what has been effected has been undertaken by the authoritative powers being urged on by Parliamentary desire, or the pressure from without. To these causes we owe increased accommodation to the British Museum, the National Gallery, Greenwich Hospital, the Tower of London, as well as the laying out of Victoria Park at Bethnal-green, and a proposed new one in Battersea-fields. Parks are, however, of slow growth; and while the trees may grow which are not yet planted in the last-named undertaking, I wish to call attention to great capabilities for healthful enjoyment on the opposite bank of the river at Chelsea.

Of all the suburbs of London where good residences abound, there is not one so ill laid out for main thoroughfares as this locality. The King's-road, leading out of Sloane-square, is obstructed on the south side by the wall of the Royal asylum, which does not leave space for a footpath even; and opposite it one might imagine a rivalry of obstructions had taken place, each inhabitant endeavouring to push his place of trade to the edge of the kennel. Beyond Church-lane, leading to Battersea-bridge, the same enmity of transit appears to have afflicted the builders. Considerable improvement was effected by making the road-way that traverses the front of Chelsea Hospital; but beyond that, at a little distance, the same inconvenience of a single footpath is occasioned by the wall of the apothecaries' garden, and a narrow dirty lane of irregular houses must be threaded before you can arrive at the fine river terrace of Cheyne-walk.

In the pursuit of this healthful recreation, on the Sunday afternoons of last summer, more than 5,000 persons have landed at the numerous piers on this spot from the river steamers. The majority of these are the quiet respectable persons of the industrious class, with their families. Few but the idle, wicked, and dissolute can venture on the opposite shore, where, on every Sunday in fine weather, a disgraceful saturnalia is held, in defiance of morality and all the decencies that honour existence.

The subject to which it is particularly wished to call attention is Chelsea Hospital with its extensive grounds. Some accommodation is granted by the officials, of a limited character: this seems not generally known; and it would be a great and desirable improvement to increase the means for its free perambulation.

Chelsea Hospital is a great monument of national benevolence. Belonging to the nation, and sustained with pride by a heavily taxed people, they may claim as a public right the tranquil enjoyment of its pleasure grounds. The edifice besides has its internal attraction of the trophies of victorious war. In the chapel are preserved the eagles of Napoleon, captured at Barrosa, Talavera, and Waterloo. In the dining-hall remain the fragments of the standards won at Blenheim, from the proud Louis the Fourteenth, surnamed the "*Grand*," besides flags of all nations, down to the Chinese, with the dragon banners.

How few have been the visitors to these mementoes of our successes on the battle field, comparatively with the affluence of the curious at Greenwich! The latter appears gay as a palace, with its myriads of strollers, while the Chelsea gardens are melancholy as a cemetery. They are but little frequented, although in a measure open to the public, but woe to the sprightly child who dares to tread on the verdant turf; that is not privileged to youthful sportiveness; the greater portion is an enclosed preserve where certain happy cows can chew the cud in undisturbed comfort.

The large area on the north of the building, with its umbrageous alleys of horse-chesnut trees, is only penetrated by a few well-dressed individuals,—for this latter qualification is rigorously enforced. The handsome gates opposite the King's-road are constantly locked; and never opened but to the governor or a grandee. The large grassplats between the alleys are railed off: no human foot ever treads here. A rick of hay in one corner marks conspicuously that the herbage is a perquisite. A stable, with outcast heaps of dung, proclaim the condition of enjoyment possessed by the proprietor of the perquisite.

The grounds on the banks of the river are open much on the same condition, that is, to be well-dressed and keep on the gravel. The principal space abutting on the hospital has a broad walk leading to a terrace on the river side, bordered by dwarfed lime trees. There is no trespassing on the grass here, for a wide ditch on each side, brimful of stagnant water, impedes the attempt; and on the other sides the spaces are strongly hedged in for the benefit of the aforesaid happy cows. There is another large space of ground adjoining this formal piece, where a greater freedom is allowed, possibly because the vast sewer that comes down from Knightsbridge runs here open by its side. This portion retains some fine trees, affording shelter from the summer sun, at the expense of inhaling the odour of a tank of mud, about 60 feet long and 30 feet wide, close by the side of the principal walk. It was formerly part of the famed Ranelagh Gardens, and leads down to the mouth of the sewer, where the filthy stream is discharged into the Thames. Here, just on the bank where its languid course becomes changed by a sharp descent into a bustling activity of emitting its foul odours before the river absorbs the precious fluid, several seats are placed, to enable visiters to inhale at their ease an ample store of the anti-olfactory scent.

If the sewers were arched over, an open terrace made to the river, the enclosed spaces thrown open, and the stagnant imitative canals filled up, the gardens of Chelsea Hospital would make, with their present plantations, one of the most beautiful parks on a small scale with which London could be adorned. The good conduct of the people has already been established where any such advantages have been made open to them.

The garden of the Apothecaries' Company is but a few paces off, and contains a variety of rare medicinal plants. Two magnificent cedars, planted in 1683, adorn the grounds, and there would be pleasant frontage to the river, if the cheering, breathing prospect were not completely shut out by two lateral walls on the bank of the stream, where all the refuse and rubbish of the garden is preserved. No stranger is admitted within its gates, excepting he is provided with an especial permission from some member of the corporate body. Yet the garden was a legacy to this society by Sir Hans Sloane, and who can doubt that the munificent bequest was intended to be a public benefit. Another large area, with a grassy lawn, on which stand some noble trees, is adjacent to the hospital grounds, namely, that of the Royal Asylum. How much space do all these offer, if opened in a proper spirit, for exercise and recreation, independent of the mental enjoyment that would arise to the multitude in the contemplation of these various establishments dedicated to science, humanity, and gratitude to the defenders of our country.

Idler in London.

Crockford's Club-house, St. James's-street, is being scraped down externally, and is about to be decorated internally, for (as we are told) a Militia Club. A correspondent remarks on the improvement to the front of this building, which has several good qualities, that would be made by the addition of a portico or porch. The suggestion is well worth the consideration of those concerned in the building.

THE "PALAZZO REZZONICO," VENICE.

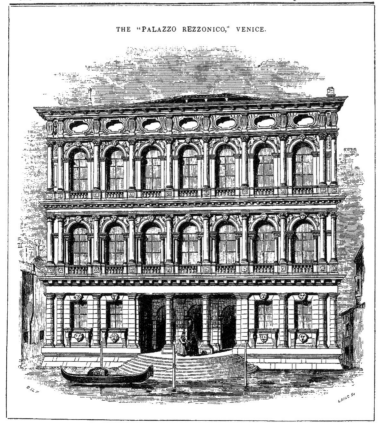

THE "PALAZZO REZZONICO," VENICE.

In our last volume* we gave a view of the Pesaro Palace, erected, from the designs of Baldassare Longhena, on the Grand Canal, Venice. Annexed is an engraving made from a sketch by Mr. Horace Jones, of another work by that master, the Palazzo Rezzonico, in the same city. The general arrangement of the two fronts will be found very similar,— the same number of stories, same number of windows, same general distribution. In the details, however, there is considerable difference. The effect of this structure is peculiarly fine, and it has an advantage over its sister edifice in simplicity.

The upper story is attributed to Carlo Massari.

Cost of Newark Corn Exchange.— I see in the *Illustrated London News*, Feb. 3, the Newark Corn Exchange is stated to have cost 4,300l. ; now I am credibly informed that the cost of that building was nearly (or fully) 7,000l. — a slight difference. Such mis-statements as these are calculated to injure the profession and to mislead the public. I send you my name.   J. B.

TOPOGRAPHY OF JERUSALEM.
MILLO.

It is gratifying to note the increased interest taken in the topography of Jerusalem and in the geography of the Holy Land.

As regards Millo, the writer in the last number goes far in clearing up a very old and great difficulty; but he might have gone further. In the Jewish economy, the house of Millo was the Jewish senate ; and at an earlier period the Jebusites had a "house of Millo," which was also the seat of judgment in both cases : but as then every man was trained to arms, and the captain of a thousand was a senator (together with the elders, or birth aristocracy), we can from "Millo" trace the terms "Miles," a soldier, and "Mill," a thousand, and better understand why the term "Millo" was used as a generic term. As thus,—"And all the men of Shechem gathered together, and all the house of Millo (the senate, *i.e.* the elders and captains of thousands of all Israel), and went, and made Abimelech king." (Judges ix. 6.)

The birthright was then in Joseph, and vested in Ephraim, at Shechem, where Joshua, who was of the tribe of Ephraim, had had his inheritance. So had also Eleazar, the high priest contemporary with Joshua. And the tabernacle was at Shiloh, not far distant from Shechem, and both within the territory of Ephraim. The remains of Joseph, brought out of Egypt, were interred at Shechem ; and by virtue of the birthright vested in Joseph by his father Jacob, the seat of government was in the territory assigned to Ephraim.

The compiler of the genealogies given in the first book of Chronicles helps us much here — (chap. v. 2), "For Judah prevailed above his brethren, and of him came the chief ruler, but the birthright was Joseph's."

In process of time, according to Divine appointment, the birthright passed to Judah ; and David took the castle of the Jebusites, on Mount Zion, "and dwelt in the fort, and built round about from Millo inward." The best writers are agreed that, in David's time, the city or castle of David (insulated from Mount Zion), was a rock or mount *per se*, with a valley all round its base. The principal gate was, as in other cities, the seat of judgment, and the house of Millo, the senate-house over, or attached, or near to the gate, from which David built inward. The valley outside was the valley of Millo. Solomon had a scruple of conscience, growing out of the circumstance that his queen's court (Egyptian, and perhaps idolatrous) was misplaced within the walls of the city of David, where the tabernacle then was, and he removed the queen's palace to the other side of the valley, on Mount Zion, thereafter better known and designated, in innumerable instances in Scripture, as "the daughter" of Zion. A better communication, historians tell us, was acquired betwixt the two localities, by filling up that portion of the valley which had separated the castle of David from the queen's palace on the daughter of Zion. In our own times, Mr. Johns, the architect, had to go down above 40 feet below the surface to reach a foundation for the Anglican Church of St. James; and I believe he went through the soil stated to have been filled in by Solomon. Solomon was instructed by God to build the temple on Mount Moriah. It is not so clear that either David or Solomon were instructed to remove the house of Millo from Shechem to Mount Zion. The children of Israel at large did not think so. They built willingly on Mount Moriah, but unwillingly on Mount Zion. After Solomon had finished the temple, he followed the queen, and built palaces and the house of the forest of Lebanon on the daughter of Zion. The latter was a new house of Millo, or senate-house, far exceeding the royal palaces in extent and splendour, which we can credit when we contrast our new Houses of Parliament with our palaces.

Solomon was seven years in building the temple, but he was thirteen years in building his own house. It did not please the tribe of Ephraim that the whole prestige of the seat of government at Shechem should thus be transferred to Mount Zion. The facts can be best stated in words of Scripture—"This is the reason of the levy which King Solomon raised; for to build the house of the Lord, and his own house, and Millo, and the wall of Jerusalem." (1 Kings ix. 15.) "He (Solomon) made him (Jeroboam, an Ephraimite) ruler over all the charge (burden) of the house of Joseph." (1 Kings xi. 28.) "And this was the cause that he (Jeroboam) lifted up his hand against the king: Solomon built Millo, and repaired the breaches of the city of David his father." (1 Kings xi. 27.) "And Rehoboam went to Shechem, for all Israel were come to Shechem to make him king." (1 Kings xii. 1.)

From these passages it is clear that Solomon had displeased the people by adding burdens or levies for buildings on Mount Zion, which the people thought excessive and unwarranted, and they simply required from Rehoboam a little breathing time, which he refused to grant, and thus lost ten-twelfths of his kingdom. Rehoboam ought to have foreseen the result of a stern resolution on the part of the authorities not to come to Solomon's house of Millo on Mount Zion, to crown him. They compelled him to come to the old house of Millo, at Shechem, notwithstanding the fact that the thrones of the house of David were set in the house of the forest of Lebanon. Joash was slain by his servants "in the house of Millo" (2 Kings xii. 20), probably when being carried in a litter, ill ("on his bed"), from his palace to Siloam, which agrees with the site assigned by Dr. Richardson [vol. ii. page 268] to the house of the forest of Lebanon, and the ruins of which he hopes will one day be excavated from beneath the surrounding and accumulated soil. There are many other references in the Old Testament to, and highly interesting details of, the house of the forest of Lebanon, or Millo, in Josephus and Adrichom. I gather from the New Testament that a building for similar purposes and uses stood on the old site in the days of our Lord.   G. H.

THEATRE ROYAL, ADELPHI.—The new Adelphi drama, by Mr. Buckstone (and an Adelphi drama is a thing per se, and has been so for as many years as we can remember, consisting of exciting mystery, injudicious love, streaks of broad fun, dreadful murder, and O. Smith), contains three very well painted scenes;—the Hall of Raynham Castle, with columns and establishments; the Hop-grounds; and a night-scene in the open country, "The Cross Roads." The disappearance of the castle on the hill, in the background of the latter, in the increasing darkness, and their re-appearance, illuminated by the moon, make a striking point, and show consideration. The wheel-tracks in the road give much completeness to the scene. Mr. Pitts is the chief artist here.

FORMS FOR WINDOW GLAZING.

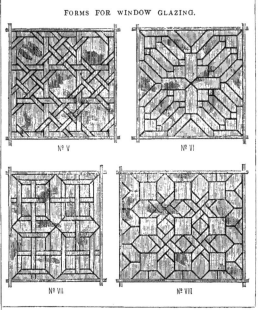

N° V   N° VI

N° VII   N° VIII

PATTERNS FOR WINDOW GLAZING.

ABOVE we add four to the patterns of glazing already given, and shall be glad to find them made use of. They are from various churches in France.

TELEGRAPHIC COMMUNICATION ACROSS SEAS.

THE proposed Dublin and Holyhead submarine line of telegraph has been estimated by Mr. Blunt, the projector, to cost about 16,000l. This sum, it was his desire, in the outset, the project being one of national importance, to obtain from the Treasury; but although he was assured that " their lordships had no wish to throw any impediment in the way of any experiment he might be disposed to make," and by the Admiralty that " they would hear of the success of this undertaking with much satisfaction," the proposal to advance the cash was declined, on the ground that their lordships " had no funds to apply to such purpose." It is under these auspices, such as they are, that Mr. Blunt proposes to carry out his design, unaided by the Treasury, but probably with the assistance of a company of shareholders. We know not whether it be intended to insulate the wires with gutta percha, but were it so, we have no hesitation in saying that such a scheme would be premature; for as yet nothing is known about the sufficiency, or even the existence, of any series of experimental tests of the capability of such an insulater to withstand even the physical or mechanical action of oceanic influences, especially the ravages of marine insects, or other of those living creatures which pervade the ocean, and, as we have already noted, bore their way through even the solid rock, consuming all that is not mineral. Moreover, the public as yet know nothing of the chemical power of gutta percha to resist various other destructive influences with which the ocean teems. In a slight experiment, instituted on the spur of the moment by ourselves for instance, we find that two at least, and not the most powerful, though in our case

the readiest, of those dissolving, penetrative, and insinuating agencies, the halogens, viz., bromine and iodine, which, with chlorine, constitute such peculiar and abundant elements in the chemical constitution of the ocean, in a very few minutes penetrate deeply into, blacken, and alter the substance of gutta percha, which does not appear to be capable, therefore, of resisting even these influences. Any appeal to the public for support should be preceded by adequate and successful experimental tests of the power of such wires, &c., as are to be used, to resist all sorts of oceanic influences, chemical as well as mechanical, for a sufficient length of time, and still to continue in good working order.

But it has even been suggested that we shall yet see the submarine electro-telegraphic communication established without conducting wires at all! and by the mere uninsulated circuit already completed between the ocean on the one hand, and the ocean bed on the other. Experiments, already made, at least give some countenance to the suggestion as a bare possibility, if not as a great probability, though many cannot even imagine the possibility of such a thing. May we be allowed to assist the fancy of the latter order of matter-of-fact minds a little without incurring the risk of being ranked with believers in the great probability of such a consummation, in place of in its mere bare possibility? We do love to dive a little into possibilities, and to put an unmitigated faith in the miraculous powers of nature, as the wonders of the nineteenth century so fully justify us in doing, without being such fools as to regard any thing as highly probable, merely because we deem it within the bounds of possibility. Our suggestion, however, is merely one of more or less slight analogy, and by no means one with higher pretensions as to explanation, &c. The possibility of such a communication, which may at least be conceived, when it is considered that an American-Indian is able to distinguish impressions produced by footsteps, &c., on the ground at immense distances and beyond the reach of the eyesight, by merely planting his ear close to the ground on which he stood. There is merely a vague analogy here, be it readily admitted, but it may give an idea of the possibility of electro-telegraphic impressions being distinguished by the apparatus of an electro-telegraphic *ear*, if we may so call it, and at an immense distance apart, without any *special* or insulated line of transmission. Indeed the analogy is not so very vague, after all, as may be supposed; for we can readily conceive the possibility of a couple of sharp-eared Indians carrying on an acousto-telegraphic communication by a preconcerted series of signal-impressions, transmitted backwards and forwards through the ground as the sole uninsulated medium. Moreover there is a stronger analogy we believe between the force called into action or excitation in acoustics, and that called into excitation in electrics, than is generally imagined.

RAILWAY JOTTINGS.

Circulating railway libraries seem to be now the order of the day, and about to have their run through all the railways, so that passengers themselves, no less than their parcels, may soon be any where "booked for a penny." The Great Western are having one with 1,000 volumes set agoing at their Paddington terminus, where passengers, for a like sum, may have the run of the whole, if they choose, or can get through them fast enough, "while waiting for the train." If this be all, however, and if it be only at the Paddington station that the 1,000 volumes are to be deposited and read, we ought rather to denominate this one a station-ary library than a circulating or a railway one, for the latter of which, duplicate thousands will be requisite at various stations to complete the circle of rotation. Messrs. Marshall and Sons have taken the contract, and retain the management, at Paddington, where the library table is also to be supplied with all the metropolitan papers, periodicals, and other publications, for sale.——The railway servants at Rugby are getting up a co-operative club, or association, for the purchase of provisions, &c., at wholesale prices, and their distribution or sale amongst the members at a trifling retail profit.——The works at the Great Western Docks, Millbay, Plymouth, were lately stopped, in consequence of some difference between the contractor and the company.——The tunnelling portion of the Manchester and Matlock line, near Matlock, is in a state of great forwardness, and the other works are proceeding steadily.——Some blasting operations of an extensive character have been effected at Bray Head, on the Waterford, Wexford, and Wicklow line of railway, by Mr. Purdon, the resident engineer. Three large drifts were lately made, 25 feet in depth, and 5 inches in diameter, with two supplemental ones of smaller dimensions. They were bored 15 feet from the surface of the rock, and about 6 feet apart. About 450 lbs. weight of gunpowder were used in charging them, principally government powder. They were connected with a 10-pair battery of Callan's, and fired. The explosive noise was not loud but rumbling, and the spalls were not driven any distance. The length of rock displaced was 45 feet, the breadth 25 feet, and depth 25 feet. Mr. Copeland, the local engineer, was the operator. Several minor blasts were made, showing, it is said, the activity with which obstacles formerly considered impracticable, are now disappearing. The long tunnel at the southern end of the head can be passed through walking upright. The original intention of crossing the deeply-indented ravines made by the sea, by means of bridges, is abandoned, and all will now be filled up at a less amount of expense, and with equal stability and safety. A Liverpool contemporary quotes rather an odd story about a recent meeting of this Irish Company in London, called, according to another authority in a Bradford paper, by the Directors themselves. "Neither the chairman nor the secretary attended," says our authority, "but the secretary's clerk (was he an Irish gintleman?) went in and ordered the shareholders to depart, insulting them most grossly, and threatening, when remonstrated with, to call a policeman to clear the room. Being asked who had authorised him to attend and dissolve the meeting, he said he would answer no impirtinent questions. Mr. Nash was called to the chair. It was resolved, that, in consequence of certain unsatisfactory matters relating to the accounts, a committee of three be appointed for their investigation, with liberty to report on the future prospects and management, or the suspension or sale of the line, and to bring these subjects before a committee of the House of Lords, now sitting on railway accounts."——The extension of the Blackwall line to Bow is now complete, as also is the alteration of gauge for the junction with the Eastern Counties line.——According to the *Leeds Intelligencer*, nearly three-fourths of the immense wooden viaduct now erecting at Mytholm Bridge, on the Holmfirth branch of the Huddersfield and Penistone Junction with the Sheffield and Manchester Railway, were lately blown down. Many of the colossal upright timber pieces composing the structure were snapped in twain as if they had been mere match-wood.——The viaduct at Comrie Den, on the Stirling and Dunfermline line, the foundation stone of which was laid on 5th February, 1847, was finished during the month just past. The length is 434 feet, width 45 feet, and height in centre from foundation-stone to top of cope-stone about 70 feet.——The works at the eastern termini of the Manchester, Sheffield, and Lincoln are being urged forward. The works at New Holland, designed by Mr. Fowler to complete the ferries on that side, have been let to Messrs. Wilson, of Leeds. They consist of an iron pontoon or floating pier of large dimensions, which is to rise and fall with the tide, and of two hollow wrought-iron girders, which will connect it with the present pier in such a way as to enable the passengers to descend, under cover, down a gentle incline from the railway train to the steam-boat. The works of the Great Grimsby Docks, as designed by Mr. Rendell, have been let to Messrs. Hutchings, Brown, and Wright.——The Great Western, says the *Gloucester Journal*, have made another retrenchment at the expense of the public convenience, by taking off several trains; amongst which is the 6 o'clock morning train from Paddington. The London papers do not in consequence reach Glocester, Bath, and Bristol until 12 o'clock, instead of 10, as formerly. What makes this alteration more remarkable is, that the train is taken off at the commencement of summer, during which it pays, though it has been continued through the winter, when it does not.——A Knaresborough correspondent, A. S. S., complains very justly of the miserable economy, or mistaken policy, whichever it be, still practised on various lines, of huddling all and sundry third-class passengers, at night, into unlighted carriages. Were these carriages lighted as they ought to be, not only would thieving and other practices be put a stop to, but, as our correspondent shrewdly observes, many who are able enough to pay for the higher classes of carriages, but who are actually induced to enter the third class under screen of the darkness no doubt intended to deter them, would be driven off to their own more befitting class-carriages so soon as they were exposed to view among third-class passengers. In general, too, there is not only a want of light but of ventilation in third-class carriages, which ought to be remedied, as it readily could be with very little expense.——A signal-light has been recently registered, "by the use of which a signal may be given by the passengers inside a carriage to the guard or attendant on the outside, whenever urgent necessity [such as the ignition of a carriage by friction or otherwise, the advent or dread of accidents from other causes, sudden illness or apparent death, ill-usage, or threats of murder, robbery, &c.] may require a communication to be opened between them." This is just another of those half measures which await the 'completion of the circle' of communication by the opening of a way of personal access *to* the carriages, whereby the guards may be the better able to judge of the urgency of the peril which such signal-lights may or may not faithfully indicate. The Government railway commissioners, it may be recollected, lately recommended to railway companies the adoption of a protected line of footboards for this very purpose. We trust the *recommendation* will not be overlooked or neglected till some serious fatality occur in which it may be proved to a jury that such a step *would* have constituted an efficient and sure preventive.——The United States' Senate have adopted a resolution, directing a survey to be made by the topographical corps to ascertain the best route for a railroad from the Mississippi to San Francisco.

NOTES IN THE PROVINCES.

The parish church of Aylsham remains closed for want of funds to render it safe. The foundations of the heavy tower had so far given way that the architect who examined them pronounced the whole building insecure till a considerable outlay shall have been devoted to it. Extensive repairs and alterations were recently made in the chancel by the vicar.——Numbers of unemployed hands have recently flocked to Portland in the hope of obtaining a share of the good things destined for the convicts. Not having made themselves eligible, they have not got "leave to toil" in accordance with their request. The supply, it appears, exceeds the demand. The works are progressing expeditiously.——Plans have been provided for the restoration of the pewing of St. Martin's Church, Salisbury. The estimated cost will be under 1,000*l.*, of which about 700*l.* can be obtained to start with, and a rate has been resolved on for the remainder, so that the restorations will be immediately proceeded with.——The modern altar-screen in Ludlow Church has been removed, and the original carved stone altar-piece again laid open to view and regilded. Mr. R. K. Penson is the architect selected to carry out the work of restoration here, for which a subscription is to be forthwith entered into.——The Swansea corporation lately proposed to borrow 50,000*l.* on corporate property, chiefly to make a wet-dock; but the Treasury, it is said, have refused to accede to the proposal.——The church of St. Peter, Everton, Liverpool, the foundation-stone of which was lately laid, will nearly form an equilateral triangle with St. George's and Christ Church, Everton. It is arranged to accommodate 1,200, mostly free. The floor will be laid with red and blue tiles, and the benches will be loose and uniform. The architecture is middle pointed, and the building will be divided into a lofty nave, with clerestory, north and south aisles, with choir and chancel. A spire, 150 feet in height, is building at the west end of the north aisle. The extreme length from east to west is 45½ yards, and the breadth from north to south 22 yards, exclusive of a large porch forming the access from Sackville-street. The amount of the contracts for its completion is 4,102*l.* Mr. Hay is the architect. An engraving of the edifice appears to have been prepared.——Amended plans for baths and washhouses at Manchester have been agreed on, and measures taken for obtaining tenders for the work.——One of the Norman windows of the south aisle of the nave of Southwell Collegiate Church has been recently filled with painted glass.——In "The Land we Live in," it is noted that a flax mill at Leeds measures about 400 feet long by more than 200 broad, and covers nearly two acres of ground. "Birmingham," adds the writer, "is justly proud of its Townhall, but this wonderful factory-room is nine times as large. Exeter Hall is one of the largest rooms in London, but it would require seven such to equal the area of this room."——Hawes Church, according to the *Leeds Intelligencer*, is now to be enlarged or a new one built.——Arrangements are in progress for the erection of a bridge across the Tyne at Ovingham.

Erection of Barracks, &c.—A circular has just been issued from the Horse Guards, inclosing ordnance regulations for the future erection and repairs of barracks in the United Kingdom. It orders that, for the future, no repairs shall be made without representation to the authorities on the subject. It would appear, says the *Morning Post*, that the expenditure of money in barrack erection and repairing has been for some time carried on in the most reckless manner. In Ireland barrack jobbing has been most wantonly carried on, although there is scarcely a barrack in the country capable of affording comfortable accommodation to the officers and men.

GLOUCESTER.

THE destruction of the noble cathedral of this city, as already noted by us, was lately threatened by a fire which broke out in the College School. The library of the school, which communicates with it, is over the Chapter-room, on the north side of the cathedral, and abutting against the north transept. But for great exertions, the fire must have extended to the north transept.

There have been several other fires in Gloucester since.

Another effort has been made in the town council to induce the establishment of a museum, and Mr. Bowly deserves credit for having done his utmost to induce the council to obtain accommodation for this purpose. We are sorry to say the proposition was negatived: that a city like Gloucester should have no museum is disgraceful to its many wealthy denizens. Not long ago a fine collection was offered them if they would but provide a proper place for its reception. Renew your efforts, Mr. Bowly, and persevere until you succeed.

THE SHIELD OF ÆNEAS—PITTS THE SCULPTOR.

SINCE you published my remark on the shield of Æneas last week, I have learned that on the death of Mr. Pitts, Messrs. Mortimer and Hunt (now Hunt and Roskill), spontaneously offered Mrs. Pitts 500*l*. for the model of the same, which offer was at once accepted by Mrs. Pitts, she reserving the right of disposing of casts in wax or plaster. At present no such casts have been made. The "Shield of Hercules from Hesiod," is still in the possession of Mr. Pitts' family. The "Pleiades adorning Night," was sold for only 50*l*., not the value of the time employed in making the cast from the model. In describing the working of the shield in silver, I ought to have mentioned that the silver plates are brought, by bending and hammering them, into form over a hard metallic cast taken from the model before they are placed on the pitchy substance for chasing and finishing. Δ.

METROPOLITAN COMMISSION OF SEWERS.

OPINION OF THE LAW OFFICERS.

A GENERAL court of the Metropolitan Commissioners of Sewers was held yesterday at the district office, Hatton Garden, Mr. Edward Lawes in the chair.

The court was held in consequence of the immense number of defaulters in the payment of sewer-rates, amounting altogether to nearly 10,000. This large number was produced partly in consequence of a practice which formerly existed in this commission, under the Local Act, 54th Geo. 3, c. 219, s. 10, to forego all sewer-rates on houses that were for any period unoccupied.

Long before the hour of commencing business, the vicinity of the office was so densely crowded with this immense number of appellants, that Hatton Garden was rendered almost impassable, and it required the assistance of a large body of police to preserve any thing like order. On the opening of the court the rush for admission was tremendous.

The New Islington Cattle Market.—The solicitor to Islington cattle market appealed against the rate, not wholly, but for such portion of it as was charged on the part appropriated as a layer for cattle, extending to fifteen acres. This part of the market had hitherto not been used for the purposes intended, or for any profitable purpose whatever. After some discussion it was agreed that a case should be drawn up by the solicitor to the company, and the subject receive further consideration.—The rest of the appeals were disposed of, the question of empty houses being reserved for future consideration.

The Closed-door Business of the Commission.—Mr. Leslie then rose and said, it became his duty to move that the case and opinion of the attorney and solicitor general, as to the mode of conducting the business of the commission by committee, be printed and circulated amongst the commissioners. The case, as submitted, consists of nearly forty sheets of brief paper, but the following are the questions embracing the main point referred for the consideration of the law officers of the Crown, with their answer thereto:—

QUESTIONS.

You are requested to advise the Metropolitan Commissioners of Sewers if they can lawfully perform their duties by such subdivision of labour as might be effected by means of committees appointed by the court, and consisting respectively of a limited number of commissioners, acting under the control of the court; and to what extent can the court delegate its authority to a committee, or sub-committee; and what, if any authority could be conferred on a limited number of commissioners to regulate works of a given kind, as, for instance, the cleansing of sewers, ditches, drains, &c., under sections 50, 52, and 58, or to regulate and manage the works of the commission generally.

If the court can make such delegation, would the orders of the committee, which might involve the entering into contracts, requiring works to be done and paid for, or imposing burdens on parties, be of force until afterwards confirmed by a court of sewers?

You will also please advise if the commissioners may appoint officers and make any regulations for the conduct of their business and appointment of committees, without previously making formal bye-laws under the 123rd section of the new Act. * * * * * *

OPINION.

We think that the commissioners may lawfully perform all duties of mere regulation and management by means of committees specifically appointed for the specific purpose under the 21st section, and of direction and superintendence of works and operations in progress by means of one or two commissioners appointed according to the 23rd section. The Act says nothing about sub-committees.

Orders for works and expenditure, decrees, rates, bye-laws, and other things which the commissioners have authority to do, must originate with the court, which speaks by its seal, and whose proceedings are public and recorded.

That original authority cannot be delegated, nor can any committee be empowered to use the seal. Under an order of court defining the purposes of the appointment, and referring the specific subject, a committee may lawfully conduct the details of business which the commissioners have directed to be done. It cannot, indeed, enter into contracts, for those need the seal, nor render works or burdens obligatory, for such obligation can be created only by act of court. The committee can originate no business, but any letters, plans, or accounts may be referred to a committee; and it may not only report on any matters referred to it for the information of the court, but also, under the 21st section, regulate and manage for every purpose indicated in their appointment all matters referred to them specifically by the court, in all details not requiring that act of court, by which alone the commissioners, as a body, can act. Practically this limitation of the powers of the committee leaves a wide scope for the subdivision of the labours of the commissioners. Committees may be empowered from time to time, by appointment for the specific purpose, to suggest plans, consider reports of officers, prepare and arrange details of works, and regulate and manage matters referred to them specifically by order of the court. Each committee should be appointed by an order of the court, fixing the quorum, and defining the mode of discharging the business referred to it from time to time by the court, and should report its acts to the court by means of the minutes of proceedings. Each court will exercise its discretion as to continuing, altering, or discontinuing the committee: and where any new matter is referred, or new purpose contemplated, it must be embodied in an express order of court. * * * *

Rules of general and permanent application would be "Bye-laws," and must be made according to the provisions of the 123rd section, and no new or additional offices can be created without a bye-law.

* * * * * * *

(Signed) JOHN JERVIS,
JOHN ROMILLY,
Temple, 10th March, 1849. J. HENDERSON.

After a few words from the Hon. F. Byng, Mr. Leslie's motion was put and carried unanimously, and the court adjourned.

Books.

Rudimentary Treatise on Geology, by Lieut.-Col. PORTLOCK, F.R.S.

Rudimentary Electricity, being a concise exposition of the general principles of electrical sciences and the purposes to which it has been applied, by Sir W. SNOW HARRIS, F.R.S.

Rudimentary Mechanics, being a concise exposition of the general principles of mechanical science, by CHARLES TOMLINSON.

Rudimentary Treatise on Well-digging, Boring, and Pump Work, by J. G. SWINDELL, M.I.B.A., with 16 plates. London: Weale, 1849.

Mr. WEALE'S series of Rudimentary Works for beginners, of which these are four, has now advanced to a considerable extent, and forms a goodly range of little red books, well calculated to be of service to the rising generation. Each subject is treated briefly but perspicuously, and the name of the author is a guarantee of the general soundness of the views advanced.

Mr. Swindell's treatise would be found particularly useful by several correspondents who have recently questioned us on the subject of well-digging and boring.

Relative to one part of the series reviewed by us some time since, namely, the treatise on "The Orders," a correspondent complains that in the second edition of it, which has been published, the definition of "copying," given in the first, is omitted.

"Copying," says the author, "is the process of converting design into manufacture, and an architect into a machine." "This (continues our correspondent) is a truth that every architect ought to know. Everybody cries out that architecture has declined, and at the present day we cannot produce such splendid works as those of our forefathers. Very true—but why? Because at the present day the principles of composition are usurped by the principles of copyism, and he who makes the most perfect copy is lauded as a genius; whereas he who attempts to produce a new work upon æsthetic principles is pooh-poohed as an innovator, a booby who presumes to think, when thought is quite unnecessary in the architecture of the nineteenth century." He calls on the publisher to restore the definition in subsequent issues, and we offer no objection.

Miscellanea.

ROYAL LYCEUM THEATRE. — A capital little piece by Mr. Planché, called "A Romantic Idea," in which Mr. Charles Mathews, Mr. Hall, Mr. Roxby, Miss Fitzwilliam, and others play admirably, has given Mr. W. Beverley an occasion for two architectural paintings of considerable excellence. The first is the ruins of a roofless hall in a German castle, with the tower at the back, and the whole bathed in the mild moon beams, a beautiful piece of effect, and in no way offending an architectural eye in the details. The second shews the hall restored; and remembering the "villanous compounds" which Gothic interiors some years ago usually presented on our stage, claims for Mr. Beverley great praise for congruous design as well as good painting. The sudden re-transformation to the ruin is very striking and effective.

QUEEN'S COLLEGE OF CIVIL ENGINEERS AND ARCHITECTS, BIRMINGHAM.—The heads of Queen's College, Birmingham, have matured a plan for the addition of an engineering department to the college on a site adjoining, recently purchased. They have resolved, in confirming a report of the committee appointed to mature the plan, that lecture rooms, model rooms, workshop, laboratory, and students' chambers be forthwith erected, and opened next October; that tutors and professors be appointed, the latter to give lectures on civil engineering, land surveying, practical mathematics, geometrical and architectural drawing, geology, mineralogy, and the arts of construction; that the system of tuition embrace a three years' course; that an engineering workshop be furnished, also a model room; that junior students be of the age of about sixteen, and those for the three years' course about eighteen; that students prepare for matriculation in the University of London end of first year, and for taking their B.A. degree in same University end of third year; and that students who have matriculated and graduated be admissible as candidates for fellowships in Queen's College.

THE BURIAL IN TOWNS QUESTION.—It will be seen, by an advertisement, that a public meeting will be held at the late Crown and Anchor, in the Strand, on the 4th of April, to petition Parliament to close burial places in cities and towns; Mr. Bond Cabbell, M.P., will preside. The great importance of the question is becoming gradually felt. The City Sewers Commissioners have been stirring actively in it, and have caused the discontinuance of burials at St. Bride's. A correspondent who forwarded to us a short time since a plan of the abominable Spa-fields ground and the neighbourhood, suggested that a plan of the town, showing clearly all these plague-spots, and accompanied by a few statistics, could not fail to have a powerful effect on the public.

HOUSE-PAINTERS' BRUSHES.—Mr. Nash, a manufacturer, has registered a supposed improvement in painters' brushes: it consists in the use of a metal binding, of circular form, flattened into a somewhat oval shape at the upper part of the brush near the flags of the bristles, with the view to cause the top of the brush to be flattened at the back and front of the same, in order to afford better surfaces for use. The asserted advantages of this arrangement are, that by the substitution of the metallic binding for strings wound round the flags of the bristles—as now in common use—or of wire, the brushes are not so liable to come to pieces or allow loose hairs to come out. Whether or not the increased strain on the workman's wrist, slight though the extra weight may be, will be found disadvantageous, remains to be seen.

COMPETITION.—Five pounds are offered for a plan (to be approved of by a committee) for the erection of a school-room at Deptford.

PROJECTED WORKS.—Advertisements have been issued for tenders, by 31st inst., for the restoration of a portion of Llandaff Cathedral (the Presbytery); by 9th April, for the erection of additional buildings to the workhouse of St. George (East), Middlesex; by 14th, for the execution and completion of the criminal court, &c., at Cardiff, Glamorganshire; by 4th, for the erection of baths and washhouses at Bristol; by 19th inst., for the complete restoration of the tower of Thurmaston Church; by 21st, for the erection of a new north aisle to the church at Great Barford, near St. Neots, and otherwise restoring the same, and building a new vestry, with other works,—also for the complete restoration of the chancel of same church, with new roof, &c. (separate tenders); by 5th April, for building a stone bridge of one arch or more, or an iron suspension-bridge, over the Ithon, at Disserth, Radnorshire; by 2nd, for rebuilding a house and offices (chiefly with old materials) at Petham, near Canterbury; by same date, for the erection of committee-rooms and offices, and the enlargement and alteration of warehouses at the Stourbridge Wharf; by 23rd inst., for the excavation of a new reservoir at North Shields, and the walling of a reservoir there, both for the North Shields Water-works (separate or together); by 26th, for the removal of a portion of the bank of the river Clyde at Glasgow; by 27th, for erecting the works of a tunnel at Islington for the Great Northern Railway; by 28th, for the erection of the stations, sheds, goods warehouses, &c., on the Shrewsbury and Birmingham line at Oaken Gates and Shiffnal, and also for the stations at Albrighton and Codsall, and for the company's offices and several shops at Wolverhampton station; and by 24th, for supplying and laying down Cornish granite kerb, Yorkshire paving, flag-paving, pebble-paving, granite cubes,—also for taking up and relaying old paving, &c., all at Greenwich.

BLIND BUILDERS.—Tenders for the erection of a new wing to the Derbyshire General Infirmary, at Derby, Mr. H. J. Stevens, architect. The quantities were furnished.

Watts, Derby	£8,750	0
Cooper, ditto	7,970	0
Freeman and Co., Belper	7,850	0
Wood, Derby	7,400	0
Clark, Sheffield	7,315	0
Thompson, Edwin, Derby	6,900	0
Slater, ditto	6,750	0
Thompson, George, ditto	6,250	0

The lowest was accepted.

A correspondent gives the following list of tenders for building and finishing a four-roomed house, with washhouse and three privies, with garden wall 6 feet high from ground, opened by the surveyor, Mr. C. Foster, on the 12th.

Essex, Islington	£283	10
Bagg, Clerkenwell	231	10
Pilbeam, Bagnigge Wells	220	0
James, Islington	218	0
Brake, Clerkenwell	215	0
Gladdie, Islington	215	10
Haswell, ditto	186	0
Kenwood, Hackney-road	180	10
Day, Caledonian-road	170	0
Pickford, Islington	138	0

THE "BURIAL OF HAROLD."—Our readers will remember a letter from a correspondent in the last number but one of THE BUILDER, on this subject. Further inquiry shows that the story given in writing (as we understand) at the bar of the house where the daub which led to the reports is, to persons who, much interested in the matter, went there to inquire, and which seemed to give colour to the case, was incorrect.* The statement now is that only eighteen months ago the canvas on which it is painted had on it the portraits of two children. We fully expected that the story could be proved wholly groundless, and gave place to the letter, finding the statement current in several quarters, with no other motive than that it should be so. Our only regret is that Mr. F. R. Pickersgill did not, instead of addressing a note to us as little marked by courtesy as wisdom, avail himself of the opportunity which was in kindness offered him, and disprove the assertions which were being made.

* The story as given was, that the present owner of the picture had bought it four months ago in the "Cut," Westminster. His attention being afterwards led to the likeness of it to the "Harold," he learnt that the party from whom he obtained it had had it about 2½ years, and that he bought it of a picture dealer in the Blackfriars-road, who had had it in his possession more than two years.

TOMB OF NAPOLEON, PARIS.—A French paper, quoted by the Athenæum, gives the following details relating to works at the tomb of the Emperor Napoleon. An immense circular crypt has been dug beneath the dome; within which, on three shafts of green marble, the sarcophagus containing the emperor's coffin will repose. The block of porphyry which the curious are now flocking to see on the Quai d'Orsay is destined to cover the sarcophagus. A lower gallery, paved in mosaics and lined with marble bas-reliefs representing the principal events in the Emperor's life, will admit the public to circulate about the sarcophagus. Twelve colossal statues in white marble—of which six are already placed—will sustain an upper gallery whence it may be looked down on and its details examined from above. These allegorical statues, from the chisel of Pradier, represent the principal branches of human activity—Science, Legislation, War, Arts, &c. A magnificent altar of black marble veined with white rises in front of the tomb. Four large and beautiful columns, also of black and white marble, support the canopy of carved and gilt wood. Ten broad steps, each cut from a single block of Carrara marble, lead up to the funeral altar. Beneath this altar is the passage to the lower gallery above spoken of, whose entrance is guarded on either side by the tombs, in black marble, of Bertrand and Duroc—dead marshals keeping wait at the door of the imperial dead. The marbles employed in the construction of this tomb cost not less than 60,000l. in the rough; the sculptures and bas-reliefs executed by Simart cost 24,000l. The block of porphyry for the covering of the sarcophagus weighs 45,000 kilogrammes; its extraction and carriage to Paris cost 5,600l.

DILAPIDATIONS.—On Wednesday last a case of considerable importance between landlord and tenant was decided in the County Court at Kingsbridge, by the judge, Mr. W. M. Pread. The plaintiff sued the defendant for 4s. 6d., being the amount paid by him for repairing the glass of the windows of a dwelling house, left by defendant on the 8th of December last, and which the defendant refused to repair. His honour inquired what agreement was made when defendant first took the house three years and a half ago? The plaintiff said that he could not recollect, but relied entirely on the custom of the country. He said he had been in the habit of letting many dwelling-houses of his own for the last twenty-five years, and had also been employed to some extent as an agent for other owners of houses, and had always relied on the custom of the country to compel the tenants to repair the glass broken by them. His honour immediately gave judgment for the defendant, observing, that a tenant was no more bound by the custom of the country to repair the glass of the windows, than the thatch or any other part of the house. Thus far the Devonport and Plymouth Chronicle. We should like to know where Judge Pread got his law from.

GUILDFORD DRAINAGE COMPETITION.—What are we to think of the proceedings of the Commissioners of Pavements with respect to the plans, &c. lodged for the drainage of the town on the 15th January last? The only information I have received has been derived from your paper of the 3rd ult., which was not of the most satisfactory description. Should the statement made by your correspondent, in the number of your journal referred to, be correct, I hope the competitors will take some steps to expose such reprehensible practices on the part of public bodies, and lead to the parties in question putting forth some explanation of what they have been about, and what they intend to do.—A COMPETITOR.

EMPLOYMENT OF THE WORKING CLASSES.—A public meeting of the trades of London has been held at the Hall of Commerce, Threadneedle-street, "To take into consideration the distressed condition of the trades of the metropolis, and the working classes generally, with a view to petition Parliament to sanction the establishment of home colonies, as a mode of giving immediate employment to the numerous but compulsorily unemployed of our population. Also to consider the propriety of petitioning Parliament for the establishment of local boards of trade." The chair was taken by Mr. Luke J. Hansard.

THE LONDON EXCHANGE CHIMES.—The bells of the Royal Exchange have caused some jangling, and have put the pipes out of several members of the Common Council. One of the Messrs. Mears, who have received the tin in exchange for their bell-metal, went to the court a few days ago, quite out of tune, objected to certain statements which had gone forth, and offered to make any alteration that might be required by the corporation. Of course he could not admit that his bells were cracked—thought perhaps that the epithet applied better to those in the court who would let their clappers run to his injury. Old citizens shake their heads, and say the new chimes would never have brought back "Whittington."

ROYAL INSTITUTE OF ARCHITECTS.—At a meeting held on the 5th inst., Mr. R. Lacon Sibley was elected an associate, and various donations of books were announced. Mr. I'Anson read a paper on the probable form and design of the Temple of Solomon at Jerusalem. The chairman announced that the council had resolved that papers read at one meeting should be open to discursive observations at the succeeding one, being of opinion that such arrangement would tend to elicit much valuable information.

DUNDEE ROYAL ARCH COMPETITION.—Competitors complain that they have as yet heard nothing of this matter. We are told that a very large number of designs have been received, and that the committee have divided them into three classes.

STATE OF HYDE-PARK.—Sir: I beg to call your attention to the curious manner in which the drainage of Hyde-park is conducted. Some time back the rain-water collected in the ditch between the Mount-gate of Kensington Gardens and the bridge at the Serpentine. This deep pond was allowed to remain a week or ten days, much to the dread of nursery-maids and children, and considerably so to pedestrians at night. Well, after a time, a pump was placed and the water drawn off, and as far as I could see no inspection made of the drain itself, which is no doubt choked up. The rain of Wednesday last refilled this ditch, and the same blind method will, I suppose, be adopted. I wish you would hint in your valuable columns, that the path running across from the Prince's-gate to the bridge is in a most disgraceful state of mud; and could you send one of your carpenters with his saw, to remove the rails, under which the pedestrian is now obliged to stoop, and perhaps break his back, it would be advantageous to do so.—COCKNEY.

SHAPE IN RESPECT OF AREA.—In THE BUILDER of 24th inst., your correspondent "B. B. Grantham," gives a calculation elucidating "shape in respect of area:" he says,—"A figure which has all its four sides equal, contains the greatest area within the same length of wall," viz., 80 feet by 4, equal 320 feet, equal 6,400 feet area. Suppose a circle 320 feet in circumference, the area thus circumscribed will be found to contain 8,145 feet, exceeding the space inclosed by a square (as above) by 1,745 feet. It is another question whether the increased space gained between circular and square enclosures (each having a like quantity of walling) would compensate for difficulties of internal arrangement, for such purposes as your correspondent alludes to.

JOHN KELLY.

TO OUR READERS.

TENDERS

For the new Fulham Union, opened at the Hammersmith Workhouse, on Tuesday (in the presence of tho builders), Mr. Gilbert, Architect.

F. Faulkner	£15,800
Kates and Chamberlin	16,613
H. W. Cooper	15,087
Edward Carter	14,897
E. B. Gammon	14,490
F. W. Costar	14,451
J. T. Barr	14,443
G. Bird and Co.	14,366
M. Patrick	14,066
T. Burton	13,931
T. Crook	13,871
S. and H. Bird	13,749
W. Filbeam	13,558
Cooper and Davis	13,382
J. Willson	13,386
W. Higgs	13,291
T. and W. Piper	13,259
J. T. Taylor	13,189
R. and K. Curtis	12,790
J. Glenn (accepted)	12,484
	12,466

MEETINGS OF SCIENTIFIC BODIES

Held during the ensuing week.

MONDAY, March 19.—Institute of Architects, 8 P.M.
TUESDAY, 20.—Instit. of Civil Engineers, 8 P.M.
WEDNESDAY, 21.—Society of Arts, 8 P.M.
THURSDAY, 22.—Royal Society, 8½ P.M.; Society of Antiquaries, 8 P.M.
FRIDAY, 23.—Archæological Association, 8½ P.M.

TO CORRESPONDENTS.

Received.—" J. K.," " J. A." (Mr. Hutchison's address is " Calverley Quarries, Tonbridge Wells." The above hand-saws appeal well worthy of (trial). " R. I.—" T. P.," " D.B.," " S V., sen.," " R. C.," " E. M." (no good end would be answered by an interview). " A Constant Subscriber." " A Subscriber." (The Recommendation for Institute of Architects must be signed by three fellows. There would be no difficulty in getting the signatures. Call on or write to the secretary at 16, Grosvenor-street). " S B.," " J. B. W.," " A. M. Z." (several recipes were given in early numbers). " Twelve Years' Clerk," " Captain N.," " W. H. S.," " N. H. K.," " R. H. S.," " W. R.," " A Subscriber," " O. H.," " M P.," " E. R." " Schedule of Contract for the Ordinary Works and Repairs to Buildings in Charge of the Department of the Woods and Forests, in London district," (Clowes and Son, Charing-cross.)

NOTICE.— All communications respecting *advertisements* should be addressed to the "Publisher," and not to the "Editor:" all other communications should be addressed to the EDITOR, and *not* to the publisher.

No. CCCXX.

SATURDAY, MARCH 24, 1849.

MONGST the new works at this moment before us is a thin folio of Illustrations of Strixton Church, Northamptonshire, by Mr. E. Barr.*

Strixton Church is a remarkably simple Early English Church, consisting of a nave 20 feet wide, and twice 20 in length, and a chancel 30 feet long, and half that in width. It has a bell-cot at the west-end, and a little porch on the north side. It will seat 200 persons, supposing one-fourth to be children, and it is given "as an ancient example, of which the general effect is pleasing and good, while it may be built at a very moderate cost,"—750l. says the estimator, including the fittings. The object of the publication is that the church may be copied. The introduction says, in tone gratulatory, that the bell-cot given in a similar publication of Wilcote Church "has been *copied* in numerous instances since," and that this of Strixton will probably "also be *followed*." The church is "an excellent model for *imitation*;" it presents valuable features "for an architect to *copy*," and so it goes on *copy*, copy, copy,—itself being only forty-five lines in length.

Here are four walls with a roof on them, two doors required for access, and a few narrow windows for light, and all we men of the nineteenth century can do, boasting such power of intellect, and such dominion of knowledge, as dark ages guessed not at, is to copy the structures these ages left, without a thought of our own, and almost without a feeling. As was asked long ago, in our pages,— " Is the fountain of the beautiful a narrow shallow well, into which our fathers dipped and drained the utmost drop at once ? Or is it a vast deep ocean, boundless, bottomless, into which they dipped and drew forth beauty, and into which we, in our turn, may dip and draw forth more,—dip with our far longer line, and reach far deeper and far denser regions in the infinite profundity of its teeming, teeming bosom ?" It may be thought that we have indeed become a race of brainless imitators.

Of the value of careful representations of ancient examples, the necessity of an intimate acquaintance with the works of our forefathers, and of full investigations of the principles on which they worked, we have too often spoken to run any risk of being now misunderstood. To re-combine these materials and produce fresh beauties,—to work on these principles under the circumstances immediately occurring, and so to eliminate new results, we may at least aspire, —exhibiting some mind, improving where practicable, and meeting modern requirements.

Mere slavish re-production, and the condition of mind to which such a course necessarily leads, are to be carefully avoided and universally discouraged.

The Architectural Publication Society have issued the first part of their volume of illustrations for the current year, containing twelve plates from drawings by Messrs. John John-

* "Elevations, Sections, and Details of Strixton Church, Northamptonshire." J. H. Parker, Oxford and London. 1849.

son, Sydney Smirke, J. M. Lockyer, C. Fowler, jun., John Davis, D. Wyatt, D. Mocatta, and T. L. Donaldson. The drawings are illustrative of the terms campanile, ceiling, chimney, corbel, cortile, loggia, pavement, staircase, &c., on which articles will be given, in such a manner as to take their place hereafter in that complete " Architectural Dictionary," at the production of which the society aim.

Under the head "Campanile," we have seven examples, inscribed Genoa (2), Lago di Guarda, Cremona, Mount Cenis, Lombardy, and Messina. "Cortile" is illustrated from the Palazzo Caprarola, by Vignola ; " Loggia," from the cathedral, at Spoleto, by Bramante ; and under the head " Staircase," there are four suggestive examples, from the castle of Bracciano, near Rome, the Church of Francesco, at Assisi, the Cathedral at Modena, and the Forum Romanum, by Bernini. The plates are executed in lithography, by Messrs. Day, on a paper, it may be well to mention, which will take colour. Of the lithography we cannot speak well ; it is unworthy of Messrs. Day's reputation, and should lead the committee to hesitate before placing another set of drawings in their hands.

The idea of "The Architectural Scrap Book," by Messrs. Butler and Hodge, of which the two first parts are before us,* would almost seem to have been taken from the announced intention of the Publication Society, to issue periodical collections of sketches of parts of buildings. If so, the idea is in bad taste. The first part contains four plates and seven subjects ; Gateway, Magdalen College, Oxford (by Pugin) ; Chimney-piece, Stowe; Oriel window, Brazennose College, Oxford ; two dormers, and two turrets. The authors point attention to the value of a Turret in composition, and remark on the neglect of this inexpensive feature in England.†

America contributes to our budget of books a very useful volume on "School Architecture," by Mr. Barnard, a commissioner of public schools in Rhode Island,‡ of which 20,000 copies have been gratuitously circulated in the States, where the author has been called upon to labour in the cause of common-school improvement, or among the friends of popular education in other parts of the country.§ This book contains a large amount of information on the subject, especially as to the modes of ventilation adopted in the American schoolhouses, and as to the fittings.

The taste displayed in the elevation of most of the schools is not great, if we may judge from the engravings given ; but a feeling of the important effect with well-ordered, well - proportioned, and fittingly - adorned buildings have in the education of children and on the character of a nation, is beginning to grow up in America. "Why," says one of their writers, Mrs. Sigourney, "why should not the interior of our schoolhouses aim at somewhat of the taste and elegance of a parlour ? Might not the vase of flowers enrich the mantelpiece, and the walls display not only well-executed maps, but historical engravings or

* " The Architectural Scrap Book, containing Sketches of Picturesque and Beautiful parts of Buildings, English and Continental."—Beaufort-buildings, Strand.
† The second part contains an old house in Aldate's-street, Oxford ; Well-house in Marquise, near Boulogne ; Gateway, Stowe (by Kent) ; Fire-place, Yate-court ; and a tomb in Beaconsfield Church.
‡ " School Architecture ; or Contributions to the Improvement of School-houses in the United States." New York : Barnes and Co. There is no English publisher's name on the title-page, but the book could doubtless be obtained at Mr. John Chapman's, Strand.
§ Mr. Barnard's labours in this field have been very extensive: copies of his works have been recently placed in the British Museum.

pictures ? and the bookshelves be crowned with the bust of moralist or sage, orator or father of his country ? Is it alleged that the expense, thus incurred, would be thrown away, the beautiful objects defaced, and the fair scenery desecrated ? This is not a necessary result. I have been informed by teachers who had made the greatest advances towards the appropriate and elegant accommodation of their pupils, that it was not so. They have said it was easier to enforce habits of neatness and order among objects whose taste and value made them worthy of care, than amid that parsimony of apparatus, whose pitiful meanness operates as a temptation to waste and destroy." The same applies in the dwellings of the poor.

And again :—" Let the communities, now so anxious to raise the standard of education, venture the experiment of a more liberal adornment of the dwellings devoted to it. Let them put more faith in that respect for the beautiful, which really exists in the young heart, and requires only to be called forth and nurtured, to become an ally of virtue and a handmaid to religion. Knowledge has a more imposing effect on the young mind, when it stands, like the apostle with the gifts of healing, at the 'beautiful gate of the Temple.' Memory looks back to it more joyously from the distant or desolated tracks of life, for the bright scenery of its early path." "But when young children are transferred from the nursery to those buildings, whose structure, imperfect ventilation, and contracted limits furnish too strong an idea of a prison, the little spirits, which are in love with freedom and the fair face of nature, learn to connect the rudiments of knowledge with keen associations of task-work, discomfort, and thraldom."

Let us all strive to cultivate a perception of the Beautiful, satisfied that it tends not merely to refine and delight, but to make better the world.

ON THE IMPORTANCE OF A KNOWLEDGE AND OBSERVANCE OF THE PRINCIPLES OF ART BY DESIGNERS.*

IN painting, the artist has to embody his ideas of scenes, persons, or incidents, by a pictorial representation of natural objects ; and in proportion to the skill of his design and the truth of the representation, must be the vividness with which his idea will be expressed. In considering what would be the most essential and universal characteristics of the subject to be depicted,—as light and atmosphere in a landscape, action and expression in a group of figures, breathing individuality in a portrait,— we arrive at once at the most important points which the painter has to attain by means of his art, and the most difficult of representation by the use of pigments on a flat surface. And here the principle that illusory imitation is not the province of painting, becomes strikingly apparent ; for can light, atmosphere, motion, breath, vitality, be imitated ? They can only be indicated suggestively by depicting their visible effects upon the scene or object ; which of course implies an accurate representation of the real forms, or rather, of their momentary appearance under the particular aspect ; for it is the apparent forms, surface, and hues of things that the painter has to depict, though he can only do this by understanding their real form and nature, and the effects of light and atmosphere upon them. A picture is (or should be) the representation of what is seen, either in reality or in the mind's eye, from one point of view, at one moment of time, and should convey the impression of an idea stamped upon the mind of the painter at that moment ; which all fine pictures do. Design gives unity and definition to the conception. But if the artist, unmindful of these principles, perverts his executive skill by imitating to *illusion* the

* See page 122, *ante.*

chair in which his sitter is seated, the table-cover on which the hand rests, or the satin dress in which a lady is attired, the vitality of the portrait is lessened, if not entirely lost; for the semblance of life in the face is made to appear unreal by contrast. So in a landscape; if a bit of rock in the foreground be painted with microscopic minuteness, unity of effect is destroyed; for it is evident that the eye, while scrutinising a near object, cannot take in remote ones at the same moment. Who does not remember to have seen instances where the sails of a windmill in a landscape, or a vessel tossing on a rough sea, have been represented so as to appear fixtures, reminding one of those sporting prints where the wheels of a chaise are depicted as spinning round with such velocity, that the spokes of the wheels are invisible, while the body of the vehicle, the horse and harness, the driver and his costume, are represented with all the minute details of still life? There is a popular coloured print of a smuggler presenting a pistol, in which it was attempted to convey an effect of reality by protruding the figure out of the canvas; a violation of the principles of art that results in making the figure appear as flat as a pancake, and the pistol to lose what appearance of projection the painter had given it. The absurd and now obsolete practice of cutting out the portrait of a child from its panel and sticking it up in a corner to deceive the eye, results in a failure; for the loss of the background renders the figure flat, and destroys the illusion. In the execution of modern pictures, too, we have so often to regret the absence of luminous brightness in the light, of transparency in the shadows, and consequently of rotundity and animation in the forms, and of atmosphere in the *ensemble*, that it is becoming evident to some of the most thoughtful and inquiring artists, that the modern painters have lost sight of the principles of colouring which were acted upon by the Venetian, Flemish, and Dutch schools, and also by our own Gainsborough.

But as design is more especially the subject of this paper; let us pass to the department of ornamental art, in which there is most need of principles to guide the inventive talent and adaptive ingenuity of ornamentists.

The value of ornament consists in its being used to add beauty to common things, and to relieve the blankness of bare walls, floors, and ceilings. Since the Puritans banished colour from English churches until the present time, decorative art has performed perpetual penance in a sheet of whitewash, and our national ecclesiastical architecture has been mutilated and deformed, not only by tasteless churchwardens, but by accomplished architects, who, in respect of English architecture, were as ignorant as their employers. But let us not forget what we owe to Wren; nor that to his discerning encouragement we owe the development of the genius of the greatest ornamentist this country has seen — Grinling Gibbons, whose wood carvings have been so well appreciated and emulated in our own day by Mr. Rogers.

In entering upon the wide field of ornament, it becomes necessary to draw a distinct line of demarcation between the several branches of ornamental design; namely, the ornamentation of architecture; of vessels, utensils, and implements; and of textile fabrics. Each of these is governed by different principles, but in all, the practice of illusory imitation is alike objectionable: true art repudiates shams. The great blank space of raw white plaster that shocks the sense as well as the taste in almost every room we enter, from the poor man's garret to the gilded saloons of the wealthy, is a relic of puritanical aversion to colour; and the drab hues that make dreary our parlours and dining-rooms, are only a Quakerish compromise. The ceilings

> "Where sprawl the saints of Verrio and Laguerre."

are bad in taste, and equally inconvenient and disagreeable to look at: even pictures, though by Rubens, Titian, or Michaelangelo, when let into a ceiling, are solecisms in point of taste; for the penalty of admiring them is a crick in the neck, even though, as in the churches and palaces abroad, you are accommodated with cushions to enable you to view them in a supine posture. Mimic balustrades and apertures in ceilings, and still more, pictured skies, are obvious anomalies; they fail as attempts at illusion, and as ornaments they are not beautiful. Ornament is indispensable in a ceiling; and whether it be moulded in relief or not,—colour, or gilding, if not both, according to the character of the apartment and its ornaments and furniture, is necessary to make it harmonize with the walls: a waste of whiteness affronting a Persian carpet and pictured walls is a barbarism that, accustomed as we are to see it, cultivated taste revolts at. Yet paper-hangings are often so ugly as to make one resigned to the drab-tinted stucco. I have a vivid impression of the effect of a particular room, of the gloomiest coldness, that colour of any kind, not absolutely discordant, is preferable. This room was painted a leaden-coloured drab, with raw-white ceilings, of course, and it was hung with sad-coloured draperies edged with black; the chimney-piece was as black as the stove; the chairs and sofa, covered with black horse-hair, stood upon a blue and black carpet; and prints in black frames enlivened the walls: it was a room in half-mourning, and its gloom fell like a pall upon a visiter. The exhilarating influence of a cheerful and elegant room is only inferior to that of a sunny day out of doors, or lively and agreeable society: black,—whether marble, horse-hair, wood, or iron,—should be inadmissible.

In painted decoration, and in the patterns of paper-hangings, curtains, or carpets, form ought to be regarded chiefly, if not merely, as a vehicle of colour. How tiresome and tantalizing is the reiteration of patterns in a paper-hanging, especially when great splotches of red, or some powerful colour, are scattered over it, or cutting lines of blue, or some other positive hue, divide the wall into strips. Intense colours ought to be used sparingly, and skilfully distributed, so as to enliven the mass of secondary tints; for a room is made to seem smaller by strong contrasts of colour or harsh lines, as ceilings are apparently lowered by deep mouldings or powerful colours; indeed, vivid colours are not essential either to the elegant or cheerful aspect of a room. The walls should form a chaste, but not dull, background to the furniture, pictures, and occupants; gaudy carpets of large patterns are therefore objectionable. If positive colours are used, these should be subdivided by the intricacies of a small and undefinable pattern, like the Persian and Turkey carpets, which have never been equalled for richness and sobriety combined.

The art of the decorator is not yet rightly understood, and therefore not duly appreciated. It should not be confined to the painting of walls and ceilings; for the effect of the richest and most beautiful decoration may be destroyed by a discordant carpet, by hangings of inharmonious hues, and by ill-chosen furniture; nay, even by the injurious contrast of a hall, staircase, or ante-room, while a house may be rendered elegant and cheerful, without any parade of ornament, by a skilful assortment of colours, suited to the aspect and uses of each apartment, and the juxtaposition of ante-rooms and lobbies. But to effect this requires practised skill and taste on the part of the artist.

In designing patterns for textile fabrics, the uses to which the drapery is to be applied requires to be more considered than is commonly the case. Obviously the pattern for a dress should not be so large as that for a curtain; yet one sees silks and satins in the mercers' windows, the wearers of which would certainly appear as if robed in window curtains, or wall hangings. The elaborate imitation of flowers in dresses is wrong upon principle, because the effect is to divert attention from the *ensemble* presented by the dress of the wearer; the nondescript patterns of India shawls, in which the effect is seen in the mass, are still superior to modern designs. A great nosegay of dowers on a shawl, or a dress sprinkled with bouquets, is only a degree less absurd than the horns and trumpets which decorate the dressing gown of Signor Lablache in "Il Fanatico per la Musica." The effect of harmonious combinations of colour is what the pattern designer should rely upon; and of these the variety is endless. The famous Swiss designer of patterns, whose fecundity of invention is extraordinary, when asked where he got the materials for his varied and beautiful combinations, replied, "The wealth of nature is inexhaustible." And he then explained that the colours of birds and insects, of lichens, of sea-weeds as well as flowers, all furnished him with harmonious contrasts of colour; but he did not content himself with picturing the objects entire—he did not sprinkle a dress with beetles or humming birds, or cover it with lichens or sea-weed, nor even with the most beautiful flowers; but he selected a particular harmony of hues, perhaps in the bottom of the calyx of a flower, on the breast of a bird or the back of an insect, and applied it by means of some arbitrary form, suggested also, probably, by a natural object. The resources of the pattern designer in nature are boundless, if he uses them aright; but to copy literally the most beautiful object is crude and wasteful error. In designing patterns for draperies of all kinds, the artist may be content to seize and adapt the suggestions of nature. In designing decorations for architecture his fancy should become suggestive of ideas. But in both, wherever colour is employed, forms are valuable chiefly as a means of varying the quantities and distribution of colour; form is the medium for displaying colour. In draperies that hang in heavy folds like curtains, it is evident that the shape of the pattern is not seen truly; its effect, as shown in the play of colour, is infinitely varied by the folds, and therefore a large bold pattern, as in damask, is preferable. In dresses where the folds are smaller, and especially in scarfs, angular patterns are not only admissible, but pleasing, because the multitude of cross-folds not only destroys the formality of pattern, but gives rise to an infinity of piquant combinations. But when large plaids are worn in the flat drapery of a cloak, the back of the wearer is squared out in chequers, and one might almost as well hang a chess-table cover over the shoulders. So in damask, to hang flat in the panels of a room or diapered walls, the pattern need be so subdued either by slight modulations of colour or smallness and intricacy, that the eye should be prevented from resting on the forms, and regard only the effect. The pattern of a carpet, by the same rule, should not provoke attention to its details: its effect alone ought to be attractive. Nothing can be a greater violation of the principles of art than the French tapestry carpets, which, to be seen properly, ought to be placed in an empty room. In modern apartments, where the floor is almost hidden by chairs and sofas, tables, and musical instruments, what are called bold and handsome patterns can never be seen; even if it were desirable. And to work coats of arms and other heraldic devices, is to trample upon the pride of ancestry and the pomp of heraldry. While noting the impropriety of applying honoured symbols to base uses, I may be allowed to throw a word of derision on the offensive impropriety of pictured handkerchiefs: sporting men may like to tie the portrait of a race-horse round their necks, and country cousins may find a map of London on cambric as useful as the dwellers in the backwoods of America, where paper was scarce, did the newspaper which the Yankees tell us was printed in clay on linen, and washed off when the news was read to receive another impression; but to dry the moisture with Jenny Lind's charming face is a very ignoble mode of complimenting the Swedish nightingale.

In designs for hardware, whether of silver or brass, glass or porcelain, form, and proportion are paramount; no ornamentation, however rich or fanciful, can redeem bad proportion or ungraceful form; while a beautiful form unadorned is itself ornament of the most refined and pleasing description. Neither should ornament be so prominent as to overlay, or prevent the full development of form; while neither form nor ornament ought to interfere with utility. The principle is so obvious that it is surprising there should be any need for enunciating it; yet if we look into the windows of our china shops, the infinite variety of ugliness of shape and proportion displayed in vases and other ornaments for mantel-pieces, is extraordinary. And the designs made by artists for Felix Summerley's art-manufactures are more admirable for fanciful ornamentation than elegance and symmetry of form. But this does not diminish the claim which Felix Summerley has upon all who take an interest in art, for giving a fresh impulse to artistic ingenuity, and directing the attention of artists, manufacturers, and the public, to the value of ornament in things of common use, more especially since it has been his aim to strike out a new style, neither classic, nor Gothic, nor renaissance, but English and original. The shapes of Greek and Etruscan vases, beautiful as they are, are not more adapted to modern pottery or hardware, than is the decoration of the fictile vases: we do not want to convert achrymatories into scent bottles, funeral urns into teapots, vases into flower-pots; nor are the forms of amphora suitable for decanters, or of pateræ for caudle cups. The material and uses of the vessel should determine its form; teapots that would not draw, jugs that cannot be washed clean, glasses and cups that one cannot drink out of comfortably, however elegant their form, are essentially defective. And the adaptation of the thing to its purpose, so far from producing ugliness, tends to beauty; for it involves fitness, which in articles of use is an ingredient of beauty, and it also induces new forms. The problem to be solved is simply this—given the use and material of the article, to find a beautiful shape. In the commonest, rudest, and oldest implements of husbandry, the plough, the scythe, and the sickle, we have examples of simple and beautiful curves. The most elementary and simple forms, if well proportioned, and of graceful contour, are the most pleasing. To enter into the multifarious details of ornamental design would require a separate paper upon each branch of ornament; and I have already, I fear, engaged attention too long a time. I will only, therefore, notice a few instances where principles are violated by misdirected ingenuity.

Each material has advantages and disadvantages peculiar to itself, and to develop its best qualities ought to be the study of the designer. In glass, for instance, the facets of cut glass produce a brilliant prismatic effect by the refraction of light; angularities, combined with curved forms in glass, therefore, are beautiful and appropriate; but angularities in pottery, vases, jugs, dishes, &c., are ugly and inappropriate. Nor are straight sides and angularities pleasing in metal, whether silver or not; swelling curves are the most beautiful forms for small articles of a polished material, whether porcelain or metal.

The eagerness for novelty, both of purchasers and manufacturers, leads to the adoption of odd and ugly shapes, and the introduction of fantastic and unmeaning or inappropriate ornament; and the necessity for the restraint of principles to prevent ingenuity from being perverted is strongly apparent in the department of ornamental pottery and hardware. The climax of skill would seem to be to achieve deception, aim at impossibility, and give to things the appearance of something which it is not. Thus we have the arum dwarfed, so as to deprive the graceful plant of its elegant form, the stem and leaves cast in bronze or brass with the flower in clouded glass, and stuck in a garden-pot by way of ornament, or converted into a gas-burner or a curtain-holder. Brass fuchsias and lilies hang pendent from cornice poles; bronze plants are made to blossom with wax lights on pier tables, and perhaps we may yet behold a cast-iron tree in a ball bearing fruit in the shape of hats and caps. These absurdities are equally as puerile as the Toby Philpot jugs and duck-shaped sauce-boats that we have come to ridicule. The beautiful paintings on Sevres porcelain, and the painted flowers in relief on Dresden china are equally objectionable in point of art, though for different reasons. In the instance of the Dresden china, the modelled and painted flowers, by their polish and brittleness, want two of the most essential attributes of the beauty of flowers, rich transparent colour and softness: people exclaim, "how natural!" but it is neither true nature nor good art. Miniature paintings on vases are very beautiful; but why injure the effect of the picture by the curve of the vase, and lessen the peculiar beauty of the form of the vase by putting on it a picture that might be better displayed in a frame? As for landscapes on dinner and dessert plates, they are still more absurd; the tart or the fruit effectually oblite-

rates the view of Windermere or Virginia-water, whose beauties are left to the admiration of the scullery maid or the housekeeper. The ornamentation of the Chinese and Japanese vases are as yet unequalled in harmonious richness of colouring, and deserve attentive study, but not imitation. The principle exemplified in their scheme of colour and style of ornament would, if differently carried out, lead to beautiful and novel results. The strange and grotesque become a valuable feature in painted ornament, because it disinclines the eye to follow the forms, and satisfies it with colour. Hence the popularity of the common "willow-pattern" ware; its incongruous and nondescript character, baffling attention, convert its bridge, and temple, and willows into merely vehicles of colour. The blurred pattern ware, where the outline appears as if it were traced in an absorbent material, was an accident; but its effect was so good that it at once became popular: another proof that forms are subordinate, not principal, in patterns.

The practice of ornamenting porcelain by giving it the appearance of marble, is another mistake: a marble jug is an absurdity, almost as great as a mahogany wash-hand basin or a rosewood ewer. Equally absurd it is to paint zinc baths like wainscot, and give to tin chamber-pails the appearance of staves hooped round. Let ornament be ornamental, and shew for what it is,—decoration; and let it be appropriate and subordinate to utility, as well subservient to elegance.

There are other points that need to be touched upon, and these that have been adverted to need fuller investigation; but enough has been said, I trust, to prove the importance of a knowledge and observance of the principles of art by designers, and perhaps to shew, also, that these principles are easily ascertainable by studious attention and rational reflection.   W. SMITH WILLIAMS.

WHAT THE SEWERS COMMISSION HAVE DONE FOR KENSINGTON.

SIR,—May I again claim your advocacy in THE BUILDER for something to be done towards remedying that nuisance, of which you have before written, the open, stinking, almost stagnant ditch which receives the whole drainage of the town of Kensington, and, passing through the Guardians' premises, has no outlet but into this ditch, which is 4 feet 6 inches above the bottom of the sewer which the Guardians have built under the direction of the Sewers Commission : the excuse now made is, and it is a mere subterfuge, that the levels are not completed. The same story was told last summer, accompanied by a promise that it was hoped that shortly some steps would be taken to remedy the evil that had been complained of, as noticed in THE BUILDER.

It is right that the public should be informed of what has since occurred. James-street and Jenning's-building have been visited by the cholera, so many as eighty cases having occurred in this locality, and even up to to-day there were three persons brought away from James-street with virulent fever, arising from this imperfect drainage. The Sewer Commissioners sent down what they called their disinfecting compounds, and the pumping apparatus. They were assisted by the parochial authorities in every possible way, and so far as any cleansing could be of any avail, it was promptly done; but all this deposit of filth and dirt now lies to the depth of several feet in the sewer which passes close to the Kensington Workhouse, in which there are between 300 and 400 inmates; and only such portion of the dirt as will float away has any chance of escape, and then only into this open ditch.

The Sewer Commissioners, under the pretence of doing something to remedy the complaints of the inhabitants, about a month ago sent a steam-engine, and at the mouth of this large and substantial sewer set it to work; but as what they pumped up had to go into this open ditch, they only produced a most awful and destructive stench,—for of course, as the ditch is 4 feet 6 inches above the bottom of the sewer, whatever was raised by the engine went back again into the sewer.

This attempt, like that of an endeavour to fill a sieve with water, was soon abandoned, and so the nuisance remains ; but it is thought right that the public should be apprised fully of the doings and not-doings of the Sewer Commissioners, and no better channel through which this information is to be conveyed is known than THE BUILDER.

Yours, Mr. Builder, ever truly,
E. H. NIXON, J. P. and Vice-Chairman of the Kensington Board of Guardians.

Bladen Lodge, Old Brompton, 22nd March, 1849.

INSTITUTION OF CIVIL ENGINEERS.

ON the 13th, the paper read was "A description of the Camden Station of the London and North-Western Railway," by Mr. R. B. Dockray. Particulars of this were given in THE BUILDER some time ago. In the first design of the railway, in 1833, this station was intended for the sole terminus of the line, and, after much discussion, thirty acres of ground were purchased, although that quantity was considered preposterously large. A very short time demonstrated the necessity for the establishment of the Euston Station solely for passengers ; and fourteen acres were there secured, and ultimately covered with buildings. The whole station at Camden-town was then devoted to goods and cattle; and, although in the original design great care was taken to anticipate the wants of the traffic, yet such has been the rapid development of the railway system, that in the space of ten years it has proved necessary to sweep away almost every vestige of the original constructions, and entirely to remodel the station. As the increase of the traffic progressed, the trains in the sidings frequently became of such length as to cause danger to the passenger trains ; it, therefore, became necessary to alter the whole disposition, which has been so done as now to give a length of double line of two thousand five hundred feet, for the goods' waggons only, entirely clear of the main line. The circular engine-house, 160 feet diameter, to contain twenty-four engines and tender, with a central turn-table 41 feet in diameter, and an iron roof, was described. Some idea of the extent of the station was given by the statement, that the length of single line of railway, exclusive of the main lines, exceeded 12 miles. There were 112 sets of points, 196 turn plates, and 110 cranes, varying in power from 1½ to 20 tons. The area of goods' sheds was upwards of 135,000 superficial feet, and that of the platforms was 30,000 feet. The annual consumption of gas exceeded six millions of cubic feet. The supply of water for the locomotive engines was treated of at some length, and exhibited some curious anomalies. The only water that could originally be used, was taken from wells at Tring and at Watford ; an attempt was, however, made to obtain a supply at Camden Station, first from the Regent's Canal, and then by sinking a well down 145 feet into the chalk, or to a total depth of 300 feet below Trinity high-water mark. The water from the sand stratum was excluded, and although only that from the chalk was pumped up, which ought to have possessed the same qualities as the water at Tring and Watford, derived also from the chalk, yet it was found to cause the locomotive to "prime," or flush water through the cylinders, with the steam, to such an extent as to seriously impede the progress of the trains. This was shown, by analysis, to arise from the excess of carbonate of soda contained in this well water, which there was an entire absence of in the waters of the wells at Tring and at Watford. The well, therefore, became useless for the engines, but the water was so excellent for household and other purposes, that it has been employed for the general uses of the station, and for the hotels and houses belonging to the company.

THE MARBLE ARCH.—As the ultimate destination of the marble arch at the Queen's Palace appears to be at present undecided, allow me to suggest the front of the British Museum (to which his Majesty George the Fourth was a most princely contributor) as an eligible situation.   J. U. S. C.

PATENT METHOD OF FACING WITH STONE.

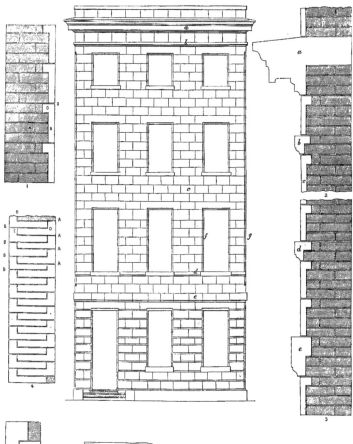

C.C.LAING Sc.

A NEW MODE OF FACING WALLS.

MR. JOHN TAYLOR, Jun., architect, has obtained a patent for a mode of constructing and facing walls, which professes to avoid the objections hitherto existing against erecting brickwork with a facing of stone, arising from the subsidence of the numerous mortar joints in the former compared to the latter, by which the stone facing unavoidably becomes injuriously weighted, and the crushing of the bed is the result. To remedy this, he carries up the brickwork, simultaneously *suspending* the facing stones thereon, and bonds in every stone, by weighting that part most adapted for it by the superstructure, but leaving the lower or bed joints open until the danger from the subsiding of the mortar joints is at an end, when the stone may be allowed to take a bearing, and become a portion of the construction by pointing up. He is thus enabled to dispense with much of the stonework hitherto necessary in the ordinary mode of construction, and reserves only sufficient for protection, appearance, &c.; and as he further proposes to obtain what is required by steam power, a saving of more than half, it is asserted, will be effected in the cost of the stone.

The annexed illustrations will explain the system:—Section No. 1. A, the brickwork, three courses of which having been carried up, and the mortar bed laid, the facing stone B is suspended thereon by the rebated part C, and in this state can be readily and properly adjusted, and when weighted by the brickwork above the bonding, is complete. The joint D is to be left sufficiently open to allow for the subsidence of the mortar joints, and where this has taken place the stone may be allowed to take a bearing by pointing.

Section No. 2 and 3 show how cornices, string courses, &c., may be applied in the same manner.

No. 4 shews the method of cutting the facing-stones out of the block. The cuts, AAA, BBB, which form the face and back of the stones, may be made in any number by one and the same operation. The cut, C, is then made and the first piece released, which, being the rough end of the block, is waste. Cut D is then made, and the first facing-stone delivered, also the second by the cut E, and in like manner till all are delivered.

Nos. 5 and 6 show the same method applied to cornices, strings, &c.

Plan No. 7, reveals of windows, doors, &c., which may be formed by notching out the rebate of the facing stone to admit that forming the reveal; any waste from the facing stones will form these.

Plan No. 8. The angles of the building formed in the same manner.

The Elevation is intended to show an ordinary building where the various parts are applied.

The italics on the elevation refer to corresponding letters on the plans and sections.

The patentee considers that the reduction which is effected in the cost of thus facing a wall with stone, together with the great facility in its erection (all the trouble and delay of procuring stone and making arrangements for working it being avoided), and the fact, moreover, that the material will be obtained and applied with no more trouble than facing bricks, will lead to its being used where otherwise cements would be resorted to.

THE ROYAL ITALIAN OPERA HOUSE.—The production of Auber's opera of *Massaniello* in a style of extraordinary magnificence and completeness (and which should be heard by all who love Beauty in sound), has led to some admirable painting by Messrs. Grieve and Telbin. The view of the Bay of Naples is worthy of Stanfield, and preservation. The market scene, before which is sung the well known "prayer," so as it never was sung before perhaps, has the church and campanile carefully and effectively painted. Perhaps the most striking scene of all, however, is that with which the fourth act opens, where two Doric porches on each side of the stage stand out against the clear blue sky, with Vesuvius in the back ground, and pleasant villas and quiet grounds at the foot, waiting to be overwhelmed by an eruption which is fearfully pourtrayed.

IMPROVEMENTS IN CONSTRUCTION.

SUGGESTED EXHIBITION.

IN a late number you referred to two important exhibitions, one for the advancement of the study of architecture, the other for the encouragement of British manufactures; but there appears to me another exhibition required in the metropolis, viz., one embodying the improvements which have been recently made in all that relates to the mechanical and scientific branches of Architecture. The numerous inventions which are constantly reviewed by yourself, and advertised in your columns, will, I am sure, without further remark, convince the architectural world of the value of such an exhibition. It requires but a slight effort to form the nucleus of a society to carry out this object.

Such an exhibition would embrace improvements of iron and timber, bridges, girders, roofs, floors, partitions, staircases, &c. Locks and fastenings of every description, and specimens of smith's work, sashes, window frames, shutters, skylights, ventilators, warming and heating apparatus, stained and plain glass, and improved modes of glazing. Water-closets, house drainage, &c. Specimens of brickwork, and improved modes of constructing chimneys. Samples of all cements and plasters, and specimens of application, and of scagliola work. Improved modes of lathing, and the best mode of using iron laths for fire-proof work. New modes of slating, also of forming flat roofs in slates, tiles, copper, lead, or iron.

Improvements in masonry, both stone, marble, and granite, especially as relates to the use of lead and iron in making joints. Specimens of architectural carving in stone and marble, pavements, paper-hangings, house-painting and graining, &c.

By reviewing this list, you will see that by far the most numerous prizes for improvement may be conferred on working men, and I know nothing that can more elevate the workman than by thus fairly rewarding his genius, and bringing him into contact with the patrons and professors of architecture. Many a poor man would by such means have a chance of raising himself in society, whose present opportunities are now indeed too few.

The spinning, weaving, printing, tool making, engineering, and other such like manufactures, require similar exhibitions, and in those parts of the kingdom best suited for such works; but I desire to begin with the art which calls all others to its aid, and by turns fosters and nourishes the whole. Δ.

*** We have on more than one occasion pointed out the advantage which such a collection would give to architects and those engaged in building.

THE CURIOSITIES OF ESTIMATING.

"THE more you knock," as the Frenchman said, "the more I wont let you in:" the more fully the system of estimating, or rather the want of system in estimating, pursued by some builders, is exposed, the more glaring are the inconsistencies exhibited. A correspondent from Chester, referring to our recent notice of contemplated restorations there, says the following tenders were submitted to the committee on the 9th, for taking down and rebuilding St. Michael's tower with white stone:—

Haswell	£1,310
Morris (accepted)	675

But this difference, striking as it may seem, is nothing compared with what is found in the following list of tenders sent in on the 14th, for building the Printers' Almshouses, Wood-green, Tottenham. Read and digest it:—

D. Bodger	£6,310
Glenn	2,480
Cripps	2,375
Carter and Ellis	2.225
Taylor	1,989
Cooper and Davis	1,940
Maxted and Harris	1,859
Walker and Soper	1,850
Roberts (accepted)	1,750
W. Lamprell	1,513

One result of such affairs as these must of course be, that respectable builders will refuse to tender, excepting with parties known to them.

RAILWAY JOTTINGS.

WHAT we want for railways, says the *Railway Journal*, "are the following things:—1st. That the shareholders should have much more power than they have in the election of good directors, and the dismissal of obnoxious and useless ones. 2nd. That railway accounts should be kept on one uniform and simple system, so that when a man understands one he may understand any. 3rd. That the accounts, and all documents connected with them, should be open to the inspection and examination of shareholders at proper times. 4th. That the capital accounts should be closed, except under very special circumstances, within two years after the railway is opened for public traffic. 5th. That all contracts should be let by public tender, and the lowest be accepted, if proper security should be preferred. 6th. A careful, proper, and impartial audit. If these things were done," adds the *Journal*, "railway property would immediately rise in value."——We understand, says the *Railway Record*, "that the reductions which the directors of the Great Western Company have made in the number of passenger trains, will effect a saving in the expenditure of the company to the extent of 100*l*. a-day, or at the rate of upwards of 36,000*l*. a-year. We have only the credit side of the account here, however.——Amongst other indications of a revival of trade, it appears that the traffic on the London and North-Western for seven weeks, since the closing of the last half-yearly account, shows an increase of nearly 17,000*l*. over the corresponding period of the previous twelve months, or an increase at the rate of 2,400*l*. per week. No new extensions have been opened.——At the half-yearly meeting of the South-Eastern, Mr. J. Macgregor admitted that Lord Torrington, for his services in Parliament, had received out of the capital account a service of plate, worth 2,800*l*., besides 1,000 No. 4 shares, given at a dinner which cost 300*l*.——A recent report of Mr. Stephenson, the engineer, states that the Britannia-bridge masonry is finished, and nearly ready for the reception of the hydraulic presses for lifting the tubes. The Carnarvon platform for the short tubes is finished, and one of them commenced. The corresponding short tube on the Anglesey side is nearly completed. The four large tubes wait only the cast-iron work to be ready for floating. The arrangements for floating, including the hydraulic presses and pontoons, are nearly complete, and will be entirely so in May. The excess in works on this line beyond the Parliamentary estimate was 254,000*l*.; in stations, 72,000*l*.; in rails and sleepers, 95,000*l*.; land, 124,000*l*.; Conway-bridge, 50,000*l*.; Britannia-bridge. 350,000*l*.,—making a total excess of 945,000*l*. on a total amount of 3,084,650*l*. The amount yet to be expended on the works is stated to be 185,000*l*. The accounts to 31st December showed that 3,418,596*l*. had been received, and 3,358,271*l*. expended,—leaving a balance of 60,379*l*. in cash and at interest.——The Lancaster and Carlisle Company have taken forcible possession of the Maryport and Carlisle Company's station and ground at Carlisle, at present leased by Mr. Hudson. By the Act of the Lancaster Company it is said they had the power to do so on paying the amount assessed by a special jury, and for the purposes of a central station. A body of navvies took possession by tearing up the rails and carrying off the station bodily! the building being a temporary one.

COLOURLESS INK.—SIR: While in the formation of an inkstand so much beauty is sometimes displayed, both in the form and the material, it is vexing to see, when it is put to its destined use, how soon it is soiled by the black liquid, and disfigured by the accumulation of dregs or dried ink. It occurred to me that, by saturating paper with one of the principal components of ink, and writing with the other, this would be avoided. The inkstand would then contain only a colourless fluid, its beauty would not be injured; and if by any accident it were spilt, no material injury would be done either to dress or furniture. I have tried this, and find it answer very well, but probably others could improve upon it, especially in the construction of the paper.—JAMES EDMESTON.

DESIGN FOR THE SMALL-POX HOSPITAL. — MR. S. A. MATTHEWS, ARCHITECT.

[TO WHICH THE SECOND PREMIUM WAS AWARDED.]

HURWOOD'S PATENT FOR MOVING WINDOWS, &c.

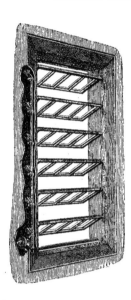

Fig. 1.

Fig. 2.

THE SMALL-POX HOSPITAL COMPETITION.

SEVERAL members of the profession have written to us expressing themselves very indignant, that in spite of the assertions of the committee that they would not select a design until assured that it could be executed for 12,000*l.*, the lowest tender for the design, by Mr. Daukes, which was selected to be carried out, amounts with the foundations, &c. already put in, to 18,700*l.* There is no occasion for us to repeat our opinion on the principle involved in this matter. The competitor who best gave the committee the required accommodation *for the sum to which they limited architects*, was the person entitled to the premium.

Mr. S. A. Matthews (a pupil of the late George Allen) has addressed a statement to us, in which he says, "My design for, the Small-Pox Hospital stood *first* in the estimation of Mr. S. Smirke and Mr. J. Shaw, the architects referred to, and of the committee, and would have been carried out, had not Mr. Daukes *guaranteed to execute his design for about the sum of* 12,000*l.* The Chairman informed me at the time he handed me the second premium, that mine was lost even then by one vote only. My design would cost about 13,000*l.*", At the solicitation of Mr. Matthews, and because we think it may not in other respects be useless, we have engraved his design, and we give his statement as affording an example how the system works.*

---

* The following is the architect's description of his design:—The entire length of the building is 385 feet, width 34 feet 6 inches; depth of wings 23 feet 6 inches by 25 feet 6 inches wide, including the thickness of the walls. The basement does not include the wings nor the entire width, is 13 feet high, contained kitchen, scullery, pantries, provision stores, domestic washhouses, laundry, coal-cellar, &c. Ground floor, 13 feet high, contained, on the left of principal entrance, Visitors' waiting-room, strong-room, secretaries'-room, board-room, and surgeons' and matron's sitting-

We are not advocating any claim of Mr. Matthews: for anything we know, it might be shown, that to carry out his design would also cost much more than the sum named. In that case, he ought not to have had even the second premium. We have nothing to do with persons, we are looking only to principles; and the right and wrong in this matter are so evident, that none can mistake who desire to go right.

HURWOOD'S PATENT FOR WINDOWS.

DURING a recent visit to Ipswich, we had the opportunity of examining some applications of a mode of moving and fastening windows (dispensing with pulleys, weights, fastenings, &c.), for which Mr. Hurwood, engineer of that town, obtained a patent some time since, and which deserves to be better known beyond Ipswich than it is. The principal feature in the invention is the application of the screw

rooms, stores, &c.; side entrance and corridor. To the right of principal entrance—patients' receiving-room and lift, surgeons' and physicians' rooms, library and museum, surgery, drug stores, and mattrass and bedding stores, and room for reception of foul linen from shoot, &c.—First floor, 15 feet high, contained, on the left of centre, two acute wards for males, of the required dimensions, baths, water-closets, &c. The wing, with a separate staircase, the surgeons and matron's sleeping and spare rooms, &c. To the right of centre, the two wards for females ditto and children's wards. In right wing, servants' bed-rooms, &c., foul-linen shoot, and coal-lift. The centre occupied by nurses' room, and two rooms on each side for male and female delirious patients; staircase at back 20 feet square (the width of the hall), and two sculleries. Second floor, 15 feet high, contained six wards for male and female convalescent patients; night nurses' sleeping-rooms In centre, with linen and other stores,—with all other conveniences as before mentioned, together with servants' sleeping-rooms, &c. The out-buildings not adjoining, which for males, of the required dimensions, baths, &c., with large airing-ground at back. The stables and piggeries are near the lodge entrance in Maiden-lane. The vaccination-room and larger lodge adjoin the principal entrance at Highgate-hill. The arch shown in advance of the principal entrance to the building leads at once to the provision stores in the basement.

working into a wheel or rack as prime mover. It is applied to windows of various forms, two of which we illustrate.

In fig. 1, it will be seen that the window is divided into as many portions as there are panes in height. Each part turns upon two pivots, one of them being sufficiently long to pass through the frame to receive a small crank. A screw and portion of a screw wheel is fixed at the bottom of the frame independent of the sashes, to which a crank is also connected: a slight flat rod is attached to the crank fixed to the same axis as the screw wheel, and also to each of the cranks connected to the window, so that when motion is given to the screw wheel by the screw being turned, the window is more or less moved.

In fig. 2 the apparatus is fixed to the centre mullion of the window. In others only the top part of the window opens. For Lunatic Asylums, and other places, where it is of importance there should be good ventilation, and that the inmates should have no control over the windows (a key, it will be observed, is necessary), this invention of Mr. Hurwood will be found particularly available.

We had written a memorandum upon the town, but must postpone it for another number.

SUPPLY OF WATER TO AMSTERDAM.—A company, managed by a board in London, is being formed, with a capital of 600,000*l.*, in 30,000 shares of 20*l.* each with 2*l.* per share deposit, to supply Amsterdam with water from the Rhine. The privilege has been conceded in perpetuity to this company, who are to be entitled to a maximum charge of twice the amount believed to be capable of yielding a return of 24 per cent. The responsibility is limited, it is said, to the amount subscribed.

THE PARKS AND APPROACHES.

WE may vaunt of the glories of our capital, its extent, commerce, river, structures, and parks; but we cannot boast of our avenues or approaches. There is no city of the modern world, inferior though it be in aggregate advantages, which does not distance us, *longo intervallo*, in the grand essential to preliminary importance—open and imposing avenues and approaches.

Who, for a moment, would compare Paris, in these particulars, to London? We have, it is true, some noble central streets and squares, such as the Fleet-street line, Oxford and Holborn, Pall Mall, and not least, Regent-street and Portland-place; but all these terminate in infinite and everlasting masses of brick, and afforestments of chimneys; we have, too, a long boulevard,—the New and City roads. Nature endowed us with a river, and we have erected bridges.

In this department of architecture, no city in the world is, I believe, comparable to London, which being placed on a site possessing every element for adornment, appears to have been planned (if ever it was, which I very much doubt) without any regard to those first postulates of grandeur.

There are few cities which some great imitators of Appius have not illustrated by cutting out noble avenues, if not arcs and portals, as well as by the erection of that inestimable desideratum, quay walls to rivers.

Paris is notable amongst all others for her notable avenues,—that of Neuilly hardly requires mention; the Boulevards, Tuilleries, Champs Elysées, various approaches and barriers of colossal dimensions, and even quay walls to its tideless stream.

Brussels, too, is familiar to English travellers in these attributes of civic consequence; and even Dublin has her granite quays of chisseled masonry to the Liffey.

It is manifest that these advantages, the products of industry and expense, under the guidance of good taste, formed no part of an original plan, but that these embellishments were added as the cities grew; and that the enterprise of the citizens effected what the advancing taste of the age demanded, or that some great potentate imagined and executed what was useful and pleasing to the time.

Some may call these things accidents; so perhaps, in some sense, they are, as is the accumulation of houses and population in any city. If so, then our metropolis is an unhappy accident,—unhappy, at least, in its peculiar meagreness and utter want of both quay walls to the parent of commerce, Father Thames, and of appropriate approaches to this overgrown mart of all nations.

Having before, in THE BUILDER, alluded to the openings of one avenue in continuation of Pall Mall, allow me now to suggest another of not less important display, although of considerably less expense, in another quarter. The line of Portland-place, terminated by the Quadrant, but drawn out *in extenso*, you may say, to the Bank—on the other end sinks in a rail and shrubbery (perhaps, rather, scrubbery,) at Park-crescent. This line is continued in a direction straight northward, by the open esplanade across Regent's-park, shewing in the distance Hampstead-hill. A very short interval of garden (most certainly a pretty one) intervenes between the top of Portland-place and the park: the distance is not more than 420 feet, and this all public ground, without an obstruction. How trifling would be the cost of making 400 feet of carriage way, and railing it in on each side, and of constructing gates and lodges if necessary? The distance hence to the esplanade, or long walk, is all open park, and is perhaps 400 yards; this would require only a firm road to the point of junction, and when opened and finished would present as fine a *chaussée* as ever Paris can exhibit, terminating southward at Langham church and spire, northward merging into the hilly undulations of Hampstead.

The cost of this whole improvement could not (under *private management*) exceed 3,000*l.*, and would bestow on this region of stately drear, now languishing in the dinge and gloom of bygone importance, a lightness and character not to be appreciated but by those accustomed to the study and practice of such plans and improvements.

No property, no house, could be injured by the change; on the contrary, the traffic must be, in a measure, diverted from the portals of the crescent by the medium route, whilst sufficient space of ornamental parterre would yet remain undisturbed for the *égaiement* of the frontages in the locality. The opening of the long walk, as an approach to the railway terminus and Hampstead, over the most elevated portion of this very pleasing, if not beautiful park, would also be a boon to the public (I mean the opening of the whole esplanade for private carriages), as beneficial to the health and enjoyment of the citizens as to the increased requirements of a teeming population. It was evidently the intention of the monarch who planned this park, and who laid out and planted this esplanade, that such adaptation should one day be made, to carry out the tasteful design of his offspring in the march of improvement—Regent-street.

Now, as to this park and the new purchase of Primrose-hill, perhaps a few words may be excused on that subject.

The Commissioners of Woods and Forests, whatever be their powers or incompetencies, have certainly the merit of having, within a few years, done work, in the plantation and embellishment of St. James's, Victoria, and Regent's parks—the purchase of 180 acres, including Primrose-hill—and in laying out plans for another park at Battersea, in order to provide lungs for a prospective town, and a generation yet to spring up in that district; but for two years all has been at a stand-still—a dead halt! Commissioners fluctuate with the Administration; they change in their goings out and comings in, with the Government of the day, and can have but little experience in the routine of office. No, the management rests with the permanent fixtures at the board. Some people call this rather mismanagement. However, the commissioners always discovered an anxiety to carry out public improvements with spirit. But who can blame the commissioners for hesitating to carry out essential public designs, if the public purse be exhausted, and that there are no funds in the exchequer of that department?

The point on which I would animadvert is the naked unplanted condition of Primrose-hill or Albert-park, which has been two years enclosed, and particularly the omission to secure a building plot on the verge of Primrose-hill-park, interposed between that and Regent's-park—which is the only spot on which a gate or entrance could be effected facing that of the latter. This plot is directly opposite the suspension-bridge (over the canal) which forms the exit from Regent's-park,—and a detour of 70 or 80 feet is now made close beyond the bridge, to the right, in order to approach the entrance to Primrose-hill.

Should this plot be built on—and it is proposed and labelled for building—a row of houses will present a bastion which will effectually cut off the view from park to park; and this is the most pleasing *coup-d'œil*, where, looking through the now matured groves, the hills are revealed merging one into the other.

This point is most pleasing, if not absolutely picturesque, but the eternal continuation of houses will mar all—not to speak of the two opposing entrances (for Park-road separates them) being 80 feet apart, and askew. Thus not only is the connection between the parks (with all view from one to the other) to be cut off, but all order violated, which should make the portals of office (if not the paths which lead to them) straight.

Above two years has this place of popular resort been paled in: so much time has been lost in its furniture by plantation—not one shrub gives note of a living Repton at the board. Yes; there is a garden—a bare garden, 100 paces square; and this is studded with miniature plants: besides there are planted here divers bare poles, and gymnastic contrivances, to exercise the athletæ; the plat so complete, and close to the open road, as to notify to all passengers the amount of official care for the amusement of the mob. What youth would there resort to be a mountebank in public view? No: place it in some sequestered nook.

Space admonishes me to leave this subject, and only to touch upon one item more—the hideous deformities in Hyde-park! Here are the serjeant's guard-barrack, the magazine, the sub-rangers' lodge, another for an underling, and a hovel for some inappreciable use—these form a sequence of five unsightly constructions that would be a disgrace to the bye-lanes of Epping or Willesden, and which occupy a space of six acres, paled off in a shapeless longitudinal section: the most beautiful and sylvan portion of Hyde-park, near the Receiving-house at the Serpentine, is thus deformed and disenchanted.

These intrusions destroy the privacy (if the term is admissible) of our national park. In this spot, at unaccustomed hours, I have ranged, and, looking toward the Serpentine, have indulged the pleasing illusion of complete sequestration; turn round two points of the compass, the elysium vanishes; the hovels, the poles, the lounging guards, at once awaken the palpable fact that you cannot indulge in a rural dream (momentary though it be) short of Richmond-park.

It would be vain to inquire the utility of these obtrusions; for all those piles are drooping in neglect, and afford only a refuge for *one humble hanger-on* and a *locus penitentiæ* for, perhaps, a refractory squad of the Coldstreams.

QUONDAM.

A LEASH OF PORTRAITS.

IT will be remembered that a subscription was raised some time ago by the Builders' Society to present a testimonial of friendship to Mr. Thomas Cubitt, and that a portrait being determined on, to be afterwards engraved for the subscribers, Mr. Pickersgill, the Royal Academician, was commissioned to paint it.

Calling at Mr. Pickersgill's last week, we found, amongst a batch of portraits going on, this "counterfeit presentment" of Mr. Cubitt next to a picture of Mr. Charles Barry, and on the other side of the latter the *vraie ressemblance* of Mr. Grissell,—a triad which, when exhibited in the Academy, will interest many of our readers. The picture of Mr. Cubitt is a full length; those of Mr. Barry and Mr. Grissell are three-quarters. Mr. Barry is in a loose morning robe of quiet colour, with a roll in his hand, and an elevation of the Royal Tower on the table near him: Mr. Cubitt stands with his hand in his vest, an accustomed position; and Mr. Grissell, out of doors, wears a cloak, the red velvet lining of which, with other accessories, produces a result sufficiently gay. As likenesses, these pictures are remarkably successful; and as works of art they are equal to any thing Mr. Pickersgill has done for a long time.

NOTES IN THE PROVINCES.

THE first stone of the new church of Stanmore parish was lately laid by the Earl of Aberdeen, in presence of her Majesty the Queen Dowager, the Bishop of London, &c. It is to accommodate 800 persons, one half free. The funds are being raised by subscription.——The foundation stone of the first Primitive Methodist Chapel and School-rooms in Bristol was laid on Tuesday week. The building will be in the Norman style, and will contain 450 sittings, and school room for 300 children.——The new church of St. John the Evangelist, Ashton Hayes, Tarvin, Cheshire, was consecrated on 9th inst. The edifice is of stone, with a spire, and contains 305 sittings, more than one half free. It has been erected, and fitted up at an expense of about 3,000*l.* at the sole cost of Mr. William Atkinson, of Ashton Hayes, who has also erected a parsonage house and schools, besides endowing the church with 1,000*l.*, and a repair fund of 150*l.*——The cost of the proposed Temperance-hall, at Leicester, lately noticed, is stated, it seems, at 3,000 guineas.——The exterior of the chancel of Whitby Church, has had its ornamental turrets restored: they were blown down in 1820.——During a recent gale the wooden beacon erected on the sand banks, near the mouth of the river Esk, below Ravenglass, was blown down.

COMPETITION.—Plans and specifications are wanted from architects and gas engineers for gas-works, at Walsall, by 7th April: the successful competitor to superintend the works.

METROPOLITAN COMMISSION OF SEWERS.

THE COMMITTEE QUESTION.

A general court was held on Thursday in last week, at the Sewers' Court, Greek-street; the Earl of Carlisle in the chair.

Mr. Hertslet, the clerk, read the voluminous case submitted to the law officers of the crown on the business of the commission, with their opinion thereon, the substance of which appeared in The Builder of last week.

Mr. Leslie then rose and said that he felt called upon, in this stage of the matter, to make a few observations. The court were aware that the opinion that had been just read had been elicited in consequence of certain resolutions as to the business of Courts of Sewers coming up from the Bye-laws Committee, and, subsequently, to the General Committee. The case, as stated, gave the different readings and different opinions taken on the subject. On the opening of the commission he objected to the words "Standing Committees," that they ought not to be permanent, and that the main business of the commission should be done in open court. Others thought that a great deal of business might be got through by a subdivision of labour, through the means of committees. Now, what were the resolutions as to the Works Committee? why, these:—"To have under their immediate regulation and management (but subject to the General Committee), all the affairs of the commission relating to works and operations of the commission, and also the immediate control over the engineers, surveyors, assistant-surveyors, and other officers and servants of the commission employed about such works and operations; and should be empowered to obtain plans, sections, and estimates of all proposed works and operations, and to employ (but subject to the approval of the court) such clerks of the works and other subordinate officers and workmen as may be necessary." Now, here it was evident that the chief functions of the commission were to originate in this committee, and on their report the court might adopt or reject their recommendations; but if the minutes of this committee were wanted, it required a requisition in writing from three commissioners to have them produced. Now, by the opinion of the law officers, they were told that no business could originate with committees, but must originate in open court; therefore, on the first occasion, he submitted that the recommendations of the Bye-laws Committee could not be adopted, in consequence of their illegality. He had told them that if they could not get through the business, they might specifically appoint committees to assist them, and that was precisely the view that had been taken by the law officers of the crown, and, as he had shown, they could not make appointments in committee, or delegate the powers of the commission to any committee whatever. This power had been usurped in the appointment of Mr. Gotto as assistant-surveyor; as they had no right to make any such appointment. Although no power could be delegated to them, yet even so recently as Monday last, and since the opinion of the Attorney and Solicitor-general had been received, which told the committee they could originate nothing, they had instructed Mr. Gotto to look out for a convenient site for trial works. The opinion said that the court must originate all the business, and that any court could alter, continue, or discontinue such committee at any court. (Cries of "No, no.")

The Earl of Carlisle said the words were, that "committees may be empowered from time to time."

Mr. Leslie resumed:—As he read the words, the court could alter or continue a committee at any court; and if any new matter was considered, it must be by an express order of court. If the rate-payers were dissatisfied with their proceedings, the matters could be removed by *certiorari* to the Court of Queen's Bench; therefore no expenditure could take place unless by order of the court. He was told that this expenditure applied only to a class of cases, where the sums did not amount to 50*l*., which was most absurd, as they might make orders for fifty such cases, and order payment for the whole without coming to the court at all. Such being the case, he felt it to be his duty to step in and save the commission from total destruction; borne out as his view now was by the opinion of the Attorney and Solicitor-General. There would be no difficulty in proceeding with the business, when they were empowered to have monthly courts, special courts, and committees for specific purposes; but it was not for the public interest that the business of the commission should be carried on as it had been lately. They had been doing nothing lately but spending hundreds of pounds of the rate-payers' money without any order of the court. Gentlemen might smile, but he saw nothing to smile at, as he was prepared to prove it. As far as useful purposes, they had had for some time two plans for the improvement of the drainage of Westminster,—one by Mr. Austin and the other by Mr. Phillips;—and yet they could not get the subject to discuss. Another question had arisen,—an application from the Improvement Commissioners for a new line of sewer; but even this matter had never reached the court, but in common had been passed over to the committee. The hon. commissioner concluded by reiterating some of his main points of objection.

Mr. Slaney remarked that he had listened with regret to this discussion. He hoped they would come to some amicable mode of carrying on the business of the commission. It appeared to be the opinion of gentlemen that some injury was about to be committed from their being excluded from certain committees. Now he, God help him, was not on any committee, and he was not in the least offended (a laugh), but he believed, that unless they delegated the details they could not efficiently carry on the business of the court. At the same time he thought there was a fault on the other side, and that a statement of the business to come on at the court should be issued, to give them an opportunity of considering it.

Mr. R. L. Jones considered the number of the court would not prevent the whole duties being properly discharged if the court met weekly, when every gentleman might attend. The officers were now called away by committees, and could not attend to their duties. The court, too, was placed in entire ignorance of what was going on, unless they came to the court and read volumes of reports, and therefore he was satisfied the business could not be done unless they met weekly, as it was at present in a complete state of chaos. As a commissioner, he had a right to be informed of what was going on, or he had no business there at all.

The Hon. Fred. Byng said that Mr. Slaney's observation was unfair as regarded himself. He had objected to the constitution of a Works Committee, even supposing it to be legal, as the thirteen gentlemen put on it formed a complete majority, rendering the opinions of the rest of the commissioners a mere nullity. He had impressed upon the committee the necessity of its being open, and had come down to the court for the purpose of moving that all committees should be open, but found that, unknown to him, Mr. Leslie had made a similar motion, which he was happy to second. The resolutions had been borne out by the opinion of the law officers of the crown. He (Mr. Byng) was not on committees, therefore he could not be charged with having "obstructed" their business. The manner of doing it had hitherto been happy-go-lucky, and it was now time to divide their districts.

Lord Ebrington thought they would act wisely to acquiesce in the opinion received, and thereby put an end to useless and fruitless discussion, while the works of the commission were slumbering. He thought it would be prudent to take this opinion as their text for the interpretation of the law. With regard to the appointment of Mr. Gotto, the choice of an assistant-surveyor was specially referred to the Works' Committee. When he heard gentlemen talk of nothing being done, and in the same breath complained they could not read the reports; he thought the objections answered themselves. It was the practice of large bodies to refer details to smaller bodies, and in this they had an example in the high court of Parliament.

After a few words from Mr. Lawes,

The Earl of Carlisle trusted that persons appointed for the public good would act in harmony together, feeling assured that no expenditure could be valid unless it was authorised by the court. Cases of emergency, however, might arise to render it necessary to depart from this rule; and whether it applied to bodies or individuals, they must rely upon the justice of the case for the approval of the act so performed. The law officers had declared that all business must originate in the court at large; and he thought they would act wisely by following the course there pointed out: yet the court might refer such branches of it as they were unable to settle themselves. As to attending weekly, he at present held more offices than he could properly discharge; but even with weekly attention, there were at present many pressing matters,—such as house-drainage, the size of sewers, and the withdrawal of pollution from the Thames, all great matters of principle,—which he thought it would be prudent to consider first, and refer to the court, believing there was no substantial difference of opinion in proceeding to the ordinary business of the court.

Mr. Bullar then submitted a string of fourteen resolutions, abolishing the general committee, converting sub-committees into committees provisionally, and defining the duties of them. The resolutions were seconded by the Rev. W. Stone.

Mr. Leslie deprecated these resolutions being brought forward without notice of motion. He reiterated his objections to the abominable practice of committees, and, having discharged his duty, if they chose to pass the resolutions, he should not say another word on the subject.

The resolutions were then put *seriatim*, and carried as a provisional arrangement, Lord Carlisle remarking that unless something of the kind was done, the whole business of the commission would be completely at sea.

Mr. Byng then withdrew from the Finance Committee, and Mr. Leslie and Mr. Lambert Jones gave notice that at the end of a month they should also retire from that committee.

At a meeting on the 22nd, the minority entered a strong protest against the legality of the resolutions.

Miscellanea.

Her Majesty's Theatre.—When Her Majesty's Theatre was decorated in 1846 we spoke of the work at some length, as one of the most successful and effective of its kind, and we gave praise to Mr. Johnson, the architect by whom it was designed, and to Mr. Marshall and Mr. Sang by whom it was carried out. It still holds its good place in estimation, and viewing it a few nights since we were more than ever impressed with the success with which a great desideratum had been obtained,—namely, *unity, with variety*. While the eye and mind find constant occupation in the always varied groups, medallions, and Raffaellesques displayed, there is a oneness and congruity about the whole which is particularly satisfying and admirable. Mr. Charles Marshall, by whom the scenery here is executed, stands high amongst the half dozen able men now painting for the London stage. We shall have an opportunity to speak of some of his works.

Electro-telegraphic Progress.—Mr. Brotherton, of Preston, has recently patented an invention for prevention of accidents on railways. It consists of an electric apparatus fixed beneath the rails, on which the wheels of the train act as they pass over it. A wire connects this apparatus with any station or junction which the train may be approaching, and at which an electric alarm is fixed. By this invention the attendants at any station or junction may, it is said, be apprised of the approach of a train any number of miles off, and in case any obstruction exists, a signal can be immediately forwarded to the train.——The projectors of the great submarine line across the Atlantic propose to construct it between the coast of Newfoundland and the nearest cape of Ireland. They state that there is every reason to believe that a submarine bank extends from Newfoundland to the British Isles, to which they propose to anchor the wires, supported in cork tubes, at intervals of 10 miles. They have appealed to Congress to aid them in the enterprise, by appropriating a public vessel for their use, to ascertain the truth concerning the nature of the bottom. Should they not find soundings, they state they could still manage to anchor the buoys by means of buckets, &c. They exhort Congress "not to allow the British Government to anticipate the United States in this sublime project."

Card-board Models.—In reply to a late inquiry from Tyro, wishing to know how to colour card-boards for models,—I have had many years' experience of the art, and find that the best plan is to procure card-board of the colour required, such as stone, slate, or lead colour, and shade it with warm sepia. In all cases where brick colour was required, I coloured the card-board with Indian red, and shaded as above, as I could not procure card-board of that colour; though I should think board of any colour could be procured in London, if required, which would be preferable.—H. W. Benson, North Shields.

Prevention of Coal-pit Explosions.—Mr. George Dunn, of Doncaster, M.D., has invented a ventilator, which he has presented to the public without appropriation by patent, and by means of which it appears from experiment at the Darley Main Colliery, where it has been tested, that such a perfectly free circulation is attainable through a pit as will obviate all chance of explosion. This ventilator, says Mr. Dunn, may be constructed of wood, zinc, tin, iron, or copper. One is to be placed, in the form of a hood or cowl, and self-acting, over the up-cast shaft, while another is placed over the down-cast shaft, with its open side or mouth to the wind, and will also be self-acting, where a down-cast shaft can be appropriated to it: by these means, a current of air is to be made to circulate through every part of a mine.

PROJECTED WORKS.—Advertisements have been issued for tenders, by April 11th, for the execution of various works for the completion of the Portsmouth station of the Brighton and South-Western Railways; by 26th, for the erection of a building for the Town-hall and Market-house Company, at Brentford; by 2nd, for dredging a shoal in the river Thames, at Woolwich; by 17th, for various works (separate tenders) for the Folkstone Water Works Company; by 26th inst., for the erection of an additional story and other alterations to the Sewers' office, No. 1, Greek-street, Soho; by 31st, for constructing dams and erecting new piers and other works, at Allington-lock, near Maidstone; by 14th April, for the execution and completion of the Criminal Court, and other works, at Cardiff; by 4th, for the erection of buildings for baths and wash-houses, at Bristol; by 12th, for the works comprised in the construction of the dry-pool basin and entrance lock from the river Hull to the Victoria dock, at Hull; by 2nd, for the erection of committee-rooms and offices, and the enlargement and alteration of warehouses, at Stourbridge wharf; by 28th inst., for the building, finishing, and completing of a lock-up, at Maryport; by 28th, for alterations and additions at Bitterne Lodge (Southampton), together with the erection of an entrance lodge and greenhouse there; by 28th, for paving and materials for the repair of the roads in St. Mary's, Islington: by 27th inst., for planning a skeleton map of the township of Nicholforest (Longtown); by 2nd April, for two several quantities of tubular glazed stoneware pipes, for Oxford; by 27th inst., for 900 yards of cast-iron pipes, and for the works of a reservoir, filter, &c. (separate tenders), for the Industrial schools, at Swinton (Manchester); and by 30th, for lead, tin, red lead, oil, &c., for Bristol Water-works.

LAVISH EXPENDITURE.—From the evidence of witnesses examined before a Parliamentary Committee, it appears, that although Pembroke dockyard, begun in 1820, cost only 6,000*l.* in construction, the mere levelling of it afterwards cost 54,630*l.*, and although many years have since transpired, the authorities are still paying nearly 1,500*l.* a-year for hired teams, in place of forming tramways at once. But even all that is nothing to the amount of private contracts for works connected with this same dockyard, and for which public competition has been either never sought for, or effectually put down by favouritism and official jobbing. One person and his brother-in-law (principal and agent), have, it is said, alone had nearly the whole amount of half a million of money in private contracts for works connected with this one dockyard: off that sum, however, they had to provide "dinners and saddle-horses," &c. for certain officers.

POWER FROM WATER IN AIR-TIGHT PIPES.—We have already alluded to this new application of power—the pressure of water in air-tight pipes. The *Glasgow Citizen* describes a model engine in the office of the Gorbals Gravitation Water Company, Portland-street, as a beautiful contrivance:—"The model is about one-horse power, with a horizontal cylinder, and having a 12-inch stroke. The water, which here has a pressure of about 210 feet, is introduced to it from a common house pipe; and such is the simplicity of the machine, that a child could work it, and regulate its speed at pleasure, by the mere turning of a handle. The great advantage of this engine consists in the fact that it can be put up in any flat of a house of any street—wherever, in fact, there is a water-pipe. It takes up very little room; it registers the quantity of water which it uses; and it may be erected in those localities in cities where steam-power is prohibited on account of danger and nuisance from smoke, and *without raising the rate of insurance*."

THE WINDOW TAX.—A meeting of the inhabitants of St. Mary, Whitechapel, was held in the vestry room, on the 8th inst., and a petition praying for the repeal of the injurious and unjust tax on light was unanimously resolved on.

FREEMASONS OF THE CHURCH.—A meeting of this society was held at Great Marlborough-street on the 13th. After the usual business the secretary read a paper, by Mr. D. Wilson, on the positions of founders' tombs in ancient collegiate churches, chantries, &c.

DECLINE OF TRADE IN SHEFFIELD.—Too little union among the masters, and too much of it among the men, appear to be fast ruining this once busy seat of trade. Every one complains, yet no one moves an amendment. No sooner does a master undertake any large or important contract than the men are ready to pounce upon him with unreasonable demands, which, if resisted, lead to the sure destruction of his machinery. Thus, while Belgium, Germany, and the United States, in which no such pernicious system prevails, are beating the English out of extensive markets, and even bearding the Sheffielder in his own den, or shaving him rather with his own weapon,—by help of the same sure instrumentality the latter is deliberately cutting his own throat—smashing his own machinery, in fact, in more senses than one. There is a talk of the necessity of some new trade. But of what use would a new trade be with the old system of 'union' and disunion? It is 'a new man' that is wanted probably still more than a new trade.

COMING WORKS.—The "Oxford Graduate" (Mr. Ruskin), advertises a new work, "The Seven Lamps of Architecture." Mr. W. Lea has in the press "Tables of the Strength and Deflection of Timber," for the purpose of determining by inspection, and therefore without having recourse to the extraction of roots or the solution of algebraical equations, the scantlings of any description of timber requisite to carry a given weight and to have when loaded a given deflection. They are designed as a kind of ready reckoner for the use of engineers, architects, surveyors, builders, carpenters, joiners, and all persons who may be interested in the subject.

CALCINED GRANITE. — Mr. Archibald M'Donald, of Aberdeen, some time ago discovered a process for reducing Aberdeen granite to a fine clay, which was moulded into form at the Seaton Pottery, and presented an article of the most beautiful and durable character. Since then, Mr. M'Donald has had an experiment tried of working the calcined granite into water-pipes.

BEQUEST TO INSTITUTION OF CIVIL ENGINEERS.—In the Rolls Court, a decision has just been come to which, if not reversed in a higher tribunal, will confirm in favour of the Institution of Civil Engineers a variety of shares in public companies, &c., bequeathed by Mr. Thomas Telford under his will, but resisted by his heir-at-law under the statute of mortmain.

IMPROVEMENT OF GLOUCESTER. — The remarks on the want of spirit displayed by the citizens of Gloucester, contained in the last number of THE BUILDER, must have been acceptable and gratifying to every individual who really takes an interest in the prosperity of the "fair city." It was observed by a local contemporary that the citizens, during the raging of the late fire at the cathedral, were so laudably sensible of the value of that noble ornament of their city, that the anxiety of the great majority to be of service only made "confusion worse confounded," and yet some days subsequently, when the principal magistrate of the city proposed to increase the efficiency of the fire engines (and no city in England of the same extent is, I am positive, more inefficiently supplied with the means for extinguishing fire), and to institute a fire brigade, persons were found who raised objections to that enlightened mode of procedure. With respect to the proposed museum, I can safely say that no city is more deficient in means of rational amusement than Gloucester, and directly an enlightened member of the town-council, like Mr. S. Bowly, for instance, proposes the establishment of a museum, up rises a member of the same body, who is not very noted for the promotion of learning, and says, "Oh, you had better engage rooms instead for the supply of mutton chops to the poor," and the proposition is negatived. Comment is needless. Mr. William Vernon Guise some time since offered a fine collection to the city, upon condition that a kind of museum should be established within a given time. That period has now elapsed, and the city has been deprived of a very choice collection through the instrumentality of the majority of its local representatives. I enclose my card. A GLOUCESTRIAN.

WAGES OF MASONS IN AUSTRALIA.—Masons find plenty of employment at from 5s. 6d. to 7s. per day. Except in the town, very little wrought stone is used for building, unless for large bridges, churches, or other substantial erections. The stone quarries near Adelaide supply this material in abundance, and of excellent quality, and many of the shop fronts and stores in town are now embellished with elegant facings. Limestone is also abundant, and of good quality. In the country, houses are built of rough stone only; but in many parts a peculiar kind of white slatestone is found, which splits off in large slabs, and can be worked with great accuracy: it is as soft as the blue slate, and breaks with a clean straight fracture. In other parts there is a kind of blue marble, which also works well, and makes substantial dwellings. Masons going should take out theirown tools, with a few good wedges and crowbars to quarry stone. A wife and children will be no drawback, but the contrary.—*A Working Man's Handbook to Australia.*

FARM BUILDINGS.—The choice of a site for a farm-yard, says *Bell's Weekly Messenger*, and the arrangement of its buildings, are questions whose importance are far too seldom regarded. The landlords of England can hardly be too often reminded of these things. "Could they," remarks Mr. Grey, of Dilston, in a valuable paper on farm buildings (Journ. R. A. S., vol. 4, p. 2)—"could they hear now and then the discussions on their management which take place among the farmers around them, they might obtain useful hints for their own benefit." It is upon a general principle only we can usefully dwell in these observations, and what Mr. Grey has in another place said so well, we need not attempt to express in any other words. In commending these things to the careful study of those who have the erection and improvement of farm buildings, we would, above all things, anxiously urge upon their attention the paramount consideration of the *health* of their inmates. It is idle to consider even the saving of labour, and the other necessary conveniences of a farm-yard, if the farmer's family are to be constantly visited with fevers, and other diseases consequent upon bad drainage; and if his live stock are to be constantly in the hands of the veterinary surgeon. Let the landowner and the architect, then, ever take for their motto the words "health and comfort," whenever the buildings of a farm are under their consideration.

TO COLOUR MONUMENTAL INSCRIPTIONS.—As Mr. C. H. Smith, in his last letter, mentions the difficulty of colouring inscriptions on monuments, I beg to state that I have found *sealing-wax, dissolved in spirits of wine*, answer the purpose admirably. Any colours may, of course, be used, and it should be laid on the same as paint.—G. T.

NOTICE.

"BUILDINGS AND MONUMENTS, MODERN AND MEDIÆVAL," being Illustrations of recently erected Edifices, and of some of the Architectural Works of the Middle Ages, with Descriptive Particulars. Edited by George Godwin, F.R.S., Fellow of the Royal Institute of Architects, &c., &c., &c., Editor of THE BUILDER.

Under the above title it is proposed to publish in bi-monthly parts, price 2s. 6d. each, the principal Illustrations of Modern and Mediæval Buildings which have appeared from time to time in THE BUILDER, with their accompanying descriptive particulars. Each part will contain about eight plates, folio size, and eight pages of letter press, with plans and details. The engravings will be printed separately, with care, on a tinted paper.

The first part will be issued in time to be forwarded with the magazines for May 1, and will contain:—

Her Majesty's Marine Residence, Osborne; with Plan.

The Carlton Club House, Pall-Mall.

Church of St. Isaac, at St. Petersburgh; with Details.

Kensington Union Workhouse.

The Liverpool Branch Bank of England; and Details.

The New Throne, Canterbury Cathedral.

The North Porch, Restored, of St. Mary Redcliffe, Bristol.

The Interior of Lincoln's-Inn Hall.

Persons desirous of becoming Subscribers, are requested to forward their names to the office of THE BUILDER.

MEETINGS OF SCIENTIFIC BODIES
Held during the ensuing week.

TUESDAY, 27.—Instit. of Civil Engineers, 8 P.M.
WEDNESDAY, 28.—Society of Arts, 8 P.M.
THURSDAY, 29.—Royal Society, 8½ P.M.; Society of Antiquaries, 8 P.M.

TO CORRESPONDENTS.

"*Brick Kilns.*"—A correspondent asks for the best and most improved plan of building brick kilns.

"*Paint for External Work.*"—A correspondent solicits "a recipe for the best external paint or colouring to effectually prevent rain penetrating brickwork in exposed situations,—economy and durability accompanying beauty of effect."

Received,—" R. C." (shall hear from us. We think better of the material than of the number of the pattern book forwarded to us, and therefore give no opinion as to this moment); "J. B." (communication shall be returned, if not used); "J. N." (the squares are mostly private property); "J. E." "F. N." "J. J. S." (paper not sent as promised); "P. E. N." (stamp being six months old will make no difference. A license is necessary); "G. N.," "J. L.," "R. L. F.," "W. W.," "F. D.," "T. B.," "F. S.," "J. H." (we are unable to give the information); "C. J. D." (shall hear from us. Well done'); "Lover of Convenient Architecture" (we are not disposed to "put down" corners, &c.); "E. S." (scarcely desirable); "W. C.," "W. B. (we do not know); "O. T." declined with thanks; "The Picture Collector's Manual, adapted to the Professional Man, and the Amateur," by James R. Hobbes; T. and W. Boone, 29, New Bond-street.

ERRATA.—Page 114, for "Jamiculan Gate," read "Janiculan;" and for "Lungo l'Arno," read "Lungs l'Arno." The examples were from drawings by Mr. Ricardo.

NOTICE.—All communications respecting advertisements should be addressed to the "Publisher," and not to the "Editor;" all other communications should be addressed to the Editor, and not to the publisher.

"*Books, Prices, and Addresses.*"—We have not time to point out books or find addresses.

ADVERTISEMENTS.

No. CCCXXI.

SATURDAY, MARCH 31, 1849.

ATTERS artistical are taking their place before the public: the works done quietly in lone rooms, with Hope for a stimulator and support, are being gathered together into the public places for commendation or sneer, sale or neglect. The harvest of the year is to be gathered. May the weather be fair for all, and the sun shine brightly on the deserving! Those who know best at what cost of time and labour art is attained, will the least willingly condemn, the most readily encourage. They will not expect to find a Michaelangelo or a Raffaelle in every striver after the beautiful; nor will they compare the works of the year of any set of men, with galleries of ancient art,—selected specimens of many masters from the works of many years.

On Monday, the *Association for Promoting the Free Exhibition of Modern Art*, opened their gallery. It contains 531 works of art, of which 15 only have been exhibited before, and is far superior, as a whole, to the collection in the same place last year.

. At the private view on Saturday the attendance of visitors was very numerous, including many distinguished names, and eighteen pictures were purchased, being more, as we understand, than were sold there during the whole of last season, leaving out the sales to the Art-Union of London. The attendance of visitors since has been much better than it was last year, and will doubtless increase as the collection becomes known.

Nos. 6 and 7, " On the Trent," and " A Willowy Stream that turns a Mill," are two nice landscapes, by F. W. Hulme, at present better known by his excellent drawings on wood than by his pictures. No. 14, " Morning Prayers," by Marshall Claxton, is more to our fancy than some larger works by the same artist. The well fed, pompous hand seen at one corner of the picture, in the curtained pew, contrasts cleverly with the meek slight girls at their devotions in the " free-seat." In No. 23 E. H. Corbould gives a possible view of " The Old Hostelrie, High-road, Knightsbridge, A.D. 1497 (anciently called Kynge's-Brygg, or King's-bridge, but more commonly known as Stone-bridge)." The dwellers in that pleasant suburb will scarcely recognise " the Green," now disgracefully disfigured by mud heaps, zinc cowls, and what looks like a very ugly warehouse or stable, but is in reality a free school, where young minds may be educated by externais (and how strong they are we all know), into due contempt of decency, order, and symmetry. No. 48, " Rugged Pastures," is by S. R. Percy, and has much excellence. The same artist exhibits five other landscapes, all possessing more or less merit.

55, " Christ teaching Humility," a finished study for a large picture, by R. S. Lauder, R.S.A., is one of the finest works in the gallery, and is calculated to raise the artist's reputation very considerably. It represents that incident in the life of the Saviour, when, in reply to the question, " who is greatest in the kingdom of heaven ?" he exhorted his disciples to become as little children. This

picture alone would justify a visit to the gallery. No. 76, " Poggio Bracciolini discovering ancient Manuscripts," by D. W. Deane, has excellent qualities, which are still further displayed in 367, " Tasso reading his poems to Leonora D'Este," and 376, " Margaret prophecies the death of Richard III.," by the same painter.

No. 82, " King Lear," by Ford Maddox Brown, is a very remarkable work, and entitles Mr. Brown to a high place in the list of British artists. It is full of thought, and in finish, a perfect marvel. Mrs. M'Ian's " Soldiers' Wives waiting the result of a Battle," No. 92, about to be published by the Peace Society: it is a touching scene, charmingly rendered. No. 100, " Highland Girls winnowing Corn, Fort William, Lochaber," is a pretty picture, by R. R. M'Ian.

J. E. Lauder exhibits two pictures, " Yorick and the Grisette,—the Pulse " (No. 103), and " Columbus " (275), which are both of great excellence. 146, " Kilns at Alfreton, Middleton Dale, Derbyshire," and 216, " Bonsall Dale, Derbyshire," are two of the best out of a number of very powerful landscapes by Niemann. If Mr. Niemann avoid falling into boldness into coarseness, he will not fail to make for himself a good reputation.

One of the best landscapes in the room is 106, " Lowering Weather,—Cader Iris," by Alfred W. Williams. This was bought by Mr. Creswick, A.R.A., showing a good feeling on the part of one connected with the Academy, which must be gratifying to the members of the association. 295, " Langdale Pikes, Westmoreland," by the same artist, is a delicious sunset amongst the hills, refreshing to the eyes of those locked in towns. No. 187 and 188 are two glittering views of the Eternal City, by W. Oliver. 200, " A Willow Bank," well painted by A. Gilbert. Mrs. Criddle, in 221, " Juliet," has a head full of deep feeling. Amongst the historical works will be noticed No. 290, " Claverhouse mortally wounded at Killiecrankie," by W. B. Johnstone, R. S. A., which although rather a picture of those who shot Claverhouse, than of Claverhouse himself, has a breadth and largeness about it which redeems some bad painting. 308, " A Highland Stronghold," by H. M'Culloch, R.S.A., of whom Edinburgh is justly proud, is not quite so good as the picture exhibited here last year, but has all that truthfulness which distinguishes this artist's works. " Moss Dale Fell," by W. K. Briggs, is a clever piece of mountain scenery. 341, " Don Quixote preparing for his first achievement," by R. W. Buss, has much character. 560, " The Ascension of the Just," is earnest and well-intentioned, though defective in execution. 368, " The Girlhood of Mary, Virgin," by D. G. Rossetti, is in the manner of the early school, finished with extraordinary minuteness and displaying a high tone of mind. It is one of the most noticeable pictures in the gallery.

. We must further mention J. D. Passmore, W. and H. Barraud (who have several excellent works), Wingfield, Dukes, Elen, Bullock (his fruit is quite faultless, better than nature and almost as good as Lance), Desanges (whose works, with much theatricality, display a mastery over some peculiar effects of light), J. T. Houlton, J. Peel, and others.

The Exhibition of the *Society of British Artists* will open on Monday. We may say, in anticipation, that it will be found above its average degree of attractiveness. Although there are no particularly striking pictures,

there are several of great merit, as, for example, Mr. Johnstone's " Mary at the Tomb," Mr. Anthony's " Lake of Killarney,", and his " Round Tower " picture; Mr. Baxter's beautiful modelling and refined feeling for colour, as exemplified in his " Gipsey Heads," this year, and his admirable pourtrayal of childhood; Mr. Dobson's praiseworthy scriptural work ; Mr. Hurlstone's gorgeous " Lady looking into the Glass ;" the " Faerie Queene" picture of Mr. Gale ; the Dutch-like transcript of the Wilsons, and hosts of sunny corners and cool green shady spots, from the pencils of Pyne, Allen, Boddington, &c. A new name to London, West, of Clifton, a natural genius, contributes a picture remarkably faithful and beautiful, executed much after the style of Creswick. These, with a very good gipsy episode, skilfully rendered by Mr. Hill ; some three or four embodiments of Mr. Woolmer's gay dreams; some good marine subjects by Mr. Brunning, a new member ; with the works of Messrs. Clint, Tennant, Herring, Clater, and members generally, constitute the nucleus of a much better collection than usual.

Most of our readers will be glad to hear that the *Free Architectural Exhibition* has hitherto more than realised the anticipations of the projectors, the number of visitors having just prior to the extremely cold weather reached to 560 and 670 in the day. His Royal Highness Prince Albert has honoured the association with a visit; and amongst other distinguished visitors have been the Marquis of Northampton, Sir Robert Peel, Lord Codrington, and others. It remains open until the 5th April,—so that there is yet time for those of our readers who have not seen the exhibition to visit it.

The subscription list of the *Art-Union of London*, will be open just long enough after the issue of our present number, to enable such of our readers to add their names to it as have up to this time postponed doing so. We may mention, as news, that the council proposes to electrotype the two rewarded bas-reliefs, and to issue a certain number of copies of them in bronze as prizes. This is an excellent step. The illustrated edition of " *L'Allegro*," having been very successful, the council determined on illustrating Goldsmith's " Traveller," and issuing it to all the subscribers. Amongst the artists who have already accepted commissions for this purpose, are T. Webster, R. A., J. Absolon, W. L. Leitch, W. E. Prost, A. R. A., C. Stanfield, R. A., E. H. Wehnert, R. Huskisson, Fk. Taylor, J. Gilbert, E. Corbould, R. Ansdell, and E. M. Ward, A. R. A.

The Art-Union of London has done good service and will do more.

ROYAL INSTITUTE OF ARCHITECTS.

At a meeting held on the 19th inst., Mr. Ambrose Poynter, V. P., in the chair, a letter was read from Mr. B. Ferrey, giving a sketch of the life of the late Mr. Miles, an associate of the Institute, who died recently at the early age of thirty-two years.

In May, 1841, Mr. Miles left England for Hamburgh, travelled through Bavaria to Italy, stayed in Italy till December, went to Sicily, Greece, Constantinople, and returned to Rome. He returned through Germany to England in 1842. During the whole of this time he occupied himself most industriously, in taking sketches and measurements of the interesting buildings that came in his way. He devoted himself more particularly, however, to the collecting of such details as might be valuable to him to consult in the prosecution of his future practice; knowing that many exquisite pictorial representations of the most celebrated edifices had already been published, and feeling that it was the more practical kind of details which the architect principally needed. This determination was creditable to him, for he was possessed of no small skill as an artist, and it must have been a struggle to him at times to act up fully to his resolution: not that he neglected perspective drawing, but that he knew the greater importance of severe outlines.

In conjunction with Mr. Sylvester, the engineer, he was engaged in erecting several works, in which the principles of atmospheric heat and ventilation required particular study; of these the flax mills at Patrington, near Hull, may be mentioned, and some conservatories in Cumberland and Derbyshire. Amongst other buildings, he erected a mansion in Hyde-park and two in Westbourne-terrace, a villa for Herbert Evans, Esq., Hampstead, and a cottage for Mr. Benj. Marshall, at Muswell-hill; at the period of his decease he was occupied on some extensive buildings in Scotland. The restoration of the chancel of Beddington Church, the national schools at Beddington, Kilburn, and West-End, Hampstead, are also amongst his works.

Mr. Charles Geoghegan exhibited a rubbing from the frieze of an Elizabethan mantel-piece, discovered lately during the alterations to Wiarton House, near Staplehurst, Kent. In the original, which is elegantly executed in the Kentish rag stone, the pattern is very slightly incised in the stone, perhaps 1-50th of an inch, and it is a question if the same has not been traced out by means of an acid, this practice having been formerly much resorted to by the local masons.

Mr. Sydney Smirke, V. P., then read a paper, "On the contents of a work by Sir Balthazar Gerbier, written in the 17th century, and entitled 'Counsel and Advice to all Builders,' together with some remarks suggested thereby."

These remarks referred to the condition of artizans now and at that period, and considering that they are calculated to be useful as shewing a progressive improvement in the condition of the working man, we give them prominence, and invite our readers of the class in question to a calm consideration of the facts set forth. To the other part of Mr. Smirke's paper we shall refer hereafter.

The Chairman said that, although this work of Gerbier's was undoubtedly one of the earliest works on the subject in our language, it was not the first. Walpole mentions a treatise by John Shute, a copy of which had recently been recovered by Professor Willis.*

Mr. Taylor, jun., then described his patent method of facing walls with stone, illustrated in our pages last week. Mr. Fowler mentioned, in connection with the subject, that the tower of Chelsea new church was cased after the brickwork of it was finished, and that the masons began at the top and worked downwards. Projecting courses had been worked in.

ON THE CONDITION OF WORKMEN NOW AND IN EARLY TIMES.

A PERUSAL of the little book written by Sir Balthazar Gerbier, in the seventeenth century, entitled "Counsel and Advice to all Builders," leads me to offer a few observations of a statistical nature, suggested by some data which the treatise affords, concerning the price of labour and materials in the latter half of the seventeenth century. Many, indeed most of the prices are stated in the book so loosely as not to admit of any safe comparison with the prices for the like work at the present day. Let me, however, take a few of Sir Balthazar's prices,—such as do admit of exact comparison, and let me place beside them what may be fairly considered as the present fair average price of the same works:—

	Present price.
Bricks, per thousand, 16s. 8d.	38s.
A rod of reduced brickwork, 5*l*.	13*l*.
Brickwork, labour, and mortar only, including arches, 33s. per rod	78s.
Chalk lime, 6d. per bushel	6½d.
Lath and plaster, set, from 11d. to 17d. per yard	21d.
Render, set, 3d. to 4d.	6d.
Lathing only, 6d.	9½d.
Iron-bars, hinges, bolts, staples, hooks, &c., 1½d. per lb.	5d. to 6d.
Lead gutters, 20s. per cwt.	22s.
Solder, 9d. to 10d. per lb.	6d. to 9d.

It is apparent, from the above comparison, that the prices of those works of which the value is composed of labour rather than of material were low as compared with present prices, whilst those prices are comparatively high of which labour forms a less important element. Sir Balthazar, unfortunately, does not give us the wages of workmen in his day; but the researches of Mr. Macaulay, in his recently published history, supply ample evidence on this subject. He shows that the ordinary pay of a skilled workman was 6s. to 7s. per week, whilst the ordinary pay of a labourer was 4s. per week. Compare these with the present wages of workmen, and we shall find that they receive more than *four* times as much as they did at the period in question.

Having thus shown how low the scale of workmen's wages was in those "good old days," let us inquire into the necessary expenses of a workman. On referring to the table given by Adam Smith of the prices of wheat, it will be seen that the average price, from the year 1637 to 1700 inclusive, was 51s. per quarter: the fluctuation was enormous, for in 1648 it was 85s., and only a year afterwards it was 35s. 6d.,—but the average was 51s. But what is the present price? About 49s.—extraordinarily low at the present moment, I am aware, but the average of the last eight years is little more than 54s.

It is therefore plain that during the Commonwealth, and subsequently, a workman must have paid about as much for his bread as he now pays, whilst he received rather less than one quarter of his present wages.

I have no data at hand as to the price of meat, but Mr. Macaulay reminds us that hundreds of thousands of families rarely, or never, touched it, and it probably did not then form an article of ordinary consumption among the working classes; indeed, the risk and expense of bringing cattle to the London market in those days, would alone justify the presumption that meat was a comparatively high-priced luxury. Mr. Macaulay has also ascertained that the prices of the following articles in 1685 were not merely relatively, but actually, higher than in 1848:—viz., sugar, salt, coals, candles, soap, shoes, stockings, and, generally, all articles of bedding and clothing. Then, as now, these commodities comprised nearly all the personal comforts of a labouring man.

If we even look back to so recent a period as the year 1800, I have it on excellent living testimony, that the wages of a good mason in London were only 16s. per week, who now receives from 30s. to 33s. In the year 1800, wheat was, on an average of five years, as appears by the tables given in Tooke's History of Prices, 90s. 6d. per quarter; and, indeed, during a year of great scarcity about that period, the quartern loaf, for which we now pay 7d. or 8d., cost 1s. 10d.*

It is, indeed, most gratifying to trace the real and progressive improvement in the condition of the working man, since times to which many are too apt to look back with a vague feeling of regret,—as if the keener competition of later times had reduced both the means of employment and the reward of labour. It seems, however, to be a law of our nature that, with the growth of all the material gratifications of life, there grows up also (and in a still greater degree) an increased wish to obtain a larger share of them; and hence it is that contentment is not found to keep pace with improvement.

I trust that my motives in making this contrast will not be misunderstood. I am anxious to shew to workmen that they have at least some grounds for satisfaction, but I am very far indeed from *regretting* their present wages. *We*, as architects, are too deeply interested in their welfare to admit of such a supposition. Our fortunes are bound up with theirs; upon their fidelity and care our professional character and credit depend. Nor can we expect them to use their energies with the same zeal and assiduity, whether we pay them with a grudging or a liberal hand. If ever it could be said with truth that a workman is worthy of his hire, it can be said now of English workmen. In all the most important arts of manufacture, machinery, and architectural construction, English workmanship is without a rival. I appeal to those architects who have examined the present state of the art of building on the continent, to testify the perfect truth of this assertion.

If, in our solicitude for the welfare of this very intelligent, sober, industrious, and loyal class of men, we look around for the means of further advancement, we must turn to those causes over which we can reasonably expect to exercise some control.

The *rate* of wages is everywhere determined by causes which it is useless to attempt to influence; nor have we any reasonable prospect of removing the mischief arising from uncertainty of employment, or from the fluctuations in prosperity or fashion. But the further reduction of the cost of all the necessaries and comforts of life, is an object clearly within the sphere of our competency. That is the quarter from which we may, with reasonable confidence, anticipate an amelioration of the labourer's lot.

Among the articles of primary necessity is that of *lodging*; and it is unfortunately one in which the condition of working people cannot be shown to have experienced much, if any, improvement. Both in this and other countries this head of expense is one which for very many years past has been found to have comparatively little tendency to decrease. In many parts it has nominally increased in a great degree.

About fourteen years ago I ventured to put in print a few suggestions for cheapening and improving the dwellings of the labouring classes. The ground I then broke was, to the best of my belief, a perfectly virgin soil: many have since entered on the same field, and much has been done; companies have been formed; many plans in various parts of the country laid down, and in part carried out, for providing cheap, healthy, and commodious dwellings. The idea, therefore, has struck root, and I trust it may continue to flourish and bear good fruit. I will now, in closing my remarks, quote the words of one of the ablest of French statesmen, M. Thiers, in reference to the defective condition of workmen as regards their dwellings—words which are certainly remarkable when coming from such a quarter. In a speech recently pronounced by him, he says:—"Il y a, je le répète, possibilité de loger les ouvriers dans les grandes villes à meilleur marché d'une maniere plus saine. Cherchez avec nous les moyens d'y arriver; mais il faut les chercher en hommes qui aiment le peuple et qui veulent faire son bonheur."

SYDNEY SMIRKE.

IMPROVEMENTS IN SHAPING METALS.—Mr. John Frearson, of Birmingham, has obtained a patent for improvements in bending or shaping. The metal as supplied hot from the rollers, is drawn by tongs with a to and fro and closing and opening motion between a pair of cutters, and slantwise, across a mandril or die. The requisite length is cut off, and then drawn by the mandril between a pair of grooved rollers, supported in levers side by side. As the iron is drawn through, the rollers approach by cams acting on the free ends of the levers, bending it completely round the mandril. The link, when completed, is removed by the mandril being made to slide back, and by the forward action of a catch interposed between the link and sliding-plate in which the mandril is supported. The different parts are worked from the main shaft by an arrangement of cams and levers far too complicated to be described without diagrams.

* John Shute was buried in the old church of St. Edmund, Lombard-street. His book was called "The First and Chief Groundes of Architecture:" he died Sept. 28, 1563. According to Stowe, his epitaph commenced as follows:—

"This monument declares, that here the corps doe lye
Of him that sought in science sight to publish prudently,
Among the rest of things, the which he put in ure,
That ancient practice and profound, that hight of architecture.
A knowledge meet for those that buildings doe erect,
As by his workes, at large set forth, is shewne the full effect."—ED.

* Some interesting facts, tending to shew the improved condition of workmen within the last fifty years, are noticed by M. Thiers, in his "Discours sur le droit au travail," pronounced 13th September last.

THE HISTORY OF ECCLESIASTICAL ARCHITECTURE IN ENGLAND.*

THE SEVERAL INFLUENCES WHICH CONTRIBUTED TO FORM GOTHIC ARCHITECTURE.

To express the difficulty of certifying the date of an invention, we might repeat a trite proverb—"that there is nothing new under the sun;", and architecture forms no exception to the applicability of the saying. We particularise the present period for poverty of invention, and not entirely without reason, but we forget how few are the years over which our observation has extended, compared with those in which gradual progress was at length consummated in the works which we admire. As we still practise those methods of construction which were described by Vitruvius near two thousand years ago, so the elements of the art are found in the very infancy of time. And as we can retrace the changes of style, and note the influence of nation upon nation, so the wonderful beauty of the Gothic cathedral was not altogether the work of the 13th, 14th, and 15th centuries; and so, even the Saxon style was the offshoot of another.—We might, indeed, have traced the spire to the Saxon period, from the illuminations of Cædmon's paraphrase.

From the degenerate architecture of the Roman empire—imitated, in its several relinquished provinces, or subsequently, as we have seen, from recollections of the "eternal city"—sprang the various phases of architecture in Europe.

But the architecture *more Romano* was composed of styles which merely indicated the common origin. The architecture of the Saxons, and the style which was introduced by Edward the Confessor, had many striking features of dissimilarity. With all its reliance to a common origin, the style of the Normans was essentially that of a different race, and it infused not only new elements but new vigour into the architectural efforts of the country. The most characteristic decorations of pointed architecture—of the early period at least—were suggested in Norman buildings; whilst those structural elements which we have noticed during the Saxon period, were more fully developed, and, generally, the several influences which contributed to form the pointed style, are to be *observed* in the durable works of the Normans, and not mainly to be gleaned from written chronicles.

The *science* of masonry has never been carried to greater perfection than during the period of pointed architecture; and the period of the Norman style is thus important, if considered merely as that of the education of the English masons. The zeal and enterprise of those who raised our cathedrals may astonish all; the beauty of the arrangement of flying buttresses and groining may delight the artist; but the rich embroidery of the roof of Henry the Seventh's chapel is merely the encrustation of a wonderful design for the adjustment of stones, towards which the first steps were taken during the Norman period.

In the great influence of continental architecture over that of this country—in which resulted the importation of the most characteristic features of the pointed style—we discover another effect of the Norman invasion.—But other influences towards the establishment of the architectural works of a later period, have to be enumerated. Of these were the very defects of construction—such as did exist, notwithstanding the merit of the Norman works compared with those which preceded them. In the extensive reparation which has taken place at Hereford, and in the accident which befel the nave of that building, we have had recent evidence of that imperfection of Norman masonry, to which we owe the earlier ruin of other important buildings. Thus from this cause alone—although in the twelfth century there were an immense number of churches and religious establishments—and excluding from consideration that continual desire to contribute to the splendour of the religious edifice, which occasioned continual changes in buildings—were produced many beautiful works, amongst which the lantern at Ely may be particularly cited.—It is perhaps to a similar want of constructive skill that we must attribute the frequent absence of groined roofs of Norman date; and the fate which has so constantly followed the cathedral at York, in which even the groining has always been of wood, attended many noble structures. But to such causes as these we owe the works which rose from their ashes.

The most important influence over the forms of Gothic architecture — referable to this period — is one of which we scarcely think Mr. Poole has taken sufficient notice. The crusades may indeed have given to Europe the pointed arch itself, and though it may be objected that, as the form is found in buildings which are not Gothic, it is not sufficient to constitute a distinct style, it remained, throughout, an inseparable element, lasting even after the principle of verticality was absorbed in the rectangular character, and being retained in arcuated forms in tracery, when abandoned in the circumscribing outline of the aperture. — It is not our purpose to pursue the inquiry into the question of the origin of the form, to justify the opinion of Sir Christopher Wren, or to revive the ingenious theory of Milner, any more than to resuscitate the picturesque fancies of Sir James Hall, respecting the origin of the style itself. All that we now show is, that in the Norman period of English history, and of the progress of architecture, we may find sufficient evidence for a certain amount of reliance upon such theories.—The effect of the crusades upon the structural arrangement of churches was important, if only from the influence of the model of the church of the Holy Sepulchre, and the theory of the eastern origin of the pointed arch is still that which presents the greatest amount of probability. With the Norman style the pointed arch was long co-existent; it was *transmitted* from the continental to the insular possessions of the Normans; but it was a form with which the English crusader was already familiar, and which had been apparent in the intersecting arches of the Norman style. And what palmer or knight, however much under the influence of the religious fervour of that remarkable age, could see "the land of the east" without deriving some impressions of the beauties of nature, from which our closet life "in cities pent" too much removes us. The carved ornaments and capitals of the Early English period have not, perhaps, the truthful adherence to natural forms which is observed in a later style; but they have so great a resemblance to well-known plants, that there can be no doubt as to their evidence of an awakened perception of natural beauties; whilst the still conventional mode in which they are treated, recals the architecturalised treatment of foliage, which the Normans derived, along with even the Corinthian capital itself, from the Roman style.

Considered as the period of the introduction of heraldry, the crusades are equally important: for between this science and Gothic architecture there has always been a very intimate connection. It would be erroneous to suppose that this connection subsisted mainly in that period when armorial bearings formed the principal sculptured decoration of buildings,—when the rose, the portcullis, and the fleur-de-lis, were planted in every imaginable position, and when the religious principle which is believed to have chiefly inspired the monumental architecture of the middle ages, was *most* obtrusively impaired by trappings and mementoes of social strife—which were intruded upon the sleep of death—or by the assertion of high lineage in the equality of the tomb. That the connection of architecture and heraldry was more subtle and intimate, is evidenced by the remarkable parallelism which may be observed in their progress. The shield was not only in constant use as an architectural decoration, but its form altered with that of the arch. Architecture and heraldry—each had a symbolical meaning, and the symbols which they employed were often the same. "But," according to Mr. Poole, "the great bond of union was the religious element. *In theory* every knight was a faithful and devoted Christian; *in theory* every architect was a servant of the living GOD. The knight received his arms and his banner at the hands of the Church, after prayer and vigil; and the rules of his order, and his vow of chivalry, were full of religious requirements and promises. And the arms which he received from the Church he desired, at his last day, to suspend over his monument, in pious acknowledgment that he had received them from GOD, that he had kept them unsullied by GOD's grace, and that he was permitted to offer them again to GOD in thankfulness and honour. And so with the architect and his work. The church was an offering, *in* the heart, and *from* the heart of all concerned,—the founder, the architect, the artisans."

But *symbolism* most deeply pervaded the architecture of the middle ages, and however little we may countenance the opinions of some who would see in Durandus the highest authority in ART, we are forced to admit, with Mr. Poole, that all who do not depart greatly from the forms of Gothic architecture—and of such there are few —"must still design their churches with submission to several laws which have no basis but that of symbolism." Our author, in his definition of intended symbolism, rejects the aspiring characteristic of the mediæval church; but he carefully excludes the application of symbolic meaning from details which there is no proof were ever accepted as symbolical, and does not convert the moral reflections of Durandus into legitimate interpretations. Symbolism, however, was of the greatest importance in determining the peculiar character of pointed architecture. We might, indeed, have discovered its germination during the Saxon period,—in the recognition of the principle of orientation,—in the division into nave and aisles—symbolic of the Trinity—and that into nave and chancel, and in at least the existence of the cruciform arrangement. But in the Norman period symbolism was fully developed. The richness of the doorways was not merely æsthetic, and suggestive of similar depth and richness at later periods. It was the distinctive principle of the Norman architect to present "the *decorated* face of every portion of the church to the advancing spectator;" and this—most completely expressed in the Norman style—was certainly a most marked characteristic of pointed architecture.

It is not our purpose here to enumerate *all* the component elements of pointed architecture, any more than we are able to touch upon the multitude of forms in which these found expression. We might, indeed, point out that the arts of sculpture and painting, in their several branches, were never more indissolubly interwoven with the whole conception of a style, than during the mediæval period, notwithstanding that it has been urged against the revival of the style, that it can give no scope for the exercise of these arts.—We might, too, have enumerated, amongst other influences, dating from an early period, that of veneration for the patron saint, such as led to entire changes of the structure of particular buildings, and consequent most important influences upon style. Thus we might instance the venerated memory of Edward the Confessor, which occasioned the erection of the entire new building of Westminster Abbey,—a work most important in the history of architecture, from the circumstance that it is believed to give the earliest date of the introduction of the traceried principle.—The bishops of the Saxon and Norman periods became the venerated saints of the later church, the reputation of martyrs brought wealth to their shrines, and the edifice increased in splendour, though at length its structural harmony was interfered with.

But it is impossible to exclude from predisposing influences the existence of the guild of Freemasons, by which that remarkable uniformity of detail in structures of the same age was communicated from one locality to another. At the same time, as Mr. Poole well observes, this uniformity is often exaggerated, although he might have added to his discrimination of national peculiarities the distinctive characteristics of more minute divisions of style, such as are observable in the works of different counties. Some of these may have arisen from difference of materials, but in other particulars, the churches of one locality are distinct from those of another of the same date.

It would be wrong, indeed, to ascribe that importance to the Freemasons which has been given to them by popular consent. That it was held an honour to belong to the craft, that their influence over the art was great, and that their mysteries contained many of the principles for which modern investigators are busily engaged in searching, seems obvious; but that

[SUPPLEMENT.

* Continued from page 111.

no merit is due to local workmen, may, after recent investigations, be doubted.

Mr. Poole falls into the mistake which we have had occasion to point out in the work of another writer. The thrust of the semicircular arch is not almost entirely vertical. The acutely pointed arch exercised much less thrust than that which preceded it. In this was its great merit. The Norman "buttresses," which were shallow pilasters having merely a decorative purpose, suggested the buttresses of the Gothic style. These were necessary, notwithstanding the greater facilities of construction which the pointed arch afforded, because in place of resisting the thrust by a continuous wall of great thickness, it was concentrated at a particular point, *at* which was placed a buttress, and this was required to resist not only the pressure of the aisle vaulting, but—unlike the preceding style—also that of the vaulted roof to the nave. As the arch became depressed, the increased thrust required that greater projection of the buttress which was given to it. The use of the buttress was dictated by sound geometry, and the most economical distribution of materials, and it rendered the thick walls of early buildings unnecessary in succeeding instances. To appreciate the full merit of the mediæval architects, it requires that this should be properly understood.

It should be remarked that during the Perpendicular Period, many of those characteristics which we have noticed, were almost wholly obliterated, and the period is, perhaps, not erroneously viewed as the long decline of Gothic art. But it was not without many distinctive excellencies; it added greatly to the resources of the art; and had not political and religious changes supervened, it is not altogether certain that the general abandonment of Gothic architecture would have taken place; at least, a return to Decorated forms is sometimes observable, which betokens—we are inclined to think—rather an independence of thought, than that poverty of invention which is mainly characteristic of the facility of decoration which attended the use of panelling. Nevertheless, the error must be guarded against, that the subversion of Pointed Architecture is to be traced mainly to the Reformation. It was not consequent upon the dissolution of the monasteries, which indeed preceded the Reformation, and it is remarked that Wolsey had dissolved and despoiled religious houses to found his own college long before that event took place.

Mr. Poole leads us through the various changes of style, during which the several influences we have enumerated were at work, and gives the history of the principal buildings in which these changes are exemplified. He has generally executed his task with ability, and has produced a work of reference, which cannot but be found useful. We are the more prone to give him credit for what he has done, because if we may judge from his concluding paragraph, *he* has not the self-sufficiency, or "little knowledge," which has too often rejected the assistance of those who devote their lives to architectural studies and practice, and because, in deprecating too severe a judgment upon what has been done in modern Gothic Architecture, he recognises "that it does not fall to the lot of the same person or the same generation, both to be first in action, and to profit by experience." There is a limit to all human ability, and time and circumstances have effected those changes in taste, over which individual architects had no power of control. We are now reaping the advantages of the labours of those who have examined and explained the characteristics of Gothic Architecture. It must not be forgotten how recently the style has received this succinct exposition; and if we are superior to our ancestors in most things, and if we regret that our *religious* architecture, particularly, is an exception to that superiority, we may confidently say that the state of architectural knowledge in England gives ground for the anticipation that the ART will again achieve great results.

BUILDERS' BENEVOLENT INSTITUTION.—Mr. Biers, the president, had an interview with the Earl of Carlisle on Wednesday last, when his lordship consented to take the chair at the anniversary dinner, which is to take place early in July.

ON COMPARISONS AND EXCLUSIONS OF STYLES IN ARCHITECTURE.*

IT will probably be thought by most of us that, of late, enough and to spare has been said concerning style in architecture; and certainly, in an antagonistic mood, much praise has been bestowed on this style, and much abuse vented against that or the other; but I have had the presumption to think that no recognised style of architecture in existence calls for either that unqualified censure, or that exclusive praise, which has been so freely and abundantly expressed concerning all styles in their turn.

For my own part, I have a strong desire to see rallied, as it were, under the banner of the grand, the beautiful, and the picturesque, all that is admirable and worthy of imitation in the various and sometimes conflicting attributes of the Grecian, the Roman, the Italian, and the Gothic styles; for that each of these does contain much that is admirable and worthy of imitation, the consent of a majority of the whole civilized world goes far to prove. Indeed, I should apologize for the assertion of so palpable a truism, were it not that the language of some amongst our architectural fraternity would tend to a contrary conclusion.

There can be no doubt of there being such a thing as bigotry in the fine arts, as well as certain other matters, and in architecture it abounds exceedingly. As one way of being convinced of this, let any individual who has studied architecture progressively, for some fifteen or twenty years, consult his own personal experience. He will remember, perhaps, that, at the outset of his career, he was taught to put faith solely in the pure and sublime triad of Grecian orders; he was to take his stand upon the Acropolis of Athens, as upon the topmost summit—the veritable Olympus—of architectural excellence, and thence look down upon Rome and upon the nations given to the heresy of Gothicism, as containing naught but debased imitations and barbarous perversions of that art which, forsooth, the Greeks alone understood.

But, as years advance, this young student begins to perceive that the ruins of the Temple of Jupiter, situated in a cowfield at Rome, will almost bear comparison with the monument of Lysicrates, discovered in one of the gardens of his beloved Athens; and thus, by degrees, he begins to perceive the existence of beauties in Rome that he had never dreamt of; nay, perhaps ultimately, like an inconstant lover, he entirely discards his first love, Greece, and attaches himself, with a new-born fervency, to Rome. But still he prides himself upon being a classicist, and that he has not defiled himself with Gothic incongruities and absurdities. As time advances, however, he finds himself compelled by self-interest, or necessity, to embrace even the Gothic, and afterwards, peradventure, the Elizabethan style, which, in the days of his innocence, he was taught to look upon as a monstrous jumble of all the abominations ever perpetrated in the name of architecture. Lastly, he throws to the dogs his early and verdant antipathies, surmounts antique prejudices, and, becoming a wiser and better man, finds beauty even in the Gothic and Elizabethan styles, and good in every one.

To my thinking nothing can be more ludicrous than the controversies that sometimes take place between the upholders of one style of architecture and those of another.

Leeds has very justly remarked that "indiscriminate and exclusive admiration of any one style is more akin to blind and ignorant prejudice, than to real sympathy with it, and to enlightened taste."

"Besides," as he further observes, "as much or even more depends upon the spirit with which a style is treated than what it is in itself; for as the noblest may be vulgarized, and be in course of time corrupted by the very means resorted to in order to maintain it in its pristine integrity, so may the poorest be aggrandized and elevated, if treated with *maestria.*"

Of late years Gothic architecture has been thrust before us so multifariously, and, with some worthy exceptions, so *shabbily*, that to confess the simple truth, it cannot be wondered at that some restive and not very deeply reflective spirits should now kick against it altogether; but, as must always be the case in these outrageous partizanships, neither side is altogether in the right, some truth and a great deal of error being on both sides.

I have said that these controversies about styles are very ludicrous, and for this reason,—that the prejudice against any particular style is invariably more or less in proportion to the want of that knowledge of its principles which is only to be acquired by diligent and impartial study and long practice.

One gentleman writes a facetious book, to prove that construction is no part of architecture. Doubtless it is a very convenient doctrine for any who will not take the trouble to acquire a knowledge of the principles of the things condemned, to excuse an inactivity. No one individual has any right to condemn that which has met with the approval of a large number of men of taste and discernment, without adducing very clear and sufficient grounds for his dissent; and I must take the liberty of saying, that all I have heard advanced by way of objection against any style of architecture now in vogue, just amounts to what may be expressed by the vulgar distich—

> "Different men are of different opinions,
> Some like leeks, some like inions."

There is a phrase in the classics to the same effect, but not quite so expressive.

I have supposed the case as of an unfavourable comparison of what has been called the Christian with the pagan styles, and the attempted exclusion or degradation of the former, but my argument would be precisely similar were the circumstances reversed; and this will readily be believed when I avow that I am much less acquainted with the principles and practice of Gothic architecture than with other styles, and that, personally, I have the greater predilection for classical architecture.

It is not in our art alone that the lack of capacity or comprehension and patient study go hand in hand with contemptuous censure and objection. Take music for example. When the grand symphonic compositions and the later instrumental quartets of the greatest composer the world ever saw, first appeared in this country, they were looked upon as being the wild emanations of semi-insanity, nobody could play them, nobody could understand them, but they have since exalted the name of Beethoven to the highest pinnacle of fame.

And, again, there are the same crude and virulent antipathies with regard to styles of music, as exist in reference to styles of architecture.

One party will take its stand upon the classical works of Haydn, Mozart, and Beethoven, and deny that any good thing can be found in those of Rossini, Donizetti, Auber, and others of the same school; and, as for the popular Jullien, he is a Goth of so outrageous a character, that they would almost sentence him to be hanged, drawn, and quartered. I trust I shall be pardoned for thus wandering into the regions of another art than architecture, for the sake of analogy and illustration.

And now I would ask, to what good end does this chaos of opposition tend? I may be told that controversy itself has its good, but I maintain the contrary, unless such controversy be conducted upon sounder and better defined principles, or, as I may say, upon some principle rather than the no-principle which at present prevails.

In a number of a periodical published a few days since appeared some remarks which, after an allusion to the unequal circumstances and contrary prejudices of certain parties to a controversy, proceed thus:—"Controversy between such men is interminable. It is not pure controversy—not the controversy that leads to the discovery of truth; for the ears and eyes of both parties being partially shut, the truth can never be perceived by either. They are both blind of an eye; their ears are stopped; neither will yield one jot or tittle; and, in the heat of intellectual battle, they very often deny that there is any truth or goodness whatever on the other side. This is not pure controversy. There can be no such thing until the ears and eyes of men are opened."

In making this quotation I would not be understood as condemning even such imperfect controversy as we can get, supposing, as I have said before, that some definite leading

* Read at a meeting of the Architectural Association on the 16th inst.

principles be primarily agreed upon, and rules laid down for our guidance in debate. Now, although it is bootless labour for any one to rise and pronounce wholesale objections against any of the styles of architecture now practised in this country, there *are* portions or particular features of any of those styles which form legitimate objects of attack or subjects for discussion, but for my own part I could not waste time in listening to that sort of crude and unsupported censure and objection to which I have before alluded.

In every case it should be imposed as a condition to the putting forth of an objection, that the objector be prepared by actual graphic illustrations to show the improvement to be gained by adopting his view of the case. You have already had an example of what I would propose, in that paper of Mr. Kerr's in which he objects to the arrangement of the pediments of Grecian Doric temples;* although, unfortunately, he did not complete his illustration by drawings, in respect to his proposal to improve the Grecian Doric column by placing beneath it a square tile to counter-balance the abacus. But, however, Mr. Kerr's mode, so far as it extended, I must maintain to be the only one that we ought for a moment to tolerate.

Let us suppose, for further example, that an objection is started against any particular feature in an architectural composition, no matter of what style, of what date, or of what degree of celebrity. We will say, for instance, that the matter objected to is the introduction of grotesque figures of animals in Gothic architecture, and that one of the turrets and flying buttresses of Henry the Seventh's chapel is selected; perhaps, also at the same time, some other features in these portions of the building are condemned.

Well, all that we should require is, that the objector, or he that condemns, should produce two faithful and intelligible drawings, the one showing the example as it exists, and the other as he would improve it. Let him accompany these by his best reasons for the suggested improvement, and we shall have at once the only tangible and instructive mode of controversy on matters architectural.

With regard to the use of the grotesque in Gothic architecture, perhaps I may be permitted to say a few words. It appears to me that those who condemn it hedge themselves in, as it were, with one principle of architectural effect, and cannot see that there are many others. Why, let us ask, did the Greek imagination introduce the repulsive satyr, side by side with the graceful Bacchante or the beauteous wood-nymph? And why, to this day, do painters delight in similar contrarieties? Why is it that the musician introduces passing discords in such a manner as to be absolutely painful to the ear until they are resolved into their succeeding harmonies? And wherefore have our most renowned poets introduced in their sublimest poems and dramas the lowest buffoonery, and made the most sudden and determined descents from the heroic to the vulgar, from the sublime to the ridiculous? May we not truly answer that it is for the sake of that principle universal throughout nature — CONTRAST? And such is the principle upon which the grotesque is made to mingle with the beautiful in architecture. To recur, parenthetically, for one moment, to dramatic poetry, it appears to me that, taking Æschylus and Euripides as the exponents of the Greeks, and Shakspeare as of ourselves, we have at once the same elements of difference between their dramas as those which exist between the architecture of the Greeks and that of the middle ages of modern Europe; and yet, so much more general is the predilection for the piquancy of contrast than for the insipidity of uniformity, that even the Greeks were not wholly free from the practice of introducing the grotesque. It is true that for the most part they dealt in the horrible instead of the comical, introducing Gorgons, furies, and so on,—but we must not forget those odd-looking horned fellows, half men half goats, that I have before mentioned. Then again, they had their Silenus: surely he was no great beauty. And be it remembered that all these have been used in the sculptured and painted decorations of classical architecture. Moreover, I would ask, what are the centaurs in the metopes of the Parthenon; and the half-human half-fishy monsters in the frieze of the monument of Lysicrates, but grotesques?

Nevertheless, we cannot deny that the Gothic architects indulged in the grotesque much more freely than did the ancients, but not a jot more than the peculiarities of their style demanded. What else could be so well adapted for giving picturesque beauty, contrast, and effective outline, to the mitres and terminations of mouldings in Gothic buildings, as those queer-looking griffins, hogs, dogs, and devils, which the chisels of our old English masons have left us?

Still, I am not here to defend, through thick and thin, everything that precedent-mongers would have us respect and adhere to in Gothic architecture. If grotesque figures cannot be introduced significantly and as an augmentation of the general effect, I say, by all means let them be dispensed with; and, as a general rule, I would submit, that however grim and angular such figures might be on the exterior portions of an edifice, internally they should exhibit solely the most graceful and purely beautiful forms.

I am fully conscious that this paper of mine is of a somewhat desultory character. In truth, I have had no time for condensation and arrangement. I will therefore proceed to impart the gist of what I would say in a few concluding remarks. I would contend, then, that it is utterly useless to attempt to exclude from favour any one of the styles which the members of our profession, collectively, are called upon to practise; that, as regards one style with another, integrally, "comparisons are," as Mrs. Malaprop would say, "odorous;" that all new applications of an existing style or combinations of the principles of one style with another, and all proposed modifications or improvements, should be illustrated and explained by drawings. This mode would also open a fine field for contrasting, by ocular demonstration, compositions in two or more different styles, for the same subject; and I cannot conceive of anything more interesting than one and the same person preparing two designs in, we will say, the Italian and Gothic styles, and exhibiting them, with his observations, on what he conceives to be their relative merits, and the advantages of one style over the other.

Take even a church, for instance (for I am by no means of opinion that the Gothic is the only fit style for such a building), and fill in, as nearly as possible, the same outlines, one with classical, and the other with Gothic forms and details. This would enable us at once to form a true opinion, whereas all the mere talk in the world will leave us as far off the mark as ever.

I feel confident that this plan of proof and illustration, by drawings, would tend materially to enhance the interest of such matters, and would equally conduce to the improvement of the reasoning power and perceptions of all—so that, in the end, we should come to regard architecture as a grand and comprehensive whole, and not a mere thing of shreds and patches.

At all events, if, through lack of opportunity, or the non-possession of an active and all-grasping intellect, any amongst us should not attain to ability in all styles, I trust that there would be begotten within us a spirit of justice and impartiality, to say nothing of charity, which would prompt us to pay due respect to every one, according to his peculiar talent, whether he be merely a worker in the Grecian style, the Roman, the Italian, or the Gothic.

Perhaps we cannot all become equally successful in two or three styles of an entirely opposite nature; but it is in the power of most, if not all of us, to do one thing well, and respect the other for doing another thing well also. Look at painters—what various styles they choose, both of subject and execution, and yet how little they clash with one another. One chooses the high historical, and another the domestic or every day life. One selects landscape, another dogs and cattle, and another simple fruit and flowers; and yet I should think that the Ettys, Mulreadys, the Stanfields, the Landseers, the Coopers, and Lances very cordially *agree* to *disagree*, and each respect the other for what one can do and what another cannot do.

Let us then be actuated by the same spirit, and a truce to all carpings and cavillings about style. Let us endeavour to improve and purify all styles, and, if possible, invent something new, rather than quarrel about what we have; and let us save ourselves from the ridicule and contempt of all reasonable men, by giving praise where praise is due, rather than be so free to condemn in cases wherein we know not what we condemn.

WILLIAM B. COLLING.

* See p. 615, Vol. VI.

BUILDERS *v.* ARCHITECTS.

DESIGNS FOR THE UNITED GAS COMPANY, LIVERPOOL.

A SINGULAR case has occurred in Liverpool. The United Gas Company there, requiring larger offices and other premises, employed an architect to prepare plans. When the estimates came in (at about 8,000*l.*), they amounted to 2,000*l.* more than the committee had reason to expect. This caused much dissatisfaction, and they determined to put the plans and specifications into the hands of another professional man to examine and report as to their sufficiency, the mode of construction, arrangement, convenience, and cost. A report was presented of a favourable nature. The committee, however, were still dissatisfied, and then came to the resolution of applying to *six builders* for designs and estimates. Four of the builders declined sending in, but two firms which profess to combine the functions of architects and builders undertook to prepare plans accordingly, which plans, if approved, they were themselves to execute.

A number of architects, hearing of these circumstances called a meeting, and drew up the following resolutions, which have been sent to the directors of the gas company and extensively circulated elsewhere.

"1st. That the profession of an architect and the business of a builder are separate and distinct occupations, and cannot be combined without lowering the moral character of both, and acting detrimentally on the public interests. That such must be the effect the following brief reasons may tend to show:

The object of the architect (besides the preparation of designs, as works of art, which are to give a character to the town and the period), is to secure the best workmanship, the safest mode of construction, and the first quality of materials. In these respects he has often to come into collision with the builder, whose interests frequently appear to be conflicting. If the architect and builder are the same individual, who is to secure the due performance of his contract? A mere clerk of works, employed to superintend the designs prepared by another, must of necessity be a person of a class ill qualified to judge of the sufficiency of the plans and specifications in the first instance, and unprepared to meet the emergencies which constantly arise on the erection of every building of any importance.

2nd. That, holding these views, we have heard with deep regret of the circular issued by the directors of the gas company inviting builders to send in plans and estimates for their intended erection in Newington. We cannot but believe that this step has been inadvertently taken, without due consideration of the injury inflicted on a respectable profession, and in ignorance of the results which must necessarily follow. The judgment between plans thus sent in, involving a complicated comparison of design, arrangement, construction, detail, kind of material used, completeness of specification, and estimate of cost (all mutually acting and re-acting on each other), could only be safely entrusted to an architect of extensive experience and first-rate standing. No respectable architect would undertake such a task with builders' plans; and the qualifications required for this purpose would be employed with more effect in preparing original designs.

3rd. That the art of architecture can only be successfully cultivated where it is liberally encouraged. That to public companies especially, the profession naturally looks for examples of enlightened support, but if public bodies become so far misled by a mistaken idea of self-interest, as to act in this short-sighted and parsimonious manner, the public cannot complain if architecture, from a liberal art, is degraded into a petty trade.

4th. That feeling satisfied that the views stated above are equally founded in justice to themselves and the public, the undersigned are resolved by every means in their power to discourage and discountenance the practices above alluded to."

This document was signed by twenty architects.

BISHOP ALCOCK'S CHAPEL, ELY CATHEDRAL.

[DATE. 1489.]

W CAPELER   LAING S.

DECORATIONS FROM ABROAD.

CIRCULAR PANEL FROM THE FRESCO PAINTINGS AT CAPRAROLA.　　　PANEL FROM THE TOMB OF CARDINAL ASCANIO SFORZA, ROME.

BISHOP ALCOCK'S CHAPEL, ELY CATHEDRAL.

Few of our English cathedrals have of late years so much engaged the public attention as Ely; and there are several reasons for this : until he opening of the Eastern Counties Railway, ts great and varied beauties were comparatively ittle known; it was not included in the noble eries of cathedrals published by Mr. Britten, ior has any other author ever given a full and iatisfactory account of it; so that when the ipening of the railroad made it so easy of iccess it possessed greater novelty than periaps any other cathedral in the kingdom. Since that time, several circumstances have ombined to increase the interest with which it vas then regarded. Some five or six years iack, it was decided by the dean and chapter hat the whole pile should undergo an entire estoration—a restoration conceived and caried out in a proper spirit,—one, in fact, that ias no parallel, with the exception of Canteriury Cathedral, the authorities of which set so jood an example in their very complete renoration of that splendid specimen of our ancient ecclesiastical architecture. The works at York ian hardly be called mere restoration; in consequence of the two lamentable fires that iccurred there, it was necessary to do more han restore, in the common acceptation of the word. Considering that the expenses of the restoration at Ely are met entirely by voluntary contributions, it must be allowed that those persons who, have aided in this very essential part of the work have been most liberal in their lonations. Perhaps the most visible improvement, or at any rate that which is most effective, is the substitution of painted glass windows for those of the commoner material so lately occupying the lantern; and although the whole of these windows are not yet completed, there can be no reasonable doubt but that they will be in the course of a short time. All these causes, and the satisfactory progress of the works, have induced architects and others to visit the cathedral year after year, and each time with increased interest,

and with the prospect of· discovering some hitherto hidden beauty.

It is quite unnecessary here to enter into a detailed description of the many points of interest to be noticed in this cathedral. We have, from time to time, as opportunities have presented themselves, illustrated some of the finest portions, such as the east front, the Galilee porch, &c. It has, however, some peculiarities that deserve a passing remark; the principal of these is the central octagon, with its lantern; this feature is quite unique. The peculiar situation, and the beauty of the lady chapel, also call for attention, although the latter is much injured by its conversion into a parish church, with the usual unsightly fittings: let us hope, however, that these will shortly be removed. This cathedral affords every opportunity for a complete study of ancient ecclesiastical architecture, as it possesses each successive style in perfection. The nave is an excellent, although rather late, specimen of Norman—no finer examples of Early English are known than those to be seen in the east front and the Galilee porch—and where can any specimens of the Decorated style be found more valuable for beauty and delicacy of details than those in the choir of Ely and the Lady Chapel? In Perpendicular work the cathedral is not so rich, but yet it has some specimens of the style that it would be difficult to excel, so far at least as elaborate and delicate details are concerned.

The principal of these forms the subject of our illustration; it is situated at the east end of the north aisle, and is known as Bishop Alcock's Chapel, having been built by that prelate in 1488. There is no chantry chapel known in England that has so much elaborate detail placed in so small a space—it is about 17 feet square, and the whole of its four sides are completely covered with the most delicate carving; it is, in fact, too small for any really good view of it to be got from the interior. The screen shewn in the illustration separates the chapel from the north aisle, and is best seen from that part: the interior of the chapel has lately been entirely restored at the cost of the fellows of Jesus College, Cambridge.

DECORATIONS FROM ABROAD.

CIRCULAR PANEL FROM THE FRESCO PAINTINGS AT CAPRAROLA.

Federigo, Ottaviano, and Taddeo Zucelin, Tempesta, and even Vignola himself, were all engaged on the decorations of this maste,piece of the great architect. This graceful composition forms a portion of the frescoes in one of the chambers ascribed to the Zuccheri. There are in the same chamber three similar compositions, all coloured in light and varied tints on a white ground.

PANEL FROM THE TOMB OF CARDINAL ASCANIO SFORZA, ROME.

THE tomb is a magnificent pile of marble, covered with elegant bassi-relievi, in the best style of the artist, Andrea Sansovino, who was invited to Rome expressly by Julius II. for this purpose. It is one of the finest examples of cinque cento in Rome, and was executed 1505—1507. Vasari mentions this tomb in high terms of praise. An elevation of the tomb (which is situated in the church Sta. Maria del Popolo) was given in our last volume, p. 318.

A MEMORANDUM IN IPSWICH.

FOR THE BENEFIT OF THAT AND OTHER TOWNS.

By what course of reasoning the shrewd clear heads of Ipswich were led to concur in placing the station of the railroad so far outside the town as it is, one can now scarcely discover. When railroads were first projected, and the word conjured up the idea of all sorts of horrid nuisances, towns in their ignorance spent thousands to drive the stations farther off, and would afterwards have spent double the amount to bring them closer. But when the Ipswich station was settled on, parties were more enlightened upon the subject; moreover it was not done without some one to point out the mistake, and urge another course; for, in an old file of the local papers, we ran against the record of how Mr. Shave Gowing, a townsman, at a public meeting called to consider the subject, spoke long, almost alone, to induce them to insist on a nearer approach. Many must have lamented since then that they allowed themselves to be so hoodwinked as to be unable to see the true state of the case, or, if they did see it, to be silent.

The new street, which was in consequence required to lead to the station, is a curious specimen of *alignement*, as the French call it, and shows greatly the want of supervision on the part of the corporation. To render the formation of the street necessary by stopping the high road—the railway—short of its destination, was a great absurdity; but not to see that this street was made properly, and with a view to the convenience and ornament of the town, shows a want of foresight, and almost a want of sense on the part of authorities which really deserves reprobation. It twists and turns about in all sorts of ways, without the slightest reason, so far as we could learn, and, instead of tending to the improvement of the place, as it ought to have been made to do, is a positive disfigurement, or rather series of disfigurements.

This is the more to be regretted and wondered at, because much has been done here recently in a right direction, and the town is increasing greatly in size and apparently in prosperity. Many of the shops recently built or altered display taste; the new custom-house mentioned by us before this, has some good features, though not without flaws, and the docks have been greatly extended and improved.

A walk through the town has much to interest. There are many curiously carved and ornamented houses, remnants of the past. One, known as Mr. Sparrow's, the date of which is 1567, is a remarkable and well-known specimen. The connection of Ipswich with Wolsey is recalled, when wandering through the town, by a brick gateway erected by him, and now much needing repair; and the river Gipping, on which the town is seated, suggests the origin of the name of the place, which was anciently written Gyppeswid, or Gippeswic, and afterwards Yppyswyche.

The churches in the town, of which there are several, are mostly of the Perpendicular period, and have been sadly disfigured by repairers and restorers. The church of St. Mary at Elms has a Norman south door; St. Margaret's has a very handsome clerestory, externally, of late character, and a curious open roof,—one of the latest; the Key Church, as it is called (St. Mary's) displays some tolerable flint-work; and in the church of St. Nicholas there are some very curious sculptures, the decorations of an earlier building, which were discovered during recent repairs. These are described by Dr. Drummond, in the papers of the "Suffolk Archæological Association,"* where drawings of them by Dr. Edward Clarke are given. Mr. Waller and others, qualified to judge, have considered them Saxon. They did not seem to us, however, to differ in any respect from some works of the same kind known to be of the Norman period.

Amongst other improvements in St. Nicholas's, the interior has been wholly reseated by Mr. Ringham, an able wood carver in the town, whose reputation is very justly extending. We saw in his workshops an oak lectern, pulpit, and altar rail, in progress, which were highly creditable to him.

At St. Helen's, an old church, where the flint and stone work have been restored externally, a slight, ugly, queen post roof has been put up, to the great disfigurement of the building and the impeachment of the taste of all the parties concerned in the work.

A museum has recently been established, and is making satisfactory progress; and there is a mechanics' institution, which has been in operation about five-and-twenty years, and has produced good fruits. There was a proposal some time since to build new premises for its purposes, but nothing has yet been done in this respect. This institution has an extensive library, and should be heartily backed up by all interested in the well-being of the town.

After examining Mr. Hurwood's ingenious arrangements for windows and greenhouses, illustrated last week, we took the opportunity to see the process of manufacturing Messrs. F. Ransome and Parson's patent artificial stone. In this, sands of various colours and degrees of coarseness are combined into a mass by flint or silica, brought into a semi-fluid state by subjecting it to the action of caustic alkali, in a boiler at a high temperature under pressure. The artificial stone, after being moulded to the required form, is submitted in a kiln to a gradually increasing temperature up to a red heat. It seems calculated to be durable, and it was proposed, in the first instance, to apply it in the production of all varieties of architectural decorations. The feeling of the time, however, is opposed to imitative *cast-work*, and at this moment, strange to say, the application of the material is nearly confined to the production of whetstones for scythes, and a patent water-purifier, and these are required in such numbers as to occupy the whole establishment.

In connection with the docks, we observed with no common gratification that an extensive piece of land, beautifully placed and commanding a charming view, has been planted and laid out as a public walking place, mainly through the influence, as we understand, of Mr. Alexander, a leading inhabitant of the town. All who have aided in this work have entitled themselves to the thanks not merely of their fellow-townsmen but their fellow-countrymen—of all who recognise the value of open areas for recreation and enjoyment, and regret the miserable deficiency of them observable in our towns generally.

We should be glad to see some of the principal inhabitants form themselves into an Improvement Society, or Board of Adornment; or some existing body might extend their purposes so as to effect the object in view. Even if they had no power to control individuals, they might do much good, by pointing out evils to be avoided and improvements which might be made, keeping a watchful eye on every step taken, and omitting no opportunity to lead public opinion in the right way. At the present moment numbers of small houses are being built in Ipswich, enclosing and damaging it, and will be found hereafter to present vexatious obstacles to the extension of the good quarters.

In a sanitary point of view, much is needed in Ipswich, and so fully was this felt by many of the inhabitants, that an engineer (Mr. H. Austin) was employed some time ago to report on the state of the town, and advise as to the improvements necessary. This was done, but from some cause or other the report did not exactly take the inhabitants with it, and nothing has been proceeded with. The drainage is bad, the paving worse, and the supply of water so ill regulated, that while thousands of gallons are constantly seen rushing down the streets to waste, producing annoyance, if not doing positive injury, many of the poorer inhabitants obtain it only with great difficulty.

It is to be hoped that steps for the improvement of the sanitary condition of the town will no longer be delayed; and with the expression of this opinion we end our present memorandum in Ipswich.

* For Nov. 1848.

PATENT METHOD OF FACING WITH STONE.

THE description of Mr. Taylor's invention, in last week's BUILDER, professes to avoid the objections hitherto existing against erecting brickwork with a stone facing, arising from the subsidence of the numerous mortar joints, in the former, compared with the latter; by which the stone facing unavoidably becomes injuriously weighted, and the crushing of the bed joint is the result: a very reasonable conclusion to arrive at, as far as theory alone is concerned; but, with here and there an exception,* the mode of constructing brick walls with a stone facing, is the same now as it has been time out of memory; the two trades go on simultaneously; as soon as the mason has fixed a course of stones, the bricklayer backs it up immediately after. If this method is known to be objectionable, why continue to practise it? why do ninety-nine architects out of a hundred adopt a plan likely to crush the bed joints of the stone? I have practically examined the stonework of the principal buildings in London, and have travelled extensively through the provinces for a similar object; yet I cannot recollect an instance of crushing, arising from the shrinking of mortar joints, not even where the most friable stone, such as that of Bath or Caen, has been used: occasionally the stone is fractured by iron cramps injudiciously inserted, as may be seen in many parts of Sir C. Wren's church at Greenwich; but this has nothing whatever to do with the subject of Mr. Taylor's patent. Buildings faced with stone are generally of a superior class, and it rarely happens that they are carried up faster than an average of two courses of bricks per day; so that an elevation 50 feet high would occupy three or four months in erection. No appreciable shrinkage takes place after the greater portion of moisture has been absorbed from the mortar, which, if the bricks are tolerably dry, becomes solidified in a few days, although induration occupies an infinitely longer time. Whatever the subsidence may be, it takes place within a week or ten days after the mortar, in a semi-fluid state, has been applied in the wall, and long before any considerable weight of masonry can be fixed, which is likely to fracture the bedding joints of the stones beneath. • S.

*** The main object of the patent is to *cheapen* the application of stone, so that it may be used instead of cement.

* At the British Museum, the brickwork was completely erected, and the stone facing afterwards fixed to the walls with cramps.

PROPOSAL RELATIVE TO THE COLLECTION AND DISTRIBUTION OF THE CONTENTS OF SEWERS, AND PROTECTION OF THE RIVER FROM POLLUTION.

IN the discussions which are now going on as to the best system of preventing pollution of the river Thames, and turning the contents of the metropolitan sewers to some practical advantage, a vast number of suggestions have been made, but none of them have been as yet, it would appear, of a sufficiently simple and useful character to meet with the approbation of the parties appointed to consider the important subject.

It will, I hope, be excused, if a party, not altogether scientific, should venture to suggest a plan; as, although very imperfect, it may give rise to better ideas on the subject. Moreover, when we consider that many suggestions, some emanating from experienced practical engineers, have been found inapplicable, either from the greatness of the expense, or from the impossibility of adapting the schemes to the necessities of the case, does it not become the more important that any proposals should be received and considered, in order to give a better chance for the development of some new light upon the subject?

These remarks are made, not from any confidence that the writer is about to propose anything new—quite the reverse—but from a conviction that, in a matter so interesting and so deeply involving the health and comfort of an immense and increasing population, every liberty should be given to the inventive mind to exercise its ingenuity, and every consideration be paid to suggestions, however farfetched and remote from practicability they may be.

The construction of branches parallel with the river, carrying the contents of the sewers towards Limehouse and Deptford, would demand too great an outlay, to be found sufficiently remunerative, besides interfering with property and business to an injurious extent.

A party has suggested that the contents of the sewers should be conveyed down the bed of the river by means of pipes, but this obviously presents difficulties, which a little reflection will show to be insurmountable. A variety of other suggestions has been made.

Taking into consideration the fact of the impossibility of uniting all the sewers in one or two main sewers running eastward—or indeed of uniting several of them together without considerable difficulty and expense—it seems to be necessary that each main sewer should have its contents collected separately, and distributed according to some simpler plan.

Can the following suggestions be made of any use?

At the end of each of the main sewers shall

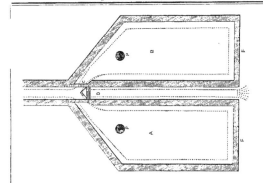

be constructed two reservoirs for receiving the contents as they flow towards the river, to be opened alternately in the manner shown in drawing. When the reservoir B is filled, the gate (c) to be closed, and that leading into reservoir A to be opened.

During the progress of filling, however, a pipe, descending from a building erected over the reservoir—having the lower part filled with holes, and susceptible of being raised or depressed at pleasure—should be made the means of conveying by suction the liquid part of the contents into a reservoir, on the top of the building—from whence it may be conveyed in pipes (p p) to any distance by pressure or otherwise.

In the course of time, a deposit of a more solid character would be formed, which, having acquired a given thickness, should be removed by mechanical means, if not by manual labour.

A small steam-engine should be at work for the purposes in question, and the lofty chimney be made, at the same time, the means for carrying off unpleasant vapours, supposing no chemical agent is available to destroy the same. This, however, I fancy, could be done in these reservoirs if they were properly constructed.

Such a plan would, of course, require that a man or two should be in constant attendance, although the time required for the raising of the one, and the lowering of the other gate, might very soon be prettyaccurately ascertained.

Under any circumstances, in case the contents, by reason of rains and storms, suddenly increase, the upper parts of the reservoir should be provided with divisions (f f), which, on a given degree of pressure being exercised by the flood within, should open to allow of the exit of the surplus to Father Thames. This would not have much effect, if any, upon the river.

A passage, D, should still be left between the reservoirs to the river, only to be used under circumstances of necessity, at the discretion of the guardian or keeper.

The upper surface of the reservoir should be just about on a level with the quays of the river, i. e., just about high tide—if the position of the sewer will admit of it : the lower part may be as deep as is consistent with the amount of liquid usually flowing from the sewer.

Smaller sewers might be turned into the greater ones, and thus as few such establishments be created as possible. But it appears to me, under any circumstances, that no plan would be cheaper, and that the profits arising from the sale of the liquid, and also from the sediment to be dug out from time to time, would be more than amply sufficient to repay any expenses incurred.

THE COMMISSIONERS OF WOODS AND FORESTS have accepted the tender of Mr. Robert Hicks, of Stangate, for the masons', carpenters,' and joiners' work required in the repairs and ordinary works to the royal palaces and public buildings of the metropolis.

RESTITUTION OF PROJECTING SHOP FRONTS WITHIN LIMITS OF THE BUILDINGS ACT.

In reply to some inquiries as to the views of the official referees concerning the re-construction of shop fronts in town at present projecting before the line of fronts, we cannot do better than place before our readers the substance of an award made a short time ago, on the information of the Marylebone district surveyor, against the owner of No. 85, Oxford-street, and the builder employed.

In this case the old shop front had projected very considerably before the line of fronts, and the house being taken down, the owner contended that he was entitle to rebuild upon the site to the full extent of the said projection. Adjoining occupiers contended that the projection would be injurious to them.

The award set forth the following :—

"1st. With reference to the claim of the said builder and owner, that as the said house had been recently rebuilt, and a projection formerly existed in front thereof upon the ground of the same owner, they are entitled to rebuild the said projection to the same extent,—we, the said official referees, considering that it is by the first-mentioned Act (section 5) enacted, that buildings shall be built, rebuilt, enlarged, or altered, in reference, among other matters, to the projections and to any other parts or appendages of such buildings, in conformity with the several particulars, rules, and directions, which are specified and set forth in the several schedules, C, D, E, F, G, H, I, K, to the said Act annexed, and considering also that certain rules are by the said schedule E specified and set forth, ' with regard to buildings hereafter to be built or rebuilt in reference to projections therefrom,' and also ' with regard to buildings already built or hereafter to be rebuilt, as to bow windows or other projections of any kind,' do hereby determine and award, that it will not be lawful to rebuild any buildings so as to retain any projection contrary to such rules, or to rebuild any projection whatsoever which it would be contrary to such rules newly to erect.*

2nd. With reference to the allegation that the projection in question is a shop front, and as such, is permitted to project beyond the general line of the fronts of the houses in any street or alley, we do hereby determine and award, that the said projection is not wholly a shop front, but that it is in part a projection made before the front of the said house as an extension of the second or ground-floor story thereof, and is not allowed by the said first-mentioned Act to project beyond the general line of the fronts of the houses, and that the face of the front external wall of the said house No. 85, Oxford-street, above the said projection, is in the general line of the fronts of the houses in that part of Oxford-street where the said house is situate, and that inasmuch as the said projection projects beyond such line, the same is contrary to the said first-mentioned Act.

3rd. With reference to the allegation that the said projection would be injurious to the owners and occupiers of the buildings thereto adjoining, we do hereby find and certify, determine, and award, that the said projection will be injurious to the owners of such houses, and that such projection will be injurious to William Swinstead, by obstruct-

* We are not to be considered as necessarily assenting to the universal application of this dictum.—ED.

ing the view of his goods when displayed in any shop window that he may lawfully make before the front of his house, and that such projection is in this respect contrary to the said first-mentioned Act.

And further, we are of opinion that in no case may any projection be made beyond the general line of fronts, under the name of a shop front, so as to be in fact an enlargement of any floor or story of the building to which it belongs, but that where the said first-mentioned Act allows shop fronts to project beyond the general line, it is to be understood of shop fronts properly so called and not otherwise, and that any projection which projects to an extent greater than the reasonable width of a stall board cannot be included in the term " shop front," and that such reasonable width may be taken to be in the case of the building in question, and of the buildings on each side of it, two feet three inches, and no more, and that any cornice to such shop front may take the reasonable projection of a cornice, so that in any case there be no overhanging or encroaching upon the public way, and so that such shop front and cornice if they project beyond the statuable width for wooden shop fronts and cornices, be wholly of brick, tile, stone, artificial stone, slate, cement, or metal, or of other proper and sufficient fire-proof materials, except the frames and sashes of the doors and windows, in reference to the necessary woodwork thereof.

And as to the proper separation of two shops, as well as to the injurious effect of shop fronts upon the adjoining owner, we do also declare our opinion that unless any two adjacent shop fronts be separated from one another by projecting brickwork, at least 8½ inches thick (which may be in two half bricks in the line of the party wall, between the buildings), or by brick built ends, clear of one another, and of the party wall, the returns of the shop fronts ought to be kept wholly within the lines of the inside faces respectively of the party wall."

The owner was accordingly directed to take down and remove so much of the projection as extended more than two feet three inches beyond the face of the front external wall of the house.

FORMATION OF THE VAULTING OVER ST. GEORGE'S HALL, LIVERPOOL.

MR. ELMES intended that the vaulted ceiling of St. George's Hall should be formed in brickwork; Mr. Robert Rawlinson, however, introduced hollow pots for the purpose, as we mentioned in our recent notes on Liverpool. The ceiling has just been completed, and the centres struck. It is 169 feet long and 65 feet in span, and according to the Liverpool Journal, the whole amount of subsidence was three-eighths of an inch at the crown, uniformly throughout the entire length of the crown. The journal in question says :—The arch has been turned with hollow tile, 12 inches in length, and 4 inches square on section, each tile being perforated, longitudinally, with a circular space 2 inches in diameter. The soffit of the arch is panelled, having two breaks, or separate sinkings of four inches each. The whole is formed and worked in with the tile, so that portions of the ceiling are 4 and 8 inches below the general line of the inner pannel, which is one tile, or 12 inches in depth. All the tiles are set as " headers " in this portion of the arch, to secure means of ventilation. The main ribs are 2 feet, or two tiles in depth, also set as " headers." The tiles were made by Mr. Scragg, of Tarporley, in Cheshire, by his drain-tile machines, and were delivered on the ground at 3l. 5s. per thousand. About 140,000 have been used in the arch. It would have taken about 230,000 bricks to construct an arch of the same dimensions and depth. The weight of the tiles in the arch is about 600 tons. Brickwork would have been about 1,000 tons—there is, consequently, a saving of 400 tons in weight by using the hollow tile. The arch has been set in mortar, made from Halkin mountain lime, excepting 5 feet on each side of the key, which is set in cement.*

The arch was keyed on the 3rd and the centres were struck on the 6th, and lowered about 6 inches. We shall probably give a section of the vault.

* Many doubts have been thrown upon the practicability of turning this ceiling, by architects and builders ; but its completion will be a full answer to all objections. Ceilings and arches have been turned with pottery-ware and tiles by the Romans, Italians, and French, but not of this magnitude and character. The successful completion of this arch will give an impetus to hollow brick and tile constructions, as the tile-making machines offer great facilities for their manufacture ; and for all purposes where combined strength and lightness are required,—as in ceilings, vaults, fire-proof floors,—the advantages are great. They will also be used for purposes of ventilation, for partition walls, and for lining external walls to prevent the admission of damp.

COSMOS.*

THE STUDY OF NATURE IN ITS RIGHT ORDER AND CONCURRENCE OF FORMS AND POWERS.

THERE may be much more in heaven and earth than is dreamt of even in Baron Von Humboldt's philosophy, and, nevertheless, that same philosophy be perfectly correct; for, compendious as is his detail of what does exist in both of these rather extensive districts, his philosophy relates not so much to what 'may be' in either, as to its proper order or arrangement when it does 'turn up.' "A proper place for every thing, and every thing in its proper place," might very fairly be adopted by the baron as his motto, were it not rather too homely for a cosmopolite so far-travelled, so far-seeing, and so renowned.

The sweep of this philosopher's mental vision is indeed a noble one,—his aim an all comprehensive one. We prefer, however, at once to occupy our space with his own plain, modest, prefatorial explanation of his own great purpose, much rather than presume to translate his ideology into any other.

"The first volume contains a general view of nature, from the remotest nebulæ and revolving double stars to the terrestrial phenomena of the geographical distribution of plants, of animals, and of races of men; preceded by some preliminary considerations on the different degrees of enjoyment offered by the study of nature and the knowledge of her laws; and on the limits and method of a scientific exposition of the physical description of the Universe. I regard this as the most important and essential portion of my undertaking, as manifesting the intimate connection of the general with the special, and as exemplifying, in form and style of composition, and in the selection of the results taken from the mass of our experimental knowledge, the spirit of the method in which I have proposed to myself to conduct the whole work. In the two succeeding volumes I design to consider some of the particular incitements to the study of Nature, —to treat of the history of the contemplation of the physical universe, or the gradual development of the idea of the concurrent action of natural forces co-operating in all that presents itself to our observation, —and lastly, to notice the specialties of the several branches of science, of which the mutual connection is indicated in the general view of nature in the present volume."

We might as well attempt to give our readers an idea of the British Museum by the exhibition of one or two of its lions or its eagles, or a 'specimen' or two of its gold or silver ores, as any correct idea of "Cosmos" from mere quotations within our limits: we must refer them to the work itself, which is now within the reach of all, at half-a-crown a-volume,—a phenomenon, the mere sight of which itself is 'well worth the money,' as an exhibitor might say of some one introductory wonder of the nineteenth century, issuing in a host of other varieties and valuables.

But we may fairly present an illustration of the author's general style, though even that is varied, ranging from what befits the calm philosopher, to even the picturesque and glowing imagery of the artistical enthusiast. As an average specimen of the whole, however, we may quote a few of his preliminary observations on the general study of natural knowledge:—

"The clearer our insight into the connection of phenomena, the more easily shall we emancipate ourselves from the error of those who do not perceive that for the intellectual cultivation and for the prosperity of nations, all branches of natural knowledge are alike important; whether the measuring and describing portion, or the examination of chemical constituents, or the investigation of the physical forces by which all matter is pervaded. It has not been uncommon presumptuously to depreciate investigations arbitrarily characterised as 'purely theoretic,' forgetting that in the observation of a phenomenon which shall at first sight appear isolated, may lie concealed the germ of a great discovery. * * * * Where all the blossoms of civilisation unfold themselves with vigour under the shelter of wise laws and free institutions, there is no danger of the development of the human mind in any one direction proving prejudicial to it in others. Each offers to the nation precious fruits,—those which furnish necessary subsistence and comfort, and are the foundation of material wealth,—and those fruits of creative fancy which, far more enduring than that wealth, transmit the glory of the nation to the remotest posterity. The Spartans, in spite of the Doric severity of their mode of thought, 'prayed the Gods to grant them the beautiful with the good.' As in that higher sphere of thought and feeling to which I have just alluded, in philosophy, poetry, and the fine arts, the primary aid of every study ought to be an inward one, that of enlarging and fertilising the intellect; so the direct aim of science should ever be the discovery of laws, and of the principles of unity, order, and connection, which every where reveal themselves in the universal life of nature. But by that happy connection, whereby the useful is ever linked with the true, the exalted, and the beautiful, science thus followed for her own sake will pour forth abundant, overflowing streams, to enrich and fertilise that industrial prosperity which is a conquest of the intelligence of man over matter."

Without desiring to institute any parallel, or to express any opinion as to relative or respective merits, we cannot conclude without reference to Mrs. Sommerville's most able work on the connection of the physical sciences, in especial juxta-position with the context of such a quotation as this. In the only special notice of Mrs. Sommerville's work which we have remarked either in text or index, the baron himself does this lady the justice to allude to her "generally so exact and excellent treatise." With the translator, or rather the editor, we have at present only one fault to find, if fault it be: why still persist in giving the new centrifugal planet 'Neptune,' as he does so prominently in *the only note*, throughout, beneath the text (Vol. I., p. 20), the controversial, and by no means co-relative name of 'Le Verrier?' even granting that it be not amiss to give the credit of the 'a-missing' planet's discovery to him and not to Adams. Is it because the colonel happens to be the *foreign* sec. of the R. S. that it is so? By the fiat of astronomers in general, Le Verrier himself included, if we mistake not, the planet in question has been already formally christened with the certainly heathen, but still co-relative, name of 'Neptune,' a much better associate for Jupiter, Saturn, and Uranus than 'Le Verrier' can ever be, at least until the nineteenth century be lost in the myths of ages, and then the already classical name of Sabine itself may, we hope, hold an honourable place, if not in the rank of Jupiter and Le Verrier, at least among the lesser stars.

* "Sketch of a Physical Description of the Universe, by Alexander Von Humboldt. Translated under the superintendence of Lieut.-col. Edward Sabine, R.A., For. Sec. R. S. Fourth edition. London: Printed for Longman, Brown, Green, and Longmans, Paternoster-row; and John Murray, Albemarle-street, 1849:"—in two Volumes.

METROPOLITAN COMMISSION OF SEWERS.

Protest against the appointment of Committees. —At a general court held on the 22nd, to which we briefly referred in our last, the Earl of Carlisle in the chair, the minutes of the last court having been read, including which were fourteen resolutions for the appointment of committees,—

The Hon. F. Byng said he rose for the purpose of protesting against the passing of these orders. When he left the last court he had little intention of returning to it, but for the astounding orders, cut and dried, that had been thrown upon the court by Mr. Bullar, apparently with the authority of law, and which were seconded by Mr. Stone, who then acknowledged that he had never seen them before. He (Mr. Byng) believed them to be nothing more than an evasion of the opinion of the law officers of the crown. Having considered the subject further, and taken good advice, he had come down for the purpose of protesting against these proceedings, and he should do so in spite of the charge of "obstruction" to the business of the court. Luckily, however, he was one of the small number by whose "obstruction" they had gained for the public open doors and a knowledge of all their proceedings. The regulation of their business had been submitted to two gentlemen, of whose ability there could be no doubt—Mr. Bullar and Mr. Chadwick, and they had submitted various suggestions. The mode of its transaction had lately become most serious and ought to be checked. He might allude to the Committee on the Ordnance Survey, from whom they had received no minutes, or any account as to what expense the commission would be put to —in fact, they had received no account whatever, except a frequent charge for wages. He then adverted to the charge for flushing, which, without curing the disease of filth and dirt, had up to December cost 14,000*l*. After some further observations, the hon. Commissioner recorded a lengthened protest against the orders, which, after detailing the grounds of objection to individual orders, concludes with a general protest against the whole:—

"Because out of the seven committees constituted or confirmed by these orders, four exclusively consist (with one single exception) of twelve of the commissioners nominated upon the Works Committee; and because the system of permanent private committees, as sanctioned by these orders, will destroy the responsibility of the officers, impair the efficiency of the court, and deprive the public of their main security against extravagance and caprice."

Mr. Leslie said he had seen the document, and had great pleasure in signing the protest, as it put fairly before the court the true construction of the Act of Parliament. At the last court he wished these orders to stand as notices of motion; but that being refused, he had no course left but to sign the protest.—Mr. Lawes also expressed his determination of signing it; and contended that referring matters in gross to committees was opposed to all principle of law.

The Earl of Carlisle said there could be no objection to any commissioner protesting against their proceedings; but as the question had been decided by so large a majority at the last court, he thought it was not desirable to reverse that decision without notice.—Lord Ebrington said no idea of secrecy existed, but only a discretion as to limiting the number, to prevent interruption to public busines.

Mr. Chadwick said on the question of publicity, so much talked of, he believed there could be no greater evil or obstruction than being called upon to pass a mass of unexamined and unarranged business in open court. He believed that it would be impossible to get through it unless by a subdivision of labour. Take, for instance, the Committee on the Ordnance survey, that had been spoken of. Now, nothing could be more ignorantly absurd than to suppose that the business of a triangular survey could be done in open court. He then took a review of that work, and said that the public were deeply indebted to the indefatigable zeal of Sir Henry de la Beche, who had given a clearness and accuracy to the works of the survey that were beyond all praise. In point of money, he had saved the public 100,000*l*.; and in point of time, several years. The county had had the best talent engaged on it; and when completed would be the greatest and most accurate work ever accomplished. He justified, next, the charge for flushing, as the only expedient that lay within their reach; and although it had cost 14,000*l*., under the former system of carting it would have cost five or six times that amount.

Mr. Bullar denied any intention of evading the Act of Parliament.

The Ordnance Survey.—Three very voluminous reports were received on the subject of the survey, in which a variety of topics were treated on. It appeared that the whole of the ground survey is complete except in some parts of Kent and Surrey, which would be complete in three or four months, and the whole of the town area would be completed by the end of the year. These documents were accompanied by reports on the subterranean survey, showing that the sewers in Soho, Fitzroy, Manchester, Cavendish, and Bryanstone squares were loaded with filthy deposit, and also those in Hyde-park-gardens and the costly streets and squares adjacent, with Berkeley and Eaton squares. In fact, the only healthy spot in the whole city of Westminster was in the neighbourhood of the Seven Dials. As regarded the sewers of Kent and Surrey, they contained deposit varying from 5 feet in depth, and several explosions of choke damp had taken place during the examination of them.

A long discussion ensued on the drainage of Kensington, and the surveyors were ordered to report on the best means of effecting this.

A proposition to employ street orderlies in conjunction with this commission in street cleansing was negatived.

It was ordered that Hammersmith and Fulham be declared a sewers district.

An application from Guildford, asking that Mr. Phillips may assist in the inspection of plans for the drainage of that town, was respectfully declined by the court.*

Various lengths of pipe sewer were ordered to be put down.

THE DUNDEE ROYAL ARCH COMPETITION. —Out of 300 designs submitted to them, the committee, described to us as being wholly incapable of judging, have selected a *Norman* design, by Mr. J. T. Roughead, of Glasgow. We are informed by a professional correspondent that it consists of a *pointed* centre arch, two semicircular side ones, three tiers, one above another, of interlacing Norman arches, two octagonal turrets with battlements terminating the main piers. The selection has caused great dissatisfaction.

* This will serve as a reply to several inquirers on the subject of this competition.—ED.

LONDON: Printed by CHARLES WYMAN, of 7, Calthorpe-street, in the Parish of St. Pancras, in the County of Middlesex, Printer, at the Printing-office of J. & H. Cox, Brothers, 74 & 75, Great Queen-street, Lincoln's-Inn Fields, in the Parish of St. Giles-in-the-Fields, in the said County; and published by the said CHARLES WYMAN, at the Office of "THE BUILDER," 2, York-street, Covent Garden, in the Parish of Saint Paul, Covent-Garden, also in the said County.—Saturday, March 31, 1849.

Miscellanea.

FIREPROOF FLOORING AND ROOFING.—Mr. G. Nasmyth has obtained a patent for "certain improvements in the construction of fire-proof flooring and roofing, which improvements are also applicable to the construction of viaducts, aqueducts, and culverts." According to contemporaries, these improvements consist in constructing floors and roofs of iron plates, which are bent into the form of a segment of a circle, or into a conical, polygonal, or other shape, by the ordinary plate-bending machinery, or by any other suitable means. These bent plates are supported on chord plates, or tension bars, which have their ends bent upwards, whereby the plates are retained in their curved position when subjected to pressure. The ends of the chords rest upon the flanges of cast or wrought iron girders, above which are cast or riveted knee pieces, which prevent the bent ends of the chords from springing; or, instead of iron plates, angle or T iron, bent into the required shape, and supported upon chords resting upon the flanges of girders, may be employed. Over these curved ribs, iron plates are bent, with their ends placed underneath the bent-up ends of the chords. The spaces above the iron plates are filled up, to form the flooring, with Portland cement, mixed with broken bricks and other suitable materials. The improved girders are formed by bolting iron plates to the sides and top of stone arches and chords, combined as before. The side plates are made with flanges to support the arches and chords, which form the joists, and have also knee pieces bolted to them to prevent the chords from springing when the arch is subjected to pressure. The arches and chords may be made of one piece each, or may be made of several pieces bolted or riveted together. Currents of air may be caused to pass in the hollow spaces left between the arches and their chords, and through perforations in the floor in the room.—*Claims*—1. The modes of constructing floors and roofs of buildings, and the beams or girders of bridges, viaducts, and aqueducts by means of metal arches, or other curved or angular figures, or both, which are supported by chords that serve as abutments to the arches.—2. The application of this flooring to the warming, cooling, and ventilating of buildings, by causing currents of air to pass through the hollow spaces left between the arched plates and the chord plates. We have not yet seen the construction. It seems similar to an arrangement we saw some time since at Mr. Porter's works, Southwark.

NEW SAW-FILING AND SETTING MACHINE.—Messrs. Norton and Cottle, of Holme's Hole, have recently patented a machine for filing and setting saws, enabling the operator to whet and set the teeth of saws in such a manner that every tooth will be equal in size and length, the proportion being graduated by an index, and so adjusted as to suit the teeth of saws of every description. Saws that have been used and become useless in consequence of bad filing, can be recut. The set is attached to the machine in such a manner, that when the filing is completed, no alteration is required in the adjustment of the saw to complete the setting. The inventors have found by experience, that the hardest saws can be set without breaking or injuring the teeth. Saws considered in a measure useless having passed through this machine are said to work perfectly easy, and perform much faster than those filed in the usual manner; and the teeth being all of an equal length, will not require filing as frequently. These machines, if not too expensive, we think, will come into extensive use.—*New York Mechanic.*

SMALL-POX HOSPITAL DESIGN.—Sir: I was surprised to see, in THE BUILDER of last Saturday, my design for the Small-pox Hospital (for which I received the 2nd premium) without my name attached to it. It should be by Moore and Matthews, and not Mathews only.—I am, Sir, yours, &c.—R. H. MOORE.

*** It was so published on the positive assertion of Mr. Matthews that the design was by himself alone. It is certain the premium was awarded to the two conjointly. We cannot enter into any discussion on the matter, and will only express the pain with which we ever view a want of good faith.

PROJECTED WORKS.—Advertisements have been issued for tenders, by 5th April, for paving the carriageway and footway of a new street about to be formed from Bermondsey-street to Griffith's-rents; by a date not specified, for the delivery in Oxford of not less than 500 tons of granite, &c., annually; by 16th, for the erection of the east wing of the Royal Berkshire Hospital; by 2nd, for putting down 2,500 feet of 18-inch glazed stone-ware pipe sewer along Hutchinson's-lane, Earl's-court-lane, and Pembroke-road, Kensington; by 10th, for the rebuilding and restoration of Kingstone Church tower, &c. (Herefordshire); by 11th, for the whole works required to complete the Portsmouth station of the Brighton and South-Western Railway; by 30th, for the execution of a new bridge over the Trent, near Newark; by 17th, for laying iron pipes through Folkstone and from reservoir, and also for formation of reservoir, and of new road, and other works (separate tenders) for the Folkstone Water-works; by 2nd, for a workhouse kitchen-range, with iron boiler, &c. at New Forest Union; by 17th, for the construction of three reservoirs, with embankments and stone work, &c., for Manchester Corporation Water-works; by 3rd, for the works in erecting a chapel, schools, &c., at Everton (Liverpool); and by 12th, for the erection of a stone or an iron suspension-bridge at Disserth, Radnor.

PATENTEES IN AMERICA.—The last annual report of the Commissioner of Patents in the United States contains the following passage:—"In my last annual report I had the honour to refer the attention of Congress to the expediency of placing the citizens and subjects of foreign governments, applying for patents in this country, on the same ground with regard to fees which our own citizens occupy. Deeming the matter of much importance to the interests of this country, I feel it to be my duty again to bring that subject to the consideration of that honourable body. At present, the subject of a foreign government who applies to this office for a patent is required to pay the sum of 500 dollars, if a subject of Great Britain, and 300 dollars if the subject or citizen of any other foreign power, before his application can be received, while the American citizen is required to pay only 30 dollars. It is true that the fees and duties required in most foreign countries are very much higher than those which our laws demanded, but they are imposed on all alike, whether subjects or foreigners. But even if it were just to make a discrimination in favour of American citizens with regard to fees for patents, I am of the opinion that the policy is injurious to the interests of this country, and therefore not expedient." We understand the recommendation is likely to be acted on.

DISCOVERIES AT FOUNTAINS ABBEY.—In a thicket of underwood, near the lady chapel, and where the river Skell is arched over, some interesting remains of the abbot's house have been discovered. In repairing the arches, and on reaching a level just above the perfect parts of the structure, the workmen came to pavements of encaustic tiles, the bases of two rows of clustered Early English columns, and broken Netherdale marble shafts, similar to those now to be seen in the choir and lady chapel. Here, too, in what appears to have been the common ash-hole, were found some Ralley or Railage coal, and a silver tea-spoon! The remains seem to be spread over an extent not much less than the nave and choir of the Abbey Church, and, from what has already been uncovered, it appears that the whole ichnography of this important building may yet be retrieved by a careful excavation.

INSURANCE OF CHURCHES.—It has been urged, that while almost every house of any respectability in the country, and nine-tenths of the corn ricks and homesteads are insured, scarcely any of the churches have had the same precaution used with regard to them. It is said that a legal opinion of a high ecclesiastical authority was given in respect of Portsmouth Church, not many years past, to the effect that "the churchwardens would be censurable, I had almost gone the length of saying punishable, for omitting the necessary precaution of insuring the parish church from fire." Churches erected under the Church Commissioners are all insured, and generally to the amount of two-thirds of their cost.

INSTITUTION OF CIVIL ENGINEERS.—On the 27th, the paper read was a "Description of the Groynes formed on the South Rocks, the site of the new docks at Sunderland," by Mr. W. Brown. These groynes have been erected for the purpose of retaining the deposited materials excavated from the new docks, and of arresting the sand and shingle which naturally travel southward, in order to form a barrier beach, that should effectually exclude the sea from beyond a given line. The three first, whose lengths varied from 326 feet to 358 feet, were erected at a height above ordinary high-water mark of 2 feet 6 inches, and 10 feet at the seaward and inner ends respectively. The exterior was composed of ashlar-work; the interior partly of the excavated magnesian limestone, and partly of rubble set in mortar: the batter of the north sides was two and a half inches to a foot, that of the south sides one to one, and the crest was formed into an arch, with a radius of 5 feet 6 inches. The four other groynes were constructed of a different form, in consequence of those first erected not retaining the deposited excavation, and accumulating other materials as was desirable, and from their having been injured by the sea during a heavy storm, which occurred at the time of the equinoctial tides, during the spring of 1848, when a breach was made in the first and third groynes, and at the same time some of the stones in the second groyne were loosened. These effects were produced at about the same point in each, namely, the intersection of the inclination of the groyne with the line of ordinary high-water mark; and it was found, from observation, that the momentum of the waves was greatest at or about the time of high water. The sides of these groynes were semi-cycloidal, each being generated by a circle of 12 feet 9 inches in diameter, and uniting at the apex; the seaward and inner ends are respectively 7 feet and 10 feet above ordinary high-water mark, and their lengths varied from 510 feet to 579 feet. The foundations of these groynes consisted of a course of freestone, laid at an average depth of 2 feet below the surface: the sides were also of coursed freestone, set header and stretcher alternately, and the hearting of large-sized rubble, closely packed, the vacancies between it and the ashlar-work being filled with small stones set in Roman cement, so as to insure a solid bed. At a depth of 6 feet below the crest of the groyne, and resting upon the rubble hearting, coursed ashlar was introduced, and carried as near to the crest as possible, the vacancy being filled with small rubble and Roman cement.

A STEAM STONE-DRILL.—Mr. Joseph J. Couch, of Boston, has invented a steam-drill, which, it is said, can be worked so as to apply the force at any angle with the requisite rotary motion, and to do the work of seventy-five to eighty hands at once by the aid of two. The "*Atlas*," in describing it, says—"The drill is attached to a shaft by means of a socket. The shaft is made to ply with great force by simple mechanism, and as the drill approaches the rock is detached as by throwing by hand, only more forcibly. At every blow a rotary motion is effected by means of a small ratchet on the drill shaft. In horizontal positions the power depends on the momentum of the drill shaft; in vertical and inclined positions the momentum is assisted by gravity. At the trial, the machine was placed in a *horizontal* position, and perforated a block of the hardest granite with a 4-inch drill at an average rate of 22 inches in the hour; with a 3-inch drill, it executed from 25 to 30 inches in the hour. A medium rate is 125 blows per minute. But by heightening the speed, not only is the number, but the force of the blows increased. The machine can be seen at Mr. J. W. Fowle's, No. 16, East Orange-street." A machine of a like nature, we may here observe, but worked by hand or by horse, with a crank and fly-wheel, has been invented, or improved rather, by Mr. E. Nicholson, of Newcastle. It appears, however, to be only capable of drilling vertically. The drill is made to rotate also, and to be detached in falling and griped in lifting. With large drills, four men, or a horse, will thus cut a 4-inch hole in hard stone, it is said, at the rate of 2½ to 3½ feet an hour, and two men, with smaller machines, a 4-inch hole in freestone, at the rate of 5 to 6 feet an hour.

A NEW RIG.—At Boston, U. S., a pamphlet on ship rigging has been lately published by Captain R. B. Forbes, who, from his numerous inventions and recommendations of improvements in ships, as to model, steering, chain-cables, pumps, windlasses, compasslights, lightning-conductors, life-boate, lifebuoys, life-preservers—seems to be, if not a perfect Ark-wright in his way, at least a firstrate ship-wright. His last achievement is regarded as his first in point of importance, and as to economy, convenience, and safety. It is not exactly "a wheel-rigged ship," for halt and blind management that the captain has thus recently invented, but a simplification of the usual troublesome process of "taking in a reef," which, indeed, as every landsman even knows who has read the thrilling strain of Falconer in his Shipwreck, becomes not only a troublesome but a dangerous, if not an impossible task in a strong gust of wind, when it is most of all essential to "take in a reef." This boast of the daring and destruction of the rash has been disarmed, it is said, of all its terrors by this captain of captains. Without reducing the surface of canvass necessary to propel the ship, he has so arranged it, that the topsails and maintop gallant sail have only a single reef in each, which, once in, renders the ship as snug as if under close reefs of the old rig; and this is accomplished by having long lower mast heads, upon which the first topsails are set. His rig, in fact, has two topsails upon each topmast, one above, and the other below the cap. The nautical reader will therefore probably be of opinion that the upper topsail can always be carried to the last moment, simply because it can be easily taken in, and that then, without reefing at all, the ship is at once equal to one of the old rig, under double reefs. His yards, too, on the fore and mainmast are, all but one, of the same dimensions, an advantage, it is conceived, of no ordinary importance in the event of disaster aloft. This new rig, it is said, has been fully tested.

THE LEANING TOWER AT PISA.—It has ever appeared to me to be an error in judgment to represent the well known tower at Pisa in a leaning position. It was originally built straight, then why not represent it so? When architects discover ruins of an interesting building, their care is to arrange them in order, and to represent the fabric in its pristine state; why, then, make an exception in the case of the beautiful structure alluded to, and represent it apparently tottering to the ground, and so seize upon an accident which greatly mars its effect? Had the building been originally constructed in a leaning position, it would have been an absurdity, on the part of the architect, not worthy of being recorded. The fact of the tower being constantly represented in elaborate drawings and expensive plates under its present unsightly aspect, has led to the belief with many that the original designer intended thereby to produce a sort of architectural tour de force: and I met persons at Pisa who were astonished, upon examining the building, to find that its leaning position was owing to a local accident, which all the towers built in that city had been more or less subjected to. The Dome of St. Genevieve, at Paris, subsided some years since, and was skilfully arrested in its fall; the oblique lines in the interior still tell the tale; but who would think of marking that defect in giving a representation of the design of that building?—A. W. H.

THE MASTER CARPENTERS' SOCIETY held its March meeting at the Freemasons' Tavern on Wednesday evening. In reply to several inquiries as to the intended New Buildings Bill, it was intimated by the chairman of the Buildings Bill Committee that it was now about to be printed, and he had no doubt that the improvements would give satisfaction. Previous to the meeting being adjourned, the whole of the members present consented to be stewards at the ensuing anniversary dinner of the Builders' Benevolent Institution.

HOLBORN HILL.—Sir: If the hill were made to start from the centre of Farringdon-street, and gradually end at Fetter-lane, there would be less hill to encounter than on the Snow-hill side. Men are now lowering the crown. I have looked at it carefully, and cannot conceive the utility of stepping off the curb, a declivity of at least 10 inches, in front of the gin-shop at the corner of Farringdon-street. * *

THE ELECTRIC LIGHT is about to shine again, after temporary darkness. Mr. Staite is announced to give two lectures on its commercial value, at the Western Literary Institution, where it was first exhibited to the public. .

ST. JAMES'S CHURCH, CLERKENWELL.—The trustees have given instructions to Mr. W. P. Griffith, architect, to take the necessary steps for the erection of a scaffolding to repair the steeple of this church, which is to be done by public contract, of which due notice will be given.

MORE MADNESS.—The following is a list of the tenders delivered for additions and alterations to the Hampstead workhouse. Mr. H. E. Kendall, jun., architect:—

Barr	£8,644
Pollock and McLennan	6,894
Glenn	6,494
Smith	5,970
Reynolds and Co.	5,691
Hill	5,656
Clowser	5,287
Pilbeam (accepted)	3,179

NOTICE.

"BUILDINGS AND MONUMENTS, MODERN AND MEDIÆVAL," being Illustrations of recently erected Edifices, and of some of the Architectural Works of the Middle Ages, with Descriptive Particulars. Edited by George Godwin, F.R.S., Fellow of the Royal Institute of Architects, &c., &c., &c., Editor of THE BUILDER.

Under the above title it is proposed to publish, in bi-monthly parts, price 2s. 6d. each, the principal Illustrations of Modern and Mediæval Buildings which have appeared from time to time in THE BUILDER, with their accompanying descriptive particulars. Each part will contain about eight plates, folio size, and eight pages of letter press, with plans and details. The engravings will be printed separately, with care, on a tinted paper.

The first part will be issued in time to be forwarded with the magazines for May 1, and will contain:—

Her Majesty's Marine Residence, Osborne; with Plan.
The Carlton Club House, Pall Mall.
Church of St. Isaac, at St. Petersburgh; with Details.
Kensington Union Workhouse.
The Liverpool Branch Bank of England; and Details.
The New Throne, Canterbury Cathedral.
The North Porch, Restored, of St. Mary Redcliffe, Bristol.
The Interior of Lincoln's-Inn Hall.

Persons desirous of becoming Subscribers, are requested to forward their names to the office of THE BUILDER.

TENDERS

For building an addition to the Euston Hotel, in Seymour-crescent: Mr. P. Hardwicke, architect:—

Cubitt	£2,950
Hege	2,511
Holland	2,599
Jay	2,567
Scantlebury	2,550
Mashman	2,549

MEETINGS OF SCIENTIFIC BODIES

Held during the ensuing week.

TUESDAY, APRIL 3.—Instit. of Civil Engineers, 8 P.M.
WEDNESDAY, 4.—Society of Arts, 8 P.M.

TO CORRESPONDENTS.

"*Galvanized Iron and Galvanized Tinned Iron.*"—We have received a very large number of letters on the subject of a recent paragraph concerning these materials, and will give them consideration.

"*To Polish Old Marble.*"—A correspondent asks,—the best means to clean and polish old marble chimney pieces.

Received.—"R.B." (we shall be very glad to see the drawings and will write), "J. B." (shall hear from us), "Ajax" (see present number), "W. and H.," "S. M.," "J. C.," "Dr. Ryan," "G. W." (THE BUILDER will be forwarded to him regularly by post on Friday, direct from the office, on receipt of money order), "O. H." (we cannot inform him), "A. F. S." (charge would be 5s. Send money order), "M. A. P." Subscriber (amount of royalty would depend on quality, locality, &c.," C. and J. G.," "E. D.," "Town Subscriber," "E. B.," "W. F. P.," "J. W. and Sons," "Old Subscriber" (Mr. Richardson's works, published by M'Lean), "A Sufferer," "J. B." (all in good time), "W. C." (block shall be sent), "J. A. J.," "J. E. T.," "S. S.," "H. H. M.," "J. F. (the contents are 10 feet 7 inches), "Parishioner," "R. T. B." (a reply without further information might mislead: we therefore profit not answering), "P. P.," "B. and B." "A His-Lofy of Architecture," by Edward A. Freeman, M.A.; Master's Bond-street), 149; "Tables and Formulæ for Computation of Life Contingencies," by Peter Gray, F.R.A.S.; Longman and Co., 1849; Beardmore's "Patent for Breakwaters, &c,"

NOTICE.— All communications respecting *advertisements* should be addressed to the "Publisher," and not to the "Editor;" all other communications should be addressed to the EDITOR, and *not* to the publisher.

No. CCCXXII.

SATURDAY, APRIL 7, 1849.

 ROM the letters received during the past week (such a varied budget, that to reply to them satisfactorily would demand an encyclopædic mind, and half a dozen pairs of hands), we select for notice those on two or three subjects of more immediate interest. Prominent amongst these are a pile with reference to our brief remark on galvanized iron, and galvanized tinned iron, in a recent number. As we have before now said, we might commend a man or a material every week for a year, and never extort a single acknowledgment from him or its owner,—they stand too well to care for or need the praise of so small a thunderer,—it is simply their due; they *have* merit, and no thanks to them who observe and admit it. On the other hand, if we but question ever so slightly the infallibility of the man, or express a doubt as to the preeminent goodness of the material, a shower of letters forthwith arrives, to prove that although our good opinion is worth nothing, our bad opinion is very differently estimated.

What we said of galvanized iron was comprised in nineteen lines and a half, and was a simple statement of the fact that specimens of the material had been sent to us, which, after two years' use, were full of holes. Now we speak under the mark when we say that we have received, in consequence of these nineteen lines and a half, twenty visits and forty letters! Intentions have been altered, orders suspended: and both the Galvanized Iron Company and the patentee of the Tinned Iron are receiving from different parts of the country constant reference to the paragraph in question. The majority of the letters are from interested parties, for and against:—from persons engaged in the manufacture or the sale of this material, and from those who consider their interests affected by it. Amongst the former, however, are several, whose testimony in its favour, to the extent of five or six years' knowledge, is entitled to every consideration. It is far from our desire to interfere with the use of the galvanized metal, if it be really a durable material; and we are quite ready to admit that the examples of its failure forwarded to us, if isolated cases, are not to be considered sufficient proof to the contrary. There may have been some peculiarity in the water in each of these cases; and we know very well that under some circumstances even lead is acted on and rapidly destroyed. Dr. Ryan, the professor of chemistry, who has addressed us on the subject, says (as we ourselves have long before this stated):—"I have known cases in which the tubes and lining of leaden cisterns have been acted upon and dissolved by water to such an extent, as to be highly injurious to health, and, in some cases, fatal. Such, also, is the case with copper, under a variety of exposures." There is, in fact, no metal but gold or platina which will resist every action, either of air or water, to which it may possibly be subjected, even in the ordinary uses of life.

The doctor continues (and by giving insertion to this, which is in truth a testimonial, we are shewing conclusively our willingness to give the material fair play)—"Speaking from my own observation of galvanized tinned iron, for now more than six years, I am of opinion that it is as little acted upon by either air or water, under the average of circumstances, as either lead or copper. There are circumstances under which the galvanized tinned iron is not applicable; for instance, when the medium in which it is placed contains acid, or acid vapours, an action takes place which must sooner or later destroy the metal.

Nor is it necessary that such acid or acid vapours be in a free or uncombined state, as by the well-known laws of chemical affinity, zinc will displace certain other bases from their combination with acids. If, for example, a piece of zinc be placed in water containing a salt of either iron, tin, copper, or lead, the zinc is dissolved by substitution, while the metal previously in combination with the acid, and held in solution by the water, is disengaged and precipitated, in most cases, in its metallic state. The applicability of the metal is, however, as easily ascertained as the applicability of any other material, under given circumstances; and it only requires the care and attention which an ordinarily prudent and intelligent person would exercise, and which must be exercised in the use of any other material whatever, to know, whether or not the metal is suitable for the purpose to which he intends to apply it."

We make no comparison between the two materials, the galvanized iron and the galvanized tinned iron, and consider the whole question still an open one with us, leaving the public to decide on the evidence before them.

The destruction of the Olympic Theatre by fire, on the 29th ultimo, has led several correspondents to refer to our repeated remarks on the necessity of commodious and safe means of access and egress in theatres and public places, and the fearfully unsatisfactory condition of many of our theatres in this respect. The wildfire rapidity with which the house was entirely consumed would have given little chance of escape to the audience. Had the fire happened when the house was full instead of previously to the opening of the doors, as was happily the case, the majority must have been destroyed,—literally roasted as they stood.

A survey of the stairs and accesses of our theatres should forthwith be made, and such alterations insisted on as might be found necessary for the safety of the public.

It is to be hoped that the fire may lead to the improvement of a part of the town much requiring it, and that the theatre, if rebuilt, will be placed on another site.

Mr. Smirke's paper of last week, on the relative condition of workmen in the seventeenth century and now, has not escaped commentators out of the class to which it was more immediately addressed. The letters, while setting forth the actual condition of many hundreds—must we not say, thousands —of intelligent artisans, are couched in a tone most honourable to the writers and the body which they represent. Our reference recently to the effect of too much union amongst men and too little union amongst masters, has led one working man, the "Old Mason" to whose lucubrations we have before given publicity, to address to us a letter calling upon the masters to *protect* those men in their employ who refuse to enter into union with others, and not to dismiss them at the dictation of their other men. He says:—

"To illustrate the truth of these remarks: —Some time since a strike took place against Mr. Trego, builder, of Lambeth, in respect of the four o'clock movement, and the members of a society were prohibited from working for him, or to allow those whom he had employed since such strike, to work with them, under a penalty of 5*l*. A mason who was at work at Mr. Trego's after the strike, having been discharged from his employ, applied at a respectable mason's in Pimlico, and obtained employment. He commenced work, by the foreman's directions: after working about an hour or so some of the masons working in the same shop, informed the foreman that he had been previously working for an obnoxious employer: they further stated their determination to strike unless this man was immediately discharged. The consequence was this man was compelled to leave his work, take his tools, and quit the premises at a moment's notice,—and that through the conspiracy of the members of this society. The foreman informed him that it was through no ill-feeling on his part that he was discharged, but that he could not think of keeping him at work and be the cause of all the others leaving their employment. This man, then, must either join a society which is obnoxious to him, and illegally combined against him and others, or he must lose the benefit of his labour, which will be to take away his means of existence.. Thus he is deprived of the liberty of an Englishman; he must only work how, when, and where others choose to dictate, and break the laws of his country to fulfil those of their making."

The same writer, a working man be it remembered, says, in another communication on the subject of equality,—" If the liberty that I take encroaches on the liberty of another, it ceases to be true liberty, and wears the aspect of oppression. There is but one method of securing universal liberty, and that is for each individual to be as anxious to promote the welfare of another as his own. We hold this true in theory, but it is a lesson the world has not yet learned to practise. Man is evidently selfish, and if allowed to have the extent of his desires, he often encroaches on the liberties and rights of others. From this we discover the necessity of law and order, without which no man's life or property would be secure. It is for the general good that laws are made and enforced; but the question arises, whether or not one individual should have dominion over many? Are not all men of the same flesh and blood, and ought we not to contend for equality?

"Those who contemplate nature may discover that the universe teems with an infinite variety. If the eye of the mind, assisted by revelation, penetrates the upper regions, powers, excelling in wisdom and authority, are represented to his view. If we descend below ourselves in the scale of creation, as far as naturalists have discovered, the meanest insects seem to have order maintained among them by a few having authority over the many. Respecting governments among men, we are expressly informed, from the highest authority, that the powers that be are ordained of God, and whosoever resisteth the power resisteth the ordinance of God. That man enjoys the truest liberty who willingly and cheerfully submits to the proper performance of his duty, rendering to all their dues,— fear to whom fear, honour to whom honour. Bind such a man with fetters of iron, his mind is still in the enjoyment of liberty."

While we find such opinions as these current amongst our operatives, we need not fear the efforts of evil-disposed agitators.

ON SIR BALTHAZAR GERBIER'S "COUNSEL AND ADVICE TO ALL BUILDERS."*

THE small volume of which I am now about to give you some account, possesses very slender claims to literary merit—nor has it much intrinsic professional value; yet it has, I think, still, great claims on our attention, as being among the very earliest of our native literary productions exclusively on the subject of our art.

The earliest edition of Sir Balthazar's Counsel and Advice is 1663. The early date, therefore, of this book gives it a value,—and a stronger interest attaches to it in our eyes, as giving some insight into the practice of architecture at the period of our great master, Sir Christopher Wren. Sir Balthazar was born at Antwerp, in 1592, and was brought up as a miniature painter. He was knighted by Charles I., and was employed by him, in conjunction with Rubens, to negotiate a treaty with Spain; he also resided at Brussels in a diplomatic character. He was subsequently employed as an architect by Lord Craven.

I must not, however, conceal that his biographers give but a sorry account of him. He failed to secure the favour of the court, and was driven to adopt a variety of means of living. It is true he fell upon evil times. The death of Charles I. deprived him of hope at court. He migrated to Surinam, where he was persecuted by the Dutch; and although at the restoration of Charles II. he built triumphal arches in honour of the young monarch, he appears never to have attracted much of the royal favour. He died in 1667. Having said thus much of our author, and having, I trust, prepared you to expect very little of value or novelty in his work, I proceed to fulfil my engagement to give you some account of its contents.

Prefixed to the treatise are no less than forty-one dedications, which, in fact, occupy about half the duodecimo volume. Although seldom, I believe, carried to so ridiculous an extent as in this case, the practice of preluding every literary attempt by these rhetorical invocations, through which it was hoped to win the favour of the great, was one of the literary foibles of that age; but the following observation in Mr. Macaulay's recently published history gives us some clue to the origin of these somewhat fulsome appeals—"The fee paid," he says, "for the dedication of a book was often much larger than the sum which any publisher would give for the copyright. Books were therefore frequently printed merely that they might be dedicated."

The treatise commences by adverting to the author's previous work, which he describes as "a little manual concerning the 3 chief principles of magnificent building—viz., solidity, conveniency, and ornament;" wherein he "notes the incongruities committed by many undertakers of buildings." He points to the Grecians and Romans as the best builders, and urges that men should not be subject to fancies nor "inslaved by weather-cock-like spirits, to make their buildings according unto things *à la mode*. He further condemns the incongruity committed by surveyors, who were minded to show that they were skilled in describing columns, cornishes, and frontispieces, although, for the most part, placed as the wilde Americans are wont to put their pendants at their nostrils."

The author then proceeds to treat more particularly of his advice to all builders. "Whoever," he says, "is disposed to build, ought, in the first place, to make choice of a skilful surveyor, from whose directions the several master workmen may receive instructions by way of draughts, models, and frames." I should here say that the author throughout uses the terms surveyor and architect as perfect synonyms; there is no indication whatever of that distinction which is now, in England at least, universally received. He then adverts to some of the requirements of architects, and especially dwells on the knowledge of perspective as essential; he teaches that the architect should consider the ground whereon the building is to be erected, and then govern himself as the ground will give him leave; or, as Pope has since more elegantly expressed it, "consult the genius of the place." He must place the front of a country house towards the east, "by which means he may shelter his double lodging rooms from the north-west." I cannot say that this piece of instruction is very intelligible. We can hardly regard the north-west as the aspect most to be shunned. The author here adds, what he quaintly calls a *nota bene* to builders—viz., he must cause all the back of his stonework (which stands within the brickwork), to be cut with a rebate 3 inches broader than the breadth of his jambs and cornish, which will hinder the rain from piercing into the inside of the wall, and through the meeting of the brick and stone. He deems it necessary to make a sort of apology for this advice, as implying that "surveyors and master workmen in this refined age which abounds in books, with the portractures of the out and inside of the best buildings, are to seek the first points of their apprentiship; of whom I ask the reason why modern buildings are so exceedingly defective; and whether it is not because many of them have been but apprentices lately, and too soon become journeymen; and that surveyors (who either affect more the building to themselves a strong *purse*, or are blind to the faults which their workmen commit), like careless postillions, hasten with the packet maile to the post-office, be it never so ill-girted, whereby it oft falls in the midway."

The author then advises how to try the capacity of a surveyor. "The readiest way to try him," he says, "is to put him to draw a ground plot in the builder's presence; to make him describe the fittest place for a seat; the ordering of the rooms for summer or winter; to contrive well the staircases, doors, windows, and chimneys,—doors and windows so placed that they may not be inconvenient to the chimneys,—the bedstead place far from the doors and windows, and of a fit distance from chimneys."

He then adverts to the "seelings of rooms," adapting their height to the size, character, and use of the room. A bedchamer of state may be 30 feet wide, 40 feet in length, and 16 or 18 feet high; whereas a closet, 10 feet square, adjacent thereto, if made of the same height, would be "preposterous, and like a barber's comb-case." The dimensions here set down for a state bedchamber seem somewhat extravagant; but it must be remembered that our author's advice is apparently addressed to royal or noble builders; and in the 17th century business was transacted, and morning visitors were received, usually in the bedchamber, a practice which, at the present day, has not fallen altogether into desuetude on the continent.

The author then proceeds to the subject of exterior architecture. He points out the necessity of cornices over doors and windows, to prevent rain from falling on them, which he illustrates in his usual quaint way, by comparing a "cornish" to "the broad brim of the good hat of a traveller in a rainy day."

"The good surveyor," he adds, "will order ornaments to the front of a palace according unto its situation: shun too much carved ornaments on the upright, whereat the southerly windes raise much dust;" also "shun those spectacle-like cant windows which are of glass on all sides, for it may be supposed that the inhabitants of such houses and rooms with cant windows (exposed to the north-west) may well imitate a merry Italian fisher, who in a winter, windy, rainy day, had been stript to his skin, and having nothing left to cover him save his bare net, wherein he was wrapt, put his finger through one of the holes, asking of passengers what weather it was out of doors." It is here to be observed, that at the period when our author wrote, classical architecture, on its revival, was still struggling with the Gothic forms that had prevailed for so many centuries previously. These cant or bow windows were peculiarly characteristic of the Tudor and Elizabethan ages, and so firmly rooted were they in the domestic habits and usages of the time, that the revivers of classical architecture were driven to make many attempts to retain the old favourite form with a new dress; and down to the present day we seem to have remained true to the old spectacle-like cant window of our forefathers, which, whilst it is almost universal in England, can scarcely be met with in modern architecture on the continent.*

Sir Balthazar then proceeds to give us advice of not a very important nature on the subject of balconies, balustrades, and cornishes. He says that the Grecian and Roman surveyors ever made the cornishes and ornaments about the windows of the upper stories to be bigger than those on the lower; and illustrates his remark by a somewhat pedantic reference to Michaelangelo, Raphael d'Urbin, and Albert Durer. He then teaches us as to the proportions of doors and windows. The chambers of a palace, he says, should have the doors wide enough for two to pass at once, and the height to be double the width; all other chamber doors should be convenient for a man of complete stature to pass with his hat on. Windows must be higher than they are wide, because light comes from above, and the middle transome should be above 6 feet from the floor, otherwise the transome would be opposite a man's eye; "hindersome," as he says, "to the free discovery of the country." The leaning-height of a window should be 3½ foot, and not so low that wanton persons may sit on them and break the glass, or that they may show themselves in quirpo to passengers. "A good surveyor," he says, "shuns the ordering of doors with stumbling-block thresholds, though our forefathers affected them, perchance to perpetuate the ancient custom of bridegrooms, who, when formerly at their return from church, did use to lift up their bride, and knock her head against that part of the door, for a remembrance that she was not to passe the threshold of their house without their leave."

Doors, he says, should be on a row, and close to the windows, that when the doors are opened they may serve for screens, and not to convey wind to the chimney.

The hearth of a chimney ought to be level with the floor; and chimney mantles ought to be of stone or marble. It is necessary to cover the top of chimneys to keep out rain and snow; the smoke holes can be very conveniently made on the sides of their heads. Had the knight lived in these times he would doubtless have been very severe, in his quaint way, upon the monstrous fashion of modern chimney-pots.

"Roomes on moist grounds do well to be paved with marble," and "a good surveyor shuns the making of timber partitions on the undermost story." "The good surveyor doth contrive the repartitions of his ground plot so as most of the necessary servants may be lodged in the first ground-story, whereby there will be less disturbance, less danger of fire, and all the family at hand on all occasions." "Finally, he ought from time to time to visit the work to see whether the building be performed according unto his directions and moulds." The author then proceeds to a chapter on clerks of works. "A clarke of the werks," he says, "must be verst in the prices of materials and the rates of all things belonging to a building; know where the best are to be had; provide them to the workmen's hands," and so on, adding that "though nails to some seem not very considerable, yet ought the clarke of the werke to be discrete in the distributing of them to some carpenters whose pockets partake much of the austruche's stomachs." "His eyes must wander about every workman's hands, as on those of the sawyers at their pit so that they waste no more than needs in slabs; on the laborers' hands in the digging of the foundation for the bricklayers, that all the loose earth may be removed and springs observed."

Some of the ordinary duties of a clerk of works are then enumerated; as, that he should prevent bricks being tumbled out of the cart; that he should suffer no sammell bricks to be made use of, and that he should not suffer the bricklayers to lay any foundation except the ground be first rammed, though it seem never so firm. "No great and small stuff," he says, "should be huddled together in the foundation, but all laid down as even as

---

* Read at a meeting of the Institute of Architects, as mentioned last week. The whole paper will probably be published hereafter in a more complete form.

* Lord Bacon, who wrote somewhat before the date of this book, had none of our author's prejudice against these embowed windows. "I hold them," says he in his well known essay on building, "of good use, for they be pretty retiring places for conference; and besides they keep both the wind and sun off, for that which would strike almost through the room doth scarce pass the window."

possibly can be, to ram it the better and the more equal, and must be of solid hard stuff with no concavities daubed over with store of mortar," and he adds here in a marginal note that these precautions were observed in building the foundations of Solomon's temple, but he does not give us his authority for this information.

The clerk of works is further to see that the line and plumb rule be often used; that the bricklayers make small scaffling holes, and never suffer them to begin scafflings in the morning, but before leaving of their work; "for, if in the morning, he says, "most of them will make it a day for the gathering of nuts."

Then follow some injunctions respecting mortar, that I scarcely need particularise—and the author proceeds to the subject of masonry. The workmen must observe exactly the surveyor's molds, and work close and neat joints, using but little mortar between them, not only because much mortar will be washed away, but that cornishes will also appear like a rank of open teeth; and they must not forget to shore up the middle part of the head of the windows, as well as the sides, to prevent an unequal settling of the work, and, consequently, cracks. There here ensue, for the next thirteen pages, detailed directions for the proportioning of the several orders. The masons "must divide the Tuscan column, or rustick base and capital (which is as much as to say, feet and head) seven times its thickness; the architrave, freeze, and cornish one-fourth-part of the column, with base and capital. If they make the said order without a pedestal, they must divide its whole height into seventeen parts and a half, which (in their vocation phrase) are called *models*, and are divided into twelve equal parts: if they are directed by their surveyor to make them *with* a pedestal, then are they to divide the whole height into twenty-two and one-sixth part, for that the perfect shape of the said order requires a pedestal which must have a third part of the column. It seldom happens that a pedestal is put to the Tuscan order, because (as it represents an atlas, and that no man will take a dwarf to reach to the first story of a building) the said order requires, not to be set as a candlestick on a cubbert; it's as a substantive, that can stand without an adjective." And then our author adds, for he loves a joke, whether in season or out of season, "some Venetian ladies must have their shoppings to stand on, and were they as strong as the Tuscan, they would not need some of their Masaras to lean upon," which no doubt conveyed a hard hit at the luxurious habits of the Venetians, then in the plenitude of their wealth and greatness, but which has lost its point now—the very terms used being obsolete.

The author then proceeds to lay down the proportions of the Doric, Ionic, Corinthian, and Composite orders: the necessity for adhering exactly to these proportions he considers paramount—"For it is a rule as certain," he says, "as that without the same, there cannot be a perfect building made, no more than a man could without good orthographie write true English."

"It is the rule of the ancient masters, whose reliques, to be seen throughout most places of Italy, make many strangers that come their gape so wide as that they need no gags."

The author now enters upon the subject of carpentry. He teaches "That the carpenters should be good husbands in the management of the builder his timber; on the cutting of the scantlings; their sparing to make double mortices which doe but weaken the summers. To lay no gerders which are needless and hindersome to the bording of a room; no summers to be laid except the ends of them are either pitcht, or laid in loam to preserve them from rotting," "and therefore in Italy, France, and Germany, and among the most prudent and solid builders, the free masons, put stone cartouches in the top of the inside walls which are bearers to the summers, as such cartouches are seen in divers churches, and some of them are carved in ornamental figures." He alludes, no doubt, here to the stone corbels upon which we sometimes see the ends of principal timbers resting: an excellent old practice which we in our own days follow, although in a much less picturesque way, by inserting the ends of our timbers into cast-iron shoes projecting from the face of the wall. The utilitarian tendencies of modern practice have been very subversive of the old picturesque ways of our ancestors, whether on costume, furniture, or architecture. An upholsterer now ascertains with precision the size of the piece of oak that will just carry his table; he seeks till he finds the safe minimum scantling, and this successful discovery is the triumph of his art. Whilst our forefathers would take a log of oak, all regardless of this politico-economical search after the greatest possible strength with the least possible stuff, and would carve it into one of those ponderous and fantastic legs which charm us by their quaintness, although they defy our efforts to lift them.

In further illustration compare the broad, deep, capacious fire-places, whereby our forefathers would warm themselves, with the scientifically constructed, snug, rumfordized stove, with bevelled cheeks, no hobs, contracted openings, all contrivances admirably adapted to meet our modern requirements of convenience and economy; but how destructive to the poetry of our grandsires' ruder arrangements!—men of a rough, bold stamp, who, provided they secured to themselves a warm chimney corner, appeared to regard with great indifference the minor evils of smoke and blacks.

Then follow many other details of the manner the carpenter is to lay his timber, and the author adds that the clerk of the works must be very careful not to suffer the carpenters to lay any timbers under the chimneys, "whereby many houses have been set on fire, and burnt to the ground." We have then a variety of scantlings for the timbers of floors and roofs, which scantlings he gives as fit for substantial structures, but which are "not usual in lime and hair bird-cage-like buildings"—a remark that leads us to the conclusion that the flimsy structure of modern speculators was not wholly unknown to our ancestors. The care of the clerk of the works must also be on "materials of weight, as sauder, wherewith an unconscionable plummer can ingrosse his bill." In this respect we see that 200 years' experience has not advanced us—we have still "unconscionable plummers." "The clerk is to see sauder weighed and well managed, and in the attesting of bills have a care not to pass his eyes *slightly* over them, lest when a plummer sets pounds of candles used about his sauder, that trick prove as insupportable as that of one who, having played away a round sum of his master's stock in a journey to the East Indies, set down in his bill to have paid a hundred pound for mustard." "He must likewise have a clear insight on the glass pains of the glazier; suffer no green pains of glass to be mixt with the white. He must with his eyes follow the measurer of the work, his rod or pole; so the line wherewith the joiner's work is measured, that it be not let slide through the measurer's fingers, since the joiner's work hath many goings in and out, and a leger-de-mayne may be prejudicial to the paymaster's purse. It were likewise better to agree with painters to have their work rated on running measure and on the straight, as the carpenter's work, who (being of an honest Joseph's profession), are as deserving to be well payd as the painters who do but spend the sweat of wall nuts (to wit, oyle), the carpenters that of their browes."

"As for coverings of buildings, lead is best for churches, for who would rob them but goths and vandals? Blue slates are most comely for a nobleman's palace," "a roof covered with them is of an equal color, when as red tiled roofs the least breaking of them makes great chargeable work for the tiler, who often removes ten tiles to lay two new ones in their place, and renders the nobleman's roof like a beggar's coat."

Our author then proceeds to some remarks on the making of bricks, and recommends the clerk of works to look well to the working of the clay, which, if not well wrought, will never make good bricks. He says, that it is usual to pay 5s. per thousand for making and burning bricks, the clay-digging therein comprehended. He then goes into some details as to the relative expense of making bricks, and purchasing them made; whereby it appears that only 6s. 8d. are saved in 20,000 bricks, by making them. He says, that of clam-burnt bricks, 500 out of 20,000 are unfit for work.

Various other details are entered into respecting the making and use of bricks. Men dig clay, he says, for 6d. the thousand; lime is burnt at 4s. per load, and costs 40s. a load. Touching the use of chalk in building walls, he says, that "those that mend the making use of chalk in their walls must be contented (if the ground hath springs) with the green mold which breaks thro' the whitened walls within doors. Walls about a parke or court may be *fited* with chalk, which may be digged for 18s. per load, and brought for 2s. 6d. the load." "Good country bricklayers do work at 27s. the rod, the bricks not being rubbed. Good London bricklayers will work the rod for 40s. with rubbed bricks; the inside for 33s., arches comprized."

Then follow some remarks about lime burning, describing the mode of burning it "in China and other parts of the Indies," wholly with wood and not in kilns.

Our author now proceeds to a new division of his work, which he heads, "As for choice of master workmen." "King Henry the Eighth," he says, "shewed a good president when the serjeant plummer, calling his workmen to caste, in his presence, a leaden medal which was given him:" the king told him, "he would have no walking master-workmen." Those, therefore, which are fit to be employed are working masters, and not those who walk from one building to another; "nor will any master workman deny to have had as much more done and well, by bestirring their hands and tools in their workmen's presence than otherwise." I cannot refrain here from calling your attention to the singular social change that has taken place since King Henry inflicted his reprimand on the *walking* instead of the *working* master. Fertile as he is said to have been in oaths, certainly no *usual* oath would have sufficed to express the royal indignation had he lived in these times, to have seen the master workmen not walk, but *drive* up to his works in as fair an equipage as that of any of his most favoured courtiers. Our author proceeds to counsel that master workmen be bound to a precise time, and to observe exactly the model held forth to them by the chosen surveyor, and to make good at their own cost what they do amiss. He further counsels "to shun the reprehending a master workman of any oversight before his men; but rather privately; since it would be to him as prejudicial as a check to a commander at the head of his troops."

We have next a division of the work entitled "As for the Builder and Proprietor." He advises the builder (by which term he always means the employer) to buy his own materials, and to have in reserve such a stock of his own as he can well spare, and also, he adds, "against the mistakes of workmen, a stock of patience;" nor to begin building walls before March, nor after the middle of September.

The next twenty-eight pages contain a variety of miscellaneous and not very well assorted notes respecting the prices of materials and workmanship.

Touching the paving of courts, to prevent the overgrowing of grass and the charge of too often weeding, he says, "it would not be amiss to lay chalk or lime under the paving, and to do the same in gardens under gravel walks"—a piece of advice which is well worthy of notice.

With respect to street paving with pebble stones, he alludes to a Mons. Le Cœur having recently introduced great improvements in paving works done under the commissioners. This French undertaker appears to have formed a company for carrying out a new invention in paving, "whereby they are not only able to make a most substantial good pavement, but are likewise capable by that same new invention to maintain it durable for twenty-one years." Our author (who, as must have been observed, is remarkable for the want of order and method in his remarks), brings his book to a close with some, what he calls *necessary* notes. "What contributes more to the fatal end of many good mother's son is ill-building: paper-like walls: cobweb-like windows: doors made fast as with packthread, purposely made to tempt men who, through extreme want, are become weary of a languishing life, and to whose fatal end, ill builders are in a manner accessory." He says that the scarcity of thieves vaunted of by the Hollanders, German, and other northern nations, is to be attributed to the defence they are wont to make against thieves: he then describes very particularly the Hollander's mode of making outside window-shutters so secure by fitting them very closely to the reveals, and by a careful arrangement of the bolts and hinges,—precautions which, however necessary, certainly do not lead us to entertain any exalted idea of Dutch honesty in the seventeenth century. Some further suggestions are then made for rendering doors and windows secure both from rogues within and without: a suggestion, even, is made for the better securing a house against "thieves who do untile houses." We have then some remarks on porches, which he says serve to distribute alms to the poor, but also prove often cumbersome, being the receptacle of foul creatures, who, as soon as they are gotten into a court, make it their rendezvous. The entrance to a hall, he says, is not so proper in the middle as at the end, or at all events, set as much as possible near the end. He urges, that the principal floor of a building should not be level with the ground; he then introduces "his story of one in authority, who, passing by a town wherein the people generally did not outlive their thirtieth year, caused all the backs of their houses to be made the front; and the windows which were forward to be made up, to free them from that infectious aire that did shorten their lives, which had its effect accordingly, and it is therefore I do so much insist on the point of placing a building where good ayre is, and that neither chimnies nor doors may be so placed as to serve for the attraction of infectious aire, which kills more than the sword, or the sea overturnes ships." A truth, which, although uttered in 1663, we seem now, in 1849, only just beginning to perceive the importance of. The book closes with some desultory remarks of no great importance as to the choice of clerks of works and surveyors, from which I need only quote the following portion:—

"Let all owners [of houses, he means] be prepared to repent, whether they build or not, for it is like the fate of many who marry, or marry not. Let both the one and the other lay, as in a scale, their several charges, vexations, cares, labours, and pleasures, they will find this to be true, viz., if they build they must be at great present disbursements, vext with as many oversights, and to be overeach'd in bargains concerning their materials. If they build not, they are subject to the inconvenience of houses built according to the fancies of [other] owners; and when they shall cast up the summs of money spent in the rent, besides many chargeable alterations, they shall finde that they might have built a better and more fit habitation for them and their posterity."

SYDNEY SMIRKE.

THE LATE MR. ROBERT SIBLEY.

WE record with regret the sudden decease (on the 31st ult.) of Mr. Robert Sibley, when apparently in perfect health, and at the age of 59. But a few days ago he wrote us on the subject of burials in towns, and the desecration of the dead, and now he himself lies in the lone grave. Mr. Sibley was the county surveyor for many years, but resigned the appointment for that of the district surveyorship of Clerkenwell. He was, besides, surveyor to the Company of Ironmongers. He was a member of the Council of Civil Engineers. Amongst the buildings which he erected were the Hanwell County Lunatic Asylum, the Light Horse Volunteer Barrack in Gray's-Inn-lane, now a refuge for the destitute, and several small bridges, among which was Brentford. He also constructed the large iron wharf at London-bridge. The interim appointment to the district surveyorship has been conferred on his son, Mr. R. L. Sibley, who is a candidate for the office permanently. The election will take place on the 19th.

ST. STEPHEN'S, WALBROOK.—The financial disputes in Walbrook are at last settled, we understand that the parish have now funds in hand to repair and adorn the church. We trust that no time will be lost in commencing this much-needed work, and that it will be done under proper direction, and thoroughly.

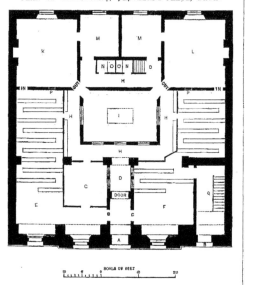

PLAN OF DISPENSARY, CLEVELAND-PLACE, BATH.

SCALE OF FEET

PLAN OF A DISPENSARY.

ANNEXED is the plan of the dispensary in Cleveland-place East, Bath, the arrangement of which seems very convenient, and may serve as a suggestive type. The annexed references will explain the appropriation of the apartments and show the modes of access.

A Public entrance.
B Private ditto.
C C Patients' ditto.
D Visitors' ditto.
E Room for physician's patients.
F Room for surgeon's patients.
H H H H Passages.
I Dispensing-room, with lantern light.
K Physician's room.
L Surgeon's ditto.
M M Private ditto.
N N Water closets.
O Stairs to hot-water furnace.
P P Ventilators.
Q House stairs.

It will be seen that the physician's patients go in on the left-hand side of the hall, and taking a seat wait their turn to be admitted to his room (K) by the door marked "IN:" having received his prescription, they retire by the door marked "Out," obtain the medicine at the window of the dispensary-room (I), and leave the dispensary by D.

The surgeons' patients take the same course on the opposite side.

The building is warmed by hot-water pipes. Above there is a large committee-room, with sitting-room and three chambers.

In few ways can the affluent better aid their less fortunate brethren than by founding and affording support to DISPENSARIES.

PUBLIC NECESSARIES.—Nothing has yet been done in this respect, and probably will not be till the Health Commissioners take up the matter. It is one of very serious import, and is necessarily denied the advantage of public discussion.

THE ROMAN PERIOD OF GREEK DECORATIVE ART.

IMPORTANCE OF SYSTEM IN STYLE, AND OF TASTE AND SUBORDINATION IN ORNAMENT.

IN pursuance of his course of lectures on decorative art, at the Government School of Design, Somerset House, Mr. Wornum proceeded, on Friday, the 25th, to follow up his remarks on the Periclean age of Greek art (vide p. 112), with some account of its progress, or decline rather, under Roman auspices.

In the last lecture, said he, we reached the culminating point of Greek decorative art, illustrated in the Parthenon, the Erechtheium, and the Choragic monument of Lysicrates. We have now to trace its decline, or point out that deterioration of style which immediately followed the period of Alexander, and which has caused this later age to be termed the period of decline.

The designation appears to be just, though, as regards the mere production of ornamental works, it exhibits not only a more profuse expenditure, but even more energetic enterprise, in, perhaps, every species of ornamental art, than any preceding age. The decline was in the art—in the manner in which the decorations were applied—not in the ornaments themselves. These were the same, and, in most cases, equally well executed; but that quality which we term taste—that is, judicious selection and arrangement—seems to have experienced a total revolution. Quantity was apparently mistaken for quality; and the whole decorative art of this period, viewed generally, well illustrates that deficiency of power in the artistic mind which Apelles so aptly exposed. If the Roman works are not beautiful, they are at least rich. When I say Roman works, I by no means allude merely to works executed at Rome, but to all efforts of this period in any part of the ancient world to which Roman influence extended. And from the time of the conquest of Greece, about a century and a half after Alexander, few great works were undertaken which did not owe their origin immediately to Rome, though perhaps in nearly all cases executed by Greek artists. The Romans even collected and exhibited works of Greek art at Rome *within* a century after the death of Alexander, as the works brought by Marcellus from Syracuse, 214 B.C.

Under these circumstances we may, perhaps, safely term this period of decline—that is, from Marcellus to Constantine the Great—about five centuries—the Roman period of Greek art. We cannot call the art of these centuries Roman art, but it was strictly Greek art under Roman influence, and its chief monuments, even in the Oriental provinces, were raised by the orders of Roman Governors or Emperors, —as at Petra, Palmyra, Baalbec (Heliopolis), Athens, Pola, and Spalatro.

The decline, then, which characterises this remarkable period is not one of poverty, but rather of luxury; it was an embarrassment of riches—an injudicious application of ornament, from the want of that proper discrimination which we term taste, or rather, perhaps, that want combined with the ostentatious rivalry of a luxurious age. And yet, with all its enterprise and boundless expenditure, this age has added but one single new form to those which constituted the elementary types of the preceding age. This new form is *the shell*, which we find cut on the modillions of the arch of Titus, at Rome. This species of net-work is not new. Net-work of gold was introduced largely in the funeral car of Alexander the Great: it appears to be a mere imitation of basket-work, or what it literally is, net-work. We have in this period, also, vertical reeding, rare in Greek art, unless in furniture.

Style and system may be looked upon as synonymous terms in ornamental art. Besides the ornaments themselves, we must have some system of applying them. And if the prominent and characteristic members of certain established styles are promiscuously thrown together, the principal features of one style applied as secondary to subordinate features of another, the value of all is diminished or lost, and the general effect has but its vagueness to characterise it. The same ornamental types may be used in the development of new styles, distinction of style depending not so much on the types themselves as on the mode of using them. But in the development of any particular historic style of ornament, we are strictly limited to the elements belonging to that style; and in combining styles, the various members belonging to the same style should preserve their relative degree of importance.

The general decorations of the Roman period, however, and especially those of Pompeii, exhibit an utter disregard of these observances; and thus all distinctions of style and consequent peculiarities of character are lost.

Systematic designing exhibits the art of the ornamentist in a highly intellectual light. Whatever style prevailed in a particular period, it is one expression of the spirit of that age; and by thus attending to these periodic or local developments of ornament, the designer affords not only the delight and gratification arising from the contemplation of a beautiful work of art, but at the same time presents an agreeable and instructive record of the past, full of the most valuable suggestions.

These remarks apply as much to furniture as to decoration, and also, though in a less degree, to designs for costume and ornamental manufactures. For unless the designer for cabinet work, papers, furniture damasks, and stuffs generally, conforms as much as the decorator with the distinctions of style, these manufactures cannot contribute anything towards that complete developement of ornamental art which it is the object of these schools to foster. There is perhaps only one department of manufactures in which this discrimination of the various styles of ornament can be considered a matter of indifference,—that is in the printed or woven fabrics for ladies' dresses. Here it should rather be avoided, as we do not wish to see our mothers, wives, and daughters look like antiques, or even as middle age ladies. For this class of fabrics, the most appropriate design is such as shall be completely unobtrusive, and while ornamental, at same time strictly subordinate. To make so conspicuous a design as to attract the attention from the lady herself to the pattern of her dress is to commit a capital error: it then no longer adorns but rivals the person. This elaboration of an accessary at the cost of the principal object, is an error too often committed in works of art, of which even the Greeks have afforded a sufficient number of examples: as Androcydes, the contemporary of Zeuxis, who painted a picture of the six-headed sea-monster Scylla, in which he gave so much care to the *fish* he introduced in the composition, that the monster herself, really the picture, was comparatively unimportant, and Androcydes was ever after ridiculed for having forgotten his art for his appetite, for he was known to have been very fond of fish. Protogenes too, the rival of Apelles, in his celebrated picture of a "Reposing Faun," had introduced a quail so admirably painted, that the first exclamation of the spectator was, "what a beautiful quail!" This so annoyed the great painter, that although the picture was already dedicated, he solicited and obtained leave to efface the offending bird.

Now, it is quite as easy for the ornamental designer to fall into this error as for the painter. His ornaments may become so prominent as completely to obscure the intention or destination of the object he has ostensibly endeavoured to adorn. Every addition by way of ornament should tend only more completely and elegantly to express the designer's purpose: otherwise what is principal is sacrificed to what is but secondary. It is the more or less strict observance of this principle which constitutes good or bad taste,—not the mere character of the design itself; for what might make very handsome carpets, oil cloths, or papers, would in most cases appear ridiculous if used for dresses.

Thus a deteriorated age may use all the elements of the most refined,—possess even the same imitative or mechanical skill in execution,—and yet by a want of discrimination in the application of design, exhibit even a barbarous character in comparison with the design of that period, in which a due attention has been paid to the propriety of application, whether in quantity or quality. And thus a barbarous style of design may, perhaps, more easily arise out of too much ornament than too little.

This, then, is the character of that period of decline which supervened upon the great age of art which attained its highest development in the time of Alexander the Great, and gave evidence of a decay even in the time of Alexander himself, the description of whose funeral, preserved by Diodorus, shows how completely the taste of the Greeks had become orientalized. Sumptuous splendour had taken the place of taste. The decline, however, was very gradual, especially in sculpture. Some of the most prized productions of ancient art are maintained by many critics to belong to a much later age than that of Alexander—as the Laocoon, the Torso of Apollonius, and the Apollo Belvedere—all of them assigned to the time of the Roman emperors. The school of Rhodes was the latest of the Greek schools that maintained a great reputation. Painting seems to have been much less enduring. Mere technical excellencies of art became prominent, and higher qualities were overlooked—*form* became paramount over *essence*. Such was the decline of Grecian art which rapidly supervened on the close of the Alexandrian age. That it never revived from this decline is not remarkable. Greece not only became a Roman province, and lost her artists, but almost every important work that could be moved was transported either to Egypt or to Italy. The Romans were not contented with removing pictures and statues, but the very walls were stripped of their plastering, and the pieces transported in wooden cases to Rome. The spoliations of the Grecian kingdoms of Asia and of Sicily continued uninterruptedly for about two centuries, yet such was the inconceivable wealth of Greece in works of art that Rhodes alone still contained upwards of 3,000 statues, and there could not have been less at Athens, at Olympia, or at Delphi. But all these were nothing compared with the myriads of works, pictures, and statues which were collected together in the public buildings of Rome. Cassiodorus says that Rome was one vast wonder, a statement we can well understand, if we are to judge from the temporary theatre constructed by Scaurus in honour of his ædileship, which he decorated with 3,000 bronze statues.

Considering this unparalleled wealth, then, in works of fine art, it is quite consistent that the Romans should endeavour to decorate their buildings in a style of commensurate splendour and profusion, and thus we find that the most florid examples of purely Greek ornament are plain when compared with the Roman treatment of the same forms, although it is very probable that Greek artists were employed to execute their elaborate designs.

By help of numerous illustrations the lecturer then proceeded to contrast the Greek and Roman orders, and to trace their variations, enrichments, transformations, complications, and confusions during their 'decline and fall.' Examples of ancient ornamental art in the forms of armour, helmets, shields, &c., and of sculpture, candelabra, and other designs, were also referred to and described, with various "preposterous combinations" and "fanciful decorations," deprecated by Roman writers themselves as illustrations of "a beautiful system of ornament run mad—a bed of flowers overrun with weeds." The barbarous forms and colours of specimens of stucco-work and other decorative details from Pompeii were exhibited in justification of such complaints. That even Pompeii, however, a small provincial town, exhibited occasional traces of a magnificent system of decoration, was freely admitted.

Having passed in review every element of classical ornamental art, continued the lecturer, or at least every element of importance, we will now briefly consider what is the exact object of this historical investigation. * * * This is the view with which we study the history of art,—to discriminate and individualize the styles of the various epochs, and, by thus developing distinct characters, to multiply to an equal extent our means of viewing nature, and our powers, consequently, of representation. The real object of historical knowledge, therefore, is not the mere copying what has been done before, but the acquisition of a power which not only supersedes all copying, but which alone will ensure the production of that variety of ornamental design which, the simplest theory must make manifest, is the ostensible effort of every designer.

A knowledge of the various styles not only gives a very great command over the elements of ornamental art, but will enable you to view what comes under your own observation in several distinct lights. For instance, take a walk in one of our fields some summer's day, and make a series of different designs out of what you find there,—say a blade of grass, or a dock-leaf, butter-cups and daisies, an ear of wheat and a poppy or any other simple plant. First throw them together in your own way, and as you would do if you had no knowledge of ornamental design. Then, for example, consider how an Egyptian would have treated these things, and arrange them into a frieze ornament, such as we have many examples of in the temples of Egypt. Then make an attempt at the Doric, and do not forget the anthemion; from that age pass to the Alexandrian, producing a more expansive and rich arrangement, bearing in mind the acanthus; and finally, try the Roman, in which you may put all the gorgeous exuberance of display of which your materials are capable, not forgetting the scroll, and that in both the Alexandrian and Roman styles fabulous animals are admissible. This is only one of a thousand useful experiments or exercises that your historical knowledge will enable you to make in the arrangement of new materials in established forms; and it is a field of enterprise that, without historical knowledge, would be wholly closed to you. I may observe that you will ensure a much greater variety by disposing the same materials in different forms than by arranging different materials in the same forms.

By following out this system, with a thorough knowledge of ornament, you cannot fail to produce variety and beauty at once,—the end of all these studies, and the object of every ornamentist, whatever may be the ultimate destination of his design.

Brick Duties.—Mr. Peto has presented a petition from Norwich, praying for a reduction of duties on bricks and windows.

ST. BARNABAS' COLLEGE, PIMLICO.

Messrs. CUNDY, Architects.

ST. BARNABAS' COLLEGE, QUEEN STREET, PIMLICO,
IN THE DISTRICT OF ST. PAUL, KNIGHTSBRIDGE.

The first stone of the college was laid on St. Barnabas' day, 1846: it includes schools for boys, girls, and infants, about 600 in all, twenty-four of whom are to be on the foundation, to be clothed, boarded, and lodged, as well as educated, gratuitously. The residentiary house is constructed to hold four clergymen, whose duty it will be to attend to the parochial duties of the district, and to minister in the church. They will also teach in the schools, and have the special superintendence of the twelve choristers on the foundation. The church is intended to be entirely free, without pews or paid seats, and will be capable of holding 700 persons in open benches.

The schools were opened on St. Barnabas' day, 1847, and at present serve the purpose of a temporary church for the district.

The residentiary house has been completed, and is now occupied, and the church is built with the exception of the upper part of the tower and the spire, which are expected to be finished by the middle of the summer, and during the following year it is probable that the completion of the church may be accomplished, so as to be ready for consecration by St. Barnabas' day, 1850.

The buildings are constructed of Kentish rag stone, both externally and internally, having dressings and a spire of Caen stone. The roof of the church, chancel, sacristy, and choir vestry are of oak.

The cost of the schools, residentiary house and church, with the enclosing walls and appurtenances, will be about 19,000l.

The freehold site of the college was the munificent gift of the Marquis of Westminster.

The funds have been provided hitherto by the voluntary contribution of the inhabitants of St. Paul's district, through the indefatigable exertions of the Rev. W. G. Bennett, the incumbent. The style of the architecture is the first Pointed (Early English), and which appeared to the trustees of the college best adapted for the poor man's church. There is yet to be collected about 5,000l. for the completion of this establishment.

The dimensions of the interior of the church are as follows:—The length is 97 feet from east to west, including the chancel, 30 feet deep; the width of the nave and aisles 51 feet; and the height of the nave 50 feet: the height of the tower and spire will be 170 feet. The general arrangement is a nave with north and south aisles, a tower at the west end of the north aisle, a south porch, a chancel with aisles, a sacristy, and choir vestry, all attached, connecting the church to the other portions of the college. The whole of the internal fittings are to be of oak; the church and chancel are to be paved with tiles, and all the windows are to be appropriately glazed with stained glass, much of which has been already offered. There is a crypt under the chancel. The architects are Messrs. Cundy, to whom praise is due for the satisfactory manner in which this interesting pile of buildings is being carried out.

In our engraving, the schools are seen on the left, and the residentiary house on the right of the church.

THE AYLESBURY COMPETITION.—The competition for the erection of judges' lodgings at Aylesbury, into which ten architects entered, has been decided in favour of Mr. Lamb. A respectable correspondent (one of the competitors) comments on an ambiguous statement made by the chairman of the magistrates, Sir Thomas Aubrey, in announcing this result to the few who were present, to the effect " that the reason which had led to their choice was known amongst themselves, and the less said about it the better for all parties concerned;" but this statement is too vague to justify any suspicion of unfairness on our part.

ARTISTS' GENERAL BENEVOLENT FUND. —The thirty-fourth anniversary dinner of this institution was held on Saturday in last week. The Marquis of Westminster presided, and about 420l. were subscribed.

LODGE, MANOR PARK, STREATHAM.

Mr. ROUMIEU, Architect.

LODGE: STREATHAM.

THE accompanying engraving represents the tower lodge on the principal entrance to the Manor Park, Streatham. The building, which is from a design of Mr. R. L. Roumieu, architect, is in the Italian style of architecture, and built of brick, covered with metallic cement: it contains four bed-rooms, two sitting-rooms, with kitchen and scullery complete.

The tower, which is 70 feet high, contains a staircase to the top, which commands a beautiful view of the surrounding country: on a clear day Epsom, Harrow-on-the-Hill, and Highgate can be seen without the aid of a glass. It was built for the residence of the agent to the estate. The park is being belted round with houses of various styles of architecture, leaving the interior open for walks and pleasure grounds.

ARCHITECTURAL SOIREE AT LIVERPOOL.

THE Liverpool Architectural Society held their first *soirée* on the 28th ult., when a nice party assembled, and the whole of the proceedings passed off with great satisfaction. The band of the 46th and an exhibition of the electric light were pressed into the service, nor were the creature-comforts wanting; in fact, one of the local papers devotes about half the space allotted to an account of the meeting to commendation of the jellies and creams then and there dispensed.

The Rev. D. James, F.S.A., was in the chair.

Mr. J. A. Picton gave an account of the origin of the society, already stated in our pages. Mr. Picton further said,—It must be admitted that great improvements might be made in building, and in architecture generally, and these would be promoted by the establishment of their society. They proposed

to form a good architectural and artistical library, but that they were as yet unable to carry out. It would also be their object to furnish illustrations of the remains of antiquity in the neighbourhood. Besides this, the society would have a great effect in calling out the energies of architects still further than they had been, and affording greater facilities for students.

Mr. Cockerell, R.A., one of the guests of the evening, was then introduced to the meeting, and expressed the gratification with which he viewed the establishment of the society. Speaking of Liverpool, he said, he did not think that in Europe there was a modern building at all equal to St. George's Hall, as regarded its structure, unity of design, and magnificence of execution. Another building, the Town-hall and Exchange, had also on all occasions excited his admiration. He was happy to learn that, during the last year, an institution had grown up which it had always appeared to him was required in Liverpool, where there was a certain grandeur of mind, arising from the enterprise and commercial spirit for which it had been, at all times, remarkable. He felt sure the art would flourish there, because they had not only many able architects, but they had amongst them teachers and guides in all the various walks of life. In the present state of progress it was highly desirable, unless the architects were to lag behind, that they should take up a position, and, by union, create a body, in order to balance the great social influence which was bearing upon them on all sides.

Mr. S. Holme said he thought that a good understanding ought to exist between the architect and the builder, as there was nothing more likely than such a course to promote permanent success. The minds of mechanical men were expanded by having the advantage of communicating with those of superior thought and intelligence, and architects themselves might oc-

casionally receive practical hints which practical men were so able to give, and by an action and re-action there would be an advantage to both. The theoretical architect would receive advantage from being operated upon by the practical architect, and practical good would result to themselves and to the society. When they looked at the achievements in science and art, at the present day, it was necessary, if architecture was to keep its place, that the members of the profession should undergo a course of study, and unite themselves together in order to promote their general improvement and experience. Unless they did so they must lag behind in that wonderful march of progress which they saw now in existence throughout the land.—Mr. Sharpe and other gentlemen also addressed the meeting.

THE SHEFFIELD TRADE.

IN last week's *Sheffield Times* is published the essay selected as the best of those presented in competition for the prize offered by the proprietors of that paper for an essay "On the Present Condition and Future Prospects of Sheffield." The successful competitor is Mr. Joseph Hutton, Saint Cross, Eckington, who appears to have had long experience in the trade as a manufacturer, and who was himself 'shelfed' by the unionist workmen no less than twenty-seven years since. His sentiments on this particular subject correspond entirely with our own. If there are to be unions, he remarks, let the masters unite as well as the men, and come, if possible, to some mutual understanding for the settlement of differences, otherwise, "as things are now in Sheffield, the masters with money, who employ workmen, will soon disappear, and leave only working masters, who, like ravenous wolves, will tear each other to rags." As to new trades that might be advantageously introduced, he says,

"I know of no natural objection; but what man of sense or company of men would lay out their money in making preparations in Sheffield, so infected with trade-unions."

The dissatisfaction of the essayist, however, with the present state of things in Sheffield, does not rest here. He exposes what he conceives to be those technical and professional causes which have tended to blast the good fame of Sheffield wares in general. These, virtually, he may be said to comprehend under the head of haste and carelessness in the production of worthless quantity, in place of care and labour in the manufacture of sterling quality. "Softness of temper is the general complaint of Sheffield wares." If hardened to a sufficient extent, in the haste and carelessness of manufacture, the goods are destroyed by wholesale. The grinder, moreover, "I have seen ram dozens into the wheel-fire, and heat them red-hot, in order to dispatch his work more quickly;" otherwise, he either destroys or returns them to the manufacturer to soften them. Haste, too, in the manufacture of steel he deprecates, recommending strongly the preparation of cast steel by the manufacturers under their own eye. "As to cast-steel," he says, "few are aware why it is so uniform in temperature; it is from being melted, which mixes the high and the low conversions, the outside and the inside, in the crucible."

On the whole, the essayist's hope for Sheffield is by no means cheering. His concluding words, which do not very clearly express his meaning, are, "That the Sheffield trade may revive and progress is the fear, but still the fervent wish of the writer." He takes care to remark, however, that if he were now a young man, about to enter into the business, he would steer clear of Sheffield by a hundred miles.

NOTES IN THE PROVINCES.

Plans for a new church at Birch, near Colchester, have been prepared by Mr. S. S. Teulon, architect. The style is Gothic, and the building is to have flint facings and Caen stone rusticated coins, a tower and spire: sittings, 600.——The sum of 3,000*l.* is to be at length borrowed, on church-rate security, for the repair and re-opening of Aylesbury Church.——The Grimsby dock area reclaimed is 132 acres, length of dam and embankment, 6,500 feet, with projection into river beyond high water 2,900 feet; bead of water against the dam at spring tides, 25 feet.——It is proposed to erect a monument to Cromwell on the site of Slepe Hall, St. Ives, where he resided at the opening of his public career.——Trinity Congregational Chapel, Queen's-road, Reading, lately opened, is in the Early English style, with a turret and pinnacle at each of the four angles, and a triplet window and slightly projecting porch at the end facing Queen's-road. Swindon stone with Bath stone dressings have been used in its construction. The exterior presents carved corbels and finials, gable and dripstone terminations, &c., so far ornamental, but there is no 'superfluous decoration.' The roof, interiorly, is of simple construction, and the principals rest on stone corbels of carved foliage. There is a gallery of timber across the northern end. The benches are all open and low backed, with *fleur de lis* terminations. The woodwork in general is of deal, stained and varnished. Mr. W. F. Poulton, of Reading, was the architect, and the contractors were Messrs. Cooper and Sons, of Maidenhead; sub-contractors, Mr. Darter, painter, and Messrs. Wheeler for masonry and carving.——The consternation and distress, says a contemporary, occasioned among the working mechanics and labourers in Plymouth-yard, as the details of the Government plan of reduction become developed, is extreme. Many who have been doing duty as leading hands over hired mechanics for years, themselves having been previously entered on the dockyard establishment, and supposing themselves on that account secure from discharge, are to be summarily turned adrift at the close of the financial year; the only alternative being the bitter one of taking the berth and pay (12s. a-week) of a labourer, and this considered a favour.——A baptismal font has just been added to the Holy Cross Church, Pershore. It was executed by Messrs. Gibbs and Son, Oxford, and cost 30*l.*, raised by the curate.——The roof of Holy Rhood Church, Southampton, is now covered in, the galleries are in progress, and the interior masonry is almost finished.——Collumpton Church is to be almost entirely reseated and repaved, and the gallery obscuring the fan tracery vaulting of Lane's chapel removed, and the nave gallery reduced. A chancel, as our readers are probably aware, was recently built.——The new church at Yardley Wood, near Birmingham, lately consecrated, comprises a nave, aisles, and chancel, with short transepts, and a bell tower.——The opening of the Manchester New Exchange, in May, is to be celebrated by a public ball, substantially for the benefit of the baths and wash-houses there——The Newcastle baths and wash-houses seem to be in busy use, not only by the class for whom they were designed, but by 'the public' generally, and those truly industrious classes of the community, the maids of all work and the professional washerwomen, are getting fast initiated into all the mysteries of hot-air closets and steam-boilers, thus, as the *Gateshead Observer* remarks, at once saving their employers' houses from damp and discomfort and their tempers from still worse evils.——Three ornamental windows have been executed and put up by Mr. J. Gibson, of Newcastle, in the church at Walker.——A subscription has been opened to purchase the late Mr. David Scott's painting, "Vasco de Gama, the discoverer of the passage to India, doubling the Cape of Good Hope," to be placed in the hall of the Trinity House at Leith. Why do not corporations and other bodies purchase some of the large pictures now spoiling in artists' studios *before* the painter dies?

RAILWAY JOTTINGS.

Sir F. Head, in his 'Stokers and Pokers,' states that 10,000,000*l.* were expended in Parliamentary inquiries and Parliamentary contests in 1845, 1846, and 1847, and that that money "would, at the rate of 20,000*l.* per mile, have constructed a national railway 500 miles in length—say from London to Aberdeen."——The cost of advertising one railway scheme in the London morning papers alone is said to have been 2,500*l.*——The Great Western Company, says the *Liverpool Times*, "have effected a saving of 15s. per annum by wafering instead of sealing their letters. What an anomaly! their income is increased by *waxing less.*" If the waferer, however, get no more a-week than the saving per annum, he will be apt to reduce the profit by eating the wafers—a circumstance which ought to be taken into consideration—though he will not wax so fat, we fear, even in such a way of faring, as to justify any further reduction of wages.——Two hundred more of the workmen on this line, besides clerks, it is said, are to be discharged on 1st May—not a very bright summer's morning to them, poor fellows.——"At length," says Herepath, "the Government has determined to try whether the Great Western Railway Company of Common Carriers are to be amenable to the laws of the land or not; whether they shall be compelled, like other Companies and individuals, to obey the Acts of Parliament granted on their own solicitation, or shall treat them as waste paper. It will be remembered that, some time ago, the case for the reduction of the Great Western fares was laid before the Attorney and Solicitor General, and that they gave their opinion that the Great Western ought, under their Act, to reduce their fares and charges. The Great Western have neglected to do so, and therefore the Crown has ordered a bill to be filed in Chancery against them to compel them."——The Copenhagen tunnel on the Great Northern is about to be let. This tunnel is about 600 yards in length: it commences at the end of Mr. Brassey's contract, towards, or rather into London. The short length, about three-quarters of a mile, between the Copenhagen tunnel and King's Cross station, has already been contracted for, so that the Copenhagen tunnel will, when let, leave the line immediately into London completely contracted for. The only work which will then remain to be disposed of at the London end, will be the King's Cross station.——A railway bridge at Stowe, near the Marton-road station, has lately given way it is said.——The *American Railway Journal* states that no fewer than 6,421 miles of railway were in actual operation within the limits of the United States at the commencement of the present year. These railways, including plant, have cost on an average about 30,000 dollars, or 6,000*l.* per mile. Of course they are not on the same scale of magnificence as the lines of this country. In Canada very few miles of railway have as yet been constructed.

ELECTRO-TELEGRAPHIC PROGRESS.

We understand, says a contemporary, that a proposition will shortly be brought before the public, having for its object such an extension of the facilities of electro-intercommunication, as to bring its use within the means of the million. It must be something extremely urgent which induces the capitalist to pay about 7s. per 100 miles for twenty words, when he can get a long detailed letter in five or six hours for one penny. The system in America has been established on thousands of miles of railway, on the principle of enabling the public generally to partake of its advantages; and a company in this country, on the same principle, charging about 6d. or 1s. per message, would soon find the decrease in price produce an enormous extent of business, and make the undertaking exceedingly popular. Increased means of never-failing power, unquestionable secresy, and great reduction in charges, are recommendations that cannot fail to prove highly attractive to capitalist, merchant, and trader.——One of the most remarkable features in connection with the transmission of President Taylor's curtailed "message," by telegraph, from Liverpool to London, was the expense. It occupied about ninety-eight lines; and the sum paid by Willmer and Smith to the Electric Telegraph Company was 21*l.* sterling. The same thing would have been done in America for as many dollars. How, says the *European Times*, can the English press, under its already heavy expenditure, endure pecuniary inflictions of this nature?——The wires of the telegraph working along the South-Western have been brought round from Fareham to the terminus at Landport, Portsmouth, and thence carried across the fortifications. The Admiralty are to communicate by cyphers, with, of course, a secret key. The old semaphore stations, however, are not to be given up, and a new one for Osborne is talked of.

METROPOLITAN COMMISSION OF SEWERS.

A general court was held on Thursday, at the Court-house, Greek-street, Soho-square; the Right Hon. the Earl of Carlisle in the chair.

The Drainage of Kensington.—A plan for the effectual drainage of the town and workhouse of Kensington, was presented by Messrs. Austin, Phillips, Gotto, and Lovick, pursuant to an order of the last court. They recommended that an 18-inch pipe sewer should be laid down to communicate with the Counters' Creek Sewer, at an estimated cost of 790*l.*, towards which Mr. Bird, the builder, was willing to contribute 300*l.*

Mr. Leslie expressed his approbation generally of the line proposed, but believed that it might be still further improved by passing it through a field on which 200 houses were about to be erected (the plan of which he produced), a straight line would be formed, and with a considerable saving of expense. He would, however, for the pipe sewer proposed, lay down a substantial brickwork egg-shaped sewer, which, by being submitted to public competition, might be executed at 10s. per foot. By the adoption of his plan, a permanent remedy would be found for every complaint at Kensington, at an expense not exceeding 1,200*l.*, a large proportion of which would be contributed by the owners of the adjoining property.

Mr. Austin, the consulting engineer, said the Counters' Creek Sewer was a most offensive ditch, and, for the sake of improvement, it was desirable to divert the sewage from it altogether. Taking a general view of the drainage area, therefore, he was not prepared to recommend any drainage into it as a permanent work.—Mr. Chadwick objected to commissioners having a local knowledge of particular districts submitting their views for the drainage of them without proper plans, as what might be proper for a single place might turn out highly improper for a whole district.—Lord Ebrington was in favour of the plans as proposed by the surveyors.

The Earl of Carlisle said it was desirable to carry the scheme immediately into effect, as the state of the workhouse [recently set forth in THE BUILDER] would admit of no delay.—The motion for the adoption of the plan was then put and agreed to.

The Salaries of the Officers of the Commission.—Mr. Bullar then moved, pursuant to notice, "That from January 5, 1849, the salary of the order clerk be 800*l.* a-year, the salary of the consulting engineer 400*l.* a-year, and the salary of Mr. Phillips, as one of the chief surveyors 600*l.* a-year. The motion was agreed to *nem. con.*

On the motion of Mr. Chadwick, it was agreed "That it be referred to the Works' Committee to obtain plans, models, specimens of soil, pan apparatus, taps, and sinks, for the completion of house drainage and providing public conveniences, in accordance with the Act, and not to expend more than 60*l.* for that purpose."

On the motion of Mr. Bullar, seconded by Mr. Chadwick, the following resolutions were agreed to:—

"That no order be given to any contractor or other tradesmen, and no other expense be incurred, with reference to any work, experiment, or investigation, without the written certificate of the order clerk, the consulting engineer, or one of the chief surveyors, of the propriety of such order or expense."

"That it be an instruction to the Finance Committee, while it continues, to require and receive, as regards orders given and expenses incurred before March 15, 1849, inclusive, the certificate as to its propriety of the officer under whose supervision the work, experiment, or investigation in question was conducted; and as regards orders given and expenses incurred with reference to works, experiments, and investigations after that day, the certificate as to its propriety of the order clerk, the consulting engineer, or one of the chief surveyors."

The Committee Question.—On the motion that certain committees appointed provisionally at the last court be confirmed as orders of court,

Mr. Leslie rose and said that on the subject of these committees they had got the opinion of the law officers of the Crown. They had also got the resolutions and a protest against them, and he wished to know which was the correct view of the case. They were now called upon to take a long string of resolutions into consideration, and were they to pass them, in a week or two they might find that they were acting illegally again. To guard against such an occurrence, he felt it to be his duty, painful as it was, to move as an amendment, that the resolution proposed, with the protest that had been signed against them by four commissioners, be referred to the law officers of the Crown.

Mr. E. Lawes seconded the amendment.

Lord Ebrington was opposed to the reference of questions not involving points of law, but of policy, and believing the present question to be one of policy he should vote against the amendment.

Mr. Bullar was not about to give his opinion as a lawyer, as he had before declined being the legal adviser of the Commission. However, since the last court he had taken the opinion of a friend residing in the Temple, and whose intelligence he believed to be quite equal to that of the Attorney and Solicitor General (as we understood), and with him they went word by word through the orders, comparing them with the statute; and it was his friend's decided opinion that these orders were quite legal. Another friend, too, to whom he had submitted them had come to the same conclusion, except as to the 3rd rule, in which a question of legality might possibly arise. He (Mr. Bullar) had no wish to criticise the protest, but he felt assured that if he sat down for the opposite side he should find no difficulty in taking 500 objections, every one of which should be as valid as those contained in the protest.

Mr. Chadwick protested against the impression that anything had been going forward that was illegal. A great deal had been said about being taken into the Court of Queen's Bench by *certiorari*. He thought on that subject gentlemen would be very unwilling to risk their own money. That the public money had been culpably misapplied in the waste of the time of the Court he believed no impartial man entertained a doubt; and as to the law of the case, he never heard of any so fundamentally bad as had been opposed to the proceedings of a sub-division of labour. With regard to the reference of these orders to the law officers of the Crown, he (Mr. C.) should as soon think of referring to the Attorney-General on the construction of a water-closet as on any one of these regulations.

After some further discussion, the amendment was put and negatived by a majority of 12 to 2, and the confirmation of the appointment of the committees was agreed to.

The Ordnance Survey.—A lengthy report was received from the Ordnance Survey Committee, which set out by giving a number of questions to Capt. Yolland, of the Royal Engineers, on the practicability of increasing the three-mile radius to a scale of 10 feet to the mile, for the purpose of laying down the details of house drainage, with his answers thereto. It also stated the fact, that although the estimated cost of the survey was 24,000*l.*, the work would be completed for 3,000*l.* within that amount, and 5,000*l.* below the estimate given in by the civil surveyors.

Sir H. de la Beche said it was very important that they had been able to save so large an amount, as it would nearly enable them to engrave the plates, and to form blocks of houses. Without much trouble they would be enabled to enlarge such portions of the survey as might be desirable from time to time. The work of the survey had been one of extreme success, and might, if necessary, be consulted by persons laying out property, and for other purposes. He believed that when their labours were closed, it would be found that the interests of the public had been well protected.——Mr. Chadwick believed that the engraving of the plates would be executed at a cost of 6*l.* per sheet, in a manner superior to that of the Ordnance maps at 10*l.* per sheet.——The report was then received, and, after some works of emergency were ordered, the court adjourned.

Miscellanea.

THE SAXON CHURCH AT STOWE.—The nave foundations are now under repair with Yorkshire stone cramped together and laid in cement. It is said, too, that Archdeacon Stonehouse has entered into contracts for the nave and chancel repairs. Unfortunately, however, the parishioners appear to be restive under the anticipated infliction of a church rate for a system of repair carried out on one principle, while an alleged preference is given to another; so that between two extreme and opposing lines of procedure, it is possible that justice may fail to be done to this venerable mother church. Those who supply the rate appear to be mere utilitarians—or rather, we may say, necessitarians—who are only willing to vote for "necessary repairs," while the executive has an eye to a special system of alteration and adornment in combination with the mere prop work, but without the sympathy of his constituents. "For the restoration of this old church," says a contemporary, "a public appeal should be made, and the repairs and restorations should be under the direction of some experienced architect."

PORTABLE STEAM-ENGINES.—The *Scottish Agricultural Journal* describes a farm steam-engine at work near Edinburgh. It is of four-horse power, and drives a six-horse thrashing mill. In length it is 8 feet, including fire-box, boiler, smoke-box, and carriage, which latter is constructed of timber, bound with iron-work, and placed on iron axles and wheels; the fore carriage working on an axle, so as to admit of its being easily turned. The breadth over the axles is 6 feet, and the height to the top of the driving-wheel 8 feet. The height of the chimney is 15 feet, but when the engine is not at work, it is lowered by a joint at 10 feet from its summit, into "a saddle." The boiler is tubular, and can be easily repaired, and the smoke-box removed, so as to clean out the soot of the chimney and the tubes: means are used to prevent any issue of sparks from the chimney. The driving wheel is about 5 feet in diameter. One of the boiler tubes is made of softer metal than the others, so that, in the event of neglect or stupidity in overloading the boiler, this tube will give way and extinguish the fire, thus preventing the chance of explosion. The engine, it is said, can do all the work generally executed by manual or bestial power on the farm steading, and may be employed in pumping water, making tiles, or sawing wood; and being "a moveable subject," it can be "sold, alienated, or disposed of" at pleasure, or used jointly by a number of farmers.

GIRDER-BRIDGE AT BARNES.—An accident occurred here lately by the giving way of a winch on a travelling frame which crosses the Thames where a new iron girder-bridge is forming, to continue the loop line from the Barnes station of the Richmond Railway to Twickenham. A girder of seven tons weight had been raised from a barge and lowered to within three inches of its place, when the connecting-rods and timber arm gave way, and the winch and platform fell, when one of three workmen jumped into the river, and was carried down with the tide and lost.

CALICO BY THE MILE. — VERY LONG CLOTH.—The cylinder printing machines in Messrs. Hoyle's print works, Manchester, print a mile of calico in an hour! If fifteen of these machines work uninterruptedly for ten hours each day, and for six days in the week, they would be able to print cotton dresses in one such week for one hundred and sixty-two thousand ladies! According to the *Birmingham Journal*, the actual number of miles of calico printed by this firm alone in a single year exceeds ten thousand, one fourth more than the diameter of our planet.

GAS MONITOR.—The assistant-secretary of the Baths and Washhouses for the Labouring Classes, Mr. Woolcott, has written to us to say that the advertisement in THE BUILDER of last week, which states that the use of the gas-light monitor has effected a saving of 10,000 cubic feet of gas, in six weeks, at the model establishment, Coulston-square, Whitechapel, is incorrect: but as the note goes on to say that the monitor is no doubt useful in regulating and saving the consumption of gas, and that the committee are about to have more of them fitted up, we do not see the value of the contradiction.

THE ROYAL CYCLORAMA.—We spoke in terms of commendation of the Cyclorama of Lisbon's Destruction by Earthquake, at the Colosseum, when it was first opened, but its effect upon us then was less powerful than it was on a second visit lately. Mr. Bradwell has the machinery more under control now than at first, especially for the management of the lights, on which much depends. The sunrise in the opening view at the mouth of the Tagus is beautifully managed, and the effect of the storm is appalling. We were somewhat surprised to hear that neither Her Majesty the Queen, nor the Prince, has yet seen this work. A visit from these illustrious personages, so well qualified to judge of its merits, and usually willing to give their countenance where it is deserved, would be a gratifying reward to those who have carried out this undertaking, and one which, considering the elegance of the building raised for the exhibition, the extent of the painting, and the costliness of the experiment, they might not unreasonably hope for.

MR. HENNING, THE SCULPTOR.—The *Art-Journal* for April contains an interesting sketch of the life of John Henning, sen., best known by his reduced and restored copy of the Elgin frieze, the chief intention of which is to raise a fund to engrave this work for the benefit of the sculptor. We cordially wish the scheme success. It was commenced by the late Mr. Freebairn, but went no further than one plate.

BUST OF FRANCIS BAILY. — At the annual general meeting of the Royal Astronomical Society, Sir John F. W. Herschel, Bart., presented to that body a marble bust of their late President, Francis Baily, D.C.L. (the gift of Miss Baily, his only surviving sister), with an appropriate address, which appears in the Society's transactions for February, 1849.

COST OF PIPES AND DRAINS.—The following is a list of tenders for 6,350 ft. of stoneware pipe, to be laid in Oxford, and 450 ft. of 3 ft. by 2 ft. 9 in. half-brick tunnel, in mortar, in the same line. The sizes of pipes were 4,100 ft. of 15 in., and 2,250 ft. of 12 in. Also a 15 in. cast-iron syphon-pipe, 20 ft. long, and a 9-in. wall, at each end of drain, for rest of mouth of pipes. Tenders opened on the 3rd of April.

For excavation and brick tunnel, &c.:—			
Yeoman, of London	£616	0	0
Winterbourne, of Oxford	534	0	0
Adams, of Oxford	520	0	0
Hope, of Oxford	465	6	0
Trebarne, of London	459	0	0
For pipes only:—			
Smith, of London	856	0	0
Stiff, of London	814	0	0
Doulton, of London	803	1	0
Green, of London	798	14	0
Doulton, of St. Helen's	769	0	0
For the whole work:—			
Pearce	1,300	0	0
Treharne, of London	1,253	0	0
Dethick, of London	1,247	0	0
Richards	1,245	0	0

Treharne's tender for groundwork, &c., accepted; J. Doulton, of St. Helen's, accepted for the pipes.

PROJECTED WORKS.—Advertisements have been issued for tenders,—by a date not specified, for the erection of a new pauper lunatic asylum (in the neighbourhood of Devizes), for the county of Wilts; also for a large quantity of cast-iron columns, sashes, and joists, to be used in the above erection; by 18th inst., for the erection of a new chapel for the Bridge Union; by 18th inst., for sundry works required in reinstating the dwelling-house and warehouses recently destroyed by fire in Addle-street, Aldermanbury; by 17th inst., for alterations and additions to Hampstead Workhouse; by 20th, for the erection of a Sunday school to be attached to Beresford Episcopal Chapel, Walworth; by a date not specified, for the erection of the chapel, catacombs, cloisters, lodge, &c., at the Leicester Cemetery; by 10th, for the rebuilding and restoration of Kingstone Church tower, Herefordshire; by 14th, for the construction of the criminal court and other works at Cardiff; by 11th, for the erection of St. Augustine's new national schools, Bristol; by 13th, for the building, &c. of a lock-up at Alston; by 9th, for forming, culverting, &c. four new streets at Birmingham; and by 17th, for the supply of wrought-iron wheels, springs, bar-iron, oak and teak for waggons for Lancashire and Yorkshire Railway.

AN IRISH SPECULATION UNDER ENGLISH AUSPICES.—It is proposed, says the *Irish Railway Gazette*, to extract the potash from the granite stone extending over a district of 70 miles between Dalkey and Wexford, whereby, with an outlay of 10,000*l*. capital, it is expected that a gross revenue of 40,000*l*., to be chiefly expended in labour throughout the Kingstown district, may be realised by the sale of 2,000 tons of potash at 20*l*. per ton in place of 40*l*., the price of that imported from America; and that moreover a further sale of the article may also be pushed in America itself. Of course, as in preparing bread out of sawdust, or soup out of whinstones, it is by means of proper chemical and other materials and operations that this, it may be much more hopeful, project is to be carried out. The potash which it is designed to extract is that which pervades the external surface of the stone. Valuable chemical substances, we all know, have been extracted from shale and other mineral strata. All, of course, must depend on the relative value of the result when compared with that of the materials and labour employed.

IMPORTANT TO RAILWAY CONTRACTORS.—On Tuesday last, at the Court House (before J. Stanhope, J. Thornely, and T. Taylor, Esqrs.), the surveyors for the township of Denby obtained a summons against the Lancashire and Yorkshire Railway Company to recover compensation under the Railway Clauses Consolidation Act, for the injury done to the roads in the township of Denby, in the making of the branch line of railway from Huddersfield to Penistone, comprising a distance, to which injury had been done, of upwards of ten miles of road. Mr. Barret, of Wakefield, solicitor, appeared in behalf of the surveyors, and Mr. Tyas, of Barnsley, and Mr. Dransfield, of Penistone, solicitors, appeared in the interest of the railway company. After a very lengthened inquiry, the magistrates made an order on the company to make the necessary repairs to the roads within the space of one month, and in default thereof the magistrates imposed the penalty of 5*l*. per day, pursuant to the above-mentioned act.

THE FIRE ANNIHILATOR.—Mr. Phillips' fire annihilator has been dug up again to afford a subject for one of the Friday evening meetings, at the Royal Institution. As we have before said, we cannot understand the policy of the inventor of this machine, who contents himself with having it talked about periodically, and gives no opportunity for its practical application.

STILL BLIND.—Tenders for the taking up the old locks at Maidstone, and putting down new; Mr. Whichcord, of Maidstone, architect.

					Extra work.		
Tassell, Maidstone..	£3,270	0	0	..			
Balston, London ..	2,800	0	0	..	£62	4	0
Diggle, Maidstone..	2,450	0	0	..			
Wood, Gravesend ..	2,120	0	0	..	170	0	0
Jarvis, London	1,746	10	0	..	41	10	0
Sutton, Maidstone (accepted)	1,376	10	0	..	22	0	0

INSTITUTION FOR THE DEPOSIT OF WORKS CONNECTED WITH ARCHITECTURE.—I am highly gratified by your correspondent's remarks on the want of an Institution of Practical Science connected with building. Some time since I attempted to effect the same object at the Mechanics' Institution of Hastings, by medals and rewards, and I shall have great pleasure in assisting to support an institution for the purpose in London, by an annual subscription of 5*l*. I give you my name.—A CONSTANT READER.

BELLS ABROAD.—Mr. Reeves, of New York, has made a valuable improvement in fire bells. The great difficulty to be obviated was in repeating the blows of the hammer in the one place, by which the bell was generally cracked. This he has done by fixing the bell on a ratchet wheel, which causes it to revolve at each stoke of the hammer. The hammer is swung by a lever, and strikes in the same place only once in every 240 strokes.——The Roman Constituent Assembly has decreed that all church bells which are not strictly necessary shall be melted down for cannon! Those of the cathedrals, parish churches, and such as are valuable in point of art, are excepted,—at present.

THE TRON STEEPLE AT GLASGOW being out of repair, a small part of the ashler work gave way, when some of the town council coolly proposed to save all future trouble and expense by razing this characteristic old feature of the Trongate to the ground. Bailie Orr indignantly expressed his astonishment at such a proposal, and the Lord Provost warmly concurred in the bailie's protest. The proposal itself accordingly fell to the ground, and the steeple was forthwith ordered to be repaired by the Finance Committee.

THE IRON TRADE.—It has been determined by the ironmasters at a recent preliminary quarterly meeting, that the puddlers and other workmen shall for the future participate in the nominal advances of price that may be declared at each meeting; and accordingly, as an earnest of the carrying out of a principle which cannot but tend to induce something like respect for the quarterly price decisions if faithfully carried out, an advance in puddlers wages of 6d. per ton on the head of the advance of price, 20s. per ton, declared in February, is now decided on. Of course if the workmen are to benefit by every rise in price, they must expect an equivalent reduction of wages whenever a fall may hereafter happen in place of a rise.

BURIALS IN TOWNS. — On Wednesday evening a meeting was held at the old Crown and Anchor, in the Strand, to petition Parliament for the immediate closing of burial places in cities and towns. Lord Dudley Coutts Stuart, M.P., took the chair; Mr. Mackinnon, M.P., Mr. G. A. Walker, Mr. Ivat Briscoe, and others spoke, and there were from 800 to 1,000 persons present. It was the most important meeting on the subject which has yet taken place, and shewed clearly the hold the question is beginning to take on the public mind. Mr. Walker spoke with the earnestness of one who feels his subject deeply.

PIRACY OF REGISTERED DESIGNS.—We learn from the *Sheffield and Rotherham Independent* that a manufacturing firm at Sheffield has been awarded by the magistrates 15*l*. and costs, payable by another manufacturer, for the infringement of a registered design for a candlestick, which was alleged to have been taken originally from some of the French patterns published from time to time in the *Art Journal*. The imitation, also a registered design, was varied in the style of ornament.

MANCHESTER PARKS' TESTIMONIAL.—Mr. Malcolm Ross and Mr. Edward W. Watkin, by whom the project was carried out, as Hon. Secretaries to the Parks' Committee, were lately presented, the former with a silver-plated épergne, and the latter a silver tea-service, in the presence of the Bishop and Mayor of the city, and a numerous assemblage, at a *dejeuner à la fourchette* given by the Mayor in his parlour in honour of the occasion.

FOREIGN WINDOW GLASS.—We understand that the importations at the present time of window glass, especially from Belgium, are very large. One vessel, the *Princess Victoria*, has just arrived in the river, from Antwerp, with 990 cases of the article on board, consigned to a firm in the metropolis.

CHURCH LEASEHOLD PROPERTY.—It is but little known that a commission is now sitting to collect information and hear the representation of parties, on the proposal for the settlement of the question between the church and the lessees holding property under the different deans and chapters. A meeting has been held in London on the subject, at which the Duke of Richmond presided, when a committee of members of both Houses of Parliament was appointed for the purpose of communicating with the lessees of church property, in order to obtain and select evidence to be submitted to the Royal Commission now sitting.

NOTICE.

"BUILDINGS AND MONUMENTS, MODERN AND MEDIÆVAL," being Illustrations of recently erected Edifices, and of some of the Architectural Works of the Middle Ages, with Descriptive Particulars. Edited by George Godwin, F.R.S., Fellow of the Royal Institute of Architects, &c., &c., &c.

Under the above title it is proposed to publish, in bi-monthly parts, price 2s. 6d. each, the principal Illustrations of Modern and Mediæval Buildings which have appeared from time to time in THE BUILDER, with their accompanying descriptive particulars. Each part will contain about eight plates, folio size, and eight pages of letter press, with plans and details. The engravings will be printed separately, with care, on a tinted paper.

The first part will be issued in time to be forwarded with the magazines for May 1, and will contain:—

Her Majesty's Marine Residence, Osborne; with Plan.

The Carlton Club House, Pall Mall.

Church of St. Isaac, at St. Petersburgh; with Details.

Kensington Union Workhouse.

The Liverpool Branch Bank of England; and Details.

The New Throne, Canterbury Cathedral.

The North Porch, Restored, of St. Mary Redcliffe, Bristol.

The Interior of Lincoln's-Inn Hall.

Persons desirous of becoming Subscribers, are requested to forward their names to the office of THE BUILDER.

TENDERS

For the erection of nine small houses at Walham-green; Mr. C. Lahee, architect, opened in the presence of the parties tendering:—

Symons, Chelsea	£3,437	0	0
Burgess, Wardour-street....	3,380	0	0
Todd, Chelsea..............	3,319	10	0
Watts, Motcomb-street	3,229	0	0
Underhill, Chelsea	2,595	0	0

For rebuilding the parish church of St. Edward, Romford; Mr. J. Johnson, architect:—

Trego	£8,490
Myers	6,900
Piper........................	6,687
Curtis, Romford..............	6,655
Kelk..........................	6,190

Quantities not furnished.

For erecting four villas at Battersea, for Mr. C. J. Spicer:—

Locke and Nesham	£3,535
Hammond and Hill	3,457
Mansfield and Son	3,440
Nicholson and Son	3,406
Trego	3,336
Harmer	3,329
Gammon	3,223
Cooper........................	3,129

Tenders opened at Wimborn, on the 20th ult., for building the new Grammar Schools and masters' houses. First division comprises bricklayer, excavator, plasterer, tiler, and slater; second division, mason and paviour; third division, carpenter, joiner, smith, ironmonger, bellhanger; fourth division, plumber, painter, glazier, and paperhanger:—

	First Division	Second Division	Third Division	Fourth Division
	£	£	£	£
C. Smith, London	3,204	2,643	2,800	945
J. Jackson, do.	2,970	2,054	3,004	778
Simmonds, Wimborn	2,944	2,620	2,735	826
Plowman and Luck ..	2,792	2,607	3,125	704
G. Brown............	2,756	2,583	2,858	755
Walker and Soper, London............	2,695	2,800	2,394	697
J. Scorer	2,691	..	..	..
G. Scorer	2,654	..	..	..
Gover and Son	2,528	2,193	2,872	834
Pollock and M'Lennan, London............	2,473	2,134	2,863	705
Green	2,464	2,010	2,975	981
J. T. Taylor, London..	2,300*	1,950*	2,409	580*
Beavans	..	2,175	..	..
Nott	..	1,995	..	..
S. Colman............	..	..	2,816	..
J. Bugden	..	..	2,323*	..
Ellgood..............	..	..	..	842
J. Sloper, London....	..	..	..	897
J. Ricks	..	..	..	696
Ellgar	..	..	..	815
S. Wallan	..	..	..	687
M. Hall, London	..	..	..	651
H. Hall..............	..	..	..	626

* Accepted.

MEETINGS OF SCIENTIFIC BODIES

Held during the ensuing week.

TUESDAY, APRIL 10.—Freemasons of the Church, 8 P.M.

WEDNESDAY, 11th — Society of Arts, 8 P.M. ; Graphic Society, 8 P.M.

FRIDAY, 13th. — Archæological Association, 8½ P.M. ; Archæological Institute, 4 P.M.

TO CORRESPONDENTS.

"*Size of Drains.*"—Several correspondents complain bitterly, that while the Commissioners of Sewers forbid the use of drains more than 4 inches in diameter, they will not take the responsibility of any derangement in consequence.

"*Copper Bronze Powder.*"—A correspondent wishes to know "the method of making copper bronze powder. I have tried the common receipts, viz., by placing bars of iron or pieces of zinc, into a solution of the sulphate, or nitrate of that metal, but this changes so rapidly into the red, or black oxide, as to be perfectly useless."

"*Constantinople.*"—A correspondent asks "whether the water, which is used in Constantinople, and brought from the forest of Belgrade, is raised to the level of Constantinople by the action of capillary attraction, in the numerous upright pipes, standing between the reservoir at Belgrade and the reservoir at Constantinople, or by the action of the syphon?"

Received.—"T. S.," "J. H.," "R. L.," "E. T. B.," "L. C." (tenders for the "Middle Level Drainage" have not reached us);" Surveyor" (there are no published precedents: so much must depend on circumstances);" G. W.,"" E. K. D.""" A Miner" (we agree with our correspondent in considering *choke-damp* not explosive. The expression of Sir H. Delabeche may have been misunderstood, or was inadvertant) ;" E. B." (we have not had time to reply) ;" G. N." (we cannot afford the time at this moment) ;" K. and Co.,"" Constant Reader,"" J. and Co." (we are sorry our correspondents were inconvenienced) ;" Scriptator" (urges that a brick sewer for Kensington, might be formed for less money than drain pipes will cost) ;" A. F.,"" Gerard,"" W. H.,"" W. B. C." (we have not heard that competitors have received any announcement from Dundee) ;" Blackwood,"" Ecclesiologist,"" Journal of Design," No. 3.," Remarks on Entrances to Docks," by J. B. Redman ;" The Ecclesiastical and Architectural Topography of England," Part II., Berkshire, J. H. Parker;" Paper on Hot and Cold Blast Iron," by H. Hartop.

"*Books, Prices, and Addresses.*"—We have not time to point out books or find addresses.

ADVERTISEMENTS.

No. CCCXXIII.

SATURDAY, APRIL 14, 1849.

N turning over the leaves of Mr. Brandon's work on " Parish Churches," the observer cannot avoid being struck by the diversity of forms and varied effects apparent in structures identical in purpose, and so similar in general arrangement as these buildings necessarily are. A nave, with aisles or without; a porch on the south side of this, at the west end; a chancel growing out of the nave, and a tower, or bell-turret, as the case may be, are the features which go to make our ancient parish churches : the same class of windows, mouldings, and decorations, was used in all churches built within particular periods;—and yet no two are exactly alike, but all present singular differences, and have beauties entirely their own. Built on the same type, representations of the same feelings, provisions for the same wants, compounds of the same details,—the result, as a whole, is still so different, that it is only within a very short period of time, that it was discovered these buildings can all be classed under four heads, according to the date of the erection, and that, knowing this date, we may with tolerable certainty predict the components of the structure,—know what we may expect to find and where to find it.

This diversity, co-existent with uniformity, resulted from able minds working on the same principles and modes, controlled by existing circumstances, and could not have been produced by slavish copying. Ideas were of course constantly borrowed : what had been done served as the point from which to start again, and there were always inferior minds contented to follow where the master minds led. Moreover, that they were in the possession of formulæ by which certain satisfactory results were invariably obtained, seems clear. Unless some system were followed, Mr. Ferguson remarks in his " Inquiry," " We must admit that between the ages of St. Louis and our Edward III., there was born, in every great town of western Europe, an architect capable of designing a great cathedral, and in every village one capable of building a parish church; and that all this myriad of architects were endowed with the same modicum of genius, for all the buildings of that age, whether great or small, bear a nearly equal impress of perfection; and that this great race perished entirely in the following century, for the art of erecting such buildings was lost soon after it reached its highest point."

We are disposed to attach more importance to the efforts of the *one man* and his influence on the works of the multitude, than the author last quoted does; but that some system was followed, and that these productions were the result of a nation's labour, and above all of the upper and most intellectual classes of society, we are fully satisfied.

Let us look back, however, to " Parish Churches," the interesting and useful volume which led us to the foregoing remarks,* and we shall see in every example an evidence of

* Parish Churches; being Perspective Views of English Ecclesiastical Structures : accompanied by Plans, drawn to uniform scale, and letter-press descriptions. By R. and A. Brandon, Architects. Bell, Fleet-street.

the diversity and originality to which we referred.

This work contains views of sixty-three churches, from sixteen counties; nearly half of the illustrations, however, are from Lincolnshire and Northamptonshire. In the first view, Little Casterton Church, Rutlandshire, the west wall is continued up, and has two arched openings in it for bells, surmounted by gables, while against the face of the wall below are two massive buttresses in the line of the belfry, which produce a tower-like form, and give character at little cost.* The plan of the nave and aisles is a square, and the chancel is a double square.

At Howell Church, Lincolnshire, the west wall, to the extent required for a similar double belfry, is made to project slightly ; and in Manton Church, Rutlandshire, with the same double belfry, one gable encloses the two openings, as it does also at Howell Church, and there is a buttress runs down the *centre* of the front.

At Herne Church, Kent, an interesting example, the tower, of massive proportions, is placed at the west end of the north aisle, and was built quite distinct from the church. The lower story, open to the church by means of arches, is groined over, and is made the baptistery. Brampton Church, Northamptonshire, is remarkable for its regularity : the tower, with broach spire, is in the centre of the west end; a porch on the south side is balanced by a porch on the north.

In Temple Balsal Church, Warwickshire, an octagonal stairs' turret, which scarcely shews at the south angle of the west front, is enlarged at the eaves of the roof to a square tower. Warmington Church, Northamptonshire, a pure Early English church, shews in its beautiful broach spire three ranges of spire lights surmounted by elegant crosses.

In Fleet Church, Lincolnshire, the tower is detached, and stands on the south side. In Donnington Church, Lincolnshire, the tower is on the south side of the nave aisle : the lower part of it is made to form the south porch. In Leckhampton Church, Gloucestershire, the tower is over the western extremity of the chancel, and in Clymping Church, Sussex, it is at the southern extremity of the south transept.

We cannot attempt to note all the observations which occur on examining the plans and views here brought into juxta-position. One more, however, we cannot avoid making, and that is, the uniformity apparent in the size of the *chancel* of a large number of the examples given, however different the size of the rest of the building. Thus the length of the chancel of Trunch Church, Norfolk, is 34 feet 6 inches ; Westwick Church, Norfolk, 31 feet 10 inches ; North Mims, Herts, 32 feet 3 inches ; Floore Church, Northamptonshire, 33 feet 6 inches ; Eston Church, Northamptonshire, 35 feet 9 inches : Brampton Church, Northamptonshire, 31 feet 10 inches ; Casterton Church, Rutlandshire, 32 feet; Long Stanton Church, Cambridgeshire, 29 feet 3 inches ; Filby Church, Norfolk, 34 feet ; Martham Church, Norfolk, 34 feet ; Deopham Church, Norfolk, 32 feet 4 inches ; Morley St. Botolph's Church, Norfolk, 34 feet 6 inches ; Woolpit Church, Suffolk, 32 feet 8 inches ; Achurch Church, Northamptonshire, 32 feet; Islip Church, Northamptonshire, 30 feet 6 inches; Gransley Church, Northamptonshire, 31 feet 6 inches ; Shiere Church, Surrey, 32 feet

* A similar arrangement is found in Long Stanton Church, Cambridgeshire.

2 inches ; Barton Church, Suffolk, 34 feet, The width is, in nearly every case, half the length.

It is much to be regretted that many of the churches named are, as we happen to know, in a miserably-neglected and decaying state. It is much to be wished that the desire to uphold and restore the evidences of our forefathers' piety and our forefathers' skill, now happily apparent in many quarters, may extend to the guardians of these,—and equally so that our architects, regarding these as proofs of the boundless variety of combinations obtainable in their art, should be led to work on the *same system* as their mediæval predecessors, rather than from the *same moulds*, and be ARTISTS instead of artificers.

ARGUMENTS IN FAVOUR OF INTERNAL ECCLESIASTICAL DECORATION.

THESE arguments, it is hoped, will remove in some measure the prejudices existing in many minds against internal ecclesiastical decoration, as well as direct the attention of the members of the Protestant church to its importance.

The desire of multiplying churches and chapels is so great, that all available funds are too frequently lavished on walls and roofing—those absolute requisites to protect congregations from the weather. If decoration be at all considered, it is only with reference to their *external* architectural features, which is farther advanced in public favour than interior adornment. The question to be considered is, whether it would not strengthen the best interests of the Protestant church, and be its wisest policy, to build fewer, and render those already built worthier their consecrated purpose? Places of worship at present exhibit too much of factory-building economy ; they awaken no reverence : designed for man rather than God, his mean and selfish nature pervades them : there is no evidence of his having devoted his highest powers to the service of the Most High. They do not burst upon the view as visible prayers ascending to the Creator, but are cold, dumb, and unthankful.

All funds are exhausted either before or at the time when internal decoration ought to be considered, so that those who may be inclined to favour it, but who do not possess sufficient influence to control the funds, are obliged to acquiesce and yield the gratification of their rational desire. This fact ought to be taken into consideration in forming any estimate of the numbers really opposed to it, and while prejudice is in the ascendant, Protestant places of worship will be left mere carcases, without the soul of internal decoration. Would it not be better to neglect the exterior rather than the interior ? Interior splendour would be typical of the Christian character, which ought not to consist in mere outward show, but in the inward and spiritual grace. It may be said by some that all decoration is mere outward show ; so it is—but surely it is an outward show preferable to that of ugliness and deformity : is not all beauty a full voiced choir of praise? A lively faith, with an unsuppressed will, is irresistibly led to manifest itself in all possible directions, compelling dumb inanimate wood and stone to echo its admiration—reconciling discordant sounds and colours into harmonious love and praise.

It is not known to the writer on what ground any Christian can reasonably, or even consistently, object to painting and sculpture in the internal architectonic decoration of churches and chapels, who admits the propriety of their external decoration, or musical performance within them. It is not known why the sense of hearing should precede sight in the holy gratification, except that it obeys the law of intellectual progression, namely, that the highest sense is the last gratified. Vision has always been considered the least gross and material of the senses ; the idea of this power is extended to express Deity, as " The All-seeing"—its relative position in the human frame is typical of its superiority. If this be true, there would be no more harm in preaching several sermons to defray the expenses of altar pictures and other decorations than to obtain funds for a carved and gilt organ. Illustrations of the proverb, "straining at a gnat and swallowing a camel," are too frequent; for, besides the anomalies referred to, there are others, such as the admission of numerous monumental effigies, combinations of variegated marbles, &c., brilliant velvet cushions fringed with gold; embellishments, denied the church, liberally bestowed on prayer-books and bibles. Again, insisting on the strict adherence to the precept, "thou shalt not make to thyself any graven image," and yet permitting the representation of Moses over the altar bearing the tablets of the law which contain it—pulling down sculptured representations of the passion, setting up the royal arms or the banners and escutcheons of noblemen and gentlemen. How long will men exhibit the capriciousness of children? To push notions to their limits, a church must have some form and colour; these are conditions which cannot be banished from being; colour is peculiarly a manifestation of health and life; the church that endeavours to banish it is pale and sickly; colour will find its way into the temple even if its walls be reduced to black and white: deny these to be colours, bright hues steal in on bonnets—ribbons—silks—reduce these to grey—the rosy tints still modestly blush on the lips and cheeks of the fair Christian; banish it from hence, and it is an unmerciful and gloomy creed—a foul blotch on nature's visage—the sooner removed the better for society.

The following are the heads of arguments, addressed to churchwardens in particular and others whom it may concern. To enunciate the law of alternation, or of action and reaction, particularly as regards the affections and disaffections of society and individuals. The expediency of meeting the reaction in favour of ecclesiastical decoration, that the advantages of the persuasive influences of painting and sculpture may not accrue to those opposed to Protestantism, by yielding them the power of attracting men from the pale of its teachings. To show that form and colour are like musical sounds, mere agencies, edifying and elevating when ordered by virtue, noxious and degrading under the tyranny of vice. To suggest to those who would admit ornamentation in churches, without sanctioning the introduction of the human figure, painted or sculptured, abhorring idolatry; that if worshipping in presence of an image be idolatry, then all worship is idolatrous; and lastly, an argument on a lower basis—the importance of church decoration to the manufacturing community and general prosperity of the country.

It appears to be a universal law of nature to oscillate between extremes, and from any condition under which it has previously existed to seek its contrasting or opposing quality. The moral world of man, like the globe he inhabits, alternates between the laxity of summer and the severity of winter, dark night and bright day, storm and calm, action and repose, life and death; the same holds in regard to his physical being, which if excited exclusively in any one direction demands its complementary reaction,—fast leads to hunger, surfeit to disgust and abstinence. The artist and musician perceive the same physiological tendency to opposite states with regard to colour and sound. Society is the aggregate manifestation of man's individual nature, and is, therefore, similarly necessitated, as witnessed in its revolutions: when oppression of one kind has reached its limit, it is succeeded by one of an opposite nature—the oppressed become the avenging oppressors—examples are too familiar, even within our own times, to need any comment, save reminding the oppressor that there will inevitably be a day of retribution. Again, when the Latin church had run into excesses, it was opposed by the austere and iconoclastic extremes of the early reformers. The awe inspired by contemplating the convulsions of the earth, or of society, is somewhat abated, however, on reflecting there is consoling evidence that every successive convulsion oscillates, as it were, in an arc less than the preceding, the antagonistic reacting extremes being the bridles which ultimately guide striving nature to that mid-point, the goal of unity and harmony.

Does not this law of alternation give the clue—the perception of the necessity of the reaction which has visibly commenced with regard to church decoration? Men begin to pall of whitewashed churches and chapels, the extreme in this direction having been indulged in long enough—the good no longer exists which pricked it onward in its course—the tide is on the turn—the antagonistic feeling which urged public opinion in this direction is fast dying, men begin to reflect calmly and rationally, whether they may not have gone too far in the spirit of opposition, and whether there be not danger in abstaining,—in fasting the senses on bare walls,—the danger of denial is, that when its gates are once unlocked, the imprisoned sense at once rushes into excess; it chafes in its chains and narrow cell impatient of restraint, and when liberated, turns its freedom to abuse till it finds itself again at the extent of its tether in the opposite extreme: men ought to have learned from experience—from historic precedent, that true social and moral liberty is alone left when their chains bang loosely about them, becoming conscious of thraldom only when they forsake the "in media tutissimis ibis" of reason—

> "Austerity, severe and cold,
> Or wild excess—
> Voluptuous ease, in halls of gold,
> Not happiness:
> They true enjoyment find alone
> Who, bound between
> The torrid and the frigid zone,
> Observe the mean."

Let the Church of England and dissenters consider this law well—consider whether there be not a probability that the multitude will be attracted within the pale of those churches and chapels which offer them—

> "Storied windows richly dight,
> Casting a dim religious light;"

the splendours of painting and sculpture, or the glorious anthem vibrating in the choir—

> "There let the pealing organ blow,
> To the full voic'd choir below,
> In service high, and anthems clear,
> As may with sweetness through mine ear,
> Dissolve me into extasies,
> And bring all heaven before mine eyes."

Let Protestantism recollect that these quotations are tributes to the influences of such powers by one of its bulwarks and chief ornaments. Are not such influences a relief to the monotony of work-day life? Is not the Protestant church relinquishing advantages which might secure to it complete victory? Would it not be good policy to adopt it as a principle of allurement as well as defence? It may believe itself too strong to require such aids—but there is a danger in the supineness of fancied security. He would be but a bad general who should consider his position strong enough when opportunities present themselves to make it stronger: "watch and prepare." The beautiful in form and colour enlisted in the worship of the Creator, might allure the indifferent with soft persuasion, within reach of argument and reason, and while softening man's grosser nature, open the gates of his understanding, that sound principles may enter freely. If such means be despised, the English church may rest assured that others will continue to avail themselves of them whose doctrines it does not esteem, and the advantages to be derived from the use of such persuasives will thus be reaped by its enemies. Is it more criminal to starve the belly on Friday, than the eye, which has been famished the work-day week, on Sunday? Will not the hungry sense have a tendency to seek those who will give it food, and willingly agree as the price of its enjoyment to abjure flesh on the Friday? Theatres owe half their attractive influence to the fulsome and meretricious excitements of form and colour which vitiate taste, wanting a presiding influence to offer pure and holy beauty to the eyes of the people. The power of such excess is the greater under the denial and limited opportunities which the public have of gratifying the higher tastes; it is no wonder, therefore, that when adverse powers offer sense-excitements, they are readily embraced. This effect of denial to precipitate in opposite extremes, is of constant occurrence in society; and 'tis pity that legislators, instructors, and parents cannot foresee the inevitable consequences of many of their acts. It may be observed, that all are more susceptible of gross influences, who have been under restraint and denial: children that have been overawed and drilled into unwilling anchorites, at last break loose; the parent mourns too often the wickedness of his children, instead of his own folly; the youth from the country often falls a victim to the seductive influences of the city; the extravagance of the sailor a-shore, and the improvidence of the poor, are proverbial; princes seek retirement and relief in the employments of their subjects; the libertine and anchorite often retrace their steps.

Forms, colours, and sounds, are mere agents, not guilty in themselves. In the service of good they should contribute to its effulgent glory, that its intense light may extinguish the fascinating eyes of the serpent. They are in one shape or another the common weapons of good and evil. Both good and bad spirits may inhabit beautiful dwellings,—the angel to awaken love to good,—the devil to seduce to evil. All that is lovely on the earth has been given for our use, not abuse.

> "For nought so vile that on the earth doth live,
> But to the earth some special good doth give;
> Nor aught so good, but, strain'd from that fair use,
> Revolts from true birth stumbling on abuse."

What evil is there in the form of the lily, the tints and perfume of the rose? Poisons may lurk in their juices, but the form, colour, and perfume may be abstracted from the noxious qualities which wear them. It is with form and colour as with gold, in a moral point of view,—all its good offices are forgotten, and only its crimes remembered; it is forgotten they are but mediums, subject to conflicting powers, and that only figuratively can we qualify them as bad or good. In this sense, with regard to gold, it is good that it has ransomed the captive—it is bad that it has purchased the slave; it may be alike used by the ministrants of charity and abettors of crime. Parallels of use and abuse might be drawn with regard to form, colour, and sound.

The Reformation, in its antagonistic fanaticism, consigned all that was beautiful in the Latin church to destruction, considering it as being tainted by its connection; but pure beauty, like pure virtue, might stand unscathed, uncontaminated, even in hell. If there had been evil in the glorious tints of flowers, the broidery on Nature's robes, Nature might, as an anchorite, have been cloaked in universal grey; and what ideal then would have been framed of heaven but cold monotony? But as we ascend from one beauty of the earth to another—as we mount up to the contemplation of its full splendour—the imagination still exclaims "excelsior." It is from things terrestrial alone that men are enabled to form some feeble idea of the aspect of heaven and revelation: still to exalt our vision within the pale of our limited understanding, brings all the splendours of earth, even gold and precious stones, to frame an idea in our minds of a heavenly city. If such means are not considered derogatory in the sacred writings, why should men abjure that which has been consecrated? Let our churches and chapels then be typically adorned with the treasures and beauties of earth, that after our utmost powers have been exhausted, the imagination may still travel beyond. The Chinese believes his celestial empire transcends all others, because there is no mental liberty and progress. The American Indian is superior in imagination, and dies in the anticipation of the delights of his beautiful hunting grounds, which having found to graduate in superiority on earth, he believes will be transcended in the next world. We smile at his credulity, at his humble notion of heaven: yet the "excelsior" of mankind, in all its grades of progression, is analogous,—it is the anticipation of a more superlative enjoyment than the most elevated experienced on earth,—is more physical in its character in the first stages of civilisation, more refined and rational in its latter or advanced condition. The more the prospect of man's intellectual vision is extended, the nearer it is to heaven.

Before dismissing this part of the subject, it may be asked what sins lurk in the hues of the prism? who will impugn that which has been consecrated in the ark—the covenant with Noah? Can men rationally then banish form and colour from ecclesiastical decoration? deny themselves walls and roofs, worship under the canopy of heaven—there will be the blue expanse, the bright sun, green trees, sparkling flowers, and incense-laden winds—are these sinful? There would be no need of church-building were the climate constant; but the bright day may be overcast—the healthful storm must sweep the infection-charged gullies, and purge nature of its rank growth and excess; Protestant churches and chapels still have the leaden aspect of the storm-cloud of the Reformation upon them, but it is visibly breaking and gradually rolling in masses away—sunshine appears in golden patches—music awakens, and the bright hues sparkle in the iris.

There are very many who would go the length of admitting ornamental decoration in places of worship, but who would still object to the introduction of the human figure in either painting or sculpture, dreading the imputation of idolatry. The worship and reliance on mere idols of wood and stone can alone appertain to the lowest condition of man; should such gross ignorance prevail in any class of society in Great Britain, the sin will be imputed to those who suffer such condition to exist when even moderate education would correct it. With the educated the image can never be more than typical—it is the embodiment of the idea formed in the artist's mind by the study of Holy Writ, which he projects out of himself, that his thoughts may become objective to others. Every body has pictures on the tablet of the mind, unseen by others; the artist is able to copy his, that his thoughts may be seen. Every Christian has graven images in his mind of the Saviour—his crucifixion—his burial—of the Apostles, and various descriptive passages of the sacred writings; the unseen Saviour to whom he bows is thus typically worshipped under the form of the image existing in his mind, designed and imprinted there by revelation. Had he the power of the artist again to reflect it out of himself we cannot see what harm there would be in worshipping in presence of the copy;—he must in presence of the original in his mind. If mankind have these painted tablets within them it may be said that they require no others; but the susceptibility of the artist's mind to receive a more vivid and correct impression than other men enables him to present mankind with a higher and more beautiful type—to replace the imperfect presentiments of ordinary minds; it is, perhaps, the rude undefined image existing in the ordinary mind that deludes it into believing it worships none—its own is so faint when compared with the reality of the artist's that the artist's completely effaces it—its own is forgotten. If men reflect calmly and dispassionately, they would find that the difference between the image of St. Paul in their own minds and that presented to them by Raffaelle is really the perfection of his compared with their own.

The embodiment, then, of the sacred personages or presentiments of the historical portions of holy-writ by a talented artist presents the community of Christians with a higher interpretation, a higher realisation of Scripture than its own, and has the advantage as an adjunct of language of impressing its precepts and descriptions more forcibly on the mind by phrenotyping it in connection with form and colour. If what has been said be true, the introduction of the human figure, deified in painting or sculpture, cannot be rationally objected to; revelation informs us that man was made in the likeness of his Creator.

The masses would acquire elevated tastes by the prevalence of ecclesiastical decoration, and the feelings imbibed on the Sunday would ultimately suffuse the productions of industry, for men are insensibly moulded by the outward circumstances which surround them. While morally elevating the people, give them increased prosperity, and, to our productions in foreign markets, besides the superiority of fabric, superiority in design, and the inhabitants of Great Britain would then present to the foreigner the aspect of a higher and happier people.

W. CAVE THOMAS.

THE GAS MOVEMENT,

IN TOWN AND COUNTRY,

HAS fairly broke away from the leading strings and the fostering care of THE BUILDER, beyond whose limits in space it has at same time so rapidly risen, that all further attempts to compress its substance within the skirts and outskirts of the few short articles in which alone we could afford to clothe its hale and hearty limbs and members, now, were vain. We are but too well pleased, however, to see our broader sheeted contemporaries of the newspaper-press so willing, and anxious to adopt its cause, and we most warmly congratulate both them and it, as well as ourselves, on the promising result, although we do not mean to desert the ranks of its future defenders, in which, on the contrary, we are ready at once to enrol ourselves even as humble 'privates' amongst the great guns in newspaper warfare.

The excitement in the city on the subject of a supply of cheap and good gas has become so intense, that those who wrongly imagine they have cause to dread its issue, stigmatize it with the name of "mania;" and so extreme, on the other hand, is that most groundless dread itself, that *it* is characterised, by the very same parties, as a "panic," the reality of which, in the meantime, however groundless its cause, is but too clearly evidenced by "the continued fall in the value of their shares at the Stock Exchange," a fall which was lately acknowledged to have depreciated the metropolitan stock in gas alone 20 per cent., or to the extent of half a million of money, but for which, we have not the least hesitation in saying, the holders have themselves and their senseless 'panic' alone to blame. And these same panic stricken stags, not satisfied with dashing their own brains out, if they have any, have of late rushed into the provinces in print, by pamphlet and circular, to spread the infection amongst their own particular flock throughout the length and breadth of the land, beseeching all and sundry gas companies, shareholders, and officials, to bestir themselves in the cause, to rouse heaven and earth, or at least the House of Commons and its shareholding constituents, to destroy that 'great central' bugbear, "the Great Central Gas Consumer's Company," by smothering its Bill in the birth, else "the principle, when once established, must necessarily extend itself throughout the kingdom," and the light, they might have added, necessarily shine, in consequence, throughout every humble dwelling.

Now, that all this pitiful panic possesses no other essentiality than that of irrational and groundless absurdity, common to it with all panics, it would be very easy to show, were it at all worth *our* while, whose interests are identified with the extension and the triumph of a totally different cause,—the cause of the million. Yet having really also at heart the cause of the administrators, themselves, of this—poor man's light and heat, for kitchen and for parlour,—as we may well and truly say that gas is, or ought to be,—we shall just recall for an instant one case nearly in point, viz., that of the enforcement of reductions in price at Liverpool; and this we shall do most briefly and concisely by a short quotation from what we have already said on that subject. The metropolitan companies are now on the eve of being forced to swallow the very pill that has already done so much good to those who kicked and sprawled as lustily at Liverpool as our metropolitan friends are now engaged in doing here. "In that case, if our readers recollect, the company, after being literally *pulled down* from 45s. to 15s., 12s. 6d., 8s., and 7s., declared that it was *utterly impossible* to make gas at a lower price,—*then to* 5s., when there was another dead stop, as *it* was declared to be *a losing price*,—then down to something less than a losing price, viz., 4s. 6d. which their own 'chief clerk' at length, in evidence, declared to be a very good reason why they should—raise it again? by no means, but —reduce it even to 3s. 6d.! And, in truth, the *ruinous, losing*, and *impossible* prices actually realised the highest dividends allowed by their Acts, viz., 10 per cent., which were shortly afterwards announced! and that, too, in the face of a constant rise in the price of coal!!" And now we may add, the expiry of another year, and even in the midst of a general depression in trade, has only confirmed the flourishing state of things brought about by the exercise of a little gentle compulsion on the part of the Liverpool gas consumers, in the administration of a pill—offensive, it may have been, as assafœtida, in prospect and administration, yet assuredly, wholesome as household bread in operation and effect.

But have we not proved, in short, to satiety, from their own returns to Parliament, that reductions in price, to an indefinite extent, have ever been attended with an equivalent increase in profit as in consumpt, and that there is not the slightest reason to think that the minimum of price, or any thing like it, has ever, as yet, been any where reached? At Liverpool itself, the price of coal has been much about the same with what it doubtless has cost the metropolitan companies. Indeed, at one of the late city meetings, as reported by a contemporary, it was declared by Mr. Pontifex, that "one ton of coals, which he could get for 12s. (a less price by several shillings than that at Liverpool when 4s. 6d. became the highly profitable charge for gas there per 1,000 cubic feet), would produce from 9,000 to 10,000 cubic feet of gas, consequently his gas cost but 1s. 2½d. per 1,000 feet, the coke and residuum paying the cost of manufacture. If proper economy were used, 1s. 6d. per 1,000 feet would afford sufficient profit when the supply was large. He was supplying the Great Western Railway Company at Swindon at 1s. 8d. per 1,000, and certainly did not lose by it." Besides, even from the statement of Mr. Lowe, engineer to the Metropolitan "Chartered Gas Company," not only is the residual matter "of so much more value in London than in Liverpool, that gas can be manufactured 5d. per 1,000 cheaper in the former place from that source alone, as the larger the quantity of gas made the cheaper the production;" but moreover, "when the quality of the Liverpool gas is tested by the quality of that burnt in other large towns and the price paid for the two, the former being 4s. 6d. per 1,000 cubic feet, and the latter 7s. per 1,000 cubic feet (as it then was in the metropolis itself)—the reference being had to quality alone,—the other—the Liverpool gas—would be relatively worth 14s. per 1,000 cubic feet." What *are* we to think of the present restive resistance and protestations of the metropolitan companies then, by comparison with past experience at Liverpool? The former are not only engaged in a repetition of the groundless panic and outcry of the latter as to "losing prices," "ruinous losses," &c. &c., but they are losing all the little remnant of discretion which their past, though perfectly cognizant silence, under the infliction of our own hard knocks with stubborn facts, appeared to indicate. Desperation and the 'panic' aforesaid have at length betrayed them into publication, or into a permission of publication, in their defence, and by their own dependants, of some very formidable-looking and would-be-proof-positively-statistical, but only too-clearly demolishable, pamphleteering and other statements, such as those to which we have before given all the notice that they merited; and we only now recur to them to prove, by a single instance, and by internal evidence of their own showing, and altogether apart from that overwhelming evidence which we have already adduced from time to time in THE BUILDER,—how truly preposterous and suicidal are their endeavours to bolster up a bad cause, and to occupy a false and untenable position. The instance in question occurs in a recent pamphlet, in the form of a Letter to Lord Carlisle, by a Civil Engineer; and is repeated essentially, though in a more curt and manageable form, in a letter signed Thomas G. Barlow, addressed, together with the pamphlet in question, to the editor of the *Morning Advertiser*,—an able defender of the good cause. In that letter, the statistical details of the pamphleteer are thus essentially put:—One ton of coals, at 17s., yields 9,250 cubic feet of gas, which give 2*l.* 0s. 10d. at an average price of 4s. 5d. (arising from the iniquitous and unjustifiable overcharge of 2s. 2d. beyond what the city street lamps are lighted at, namely, 3s. 10d., or 2d. less than the sum which the citizens in general are willing to give for their own supply). To this 2*l.* 0s. 10d., add for coke, tar, breeze, &c., 8s. 10d., and the whole proceed of the ton of coals is 2*l.* 9s. 8d. Now, over and above the exagge-

HINTS FOR STREET ARCHITECTURE.

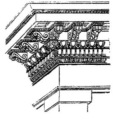

CORNICE, OR CORNICIONE, OF THE COLONNA PALACE, AT ROME.

CORNICE OF A HOUSE IN ROME.

CORNICE OF THE PALAZZO BORGHESE, ROME.

---

rated wholesale price of the coal itself, namely, 17s., a sum of no less than 1l. 0s. 8d. is added to the expense on *every ton of coal*, for wages or salaries, loss, repairs, and other incidental items of outlay; and that, too, altogether exclusive of interest on capital or expense of works and pipes no less than of cost of coal itself. In other words, it is alleged that for every ton of coals converted into gas, a City Company has to expend 1l. 0s. 8d. for mere wages, loss, repairs, and other incidental charges. It is to this sum of 1l. 0s. 8d. that we mean to restrict our present remarks. In the same pamphlet we are told, that in the metropolis "the quantity of gas made and distributed, or lost by leakage, in the year 1848, was 3,200,000,000 cubic feet,"—to produce which, it informs us, 350,000 tons of coal were used. Now, 350,000 tons of coal, at 1l. 0s. 8d. a ton, amounts to about 361,666l. —a sum which we are to believe that the metropolitan gas companies pay every year for mere salaries, repairs, and other incidental charges! If such really be the case, we can only say that it affords one of the strongest arguments that can possibly be urged in favour of a thorough reform in the administration and supply of this public and poor man's invaluable property—gas-light.

As to the general progress of the gas movement, both in town and country, we had much more to say, but our limits impel us to reserve it till further opportunity; meantime we have only room to remark, that while the metropolitan companies, or their representatives or defenders, are renewing the delusive estimates of apparently moderate profit or percentage on their capital, estimates founded, as we have already showed, not on the capital actually laid out in necessary works, but on the whole of the enormous amounts authorised by their respective Acts of Parliament;* and while they are refusing, on many repeatedly disproved and delusive grounds, to reduce their present charges, we observe that one of them, the Phœnix, is at present offering to supply gas at Bedford for 5s. per 1,000 cubic feet, on a small and comparative expensive scale, and with coal there at 17s. 6d. a ton; and that the same company has already erected works at the Stratford station of the Eastern Counties, and contracted to supply the same article there, on a probably still smaller scale, for fourteen years, at a price beginning with 5s., to be afterwards reduced to 4s. and 3s. 6d., although unquestionably coal will there also cost considerably more than the same company can have it for in the metropolis, where the price of gas on an immensely larger scale cannot be reduced below 6s. without a "ruinous loss!"

* And exclusive of all allusion, of course, to the important but secret system of bonuses, which we have occasionally exposed, so as to show that It averaged at least 30 per cent. of the dividend itself. Mr. Barham, of the Great Central Gas Consumers' Company, recently speaks of one of the two city companies, "whose 80l. shares have for years, before the recent panic in shares, been quoted at 200l., and which pays 10l. per share, besides a frequent bonus, which, it was offered to be proved in a court of justice, renders the annual profit of the 80l. shares equal to 16l." Were we inclined we could also say something more about bonuses from our own private knowledge, but that is unnecessary.

HINTS FOR STREET ARCHITECTURE.

CORNICE, OR CORNICIONE, OF THE COLONNA PALACE, AT ROME.

The exterior of this palace has little to attract attention, though the details are all very handsome. In the interior the noble picture gallery is perhaps unrivalled for the beauty and splendour of its proportions and decorations.

CORNICE OF A HOUSE IN ROME.

This design has been attributed to Raphael Sanzio, but it is not at all similar to his other works, which have all a marked character, and are easily to be distinguished.

CORNICE OF THE PALAZZO BORGHESE, ROME.

This enormous palace was commenced in 1590, by Cardinal Borghese, and was finished by Paul Vth about the year 1615. The first architect was Martino Longhi, and it was completed by Flaminio Ponzio.

BLINDS TO SHOPS WITHIN LIMITS OF BUILDINGS ACT.

WITH regard to a house in the Quadrant, Regent-street, in the district of St. James, Westminster, Mr. Pitt, a blind-maker, was about to fix on the top of the shop front a blind-box, framed of wood, which was to extend in a line with the shop front, and to the same extent at one end, and which shop front continued over the whole thickness of the party wall, or nearly. The district surveyor objecting, the parties required the official referees to determine the following questions, viz.:—

1st. Whether the said blind-box, which they consider only a tenant's shop fixture, would form a part of the shop front, it being intended to fix the same on the lead-flat over the said front, without altering the same, with iron brackets screwed thereto?

2nd. Whether such blind-box would be at all subject to the rules of schedule E. of the said Act first above mentioned?

And 3rd. Whether if the entablature of a shop front be merely altered for the reception of a blind-box within it, it would require such entablature to be wholly made in conformity with the said schedule, by keeping all woodwork the required distance from the centre of the party wall, or stopping it with a pier or corbel of incombustible material?

The referees awarded,—"1st. That the said blind-box, if fixed on the lead flat over the said shop front, will form a part of the said shop front. 2nd. That the said blind-box will be subject to the rules of schedule E. of the said Act first above mentioned. And 3rd. That if the wooden entablature of the said shop front be altered for the reception of a blind-box within it, such entablature must be wholly made in conformity with the rules of the said Act, and such blind-box, entablature, and every other part of such shop front, must not be fixed nearer than 4½ inches to the centre line of any party wall or party walls; and if it be fixed at such distance of 4½ inches, then a pier or corbel, butt of stone or of brick or other incombustible material, and of the width of 4½ inches at the least, must be fixed in the line of the party wall, so as to be high as the woodwork, and so as to project one inch at the least in front of the face thereof."

THE BRITTON TESTIMONIAL AND CLUB.

MANY of our readers are interested in the testimonial to Mr. Britton, and will be glad to learn what progress has been made in it. The "Club" which grew out of it had their first dinner (given by Mr. N. Gould, F.S.A.) on Tuesday last, and on the health of Mr. Britton being drunk, one of his friends read a short reply that he had written, being not sufficiently well to speak. We give the following portion of it, as affording the information desired :—

"On the 22nd of August, 1846, nearly a hundred of my kind and partial friends invited me to a public dinner at Richmond, as a compliment for my archæological and literary labours, promoting at the same time a general subscription, as a TESTIMONIAL of those exertions. Some of these friends knew that my gains in the literary market were never great, and that the profits on book-making, or authorship, are rarely commensurate with its toils and anxieties; for the phrase "a poor author" is proverbial. At the same time I must endeavour to disabuse your minds of a popular prejudice, by assuring you that any professional author, whether man or woman, possessing but a fair proportion of talent, industry, and prudence, may obtain a respectable income by a judicious exercise of the pen. The little I have acquired has arisen from other sources than writing and publication; and, although not *rich*, I am happy to acknowledge that I have saved enough to secure the comforts and some of the luxuries of life. Amongst the latter I include the cordial companionship and confidence of friends, whose talents, tastes, and characters render them valuable members of society at large, and examples to their families and associates. From an intercourse with such individuals I have derived much happiness; and as long as life may be granted to me I hope to deserve and enjoy their unreserved friendship and cordial sympathy. I have not yet mentioned the "unprecedented circumstance" belonging to this club, and the testimonial to which I have awarded. Sums of money, pieces of plate, and other honorary rewards have been often awarded to heroes, statesmen, and the officers of great public companies. In my own case the subscription already referred to commenced in the warm hearts of a few esteemed and estimable friends, who know the extent of my literary works, and the industry devoted to their production, together with the comparatively humble station in which I was contented to live. They enlisted their immediate friends in the cause, and the amount connected has far exceeded my most sanguine anticipations,—for there has been no public appeal, through the medium of the newspaper press. The total will be at least 800l.,—the whole of which will be expended in the preparation of an illustrated volume, which I am writing and preparing for publication, and which I trust, according to the market price of such articles, will be at least of equal value to the amount subscribed by each individual. Hence there will be a reciprocity of obligation between the giver and the receiver. By this engagement I have entailed upon myself an amount of personal and mental labour, which I little anticipated when I pledged myself to the task. If, however, life and health be granted me for a few months more, I hope and expect to see a volume completed, which will neither reflect discredit on the head nor heart of the author, nor impeach the taste or generosity of those kind friends, on whose account, and for whose gratification, it has been written."

Captain Smyth, director of S. A., in replying for the Astronomical Society, pointed to Mr. Britton as the founder and first secretary of the Geographical Society. Mr. W. Tooke, F.R.S., replied for the Royal Society; Mr. James Walker for the Institution of Civil Engineers; Mr. W. Cubitt, M.P., for the Building Interests, and Mr. Cunard in connection with Steam Navigation. Mr. Burgess, Mr. Cunningham, Mr. Ex-Sheriff Hill, Dr. Ure, Mr. Wansey, F.S.A., and others were also present.

THE WOODEN ROOFS OF OLD ENGLAND.

At a recent meeting of the Hereford Archæological Society, after other communications (reported at length in the local papers), Mr. Beloe read some remarks on wooden roofs.

Mr. Beloe observed that the timber roofs of the ancient regal and baronial halls merited in an eminent degree the attention of all to whom the science of construction is an object of interest, although he was unable to enter into it, then, at the length which its importance demanded. He could then only furnish a few observations, which might prove not uninteresting. He remarked that the artificers of the early Saxons appeared to have been, for the most part, either monks or slaves. They were in fact nothing more than mere necessity made them; and they lived and died poor, unhonoured, and unimproved. Mr. Sharon Turner, the historian, had remarked that "the habits of life were too uniform, its luxuries too few, its property too small, its wants too numerous, and the spirit of the great mass too servile and dull, to have that collection of ingenious, respected, and inventive men, who make and circulate our internal and external commerce, with eager but not illiberal competition, or to have those accomplished artificers and manufacturers, whose taste in execution equals the most elegant fancy of its invention." Mr. Beloe went on to remark that the Anglo-Saxon carpenter was considered as part of what we are accustomed to call the *plant* of an estate, transferable with the land. He was called the *Treow-wyrta* (tree or wood workman), and the Anglo-Saxon verb used in speaking of building is *getymbrian* (to make of wood). It was well known that churches were at times constructed of wood, one of them —Greensted, Essex—still remaining.

The Norman period was touched upon by the lecturer, who observed that it was marked by the introduction of more durable materials, which were used for several centuries before the construction of any wooden roof. This art the Norman architects practised with such admirable skill and effect, that their works have not unfrequently been considered beyond the pale of *modern* imitation. After alluding to various instances of this style, the lecturer passed to the Semi-Norman (1154 to 1189), which he remarked possessed all the characteristics of the Norman, combined with the pointed arch. Castle Acre Priory was selected as an example. The Early English or Lancet (1189 to 1272) was next explained, the illustration being a door-way at Paul's Cray, Kent, and the lecturer referred to the beautiful windows of this style in our cathedral, as well as at York, Salisbury, &c.

The lecturer then proceeded to explain the form and idea of the open-timbered roof, remarking that the upright strut or queen-post, which rises from the extremity of the hammer-beam, in most of these roofs, suggested the idea of a pillar being cut away at that point. The whole roof, therefore, reminded one of two rows of pillars, dividing the area into three aisles. He observed that the palace of the Bishop of Hereford, and Westminster Hall, as originally built by William Rufus, were built on this plan, which indeed seemed to be the usual mode of constructing halls of large dimensions previous to the fourteenth century, when an improved manner of constructing arched roofs of timber superseded the necessity of columns.

The Decorated period, including the greater part of the fourteenth century, was next referred to. After explaining the architectural characteristics of the style, the lecturer remarked at length upon the timber roofs of Nursted Court, Kent; Balsall Temple, Wor-

cestershire; Coventry School; Croydon Palace, &c. The roof of Crosby Hall, and other buildings, though erected in that period, was perfectly distinct in principle from those yet considered, being based on the property of the triangle to resist racking or change of form.

He then passed on to consider the Perpendicular style (1377 to 1485), illustrating the architecture from a sketch of a doorway in St. Mary's, Beverley, and explaining its characteristics. In considering the timber roofs of the period, he gave a detailed description of that of Westminster Hall. That edifice was rebuilt by Richard II., almost from the foundation; he said *almost*, because Mr. Pugin says that some of the lower portions of the side walls are the original works of the time of William Rufus. As it now stands, the span of the roof is nearly double the ordinary width of Gothic groined roofs, which seldom exceeded 35 feet. Numerous obstacles to the erection of a stone roof in that case must have presented themselves, and the builder was thrown upon the resources of his art. The result was a novel as well as elegant application of that great element of lightness and beauty in the arch. The former ponderous and friable material was exchanged for one equally susceptible, and greatly superior in both tenacity and tractability. The lecturer went on to refer to the roof of Romsey Abbey Church, and that of Eltham Palace. The nearest example to the latter in this locality was the roof of St. Martin's Church, in this city; but the idea was not carried out to its fullest extent of beauty, some parts being plastered over. The lecturer then referred to the Guard-room, Lambeth Palace.

At that period, he remarked, ceilings were valued ornaments of palaces. They usually contained representations of memorable actions, but our azure church ceiling with stars occurs in ancient crypts; in other cases the ceiling in black, with painted and gilt lattice-work, and grotesque heads, &c.; and others were of wood, painted or plastered in panels. After explaining the construction of the roof of King's College Chapel, Cambridge, the lecturer went on to allude to the interesting specimen of the roof of the cloisters of Hereford Cathedral, at the same time expressing his acknowledgments to the Very Rev. the Dean, for having drawn his attention to that roof, and to the President, for a specimen of carving. In speaking of the Tudor period, the lecturer referred at some length to Wolsey's Hall, Hampton Court, perhaps the most elaborate specimen extant of the style. As a scientific construction, it was much inferior to the roof of Westminster Hall, although it displayed much ingenuity. Reference was then made to Westminster School, the Middle Temple Hall, and other excellent specimens of the period.

The lecturer proceeded to glance briefly at the general heaviness [and inelegance of the Debased style (1547 to 1640). The illustration was from St. Peter's-in-the-East Church, Oxford. An interesting roof of this period exists in the chapel on the estate of Mr. C. T. Bodenham, of Rotherwas.

He concluded by dividing Gothic roofs into four classes:—first, those of simple arched ribs; second, those which have a grand arch spanning the entire width; third, those that have the arch supported on brackets; fourth, such as are formed of two intersecting triangular frames, in which the lateral pressure is counteracted by the longitudinal stress upon the connecting beams. After that period it became very difficult to trace the principle of the style at all.

BEDFORD ARCHITECTURAL SOCIETY.—At a committee meeting held on Monday, the 26th ult., Sir H. Dryden, Bart., in the chair, a grant of 4l. was made to be placed in Mr. Hartshorne's hands, for the purpose of securing plans to be made of an ancient barn, near Peterborough, called the Saxon barn, which is about to be pulled down for some railway works. A donation of 1l. 1s. was made towards the spire of St. Edmund's, in memorial of the late treasurer of the society, Mr. Percival.

THE THAMES TUNNEL.—It is said that the number of passengers who passed through the tunnel in the week ending March 31, was 43,761. Amount of money received, 182l. 6s. 9d.

It says something for our own and other efforts to set before the public the merits of some of the scene-painters of the day, when we find the much greater attention to the scenery of our theatres which is now paid by the periodical press generally, than was the case not long ago. The Easter spectacles produced at the various houses have given opportunities to the artists, which they have not failed to take advantage of in a greater or less degree. We shall glance at them as we have heretofore done, when an opportunity occurs, to glean any point that may interest our readers, but at this moment confine ourselves to a few words on the piece at the *Lyceum*, "The Seven Champions of Christendom," written by that arch-magician, J. R. Planché, to whom the public have reason to be grateful for realising, though temporarily, many bright dreams, and pleasant myths, without taint of immorality or coarseness.

Mr. Planché has the talent of seizing on the things of the day, and while turning them to use, shews their absurdity. He must rank amongst the opponents of "sham" in architecture, for in the new piece, Mr. Charles Mathews sings (in the way that is his own),—

" O such a town, such a wonderful metropolis,
With mysteries and miracles all London teems;
Humbug has there got the snuggest of thoroughfares,
Every thing is any thing, but what it *seems*,
You sleep upon an iron bed, and fancy it a feather one,
You think your ceiling's carved in oak—why, bless you, its a leather one;
Your marble mantle-piece turns out of slate, if you're a scrubber, Sir,
And paving stones are made of wood, or else of india rubber, Sir."

He touches very cleverly the love of Latin and Greek names,—

" Here is a Pantechnicon, and there is an Emporium,
Your shoes are ' antigropelos,' your boots of ' pan-nus-corium ;'
' Fumi-porte chimney-pots,' ' Eureka shirts ' to cover throats,
' Idrotobolic hats,' and ' patent aqua-scutem ' over coats."

And then gives an immense amount of information on art, & reference to the weak state of our School of Design, and the improper manner in which the Vernon collection has been treated, all in the space of eight lines :—

" O such a town, such a picturesque metropolis,
Taste is polychromical for painting wild ;
Frescoes for peers, and Art-unions for the populace,
Schools where young designers learn to draw it mild.
Dioramas, Cosmoramas, Cycloramas, charming ones,
Missisippi panoramas, four miles long—alarming ones!
A national collection, where they never ask a fee at all,
Besides the Vernon Gallery, a sight no one can see at all."

We must not forget the scenery. Mr. Beverley has quite maintained the character we have before this given him. " The Fairy Lake and Grotto of the Swans " is a beautiful piece of imaginative rock work; the " Ruins in the Valley of the Nile," is a morsel of David Roberts,' magnified (which might have been made a little more of), and as to the " Camp of the Champions," the last scene, we are quite willing to adopt the lines of the epilogue—

—— " Own it is a joyous decoration,
And be kind enough to say, in our usual good-natured way,
That the scenery by Mr. Beverley,
Has been painted very cleverly."

ROMAN REMAINS FOUND NEAR COLCHESTER.—On ground belonging to Mr. J. Taylor, of West Lodge, about 250 funeral vessels, and a great variety of other remains, have been found in such circumstances as lead to the supposition that there are at least twelve times as many urns in the same ground still unexhumed. Mr. R. Smith and some other members of the Archæological Association have been at Colchester inspecting these remains.

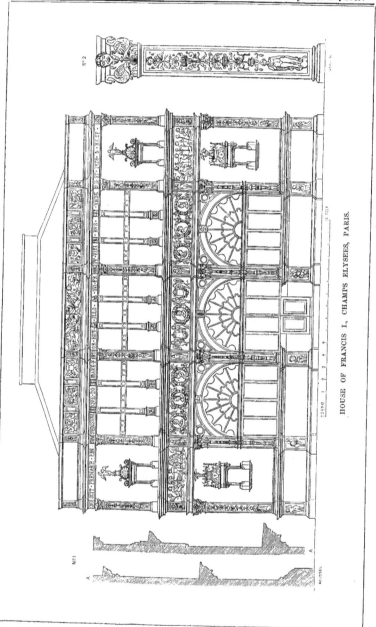

HOUSE OF FRANCIS I, CHAMPS ELYSEES, PARIS.

DETAILS: HOUSE OF FRANCIS I., CHAMPS ELYSEES, PARIS.

HOUSE OF FRANCIS I., CHAMPS ELYSEES, PARIS.

This house, formerly under the name of "Maison du Tonnelier," was, according to tradition, built at Moret, by Francis I. The little town of Moret, of very ancient origin, is situated two leagues from Fontainbleau. As forests bound it on all sides, Francis I. had an idea of establishing there a meeting place for hunting; and he caused the elegant edifice, which our drawings illustrate, to be erected. Its interior clearly shows for what object it was constructed. The three great arches which decorate the front occupy nearly the whole space of the ground-floor.

This house being sold in 1826 by the Government, it was bought by a lover of the arts, who caused it to be transferred, stone by stone, to Paris, where, in the *Champs Elysées*, the house of Moret was rebuilt, uninjured, with its own debris. The sculpture is attributed to Jean Goujon.

A section of the cornices, strings, &c., on the front wall is given, and some of the details to a larger scale. The date 1828, in the frieze, refers to the installation of the rebuilt structure. This house is an excellent example of the Renaissance period in France.

BEAUTY IN TOWNS AND VILLAGES.

The following extracts from Mrs. Tuthill's American "History of Architecture," reviewed by us some time since, are interesting as affording evidence of the growth of a right feeling in America, in respect of *beauty*, and, moreover, may have their use in England:—

"The public squares of Philadelphia are incalculably important to the health of the city. Beneath the dense foliage of Washington-square, crowds of merry children enjoy, unmolested, their healthful sports. Within the enclosure of Independence-square, was first promulgated the Declaration of Independence. Franklin-square has in the centre a fountain, falling into a handsome white marble basin. Penn, Logan, and Rittenhouse-squares are also ornamental to the city.

The New-Haven-green has been justly celebrated as one of the most beautiful public squares in this country. Its elms are remarkably fine; it has recently been enclosed with a light and tasteful iron-railing, which adds much to its beauty.

Many of our large cities are entirely destitute of such green retreats. Gardens and squares are so necessary to the health, as well as the enjoyment of those who are shut up in the close streets of a city, that it should be considered an imperative duty to provide them for all classes of the inhabitants. It may be urged, that if left open and free, the decorations would soon be destroyed by the populace; some few rude hands might occasionally make sad havoc among them, but when the people have once learnt how much such places of resort contributed to their health and pleasure, they would carefully protect them from injury.

'The beauty of the edifices constitutes the principal beauty of the streets, squares, and city in general. And who should preside over this department? Every city should have its Academy of Architecture, without whose approbation nothing should be erected.' (The independence of American taste would not submit to such dictation.) 'The height of the houses should never be more than three stories, their façades regular and well proportioned, all equally simple, but differing in their style and ornament. Uniformity should be admitted in the squares only.'

The public edifices should be so placed as to suit public convenience. The university, colleges, and high schools, should stand upon commanding situations, with squares and courts about them, planted with trees and ornamental shrubbery, excluding as much as possible the noise and dust of the city. A correct taste would thus be early implanted in the minds of the young, and a love of the beautiful 'grow with their growth and strengthen with their strength.' Banks, exchanges, and custom-houses should be built where 'men most do congregate;' and have the expression of richness and durability.

Markets, with abundant space about them, should be as near the suburbs as convenience permits, and should stand at the termination of some of the principal streets. The Boston market-house is finely situated, and is a beautiful building.

Hospitals, manufactories, and magazines, should be without the city, in open elevated places, where they can enjoy a free, fine atmosphere. Cemeteries should be laid out with taste; planted with suitable trees and evergreens, and kept with scrupulous neatness. Architecture ought to be displayed with the greatest sublimity in churches, which neither on the exterior nor within should have anything mean or inelegant. They should stand upon an open square, or at the termination of a street presenting the whole façade to close the vista.

Villages.—Bad judgment and bad taste have prevailed in the laying out of many of the villages in the United States. The New England villages have been much admired for their neatness and beauty. An observing and venerated author,* whom we have once or twice quoted, thus contrasts the villages, or towns, in the Connecticut Valley with those on the Hudson River:—'They are not, like those

* President Dwight.

along the Hudson, mere collections of houses and stores, clustered round a landing, where nothing but mercantile and mechanical business is done, where the inhabitants form no connections nor habits beside those which naturally grow out of bargains and sales; where the position of the store determines that of the house, and that of the wharf often commands both; where beauty of situation is disregarded, and every convenience, except that of trade, is forgotten. On the contrary, they are villages destined for the reception of men busied in all the employments existing in this country. The settling in them is not merely to acquire property, but to sustain the relations, perform the duties, and contribute to the enjoyments of life. Equally, and, to my eye, happily, do they differ from most European villages. The villages on the other side of the Atlantic are exhibited as being generally clusters of houses, standing contiguously on the street, built commonly of rough stone, clay, or earth, and roofed with thatch, without court-yards or inclosures, and of course incapable of admitting around each house the beautiful appendages of shrubs, trees, gardens, and meadows.

New England villages, and, in a peculiar degree, those of the Connecticut Valley, are built in the following manner.

'The local situation is pitched on, as a place in itself desirable; as a place, not where trade compels, but where happiness invites to settle. Accordingly, the position of these towns is usually beautiful.' One wide street, planted with trees, generally passes through the whole length of the village. 'The town plot is originally distributed into lots, containing from *two to ten acres* (not twenty feet by fifty!) In a convenient spot, on each side of these, a house is erected at the bottom of the court-yard, often neatly enclosed, and is furnished universally with a barn and other convenient outbuildings. Near the house there is always a garden, replenished with culinary vegetables, flowers, and fruits, and very often also, prettily enclosed. The lot on which the house stands, universally styled the home-lot, is almost, of course, a meadow, richly cultivated, and containing generally a thrifty orchard. It is hardly necessary to observe, that these appendages spread a singular cheerfulness and beauty over a New England village, or that they contribute largely to render the house a delightful residence.'

These villages have been the models of many in the western part of New York, and still farther west. The buildings in some of these villages, especially in the State of New York, are superior to those of New England. Who has not admired the beautiful location of Canandaigua, Geneva, and Skaneateles, upon their lovely lakes? The refined taste exhibited in their style of building, too, has excited the surprise and pleasure of travellers. We have been accused of a want of patriotic and generous feelings as a nation; of possessing strong individuality of feeling and interest, amounting to absolute, controlling selfishness. This accusation may, or may not be true; it is perhaps as difficult for us to know ourselves as a nation, as the wise Milesian considered it for each one to be acquainted with himself. It is certain that we have too few objects of common interest. Every state, county, and even village, is divided into innumerable jarring and contending parties and sects. Though a prosperous, we are not a cheerful people. Anything that would contribute to unite public feeling, by bringing men to act together for the general good, would be a great benefit to a community. Suppose it to be a public garden and promenade, open and free to all. Every villager contributes according to his means to this object. Some suitable persons are chosen to lay out the grounds, others to keep them in order. It belongs to the village, it must be beautiful, for the good of the village. It is a common object of thought, feeling, and action. The moral influence of it will soon be felt. The man, instead of going to the tavern for the news, may walk out at the sweet hour of summer twilight, and beneath spreading trees enjoy the society of his neighbours, and at the same time have his children under his eye.

If this public garden or promenade were richly and tastefully arranged and ornamented, a desire for neat and pleasant dwelling-houses would naturally arise among the villagers. Lord Kames, in his 'Elements of Criticism,' remarks, that, 'In Scotland, the regularity and polish even of a turnpike-road has some influence of this kind upon the people in the neighbourhood. They become fond of regularity and neatness; which is displayed first upon their yards and little enclosures, and next within doors. A taste for regularity and neatness thus acquired, is extended by degrees to dress, and even to behaviour and manners.' Two little girls from a city had one day taken a long walk beyond the city, upon a public road. A sudden shower of rain threatened to drench them to the skin. Several houses upon the road offered themselves as places of shelter; the youngest girl proposed to enter the nearest one. 'No,' said the elder, 'we will not go in here, nor into the next, but yonder is a neat, pretty cottage, with flowers in the front yard; I know they will be kind there.' 'But this is the biggest house,' urged the younger sister. 'Oh! but I am afraid to go in here, it looks so dirty and careless; hurry, hurry, sister! for I know they will treat us well where they take so much pains with their neat house and garden.' And the girl's reasoning was correct. There was gentleness and kindness within, as well as neatness and taste without.

Would it not be well if some of our statesmen would condescend to pay more attention to this subject? How often might they become public benefactors, at a small expense of time and money, if they were men of cultivated taste and generous public spirit! Those beautiful avenues of elms in the city of New Haven, are they not graceful, magnificent monuments to the memory of the noble statesman who placed them there? Who can estimate the influence that his tasteful benevolence has exerted upon the community to which he was so great a benefactor?

On a review of this subject, it may be urged, that we are a business people, an industrious people; we have no time to devote to amusements; besides, we are a serious people, and such objects as are here proposed, are not in unison with our habits and feelings. Our cities must grow up and increase as they have done hitherto, without the fostering hand of taste; we are young, and not yet prepared for such improvements, if indeed they are improvements. With due deference to those who differ, and with becoming modesty, we must still urge that the purity of morals, the simplicity and sobriety of the citizens of the United States, would not be endangered by suitable attention to the cultivation of a taste for architecture, and the beautifying of cities and villages. It is as easy to plan a city, a village, or a building, in good taste, as in bad taste, and as cheap too, since that is an all-important consideration. Simplicity of style in architecture is in itself a beauty. A Doric temple is perfectly simple, yet what object of art is more imposing and beautiful? We have wealth enough, if we have only taste to use it, to render our country as superior in artificial, as it is in natural beauty, to almost any country in the wide world. When Athens was at the height of her glory and splendour, she had not one quarter of the population or the wealth that the State of New York now possesses. And New York is arousing herself like a giantess, and soon, we trust, will exhibit to the world buildings which, for, 'nobleness of design, vastness and grandeur of conception, proportion and harmony of parts,' shall rival the decaying glories of republican Athens.

But this is not what we would mainly urge. There may, and ought to be, taste, and even elegance, where there is but little wealth. Every town and village may appear beautiful, if proper attention be paid to the houses and grounds. A rustic farm-house may be convenient and picturesque. A turnpike gate, now a most unsightly object, might be made even ornamental. If we are not yet prepared for these things, we ought to be. Professing ourselves free, liberal, enlightened, refined, without any perception of beauty!

'Beauty was sent from Heaven,
The lovely ministress of truth and good,
In this dark world; for truth and good are one,
And Beauty dwells in them, and they in her,
With like participation. Wherefore then,
O sons of earth! would ye dissolve the tie?'"

THE BURIAL GROUND QUESTION.

SIR JAMES MURRAY, the physician, of Dublin, in a letter to a friend on this subject, says, "I remember during many years when I resided in Belfast, there was an extensive graveyard along the east side of Church-lane, from one end to the other of that narrow street. The back windows of all the houses opened into that damp Golgotha, so low as to be on a level with the neighbouring docks and quays. I well recollect that scarcely a house on the cemetery side of the lane was ever free from some kind of low sickness, or its consequences, whilst the south side was comparatively exempt from disease.

At length, burial was prevented in that ground, and a handsome church was erected on it. I understand the adjoining families are now as healthy as any in that vicinity. You are aware, that during thirty years I have been making experiments upon the insalubrious effects of localities where damp, variations of temperature, and decomposing bodies form what I call vast galvanic troughs. Fens and marshes, low and filthy streets, crowded lanes and moist situations, are all batteries, emitting disturbed galvanic emanations around. But if you insert deep wires into festering graveyards, and bring them into electrical contact, you will find that there is no battery whose communications are so lethal, as the break of galvanic equilibrium inflated by the vast and continued decomposition evolving in burial-places."

As Lord Dudley Stewart said, at the public meeting mentioned by us last week :— We are proud of our riches, of our talents, of our civilisation, and of our progress in commerce and in all the arts and sciences, and we should be offended if any person presumed to say that this country was not the most moral and most religious in the world, and yet, gracious Heaven! we suffer such things to be in the midst of this great metropolis. But when I mention to you the shocking state of things to which I have alluded, and which is of a nature to harrow up your feelings, and, as I must think, to blunt the sensibilities, and make men careless of the respect to the dead, and also irreligious,—when I mention these things I have not told you all, for a very great deal remains behind. If burials amidst crowded cities are injurious to the morals, they are also fraught with deadly poison to the public health. No subject has engaged the attention of the public or of the Legislature of late years to a greater extent than that of the public health. Sanitary measures have engrossed much of the attention of Parliament, and have occupied the minds of men throughout the country; writings have been poured forth from the press on the subject; meetings have been held again and again, and information to a great extent has been supplied, with the hope of improving the health of the public,—but it may be said that all these endeavours will be in vain, as far as regards the health of towns, as long as the system of burying in the heart of towns is permitted. You say, let us have good sewerage, let us have good ventilation, let us have fresh air and a good supply of fresh water; and I say so too. I know nothing more important; but, alas! it is in vain to have improved sewers, good supplies of water, and fresh air; it is in vain to make the attempt which has been made, and will be renewed, to give poor people an unstinted supply of light by the repeal of the window-tax, if with these advantages we do not also succeed in rooting out and drawing away all interments from the heart of the metropolis. For what would be the use of breaking open the small cramped-up windows of the poor to let in light and air, if that air brought in with it poison? Men say give us air—aye, but give us fresh air —don't give us polluted air, charged with miasma and poison from reeking bodies in a state of putrefaction, which are heaped up at our very doors.

Mr. Walker, in the course of his speech, observed,—The other day I saw a gentleman just returned from Constantinople, who told me that the plague invariably broke out in Turkey in the neighbourhood of burial-grounds. Madden, in his travels in Palestine, says that plague miasma originates in the putrefaction of animal matter; and decidedly

the best authority who has ever written on this subject, M. Pariset, whose name is well known, and possesses a European reputation, says, that with pure air and water, with healthy food in moderate proportions, none of the singular mutations, productive of death in man and animals could exist. He says, as the result of his long experience and observation in the Levant, that there is only one country in the world in which the plague is permanent, and that country is Egypt. He states further, as the result of his observation, that he believes its origin is entirely due to the emanations from human and animal corpses, but especially from human bodies.

How much longer shall we refuse to listen?

DWELLINGS FOR RICH AND POOR.

UNION OF CLASSES.

THE arrangement of towns has been but too little attended to; as it must tend very considerably to alter, for better or worse, the character of the city, it should meet with more consideration. An evil is now growing around us of large districts entirely destitute of dwellings for the poor; the consequence is, they lose the advantage of the example of those of superior education; the rich, on the other hand, have not that control over their indulgences by the constant exhibition of poverty; these two classes, instead of growing up together on each other's sympathy and support, are so entirely estranged as to become dangerous to each other (this is clearly shown in the July riots in Paris, when faubourg fought against faubourg): another evil is also very pressing, viz., the poor's-rate. In the more wealthy parishes it is diminishing, while in the less fashionable quarters it is increasing to a most frightful extent.

As new communications are about to be opened in districts that are crowded with poor, who must necessarily be driven to the outskirts of London, or press more closely upon the already too densely inhabited rooms of their former haunts, this is a subject not unworthy of the architect's profession, as to how far these evils may be alleviated, and these new thoroughfares be made available for the amalgamation of the rich and the poor. The problem is this, can houses be built in leading streets which will pay better than mere houses over a shop, the present usual mode of building a new street? The plan the writer would suggest is, that a block with a frontage, say 300 feet, and 60 feet deep, should be built on the following plan :—The ground floor to consist of a shop, and over that an entresol; this portion of the building to be entirely separate, so that a tradesman should be enabled to have a good frontage without the risk of lodgers, the entresol of course forming the dwelling of the shopkeeper. In an artistic point of view this would be a gain, as the proportion of base would be better than in the more ordinary mode, and the piers would be of a more solid construction. The shop decorations would by that means become accessories to the construction, and not form part of the building. Over this might be placed four stories, to be thus arranged. The two first floors to be inhabited by small gentlemen's families or single persons, each set of chambers forming a complete small house within one door: the two next floors would be occupied by clerks, or the superior artizan. Two staircases would be sufficient for 300 feet frontage; these might be so constructed that two staircases should occupy one well, one leading to the drawing-room and first floor, the other the full height. The whole building to be fire-proof, and warmed and ventilated on the plan of public buildings, say a temperature of 55 degrees. This class of building would suit a principal thoroughfare, and inferior classes would occupy the side street. It is a matter that cannot be too often enforced upon the public, that an ordinary mechanic cannot obtain, even at the high rate he pays in proportion to his income and quality, a really wholesome apartment. It should be enforced upon the profession to make their art popular; many of our most wealthy districts have grown up almost without their aid. It is but too generally thought that the architect designs only public buildings and country mansions; let it be shown that his science can administer to the comfort of all classes, and that all art is only good as it is utilitarian, not in the ordinary acceptation of the term, but as it is productive of good. Painting and sculpture are useful not only as affording pleasure; but while the eye is pleased, so is the mind elevated and raised to purer and holier thoughts. So let the architect, the professor of the chief sister's art, endeavour by his skill to allure even the humblest of his fellow citizens from the baneful influence of an ill-regulated home; let his science penetrate to every part of the house, in warming, ventilation, drainage, and arrangement; it is then that the world will begin to appreciate architecture, and clearly understand the duties of its professors. T.

SUPERVISION OF BUILDINGS IN VIENNA.

DIPPING the other day into Thompson's new work on "Austria," we fell upon some particulars of the means taken in Vienna to control new buildings, which will probably interest our readers; and here they are:—

"Attached to the staff of the police is a board of architects with numerous employés to attend and enforce the different regulations laid down to insure the health and security of the inhabitants by sufficient drainage and ventilation. Three plans of a house to be built must be lodged at a magistrature, when a commission is appointed to examine them, and if no objections present themselves the work is allowed to proceed. The chief points insisted on are, that the scaffolding shall be so constructed that nothing can fall through it into the street, and that it shall not project more than 6 feet; that though the cellars may be carried to any depth, the foundation must be laid one-sixth as deep as the house is intended to be high, the maximum height being restricted to four stories. The ground-floor must be arched, and the walls of the upper story must be 2 feet thick, while each one above the ground-floor increases 6 inches, so that in fact a house of four stories high must be 4 feet thick at the ground-floor. No story may be less than 9 feet 6 inches high, and the ground-floor must be at least 6 inches above the pavement of the street. All kitchens, on whatever floor, must be arched; and as each floor is usually occupied by several sets of tenants, each stove, to prevent annoyance, must have its separate flue, of at least 7 inches in diameter, carried up at an angle of 60 degrees, to facilitate cleaning, into the main chimney, which must be at least 4 feet above the roof, and be secured both above and below by an iron grating. The staircases must be entirely of stone, and the window frames of either stone or brick; and a drain, at the expense of the proprietor, must be carried into the main sewer. The houses are built of brick, cemented over, which, besides presenting a more uniform appearance, is necessary, as the bricks are coarse unsightly affairs; they are of large dimensions, measuring, by statute, 11½ inches by 5½ and 2½ inches thick, and cost about 30s. the thousand.

The value of land in the best parts of the city ranges from five to six hundred florins 50*l.* to 60*l.*) the square fathom, and in other parts from two to three hundred; but in the suburbs it is much less, and ranges from five to fifty florins. In the rebuilding of a house the magistrature has the power of setting it back, to widen the street, on paying for the land at the average value of that in the district. Leasehold property is unknown; and thus the owner of the land, even if another person should build the house, is registered as the proprietor in the *Grundbuch*, which is the complete record of all the household and landed property in the empire. In all towns this register is kept by the *grundgericht*, a peculiar kind of magistrate, and in country places by the landowners, or *herrschaft*. In Vienna there are four of these registers, two civil and two ecclesiastical—one of which latter belongs to the metropolitan diocese, and is under the charge of the archbishop, and the other to the clergy of the Schotten order. All amounts of money advanced on mortgage, or otherwise on houses and lands, must be entered on these records, to make the transaction valid, and to prevent fraudulent practices."

CONSTRUCTION OF LIGHTHOUSES.

LIGHTHOUSE ON COHASSET ROCKS, U.S.

FROM the official report of Captain Swift, under whose direction this lighthouse is being constructed for the American Topographical Bureau, we learn that the form of the lighthouse frame is an octagon, of 25 feet diameter at the base; the structure is formed of eight heavy wrought iron piles, or shafts, placed at equal distance from each other, with one also at the centre. The piles were forged in two pieces each, and are connected together by very stout cast-iron or gun metal sockets, the interior of which is bored, and the pile ends are turned, and secured to the sockets by means of large steel keys, passing through the piles and sockets. Above and below the joints or sockets, and connecting the middle pile with each outer pile, there extends a series of wrought iron braces, and the outer shafts are connected together by similar braces, extending from one to the other,—and thus the whole structure is tied together.

The keeper's house is octagonal in shape, and 14 feet in diameter; the uprights, or stanchions, are of cast-iron, and rest upon the cap immediately over the pile heads, where they are secured with bolts and keys. These uprights are cast with double flanches, between which 2-inch plank, grooved and tongued, are to be fitted horizontally: and at right angles another series of plank is to be set on end vertically, and, together, these form the side or frame of the house; upon this frame the roof will be placed, and, finally, upon this, the lantern will be set up.

The drilling of the holes for the lighthouse occupied the better part of two seasons. The erection of the iron structure in place, it may be conceived, was comparatively a work of much less difficulty, and, with favourable weather, an undertaking not requiring much time. The triangle and drilling machine was swept from the rock twice during the first season's operations, and the men were frequently washed from the rock, but happily no lives have been lost. The holes were all finished on the 16th August, that is to say, nine holes of 12 inches diameter and 5 feet deep.

The entire height of the structure from the surface of the rock to the top of the lantern will be about 70 feet, and upwards of 50 above the line of the highest water.

The entire weight of the iron work is about 70 tons; of this upwards of 40 tons is wrought iron, the residue of cast iron. The average weight of each complete shaft is about 8,200 lbs. The cast-iron couplings for connecting the upper piles with the lower are 3 feet long, and weigh nearly 800 lbs. each; they are made of the best gun metal. The weight of the lantern and illuminating apparatus is about 4½ tons.

RAILWAY JOTTINGS.

THE contracts for the execution of the Bishop Auckland and Fensher and Sunderland branches of the York, Newcastle, and Berwick line, have been let to Messrs. Rush and Lawton—the former for 235,000*l.* and the latter for 63,000*l.*——The strengthening of the permanent way of the Bristol and Birmingham line from Gloucester to Birmingham has been completed to an extent of 16 miles. The rails are of a weight of 84 lb. to the yard, in the place of 40 lb. as heretofore. ——A range of old buildings at Wolverhampton, have been removed preparatory to the erection of the entrance to the station of the Shrewsbury and Birmingham line. Besides the offices, a double row of new shops and houses will be erected, so that with the removal of unsightly buildings, a twofold improvement of that part of the town extending from Railway-street towards the canal will be thus effected.——A new axle-box has been tested on the North-Western carriages. The escape of grease and the admission of grit or dust are both obviated, it is said, in this invention, so that a carriage has been found to be capable of running 4,000 miles without either renewal of grease, access of dust, or hot axles. The grease is supplied through a screw opening, and a valve acted on by vulcanized rubber springs is fitted to the axle at the end of the box usually left open, so as to prevent either the waste of grease or the access of dust. A saving of several thousands of pounds a-year is anticipated from the adoption of this axle-box, which is an invention of one of the company's engineering officers, Mr. Normanville. ——The *Daily News* states that a discovery has been made of fraudulent practices or intentions with reference to the South-Eastern Company's passenger tickets, on the part of a subordinate officer on the North-Western.

LAUNDRY DRYING-CLOSETS.

A CURRENT of air having been long considered essential to the evaporation of moisture in laundry drying-closets, I beg to send you the result of some experiments tried with the new closet at the Middlesex Hospital, which prove that at high temperatures an external air-drain may be entirely and advantageously dispensed with.

The closet alluded to is 6 feet wide, 7 feet high, 8 feet long, and is heated by the direct radiation of the heat produced by the flue of the ironing stove passing through it, by which means it is kept at a temperature varying from 180° to 200° Fahrenheit, with little more fuel than would be required for the working of the ordinary ironing stove. The closet was originally constructed with an external air drain, but the drying not being satisfactory the drain was closed, and the following result obtained:

	Weight when put in.	Weight when taken out.	Water evaporated.	Time in evaporating.	Temperature of the Closet when rugs, &c. were put in.	Temperature when taken out.
	lbs.	lbs.	lbs.	h. m.		
Six Blankets..	44	23½	20½ }	1.35	200°	160°
Eighteen Rugs	169	87½	81½ }			

The closet, after the linen was taken out, gradually rose to the temperature of 200°. The quantity of fuel required to keep the closet and ironing stove in full work was found to be about 16 lbs. weight of coke per hour.

It will be observed that the water evaporated from this closet is equal to 1 lb. per minute, and the fuel consumed about one-fourth of the weight of water evaporated.

WM. JEAKES, Jun.

Miscellanea.

TENDERS FOR HAMPSTEAD WORKHOUSE. —Sir: I observed in your journal a striking example of the contracting monomania exhibited in the amounts of the several tenders sent in for the proposed alteration to Hampstead Workhouse. The lowest tender, Mr. Pilbeam's, was accepted, but in a day or two, I heard that Mr. P. had discovered a trifling, and of course, accidental error, of some 1,500*l.*; the guardians declined accepting his amended tender, but to my great surprise I have seen an advertisement calling for more tenders. Were there none of the other contractors responsible men, or are the guardians so very ignorant of the usual method of proceeding in such a case? Is there no man of business among them to set them right, or do they imagine that it is no trouble to builders to take out their own quantities and estimate for such works for the amusement or instruction of Boards of Guardians? May I beg the favor of your inserting this, as I think it will only be carrying out the great principle of fair play to all which you have so long and so fearlessly advocated.—A LOOKER ON.

THE GAS MONITOR.—Sir: My object in pointing out the incorrectness of the advertisement of the Gas Light Monitor, was to avoid contributing by my silence to misleading the public. I cannot exactly ascertain the saving of gas effected at the Model Establishment, but instead of its being 10,000 feet in six weeks, as stated in the advertisement, I do not think it could have been much more than one-tenth of that amount.—GEORGE WOOLCOTT, Assistant-Secretary to the Committee for Promoting the Establishment of Public Baths and Washhouses.

PROJECTED WORKS.—Advertisements have been issued for tenders,—by May 26th, for the erection of sundry buildings and works, at the new barracks, at Awlerton, near Sheffield; by April 14th, for sundry earthwork to be done in the removal and levelling of ground at East Hill, Wandsworth; by 25th, for the erection of St. John's Church, Kingsdown, near Walmer, Kent; by May 2nd, for the erection of additional buildings at the Queen's College, Birmingham; by 23rd instant, for certain works and additions to the laundries and drying rooms of the workhouse at St. Martin's-in-the Fields; by 26th, for the erection of an infirmary and other works, as an addition to the Wandsworth and Clapham Union Workhouse; by a date not specified, for the erection of a new Pauper Lunatic Asylum, for Wilts, at Devizes, and for a large quantity of cast-iron columns, sashes, and joists for same, separate tenders; by 30th, for the erection of the Normal College for Wales, at Swansea; by 24th, for the erection and completion of a brick warehouse at Bolton; by same date, for the supply of boiler plates, bar and angle iron, spring steel, copper, brass tubes, &c. for Lancashire and Yorkshire Railway, also for materials for waggons for same; by same date, for various articles in iron, copper, brass, &c., and for paints, glass, &c., for Glasgow and Ayr Railway Company; by 2nd May, for the supply of materials for the metropolitan roads; and by 24th April, for a supply of English tough cake copper at Chatham.

COMPETITION.—Resident architects in St. Martin's-in-the-Fields are invited to compete "for the erection" of new national schools in that parish.

THE ORDNANCE SURVEY OF THE CIVIL SURVEYORS.—Sir: In your paper of last week, under the heading "Ordnance Survey," is the following paragraph:—"It also stated the fact, that although the estimated cost of the survey was 24,000*l.*, the work would be completed for 3,000*l.* within that amount, and 5,000*l.* below the estimate given in by the 'Civil Surveyors.'" In this there must be some mistake, as on referring to the published papers of the "Surveyors' Association," I find, that while the estimate furnished by the Ordnance Department to the Commissioners of Sewers for a block plan and levels of London, within a radius of eight miles round St. Paul's, was 19,945*l.*, exclusive of 4,270*l.* for the triangulation, making together 24,215*l.*; the estimate of the Civil Surveyors was 18,200*l.*, at which sum they were very desirous to undertake the work, and offered to give approved security, and suffer heavy penalties if it was not completed within six months of the date of contract. By your paragraph we are to assume that the survey will be completed by the "Ordnance Surveyors" for about 21,000*l.*, and my object is to show, that that sum is not 5,000*l.* below the estimate of the "Civil Surveyors" but, on the contrary, exceeds it.—EDW. RYDE, Upper Belgrave-place.

LEARNED DISQUISITION ON GUTTA PERCHA.—A lively controversy has been going on in the Edinburgh journals between Professor M'Lean, 'the well-known linguist,' and Mrs. Jamieson, on the pronunciation of the 'percha' in 'gutta percha.' It is 'perka' according to the lady, 'persha,'—the linguist. Now, we are greatly mistaken if both be not wrong. The word is native Malay, and not only the original importers of the article, but the Malays themselves are said to have declared it to be 'pertsha,' and if so, not being very profoundly versed in the Malay lingo, we certainly prefer following the authority even of a native barbarian rather than that of the best known 'linguist' in the north. But the professor of botany, then, must be supposed to know something about it, seeing that the tree which yields it holds, or ought to hold, a place in his 'album,' and the professor, as an umpire, authoritatively declares in favour of his fellow professor, stigmatising the lady's dictum—moreover, as "an unadulterated cockneyism." The cockney naturalist, however, whose researches led him to the fishmongers' museum of piscatorial history on the look out for gutta percha soles, must have ranked the gutta percha with the sole tribe as a hybrid with the 'perch,' and, being doubtless versed in Latin terminology, must have asked for "gutta *pertsha* soles."

DOCKYARD REDUCTIONS.—"From every dockyard," says the *Morning Herald*, "we have the most lamentable statements of reductions on Saturday last—hundreds of poor fellows left her Majesty's service to starve, or to become chargeable to the parish; whilst others—the very best men of the establishment, and quite as good as those left behind—men who have 'borne the heat and burden of the day'—were seen, with heavy hearts, lugging their chests of tools out of those gates which they have been accustomed to enter for the last thirty years. The Government have much to answer for in respect of these reductions, which should have been gradually, and not so summarily made. Confidence is utterly shaken throughout the Royal establishments, and the result is, every good man without influence, will try to better himself out of the service the moment he sees there is an opportunity."—"One of the consequences," remarks the *Hampshire Advertiser*, "must be an increase of the poor's-rates. We think, if reductions are inevitable, and we fear they are, they might have been made in a different way. In all cases of this kind, Government invariably begin at the wrong end. Why not cut down high salaries? abolish useless offices?" Between 600 and 700 men are here thrown out of employ, whereas by the course suggested probably not even a dozen might have been deprived of their sinecures, and yet have had abundant other means of upholding life, not only in all its essentials, but in all its comforts and luxuries too. Here is the way in which the heart of the poor man is soured and disgusted with his rulers—one and all, and the prolific seeds of Chartism and crime but too abundantly sown,—not amongst discharged officials alone, but amongst all of the same class, ay, and of others also, who sympathise with them.

WANT OF AMBITION AMONG WORKING MEN.—There is no such startling difference in the emoluments of classes, as in their habits and social peculiarities. The half-pay officer, the dissenting clergyman, or curate of the establishment, the government or mercantile clerk, draw salaries which are often exceeded by those of working men, yet they do not consider it their duty to appear in filthy attire, or to expend a third of their income at the tavern; and, on the other hand, they do not give testimony to their utter want of self-command by requiring that their wages should he paid weekly. It is an appalling thing to reflect how large a fund, if we look on it merely as a pecuniary question, is sunk in that unfortunate peculiarity which prevents the workman from raising the tone of his mind, and the character of his habits, above the level of the lowest of his fraternity. It is natural to anticipate that when accident throws enlarged funds into the possession of the more unskilled hand-labourer, they should be wasted and misapplied; but the class influences rise higher, and are found so tainting the able and accomplished workman, as frequently to make his ingenuity and energy contribute to demoralise and degrade him. An employer of skilled workmen lately told the author of these remarks that he gave out work occasionally to a man who could make 1*l.* a-day, and who, both by his skill and his income, might be expected to take his rank among professional men. But nominally he was a worker; he stuck to his order, and would not permit his capacities to raise him above his brethren, so that he never saved a farthing from the tavern, and was then lying penniless in a public hospital.—*Burton's Political and Social Economy.*

SUPPLY OF WATER.—At the last returns there were 70,000 houses out of 270,000 that had no water supply whatever; and though it is asserted that the number has since diminished, the supply of water to the poor in general is so exceedingly scanty in many districts, that it is practically a perfect mockery. Seventy thousand houses inhabited by the poor, with an average of only two families to a house, would give 700,000 persons who have to beg or steal water every day for the ordinary necessities of existence. Although the practice of reducing to figures and to a money value, the sanitary ills endured, is to a certain extent a pandering to the vicious system which prompts an Englishman always, when first considering a new project, to regard it in a mere money point of view, still it has its benefits in being an *argumentum ad hominem* of no inconsiderable value, in determining speedy conclusion. Now, if the very hardness of the water of London alone leads to an outlay of soap and soda of, at the least, double the amount absolutely requisite, and that amount be 630,000*l.*, it is surely worth while to determine whether an actual waste of 315,000*l.* should be annually tolerated in the metropolis. But if we embrace the moral and physical evils, and combine with them the sum of the pecuniary loss entailed by the present scanty and intermittent supply of impure, often dirty, water to London, such an array of facts would stand forth as to cause every inhabitant to cry shame upon those whose duty it should happen to be to present a remedy for such a condition of things.—*Health of Towns Journal.*

NEW CALCULATING MACHINE.—Two miserably poor young men, residing in an obscure village in the department of the Isere, in France, have succeeded, it is said, after ten years' labour, in completing a machine declared to be superior to any yet invented. The Academy of Sciences have issued "a most eulogistic report" on it. What has become of Mr. Babbage's machine? The only calculation of any importance yet effected by it, we fear, is a never-ending multiplication of expense to the country. What *has* the calculator been about for so many years, while young men have been growing old and grey, and the middle-aged falling into second childhood—all forgetting that Babbage or his machine ever existed. We will be bound to say that thousands of intelligent young men have sprung up from childhood since this hopeful machine was produced, and are at this moment ignorant of the fact that it ever *was* produced, far less of the hope that it ever will come to maturity.

THE BRISTOL WATER-WORKS are in an advanced state of progress, and the directors report that the engineer expects to bring the water from the Harptree Coombe springs into the city in the ensuing autumn, and from those at Chewton Mendip in the spring of 1850. More than 50 miles of pipes are laid through the city and suburbs.

WINDOW DUTIES.—The amount of window duty assessed during the year 1847-48 was 1,880,325*l.*; the amount received, 1,811,742*l.*; the number of houses charged to 485,143; and the number of surcharges made to 2,166.

THE SUBTERRANEAN MAP OF PARIS, commenced in 1844, is said to be nearly completed, and will form an atlas of forty-five sheets. It will exhibit, quarter by quarter, all the labyrinthine sinuosities of the ancient quarries and catacombs over which Paris is built, with the corresponding edifices, squares, and streets, above ground.

NOTICE.

"BUILDINGS AND MONUMENTS, MODERN AND MEDIÆVAL," being Illustrations of recently erected Edifices, and of some of the Architectural Works of the Middle Ages, with Descriptive Particulars. Edited by George Godwin, F.R.S., Fellow of the Royal Institute of Architects, &c., &c.

Under the above title it is proposed to publish, in bi-monthly parts, price 2s. 6d. each, the principal Illustrations of Modern and Mediæval Buildings which have appeared from time to time in THE BUILDER, with their accompanying descriptive particulars. Each part will contain about eight plates, folio size, and eight pages of letter press, with plans and details. The engravings will be printed separately, with care, on a tinted paper.

The first part will be issued in time to be forwarded with the magazines for May 1, and will contain:—

Her Majesty's Marine Residence, Osborne; with Plan.

The Carlton Club House, Pall Mall.

Church of St. Isaac, at St. Petersburgh; with Details.

Kensington Union Workhouse.

The Liverpool Branch Bank of England; and Details.

The New Throne, Canterbury Cathedral.

The North Porch, Restored, of St. Mary Redcliffe, Bristol.

The Interior of Lincoln's-Inn Hall.

Persons desirous of becoming Subscribers, are requested to forward their names to the office of THE BUILDER.

TENDERS

Given in for the erection of a new church at Mansfield, Nottinghamshire, Mr. H. J. Stevens, architect. The quantities were furnished.

Brooke and Adlington, Mansfield	£4,720
Hall, Nottingham	4,000
Watts, Derby	3,900
Lindley, Mansfield (accepted)	3,800

For St. George's (East) Workhouse addition. Mr. Hammock, architect.

Wood	£10,894
Cooper	9,338
Hall	9,280
Ashby	9,236
Wilson	8,988
Nicholson	8,850
Colbatch	8,777
Piper	8,596
Jay	8,437
Hill	8,282
Higgs	8,145
Wilson, Southwark	8,120
Burton	7,911
R. and E. Curtis (accepted)	7,894
Crook	7,830

MEETINGS OF SCIENTIFIC BODIES

Held during the ensuing week.

MONDAY, April 16th.—Institute of Architects, 8 P.M.
TUESDAY, 17th.—Institution of Civil Engineers, 8 P.M.
WEDNESDAY, 18th.—Society of Arts, 8 P.M.
THURSDAY, 19th.—Royal Society, 8½ P.M.; Society of Antiquaries, 8 P.M.

TO CORRESPONDENTS.

Received.—"J. L. P." (thanks), "Bart," "A. Y. C.," "J. C." (Ipswich), "S. C." (shall hear from us), "S. and P.," "M. P.," "G. N.," "W. S.," "Rev. V. H.," "H. P. H.," "E. H." (the cuts are in the hands of Mr. B., jun.), "Rev. W. S." (if we can find time, we will call), "E. W.," "J. J.," "J. E." (declined with thanks), "Reader of THE BUILDER," "T. B." (Chantrey was a sculptor, Mr. Chantrell is an architect), "W. S.," "J. E.," Bath (letter shall be attended to), "R. H. S." "Form and Sound, can their beauty be dependent on the same physical laws?" by Thomas Purdie (Edinburgh: A. and C. Black, 1849). "Algebra of Ratios," by H. B. Browning, Architect, Stamford (Cambridge: Macmillan. London: Simpkin and Co., 1849).

"*Books, Prices, and Addresses.*"—We have not time to point out books or find addresses.

ADVERTISEMENTS.

CATHEDRAL of COLOGNE and ROUEN.—Now exhibiting, the inimitable and colossal model of the Cathedral of Cologne, which has been honoured with the unqualified approbation of her Majesty and Prince Albert. The dimensions are 8 ft. long, 8 ft. high, and 4 ft. 8 in. broad, modelled by C. SCHROPP, in wood and iron. The above splendid piece of workmanship was completed in eight years and seventeen days. Also a magnificent model of the Cathedral at Rouen. At the Cosmorama, Regent-street, from Ten in the morning till dusk. Admission, 2s. 6d. Children, 1s.

ROYAL POLYTECHNIC INSTITUTION.—The collection of Models of Agricultural Implements has been greatly increased by additions deposited by the Royal Agricultural Society and other scientific parties. The use of these Models, as well as all others in the Institution, is explained from day to day. Lectures, by Dr. Bachhoffner, on the Ventilation of Mines, &c., by means of a Jet of Steam, daily at Two o'clock, and on alternate Evenings. Lecture on Chemistry, daily at half-past Three, and on alternate Evenings. The Microscope. The new Dissolving Views include Scenes in Van Dieman's Land, from Original Drawings taken on the spot by J. Skinner Prout, Esq. New Chromatrope. Diver and Diving-bell, &c. &c. The Music is under the direction of Dr. Wallis.—Admission, 1s.; Schools, half-price. The New Catalogue, 1s.

IRON SHUTTERS.—The PATENT CONVEX REVOLVING IRON SHUTTERS are cheaper, twelve times stronger, work easier, cannot run down, and roll up in one-third less room than any other shutters made. Harcourt Quincey, Patentee.

CLARK and Co., Sole Manufacturers, and of IMPROVED DRAWN ORNAMENTAL METALLIC SASH BARS, ASTRAGALS, MOULDINGS, STALL-BOARD PLATES, &c. &c., in brass, copper, and zinc. WROUGHT-IRON GIRDERS, HOT-WATER APPARATUS, and metal works of every description connected with buildings. Steam engines, millwork, and machinery. CLARK and Co., Engineers, 218, Wapping. Models can be seen and every information obtained at 458, Oxford-street, and 4, Moorgate-street, City. Agent for Scotland, Mr. G. BRIGSTOCK, 17 George-street, Edinburgh.

SNOXELL'S PATENT SAFETY REVOLVING WOOD SHUTTERS, Manufactory, 96, REGENT-STREET and 121, CHANCERY-LANE. Patent sealed on the 4th day of February, 1845, for Fourteen Years, for Improvements in Revolving Shutters of WOOD and IRON, consisting of Six Methods of Raising and Lowering Shutters, without Machinery, and Two for Hinging and Sheathing the Edges of Wood laths with Iron.—The Patentee having fixed up some hundreds, will feel pleased in forwarding the Testimonials of Architects, Principals of large Establishments, and others, having them now in use, which fully guarantees the Patentee in stating they are beyond dispute superior to any other Revolving Shutter for durability, security, and simplicity, without the use of cog-wheel worm and screw gear, or any other complicated machinery employed by other makers.

BUNNETT and Co., ENGINEERS,
Patentees of
REVOLVING IRON AND WOOD SAFETY SHUTTERS,
and of
ORNAMENTAL METALLIC SASH BARS, MOULDINGS, &c.,
IN BRASS, COPPER, ZINC, &c.
FOR SHOP-FRONTS, SKYLIGHTS, &c.

Shop-fronts completely fitted and fixed in a superior style, either plain or ornamental, also glazed with best plate glass. Strong moulded stallboards handsomely engraved. Metal works and machinery of all kinds in connection with banking-houses, shops, warehouses, &c. &c.

B. and Co. challenge competition as to either quality or price. Designs furnished and estimates given.

IMPROVED PATENT BENCH AND FLOORING CRAMPS FOR BUILDERS.
SOLE LICENCEES FOR MARVIN and MOORE'S PATENT DIAGONAL GRATINGS.
Office of the Patentees, 26, Lombard-street, London; and at the Works, Deptford, Kent.

CAST-IRON PIPES, IRON WORK FOR OVENS, &c.

RAIN PIPES, &c.—F. A. TIDDEMAN, Purfleet Wharf, Earl-street, City, near Blackfriars-bridge, keeps a large stock of Rain Pipes, Heads, Shoes, Elbows, &c., half round and O. G. Gutters, Socket Pipes for Water or Gas, Flanch Pipes, Sash Weights, and other Castings; Iron Work for Baker's Ovens of every description, fitted complete, to be had in sets or in parts.—Prices equal to all competition. Contracts taken to any extent.

MINTON and CO.'S ENCAUSTIC and other PATENT TILES for Churches, Entrance Halls, Conservatories, Balconies, &c., Antique, Geometrical, and Alhambric Mosaics, manufactures of a highly decorative character and extreme durability. Slabs and Tiles for Fireplaces, Hearths, and Covings for Grates, Door Furniture, White Glazed and Ornamental Tiles for Baths, Dairies, and Kitchen Ranges may be had in great variety at their Warehouse, 9, Albion-place, Blackfriars-bridge, London, and at their Manufactory, Stoke-upon-Trent, Staffordshire.

TO ARCHITECTS, BUILDERS, AND RAILWAY CONTRACTORS.

BRICKS and TILES, plain and moulded, manufactured in a superior manner, from fine beds of clay on the Earl of Leicester's estate at Holkham, of red, blue, and Bath stone colours, both for plain and ornamental work. Specimens to be seen at Blashfield's Wharf, Commercial-road, Lambeth (near Waterloo-bridge), consisting of plain bricks of the usual size for building purposes, moulded bricks for forming Tudor chimney shafts, of various designs, label mouldings, cornices, copings, window sills, dressings for windows and doors, mullions, ridges, skirtings, &c. Also roofing and paving tiles of an ornamental character in the same materials. The moulded bricks are fully equal to the best specimens referred to under the articles "Brickwork," in Nos. 280 and 281, of "The Builder."

SMOKE NUISANCE.—HAZELDINE'S PATENT FURNACE has now been in operation, giving the utmost satisfaction, for the last twelve months, and is found to be a perfect SMOKE CONSUMER. It is simple in its construction, burning the screenings from coals, and is erected at half the cost of any other patent, effectually answering the same purpose.—Address, 45, Brudenell-place, New North-road, Hoxton.

SIR HENRY HART'S CHIMNEY PUMP, FOR THE CURE OF SMOKY CHIMNEYS, and the constant ventilation of apartments. It has been in successful use at Greenwich Hospital for several months.

SOLE AGENTS.
DENHAM and SONS, 19, Wigmore-street, Cavendish-square, and G. and J. DEANE, opening to the Monument, London Bridge.

A liberal discount to Ironmongers and Builders.

DR. ARNOTT'S VALVES for thoroughly VENTILATING APARTMENTS of every description. F. EDWARDS having had the advantage of making them under the immediate direction and patronage of Dr. Arnott, enables him to present the public with Valves of the most approved principle for general use. Prices from 7s. 6d. to 20s. and upwards. A prospectus, containing every information, to be had on application to F. EDWARDS, 42, Poland-street, Oxford-street, London.

DR. ARNOTT'S VENTILATING CHIMNEY VALVE,

For carrying off Heated and Impure Air from Bed-rooms Sitting-rooms, Counting-houses, and Apartments generally.

LIST OF PRICES.

	First size, 11 by 8.	Second size, 16 by 9
Plain Iron Valve	7 6	12 0
Bronzed and Leathered	9 0	14 0
Japanned, white with Gold lines	15 0	21 0
Brass Front	17 0	24 0

Packing Cases (if required), 1s. 3d. each.

Manufactured by HART and SONS, 53, 54, 55, Wych-street Strand, London.

IMPROVED SELF-ACTING CHIMNEY VENTILATORS,

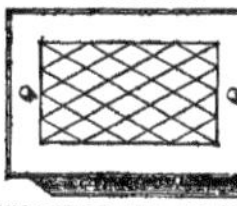

FOR CARRYING OFF HEATED AND IMPURE AIR from drawing-rooms, sitting-rooms, bed-rooms, nurseries, offices, &c. &c., from 5s. each.—BURT and POTTS, Manufacturers and Ironmongers, 65, York-street, Westminster, London.

Stoves, ranges, rain-water pipes, gutters, and builders' ironmongery, as low as any house in London. Delivered free within 5 miles.

PATENT GALVANIZED TINNED IRON and ZINC WORKS, 5, Quickset-row, New-road.—ANDREW WHYTOCK begs respectfully to acquaint the customers of Mr. C. GELL, Jun., and the Public, that, having succeeded Mr. Gell in the above business, he will feel obliged by a continuance of the favours so liberally enjoyed by Mr. Gell, and trusts, by prompt attention to orders and sound work, to merit patronage and confidence. The Patent Metal being fire-proof, and free from all liability to corrosion or oxidation, is peculiarly well adapted for roofing of every description.

The Advertiser begs to call the particular attention of Builders to the Patent WELDED GALVANIZED TINNED IRON WATER PIPE, which is free from many troublesome objections to which lead pipe is liable,—amongst others, it is proof against bursting, and cannot be cut through by workmen in repairing the roadway; with regard to public health it is of the first importance.

Dr. Ryan, M.D., LL.D., when writing of the above pipes, says,—"Whereas, after passing through pipes of Galvanized Tinned Iron the water is perfectly unchanged. Some time since I was called upon, professionally, to examine the water conveyed through lead pipes, for the use of the royal hounds at Windsor, in consequence of the great mortality which had occurred amongst the animals; and, on analysis, I found that the cause arose from the water becoming impregnated with lead in its passage through the tubes made of that metal. Had your Galvanized Tinned Iron Tubing been then in use, I have no hesitation in saying that no injurious consequences could have occurred, under the like circumstances. This is but one instance out of many in which injurious and even fatal consequences have resulted from the use of water which has passed through lead tubing, or been kept in leaden vessels."

A. WHYTOCK is enabled to supply Tube, in large or small quantities, on the same terms as the Patentees.

London, April 12, 1849.

TO ARCHITECTS.—COMPETITION AND OTHER DRAWINGS.

MR. THOMAS S. BOYS, Member of the New Society of Painters in Water Colours, and author of "The Picturesque Architecture of Paris, Ghent, Rouen, &c.," and of "London as it is," offers his services in Tinting Backgrounds, Landscapes, Perspective Views, Interiors, &c. From the long experience he has had in such subjects, he is fully aware of the points essentially necessary to be attended to. Drawings and designs lithographed in a superior manner.—Address, Mr. BOYS, 81, Great Titchfield-street, Oxford-street.

FIRE-PROOF BUILDINGS.—PORTER'S PATENT.—By an improved mode of applying Corrugated Iron in the construction of Floors, Roofs, &c., for which Patents have recently been granted to John Henderson Porter, Buildings of every class can be rendered Fire-proof at a very trifling increase of cost, and without any increase of weight,—while from the absence of cast-iron and timber greater security is obtained, in point of strength, than by the ordinary method of construction.

PORTER'S PATENT BEAMS and GIRDERS of CORRUGATED IRON, on account of their remarkable stiffness, are particularly suitable for buildings and bridges; they are 30 per cent. lighter, and 20 per cent. cheaper, than other wrought-iron beams of equal strength.—Manufactory, Iron Building and Roofing Works, Southwark; Office, 2, Adelaide-place, London-bridge, City.

INCREASED ECONOMY in BUILDING, combined with PROTECTION from FIRE, &c.—The following advantages result from the adoption of the "PATENT FIRE-PROOF FLOORS and ROOFS, viz.:—

Security from Fire.
Great Economy of Construction.
Increased Durability.
Protection from Dry rot and from noxious Insects and Vermin.

The economy of this system is very considerable; its cost, as compared with the common method of fire-proof building, being about one half; while, as compared with the ordinary timber floors, it effects a saving of from 10 to 35 per cent. The entire freedom from lateral thrust, in this method of building, gives it a further advantage over the plan of iron girders and brick arches. The system is applicable to all classes of buildings. It has been introduced at the Middlesex Hospital, where it can be seen at any time, and all information obtained of Messrs. FOX and BARRETT, Leicester Chambers, 46, Leicester-square.

CHUBBS' LOCKS, FIRE-PROOF SAFES, AND CASH BOXES.

CHUBBS' PATENT DETECTOR LOCKS give perfect security from false keys and picklocks, and also detect any attempt to open them. They are made of all sizes, and for every purpose to which locks are applied, and are strong, secure, simple, and durable.

CHUBBS' PATENT LATCH, for front doors, counting-house doors, &c., is simple in construction, low in price, and quite secure. The keys are particularly neat and portable.

CHUBBS' PATENT FIRE-PROOF SAFES, BOOKCASES, CHESTS, &c., made entirely of strong wrought-iron, so as effectually to resist the falling of brick-work, timber, &c., in case of fire, and are also perfectly secure from the attacks of the most skilful burglars.

CHUBBS' CASH and DEED BOXES, fitted with the Detector Locks.

CHUBB and SON, 57, St. Paul's Churchyard, London.

LEADBEATER, FIRE-PROOF SAFE AND DETECTOR LOCK MANUFACTURER TO HER MAJESTY'S BOARD OF ORDNANCE.

CAUTION to Purchasers of FIRE-PROOF DOORS for Strong Rooms, Safes, Chests, and Detector Locks, &c. &c. LEADBEATER, many years manufacturer for Chubb.

LEADBEATER begs most respectfully to inform Architects, Surveyors, Builders, &c., that he can supply them with IMPROVED DETECTOR LOCKS for universal purposes. STRONG WROUGHT IRON FIRE-PROOF DOORS, SAFES, and CHESTS, &c., on the most improved principles of security against FIRE and THIEVES, without the aid of "expensive machinery," which is employed by some inexperienced makers, but must be paid for; at prices 25 per cent. under any other house in London.

LEADBEATER offers ONE HUNDRED POUNDS reward to any person who can pick his improved detector locks or latches. Some thousands of Leadbeater's strong-room doors and safes have now been put up without a SINGLE COMPLAINT, and fifteen years' practical experience, during which he has adapted every possible improvement to real security, enables him to challenge competition with any house in London. A large assortment of all sizes on sale and made to order. A pair of extra strong wrought-iron fire-proof folding-doors with ventilating gates, made expressly for a banker's strong room, may be viewed at his manufactory. Strong wrought-iron doors for party walls, with wrought-iron rabitted frames, and secured by the BEST DETECTOR LOCKS in ENGLAND, 6 feet high by 2 feet 3 inches wide and upwards, price 10l. each, always on hand at LEADBEATER'S MANUFACTORY, 125, ALDERSGATE-STREET, LONDON.

ZINC, from the VIEILLE MONTAGNE MINING COMPANY, is the purest known, free from alloy of iron, lead, or sulphur. It is supplied in spelter for brass founders, &c., and in sheets for ship sheathing and roofings of all kinds, and nails of all dimensions. It may be had at the following Agents', who have always a large stock in hand:—

London—Messrs. Charles Devaux and Co.; Mr. Charles Jack Mr. William Skirrow.
Birmingham—Mr. John Barwell.
Liverpool—Messrs. E. Zwelchenbart and Co.
Manchester—Messrs. Richard Johnson and Brother.
Leeds—Messrs. J. G. and T. Heaps.
Hull—Messrs. J. Parker and Sons.
Newcastle-upon-Tyne—Mr. Benjamin Plummer.
Leith—Messrs. Robert Anderson and Co.
Glasgow—Messrs. A. G. Kidston and Co.
Bristol—Messrs. Morgan McArthur and Co.
Plymouth—Messrs. Luscombe, Driscoll, and Co.
Southampton—Mr. W. J. Lefeuvre.
Yarmouth—Messrs. John Shelley and Co.

Zinc from 20 to 21 oz. per square foot is generally used for roofings, which come at least one-third cheaper than slate coverings; and the ship sheathing, which lasts from five to six years, comes two-thirds cheaper than copper or yellow metal. And if the zinc coverings are made of the Vieille Montagne Zinc, and under the superintendence of Mr. Geyelin, the surveyor of the Company (for which no charge whatever is made), a guarantee of ten years will be given of its durability.—For further particulars and prices, apply to Mr. H. F. SCHMOLL, General Agent for England, at the Company's Offices, No. 12, Manchester-buildings, Westminster-bridge, London.

By Her Majesty's Royal Letters Patent.

PITT'S PATENT SELF-ADJUSTING DOOR KNOBS AND LOOSE SPINDLES.

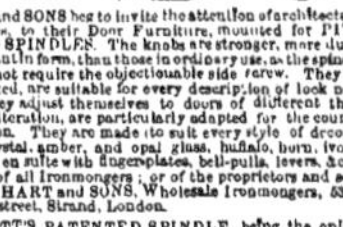

HART and SONS beg to invite the attention of architects, builders, and others, to their Door Furniture, mounted for PITT'S PATENTED SPINDLES. The knobs are stronger, more durable, and more elegant in form, than those in ordinary use, as the spindles, being loose, do not require the objectionable side screw. They are more readily fixed, are suitable for every description of lock now in use, and, as they adjust themselves to doors of different thicknesses, without alteration, are particularly adapted for the country or for exportation. They are made to suit every style of decoration in China, crystal, amber, and opal glass, buffalo, horn, ivory, ebony, brass, &c., en suite with finger-plates, bell-pulls, levers, &c.—May be obtained of all Ironmongers; or of the proprietors and sole manufacturers, HART and SONS, Wholesale Ironmongers, 53, 54, and 55, Wych-street, Strand, London.

N.B. PITT'S PATENTED SPINDLE, being the only one that does not require a screw in the side of the knob or mounting, the use of any lock furniture without such side screws would be an infringement of the patent.

No. CCCXXIV.

SATURDAY, APRIL 21, 1849.

 E are anxious that the committee of the House of Commons appointed to investigate the [want of] constitution, [mis] management, and [strange] proceedings of the Schools of Designs, should get earnestly to work; and, still more so, that the result of the inquiry may be reformation and satisfactory progress. For some years we have endeavoured strenuously and continuously, by directing attention to abuses in the schools, and to the lamentably small results of a large outlay upon them, to lead to improvement. We were very unpopular in some quarters in consequence,—THE BUILDER was positively a forbidden book at one time in Somerset House,—but our opinions became ultimately the universal opinions, and a certain amount of good was done.

We will not compare the present condition of the London school with what it was at the time to which we are referring, when undisguised incompetence reigned, and entire disorganisation resulted. Still, the proceedings appear to be far from satisfactory in some respects, and the issue unsatisfactory in all. In architecture we want artistical operatives, and we have been looking to our schools of design to produce them. Where are they? Echo derisively answers, where? The *Journal of Design*, which has commenced an onslaught, says,—

"What a specimen these schools afford of Government administration, when we recollect that there has been expended, in one way or another, by Parliamentary grants and local subscriptions, &c., something near 100,000*l.* on these schools, and that it is a doubt whether it be possible to instance, out of all last year's manufactures, any ONE single useful article of *first-rate* quality which is the unassisted design of a pupil who has been *wholly* educated in these schools! We may be wrong in the sweeping doubt here implied, and we shall be glad to be proved to be so; and we shall be greatly obliged to manufacturers and designers who will point out to us any articles of manufacture of original design, produced within the last twelve months, as the best fabrics of their class, which have been designed by a student educated altogether in the school,—one who has studied in the school, say not less than four years, and who does not exceed the age of twenty-five years. We do not want to be informed of the designs of those who were practising designers before they entered the school, and had mastered the difficulties and rudiments of their profession before they entered it. We want to know the works of the real scholars of the school."

We have again and again shown that to call the establishment a School of Design was ridiculous, it was simply a drawing school—design was not thought of; it was even asserted by some in authority that to consider it in the system of instruction was quite unnecessary,—drawing, and merely drawing, was all they had to think of.

That this is not the opinion there now, may be gathered from some of the very good lectures recently delivered to the students. Thus, Mr. Dyce said;—

"The power of imitation, that is to say, skill in drawing, painting, modelling any given object,—although to a great extent the ultimate purpose of the instruction in an academy of fine art, is, in a School of Design, but *the means to an end*. The opposition formerly made to introducing into this school certain branches of instruction, which were reckoned proper only to academies of fine art, was partly grounded on the supposition that, if the means of elementary study were unlimited, the effect of the school would be to overflow the country with artists; and so it was thought that if these branches were excluded, or if not excluded, were taught only up to a certain point, the school would be made to keep its due place in the scale of art. Now, although these views arose from an indistinct apprehension of the purpose of the school, and of the means required to effect it, it must be admitted that the fear lest the means should be mistaken for the end, was not without reason. If the school were to stop short at the point of having taught the art of drawing, painting, or modelling—that is to say, if the studies terminated in a purpose which is common to it and general drawing-schools, not only would the fears I have spoken of be realised, but the school would, in point of fact, have abandoned its specific claim on public support. It was established by Government, *not to afford general instruction in art, but to teach the special art of designing ornament, and its application to manufactures and decoration.* The proper business of the school, indeed, may be said to commence where other schools of art leave off; at all events, however much, in certain respects, the school occupies ground common to it and to general drawing-schools, it has beyond this the definite and specific object of *cultivating ornamental art. This is its peculiar province: this is its primary business and occupation.*"

It is something to find that this apparently obvious fact has been at last arrived at. We shall keep an eye on the course of proceedings before the committee.

We should be glad to know what has become of the Female School, formerly of Somerset House. It was sent into lodgings somewhere in the Strand,—on the same grounds, it would seem, which led boards of guardians to send pauper children to Tooting, and has never been heard of since.

Concerning the provincial schools we have lately received several communications, including an amusing budget of complaints from *Paisley*, written by a resident manufacturer; but as they are wholly *ex parte*, they need inquiry before publication.

In Glasgow, a fortnight ago, the annual meeting of the School of Design was held, and the committee said in their report that the number of students had increased (there are now 856, male and female), that the works of art had been arranged by the present master (Mr. Wilson), and that arrangements had been made to render the Library of Reference there accessible to designers, for whom a commodious apartment had been appropriated, where they might study four days in the week.

To the Sheffield School of Design the Government grant has been increased from 200*l.* to 550*l.* per annum, if our informant is correct, and two assistant masters have been appointed in consequence.

We are so little used to Government grants in aid of art, that the sums appropriated to the School of Design seem large. If it were well applied, however, and produced due fruit, the public, so far from objecting to such votes, would willingly see them increased. A correspondent of the *Literary Gazette* gives a list of sums just voted by the National Assembly of France, for the encouragement of science and art, including the following, which contrasts strongly with the doings of our own Government in that respect :—

	Francs.
"*Etablissement des Beaux Arts*	447,000
Personnel of the National Museums	148,700
Matériel of ditto	151,700
Works of art and decorations of public edifices; *including* the purchase of pictures and statues for the Louvre	950,000
Preservation of ancient historical monuments	750,000
Encouragements and subscriptions to the Fine Arts	186,000
Annual indemnities or temporary assistance to artists, dramatic authors, musical composers, and their widows	137,700
Institut National	581,300
Museum of Natural History	486,350
Astronomical establishments	121,760
Bibliothèque Nationale...............	283,600
Ditto, extraordinary credit	60,000
Service of public libraries.............	222,300
Literary subscriptions	170,000
Learned societies	50,000
Voyages, scientific missions, public lectures	112,000
Encouragement and assistance to men of science and literary men	197,400
Unpublished documents on natural history	150,000
Subvention to *Caisses de retraite*	500,000
Re-impression or publication of scientific works...........................	1,939

with much more for public education, faculties of theology, medicine, law, &c."

In other parts abroad, they seem more inclined to dissipate than to collect works of art, —to knock down rather than build up. The revolutionary government of Rome are said to be in treaty for the sale of the Apollo Belvidere to American agents, and of many other treasures of art garnered in the Eternal City, to English and French speculators. The *Times*, in a leading article, deprecated the removal of the inestimable monuments which form the chief glory of that city, and with the view of preventing Englishmen from being a party in the disgraceful proceeding, urged, that should the legitimate government be restored, it would be difficult to defend a possession which had been acquired with a full knowledge of the circumstances attending the sale. "It appears to us," continues the journalist, "that the purchase of these monuments from Mazzini's committees can no more be justified than the purchase of diamond necklaces from those gentry who at this season of last year were so comfortably housed in the Tuileries. The buyers of this stolen jewellery were unhesitatingly prosecuted, and if the buyers of pictures and statues escape a similar summons, it will be owing less to the essential difference of their acts than to the fortunate difference of their position. It would be the height of injustice if through the interested concert of those who should be more uprightly minded, such a gang of desperadoes as that which now lords it over Rome, should be enabled during their ephemeral usurpation to inflict so grievous a loss upon their country, and to damage so irreparably the government which will presently supersede them. We hope better from the generosity, if not from the prudence of Englishmen."

A friend writing us on the subject of art, says, with reference to these remarks,—" I was amused the other day with reading the leading article of the *Times* on the shameful proceedings of the anti-papal government of Rome in disposing of the 'works of art, just as if these works had been indigenous productions, and not the collective plunder of other countries. If King Otho had purchased the Apollo surely it would have been no extraordinary act of vandalism to have transported it to Greece and set it up in Athens? What gives Italy the prescriptive right of possession in the higher productions of the art of foreign nations? Some day or other, some thousand years hence, we may have an American editor lamenting that the confederated republics of Greece have repurchased from the Provisional Government of Britain the Elgin marbles, and certainly they are as much art-products of England as the Apollo of Rome."

We cannot agree with our excellent correspondent in regarding this lament as an evidence of "untimely sensibility;" but join in deprecating earnestly any steps which should tend to break up the museums and galleries of Rome.

When the collections of private individuals, gathered together with time, discrimination, and pains, are distributed and sent east, west, north, and south, it is matter for deep regret. How much more so would it be in the case of those wonderful agglomerations of the results of human skill in Rome,—connected with it by so many associations, and which have formed for so long its chief glories!

If they are destined to be distributed, we should desire that they might come to England rather than be sent elsewhere, but so long as that can be prevented, we hope to see no inducements offered by our countrymen.

The newspapers say that the Edinburgh artists have been deprived of the opportunity of exhibiting their pictures this season at the Royal Academy, through the detention of the steamer which carried them. They did not arrive in London until the 9th, the day after the time fixed for receiving at the Academy, and the statement is, that the council considered the regulation imperative, and declined to receive them. If it were shown that the delay occurred through no fault of the artists, it may be thought that the council would have been justified, by the peculiar circumstances of the case, in overlooking the few hours by which the date had been exceeded. It is a hard thing for the artists, as the chance of obtaining a return for their labour is, in all probability, postponed until next season.

Apropos of which, we may mention that the general meeting of the Art-Union of London, for the reception of the annual report, and the distribution of the funds for the purchase of works of art, will be held in Drury-lane Theatre on Tuesday next, and will be open to all members and their friends. We shall give, as usual, a full report of the proceedings, and a correct list of the prizeholders.

As our gossip has fallen on matters of art, we may mention as amongst the works now exhibiting at the Cosmorama, in Regent-street, a remarkably beautiful model of Cologne Cathedral, with its spires completed, and forest of 5,000 pinnacles. It is the work of a German, Herr Charles Schropp, and is formed in wood and iron coloured; the niches are filled with their statues, and the windows with painted glass. It is 8 ft. 8 in. in length, 4 ft. wide, and 8 ft. high, and was completed, the modeller says, in eight years. It gives an admirable idea of this wonderful structure, and deserves a visit.

The last time we saw the cathedral of Cologne, thousands of persons were crowded

around it, from all parts of Germany and many parts of Europe. The King of Prussia was about to lay the first stone of the new works, and the words he used on the occasion are still ringing in our ears. "Here where the ground-stone lies," said he, "here by these towers, with all God's will, the portal in the world. Germany builds it,—may it be for her, with God's will, the portal of a new era, great and good! Far from here be all wickedness, all iniquity, and all that is ungenuine and therefore un-German! May dissension between the German princes and their people, between different faiths and different classes never find this road; and never may that feeling appear here, which, in former times, stopped the progress of this temple,—aye, even stopped the advance of our fatherland! Men of Cologne, the possession of this building is a high privilege for your city, enjoyed by none other, and nobly this day have you shown that you recognise it as such. Shout, then, with me, and while you shout will I strike the ground-stone;—shout loudly with me your rallying cry, ten centuries old, ' Cologne for ever !' "

And loudly was it echoed far and wide, " Cologne for ever !"

Since then great changes have taken place in Germany, calculated, we fear, to retard the progress of this important work.

ROYAL INSTITUTE OF BRITISH ARCHITECTS.

AWARD OF MEDALS.

At an ordinary meeting of the Institute held on the 16th inst., Mr. Sydney Smirke, V. P., in the chair, the following report from the council, on the award of the royal medal, and the essays and drawings submitted in competition for the other medals, was read :—

" The council have to report to the meeting, that pursuant to the notice publicly given, they proceeded, on the 29th of January last, ' to take into consideration the awarding of the Royal Medal for the year 1848, to the author of some literary publication connected with architecture; and having received and examined the several claims submitted, at a subsequent meeting, on the 12th of March, it was resolved, That the Royal Gold Medal be awarded to the Signor Cavaliere Luigi Canina of Rome, as the historian of architecture from the earliest period, and for his antiquarian researches; he having published a series of important works on the various styles of art, and likewise on the tombs of Etruria, the cities of ancient Latium, and other antique remains.'

This resolution of the council having been duly notified to her Majesty the Queen by the president, his Lordship was authorised to express to the council the full approbation by her Majesty of the award.

For the medal of the Institute offered for the best essay ' On the Peculiar Characteristics of the Palladian School of Architecture, and a comparison and contrast of its elementary principles and details with those of Ancient Roman Art,'—three essays were submitted in competition, distinguished by the following mottoes and marks :—No. 1. ' There's something of Magnificence about us we have not seen at Rome;' 2. ' How different, yet how like the same;' 3. ' The Letter X.' The council are of opinion that the essay designated by the motto, ' There's something of Magnificence about us we have not seen at Rome,' possesses considerable merit, and is entitled to the reward offered, and they therefore recommend that the silver medal of the Institute be awarded to it accordingly.

For the medal offered for an essay ' On the best manner of covering the roofs, and forming the flats and gutters of buildings,' &c., there are two competitors: one essay bearing the motto ' Finis coronat opus,' and the other ' Spe,'—but neither of them possesses sufficient merit to justify the council in awarding the medal on this occasion.

For ' the Soane Medallion,' the subject being, ' A Design for a Building to serve as a national Repository and Museum for the illustration and exhibition of the productions of the industrial arts, with all suitable accessories, &c;' six designs have been received, thus distinguished :—1. ' Simplicitas,' 2. ' Solidity, Convenience, Delight,' 3. ' Endymion,' 4. ' Esticot,' 5. ' Justitia! imploro

Fidem,' 6. ' Usui populi decori Regni.' It is with feelings of sincere regret the council announce that they cannot recommend the award of the Soane Medallion on this occasion. They deem it proper to state that the designs submitted exhibit generally a surprising deficiency of the recognised elementary principles of architectural composition, together with a lamentable want of constructive knowledge. In some, prominent and integral portions of the structure are impracticable as to execution ; in others, the most glaring discrepancies are apparent between the plans, sections, and elevations, and although it may be thought of minor importance, the drawings in general exhibit great negligence in execution, both as regards outlining and shading. The council consider that with a just regard to the best interests of those who aspire to be distinguished for their education and taste in the art, they are necessitated to withhold the reward offered, lest it might be inferred that the institute adopts, as a standard of merit, either of the productions now submitted."

Mr. C. Fowler said he thought it desirable that the award of the medals should be the act of the Institute, and not of the council alone : but in this case, as the report must be put to the meeting for confirmation, it would also be open to objection.

Mr. Godwin said, that to alter the award now was, of course, out of the question, as it had been communicated to her Majesty, and had received approval; but he would nevertheless strongly express his dissent from the policy of the council in sending the Royal medal abroad so early, considering how few honorary rewards were open to English architects and architectural investigators.

It was ultimately ruled that the award was in the hands of the council, and did not need the confirmation of the meeting. The report, therefore, was not put for reception by the meeting, a departure, to the best of our recollection, from the proceedings in similar cases before.

The letter which accompanied the selected essay being opened, the author was found to be Mr. Wyatt Papworth.

Mr. Robert Rawlinson, one of the superintending inspectors in the General Board of Health, then read a paper, prepared for our columns, and which follows this notice, on the hollow brick ceiling recently turned over St. George's Hall, Liverpool, and on hollow brick constructions generally.

During the discussion which afterwards ensued, the Chairman said that, as to the use of terra-cotta, we were quite in our infancy, and might with advantage look back to the works of the ancients. Some time ago he had applied to the principal drain-pipe makers respecting some tubes 3 feet in diameter, and found they could not be had. Twenty years ago he had seen abroad earthenware pipes of this diameter, lining a well 3,500 years old, with holes for the tree in the event of desiring to descend.— Mr. Garling reminded the meeting that hollow bricks had been used by Soane and others, and were probably abandoned because of expense.—Mr. Fowler spoke of their use for doors in Berlin.

Mr. Edwin Chadwick said the expense now was much lessened : 1,000 tiles made by the machine cost about ten or twelve shillings, and it was thought 1,000 bricks could be obtained for 2s. more. Wherever tiles were made, these bricks could be made. As to strength, the hollow brick was stronger than the solid, probably because more dense and better burnt.

The Health of Towns Association held their annual general meeting on Tuesday at the house of the Statistical Society, St. James's-square, the Hon. Frederick Byng in the chair. The meeting was addressed by the president, by Dr. Guy, Dr. Aldis, Mr. Joan Gunter, Mr. Mackinnon, M.P., Mr. P. H. Holland, Dr. Oliver, Mr. Grainger, Mr. Liddle, the Hon. H. Melville, and Dr. Melroy. The usual business of the year was moved and adopted, and a vote of thanks to the chairman passed before the meeting separated. An appeal to the public for subscriptions was made, and ought to be listened to.

Great Grimsby Docks.—On Wednesday the first stone of the Great Grimsby Docks (weighing 11 tons !) was laid by his Royal Highness Prince Albert. We shall give some particulars of this undertaking next week.

REMARKS ON HOLLOW BRICKS,

AS USED IN THE GREAT ARCH CEILING OVER ST. GEORGE'S HALL, LIVERPOOL, AND ON BRICK AND ARCH CONSTRUCTIONS IN GENERAL.

IN the following brief and imperfect remarks, on the peculiar structure of the ceiling of St. George's Hall, I beg to disclaim any pretensions to originality in the matter. My only desire is, to give a plain statement of facts. The use of bricks and tiles, solid and hollow, appears to be as old as the records of history. They are dug from the buried ruins of a forgotten civilization in Asia; the Egyptians converted their manufacture into an intolerable burden to the enslaved Jews; the Etruscans and Greeks were skilled in the art of working clay, to an extent even now considered almost perfect; the Romans constructed vast works with bricks and tiles, moulded into forms of use and beauty, unknown even in this age of invention; and the Italian architects have used bricks and tiles in their buildings, following the examples set them by their Roman predecessors. There are many old examples of brick and tile work where the material has been moulded into forms of ornament as well as utility of construction.

In the fifth and sixth centuries, bricks were used in walls and arches as a facing to rubble and concrete, as seen in the sections given of palaces, churches, and other constructions of the time of Theodoric, at Terracina. The ancient temple of the Caffarella, two miles from Rome, one of the earliest examples of a pagan temple consecrated to the Christian religion in the fourth century, is of brick, and the cornices, which are hold in their projection and elaborate in relief and ornament, are also of brick, and terra-cotta ornaments adorn the structure.

St. Stephen's, the round, at Rome, was ceiled with small vases or tubes of terra-cotta; these tubes were from six to seven inches in length, three inches in diameter, the exterior surface spirally channelled to give greater hold to the mortar. This building was converted from a heathen temple to a Christian church, in the fifth or sixth century.

The church of St. Vitali, at Ravenna, built under the reign of Justinian, and from drawings brought from the East, in the sixth century, has a dome constructed in spiral lines with small terra-cotta vases, seven inches long and two inches diameter, the lower part of the structure being built with vases of terra-cotta twenty-two inches high and eight inches in diameter.

The house of Pilate, at Rome, eleventh century, exhibits a knowledge of construction and adaptation of brick and tile to the purposes of ornament and use, for which we shall look in vain to find many modern examples to compare with it; there is beauty, utility, fitness, and variety combined, so as to give strength and grace to the structure. If we would learn how to construct arches for durability, we must (except in rare cases) most certainly refer to the works of men two thousand years dead and buried. We shall assuredly not find in their great works any examples of flat lintels over openings, with parallel bricks, set in parallel beds, until the courses meet in a point on the under side, leaving a triangular space for the key, which is fitted in with similar parallel courses, and yet this abortion of an arch is the modern mode of construction in too many instances throughout this country; examples of it may be found in new houses and public buildings not six months old; the cement and stucco-fronted shams of modern London have rarely any other form of construction, and the result is exhibited in ugly cracks and rents over the door and window openings.

I would beg to mention, incidentally, that fitness and propriety are not so much considered as they ought to be in the construction of arches for architectural purposes, and I could bring hundreds of examples, even from those termed our finest buildings, to prove this. The purpose of an arch is to span and cover in a space not attainable by horizontal lintels. This may be termed its prime purpose on a great scale, such as in the ceiling immediately under notice; this is only accomplished by a judicious distribution of strength and weight, so as to balance equally all the parts. At the springing line, the arch must be the deepest on bed; at the crown, or key, it ought to be the lightest and thinnest, so that if it was divided along the line of key and erected into a wall on each abutment there would be a gradual diminution of thickness and strength from the base to the summit. I would ask, is this the mode of construction generally used? Do we not see all forms of arch, the semi, the segment, and the elliptical, with a bed at the springing several times less than the depth at the key. Divide such arches, and rear them up on their abutments, and we should have the pyramid on its apex. Then we have faulty jointing; the beds of an ellipsis all drawn to one point, as seen in the arch at Temple Bar; or the inner and outer line is equally divided to produce the bed lines; archstones bent in the form of an Γ, as seen in semi's, &c.

The bent joint, or bed, in masonry ought never to be used. All masonry must depend, principally, up onits gravity, for stability; stones cannot, legitimately, be hung together; they may, however, be joggled for some purposes of strength in their vertical joints and horizontal beds, but no form of arch should depend upon joggles. Stone ought to be considered as having no tensile strength, and be treated and used accordingly. Bricks should be made subject to the same rule.

In bridge-building we frequently see a heavy ponderous key-stone, and over it a break in the cornice, with a massive solid pedestal in an otherwise open balustrade, on which, at times, a lamp is placed. All this is false; the pedestal should be over the pier or abutment, and not over the key, where all should be light and graceful: unbroken lines over an opening always have the best effect; there should be no massing or adding of weight at the crown of an arch.

The bridges of Telford and Rennie display constructive skill of the highest order; Mr. Buck, the engineer, has studied bridge construction thoroughly, and his examples may be considered perfect. Some of his bridges can be seen in Manchester, near the Birmingham and Sheffield Railway Station. The great bridge over the Dee at Chester, designed by the late Mr. Harrison, and constructed by Mr. Jesse Hartley, Engineer of the Liverpool Docks, is one of the finest examples of masonry in the world. Mr. Hartley is perhaps one of the most perfect masons and constructive engineers of the age, of which his Liverpool dock-works are an enduring testimony; he is always perfect in his arrangement of masonry beds and joints. There are also good examples by other architects and engineers.

Columns and architraves, forming the appearance of a door or porch, have no business with the abutments or piers of bridges; they are not useful, and most certainly are not ornamental, and yet we find them added to the finest bridges in the world; some of those over the Thames.

In making these remarks I may be considered bold, and presumptuous; but I must dare the censure in advocating propriety and fitness in construction, and asserting that construction must be the first consideration. If ornament will not harmonize with construction, ornament must give way; if precedent rebels against construction, precedent must be abandoned.

It has been shown from the ancient examples quoted, that the use of hollow bricks, tiles, and terra-cotta vases for arch and dome structures, is at least 2,000 years old, and that some of the work is now perfect; an enduring testimony to the constructive skill of the architects and builders. We may not then claim the honour of invention in the use of hollow brick or tile; but we may follow the example set to us, and, with modern means and appliances, improve upon our models. We have clay in abundance, fuel cheap, tile and brick-making machines to economise labour, &c. There has hitherto been one great drawback to improvement in brick and tile construction, the excise duty. This in a great measure has arisen from an idea that the law dictated the form and size, namely, 10 inches by 5 inches, by 3 inches, or, 150 cube inches. The 150 cube inches the law does dictate as the largest size for single duty; but any form may be given to that cubic capacity; and, if the brick does not displace, in water, more than this number of inches, it will be allowed at the single duty. But even with this relaxation, the law is more fitted for China than for Great Britain, as it cripples invention and cramps construction.

I will now quote some passages, from a MS. volume by Mr. Edwin Chadwick,* on the subject of hollow bricks:—

If we suppose that improvement were to stop at the adoption of constructions of hollow brick, made of the common sizes and shapes, so that they might be worked by the common bricklayers without change of their practice in any other respects, the gain would be considerable in getting rid of a large proportion of the absorbent qualities, and the damp incident to the use of common bricks, apart from the gain in the more economical manufacture of the hollow bricks.

There appears to be no reason to doubt that all the observations which we have collected, in respect to the superior warmth of double walls, and of walls made hollow as described by means of half bricks, of battened walls, and of hollow walls of wainscot, will be found applicable to walls of the proposed hollow brick construction. In reducing the amount of heat requisite to repel extraneous damp, we economise the labourer's fuel, in other words, increase its power and his means of comfort.

Suppose the walls of a cottage constructed 9 inches thick with 9-inch hollow bricks, the possible absorbent power of the walls of a cottage, say of 500 cubic feet, will be reduced from 306 gallons to 102 gallons of water.

Any gentleman who has a tile-machine and a kiln, may with it use almost any description of clay, and more conveniently apply it to the manufacture of hollow than common bricks for the construction of dwellings for his labourers; which dwellings will be drier and warmer, and he may afford to let them at a lower rent than the common cottages.

For farm steadings, also, and for garden walls, the less absorbent and drier walls, constructed with the harder-burnt and less porous hollow bricks, will be found of great advantage.

But the remaining absorbent power of the hollow bricks, it may be submitted, is an ill quality, for the removal of which it is worth while to make exertions. To this end I have requested a trial to be made of a machine, for giving additional density by additional pressure to the bricks made by the machine. The trials are very satisfactory, and the work is promised to be done at a very cheap rate.

I propose to have the bricks glazed, to save whitewashing and paint inside the house, and to give a cheerful appearance on the outside, and to repel the weather. The process, judging by that for pottery, need not be an expensive one. It would, moreover, be worth the while to increase the density of the clay, by a careful preparation of it in the mode of potter's clays.

By the additional pressure, greater exactitude to form will be given, and larger bricks made, fit for a construction of the nature of ashlar or stone construction.

To keep, however, to the construction of walls, there appears to be no reason for supposing that a 5 or 6-inch wall may not be made by means of hollow bricks sufficiently dry and warm, to render any further increase of thickness of little moment compared with the expense.

In towns, space in houses is of the greatest consequence. There, the space for the houses of the poorer classes may be taken as small and fixed; and this being so, all that can be gained from the thickness of walls, within that fixed area, is gained as breathing space.

Thus, the difference between a 9-inch and 5-inch wall, in a fourth-class two-story house, is about 500 cubic feet, equal to the space for two bed recesses, or one small sleeping room.

The improvement in the manufacture of bricks so as to ensure to a thick wall greater dryness and warmth than to a practically thick wall, is a highly important object.

Hollow bricks, it may be stated, from the experience of hollow walls, will transmit far less sound than solid walls. Partitions may be made of 3-inch hollow brick, which will not only attain this end excellently well, but another,—that of superseding the hollow wooden partitions, which give dreadful facilities for the spread of fires.

In confined space and crowded apartments, the noise and disturbances from the tread of adults (not to speak of children or their noises) is the occasion of much irritation, and, in the cases of sickness, of pain and injury.

To prevent this, and to isolate as far as possible one family from another, and the living rooms from the sleeping rooms, the floors of some of the improved dwellings for the labouring classes at Birkenhead were constructed of brick in flat arches of about 6 feet span. The arches were

* "On the chief evils affecting the health and comfort of the population, which appear to be preventable by improvements in the materials and for the construction of dwelling-houses, more especially of the dwelling-houses for the poorer classes."

tied together by iron ties, and abutted in the centre on an iron beam. The spaces between the upper surface of the arches and the spandrils were filled in by mortar, on which flat tiles were imbedded. They answered the purpose perfectly; but the weight of a floor of such a construction must be very great. Observing this construction, and, generally, the economy of constructions of groined arches in brick, where the same centreing was used successively for many arches, it occurred to me to propose the construction of such floors of hollow brick, moulded in form for the purpose. The precise thickness, and the best forms of bricks for the purpose, may not be readily determined. The expense of an ordinary wooden floor, of 12 feet square, would be about, I am informed, *7l.*; the expense of an arched floor of the hollow brick construction, tied together with iron ties, taking the hollow brick at one-third less price than the solid bricks, is estimated at *4l.*

With constructions of these hollow bricks experiments were made—

1st. For a series of arches of small curvatures without iron ties.

2nd. For circular arches without iron ties.

3rd. Elliptical arches with iron ties. The experimental arches were 2 metres, or 6 feet 6 inches wide, or 43 square feet, being a portion of a surface of 690 feet.

The ordinary weight of a common wooden floor of that extent, as constructed in England, would be about 700 lbs., and it would be expected to bear say 2 tons. Each ton would be equivalent to the average weight of say fifteen adult persons, at least, in England. The results were—That the elliptical arch made of earthenware pots or hollow bricks, $6\frac{1}{2}$ inches high and $3\frac{1}{2}$ inches in diameter, without iron ties, supported, besides its own weight, a load of about 2 tons 10 cwt. on each 10 superficial feet.

That an arch of small curvature, made of hollow bricks $9\frac{3}{4}$ inches high and $5\frac{1}{2}$ inches diameter, supported besides its own weight a load of 3 tons 18 cwt. on $10\frac{3}{4}$ superficial feet.

That a portion of a circular arch, constructed with earthenware pots $12\frac{1}{2}$ inches deep and $5\frac{1}{2}$ inches in diameter, supported besides its own weight a load of upwards of 5 tons, or the weight of more than 67 adult persons of 165 lbs. each; that a floor of earthen pots, 4 inches high and $3\frac{1}{2}$ inches in diameter, tied with iron ties, supported besides its own weight a load of 2 tons per square foot; that a floor, formed with earthen pots $7\frac{1}{2}$ inches high and $4\frac{1}{2}$ inches in diameter, and tied with iron ties, supported more than 3,994 lbs., or the weight of 24 adult persons, besides its own weight.

The experiments and practical experience in private and public buildings of the Parisian architect corroborate the general conclusions which are submitted as established in relation to the hollow brick construction, as being superior to the common stone and brick construction:—

In preventing the passage of humidity and being drier.

In preventing the passage of heat, and being warmer in winter and cooler in summer.

In being a security against fire.

In preventing the passage of sound.

In having less unnecessary material and being lighter.

In being better dried and burnt harder and stronger.

In being more cleanly.

In being cheaper.

The extent to which these qualities are attainable must depend upon the extent of demand for them, upon further attention and experience been brought to bear upon them, and on the approved application of machinery to the construction of the various eligible forms of hollow bricks.

So far Mr. Chadwick.

The modern French architects use a kind of pottery vase in construction for partition walls, floors, stairs, and ceilings; but they depend more upon the lightness of the material and the strength of their mortar and cement, for the stability of their works, than upon skill in constructive adaptation of their hollow pots. If fact, the stability of their work depends upon the strength of the mortar or cement (gypsum), and iron bond, altogether, as a glance at their forms of hollow ware will show. We are not without some modern examples of hollow brick or tile work even in London—floors and arches have been found of such material, as when the old Carlton Palace was taken down, as mentioned in the manuscript volume already referred to. It is difficult in this our day, to settle satisfactorily where or how an idea is obtained. "Necessity is said to be the mother of invention," and no doubt many inventions are new to the person, which are old to the world; the faculties of the mind are infinite for purposes of combination in thought, but frequently similar in their results. Two men, wide apart, in distant regions, may strike at the same idea, when investigating the same causes; and we, consequently, have every great invention disputed by rival claimants. It was so with Franklin and electricity; and one of the most recent instances is the discovery of the planet Neptune, in astronomy. If, however, all men were honest to themselves, they would care little about priority of discovery, as the man who is anxious to earn fame from one lucky thought or invention, is seldom deserving of the honour. True genius will not rob for an idea, and has no fear of robbery from others; but it will adapt, mould, and use the ideas of every age, for purposes of utility, ornament, and truth.

The ceiling now turned over St. George's Hall, Liverpool, was designed by my late friend, Mr. Elmes, a bill of quantities for which was made out by him in March, 1843. The arch was to be of solid brickwork. Patent compressed bricks were specified for, and for this mode of construction the contract was let to Mr. Tomkinson, the builder. I had many conversations with Mr. Elmes from time to time about the arch, and I always expressed myself confidently as to its practicability. Several forms of section were made, and Mr. Elmes sought up all the known examples of great ceilings to guide him in the construction of his own. The form and sectional strength settled, another difficulty presented itself. The room must be ventilated according to plans devised by Dr. Reid, and the doctor required 400 square feet of open space, as equally diffused throughout the arch as possible.*

When the time for preparation to commence the work came, Mr. Elmes was stricken with his fatal malady; his strength was failing, and the physicians had ordered him abroad: he sent for me to come and see him, and as I was not at the time much engaged, I commenced some sections of the arch to provide for the required space for ventilation; and the plan decided upon at the time was, to leave out alternate headers, as frequently seen in the sides of a barn.

I had quite forgotten seeing hollow bricks in Mr. Chadwick's office at Somerset-house, although I had written to Mr. Elmes at the time recommending their use. But it was certainly with Mr. Chadwick that I first saw them. These were of the ordinary size.

Mr. Elmes left England never to return, and as the time for commencing the arch drew on, I was constantly turning the subject over in my mind how I could obtain lightness, open space, and strength. About this time I was called over to Castle Howard on professional business; and, in the steward's office I saw some beautiful drain-tiles, 12 inches long, with a bore of 2 inches in diameter. I took one up, examined it, and asked how and where it was made, when I learned that they had machines which made them on their own estate. My first idea was, why not construct an arch of circular tile, set in cement? My next question was, will the machine make other shapes than the circle? and the answer was, "any shape you like." I then thought of hexagons, and finally adopted the square, and settled the present dimensions, four inches by four inches, by twelve and a half inches, for purposes of bond. On my return to Liverpool, I wrote to Mr. Scragg, the maker of the machines, and asked him to meet me on the ground at St. George's Hall. I shewed him the sections, and the building, explained what I required him to make, and ordered fifty tiles to be made of the dimensions above stated; half with a longitudinal perforation of three inches, and half two inches. I then weighted them singly, and decided upon the two-inch perforation. I drew up a report,* and presented it to the committee, when they decided at once to adopt the hollow tile. I consulted Dr. Reid about them, and had his full concurrence for their use. I loaded four of the tiles, placed singly, with upwards of thirteen tons, without their shewing any tendency to fracture, and I left them loaded as an answer to all objections to their use on the score of strength (and there were many), intending to have loaded them to crushing, but they were removed without my knowledge. For equal drying, I had fifty thousand moulded with square perforations, but the maker said he found little or no advantage over the circle. Not only was the great hall ceiling intended to be of brick, but the ceiling over the two courts, which are about fifty feet square. These, however, have been formed of timber, notwithstanding the order of the committee to the contrary, and although the hollow bricks for their construction were delivered on the ground.

The great arch is struck from three centres, and the soffit is divided into panels, the ribs to form which are worked in the tile. These longitudinal ribs are bonded with York paving, four inches in thickness, cramped together at the joints. The main ribs of the arch are two tiles, or two feet in depth; the plain portions of the panels are twelve inches, or one tile in depth, so that the strength of the arch, of sixty-five feet span, is reduced to twelve inches in depth, with the weight of the panel ribs added. The accompanying section † will further explain the construction.

That hollow bricks may be used in arches, with perfect safety to the structure, is, I think, fully proved, and I have no doubt but that the researches of Mr. Chadwick will soon be brought into practical use. The machines are an advantage unknown to the ancients, and we may obtain from them a truth of form which shall not depend upon the strength of the cement alone for the stability of the structure. It was the custom formerly to score, or reed, the surface of all pulleys to make the driving strap adhere. This not only lost power, but it rapidly wore out strap and pulley; so we shall find in another way, with our brick and tile work: mould the correct forms, put them together in a proper manner, and we shall require mortar to bed them, but not to be also the sole means of stability and support.

In these modern times we are too much wedded to "precedent," without always fully considering if it is worth imitation, and we are apt to make "ornament" the first consideration, when, in all cases, it ought to be construction. Nature, in this, should be followed. The skeleton of the building ought to be perfect; then clothe and beautify in accordance with that skeleton structure. Nature is ever beautiful because most perfect; but the beauty of nature is not always for the sight. The external forms of grace alone, are present to the eye, but that which is hidden is frequently more complex, wonderful, and beautiful than that we see. Take the skeleton of any animal, and what a combination of structural beauty does it unfold; joint fitted to joint, bone adapted to bone, solidity where solidity is required, tubular where advantageous; notice the graceful curves, the swelling joints, the arched spines, the flattened blades, the serrated skull, and answer if the build of any creature could be improved by all the ingenuity of the skilled mechanic, or the calculations of the most profound mathematician. Take the graceful nautilus, examine its plated chambers,

* Elmes was seriously perplexed by the requirements insisted on for ventilation. As to some alterations in the external appearance of the building in consequence, a correspondent from Liverpool wrote thus last week:—"I was surprised to observe that, in a recent notice of *Elmes's* magnificent pile, the St. George's Hall here, you had not remarked that the 'sky line' of the admirably designed central mass was broken and destroyed by the projection of a huge louvred structure, rising above the intended ridge of the main roof, and that the circular termination to the north, containing the concert-room, is shockingly disfigured by a polygonal boarded lantern, which has been aptly compared to the ventilator of a common brewery. Both these blots are the result of the adoption of the method of ventilating, and were never contemplated by the architect in the first instance, as may be seen by examining the model kept on the works; and though I believe every exertion was made by that lamented artist to save his beautiful design from such injury, he strove in vain; the inexorable doctor would not give way, nor would the corporation authorise a departure from his project. An additional couple of courses in the stonework of the centre would have hidden the eyesore *there*, though certainly at some sacrifice of its deeply-studied proportions, but cure for the northern excrescence there was none, but by making it, if possible, a sightly, since it would never be an ornamental, adjunct. Neither of these remedies has been applied, the economy imposed upon the building committee by the accession of several heavy items beyond the contemplated cost of the building, preventing the further addition which would have been thus incurred. It is needless to say that to a man of Elmes's fine taste such unsightly projections on his intended outline were a source of great annoyance, or that they will have a like effect on every one with a feeling for the beautiful in architecture; but that they are indispensable to the proper ventilation of the buildings, or that the same area of exit could not have been provided in some less obtrusive manner, would, I venture to think, be less easy of proof."—ED.

* This we will give, with the specification, next week.—ED.

† The section is to a scale of 1-16th of an inch to 1 foot. We likewise give a plan of the great hall and adjoining apartments, which serve as abutments, (see page 186). The spaces marked A A on plan are for ventilation.—ED.

see how they are curled over, backwards and forwards, to give the greatest quantity of support, with the least expenditure of material, over the greatest external surface. Look at the more graceful fossil ammonite, and consider the enriched markings of its air chambers, varied to every form of section, and then say if man has not much to forget, and more to learn in his structural arrangements. The bee has constructed, age after age, and in all countries where it can exist, the same perfect hexagon, which is proved to be the best form for economising space, and giving strength with the least expenditure of material.

Used with iron, wrought and cast, hollow bricks may be combined for purposes where, at present, wood alone is introduced. Palaces and churches may own their adoption with singular advantage. In hospitals, gaols, workhouses, and asylums they will give ready means for a general diffusion of warmth and ventilation; barracks in tropical climates, so constructed, with hollow walls, would resist the intense action of the sun, and the solid material of the tile the attacks of insects, and, what is almost of as much consequence, their carriage would be about one-third that of solid bricks. Factories and warehouses would be made fireproof at the least cost, as much weight in the floors would be avoided. Museums and picture galleries would be freed from damp and rot, to the preservation of the wonders of nature and the glories of art; the dwelling-houses of the wealthy may have, in every room, a completeness of ventilation at present unattainable with solid bricks. The humblest cottage may have walls, stairs, floors, and roof of the same hollow material; they may be made dry, warm, and fireproof; ventilation may be simple and effective, and fuel may be economised to an extent not at present practised, by expending much of the heat of the fire in the hollow walls and floors. With these advantages, Mr. Chadwick proposes to combine extreme-solidity of substance and colour: solidity and finish he will obtain by mechanical pressure; colour by thin layers of tinted clay pressed on the surface, or by washing the semi-dried brick or tile in a mineral solution. The tile making machines will press out any form of section, plain or moulded; and any raised form, not undercut, may be obtained by pressure, as practised in terra-cotta. Hollow bricks can be made subservient to improved construction; they may be worked and combined with stone, solid brick, iron, and timber; they may be made to serve in numerous instances all the purposes of solid material, with advantages peculiarly their own. Much more may be said on the subject—in fact is said by Mr. Chadwick in his volume, which I trust may ultimately be laid before the public.

Before leaving the subject, I beg distinctly to remark that I do not contemplate a superseding with hollow bricks all practised forms and modes of construction, but an adaptation where reason can clearly demonstrate an advantage. One material and one method is the project of a theorist of one idea, or of a quack.

Nature revels in infinite variety of structure, but is always perfect in adaptation and usefulness: let us break the shackles of precedent, and try to imitate nature in her economy, use, and beauty. To do this, construction must ever be our first consideration; this must be adapted to utility, and we may then add ornament for beauty, but ever with consistency.*

Robert Rawlinson.

Monument to Mr. Peter Nicholson, Architect, at Carlisle. — In respect to the statue, or other suitable and lasting memorial of this useful member of our profession, which it is proposed to erect in Carlisle, a correspondent, "Alpha," suggests that the fact ought not to be lost sight of that he died in very poor circumstances. It is to be hoped, therefore, that while his talent is honoured his family will not be neglected, otherwise a monument to his memory would be but a sorry mockery of the man.

* The great arch was keyed on March 3rd, 1849, the centres were lowered on the 5th, and it had deflected 3-8ths of an inch by the 12th, and was found in precisely the same position April 14th. The whole of the timbering forming the great centres will be taken down by the first week in May. The arch, however, stands perfectly clear of everything.

NOTES IN THE PROVINCES.

The repairs of the rood tower of Lincoln Cathedral are proceeding. The south and west sides have been repaired, and the east side is in progress.——A hotel, built by Messrs. Grissell and Peto, near the Colchester Railway station, at a cost of 12,000*l.* to 15,000*l.*, has been charitably converted by Mr. Peto into an asylum for infant idiots.——The new Wesleyan Chapel in Hobson-street, Cambridge, is of white brick with stone dressings; the portico, Corinthian columns, and antæ, are of Ketton stone. The length of the building is 61 feet; width, 45 feet 4 inches; accommodation, 1,000 sittings,—400 free. Mr. Trimer was the architect, and the builders were Messrs. Quinsee and Attack, of Cambridge. The final cost was 2,100*l.* There are school-rooms under the chapel.——The new building near the Sussex County Hospital, Brighton, intended for the Brighton College, the first stone of which was laid on 27th June last, is rapidly approaching completion. Mr. G. G. Scott is the architect, and Messrs. Wisden and Anscombe are the builders. The style is collegiate of fourteenth century, with cloisters along the front of the building. The principal front of the design only has been hitherto undertaken. The class-rooms, however, will accommodate 300 pupils. The plan includes a school-room, dining-room, and chapel; the whole to form three sides of a quadrangle, with houses for the master and wardens arranged about the front.——The market improvements at Worcester, in the conversion of a space of ground, recently occupied as a market for green-grocery, into a butchers' and fish market, are rapidly progressing, under the superintendence of Messrs. Rowe and Son, architects, of that city. The butchers' market will be 112 feet in length by 40 feet wide, and fitted up with four rows of stalls, and lighted by side lights. The fish market will be divided from it, and lighted from the roof. The height of the market to the apex of the roof will be 31 feet, and the timber supporting the roof will be exposed to view. The *Journal* speaks favourably of the design. ——The church at Heywood, Westbury, built at the expense of Mr. H. G. G. Ludlow, of Heywood, was consecrated on Thursday week. The building is in the early English style, with open benches for about 360 persons. The old parish church has lately been restored at the cost of 2,000*l.*——The new chapel at Copston, near Monk's Kirby, Warwickshire, was consecrated on Tuesday week. It is in the decorated style of architecture, and capable of holding two hundred persons. It has been built at the expense of the Earl of Denbigh. The cost was 1,000*l.* exclusive of carriage of materials by the Earl's tenants, free.——On Thursday week the inscription stone of the Birmingham Free Industrial Schools, in Gem-street, was laid with the usual ceremonies. The cost of the erection will be upwards of 2,000*l.*, and the accommodation sufficient for 200 children of both sexes.——The new Concert-hall, in Hope-street, Liverpool, noticed by us lately amongst buildings in progress there, is about to be formally opened with a series of grand musical performances.——Mr. Samuel Addison, banker, Wednesbury, has contributed 700*l.* for the completion of the tower and spire of the new church there. The same gentleman gave 500*l.* in addition to the site, towards the erection of the church itself.——At the Jarrow Docks the operations commenced by the contractors have been suspended, and the workmen discharged, owing to the unsettled state of the affairs of the Railway Company, and the probability of such schemes being, for the present, abandoned. It is said that the arrangements for purchasing the land in the locality were not completed.——The first stone of St. Peter's Church, Ascot Heath, was laid last Monday by the Bishop of Oxford. Mr. Perrey, architect; Messrs. Higgs and Sons, builders. It is in the Decorated style, and is to cost about 1,400*l.*——The time for lodging plans in competition by certain architects, for the Essex County Lunatic Asylum at Brentwood, has been extended to 1st May.——A site for a new asylum at Hampshire has been selected at Titchfield.——The church of St. James, Lower Gornall, has been enlarged and refitted. The chancel, entirely new, is laid with encaustic tiles. Mr. Bourne, of Dudley, was the architect employed.——A large building in Great Ancoats-street, Manchester, according to the local *Spectator*, is to be fitted up, under the direction of a competent architect, as a model lodging-house.——A sum of 1,600*l.* has been voted, at the West Riding sessions, for the enlargement of the second court of the Wakefield Court-house.——The foundation stone of the Durham Mechanics' Institute was laid, on the 30th ult., by the leader of a procession of Freemasons.——The chancel window of Crosscannonby Church, near Maryport, has been filled with stained glass, supplied by the parishioners. The window consists of three lancet lights; in the centre one of which is represented the Crucifixion. In the left lancet is St. Peter, and in the right, the saint to whom the structure is dedicated. The remainder of the window is fitted with dowered quatre-foils, enclosed in circles. The designs were furnished and the work executed by the Messrs. Scott, of Carlisle.

A NOTE TO WORKMEN.

Observing in your publication of last week some remarks on the want of ambition among working men, I beg to make a few observations on the subject. The statements in the article are certainly lamentable facts, the extent of which is very considerable. The evils resulting from them greatly impoverish the nation, and entail misery and wretchedness on posterity. The following remarks relate alone to myself. They are not given as a boast, neither as reproof, but rather to excite an honest ambition in the minds of the working classes. I am a married man, with a wife and five children, who are dependent on my exertions for their support. Being a working mechanic, my income is (when employed) 1*l.* 10s. per week. My parents, thirty years ago, were similarly situated, with about one-third of this income. From them I learned a lesson of economy. The great question with me is, what quantity and quality of the necessaries of life are most conducive to promote health, strength, and happiness. Guided by the wise in former ages, and by my own experience, I have long since come to this conclusion—that man's real wants are comparatively few. I have found, therefore, in past years, that two-thirds of my income will sufficiently supply myself and family with the necessaries of life; the one-sixth of the same will meet the casualties of loss of employment; the other sixth, which is 5s. per week, or about 10*l.* per year, is laid by for sickness or age. This trifling sum, with interest and compound interest, in a few years will make a poor man comparatively rich. Now, I am persuaded that there are thousands of working men, if they would make an honest statement of what they spend foolishly, the amount of money so spent would be more than I pretend to save, and they are often laying themselves under the necessity of giving 20 per cent. for pledges of their property, when at the same time they might, by resolution and good management, be receiving instead of giving interest for money. Let these hints be received in the spirit they are given. Let them excite an honest ambition to raise ourselves from that state of degradation in which too many of us are found. Better times approach but slowly to the sluggard and profligate,—I might rather say, they are always retreating from him, while the industrious and frugal are overtaking them every day.

A Working Man,
Formerly an "Old Mason."

Bursting of a Reservoir near Keighley.—At Cowling, on the top of a moor, a reservoir, which supplied a small cotton mill with water, lately gave way, and carried all before it with a stream occasionally 15 to 20 feet deep; but fortunately without the loss of a single life, though several were in imminent jeopardy. A bridge was carried away, and rocks of several tons weight were bowled along with a noise like prolonged thunder. It is even alleged, that "in one place the living solid rock has been scooped away to such an extent that a basin big enough to contain a large house has been formed in one hour."

ST. GEORGE'S HALL, LIVERPOOL.*

PLAN OF HALL, &c.

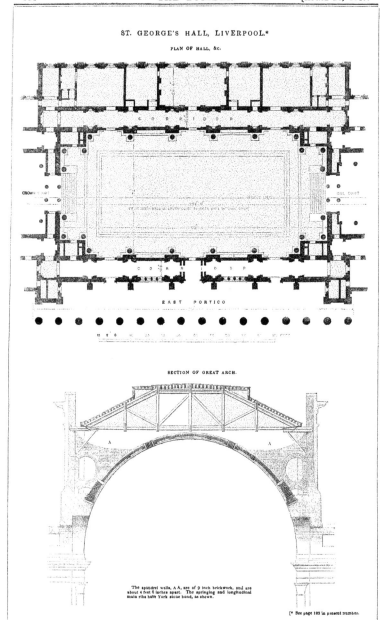

SECTION OF GREAT ARCH.

The spandrel walls, A A, are of 9 inch brickwork, and are
about 4 feet 6 inches apart. The springing and longitudinal
main ribs have York stone bond, as shewn.

[* See page 183 in present number.

ENTRANCE FRONT OF THE BRITISH MUSEUM.——SIR ROBERT SMIRKE, R.A., ARCHITECT.

THE NEW BRITISH MUSEUM.

On the preceding page we place before our readers a perspective view of the entrance-front of the British Museum, now nearly completed. In the second volume of our journal a view was given of the old Museum, known as Montague House, together with some historical particulars.*

The order of architecture adopted throughout the exterior of the new building is the Grecian Ionic. The southern façade consists of the great entrance portico, eight columns in width, and two intercolumniations in projection. On either side is an advancing wing, giving to the entire front an extent of 370 feet, the whole of which is surrounded by a colonnade, consisting of forty-four columns, raised upon a stylobate five feet and a half high. The columns are five feet at their lower diameter, and forty-five feet high; the height from the pavement of the front courtyard to the top of the entablature of the colonnade, is sixty-six feet and a half.

The principal floor of the building is reached by a flight of twelve stone steps at the foot of the portico, one hundred and twenty-five feet in width, terminating on either side with pedestals intended to receive groups of sculpture.

The tympanum of the portico is proposed to be enriched with historical or allegorical sculpture in full relief, and colossal statues are to surmount the pediment. These are not yet executed.

The principal entrance to the museum under this portico is by a carved oak door, hung to a door-frame of stone, nine feet six inches wide, and twenty-four feet high, through which we shall pass next week, and give a view of the great hall and staircase.

The majority of our readers know that the Museum has been erected from the designs of Sir Robert Smirke, but that since 1846, in consequence of the ill-health of Sir Robert, his brother, Mr. Sydney Smirke, has been engaged in completing it.

* In the same Volume of The Builder, p. 324 and p. 360, will be found two Views of the entrance gateway, now about to be removed.

RECOVERY OF EXPENSES INCURRED BY OVERSEERS IN PULLING DOWN RUINOUS STRUCTURES UNDER THE BUILDINGS ACT.

Last week a case was heard at the Thames Police-office, arising out of a suit for the recovery of 13*l*. 16*s*. from Sarah Moncar, of Shipwrights'-terrace, Poplar, being the residue of expenses incurred by John Coombs, overseer of the parish of All Saints, Poplar, in respect of a certain building.

The defendant was the owner of a small tenement in a place called Cold Harbour, Blackwall, which has been for many years in a ruinous state, and was inspected by the district-surveyor so far back as 1845, when, it is stated, he reported to the official referees that it was in a dilapidated and dangerous condition, and that it was expedient and necessary that the building should be taken down, and a hoard put up for the safety of passengers. Nothing, however, was done beyond shoring up the building until February last, when, owing to repeated complaints from various persons, the law was set in motion and the Act was brought into operation. The defendant was first waited upon, and the ruinous and perilous condition of the building was fully represented, but without effect. The overseers, accompanied by the surveyor of pavements and the vestry-clerk, surveyed the premises on the 12th of February. The roof had then fallen, and the tenement was in the most dilapidated condition imaginable, and in danger of falling and burying the defendant, the only occupier, in the ruins. The next step was to send a notice to the official referee of metropolitan buildings, who gave Mr. Good, the district-surveyor, orders to make a survey, and he did so, and certified that the premises required to be wholly pulled down. After the various other formalities required by the Act, and a copy of the surveyor's report had been served on the overseers, a notice was served on the defendant to pull down the premises at the expiration of fourteen days from the date thereof. The defendant still refused, and after repeated notices had been given to her by Mr. Kemp, the overseers employed a builder to raze the building to the ground, caused the materials to be sold by public auction, and now sued the defendant for the balance of the expenses, amounting in all to 21*l*. Credit had been given to the defendant for 7*l*. 4*s*., the sum which the old materials realised by the sale, and proof was given that a formal demand of the balance now sued for had been made. The payment of the district surveyor's fees, auctioneer's expenses, the solicitor's costs, and the services of notices, &c., were proved by numerous witnesses, and there was no question raised by the defendant's solicitor as to the ruinous condition of the building. An objection was taken to the service of a notice, thrust through a broken window-pane, which was overruled. Likewise to the charge of a guinea made by Mr. Kemp, the vestry clerk, including 4*s*. for coach hire. It was said that Kemp was paid a salary, and it was part of his duty to advise the overseers, and that when he attended the court, or went to the premises in question, he was on parish duty. Mr. Kemp insisted that the duty was special, and had nothing to do with his appointment as vestry clerk, and that he laid out 10*s*. 6*d*. for coach hire and fees of court.—The magistrate was at first disposed only to allow Mr. Kemp the money he had actually expended, but finally waived the objection, and 21*s*. was awarded to him. He directed a warrant to issue to distrain the goods and chattels of the defendant for the sum claimed.

INSTITUTION OF CIVIL ENGINEERS.

LIGHT.

At a meeting on April 17, Mr. R. Stephenson, M.P., in the chair, the paper read was, "On an application of certain Liquid Hydrocarbons to Artificial Illumination," by Mr. C. B. Mansfield, B.A. The paper first noticed that liquid hydrocarbons had been comparatively little used for the production of artificial light; and that in the instances in which they had been applied, their liquidity, and not their evaporability, had been turned to account.

The paper represented that a difficulty had been solved by the discovery of a liquid hydrocarbon as volatile as spirits of wine, but containing sufficient carbon for the most perfect light, and obtainable in any quantity. This hydrocarbon was procured from coal tar, and was called "Benzole." Its volatility was such as to enable it to napthalise atmospheric air as effectually as ordinary naptha did coal gas.

The system proposed by the author (which was illustrated in the room by a working apparatus) consisted in conducting a stream of almost any gas, or even of atmospheric air, through a reservoir charged with Benzole or some other equally volatile hydrocarbon; the gas or air so napthalised being then conducted like common coal gas through pipes to the burners. It was stated that the system was applicable on any scale, from the dimensions of town gas-works to the compass of a table lamp. In the apparatus exhibited, a small gas-holder, filled by a pair of bellows, supplied common air through pipes. The gases formed by passing steam over red-hot coke would answer well for this purpose, and it would depend on local circumstances whether this mode of generating the current would be preferable to the expenditure of the mechanical force necessary for driving atmospheric air through the pipes. Pure oxygen charged with the vapour would explode on ignition; it was therefore suggested that this might prove a useful source of motive force. The system was shewn to be a great simplification of the ordinary system of gas-lighting, as no retorts, refrigerators, purifiers, or meters were required, and the products of combustion were as pure as those from the finest wax.

The apparatus and conditions necessary for the success of the method were, a flow of cheap gas, or of air, driven through pipes by any known motive power, and a reservoir of the volatile spirit through which the main pipe must pass in some convenient part of its course; these pipes and reservoirs being protected from the cold.

It was stated that a gallon of Benzole, of the degree of purity requisite for the purpose, would cost about 2*s*. 6*d*.; to this, the expense of the air-current and the interest of the original outlay on apparatus, was to be added. This, the author presumed, would not raise the cost to more than 4*s*. for the consumption of a gallon of Benzole. It was stated that one ounce of that liquid would give a light equal to four wax candles of four to the pound, for one hour, or one gallon for about one hundred and twenty hours. It was inferred that a gallon of this material was equivalent to about 1,000 cubic feet of coal gas.

SCIENCE AND SCENERY AT HER MAJESTY'S THEATRE.

In the last scene of a beautiful ballet, called *Electra, or the Lost Pleiade*, played for the first time at Her Majesty's Theatre, on Tuesday night, an effect quite wonderful is obtained by the introduction of the electric light, opening new views in stage arrangements, and hearing strongly on some ideas as to the lighting of theatres expressed in a previous volume of our journal.

The story of the ballet is one that has often been used in other forms, and often will be,—it symbolises the struggle in man's mind between the *real* and the *ideal*,—the thought, and the thing. We have only so much to say of it, however, as will serve to explain the particular incident in question: although looked at philosophically, a ballet is not without its teaching.

One of the *Pleiades* becomes enamoured of a mortal on the eve of his marriage, and leads to the struggle to which we have referred. By this act the Star is deprived of her station, but is ultimately forgiven and restored. The scene is a lake, in the bright moonlight, a charming piece of deception, by Mr. Charles Marshall: it changes to the Empyrean, the "highest Heaven" of the poets, where the pure element of fire is supposed to exist. The six *pleiades* rise amongst the clouds, with each her bright particular light, and the seventh, the forgiven, is then seen sailing up and forwards to the front of the stage, with a star so brilliant and far-piercing, that the gas, as sporting men say, is "no-where." Hyperbole apart, however, the effect when we saw it was very striking and very beautiful.

Some of the previous scenes and effects, a forest, and a Norwegian view with torrent and bridge, are creditable specimens of Mr. Marshall's art.

DILAPIDATIONS.

Sheriffs' Court.—*Birch* v. *Edgecumbe*.—This was an action to recover damages for dilapidations, &c., under peculiar circumstances. The facts were these:—The defendant took the premises, situate in St. Anne's, Soho, on a lease, in which was a covenant to keep the premises in repair. After being in possession four or five years, defendant set about performing some repairs, but in the hurry gave no notice to the district surveyor, and as the alterations were not in conformity with the new Building Act, and in consequence the house was condemned, and almost wholly pulled down, the expense in rebuilding was about 500*l*., which was now sought to be recovered.

The Under-Sheriff (Mr. Burchell) said this was not a repairing lease, but the covenant was merely to keep in repair; that was, he was to keep it in repair according to the length of time he occupied, but not to make the house perfect.

Mr. Prentis, for the plaintiff, submitted that the damage had been wholly caused by defendant's negligence.

Mr. Wiltshire, surveyor, was called, and made a calculation that the house, if properly repaired, would have lasted for twenty-one years; but taking the difference of value in the old and present house, he thought 150*l*. a fair equivalent for the loss.

The jury, after a short consultation, gave a verdict for 150*l*. damages, and 20*l*. for rent—in all 170*l*.

The New City Prison at Holloway.—We understand that the contract for the building of the new city prison at Holloway has been regularly signed by the contracting parties, and that operations are to commence on the ground. The first stone will be laid at Midsummer.

STATE OF WESTMINSTER ABBEY.

SIR,—It has been stated that the Dean of Westminster has, with his well-known liberality and enthusiasm, resolved to apply a considerable portion of his income to the repairs and improvements of the Abbey; but the following extraordinary circumstances have not yet been made known to the public, though they are deeply interesting.

Dr. Buckland having determined to set a noble example, very judiciously began by a close investigation of the actual state of the edifice; and lo! it has been discovered that buttresses and other essential parts of the building are in a dilapidated, and even imminently dangerous condition, so as to threaten with destruction some of the venerable Royal chapels, and the unequalled national relics they contain. It is, indeed, fortunate that the appointment of a dignitary alike remarkable for rare acquirements in science and a generous disposition, has saved the country from the impending misfortune, and the abbey authorities from unavailing reproaches. But the case naturally leads to the question,—how it happened that the ruinous condition of parts of the admired structure was not observed and remedied by others previous to the present Dean's appointment. Appended to a return, printed by order of the House of Commons, on the motion of Mr. Hume, 25th July, 1845, and signed by the auditor of the Dean and Chapter, is a declaration that the moneys received at the entrance are appropriated to "such ornamental improvements of the Abbey and buildings belonging thereto, as do not fall within the ordinary repairs of the fabric (which is maintained out of the funds of the Dean and Chapter, usually appropriated to that specific purpose), or in any manner at the discretion of the Dean and Chapter, so that it be not made use of for any other object for which the Dean and Chapter collectively, or the Dean and Canons individually, are bound to provide."

Four years after this declaration, we learn that the funds usually appropriated to that specific purpose have not been applied to the necessary repairs of the fabric; that the objects for which the Dean and Chapter are bound to provide have been miserably neglected, and at last it devolves individually on a new dean, and he a rare example of liberality and science, to stop the onward course of ignorance, neglect, and utter ruin to the most important of our national antiquities. Surely it would become Mr. Hume or Lord John Russell to ascertain the cause of these inconsistencies; nor should our archæologists cease agitating until similar neglect is rendered impossible throughout the land.

A TRUE ENGLISHMAN.

RAILWAY JOTTINGS.

From official returns it appears that the amount of traffic for the last week, on 4,432 miles of railway, was 186,473*l*., thus accounted for:—81,461*l*. for the conveyance of passengers only; 55,942*l*. for the carriage of goods, and a remainder of 49,070*l*. for passengers and goods together, not respectively apportioned; being an increase of 27,842*l*. over the corresponding week of last year, when the mileage was 3,543. The average earnings per mile were 42*l*., whilst last year they were 44*l*.——The increase of receipts on the London and North-Western for the last eleven weeks, over and above the corresponding period of last year, amounts to 26,845*l*., or 2,444*l*. per week. The gross receipts for the eleven weeks have been 405,635*l*., or at the rate of nearly 2,000,000*l*. per annum.——The London and Brighton have made considerable reductions in the charge for periodical tickets, with the view of encouraging building, and extending facilities for suburban residence in connection with the short stations between London, Croydon, and Epsom.——In place of bells, clocks, &c., as time signals at stations, Mr. J. S. Torrop, of Edinburgh, has devised a new one, or rather adopted an old one, as a railway-train-monitor, namely, a moveable ball mounted on a lofty pillar, wound up to the top by clock-work, and taking a definite time to descend. This time is set to ten minutes. When the ball is seen at the top of the pole or pillar, passengers approaching the station are informed that they have ten minutes; if half down, five minutes, and so on. Being capable of being made a conspicuous object, its indications can be distinguished at a considerable distance by intending passengers, who may be thereby saved all unnecessary excitement and uncertainty in making their way to the station, while the officials will be also saved from the annoyance of questioning as to the time the train is due. ——Mr. Bushby, of Littlehampton, has contracted for the erection of the railway terminus at Landport. We understand the sum is between 10,000*l*. and 11,000*l*. The entire works are to be completed within five months. ——The Admiralty have assented to the proposed South-Western extension line from Richmond to Windsor, on condition that the navigable channel of the Thames be crossed by bridges of one span, with as much headway as the limits of deviation will allow. The point at which the line is to cross the river is about three quarters of a mile below Windsor-bridge. ——The past week has been an important one in the modern history of Gainsboro', from the opening of a line of railway, which places the town within an hour and three-quarters of Hull. The Great Northern line to Lincoln, also lately opened, will be felt as a still greater convenience.

SALE OF JOHN OF GAUNT'S PALACE, LINCOLN.

THE old mansion called "John of Gaunt's Palace" has lately been sold, and the beautiful oriel, or bay window, at the south end of the building, was offered for sale separately. It has not, however, been taken down, nor has any part of the building been pulled down or altered, and it is to be hoped that the destruction may be prevented. There is a view of this old mansion, done by Nathaniel Buck, in 1726, which gives a general idea of the whole eastern front. A great part was taken down soon afterwards, but the oriel, and a window which is engraved in Pugin's Specimens, from sketches by Mr. E. J. Willson, of Lincoln, were left standing, and are yet remaining. The former is blocked up, and a modern chimney stands behind it.

Part of the eastern front remained standing until the early years of the present century, and a drawing of it is in the British Museum. This was made by Mr. Grimm, an artist who was employed by Sir Richard Kaye, Bart., when Dean of Lincoln. It is to be feared that the beautiful *oriel* (to use a common term, if not strictly a correct one,) will tempt some amateur to a purchase, and then it may be pulled down and stuck into a modern villa, and thus be deprived of its real value. It has never been thoroughly examined withinside, and, consequently, the delineations that have been made are imperfect. It is unequalled for richness and elegance.

The other window is also very elegant; it has been adopted, by the late Mr. Wilkins, at Cambridge.

Miscellanea.

RE-ERECTION OF THE OLYMPIC THEATRE. —We urged a short time since the impolicy and impropriety of rebuilding the Olympic Theatre in Wych-street. The *Athenæum*, taking the same view, says,—"We regret to hear that it is proposed to rebuild the Olympic Theatre on its recent site,—the front, for the better convenience of carriage approach, being turned towards Newcastle-street. We wish there were somewhere an authority to prevent this; and are of opinion that had the fire by which this edifice was recently destroyed taken place two hours later in the evening than it did, this authority would speedily have been found. There have surely been calamities and warnings enough of late to point out the pressing necessity of providing ample passages of egress and spacious approaches to buildings in which multitudes of human beings congregate.—Covering an insufficient area of ground and hemmed closely in on every side, the site of the old Olympic seems well chosen for converting such another accident as that which has just destroyed it into one of those terrible events that startle public remorse into such measures of prudence unaccountably neglected on any milder suggestion."

PROJECTED WORKS.—Advertisements have been issued for tenders,—by a date not specified, for the erection of a district church at Brompton, Middlesex; by a date not specified, for the whole or either of the following churches: a district church at Clay Cross, Northwingfield, and a district church at Belper, in the county of Derby, and a parish church at Bulwell, in the county of Nottingham; by May 8th, for the several works required in erecting the general station at Wolverhampton, with carriage-sheds, platforms, &c.; by 27th inst., for the erection of a new Wesleyan Chapel at Witney, Oxfordshire; by a date not specified, for the erection of a gas-holder, &c. for the Sheerness new gas works; by 27th, for the several works to be done in the erection of a parsonage house at Chapel-en-le-Frith, Derbyshire; by 5th proximo, for filling up the site required for the cattle market in Shrewsbury; by 25th, for the erection of farm-buildings for Mr. Adam Eve, Jun., at Hangham, near Louth; by 28th, for the erection of a rectory house at Lambley, Nottingham; by 24th, for the erection and completion of a brick warehouse at Bolton; by 26th May, for the erection of sundry buildings and works at the new barracks at Owlerton, near Sheffield; by 7th May, for about 5,000 tons of cast-iron pipes, from 2 to 26 inches in diameter, for the Manchester Corporation water-works; by 23rd inst., for certain works and additions to the laundries and drying-rooms of the workhouse, Leicester-square; by 8th May, for certain alterations and additions to the kitchen of the Bedford Lunatic Asylum; by 2nd, for the erection of additional buildings at Queen's College, Birmingham; by 15th, for paving and repairing carriage ways and foot-ways in St. Clement's Danes parish; and by 30th inst., for the execution of the cast and malleable iron-work required for the shed and roof of the central station at Newcastle-on-Tyne; also for building a small station-house at Gateshead, and another at Newcastle. A large contract for sheet copper is shortly expected to be announced by the French Minister of Marine for sheathing a great portion of the national navy.

THE FOUR-MILE PANORAMA.—Sir: On paying a visit last week to the Mississippi panorama in Leicester-square, it struck me that it would be worth while to test the accuracy of its alleged dimensions, viz., four miles. I therefore noticed how many lengths of canvas of the *size* of the disc passed *across* it in three successive quarters of an hour: the average for each fifteen minutes was ten lengths. The exhibition lasted 1½ hour. The width of the disc was then paced, and found to be about 20 feet; consequently, 20 × 10 × 6 gives 1,200 feet as the real length; so that if even 120 feet be added as compensation for any possible error, the result is still only ¼ of a mile, or 1-16th of the pretended length. This is too palpable a Jonathanism. Of course, if the advertisement be correct, the canvas must, during exhibition, be constantly travelling across the stage nearly at the rate of 3 miles an hour, which would hardly allow the painting to be seen at all, and certainly would give no time for the lengthy stoppages and explanations that actually take place.—A.

NATIONAL GALLERY OF ART FOR IRELAND.—At the last meeting of the committee of the Royal Irish Art Union, Mr. Blacker announced that a munificent donation had just been made to Dublin, being no less than two cartoons of Raphael. The subjects were, "St. Peter and St. John Healing the Lame Man at the Beautiful Gate of the Temple," and "Elymas, the Sorcerer, Struck Blind." Early in 1847, he (Mr. Blacker) had some correspondence with Mr. Nicolay, of Oxford-square, London, when getting up the exhibition of the works of ancient masters for relief of the then general distress. He received the other day a letter from Mrs. Nicolay, saying that she was but carrying out the wishes of her late husband in asking him, Mr. Blacker, to take charge of two cartoons of Raphael, which he prized most highly, and was desirous should be presented for the formation of a permanent gallery of art in Dublin. Mrs. Nicolay, as an Irishwoman, felt peculiar, although mournful pleasure in carrying his wishes into effect. Mrs. Nicolay accompanied the gift with a short statement of their history, and how they came into Mr. Nicolay's possession, which appears to have been simply this:—These specimens of the Italian school of art were picked up by Sir Joshua Reynolds during his tour in the Low Countries, in one of the towns where they had been originally sent for the purpose of manufacture into tapestry. At Sir Joshua's death, and at the subsequent sale of his effects, they passed with one intermediate hand into the possession of Mr. Nicolay. A committee was appointed to consider the propriety of having forthwith an exhibition of old masters in connection with the newly-arrived cartoons, the proceeds to form a reserve fund for a permanent public gallery and studying school, and are proceeding to carry this desirable project into effect.

SEPARATION OF PAUL'S WHARF SEWAGE FROM THE RIVER.—Mr. Moffat, C.E., formerly engineer to the London Sewage Chemical Manure Company, has offered to the City Sewers Commissioners 2s. 6d. per ton of dry manure, to be manufactured by him from this sewage in premises to be erected at his own expense near the mouth of the sewer. He proposes to sink an intercepting well, with a shield to prevent the ingress of the tide, and to raise the sewage out of this well by steam-power into tanks, where it will be chemically treated by mixing it with hydrate or milk of lime, so as to precipitate many of the matters in solution, along with those in suspension, to the bottom, after which the water will be allowed to flow off into the Thames, and the residual matter removed and dried, and moulded into portable shape. In storms, when the sewage will be greatly diluted, there will be an intermission of the process. The medical officer of health, and the surveyor to the City Commissioners, have reported rather favourably of the proposal,—recommending, however, that such works should only be allowed as an experiment for one or two years, in case of turning out either a nuisance, or a hindrance to the realization of any more complete or comprehensive measure. In their report they also point out the fact that objections had been taken by adequate chemists to much the same proposal when made by the late Sewage Chemical Manure Company, and that, although such a measure would tend to clear the river of deleterious matter, much of its more subtle essence would still remain in the water ultimately turned into a heretofore. Mr. Moffat proposes, of course, to dispose of his own advantage, in fertilising Plumstead Marsh, or otherwise.

GRANARIES, &c., AT MANCHESTER.—In connection with the lately opened extension of the Manchester, Sheffield, and Lincolnshire Railway to Gainsborough, and for agricultural traffic, arrangements on a large scale are being made. The goods station is on the level of the street, and some 20 feet below the passenger station. But the goods warehouses, as well as the corn warehouses, will be connected by a viaduct, on the same level with the railway, and thus save the cost of "lifting." At present every truck of goods is lowered and hoisted by steam, worked on the locomotive principle, for the sake of economising the working. The arches below the station are arranged and subdivided for the different local traffic, which has grown so much of late, that the company uses them itself, and foregoes a rental of 300l. a-year on each of seventeen such arches. Of these, eleven or so are used by the London and North-Western, and the rest by the Lincolnshire line. For the corn stored in the warehouse, no one is directly charged with rent. The warehouse more particularly used for this purpose consists of a series of flats, about 9 feet high, supported by cast-iron columns. The sacks are lifted in and out by steam power. Each flat is about 180 feet long. The mere fact of making a connection between the stations of the two companies at Sheffield, says the *Railway Chronicle*, at once created a corn traffic in Manchester, which has steadily increased. It has heretofore come from Nottingham and Lincolnshire either by canal, or by the more circuitous course of the Manchester and Leeds Railway.

THE BENTINCK TESTIMONIAL.—Workmen have been boring near the centre of Mansfield Market-place, to ascertain the nature of the proposed foundation of a structure which is to be erected from a design by Mr. Hind, after an early English market-cross.

THE WONDERS OF GUTTA PERCHA are by no means at an end. Its Protean purposes appear to be themselves outvied by its singular properties. Several new ones have been recently discovered. Mr. Torrop, of Edinburgh, has communicated to the Royal Scottish Society of Arts, a notice of one peculiar property. When cast and rolled into sheets, it assumes the nature of a fibrous substance—it acquires tenacity in a determinate direction. When in the roll or sheet this tenacity is longitudinal. But if a strip be cut from the breadth, two peculiarities occur : the strip is susceptible of a definite elongation to nearly five times the original length, and its direction of tenacity is reversed. When it is considered that gutta percha is originally a fluid substance, or gum, these peculiarities are indeed curious and remarkable. In fact, when we keep its multiform uses and its other properties in view, together with such a peculiarity, it assumes all the importance, or at least the simulative form, of a sort of vegetable iron ; an idea, however, fanciful as it may be, which another contradictory property, also newly discovered, only tends to upset ; for it is said to be, like glass, an electric, only it far excels glass itself as such. A Liverpool correspondent of the *Carlisle Journal*, drawing attention for the first time to this peculiarity of gutta percha, says—" Its electric properties, so far as I am aware, have not been publicly noted ; and I venture through your columns to call attention to this quality, which it possesses in a remarkable degree. If a piece of sheet gutta percha be laid upon a table-cloth or silk handkerchief, and stroked quickly with the hand, and then lifted from the table, it emits brilliant flashes of electric light, and considerable sparks may be drawn from it by any conducting substance. The ease with which gutta percha is excited contrasts strongly with the difficulty of exciting glass and resinous substances, especially in damp atmosphere ; and there can be no doubt that it may be successfully employed to produce large quantities of electricity. The machine for this purpose may be extremely simple : an endless band of sheet gutta percha stretched over two rollers (one of them turned by a winch), pressed slightly by a cushion and having a rod or wire touching the revolving band and in connection with the conductor of an ordinary electrical machine, would produce a constant supply of electricity, in a quantity proportioned to the surface employed, which may be very considerable ; and I shall not be surprised if, by these simple and economical means, effects are produced equal to those attained by the largest electrical machines now in use. I may add, as a useful hint to experimenters with the sheet gutta percha, that it may be readily joined by laying the edges together, and cutting off a shaving with a pair of scissors moderately heated."—The supply of the article is still going on. The vessel *Duke of Bronte*, arrived from Singapore, has recently brought 36 bags, 112 bales, 11,347 blocks, and 1734 other packages, as a portion of her cargo, consigned to order ; and the *Anne Watson*, also from Singapore, has brought 7,402 packages, 120 blocks, and 3 baskets to order.

USE FOR THE PITCH LAKE OF TRINIDAD. —An important communication has been made by Earl Dundonald to Lord Harris, governor of Trinidad, on the substitution of bitumen from the pitch lake of La Brea, in place of coal, to the extent of two-thirds of this fuel, for the generation of steam, in the manufacture of sugar, &c. ; thus also restoring to the soil, in form of manure, the refuse of the cane fields now used for fuel. In a furnace, in which it has been successfully used, the bitumen, it appears, is poured into a recess, or pit, just below the fire-bars, leaving sufficient room for a rapid current of atmospheric air, and as it is decomposed, the dense smoke and gases are carried through the incandescent fuel, and go off in flame and great heat. Earl Dundonald has forwarded a plan of this furnace to the governor. The *Port of Spain Gazette* expresses a hope that the subject will attract the attention of the Royal Mail Steam-packet Company, whose intercolonial steamers consume a vast quantity of coal, conveyed at great cost from England to the several depôts, for the whole of which, under a proper adaptation of their furnaces, the pitch might prove a cheap and effectual substitute.

ELECTRO-TELEGRAPHIC PROGRESS.—The admiration excited when first the locomotive express went ahead of all other conveyance of intelligence was only lately excelled, we may say for the first time in this country, by the transmission of a full report, three close columns in length, of the Cobden banquet proceedings, at Wakefield, per electric telegraph, to the *Times*, in which the whole, down to their close, on the way to 12 p.m., was published by 3 a.m. ; the whole process of reporting, transcribing, telegraphing, retranscribing, type-setting, and printing, being accomplished,—actually finished—at one end of the country in less than four hours after the words were spoken almost at the other end of it. The telegraph is now beginning in earnest to do its duty ; and it is to be hoped that this only drag upon its lightning speed that now remains, viz., extravagant and impracticable charges, will ere long be cast off as an incubus that can no more profit the conveyancers of intelligence than its publishers.—So constantly is the telegraph in requisition for the purposes of the press on the other side of the Atlantic, that one of the New York papers is about to have an "independent" track constructed from New York to Washington and Boston, for its own exclusive use. The eastern route will be 245 miles, and the southern 225 miles.

YORKSHIRE ARCHITECTURAL SOCIETY. At the meeting of this society, the Hon. and Rev. P. Y. Savile, rector of Methley, gave notice, that at the next meeting he should ask for a grant of 10l. for the restoration of a fine oak roof, which he had discovered during certain repairs in his church, concealed above a flat plaster ceiling, and he also particularly invited the attention of the members to the peculiar features of the building. It was accordingly resolved that a special meeting of the society should be called at Methley early in May, for the purpose of examining the church. A paper was read by Mr. W. H. Dykes, architect, of York, "On the form and Management of Churches," giving some account of the various types of churches which had been common in different ages, through the Christian world, and showing that, nevertheless, they had all agreed in certain peculiar features, and especially in their having had a distinct chancel, separated by screens from the body of the church.

THE TYNE GLASS TRADE, according to the *Newcastle Guardian*, is only now reaching the climax of its decline. Out of the numerous firms formerly engaged in the window-glass trade, two only remain, and these appear to be not only languid but expiring also. Ridley and Co., a firm of a century standing, have suspended their works, and will probably not resume them. Only two of the flint-glass works remain. Various causes, none of them our authority thinks sufficient, are alleged for the depression of this trade.

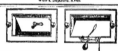

NOTED TERRA COTTA STONE GLASS LINED PIPES

The Builder.

No. CCCXXV.

SATURDAY, APRIL 28, 1849.

DRURY-LANE THEATRE was, as usual, crowded to receive the report of the Council of the Art-Union of London, and to distribute the funds, on Tuesday last, the 24th. The Duke of Cambridge, the president, being confined to his room by indisposition, was unable to take the chair, and Lord Monteagle, one of the vice-presidents, had arranged to do so. A summons to attend the Select Committee on the Operation of the Irish Poor Laws, of which his lordship is chairman, and which circumstance was communicated to the council only at the moment for opening the meeting, prevented him, however, from presiding. Under these circumstances, the letters from Lord Monteagle, and Baron Knesebeck on the part of the duke, were read; Mr. Serjeant Thompson, a member of the council, was voted into the chair, and Mr. G. Godwin, the honorary secretary, then read the following

REPORT.

According to annual custom, the council of the Art-Union of London proceed to lay before the subscribers an account of their operations during the past year, the present position of the society, and their views and anticipations for the future. In commencing this report, the thirteenth which the council have had the pleasure to make, they consider it their duty to state the substance and issue of the renewed correspondence with the lords of the Committee of Privy Council for Trade since the date of the last report. It will be remembered that at the general meeting in 1848, the question between the Board of Trade and the council was,—whether the *council* should select the prizes for the prizeholders, or the *prizeholders* select them for themselves, in accordance with the characteristic and foundation law of the association, recognized by Act of Parliament and confirmed by the royal charter, and that the council, strengthened by the unanimous opinion of the meeting, had determined to omit no effort to maintain for the prizeholders this right of choice. In the month of May following, a meeting was called by the Institute of Fine Arts, and a memorial to the Board of Trade, setting forth their opinion that "if the prizes were to be chosen by a committee instead of each prizeholder being at liberty to select for himself, the society would be virtually destroyed," and praying that "the Art-Union of London might be permitted to pursue untrammelled that course which has hitherto been so conducive to the interests of art and artists," was unanimously agreed to. This was afterwards signed by more than 300 artists, including twenty-four royal academicians, and was taken up by a deputation representing the Royal Academy, the Institute of the Fine Arts, the old and new Water Colour Societies, and the Association for Promoting the Free Exhibition of Modern Art.

The Incorporated Society of British Artists had previously, by a separate memorial and deputation, addressed the Board to the same effect.

In July the council were informed, by a communication from Sir Denis Le Marchant, that their lordships proposed to withdraw for the present their requisition that the prizes should be selected by a committee, "and to postpone the question to another year," but that they should require that so long as the right of selection remained absolutely with the prizeholders, they should be allowed to exercise it freely, by such an alteration in the laws as would enable them to give commissions to artists, or to purchase any works excepting portraits, being the productions of a living artist and in his possession at the time the selection was made,—instead of being confined, as now, to the public exhibitions of the year, and that the Board could only consent to withdraw the regulations previously forwarded, on the understanding that such freedom would be secured.

Outlines of proposed new regulations to effect this were forwarded, to enable the council to judge of them more easily.

The council required little consideration to arrive at a conviction of the inexpediency and destructive tendency of the proposed alterations, and a letter was accordingly addressed to the Board of Trade, setting forth their objections, and containing the following passages:—

"The council of the Art-Union of London are anxious, with their lordships, to give to the prizeholder the most perfect freedom of choice, with such limitations only as may be necessary to guard against fraudulent transactions.

The regulations of the society, the result of twelve years' experience and constant attention to the subject on the part of the council, have been made with reference to the prevention of the perversion of the funds to individual advantage, without interference with this freedom of choice desired for the prizeholders.

The regulation binding the prizeholders to select from specified public exhibitions works of which the prices have been recorded, have this end especially in view, and appear to the council to meet the case. The field of selection thus given is large; it has been increased as opportunities occurred (as by the addition of the 'Exhibition of the Royal Commissioners of Fine Arts,' and of the 'Free Exhibition'), while, by the previous record of the price, and the publicity which attends the transaction, the possibility of fraudulent proceedings is rendered very small, if not altogether prevented.

Should the regulation proposed by their lordships be brought into operation, this check would no longer exist, and the opportunities for collusion and improper arrangement would be so greatly increased as to *lead* to these irregularities, and ultimately to destroy the society.

Under the present arrangement, the knowledge that a certain number of pictures must be purchased from the current exhibition serves as a stimulus to artists, which, of course, would no longer exist: the prizes awarded each year are in fact so many premiums for competition open to all artists.

Under the arrangement proposed, private friendship, in the absence even of improper motives, would often lead to the perversion of the funds.

The council are quite unable to reconcile the regulation now suggested by the Board of Trade with the desire expressed by their lordships, in proposing the regulations since withdrawn, to narrow the field of selection so that the choice of the prizeholder *should be confined to works of real merit.*

The authorities of the various bodies of artists exercising a discretion in the admission of pictures, each exhibition has, to a certain extent, the character of *a selection of works of merit*; but if the prizeholder is to be permitted to select any work of art anywhere, provided it is 'the production of a living artist and in his possession at the time,' and, further, to give commissions to last a twelvemonth, if not more, the field of selection will be so widely extended that it would be impossible to embrace it by any sufficient regulations."

Soon afterwards a deputation of the council had an interview with Lord Granville, at the Privy Council office, further to explain the grounds of objection, and the result was, in January last, a letter from Sir Denis Le Marchant, which, after reiterating the opinion of the Board, that either of the courses which they had suggested (opposite enough, it must be confessed), would be preferable to the present system, concluded thus:—

"Their lordships, however, are reluctant, at least at present, to urge their views against the strongly expressed and deliberate sentiments of the committee of the London Art-Union, with whom they have been all along most anxious to co-operate. They have, therefore, directed me to inform you that they shall not now insist upon their proposal, but it must be distinctly understood that they do not relinquish the right of subsequently requiring these, or any other amendments, in the existing system, as circumstances may appear to them to render expedient."

This, then, is the position of the matter at present, and here, it is to be hoped, it will be allowed to rest. As the council have already said to the Board of Trade — Regarding the successful progress of the Art-Union of London as of great national importance, they would view with fear the possibility of a renewal of a discussion which tends to unsettle the public mind in respect of the association, and is greatly opposed to its success, and they feel it to be their duty, therefore, in consequence of the wording of the communication, respectfully but most earnestly to express a hope that their lordships will not again raise a question on which the well-wishers of the society and the great body of English artists and art-lovers have so unanimously and unmistakeably expressed themselves.

An examination of the published reports for several years past will convey to the subscribers some idea of the extent to which the time and attention of the council have been occupied by legal objections and fruitless interference. When Acts of Parliament had removed all doubt as to the legality of the system adopted by the Art-Union of London, and the association had been incorporated by charter, the council anticipated that they would be enabled to apply themselves wholly to the furtherance of its great objects.

They still look forward to this, and deprecate earnestly any renewal of the unnecessary obstructions which have been thrown in the way of their progress.

Before concluding this part of the subject the council would remark that, harassing and injurious as the proceedings in question have been, they were not wholly without advantage, since they served to elicit from various quarters expressions of good will and consideration, very gratifying to those who have the welfare of the association much at heart.

Foremost amongst these expressions they place the communication, that at the meeting of artists at the Institute of Fine Arts in May last, already referred to, it was unanimously resolved,—"That this meeting take this opportunity of expressing the warmest thanks of the body of artists to the Council of the Art-Union of London, convinced that the council have manifested at all times an anxious desire, in the face of many difficulties, to promote the diffusion of a love of art among the people, and the elevation of the position of the artist, and more especially for their disinterested and determined resistance to the measures proposed by the Board of Trade, which would inevitably place in the hands of the council a vast amount of patronage."

Turning now to the financial position of the society,—the council have to report that the total amount subscribed for the current year is 10,391*l.* 17*s.*

The commercial depression which has universally prevailed, political excitement, and the distrust which was for a time produced, have effected seriously all the institutions throughout the country which depend on the co-operation of the public, but have no absolute claim on it. When the council say that the revenue of the Art-Union of London has suffered, it is simply stating, therefore, that this society is not an exception amongst its contemporaries.

Other causes have probably aided in producing the diminution,—the check which was given last year, and the lessening of zeal on the part of some of the numerous voluntary and unpaid co-adjutors, to whose continued exertions for several years the society owes so much. It is satisfactory to the council to know that no share in the diminution of subscribers can be attributed either to the character of the engraving and illustrated work obtained by each subscriber of the past year, or to delay in issuing them. The "Prisoner of Gisors," and the "Allegro" and "Penseroso" of Milton, which have been distributed, have elicited none but gratifying expressions.

It may be mentioned as a striking illustration of the result of association, that 6*s.* 5*d.* of each subscriber's guinea sufficed to produce these works,—works which if published in the ordinary way could not have been purchased for the whole amount of the subscription; and that after paying for illustrating and printing the report, printing almanacs and prospectuses, the cost of the general meeting and the exhibition of prizes, a proportion of the cost of the charter, the reserve of 2½ per cent. to provide a gallery hereafter, and the expenses of carrying on the large operations of the society,—half the total amount subscribed was distributed in the shape of prizes at the annual meeting, and in which distribution every member had, of course, one or more chances.

With the funds then allotted, 137 works of art were purchased from the various public collections, and were exhibited in the Suffolk-street Gallery, by the kind permission of the Society of British Artists. The exhibition was open for four weeks, and was visited, as heretofore, by an immense number of persons, without any accident or injury.

The engraving for the current year, "Sabrina," by Mr. Lightfoot, from the painting by Mr. Frost, A.R.A., is ready for electrotyping.

In addition to an impression of this, each subscriber will receive an engraving after a design in *basso relievo*, by Mr. John Hancock, "Christ entering Jerusalem," submitted in competition for a premium of 100*l.*, offered by the council for the best design in *basso relievo*, for this purpose.

In reply to the advertisement of this premium, twenty-five designs were sent in, several of them having great merit. To one of these, "The Death of Boadicea," by Mr. Armstead, the council awarded an honorary premium, and have arranged to produce a certain number of copies of it in bronze, by the electrotype process, to be distributed hereafter as prizes.

Copies of the prize design in bronze will also be made.

The council take this opportunity to thank the various artists who responded to their invitation.

The satisfaction with which the illustrations of Milton have been received, has led the council to determine on producing a similar volume for the subscribers of the ensuing year. The poem selected is Goldsmith's "Traveller," which will be illustrated by thirty engravings on wood. Messrs. Richard Ansdell, John Absolon, Edward Corbould, Frederick Taylor, W. E. Frost, A.R.A., John Gilbert, F. Goodall, John Martin, R. Huskisson, W. L. Leitch, Clarkson Stanfield, R.A., E. H. Wehnert, E. M. Ward, A.R.A., J. D. Harding, G. Dodgson, F. W. Topham, E. Duncan, E. Armitage, and Thomas Webster, R.A., have already accepted commissions for the drawings.

The engraving of "The Crucifixion," by Mr. W. Finden, after Hilton, is advancing towards completion.

Messrs. Bacon, Edward Goodall, and Shenton, are making progress respectively with "The Burial of Harold" (after Mr. F. R. Pickersgill); "The Irish Piper" (after Mr. F. Goodall); and "Richard Cœur de Lion forgiving Bertrand de Gourdon," after Mr. John Cross.

In addition to these, which, as mentioned in the last report, are being engraved on *steel*, as an experiment on the practicability of ceasing to electrotype the same plate for all the subscribers, the council have placed "The Villa of Lucullus," by Mr. Leitch, in the hands of Mr. Willmore, to be engraved for the society. Each subscriber of the ensuing year will be entitled to obtain an impression of one of these engravings,—the particular print which each will receive being decided by lot.

Statuettes in porcelain of "The Dancing Girl reposing," allotted last year, are in the course of completion, and will shortly be distributed to the prizeholders entitled to them.

The engraving of "Queen Philippa interceding for the Lives of the Burgesses of Calais," by Mr. H. Robinson, after Mr. Selous, is in progress. It is proposed to allot to-day the right to 282 proof impressions of this work.

The bust of her Majesty the Queen, in bronze, after Chantrey, being coveted by many of the subscribers, it is proposed that twenty additional copies of it shall be distributed today as prizes. The greater number of those allotted last year are in the hands of their respective owners.

The figure of "Thalia," in cast-iron, already mentioned on several occasions, is now so near completion that the members to whom it was allotted may expect to obtain it forthwith. The council, although in nowise accountable for the delay which has attended the publication of this figure, feel indebted to the prizeholders for the patience with which they have waited for it. The council mention as a subject of gratification that they received intimation, some time since, on the part of the Prince Albert, that his Royal Highness would be glad to have a copy of each of the bronzes issued by the Art-Union, and wished that they might be prepared at his expense. Copies of the majority of them were accordingly obtained and forwarded, and the remainder are in course of execution. The council, who view with deep interest every event affecting the progress of the fine arts in the United Kingdom, congratulate the country on the enlightened desire uniformly displayed by his Royal Highness to assist in this important object.

The impulse that has been given to the production of bronzes in this country, by the efforts of the Art Union of London, and which has since extended to the manufacture of statuettes in other materials, is so obvious and so fully recognised, as not to require assertion. To lead the arts to the aid of our manufactures, has been one of the objects kept steadily in view by the Council of the Art Union of London from the date of its establishment. Apart from the increased commercial value thereby given, it is much to be desired in an educational point of view, that all articles of furniture and in daily use, should have the forms of beauty which art can give. As these become familiar to the eyes of all, that which is inelegant and unsymmetrical becomes unpleasing, and the general standard of taste is necessarily raised. Art can give value to the meanest material, and make a lump of clay, a "joy for ever."

The things which are around us mould and influence the mind more powerfully than some suppose. Homes are the manufactories of men, so to speak;—the well ordering of them is surely a matter of no trifling moment.

The die for the reverse of the "Wren" medal has been completed by Mr. Benjamin Wyon, and is now being hardened to supply the necessary number of impressions.

The medals commemorative of Hogarth, allotted at the last meeting, have been delivered to those entitled to receive them.

The Flaxman medal, allotted some time since, and delayed by circumstances which the council were unable to control, has been undertaken by Mr. W. Wyon, R.A. It has been already stated that prizeholders entitled to this medal, who may prefer to obtain at once, in lieu of it, either of the medals already published by the Society, are at liberty to do so.

Dies for a medal in honour of Inigo Jones are in course of execution, by Mr. C. F. Carter; thirty impressions of this in silver will be allotted to-day.

The council mention with regret, that within the last few days they have been deprived, by death, of the services of Mr. Collard, who, for several years, had given his continuous attention, as a member of the council, to the financial affairs of the society. James Stewart, Esq., assistant secretary of the Bank of England, has been elected to supply the vacancy thus caused. Further, to complete the number of the council limited by the charter, and comply with the regulation which requires that four new members shall be appointed annually, Dominic Colnaghi, Esq., John Martin, Esq., M.P., and C. R. Beauclerk, Esq., have been elected.

The reserved fund now amounts to the sum of 3,409*l.* 1s. 5d.

Details will be given in the printed report. And it may here be mentioned that arrangements have been made for issuing this report, with the list of subscribers, much sooner after the distribution than has heretofore been the case.

The following is a statement of the receipts and expenditure:—

Amount of subscriptions........	£10,391	17	0
Set apart for purchase of pictures, busts, statuettes, medals, proof engravings, and lithographs........	4,158	0	0
Cost of engravings of the year......	3,372	9	2
Expenses and reserve of 2½ per cent	2,861	7	10
	£10,391	17	0

The accounts have been audited by three members of the Finance Committee and two gentlemen from the body of the subscribers, viz., Mr. J. H. Mann and Mr. G. Gillott, to whom thanks are due.

The sum set apart for the purchase of works of art by the prizeholders themselves (3,205*l.*) will be thus allotted:—

		Each.
16 works, at	....	£10
15	,, ...	15
12	,, ...	20
12	,, ...	25
12	,, ...	40
7	,, ...	50
5	,, ...	60
4	,, ...	70
4	,, ...	80
2	,, ...	100
1	,, ...	150
1	,, ...	200

To these are to be added—

20 bronzes of "The Queen,"
50 statuettes of "Narcissus," after Gibson,
282 proof impressions, "Queen Philippa interceding for the Lives of the Burgesses of Calais,"
282 lithographs of "St. Cecilia," by Mr. Maguire, after Mr. Tenniel, and
30 medals, commemorative of "Inigo Jones;"—making in the whole 755 prizes.

The total sum appropriated to the purchase and production of works of art, including the estimated cost of the engravings, is 7,530*l.* 9s. 2d.

The bronzes will be allotted to the first twenty names drawn consecutively at the close of the general distribution; the statuettes to the next fifty similarly drawn; and the medals to the following thirty. The proof engraving of Queen Philippa will be appropriated to the names standing fiftieth in the list preceding and succeeding that of each prizeholder in the general distribution, and of each of those entitled to a porcelain statuette. The lithographs will be appropriated to the names standing in a similar manner one-hundredth preceding and succeeding those above mentioned. Notice will be sent to the subscribers entitled to the statuettes and proofs in the course of two days; the other prizeholders will receive intimation of the result by to-night's post.

Passing from the present to the future—the year which is to come—the council are most anxious to re-awaken the zeal of the numerous friends scattered over the kingdom and its colonies, to whose cordial co-operation and gratuitous exertions in the cause of art and artists the great extension of the society is mainly owing. Simply as an evidence of appreciation, the council have recently determined on presenting to each local honorary secretary who forwards the names of forty or more subscribers, one of the porcelain statuettes produced by the society. They would not have it supposed that they appreciate less the exertions of those coadjutors who, with equal good will and energy in the cause, are unable to obtain this number of subscribers, but some limit seemed necessary. The council earnestly invite the renewed co-operation of all former friends and the assistance of new, and feel assured that the subscribers at large will agree with any step which may hereafter be taken to acknowledge, in some fitting manner, these services, without reference to their results.

Desiring to avoid the appearance of invidiousness, the council do not propose to particularise the efforts of local secretaries, but they cannot avoid stating that from Boston, in the United States, through the exertions of Mr. Dennet, more than 200 subscribers have been obtained. The council have before this expressed their sense of the importance of thus connecting our trans-atlantic brethren with us in furtherance of the arts of peace and refinement.

It may be mentioned that there are now three Art-Unions in the United States, namely, those of New York, Philadelphia, and Cincinnati. The effect of their operations is thus stated in one of their leading literary journals:—

"It is hardly necessary," says the writer, "to speak of the great good the Art Union has accomplished; it is too evident to need to be insisted on; its effects are so palpable that he who runs may read. It has raised art from the lowest depths of degradation; it has taught the people, by making them familiar with it, to reverence and appreciate it. Ten years ago, what was art among us? It is true that really fine pictures found, among the few of wealth and taste, an occasional purchaser, but the young artist who felt that he must creep before he could walk, had no encouragement to begin. He must smother his aspirations or starve. All this it has remedied. Then our men of wealth filled their walls with counterfeit originals, and bad copies, the refuse of European markets.

Amongst the mass art was not understood at all. Pictures were merely things in frames pleasant enough to look at once. The prettiest were always the best, they never studied them, they never saw any relative merit in them, least of all did they desire to spend money for them. There was no taste among them, but the Art-Union has created one, and now almost every man we meet can say something about pictures, and likes to talk about them, and see them. In the increased attention to the subject of painting; in the improved taste and discrimination in judging of the merits of pictures, and in the numerous and beautiful works of art that now adorn the houses of many of our citizens, we see ample proofs of the good the institution has already done, and strong indications of the further benefit it is destined, under proper management, to confer on our country."

The council have so often dwelt on the objects and plan of the Art-Union of London, that it would seem unnecessary again to refer to them, nor can they say more than has been said in former reports, to impress upon those who may gain to-day the right of purchasing works of arts, the importance of using the greatest care and judgment in the selection.

The Art-Union of London has not worked in vain: a love and knowledge of art are spreading, the real purpose and value of art are beginning to be understood, and the artist is more properly appreciated. Much, however, is yet needed to be done to place the arts in their position amongst us, and the council feel that they cannot dwell too often or too forcibly on their importance.

Is there one of us who has not had his views cleared, his thoughts elevated, his heart lightened by the presentments of genius—by genius whose power it is to discover everlasting beauty beneath deepest disguises, and make it clear to the minds of commoner men? Great are the victories of the true artist—greater and more enduring than those of the warrior, and equally worthy of reward.

Art teaches us to see nature, and opens fresh views to the mind, providing "An endless fountain of immortal drink," and high inducements for exertion. But for art, the most perfect form of man, and some of his highest powers, would be unknown, for art, from specialities and incompleteness, has produced the general and the perfect. This is the true province of art, to set forth thought. "Always and universally," says Schlegel, it is thought, the idea of some subject or form as the inner sense or significance thereof, that constitutes the essence of a work of art, and with which art in general is concerned."

We would urge this as well on our younger and rising artists as on those who are to judge and aid their efforts, and, suggesting to them that little minds cannot produce great things, nor vulgar minds pure things, would bid them pursue their art not as a plaything or a trade, but thoughtfully, earnestly, and with high motive, for the enjoyment, instruction, and elevation of mankind.

Let it be the province of the Art-Union of London to provide a public capable of appreciating such efforts, and willing fittingly to reward them.

On the motion of Mr. John Rannie, seconded by Mr. T. C. Harrison, the report was received unanimously, and the Chairman then addressed some observations to the meeting, in the course of which he said,—As for the matter of the lottery, people have found out that it is a very different thing to seduce people to throw away their money on foolish schemes, and to take their money and so place it out as to produce an effect advantageous to the fine arts in this country. Many men of genius are not men of opulence; many who have great talent in art have no opportu-

nities of making that talent available,—or had none rather till the Art-Union was instituted; and, certainly, if the public could have seen what the council had seen in some instances, and what they have oftener had great reason to suspect,—if they had seen the struggles with which artists have to contend, against the effect of poverty in many instances, and those other circumstances of adversity which press upon them, they would know that this ranks not only among those societies which are intended for the entertainment of mankind, but amongst those whose object is of a solid and useful character. And I would impress upon those ladies and gentlemen especially, who have come to the metropolis at this time of the year, for the sake of seeing those specimens of art which are now generally exhibited, to consider when they go back to their homes, and to deliberate upon the fact, that the artists whose works they have seen are not all of them in the same opulence as the spectators of them; and may you reflect also, that a very small sum given to the Art-Union would be the most effectual means of aiding them; for these effects can only be produced by union and strength among people who have the same object before them. No one can have seen the effects which have been produced by the genius of the artist without having the mind carried along with them into a region which certainly is favourable both to virtue and to happiness; and if those ladies and gentlemen who have witnessed these effects will reflect when they return to their homes, that a very small sum at that time would be the means of encouraging art, raising probably the struggling mind when it is almost yielding to the effects of adversity, they will see one of the advantages in giving their mite to the Art-Union.

The Rev. Mr. Blaithwaite objected to the character of the engravings which had been issued, and, admitting that in this respect the council were greatly in the hands of the engravers, thought some means should be adopted to ensure a better result.

The Chairman and the Honorary Secretary having reiterated what was contemplated in this respect, and explained the position of the council,

Mr. F. Y. Hurlstone moved, and Mr. J. H. Mann seconded a vote of thanks to the council, which was carried unanimously; as was also a vote of thanks to Mr. Lewis Pocock and Mr. Godwin, on the motion of Professor Donaldson, seconded by Mr. G. R. Ward.

Miss Loudon (her father's name was not forgotten by the meeting) and Miss Susan Bagueley undertook to draw the prizes, and Mr. J. H. Mann and Mr. Seddon to act as scrutineers, and the drawing of the prizes commenced. The following is a correct

LIST OF THE PRIZEHOLDERS ENTITLED TO SELECT FOR THEMSELVES.

Entitled to a Work of Art of the Value of Two Hundred Pounds.
Appleyard, G., 27, St. James's-place.

Entitled to a Work of Art of the Value of One Hundred and Fifty Pounds.
Lane, Rev. C., Wrotham.

Entitled each to a Work of Art of the Value of One Hundred Pounds.
Biggs, W., Conduit-street.
Martin, J. U., East Dereham.

Entitled each to a Work of Art of the Value of Eighty Pounds.
Jenner, Mrs., Bridgend, Glamorgan.
Jennings, Miss, Caldbeck, Wigton.
Lamb, Miss Jessie, Liverpool.
Stones, J., Bolton.

Entitled each to a Work of Art of the Value of Seventy Pounds.
Fletcher, S., Manchester.
Hanbury, P., Lombard-street.
Hardman, H. H., Manchester.
Newman, Rev. Dr., Magdalen College, Oxford.

Entitled each to a Work of Art of the Value of Sixty Pounds.
Dodd, G., M.P., Grosvenor-place.
Doyle, M., jun., Old-square, Lincoln's-inn.
Lambton, William, Brompton.
Minton, H., Stoke-on-Trent.
Strange, J. C., Streatbly.

Entitled each to a Work of Art of the Value of Fifty Pounds.
Allan, T., Alnwick.
De la Costa, J. B., Bolivar.

Hall, Mrs. Colonel, Chertsey.
Mould, J. T., Brompton.
Smith, W., Wisbeach.
Sthamer, Dr., Whitefriars.
Thorne, C., Upper Holloway.

Entitled each to a Work of Art of the Value of Forty Pounds.
Bailey, H., Gracechurch-street.
Boardman, C., Blackburn.
Briggs, J. H., Gloucester-road.
Carpenter, Lieut.-Col., Potter's-bar, Barnet.
Christian, W., Baldock.
Dymock, Dr., Louth.
Hesseltine, R., Hamilton-house, Thirsk.
Hull, Mrs. R., Hampstead.
Homer, J., Hackney.
Richards, E. P., Cardiff.
Taylor, J. Windsor Castle.
Wheeler, Mr., New-hall Inn, Birmingham.

Entitled each to a Work of Art of the Value of Twenty-five Pounds.
Bentley, J., Shoe-lane.
Buckland, Rev. J., Laleham, Chertsey.
Field, Henry, Cambridge-heath.
Fox, G. J., Atherstone.
Gerdes, J., Liverpool.
Guthrie, Dr., Brechin.
Harrison, T. R., St. Martin's-lane.
Heginbottom, G., Manchester.
Hickson, S., Welbeck-street.
Northampton, the Marquis of.
Payne, E., St. James's-place.
Rickards, C., Piccadilly.

Entitled each to a Work of Art of the Value of Twenty Pounds.
Ackworth, Mrs., Chelmsford.
Bacon, Thos., Woburn-square.
Baiston, W., Jun., Maidstone.
Chapman, J., Edmonton.
Cornwall, Miss, Holland-place, Camberwell New-road.
Faulkner, W. C., North Hinsley.
Power, R., Atherstone.
Proctor, Thos. Cathay, Bristol.
Reynard, E. H., Sunderland-wick.
Salt, J., Lombard-street.
Spencer, Mrs., Stockwell.
Triscott, H. T., 33, New Bridge-street, Black-friars.

Entitled each to a Work of Art of the Value of Fifteen Pounds.
Armstrong, H. H., St. George-street, East, Wellclose-square.
Bennett, J., Pall-Mall.
Boddington, R., Ditchling.
Brooks, J. H., Farringdon-street.
Erskine, Lady, Conway.
Gandy, G., Kendal.
Hancock, J. L., Goswell Mews.
Hees, J., Throgmorton-street.
Light, J. D., Prerogative Court.
Miller, R., Glasgow.
Mills, C. H., Oxford-street.
Shaw, R. A., Selsy.
Sherriff, H., Aylesbury.
Stacey, R. H., Carmarthen.
Taylor, J. L., Saffron Walden.

Entitled each to a Work of Art of the Value of Ten Pounds.
A. Z., Halifax.
A. Z., Halifax.
Arklay, P. Boston, U.S.
Barry, R., Cork.
Brassey, Mrs., Lowndes-square.
Coltman, L. W., Curzon-street.
Copley, G., Pontefract.
Crook, S., Melbourne, Port Philip.
Davenport, C. Mark-lane.
Gale, W. F., Kew.
Grey, Hon. W. B., Charles-street, Berkeley-sq.
Hawkins, C. Petworth.
Lyon, Mrs., Hull.
Nilkens, Mrs., Coblentz.
Twentyman, A., Croydon.
Wiggins, W., Horley.

The following were entitled each to a bronze from Sir F. Chantrey's Bust of "The Queen:"— Messrs. Brooks, G. B. Bryden, A. Chabhot, Miss Churchill, Mr. John Cragg, Dr. Dickson, Messrs. T. T. Drinkald, R. C. Dunn, W. Greenwood, C. Lawrens, J. Lumaden, J. G. Lynd, E. J. Mawley, W. T. Mitford, H. Pilkington; Major-General Taylor, Messrs. J. Thompson, R. Thompson, J. H. Walker, and Moses Ward.

LICENSED VICTUALLERS' ASYLUM.—The PROPOSED "LADIES' WING."—Prince Albert is to lay the first stone of the increased number of habitations which have been determined to be added to this institution, on Tuesday, 29th May next.

DECORATIONS, &c., FROM ABROAD.

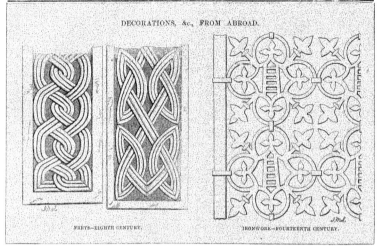

FRETS—EIGHTH CENTURY.   IRONWORK—FOURTEENTH CENTURY.

DECORATIONS, &c., FROM ABROAD.

FRETS FROM SANTA MARIA, IN COSMEDIN, AND SAN CLEMENTE, ROME.

The first of these churches was restored by Hadrian I., in 782, to which period this ornament must be ascribed. San Clemente was restored by the same Pope ten years earlier. The second fret forms a portion of the architrave of door to the ancient porch leading from the street into the Atrium, or quadriporticus, in front of this church. These two frets are precisely similar in style and execution (the triple band is a very common ornament of the period), and undoubtedly of the time of Hadrian I., 772—798.

IRON TRELLIS WORK OF ENCLOSURE TO TOMB OF CAN SIGNORE (1359—1375), VERONA (QUARTER FULL SIZE).

A beautiful example of mediæval iron-work, in which the canting arms of the family (Scala-Scaligeri), a ladder, is happily introduced.

These engravings, with two others already given under the same general heading, are from the sketch-book of Mr. J. M. Lockyer.

SOME MATTERS ARCHITECTURAL.

The Birmingham Workhouse Competition.—The Birmingham (late) board of guardians have entailed upon their successors much trouble and arnoyance by their proceedings in respect of the competition designs for the new workhouse, which were reported in our pages. If we may believe local informants, the board themselves lost their re-election to office through it, and have been succeeded by an entirely fresh set of men.

The selected design, by Mr. Hemming, had been sent to the Poor-law Board, and returned with various suggestions. These had been attended to, and fresh plans, we believe, made, but, nevertheless, at a meeting of the new board on the 18th instant, a motion that these plans be adopted was lost by 78 to 2. An amendment to the effect that the *six* selected plans should be forwarded to the Poor-law Board for their opinion upon them; and another, to the effect that these six should be submitted to three London architects for their decision, shared the same fate.

It was then moved by Mr. R. Wright, "That all the resolutions of the late board of guardians, and of its special committee, respecting the erection of a new workhouse, since the 30th of October last, be rescinded, and that the present board proceed as if no such

resolutions had been passed; and the clerk be directed *to advertise for plans*, specifying the conditions required; that such advertisement should set forth that the cost of such erection is not to exceed 25,000*l.*; and that the plans sent in should be referred to three architects, to be selected by the guardians, to examine the same, and report their opinion thereon to that board."

This was to be discussed on the 25th. If the board had followed our advice in the first instance, and obtained proper professional assistance in the selection, they would have spared themselves much obloquy, their successors much trouble, and their constituents much expense. According to the *Birmingham Journal,* Mr. Hemming has a claim of nearly 500*l.* on the parish, for the expense to which he has been put, and this will probably have to be settled in a court of law. We shall be glad if other boards are led by this occurrence to consider what they owe to architects who, confiding in their honour, submit plans in competition at great cost of time and of money, and so be induced not merely to act without reference to local connections or private friendship, but distrust their own capacity in a matter out of their usual course, and call to their assistance properly-qualified men.

The Bentinck Testimonial has been already mentioned by us to the effect, that the design selected is a Gothic cross, and is to be placed in the centre of Mansfield market-place, which is about half-way between Nottingham and Welbeck Abbey. The memorial is to be about fifty feet high, of the style that prevailed in the fourteenth century. A local paper gives the following particulars :—" It is square upon the base, and occupies a space, including the steps, of twenty feet square. The whole is divided into three compartments, or stages, the lowest forming the pedestal; the centre a gabled canopy, supported on pinnacled buttresses and clustered columns; the highest a lofty spire roof, pierced with traceried and gabled lights, terminating with a gilded vane. The lowest stage consists of a flight of steps, surmounted by an arcaded pedestal containing shields with the armorial bearings of the family of Lord George, and a deeply-weathered set-off to receive the buttresses and columns of the canopy. At the four angles of the set-off are pedestals surmounted by lions in a sitting posture, supporting vanes, upon which also will be embiazoned the arms of the family. The gables of the canopy are filled with diaper work, and contain carvings emblematical of the interests which his lordship specially advocated. The

whole of the pinnacles, gables, and spire-lights are covered with crockets." The architect is Mr. T. Hine, of Nottingham.

The Exit Eastward from Long Acre.—Commenting on the error which was committed (for no want of protest on our part), when the destroyed houses which form the abominable obstruction known as Middle-row, Holborn, were permitted to be rebuilt, the *Morning Herald,* says—"Just in like manner, only a few weeks since, two houses were removed, exactly opposite the eastern end of Long-acre. That the site on which they stood ought to have been thrown into the street, so as to form a convenient sweep from Long-acre into Queen-street, was obvious to every passer-by. But no one took any step in the matter, and new houses are rising where the old ones stood,—just as if there was no eye or mind in the whole metropolis, to take the least interest in the improvement of the public thoroughfares."

As respects ourselves, it happens that we are personally interested in this property, and were therefore forced to be silent, to avoid personal imputation. Our interests, in a pecuniary point of view, would probably have suffered rather than have been benefitted by the purchase of the property to widen the road, but others might have asserted differently, if we had advocated the enlargement.

To say that no one took any steps in the matter, however, is scarcely correct. Various strong representations were made to the parish authorities, and a deputation of the Bloomsbury Paving Board, a very influential body, attended the Commissioners of Woods and Forests, to induce them to take advantage of a good opportunity to remove what has ever been a great obstruction, and to effect, comparatively cheaply, an improvement which has been so often planned and desired. The commissioners told their surveyor to look at it, but beyond this nothing has been done, and new houses are now rising, which will probably have to be bought and pulled down before many years have passed away.

In connection with the condemnation of the houses here, entailing a large outlay and loss on individuals, we would urge on district surveyors the importance of always well considering such cases, and exercising the power given to them by the Act with the greatest caution. We do not wish it inferred that any want of caution or unwise exercise of power was shown here by our friend, Mr. Pownall, but simply take advantage of the occurrence to make the remark. And *à propos* of district surveyors, we may mention that the election for the Clerkenwell surveyorship, on the 19th, terminated in favour of Mr. R. L. Sibley, son of the late surveyor. He had 44 votes. The other candidates who went to the poll were Mr. Thos. Little (26), Mr. Jennings (22), Mr. Groves, and Mr. East.

ON THE NATURE AND PROPERTIES OF THE METALS USED IN THE BUILDING TRADES.

IRON.

ITS intimate and essential relationship to the earth's magnetic polarity even alone would entitle iron to be regarded as, without exception, the most remarkable and important metal on the surface of our own little magnet, the earth. And, in fact, the consideration of this peculiar relationship led, very naturally, to the idea, that either the whole nucleus of the globe consisted of iron, or that an immense cosmical mass of it, at least, imbedded within the crust, could alone explain the phenomena of the polar needle; and even yet, though the modern wonders of electro-magnetism have considerably modified our ideas on this subject, it is certain that the crust itself, at all events, is so universally pervaded and impregnated with ferruginous substance, that there is scarcely a single mineral combination of which it can with certainty be anticipated that it will not be found to contain more or less iron. And not only in the mineral but in the vegetable and animal creations does it equally prevail. "It is probably generated at the first breath of the youngest creature in the world, and it is abundant in the oldest granite." It exists in the blood and tissues of animals, and in the texture of plants. "It constitutes a large proportion of mica, hornblende, and clay-slate, which, with quartz and felspar, that are seldom altogether free from iron, compose almost the whole crust of the earth. Besides this there are immense deposits of iron-ore, both in primitive and secondary countries, and some very learned philosophers have thought that the quantity of iron in the interior of the earth must be immense. It enters also, as colouring matter, into most bodies which possess colour. It is found in the ashes of vegetables and in the fluids of animals. Ferruginous dust and pyritic hailstones are sometimes showered down from the skies; and from these regions there have fallen hundreds of masses chiefly composed of iron, several of which are of great magnitude." To such evidence of truly cosmical properties in iron we might go on adding in almost endless detail,—considering that it is found in mineral waters and in the ocean,—in the most lustrous gems, in the colours of which it forms an essential element, &c. &c. But even when all natural productions are exhausted, do we not find it reappearing throughout every artificial production, manufacture, art, trade, science, and invention of the human race within the bounds of civilization, and even beyond these bounds? What article of clothing, ornament, furniture, or shelter, is it that—directly or indirectly—is not beholden to iron in its manufacture? Iron seems, as a recent chemical writer remarks, to be somehow an essential ingredient in the process of civilization. What even the golden age would be without it were hard to say, but certainly the era of natural progress is, in a much more amenable and noble sense than usual, the age of iron.

Is it to be wondered, then, that the retrospective thread of human history in the art of working iron has been lost in the myths of the most remote antiquity? Even in the theocratic era of Moses, iron was used in the manufacture of knives and swords, of axes and of tools for cutting stone; and even the furnaces for extracting the iron from its ores are spoken of as then, as now, the source of its acquisition and its manufacture. Thus, it needed not the intimation of a still earlier period, when the antediluvian Tubal-Cain was "the instructor of every artificer in brass and iron," —or, in short, "the earliest iron-master on record,"—to assure us that at least centuries previous to the time of Moses (B.C. 1635) the iron manufacture was a regular branch of trade. In Egypt, Phrygia, Phœnicia, and subsequently Greece—into which it was introduced from Phrygia by the Dactyli,—we have records of its use in very early times, but more especially in Egypt, whence the Jewish leader Moses drew his natural "wisdom and knowledge." Yet, though Egypt then was old and used to the science, two hundred years after the Dactyli settled in Crete (B.C. 1431), and brought with them the knowledge of iron into Greece, we find that so slowly had it progressed that, during the Trojan war, no weapons were formed of iron, although then the substance itself was so highly esteemed that Achilles, at the funeral obsequies of Patroclus, offered a ball of it as a prize. Homer's knowledge, however, of its usual processes, may be seen from his striking but homely comparison of the hissing of the burning brand, when thrust by Ulysses into the eye of Polyphemus, to the effect of red-hot iron quenched in water by the smith,—that ancient son of *Vulcan* whose identity with *Tubal-Cain* is obvious enough, whether we regard him as an earth-born god, or as one of the "giants in those days—the mighty men of old," of whom King Og, of Basan, whose iron bedstead measured 9 cubits in length by 4 in breadth, appears to have been '*ultimus gigantum*'—the latest posterity.

Thus much, then, and more than enough, of the ancient history, or rather the antiquity and mythology, of the mineral *Mars*—as the ancient chemists styled this even modern essential in military warfare. Our further remarks must be moulded, as far as possible, on a practical exemplar, although we only pretend, in the present series of articles, to give a mere compilation, from the best available professional and other authorities, of the main features and peculiarities in the nature and properties of those metals more particularly used in the building trades, and not so much to afford any direct or explicit instruction as to their practical uses in these trades. But while as practically useful as possible, we shall not hesitate to bring to notice several facts of a curious, rather than a practical tendency, and more especially facts over which the element of beauty, either in form or colour, quantity or number, cannot but shed an interest in the thoughts of every intelligent mind.

But first of the sources whence this particular metal are derived, and of its more obvious and essential properties. It exists in nature almost exclusively in the state of ores, and rarely in the metallic state, a fact which only renders it the more remarkable that its production should have formed a branch of business almost as early as the fig-leaf manufacture. The principal ores of iron are its oxides and carbonates. Others are its sulphurets, one the magnetical pyrites, the other, in which a larger quantity of sulphur contaminates the metal, yellow pyrites — "fool's gold," as it has been called, from the fact that it has frequently, even in California, been mistaken for gold, as indeed it was by Columbus himself and the Spanish grandees who bore it in triumphal procession into Madrid, and preserved it as heir looms, some of them for several generations. Pyrites is often round as an apple and concentradiate in interior crystallization. This form of it used to be called Jove's thunderbolts forged by Vulcan—fire, or sulphur—and hence called pyrites, the stone of fire. It is so hard too as to strike fire like flint. In the chemical action of its elements under ground, it is capable of simulating earthquakes. Beautiful fac-similes of leaves and other vegetable and even animal remains are often found entirely composed of pyrites, by which the organic particles have been replaced. This ore, however, is never used in the manufacture of iron. The best of all ores for that purpose are those in which the metal is simply oxidated. The ore of most abundance in the primary or oldest formations of the earth's crust is the black oxide or magnetic ore—the loadstone itself in fact, which affords the most celebrated and valuable ores of Sweden and the north of Europe, but of which the use is greatly circumscribed from its not being associated with coal. In the secondary and tertiary formations the anhydrous and hydrated peroxide—red and brown hæmatite, or blood-stone—occur occasionally in considerable quantity. It is employed in this country to some extent for mixing with the commoner ore. The ochres belong to this class of ores. When fully hydrated these are of a yellow colour, and as the water is expelled the ochre becomes gradually redder as it approaches the state of colcothar of vitriol, or calcined copperas or sulphate of iron. Hence, by various roastings, various pigments may be thus procured from one natural substance. Peroxide of iron, too, is that form of iron which pervades the blood, at least the arterial, while, on Liebig's beautiful theory, the venous, or black blood, carries off the carbon consumed in the production of animal heat, in the form of carbonate of the protoxide or black oxide of iron, to be liberated in the lungs in form of carbonic acid, while the iron protoxide is again converted there, by the oxygen of the atmosphere, into the red peroxide of the arterial blood, as a vehicle of oxygen to the carbon of the tissues, in burning which into carbonic acid, it keeps up the animal fire or heat. Thus, the oxides of iron are, to the whole animal creation, a fountain of vital heat and living energy; and iron is the only truly sanative metal in existence. So much of it exists in the blood, indeed, that the strange idea of converting it into memorial rings is said to have actually been adopted in France.

The ore that is chiefly used in the manufacture of iron, at least in this country, is the clay iron stone of the coal measures. This is essentially the carbonate of the protoxide, though mixed with variable quantities of clay and carbonates of lime, magnesia, &c. It is nodular, and often called the argillaceous carbonate of iron. It occurs in strata, beds, or bands, from two to ten and fourteen inches thick, alternating with beds of coal, clay, bituminous schist, and often limestone. The fuel and flux with which it is to be smelted are thus ever at hand. The proportion of iron in this ore varies considerably, but averages about 30 per cent.; and after calcination or expulsion of water, carbonic acid, &c., 40 per cent. A crystallized carbonate, or spathic iron, is smelted in some parts of the continent, and gives an iron often remarkable for a large proportion of manganese. The celebrated iron of Elba is derived from a specular or oligistic iron, a crystallised peroxide, forming a beautiful mineral, which Fourcroy states that Duke d'Ayen, a French chemist, once artificially produced while decomposing the green muriate of iron by heat, during which same process were yielded crystals of sublimation of the clearest and most pellucid lustre, in the form of blades of razors, with tinges of iridescent colours, bright as those refracted by the best of prisms.*

Having thus given some account of the sources whence iron is derived, we shall, in the next place, treat more particularly of its nature and properties, and of its three chief varieties—cast-iron, wrought-iron, and steel.

ST. DAVID'S CATHEDRAL.—According to *Archæologia Cambrensis*, the restoration of this venerable structure has been going on since the subscription for that purpose in 1846. The stone rood-screen has been restored, and the unsightly wood-work which surrounded it cleared away, and replaced, where necessary, by parcloses of wrought-iron. A projecting cornice of oak has been substituted for the balustrade which formerly disfigured the rood-loft. The choir arch, before walled up, has been partially opened, and the large platform before the screen and the passage into the choir, have been laid with encaustic tiles.

BRICKS.—A return obtained by Mr. Cocks, M.P., shows the duty paid on bricks in the several excise collections of England in the year 1848 to have amounted to 448,310*l.*, of which 10,386*l.* were paid in the metropolis alone.

* We may here observe that we have repeated Duke d'Ayen's experiment, but with pure muriate of iron have failed to observe the prismatic lustre. Crystals of the precise form and texture of fishes' scales were sublimed. In an experiment with other elements altogether, however, there occurred precisely such crystals as those described, some of them with stripes of the richest rainbow colours, and others of a single hue of the purest brilliancy; but what was most remarkable, these crystals, even when each of a single hue, were of every imaginable colour, from the deepest blue and purple through the brightest reds and flame colours, with greens and yellows,—sublimed, all at once from one and the same material, with the same degree of heat, and simultaneously in every respect, the whole sparkling like a diadem,—certainly as singular a phenomenon in optics as it still appears to be in chemistry. It is probable, therefore, that the ingredients used by Duke d'Ayen were not pure: hence his process does not appear to have even till now been successfully repeated, and, in all probability, the production of the specular ore itself was assisted by the impurities mixed up with the muriate.

HALL AND STAIRCASE OF THE NEW BRITISH MUSEUM.
SIR R. SMIRKE, ARCHITECT.

THE HALL AND STAIRCASE OF THE BRITISH MUSEUM.

ABOVE is a representation of part of the Hall, in the British Museum, and the staircase,—one of the most effective portions of the new structure.

The order is Grecian Doric. The ceiling is trabeated and deeply coffered, and is enriched with Greek frets and other ornaments in various colours, painted in encaustic. On the east side are the apartments devoted to the MS. department. On the west is the principal staircase, and a gallery which forms the approach to the collection of antiquities. The centre flight is seventeen feet wide, flanked by two pedestals of grey Aberdeen granite, intended to receive colossal sculpture. The walls on either side of this centre flight are cased with red Aberdeen granite, highly polished. On the first landing are pedestals and carved vases of Huddlestone stone. The balustrades are of the same. The ceiling and walls are painted partly in oil and partly in encaustic colours, the former being trabeated and coffered to correspond with the entrance hall, and similarly decorated.

The polychromatic enrichments have been applied with very considerable success. The sunk panels are blue, with a yellow star in each; the enrichments are variously coloured,—red and white predominating ; and the stiles, beams, &c., are covered with frets, guilloche, and scrolls, in flat colours, for all of which precedents were sought in the museum collection. These decorations were executed by Messrs. Collman and Davis.

Our engraving is from a larger drawing by Mr. Collinan, which was exhibited some time since.

Knowing that comparatively few of our readers possess the early volume of our journal in which, as mentioned last week, was given a view of the building that occupied the site of the new structure, we have, at the request of several correspondents, reproduced the engraving as an interesting record.

THE HOLLOW BRICK CEILING OVER ST. GEORGE'S HALL, LIVERPOOL.

THE following is the specification for the construction of the ceiling over St. George's Hall, under which the work was executed. It will be found suggestive for other matters :—

1. The contractor must furnish, at his own cost, all labour, mortar, cement, and bond-timber, as hereinafter described.

2. The centres have been put up and the panelling set out, and hollow bricks will be furnished to the contractor on the ground, for the full and complete performance of the work.

3. The contractor is to find all staging and implements necessary for the execution of the whole work.

4. The mortar must be made from the best Halkin mountain or blue lias lime, fresh burned, composed of one part, by measure, to two parts of perfectly clean-washed fresh-water sand, free from dirt, clay, or saline particles. The character of the sand must be most particularly attended to. The mortar must be well mixed in a steam mortar mill, and must be made and delivered on the ground as to insure its being used perfectly fresh. On no account must mortar once set be remixed for use on this work.

5. The cement must be the "patent lithic," fresh and good, and mixed, by measure, with an equal proportion of sand, as described for the mortar. The cement must be used immediately it is mixed ; softening or re-tempering will not be allowed. All cement once set, before use, must be immediately removed from the work.

6. The arch and spandrils must be formed and bonded according to the plans and sections furnished, and in strict conformity with such instructions as shall from time to time be given during the progress of the work.

7. In setting the bricks, the straightest and truest sides must be chosen for the beds, and the thickest end placed outwards. Where the arch is more than one brick in depth, they must be carefully and truly bonded according to section, and instructions furnished at the time. The bond, in all cases, must be set in cement ; and, if required, hoop iron, stone, wood, or flag, is to be used, as shall be directed.

8. The work must be carried on equally, and regularly, in perfect courses on each side of the centres. The spandril walls are to be carried up with the arch.

9. When the arch shall have been raised 10 feet, on each side of the centres, the crown must be regularly and evenly loaded with dry bricks, so as to give the centres their full weight. These bricks will be for use in that portion of the arch to be completed. The bricks must be so stacked as not to injure themselves or the centres, and they must be taken gradually and regularly from thence, and used in the arch, on each side, so as to keep the new work in equal course, and the crown of the centres regularly loaded at the same time.

10. Where the double brick ribs are liable, from their depth, to come into contact with the principals, the rib must be reduced in depth, by bond, to one and a half brick.

11. For 5 feet on each side the horizontal centre line of the arch, the whole work is to be set in the best "Patent Lithic Cement," mixed and used as specified.

12. The whole of the work must be full bedded and jointed throughout the entire area of all the beds and joints, whether mortar or cement be used. The beds and joints must be evenly spread, not less than one-eighth of an inch in thickness, in the thinnest

THE BRITISH MUSEUM OF OLD TIME.

part, and each brick pressed well home into its place, so as to cause the mortar or cement to curl out full and flush along the whole line of each bed and joint.

13. The openings in the spandril walls must be set out fair and true with each other, and the entire rings of all set in cement. The triangular 4-inch portion of each spandril must also be set in cement.

14. The mortar and cement flushed out of the beds and joints must be cut off clean with the trowel while wet, and the joints filled and rough pointed with the trowel at once.

15. The bond, and joist timber, must be of the size and scantling figured, and must be cut out of the best crown Memel or Baltic timber, perfectly free from sap, shakes, or large dead knots.

16. The work must be estimated for in one lump sum. Any hoop iron, bond stone, or flags, required for purposes of bond, will be provided to the contractor on the ground; but he must take them from thence and set them in the arch for the sum named in his general estimate.

17. The plans, specification, and sections must be taken according to the full bearing of each on each; and where any discrepancy shall be found to exist, the engineer shall decide its proper meaning.

18. Any alteration in the bond, depth of ribs, form, and number of spandril walls, or any other portion of the work, shall not vitiate this contract; but should more or less work be put into the arch than is shewn by the plans and sections, it shall be ascertained by measurement, and then be added to or deducted from the amount of tender, according to the schedule of prices annexed.

Robert Rawlinson.

N.B. In the report to the Committee, January, 1848, the term, "hollow tile" is used; in this specification, "hollow brick" has been adopted instead.

In that report was given an,—

ESTIMATE OF THE COMPARATIVE COST OF BRICKS AND TILES.

Ceiling of Great Hall.

	per thousand.					
163,973 bricks at 66s...	£541	3	3¾			
100,682 tiles at 65s...	359	14	3¾			
In favour of tiles......				181	9	0

Ceiling of two Law Courts.

	per thousand.					
52,800 bricks at 66s...	£174	4	9½			
35,640 tiles at 65s...	115	16	7			
In favour of tiles......				58	8	2½
Tiles cost less than bricks				239	17	2½

ESTIMATE OF COMPARATIVE WEIGHT OF BRICKS AND TILES.

Ceiling of Great Hall.

	tons.	cwt.	qrs.	lbs.				
163,973 bricks weigh	635	17	3	25				
110,682 tiles weigh..	409	8	0	23				
					166	9	3	2

Ceiling of Two Courts.

	tons.	cwt.	qrs.	lbs.				
52,800 bricks weigh	223	18	2	8				
35,640 tiles weigh..	151	3	0	4				
					72	15	2	4
Tiles weigh less than bricks........					239	5	1	6

Thus, 146,322 tiles will cost 239*l.* 17s. 2½d. less than 216,773 bricks; the quantity required to do the work of the tiles and the building will be relieved of a straining weight to 239 tons 5 cwts. 1 qr. 6 lbs.

The greatest pressure the tiles can have to sustain in the great arch is equal to 30 lbs. to the square inch.

I have subjected them to a test of 90 lbs. pressure to the square inch, under which they did not fracture.

N.B. Each hollow tile occupies in construction 192 cube inches of space, and weighs 9¼ lbs., having 37.7 cube inches of space in the circular perforation. Each solid brick occupies in construction 121¼ cube inches of space, and also weighs 9½ lbs.

Abstract of space occupied and weight.

Hollow tiles	192 cube inches	9¼ lbs. weight
Solid brick	121¼ cube inches	9½ lbs. weight
	70¾ cube inches in favour of hollow tile,	

Or, rather more than one-third of the weight will be avoided in the arch by the use of hollow tile.

The arch, as executed, required more tile than is specified in this report, on account of the paneling which has been formed in the construction adopted.*

HOLLOW BRICK CONSTRUCTIONS.

In your last week's paper, Mr. Robert Rawlinson mentions that he first saw specimens of the hollow bricks in Mr. Chadwick's office. I imagine that the bricks he there saw were those left by me in the Sanitary Commissioners' office about eighteen months since. The idea of using hollow tubes of clay of large size in construction occurred to me seven or eight years ago. At that time I proposed it to a client of mine, who was about to erect a large quantity of walling, but the misfortune which overtook him lost me that oppor-

* We know so little of Mr. Elmes, beyond his noble work at Liverpool, that the following extract from a letter addressed by him to Mr. Rawlinson may interest our readers. He says, with reference to some observations on painting made by Mr. R.,—"I wish you would try your hand at architecture, and stir up a little spark of feeling for it. Although, in a domestic sense, it must yield the palm to painting, at least when carried beyond mere utility, yet the pleasurable sensations, indescribable almost, produced in a well-proportioned and symmetrically arranged room, to go no further, are worthy of appreciation. Architecture, as a noble science and beautiful art, in the highest sense of those terms, exists, unfortunately, at present, only in ruins or in history and imagination; but utility, and utility alone, will ever save it from utter oblivion, and in all ages it must be acknowledged as indispensable to human existence. These observations *cannot* apply to painting or sculpture, not that I would part with our handmaidens, but only claim an equal rank and equal consideration. Consider, too, the effect produced by painting and sculpture as auxiliaries to architecture; the first, by rendering the massive wall rich with varied colours, and indicating *space beyond* so delightful to anticipate, thus charming the eye while the noble subject may interest and instruct the mind;—the latter, devoid of colour, yet pre-eminent in form; the material harmonising with the architecture in massive durability, while the gracefully flowing drapery, the marked expressive countenance, and the apparent capability of motion, all contrast with the greater severity of the architectural frame work. Were this feeling general, alas for gilt frames and watch boxes for statues! The predicted fall of my vaulted ceiling made in Liverpool I find has not been confined to that town; it has been reported in London to have been abandoned. Notwithstanding these idle reports, I am proceeding steadily in my purpose, and with due care and attention, I entertain very little doubt of ultimate success. I shall, however, like to have a little talk with you upon it when we meet."

tunity of trying my plans; and it was not till about two years and a half ago that I again turned my attention to the subject. Deeply impressed with the conviction of the vast importance to this nation that her labouring poor should possess homes fit for human beings to dwell in, it struck me that a system of constructing such buildings of hollow tube was practicable, and having expressed this opinion to the Duke of Richmond, whose architect I have the honour to be, his Grace desired me to send him my plans, which I did, accompanying them with a written statement of the advantage likely to accrue from the use of such a material, not only in building cottages, but in the erection of farm buildings, and suggesting that, as the cost of such works was thus, wherever clay existed on an estate, resolvable into labour and fuel, my plan of construction would afford a great amount of employment to the Irish poor, the result of whose labour thus directed would tend to raise them in the scale of civilised beings.

His grace, whose ear is ever open to any practicable plan of improving the condition of his poor neighbours, told me at once that he would give my scheme a trial, and that the tubes should be made at his tile-yard, and a cottage built with them. Mr. Webster, of Hounsdown, was kind enough to lend me one of his hand tile machines, and with one of them the tubes I employed were formed; some of them being 20 inches long and 7 inches square, weighing, in proportion to an equal cubical quantity of solid brick, about four-fifths less. It was part of my original purpose to form roofs, walls, floors, and partitions of these tubes; but in the first experiment the roof and walls only of the cottage were constructed; and as a piece of construction it answered admirably; but the form I then used I should not employ again, as the wet, not from any leakage, but owing to capillary attraction, finds its way in at the haunch of the arch,— a defect which I believe I can wholly obviate in my next essay. Mr. Rushidge, the duke's agent, who gave me every assistance in carrying out the work, prognosticated a failure in this point, and his judgment proved better than mine; still, as a first experiment, it must be considered a successful one, and I feel assured that it will be the commencement of a new era in the system of constructing cottages. Lord Robert Clinton, who was staying at Goodwood at the time, appeared much interested in the subject, and by his request I made a series of designs for cottages to be constructed with these tubes, which designs, and specimens of the tubes, he sent to the president of the Royal Agricultural Society in Ireland. I also called on Mr. Chadwick, and left him an essay of mine on the subject of cottage construction, and also gave him specimens of the bricks made at the Duke of Richmond's works. I am about to make experiments to determine the best forms for the various purposes to which these tubes are applicable, the result of which I shall be happy to communicate to you. Such a method of construction will be as durable as it is economical, and will thus remove one of the obstacles to a legislative measure which shall relieve from the cottages of this country the stigma of being nurseries of vice and pauperism.

Southampton, April 24. JOHN ELLIOTT.

CITY COMMISSIONERS OF SEWERS.—At a meeting of the Commissioners of Sewers, on Tuesday, Mr. Deputy Peacock in the chair, measures were taken to improve the condition of the carriage-way in Leadenhall-street. Several persons were fined for cesspool nuisances, and, in consequence of a report from the surveyor, a stricter rule as to the emptying of these into the sewers was ordered in future to be adopted. A conversation then ensued upon the position of the Great Central Gas Company, which was originated by a letter from the secretary. The communication stated that "this company's mains will be laid under the superintendence and control of the commissioners, and the directors are most anxious to acquire information on the mode of effecting these necessary operations in a manner which shall provide for the public convenience in the most ample manner." The letter was referred to the General Purposes Committee.

ARCHITECTURE AND THE ROYAL ACADEMY.

SIR,—Of four designs which I had sent to the Royal Academy for their exhibition, three have been rejected, and among them that which I had made myself sure of being accepted, it being by far the best in regard both to subject and execution—in the latter respect fully wrought up to exhibition proof as a drawing. I cannot help thinking, therefore, that great error as to selection has been shown by those with whom the selecting works for exhibition rests. Very probably the drawing which is admitted is so merely because it happens to fit in conveniently among others, and it is as likely as not that I shall find it where, being a small one, it can scarcely be seen at all.

Certain it is that at the Academy not even decent attention is paid to the arrangement of the architectural subjects, which was last year more than usually unsatisfactory, for while an interior of the new coffee-room at the Carlton club-house was hung in the topmost row, so that it was quite impossible to make any thing out of Mr. Sang's decorations, several very uninteresting subjects—some of them not designs at all, but merely views consisting of bits of ruins and trees—were placed just upon the line. There being at the best so very little space at the academy for hanging architectural drawings so as they can be properly seen, surely the least that can be done is to make the most judicious use of that space, and it is nothing less than preposterous to give up to oil pictures any part of "the line," as it is termed, or, indeed, any other situation where the larger architectural subjects would show themselves at least tolerably well. To the upper part of the walls being covered with oil pictures,—since, it seems, covered they must be,—there can be no particular objection, it being better that it should be so, than that, under the pretence of being exhibited, designs should be put out of sight.

What is the Professor of Architecture about, that he does not at least remonstrate? and, if such be really the case, give us to understand that he has no authority, and remonstrates to no purpose. At any rate, we architects look to you, Mr. Editor, for upholding, as far as may be in your power, the interests of architecture, by protesting against the slights and indignities put upon it at the Academy's exhibitions. It has been suggested before now, that it would be an improvement were there to be at least one screen for the reception of smaller architectural drawings. But as it seems screens must not be thought of,—perhaps because the Academy do not wish to appear to screen themselves either in that or any other way,—allow me to point out a different and still better mode by which so many drawings might be accommodated, that, perhaps, all the walls of what is now called the architectural-room might be given up to oil pictures. It is simply this: let there be in each room a long but narrow show-table or desk, with two sloping sides, upon which the drawings have merely to be placed, their frames resting against the ledge of such desk. Tables of the kind placed in the rooms, would be no more an obstruction than forms now are, therefore free from the inconvenience, or supposed inconvenience, attending screens, while, at the same time, they would be better for looking at the drawings placed on them.

There is, indeed, one thing which such plan would render necessary, viz., that the frames must not exceed in their upright dimensions the width of the sloping surfaces of the desk. That would be the only regulation required; for the frames—and perhaps mere narrow beadings, similar to those used for prints, would be better than "picture-frames"—might be wider or narrower, as might happen, and also shorter than the breadth of the slope on which they would be placed. Of course the necessary regulation must be properly announced to those whom it concerned. As matters are managed at present, it looks as if the Academy were anxious to get rid of architecture, not, indeed, by actually kicking it out of doors—for were they to do that, they might chance to get some hard kicks in return,—but by "bowing it out," in a sort of fashion which plainly tells a person that his speedy departure will be more agreeable than his stay.

It is a pity there cannot be an election for representatives of architecture in the academy, —for in that case I do not think that any of those who now sit for it would be returned; most assuredly not out of gratitude for their past services and zeal.   OUTIS.

THE NEW SOCIETY OF PAINTERS IN WATER COLOURS.

THE report of the Art-Union of London occupies so much of our space, that we can afford but little more in our present number to matters artistical. We must say, however, to those who through these proceedings have gained the right of selecting pictures, that they will find in the New Water Colour Gallery some charming works. Although there are, perhaps, fewer prominent pictures than usual, the whole are more evenly good than is sometimes the case. In the landscape department especially, there is a great improvement. Mr. L. Haghe has a remarkably fine picture, "Vespers in the church of St. Anne, Bruges" (102); and Mr. H. Warren's "Joseph's Coat brought to Jacob" (276), displays some of the highest qualities of the art, and has narrowly escaped the epithet "grand." Mr. Edward Corbould's chief work "The Murderers of Thomas Chase, of Amersham, drawing up 'the Letter to the Clergy,'" displays a wonderful depth of colouring, and is in other respects a picture of great merit. Mr. Absolon, always excellent, is not quite up to his own mark in his nevertheless charming picture of harvesting, under the title of "Plenty" (55). Mr. Vacher has some beautiful views in Rome and Sicily.

Mr. Weigall has deserted his "poultry," and given a pleasing companion to his "Rape of the Lock" last year, called "Philandering." Mr. Wehnert's "Precincts of a large City, Evening," is an agreeable and clever drawing, but we miss the more ambitious works he has been accustomed to exhibit. Mr. Fahey, Mr. Kearney, Mr. W. Lee, Mr. Davidson (for some nice green landscapes), Mr. Mole, Mr. Riviere, Mr. Howse, Mr. M'Kewan, Mr. Harrison Weir, Mr. Rowbotham, jun. (for a clever drawing of Rouen), Miss Fanny Corbaux, &c., should all be named.

LORD ROSSE'S SOIREE.

THE new president of the Royal Society, the Earl of Rosse, gave his first conversazione on Saturday evening last, which was attended by a large number of persons. The president having no house in town, it was held in the suite of rooms occupied by the Royal Society and the Society of Antiquaries, in Somerset House. This change, from the private residence of the late president, Lord Northampton, is not by any means an improvement: it gives the entertainment the character simply of some special meeting of the society itself, and takes away the charm of a private reception. This feeling was increased by the circumstance that the Prince Albert, who was present, came early, and being necessarily attended round the rooms by the noble host, the latter could not personally receive his guests, so that it became simply a public assembly where a number of celebrities might be met.

In other respects the arrangements were the same as at Lord Northampton's.

Amongst the many interesting objects in the rooms were models of the president's colossal telescopes, a clever machine for cutting ship-timber, Mr. Whishaw's telegraphic arrangement for obtaining uniformity of time, a number of the best daguerreotypes we have yet seen, and some of Mr. Rogers's most recent carvings.

There was also an extraordinary and beautiful tryptych, painted at the commencement of the sixteenth century, and attributed to Lucas de Cranach. Cranach was the contemporary of Albert Dürer, and in some respects not inferior to him.

PROGRESS OF LITERARY AND SCIENTIFIC INSTITUTIONS.—A return obtained by Mr. Scholfield, M.P., shows that applications have been received from upwards of 100 literary and scientific societies or institutions for certificates of exemption from local rates.

THE COLLECTION OF ANIMAL REFUSE OF TOWNS.

At a meeting of the Society of Arts, on the 11th, Mr. B. Rotch in the chair, Dr. Ayres read a paper on the importance of the animal refuse of towns as a manure, and the methods of rendering it available to agricultural purposes. The author commenced his paper by calling attention to the necessity of preserving the animal refuse of towns, and the importance which is attached to it in China and Flanders, in many departments of France, Tuscany, &c., and also to the various forms in which it is applied to the earth.

Having alluded to the importance of this subject in connection with the improvement of the sanitary condition of towns, and the injurious effects upon the inhabitants of London in particular, by allowing the putrid matter to be carried into the Thames, there to be tossed upon the waves and left exposed upon the shores at each retrocession of the tide,—he proceeded to consider the contents of the cesspools of London alone, which he has calculated cannot yield less than 46,500 tons of perfectly dry matter annually—a quantity, according to the analysis of Liebig, sufficient to fertilise at least a million acres of land, and the monetary value of which cannot be stated at less than 340,000*l*. Having next alluded to the plans which have hitherto been proposed for drying and rendering this great mass of matter portable and available for agricultural purposes, he proceeded to describe a plan which he has recently patented for effecting so desirable an object.

My process (he observed) essentially depends on the fact, that all the gaseous and volatile products of putrefaction are combustible, and are resolved into the ordinary products of combustion when carried over any incandescent surface, or over or through burning fuel, when mixed with atmospheric air. Thus, ammonia is resolved into nitrogen and water; sulphuretted hydrogen into sulphurous acid and water; carburetted hydrogen into carbonic acid and water; phosphoretted hydrogen into phosphoric acid and water; the volatile organic matters associated with the gases are completely destroyed; carbonic acid alone passes through the fire unchanged. All these gases, with the exception of ammonia and carbonic acid, exist only in very small proportions in putrescent animal matter. It follows, from what has been stated, that all the volatile products of putrefaction are thus resolvable into the ordinary products of combustion, which are well known to be innocuous. It suffices to conduct these gases and vapours through a fire to effect their entire decomposition and destruction.

The apparatus by which this process may be worked, he thought susceptible of many modifications; but that to which he particularly desired to direct the attention of the society consists in drying the animal refuse by the application of heat, either obtained from steam-pipes or otherwise, and at the same time destroying the volatile products of putrefaction by burning them.

NOTES IN THE PROVINCES.

Another obituary window has been put up in Chichester Cathedral. It is the work of Mr. M. O'Connor, of London.——The restoration of the west front of Gloucester Cathedral is about to be resumed, it is said, with vigour.——The new dock at Gloucester was opened on 18th inst. The new basin nearly doubles the quayside accommodation, and there are two additional cranes, each capable of lifting upwards of 20 tons. At present the basin will be appropriated to the discharge of cargoes sent by rail.——The foundation-stone of the Lazarus Almshouses was laid last week, at Hereford, by Lady Emily Foley.——A new church, says the *Hereford Times*, is about to be erected in the parish of Clifford.——The new Exchange Market at Bristol was opened on Saturday week.——The architect of the projected Wilts County Lunatic Asylum, on Wednesday week exhibited the plans, &c., and pointed out the site to builders, ironfounders, and others intending to send in estimates for the construction of the building. Amongst those present are said to have been several London firms, with Messrs. Willcox and Son, Bristol; Messrs. C. and R. Gane, and Mr. W. Hancock, Trowbridge; Messrs. Simpson and Bennett, Lyme; Messrs. Daniel and Charles Jones, Bradford; Messrs. James and John Hodges, Doulting, Shepton Mallet; Messrs. Young and White, Devizes; Mr. John Mitchel, Pewsey; Mr. H. B. Hale, Warminster.——The Lion Barracks, at Portsea, are to be given up to the authorities in a finished state on 1st May, or within the time specified by the contractors, Messrs. Locke and Nesham.——The following tenders, according to a provincial authority, were given in for the restoration of the parish church of Atherstone:—Messrs. Broadbent and Hanley, of Leicester, 2,845*l*.; Mr. Spencer, of Lutterworth, 3,298*l*. 10s.; Mr. Lilly, of Measham, 3,288*l*. 2s.; Mr. Lloyd, of Atherstone, 3,312*l*. 7s.; Mr. Spencer, of Atherstone, 3,452*l*. 7s.; Mr. Hardy, of Coton, 3,470*l*.; Messrs. Miller, Fox, Pullon, and Stanton, Atherstone and Hilton Building Company, 3,973*l*.; Mr. Cooper, of Derby, 4,272*l*. The lowest tender, that of Messrs. Broadbent and Hanley, accepted.——The cost of the recent alterations and additions at the Bedford Lunatic Asylum, affording accommodation for about seventy additional patients, besides offices, enlargements of airing yards, warming and ventilating, and a supply of hot and cold water apparatus, is upwards of 5,000*l*.——On Tuesday week the foundation stone of St. Alban's Church, Liverpool, was laid at the end of Bond-street. The building is to accommodate 1,000 persons, at a cost of 5,000*l*.—St. Matthias's Church, Great Howard-street, designed by Mr. A. Holme, with accommodation for 1,000 persons also, was consecrated on same day.——St. Jude's Church, Bradford, is at present under repair and renewal.——The sewerage of Gateshead is about to be commenced by call for tenders for a main sewer.

SUPPLY OF WATER TO CONSTANTINOPLE.

I beg leave to send you the following reply to the query of your correspondent relative to the supply of water to Constantinople. The numerous erections which he terms "upright pipes," are called "souterazi," or water towers, and are used for the purpose of passing the water across the valleys upon the principle of the syphon, instead of the more expensive construction of aqueducts. These towers, it is stated, were erected at about one-fifth of the expense of aqueducts, and are generally attributed to the ancient Greeks. The supply of water to Constantinople is obtained from the mountains, bordering on the Black Seas, where it is collected in reservoirs, which are situated about 15 miles from that city, and is conveyed by means of four conduits, composed of earthern pipes, having at intervals the "souterazi" to the central reservoir contiguous to the city, and from whence it is distributed by conduits to the seraglio, and the fountains that are established in almost every street.

These "souterazi" form a regular inclined plane from the mountains to the city, and they also have the same effect as the "columnana" of the ancient Romans, in relieving the hydraulic pressure on the pipes, and at the same time allow the escape of the air, and the basin on the top serves as a place of deposit for any sediment or feculent matter.

B. Baylis.

METROPOLITAN COMMISSION OF SEWERS.

A general court was held on Thursday, the 19th inst., at the Court House, Greek-street; Lord Ebrington, M.P., in the chair.

The Retirement of the Hon. Fred. Byng from the Commission.—Upon a recommendation from the Works Committee being read, that 455 feet of pipe sewer be put down in Parker-street, Drury-lane, and 135 feet of invert of the existing sewer be lowered, at an expense of 140*l*.,

Mr. R. L. Jones briefly complained that this question was now brought before the court for the first time, and protested against such a system.

Mr. Bullar rose to order. This was going into the old question of committees.

The Hon. Fred. Byng then rose and said, that he hoped the court would hear a few observations from him, and probably they would be the last he should offer in that court. Mr. Chadwick had charged him with "obstructing" the business of the court, but he felt that the Works Committee had almost become the court, and he was useless there unless it were to hold up his hand for the confirmation of their proceedings. That committee, from the very large number of which it was composed (13) was in effect, though not quite in number, a majority of the court, and when himself and other commissioners came down to the court they knew nothing about what was going on, the business having been done by the Works Committee. Mr. Chadwick had frequently boasted of the sub-division of labour, but the term was most extraordinary, and the application of it rather droll. The Works Committee had taken or imposed upon itself duties as regarded "all complaints and applications for works and operations, and leave to execute works and operations as to sewers and sewerage—as to house drains and cesspools—as to surface drains and gullies—as to paving, water supply and cleansing—and as to miscellaneous matters relating to works," matters enough to overwhelm an ordinarily-constructed committee. Call this a sub-division of labour!—he called it a concentration of labour. It was a most extraordinary sub-division of labour, for he found that the attendance at the Works Committee was not numerous, taking the average; but what appeared to him most extraordinary with reference to it was the fact, that the persons most frequently present at it, were persons who, like his lordship in the chair, and Mr. Chadwick, held overwhelming appointments under the state. He believed, also, that the appointment of officers was illegal. By the course that had been adopted, he found his attendance extremely irksome, and he felt compelled to take a similar step to that taken by an excellent commissioner (Mr. Hutton), with whom he acted for fifteen months, and who had expressed his determination to attend no longer. He had waited upon that gentleman to ascertain his reasons for so doing, and found the grounds for his retirement to be similar to his own. He had come to the same conclusions that had induced Mr. Hutton not to attend, and should now follow his example. He had, for his opposition, been threatened to be superseded, and had been recommended by Mr. Chadwick to withdraw if he was dissatisfied with the order of proceedings. He (Mr. Byng) could not agree to take his advice, but should take his own, and he had come to this conclusion because he believed the Government approved of the views of Mr. Chadwick, and the manner in which measures for the public service were carried out in that court. However, he could only see in their proceedings an illegality and an unwarrantable outlay of money by the court in a way that had never been intended. He held in his hand two publications,—one given by his friend Mr. C. Johnson, the other by Mr. Chadwick, on agricultural subjects,—clever pamphlets, certainly, in their way, but not of pressing importance, and, therefore, he contended, they ought not to have been entertained by the court. The one had been ordered to be printed by the court; but he found the other had been ordered by the Works Committee, to be printed exclusively for their use, having no regard whatever to the rest of the commissioners, and he believed they were not at all justified in going into any expense of this kind. He intended, after the present meeting of the court, to withdraw from any active interference in the affairs of this commission, which he regretted sincerely, as it might deprive him of his share of the applause if success should attend the action of the commission for the benefit of the public; but he believed they acted illegally, and that their acts would bring them into the Court of Queen's Bench.

Lord Ebrington hoped the court would not re-open the long-vexed question as to the business of the court.

Mr. R. L. Jones believed every question ought first to be brought before the court, for the mode of carrying on the business was the most irregular he had ever witnessed. In fact, those commissioners who were not on the Works Committee were a mere non-entity.

No other commissioner rising to address the court, the chairman put the motion for the adoption of the recommendation of the Works Committee, which was passed without opposition.

The Jurisdiction of the Commission.—A long report was presented on the subject of the recent fine imposed by Mr. Burrell, the magistrate at the Westminster Police Office, on John Merry, a foreman of pumps and hose, for having created a nuisance during the process of emptying a cesspool in York-street, Westminster, the odour being so great as to compel the tradesmen to close their shops and windows. In giving judgment, under the provisions of the Police Act, the magistrate contended, notwithstanding the extraordinary powers vested in the Commissioners of Sewers, they had no right to relieve the cesspools in the day-time, or to create a nuisance in so doing, and thereupon fined the defendant in the nominal amount of 10s. to try the question, as Mr. Smith, the solicitor to the commissioners, had signified his intention, on their behalf, of appealing against this conviction.

It appeared that the information had been laid by

Mr. Sngg and Mr. Crow, inspectors of pavements and nuisances for the parishes of St. Margaret and St. John, Westminster.

Mr. Chadwick, in reference to the evidence given by Mr. Crow before the magistrate, as to the annoyance received by the inhabitants from the use of the pump and hose, read the evidence of the same person on this subject contained in the third report of the Sanitary Commissioners, in which he stated that he had introduced the use of the pump and hose in emptying between 300 and 400 cesspools; that it was cleaner, and cheaper by one-third; that he had had his own house cleansed by this means, and that the only dissatisfaction expressed by any party was that it would not remove the hard and solid substances. In conclusion, he remarked that if cholera appeared in the neighbourhood, and he was left to himself as to what was to be done, he should apply the pump and hose as actively as possible.

This report led to a long desultory conversation, in which it was asserted by Dr. Southwood Smith that if any odour escaped in the night more danger was to be apprehended from it than if the work was performed by day, to say nothing of the additional expense that would be incurred in having it removed by night. But if the work was properly performed that no odour whatever could be detected, and that it might even be performed in a drawing-room. It was also necessary that the commissioners should have the entire control over these works, to carry them out in the way most conducive for the public interests.

John Merry, the foreman, was suspended from his duties until further orders, and a committee appointed to investigate his conduct.

Mr. John Grant, of Exeter, was appointed an assistant-surveyor at a provisional salary of 250*l.* per annum. After some severe comments from Mr. Leslie and Mr. Jones that no information was received from the Committee of Works as to the eligibility or qualifications of any of the other candidates for that appointment, some works were ordered, and the court adjourned.

MISCELLANEA.

INSTITUTION OF CIVIL ENGINEERS.—At a meeting on Tuesday, 24th, Mr. W. Cubitt, Vice-President, in the chair, the paper read was "On the Construction of Locomotive Engines, especially those modifications which enable additional power to be gained without materially increasing the weight, or unduly elevating the centre of gravity," by Mr. T. R. Crampton. It was contended that the durability of the working parts of the engine, the stability of the permanent way, and the freedom from oscillation, so essential for the comfort of travelling, all depended upon the steadiness of the engines when at high speeds. This consideration led the author to introduce several modifications of the ordinary construction of locomotives; the driving-wheels were removed from the centre of the engine to behind the fire-box, placing all the weight on and between the extreme points of support. The centre of gravity was so reduced, that on the narrow-gauge railways the angle of stability equalled that of the broad-gauge engines. All the moving parts of the machinery were removed from beneath the boiler and placed on the two sides, within the easy inspection of the workmen, and enabling the repairs to be effected with ease and despatch. These dispositions had the effect of enabling a larger amount of heating surface to be given in the boiler, within a certain length of engine, than even in the larger class of engines of much heavier weight; thus, in fact, simultaneously concentrating the power and reducing the weight.

PORTLAND.—We are happy to observe that within this past week the Breakwater begins to show itself, so that from the road leading to Portland it now forms a conspicuous object. The "navvies" are putting their best leg foremost; in fact, all hands are putting their shoulder to the wheel in good earnest.—*Somerset Herald.*

INDIA-RUBBER RIGGING SPRINGS.—Mr. Newall, wire rope manufacturer, has patented an elastic support for rigging. It consists of a long box of iron plates, at each side of the ship, containing square blocks of India-rubber, divided by thin plates of sheet-iron. By a regulating screw the rigging can be strained to any degree of tightness, and whatever strain is afterwards produced by winds, lurching of the vessel, or other cause, the spring, by its reaction, pulls the rope back to its place when the strain is removed

PROJECTED WORKS.—Advertisements have been issued for tenders,—by May 7th, for the erection of an additional wing to the Licensed Victuallers' Asylum, Old Kent-road; by 9th, for the erection of the Seamen's Infirmary, Ramsgate; by 11th, for the erection of dwelling-house and farm buildings upon the Bedlam estate; by 11th, for the erection of an infirmary at Uxbridge Union Workhouse, Hillingdon, Middlesex; by 30th April, for taking down and rebuilding Upper Chapel, at Idle, Bradford; by 5th May, for fitting up site required for cattle market, Shrewsbury; by 14th, for erection of proposed lock-up house, &c., at North Sunderland, Bamburgh; by 8th, for extensive alterations and additions to St. Ives Union workhouse; by 8th, for the conversion into embankment of present pileway of Preston and Wyre Railway into Fleetwood; by 14th, for completion of works of Plymouth Great Western Docks; by 1st, for works in remodelling fittings of lecture-room of Portsmouth and Portsea Literary and Philosophical Society; by a date not specified, for erection of gas-holder and station meter, also for setting up retorts, and for other gas works for Western Gas Light Company; by a date not specified, for erection of gas-holder and other works, and for supplying and laying down necessary mains and pipes in Blue and Mile-towns, Sheerness, for new gas company there; by 1st May, for lamp-posts, to contain hydrants or water valves, for borough of Liverpool; by 2nd, for excavation and formation of public sewers at Gateshead; by 4th, for construction of new road, embankments, culverts, fencing, &c., at Stafford-bridge (Bedford); by 1st, for 36 mile-stones, with cast-iron plates, for Hereford Turnpike Trust; by 8th, for the supply of soft melting pig-iron, for the dock-yards at Woolwich, Chatham, and Portsmouth; by 1st, for the supply of works and articles in numerous branches of the building trades, including gas fitters, iron founders, painters, &c., for Shoreditch parish; also by 7th, for lighting St. Paul's, Deptford, with gas, for three years.

COMPETITION.—Plans and estimates are required for the erection of a new workhouse for the parish of Birmingham, to contain 1,550 inmates. Premiums of 150*l.* (for the plan finally adopted), and 50*l.* for the second, as advertised.

SHAKSPEARE'S HOUSE.—It appears that the sum of 478*l.* is yet required to make up the amount for the purchase of the house, and that this has been borrowed on the usual terms, of the Stratford bank, on the *security of the deeds of the property.* The amateur performances have realised 1,500*l.* for the endowment of a custodianship, and this sum has been invested in the funds. Would it not be better and safer to borrow the 478*l.* from this amount, and pay the interest to the fund instead of to the banker's?

NEW CHURCH, WESTMINSTER.— It is stated that another new church is about to be built in Westminster, at the cost of the Rev. W. H. E. Bentinck, one of the canons residentiary of Westminster.

BURIALS IN TOWNS.—A public meeting, to petition Parliament to close burial-places in towns, will be held this (Friday) evening, at the Western Literary Institute, Leicester-square.

COMMONS' COMMITTEE ON SCHOOLS OF DESIGN.—This committee began its labours on Friday, the 20th, by electing Mr. Milner Gibson its chairman. The examination of witnesses commenced on the following Monday, and Mr. Stafford Northcote was summoned to give the best account he could of the recent management of the school by the Board of Trade direct. We have understood that he at once admitted that the schools were too elementary, and that he was rather puzzled to say what progress had been made in actual "design!" He did not appear very well informed about the state of the finances, although he said he was one of the managers of them. Sir Robert Peel was present during the examination, and seemed most attentive, and taking an evident interest in the subject. Indeed, all the members present seemed thoroughly interested, and they mustered strongly. Besides Sir Robert, there were Sir G. Clerk, Mr. Labouchere, Mr. Rich, Mr. Scholefield, Mr. Moffatt, Mr. Hastie, Mr. H,

Hope, Mr. Baring Wall. So that there is every promise of the committee being tolerably effective. We understand some questions were ordered to be sent to the principal manufacturers, soliciting information as to the benefits they have derived from the schools, and asking to have specimens of designs forwarded.

THE LATE TRADES' CONVENER, DAVID SMITH, OF LEITH.—A correspondent has forwarded the following paragraph, recording the death of this gentleman, who was a master builder in Leith, and convener of the trades, and departed this life there on the 21st ult., after an hour's illness, aged fifty-one. Few public men in Leith, of late years, have been more universally regretted. Energetic in business, affable in manners, and humane in his disposition, it may safely be affirmed of Mr. Smith that he belonged to that honourable class of men, who, from their conciliatory spirit, "sweeten the breath of society." Within the last twelve or fifteen years, in conjunction with his late partner, Mr. Watson, he contracted for and erected the martyr's monument on the Calton Hill and Professor Dick's class-rooms and residence in Clyde-street, Edinburgh; and besides being engaged in the extensive improvement of the old harbour, in Leith, he built the Rev. Mr. Lewes' church and tower, in Constitution-street, Dr. Bell's public seminary, in Junction-street, and very recently he completed the renovation of the ancient cathedral church of St. Mary's, in South Leith.

" COLD-HARBOUR," AGAIN.—At a meeting of the British Archæological Association on the 13th, Captain Shortt asked permission of the chairman (Mr. Crofton Croker), to make an observation on the meaning of the term 'cold-harbour,' which he perceived had engaged the attention of the Society of Antiquaries. He considered it to be derived from the Saxon "*yld hereborga,*" the old mansion or resting-place of the soldiers, with the Scandinavian prefix, e.; or it may be from *ceol yld hereborga,* the cottages, or *ceold* of the soldiers' halting or resting-place.—Mr. Gould said that he had hoped the discussion on this word had ended; for his part he thought it a pity to go away from that which was obvious and at hand, to that which was abstruse and far-fetched. He believed the word to be what it expressed,—a harbour, or shelter, or dwelling of some sort, in a cold, exposed, or barren situation,—that he was acquainted with about a dozen cold-harbours, and nearly all of them sufficiently established their name from their locality. In the ridge of hills beyond Guildford he remembered half-a-dozen such places. The word arbor or arbour is one common to the languages of German or Saxon affinity; in the Dutch language *herberg* is a shelter, a cover, a public house, and in French we have also "herberg," now written "Auberge," for the same; and even in Italian "albergo." Johnson, an authority he was not generally fond of, however, gives harbour and harbinger as derived from the Dutch word. From the little he had acquired of the Gaelic language he did not believe that anything could be got from it, without a stretch of imagination, and the same of the Latin language. Mr. Windus considered that the term was derived from the burning of charcoal.

MEETINGS OF SCIENTIFIC BODIES

Held during the ensuing week.

MONDAY, April 30th.—Institute of British Architects, 8 P.M.

TUESDAY, May 1.—Institution of Civil Engineers, 8 P.M.

WEDNESDAY, 2nd.—Society of Arts, 8 P.M.

THURSDAY, 3rd.—Royal Society, 8½ P.M.; Society of Antiquaries, 8 P.M.

FRIDAY, 4th.—Archæological Institute, 4 P.M.

TO CORRESPONDENTS.

Received.— "F. B.," "J. L.," "C. E. L.," "S. H." (we have already briefly alluded to these works, and hope to pay a visit), "J. G. G.," "J. B." (declined), "R. R." (shall hear from us—we have handed advertisement to the publisher), "R. U.," "C. C. C." "Journeymen Cabinet-maker," "J. B." (Newark), "H. H.," "Mr. H." (City), "J. G.," "E. O. R." (we believe that nothing is positively decided, even yet), "W. T. G." "Young Friend," "J. D.," "G. W." (Dundas), "W. M. B.," "Scripio," "F. B.," "A Carpenter" (take proper advice), "Capt. N.," "G. C." ("Buildings and Monuments" may be ordered through any bookseller—King's College is in the Strand), "F. C.," "J. H.," "Prize Model Cottages" (Dean and Son).

*Erratum.—*The advertisement last week as to Metals, Institute of Architects, reads that "each essay is to be distinguished by a motto, *with any name attached thereto*:" it should have been *without any name*.

*"Books, Prices, and Addresses."—*We have not time to point out books or find addresses.

NOTICE.— All communications respecting *advertisements* should be addressed to the "Publisher," and not to the "Editor;" all other communications should be addressed to the EDITOR, and *not* to the Publisher.

ADVERTISEMENTS.

No. CCCXXVI.

SATURDAY, MAY 5, 1849.

HE summer weather is coming, with light mornings and long days, and our student readers will do well to avail themselves of it, whenever opportunities occur, to see all that is to be seen in their respective neighbourhoods, by which habits of observation may be formed, their store of knowledge increased, their taste formed, or their judgment strengthened. See all the best pictures, and the best buildings you can find: by accustoming the eye to what is good, it will soon be led to reject what is bad. When you have a leisure day, get off to some of the old churches near you, or to one of our noble cathedrals, and fill your sketch-book and your note-book with records of what you see and what you think. Make it an enjoyment; a relief from stricter study. Even without reference to the " good " that is to come from such jaunts, in the work-a-day sense of the word *good*, they give tone to the mind, fill it with pleasant memories, enlarge the store on which thought may afterwards draw, and invigorate the body.

And these are not trifles. As we have before now said, to make a good architect or a good builder is something; but to make a healthful, well-judging, virtuous, and happy man, is something more. Recreation is necessary for all; and it is most desirable that we should so tutor ourselves as to find this in pursuits which, so far from being hurtful, are advantageous as well as innocent.

When we took up the pen it was for the simple purpose of introducing to our readers a view of that extraordinary architectural production, ROSLIN CHAPEL, near Edinburgh; and we were led to make the preceding remarks by the recollection of the enjoyment which the jaunt to this very curious and interesting remnant of the fifteenth century had afforded us.

The vale of Roslin, a sequestered and beautiful spot, varied by wood and waterfall, is on the north Esk, and about 7 miles south from Edinburgh. The day was superb, our companions (one of the best of the modern Scotch song-writers, and a well-known sculptor,) abounding with information and good feeling, and the road so sequestered and romantic, that a notice, which we saw on a board in a hedge, — " Beware of thimblers and chaindroppers," seemed singularly out of place and uncalled for.

It is not our intention, however, to chronicle the journey, beyond alluding to a remarkable natural amphitheatre (forming part of the valley of the Esk), with a paper-maker's house at the bottom of it, and pointing out, as a warning to those who would design without constructive skill, a monument to James Lockart Wisheart, of Lee, which was built in 1790, and is passed on the road. This structure consists of four piers, enclosing a small square area, in the centre of which is the memorial. Four pointed arches connect the piers, and were to carry the covering, but for having no abutment, and being constructed without reference to *statics*, they failed, and were a ruin before they were perfect.

Roslin Chapel (or Collegiate Church as it was), was commenced in 1446 by William St. Clair, Earl of Orkney. " Age creeping on him," says a MS. in Hay's Collections,* " made him consider how he had spent his time past, and how to spend that which was to come. Therefore, to the end he might not seem altogether unthankfull to God, for the beneficies receaved from him, it came in his minde to build a house for God's service of most curious work, the which, that it might be done with greater glory and splendor, he caused artificers to be brought from other regions and forraigne kingdomes, and caused dayly to be abundance of all kind of workmen present as masons, carpenters, smiths, barrowmen, and quarriers, with others. The foundations of this rare work he caused to be laid in the year of our Lord 1446 ; and to the end the worke might be more rare, first he caused the draughts (or designs) to be drawn upon Eastland boards, and made the carpenters to carve them according to the draughts thereon, and then gave them for patterns to the masons, that they might thereby cut the like in stone. Because he thought the masons had not a convenient place to lodge in, near the place where he builded this curious colledge (for the town then stood half a mile from the place where it now stands, to wit, at Bilsdone Burne), therefore he made them build the town of Rosline, that is now extant, and gave every one of them a house and lands answerable thereunto."

The founder died in 1479, and left the building unfinished: the completion of it is attributed to the end of that century.

This chapel is an extraordinary combination of the massive and the minute, some of the parts being large and coarse, while the decoration over the whole is most elaborate and continuous. But for documentary evidence it would be ascribed to the following century, when Gothic ran mad; it is like nothing else,—cannot be classed,—and ought not to be imitated. Externally, some of the pinnacles have a Chinese aspect, and other parts are Indian; there are flowers carved on the face of the buttresses, and a semi-circular arched porch over the south door.

The character of the inside is conveyed by our engraving, which shews the east end of the building, with the aisles beyond.† All the parts, roof, jambs, strings, arch mouldings, are sculptured, and much of the carving is well executed and now in a good state, considerable works having been done there eight or nine years ago, at which time the east window (not seen in our view), was put in. The effect would have been better if, instead of this window being, as it is, one of the existing windows enlarged, and having consequently only one mullion, the opening had been more subdivided by tracery.

The vaulting of the aisles is received on straight lintels, which run from the main columns to the aisle wall. These lintels are all sculptured ; one of them displays the Vices, with the Evil One looking on out of the jaws of hell. In the arches at the east end, where there is the greatest luxuriance of carving, the Dance of Death is represented.

At this end a striking peculiarity occurs, which has been already noticed in our pages.‡ The vaulting here terminates next the wall on large corbels of singular design, which

project to such an extent as to have led to the supposition that the east wall was pulled down after the groining was finished, and set further eastward, to give 3 feet more room, and that the corbels were then put in to prevent the necessity of pulling down the vaulting. We are not disposed, however, to coincide in this theory, but regard the arrangement in question simply as one of the many ingenious vagaries which distinguish this remarkable, and, in its general effect, beautiful building.

The " Prentice's Pillar," as it is called, with its sculptured decoration around it, is seen in our view,* also the entrance (to the right) to the crypt-like chamber at the east end, where, according to tradition, made current by Sir Walter Scott,

" Twenty of Roslin's barons bold
Lie buried, ————"

in their mail :—

" That chapel proud,
Where Roslin's chiefs uncoffined lie,
Each baron, for a sable shroud,
Sheathed in his iron panoply."

Mr. Burn, the architect, disproved the story in a degree by excavating both in this chamber and in the chapel. But those who are unwilling to give up the story suggest, that the bodies were placed on the ground, and not under it; and were carried off when the chapel was desecrated.

Nearly every stone in this chamber bears a " mason's mark," and in the chapel above, also, the marks are very numerous.†

Roslin Castle, with its strong walls, curious outer buttresses, and singular series of vaults, increased the pleasure of the visit: we returned by way of Lasswade; and it was light enough when we got back, to see the glorious picture which Edinburgh presents viewed from a short distance.‡

THE LATE MR. AUSTIN,
THE RESIDENT ARCHITECT OF CANTERBURY CATHEDRAL.

FOR many years up to about 1819, the cathedral of Canterbury had been allowed to run to decay, the only moneys laid out on the fabric being those barely sufficient to keep the roofs dry and the main walls from falling. Some of the most beautiful portions of the cathedral, as they became decayed, requiring more skill or outlay to repair them than was possessed by the director of the workmen, or was approved by the treasurer, were gradually swept away : amongst the latest destructions we may mention the beautiful turret, which surmounted the staircase of the north-west transept.

It was at this time that Mr. Austin, being a resident in Canterbury, suggested the absolute necessity of some repairs and works, in order to save the main fabric from falling into such a state as would endanger its existence ; and by the praiseworthy exertions of the Bishop of Carlisle, then Archdeacon of Canterbury, the building was afterwards placed under his care, with directions for the suggested works to be carried out.

It would be impossible in the space of a short notice to recapitulate the various works found necessary and undertaken by Mr. Austin, or the many ingenious methods adopted to overcome the difficulties which surrounded

---

* The story (which probably every one knows), is, that the master mason, being unable to execute this pillar, went to Rome to see one of a similar description there. During his absence, his apprentice proceeded with the execution of it, and the master on his return found the column as we now see it. The story runs that envy led the master to kill his apprentice on the spot with his mallet. This story is told at other places besides Roslin, and is probably equally refraction at all.

† In connection with the subject of " masons' marks," Mr. Handyside Ritchie showed us, when in Scotland, a copy of an old document, dated 1598, purporting to be the charter of St. Mary's Chapel Lodge, Edinburgh, wherein the signature of every member is followed by his masonic mark.

‡ In " Britton's Architectural Antiquities," vol. iii., will be found a ground-plan of Roslin Chapel, with views and details.

* Quoted by Mr. Britton, in a paper read at the Institute of Architects. See Vol. IV., p. 27.
† See p. 210 in present number.
‡ See p. 51 and p. 64, Vol. IV.

him, with a comparatively small annual sum to lay out, and a building of such extent and magnitude, requiring extensive repairs in every part,—but amongst them we may mention, that the south-eastern transept, through long neglect, and worse measures adopted for its relief (as, for example, a number of massive unsightly wooden pillars in the interior of the cathedral), was found to be in a very alarming condition,—so much so that it was considered necessary that it should be pulled down, in order to save the surrounding portions of the cathedral, but no workmen had been found who would venture on the work of demolition. By an ingenious mode, Mr. Austin removed the superincumbent weight from the walls, forced them into an upright position, and firmly fixing them there, reset the large oriel and other windows, which had assumed all kinds of shapes; and, taking off the massive groining of the roof, re-turning the arches, replacing such portions of the ribs as had fallen, and removing the wooden supports in the interior, restored the transept to its former beauty. After some years, the Norman gable, which had been taken off years before to relieve the crumbling walls, was rebuilt, and the walls are now firm and strong.

The whitewash, accumulated for centuries on the interior of the building, was removed, and the whole face of the walls and pillars restored, including the innumerable small purbeck pillars, which were refaced by a composition made by the architect; and the bosses and ornaments of the roofs and tower were gilded and painted, according to their former state.

During these works, a great number of half-destroyed wall paintings were discovered, drawings from which were made, and are now in the possession of his family. At this time the stained glass of the cathedral, which stands unrivalled for its beauty, was much in need of repair, having suffered greatly from ignorant workmen; but the art of staining glass being considered at low ebb, it was thought irreparable. Mr. Austin, however, undertook himself to restore some of the worst lights, and the vacancies of one or two other lights of figures he filled with new glass,—though without the slightest previous knowledge of the art; and it is told to us (we do not remember to have noticed the fact ourselves) that the imitation is so curiously correct that many artists, when asked to point out the new glass, have failed to fix on the right lights.

The most difficult work of Mr. Austin was perhaps the north-western tower. The ancient Norman tower which originally occupied this site, and against which the present nave was built, had long been found to be in a dangerous condition; and in order to relieve the walls, the spire which once surmounted this tower was removed about a century since. This tower had at last become so ruinous that portions fell during every storm, and it gave unmistakeable signs of falling towards the north, in which direction the wall of the nave, deprived of its support on that side, began to heel over, and the groining in consequence was much crippled. At this juncture Mr. Austin, by a combination of mechanical power, after separating the nave walls from the failing tower, raised the crippled groining, and strained the walls into their upright condition, fixing them there until the new tower might be built and be sufficiently set to withstand the lateral pressure. The old Norman tower was then taken down, and the present tower erected,* for which the foundation required care, the site having been once a bog or marsh, which was clearly proved by the remains of plants, &c., there found; and lower down, 16 feet from the surface, were discovered the entire skeletons of a man and an ox, in such positions as to render it almost certain they had been smothered by sinking in the soft soil.

In the interior of the cathedral many restorations were executed by Mr. Austin. The old painted organ, the case of which entirely stopped up the fine arch between the choir and the central tower, was removed, and the various movements of the organ and its multitudinous pipes were arranged in the triforium—thus opening the view from the westernmost end to the extreme east.

* We do not enter into the question which arose as to the propriety or otherwise of retaining the early design.

The incongruous oaken screen and altar-piece which surrounded the choir, and reduced it to half of its ancient proportions, was removed, and the beautiful screen of Henry d'Estria brought to light and restored, and the altar carried back to its ancient position. The present altar screen was then designed and erected, forming a veil, through the fretted openings of which the most beautiful and interesting portions of the cathedral are seen. In clearing away the rubbish for the foundation of this screen, and directly beneath the spot fixed upon by Mr. Austin for the altar table, were discovered the remains of the ancient high altar, surrounded by the jasper pavement, the destruction of which, in the fire of 1174, is described by Gervase, the contemporary of Becket. This would serve to shew the correctness of Mr. Austin's views as to the restoration.

The new throne, illustrated by us some time since, was the last addition to this cathedral by Mr. Austin. The design is in character with that of the altar screen, and also with a design for the erection of stone stalls, which were proposed to be substituted for the present oaken ones (a design which was preferred to those of Mr. Blore and Mr. Rickman, who also sent in drawings), but which were afterwards abandoned by the dean and chapter for want of funds. The throne was designed, and for the greater part erected, in the short space of about six weeks, in order that it might be ready for the triennial visitation of the archbishop. The ornamental parts were prepared by workmen who had been employed in the cathedrals of Brussels and Cologne, as Englishmen could not be obtained at the moment. It was erected at a cost of about 1,200*l.*, which was defrayed by the late archbishop, whose armorial bearings ornament the interior of the throne. It has been proposed to paint and gild some portions of the throne and altar screen, but we are not anxious that this should be done.

In justice to Mr. Austin it should be stated that the stone pulpit which has been lately erected opposite the throne was *not* erected by him or from his design, though some portions of it were afterwards altered and adopted by him.

Mr. Austin, to whom it may be justly said all admirers of ecclesiastical architecture are indebted, died in October, 1848, having held office under the dean and chapter for thirty years; and it was a graceful act of the dean and chapter, by which even his death was rendered a continuation of the services of his life in beautifying the cathedral, that they have directed the large window in the north-western tower to be filled with stained glass to his memory. Mr. Austin died at the age of 62, and was a native of Woodstock, being born in "Chaucer's house." It should be remembered, when estimating the merit of his work, that he was one of the earliest of those who gave attention to the restoration of our cathedrals, and began the good work which has of late years been so largely carried out.

"PERFECTION IN BUILDING—A WORK OF PROGRESS."

IT is an undeniable fact, that thousands of houses are rapidly built, tenanted, and sold in this London of ours, devoid of anything like comfort or novelty of arrangement, though in a scientific age like unto the present, when numberless improvements are being patented, or at least registered (and none are brought to more perfection or in greater number than those connected with building), yet is the tradesman or clerk content to go on year after year, in the occupation of the ill-arranged and scantily-constructed dwellings with which the metropolis swarms. Scarce a district where, but a short space since, notice boards said, "*Horses taken in to grass*," but now, alas! the fashion's changed, and "*Apartments for single gentlemen*," with houses to let, or perhaps to sell, with the temptation of paying a large per centage, take their place. That argument of the purchase or sale of house property to pay a "*per centage*," annoys me! Examine some of the lists put forth by auctioneers, and property will be found to pay from 4 to 20 per cent.; surely the one must be too cheap, while the other must be too dear. Take an intermediate, say some ready-built tenements to be sold to pay 10 per cent.; now, without reference to whether they are well or ill built, I would wish the question to be canvassed—whether the materials of which the house is built, together with the labour, and with these a fair tradesman's profit, should not rather be the basis for calculation of value, adding value of land, than by extorting an exorbitant rent in order to make the purchase-money larger! How the houses ever find tenants at all is astonishing, were it not a known fact, that as soon as they are finished, the builder will let them to *any one* who will agree to pay a high rent; he, intending to dispose of the property, cares not to see quarter-day, to ascertain the stability of the occupants, but is then in a position to sell "the desirable house, let to a most respectable tenant, at a low rent, and the investment will pay the purchaser 10 per cent."

How forcible are the truths of old Gerbier, who, as far back as 1660, said, "Let all owners of houses be prepared to repent, whether they build or not; for it is like the fate of the many who marry and who marry NOT: let both, the one and the other, lay as it were in a scale their several vexations, cares, labours, and pleasures, they will find this to be true, viz.,—if they build, they must be at greater present disbursement; while if *they* build NOT, they are subject to the inconveniences of houses built according to the fancies of *others*; and when they cast up the sums of money spent in rent, besides many chargeable alterations, they will find that they might have built a better and more fit habitation for them and their posterity." Well, nearly two hundred years ago do we find advocates were to be found trying to teach the public that the art of building was intimately connected with the convenience and comfort of life, and, as such, was most deserving of the best attention of all.

Building is essentially a work of progress, not positive inaction, letting what was before be now but the reducing of a system by which stability and elegance are blended, and also a judicious choice and application of all materials. Many parts of the globe present strong pictures of from what a mean original buildings arose; for instance,—the necessity of providing protection from the changes of the weather led men, in the first instance, to select natural cavities or grottoes; but when a colony of men joined together, these natural dwellings became insufficient: then, *stern necessity* compelled them to unite in erecting a sort of hut,—and of this primitive type the Indians of the present day have striking examples, being constructed of boughs and trees tied together by bands uniting at the top, not unlike in outline our tents. From this we can conceive the origin of building; and though the first efforts may (to us moderns) appear rude, still they were such as answered the wants of the inhabitants,—more than can be said of many a noble erection built in the age of refinement and civilisation. We could go on suggesting and imagining that the different productions of old dame Nature began to be regarded and eagerly sought after, and that stone began to take the place of boughs and trees in walls. Then the erections first began to have an appearance of regularity and strength; then this was further assisted by the ambition of each endeavouring to excel his neighbour in his dwelling, and this rivalry must have materially aided the introduction of ornament. Then commenced and progressed civilisation, and, perhaps, even proportion was not lost sight of: certain it is that many of the former rude appliances came to be suggestive of ornament. Thus, the bands, encircling and keeping the trees together, when copied into stone, became mouldings. Again, the stone under the tree, placed to prevent it driving into the ground, may have given the first idea of the base of the column. The early knowledge of our forefathers must be estimated by the fact, that bricks were known, as also a composition like our mortar, soon after the deluge.

Look at the ponderous works raised by the mighty Egyptians four thousand years ago! Do not their remains, even in a ruinous state, still show a boldness of outline and a truly impressive appearance? But grand as the works in Egypt were, they were improved upon in succeeding ages by the Greeks, who, though not producing works of the same astonishing magnitude, still formed successful rivals, by adding perfection of proportion and simplicity of form; and the Romans subsequently, though adopting the architecture of the Greeks, still further advanced the arts by adding magnificence. Perhaps they did not make so distinct a step to originality of conception as the Greeks did, when borrowing from the parent source, Egypt. On the decline and fall of Roman power, purity and perfection in the art became entirely disregarded, giving place to a most curious mixture of arches, columns, and ornament, without any certain rule to determine the proportion. Then flourished, in more or less perfection, all the several styles and stages of Gothic architecture, which was likewise without precedent; sometimes expressing durability and strength by circular arches and large columns—at others, with pointed arches with groups of columns tied together, models of lightness and marvels of construction. And all these, singularly incongruous one with another, have been adopted by us moderns; in fact, this London has copies, or at least representatives, of every known building peculiar to every age and country, though some are such vile productions, that one is tempted to wish that

"The Goth, the Christian, time, war, flood, or fire"

would relieve us of their presence. In speaking of the architecture of any country we usually hear something about the "Augustan age," or that period when the arts were cultivated in the most pure style; now, whether England has ever seen that age, or if it is in the good time coming, it would be difficult to say, for it is not a little amusing to find each wishing to claim his own as the period. Elmes was for fixing the reign of George IV., when Nash and others produced works that have since been pulled down, or new fronted, perhaps, with no greater reason than that the fashion has changed. Thirty years ago it would have been positive madness to have proposed a Gothic church, and now it would be equal madness to propose one in the classic style. Every dog has his day, so truly has every idea. Professor Cockerell made mention in one of his lectures that he himself had known four distinct changes. We have shown, then, that building should be a work of progress, not inaction, but this has hitherto more particularly referred to public buildings alone, not to our private dwellings. Hence is it that old houses find more respectable tenants than the modern fashionable residences. The fact is, in the erection and arrangement of these houses, no new idea is thought of, because of the expense, but they are modelled after the "what was before," with this exception, that every part is to be cut down and reduced to a marketable price, and to pay the good per centage.

It will be noticed that our remarks apply to the numerous small houses erected by builders on the speculation of finding a purchaser; in fact the ready built houses are the stock in trade of these builders, built expressly for sale, with dashing fronts, ornamented enough to produce the "how nice!" from the public,—such as those who occupy and who are the patrons of houses with porticoes of two Doric columns, perched on a flight of steps high enough to serve for an ancient temple, and finally, in the entablature, Gothic battlements for a cornice, guarded by sphinxes or curious lions, anything but thorough-bred. Depend upon it, however small the edifice may be, it will be best to consult some person to make a plan, and then abide by it, rather than purchase the work of men which is the result of but "little knowledge," which is admitted to be "a dangerous thing." Does not the following speak for itself? "T—— S——, bricklayer and plasterer; jobbing in all its branches; buildings designed in all the five orders of architecture." This is to be seen suspended in very large letters in front of a house in Tottenham, and this perhaps is notified to the public on the strength of having spent a month in some engineering college, where everything is taught at first sight. Depend upon it, so long as the public remain indifferent to becoming judges of building, there exists but little prospect that better houses will be brought into the market. The utility is surely self-evident, in fact it is a point of *self interest*. Let the study be taken up by educated people, and instead of being, as now, simply a professional one, it would acquire a popularity that would have a most beneficial and salutary effect on the art itself;—then would this ennobling art find a refuge from those who play such fantastic tricks with bricks and mortar, as make us "wipe the tear of pity from our eyes."

FRANCIS GROSS.

NEW GAOL IN THE CITY OF BOSTON, U.S. FOR SUFFOLK COUNTY.

A NEW gaol is about to be built in the city of Boston, from the designs of Mr. G. J. F. Bryant, architect. As it differs greatly from any arrangement yet adopted in England, we annex a plan of the ground-story, and a description by the architect.

The gaol will be cruciform in plan, and will consist of a centre octagonal building, having four wings radiating from the north, south, east, and west sides thereof; the north, south, and east wings will contain the cells for the use of the prisoners, and the west wing will be appropriated for the jailor's family, officers' quarters, and the necessary incidental offices and apartments required for the building, together with a chapel and hospital.

The three wings containing the cells are to be constructed upon the "Auburn plan," so called (being a prison within a prison), the north and south wings will each measure 80 feet 6 inches in length and 55 feet in width, and 56 feet in height above the surface of the ground; the block of cells within each of the north and south wings will measure 63 feet 6 inches in length, 21 feet in width, and 54 feet in height, and will be divided into five stories; each story will contain ten cells, each of which will measure 8 feet by 11 feet, and 10 feet high, thus giving to each of these two wings fifty cells.

The east wing will measure 164 feet 6 inches in length, 55 feet in width, and 56 feet in height above the surface of the ground. The block of cells within this wing will be 147 feet 6 inches long, 21 feet wide, and 54 feet high; it will also be divided into five stories in height, each story will contain twenty-four cells of uniform size, with the cells of the northern and southern wings, before described, thus giving to this wing 120 cells.

The spaces around the outside of each block of cells in each of the before described wings (between the cell walls and the exterior walls of the wings) are to be appropriated as "areas," which are to be open from the floor of the lower story of cells in each wing, up to the ceiling of the upper story of cells in the wings; galleries of iron will extend the entire length of each of these spaces, outside of the cells, on a level with each of the floors; these galleries will form a communication with other galleries which are to encircle the interior of the "centre octagonal building" aforesaid, on the same uniform level with the first-named galleries. Each cell will contain a window and a door communicating immediately with the galleries of the "areas." The west wing will measure 55 feet in width, and 54 feet in length, and be of uniform height with the three first named wings: it will be four stories in height, the lower one of which will contain the family kitchen and scullery of the gaoler; the second story will have the gaoler's office, officers' rooms, and gaoler's family parlours; the third story will be devoted entirely to the sleeping rooms of the gaoler's family and officers; and the fourth story will be appropriated for the hospital and chapel of the prison.

The "centre octagonal building" will measure 70 feet square, and 85 feet in height above the surface of the ground. It will be but two stories in height, the lower one of which will contain the great kitchen, scullery, bakery, and laundry, and will be on a uniform level with the lower story of cells in each of the three wings which contain the same. The upper

---

GROUND PLAN OF NEW GAOL, BOSTON, U. S.

A Gaoler's family parlours.
B Stairway to first story.
C Gaoler's entry.
D Closets.
E Stairs to third story.
F Gaoler's eating room.
G Gaoler's office.
H Guards' eating rooms.
I Eylets.
K Privilege rooms.
L Cells.

M Galleries to cells, doors, and windows.
N Guard room.
P Prisoners' entrance to gaol.
S Open areas.
T Gaoler's family and visitors' entrance.
V Vestibule and entrance to office.
N.B. Ventilator in centre wall to each cell.

story will be finished as one "great central guard and inspection room," reaching from the ceiling of the first story up to the roof of the building; this room will measure 70 feet square, and will contain the galleries and staircases connected with the galleries around the outside of the cells in the three wings.

All the areas around the outside of the cells of the north, south, and east wings will receive light from the great windows in the exterior walls of the wings; these windows will be thirty in number, each measuring 10 feet in width, and 33 feet in height, beneath which other windows, 10 feet wide and 9 feet in height, will be placed, thus yielding an amount of light to the interior of the cells probably four times as great as that in any prison yet constructed upon the Auburn system.

The cost of this prison is estimated at 150,000 dollars, but, according to our informant, it will probably cost *three* times that amount.

THE CHARGES OF THE ELECTRO-TELEGRAPHIC COMPANY.

WE have received a letter from Mr. J. Lewis Ricardo, M.P., chairman of the Electric Telegraph Company, calling our attention to a paragraph of our own regarding the telegraphed report of the Cobden banquet at Wakefield, wherein, after doing justice to the expedition with which that first and only great effort in this country was accomplished, we expressed a hope, "that the only drag upon the lightning speed of the electric telegraph that now remains, viz., extravagant and impracticable charges, will ere long be cast off as an incubus that can no more profit the conveyancers of intelligence than its publishers." Mr. Ricardo enters into a lengthened and interesting explanation of the heavy outlay and expense attendant on the construction and maintenance of the extensive apparatus and property of his company; an explanation we would the more regret our inability to offer in full, were it not that the same explanation has already appeared in the *Times*, and more or less fully in other papers, through which our paragraph had previously circulated. Of course Mr. Ricardo's object is to shew that, every thing considered, the company's charges are moderate, and that therefore our accusation is unjust and unmerited. "As I am quite satisfied," he says, however, "that you had none but public motives in the charge made against us, I am anxious to set ourselves right with you, and through you with the public, on a charge which is calculated to do serious damage to our undertaking, the importance of which you have fully and handsomely acknowledged."

We should be exceedingly sorry indeed to do even the slightest damage to so important and almost national an undertaking. Our sincere intention, on the contrary, was to do good service to the company no less than to the public, and it still remains to be seen, whether a very considerable reduction of the present charges for the conveyance of intelligence,—even of mere messages, though we principally alluded to such lengthened reports as that to which we had just referred,—would not very considerably increase the company's profits, even while additionally benefiting the public. Mr. Ricardo himself, while limiting the very design or purpose of the telegraphic system at large to *important and urgent messages*—thus plainly showing that the eyes of the company are not even yet opened to those wider and more extensive purposes recently displayed in their own striking and meritorious achievement for the *Times*,—admits that "many of our wires are in far from complete and continuous employment." Why should this be still the case, if the charges, even for messages, be not to a greater or lesser extent impracticable? Nay, why should the company calculate their charges by any exclusive reference to *urgent* or even *important* messages at all? It is certain, that so long as the charges are so estimated, messages of a less urgent or a less important nature *will* be permanently excluded. Does not the very fact that many of their wires, even though only capable of conveying a certain more or less limited number of messages in a given time, are in far from complete and continuous employment, clearly prove that the company pitch their charges at too high a figure for those less urgent or less important messages, which otherwise *would* keep their wires in complete and continuous employment? Ay, and in all probability, call for duplicates, triplicates, or manifold repetitions of separate sets of many of them for separate and simultaneous purposes? It is not such mere "statements" as ours alone that may "have the effect of preventing the public from making the full use of the telegraphic accommodation provided for them," or be calculated to "impede an extension of that accommodation;" and the company may depend on it that the initiative in "diminishing the cost at which it is provided" rests, not with the public who do not fully patronise their wires, but with themselves, who do not afford them a sufficient temptation to do so.

In allusion to the magnitude and expense of the establishment,* the numerous staff of clerks, mechanics, batterymen, and higher officials, kept up, the tear and wear, improvements, substitutions, &c., continually going on, Mr. Ricardo says, if these things be considered—

"I submit that a maximum charge for a message amounting to 1d. per mile cannot fairly be considered as an exorbitant demand for the accommodation afforded to the public in keeping open so many receiving stations, and the maintenance of the expensive establishment to which I have adverted. The telegraphic system is designed for important and urgent messages, and could I violate the secrecy which I feel bound strictly to observe, I could show that not one despatch in a hundred has been forwarded which has not been worth many times the amount paid for it by the sender. A commercial house at Liverpool will scarcely grudge 8s. 6d. for a communication by which a necessary payment may be made, an important order given, or a profitable operation facilitated in London; and the message from Glasgow, which traverses a distance of 520 miles in an instant, to summon a son from the metropolis to the bed-side of a dying parent is scarcely to be judged overpaid at a charge of 14s.—considerably less than a halfpenny per mile. An express message, sent by porters or by a cab from the city to the west end of the town, say from this office to the House of Commons, a distance of four miles, will cost 2s. 6d.; and if the same message can be sent from Manchester to Liverpool, a distance of thirty miles, for the same sum, and in a shorter time, it cannot surely be deemed an extravagant demand."

Now, over and above what we have already said as to the design or purpose to which the Electric Telegraph Company seem to desire to limit their ramifications throughout the country, it appears to us that they are not very much entitled to compare or contrast their charges in this way. What would they say to such an argument as this, by way of contrast, against themselves?—Your charges are exorbitant, for while you are exacting 1d. per mile for the mere conveyance of twenty words through a wire not a quarter of an inch in diameter, railway companies are conveying passengers themselves, even though they be 20 stone weight, at that very charge, and even at considerably less, in heavy and expensive carriages, and by steam-power, along a vastly more expensive line of massive rails, and levelled, tunnelled, bridged, embanked, and stationed and officialed railways: and this they do, however urgent and important the object may be which the passenger has in view, or however much he may benefit by his journey! But let us see what they do say at Liverpool to all this special pleading of our correspondent.

"Several Liverpool merchants on 'Change," says the *European Times*, "called our attention to a letter in the *Times* of yesterday from Mr. J. L. Ricardo, chairman of the Electric Telegraph Company, upon which we would at present merely remark that it is not surprising that the electric telegraph is but little used in England, when the company demanded, on the 26th inst., 13s.! for transmitting from London to Liverpool the following short message:—

Lit. Hl. Db. Sixty-eight half Nine-fourth.
E. Ayax. O. G. S. T. Three-ten.

Only forty-eight letters. And at this exorbitant rate they say they do not guarantee the correct transmission of a message unless paid for as a "repeated message;" so that under that infliction the public would have been mulcted of 21s. for sending forty-eight letters. See how the thing is done in America. We lately sent a message of greater length from New York to New Orleans and back, about 4,000 miles, for 8s., and it was accomplished in 70 minutes. Here is another fact. We had, on the same day, a message, containing more than forty-eight letters, sent from Philadelphia to New York. On its delivery we paid one shilling for its transmission, and (one penny) for delivery. In these two American messages there was not a single mistake!* As this is a subject of great public interest, we will prepare and publish a full statement of our business with this company for the 117 days of this year."

But, again, we must remark, that our allusion to impracticable prices bore direct reference to the charges made to newspaper proprietors for the conveyance of general intelligence in such reports as that which appeared, we may say, for the first and only time in this country. And it is a remarkable circumstance that in so elaborate a reply to so incidental an allusion, not one word relates to this our real complaint against the company. Charges of one halfpenny, or even one penny per mile, for a message of twenty words, *might*, after all, be unobjectionable, though even these, it appears, ought to have come within the sweep of our denunciation of extravagant and impracticable prices; but, even otherwise, such charges, for every twenty words, in a long report of a meeting, must be preposterous, even were they moderate for mere brief messages of urgency and importance. It cannot be denied that the first announcement of their charges by the Telegraph Company completely damped the hopeful prospect of mutual benefits in constant intercourse between these conveyancers of intelligence and its publishers, and pre-determined the latter against the former altogether. Thus it seems to be that the promotion of public and general intelligence of more or less importance, by newspaper report, is not even comprehended in the category of the purposes or design of the telegraphic system at all,—whereas, until it be so, and until temptations in the shape of considerable reductions in charge be offered to the public and the press itself, to transmit intelligence of second, third, or even fourth-rate, far less of first-rate, importance or urgency, we do fear that there will be no such profitable return as we would desire to see reaped in so spirited and large an undertaking as was the establishment of the Electro-telegraphic Company.

THE NEW DOCK AND WHARVES CONSTRUCTING AT GREAT GRIMSBY.

THE plan of these works includes an entrance basin, area 19 acres, accessible for the largest vessels at all times of the tide, with piers suitable for all vessels not requiring to enter the docks. The great lock is 300 feet long, and 65 feet wide. The small lock 200 feet long, and 45 feet wide. The dock, area 29 acres, is accessible for all vessels for twenty hours out of the twenty-four. The east wharf is 2,000 feet long, and 670 feet wide, to be appropriated to warehouses and a goods station, with railways laid to every part, area 42 acres.

Great Grimsby has every prospect of becoming a very important harbour and port, and when

* We may here give a summary of this part of Mr. Ricardo's letter. The wires of the company stretch from Glasgow on the north to Dorchester on the south, from the east coast at Yarmouth to the west at Liverpool. They have brought upwards of 150 towns into instant communication with each other. Besides a central office in Lothbury, and five branch receiving-houses in various parts of the metropolis, from the main station at Lothbury their wires (carried at great cost in iron pipes under the streets) diverge to every town of importance in the country. In the metropolis alone they have upwards of sixty persons in their employment, and at each of their country stations they have, independently of messengers, not less than two, and in many cases as many as ten, signal clerks, all of them skilled in manipulating and interpreting the telegraph. The wires which they have set up for the use of the public alone are upwards of 9,800 miles in length, and extend over a distance of 2,060 miles, and, exclusive of those running underground and through tunnels or rivers, are stretched on no less than 61,800 posts, varying from 16 feet to 30 feet in height, and of an average square of eight inches, with an expensive apparatus of insulators and winders attached to each.

* Here we must observe that the Americans might have urged the very argument adduced by Mr. Ricardo in favour of his higher charges. Yet no one can doubt brother Jonathan's perfect competency to mind the main chance. Some further illustrations of the contrast between American and English charges are given in the *Times*.—Messages of ten words or under are as follows:—from New York to Boston, 50c.; New York to Philadelphia, 25c.; Baltimore to Washington, 10c.; Washington to New Orleans, 150c.; Baltimore to Cincinnati, 90c.; Baltimore to St. Louis, 135c.; Baltimore to Philadelphia, 25c.; and from Philadelphia to Washington, 30c. From New York to Boston the distance is 200 miles, for which the charge is 2s. (English). For every additional word 1d. is charged, *and with these remarkably low prices the company makes a good profit, because the public continually use this wonderful medium of communication.*" And why *do* they so use it, but *because* the prices *are* so low?

its spacious tidal basins and large floating docks are completed, there will be every advantage which a port can possess afforded to the shipping which carries on the eastern commerce of the country. Even at present the harbour of Grimsby affords shelter to a large traffic; the natural advantages have already rendered it an extensive port, and the floating docks, although not on a large scale, are oftentimes full of ships, chiefly from foreign countries.

Mr. Rendel is the engineer-in-chief, and Mr. Adam Smith, the resident engineer.

At the lunch which followed the ceremony of laying the first stone on the 18th, the Earl of Yarborough, who presided, said in the course of his speech, Perhaps strangers may not be aware of the enormous quantity of timber necessary to construct these docks. That timber has been imported from the Baltic. We have succeeded, though it was prognosticated that we could not, in shutting out the water as you have seen to day, and we may consider it fortunate, as I believe we are at this moment 19 feet below the level of the water. The first pile of this timber was driven in 1846, and I recollect that it was stated in a neighbouring port that there was an end of the Grimsby docks. It was said that when the first pile got tapped on the head by the engine it went through the quicksand, and was no where to be found. But it was a mistake, for since that time the coffer-dam has been extended to the length of 1,600 feet, and to construct it there have been obtained 70,000 pieces of Memel timber, of the average length of 50 feet. The measurement of these works is in circuit a mile and three quarters.

We may probably lay before our readers a notice of some of the peculiarities observable in the construction of these docks.

"WONDERS IN LOCOMOTION: NEW MOTIVE POWER."

IN this age of spanking locomotives, such an announcement as that now quoted from the columns of a contemporary is, to say the least of it, somewhat startling. Yet it turns out that the "new motive power" by which these wonders are to be accomplished is by no means very new, even as a motive power; and although the author of the announcement, "Adolph Count de Werdinsky," intimates that this new motive power has been patented, he will find, by reference to No. 230, Vol. V. of THE BUILDER, that even that fact is not very new, the same power, or "patented ingredient," having been patented in this country, by Mr. Fox Talbot, as a motive power, previous to 3rd July, 1847. In short, this great discovery consists in the use of gun-cotton, xyloidine, pyroxyline, or whatever it is to be called, as a motive power. Amongst various modes of adapting it, says the Count, it may be applied directly under the piston, and fired by electricity, so as to supersede the necessity of boiler, furnace, or other cumbrous apparatus. Such is the very nature and description of Mr. Fox Talbot's patent. The explosive material is supplied by a tubular slide under the piston, and that portion of it which protrudes or is pressed through the slide into the piston is to be fired by a platinum wire, thrust through the cylinder,—xyloidine, it appears, having the peculiar and invaluable property of exploding only when and where not under pressure. The Count is hopeful that this new patent will be applied even to street cabs, old ladies' Bath chairs, and dandy's velocipedes, far less to omnibuses and mail-coaches, or common-road locomotives in general,—the economy of it being, as he remarks, enormous, when it is considered—that "all kinds of vegetable fibres or lignine, such as cotton, flax, hemp, tow, sawdust, straw, hay, rags, paper, &c., can be rendered explosive by their being merely dipped for eleven to fifteen minutes in nitric acid, strengthened by an admixture of an equal quantity of sulphuric acid, then well washed in water, and dried for about two hours,"—and that "for an engine of two-horse power [thus supplied (see *Manchester Examiner* of 6th March, 1847) at New Jersey] a thread not larger in size than ladies' sewing cotton is quite sufficient." But not only so: for although "small and compact xyloidine engines are easily attachable to carriages, street cabs, tradesmen's cars, farmers' waggons, dandy's velocipedes, or old ladies' Bath chairs," the Count tells us that since writing the above he has "made a further discovery, and this last one is verging almost on a miracle"—the most prominent of its features being, that not even engines are necessary! far less boilers, "steam, fire, water, magnetism, air, or animal power;" so that if "a thread not larger in size than ladies' sewing cotton" be quite sufficient to propel with a power equivalent to a couple of horses, and without even an engine, we are likely to see *Punch's* ingenious idea of propelling 'old ladies' with gun cotton 'stay laces' briskly drawn through 'pie holes,' and even without Bath chairs, any more than engines, in one sense realised, or more than realised; indeed, by all the difference between the power of a cotton thread and that of a stay lace. Moreover, by the same wonderful means—or want rather of apparently adequate means, ships may be propelled "without paddles, or any propellers whatever,"—pyroxyline, as the naked "propeller" itself, we presume, excepted. After all this, it is useless urging the objection already started, that the gaseous proceeds of gun cotton may corrode the pistons of engines; the Count does not even admit that. But, however ultra-enthusiastic he may be in hopes which themselves remind one of the like, heretofore entertained as to other expansive forces, that wonders may yet be excusably anticipated from the compaction of such forces into forms so convenient as those of which gun cotton is capable, can scarcely be denied, when it is considered, that while, in a simple and most economical way, "all the vegetable fibres in the creation become highly explosive;" they nevertheless remain perfectly tractable and manageable by mere matting compression.

NOTES IN THE PROVINCES.

THE foundation-stone of the new buildings for the Farm School at Redstone-hill, Reigate, for the reformation of juvenile offenders intrusted to the care of the Philanthropic Society, was laid by H. R. H. Prince Albert on Monday last. The new buildings will accommodate 120 boys, besides 50 in the old farm buildings: an increase to 500 is expected in a few years. A chapel and school-room are to be built.——St. Lawrence's Church, Winchester, is being re-opened, after a closure of nine months, during which a new east stained-glass window has been put up, at a cost of 200*l*., by Miss Littlehales; the old pews have been replaced by others, and the old flat ceiling taken down, and the roof timbers thrown open.——Upwards of 1,200*l*. have been subscribed for the repewing and other restoration of the ancient church of St. Martin, Salisbury. Two of the principal windows, stopped up some years since, are also to be re-opened, and the spire is to be partly rebuilt, and other improvements effected.——An infirmary chapel is to be built at Worcester, at an outlay of 1,200*l*., partly obtained (300*l*.) from the Jenny Lind fund, and from a subscription list headed by 100*l*. from the dean.——The foundation-stone of the Cheltenham Church of England Training Institution was laid by Lord Ashley on Thursday week before last.——Thornbury Church was to be re-opened on the 1st inst. It has been new roofed, new pewed, new clerestory windows put in, the gallery removed, the interior of the tower restored, and the west window thrown open to view. The floor of the chancel has been relaid with encaustic tiles; and a five-light decorated east window, by Mr. George Rogers, of Worcester, inserted. The architect employed was Mr. F. Niblett, of Gloucester; and the contracting builder, Mr. John Brown, of Bristol.——The new church of Upton, parish of Tormoham, Torquay, lately consecrated, accommodates about 1,000 persons. All the seats are open. The style of the building is Early English, and the material, grey lime-stone, with wrought quoin-stones and carved work and dressings of Caen stone. The elevation is massive, consisting of a nave and aisles, with circular chancel, and the foundation of a tower and spire for the complete design. Total length of interior, with chancel, 120 feet; breadth, 60 feet; height, 70 feet. The chancel and west windows are decorated. A row of circular pillars runs between the aisles and nave.——The lower compartment of the Phœnix tower at Chester is being put into a state of repair.——At Chowbent, a locality not long since notorious for barbarous usages, a mechanics' institute has just been opened, with a lecture by Dr. Hodgson.——Miss Sharpe, of London, has presented additional decorations for the completion of the two chancel windows of the church at Tibshelf.——A public subscription has been announced to be made for repairing the roof of Honiton Church, at an estimated cost of 800*l*.—one-half of which has been contributed, chiefly by the parishioners.——On 24th ult. the foundation of the new congregational church at Leamington was laid.——A corn exchange is about to be established at Dumfries.——Nine new churches are to be erected at Glasgow, and 6,000*l*. have been subscribed for the purpose.——The foundation stone of Patrixbourne and Bridge new schools was laid on Friday, the 27th ult., by the Dowager Marchioness of Conyngham. Mr. Hezekiah Marshall is the architect.

THE OLD WATER-COLOUR SOCIETY.

THE current exhibition of the Society of Painters in Water Colours contains 365 pictures (one for every day in the year), and is as a whole one of the most perfect annual collections ever seen. The sales have been proportionably great, the blue ticket meets the eye in every direction.*

Prout, Copley Fielding, Gastineau, D. Cox, P. De Wint, G. Fripp, Frederick Taylor, J. M. Wright, V. Bartholomew, F. Mackenzie, W. Hunt, have all done their best, and the picture-loving public know well what that is. Cattermole has several small works of great excellence,—amongst them "The Exhortation" (283), and "The Goldsmith" (328), may be pointed out as two of the most perfect things in the room. Oakley has fallen into a manner (the one fault with many of the members), and will need an effort to retrieve himself.

Amongst the seceders from the new society, J. J. Jenkins appears to have made the greatest advance upon his former productions. Topham has several charming drawings,—but, to our mind, less so than some of his previous admirable works. Duncan is, as usual, excellent. Branwhite's 183, "On the East Lyn, North Devon," is a wonderful piece of distemper painting.

Mrs. H. Criddle, who has but recently turned her attention to water colours, exhibits several pictures of considerable pretence and power, and will be found an acquisition.

LAUNDRY DRYING CLOSETS.

GREAT attention being now called to the subject of drying clothes and linen, in consequence of the number of public laundries and asylums requiring improved means of effecting that object, I am induced to trouble you with a few remarks, which I trust may be considered of public interest.

It has always been a received opinion (and very justly), that a current of pure fresh air is an important part of the process of drying, but which would appear from the remarks of Mr. Jeakes in your last number to be unnecessary. I have recently erected two very powerful drying closets at the Surrey County Lunatic Asylum, one 20 feet long, 15 feet wide, and 10 feet high; the other 20 feet long, 10 feet wide, and 10 feet high. In each of these a temperature of 230 degrees can be easily attained. Mr. Jeakes's closet, according to his statement, contains 336 cubic feet of space: the smallest of mine is equal to 2,000 cubic feet, and the largest 3,000 cubic feet of space. The usual working temperature of these two large closets is 180 degrees *with ventilation constantly going on*. I should judge the reason Mr. Jeakes's closet does not dry satisfactorily *with ventilation*, is on account of deficiency of power in the heating apparatus, as with each of mine there is at least 144 inches area of ventilation always acting, notwithstanding the high temperature maintained.

WM. HEALY.

* Many of the drawings are bought by dealers to sell again.

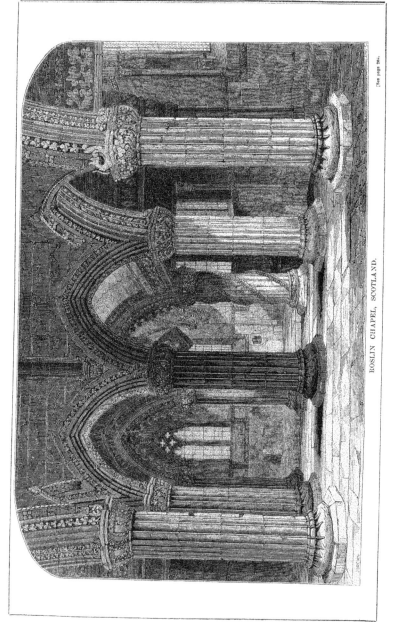

ROSLIN CHAPEL, SCOTLAND.

[See page 204.

HINTS TO THE WORKING CLASSES.

WE have received a number of letters from working men, relative to a "note" which appeared a fortnight ago in our pages. They deny that a mechanic with a family can save money out of 30s. a-week, and seemed to conclude that the object of the note in question was to cut down wages. This, however, was not the case. The intention of the writer,—a mechanic like themselves,—was to induce men of his class to spend less than they get. We will let him further speak for himself. Personally, we will only say, that, so far from making any endeavour to lower wages, or countenancing any endeavour to do so, we would most gladly assist in getting for the workmen better times, consistently with justice to others. Whatever the wages may be, however, we must always urge our readers to spend *something less* than their amount, if possible. "Another Working Man," or "A Young Joiner," may live very economically, and yet find it impossible to save anything out of 30s. a-week; still, if he look round, he will find thousands who are *compelled* to exist with a family on 20s. a-week. It is not that we would see our artizans in such a strait,—far from it—but, being there, we would have them guard against a worse.

The poverty, wretchedness, and want of employment prevailing so largely at the present time, demand the attention of all parties, but more especially of the working man himself.

If working men were placed in their proper position, they ought to be enabled, during the thirty or forty years' toil they have to pass through, to secure to themselves something like an independence for old age.

It is to the interest of the public at large that every man should have a fair day's wages for a fair day's work; for if the honest and industrious are not sufficiently remunerated to support themselves, they must be supported as paupers, vagrants, or convicts; and when the latter are better supported than the former, it is not surprising that the numbers of the latter should be considerably augmented.

But the difficulty arises in giving any definite sum that may be considered as fair between the employer and the employed. That man who receives 15s. per week complains, and justly too, that it is not enough; the man who receives two or three pounds per week finds it too little; but let a man who has been accustomed to receive only 15s. per week be raised to 30s. per week, he deems himself raised to affluence and plenty; reduce the man who has been accustomed to receive 3*l.* per week to the same standard, he deems himself reduced to starvation: such are the different views of different individuals.

But these remarks are not intended to show what is too much or what is too little, or what is enough; but rather to improve that which we receive, which is the surest way to get more.

We take the average wages of mechanics to be about 1*l.* 10s. per week; but the fluctuation of trade renders their employment uncertain. No work, no money; consequently, with many, little or no bread. Now supposing a man to calculate upon working ten months during the year, and every month he lays by 1*l.*,—he saves 10*l.* for the two months he expects to be unemployed, making an average income of 1*l.* 5s. per week. But many may object to this rule of saving the sum proposed: I see a greater objection in endeavouring to live without any income when unemployed.

There is another stage of life which should excite our attention, viz., old age. Old age is not so tardy in his approaches as many of us imagine. Our abilities for labour soon become enfeebled. The services of the young and active are preferred to ours, and long before we are prepared or willing we are obliged to give place to them. Now that man's case is truly pitiable who has toiled for thirty or forty years and always lived up to his income, and when he most stands in need of the comforts of life, has little or nothing for his support: it is a hard case to supplicate the tender mercy of others, and to receive for his miserable pittance only about the sixth or seventh part of his former money, and that to be doled out with a grudging hand and a reproachful look.

Forseeing such evils as these, which every working-man without a capital has reason to expect, can it be unwise to make a provision for this season of life? If we take another 5s. per week it reduces the mechanic's calculated income to 1*l.* per week; the money so taken makes 10*l.* per year for old age. Now let us look at the benefits resulting from such conduct. The man who saves 10*l.* per year out of his wages has very soon a little capital at command, with this advantage, his pound per week is worth or equal to 1*l.* 5s. of that individual who runs in debt. He can save all this in his purchases by his former savings. By adopting this plan, in the course of thirty years he may calculate on saving sufficient to obtain comforts for his old age. Let young men take the hint; they have a fair starting point.

Further, if this plan were generally adopted it would cause a great increase of trade, which is just what we want. We cannot suppose working men in the possession of a small capital would consent to live in hovels stinking with filth and vermin, and paying after the rate of ten or twelve pounds per year for the same, when they themselves could build respectable cottages, the rent of which would not cost them half that sum. Old ruinous houses would then be forsaken, new ones built, and inhabited by the respectable working classes; we might then calculate on having full employment, which would restore us our other 5s. per week. We hear that poverty and crime are increasing; if so, labour will decrease accordingly. Poverty and crime are like the overflowings of water; as the torrent increases, the embankment yields to its fury; so by the increase of poverty and crime, a nation is involved in ruin.

Further, if this plan were adopted generally, it would be the surest way to keep up good wages; working men would be in a position to resist any encroachment on their rights, but in a state of poverty, they are compelled by circumstances to accept any and every unreasonable offer that is made to them for their labour. I might continue to enumerate advantages; everything reasonably desirable might be gained,—nothing lost but poverty and disease. It is the shortest way, the smoothest passage, to the gold regions of California.

AN OLD MASON.

PISE AND COB WALLS.

THE substance of cob is loam or clay mixed with straw; it is put on in a moist state by means of shovels, so that a course can hardly be raised higher than 1 foot or 1½ foot at a time, without risk of bulging, and then must be left some time to dry and become consolidated, before a second course can be imposed upon it; and when the whole wall is built up it must be pared down to make the surfaces true and even, whereas the Pisé gravel is rammed in frames, is perfectly dry, and comes forth from the frame a hard, and solid, and dry mass, and the wall may be carried to its full height without any interruption or delay, except what arises from moving the frames: the surfaces are quite even and perpendicular; and nothing remains to be done but to fill up the holes where the bolts passed, which is done by ramming in fine Pisé gravel on both sides at the same time,* with cylindrical pieces of wood of the size of the bolts.

The cob walls being put up wet, no bond timber can be inserted for door-posts, window-frames, or floor-joists; but in the Pisé walls these may be put in, as the work rises, wherever they are wanted. One could pull down a cob wall with the hand; but it requires iron to pick down the Pisé gravel, unless it be previously wetted: vermin can make their way through cob, but no animal can penetrate the Pisé; the one kind of work is tedious, from the necessity of allowing the different courses time to dry, and is often unsatisfactory from the fissures which occur from the inequality of the substance that is used, according as it is worked up more or less stiff; the other suffers no interruption; and if there be any fear of fissure, it can easily be guarded against by laying strips of deal 3 inches wide, and ½ or ¾ inch thick; the one is feeble and perishable in comparison, the other is said by Pliny to be eternal. The only thing I can compare with Pisé is the old grouting which was formed by filling frames, such as the Pisé frames, with flints or other stones, and then pouring in upon them hot mortar, so liquid that it will make its way into the interstices, and form a compact mass.

Directions for making cob walls 2 feet wide.—The quantity to build a perch of work, that is to say, 18 feet long and 1 foot high, and 2 feet wide,—two loads of clay, and one load of coarse shilf* mixed and wetted, and trodden together to lump, just the same as clay for brick before it is put in the mould. Then take three bundles of barley straw, and turn in on straw part of the above mixture, well treading in the three bundles of straw into the above mixture of three loads of clay and shilf; then build it on the stone wall, about 6 inches at a time, treading every layer down well and solid. The stone wall under the cob ought to be 2 feet in height from the foundation, to keep the damp off from the cob. The cob wall should project over the stone wall about 1½ inch. If the weather be dry, you may build about 5 feet in height at a time; then it may rest about three weeks, till the wall is got dry to build on again, then bind on 5 feet more on the top, if required.

* I doubt whether they have Pisé gravel in Cornwall; what was used at Enys and Penrose I think was artificial.

* [*Shilf* means broken slate, in small pieces, such as is used for mending roads in parts of Cornwall.—ED. *Ecclesiologist.*]

EFFECT OF OXYGEN ON COLOUR OF GLASS.

AT the Society of Arts, on the 18th, Mr. F. Pellatt read a paper on the supposed influence of oxygen on the colour or tint of flint glass.

The author, in commencing his paper, stated that the remarks contained in the same are entirely the result of experience in the manufacture of glass in large quantities, it being only under such circumstances that many of the changes there noticed can be observed, because they are so minute, that in dealing with small quantities, their occurrence would not be perceptible. In speaking of white glass the term is comparative, as no glass is perfectly colourless, and to the practised eye of the glass maker there exist no two pieces of the same tint or shade; the word colour, therefore, is used to denote that particular tint or shade, whatever it be, which all white transparent glass possesses. With these remarks the author proceeded to consider the action of oxygen as affecting the colour of flint glass in two distinct particulars. First, its action upon the glass mixture during its melting or founding whilst in a state of fusion; and secondly, during its annealing or gradual cooling.

The constituents of flint glass are silica, lead, carbonate of potash, and nitrate of potash. The silica is found sufficiently pure as fine sand, which abounds in some districts,—that from Allum Bay, Isle of Wight, is much esteemed. The protoxide of lead—litharge, or the deutoxide—red lead, is the state in which the lead is used, and the potash is the ordinary curl and nitrate of potash of commerce. These, when mixed in certain proportions, and subjected to a strong heat for sixty or seventy hours, produce flint glass. The purer the metal the more transparent the glass, but although all the materials be chemically pure a colourless glass is not the product; owing to some chemical change which takes place during the melting, the glass is tinted with green. This is generally stated to arise from the presence of oxide of iron, but the author believes that in most instances it is owing to the want of a necessary proportion of oxygen in the mixture, which the following experience will go far to prove. The tint of green is always minus when the lead in the glass mixture is in the highest state of oxygenation, that is, when red lead is used, and lowest when litharge is employed in the mixture. When an excess of carbonate of potash is used the green tint is deep, but it may be entirely overcome by the use of the nitrate of potash, and superseded by a purple tint when no metal but lead is present.

Oxygen being the agent by which these changes in the colour of the glass are effected, the glass-maker, in order to overcome the green tint always present when oxygen is minus, uses the oxide of manganese, which has the property of giving off its oxygen very slowly. An excess of manganese gives to glass a purple tint, and where altogether absent the glass is always green.

Having thus called attention to the peculiar composition and mode of manufacturing flint-glass, he proceeded to describe the changes which take place in the colour or tint of glass, and the methods employed by the glass-manufacturer to convert the mass from a green, purple, amber, or other tint, to a pure or colourless metal, and brought forward examples tending to prove that the changes in the colour of the glass are due to the presence or absence of a given proportion of oxygen. Manganese, as a metal, gives no colour to glass, although by the oxygen it yields to the lead in the mixture, a purple colour is produced, because by reducing the quantity of oxygen, either by poling or subjecting the glass to a long-continued heat, or by submitting it to the action of carbon, the purple colour is removed, though the manganese still remains. Iron and copper also assume different colours when combined with different proportions of oxygen. If this be true, may not all colours of the oxygen of other metals, such as iron, copper, and lead, be due to the combination of certain proportions of oxygen with the metal or metals present, so as to induce a particular molecular arrangement, from which the glass has the power of absorbing a particular colour?

THE MANCHESTER SCHOOL OF DESIGN.

AT the annual meeting of the Manchester School of Design, held on Tuesday in the week before last, the Bishop of Manchester, who presided, said the advantages of schools of design, in whatever point we looked upon them, stood out pre-eminently conspicuous. Whether we regarded them as a means of improving the manufactures, and consequently the trade of this country,—there they stood pre-eminent; whether we looked upon them as means of raising the lower classes in the scale of civilisation,—there again they were most effective; whether we regarded them as a means of opening a source of happiness to every class of our fellow-creatures, who had hitherto had the study of art placed out of their reach,—there again they were most valuable. But he could take even higher ground. He had found, from experience, the school of drawing and design most valuable in providing a means of innocent, useful, and valuable instruction to the lower classes, at a time when temptations of a diametrically opposite character were calling them from their homes to vice and indulgence; he had found that, independently of enabling them to carry home a new feeling and sensation to their dwellings, it had rendered them more keenly alive to the beauties of nature, and more capable of understanding and admiring the wisdom and benevolence of their God.

The report, which was read by Mr. Gregan, expressed regret that the great body of the manufacturers engaged in that particular branch of trade to which the school is so decided an auxiliary, still continued to manifest so small an interest in its proceedings, and to contribute in so slight a degree to its support. "We are all sensible enough of the importance of good design in our industrial productions, and it is surprising that so little pains should be taken by those most nearly concerned to secure it. In many cases, indeed, corporations and town councils have publicly supported these schools, while, in the manufacturing metropolis of England, no public aid whatever is granted to an institution, which, if endowed with more extended means of usefulness, is calculated so much to enhance the commercial value of our manufactures."

From the treasurer's statement it appeared that the receipts for the year ending December 31, 1848, were:—Government grant, 390*l.*; annual subscriptions, 302*l.* 8*s.*; students' fees, 142*l.* 10*s.*; fees from private classes, 87*l.* 3*s.*; balance due to treasurer, 212*l.* 1*s.* 11*d.*; total, 1,134*l.* 5*s.* 1*d.* The expenditure amounted to 1,134*l.* 5*s.* 1*d.*, of which the principal items were:—salaries of masters, 465*l.* 17*s.* 9*d.*; secretary's salary, 50*l.*; rent of rooms, 220*l.*; printing and advertising, 41*l.*; gas rent, 50*l.*; books and works of art, 31*l.* 10*s.*

Mr. F. C. Calvert contended that the School of Design had not hitherto flourished, simply because of the system of working adopted, which he believed neither met the hopes of the pupils nor the wishes of the supporters. He suggested that, after three years' study, five of the most proficient pupils in the institution should be selected, to whom assistance should be given if they were not able to support themselves, while they were advancing themselves in their studies; afterwards the most proficient of them should be sent upon the continent, under the protection of the school, to study in France, at Rome, or any other great centre of art, where those arts might be cultivated which would be most beneficial to that district.

ARCHED BRICK FLOORS, BIRKENHEAD.

IN a report, in your valuable journal, of the paper read by Mr. Rawlinson, that gentleman, quoting from a manuscript by Mr. Chadwick on the improvement of building materials, mentions that the floors of the "improved dwellings for workmen erected at Birkenhead were constructed of brick, in flat arches about 6 feet span. The spaces between the upper part of the arches and the spandrels were filled in by mortar, on which flat tiles were imbedded."

As the architect of these dwellings, which were designed by me and commenced in 1845, you will perhaps allow me to make a slight correction in this statement. The arches, some of which were 7 feet in span, were turned in what is termed half brick, except at the springing and the skew backs, I caused also a certain number of three-quarter and other parts of bricks to be inserted, so as to form a toothing or vertical bond with the *concrete* with which the spandrels were filled in, and *not with mortar*. The six or seven crown courses were wedged in with slate while the mortar was wet, and the consequence is, that in no one instance has the least subsidence taken place at the crown, although subjected to very severe trials,—the stairs having been used by the labourers for carrying up all the materials, and the men often jumping from the walls upon the arches. I think, however, 7 feet is the limit of a half-brick arch turned in mortar with the ordinary rough brick. The arches rise about one inch to every foot in span. The tiles were laid in mortar on the concrete, which made the thickness of the floor at the crown of the arch about 5¾ inches. There were altogether about 1,200 arches of this kind turned, and without the slightest accident.

CHAS. EVANS LANG.

USE OF HOLLOW BRICKS.

As much attention has been drawn to the subject of hollow bricks or pots, by your notice of the erection of the great arched ceiling at Liverpool, I beg to observe they were, I believe, first introduced in England about 55 or 60 years ago, by Henry Holland, the eminent architect of his day, at Drury-lane theatre, Carlton House, and other of his buildings.

I am not aware of any reason for their not being generally adopted, but that they were probably more expensive, and also were something out of the common way, and required more attention and care in execution, and therefore gave trouble to the operative builder, who would in consequence perhaps discountenance and shirk them.

The building world was sleepy in those days compared with the present, and were content to follow in the footsteps of their forefathers without much thought. But "we have changed all that," and as in the political world so in buildings, there is a rage for new things, and the difficulty is in steering clear of extremes. "There is a moving power and a steadying power—there is the sail and ballast; without the former there would be no progress, without the latter little safety." This has been said in a well-known Review of Whig and Tory in politics, and may be applied to all matters where much change is contemplated.

With reference to large arches, it may not be irrelevant to observe that the Adelaide Gallery, in the Strand, is arched with three or four courses of plain tiles in cement, forming at once roof and ceiling. It was thought a bold novelty at the time, and particularly as it is perforated with circular openings for skylights.

This was done, I believe, by a builder, Mr. Herbert; the principal thing, however, that the world looks at is

"NON QUO SED QUOMODO."

COMMONS' COMMITTEE ON SCHOOLS OF DESIGN.

ON Friday, the 27th ult., the examination of Mr. Stafford Northcote was resumed. It was somewhat vague. He knew nothing of the proportionate value or importance of the various classes of manufactures in this country. He approved of public exhibitions of designs, but there had been none for more than two years: they had been overlooked. Mr. Poynter followed. He thought the provincial schools "mere drawing schools," as late as 1847; but that this defect was remedied by Mr. Wornum's lectures, and he could suggest no further improvements.

On the 30th, Mr. Dyce was examined. He showed, that at one time design was really cultivated in the school, and then abandoned. He thought the present system impracticable, and had resigned in consequence. The present committee of management ought to be changed. The responsibility was divided and uncertain. Mr. J. C. Horsley, formerly a master, followed. His evidence proved that the present system was wrong and impracticable, and that he had resigned because he found it so. There had been constant changes and no fruits.

May 2nd. Mr. Wakefield, one of the largest garment fabric printers at Glasgow, proved that the school had not influenced the designs in his trade. He was friendly to the schools; but thought them failures in that respect. The masters ought to know the practical working of manufactures. The evidence of Mr. Nickisson, an agent for manufacturers, was to the same effect: he had been a student in the school for five years, and did not think "design" was properly taught.

RAILWAY JOTTINGS.

THAT tricks *can* be played with railway tickets appears but too plainly, from the detection of a clever system of fraud practised on the Yorkshire and other lines, by a traveller to a London chemical firm. He appears to have been allowed to retain his legitimate tickets by wholesale, eighteen having been found in his possession, with chemical erasures ready for future occasions, besides an altered one, by means of which he was detected. Types were also found in his pocket. With these he appears to have managed to make all the requisite alterations which enabled him to 'come over' the officials again and again in his travelling trips from one town to another. The only question in his prosecution was whether to charge him with fraud or forgery, for the latter of which it was ultimately decided that he shall stand his trial at the next York Assizes.——Another system of fraud with tickets by conspiring officials themselves was lately discovered on one of the Northern lines. By connivance with the issuer of the tickets, a guard returned so many to his confederate at every trip for reissue, the parties sharing the proceeds between them to a heavy amount.——The London and North-Western Company conceiving themselves entitled to open carriers' parcels of parcels, and charge separately for each separate article in the aggregate package, did so in the case of a Mr. Crouch, who brought an action against them lately at the Warwick Assizes. The Judge (Chief Justice Wilde) said the defendants were bound to charge an equal price to all alike, and he could not see what other conclusion could be come to but that in the present case they had made an excessive charge. Verdict for the plaintiff; damages, 49*l.* 4*s.* 2*d.* A special jury case, in the Court of Exchequer, stands adjourned to Trinity term, in which Mr. Crouch, the plaintiff in this action, sues the company for special damages.——In a case of compensation at Bradford, to Messrs. Ripley, dyers, by the Lancashire and Yorkshire Company, the evidence for the claimants went to prove that they would suffer to the extent of from 1,000l. to 1,500l. by the loss of light and ventilation; that the value of 4,190 yards of land required by the Railway Company would be 838l., being 4s. per yard; and that the loss by severance, upon the rest, 11,673 yards, would be 875l. 9s.; being 1s. 6d. per yard. An arrangement was come to with respect to the loss of light and ventilation, and the jury, in reference to the land required, gave a verdict for the claimants—damages, for 4,190 square yards of land, 2s. 6d. per yard, or 523l. 15s., and for injury by severance, 150l. —— What will competition do? says a contemporary. The London and North-Western and the East Lancashire are rival lines. The North Union used to charge 5s. first class, 4s. second-class; 3s. 3d. third-class. The present fares are 1s. 9d., and 6d. ——Perhaps many are not aware that the Great North-Western have still competitors in the shape of canal fly boats which ply regularly between London, Birmingham, Wolverhampton, Liverpool, Manchester, Stafford, " and all parts of the kingdom."——It is said that the engine manufactory of the North-Western at Crewe, turns out a new locomotive and tender every Monday morning——The atmospheric tubes on the South Devon line are about to be sold as old iron.——A novelty in railway excursions is to come off in May, namely, a trip between Dublin, London, and back, for two guineas, viâ the Chester and Holyhead and the North-Western.——It is stated that one half the receipts of the Bristol and Exeter have been offered to the Great Western if they would work the traffic, but that the proposition was not entertained by the Paddington authorities. ——The directors of the Great Western, says the Times, have at length found that the abolition of ' return-tickets,' more especially on short distances, has tended considerably to decrease the traffic on the line, and on and after the 1st of May it is their intention to re-issue return-tickets, for the day only, to be available until 12 o'clock at night. The re-duction will be 25 per cent. on the single journey, that is, the cost will be a fare and a half for a return-ticket. No return-tickets will be issued for third-class trains.——The South-Western have adopted the system of second-class season tickets, and made a reduction in charge on first-class tickets, ' to encourage residents in the vicinity of their railway.'—— While clearing away old buildings at the Landport joint terminus, Portsmouth, four workmen were lately buried under the wall of a house, which they persisted in further under-mining, although warned of the risk.—— The opening of railway communication between Edinburgh and Galashiels has had the rather odd effect of opening up an insatiable demand at Galashiels for milk from Edinburgh: think of London supplying a country town or village with milk! Coal and other articles of general consumpt have also been greatly cheaper at Galashiels, since it has had the advantage of railway communication. ——The post-office authorities have authorised the opening of post-office letter-boxes at every ' first class' railway station in the kingdom. ——With reference to late proceedings, there has been some talk in the Houses of Parliament about the appointment of a more effectual system of auditing railway accounts. Mr. Labouchere stated, that if a measure did not emanate as he expected from a Committee of Lords now sitting, he should himself submit to the Commons a measure on the part of Government to that end. Some of the disclosures recently have been startling.

PARIS EXHIBITION OF MODERN ART.— The National Assembly has determined that the annual exhibition of the modern productions of art shall take place in the ci-devant palace of the Tuileries, now named the " Palais National." It will not open before the 15th of June. The Exposition of Industrial Art will open June 1.

COAL TAR.—Mr. R. A. Smith, of Manchester, has obtained a patent for some improvements in the application and preparation of coal tar, which are described to consist in the preparation and application of coal tar to coating the interior surfaces of water-pipes.

THE MINER'S LIFE.

WE take the following graphic sketch of the discomforts and perils which environ the miner, from a recent article in the Times :—
A large and increasing part of the British population lives a hazardous, uncouth, and cheerless life in the bowels of the earth, further than Lynceus ever saw, and deeper than Cyclops ever descended. So little are we, of this upper earth, accustomed to dive below the surface, that in order to form any idea of the level at which a collier does his daily work, we must measure it by something above our heads. We must suppose our wives and children on a level with the cross of St. Paul's, perhaps twice or even three times higher, and ourselves daily descending by ropes to the sewers of this city. We shudder at the thought of hardy islanders suspended over the precipice in quest of birds' eggs. The collier's descent is often deeper, and his doom, should he fall, more certain. Should he miss a step at the " bank," should the rope break in his descent, should a wheel in the engine be out of gear, or a peg out of place, or should the boy at the pit's mouth be inattentive for a moment, the next instant basket, rope, and man lie an undistinguishable mass at the bottom of the shaft. But that is only one, and not the greatest of his dangers. The miner moves in an atmosphere into which a million chinks and pores distil a deadly vapour. The very air he breathes is a magazine of destruction. Wherever he extends his labours he lays bare a new surface, and starts a fresh foe. In these upper regions the natural currents of the air diffuse and carry off all noxious effluvia as fast as they arise; but the natural atmosphere of these wonderful vaults is itself a poison, and the vital air we breathe must be artificially introduced, in quantities sufficient, not only for human consumption, but for the expulsion of local gases. A strong current of fresh air must be brought down a shaft, conducted through the whole mine, carefully sweeping every corner and recess, and so passed up another shaft to the surface. If this current is insufficient, or accidently interrupted, the foul vapours accumulate, and a naked candle, a spark, or a lighted pipe explodes the whole mine, burning, suffocating, or dashing to pieces every living being in its range. The explosion which drives out by the pit's mouth the whole mass of air within entails a reaction not less deadly. The " after-blast " finishes the work of destruction. The list of perils is not complete unless we add that everywhere are suspended over the collier's head vast masses of material ready to fall and bury him at his work.

THE AMERICAN BOWLING SALOON.

DECORATION.

A LARGE apartment at the back of 393, in the Strand, formerly an auction room, has been suddenly converted, at some cost and with considerable taste, into a handsome saloon for bowling on the American system. The walls are formed into panels, containing pictures and glasses, by pilasters, with other segmental panels above, containing children and scroll-work on a maroon ground. The ceiling is in panels and painted medallions,—bas-reliefs, wreaths of flowers, &c. fill various spaces. It is lighted by skylights, and tastefully fitted up. At the far end are casts of the Graces and the Nymphs of Canova, Diana, Ceres, &c. It is altogether a clever piece of decoration of its kind, and very creditable to Mr. C. Norwood, of Hoxton, by whom it has been executed.

THE LOUVRE.—The wing of the Louvre called the Gallery of Apollo is undergoing extensive repair, and a great number of workmen are employed in it. The timbers of the roof were found so much decayed that the entire reconstruction became necessary. Visitors to Paris before the Revolution of February may recollect the statue of the unfortunate son of Louis Philippe, the Duke of Orleans, adorning the centre of the Court of the Louvre. This has been removed, as offensive to republican notions, and preparations are making to transport the fountain of the " Marché des Innocens " to replace the statue, which is, for the present, condemned to oblivion.—Art-Journal.

Books.

The Ecclesiastical and Architectural Topography of England. Parts I. and II.— J. H. Parker, Oxford and London.

IN Mr. Parker's late excellent edition of Rickman's work, the brief notices of churches which were given by that author were omitted, with the intention of publishing them separately, with such additions as should render the list a complete dictionary of the ecclesiastical edifices of England. This intention is now being carried out under the title at the head of this notice. Each part contains one county (No. I., Bedfordshire; II., Berkshire), and it is intended to publish the succeeding parts at the rate of four in the year. Buckinghamshire will form No. III.

Outlines of General Knowledge. By H. INCE, M.A. Ince's Outlines of English History. Ince's Outlines of French History. Gilbert. Paternoster-row.

Very useful little books, well deserving the circulation they have obtained.

Miscellanea.

THE METROPOLITAN SEWAGE MANURE COMPANY held their usual half-yearly meeting on Tuesday last, when the reports of the directors and engineer were read and adopted, after a somewhat lengthened discussion. The report of the directors congratulated the shareholders on the amicable relations established between the company and the Metropolitan Commission of Sewers, and the permission given them to communicate, by means of a pipe, with the Ranelagh sewer, and with the Eel Brook and Stamford Villa sewers. By these arrangements the company would be enabled forthwith to carry out its operations within the Fulham district, without incurring the large outlay that would have been required had they proceeded to the construction of the tunnel sewer. Contracts had been entered into with market gardeners for the supply of about 100 acres, for 70 of which service pipes were being laid. Recriminations and explanations were entered into as to the treatment of Mr. Moir, the late secretary of the Company, who had been defied, it was alleged, to ' do his worst,' and who accordingly did his worst, by taking the company to law, at a cost to them of 600l. to his legal supporters, besides several hundreds to their own solicitor, and 400l. a-year as salary to himself. He had then, as a shareholder, thrown the company, for contravening their Act of Parliament, into Chancery. During the discussion it was elicited that more than half of the nominal capital of 175,000l. had been taken up. On the whole, although the ' bandying of reproaches,' as one shareholder termed it, was still considerable on various points, there did not appear to be so strong an animus against the proceedings of the directors as at the last general meeting.

THE DIORAMA.—The new view at the Diorama, " the Valley of Rosenlaui " in the southern part of the canton Berne), painted by M. Diosse, is a pleasing picture of mountain scenery, diversified by the effects of a storm in the Alps. When the clouds are clearing off and the returning sun gilds the highest peaks of the mountains, the view is at its best and exceedingly effective. The second picture, " the Church of Santa Croce," at Florence, was exhibited some years ago, but is none the less deserving of a visit. The changes in light and shade are quite marvellous. From the broad light of day, shewing every tile with which the immense area is paved, and every stone of the Corinthian columns which form the numerous chapels down the aisle, to the deep darkness of midnight, when a few candles bring into view merely one altar, the figure of the Virgin, and a few projecting cornices, the various gradations are exhibited with such surprising effect that it is difficult to believe we are gazing on a picture painted on a perfectly flat surface of canvas.

ROYAL ACADEMY.—The following gentlemen have been recently admitted as architectural students, namely, Messrs. F. C. W. Anderson, James Brooks, Richard Norman Shaw, Horatio Nelson Goulty, Harry Robert Newton, John Nicholls, Cyril Jackson Stafford, and Sidney Godwin.

Projected Works.—Advertisements have been issued for tenders,—by dates not specified, for the erection of parsonage-houses at Maplebeck, Rihoulton, and Nottingham, and for a church and parsonage-house at Hasland, Derby; by 16th inst., for rebuilding the upper part of the spire of St. James's Church, Clerkenwell; by 31st, for the erection of judges' lodgings at Aylesbury; by 16th, for repaving and repewing Cowbridge Church, Glamorganshire; by 11th, for the erection of a block of dwellings near Spicer-street, Spitalfields; by 12th, for the various fittings required for lighting with gas the Borough Asylum for insane paupers, at Birmingham; by 8th, for deepening the bed of the river Medway; by 23rd, for the erection of an asylum for pauper lunatics in the county of Warwick; by 11th, for the erection of an infirmary at the Uxbridge Union, Hillingdon, Middlesex; by 21st, for the erection of five small houses near Blackheath; by 14th, for the erection of the Normal College for Wales, at Swansea (extension of time); by 16th, for the construction of brick arches and piers, &c., in widening Manchester station of North-Western Railway; by same date for the construction of an iron viaduct for same; by 12th, for the erection and completion of portion of an extensive range of farm steading, near Warrington; by 8th, for the erection of a farm-house at Broom, Warwickshire; by 10th, for the labour in erecting farm buildings at Preston-upon-Wye; by 30th, for the execution of cast and malleable iron work for passenger shed and roof of central railway station at Newcastle-on-Tyne, and for supplying the glass for roof and other parts of same; by 7th, for the erection of a third portion of market avenue at Ashton-under-Lyne; by 26th, for the erection of sundry buildings and works at the new barracks, Sheffield; and by 9th, for a supply of pig-iron, pig-lead, ironmongery, &c., for the East-India Company.

Competition.—The time for receiving plans for the restoration of Bridgewater Church is extended to 14th inst.

Land Surveyors' Association.—The general association, some time since noticed in The Builder, has given rise to a more select institution, under the title of "The Surveyors' Association," with rules of a more or less stringent order for the admission of members, the regulation of the affairs of the association, and the protection and promotion of the interests of the legitimate members of the profession. By section III. of the published code of regulations, it has been resolved that the association shall consist of three classes—viz., members, graduates, and honorary members. Every candidate for admission as a member must be twenty-four years of age, and have been regularly educated as a land surveyor, according to the usual mode of pupilage, or have acquired a knowledge of the profession in the office of a land surveyor for three years, and had a subsequent employment as such for three years further, one of them at least on his own account. — Graduates must be eighteen years of age, and have been two years in the office of a land surveyor, or under a course of instruction as land surveyor, and still in the profession. By section V. it is appointed that each member shall pay an annual subscription of one guinea, and each new member an entrance fee of one guinea. Each graduate shall pay annually half-a-guinea, and each new graduate an entrance fee of half-a-guinea. Members may compound for seven years by payment of five guineas, or for life, twenty guineas. The association already numbers fifty members, admitted in accordance with the regulations. Mr. Thos. Thurston, Ashford, is the chairman for the current year, and Mr. William Murray, 21, University-street, is the hon. secretary.

Yorkshire Union of Mechanics' Institutes. The Earl of Carlisle has consented to preside at the evening meeting of the Yorkshire Union of Mechanics' Institutes, which will be held at Hull, on Wednesday, the 30th of May. There are now seventy-nine institutions in the union, and nine more seeking to be admitted at the annual meeting—making a total of eighty-eight institutions, containing about 16,000 members. On the day after the meeting there will be an excursion to Flamborough Head.

The Steam Docks at Keyham, Devonport.—It appears from a late debate on ways and means, that Government, about six years since, proposed an expenditure of 400,000*l.* for steam-dock accommodation, whereby, it was alleged, no less than 25 per cent. would be saved on repairing contracts. First, therefore, the comparatively modest instalment of 30,000*l.* was called for and voted; but the appetite for more appears to have grown, as did the estimate, with what it fed on, even down to the present moment: the following summary will shew the past and present state of these works of economy and saving:—

	Total estimate for New Steam Basin.	Instalment granted for the year.	Leaving still due.
1844-45 ..	£400,000 ..	£30,000 ..	£370,000
1845-46 ..	675,000 ..	100,000 ..	545,000
1846-47 ..	675,000 ..	133,000 ..	412,000
1847-48 ..	675,000 ..	120,000 ..	292,000
1848-49 ..	1,225,000 ..	150,000 ..	692,000
1849-50 ..	1,225,000 ..	120,000 ..	572,000

And, moreover, it is now said that the works were so hastily and injudiciously begun, that their chief utility will be entirely neutralized by their very situation, on a lee shore, with a depth of water too small to admit large steamers at ordinary full tide. Of course, with 572,000*l.* still to follow the 653,000*l.* already paid out, the works are as far from completion as they appeared to be when founded.

Blind Builders.—Tenders delivered for the New Market House, Brentford, April 27.

Figg	£4,725
Burton	3,777
Burchett	3,648
Glenn	3,490
Nye (accepted)	3,453
Taylor	3,197
Higgs	2,929
R. and E. Curtis	2,887
Tombs	2,786

Improvements in Chisels and Gouges.—Mr. H. Wilson, a foreman at Sheffield, has obtained a patent, in the specification of which he states, that in the manufacture of chisels and gouges it has been the practice to make some with sockets and others with tangs, for the purpose of affixing the handles to the same, the tangs and sockets in each case being used alone. The object of this invention is to combine the use of a socket and a tang with the same chisel or gouge, whereby each of such tools may be applied to the ordinary uses of a chisel and gouge, and to morticing, so that the workman will not require to have a tool for each purpose. The old socket-chisels and gouges have wooden handles inserted into their sockets; these handles, when the tool is being used, receive the blows or strokes of a mallet, and often those of a hammer, and are much subjected to lateral strain, from which circumstances the handles are liable to break off at the upper edge of the sockets, and the patentee considers that the addition of tangs to such tools will give greater stability to the handles. The ordinary tanged chisels and gouges also have wooden handles, which are drilled, and the tangs are driven into them, and in some cases ferrules are applied to the lower parts of the handles. The handles of these tools are liable to be split, not only by the side strain to which they are subject when in use, but also by reason of the tools being often driven by a mallet or hammer, and it is to obviate these defects that the patentee proposes to combine sockets with the tangs.

Steam 'Cutters' for Frozen Seas.—Commander Joseph West, an officer of experience and skill, says the *United Service Gazette*, has proposed the construction of ice hammers and saws, to be worked in steamers by the engine shafts. The main object appears to be the navigation of the arctic region in search of Sir John Franklin's expedition; but the like invention seems to be feasibly applicable to the rapid opening of a way for shipping and commerce in northern ports when frozen up, and at a stand in winter. Ice 4 to 5 feet thick, it is calculated, may thus be broken up by hammers of 15 to 20 cwt., working alternately on each side before the stem of the vessel, which may be worked either by screw or paddle.

Battle Maps. — With singular rapidity Mr. Wyld has published plans of the last battles in India, which will be examined with interest by those interested in military tactics, or who have friends fighting there.

Bridges in China, &c.—The bridges ar variously constructed: some consist of a singl arch, others of three or more arches, and som are merely a series of stone piers, with larg stone slabs laid across them, as described b us in our account of the famous bridge at Foo chow-foo. Some bridges are built of re granite, and others of a greyish marble, cu into blocks 5 feet or more in length, which ar laid alternately end-ways and cross-ways. Th arches are very high, are semi-circular, circula and polygons in shape, and the bridges hav steps at either end. Some are very handsom structures, particularly one a few miles to th west of Pekin, which is composed of whit marble, beautifully cut and ingeniously de vised. The balustrades are composed of 7 small pillars, on either side intermixed wit marble tablatures, carved with birds an animals, foliage, and flowers.—*China and th Chinese.*

Ripon Diocesan Church Buildin Society. — The half-yearly meeting of th Central Committee was held the week befor last, at Ripon, when grants were made toward the following objects:—400*l.* for the erectio of a new church at Gomersal, which will con tain 466 free sittings; 200*l.* for the endowmen of St. John's Church, Bradford, and a lik sum for the endowment of St. Mary's Church in Sowerby, near Halifax; 200*l.* each for th erection or purchase of parsonage houses fo Holy Trinity, Ripon, St. Jude's, Bradford and Ingrow-cum-Hainworth, near Keighley.

Institute of British Architects. At a meeting on the 30th April, Messrs. R. C Baxter and R. J. Withers were elected ass ciates. The first part of the following pape was read by Mr. J. W. Papworth:—" O some features of the connection between th Architecture and Chronology of Egypt; wit an account of the Work lately presented to this Institute by Mr. J. B. Le Sueur, Architect, of Paris, being his Essay 'On the Obronology of Egypt illustrated by its Monuments,' to which the medal of the Institute of France was awarded in 1847."

Exhibition of Machinery at Ghent. —A special exhibition of machinery, frames, looms, and implements of trade (of Belgian or *foreign* make) employed in the manufacture of yarn and tissues of all sorts, is to be opened at Ghent (on the occasion of the exhibition of the produce of the industry of Flanders) in the month of July. Special rewards, consisting of commemorative medals, of gold, silver, and bronze, will be awarded to such exhibitors as shall appear to merit such a distinction.

Bedfordshire Architectural Society. —A joint meeting of the Northamptonshire Architectural Society and the Bedfordshire Architectural Society is appointed to take place at Higham Ferrers, on Tuesday, the 8th. The Marquis of Northampton will preside, and an excursion is proposed to some neighbouring churches on the following day.

Rating Railways.—We understand that the South-Western Railway have successfully appealed against the rating of their line by the parish of Romsey. The parish wanted 200*l.* per mile, the court gave 25*l.*

The Iron Trade.—At present the prices of wrought and pig-iron are pretty well sustained, though we fear very little of the former has realised the nominal price of 7*l.* 10s. per ton.

NOTICE.

On Tuesday was published, Part I., price 2s. 6d., of "Buildings and Monuments, Modern and Mediæval:" being Illustrations of recently-erected Edifices, and of some of the Architectural Works of the Middle Ages, with Descriptive Particulars. Edited by George Godwin, F.R.S., Fellow of the Royal Institute of Architects, &c.

The first part of this work (to be continued every alternate month) contained Engravings on Wood, folio size, of—

Her Majesty's Marine Residence, Osborne; with Plan.

The Carlton Club House, Pall Mall.

Church of St. Isaac, at St. Petersburgh; with Details.

Kensington Union Workhouse.

The Liverpool Branch Bank of England; and Details.

The New Throne, Canterbury Cathedral.

The North Porch, Restored, of St. Mary Redcliffe, Bristol.

The Interior of Lincoln's-Inn Hall.

Published at the Office of "The Builder," 2, York-street, Covent Garden.

TENDERS

For the parsonage house and enclosures for the district of Saint Bartholomew, Bethnal-green. Mr. Alfred R. Mason, architect.

Hicks	£1,360
Holland	1,258
Lock and Nesham	1,250
Piper	1,222
R. and R. Curtis	1,173
Hill and Co.	1,154
Joshua Wilson	1,133

MEETINGS OF SCIENTIFIC BODIES

Held during the ensuing week.

MONDAY, May 7th. — Institute of British Architects (Anniversary.)
TUESDAY, 8th.—Institution of Civil Engineers, 8 P.M.; Freemasons of Church, 8 P.M.
WEDNESDAY, 9th. — Society of Arts, 8 P.M.; Graphic Society, 8 P.M.
THURSDAY, 10th.—Royal Society, 8½ P.M.; Society of Antiquaries, 8 P.M.
FRIDAY, 11th.—Archæological Association, 8½ P.M.

TO CORRESPONDENTS.

Received.—"Spectator" (we agree with our correspondent in preferring reality to sham), "R. S." "W. H." (can our correspondent send us a report?), "J. H. L." (we shall be glad to receive remainder of the article), "A Constant Reader," "W. P. M." (we shall be glad to receive particulars), "J. C." (Warrington), "J. M.," "W. F. and T. W.," "V. W." jun.," "J. W. B.," "A. G." (we have no " antipathies" or " prejudices," but we have convictions), "F. G." (inquire of Mr. Abrahams, as the Westminster Improvement Office, Great George-street, Westminster), "J. B." (Newark), "Scriplo" (we are not friendly to such expansion of classes), "Mr. G." (one act of THE BUILDER, complete, in green cloth, can be had at 21s. per volume), "W. T.," "J. B.," "Jacobus" (we have reason to believe the Dundee arch competition is scarcely settled even yet. We have no precise information beyond what has appeared in our pages). "Dolman's Magazine," "Blackwood's," "The Art Journal," "The Journal of Design," No. III.; "Con Cregan," No. V. (Orr and Co.); "Journal of the Franklin Institute."

"*Books, Prices, and Addresses.*"—We have not time to point out books or find addresses.

NOTICE.— All communications respecting *advertisements* should be addressed to the "Publisher," and not to the "Editor:" all other communications should be addressed to the EDITOR, and *not* to the Publisher.

ADVERTISEMENTS.

No. CCCXXVII.

SATURDAY, MAY 12, 1849.

HE aggregate number of works of art exhibited in the six galleries open in London at this time last year was 4,023, and the total number produced, calculating that at least 1,500 were returned to the artists, 5,523, without counting those exhibited only in the provinces. In the present year the number exhibited is rather less, namely, 3,796, and is thus made up, namely—at the British Institution, 518 ; the Society of British Artists, 639 ; the Free Exhibition, 531 ; the Water-Colour Society, 365 ; the New Water-Colour Society, 402 ; and at the Royal Academy, 1,341. The number produced, however, was doubtless as great, if not greater: from the Academy alone, we understand, 1,300 pictures were sent back,—many of them, as we can assert of our own knowledge, very meritorious productions.

In consequence of the size of some of the works which are hung, and the arrangement generally, there are 110 works fewer than were exhibited there in 1847, and 133 less than last year. More space is needed. The rejection of an artist's picture involves anguish and trouble of which the public have scarcely any idea. Many of our readers have already seen the particulars of a brutal attack made on Mr. J. P. Knight, the worthy secretary of the Academy, by an artist who had received an official letter from the secretary, stating that his picture could not be hung. The assault was infamous and indefensible, and we would not say a word which would seem to make it appear less so. It may serve as an illustration, however, of the effect of rejection on exciteable minds, even where serious pecuniary interest, so far as we know, was not involved.

The exhibition, as a whole, is fully of the average degree of merit, and creditable to the country. Attempts at the highest style of art are rare, but this is less the fault of our artists than of the state of education in art generally. The elder artists, for the most part, maintain their ground, and the younger and rising painters give evidence of a decided advance.

In the architectural room, to which we must first direct our attention (though at present we can go no further than the door, so many matters have pressed upon us), there are 105 works, which specially belong to it,* mixed with very nearly the same number of oil paintings. They are better disposed, however, than they were last year, the architectural drawings occupying the lower part of all four sides of the room, and the paintings the upper part.

It is small space to afford to the big-sister-art, and admits of but trifling illustration of what is doing in architecture among us. As one of our correspondents observed in a recent number, few thanks seem to be owing to the present architect-academicians for the provision for and honour there of the art they profess.

There are no models, and it is desirable that the refusal of the academy to receive them should be known, to save architects unnecessary expenditure and annoyance. Ignorance

Last year there were 113.

of this led to the preparation of a model of a large building now being erected under a government department, for exhibition at the academy, and the annoyance ·to the architect will be better conceived than described when he found that, after all the pains and expenditure, admittance was refused to it. It is sufficient to say that the model was made by Mr. T. D. Dighton, to prove that its rejection is not to be attributed to want of excellence as a work of art.*

Mr. Cockerell, R.A., has a very remarkable drawing, called "The Professor's Dream" (1,102), and which is a synopsis of the principal architectural monuments of ancient and modern times, drawn to the same scale, in forms and dimensions ascertained from the best authorities, and arranged on four terraces—Egyptian, Grecian, Roman, and Mediæval and Modern ; the last of these shows more particularly the comparative heights. The Egyptian temples and propylea form the foreground, including also the sphynx, the Memnon, &c. Then come the Athenian wonders ; and the Roman Coliseum, Pantheon, and (once called) Jupiter Stator : the Pisan Tower, the Cathedrals of Cologne, Strasburg, Antwerp ; the Brussels Town Hall, &c., represent the mediæval skill. The Italian domes of the Revival, with St. Paul's and other of Wren's works, are crowned by St. Peter's, and the whole are backed by the dim pyramids, which, as old Fuller says, have outlived their makers' names. The buildings are brought into combination most artistically, and the result is an extraordinary work.

Mr. Pugin, who is not usually an exhibitor, has sent four prominent drawings,—No. 1,057, "An Elevation of St. George's Catholic Church, Lambeth," showing the tower and spire as they are intended to be finished ; No. 1,013, "New Dining-hall, now erecting for the Earl of Shrewsbury, at Alton Towers ;" No. 1,085, "A View of St. Augustine's, Ramsgate," and No. 1,117, "A View of Bilton Grange, Rugby," the seat of Washington Hilbert, Esq. St. Augustine's is the residence of the architect, and includes a church, now building, cloisters, school, &c., all shown isometrically in this "true prospect." Around the main drawing, in compartments tied together by foliage, admirably drawn, are small views of the interior of the church, the "Herbert" Chapel, &c. The style is Early Decorated : propriety rather than ornament is studied. The view of Bilton Grange is finished in the same manner as the last : the interior of the library, the conservatory, the long gallery, &c., occupy the sides. The building itself is Tudor, of red brick and stone, and has an entrance-tower open on three sides, to admit a carriage-drive. The elevation of St. George's tower and spire is several feet in height. The straight heads of the windows in the second story deserve reconsideration.

Mr. Perrey has three designs,—No. 1,140, "The Training and Middle School for the Diocese of Worcester ;" geometric in style, plain and appropriate in appearance ; No. 1,173, "Some Additions made to the West

* We have received some complaints as to errors and omissions in the catalogue. Mr. F. E. H. Fowler says, the title of his drawing, No. 1,139, which stands thus—"Design for the Army and Navy Club-house, to which the second premium in the first competition was awarded," was further described as—" modified to suit the extension of the frontage afterwards made by the committee, given as that which might have been submitted (in lieu of that actually sent in.) In the second competition, had the instructions prescribed in that case not been adhered to, or had they been rescinded in the instance of each competitor." Mr. Talbot Bury's drawing, No. 1,156, has both an incorrect description and name. It ought to have been—" View of the chancel of Aldenham Church, Herts, as rebuilt from the designs and under the superintendence of Talbot Bury."

Front of the Episcopal Palace, Wells ;" and No. 1,187, "St. Stephen's Church and Schools, Westminster," of which we gave an engraving some time ago.

Mr. Daukes, who seems to be one of those fortunate individuals graphically described in the old saw, as having "somebody else's luck and his own too," exhibits most of the works which have recently fallen into his hands,—No. 1,036, "Church of England Training College at Cheltenham ;" No. 1,075, "The Middlesex County Lunatic Asylum, Colney Hatch ;"* and No. 1,141, "Aged Freemasons' Asylum, at Croydon" (a very every-day affair) ; while Mr. Webnert exhibits a "View of St. Peter's Church, Cheltenham (No. 1,032), and Mr. Coe, a drawing of St. Stephen's Church, Avenue-road, Regent's-park" (in the Decorated style), both in course of erection by the same architect.

TRAVELLING NOTES IN ITALY.
BY AN ARCHITECT.
PÆSTUM.

HERE we have more stupendous and more mysterious memorials of the Italo-Greek race. These Greek colonists seem to have selected the most enchanting spots for their cities. The site of Pæstum equals, almost surpasses, that of Pompeii ;—on the shore of a fertile plain, spreading itself at the foot of the lofty snow-capped ranges of the Calabrian Apennines, and laved by the blue waters of the magnificent Gulf of Salerno—a gulf at least equal in beauty to that of Naples. These three temples of Pæstum, like those of Baalbec, stand like solitary rocks in the chart of ancient history. The annals of the races that founded them have perished. History has not a word to say in regard to their origin or their object. Doubtless they were already ancient when Pompeii was overwhelmed, and they may have been visited by the Pompeiians as vestiges of remote antiquity. There they stand in silence and solitude, like the great triad of pyramids on the rocky edge of the Egyptian desert, lone monuments of the genius of their aspiring founders, whose bodies have ages ago been re-united to the dust of their native plain ; and still they greet successive generations of travellers with that same august and tranquil aspect they have ever worn.

If the traveller were to select from the thousand objects that challenge admiration in Italy those which had most moved his soul at the moment, and had traced the most indelible images on his memory, he would probably name the interior of Milan Cathedral, the cupola of St. Peter's looking up from the pavement, the Coliseum by moonlight, and the temples of Pæstum. Of these the dome of St. Peter's is emphatically a monument of the towering genius of the great architect ; but the other three may be regarded as bodying forth the spirit, and genius, and habits of thought of the three great ages of Italian civilisation—the Hellenic, the Roman, and the Mediæval age. At the Duomo of Milan, that sublime vista of piers and arches, those gorgeous stained windows, that high embowed roof, and those unparalleled effects of chiaroscuro, how exactly adapted are they for priestly pageantry, for awakening all the fervour of devotion, or at least of devoteeism, for which that age is remarkable. At the Coliseum the grandosity of the design, the rapidity of its execution, the bloody associations of its vast arena, where ladies would sup while it was still reeking with the blood of the gladiator or the Christian martyr, all vividly recall the characteristic traits of the Roman mind. Then recur to Pæstum. How dissimilar are these monuments to the other two. In that sublime unity of conception, that severe simplicity of mass com.. bined with finish of detail, above all, in that

* This was described in our pages at the time of the com.. petition. The first stone of the building was laid by Prince Albert, a few days ago. According to the newspapers, the extreme length of the building will be 1,893 feet 8 inches, greatest breadth 143 feet 10 inches. There will be two wings, the right for females and the left for males, to each of which will be attached a surgeon's residence and an in.. firmary. The descent to the basement story is to be effected by a corridor of inclination, instead of steps. The roofing and flooring are to be covered with metallic lava.

faultless elaboration of the original idea, you have the qualities that mainly characterise every production of the Greek mind, where all had to undergo the ordeal of fastidious criticism from a nation of critics.

The Pæstum temples differ from those of Greece, chiefly in the greater massiveness of their columns and the flatness of the mouldings. One of them has a column instead of an interspace in the centre of the portico, and a range of columns up the middle of the interior. This peculiarity of plan, which has caused so much speculation, is satisfactorily explained by a reference to the temple of Kom Ombo, in Upper Egypt. There, too, the portico has an odd number of columns in front, and two entrances lead to two suites of inner doorways. An inscription still extant explains the cause of the peculiarity: it was a *double* temple dedicated to two gods.

THE BAY OF BAIÆ.

While the cities of the Greek colonists were flourishing along the gulfs of Sorrento and Naples, the shores of the bay of Baiæ became, under the empire, the favourite retirement of the patricians of Rome. It was, in fact, to them what the Lake of Como is to the magnates of modern Italy. Its beauties are of a more ordinary and homely kind, and more circumscribed in extent, than those of the two larger bays. Its vicinity to the harbour and arsenals of Misenum may have contributed to render it so favourite a haunt with the Romans. Every beautiful point and headland became the site of some aristocratic villa, the walls and terraces of which were washed by the ripple of the landlocked bay; and fragments and substructions of these villas are still seen all along the now deserted coast, standing in the water and under it. As every ruin must have some name, the ciceroni have affixed to these shattered fragments the high sounding names of Marius, Sylla, Pompey, Cæsar, &c.

Under the empire magnificent public structures arose around the bay, usually octagonal or round in plan, and roofed with vast hemispherical vaults of tufo, which, from its lightness, is admirably adapted for the purpose. Although the whole coast has been rocked and rent by earthquakes, some of these immense *rotondos* still remain tolerably perfect; others having been riven by earthquakes, huge rock-like fragments have fallen from the vault, and thus let in glimpses and stripes of the blue sky, the ragged edges of which are beautifully fringed with shrubs and pendant foliage. It were equally easy and unprofitable to descant on the object and purpose of these structures. Local antiquarianism styles them temples. They have more analogy to the immense circular *exhedræ* of the imperial baths than to any other buildings in Rome. They are constructed with brick quoins and courses, filled in with reticulated work in tufo. The vault is solid, and narrows in substance as it ascends. The tufo has been corroded by the sea breeze, but the brick and cement resist it. Within the solid of the walls are arches of construction, with voussoirs formed of immense tiles, the wide intervals between which are filled with brickbats. Though the walls have been riven asunder and sometimes thrown down by volcanic or some other terrific agency, they stand as hard and compact as rocks, it being easier to fracture than to disunite the materials.

One of the octagonal temples of Baiæ is remarkable as offering probably the only ancient examples of a balcony supported by small arches, on brackets or corbels. These project from large openings, one on each side of the octagon. They are doubtless the prototypes of the arched balcony now so common in southern Italy.

At half an hour's distance from Baiæ, on the promontory of Misenum, is the Piscina Mirabile, a square block of massive and lofty vaulted galleries in brick, still perfect. In the palmy days of Rome they formed the reservoir which supplied water to the Roman fleet lying at anchor in the port below. This magnificent cistern is worthy of the people whose stately aqueducts strided over the plains of the Campagna to supply their capital with the purest water from the distant mountains. The great architectural monuments of Greece and Egypt were sepulchral or religious; but the most original and wonderful works of Rome were utilitarian,—roads to unite the distant provinces to the metropolis and heart of the empire, aqueducts and cisterns to supply fleets and cities with water, baths to promote the health of the myriads of a crowded metropolis.

Not far from the Piscina Mirabile are the prisons of Nero, an extensive range of subterranean excavations.

At Pozzuoli, on the opposite side of the bay, are several remains of the ancient Puteoli, which stood on the same site. The most interesting are the mole or pier, the temple of Serapis, and the amphitheatre. The plan of the Serapeon is unlike that of any other building existing in Italy, or in the world. A quadrangular court was inclosed by colonnades; in the middle of the quadrangle stood a circular temple on a raised basement which still exists. A portico of taller columns occupied the centre of one side of the quadrangle, and seems to have formed the entrance to the temple. There were also numerous small chambers and cells, which appear to have been indispensable to all Egyptian temples. It is thought that some of these were baths, whither patients resorted to bathe in consecrated water. The pavement of the quadrangle is now flooded by the sea. The marble columns of the palace of Caserta were taken from this building.

The *Amphitheatre*, which for ages had been half-buried under a diluvial deposit, has been recently disentombed in excellent preservation. Like all other Roman ruins in the vicinity, it is built of bricks and tufo. It had seats for 45,000 spectators. There were vaulted chambers and galleries under the arena, lighted by large square openings in the vault, which were covered with planks when the arena was used for the shows. An inclined plane, passing under the chief, or Consular entrance, gives access to these subterranea. It was at Puteoli that St. Paul first set foot on Italian ground, whence he proceeded towards Rome.

Along the whole of this wonderful coast the action and effects of subterranean fire meet you at every step. No fewer than 20 craters have been counted here. At one of these, the *Solfatara*, the fire is rather smouldering than extinct. The Solfatara is a small sandy sulphurous plain, in a basin of white sulphurous rock, and resembles, except in size, that most arid of deserts, the Desert of the Dead Sea. Hot vapour issues from crevices in the rocks; when you stamp on the ground, it reverberates with a hollow sound—and hot water was found at the depth of 100 feet when the basin was bored by the French. A natural sweating-bath may be immediately formed by constructing a low building around one of the perforations in the rock, and thus confining the vapour. Such are the baths of S. Germano. Alum and sulphur are prepared at the Solfatara, and there is also a manufactory for the famous Pozzulana cement.

The host of travellers that resort to the Bay of Baiæ from Naples to visit the wonders of nature and art in its neighbourhood, have called into being a troop of hungry *ciceroni* and showmen, who hold a kind of vested interest in old ruins, steaming fountains, and sulphurous caves. Some lie in wait for the tourist in the vicinity of the Sybil's Cave, lead him along a narrow, dark, rock-hewn gallery, to two or three subterranean grots filled with water, through which you are carried and landed in what they gravely assure you was the sybil's bath! The flaring torches throw a wild and fitful light through these gloomy shades; but the loud laugh, the merry nonsense, the genuine English and the bad Italian with which the dark galleries resound, banish all ideas of the supernatural and the ghostly.

At the baths of Nero, on the margin of the bay, another exhibition awaits you. The *custode* having stripped to the waist and lighted a torch, runs with it down a subterranean adit, intensely hot with vapours from a spring at the extremity; in two or three minutes you begin to hear the groans of a dying man along the adit; they grow more and more distinct, and presently the poor fellow reappears, streaming with perspiration, his face wild, haggard, and deeply furrowed,—in his hand a small vessel of hot water, containing an egg, which be has brought from the hot spring. He throws himself on a seat, half dead with heat and exhaustion. The egg is presently boiled. In the outer cave, where we stood, the air under the roof was very hot, while the lower stratum was cool, so that when stooping low you might walk without inconvenience.

At the Grotta del Cane a dog is made the victim to scientific curiosity. The poor beast is held over the poisonous gas as it issues from the rock, and in a few seconds becomes stupified and senseless; but on being removed to fresh air, presently recovers, to be again similarly tortured before another audience.

The low headland between Naples and the volcanic plain skirting the bay of Baiæ, is pierced by the ancient gallery called the Grotto of Posilipo, about half a mile in length, and at present upwards of 100 feet high. It still forms part of the high road between Naples and Pozzuoli. Two or three similar tunnels, through this ridge, have recently been re-opened by Government.

MOVEMENT AT THE ROYAL INSTITUTE OF ARCHITECTS.

THE ANNUAL GENERAL MEETING.

THE annual meeting was held on the 7th inst., Mr. Bellamy, V. P., in the chair. On the motion to suspend the bye-law 23, that "No member who has filled the office of president for two successive years shall be again eligible to the same situation until the expiration of one year from the termination of his office," with a view to the re-election of the Earl de Grey,

Mr. Tite said, no member entertained greater respect for their noble president than himself, or had a fuller sense of the obligations conferred by him on the Institute; he should not be misunderstood, therefore, when he said it appeared to him important to inquire whether or not they should have for president some distinguished member of the profession. A certain degree of success had attended the establishment of the Institute, but in his opinion it did not occupy the ground it should. The principal architects did not support it as they should, and it occurred to him that if the honour of the presidency were open to them it would be an additional inducement for them to come forward. Other societies had found such a course desirable. There were some reasons why the Institute had not taken the ground it ought, and it seemed to him worth inquiry if this were one of them. He threw this out without any reference to the present election, but for a future year, and renewed his desire to have his motive properly understood.

The chairman, and Mr. Kendall after him, agreed in thinking the inquiry desirable.

Mr. Godwin said, that without expressing an opinion at that moment on the particular question which had been raised, he entertained a strong conviction that a fuller and more searching inquiry into the position and scope of the Institute was necessary. He could assert of his own knowledge, that it did not occupy that position in the opinion of the great body of the profession throughout the kingdom which it should do. The number of members was not half what it ought to be, and its usefulness was not universally admitted. He attributed it himself to an exclusive spirit which pervaded the laws; he desired to see the opportunity given for other classes immediately connected with architecture to become co-operators. In the Institution of Civil Engineers this was the case, and great advantage had resulted from it. That some alteration was necessary seemed to him evident, if only from the existence of the *Architectural Association*. If the Institute were liberally constituted and did its duty, surely there could be no occasion for this second society: the gentlemen forming it ought to be able to find within the walls of the Institute greater advantages for the same amount of subscription than they could provide for themselves. He felt so strongly the necessity of some change, that if no other member took any step in the matter, he would move for the appointment of a committee of inquiry.

Mr. Pownall quite agreed with the last speaker that an extended inquiry was necessary, and that more liberal views should prevail. The laws as they then stood, excluded all who measured for tradesmen. It was well known that many educated and properly qualified architects also practised measuring, and for this they were to be excluded from the

Institute. Instead of putting a ban on measurers, the object should be to elevate their character as a body. The Institute could discriminate between the worthy and unworthy; but to exclude every man simply because he practised as a measurer, seemed to him most unreasonable.

Mr. Tite was convinced that the suggested inquiry was the right step. Putting the Institute on one side, architects, as a body, did not occupy the position they should. Most people knew that he had no reason to complain of lack of employment. Still he did not hesitate to say that persons moving in the upper circles of life, did not employ architects as they should do, nor did they properly rate their services. Architects must take a place for themselves and maintain it, or the world would not do so.

Mr. C. Fowler, as one of the original founders of the Institute, could say that some of the principal members of the profession made exclusion the condition on which they gave their support. For himself, he thought the subject well deserving investigation; and, moreover, was satisfied that something must be done.

Ultimately, on the motion of Mr. Tite, seconded by Mr. Godwin, a resolution was passed unanimously, requiring the new council to examine to what extent the objects of the founders of the Institute had been effected, and if any and what alterations in the laws were desirable.

The motion for suspending the regulation as to president having been carried unanimously, Mr. G. Bailey, Hon. Sec., read the report, which showed, amongst other things, that the receipts for the current year were 857l. 12s., and that there was a balance of 267l. at the bankers'.

A discussion ensued as to the award of the royal medal, in which Mr. Fowler, Mr. Woodthorpe, Mr. I'Anson, &c., took part; and it was shown conclusively that the council, by committing the institute to their award, by applying to her Majesty before coming to the general meeting to confirm their report, had exceeded their powers.

The report having been received, thanks were voted by acclamation to the president, Earl de Grey, and afterwards to the vice-presidents.

Mr. Bailey, who had acted as honorary secretary for seven years, having expressed his intention of not serving again, a vote of thanks was passed, expressive of the high sense of the institute of his services.

Other complimentary motions having been carried, the ballot was taken, and the following were elected the officers for the ensuing year :—*President,* Earl de Grey ; *Vice-presidents,* Messrs. Bellamy, Salvin, and Sydney Smirke ; *Honorary Secretaries,* Messrs. T. L. Donaldson and Scoles ; *other members of council,* Messrs. Donthorne, Kendall, Mayhew, Mair, Mee, Mocatta, Nelson, C. Parker, Penrose, and Wyatt ; *Auditors,* Messrs. Kendall, jun., and C. Barry, jun.

SELECT COMMITTEE ON SCHOOL OF DESIGN.

ON the 4th inst., Mr. R. Solly, chairman of the Sheffield School of Design Committee, was examined, also Mr. Young Mitchell, the master of that school. The latter produced some designs made by pupils, and showed that public taste, with regard to designs, is so bad in Sheffield, that a pure design has every chance of being rejected by the manufacturers.

Mrs. M'Ian, being examined, said the progress of her pupils had been less satisfactory since their removal to the lodgings in the Strand, and that if the committee had desired to find a place that was ill-adapted for the school, they could not have succeeded more eminently.

Mr. C. J. Richardson, one of the masters, said he was convinced, if the school were made more practical and the masters in each class allowed to instruct their pupils in design, that it would be much more frequented by artisans than it is. He considered the school in its practical results a failure, and thought the control exercised by the committee injurious.

THE SUSPENSION BRIDGE AT PESTH, it is said, has been destroyed by the Austrians, in order to cover their retreat before the Hungarians ; the bridge of boats is also said to have been burnt for the same purpose.

DRYING CLOSETS.

MANY experiments have been made by Mr. Baly, the engineer to the Committee for promoting the establishment of Baths and Washhouses for the Labouring Classes, and recently under the immediate superintendence of Mr. William Hawes, the deputy-chairman of the committee, for the purpose of ascertaining the best mode of drying clothes, &c., *quickly and economically.* For some time past Mr. W. Hawes, as one of the board of the Middlesex Hospital, has been superintending such experiments for the purposes of that institution, as well as for those of the Model Establishment of Baths and Washhouses. Mr. Jeakes's letter to you announces the result of one of the experiments suggested and superintended by Mr. Hawes, and which appears likely to insure economy as well as rapidity in drying. The previous experiments were generally, and some of them were strikingly successful, as regarded quickness in drying clothes,—it being found that a clothes'-horse load could be well dried in half-an-hour ; but the committee were constantly foiled in their endeavours to do the work with a small consumption of fuel.

The subject is one of considerable importance ; and perhaps Mr. Jeakes and Mr. Healy would be so obliging as to state what are the quantities of fuel necessary for evaporating, in given times, by their respective plans, given weights of water,—for the more light from experience that can be thrown on the matter the better.

In order that washhouses for the labouring classes may, with low charges, be self-supporting, the greatest economy of fuel is most desirable. The dilatory habits which those who have been forced to boil their water for washing by the half gallon or the quart at a time, have unavoidably acquired, cannot be corrected immediately ; but by enabling them to wash and dry quickly, they may be led to use more dispatch. For such institutions as hospitals, workhouses, &c., economy may be the chief requisite, while for many manufacturing processes rapidity is of more importance. The great object of the committee is to combine rapidity with economy, and they have not hitherto found any existing practice sufficient for insuring the combination. It may be of service to give publicity to a hint, for which the committee are indebted to Mr. Brunel, that drying would, in some cases, be effected much more quickly and better by high-pressure steam than by hot air. Mr. W. Hawes's plan makes an approach towards the high-pressure steam plan.

I may add that the experimental labours, expenditure, and failures of the committee promise to bear the good fruit of eventual success, and fully to reward the generosity with which their perseverance has been supported by the public. The success which has attended the adoption of the plans of the model establishment for the St. Martin's baths and laundries, may be referred to as an illustration of the beneficial results of that perseverance. Even during the winter months the receipts at those baths have yielded a decided profit over the working expenses. It cannot be too strongly impressed on those who have to design baths and washhouses that it is true economy to spend 200l. or 300l. extra, for the purpose of enabling the services of a single attendant to be dispensed with, or for making one ton of coals a-week do the work of three.

                       JOHN BULLAR, Hon. Sec.

*** We have great respect for the intentions of the committee, but we cannot, even by silence on the point, justify the extraordinary waste of time and money which has taken place at the model establishment. Some of the statements forwarded to us by parties who ought to be correctly informed, would almost justify a committee of inquiry on the part of the subscribers.

Mr. Jeakes's notice under this head in your number of April 14th states, that his experiments on a small closet " prove that at high temperatures an external air-drain may be entirely and advantageously dispensed with ;" and leads to the inference that a change of air in drying-closets is not an assistance, but an impediment ; which is so much at variance with received theory and successful practice,

that I am induced to think there must be something in the case which has been overlooked.

In your last number (May 5) Mr. Healy correctly gives it as a received opinion, that a current of air is an important part of the process of drying,—perhaps as important as heat ; for linen may be dried out of doors, where it will be subject to constant change of air about its surface, without artificial heat at all ; but if hung in a saturated medium, it will not dry though at a high temperature. Any laundress practising open-air drying, will say that the difference between a good and a bad drying day lies here : in the former, the atmosphere is in brisk *motion,* and *dry ;* in the latter, it is *still* and *moist.* In other words, the linen dries most quickly, when there is a rapid succession of dry particles of air passing over its surface.

Artificial drying is in fact a two-fold operation. By heat, the moisture is quickly converted into vapour ; by ventilation, that vapour is carried away, and replaced with dry air. If no fresh air were introduced, successive charges of wet linen would soon saturate the atmosphere of the closet, at which point drying must altogether cease.

But ventilation may be in excess. The utmost effect will be obtained from a closet and heating apparatus, of given size, when the air admitted bears a definite and not to be exceeded proportion to the quantity of vapour to be evolved in a given time,—to the temperature,—to the thickness of the textures,—to the state of the atmosphere at the time as regards dryness and motion. Hence, there should be area for ingress and egress, sufficient for the greatest required quantity of drying under the least favourable state of the external air, with means of reducing that area for smaller quantities and a drier or less stagnant atmosphere.

In many drying closets which I have been engaged on in this district, on the large scale for manufacturing purposes, rapidity of drying has been materially promoted by increasing the ventilation : in some cases where the textures were very thick, and introduced in a very wet state, still greater acceleration has been produced by the application of powerful forcing-apparatus, such as air-pumps or fans, worked by a steam-engine.

At the Lancaster County Lunatic Asylum, I have recently completed a closet for drying all the linen, bedding, &c. for 700 to 800 patients. The textures are unusually thick and heavy, and not easily wrung by female hands, and hold, on the average, twice their own weight of water when placed in the closet, thus :—Weight of a dry rug 4½ lbs., wet 13 lbs.; weight of wet clothing dried daily in twelve hours, 4,006 lbs; water evaporated in the same time, 252 gallons; temperature, 120° when the clothes are put in, increasing to 170° when dry ; cubic contents of closet, 5,040 feet ; constant ventilation, 288 square inches, with means for increasing it in moist heavy weather.

The foregoing considerations applied to the case in question lead to the conclusion :—1st, that the quantity of air admitted was too great for the size of the closet and for the heating power. 2nd, that though the original provision has been abandoned, there may still be left crevices or accidental openings, permitting sufficient change of air for so small a closet.   Manchester.   W. WALKER.

My remarks on the drying closet at the Middlesex Hospital have been entirely misconceived by your correspondent in the last number of THE BUILDER. By repeated experiments on that closet, it has been proved capable of evaporating 1 lb. of water per minute by employing merely the waste heat derived from the flue of the ironing stove; and although containing, as your correspondent observes, but 336 cubic feet, dries with ease the whole of the linen for 250 patients!

That this great effect is owing to the absence of the cold-air drain, has been satisfactorily proved by experiments tried before this drain was closed. Its economy cannot be disputed ; for assuming your correspondent's statement of having an air-drain containing 144 inches, and allowing the air to travel at the rate of 3 feet per second, 180 cubic feet must then be heated per minute from the temperature of the external air to that of the closet, which, in the case of the closet at the Middlesex, is dispensed with.   W. JEAKES, Jun.

THE ARCHITECTURAL ADVANTAGES AND DEFICIENCIES OF LONDON.*

THAT there are certain sites so admirably suited by nature for the development of a city, that so long as the district where they exist be civilised or even populated, they must form its foci, is a fact historically demonstrated. Of such sites, perhaps the one most remarkable is that spot where two large political divisions of the earth's surface are only separated by a narrow tranquil strait. On Europe's side a platform but a few feet above the level of the sea, with a soil exuberantly fertile and a climate unexcelled, protected from the attack of either man or the elements by a forest-covered range of mountains commanding the resources either of the Mediterranean or the Euxine, receiving its merchandise from all parts of the world upon an almost unexcitable sea,—Constantinople, whether its rulers be Frank or Turk, will never cease to rank the 'queen of cities.' So in Italy, where Greek, Goth, Italian, all have stood in turn as conquerors, all have consented to the supremacy of Rome; but where, on the contrary, an uncongenial site, destitute of natural qualifications, has been selected, as in the old cities of Assyria, in Carthage, or the modern Munich, imbedded in a barren sandy plain, and relying solely on the acquired wealth or warlike character of its inhabitants, although raised to a dazzling but ephemeral splendour by the munificence of some imperial master,—on the first reverse of fortune they fall, never to re-appear. And when we consider attentively the site of London, although superior in comparison with those last mentioned, yet, should its dissolution be decreed and another race tread over the earth in which its ruins are entombed, they would pass it by and find in England many sites far more naturally pointed out as its metropolis.

The chance-favoured Romans, on whom devolved the task of selecting a position for their intended fort,—for we must not suppose them as foreseeing its growth even to a town,—guided by their warlike wants alone, pitched their camp as the sea-wave raises a rim upon the stony beach, that they might halt, return, recruit, and sweeping it before them, impress their brand higher up upon the conquered country. It chanced otherwise; the stragglers who remained, while the main army returned to a more congenial home, unable, with the trifling shelter of a camp, to resist the cold wet winter of the then, as now, inhospitable clime, felled some trees around them, and, with a process the same as, at the present day, goes on in some embryo empire of the far west, they raised unconsciously the first germ of the future London.

As architects—as artists—aiming at beauty and picturesqueness equally with practical materialism, we must confess nature has done but little for London. The atmosphere, misty and rarely clear in any part of England, is still less so in London; at the bottom of a natural basin, all the dense clouds from the neighbouring hills gravitate towards it, and the east wind never reaches unless burdened with the damp evaporation of the marshes which form the border of the Thames so many miles eastward. The sea, which like a bright and sparkling eye to a face otherwise but plain, animates and gives expression and brilliancy to the scenes of nature it adorns, is far distant. We cannot boast, like Naples and Constantinople, of a bay reflecting as a mirror the bright mass which seems to float so calmly on its surface. Neither, as in the cities of antiquity, can we point to a natural capitol which should form a dome—a culmen—to the whole, giving to the spectator, on whichever side he stands, the full command of all the beauties which are around him. With us no seven hills give the variety of undulation to our too monotonous levels; no quarries are at hand to yield the only beautiful and permanent material for its buildings, to give to each one not the appearance of being raised up piece by piece with mortar and with sand, but to have been at once carved out—sculptured from the native rock—resting upon the earth as a block that has issued from its bosom, and promising an almost coeval existence. But, although we must come to the conclusion that the site of London is far from naturally beautiful, let us remember, in the words of Macaulay, lately, at Glasgow—"It is not on the fertility of the soil, it is not in the mildness of the atmosphere, that the prosperity of a city or a nation will depend,—slavery and superstition can make Campania a land of beggars, can change the plain of Enna to a desert; nor is it beyond the power of human intelligence and energy, developed by civil and spiritual freedom, to change sterile rocks and pestilential marshes to magnificent cities and luxuriant gardens." Let us see, then, what man has done as his share to supply these natural deficiencies, and by the creation of his art transform the disadvantages he labours under till they become the basis of a new peculiar character. Atmosphere must ever be the primary consideration. The Londoners found theirs naturally foggy: how have they endeavoured to improve it? Alas! day by day the refuse of 2,000 tons of coal is added to its foul burden. The Englishman is proud of the possession of that gloomy mineral, but what an enemy is it to the English architect,—through what a dirty glass does he behold his pretty picture when it is executed,—with what obstinacy do its foul black stains counteract the well-studied lights and shadows of his design! Let us take the south side of St. Paul's any time that the sun may have discovered that magnificent pile, and then examine the anomalies presented to our view, every projection probably with each side in shadow, as though all its illumination proceeded from the parallel gas-lamp in the street below,—mouldings and ornaments filled up and lost,—every variation of shadow that should constitute superficial effect in architecture, reversed, perverted, or obscured. And is there no remedy for this? Chemically, there is no portion of that sooty refuse incombustible: why should there be practically?

We have seen that London has no natural capitol; it were well, then, to supply its place with such a concentration of public buildings, as should afford a resting place for the wandering eye, and give the epithet magnificent to at least one quarter of the city; but, alas, how are they scattered! We fail upon them with such intervals, that our first idea must be they are few and insignificant; nor is such an idea far from the fact. If there be such a principle as proportion in art, it would follow that the public edifices in our cities should have some relation to their extent, and since London is in reality the largest of any city, it follows it should show an equally unexcelled array of public buildings. It is notoriously otherwise. Rome, Paris, Naples, very far exceed us even now, and how many of our noblest buildings date no farther back than the last ten or twenty years! London has but one character, that of extent, wearisome, monotonous extent: the complex arrangement of its streets, the smallness of its component parts, all contribute to this effect. But this extent must not be taken as implying grandeur, or vastness. It is not a city, but rather a mass of towns joined one to one, — respectable when viewed independently, but meagre and tame when considered in relation to the harmony and proportion of the whole. Nothing adds so much to this apparent petiteness as the jagged varying broken outline of our roofs; how have we jumbled together the horizontality of Italy and Greece with the high picturesqueness of the German roof, and produced a mongrel, destroying all beauty, dishonouring all architecture!

Hamburgh, considerably nearer the cold north than London, affords an example of the practicability and beauty of flat roofs, worthy of our attention; there, since the late fire, the roofs have become, as in the cities of the East, the gardens of the town, with the air purer than below, less disturbance from the traffic in the streets; may we not hope at some early period having enticed 'rus in urbe,' to rival the mystic Babylon in our hanging gardens.

And here one word against the projects broached of late against the existence of our quiet tranquil squares, the only feature we can really mention as peculiar to London. "Naturam expellas furcâ tamen usque recurrit" was the taunt of the Roman poet to his city-loving fellow citizens, and does it not apply to us? in vain do we imbed ourselves in material of our own creation; in vain smother all the yearnings of an innate love of nature: how often has not the view, even of the perverted green of our melancholy squares, thrown a ray of cheerfulness over our moody mind, and touched the spring which lets loose at once upon us a crowd of happy associations and inspiring hopes! Mark the most dirty and neglected streets, you will still find some window where the poor inmate, with grateful heart, puts forth his humble offering to the shrine of nature. Better our squares, exclusive as they are, and selfishly enclosed from the tread of those who would enjoy them without thought of injury, than see them transformed into barren arenas for the strut of policemen, the nurseries of the mendicant and the thief, the noisy playground of the idle and the vagabond, the blank and meagre site of still more meagre statues.

Hamburgh is perhaps the chief instance of a city rising from its ashes in greater splendour than it descended to them. The opportunity is generally lost, and for this reason, that the hurried and unexpected demand thus made upon the architectural talent of the time must produce much that is commonplace and unstudied; that men half ruined by their misfortune, and waiting for a sheltering roof, care little for its decoration, and would be sadly disposed, in their rebuilding, to merge every other consideration in that of economy.

The fire which in 1666 gave London an opportunity of regeneration on the grandest scale, gave, alas! that chance in vain; and although the loss was greatly qualified by the impetus thus given to the genius of Wren, there was but one Wren; and, worried as he was by the stupidity of the officials of his time, it is but natural that smaller works, left to the unguided rawness of a pupil, suffered accordingly. It is true he formed a comprehensive project for the rebuilding of the city,—a project of which it is idle to regret the execution. A time of unparalleled misery, discord, and selfishness, was not the fittest to ask of men that they should merge the right of property and frontages, the advantages of established business, for the chimerical compensation the new project offered. A vast and firm government would have been the only chance of appeal. The government of Charles II. and his ministers was never otherwise than careless and indifferent; nor was Wren's project faultless. I question, if carried out, whether it would meet the approbation it receives on paper.

A peculiar feature is the frequency of certain points, where six or eight converging streets constitute an arrangement, of which almost the only perfect type we possess is Seven Dials,—an idea excellent and highly admissible when the project is a labyrinth: but the few specimens we are acquainted with warn us against its adoption, save as an occasional curiosity. The traffic of each wide street poured at once into the central space would produce a jumble and confusion unparalleled even in the narrow crowded thoroughfares of the present day; besides that, the triangular wedge-shaped pieces left by this convergence are the most extravagant and ill-judged areas for building. The plan of a large collection of buildings should be as simple as practicable, adhering to straight lines, not only from the convenience of the parallel building areas, but from the greater grandeur produced by an arrangement of vistas and long-continued façades, than when the view is interrupted and checked by angles or abrupt curves; not that an occasional violation of this rule, where it is truly occasional, as in the Quadrant here, does not form, from its agreeable contrast, a beautiful and striking feature. And this leads us to the consideration of the cause of the apparent insignificance of London—the scarcity of continuous horizontal façades: each separate slice of our principal streets seems to pride itself upon its independence as a house, piled up like books of all sizes and all bindings on a library shelf; the elaborately decorated front, 60 feet frontage and the same in height, abuts upon a mean and narrow shop one-third the width, and with its parapet in line with its proud neighbour's first-floor windows—the chrysalis by the side of the gay butterfly, taunting it with its origin. A few continuous string-courses, ranging windows far apart, and a bold crowning cornice, give an effect of grandeur unattainable by far more extravagant superficial decoration. In our

* The following forms part of a paper read at the Architectural Association on Friday, the 30th ult.

quiet streets, too, there is the same character of exclusive meanness to each house. What strange pride it is to forego so much extra comfort, to pay double rent, and live in sordid shabby state, for the mere satisfaction of being dubbed a householder, paying rent and taxes and possessing unshared, unquestioned, the key of one's own street door! Let us not believe such is the selfish disposition of the Englishman; it is not the will, but only the opportunity he lacks. When he has seen more of his continental friends, he will not scorn to take a note from them, and adopt their far more rational, far more economical system of habitation. It is statistically a fact that 75 per cent. of London houses are inhabited by more than one family: built upon the narrowest frontage, the smallest of them must be still too large for many of the poorer house seekers; they divide it, and how awkward, how inconvenient this division,—the one kitchen and one entrance are the scenes of perpetual contests for precedence, till the one party falls into the position of the victimised and ever-grumbling lodger,—the other ranks as the grinding and exacting landlord; and yet the remedy for this is easy. The poor-law union of the present day boasts the façade of a palace, why should not the dwelling of the honest workman claim some share of beauty and architectural effect,—suites of rooms, neatly, plainly furnished, well drained, well ventilated, opening to public corridors, and occasional staircases, might be encased in a front truly palatial, and yet form a safer investment for the capital of its proprietor than the trumpery house property of the present day. And there is another advantage in this: all the London houses of the present day are built upon erroneous constructive principles; the ground-floor is necessarily the least subdivided by partitions, the first floor more so, and the second most so; consequently it is impracticable, without great expense, to construct these partitions, hanging over voids, fireproof, or even so far substantial that they should intercept the passage of sound; but when one range of chambers stand perpendicularly upon another these difficulties vanish, and the brick partition goes up cheaply, and solidly, to the roof.

London is yearly spreading wider the huge net of its entangled streets; one by one the fields and gardens of our suburbs merge into the brickfield, and soon into the little colony of villas: once the colony established, a market becomes its natural demand,—and it is the formation of this market that increases so visibly the size of London. The suburb, boasting its long rows of small but comfortable tenements, once the humble retreat of the retiring tradesman, in comparison with the colony beyond, soon loses its rustic reputation; the owner finds it his interest to seek more adventurous tenants, and one by one each house casts a proboscis forth, and in the shape of a long, low, narrow shop, covering the dull patch that once was dignified as the front garden, opens its greedy mouth to snatch the passing customer; and when in course of time each shop has thus stepped forth, the first has thrived so much that, taking down the little origin of all, he raises in its place another specimen of the gaudy compo-bedecked modern shop-front, and very soon the once wide foliated road becomes a narrow, money-grabbling street.

But London is already too extended for convenience or sociality; and it is with regret that we behold every fresh encroachment on the country round, unless, indeed, we could discover something superior to the slow, tedious system of communication of the present day. It were easy to imagine an Utopia of London, to build its river-terraces and palaces upon them, to project large thoroughfares for the relief of its over-crowded traffic, and to line them with public buildings, museums, and galleries of magnificent façades: but as easy in imagination so much the more impossible in execution; we must proceed in slower, surer steps—blunder no more over our public buildings—lose no opportunity of widening and straightening our streets—and, last of all, inculcate in the shop-keeper and petty landlord a sense of the advantage he will derive from the decorative improvement of his property; for it is useless to talk of art to those who regard as everything the world palpable and material, resolving itself to system, to interest, to calculation, and despise those who would preserve in it some worship of the beautiful and ideal, and interpret some few words of that mute language which so mysteriously connects the world invisible with the world revealed.

F. CHAMBERS, JUN.

NOTES IN THE PROVINCES.

THE exterior of the tower of Trinity Church, Colchester (a very early work), has been partly stripped of its old coat of plaster: but it has been found that some of the material of which it is built, is so decayed, that the plaster must either be restored or a more substantial repair subscribed for. "The building," says the *Chelmsford Chronicle*, "now stands half stripped and in a very doleful predicament."——The restorations in the parish church of Elsenham have been completed. The flat ceiling has been removed and the roof laid open from the interior. The pews have been replaced by benches with carved oak ends. The quaint old carved pulpit has been restored. The south porch, roofed to correspond with the church, has been renovated. The church and chancel floors have been laid with chequered Derbyshire tiles, black and red. These and other renovations have been made under the superintendence of Mr. Ollett, carver and builder, Norwich.——In laying down the water pipes at Boston, according to the *Lincolnshire Times*, the workmen have in several places met with the remains of the wooden pipes formerly used for the same purpose. Nothing is known of the time when these pipes were laid, but there can be but little doubt, it is thought, that more than 150 years have elapsed. The pipes appear to have been merely trunks of trees, hollowed in the centre, and made to fit into each other at the ends, where they were fastened together by some kind of cement.——Advertisements have been issued announcing the opening of a subscription for the restoration of Felmersham Church, Beds., at an estimated expense of 500*l*., independently of the chancel and those necessary substantial repairs which will be borne by parish rate.——Trinity Church, Penn, Bucks., was consecrated on 1st inst. It is in the decorated style and cruciform in structure, with nave, chancel, two transepts, and a central tower surmounted by a spire, in all 135 feet high. Mr. Perrey was the architect. The building has the advantage of a site on the verge of a large collection of beech trees, named Penn Wood. The east window, a decorated one, was presented by the Queen Dowager. There are also two other stained glass windows, executed by Mr. Willement, in the chancel.——Widley Church, Winchester, is about to be rebuilt in the Norman style, a sufficient sum (nearly 700*l*.) having been already subscribed. The architect is Mr. J. Colson, of Winchester, who, by the way, has just completed a school and master's house for Widley and Wymering, towards which Mr. T. Thistlewayte subscribed 300*l*.——A painted window in the chancel of Almondsbury Church, Gloucestershire, has just been put up by Mr. O'Connor, of Berners-street.——A stained glass east window has lately been placed in Wilton Church, near Taunton.——The temporary church, recently erected in the district of St. George, Kenwin, was opened on St. George's day. It is built of wood. The design is first-pointed, and consists of a chancel and nave, with sacristy on the south side. The exterior is plain. The dimensions are —Chancel, 19 feet by 20 feet; nave, 56 feet by 20 feet; height throughout 10 feet to the eaves, and 25 feet to the ridge. It will accommodate about 330 persons. The entire cost, we understand, will be, when completed, about 250*l*. The architect was Mr. White, of Truro.——On lately removing the floor within the altar-rails of Sithney Church, Cornwall, the old Norman font was discovered. This piece of antiquity will probably be restored to its original purpose.——The Vicar of Whitchurch Canonicorum, is to restore the parish church, which is a specimen of the architecture of twelfth century.——Mr. S. Hemming claims 382*l*. 17s. from the Birmingham workhouse authorities, as remuneration for his plan of the new workhouse, accepted by the late board.——A plan for an erection for shelter on the new landing stage at Liverpool, at an estimated cost of 1,000*l*., is about to be carried into execution. A portion of the building will be let off as a refreshment room, and so nearly redeem the interest on the whole expense.——In addition to the large hotels forming the crescent at Buxton, an extensive inn is in course of erection there on the site of the old Angel Inn. The corner stone was laid on 1st inst., in presence of Mr. S. Worth, of Sheffield, architect, and others. The elevation will form a frontage of 150 feet, in the richest Italian style.——An individual has just presented to St. Peter's Church, Derby, stained glass for the chancel window, which is of five lights, in the perpendicular style, and richly traceried.——A new church is about being erected at Derby on a portion of inclosed land formerly called Nunn Green. To judge from the plan, it will probably accommodate, without galleries, about 500 persons. Subscriptions are afloat for another new church, training-school, and national school, to each of which two gentlemen have handsomely contributed 100*l*. each, making 600*l*. A new entrance is about being formed to the Arboretum, at which a lodge will be erected. An extra room for the accommodation of visitors is also being built.——A portion of the foundation of the walls of the Victoria Dock entrance lock into the Humber has settled down into the ground, and until the water is again drawn off, the extent of the repair which will be needed cannot exactly be ascertained.——The works for a new congregational church to be built at Berwick were let on the 23rd ult. The building is to be erected under the superintendence of Mr. T. Oliver, architect, Sunderland. It is in the Early English style, and has a bell-turret on the west gable. The following is a list of the tenders, and a pretty specimen of estimating:—

1st class	£1,428	15	0
2nd ditto	1,134	0	4
3rd ditto	1,032	13	6
4th ditto	979	5	0
5th ditto	949	2	0
6th ditto	793	15	9

As the works were tendered for separately, and not in all cases by the same parties, the sums have been classified. The lowest estimates have not been accepted.

IRON HOUSES.

A CONSIDERABLE number of iron houses and warehouses have been lately shipped to California from Liverpool and other towns. One of these structures has just been erected by Messrs. Edward T. Bellhouse and Co., of Manchester, for Messrs. Pim and Roberts, who are proceeding to San Francisco.

The total length is 60 feet, the width 24 feet, the height to the eaves 10 feet, and to the ridge 17 feet. There is a partition of iron 15 feet from one end, forming a compartment for a dwelling-house; the remainder is for a warehouse, 45 feet by 24 feet. The foundation is formed by a strong framework of timber, upon which is screwed a moulded base of cast-iron, rising 6 inches. The uprights and principals of the roof are formed of wrought iron of the T section, the roof principals being strongly trussed. The plates, in lengths of 4, 5, and 6 feet, by 2 feet 6 inches in width, and ⅛ of an inch in thickness, are bolted to the uprights and to the principals of the roof by ⅜ bolts, and to each other by lap joints with bolts ¼ of an inch in diameter.

The doors are of wrought iron, framed with angle iron, and the windows and skylights are of cast-iron. The mode of construction, and the care taken in the execution of the work, make it a remarkably stiff and substantial edifice. This is an example of the celerity with which these erections can be fitted up, as the iron of which this house is made was received only a fortnight before the day of completion of the work.

VERY MODEST.—A petition has been presented to the House of Commons from certain parties, stating that great injury was done to the public morals in consequence of the objectionable character of some of the pictures in the National Gallery, and praying that the objectionable portions might be painted over or expunged.

DORIC PORTAL OF THE PALAZZO, SCIARRA COLONNA, ROME.

[A.D. 1603.]

PLAN.

DORIC PORTAL OF THE PALAZZO, SCIARRA COLONNA, ROME.

This fine doorway, which graces the façade of a simple but noble palace on the Corso, has been attributed to Vignola, but is more probably the work of Flaminio Ponzio, who, in 1603, was employed to build the palace. The great projection of the keystone is a peculiar feature, and the management of the triglyphs at the ends of the entablature is worth observation. Quatremère de Quincy, in his *Histoire des plus célèbres Architectes*, speaks of this doorway as one of the best examples of its class. The whole height is about 34 feet, and the width, from centre to centre of column, is 17 feet. The drawing was made on the spot by Mr. Lockyer.

Amongst the other works of Flaminio Ponzio are the great double staircase of the Quirinal Palace, and the restoration of the Church of St. Sebastian, beyond the walls.

A BLOW AT INTRAMURAL BURIALS.

WATERFORD—GLOUCESTERSHIRE.

THE following memorial has been signed by the leading medical men of Waterford :—

We, the undersigned, declare it to be absolutely necessary to the safety of the public, that no more interments should take place in the church-yards of this city. The state of them, and especially the older ones, is at once an outrage on public decency, as well as detrimental to the public health. In the cathedral churchyard, which is altogether uninclosed, and a public thoroughfare, as well as the resort during the night of bad characters, the earth is continually falling into the old graves, leaving passages or vents which lead to the remains deposited below, and serve for the escape of noxious gases ; and when the earth is thrown up to form fresh graves, it is found so loaded with animal matter, as to be actually offensive to the nose as well as eyes. In Olave's Churchyard, the bodies have of late years been deposited in tiers, above each other, just under the east window of the church, till they are within less than 3 feet of the surface, and

actually above the level of the ground within one or two yards adjacent ; whilst at certain periods, and in certain states of the atmosphere, a putrid smell can be distinctly perceived in the neighbourhood. John's and Patrick's Churchyards are in much the same state ; and we therefore submit, that it is the duty of every one, and especially of public bodies, to co-operate for the abatement of a nuisance so dangerous and disgraceful to our city.

In Gloucestershire, also, the medical men are bestirring themselves. Last week Mr. Mackinnon presented a petition to the House of Commons from the president and council of the Gloucestershire Medical and Surgical Association, representing a large body of practitioners. It sets forth,—

That your petitioners are of opinion that the interment of the dead in towns and populous districts is highly injurious to the public health, and that no measure of sanitary reform is complete unless this obnoxious system is at once and for ever abolished by legislative enactment.

That your petitioners cordially support the efforts

DESIGNS FOR KNOCKERS.

M. DUBAN, Architect.

AT THE HOTEL PORTALES, PARIS.　　　AT THE HOTEL ROTHSCHILD, PARIS.

now making by the "National Society for the Abolition of Burials in Towns," and they desire respectfully to add their testimony and influence as experienced medical practitioners, in aid of a measure at once politic and humane, and worthy of an advanced civilization.

DESIGNS FOR KNOCKERS.

THE accompanying engravings, from drawings made for us by Mr. Roussel, represent two metal knockers cast from the designs of M. Duban, architect, and put up in Paris. The first is at the residence of Count Portales, Rue Tronchet ; the second at the Hôtel Rothschild, in the Rue Laffitte. They are drawn one-third the real size.

DECORATIONS FROM ABROAD.

MARBLE PANEL FROM SAN MARCO, ROME.

THE church of San Marco (which immediately adjoins the Palazzo di Venezia) is said to have been founded as early as the fourth century. In 833 it was rebuilt by Gregory IV., but, with the exception of the tribune, and a few scattered fragments in the portico, there are now no remains of these earlier constructions. In 1468, the Palazzo di Venezia was built by Paul II. (a Venetian), and at the same time San Marco was entirely reconstructed ; the ancient tribune alone, on account probably of its fine mosaics, was suffered to remain.

The accompanying panel, which is in white marble, appears to have formed a portion of the enclosure to the presbytery of the church as rebuilt by Gregory. These enclosures (of which the most perfect example now remaining is in the church of San Clemente on the Esquiline) were usually richly decorated with sculptured marble panels, often inlaid with mosaic. The design before us might be successfully adapted to iron-work.

THE WELFARE OF WORKMEN.

WHEN, in the shape of abstract and impracticable theories on government, there are so many injurious influences operating to disturb the mind of that large and important section of the population called mechanics, it is gratifying to read such sound, practical remarks as those expressed in THE BUILDER, by your correspondent "An Old Mason." I am a working man myself, and feel deeply interested in any thing which will tend to the intellectual and moral advancement of my fellow workmen. I will, therefore, if you will

MARBLE PANEL, SAN MARCO, ROME.

allow me, strengthen his "assertion" that mechanics who are receiving 30s. per week may contrive to save a trifle out of that sum, which, in the course of a few years, would accumulate to something important. It is well known that in the country a carpenter, or mason, seldom gets more than 22s. per week, and yet I know many a man, with a wife and two or three children, who lives respectably and contrives to save a trifle out of that; and there are many young men who, with 20s. per week, save a sum which would scarcely be credited. But they are, of course, steady and economical; they are not addicted to morning drams, nor do they spend their evenings and Sundays in dissipation at the alehouse; and while you would see them attired with good and enduring apparel, you would not see in their dress an attempt to mimic the folly of some above them. Now, if my fellow-workmen would study the first principles of *economics* as well as "mechanics;" if they would see what they could do with, and what they could do without, they would find that their present wages (which, in my judgment, are not at all a just and equitable remuneration for their skill and labour) could be used, so as to put them in a much more respectable position than that in which too many, alas! are now to be found. That happiness which is sought ineffectually at the tavern, may certainly be found at the reading-room, or in the private study of those great principles which stamp the building art with such interest and importance. Self-culture, mental discipline, the development of the finer feelings of humanity, will doubtless make us better and happier men, if it will not make us better mechanics. It is only by making the best possible use we can of our present means that we can hope for a better future. Let our skill and intelligence, together with a high moral influence, solicit a more equitable adjustment of our time and wages, not—any farther than can be avoided—our poverty and destitution demand it. Of all reforms, individual reform is the most valuable, and is the surest and safest road to governmental reform.

A YOUNG CARPENTER.

BUILDERS' RIGHTS AND FOLLIES.

TENDERS, ST PETER'S CHURCH, CHESTER.

YOU will much oblige several individuals by inserting, in your valuable paper, the following note respecting the estimating for a new gallery, and three new windows, in St. Peter's Church, Chester, in the decision on which there is something too much savouring of unfairness, to be passed over unexplained. A number of respectable tradesmen were invited to give in tenders. The two lowest tenders were from first, a citizen of thirty-five years' standing, and, secondly, a builder who had done the whole of the carpenter's and joiner's work at the new station, and many other large works.

The last was invited by Mr. Harrison, the architect, who, unsolicited, sent him the plans and specification, desiring him to give a tender. He complied with the architect's request, and gave in an amount 27*l.* lower than the *accepted* tender. The public and the two lowest competitors are at a loss to account for such a digression from fair play. If the Committee have a surplus fund at their command, will there be any impropriety in allowing the unsuccessful competitors a fair remunerative per centage for their trouble, expense, and loss of time, in taking off the quantities, and estimating for the works?

TWO OF THE VICTIMS.

Amounts of the Tenders.

Blower	£320	0
Royle	239	0
Ingram	235	0
Hughes	230	0
Harrison	210	0
Bellis and Williams (accepted)	197	0
Wynn	178	10
Freeman	170	0

LOWTON CHURCH, LANCASHIRE.

To show the state of the contract system in the provinces, I beg to send you the following particulars. The parish church of Lowton (Lancashire) had to be painted outside, and papers were printed and distributed in four or five townships: the several estimates ran thus—

No. 1	£13	0	0
,, 2	9	6	0
,, 3	8	0	0
,, 4	7	0	0
,, 5	4	15	0

The lowest estimate was accepted.

There is much business done upon this principle: men who have nothing to lose compete with respectable tradesmen, send in one contract after another, always doing the work lower, and gain much trade in a short time. The system tells its own tale, and their goods are brought to the hammer, and yet there are those who will come forward, and will offer them sympathy, and say—"Poor fellow, he worked hard when he had it to do, but did not take sufficient care of himself, for we know he worked very low;" and they, under the impression that another body of men are "dear," employ this "cheap" man, and recommend him to their friends out of charity. What a pity but that they could see behind the scene, and find out the motives actuating such proceedings,—proceedings not only morally wrong and unjust, but dishonest! If the multitude acting upon the principle of "cheap work" would look a little to the private character, it might convince them that high chargers are not necessarily knaves, but that the very low chargers must be fools,—*i. e.* to work for less than it costs them,—or knaves, to use material for which they never intend to pay. This is no exaggerated case, but a simple every day fact, and one which I could illustrate by many examples that have come under my own eye.

A. B.

Estimates for the Leicester Cemetery, under Messrs. Hamilton and Medland.

Greenock, Leicester	£9.940
Booth, ditto	9,820
Wykes, ditto	8,575
Burton, London	8,294
Herbert, Leicester	7,700
Farrow, ditto	7,073
Norman, ditto	7,036
Clarke, Sheffield	6,806
Piper, London	6,930
Broadbent and Hawley, Leicester	6,651
Hull, Holland, and Smith, Leicester (accepted)	6,597

RAILWAY JOTTINGS.

THE returns called for by the House of Lords, on the motion of Lord Brougham, are to embrace a return of the share capital, dividends, costs, receipts, expenditure, and other accounts, of every railway in the three kingdoms, and will be the most comprehensive, searching, and complete exposure possible, so far, at least, as the order itself intends it to be. ——It is stated, in reference to the Eastern Counties accounts and investigations, that the sum of 62*l.* per share has been paid as dividends from 1845 to 1849, while the earnings applicable to dividends (nothing, however, having been allowed for wear and tear of locomotive stock,) have only reached 28*l.* per share for the same period of four years. Arrangements are said to be in progress for working this line by contract instead of by the Company itself, and it is alleged that the saving to the Company thus will be 90,000*l.* a-year.—— A letter, lately published, as to the doings of others than the noted prime mover of 'directors,' adds another argument in favour of an improved system of auditing railway accounts. One object of the writer is to show that shareholders are kept in ignorance of the real state of things until fresh calls for money become necessary; and that, as he contends, is the case with the Chester and Holyhead Company, their original capital is to be mortgaged, and even sacrificed, in favour of what are called "preference shares." He states that there has been a sytematic concealment of the amount required to complete the undertaking, and that the traffic and receipts are utterly insufficient to make any return on the original capital, while the directors are assuring the shareholders that the information they have received has "tended to establish the merits of the Chester and Holyhead Railway as an investment." The writer shows that 80 miles of the railway are open out of 84, and that the gap of 4 miles at the Menai-bridge is travelled by a well-appointed omnibus. "If, then, they do not [...] all the traffic they should, it is owing to c[...] causes than the so-called partial opening. [...] is because travellers go cheaper another [...] Now, credulous shareholders," he adds, "[...] to your liabilities, as swelled by gross [...] management. Capital required, 4,427,6[...] will require for interest 232,702*l.*, or upwar[...] 4,000*l.* per week;" while the total profits, he c[...]tends, are but 20,800*l.* per annum, or "4[...] per week to pay interest amounting to 4,0[...] per week." Among other charges against the [...]rectors he brings that of "deluding the sha[...]holders with the prospect of 6 per cent. d[...]dend on the original shares, whereas they [...] get no dividend at all."——The tender [...] Messrs. Abbot and Co., of the Gateshead P[...] Ironworks, for the cast and malleable ironw[...] required for the shed and roof of the cen[...] station in Newcastle has been accepted; also t[...] of Mr. C. J. Pearson, Gateshead, for the in[...] station at the eastern entrance to Newcast[...] and of Messrs. Wilson and Gibson, for [...] small station in Halfmoon-lane, Gateshead. On 28th ult., the ironwork of the High Le[...] Bridge was brought into connection from [...] to end. By 1st August, according to [...] *Gateshead Observer*, it will stand compl[...] ——The only unlet portion of the Dumfr[...] and Carlisle line was lately advertised for c[...]struction. The length embraced in th[...] contracts is stated to be about 14 miles, [...]tending from Old Cumnock to Sanquh[...] Great exertions are making to complete [...] line between Dumfries and Thornhill, and [...] contractor expects to have it ready for openi[...] in July next.——In East Lothian, such [...] the effects of the opened railways on farmi[...] that there is a rise of rent about 10 per ce[...] The railways enable the farmer to send [...] grain crops to Edinburgh to compete with t[...] farmers around the city; he is able to h[...] manure cheaper; the whole of his crops a[...] live stock can be sent at less expense to m[...]ket, and the live stock in much better con[...]tion. Mr. Smith, of Deanston, in his e[...]dence before the House of Commons, gives as his opinion that all good land from ten [...] fifty miles from a large town, on a line [...] railway, will be worth 10s. more per acre.

METROPOLITAN COMMISSION OF SEWERS.

A GENERAL court was held on Thursday, th[...] 3rd inst., at the Court-house, Greek-street, Soh[...] square; the Right Hon. the Earl of Carlisle in th[...] chair.

The Jurisdiction of the Commission.—A repo[...] was presented from the special committee ap[...]pointed to consider the conduct of John Merry, th[...] foreman of pumps and hose, who was suspended f[...] alleged misconduct in the use of that apparat[...] in Westminster, and who, for the nuisance occa[...]sioned, had been fined 10s. by Mr. Burrell, th[...] sitting magistrate. The committee now reporte[...] that they had fully investigated the subject, and th[...] the great balance of the evidence obtained was i[...] favour of Merry; that the temporary nuisance wa[...] occasioned by a defective hose, which was imme[...]diately replaced by a proper one; and that larg[...] quantities of the deodorising fluid were used in th[...] course of the operation. Therefore they recommende[...] that the order for his suspension should be with[...]drawn, and that he be restored to his employment.

Mr. Hertslet, the clerk, in reference to this sub[...]ject, reported, that since the last court a reque[...] having been received from Messrs. Evans, of Par[...]liament-street, for the relief of a cesspool on the[...] premises by the pump and hose,—on their servant[...] proceeding to the place with their apparatus, the[...] were seized by the authorities of St. Margaret'[...] parish, who expressed their determination to do s[...] on every occasion where it was used in the daytime[...] viz., before eleven o'clock at night, or after five [...] the morning.

Mr. Lawes said this subject had occupied th[...] attention of the Bye-Laws Committee, and the[...] thought that to give the court a greater probabilit[...] of success in their appeal against the magistrate'[...] conviction on this subject, they should make a bye[...] law in reference to it. If the court at present pos[...]sessed the power of cleansing cesspools in the day[...]time, that power would be strengthened by makin[...] the bye-law. The Public Health Act regulated th[...] time and manner of emptying cesspools, by day a[...] well as night, and it was highly necessary for th[...] public interests that the Sewers Commissioner[...] should exercise a similar power. He thought th[...] best course was to give notice of a bye-law, and a[...] the proper time to move its confirmation. He con[...]cluded by proposing a resolution to that effect.

Mr. Bullar seconded the motion.

Mr. Leslie remarked that, at a former court, he ad urged the necessity of the court giving a written uthority to their officers to cleanse a particular esspool. He considered the shortest way was the est way, as they could arrive at the point much uicker to try their right. The parish authorities aid they had no power, but he believed they were illy authorised under the 49th section; therefore he rged the court to make the order at once, and if he parties were dissatisfied, they could remove the uestion to the court of Queen's Bench. They ould make no bye-laws that were repugnant to the aws of this country, and without any, he believed hey had full power under the 49th section to order ny cesspool to be at once cleansed.

Mr. Grove said that a bye-law must be reasonable nd in conformity with the laws of the land; and what they were unable to do by their Act they could iot do by a bye-law. They could not take to themelves that power that Parliament did not give them. As he found a provision on this subject was conained in the Public Health Act, and was not in heir own, he thought the less they said upon the ubject the better.

Mr. Chadwick believed, if they were compelled o discharge their cesspools in the night-time, it vould occasion great additional expense upon the ate-payers. He thought they might stand by the easonableness of the order and of the bye-law.

The Earl of Carlisle suggested, as doubts had risen on this point, whether it would not be desirable to have the opinion of counsel as to whether it vas necessary to have a bye-law, or could the work be done without it. If there were doubts, he rusted they would not unnecessarily get into law, but do such works as were pressing by night, and n the meantime go to the Legislature for fresh powers in an alteration of the law.

The mover and seconder of the resolution expressed their readiness to withdraw the same, and the suggestion of the Earl of Carlisle was embodied in a resolution—"That, until further orders, all cesspools be cleansed at night." The resolution was unanimously adopted.

Public Conveniences.—On the motion of Mr. Bullar, the following resolution was carried:—"That the officers of this commission do report on the most eligible sites for public conveniences; and that they do place themselves in communication with the parochial officers for that purpose."

The Ordnance Survey.—A report was presented from the Ordnance Survey Committee, recommending that the maps of the three-mile radius of the survey, on the enlarged scale of 16 feet to the mile, should be engraved or lithographed, as the original plans would be greatly injured by frequent tracings.

Sir H. De la Beche produced a sheet on the enlarged scale, prepared, according to the order of the court, on the scale of 16 feet to the mile, executed by their own officers,—and a more beautiful work, he said, he had never witnessed. This work would be not of value alone to themselves, but would afford the greatest facility in all parochial matters for the supply of gas and water, and in the valuation of property. They would be no longer in the dark as to the fractional part of an inch, and could at once lay down, where desirable, drainage for any part of the metropolis. They would secure these enlarged plans at an extra expense of 1*l.* per acre, and that charge would be distributed over a series of years.

Mr. Chadwick said these plans would be very useful, even for the purpose of house-drainage.——Mr. Leslie expressed his entire approbation of the work.

Proposed Drainage for Jennings's Buildings, Kensington.—An elaborate report was presented to the court by Mr. Gotto, surveyor, on the state of the above locality, with a plan for its relief. This place is remarkable from the fact that, in January last, from the 17th to the 29th, twenty-two cases of cholera occurred, of which ten were fatal, many of the houses being very crowded, five or six persons occupying the same bed, and frequently two or three families the same room. This overcrowding would naturally predispose the inhabitants to cholera, yet, in addition to this evil, there was scarcely any drainage, producing atmospheric impurities inviting disease, and upon which it may be said to feed. This locality is occupied almost exclusively by the lower class of Irish, and its dangerous condition has been several times reported upon by Dr. Grainger to the Board of Public Health. Mr. Gotto proposed to lay down a drainage at an expense of 285*l.*, to be paid for by an improvement rate (the first application of this part of the new Act), spread over a period of twenty years, which would amount to only 4s. 4½d. per annum, or about 1d. per week per house.

This report led to a conversation, in which the Earl of Carlisle, Mr. Chadwick, Mr. Slaney, Mr. Leslie, and Mr. Bullar took part; when it was resolved, "That the recommendations of the surveyor as to works, improvement rate, &c., in Jennings's Buildings, Kensington, be received, and copies of the report be distributed among the owners and occupiers of the property."

It was agreed that separate sewerage districts be formed, under the 34th section, Lord Carlisle urging the necessity of measures being taken to prevent the further pollution of the Thames.

It was ordered that 800 feet of sewers be laid down in the main line of the Counter's Creek Sewer.

Books.

The Historic Lands of England. By J. B. Burke, Esq., author of the "Landed Gentry," &c. 2 vols. imp. 8vo. London, 1849. Churton.

This new and kindred effort of one already so well known as Mr. Burke is for his interesting labours in genealogy and other cognate subjects, is likely not only to sustain but to enhance his reputation as an antiquarian chronicler, while it also affords us evidence of other powers than those of a mere chronicler, the text being full of descriptive imagery, the well-told tale, the quaint quotation, and the poetic fragment of the olden time. That the author is deeply imbued with the right spirit for such a task, and that his labour is one of love, is evident. He chooses his subjects with discrimination, in general avoiding all that is not mellowed by historic interest,—no more allowing his course to be arrested by mere modern topics, "than the epicure," to use his own simile, "would pause in a well-filled wine-cellar on a pipe of new wine, when so many others of older vintage were demanding his attention." And many choice old tuns he taps. But, in the meantime, all that we can offer our readers is a sample of the introductory foretaste.

"The subject we have undertaken to illustrate," he with truth remarks, "is one of great national interest. There is scarcely a village or nook in England that has not its local tradition or historical association; and numerous, indeed, would be the volumes necessary to do justice to so important a theme. All we can attempt in the following pages is to afford a rapid glance at the more striking spots of this fair realm, around which the halo of departed greatness sheds a peculiar attraction; and to give a description of some of the most important 'historic lands,' referring, as copiously as our limits will permit, to the annals and ultimate fate of the various families which, in the course of time, succeeded to their possession, and enlivening the narrative with anecdotes and traditional reminiscences. If this endeavour be received with public favour, we hope, in subsequent annual volumes, to carry out the plan fully and completely; and thus to produce an amusing and comprehensive history of the celebrated estates of the kingdom."

The work is of course full of illustrations (some of which might be better), the type is clear and good, and with the general style of the 'getting up' of the book, does credit to the publishers.

Miscellanea.

Military, Naval, and County Service Club-house.—The club-house at the Piccadilly end of St. James's-street, formerly known (not *well* known) as "Crockford's," has been taken by a club of military, naval, and militia officers, and has been decorated and furnished in a costly manner. The walls of the library are sage-green, with the mouldings gilt; the drawing-room cream-colour, mouldings very heavily gilt (the old ceilings, also heavily gilt, remain); and the writing-room has a deep blue paper on the walls, cream-colour woodwork, and more gold mouldings. On the staircase, too, with very good marblings, it is gold, gold, gold; so that it might be thought, whether originally or now, that the tradesman, rather than the artist, had been the director of the works. The effect, nevertheless, is one of magnificence.

Emerson's Patent Mineral Paint.—Some who have used this "Patent Mineral Paint" in place of tar for outhouses, fences, &c., give it so good a character, that we are led to name it to those of our correspondents who have inquired for some such cheap material.

Mahogany.—On Friday a sale of Honduras mahogany took place at Birkenhead. It was well attended, and the spirit of competition ran high. One of the cargoes offered, and sold without reserve, realized the high average value of 8⅞d. per foot.

Electro-telegraphic Progress.—A gentleman formerly in the service of the Electro-telegraphic Company, who, he says, dismissed him in consequence of matters arising out of inventions of his which he calls "current deflectors," for the improvement, we presume, of the electric telegraph, has been lecturing of late against the electric telegraph altogether, and in favour of the hydraulic telegraph,—an invention, we believe, of Mr. Whishaw. The charges brought against the telegraph in ordinary use are, that it is liable to continual disarrangement and uncertainty from fluctuations in the galvanic circuit, and the interference of atmospheric and terrestrial electricity, producing oscillations and variations of the needles, so that "a certainty of accuracy is what cannot be attained so long as the letters of the alphabet are signalled as they now are." The evidence of this brought forward by the lecturer is said to have been very convincing. Perhaps, too, he might have adduced the costly practice of repeating messages without which the company are said to refuse to guarantee the accuracy of their transmission. It seems to be a grave question, however, whether on the whole the hydraulic telegraph would be a desirable substitute, even keeping in view the various other difficulties to contend with in the working of the electric, as also pointed out by the lecturer, such as accidents by high winds, breakage of posts, twisting of wires, and loading and derangement of same with hardened snow, &c.; or the complex arrangement of signals, and accidents in the use of the battery. The hydraulic telegraph, described by him, consists of two cylinders, one at each of two stations, connected by a water-tight tube. In each cylinder is a free moving piston surmounted by its rod, connected to which is the index or pointer, running up and down a graduated scale. That used by the lecturer was the complete alphabet of twenty-six letters, a sign for 'stop,' and the ten numerals. He pointed out how words were to be spelt and read off with scarcely the probability of error. It was also possible to represent entire words, and every letter might be used as a station signal. Modes of preserving the water from frost, and of ascertaining the point at which any accident may have occurred, and leakage taken place, were alluded to, and a patent for a plan by which he should be able to print, not, as by Mr. Brett, merely with marks in a straight line and requiring the assistance of several persons, but so as to be carried on, although no person was at the station to which the message was to be sent. He could also communicate with any number of stations, or select any particular one from the whole. He said the expense of the electro-telegraphic system, where the wires were suspended, had been about 260*l.* per mile, and was now, he believed, about 200*l.*,—cost of street work, 616*l.* The hydraulic system, however, would only cost 60*l.* per mile, and would not be a suspension but a subterranean plan.

Speedy Suppression of Fire in a Coal Mine.—The proprietor of a mine near Manchester describes, in the *Times*, the means whereby Mr. Goldsworthy Gurney has lately effected this important object. In place of either shutting up the mine and keeping it so for months, sometimes for years, and but too often after all unavailingly, or filling it with water at an enormous loss,—Mr. Gurney, by means of a furnace, tank, cylinders, and other apparatus, filled the mine and its galleries and lateral workings, three miles in length, with carbonic acid and nitrogen gases, or, almost literally, with choke damp,—completely extinguishing all vestige of fire. An equal quantity of fresh air was then thrown in by help of the same apparatus, and the choke damp thus expelled, and the mine so well ventilated, and rid of fire-damp as well as choke damp, that in two days from the commencement of the operations the miners were at work throughout the mine with naked candles! It is "a public remedy for a national loss," as remarked by the grateful owner of the mine in which this invention has been thus for the first time so successfully tested. And henceforth "the mineral property of the kingdom has been insured against the destructive element of fire." Our readers will remember a suggestion to this effect, as referring to ships, discussed some time ago in our pages.

PROJECTED WORKS.—Advertisements have been issued for tenders,—by 19th inst., for the erection of a district church in Brompton, Middlesex; by 21st inst., for the erection of a new vicarage-house, &c., at St. Neot's, Huntingdonshire; by 21st inst., for building 800 feet of brick sewer at Notting-hill; by 16th inst., for sinking a well, and other works, in High-street, Norton-tolgate; by 28th inst., for the erection of an engine-house, boiler-house, &c., at the water-works, Stone Ferry, near Hull; by 28th inst., for the construction and erection of pipes and fittings for the baths and wash-houses now building in Treppet-street, Kingston-upon-Hull; by 21st inst., for the erection of additional buildings at Hambledon Workhouse; by 24th inst., for the supply of granite, gravel, &c. to the parishes of St. Giles-in-the-Fields and St. George's, Bloomsbury; by a date not specified, for the erection of a chapel at Gunthorpe, in connection with the parish of Lowdham, Nottingham; by 17th inst., for repairs to Middle-bridge, Romsey Infra; by same date, for executing certain works at various public building in Southampton; and by 16th, for the supply of British iron, bellows, &c., for the East-India Company.

COMPETITION.—Premiums of 15l. and 10l. are offered for the two best plans for repewing that portion of Northfleet Church, Kent, at present pewed, and pewing that portion not hitherto pewed.

INSTITUTION OF CIVIL ENGINEERS.— On the 8th inst., the discussion on Mr. Crampton's paper, "On the Construction of Locomotive Engines," was continued, without arriving at any definite result, other than that it was desirable in all engines to lower the centre of gravity, in order to establish a great angle of stability, and to arrive at a ratio between the circumference of the driving-wheel and the cubic content of the cylinders, such as whilst the greatest speed might be maintained with an economical consumption of fuel, every facility should be afforded for starting rapidly. A short paper was read, describing a kind of permanent way, which had been somewhat extensively laid down on the Lancashire and Yorkshire, and other railways, in the north of England, by Mr. Hawkshaw. The principle was that of a bridge rail, weighing seventy-five pounds per yard, placed upon continuous longitudinal timber bearing, and the novelty consisted in having at each joint a malleable iron plate chair, with a projection on the upper surface, fitting within the interior of the rail, and the flanches, which were fourteen inches long by eight inches wide, and half an inch in thickness, attached to the rail by rivets in such a manner as to fix them firmly together, and yet to allow for the expansion and contraction caused by the variations of temperature. The paper announced to be read at the next meeting of Tuesday, May 15th, was "On the Theory of Transverse Strain of Cast-iron Beams," by Mr. W. T. Doyne.

FREEMASONS OF THE CHURCH.—A meeting of this institution was held on May 8th, the Rev. George Pocock, Vice-President, in the chair. Mr. W. H. Rogers exhibited two elaborately carved boxwood friezes executed by his father for her Majesty the Queen; also a curious ancient vase of "faience de Nevers" and a Byzantine figure of the Blessed Virgin, of the 12th century, both the property of Messrs. Falcke, together with an enlarged drawing, taken by himself, from the coronet of the figure, showing the care and taste which in the middle ages were expended on the minute details of works intended for sacred use. Mr. C. H. Smith offered some observations on the great importance, for the sake of truth, of preserving all records of date or origin which may attach themselves to such relics as the figure contributed by Messrs. Falcke, and urged it as the duty of the society to inquire into the histories of any similar objects exhibited at its chapters. Mr. G. R. French then delivered a discourse on "Roman Architecture."

A VALUABLE PICTURE has been discovered at Leeds, according to the local *Intelligencer*, in one long deemed valueless. It is said to be one of Gerard Lairope's. The subject (the Abduction of Ariadne, by Bacchus), consists of twenty-two figures, grouped and painted in the manner of Nicholas Poussin.

BRICK DUTIES.—I was glad to see, in a late number, the smallness of the amount received from the duty on bricks. I hope that it will induce the Government to relinquish the duty as early as possible, as it causes the bricks to be twice the price they would be if free from duty, and prevents persons making them where they intend building, which would be done in many cases if it could be done without having the exciseman to contend with, which few men with small capital choose to risk. I have many times carted brick-earth away from places where there has been a basement story with cellars to the buildings, and had bricks brought 70 miles, by water, besides having to pay for unloading, cartage, &c., which cause great waste of time and materials. We know that it is the wish of most persons to improve the condition of the working man, and many plans have been mentioned as likely to do so: I know of no step so likely to do this as the repeal of this duty, as we know that most of the working classes are laudably anxious to have a house of their own, and would exert themselves every way to get one, which is proved by the number of building societies established amongst us. It would also benefit the ground landlords very materially, by causing land now letting as grass land for 5l. or 6l. per acre to be worth 50l. or 60l. per acre, besides the reversion, which would be the case if the cost of building was lowered, as it would enable persons to make roadways to ground lying a distance from the public roads. It would also give scope to the enterprise of our industrious middle classes, and instead of calling upon them to leave the land of their birth to improve other lands, they might benefit their own.—* * *

EXCISE INFORMATION AGAINST A BRICK-MAKER.—On Wednesday, at the Wolverhampton Public Office, before John Leigh, G. B. Thorneycroft, and John Barker, Esqrs., Mr. John Guest, brickmaker, of West Bromwich, was charged by Mr. Coomber, Supervisor of Excise, with wilfully concealing about 7,000 bricks, with intent to defraud her Majesty's revenue. Besides the penalty, the information sought a forfeiture of upwards of 20,000 bricks, which were alleged to have been used in concealing the 7,000. The magistrates, however, did not consider the proof on this point sufficient to warrant them in declaring the bricks to be forfeited, and after hearing Mr. T. M. Whitehouse for the defence, fined the defendant in the mitigated penalty of 25l.

INSTITUTION OF MECHANICAL ENGINEERS.—The general meeting of the members of this institution was held in the theatre of the Birmingham Philosophical Institution on Wednesday week, Mr. Robert Stephenson, M.P., the newly-appointed president, in the chair. Mr. Baines, of Norwich, entered into explanations relative to his improved railway chairs and switches. A paper by Mr. Weallens, of Newcastle, "On an Express Locomotive Engine" was read, and was followed, as some of the other papers were, by a lengthened discussion. A paper, by Mr. Henry Smith, of West Bromwich, "On a new Solid Wrought-iron Wheel," was then read, and a vote of thanks accorded. The next paper was "On the Construction of Permanent Way," by Mr. Hoby, of Brighton. "A paper, by Mr. Ramsbottom, of Manchester, "On an Improved Locomotive Boiler," was postponed till next meeting. A number of new members were ballotted for and elected.

BRIDGEWATER CHURCH COMPETITION.— I observe in a retired page of your journal, which sometimes does not in the far west reach us till three or four days after publication,* an extension of time in Bridgewater Church competition. Being one of the parties who hurried his plans in by May 1, I naturally demand what is the use of this public advertisement on the 5th, unless to advantage some favoured individual. The time given was ample, even for designing a new church. Pray, Mr. Editor, plead for fair play for us in that voice wherewith you are wont to espouse the cause of competing architects generally, and for which you have the cordial thanks of yours faithfully, A GREAT WESTERN.

* This is the fault of the parties through whom it is obtained.—ED.

SANITARY INQUIRY AT BIRMINGHAM Mr. Rawlinson proceeded on Monday week complete his adjourned inquiry, as survey inspector for the Board of Health. Vari parties were heard as to local nuisances, an discussion took place as to boundaries. T state of the Worcester Canal and its vicin was complained of, and Mr. Beilby blan "parties so indiscreet as to take land at a hi price for building purposes, without requir the owner to make any provision for draining A deputation from the new board of guardi attended. The inspector, in asking for retur &c. from them, observed that as we had carr our civilisation so far as to take good care our paupers and criminals, the Board of Hea would now take good care of those who we honest. The inquiry itself was formally clos on Wednesday, but during the rest of t week Mr. Rawlinson was engaged in a perso inspection of the town and outlying haml more especially with a view to determine t boundaries within which the Sanitary Act sh be brought into operation.

SALE OF WORKS OF ART AT ROME. It is said that upwards of 40 boxes, containi sacred vases, marbles, statues, and pictur have been sequestered by the French custo office. These articles were purchased at Ro by an association of German Jews, formed Frankfort, under the direction of M. Bruck The advantageous terms on which M Francis Warton had obtained the Virg and Angels of Benvenuto Cellini had excit the cupidity of all the merchants of works art. The catalogue of articles sold by t Revolutionary Government of Rome amoun it is said, to 2,500; they only produc 3,000,000l., although worth 10,000,000l. least. Their restitution will not be easi effected, though the names and addresses of t buyers are inscribed on the margin of th catalogue.

IMPORTANT TO HOUSE-AGENTS.—At N Prius, before the Chief Baron, a case was r cently tried which mainly turned on the fa that the plaintiff, proprietor of a furnishe house to let, while employing a house-agent also made personal inquiries as to the suffi ciency of the means of a tenant, and expresse herself satisfied; on which the agent, afte also making inquiries, let the house. It shortl afterwards appeared that the tenant was in solvent, and had even been in confinemen immediately previous to the letting. Plainti therefore claimed compensation for neglect o the part of defendant; but the judge appeare to be of opinion that the plaintiff was quit out of court, having inquired herself, and th jury returned a verdict for the defendant.

GUILDFORD DRAINAGE PLANS.—Afte long hesitation, the various plans for th drainage of Guildford, sent in competitio were submitted by the Committee to Professo Hosking for examination, to assist them i making the award. It will be seen by a advertisement that three plans have bee selected for final consideration, marke "Pioneer," "Specula," and "C. Engineer."

MEETINGS OF SCIENTIFIC BODIES

Held during the ensuing week.

TUESDAY, May 15th.—Institution of Civil Engineers, P.M.

WEDNESDAY, 16th.—Society of Arts, 8 P.M.

THURSDAY, 17th.—Society of Antiquaries, 8 P.M.

TO CORRESPONDENTS.

Received.—" J. B.," Brewer-street (there are no lectures going on now at the Society of British Artists), " G. B.," " W. T.," " " Subscriber from the First " (expenses in lay- ing first stone should be paid by the employer)," T. H. ," " A Thinker," " Spec.," " J. B., Newark (we are led believe with an appeal would not be agreeable to the cities)," " M. P." " C. W. O.," " Cosmopolitan " (we are liable to comply)," " E. A.," " M. P.," " A Baronet," " S.," " J. J.," " C. N.," " H. B." (Paddington), Mr. John Tombs, of Millbank, requests us to state that it was who tendered for Brentford Market-house.

"*Books, Prices, and Addresses.*"—We have not time to point out books or find address a.

NOTICE.—All communications respecting *advertisements* should be addressed to the " Publisher," and not to the " Editor;" all other communications should be addressed to the EDITOR, and *not* to the Publisher.

HART and SONS beg to invite the attention of architects, builders, and others, to their Door Furniture, mounted for PITT'S PA-TENTED SPINDLES. The knobs are stronger, more durable, and more elegant in form, than those in ordinary use, as they seldom, being loose, do not require the objectionable side screw. They are more readily fixed, are suitable for every description of lock now in use, and, as they adjust themselves to doors of different thickness, without interference, are particularly adapted for the country or for exportation. They are made for suit every style of depression) in China, dry-flat, amber, and opal glass, buffalo, horn, ivory, glazed, brass, &c., en suite with finger-plates, bell-pulls, levers, &c.—May be obtained of all ironmongers; or of the proprietors and sole manu-facturers, HART and SONS, Wholesale Ironmongers, 53, 54, and 55, Wych-street, Strand, London.
N.B. PITT'S PATENT SPINDLE, being the only one that does not require a screw in the side of the knob or mounting, the use of any lock furniture without such side screws would be an infringement of the patent.

No. CCCXXVIII.

SATURDAY, MAY 19, 1849.

HE announcement of a new book on architecture by Mr. Ruskin, the author of "Modern Painters," at first known only as "an Oxford Graduate," has, doubtless, excited the curiosity of such of our readers as are acquainted with the latter remarkable and interesting work. Mr. Ruskin has long given attention to the picturesque in architecture. He wrote the series of papers "On the Poetry of Architecture," signed *Kata Phusin,* in *Loudon's Magazine* (if we remember rightly), and we anticipated much gratification in the perusal of his more extended observations and matured opinions.

The volume has come into our hands too recently for a careful examination of all the writer's views on the present occasion, and we must content ourselves mainly with giving some idea of the contents of it.

The title is a taking one,—"The Seven Lamps of Architecture."* It sounds romantic, recalls Aladdin, and, moreover, is not at once understood, and so whets curiosity. What *are* these lamps? say many:—they are lamps which, of themselves, throw no light on the author's meaning. Let us give them some oil. The author's endeavour has been to extricate from the confused mass of partial traditions and dogmata with which the art of architecture has become encumbered, those large principles of right which are applicable to every stage and style of it,—to determine, as the guides of every effort, some constant and general laws of right, based upon man's nature, and not his knowledge. To do this would indeed be something. "Their range," he says, "necessarily includes the entire horizon of man's action. But they have modified forms and operations belonging to each of his pursuits, and the extent of their authority cannot surely be considered as a diminution of its weight. Those peculiar aspects of them which belong to the first of the arts, I have endeavoured to trace in the following pages; and since, if truly stated, they must necessarily be, not only safeguards against every form of error, but sources of every measure of success, I do not think that I claim too much for them in calling them the Lamps of Architecture."

And thus the author names them,—The lamp of Sacrifice, the lamp of Truth, the lamp of Power, the lamp of Beauty, the lamp of Life, the lamp of Memory, and the lamp of Obedience; or, as they stand on the cover of the book, *Religio, Observantia, Auctoritas, Fides, Obedientia, Memoria,* and *Spiritus.* From this the tone of the work may be pretty correctly guessed at; this is a brick from which the character of the house may be judged.

Enthusiasm, strong convictions, and high religious feelings, mark the work; and though we are disposed to think they have carried the author in parts out· of the regions of plain sense, claim attention and consideration. He enters upon the task almost solemnly; says the aspect of the year is full of mystery, the

---

weight of evil against which we have to contend, increasing like the letting out of water, and that it is no time for the idleness of metaphysics, or the entertainment of the arts. There is no action so slight that may not be done to a great purpose, nor any purpose so great but that slight actions may be so done as to help it much, "especially that chief of all purposes, the pleasing of God." To the strength of this motive, desire to please God, he attributes the excellence of the mediæval structures; on this ground he calls for "the offering of precious things, merely because they are precious, not because they are useful or necessary," and condemns, as others have done before him, the "nicely calculated less or more," in church building. It is not the church we want, but the sacrifice; not the emotion of admiration, but the act of adoration; not the gift, but the giving." Without advocating meanness in our own dwellings, he would get rid of "cornicings of ceilings and graining of doors, and fringing of curtains, and thousands such; things which have become foolishly and apathetically habitual—things on whose common appliance hang whole trades, to which there never yet belonged the blessing of giving one ray of real pleasure, or becoming of the remotest or most contemptible use,—things which cause half the expense of life, and destroy more than half its comfort, manliness, respectability, freshness, and facility." And he says that "the tenth part of the expense which is sacrificed in domestic vanities, if not absolutely and meaninglessly lost in domestic discomforts and incumbrances, would, if collectively offered and wisely employed, build a marble church for every town in England; such a church as it should be a joy and a blessing even to pass near in our daily ways and walks, and as it would bring the light into the eyes to see from afar, lifting its fair height above the purple crowd of humble roofs. I have said for every town: I do not want a marble church for every village; nay, I do not want marble churches at all for their own sake, but for the sake of the spirit that would build them."

The two conditions which he considers enforced by the spirit of sacrifice, are, first, that we should in everything do our best; and, secondly, that we should consider increase of apparent labour as an increase of beauty in the building.

"For the first: it is alone enough to secure success, and it is for want of observing it that we continually fail. We are none of us so good architects as to be able to work habitually beneath our strength; and yet there is not a building that I know of, lately raised, wherein it is not sufficiently evident that neither architect nor builder has done his best. It is the especial characteristic of modern work. All old work nearly has been hard work. It may be the hard work of children, of barbarians, of rustics; but it is always their utmost. Ours has as constantly the look. of money's worth, of a stopping short wherever and whenever we can, of a lazy compliance with low conditions; never of a fair putting forth of our strength."

The extent to which the author would carry this out is shown by his remark, "that whenever, by the construction of a building, some parts of it are hidden from the eye which are the continuation of others bearing some consistent ornament, it is not well that the ornament should cease in the parts concealed; credit is given for it, and it should· not be deceptively

---

withdrawn: as, for instance, in the sculpture of the backs of the statues of a temple pediment; never, perhaps, to be seen, but yet not lawfully to be left unfinished."

It is scarcely necessary to say that all imitations and architectural deceits are denounced, as positive sin: and though we do not view the question in quite so serious a light (we have more than once fully argued the subject), we go with him when he says,

"For, as I advocated the expression of the Spirit of Sacrifice in the acts and pleasures of men, not as if thereby those acts could further the cause of religion, but because most assuredly they might therein be infinitely ennobled themselves, so I would have the Spirit or Lamp of Truth clear in the hearts of our artists and handicraftsmen, not as if the truthful practice of handicrafts could far advance the cause of truth, but because I would fain see the handicrafts themselves urged by the spurs of chivalry; and it is, indeed, marvellous to see what power and universality there is in this single principle, and how in the consuiting or forgetting of it lies half the dignity or decline of every art and act of man."

We may convey·our author's opinion on the limits of license, by saying that if graining be so ill done that no one can mistake it for the wood it represents, it is lawful, but if so good as to deceive it is illegal and a lie!

The use of cast work he considers a downright and inexcusable falsehood. "You use that which pretends to a worth which it has not, which pretends to have cost, and to be, what it did not, and is not: it is an imposition, a vulgarity, an impertinence, and a SIN. Down with it to the ground—grind it to powder," &c. &c. Down with it to the ground if you like, when you can put something better in its place. We have no love for cast work, generally speaking; but we cannot afford to give it up altogether, and as to calling it a *sin* (except in many cases against good taste and propriety), we would not venture on such a step.

No one is ever deceived into taking "compo" for stone: it is exactly what it seems to be —"compo," and (like Wordsworth's yellow primrose) nothing more. It has many sins to answer for; but still it would not be wise to give it up.

The use of cast-iron he considers one of the most active causes in the degradation of our national feeling for beauty.

In designing, the author thinks light and shade the great points to be considered: "after size and weight, the Power of architecture may be said to depend on the quantity (whether measured in space or intenseness) of its shadow;" and he urges, that among the first habits that a young architect should learn, "is that of thinking in shadow, not looking at a design in its miserable living skeleton; but conceiving it as it will be when the dawn lights it, and the dusk leaves it."

No matter how common or clumsy the means,—so that shadow be got, our author is satisfied; he seems to attach little value to the beauty resulting from proportion, fitness, and propriety;—he finds charms only in the massive, the rude, or the ruined.

In treating of beauty, Mr. Ruskin, insisting on the fact that "all most lovely forms and thoughts are directly taken from natural objects," assumes the converse of this, namely, "that forms which are *not* taken from natural objects *must* be ugly," and then attacks the Greek fret, on grounds which cannot be admitted as valid. He says, —"The first so-called ornament, then, which I would attack is

---

* "The Seven Lamps of Architecture." By John Ruskin, author of "Modern Painters." London, Smith, Elder, and Co. 1849.

that Greek fret, now, I believe, usually known by the Italian name Guilloche (!), which is exactly a case in point. It so happens that in crystals of bismuth, formed by the unagitated cooling of the melted metal, there occurs a natural resemblance of it almost perfect. But crystals of bismuth not only are of unusual occurrence in every-day life, but their form is, as far as I know, unique among minerals; and not only unique, but only attainable by an artificial process, the metal itself never being found pure. I do not remember any other substance or arrangement which presents a resemblance to this Greek ornament; and I think that I may trust my remembrance as including most of the arrangements which occur in the outward forms of common and familiar things. On this ground, then, I allege that ornament to be ugly; or, in the literal sense of the word, monstrous; different from any thing which it is the nature of man to admire: and I think an uncarved fillet or plinth infinitely preferable to one covered with this vile concatenation of straight lines: unless indeed it be employed as a foil to a true ornament, which it may, perhaps, sometimes with advantage; or excessively small, as it occurs on coins, the harshness of its arrangement being less perceived."

First, the fret is not known as the *guilloche:* the two are quite distinct, the latter being no "concatenation of straight lines" at all ("vile" or otherwise), whatever the fret may be.

The fret, our readers will scarcely need to be told, is formed of one or more fillets meeting each other *vertically* and *horizontally*, whereas the Guilloche is formed by two or more bands twisting over each other so as to repeat the same curved figure by the spiral returning of the bands.

Passing over this, however, are all geometrical patterns to be condemned as "monstrous," if not taken from natural objects and composed of curves?

Architecture, as the author is forced to admit, deals necessarily with straight lines, and with forms which have no precedent in nature.

Mr. Ruskin lays down as "a law of singular importance in the present day, that we are not to decorate things belonging to purposes of active and occupied life." "Wherever you can rest, there decorate; where rest is forbidden, so is beauty." Adorned shop-fronts are abominations in his eyes; and as to railroad stations,—but let him speak for himself:—

"Another of the strange and evil tendencies of the present day is to the decoration of the railroad station. Now, if there be any place in the world in which people are deprived of that portion of temper and discretion which are necessary to the contemplation of beauty, it is there. It is the very temple of discomfort, and the only charity that the builder can extend to us is to show us, plainly as may be, how soonest to escape from it. The whole system of railroad travelling is addressed to people who, being in a hurry, are therefore, for the time being, miserable. No one would travel in that manner who could help it—who had time to go leisurely over hills and between hedges, instead of through tunnels and between banks: at least those who would, have no sense of beauty so acute as that we need consult it at the station. The railroad is in all its relations a matter of earnest business, to be got through as soon as possible. It transmutes a man from a traveller into a living parcel. For the time he has parted with the nobler characteristics of his humanity for the sake of a planetary power of locomotion. Do not ask him to admire any thing. You might as well ask the wind. Carry him safely, dismiss him soon: he will thank you for nothing else. All attempts to please him in any other way are mere mockery, and insults to the things by which you endeavour to do so. There never was more flagrant nor impertinent folly than the smallest portion of ornament in any thing concerned with railroads or near them. Keep them out of the way, take them through the ugliest country you can find, confess them the miserable things they are, and spend nothing upon them but for safety and speed."

We have great respect for our author; his eloquence and earnestness in parts have warmed and delighted us: but we cannot avoid saying that, to our poor comprehension, this last paragraph is simply nonsense.

THE ROYAL ACADEMY EXHIBITION.

Such an exhibition as the present ought to prove a source of gratification to all interested in the progress of British art. Each successive visit brings fresh conviction of its excellence. Notwithstanding the observable absence of Maclise, and the weakened efforts of Etty, no other nation could produce in a collection of the year so large a number of works of art of such pretensions. High art is ably supported by Mr. Herbert and a few others this year, whilst the poetry of Messrs. Stanfield and Danby's noble landscapes, and the intense feeling and elevated intention so elaborately yet graphically worked out by Mr. E. M. Ward, in his picture of "De Foe," almost entitle them to be considered in the same category. A feeling seems obviously to have arisen that *a dip* into past catalogues, or a selection from the old *repertoire* of subjects, will no longer pass current with the public, who are becoming *discerning*.

Amongst the strictly historical pictures, Mr. Egg, A. (8), "Henrietta Maria in distress, relieved by Cardinal de Retz," has high claims to praise; in fact, as far as colour and painting are to be considered, it is perfectly wonderful, but the conception of the desolate queen does not please us. The same artist has another extraordinary picture for colour and execution, evidently founded on Paul Veronese,—(473), "Launce's substitute for Proteus's dog." Mr. Egg exhibits painstaking and research in all his productions, in these last particularly, and great power over the mechanical part of the profession.

(13) "The Desert,"—a dead lion, painted with Landseer's sweeping pencil, has not that charm which belongs to the majority of this artist's work. Through accident, portraits of M. Guizot and Prince Metternich form pendants on either side of this dead representative of royalty. (23) "Religious Controversy in the time of Louis XIV.," A. Elmore (A.), is a work of art creditable to any age, characterized by qualities of the highest order. The head of the Protestant clergyman,—indeed, the whole figure,—is finely conceived; the composition of the heads to the right of the spectator, strikingly beautiful; and the drapery of the cardinal, to the left, is painted in a masterly manner. The figure of the boy whispering to the gorgeously-attired lady, and, amongst the accessories, the table-cloth and carpet, with the back ground generally, exhibit great facility and knowledge. (378) Subject from Tristram Shandy, out of the artist's way, is not equal to some other productions; whilst (471) "Lady Macbeth," though melodramatic and exaggerated, is an extraordinary piece of painting. (43) "Omnia Vanitas," W. Dyce, R.A., represents a female in the zenith of her charms, with a skull on which her hand is resting. It is beautifully painted: the drawing of the arm seems questionable.

(60) "Amoret Chained," by Etty, R.A., may not be compared with former works by this master; nevertheless the flesh tints are scarcely to be surpassed. (72) "Lear Disinheriting Cordelia," by J. R. Herbert, R.A., in progress in fresco in the new Houses of Parliament, is wonderfully grand in treatment, and brings back to memory some of the past great ones. Such a production is an honour to the time. The austere old king, devoid of strained exaggeration, presents the crown to the already struggling and quarrelling husbands of Goneril and Regan; whilst the dutiful and ill-treated Cordelia stands regardless of personal loss, half conscious of her father's impending fate, heedless of the honest Kent's remonstrating at the king's injustice and blind credulity.

A picture on a loftier theme (489), "T Outcast of the People," by the same paint is still more elevated in its character, a may almost be called sublime.

A covetable and delicious picture is (10 "The Forester's Family," by E. Landseer, R.. A lovely heather belle feeding fawns, th assemble around her with all their chara teristic half-timidity and half-confidence, ru bing the fodder she is loaded with, whil others are trotting up to receive the accu tomed caress from the well-known hand. T upper part of the girl's figure seems somewh small for the size of her feet and length limb. (196) "The Free Church" is anoth beautiful contribution by the same painter; t head of the girl in this is a sweet study of brunette. (127) "The Syrens Three," W. Frost, (A.), is scarcely up to the usual mark notwithstanding its many excellences ar beauties, whether from its being in juxt position with Mulready, it looks blacke than usual, and cold compared to the luminou back view (135) "Women bathing." M Mulready in this walks out of his beaten path t exhibit his proficient knowledge of art in a its branches. Perfect drawing and close ob servance of natural action are the most appa rent qualities of this masterpiece,—a sever lesson to the student of the nude figure.

Professor Leslie produces a picture fro his favourite "Don Quixote," wherein his taste humour, learning, and the apparent ease wit which he works pre-eminently shine forth.

(141) "The Duke's Chaplain, after attackin Don Quixote for his devotion to knigh errantry, and Sancho for his belief in hi master, reprimands the Duke for encouragin their fancies, and leaves the company in passion." The expression of extreme disgus and contempt of the choleric chaplain, th refined mirth of the duchess, the ill-conceale laughter of the duke, the affronted dignity o the chivalric knight, and the astonishment o Sancho, are rendered with astonishing truth, whilst the suppressed risibility of the domestics inclines the spectator to wait until they gave vent, so truthfully is it portrayed. Mr. Leslie is the leader in *genre* painting, and has made Cervantes and Le Sage almost his own by strictly working out their texts. A smaller picture from Henry VIII., by the same painter (55), is a genuine embodiment of Shakspeare.

THE ARCHITECTURAL ROOM.*

(1015) "Private chapel and cemetery recently erected at Carnsallock," by E. B. Lamb, is designed with Mr. Lamb's usual propriety. It is decorated in style; and the pointed arch over the doorway is filled with tracery, and serves as a window. The same architect exhibits "The selected design for the Judges' Lodgings, about to be erected at Aylesbury," a plain substantial building of brick, in appearance as close upon a prison as a judge is to a prisoner. (1021) and (1022), two interiors of "Ormond Quay New Church, Dublin," are perfect abominations. On what grounds they were admitted, to the exclusion of better things, and moreover placed in one of the best situations, it is difficult to guess. (1038) "Design for the Normal College, Swansea" (to which the second premium was awarded), by R. A. Potter, is Tudor in character and not without merit. The title of (1043) "Proposed Foundation of an Archway in the front of St. Benet, Gracechurch-street," by E. I'Anson, jun., seems scarcely a right description, if the drawing show, as we understand it to do, the alteration proposed to be made in the lower part of the tower itself, so as to admit of a public passage-way through the side and front of it, for the improvement of the thoroughfare. Mr. I'Anson has a second drawing, "The Front of the Branch Office of the Argus Life Office, Pall-mall" (1118).

(1044) "Meanwood Church, erected near Leeds," by W. Railton, is Early English, with high-pitched roof, and of better character than some of this architect's other works in the same style. (1064) "The New Chapel of Ripon Palace," by the same, is Perpendicular, and includes carved throne, reading-desk, and altar rail. (1050) "South-east View of a Design, *Celsus*, for the Small-pox Hospital," by G. Low, represents a building which is exhibited in another part of the room as by R. H.

* See p. 217, *ante*.

ihout (1,148): it is Elizabethan, with *ortile;* has a square turret at each end, ctagonal lantern in the middle, and two projecting buildings in centre of the long front, vith entrance gateway between them.

(1060) "The Terrace now erecting at Windsor, on the road to Ascot," by S. S. Teulon, s of Tudor design (with range of gables), and red brick construction. (1103) "Schools recently erected in the Village of Roby, Lincoln," and (1161) "Schools recently erected at Elvetham Park, Hants," are by the same architect and in the same style, cleverly treated. (1073) "A Design for the proposed Restoration of the Poultry Cross, at Salisbury," is nicely drawn by O. B. Carter. 1074) "Interior Part of the New Buildings at East Sutton, Kent, the seat of Sir Edmund Filmer, Bart.," by C. J. Richardson, is so placed that it can scarcely be examined, but being in the style with which Mr. Richardson s thoroughly embued, may safely be pronounced satisfactory. (1179) by the same, 'Designs for Villas in various Elizabethan Styles," would delight old Thorpe, but are not what we wish to see revived. (1091) "Design for a building for the reception of the Vernon gallery, and other productions of modern painters," by R. M. Phipson, must surely be miscalled; it has a rustic character, and might be taken for the market-house of a provincial town. (1108) shows the "North end of the great hall, Euston station," by P. C. Hardwick, whereof we in our present number give a representation, and express an opinion.

Enough for the present.

THE HIEROPHANTINE FRAGMENTS.

THE following are eight fragments from the archives of Hierophantus, master architect of the pre-Adamite schools of the Dom-Daniel:—

I.

Whatever ye do,
Work solid and true,
Go thorough and through.

II.

If a zealous Fellow-craft have not the patience of a dog, he will lead the life of one.

III.

Never ride the free horse down.

IV.

He that would keep a fortress this must do,—
Casemate his flanks, and flank his casemates too.

V.

Consider what you undertake,
And analyse it well;
And ever work from *Whole to Part*—
Grand principle of *master* art—
That makes that work to tell.

VI.

Tell me not "I have no ground!"
"There's no foundation to be found!"
If the ground is there,—you take it;
If the ground is not,—you make it.

VII.

Hold on in office—just as long
As health is good and nerves are strong:
That is, for health; whilst the complexion
Hath yet the "Carrot" in perfection:
Parsnips' or parchment's neutral tint
Cadaverous, give more than hint
. . . . . *
Mistake the knowledge of routine
For deep and sage experience . .
. . . . . a last farewell
To thought deliberate and cool reflection.
Patient endurance . . . .
. . . . . fibre, ligneous, or of nerve—
Passed Tension's modulus . . verve—
. . . . .
As Tredgor † hath it . . .
"Permanent flexure is incipient rupture."

VIII.

Eschew the hollow work! ‡—head, heart, or wall—
Folly or fraud involve the certain fall.
How stands the torrent's force, the flimsy dam?
How stands the ill-built wall, the battering ram?
Low though the *stated* cost,—low the deceiver's bow;
Smooth though the offer be,—smooth as the servile brow;—
The CRAFT'S dishonoured! by the crooked bent
Of knaves who from the first unfairly meant
To carry out the ill-conceited pact
In towers tumbling, and the walls all cracked,—
Crumbling cement,*—a quick-sand treacherous base,—
A heart of rubbish, and a shiner† face,—
Their own vile image and (unfelt!) disgrace.

* . . . denote lines so blotted and fishbeaten as to be illegible.

† An ancient and venerated predecessor of Hierophantus, celebrated for his constructional knowledge.

‡ No offence to patent hollow bricks of all sorts.

These are all the fragments that our diving-bell swept over; and they owed their protection to having been encased and petrified in a huge *pinna* that had contrived to bolt, though it could neither masticate nor digest them.

Judging from circumstances, it would appear that the last of these lines were written not many centuries before the Dom. Daniel vaults were blown up by Thalaba.

Dr. Southey has been at much pains to mystify this Thalaba, the mystic and professional progenitor of Major-General Sir C. Pasley, of voltaic and otherwise well-earned celebrity. The Dom-Daniel fell from a schism in the worshipful body-corporate; they broke gradually and virtually into "conservatives and abolitionists."

Now, young Thalaba was sub-prefect of the demolitors, corresponding, I presume, to a major of miners and sappers and engineers—(is that one regiment or two? I can't make it out at all ‡)—who engaged to play the Guy Fawkes to the old "conservatives" when assembled in conclave under the august presidency of that Megatherium of self-impostors, the imperative, the potential, and pot-bellied Magnarch,—HURLOTHRUMBO SMELLFUNGUS SAP,§—very limited, and therefore very conceited: *ex officio, privileged* to be dictatorial and pragmatic.

This dignitary, by the way, was the son of a dirty servile election-jobber, who contrived to force his scion into a place unsuited to his age, education, or natural ability:—hence this piece of sappy "alhern" albernum, was constantly verging towards the dry-rot and dotage so remarkable in unsound beech:—from under a pair of ragged bushy eye-brows and enormous round spectacles, he was fond of proclaiming himself to be a "matter-of-fact man of plain-sense, and v-a-i-r-y few words indeed!" His answer in all cases beyond mere routine, was a negative, in a portentous oracular tone, delivered slowly over a double chin from the back of his throat and the bottom of his belly, to the following effect: "It-is-un-u-su-al, and THEREFORE cannot be re-com-mend-ed!" He was just the type of that curse of so many public offices,—the class of man specified in Fragment VII. as ever confounding the knowledge of mere routine with experience.

Thalaba, in order to destroy his opponents, condensed several cubic miles of etherial imagination by "surface action" on the central point of a spongious syllogism. On this was to be brought to bear suddenly the moonshine of the lunar caustic of the angry but silly remarks of the Magnarch, concentrated by lanticular form and power of an approximate and preceding lucid interval.

The "imagination" thus condensed into what Thalaba's utilitarian impertinence called "the semblance of a single solid grain of common sense," was slightly but carefully dusted over with humbug and mill-puff: the intended 'fuse' for the sudden development of the 'moonshine' was the short ironical and inflammatory speech with which it was delivered to Mr. Magnarch. But here he failed,—he cut his fuse, and thereby his stick,—too short: Magnarch took fire too soon, and, by a premature thump of indignation on his desk (always his resource when he felt very angry or very empty), 'detonated' and exploded the whole chamber and sub-prefect, Thalaba, submarine vaults and all, into an inconceivable state of atomic comminution. The "Dom-Daniel cavern under the Root of Ocean," was simply an enormous series of caves in the mountain limestone formation; and the lifting of a remote corner (at a considerable depth under the surface) produced the bank at Spithead, on which Gen. Pasley operated so successfully in later days; but his explosions were but the

Gentle breath of Zephyr, o'er the swell
Of Ocean's bosom as it rose and fell—

to that of the unlucky Thalaba. So much for Dr. Southey's mystification!

"I like good plain prose," said a hard-fighting old soldier to me one day, "but as to pott'hery—'tis all GAMMON!"

X + Y + Z.

* No offence to Dr. Parker's ghost, or present makers of Roman cement, notwithstanding its eclipse by Mister White.

† Teutonic? "Scheinen?" No offence to Mister Taylor's patent facing.

‡ X + Y + Z stands corrected. "Royal Sappers and Miners," and "Royal Engineers"—two distinct corps: the former has no officers of its own: and the latter has no men, though they always command the sappers on a footing of temporary attachment. Hence the former is a regimental corps,—the Royal Engineers a staff.—ED.

§ We have suggested to X + Y + Z the probability of this being considered as a personality; but he assures us that, like the Magnarch, the character has no specific originality,—a thing of threads and patches,—a compound old goose of many giblets, collected from many birds in John Bull's large official farmyards—civil and military.—ED.

ELEVATION OF THE WORKING CLASSES.

IT must be a strong motive to make a toiler, like myself, set aside the chosen pursuit for his leisure evening time, and task himself with "the stringing together of sentences," but the truth is, I cannot well help it. The pith of the communications of the "Old Mason," has warmed my dull phlegmatic nature into nervous life; and having given insertion to his advice, perhaps you will spare me a little room for a few comments upon it.

Simplify your wants. Do as I have done. I have kept myself, wife and children, upon 1*l.* per week; and thus out of my weekly stipend of 1*l.* 10s., saved 10s. This, I think, is the cream and marrow of his advice.

I shall not inquire how much, or how little, they eat or drank; how often sickness, with its gloomy shadow darkened their homestead; how often he was out of work; what rent they paid, &c.; such details would be quite unfit for publication. But I must say, is this a time to be chosen to talk to us of saving 10s. out of 30s.? Where are the 30s.? Not one-half of us engaged in the building trade in London, have had it for these last eighteen months; we have either been "totally without employment, or working short time."

My first objection to his advice is founded upon the negative of the following question—: Ought we, for a contingent evil, to sacrifice a certain good? I think not; the evil in this matter (want, dependence in old age) is in time future, and therefore contingent. The certain good I shall now explain.

Let any man take 30s. Let him find the bread necessary for the sustaining of the animal natures of himself and family. This done, let him think of that other nature which God hath given them; let him consider this second want—this bread-finding for the intellectual—for the spirit nature, and God help him in his sore trouble; God forgive him for the bitterness which venoms his soul, when he sees in what poor doles he must mete it out to the children of his own blood, whose very sympathies are his own; and for whose well-doing he must face to face with them answer to his God.

And let this not be forgotten (suppose those children are sent to a good school, there they acquire the means, the tools of education), it is the parent who ought and must be the trainer; he must teach the application, he must mould their minds, and lead them forward towards ultimate results. And to do this, his own soul-work—his own education—must be pursued, and this will be another cause of expense; it is true, in one sense, books and education are cheap enough now-a-days. Yes, and always were—even worthy the shedding of one's blood to obtain; but, alas! dear, very dear, to a man with only 30s. per week; for of a surety there will come a time to every brain-worker, who works truly and well, when his mind will need something not quite so *elementary* as penny magazine treatises; and then, woe—woe to his saving, he has crossed the rubicon—his march of education is, in other words, *eternal* progression (*i. e.* an endless expense). Good books, such as he may now require, are only to be purchased with large sums. And here let every man think over his own mind's progress, and think over a few of the tortuosities he has been forced into, by wanting a book that he could not afford to procure. Talk of saving for old age!—the "Old Mason" has never witnessed the feverish anxious thrift of a working-man saving to buy a book.

A little while agone, back in the winter-time, a fellow-workman lay upon his death

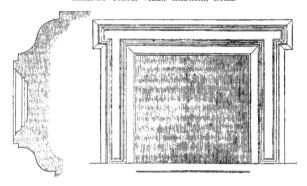

bed; but in death as in life, his thoughts were of his children, and his cry was, "My poor Willy, my poor Mary! what will become of them?" And friends came—and the minister amongst them—and with the grief gurgling in their throats, tried to administer peace, consolation, to the dying man; but in vain—between himself and consolation he saw his pale-faced children fatherless! At last one friend came and said, "Fear not, you leave them a rich legacy,—rest assured your teachings will not be forgotten: the seed you have sown will not be lost. And your books—which to you have been such household gods—will be the same to them, and open their minds, and through them minister lovingly to the Great God of all!"

Oh peace—consolation, said the dying man, and he spoke no more.

Would that every working man, whose hour was come, had as rich a legacy to leave!

Besides this error of sacrificing the present to the future, there is another which should be noticed. It cannot be doubted but that the simplification of our wants is an end worthy the striving for; but is it not one of the results of pursuing a system of morality?—a consequence, not a beginning? Diogenes had seen and thought much before he retired to his tub; and there he had cogitated much before, in reply to Alexander's offer to grant him a favour, he mildly replied, "Stand aside, that the glorious sunshine may reach me."

It is a very great but common error that the working classes must be written "down to"—that we need a particular literature, or a literature of a particular style. No; train us to habits of thought,—teach us to think, and to try to think aright; this is all we want,—it is all every class wants; in this particular we are not peculiar.

From the time of Franklin to the "Old Mason," one particular style has been adopted towards us—a style that we especially dislike. Philanthropists and economists come into our habitations, ransack and take an inventory of the contents of our cupboards, how much we eat and drink—in short, study our habits as they would wild animals—and then publish a little truth sometimes, but always a great deal of error about us. Would this be endured by any other class? Would John, duke of Plantagenet, endure it? Then why John Noakes, the mason? However well-intentioned this philanthropy may be, it always has failed—it always will fail; because the writers seek to eradicate an effect, and leave the cause to germinate afresh. Admitting that waste and extravagance exist among the working classes, it is but the necessary and inevitable effect or consequence of a cause. And what is that cause? I think but few will doubt that it is ignorance. Then, decrease the power of the

cause, and the effect will, in a like ratio, also decrease. And let him who would benefit us set to work, and hew and cut slashingly, like another St. George, at the dragon Ignorance; let him shew the mechanics upon what beautiful mathematical principles their crafts depend—what they know (without being sensible of it) practically, let him teach them theoretically, and so set them thinking—as they will when this is done—and trying to work out new results from old Euclidian and Archimedian principles; for, of a certainty, it is strange if we have arrived at perfection in joinery, or even masonry. And further, he may show us how our lives, which too often pass so wearily, may be made pleasant—aye, hard muscle-tearing work pleasant—*by teaching us to work intelligently.*

Do you think that the Theurgic brotherhoods—the "masonries" of architecture—the architects who individually and collectively dotted Europe in the twelfth and thirteenth centuries with churches and cathedrals of wondrous beauty and varied design, had often to complain, like the architects of the present day have, of bad and indifferent workmen? Oh, no; the Celtic nations, fresh from their woodland haunts, with the remembrance of nature mingled with a strong passionate faith in their new religion, were true and intelligent workers; they felt the ideas of the architect, great as his genius might be; there was a sympathy between them, that, alas! is in a great degree wanting now; and unity, harmony of design, from the spires to the slightest ornament, was the consequence of this intelligent working.

Then, up and to work, good spirits! Teach, teach; lessen our ignorance—be it never so little, do something towards it; believe me, it will be far better, nobler work, than teaching us to hoard pence; and should you be discouraged, think into how many poor, dark, benighted souls this Publication has shed a little light, and how that light is increasing, growing brighter and stronger, and what a glorious army of workers we may have in the future time. See to this; begin—there is a magic in beginning—and no cheer will be heartier, no prayer more fervent, than the "God speed you" of

BEOWULF, Yᵉ CARPENTER.

*** "Beowulf" and the "Old Mason" are not opponents, but fellow-workers in a good cause: and most sincerely do we hope that both may be listened to. Prudence, forethought, avoidance of evil and improvident habits, self culture, and an honest ambition to advance in the scale of society, are the objects sought to be inculcated.

We have received several other letters on the subject from working men, the majority of them most creditable to their writers. We

hope they believe us when we repeat, that w have no desire to keep down wages—quite th reverse: or even, at this moment, to discus what are and what are not sufficient. We would assist in leading the working classes to do the best that can be done with what *they* have, improve the present, and be not forgetful of the future. We heartily wish their position was better than it is, and would gladly aid in improving it. We have good reason to know that great distress prevails in parts.

CHIMNEY-PIECE, VILLA MADAMA, ROME.

THE villa was built for Giulio, Cardinal Medici (afterwards Clement VII.), by Giulio Romano, who, as Vasari says, had 'il carico di tutto' connected with the place, and accordingly was both architect, landscape gardener, and house decorator, to his eminence. The clear opening of this chimney-piece is 5 feet by 4 feet 8½ inches, the effect of the mouldings very good. Chimney-pieces of this description were common throughout Italy at that period.

SMALL DRAINS.

LAST week Mr. Freeman, of Kennington-road (from whom a letter as to trapping-drains appears in our present number) applied to the magistrate at the Lambeth office for his advice under the following circumstances.

From the statement of Mr. Freeman it appeared that, in the early part of the month of February last, he had applied to the Sewers Commissioners to have a drain or communication from his premises with the common sewer in the Kennington-road, and on the 27th of that month persons were set to work to make the required communication. The small tube piping of 4, or rather 3½-inch diameter, lately adopted, was laid down for the purpose, but on the 14th of March it was found to be stopped up, so that the trenches had to be re-opened, and the same pipes relaid, but with a greater fall. A second stoppage, however, took place, and the applicant, in consequence, had communicated several times with the Earl of Carlisle on the subject, and the result was that the principal surveyor to the board was called on twice to report on the subject. The drains were opened a third time, and had remained so from the 24th March to the present, to the greatest annoyance and imminent danger to the health of himself, his family, and servants. After some conversation, the magistrate said he had no power to assist him.

TRAPPING DRAINS.

I BEG to call your attention to one of the serious errors daily committed by the Commissioners of Metropolitan Sewers, which is, in having a trap fixed at the end or outlet of every house drain in the sewer, for the purpose of keeping the poisonous air and gas of the sewers out of the house: but instead of doing so, it insures a regular supply of the obnoxious fluid into the houses. To explain, when a pailful of water enters a drain, a pailful of air must escape out, and does so where there is the least resistance, and this is at the sink trap or the closet pan trap. When the water reaches the end of drain, and opens the trap, as it runs out the same quantity of air must go in over the stream from the sewer, the inlets being closed with water traps; so that for every separate pailful of water which enters the drain, the same quantity of air is measured out into the house. I think you will see it is evident drains can be trapped only at the inlets; and where back-water is troublesome, each inlet might have the same trap which is now used for the outlet.

Kennington-road. RD. FREEMAN.

SCENIC ANACHRONISMS.

ROYAL ITALIAN OPERA HOUSE, COVENT GARDEN.

AFTER seeing and listening to the truly magnificent *ensemble* presented by Mayerbeer's *Robert le Diable*, as given at the Italian Opera House, Covent Garden, it seems almost ungrateful to those who have done so much for the gratification of the public to find fault on what may be considered minor points. If we thought that doing so would keep away one intending visitor, it would probably remain undone, but so far from this being the case, the admiration we can honestly express, in making the observation, may, perhaps, lead some to go there who had no such intention previously.

What we have to say, then, is this:—Robert, surnamed the Devil, is an historical personage, and belongs to the eleventh century,—the Norman period; yet in the scene of the second act, a stone screen, the whole width of the stage, is shown of fourteenth century Gothic, and, worse still, in the back ground is seen an Italian palace of the sixteenth century.

Every one now appreciates the absurdity of playing Julius Cæsar in a modern court dress, but what we are now speaking of is, in reality, no less absurd to the discriminating portion of the public. Messrs. Grieve and Telbin are masters in their art, and it is therefore the more important that their attention should be kept to the importance of chronological accuracy. The first scene, a view of Palermo, is charmingly painted. The opera itself is magnificent.

REMOVAL OF SMOKE, AND VENTILATION OF SEWERS.

WE make the following extracts (which have been for some time in type) from a pamphlet by Mr. W. Flockton, surveyor to the town trustees of Sheffield,* not because we think the scheme practicable, but that our readers, who are interested in the questions to which it refers, may know what others are doing.

"We propose to carry away and disperse or consume smoke, noxious gases, and foul air, and, instead of permitting them to injure and destroy, to turn them, or at least the heat that accompanies them, to a very useful and valuable purpose. It may be well to state the considerations which first suggested our plan. Observing an ordinary house fire, we were led to a conclusion which no doubt many persons have arrived at before, viz., that probably as much heat was discharged up the chimney as into the room: it also occurred to us, that in the case of furnaces, and gas and other retorts, considerably more in proportion passed up the chimneys. As a striking instance of this, we may remark that the heat at the top of a steel-melting furnace flue, which may probably be ten yards from the furnace, is so intense that the colour of the flame is nearly white. Then in the case of fires used to generate steam, although a considerable quantity of the caloric is carried off by the water, it is well known that the heat is very great after it has passed through the boiler flues and entered into the stack or great chimney; indeed, this is proved by the necessity of lining all those chimneys with firebrick from the bottom to some considerable distance upwards; but without referring to other cases, we were, from noticing these facts, led to believe that the total quantity of heat which is constantly being discharged from the chimneys in a large town must be enormous, and that if it could be collected and concentrated it would place at disposal an immense power, which might be used to remove and probably destroy its accompanying and disagreeable partners—smoke and sulphur and noxious gases; and, at the same time, furnish the best, the most powerful, and cheapest means of effecting ventilation that has yet been discovered, and that, too, on a scale commensurate with the wants of a town—no matter whether large or small, for in proportion to the number of houses and other buildings would be the number of fires, and in the like proportion the extent of ventilation required and the power to accomplish it. Reflecting on the fact that the powerful agent which is so admirably adapted for the purpose was in such abundance that every contrivance the ingenuity of man could invent had been tried to carry it over our heads, there to mingle with and poison the air, producing disease and premature death, we were led to the conclusion that, if it were passed under our feet and properly applied, it would not only greatly assist in purifying our dwellings and work rooms, but while performing these important operations, be instrumental in destroying smoke, and probably prove as great a blessing as it is now an evil to the inhabitants of towns.

The arrangements of the plan are as follow:—

Under the footpaths along each side of every street and lane, it is proposed to construct flues of sufficient capacity to carry off all smoke and other atmospheric impurities from the buildings of a given district. The flues and their dimensions to be arranged on one general plan, so that they shall increase in capacity as they approach the outlet, in the requisite proportion to the increase of the smoke, &c., intended to pass through them; and so also that a flue may at any point be closed up for the purpose (if such stoppage be necessary, which it is thought it will not) of making fresh communications with it, or for repairs, or any emergency that may arise, and the current either turned in two opposite directions, or across the street to the flue on the other side, but, of course, always providing that there be but one way for the general current to the outlet at any time. In towns of moderate size, it is proposed that the main flues be carried out of the town, in as many and such directions as shall be most convenient, terminating in each case with lofty towers or stacks: in which it is confidently expected that, after being once ignited, a fire, produced by the combustion of the inflammable gases accompanying the smoke, &c., would burn spontaneously, in a similar manner to the combustion of foul air from some old shafts connected with coal mines. That this would be the result, there can be very little doubt, taking into consideration the nature of the gases drawn from various sources, together with the large quantity of unconsumed carbon accompanying the smoke—and that both gases and smoke being supplied at the base of the tower with oxygen to any required extent, so as to produce perfect combustion, would, in all probability, produce a constant flame of such magnitude and brilliancy as to assist materially in lighting the district by night. However, should this not be so, the combustion might be assisted by jets of coal gas, or a fire of coke, as the case might require or circumstances permit.

It is submitted that the draft caused by the great length of the flues, and height of the towers, combined with the impetus given by the furnaces in the towers, and the vast body of heated air poured into the flues from the whole of the fires in the district, would form an immense power, much more than equal to the ventilation of a town to any possible extent; and would, at the same time, insure a regular and constant draft through every flue into the street mains, which might be increased or diminished by valves or dampers at pleasure, rendering a smoky chimney a thing unknown; for it may be fairly presumed, that neither the variable state of the atmosphere, nor the changeableness nor violence of the wind, would have any effect on the dues and great towers.

The next important feature of the plan is, its connection with the sewers. Communications are proposed to be made at proper intervals between the sewers and the street flues, sufficient in size to carry off the sulphuretted hydrogen, and other noxious gases, generated in or passed through the sewers, and thus effectually prevent their transmission into the houses through cellar drains, and into the streets through the gulley holes.

It may be imagined that an enormously large flue would be required to carry off all the smoke from a district, but we submit that, when the velocity of the current is increased to the extent which may reasonably be expected, a flue will carry off a very much greater quantity of smoke, in a given time, than under existing circumstances.

We therefore apprehend, that a house flue, as at present constructed, is of at least ten times as great a sectional area as would be necessary with the powerful draft we propose to apply; and that a flue of the present size, would be capable of carrying off the smoke from perhaps ten, or more, house fires, and the reduction would apply in the same degree to furnace and other fires."

* Published by Hamilton, Adams, and Co. London, 1849.

THE NEW BOROUGH PRISON AT PLYMOUTH.

THIS building, which has been erected under the superintendence of Messrs. Fuller and Gingell, of Bristol, is now complete, and is about to be delivered over to the corporation. A correspondent sends us the following particulars:—It is built of the blue limestone from the quarries at Catdown, relieved by Caen stone, and the sashes are all of cast-iron, glazed with plate glass, a quarter of an inch in thickness. The governor's house and porter's lodge, are detached from the prison buildings—the former being on the right and the other on the left of the entrance gate. The main building comprises offices for the governor, and apartments for the matron, in case she should not be the governor's wife,—a chapel and surgery, reception cells, visiting cells, convalescent rooms, bath room, and cells for sixty prisoners. The female prisoners will be confined in one wing of the building; their airing yards and punishment cells (which are so constructed as to admit air, but not one particle of light), are entirely distinct from those appropriated to offenders of the other sex. The debtors will occupy a distinct portion of one wing of the building—and will be divided into two classes, each of whom will have an airy and comfortable day-room, but their sleeping cells do not differ from those of the other prisoners. The arrangements have been made with a view to carrying out the separate system of confinement, in all its completeness. Each cell is fitted with a water-closet and washing bowl, a bed and bench; and the gas and water are introduced into each. The airing-yards are twenty-four in number, radiating from a common centre, and each one of them will be occupied but by one person at one time: an officer of the prison will be so placed as to have the command of all the yards at one and the same time. A similar arrangement is carried out in the chapel. The buildings are 270 feet in length, and 150 in breadth, and they have been completed in less than fourteen months from their commencement. Messrs. Clift and Goodyear were the contractors.

BLIND DREDGERS.—A correspondent sends the following list of extraordinary tenders for deepening the bed of the River Medway, near Maidstone; Messrs. Whichcord, architects:—

Couchman (Sheerness) ..	£3,199	0	0
Jarvis (London)	873	5	0
Diggle	750	0	0
Court	750	0	0
Rook, Thomas (London)..	748	0	0
Cooper (Maidstone)	730	0	0
Sampson, R. (Maidstone)	376	0	0

THE GREAT HALL AT THE EUSTON STATION.

Mr. P. C. HARDWICK, Architect.

THE GREAT HALL AT THE EUSTON STATION,

LONDON AND NORTH-WESTERN RAILWAY.

THE public are aware that very considerable works have been in progress at the Euston station of the London and North-Western Railway for some time past. These are now drawing to a close, and the new building will be opened to the public in a few days. It comprises two booking offices: the one to the east occupies the site of the old one, and will be used for the principal part of the traffic; the other is quite new, and is intended chiefly for the smaller trains. These open from a Hall of large size, which is the great public *ante-room* to all those apartments which are appropriated to the passenger traffic. Into it will be wheeled all the luggage from the quadrangle in front, and here or in the waiting-room (which opens from it), passengers may remain if they are too early for their train. On the piers between the arches will be large boards, on which will be placed notice of the destination and time of departure of the train next leaving the station, so that a passenger can at once see to which booking-office he is to direct his steps. In the centre of the hall will be a large refreshment counter, and it is intended that persons may be served in the waiting-rooms, which will be fitted up accordingly.

Opening from the hall is the lost-luggage office, and access to other departments,—all more or less connected with the passengers. A very necessary part of the arrangement of such a building is the clear division of the passengers from the transfer and other business of the company; and, in this case, such a separation is effected by means principally of the great hall. Immediately opposite the entrance of the hall will be placed the electric-telegraph office, easy of access alike to the public and the officers of the company.

In the four angles of the building there are four staircases leading to the secretary's, transfer, engineers', and other offices, committee-rooms, board-room, and the various branch railway offices.

Annexed we give a view of the public hall, an apartment of large proportions and striking effect, and we will now speak a little more in detail of that and the other parts of the new building. The length of this vestibule is 125 feet 6 inches, the width 61 feet 4 inches, and the height 60 feet;—or as nearly as may be two cubes. It will be seen that the ceiling is panelled, deeply recessed, with all the members fully enriched. It is connected with the walls by large ornamented consoles of bold design. The walls, which are rendered with grey Martin's cement, are splashed as granite, and the Ionic columns, seen in the view, and attached to the wall at the other end of the room, are painted like red granite, with white caps and bases.*

A bold flight of steps at the end of the hall leads to the vestibule of the general meeting-room, and the board-room, and forms a striking and original feature. The door of the general meeting-room, seen at the top of the stairs, is surmounted by a group of sculpture, ably executed by Mr. John Thomas. It represents Britannia, with Mercury on one side, and Science on the other. The light comes down on this group very effectively. In the angles of the great hall, immediately under the ceiling, are eight panels in *alto relievo*, by the same sculptor. These represent by symbolical figures London, Birmingham, Manchester, Chester, Northampton, Carlisle, Nottinghamshire, and Liverpool.

There is a gallery all round the hall; the area is paved with Craigleith stone (a good specimen), and it is heated by hot-water pipes on Perkins's system. Some of the panels in the ceiling are perforated; and behind these are disposed other coils of hot-water pipes to promote ventilation. The same arrangement is made in the general meeting-room; and in the whole there are some miles in length of these pipes.

Of the general meeting-room we shall give an illustration hereafter. It is a handsome apartment, 75 feet long, 45 feet wide, and 40 feet high, calculated to accommodate 400 persons. Around the wall are coupled Doric columns on a podium. The coved and panelled ceiling is cleverly managed. There are windows on one side of this room, and lights in the cove of the ceiling on both sides.

The board-room, adjoining the last, is wholly of wainscot, with the exception of the ceiling, and has Corinthian columns of the same material. The size of it is 34 feet 6 inches, by 27 feet 2 inches. Two large rollers with connecting straps, have been fitted up here for a remarkable map of all the railways which belongs to the Board. The ceiling is coved, and has one rectangular panel, formed by flowers and fruits, subdivided into three.

The booking-offices, are, one 56 feet by 39 feet 10 inches; the other, 60 feet by 40 feet 6 inches, and have each a domical skylight of cast-iron, 28 feet in diameter. The pendentives of the ceiling are received on double consoles, which have the head and body of a lion between them and the pendentives. There is a gallery all round each office.

In the rooms on the second floor are some offices for branch lines, and a number of rooms to be occupied in a short time for similar purposes. In the basement are numerous store and other rooms, most of which are in use.

The whole of these works have been executed from the designs of Mr. P. C. Hardwick, to whom they are highly creditable. Messrs. W. Cubitt and Co. were the contractors. The total amount expended is not yet arrived at, but will probably not be less than 125,000*l.*!

* These columns are of brick, with iron stanchions running through them. An accident which happened to these columns during their first erection, and led to an inquiry, fully reported in our pages at the time, will be remembered by many of our readers.

NOTES IN THE PROVINCES.

Mr. Petrie's ingenious mode of protecting premises by the aid of electric shocks, as first suggested in The Builder, is about to be applied, it appears, to an extensive factory at West Ham. The battery will be a very powerful one, and will effect the two-fold object of ringing a large alarm bell, and prostrating all who may attempt to enter the premises. The application of such an apparatus is suitable for banking houses or the mansions of the nobility and gentry as well, and may be applied to one room or the whole dwelling.——The repair of Salisbury Cathedral spire has been resumed. ——A recent report of the boring at Northam for the Southampton Artesian well states the depth arrived at to be 286 ft., and that the workmen could not bore any further with safety till they had iron piping to the depth of 290 feet, and the present depth of the bore was 296 feet in hard clay.——Some further improvements are now being carried out at Southsea in the drainage and planting of 100 acres of ground, called Webb's marshes. A number of villas are to be afterwards erected on the site.——The old mansion named Bourne-park House, near Bridge, in Kent, is at present undergoing a thorough restoration, under the superintendance of Mr. J. Shaw, architect, and by Messrs. Locke and Nesham, builders. The building had been very much decayed, and almost uninhabitable. The ceilings, carvings, &c., have been renewed, a stone portico added to the doorway, the basement lowered and vaults constructed, the exterior tuck-pointed with stone dressings, and the grounds laid out with artificial water, garden, and other arrangements. —— St. Margaret's Church, Whalley Range, in the parish of Manchester, was consecrated on the 29th ult. It is geometrical in style (the transition from Early English to Decorated), has a tower and broach spire, and was built from the designs of Mr. James P. Harrison.——The rational mode of self-employment by some of our surplus hands, in the production of a subsistence for themselves out of the bounties of nature in spade cultivation, is being carried out at Huddersfield, where 75 workmen have lately formed an association, and purchased an eight-acre field for this purpose. Whenever any of the members are out of employment they will receive a ticket for six days' work, or twelve days' work, and be paid a fair day's wages for a fair day's work, and thus be prevented from becoming burdensome to the town, and having pauper relief. There are two such societies in the town already: this is the third. There is now hardly a village within 7 miles of Huddersfield, says the *Leeds Intelligencer*, but has its allotment society or industrial farms.——A meeting was to be held at Gainsborough last week, to prepare the way for the erection of a corn exchange.——The construction of the first of two extensive sheds on the sides of the Humber Dock Basin has been commenced by the Dock Company. Each is to be 150 feet long and 40 feet wide. Fourteen cast-iron pillars, embedded in solid masonry, and rising about 12 feet, are to support each of the sheds.——"Mr. John Pearson, the contractor for the execution of the great sewer in the High-street of this borough," says the *Gateshead Observer*, "made a beginning of the work on Wednesday, on the site of the departed tolbooth, nearly opposite the departed almshouses of the late Mr. Powell. The excavations have laid bare the foundations of the old prison, which stood in the middle of the street, and appears to have commenced in a line with the south end of the almshouses. The contractor has also had the luck to hit upon the 'high main' seam of coal; and this, we presume, he may appropriate as a perquisite, and vend under the name of 'Pearson's Wallsend' [or what says our cotemporary to 'Pearson's Godsend?'] At the foot of West-street, Messrs. Wilson and Gibson are about to begin the erection of the new railway bridge across Slant-street (which, we hear, has been rechristened by the less expressive name of 'Hills-street.') Thus, both underground and aboveground, the work of improvement goes on in our ancient borough." —— Public attention in Sunderland being directed to the establishment of public baths and wash-houses, we, says the *Sunderland Herald*, give publicity to the following results of the institution in Newcastle:—During the two last months, 1,200 warm baths have been taken, showing (if the average be taken individually) that one in every 84 of the entire population of Newcastle and Gateshead has had a warm bath within the last two months. The average weekly number of houses occupied by those who got their clothes washed, dried, and ironed, in a very few hours, during the same period, amounts to 4,300. The receipts amounted to 28*l.* 15*s.*; and if March and April could fairly be taken as average months, the annual receipts in that case would be 172*l.* 10*s.* It is confidently asserted that the baths will be self-supporting this year, and yield a profit afterwards.

IMPROVEMENT OF POOLE, DORSETSHIRE.

Our attention has been lately called to a port on the south coast of England, possessing great capabilities, and although long used by merchants trading to the North American colonies, nevertheless not so extensively known as from its position and convenience it deserves. We allude to the port of Poole, in Dorsetshire. The harbour is an extensive estuary of about 60 miles in circumference, the quays are large, with the advantage that vessels lie afloat at all times of the tide. The dues are nominal; the neighbourhood abounds in clay and stone, the former forming the chief ingredient used in the Staffordshire Potteries, and supplying London with the entire material used in the numerous potteries springing up in that locality. On the completion of the Wilts and Somerset Railway, a direct opening will be effected through the port of Poole, between the English and British channels, a convenience desiderated for the last half century, and first recommended by the late Sir Thomas Telford.

We hear that potteries on an extensive scale are contemplated on the estates of Sir J. J. Guest, Bart., in the neighbourhood. Lord Eldon is also outlaying a large sum of money within the harbour, principally for the purpose of bringing the most valuable of the Purbeck stone from the surrounding hills. It certainly appears strange that efforts have not been sooner made to develope the resources of this country, it can only be accounted for from the want of enterprise in the county of Dorset. It is said that Sir J. Guest has lately become the possessor of the greater part of the country near the port, and if so it may be prophesied that its resources will very soon be developed.

THE CHELTENHAM GENERAL HOSPITAL AND DISPENSARY.

This building, lately erected in Sandford-fields, Cheltenham, by Mr. Darby, builder, from plans prepared by Mr. D. J. Humphris, architect, and recently opened to patients, has an entrance front on the ground-floor, beneath a portico supported by four fluted Ionic columns, and approached by nine steps. The entrance hall is 24 feet 10 inches by 16 feet. It is separated from the corridor by two pillars. Branching off from the hall are various official apartments, and in each wing there is a ward 42 feet by 21 feet 6 inches, and 14 feet high. There is a museum 33 feet by 21 feet 6 inches in the front of the east wing. The basement story contains kitchens and other offices. On the next floor above the ground range there are also two wards, with a bath room, matron's and other apartments, and in each of the front wings is another ward. At the back of the centre is an extra floor (contrived by reducing the height of the rooms beneath), containing an operating room 24 feet 10 inches by 16 feet 4 inches, a room 20 feet by 11 feet 6 inches, and other apartments, with hot and cold water cisterns. The whole of the rooms are supplied with gas and hot and cold water. There is a corridor on each floor extending the entire length of the building, and 9 feet in width. Around the building is an area of two acres in garden ground.

RAILWAY JOTTINGS.

THE Commissioners of Railways have issued their report, dated 1st inst. Amongst other statistical details, it states that probably one-half at least of the 4,800 miles of authorised railways, of which the works are not in progress, will never be completed under existing Acts of Parliament; that at end of last year rather more than 200,000,000l. had been expended on railways,—besides which companies retain power to expend, in authorised lines, about 140,000,000l. more, within five or six years. 50,000,000l. of which, however, will probably not be required; and that the average depreciation of the stock of four great lines,—the North-Western, the Great Western, the South-Western, and the Midland,—during the last two years, has been 53½ per cent. "Confidence in the managers and directors of railways," they state, "is now so generally and so justly shaken, that the commissioners consider the appointment of competent and impartial auditors, and the adoption of an uniform system of accounts and vouchers (carefully adapted to each other), indispensable to the restoration of that confidence."——The mails are now conveyed between London and Dublin within 17 hours; and when the tubular bridge across the Menai Straits is completed, another hour will be saved. The mason-work of the pier for the first of the tubes is progressing, so as to enable the tube to be placed across the straits early in June at latest. Other preparations are also being made, the tubes are nearly all ready, and the other mason work is quite finished.——The first stone of the paddock viaducts on the Huddersfield and Sheffield line was laid on Thursday week before last, " by the infant son of Mr. Frazer, resident engineer on the works." The viaducts, says the Leeds Intelligencer, will be a work of immense labour, and when completed, will connect the Huddersfield and Sheffield with the Huddersfield and Manchester line, in an open cutting in Spring Wood Tunnel. In order to make way for these viaducts, a mansion, which had been erected within the past few years at a cost it is said of 1,400l., and four other large and respectable houses, have been razed to the ground.——Three individuals from Edinburgh, detained on a pleasure excursion at Burntisland till too late to proceed to their proposed destination, were lately found entitled, under a judgment of the sheriff, to repayment of the price of their tickets for the whole distance.——A new locomotive for burning anthracite or hard and ultramineralized coal, has been built in America by Hinckley and Drury, for the Fitchburg Company. It is a freight engine, and is said to " work well so far" with a heavy train.

ELECTRO-TELEGRAPHIC PROGRESS.

THE hydraulic telegraph, it is said, is to be tried on a line of railway at Nottingham.——On 13th ult. the Baltimore Telegraph Company declared a dividend of 4 per cent. on the previous three months' working.——From Boston to New York, a trade circular, containing 1,300 words, was lately transmitted, and re-written, in forty-five minutes.——Some of our contemporaries of the past week have been following up and fully exonerating our previous remarks, not only on the impracticability of the present prices of our metropolitan, or rather national, company, for general utility to the public, or even for adequate profit and prosperity to the company,—but also on the prudence of centering so much power in one company as this one possesses, without some limit, restriction, or regulation by Government, such as we suggested with reference to a circumstance that occurred some time ago at Manchester. As to the former point, one contemporary says,—We called attention, in our journal of 28th April, to the outrageously extravagant terms which the Telegraph Company impose on the public, and the necessary consequence resulting from exorbitant charges, either by individual tradesmen or public Companies,—the loss of business by the former, and the indignation and neglect of the public in the latter to whatever useful purposes the company may have been established. We have since received considerable information

on the charges and working of the American telegraphs; and from the smallness of the charges and the general civility and accommodation afforded in the working, all the American lines have already paid dividends exceeding those of other enterprises or of ordinary stock. No wonder that the telegraph should have made such rapid strides, or that it should be still rapidly extending, in all parts of the Union. We have before us a list of twenty-seven distinct systems of telegraphs, the longest of which is from Washington to New Orleans, a distance of 1,716 miles, and the aggregate being 6,768 miles; these are all in daily use, and several in the western states which were to have been completed last year, extend over several hundred miles.

SUPPLY OF WATER TO CONSTANTINOPLE.

THE account given in a late number of THE BUILDER, page 201, of the " Souterrazi " of Constantinople, seems to me unsatisfactory. The " Souterrazi" are rows of towers, with cisterns on the top of each, communicating through inverted syphons; and your correspondent states that this construction " relieves the hydraulic pressure on the pipes." Now any one acquainted with the principles of hydraulics must see that the pipes are relieved from an amount of pressure quite insignificant, that cannot possibly exceed the pressure of a column of water which would reach from the level of each cistern to the level of the original source. The result is, that the Turkish system, though much less expensive than an aqueduct, is much more expensive than a continuous line of pipes, over which latter system it has no adequate advantage. If your correspondent had explained how earthen pipes are made large enough to supply a great city with water, and how the joints are made tight against the unavoidable great pressure, he would have rendered an acceptable service.

The following show the greatest possible pressure at different points, on the supposition that each tower is one foot lower than the preceding tower,—and also what the pressure would be if the towers were swept away and a continuous line of pipes substituted :—

	At foot of 1st tower.	At foot of 2nd tower.	At foot of 3rd tower.
Pressure on the Turkish system	39 ft.	83 ft.	87 ft.
Pressure on continuous pipes	40 ft.	85 ft.	90 ft.
Difference	1 ft.	2 ft.	3 ft.

SPEC.

METAL WORK AND ITS ARTISTIC DESIGN.

AT the Society of Arts, on May 9, Mr. W. Tooke, F.R.S., in the chair, Mr. D. Wyatt, arch., read a paper on " Metal Work and its Artistic Design." He commenced with some remarks on the absolute necessity of the study of specific design, in order to confine the errant imaginations of artists within reasonable bounds, and in order fully to take advantage of all the natural properties, mechanical capabilities, and recorded experiences, peculiarly belonging to all materials, in the elaboration of which it is requisite that an alliance between use and beauty may be effected. The author maintained that all propriety and perfection in manufacturing design were derivable from the result of such studies,—and that the more clearly the objective individuality of every ingredient was preserved and enunciated in the finished article, the more satisfactory to both eye and mind would the character of its ornamentation appear.

The specific design of metal work was described as based on three great studies, a thorough knowledge of which was requisite to all who would either manufacture, compose, or criticise, in any one of its various ramifications. The first of these was that of the distinctive characteristics and appliances of each metal; the second, its form as modified by all the mechanical processes of manufacture; the third, a thorough analytical and critical acquaintance with all the best models in which reasonable and good principles of art can be traced, and through modifications of which pleasing associations of idea may be commanded at the will of the designer. In accordance with his scheme thus laid down, the

author proceeded to deduce the correct theory of the manufacture of each metal, from the properties with which it had been endowed by nature. He then described, at considerable length, the process by which almost all objects in metal must be produced, dwelling on those best harmonising with the character of each substance, and the accredited conventionality of its use. Thus he emphaticised the refining, beating into sheets, wire drawing, stamping, and torsion of gold; the beating in a plate, gilding, dead silvering, parcel gilding, soldering, &c., of silver; the hollow casting of bronze by means of wax and of moulds, " à bon creux;" and the solid founding of iron in complex forms. Having disposed of the structural processes, the author rapidly analysed the decorative or superficial, enumerating and sketching out the leading peculiarities of engraving, matting, niello, cooking, burnishing, the six chief divisions of enamel, and three or four varieties of damascening. The mechanical limits of the art being thus pointed out, the impressions suggested by the history of past chefs-d'œuvre were then cursorily examined. The extreme antiquity of metal work, and its details among the Jews, Egyptians, Assyrians, Persians, Greeks, Eturians, and Romans, were demonstrated from descriptions furnished by various authors, and by monuments of wonderful merit still existing. The speaker then passed over the mediæval portion of the subject, and concluded by calling attention to the examples by which he was surrounded, and urging a systematic recognition of first principles and practical details, to be superadded to the study of beauty and fine art in the abstract.

IRON STEAMERS.

IRON steamers seem now destined to carry the sway in our steam marine, not without reason, for the advantages they possess over vessels constructed of wood are manifold and momentous. They are much less susceptible of injury from getting ashore than vessels built of wood, not simply on account of the toughness and tenacity of iron, but in consequence of the plan of separating the hold into compartments, by means of water-tight bulkheads, being carried into effect with the greatest ease and efficacy. Iron vessels are much stiffer than wooden ones, not in a nautical sense, but in their capacity of resisting working and vibration. There is no play of joints, no opening and closing of seams, as in a wooden vessel; and in the case of a steamer there is scarcely any tremulous motion: there is but little smell from bilge water, no rats eating their way through the vessel, and no dry rot. There are, however, certain evils peculiar to iron vessels, though not insuperable. Some of the most conspicuous may here be enumerated. The most formidable of these by far is corrosion. Iron, when immerged in water, and especially in sea water, will rust very quickly if left unprotected, and, although its surface may be protected by a paint, yet this is not an effectual safeguard. In passing up and down rivers, and, indeed, in other situations, steamers will sometimes get aground, and the protective paint may thus be rubbed off the bottom in particular places, leaving the iron exposed. But, independent of this objection, there is another arising from the want of a soluble poison on the bottom of iron vessels, in consequence of which the bottom is liable to be covered with seaweeds and barnacles. A poisonous paint, into which arsenic has been introduced, is sometimes used as an antidote to barnacles, and operates for a time satisfactorily. But, after a certain period, the poison on the surface of the paint is all dissolved away, leaving only an insoluble stratum for the water to act upon, and the effect then is just the same as if no poison had been intermingled.

It would appear that both of these evils might be effectually prevented, if it were possible to plate the bottom of the vessel by means of the electrotype process, with a metallic alloy of arsenic and zinc; but it seems doubtful whether this could be accomplished, as the electrotype seems to show a preference for pure metals. If this cannot be done, it would suffice to work zinced plates into the bottom of the vessel, during its construction, and then to paint the bottom with a compound formed of marine glue, and the ordinary proportion of arsenic.

Another rather important objection to iron vessels is, that they are liable to break in the middle, and a long list of steamers could be named that have cracked in that part, and some of them have foundered. This has arisen not from the direct tearing of the iron, but from its buckling in a sea way, and it has been rent by bending it first to one side, then the other, just in the manner pursued in breaking a piece of tin. The remedy for this evil is good strong keelsons, good stringers, and a strong wide iron covering board running entirely round the ship, and stretched for several feet in width between the main deck. It is also a good plan to have diagonal plates running between the main deck and the beams. G. J. RHODES.

Miscellanea.

INSTITUTION OF MECHANICAL ENGINEERS, BIRMINGHAM.—At the general meeting, already mentioned by us, Mr. Robert Stephenson, on taking the chair, said, it was necessary that he should express to them how apprehensive he was—at least that he had apprehensions—of an institution of that kind failing for want of energy on the part of its members. What had hitherto been the character of almost every institution of this kind in this country? almost universal failure. It was a remarkable circumstance, that in a country like Great Britain, whose wealth and power are so closely connected with the development of the mechanical arts and sciences—it appeared to him, in fact, a complete anomaly—that institutions of that kind should not appear to reach a higher standard than they now had. They saw astronomers cultivate and maintain a society for extending their knowledge of the movements of the heavens. They saw geologists maintaining and extending societies for investigating and developing the structure of the earth. They saw physiologists and botanists maintaining and extending their societies for investigating and developing the knowledge of the animal and vegetable productions of the earth: yet they had witnessed only languidness and inactivity in the pursuit of those arts and sciences on which the nation's wealth absolutely depended. That it should be the case was to him the more remarkable, because the nation stood pre-eminent for their mechanical abilities. It was not egotistical in him to say this in Britain, because all foreigners conceded to them an unmeasured pre-eminence in those particular arts. Without despairing therefore of the success of the institution, he felt that in undertaking the task he was now doing, it was necessary that he should impress upon the members the absolute necessity of co-operating with him with energy in the further development of the institution. With that strong conviction on his mind, he wished also strongly to impress it on them; for without energy and industry they must fail as heretofore.

YORKSHIRE ARCHITECTURAL SOCIETY.—A special meeting of this society was held on Monday last, at Methley, for the purpose of examining the church of this village, which is now in the course of restoration. A fine oak roof over the nave, which had been discovered during the progress of the works, concealed above a flat plaster ceiling, excited admiration, and several other features of the church were considered as singular and interesting.

BRIDGEWATER CHURCH COMPETITION.—Sir: Will you permit me to explain to "A Great Western," that the advertisement for an extension of time for receiving plans for the restoration of the above church was forwarded by me to your office, on the 26th ult., for insertion in THE BUILDER of April 28th; its non-insertion is for the publisher to explain. I trust your correspondent, after this explanation, will be assured that its non-insertion at the proper time was not for the purpose, as he insinuates, "to advantage some favoured individual."—H. C. HEARD. Bridgewater, May 15.

*** The advertisement in question, dated 26th, did not reach the publisher till after the publication of the paper on the 27th. THE BUILDER, it should be remembered, is published early on *Friday* morning.

TRADE IN BIRMINGHAM AND LIVERPOOL.—The prospects here, says the *Birmingham Journal*, "are not so cheering as previous to Christmas. The diminished duty on glass caused such an increased make as inundated the market, and it remains so glutted, that the demand, at the manufacturers, even at low prices, is very limited. Low prices alone will not bring an article like glass into universal use at once. We require to be educated to perceive its advantages. Hence the mistake. With respect to the general ironmongery business, our reports are more favourable; nor do we believe all we hear, that, notwithstanding the low price at which it is said the Germans can manufacture tools (such as files, vices, nippers, &c.), any quantity of foreign make has yet found its way, or can find it, into the markets of this country. We are aware that pattern cards of German manufactures are in circulation in Birmingham, and that after paying an import duty of about 10 per cent., the brokers and their agents profess to supply English dealers and consumers with articles of equal quality, at 40 per cent. less than the articles in question are now made by the British manufacturers. The artisans of Birmingham dispute these assertions, and it would be strange if, while Stubb's files bring high prices on the continent, German manufactures should supersede them in England." At Liverpool, the disorganized state of the continent affects unfavourably the market for timber. Prices, however, since 1st instant, continue without much change. During the week two cargoes of St. John's spruce deals have been sold on the quay at 7*l.* 15s. and 7*l.* 10s. per standard. By auction, 14,864 St. John's spruce deals and battens, &c., at from 7*l.* 10s. to 8*l.* 5s. per standard; 2,665 St. Stephen's spruce deals, at from 7*l.* 17s. 6d. to 8*l.* 2s. 6d. per standard; 378 Quebec, third quality, inferior pine deals, at 7*l.* 17s. 6d. per standard; 300 logs St. John's pine, averaging 19¼ inches calliper, at 18d. per foot, and 50 logs at 18½d. per foot; 28 logs elm, at 16½d. per foot; 35 logs ash, at 14d. per foot, 78 logs oak, at 1s. 8d. to 2s. per foot; 110 logs Savannah pitch pine, at from 2s. 1d. to 2s. 4½d. per foot; planks ditto, 3⅝d. to 3¾d. per foot 2 inches. Iron continues dull of sale, and a further decline to a small extent has to be reported. For common bars 6*l.* is now the highest obtainable rate; whilst for cargoes in Wales, the rates are nominal, with a wide range from 5*l.* 15s. to 5*l.* 7s. 6d. Copper is steady and in fair demand."

SILVERING GLASS BY AID OF GUN-COTTON.—M. Vohl has recently discovered that a solution of gun-cotton, in a caustic ley, possesses, in a high degree, the property of precipitating silver from its solutions in the metallic form. On pouring into it a few drops of a solution of nitrate of silver, and adding ammonia until the oxide of silver formed is redissolved (the mixture being slowly heated in a water bath), the liquor will, at a certain period, assume a deep brown colour, and effervesce, the whole of the silver being precipitated on the sides of the vessel. The mirror thus produced is much superior in brilliancy to those produced by means of etherial oils or ammoniacal aldehyde; and the facility with which it is produced will doubtless render it of practical importance.—*Technologiste.*

OUR 'WOODEN WALLS' IN DANGER.—On Monday evening, there was a considerable concourse of persons on Tyne Bridge, and on the shores of the river, to witness a race between an ordinary wooden skiff, or gig, and one made of *gutta percha*, 26 feet long by 3 broad. When first we caught sight of the competitors struggling for the goal, '*Gutta Percha*' was several lengths in advance, and she kept her 'proud position' to the end. Our old 'wooden walls' were thus defeated by an innovation in nautical architecture, built of a mongrel material, half leather, half India rubber. What with a reverse like this, following upon the use of iron in shipbuilding, our good old English 'heart of oak' may well be heart-broken. Mr. Taylor, having won the boat race, next made trial of a *gutta percha* 'life buoy.' A lad, who had consented to have his life saved and his clothes spoiled, jumped into the river in 'full dress,' and was rescued, as we understand, by the buoy.—*Gateshead Observer.*

ARCHITECTURAL AND ARCHÆOLOGICAL MEETING.—The spring union-meeting of the Northampton and Bedfordshire Societies was held at the Town Hall, Higham Ferrers, on Tuesday week, the Rev. Sir George Robinson in the chair, in place of the Marquis of Northampton, who was indisposed. The Rev. H. Rose, rector of Brington, read a paper "On the Chicheley days of Higham Ferrers," and one, by Lord Alwyne Compton, "On encaustic tiles." The Rev. H. J. Rose, rector of Houghton Conquest, then read a paper "On Hebrew shekels, and on some architectural devices found in coins."—Mr. Matthew H. Bloxam, one "On an ancient stone offertory box in Bridlington Church, Yorkshire, and on an ancient stone offertory bason in East Kirby Church, Lincolnshire;" and Mr. G. G. Scott another, "On the principles of church restoration;" in the course of which he made some remarks upon the injudicious manner in which some attempts at restoration had been made. In these attempts more had been done to obliterate good examples than if they had been left in the mutilated condition in which the "restorer" found them. Sometimes well-meaning, but crotchetty individuals would take upon themselves to alter that which was old, because it did not suit their taste, and so destroyed the authenticity of the work; and many had destroyed portions of really choice works of art to make room for their own. Against such "restoration" as this he vehemently protested. This style of thing must be prevented, or much mischief would be done even under good intentions. The great danger was in doing too much, and it required some considerable skill to tell where to stop. On the following morning an excursion was made to some of the neighbouring churches.

FOUNTAINS ABBEY.—The excavations of the site of the Abbot's house at Fountains Abbey are proceeding very satisfactorily. The arches on which the house has been built cover the river for nearly 300 feet; but how far the building has extended north and south it is at present impossible to say. According to the *Times*, the most interesting apartment brought to light within the last week or two is the private oratory of the Abbot, near the eastern portion of the remains. It has been an elegant little chapel, of a style of architecture different from any hitherto noticed at Fountains, viz., the dog-toothed Early English, and has been, no doubt, as Mr. Walbran, of Ripon, states, the work of an immediate successor of the three Johns, som etime between 1245 and 1290.

BRITISH ARCHÆOLOGICAL ASSOCIATION.—The congress will be opened at Chester on the 30th of July. An influential local committee has been formed.

THE DUNDEE ARCH COMPETITION.—Can you afford me any information relative to the Dundee Arch Competition?—for from Dundee itself I can obtain none. Understanding that a design had been selected, and not receiving back the one that I had sent in, I wrote to request that it might be returned to me. Not obtaining either my drawings or any reply, after waiting about a fortnight, I wrote again in somewhat peremptory terms, but without any better success. Another competitor has experienced just the same treatment, or even worse, for he has written no fewer than four times, yet has not been able to obtain a single syllable in reply!—which is surely highly monstrous. There ought to be no occasion for writing at all, but designs ought to be returned to the respective competitors as matter of course. The only reason there can possibly be for detaining them is that the Committee have, like that of the Army and Navy Clubhouse, rescinded their first decision, viz., that in favour of a Norman Arch, and not yet come to any other. Yet if such be really the case, wherefore, in the name of common sense, is not such reason assigned, in answer to the first inquiry. Neither common sense, however, nor common decency, seems to be regarded on such occasions.

COMPETITOR.

*** To this question, put also by five other correspondents, we are unable to reply. The competitors have just reason to complain of want of courtesy: we hope the cause of complaint may be *confined* to this.

ECCLESIASTICAL DILAPIDATIONS. — A writer in the *Carlisle Journal* draws attention to the great expense often entailed on clergymen by the size of the glebe house, and the repairs consequently required. Every unnecessary building entails a burthen upon the succeeding clergyman. "Very great disputes," he continues, "often arise about dilapidations. I will give you an instance of a case in Cumberland which took place not many years ago. A clergyman came upon his predecessor for dilapidations; valuers were employed from different parts to ascertain the amount of damages. One valuer's estimate amounted to 147*l.* 0*s.* 6¾*d.*, the second to 147*l.* 2*s.* 9*d.*, the third to 155*l.*—none of which values proved satisfactory. The case came before a jury, whose verdict was, I believe, 50*l.*! A case of dilapidation came before the late Judge Bayley. The mode of valuing was stated—the first plan was, including papering, whitewashing, and painting, 399*l.* 18*s.* 6*d.*; the second, exclusive of the above three articles, was 310*l.*; the third, similar to an outgoing tenant, was 75*l.* 11*s.* His lordship said that none of the rules were precisely correct, but the middle one seemed nearest the truth. He said that papering, whitewashing, and painting, except for preserving the wood from the external air, were luxuries, not properly dilapidations."

INSTITUTION OF CIVIL ENGINEERS.—On Tuesday, May 15, 1849, the president in the chair. The discussion on Mr. Hawkshaw's paper, "On a longitudinal continuous bearing permanent way," was continued throughout the evening, to the exclusion of every other subject. Some interesting observations were made on the actual destruction of the cast-iron chairs and double-headed rails, and the advantages that would result from the more general substitution of continuous longitudinal timber bearings for the present transverse sleepers and cast-iron chairs. The system of inserting a piece of hard wood between the rail and the main timber, as on the Great Western Railway, was much approved, as was also the plan of side transoms halved into the main timbers, as it enabled a better system of drainage to be employed than had been usual with that kind of permanent way. The general opinion seemed to be in favour of the longitudinal bearing.

SCHOOL OF DESIGN.—The following has been sent by Mr. Milner Gibson, as chairman of the committee, to several eminent manufacturers. A request for "a general return, applicable to all classes of manufacturers (addressed to certain manufacturers in each class), to be filled up according to the peculiarities of each class of manufacture. A return of the numbers of designers, drawers of patterns, putters on, modellers, chasers, and other artisans engaged in the production of ornamental designs, requiring artistic ability, at present employed by you; distinguishing them into two classes:—Class I. Numbers of those who have *not* attended any School of Design; Class II. Numbers of those who *have* attended any School of Design; with the following details, so far as applicable to Class II. only:—Designer's, &c. name; age; whether designer, &c. or before he attended any School of Design; name of school he has attended; length of time he has attended the school; how long employed by your firm." The results will show to a certain extent how far the school is practically at work.

A NOVEL EXPORTATION.—There is a story current that some short time since a whole army of "Lord Broughams," executed in lead, and of colossal proportions, disembarked in the United States, and were drawn up on a public quay in two lines, resembling an avenue of Egyptian statues. The Custom-house officers were lost in wonder at the sight of so many giants turning up their noses at Brother Jonathan, and inquired what the monster importation meant. "Statues of Lord Brougham," replied the skipper; "one for every city in the union; being the gift of his lordship's English admirers to the American Republic." Lead, as such, is subject to a heavy import duty, but "works of art" are admitted free. What could the officers of customs do? They did not swallow the skipper's story, but they could not detain his statues; and in a short time Lord Brougham was in the melting-pot, and "cast into bullets for the Mexicans."

PROJECTED WORKS.—Advertisements have been issued for tenders,—by June 7th, for the repairs, repewing, &c., of West Ham church, Essex; by June 4th, for the construction and erection of the pipes and fittings connected with the baths and washhouses in Tripp-ett-street, Kingston-upon-Hull; by date not specified, for the erection of twenty semi-detached villa residences, about three miles from the bridges (Surrey side); by June 1st, for the erection of schools, &c., at Minera and Brymbo, for the trustees of the Wrexham Charities; by 21st instant, for the erection of a vicarage-house, offices, and boundary wall, at St. Neots; by 23rd, for the erection of a detached station for constabulary, near Newbury; by 25th, for the several works required in the erection of a Presbyterian church in Grosvenor-square, Manchester; by 24th, for the erection of a bakehouse and store-rooms, and enlargement of washhouse in Chorlton union workhouse, Hulme; by 26th, for the erection of a warehouse at Salford, of brick or stone; by 21st, for sewering, paving, &c., at Chorlton-on-Medlock; by 21st, for 800 feet of brick sewer at Counter's Creek sewer, Notting-hill; by 14th June for 2,800 tons of granite, 1,800 tons of flint, &c., at Paddington; and by 26th inst., for the erection of a steam-engine and engine-house at Marshland Fen.

COMPETITION. — Plans and specifications for a church at Bracknell have been advertised for, to be lodged by 28th instant: the usual commission offered for the selected design.

ARCHÆOLOGICAL DISCOVERY.—We learn from Winchester, that during the progress of the restoration of the church of Stoke Charity, now in hand, a very curious discovery was made, namely, a sculpture representing a bishop celebrating mass, he holding the host in one hand and the chalice in the other, above whom is a representation of the deity, attended by angels. It was found concealed in a niche in the chancel, which had been bricked up for the probable purpose of concealing the sculpture, which doubtlessly occupied in Catholic times some other situation in the church. Mr. F. Baigent, of Winchester, has taken a sketch of it, which he has forwarded to the Archæological Association. Stoke Charity is about seven miles' distance from Winchester, the church is of Norman structure, and contains, in addition to the above, several curious monuments and sepulchral brasses.

ARCHÆOLOGICAL INSTITUTE.—At a meeting on the 4th, the Hon. Richard Neville communicated a memoir on his investigations at a Roman site on Lord Braybrooke's estates, near Billingbear, Berks. The remains of a Roman structure had been first noticed there, at Wey-cock, in the parish of Waltham, by Camden, and subsequent discoveries are slightly recorded by later antiquaries. The excavations directed by Mr. Neville have laid open the ground plan of the building, which seems to have been an octagonal tower, about 20 yards in diameter. Numerous vestiges of Roman occupation had been found. Mr Neville gave an account also of a curious discovery of numerous interments, discovered near Waltham, in the course of construction of the Great Western Railway; with a line of shafts resembling wells, such as have been recently described in the neighbourhood of several Roman sites in England,—as at Ewell, Chesterford, &c.

THE ADELPHI THEATRE.—We are glad to see that, prompted by the late occurrence at the Glasgow theatre, the proprietor of the Adelphi Theatre has formed an additional outlet, from both boxes and pit, into Bull Inn-court, Strand. It was greatly needed. We hope the example will be followed. There is some pretty scenery in the new burlesque here, "The Revolt of the Flowers."

DECORATIVE ART.—Miss Wallace, a lady of fortune, has discovered a mode of gilding and colouring the interior of glass tubes, which, when so prepared, form a heading for the decoration of rooms.

CAUTION TO ARTISTS.—Mr. A. F. West, a young artist, died on the 23rd; and after a *post mortem* examination, a jury returned a verdict, "That the deceased died from the effect of carbonate of lead." It appeared that he was in the habit of drawing his brushes through his lips.

THE AMPHITHEATRE AT ARLES.—A writer in the *Athenæum* says, the care expended by the city of Arles on the preservation of its monuments—the memorials of its palmy state when it was the Rome of Gaul, as Ausonius calls it—is highly creditable. Its exquisitely proportioned little amphitheatre, a veritable miniature Coliseum, is still under the hands of the masons. Indeed, the only fear seems to be lest the authorities should fall into the fault so common to the French in such matters, and push the indispensable work of preservation too far towards an attempt at restoration. It has been at length thoroughly isolated from the mean surrounding buildings, which well nigh suffocated it; the interior has been well cleared out; and a light iron railing as a defence from wanton injury has been erected around it. Evidently, the good city has not spared cost in the matter.

THE LINCOLNSHIRE ARCHITECTURAL SOCIETY held a meeting in the manor-house rooms, Gainsboro', on Wednesday. Amongst other papers was one by Sir Charles Anderson, Bart., on Lea church, which has been almost rebuilt by Sir Charles himself.

AN ORDER OF MERIT.—I believe it has been already suggested, though not yet acted upon, to establish an order of merit to be conferred on distinguished individuals in this country. That such a mark of distinction would be appreciated, and is wanted, there can be but little doubt, but then let it be an order of merit conferred solely on those who have distinguished themselves by their talent in the arts and sciences, for great learning, and those who are at the head of the several learned institutions. They have such a mark of distinction in Paris, why not in this great country?

A SUBSCRIBER.

MEETINGS OF SCIENTIFIC BODIES

Held during the ensuing week.

MONDAY, May 21.—Institute of Architects, 8 P.M.
TUESDAY, 22.—Institution of Civil Engineers, 8 P.M.
WEDNESDAY, 23.—Society of Arts, 8 P.M.
THURSDAY, 24.—Royal Society, 8½ P.M.; Society of Antiquaries, 8 P.M.
FRIDAY, 25.—Archæological Association, 8½ P.M.
SATURDAY, 26.—Institute of Fine Arts. 8 P.M.

TO CORRESPONDENTS.

"*Analysis of Clay.*"—A correspondent asks for "the analyses of the best fire-clays, Co. clays, and pot and china clays, presently used in England for manufacturing the various articles made of these clays."

Received.—"W. G. R." (too late for present number), "W. J., Jun.," "J. and G.," "W. P. M.," "A Middle-aged Millwright" (will see that his object is answered by a letter from another correspondent in our present number), "A. B. D. A.," "J. D." "J. T." ("Railway Reform"), "Examples of Ancient Pulpits existing in England," by F. T. Dollman, architect (London, Geo. Bell, and the author, 37. Mornington-road, Hampstead-road), 1849. T. Wright's "History of Ireland," Part II. (London, Tallis). "A Manual of Logic," by B. H. Smart (London, Longman), 1849. "Form and Sound: can their Beauty be dependent on the same Physical Laws?" by Thos. Purdie (Edinburgh, Black), 1849. "Antiquarian Gleanings in the North of England," Drawn and Etched by W. B. Scott (London, G. Bell). "The Philosophy of Painting: a Theoretical and Practical Treatise," by Mr. Henry Twining (London, Longman, Brown, and Co.), 1849. "An Historical and Descriptive Account of Life Assurance," by Mr. Alfred Burt, secretary to a Life Office. "Popular Rhymes and Nursery Tales: a Sequel to the Nursery Rhymes of England," by Mr. Jas. Orchard Halliwell (London, J. R. Smith, Old Compton-street), 1849.

Note.—The statement in respect of Mr. J. Tombs, of Westminster, last week, should have been to the effect that he did *not* tender for Market House, Brentford.

"*Books, Prices, and Addresses.*"—We have not time to point out books or find addresses.

NOTICE.— All communications respecting *advertisements* should be addressed to the "Publisher," and not to the "Editor;" all other communications should be addressed to the EDITOR, and not to the Publisher.

ADVERTISEMENTS.

No. CCCXXIX.

SATURDAY, MAY 26, 1849.

EVERAL points of considerable interest, as respects our antiquities and the history of architecture, were discussed at some length at the last meeting of the Institute of Architects, held on the 21st inst. The conversation began with the announcement of donations, and ran on till the meeting was adjourned. Mr. Donaldson, who took once more his old seat as one of the secretaries, commented in his usually good-natured, rose-coloured way on the various books and drawings which were presented (including a new work by Mr. Fergusson, on fortification, Mr. Brandon's nice volume of parish churches, the second collection of sketches issued by the Architectural Publication Society,* and a drawing by the late Mr. Dance, giving the measurements of old London-bridge), and did not omit a few words of commendation, afterwards repeated by the chairman (Mr. Bellamy), of the first part of our "Buildings and Monuments." A little volume relative to the city antiquities, the secretary said he should leave in the author's own hands, in order that he might make some statements on the subject. Accordingly up got Mr. Tite, and presented "A Descriptive Catalogue of the Antiquities found in the Excavations at the new Royal Exchange, preserved in the Museum of the Corporation of London,"† and he did so in order that he might remark how easily public bodies might be impugned without cause, and to show that the citizens of London had never been unmindful of their antiquities, even at a time when they were held in little esteem elsewhere. The catalogue itself, the speaker said, was written by Mr. Thompson, of the London Institution, but the introductory essay was written by himself, and he would read a few passages to show, first, that he did not consider Roman London was so important a place as some believe; and secondly, to answer what he thought the inconsiderate and gross attacks which had been made on the officers of the corporation.

The chairman took the same view, and said Mr. Tite's book would have the effect of disabusing the public mind; and if for that effort alone, could not be too much applauded. He afterwards made some observations as to the universally erroneous nature of the statements of the periodical press, which it would be difficult to maintain. As to the "city" question there are certainly two opinions upon it. It will be remembered that it was the subject of a sharp correspondence in our pages some time ago, between Mr. Tite and Mr. C. Roach Smith; and as the corporation book will probably not get into the hands of many of our readers, we turn to it and give the portions which were read.

Speaking of the first collection of London antiquities, the author says,—

"These reliques must always possess a con-

siderable intrinsic value as illustrations of society and manners, and also a peculiar local interest, as indicating the condition of the place and people where they were found; though they cannot always be implicitly relied on as conclusive evidence of the nature of the buildings formerly standing on the spots where such antiquities were discovered.

The Tradescant family is usually regarded as having formed the first considerable collection of natural and artificial curiosities in England; but, with the exception of coins, only six Roman articles occur in the catalogue of the Museum published by John Tradescant, junior, in 1656, and only one of these is distinguished with the name of the place where it was found. After the collection passed into the possession of Elias Ashmole, it was very considerably increased; and, as it was not transmitted to Oxford until 1682, he probably added to it many specimens of London antiquities discovered after the great fire.

From the time of the rebuilding of the city, the importance of preserving such reliques, especially Roman remains, appears to have begun to be rightly perceived; and one of the first and most successful collectors of such specimens was Mr. John Coniers, an apothecary of London, who was living at the period. By his researches and industry were brought together most of those numerous Roman vessels and articles of every kind which, afterwards formed the extraordinary museum of Dr. John Woodward, who bought the principal part of the collection. After his death in 1728, such parts of his museum as were not bought by the University of Cambridge were sold by auction at Mr. Cooper's, in the Great Piazza, Covent Garden,' in a thirty-three days' sale, the last three of which were occupied by the celebrated Roman shield and the miscellaneous antiquities."

Three other contemporaneous collectors of London antiquities were Dr. Harwood, John Bagford, a bookseller, and John Kemp.

"From the time of these original preservers of London antiquities, the custom of observing and recording their discovery appears to have generally commenced, with more or less of intelligence and accuracy in the description and delineation of such remains. At the present time, however, the practice has been long since established in a highly improved form; and the reports which are now so frequently published, in illustration of the ancient reliques of all periods, often exhibit such an amount and variety of antiquarian learning as seemed in the last century to be almost unknown. This increased intimacy with the nature and value of antiquities has led to their more careful preservation and better exhibition, as well in public local depositories as in private collections. One of the former is the museum established in connection with the Corporation Library at Guildhall, for the reception of antiquities relating to London, especially such as may be discovered in the execution of civic public improvements, which it is certain cannot rightly belong to any other depository."

The author says, in concluding his "attempt to illustrate a series of antiquities, full of interest at the present time as being the types of places and manners long since departed,"—

"It has been also attempted in this sketch to show that the citizens of London have never been unmindful of their ancient civic remains; and even in times when such memorials were held in little estimation, and the nation had no national museum, they possessed in Gresham College not only such a receptacle, but apparently a niche for local antiquities. The liberal willingness with which every suggestion has been met, with reference to the preservation of these reliques, also shows the inconsiderate injustice of those gross attacks on the corporation and its officers in this respect, which are so constantly made, and which it is impossible to reconcile either to candour or to truth."

We must leave this to those who are personally concerned, but are compelled to admit a strong impression that the corporation, as a body, have done grievously little towards the preservation and collection of their antiquities, whatever they may be disposed to do now.

To confine ourselves, however, to the proceedings of the meeting. Mr. John W. Papworth then read the conclusion of his paper on some features of the connection between the architecture and chronology of Egypt, with an account of Le Sueur's essay "On the Chronology of Egypt, illustrated by its Monuments." Afterwards Mr. Papworth laid before the meeting the opinions of the learned Dr. Lepsius, "On the relation of the later Egyptian orders and the Greek column," and as the discussion which followed referred chiefly to this, we must for the most part confine ourselves at this moment to it. We give the reader's own words.

I hope to be excused, he said, if I venture to add what Lepsius himself says on the subject, at the end of the valuable paper which I have so often quoted, containing the grounds for the conclusion, in which he is supported by the authority of Barry and Jomard,—a conclusion in which I humbly concur, although for very different reasons to those which he gives as the steps by which he attains his object; and I beg it may be understood, that what I am about to read are *his* opinions, and not *mine*.

At the first glance, says Lepsius, it is evident that the division of the Greek column into base, shaft, capital, and abacus, supposes more than a natural analogy founded upon mathematical laws, or the practice of architecture in general, and consequently necessarily seen wherever there is an architecture with ceilings, and supports to those ceilings. In vain will "historic relations" be denied; they are relations which manifest themselves the more that the several parts are taken into consideration.

To commence with the capital: we have no need to go further than that of the Corinthian order, to find, with Jomard, its type in the Egyptian leafy capitals.*

The echinus of the Doric order corresponds altogether as evidently with the large expanded calix of Egyptian columns. This is not only proved by the analogy of the principal forms, but also by the ornament, which, according to Semper's researches, appears to have been generally *painted*, but of which we have seen one *sculptured* example in the columns of the great Portico and of the small Temple at Pæstum.

So, too, the colors of these ornaments, which are blue and red, with green leaves interposed, are the same which are ordinarily employed in Egyptian columns. But that which appeared to Lepsius decisive for his connection of the calix cap with the Greek echinus, was the existence of the listels, or annulets, below the echinus, and the groove so often seen at the necking or hypotrachelion of the Doric and other columns. These listels, or annulets, he thought, evidently corresponded with the Egyptian ribbons which tie the bundles of stems, and which annulets are generally found three in number, or, as at the Parthenon and elsewhere, so many as five, the ordinary number of Egyptian bands.

Above the plant-capital we have the abacus, square in Greece as in Egypt, with the single difference that, while the Egyptian die remains of the same width with the architrave, the Greek abacus advances beyond it.

Other points of relationship present themselves in the shafts of the columns. Here we recall the entasis, corresponding exactly to that of the Egyptian plant column, which also finds itself greatest at one-third of its height in many cases, but frequently, nay, generally, lower, at one-seventh, which indeed agrees better with the swelling of the aquatic plants which it was the intention to imitate.

In saying of channelling—that habitual ornament of the three Greek orders—that it is never wanting in the Doric (the Roman and Etruscan examples are not forgotten), the temple at Segeste might be cited as a contradiction; but then this has never been finished, as is evident from the cases in the great temples at Eleusis and Rhamnus, and from those at Delos and Thoricus, all which have the channelling at top and bottom, because the remainder was to have been worked in place.

---

* The second part issued by the Architectural Publication Society is full of valuable hints. We will look to it next week.

† "Preceded by an introduction, containing an account of their discovery, with some particulars and suggestions relating to Roman London." By W. Tite, F.R.S., F.S.A., Architect of the Royal Exchange. Printed for the use of the Corporation of the City of London.

* The preceding paper mentioned several capitals as being probably borrowed from the Corinthian capital in the Ptolemaic period.—Ed.

But in this very fact of channelling at all, Lepsius thinks that he has found a new and very clear proof of "historical relationship" to the Egyptian works. The general number of Doric channellings is 20, but instances of 16 (the ordinary number in Egypt) are not rare; they are found in the Temples of Minerva at Sunium, and of Jupiter at Syracuse, in the interior of the great temple at Pæstum and of Jupiter at Ægina, in the theatre at Segeste, and in many other places.

Polygonal columns intended to remain without channels, are scarcely found in Greece, to his knowledge, by the side of channelled columns, as in Egypt, though there may be examples in private houses at Pompeii. As to the isolated instance of octagon brick columns in the Roman temple of Redicolus, it would seem that they had anciently a channelled stucco which had at a later period fallen away.

Still less are pilaster columns, or pillars with four faces, known in Greece, or in Greek art; for the only example known is found in the Temple of Minerva, at Priene; for the pillars of the Temple of Jupiter Olympius, at Agrigentium, so extraordinary in many other respects, are joined by walls up to the very top.

But the intimate relation of Greek channelling to plain facets is not the less true; it is, first of all, stated by these words of Vitruvius, lib. iv., c. 3 :—

"Columnas autem striari viginti striis oportet quæ si planæ erunt angulos habeant viginti designatos. Sive autem excavabuntur sic est forma facienda ut quam magnum est intervallum striæ tam magnis striaturæ paribus latiribus quadratum describitur;" words which, at the least, prove that he knew that, before Doric columns were channelled, they must be facetted; at the Theatre of Segeste, columns with sixteen channels by the side of others with as many faces, would seem to show that these last once were intended to have been channelled; and, lastly, there are cases where a third part from the base upwards has been left polygonal; whilst the remaining portion is channelled, as in the Temple of Hercules, at Cori; and in that called " of Philip," at Delos, in both cases twenty channels above and twenty facets below.

The form of the Egyptian channels is very slightly hollow, and is not always a pure segment; at Amada they are almost flat in the middle, in which feature is conveyed another point of resemblance in the Doric channels, which are also not hollowed in a purely circular form, but pretty frequently are almost flat in the centre, with a much more perceptible curve toward the arrises, as in the Propylæa of Sunium, and of the Temple of Diana, at Ephesus, in the great Temple at Rhamnus, and in the Temple of Minerva, at Sunium. There is only a difference in their depth ; for instance, at

Sunium it is to the width as	1 to	6·625
At Barry	1 to	6·000
At Beniassan, according to Wilkinson	1 to	16·000

It seems, continues Lepsius, that this resemblance in general portions, and these striking analogies in the most special peculiarities, between the Greek and Egyptian columns, can admit no doubt as to their "exterior and historic relation."

But it seems also evident, in the second place, that the Greek column* is composed of two orders, which in Egypt are very distinct, and which never mix, that is to say, of pillar-columns and plant-columns.

We have seen that since channels can only be found in pillar columns where, on principle, they are perfectly proper and natural, they must be exotic and incompatible in plant columns.

In Greece they are seen employed as a constant ornament for Doric columns, together with the echinus corresponding to the Egyptian calix, with listels representing the Egyptian ribbons, and with the entasis, whose prototype is found in that of the Egyptian columns, which imitate aquatic plants : in short, the channels of pillar columns are seen applied to the shafts of plant columns ; for at the least, no one will pretend that the Greek channels, which show themselves in the same numbers, 16 and 20, and of the same difference of curvature, have no connection with the Egyptian channellings, and are an ornament which

* Of all orders.—Ed.

could develop itself at entirely different periods, and from entirely different origins, in two separate nations, and without the supposition of "historic relations."

On the other side, Lepsius himself urges that it is not to be thought, with Jomard, Rosellini, and Wilkinson, that the mere identity of these channels would suffice to authorise the denomination " Protodoric," which Champollion wished to give to the second Egyptian order; for we see that, on consideration of the actual elements which exist in all columns, the three Greek orders form but one, in opposition to the two styles of Egypt; and that the Doric order, as well as the two others, presents a mixture of plant and pillar columns.

Now, if it be considered that success has attended this attempt to prove that the mixture of the two styles exists, there remains a final result, viz., that principles confounded and misunderstood from very ancient times, carry always in themselves a very sure proof that they are of exotic origin, and that their true birth must be sought in that country where they are still to be seen pure and simple, and easily to be recognised and understood; that is to say, that it is necessary to seek the origin of the Greek column, not in Greece, but in Egypt,—an opinion not enunciated as original, but which he thinks he has established for the first time, by arguments which sound criticism will not be able entirely to blame.

Mr. Tite, after complimenting Mr. Papworth, proceeded to make some comments on Lepsius's theory, first saying a few words as to Le Sueur's book, which was the first product of the French national press, and was remarkable as having the hieroglyphics printed in moveable type, showing that, although apparently so arbitrary, these consisted of only a limited number of forms. Egyptian chronology was an obscure and difficult subject; looking at some of the early cosmogonies, they reminded him of the Welsh pedigree which midway contained,—"About this time the world was created." Confining himself, however, to the Protodoric theory,—the development of Greek architecture from that of Egypt,—he believed nothing of the sort. It was true that the Greeks were a colony of Egyptians, but they had nevertheless borrowed nothing. Egyptian architecture was that of a people who excavated, the Greek the architecture of those who built. If Lepsius had been an architect, he would have made no such mistake. Much stress had been laid on the tomb of Benihassan, given from a sketch by Mr. Barry, in Mr. Gwilt's edition of " Chambers,"* but he could not, from that one coincidence alone, believe that Greek architecture was indebted to Egyptian architecture. Although there was communication between the countries, and Cadmus came from Egypt, it was 300 or 400 years after that event before there was anything like government in Greece, and 700 years before Doric architecture grew up. The interval was so long, he could not connect one with the other.

Mr. Donaldson gave an interesting account of the circumstances which had led M. Le Sueur to devote attention to Egyptian chronology. He said he fully agreed with those who denied that Greece owed anything to Egypt in architecture. Egyptian architecture was purely that of the cavern, Greek that of the cabin. The proportion and refinement of the latter showed quite a different sentiment.—Mr. W. Pocock said he was satisfied that Greek architecture originated in wood. In a decree by Lycurgus the builders' tools mentioned were the axe and the saw, showing that the buildings were of wood.

A Visitor argued, with sound reason, that

* The engraving of Benihassan occurs at page 38 of the introductory essay. The tomb is excavated in the rock, and presents fluted columns, and a approximation to mutules.

genius, although prompted by what is around, and making use of others' materials, so assimilates them and makes them so entirely his own, that it is scarcely possible to say whence they came. The influence of one nation upon the other was not to be doubted, he thought. He would point to the Gothic and the Greek. Surely there was more apparent difference between these than between Greek and Egyptian architecture, yet one had grown out of the other.

Mr. Wathen (whose work on Egypt is known to many of our readers) thought that the age of Benihassan had been greatly overstated, and that it was imitated from the Greek Doric. It was the practice with the Egyptian to put before their own names the title of their most distinguished ancestor,—this was called the prenomen. The title of Orsotosen having been found on the tomb of Benihassan, the tomb had been ascribed to his reign; but he (the speaker) would maintain, that this tomb had been formed by the latest of the Pharaohs, and that the title of Orsotosen was merely the prenomen. This view was confirmed by the fact that an obelisk, indisputably of a more recent period (fifty years before the conquest by Alexander), had also upon it the title of Orsotosen.

Mr. Papworth, in the course of his reply to some of the objections, said the Greeks certainly used wood construction, as they were necessitated, and so it appeared in their later buildings, but they began with a stone idea; and Wilkins constantly speaks of temples which were burnt being restored, i. e. not rebuilt, but repaired. Further, if Cadmus left Egyptian Thebes for Phœnicia and Crete, at the period fixed by the Arundel marbles, and if after that time Athens was Cretan, a colony tributary to Minos, where would be the wonder that a general notion of a column should have gone thither with the emigrants, which grew up afterward, under their scientific progress in every department of the fine arts, into principles self developed ?

We do not agree with those who deny altogether the obligation of the Greeks to the Egyptians, although we would in no way depreciate the merit of the Greeks. The influence of one over the other has always seemed to us too evident to be questioned. A large number of the early inhabitants of Egypt dwelt in constructed cabins, from which a system of architecture was developed quite distinct from that which grew out of their excavated structures, and it is undeniable that the earliest temples of Greece are the most like Egyptian work, and the least like the timber hut, a fact which was not brought into view during the discussion.

What we have written will suffice to shew that the evening was passed pleasantly.

BURIAL IN TOWNS.—A public meeting of the national society for the abolition of burial in towns, was held on Wednesday, last week, at the royal national schools, Cowper-street, City-road, to petition Parliament for the immediate closing of all burial places in cities and towns; Mr. George Thompson, M.P., in the chair. The meeting was very numerously attended, and its more immediate object was explained by the chairman, who remarked, that as the evil, though a great one, and an outrage to public decency, and to the holiest feelings of humanity, was likely, nevertheless, to be defended by some who thought they had a vested interest in the abuse, its remedy could only be applied by the Government with the aid of the Legislature, backed or enforced by a pressure from without. After a detail of the grievance to some extent, the meeting was addressed by Mr. Walker, Mr. Luke Hansard, and others, and resolutions unanimously adopted.

CHRONOLOGICAL ACCOUNT OF BUILDINGS IN ITALY AND SICILY.

In tracing the dates of buildings solely from the records of the most accurate historians, many and great difficulties are presented to the careful inquirer.

We find, to take an instance, in Severano's "Rome," that S. Giovanni Laterano was built by Constantine, restored "almost from foundations" in 772-95, after an earthquake; added to by Leo IV. 847-55; repaired in 1183, 1276, 1290, and 1300, besides being embellished at various other times. Now this, at first sight, seems tolerably exact, as giving the chief part of present building the date of c. 772. But how are we to say how much, if any, of its predecessor still remains? How far its plan and arrangement were followed, what precise parts were added, and how much escaped intact during the after repairs and alterations? We know too well what *restorations* often mean with us. The works in 772 might have been executed quite unlike their originals, as the rebuilding of Canterbury by the Williams, or of St. Paul's by Wren,—or after their model, as so many of the late restorations in England. The additions and repairs might have been done as they were by Jones to St. Paul's, by Wykeham to Winchester. The building might have been *restored* and spoilt as Wren spoilt Westminster, and some ignorant person the nave of St. Saviour's.

Yet, to shed upon us a ray of hope, we are told that in one particular instance (and from the care with which the fact is noted we fear an exception), viz., S. Clemente, Rome, the chief part was actually rebuilt in the likeness of its predecessor from the very ground.

Thus it is seen that the church historian must fall back for assistance on the architect, and that a critical examination of the works themselves is necessary before any good judgment can be formed as to the changes they have undergone. A personal examination is the more necessary, as very few Italian writers furnish any accurate details of mouldings ornaments, or construction. Very many excellent works are, indeed, to be met with among them, which enter, with great research, into the various documents and histories connected with the buildings, so as to arrive at as accurate a knowledge as can be obtained, by that means only, of their eras. Such are Fabri's "Ravenna," Rossi's and Severano's "Rome," Richa's "Florence," &c. But very few have brought architectural knowledge to their assistance, sought information on doubtful points from the buildings themselves, or given details such as might have allowed others to work on. Except Cicognara, the Duke di Serradifalco, and D'Agincourt, I am not aware of any Italian work giving such information; and even there it is meagre. In fact, I know of no work of the sort in Italy itself that gives any thing like the real information drawn from the buildings themselves that is supplied by Professor Willis in his work, intended merely as a sketch, of the Italian mediæval architecture.

It was trusting too much to written authority, and too little to the clear evidence of the edifices themselves, that led that enthusiastic writer and brilliant theorist, Hope, to assign to the tenth and eleventh centuries the use of the pointed arch, by reference to its introduction at S. Ambrogio, S. Ciriacco, and S. Giovanni Laterano, when a careful examination would have shewn it due to the additions in the fourteenth.

The following gives an abstract of the dates of building, restoring, &c., the principal edifices in Italy and Sicily, together with the authorities for the same:—

Nocera Baptistery.—330 (D'Agincourt). Converted from an antique temple.

S. Constanza, Rome.—334 (D'Agincourt) "Oxford Glossary," and Nardini, who supposes it to have been built as a baptistery to S. Agnese. Hope believes it to have remained almost unaltered. Nothing certain known of its date, except that, in 1256, it was dedicated to S. Constanza (Vasi).

S. Giovanni Laterano Baptistery.—334 (Severano); 330 (Vasi; the columns under cupola added 1475); 440 (H. G. Knight); 462 and 638, the chapels added (Severano); but restored almost from foundations, 1600 (Vasi); 1153 (Knight). Baptistery much altered and walls raised. Constantine was *not* baptised at Rome (Gibbon); 330 (Vasi). He says the second row of columns under cupola was added 1480. The chapel of S. Venanzio added, 640; S. Ruffina, 1253; that of S. Ilario restored, and the fourth rebuilt from foundations, c. 1600.

[All these baptisteries seem to have been built in the same way. The builders got some old columns, on which they put as many old capitals as they could find, without much regard to fitness. A large base made amends for a small capital. Where enough old capitals were not to be found, new ones, in rude imitation, were made. The columns were then arranged in circles, arches turned from column to column, without mouldings or ornaments of any kind; a flat roof put over aisles, and a dome over the centre. Yet, rude as they are, these old baptisteries, from their fine circular outline, have a vastly picturesque internal effect.]

S. Maria Maggiore, Rome.—432 (Severano). He says it was originally built 353; restored and enlarged, 442, as now (1675) seen, except some chapels; altered, and roof, &c., restored, 732; tribune rebuilt, 1295; porch, 1145—1575; present roof formed, c. 1500; chapel of S. Cosmo e Damiano, 498. [Altar to north-west. The general plan gives scarcely any idea of a cross. No mention is made of any atrium.] Rossi says porch was reconstructed, 1150; great repairs done to church in 1288 and 1450; it was rebuilt from foundation in 432, and enlarged. Vasi dates the campanile, c. 1275. Rycaut and Severano give its date as 1376; Rycaut says the porch, tower, and roof were constructed in later times than the rest. [This tower is clearly very late in date. The lower arches are pointed, and all the mouldings more elaborate than usual. Were it not for the ugly steeple, this would be, perhaps, the finest tower in Rome.]

Duomo Ravenna.—380 to 398 (Fabri), consecrated 381; entirely rebuilt, 1734—45; supposed to have been built by S. Orso with remains of Temple of Jove.

[Apsidal end, two rows of columns on each side, forming aisles, going right up to end wall, without any triumphal arch or sign of the cross on plan. It has its old circular tower diminishing towards the top (much ruined), but seems of about the same date as the square Roman brick ones.]

SS. Silvestro and Martino, Rome—320 (Filippini). This is the date of oratory, which was built in the baths of Titus; 498 (Filippini), church restored, 780 and 844; c. 500 (Rossi), was rebuilt from foundations. The roof by S. Carlo Borromeo; 845 (Rycaut), church rebuilt; 1200 (Milezia), was restored by Marchione of Arezzo.

S. Lorenzo Basilica, Rome.—(Severano and Nardini), built by Constantine; 579 to 590, rebuilt from foundations. It had been altered and restored 435, 450, and afterwards 720 and 780 (Rossi and Severano).—Again from foundations, 1220; when porch was built with twenty-two columns. The work in 578-90 included rebuilding the church from foundations, the part then built being the present tribune end. In 780 the form was changed, aisles being added, and the entrances altered; and in 1220 the orientation was changed. 780, old nave formed into choir. New nave added, 1220 (Hope).—The cloisters are clearly of the same date as the Roman brick towers, the columns being precisely similar to those in the towers. Much of the ornamental work of choir is well done; but some of the pilasters, capitals, and scrollwork are badly executed. The Ionic capitals of portico equal in freedom and beauty of carving, almost any existing.

S. Giovanni Laterano, Rome.—By Constantine. Rebuilt almost from foundations, 772. The ambulatory behind tribune, 850. Restored or repaired, 1130, 1183, 1276, 1290, 1305, &c.; 1140, Campanile; rebuilt 1560; 1500, principal arch of nave supported by two great columns (Severano); 1290, being ruined by heretics was restored (Rossi); 1308, being burnt was restored (Vasi); 750, tower and porch (Rycaut).

S. Giovanni e Paolo, Rome.—398, nearly rebuilt, 770 (Rondinino); 398, originally built towards the east, the present tribune being in site of old façade (Rossi); the church is on the site of the Curia Hostilia (Nardini and Rossi); the tower c. 1200, Hope; 1570, porch rebuilt on grander scale (Rondinino). The tower is one of the peculiar brick ones, and a string course, similar to those of tower, is used as a cornice to the ionic columns of portico. It has an egg-shaped ornament, being the only instance of its use I recollect. Altar to west.

S. Pietro in Vincoli, Rome.—400, anciently the Basilica Eudoxiana (H. G. Knight); 440, rebuilt, its original date being very ancient; restored, 555 (Vasi); eighth century restored (D'Agincourt and Willis); 442 (Bunsen); 1500, restored (Rossini). Altar to north-east.

S. Clemente, Rome.—c. 450: in eighth century rebuilt nearly on the old plan (H. G. Knight, Rondinino, and D'Agincourt); in 872 rebuilt nearly on the old plan (Bunsen); 1112, repaired (Rondinino); 1112, amboni added, and cathedra in 1123 (Crescembini). Altar to the west.

S. Saba, Rome.—Fourth century; west front, 770 (Willis). Altar to south.

S. Agnese Maggiore, Ravenna.—400, on site of Temple of Hercules (Fabri).

S. Agata Maggiore, Ravenna.—434 (Fabri); 400 (D'Agincourt).

S. Andrea Maggiore, Ravenna.—440: the pulpit 660. The church much ornamented 553, with Greek marble columns still there, 1664 (Fabri).

S. Apollinare Nuovo, or Di Dentro, Ravenna.—Fifth century, by Theodoric, king of the Goths. The twenty-four marble columns brought from Constantinople (Fabri). It has a round tower, with openings almost exactly like the Roman ones, having also the flush archivolt, not very common in Ravenna. The old pulpit still remains on its five columnar supports. The capitals of columns all alike.

S. Giovanni Evangelista, Ravenna.—425: once adorned with most splendid marbles and mosaics. Built by Galla Placidia (Fabri). It has a square tower like the Roman brick ones. The capitals of columns inside church are all alike.

S. Croce, Ravenna.—449, by Galla Placidia (Fabri).

S. Giovanni Battista, Ravenna.—440, by Galla Placidia. The entrance was by a long portico of eighteen little columns. They were removed in 1634, and a new piazza formed (Fabri). Has clerestory of three arches on columns under one large arch (D'Agincourt).

S. Nazareo e Celso, Ravenna.—440, by Galla Placidia (Fabri).

S. Sabina, Rome.—c. 430, restored 795 and 825 (Severano); 424, restored 795 and 1683 (Ciampini); c. 340 (Crescembini). Supposed from Temple of Juno Regina (Nardini); 425, rebuilt from foundations, and consecrated 435. Rebuilt in 824 and 1441, and much embellished and repaired in 1587 (Rossi); 425, 824, 1238 (Willis). Altar to north-east. Built c. 430 (Vasi).

S. Crisogono, Rome.—400, supposed, but date unknown. Restored in 741. Again from foundations in 1119 and 1124. Again restored 1624 (Severano); 730 (Bunsen); 741, roof, &c. restored, (Rycaut). Supposed by Constantine. Restored 730 and 1500 (Vasi). The columns are from the baths of Severus. The plan like S. Paolo fuori. Altar to the west.

S. Giovanni de Calene, Ravenna.—438. It has a circular tower with openings like the Roman brick ones.

S. Francesco, Ravenna.—450: first dedicated to S. Pietro Maggiore (Fabri).—It has a square brick tower like the Roman.

S. Stefano Rotondo, Rome.—467: restored and dedicated, it having been an old temple; again restored 780; altered to present form 1450 (Rossi and Severano).—c. 475, and repaired 1450 (Vasi and Bunsen).—c. 1450, reduced to form now seen, it having, before that time, been larger, and with three rows of columns; what it originally was is not well proved (Nardini).—470: not an old temple (Hope).—The outer columns were *not* walled up in 1450 (*Quarterly Review*).—All the Ionic capitals are execrably carved, the outer row (blocked up in wall) especially.

S. Bibiano, Rome, 363, by Olimpiana; restored 467, 1216, 1560 (Severano).—Built, 470 (Rossi).—Very ancient; rebuilt, 1216; restored, 1630 (Vasi). Altar to east.

S. Agata, in Trastevere.—714, 717 (Rossi and Severano).

S. Agata in Suburra, or de' Goti, Rome.—500 (Rycaut).—Reconstructed 600; being ruinous, was restored and embellished in 17th century (Rossi).—714 (Severano).—Very ancient; restored, 600, having been profaned by the Goths (Vasi).—472 (Ciampini).

Theodoric's Tomb, Ravenna.—490; consecrated 1221 (Fabri).—Its use is disputed and date uncertain (D'Agincourt).—The workmanship is so very much better than that of cotemporaneous buildings, that one almost suspects the correctness of the date usually assigned to it.

Theodoric's Palace, Ravenna.—490 (Fabri).—Date very doubtful (*Quarterly Review*, 1845).—The general appearance of the façade gives the idea of its being of about the same date as the Roman brick towers.

S. Pancrazio, Rome.—360: rebuilt 500 (Rossi). 500: repaired 630; rebuilt 1630 (Rycaut).—There was a small chapel here 272; enlarged, 360; in 510 as now seen; restored, 630 and 1609 (Vasi). 1249: the Ambone. Date sculptured on it (Ciampini).

SS. Cosmo and Damiano, Rome.—528 (Crescembini, Vasi, Rycaut, Ciampini): 780—restored and rebuilt 1630 (Vasi): converted from temple of Remus and Romulus (Nardini): the bronze gates brought 780 from Perugia (Rossi).

Parenzo.—540 (Hope and D'Agincourt).—The plan is interesting, shewing the complete arrangement of the early churches.

S. Maria Maggiore, Ravenna.—541 (Fabri): circular tower with openings in it, like the Roman brick ones.

S. Michele, Ravenna.—545: the front and campanile afterwards added (Fabri).—545 (Ciampini).

S. Apollinare in Classe, Ravenna.—545: embellished 748-69 ; injured by Saracens, 850 (Fabri) ; 549 (Hope, Willis).—The capitals are all curious middle-age imitations of the antique, and all alike.

S. Andrea Maggiore, Ravenna.—440 : rebuilt 550, when the Greek columns, still there, were added (Fabri).

Altars.—Up to this time we find no vestiges of side altars, and little or no attention paid to orientation.

Apse.—The chancels were no farther distinguished than by the semi-circular apse, except at S. Apollinare Nuovo, where the apse is thrown back nearly its own diameter. I am aware of no church having apse at each end. Some, but very few, have apses to aisles as well as nave ; but then the cross arms are given up.

Chapels.—Side chapels were scarcely known. Severano says, indeed, those of S. Giovanni Batt. e Evang. were built 462 ; but they are almost distinct, though small, churches.

The arches are, I believe, invariably unmoulded. I remember none having mouldings except those of S. Clemente, and this was rebuilt in later times.

In the two centuries after Constantine, the greatest simplicity prevailed in form and arrangement. The only appearance of any marked change shews itself at Ravenna, where S. Nazarea e Celso shews a bold change of form, and the brick towers (if, as I believe, of this date) of outline.

With this ends the list of the fine Ravenna basilican churches. They contain, usually, a very great quantity of middle-age sarcophagi, rounded or coped at top. Few have inscriptions. I saw no capitals in any of the churches earlier than the lower empire, and in almost every case the capitals in each one church are all similar.

The windows in the towers, square and round, are almost all similar in the peculiar deeply-recessed columns and small arches above to the Roman brick ones. Few, however, have the small archivolt, and none the imposts. There are very few strings, and those few are formed merely of bricks laid anglewise between two plain rows of bricks, almost flush with the face. They have no dentils. The crowning cornices are in similar style, but larger and bolder. The columns have, sometimes, slightly carved capitals in the Norman style.

Altogether, these Ravennese towers are less finished, and seem earlier than the Roman.

It is worthy of notice, that the churches in Greece have the windows formed on the same principle as those of the above towers.

T. H. L.

ST. MARY-AT-HILL, THAMES-STREET, CITY.

WE spoke some time ago of the internal restoration of this church, if we may use the word, in the style of Wren's period. The original church was greatly injured though not destroyed in the great fire of 1666, and the interior and the east end were rebuilt by Wren between 1672 and 1677. The west end and tower which remained were in recent times taken down and rebuilt.* The whole area of the building is an oblong figure, about 96 feet by 60 feet : an ambulatory is formed at the west end of it by a screen, and the body of the church is thereby rendered nearly square. Four Italian Doric columns support entablatures, proceeding from pilasters against the side walls, so as to produce a cruciform arrangement of the ceiling. The centre space between the four columns is covered by a cupola, in which an octagon lantern has been introduced.

The building was gutted : the ceiling is entirely new, and the wood work, comprising the pulpit, priest's desk, organ gallery, displays such an extent of carving in this particular style, as has not been executed before in the city for many years.

To the organ gallery have been added new wings, which are supported by square pillars rising from the churchwardens' pew, and ornamented with fruit and flowers. The great screen is entirely composed of plate glass, in a framing of oak. The rector's pew and reading desk are enriched with carved open tracery, and brackets surmounted with the royal supporters, bearing shields with V. R., 1849.

The pulpit is entirely new, and is very elaborately carved. In the sounding-board are bosses of flowers of 12-inch projection. On the back of the pulpit are two carved trusses. From the eyes of the volutes garlands of flowers

* Godwin's " Churches of London." Vol. II.

---

are suspended, which pass through the split trusses, and fall down, crossing and uniting behind. Within the pulpit, at the back, there is a well-executed drop, composed of fruit and flowers. The stairs are of unusual extent, and show that neither cost nor pains have been spared.

On the front of the organ-gallery there are clusters of very bold carving, consisting of musical trophies and garlands of flowers, with birds and fruit. The Royal arms, with a mantle scroll, is about 10 feet long, and forms a perforated screen on the top of the organ-gallery. The organ was built by Mr. Hill.* The whole of the pews are cushioned and carpeted. The fittings of the altar-table, pulpit, &c., were executed by Mr. Geo. Haines.

All the carved work is by Mr. William Gibbs Rogers.

The works were executed under the direction of Mr. James Savage, Architect ; the builder employed was Mr. Ryder; and the plaster work was by Mr. Newport. A very large sum of money must have been spent ; and such is the good feeling on the subject prevailing in the parish, that the windows are about to be filled with stained-glass at the expense of individuals.

CURE FOR THE CORN WEEVIL.—In granaries with damp walls, it has been found that the weevil breeds in incredible numbers ; while the adoption of means to insure dryness in the construction of the building, otherwise so necessary to the preservation of the corn itself, will also prevent the generation of the weevil, or destroy it if previously generated.

* This organ is constructed on the German plan, and contains two manuals and a pedal organ. The compass of the manuals is from C C to F, the pedals from C C C to E, 2⅔ octaves. The great organ contains:—1. Open diapason, 16 feet ; 2. Open diapason, 8 ditto ; 3. Gamba, 8 ditto ; 4. Stopt diapason, 8 ditto ; 5. Quint, 6 ditto ; 6. Octave, 4 ditto ; 7. Wald flute, 4 ditto ; 8. Octave quint, 3 ditto ; 9. Super octave, 2 ditto ; 10. Flageolet, 2 ditto ; 11. Sesquialtra, 3 ranks ; 12. Mixture, 3 ditto ; 13. Posaune, 8 feet ; 14. Clarion, 4 ditto ; 15. Krum horn, 8 ditto. The swell organ contains :—1. Bourdon and open diapason, 16 feet ; 2. Open diapason, 8 ditto ; 3. Hohl flute, 8 ditto ; 4. Stopt diapason, 8 ditto ; 5. Octave, 4 ditto ; 6. Octave quint, 3 ditto ; 7. Super octave, 2 ditto ; 8. Suabe flute, 4 ditto ; 9. Sesquialtra, 3 ranks ; 10. Cornopean, 8 feet ; 11. Hautbois, 8 ditto ; 12. Clarion, 4 ditto. The pedal organ contains :—1. Open wood diapason, 16 feet ; 2. Octave, 8 ditto ; 3. Trombone, 16 ditto. All the stops in the great organ extend through the whole compass of the manual.

DOOR HANDLE AND KEY-HOLE, HALLE AUX LAINES, BRUGES.

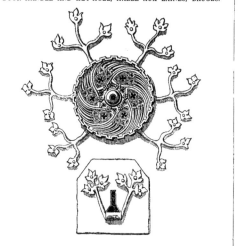

GOTHIC IRONWORK.

ANNEXED is a representation of all that is left of the door-handle and key-hole at the *Ancienne Halle aux Laines*, Bruges ; the knob (or ring) has been broken off. The diameter of the circle is 9 inches. The variety discoverable in medieval metal-work is quite extraordinary.

THE ROYAL ACADEMY.

(144) " Helena," the only contribution of Mr. Eastlake, R.A. The character and expression of the features beautifully realise the poet's conception ; it is painted in a manner suggestive of the combined styles of Titian and Raffaelle.

(159) " Circe with the Syrens three," F. R. Pickersgill, (A). A composition signalised by much beauty, although not a favourable picture for an exhibition, from its delicacy of colour, verging on weakness. Few artists, however, could put together a like number of figures with more masterly arrangement of beautiful lines.

The same appearance of weakness is observable in (463) " The Maids of Alcyna, the enchantress, endeavouring to tempt Rogero," by the same artist, but this also is an elegant composition.

(171) " A Slide," T. Webster, R.A. An essentially English picture, and the most perfect of its class in the collection. The genuine humour, natural treatment (although refined), and probable disposition of the performers in the scene,—the sunny little face of the red-cloaked girl, placed as she is, are beyond all praise. The individuality of the figures and heads is something surprising, as well as is the absence of conventionality ; the only drawback to its exciting unqualified pleasure is the truth with which the cracked ice is painted : one imagines momentarily to perceive it give way, and expects to lose sight of the failing and fallen together. Mr. Webster's lesser performance, entitled (91) " A See-saw," wherein a small boy is elevated above his expectations, to his no small uneasiness and the heavier one's enjoyment, is also a charming production.

(174) " The Stream at Rest," and (392) " The solitary Pool," R. Redgrave, (A.) are astonishing facts to certify that the artist has

hitherto mistaken his walk. "The solitary Pool," particularly, is second to nothing of the sort; it is painted with the precision of a daguerreotype as to form, and in colour, is nature reflected.

(177) "The Chevalier Bayard wounded at Brescia." This is the best of three excellent productions by J. C. Hook, which satisfactorily prove a continental tour is not always an artist's ruin. Exquisite in colour throughout, the head of the Chevalier is remarkably fine in conception; whilst the delicacy of character and execution of the virtuous, fair, and well-trained damsels bespeak a refined taste, free from all taint of prettiness. A little more confidence and decision would perfect it. The same remarks will apply to a smaller but no less excellent contribution, (382) "Othello's first Suspicions," which exhibits great feeling for the first order of art. (517) "Bianca Capello," the last and least original of the three, has, nevertheless, traits of great excellence. Mr. Hook promises to be an honour to the school.

(8) "The Wreck Buoy," and (206) "Venus and Adonis," painted in imitation of the old Venetians, are specimens of the wonderful art of Mr. Turner, R.A.,—superior to many of his late works. For years he has not been so *strong*, and in two opposite manners.

(207) "The First-born," C. W. Cope, R.A. A sleeping child, and its young mother bending over it in happy contemplation of its loveliness, with the fond husband, painted in the manly style of this artist: it demands the appreciation of all. The grey and general tints of the girl's neck and shoulders vie with the colours of Etty.

(117) A coloured study for fresco in House of Lords—"Griselda's first Trial," and (903) cartoon of the same, wherein all the ample resources of the artist have been called into requisition, promise the fresco to be not inferior to what might have been expected from the painter of "Cardinal Wolsey." The drawing of "Griselda," the arms in particular, is marvellously beautiful, as is the composition.

The six productions of Mr. Stanfield, R.A., set forth his characteristics to advantage. (498) "Moonlight off the Reculvers," is to us his most extraordinary work, being accurate delineation of a most difficult natural effect. The cloud that seems to float over the middle distance startles the spectator from its truth: there is a freedom too from the coldness and blueness, so often pervading moonlight pieces, that renders it remarkable. (12) "Tilbury Fort—Wind against Tide;" (151) "Lugano;" (211) "Salvator Rosa's Studio" (less worthy of the master); (325) "Lago Maggiore;" and (331) "Near Miori, Gulf of Salerno;" are the other works of this our best marine painter.

(242) "The Cup found in Benjamin's Sack," Sir W. Allan, R.A., gives proofs of labour and research during the artist's sojourn in the East.

(284) "Drawing for the Militia," J. Phillip, full of the incidents belonging to the scene, and, from what we can see of it, replete with the fruits of exercised talent, skilful perception of character and expression, and an education in the manual part of the profession of no small limits. Surely the producer of the "Presbyterian Catechists," and the "Scotch Fair," deserved more consideration than the position of his picture shows he had.

(286) The duet, "Andante con Moto," F. Stone, remarkably pretty and *Mr. Frank Stone-y*.

(290) "The Destruction of Jerusalem" by the Romans, under the command of Titus, A.D. 71, D. Roberts, R.A.—a concentration of topographical, professional, and historical knowledge, forming a really grand work—the only exhibited one of the artist, and, perhaps, his *chef-d'œuvre*.

(303) "Benjamin West's first Effort in Art," E. M. Ward (A). Little Benjamin, the embryo President of the Royal Academy, is represented intently bent upon committing to paper the transient smile of his sleeping nephew, struck with its beauty whilst sleeping. The earnest desire to consummate his intention, and the quiet admiration depicted in his expression, are beautifully pourtrayed. The sleeping infant is a nice study; and the treatment and composition of the work, as a whole, bespeak an advance upon any of his preceding pictures. In Mr. Ward's productions may be always discerned research and persevering industry: few possess more determination to think for themselves, or labour more zealously to find novelty in choice of subject,—still fewer who determine to leave as little undone as possible, and invest such an amount of thought in one performance. (318) "Daniel Defoe and the Manuscript of Robinson Crusoe" is a striking instance; his perception of the human feelings, and power of expressing them, have never been brought into play with more success; the despair of the poor author, who has hawked about his work until almost ashamed of it—the sympathy of his wife and child—the *nonchalance* of the dandy bookseller, who is extinguishing the smouldering wick of the taper with the nib of his pen—the assumption and egotism of the fashionable authoress of namby pamby odes to expiring bullfinches, fickle butterflies, and arched eyebrows—the sycophantic and complimentary senior partner,—are to the life.

(311) "Isabella," J. E. Millais, is a singularly clever reading of Keats's poem: the personages are a succession of well studied and portrayed individuals, every one of them distinct. As the work of a young artist, it may be called extraordinary.

(324) "Rienzi vowing to obtain Justice for the Death of his young Brother, slain in a skirmish between the Colonna and Orsini factions," W. H. Hunt, is much in the same style as that of Mr. Millais, and scarcely less clever; perhaps there is even a higher feeling about this that promises well for the hereafter.

(326) "The Fountain, a Scene at Mola di Gaeta," P. Williams, a repetition of one of the artist's most pleasing and elaborate engraved works. Several other transcripts of Italian life contributed by him this year will amply repay inspection.

(131) "A Glade in the Forest," (343) "A Stream in the Hills," (371) "Passing Showers," (417) "The Shade of the Beech Trees," and (544) "The Quiet Lake," are some of the most successful attempts of Mr. Creswick (A.) to show nature as it is; he affords one of our strongest arguments when the superiority of English landscape painters over all others is asserted—no one represents nature in truer colours; it is quite a treat, requiring little imagination, to take off your hat and fancy yourself in the enjoyment of the invitingly cool shade ever present in his delicious pictures,—a welcome escape from the heat and glare of a crowded exhibition room.*

* We are compelled to postpone continuation of notice of the Architectural-room.

LAUNDRY DRYING CLOSETS.

The great importance of the subject induces me to attempt an elucidation of the two systems of drying; viz., with and without a current of fresh air; and I trust that although both practice and prejudice are strongly in favour of the former, I shall be able satisfactorily to prove the latter system to be not only the most economical, but the most effective.

As your correspondent Mr. Walker observes, "Artificial drying (has been) in fact a two-fold operation. By heat, the moisture is quickly converted into vapour; by ventilation, that vapour is carried away, and replaced with dry air;" or in other words, drying has been effected by the joint action of a radiating surface, and a current of heated air, distributed in such a manner as to bring it as nearly as possible in contact with the linen suspended in the chamber. By these means, the temperature was raised from 50° or 60° to about 200°, according to the extent of the heating surface, and the quantity of air admitted. Now, supposing the air in its passage to be perfectly heated to the temperature of the chamber, then *every particle passing off represents a waste of fuel* equivalent to the raised temperature; and if any air enters the chamber, and passes through *without* being sufficiently heated, the effective power of the chamber is then lessened, and *time*, a most important element, is lost in the drying. By placing thermometers in different parts of a chamber thus heated, after it has been filled with wet linen, the unequal temperature of the stream of air may be shewn; and that it is so, will be proved by the rate of evaporation varying in different parts of the chamber; but if you *close* the air flues, and expose your heating surfaces, whether of brick or iron, to the linen of the chamber, with only a slight net work of wire between them and the linen to prevent accidents, then the temperature of the chamber will quickly rise above the boiling point of water, and evaporation will take place rapidly; not a particle of heat will be wasted, and nothing but the steam produced by the evaporation of the water will escape from the outlet, which ought to be small, and capable of regulation. By this mode, the heat radiated from the flues acts through a rarified medium, *directly* on the water in the linen. *All* the heat is employed, and none escapes except charged with vapour; and as water evaporates at the boiling point much more rapidly than at any lower temperature, so will a chamber thus heated and closed (and which may with strict truth be compared with a steam boiler, or evaporating pan), dry the linen more economically and rapidly than if supplied by "*an ample current of fresh air*."

Everything in this arrangement tends to economy, and the whole of the heat derived from the fuel is employed.

The difference between the two methods is this:—in the one case, you are constantly heating a large volume of air, and by thus altering its hygrometric capacity, you enable it in its passage through the chamber to take up the water converted into vapour by the radiant heat of the flues,—every atom of air thus passing out at a raised temperature being a waste of fuel. In the other, you employ the whole of the heat derived from the fuel, directly to evaporate the water in the linen, which passes from the chamber in the form of vapour, *robbing the flues only of so much heat as is due to its conversion*.

The object of either method being to evaporate water, the question is, by which means it can be evaporated most rapidly and economically. Were there not experiments to prove the efficiency of the one method over the other, the question might easily be decided by reasoning upon the respective plans. But that is not necessary.

In a chamber with a given heating surface supplied with fresh air, and maintained at a temperature of 200° before it was filled with wet linen, it was found that not more than one-third of a pound of water per minute could be evaporated. The same chamber with its air-flues closed, and maintained at the same temperature, regularly evaporated one pound of water per minute. To ascertain whether the whole of the heat given off by the fuel was radiated in the chamber, a sheet of writing paper was introduced into the flue at its exit from the chamber. After being there ten or fifteen minutes it was removed, and found discoloured, but scarcely scorched. Now, as economy is so large an element of success as applied to the "Laundries for the Working Classes," the importance of this subject to them cannot be over-estimated, and it is to the pertinacity with which the committee and engineer adhered to the old system of drying that the expense on this part of the model establishment at Goulston-square is to be attributed. Had it been known that drying could be accomplished by the simple radiation of heat in a close chamber, and *with the conditions required for such an establishment*, much time, money, and anxiety would have been saved. The "close" system of drying has now been adopted there, and I have no doubt will be followed in all public establishments where economy is studied.

Wm. Jeakes, Jun.

Holborn-hill and its Vicinity.—A meeting of the ward of Farringdon-Without was held on the 16th inst., for considering the propriety of applying to Government for aid in carrying out the improvements on Holborn-hill and Victoria-street,—the Lord Mayor in the chair. The meeting was addressed by his lordship, and by Messrs. Walker, Barnard, Galloway, Williams, Taylor, Herepath, Meeking, Buckmaster, Lamplow, and others. Resolutions were unanimously adopted in accordance with the objects of the meeting, and a committee was appointed to carry them out.

Surveyor to Ironmongers' Company.—Mr. G. R. French has been elected surveyor to this Company in the place of the late Mr. Sibley. There were eight other candidates. Four of them went to the poll.

GENERAL MEETING ROOM, EUSTON STATION.

Mr. P. C. HARDWICK, ARCHITECT.

THE GENERAL MEETING ROOM, EUSTON STATION.

LONDON AND NORTH-WESTERN RAILWAY.

WE said last week in our notice of the great hall at the Euston Station, that the new general meeting-room was a handsome apartment, 75 feet long, 45 feet wide, and 40 feet high, calculated to accommodate 400 persons; and we now give a view of the apartment, which will be found, we think, to justify the epithet.

The walls, columns, &c., are formed in grey Martin's cement, painted in imitation of granite. There is a fire-place at each end; the chimney-piece is of dove marble.

THE SEVEN LAMPS OF ARCHITECTURE.*

THE following detached passages, marked when reading the book, will further elucidate Mr. Ruskin's views :—

Position of Buildings.—It would not be well to build pyramids in the valley of Chamouni; and St. Peter's, among its many other errors, imagine it placed on the slope of an inconsiderable hill. But imagine it placed on the plain of Marengo, or, like the Superga of Turin, or like La Salute at Venice! The fact is, that the apprehension of the size of natural objects, as well as of architecture, depends more on fortunate excitement of the imagination than on measurements by the eye; and the architect has a peculiar ad-

* See p. 229, *ante.*

vantage in being able to press close upon the sight, such magnitude as he can command. There are few rocks, even among the Alps, that have a clear vertical fall as high as the choir of Beauvais; and if we secure a good precipice of wall, or a sheer and unbroken flank of tower, and place them where there are no enormous natural features to oppose them, we shall feel in them no want of sublimity of size. And it may be matter of encouragement in this respect, though one also of regret, to observe how much oftener man destroys natural sublimity, than nature crushes human power. It does not need much to humiliate a mountain. A hut will sometimes do it; I never look up to the Col de Balme from Chamouni, without a violent feeling of provocation against its hospitable little cabin, whose bright white walls form a visibly four-square spot on the green ridge, and entirely destroy all idea of its elevation. A single villa will often mar a whole landscape, and dethrone a dynasty of hills; and the Acropolis of Athens, Parthenon and all, has, I believe, been dwarfed into a model by the palace lately built beneath it. The fact is, that hills are not so high as we fancy them; and, when to the actual impression of no mean comparative size, is added the sense of the toil of manly hand and thought, a sublimity is reached, which nothing but gross error in arrangement of its parts can destroy.

Our Street Architecture. — Of domestic architecture what need is there to speak? How small, how cramped, how poor, how miserable in its petty neatness is our best! how beneath the mark of attack, and the level of contempt, that which is common with us! What a strange sense of formalised deformity,

of shrivelled precision, of starved accuracy, of minute misanthropy have we, as we leave even the rude streets of Picardy for the market towns of Kent! Until that street architecture of ours is bettered, until we give it some size and boldness, until we give our windows recess, and our walls thickness, I know not how we can blame our architects for their feebleness in more important work; their eyes are inured to narrowness and slightness: can we expect them at a word to conceive and deal with breadth and solidity? They ought not to live in our cities; there is that in their imaginations, as surely as ever perished forsworn nun. An architect should live as little in cities as a painter. Send him to our hills, and let him study there what nature understands by a buttress, and what by a dome. There was something in the old power of architecture, which it had from the recluse more than from the citizen. The buildings of which I have spoken with chief praise, rose, indeed, out of the war of the piazza, and above the fury of the populace; and Heaven forbid that for such cause we should ever have to lay a larger stone, or rivet a firmer bar, in our England! But we have other sources of power, in the imagery of our iron coasts and azure hills; of power more pure, nor less serene, than that of the hermit spirit which once lighted with white lines of cloisters the glades of the Alpine pine, and raised into ordered spires the wild rocks of the Norman sea; which gave to the temple gate the depth and darkness of Elijah's Horeb cave; and lifted, out of the populous city, grey cliffs of lonely stone, into the midst of sailing birds and silent air.

THE HOP IN DECORATION.

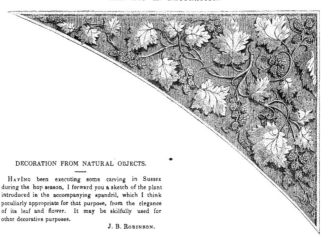

DECORATION FROM NATURAL OBJECTS.

Having been executing some carving in Sussex during the hop season, I forward you a sketch of the plant introduced in the accompanying spandril, which I think peculiarly appropriate for that purpose, from the elegance of its leaf and flower. It may be skilfully used for other decorative purposes.

J. B. Robinson.

Proportion.—I believe that all that has been written and taught about proportion, put together, is not to the architect worth the single rule, well enforced, " Have one large thing and several smaller things, or one principal thing and several inferior things, and bind them well together." Sometimes there may be a regular gradation, as between the heights of stories in good designs for houses; sometimes a monarch with a lowly train, as in the spire with its pinnacles: the varieties of arrangement are infinite, but the law is universal—have one thing above the rest, either by size, or office, or interest. Don't put the pinnacles without the spire. What a host of ugly church towers have we in England, with pinnacles at the corners, and none in the middle! How many buildings like King's College Chapel at Cambridge, looking like tables upside down, with their four legs in the air! What! it will be said, have not beasts four legs? Yes, but legs of different shapes, and with a head between them. So they have a pair of ears: and perhaps a pair of horns: but not at both ends. Knock down a couple of pinnacles at either end in King's College Chapel, and you will have a kind of proportion instantly. So in a cathedral you may have one tower in the centre, and two at the west end; or two at the west end only, though a worse arrangement: but you must not have two at the west and two at the east end, unless you have some central member to connect them; and even then, buildings are generally bad which have large balancing features at the extremities, and small connecting ones in the centre, because it is not easy then to make the centre dominant. The bird or moth may indeed have wide wings, because the size of the wing does not give supremacy to the wing. The head and life are the mighty things, and the plumes, however wide, are subordinate.

Colour in connection with Architecture.—I do not feel able to speak with any confidence respecting the touching of *sculpture* with colour. I would only note one point, that sculpture is the representation of an idea, while architecture is itself a real thing. The idea may, as I think, be left colourless, and coloured by the beholder's mind: but a reality ought to have reality in all its attributes: its colour should be as fixed as its form. I cannot, therefore, consider architecture as in any wise perfect without colour. Farther, as I have above noticed, I think the colours of architecture should be those of natural stones;

partly because more durable, but also because more perfect and graceful. For to conquer the harshness and deadness of tone laid upon stone or on gesso, needs the management and discretion of a true painter; and on this co-operation we must not calculate in laying down rules for general practice. If Tintoret or Giorgione are at hand, and ask us for a wall to paint, we will alter our whole design for their sake, and become their servants; but we must, as architects, expect the aid of the common workman only; and the laying of colour by a mechanical hand, and its toning under a vulgar eye, are far more offensive than rudeness in cutting the stone. * * *

Whatever harmonies there may be, are distinctly like those of two separate musical parts, coinciding here and there only—never discordant, but essentially different. I hold this, then, for the first great principle of architectural colour. Let it be visibly independent of form. Never paint a column with vertical lines, but always cross it. Never give separate mouldings separate colours (I know this is heresy, but I never shrink from any conclusions, however contrary to human authority, to which I am led by observance of natural principles); and in sculptured ornaments do not paint the leaves or figures (I cannot help the Elgin frieze) of one colour and their ground of another, but vary both the ground and the figures with the same harmony. Notice how nature does it in a variegated flower; not one leaf red and another white, but a point of red and a zone of white, or whatever it may be, to each. In certain places you may run your two systems closer, and here and there let them be parallel for a note or two, but see that the colours and mouldings do; the same for an instant, but each holding its own course. So single members may sometimes have single colours: as a bird's head is sometimes of one colour and its shoulders of another, you may make your capital one colour, and your shaft another; but in general the best place for colour is on broad surfaces, not on the points of interest in form. An animal is mottled on its breast and back, rarely on its paws or about its eyes; so put your variegation boldly on the flat wall and broad shaft, but be shy of it in the capital and moulding; in all cases it is a safe rule to simplify colour when form is rich, and *vice versâ*; and I think it would be well in general to carve all capitals

and graceful ornaments in white marble, and so leave them.

Value of Architecture.—We may live without her, and worship without her, but we cannot remember without her. How cold is all history, how lifeless all imagery, compared to that which the living nation writes, and the uncorrupted marble bears! how many pages of doubtful record might we not often spare, for a few stones left one upon another! The ambition of the old Babel builders was well directed for this world: there are but two strong conquerors of the forgetfulness of men, poetry and architecture; and the latter in some sort includes the former, and is mightier in its reality; it is well to have, not only what men have thought and felt, but what their hands have handled, and their strength wrought, and their eyes beheld, all the days of their life. The age of Homer is surrounded with darkness, his very personality with doubt. Not so that of Pericles: and the day is coming when we shall confess, that we have learned more of Greece out of the crumbled fragments of her sculpture than even from her sweet singers or soldier historians. And if indeed there be any profit in our knowledge of the past, or any joy in the thought of being remembered hereafter, which can give strength to present exertion, or patience to present endurance, there are two duties respecting national architecture whose importance it is impossible to overrate: the first, to render the architecture of the day historical; and the second, to preserve, as the most precious of inheritances, that of past ages.

The late Affray at the Royal Academy.—Mr. Evans, who assaulted the secretary on the rejection of his artistic labours, was sentenced lately at the Middlesex Sessions to pay to the Queen a fine of 25l., and enter into his own recognizance in the sum of 40l., with one surety in 20l., to keep the peace for six months. The fine was paid, the recognizance entered into, and the surety given, on which the defendant was liberated. The case appeared to excite great interest.

Electro-telegraphic Progress.—The Common Council of the City have agreed to offer no hinderance to Messrs. Blunt, C.E., in their intended deposit of the wires for their projected coast line of telegraph in the Thames, unless they prove a nuisance either to the public or to individuals.

EARLY CHRISTIAN ART.

HAVING completed his review of ancient art, Mr. Wornum proceeded, on Friday week, at the School of Design, Somerset-house, to lecture on art in the middle ages—the "dark ages,"—so called, said the lecturer, because we are pretty well in the dark concerning them This period he comprised in the interval between the establishment of Christianity and the renaissance or revival of art,—a period of about 900 years, from the fourth to the thirteenth century. He proposed, therefore, to devote to this period three lectures, including the consideration of the various styles of Gothic ornament, comprising, of course, architecture. In this first of these, however, a general historical view of the period merely was taken, and the character of its ornaments and symbols examined in detail.

Ancient art, he proceeded, might be said to have ceased when Rome ceased to be the capital of the world, namely, from the time of Constantine, in the fourth century. The establishment of Christianity, the division of the empire, and the incursions of barbarians, were the chief causes of the important revolution experienced by the imitative arts, and the serious check they received; and the foundation of Constantinople, and the Exarchate, were equally fatal to the magnificence of Rome.

Byzantium, the Rome of the East, became more rich in works of art than Rome herself: Europe and Asia were despoiled to enrich the new city of Constantine: its great thoroughfares were adorned with colossal figures in bronze; and before the church of St. Sophia alone were disposed many hundred statues, the masterpieces of ancient art.

But nearly all these works, and many more in the various capitals of Europe, Asia, and Africa, became a prey to religious fanaticism, or were carried away for the value of the metal by the many hordes of Huns, Goths, and Vandals, by whom nearly every trace of ancient grandeur was swept from the earth. The volcano, even, was a protection compared with the destructive fury of those middle-age fanatics, the iconoclasts, whether Christian or Mahomedan. So effective was their system of destruction, that but for the fortunate preservation of Pompeii, by Vesuvius, we should have had to glean our knowledge of ancient manners and customs almost entirely from books. In the third century, however, as the church became more general, and accordingly more firmly established, the antipathy and dread of images proportionately declined.

During the first and second centuries, Christian works of art were limited to symbols, and were then never applied as decorations, but as exhortation to faith and piety; such we find, for instance, on their tombstones. The first of all symbols was the monogram of Christ. It was sometimes combined with the figure of the cross, with the letters *alpha* and *omega* on the sides. Another very common symbol was the fish; it is what is called an acrostic symbol: the Greek word for fish, ιχθυς, being composed of the initial letters of the words of the following Greek sentence—Ιησους Χριστος, Θεου Υιος, Σωτηρ,—Jesus Christ, of God the Son, the Saviour. This is the origin of the common symbol known as the *Vesica pisces*, which is the shape of the glory that we find occasionally surrounding the whole figure of Christ, especially in representations of the transfiguration in Byzantine MSS. The five letters of the word occur as well as the fish, but in this case written vertically. Other symbols employed in early decoration were then adverted to by the lecturer, together with the pictorial and plastic representations mixed up with them in and after the third century. The most ancient figure of the Saviour depicted in the catacombs at Rome and copied by Raffaelle, and others of a subsequent date, with the nimbus, or glory, introduced only in the fourth century, were then described; and the mosaics of the old Christian churches or basilicas in Rome, Ravenna, and other parts of Italy, pointed out as our principal monuments of early Christian painting. As works of art, he remarked, these latter decorations have little value, but their interest is great as historical and ecclesiastical monuments.

The basilicas, which mean literally, houses of the king, or lord, spiritual or temporal, were originally used as halls of justice; and the upper end is called the tribune or tribunal, from the seats of the judges and magistrates, the tribunes, who held their official sittings in that part. The tribune is frequently built in the form of a large semicircular recess, surmounted by a semi-dome. The altar was sometimes placed in the recess, and sometimes before it. The whole upper concave surface (called the apsis) was gilded and adorned with figures of Christ and the apostles, variously arranged, though generally similar in the essentials, and nearly always executed in Mosaic work.

In the large basilicas in which a transept is introduced before the tribune, the ground plan thus forming what is called the Latin Cross, the transept is divided from the nave by a large arch, called the arch of triumph; and in this case subjects from the Apocalypse are frequently represented on the arch. Other subjects from the various religious cycles were introduced in other parts of the church.

These mosaics, mostly executed from the fifth to the ninth centuries, are similar in character to the illuminations of the MSS., especially those of the Byzantine school.

As regards pavements, less change, perhaps, took place than in any other class of ornamental designs; that is, the purely geometrical patterns, which, even though heathen works, could present nothing offensive to the most scrupulous Christian. We accordingly find, in many churches of the middle ages, mosaic pavements nearly identical in pattern with those lately discovered in Pompeii.

Some interesting remarks on embroideries, representations of the Divine Trinity, &c., then followed, and reference made to the "Guide to Painting," by the monk Dionysius, recently translated and published at Paris as a manual of Christian iconography.

In the extraordinary peninsula of Mount Athos—the 'holy mountain,' as it is called, there are no less than 935 churches or chapels, every one of which is either covered in the interior with frescoes, or ornamented with pictures on panel, and occasionally with mosaic, and many of these works, said the lecturer, date from the early period of which we are now treating. The monasteries of Mount Athos also possess many ancient relics of the jeweller's art, as the magnificent triptic of St. Laura, presented to that monastery by Nicephorus Phocas, in the tenth century. It is set externally with emeralds, pearls, and rubies as large as sixpences, and a double row of diamonds. The most singular peculiarity of this remarkable peninsula is, that no woman is allowed to enter it—no female has ever trod in one of its 935 chapels, and yet these chapels are decorated with the figures of female saints, by painters who perhaps never saw a woman from the time of their infancy: this is, however, of little consequence, as the images of the saints are strictly traditional. Such, continued the lecturer, is the nursery of the Byzantine school, until lately without a rival where the Greek Church prevails, and formerly of almost equal influence in the west.

A point which the educated artist ought to know, relates to the representation of the divine Father, by the hand in the attitude of benediction,—a very common symbol in early Cristian art,—but differing in the Greek and Latin churches, so as at once to determine the origin of a work of art; for where the Greek form occurs, it is infallibly a sign of the Byzantine School. The Greek form represents the monogram of Christ, IC XC,—the first finger or index pointing upwards, the second slightly curved, the thumb and the third crossed, and the fourth or little finger also slightly curved. The Latin shows the thumb and the two first fingers, a symbol of the Trinity. The artist will find this distinction of frequent use in studying old monuments: it throws a light on the origin of several so-called Gothic works.

The memorable image controversy between the emperors in the east and the popes in the west, which ultimately separated the eastern and western churches, and indeed convulsed the whole of Christendom for a century and a half, commenced shortly after the Council of Constantinople, in the eighth century, deprecating symbols,—as the Council of Illiberio, nearly four centuries earlier, had prohibited the decoration of churches with images. Into the particulars of this controversy the lecturer entered pretty fully, and afterwards proceeded, with the help of illustrations, to examine more in detail, the character of the ornaments, or symbols rather, of the whole of this period of art, apart altogether from its architectural arrangements. Here, said the lecturer, a new world as it were presents itself to the ornamentist, and one wholly unintelligible to him without some slight knowledge of symbolism, though much is not required, it being sufficient to point out the leading forms, and before all the cross and dome or circle; the latter, the dome or circle, referring to heaven and eternity, and the former, the cross, to the means of attaining them. These forms pervade almost every ornamental design of the middle ages, especially of the earlier periods; and they are still further developed by a host of secondary symbols, some of them already explained. In architecture too, though we cannot enter into it at present, the cross and dome supplanted every other form, and constitute the great elements of the Byzantine style, completely illustrated in St. Sophia of Constantinople, San Vitale, of Ravenna, and St. Marks, of Venice.

The symbolism of middle-age art gives its ornaments no beauty; their effect in most cases is to be attributed to the richness of their colouring and materials. But we shall find as we proceed, that in one subject at least—in geometrical design—the artists of the middle age are yet unapproached; and it is not to be overlooked that the whole range of mediæval monuments offer a vast source of suggestions to the decorator and designer, which he cannot too frequently consult, not for imitation, but for hints.

In my next, concluded the lecturer, I shall treat of some of the middle-age mosaics, and of Romanesque, Lombard, and Saracenic architecture, and their characteristic decorations.

NOTES IN THE PROVINCES.

THE colossal statue of Dr. Jephson, by P. Hollins, is to be publicly inaugurated at Leamington on 28th inst.——The new ship dock at Portsmouth, opening into the lately-finished steam-basin, has been completed by the contractor, Mr. Rolt. Its dimensions are —length on the coping, 300 feet; width, 90 feet; length at bottom of dock, 260 feet; width, 35 feet. It is capable of receiving the largest modern-built ship afloat.——A sum of 10,000*l.* has been bequeathed by a Mr. Parsons, of Dudley, for the establishment of a free school for poor boys and girls of that town and parish.——The restoration, as it is still called, of St. Michael's Church, Gloucester, the idea of which had been abandoned, is about to be carried out by "taking down the whole of the present edifice except the tower, and erecting a new building, composed of a nave and two aisles with a chancel." Messrs. Fulljames and Waller had prepared a plan of restoration, and made an estimate, which has been modified in cost from 3,000*l.* to 2,000*l.* The walls are to be slighter, and the aisle pillars lighter than those of the present edifice. From a re-arrangement of the seats, increased accommodation (for 50 persons) will be provided.——The corner-stone of a new Unitarian Chapel has been laid at Tipton.——The bank of the Oxford and Coventry Canal, at Rugby, lately burst and inundated the village: what was the cause we have not yet ascertained. ——A small edifice, to be called St. Alban's Church, is in course of erection by the Liverpool Church Building Society, in Bevington district. The chief stone was laid on Tuesday week. The design is by Mr. A. H. Holme, and the building is to be of rock-faced Yorkshire stone. It is to be in the Early English style, 108 feet long and 48 feet wide; height of the roof, 55 feet; spire, 120 feet in height from ground. There will be 1,000 sittings, and the cost will be 5,000*l.* Messrs. J. and R. Duckworth, G. Glaister, T. Mackerell, P. E. Weber and Co., J. Crellin, and W. Goodall, are the contractors.——The foundation-stone of the Manchester Baths and Washhouses is to be laid on Whit-Monday with all due ceremony.——Some alterations and improvements are about to be made at the Salford Townhall, from plans by Messrs. Travis and Mangnall, at a cost of about 500*l.*, according to estimates sent in.——The South Cliff

Building Company at Scarborough have applied to the town-council there for leave to build a bridge over Ramsdale Valley, and to make a carriage and foot road from the pavilion adjoining the railway station to the South Cliff. Opposing interests are astir against the project.——The whole work of restoration at Scarborough Church is to be continuously prosecuted, in place of being stopped and resumed, as was intended.——The new district church of All Saints, Monkwearmouth, Sunderland, was opened on Sunday week. This church was built from a design by Mr. Dobson, of Newcastle, and is calculated to hold 500 people. A great portion of the sittings will be free. The cost of the erection is upwards of 2,000*l.*, chiefly public subscription.

LIFE ASSURANCE.

THE Manchester agent of the British Mutual Assurance Company (a respectable life office, in the success of which we feel interested), gives the following curious results of a personal canvass at 1,349 houses, in 70 streets, in the districts of Hulme and Charlton, chiefly rentals from 12*l.* to 24*l.* per annum. The inquiry showed that there were 29 insured; 8 persons too old; 11 who never heard of life assurance, and who were anxious to have it explained to them; 471 who had heard of it, but did not understand it; 419 who were disinclined to assure; 19 favourable, if their surplus incomes were not otherwise invested; 89 persons who had it under consideration, with a view to insure as soon as their arrangements were completed, and who appointed times for the agent to call again; 21 refused the circulars, or to allow an explanation; 171 doors not answered; 102 houses empty; 3 had sufficient property not to require it; 1 favourable, but afraid of litigation; 1 preferred the savings' bank; 1 used abusive language; 2 would trust their family to provide for themselves; and 1 had been rejected by an office, although he never was unwell, and was consequently afraid to try again, although very anxious.

LANDLORDS AND TENANTS.

IMPORTANT DECISION UNDER THE COUNTY COURTS' ACT.

Garrett v. *Saunderson.*—In the Brompton County Court on Friday, May 18, the defendant (a widow) appeared to a judgment-summons requiring her to shew cause why an order of the Court, which was made on the 16th of February last, for the payment of 5*l.* 5s. for a quarter's rent, had not been complied with.

Mr. Dodd, the plaintiff's solicitor, said he should be able to satisfy the Court, that the defendant was not justified in taking the house, and submitted that by refusing to give up possession, she had contracted a debt without reasonable means of payment. The plaintiff had offered to forgive the defendant the rent if she would give up the key, but she refused to quit the premises on the ground that she had no place to go to. The 122nd clause of the 9th & 10th Vic. cap. 95, empowered his Honour to issue a warrant requiring the defendant to give up possession; but he (Mr. Dodd) would submit that this was a case which clearly came within the meaning of the 99th clause of the same statute, which enacts that if it shall appear to the judge that the defendant has incurred a debt under false pretences, or has wilfully contracted such liability without reasonable expectation of being able to pay the same, the judge may order such defendant to be committed to the House of Correction for any period not exceeding forty days. He should be able to show that the defendant did incur this debt under false pretences, having represented herself to be a person of property when she took the house, and that she would shortly come into possession of 1,000*l.* through the death of a brother. At that time she was, and has since been, in the receipt of parochial relief. In proof of that fact, he had obtained the relieving officer's certificate. It was perfectly clear that the defendant had no right to keep possession of the house, not being in a condition to pay the rent; and by so doing, coupled with the facts he (Mr. Dodd) had stated, she had evidently incurred a debt without any reasonable expectation of payment, and had subjected herself to imprisonment.

This statement having been borne out by evidence, the Court held,—that the defendant remaining in the house was equivalent to a representation of being able to pay, and ordered her to be committed for seven days.

METROPOLITAN COMMISSION OF SEWERS.

A GENERAL court was held on Thursday the 17th, at the Court House, Greek-street, Lord Ebrington, M.P., in the chair.

The Ordnance Survey.—A recommendation was read from the Ordnance Survey Committee, "that an application be made to the Ordnance Survey Department for levels, &c., of the area from the Counters Creek Sewer to Brentford, &c.—Mr. Chadwick, in support of the motion, said that the inhabitants of this district were most anxious for the active operation of the powers of this commission for a system of improved drainage.—Mr. Leslie, seeing Sir John Burgoyne present, wished to ask of him whether by consenting to the requirements of this new district, it would not have the effect of impeding the works required most urgently for the metropolis itself?—Sir John Burgoyne gave it as his opinion that the placing this district under their active operation, might be effected with but trifling delay, and at a very small expense.

Mr. R. L. Jones wished to be informed whether the proposed increased scale of ten feet to a mile was to apply to the whole of their districts; for if so, the expense of it might become a very serious consideration.—Mr. Chadwick said that it would be undesirable that the whole of their districts should be laid down on that scale, as in many parts, consisting mainly of fields, they should present but so many sheets of paper with scarcely a line upon them; but that they should have the enlarged scale for the closer and more densely populated districts. He might now mention that for sanitary purposes in Liverpool, it had been found necessary to have their maps enlarged to the 20 feet scale.

The motion was then put and unanimously agreed to.

A further recommendation from the Ordnance Survey Committee was read,—" That 281 acres of the Ordnance plan of Westminster be enlarged to the 10 feet scale."—This recommendation, it was stated, was brought forward at the pressing solicitation of the Westminster Improvement Commissioners, who were unable to proceed with their works until a defined and settled plan of drainage was laid down.—Mr. Slaney said that there was not a more unhealthy district than this city.

Mr. Leslie expressed an opinion that these works ought to be effected for the benefit of the public at large.—It was explained, in reference to the application, that the Westminster Improvement Commissioners had no interest in the question but for public benefit. It was proposed and agreed to unanimously.—" That in consequence of the pressing representations of the Westminster Improvement Commissioners, and the urgent requirements of the district, the recommendation be agreed to."

It was also proposed,—" That 300 sheets of the Ordnance plan of the town area and suburbs be engraved by the Ordnance Map department, their estimate for an average sheet being 8*l.* 15s. 7d.

In support of this recommendation, Mr. Chadwick stated that the whole cost of the engraving of these plates would be defrayed within the estimate proposed for the Ordnance Survey alone, and no new charge would be incurred on that account.

The motion was put and agreed to unanimously.

A report was received from the Bye-laws Committee, to the effect that the commissioners had no right to dispose of any earth, stones, or gravel remaining after making good the ground for a sewer. This subject led to a long conversation, and, on the motion of Mr. Bullar, it was agreed that the doubtful points of the Act of Parliament should be referred to the Bye-laws Committee, with a view, if necessary, to obtaining fresh powers for the amendment of the same.

A communication was received from the Kent and Surrey Waterworks Company, on the subject of a definite and formal arrangement for a supply of water for the use of the sewers. Mr. Chadwick said it was a question open to them to consider whether they should provide water for themselves, or make arrangements with any of the existing companies. Several of the commissioners expressed opinions that no definite arrangement could be come to until it was ascertained what quantity of water would be required.

It was agreed that terms for a provisional agreement for a supply of water be drawn up between the commissioners and the water companies.

It was agreed that application be made to the London, Brighton, and South Coast Railway Company, for a contribution of 500*l.* for proposed new works in the neighbourhood of Weston-street, Southwark, the company having accepted the offer made to them.

The Salaries of Officers.—On a recommendation from the Works Committee—that the salaries of Mr. Lovick and Mr. Donaldson, assistant surveyors, be from the end of the first year's service at the rate of 350*l.* a-year—being read,

Mr. Chadwick moved the adoption of the report in the case of Mr. Lovick, who, he stated, had been appointed to the office from a perception of his worth alone, which was a rule he hoped to see followed in every other instance. He moved the adoption of the recommendation. Mr. Bullar seconded the motion.

Mr. Hawes wished to know whether this advanced salary was to include all charges made on account of their surveyors?

Mr. R. L. Jones complained of the large amount expended by their officers in cabs and other vehicles, in one case reaching 13*l.* in the quarter for this item alone. He could not, therefore, but again complain of the manner the business was being carried on in that court, by the officers being so continually called away from their duties in their attendance on committees. He then referred to a report made by Mr. Grant, their new assistant-surveyor, on a system of tubular drainage laid down by Mr. Phillips, their chief surveyor, a work that any common bricklayer could have performed. Here he was set to watch the work of their surveyor—they called upon a subordinate officer to give them that information they could have obtained from Mr. Phillips himself. It was quite idle to make such a reference at all.

Other commissioners having complained of the officers' charges,

Mr. Leslie believed that the purchase of two silver watches for the officers was the point some gentlemen were aiming at, but they were unwilling to say so.

Mr. Bullar said these watches were the property of the commission. They were stop-watches, to be used for experimental purposes; they were mere tools required to be used in their business, and the officers had as much right to order them as they had a spade or a pickaxe.

Lord Ebrington protested against it going forth to the public that they were squandering the public money. He had, however, heard of a pennyworth of wisdom and a poundsworth of folly.—Mr. Chadwick said the chief part of the expense of cab-hire was incurred during the raging of the cholera, when time was of the greatest importance, and even human life was at stake.

Mr. R. L. Jones thought these charges were highly improper, as they might as well furnish all the officers of the Ordnance with watches. He found one charge of 13*l.* 13s. for a quarter's cab-hire, and believed that the area of their district was not so large that there should be any necessity for these charges.—After some other observations, the recommendation as regarded Mr. Lovick was agreed to.—A similar motion was agreed to in the case of Mr. Donaldson.

On the motion that 800 feet of half-brick sewer, 3 feet 6 inches by 2 feet 3 inches, and 158 feet of 12-inch pipe sewer be laid down in St. George and Gloucester-terraces, Kensington, it was stated by Mr. Hartslet, the clerk, that the work would be done entirely at the cost of Mr. Inderwick. That gentleman had hitherto resisted the applications of the late Westminster Commissioners, to contribute a proportion of the expense of the drainage of that locality, but he now came forward and was willing to pay the whole amount.—Agreed to.

It was proposed that 705 feet of 12-inch pipe-sewer be put down in the open ditch at the back of Marlborough-place, Old Kent-road. It appeared that the market gardeners had been in the habit of damming up the waters of this ditch for the purpose of irrigating the adjoining land, through which refuse accumulated, and it now contained upwards of 4 feet in depth of filthy deposit. In the plan for its improvement, certain apertures were to be left in the pipes, from which, if desired, the sewage water could be withdrawn. The plan was agreed to.

The following resolution was agreed to on the question of detailed estimates for works:—" That the order of court of April 19th, 1849, No. 42, as to detailed estimates, be rescinded, and that all future estimates for works be made on detailed calculations as to separate cost of work and materials; and that the surveyors be prepared whenever called upon by the court or any committee to support their estimate by such calculations."

The Drainage of St. James's Parish, Westminster.—It being stated to the court by the Paving Board of St. James's parish, Westminster, that as they were about to expend 3,000*l.* in the paving of that parish, they wished to know whether this commission contemplated making any new sewers in that district, as a new sewer for Pall Mall had been spoken of. The question was referred to the surveyors, who reported that the sewers in Pall Mall, Bentinck-street, Berkeley-street, Sherrard-street, Queen-street, Blenheim-mews, and Marlborough-mews, were in bad condition; that particularly the sewer in Pall Mall was defective, being flat-bottomed with upright sides, 7 feet in height and 6 feet wide, but that a new sewer there could be effected without disturbing the pavement. Other improvements were proposed, on a minor scale, for the rest of the district.

Miscellanea.

PURIFICATION AND SOFTENING OF WATER.—By means of a union of chemical and mechanical processes, patented by Mr. Horsley, of Ryde, Isle of Wight, chemist, it is proposed not only to purify water, as in filtration, but to soften it by the withdrawal of its sulphates or other 'hardening' salts, if not also to deprive it of all animal or vegetable impregnation, and thus to render it wholesome for human and animal use, and economical and useful for domestic purposes and for many processes of art and manufacture, as well as for the prevention of incrustation in steam and store boilers, which arises chiefly from the deposit of the sulphate of lime during the evaporation of the water into steam. For this latter purpose, we remember, a patent was some time since taken out, under which sal-ammoniac was inserted into the boiler and became decomposed, the sulphuric acid of the incrustation uniting with the ammonia of the sal-ammoniac, and its lime with the muriatic acid forming a very deliquescent salt in place of the incrustation. It may be by some combination of an analogous process with the other means alluded to that Mr. Horsley's patent operates. And at all events, the idea is a very important one, and its realization most desirable, especially in localities where there is good reason to believe that calculous and other diseases are generated by hard or impure water.

RAILWAY GUARDS' AND BREAKSMEN'S FRIENDLY SOCIETY.—A numerous meeting of the guards and breaksmen of the various metropolitan railways was held lately for the purpose of establishing a "Railway Guards' Universal Friendly Society." The object in view is to provide a sick fund; a sum to the family of a member killed; a pension fund for disabled members; but especially a fund for relief of widows and orphans of deceased members. The society has been originated by the guards of the London and North-Western; and Mr. G. C. Glyn has given his earnest support to it, and become one of the trustees. Upwards of 1,000 guards and breaksmen have signified their willingness to become members. The preliminary rules and regulations were approved of, and the rates of weekly payment to recipients of relief are under the consideration of Mr. Neison, the actuary.

INSTITUTE OF GAS ENGINEERS.—We are informed by a correspondent that a new institute, or college, is about to be established, for the collection and discussion of all data relative to the manufacture, price, purification, and distribution of gas, and the best mode of regulating the supply, so that it may be conveyed to consumers at a cost much less than that at present charged, and on more consistent and equable terms than those anomalous and variable ones which still prevail throughout the country. The adaptation, if possible, of the many new and improved methods of manufacture to old works should also be considered, for behoof of those companies who find the expense of such adaptation a hinderance to their adoption. Another important object is the regular training and instruction of gas engineers, so as to reduce to one uniform system and science that diversity of modes which still prevails together with extravagant and ill-directed expenditure. The projectors of this new institute are said to be Professor Wilson, of the Andersonian University, Glasgow, and Mr. Angus Croll.

THE IRON TRADE.—Scarcely were the promising arrangements for a rise of workmen's wages, with an increase of nominal prices, *settled* at the quarterly meetings, when everything as usual has been unsettled again in the interim, by the lowering both of wages and of prices to their previous standard. This renewed exposure of the vain attempts to impose fictitious and impracticable prices at the quarterly meetings, has at length induced the *Times* and other of our contemporaries to confirm the truth of our repeated exposure of so hollow and unavailable a practice, by a declaration that they now perceive that "no dependance is apparently to be placed in the decision of quarterly meetings."

THE LATE MR. VERNON.—Our readers will hear with regret that Mr. Vernon has passed away from amongst us, before receiving any fitting acknowledgment of a nation's gratitude.

ECCLESIOLOGICAL LATE CAMBRIDGE CAMDEN SOCIETY.—The tenth anniversary meeting of this society was held on Thursday, May 10, in the school-room of Christ Church, St. Pancras, in Albany-street,—Mr. A. J. B. Hope, M.P., in the chair. The report read by the Rev. B. Webb, honorary secretary, stated that fifteen new members had been added to the society during the year, and that the rooms in Bond-street had not been found practically useful. It mentioned that the New York Ecclesiological Society had established a magazine, entitled the "New York Ecclesiologist," conducted with much ability and principle. Le Père Martin, a French ecclesiologist, read, in French, two short papers, one of them on the "Stone Chair," at Canterbury, to which he assigned no earlier date than the time of Cardinal Langton. A paper on the "Draining and Drying of Churches," was read by the Rev. B. Webb. The Rev. J. M. Neale, another of the secretaries, read a paper on "Ecclesiastical Ironwork," showing how village smiths might be taught to execute it, and exhibiting examples in proof.

NEW CHURCHES.—The number of additional churches erected during the last thirty years is variously estimated at from 1,000 to 1,400; the latter amount probably includes the whole number consecrated, many being churches rebuilt only. In the diocese of London, 161 new churches were consecrated (to 29th of July, 1847). In the diocese of Winchester, 155, of which 55 were rebuilt (to November, 1847). In the diocese of Lichfield, 135 new churches were consecrated (to October, 1847). In the diocese of Chester, during the twenty years it was held by the present Archbishop of Canterbury, 230 new churches were built.

RESTORATION OF BRIDGEWATER CHURCH COMPETITION.—On Monday in last week being the day appointed for receiving designs for the restoration and re-pewing of Bridgewater Church, nine were received by the vicar and churchwardens. The *Bridgewater Times* says, "we apprehend the next step will be to select from these, and we believe that if any difficulty should arise in the selection of a design, it is the intention of the vicar and churchwardens and the gentlemen nominated to co-operate with them in carrying out the work, to call in the assistance of an able architect wholly unconnected with the town and with the different competitors who have forwarded designs." The following are the mottoes attached to the various designs received: "Venerator Temporis Acti." "Nil sine magno vita labore dedit mortalibus." "Laus Deo." "Delectare in Domino." "Spe." "F." "A Cross." "A double triangle." "Suum cuique."

CONVERSAZIONE AT THE INSTITUTION OF CIVIL ENGINEERS.—On the 22nd, Mr. Field, the president of the institution, held his annual conversazione, and was efficiently assisted by Mr. C. Manby, the secretary, whose general arrangements, and distribution of the works of art and the models, claim praise. The visitors were very numerous, and the collection of works of art and science large. Mr. Thomas contributed a marble chimney-piece, intended for Mr. Peto, including in the design figures of Science and Art. Mr. Dighton's model of the Kneller Hall training school, designed by Mr. Mair, excited attention.

THE WORKING CLASSES.—On Tuesday, Mr. Slaney moved the appointment of a standing committee, or unpaid commission, to consider and report from time to time on practical measures (unconnected with political changes) likely to improve the condition of the working classes, to encourage their industry, and increase their contentment, but notice being taken that forty members were not present, the House was adjourned.

CRYSTALLIZATIONS ON NEW WALLS.—Sir,—In walls of old habitations, the nitrate of lime is formed from whence nitrate of potash is subsequently manufactured. Will some of your readers say, what is the efflorescent crystallization that forms so rapidly on walls of new houses long before they are fit for occupation? The taste is powerfully alkaline, generally sodaic. It is proposed to remedy the mischief of the latter by covering the surface affected with tin-foil, fixed to the place by copal varnish. N.

PROJECTED WORKS.—Advertisements have been issued for tenders,—by June 1st, for supplying and laying down about 1,800 yards of 3-inch tooled York paving, 1,100 yards of quarry-worked Purbeck curb, and 560 yards of quarry-worked carlinose, or Aberdeen curb; by 4th June, for building 800 feet of brick sewer, and 158 feet of glazed stone-ware pipe sewer, in the parish of St. Mary Abbots, Kensington; by 31st, for the erection of a Wesleyan chapel at Kingswinford; by 2nd June, for the erection of a warehouse at Salford; by 4th, for the construction and fitting up of pipes, &c., connected with the Hull baths and washhouses; by 29th inst., for the erection of school-houses at Norwood; by same date, for the maintenance of the permanent way of the Blackwall Railway; by 6th June, for the construction of the works of the Waterford and Kilkenny Railway from Thomastown to Knockwilliam, county Kilkenny; by 29th inst., for making 200,000 stock bricks at Buxton; by 30th, for painting and whitewashing the Ecclesall Union Workhouse; by 26th June, for the supply of 2,600 loads of English elm timber for the navy; by 7th, for repairing, repewing, and other works, at Westham Church, Essex; by 4th, for a gasholder and cast-iron tank for the Richmond Gas Company, also for the erection of a retort stack and setting 23 retorts for same; by 7th, for alteration and improvements to five houses at Poplar; by 1st, for paving and repairing carriage and footways of St. John's, Clerkenwell; by 31st inst., for the excavators', masons', and bricklayers' works, in erecting a large gas holder tank at Sheffield; by 31st, for taking up and repaving the High-street of Bridgnorth; by 5th June, for the performance of bricklayers', carpenters', masons', painters', paperhangers', paviers', plasterers', plumbers', and other works at Birmingham, Coventry, Weedon, Northampton, Nottingham, Mansfield, Burslem, Newport, Brecon, and Carmarthen, for the Ordnance department.

EMPTY HOUSES IN LIVERPOOL.—An official return of the unoccupied houses in Liverpool, of a rental of 30*l.* and upwards, gives the extraordinary number of 5,900; and yet the population, it is said, has not decreased. Rents are beginning to fall; and a shop in Bold-street, which let for 120*l.* is now, says the *Manchester Guardian*, untenanted, though only 70*l.* is asked.

METHOD OF SOLDERING CAST-IRON WITH WROUGHT IRON.—The following process has been recommended for this purpose: —First melt filings of soft cast-iron with calcined borax in a crucible; then pulverize the black vitreous substance which is thereby produced, and sprinkle it over the parts which are intended to be united; after which, heat the pieces of cast and wrought-iron and weld them together on an anvil, using only gentle blows. This method is peculiarly applicable for the manufacture of iron articles which are intended to be made red hot, and are required to be impervious to fluids or liquids, as such a result cannot be obtained by simple fastening.—*Sheffield Times.*

SOMERSETSHIRE ARCHÆOLOGICAL AND NATURAL HISTORY SOCIETY.—A society bearing this title has been formed. Its objects are—the cultivation of, and collecting information on, archæology and natural history, in their various branches, but more particularly in connection with this county. One of the objects of the society is to collect, by donation or purchase, a library and museum, more particularly illustrating the history, natural, civil, and ecclesiastical, of the county of Somerset.

THE GYMNETRUS NORTHUMBRICUS.—A remarkable specimen of the *Gymnetrus*, caught off the coast of Northumberland, is now exhibiting at the Cosmorama Rooms in Regent-street. Its form and the peculiar arrangement of the dorsal fin, lead its owners to exhibit it as coinciding with the description of the *sea serpent*. Those who go to see it as this hypothetical being will be disappointed: simply as a specimen of a rare and curious fish it is very interesting.

DUBLIN SCHOOL OF DESIGN.—Mr. M'Manus, who was so unceremoniously bowled out at Glasgow, as some of our readers will remember, has been appointed head master of the Government School of Design in Dublin, with full power to carry out the objects of the institution.

ARCHITECTURAL LENDING LIBRARY.—
A correspondent mentions that an architectural subscription library is forming at Edinburgh, and thinks that Londoners ought not to be behind-hand.

MEETINGS OF SCIENTIFIC BODIES
Held during the ensuing week.

WEDNESDAY, May 30.—Society of Arts, 8 P.M.
FRIDAY, June 1.—Archæological Institute, 4 P.M.

TO CORRESPONDENTS.

"*St. Peter's Church, Chester.*"—Mr. James Harrison, the architect, has written to deny that he specially invited Mr. Freeman to tender for the work at St. Peter's Church.

"*Bedford Corn Exchange Competition.*"—We have no information yet as to the result.

"*J. J. D.*" (Kent).—Our remark on Nos. 1021 and 1022 applied, as a matter of course, to the design, and not the drawing. We appreciate the feeling which led our correspondent to address us. Had the catalogue given any intimation that the exhibitor was not the designer, we should have drawn a distinction.

Received.—"J. B." (lock shall be looked at), "A. P. M.," "W. J. D.," "H. S.," "F. P. D." (we have no reason to doubt the good faith of the advertiser. Some mistake must have occurred), "J. L. P." (in the engraver's hands), "J. D.," "T. S." (no personal offence meant), "W. T. C." (the charge appears enormous, but we should be wrong to express an opinion without full knowledge), "An Old Subscriber," "J. B.," "S. H," (shall appear), "A Constant Reader," "T. B. H.," "T. H. L.," "R. H. P.," "G. B. T.," "Subscriber from the Beginning," "R. N.," "G. W.," "E. B.," "L.," "T. S.," "W. J. W.," "J. C. W.," "A. J."

Note.—In list of tenders for model dwellings last week, the amount of Messrs. Haynes' tender should be 11,950l., instead of 11,450l. The error (of the press) is obvious.

"*Desks, Prices, and Addresses.*"—We have not time to point out books or find addresses.

NOTICE.—All communications respecting *advertisements* should be addressed to the "Publisher," and not to the "Editor;" all other communications should be addressed to the EDITOR, and not to the Publisher.

ADVERTISEMENTS.

No. CCCXXX.

SATURDAY, JUNE 2, 1849.

OME of our readers have expressed surprise that we have not made more specific remarks on the recent exposures in connection with the railway system, the dethronement of the railway potentate, and the present state of the railway world, than have been given occasionally in our weekly budget of notes connected with the subject generally. We have avoided doing so, simply because we did not see that any positive good was then to be achieved by such a course; it was not because we had formed no decided opinion upon recent disclosures, or that we had joined in an absurd adulation and were ashamed to spurn what we had worshipped, or that we had words to eat and no stomach for the task. A reference to our past volumes would justify some amount of self complacency in this respect. We have uniformly discouraged reckless expenditure by railway directors, and the want of efficient supervision of works and expenditure; while discountenancing jobbing in shares, we have urged the value of railways as an investment, if economically constructed and wisely managed; and, at a time when all England was bowing at the feet of Mr. Hudson, and subscribing their thousands for a permanent testimony of admiration, we pointed out the absurdity of such a proceeding, sketched in different colours from those which were being employed for the same purpose, what he was and what he really had done, and contrasted his reward with the treatment received by men who had, with self sacrifice, benefited their fellow creatures.[*]

At that moment the public, who will not give themselves the trouble to investigate for themselves, or even to judge, had taken Mr. Hudson for their guide. When he joined a line the shares rose; if even seen on the site of a proposed railway, it had an effect on the value of the scrip, and he bought and sold, and all went on swimmingly. We then remarked—"The career of Law of Lauriston, the projector of the Mississippi scheme, forces itself as a parallel on the recollection. Let us hope," we said, "that Mr. Hudson may never equally abuse the power that public weakness has placed in his hands."

He took too high a place, and we looked for a fall. It came! The honours were not borne too meekly, and the fall has been received with a yell, which is as little creditable to the utterers as their blind and selfish adoration was at an earlier period.

We will not, however, underrate the magnitude of the evil which has been committed, though we say that much of it attaches to a degrading system rather than to the individual, and that, if we mistake not, a strict investigation would convict many others of similar acts. It is even greater in its consequences than many suppose, much greater. "Cooking the accounts," as it has been termed, does not seem a frightful charge to make,—declaring a dividend of 9s. per share when the earnings would not justify one of 3s., and paying the difference out of capital, perhaps borrowed

[*] Vol. III., Supplement, p. 5 (1845).

for the purpose, appears to some simply unbusinesslike and well calculated to lead to bankruptcy. But it is much more than this. The dividend declared by a body of Directors, supposed to be honest and honourable men, is taken by the world implicitly as evidence of the state of the undertaking, and this regulates the price of the shares, and quickens or lessens the demand. On the faith of this, trustees invest the dependence of orphans and widows,—the thrifty father, his savings. The declaration of a dividend greater than the earnings of the line will pay, is a fraud of the grossest kind, meriting the severest punishment.

Such, however, is the laxity of principle which has been induced by share-dealing, that those who have been party to such an act, have viewed a resort to it, with a dozen other equally dishonest modes of raising the price of shares, as perfectly legitimate. Inordinate desire to make money is a blot on the English character, and leads to such acts as would be otherwise shrunk from. When we think of much that we have seen and heard of in connection with railway schemes and the share market, we blush for our countrymen, and ought to say, countrywomen too.

Dealing in shares since 1845 has been mere hocus-pocus :—nothing was known, the data were untrue. The change which has taken place in the value of shares since 1847, is very striking. It has been shown that the average depreciation since that date, taking ten of the leading lines, amounts to 65 per cent. In the case of the South-Western, it is 91¼ per cent., that is, 50l. shares were at 28 5-8ths premium in 1847, and are now at 17 discount : 20l. Eastern Counties are depreciated 106 per cent. and 50l. North Midlands, 139 per cent. Even with the London and North-Western there is a difference of 76 per cent.; 100l. shares were then at a premium of 102, and are now at a premium of but 26.

The expenditure on most of the lines has been much greater than it ought to have been; money has been squandered thoughtlessly and uselessly : in obtaining Acts no amount of money was allowed to stand in the way of success, and in their after works no thought as to the extent of traffic which would be required to pay the interest of the money expended, seems to have crossed their minds. Take a recent instance, and one for which an excuse could be found more easily than in most other cases. The cost of the new hall and offices at the Euston Station of the London and North-Western is understated at 125,000l., the interest of which, at 5 per cent., is 6,250l. per annum. The company must therefore earn more than 17l. per day for every day in the year, including Sundays, simply for the use of these new buildings, exclusive of the cost of repairs.

It is scarcely necessary to say, that public opinion is now very different from what it was when these extensive works were commenced.

Advantages can scarcely fail to result ultimately from the stop which has been put to the present system. Various suggestions are now occupying attention : amongst them, one to work railways by contract,—a suggestion which has been received with considerable favour. The Eastern Counties, it is said, are about to effect an arrangement of this sort, and some other companies have already done so.

An honest and searching inquiry must be made into the affairs of all the Companies; Boards of Direction must be weeded and reformed, and where new lines are to be constructed, the works must be done with due regard to economy, and with a view to a sufficient return for the capital invested.

When we remember that up to the end of last year more than *two hundred millions of pounds sterling* had been expended on railways, and that Companies have power to expend on authorised lines one hundred and forty millions more (the sums are too large to grasp at once), it will be seen, that this is a question affecting the prosperity of the whole community in a remarkable degree.

The reign of pompous mystification, humbug, and fraud, must be brought to an end.

LECTURE ON ROMAN ARCHITECTURE.

In previous papers we have traced architecture from its infancy to its prime—we have noticed the first rude attempts as seen in the unhewn monuments of the patriarchal ages and of Druidical times—we have contemplated the colossal splendours of the Egyptians, those vast and enduring remains which yet stand the gigantic spectres of departed greatness, the Titan progenitors of future ages—and we have seen the perfected greatness of art and science in the unrivalled glories of Greece—glories which yet shed their lustre, although somewhat dimmed, upon the nations of the earth. We are now to record some of the architectural wonders of Rome—

> " The city that so long
> Reigned absolute, the mistress of the world."

We shall not, it is true, find in Roman architecture the massive solidity of the Egyptians, nor the chaste simplicity of the Greeks, but we shall see the utmost height to which the art could reach in sumptuous decoration, in vastness of design, in great and varied applications, as beheld in those magnificent structures, which made the seven-hilled city indeed

> " A dream of glory; temples, palaces,
> Called up as by enchantment; aqueducts
> Among the groves and glades rolling along
> Rivers, on many an arch high over head;
> And in the centre like a burning sun
> The Imperial city."—*Rogers.*

In no one spot were so many splendid buildings congregated, as we are assured were collected in Rome, when the enormous wealth of which her citizens became possessed was lavished on the sister arts. The stern simplicity which marked the habits of the earlier Republicans gave way before the enervating effects of the riches which poured in like a flood upon the conquering Romans, and thus Horace complains in his fifteenth ode of the increasing fondness for architectural splendour at the expense of humbler pursuits—

> " In royal pride our buildings rise,
> The useless plough neglected lies;"

and he still further inveighs against Roman luxury in his eighteenth ode :—

> " No walls with ivory inlaid
> Adorn my house, no colonnade
> Proudly supports my citron beams,
> Nor rich with gold my ceiling gleams :
> Nor have I, like an heir unknown,
> Seized upon Attalus's throne."

Indeed, there was a wide contrast between the aspect of Rome in the Augustan age and that which marked it in the days of her early kings, when the temples were only large enough to contain a statue of the god, and when the houses were only cabins, with their walls of mud and their roofs of straw, so that Ovid calls the palace of Romulus a cottage, which it must really have been.

But the Roman consuls and pro-consuls, who, going forth as private citizens, returned from their conquests and vice-royalties with the revenues and the tastes of kings, could not be satisfied with the simple habits and unadorned dwellings which contented their ancestors, the Decii and Fabricii of old; and, although even Julius Cæsar, in the height of his power, obtained with great difficulty permission to ornament his house with a pediment —an architectural luxury till then denied to private dwellings, and considered worthy of a place on buildings in Olympus—the restrictions against the indulgence of expensive tastes in art must soon have been swept away, since we find even in the Julian period a record of the sumptuous palaces that were raised by the illustrious citizens of Rome, vying with each other in the display of all that wealth could procure or art produce. The union of architecture, painting, and sculpture could never have been surpassed, as seen in some of the palaces, as we should call them, or villas, as they were termed by the Romans, when we find that even the house of Sallust, who could hardly have possessed much wealth, was adorned with such figures as the Dying Gladiator, the Silenus, and Infant Hercules, as discovered in the ruins; and the astonishingly beautiful fresco paintings on the walls of the exhumed city of Pompeii, a fourth or fifth-rate town, lead us to conclude that not less valuable works of art ornamented the residences of a Mecænas, a Lucullus, or a Hadrian in the capital of the world; and we know that Hadrian possessed those matchless triumphs of the sculptor's power, the Venus de Medici, the Faun, the Flora, as found in the ruins of his villa, and of course the Antinous.

These sculptures and paintings, however, were the productions of Greek artists, and there can be no doubt that much of the best architecture of Rome was also the offspring of Greek taste. Sylla is said to have first introduced Greek architects in Rome; in the time of Pompey and Cæsar the Grecian artists Arcesilaus, Pasiteles, Zopyrus, and Criton resided in Rome. The architect who planned the temple of Jupiter Stator, was Hermodorus of Salamis; many temples were designed by two natives of Laconia, Saurus and Batrachus, who have perpetuated their fame by the lizard and frog, the symbols of their names, still to be seen sculptured on the columns in some of the churches* of Rome, which once belonged to Pagan temples, whilst the two architects, Chrysippus and Cluatius, employed by Cicero, were also Greeks.

Certain it is that after Greece became a Roman province in the year 145 B. C., we begin to find architecture employed by the conquerors of the world to record their triumphs in the temples to which they consecrated their spoils, in the theatres in which the wild beasts, or men as wild, of far distant climes, were exhibited to the admiring multitudes, in the arches under which the proud victors entered the city.

> " With acclamation, and the martial clang
> Of instruments, and cars laden with spoil,"

or in the private dwellings which yet contained within their walls treasures which kings might envy, yet hardly purchase, those beautiful creations of the sculptor's chisel and the painter's pencil, of which, though the latter are lost to us, many of the first still survive the admiration, almost the homage of pilgrims to the shrines of art in the eternal city; when to the actual possession of the matchless works of art with which Rome abounds, we add the charm which the memory of her great men imparts to the localities, where

> " The very dust we tread stirs us with life,
> And not a breath, but from the ground sends up
> Something of human grandeur."

When we recall the mighty names of Pompey, Cæsar, Brutus, Cato, the Scipios, the Decii, and the softer shades of Virgil, Horace, and Ovid, we cannot wonder at the profound interest which has always been attached to her who was once the mistress of the world, but is now the Niobe of nations.

In addition to the magnificent buildings erected in the time of the Cæsars,—

> " When Rome in noon-tide empire grasp'd the world,"

modern Rome attracts the observation of the visitor by the scarcely less splendid structures which arose under the auspices of the popes, who, calling themselves the servants of servants, in the pride of humility, assumed a power scarcely inferior to that of the former imperial masters of Rome. But, whilst we condemn their presumption in arrogating to themselves universal dominion, we must do them the justice to admit that they patronized the fine arts, encouraged learning, and promoted taste. The religious structures erected under their auspices were adorned with the performances of men "whose pencil had a voice," and which have made the names of Michael Angelo, Raffaelle, and Correggio, immortal.

The chief, if not almost the only public buildings on which the Greeks delighted to bestow the graces of architecture were temples, as if to none but the divinities were its glories appropriate. But the Romans applied architecture in all its pomp to a great variety of purposes unknown to the Greeks, and not only to magnificent temples for worship, and to stately porticoes for recreation, but to colossal theatres and hippodromes for amusement, aqueducts of wondrous length, triumphal arches, lofty columns of commemoration, and palaces rivalling towns in extent, and public baths of astonishing splendour and size, and halls of justice.

The Romans adopted chiefly in their public buildings, the latest and richest of the Greek orders, the Corinthian, on which they grafted another order, the Composite, which has only the distinction of being encumbered with a profusion of ornament conceived in a taste far removed from the purity of the Greeks. The Doric order, which was brought to such a height of perfection in Greece, was evidently no favourite with the Romans, to whom its severe requirements were a restraint in the way of indulging in a fondness for gorgeous embellishment.

With the exception of the Trajan and Antonine pillars, I am not aware that Rome possessed any specimens of the Doric order in the manner of the Greeks, and even these can hardly be considered as specimens of attic taste and simplicity, since they have moulded bases, and the capitals have the Ionic ovolo cut in the echinus, whilst the lowest stages in which the Coliseum and theatre of Marcellus are divided, are adorned with columns after the fashion of the so-called improved Roman Doric style.

The examples of Ionic also are not numerous in Rome, nor are these in the best taste:—the temples dedicated to Manly Fortune and to Concord are proofs of this assertion, and, in fact, only deserve to be mentioned, that imitation should be avoided.

But if we cannot award any praise to the Romans in their employment of two out of the three ancient orders, we must admit their claim to admiration for the manner in which they introduced the third. This, the latest order among the Greeks, was only making a place for itself in Athens at the time of the Roman conquest, and our specimens of the style are limited to very few examples, and those of very small buildings; and it is rather remarkable that Corinth, whence the name of this order is derived, should not only have no specimen remaining, nor is it known ever to have possessed one, but exhibits in its temple perhaps the oldest example of the Doric order in Attica.

The temples built at Rome of the Corinthian order were the stateliest examples ever raised; those dedicated to Jupiter Stator, to Jupiter Tonans, and to Mars Ultor, of which only fragments remain, must have been truly magnificent buildings with columns nearly 50 feet high, and 5 feet in diameter, and evidently they were designed by Greek taste before the lines of the entablature were broken, or other derelictions from purity were introduced.

The great distinction between the pure Greek styles, and the later or debased Roman orders, was caused by the introduction of a feature which has had a wonderful and salutary influence upon architecture. The origin of the arch, like other vexed questions, may serve to amuse and bewilder the learned, who seem to find glimpses, rare indeed, and almost isolated, of its existence among the monuments of Egypt, of India, of Assyria, and of early Greece. But these few instances only prove that the arch, if known, was not used in general among these nations. But the Romans, although not strictly entitled to the parentage of the arch, have, by their adoption of that feature, earned for themselves as much honour as if they were discoverers; and to them alone is clearly due the merit of first appreciating and employing its wonderful properties. And if in some instances we must regret to see its application, as in cases where the continuous architrave is dispensed with to make way for arches springing at once from column to column, yet in others we cannot but applaud the daring ingenuity with which wide spaces are vaulted as in the Temples of Peace and Minerva Medica. We must admire the invention which enables us to cross mighty rivers,—to hang the lofty dome in air,—and above all, instead of being obliged, as in former times, to employ ponderous blocks for imposts and architraves from the difficulty of otherwise spanning large spaces, we must confess our obligations to a feature which can be formed into the most magnificent proportions by small and convenient materials, accessible in all climates and in all situations; and more than all, it may be safely asserted that, to the employment of the arch by the Romans, afterwards by the Byzantines, and again returning to its first country, by the Italians, we are indebted for the introduction of a system of architecture which has enchanted the world for several centuries with its beautiful conceptions, and which has enriched Europe in particular with so many splendid cathedrals and churches and which now, by common consent, is looked upon as most suited to edifices of a religious character.

In the limited space to which, of necessity a paper of this nature must be confined, only a few of the important works of the Romans can be noticed, for the bare enumeration of them would fill a volume. The most striking monuments of their taste are temples, theatres, aqueducts, triumphal arches, and commemorative columns.

Very few, if any, remains can be found in Rome of buildings before the time of Julius Cæsar, who, as well as his great compeer, Pompey, built many temples. The latter built the Temple of Minerva out of the spoils of the Mithridatic war (B.C. 60), and a temple in honour of Venus close to the theatre, which he also erected. Cæsar built temples in honour of Venus and Clemency; and it is a curious trait to observe these stern warriors dedicating temples to the benignant divinities. Cæsar besides projected many magnificent and useful works which he might have carried out, had not his great career been stopped by a violent death, when

> " The foremost man of all the earth"

fell under the daggers of the conspirators.

But it was to his successor, the fortunate Augustus, that Rome owes the commencement of its architectural greatness; his was not an empty boast, that he found it built of brick, but would leave it of marble. Three such illustrious patrons of the arts have rarely been found at the same time as Augustus and his celebrated friends Mecænas and Agrippa. As Gibbon well observes, "The example of the sovereign was imitated by his ministers and generals, and his friend Agrippa left behind him the immortal monument of the Pantheon."

Augustus built a temple in honour of Apollo of white marble, in which the Sybilline books were kept; another magnificent temple in honour of Mars the Avenger, in which he directed that the Senate should always hold their consultations on the affairs of war. He reared another temple to Jupiter the Thunderer; a superb memorial of his gratitude for his escape from the lightning which killed his armour-bearer at the side of his litter. With the exception of the temple of Jupiter Stator, the two temples just mentioned were the most stately and magnificent in Rome; they are of the Corinthian order: that dedicated to Mars as the Avenger on the occasion of Augustus going forth to avenge the death of Julius Cæsar, consisted of a noble portico of eight columns in front, and eight on each flank, and occupying an area of 116 feet by 73 feet. These columns were 6 feet in diameter, and 58 feet high, the loftiest of their kind in Rome. Ovid in his Fasti (v. 549) alludes to this temple and its place in the Forum:

> " Ultor, ad ipse suos cœlo descendit honores
> Templaque in Augusto conspicienda foro."

The temple of Jupiter Tonans has only three fluted columns remaining to attest its former magnificence. They are of white marble, 46 feet high, in three blocks; the diameter is 4 feet 8 inches. It appears to have resembled the temple of Mars in its general plan, except that its portico consisted only of 6 columns. Those which remain were buried nearly up to their capitals when Camporesi reduced the hill and laid them open.

But the most splendid example of architec-

* The church of St. Eusebius, and of St. Lorenzo beyond the walls, have these interesting relics of the sculptor's genius.

ture in Rome, or in any other capital, was the temple of Jupiter Stator, the name by which it is best known to us; its era is not exactly ascertained, but from the fine character of its design and execution, it may with great probability be ascribed to the Augustan age. Its destination has been the subject of great variety of opinions. By Albertino (1510), Labacco, Palladio, and Pomponio Leto (1520), it was considered to be a temple of Vulcan. Nardini, Versuti, and others contend that the columns belonged to the Comitium. Gamucci (1565), Fauno (1553), and Ficoroni, held that the columns were part of the Temple of Jupiter Stator, which is the opinion held by Piero Ligorio and Marliani. Of this superb edifice only three columns remain, of white marble; and of these remains Valadier justly remarks, that "they are a monument of the best age of Roman architecture, in which are united magnificence with beauty, sublimity of idea with perfection of execution, the acme of architecture with that of sculpture." These columns were 4 feet 10 inches in diameter, and 40 feet high in the shaft alone, and eight columns formed the portico. The capitals of these columns are the richest that were ever executed: they differ from all others of the Corinthian in that the central caulicoli are intertwined: they were imitated with the entire entablature in the portico of Carlton House, the columns of which now form part of the façade of the National Gallery, but with a plainer and therefore less appropriate entablature. Sir John Soane also copied them in his façade of the Privy Council and Board of Trade in Whitehall, where the architectural public have seen the late profeso 's columns cut in halves to perform double duty.

The Campo Vaccino, or ancient Forum Romanum, was crowded with magnificent temples and edifices, built by successive emperors. One of these, in the best taste after those we have just noticed, was built by Marcus Aurelius, and dedicated in honour of Antoninus, and Faustina, daughter of the latter and wife of the former emperor. It has a portico of six Corinthian unfluted columns, with three on the returns, of good proportions. The frieze in front is plain; but on the flanks of the temple it is adorned with sculptured griffins and candelabra.

In front of this temple was placed the bronze equestrian statue of Marcus Aurelius, now in the square of the capitol, and which so excited the admiration of Michael Angelo that he cried out to the figure, "Cammina!"

This ancient temple, like many others of pagan origin, is now a church dedicated to St. Lorenzo, in Miranda; and to the care of the pontiffs in thus consecrating such structures, we are indebted for much that remains of Roman art.

With the exception of the little gem of the choragic monument of Lysicrates, at Athens, we are not acquainted with any specimens in Grecian architecture of circular buildings, whilst we have many examples amongst the Romans: two of these, though small, are very beautiful; one was in Rome itself,—a Corinthian temple, dedicated to Vesta, and it was considered that the circular form of building was appropriate to the goddess who personified the earth.* This temple consisted of twenty fluted columns, one only of which is wanting, but the entablature is entirely gone. It appears to have been repaired at different periods, as the capitals vary in their design and execution. It had two windows; and the building is now used as the Church of La Madonna del Sole. The whole height of the columns is 34 feet 7 inches, and their diameter 3 feet 2 inches.

About 18 miles from Rome stands the relic of one of the most graceful temples ever erected: Tivoli, the ancient Tibur, immortalised by the pencil of Turner, recals some of the most famous names of Roman story. Here the illustrious Mecænas had a villa, where he was often visited by his imperial friend Augustus, in company with Horace, who is said to have also had a residence here, a legend so happily alluded to by the author of "Italy" when speaking of this locality—

"Where the precipitate Anio thunders down,
And thro' the surging mist a poet's house
(So some aver, and who would not believe?)
Reveals itself."

* "La forma obicolare de' tempj è propria di questa dea."—*Valladier.*

Tibur also served as a refuge to those great spirits who were checked in their ambitious enterprises. Thus we find that Cinna, the consul, came here in a temporary exile, as did Brutus and Cassius; and therefore Ovid says—

"Quid referant veteres Romanæ gentes apud quos
Exilium tellus ultima Tibur erat."

Here also the Romans sent some of their noble captives into an honourable retreat, among whom were the Numidian Emperor Syphax and the celebrated Queen Zenobia. The villa of Hadrian, at Tivoli, resembled a town in extent, and here also were the residences of Caius Marius, of Scipio Æmilianus, Virgil, Catullus, and Vopiscus, whose porphyry pillars were celebrated in song.* Of the beautiful temple itself ten columns remain of the eighteen which formerly surrounded the cell, which is only 24 feet in diameter; it was built of travertine stone, and the Corinthian capitals of the columns are very original, and this example was finely, and for the first time, imitated by Sir John Soane in the exterior of the Bank of England, and the small circular corner next Lothbury may serve, and that very happily, to convey some idea of the temple itself, since its peculiar ornaments of ox skulls and garlands are introduced on the frieze.†

GEORGE R. FRENCH.

* These names prove that Tivoli was a favourite retreat when the summer heat of Rome compelled her emperors, her stern warriors, her wise statesmen, or her gentle poets, alike to seek amidst the cool groves and matchless scenery of the Tiber, and silver waters of the Anio, a temporary refuge from the cares and turmoil of the busy capital.

† To be continued.

THE ROYAL ACADEMY EXHIBITION.

MR. FRITH (A.) is another of those few artists whose works bear evidence of great perseverance. He seems properly impressed with the necessity of labouring to improve the power he has. His picture this year (349), "Coming of Age," shows great research, and no sparing of trouble and pains. The diversity of incident attendant on such a scene is well calculated to allow scope to the painter's imagination; each individual is conceived with great delicacy of perception, from the mumbling old reader of the address, to the difficult but beautifully conveyed expression—half smile, half tear—of the happy mother; the noble old grandmother, proud in ancestral rights; the jollity of the retainers; the busy importance of the cook (a head worthy the best of Dutch painters) carving from an ox roasted whole; the simplicity of the children, one of whom, on the shoulders of perhaps its father, in order to insure its position, has twisted its little fingers amongst the shaggy hair so redundant on the boor's head, quite unconscious of the grimaces that bear witness to his discomfort; another dropping the flowers brought to strew the young lord's path, with its mother stooping to pick them up, forms a sweet little episode. The conception of the principal figure is not the most successful; it presents that nervous determination of going through the necessary ordeal with as much ease and grace as possible, but the youth is too old for one who had but just attained majority.

(383) "Ferdinand declaring his love to Miranda;" (384) "The Conspiracy of Sebastian and Antonio;" (385) "Ferdinand and Miranda discovered by Alonzo, at the entrance to the cave, playing at chess" (a picture in three compartments), all by P. F. Poole (A.), are marked by originality of treatment. The admirable arrangement of colour in all three productions, strikes the spectator at once, but where Mr. Poole finds his authority for introducing female courtiers attendant on the king, is a theme of astonishment to all readers of Shakspeare. He has certainly made great use of this artistic liberty, and the sleeping ladies in the middle compartment cause one to forget the deviation in admiration of their *pose*, and the unusually nice drawing for this colourist. The "Blackberry Gatherers" (514), demands praise for effect and colour: the head of the girl is lovely, and the painting of the red petticoat is very remarkable.

(397) "Innocence and Guilt," A. Rankley. An unaffected relation of an eloquent story. The picture represents the interior of a country church; the right-hand side presents an open pew, wherein are seated a gay young spendthrift squire and his courtezan; he is struck with remorse,—the effect of the honest pastor's words is visible in his whole deportment; his companion perceiving it, is bantering him; but the sense of having erred too strongly affects him; he remains transfixed in self-examination and mental trouble. Before these, sitting on the free-seats, are two rustic lovers. The beautiful girl,—beautiful in her confidence and innocence,—kneels reverently; whilst her lover, manly devout, nevertheless hardly able to resign his whole thoughts to the time and ceremony, reads from the same book. The father and mother, who accompany them, are intently bent upon the responses. To the left of the spectator is a long row of charity girls, arrayed in the white capes and caps, leading perspectively into the picture, capitally managed. It is certainly a charming work, and displays an amount of thought that is highly commendable.

(404) "Sand-pits." This unpretending title applys to a marvellous production by Mr. Linnell. It defies criticism, further than claiming the observation of its being nature in her best colours. The "Sand-pits" of J. Linnell, and the (531) "Morning on the Banks of Zurich Lake" of F. Danby (A.), are, without question, two of the finest landscapes in the collection: the total absence of the appearance of paint is one of the minor characteristics of the latter. (407) "The Wise and Foolish Builders" of G. Harvey, had much better have returned to Edinburgh than have been placed where it is. In 413, "The First Pair of Trews," by R. McInnes, much that is clever is counteracted by the disagreeable smoothness of style so applicable to snuff-box pictorialising. (420) is a charming North Welsh landscape, entitled "Crafnaut Mountain," by T. Danby. (434) "Evangeline in the Church," C. Lucy. An advance upon former works, but few youths would have fixed their eyes upon any thing *quite* so plain as the heroine, much less have considered her

. . . "as the saint of his deepest devotion."

(447) A picture without a title, by E. Armitage, accompanied by a long extract from Thierry's "History of the Norman Conquest," is utterly unworthy of De la Roche's pupil, who has eminently distinguished himself in the Westminster Hall competitions. It is ill drawn, and trite in general treatment.

(470) H. Pickersgill, jun. "The First Interview of Robert, surnamed 'the Devil,' with the young Girl of Falaise, who was afterwards the Mother of William the Conqueror." A very clever picture from Thierry's history, evincing both painstaking and ability, but placed somewhat too high for close inspection. Mr. Pickersgill (the son of the veteran academician), is a very accomplished man, but too modest and retiring for these pushing days.

(474) "Malvolio," J. C. Horsley. Not what might have been expected from the author of many first-rate poetical compositions.

(488) "Mozart's Last Moments," H. N. O'Neil. A fine subject, and, as far as discernable, well treated. Much labour and study are observable here, although it is badly placed: it is evidently the work of a musical enthusiast.

(497) "Academy for Instruction in the Discipline of the Fan, 1711." One of those quaint subjects of which Mr. A. Solomon, with his nice perception of beauty and clean painting and drawing, knows so well how to make the most of. This also is badly hung.

(538) "The Wolf Slayer," R. Ansdell. A very powerful picture, richer in colour than Mr. A.'s works are ordinarily, approaching the grand in composition. The foreground group of dogs and wolf would not have been unworthy of Snyders. The wolf-slayer is the least best part; but the work, as a whole, claims the highest praise.

(612) "The Orphans of the Village—Harvest Time," T. F. Marshall. A refined and well thought-of subject, from "Thomson's Seasons," deserving of a much better situation than that assigned to it. From what can be seen of it, it is evident great care has been bestowed upon the arrangement and execution; it is a striking advance upon former works, and, from its nice sentiment and agreeable *ensemble*, a very favourable specimen of the painter.

THE ARCHITECTURAL ROOM.

Resuming our notice of the works exhibited in the Architectural Room, we may point to a satisfactory "Design for School and Master's House about to be erected near Trinity Church, Tonbridge Wells," by E. N. Stevens (1063). The materials are flint and stone, with tiled roof. If the interesting old church, St. Giles's, Cripplegate (where Cromwell was married and Milton buried), is to be restored in accordance with the drawing 1072 (A. D. Gough), the flanks of nave will look bare and little accordant with the tower. (1114), by the same, "St. Matthew's Church, Denmark-hill, Camberwell, in course of erection," has a very attenuated tower, too telescopic in outline. The west end is polygonal, with gablets. In 1100 we have a view of "The lower market at Exeter, from the northern entrance," by C. Fowler. Mr. Fowler also exhibits a drawing of the "Conservatory at Syon, erected for the late Duke of Northumberland" (1156), some years ago. 1120 is the selected "Design for the Savings Bank at Newbury, Berkshire," by G. Truefitt. It is Tudor in style, standing on open arches, red and white in colour, and has much of the right feeling.

(1122) "The new library at Mostyn Hall, North Wales," by A. Poynter, is Elizabethan, with an elaborately panelled ceiling (of good design) fully chromatised: the larger panels are blue, the smaller red. The chimney-piece is carried up to the ceiling, and ornamented with shields of arms. (1123) "View of a Design for a County Lunatic Asylum," by F. W. Porter and W. A. Boulnois, is clever and original: the style is Italian, with a campanile.

(1129) "Interior of St. James's Church, to be built at Hatcham, Old Kent-road, one of the new districts of the metropolis," by W. L. B. Granville, is of the Geometric period, and would seem to be a large and imposing structure. There is a rose window in transept, the tracery of which is scarcely so elegant as it might be. 1157 is the "South-east view of the Derby County Lunatic Asylum," now in progress of erection, from the design of Henry Duesbury. This design, which is Elizabethan in character, has a nice play of outline, and is free from some of the vulgarities of the style occasionally indulged in. 1172 is a view in the nave and transepts of Sherborne Abbey Church, Dorset, shewing the proposed restoration and arrangement," from the designs of R. C. Carpenter; and 1189 is a view of the choir of the same fine building. The organ is to be placed in the upper part of north transept, with a circular staircase up to it: the sittings are to be open. In the choir a good coronal is shown. Amongst the designs for churches beyond those already noticed, may be mentioned (1159) for the West of Ireland, by C. Geoghegan (early English), (1169) by H. Wyatt (decorated), and (1144) "Church of St. Mary the Virgin, Biscovey, Cornwall," by G. E. Street (tower of which is somewhat disproportioned). The "Church of the Confraternità di San Bernardino, at Perugia," of which a nice view is given by J. M. Lockyer, is a curious example of polychromic architecture produced by marble and glazed blue and white porcelain.

VANISHING LINES IN PERSPECTIVE.

Most professional readers are no doubt acquainted with the use of proportional scales on each side of their picture, for obtaining the direction of the vanishing lines where the points of distance lie a long way out of the picture. The rules for fixing the proportion of these scales are not always simple. The following method may prove useful to many, especially on an emergency, when a long drawing-board or long rule is not at hand.

Obtain as nearly as may be, by a tape, or pocket-rule, the distance of the point in question beyond the margin of the picture, and the intersection of any one of the principal lines with the edge of the picture. Any one used to perspective sketching will readily do this. All that remains to be done is a very simple rule-of-three sum.

Upon the common principle of similar triangles, AB and *ab* will be in the same proportion to each other that AV and *av* are to each other.

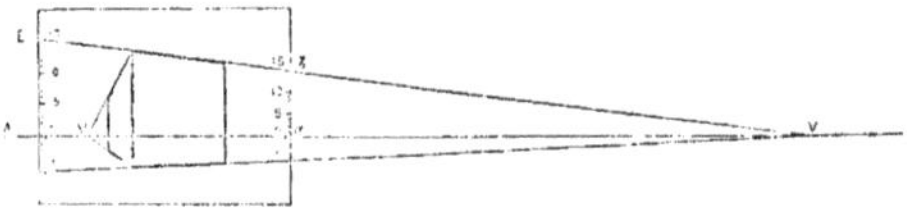

Hence, if in the above figure V is 4 feet beyond the margin of the picture, the picture being 2 feet in width, AB : *ab* :: 6 : 4; or *ab* will be two-thirds of AB.

So, if *ab* is 6 inches, AB will be 9 inches; and if a length of nine inches set upon the horizontal line be divided into fifteen parts on the left hand side, and a 6-inch length be divided into fifteen parts on the other side, or into any equal number of divisions, the lines which connect any two corresponding divisions will be lines in the direction of the vanishing point. The same principle applies below the horizontal line.

The convenience of this method is, that the length of the scale (as AB) for one side can be calculated readily from the other (*ab*) in any case where it might be difficult (and it often would be) to lay down in the first instance the entire line, B*b*.

CHRONOLOGICAL ACCOUNT OF BUILDINGS IN ITALY AND SICILY.*

S. Vitale, Ravenna.—Not the least trace of the cross form is here apparent. There is a marked peculiarity of the capitals, not only in their shape and carving, but in the method of working them. Those nearest the altar are like basket-work, so cut away from the stone block as to seem formed of cast-iron, kept away a few inches from it. The few external mouldings are like those of the Roman brick towers; 550; consecrated 555 (Fabri); 510 (Cockerell); 547 (H. J. Knight).

Monza Cathedral.—595; façade, 1350 (Hope).

S. Balbina, Rome. — 366, founded; restored in 600, 731, 1464, and 1600 (Rossi); 600 and 720 restored (Vasi.) Altar to south-west.

SS. Quattro Coronati, Rome. — 311; restored 775, 847, and 1099, after that quarter was fired by Robert Guiscard (Rossi); 625 (Bunsen); 625, but rebuilt 1105 (Nardini); 311, but rebuilt from foundations 1105 (Vasi). Altar to west.

S. Adriano, Rome.—626 (Crescembini); 630, rebuilt; again 911, it being in a ruinous state. The bronze gates brought, 780, from Perugia (Rossi); 600; restored in 1586. It was an ancient temple, used as a church until 600 (Vasi).

S. Anastasia, Rome.—630 (Rycaut); it is known to have been originally built before 500; restored 1120, again 1471; repaired 1605; the façade, 1636 (Rossi and Vasi). Altar to south-east.

S. Agnese, Rome.—Fourth century built; restored 500 and 621 (Rycaut and Rossi); 621; no part considered older than this (H. G. Knight); 625 (Bunsen).

S. Tomaso in limine, Bergamo.—Seventh century, supposed (H. G. Knight); eleventh century, supposed (Quintiliano).

S. Michele, Pavia.—660 supposed. In 916 and 1004 it was repaired (H. G. Knight); c. 1000 (St. Quintino).

S. Frediano, Lucca. — 670; the campanile c. 1150 (H. G. Knight).

Florence Baptistery.—c. 550 (Cicognara); c. 675. This date is supposed, but is uncertain. The church is known to have been finished before 725 (H. G. Knight). The lantern built 1150, by Lombards; façade covered with marble, by Arnolfo, 1293, when the new doorway was made. It is supposed to have been an old temple of Mars, and open at top. The internal decorations, cupola, &c., done under Constantine. The pavement raised, hiding the steps, 1288. Originally there was only one door, which was where tribune now is. This was closed, and three new opened c. 1200 (Richa).

S. Giorgio in Velabro, Rome.—600; built before this date; restored and adorned 682 to 742 (Severano); 682, restored; repaired 741 and 1611 (Rossi); 740 to 750, built (Rycaut); 682 (Bunsen); 827 to 844, enlarged, and porch added; repaired 1610 (Crescembini); 682: at this date rebuilt almost from foundations, having been previously restored, 600; again restored 745 and 1611. It is on site of Sempronian Basilica (Vasi). The cornice and antæ seem of the same date as the brick towers.

S. Stefano, Bologna.—Eighth century (Knight).

Brescia Cathedral.—662 to 671 (Knight).

S. Teodoro, Pavia.—Before 750 (Knight)

S. Nicolo, Ravenna. — 768: the convent, &c., 1256 (Fabri).

S. Maria in Cosmedino, Rome.—c. 270: originally founded on ruins of temple "della Pudicizia patrizia." Rebuilt 772, from foundations; 860, porch restored. The amborni 1123 (Crescembini); 772: the founder unknown. Porch built 858; the church adorned 858 and 1118 (Severano); 790 (Bunsen). The mouldings of tower are similar to those of S. Giorgio in Velabro, but much dilapidated. Altar to west.

S. Pudenziana, Rome.—51 (by S. Pietro); rebuilt 772; also restored 1075, and being ruinous, rebuilt in 1600, from foundations (Rossi). This date, 772, is probably that of tower. Its mouldings are similar to those of S. Giorgio.

S. Croce, Rome.—By Constantine, who threw down part of Temple of Venus to build it. Chapel of S. Elena restored 426; the church restored c. 720 and 976; the roof rebuilt 1493 (Severano). Altar to east.

S. Vincenzio alle tre fontane.—790 (Bunsen); c. 790, restored from foundations after a fire (Ciampini); 780, restored from foundations (Crescembini and Severano).

S. Giovanni a P. latina.—790 (D'Agincourt and Bunsen). Altar to south-east.

S. Nereo e Achilleo, Rome.—498: date of erection unknown, but mentioned at this time; restored 795 from foundations; again restored, it being in ruinous state, in 1480 and 1596 (Severano). Once a temple of Isis. Restored 526 and 1595, according to the ancient forms (Vasi). Altar to south-west.

S. Vincenzio e Anastasio, Rome.—625, originally built; rebuilt from foundations in 795 (Severano); 625, rebuilt from foundations, and in 800 restored. Splendidly enriched by Charlemagne (Rossi).

S. Maria in Navicella, Rome.—817, rebuilt from foundations. Its original date is unknown. Restored 1500, when porch was added (Rossi and Severano); 817, rebuilt, with two orders of columns (Vasi). Altar to west.

S. Cecilia, Rome.—745 (Rycaut); ninth century (D. di Serradifalco). Its date unknown, but before 552. Restored 600 and 821 as now seen (Vasi); 1518, much ornamented (Rossi). Altar to west.

S. Lorenzo, Verona.—813 (Maffei).

S. Prassede, Rome.—160; rebuilt 817, with chapel of S. Zeno (Vasi); 820,—Bunsen, Rycaut, Severano, &c., agree that it was then entirely rebuilt. Original date unknown, but spoken of in 499. Chapel of S. Zeno, 820; sacristy, 1605 (Severano). S. Carlo Borromeo rebuilt porch and façade, decorated interior, altered altar-steps and the balustrades, restored the ancient seats round choir, and the ancient marble tables (Rossi).

S. Marco, Rome.—833, from foundations; in 1468 restored; 336 first built (Nardini); 772, the third part rebuilt and enclosed with porticoes all round; in 833 rebuilt from foundations; in 1468 palace adjoining built (Rossi). This church is very curious. It is very small, and built on basilican plan. The aisle columns Roman, with circular arches over. The clerestory windows are Gothic.

Subiaco.—847: the pointed arches clearly belong to this date (D'Agincourt). The chapels much injured 1299 and 1350 by earthquakes, and the pointed arches introduced at the restorations (Knight).

Gt. Cuba, Palermo.—Ninth century. These are the first pointed arches in Europe (Cavallari).

Cast. di Zisa.—Ninth century: the Norman additions in 1154—69 (Knight).

L. Cuba.—Ninth century: the masonry of all these buildings is of small squared stones, just like the Norman.

S. Francesca Romana, Rome.—c. 850: the tower is supposed of this date, but it is uncertain (Knight).

S. Ambrogio, Milan.—800 to 861; the vestibule 861 to 882. One campanile 850, and the other 1143. The pointed arches introduced 1300 (Knight). The capitals of the vestibule columns are, generally, very flatly carved, partly of foliage and partly of animals. The general appearance of the interior is decidedly Norman.

S. Ciriacco, Ancona.—950 (D'Agincourt, Hope, Serradifaico); 1100, supposed by Greeks (Knight); 1300, Milezia—(Is this the date of the porch ?).— The transepts floor is raised seven steps, and was so built. The south doorway under porch, the porch itself, and all the west front have every appearance of having undergone extensive repairs. The roof is of later date than the church, as the front and transepts have false gables. The principal front has also undergone very extensive alterations. This church seems worthy of very attentive study. Its plan, the arrangement of its dome, and its general details are very interesting. It may be classed with S. Pietro and S. Maria della Piazza, Ancona, and

* See page 244, *ante*.

ike a plan or scheme for forming it; and both
Smyth and Stratford lamented that such a
desideratum was not promptly and substantially adopted. I ventured to remark that it was
a subject I had often meditated on, and that I
had, at one time, penned something of a pro-
pectus, expressly on the subject, and if they
would breakfast with me the next morning
I would show them what I had written, or at
all events explain my opinions on, and wishes
to see, a practical society formed to promote
and give additional interest to the science of
geography. Five of our friends assembled the
next morning, when resolutions were passed
and written down; and I volunteered to act as
secretary *pro tem.*, and write a more matured
prospectus than the one I had previously and
hastily prepared, and that it should be submitted to each person then present for comment, improvement, and adoption. I had it
set up in type, and sent a copy to each gentleman. They were returned with various suggestions, &c., and a proof combining the whole
was sent to the printer: revised proofs were
soon provided, and clean copies sent to the same
parties. One of them was shown to Mr.
Barrow, secretary to the Admiralty, who soon
manifested not only angry hostility to the
scheme, but wrote intemperate letters to one
or two of the officers who were and are con-
ected with the Admiralty. The language
used by the secretary was very irritating to the
gentlemen he addressed, and it was feared that
serious consequences might ensue. A meeting
of our preliminary committee assembled, and
it was agreed that the prospectus should be
issued, and an appeal made to the public,
to ascertain who were willing to co-operate
in forming a new society therein explained.
The secretary, who was prompt, peremptory,
and resolute, instead of asking the advice and
aid of friends, issued a prospectus, named a
committee, and told the public that such a
society was formed, and invited members to
join it.

Too much engrossed with the literary works
I had in hand, I did not feel disposed to enter
the field. I declined to involve myself in a
paper contest, but both I, Captain Smyth,
and Mr. Baily were named on the first committee, where we both saw and lamented,
that a man of such rough bearing and manners should overawe and govern the society
which had thus been formed.

In the autobiography which I am now printing, I may be induced to give a further explanation of this public subject, from papers and
dates of the time; as the *Literary Gazette* of
May 26th has endeavoured to invalidate my
claims to credit in the origination of the
Geographical Society.   J. BRITTON.
May 29, 1849.

GUTTA PERCHA.

IN a late number of your journal, No. 323,
page 178, you have some remarks as to the
right pronunciation of the word "percha,"
the article "gutta percha." As I have
before me two letters relating to the subject,
which may, I think, be considered good authorities, (one from my brother, for many
years resident at Sumatra and the adjoining
settlements, and a perfect Malay scholar, and
the other from a native of that island, a lady,
whose husband holds a responsible situation
in the spot in the East-India Company's
service, and who has also published an essay
on the properties and uses of the substance),
take leave to send you extracts for the information of your readers; and I would beg
attention to the very injudicious method at
present in use for procuring the article, in
the hope that a practice so injurious to its
future supply may be abandoned before its
effect is felt in the market. "The gutta
percha is in our forests,* but the people are
too indolent to procure it. At Singapore, considerable quantities are brought from the
neighbouring islands, but from the injudicious
mode of collecting it, that of felling instead of
tapping the trees, the supply is likely to
decline, unless measures are speedily adopted
to remedy the evil." Gutta is the Malay for
gum, and percha is properly " runnant,"† but

<small>* " Our forests." The letter is dated Penang, in the
"walls of Malacca.
† " Runnant." I do not at present know the meaning of
this word as here used, though it may be surmised.</small>

the gutta having been first introduced from
Sumatra, which the Malays call " poolow
percha," it has gone abroad as Sumatran gum.
Gutta percha is *soft*, as in perch, the fish of
that name, and is pronounced by the natives
thus, gutta-perch-a.

                              HENRY GARLING.

BISHOP DUPPA'S ALMSHOUSES.
RICHMOND, SURREY—1661.

THESE almshouses, affording accommodation to ten poor women (each inmate having
two rooms), were erected by Bishop Duppa,
tutor to Charles II., on the spot where his life
was saved, when that prelate was pursued by
some of Cromwell's adherents. On that occasion the Bishop made a vow that, if the King
were restored to his throne, he would perform
some work to the honour of God ;—hence this
pious work. The charity is under the management of trustees, the present receiver and paymaster, Mr. Wm. Smith, having held that
capacity for the last forty years.

The entrance doorway here represented is a
correct and graceful example of Italian architecture, and constitutes a leading feature of the
above-named structure, which bears the date
of 1661. Sir Wm. Chambers, in his treatise,
describes this style of doorway, and says " it
is a disposition of Michelangelo. The windows
of the capital are of this kind; and Sir

Christopher Wren hath executed doors of this
sort, under the beautiful semi-circular porches
in the flanks of St. Paul's."

The almshouses of this period are well worthy
of attention: freed from all ostentation of design,
these structures are generally wisely planned and
substantially built; and if any display of art
is made to enter into the composition, it is ever
accompanied by a marked sobriety of feeling.
It is to be regretted, in this instance, that the
front wall, which had a picturesque appearance,
has been pulled down, and a common brick
one substituted, and built in a direction wholly
irrespective of the building, to which it serves
as a screen. Such manifest indifference for
works of skill and taste is too frequently exhibited amongst us. When, through imperative
necessity, an interesting structure of by-gone
times must be demolished, would it be requiring too much at the hands of the destroyers
that they should deposit in the public archives
of the neighbourhood a correct representation
of the doomed structure? For the want, in
this instance, of the information which such a
document would supply, it is not possible to
learn the true character of the demolished portion of the building,—a circumstance the more
to be regretted, since it appears to be not improbable that the work in question is from the
hand of Inigo Jones. There is something very
barbarous in thus consigning to oblivion the
thoughts of those whose names are revered by
posterity.   A. P. HAKEWILL.

BISHOP DUPPA'S ALMSHOUSES, RICHMOND.
A.D. 1661.

VIEW FROM ROAD

DEO ET CAROLO

VOTIVA TABVLA

SCALE TO   ELEVATION

BUILDING

CARDENS   COURT   GARDENS

ENTRANCE
ROADWAY

THE CITY ANTIQUITIES.

In a report of the proceedings at a meeting of the Royal Institute of Architects, which appeared in your paper of last week, Mr. Tite (who seems to have taken up the cudgels and become the champion of the City authorities) endeavours to prove that the citizens have never been unmindful of their antiquities, and that they have been impugned without cause. To support this assertion, he goes on to state that Gresham College has always possessed a niche devoted to local antiquities. I have now before me "A Catalogue of the Rarities preserved at Gresham College," by Nehemiah Grew, Esq., F.R.S., extending over nearly 400 pages, with plates of the more curious specimens, dated 1681, in which are enumerated many antiquities presented by Sir Christopher Wren, John Aubrey, Esq., and other distinguished antiquaries of that day, such as tesselated pavements, Roman urns and coins. The museum also contained some valuable gems; and, amongst these, "a rock of diamonds," amethysts, sapphires, emeralds, &c.; specimens of natural history, plants, metals, minerals, &c. Perhaps the architect of the Exchange can inform me what has become of this collection? I have in vain endeavoured to ascertain its fate; and as he has instanced this "local antiquity niche" as a proof of the "regard the citizens have always had" for the remains of our ancestors, he can, or ought to give us some little information relating to it. I certainly do remember a "local antiquity niche" in Guildhall, about 3 feet by 6 feet in size (with about as many inches of dust and dirt), illumined by a pane of glass at the top of one of its sides, admitting just enough light to make *darkness visible*, which appeared as if, in remote times, it had been a temple dedicated to the goddess Cloacina. These isolated antiques are now removed from this apartment, and, with others discovered on the site of the Royal Exchange, placed in a larger room, and, within the last month or two, have been arranged in a glass case, protected by sheets of cartridge, to prevent the rays of the sun from injuring the crimson hue of the paper on which they are laid. Since 1841 (the time the Exchange antiquities were discovered) I have been year after year looking for their production, and at last we are favoured with a sight of them. But to whom are we indebted for this one room, now allotted to the reception of local antiquities, save to Mr. Lott, the only member of the corporation who, through a series of repulses and oppositions, which would have daunted a less enterprising man, at last prevailed upon the Common Council to devote this space? Should it be requisite in any public manner to detail the long account of negligences on the part of the corporation towards their antiquities, as well as numerous glaring instances of the manner in which valuable remains have been destroyed, I am certain abundant evidence will be forthcoming. But who are to be the judges? I think the best tribunal is the public press—the best judges, the public.

A London Antiquary.

PAINTINGS BOUGHT BY THE ART-UNION OF LONDON.

The following is a list of the works of art purchased by the prizeholders up to this time:—

"A Mountain Chieftain's Funeral in Olden Times," F. Danby (B. I.), 300*l.*; "River Scene, N. Wales," F. R. Lee, (R. A.), 126*l.*; "The Solitary Pool," R. Redgrave (R. A.), 99*l.* 15*s.*; "Soldiers' Wives waiting the Result of a Battle," Mrs. McIan. (Free Ex.), 80*l.*; "Horses' Heads after Nature," J. F. Herring (S. B. A.), 80*l.*; The Holy Well, Brittany, J. J. Jenkins (S. B. A.), 80*l.*; "The Orphans of the Village," T. F. Marshall, (R. A.), 105*l.*; "Wyndings of the Wye," G. B. Campion (N. W. C. S.), 69*l.* 6*s.*; "Harwich from the Stour," C. Bentley (B. I.), 73*l.* 10*s.*; "Preparing for the Festa," F. Y. Hurlstone (S. B. A.), 80*l.*; "Bianca Capella," J. C. Hook (R. A.), 73*l.* 10*s.*; "Hessian Girl and Cows," J. W. Keyl (R. A.), 73*l.* 10*s.*; "Wood Scene with Cattle and Figures," W. Shayer (S. B. A.), 60*l.*; "The Alarm Signal, Smugglers off," H. P. Parker (F. E.), 50*l.*; "The Curassier's Forge at Caen," E. A. Goodall (R. A.), 55*l.*; "My Wife this day puts on first her French Gown," &c., J. Noble (S. B. A.), 52*l.* 10*s.*; "A Game at Marbles," G. Smith (R. A.), 50*l.*; "Age and Infancy," J. F. Marshall (B. I.), 50*l.*; "Hagar," Miss F. Corbaux (N. W. C. S.), 63*l.*; "A Fishing Boat putting about for her Rudder," W. A. Brunning (S. B. A.), 60*l.*; "Near the Deer Leap, New Forest," W. Shayer (S. B. A.), 40*l.*; "A Shady Stream, N. Wales," H. J. Boddington (S. B. A.), 40*l.*; "Davie Deans," T. Clater (S. B. A.), 50*l.*; "View from the Moors above Taynuilts," C. Fielding (W. C. S.), 42*l.*; "Undercliff, Isle of Wight," W. Shayer (S. B. A.), 45*l.*; "The Scene at the Mermaiden's Fountain," G. E. Sintzenick (R. A.), 42*l.*; "A Poaching Terrier," J. Bateman (S. B. A.), 20*l.*; "A View near Brighton," G. B. Willcocks (F. E.), 25*l.*; "Domestic Ducks, after Nature," J. F. Herring (B. I.), 30*l.*; "St. Michael's Mount, Normandy," C. Bentley (W. C. S.), 26*l.* 5*s.*; "The Interior of the Fisher's Cottage," Miss J. McLeod (B. I.), 25*l.*; "A Peep under Westminster Bridge," W. A. Brunning (S. B. A.), 25*l.*; "Entrance to a Village," H. J. Boddington (S. B. A.), 20*l.*; "Flowers of the Forest," R. Sayers (F. E.), "A Shady Lane, Banks of the Conway, N. Wales," A. Vickers (R. A.), 20*l.*; "Piedmontese," A. H. Taylor (N. W. C. S.), 20*l.*; "A Mountain Stream," H. Jutsum (R. A.). 15*l.*; "The Morning of Life," R. Sayers (F. E.), 15*l.*; "Fall of the Machin, and Pandy Mill, N. Wales," T. L. Rowbotham (N. W. C. S.), 17*l.*; "On the Frontiers of Holland," C. Adloff (R. A.), 15*l.*; "The ancient Rath Haus of Coblentz," Mrs. Phillips (R. A.), 15*l.*; "Near Chidingstone, Kent," A. W. Williams (B. I.), 15*l.*; "At Bait; a Road-side Scene," H. B. Willis, (R. A.) 15*l.*; "On the Lake of Orta," G. C. Herring (B. I.), 25*l.*; "Desecrated Chapel of St. Jacques, Orleans," S. Frout (W. C. S.), 10*l.* 10*s.*; "Mill at Shere, near Guildford," C. Pearson (S. B. A.), 10*l.*; "Voreppe," H. Gastineau (W. C. S.), 15*l.* 15*s.*; "Interior at Dieppe," S. Prout (W. C. S.), 12*l.* 12*s.*; "Michaelmas Day," J. Poulton (B. I.), 10*l.*

NOTES IN THE PROVINCES.

A drawing and designing class has been formed at the Literary and Mechanics' Institution, Chelmsford, and the authorities at Somerset House have presented their elementary course for the use of the students, twenty in number, and almost all operatives.——Mepal Church is about to be restored at an estimated expense of about 600*l.*——The example of Sir C. Anderson is about to be followed in the erection of stained glass memorial windows in Lincoln Cathedral.——The public baths at Hinckley are in an advanced state. The building is in the Tudor style, and has been erected by Mr. Harrold, builder, who is also to form a swimming bath, 60 feet long by 20 feet wide.——Brighton appears to be on the increase. According to the *Sussex Express*, Baron Goldsmid is to complete Adelaide-crescent forthwith, and to form a square at the top, similar to that at Kemp-town, the road for which is partly laid out. The whole of the west side of Lansdowne-place has been built on. Opposite the Wick Inn detached villas are to be built. A great number of houses have also sprung up east of Montpellier-crescent, forming quite a new town.——The restoration of Romsey Abbey Church is still going on. The outside of the north transept is now under repair.——The Hon. and Rev. W. H. Scott has taken in hand the repair of Maiden Newton Church, according to the *Poole and Dorset Herald*, on condition that the parish contribute 100*l.*, according to estimate.——An asylum for middle class lunatics is about to be erected near Stafford, at a cost of 10,000*l.* besides funds in hand.——The consecration of a new church, erected at Tixall, Staffordshire, at the expense of the Hon. J. C. Talbot, was to take place on the 28th instant.——The nave of Atherstone Church, Warwickshire, having been taken down, the first stone of the new building is to be laid on the 2nd of June. The accommodation provided is for between 1,200 and 1,300 people, including children.——Two painted windows have been put up in the chancel of St. Mary de Lode Church, Gloucester, at the expense of Miss Goglan, sister of the Vicar. The artist was Mr. Rogers, of Worcester.——The completion of the extensive buildings at the Manchester Exchange (already described by us) was celebrated on Friday week, by a ball in aid of the baths and washhouses funds.——Methley Church has been extensively repaired, and was to be opened on Thursday last. The oak ceiling has been restored. Messrs. Vickers and Hugall, of Pontefract, were the architects employed.——The first stone of a new Baptist chapel at Kirkstall was laid on Tuesday week. It is to be a plain building, at an estimated cost of 450*l.*, already subscribed.——The grammar school at Richmond, says the *Hull Packet*, is to be rebuilt by subscription of 1,200*l.*, realised, in honour of the late headmaster, Mr. Canon Tate. The plans of Mr. Andrews, of York, have been adopted, and the sub-structures were commenced in April,—the chief stone on 19th May.——The foundation-stone of Holyrood Free Church, at Edinburgh, was laid on Thursday week, at the site at head of Horsewynd, near St. Ann's-yards.

DUNDEE ARCH COMPETITION.

I send you a printed circular which I have this morning received from Dundee, after waiting upwards of a month without being able to obtain either my drawings or any reply to my inquiry respecting them. No doubt, better late than never is quite Shaksperian; nevertheless a little more promptitude in issuing these circulars would have been better still. After all, too, mystery and suspense are protracted very unnecessarily. It is not even quite clear that the design first chosen will be set aside, but merely that it possibly may be, and that "another may yet be preferred." It is not, however, at all likely that there can be many others,—perhaps not above three or four,—between which the choice in the second instance would lie; therefore those designs which are already finally rejected might as well have been returned, instead of being very needlessly detained, merely in order that those who sent them may have the trouble, or, as the committee seem to think, may have the pleasure, of applying for them again.

Possibly, the keeping all the designs a few weeks longer has been determined upon with the good-natured view of also keeping the competitors in good spirit, each of them being thus left to suppose that *his* design has still a very fair chance of being selected,—that is, should there really be any second selection. Surely committees must have more of feline playfulness than of feeling in their nature,—of feeling at least for the feelings of unlucky competitors, with whom they sport, just as cats do with mice, instead of inflicting the *coup de grace* as quickly as possible.*

Competitor.

Books.

A Manual of Logic. By B. H. Smart, author of "Beginnings of a New School of Metaphysics," "Grammar on its True Basis," &c. London, 1849. Longman and Co.

Mr. Smart completely, and we think very properly, discards the old wordy Aristotelian logic, and substitutes a new logic in which there is something more than a mere play of words—the shadowy signs of thought. He would have us reason *by means* of words, but not altogether with and about words. Mr. Smart confesses himself a disciple of Locke and Horne Tooke; yet we very much mistake if he is not far more apt to be regarded as an adapter to logical purposes of Dr. Brown's admirable, though still imperfect, theory of *relationism.* He wonders why Morell, in his able "History of Philosophy," places him in the class to which this very metaphysician belonged: he may depend on it that Morell

* The circular (dated May 26) says:—"In reference to the competition designs received for the proposed Royal Arch at Dundee, I think it necessary to inform you why the committee has not yet been able to come to a final decision regarding them. A design has been selected as the most suitable, but as it is yet uncertain whether it can be erected for the sum originally fixed, another design less expensive may yet be preferred; in a few weeks, however (say two or three), this point will be ascertained, and, in the meantime, the committee will use every despatch, and will give notice in *The Builder* and *North British Advertiser* newspapers, when the unsuccessful competitors may apply for their designs."

had Brown in his eye when he did so. Yet Mr. Smart may not be indebted to the latter, even for his relationism, and indeed he displays a want of familiarity with Brown's doctrines, as where he calls the idea that tactual not visible impressions are the early inlet of all our fundamental knowledge a *new one*, suggested by an anonymous correspondent of his own. Familiar or not, however, he is plainly on the right tack, and has obtained a glimpse of the concentradiative nature of the mind, as yet so little known. The capability and tendency in the mind to pass inwards from subjective terms to relations in common, more or less abstract, is so far worked out in his theory of inductive logic, as is its perfectly parallel capability and tendency to repass outwards from relations, so begotten, to subjective terms, in his theory of deductive logic; and the threefold distinction of the faculties in general into the potential, the sentient, and the sciential, we trace in his definition of the difference between grammar, rhetoric, and logic, in the outset.

"Logic," he remarks, "is a branch of learning connected with grammar and rhetoric. While grammar looks only to correctness of *construction*, or putting properly the parts of speech together so that they shall be accurate *forms* of language, and rhetoric varies those forms in order to make them expressive of *emotion*, logic looks to the *sense* which language has to convey, clear from any emotion which may or may not be its effect.......

The process of the understanding by which knowledge is accumulated and included under a sign, is called Induction; the process by which the knowledge so accumulated is spread again before the understanding in words, which being joined together make evident *sense*,—that is to say, make one expression with one meaning, is called Deduction."

In the form of an Appendix, the work contains an introductory course for students, and there is also an instructive Index of terms, &c.

Digest of Evidence taken before a Committee of the House of Commons appointed to inquire into the Agricultural Customs of England and Wales, in respect to Tenant-Right. Compiled and arranged by WILLIAM SHAW, Editor of the "Mark-lane Express," &c., and HENRY CORBET, Secretary of the London Farmer's Club, &c. London, 1849. Rogerson, Strand; Ridgway, Piccadilly.

This is a book that ought to be in the hands of every landlord and every tenant-farmer in the three kingdoms. We have long advocated the cause of land tenant-right, which in fact (pity it had not a better name) is just another term for mutual-right and advantage between land-owner and tenant. To deprive an outgoing tenant of all due compensation for improvements made by him on his landlord's estate, so far from benefiting the latter, or enabling him to grasp at anything of essential value, can only tend to injure his own interests. It is virtually to insist that his tenant shall *not* improve his property. Whereas, if duly compensated, every outgoing tenant with capital and enterprise would leave the land in a higher state of cultivation and improvement, yielding increased produce and higher rents. Yet from this excellent digest of important evidence, it appears that an immense proportion of England is without such tenant-right at all, either by custom or law. Indeed two-thirds of it is held by the proprietors themselves on life-lease only, or by entail, so that no adequate security at present *can* be afforded for improvement of the property of heirs not bound to pay for it. The landlords even thus, then, have as deep an interest as the tenants in the adoption of means for the establishment of 'tenant-right' as the law of the land. Without security to his capital, either by tenant-right or lease, it is clear that the farmer cannot prosecute his calling with energy and confidence, or bring the land to so high a state of cultivation as he is perfectly capable of doing. The Committee, themselves landowners, have unequivocally admitted the soundness of the principle (see 13th clause of report), and indeed the highly cultivated state of Lincolnshire and part of Scotland, where this form of tenant-right (not the Irish of course), prevails by custom, speaks for itself still more unequivocally in its favour. The Committee, too, have recommended an Act of Parliament applying it to entailed estates (see 15th and 16th clauses).

In fine, we cannot but recommend such a digest as the present, as a capital improvement on the horrid blue books, through acres of which one may wade without gleaning more than a mere handful of the really valuable matter which they generally contain.

Popular Rhymes and Nursery Tales: a Sequel to the Nursery Rhymes of England. By Mr. JAMES ORCHARD HALLIWELL. London, 1849. J. R. Smith.

THAT the nursery has an archæology, the study of which may eventually lead to important results, and thus redeem the songs and jingles of our childhood from the imputation of exclusive frivolity—as, indeed, it has already done in not a few isolated instances,—is what we quite agree with the author of this little work in thinking. But, as he observes, those who have the opportunity, and do not consider it a derogatory task to add to such memorials, must hasten to the rescue. The antiquities of the people are rapidly disappearing before the spread of education; and before many years have elapsed they will be lost, or recorded only in the collections of the antiquary, perhaps requiring evidence that they ever existed. Let it not be thought, however, that it is from any comparative paucity of those interesting little subjects of universal reminiscence in the present collection, that the early recollections, or the mannikin acquaintance, of others are thus appealed to. On the contrary, this first endeavour of any gifted mind to gather together the decaying fragments of the literature of the little men and women of England, is—all obstacles considered—a perfect monument of industry. This could only be realized by the *con amore* help of others, and hence a further appeal for information, to which we gladly give increased publicity.

The learned and able author has, moreover, another purpose in view besides a merely archæological one. "It were greatly to be desired," he remarks, "that the instructors of children could be persuaded how much is lost by rejecting the venerable relics of nursery traditional literature, and substituting in their place the present cold, unimaginative—I had almost said unnatural—prosaic good-boy stories." And, indeed, he might have altogether said so; for the imagination is one of the most vivid of all faculties in the little, wondering, radiative, souls of children, and is hence the main material or ground on which to work, in rearing them into orderly maturity of mental structure.

But although even architects and archæologists have, doubtless, once been fellows of the peculiar and extensive literary and scientific society, a volume of whose varied records now lies before us,—and, although we believe that many of our readers are now *patrons*, or at least honorary members, of that interesting community to which they once more exclusively belonged,—nevertheless any further encroachment on the really refreshing pages of Mr. Halliwell would be scarcely within our province—unless, indeed, his archæological researches into the foundations of the house that Jack built, be a legitimate exception: even the discussion of that important question, however, we must postpone for the present, *sine die*.

Miscellanea.

A WHOLE TOWN AND GREAT PART OF ANOTHER GOING BY AUCTION.—Amongst the items of 284 lots of a 'momentous sale' of property by auction, in Cheshire, beginning on the 4th inst., by Messrs. Churton, of Liverpool, as advertised in the *Albion*, are "the whole town of Parkgate, and the greater portion of Great Neston," with lots of "brick clay, sand, building stone," for preparing a few more of such subjects for the hammer of some future wholesale knocker-down of towns and villages.

PUBLIC RECORD OFFICE.—Mr. Monckton Milnes has given notice of a motion—That a humble address be presented to her Majesty, praying that she will be pleased to give directions for the immediate commencement of a building suitable to contain the public records and State papers, and relieve them from that dangerous condition to which Mr. Braidwood, superintendent of fire brigade, has stated in evidence—"no merchant of ordinary prudence would subject his books of account."

TO FIX DRAWINGS IN CHALK AND CRAYONS.—The Marquis de Varrennes has discovered a method, which is equally simple and ingenious, of giving to drawings in pencils and crayons the fixidity of painting, and without injury. He succeded in obtaining this result by varnishing them on the back; that is, by spreading over the back of the paper an alcoholic solution of white gum-lac. This solution quickly penetrates the paper, and enters even into the marks of the crayon on the other side. The alcohol rapidly evaporates, so that in an instant all the light dust from the crayons and chalk, which resembles that on the wings of a butterfly, adheres so firmly to the paper, that the drawing may be rubbed and carried about without the least particle being effaced. The following are the accurate proportions of the solution:—10 grammes of common gum-lac are dissolved in 120 grammes of alcohol; the liquid is afterwards bleached with animal charcoal. For the same purpose may be used even the ready-made paint that can be purchased at the colour shops, containing a sixth of white-lac, and adding two-thirds of rectified spirits of wine. After it has been filtered, there is nothing further to be done than to spread a layer of either of these solutions at the back of the drawing, in order to give them the solidity required.

THE RE-ADORNMENT OF LINCOLN CATHEDRAL.—With pleasure we desire to draw the attention of our readers, especially those of "the nobility and others, owners of property, or residents in the diocese of Lincoln," to an endeavour of the dean of the cathedral, by letter, to raise by subscription the balance of a sum of 1,500*l.* (of which 500*l.* have been already provided by the Dean and Chapter themselves, and others), in order to restore the east window to its pristine glory, by replacing the present inferior material with "glass in the best and most splendid style of modern art." We agree with the dean in thinking that "for the honour of Almighty God in this his glorious house," the present opportunity of manifesting good-will in such a cause will be promptly embraced by a number of the wealthier sons of the church, even to a greater extent than sufficient to complete this really trifling sum.

LUMSDEN'S MODEL DWELLINGS FOR THE WORKING-CLASSES.—On the 25th ult., these dwellings, situated in Garscube-road, Glasgow, and already described by us, previously to being occupied by the tenants, were visited and inspected by the magistrates and other members of the town council, as well as by numerous other gentlemen interested in the prosperity and comfort of the working-classes. Mr. Lumsden himself was present, and, aided by Mr. Wylson, the architect, afforded every information and explanation to the visitors, all of whom expressed themselves in a high degree gratified by the many admirable arrangements for the accommodation of those by whom domestic comforts of the humblest kind have been hitherto all but unattainable. The houses have been long since all let. The scheme is worthy of imitation, and reflects lasting credit on all concerned.

QUEEN ELIZABETH'S GRAMMAR SCHOOL, SOUTHWARK.—Painters have been busily employed marking the stonework and other portions of the buildings situate not far from the Railway terminus at London Bridge, and known as the grammar school of Queen Elizabeth for the parishes of St. Olave and St. John, Southwark, in order that they may be taken down and re-erected in the same form elsewhere. Neither does there appear to be any excuse for such parsimony on the part of the institution. A correspondent, who says that it is possessed of immense property, and has received a large compensation from the Brighton and South Coast Railway, calls upon us to object to this course as niggardly and inexpedient. It does not seem to us, however, a case calling for interference.

HYDE PARK GALLERY OF MODERN ART.—We are much pleased to hear that the committee of the "Hyde Park Exhibition," have granted free admission to their gallery to the students of the Government School of Design, Somerset House. This is an example we hope to find followed by other exhibitions in this metropolis, as such a step is well calculated to improve the taste of our designers.

The Patent-Eater. — Dickens' Model Patent-Eater is graphic: "The Patent-Eater is of a peculiar species—he is a '*chance*' child —of foundling descent—sharp and thief-like— no teeth—(glass corrodes the Enamel)—Cambridge bred—quick at L. s. D.—a smatter of the law—particularly, bankruptcy—*meum* and *tuum* not in his vocabulary—a breed of them was lately imported from Bristol to Birmingham, where they thrive marvellously well in a *lane* a few miles out of town, *vid* canal." The Patent-Eater has various plans laid for indulging in his favourite appetite since the repeal of the glass duties. We know one case in point which occurred a few years ago. A patentee in the glass trade, who had expended his hard earnings and a number of years' labour, in bringing out a very useful patent for ornamenting glass, by "*chance*" fell in with one of these gentlemen. A protection of his patent, and large promises of reward were held out to the patentee, if he would join the Patent-Eater, to establish a connection and set the process a-going, of which the Patent-Eater had no knowledge whatever. The young patentee, open, generous, and confiding, was very easily persuaded, and a written agreement was entered into. The process was set a-going, a demand for the article created, and a good trade in prospective, certain. Then the cloven foot began to show itself. The junior partner has his part of the game to play. *Jacques* (hopeful youth, half-way bred between Cambridge and Billingsgate) is sent to annoy the patentee in every possible way, and to assail him with such names as liar, &c. The patentee begins to smell a rat (in reality), and on referring to his agreement (written by *Jacques*), he finds that it is not worth one straw. The result may easily be guessed at. The patentee is turned adrift without a penny, and the noble Company enjoy a flourishing business with forty or fifty hands employed in it. This is what is technically termed "scotching a patentee," and is of frequent occurrence. You will ask, honest reader, is there no remedy? There is, virtually speaking, none whatever. It would be a fruitless waste of money. The Courts of Chancery, Exchequer, Old Palace, Bankruptcy, or any other court, are all one and the same thing to Rob Roy, "the Paten-tEater." Surely the patent laws might be amended so as to prevent and punish such base injustice.—*Cooper's " Glass Manual.*"

The File Trade.—We have learned with very great pleasure that there are some palpable indications of an improvement in this trade at Sheffield.

Removal of Vitiated Air.—The article under the head of Removal of Smoke and Ventilation of Sewers, which appeared in a late number of The Builder, has suggested to me the idea of a cheap mode of carrying the vitiated air from dwellings by means of tubes leading from the rooms to the gas-lights in the street, the heat from which would cause the confined air to pass off with great velocity, by which a constant fresh supply would be insured to the inmates, and at a time, too, when they most need it. The same principle might, to a certain extent, be applied to the ventilation of sewers.—A. B.

Bookbinding.—Some idea may be formed of the extent of the London bookbinding trade from calculations which have been made, to the effect, that the weekly consumption of leaf gold, for enriching the exterior of books, amounts to about 3,600,000 square inches; and that 350 tons of paper shavings from book edges are sold annually by the London binders.

Astounding Liberality to preserve Ancient Works of Art.—The Earl of Guilford has ordered that the beautiful frescoes (?) which literally cover the walls of the Church of St. Cross (Winchester), shall next week receive an additional coat of whitewash! —*Hampshire Independent.*

St. Paul's Church, Camden-town.— The first of several churches proposed to be built in St. Pancras parish was consecrated on Thursday in last week. It is in the Pointed style, from designs by Messrs. Ordish and Johnson, and accommodates 1,200 persons. The vicar and his active coadjutors in committee are responsible for a considerable amount, yet to be subscribed in order to defray the cost.

Projected Works.—Advertisements have been issued for tenders, by 7th inst., for the erection and completion of a large building at the Infantry barracks, Manchester; by 21st, for the erection of a new chapel to the hospital for consumption, Brompton; by 14th, for the erection of additional wards to the St. Saviour's Union, Southwark; by 11th, for the erection of a farm house at *Hermitage*, Dorset; by 26th, for the erection of a farmery at Arsley, Bedfordshire; by 30th, for the erection of a church in the district of St. Paul's, Devonport; by 6th, for alterations and improvements to five houses in the parish of All Saints, Poplar; by a date not specified, for covering a large tavern with 1½ inch planed slates, rabitted together; by 12th, for the erection and completion of a stone warehouse at Bradford; by 5th, for the erection of farm-buildings, near Leicester; by 4th, for building 800 feet of brick sewer and 158 feet of glazed stoneware pipe sewers at Kensington; by 5th, for repairing sewers, &c., in the City; by 6th, for painting and repairing lanterns and fittings of gas-lamps at Islington, and painting lamp-posts, &c.; by 5th, for the supply of 670 yards of iron water-piping for the Lancashire and Yorkshire Railway; and by 7th, for 50 fathoms yellow deal ends at Kensington Workhouse.

Richborough Castle.—Mr. Rolfe has been excavating the *castrum* at Richborough, and has laid open some square towers and two circular ones at the angles.

A curious Encaustic Tile, richly embossed, was found a few days since in excavating for a new sewer in Broad-street, City. It was presented by Mr. Haywood, the surveyor, to the Commissioners of Sewers. The design, we are told, represents an empress wearing a crown, the hands being uplifted as if in amazement.

The Porcelain Tower of Nankin.— The great Porcelain Tower at Nan-kin, in the province of Kiang-nan, is the most extraordinary building in China; it was built by the Emperor Yong-lo, and is called by the Chinese the "Temple of Gratitude." The tower is erected upon a pile of bricks, and is formed upon a most substantial timber framework; it stands about 200 feet high, and is of an octangular shape. It is surrounded by a very thick wall of the same form, over which a roof is thrown from the tower, covered with green porcelain tiles, which make a very handsome promenade, the walls and roof being painted in arabesque. On the eastern side a marble staircase leads to the first floor, which is surrounded by a gallery or verandah, the roof of which is covered with green tiles, being supported by several pillars; on the top of the marble staircase there are three large doors leading into the hall or temple, which is on the first floor, and measures 40 feet across, which gives 15 feet for each of its sides. The floor is of marble, which has the appearance of projecting through the wall, as a cornice of marble 2 feet thick runs round the building on a level with the floor. The temple or hall is 100 feet in height, and is only lighted by means of the three doors we have already described. The tower is composed of nine stories, each one above the hall being of equal height, but the diameter of each succeeding one decreases in equal proportion up to the top. The walls externally and internally are covered with porcelain, and a verandah surrounds each story covered with porcelain tiles, while small bells are pendent to every corner of them. The beautifully sloped roof is appropriately finished by means of a very thick spar, which is planted in the floor of the eighth story, and passing through the centre of, and extending above, the roof some 30 feet. This spar is surmounted with a large golden ball, and from its junction with the spar, a thick gilt wire is carried down like a screw in a conical form, which gives a novel and light appearance to the building; the second, and each succeeding story, has a window on each of its sides; the floors are laid upon thick cross beams, which are carved and painted in arabesque to form the ceilings of the rooms below them. The walls are covered with porcelain tiles, stamped with various figures and devices; small niches are filled with figures in *basso relievo*, and rich gilding adorns the whole of the interior; a winding and inconvenient staircase runs up to the ninth story.— *China and the Chinese.*

New Gas Works at Walsall, near Birmingham.—The Corporation of this borough lately determined to erect new gas works, and having selected an eligible site requested that plans might be laid before the Town Council for their approval. Eleven designs were submitted, out of which they selected the design jointly made by Mr. H. C. Saunders, Wolverhampton and Stratford, and Mr. Ewinson. The buildings will cost upwards of 5,000*l.*

District Surveyor's Fees. — I have been called on to pay a fee of 10s. by the district surveyor of ——, for rebuilding the eight upper courses of a chimney stack and reseting the pots. Is this the spirit of the Building Act? The work has cost something less than 40s., and I do think it very unreasonable to pay a fee for such an operation. The chimney-stack is not in party; that is to say, belongs exclusively to one house. I have paid the fee under protest.
W.

MEETINGS OF SCIENTIFIC BODIES
Held during the ensuing week.

MONDAY, June 4.—Institute of Architects, 8 P.M.
TUESDAY, 5.—Institution of Civil Engineers, 8 P.M.
THURSDAY, 7.—Society of Antiquaries, 8 P.M.
FRIDAY, 8.—Archæological Association, 8½ P.M.

TO CORRESPONDENTS.

"*Cement.*"—A correspondent asks to be "furnished with a receipt for the best composition or liquid cement for piecing Yorkshire blue stone, without having the stone to make hot; the same to have no kind of oil mixed with it."

Received.—"W. C. L.," "G. W." Subscriber," (four lines over). "H. R." (we will wait). "J. W.," "Mr. G." (see to the breakwater, and show yourself *Abel*). "T. H. L.," "G. G." (Denton). (Don'tyou might be mudfied for the purpose named, but would scarcely suit as it is). "J. N. C.," "E. P.," "G. P. K." "The Open Timber Roofs of the Middle Ages: illustrated by perspective and working Drawings of some of the best Varieties of Church Roofs," by R. and L. A. Brandon, Architects (Hogue, Fleet-street), 1849. Wright's "History of Ireland," Part II. (London, Tallis). "Gibbon's "Law of Dilapidations and Nuisances," 2nd Ed. (Weale, Holborn), 1849. "A Book of Ornamental Glazing Quarries, collected and arranged from Ancient Examples," by A. Woollaston (Franks, B. A.; J. H. Pafterf, Strand and Oxford), 1849.

"*Books, Prices, and Addresses.*"—We have not time to point out books or find addresses.

NOTICE.—All communications respecting *advertisements* should be addressed to the "Publisher," and not to the "Editor;" all other communications should be addressed to the EDITOR, and not to the Publisher.

ADVERTISEMENTS.

ROYAL ACADEMY of ARTS, TRAFALGAR-SQUARE. The EXHIBITION of the ROYAL ACADEMY is now OPEN.—Admission (from eight o'clock till seven), 1s.; catalogue, 1s.
JOHN PRESCOTT KNIGHT, R.A., Sec.

THE NEW SOCIETY of PAINTERS in WATER-COLOURS.—The FIFTEENTH ANNUAL EXHIBITION of this Society is now Open, at Duff Gallery, 31, Pall-mall, next St. James's Palace, from Nine o'clock till Dusk.—Admission 1s.; Catalogue 6d.
JAMES FAHEY, Secretary.

ROYAL POLYTECHNIC INSTITUTION—A Lecture, on Floral Botany, by Thomas Graham, Esq., M.R.A., on Monday, Wednesday, and Fridays, at half-past Three. Lectures, by Bartholomew, on the various modes of producing Artificial Light, in which the Drde Light, the Oxy-hydrogen Light, and the Electric Light, will be exhibited in juxtaposition. A Lecture on Chatterêl, with Musical Illustrations, by J. Russell, Esq., every evening at Eight o'clock. Lectures on Experimental Philosophy. The Microscope. The Dissolving Views include Scenes by Various Memen's Land, from Original Drawings taken on the spot by J. Skinner Prout, Esq.; also a New Series of Diptamic Effects, by Mr. Childe. New Chromatrope. Diver and Diving Bell.—Admission, 1s.; Schools, half-price.

COMPETITION DESIGNS prepared, coloured in Perspective, and Tinted with Backgrounds, &c., by an experienced Architectural Draughtsman.—Address, O. B., Publisher, Ledg's-street, Burton-crescent.

MR. EDWARD is desirous of meeting Gentlemen who require Coloured Architectural Designs, Perspective, got up and coloured in the neatest style at moderate terms. Mr. E. further begs to state that he makes a speciality also in this matter, should the competition prove ful successful.—Address, Mr. EDWARD, 16, Woodstock-street, Bond-street.

TO ARCHITECTS.—COMPETITION AND OTHER DRAWINGS.

MR. THOMAS S. BOYS, Member of the New Society of Painters in Water Colours, and author of "The Picturesque Architecture of Paris, Ghent, Rouge, &c," and of "London as it is," offers his services in Tinting Backgrounds, Landscapes, Perspective Views, Interiors, &c. From the long experience he has had in such subjects, he is fully aware of the points essentially necessary to be attended to, Drawings and designs thus graphed in a superior manner.—Address, Mr. BOYS, 81, Great Titchfield-street, Oxford-street.

TO BUILDERS.
MONEY ADVANCED.—230 feet, or less, of eligible BUILDING LAND, TO BE LET reasonably, for 80 years, at Camberwell, and the freeholder will contribute one-third, and provide benefits building thereon.—Apply at 12, Wandsworth-road, Piece, Knightsbridge, (the small house at two of one quarter.)

DRYING for BATHS and WASH-HOUSES, ASYLUMS, LAUNDRIES, &c.—The Patent Dissipating Company can dry, by itself process, at any rate of speed, rapid any amount of moisture; at the same time, in drying, cleanse or clothing, &c., altogether unaffected by means of cookies, steam. Hot-water pipes, &c.—For full particulars, apply at the offices of the Patent Dessicating Company, 41, Greenchurch-street, City.   ANGUS JENNINGS, Secretary.

BATHS and WASH-HOUSES for the LABOURING CLASSES.—A GENERAL MEETING of the Committee for promoting the establishment of Baths, and Wash-houses for the Labouring Classes, the subscribers and their friends, was held at the London Tavern, Bishopsgate, on Friday, May 25, 1847.

The late Sir H. B. DUKINFIELD, Bart. (the chairman of the committee), in the chair.

When it was moved by Mr. Samuel Jones, Lord, seconded by Mr. William Moore, and Resolved unanimously.—
That the Seventeenth Report of the Committee of Works, then read, should be printed and circulated.

And it was moved by the Right Hon. Lord Baddock, seconded by Mr. Arthur Currie, and Resolved unanimously.—
That the Trade Report of the Finance Committee, then read with the balance-sheet, and recommendation to the subscribers (which had been drawn up by Mr. Baguke, of Coleman-street), should be printed and circulated.

And it was moved by Mr. T. M. Weguelin, seconded by Mr. D. Lankester, and Resolved unanimously.—
That this meeting of previously Recommend that the utmost efforts be made by the friends of the institution to raise an additional subscription of funds, in order that the object of the Committee may be fully carried out with all possible speed.

The most sincere thanks of the meeting to the Chairman, the Rev. Mr. H. Dukinfield, Bart., with a cordial recognition of the noble and valuable and efficient exertions in promoting the establishment of Baths and Wash-houses for the labouring classes, were then proposed by Mr. P. Cazenove, seconded by Mr. S. J. Loyd, and carried by acclamation.

JAMES JULLIAN | Hon. Secs.
JOHN BULLAR |

Donations and subscriptions will be received at the Bank of England in the credit of "Samuel Jones, Loyd" and others; by the following bankers:—Messrs. Coutts and Co., Smith and Co., &c. Also with the following named gentlemen:—Messrs. Curtis and Co., Strand; Messrs. Drummond, Charing-cross; Messrs. Gosling and Sharpe, Fleet-street; Messrs. Glyn, Mills, Co., Lombard-street; Messrs. Hanbury, Taylor, and Co., Lombard-street; Messrs. Heywood, Parrish, and Co., St. James's-street; Messrs. Jones, Loyd and Co., Lothbury; Messrs. J. T. Ladbroke, Bart. and Co., Bankers; Messrs. Twining and Co., Strand; Messrs. Williams, Deacon, and Co., Birchin-lane; London and Westminster Bank and its branches; by any of the members of the Committee; and by the Assistant Secretary, at the Committee-room.

GEORGE WOOLCOTT, Assistant Secretary.
Committee-room, 5, Exeter Hall, May 26, 1849.

PUBLICATIONS.

ARCHITECTURAL PUBLICATION SOCIETY.—The SECOND PART of the publications for the year 1849, is NOW ISSUED. The Third Part, consisting of Illustrations, will be ready about the end of July; and, after its delivery, the Committee cannot guarantee these publications to Subscribers of future years.
Subscriptions for the Volumes, paid in advance for the year ending 30th April, 1850, will now be received by the honorary Treasurer, THOMAS L. DONALDSON, Esq., Bedford-square, or the local Honorary Secretaries; or by
WYATT PAPWORTH, Honorary Secretary.
19, Carolina-street, Bedford-square, May 31, 1849.

MR. WEALE has just Published.
A TREATISE on the LAW of DILAPIDATIONS and NUISANCES. By DAVID GIBBONS, Esq., M.P. New and extended edition, large 8vo, price 10s.

WEALE'S PAPERS on ENGINEERING. Part XII. (completing Vol. I.), 4to., with plates of Water-wheels, price 16s.

ILLUSTRATIONS of the PUBLIC BUILDINGS of LONDON. Large 4to. Part IV., with 24 plates, price 3s. 6d. Parts I., II., and III., to suit.

TREDGOLD on the STEAM-ENGINE. Part X., plates, 4to., price 3s. 6d.
No. 59, High Holborn.

THE FINE ARTS.—To Artists, Architects, Antiquaries, Connoisseurs, and others.—A genuine Roman Edition of "PIRANESI," consisting of Twenty-six Volumes. To be sold a bargain, this exceedingly scarce and valuable work, perfect, complete, and in as good condition as when struck off.—May be seen and fully examined any day, from two to six o'clock, at Mr. PETER BROAD'S Offices, 92, Tavistock-street, Covent Garden.

TO BUILDERS and CARPENTERS.—Elliptic Stoves, double backs, 3d. per inch. Registers, 9½d. and 4d. per inch.
Colcase Ranges, with Ovens and Boilers, 2 ft. 3 in. 40s., 3 ft. 4 in. 50s., 3 ft. 6 in., 60s.
Self-acting Ranges, with Circular Oven and Back Boiler, best in Wought Iron and Bright Fittings,
3 ft. 3 in. 50s.   3 ft. 6 in. 66s.
Best Patent Cut Clasp.   1s. 10d. per 1,000
9d.   6d.   4d.   3d.   2d.
Best Sheet Floor Brads 10s. 6d. per cwt.   6½d.
Best Town Glue 38s.   Do. Scotch, 24s. per cwt.
3s. 3d.   6d.   3s. 4d.   7s. 6d.   19s. per gross
At F. R. WILLIAMSON'S IRONMONGERY and STOVE WAREHOUSE, 36, Oxford-street, five, City-square.
Lists of Prices had on application at the Warehouse, or by letter pre-paid, inclosing postage stamp.—Warehouse closes at 7 o'clock

TO ARCHITECTS, BUILDERS, &c.
HAYWARD, BROTHERS, late H. HENRY and Co., WHOLESALE IRONMONGERS and Manufacturers of KITCHEN-RANGES, STOVES, &c., 199, Blackfriars-road, and 117, Union-street, Borough.
Strong Self-acting Kitchen Ranges, with Back Boiler and Oven and Wought Bars:—
2 ft. 3 in.   3 ft. 6 in.   3 ft. 9 in.
£3. 15s.   £3. 15s.   £4. 4s.   £4. 14s.
Healy's Patent Improved, with back Boiler and Wrought Iron Oven:—3 ft. 3 in.   3 ft. 6 in.   3 ft. 9 in.   4 ft.
£3. 3s.   £3. 13s.   £4. 4s.   £4. 14s.
Best Register Stoves, at 7d. 3d., and 9d. per inch.
Do. Elliptic do., at 8d., and 4d. do.
Manufacturer of WOLFASTON'S PATENT REGISTER STOVES, a certain cure for SMOKY CHIMNEYS, and effecting a great saving in fuel. To be seen in use daily. Orders from the country, accompanied with a remittance or reference, will meet with prompt attention.

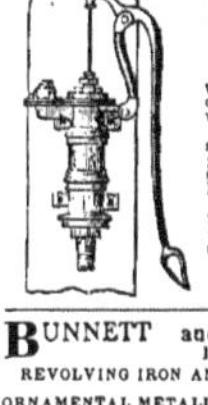

TO BUILDERS, CARPENTERS, &c.—The undermentioned are the PRESENT PRICES of IRONMONGERY at YOUNG'S, 104 Oxford-street. Every other article equally low. Offices executed upon receipt of remittance or a respectable London reference.
                         3 ½   3   3 Inches.
Cast Butts .... 5s. 3d. 7s. 6d. 11s. per 5 dozens.
Cut .... 4s. 6d.   3s.   2d. per 100.
Clasp .... 3s. 6d   4s.   3s. 6d. / 1,000.
Nus. .... 3½os.   2   s   3   8
Patent Lins .... 6s. 0d. / 3d. 9s. 10d. 10s per gross
                      9   7   6   5   3 inches.
Rule Pipe .... 1s. 1d.   1s. 3d. 1s. 5d. per yard.

BRITANNIA NAIL WAREHOUSE.—
Best cut clasp.
5d.   4d.   3d.   2d.   1s. 10d. per 1,000.
3d.   6d.   4d.   10d.   20d.
Cast butt hinges .... / 10d.   1s. 5d.   1s. 10d per dozen.
                            9 in.   12 in.   10 in.
Best wrot iron Ps. per pair, 8d. per doz.
Difile Offile halves, 2s. to 3d. per dozen.
Air bricks, 1s. per dozen.
Dr. Arnott's patent Ventilators, 11 by 9, 6s. 6d.; 10 by 9, 10s. 6d. each.
Every article of General and Furnishing Ironmongery equally reduced in price, as DENNE and PEIRCE, Wholesale Ironmongery Warehouse, 44, Farringdon-street. Lists of prices can be had on application. Contracts given for Bell Works, &c.

IRONMONGERY WAREHOUSE.—
1k. and W. PRICE, 16, Newington-causeway, Southwark, opposite the Elephant and Castle.
Self-acting Ranges, with circular ovens and back boilers, a feet, £2. 5s.; 4 feet, 4 inches, 70s.
Dillo. ditto, with best wrought bars and bright fittings, 3 feet, 55s.; 3 feet 4 inches, 80s.
Register Stoves, 1½d. per inch, and upwards. Elliptic Stoves, with double backs, 3d. per inch.
Best Cut Clasp, per cwt, at 17s.; 6d.; 14s.; 10d.; 15s.; 20l.; 1s. 10d. per Bush and super roof, 3 in. 2d.; 90 in., 1s. 7d.; 4s. 3d., 3d.
Sheet Floor brads, per cwt, 10s. 6d.
Sash Pulleys (bush'd), 7s. 9d. per gross.
Best rich Coach-wrench, Bell-hangers, and others, supplied with every description of Ironmongery and Brass Foundry of superior quality, at Birmingham prices.

CHEAP IRONMONGERY WAREHOUSE.—
GEORGE BANDSMAN, 92, York-street, Borough, leading to the Borough Market.
Elliptic stoves, with double backs, 3d. per inch.
Register stoves .... 9½d. per inch.
Patent cut clasp .... 9d., 6d., 3d., 2d., 1½d.
per thousand .... 3d.   1s. 3d.
Best sash line, 5s. per gross.
Best Patent Sash Line.
No. 1 2   3   5
Per gross—1s. 3d.   9d.   11½d. per doz.
Sash weights, 6s. per cwt.
Cast butts, 11   9   8½ inch.
Per dozen, 8d   11½d   2s. 4d
Every description of Ironmongery at the lowest prices. Warehouse closes at Seven o'Clock.

OLD-ESTABLISHED WHOLESALE IRONMONGERY WAREHOUSE, Kitchen-Range, and Stove-grate Manufactory, 16, Crooked-lane, Eastcheap.
JOHN GRICE most respectfully solicits the attention of Architects, Builders, and Carpenters, to his Stock of Black and Bright Stoves, Kitchen Ranges, &c., &c.
Black Registers, 5s. 6d. per in. and upwards.
Best Brights Register, 4s. 3d. per inch, and upwards.
Self-acting Kitchen Ranges, with Oven and Back Boiler:—
3 ft. 3 in. 3 ft. 6 in. 3 ft. 9 in. 4 ft.
Elliptic Stoves, with double backs, 3d. per inch.
All articles made on the premises and warranted, and delivered free of expense within five miles of London. Bell-hanging in superior style, hung in secret, 6s. per pull.

No. CCCXXXI.

SATURDAY, JUNE 9, 1849.

 OTHIC exemplars multiply apace, and architects are ensured a *safe* road, though it be a low one, and are saved the trouble of thinking. Soon there will be nothing left to draw but the nail-holes, and this will probably be done, so that the mediæval disposition of these may be rigorously followed.

Regarded as evidences of the spirit in which the Gothic architects proceeded, and illustrations of the principles which guided them,—as materials for us to work with, and suggestions by means of which we may proceed onwards, these illustrations are of great value; but, if used only for the purpose of servile imitation, as is too much the case, so far from advancing architecture amongst us, they will necessarily tend to stay its progress. Nothing great in art can be done without *progressive* efforts: retrogression, except so far as may be necessary to get out of a wrong road into the right one, is not the way forward.

We have several works of the class to which we have been alluding, now before us, some of them of great excellence and beauty. Amongst these we will name Dollman's "Examples of Antient Pulpits," just now published by Bell,* and Brandon's "Open Timber Roofs of the Middle Ages," published by Bogue.†

Up to this time there was no series of delineations of the ancient pulpits remaining in England. Mr. Dollman has given on thirty plates twenty-three specimens, mostly to the scale of one inch to a foot, with details a quarter the real size. Thirteen of these are stone pulpits, and ten of wood. The former are from St. Werburga, Chester (*circa* 1270); St. Peter and Paul, Shrewsbury (1320); All Saints, North Cerney (1460); Holy Trinity, Nailsea (1500); St. Peter, Winchcombe (1520); St. John Baptist, Cirencester (1450); St. Mary, Totnes (1500); St. Mary, Frampton (1450); St. Benedict, Glastonbury (1500); St. Peter, Wolverhampton (1480); St. Andrew, Cheddar (1500); St. Andrew, Barwell (1460); and St. Saviour, Dartmouth (1530).

Those of wood are from St. Michael, Coventry (1400); St. Mary, Wenden (1440); St. Mary, Fotheringhay (1435); Holy Trinity, Cold Aston (1500); St. George, Brockworth (1520); Holy Trinity, Long Sutton (1530); All Saints, Sudbury (1500); All Saints, Hawstead (1540); St. Mary de Lode, Gloucester (1480); and St. Mary, North Petherton (1500). They are all very carefully and beautifully drawn in outline (Mr. Dollman's careful style of drawing is not unknown to the readers of THE BUILDER); and the examples from St. Andrew's, Cheddar; Holy Trinity, Long Sutton; and St. Saviour's, Dartmouth, are coloured and gilt in imitation of the originals.

It will be observed, that with the exception of the subjects from Chester and Shrewsbury,

both *refectory pulpits*, with characteristic features of their own, the examples given are of the Perpendicular period. This, the author remarks, could not have been otherwise, "inasmuch as it was not till the fifteenth century that the pulpit appeared as a distinct feature of interior church arrangement." He says, in the course of his introductory remarks,—

"As soon as the rood-loft became a feature of importance in church arrangement, it supplied in a great measure the place of the ancient ambo; and from it the epistle and gospel were read by the dean and sub-deacon. Owing to the depth of the chancels, the view, as well as the hearing, must have been considerably impeded by the intervention of the rood-loft; and therefore it may fairly be assumed that from the necessity of the case originated the pulpit as best suited for its distinctive use, viz., that of preaching; and the part of the building that appeared most adapted for the purpose was the east end of the nave, immediately westward of the rood-screen. Possibly also the increased attention devoted to preaching in the fifteenth century may have been a reason. Since that period pulpits have been almost universally adopted, and the examples prior to the Reformation are far from uncommon, but previous to the year 1400 few, if any, are known to exist; one of about the date of 1340, at Fulbourn, in Cambridgeshire, which is figured in Part VII. of the "Instrumenta Ecclesiastica," being an exception. By a canon of 1603, every church was ordered to have a pulpit; a requirement to which the undue exaltation of preaching, which characterised the succeeding period, responded in the great number of pulpits erected in what is known as the Jacobean style. Of their kind these last are often very rich, though debased in style and more than questionable in detail. Among the most elaborate are examples in the churches of St. Cuthbert at Wells, and St. Thomas at Newport, in the Isle of Wight. They are mostly of wood; but, of examples in stone, are to be found one at Dinder, near Wells, bearing date 1621, with the inscription, 'Blessed are they that bear the word of God and keep it,'—and another on the south side of the nave of Wells Cathedral (the entry to which has been made through Hugh Sugar's chantry), on which are inscribed the words, 'Preach thou the worde; be fervent in season and out of season; reprove, rebuke, exhort with all long suffering and doctrine.'"

Mr. Brandon's subject, the open timber roofs of the middle ages, affords wider scope than that last mentioned, and has received ample justice at his hands. Mr. Brandon, in conjunction with his late brother, has already done good service: his "Analysis of Gothic Architecture," and his "Parish Churches," are excellent works, and this, his last production, is worthy to stand on the same shelf with them.

In some places they would of themselves "set up" a Gothic architect, as times go. "Parish churches" would give the general arrangement; the "Analysis" supply doors, windows, mouldings, ornaments, sittings, and fittings; and the book now before us enables our artist to roof the whole in the most improved and effective manner. We sincerely hope, however, as the author himself urges, that they will be used to better purpose.

The book contains 43 quarto plates, and illustrates 35 roofs, 18 of which are supplied by Norfolk and 7 by Suffolk. Two of the roofs are coloured, and serve to illustrate different methods in which colour was introduced. Our own experience coincides with that of the author, in leading us to consider it almost a rule that

"Where the windows of a church present any remains of stained glass, other portions of the edifice have likewise been enriched with colouring. This style of embellishment, which dates from the remotest antiquity, appears to have been held in deservedly high estimation by the mediæval architects, nearly every portion of whose structures admitted of and profited by

its application; and there is scarcely a church of their times that does not bear witness to this favourite style of decoration. We see it in the mosaic pavement, the frescoed walls, and the brilliant hues of the stained-glass windows; in the rood-loft and screen, rich in gold and gorgeous colouring, the lower panels adorned with paintings of the apostles and saints; in the sepulchral monuments, the pulpit, and lectern, and the font and cover, and finally in the roof itself, the crowning ornament of the whole edifice."

Our author classes the roofs in four main divisions, namely:—roofs with tie-beams; trussed rafter, or single-framed roofs; roofs framed with hammer beams and braces; and roofs constructed with collars and braces, or with the latter only. In speaking of the first division, he remarks:—

"In the churches of the Middle Ages, a perfectly horizontal tie-beam is of extremely rare occurrence; where a tie-beam is used, we almost invariably find it cambered, as are also the collar-beams; even the hammer-beams will incline upwards from the walls. The disagreeable effect of a straight tie-beam was often further counteracted, by having curved braces framed from its underside connecting it with the wall-pieces, thus forming an arched support for it, as at Outwell Church, Norfolk. In roofs of higher pitch the builders still endeavoured, with varied success as to effect, to retain the arched shape in conjunction with the tie-beams: a curious specimen exists at the church of St. Mary the Virgin, Pulham, Norfolk, where the beam literally divides the arch in two, and a similar instance is met with over the nave of Morton Church, Lincolnshire; the effect, however, is anything but agreeable or satisfactory."

Of the curved braces he says :—

"The curved braces in all the foregoing descriptions of roofs, besides binding the different timbers together, serve two other highly important purposes; in the first place, that of conveying the thrust or strain of the roof lower down on the walls, where of course they can offer a greater resistance to any lateral pressure; and, in the next place, serving as a great steadiment to the walls; this latter being by far the most important part of their services, for they are to be met with in roofs where no lateral thrust occurs, such as most tie-beam roofs. or the flat roofs which cover the late perpendicular clerestories of many of our churches: in neither of these cases is there any danger to be apprehended from an outward thrust of the roofs, and though the arched braces act as a great support to the massive beams, yet in conjunction with them they form a most effectual counterfort to the walls themselves—a very necessary provision when we contemplate the lofty clerestories, so perforated as to present almost the appearance of one long window opening, and call to mind that these are not supported on a solid foundation, but nicely poised on slender shafts placed at wide intervals apart."

This book is a very valuable contribution to the architectural library.

"A Book of Ornamental Glazing Quarries," by A. W. Franks, B.A., is another collection of examples, just now published by J. H. Parker.* This is a handsome octavo volume, in red, nicely got up, and ranging with Mr. Winston's excellent "Hints on Glass Painting." Whether the subject justifies the cost and pains seems to us doubtful. By quarries are meant the lozenge-shaped panes with which windows in old buildings are generally glazed. "The word is apparently derived from the French *carré*, or *carreau*, meaning a four-sided figure; or perhaps it is a corruption of the older word *quarrel*,† which seems to come from *quadrellum*, a small square."

---

* "Examples of Antient Pulpits existing in England, selected and drawn from sketches and measurements taken on the spot, with descriptive letter-press. By Francis T. Dollman, architect. London; G. Bell, Fleet-street, and by the author, 27, Mornington-place, Hampstead-road.

† "The open timber roofs of the middle ages. Illustrated by perspective and working drawings of some of the best varieties of church roofs, with descriptive letter-press." By R. and J. A. Brandon, architects. London: D. Bogue.

* "A Book of Ornamental Glazing Quarries, collected and arranged from Ancient Examples." By Augustus Wollaston Franks, B.A. London and Oxford. J. H. Parker, 1849.

† This word appears in the account of Little Saxham Hall (*vide* "Glossary of Architecture,") in the account Rolls of the reign of Edward III. ("Hints on Glass Painting," vol. i., p. 337). In the latter case it may possibly be in-

One hundred and twelve of these quarries are given full size, on 112 pages, bearing ample testimony to the industry and perseverance of Mr. Franks, who adopts for his motto on the title-page a line from George Herbert,—" If studious; copy fair what time has blurred." It should be taken, however, with this condition, that it be *worth* copying, which is certainly not the case with a number of the patterns here figured; while the majority of the best of them have been reproduced by Messrs. Powell in their patent stamped quarries, which, by the way, make excellent work.

In an introductory chapter the author sets forth, when showing how to determine the date of different examples, that the chief characteristics of *Early English* quarries consist in the stiff and conventional character of the foliage, the cross lines with which the ground of the pattern is usually covered, and the breadth and distinctness of the outlines. To these may be added the absence of the yellow stain, and the almost universal presence of bands or borders at the edges of the pane.

In the quarries of the *Decorated* style the hatched ground very generally disappears, and the foliage becomes more natural and flowing. About 1310 we find the yellow stain introduced, and it generally appears in quarries after this date.

In the *Perpendicular* style the lines are generally thinner and less elegant than those of Decorated quarries. The yellow stain is almost universally employed to heighten the effect of the patterns, and elegance is replaced by rich and elaborate workmanship. In later examples the patterns are frequently shaded, and the enamel is of a purple black instead of a rich brown. None of these characteristics, however, can be wholly depended on.

LECTURE ON ROMAN ARCHITECTURE.*

THE noblest circular temple in Rome, as well as in itself a fine example of the Corinthian order, is the unrivalled Pantheon, the splendid monument of the taste and munificence of the illustrious Agrippa—friend, general, and son-in-law of Augustus, patron of Horace, and the theme of Virgil,—this great man, and who had the magnanimity to refuse the honours of a triumph, is yet rendered greater by the superb building which was raised by him. For his victories at sea over Sextus Pompey a mural garland was decreed him, the second ever bestowed, to which honour Virgil alludes :—

" Agrippa seconds him with prosperous gales,
And with propitious gods his foes assails,
A mural crown that binds his manly brows
The happy fortune of the fight foreshows."†

We may form some notion of the magnificent scale on which the Romans delighted to construct all their public buildings, when we find that the splendid portico of the Pantheon, and the noble circular hall behind it, were only intended as an approach and vestibule to the baths which Agrippa projected. Some writers have supposed that the Rotunda was erected in the time of the Republic, with a very plain interior, but the portico was certainly the work of the great man whose name it bears, as the inscription of the frieze, and which records his having been thrice consul,‡ informs us. This superb temple is well apostrophised by Lord Byron :—

" Simple, erect, severe, austere, sublime—
Shrine of all saints and temple of all gods,
From Jove to Jesus—spared and blest by time;
Looking tranquillity, while falls or nods
Arch, empire, each thing round thee, and man plods
His way through thorns to ashes—glorious dome!
Shalt thou not last? Time's scythe and tyrants' rods
Shiver upon thee—sanctuary and home
Of art and piety—Pantheon!—pride of Rome!"
—*Childe Harold*, iv. 146.

The only light to this vast edifice is by the circular eye, or opening, in the apex of the dome, 27 feet in diameter, by which a soft and agreeable and sufficient light is diffused throughout. The hall itself is 139 feet in diameter, and the magnificent vault springs from the walls at the height of 75 feet from the ground, and is divided into coffers, or panels, in five rows. The lower part of the interior is supposed to be of more modern date than the outer walls.

The portico consists of sixteen columns in all, whereof eight are in front; each shaft of granite is in one block 46·5 high and 5·0 in diameter; the capitals and bases are of white marble; the architrave and frieze form together one block in height, each being 15 feet long, extending from centre to centre of the columns. In one of the two great niches at the back of the portico was placed the statue of Augustus, who would not permit it to be set up inside the temple, and in the other that of Agrippa; this is now in the Palazzo Grimani in Venice.

The ceiling of the Pantheon, if the superb vault may be so termed, was formerly covered with bronze, which was taken away by Pope Urban VIII. (whose family name was Barberini), for the double purpose of making the four colossal twisted columns of the baldacchino, or canopy, over the high altar of St. Peter's and the cannon of the castle of St. Angelo, and this spoliation gave rise to the bitter taunt of the Pasquin of the day,

" Quod non fecerunt Barbari Romæ, fecit Barberini."

The columns of the portico are unfluted, differing in this respect from the uniform practice of the Greeks, and also from other examples of the Augustan age. Two great masters of their art, the divine Raphael, and the tender Metastasio, are buried under the pavement of the Pantheon.

From its name and dedication we may presume that the statues placed in the temple, and which were of bronze and silver, were those of the gods or deified emperors; that of Julius Cæsar was in the most conspicuous situation, and many emperors seem to have taken a delight to enrich it in a costly manner, and it is said to have been originally covered with silver tiles.

The east front of the New Royal Exchange is an imitation of the portico of the Pantheon, with the omission, however, of some of the internal columns,

In noticing specimens of Roman magnificence in temples of the Corinthian order, we must glance at one, although it adorned the plains of Athens instead of the streets of Rome. This is the temple of Jupiter Olympius, of which now only sixteen columns remain,—sufficient, however, to prove that the temple in its integrity, must have been the most splendid of all the sacred structures of antiquity, and only second in size to the temple of Diana at Ephesus, and a superb proof of the taste of the architect Cossutius, who commenced, and of the imperial Hadrian, who finished it. The temple, in which stood the masterpiece of Phidias, the statue of Olympian Jove, was surrounded by 148 columns, more than 6 feet in diameter, and exceeding 60 feet in height. Many of the original columns were carried away by Sylla to adorn the temple of the Capitoline Jupiter, at Rome.

The other temples, of which remains still exist in Rome, have little to recommend in them for imitation. In the temple of Manly Fortune of the Ionic order, although the entablature is continuous, we see engaged or only half columns to the flanks; and in the Temple of Concord, the columns, also Ionic, are actually of different diameters. It is supposed to be of the time of Constantine, and is a restoration of an earlier building.

Many noble structures were raised by the different Cæsars, of which we shall only be able to notice a few. One of these was the largest building of its kind, the Coliseum, or amphitheatre of Vespasian. Among the refined Greeks, the theatre was used for the enjoyment of intellectual pleasure: there the met to hear and see represented the gloriou works of an Æschylus, a Sophocles, or a Euripides. Confined entirely to dramatic re presentations, we associate none but pleasin recollections with a Greek theatre, for the mu ders committed therein were only of a mimi nature. But the very mention of a Roma amphitheatre calls up visions of cruelt slaughter, and ferocity, the more lamentabl because the offspring of pastime, in which tha mighty, but in many respects barbarous peopl indulged their appetite for spectacles, in thos vast receptacles of crowding thousands, whe

" The buzz of eager nations ran
In murmur'd pity or loud roar'd applause
As man was slaughter'd by his fellow man."
Byron.

Julius Cæsar erected the first regular am phitheatre, which was of wood, whilst Statiliu Taurus erected the first which was built o stone, although by some writers it is said tha Pompey was the first who built in that material Afterwards Augustus raised the theatre calle after his much loved nephew, the early-doome Marcellus—immortalized in the verse of Virgil

" Heu miserande puer! si quà fata aspera rumpas
Tu Marcellus eris."—*Æn.* vi. 882.

But all the theatres, whether that built b Curio, which turned round on hinges so tha two separate entertainments could be carrie on at the same time, or that of the grea Pompey, with its statues of celebrated mal and female persons, or that magnificent one i honour of Augustus by Cornelius Balbus, o that of the Ædile Æmilius Scaurus, for 30,00 spectators, with its 360 marble columns, an 3,000 brazen statues, all fell short of th mighty structure which we are now consider ing, and which in its vast circumference ex hibits—

" Arches on arches! as it were that Rome
Collecting the chief trophies of her line,
Would build up all her triumphs in one dome,
Her Coliseum stands."—*Byron.*

It was built over the marshes of Nero, as appears from the lines of Martial :—

" Hic ubi conspicuè venerabilis amphitheatris
erigetur moles,
Stagna Neronis erant."—*Epig. II.*

The Emperor Vespasian demolished the golden house of Nero, and from the materials constructed the Coliseum, which was finished by his son Titus. It is of an oval form, the conjugate diameter being 620 feet, and the transverse 513 feet; the height is 157 feet, and it occupies a space of 6 acres. It is decorated with four orders of Roman architecture, the Doric, Ionic, Corinthian, and Composite, forming as many stories in height. Arches to the number of eighty are placed between the columns in each story; those of the second and third stories were originally filled with statues. Nothing can be better planned than the arrangement of the seats around the arena, whose longest diameter was 287 feet, and the shorter 180 feet. Rising in symmetrical rows, the seats were appropriated to the degrees of rank, the lowest being the most honourable. Next the podium, which separated the spectators from the arena, were the seats for the emperor, the senators, ambassadors, and persons of distinction; above these were ranged the equestrian order, the civil and military tribunes.

In the upper rows were persons of inferior rank, and females; and above these again were the common people. In the seats and lobbies, and what we should term the standing-room, altogether, 109,000 spectators could find accommodation; yet so admirably contrived were the means of ingress and egress by the appropriate entrances without, all being numbered, and the numerous passages and corridors within, that the vast multitude could leave the amphitheatre without confusion or delay. Although open to the sky, yet at times an enormous velarium or awning was spread over the vast surface, supported on 240 masts or poles, placed on the outside. Beneath the seats were ample vaults for the wild beasts collected for the shows. At first, in the amphitheatres, the spectacles were confined to exhibition of animals, collected from the various parts of the globe to which the Roman arms had carried their conquests. Titus, at the dedication of this amphitheatre,

tended for the small openings in the heads of the windows, as the word is so employed in the agreement for glazing the Beauchamp Chapel, Warwick, printed in Nichols's description of the building,—" *Item*, all the katurs (quatrefoils), quarelles, and oylem'nts." In France, the common paving bricks still used in houses are called *carreaux*.

* See p. 253, *ante*.

† " Parte aliâ ventis et Diis Agrippa secundis,
Arduus, agmen agens: cui, belli insigne superbum,
Tempora navali fulgent rostrata coronâ."—*Æn.* viii. 682.

‡ M. Agrippa L. F. Cos. Tertium Fecit.

entertained the people of Rome with shows for 100 days, and 50 wild beasts were slaughtered each day; and battles on foot and in boats were represented by hired gladiators. Afterwards the ferocious nature of the Romans was gratified by contests between animals and men, and Christians were chiefly selected for this cruel and generally unequal combat, and, lastly, man was pitted against his fellow. As Cassiodorus properly observes, "the people went with pleasure to see what human nature ought to have looked upon with horror."

There is no doubt that much of the excellence of the antique sculpture was owing to the opportunities afforded to artists of studying the human form in the different games which, as the parties engaged in them were always naked, where thence called gymnastics. Two of the finest works of art which have been preserved to us are the "Fighting Gladiator," discovered at Antium, and the figure still better known under the title of the "Dying Gladiator," ascribed to Ctesilaus.

The gladiatorial combats, in which even emperors could sometimes take an active part,* were continued to the year 404, A.D., when a monk, Telemachus, rushing in to separate the combatants, was killed, and the inhuman shows were immediately abolished by the Emperor Honorius.

When it was abandoned for the purposes of display and spectacle, it seems to have been regarded as an exhaustless quarry for building uses, and accordingly we find that, among other palaces, the Farnese palace, erected by the nephew of Pope Paul III., and designed by Michael Angelo, was built almost entirely from the Travertine stone of the Coliseum, and so also was the palace of the Cancellaria, by Bramante. This spoliation was at length checked by Benedict XIV., who erected altars and a cross within the area, consecrating the place to the memory of the martyrs who perished in it during the persecution of the Christians. It is therefore at this moment very much reduced in size, and is, indeed, become

"A ruin—yet what ruin! From its mass
Walls, palaces, half cities, have been rear'd.
Yet oft the enormous skeleton ye pass,
And marvel where the spoil could have appear'd.
Hath it indeed been plunder'd, or but clear'd?"
Byron.

Every considerable town had its amphitheatre, in which the inordinate passion of the Roman people for spectacles could be gratified, and important remains are still to be seen of amphitheatres at Pompeii, at Pola, at Puzzuoli, at Capua, at Nismes, and Verona; this last is of very large dimensions, and in tolerable preservation, especially in the noble ranges of marble seats; and, if I recollect rightly, the Emperor Napoleon held spectacles within its walls. It was probably built either by Domitian or by Trajan.

We must now take some notice of another kind of building, and one peculiar to the Romans, who gratified their love of architectural splendour at the same time that they paid homage to the illustrious deeds of their imperial leaders, in the erection of triumphal arches. Simple at first, consisting only of one arch, with a statue placed above, by degrees these portals of triumph became imposing from their size and magnificence. At Susa we find that a triumphal arch, with the opening, was dedicated to Augustus: at Rimini was one in like manner to him. At Ancona, that in honour of Trajan, a fine example, has only one opening, as had the arch at Vicenza, a simple and elegant design; that at Beneventum, to the same emperor, is pronounced by Sir R. C. Hoare to be superior to any in Rome; and it deserves this commendation, and its name of Porta Aurea, and is supposed to be the design of the great Apollodorus, with whom the Emperor Hadrian even condescended to enter the lists as an architect, though met by the rebuke, more honest than courteous,—"Go and paint gourds," when he submitted a design from his own imperial hand.

The Arch of Titus at Rome is highly interesting from its association with the conquest of Jerusalem; it consists, also, of only one opening; it is built of the white marble of Paros, and had four columns on each front, of the Composite order—the first instance of its application; the sides of the archway were decorated with bas-reliefs, in which are seen representations of the spoils of the Holy Temple, the golden candlestick of seven branches, the table of shewbread, the silver trumpets, the cups (the symbol of the river Jordan), which were actually carried in the procession at the triumphal entry of Titus into Rome, and therefore we can well believe that the Jews will never pass under this arch, which must constantly remind them of the disasters which befel their fatherland.

At Verona there is a triumphal arch, called the Gate of the Lions, of two openings, the only example which occurs to me of this arrangement, and which was said by Palladio to be exceedingly beautiful, whilst of arches of three openings the specimens were very numerous. That of Trajan, in his forum at Rome, was barbarously stripped of much of its decorative sculpture to enrich the triumphal arch of Constantine, for the reason which Gibbon gives—"that it was not possible to find a sculptor in the capital capable of adorning the arch of Constantine," and therefore we see the glaring discrepancy of bas-reliefs commemorating Trajan's defeat of the Dacians placed on a building erected in honour of an emperor who lived so long after him.

The arch of Constantine, like that of Septimus Severus, both at Rome, consists of three arches, that in the centre being considerably wider and higher than those at each side. In these structures we see departures from the simplicity of the Greek school, in the entablature broken over the columns, and in many other respects, as the coupling of columns, and placing them on stilted pedestals, confused and redundant mouldings.

Noble arches of three openings were raised in many of the provinces, one at Orange, called the arch of Marius, a good composition; at Rheims are the remains of one which appears to have three equal openings, not a common arrangement, and in the city—little known, but wonderfully rich in architectural ruins—of Geraza, in Palestine, a splendid arch of triumph of three openings leads to the principal street.

Another specimen of magnificent commemoration is the lofty single column erected to the emperors, a mode of honouring the memory of departed greatness, which has much imitation in modern times, although its architectural propriety is very questionable. The first which we shall notice is the column of Trajan, which rose in majestic dignity from the midst of his forum, the pavement of which is discovered to be 15 feet below the level of the modern streets; this forum was 180 feet wide, and was divided into five avenues by four rows of columns, traces of which have been found, and it is believed that the whole of this forum was under cover, and paved with squares of different marbles, viz., white, veined, giallo antico, and pavonazetto. In the centre stood a noble equestrian statue of Trajan, and on the top of the porticoes were statues and military ornaments, whilst the forum was surrounded by a library, a basilica, and a temple, the triumphal arch being on the fourth side.

Apollodorus designed this column, and we may presume its surrounding accessories, in honour of him whom Byron calls

"The last of those who o'er the whole world reign'd
The Roman globe, for after none sustain'd,
But yielded back his conquests."

This superb object is, with its pedestal, of white marble: the latter is 17 feet 11 inches high, and the column is 97 feet 9 inches; the lower diameter is 12 feet 2 inches; the order is Doric; it is fluted a few inches at top and bottom, the rest of the shaft being entirely covered with sculptured figures, which proceed in a spiral direction from the base to the capital, commemorating the exploits of Trajan in his different expeditions: there are but nineteen blocks in the column.

The Antonine column was erected by the Emperor Marcus Aurelius, in honour of the victories obtained over the Germans, Armenians and Parthians, and dedicated to Antoninus Pius. It stands in the square, which is from it called the Piazza Colonna. In height it is only 6 inches less than that of Trajan, but its diameter is nearly a foot more at the base, whilst the upper diameter is only 1 inch less than the lower diameter of Trajan's pillar, consequently its proportion is not so good. Including the pedestal, which is loftier than that of the other column, the Antonine pillar is 123 feet. It is also sculptured in a spiral direction, with figures in imitation of the other column. On each of these pillars the summits had statues of the emperors, to whose honour they were raised; these have been superseded by figures of saints: that of Trajan has given way to St. Peter, whilst St. Paul has displaced the Emperor Aurelius, whence the sarcasm of the noble poet,

"And apostolic statues climb
To crush the imperial urn whose ashes slept sublime."

The column of the Emperor Phocas is a simple Corinthian fluted column, about 4 feet in diameter, and its whole height, including the pedestal, is 54 feet.

By way of comparison, we may remark that the single columns erected in England, if not so decorated as those in Rome, yet carry off the palm in respect of size. Nelson's column, at Yarmouth, of the Doric order, is 144 feet high; but the column in London, called the Monument, by Sir Christopher Wren, is 202 feet, or nearly 80 feet higher than the Trajan and Antonine pillar, whilst its diameter is 15 feet, and being fluted throughout, this noble pillar, the finest in the world, has a greater air of simple grandeur than its Roman rivals; and I may here remark that the Duke of York's column, in Waterloo-place, has a very cold and naked appearance, from the absence of flutings in the shaft,—this is the more to be lamented since the situation is so fine.

The edifices we have lately noticed were the offspring of the vanity and love of display of the Romans; but there were others in which, though these qualities may also have had some share in instigating the erection, we must also admit their usefulness—these were their bridges, their aqueducts, and their baths. For the former the arch was a mighty invention, for which we cannot be too grateful to the Romans, who seem to have had as splendid notions in bridge-building as in all other instances. Trajan threw a bridge, designed by Apollodorus, over the Danube, whose piers were 150 high whilst the arches were 170 feet wide, and the bridge itself was 60 feet in width and upwards of a mile in length. This was destroyed by Hadrian, it is asserted, through jealousy of his imperial predecessor.

Quite as wonderful as noble works of art were the aqueducts, of which there were several to supply Rome. The first was built by Appius Cæcus, whose name has been immortalised by the splendid road called, after him, the Appian way—which has been appropriately called "the Queen of Roads."*

The second aqueduct was constructed by the censors Papirius Cursor and Curius Dentatus, and the water was brought from a distance of more than 20 miles. The Aqua Julia and the Aqua Virgo were introduced by Agrippa, that munificent benefactor of the Roman people. The purest water was that brought in by the aqueduct of the Prætor Marcius from Subiaco, of which Pliny says, "We may esteem this water for one of the greatest gifts that the gods have bestowed upon our city." To its agreeable coolness, Statius alludes,

"Marsasque nives et frigora ducens Marcia."

The aqueduct introduced by Augustus was chiefly for supplying water for the sea-fights which he had formed in the fourteenth region. The last aqueduct was the work of Caligula, and finished by Claudius, after whom it was called.

The eight aqueducts by which Rome was supplied were carried over valleys by tiers of arches, two, three, and four in height, or brought through hills; and in some of the provinces the aqueducts are really astonishing works of construction. The celebrated Pont du Gard, where it crosses that river, is 160 feet high, with arches in three tiers, some of which are 60 feet wide and 70 feet high. That of Nismes is another famous work, and believed to be the production of Agrippa when he was governor of that city, and even now rich in Roman remains, of which the famous Maison Carrée is a noble instance.

The time would fail to speak of the other works which were raised by Roman wealth and enterprise. Of much that has been described we have now only ruins, so that old Tiber

* As Commodus.

* "Regina Viarum."

indeed flows " through a marble wilderness."
We have not time to speak of that "stern
round tower of other days,"* nor of

" The mote which Hadrian rear'd on high.
Imperial mimic of old Egypt's piles."†—*Byron*.

We have not time even to glance at the 850
baths, the 300 palaces, the basilicas, the
forums, nor at the domestic architecture of the
Romans, as made clear to us in the buried
cities, Pompeii and Herculaneum; but we
must always feel unbounded admiration at the
genius of a people who have left behind them
such records of their power,—whose noble
roads and walls we find even yet in Britain,
the *ultima Thule* of their conquests; whose
arches and pillars are to be seen in Africa;
whose

" Temples, palaces,—a wond'rous dream,
　That passes not away, for many a league
　Illumine yet the desert."—*Rogers*.

And still gleam in Tadmor, in the wilderness, and Gerasa in Palestine, relics of that
Rome, who, if she conquered the world, also
diffused with liberal hand the blessings of
peace in works of usefulness and beauty.

" She who was nam'd Eternal, and array'd
　Her warriors but to conquer—she, who veil'd
　Earth with her haughty shadow, and display'd,
　Until the o'er-canopied horizon fall'd,
　Her rushing wings."—*Byron*.

And if, in the song of the Italian peasant
of the day,—

　　" Roma ! Roma ! Roma !
　　Roma non è più come era prima,"

we hear the mournful dirge of a mighty race,
we, who have still their wonderful works to
gaze upon, must feel gratitude to those great
spirits of the past, who, in their architecture,
have raised up immortal trophies of their
enterprize, their dominion, and their taste, and
bequeathed them as a rich legacy to after
ages.　　　　　　　G. R. French.

BUILDERS' BENEVOLENT INSTITUTION.

We would direct the attention of our readers
to the circumstance, that the anniversary dinner
of this valuable institution is fixed for Wednesday, July the 18th, and we would, further, solicit
them to assist in the objects of the institution.
The Earl of Carlisle has promised to take the
chair, and the advertisement in another column
shews that the list of stewards is already very
strong and influential. We are disposed to anticipate a brilliant meeting.

Some alterations have been made in the
laws, with the view of enabling the committee
to grant pensions sooner than was at first proposed, and they hope before long to get into
work. We sincerely wish them success.

It is worth noting, as supplying a sign of
the times, that to fulfil the duties of secretary
to this institution, which demand the whole
time of the officer, and are paid for by a salary of
50l. per annum, the committee had no less
than 105 applicants.

AMENDMENT OF THE BUILDINGS' ACT.

At a meeting of the Carpenters' Society,
held on the 30th ult., Mr. Nesham, the president, in the chair, it was resolved, "That
owing to the uncertainty which prevails as to
the progress of the intended New Buildings'
Bill, the president be requested to address a
letter, on the part of the society, to the Earl
of Carlisle, representing the urgent necessity
for its introduction during the present session
of Parliament." A letter has been accordingly addressed to his Lordship, and it is to
be hoped that the new Bill will be no longer
delayed. The seventy-fourth anniversary
dinner of this old established society is about
to take place.

The Paris Exposition was opened on the
4th inst., and comprises 4,500 exhibitors. The
building is 800 feet long and 350 feet wide,
containing three courts, one of which is filled
with metal work, chiefly cast-iron and zinc.
The erection of the building alone is said to
have cost 36,000l., but this seems scarcely
credible.

* The tomb of Cecilia Metella, called Capo di Bove.
† Now the castle of S. Angelo.

[16th CENTURY.]

LAING' Sc

CARVED STALLS FROM FIEZOLE, TUSCANY.

The stalls in the cathedral of Fiezole were
executed in the sixteenth century, and are
good specimens of the art of that epoch. We
give a representation of one division from a
drawing made purposely for us. The heights
are figured in inches.

The sketch added by our artist in the lower
part, appears to represent the disposition of
another portion of the stalls, but is not clearly
explained.

NOTES IN THE PROVINCES.

A new stained glass window has been presented to Ely Cathedral, by Mr. Warrington:
subjects, the Nativity and the Annunciation.
It is put up near the font.——Halstead old
church is now, it seems, about to be repaired.
Estimates have been got, and the requisite
means, it is thought, will be provided altogether by voluntary subscription. In the interior the pews are to be replaced by open
benches.——The Independents are about to
build a new college in St. John's Wood, in the
place of the Homerton, Highbury, and Coward
Colleges, the sale of the two former of which
was lately announced.——The yearly receipts
at the Canterbury Museum, since the charge
was reduced to one penny, have been double
the amount realized when the charge was sixpence.——Some large factory buildings have
been erected at Northam, by Mr. Gambling,

builder, for Messrs. Summers, Day, and Baldock, steam engineers and boiler makers, who
already possessed an extensive series of factories, shops, &c., there. The slate roofing of
the new erections alone comprises 500 slaters'
squares of 100 square feet to a square. It includes foundries, smith's shops, turning factories, &c. The blasts to the whole are produced by two fans, making 1,270 revolutions
a-minute, and these, with the lathes, &c. are
worked by a steam engine of 10-horse power.
Northam is now all new bricks and mortar:
the river side path is covered with factories.——
St. Mary's Church, Truro, is re-opened. The
pews have been replaced by low open seats of
oak, with ornamented ends. The passage-
flooring throughout is laid in patent tiles of
warm colouring. The organ has been removed
from the nave gallery to the western arch of the
north aisle, a portion of the north gallery having been taken away to make room for it. A
western window of stained glass, it is said, will
be provided in connection with alterations in
that part of the church.——A new church is
in contemplation for the hamlet of Charlton,
parish of Downton, Wilts, at an estimated cost
(including a sum for repairs) of about 1,250l.
The endowment has been provided conjointy
by Lord Nelson, the warden and fellows of
Winchester College, and the vicar of Downton;
and a site offered by Mr. Newman, of Charlton.
——It is proposed, in commemoration of the
three hundredth anniversary of the institution
of the English Prayer-book, to erect a stained-
glass window, of appropriate design, in Chester

Cathedral.——The foundation stone of the new free grammar school of Queen Mary, at Walsall, was laid on Wednesday week. The building will have two fronts, one to Lichfield-street, the other to Littleton-street, and will be built in the light Elizabethan style of the South Staffordshire railway station at Walsall, and composed of brick, with stone facings, from a design by Mr. Edward Adams, of Westminster, architect. In addition to the school will be houses for the head master, second master, and master of commercial department. Mr. J. Highway, of Walsall, is the builder.——An Odd Fellows' Hall is now in progress of building in Temple-street, Birmingham: architects, Messrs. Coe and Goodwin, Lewisham; builders, Messrs. Branson and Gwyther. Amount of contract, with commission, 2,600*l.* It will consist of a suite of rooms for secretary, library, and reading-rooms, cloak-rooms, &c.; a large room to accommodate 120 persons, and a hall to seat 1,000 persons.——The stones for the church and dissenting chapels at the Leicester cemetery are about to be laid. A town museum and school of design are also about to be opened.——The foundation stone of a methodist chapel was laid at Kingswinford on 29th ult. The design of it is by Mr. Robinson, of Stourbridge, architect.——On Saturday week the foundation stone of a new church was laid at New burgh, near Wigan. The Earl of Derby pays the cost of this and another about to be built in that quarter.——The foundation-stone of another church was laid at Clayton on 29th ult. It is to be dedicated to St. John the Baptist, and has been "talked about for thirty years last past," according to the *Leeds Intelligencer*. The site has been given by Mr. John Hirst, of Clayton House. Messrs. Mallinson and Healey are the architects. The edifice is to consist of a west tower, nave with clerestory, and aisles and chancel, and to accommodate 800 persons. The dimensions are to be as follows:—tower: height, 67 feet; east to west, 20 feet; north to south, 20 feet. Nave: length, 70 feet; breadth, 20 feet. Aisles: length, 86 feet; breadth, 10 feet. Chancel: length, 29 feet; breadth, 18 feet. It is to be in a style of what the vicar calls 'decent simplicity,' a—village church devoid of ornamental decorations; the pecuniary means at the disposal of the architects being apparently very limited.——Of the sum requisite to the erection of a corn exchange, as designed at Gainsborough, namely, 4,000*l.*, scarcely a fourth can be mustered, and there is some talk of converting the theatre into a substitute for the new structure.

SCENERY.

HER MAJESTY'S THEATRE.

THE production of Mozart's immortal opera, "Don Giovanni," at her Majesty's Theatre, having been long contemplated, and delayed by the "Lind rage," Mr. C. Marshall was enabled to give more time and thought to the preparation of the scenery for it than is usually the case, and has succeeded in producing a very fine work. The locality is Spain, and Spain, accordingly, he has depicted; but, in order to obtain variety, he has assumed that Giovanni occupied a palace erected during the dominion of the Moors. The fifth scene of the first act—the hall of the palace illuminated for the ball,—and the last scene of the second act, are accordingly Moresque — Alhambra-ish, — capitally drawn and brilliantly coloured.

The opera is altogether produced with great completeness.

ROYAL LYCEUM THEATRE.

The second scene in the successful comedietta, "A Wonderful Woman,"—a view of a French road, tree-bordered,—is a charming piece of landscape painting, by Mr. Beverley.

NEW WING OF LICENSED VICTUALLERS ASYLUM.—His Royal Highness Prince Albert laid the first stone of the addition to the Asylum, which is to be called "The Ladies' Wing," on the 2nd instant. It is to cost about 4,000*l.* We were not present on the occasion; and if the statement forwarded to us be correct, have little reason to regret this, small courtesy having been shown to those gentlemen connected with the periodical press who took the trouble to attend.

COST OF SEWERS IN CHESTER.

THE following are the results of a recent competition for the sewerage of some of the streets in the city of Chester, under Mr. Baylis, borough engineer:—

	St. Anne-street.	* Castle-street.	* Bunce-street.	Charles-street.	*Common-hall-street.	Henry-street.	Lyon-street.	Pitt-street.	Tower-street.	* Weaver-street.	Welling-ton-street.	* Olave-street.	Back Brook street.	Cuppin-street.	
	2' 4" by 1' 9".	2' 0" by 1' 6".	2' 0" by 1' 9".	2' 4" by 1' 8".	2' 4" by 1' 9".	2' 0" by 1' 6".	2' 9" by 2' 3".	2' 0" by 1' 6".	2' 0" by 1' 6".	2' 4" by 1' 9".	2' 4" by 1' 9".	2' 0" by 1' 6".	12" Glazed Pipes	1' 9" Brick Drains.	12" Glazed Pipes.
	s. d.	s. d.	s. d.	s. d.	s. d.	s. d.	s. d.	s. d.	s. d.	s. d.	s. d.	s. d.	s. d.	s. d.	s. d.
E. Jones......	15 2	21 10	20 5	15 5	21 7	14 9	17 10	13 3	15 5	29 6	15 5	20 5	14 1	8 10 ..	13 3
G. Lunt......	†7 3	10 6	6 0	7 0	10 6	†6 0	7† 6	†6 0	†6 0	10 6	†7 0	6 6	†6 0	.. ..	6 6
— Townshend..	11 0	13 0	13 0	11 0	13 0	11 0	11 0	11 0	11 0	13 0	11 0	13 0	7 6	.. ..	9 0
W. Andrews ..	..	12† 6	10† 0	..	..	..	..	..	..	10 3	..	10†0	..	8 6 ..	7 0
R. Evans......	12 0	..	..	11 0	..	10 6	13 0	10 6	10 6	..	11 6	..	9 6	.. ..	..
P. Jones......	8 9	12 9	12 0	9 0	11†0	7 6	8 9	6 9	7 6	11†0	9 0	12 0	7 0	7† 6 ..	†7 3
R. Roberts....	7 9	13 6	13 0	7 3	14 0	7 0	8 0	7 0	7 0	12 0	7 8	9 9	6 6	7 6 ..	6 6
J. Knight.....	9 8	14 0	12 8	9 8	12 0	8 6	10 0	8 6	8 6	10 6	9 6	11 0	6 6	.. ..	8 0
J. Mulligan....	8 6	..	..	..	..	8 6	8 6	8 6	8 6	..	8 6	..	8 6	.. ..	..

The streets marked thus * are in rock.

The tenders marked thus † were accepted, founded upon a schedule of prices (at per linea yard), and including excavation.

CHURCH ARCHITECTURE.

AT the opening of Thornbury Church, Gloucestershire, recently restored, as already mentioned, under Mr. Niblett,* the Rev. George Madden, the rural dean, said in the course of his sermon—"We should recollect the purposes for which we build churches. We should make them suitable for Christian worship. We should make them in all their design, arrangements, furniture, and ornaments, such as may meet the requirements of devout members of Christ's church, who desire to meet together for public worship. We should recollect the various parts of Christian worship—confession, prayer, praise, preaching, and administration of the sacraments, and we should make our churches, in all their parts and arrangements, suitable for these holy purposes. Whatsoever is calculated to remind us of our faith and of our duty—whatsoever is calculated to excite feelings of awe, and reverence, and devotion—whatsoever is calculated to help us in raising our hearts and thoughts to God—that should meet our eyes when we enter into the House of God! * * * *

We all know, brethren, that God will hear a Christian's prayer at all times and in all places. From our beds and from our fields—from the shop—from the market—from the highway, may prayer rise acceptably to the Throne of Grace. The poor settler, in the wild forests of America, may rest from his work, and kneel down and make his voice to be heard on high, as easily as the queen of this land in our noblest cathedral; but still both reason and piety teach us that whatever we offer to God should be of the best which our circumstances will enable us to obtain. David refused to offer unto God that which cost him nothing. Let all church building and church restoring be carried on in the same excellent spirit. Next, as to the internal arrangements of our churches. The time will not allow me to notice many, but I will say a few words concerning the chief. Our Lord commanded his apostles to go and teach all nations, baptising them in the name of the Father, and of the Son, and of the Holy Ghost. In every church, therefore, the first object which should meet the eye upon entering is the font. It is placed generally near the principal entrance, to signify to us that by baptism we enter into the church, and that until we have been baptised we are unfit to join in Christian worship: it should be raised somewhat higher than the ordinary seats, in order that every one may see infants baptised, and thus be reminded of his own Christian profession, and urged to live according to it; and it should be large enough to allow of an infant being baptised by immersion,—because though, in this cold climate, the practice of the church is generally to baptise by sprinkling (which is doubtless sufficient), yet if any one is scrupulous upon this point he may have his scruples satisfied, and no unnecessary stumbling-block thrown in his way.

Next, at the entrance of the chancel, either in it or near to it, should be seen the prayer-desk at which the minister is to stand or kneel in leading the devotions of the assembled congregation. Among those objects which constitute Christian worship, and for which we assemble ourselves in the house of God, are—confessions of sins, confession of faith, prayer, praise, thanksgiving. In these, the office of the minister is to lead the congregation, not to pray to them, or for them (himself alone), but with them. Prayer and praise is addressed to God by the whole congregation; and though the minister alone utters the words of the prayer, the whole congregation are to join mentally, and make it their own by saying Amen at the end of it. In many churches, especially small ones, where there is no objection on the ground of hearing, the prayer-desk may be turned to the east end of the chancel, or, at all events, not towards the people, in order to remind us that our prayers are addressed to God by all, both minister and people,—that they are not what the congregation are merely to sit and listen to, but to join in and offer up, on their knees, as their own humble supplications before the throne of God. The pulpit, on the contrary (which is generally placed near it), is invariably turned towards the congregation, because the sermon is an address to the congregation. When a person speaks to others, he naturally turns to them, so that he may best be heard by them. On this account the pulpits in our churches are generally raised somewhat higher than the prayer-desks, and are so placed that all present may best hear the words spoken,—not unnecessarily high, so as often to exalt preaching above prayer and the sacraments, and to encourage the notion (which is, alas! too common among ignorant persons,) that the sermon is the most important part of the service, but sufficiently high, so as best to answer the purpose intended, and to give to preaching its due place and importance among the ordinances of Christ's Church. The communion-table is allowed by the rules of the church to be either in the body of the church or in the chancel, but it is almost universally placed at the east end of the chancel. The receiving the holy communion of Christ's body and blood being the highest mystery of our faith, and the most solemn religious act which we can perform, it is natural and reasonable to choose for its administration the more quiet and sacred part of the building, designed especially for that sacred purpose."

* The author of the "Church Goer," an interesting series of papers published in the *Bristol Times*, says,—"Thornbury church is one of the most ancient in the neighbourhood, and was for a long time previous to the Reformation in the patronage of the Bishop of Worcester, by whom, we believe, it was appropriated to the profit and use of the Abbey of Tewkesbury. In the reign of Henry the Eighth, Stafford, Duke of Buckingham, selected the adjoining land for the site of his castle, and the bluff king and his consort were at one time, for several days, the distinguished guests of his grace; so that we have good grounds for presuming that the royal personages attended prayers in the building which has been just restored. The habitation of human greatness, the monument of this world's pride and grandeur, is in ruins; the wild birds build their nests in the ivy which clothes the walls of what were once tapestried chambers and suites of banquetting rooms; but the sacred edifice whose battlements were raised long before the foundation stone of the castle was laid, still stands, as it were, to show how fabrics appropriated to sacred purposes will outlive those dedicated to the pomps and vanities of this world."

PRINTERS' ALMSHOUSES, WOOD GREEN, TOTTENHAM, MIDDLESEX.——MR. W. WEBB, ARCHITECT.

PRINTERS' ALMSHOUSES, WOOD-GREEN, TOTTENHAM, MIDDLESEX.

THE working printers of the metropolis, as a body, are a thinking, well-informed, and sensible set of men. "Who slays fat oxen" need not "himself be fat," but he who ponders over and communicates the best thoughts of others, possessing too the amount of preparatory education which the occupation requires, may well be expected now and then to get some good thoughts of his own, or at all events to have his comprehension enlarged and his perception sharpened.

It was reasonable to expect that amongst men of this class a desire would grow up to provide for such of themselves as should be stricken by misfortune, a refuge in their old age,—and such was the case. For several years past accordingly a committee has been at work with this object in view. The master-printers approving their intention afterwards lent their aid* (Messrs. Baldwin, Clowes, Cox, Hansard, R. Taylor, and other of our most influential printers, are amongst the subscribers), a plot of ground at Wood Green, Tottenham, has been purchased, and on Monday next the Right Hon. Lord Mahon, M.P., president of the Society of Antiquaries, will lay the first stone of the proposed Asylum.

Connected as we are with printers, and knowing, moreover, that they are eminently entitled to the consideration of all classes, we feel a pleasure in calling the attention of the public to the claims of this institution.

Annexed we give a view of the proposed building, designed by Mr. Wm. Webb, architect, and which is to be erected by Mr. Roberts, builder, for the sum of 1,750*l*.†

The building is intended to accommodate twelve persons; it is to be in the Tudor style of architecture, and will be effective and picturesque in its character. The foundation-stone will form a large buttress in the centre of the building, under the bow-window, bearing the name of the institution and the arms of Lord Mahon. On the ground-floor of each house two rooms and a scullery will be provided, namely, a sitting-room in front about 12 feet square, a bed-room about 11 feet square, and scullery about 9 feet square, with other conveniences: and the same on the floor above. Each floor will be 10 feet in the clear height. There will be a separate entrance to each person's apartments, the upper floors having their entrance by means of an external gallery with iron railing in front, and steps at each end. This gallery will have the advantage of not only affording separate entrances, but can be used as a terrace for exercise, similar to that on the ground-floor, on which the building will stand elevated about 4 feet. All the doorways on the ground-floor will have a comfortable seat on each side, under cover.

The centre building will contain a large room, with a bow-window and open roof, the latter stained oak colour, to be fitted up and used as a library and general meeting-room. This will be approached by a staircase in the old style, in the tower adjoining. On the right there will be a secretary's or waiting-room, and stairs leading to top of tower, with other conveniences. On the ground-floor will be an open hall, with a lavatory, stores, &c.,—the open hall being used to distribute coals, &c., to the inmates.

The whole of the buildings, front and back, are to be faced with red bricks, with dark-coloured mortar, and Bath-stone dressings (mullions, jambs, quoins, plinths, strings, and copings), and roofed with the Delabole slating, of a greenish colour.

On the other side of the road stands the Fishmongers and Poulterers' Institution, for a similar benevolent purpose, and which was designed by the same architect. The two buildings are separated by the village church, and will, when complete, form a very pretty whole. Each person in this latter institution has a house to himself,—sitting-room and scullery on the ground floor, and bed-room on the first floor; the whole of the principal rooms being in the front.

Confining ourselves, however, to the printers, —a few years ago much stir was made respecting a monument to the memory of William Caxton, as the first English printer, but although many subscriptions were announced, no definite result ensued. Now, here, we think, is an admirable opportunity for the subscribers to that monument to carry out their views. A large plot of ground in front of this institution is unappropriated; it will be devoted to an ornamental arrangement of shrubs, unless the aforesaid subscribers to the monument come to an arrangement for placing a statue of William Caxton in front of the almshouses designed for the needy professors of the "divine art" which he was the means of introducing into England. Or, what would be better still, let the funds subscribed be applied to double the number of almshouses proposed to be built, and endow them as

The Caxton Asylum.

We commend this suggestion to the consideration of all parties concerned.

Our sympathies are enlisted in the cause of the printer, and we shall be glad to be the medium of conveying any subscriptions from our readers, to aid the committee in the prosecution of their object.

* Although not to the extent which may yet be hoped for.

† Our readers will remember that there was a startling difference in the amounts of the tenders sent in by builders.

LONDON ANTIQUITIES AND THE CORPORATION.

I AM sure any lover of antiquities will feel grateful to Mr. Tite for his services in securing for the Guildhall the fragments of Roman vases and other objects found on the site of the new Royal Exchange. I cannot say *museum*, for it would be absurd to dignify a mere cupboard by such a title, or to designate a few cases of relics from a few yards of the great area of the city as "antiquities illustrative of Roman London."

Neither, while I thank Mr. Tite for saving some scraps from the general wreck, can I admit that our citizens have ever been mindful of their antiquities. They never knew aught about them, or cared to know. I am anxious to read the answer to the questions put to Mr. Tite by "A London Antiquary;" and, at the same time, I should like to know whether, within the last few years, a most valuable series of documents relating to the management of the city property by Henry IV. was not sold out of the Guildhall *as waste paper?* Secondly, whether the Common Council did not give up the ancient wall on Tower-hill to be pulled down? And, thirdly, I should like to be informed by Mr. Tite where all the antiquities discovered in making the approaches to new London-bridge are deposited?

Mr. Tite accuses public opinion of wronging the Corporation. Let these three questions be fairly answered, and we shall then be better able to judge whether Mr. Tite or the general voice be correct.

I am also sorry to see the name of Mr. Thomas Lott, F.S.A., omitted in Mr. Tite's *brochure*. To him, and to his dauntless perseverance, is owing the grant of the trifling sum which the corporation have given for this apology for a museum. And, last, not least, how could Mr. Tite avoid mentioning the tesselated pavements discovered near the Royal Exchange, and excavated and deposited in the British Museum by the late Mr. Moxhay, or rather, at his private expense? In fact, every object of ancient art that has been preserved has been saved by individual exertion, and not by any provident care exercised by the corporation,—except, perhaps, the few remains found on the site of the Royal Exchange.

AMOR VERITATIS.

SOLUBLE GLASS.—What is called soluble glass is now beginning to come into use as a covering for wood, and other practical purposes. Some of our clever artisans may like to experiment upon it. It is composed of fifteen parts of powdered quartz, ten of potash, and one of charcoal. These are melted together, worked in cold water, and then boiled with five parts of water, in which it entirely dissolves. It is then applied to woodwork, or any other required substance. As it cools it gelatinizes, and dries up into a transparent colourless glass, on any surface to which it has been applied. It renders wood nearly incombustible.—*New York True Sun.*

RAILWAY JOTTINGS.

THE works on the Direct Northern line, in the neighbourhood of the metropolis, are progressing rapidly towards completion. The line as far as the Caledonian-road, above the Caledonian Asylum, has been excavated, and a bridge is constructed across the railway on a line with the Caledonian-road. Above 100 men are now employed on Copenhagen-fields, under which a tunnel will be formed several hundred yards in length, to the Regent's Canal, passing under Maiden-lane. For this purpose three shafts are in course of formation, at equal distances from each other. Between Holloway-road and the Seven Sisters-road, an embankment is being raised, the materials being supplied from extensive cuttings between Hornsey Wood House and Wood Green. The line after passing under Copenhagen-fields and Maiden-lane, will be taken under the Regent's Canal, and it is intended that the water of the canal shall be carried by an iron viaduct over the railway.——The great tunnel on the Leeds and Thirsk line, under Bramhope-ridge, which has been in progress since November, 1845, is so far completed that a locomotive and train passed through it on Thursday week with some of the Directors, Mr. Bourne, the Company's engineer, and others, among whom were Mr. Bray, the contractor; Mr. Watson, the contractor's engineer; Mr. Champion, the contractor's superintendent of tunnel works; Mr. Naylor, the company's resident engineer; Mr. Thornton, contractor for the Leeds contract, &c. The tunnel was designed originally to be two miles in length, but the 'greasy' nature of the ground has induced its extension 200 yards further. There were nineteen working shafts sunk, besides four permanent ones. Where deepest, almost under Bramhope village, three of the working shafts were sunk, over and above the number originally designed, on account of obstacles to progress arising from an influx of water. The debris is not yet all cleared out, but the whole will be completed during the present month. The interior is being sheathed with galvanized iron where the water oozes out to any extent. This line of railway throughout will be opened in the autumn.——The opening of the Burnley branch of the Lancashire and Yorkshire is retarded by another earth slip at the Holmes Chapel tunnel. This last fall has rendered fruitless the labours of many months. The fall was so sudden that the men had to leave their working implements behind them in escaping with their lives.—— It is only of late years, says the *Gateshead Observer*, that Whitsuntide has been much observed at Stockton as a holiday. But the Stocktonians—and, indeed, Englishmen generally—are becoming more of a holiday-making people. Thanks, partly, to the railways, which afford the means of rational, healthful enjoyment—and where should the advantages conferred by steam locomotion be enjoyed, if not at Stockton, the birthplace of the passenger railway? This year, on Whit-Monday, the town was turned inside out. Nobody was at home but the letter-carrier and the town-pump. The iron horse ran off with the inhabitants in all directions—to Ripon and Studley Park—to Redcar and Kirkleatham—to Seaton and Hartlepool—to Durham, Sunderland, Newcastle, &c. Though the rail in truth, even while saving so much of our 'valuable time,' makes most of us occasionally grudge still more the loss of the smallest portion of that precious saving, which now often renders barely possible what heretofore was not to be seriously thought of at all, it is pleasant indeed to think that nevertheless it is thus begetting such a national disposition to expend a little of its own wondrous savings in healthful holiday recreation to the people at large, whose life of labour so much requires it, even for the sake of that labour and their power to sustain it with spirit and profit to all.——The Shropshire Union line of railways has been publicly opened. This line will now enable a passenger to take his seat at Euston station and reach Shrewsbury direct (160 miles), by express train, in five hours. The Union line is 30 miles long from Shrewsbury to Stafford. The total cost of it has been 500,000*l*. It is to be worked by the London and North-Western. ——Some of the leading Staffordshire iron-masters have had an interview with the North-

Western authorities as to the manufacture of metal for the rails. The ironmasters undertook to guarantee their rails for two years, and to institute a series of experiments for the purpose of producing iron of a quality best suited to the wear and tear of railway traffic.

——It appears from a return of French railways, that the estimated cost of constructing eighteen lines amounted to 917,410,000 f. (37,096,400*l.*), of which thirteen were estimated to cost 624,110,000 f. (24,964,400*l.*), and it has since been ascertained that they will cost 849,422,000f. (33,976,880*l.*), being on the average 36 per cent. above the estimates. Some of the lines cost between 60 and 75 per cent. above the estimates, while others cost no more than from 2½ to 16 per cent. above the sum specified. Two of the lines were completed within the estimates — viz. : the Paris and Rouen, and Boulogne and Amiens.

ELECTRO-TELEGRAPHIC PROGRESS.

ANOTHER matter-of-fact proof of what the telegraph *can* do, and ought to be now daily doing, together with the co-operative aid and expedition of the press, has of late occurred in the transmittal to London of a verbatim report of a public meeting at Liverpool, held on 18th ultimo, from two till four o'clock, p.m., and in which ten speeches and four resolutions were read and reported, besides a petition. The whole, by piecemeal, was reported, transcribed, dispatched, telegraphed, re-written, type-composed, corrected, printed, and published in London, by the *Shipping Gazette*, at *thirty-three minutes past four o'clock*—the very hour when the proceedings closed at Liverpool, 200 miles across the country.*

COMPETITIONS.

Restoration of Bridgewater Parish Church. —We learn that the committee appointed to adjudicate upon the designs sent in for the restoration of this parish church, have decided in favour of those bearing the motto " Suum Cuique," and which prove to be the production of Messrs. Dickson and Breakspeare, of Manchester.

Bedford Corn Exchange.—Forty designs were received and the committee have selected one by Mr. Abbot. The style is Italian.

For laying out Ground at Coventry.—Correspondents complain of the length of time which has elapsed since these plans were sent in, and that no decision has been announced.

Asylum for Aged Governesses.—The new asylum erected for this purpose in Kentishtown will be opened on the 12th, with a fancy-fair in aid of the building fund. The object is a noble one.

---

* What a pity it is that while thus doing all due justice to our really magical "electro-telegraphic progress," truth compels us to turn up the adverse side of the picture, such complaints and capitulations as the following (from the *Morning Herald*), which still prevail. and which more than eXonerate us, as others also have done, for all that we ourselves have said, as well as for the public attention which we were the first to call to this disagreeable subject. In doing so, too, we must remark, that one of the latest instances of delay or neglect alluded to has been brought under our notice also by Messrs. Wilmer and Smith of Liverpool. "The numerous cases of gross neglect and inattention which are continually occurring in the management of the Electric Telegraph Company call for reprehension in the strongest terms. This company, avowedly established for the convenience of the public, the facilitation of business, and quick transmission of intelligence, has departed from all these professions in more than one instance. The latest case which has been brought under our notice is that of Messrs. Wilmer and Smith, of Liverpool, who ought to have had the intelligence of the dastardly attempt to seriously alarm the Queen on Saturday evening last, for the purpose of setting at rest the loyal fears of the inhabitants. The message, however, was not delivered until Monday morning, the eXcuse made being that the house of business of Messrs. Wilmer and Co. was closed. The direction of one of the partners of the firm was. however, painted on the door, and messages per telegraph had in many instances previously been left at the private residence. On such an occasion, when mere loyalty ought to have been a sufficient inducement to rapid motion, that lengthened delay took place. Not only, however, has the public to complain of manifold delays and inaccuracies, but also of the eXorbitant rates charged for the transmission of messages. ' Carpe diem' appears to be the motto of the Company, and whilst there is no competition, the disposition to act up to it is fully developed. Such a state of affairs cannot, however, be suffered in a commercial community ; and unless the eXtant company take timely warning and a practical lesson from the Transatlantic Telegraph Companies, as regards accuracy, speed, and moderate charges, they may probably find ' another Richmond in the field.' " For the honour and glory of our electrifying favourite *Punch*, we trust, now that we know somewhat of the real *modus operandi*, that he will not erroneously attribute the contrast between the celerity of the transmittal of the " electricity " *eastward*, and its tardiness *westward*, to some *recherché*, but imaginary electro-magnetic facilities in the one case, and obstacles in the other, respectively connected with our diurnal rotation from west to east.—from Liverpool to Lon. don. But, however wilfully mistaken as to cause, commend us to *Punch* for *effect*, as the Electro-Telegraphic Company may come to know as well as to cuure, unless they look sharp with their—N. E. W. S.—north, east, west, and south.

MOULD TO RUN THE MITRES OF CORNICES.

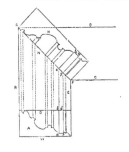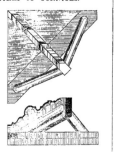

MOULD TO RUN THE MITRES OF CORNICES.

HAVING had occasion to complain of the imperfect manner in which plasterers finish mitres in moulded cornices, &c., I was led to seek for a remedy in the form of a mould that would run them perfectly, in lieu of the old system of hand-working ; and, as you are always ready to give publicity to any thing advantageous to the building classes, I beg to submit the inclosed sketch and explanation for a mould, *horsed*, that will run a moulding at right angles, and leave the mitre as perfect as any other portion of the work. Another advantage it has is a great saving of time, as, instead of taking off the mould at the mitre (according to the old system), it is taken off in the straight part of the work and finished with a small joint-rule, the same as floating a plain piece of work, and the moulding each side of the vacuity would form a *screed* for the rule to work against.

The first thing to be done is, to trace the required mould from the given mould at the angle you wish, in the same manner as an angle bracket is traced. But as the generality of plasterers are but little acquainted with geometry, it may not be out of place to show the method for laying down a section of the given mould (which lays no claim to architectural beauty, but merely to illustrate the subject), and tracing the mould required for a right-angle from it.

Let A be the section of the given mould, and from it draw the line B at pleasure, and on the line B erect the perpendicular D, then from the section A draw the line E parallel to B ; on the line E erect the perpendicular C the same distance from D as E is from B ; then connect the angles F G with the line N, which will be the mitre line ; draw the line O parallel to W, then draw the lines *ab, cd,* &c. to the line N, but parallel to E B ; on the line N erect perpendiculars, and make *ef, gh,* &c., equal to *ab, cd,* &c. (the more lines drawn, the nearer truth will be the mould), then will the moulding H be the moulding required.

The mould thus traced is then *horsed* at a right-angle mitre, on a double *horse,* forming a right angle, as the lines B, G, D, and the mould is in the same position when *horsed* as the line N stands with the lines B, G, D : the sketch P is the plan of a mould *horsed* and R the elevation.

Before commencing to run the moulding, the *running* rules must be fixed on each side of the mitre, so that when the mould is run up at the mitre the rule on the other wall is in its place to take the mould along the wall, and to finish the mitre, and on any part of the wall take off the mould and turn it ; then it will be in its work for the next angle, those being the places that I before mentioned that will have to be finished with the joint-rule. For running external angles there must be a stop fixed to the *running* rule at the mitre, to keep the mould from cutting the " throats " of any undercut mouldings.

It must be understood the above mould will only run a moulding at right angles, that is, to finish the mitre. If, for instance, it was required to run the same moulding in an obtuse angle, the mould before you would be too long, and if to run an acute angle it would be too short; consequently, if you wish to run a mitre clean, the mould must be traced and *horsed* accordingly, but in the same way as I before described.

It must be understood, that whatever angle the mould is traced for, the *horse* must be made to the same angle, so that they be in conformity with each other.

JAMES DRAKE.

DOUBLE TRAPPING DRAINS.

WITH reference to the letter on this subject, p. 233, *ante,*—if your correspondent will invert an empty wine-glass, and keeping the mouth erect just below the surface of some water, in a tumbler, he wiil see that a considerable quantity of water wiil enter the wine-glass, without any of the air escaping ; and, therefore, that it is possible for a painful of water to pass *through* a trap, along a drain, beneath the gas, *through* another trap, without measuring a painful of gas into the house. Double trapping drains is not new—the fact, the probable evil, and the effectual remedy, are given in THE BUILDER, vol. iii., p. 453, as an extract from the " Penny Cyclopædia." I have no doubt but that the *necessity* for the ventilation of all receptacles, where decomposition takes place, is fast forcing its way. Professor Hosking, in his admirably suggestive work on the " Regulation of Buildings in Towns," points out the necessity very clearly, but it occurs to me, his barrel of beer illustration, p. 234, a little modified, would illustrate the retort formed by a double trapped drain, for it is (unless perfectly clean from deposit of every kind) a retort of certain capacity, in which gas is generated, but confined by the trap at each end, until a sufficient quantity is evolved, to overcome, by its elasticity, or expansive force, the combined resistance of the trap and atmosphere : an escape then takes place, at the highest point of communication, where there is least resistance, until equilibrium is restored ; and will continue to do so at intervals, unless no gas is generated, or provision is made for its harmless escape.

The article, p. 232, respecting small drains, appears opposed to the evidence given in favour of them (THE BUILDER, vol. iii., p. 523, and vol. iv., p. 109), but how often it occurs that the blame attached to an instrument should be attached to individuals. I have no doubt a 6-inch pipe would be stopped at one house when a 2½-inch would suffice at the next, entirely from the difference in the habits of servants. If parts of heath-brooms, mops, flannels, and hair are to pass through traps and drains, then greater capacity must be allowed than is necessary where ordinary sewage passes.

If any one of your readers interested in the

subject will rule about half-a-dozen columns in their common-place book, and, under the head of drains and sewers, collect and enter in their respective columns the pages in THE BUILDER referring to those heads which are important (and the index will help them much), they will find they have a map of valuable information on the subject, which I do not think they can find elsewhere; they will find, I think, that facts are the things we want collected now,—other parts have been pretty well sifted; but why what answers well in fifty cases does not in the fifty-first, wants exposing, so that the right remedy may be applied.

A. P. M.

DOINGS IN DERBY.

A MEMORIAL has just been placed in All Saints' Church, Derby, to the memory of the late Mr. Rawlinson, artist of that town; it consists of a tablet surmounted by a figure of Faith; executed by Mr. Loft, of London.——The second experimental trip on the Manchester, Buxton, Matlock, and Midland Junction Railway took place on Monday, in last week, under the direction of Mr. G. R. Stephenson and Mr. Campbell, the resident engineer. The trains consisted of one first-class and one second-class carriage. The whole length run over was in excellent working order, and the train ran very smoothly. On passing through the Willersley tunnel some blue and crimson fire was lighted, which had a fine effect. The line is now open for traffic.——A new bridge of two arches has just been completed across the large brook running through Derby. A new bridge is also in course of erection at the same place, spanning the river Derwent. Towards defraying the cost of the latter, Mr. Alderman Moseley has contributed 500*l*.——A new gallery has just been erected in St. Mary's Church, Little Darley! —— The stained glass in the chancel window of St. Peter's Church, Derby, consists of a figure of our Saviour on the Cross; on his right, those of St. Peter and the Virgin Mary; on his left, St. John and Bishop Chad. Some of the good people ask why they should have a Romish bishop made so prominent. They also object that the Saviour is represented smiling, when we know that his sufferings on the Cross were of the most agonizing description. The window was put up by Mr. Barker, of York. The tracery above is to be filled in with plain yellow stained glass, and the whole (with exception of tracery) is the gift of a lady.

REMOVAL OF SMOKE OF TOWNS.

I OBSERVE in a recent number a notice of a recently published pamphlet by Mr. Flockton, on a proposed method for obviating the discharge of smoke into the atmosphere from dwelling-houses and manufactories by means of underground flues in the streets, leading to lofty towers or chimney stacks out of the town; and for readily obtaining in this way a more perfect ventilation of sewers.

Perhaps you will permit me to trespass on your columns with a suggestion on this subject which has long occupied my thoughts, viz., that the sewers themselves should be made use of for the purpose of such underground flues, by employing the upper part, now the receptacle of the noxious gases generated in them, for the underground passages for smoke, in passing along which the coldness of the water beneath would cause part of the soot to precipitate, and be carried to the outlet of sewage water, with the other refuse; while the uncondensed smoke would be drawn out by mechanical or other means, and discharged at chimney shafts erected in the most convenient places at a distance from the town.

A paper on this subject was drawn up by me in January last, without any previous knowledge of Mr. Flockton's, or any other such plan; and with the view of obtaining a more competent opinion of its practicability before venturing to publish so seemingly extravagant an idea, I submitted it to an eminent engineer, Mr. Farey. The method of procuring a sufficient draught by the heat contained in the smoke itself was considered by that gentleman wholly impracticable,* owing to the cooling effect of long underground flues, and particularly of damp sewers, upon the smoke passing through them. The general idea, however—one which had many years ago occurred to Mr. Farey himself—was thought not unworthy of consideration, and, to a certain extent, practicable, provided adequate means for producing the draught were employed; such, for example, as are adopted in the ventilation of extensive mines.

I hope the desire to avoid encroaching too much on your space has not rendered this communication obscure. I make it that "those of your readers interested in the question to which it refers may know" what others are contemplating, and in furtherance of the object—the public benefit—evidently aimed at by you, which appears also to be the laudable aim of Mr. Flockton.

GEORGE DEVEY.

* This, I perceive, is also your opinion. BUILDER, No. 328, page 233.

CONVEYANCE OF WATER. CONSTANTINOPLE.

YOUR correspondent "Spec.," p. 236, misunderstands the nature of the question asked in a former number of THE BUILDER, and the reply given; the allusion to the hydrostatical pressure referred to the earthern pipes connecting the souterazi together, and not to the leaden pipes in the souterazi themselves.

The cistern or reservoir formed at intervals must necessarily relieve the hydraulic pressure; as, if water is to be brought from an altitude of 1,000 feet, and it descends in stages of 100 feet into reservoirs at those intervals, your correspondent must admit that the pressure upon the pipes connecting the reservoirs together will be less than if the water is conveyed down in one continued conduit.

Although the stone-ware pipes of the present day will bear a pressure of a column of water equal in altitude to from 300 to 400 feet, I imagine that in those days (probably in the year 404), the ancients were not so well acquainted with the manufacture of those articles as in the present day, although they show by their works they were not totally unacquainted with the science of hydraulics.

There is a tendency to return now to the use of earthen pipes as conduits for water in preference to iron, probably on the ground of economy; but if it be true, as I hear from Aberystwith, that vegetation occasionally takes place inside them, it will be an obstacle fatal to their use. For the information of your correspondent, I may further state that earthenware pipes can be manufactured 3 feet diameter (although manufacturers prefer making the smaller sizes), and their use must be regulated by the hydrostatical pressure they will bear, which has a limit in that material as well as iron; the joints of the pipes in towns where they have been used, were made secure with cement.

B. BAYLIS.

Miscellanea.

DRYING CLOSETS.—Amongst other letters received by us on this subject is one from Mr. A. Jennings, on the part of the Dessicating Company, objecting *in toto* to the *close* system, but containing nothing to controvert the experiments of former correspondents. He says, "it does appear to me most extraordinary that such a principle should for one moment be contended for. The water (in probably foul or infected blankets) converted into noxious vapour, for want of a proper current to carry it away, is to a great extent dried up in the articles themselves! Is this the way to obtain pure linen? Those who happen to be of such opinion had better consult the works of Dr. Henry, of Manchester, Dr. Copland's Medical Dictionary, vol xi., page 245, and, more recently, the Medical Gazette of Feb. 2, 1849, where they will find that impelled rapid currents of dry heated air are the requisites for insuring perfect drying as well as perfect disinfecting. As to a chamber of 300 feet or even 5,000 feet cubic capacity, it is as nothing compared with those now in daily use upon the desiccating principle in the manufacturing districts and elsewhere. In some cases these chambers contain upwards of 30,000 cubic feet."

PROJECTED WORKS.—Advertisements have been issued for tenders, by 9th inst. (extension of time), for the works required for West Ham Parish Church; by 11th, for building about 100 feet of wall round the head of the Middle Dock, Rotherhithe; by 18th, for making two oval sewers at Bristol; by 19th, for the erection of a new congregational church in the City-road; by 25th, for the erection of the new York County Hospital; by 12th for rebuilding St. Mary's Church, Foulness Island, Essex; by 29th, for the erection of a stone bridge at Vowchurch, Hereford; by 12th, for the erection and completion of a stone warehouse at Bradford; by 21st, for the erection of a police station at Ormskirk; by 23rd, for alterations and additions to the Peterborough Union Workhouse; by 11th, for the erection of extensive farm buildings at Kirtling, Cambridgeshire; by 22nd, for building a sewer at Birmingham; by 12th, for sinking an engine shaft at the Dudley Waterworks; by 12th, for supplying and fixing a galvanized corrugated iron roof to a large tank at St. Pancras Workhouse; by 19th, for hewed wedges of beech for the navy at Portsmouth; by 12th, for mineral black for paint for the navy; by 16th, for various works in churches, &c., in St. Marylebone, and for flints, cement, lime, hammers, &c., for same parish. Tenders also wanted by 21st for surveying and mapping a township in Whalley Parish, Lancashire.

INSTITUTION OF CIVIL ENGINEERS.—On Tuesday, June 5, Mr. Field, president, in the chair, the paper read was a "Description of a Method of Rolling Bars for Suspension Bridges, and other-like Purposes," by Mr. Thomas Howard. It was described that by the ordinary process of manufacture, the head, or end of the link, out of which the eye, or hole for the connecting pin, was bored, had been sometimes welded on to a parallel rolled bar, or, at other times, been hammered to the required form; both these methods were, however, objectionable, owing, in the former case, to the insecurity, and in the latter to the tediousness and expense. By the method introduced by Mr. Howard, the bars were rolled at once into the requisite form; the shingle, or faggot, was first passed longitudinally, at a welding heat, through grooved rollers, in the ordinary manner, and then, before being drawn down to the intended thickness, was carried to rollers having bosses, or incr. ased diameters at the places corresponding to the heads to be produced, and there passed to and fro between the rollers transversely, or across the breadth of the bar, thus receiving a pressure only at the enlarged parts of the rollers, which gave the necessary increase of breadth at the heads; it was then taken to plain finishing rollers, and drawn out longitudinally in the usual manner, until it attained the required length and thickness; the heads being afterwards trimmed by machinery to the exact dimensions, and the holes drilled for the pins. It was stated that the chains of the large suspension bridge, erected by Mr. W. Tierney Clarke over the Danube, at Pesth, which lately so satisfactorily withstood the heavy strain brought upon it by a retreating army, were constructed on this system.

SMITHFIELD MARKET.—The protracted inquiry of the Parliamentary committee into the eligibility of Smithfield-market is about to be brought to a close. The last few sittings of the committee have been principally occupied with the evidence of some of the principal butchers, graziers, and salesmen of the metropolis and the market, who are in favour of the continuance of Smithfield, on account mainly of its central situation, and its proximity to their premises and slaughter-houses.

THE METROPOLITAN ROADS.—The twenty-third report of the Commissioners of the Metropolitan Roads states that the receipts from tolls during the past year amounted to 64,019*l*. and the total receipt from all sources of income, including the balance in hand on the 25th of March, 1848, to 71,036*l*. The total concurrent expenditure amounted to 68,773*l*., including the interest and the instalment of the mortgage debt. The state of the roads on Sunday last, at the west end of the metropolis, for want of watering, was abominable. Why health and property should not be protected on a Sunday as on another day, it seems hard to say.

THE BRICKLAYING LEGISLATOR.—Naudaud, a steady hard-working fellow from Creuse, whence all Paris is supplied with masons, came trudging to the capital with hod and trowel as his only capital, some short time previous to the revolution. Madame Naudaud accompanied him with her frying pan, wherewith to supply with fried potatoes all the *bons camarades* of Naudaud, at the same time honestly earning more in a single day, as it turned out, than poor hard working Naudaud could do in a week. The grand revolution came, and made all the masons gentlemen at once, so far as work was concerned. But their stomachs were light as well as their pockets, and though they could fill the latter with their idle hands, they could not do that with the former. In this dilemma Naudaud made a speech. "Madame Naudaud," said he, "has saved 6,000 francs. Had you not been honest *bons camarades* we would have been poor like you: come, let us live together and divide the proceeds till better times." Notwithstanding Naudaud's latter fling at the grand revolution, his proposal was deemed not only a fair one, but worthy of all acceptation. Naudaud's wife, however, was not only a prudent woman but an ambitious one. She, therefore, under the rose, appended what she conceived to be a reasonable condition to her husband's truly generous offering, namely, that in return they should elect him a member of the Legislative Assembly! Naudaud *was* so elected, and he almost merited the distinction, all the more indeed that he knew his own unfitness to fulfil its duties. To oblige his *camarades*, however, and to please his wife, he laid down his hod, with reluctance, and not till the very day of meeting, when he presented himself in his ordinary blouse and casquette. The huissier on duty refused to admit him. Do as you please, *mon ami*, said Naudaud. I'll go to work again. "What a good excuse I'll have! They won't admit me!" Naudaud's soliloquy, however, was rather premature, for the huissier on second thoughts called him back, and ushered him forthwith into the midst of his new *camarades* of the Assembly, one of whom, inquisitive as to his speechifying powers, he sensibly assured that he did not mean to open his mouth at all, contenting himself with voting amongst those who upheld the constitution. Such is the substance of a little gossip by the Paris *Correspondent of the Atlas*.

HUDDERSFIELD AND PENISTONE RAILWAY OPENING.—Mr. Miller, of Miller, Blackie, and Co., the contractors, ran an engine throughout this line on 25th ult. The length of the whole is only 13 miles, but in the course of it there are no less than four great viaducts; six tunnels, one nearly a mile in length and another half a mile; twenty excavations, many of them very deep and long, and as many embankments, many of equally laborious formation; with 30 bridges, some of great expense, others varying from 200 to 2,000 cubic yards of masonry in each. One of the viaducts, the Paddock, first from the junction with the Manchester line, at Huddersfield, by a deep cutting in the Spring Wood tunnel, is not yet erected, owing to an arbitration for half an acre of ground, near some silk mills. For this the claim of 10,000*l*. has been allowed. Another of the viaducts, that in the Lockwood valley, 478 yards long, and 146 feet high in the centre, with 32 arches of 30 feet span, and two skew arches, one 70 feet span, at an angle of 330,—is wholly built of rubble, excavated near the spot, and is thought to be a fine specimen of workmanship. It contains 34,000 cubic yards of masonry, and cost 30,000*l*. A third viaduct, at Denby Dale, 400 yards long and 109 feet high above a rivulet, is of timber, of great lightness of aspect. A branch line is nearly completed between Brockhole's embankment on this line and Holmfirth. It also contains some rather heavy works. None of the stations have yet been built.

THE IRON TRADE.—BIRMINGHAM.—The reduction of 1*l*. per ton in the price of iron has been generally adopted, and it now appears that many of the masters never sold at the advanced rate resolved upon at the January quarterly meeting. Some dealers are of opinion that it will be difficult to maintain even the present price, and that a further reduction may be expected at or before next quarter-day.

CARBONIC ACID GAS ENGINES.—In lately recommending Baron Von Rathen to try the condensation of carbonic acid gas in his locomotive air-bottles, generating it from such carbonates of lime as marble or chalk, we scarcely expected to hear so shortly of a definite invention for the very purpose. Such is the case, however; and it is proposed, in order to cheapen the process and render it all the more likely to be economically practicable, that the condensed or liquified carbonic gas, after the expenditure of its power in expulsion from the air-bottles or reservoirs, should be reabsorbed by quicklime, so as to be as ready for re-agency, with the help of sulphuric acid and the air-bottles, as ever; leaving sulphate of lime as a marketable residuum. It is calculated that, as a mere auxiliary, a steam-engine of 50-horse power, by aid of such a carbonic acid engine, would be equivalent to one of 95-horse power; and that, from the saving of fuel, both marine and locomotive engines could be worked with it to great advantage.

THE JEPHSON STATUE AT LEAMINGTON was inaugurated on Monday week by Mr. Serjeant Adams, at the ornamental temple in the Jephson gardens, erected for its reception. At a convivial meeting in the evening, Mr. Hollins, the sculptor, explained the reason of the temporary want of likeness in the features when the statue was got ready for exhibition at the Royal Academy, and defended the Committee and himself against objections made to the enclosing of it in a temple, where it had all the advantages of a preconcerted arrangement of light and shade.

NAIL-MAKING.—Mr. Moses Poole has obtained a patent for some improvements in machinery for making nails. The metal is passed between the edges of a top and bottom roller, to split it into rods of the requisite thickness, which are then passed between the edge of a second top roller and the other edge of the bottom roller, whereby they are formed into a succession of rectangular triangles. These triangular-shaped rods are then forced between a pair of vertical or horizontal matrices, to point them, and likewise a pair of cutters to separate them, and subsequently through a punching machine, by which the heads are formed. *Claim.*—The mode of arranging machinery for making nail-rods, by first splitting the metal and then shaping it. Making nails by means of the matrices in combination with the heading machine. The application of the machine last described.

NEW YORK AS IT IS TO BE.—We know nothing more frightful (says the *Daily News*) than to look at a plan of New York, and fancy what it will be when the whole island is built upon. Never was so noble a gift of nature so sacrificed to mathematical precision and utilitarian caprice. Let the reader imagine a dozen of Harley-streets, Baker-streets, and Edgeware-roads, all parallel to each other, and extending in a straight line from six to ten miles in length, without a Hyde-park, a Regent's-park, or a Hampstead intervening, and intersected rectangularly at unvarying intervals by a couple of hundred cross streets, all the ditto of each other, and he will have some notion of what New York is to be.

THE METAL TRADES PENSION SOCIETY held a general meeting, on 28th ult., at the London Tavern, for the election of six additional pensioners and other business. There are now 25 annuitants on the roll of this useful society, with pensions, as we understand, of twenty guineas each per annum. More than 200 names of new subscribers or donors appear in an appendix to the report, and 100 more are greatly desired before 1st August, to enable six more pensioners to be added to the list.

THE CORROSION OF IRON RAILINGS.—Where they are united to their sockets by lead, it may be lessened in the following manner:—The cause of the corrosion, as is well known, is the galvanic action which goes on between the two metals, through the medium of the water collected at the angle of juncture by capillary attraction. If, then, the lead, instead of being flush with the stone into which the iron is fixed, were to be levelled from the iron to the stone at an angle of about 60 degrees, all the water would drain off, and, consequently, the galvanic action would be stopped.

J. C. W.

THE CAMPANILE OF GIOTTO AT FLORENCE—I remember well how, when a boy, I used t despise that Campanile, and think it meanl smooth and finished. But I have since live beside it many a day, and looked out upon i from my windows by sunlight and moonligh and I shall not soon forget how profound an gloomy appeared to me the savageness of th Northern Gothic, when I afterwards stood, fo the first time, beneath the front of Salisbury The contrast is indeed strange, if it could b quickly felt, between the rising of those gre walls out of their quiet swarded space, lik dark and barren rocks out of a green lake with their rude, mouldering, rough-graine shafts, and triple lights, without tracery o other ornament than the martin's nests in th height of them, and that bright, smooth sunny surface of glowing jasper, those spir shafts and fairy traceries, so white, so faint so crystalline, that their slight shapes ar hardly traced in darkness on the pallor of th eastern sky, that serene height of mountai alabaster, coloured like a morning cloud, an chased like a sea shell. And if this be, as believe it, the model and mirror of perfect ar chitecture, is there not something to b learned by looking back to the early life o him who raised it? I said that the power o human mind had its growth in the wilderness much more must the love and the conceptio of that beauty, whose every line and hue w have seen to be, at the best, a faded image o God's daily work, and an arrested ray of som star of creation, be given chiefly in the place which He has gladdened by planting there th fir-tree and the pine.—*Ruskin*.

EAST ANGLIAN ARCHITECTURAL SOCIETY—On Monday last, a number of the members o the East Anglian Architectural Society had a excursion, upon which occasion they visite Ely Cathedral, when the Rev. Mr. Boutell, o Downham Market, delivered a lecture on th various styles of architecture.

SKETCHES AND STUDIES FROM NATURE—An exceedingly interesting collection o sketches and studies from nature by Englis painters, 239 in number, is now being ex hibited by Mr. Hogarth, at his gallery in th Haymarket.

THE MARBLE ARCH.—In reply to som remarks by Mr. Osborne in the Commons, o the 'ways and means' to be voted for takin down the arch at Buckingham Palace, th Chancellor of the Exchequer confessed tha where it was to be put was even yet no quite decided.

TENDERS

For Chiswick Station, South-Western Railway; Mr. W Tite, Architect.

Grimsdell	£1,635
Jay	1,617
Lee and Son	1,600
Piper	1,592
Nicholson and Son	1,487

For Parsonage-house, Lower Tooting; Mr. D. Ferre Architect.

Nicholson and Son	£2,070
Smith	2,044
Piper	2,035
Higgs	1,994
Rigby	1,893
Hicks	1,865
Kelk	1,820
Holland (accepted)	1,797
Carter	1,775

For St. Peter's Hospital, Wandsworth; Mr. Sutel Architect.

Nicholson and Son	£21,400
Knight	20,760
Lee and Son	20,352
Locke and Nesham	20,300
Curtis, R. and G.	20,284
Munday	19,975
Kelk	19,894
Costar	19,800
Ashby and Holmer	19,783
Grimsdell	19,422
Hicks	19,400
J. Wilson	18,955
Hayward and Nixon	18,870
Piper	18,745
Marsh and Colebatch	18,647
Jay	17,142

For the Judge's Lodgings, Aylesbury; Mr. E. B. Lanc Architect.

Cooper and Davis	£2,247
Birkenshaw	2,194
Green (Aylesbury)	2,126
Bracher	1,893
Patrick	1,845
Burton	1,829

MEETINGS OF SCIENTIFIC BODIES

Held during the ensuing week.

TUESDAY, June 12.—Institution of Civil Engineers, 8 P.M. Freemasons of the Church, 8 P.M.

THURSDAY, 14.—Royal Society, 8½ P.M.; Society Antiquaries, 8 P.M.

SATURDAY, 16.—Institute of Fine Arts, 8 P.M.

TO CORRESPONDENTS.

Received.—"A Subscriber," "Witt's Lunatic Asylum." We are asked to say that the tender for ironwork given last week as by "Cole," was from "Swift and Cole." " C.J." (either "Laxton's" or "Taylor's," may be obtained at 2, York-street). "M. B.L." (we should be disposed to try the syphon trap). "B. and B." shall appear, if not given elsewhere). "A.J.," "C.H.S.," "Mr. K.," "T.P.," "T.E.L.," "G.J.R."

NOTICE.—All communications respecting *advertisements* should be addressed to the "Publisher," and not to the "Editor;" all other communications should be addressed to the EDITOR, and not to the Publisher.

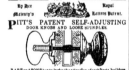

No. CCCXXXII.

SATURDAY, JUNE 16, 1849.

AST week we endeavoured to make known to our readers the nature and character of some of the more recently published collections of Gothic Architectural Exemplars. In our present number we would in like manner bring before them two or three new books connected with the art of painting, to which we have not yet had an opportunity to refer, namely, Mrs. Merrifield's translation and notices of ancient " Original Treatises on the Arts of Painting," published by Murray; "The Picture Collector's Manual," by Jas. R. Hobbes, published by Boone; and Mr. Henry Twining's " Philosophy of Painting," published by Longman.

Hazlitt scoffs at the " ambiguous quackery of rules " for the production of beauty; they have been called the " fetters of genius," and many inquirers who do not repudiate them altogether, are undetermined as to what extent they may be made available. There can be no reasonable doubt, however, as to the utility, and indeed necessity, of guiding principles. Rules are no substitute for genius, but without them genius may waste itself or be perverted; and as to their being fetters, says Reynolds, " They are fetters only to men of no genius, as that armour, which upon the strong is an ornament and defence, upon the weak and misshapen becomes a load, and cripples the body which it was made to protect."

We are glad, therefore, to find the theory of art occupying the attention of competent minds, and augur from it much advantage. "Theory," remarks Mr. Twining, " would indeed be worse than useless in the art of painting, were it to claim, as its special office, to rule the inspired thought, and to assert principles of grace in the lively creations of the fancy. Its advantages are chiefly shown in correcting the errors, and in chastening the productions, of those who want the penetration and experience necessary to proceed unguided. A more extended knowledge of the principles on which art is founded, might not add many to the best of the yearly productions of our artists, although it might diminish immensely the number of the inferior ones; and by thus rendering the attainment of that which is at least genuine and good, more easy and certain, it doubtless confers a benefit on art in general, which ascends less obstructed, and it may be, to a loftier position, when seated on the foundation of truth, than when based on inconsistency, chance, or extravagance."

Mrs. Merrifield's work relates to the *technical* part of painting, and is a most satisfactory testimony to the learning, accomplishments, and ability of the author.* Mrs. Merrifield was deputed in 1845 to proceed to the north of Italy for the purpose of collecting MSS. relative to painting, with the view, principally, of ascertaining the processes and methods of oil - painting adopted by the Italians. On Mrs. M.'s return, Sir Robert Peel entrusted to her the publication of the MSS., with an intimation that part of the expenses would be defrayed by Government; and this book is the result. As a matter of course, much of the information given in these MSS. is practically useless, although in an antiquarian and historical point of view the whole are valuable.

Prefixed, Mrs. Merrifield has given an interesting sketch of the history and technical processes of the different kinds of painting and other arts which are alluded to in the manuscripts.

The MSS. given are those of Jehan le Begue (fifteenth century); Petrus St. Audemar (thirteenth and fourteenth centuries); Eraclius, Archerius (fourteenth century); the Bolognese MS. (fifteenth century); the Paduan MS. (beginning of seventeenth century); the Brussels MS., written by P. Lebrun, 1635, and some others.

Mrs. Merrifield has executed the task confided to her very satisfactorily, and fully justified Sir Robert Peel's selection.

"The Picture Collector's Manual,"* besides being a Dictionary of painters, supplies an omission which has long been felt, namely, an alphabetical list of the various pupils, imitators, and copyists, arranged under the heads of the different masters. There is also a classification of subjects, showing the names of those who painted in the several departments of art, thus affording, as the author says, "in all uncertain cases, a clue by which the judgment may be guided, the opinion strengthened, and the doubt [sometimes] removed." A want of care in the collation of dates is observable, and is to be regretted. Thus the death of Lucas de Cranach, who was born 1472, is put in the year 1586, but in truth took place in 1553; and Cuyp appears to have been born in 1768, and to have died in 1649!

In plan, however, the work is excellent, and, in spite of what we have said, we do not hesitate to recommend it for purchase.

The author concludes his introduction, which consists of a brief description of the various schools, with the following outline of the characteristics of a few of the principal masters :—

" Titian's lights are generally in the centre; his shadows are broad and extended; his middle tints in the extremities of his figures, such as the hands, feet, &c., are of a reddish brown; those parts most distant from the light, are weakened in colour, and have a dusky appearance; his receding figures, and those on the outside of his groups, are always the most obscure; his dead colours are made with cold middle tints, and finished by laying on warm colours, extremely thin, light, and transparent; his middle tints of shadows are thinly covered with yellow, and in the darker parts with red and black; he used but little white in his lights, and none at all in obscured parts of his pictures: whilst Raffaelle used it largely, he is neither so bright in his lights, nor dark in his shadows as other masters; and in the old men of Rubens and Titian the principle appears to be the same, little or no white in the carnation, and a sort of orange colour, made up with yellows and reds; in historical compositions, his great light is in his skies and behind his figures,—he does not affect a whiteness and glitter when the light is thrown upon the fleshy part in his female figures; it shines but is subdued, and not opposed to dark shadow in obscure parts. Conceive a scale of colouring between the chalky hard manner, and the opposite extreme of obscurity, the strongest light being at No. 1; we then arrive at this comparison : Guido's strongest light on the flesh is at No. 1, his middle at No. 3, and his dark at the extreme; Titian's strongest light is at No. 2, his middle at 3, and his dark at the flesh; Agostino Carracci's are at 3, and his middle at 1; and Vandyck's are almost as strong as those of Guido, but his strongest shadows are off the flesh, and in the draperies and backgrounds."

" The Philosophy of Painting "* is a continuation of a work by the same author, Mr. Twining, entitled " Elements of the Picturesque," printed originally for private distribution only, and which was reviewed in our columns some time ago. The present volume is divided into three parts. The first is appropriated to remarks on the elementary principles which constitute the Beautiful, and those conducive to the perception of the Beautiful, and includes an analysis of the views entertained by various authors on the same subject. The second part comprises the consideration of subjects connected with imitation in painting, such as composition, expression, light and shade, styles, &c.; and the third part treats of linear perspective, projected shadows, and the perspective of reflections.

This work is the result of personal observation and thought, rather than of reference to the writings of others, and requires, for its due mastery, the corresponding exercise of thought by the reader. Those who will give this will find it eminently suggestive, and will not fail to derive from it much advantage. Mr. Twining is an enthusiastic lover of art, and for his disinterested efforts to advance the knowledge of it, is entitled to our praise,—he has his return, however, in the enjoyment the pursuit affords.'

To all our readers we say, as we have often said before, cultivate a knowledge of art,—improve your taste,—and as one of the best means of doing this, lose no opportunity of exercising the eye by examining fine specimens of art. As Leigh Hunt remarks, in his pleasant " Book for a Corner," " We have reason to regard the having been conversant with a house full of paintings during childhood, as one of the blessings of our existence. We have never since entered a room of that sort without a tendency to hush and move softly, as if in the presence of things above the ordinary course of nature, of spirits left behind them by great men, looking at us with divine eyes, or informing the most beautiful visions of nature with art as wonderful."

ON THE BUILDING MATERIALS EMPLOYED IN PARIS AND IN THE VALLEY OF THE LOWER SEINE.

At the present day, when the attention of the profession has been so powerfully directed to what may be called the physiology of the materials employed in the execution of the works committed to their charge, it may be interesting to examine the practice of the architects in the neighbouring capital. Such an examination, moreover, becomes more interesting from the comparatively superior attention paid by the French architects and engineers to the study of the philosophy of the mechanical parts of their pursuits. With the glorious exceptions of Rennie, Tredgold, Barlow, and Hodgkinson, nearly all that we know of the chemical and mechanical nature of the materials we have to employ is derived from the works of the French authors. The practical lessons they have drawn from their researches become, therefore, of much more immediate importance; and, although the geological nature of the country in which they are applied differs so entirely from that of our

---

* " Original Treatises, dating from the Twelfth to the Eighteenth Centuries, on the Arts of Painting in Oil, Miniature, Mosaic, and on Glass; of Gilding, Dyeing, and the preparation of Colours and artificial Gems; preceded by a general Introduction, with Translations, Prefaces, and Notes." By Mrs. Merrifield. In two volumes. London, John Murray, 1849.

* " The Picture Collector's Manual, adapted to the Professional Man and the Amateur; being a Dictionary of Painters, containing 1,500 more names than in any other Work." By J. R. Hobbes. 2 vols. London, 1849. T. and W. Boone.

* " On the Philosophy of Painting: a Theoretical and Practical Treatise; comprising Æsthetics in reference to Art, the application of Rules to Painting, and general Considerations on Perspective." By Henry Twining, Esq. London: Longman and Co. 1849.

own, yet the mode of analysis adopted, and the conclusions arrived at, are as applicable here as elsewhere.

Building materials may be separated, for the purposes of classification, into the following groups:—1st, stone; 2nd, bricks; 3rd, limes; 4th, woods; 5th, metals. Under the head of bricks are included tiles, pottery, and artificial stones; under that of limes are included plaster, cement, sand, stuccos, &c. These materials are to be examined, firstly, as to the nature and qualities of their constituent parts; secondly, as to the manner of their use.

1st. Stones.—The stones employed in building are grouped thus—1st, the argillaceous; 2nd, the calcareous; 3rd, the gypseous; 4th, the silicious; 5th, the volcanic and divers natures.

The Argillaceous Stones.—These are comprised of a base of alumina, generally combined with silicates and the oxides and sulphurets of iron. They do not effervesce with the acids, and are composed of successive layers, easily separated. The schists and slates are of this class.

The slates used in Paris are extracted at Angers, in the department of the Maine and Loire. The quarries are opened in a bed of silurian argillaceous schist of an enormous thickness, which outcrops for a length of ten miles, between Avrillé and Treluzé, passing under the town of Angers, where the Mayenne cuts the direction of the formation at right angles. There are eight quarries opened in a direction from east to west. Immediately under the vegetable soil is found a bed of incoherent schist, named in the country "cosse." This is followed by a bed difficult to cleave, and, therefore used locally as a rubble building stone; and lastly occurs, about 14 or 15 feet from the surface, the useful slate. It is worked in patches about 400 feet wide, leaving underneath an unknown thickness, though the depth quarried in many cases extends to 300 feet.

The quarries of Angers furnish a slate of a very fine grain, remarkably thin and light; although the specific gravity of the slate itself is very great. It is 3·000, water being 1·000, or 188 lbs. per foot cube. Four sizes are worked for the Paris market, viz.: the "grande carrée forte," $11\frac{1}{2}$ long by $8\frac{1}{4}$ wide, and $\frac{1}{8}$ thick ($0^{m}.293 \times 0^{m}.217 \times 0^{m}.003$); 2nd, the "grande carrée fine," of the same dimensions as to length and breadth, but of about half the thickness; 3rd, the "cartelettes." $8\frac{1}{4}$ long by $6\frac{1}{4}$ wide by $\frac{1}{8}$ thick ($0^{m}.217 \times 0^{m}.162 \times 0^{m}.003$); and 4th, the "cartelette fine," of about half the thickness. According to the statistical returns of the Ingénieurs des Mines, the value of the slates extracted at Angers in the year 1845, was at the pit's mouth 1,420,036 f. (56,400*l.*); and there were employed in the quarries 2,366 workmen.

The quarries of Charleville, in the department of the Ardennes, are worked upon a larger scale for the supply of slates for the east of France, Holland, and the Low Countries; but the expensive land carriage prevents their being employed in the capital. The value of their produce is about 1,793,945f. (72,000*l.*); they employ 2,843 men. The slates are somewhat softer than those of Angers, consequently they decayed rapidly in the damp countries where they were usually employed. M. Vialet, Ingénieur des Ponts et Chaussées, overcame this objection by roasting the slates until they assumed a red tinge; their durability was doubled by this process. In the neighbourhood of St. Lô, in the department of Calvados, are some slate quarries in the Cambrian strata, which are used to a considerable extent in the neighbourhood, and which, if the land carriage were not so ruinous, would doubtlessly be formidable rivals to those of Angers. The cathedral of Bayeux is covered with the former; but even there, the price of the Angers slate is so much inferior to that of St. Lô, as to ensure the preference for general use, in spite of the superiority of the latter. The value of the slates extracted in the department of the Calvados in 1845 was 10,360f. (414*l.*)

The usual practice in Paris and in the departments of the Lower Seine, is to nail the slates with two nails upon battens half an inch thick, and from $4\frac{1}{2}$ inches to 7 inches wide, that is to say, either of deals cut in two, or of battens. Some times these "voliges," as they are called, are of poplar or sycamore, but they decay very rapidly. The slates lap over one another two-thirds of their length, leaving a "pureau" of one-third, when the inclination of the roof is not above 33°: at 45° the pureau is one-half of the slate; at 60° two-thirds. The battens are rarely laid close, for the slates are found to decay more rapidly if there be no circulation of air. The usual space between the battens is about $1\frac{1}{2}$ inch. Hips, ridges, valleys, and gutters are executed as in England, with the trifling exception, that step-metal flashings are unknown; the slates are made good to the Pignon walls by merely covering the meeting angle with plaster.

The Calcareous Stones.—The formations which furnish the building stones of this class occur in the neighbourhood of Paris, and of the basin of the Lower Seine, in vast deposits. The ease with which they are extracted, and the proximity of the quarries to the places in which the stone is to be used, render their employ almost imperative; and it is to the use of these materials, that the monumental character of Paris is in a great measure to be attributed.

The nature of this class of stone is too generally known to render it worth while to dwell upon it at present. Our geological observations will therefore be merely confined to an enumeration of the great sources of supply. These are, for Paris itself, the vast tertiary formation, which nearly covers the whole of the departments of the Seine, Seine and Oise, Seine and Marne, l'Oise, and extends into those immediately around. Rouen, and some of the small towns above and below it, use large quantities of an indurated chalk met with on the banks of the Seine, whilst Havre and the intermediate towns derive their building stones principally from the oolitic formations of the department of Calvados.

Nearly the whole of the department of the Seine in which Paris is situated, may be considered as capable of furnishing calcareous stones for building purposes. The excavations which have been, and still continue to be, made, in and around Paris, are immense. About one-sixth of the town is built over the abandoned quarries, which are known under the name of the catacombs. The quarters St. Marcel, St. Jacques, St. Germain, and Chaillot, are in this condition; and it is calculated that the mass of materials extracted thencefrom is not less than 385 million cubic feet. At present the bulk of the superior stones furnished by the department, comes from the quarries of Arceuil, Bagneux, Montrouge, and St. Cloud, which lie to the south-west of Paris.

The department of the Seine and Oise, is rich in quarries. Amongst them may be cited those of Saillancourt and Conflans, near Pontois, of Poissy, St. Nom, St. Maure, l'Ile Adam, and Chèrence, near Mantes and upon the borders of the chalk. The department of the Oise furnishes the lias of Senlis, and the Vergelée of St. Leu. The Seine and Marne furnish the very beautiful stone called the Chateau Laudon.

This stone of the Chateau Laudon is the hardest, densest, and, consequently, heaviest, employed in Paris. It is nearly a pure carbonate of lime, containing in 1,000 parts 18 only of magnesia, and eighteen of silicate of alumina. Its colour is a grey, slightly tinged with yellow; it is subcrystalline, resists the action of the atmosphere, and bears a kind of polish. The quarries from which it is extracted are about 63 miles from Paris; yet the great superiority of the stone causes it to be preferred wherever great solidity is desired. It was first employed in the erection of the bridge of Nemours; subsequently Rondelet used it for the paving of the Pantheon. The Barrière de l'Etoile is faced with it; the pedestals of the Pont d'Iéna, the large basins of the Chateau d'Eau, and of the fountain of the Innocents, and the parapets of the terre-plein of the Pont Neuf are executed of this stone, as are also the steps, parapet walls, and balustrades of the church of St. Vincent de Paul.

The specific gravity is 2·605; its weight about 163 lbs. Eng. to a foot cube; and it is able to resist a crushing weight of 332 kilo. per centimètre square.

The lias, which was formerly extracted to the south of Paris, was an excessively hard stone, but the quarries are nearly exhausted. The name is still retained amongst the quarrymen and is by them applied indiscriminately to the hardest beds of the *calcaire grossière*, which rarely occur in any great depth. At Arceuil, Bagneux, Montrouge, &c., the lias is fine grained and compact, but is rarely raised in blocks of more than a foot thick. At Montereau it is occasionally 2 feet thick. At St. Cloud, it is soft; at Maisons, in the south-west of Paris, it takes a rose tint, and occurs in beds of from 9 to 10 inches thick. The specific gravity of the lias is, on the average, 2·439; the foot cube weighs 152 lbs.; the crushing weight per centimètre square is even greater than that of the Chateau Laudon; it is 445 kilog. It was doubtlessly for this reason that it was chosen for the execution of the columns of the exterior of the Madeleine and of the Bourse. The crown moulding of the large pediment of the Louvre is executed in lias, extracted at Mendon; it is of two pieces each 16 m. 24 c. long, by 2 m. 60 c. wide, by 46 c. high (53 feet 3 inches × 8 feet 6 inches × 1 foot 5 inches).

The "cliquart" extracted at Vangirard and Mendon is a species of lias of a rather loose texture.

The stones called the "roches" are hard of a coarse grain, very shelly. They occur in beds varying in thickness from 1 foot 4 inches to 2 feet 2 inches; their specific gravity is between 2·415 and 2·305, the heaviest being as usual, the best. The foot cube weighs between 151 lbs. and 141 lbs.; the crushing weights 302 kilogs. and 283 k. p. c. square. The roche of St. Cloud is red and shelly, but of a very superior quality; it occurs in beds from 18 inches to 2 feet thick, and has the peculiar quality of being able to be employed on the wrong way of the bed. The isolated columns of the court of the Louvre and of the garden front of the Tuileries are of this stone, and have stood well for upwards of two hundred years. We shall have occasion to revert to this apparent anomaly on some future occasion. The basements of the Madeleine, St. Vincent de Paul, Notre Dame de Lorette, of the Palais du Quai d'Orçay, and of the Bourse, are executed in the "roche de Bagneux."

The bridges of Neuilly, the Pont d'Iéna, of Louis the 16th, and numerous similar constructions, are built of the "roche" of Saillancourt. At Rouen large quantities of the roche of Chèrence are employed in works which require solidity: for instance, the stone bridge and the basement of the Custom House. The rubble filling of the bridge is, however, of the Vetheuil stone, one of the lowest members of the tertiary formations. At Havre, the plinth of the Museum is executed in the Chèrence stone. The practice of the French architects is never to employ the softer materials, such as the Caen oolite, near the ground.

The "pierre franche" is a fine, close-grained stone, less dense and hard than the "roche," but preferable for the decorative purposes of architecture, on account of the superior homogenity of its grain. Its specific gravity is about 2·130; the foot cube weighs 133 lbs. nearly; the crushing weight is about 126 kilogs. per centimètre. The lower parts of the Pantheon are of this stone, extracted at Arceuil. The angle stones of the façade of the same building are executed in blocks from the banc royal of Conflans, of the same nature; they were 10 feet square by about 6 feet 6 inches high, and weighed about 24 tons. The arches of the portico and of the interior of the church and the dome, the entablature, and the capitals of the exterior order, are of the same stone. The Vergelée and the St. Leu are of the same category, as is also the stone of l'Ile Adam; they are extensively used in Rouen and the neighbouring cities, on the banks of the Seine and the Oise, in those of the canal, and on the Northern Railway. The exterior dome of the Pantheon is in Vergelée stone.

The lambourde is a soft stone of an even, coarse grain; it decomposes when exposed to moisture, and is therefore only used in positions in which the action of the atmosphere is the slightest. The best stone of this description is extracted at St. Maur, where it reaches 1 foot 8 inches in thickness. Some beautiful stones for internal works are obtained in this series at Conflans and at St. Leu, which attain 2 feet 2 inches thickness. The specific gravity varies between 1·897 and 1·709; the weight per foot cube is between 113 lbs. and 107 lbs.;

; crushing weight is about 59 kilogs. per st. square.*

At Vernon, in the department de l'Eure, a ecies of indurated chalk is largely quarried local uses. The church of Vernon, and it of Louviers, are executed in this kind of ne, as are also those of Pont de l'Arche, d of les Andelys. When fresh from the arry these stones are soft, but they harden exposure to the atmosphere; so much so to resist atmospheric action in a very extra-linary manner. In the instances of the three st-named churches, all the external orna-ntation is of the most elaborate character of "flamboyante" architecture; and in all es where the water does not lodge, the de-ls of the foliage, and the arrises of the ouldings, are preserved in a very remarkable nner. The blocks are sometimes 3 feet 4 in. gh; their specific gravity is 2·155; the foot be weighs 135 lbs. nearly, the crushing ight is about 220 kilogs. per centimètre uare.†

A similar description of indurated chalk is tracted at Caumont, in the Seine Inférieure, the north-west of Rouen. This, or a like ne from St. Etienne, nearer still to the wn, was much employed in the middle ages the buildings of Rouen. The cathedral, . Ouen, St. Maclou, the Archbishop's pa-e, may be cited as instances.

The lateral elevations of the Madeleine are of e Pierre Franche of l'Ile Adam, the upper rts of St. Vincent de Paul, of N. D. de Lorette, Vergelée de St. Leu; those of the Palais du uai d'Orçay, are a mixture of the pierres nches of Carrières St. Denis, Montesson, d Carrières sous bois, near St. Germain. e façades of the Bourse are in stone of l'Ile dam and of Conflans. The restoration of e Palais de Justice, the completion of St. uen, the upper parts of the Douane and of ntrepôt des Sels, at Rouen, are in Vergelée St. Leu.

At Havre, and generally in the embouchure the Seine, the calcareous stones of the lvados are used. An examination of them ould lead us into too many details at present; it they have become so interesting to us, om the extensive use made of them in Eng-nd, that it is much to be desired that a more aborate examination be made than we have at esent. The notices contained in THE UILDER, notwithstanding their undoubted erit, present questionable points. The chemical alysis, firstly, I am convinced, is not correct; asmuch as the Caen stone is stated only to ntain *a trace* of magnesia, whilst it is noto-ous that the lime it yields is thin, without ing hydraulic, which would not occur less there were present a very consider-le quantity of magnesia.‡ The use of the anc banc is justly objected to, but the use of e stone from the quarries of la Maladrèrie is uch more dangerous, and this, I observe, is nt over to London in very large quantities. It if not asserted, at least given to be under-od, that no inconvenience would arise from e use of Caen stone placed the wrong way the bed; whereas all the most accurate and ientific observers who have made any re-arches into the subject—namely, Rondelet, ufflot, Peyronnet, Ganthey, Sganzin, Reibel, d Vicat,—all agree in asserting that the resistance of stones is much greater when they are employed upon their natural bed. As to the action of the sea water upon the Caen stone, it is universally received amongst the French practical masons that the sea water destroys it very rapidly; and chemistry teaches us that the muriates and sulphates of magnesia, present in the sea water, enter into energetic combination with the salts contained in the limestones, and produce rapid disintegration.*

Practically, at Paris, where from the nature of the subsoil it is expensive to form cellars, and where the bulk of the houses are built upon the ground, without deep foundations, where the land is all freehold, building leases are unknown, and consequently where the interest of the proprietors is evidently to obtain the greatest number of dwellings upon the least possible surface, and the houses, therefore, are generally from six to seven stories high, the lower parts of the houses are built of the roche stone, towards the street and up to the first floor; from thence two stories are carried up in la pierre franche; and the remainder is executed in lambourde. The party walls are mostly executed of moellon, or small coursed stones, of similar natures to the corresponding parts of the façade. The back walls and partitions are of wood, filled in with light rubble, and plastered. Such construction is about as bad as can be: the front wall, built of carefully-squared ashlar, sinks very little. The party walls, of rubble and plaster, not only sink more than the front, but, from the fact that the plaster in setting expands, it becomes necessary to build these walls totally independent of one another. The back walls, of wood framework, shrink still more. It is therefore almost impossible, in the new quarters of Paris, where this style prevails, to find a house which is not disfigured in all directions with cracks and settlements of every kind and size imaginable.

The mode of using the stone is, however, logical, and merits imitation. The harder and less hygrometric stones are placed at the bottom, as being the most fit to resist the crushing weight and the capillary action of the stone upon the humidity of the soil. The finer grained stones are employed at the heights destined usually to be ornamented; the lighter and more perishable stones are used above, where they load the foundations less than the others would do, and where they meet with the atmospheric conditions the most adapted to their own preservation.

In Rouen, the Chèrence stone, or that of Vernon, are used in the situations where the roche is used at Paris; the upper parts are of the softer stones. At Havre the same rule is observed: the Chèrence, Caumont, Ranville, or granite, are used in all cases where there is danger to be feared from humidity; the Caen stone is only used in the upper works. Wherever I have seen the Aubigny stone used, it has decayed rapidly. Indeed, the French architects do not much advocate its use externally.

3rd. *The Gypseous Stones.*—These stones, from their soft and friable nature, and the facility with which they decompose in the atmosphere, are not allowed to be used as building materials in Paris. Sometimes enclosure walls are built of them, employed as moellon. The principal use is in the fabrication of plaster.

The chemical nature of these stones as found at Montmartre, Belleville, Charonne, Menilmontant, le Calvaire, Triel, and Meulan, is, according to Fourcroy, 32 parts oxide of calcium, 46 parts of sulphuric acid, and 22 parts of water. They differ from the gypsums of other countries in the large quantities of lime they contain, which gives them greater powers of resistance to the action of the moisture of the atmosphere. The operation of burning consists simply in driving off the water of crystallization. In this state the plaster has a remarkable avidity for water, and immediately that any is presented it absorbs it, and crystallizes around the bodies in its immediate vicinity. I noticed previously the singular fact of the swelling of the plaster during this process; it is one that requires great attention in the employ of the material. Another fact worthy of notice is cited by Rondelet, namely, that two bricks set together with plaster adhere with one-third more energy than bricks set with lime during the first month; but that afterwards their adhesion diminishes, whereas that of the bricks and mortar increases almost indefinitely.*

4th and 5th. *The Silicious Stones, &c.*—They comprehend the grés, flint nodules, the meulières, the granites, porphyries, and the basalts.

The grés is a species of imperfect sandstone formation, at least as it occurs near Paris, and in the department of the Lower Seine. It is composed of a fine sand of a whitish tinge, cemented together by a silicious cement. Generally speaking it occurs in detached nodules, named "rognons;" sometimes it occurs in layers of different thicknesses. The quarrymen observe that the lower they descend the softer the grès becomes, and that the harder nature of stone is the most easy to quarry in regular forms. It has no definite planes of stratification or crystallization, and is therefore easily worked into any shape required. The streets of nearly all the towns between Paris and the sea-board are paved with these tertiary grès, which occur in isolated patches along the whole course of the river. At Havre, of late, the red sandstone of May, near Caen, a member of the Cambrian system, has been employed instead thereof, with remarkable success. The usual size of the paving stones is 9 inches square; but some of the last works of this kind have been executed with narrower stones, about 4 inches wide.

The flint nodules are sometimes used for rough rubble masonry. They occur in chalk and in the gravels overlying the tertiary formations.

The meulière is a species of quartzose concretion, with numerous small holes. It is met with in two forms; one which occurs in masses sufficiently large to form millstones of one piece; the other in detached nodules scattered over the country. The principal quarries of the first, for the supply of the Paris market, are at Montmirail (Marne) and la Ferté sous Jouarre (Seine et Marne). The second sort are found nearer Paris, and in the department de l'Eure.

As the meulière is excessively hard, and resists all external action in the highest degree, it is much used by engineers and architects in situations where those qualities are required. The fortifications of Paris and of the detached forts are faced with it. Many of the works of the Canaux St. Martin, St. Denis, and de l'Oure, the sewers of Paris, and the abattoirs also, are faced with the meulière; for all these works it is admirably adapted. One species is, however, to be avoided,—"la caillasse;" its surfaces are so perfectly even that they offer no key to the mortar.

The granites, a description of which would here be unnecessary, are only used in Paris and the other towns in the interior as borders for the foot-paths, and occasionally as flagging. That used in Paris is mostly extracted at the island of Chaussey, and is of a nature closely resembling the best Devonshire granites. The plinths of the columns of the Law Institution in Chancery-lane† are of this granite, and may give a correct idea of its nature. The enormous cost of the granite, owing to the land carriage, must at all times limit its use in the interior. At Havre, however, and at Honfleur, it is much used in the different docks, and the fortifications towards the river are entirely faced with it.

The porphyries are very little used, nor do they occur abundantly in any position suitable

The chemical type of the building stones of Paris may regarded to be that of the stones found near Marly; they thus composed—

Carbonate of lime	89
Magnesia	1
Silicate of ammonia	10
Total	100

netimes the magnesia disappears, and the quantity of clay l flint diminishes considerably: thus it is—

Carbonate of lime	0·985
Silex and clay	0·015
	1·000

Berthier.

The most correct chemical analysis of the chalk in the artment of the Lower Seine was made upon some ex-ted at St. Catherine. It is more fissured than at Ver-, St. Etienne, or Caumont, but may be regarded as of same mineralogical type. It contains—

Carbonate of lime	68
Silicate of ammonia	12
Sand	6
Oxide of iron	2
Water	12
	100

The name of Professor Phillips, by whom the analysis made for us, should be a sufficient guarantee of its ectness.—ED.

* The calcareous stones when first extracted are certainly in a very different state to that in which they appear after losing the quarry damp, to use the expression of the quarrymen. I suspect that they exist in the quarry only as a sub-carbonate of lime; at any rate, it is certain that they are hydro-carbonates. In either case the lime is, comparatively speaking, free to enter into new combinations. If sea water be introduced, the magnesia enters into combination with the lime, the more readily if carbonic acid be present, giving rise to the formation of a magnesian carbonate of lime. The sulphuric acid gas also enters into combination with the lime, giving rise to the formation of sulphate of lime. These combinations take place with the commencement of a confused crystallization, the mass is disintegrated, and falls to powder.

* The value of the building materials extracted in 1815 was, for the departments before cited, as follows:—

	Building Stones.		Plaster.
Seine and Marne	F.647,000	....	F.750,000
Seine	2,413,212	....	1,295,067
Seine and Oise	1,375,576	....	504,509
Seine Inférieure	109,593		
Eure	222,958	....	182,784
Calvados	837,551		
Oise	300,400	....	148,350

besides the value of the slates, quoted previously.

† That is to say, of the columns of the portico.

CARVED BENCH ENDS.

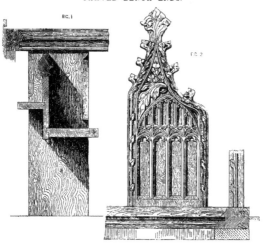

FIC. 1

FIG. 2

FIG. 5

2 FEET

---

to their being worked for the Paris market. The basalts also are rare, at least for practical building use. They are, however, occasionally used for flagging, as in the Rues de la Paix, de Richelieu, &c.*

GEO. BURNELL.

CARVED BENCH ENDS.

WE add to our collection of bench ends, Figs. 1 and 2, from Atherington Church, Devon, with section showing seat and bookboard; and Fig. 3, from Plympton Church, in the same county. The form of the capping in Fig. 1 would not conduce to the comfort of the sitter.

* To be continued. The foregoing paper was read at a meeting of the Institute of Architects on the 4th instant.

ETTY'S WORKS—AN HONOUR TO THE NATION.

IN conformity with the proposition made by the Society of Arts, in 1848, to "assist in the formation of a National Gallery of British Art, by means of *public voluntary contributions*, arising from donations and annual subscriptions, and from the proceeds of an annual exhibition of the pictures and studies of some one eminent artist," a collection from the finished works and studies of Mr. W. Etty, R.A., has been opened in the Adelphi, wonderful for its richness in all the attributes and excellencies of art, as for the evidence it affords of the untiring perseverance exhibited by this great artist through the ups and downs of some thirty years, the manly energy that characterised his determination of succeeding, in spite of the many difficulties that beset his early career. The repeated rejection of his pictures (as we hear from himself in his own

unvarnished biography*), the heart-burnings o disappointed ambition, seem only to have stl mulated him to further efforts. When it i seen that such pictures as his "Judith and Ho lofernes," "Mercy interceding for the Van quished," and "Benaiah," could meet with n purchasers until bought by the Scottish Aca demy for a comparatively trifling sum, ou young artists will be encouraged against simi lar disheartening freaks of fortune. The pos sessors of such treasures may well congratulat themselves,—certainly, few could place then better.

The variety in the collection is not the leas striking feature of the exhibition; one woul imagine, from surmise, that it would be impos sible for one man to produce so many dissimila works, particularly taking into consideration th repetition of *materiel*; and although at first glanc

* In the *Art-Journal*.

the walls present the appearance of a dazzling *melée* of flowers, fruit, jewels, and rich draperies, indiscriminately but beautifully associated, each work on inspection displays a study and arrangement of colour perfect in itself. The earlier productions are easily distinguishable from their marked care and study. What amazement will the glorious inspiration of "Judith" excite in those who behold it for the first time!—those who hardly glance at the marvellous blots with which his name has of late years been associated, will hardly recognise Etty in it, or in the still more sublime conception of "The Listening Maid," which compartment is to us the most extraordinary of the three. Who of the ancients produced a finer "Mercy interceding for the Vanquished?" wherein the most perfect drawing is combined with scarcely approachable colour. The entreaty so beautifully depicted in the female, the ponderous strength of the victor, and the horror and despair of the vanquished, are too well known to call for remark. This glorious allegory is priceless. "Benaiah, one of David's chief captains," allegorical of valour, is another foundation-stone of Etty's "high-piled" fame.

Who, past or present, depicted more in accordance with Homeric text, and yet with more original fancy, "the Syrens three," an exemplification of *the importance of resisting sensual delights?*—the voluptuous loveliness of the nymphs, whose

"Song is death, and makes destruction please,"

modelled with the grace and truth of a Phidias, and coloured in such a manner as to preclude all possibility of mistaking the author, —the positive grandeur in treatment of the infatuated Ulysses struggling with his soldiers, and the whole of the background. Who, in any case, combined so many of art's highest excellencies with so little to detract? and what further proof is requisite of Etty's greatness than that existing in this masterpiece? One is inclined almost to regret the exhibition of "Joan of Arc" placed in juxtaposition with his noblest triumphs; but considered as a consummation of his desire to paint "three times three" colossal pictures, it is a necessary and interesting appendage.

As evidencing the careful study and perfection present in his earlier compositions, (25) "The Storm," worthy of Michelangelo in feeling, and of Etty in colour (painted in 1831); "Venus and Cupid descending" (32), exquisite beyond expression (painted 1822); (42) "Pandora," another fine specimen, to which the remark that, if "pricked with a pin the flesh will bleed," applies; (44) The Parting of Hero and Leander," a miracle of moonlight painting (painted 1827); (46) "A Composition from Paradise Lost," the prototype of many a later picture by *other* hands; (102) "The Choice of Paris;" (104) "Sabrina," exquisitely chaste, and a perfect gem (exhibited 1831); (105) "Cleopatra's Arrival in Cilicia," another perfect work of art (painted in 1821); (112) "Cupid and Psyche descending," radiant with mythological loveliness; and (128) "Britomart redeeming fair Amoret," may be mentioned. They all show how unceasingly industrious and studious he was, and how he gloried in his profession. The elaborate finish, attended with so much success, determines that, to acquire the freedom so conspicuous latterly in all his contributions to art-exhibitions, a devoted attention to every minor detail, attended necessarily by hard work and perseverance in finishing to the utmost, is indispensable.

(39) "Study of a Little Girl," (61) "Portrait of Miss Wallace," and (81) "Preparing for a Fancy Dress Ball," evidence, beyond a doubt, his admiration of the style of Sir Thomas Lawrence, his master.

(14) "Diana and Endymion;" the poetic notion of Diana assuming the crescent form is strikingly beautiful, as is the general tone consistent with a moonlight effect.

(22) "Samson betrayed by Delilah" is signalised by many incongruities, but by more excellencies.

(27) Pluto carrying off Proserpine;" the two principal figures are as fine as anything in the collection. (33) "Waters of Elle;" a beautiful bit of pathos charmingly rendered; exhibited some ten years back at the British Institution. (40) is a powerful bit of colour, "The Bridge of Sighs." (41) "The Good Samaritan;" a beautiful specimen, abounding in fine points, never excelled in colour. (45) "Phœdria and Cymochles"—a bouquet of flowers.

(50) "The Repentant Prodigal's Return to his Father." The expression of the son is exquisitely appropriate, and the painting and colour inimitable; a little bit of still life painting is particularly attractive from its truth and apparent finish.

(60) "The Sea Bather;" a finely coloured half length figure of a female, in the recollection of all, from its being but five years ago in the Royal Academy.

(62) "The Saviour;" wrongly entitled, but a beautiful work of art, remarkably slight in execution.

Every lover of art ought to pay at least one visit to this most interesting exhibition.

BITS FROM BRISTOL.

The Bristol and West of England Architectural Society held their annual meeting on the 21st ultimo, when Mr. Norton read a paper on the Bristol High Cross, of which a *fac-simile* is about to be erected in College-green. It is now at Stourhead, in a miserable state of decay, the cause of which the reader thus explained:—The material used is a very coarse-grained oolite, the ova being large and distinct, and readily absorbing moisture and frost. This, however, was remedied for many centuries by the application of polychromatic colouring, which evidently formed an effectual preservative against the weather. It presents, in its mutilated state, sufficient proof that originally not the figures only, but the entire surface of the stonework, was thus enriched: the figures have best preserved these remains of colouring. The colours used were vermilion, blue, and gold. The gilding may be traced in every part,—on the ribs of groining, &c., &c.; but the vermillion is by far the best preserved, being even now of a rich hue; the blue has faded to a pale gray. The dresses of the figures are usually painted vermillion; mantles, and such portions of dress, blue; borders, and other subsidiary ornamental parts, being relieved with gold. This surface of painting has long fallen to decay, and hangs in loose flakes. Generally one of the above-named colours may be seen in an intermediate coat or stratum.

In addition to this cause of decay (the neglect of repainting the surface), another very fertile one is discoverable in the use of iron cramps; whether these are original, or only placed on the removal, cannot easily be determined; but in many instances the iron has become oxidated and increased in size to such an extent as literally to heave and thrust the stones off their beds, and a fissure thus commenced has ended in the disruption and fall of large masses of stonework. Lead is also very generally used, both constructively, between the joints, and as flashings above the canopies, &c., and in the case of the ogee arches, circular bar iron is placed within a circular roll of lead, thus forming a kind of continuous tie or bond. The lead has affected the iron in a very extraordinary manner, and from some chemical cause has completely pulverized it; in other cases the expansion of the iron has burst asunder the lead roll and the stonework in its turn,—a practical lesson we may all profit by.

The exhibition of *The Bristol Academy for the promotion of the Fine Arts* is now open, and consists of 244 works of art. The principal feature of the exhibition is Wilkie's fine picture "Columbus explaining to the Prior of the Convent of La Rabida his plan for the discovery of a new continent." Lucy, Townsend, Herbert Smith, Joy, Branwhite, and others, exhibit pictures which have been seen in London before, and there are several nice landscapes by local artists. Amongst the latter W. West has several, which are very clever, 32, "On the Conway" (figures not so good as the landscape), and 43, "Deep Shade" (something like Cresswick); and there are some good pieces of foliage, by Tucker, 114, "In the New Forest," and 132, "Wood Scene." There is a good likeness of a good antiquary, Mr. Thomas Garrard, ("the Chamberlain") by Curnock, and a painting of the "St. George, at anchor, off Devonport," by Colling-wood Smith, which has much poetical feeling, and with a little more care, would have been a fine picture. "The Normal College for Wales, to be erected at Swansea," by Fuller and Gingell (231), is Tudor in style, with an octagon tower in centre.

There is an Art-Union in connection with the exhibition.

A *new church* is being built, dedicated to *St. Jude*, which promises fairly. It is in the decorated style, and has a tower. The roof, of course, is open.

St. Mark's, Easton, recently finished, is imitation Norman, and has a tower and low flat spire (or rather high stone roof), with grotesque animals creeping down the angles. There is a semi-circular absis, and within, the building is decorated in what seemed to us a somewhat tawdry and flaunty manner. We are glad to see a desire abroad to apply colour to the interior decoration of our churches, but it is absolutely necessary, if used, that it be applied artistically and with discretion.

At *St. Simon's*, an early English church (having a north aisle), with open roof, and stalls in chancel, the pulpit and desk are placed at the south-east angle of the nave, so as, very properly, not to obstruct the view of the altar, but a large stove is nevertheless erected in the centre of the chancel arch, and, with a monstrous smoke pipe, sadly disfigures the interior. This and an ugly common street lamp affixed to the outside of the porch, should be sent to the right about. The church has a tower and broach spire, the outline of which is not very elegant. Two or three Independent and Wesleyan Chapels are about to be built in the neighbourhood of Bristol, under the direction of Mr. Austin, of that city.

THE DUNDEE ARCH COMPETITION.

Some of your correspondents may feel relief by knowing that the Dundee Arch affair is now closed. The architect whose design was selected brought three estimates from Glasgow and obtained two in Dundee; and that of a Mr. Harvey, of Hamilton (a village near Glasgow), amounting to 2,173*l*., is accepted. The estimate seems close to the sum prescribed,—but here's the rub: the stones are to be taken from a quarry in Fifeshire, and are so soft and easily worked, that by using them instead of the Dundee stones a saving of between twenty and thirty per cent. is effected. So that, had the design in the "Enriched Saxon" style (thus the architect designates it) been executed of the stone which the Committee not only specified, but sent the prices of to the competitors, to enable them to make up their estimates, it would have cost above 2,700*l*. In the discussion on the subject it was stated as a reason for the change, that the architect had inspected some of the balustrades in Reform-street, of Lochee stone, and found symptoms of decay, which were also already visible in the masonry of the new churches. The churches, curiously enough, are not built of the stone in question at all; and even admitting that Lochee stones are ineligible, which is rather startling, why are the Mylnefield stones rejected, the durability of which it would be folly to question while the old tower, after seven centuries, exists in such good preservation? "Expositor" can now proceed, albeit his terms are not greatly relished by some of the competitors here. M. N.

⁂ Competitors will find an advertisement from the committee in our present number. The Chairman, Mr. Neish, informs us, as to the delay complained of, that it "arose from the competitors not complying with the terms stated in the first advertisement, as inserted in The Builder. The competitors were 151, and the designs sent in (from England, Ireland, and Scotland) about 300. The one preferred is by Mr. J. T. Rochead, of Glasgow, and is of the Saxon style."

London Antiquities.—There is a trifling error in my letter addressed to you on the subject of the City antiquities, which, although of no great consequence, and not affecting the question, should be corrected. I intended to say that some of the City documents, alleged to have been sold from the Guildhall, are believed to date as early as the time of Henry IV.—Amor Veritatis.

ST. MARY'S CHURCH, WEST BROMPTON, MIDDLESEX.——George Godwin, F.R.S., Architect.

ST. MARY'S, WEST BROMPTON.

Additional church accommodation being required for the western portion of Brompton, in Middlesex, the incumbent, the Rev. W. J. Irons, B.D., took steps to obtain it; Mr. Gunter, a wealthy and liberal proprietor, of the neighbourhood, generously presented a plot of land for the site of a new building, situated between the Fulham-road and Earles Court-road; and an energetic coadjutor being found in the Rev. Hogarth J. Swale, plans were prepared by Mr. G. Godwin, architect, and being approved of by the Lord Bishop of London and the Church Commissioners, are about to be carried out forthwith, although, as yet, the amount subscribed by the neighbourhood is small.

Our engraving represents the church as it will appear seen from the south-west, when completed. It is a cross church without aisles, with an octagon lantern at the intersection, open to the building, ornamented by kneeling angels on the parapet, and surmounted by a spire with ball flowers at the angles. In the first instance, however, it is proposed to build the nave and south porch only, with the lower part of the tower, which is to be roofed to form the temporary chancel, and a bell cot is therefore provided at the west end. The length of the nave is 86 feet, and the width 33 feet; the temporary chancel about 18 feet square. The height to the ridge is 46 feet. There is a small open gallery of wood for children at the west end (the turret seen in the view contains the stairs to it), with screen beneath; and there is accommodation in the part now to be built for about 500 worshippers.

The style of architecture adopted is the Decorated; the materials, Kentish rag with Bath stone (from the Coombe Down quarries) for the dressings. The walls are 2 feet 3 inches thick, on a concrete bottom. The roof is open, of course, having arched ribs at intervals springing from carved stone corbels: the covering of green slates. All the seats are open, and have ornamental ends.

The following tenders were sent in for the execution of the work:—

Carter and Ellis	£3,297
Glenn	3,251
Haward and Nixon	3,240
J. Barr	3,096

Considering that each builder took out his own quantities, their close approximation is somewhat remarkable.

The estimated additional cost of Caen stone for the dressings in lieu of Bath stone varied from 130*l.* to 100*l.*

The church will occupy the centre of an ornamental enclosure, which will have detached villas, in a crescent form, around it.

POPULAR EDUCATION.

YORKSHIRE MECHANICS' INSTITUTES.

At the Hull Athenæum *soirée*, held on the 30th ult., after a meeting of the Yorkshire Union of Mechanics' Institutions,* some admirable addresses were delivered by the Earl of Carlisle, who presided, the Earl of Yarborough, the Dean of Ripon, Dr. Hodgson, Mr. E. Baines, Mr. Clay, M.P., the Rev. James Aspinall, and others.

Lord Carlisle, in the course of his speech, said, I should think that person a very injudicious friend of mechanics' institutions who should pretend that in your reading rooms and lecture rooms, the means were afforded of turning all your members at once into finished scholars, or ready-made philosophers; or should say that they put it in your power to grasp that eminence which must always be the reward of the midnight toil of the student, or the life-long research of the experimentalist. But if it be the object how to raise the toiling masses of our countrymen above the range of sordid cares and low desires—to interweave the daily drudgery of life with the countless graces of literature, and the glowing web of fancy—to clothe the lessons of duty and of prudence in the most instructive as well as the most inviting forms—to throw open to eyes, dulled and bleared with the irksome monotony of their daily task-work, the rich resources and the boundless prodigality of nature—to dignify the present with the lessons of the past and the visions of the future—to make the artizans of our crowded workshops and the inmates of our most sequestered villages alive to all that is going on in the big universe around them—and, amidst all the startling and repelling inequalities of our various conditions, to put all upon a level in the equal domain of intellect and of genius; if these objects, and they are neither slight nor trivial—if these objects are worthy of acceptance and approval, I think they can be satisfactorily attained by the means which mechanics' institutions place at our disposal, and it is upon grounds such as these that I urge you to tender to them your encouragement and support.

His lordship mentioned that the London School of Design has consented to give elementary drawing books to all mechanics' institutes which may choose to enter into the proper arrangements for obtaining them, and that drawing is taught in 27 institutes to 682 pupils.

In concluding, the speaker said,—There is hardly a country, hardly a community, which is not disastrously suffering from the evils of the revolutionary wars which are now going on. Look at the condition of Europe at this moment—the Russians on the Danube, the French on the Tiber—why, it would really seem as if the nations of Europe, in some species of wild bacchanal, were seizing the torches of civil discord and foreign war, and throwing them in furious glee from frontier to frontier, river to river, rampart to rampart,—scaring the homes of peace and the haunts of industry with uncouth dissonance and hideous glare. While such are the appalling sights and sounds of which we catch the reflection and the echoes here, let us in Yorkshire,—let us in England,—while we in our accustomed occupations move on in our allotted spheres in the broad and equal light of freedom, let it be our care to light the genial lamp of knowledge, and to transmit it from hand to hand, from institution to institution, from wold to plain, from college to college, from the workshop to the cottage, through every portion of our land, till there shall be no haunt of human revelry unrebuked, till there shall be no abode of ignorance unenlightened, till there shall be no haunt of peaceful industry uncheered.

The Dean of Ripon mentioned three individuals who had recently gone out of the Ripon Institution:—One of them, a common bricklayer, came to seek for instruction and the advantages to be derived from the school in that place. He is now a person of considerable comfort and station in Australia, and he subscribed 5*l.*, said the dean, for our new building, and states that he owes all that he has from having had an opportunity of entering our Mechanics' Institute. Another man came in, whose abilities became quickened, his ambition turned, and his full purpose of mind excited. He is now in most comfortable circumstances in Sweden, and writes continually with a bosom full of gratitude for the benefits he received. Another individual who came into the institution first got education himself; then he became a teacher; afterwards he put himself forward, until he was made master. He is now an engineer in a most important situation, and rising rapidly in the comforts of life. I may just add, continued the rev. gentleman, two other cases, which I think were exceeding good: they were two poor "navvies," who came to the institution, after working fourteen hours in wheeling and labouring at a railway, to learn to read, write, and to cypher. These men, at the conclusion of the railway work, came to the institution, thanked the secretary for the knowledge they had acquired, and for what was of more value to them,—the habits of sobriety, temperance, and retirement, apart from the evil ways of their companions. They were both going to America, and came to take their leave. One had saved 80*l.*, and the other 100*l.* These are the practical every-day events, which I believe are taking place in the bosoms of our institutions.

And then chimed in Mr. Baines, and said,—It is not poverty that is vulgar. Poverty may be most honourable and most highly to be respected. But it is ignorance that is vulgar,—it is vice that is vulgar. It is the habits of a low, sensual, and degrading kind, which are vulgar. These are things which, if a man carries with him from a lower station to a higher, will make him vulgar in spite of all the dignity his position may give him. Our object is very unambitious. We have to labour by most homely means, and to labour in a very elementary way upon the very humblest classes, and there it is that we do our good.

* The total number of Mechanics' Institutions, as comprised within the Yorkshire Union, amounts to 94, and the aggregate number of members thus united is 16,728. Within the period of this last year there has been an addition of five institutes and of 1,623 members to the ranks of the institution.

NORTHAMPTON CORN-EXCHANGE COMPETITION.

Many of your readers will doubtless be glad to know how this affair is progressing. Between fifty and sixty very elaborate designs have been sent in, the mere cost of which, wholly irrespective of the labour of each individual competitor, cannot have fallen far short of a thousand pounds, or one-eighth of the actual sum required to erect the building,—so that there is, I think, a strong case for assuming, as a friend of mine did the other day, that, take them on the whole, architects are a very wealthy, public-spirited body of men. Henceforth, Sir, let us hear no more of *poor* architects, since this is the every-day style in which we respond to advertisements for competitions; and, in fact, you may say, why should we trouble you with our individual complaints of the mode in which competitions are conducted and decided, since it is evident, from our torpidity as a body, that we are extremely well satisfied with the system?

In the present case I understand the committee have selected three designs, one of which they propose to adopt. The rest may be seen, not hung up (for even simplicity's sake), but laid out flat upon tables, one drawing upon another, or, as the case may be, one design upon another; so I leave you, Sir, to judge what must have been the expertness, discernment, and not merely mental but downright manual exertion of these gentlemen, to have thoroughly examined in so short a time (for their meetings are few and far between), this vast and cumbersome stratified surface of architectural drawing.

> They'll settle the mystery *sine timore*,
> And (as we *must* all suppose) *sine favore*;
> But *both* things they'll never do, *sine sudore*.

But to be serious (and it is indeed a serious matter): How was it possible thus to do justice to the very many competitors, some of whom I know to be eminent men?

I write to The Builder because this affair is still undecided; and your journal will be again published ere the next meeting of the committee can take place. I do not at all assume that these gentlemen would knowingly act unjustly in this matter; the blame, in fact, lies at our own doors; for architects, and they alone, have the power to remedy this state of things. I must add, that although the Committee have thought themselves competent to select the three best designs out of the fifty or sixty, and have ascertained the names of their respective authors, they are completely at fault as to which one of these few to choose; and they have therefore called in a F.R.S. from London to decide which is the best of all the three. Whoever this gentleman may be, his being called in at all speaks well, I think, for the good intentions of the committee; and I entertain a hope that he will explain to them that if they really desire their project to be benefited by his professional experience and ability, they will at once take his opinion, not merely of these *three* designs, which, by the by, they will not admit any competitors to inspect, but of the entire fifty or sixty submitted.

By publishing these particulars the adjudication of this competition will become more or less what that of all public architectural competitions ought to be, a public transaction, open to the face of day; and I am convinced that the more they are made so the better it will be, not for architects merely, but for our public buildings, and still more especially the interests of those most mysterious, invisible, and much-abused gentlemen, the architectural competition committees.—I am, &c.,

W. Y.

The Royal Academy of Fine Arts at Berlin have elected Mr. Donaldson an honorary and foreign member of that body.

LORD LOVELACE'S COLLAR ROOF.

INSTITUTION OF CIVIL ENGINEERS.

AT the meeting on Tuesday, June 12, Mr. J. Field, President, in the chair, " A description of the construction of a collar roof, with arched trusses of bent timber, at East Horseley Park," by the Earl of Lovelace, was read.

The roof, which covered a hall of 56 feet long by 24 feet wide, was described as being sustained by four arched trusses, springing from stone corbels. The ribs of these were each composed of four layers of deals, 3 inches thick, bent to the required form by steam heat. All the mouldings surrounding the tracery were also bent to the required forms in the same manner, thus giving, as was thought, great strength and lightness, as well as performing the work with greater economy of labour. The tracery was cut out from two thicknesses, half-an-inch each, of tub-stave oak, glued together, with the fibres at right angles to each other, which facilitated the carving, and gave greater strength to the minute tracery.

The ceiling was formed of half-inch diagonal boarding, and as the slate battens crossed it in a horizontal direction, the roof was strongly braced against the action of wind, and the staining of the alternate boards gave a pleasing variety of effect.

This kind of construction was first suggested by Colonel Emy, in his work on Carpentry, but he had applied it to much flatter roofs of large span, whereas Lord Lovelace's intention was to demonstrate its applicability to roofs for edifices in the Pointed and Tudor styles, and to show that great advantage would result from bending timbers rather than cutting them to the requisite forms; that the thrust of the roof might be entirely taken from the upper part of the walls, and carried far down them, and that such a construction might be adopted as would satisfy every condition of solidity, and, at the same time, admit of considerable decoration.

THE DOVER BREAKWATER.

THE formation of the breakwater at Dover appears to be proceeding satisfactorily. It commences near the look-out house, and will run out into the sea, in cants about 800 feet, so as to form a harbour. A length of about 270 feet is done, and about 100 feet more will be added this season : the progress is regulated by the amount of money voted.

The outer faces of the breakwater are of Yorkshire stones (Bramleigh Fall), backed up with a course or two of Portland stone. The stones are very large, measuring above 80 feet cube in each. The space between the two walls is filled in solid with concrete. Large blocks of concrete are prepared (hard and dry), ready to use as they get out more into the sea, and two diving-bells are in daily use by the workmen. There is a steam-crane to take the stone out of the ships, and the mills to grind lime for concrete, and brick-earth burnt for mortar, are worked by steam power. There is a large quantity of stone ready for setting.

The work appears to be well and carefully done, and is creditable to the contractors, Messrs. Lee, of Chiswell-street. Mr. Walker is the engineer.

BREAKWATERS AND LANDING PLACES. —We have lately inspected models of some inventions connected with landing-places, which seem to deserve the inspection of those whose attention is directed to such matters. They consist of a floating pier and buoys, double action yielding moorings, also an attached self-adjusting tidal ladder, constructed on a new principle, and which seems well suited for the purposes intended. The inventor has also constructed a life-boat and travelling crane, for the preservation of life from stranded vessels : this is attached to his floating pier,—which, from its construction, he considers will be enabled, at all times, and in all weathers, to maintain its position. The name of the inventor is Savage. A floating bath and breakwater, a floating light, and a plan for extinguishing fires on board ships, by the provision of a series of perforated pipes under the decks, bear further testimony to his ingenuity and skill.

MULTIPLICATION OF THE CUBE.

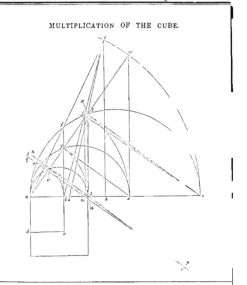

THE attention of the writer was directed to this subject by the following passage, in the *Mechanic's Magazine*, for the 7th of last October, page 355 :—" At this time Mr. Mackie, a Roman Catholic priest, published a duplication of the cube, the plausibility of which attracted attention, and, it is said, even obtained the assent of the teachers of Maynooth. Young Murphy, then eighteen years of age, answered this duplication in a pamphlet, entitled " Refutation of a pamphlet, written by the Rev. John Mackie, R.C.P., entitled ' A method of making a cube double of a cube on the principle of elementary geometry,' wherein his principles are proved erroneous, and the required solution not yet obtained." By Robert Murphy, Mallow, 1824, (20 pp.)

Let *abcd* be equal to one of the sides of the cube to be multiplied. Make the line *ae* as many times greater than the line *ab* as the required cube is to be greater than the given one ; *ab* is the linear unit, *abcd* the square unit.

Upon *ae* describe the semicircle *aef*, draw *bf* at right angles to *ae*, with radius *ae* describe the arc *eg*, through the point *f* draw *ag*, draw *gh* parallel to *fb*, bisect the angle *agh* by the line *ig*, from the unit point *b* draw *bg*, from the points of intersection *j* and *k* draw *jm*, and *ki* parallel to *fb*, draw *ke* and *je*, draw *no* and *pq* respectively parallel to *ke* and *je*, with *ab* for a radius describe the arc *br*, from the point of intersection *s* draw *st* tangential to the arc *br* ; the square described upon *au* is equal to one of the sides of the required cube.

Demonstration. Upon *au* describe the semi-circle *auv*, cutting the tangent *uv* and the arc *rb* in their common point *v*, through *v* draw *aw*, draw *uz* at right angles to *ae*, and complete the figure.

The apex *x* of the triangle *aez* in one particular case, will coincide with the points *j* and *k* ; in all other cases, it must lie between them ; the angles *jek* and *qsn* (formed by corresponding parallel lines) are equal, and are similarly divided by the parallel lines *ze* and *vs* (the last by the construction at right angles to the unit radius *ae*); the right-angled triangle *auv* inscribed in its semi-circle is equal to the right-angled triangle *aby*, and the hypothenuse *au* is equal to the hypothenuse *ay* ;

the right-angled triangle *awx* is equal to the triangle *aez* inscribed in its semi-circle, and the side *az* is equal to the side *ax*.

By similar triangles,

$$av = 1 : ay = au : : au : ax = az = au^u$$
$$av = 1 : az = au^2 : : au : ae = au^3$$

Numerals. Cubes.
$$ab = 1$$
$$ab^2 \qquad = 1^3$$
$$ae = au^3 = ae \times 1^3$$

The cube represented by the numeral au^3 as many times greater than the cube denoted by ab^3 as the line ae is greater than the line ab.

$$bz = ax - 1 : by :: by : ab = 1 . by = \sqrt{ax -}$$
$$ab = 1 : by = \sqrt{ux - 1} :: au =$$
$$\sqrt{au} : uz = xy = \sqrt{ax} . \sqrt{ax - 1} .$$
$$ay = \sqrt{ax} .$$
$$xy^4 + ay^x = az^x - ax + ax$$

Squares described upon *xy* and *ay* are together equal to the square described upon the hypothenuse *ax*. J. P. W.

⁎ The above is to be regarded merely an approximation, our correspondent's demonstration being incomplete.—ED.

METROPOLITAN COMMISSION OF SEWERS.

A GENERAL court was held on Thursday, the 7 instant, at the Sewers Court, Greek-street ; t Earl of Carlisle in the chair.

The Sewage Manure of the Metropolis.—A r port was read from Mr. Donaldson, assistant-su veyor, on recent experiments made by him wi sewage manure at Brentford, Hanwell, &c., as with very satisfactory results. The operations ho been conducted by the use of the hose and jet. T average quantity supplied was 110 tons per acr the time occupied being one hour and five minut per acre, and the cost 1s. 8d., exclusive of its co veyance. In reference to this repo.t, a reco mendation was received from the Sewage Manu Committee that advertisements be issued, invitir offers from the owners and occupiers of land at moderate distance from town to take the sewag the supply to be at the rate of eighteen irrigatio per annum of 250 tons each, and stating that th metropolitan districts would yield sewage matte equal to the irrigation of 150,000 acres.

Mr. Chadwick rose to move the adoption of th recommendation, and in doing so, remarked o the important results arrived at by the use o sewage manure in Edinburgh, in Milan, and the whole of Belgium; and hoped they were now in a condition to bring those advantages nearer home, not only in converting the sewage to the use of lands near to the metropolis, but to offer it to farmers, on very low terms. The results showed, by the use of the manure they obtained double the quantity of grass, and from other results they were fully satisfied that through its use the metropolis might be amply supplied with grass-fed lamb, at least one month earlier than heretofore. In confirmation of this statement, Mr. Chadwick read an extract from a letter received from Mr. Roe, the former surveyor to this commission, which stated that by the use of liquid manure, he was last year enabled to cut five crops of grass, leaving besides a good feed, and that this year he expected to cut seven crops, worth to cowkeepers from 6*l.* to 7*l.* per acre each crop. He might mention Edinburgh as an example of the productiveness of sewage waters, and also the waters of Milan. Experiments of a most important nature had been made, not noticed in Mr. Donaldson's last report, as it was of the first consequence to surmount the difficulty of the removal of the manure, and the cost of its conveyance. By Mr. Donaldson's plan, the top dressing of an acre of land would cost but 1s. 8d., while the usual expense was 1*l.* 7s.

The Earl of Carlisle—Does that include the cost of the article?

Mr. Chadwick said that was only the cost of the delivery, but it was an established fact that they should be able to supply it at one-sixth its former amount, or to give six times the number of doses for the same charge, and the labour of an acre could be performed by a man and a boy in about forty-five minutes, and in the course of half an hour no person could distinguish in walking over the land that anything had taken place. This was an immense gain, as it did away with the question of its offensiveness, and removed the objection in a sanitary point of view to the use of this manure. With these advantages, it might be asked, why not advance the state of the land in the vicinity of the metropolis? Mr. Donaldson had stated that on all the lands irrigated he found the crops look better, except on the undrained lands, of which there was a great deal in the vicinity of London, of pestilential marshes in almost their primitive condition. The consumption of this manure would not be impeded by a distance of twenty or thirty miles, provided large quantities were used, for beyond the metropolis, in the sandy lands it might be used with advantage, and a strong manure obtained for about 2s. per acre. There had, unfortunately, been great obstacles to their proceedings in various ways, and necessarily a corresponding delay in their operations; but great works were now in progress, and with the most promising results. A committee had been formed, consisting of Sir John Burgoyne, Sir H. de la Beche, Captain Dawson, and Captain Veitch, of the Royal Engineers, who were considering the best means available of getting rid of the pollution of the Thames, and were seconded in their labours by the Sewage Manure Committee. He hoped, therefore, on the completion of the survey, they should be enabled to distribute the sewage that at present flowed into it at a distance of 20 or 30 miles from the metropolis. There were many persons who could not see what relation these measures, or agricultural land drainage, had to do with the sewerage of the urban districts; but he contended that the health of the metropolis was mainly dependent on the external operations. There were other questions under consideration, and amongst them a plan for intercepting the sewage, and conveying it to an immense reservoir at the Isle of Dogs; and as to how they could get by the docks;—all subjects of considerable importance. However, the whole question would be examined, and fully reported upon by the officers and engineers of the commission. He concluded by moving the adoption of the recommendation of the Sewage Manure Committee.

Mr. C. Johnson seconded the motion, and said that the grand object in the interception of the sewage of the metropolis was, that there was sufficient of it poured into the Thames to irrigate 1,000 acres of land daily, allowing at the rate of 250 tons per acre; which would yield a great return of revenue for any expenses incurred. They must, however, look forward to the day when they could remove this sewage to a greater distance from London than they were now justified in announcing, and this might be done without putting the public to any expense. There were large breadths of land in Sussex, on the banks of the Crouch in Essex, and in Hertfordshire, where it might be used with the most advantageous results. They proposed to carry it through open or closed pipes, according to the facilities given. At present all sewage was carried through closed pipes.

Mr. Chadwick remarked, that having taken the average drainage of 1,000 houses for sixteen hours, they found that, with an ordinary flow, *the whole of the sewage of the metropolis could be passed through a three-feet pipe.*

Mr. Slaney felt the deepest interest in the question, and had the greatest respect for the opinions of his friend Mr. Chadwick; but thought that it was extremely desirable, for sake of the success of their endeavours, that the advantages should not be placed in too broad or too favourable a point of view. He had no objection to the form proposed, and that they should receive tenders for the sewage, but that it would not be wise to go to large expenses until they were well assured of the success of their experiments. The statement that had been made by Mr. Chadwick, and supported by Mr. Johnson, would go before the public, and no doubt its merits would be well sifted and tested, and then, if satisfied with the practicability of the plan, it would be taken up by enterprising individuals, not alone in the metropolis, but in many provincial towns, whose situation for its use was much better than the lands near to London. In the high lands particularly it would be of great value. It appeared that 18,000 acres of land could be manured with 250 tons per acre, and taking this to increase its value but 10s. per acre, at 6 per cent., it would then yield an annual increase of 200,000*l.*, and therefore he believed that numerous parties would be found willing to come forward, and by themselves carry out these important results and advantages.

Lord Ebrington was as desirous as Mr. Slaney to understate, rather than otherwise, the advantages to be derived, but must altogether demur to the estimate of 10s. per acre as the increased value from this irrigation. He was cognizant of a fact that, in Devonshire, a clear stream of water merely being passed through a track of land, increased its value from 2*l.* to 3*l.* per acre; but to give but 10s. per acre as the increased value from sewage manure was quite out of the question. He would mention that the Duke of Portland had converted land worth not more than 7s. per acre into water meadows, by means of the sewage received from the town of Mansfield, which was not very strong, and its value had been increased to 14*l.* per acre. In Edinburgh, too, the value had been raised from 5s. to 25*l.* per acre. Such being the case, he believed the calculations of Mr. Johnson were not overstated in giving the increased value at 10*l.* to 12*l.* per acre. He found that water could be conveyed 5 miles at 2½d. per tun, and therefore the charge of conveying fresh water to towns need hardly differ from the cost of conveying the dirty water back. Pure water was not more necessary in towns than the fertilizing fluid was to the farmers for the purposes of vegetation.

Dr. Southwood Smith said as to the operation of the fluid in a sanitary point of view, he found that the deodorising fluid entirely destroyed the offensiveness of the manure, increasing at the same time its value to the land. He had himself tried experiments upon two acres of land, and had used a great deal of the most offensive manure, but by applying deodorisers, in half an hour not the slightest odour was perceptible. He used nitrate of lead, which was very cheap.

The motion was put and unanimously agreed to.

Amendment of the Sewers Act.—A recommendation was received from the Works' Committee, "To consider as to representing to her Majesty's Government the necessity of applying to Parliament for amended powers."

Mr. Bullar, in support of this recommendation, said the cleansing operations in one district were brought to a complete stand. By the decision of Mr. Burrell, under the provisions of the Police Act, they were prevented from cleansing cesspools in the day time, and in their endeavours to conform to this decision by cleansing them at night, they were met with a fresh difficulty, the Chelsea Water Company then refusing to supply them with water; so that they were prevented from doing the work either by night or by day.—This subject led to a short conversation, and it was agreed that the heads of a Bill be drawn up by the Bye Laws Committee, and transmitted to her Majesty's Government for presentation to Parliament.

A resolution was passed that all fossils, coins, &c., found in the excavation of works under the commission, be the property of the commission.

THE NEW BUILDINGS' BILL.—Your remark last week was loudly called for. It is exceedingly desirable that the intended Buildings' Bill should be passed through Parliament without further delay. When we know that the amendments proposed occupied a commission, supposed to be well able from their practical experience to deal with them, several months, that this commission was appointed by the noble lord at the head of the Woods and Forests, there would seem to be little cause for delay, and I cannot but think that somewhere or other there must be apathy or inattention to the wishes of those interested in the amendment of the present inadequate piece of legislation. A. B.

Miscellanea.

PROJECTED WORKS.—Advertisements have been issued for tenders, by 19th inst., for the erection of baths and washhouses in Kent-street, Birmingham; by 25th, for certain repairs, and painting, whitewashing, &c., at St. Martin's workhouse; by 3rd July, for constructing a new sluice, and other works at Outwell; by 6th July, for relaying the carriage way, &c., of High-street and Spital-square; by 30th inst., for putting up new roof on Kirton in Lindsey parish church; by 25th, for the various works to be done in erecting the York county hospital; by 25th, for the erection of a granary and dwelling-house at Huntingdon; by 23rd, for alterations and additions at Peterborough union workhouse; and by 26th, for copper, gas-fittings, &c., lead, zinc, glass, nails, screws, and other stores, for the Lancashire and Yorkshire Railway.

CHURCH DECORATIONS.—At the last meeting of the Archæological Institute, held on the 1st inst., drawings of two ancient reredos, recently discovered during some alterations in the church of St. Cuthbert, at Wells, Somerset, as mentioned by us some time since, were presented, and detailed descriptions given. One reredos was found in "Tanner's Chauntry," and presents a series of nineteen gorgeously carved and gilded and elaborately groined canopied niches, some of which contained mutilated figures, with scroll and descriptions, such as are usually represented in the history of Jesse. The other is of a still more highly enriched character, and was found in the Lady Chapel: it has two rows of niches and pedestals, five in each row. Previously to these discoveries, a fine painting of the "Salvator Mundi" had been found on the walls of the chapel of the Holy Trinity in the same church. The Marquis of Northampton in some observations on the frequent discovery of the ancient decorations of our churches, mentioned to the meeting some wall frescoes (?) which, on removing some plaster in the church at Castle Ashby, he had found decorating the splay of one of the chancel windows. These were in outline, and bore no traces of having been coloured originally. The style of art was of about the date of the fifteenth century.

SOCIAL IMPROVEMENTS.—Under this head Mr. Charles Cochrane has published a sensible address on a broad-side, drawing attention to the Acts of Parliament which afford to the public a power to remedy most of the evils relating to bad drainage, overflowing cesspools, nuisances of every kind, offensive privies, filthy streets, courts, and alleys, expensive means of bathing and washing, impure and expensive water, fetid and expensive dwellings for the poor, the overcrowding of churchyards, &c., evils which tend to retard the social progress of the human race. In conclusion, he says wisely, "local meetings will prove of service; but care must be taken that the discussions are conducted free from any angry or personal feelings. A temperate, conciliatory, course is almost sure finally to win over the most prejudiced or the most obstinate. Above all things, never allow party or political questions to be obtruded on your meetings convened for social purposes."

RAILWAY JOTTINGS.—The first tube of the Britannia-bridge is to be floated on Tuesday, 19th inst., at an early hour, unless the weather induce a postponement till next morning.——The works of the Tunbridge Wells and Hastings Railway are now in active progress from Tunbridge Wells southwards, to near Ticehurst. Gangs of men are working night and day the heavy tunnels at Wadhurst and Strawberry-hill, which give employment to upwards of 1,000. Tunnel bricklayers seem much in request, getting high wages. Eight large brick-fields are in full operation.——A correspondent of the *Gateshead Observer* describes the railway bridge at Yarm as spanning the river Tees "by two oblique arches of 66 feet span each, built entirely of stone (and not a suspension bridge, as the *Herald* says.) There are at the north side of the river arches three land arches, and at the south side thirty-eight, making altogether forty-three arches. The land arches are 39 feet span. The height from low water to the rail is about 68 feet; and the average height of the land arches, from the surface of the ground to the rail, about 56 feet."

The High Level Bridge on the Tyne, at Newcastle, on the York and Berwick line of railway, will, it is expected, be opened with great ceremonial on 1st August. The key of the last arch was driven home on Thursday week, by the Mayor of Gateshead, Mr. Hawks, of Hawks, Crawshay, and Co., the contractors for the ironwork. His worship stripped for the occasion, and in a business-like manner, as became a captain of industry, with a rosewood handled brass-headed hammer, struck the last few blows that united this great work from end to end. The first pile, according to the *Gateshead Observer*, was driven on 24th April, 1846, in presence of its designer, Mr. R. Stephenson, M.P.; and the first segment of the first arch was placed so lately as 10th July last. The iron work rising to a height of 120 feet above the bed of the river, much caution was called for, and from the careful and expensive arrangements therefore made, there has been neither loss of life nor limb in the fixing of the six massive arches, many of the castings of which weighed from 10 to 12 tons each. The cost of the bridge when completed is estimated to be 243,096*l*.; the viaduct through Gateshead and Newcastle, 113,057*l*.; land, compensation, &c., 135,000*l*.; total 491,153*l*. Large as this sum is, however, it is only half the amount that rumour assigned as the cost of the bridge alone.

A Tread-wheeled Coach.—We have already had schemes for the complete inversion of the railway system, with wheels on the sideway and rails on the train,—so that no one need now be surprised to hear of an inversion of the old jog-trot highway system, with the horses *riding* in the coach, and the passengers hanging on by the wheel. Such is literally the fact alleged to have been recently realized in Ohio, U. S., where a single broad wooden wheel or roller, 14 feet in diameter, and 6 feet in breadth, has been fitted up with tread-boards for the horses within, and an axle whence seats are suspended for 24 passengers. Iron stays stretch from each axle upwards, and meet above in a seat for the driver, who, it would appear, can turn about and wheel about as quick as Jim Crow, or at least much quicker than a coach and six. We should prefer seeing it running straight on up-hill, however. Two heavy draught horses, it is said, can easily bowl along two dozen passengers (on a level, we presume), at the rate of one dozen miles per hour, and win easy too, their work on the tread-mill being mere amusement.

Mural Paintings at St. Cross.—Coloured drawings of these paintings, recently discovered on the walls of the Church of St. Cross, were exhibited by Mr. Francis Baigent, at a recent meeting of the Archæological Association. Some are exceedingly elegant in design, and apparently of the early part of the fifteenth century. Mr. Baigent was stopt in his efforts to obtain complete sketches, as the Earl of Guildford ordered the walls to be immediately re-whitewashed, as already mentioned.

Royal College of Chemistry.—It seems but yesterday since we had the plan and elevation of this new college in The Builder, as a novelty not yet realized, and now we have before us a goodly volume of the "Researches conducted in the Laboratories,"* with an able 'Introduction' and 'Remarks,' by Professor Hofmann, their presiding genius. The institution is now in a flourishing state, free of debt, and already nearly independent. The lecture theatre, however, of the original design (cost 1,800*l*.) is much wanted, together with some further temporary assistance, which we hope will not be denied to so thriving and hopeful a germ of future scientific greatness. We are pleased to observe amongst the items of chemical advancement within the last year or two, enumerated in Professor Hofmann's introduction, one in the reception and establishment of which The Builder may justly claim some little credit, namely—"the happy substitution of the stable and innocuous oxide of zinc, as a pigment, for white lead, which is so easily injured, and so frequently gives rise to serious diseases."

* "Reports of the Royal College of Chemistry, and Researches conducted in its Laboratories, in the years 1845-6-7; London, 1849."

The Iron Trade.—On the only few occasions on which we have felt inclined to put the slightest trust in quarterly meetings, namely, on a recent show of onerous motive in the raising of wages along with prices, our partial confidence has very speedily proved to be misplaced. The present state of the trade is thus announced by the *Birmingham Gazette*,—one of the staunchest upholders of the masters' interests:—"The depression in every branch of this trade still continues, nor has the declared reduction of 20s. in price been followed by the slightest revival of demand. On the contrary, it seems to have had a prejudicial effect; and, combined with *the astounding disclosures that sales of manufactured iron had been previously made from 20s. to 30s. below the nominal rates*, and that good mine pigs were in the market under 3*l*. per ton, has done much to impair general confidence, and to prostrate any expectation of an early revival of business. The workmen, as was expected, have quietly acceded to the proposed reduction in their wages."

The Buckingham Estates in Ireland.—A renewed attempt was lately made to sell these estates by auction. They are situated in Westmeath, and consist of 4,270 acres of land, with 121 labourers' and other houses, mills, &c., producing in all a rental of 2,300*l*. a-year. The whole was divided into four lots, for the first of which—653 acres of 'very excellent' land, with fourteen houses, rental in all 430*l*. a-year,—6,100*l*. had been previously offered and refused. The only offers now made were 4,500*l*. and 5,000*l*., by one bidder—also refused. For the next two lots,—one of 1,279 acres 'of a very superior quality,' with 23 houses, and a corn-mill, rental 579*l*. a-year, upset price 7,000*l*.; and the other of 1,001 acres, 'average quality,' with thirty-nine houses, rental 526*l*.—upset price 4,000*l*.—there were no bidders. Lot No. 4 contained 1,338 acres, a moiety of 'the most superior quality,' with forty-five houses, and a 'well-paid rental' of 766*l*. 17s. a-year. For this lot 11,000*l*. were previously offered and refused. The previous bidder, Mr. Gibbings, now offered 9,000*l*. for this lot, but it also was bought in, as were all a second and third time without further offer. The sale was then adjourned *sine die*.

Exemption of Literary and Scientific Societies from Local Rates, &c.—A meeting on this subject, consisting of delegates from a large number of these societies, was held at the City of London Literary and Scientific Institution, on Wednesday, the 6th instant; Mr. W. Brown, M.P., in the chair. The report of a committee appointed at a former meeting was read, setting forth the difficulties and injustice which attend the administration of the present Act; and stating, that a measure had been prepared, which, providing for the annual issue of a certificate of exemption, founded on an annual return, and simplifying the legal procedure in cases of litigation, would, it was believed, secure to these institutions the immunity intended to be conferred by the 6 and 7 Vict., c. 36. It appeared, that influential deputations had waited on Sir George Grey and Lord John Russell, and that the Government had promised to give immediate attention to the subject. The meeting was addressed by Lord Wriothesly, Mr. Wyld, M.P., Mr. Lacey, M.P., Mr. Birkbeck, Mr. Toulmin Smith, and other gentlemen; and it was determined to take active means to secure an efficient Bill.

Dartmouth Park.—Lord Dartmouth, under the directions of his agents, Messrs. Pearce and Thynne, has laid out a large area of land at the Forest Hill station of the Croydon and Epsom Railway (close to Sydenham), as a park, with the view of inducing the erection of villas, and builders have already commenced operations. Several thousands of trees and evergreens have been planted, and a site has been appropriated for a church, much needed in the neighbourhood. The beauty of the locality, its reputed healthiness, and close proximity to London, are strong claims in favour of this new "settlement."

Bracknell Church Competition.—Fifty-one designs were sent in, from which three were at first chosen. Ultimately the committee decided upon one by Messrs. Coe and Goodwin.

Competition.—Plans and specifications are wanted for the widening and improvement of Bristol bridge; premium 25*l*., as advertised.

Artificial Mahogany.—The following method of giving any species of wood of a close grain the appearance of mahogany in texture, density, and polish, is said to be practised in France with success. The surface is planed smooth, and the wood is then rubbed with a solution of nitrous acid; 1 oz. of dragon's blood is dissolved in nearly a pint of spirits of wine; this, and one-third of an ounce of carbonate of soda, are then to be mixed together, and filtered, and the liquid in this thin state is to be laid on with a soft brush. This process is to be repeated, and in a short interval afterwards the wood possesses the external appearance of mahogany. When the polish diminishes in brilliancy, it may be restored by the use of a little cold-drawn linseed oil.

Incised Inscriptions.—Mr. J. Williams, an ingenious stone carver, of Ipswich, has submitted to us some specimens of a mode of inscribing stone which seems entitled to encouragement. The letters are incised and filled in with a composition (either black, or coloured for the capitals, as the case may be), and the whole face may then be either varnished or not. He has put up several Tables of Commandments in this way, and says he can execute them as cheaply as a competent painter could write them. The mode would seem to be applicable to other matters.

The Valley and City of Kashmir.—The view of the Valley of Kashmir, painted by Mr. Burford, and now exhibiting at his establishment in Leicester-square, is a very successful and interesting work, the merit of which, as of other paintings by Mr. Burford, is not sufficiently appreciated by the public although they visit them. The rapidity with which, assisted by Mr. Selous, he produces what are in reality well-finished oil paintings, full of nature, is quite marvellous.

The old Market-house, Berkhempstead.—A correspondent is anxious to draw attention to the old market-house at Berkhempstead, in order, if possible, to induce its repair, before it finally falls to the ground. It is one of those quaint timber erections of the Tudor age which are so picturesque, and which we do not desire to lose. A few well-timed repairs to the roof and posts which carry the building, and form a covered-way, may supersede the necessity of erecting a new one, and at present it accords well with the Grammar School.

Labourers' Cottages Prize Essay.—We understand that the Council of the Royal Agricultural Society of England have awarded the society's prize of 50*l*. "For the best Essay on the Construction of Labourers' Cottages" to Mr. Henry Goddard, architect, of Lincoln.

An Architectural Society at Chester has been formed, combining archæology and history. The Marquis of Westminster, lord lieutenant of Cheshire, the bishop of the diocese, and other influential persons have joined it.

TENDERS

For building Chapel and Schools in the Bethnal-green-road, for the Rev. J. Viney and others. Quantities furnished; Mr. Tarring, Architect.

Little and Son	£7,440
Ward	6,173
Holland	5,970
Curtis	5,953
Higgs and Son	5,896
Ashby	5,733
Wood	5,640
Grimsdell	5,612
Haynes and Co	5,537
Myers (accepted)	5,489

For House in Red Lion-street, Whitechapel, for Mrs. White; Mr. F. R. Beeston, Architect.

Wilkinson	£1,453
Rider	1,384
Saunders and Woolcott	1,348
Grimsdell	1,289
Wilson	1,275
Rivets	1,195
W. Hill	1,093

For Messrs. Charrington, for Clerk's Dwelling, Principal's Dwelling, Boundary Walls, Drains, &c.; Mr. A. R. Mason, Architect.

Trego	£3,545
Pritchett	3,471
Wilson	3,271
Jay	3,072
Ashby	3,002
Holland	2,990
Locke and Nesham	2,953
Lawrence	2,897
Piper	2,889
Grimsdell	2,829
Curtis	2,695
W. Hill (accepted)	2,598

[Sad work. Comments seem useless.]

MEETINGS OF SCIENTIFIC BODIES

Held during the ensuing week.

MONDAY, June 18th.—Institute of Architects, 8 P.M.
TUESDAY, 19.—Institution of Civil Engineers, 8 P.M.
THURSDAY, 21.— Royal Society, 8½ P.M.; Society of Antiquaries, 8 P.M.
FRIDAY, 22.—Archæological Association.

TO CORRESPONDENTS.

"*Contract for Tooting Parsonage.*"—"I beg to inform you that my tender was accepted, and I am now progressing with the works.—EDW. GARTER."

Received.—"G. H. W.," "Messrs. W. and B." (Berlin), "T. B.," "J. F. C.," "Mons. A. L." (shall hear from us), "E. C." (notice was in type), "W. H." (some of the best published examples of Elizabethan chimney-pieces are in previous volumes of THE BUILDER) "H. B.," Dublin (nitrate of lead is recommended), "J. B. R.," "T. H.," Leeds (it is against our practice to give praise on hearsay), "Pioneer," "J. J.," "Square" (look in any "arithmetic"), "W. A. L.," "An Architect," "M. P." "A Treatise on the Theory and Practice of Landscape Gardening, with a view to improvement of Country Residences." By A. J. Downing. (London, 1849. Longman). "Gas Lighting; its progress and prospects." By J. O. N. Rutter. (J. W. Parker, London, 1849). "Veritas," a poem. (Longman, 1849).

"*Books, Prices, and Addresses.*"—We have not time to point out books or find addresses.

ADVERTISEMENTS.

BRITISH MUTUAL LIFE OFFICE.—The Public are invited to examine for themselves the advantages gained for Assurers by the plan on which policies are granted by this Office.—Apply to CHARLES JAMES THICKE, Secretary, 17, New Bridge-street, Blackfriars.

ARCHITECTS', BUILDERS', and GENERAL FIRE and LIFE INSURANCE COMPANY, 69, Lombard-street, London.

CHAIRMAN, SYDNEY SMIRKE, Esq., A.R.A.
TRUSTEES.
T. L. Donaldson, Esq. | A. Salvin, Esq., F.S.A.
S. Grimsdell, Esq. | G. Smith, Esq., F.S.A.

The rates for both Fire and Life Insurances are as low as can with safety be taken. Those for Life Insurance may be paid either yearly, half-yearly, or quarterly; one-half the annual premium may be left unpaid for seven years, or one-third to the end of life. Thus large sums may be insured at the smallest present outlay.
Prospectuses, forms of proposals, &c., may be had at the Office 69, Lombard-street, or of the agents.
JOHN REDDISH, Manager.

LONDON ASSURANCE CORPORATION, established by Royal Charter in the Reign of King George the First, for LIFE, FIRE, and MARINE INSURANCES.
Offices:—7, ROYAL EXCHANGE, CORNHILL, and 10, REGENT-STREET.
The expenses of managing the Life Department are defrayed by the Corporation, and not taken from the Premium Fund.
Profits are added as a bonus to Policies, or paid in cash, or applied in abatement of the Annual Premiums.
The assured are exempt from all liability of partnership.
A low fixed rate without participation in profits.
Parties proceeding out of the limits of Europe are liberally treated.
FIRE INSURANCE on every description of property at moderate rates, and MARINE INSURANCE at the current premiums.
Prospectuses free on personal or written application.
JOHN LAURENCE, Secretary.

DESIGNS for FURNITURE, MANUFACTURES, SHOP FRONTS, EMBELLISHMENTS, &c., are prepared by and under the superintendence of Mr. DWYER.—Devisors' Offices, 17, Poland-street, London.

WRIGHT'S PLASTER OF PARIS.—Builders and Others are respectfully invited to make trial of this well-known plaster, as manufactured by the original maker and of improved quality. This firm has no connection with any other, and the only manufactory of Wright's Plaster is at the old established Works, 3, Upper Ground-street, Blackfriars.
N.B. Very superior Roman Cement.

FLEXIBLE INDIA-RUBBER PIPES AND TUBING. For Railway Companies, Brewers, Distillers, Fire Engines, Gas Companies, Gardening and Agricultural Purposes, &c.—J. L. HANCOCK'S patent VULCANIZED INDIA-RUBBER HOSE-PIPES are made to stand hot liquor, and acids without injury—do not become hard or stiff in any temperature (but are always perfectly flexible) and as they require no application of oil or dressing, are particularly well adapted for Fire Engines, Pumps, Gas, Beer Engines, Gardens, Liquid Manure, and all purposes where a perfectly flexible pipe is required. Made all sizes, from ¼ inch bore upwards, and of any length to order. Vulcanized India rubber garden hose fitted with brass-taps, copper branch and roses complete, ready to be attached to pumps, water-butts, or cisterns. Sole manufacturer, JAMES LYNE HANCOCK, Goswell-mews, Goswell-road, London.
JAS. LYNE HANCOCK invites the attention of parties using long lengths of FLEXIBLE GARDEN HOSE to his SELF-ACTING HOSE-PIPE REEL, which will be found a most convenient machine for readily winding up and conveying away the hose when out of use. By it also liquid manure is easily distributed from tanks.
N.B. Vulcanized India-rubber washers of all sizes for joints or hot-water and steam pipes, and Vulcanized sheet rubber any thickness for all kinds of joints, and other purposes.

DAMP and GASEOUS EXHALATIONS.
SANITARY MEASURES.
MEMBERS of BOARDS of HEALTH are especially directed to the most EFFECTIVE MEANS which they can adopt to prevent the injurious and often FATAL EFFECTS upon the HEALTH of the COMMUNITY, arising from exhalations that are produced from moisture, decayed animal matter (as in grave-yards), stagnant water, and collections of fœtid refuse, tending to produce a miasmatic state of atmosphere. In situations so affected, the impervious quality of the ASPHALTE of SEYSSEL renders it the most perfect PAVEMENT or COVERING that can be relied upon for hermetically closing, and thereby preventing, the rising of moisture and the escape of noxious Vapours. The present extensive application of this material for covering roofs, terraces, and arches, for preventing the percolation of wet, is strong evidence of its effectiveness for the above purposes, which is further confirmed by the following extract from the Report of the COMMISSIONERS on the FINE ARTS.
L. FARRELL, Secretary.
Seyssel Asphalte Company, Stangate, London.
"In 1839, I superintended the construction of a house of three stories on the Lac d'Enghien. The foundation of the building is constantly in water, about 10½ inches below the level of the ground floor. The entire horizontal surface of the external and internal walls was covered at the level of the internal ground floor with a layer of SEYSSEL ASPHALTE,* less than half an inch thick, over which coarse sand was spread. Since the above date, no trace of damp has shown itself round the walls of the lower story, which are for the most part painted in oil, of a grey stone colour. It is well known that the least moisture produces round spots darker or lighter, on walls so painted. Yet the pavement of the floor, resting on the soil itself, is only about 2½ inches above the external surface of the soil, and only 10½ inches, at the utmost, above that of the sheet of water. The layer of Asphalte having been BROKEN AND REMOVED, for the purpose of inserting the sills of two doors, spots indicating the presence of damp have been since remarked at the base of the door-posts."
* This method has been adopted at the new Houses of Parliament.

ROYAL ARCH, DUNDEE.—A Design for this Building having been selected, the other Competition Plans are now ready to be returned to the gentlemen by whom they were sent in. Those wishing their designs forwarded by any particular conveyance, are requested to intimate accordingly, and to state their mottoes. The packages for London, Hull, or Leith, can be sent per traders, freight free, but at the risk of the competitors.—By order of the Committee,
Dundee, 12th June, 1849. THOMAS NEISH, Chairman.

CHEAP ORNAMENTAL GLASS.—I beg to inform my friends and the public, that I have now completed a new ENGINE, and, owing to the facility with which I can execute orders, I am enabled to reduce my former prices considerably. The prices are now from ONE SHILLING PER FOOT SUP., and borders from SIXPENCE PER FOOT RUN. A large quantity of the cheapest patterns always in stock. Embossing and painted work on the most moderate terms.—CHARLES LONG, No. 1, King-street, Baker-street, Portman-square.—Cash only.

E. and W. H. JACKSON beg to call the attention of Builders and the trade to the reduced prices of their PATENT PLATE GLASS, which, from its cheapness, is now superseding crown in all respectable dwelling-houses. BRITISH and ROUGH PLATE, CROWN, SHEET, STAINED, and ORNAMENTAL GLASS, supplied of the best manufacture, and at the lowest terms. List of prices, estimates, and every information can be had on application at their warehouse, 315, Oxford-street.

PATENT PLATE GLASS.—CLAUDET and HOUGHTON beg to announce to Architects, Builders, and the trade, a further very considerable reduction in their prices of PATENT PLATE, SHEET, and CROWN GLASS. Their new lists of prices are now ready and will be forwarded free on application.—Wholesale and Retail WINDOW GLASS and GLASS SHADE WAREHOUSE, 89, HIGH HOLBORN.

PLATE GLASS.—THOS. MILLINGTON begs to inform the trade that he has now ready for Sale, a large quantity of BRITISH PLATE GLASS, which he can offer at the following low prices:—In sizes, under 1 foot super, 1s. 2d.; under 1 ft. 6 in., 1s. 6d.; under 2 ft., 1s. 9d.; and under 3 ft., at 2s. per ft. super. Also, Roughed Plate, in various substances, from 1-8th in. upwards. Observe the address—87, BISHOPSGATE-STREET WITHOUT.

THE UNION PLATE GLASS COMPANY beg to call the attention of architects, surveyors, builders, large consumers, and the trade generally, to the quality, colour, and substance of their highly-finished glass, and as the discounts vary according to size, they prefer giving a special estimate for each quantity required. To encourage the use of Plate Glass for glazing purposes, the price is considerably reduced, which will, for its durability and appearance, insure the preference to any other description.
ROUGH PLATE GLASS supplied for skylights, warehouses, workshops, and flooring, 3-8ths, ½, ¾, and 1 inch thick.
London Warehouse, 99, Hatton-garden, Holborn.
H. CHRISTIE, Agent.

REGISTERED
SOLID AXLE SASH PULLEY.—This pulley, after having been submitted to the most severe test, is allowed to be superior to every other made for strength and durability. It is fixed with the same facility as the common axle pulley, and comes equally low in price. May be had from any of the Birmingham or Wolverhampton factors. The Crane Foundry Company, Wolverhampton, Proprietors and Sole Manufacturers.—No. 8 is all iron; No. 9, brass front and wheel with iron axle; No. 10, brass front and wheel with brass axle.

CHAS. WM. WATERLOW,
MANUFACTURER
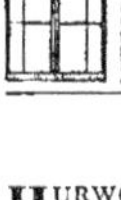
of Sashes and Frames, and Joiner to the Trade, 121, Bunhill-row, Finsbury-square.—Well-seasoned materials, superior workmanship, lowest prices.—Upwards of 400 DOORS, and a large variety of Sashes and Frames, always on sale. Glazed goods securely packed for the country. Steam-struck Mouldings in any quantity.—N.B. This Establishment is worth the notice of all engaged in building.
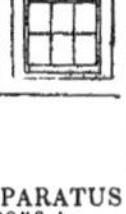

HURWOOD'S PATENT APPARATUS for MOVING and FASTENING WINDOWS, &c.
GENERAL DESCRIPTION.—This invention recommends itself in all its applications by its simplicity, efficiency, and certainty of action, and entirely dispenses with all pullies, weights, cords, springs, set-opes, fastenings, &c. A principal feature in the invention is the application of the screw, or worm working into a wheel or rack, as a prime mover. The apparatus moves with ease and certainty; is very durable, not likely to be out of order; is perfectly secure in every position, and is applicable to conservatories, French casements, folding shutters, stables, ventilators, skylights, ship scuttles, deck and stern lights, and to all descriptions of windows, and is particularly adapted to public buildings, where security is an important object, as in lunatic asylums.
Further particulars may be had upon application to the Patentee, and also the terms upon which licenses are granted.
\. Illustrative Catalogues may also be obtained from the Patentee, Ipswich, by inclosing twelve stamps, to cover postage.

TODD'S PATENT PROTOXIDE PAINT, at a very considerable REDUCTION of PRICE.—This article is extensively used by the principal Railway and Gas Companies, and by Builders and others for painting Stucco. It prevents iron from rusting, wood from decay, masonry from damp, and the hottest sun has no effect upon it.—Manufactured by CHARLES FRANCIS and SONS, Cement Works, Nine Elms London.

PAINTING WITHOUT SMELL; a fact accomplished by the use of the newly-discovered SWEET OIL of TURPENTINE, instead of the deadly abomination called oil or spirits of turpentine. Paint mixed with it is free from smell, is improved in brilliancy of colour, and the baneful properties of the lead being neutralized, does not emit those noxious exhalations which have hitherto been so universally associated with painting. By this really valuable discovery house painting is now converted into a sanitary operation, that may be effected at any season of the year, being productive of health and comfort, without causing the slightest derangement to the domestic economy. Sold by the gallon, cwt., or ton, by every respectable oilman in the kingdom, and at the depot, 1 Bream's-buildings, Chancery-lane, where may be seen, and copies had of, the original certificate of Dr. Berny, a senior member of the College of Chemistry. Sold also in sample bottles, 1s. and 2s. each, bottles included.

THE PATENT ALKALI COMPANY'S METALLIC BLACK and PURPLE-BROWN PAINTS are applicable to every kind of Iron and woodwork, farm, and other out-buildings, shipping, &c. &c., and are pre-eminently superior to all the ordinary descriptions of white or red lead, or so-called "Mineral Paints," in point of economy, durability, and preserving quality.

	Prices
Black	£25 per ton.
Rich Purple-Brown	23 "

Delivered in London or Liverpool, exclusive of packages, which are not returnable, except to be refilled, free of expense to the company.
AGENTS.
Messrs. Evans, Brothers, London; Messrs. Matthews and Leonard, Bristol; Messrs. Evans and Hodgson, Exeter; Mr. S. J. Fill, Yarmouth, Norfolk; Mr. D. Sandeman, Glasgow; Mr. G. Sandeman, Dundee; Mr. R. Newby, Bradford, Yorkshire; Mr. R. S. Farr, Edinburgh; Mr. W. Bailey, Wolverhampton; Messrs. Vint and Co., Newcastle-on-Tyne, and Sunderland; Mr. Robert Oxland, Plymouth; Mr. Joshua Fox, Tregedna, near Falmouth; Messrs. Bryant and May, Tooley-street, London.
To be obtained (also with testimonials) on application to the offices of the company, 20, Fenchurch-street, London.
JOHN A. WEST, Secretary.

TO CAPITALISTS.
WANTED, a Person with 500l. to assist the inventor in preliminary expenses in carrying out a plan for extinguishing fire in ships and houses; plans of the same are now under the consideration of the Lords of the Admiralty and the Master-General of the Ordnance.—Apply, by letter, to Mr. FENWICK, 9, Kennington-green, Kennington-common.

TO MANUFACTURERS OF CORRUGATED IRON, BUILDERS, &c.
THE Advertiser, who is the Author of an important invention in Shop Shutters, by which corrugated iron or wood laths may be made to supersede every other kind (possessing all the advantages of revolving shutters at one-third the cost), wishes to DISPOSE of his RIGHT in the INVENTION.—Apply, under cover, to L. W., care of Simpkin, Marshall, and Co.

TO ENGINEERS AND OPTICIANS.
WANTED, a DUMPY LEVEL, complete and in good condition (Troughton and Sims' make preferred).—Address, stating price, which must be moderate, to X. Y. Kirton's Coffee house, City-road.

TO ENGINEERS, IRONFOUNDERS, CONTRACTORS, AND OTHERS.
LONDON AGENCIES WANTED.—A Gentleman, by profession a Civil Engineer, resident in London, wishes to make an arrangement with either of the above, residing at a distant part of the country, in forwarding particulars of contracts, with accurate tracings of drawing and specifications relating thereto, soliciting orders, &c.; is also a good draughtsman, and would not object to occasionally assist in the office.—Address, G., care of Mr. Powell, Optician, 121, Gray's Inn-lane, Holborn.

S. POWELL (from ELLIOTT'S), Manufacturer of Engineers' and Surveyors' Instruments, REMOVED from 112 to 121, Gray's Inn-lane (one door from Holborn), where he hopes to meet with the liberal patronage he has hitherto received.

TO ARCHITECTS, BUILDERS, AND DECORATORS.
COMPOSITION ORNAMENTS, PROJECTING LETTERS, and CEMENT TRUSSES, of first-rate quality, are manufactured at the lowest possible remunerative prices by J. and E. CHILLINGWORTH, Ornamentors, 1 and 2, Dover-road, Borough. Counter trusses 9s. per dozen. Ceiling flowers 6d. per inch up to 24 inches. A stock of well seasoned cement trusses always on hand ready for fixing.

HEAL AND SON'S LIST OF BEDDING, containing a full description of Weights, Sizes, and Prices, by which Purchasers are enabled to judge the articles best suited to make a good Set of Bedding, sent free by Post, on application to their Factory, 196, (opposite the Chapel,) Tottenham Court Road, London.

BUILDERS AND CONTRACTORS.
TARPAULINS for COVERING ROOFS during Repairs. SCAFFOLD CORD and every description of ROPE used by Builders upon the lowest terms. Marquees and temporary awnings on sale or hire. Orders per post receive the most prompt attention.—WILLIAM PIGGOTT, 115, Fore Street, City, Manufacturer, by Appointment, to Her Majesty's Honourable Board of Ordnance.

CAST-IRON PIPES, IRON WORK FOR OVENS, &c.
RAIN PIPES, &c.—F. A. TIDDEMAN, St. Ann's Wharf, Earl-street, City, near Blackfriars-bridge, keeps a large stock of Rain Pipes, Heads, Shoes, Elbows, &c., half round and O. G. Gutters, Socket Pipes for Water or Gas, Flanch Pipes, Sash Weights, and other Castings; Iron Work for Baker's Ovens of every description, fitted complete, to be had in sets or in parts.—Prices equal to all competition. Contracts taken to any extent.

DRYING for BATHS and WASH-HOUSES, ASYLUMS, LAUNDRIES, &c.—The Patent Desiccating Company can dry, by their process, at any rate of speed, expel any amount of moisture; at the same time disinfect and give a sweetness to clothing, &c., altogether unattainable by means of cockles, steam, hot-water pipes, &c.—For full particulars, apply at the offices of the Patent Desiccating Company, 41, Gracechurch-street, City. ANGUS JENNINGS, Secretary.

PAPER-HANGINGS by MACHINE and BLOCKS.—The trade supplied in town and country, with machine goods, from first-rate new designs, at the lowest prices they have ever been sold in this country; and block goods, for style and quality, not to be surpassed by any house in England. All the patterns are registered, and can only be supplied by HENNELL and CROSBY, Queen-street, Southwark-bridge-road. Cheapest house in London for oak, marbles, and panel decorations. A set of patterns, 5s., to be deducted off an order of 5l.—Terms, cash.

PAPER-HANGINGS, MANUFACTURED UNDER HER MAJESTY'S ROYAL LETTERS PATENT.
E. T. ARCHER, 451, Oxford-street, solicits an inspection of the various DECORATIVE PAPERS, fitted up in panels on the walls of the extensive range of apartments, built expressly for that purpose; where also is kept an extensive stock of every variety of Paper-hangings, at the lowest possible price and of the best manufacture, in English and French Designs, by the best Artists; and where may be had a large assortment of French and other Continental Paperhangings always on hand.—Builders and large Consumers are particularly invited to the above.—451, Oxford-street.

DAMP WALLS PERMANENTLY CURED BY MORRIS'S IMPENETRABLE METALLIC COMPOSITION.—This discovery, so long a desideratum, after years of persevering and unwearied application, is now perfected. The composition adheres to, and dries hard and quick on, the wettest wall, no matter of how long standing, or from what cause damp may arise. From its drying and antiseptic properties, new walls whilst wet can be immediately papered after its application, as in numerous instances can be shown. It requires no preparations, and can be used by the most unpractised workman. One quart will cover twenty yards. Sold, with directions for use, in tins of one quart, 3s. 6d.; half-gallons, 6s.; gallons, 11s. 6d. Sold wholesale by Messrs. PILCHER and SONS, Morgan's-lane, Tooley-street, London; Hibberts, Russell-street, Wednesbury; Hudson and Son, 12, Dock-street, Leeds; J. Roberts and Co., Bourn, Lincolnshire; and Mush and Co., 47, Cross-street, Manchester.—A liberal discount to large consumers.

By Her Majesty's Royal Letters Patent.
PITT'S PATENT SELF-ADJUSTING DOOR KNOBS AND LOOSE SPINDLES.

HART and SONS beg to invite the attention of architects, builders, and others, to their Door Furniture, mounted for PITT'S PATENTED SPINDLES. The knobs are stronger, more durable, and more elegant in form, than those in ordinary use, as the spindles, being loose, do not require the objectionable side screw. They are more readily fixed, are suitable for every description of lock now in use, and, as they adjust themselves to doors of different thicknesses, without alteration, are particularly adapted for the country or for exportation. They are made to suit every style of decoration in China, crystal, amber, and opal glass, buffalo, horn, ivory, ebony, brass, &c., en suite with finger-plates, bell-pulls, levers, &c.—May be obtained of all Ironmongers; or of the proprietors and sole manufacturers, HART and SONS, Wholesale Ironmongers, 53, 54, and 55, Wych-street, Strand, London.
N.B. PITT'S PATENTED SPINDLE, being the only one that does not require a screw in the side of the knob or mounting, the use of any lock furniture without such side screws would be an infringement of the patent.

No. CCCXXXIII.

SATURDAY, JUNE 23, 1849.

HE superintending inspectors under the Public Health Act, are making their reports to the general board, on the preliminary inquiries instituted in various towns; and a few of these, namely, the reports on Whitehaven, Fareham, Ware and Amwell, Uxbridge, and Croydon, are now before us. A large section of our readers look to know something of the result of these inquiries, and, although we cannot pretend to put before them any complete view of the matter, we will endeavour to satisfy them to a certain extent. The reports are printed in an octavo form,* and consist of from twenty to forty pages each. They one and all give a miserable picture of the existing state of things, and show "that the application of the Public Health Act is not only imperatively necessary, but will be of the greatest advantage, morally, physically, and pecuniarily, as the benefits will be reaped alike by rich and poor. The labourer will be relieved from much preventible sickness, poverty, and despair; the health of all classes will be improved, and the present oppressive rates reduced."

To the statement, as to the pecuniary advantages,—"that the requisite measures may be carried out at a positive saving to the inhabitants,"—the said inhabitants do not all seem disposed to give credence, whatever may be their opinion of the report in other respects. Of this, however, hereafter.

Looking to one of the fullest of the reports (that on Whitehaven), we find the inspector (Mr. Rawlinson) saying, that in every town he has visited, "few beside the medical gentlemen know any thing of the utter wretchedness and misery produced by a want of proper sanitary regulations;" that this particular town has a great excess of disease distinctly traceable to preventible causes; and that the health of the inhabitants may be improved, and the poor-rates reduced by, "first, a full and constant supply of pure water laid on in every house and in every room-tenement. Secondly, by a system of sewers laid down in the town, and of drains properly arranged and taken into every house, back street, court, yard, and alley. Thirdly, by the general adoption and use of water-closets or soil-pan apparatus, fitted up with proper tubular drains to convey away the refuse from each, and by the removal of all liquid refuse in similar drains laid at such a depth as shall insure, by means of the same excavation, the perfect drainage of the foundations of all dwelling-houses. Fourthly, by opening out blind courts and alleys, by removing all open middens in confined places, and forbidding their accumulation, by closing all objectionable cellar and room-tenements, by improved paving of all yards, courts, and alleys, and by a regular system of surface cleansing with water."

He further recommends that a cemetery should be provided, the existing burial grounds being amidst houses, and unduly crowded; that the place should be better lighted, and that the refuse of the town, by being applied to agricul-

tural purposes, might be made to lessen the rates, and produce a fund for improving the place. There is a public school here, the yard and convenience of which are in an indescribable state; "the children have to pick their way in and out of it as best they can." The inspector found it difficult to choose his way in broad day-light!

A pretty place in which "to rear the tender mind, and teach the young idea how to shoot," —to induce careful habits and love of order! The effect of external circumstances in the formation of character is ignorantly overlooked by all classes of society. What is attributed to disposition (and the Inevitable) in after days, and affects not merely the well-being and happiness of the individual through life, but of society generally, is oftener the result of the circumstances under which he was placed, and might, without difficulty, have been changed or regulated.

In Whitehaven the habitations of the labouring classes are most injuriously crowded together, and unfit cellars are used as dwellings to a great extent. A report made to the local Board of Health there says properly :—

"Your committee cannot condemn in terms too strong the habitation of cellars, which exists in many parts of the town to a great extent. Nothing can be more injurious to the health of a labouring community than being obliged to occupy abodes of such a nature. Deprived alike of the cheering and invigorating influence of light and fresh air, it is in these dens of misery and wretchedness that disease, particularly of an infectious nature, seizes upon its unresisting and helpless victims. From these, fresh sources of infection spring up, and a neighbourhood that might otherwise be healthy is rendered the reverse of this, from the habitation of cellars being permitted to exist."

And not merely is it rendered less healthy bodily, but less happy, less good. A moral infection spreads, even more disastrous in its results !

The cost of such districts to the community is placed beyond cavil. "Bad sanitary regulations, excessive sickness and mortality, with burdensome and oppressive poors'-rates, must ever be associated. They are cause and effect."

A statement as to the gas-lighting of the town bears out the truth of our often repeated assertion (so often repeated that the echo of it is now to be heard in all quarters), that with reduced prices comes increase of consumption, and advantage as well to the shareholder as the public. The price charged for gas here, when the works were first established, was 12s. 6d. per 1,000 cubic feet. This was reduced, the chairman of the company said, "as the consumption increased, to 10s., 8s., and, in 1847, to 4s. per 1,000 feet. Since the last reduction, a very considerable increase has taken place in the consumption, and ground has been purchased to increase the works, which will be commenced immediately. Generally speaking, we divide an annual dividend of 10 per cent. But after the price was reduced to 4s. per 1,000 feet we did not divide so much. The first year was only 5 per cent., but for the last half-year we did divide 10 per cent."

"The gradual reduction in price detailed by the chairman," says the Inspector, "is a strong incentive to comprehensive and liberal measures, as the increased consumption consequent upon a reduction of 4s. from 8s., in the space of one year, raises the per centage up to the same rank, namely, 10 per cent., and there is no proof that this is the final limit of reduction."

Existing evils are said to be frightful, and the inspector remarks that those who have hitherto had the management of the town affairs must have thoroughly neglected the condition of the inhabitants, or such an amount of human misery and degradation as is there found could not have been accumulated.

Will succeeding trustees commit the crime which a continuation in such a course, now that the evils of it are known, unquestionably involves ?

The report on Fareham, by the same inspector, shows, amongst other things—

"1. That the town of Fareham is not so healthy as from its pleasant and open position it ought to be. That, in a great measure, this arises from the want of proper sewers and drains. That the stagnant ditches and open dung-heaps render the inhabitants liable to any epidemic disease whenever such unfortunately prevails.

2. That, according to the medical testimony, excess of disease and fever may be distinctly traced to this want of drainage, and to an imperfect and impure water supply; and that a low state of morality is ever attendant upon bad or imperfect sanitary regulations, as stated by the vicar.

3. That many grievous public and private nuisances exist, such as open and stagnant ditches, privies, and pigsties, in contact with dwelling-houses, exposed middens near open and shallow wells of water, and cesspools in confined yards and houses.

4. That the present churchyard burial-ground should be closed, and another cemetery provided."

It maintains that the health of the inhabitants would be improved and their moral condition raised, by a perfect system of drainage, a constant and cheap supply of pure water, the use of soil-pan apparatus, improved roads properly cleansed, and the application of the Public Health Act to the town.

The inhabitants, however, or a section of them, decided, at a public meeting held two or three days ago, against the introduction of the Act. The vicar of Fareham, the Rev. Wyndham Madden, and an intelligent minority, sought to prevent a hasty decision, but the resolution was nevertheless carried.

In the report on Ware,* the inspector, Mr. W. Ranger, dwells on the importance of ventilation in preventing disease, and mentions the following illustrative facts which occurred at Aylesbury :—

"Soon after the formation of the union in 1835 and 1836, the parish workhouse, which then stood in a meadow, was purchased by the guardians of the union : the building itself underwent much alteration and considerable enlargement, so that the space around, which before was free and open, became occupied by new buildings, outhouses, &c., and a high boundary wall was erected. In these premises the inmates of the union-house year after year were severely and fatally affected with gastric fever, diarrhœa, and dysentery; this state of things led to various measures, and all that were practicable were in succession adopted, but without effect, so that it became necessary to decide on abandoning the building as unfit for the purposes of the union (after having expended a considerable sum on the additions, &c.), solely from its insalubrity. A new union-house has since been erected on an open elevated situation; and in this building, which has been occupied since 1844, dysentery has never arisen, and the autumnal gastric and intestinal affections are far milder and infinitely more rare than in any other part of the district, though no alteration of the diet of the inmates has been made. The union-house hospital is made the receptacle of most of the chronic and protracted cases for different parts of the union, and in the winter months nearly all the beds are often thus occupied. The new union-house is thus made subservient to the interests of the union, and the hospital a benefit to the sick poor instead of being the hot-bed of disease, which the old union-house most assuredly was. That building being sold, it was partly pulled down and converted into distinct dwellings, and other detached houses have been erected on the same site: by clearing some of the ground and attention to drainage (although the latter is very imperfect), and by rendering the place more open, it has been restored to an equal degree of salubrity with the rest of the vicinity. Exemplifications of similar causes of disease (*i.e.* want of adequate ventilation) abound in Ware, particularly Cage-yard, Blue Coat-yard, and the courts of Amwell-end."

The inspector comes to the conclusion that "a very large amount of excessive sickness, and the great excess of premature mortality, and the expense contingent thereon, may be materially alleviated by the application of the provisions of the Health Act to the township of Ware and that portion of Great Amwell immediately adjoining." He recommends that powers be taken for carrying out the following measures:—

"First—For an abundant supply of pure water upon the constant system, filtered and carried into every tenement, for domestic use, for cleansing, and household purposes, the cost of which, I am of opinion (judging from the cost of existing water-works), will not exceed the amount of 1d. per house per week.

Second—For converting existing privies into water-closets, and, in the numerous instances where neither privies nor water-closets exist, for erecting water-closets, which have been estimated at the cost of 3*l*. per closet, or 4s. per annum.

Third—That powers be taken for systematically draining, by means of tubular or other efficient drains, houses, courts, areas, and roads.

Fourth—That powers be taken for daily cleansing the carriage and foot ways, so as to prevent the accumulation of mud and filth.

Fifth—That powers be taken to render the manure of the town productive, which, I am of opinion, may be done in a way alike beneficial and profitable to all parties—the farmers as well as the inhabitants—when the necessary arrangements are made for its distribution.

Sixth—That all blind alleys, where practicable, be converted into thoroughfares, in order that the noxious vapours may be dissipated by currents of air, or diluted by access to large open spaces. In furtherance thereof I am of opinion that all dead walls should be taken down or made as low as possible, and open fencing substituted.

Seventh.—That powers be taken for insuring a complete system of ventilation of the several rooms of tenements and parochial and other schools for the children of the poor, and also for preventing overcrowding by regulating the number of persons sleeping in rooms, according to their sizes."

In the report on Croydon, also by Mr. Ranger, the writer urges, as he does in others, that benefits would be derived by the ratepayers from general contracts for the erection and repair of drainage and water apparatus.

"Under ordinary circumstances, when accidents happen within or without a building, the tenant has to consider in what manner the repair is to be done, and, not unfrequently, how he is to pay for it: but the first question is, who is to be sent for? The men when they arrive make the repair in their own way, and regardless of any system. In a majority of cases where the plumber is sent for, more than one-half of the time is absorbed in journeys. It is suggested that much of the loss arising from the journeys, &c., would be saved, and the inconvenience much more speedily remedied, if general contracts for the repairs were adopted.

There can be no doubt of the fact that by general contracts the rate-payers would derive a very considerable benefit. By the present mode separate plumbers are employed, each doing the work in his own way; by the plan of general contracts a considerable saving of capital would be made, and the work done on principle, in a superior manner, and at a much less cost. If the apparatus for each house require an expenditure, say of 5*l*. from the owner, then, instead of enforcing an immediate outlay from him to that amount, or of obliging him to send for a plumber and bricklayer, the whole might be commuted for an improvement-rate, say 1d. or 2d. a-week, payable half-yearly by the tenant."

It appears that there are in Croydon forty-five public-houses and thirty-three beer-shops. "Taking the receipts at 6*l*. per week on the average for public-houses, and 2*l*. per week at the beer-houses, the total annual expenditure of the parish at such houses will amount to 17,272*l*."

This is a suggestive sentence. Let some of our readers think over it.

It will not be difficult for those who are blindly opposed to the movement to cavil at parts of these reports, but that is not our *rôle*: we would by every means in our power help it forward, and aid in leading to the adoption of measures calculated to lessen suffering, and lengthen life; to save money, and elevate the moral character of the community.

ON THE HISTORY OF THE POINTED ARCH.

IN attempting to trace the history of the pointed arch, it is not my intention to enter upon the various theories which have been proposed to account for its invention: it would be irrelevant to my present purpose to discuss whether it arose from the intersection of two round arches, as proposed by Dr. Milner, or whether it was suggested by the intertwining branches of a grove of trees, as proposed by others, even if it could be shown that it arose from any such circumstance, which I do not myself believe it can. As the question was very distinctly stated by Dr. Whewell, in his notes on German Churches,—"These only tend to show how the form itself, as an arch, may have been suggested, not how the use of it must have become universal." It appears to me that the discussion of such questions can lead to no really practical result, and, on the contrary, tends to do harm,—as, while men are discussing purely theoretical points, their attention is diverted from the real facts of the case. The tendency to theorise instead of observing, seems to have been the first great mistake committed in treating this question; but a second has been, confining the question to the eleventh or twelfth centuries, and discussing only whether it was then invented by the French, English, or Germans, instead of treating the question as a whole. What I propose is, to widen the base of the inquiry, by placing the whole history of the pointed arch before you; and if I succeed in doing this distinctly, though it must be very succinctly, you will be as able as I am to answer the previous question for yourselves, as the whole will resolve itself into a question of probability. The principal point, however, is to place the facts of the case before you. In doing this, I shall have to bring before you four different series of pointed arches.

The first, commencing with the ancient known buildings, and extending down to the period of the Roman empire.

The second, commencing with the decline of the Roman influence, and extending to the present day,—in the countries of the east, to which these two classes of arches are confined.

The third class appears in the south of France alone, in the age of Charlemagne, and extends to the eleventh century, when it was superseded by the round-arched, or Norman or Lombard style; which last again gave way, in the twelfth century, to the true Gothic pointed arch, which forms the fourth class, and which prevailed almost universally over the whole of Europe till the time of the Reformation, in the sixteenth century.

There may, perhaps, at first sight, be some difficulty in admitting the four series into the category of arches at all, as none of them are constructed on the radiating principle; and in modern times, at least, the usual definition of an arch is,—"A curvilinear archivault, con posed of two or more stones radiating fro one or more centres, and so placed as to reta their position from their force and gravit without the aid of cramps or other subsidia means." We never build arches on any oth principle, and consequently restrict the ter to them. In the east, however, the case different, and the word 'radiating' must l omitted, as there the arches are as often, pe haps more frequently, constructed by placi the stones horizontally, rather than in a rad ating position; and I am not quite certain in some cases, we would not do well to imita the practice, as it has the advantage of gettir rid of the lateral thrust, to which I attribu mainly the durability of the specimen I a about to allude to; but be this as it ma and whether it is determined to call the only pointed *openings*, and not pointed arche the history of the subject will never be co rectly understood till we take both into a count—for the second, I think, almost ce tainly arose out of the first.

The specimen I will name is from tl third pyramid of Gizeh, and from the ro of the sepulchral chamber. It has pe haps less title, in one respect, to be co sidered as an arch than any of the other as it consists only of two stones; but it is in teresting, as showing how early the curviline form, with a point in the centre, was use and, consequently, how familiar it must hav been to the architects of all ages.

The second example is from the pyramid of Meroe. Its age is not very well dete mined, but I do not think it can be far fro the period I have assigned to it, or abo 1000 B.C.; at all events, it is anterior to th age of Greek or Roman influence, which is a that is necessary for my present purpos Mr. Hosking is quite positive about its bein a radiating pointed arch; though, without h distinct testimony, I would have been rath inclined to believe that it was horizontal constructed; at least, I do not know of an other of that age built on the same principle But assuming it to be as described, if radia tion and thrust are the true characteristics an arch, these two have, in this respect, mor title to be considered as arches than the fol lowing, the first of which is from a tumulu near Smyrna, in Asia Minor, and interestin as being, both in size and purpose, almost counterpart of the chamber in the thir pyramid. The form of the vault, however, an the mode of construction, vary considerabl in the two examples, though they are still similar as to admit of their ascribing them t the same idea at least, though not, perhaps, t the same people.

The next example is of a gateway nea Missolonghi, an instance which I quote here serving to explain the mode of constructio adopted in these buildings, which is simpl that of allowing the corners of masonry project beyond one another till they meet i the centre, thus bridging over the opening t be spanned.

Another example, from the tombs of th Atridæ, at Mycenæ, combines the metho shown in the two last, the curvilinear for being retained for the vault as in the fir instance, the straight-lined for the opening but with the addition of an architrave cuttir across the opening at a certain height, whi was, no doubt, a great improvement on t preceding mode.

A further example, from a city gateway Arpino, in Italy, shows the curvilinear for adapted to an opening, which, in the previo examples, was only applied to vaults, and w so obvious an improvement, not only from i greater beauty, but from its convenience, th the straight-lined form was never afterward so far as I know, adopted.

In an example from an aqueduct Tusculum, we have a further innovation, i asmuch as the horizontal construction is not co tinued to the summit, but an Egyptian arch used to complete it. It is evident that the ne step to this would be using the radiating arch, we now use it, but it seems to have stopp there, for some time at least, as I shall ha occasion to show in speaking of the Saracen style in India.

The last of this series I shall name is fro a gateway at Apos, in Asia Minor, whic from the character of its masonry and oth circumstances, is known to belong to the best period of Greek art, and is, in fact, coeval, or nearly so, with the Parthenon. Notwithstanding, however, the perfection of its masonry, it retains all the constructive peculiarities of the preceding examples. The opening is roofed, if I may use the expression, by a horizontal architrave, and a horizontal arch placed over it to discharge the superincumbent weight, as in the tomb above quoted, and the well known Gate of Lions, at Mycenæ. One, however, of its most singular peculiarities is, that on the inside the discharging arch is semicircular, though constructed horizontally, and of the same course of stones as the outer or pointed arch, showing, I think, evidently, that though the architects used the horizontal construction, they could not be ignorant of the principles of the radiating arch, for nothing can be more clumsy and unscientific than an unbroken circular form and horizontal construction, and I am convinced it never would have been adopted in this instance, but from its familiarity rendering it beautiful in the eyes of the architects.

These examples are, I believe, sufficient to explain all the peculiarities of this mode of construction; though, if it were worth while, their number might be multiplied to almost any extent, for they exist not only in Asia, but in Italy and Greece, and indeed in all those countries inhabited by those races whom, in my "Historical Inquiry into the True Principles of Beauty," I have called Pelasgic, and they seem to have formed a substratum to all the other nations of Europe, and to most of those in Asia also.

With the appearance of Rome, however, this form entirely disappears from the countries to which her influence extended, and is universally supplanted by the circular radiating form, which, whether she invented it or not, she introduced everywhere, and left it in every country to which her dominion extended, as one of the most marked and distinguishing architectural memorials of her sway. So completely did the Roman form supplant the older Pelasgic one, that I do not know of a single instance of pointed arch of any form or mode of construction during the period of her supremacy, in any of the countries to which her influence extended.

The moment, however, that her power declined, the pointed form re-appears; but it is not in Italy or Greece, where her influence had been so innate and so long felt, that the previous civilisation and races had been entirely obliterated, but in Asia, its native seat; and I am convinced it would also be found in Egypt, if we had a single building of the period; but, as none exist, we are forced to recur to the very few that remain in Syria and Western Asia for our examples.

The first of these that I shall quote is from the church of the Holy Sepulchre, built by Constantine the Great, now known as the mosque of Omar. Its arches are throughout pointed, but so timidly as to be scarcely observable at first sight, as might indeed be expected at the first revival of a long obsolete form. You will observe, also, that besides the pointed arch which looks so strange mixed with Roman details, as we here find it, it contains reminiscences of another Pelasgic form, inasmuch as the architrave rests freely on the supports, relieved from the superincumbent masses by a discharging arch, as pointed out before.

This is the only specimen of an architectural building with pointed arches of the age to which I am able to refer on this occasion,—a deficiency which arises from two causes; first, the paucity of buildings of any class erected in these countries during the period that elapsed between the age of Constantine and that of Mahomet, so that whether we are looking for round or pointed arches, we would be almost equally at a loss to find examples. The church in Bethlehem, which has no pier arches at all, is the only other building I know of. In Syria and in Egypt not one specimen of any such remains; nor do I know of one in Asia Minor; and, of course, it will not do to look for pointed arches either in Italy or Greece, where the Roman influence remained paramount far beyond the limits of the period we are now speaking of. Another cause of the want of examples is, that they have not hitherto been looked for, but wherever a pointed arch is seen it has hitherto been put down at once as belonging to a Saracenic edifice or to some other epoch; but once it is known that the pointed arch is a characteristic of the age, and antiquaries open their eyes and look for them, I am convinced many will be found. In the meanwhile I am happy to be able to quote so valuable an authority as the Baron Texier in support of my views. I need scarcely remind you that the baron was employed by the French Government for many years in exploring the countries of the East, and is now publishing the result of his researches, under the direction of the Minister of Public Instruction, and I believe, that both from his experience and his character, there is no man living more qualified to give an opinion on the subject than he is.

In speaking of the Cathedral of Am, which is built with pointed arches throughout, he says, after quoting an inscription, which proves that it was finished in the year 1010, "It results from this document, that at a time when the pointed arch was altogether unknown, and never had been used in Europe, buildings were being constructed in the pointed arch style in the centre of Armenia.

At Diarbekr there is an extremely remarkable building now converted into a mosque, which is also constructed with pointed arches. The Armenians call the building the palace of Tigranes, and there is nothing to show that it may not have served as a residence to that prince. The lower story of the palace is ornamented with columns, Roman in style, and with capitals of the Corinthian order, tolerably well executed. These columns support pointed arches. The order of the upper story is also of a very ornate Corinthian order. The friezes and cornices are executed according to the principles of Roman art of the fourth century; nevertheless the pointed arch is found everywhere mixed with the architecture as if it was currently practised in the country.

I have already spoken of the palace at Modain, the ancient Ctesiphon, a building of the sixth century, whose gigantic portal is also of pointed architecture."

The baron then proceeds to remark, "Although it is difficult to fix exactly the period of the introduction of the pointed arch into architecture, it is impossible to draw any certain conclusion regarding the date of a building from its being used in it. The question is at present far from being solved in a satisfactory manner. One thing, however, is certain, that the pointed arch is an eastern invention, and was employed in Mesopotamia long before it was known in Europe."

From the above description it is evident that the upper story at least of the mosque at Diarbekr is a building identical in age and style with the so-called mosque of Omar at Jerusalem, for the words the baron uses in speaking of it apply as correctly and graphically to the one as to the other, and if he is correct in ascribing the lower story to Tigranes we have at least three specimens on the Tigris, extending from the Christian era to the Mahometan conquest, and, though few and far between, it must be confessed, I have no doubt but that with a little industry more may easily be discovered, and the lost links in the chain thus supplied.*

JAMES FERGUSSON.

OSBORNE.—LIGHTNING CONDUCTORS.—We learn that on the 8th a heavy electrical discharge fell on her Majesty's palace at Osborne, and did some damage to the new tower now about being completed at the east end of the building. Some of the cornice was destroyed, the windows shattered, and three men struck down. The high tower and flag-staff at the west end, fitted with lightning-conductors, was unharmed. The tower which suffered, not being complete, had not any such protection, and was about 200 feet distant from the more elevated tower at the west end, and which escaped damage, thus furnishing an illustration of the advantage derived from a system of electrical conductors in disarming the thunder-storm of its terrors.

* The paper, of which this is the commencement, was read at a meeting of the Royal Institute of Architects on the 18th instant. We shall give the remainder hereafter, together with a report of the discussion which followed.

AN ATTEMPT TO EXHIBIT THE TRUE PRINCIPLES OF ARCHITECTURAL AND PICTORIAL EFFECT IN REFERENCE TO STREETS, AND TO TOWNS GENERALLY.

BEFORE proceeding to our immediate subject, it will not be amiss, briefly to remind you what is the real nature and influence of architecture generally, and its rank among the arts.

Architecture, in its largest sense, comprises a scientific and mechanical department, as well as an artistic; and they are most intimately connected; the latter arising in a great measure out of the former; but it is with the profession as a fine art that we have chiefly to do in this paper. Architecture as such is worthy of the consideration of the most exalted intellects; it has an influence from infancy upon our daily life, entwines itself with household virtues, and excites in our breasts a love of country and home. In its loftier effects, with painting and sculpture (from which it differs only in mechanism and application), it hallows and ennobles the mind, elevating it above trifling and vicious pursuits, and becomes, in the words of Fuseli, "the highest degree of education—the ultimate polish of man." For in the architectural pile, no less than in the poem, may be enshrined "undying thought." York Minster and St. Paul's Cathedral are equally exponents of mind with the volumes of Shakespeare and Milton. A piece of genuine architecture may be *read*, and become productive of the loftiest emotions of which the heart is capable. Erecting an edifice then, artistically, is the expressing of a sentiment, giving to stone and wood an idea, "fixing" as Bulwer has it, "into substance the invisible." Coleridge calls a Gothic church, "a petrifaction of religion." Goethe terms architecture, "frozen music." Madame De Stael has the same beautiful conceit, and Lamartine in his "Memoirs of my Youth," calls St. Peter's church "an apotheosis in stone, a monumental transfiguration of the religion of Christ."

We run counter to analogy if we deny this, and suppose that the spirit of beauty embodied in the creations of the artist, is intended merely to please the eye while it continues a novelty. It is opposed to the whole economy of nature, of which art is a reproduction; "A thing of beauty," sings the poet—

> Is a joy for ever;
> Its loveliness increases, it can never
> Pass to forgetfulness.

There is an instinctive yearning after the beautiful in the breast of every man, and the mission of the architect is, with the poet, the sculptor, and the painter, to co-operate with nature in ministering to that want.

Houses were so arranged in cities as to form regular streets, from the earliest time; frequent mention of them occurs in Scripture (the earliest in reference to Sodom in the days of Abraham), where much figurative use is made of the word. "The golden streets of the New Jerusalem" are familiar to all readers of the bible.

The streets of Babylon are the first of which we have anything like description. They are said to have been in straight lines, fifteen miles long, and at right angles to each other. The houses were detached and richly ornamented towards the streets. The streets of Athens were not remarkable for beauty; the houses were ill-constructed and mean, the lanes dark and narrow; some, as may be gathered from ancient authors, were tolerably spacious; of a few mention by name has been made, as the street of Theseus—the way which led to Eleusis,—Tripodian-street—a way near the Prytanæum,—and some others.

However erroneous the principles on which streets in various times and cities were formed, the subject was generally deemed one of importance; street magnificence having not unfrequently been an object of ambition to kings and conquerors, not only in ancient but in modern times; and so much talent and wealth have of late been expended, and are now expending, on improvements in our large towns, that an inquiry into the true principles of effect in reference to street-formation is not without importance, and cannot be altogether void of interest to the present meeting.

It has been the practice, as is well known, in the improvements alluded to, in London, Liverpool, Birkenhead, and elsewhere,—in fact it is a feature of the day, to form the new streets invariably in straight lines, with long double rows of attached houses, exactly alike, and frequently to unite under one design, in the form of terraces, a number of dwelling-houses, giving to a dozen or more of such the appearance of one large mansion or palace. The object of the following paper is to show that these and some other practices have not been adopted in conformity with correct principle. With respect to the straight line, its use, I apprehend, originated in a just aversion to the crooked, jagged, tortuous forms, with sudden (almost right-angled) bends, so much reprehended in the old cities, and under the impression, on the part of the projectors, that by introducing a form the antithesis of all these, they would doubtless be right. In other words, the re-action in favour of a better practice was not attended by a due consideration of the laws upon which beauty depends. They took the course diametrically opposite to the rejected one, instead of instituting an inquiry into natural principles. In the practice of invariably joining houses together, and putting them in "uniform," principles everywhere manifested in nature have been unheeded, viz., individuality and diversity. Between human habitations and human beings an analogy exists, and if we look into nature in reference to the latter, we find a plan pursued very different to that of builders; nature never loses sight of individuality; she does not occasionally usher into the world, to lighten, as it were, her task of invention, half a dozen or a dozen men, exactly alike in size, form, and feature—fac-similes of each other; and we should shrink with horror at the sight of a dozen corporeally attached men; yet the practices to which I have alluded in reference to houses, are no less opposed to the dictates of good taste and enlightened judgment than such phenomena would be to the usual course of nature. In short, it cannot be disputed, if we follow the analogy of nature, that in dwelling-houses, as in the human species, there should be individuality, and that houses for different persons to inhabit should be of different designs, if not suiting the varied tastes of the occupants, at least symbolising the peculiarities of human character; and, in reference to street formation, that every house should not only be a picture in itself, but that the houses collectively should form a picture of greater variety, and that they should be, where possible, arranged with respect to composition, light and shade, breadth, colour, union and harmony with the ground, variety, and other qualities, just as a skilful artist composes his picture.

We shall, however, look in vain for the highest attributes of street perspective in the straight line, however beautiful and varied the buildings, individually, may be; that continuity of charm, or series of fine effects, of which a street is capable, cannot, I consider, be given to a straight line, however great the means employed. I am not insensible to the graces of columnar perspective as exhibited in an avenue formed by colonnades, whether interior or exterior. The long drawn aisle also of our Gothic cathedrals awakens ideas of the sublime. Than the vista of the pointed nave, continued by that of the choir, combined with chantries, screens, and shrines, nothing can be imagined more overwhelming in effect, or more in keeping with the sacred destination of the edifice. They symbolise infinity, and are productive of mysterious and sublime sensations. I mention these, because I have heard them cited in support of the straight line in reference to streets; but the office of such, I consider, is confined to a surprise—to a single and occasional view,—and look upon that office as fulfilled when they have produced their first overwhelming effect upon the spectator, to which end every means has been directed. Whilst streets, on the contrary, are for promenade and constant use, and a succession of effects and ideas are required.

The line I would suggest as most conducive to this, is one in which nature may be said to revel, viz. the winding serpentine line of a very gentle sweep; or the simple arc of a circle. Streets so formed, I consider, would not only be susceptible of the highest architectural beauty, but possess that exhaustless charm, that endless variety of effects which I have endeavoured to describe.

It will be understood, I trust, that I do not recommend these curves for the beauty of the lines themselves, as in a picture,—their own immediate beauty could not appear, except upon the map; the merit of the curve consists in its continually altering the point of view, and in the variety and beauty it thus produces. In such streets, the spectator of intellect and susceptibility would find a continued development of beauty, and as the disposition of light and shade, and atmospheric effect, is never the same for two minutes together, the variety will seem infinite, the pleasure endless; whilst on the other hand, a straight street flanked on either side by columns, however lavishly the riches of architecture may have been expended on it, must soon, not only cease to please but grow wearisome to the eye.

The mathematical fact that the straight line is the shortest distance between two points, cannot, I consider, be urged against this in reference to utility. In giving a winding line to a leading thoroughfare running through a town, as a trunk for branch streets, no ground would be lost. The gentle curvature which I recommend, would make but little difference in the length, and the passenger would be recompensed for a longer walk by its containing a proportionately greater number of shops or places of business, while its devious course would enable it to embrace a greater number of distinct points or localities necessary to be united.

I do not insist, however, upon the curve as a form that should be invariably employed; there are circumstances under which the straight line would be more proper. In short streets, for instance, running from one great thoroughfare to another, the latter form would be most befitting, as no purpose could be answered by the curve. *Width* is the chief means of giving effect to these. Neither can the detached principle be insisted upon, except in streets where magnificence is the leading aim. The high value of land in the centre of a town would forbid it. What I would invariably insist upon, is the detaching of character—individualizing the houses; and, after all, that is the most important point, as it immediately produces the great desideratum—variety; while the other qualities for which I contend, do it but in an indirect manner.

To a curved street, distinct character to the houses is an advantage which should not be dispensed with; it is requisite to the full development of that variety which the eye requires, but in a straight street it is *absolutely necessary*, as an escape from the most wearisome and complete monotony: in such a street the houses should present every variety of form, size, hue, style, and design, and thus produce the greatest possible change of sky-line.

There are four streets in the city of Oxford that will serve as examples here—two ancient and modern; of either kind one is curved, the other straight; in the ancient ones the houses vary in character, in the modern ones they are all alike. To any unprejudiced mind that examines and compares the several effects of these streets, the general truth of the remarks I have made, will, I think, be apparent, without further comment of mine.*

I am aware that the projectors of modern streets in adopting the straight line have had ample precedent. If we turn to the great cities of ancient and modern times, which have been executed throughout or for the most part upon a complete and digested plan, we find, though magnificence has been the leading aim, that this principle has been followed. Babylon, as I have said before, was built in straight lines, each street crossing the other at right angles. It had, however, one quality conducive to the pictorial—the houses were detached.

In Washington, evidently intended by its founders to unite in its plan all the beauties of which a city is capable, the same principle has guided, though in many respects it is an advance upon Babylon and others: besides its intersection by the principal streets running due north and south, from the president's house, the capitol, and other important points of the city, run diagonal streets, east and west, connecting them with other ornamental and imposing objects, which with the former close the perspective at either end: this arrangement is well worthy of notice, it tends greatly to promote diversity of view, and is highly conducive to grandeur of general effect. There are open areas at the intersection of the principal streets, formed into various regular figures, destined for the reception of statues and obelisks to their eminent men; the great leading streets are 160 feet wide, with not only a foot walk and carriage way, but also a gravel walk, planted with trees on each side. St. Giles's-street, Oxford, in all probability suggested this arrangement.

The streets of Philadelphia, and of most of the new towns of America, are straight and cross each other at right angles.

In Rome, some of the principal streets are of considerable length, and by dint of churches, palaces, and fountains, have an imposing effect: the Corso, which contains several palaces ranging in a line with the houses, is perhaps the finest; but the streets are perfectly straight. The streets of the principal towns of the Romans were straight, and Tacitus informs us that for protection from the sun they are so narrow that Pompeii was called a city of lanes. Antinöe, built by Adrian, and considered a perfect model of the Roman city, had its streets straight. The principal ones had on each side of the way piazzas 5 or 6 feet broad, and running the whole length of the street, by means of which the city from one end to the other might be traversed without exposure to rain, or to the heat of the sun.

In Mexico, almost entirely rebuilt after its conquest by the Spaniards, the streets are straight, and so regularly arranged, that, if uniformity were identical with beauty, it would perhaps bear the palm over all other cities.

I can, however, refer to cities whose chief beauty may be traced to the agency of the principles for which I am contending. The amphitheatrical form of Naples is evidently the secret of its beauty, and no street in Washington, Rome, or in any other city, where the straight line prevails, can vie with the Strada di Toledo, or with the beautiful streets upon the bay.

Venice also, beautiful as a dream, may be cited for the same reason. The Grand Canal, of an expansive width, takes a serpentine course through the sea-girt city. The view from the Rialto along this canal, flanked on either side by the most gorgeous palaces, churches, domes, and spires, with their sculptured arabesques, and purple marble, where the beauties of art as reflected on the pictures of Claude and Canaletti and our own Turner stand forth as rivals to those of nature, must, to those who are capable of appreciating the glories of sunshine and shadow, have an effect that words are inadequate to describe. "Detail after detail," says an eloquent writer, "thought beyond thought, you find and feel them through the radiant mystery, inexhaustible as indistinct, beautiful but never all revealed, secret in fulness, confused in symmetry as nature herself is to the bewildered and foiled glance, giving out of that indistinctness and through that confusion, the perpetual newness of the infinite and the beautiful."

But I have an example to refer to nearer home, in the interesting city of Oxford beforementioned, where though architectural beauties meet the eye at every step, and there is perhaps a greater amount of architectural wealth, in proportion to its size, than in any other city of the kingdom,—though colleges, churches, and halls are the chief objects in the view, the whole charm may be traced to that wonderful variety of form, hue, disposition, and style, that harmony with nature, and obedience to her laws, which is seen around.

The High-street, like the Grand Canal, is an embodiment of Hogarth's line of beauty. It is of a gentle flexuous curve, meandering through the city, and exhibiting beauties confessedly beyond what any other European city can boast; beauties which have at least been felt by Wordsworth, who in a sonnet on Oxford, forgets not the "stream-like windings of that glorious street." "Sweeping along," observes an old writer, "in a gentle curve of a most expansive width, and bordered by a picturesque assemblage of public and private edifices, it is indeed, perhaps, without a rival. In viewing it the eye does not repose on splendid uniformity, but on an enchantingly varied whole, and when, satisfied with viewing the entire perspective, we commence an examina-

* The four streets of Oxford are, High-street, St. Giles's-street, Beaumont-street, St. John-street.

THE FARNESIAN GARDENS, ROME.

VIGNOLA AND MICHELANGELO, ARCHITECTS.

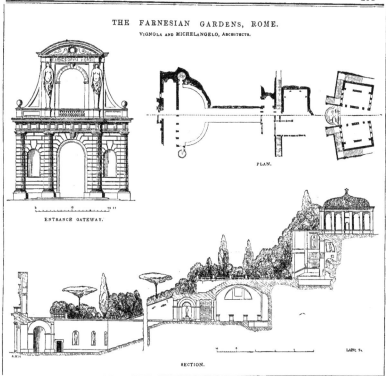

ENTRANCE GATEWAY.

PLAN.

SECTION.

race, with its semi-dome and rock-work basins are considered to be the work of Michelangelo, as also the flights of steps which, winding round on either side of the pavilions, lead to the upper terrace. The pavilions themselves, which served as aviaries, and crown the summit of the gardens, are the work of Rainaldi.

It will be remarked, that these buildings are placed obliquely, in order to enhance the beauty of the perspective view, as seen from the entrance gateway below.

It may be observed, that the Italian architects frequently adopted this peculiar mode of grouping buildings, with the view to add to their picturesqueness of effect, and that Bernini, in particular, often had recourse to this expedient both in the interior as well as in the exterior of the edifices which he erected.

The gracefulness of the entrance-gateway, and its fitness of expression as an entrance to a garden, cannot fail to strike the beholder. The graces of art have been lavished with a profuse hand upon this agreeable retreat, which must, in its pristine state, have resembled those enchanted abodes which are supposed to exist in fiction only. The whole composition, in fact, is the realisation of a poetical idea: its contrivers and designers were poetical beings. Those who visit Italy are made to feel how often the beauty of her landscape is increased by the magic of her architecture. Terraced or hanging gardens form a conspicuous feature in Italian landscape; and the Farnesian gardens are amongst the most beautiful of those which abound in the neighbourhood of Rome; and though now in a neglected state, afford valuable suggestions to those persons whose taste or calling leads them to attempt similar undertakings.

A. W. HAKEWILL.

PRODUCTION OF THE IONIC VOLUTE.

A MEMORANDUM.

June 5th.—This day I first drew a spiral revolution for a volute on the principle of having the apparatus fixed to the eye or centre. I had, however, known for a year, the motion which produced it; but I had no apparatus to carry it out, nor had it occurred to me, to *fix* one part in the centre of the eye. On the same day that this idea was presented to my mind, I first connected some sliding pencil sockets with strips of wood, and short pieces of pencil, and then attached a part to a fixed point to represent the centre of the eye of the volute. I now saw that it would do, and various ideas of a fixed centre occurred to me.

In the Grecian volutes it has been found that a separate piece has been inserted in the eye; and it has been conjectured from this that something had been previously introduced into the hole—it has been supposed a spiral shell, and that the volute had been formed by the unwinding of a string.

I therefore thought of a hole in the *drawing* board, in a *slate*, or in a *copper plate*, in which to fix a pin for a centre. Then in all these cases, I considered that the centre might be fixed by means of cement, without a hole, which in many cases and materials would be objectionable. I did not like to make a hole in my drawing board, and I had not anything handy or fit for the others. Next the "*weight of a pentagraph*" occurred to me. I took it out of the case, but the pin was too small for the hole in the pencil socket, but for a trial I thought it might do. I therefore cut off some slips from a card to fill the space the pin did not occupy. I then arranged my temporary apparatus, and drew the first revolution of a spiral by this means.

As soon as I had drawn this *one* line, I reflected, and considered that I ought to stop a while, and record my first impressions. I looked at the line, and at the apparatus by which it was produced; the one was so beautiful, and the other was so simple and obvious, that I felt as if I had seen it, and must have known it all before. It was so clear, that if a centre was thus fixed to a block of marble or stone, intended for a volute, a line, or part of a line might be drawn without any mould, and worked, and its accuracy tried with the greatest ease as often as might be wished; and, in fact, that the line could be continued, left off, or introduced when and where the sculptor might wish,—in short, that he or an artist on any material might design with the apparatus as he proceeded, bit by bit, in the execution of the work, during which the apparatus need never be in his way.

It was equally obvious that, where a centre could be fixed in the eye of any example of a Grecian volute in the British Museum, an apparatus might be adjusted so as to compare the path of the motion with any line, and thus prove, beyond a doubt, whether this is the identical method that was used by the Grecians or not.

It is strange, that man should know the motions in the heavens and not know this!

Professor Donaldson may perhaps remember that I measured a cast of a volute in his possession many years ago. The paper with *sixteen* radiated openings, on which the centre was marked, was applied to the centre of the eye of the volute, and then *seventeen* points in one revolution were obtained. This paper has been long lost, but I still have a slip of paper, on the edge of which, at the time, I formed a scale of the radii, and which indicated an error in one of the marks first made on the radiated paper; and that was then proved to be an error, by placing the paper again on the cast, and then correcting it. The measures on this scale, some time ago, I transferred from a centre to sixteen radiating lines; and, on turning over some papers and seeing it, I considered that, without going to the "British Museum," I could make one comparison. I therefore placed the "pentagraph weight" in the centre, and adjusted my temporary apparatus to it; and it has thus become the *first*, and a most powerful, evidence of the great probability that this is the identical method used by the ancient Greeks. Indeed, nothing but the most inveterate prejudice could blind the eyes of any person who would give the least attention to the subject.

The particular adjustments of the apparatus also clearly indicate that the ancient architects worked by rule: the adjustments for the apparatus in this case being, in their proportions to each other, as 2, 6, and 12,—each being a little more than so many English inches.

The application of forms produced by varying motion was not "problematical" to the "ancient Greeks," whatever it may appear to be to Mr. Cockerell,—who by such imaginations, has perhaps contributed to prevent such simple facts being known.

The spiral lines now produced have in their general character, when compared by scales of radii, a similar appearance to the variation in the lines which I had previously supposed, from that circumstance, and from the equal simplicity of motion, to have been the Greek spiral; although no one, to my knowledge, has attempted to disprove the correctness of such a supposition, and it may yet be found to be a variety, but in this instance it must give way to this *new* (*doubtless very old*) character of motion; and the variation of adjustments which this motion admits of, furnishes such strong presumptive evidence that it has been the *origin* of *all scrollwork;* and this will not appear the less obvious when it is known and seen, that by the most simple variation in the adjustment, every variety of "*inflected* lines," —"*lines of beauty*" for connecting the two scrolls at the ends of a map,—whether equal or unequal,—can be obtained.

I had ascertained how to produce these "*lines of beauty*" about a year ago, although I had not an apparatus to draw one complete on this principle. I should be ashamed of saying this, if this simple principle of motion had not also escaped the observation of, as far as I know, all others, even mathematicians.

Professor Willis has not included it in his attempt at classification of motions. Nothing is more easy than to build up complicated apparatus, or to hide, to common observers, imperfections in form, by colour and ornament; while experience daily proves that the most simple principles, which, when known, require no demonstration to make them obvious, have not been so easily discovered.

Upon the whole, I am not sorry that the present race of architects, and especially the professors, have looked upon my endeavours with so much prejudice and indifference—perhaps I may say absolute contempt—although they have been incapable of offering anything as a substitute.

Had it been otherwise, and had they given just so much attention to my discoveries, as to understand the subject, they might then, before me, have discovered some of the most important and interesting adjustments in the septenary system, which I had hitherto passed over. This, however, they have not done, and Mr. Cockerell may long look at the object in the wall—"*a fossil of beautiful spiral outline*,"—before he discovers a simple practical method equal to "*those refinements which marked the smallest productions of the Grecian chisel, testimonies of the science of the Greek architects*," for producing true lines in the actual execution of a volute, with the facility the apparatus now before me is capable of. To incur the cost, however trifling, of getting an apparatus made to work very accurately, would be a risk that the invention would be at once copied; and it would be the same if even the temporary apparatus was applied, for additional proof, to a volute in the British Museum.

All, therefore, that I can do is to draw a few lines, and to exhibit an example of a volute, drawn with the temporary apparatus, at the Polytechnic Institution, and invite architects to look at them, and to invite all to ask architects the question,—whether they can produce as correct a specimen by simple continuous varying motion, either for volutes or entasis, and what they really know of the septenary system?

JOSEPH JOPLING.

NOTES IN THE PROVINCES.

THE Fitzwilliam Museum at Cambridge is now open to all respectably-attired persons on Wednesdays and Saturdays, from twelve till four o'clock.——A new chapel has been opened at Prickwillow, Ely. It is built on a site near the bridge on the Dark river, and is of flint, with stone and brick dressings and slate roof. ——The restoration and repair of the chancel of the old church at Soham have commenced, on plans by Messrs. Bonomi and Cory, of Durham. Carved oak stalls will run round the two sides; the floor will be relaid with encaustic tiles. The repewing of the whole body of the church is thought desirable.——The repairs and restoration of Melton Mowbray Church by the contractors, Messrs. Broadbent and Hawley, of Leicester, are in progress. The large window on the west side of the church is to be repaired, it is said, and replaced with new stained glass.——A tomb of Caen stone, representing a railway arch or tunnel, surmounted by embattled towers or lanterns, has been built in the parish church of Otley, in memory of the thirty-four unfortunate workmen killed at the Bramhope tunnel during the progress of the Leeds and Thirsk Railway works.——The harbour of Lowestoft has now cost 177,385*l*., and when completed will cost about 200,000*l*. It is capable of containing 200 vessels, independently of the outer basin. At its entrance at low water there is a depth of 19 feet 6 inches. The dues for last year amounted to 3,954*l*., and the present are 60*l*. per week higher than the average of the past year.——The Bristol council have commenced rebuilding the landing-pier of Portishead; Messrs. Charles Emett and John Gay, contractors: plans by Mr. Joseph D. Green, engineer to the Bristol Docks, under whose direction the works are now in progress.——The Albion Chapel, Southampton, was opened on Wednesday week. It is 80 feet in length, 50 feet in width, and 32 feet 6 inches in height from door to ceiling. The entire cost is between 5,000*l*. and 6,000*l*. Mr. W. Hinves, of Southampton, was the architect, and Mr. T. A. Gates the builder: plasterer, Mr. C. Scorey. The building is described as "a structure in the Ionic order of classic architecture." The front is of white brick, with columns, &c., faced in Portland cement. A flight of stone steps ranges the entire length of the front, and the whole is inclosed by an iron railing from the street. ——The Brighton Commissioners, with reference to the projected sale of the Pavilion, &c., have passed a resolution that it would be highly injurious to the town of Brighton to suffer the lawn and pleasure-grounds to be built over.——The first stone of a church, to be built at Wickham Bishops, was laid on Friday in last week. It is in the perpendicular style: cost, when finished, about 3,800*l*. The church is the gift of a lady,—Mrs. Lee, of Wickham Bishops, Essex. Mr. Christian is the architect.——Fifty acres of Wimbledon Common, it is said, are to be enclosed, and an establishment for pauper children, from the Surrey Union, erected there.——St. Peter's Church, Canterbury, according to the *Dover Chronicle*, is about to be placed under a process of restoration, which it much requires. The plaster covering the flint is being cleared off, and the work fresh pointed.——The Rochester-bridge wardens have resolved on the erection of a new bridge forthwith. The plan is not yet determined.——A temporary church, in the form of a spacious tent, to hold between two and three hundred persons, has been erected in Datchet-lane, Windsor, under the Castle walls, for the families of labourers engaged in forming the branch railway to the Great Western, at Slough, and the continuation of the Richmond line from Datchet.——The Macclesfield baths and washhouses for the working classes have been formally opened. ——On Monday week the Bishop of Manchester laid the first stone of Christ Church, Friezland, near Ashton. The edifice is to be in the early English style, from a design by Mr. G. Shaw, of Upper Mill, Saddleworth, to accommodate 500 persons, and to consist of a chancel, nave, and north aisle, a tower and spire, and a south porch, the vane of the spire to rise 180 feet from the base course. A school has been already erected in the same style, and there is to be a parsonage and a house for the schoolmaster, also in the same style: estimated cost, schools, 1,000*l*.; church, 3,000*l*.; parsonage, 1,500*l*.; master's house, 300*l*. The whole are to be built of irregular coursed parpoints, and ashlar coigns. The contractor is Mr. Wade, contractor for part of the Huddersfield Railway.——The Doncaster New Market, erected by the corporation, was recently opened. It is a long, wide building, in the shape of the letter L, placed on the site of the old Town Hall, in the centre of the Magdalens. There are eight public entrances into it. Round the inside are fifty-five shops, and up the centre at one end thirty-nine stalls: the other end is used as a butter and poultry market. The whole is already let, and at present rents, upwards of 500*l*. annually will be realized.——Eldon Church, to be consecrated on 16th inst., will accommodate 800 persons. The font is of Roche Abbey stone, and the pulpit is moulded. A tower is much wanted, and the unfinished state of a street close by is an eyesore in the view of the whole.——Messrs. Wilson and Gibson, the contractors for the southern approaches of the High Level Bridge, at Newcastle, and for the new Durham Infirmary, and other buildings, have got the contract for the erection of the new Public Hall in the city of Durham, under Mr. Hardwick, architect.——Some workmen having been employed in taking down a portion of the screen in front of the Register-house, at Edinburgh, preparatory to the erection of the equestrian statue of the Duke of Wellington, an interdict was immediately obtained, on its being learnt that the Government had no intention to allow the whole screen to be thrown back as desired by the citizens.——The Marchioness of Waterford is building, at her own cost, a new church at Guilcoh, in the diocese of Waterford. The first stone has lately been laid. The inscription on it is,—"To the Glory of God. Laid May, 1849, by George Wilson, aged 106 years; erected by Louisa, Marchioness of Waterford."——On Tuesday, June the 5th, the chapel lately built in the hamlet of Frieth, in the parish of Hambleden, Bucks, was, with its burial-ground, consecrated by the Lord Bishop of Oxford. It is dedicated to St. John the Evangelist, and contains seats for 150 persons. Mr. J. P. Harrison is the architect. At the east and west ends are memorial windows of stained glass: the west window, in memory of the Rev. H. C. Ridley, is the work of Mr. Hudson, of Pentonville; the east window was executed by Mr. Hardman. The carpet for the chancel is a joint contribution from the labours of several ladies. The chapel is well placed on the slope of a hill, and is built of flint, with Bath and Caen stone dressings. The roof is of deal, the seats of cedar, the lectern of oak, and the altar-fence, pulpit, and prayer-desk of oak and cedar intermixed. The belfry is of oak, filled in with decorated work. The cost of the church and its fittings is about 1,200*l*. Mr. Bond, of Marlow, was the builder.

METALS.—Returns for 1848 show that 3,788 tons of pig and sheet lead were imported into the United Kingdom, together with 1,298 tons of lead ore, and 64 tons of white lead. Export of lead ore, 134 tons, of pig and rolled lead, 4,977 tons, white lead, 1,168 tons, red lead, 842 tons, and pig and sheet lead, 3,747 tons. Copper ore imported, 50,053 tons. Value of copper manufactures imported, 9,200*l*. Copper ore retained for domestic use, 51,307 tons; duty, 10,227*l*. net. British copper exported, 13,466 tons. Zinc or spelter imported, 13,529 tons, duty free. Zinc exported, 562 tons British, and 3,766 tons foreign.

SALISBURY CATHEDRAL.—It is reported in the neighbourhood, that the dean and chapter have it in contemplation to throw Salisbury Cathedral open to the public. We sincerely hope that the report in question is founded in truth.

EXEMPTION OF EDUCATIONAL INSTITUTIONS FROM TAXES.

OBSERVING in your able periodical of last week a paragraph relative to the exemption of literary and educational institutions from the payment of rates, permit me to draw attention to the want of equity, under the present Act, in saddling a particular parish with the entire loss of rate. In a country town, for instance, with some dozen parishes, why should the parish in which a museum or mechanics' institute happens to be located be alone taxed by the loss of a rate on a large property, and the other eleven, which derive equal benefit from the institutions, be exempted?

Could not this injustice be obviated by directing the treasurer of the union to CREDIT the *individual parish* in which an institution might be situated with the amount of rate which would, but for the special exemption, be due to it, and DEBIT *the union account* with the same sum? I believe some such arrangement as that suggested would obviate much of the objection and opposition with which the working of the Act has been impeded.

Of course this is only suggested in the absence of a "national poor rate,"—the only effectual remedy for this and many other more important and equally inequitable anomalies.

T. S. G.

LIVERPOOL ARCHITECTURAL AND ARCHÆOLOGICAL SOCIETY.

THE annual excursion of this society took place on Saturday, the 16th inst. The locality fixed upon was the village of Gresford, in Denbighshire, famed for its beautiful church and the picturesque scenery in its neighbourhood. The party from Liverpool was joined at Chester by a deputation from the Chester Archæological Society. On their arrival at Gresford they were conducted over the church by the reverend vicar. The church is a fine specimen of late Perpendicular work, the tower being particularly rich in panelling and niched and canopied buttresses, the statues, for the most part, still remaining. After staying a sufficient time at Gresford, to sketch the most interesting portions, and to delineate the details, the party proceeded to Wrexham, and made an inspection of the church there, which is generally considered the pride of North Wales, after which they sat down to an excellent dinner at the Wynnstay Arms Inn. Covers were laid for forty. The chair was occupied by Mr. J. A. Picton, F.S.A., vice-president of the Liverpool Society; the vice-chair was taken by Mr. C. Reed, the secretary, and the meeting was addressed by them, by the Rev. Mr. Massie, rector of St. Mary's, Chester, Mr. John Hicklin, secretary to the Chester Society, and editor of the *Chester Courant*, Mr. R. Alexander, editor of the *Liverpool Mail*, and other gentlemen.

ARCHED TRUSSES OF BENT TIMBER.

I OBSERVE in your Saturday's number a report of a description of the construction of a collar roof, with arched trusses of bent timber, at East Horseley Park, read by the Earl of Lovelace.

I have never heard of, or seen Col. Emy's work on Carpentry, but the idea of bending the timber in laminæ occurred to me in the beginning of 1843, when plans were wanted for temporary churches for the clergy that left the Established Church of Scotland, a model of which I had prepared and deposited in the studio of Handyside Ritchie, the sculptor, which was examined and highly approved of by a great many scientific gentlemen in Edinburgh. Since that time I have designed and carried out several churches in the pointed style, with the ribs of the trusses bent, and I have at this moment six churches in hand erecting on the same principle as regards the roof, in different parts of the kingdom. Independent of the beauty of appearance and unquestionable strength gained by such a mode of construction, the great economy is, perhaps, the most striking.

About twelve months ago I was called upon to prepare a design for re-roofing a church in Cheshire, 48 feet wide, built in a sort of bastard Norman style, and I adopted the semi-circle, as more in keeping with the rest of the work, the inner angles of each rib moulded with a notched billet. Another architect prepared a design, consisting of the common tie beam and king post, and both were estimated by the same tradesman; for the former his tender was 420*l.*, for the latter 730*l.*, showing a difference of 310*l.* in favour of this system of construction.

In no case have I had the slightest accident or giving way of the work.

The notice in THE BUILDER is the first intimation of this principle being applied by any one but myself to the purposes of roofing, and in a new edition of Nicholson's Carpenters' Guide, now publishing by Virtue, of Ivy-lane, under my revision, I intend to embody this mode of roofing in the work, illustrated by drawings and details.

Liverpool.   JOHN HAY.

NINEVEH.

SYRO-EGYPTIAN SOCIETY.

AT a meeting of this society, on the 12th, Mr. Ainsworth, the secretary, read a communication "on the topography of Nineveh." After pointing out the received distinctions of Assyria proper and of the Assyrian empire, the writer proceeded to argue, that whichever of the disputed versions of Genesis x., 11, is adopted, it still remains certain that there was an Assur, or Athur, existing before the foundation of Nineveh. That the Arabian geographers Yakut, Abulfeda, and Ibn Said describe the ruins as the modern Nimrud, as those of the said Asshur, or Athur (sometimes Akur, with a *kaf*). That Mr. Rich, in his "Kurdistan" (vol. ii., p. 129), the Rev. N. Morren, in art. Assyria ("Cyclop. of Bib."), and Dr. Layard, in his "Nineveh, &c.," vol. ii. p. 245, admit that all well-informed natives designate Nimrud as Al Asshur, or Athur. That the name which occurs in the inscriptions found in the north-west edifice at Nimrud has been read by Major Rawlinson as that of the Asshur of Genesis, and that Dr. Hincks has also published his conviction that the first word of the inscription is either the name, or an abbreviation of the name of Athur; but the Doctor also adds, which is a *non sequitur*, that the same name stands for the city, of which the historical name is Nineveh.

That Dr. Layard's archæological investigations have already shown that the builder of the central palace—the second in succession of time—at Nimrud, also erected edifices, if he did not found the sites of what are now called 'Ba'asheikba and Kaláh Skirgat; that Dr. Layard also admits that the more modern Assyrian ruins at Koyunjuk, Khorsabad, and Karamles, represent the Nineveh of the Books of Jonah and Nahum, and of profane history and of travellers. But Dr. Layard also comprises within the same denomination, a palace of the same age that was erected upon the ruins of Asshur.

Mr. Ainsworth showed, upon a map of Assyria on a large scale, which he had drawn up, that no arbitrary grouping of the Assyrian ruins would be satisfactory at the present moment, and that in the present state of the inquiry there are no other data than that Nimrod or Ninus, or his or their successors, erected and continued to erect edifices at Athur, one of the oldest cities of Assyria proper, and that the second dynasty also erected edifices at the same spot after its fall and the rise of the historical Nineveh, to identify the one with the other; but that the greater number of probabilities, at least topographically speaking, are that the two sites were always distinct, and that Athur or Nimrud was a separate site from the abode of Ninus, as well as from the historical Nineveh.

ST. MARY'S CHURCH, WARE, will be re-opened for service on Thursday, July 5, and a sermon will be preached to aid the restoration fund, by the Rev. Henry Melvill. The restorations here, which commenced with the outside, have been carried out very extensively inside, through the zeal of the vicar and parish officers and the liberality of the inhabitants. Although personally concerned, we shall be tempted to give hereafter some little description of the alterations effected.

Books.

The Architectural Scrap Book, containing sketches of parts of buildings, English and Continental. By J. BUTLER and H. HODGE, architects, Beaufort-buildings.

THE north aisle of Hallaton Church; Churchyard Cross, Houghton; Turrets from Bologne and Oxford, and two Elizabethan doorways, constitute No. 3 of this work, and in No. 4 are brick chimneys, at Assington and Terling, an oriel window from Colmar, France; and two wooden porches, from Trowlesworth Church, Leicestershire, and Heston Church, Middlesex. The last number is an improvement on those which precede. The oriel window from Colmar, belonging to the seventeenth century, is a curious renaissance version of the mediæval period abroad. "The plan of the window is a parallelogram, placed on the angle-house of a street, offering facilities for seeing up and down four streets; it looks remarkably picturesque and rich."

Touching our remark on a previous occasion that "the idea of the 'Architectural Scrap Book' would almost seem to have been taken from the announced intention of the Architectural Publication Society," the authors have written us to say that "whatever might be inferred from appearances, the prospectus of the work was written and printed many months before they were aware of the Publication Society's existence, and that they have too much respect for the praiseworthy efforts of the society to interfere with their work or intentions."

Antiquarian Gleanings in the North of England. Drawn and Etched by W. B. SCOTT, of the Newcastle School of Design. No. I. Bell, Fleet-street.

THIS is the commencement of a laudable attempt by Mr. Scott to preserve records of the moveable antiquities of "the Nor-Humbrian province." It includes the carved reading-desk in Jarrow Church, various cinque-cento cups, a carved chimney-piece in the Guild-hall, Newcastle, chairs, and wall paintings.

The History of Ireland, from the earliest period of the Irish Annals to the present Time. By THOMAS WRIGHT, M.A., &c. London: Tallis. Nos. 10 to 12.

MR. WRIGHT is advancing with his history, the last number (12) bringing us to the year 1601. It seems to be carefully written, and is well calculated to supply an existing deficiency.

Miscellanea.

JOHN KNOX'S HOUSE AT EDINBURGH.—The old house in the Netherbow, in which the stern old Calvinist lived and died, is now so dilapidated that the dean of Guild-court has ordered its removal, notwithstanding an endeavour of Mr. R. Chambers and other members of the Scottish Society of Antiquaries to prevent it. Some time ago it was proposed to erect on this spot a monument to the memory of Knox, to consist of a tower and two churches. It is to be hoped that nothing worthy of preservation in this ancient edifice will be destroyed.

A FORTHCOMING PANORAMA.—Mr. Henry Warren, Mr. Haghe, Mr. Bonomi, and other good men and true, are engaged on a panorama of the Nile, of very considerable extent, and will soon bring their labours to a close. The novelty of the subject,' and the goodness of the authorities consulted, can scarcely fail to obtain for it a large amount of popularity, if the idea be carried out as efficiently as the names above-mentioned give us reason to believe it will be.

A NEW STREET WATERER has been patented by Mr. Salter, of Birkenhead. The tank is of cast-iron, mounted on cart wheels, which in rotating work a force pump, projecting the water into an air chamber, and thence in a steady stream into pierced pipes as usual. A breadth of 30 feet, or only one-half, can thus be effectually watered, or the force pump thrown altogether out of gear, by treadles at the driver's feet and handles at his side. The cost of the forcing apparatus is 15 guineas, and of the whole 45 guineas. The machine, it is said, can do the work of three ordinary water carts.

PROJECTED WORKS.—Advertisements have been issued for tenders, by 30th inst., for building a covered corn-exchange at Bedford; by July 2nd, for the erection of a bank at Darlington; by 4th, for the erection of schools at Margate; by 10th, for the erection of town-hall, county court, and mechanics' institute, at Stonehouse, Devonport; by 11th, for the erection of a pensioners' establishment at Regent's-park barracks; by 10th, for the erection of the Welsh Educational Institute, at Llandovery; by 29th inst., for the erection of a vicarage and offices at Bardsey; by 27th, for the erection of extensive farm buildings at Kirtling, Cambridgeshire; by 3rd July, for cutting trenches for water mains near Manchester; by 28th inst., for the whole or any portion of the works in erection of a north wing and additions to Manchester Royal Infirmary; by 3rd July, for the erection and completion of a warehouse at the Huddersfield Station of the Lancashire and Yorkshire Railway; by 3rd, for constructing a sluice at Outwell and for excavating the canal from Wisbech to Outwell; by 6th, for relaying carriage way in High-street and Spital-square, and other works; by 26th inst., for building sewers in Little Moorfields, &c., City; by 25th, for the construction of an outlet sewer at Toxteth-park, Liverpool; by 27th, for making roads and footpaths in Walthamstow parish; and by a date not specified for improving turnpike roads at Worcester.

COMPETITIONS.—Advertisements have been issued for plans, &c., of a church for Cheltenham; and for workhouse accommodation at Chelsea: particulars as advertised.

SOCIETY OF ARTS.—On Thursday in last week, the annual distribution of prizes took place, H. R. H. Prince Albert, the president, in the chair. In his speech, the prince stated that he had been induced this year to offer two medals on his own account, to be competed for on two subjects, very different in themselves, but appearing to ask for competition, and to be particularly eligible as subjects to which public attention should be drawn. The first was for making a good cement to bind glass together. The substitution of glass for metals was a matter of great importance as regarded cleanliness, and consequently the promotion of the public health, and that had been prevented to a great extent by the want of a cement that would hold. All connected with the manufacture of glass well knew that slipperiness of surface was a great cause of the difficulty experienced. But the subject of the next medal was one of national importance, and was intended to promote an improved system in the production of sugar. His Royal Highness then entered more fully into this question, which is out of our province. He expressed his satisfaction to see in the Colonial Secretary's presence a proof of the importance attached by the Government to this subject. The latter medal was awarded to Dr. Mitchell, but the former was not conferred on any one. The report read by the secretary stated that the revenue had increased during the past year from 800l. to 1,600l. per annum, and that the society had applied to the Board of Trade and the Woods and Forests for a space of ground for exhibitions of manufactures, the first of which it was proposed to hold in 1851. The prizes were then distributed, and the meeting was addressed by the Bishop of Norwich, Chevalier Bunsen, Sir E. Codrington, and others, and a vote of thanks accorded to the president.

THE PARISIAN PORTABLE ALARUM.—A cheap portable alarum has been submitted to us by Mr. Adams, and seems worthy the attention of those who require occasionally to rise early. The all-important point in an alarum is, of course, that it should go off at the desired moment; and if all comply with this condition as well as the specimen now in our hands does, buyers will have no reason to complain.

THE PARIS EXHIBITION OF THE WORKS OF LIVING ARTISTS was opened on the 15th, at the Tuileries. As might almost be expected, it is not of high character.

MURAL PAINTINGS AT ST. CROSS.—Mr. Baigent wishes us to state that the report that he was stopped in his efforts to obtain complete sketches of these paintings is not correct, as "nothing was done to the walls until several days afterwards."

BREACH OF CONTRACT IN THE IRON TRADE.—A case was recently tried in the Court of Exchequer, in which Baron Parke held that a firm-offer, authorising a party to sell at a stated price "till" a specified date, included the date so specified, till the evening of that day. But such an offer, he held, was not a binding contract till the bought and sold notes were communicated, and in this case that was not done till the day following. Evidence of this being the usage of the trade he did not think satisfactory, as offered in this case. A majority of the Jury, however, held it to be so. But the Baron started another difficulty. The contract he was of opinion was revocable, and in this case it was revoked by the defendant in due time, namely, on the last date specified in the offer, on its acceptance by the plaintiff. His lordship, therefore, directed a nonsuit in the claim of 187l. 10s. paid to another party on 300 tons of bar iron, on a rise in price from 5l. 7s. 6d. to 6l.,—with leave, however, to move to enter a verdict for the sum claimed. Eventually, to prevent further litigation, a juror was withdrawn, and the judge asked to decide whether the plaintiff were entitled to recover any, and if any, what sum. His lordship approved of this on account of various legal difficulties in the way, and awarded half the sum claimed.

BATHS AND WASHHOUSES. — TIMELY ADVICE.—A foreign visiter to some of our public baths, the Baron de Suarce, while honouring the English of all classes for the establishment of such noble institutions, advises the exercise of great and even scientific care in the cleansing of towels and flannels, particularly in such a season as the present, and, above all, in the metropolis, "whither crowd strangers from every quarter of the globe, many of them from countries deplorably unhealthy, and where disease has an increased malignity." It is not sufficient, as the Baron urges, that the towels be boiled in alkaline water—the ordinary mode of cleansing,—for thus "the corrupt humours of the diseased may be enfixed in them. That," he adds, "is what your medical men, agreeing with me, will tell you, and particularly your manufacturers in wool and cotton. At Leeds, and in the west of England, the operation of cleansing the wool is known to require a wash possessing a certain precise amount and no more of alkali and heat, as the slightest deviation irremoveably fixes the oil in the texture, instead of separating the two."

IMPROVEMENT AT PRINCES-STREET GARDENS, EDINBURGH.—Arrangements are in progress between the Government and the Edinburgh Town Council for a grant of ground on the mound, Princes-street, for the purpose of erecting buildings for the annual exhibitions of the Royal Scottish Academy, the extension of the Schools of Design, and the institution of a National Gallery of Painting and Sculpture. A design by the city architect, Mr. Cousin, has also been favourably considered by the council for the appropriation of a sum of money paid by the Edinburgh and Glasgow Railway Company, in the adornment and public opening of the gardens across which the mound runs. The scheme includes a terrace 95 feet wide along the eastern division, with the Scott monument in the centre, on the side next Princes-street, and a range of statues on pedestals. The plans, which comprise further improvements, are to be submitted for suggestion to other architects or artists.

RAILWAY JOTTINGS.—Contracts have been entered into at Glasgow, for the construction of part of the Nithsdale line between Sanquhar and Cumnock, a distance of 14 miles. Mr. Ritson is contractor for one-half the distance, and Messrs. Jeffs for one-fourth. The works are not heavy, and as the labour is cheap, they have been taken at 56,100l., to be completed in eighteen months. At the Drumlanrig tunnel there is now a drift through the whole excavation.——Another fatal accident has occurred at the Bramhope tunnel, where a stone from a blast in one shaft entered another 210 feet apart, and killed one of the workmen.—— Large sales of rails, to the extent of some 13,000 tons, are rumoured to have been charged to the York and Berwick Company, at 3l. or more per ton than they cost. It is said that a large iron house will undergo close examination on this point.——The

railway clocks on the Great Northern and other principal lines in France are now regulated by electricity, the mean time emanating from one regulating clock on the Great Northern.—— In Massachusetts there are 37 railway companies, with a capital stock of 50,004,100 dollars. The length of road is 954 miles, besides 88 of branches, cost 46,777,009 dollars. The earnings for last year were 6,057,154 dollars, working expenses 3,284,931 dollars. Only 220 miles are of double track Mean speed of passenger-trains about 23½—0 luggage-trains about 12½ miles. Return of casualties,—56 persons killed, and 65 injured During the year 300 miles of new road have been put in operation on the lines leading to Boston. The total mileage in the United States being 6,421, nearly one-sixth is in Massachusetts setts.

LORD ROSSE'S LAST SOIREE.—At the fourth and last conversazione given by Lord Rosse to the Fellows of the Royal Society on the 16th inst., there was a considerable attendance of men eminent in art, science, and literature. Amongst the matters exhibited which more particularly bore on our speciality was an extraordinary model of the Go Prum, or great gate of the Pagoda at Cimbaconum, near Tanjore, in the East Indies. This singular work is of pyramidal form above the gateway, in twelve stories, and displays about 300 carved figures. Mr. Perigal exhibited his instrument to develop a peculiar law of compound motion generating "retrogressive" curves, which has been seen before at similar meetings; and Mr. Scriven exhibited a model of the Ainslie Tile Economic Kilns, wherein the heat, generated in one kiln, and having there done its work, is made to pass into another, and advance the ware a certain stage. There were some pretty specimens of the vitrified lace-pattern glass, and an admirable collection of photographs by Messrs. Henneman and Co., of Regent-street, and Mr. John Woolley, an amateur. The architects mustered strongly, and the builders were not unrepresented.

VULCANIZED INDIA-RUBBER JOINTS.— In reply to inquiries, we have had no personal experience in the durability of Mr. Brockedon's vulcanised joints. There are reports, however, on the subject by Mr. Wicksteed and Mr. A. Aikin, which are strongly in their favour. Caoutchouc is vulcanised by combination with a certain small proportion of sulphur.

SOCIETY OF ARTS; LABOURERS' COTTAGES.—We have received several letters, complaining, in strong terms, of the non-adjudgment of the premium offered by the society for the best design for labourers' cottages. The society assert that the condition as to cost (100l. for each five-roomed cottage) was not adhered to.

A WORD IN SEASON.—Never be cast down by trifles. If a spider break his thread twenty times, twenty times will he mend it again. Make up your minds to do a thing in compass, and you will do it. Fear not if trouble comes upon you; keep up your spirits, though the day be a dark one.

Troubles never stop for ever,
The darkest day will pass away.

Fight hard against a hasty temper. If anger come, resist it stoutly. A spark may set a house on fire. A fit of passion may give you cause to mourn all the days of your life. Whatever you do, do it willingly. A boy that is whipped to school never learns his lesson well. A man that is compelled to work, cares not how badly it is performed. He that pulls off his coat cheerfully, strips up his sleeves in earnest, and sings while he works, is the man for us.

A cheerful spirit gets on quick;
A grumbler in the mud will stick.

BUILDINGS AND MONUMENTS,

EDITED BY GEORGE GODWIN, F.R.S., &c.

Part II., containing views of the Army and Navy Club House, Pall Mall; St. Stephen's Church and Schools, Westminster; Interior of the Museum of Economic Geology, with details; Chapter House of Lincoln Cathedral; New Hall, Pembroke College, Oxford; South Hackney Church; Interior of the Royal Italian Opera House, and University Galleries and Taylor Institute, Oxford, will be published on Saturday next.

TENDERS

Received by the Society for the Improvement of the Labouring Classes for building the New Model Lodging House for families in George-street, Bloomsbury; Mr. Roberts, honorary architect. The estimates provide for two modes of constructing the floors and roof; that consisting of hollow tile arches is to be the method adopted. The quantities were supplied.

	General estimate exclusive of floors and roof.	Floors and roofs constructed in the usual manner.	Floors and roof constructed with hollow tile arches.
Mansfield	£7,650	£1,365	£1,526
W. Cubitt and Co.	7,484	1,260	1,497
G. Bird	6,644	1,222	1,302
Ricks............	6,645	1,217	1,319
T. Piper and Co...	6,457	1,218	1,246
Hayward and Co..	6,262	1,120	1,180
Grimsdell.	6,268	1,043	1,148
Holland (accepted)	6,148	1,180	1,222

TO CORRESPONDENTS.

"*Smoky Bricks.*"—"G." (Canterbury), will find some advice on preventing stains from old smoked bricks, in our fourth volume, p. 465 (September 26th, 1846).

"*Building Materials in Paris.*"—Conclusion next week.

Received.—"G. D.," "A Competitor," "J. B." (Spring Gardens); "Mr. R.," "A. B.," "Old Subscriber," (Norwich: many thanks for kind words, always grateful and stimulating); "J. J. C." (ditto); "A Competitor" (the prize is withheld); "Architect in Embryo," "B. and B." (accidentally delayed. Were there other tenders? Can you explain cost); "W. W." (we have not space); "W. J.," "H. M'C." (note shall be forwarded); "J. T.," "R. J. M.," "A. B. S." (we hope to use it); "O. G.," "Expositor," "J. K.," "G. J. R.," "J. L.," "J. H. L.," "W. M.," "A. B. S.," "A Subscriber," "J. Q.," not arrived); "Messrs. W.," Mr. L." (declined): "J. F. (Ipswich); "E. S.," "Double Trapping," "G. G. (Saffron Walden); "J. W." (the subjects sent scarcely warrant engraving, but make us wish to see the other sketches); "Hints on Public Architecture." By Robt. Dale Owen, Chairman of Smithsonian Institution. (Putnam: New York, and Strand, London, 1849.) "A Hand-book for London, Past and Present." By P. Cunningham. 2 vols. London: (John Murray, 1849.) "Observations on the British Museum, National Gallery, and National Record-office, with suggestions for their improvement." By Jas. Fergusson, M.R.I.B.A. (Weale, Holborn, 1849.)

NOTICE.—All communications respecting *advertisements* should be addressed to the "Publisher," and not to the "Editor:" all other communications should be addressed to the EDITOR, and *not* to the Publisher.

ADVERTISEMENTS.

ARCHITECTS', BUILDERS', and GENERAL FIRE and LIFE INSURANCE COMPANY, 69, Lombard-street, London.

CHAIRMAN, SYDNEY SMIRKE, Esq., A.R.A.

TRUSTEES.

T. L. Donaldson, Esq. | A. Salvin, Esq., F.S.A.
S. Grimsdell, Esq. | C. Smith, Esq., F.S.A.

The rates for both Fire and Life Insurances are as low as can with safety be taken. Those for Life Insurance may be paid either yearly, half-yearly, or quarterly; one-half the annual premium may be left unpaid for seven years, or one-third to the end of life. Thus large sums may be insured at the smallest present outlay.

Prospectuses, forms of proposals, &c., may be had at the Office 69, Lombard-street, or of the agents.

JOHN REDDISH, Manager.

BUILDERS' BENEVOLENT INSTITUTION.—SECOND ANNIVERSARY DINNER to be held at the London Tavern, on WEDNESDAY, the 18th of July, 1849.

The Rt. Hon. the Earl of CARLISLE in the Chair.

STEWARDS.

THE RIGHT HON. EARL MANVERS.
THE RIGHT HON. LORD ROBERT GROSVENOR, M.P.
THE LORD DUDLEY COUTTS STUART, M.P.
GENERAL SIR DE LACY EVANS, K.C.B., M.P.
SIR BENJAMIN HALL, Bart., M.P.
WILLIAM CUBITT, Esq., M.P.
SAMUEL MORTON PETO, Esq., M.P.
DAVID SALOMANS, Esq., Ald.
SIDNEY SMIRKE, Esq., A.R.A.
THOS. GRISSELL, Esq., F.R.S.
WILLIAM TITE, Esq., P.R.S.
GEORGE GODWIN, Esq., F.R.S.

Abbott, Mr. James.
Adams, Mr. Thomas.
Aitchison, Geo., Esq. (Dist. Surv.)
Allen, Mr. Thomas.
Angell, Samuel, Esq. (Dist. Surv.)
Armstrong, J., Esq.
Ashby, Mr. Henry.
Austen, Henry, Esq.
Austin, Mr. H. D.
Biers, Hugh, Esq., President.
Baker, Henry, Esq. (Dist. Surv.)
Banting, J., Esq.
Bardwell, Mr. Wm.
Barnett, John, Esq.
Barrett, Mr. G.
Beaumont, A., Esq.
Bennett, Jos., Esq.
Bennett, Mr. Wm.
Betts, E. Esq.
Bird, Stephen, Esq.
Bird, Mr. Joseph.
Bird, Mr. Henry.
Bird, Mr. G., Treas.
Bosse, Mr. John
Bott, Arthur, Esq.
Boulting, Mr. John.
Brown, Mr. Edm.
Brown, Mr. George.
Burton, D., Esq.
Burton, Mr. Henry
Carter, Mr. J.
Cisto, Mr. William.
Coleman, Mr. J.
Collins & Stanbury, Messrs., Birmingham.
Cooper, Rd., Esq.
Cooper, Mr. H. W.
Coote, Mr. W., jun.
Cozens, Mr. Thos.
Crake, Wm., Esq.
Curtis, Mr. Robert.
Curtis, Mr. Edward.
Day, Mr. Ebenezer.
Dent, Wm., Esq.
Dobson, Wm. Esq.
Donaldson, Thos. L., Esq. (Dist. Surv.)
Eales, Chris., Esq.
Eales, Mr. William.

Ebbs, Mr. John.
Edser, Mr. James
Eldred, John, Esq.
Ellis, Mr. William.
Eyre, Walpole, Esq.
Ferguson, Mr. D.
Ferrey, B., Esq.
Field, James, Esq.
Francis, F., Esq.
Freeman, W., Esq., Jun.
Gotto, Edward, Esq.
Gutch, George, Esq. (Dist. Surv.)
Gough, B., Esq.
Gooch, Mr. W.
Grayson, C., Esq.
Greaves, Rich., Esq., Stratford-upon-Avon.
Hardy, J., Esq.
Harris, Mr. William
Halvey, J. W., Esq.
Hertslet, Lewis, Esq.
Heywood, Geo., Esq.
Higgs, Mr. Joshua.
Hosking, Wm., Esq. (Official Referee).
Hodson, W. M., Esq.
Howard, Mr. Thos.
Hutchons, Mr. Wm.
Hold, William, Esq.
Jackson, Mr. John.
Jenkins, W., Esq.
Kendall, H. E., Esq. (Dist. Surv.)
Kendall, H. E., Jun. Esq. (Dist. Surv.)
King, William, Esq.
Knight, James, Esq.
Knight, J. G., Esq.
Knowles, J. T., Esq.
Laxton, W., Esq.
Lee, William, Esq.
Lee, Charles, Esq.
Leonard, John, Esq.
Lever, Mr. George.
Little, Mr. B. J.
Lloyd, L. W., Esq.
Lomax, E., Esq.
Long, J., Esq.
Lovick, Mr. T.
Manning, J., Esq.
Mather, Mr. Alex.

Mayhew, Chas., Esq. (Dist. Surv.)
McGill, James, Esq.
Moon, James, Esq.
Munday, Geo., Esq.
Nesham, Thos., Esq.
Oldfield, C. F., Esq.
Outhwaite, Mr. J.
Parker, T. R., Esq.
Parsons, John, Esq.
Pearse, Peter, Esq.
Pennethorne, J., Esq.
Phillips, John, Esq.
Potter, Mr. George.
Poynter, Amb., Esq. (Official Referee)
Reynolds, Mr. Wm.
Richardson, R., Esq.
Roberts, R., Esq.
Rowe, Edward, Esq.
Rudd, G. P., Esq.
Salvin, A., Esq.
Sarson, Michael, Esq.
Shee, Mr. Serjeant.
Simmonds, G. H. Esq.
Smith, C. S., Esq.
Sterling, J., Esq.
Stephens, Mr. S. J.
Stewart, W., Esq.
Stone, Coutts, Esq.
Symonds, A., Esq.
Tarring, J., Esq.
Taylor, G. V., Esq.
Taylor, Mr. J. T.
Taylor, Mr. Joseph
Thorn, Mr. John.
Thorpe, Mr. John.
Tillott, J., Esq.
Timpson, Mr. M.
Todd, Mr. W., jun.
Trego, Wm., Esq.
Tress, W., Esq.
Turnbull, Mr. T.
Tyerman, T., Esq.
Unwin, Mr. Isaac.
Wade, Rich., Esq.
Warrington, E., Esq.
Webb, Wm., Esq.
West, Mr. William.
White, J., Esq. (Dist. Surv).
White, J. A., Esq.
Williams, Mr. J.
Wing, C., Esq.

Gentlemen desirous of forwarding the views of the Institution by becoming Stewards, will be pleased to forward their names to the Secretary, Mr. A. G. HARRIS, at the Office, 13, Broad-street, Golden-square.

CROGGON'S PATENT ASPHALTE ROOFING FELT and INODOROUS FELT, for DAMP WALLS. Sold in rolls, 32 inches wide, price one penny per square foot. Also, Dry Hair Felt for preventing the radiation of heat and deadening sound. Samples, directions, and testimonials sent by post, on application to CROGGON and Co., No. 2, Dowgate-hill, Walbrook.

DRYING for BATHS and WASH-HOUSES, ASYLUMS, LAUNDRIES, &c.—The Patent Dessicating Company can dry, by their process, at any rate of speed, expel any amount of moisture; at the same time disinfect and give a sweetness to clothing, &c., altogether unattainable by means of cockles, steam, hot-water pipes, &c.—For full particulars, apply at the offices of the Patent Dessicating Company, 41, Gracechurch-street, City. ANGUS JENNINGS, Secretary.

PARISIAN PORTABLE ALARUMS (Sonnerie très-bruyante), indispensable for architects, builders, employés, &c., and all whose professional pursuits require occasionally very early rising. They are exceedingly small, measuring only 2½ inches diameter by 1½ inch thick; so simple in construction that they cannot well get out of order. They may be set to any required time, and will not fail to awake the soundest sleeper. Price, 20s. each; electro silver plate, 22s. 6d. Forwarded by post to any part of the kingdom, upon receipt of a post-office order, including one shilling extra, payable at Charing-cross.—Agent—WILLIAM S. ADAMS, furnishing ironmonger, 57, Haymarket.

BIELEFELD'S PAPIER MACHE.—The superiority of which, for Architectural Decorations, is proved by the fact of its extensive application in this and other countries. A quarto volume is published, price 1l., with a Tariff, containing upwards of 1,000 designs, most of them executed for works designed by eminent Architects. Patronised by the Hon. Commissioners of Her Majesty's Woods and Works.

"This is unquestionably a most valuable invention."—*Literary Gazette.*

Works, 15, Wellington-street North, Strand.

PAPIER MACHE and CARTON PIERRE ENRICHMENTS MANUFACTORY, 49 and 50, Rathbone-place.—GEORGE JACKSON and SONS beg the attention of Architects, Builders, Decorators, and others, to their large assortment of ENRICHMENTS in every style, executed in the highest class of art.

The facilities and repeated enlargement of means enable GEORGE JACKSON and SONS to announce the execution of works of the above descriptions in these advantageous materials at a cost considerably below any known method, while for quality, relief, and finish, they flatter themselves they stand unrivalled.

Just published—a large Quarto Work of their ENRICHMENTS, with dimensions for reference and price.

MINTON and CO.'S ENCAUSTIC and other PATENT TILES for Churches, Entrance Halls, Conservatories, Balconies, &c., Antique, Geometrical, and Alhambric Mosaics, manufactures of a highly decorative character and extreme durability. Slabs and Tiles for Fireplaces, Hearths, and Covings for Grates, Door Furniture, White Glazed and Ornamental Tiles for Baths, Dairies, and Kitchen Ranges may be had in great variety at their Warehouse, 9, Albion-place, Blackfriars-bridge, London, and at their Manufactory, Stoke-upon-Trent, Staffordshire.

TO ARCHITECTS, BUILDERS, AND RAILWAY CONTRACTORS.

BRICKS and TILES, plain and moulded, manufactured in a superior manner, from fine beds of clay on the Earl of Leicester's estate at Holkham, of red, blue, and Bath stone colours, both for plain and ornamental work. Specimens to be seen at Blashfield's Wharf, Commercial-road, Lambeth (near Waterloo-bridge), consisting of plain bricks of the usual size for building purposes, moulded bricks for forming Tudor chimney shafts, of various designs, label mouldings, cornices, copings, window sills, dressings for windows and doors, mullions, ridges, skirtings, &c. Also roofing and paving tiles of an ornamental character in the same materials. The moulded bricks are fully equal to the best specimens referred to under the articles "Brickwork," in Nos. 290 and 291, of "The Builder."

FIRE BRICKS.—To Builders, Gas Companies, Engineers, &c. &c. WARD and CO., Honduras Wharf, Bankside, have now on hand an extensive and well-selected Stock of every description of Fire Bricks, Lumps, Tiles, Clays, &c., used in Gas Works, Coke Ovens, Furnaces, Kilns, &c., which they are offering on very liberal terms to consumers, and the trade in general; also, Malm Paviors, Stock Bricks, Patent Malting Tiles, Pan, Plain and Ridge Do., Windsor and other Oven Tiles, Sand, Gravel, Lime, Cement, Windsor and other Loams, Red and White House Sand, Dutch Clinkers, Sanitary Pipes, and every article connected with general Building. Goods made to pattern on the shortest notice. Country buyers and consumers will find this the best and cheapest market.

DR. ARNOTT'S VALVES for thoroughly VENTILATING APARTMENTS of every description. F. EDWARDS having had the advantage of making them under the immediate direction and patronage of Dr. Arnott, enables him to present the public with Valves of the most approved principle for general use. Prices from 7s. 6d. to 90s. and upwards. A prospectus, containing every information, to be had on application to F. EDWARDS, 42, Poland-street, Oxford-street, London.

DR. ARNOTT'S VENTILATING CHIMNEY VALVE.

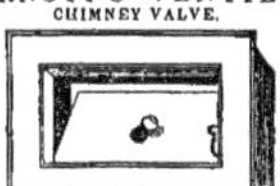

For carrying off Heated and Impure Air from Bed-rooms Sitting-rooms, Counting-houses, and Apartments generally.

LIST OF PRICES.

	First size, 11 by 8.	Second size, 16 by 9
Plain Iron Valve	7 6	12 0
Bronzed and Leathered	9 0	14 0
Japanned, white with Gold lines	15 0	21 0
Brass Front........	17 0	24 0

Packing Cases (if required), 1s. 3d. each.

Manufactured by HART and SONS, 53, 54, 55, Wych-street Strand, London.

IMPROVED SELF-ACTING CHIMNEY VENTILATORS.

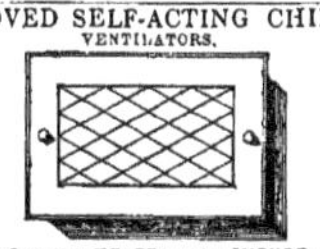

FOR CARRYING OFF HEATED AND IMPURE AIR from drawing-rooms, sitting-rooms, bed-rooms, nurseries, offices, &c. &c., from 5s. each.—BURT and POTTS, Manufacturers and Ironmongers, 65, York-street, Westminster, London.

Stoves, ranges, rain-water pipes, gutters, and builders' ironmongery, as low as any house in London. Delivered free within 5 miles.

BUILDERS and CARPENTERS' IRONMONGERY WAREHOUSE, 18, Blandford-street, Manchester-square, leading out of Baker-street, Portman-square. Lists of prices may be obtained on pre-paid application.

JOHN and EDWIN YOUNG, Proprietors.

LAP WELDED IRON TUBES.—W. H. RICHARDSON, Jun., and Co., MANUFACTURERS of every description of WROUGHT IRON TUBES for Locomotive and Marine Boilers, Gas, Steam, and other purposes.

PATENT TUBE WORKS, DARLASTON, STAFFORDSHIRE.

HOT-WATER APPARATUS.—The attention of architects, builders, and others is respectfully requested to BENJAMIN FOWLER'S superior method of heating churches and chapels, halls, staircases, conservatories, forcing and greenhouses, manufactories and warehouses, kilns, rooms for drying timber, &c., and every variety of purpose for which artificial heat is required. Within the last twenty years some hundreds of buildings have been heated upon this plan, and the parties for whom they were executed are constantly expressing their satisfaction, also their willingness to vouch for their efficiency.

BENJAMIN FOWLER, late of 63, Dorset-street, removed to the new factory, Whitefriars-street, Fleet-street.

IRON FOUNDRY, 80, Goswell-street (late of Brick-lane, St. Luke's).—J. J. JONES having made great additions to his STOCK of PATTERNS, begs to inform the Trade, that he can now supply them with Plain and Ornamental Iron Columns Girders, Railings, Gates, Iron Coping, Balconies, Window Guards, Verandahs, Ornamental Staircase Panels, Iron Staircases, Tomb Enclosures, Trellis Panelling, Lamp and other Brackets, Cantilevers, Newel Bars, Water Closet Work, Area Gratings, Fly and other Wheels, Wheel Plates, &c.

BAKER'S OVEN WORK, Forge Backs and Troughs, Rain Water Pipes and Gutters, Sash Weights, Furnace Bars, Stoves Ranges, &c., always in stock.

IRON FOUNDRY,
68, DRURY-LANE, and CHARLES-STREET, DRURY-LANE
JOSEPH GLOVER,

Solicits the attention of the Trade to his extensive Stock of PATTERNS for CASTINGS of EVERY DESCRIPTION, consisting of those for every purpose, either structural or ornamental.

Wheel Pinion and Steam-Engine Patterns; Range Stove and Hot Plate Metal.

A stock of Rain-Water Pipes, Plain and O G Guttering, Air Bricks, Sash Weights, &c. &c.

A very superior description of Soot Door, particularly suitable for internal work, being perfectly secure, and not unsightly.

ESTIMATES given for IRON ROOFING and every description of Ironwork, complete to specification, and the work executed with every attention to quality and dispatch.

GLOVER'S FOUNDRY,
168, DRURY-LANE, and CHARLES-STREET.

IRON SHUTTERS.—The PATENT CONVEX REVOLVING IRON SHUTTERS are cheaper, twelve times stronger, work easier, cannot run down, and roll up in one-third less room than any other shutters made. Harcourt Quincey, Patentee.

CLARK and Co., Sole Manufacturers, and of IMPROVED DRAWN ORNAMENTAL METALLIC SASH BARS, ASTRAGALS, MOULDINGS, STALL-BOARD PLATES, &c. &c., in brass, copper, and zinc. WROUGHT-IRON GIRDERS, HOT-WATER APPARATUS, and metal works of every description connected with buildings. Steam engines, millwork, and machinery. CLARK and Co., Engineers, 236, Wapping. Models can be seen and every information obtained at 434, Oxford-street, and 4, Moorgate-street, City. Agent for Scotland, Mr. G. BRIGSTOCK, 17 George-street, Edinburgh.

BUNNETT and Co., ENGINEERS,
Patentees of
REVOLVING IRON AND WOOD SAFETY SHUTTERS,
and of
ORNAMENTAL METALLIC SASH BARS, MOULDINGS, &c.,
IN BRASS, COPPER, ZINC, &c.
FOR SHOP-FRONTS, SKYLIGHTS, &c.

Shop-fronts completely fitted and fixed in a superior style, either plain or ornamental, also glazed with best plate glass. Strong moulded stallboards handsomely engraved. Metal works and machinery of all kinds in connection with banking-houses, shops, warehouses, &c. &c.

B. and Co. challenge competition as to either quality or price.

Designs furnished and estimates given.

IMPROVED PATENT BENCH AND FLOORING CRAMPS FOR BUILDERS.

SOLE LICENCEES FOR MARVIN and MOORE'S PATENT DIAGONAL GRATINGS.

Office of the Patentees, 26, Lombard-street, London; and at the Works, Deptford, Kent.

CHUBBS' LOCKS, FIRE-PROOF SAFES, AND CASH BOXES.

CHUBBS' PATENT DETECTOR LOCKS give perfect security from false keys and picklocks, and also detect any attempt to open them. They are made of all sizes, and for every purpose to which locks are applied, and are strong, secure, simple, and durable.

CHUBBS' PATENT LATCH, for front doors, counting-house doors, &c., is simple in construction, low in price, and quite secure. The keys are particularly neat and portable.

CHUBBS' PATENT FIRE-PROOF SAFES, BOOKCASES, CHESTS, &c., made entirely of strong wrought-iron, so as effectually to resist the falling of brick-work, timber, &c., in case of fire, and are also perfectly secure from the attacks of the most skilful burglars.

CHUBBS' CASH and DEED BOXES, fitted with the Detector Locks.

CHUBB and SON, 57, St. Paul's Churchyard, London.

CAST-IRON PIPES, IRON WORK FOR OVENS, &c.

RAIN PIPES, &c.—F. A. TIDDEMAN, St. Ann's Wharf, Earl-street, City, near Blackfriars-bridge, keeps a large stock of Rain Pipes, Heads, Shoes, Elbows, &c., half round and O. G. Gutters, Socket Pipes for Water or Gas, Flanch Pipes, Sash Weights, and other Castings; Iron Work for Baker's Ovens of every description, fitted complete, to be had in sets or in parts.—Prices equal to all competition. Contracts taken to any extent.

TO ARCHITECTS, BUILDERS, AND BRICK-MAKERS.

PUMPS of Superior CONSTRUCTION, bored perfectly true by improved machinery, in various plain and ornamental patterns for Conservatories, Squares, Market Places, Roads, Gardens, and for Liquid Manure. BRICK-MAKERS' PUMPS, in Wrought and Cast Iron, HYDRAULIC LIFT PUMPS, and ENGINES for Wells of any depth. SINGLE and DOUBLE PUMPS up to twelve-inch bore, kept for Hire.

BENJ. FOWLER (late of 63, Dorset-street), removed to the new Factory, Whitefriars-street, Fleet-street.

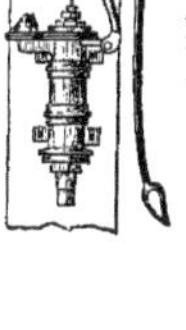

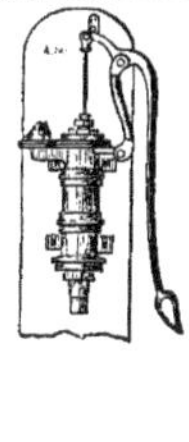

TO BUILDERS AND PLUMBERS.

THE attention of the Trade is called to JOHN WARNER & SONS' PATENT VIBRATING STANDARD PUMP, which is recommended for the simplicity of its construction, and the ease with which it works.

By the introduction of the vibrating standard the cumbrous carriage and expensive slings and guides are unnecessary, rendering the price considerably less than pumps made on the old plan.

Beer and Water Engines for raising fluids from a depth not exceeding 28 feet; also, Garden Engines constructed on the same principle.

JOHN WARNER & SONS,
8, Crescent, Jewin-street, London,
Manufacturers and Patentees.

		Thick.			
	1 in.	1½ in.	1½ in.	2 in.	2½ in.
	d.	s. d.	s. d.	s. d.	s. d.
Under 4 ft. long, or 3 ft. wide	3½	5	6	7	9	1 ft. sup.
Ditto 5 ft. do., or 3 ft. do.	4	5½	7	8	11	do.
Ditto 6 ft. do., or 3 ft. do.	4½	6½	8	10	1 0	do.
Ditto 7 ft. do., or 3 ft. do.	5	7	9	11	1 2	do.

Larger Slabs in proportion.

		Thick.			
	1 in.	1½ in.	1½ in.	2 in.	2½ in.
	d.	s. d.	s. d.	s. d.	s. d.
Cutting to order	1	1½	2	2½	3	1 ft. sup.

No. CCCXXXIV.

SATURDAY, JUNE 30, 1849.

ONDERFUL LONDON! "London;—opulent, enlarged, and still increasing London! Babylon of old, nor more the glory of the earth than she, a nore accomplish'd world's chief glory now."
'If you wish," said Johnson, "to have a ust notion of the magnitude of this :ity, you must not be satisfied with seeng its great streets and squares, but must urvey the innumerable little lanes and courts. t is not in the showy evolutions of buildings, ut in the multiplicity of human habitations which are crowded together, that the wonderful mmensity of London consists." And Byron 1as the same idea of it when he says—

' The man who has stood on the Acropolis,
And look'd down over Attica ; or he
Who has sall'd where picturesque Constanti-
        nople is,
Or seen Timbuctoo, or hath taken tea
In small-eyed China's crockery-ware metro-
        polis,
Or sat amidst the bricks of Nineveh,
May not think much of London's first appear-
        ance ;—
3ut ask him what he thinks of it a year hence ?''

That he may answer with truth, however, even hen, he must have looked a little beyond the urface, and have seen, as well as the town, the ast and complicated operations going on in it— 's trade and commerce, administration of jus- ice, monetary system, legislature, machinery, raffic, markets, clubs, places of worship and musement, scientific and literary associations, he habits and manners of the people. Its old streets are all histories—

" The stones have voices ; and the walls do live ;"

.nd its new squares are most eloquent utter- .nces of the present time, to those whose eyes .nd ears are open. Far outstretching on every iide, long strings of residences tie it to the .djacent country, and render its limits inde- inable. The Thames links the world to it : ts institutions have made it the focus of civi- ization : ability from whatever clime there will iave reward, and deposed kings, exiled minis- ers, and flying " red republicans " find refuge iide by side,—

" Where London streets ferment in full
        activity,"—

ecure so long as they respect the laws. A 'ear may give a good notion of London, but o know it requires much more time than his.

Even those who have lived in it all their ives, if they will glance through Mr. Cun- iingham's " Hand - Book," just now pub- ished,* and which being before us has led to he foregoing observations, will see how much here is in London of which they know iothing, and how full of interest and wisdom .re scores of places that they have passed istlessly scores of times. To those who see ightly, London is much fuller than it is to he unknowing, who see only with the eye.

Horace Walpole has this memorandum,— " There is a French book, called ' Anecdotes ies Rues de Paris.' I had begun a similar vork, ' Anecdotes of the streets of London.' intended, in imitation of the French origi-

nal, to have pointed out the streets and houses where any remarkable incident had happened ; but I found the labour would be too great, in collecting materials from various streets, and I abandoned the design, after having written about ten or twelve pages." Some years ago, we fell upon the notion ourselves, as probably many others have done, before meeting with it in " Walpoliana," and began " Stories of the Streets,"* but the intention went to pave a nameless place. Mr. Crofton Croker, in a series of most interesting dissertations, printed in " Fraser's Magazine," two or three years since, under the title of " A Walk from Hyde- park Corner to Fulham," showed to what an extent the idea might be carried out by intelli- gence and industry. And now, in the volumes before us, Mr. Cunningham has made Wal- pole's remark the motto on his title-page, and has to a considerable extent, but necessarily in this " Handbook ;" and he has brought to bear upon it an immense amount of reading, espe- cially of the poets and essayists of the two last centuries, showing industry and powers of research in the examination of parish papers and other MSS., and discrimination and skill in the use' made of the matter col- lected. The book is in the dictionary form, similar in that respect to Elmes's " Topo- graphical Dictionary of London :" it contains a great deal of new matter, and must have cost its author much pains and labour during the seven years it has been in hand.

Mr. Cunningham commences his work with an interesting " Chronology of London Occurrences," brought up to the present time ; and from this, without stopping to check the dates, we have selected some of the events relating to buildings :—

" 886—London repaired or rebuilt by Alfred the Great.

1078-81—White Tower, in the Tower of London, built by Gundulph, bishop of Rochester.

1083—Old St. Paul's (the church described by Dugdale) began to be built.

1097—Westminster Hall built by William Rufus ; part of the building still remains.

1133—St. Bartholomew's Church founded by Rahere.

1176—London-bridge " began to be founded."

1185—Temple Church, dedicated by Heraclius, patriarch of Jerusalem. The inscription recording the circumstance was destroyed in 1695.

1189—In this year it was directed that all houses should be built of stone up to a certain height, and covered with slate or baked tile.

1208—The church of St. Mary Overy in South- wark " begonne."

1221—The foundation-stone of the Lady Chapel in Westminster Abbey laid by Henry III.

1222—St. Paul's steeple built and finished.

1245—Henry III. ordered the east end, the tower, and the transepts of Westminster Abbey Church, to be taken down and rebuilt on a larger scale, and in a more elegant form, at his ' own expense.'

1245—Savoy Palace built.

1285—The great conduit in West Cheap com- menced building ; this was the first cistern of lead castellated with stone erected in London ; the water was conveyed by leaden pipes from Tyburn.

1290—Stone cross in Cheapside erected by Edward I. to Queen Eleanor.

1397—Westminster Hall repaired by Richard II. ; the walls were carried up 2 feet higher ; the windows altered ; a stately front and a new roof constructed, according to the design of Master Henry Zeneley.

1431—Fleet-bridge repaired or rebuilt ; this was the bridge standing in Stow's time.

1503-4, Jan. 24—First stone of Henry VII.'s Chapel laid.

1505—Henry VII. rebuilds the Savoy, as an hospital of St. John the Baptist, for the relief of a hundred poor people ; Stow says about 1509, but Weever tells us that the date 1505 was over the gate.

1518 — Lincoln's - inn Gate, Chancery - lane, erected.

1540-41—High Holborn paved.

1548-49 — Old Somerset House commenced building.

1552—May, Covent Garden and Seven Acres, called Long-acre, granted to John, Earl of Bed- ford, Lord Privy Seal.

1561—June 4, the steeple and roof of old St. Paul's consumed by lightning.

1566—June 7, the first stone of the Royal Ex- change laid.

1571—Whitechapel first paved.

1572—Middle Temple Hall built.

1580—July 7, the Queen's proclamation dated, prohibiting the erection, within three miles of the city gates, of any new houses or tenements " where no former house hath been known to have been."

1582—Thames water first conveyed into men's houses by pipes of lead from an engine near London- bridge, made by Peter Morris, a Dutchman ; this engine supplied the Standard in Cornhill, which was first erected this year.

1586—Lodgate rebuilt, and the statue of Queen Elizabeth, now at St. Dunstan's, set up.

1594—An engine erected by an Englishman (Bevis Bulmer) to convey Thames water into West- cheap and Fleet-street.

1603—Sept. 16, Proclamation issued by King James against inmates and multitudes of dwellers in streets, rooms, and places, in and about the City of London.

1606-7—Moorfields drained.

1608—June 10, first stone of the New Exchange in the Strand laid.

1609—April 11, New Exchange in the Strand opened.

1617—July 7. Church of St. John's, Wapping, consecrated by King, bishop of London.

1618-19—Jan. 12 (Tuesday,) the old Banquetting House at Whitehall burnt down (Howes, p. 1031).

1619—June 1, Inigo Jones's banqueting-house, at Whitehall, commenced building.

1620—Sept. 20, New River finished by Sir Hugh Myddelton.

1630—July 24, proclamation dated " concerning new buildings in and about the Cittie of London, and against the dividing of houses into several dwellings, and harbouring inmates ; forbidding the erection of any building upon a new foundation, within the limits of three miles from any of the gates of the city of London or Palace of Westminster."

1632—Sept. 14, first stone of the chapel at So- merset House laid by Henrietta Maria (Ellis's Letters, iii., 271, 2nd series).

1633—Church of St. Paul, Covent Garden, built ; it was not consecrated till 1638, owing to a dispute between the Earl of Bedford, at whose expense it was built, and the vicar of St. Martin's-in-the- Fields, who claimed the right of presentation.

1633—Inigo Jones's classic portico to Old St. Paul's commenced.

1635—Lincoln's-Inn Fields laid out according to the plan of Inigo Jones.

1638—Sept. 27, Church of St. Paul's, Covent Garden, consecrated.

1643—London fortified : Mount-street, Gros- venor-square, derives its name from one of the fortifications.

1652—July 21, Inigo Jones died.

1657—June 20, " Much debate was upon the Bill for restraint of new buildings in and about London" (Whitelocke, p. 661).

1657 — Portugal - row, Lincoln's Inn - fields, erected.

1662—July 17, supervisors appointed by the Commons for repairing the highways and sewers.

1662—Nov. 15, Hugh Audley, " the rich Aud. ley," died ; North and South Audley-streets were called after him.

1666—Sept. 13, proclamation dated for the re- building the city.

1667—May 8, Order in Council for rebuilding the City dated.

1667—Oct. 23, first stone of the second Royal Exchange laid.

1667—The Rebuilding Act passed (19 Car. II., c. 3) ; a monument to be erected in memory of the fire, near the place where it broke out (sec. 29).

1670—An additional Act for the rebuilding of the City passed (22 Car. II., c. 11). Water from the tops of houses to be conveyed down the sides of houses by pipes.

1670—Temple Bar built.

1671—The Monument commenced building.

1671—Bow Church commenced building.

1674—Charles I.'s statue at Charing Cross erected.

1675—June 21, first stone of St. Paul's laid ; warrant to commence dated May 1st, 1675.

1678—Parish of St. Ann, Westminster, made.

1680—St. Bride's Church, Fleet-street, built.

1682—March, Charles II. laid the first stone of Chelsea Hospital.

1682—First fire insurance established ; the Phœ- nix, at the Rainbow Coffee-house, in Fleet-street.

1684—July 13, St. James's Church, Piccadilly, consecrated.

1684—Dover-street built.

1686—March 21, Church of St. Ann, Soho, con- secrated by Compton, bishop of London.

---

* A Hand Book for London, past and present. By Peter Cunningham. 2 vols. London ; 1849. John Murray.

* Under this same title, if we remember rightly, Mr. Leigh Hunt wrote some papers not long ago.

1696—June 30, first stone of Greenwich Hospital laid.

1698—First workhouse erected in London; erected in Bishopsgate-street, next door to Sir Paul Pindar's.

1705—Tottenham-court-road first paved.

1709—Marlborough House built.

1714—Feb. 25, first stone of the church of St. Mary-le-Strand laid.

1715—Cavendish-square commenced.

1720—House designed for the Duke of Chandos, on the north side of Cavendish-square, began to be built.

1721—Present church of St. Martin's-in-the Fields built.

1723—Feb. 25, Sir Christopher Wren died.

1724—March 23, church of St. George's, Hanover-square, consecrated.

1732—Aug. 3, first stone of Bank of England laid.

1732-33—March, Saville-row, Burlington-gardens, laid out.

1735—Westminster Abbey towers completed.

1735—June 2, the area of Lincoln's Inn-fields railed in.

1738-39—Jan. 29, first stone of Westminster-bridge laid.

1753—Horse Guards built.

1753—Mansion House finished.

1764—Portman-square commenced.

1775—The present Somerset House commenced building.

1777—Portland-place built.

1778—Marybone Gardens closed and the site let to builders (*Lysons*, iii. 245).

1790—April 9, first stone of Novosielski's Opera House laid.

1795—Sept. 17, Covent Garden Church, built by Inigo Jones, burnt down.

1807—Jan. 28, gas first employed; Pall Mall the first street lighted with gas, through the sanguine perseverance of a German named Winsor; Bishopsgate-street was the second street in London lighted with gas.

1811—Oct. 11, first stone of Waterloo-bridge laid; it was then called the Strand-bridge."

In seeking to give an idea of the book, our object must be to extract those portions which may be most interesting to our readers.

Speaking of *Aldersgate-street*, and first quoting Howell, who, in his "Londinopolis," published in 1657, said this street resembled an Italian street *more than any other* in London, "by reason of the spaciousness and uniformity of buildings, and straightness thereof, with the convenient distance of the houses," he says,—

"On the east side (distinguished by a series of eight pilasters) stands Thanet House, one of Inigo Jones's fine old mansions, the London residence of the Tuftons, Earls of Thanet. From the Tufton family it passed into the family of Anthony Ashley Cooper, Earl of Shaftesbury (d. 1682-3); hence Shaftesbury-place and Shaftesbury House, as Walpole calls it in his account of Inigo Jones. In 1708 it was once more in the possession of the Thanet family; in 1720 it was a handsome inn; in 1734 a tavern; in 1750 the London Lying-in Hospital; and in 1848 a general dispensary.* A little higher up on the same side, where Lauderdale-buildings stand, stood Lauderdale House, the London residence of John Maitland, Duke of Lauderdale (d. 1682), one of the celebrated cabal in the reign of Charles II. On the same side, still higher up, and two doors from Barbican, stood the 'Bell Inn,' 'of a pretty good resort for waggons with meal.' From this inn, on the 14th July, 1618, John Taylor, the Water Poet, set out on his pennyless pilgrimage to Scotland.† On the west side, a little beyond the church of St. Botolph, Aldersgate, is Trinity-court, so called from a brotherhood of the Holy Trinity, licensed by Henry VI., suppressed by Edward VI., and first founded in 1377, as a fraternity of St. Fabian and Sebastian. The hall was standing in 1790."‡

Under the head, *Bow-street, Covent Garden*, built 1637, we hear something of Grinling Gibbons, the carver, who "lived in a house on the east side (about the middle of the street), from 1678 to 1721, the period of his death. The house was distinguished by the sign of 'The King's Arms.'* 'On Thursday the house of Mr. Gibbons, the famous carver, in Bow-street, Covent Garden, fell down; but by a special Providence none of the family were killed; but 'tis said a young girl, which was playing in the court [King's-court?], being missing, is supposed to be buried in the rubbish.'—*Postman of Jan.* 24, 1701-2."

* Hatton, p. 633. Strype's Stow, B. iii. p. 121. Ralph's Crit. Rev. Pennant.

† Taylor, in his Carrier's Cosmographie (4to., 1637) mentions four inns in this street—the Peacock, the Bell, the Three Horse Shoes, the Cock.

‡ There is a view of the old Hall in Brayley's Londiniana, 4 vols. 12mo., 1829.

In a house at the upper end of this street, Bonnell Thornton "opened an exhibition of sign paintings,—a piece of inoffensive drollery, taken from the annual exhibition of pictures made by a society of artists, previous to the institution of the Royal Academy."

Of *Covent Garden* Mr. Cunningham says,—

"Covent Garden, particularly so called, is the large and well proportioned square in which the market stands; with the arcade or piazza on the north and north-east side, Tavistock-row on the south, and the church of St. Paul's, Covent Garden, on the west. The square was formed (circ. 1631) at the expense of Francis, Earl of Bedford (d. 1641), and from the designs of Inigo Jones† (d. 1652), though never completed or even perhaps designed in full. The arcade or piazza ran along the whole of the north and east side of the square; the church completed the west; and the south was girt by the wall of Bedford House garden and a grove or "small grotto of trees most pleasant in the summer season,"‡ and under which the first market was originally held. In the centre of the square was a column surmounted by a dial (but this was subsequent to Inigo Jones's time§), and the whole area was laid with gravel, and dry and well kept. The scene of Dryden's 'Sir Martin-Mar-All' is laid in this once fashionable quarter of the town, and the allusions to the square, the church, and the piazza, are of constant occurrence in the dramas of the age of Charles II. and Queen Anne."

Speaking of Cheapside, our author thus epitomises the history of the "Cross" which formerly stood there:—

"The Cross (one of the nine crosses erected by Edward I. to Eleanor his queen) stood in the middle of the street, facing Wood-street end. Eleanor died at Hardeby, near Lincoln, in the year 1290, and the king caused a cross to be set up in every place where her body rested on its way to Westminster Abbey. Cheapside was the intermediate resting-place between Waltham and Charing-cross, and 'Magister Michael de Cantuariâ, cementarius,' was the mason employed in the erection of the Cross. Its after history is interesting. John Hatherley, mayor, 're-edified the same in more beautiful manner' in 1441. It was new gilt over in 1522 against the coming of the Emperor Charles V., and again in 1533 against the coronation of Henry and Anne Boleyn; new burnished against the coronation of Edward VI.; new gilt in 1554 against the coming in of King Philip; 'broken and defaced,' 21st June, 1581; 'fastened and repaired' in 1595 and 1600; again defaced in 1600, and finally demolished Tuesday, May 2nd, 1643, in the mayorality of Isaac Pennington, the regicide; 'and while the thing was a doing,' says Howell, 'there was a noyse of trumpets blew all the while.'"

The new *Houses of Parliament* are somewhat fully described, and a plan of the buildings is given.

* Black's Ashmole MSS., col. 209.

† "They show, at Wilton, Inigo's designs for the piazzas of Covent Garden and Lincoln's-Inn. They are not Inigo's, I think, but interesting, and of a later date."

‡ Strype, B. vi., p. 89.

§ 1668. Dec. 7. Received of the Right Honourable the Earle of Bedford, as a gratuity towards the erecting of ye Column	£20	0	0
Ditto. Received from the Honourable Sr Charles Cotterell, Master of the Ceremonys, as a gift towards the said Column	10	0	0
1669. April 29. Received from the Right Honourable the Lord Denzill Holles, as a present towards the erecting of the aforesaid Column	10	0	0
27 Nov. 1668. For Drawing a Modell of the Column to be presented to the Vestry	0	10	0
2 Dec. 1668. To Mr. Wainwright for the 4 Gnomons	0	8	6

Churchwardens' Accounts of St. Paul's, Covent Garden.

Respecting *Whitehall* the author has m curious information—

"The old Banqueting House was bu down on Tuesday, the 12th of January, 16 19, and the present Banqueting House, signed by Inigo Jones, commenced on the of June, 1619, and finished on the 31s March, 1622. 37*l*., it appears, was paid Inigo Jones, upon the Council's warrant June 27th, 1619, 'for making two sev models—the one for the Star Chamber, other for the Banqueting House.'* This p ment to Jones escaped the researches Vertue, and the inquiries of Walpole; bu still more curious discovery which I have the good fortune to make connected with great architect, is the roll of the account of Paymaster of the Works, of the 'Charges building a Banqueting House at Whiteh and erecting a new Pier in the Isle of Po land, for conveyance of stone from thence Whitehall.' The sum received by the P master 'for the new building of the Banqu ing House, and the erecting a Pier at Po land,' was 15,648*l*. 3s. The expense of Pier was 712*l*. 19s. 2d., and of the Banqueti House, 14,940*l*. 4s. 1d.; the expenditure ceeding the receipts by 5*l*. 0s. 3d. The count, it deserves to be mentioned, was n declared (*i. e.*, finally settled) till the 29th June, 1633, eleven years after the completi of the building, and eight after the death King James; a delay confirmatory of the u willingness of the father and son to bring works at Whitehall to a final settlement. T Banqueting House at Whitehall is described this account† as 'a new building, with a va under the same, in length 110 feet, and width 55 feet within; the wall of the fou dation being in thickness 14 feet, and in dep 10 feet within ground, brought up with bric the first story to the height of 16 feet, wroug of Oxfordshire stone, cut into rustique on t outside, and brick on the inside; the wa 8 feet thick, with a vault turned over on gre square pillars of brick, and paved in t bottom with Purbeck stone; the walls a vaulting laid with finishing mortar; the upp story being the Banqueting House, 55 feet height, to the laying on of the roof; the wa 5 feet thick, and wrought of Northampto shire stone, cut in rustique, with two orders columns and pilasters, Ionic and Composi with their architrave, frieze, and cornice, a other ornaments; also rails and ballaste round about the top of the building, all Portland stone, with fourteen windows each side, and one great window at the upp end, and five doors of stone with frontispie and cartoozes; the inside brought up wi brick, finished over with two orders of colum and pilasters, part of stone and part of bric with their architectural frieze and cornic with a gallery upon the two sides, and t lower end borne upon great cartoozes of timb carved, with rails and ballasters of timber, a the floor laid with spruce deals; a stro timber roof covered with lead, and under it ceiling divided into a fret made of great co nices enriched with carving; with paintin glazing, &c.; for performance thereof great quantity of stone hath been digged Portland quarry, in the County of Dorset, a Huddlestone quarry, in the County of York The masons' wages were from 12d. to 2s. 6 the man per diem; the carpenters were paid the same rate; while the bricklayers receiv from 14d. to 2s. 2d. the day. The mast mason was Nicholas Stone, the sculptor of t fine monument to Sir Francis Vere in Wes minster Abbey. His pay was 4s. 10d. t day."‡

When the reader has been through M Cunningham's book he will be quite ready exclaim with us,—Wonderful London!

Importation of Zinc.—Rods rolle for bolts being considered chargeable wi duty as being in a partly manufactured sta importers recently urged the authorities f their decision. Directions have according been given for the free admission of zinc rod

* Revels at Court, p. 45.

† Preserved in the Audit Office.

‡ Walpole, by Dallaway, ii. 58.

TILE PAVEMENT: CAPRAROLA.

TILE PAVEMENT FROM CAPRAROLA.

THE palace at Caprarola possesses a great variety of ornamental pavements in tiles; the one in the chapel (in which marble-pateræ are introduced) is especially handsome. The one here engraved is a simple and useful example from an apartment, on the "piano nobile." It is in red and white tiles. These are mostly square, 5¼ inches diameter; circular and other forms are sparingly employed, and then always adjusted with nicety and care. The dimensions of this pavement are 27 feet by 19 feet.

ON THE HISTORY OF THE POINTED ARCH.

As I said before, it is needless to look in those countries where Roman influence was strong for specimens of pointed arches—in decorative art, at least. Like our forefathers some fifty years ago, the Romans believed that the pointed arch was an ugly thing in itself, and never used it when they could help it. In some of their engineering works, however, when they were off their guard, and thinking more of the use of the construction than the effect it was to produce æsthetically, we find them reverting to the native form; as, for instance, in the aqueducts that supplied Constantinople with water. These were commenced under Constantine, indeed, must have been one of the first works undertaken after founding the city, though their completion seems to be due to the Emperor Valens (364 and 78 A.D.) Throughout these constructions generally, in the lowest story, and always in the oldest parts, we find pointed arches used, in the instance of the aqueduct near Pyrgos, where you see two stories of round arches used over a lower range of pointed ones; or in this other example from the same place where the pointed arch is used throughout, except in the decorative parts of the structure, where the round arch is reverted to, as might be expected.

In speaking of the aqueduct of Valens, in the city, General Andreossy remarks,—"That here is an older part of a better construction than the new,—the latter being so carelessly built that it is now falling to ruin; besides, the newer part is not constructed on the same plan as the older, all the arches of which are of the pointed style, while those of the newer part are semi-circular." The lower and older part he ascribes to Valens, or to the years 366 and 368.

In this instance, it is true, the pointed arch is more an engineering than an architectural peculiarity,—but it shows, at least, that it was known and used during the age of which I am now treating.

These specimens are, I trust, sufficient to show that the pointed form of arch was not unknown at the period of which we are speaking; but even if I had not a single example to adduce, I would have no hesitation in asserting its existence and general use in these countries, from the fact of its being universally used by the Mahometans from the earliest years of their existence to the present hour.

The Arabs, it must be recollected, when they left their deserts to subdue the world, were mere nomadic tribes, who had no cities, no temples, and, indeed, no buildings worthy of the name; they were warriors, not architects, and consequently were obliged to employ the natives of the conquered countries to erect their mosques; yet, with scarcely a single exception, all their edifices are erected with pointed arches.

I have here, for instance, a drawing of the oldest part of the Mosque of Amru, at old Cairo, enlarged from a daguerreotype made by Girault De Prangey, in which the pointed arch is used, not only in the built-up arcades, but also in the smaller windows; yet this portion of the mosque, at least, was erected in the twenty-first year after Hegira, A.D. 643, or only twelve years after the death of the prophet. In speaking of these arches, M. de Prangey says,—" The pointed arch, therefore, appears in the Mosque of Amru certain and indubitable, but, at the same time, only exceptionally—in some five or six arcades; and, perhaps," he adds, " even this may not be the work of the Arabs, if we admit the testimony of Edrisi regarding the pre-existence of a Byzantine church on the spot, of which these may have made a part."

Judging from my own knowledge of the building, I should say they were the work of the Saracens; but whether they were or not, is immaterial to my argument. The Saracens certainly copied the pointed arch from the Byzantines, and whether, then, these are the work of the former or of the latter, is of little consequence; it certainly is of the date quoted, or antecedent to it, which is all that is contended for. Except the mosques of Amru (there are two in Egypt), I do not know of any erections of the Saracens anterior to the end of the century. I have here, however, a specimen of one erected by the Calif Walíl, at Jerusalem, in the year 87, or about A.D. 705, in which the pointed arch is used throughout. The great mosque at Damascus is of the same age, and from this period to the present time there is no difficulty. The mosques of Cairo and Bagdad, and generally the buildings of Egypt, Syria, and Mesopotamia afford an uninterrupted series of examples, and all are executed in the pointed arch style; indeed, I scarcely know of a single round arch in any erection of this people in these countries; or if one does appear, it is so singular and exceptional as not to bear upon the argument, for round arches

are found in the Gothic buildings of the fourteenth and fifteenth centuries, but they, too, are so few that no one thinks from their existence of denying the universal prevalence of the pointed style. In Sicily, too, which the Saracens occupied for two centuries preceding 1037 A.D., they used the pointed arch in all the monuments they have left there. I need scarcely refer to the well known examples of la Cuba and la Ziza in support of this assertion.

The exception to the rule, that will occur to every one, is Spain. It is true that pointed arches are found in the baths at Gerona, at Barcelona, and other places in the north of Spain, whose date is tolerably well ascertained to be of the ninth or tenth centuries; but, as a general rule, the Moors used the round or horseshoe arch almost universally in their erections in this country. But this is just one of those exceptions that prove the rule, and is one of the strongest arguments I can use to prove the prevalence of the pointed arch in the Byzantine period; for it shows, that when the Saracens entered a Roman province, where the pointed arch never had existed, they adopted the Roman form with the same facility as they had adopted the Pelasgic one, and having no style or predilection of their own, used what they found and worked it eventually into those forms which suited their purposes, but retaining the local germ throughout all the variations to which they subjected it.

The universal prevalence of the pointed arch in Saracenic countries being so indubitable, I shall not detain you by dwelling longer on it here. There is, however, one other example to which I would wish to refer before leaving this part of the subject,—the celebrated mosque at the Kutub, at Delhi.

When the Patans conquered India, in the beginning of the thirteenth century, they brought with them their own style of architecture, and, as was then the custom, commenced erecting edifices to commemorate their triumphs. The example I am now referring to was commenced by Shems-ood-deen Altemsh, about the year 1230, and was completed by him during the ten years of his reign. The principal arch, though of the pure equilateral Gothic form, and 22 feet span, and about 40 feet high, is erected with horizontal courses to nearly the summit, when courses of stones are placed on their ends, forming an Egyptian arch, exactly in the same manner as is done in the aqueduct at Tusculum, before quoted.

It is this peculiarity of construction that induces me to draw attention to it, as showing a persistence in a certain primeval mode of construction during more than 2,000 years, and long after the radiating or common form of arch was known and commonly used, and showing how we must extend our definition of an arch, if we would understand these eastern styles. For it would be evidently absurd to say that these Indian examples were not arches, because not constructed according to our principles; yet if we admit them we must admit the whole of the first series alluded to.

To return, however, from these eastern styles to those of the west. The first series I have to bring to notice is, as I said before, that found in the south of France, for which the nonce I shall call the Provençale style. It exists to the south of the Loire, to the north of the Garonne, and extends from about the gulph of Nice to the shores of the Bay of Biscay, and its date extends from about the age of Charlemagne till about the middle or end of the eleventh century, when it was superseded by the round arch styles.

I shall perhaps startle most readers by such an assertion, as it has been singularly overlooked, or, at least, misunderstood hitherto; but the facts of the case appear to me to admit of no doubt, and that they would long ago have been received as well-established facts had it not been for the pre-conceived opinion that no pointed arch existed in Europe anterior to the twelfth century, and, in consequence, they have been ascribed to repairs or alterations, or, indeed, to anything but what they are, which is, integral parts of the original design of the edifices in which they are found.

One of the best known examples is that of the Cathedral of Avignon,—Notre Dame de Doms, as it is called. The porch and general details of the church are so nearly classical, that they are usually ascribed to the age of Charlemagne, and by some thought to be even earlier; but though the same details are continued around and in the roof, it is said it must have been a repair, and that these details are imitations of the original part of the edifice. If they are, they are the only instance of imitation in that age I ever heard of.

At Vaison, not far from this, are two well known churches, so classical also, that they are often called by antiquarians, Roman temples, and are so described in La Borde's great work. This, however, they certainly are not, but Christian churches, though of a very early age: both are roofed throughout by waggon vaults of a pointed form; and as Vaison was destroyed and deserted about the middle of the twelfth century, before the Gothic pointed arch came into vogue, these vaults must at all events be anterior to this period; and if you once admit that they are ante-Gothic, there can be no difficulty in ascribing them to any age the other circumstances of the case seem to indicate. To me there appears to be no doubt but that they are coeval with the church they cover, and probably therefore of the ninth or tenth centuries. The same remarks apply to the churches at Pernes, at Souillac, Moissac, Carcassone, and many other churches of that age, all of which are covered with pointed vaults, but of a form extremely different from the true Gothic vaults of the thirteenth and sixteenth centuries. There is not for instance a single example of an intersecting vault in this style; the roofs are either waggon vaults with or without transverse ribs, or they are transverse arches supporting domes on pendentives, as used in the Byzantine and pure Saracenic styles: but such as never were used in pure Gothic edifices.

There is a church in the Castle of Loches, in the Loiraine, which will explain most of the peculiarities of the style. The original building was founded by Geoffrey Grise Gonnelle, Count of Anjou, in the year 962; and the western tower certainly belongs to him. The nave is either a part of the original edifice, or was erected by Foulques Nerra, between 992 and 1040. The supposition that it belongs to the latter receives confirmation from its singularly eastern aspect, and the fact that this Count three times visited the Holy Land, and died there in the year above quoted. If this were the only instance of the style in this country, this evidence might have some weight, but the churches of Moissac and Souillac, S. Frout, Perigueux, and several others in this country and of this age are even more eastern in their appearance than this, so it would not do to lay any stress on such evidence.

The choir was erected between the years 1140 and 1180, by Thomas Paotius, prior of the church, and is in the late and elegant Norman style, universal in that country just anterior to the introduction of the true pointed style.

We have, therefore, in this edifice a pointed style anterior to a round arch style; and though the drawing may not make this quite evident, an examination of the building itself leaves no doubt on the subject. Indeed, the French antiquaries almost all admit that this early pointed style did precede the round arch style in the south of France; but they bring the latter so far down into the period of the middle ages—and they are correct in so doing—that they are *almost able*, even with this admission, to squeeze the pointed style into the place they wish to assign to it. But the only true solution of the problem, I am convinced, is to ascribe it to the period I have assigned to it.

Indeed, I think the inspection of the drawing alone will show you that the pointed part of the edifice is not of that form which we find in France and England growing out of the Norman and Lombard styles. It is something totally different; the pendentives in particular are singularly eastern in their construction, and though the vault is pointed, it will be observed that in this, as in every example of this style I am acquainted with, all the openings, whether for windows or doors, are round-headed, whereas in the true Gothic the openings became pointed almost before the vaults assumed that form. Indeed, so different are they in every essential respect, that I do not think there is any danger of any one familiar with the two confounding this proto-Gothic, if I may so use the expression, with the true Gothic that succeeded the Norman, which I shall now notice, but dismiss with as few words as possible.

It appears to have been introduced in the north of France, about the year 1150, and was used at first timidly, and mixed with round arches, in all the great cathedrals and churches erected in that country, whose date is ascertained to be between the years 1150 and 1200. Before the latter date it had entirely superseded the round arch, and the style may be said to have been then perfected in all its essential particulars. In this country it was in every respect above twenty-five years later. The first really authentic example of its use is in Canterbury Cathedral, where it is found in new works erected after the great fire in 1175, apparently introduced by William of Sens, who was the architect employed to reconstruct the edifice at that period. With us, as with the French, it took nearly half a century before it can be said to have entirely superseded the Norman, and acquired a fixed and certain character of its own. In Salisbury Cathedral, however, we find it so certainly and surely established, that no relapse or backsliding of any sort marred its future onward course to that perfect development of beauty which it afterwards reached.

In Germany it was somewhat later; and I do not know of any authentic specimen of the pure Gothic anterior to the commencement of the thirteenth century; and even then it was nearly half a century longer before it entirely superseded the round style. As is well known, the church of St. Martin at Cologne was finished in the round arch style only the year the first stone of the celebrated cathedral was laid. And during the whole of the first half of the thirteenth century we find round arches mixed up with the pointed ones, which were then coming into fashion.

Before concluding, I would wish to say a few words regarding another branch of my subject, viz., as to the *invention* of the pointed arch, though if I have made myself understood in what I have stated regarding its *history*, that ought not to be a matter of difficulty, and every one may form almost as correct an opinion on the subject as I can myself. The eastern invention, as I think is nearly self-evident, arose from the mode above pointed out of building arches horizontally, which requires the adoption of some such form as this.

The question of the western invention is very similar to one discussed at the Institute a few weeks ago, as to the invention of the Doric column. The facts of the case were—that Doric columns were found existing in Egypt at least 1,000 years before they were used in Greece. At the time the Greeks first used them they were in constant communication, as traders and travellers, with Egypt, and consequently numberless citizens of Greece saw these columns before they thought of using them in their own country. This being the case, are they entitled to be called the inventors of the order? The entablature is of course their own; so is the use they made of them, and so are the refinements and improvements they added; but it appears to me singularly bad logic to call them the inventors of what existed so long before their day.

The same is the case with regard to the pointed arch; it existed in the east for centuries, and I may say for thousands of years before it was adopted in the west, and was used by the Saracens in Europe,—in Sicily, and in Spain, if not in France,—before adopted by the Christians in the latter country. I think, therefore, they have no right to claim it as an invention. At the same time, it must not be understood that they copied it for mere copying sake; on the contrary, they certainly would not have adopted it unless they had conceived it to be the best possible form for the purposes to which they applied it.

In the case of the waggon vaults of the Provençale style, it is not difficult to see what that purpose was. The object of the architect in adopting it was twofold. First, to get rid of a certain amount of thrust in his roof, as is well known was one of the principal causes of its universality in the true Gothic. The other, and perhaps more important object, was to enable him to dispense with the wooden roof by laying his tiles directly on the vault with a circular form this would be impossible as he would be obliged to load the crown of it to such an extent, to get the necessary water-shed, that it would certainly bulge at the haunches and fall. Notwithstanding this however, it was used unwillingly, and abandoned afterwards, as soon as improved modes of construction and the introduction of wooden roofs enabled the builders to dispense with it.

With regard to the other class of roofs belonging to the Provençale Gothic style, those namely, whose vaults are domes resting on pendentives, such as those of Loches, Souillac, St. Frout, Perigueux, and others in that country —their form is so complicated and their construction so scientific, that it must have taken centuries of experiments and trials to elaborate their complication, and as none of the steps by which the form was arrived at have been traced in France, I think we must allow that it is an importation, more or less direct, from the east. As such, however, it seems never to have been admired, certainly never took root in the country where it is found; and as, in the other instance, as soon as improved skill and improved modes of construction enabled the architects to dispense with it, they returned at once to their favourite round arched forms, and continued to practise them till the growing influence of the north induced them to abandon them again, and adopt the true Gothic, which had in the mean time been perfected in the north. There is, however, no early true Gothic in the south of France; the style did not arrive there till it was full blown and then soon degenerated in the flamboyant and after Gothics of the later age.

With regard to the true Gothic, the view I take of the question is this:—As every one knows, who is at all familiar with the Norman or round Gothic styles, the architects tried numberless expedients to get over the difficulties of using intersecting vaults with round arches; they stilted the smaller arches, depressed the larger ones, they tried quadripartite, sexapartite, and domical vaulting, and fifty other expedients, but without ever attaining perfect or even satisfactory success. The curves of the ribs of the vaults were generally unpleasing, frequently waving, and apparently crippled; and indeed the problem seemed almost insoluble. Still they seemed determined to persevere in same path rather than use the broken or pointed arch in lieu of the graceful sweep of their own unbroken curves.

When things were in this state, the Crusades took place; half Europe visited the east, and a Latin kingdom was established over the pointed arched people of the Levant; and when they had thus become familiar with it, there can be but little doubt but they would perceive that so far from being necessarily ugly, the pointed arch could be worked into forms of as great beauty and elegance as the circular one, and had besides a lightness and, for some purposes, an appropriateness the other did not possess.

Once convinced of the fact, the problem was solved, the pilgrim architects returned from the Holy Land and immediately applied this discovery to their western churches; once the prejudice was overcome they adopted it every where and in every thing, and I need not add with what success.

In adopting such a view of the question as this, there are two things to be guarded against: the first confounding the invention of the Gothic style with that of the pointed arch,—a mistake too often fallen into. The first, however, is a purely indigenous and native elaboration from Roman art, without any trace of copying or even imitation. The latter is a mere subordinate characteristic of that style, and not at all entitled to the rank it has hitherto assumed in the controversy.

The other mistake is to assume that it was copied from the east for copying sake; the truth being, if we admit the above view, that the hint was given by the east, but nothing more: it was applied to Gothic buildings in a manner in which it had never been used in the east, and was so incorporated with and worked into the native style, that it soon lost all trace of its origin, and became as native as any other part of the true Gothic.

Though, therefore, I do not think it can be denied but that the origin of the pointed arch is from the east, it must, I think, at the same time be admitted that all its appropriateness and all its beauty, as found in our mediæval cathedrals, is wholly due to the talent and ingenuity of our northern architects, who wrought it into those forms of beauty and grace which we all now so fully appreciate and so universally admire.*

JAMES FERGUSSON.

STIR IN METROPOLITAN COMMISSION OF SEWERS.

THE following report of the proceedings of the court will be read with more than usual interest. Mr. Hertslet has resigned his appointment; Mr. Phillips, the surveyor, has thought it necessary to denounce the proceedings of the commission, and a general disorganization prevails. The length of the report, and of some other papers in our number, prevents us saying any more at this moment than that circumstances have since occurred which prove strikingly the justness of our opinion, before this expressed, that the constitution of the commission is not exactly in all respects what it ought to be.

A general court was held on Thursday, 21st, at the Court-house, Greek-street, Soho-square; the Earl of Carlisle in the chair.

The Drainage of Goulston-street and the Neighbourhood of Whitechapel.—A long report was presented by Messrs. Phillips and Gotto, surveyors, on the state of Goulston-street, and the neighbourhood of Whitechapel, which stated that their attention had been especially directed to an area of about 9 acres in that vicinity, with a population of 3,674 persons, or about an average of 9 to each house. The consequence of this over-crowding was the accumulation of more than the usual amount of filth, and the cause of much disease, vice, and misery. Very many of the houses have neither yards, sinks, nor other conveniences, and no sort of provision for drainage or ventilation. The effect upon the constitution of the inmates was evidently indicated in their countenances, and rendered them susceptible of those fearful diseases which were accustomed to attach themselves to such spots. Being aware that cholera had in many places recently re-appeared, and that several malignant cases had occurred in this place, they urged upon the commissioners the importance and necessity of enforcing sanitary regulations without delay. To effect this they recommended that notice should be given immediately of making a special sewers-rate, under the 91st section, to lay down sewer-pipes, and to serve notices upon the occupiers to empty and destroy the existing cesspools, to substitute water-closets, and to construct efficient drains into the main pipe sewer.

Mr. Chadwick moved that the report be received and adopted.—Sir H. de la Beche supported the motion, and said that the Ordnance Survey Committee were using every effort to carry out the wishes of the Court, by a progress of the subterranean survey, in connection with the Ordnance survey, and in a very short time they hoped to bring forward a large area of the metropolitan district:—viz., the Westminster district. The maps were now in a proper state, and they had taken into their serious consideration the necessity of adopting certain principles in lieu of the present mischievous system, and thus give in their operations relief of a very substantial kind. Although the whole of Westminster was below high-water tide, they had no doubt whatever as to rendering the drainage of it as perfect as that of any other district in the metropolis, and at the same time to utilise the sewage here collected. The present lines of railway would afford them great facilities for such a purpose to get rid of their sewage, and concurrently with the purification of the river Thames. For the suburban district, too, of Hammersmith, means would be devised for altogether removing the sewage from it, to throw it back into the country, instead of, as at present, falling into the Thames. The district comprised between Battersea and Deptford had also received their most anxious consideration: they were collecting all the information requisite and essential for these plans, and they had required their consulting engineer, who was conversant and acquainted with these principles, to give a general statement, plan, and estimate for carrying out these views. That nothing might be done hastily, these plans would be submitted to the Court, and he might now observe that the Sewers Committee were unanimous in their desire to relieve the Thames, and to throw the sewage into the country. He trusted that not more than a month would elapse before they should lay before the Court a plan for the entire relief of the whole of Westminster.

Mr. Slaney urged the adoption of immediate measures for the relief of the poor.

Mr. Chadwick said there was every disposition to afford immediate relief to the poor, but in many cases when relief had been brought to their doors the landlords would not avail themselves of it by making the necessary junctions.

Lord Ebrington said that legal proceedings occupied a considerable time. As regarded, for instance, the Bermondsey district, belonging to the Surrey and Kent division, there were upwards of 70 miles of open ditches, 5 feet in width, exhaling the most noxious and pestilential gases, which embraced a vast area, and even were they to afford only temporary relief, it was not so short a proceeding as Mr. Slaney might imagine.

The Earl of Carlisle thought they should consider how far it would be safe to undertake these works without the chance of the ground having to be gone over again.

Mr. Chadwick replied, that in this district there was a very good outfall, and the drainage might be effected with little variation as a permanent work.

Mr. Hertslet, with great submission, hoped he might be allowed to state, that the officers of the commission were *not in a position to carry out these works.*

Mr. Slaney was of opinion that they should use great caution in their proceedings.

Mr. Chadwick said, if they waited for a perfect combination, they might postpone all their works to an indefinite period, and in every step a difficulty was to be encountered. One of these difficulties was as to a supply of water, and he thought that should be met at once.—A long discussion ensued on the legality of the commission obtaining a supply of water, independently of the water companies.—The motion that the works recommended be adopted was then put and agreed to.

Resignation of Mr. Hertslet, the Clerk.—Mr. Hertslet said, in the course of the discussion he had taken the liberty, respectfully, of offering a few observations; but now, in consequence of the vote they had just come to, he felt that he had no alternative but to tender his resignation of the office he had the honour to hold. Mr. Hertslet then read the following document:—

"My lords and gentlemen,—After a public service of eighteen years, thirteen of which have been passed in this department, I take leave most respectfully to tender you my resignation. For the great kindness and consideration which you have shown me, and especially for that signal mark of your approval with which you were recently pleased to honour me, I most sincerely thank you, and I trust that I may carry with me into private life the kindly feeling of which I have had so many proofs.

The affairs of life are so very unstable, that I hope you will consider that, as a family man, it is only proper caution on my part to request that, although I do not now present, I may not be considered thereby to have waived, any claim I may have to a pension under the Metropolitan Sewers Act.

I had appended a few remarks setting out some of my reasons for the step, but as they contain an expression of opinion upon the working and future management of the commission, which might be considered out of place, I have withdrawn them.

It remains for me only to request that a successor may be appointed as soon as possible. I shall, of course, be most happy to render every assistance which my health will permit until the appointment is filled up."

Mr. Bullar expressed his surprise at this sudden step, and his regret for losing so efficient an officer as Mr. Hertslet.

Mr. Slaney regretted that the communication had been made without notice, and the loss of so excellent an officer. The commission had had the benefit of Mr. Hertslet's experience, and they had hitherto worked well together. If he persisted in his determination, they must, of course, accept it; but he hoped he might be induced to withdraw it; for considering the difficult and arduous situation in which he had been placed, he must say that Mr. Hertslet's services had given great satisfaction.

Mr. Chadwick thought that this subject might be much better and fully discussed in a committee.

Mr. Hertslet said that the establishment was not equal to carrying out their duties efficiently, and however willing he might be to go fast, he could not keep pace with them consistently with the opinions he entertained. He was willing even to gallop with them if it were necessary, but he was determined not to do so blindfolded.

The Earl of Carlisle said there could be but one opinion as to the value of Mr. Hertslet's services.

The further consideration of the subject was referred to a committee of the whole court.

The Ordnance Survey.—On some resolutions of the Ordnance Survey Committee being read,

Mr. Phillips, the surveyor, wished to be allowed to make a communication upon the subject, and upon leave being granted, a startling document was read; which stated that an assertion made at the last court, that a three-feet pipe would carry off all the sewage of the metropolis, had gained currency through the public press, and was now passing through the provinces with great rapidity. Such a statement, bearing the authority of the commission, which was wholly impracticable, and so contrary to fact, was calculated to bring the commission into ridicule, and destroy public confidence. It also condemned the converging system of drainage recommended for Westminster, and pointed out how, by a mere nominal sum per annum, payable for 20 years, a tunnel sewer might be constructed from Hammersmith to Woolwich Marshes, to take off the whole drainage of the metropolis by a regular and steady fall, and by this means the River Thames would be rendered as pure as it was 300 years ago. He said a just dissatisfaction was spreading, and he thought it time for him to speak out for the credit of the court and the reputation of its officers.

Sir H. de la Beche considered this course of proceeding on the part of an officer both unprecedented and unjustifiable, as the committee had come to no decision upon the subject. Until the Survey Committee had reported, these remarks were entirely out of place.

Mr. Chadwick said, the statement as to a three-feet pipe he had made on the authority of experiments made by Mr. Lovick, but that was only to apply to house-drainage, independently of storm or rain waters. Two reports, from Mr. Austin and Mr. Phillips, had been for some time before them, and they had taken the opinion of impartial engineers on their respective merits; but the present plan of Mr. Philips was totally different, and of which they now heard for the first time.

Captain Dawson and several other commissioners reprobated the course taken by Mr. Phillips.

A motion was then proposed and carried, that the letter should be referred (with that of Mr. Hertslet) to a committee of the whole court.

Reports were presented by Mr. Gotto on the drainage of Sydenham, and by Mr. Grant on the open ditches of the Kent and Surrey district.

The Cholera at Bermondsey.—A deputation of the Improvement Commissioners and ratepayers of Bermondsey attended the court on the subject of the recent cases of cholera in that parish. It having been represented to the Works Committee that the open ditches and mill streams were the main cause of the raging of this malady, the chief surveyor was ordered to attend immediately to the same, and he now presented a report, which shewed that,—"The artificial streams are upwards of a mile in length, belonging to private persons, and have existed for upwards of 300 years. The tide is admitted into them in order to provide power for working the St. Saviour's Mill, Dockhead, and consequently they are periodically left dry. A branch running along Horney-lane, a length of about 700 feet, and averaging 10 feet in width, contains an accumulation of putrid animal and vegetable matter, the refuse of house drainage and chemical works, and exposing an evaporating surface of 7,000 feet in the midst of a densely populated neighbourhood. Another branch running at the back of, and receiving the foul drainage of Albert-street, Bermondsey New Town, of about the same length and width, and more prejudicial to health than the branch above described, being immediately under the windows of the houses."

Mr. Dykes, one of the deputation, said there had been nine fatal cases of cholera in this neighbourhood within a few days; it was an insufferable nuisance, and highly dangerous to the public health.—Mr. Raines, owner of a paper mill, admitted that the stream was a nuisance, but if the supply of water was cut off, his mill would be stopped, and his workmen thrown out of employ.

Dr. Southwood Smith said he had the assurance of a medical practitioner, that he had under his charge twenty cases of cholera in this district, nine of which were fatal, within fifty yards of each other.

On Monday the deputation again attended the sitting of the Committee; Lord Ebrington in the chair. Several owners of property on the banks of the stream presented plans, showing how, if the water was withdrawn, their property would be injured, while the Improvement Commissioners contended that as steam power was now used, the water was only occasionally used to preserve a right to it, and to claim a compensation on the abolition of the streams.

It was suggested that an 18-inch pipe would carry sufficient water to supply all the parties concerned, which suggestion was agreed to.—Mr Martin, the medical officer and registrar of the district, said that five cases of cholera had occurred since Thursday last, three of which were fatal.

It was ordered that the surveyor do take such steps as he may deem necessary, and specially report on the subject forthwith.

PAWNBROKERS' ALMSHOUSES.—The first stone of the Pawnbrokers' Almshouses was laid (at Forest Gate, Essex) on the 22nd, by the Lord Mayor. The architect, in the newspaper accounts, is said to be Mr. Francis. Some of our readers will remember the particulars given by us some time ago, when the selected design in the public competition which took place was thrown overboard, the estimates exceeding the amount stipulated in the conditions.*

* The remarks which followed the reading of the foregoing paper at the Institute are necessarily postponed. In the first part of the paper, p. 290, col. 3, for "Mr. Hosking's testimony" read "Mr. Hoskins'." The name of the professor is better known to our printers than that of the Ethiopian traveller,—whence the mistake.

* Vol. vi. p. 133.

VIEW OF STOKE GREGORY CHURCH.

STOKE GREGORY CHURCH, SOMERSETSHIRE.

Annexed i send you rough sketches of Stoke Gregory Church, in Somersetshire.* I quite agree with you in condemning, as a general practice, the substitution of servile copies for original designs ; still i cannot think that the occasional reproduction of a beautiful specimen, undertaken by an architect capable of appreciating its merit, as well as its fitness for the locality he may select, would be injurious to his own professional character, or to the interests of his employers, or the advancement of art. And it is easy to imagine cases where such reproduction would be more practicable or desirable, than an elaborate restoration of the building itself.

But however sparingly we would admit of close and accurate copies, i believe no one will deny the right of an architect to appropriate any feature that pleases him in the works of his predecessors. At least, his claim is only invalidated by his own want of judgment in selection, or his incapacity to carry out the idea.

The church of which I send you a notice, though it presents nothing very complicated in its construction, might furnish a useful hint to builders of modern churches. It has a central octagonal tower, springing, you will observe, as it were from the roof of the building itself, and not from a square base or stage,

* Our engraving is made from these.—Ed.

appearing above the parapet, like those of Stafford, Tong in Shropshire, and, if I rightly remember, Nantwich. There may have been examples at Lynn and Coventry, where the towers are all that is left of the original work. But in Somersetshire we notice South Petherton, North Curry, Barrington, and Doulting (which last has a spire), similar in this respect to the example under notice. The feature must be familiar to the traveller through Rhenish Germany, and some parts of the south of France.

The continental architects knew the value of the octagonal tower. This consists, I conceive, in the circumstance of its proportions appearing unvaried, or nearly so, in whatever point it is viewed. With a square tower, the character of the outline is often materially altered, according as it is viewed cardinally or diagonally. And when the tower is crowned with an octagonal spire, the change of proportion between the two, as seen in front, or at an angle, is very manifest. i was much struck with this in Chichester Cathedral, where the effect is somewhat increased by the oblong plan of the towers. It is probably from this feeling on the part of the architect that some of the most beautiful steeples on the continent spring from towers of which the upper stages are octagonal, which ensured the keeping of the proportions intended from whatever point the building might be viewed. Freyburg is an exquisite example of this arrangement.

I will now point out the peculiarity of con-

struction which might be adopted with advantage in the present day. The central octagon in the specimen before us is narrower than the chancel, or the nave between its piers. It might almost spring from the floor without touching any of the walls. Now its eastern and western arches pretty well span the church, without any great projection of the piers into its area. The transepts are not so wide ; these nearly represent the width of the tower. But that their arches may correspond with its northern and southern sides, their faces must of necessity somewhat overhang the springs of the other arches ; that they may not, however, lose their natural abutment, namely, that given by the walls of the body of the church, they consist of a series of receding orders, of which the outer or upper one is properly placed for the support of the tower, and the lowest, or innermost one, for the abutment of the walls. A somewhat similar arrangement occurs in the cathedral of Avignon, which has a small Romanesque central octagon, but no transepts. At Hempstead, near Gloucester, the tower, which is central, and narrower than the nave and chancel, has much the same kind of arch under its northern and southern sides.

The western arch (at Stoke Gregory) has three chamfered orders to the westward, and two to the eastward. The eastern arch, two to the westward, three to the eastward. The transeptarches, four towards the area of the tower, two towards the transepts. The imposts of the eastern and western arches are continuous, without capitals, he squinches form pointed arches, of two chamfered orders. The style of the church is Perpendicular, and the whole appears to be of nearly the same date; probably about the middle of the fifteenth century. The nave has aisles and a clerestory, and is divided into four bays by shafted piers. The chancel and transept are low and short as compared with the nave. The aisles, south porch, and north transept, have an elegant parapet of openwork, a feature very common in this county. In the angle between the chancel and north transept is a low square stair-turret, communicating with the tower by a passage. The tower has two tiers of windows, the upper ones of two lights with a transom, the lower, single lights with a very deep splay. The parapet is embattled, and the whole is finished with a small low spire covered with lead. The font is rather curious.

Stoke Gregory is about 9 miles south-east of Bridgewater. On our way we notice the fine western tower of Weston Zoyland; by a slight detour we may take Middlezoy, which has also a handsome tower, Othery, a cross church with a lofty central tower, and the picturesque ruined chapel of Burroughbridge, situated on an abrupt mound near the junction of the Thone and Parret. About 4 miles beyond is North Curry, which has been mentioned, and from this the route may be continued, in one direction to Ilminster, or in another to Taunton, both affording specimens of the highest architectural richness and beauty.   JOHN LOUIS PETIT.

INAUGURATION OF THE WEST LONDON SYNAGOGUE OF BRITISH JEWS.

A NEW synagogue has just been erected from the designs of Mr. D. Mocatta, in Margaret-street, Cavendish-square. It appears that this congregation, formed in 1842, and located until the present time in Burton-street, have adopted changes in the ritual which, if they are as was explained in a discourse delivered on the occasion by the Rev. D. W. Marks, are certainly improvements. The increasing number of the congregants who have joined this body, has been the cause of a new building being necessary. The inauguration service, which was performed a few days ago, consisted of chaunting of hymns by the choir, the introduction of, and depositing, the rolls of the Law in the ark, &c., and was not without interest.

The present building is divided into two parts for the sittings,—wide galleries round three sides, for the ladies, capable of holding 150 persons,—and the ground floor for gentlemen, arranged with benches, in rows on both sides, leaving the space in the centre open, accommodates 250 persons. The synagogue has residences connected with it for the two ministers, besides other conveniences. The design is simple, in the form of a square, and consists of Ionic columns, supporting the gallery, from whence rises a second order of columns, which receive semi-circular arches. These are crowned by a bold cornice, over which is a lantern light. Although the general character of the edifice is modest, yet most of the parts which form the architectural features are ornamented. The ark has features of design that are new, and composes cleverly with the semi-circular arches which hang as pendants before it, and complete the fourth side of the building; the steps, platform, stylobate, and columns which form the design, are all of scagliola, surmounted by a decorated entablature, which supports a niche head, in which is placed the tablets of the Ten Commandments, surrounded and shadowed by the palm leaf.

The total cost of the building, including the repairs and part rebuilding of the houses, was about 4,000l.

LONDON UNIVERSITY.—After the delivery of Mr. Donaldson's concluding lecture on the 19th inst. to the students in the classes of architecture for the present session, the senior student of the classes made a gratifying address to the professor, and offered to him, in the name of the class, a parallel ruler, with silver mountings, as an earnest of their appreciation of his exertions and kindness.

ST. PAUL'S CHURCH, DERBY.
MESSRS. BARRY AND BROWN, ARCHITECTS.

ST. PAUL'S CHURCH, DERBY.

ON the 11th inst., the first stone was laid of a church in memory of the late Dr. Shirley, Bishop of Sodor and Man. Our engraving gives a view of the church as it will appear when completed. It is in the decorated, or middle pointed style, cruciform in plan, and consists of a chancel, nave, north and south transepts, north aisle, north porch, and tower at north-east angle of chancel and transept, with vestry at south-east angle. It is intended to seat six hundred worshippers on the ground floor, without a gallery.

The church will stand east and west, having the chancel and north-east tower facing the road.

Owing to the marshy nature of the site, a substratum of concrete is formed under all the walls; and this, as we are told, is laid on the surface without removing the turf.

The walls are to be built of Little Eaton stone, with Duffield stone dressings and window tracery. The roofs are all to be open-timbered, stained, and varnished.

Messrs. Barry and Brown, of Liverpool, are the architects. The execution of the works has been undertaken by Mr. Wood, a townsman, for the inadequate sum of 1,750l. The contractor would seem to be actuated by another motive than that of making money.

BOILER EXPLOSIONS: CAUTION TO STEAM-ENGINE TENDERS.— At Bishopwearmouth Iron-works, recently, a boiler exploded, ascending 60 feet in the air, the roof above it being scattered in all directions, and several of those in the streets adjoining riddled with stones and brick. The engine-man was killed.—— At Wolverhampton, lately, an engine tender, employed at the Shrubbery Iron-works, was committed to hard labour for a month, on evidence led that he had got drunk, and allowed the water to get so low in the boiler as to render an explosion probable. It was his first offence, and he had promised it would be his last. The magistrate threatened a severer punishment should a similar case be hereafter proved before him.

ON THE BUILDING MATERIALS EMPLOYED IN PARIS AND IN THE VALLEY OF THE LOWER SEINE.*

2nd. *Brick and Tiles.*—In Paris, the use of bricks is entirely confined to carrying up the flues, and turning the trimmers to the hearths. The best that are employed are the bricks made in the department of l'Yonne, known under the name of the "Brique de Bourgogne;" it is 1 foot long, 4 inches wide, by rather more than 2 inches thick. It is burnt to a very high degree. The colour is a pale rose, leaning towards the violet. The thousand weigh about 2½ tons. Rondelet found that the force necessary to crush them varied between 73 lb. and 80 lb. per centimètre square.

The bricks made at Montereau are very nearly as good as the briques de Bourgogne; they are of the same size and colour; resist nearly as well. The thousand only weighs 2 tons ½ cwt.†

The bricks of Sarcelles are those most used, but they are extremely brittle: they are about 8 inches long by 4 inches by 2 inches; the thousand weigh nearly 1 ton 14 cwt.

Some bricks are made of the clays which occur in the gypseous formations immediately round Paris. They resemble those of Montereau in quality, but differ a little in colour, being of a deeper red, and they are rather thinner and narrower. The thousand weighs 1 ton 18 cwt.‡

In the neighbourhood of Bonnières, in the valley of the Seine, a mass of clay occurred, from which the white bricks used on the Paris

* See page 277, ante.

† The composition of the Montereau clay is as follows:—
Silex, per cent. .... 0·644
Alumina .... 0·246
Magnesia ....
Oxide of iron .... trace
Water .... 0·100
                                    ——
                                    0·990

‡ The composition of the St. Ouen and Pantin clays is as follows:—
	St. Ouen.	Pantin.
Silex, per cent.	0·510	0·505
Alumina	0·140	0·105
Magnesia	0·134	0·072
Oxide of iron	0·030	0·057
Water	0·182	0·300

and Rouen Railway were made. Generally, the bricks used between Paris and Harfleur are, however, of a red colour, and made of a ferruginous clay. At Harfleur and Havre they are white, the clay being calcareous and impregnated with the marine salts. The mode of burning usually employed is in kilns; but of late, near Rouen, many brickmakers have begun to burn in clamps. Their success hitherto has been very equivocal.

Of late years wooden floors have become general in Paris, but the houses of the poor, and all the offices, passages, and kitchens of the best lodgings, are still paved with tiles; and it may, perhaps, be owing to this custom that Paris is so comparatively free from fires. The tiles are of four sorts for flooring purposes—viz., the large hexagon, of 6¾ inches over the angles; the bastard hexagon, of 5⅛ inches over the angles; and the square tiles, 6¼ inches, and 8 $\frac{1}{16}$th of a side: the thickness varies from $\frac{11}{16}$ths to $\frac{12}{16}$ths. The square tiles are used for the hearths, the hexagonal tiles for flooring. The best are made at Montereau, but their price is so high that the preference is generally given to the tiles made at Massy, near Palaiseau. Almost all the brickmakers of the neighbourhood of Paris, however, make tiles at the present day, both for flooring and roofing purposes.

Many of the houses of Paris and the neighbourhood are covered with tiles, though the use of this material is rapidly going out of fashion. The best are made at Montereau, as is the case with flooring tiles. They are of two sizes; for it is to be observed that there is only one shape in general use—the pan tile. *Le grand moule* is about 1 foot long by 9 inches wide and ⅝ inches thick; the part left uncovered is about 4½ inches. *Le petit moule* is about from 5½ to 7¼ wide, by from 10 inches to 11 inches long. The ridge tiles are 1 foot 3 inches long by 1 foot 1 inch development.

A very great number of glazed tiles and common pottery chimneys and stoves are used throughout France. The dearness of combustibles renders the use of open fire-places too expensive for the lower classes. Iron also is too dear to be employed for grates, stoves, ranges, cheeks, and the thousand uses we make of it in England.*

One of the most ingenious use made of pottery was in the construction of the floors of some houses in a street recently erected in the centre of the grounds of the ancient hotel Rougemont. At the time of the erection of these houses, there was a strike amongst the carpenters. The contractor adopted this manner of executing the floors simultaneously with the walls,—that being the invariable mode of proceeding adopted in Paris. These floors, however, cost more than those executed in the usual manner, and, consequently, have not been imitated. They were executed about 1845.

3rd. *Limes and Cements.*—All calcareous stones, when exposed to a sufficient heat, part with the carbonic acid gas which enters into their combination; but the limes resulting from the calcination assume different appearances, according to the chemical composition of the stones. These appearances are four in number,—at least of those sufficiently frequent in their recurrence to form the basis of a commercial classification. They are:—Firstly, as regards the manner of taking up water, divided into fat or thin limes. The fat limes are those which, in slacking, augment at least one-fourth in volume; the thin limes are those that remain constant in their bulk. Secondly, as regards their setting properties, limes are divided into the hydraulics and the non-hydraulics. The hydraulic limes are invariably thin,—but all thin limes are not hydraulic.

An examination of the elaborate discoveries and researches of the French chemists and engineers into this still very little cultivated branch of the chemistry of building, would lead us into far too long a discussion at present. Suffice it to say, that the practice of the best architects, and of all the engineers in France, is to use hydraulic lime to the exclusion of others, unless almost insuperable difficulties, owing to their price, occur. In so damp a climate as our own, we should do well to imitate their example; the more especially as we have at hand the means of procuring both natural and artificial hydraulic limes in unlimited quantities.

The fat limes used in Paris are made at Senlis, Melun, Essone, Champigny, Marly, Sevres, &c. The natural hydraulics are made at Senonches, and of late years at Meudon; the artificial hydraulics are made wherever chalk is found, in the proximity of clay, as at Marly, Mantes, and in the neighbourhood of Rouen.

The Lower Seine, from the neighbourhood of Mantes at least, runs through the chalk formation; the country, right and left, is of the same geological character for a great distance. Natural hydraulic limes do not occur until we reach Havre, and all the local consumption is therefore supplied by the factories of artificial hydraulic limes. The most important of these are at Rouen, where they assume very great importance, from the chemical and mechanical skill employed. The materials used are the chalk from the Mount St. Catherine, and the argillaceous deposits of the neighbourhood; the proportions of the different ingredients, and the degree of burning, depending upon the rate of setting required.

At Havre, upon the outcrop of the chalk, or rather at the junction of the chalk and the Wealden formations, a bed of argillaceous limestone is met with, which yields a very superior hydraulic lime. In the valley of Harfleur a large establishment has lately been formed for the making of artificial hydraulics; and all the immense dock or fortification works executed at Havre have been constructed with either one or the other. Cement is only used for pointing, or, on extraordinary occasions, for rendering works exposed to the action of the sea immediately after being finished.

The cements used in Paris are principally made in Burgundy, at Pouilly. They participate of the nature of our Roman cements; but do not acquire so great a degree of hardness. The same objection is to be made to the Vassy cements; and to the artificial cements made at Rouen with chalk and pounded bricks. The French architects and engineers do not advocate the use of cement to the same extent we do in England. Personally, I think they are nearer the truth than we are. It is much to be feared that materials which set so rapidly may decay in the same manner. The processes of nature are slow, at least where great duration is its object; and we are most likely to succeed by following the same course. The competition, moreover, in the supply of cement is so great, that the article, as usually sold, is little better than sand. Even the extreme rapidity of the setting of cement is an objection to its use in many ordinary cases, for it requires so much care in its manipulation as to render it liable to be slighted where the interest, or even the carelessness of the workman, may oppose its receiving proper attention.

Occasionally, in the neighbourhood of the large towns, the houses are entirely built with rubble-stone, or of bricks, and covered with a coat of plaster. Cement is never used for this purpose, nor does there appear to be any necessity for its introduction; the climate of France is sufficiently dry, and the plaster, as usually employed, is sufficiently capable of resisting the atmospheric changes, to render the use of the more expensive material unnecessary. Precautions require, however, to be taken in the application of plaster. The tops of cornices, and all weatherings, require to be covered with zinc; the parts of the houses near the ground must be rendered with a less hygrometric material; but for all other positions plaster succeeds remarkably well. Internally, it is the only material used in any part of France within reasonable distance of water-carriage from the gypsum-quarries. Stuccoes and imitations of marbles are sometimes employed in public buildings, but very rarely in private houses.

4th. *Woods.*—The practice of the French architects in the use of wood differs little from our own. On the sea-board, and in the large commercial towns, Swedish and Baltic fir is principally employed; in the interior oak is cheap enough to insure the preference. The oak used in Paris comes principally from Champagne and Burgundy; lately, however, the Prussian oak has been imported in considerable quantities. For large roots, Dantzic and other Prussian fir is used; but the architects pay such very low prices that the best woods invariably are sent to England. Indeed, there are few architects who seem to be able to distinguish the Swedish from the Prussian timber, for in all cases I have noticed that for roofing purposes the former is employed where the latter is demanded by the specifications. Indeed, so small is the supply of Baltic timber in France, that in 1848, after the bridges over the Seine had been burnt down by the mobs, it was impossible to find 50,000 cubic feet in all the markets of Dieppe, Fecamp, Havre, Rouen, and Paris.

Norway timber is used largely for purlins, and for partition stuff. The deals and battens imported are of the second and third quality; but as all the better class of joiner's work is executed in wainscot, this becomes of less moment. Some of the French oak is very beautiful, and admirably adapted for joiner's work; but its gradually increasing price, owing to the clearance of the forests, renders necessary the importation of the German, or, as we commonly call it, the Dutch, wainscot. Mahogany is only imported for cabinet-making: its use for joinery, or for ship-building, is almost unknown. Rosewood and ebony are also imported for cabinet-makers. American timber, *e.g.*, pine, spruce, &c., rarely enters France, except for the purpose of making masts and spars of ships; teak is totally unknown, as are the whole tribe of African or Australian woods.

France furnishes very beautiful poplar, ash, and beech timber, which are much used in building. Almost all the slate battening for provincial use is made of poplar; the ash serves for cart-building and carriage-works; the beech is principally employed for piles and gratings, &c., under water. The department of Calvados furnishes some of the finest beech-trees I have ever seen.

In practice the French architects are much behind our own as far as carpentery is concerned. There are, certainly, exceptions. Some of the roofs in Paris are light, elegant, and strong, the thrusts well balanced, the resistances most skilfully calculated; but, as a rule, the scantlings are far too heavy, the framing clumsy, the affectation of mathematical construction too glaring. Little or no precautions are taken to prevent the decay of the timber from the moisture of the walls; the wood itself is often used full of sap, and thoroughly wet—an objection, by the way, which may be made to carpentery in London, for we often see the wood taken from the river, cut up, and placed in buildings long before it can have dried. It is, however, to be observed with reference to the heavy scantlings used by the French architects, that the price of woodwork is about 25 per cent. higher with them than with us. Motives of economy serve as vast incentives to scientific investigations in all countries.

5th. *Metals.*—The metals used in building are iron (cast and wrought), lead, copper, zinc, and some of their compounds.

1 (*a*). The greater part of the cast-iron used in the valley of the Seine is derived either from the mines upon the Belgian frontier, from the province of Berri, or from England; the importation from our own country being principally for the supply of the markets of Rouen, Havre, and the north-west of France. The wrought-iron comes from Berri and Flanders, and there are some scrap-iron-factories at Paris and Havre.

The great distance the iron has to be transported, and the dearness of fuel, render its use in the prodigal manner we are accustomed to, quite out of the question. At Paris cast-iron costs about 50 per cent. more than in London; at Havre it costs about 33 per cent. more. Its use is therefore avoided as much as possible, the more especially as wood and stone-

---

* The clay of Forges of la Seine Inférieure are composed of—

	Forges.	Vanvres.
Silex, per cent.	0·650	0·540
Alumina	0·240	0·250
Oxide of iron	trace	0·100
Water	0·110	0·100
Magnesia	—	trace
	1·000	0·990

The clay of Forges is used for pots for glass-making, and similar purposes; that of Vanvres for kitchen-tiles.

The firebricks used in Paris are either made at Stourbridge, or at Hayange, on the Belgian frontier; some few are made in Burgundy, but they do not resist well.

work are so much cheaper than with us. The French founders are, however, very skilful, and some very remarkable works are to be met with in Paris, executed in cast-iron. The northern gate of the Madeleine, the fountains and lamp-posts of the Place de la Concorde, may be cited as illustrations.

1 (*b*). The best commercial wrought-iron is that from the province of Berri; but it is very unequal in quality, sometimes as tough as our best Welch iron, at others as short as the very commonest Staffordshire, owing to the bad manipulation in the factories. The very high price of iron, also, prevents so much attention being paid to the details of its production as is the case where its economy renders its use a matter of every-day necessity. Indeed, the state of the ironworks in France is a singular illustration of the evils of the protective system. The manufacturers have a monopoly; they fear no competition, and make a bad iron. The public pays dearly, and therefore uses as little iron as possible.

Since railways have been in fashion, however, the use of iron for roofs has become more general, and there are in Paris certainly some of the finest roofs in Europe. Amongst them may be cited the roofs over the Entrepôt réel des Marais, of the Halle aux Blés (in cast-iron), of the St. Germains and Rouen Railway, executed by M. Eugène Flachat.

The plate-iron box-girders are at present unknown; corrugated iron is but of very recent introduction, nor do the French architects appear to approve much of it.

Owing to the very high price of wrought-iron, the use of iron wire for suspension-bridges has been pushed to a very great extent throughout France. There are upon the Seine many very remarkable bridges executed with this material, such as the bridges atT riel, Gaillon, and Rouen. The iron wire is exposed to this inconvenience, that with all possible care in the fabrication of the chains, the separate threads cannot be drawn out to the full; the chains, therefore, always stretch, and the platform of the bridge necessarily sinks. Wire chains, however, bear a greater weight in proportion to their sectional area than square bars, and are more likely to be homogeneous in their strength. They avoid, moreover, the necessity for the coupling-links, which, on the latest suspension-bridges executed, augment the weight of the chain 31 per cent. beyond that absolutely necessary, supposing the chain to be of one piece. The surface of oxidation is greater for the wires than for the bar-iron chains, nearly in the proportion of 40 to 1, and this becomes one of the greatest practical objections, for not only does it necessitate frequent painting, but it diminishes, in time, the real strength of the wire cables. The practical strength of these is found, in fact, to be as 0·70 to 1·00 of the theoretical strength; after a few years it falls to 0·66. The voids in the wire cables, according to theory, should be to the solids as 0·1025 to 1·0000; in practice they are found to be 0·25 to 1·00. On the suspension-bridges, the Government engineers enforce a proof of 17 kilogs. per millimètre square of the sectional area of the iron-wire chains, to insure a surplus of strength as a guarantee against deterioration; on the bar-iron chains the proof is only 12 kilogs.

A very beautiful bridge was erected at Suresnes, by M. Flachat, of hoop-iron bands to form the main chains, which answered remarkably well. This application attained a sort of medium result, both as to cost and strength, between the systems hitherto employed.

There is a very beautiful adaptation of the use of the suspension principle to roofing purposes in the Panorama in the Champs Elysées, at Paris. The chains are of wrought-iron wire.*

2. *Lead.*—For building purposes, the bulk of the lead used is imported from England, Spain, and America. It is dearer than with us, consequently its use is not so general, zinc being generally substituted for it. The use and modes of fabrication, wherever it is employed, are precisely the same as in England.†

3. *Copper.*—France also draws the bulk of its copper from foreign countries, at very considerable expense; its use is therefore very much restrained in building. The only instance I know of its application on a large scale is at the Halle aux Blés, which was covered with copper in the year 1812, and I think at the Bourse.*

4. *Zinc.*—The high price of the two last-noticed metals has given rise to the use of zinc upon a very large scale throughout France. It is imported from Belgium and Germany in very large quantities, to the extent of 13,000 tons, worth 280,000*l.* Except upon the borders of the sea, it stands well in France; for the atmosphere does not contain (as in England, where so much coal is consumed) the carbonic acid gases which destroy zinc. On the contrary, in the interior, an oxidation of the external face of the zinc takes place, which prevents its decay. The roof of the palace on the Quai d'Orçay, the Northern, and some parts of the Rouen Railway Station, the Orleans Station, and a crowd of other buildings, are covered with zinc, to the perfect satisfaction of the architects.

The sizes of the metals usually employed for roofing are as follow:—Lead in sheets, 12 feet 3 inches long, by 6 feet 1½ inches wide; the thicknesses are either a full eighth, or a short 3-16th of an inch: the first weighs 89 $\frac{71}{100}$lbs. per yard square; the second weighs 118 $\frac{88}{100}$lbs. per yard square. The lap is generally made from 3 inches to 6 inches longitudinally.

The sheets of copper are made 3 feet 6½ inches long by 3 feet 3 inches; the thicknesses are 0·0021236 and 0·0024526 of a foot, the respective weights 13$\frac{71}{100}$ and 17·15 lbs. troy per yard superficial.

The sheets of zinc are made 6 feet 4 inches long by 3 feet 2⅝ inches, the thickness varying from a short $\frac{1}{17}$ to a very full $\frac{1}{14}$; the weights are respectively 17·15 lbs.; 19·06 lbs.; 20·80 lbs. troy per yard superficial. The sheets of less thickness than these are rarely used in good buildings. Of late years, in the neighbourhood of Paris, zinc tiles have been much used; they are made from 14 inches to 16 inches long, by 12 inches to 14 inches wide; nailed at top, and fastened by books to the slates, which lie immediately beneath them.

The compound metals used are brass, bronze, and the galvanized iron. No difference exists in the mode of preparing these compounds from that observed in England. The bronze is, however, much more often employed than with us. For instance, the columns of the Place Vendome, and of the Bastille; the gates of the Madelaine and St. Vincent de Paul; the fountains of La Place Louvoise and the numerous statues which adorn all the quarters of Paris are in this metal.

Painting and Glazing.—The modes of house-painting employed in Paris are similar to those we employ, except that the oils are better, but the colours and white lead immeasurably worse. Indeed, there is not the same necessity for excellence in the painter's art, so far at least as mere flat tints and common graining are concerned, in a country where oak is so universally employed for joinery. For all objects of luxury, however, we are frightfully behind our neighbours. The decorations of Notre Dame de Lorette, the Madelaine, the former Chamber of Peers, the Louvre, and the Sainte Chapelle, cease to be mere decorations, to pass into the higher walks of art. St. Vincent de Paul, St. Germain l'Auxerois, offer illustrations of polychromic decoration, which contrast painfully with the attempts we see in London.

These two last-named churches may also be cited as specimens of the excellence our neighbours have attained in the art of painting on glass. For drawing and colouring, the windows of St. Vincent de Paul are superior to anything, either ancient or modern, it has ever been my fortune to examine.

The decorations, painting, and glazing of the cafés and shops might afford useful lessons to the architectural student. Great attention is shown to the distribution of the light, and the general tone of the colouring, so as to suit the goods exposed. Glass is cheaper than in England, and in consequence is more prodigally used. The window glass is, however, bad, both in colour and in its powers of resistance; it is thin, green, and wavy.

Although the above notice of the building materials employed in Paris, &c., has grown to a very great length, I have been forced to pass over some of the most important and interesting subjects the review suggests. The chemical process, called by the workmen salt-petring, and its action upon stones when laid bedwise, or against the bed; the manner in which stones are affected when exposed to the various strains; the composition of mortars and cements, and all the phenomena which attend their use in the air, or under water—salt or fresh; the qualities of woods and metals—have all glided before us; but from the limited time we can here devote to them, these subjects have not met with the attention they merit. Indeed, this remark holds good not only here but elsewhere. Very little is known, comparatively speaking, of the chemistry of our profession; what little we do know may principally be sought for amongst the French authors. Perhaps I may not have occupied your attention in vain, if my remarks should call attention to subjects so full of interest to us, but at present so involved in obscurity.

GEO. BURNELL.

* France imported in 1845, 80,000 tons of cast and wrought iron, or steel.

† France imported in 1845, 22,000 tons of lead, of a prime cost value of 400,000*l.* sterling.

* France imported in 1845, 8,500 tons of copper, worth from 320,000*l.* to 400,000*l.* sterling.

BISHOPP'S DISC ENGINE.

PAYING a visit the other morning to the *Times* Printing-office, we saw the new *Disc Engine* that has been put up there to drive Applegarth's two rotary printing machines, by which the 36,000 copies, or thereabouts, matutinally required,* are whiffled off at the rate of about 5,000 complete copies per hour. In this engine, the advantages of which have been long known, the objections that alone kept it out of general use, appear to have been successfully overcome. It is a 16-horse power engine, on the high-pressure and condensing principle: it is, however, equally suitable to be worked as a simple low-pressure condensing engine.

It stands in the machine-room close to a wall, and occupies a singularly small space.† The shafting for driving the printing machines is carried by brackets fixed to the wall over the engine, and is driven by two bands: the drum on the engine-shaft is 30 inches diameter, and the two pulleys overhead 4 feet diameter.

Our impressions in favour of the engine were confirmed by inquiry. It seems that, before being erected at the *Times* office, it was tested, during a month, by Mr. Penn, of Greenwich, and Mr. Farey (both good authorities), in a corn-mill belonging to the former. The comparison was made with a beam-engine of the best construction; and, under similar circumstances, there was an important difference in favour of the disc engine, the engines driving alternately the same machinery, at an equal speed, from the same boiler.

Several disc engines have been fixed in various parts of the kingdom during the last eight years, but the arrangements lately patented by Mr. G. D. Bishopp have so much improved it, as to open to it a much larger sphere of action. This at the *Times* office was manufactured by Messrs. Joseph Whitworth and Co., of Manchester.

The peculiarity of the disc engine is, that it gives *direct motion* to a crank on the engine-shaft, and exerts a perfectly uniform force on it throughout the revolution. There are, therefore, no "dead points;" and when driving by gearing, without a fly-wheel, there is no back-lash in the wheels. Moreover, the steam can be cut off at a very early part of the stroke, without materially affecting the regularity of the driving force.

Other advantages besides the little space occupied are, that it can be fixed on the beams of a floor, or on a slight foundation, and that, although the speed of the piston (*i.e.*, of the disc rings) is only 200 feet per minute, the engine makes three times as many revolutions per minute as a common engine, and consequently, in most cases, much expensive gearing is dispensed with. It appears to us admirably

* On the last day of Rush's trial, 44,500 copies were sold. On the day the Royal Exchange was opened by the Queen, 54,000 impressions were sold,—the largest number ever struck off.

† Seven feet long and four feet wide; and the highest part of the engine is only three feet above the floor of the room.

adapted for driving the screw propeller direct, as the engine shaft has only to be extended through the vessel, and have the propeller fixed to it; it would thus enable sailing vessels which cannot spare much room to adopt the screw as auxiliary power. The disc engines are now made entirely from wooden patterns, and every wearing surface, it is said, can be refaced, or renewed, as in engines of the common construction. We cannot but think that this engine ought to come into general use.

Miscellanea.

PROJECTED WORKS.—Advertisements have been issued for tenders, by 5th July, for the enlargement of the British Orphan Asylum, Clapham Rise; by dates not specified, for the erection of the St. Martin's Northern Schools, and for the erection of Sketty new church; by August 6, for the enlargement of the London-bridge station of the London and Brighton Railway; by July 11, for the erection of St. Matthias's Church, Weir district, Bristol; by 7th, for the restoration and additions of the masonry, carpenter, slating, and plaster works of the parish church of Irthington; by 30th inst., for the erection of a butter cross, at Knighton (Hereford); by same date, for building a covered corn exchange, at Bedford; by 2nd July, for the erection of a national school-room and master's house, at Beverley; by 2nd, for building a sea wall at Bowness; by 16th, for the erection and completion of bath rooms at the Shaw Heath Union Workhouse, Stockport, and for making drains and main sewers there; by 11th, for keeping in repair the public conduits and other waterworks at Southampton, for two years; and by 10th, for 400 waggons for the Great Northern Railway.

COMPETITIONS, &c.—Advertisements have been issued for plans by July 18, for additional accommodation for 300 inmates, at St. Luke's workhouse, Chelsea. Premiums, 25*l*. and 10*l*. Also for plans, drawings, and estimates, by September, for a church at Cheltenham, to contain 1,000 persons, at a cost of 4,000*l*.—The London and South-Western Railway Company require a principal resident engineer experienced in designing and constructing railway works, and stations, &c.

THE CHURCH BUILDING SOCIETY held its usual meeting on Monday week, when grants were made in aid of the erection of new churches at the new district of All Saints, Leeds; at Gravesend, for a district of that parish; towards rebuilding the churches at Virginstow, near Launceston, and East Walton, near Haverfordwest; enlarging the churches of St. Stephen, Islington, and Compton, near Petersfield; re-arranging the interior of the churches at Llanfihangel-Rhos-y-Corn, near Lampeter; Halstead, Essex; Hinton Charterhouse, near Beckington; Brooke, near Norwich; Sutton, near Stalham; Grately, near Andover; and Cheam, Surrey.

EXEMPTION OF LITERARY INTITUTIONS FROM LOCAL RATES.—In reply to a question from Mr. W. Brown, the Attorney-General said that a bill had been proposed to him on this subject, to two of the provisions of which he entertained considerable objection. The one was that adjustment of disputes should be effected by trial at sessions, a course which would lead to litigation and expense; the other was to the creation of a new office for registration. He thought the machinery of the registry of friendly societies should be made available.—In reply to questions by Mr. M. Gibson and Mr. Bright, the Attorney-General said he would do all he could to promote a measure which did not contain the clauses to which he objected, but whether the Government would think it expedient to introduce the measure was another question. He could not say whether such a measure would be introduced or not.

METROPOLITAN.—The principal figures in the mould of Mr. Carew's "Death of Nelson," for the monument at Charing-cross, have been safely filled with molten bronze from some of the cannon taken by the hero himself in action. ——The first stone of the new Fishmongers Almshouses, at Wandsworth, was laid on Saturday last.——Two new churches are to be erected at Lambeth.

BIRMINGHAM SCHOOL OF DESIGN.—On Friday in last week the annual exhibition and distribution of prizes took place at the Society of Arts, New-Street, and was very numerously attended. The Bishop of Manchester was in the chair, and congratulated the donors and subscribers on the progress made since last year. The number of students, as well as their proficiency, had much increased. In the female school the classes are full. Announcement was made of the increase of the Government grant, and the appointment of Mr. Kidd, a modeller, as second master, and of a pupil of last year, Mr. W. O. Williams, as third master. The drawings, models, &c., have since been publicly exhibited.

THE BEDFORDSHIRE ARCHITECTURAL AND ARCHÆOLOGICAL SOCIETY held their annual meeting at Bedford on Thursday in last week, the Archdeacon of Bedford in the chair, when a number of objects of interest were exhibited, the report read, and papers also read, by Mr. M. H. Bloxham "On Conventual Arrangements;" by Mr. T. Bernard "On the Basilicæ of Rome;" and by Mr. Jackson "On Felmersham Church." Others by the Rev. H. J. Rose and the Rev. B. Bridges were deferred till another meeting. Votes of thanks were accorded, and a committee appointed to alter some of the rules of the society.

FLOATING THE TUBE FOR BRITANNIA-BRIDGE.—Tuesday week was appointed for the transport of one of the central and largest tubes of this great work to its place across the Menai straits, near Bangor. From the breaking of a capstan, however, the process was postponed till next day, when it was safely accomplished, in the midst of the acclamations of thousands, mingled with the appropriate and stirring music of the sea-song, "I'm afloat." This tube is 470 feet long, 30 feet high in the centre, and diminishes in height to 22 feet at the extremities. The clear span between the towers, on which it is to rest, is 12 feet shorter. The weight of wrought-iron in the whole is 1,600 tons. It is painted stone colour, and protected by an arched roof of thin corrugated zinc. The masonry work is of as gigantic a character of course as the iron work. The abutment on the Anglesey side is 143 feet high and 173 long. The wing walls of both terminate in pedestals, on each of which are two colossal couched lions of Egyptian design, lifting their lime-stone foreheads in the face of every train, with bullet eyes as large as human heads. The bodies are each 25 feet long and 12 feet high, though crouched; the weight of each is 30 tons. There is some intention of surmounting the central tower with a colossal figure of Britannia, 60 feet high. The great Britannia Tower in the centre of the straits is 62 feet by 52 at its base; total height, 230 feet; it contains 148,625 cubic feet of limestone and 144,625 of sandstone; weighs 20,000 tons; and contains 387 tons of cast-iron built into it in beams and girders. The total quantity of stone contained in the bridge is 1,500,000 cubic feet, in a total length of 1,849 feet. In the scaffolding used there are 570,000 cubic feet of timber and 20 tons of iron bolts. The tube launched on Wednesday week has been compared to the Burlington Arcade. If placed on end in St. Paul's Churchyard it would rise upwards of 100 feet above the top of the cross. Fifteen miles of rope were required in the management of this Gulliver in Lilliput. The slightest change in temperature, gleam of sunshine, or shower of rain, is said to act on these tubes *in situ* in appreciable expansion or contraction and deflection. The cost of the whole structure has been estimated at 600,000*l*. to 700,000*l*.

PUBLIC MUSEUM AND LIBRARY AT SALFORD.—The town council have resolved to provide and keep up the requisite accommodation and attendance for donations, &c., in a mansion-house, in Peel's Park, to which the public will have free access at all reasonable times. A rate of ½d. per pound may afterwards be authorized.

BLIND BUILDERS.—Tenders sent in for pulling down and rebuilding four third-rate houses in George-yard, Whitechapel:—

Palmer	£1,145
Cole	1,050
Toiley	929
Jacobs	908
Hall and Son, Whitechapel	735

HAND WORK.—I said, early in this essay, that hand-work might always be known from machine-work,—observing, however, at the same time, that it was possible for men to turn themselves into machines, and to reduce their labour to the machine level; but so long as men work *as* men, putting their heart into what they do, and doing their best, it matters not how bad workmen they may be, there will be that in the handling which is above all price: it will be plainly seen that some places have been delighted in more than others—that there has been a pause, and a care about them; and then there will come careless bits and fast bits; and here the chisel will have struck hard, and there lightly, and anon timidly; and if the man's mind as well as his heart went with his work, all this will be in the right places, and each part will set off the the other; and the effect of the whole, as compared with the same design cut by a machine or a lifeless hand, will be like that of poetry well read and deeply felt to that of the same verses jangled by rote. There are many to whom the difference is imperceptible; but to those who love poetry it is everything—they had rather not hear it all, than hear it ill read: and to those who love architecture, the life and accent of the hand are everything. They had rather not have ornament at all, than see it ill cut—deadly cut, that is. I cannot too often repeat, it is not coarse cutting, it is not blunt cutting, that is necessarily bad; but it is cold cutting—the look of equal trouble everywhere—the smooth, diffused tranquillity of heartless pains—the regularity of a plough in a level field.—*Ruskin.*

INSTITUTION OF CIVIL ENGINEERS.—On Tuesday, 19th, Mr. Joshua Field, President, in the chair, the paper read was "On the employment of high-pressure steam, working expansively, in marine engines," by Mr. John Seaward. In the course of the evening, the Earl of Rosse, President of the Royal Society, was presented, by Mr. Rennie, to the President of the institution, on his election as an honorary member. On the 26th, the paper read was "Observations on the Obstructions to Navigation in Tidal Rivers," by Mr. J. T. Harrison. This was the last meeting of the session.

ESSEX COUNTY LUNATIC ASYLUM COMPETITION.—The committee of magistrates appointed to receive designs and carry into execution the erection of the above asylum, have chosen that of Mr. H. E. Kendall, jun., for adoption. It is in the Tudor style,—to accommodate 400 patients,—and is to be erected near Brentwood.

TENDERS.

For repairs and repewing West Ham parish church, Essex; Mr. C. Dyson, surveyor.

Heed	£1,992
R. and E. Curtis	1,898
Revett	1,789
T. Burton	1,669
Kirk and Parry (accepted)	1,620
Glenn (omitted to comply with the form of tender)	1,616

For a new church to be built in the Bethnal-green-road.

Little	£7,440
Ward	6,173
Holland	5,970
Curtis	5,953
Higgs	5,896
Ashby	5,733
Wood	5,696
Grimsdell	5,612
Haynes and Co.	5,537
Myers	5,489

For rebuilding a farm (burnt down in March last) belonging to Mr. Clover, of Kirklington, Cambridgeshire; Mr. C. Clark, architect:—

Frost	£1,297	10	6
Reid	1,095	0	0
Quinsea and Co.	1,045	0	0
Trevethan	1,020	0	0
Andrews	988	0	0
Erswell	983	11	0
Westley	980	0	0
Davy	966	16	0
Allen	930	0	0
Grainger	845	0	0

BUILDINGS AND MONUMENTS,

EDITED BY GEORGE GODWIN, F.R.S., &c.

Part II., containing views of the Army and Navy Club House, Pall Mall; St. Stephen's Church and Schools, Westminster; Interior of the Museum of Economic Geology, with details; Chapter House of Lincoln Cathedral; New Hall, Pembroke College, Oxford; South Hackney Church; Interior of the Royal Italian Opera House, and University Galleries and Taylor Institute, Oxford, will be published on July 1st.

TO CORRESPONDENTS.

Rockford.—"G. S.," "J. M. W.," "H. B. M.," "E. A.," "H. B.," "Quondam," "J. B." (next week), "H. A." (thanks for note). "An Architect." "A Subscriber" (the discreditable condition of old Upton Church has been urged by us at some length), "J. T.," "S. H." (shall be attended to), "J. Q." (it has not reached us), "One of the Contractors," "I. L.," "E. A." (St. Mary's Church is in Kensington parish; the site is behind what used to be called "Little Chelsea," and now "West Brompton"), "J. B.," Lisson-green (you cannot oblige your neighbour to take the course pointed out), "W. M. G." (had better consult the Act, which is a very short one), "E. A.," "J. L.," "B. W." (may practise the process without license, if not for profit), "F. H. S.," "R. J. W."—Rudimentary Architecture," by Talbot Bury, Architect (Weale, 1849); "Holland's Wages and other Tables," by J. T. Holland, Accountant (Bradshaw's office, Fleet-street); "Past and Present Views of Railways," by Alexander Gordon, C.E. (London, Dalton).

"Books, Prices, and Addresses."—We have not time to point out books or find addresses.

NOTICE.— All communications respecting *advertisements* should be addressed to the "Publisher," and not to the "Editor;" all other communications should be addressed to the EDITOR, and *not* to the Publisher.

No. CCCXXXV.

SATURDAY, JULY 7, 1849.

HE stern warning given to the Metropolitan Commission of Sewers by Mr. Phillips, their chief surveyor, and his proposal to construct 20 miles of tunnel sewer at such a depth from the surface, say " 100 feet below the bed of the river," as would render it independent of all barriers,—have excited considerable attention, and seem to call for some observations on our part. We have watched the proceedings of the new commission with much solicitude from the first, and in our pages will be found *the only continuous public record of their proceedings in open court.** The space which this record occupies is large, and we have, out of consideration for that section of our readers who may not feel immediately interested in the matter, avoided enlarging it by observations. The present position of the commission, however, is so extraordinary, that to pass it by without comment is impossible.

We need not remind our readers in other than the shortest sentence, that the old Westminster Commission was superseded (and the other commissions went with it), mainly through the efforts of Mr. Leslie and Mr. Byng, two of its members, and the statements made, at what then seemed great pecuniary risk, by the clerk of the commission, Mr. Hertslet, and the surveyor, Mr. Phillips. About a year and a half ago the new commission was appointed, and these two members of the old body and these two officers were, as a matter of course, put on it. This was done, we say, but a year and a half ago, and we now find the new commission exactly in the position of the old one previous to its dissolution. Mr. Byng has withdrawn himself; Mr. Leslie has ceased his regular attendance ; the surveyor considers it "time to speak out, both for the credit of the court and for the reputation of its officers," and to prevent proceedings "calculated to bring the commission into ridicule;" and Mr. Hertslet, whose ability, courtesy, and fitness for his office all have acknowledged, says he can no longer go on with the commissioners, and gives evidence of the strength of his conviction by the surrender of nine hundred good pounds a-year.

This surely is a conjunction of circumstances which should lead to a careful and searching self-examination on the part of the commission. Without expressing any decided opinion at this moment, we earnestly invite them to it, our anxiety simply being to see the commission working unanimously and well for the public good ; and this, we are quite sure, is the desire of the excellent nobleman, the Earl of Carlisle, who presides. The majority of the commissioners scarcely appreciate the magnitude of their task, or see, what is the fact, the utter impossibility of effecting it satisfactorily by the mode they are now pursuing : some few of them, indeed, we have no hesitation in saying, re quite unfit for the office. The establishment of principles has been sadly neglected ; the—but we will not now speak harshly—the commission has had difficulties to contend against, and may yet claim our indulgence for a time.

To add to the present troubles of the commissioners, they have been thrown into Chancery. In pursuance of a recent order, the officers of the commission proceeded the other day to fill in the putrid and offensive ditches at Bermondsey, in the vicinity of which many fatal cases of cholera have recently occurred, and in consequence of this proceeding Mr. Rains, the owner of the property, has filed a bill in Chancery to restrain their operations ; in which he prays that the commissioners may be decreed to give notice of the intended nature of their operations, that he may be enabled to make a proper claim for privilege and compensation money, or to make the necessary deposit in the Bank of England, according to the Lands Clauses Act, 1845, and that in the meantime the Metropolitan Commissioners may be restrained from doing any works which may affect his interests. The Vice-Chancellor gave the plaintiff leave to move on Thursday morning last for the injunction as prayed by the bill.* On that day, the subject having been partially discussed, was postponed till Saturday, in order that the commissioners, should they think fit, might have the opportunity of exhibiting their plan of operations. The Judge, however, stated his decided opinion to be, that their proceedings were illegal, unless protected by the 61st section of their Act, enabling works of haste to be done without notice. The plaintiff's counsel responded, that this was a work that would occupy *three months*, and to proceed with it without notice, therefore, must be illegal on his honour's showing : the 61st section did not apply to such works at all. We shall see.

Now, as to the proposed tunnel sewer. The surveyor's letter, which has caused such commotion, is one result of the *committee system.*

Two plans for the improvement of the drainage of Westminster,—one by Mr. Austin, the other by Mr. Phillips,—were made sixteen months ago, and appear to have been referred to the "Survey Committee." Members of the commission have asked for them at various times,—but the court, as a court, has heard nothing of them. On the 15th of June, according to Mr. Phillips, the Survey Committee passed resolutions "approving in effect the suggestions of Mr. Austin's report ;" and then, forthwith, comes out Mr. Phillips's letter, warning the commissioners " against attempting to execute the works therein contemplated," and stating that these are "wholly impracticable, and unworthy the objects which should be kept in view for the perfect drainage of this great metropolis ;" containing, moreover, an entirely fresh suggestion for improving the drainage,—that is, fresh so far as the commission is concerned. Now, this certainly does seem rather a pre-

cipitate proceeding on the part of the surveyor, scarcely warrantable; unless, indeed, those who are behind the curtain see that the resolution of a committee is in effect tantamount to a decision of the court, in which case the object might be to prevent the committee from bringing up their report in the threatened shape.

Mr. Austin's plan, which has been called the "converging system," is to divide the locality into certain districts, and to construct in each an enormous cesspool, or "sump," as he terms it, to which the drains of the district are to concentre. The contents, thus accumulated, are to be raised by steam-engines, and distributed from time to time, through subterranean pipes, over the country, or into the Thames. This plan, with every consideration for the ability of Mr. Austin, and the eminent engineers said to have been consulted upon it, is exceedingly unsatisfactory and objectionable. The great desideratum is to remove the refuse from us, not to accumulate it amongst us, and, moreover, to do this without contaminating our noble river, or transforming what should be a means of purification and a source of health, into a stream of corruption and the fruitful parent of disease.

All are now agreed as to the necessity of this latter condition, the preservation of the Thames : to persevere in the present course would show insanity, and all honour should be given to Mr. John Martin and others, who have been urging this point for years, before the public mind was awakened to its importance.*

The deep sewer proposed by Mr. Phillips is to be constructed in a slightly and uniformly curved direction, from Kingston on the western to the Kent or Essex marshes on the eastern extremity of the jurisdiction of the court, and there suitable reservoirs are to be provided, whence the refuse could be pumped up by steam power, and used either in a liquid or a solid state. It is to take off the whole of the house-drainage and other waters which at present compose the ordinary flow of the London sewers in fine weather, and the capacity of a tunnel for such a purpose he estimates would be 8 feet at Greenwich and 6 feet in diameter at Pimlico. In its passage it goes under the West India Docks. The cost of 6 miles proposed to be immediately done he puts at 200,000*l.*

The general idea is not a new one, and for the purposes of the public it is none the worse for that.

In 1843 Mr. Thomas Cubitt published a short pamphlet, entitled " Suggestions for improving the state of the River Thames and the Drainage of London" wherein, after pointing out the injury done by discharging the sewers into the Thames, he says,—

" My idea is, that the best means of obviating this evil would be to conduct the sewer drainage at once from the west and north parts of London, by the shortest and straightest lines that can be found, to a place to the east of the town (and perhaps the low lands of Plaistow would be required. at an expense of 470*l.* These works would enable one branch of the mill-stream to be filled up as far as George-row, as also another branch from Little George-street to Dockhead, leaving the mill-ponds to be lated for the purpose), and there, near to the river, to form one or more very large reservoirs to receive the discharge from the sewers, where it should remain during the flow of the tide, having gates or sluices to be opened as-

* A meeting of the court was held at a very short notice on Monday last, when the following resolution was passed :—" That whereas it is of the greatest importance that the works in progress should not be stayed ; and whereas an Act of Parliament provides for compensation to parties sustaining damage,—the application to the Court of Chancery, of which notice has been given by Mr. Henry Rains, be opposed, and that the solicitors of the commissioners have authority to give or accede to such undertakings or terms as the Court of Chancery, on the hearing of the motion, may require or approve in reference to the supply of water, or otherwise, and to agree to any reference, and to the plaintiff's right being tried at law, or otherwise." The chief surveyor presented a report, which set forth that it would be necessary to lay down about 2,300 feet in length of 12-inch pipe, for the purpose of supplying the tanneries and other works with water, the expense of which would be 350*l.* ; and to accommodate the drainage of the houses and premises draining into the streams, about 3,780 feet of 9-inch pipe dealt with hereafter. Other resolutions were passed showing that the commissioners are determined to proceed with the works.

* Mr. Martin has recently issued several pamphlets and reprints, showing a number of important suggestions made, by him from time to time,—" Thames and Metropolis Improvement Plan," by John Martin, K.L. London, Lindsay House, Chelsea. 1849 ; " Reprint of Reports of a Committee appointed to take into consideration Mr. Martin's plan for rescuing the Thames from every species of pollution," 1835;—and some others. Mr. Martin deserves the best opinion of his countrymen.

* Whether it is desirable to continue this may be open to question.

the tide goes down; so that it would only be allowed to mix with the river when on its passage to the sea, the gates being closed before the tide changes. By this plan none of the sewer water could travel back to London. With this view very deep sewers might be made, of sufficient capacity to take a large quantity of water in the most direct way, and to receive the contents of all the sewers crossing the lines. For example: one great line might be made to commence at Paddington, going along the New-road by King's Cross (or Battle-bridge), and there taking the Fleet Ditch; from thence, running towards the east by Islington, passing under the New River and the Canal, through Hackney and Bromley, and passing below the river Lea to its great receptacle: the distance from Paddington by this route would be only about 12 miles, being 6 miles less than the present course, which has to travel with the river, by all its windings and bendings, round the Isle of Dogs, and all other obstructions. Another great line might be carried along Oxford-street to the bottom of Holborn, where it could be made sufficiently deep to take the contents of that part of the Fleet Ditch, and which might be lowered from the river to run in that direction; then to continue across Smithfield, the grounds of the Charterhouse, along Old-street by Bethnal-green, and so eastward, to join the great outlet. This would give an opportunity of draining many parts that are in a very crowded state, and at present without sufficient means of drainage."

For the south side of London he proposed a similar deep sewer running towards the east, on the other side of the Thames.

The writer afterwards makes some observations on the means this arrangement would afford of trying experiments as to extracting some part of the immense quantity of fertilizing matter that is now wasted, but he very properly urges that the first consideration is to get rid of the refuse, without poisoning the river.

A meeting of the commissioners was held on Thursday, the 5th, and it will be seen in the report of their proceedings which is appended, that they directed the surveyor to submit full details of his plan to a special court to be held on the 23rd. Every willingness was professed to give it fair play, and, although some of the commissioners are very angry with the surveyor, and threaten his dismissal unless the first letter be withdrawn, they have agreed to postpone the consideration of his offence till his plan is fully before them.

The tunnel sewer is not without its difficulties and objections, but we are disposed, nevertheless, to think that the idea (however it may be modified) must be carried out now or hereafter. Lord Ebrington presided, and we would compliment his lordship on the good feeling and pleasant manner which he exhibited.

July 5.—A report was received from Mr. Gotto, assistant-surveyor, on the subject of a complaint that had been made by the Speaker of the House of Commons, of the offensive odours arising in the neighbourhood of the Houses of Parliament. He attributed a portion of the same to St. Margaret's churchyard, which was completely filled up with bodies in a state of decomposition, having saturated the soil with gases penetrating into the sewers; and from the inquiries he had made, it appeared that particular gullies were offensive at one time and not at another, which might be accounted for by the wind down one grating forcing the gases up another.

Mr. Chadwick moved that the subject be deferred to the next court, which was agreed to.

Sir Edward Milne, from the Westminster Improvement Commissioners, attended the court, and wished to know the views of this commission as to the general system of drainage that would be finally adopted for this district, as they were unable to commence operations until some general plan should be laid down. They should be very shortly in a position to open the new Victoria street, but no builder would look at it until such plan was laid down.

Lord Ebrington promised speed.

On the resolution of the general committee of June 28 being read—"That the communication of Mr. Phillips to the court, without reference to the merits of any scheme alluded to therein, is wholly unwarrantable; and that unless the next court shall receive an assurance from Mr. Phillips, that his letter is unequivocally withdrawn, and regret be expressed to the court for the nature of the communication, it be recommended to the court that Mr. Phillips should not continue in the service of the commission,"

Lord Ebrington said that this subject involved two questions, viz., the suggestion of a plan by an officer who had devoted much time to the subject, having had great facilities of local knowledge and experience; and secondly, certain expressions he had used at the time. Before inquiring into the latter, it would be for them to consider whether the outline of the plan so drawn out should be accompanied with details and estimates. He understood that Mr. Phillips had already got a sketch drawn out, and therefore he (Lord E.) thought the best course would be that a separate day should be fixed for their consideration. They should take care that the public service should not be damaged by any personal matters, however unfitting those feelings might be for the dignity and proper working of the commission. He would accordingly move, that the details of the plan should be brought up on the 23rd, and that the same be previously printed.

Mr. Leslie seconded the proposition of the chairman, without then expressing any opinion on the plan.

Mr. Byng hoped that before proceeding in the question, they should have both plans (Mr. Austin's and Mr. Phillips's) laid before them.

Mr. Chadwick said Mr. Austin had produced no plan for the entire drainage of London.

Sir H. de la Beche vindicated the acts of the Survey Committee, who, he contended, had given no opinion whatever on any particular plan. Whatever was proved to be the best would be adopted. They were merely the trustees for the public, to do that which was the best for their interests.

A long desultory conversation ensued on the subject, in which Mr. Chadwick, the Rev. W. Murray, Mr. C. Johnson, Mr. Slaney, and Dr. Arnott took part, and the motion was finally carried.

The following resolution of the General Committee was then read:—"That it be reported to the court, that the committee, taking into consideration the zealous and efficient services of Mr. Hertslet to the present and past commissions of sewers, would be happy if Mr. Hertslet would feel willing to continue in their service; but in any case, for their own satisfaction, the commissioners would wish to receive from Mr. Hertslet any communication he may think useful to make for their information."

Lord Ebrington moved its adoption by the court, and expressed the happiness he should experience if Mr. Hertslet should continue in the service, but would not press him to do so against his better judgment, or with any sacrifice of his health. Should he persevere in his determination to retire, he trusted they would follow the same course in the question of his retirement as they had formerly adopted in the case of Mr. Roe.—Mr. Byng condemned such a course, in the formation of a nondescript office; he had the word of Mr. Hertslet that he now sought no pension.—Mr. Hertslet said he had not waived his right on that ground, but in his present position he was too proud to receive a pension out of the ratepayers' money.

Mr. Bullar said if by any modification of the onerous duties Mr. Hertslet could be induced to remain in the commission, he was sure it would receive their unanimous approval.

After a few words from Mr. Slaney, the motion was put and carried unanimously.

Mr. Hertslet believed such a course would be attended with delay. He had drawn up some reasons for his retirement, which he now had in his pocket, but as they might apply to the future operations of the commission, he begged at once to retire from the service, and that they should appoint his successor.

After a long discussion, the following resolution on the subject of improvement rates was agreed to:—"That a separate department be constituted for the purpose of calculating and preparing improvement rates for all the works performed for the benefit of ratepayers, in such a manner as to diffuse the cost of each over a series of years, and apportion the amount to each ratepayer in the measure, as nearly as possible, of the benefit he derives from them."

St. Martin's Church, Birmingham.—An architect, through the local *Journal*, calls attention to the dangerous state of the spire of this church, and its rapid decay. On examination, he finds its departure from the perpendicular to be far greater than it was, and its vibration during bell ringing to be rather alarming. The whole edifice is thought to require restoration or rebuilding, which there are surely people in Birmingham quite rich enough and ready enough to do.

AN ATTEMPT TO EXHIBIT THE TRUE PRINCIPLES OF ARCHITECTURAL AND PICTORIAL EFFECT IN REFERENCE TO STREETS, AND TO TOWNS GENERALLY.*

I have pointed to natural principles in reference to streets, but it must be added, that on these principles the art itself is based; for architecture, rightly considered, is an ideal imitation of a prototype, which may be found in the works of creation, which furnishes it with analogies. It is not the literal forms that architecture copies, but the principles they disclose; these are the rules of art, the geometry of which is but an instrument in its hands. In nature, designs may be everywhere discovered, and a secret rule which, like the laws of the Medes and Persians, altereth not. The first business of the student is to study these laws, and trace her beauty to its spring. Nature presents us with models eminently fit for our purpose; scarcely any of her objects, her groupings, or her combinations, but what are suggestive of principles for our guidance in architecture. "There is not one single object in nature," says an eloquent writer upon art, "which is not capable of conveying ideas of beauty, and which, to the rightly-perceiving mind, does not present an incalculably greater number of beautiful than of deformed parts."

To this appropriating of the principles of nature true art owes her origin, and it is essential to her existence and progress. Nature is the true genius of architecture; her beauty is the muse—the inspiration of the architect: by a close study of nature, I consider the resources of the art may be greatly extended, its capabilities increased and enriched, and effects produced beyond anything that now exists or that the world has yet seen;—whilst, on the other hand, if we lose sight of these principles, all must become anarchy in the mind, which will be a prey to the most incongruous and whimsical associations.

Versed in these principles, and enamoured of their beauty, the student will have no difficulty in applying them to art. He will perceive that unity and variety are the ingredients of beauty; that a building or street should have its various component parts strictly subordinate to the general design, and harmonizing one with the other, though each a distinct composition in itself; and in designing what in stone and wood is to give pleasure to the mind, he will consider the relative effects of form, proportion, and arrangement, as they exist before him in creation, and work in accordance with those principles of beauty and harmony which are developed there.

If I am correct in this, I shall not be deemed hasty in my condemnation of the invariable use of the straight line in streets at the present day. What, I would ask, forms the chief beauty of a river or stream? Do those splendid phenomena, the magnificent characteristics of mountain scenery, owe their beauty to the straight line? The rocky pass, the verdant valley, the interesting combination of glade and thicket, woods, groves, hills, and lakes,—have not these been looked upon by the architect in vain? Nature seems to abhor a straight line as she is said to do a vacuum. Yet while every leaf, every blade of glass, every part of the human body, presents us with some beautiful curve for imitation in works of art, both streets and houses might be pointed out in which scarce any line but the straight one can be found.

If I wanted an example of a street in which every precept of nature had been unheeded, I could not do better than instance a well-known one in Liverpool, viz., Shaw-street, than which, perhaps, nothing more monotonous could be found. Formed on level ground, or nearly so, of one straight line, and, what is the most strange, though the houses are not enlisted under one design in the shape of a terrace, with the usual arrangement of centre and wings, the houses, as if cast in one mould, are from end to end fac-similes of each other. I appeal to any gentleman who has made the observation, whether he ever experienced in that street any of those sensations of pleasure that a fine street is calculated to awaken in every cultivated mind. With the exception of a couple of Ionic columns as a door-case to each house, it is one dead merely perforated wall from end to end, devoid of all provision

* See p. 293, *ante*.

igbt and shade, innocent of anything that relieve the wearied eye, or awaken a spark iterest in the mind. I mention this street use it is one of those in the design of :h (if we are to have beauty in street itecture), from the cost and size of the ies, we have a right to expect some iowledgment of the influence, and some iience to the laws, of the beautiful. But it e fault, in a greater or less degree, of y other streets, and arises from the preinance in point of influence, of men who ider the beautiful incompatible with the ul, and have no idea of the moral agency rt. On such a street, as far as all æsthequalities are concerned, those of London ie fourteenth century might have looked idly down!

'en have hitherto been too prone to copy foregone, to kneel at the shrines of their 'athers, afraid of striking out into new s, however clearly pointed out by the ır-posts of nature and judgment. The ectors of Washington and the new cities ated Babylon and other great capitals, in-l of going to nature, a reference to which t at any time have a regenerating influence ı the art, renew its exhausted resources, remove the corruptions to which it is e from the fetters of prescription, the ing whim of fashion, and other destructive iences.

his beauty I am aware should be subordi-to constructive requirements, and to the ites of utility, and should in a great mea-arise out of them: but it does not entirely ırise,—when these have performed their , there is something still left in the way of ıration, which must be done under the lance of judgment and enlightened taste.

have hitherto considered the picturesque e as to the arrangement and diversity of ses than as regards their individual forms, the latter is an essential consideration; there was perhaps never a time when the iitect was more thickly surrounded by ients yielding hints and suggestions for inating the picturesque than at present; though it is independent of styles, yet, ur present ideas of it, we are, I consider, .ly indebted to the rise, development, and of the latter.

e Romans, infinitely inferior to the Greeks ırity of style, were superior to them in the rial: while less severe in taste and correct xpression, Rome exhibited more variety richness, and produced greater magnifi-e than Athens had known. That this was case her relics attest: the still glorious s of her temples, palaces, baths, and tri-hal arches (spoils of time yet trophies of us at which travellers still pause and ler), bear witness to her architectural dis-in the days of Adrian. But beautiful and as was the Greek architecture, and rich ust have been that of the Romans, who ributed largely to the riches of the art by introduction of the arch, and by that ning glory of the art—the dome,—it is the ırns that have produced the grandest ›inations, and most striking effects: the ronement of the Pantheon on the temple eace was a triumph reserved for Brunel-i, Bramante, Michelangelo, and Wren; ıo, with Palladio, Inigo Jones, and others, :d the Greek and Roman elements to pro-edifices, which, however far behind the ınt masters in purity of style, marked an ncement of the art in many qualities h nature suggests, and judgment sanc-ı.

ıe rise of Gothic architecture, remarkable he variety of its forms, its profound scien-knowledge, and mechanical skill, intro-d an entirely new feature into architecture urope, which gave an impulse to the study, added to the resources of picturesque gn. The inferiority of sandstone to marble ›int of beauty must have given the new ›tus to the struggle for decoration which it lved.

was the genius of pointed design that first urope, leaving the horizontal principle of ›uity, introduced the vertical, which, ac-ing to the theory of some, was intended to ›t the mind heavenward, and the whole , in various particulars, to be a sort of ›glyphical exponent of theological doc-s and ecclesiastical usages. Indeed, its aspiring outlines, its bold projections, and deep recesses, its prominent and deeply-cut ornaments, render it highly capable of the most elaborate expression. And, though much of such particular expression, admitting it to exist, must necessarily refer to doctrines and systems which have passed away, and be so far powerless, yet all must acknowledge that sufficient remains of a purely abstract character, capable of stirring, in no slight degree, the chords of the heart and imagination.

The most perfect examples of pointed design were produced in the thirteenth and fourteenth centuries; some of the cathedrals of that period here and on the continent, in their decorations, seeming to vie with the infinite variety of nature herself; but the picturesque was perhaps never more perfectly embodied than in the ecclesiastical, monumental, and domestic Gothic of the later periods. Our old English, or Tudor, manor-houses houses and cottages, with their bay and oriel windows, turretted and pinnacled gables, niches, ornamental chimney-shafts and embattled porches, are the buildings, which, in their forms, beyond any others, harmonise with those of nature.

The introduction of Italian architecture into England gave a fresh impulse to our ideas of the picturesque, and produced in domestic buildings effects unseen before. The love of the picturesque, as embodied in Gothic buildings, prevented the native architect on its introduction from adopting it entire; the continuous entablatures and flat pediments of the classic architecture, as exhibited at Rome, compared with the bold and varied composition, and endless decoration, of the Gothic, must have had much of the effect of humble prose beside the lofty flights of the poet: perhaps association and other causes attached him to his native style: however that may be, by uniting the general principles of design and composition of the Tudor with the elements of the Palladian architecture, together with something of the quaint decoration of the German and Flemish schools, the style called the Elizabethan was produced.

For some time it was a mere parody on the classic; novelty and error went hand in hand, but something abstractly valuable to art, I consider, was gained; the study of picturesque beauty in connection with the antique orders was advanced, the wholesome effects of which were visible in the designs of Sir John Vanbrugh and others, who endeavoured to call back to the architecture of Palladio something of the spirit of the native Gothic.

Whilst speaking approvingly of the Elizabethan architecture, I wish it to be understood that I do not refer to that mixture of Gothic and Italian detail that is seen in some old buildings,—these were merely transitional; what I understand by Elizabethan is the style that was presented when the transition was complete, and then no Gothic details existed in it; and, consisting of Italian details, implanted on Gothic design and composition only, it is worthy of attention. It was, in regard to the picturesque, a step in advance of the Italian,—which presented in general a straight outline, and suggestive of new combinations of the antique elements, more striking and beautiful than had yet been seen.

It was unfortunate for the art that the love of the picturesque, as engendered by this state of things, united to the most successful efforts to introduce it into the architecture of the ancients, should have been condemned as faults, and have gained for the architects little else than abuse, both from their contemporaries and successors. Vanbrugh, who had an intense feeling for the picturesque, who displayed the most original and inventive genius, and the most consummate skill in composition, was derided and lampooned by the first critics and poets of the day, and regarded almost in the light of an impostor, because he would not reproduce Roman and Greek temples in this country, but attempted to weave into picturesque forms, adapted to native requirements, the elements of the classic, and infuse the most striking features of our own into the architecture of the ancients. His chief works, Blenheim and Castle Howard, though not without faults, sufficiently attest his possession of the qualities which I here attribute to him. There are others who suffered martyrdom in their reputations to their love for the truth in architecture, convinced that whatever the style of a building, whatever the character of its details, the composition may be picturesque.

I am aware that numberless whimsicalities and absurdities have been perpetrated in the name of the picturesque, but maintain, notwithstanding, that the picturesque is not, as has been supposed by many, inimical to purity of style, and that it can be obtained in the antique styles without violating their essential laws. The Greek architecture was for a different purpose to ours,—one which called for simplicity and solemnity. The source of the grand style of Greece was religion. Had they applied their architecture to domestic and other purposes, they would doubtless have engrafted new features thereon, and have drawn upon other principles. St. George's Hall, of this town, though pure Greek in style, and a new erection, is not unpicturesque. Many architects, celebrated in their day, in order to produce picturesque forms and combinations, perverted principle; they sacrificed propriety to the pictorial, but the pictorial demanded no such sacrifice. The picturesque is of no style, but it may be obtained in any. It reigned in Greece and Rome, and may be found in India, and Egypt, and China, at the present day; and though the hand of time may be useful in producing its most affecting associations, it may be had in the newest building, where outline is attended to—where the laws of natural beauty are consulted.

Many of the old towns of the continent, and some nearer home—in Wales, for instance—strangers to the spirit of improvement that has elsewhere been busy in the land, though certainly not models for imitation in this improved age, could not be looked upon by the architect of taste without suggesting to his mind valuable hints for originating the picturesque in houses and streets. The streets of London, so far back as the fourteenth and fifteenth centuries, as exhibited in old prints, with their pointed gables and overhanging stories, though affording no lesson in constructive science, are instinct with beauty: many of them develop principles, and yield striking hints as regards relief, and are highly suggestive of the conditions on which beauty may be obtained.

Time is certainly an agent in producing the picturesque: however injurious in other respects to works of art, he increases their pictorial beauty. To his hand the outlines of a building yield their stiffness: he varies its tones of colour, melting them as it were into more perfect keeping with the local scenery, and assimilating the whole to the condition of creation around. A building grows into harmony with nature by the effect of climate; it becomes adopted as it were by the *genius loci*, and they are united under the influence of the same causes; and when originally constructed in forms that harmonise with the works of God around, "they remind the spectator," to quote the language of Wordsworth, "of a production of nature, and appear to have grown rather than to have been erected; and, when clothed in part with a vegetable garb, appear to be received into the bosom of the living principle of things, as it acts and exists among the woods and fields."

The older towns and cities, therefore, assume more of the picturesque. A town erected at a variety of periods, and in which we behold the work of centuries, presents a proportionately greater variety in style, hue, and shape,—and most towns have in this particular the advantage of the one in which our lot is cast.

I have said that picturesque beauty of design is independent of style. In this I might be borne out by the beauty of most Mahomedan cities, which present, with their array of mosques and minarets (notwithstanding the inferiority of the architecture in the higher principles), an entire result superior to what we see in many of their European compeers. Fancy and feeling, it is true, have been more consulted than judgment, but they have produced a wonderful effect, and are very suggestive to us.

It would be improper, in a treatise of this nature, to omit all mention of sculpture, which ranks high as an element of the picturesque in architecture. Statues were a crowning magnificence introduced on the apex of the temple pediments, as if the genius of the art, or the spirit of beauty itself, had alighted upon it. Sculpture some one has aptly called " the voice of architecture : " without it, the art is not complete : if it be not a breathing into it the breath of life, it is at least an awakening of it to a higher life, and rendering it capable of a more complete and divine expression. When we contemplate the result of a judicious application of statuary in architectural embellishment, we cannot but regret that so many empty niches should surround our public buildings. This is characteristic of English edifices. It would seem that English people have an antipathy to statues. The expense is, perhaps, one bar to their more extensive employment; but the chief one, I suspect, might be found in influences which had their birth at the Reformation.

There is a fault of modern streets which I have not before mentioned,—they too much resemble each other. I have heard travellers complain of the streets in some continental cities being so much alike that it was impossible for a stranger to thread his way through them. I would give diversity of character to streets as well as to houses, and for this there are resources in architecture. Public buildings, whilst they give life and dignity to the view, play a conspicuous part in producing this desired variety, and characterising their respective streets; and, fortunately, these are greatly increasing in number, both in the metropolis and in the leading provincial towns, where, it must be confessed, despite the neglect of some important principles of beauty, a great deal has of late been done conducive to pictorial effect. In London, though but few fine streets could be named, there are many beautiful spots and interesting views,—many a picturesque nook that the artist would delight to sketch, and that the most uninformed spectator would feel and admire, though perhaps, in the words of Sterne, " without knowing why, or caring wherefore."

But the streets themselves are improved. If we compare London of the present day with London of thirty or forty years ago, we must confess that great is the advantage of the former over the latter; and Liverpool has perhaps advanced in a similar ratio. Streets have been swelling into ampler width, and other provisions of beauty and usefulness becoming more abundant. What I chiefly complain of is, the non-acknowledgment of those principles by which the greatest amount of pictorial beauty would be obtained from any given means; and maintain that the rage for uniformity that has been exhibited in the new streets had its origin in a mistaken notion of beauty; that whatever other advantages that and the straight line may possess, yet to that quality which gives pleasure to the eye, and exhilaration to the mind, they must fail in contributing. I mean no disparagement in other respects to late efforts, by any remarks I have made; I am merely contending for a principle that appears to me to be lost sight of, or at least neglected. I am aware that any errors I may have pointed out are seldom to be charged upon architects. The opportunity seldom occurs for putting in practice such principles as refer to the general form of thoroughfares in towns and cities; and I am also aware that there are circumstances connected with the planning of streets to which they must succumb,—circumstances of so much importance, that this paper may be deemed by some more artistic and theoretical than practical and useful: that it may be suggestive, however, of something advantageous to the art, I am not without hope.

But there are other considerations besides those of architectural and philosophical propriety and pictorial effect, which should have weight in the formation of streets: there are considerations of a sanitary nature, though those principles for which I contend have something indirectly to do with the health; they affect the spirits, and through that medium the body; for what gives interest and pleasure to the mind will, I need scarcely say, have no slight influence in maintaining and improving the physical organs.

Respect should be had in laying out a town and determining the bearing of the streets, to the direction of the prevailing winds. In Liverpool, where the winds are chiefly from the west, the healthful breeze, for a great portion of the length of the town, is excluded by a wall of lofty warehouses, running north and south, and intersected by a very insufficient amount of opening. A good sanitary provision in the arrangement of a town would be the forming of large squares at the intersection of the main streets, and communicating with each other in the direction of the prevailing winds. But this is a subject into which I cannot enter now; it is one upon which alone volumes might be written, and I leave it to those who are better prepared for its discussion. It is every day receiving more and more of that serious attention to which it is entitled.[*]

SAMUEL HUGGINS.

A SAW ABOUT A SAW.—A man sawing with a saw, that was not the sharpest in the world, after vainly trying to use it, broke out at last into the following wise saw :—" Of all the saws that ever I saw saw, I never saw a saw saw as that saw saws."

BLIND GAS-FITTERS.—Tenders for Messrs. Welch and Margetson's new warehouse, Cheapside. Quantities supplied by Mr. O. Tillott.

	£	s.	d.
Edge	133	12	3
Meacock	114	8	4
Bownes	105	19	1
Strode	95	16	0
Debauffer	90	15	9
Cowan	90	5	7
T. Ledger (accepted)	69	18	0

[*] This paper was read before the Literary and Philosophical Society of Liverpool.

WINDOW FROM FLORENCE.

WINDOW FROM FLORENCE.

THE window represented by the accompanying engraving, made from a drawing by Mr. Lockyer, is novel and not inelegant. I is from a palace in the *Via dei Servi*, Florence and is drawn to the scale of 1-6th of an inch to a foot. It may go amongst our hints to street architecture.

THE INTRODUCTION OF THE POINTED STYLE.

AT the close of Mr. Fergusson's pape " On the Pointed Arch," read at the Institut of Architects on the 18th June, and which w have already printed in full,[*] a discussion ensued, in the course of which Mr. Tite re marked that the question as to the invention o the pointed arch, and that as to the time o the introduction of the pointed system wer quite distinct, and he thought the most in teresting part of the inquiry would be, hov was it, and when was it, that the rude archi tecture of the Romanesque period grew into th pointed style.

Mr. Sharpe acquiesced in the propriety o Mr. Tite's suggestion, that the discussion should be limited to the consideration of tha period of architecture in which the pointe arch first made its appearance in Europe. H preferred the architectural rather than the an tiquarian view of the question; and to conside the causes that led to the early use and th rapid adoption of the pointed arch in Europe

[*] See p. 290 and p. 303, *ante*.

rather than the origin of its form and the country in which it first appeared. He did not wish, however, that it should go forth that that meeting adopted all that they had heard from Mr. Fergusson of the early use of the pointed arch in the east; he begged to enter his protest against the high antiquity proposed to be given to those parts of the buildings referred to which contained it. As regarded the whole of the illustrations of the first class referred to, with one exception, the term arch was altogether inapplicable—the principle was wanting—the form was there; so it was in the first book of Euclid; but forms were not arches: these examples were simply openings formed by stones overlapping one another, and such as any one might make in a common ashlar wall by knocking out the stones. Mr. Fergusson had applied the term "horizontal arch" to this form; he (Mr. S.) understood a very different form under that term—a form very common in Gothic architecture, consisting of a stone beam formed of several pieces joggled together; there you had the principle of the arch. As regarded the buildings of Cairo, there were no doubt a great number which contained pointed arches, but the important question was, what was their date? The proof that was necessary to establish their antiquity was to be sought for under this head, rather than from the frequent occurrence of the feature. Again, Mr. Fergusson had said that the mosque of Amrou had been much pulled about and altered; how could it be proved at this day that the parts in which the pointed arches occur were not amongst the very parts that had been so altered? We should be very chary in receiving assertions as to date, and look very carefully at the proof: if proof most conclusive and satisfactory be wanting, this theory falls to the ground. As regards the question of the introduction of the pointed arch in Europe, he held the opinion that no new feature was adopted in the architecture of the middle ages, which had not some *useful* property contained in it. He believed he might go further and say that, in proportion to the utility of a member was the degree of ornament it received; he would content himself, however, at present, with the former axiom. Of the sixty-six theories contained in Britton's fifth volume of the "Architectural Antiquities," only two attempted to account for the introduction of the pointed arch on this ground. One of these was the well-known theory, due to Dr. Whewell, and enlarged upon by him in his interesting work on the German Churches, which attributed the introduction of this form to the exigencies arising out of the difficulties of vaulting an oblong space, with circular arches, in horizontal courses, as exemplified in the buildings on the Rhine. The other was that advanced by Dr. Young and Mr. Weir, namely, that the use of the pointed arch was originally due to a discovery of its usefulness in diminishing lateral pressure. He (Mr. S.) was disposed to take the latter view; and for reasons that he was about to give at large, in a work now in the press, on the "Early History of the Pointed Arch in the south of France," and which he would shortly explain, with the assistance of some of the plates which he had with him, and which included views and sections of some of the very buildings which Mr. Fergusson had referred to,—the whole of which he had himself visited and measured. In the first place, he must join issue with Mr. Fergusson in reference to his assertion that the pointed arch occurred generally under the circular arch in those buildings, and that its use was therefore anterior to the latter in point of time. He was prepared to maintain that there was a law which regulated the use of the two forms in the same building, and that a very important one,—but one very different from that laid down by Mr. Fergusson, and one evidently traceable to the cause already alluded to. The arches used in the churches of the middle ages might very properly be divided into two classes,—those used for the large openings, such as the vaulting arches, the arches of the crossing, and the pier arches, and which may be said to constitute the framework of the building; and those used for the smaller openings, such as the doorways, the windows, the arcades, &c., and which might be said to belong to the panelling of the structure;—the former class might be properly termed arches of construction, and the latter arches of decoration. In the buildings of the transitional period,—and he was disposed to accept that term, as belonging *par excellence* to those buildings which exhibited the transition from the circular style to the pointed style,—he was prepared to assert, that for nearly half a century the pointed arch was used in the arches of construction, and the circular arch in arches of decoration. This rule was not laid down upon the authority of a few isolated examples; he had a list of no less than eighty buildings in England, France, and Germany, which he had himself visited, in which this law obtained; and he had no doubt that the attention of the members of the Institute being called to the fact, this list would be hereafter very considerably increased; he spoke only of what had fallen within his own personal observation, and he thought that a good rule for every one to follow. Mr. S. then read part of the list of examples to which he referred, and explained that a few exceptions existed, but that they were not of that nature, or to that extent, as in the least to invalidate the law as applied to the whole of the earlier buildings of the transitional period. He stated that the number of buildings belonging to this period was much greater than was generally supposed, even in this country, and that they abounded on the continent; that they possessed peculiar details and characteristic marks perfectly distinct from those which belonged to the Norman, as well as the Early English period, and such as entitled them to separate classification. He explained, that in the latter part of the period the pointed arch began to find its way into the arches of decoration, as in the choirs of Canterbury and Ripon Cathedrals, the former of which belonged to the years 1185-1190; and immediately afterwards rapidly and universally in this country superseded the circular arch. As regarded its introduction into other parts of Europe, he believed that it was in the south of France that its earliest employment was to be looked for; the most usual mode of roofing the large spaces in that country in the Romanesque period was by a longitudinal barrel vault, or semi-cylinder, running the whole length of the building; this plan obtained in most of the large cathedrals, as St. Saturnin, at Toulouse, and the Cathedral of Valence, both of which belonged, upon unquestionable evidence, to the middle of the eleventh century. This was, therefore, naturally the place where we should look for the first appearance of the pointed arch; and here it is in fact that we first find it. We find it accompanied, or rather almost immediately followed, by that slight alteration of detail in the moulding and sculpture which accompanied its introduction in other countries,—and, as a natural consequence, by that reduction in the solid thickness of the walls, and that concentration of abutment at particular points, which indicated here, as elsewhere, the progress of science in construction. To premise, as Mr. Fergusson did, that this style preceded the other; that the pointed arch, in these countries, was anterior to the circular; that the builders went back, in fact, from this advanced point to earlier and ruder principles, was impossible, and was certainly unsupportable by documentary evidence of any kind. Mr. Sharpe then exhibited views and sections of the Cathedral of Vaisson, to which Mr. Fergusson had referred; the Cathedral of Sisteron; the Abbey Churches of Cadouin and Notre Dame, at Digne, and other buildings containing the pointed barrel vault, in support of his assertions,—the actual ascertained dates of which, he stated, bore out what he had said; and in the whole of which the pointed arch was used not only in the vaultings to which Mr. Fergusson supposed it was confined, but in all the other arches of construction, whilst the circular arch prevailed uniformly in the arches of decoration. The speaker then proceeded to notice a class of buildings in which the pointed arch occurred, of a very early, interesting, and peculiar kind, in the west of France, limited both as to number and the district in which they were found, which had been mixed up with those he had just been describing, but which were totally distinct from them, and, in fact, unlike anything else that he knew of in the western parts of Christendom. The type after which these buildings were planned was that of the Church of St. Mark, at Venice—or to go higher still, that of St. Sophia, at Constantinople—and consisted of five large square compartments, forming the Greek cross, and covered with five large hemi-spherical domes, supported by pendentives resting on enormous square piers. This was the type of the plan of the whole of them. In some the design had been mutilated, in others never entirely carried, and in others slightly modified, to suit western requirements; but in the Cathedral of St. Front, at Perigueux, the genuine Byzantine design is presented in its unmitigated Eastern aspect. He then exhibited parallel views of the interior of St. Mark's, Venice, and the cathedral of Perigueux, taken from the same point of view, which presented, with one exception, identically the same features, that exception being the occurrence, in the French building, of the pointed arch in place of the circular arch of St. Mark's, in the large arches which support the domical vault. He exhibited also views and plans of the cathedral churches of Cahors and Angoulême, and the abbey church of Souillac, all similar in their main features to St. Front. To the earliest of these buildings he was disposed to attach a very early date, not only on account of the extreme simplicity and rudeness of the work, and the nature of their details, but also, in the case of St. Front, on account of a certain striking correspondence of fact between the internal and external evidence of the building. He declined, however, to enter into this part of the question, or to make any assertion at that moment as to the period at which the pointed arch was thus used in this part of France, further than to declare his belief that these buildings were earlier than the class he had previously noticed; and, therefore, in his opinion, the earliest not only in France but in the west of Europe. The question still remained for solution—How came these buildings, so unlike any thing that remains in the countries uninfluenced by the Greek church, to be planted in this foreign soil? Was the pointed arch, as seen in these buildings, introduced along with the plan, or was it a local adaptation? We find it neither in its type (St. Mark's), nor its archetype (St. Sophia's). But is it likely that so important a feature was an insertion in a design which displays in every other part so unequivocally its foreign origin? He (Mr. S.) was not disposed to think so. He looked upon the determination of this question as one of no small interest in the history of the pointed arch, and one which might possibly lead to the conclusion that this form did in reality come to us from the East; but it was to be entered upon in a spirit of careful inquiry, and the facts were to be proved, step by step, in a manner which should leave as little room as possible for speculative opinion, or mere conjecture; and, above all, without hastily accepting or rejecting the dates which we might find handed to us by previous inquirers; and never, if possible, without reference to the original records or the earliest existing documentary evidence, bearing upon the history of the building in question.*

FIRE-PROOF CEILINGS OF WIRE-WORK have been successfully applied, in place of lath, with plaster and stucco as usual, at the Chester Lunatic Asylum. The wires are about ¼ in. apart, and the plaster forms an adhesive and serviceable mass, even on both sides. The wire is galvanized, or japanned, to prevent corrosion. Not only ceilings, one would think, but thin partitions and walls in general, might be wired in place of lathed, and risk of fire thus greatly diminished by a process neither patented nor costly.

THE NORTH KENT LINE OF RAIL, which will bring London into immediate railway communication with Lewisham, Woolwich, Dartford, Gravesend, Strood, Rochester, and Chatham, is now about completed, and is to be opened for passengers about the middle of July. The new portion, between London-bridge station and Gravesend, is 23½ miles in length, and, exclusive of rails and stations, the cost of construction—the original contract estimates for which were fixed at 638,000*l.*—will amount, it is stated, to 400,000*l.* only.

* At a meeting of the Institute, held on the 2nd inst., Professor Cockerell read an important paper on the present position of architecture, to which we shall give due attention.

LINCOLN CATHEDRAL——EAST END.
[13TH CENTURY.]

EAST END OF LINCOLN CATHEDRAL.

ABOVE we have the pleasure to place before our readers a view of the east end of Lincoln Minster, one of the finest of our mediæval buildings, and concerning which we have at various times spoken. Illustrations of the south porch, the fine rose window in transept, and of the chapter-house, a beautiful specimen of pure Early English, have been already given.

We may remind our readers that Lincoln Minster was commenced by Bishop Hugh, at the close of the twelfth century, and was completed by Robert, called Grosse teste. The portion here represented is of the Geometrical style, or late Early English, so to speak,—the forerunner of the Decorated.

The engraving is from a drawing by Mr. Caveler, made for the purpose.

CHRONOLOGICAL ACCOUNT OF BUILD-INGS IN ITALY AND SICILY.*

Palermo Cathedral.—1170 to 1185, by Walter of Hamell, an Englishman (Knight). Altar to north-east. Little remains of the original building but crypt and portions of south side and east end. The arches of crypt are pointed. 1420, great west door; south door, 1426; and porch, 1450 (Knight).

Montreale Cathedral.—1174 to 1182; the bronze doors, 1186, by Borumano.

S. Eustachio, Rome.—1196; founded in Constantine's time (Rossi and Vasi); has one of the brick towers.

S. Michele, Lucca.—1188, façade by Guidetto (Knight).

S. Sisto, Rome.—1200, restored. Founder unknown, but church mentioned by S. Gregory 600 (Severano); 1200, and restored in 1464-71 (Rossi); 1200, greatly repaired (Rycaut).

Torre dei Conti.—Twelfth century, D'Agincourt, c. 1200 (Rycaut).

S. Maria Toscanella.—c. 1206 (Knight).

* See page 256, ante.

S. Maria Plebe, Arezzo.—1216, tower. It is quite like the Roman (Knight).

S. Andrea, Vercelli.—1219, by Thomas, a French ecclesiastic (Knight).

Parma Baptistery.—1196 to 1281 (Knight); 1196 to 1260 (Hope).

Padua Great Hall.—1218, finished. Supposed to have been begun 1172; damaged by fire, 1420; and by storm, 1756 (Milizia).

S. Giovanni in Monte, Bologna.—1221; the campanile in 1286 (Willis).

S. Francesco, Assisi. — 1228, by a German architect (Knight).

S. Antonio, Padua.—1231, begun (Knight).

Ponte delle Grazie, Florence.—1236 (Richa).

SS. Trinita, Florence.—1250, by N. Pisano; enlarged and embellished 1383; campanile 1395; façade 1593 (Richa); altar nearly west.

S. Chiara, Ravenna.—1250 (Fabri).

S. Caterina, Pisa.—1253, by Guglielmo Agnelli, pupil of Nicolo da Pisa. Injured by fire 1651, after which transept was added (Grassi). The upper arches are pointed, but details in general are Italian.

S. Maria della Spina, Pisa.—1230: enlarged 1300 (Grassi); 1230: enlarged and enriched 1323

). This is the most Gothic-looking build-
Pisa, but all the details throughout are
.ed.

.tonio Abbate, Rome.—1259 (Vasi, Rossi,
.erano); originally dedicated 467 (Rossi);
north. [At this era the pointed style seems
got a decided footing in Italy, as may be
Ferrara, Assisi, Pisa, Vercelli, &c. But
.ecimens all seem the work of strangers;
.ils are all Italianised; and we look in vain
of the beautiful arrangements or details of
.rly English or even Norman Cathedrals.
nothing in Italy of this date which gives
a of the beautiful scroll-work and other
.ts of the Early English period, nor of the
.eak, the zigzag, or other Norman pecu-
.]

i Santa, Rome.—1216 to 1277, rebuilt from
.ons as now seen (Severano); 1585' re-
Vasi).

.acomo Magno, Bologna.—1267; roof 1497

.taria Novella, Florence.—1278, by Fra
.and Fra Sisto; façade 1349 to 1470; nave
.1307; campanile c. 1330; struck by
.g 1358 (Richa); altar to north.

.taria del Popolo, Rome.—1277, rebuilt,
.been built 1099; restored 1660·(Vasi);
.east.

.to Santo, Pisa.—1278 to 1283, by Gio.
.arches filled in 1464 (Grassi).

Publico, Piacenza.—1281, begun (Knight).
.an Michele, Florence.—1284, by Arnolfo di
.added to and decorated in 1337-1352, when
.a was employed (Richa).

.oce. Florence.—1295, by Arnolfo di Lupo;
.1320. The façade from Porta Maggiore to
.r of cloister commenced only in black
.ite marble, by Cronaca; tower and roof
.lestroyed, 1514; sacristy built before 1330;
.; by Arnolfo, son of the stranger who built
.church at Assisi (Knight); 1294 (Vihani);
.lope); altar nearly to east.

.dei Mercanti, Bologna.—1294 (Willis).
.nce Cathedral.—1298, begun by Arnolfo di
.da Colle. Altar to east.

.astasio, Verona.—c. 1300 (Maffei).
.rmo Maggiore, Verona —1313, the sub-
.n church spoken of as old in 775 (Maffei).
.ale Grande, Palermo.—1330, built in one
.night).

.aria delle Scale, Verona.—1328 (Maffei).
.i Campanile, Florence.—1330 : half pulled
.y populace 1307, and rebuilt as now seen;
.rch has been much injured by fire at various
.Richa); altar to south.

.ccolo, Florence.—1332 (Richa); altar to

.imone, Florence.—1333 (Richa); altar to

.anile, Florence.—1334, by Giotto.
.icordia, Ancona.—1349; " Hoc templum
.pestem sedanti unico die civitas fidei
.ntum eresit. 23 Oct., 1349" (Inscrip-

Ducal, Venice.—1350, canal front, and six
.olumns; rest of return front 1423-39; by
.colomeo; porta della carta, 1439; internal
.nd façade over, 1485; 1500, by Berga-
.centre window towards piazza, 1523-1538
.ara).

.i Oro, Venice.—1350 (Quadri), Cicognara
. date is uncertain.

.a Cathedral.—1359, front (Hope); four-
.entury (Willis).

.aria sopra Minerva, Rome.—1370 (Bunsen
.i), 1275; the convent adjoining stands on site
.s of temple of Minerva (Rossi).

.i Cathedral.—1386 to 1411 (Oxford Glos-
.387, doubtful whether by Arler, a German,
.ampione, an Italian; but nearly all archi-
.t employed on it were German; 1388, great
.dow by French architect (Knight); altar to

.ronio, Bologna.—1184, consecrated(F.bri);
.lar to south.

.ia, Pavia.—1396, begun; west front by
.i 1473 (Pettit).

.ofvio, Rome.—1439 (Pistolesi e Vasi); the
.groined, the apse semi-octagon, with pointed

.sirito, Florence.—1435 to 1481, by F.
.schi (Richa); altar nearly north.

.susanna, Rome.—Originally by Constan-
.built, 800; restored, 1475 and 1600, when
.is built from foundations, also gilt ceiling
.ide (Rossi); c. 290, rebuilt 800 (Vasi);
.iorth.

.ostino, Rome.—1480 (Bunsen and Vasi),
.ntelli; altar to north.

.Vendramin, Venice.—1481, by one of
.bardi (Cicognara).

Foscari, Venice.—1390 (Cicognara), 1439

.ips the most marked feature of Italian
.the capital; six distinct styles may be
.sed on careful investigation.

DECORATIONS FROM ABROAD.

FROM ARCHITRAVE, SPOLETO CATHEDRAL.

1. Imitation of the Roman, generally Corinthian, often Composite, and sometimes,
but seldom, Ionic (S. Stefano Rotondo). This
style, as might be expected, occurs in buildings
of all ages, from the earliest time to the latest;
from Ravenna, in the fifth century, to S. Caterina, Pisa, 1253.

2nd. The peculiar corbel capitals, as in the
Roman brick tower, or in many of our Saxon
churches. These have no dates which can be
strictly relied on, but from their great prevalence at Ravenna, their presence in the ancient
church of S. Vitale, and other indications, we
may imagine them to be of Greek origin, more
especially as the churches in Greece have their
windows and domes formed with columns in
this style, though rather more ornate.

3rd. Those clearly Greek, the characteristics
whereof are so clearly seen at S. Vitale, S.
Fosca, S. Marc's, S. Donato, &c.

4th. Wherein the capitals are formed either
of foliage cut out in the peculiar hard, flat
style; or of animals, or of blocks, with the
angles worked out in some ornamental way.
These I imagine to be northern importations.
They are first seen, so far as I can recollect, at
S. Michele, Pavia, and are used at S. Stefano
in Bologna, at S. Ambrogio in Milan, Pisa,
Modena, S. Zeno in Verona, Palermo, Parma,
&c.

5th. Where the Norman seems to have
gained somewhat of the lightness of the Gothic,
as seen in some of our transition work, as at

Lentini, Sciacca, Syracuse, Messina, Ferrara,
&c. I look upon these, also, as Transalpine.

6th. Where the intention has been, obviously, to give somewhat of a Gothic character, the sculptor understanding only Italian
detail, as at Pisa, Florence, Bologna, &c. At
Milan the capitals are tolerably good Gothic.

             T. H. L.

ORNAMENT FROM DUOMO, SPOLETO.

THE cathedral at Spoleto dates from a very
early period, having been originally erected
under the Lombard dukes. Numerous, however, are the alterations and additions since that
date. The sculptured piece of ornament here
represented is taken from the architrave (in
marble) of the central doorway of the principal
façade, now, with the two side doors, masked
by Bramante's elegant picturesque portico
(which, by the way, was given by the "Architectural Publication Society" in their first
issue of plates).

THE IRON TRADE.—At a preliminary meeting of masters, on Saturday last, a further reduction of 10s. per ton was resolved on, and it
is considered to be very doubtful whether even
the prices that now remain after the deduction
of 30s., can be maintained. A notice of further
reductions in wages has also been given.

NOTES IN THE PROVINCES.

THE old church at Halstead, lately decapitated by the removal of its spire—the materials of which were sold to pay the expenses of removal—begins to show other serious signs of decay. The props in the nave have begun to bend under pressure of the roof, and the edifice has been pronounced by the diocesan architect, Mr. Clark, to be quite unsafe, so that the Bishop has ordered it to be closed. According to an estimate by the architect the cost of restoration will be 2,630*l.*; but the parochial resources being exhausted in the building of a new church, 800*l.* alone can be mustered, and the authorities now appeal to the public for aid.——A new font, octagonal and decorated in style of fourteenth century, has been presented to St. Martin's Church, Leicester, by Mr. T. Combe, of Oxford.——Workmen have been engaged at Mansfield in preparations for laying the foundation-stone of the Bentinck monument. —— New parochial schools were founded at Foxearth, Essex, on 12th inst. The design is by Mr. J. Clark, and the cost will be 500*l.*, chiefly defrayed by the rector.——In the little church of Bartlow the pews have been replaced by open benches, and the arch in the round tower re-opened; other restorations and repairs have been completed, and the church is re-opened.——The large west window of Holy Rhood Church, Southampton, has been fitted with thick plate glass to exclude noise. Subscriptions are in progress, which it is hoped will enable the authorities to fill the east and chancel windows with stained glass. The gurgoyles, which were objected to, are to be reduced to small appropriate ornaments. ——A stained glass window of three compartments has been put up in the eastern chancel of the church of Mathern, Chepstow.——The new town hall at Yeovil was opened on Wednesday week. The hall is 56½ feet long, 35 feet broad, and 25 feet high. It is approached from the market-house by iron gates and stone steps with cast-iron balustrades.——Statues to Nelson and Wellington are to be placed on Southsea Common, where Nelson trod his native land for the last time, and where Wellington first stepped on British ground after his last great triumph.——Mangotsfield Church is to be repaired and renovated at a cost of about 850*l.*, besides that of restoring the chancel by the lay impropriators and other offerings. Messrs. Pope, Binden, and Clark, of Bristol, have furnished plans for the work.——The Walsall Town Improvement Commissioners, in choosing from the tenders for buildings, excavations, and gas holder for new gas works, have decided on the tender of Mr. Hale, of Walsall, for buildings and excavations, at 1,493*l.*, with deduction of 10*l.* if base to chimneys brick; and Messrs. Smith and Co., of West Bromwich, for making gas holder and removing old one, at a cost of 808*l.* 10s. The works are expected to commence the manufacture of gas at Christmas. ——The Sheffield Water Company have caused blocks of gypsum to be deposited in their culvert, in order to prevent the water from imbibing poisonous impurities from the lead cisterns and service-pipes. This may be expected to take place by the water firstly imbibing the gypsum or sulphate of lime, of which it is to be presumed the analytical chemist, Mr. Haywood, who made the suggestion, has found the water to be deficient. —— A stone tower, with a spire, is to be built on the church at Bootle, in place of the two unseemly towers, which have been removed. Other alterations are to be made, and seat-room for 400 additional sitters provided.——A German Lutheran Church is to be built at Hull.——The inhabitants of Brigg, in that vicinity, have resolved to erect a Corn Exchange by joint stock shares of 10*l.* each.——A monument has been placed in the east aisle of the north transept of York Minster, to Dr. Beckwith, who bequeathed 45,000*l.* to the cathedral, the Yorkshire Museum, the York Charity Schools, and and other laudable objects.——The repair of Knox's house in the High-street of Edinburgh being declared to be impossible, it is proposed to mark the stones, remove them piecemeal, and rebuild the house.——The repair of Jedburgh Abbey has been resumed by the Lothian family trustees. The east wing is now being restored.——Mr. Mackenzie, architect, Elgin, has constructed a design for the Culloden monument. The model represents a large, irregular, conical mass of rock, with a rough road winding through clefts, &c., to the summit, where, crowning a precipice, is a female figure, leaning on the rock, and mourning, along with her children. At prominent points are tablets, to be erected by clans, or in memory of individuals.——A church in Great Charles-street, Dublin, has been destroyed by fire.

RAILWAY JOTTINGS.

ON the Oxford, Worcester, and Wolverhampton line several hundred labourers, bricklayers, and miners have been discharged from the Mickleton tunnel from want of funds. Only forty men are now employed, and the works will shortly, it is said, be brought to a standstill.——On Wednesday week, in springing two arches of the bridge now building over the Teviot at Roxburgh, on the Kelso and St. Boswell branch of the Edinburgh and Hawick line, the pier gave way, and eight men were buried in the ruin, and killed on the spot.——The North Staffordshire Company have entered into a contract for the working of their whole line. An extensive coach manufacturer at Saltley, near Birmingham, is the contractor. There were fourteen tenders. The contract, however, is limited to the general traffic, rolling stock, and maintenance of permanent way, and does not interfere with the stations, clerks, and receipts. The company's engineer has the power to inflict a penalty of 10,000*l.*, if not satisfied with the fulfilment of the contract. The mileage rate for working and maintaining the locomotives, &c., is about 10d. for passenger trains, and 1s. for goods trains, and penalties will be incurred by late arrivals or departures.——A scramble for the Pickfordian or carrier class of pickings on the London and North-Western seems to be in progress. The company, it is said, take the singular liberty of breaking open such packages or parcels as they may suspect to contain goods for different parties separately directed, and themselves deliver the goods so separately packed, and appropriate the charges for delivery. Some carriers have had an interview with the Railway Board on this subject, and Mr. Labouchere is said to have admitted that a remedy must be provided. The company, it seems, defy the law, which saddles complainers with heavy expenses, even while they obtain favourable verdicts. Why should *small* carriers be treated on a different principle from the *great* carriers at St. Martin's-le-Grand? The post packages and mail bags are not broken open for the sake of such plunder: why should others be so,—and that, too, *ex facie*, on the mere *a priori chance* of twice chargeable contents? Should other railway companies follow such an example, why not steam and other shipping companies, coach and omnibus proprietors, and other carriers themselves of all kinds inclusive? And if so, what seal would be safe and sacred from such an universal parcel hunt? No parent even could safely send a lot of ticketed toys to each of his children, no friend enclose a few presents, without the chance of separate charges for the delivery of each, and none whatever *any* parcel or package, without affording a feasible pretence, on the part of carriers of all sorts, for breaking it open and examining its contents. It is for Government Custom-house authorities alone, with any show of propriety or right, to be allowed such a license, as that so cavalierly practised and insisted on by these North-Western Railway authorities—great though they be—in this free country.——There are two million of rivets in the tubular bridge over the Menai Straits, each an inch in diameter.——A hollow girder bridge, of make similar to the tubular, but with the rails fixed above in place of in the interior, is in course of formation, to cross the Trent at Gainsborough on the Manchester, Sheffield, and Lincolnshire line. Two principal hollow girders form the parapets, and the roadway is supported by transverse wrought-iron hollow beams, or tubes, rectangular in section. This bridge was designed by Mr. W. Fowler, and the tubes have been constructed by Mr. Fairbairn. The stone-work consists of a centre-pier, and two elliptical arches of 50 feet span each, terminated by the usual land abutments. The iron-work consists of two spans, together 308 feet, which gives a total length to the bridge of 460 feet. The principal girders are each 336 feet long, 12 feet high, and 3 feet 1 inch wide, having their tops formed of cells 18 inches wide, and 12 inches deep, to resist compression, and the bottom of double-rivetted plates, to withstand tension. They are fixed on the middle pier, and supported on the land abutments by rollers, resting on cast-iron plates embedded in the masonry, thus admitting of expansion and contraction. The first girder, if not now also the other, is already fixed.——Mr. Hennett, of Bristol, has just completed a wrought-iron bridge, which weighs 450 tons, and is intended to cross the Thames, at Slough, from the branch line of the Great Western to Windsor.

BENT TIMBER FOR ROOFING.

I OBSERVE that in your journal of the 23rd of May, Mr. John Hay, of Liverpool, has inserted a letter, the purport of which is to claim the merit of the application of bent planks for roofing purposes. His letter is a singular instance of forgetfulness. May I trespass upon you to set him right as to the originality of his discoveries?

Mr. Hay was employed as an architectural assistant upon the Rouen Railway, by Messrs. Mackenzie and Brassey in the year 1843. Whilst engaged on these works, he had the opportunity of examining the bridges of Bezons, Maisons Laffitte, Manoir, and Oissel, which were constructed under Mr. Locke's direction, with main ribs of bent plank.

To proceed to the use of such ribs in roofing did not require a great stretch of imagination. Such as was necessary was, however, made firstly by the foreman of the Rouen station, Mr. John Milroy. He made a model of a rib roof to cover the large shed of the station, building up the ribs with bent planks. This model Mr. Hay saw before he made his designs for the Scotch churches. Mr. Milroy's model was made in the spring; Mr. Hay's designs were made in the winter following.

Like all discussions upon the merit of inventions, the last comers have painful reminiscences "that the ancients have stolen our good things." Whether Mr. Hay knew of Col. Emy's work, or not, he had seen several of Mr. Locke's timber bridges; and he was well aware that a bridge upon the same principle had been constructed near Newcastle some years previously.

Mr. Tite executed a very beautiful roof over the Rue Verte station of the Rouen and Hâvre line with the main ribs of bent planks. Mr. Drake executed the roof of the station at Dieppe with elliptical ribs built in the same manner. I used similar ribs to support the intermediate principals in a large goods shed I built at Hâvre, so that there is far from being any novelty in the plan. Indeed, when the French possess two elaborate works upon the subject, one by Col. Emy, the other by Col. Ardant, and a multitude of memoirs, one of which is by Navier (a man gathered to his fathers seven years since), it is the height of absurdity, if nothing else, to claim the merit of the invention.

Paris. GEO. R. BURNELL.

ARCHITECTURAL MATHEMATICIANS;

OR, MATHEMATICAL ARCHITECTS.

A WANT of mathematical acumen and lore has been, with some, a standing reproach against the architectural profession. Let such lovers of the abstract in form and number, if they be such, purchase and digest a recent work of Mr. H. P. Browning, architect,* and probably by the time they have mastered all its articles, definitions, and corollaries, they may be inclined to suspect that, after all, architects do know how to fathom the profundities of algebra and geometry, although they make no great boast of their powers and acquisitions. The profession are certainly deeply indebted to Mr. Browning for his most able contribution towards the removal of even the shadow

* "An Algebra of Ratios, founded on simple and general definitions, with a theory of exponents extended to incommensurable ratios, and the propositions of the fifth book of Euclid easily and symbolically deduced." By Henry P. Browning, Architect, Stamford. Cambridge: Macmillan, Barclay, and Macmillan. London: Simpkin, Marshall, and Co. 1849.

of a ground for such reproaches. The more immediate object of his work, however, is to establish an algebra of ratios, on the same footing as that of abstract numbers, and thus to dispense with the unmathematical expedient of regarding all magnitudes as commensurable with each other, and to furnish *definite notions* of the powers and roots of ratios in their most difficult and comprehensive forms. These purposes, in our humble opinion, he has accomplished in that efficient manner which might have been anticipated from his growing talent. "The application of algebra to geometry," as he observes, and "which is the great object of all who study mathematics with a view to the purposes of life, will thus be rendered more satisfactory, if not more conclusive, in its results; and the doctrine of proportion, as taught in the fifth book of Euclid, will be relieved of the circumlocution and tedious repetition in which his theory abounds."

Taking for granted that a certain degree of mathematical experience is requisite fully to comprehend the subject, he has assumed the results of arithmetical algebra, and notwithstanding the prejudices of some, has adopted the definitions and language of limits, being persuaded that a studied avoidance of the use of limits in the treatment of continuous magnitude is of no advantage to the student, and introduces difficulties equal at least to those it professes to remove. A few propositions, treating principally of the limits of concrete quantities, though apparently foreign to the work, have been introduced by way of furnishing concise and easily-remembered proofs of relations afterwards deduced; and having fully considered the ratios of concrete quantities, in the conclusion of the work, a definition of the notion of a ratio of ratios is appended.

We would willingly give a citation of the author's mode of dealing with his subject, but its subdivisions are so consecutively and logically linked, that it would be no easy matter to occupy a small space without being betrayed into yielding up a larger than our own geometrical limits will fairly allow.

AN ACCOUNT OF AN EXTRAORDINARY INSTANCE OF THE RAPID DECAY OF TIMBER, FROM DRY ROT, WHICH OCCURRED IN THE CHURCH OF THE HOLY TRINITY, AT CORK.*

So many naturalists and men of science having endeavoured to account for the origin of dry rot, I shall not advance any theory of my own on the subject, although I believe that much still remains to be inquired into respecting its causes and consequences; but with the view of attracting to it that attention which its importance demands, I beg leave to submit to the institution an account of an extraordinary case that occurred in Cork; at the same time urging on my professional brethren to record any other instances which may come within their knowledge, in order that those who may be disposed further to investigate the subject, may have the benefit of facts, given on the authority of practical men.

The parish church of the Ho'y Trinity in Cork, in the year 1827, having been found to be in a bad state of repair, and quite deformed from bad and unequal foundations, the parishioners resolved on building a new church; but through want of funds, not being able to carry their design into execution, an extensive repair was decided on. The tower was taken down, and one side wall and the end of the church was rebuilt.

This church is 100 feet long by 50 feet wide, divided into a nave and aisles by double tiers of columns, the lower tier being of solid timber, supporting galleries, and resting upon rude rubble stone piers in the vaults below, the upper tier being of built timber columns supporting the roof. It is necessary to describe the building, in order to show that from retaining a part of the old timber-work the evil of dry rot emanated.

For years there had not been anything intervening between a great part of the body of the old church and the burial vaults beneath, except a timber floor, and though the interior was spacious, and even handsome, this abomination long continued.

Immediately under the floor of the church, and open to the vaults, longitudinal beams of Irish oak of from 12 to 14 inches square had been placed, resting on piers, and forming supports for the joists. Though these oak beams were decayed for an inch deep at their surfaces, sufficient of the timber (as it was thought) remained sound, and it was decided that neither they, nor the piers upon which they rested, should be removed. The vaults are arched over; memel joists, 6 inches by 4 inches, were placed on the vaulting, and connected with the oak beams which rested on the piers; the floors were removed; the old pews were replaced; new columns, coated with scagliola, were erected over the galleries, the old ones in the lower tier retained; and the whole repairs having been thus completed, the church was re-opened for divine service in April, 1829.

In November, 1830 (but eighteen months afterwards), the congregation was annoyed by an unpleasant smell, which, on examination, was found to proceed from dry rot of the most alarming nature.

On opening the floors under the pews a most extraordinary appearance presented itself. There were flat fungi of immense size and thickness, some so large as almost to occupy a space equal to the size of a pew, and from 1 to 3 inches thick. In other places fungi appeared, growing with the ordinary dry rot, some of an unusual shape, in form like a convolvulus, with stems of from a quarter to half an inch in diameter. When first exposed, the whole was of a beautiful buff colour, and emitted the usual smell of the dry rot fungus.

Whatever may have been the surprise at the rapid growth of the plant, its action on the best Memel timber was a source of greater astonishment. I took up, with nearly as much ease as I would a walking cane, that which eighteen months before, was a sound piece of timber (one of the joists) from 12 to 14 feet long, 6 inches by 4 inches scantling; the form of the timber remained as it came from the saw, but its strength and weight were gone. The timber of the joists and floor over the new brick vaulting was completely affected by the dry rot, which was rapidly spreading to the lower part of the columns under the galleries, so that at the rate the infection proceeded, the total destruction of the building would soon have been effected.

During a great part of the time occupied in the repairs of the church the weather was very rainy. The arches of the vaults having been turned before the roof was slated, the rain water saturated the partly decayed oak beams, before described. The flooring and joists, composed of fresh timber, were laid on the vaulting before it was dry, coming in contact at the same time with the old oak timber, which was abundantly supplied with the seeds of decay, stimulated by moisture, the bad atmosphere of an ill-contrived burial place, and afterwards by heat from the stoves constantly in use. All these circumstances account satisfactorily to my mind for the extraordinary and rapid growth of the fungi.

The large sum of 4,000*l.* having been so lately expended on the church, caused great anxiety to the parishioners. The opinions of the most experienced professional men were taken, and all agreed that the first effort should be to cut off the communication with the galleries, the disease having already extended 3 feet upwards on the lower columns.

The new brick vaulting was found penetrated by the fungi, imposing the necessity of having the vaulting, as well as all the timber work in the lower part of the church, entirely and carefully removed. Newer and thicker vaulting was then substituted for that which was taken down, and the whole of the floor over it was laid with Yorkshire and Shannon flags set in Roman cement. New pews were erected, resting on iron chairs let into the flagging; the flooring of all the pews was constructed so as to be occasionally removed for inspection; Roman cement was internally used next to and at the bottom of the walls, and iron columns were substituted for those of timber in the lower tier. Here I must notice the clever plan of my friend, Richard Beamish, Esq., C.E., who caused a screw to be placed in the head of each iron column, which was screwed up, so as to take the load before the temporary supports were removed, thereby avoiding the fracture consequent on ordinary wedging, so that all was effected without any disturbance or sinking of the galleries, and the columns which supported the roof, &c., the screws in each column being accurately adjusted, so as to meet the pressure from above.

The expense incurred by these repairs was very considerable; but it is satisfactory to state that there has not been a re-appearance of the dry rot since that time, now a period of sixteen years.

Of late the subject has been diligently investigated by men of science, including the chemist and the naturalist. It is not my intention to dwell on the merits of the various preventative processes that have been suggested, or for which patents have been taken out, as my object is only to give a simple account of a very peculiar case of the disease, the facts of which strengthen me in my opinion, that the best economy in extensive repairs is to be cautious in the use of old timber, and if it must be used, not to permit new timber to come in contact with it.

I shall conclude by observing that the seasoning of timber is seldom sufficiently attended to, and that the characters of professional men are frequently injured by not being more stringent in demanding proof of the stacking and seasoning of timber for a sufficient time.

* By Sir Thomas Deane. From the "Transactions of the Institution of Civil Engineers of Ireland." Vol. II. Dublin, S. B. Oldham; London, Whittaker.

Miscellanea.

OXFORD ARCHITECTURAL SOCIETY.—At the tenth annual meeting of the society, which took place in the society's rooms, Holywell, on Wednesday, the 20th of June, the Rev. W. Sewell, president, in the chair, a hope was expressed that the society might be of use in giving plans for almshouses, schools, &c., which would assist a parish clergyman when unable to employ an architect. The chairman stated that the committee had it in contemplation to establish some elementary lectures in architecture. The Rev. Mr. George Williams, President of the Cambridge Architectural Society, then read a paper on the church of St. Sophia, at Constantinople. The secretaries intimated that they would be glad if any architect or parish clergy would furnish them from time to time with plans of schools, &c., with the actual cost of erection. We are the last persons in the world to attempt to prevent generous actions. All we have to say is, that if the Church Commissioners and other bodies obtain gratuitous plans of *churches*, to forward to those parishes who wish to build such,—the Poor-law Commissioners, plans of *workhouses*,—the Inspectors of Prisons, plans of *jails*, &c., there will be little employment for poor architects.

ST. ANDREW'S, TRENT, SOMERSET.—The present rector of this church, the Rev. W. H. Turner, a few years since lengthened the nave one bay to the westward, at the same time adding a little chapel on the north side of the nave to contain the organ, and a new roof to nave and chancel, unfortunately, groined with plaster ribs and spandrils; the whole of the seats are rendered uniform and copied from existing specimens; the lower part of the tower, which forms the south transept, is filled with plainer ones; a pulpit was given by the rector, and the chancel seats placed stallwise. The effect of the chancel, perpendicular in style, is entirely destroyed by the plaster roof, &c. Series of arches run in plaster beneath the windows immediately surrounding the sanctuary, the easternmost filled with the Decalogue written on porcelain. The screen still remains. All the windows, save in the tower, are filled with stained glass, those in the nave by Wailes. The tower with spire is of the geometrical decorated style, and is built at the south-east end of the nave, forming a transept: on the west side, and abutting against the tower, is a porch of the same date. During the last year, the pinnacles on the parapet of the tower have been renewed, together with the tracery of the windows, the sanctuary paved with Minton's tiles, and a brass, by Waller, placed in the chancel to the memory of a former rector of the parish. The latter works have been carried out under the superintendence of Mr. Withers.

PROJECTED WORKS.—Advertisements have been issued for tenders, by 21st inst., for the erection of the Towcester National Schools; by 17th, for building the new Unitarian Chapel, at Banbury; by 11th, for the erection of the new church of St. Peter, at Croydon; by 23rd, for the construction of the drainage and water supply, and other sanitary works, at the workhouse premises, Amersham, Bucks; by 24th, for the erection of Harlow new schools; without delay, for the execution of the works of Sketty new church (Swansea); by 14th, for the erection of a school house and master's residence at Abergwessin (Hereford); by 10th, for the erection of the Welsh Educational Institution at Llandovery; by 9th, for the erection of the Literary and Scientific Institute, Town-hall, and County-court, at Stonehouse (Devon); by 6th August, for the execution of contract No. 1 of the London-bridge station enlargement, comprising substructure of new station, ballast, permanent way, &c.; by 10th inst., for the erection and completion of a goods shed at Mirfield station of Lancashire and Yorkshire Railway, and by 17th, for passenger-station at Bradford, on same line; by 20th, for making new line of road in parish of Leigh (Worcester); by 7th, for bricklayers', joiners', stone-masons', slaters', plumbers', and painters' works in repairing buildings for Trinity House; by 11th, for repairing public conduits and water-works at Southampton; by 9th, for construction of service reservoir for Sunderland Water-works; by 18th, for fitting up large gas-holder at Paisley; and by 11th, for the several works in building St. Matthias's Church, Bristol.

THE POSITION OF RAILWAYS.—Mr. A. Gordon, C.E., has recently republished his past anticipations of the present state of things, from which it does appear that since the outset of the railway system he has repeatedly warned the public of the false principles on which its direction and conduction were being carried on. As to recent disclosures, he estimates that even admitting the railway capital at large (200,000,000*l.*) to be now depreciated, so as to be only 100,000,000*l.*, "the grand railway account would not show quite 1 per cent. per annum from which to pay dividends." And "still," he adds, "there is no provision made for replacement of capital." The high-blown bladder, which he appears to regard as still poised on high in full inflation, "must ere long burst," he believes; and, accordingly, he once more warns all and sundry not *yet* shareholders, "that pending the requisite remedial measure, the owners and representatives of the two hundred millions are not term-tied partners, but fluctuating shareholders, whose best chance of escaping from the dilemma is by keeping up the apparent value of the shares *till some other parties take their places.*"

TANN'S RELIANCE DETECTOR LOCK.—In this, which is a lever detector lock, a new feature has been introduced, namely, the protecting one or more of the levers *by a guard.* The guard is placed on one of the levers, and protects the lever either above or below it, so that even if a false key or pick succeeded in lifting to the proper height all the levers with unprotected fronts, it could not raise the one *behind* the guard, and the slightest extra lift of the guarded lever at once fixes the detector, and then the proper key only can regulate it. The addition seems to give much increased security.

THE MARBLE ARCH.—We have no faith in the statement of some of our contemporaries that the marble arch is going to Windsor. One correspondent puts before us the suggestion made in the *Athenæum*, that it should be erected in front of the British Museum. We incline much more strongly to the suggestion in our own pages (among twenty others), that it should be made to form a fitting entrance to St. James's-park at Spring-gardens, where such is much needed.

BRITANNIA AND CONWAY TUBULAR BRIDGES.—At this moment, our readers may be glad to know of the publication of a brief description of these bridges.* Of a more important work on the same subject, by Mr. Fairbairn, just now issued,† maintaining the right of Mr. Fairbairn to a share of the public applause, we shall take an opportunity to speak.

* Chapman and Hall, Strand. † Weale.

ELECTRO-TELEGRAPHIC PROGRESS.—The *modus operandi* of the copying telegraph has at length been revealed. According to the specification of the patent, two cylinders are made to revolve by clockwork, regulated by an electro-magnet four times in each revolution, so as to be perfectly coincident in time of rotation. On one is rolled a sheet of tin foil, and on the other a sheet of paper saturated with a solution which electricity will easily decompose and blacken through a metallic pointer, which presses on it and conducts the current to the paper after it passes from the tin foil on the other cylinder, through a similar metallic pointer pressing on it. The apparatus thus prepared, and the cylinders made to revolve, with the electricity in action,—the pointers are carried gradually from one end of the cylinders to the other, so that a spiral series of dark lines, closely continuous, is described on the paper from end to end, *unless the current of electricity be intermitted*, which it is by means of writing, or other characters or forms, on the conducting tinfoil round the other cylinder, traced with a nonconducting varnish in place of ink. It is thus manifest that an exact copy of the tracing will be picked out as it were by blank intervals in the black or blue lined spiral tracery on the papered cylinder, the pointer ceasing to blacken the paper wherever its fellow passes over or across the varnish on the tinfoil; and thus, by a contrivance of the most ingenious and simple description, accomplishing one of the most astonishing miracles of this age of wonders. With a single wire, 400 letters per minute can thus be transmitted. And the wonder does not end here, for the message or letter transmitted by correspondents (*to their own paper and from their own tinfoil, of course, if desired*), with its signature, &c., is a perfect fac-simile of the original in form or tracery, only written, as it were in white ink, on a dark ground like line engraving. Drawings, it is clear, too, or even portraits, plans, &c., may as readily be thus not only copied, but transmitted hundreds of miles at one and the same moment. The name of the inventor of this triumph of genius is Blakewell. The specification of the patent includes improvements in opening and closing communication with different stations by means of one wire, and points to the establishment of a system of half-hourly dispatches. The facilitation and cheapening of newspaper reports too by such means are very obvious, especially as shorthand can thus be still more readily and rapidly copied than ordinary writing.

GUTTA PERCHA TUBING.—A series of experiments have just been concluded at the Birmingham Water-Works, relative to the strength of gutta percha tubing, with a view to its applicability for the conveyance of water. The experiments were made under the direction of Mr. Henry Rofe, engineer, upon tubes of three quarters of an inch diameter and one-eighth thick of gutta percha. These were attached to the iron main and subjected for two months to a pressure of 200 feet head of water, without, as we are told, being in the slightest degree deteriorated. In order to ascertain, if possible, the maximum strength, one of the tubes was connected with the Water Company's hydraulic proofing pump, the regular load of which is 250 lbs. on the square inch. At this point the tube was unaffected, and the pump was worked up to 337 lbs., but, as we are informed, it still remained perfect.

FOLEY'S "INO AND INFANT BACCHUS."—In the Court of Queen's Bench on 29th ult., Lord Charles Townsend sought to recover from Mr. Foley 250*l.* had and received to form a group in marble on the model exhibited at Westminster Hall as "Ino and the Infant Bacchus," to be executed for 550 guineas. His lordship, however, during its progress, regretted he had not commissioned a single figure, and ultimately, on an understanding with Mr. Foley's brother, claimed the "refusal" of the group. Mr. Foley thereupon sold it to Lord Ellesmere for 750 guineas, and Lord Townshend applied for a return of the 250*l.* advanced. The defendant urged the usual practice of bargains with sculptors in cases where the result of their commissioned labour was rejected, namely, payment of one-half the price in advance and no repayment, leaving, in this case, 38*l.* 15*s.* due to the defendant, who, however, had offered to refer the matter in dispute to Sir Robert Peel or other competent arbitrator. Lord Denman recommended Lord Townshend to commission a single figure,—a proposal at once acceded to by both parties. After withdrawing a juror and entering a nonsuit, with costs to neither, Lord Denman decided, as requested, that the value be fixed by an arbiter, mutually agreed on, either party paying the difference to the other, if above or below 200*l.*

CHESTER.—Curiosity has been awakened by some archæological discoveries in Common-hall-street, Chester. The workmen engaged in excavating for the public sewers first came across a footpath with curb stones set on edge at a depth of 7 feet, and afterwards laid bare what appeared to be the foundations of a row of columns three or four yards apart, set on a strong bed of concrete, 10 feet below the level of the present street. On the fourth of these foundations there still remained the base of a column. Many fragments of Roman bricks and tiles, with Latin letters on them, were found at the same depth. They have crossed, also, another of those mysterious passages in Common-hall-street, about 5 feet by 5 feet, cut out of the rock 11 feet 6 inches below the surface, but whether it has been used as a subterranean passage, or for the more ignoble purposes of a drain, there seems to be a difference of opinion. The borough engineer is using every exertion to collect and preserve these antiquities. As we hope to be present at the meeting of the British Archæological Association, to be held here at the end of the month, we may have something more to say of this hereafter.

THE SHANNON IMPROVEMENT WORKS.—On Monday from 600 to 700 men were placed upon the works, which consist in deepening the bed of the river, and clearing away the remains of the ancient bridge which formerly connected the provinces of Leinster and Connaught. A good deal of disappointment was felt by those who had been rejected, many of the starving creatures having travelled a long distance with the hope of being engaged. Yesterday and to-day the number of hands has been considerably increased, and now upwards of 1,500 men find employment on these works. —*Athlone Independent.*

WALL PAINTINGS, CULLOMPTON CHURCH.—The walls of Cullompton Church, Devon, now being restored, are found, upon partially scraping off the white lining, to be covered interiorly with paintings in distemper. In the north aisle is a figure of St. Christopher, 9 feet high, with hsbes and a mermaid at his feet, and his green twisted palm staff: other figures on an equally gigantic scale are sadly cut up by marble monuments; one of these is St. Michael weighing departed spirits: a demoniacal horned head is grinning between the cords of the lighter scale. There is another figure with a sort of pontifical crown, and bearing a wand, cruciform at its termination. On the north side of the nave clerestory is St. Clara in an orange-coloured robe, with a mitre terminated by a ball: her name is on a ribbon beneath. There are other specimens of the colourist's art in foliage adapted to spandrels, which, as well as the dresses of the figures, also the mouldings of the pier arches, are chiefly of an Indian red colour. It is a matter of regret to many that our antiquaries do not unveil more of these figures and their inscriptions before the decayed plastering is renewed, which it necessarily must be very shortly.

E. ASHWORTH.

TENDERS.

For building new farm house, and rebuilding farmery at Arlsey, Beds, for Mr. S. B. Edwards: Mr. Goddard, architect:—

Betts and Warren, Stevenage	£3,020
Patrick, London	2,870
Cobb, Bedford	2,500
Francis and Bryant, ditto	2,468
Newton, Hitchin	2,358
Burford and Jackson	2,195

For erecting a new church at Skewen, near Neath, stated to be an enlarged copy of the Roman Catholic Church erected in Swansea a few years since, in the Early English style:—

Hughes and Davies	£1,057
Powell	999
Townsend	787

The tenders for the Catholic Church, 10 feet less in length and 3 feet in width, were—

Jones	£1,470
Pilditch	1,350
Morris	1,350
Strawbridge	1,109
Rayner	1,054
Taylor (accepted)	1,040
Prater and Dyer	885

TO CORRESPONDENTS.

Received.—"E. B.," "T. B. S.," "H. R.," "A Subscriber (we know of no none. THE BUILDER contains the most information on the subject of drains), "W. M. B.," "One of the Shelved," "H. F. S.," "J. K.," "J. J.," "J. C.," "F.," "J. B. A.," "T. M.," "J. T. W." (thanks), "Old Architect" (will find letter on the subject in present number), "W. L." (we may yet use it), "J. W.," Derby (must allow us to retain our opinion: no offence was intended). "An Account of the Construction of the Britannia and Conway Tubular Bridges, with the complete history of their progress from the conception of the original idea to the conclusion of the elaborate experiments which determined the exact form and mode of construction ultimately adopted," by Wm. Fairbairn, C.E. (London, John Weale, 1849); "On Copyright in Design in Art and Manufactures," by T. Turner, of Middle Temple (London, F. Elsworth, 1849); "The Drainage of Towns: a Lecture delivered at the Athenæum, Plymouth, January 25, 1849," by A. Hamilton Bampton, Engineer to the Devonport Water Company (London, Whittaker and Co., 1849); "Morris's Tables for Sawing, Planing," &c. (Miller and Field, Lambeth.)

"*Books, Prices, and Addresses.*"—We have not time to point out books or find addresses.

ADVERTISEMENTS.

PAPER SPLITTING.—Artists, Amateurs, and others desirous of learning this novel and interesting Art, may receive FULL INSTRUCTIONS, by letter, by which they may SPLIT PAPER with the greatest accuracy and expedition, so as to separate engravings from letter-press, &c., on application by letter, prepaid, inclosing 5s. in postage stamps, to "ZETA," 8, Walbrook-street, New North-road, London.

CROGGON'S PATENT ASPHALTE ROOFING FELT and INODOROUS FELT, for DAMP WALLS. Sold in rolls, 32 inches wide, price one penny per square foot. Also, Dry Hair Felt for preventing the radiation of heat and deadening sound. Samples, directions, and testimonials sent by post, on application to CROGGON and Co., No. 2, Dowgate-hill, Walbrook.

PAPER-HANGINGS by MACHINE and BLOCKS.—The trade supplied in town and country, with machine goods, from first-rate new designs, at the lowest prices they have ever been sold in this country; and block goods, for style and quality, not to be surpassed by any house in England. All the patterns are registered, and can only be supplied by HENNELL and CROSBY, Queen-street, Southwark-bridge-road. Cheapest house in London for oak, marbles, and panel decorations. A set of patterns, 5s., to be deducted off an order of 5l.—Terms, cash.

PAPER-HANGINGS, MANUFACTURED UNDER HER MAJESTY'S ROYAL LETTERS PATENT.

E. T. ARCHER, 451, Oxford-street, solicits an inspection of the various DECORATIVE PAPERS, fitted up in panels on the walls of the extensive range of apartments, built expressly for that purpose; where also is kept an extensive stock of every variety of Paper-hangings, at the lowest possible price and of the best manufacture, in English and French Designs, by the best Artists; and where may be had a large assortment of French and other Continental Paper-hangings always on hand.—Builders and large Consumers are particularly invited to the above.—451, Oxford-street.

TODD'S PATENT PROTOXIDE PAINT, at a very considerable REDUCTION of PRICE.—This article is extensively used by the principal Railway and Gas Companies, and by Builders and others for painting Stucco. It prevents iron from rusting, wood from decay, masonry from damp, and the hottest sun has no effect upon it.—Manufactured by CHARLES FRANCIS and SONS, Cement Works, Nine Elms London

EMERSON'S PATENT LIQUID CEMENT is ready for use, is simple in its application, and only ONE-EIGHTH the cost of oil paint; for beauty it is pre-eminent over all other materials used on the fronts of houses, giving the exact appearance of FINE CUT STONE; can be used at once on fresh Roman cement or other plastering; is particularly calculated for country houses, villas, or gate entrances that have become soiled or dingy, which can be beautified in any weather, at a trifling cost.—Sold in casks of 1, 2, and 3 cwt., at 8s., 15s. and 21s. each.

PATENT MINERAL PAINT.

Invaluable as a coating for SHIPS' SIDES AND BOTTOMS all kinds of WOOD or METAL work, roofing felts, leaky roofs, spouts and gutters, doors, sheds, railing, and all kinds of out-door work, and being perfectly waterproof, will preserve their surfaces from atmospheric influence and decay,—requires no preparation, and will dry in a few hours.—Sold in casks, 2 to 50 gallons. Brilliant Black, 2s.; Rich Brown, 2s. 0d. per gallon.

BELL, LEAR, and Co., No. 16, Basing-lane, Cheapside.

METALLIC FIRE-PROOF PAINT.—This extraordinary substance is found in Ohio (United States), in a stratum of rock of basin formation. When taken from the mine it resembles in appearance the finest Indigo, and has about the consistency of cold tallow; but on exposure to the atmosphere, in a short time it turns to slate or stone.

Its principal ingredients are silica, alumina, and protoxide of iron, which, in the opinion of scientific men, satisfactorily accounts for its fire-proof nature—the two former substances being non-conductors, and the latter acting as a cement to bind the whole together, and make a firm and durable paint.

For use it is mixed with Linseed Oil, and applied with a brush, the same as ordinary paint, to wood, iron, tin, zink, canvas, paper, &c. It hardens gradually and becomes fire-proof. It is particularly suitable for roofs of buildings, steamboat and ship decks, railroad bridges, fences, &c. A roof coated with this article is equal to one of slate, at a vast saving of expense. It makes the most durable covering for ironwork exposed to the weather; and, as it is susceptible of a high polish, has been used to great advantage by coach and cabinet-makers in America.

Specimens may be seen, with testimonials, at the office of H. STARK, 48, Paternoster-row, London.

THE PATENT ALKALI COMPANY'S METALLIC BLACK and PURPLE-BROWN PAINTS are applicable to every kind of iron and woodwork, farm, and other out-buildings, shipping, &c. &c., and are pre-eminently superior to all the ordinary descriptions of white or red lead, or *so-called* "Mineral Paints." In point of economy, durability, and preserving quality. Prices — Black, 23l. per ton; Rich Purple-Brown, 22l. Delivered in London or Liverpool, exclusive of packages, which are not returnable, except to be refilled, *free of expense* to the company. Agents:—Messrs. Evans, Brothers, London; Messrs. Matthews and Leonard, Bristol; Messrs. Evans and Hodgson, Exeter; Mr. S. J. Fill, Yarmouth, Norfolk; Mr. D. Sandeman, Glasgow; Mr. G. Sandeman, Dundee; Mr. R. Newby, Bradford, Yorkshire; Mr. R. S. Farr, Edinburgh; Mr. W. Bailey, Wolverhampton; Messrs. Vint and Co., Newcastle-on-Tyne, and Sunderland; Mr. Robert Oxland, Plymouth; Mr. Joshua Fox, Tregedna, near Falmouth; Messrs. Bryant and May, Tooley-street, London. To be obtained (also with copies of testimonials) on application at the offices of the company, 20, Fenchurch-street, London.

JOHN A. WEST, Secretary.

PAINTING WITHOUT SMELL; a fact accomplished by the use of the newly-discovered SWEET OIL of TURPENTINE, instead of the deadly abomination called oil or spirits of turpentine. Paint mixed with it is free from smell, is improved in brilliancy of colour, and the baneful properties of the lead being neutralized, does not emit those noxious exhalations which have hitherto been so universally associated with painting. By this really valuable discovery house painting is now converted into a sanitary operation, that may be effected at any season of the year, being productive of health and comfort, without causing the slightest derangement to the domestic economy. Sold by the gallon, cwt., or ton, by every respectable oilman in the kingdom, and at the depot, 1, Bream's-buildings, Chancery-lane, where may be seen, and copies had of, the original certificate of Dr. Serny, a senior member of the College of Chemistry. Sold also in sample bottles, 1s. and 2s. each, bottles included.

ARCHITECTS', BUILDERS', and GENERAL FIRE and LIFE INSURANCE COMPANY, 69, Lombard-street, London.

CHAIRMAN, SYDNEY SMIRKE, Esq., A.R.A.

TRUSTEES.

T. L. Donaldson, Esq. | A. Salvin, Esq., F.S.A.
S. Grimsdell, Esq. | C. Smith, Esq., F.S.A.

The rates for both Fire and Life Insurances are as low as can with safety be taken. Those for Life Insurance may be paid either yearly, half-yearly, or quarterly; one-half the annual premium may be left unpaid for seven years, or one-third to the end of life. Thus large sums may be insured at the smallest present outlay.

Prospectuses, forms of proposals, &c., may be had at the Office 69, Lombard-street, or of the agents.

JOHN REDDISH, Manager.

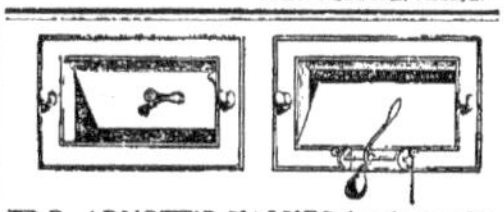

DR. ARNOTT'S VALVES for thoroughly VENTILATING APARTMENTS of every description. F. EDWARDS having had the advantage of making them under the immediate direction and patronage of Dr. Arnott, enables him to present the public with Valves of the most approved principle for general use. Prices from 7s. 6d. to 20s. and upwards. A prospectus, containing every information, to be had on application to F. EDWARDS, 42, Poland-street, Oxford-street, London.

DR. ARNOTT'S VENTILATING CHIMNEY VALVE.

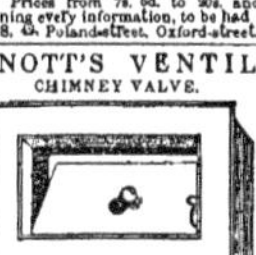

REDUCED LIST OF PRICES.

	First size, 11 by 8.	Second size, 16 by 9
Plain Iron Valve	6 0	9 6
Bronzed and Leathered	7 0	10 6
Japanned, white with Gold Lines	11 6	16 6
Ditto with Trellis-work	17 0	25 0
Brass Front	13 6	19 6
Ditto with Trellis-work	19 0	27 0

Packing Cases (if required), 1s. 3d. each.

Manufactured by HART and SONS, 53, 54, 55, Wych-street Strand, London.

IMPROVED SELF-ACTING CHIMNEY VENTILATORS.

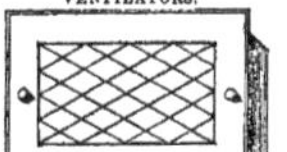

FOR CARRYING OFF HEATED AND IMPURE AIR from drawing-rooms, sitting-rooms, bed-rooms, nurseries, offices, &c. &c., from 5s. each.—BURT and POTTS, Manufacturers and Ironmongers, 65, York-street, Westminster, London.

Stoves, ranges, rain-water pipes, gutters, and builders' ironmongery, as low as any house in London. Delivered free within 6 miles.

TO BUILDERS, CARPENTERS, JOINERS, &c.

MORTIMER'S PATENT MORTICING MACHINE.—ALEXANDER RUST invites the attention of the trade to the above MACHINES, which can be seen at work daily from 12 noon till 7 P.M., at 20, Thavie's Inn, Holborn-hill, where orders are respectfully requested to be sent; or to the Manufactory, 49, John-street, Aberdeen.

"A more simple, substantial, and unique contrivance for cutting mortices could not be conceived. The machine contemplates every variety of work, and meets it by the easiest and simplest changes. To builders, carpenters, and joiners, this will prove a desideratum."—*Sheffield Times.*

"By this machine the work is done with perfect accuracy, and so simple that it cannot be said to require skill on the part of the workman. The amount of time which one of those machines would save in the course of a year, would be a very important object to the employer."—*Sheffield Independent.*

TO BUILDERS, CABINET-MARERG, AND OTHERS.

LEA'S PATENT MORTISE LOCKS and BOLTS

are a great improvement over the present mode of fastening all doors, internal and external; they are also much better and cheaper than the espagnolette fastening for French and other casements?

THE USE OF FLUSH BOLTS IS ENTIRELY SUPERSEDED,

and both doors are ingeniously and effectively rendered secure.

Prices, and every information, given at the Agents, A. L. PFEIL and Co., Wholesale Ironmongers, 5 and 6, Broad-street, Bloomsbury.

By Her Majesty's Royal Letters Patent.

PITT'S PATENT SELF-ADJUSTING DOOR KNOBS AND LOOSE SPINDLES.

HART and SONS beg to invite the attention of architects, builders, and others, to their Door Furniture, mounted for PITT'S PATENTED SPINDLES. The knobs are stronger, more durable, and more elegant in form, than those in ordinary use, as the spindles, being loose, do not require the objectionable side screw. They are more readily fixed, are suitable for every description of lock now in use, and, as they adjust themselves to doors of different thicknesses, without alteration, are particularly adapted for the country or for exportation. In addition to an extensive stock of door furniture in china, crystal, amber, and opal glass, buffalo horn, ivory, ebony, brass, &c., on suite, with finger-plates, bell-pulls, and levers, new patterns of original design are constantly being added, and an order either to sketch or pattern supplied very promptly. A simple one, for example, in three days, and a more elaborate one in less than a week.—May be obtained through any ironmonger, or direct from the proprietors and sole manufacturers, HART and SONS, Wholesale Ironmongers, 53, 54, 55, Wych-street, Strand, London.

A list of prices sent on application.

MODELLING and SCAGLIOLA done by P. DOWLING. Architects, Builders, &c., supplied with all sorts of Ornament in the different Cements on the most reasonable terms and shortest notice. P. D.'s style of making Scagliola with his new-invented brilliant polish far surpasses anything yet offered to the public. Specimens to be seen at No. 12, Drury-lane.—Royal Coats of Arms, of very superior quality, for half the original cost.

BUILDERS and CARPENTERS' IRON-MONGERY WAREHOUSE, 18, Blandford-street, Manchester-square, leading out of Baker-street, Portman-square. Lists of prices may be obtained on pre-paid application.

JOHN and EDWIN YOUNG, Proprietors.

CAST-IRON PIPES, IRON WORK FOR OVENS, &c.

RAIN PIPES, &c.—F. A. TIDDEMAN, St. Ann's Wharf, Earl-street, City, near Blackfriars-bridge, keeps a large stock of Rain Pipes, Heads, Shoes, Elbows, &c., half round and O. G. Gutters, Socket Pipes for Water or Gas, Flanch Pipes, Sash Weights, and other Castings; Iron Work for Baker's Ovens of every description, fitted complete, to be had in sets or in parts.—Prices equal to all competition. Contracts taken to any extent.

LAP WELDED IRON TUBES.—W. H. RICHARDSON, Jun., and Co., MANUFACTURERS of every description of WROUGHT IRON TUBES for Locomotive and Marine Boilers, Gas, Steam, and other purposes.

PATENT TUBE WORKS, DARLASTON STAFFORDSHIRE.

IRON FOUNDRY, 80, Goswell-street (late of Brick-lane, St. Luke's).—J. J. JONES having made great additions to his STOCK of PATTERNS, begs to inform the Trade, that he can now supply them with Plain and Ornamental Iron Columns Girders, Railings, Gates, Iron Coping, Balconies, Window Guards, Verandahs, Ornamental Staircase Panels, Iron Staircases, Tomb Enclosures, Trellis Panelling, Lamp and other Brackets, Cantilevers, Newel Bars, Water Closet Work, Area Gratings, Fly and other Wheels, Wheel Plates, &c.

BAKER'S OVEN WORK, Forge Backs and Troughs, Rain Water Pipes and Gutters, Sash Weights, Furnace Bars, Stoves Ranges, &c., always in stock.

IRON FOUNDRY,
69, DRURY-LANE, and CHARLES-STREET, DRURY-LANE
JOSEPH GLOVER,

Solicits the attention of the Trade to his extensive Stock of PATTERNS for CASTINGS of EVERY DESCRIPTION, consisting of those for every purpose, either structural or ornamental.

Wheel Pinion and Steam-Engine Patterns; Range Stove and Hot Plate Metal.

A stock of Rain-Water Pipes, Plain and O. G. Guttering, Air Bricks, Sash Weights, &c. &c.

A very superior description of Soot Door, particularly suitable for internal work, being perfectly secure, and not unsightly.

ESTIMATES given for IRON ROOFING and every description of Ironwork, complete to specification, and the work executed with every attention to quality and dispatch.

GLOVER'S FOUNDRY,
168, DRURY-LANE, and CHARLES-STREET.

HOT-WATER APPARATUS.—The attention of architects, builders, and others is respectfully requested to BENJAMIN FOWLER'S superior method of heating churches and chapels, halls, staircases, conservatories, forcing and greenhouses, manufactories and warehouses, kilns, rooms for drying timber, &c., and every variety of purpose for which artificial heat is required. Within the last twenty years some hundreds of buildings have been heated upon this plan, and the parties for whom they were executed are constantly expressing their satisfaction, also their willingness to vouch for their efficiency.

BENJAMIN FOWLER, late of 63, Dorset-street, removed to the new factory, Whitefriars-street, Fleet-street.

CHEAP

IRONMONGERY WAREHOUSE, 2, York-street, Borough, leading to the Borough Market—GEORGE SANDEMAN and Co.

Elliptic stoves, with double backs, 3d. per inch.
Register stoves, ... 6½d. per inch.

Patent cut clasp	4d.	6d.	10d.
Per thousand	6d.	8d.	1s. 3d.

Best sash line, 5s. per gross.

Best Patent Sash Line.

No.	1	2	3	4	5	6
Per gross—	4s. 3d.	5s.	5s. 6d.	7s. 6d.	10s.	12s.

Sash weights, 6s. per cwt.

Cast butts,	1½	2	2½ inch.
Per dozen,	8d.	11d.	1s. 4d.

Every description of Ironmongery at the lowest prices.
Warehouse closes at Seven o'Clock.

TO BUILDERS and CARPENTERS.—Elliptic Stoves, double backs, 3d. per inch. Registers, 6½d. 7d., 8d. per inch.

Cottage Ranges, with Ovens and Boilers, 3 ft. 2 in. 40s.; 3 ft. 4 in. 42s.; 3 ft. 6 in., 44s.

Self-acting Ranges, with Circular Oven and Back Boiler, best Wrought Bars and Bright Fittings.

3 ft., £2. 18s. 3 ft. 6, £3. 7s. 4 ft., £3. 15s.

Best Patent Cut Clasp.

4½d.	5d.	7d.	10d.	1s. 2d.	1s. 8d. per 1,000
3d.	4d.	6d.	8d.	10d.	20d.

Best Sheet Floor Brads, 12s. 6d. per cwt.
Best Town Glue 38s. Do. Scotch, 52s. per cwt.

Best Patent Sash Line.

4s. 3d.	5s.	5s. 6d.	7s. 6d.	10s.	12s. per gross.
1	2	3	4	5	6

At F. R. WILLIAMSON'S IRONMONGERY and STOVE WAREHOUSE, 35, Chiswell-street, Finsbury-square.

Lists of Prices had on application at the Warehouse, or by letter pre-paid, inclosing postage stamp.—Warehouse closes at 7 o'clock.

TO ARCHITECTS, BUILDERS, &c.

HAYWARD, BROTHERS, late R. HENLY and Co., WHOLESALE IRONMONGERS, and Manufacturers of KITCHEN-RANGES, STOVES, &c., 196, Blackfriars-road, and 117, Union-street, Borough.

Strong Self-acting Kitchen Ranges, with Back Boiler and Oven and Wrought Bars:—

3 ft.	3 ft. 3 in.	3 ft. 6 in.	3 ft. 9 in.	4 ft.
£3.	£3. 10s.	£3. 15s.	£4.	£4. 10s.

Henly's Patent Improved, with back Boiler and Wrought Iron Oven:—

3 ft.	3 ft. 3 in.	3 ft. 6 in.	3 ft. 9 in.	4 ft.
£5.	£5. 15s.	£6. 5s.	£6. 10s.	£7.

Best Register Stoves, at 7d., 8d., and 9d. per inch.
Do. Elliptic do., at 3½d., and 4d. do.

Manufacturer of WOLFASTON'S PATENT REGISTER STOVES, a certain cure for SMOKY CHIMNEYS, and effecting a great saving in fuel. To be seen in use daily.

Orders from the Country, accompanied with a remittance or reference, will meet with prompt attention.

CHUBBS' LOCKS, FIRE-PROOF SAFES, AND CASH BOXES.

CHUBBS' PATENT DETECTOR LOCKS give perfect security from false keys and picklocks, and also detect any attempt to open them. They are made of all sizes, and for every purpose to which locks are applied, and are strong, secure, simple, and durable.

CHUBBS' PATENT LATCH, for front doors, counting-house doors, &c., is simple in construction, low in price, and quite secure. The keys are particularly neat and portable.

CHUBBS' PATENT FIRE-PROOF SAFES, BOOKCASES, CHESTS, &c., made entirely of strong wrought-iron, so as effectually to resist the falling of brick-work, timber, &c., in case of fire, and are also perfectly secure from the attacks of the most skilful burglars.

CHUBBS' CASH and DEED BOXES, fitted with the Detector Locks.

CHUBB and SON, 57, St. Paul's Churchyard, London.

No. CCCXXXVI.

SATURDAY, JULY 14, 1849.

N Thursday, the 12th inst., the Society for Improving the Condition of the Labouring Classes held their annual meeting at Willis's Rooms, St. James's, when rd Ashley presided, and a fair audience embled to hear what progress had been de since the last anniversary. On that asion, it will be remembered, Prince Albert, o was in the chair, made a speech which :ead with electrical rapidity over the king-m, quickening good impulses, inducing kind lings, prompting noble acts. We went into the hall of the Freemasons' Tavern (where the eting was held) accidentally ; the president s speaking, and his words ring in our ears m now. "You may depend upon it," said he, hat the interests of often-contrasted classes identified, and it is only ignorance which ivents their uniting for each other's advan-:e. To dispel that ignorance—to show how n can help man, notwithstanding their com-cated state of civilized society, ought to be t aim of every philanthropic person ; but it more peculiarly the duty of those who, under blessing of Divine Providence, enjoy sta-o, wealth, and education. Let them be eful, however, to avoid any dictatorial inter-ence with labour and employment, which ghtens away capital, destroys that freedom thought and independence of action which ast remain to every one if he is to work out own happiness, and impairs that confidence der which alone engagements for mutual ieflt are possible. God has created man perfect, and left him with many wants, as it re to stimulate each to individual exertion, d to make them all feel that it is only by ited exertions and combined action that se imperfections can be supplied, and these nts satisfied ;" and this the Prince said so nestly that if it were not the honest, real iviction and sentiment of his heart, it was much like it that every other heart re-nded to it and admitted its force.

Since then the society has not been idle, as s shown by the report on Thursday ;* they re commenced a block of new Model Houses 48 families in Streatham-street, Bloomsbury; l with the view of showing how old and ill-anged buildings may be renovated and fitted , although not in such a way as to attain the ndard of accommodation suppliable in new ildings, still, to effect a great improvement on the existing state of things,—they have med a lodging-house for men out of what

were three tenements, in Charles-street, Drury-lane; and one for women at 76, Hatton-garden.

The tenements in Charles-street were taken at a rent of 45l. per annum, were thrown into one house, the greater part of the yard was covered over and formed into a living room, and a scullery and offices, with a bath, were added—the whole of which, together with the fittings, furniture, &c., cost 1,163l. The tenants pay 4d. for each night, but if they remain a week, 2s. (the society do not profess to lower the ordinary price, but to improve the character of dwellings) ; and it seems that this has been the most profitable of their undertakings.

We annex a plan of the house in Hatton Garden as it originally stood, and another as similar adaptations.

Of the model houses in Streatham-street, designed by Mr. H. Roberts, the society's honorary architect, we give a view, serving to show as well the number of floors as the appearance of the building, a plan of the ground-floor, and one, on a larger scale, of a tenement or set of apartments.

In undertaking to provide in one pile of building for the accommodation of a large number of families, amongst the most important considerations was that of preserving the domestic privacy and independence of each distinct family, and so disconnecting their apartments as effectually to prevent the communication of contagious diseases; this, it will be seen, on reference to the plan, is accomplished by dispensing altogether with separate staircases and other internal communications between the different stories, and by adopting one common open staircase lead-

ing into galleries or corridors, open on one side to a spacious quadrangle, and on the other side having the outer doors of the seve-ral tenements, the rooms of which are pro-tected from draught by a small entrance lobby. The galleries are supported next the quad-rangle by a series of arcades, each embracing two stories in height, and the slate floors of the intermediate galleries rest on iron beams, which also carry the inclosure railing. The tenements being thus rendered separate dwel-lings, and having fewer than seven windows in each, it is hoped that they will not be liable to the window duty,—that abominable tax on light, health, architectural fitness, and mora-lity.

The question of rendering the building fire-proof had much consideration, and a plan was finally adopted to secure this. The floors and roofs of the houses are to be rendered fire-proof by arching with hollow bricks slightly wedge-shaped, 6 inches high and 4 inches wide on the top part.

The rise of the arches will be from ½ inch to 1 inch per foot on the span, and they will be set in cement. The arrangement of the build-ing is such as to render these arches a conti-nued series of abutments to each other, ex-cepting at the extremities, where they will be tied in with iron rods. The floors of all the bed-rooms will be boarded.

The tenders for the erection of this building, which we gave a few weeks since, show it is to be erected with the fire-proof floors and roof for 7,370l., and that the extra cost of the fire-proof construction will be only 42l., or about 12s. per hundred pounds !

The plan fully describes the general arrange-ment of the principal floor; and that in the

MODEL LODGING-HOUSE, HATTON-GARDEN,
To accommodate Fifty-Seven Single Women.

Dressing Room.

Bed Room.

Staircase.   Cupboard.

Sitting Room.

Dormitory.

Dormitory.

Staircase.   Lavatory.

First Floor of the House when taken by the Society.

First Floor of the House when enlarged and fitted up.

MODEL HOUSES FOR FAMILIES, STREATHAM-STREET, BLOOMSBURY.

Mr. H. ROBERTS, Honorary Architect.

PLAN OF GROUND FLOOR.

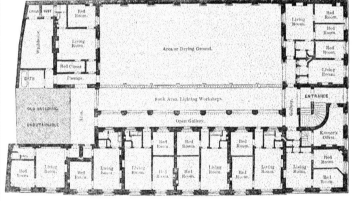

GEORGE STREET.

Scale of 10   0   10   20   30   40   50   60   70   80   90   100 feet.

next page shows, at a larger scale, one tenement or set of apartments, with the fittings requisite for a well-ordered family : in addition to the bed-rooms there is provision for an enclosed bed in the closet out of the living-room.

The nature of the foundation rendering excavation to a considerable depth indispensable, a basement story is to be formed, with a range of workshops. We may mention that the site was granted to the society on lease for 99 years, at a rent of 50l. per annum.

The Royal Patriotic Society of Scotland is endeavouring to carry out objects similar to those of this society, at Edinburgh, Perth, Inverness, and other neighbouring places, as well as promoting field gardens, fisheries, and agricultural education; and they publish periodically an *Industrial Magazine* of information bearing on the means of improving the circumstances of the lower classes. They appear to be strenuously striving to do their amount of good, and we cordially wish them success.

The competition opened by the Society of Arts for the best design for labourers' cottages was not successful; at all events the council refused to award the prize to any competitor, the designs were not equal in merit to those submitted last year, or that the stipulated sum, 100l. for each five-roomed cottage, had been overpassed. Several competitors wrote to us indignantly on the subject. Three said, candidly, they found it quite impossible to give the accommodation required for the sum named. Another said,—" If I can show that my design has all the comforts that can reasonably or possibly be expected for a cottage that is to be built for 100l., have the Society of Arts any right to hold out a bait to take up the time, money, and may I say talent, of any person capable of competing, without taking sufficient pains to ascertain whether there was not on did they advertise merely with a view to decorate their walls on occasion of an exhibition of arts and manufactures ?"

We do not remember the terms of the adver

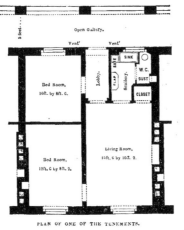

Open Gallery.

Vent'　　　Vent'

SINK

W.C.

BUST

CLOSET

Lobby.

FLAP

BAKE

Scullery.

Bed Room,
10ft. by 8ft. 6.

Bed Room,
12ft. 6 by 8ft. 2.

Living Room,
15ft, 6 by 10ft. 2.

PLAN OF ONE OF THE TENEMENTS.

10　　　0　　　10　　　20

int, but doubtless the society reserved ght of withholding the premium if the ng standard were not passed, or at all reached. Those who did not adhere e regulations have no ground for aint. It is quite true that in the ry modes of construction a labourer's e, containing five rooms, cannot be pro- built for 100l. The question is, by what ode, materials, or arrangement, can this e, and to induce the discovery of this the y of Arts are quite justified in offering a um? Most persons could build a cottage ning the requisite accommodation for, 0l. The desideratum is, to know how be done for 100l., as the labourer can only a certain sum for rent, and money t be invested without a prospect of due for it.

designs for cottages by Mr. Hine and Nicholl, to which the Society of Arts ed prizes last year, have been published, working drawings and specifications, and be found very useful by proprietors.*

each contained five rooms, pantry, and closet, and are estimated respectively 5l. and 299l. the pair, exclusive of ary walls.

mentioned some time since Mr. Chad- MS. collection on the subject of hollow floors, and roofs, with the view of lead- the cheap production of sound, dry, and fire-proof residences. The import- f the inquiry cannot be over-rated; no hould be lost in pursuing it.

RMINGHAM WORKHOUSE COMPETITION. ty-three sets of plans have been received petition, and Mr. John Shaw, London, Edge, Birmingham, and Mr. Stevens, , have been requested to act as selecting ects.

*rize Model Cottages," by Mr. T. C. Hine, Notting- nd Mr. S. J. Nicholl, London. Dean and Son, needle-street.

HAMPTON COURT PALACE.

THOSE of our readers who want an instruc- tive as well as pleasant day's recreation, and have not seen the

　　　　　" structure of majestic frame,
Which from the neigh'b'ring Hampton takes
　　　　　its name,"

as Pope sings, may find it there if they look for it with their eyes open. Those who have visited it do not need to be told that another and yet another visit will give fresh pleasure and fresh information. It is not the first time this has been urged in our pages; but the remembrance of a delightful day spent there last week impels us to say it again. Our party was not a common one,—chiefly men capable of getting the utmost enjoyment out of what can be seen, and throwing light into a dark corner,—and we had the advantage of the running comments of Mr. Jesse, whose pleasant books every one knows; but it does not need these additions to make a visit to Hampton Court Palace suggestive, edifying, and delightful; the latter more especially if it be on a summer's day. Raffaelle, Wolsey, Henry VIII., Queen Elizabeth, William III., Christopher Wren, Alexander Pope, who—

　　　" —— lisp'd in numbers, for the numbers
　　　　　came,"—

are some of the names which flash into the memory when walking round its cool courts and exquisite gardens. The picture-galleries read a historical lecture more valuable to impress the mind than many pen-written books. Efforts should be systematically made to render the collection here more complete, and to obtain a better arrangement of it. The Woods and Forests, by whom some time since a few very interesting pictures were purchased and hung, including the "Embarkation of William III." and seven curious views of old London, should appropriate a certain sum annually towards ren- dering the collection perfect; and individuals having isolated pictures, historically valuable, might be led to present them, if they were certain of a gracious reception;—pictures which alone are of little or no worth, may be exceedingly important as part of a series.

In several of these paintings at Hampton Court will be found fountains, furniture, lamps, &c., useful as suggestions for designers. Especially interesting, however, in this respect are the tapestries in the great hall and withdrawing-room,—some of which are as-

cribed by Evelyn to Raffaelle, while others may be by Albert Durer. These tapestries would of themselves furnish sufficient materials for an interesting work.

The coloured and gilded decorations in the Great Hall have a better effect now than they had at first, time having toned them. The roof of the chapel, an elaborate piece of groining with pendents of mongrel design, characteristic of the period (about 1536), has been decorated at great cost, but with little good effect, inasmuch as the rest of the apartment is not brought into harmony with it. The windows especially need stained glass. With less gilding on this roof (the upholsterer's resource), and conse- quently at less cost, we are disposed to think a better effect might have been obtained, and with the money saved, the rest of the chapel might have been made harmonious. That the whole was decorated previous to the Common- wealth, is made clear by contemporary records. The fittings of the chapel are by Wren.

Throughout the palace the contrast of the styles of two periods, those of Wolsey and Wren, is very striking and suggestive.

In Mr. Crofton Croker's collection of MSS. relating to Royal palaces, is a letter signed "Wm. Talman," who had the charge of Hampton Court, dated September 12, 1699, which shews what works were then going on, and is in other respects interesting. We steal the principal part of it for the benefit of our readers.

"The 5 roomes (the writer says) are almost finished, the great stone staires is done, and the iron work putt up; the gallery for the cartoones of Raphell is soe forward, that I shall fix up the pictures in a week; the King's great bed- chamber and two clossetts are in hand, that his Ma'tie will find I have made use of my time; for it proves a greater work than I ex- pected, and I hope it will be to his Ma'ts satis- fac'ion. Wee are making a road of 60 foot broad through the middle park, and a bason of 400 ft. diameter in the middle of the circle of trees, which will be very noble; wee have abundance of projects (if his Ma'tie will like them) by several noble Lords that wee here call the critiques.

S', as to Derham, Mr. Wilcox came lately from thence, and tells mee all things there hee hopes are to yo' satisfac'ion. Mr. Watkins acquaints mee the same, and that you were thinking of goeing on with the ffoundacons of the garden front this season, but I believe beginning early in the spring will doe better; but that is left to your better judgement.

S', as his Ma'tie had given mee power to finish his lodgings at Hampton Court, I con- cluded I was to take care of every workman there employed, should be sufficient artist in his way: I find one Greenoway, his Ma'tie lock- smith by warrant, who pretends hee haa made the locks for all the lodgings ever since the Queen's death for Hampton Court,—the truth is, the man is a very dull smith, not brought up to that trade, but of late years has taken it up, and has becne several trades. I have no prejudice to the man, but hee is an ignorant fellow; my Lord Ranelagh has desired me to employ one Keys, who is the most ingenious man in Europe, and for whose work I will answer; hee is making ten locks for the gallery, King's bedchamber, little bedchamber, and the two clossetts, that the locks of these rooms might answere the rest of ye finishing, but S'John Stanley has sent mee a very sharp letter, that if I entrench upon my Lord Chamber- laine's office, hee must complain to ye king. S', there is as much difference between the two men in their art as between Vulcan and Venus. S', if it is not improper to desire you to know of his Ma'tie whither I may goe on with those locks (they being already half done), and the other may doe the rest, for what I undertake I would have it of a peice, I should be glad of the favour of an answere, and am, with the profoundest respect S' your &c."

The letter is endorsed, "From Mr. Talman For y' king;" and may have been directed to Wren, but this does not appear. If any of our readers are led by it to notice the locks on the doors in the gallery made by this "Keys," they will find them nice pieces of work.

Respecting Raffaelle's cartoons here, Dr. Waagen, in the last number of the Art-Journal, makes a suggestion which we gladly echo. He is speaking of the importance of spreading abroad good works of art, and says,—

"This might be effected in your country, where the feeling is so strong and general in favour of enterprises of public utility, by the association of a number of benevolent friends of art and the people, who might employ a number of skilful artists to lithograph the famous cartoons at Hampton Court, in order to render them accessible, at a small price, to the lower classes. In England the knowledge of Scripture is so widely disseminated, that the exalted and noble interpretations of apostolical history would meet with an extraordinary reception. At the same time the people would have a scale whereby to enable them to determine the truly great and beautiful, and to teach them to despise the base and ignoble. In this manner, by degrees, the choice productions of the immense treasures of art, foreign as well as native, which Great Britain possesses, might become the common property of the nation."

But we may not afford more space to the subject just now; our intention is not to write an account of the place, but simply to say to our readers,—take a holiday and go to Hampton Court.*

ROMANESQUE AND SARACENIC ART.

MOSQUES AND MOORISH PALACES.

THE subject of the last lecture by Mr. Ralph Wornum, at the Government School of Design, Somerset House, was the Romanesque and Saracenic art of the middle ages.

In the preceding, said the lecturer, I introduced the subject of Christian symbolism and Byzantine art; and you will find, as we advance, that the elements then pointed out perform a very prominent part in the whole system of decoration throughout the middle ages, until the establishment of the cinque-cento, when all symbolic elements were utterly discarded, even in Germany. Gothic art itself ceased to be practised. The Elizabethan in England—our version of the Italian Renaissance—and the Louis Quatorze in France, superseded all other styles in a later period. The symbolic elements, however, of the Romanesque styles were not limited to the Christian world; they entered originally largely into Saracenic art, as I shall presently show: they are prominent at Cairo, and they can be slightly traced even in the later works of the Alhambra.

By the term Romanesque (on the utility of which the lecturer made a few remarks) we designate all the middle-age architecture of Europe not *Pointed* or *Gothic*, its development being horizontal rather than vertical. The Byzantine, Lombard, Norman, and even our own Saxon, are Romanesque in style. The Egyptian Romanesque presented a modification of the semicircular with the pointed arch. For many ages all ecclesiastical architecture was either Romanesque or Gothic: the Italian and classical styles were not applied to ecclesiastical purposes before the sixteenth century. The cross and dome were the only elements of the earlier style of decoration that were preserved, and though as architectural designs the cinque-cento styles surpassed the earlier in their forms, more especially in exterior, it is only in rare exceptions that they have even equalled the gorgeous decoration of the early Romanesque works, and more especially the Byzantine, as St. Sophia's at Constantinople, San Vitale at Ravenna, St. Mark's at Venice, or even the cathedrals of Pisa, Monreale, or Messina.

The description of St. Sophia may suffice for all. Forty thousand pounds weight of silver were expended over the altar alone. The whole vault or ceiling of the church was gilded and decorated with the richest mosaics. The walls and pavements were of different coloured marbles, arranged in a variety of geometrical forms. The numerous columns, with their gilded capitals, were all composed of single blocks of the most precious marbles—the pink and white-veined of Phrygia, the dark red of the Nile, the green of Laconia or of Thessaly, the saffron of Lybia, the black and white of Italy or the Bosphorus, and the red porphyry of Egypt. But most of these columns were from the ruins of heathen temples. The whole interior presented one blaze of magnificence; and Justinian, when he first looked upon his finished work, exclaimed, "Solomon, I have excelled thee!" Yet the exterior was completely plain—not even decorated with the common symbols of the later Romanesque, which prevailed throughout the whole ornamentation of the middle ages.

The most remarkable feature, perhaps, of Byzantine architecture in general, is its rich interiors as contrasted with its plain exteriors. The whole inner space is covered with ornament, the holy liturgy, or the glorification of Christ, being the subject generally illustrating the dome. The "Majesty" of the west—that is, Christ in a glory with his hands raised, or in the attitude of benediction, is only a summary treatment of the "Liturgy" of the Greeks.

The architecture of Byzantium, or Constantinople, spread in all directions. It extended in this country as far north as York and Hexham; it is still the standard style in Russia, and the exclusive model of the Mahomedans from Benares to Cadiz—from Cairo to Damascus; which last leads us to the second great art-development of the middle ages—the Saracenic—a magnificent system of decoration, and one, perhaps, better than all others suited to the general purposes of ornament,—to furniture, carpets, papers, dinner-services, cabinet-work, and the better materials for costume.

The earliest Saracenic works existing are the great mosques of Cairo in Egypt. The most ancient is that of Amrou, formerly of great magnificence, the whole being painted and gilded, but it is now deserted and a comparative ruin. It is the first building in which the pointed arch was adopted in preference to the round—the common Byzantine form, and, indeed, the universal form up to that time.

A mosque ordinarily consists of a square court surrounded by colonnades, with a basin or laver for ablutions in the centre. This basin is sometimes of itself a handsome building, and is often covered in with a circular or ogee-vaulted dome, surmounted by a crescent. Public baths and schools adjoin the great mosques. Niches in the wall and pulpits indicate the side next Mecca. These are sometimes ornamented with the utmost attainable splendour. The roof of the Mosque of Amrou, supported on 250 columns of precious marbles, is flat, and was painted and gilded after the Egyptian fashion. The columns were mostly taken from ancient edifices; and to show the respect the Arabs had for classical precedents, some of the bases of the columns are composed of capitals turned upside down. Every night the mosque was illuminated by 18,000 lamps, for the study of the Koran, many of the 1,300 copies of which in this one mosque were written entirely in gold.

Another great mosque at Cairo is that of Touloun, built in 876, and still in good preservation. It was designed by a Christian artist in prison. It is one of the most tasteful monuments in the world for stucco-work; and is, perhaps, the most characteristic example of Saracenic art, though the work of a Christian. It is also, thus, a sufficient corroboration of the belief that Saracenic art is only a Mahomedan development of Byzantine art. This mosque is like that of Amrou in plan: but the roof is supported on piers ornamented with four engaged columns. It is of brick, covered with cement; and all the ornaments are in relief, in stucco-work, but uncoloured, except in the sanctuary. The windows are not glazed, but are filled in with a very elegant geometrical tracery of calcareous stone. The whole was erected in two years, at a cost of 100,000 dinars, or nearly 50,000*l.*, and Ahmed Ben Touloun rewarded the architect with 10,000 dinars, or nearly 5,000*l.* (a tenth of the whole cost), for his two years' services.

The Mosque El Azar, or "The Brilliant," is another great early work at Cairo. It was built in 981. The flat roof is supported on 380 marble columns. The principal entrance is ornamented in a style (of later date) at once simple and magnificent in the highest degree. Many of the ornaments are familiar Byzantine forms,—as the trefoil, lily, and scrolls of foliage, in disguise,—the guilloche, fret, zigzag, &c.

These three mosques are the chief types of Saracenic art, and the only monuments of its original development. Grand mosques, however, continued to be built at Cairo till as late as the fifteenth century, much in the same style, though somewhat more ornamented, as the Mosque Barbauk, of the twelfth century; Kalaoun, of the thirteenth; Hassan, the grandest in the East, of the fourteenth; and the exquisite Del Maged, of the fifteenth century.

The pointed arch is the prevailing form throughout all these structures; but the semicircular, the horse-shoe, ogee, stilted, trefoil, cinquefoil, and scalloped arch also frequently occur.

All were, probably, originally designed to be coloured; those left plain were so, simply, from want of funds. The sum required for gilding and colouring such works, with their myriads of forms, was not much short of that required for their original construction. The grounds were generally blue or red, and the ornaments gilded.

The Arabs, like the Egyptians of old, also coloured the outsides of their houses. At Cairo it was a mark of distinction allowed only to Mecca pilgrims. The prevailing colour in these decorations is vermilion.

Sicily is another great repertory of Saracenic art. The principal remain at Palermo, the capital, is the palace of La Ziza. It is richly gilt and decorated, and is very profusely ornamented with geometrical mosaics. Nor were the Saracens less active in Spain. Already, in the tenth century, Cordova was the rival of Damascus or of Cairo. The Arabian writers give an extraordinary account of the palace of Abdu-r-rahman III., at Azzahra, near Cordova. Its roof was supported by upwards of 4,000 pillars of variegated marbles, brought from Carthage, Sfax, and other places in Africa. The floors and walls were decorated with the same material, and the chief apartments with porphyry vases from Greece. In one apartment a fountain of quicksilver reflected in a thousand lights the rays of the sun. The hall of the Khalifs, or Audience Chamber, was of fairy magnificence. The ceiling and walls were of brilliant mosaics, in glass and gold. The tiles of the roof were of pure gold. In the centre of the hall stood a splendid gilt bronze basin, a present of the Emperor Leo, sent from Constantinople. Within the palace was a mosque, not less magnificent, though smaller than that of Cordova itself.

The Alhambra, at Granada, though a much later work, is of sufficient splendour to justify us in believing almost any account of these Moorish palaces, however apparently extravagant. Much of it is still in good preservation. Ibnu-l-ahmar began it in the earlier part of the thirteenth century, and it was only completed by Yusuf I., about a century after. The name Alhambra signifies 'the Red Castle.' It was originally a fortress. Different monarchs completed different portions of it. Yusuf repainted and gilded the whole at an enormous cost. This gorgeous palace was built chiefly by means of tributes paid by Christians for protection. In the opinion of the Moorish architects, it was unrivalled in the whole world; but in comparison with some of the grand works of Cairo, or even of Sicily, there is a gaudy littleness of style about the decoration of the Alhambra which detracts greatly from the due effect of its grander features. The details are very much repeated; a species of lily form incessantly recurs. There is not that Byzantine character about these details which we find in the Cairo mosques. The beauty of this palace is in its general richness of effect, and its endless combinations of columns, arches, and gorgeous surfaces, its gold and silver flowers and its intricate tracery, which all combine to give the impression of extraordinary splendour as a whole, while no particular part commands any special admiration. The principal features are its tracery, its multiplicity of rich columns, the variety and intersection of its arches, and their gilt and gaudy spandrels. The horse-shoe arch is supposed to be characteristic of the Alhambra and of Saracenic art generally; it prevails at Cordova, but I believe nowhere else; certainly not in the Alhambra, where the ordinary, and stilted, pointed, and semicircular arches largely predominate. The scallop is the only approach to the form of the crescent in Saracenic art, except in the crowning and symbolical ornament of domes.

* Two Papers on Hampton Court Palace read before the Decorative Art Society, will be found in our 6th volume, p. 671, and p. 628.

Some of the Alhambra diapers are very effective. The general form of the capitals of columns is Byzantine. They are all coloured, generally in red grounds, with blue leaves and ornaments, bands and inscriptions in gold or white, in marble, on a blue ground,—sometimes the reverse.

Much as has been done, there is one great province of natural materials hitherto wholly unexplored, namely, the insect tribe. The student could, perhaps, nowhere see so beautiful a display of brilliant colours as in the glass cases of the entomological collection in the British Museum, where he will see no false combinations of colours, and where every form has all the conditions of symmetry, nearly all being forms of three thicknesses, which is the most important element of a good diaper material. Not that you ought to *imitate* these insect forms, but *use* them, as the Saracens have used flowers, merely as the base of the design.

THE PARKS AND PERIPATETICS.

To men of business who cannot quit London and its immediate precincts—and one million, at least, of the population are in this predicament—open and elevated spaces are of inestimable value; the Government of the country is fully alive to this fact, as is attested by those parties, of all shades of politics, who have been in office during the three last reigns —but particularly that of our present gracious sovereign. By them Victoria Park has been bought, enclosed, planted, and embellished; Battersea-fields have also been appropriated, if throwing 300 acres into wilderness be an appropriation, and Primrose-hill has been encircled with a fence and dedicated to public recreations.

These preliminary measures bode well for the people, and discover a forethought for the requirements of this leviathan metropolis which, notwithstanding the emigration from other parts of the kingdom, is increasing in a ratio that makes one tremble for our atmosphere of fog and smoke, so ungenial for at least vegetable life. These open spaces are the sanatoria of the tradesman, the mechanic, and the artisan; they conduce to the health, the enjoyment, and the morality of the people, and are now become so essential to their greatly improved habitudes, that every item which relates to the plantation and ornament of those *liberties* is of paramount importance.

Who that walks an evening's hour within the floral bosquets of St. James's Park and Kensington Gardens, can view the innumerable groups of gratified promenaders, and the knots of noisy sportive children, and not be struck with the sweet influence of these charming and sylvan places of resort (perhaps hardly to be called retreats) on the expanding minds of the rising generation, and their sedative and consoling effects on the more adult. These fair scenes of cultivated nature harmonise and improve the hearts of all who take relaxation there, instead of in the bowling-yard or pothouse, when fatigued by the business or toils of day; they are as consecrated ground, inalienable from the great objects of general good, and to curtail their extent by a single rood, would be a crime against reason and religion.

For the adornment of these spaces great credit is due to the men in office, under whose auspices such improvements have been achieved. And here I may be permitted to indulge a recollection of gratitude and thankfulness to the genius and industry of Loudon, to whom the world is indebted for the perfection of landscape gardening.

Any one who remembers the bleak, housebound, russet and waste-looking superficies of Hyde-park, fifteen years back, must admit the great amelioration of its appearance, from the plantations which skirt its margins: how softened and tranquil is its look now,—how like an unheeded common then! Surely the promoters of so much general happiness—the implanters of so much taste, are entitled to public gratitude, if not to a testimonial as lasting as the stern brazen Achilles. But these are the works of peace: peace, then, to the originators.

Whilst admitting all this, the reflection comes that the hand of gentle improvement is staid, and that the spirit of studying and providing for the quiet enjoyment of those who are yet to range the new enceintes of Battersea-park, but chiefest of Primrose-hill, is laid or slumbering.

In this latter inclosure (about 160 acres)—one of the most beautiful as to position, and most apt for arborage,—not a tree has been planted, although it has been encircled for now three years with wood,—that is to say, a wooden park-paling!

The land has been bought at a great cost—it has been presented to the public—five or six bare poles have been erected there for the amusement of climbing boys, just chuck up by the public road, as a sort of mock sanatorium,—but not a shrub, nor tree, nor flower —not a twig, as much as would perch a sparrow, has yet been planted; no—three years have been lost!

It might perhaps appear ungracious to allude to the deficit in the Woods and Forests exchequer, or to refer to the unhappy barrenness of crown lands which yield no usufruct, or next to nothing, to the national purse; but this liberality of serving up to the refection of John Bull and his family a coarse treat in quantity, resembles the ill-judged liberality of the host who dished his beef fresh, but without salt: so Primrose-hill is plain enough, but wants the garnish.

This is really pitiful, paltering, but it is not all; and to this subject I have before alluded in THE BUILDER. A road (the external park road) divides the hill plot from Regent's park; the latter is closely planted along the margin, and the only open space through which a view is obtained of Primrose-hill is just at the point where the suspension-bridge conducts to the new park across the dell of the canal: here, having crossed the bridge, a detour of about forty yards must be made to the right to get access (to cross the road only) to the inviting hills; whilst, immediately opposite the bridge, in the eye of the vista, intervenes a building plot of ground of only two acres, which is labelled "to be let for building." When built on, a long row of houses will intercept the sight of the rising verdant hills, and repel the wanderer back from a bastion of wall to repose on the green sward within.

Then, indeed, will the beauty of this only rural and hilly landscape within many miles of town be totally disenchanted. Lord Morpeth considered the point, agreed that it was essential to the design (or rather to prevent the two parks from being marred), that for the purposes of opposing entrances from one to the other it was indispensable; but there was no money to buy the two acres, as all had been expended on the 160; verily the management that built a house, and forgot the stairs, was wisdom to this.

So much for the stagnation impending over the new parks. Now, again, a word to the old one: the Regent's (which was planted and complete some twenty years back), with timber grown to wood, happened to contain within its limits five houses, to each of which belonged a private reserve of about seven or eight acres. These mansions were ornamental, and although the public was excluded from these reserves, yet the floral shrubberies gave a private park aspect to each holding.

A few years back, for some reason not palpable to the uninitiated in official forms, large portions of the park were again fenced off, and added to the private grounds of the favoured residents—and thus an extent of from fifty to sixty acres of this now nearly central park (central to the west-end) was excised from the national liberty, closed against the public, and devoted to the lucky denizens of the inner circle.

We know not whether this alienation of crown lands much swelled the exchequer, or turned the balance of royal domains for even one year to the crown side; but setting aside the royalties on minerals, it is quite clear, that for every acre of crown lands in official management, the state is some shillings the poorer. How would his grace of Sutherland or any great landlord contrive to live if the produce of their acres were in this inverse ratio?

There is but one more fact relating to Regent's Park to be noticed just now, and that is that the whole margin of the canal from St. John's Wood Chapel for a quarter of a mile, has been granted to the use of an individual living outside the park, and opposite that chapel; and he also has had another portion of about 1½ acre fenced off (within two years) for his use inside the park, at the extremity of the long strip forming the dell opposite Lord Dundonald's, to which slice of the park a bridge conducts across the canal opposite to the end of Charles-street, Portland-town.

Over this bridge there ought be an entrance to the park for the accommodation of Portland and Titchfield-terraces (which front full the said dell and strip for upwards of 300 yards), as also for the now dense population of Portland-town; and this entrance is more particularly requisite, as the distance between Hanover and Macclesfield park gates exceeds half a mile!

One might suppose this park had been private and not public property,—it has been so frittered, and the public so unceremoniously excluded.

If it be public or crown land, wherefore has one rood been alienated and desecrated? or why has an overgrown population been debarred access to the park for three-quarters of a mile?

The inhabitants feeling aggrieved, petitioned the Woods and Forest. Lord Dudley Stuart presented their petition; yet although the popular gales blew a hurricane, the Woods and Forests nodded not—no reply has been obtained!

Sir, if your province be to encourage architecture, every unwise change which tends to depreciate the value of buildings (and they are not ungraceful) encircling this beautiful park, must meet, as it merits your reprobation:—every restraint on the liberty of Englishmen to enjoy the little of rural scenery that is of right theirs, and in distance available, must meet your support.

These facts are palpable and indisputable, your advocacy is therefore sought by the public, which acknowledges with some proofs of its approbation your merits, whatever may be the regards due to the desultory remarks of QUONDAM.

THE ARCHITECTURAL PUBLICATION SOCIETY.

THE second part issued by this society for the year 1849 is a very good one. It contains, as the first did, twelve plates, and is accompanied by a "loose sheet" of descriptive matter, judiciously drawn up by Mr. J. W. Papworth. The subjects include further illustrations of the Italian Campanili; an interesting collection of chimney-tops; brick cornices, comparatively little known, and likely to be suggestive; doorway from Loreto; a Gothic façade at Delft; metal work from Florence and Sienna; inlaid pavements; staircase, San Georgio, Venice; stained glass, Assisi; and window coronets, of Jacobean period, from Glasgow. The contributors are Messrs. J. Johnson, J. M. Lockyer, H. Parke, Heneker, D. Wyatt, C. Fowler, jun., Garling, T. Davies, Donaldson, Mocatta, and J. Wylson.

It was anticipated that the third part, containing letter-press, would be issued in the course of this month, but depending as this necessarily does on the leisure of men mostly fully occupied, it cannot be hoped for so soon. The subscribers, however, have every reason to be satisfied with what is done, and we would hint to them that the subscription for the next year should be paid forthwith, to enable the council to make the necessary provision.

MAP DECORATIONS FOR THE NEW HOUSES OF PARLIAMENT.—At a meeting of the Geographical Society, held on the 25th ult., Capt. Smyth, R.N., in the chair, a proposal for the construction of maps upon the walls of the corridors and committee-rooms of the new houses of Parliament, by Mr. Saxe Bannister, was read, with remarks upon the subject by Mr. G. B. Greenough. Mr. Bannister proposes the construction of maps on a large scale as useful decorations to the new palace at Westminster; such as that constructed by Sebastian Cabot, suspended in the gallery at the palace of Whitehall, and as are in the Gallery of Geography of the Vatican. The idea is capable of very extensive amplification.

ENTRANCE TO MONTACUTE HOUSE, WILTSHIRE.

MONTACUTE HOUSE, WILTSHIRE.

WE have previously given illustrations of Montacute House, near Yeovil, in Wiltshire; but the oldest, and, as far as architectural style is concerned, the best portion, has never been given by us, nor has it, indeed, been ever fairly illustrated in any work. Our view shows the north entrance to the building, which was commenced in 1580, and finished in 1601, for Sir Edward Phelips, serjeant to Queen Eliza-

beth. The screen, or entrance, shown in our view, is of the latest Tudor-Gothic style,— much older than the building itself. It is a fine example of the style, and such specimens are very few in number. This screen was an addition to the building about the time of Charles the Second, on the occasion of pulling down an ancient Gothic residence belonging to the family. The front was brought to Montacute, and placed so that a passage was obtained, connecting the two wings, the centre

being only one room in depth. The house must have been very inconvenient (at least to modern notions) before this addition.

The old house must have been a very elegant specimen of the beautiful English Tudor-Gothic style. That the front of it was much larger than the present screen, we see by the numerous fragments of the turrets, placed as ornaments in various positions of the present building. The shield over the entrance gateway, held by children, boldly carved and sur-

DETAILS OF ENTRANCE TO MONTACUTE HOUSE.

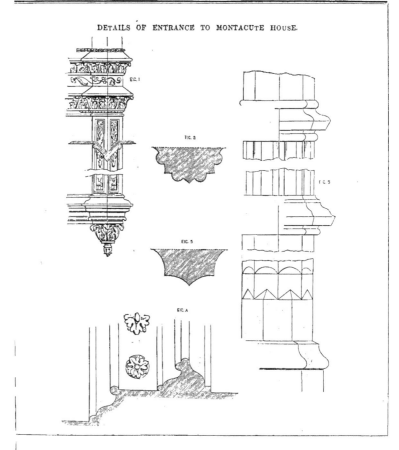

ided by foliage, is very effective, and well
erving study.

References.

Fig. 1. Compartment containing shield.
    2. Plan—upper string.
    3. Plan—lower string.
    4. Section through panel, containing
       shield.
    5. Angle buttresses.

E CULTIVATION OF ARCHITECTURAL KNOWLEDGE.

AT a time when unparalleled progress is
ng made in every department of art and
nce, when literature has assumed universal
y over the mind of mankind, and conse-
ntly that the development of the human
llect is making the most rapid onward
des, a few words may be said on the general
elevating moral tendencies of architecture.
n talk of the poetry of painting, and of the
try of sculpture (and well I own are they
thy of such terms); is not that, then, which
duces on the human mind such an idea of
ndeur and sublimity as a magnificent
litectural pile, worthy of an equal title?
s not his a master mind, and one endowed
he highest degree with poetical refinement,
suspended in air the stupendous dome of

St. Peter's? And they, who earlier reared
those mighty edifices, the cathedrals of our
country, so grand and so sublime in their conception, and for a purpose worthy the noblest
efforts of the genius which He, for whose
glory they were raised, has bestowed upon
mankind,—is there not displayed in their works
ideas equally noble and exalted, as in the
mighty basilica which Buonarotti raised in
the capital of the Christian world? Do
they not produce on the beholder a religious feeling of awe and devotion, which such
places ought to inspire? Is not, then, the
science of architecture worthy the cultivation
of the most exalted intellects? I think that no
one will deny that such is the case, and that
such are the sentiments which it inspires and
infuses in the human breast. The beautiful,
the grand, and the sublime must tend ever to
exalt the mind of the beholder, and must,
therefore, tend vastly to humanize mankind,
and be productive of the happiest results on
the pursuits, and, consequently, on the character of a nation. Why, then, I ask, not pay
greater attention to the more general cultivation of so intellectual and refining a pursuit?
If, in the history of the past, we study
the general and gradual development of the
social condition of man, do we not in architecture study history itself, and the causes which

progressively led to that development? Are not
the pyramids of Egypt ever-enduring examples? Do not the long-buried cities of
Herculaneum and Pompeii convey to us distinctly the character and customs of their
inhabitants? If such, then, are its attributes
and tendencies, why not, now that the question
of the establishment of schools of design, &c.
has been taken up by those connected with
the legislature of this country, establish also
colleges and schools to be devoted to the
study and cultivation of the science of architecture? Is not the design of a building
equally worthy attention as its decoration?
Surely the latter is but a subordinate part, and
ought, therefore, to be considered as merely
a branch of the former. No doubt that
annually many gifted minds, which might
rank with the most talented men of the day,
and reflect honour on the country, are suffered
to be neglected from the want of such an institution to call their latent talents into action.
Now that private architectural institutions are
springing up in most of our large towns and
cities, and that private enterprise is doing so
much to promote the best interests of that
art, would it not be worthy the legislative
government of the "queen of nations" to
take some steps towards its advancement and
cultivation?

In common with every true and sincere admirer of the art, I shall hail with delight the day when the cultivation and improvement of architecture shall be deemed an object of sufficient importance to occupy the attention of the legislature: when, instead of the mis-shapen mass, we shall see arise the classic and magnificent pile, such as shall hand down the enduring fame of our country to remotest posterity, and confer upon her children an elevation of character and nobility of soul, which shall pass unimpaired from generation to generation, and shine the brighter through the lapse of ages.

W. M. BUCKNALL.

INTERFERENCE WITH ARCHITECTS' WORKS.

THE WELLINGTON STATUE, EDINBURGH.

WHATEVER may be the practice on the other side of the Atlantic, there is, in the old world at least, a peculiar sacredness attached to the literary works of meritorious men, which effectually protects them from the hand of the interpolator. We have just to imagine such an announcement as "The Lady of the Lake," or "Marmion," with additions and improvements by John Wilson, or the professor's own beautiful poems altered to suit the fashion of the times by a poet of some future age; and our whole nature seems instinctively to recoil from the very thought of such a sacrilege. Nor is this sentiment confined to literature alone. Painting and sculpture are also alike protected by this most salutary principle: Zeuxis may not add from his treasures to the canvass of Apelles; and the choicest tints of even *his* palette would be more obnoxious than the very blemishes of age and neglect upon the marble of Praxiteles.

Might I ask why it is that our "modern Athenians" so readily tolerate the infringement of this same morality in regard to the sister art of architecture? Can it be that we are as yet æsthetically blind to the merits of this noble art, and that in this particular instance our moral sense requires still to be awakened? Every noble building is a *poem* in stone and lime. Upon what principle, then, can we take it upon us, not only to endanger the reputation of two *architectural authors*, but actually to break in upon and destroy those grand criteria of unity and propriety, which it is the highest ambition of every artist, whether poet or painter, sculptor or architect, to attain, by forcing into one incongruous result two distinct compositions, each in itself a completed design, and in nowise akin to the other?

"Humano capiti cervicem pictor equinam
Jungere si velit, risum teneatis, amici?"

We have been guilty of doing this in times past; and now it would appear that we are again about to repeat the offence.

Look at the Royal Institution, Edinburgh. Here is an instance in which the sculptor is obviously made amenable, in spite of himself, to architectural rules, and *as* an architect, or at least *with* the architect, he is accordingly made to stand responsible to public judgment and criticism for the rank which that building occupies in the scale of merit as a completed work of art.* I do not hesitate to say that in consequence of this, a great injustice is done both to Mr. Playfair and to Mr. Steele; and I object to this *interlineation* or *cross-reading*, so to speak, of two *architectural authors*, just on the same principle that I would object to the introduction of a lyric ballad of one author into the epic poem of another. What is more beautiful, in its own place, than Moore's "Believe me if all those endearing young charms," &c.? yet how should we like in a new edition of Milton, to find it put into the mouth of Adam, in the course of his rapturous address to Eve in the garden of Paradise! Assuredly the elegance of the composition introduced, whether it be in literature or in art, will never justify the bad taste of such interpolations; far less will it compensate for the absence of those sentiments of veneration and of justice which ought at all times to protect the memorials of genius, whether living or departed, from such violent and unseemly abuses. This objection applies with equal force to the contemplated alteration of the Register House. This building, second to none in Edinburgh in point of symmetrical elegance and just proportion, so broad and spacious, yet withal so light and graceful, is about to undergo a change. It is not my present purpose to discuss the question whether that change, so far as effect is concerned, is likely to be for the better or for the worse; although it certainly does appear to me to be an arrangement quite at variance with all propriety both in art and in sentiment. It is less to the æsthetical than to the *moral* view of the question, as being that to which, with all its importance, we seem hitherto to have been scarcely, if at all, alive, that I would apply the preceding argument in giving in my humble protest against this contemplated innovation. Every great work of art is sacred to the memory of its author. The Register Office is Robert Adam's monument—the most beautiful of all the works of that eminent architect—"*si monumentum quæris, circumspice.*" It is the temple of his name and fame, and upon its preservation his professional reputation with posterity mainly depends. Let all, therefore, who have any respect for the feeling which reveres at once the memory and the works of the departed sons of genius, and especially let those influential men amongst us, who are now engaged in the fields of literature, art, and science, in rearing up their own honourable memorials, concur in this act of justice to the memory of Robert Adam, by preserving from the hand of a needless and indiscreet innovation, this edifice, which is his best and crowning work.

For my part, I should be disposed to remove the shabby railing in St. Andrew's-square, and, in the open *Place*, to set down the Wellington statue on the west of Melville's pillar, facing along George's-street; while, in a corresponding position on the east, might be placed the Earl of Hopetoun, who is at present certainly "lost to sight," however "dear to memory;" and, on the north and south, the statues of Queen Victoria and the Duke of York, both of which are at present in unfavourable positions. With such an arrangement, and a few more buildings like the Bank of the British Linen Company, this square might be made one of the finest in the world.

Edinburgh. VITRUVIUS.

* The architect and the sculptor should work together.—ED.

ARCHITECTURAL COMPETITIONS.

PROPOSED CHURCH, SANDFORD DISTRICT, CHELTENHAM.

THE *instructions* furnished to architects by the committee for erecting a new church at Cheltenham, are of such an extraordinary character, that I venture to trouble you with a few remarks thereon, hoping that this, after the many warnings of a somewhat similar nature, though not so gross, that we have witnessed, may arouse the members of our profession to a knowledge of their own dignity and proper position, and to a determination not to suffer themselves to be dictated to by persons, who are either wholly ignorant of the subject they pretend to adjudicate upon, or else who insult the whole profession by issuing such instructions.

I enclose you a copy, by which you will perceive that accommodation is required for 1,000 worshippers in a church, to be built of stone, for the sum of 4,000*l*., including all internal fittings and fixtures, a dwarf boundary wall with two entrances, proper flues for warming and ventilating, architect's charges for plans, working drawings, superintendence, travelling expenses, &c. This is simply an impossibility. To build a church as a church should be built, in the severest manner, would cost at least 6,000*l*., and this amount would not allow of oak being used either for the roofs or seats. That buildings sometimes are erected at a cheaper rate than this I cannot gainsay, as I saw a specimen of one a few weeks back, in the neighbourhood of London; and I may say that I never before witnessed more disgraceful workmanship. The walls were built in two thicknesses, the inner of brick and the outer of Kentish rag stone, without any bond, and the brickwork looked more like rubble work than anything else; all the dressed stone base mouldings were just sufficiently let into the wall to hide the joint—at the utmost an inch—and without a single bond-stone. Had it not been that the m
sonry beneath was thicker than that abov
they could not have stood at all; and the re
of the work was of a similarly bad descriptio
On asking who the architect was who cou
allow such work, and who the builder, I w
informed that they were one and the san
person.

Is it such a building as this that the Che
tenham committee require, or have they a fe
thousand pounds in reserve to place at t
disposal of the architect they may give t
work to? If the latter, I do not hesitate
say that they act unfairly to the other con
petitors; and if the former, they would
better to advertise for a temporary church,
be used until their funds allow of their buil
ing a permanent one. The fault of the absu
expectations of building committees, howeve
must in some degree, I am sorry to say, re
with some of the members of our profession.

I heard of an instance the other day in whic
a building committee called for designs for
church to accommodate 300 worshippers, f
the sum of 1,300*l*., to include every possib
expense, and I am credibly informed that fro
the plans they received for the same, they s
lected a set which professed to give them wh
they required, and a tower and spire, near
100 feet high, into the bargain. Now, in th
case, the Committee can scarcely be blam
for wishing to get the best they could for t
money they have at their command; they act
no doubt in perfect ignorance as to the expen
likely to be incurred in carrying out such
design, and relied on the architect having pr
pared his design in accordance with their i
structions; but is it possible the author of t
design could be ignorant himself about t
probable cost of such a building? Let us s
what chance there is of the sum named suf
cing. First deduct the architect's commissio
which would amount to about 65*l*., and h
travelling expenses, say 25*l*., and there remai
very little more than 1,200*l*. for the buildin
one-half of which, at least, would be requir
for the tower and spire, if properly buil
leaving 600*l*. for the erection of chancel, nav
aisles, transept, and porch, together with
fixtures and fittings!

Such cases could not occur if compete
judges were called in to make a selection.

The value the Cheltenham Building Co
mittee set upon an architect's profession
services is another point to which I wish
call attention; in their instructions they "r
serve to themselves the full right and power
delay or suspend, after commencement, t
erection or completion of the works," which
very advisable that they should; but then th
add, that "in case the building shall not
commenced within twelve months after noti
to the architect that his plans are approved,
shall be entitled to receive for his plans, d
signs, and drawings, the sum of 50*l*., and
more, in full discharge of all claims for su
plans, &c., which are then to become the pr
perty of the committee"—that is to say, th
have only to delay the works a twelvemonth
become entitled to a full set of working dra
ings and specification, together with the desi
itself, for the sum of 50*l*. Such a set wou
comprise at least 100 drawings, which must
have been copied, and two copies of the spe
fication. This, one would imagine, was b
enough; but should the works have been co
menced the architect's position might be s
worse, for should they be suspended wh
1,000*l*. worth had been executed, he wo
have furnished the above-named drawings, &
and still only receive 50*l*., so that for his ti
in setting out and superintending the wor
and his travelling expenses, &c., he would r
be remunerated at all.

Surely it is time that the architects shou
bestir themselves, and put a stop to such
sults being offered them; how this is to
done can best be determined by themselve
I would only suggest that they should m
together and lay down a set of regulations
to on what terms they would furnish desig
in competition.

It always appears to me that these co
mittees consider that they confer a favour
the profession by calling for a competiti
whereas, in reality, the great advantage is
themselves. If there was no such thing
competition, and a building committee
quired a design, they would have to apply

some architect or other to furnish them with one, for which they would have to pay a fair price. If they approved of the design, well and good; if, however, he did not suit them at all, as might be the case, they would either be obliged to obtain the services of some other architect or else carry out a design with which they were not pleased; now, this difficulty they overcome by calling on architects to submit designs for approval, in many cases offering no remuneration whatever for the trouble they give. What they seek by competition is not to bring forward the most talented, who, perhaps, for want of connection or some other cause, may not be able to make his name known, but to obtain the best advice for themselves at the least possible cost. The present system is bad, and requires amendment; it has long been cried out against, but that is not sufficient; one or two members of the profession cannot effect what all might easily do; it rests with ourselves, then, to apply the remedy. If your influence can effect this you will be rendering a lasting obligation on the profession. RAPHAEL BRANDON.

THE GAS MOVEMENT

HAS now an impetus that will carry it through all obstacles. It needs no further fostering care from any one. The public, everywhere, have been enlightened as to its merits and its purposes, and there is no longer any attempt to throw dust in their eyes, or even sterner obstacles in the way of a steady, prudent, yet determined and not very slow reduction of cost, and a consequent wide-spread diffusion of the benefits of good gas-light throughout the dwellings of the people at large. Our next crusade may even be one more obviously on the side of the diffusers of the light themselves, in aiding them—now that their own groundless fears and their own inveterate obstacles are being and have been overcome—in battering down those—it may be no less stubborn—fortifications of inertia and old habit which may still oppose the access of the light, even when available in cost and purity, within the domestic sphere of the million, where there is so vast a field for its profitable diffusion.*

That our systematic, matter-of-fact, reiterated, proofs that reduction of cost has ever been, and will yet for a long time ever be, the sure forerunner of an equivalent rise in profits to the companies themselves, are now beginning to be duly appreciated, even where there is not the candour to give the credit of it to our own demonstrative and persevering exertions, may be gathered from the recent published opinions of parties interested on behalf of the companies, as well as in that diffusion of the article to which we have proved, by repeated instances, that such reductions surely and inevitably lead. From a book of this class on gas-lighting, by Mr. J. O. N. Rutter, recently published by Parker, West Strand, we may quote the following remarks, in the truth of which we all the more cordially agree, inasmuch as they constitute the burden of that very outcry which we dinned for so long into deaf ears.

"The tide has turned. Men are growing wiser. Large profits, on limited transactions, and from few customers, have had their day. The reverse of all this has now to be tried. Small profits, on extensive transactions, and a great number of customers, are in the ascendant. Better had it been if the adoption of these views had not been so long delayed. Most of the large provincial towns have passed, or are now passing, through the ordeal of low prices. Whatever at first may be the difficulties, there needs only courage, and patience, and perseverance [on the part of the companies he is advising of course], and all will come right. There may be fears; but there ought also to be a bold margin allowed for confidence. The efforts of those who led the way in reducing prices have been abundantly rewarded. Whilst some companies have been looking on, struggling, and deliberating, doing nothing, and not knowing what to do, the business of others has increased so rapidly as to have outgrown all their expectations. In every instance where the experiment has been fairly tried, it has been successful. There is an elasticity about gas-lighting understood only by those who have experienced its effects. Relieve it from the pressure of patronage and privileges, from protection and, its constant attendant, high prices, and it will soon exult in its freedom from such unnatural restraints. * *

A movement in the right direction has been commenced. It needs all the aids, and energies, and other appliances of persuasion and explanation to help it forward. The advantages of gas-light in private houses are beginning to be understood. It is still only a small beginning, and, in numerous instances, it has not even come to that. Gas companies must extend their operations. Low prices, and a small rate of profit, require large returns to pay satisfactory dividends. Here is a field so extensive, that all may labour in it, and in which the ground is so well prepared, that the results will be immediate, and in exact proportion to the energies put forth. The difficulties are but trifling, and many of them imaginary. By devoting constant and special attention to the lighting of private houses, a new business might be created. * * *

Amidst the changes which are in progress, and the new light which is breaking in upon trade and manufactures, something must be ventured, or nothing great will be achieved. There must be confidence as well as hope—effort as well as expectation. In gas-lighting, low prices, within safe commercial limits, *are the secret of success*. Of this the examples are so numerous, and the illustrations so decisive, that they all point in the same direction. There is no longer either occasion, or excuse, for doubts, and fears, and forebodings. Those who were most frightened acknowledge they have been more frightened than hurt; and others, who were very lately brooding over anticipated losses, have begun already to reckon their gains."

* A correspondent ("X.") has sent us some very pertinent remarks on the domestic advantages of gas. The proper place for these, however, will be in the assault which it may be necessary or desirable to make in aid of its inundation throughout all the dark corners of domestic retirement.

NOTES IN THE PROVINCES.

THE first stone of the new church at Birch was laid on 26th ult. It is to be in the Middle Pointed style, and to consist of nave and aisles, chancel, tower, and spire,—material, flint with Caen stone quoins: accommodation for 500; cost about 3,000*l*. Mr. S. S. Teulon is the architect, and Messrs. Baldiston and Son, of Ipswich, are the builders.——The rebuilding of Cranoe Church in the Early Pointed style, with nave, chancel, and porch, has been completed, and the edifice opened for service. It is roofed with red and black Newcastle tiles, with crested ridge: the old tower has been retained. The nave is 37 feet long, 21 wide, and 27 high: chancel, 13 feet long, 14 wide, and 24 high: architect, Mr. Bland; builders, Messrs. Rudding and Thompson. The chancel windows are filled with stained glass by Messrs. Powell and Co.——A new organ has been built in Barkby Church, by Messrs. Forster and Andrews, of Hull, at the sole cost of Mr. Pochin, of Barkby Hall. The occasional absence, or want of an organist, is supplied in this instrument by 'a dumb organist,'—an apparatus which plays thirty tunes without interfering with the internal arrangements.——The foundation-stone of a new town-hall and market-house was laid at Brentford, by Lord Robert Grosvenor, on Thursday week before last.——The restoration of Salisbury Cathedral spire is far advanced towards completion. The vane has been replaced. —— The General Hospital burial-ground, opposite the Commercial-rooms, Bath, has been covered with concrete 5 inches thick. ——The Chester Baths and Washhouses were opened on Monday week before last, and during the first three days 2,406 persons availed themselves of the baths, 2,184 being admitted at the charge of one penny.—— The nave roof of Hatton Bonville Church, near Northallerton, for some time in a precarious state, fell, lately, and broke the pews and seats to pieces; a boy was much hurt, but the workmen employed in making a new roof were fortunately absent.——The foundation stone of a new congregational church was laid at Cockermouth on 27th ult. It is to be of white stone in the Pointed style, from a design by Mr. C. Eaglesfield, of Maryport. Length 72 feet 6, breadth 45 feet 6, height 60 feet. There will be seats for 550 adults and 200 children. Cost 1,700*l*., of which 700*l*. is yet to be subscribed.——The foundation stone of a new parish church was laid at Drigg, according to the *Carlisle Journal*, on Friday week.——The Lord Provost and magistrates of Edinburgh are determined to use every exertion to have the Wellington monument, designed by Mr. Steele, and destined for the front of the Register House, placed in preference on the grand terrace to be laid out with statues, &c., along the Princes-street Gardens, at the Scott monument, certainly a very eligible site for such a monument. Some remarks on the subject will be found under another head.

METROPOLITAN COMMISSION OF SEWERS.

IN the strictures you have made in your last number on the proceedings of the Metropolitan Commission of Sewers, you have hardly, I conceive, gone so far as the public interest would have warranted you in going. The fact is, the present commission is incapable of transacting properly the accumulated and accumulating business of the whole of the metropolitan district. It was the opinion of all practical men, that the business could not be carried on by one commission, but their evidence was excluded from the reports, and none but evidence on one side of the question taken. What is the fact as proved by a year and a half's experience? I can speak from personal knowledge of one district; it is left in the hands of one of the inferior officers of one of the late commissions,—one of their least efficient officers,—with no one to appeal to who has any knowledge of the locality; whilst I and others feel that we are left without our old protection against partiality and injustice. Can anything be worse than the proceedings of the commission? One commissioner has seceded because the acts of the commission are illegal; all the chief officers resign because the statements and proceedings of the commissioners tend to draw down ridicule and contempt upon them as officers of the commission.

I feel convinced, Sir, we must return to local commissions, and have a general committee deputed from the local commissions, with proper powers conferred upon them, reversing the present ill-considered and hasty piece of legislation. What is the practical effect of the present commission? All business is transacted by two or three in committee, whilst so much presses on the court at large, that virtually there is no check upon the committees, and the public is without that safeguard that ought to exist. The act is one of those pieces of legislation that is termed *smuggled* through Parliament; only thirty-five members were present when the bill passed the House of Commons. I foresaw and placed on record the evils likely to accrue from the present system; and every evil that I foresaw is now in active operation.

I will not trespass further on your time except to add, that I have fully appreciated your publication as being the only one that contains regular and full reports of the proceedings of the commissioners, which reports I trust you will continue for the present at least, as well as your own occasional remarks. T.

LAW OF CONTRACT.

BURTON *v*. TRUSTEES OF ADELPHI CHAPEL, HACKNEY.

ON the 7th, an action was tried in the Court of Common Pleas, brought by Thomas and Henry Burton, builders, of Aldersgate-street, against the trustees of the Adelphi Chapel, West Hackney, to recover the sum of 6,405*l*., for extras, beyond the sum of 2,340*l*. agreed to be paid for the building of the chapel,—such extras having been ordered in writing by Mr. Owen, the defendants' architect.

For the defendants, it was contended that there was no case to go to the jury, for the contract and specification stipulated that no alteration should take place in the building unless its cost was laid before the trustees and they consented to it by signature; and that, also, their architect and surveyor, Mr. Owen, was bound by the contract to certify that he was satisfied with the execution of the works. Neither of these stipulations had been complied with.

The plaintiffs were non-suited.

GRANITE.—A block of granite was lately blown out at the Dartmoor works, the length of which was 30 feet, breadth 23 feet, height 24 feet; cubical contents, 16,500 feet; it weighed no less than 1,330 tons. It is intended for the Government works at Morice Town.

Miscellanea.

PRIZES IN CLASS OF ARCHITECTURE: UNIVERSITY COLLEGE.—The distribution of the prizes and certificates of honour in Mr. Donaldson's classes of architecture, at University College, for the session 1848-49, took place on the 30th June. We give a list of the recipients. *Fine Art*, 1st year: prize and 1st certificate of honour—Thomas Gundry, of Soho-square; 2nd certificate—W. Howden; 3rd certificate—Joseph James; 4th certificate—G. Legg. *Fine Art*, 2nd year: prize and 1st certificate—W. R. Alchin, of Gray's Inn-road; 2nd certificate—T. Hill; 3rd certificate—A. S. Goodridge; 4th certificate — Henry Wood. *Construction*, 1st year: prize and 1st certificate—William Allingham, of London; 2nd certificate—Thomas Gundry; 3rd certificate—T. C. Tarring; 4th certificate—W. Howden; 5th certificate—B. W. Betts. *Construction*, 2nd year: prize and 1st certificate—James Knowles, of Clapham; 2nd certificate—W. R. Alchin; 3rd certificate—Thos. Hill; 4th certificate—Henry A. Darbishire.

RAILWAY JOTTINGS.—A comparison of the earnings of the principal lines for the last half-year contrasts very favourably, it appears, with those of the first half of last year; and there is said to be a large increase in particular during the last few weeks.——A bright summer's day was Monday week in the dark destiny of hundreds of the poor creatures who burrow in the miserable holes and corners of the parish of St. Matthias, Bethnal-green. On that day 1,400 of them, under the *truly pastoral* care of their clergyman, Mr. Joseph Brown, were whirled out of town by special train on the Eastern Counties line, to Havering-atte-Bower, where they spent the most part of a sunny day in health-yielding holiday-making in the open held and under the green-wood tree. There the tattered and torn and weary and worn lay scattered about in groups that would have formed at least as interesting and picturesque a subject for the daguerreotype or the pencil of the artist of feeling as Ascot or Eton in all their glory.——A ' station clerk,' on the part of nearly 4,000 of his fellows, earnestly beseeches the aid of the press in procuring them a few days annually by way of holiday. From early morning till bed-time—Sunday and Saturday—seven days in every week—year after year—he complains—and without a single holiday—are such as he obliged to be at their posts ; and with this result, as he insinuates, that in spite of the best intentions and the most watchful energy, a listless habit of loose management inevitably supervenes, in the obviation of which the public itself has a special interest. There appears to be some reason in such a complaint, although the public certainly have also a special interest, in being assured that railway stations are not to be left even for a single day, far less a week, in the hands of inexperienced clerks or managers. Two or three experienced hands, however, might surely be easily engaged as circuit clerks, to take the place of a stationed clerk, should he desire it, for a week ; and we dare say many of the latter would willingly allow them to be paid out of *their* week's salary for doing *their* week's work, much rather than have no holiday at all. A plan such as this may be their only chance of amendment under present circumstances.——On Monday week the Act of Parliament, incorporating a Company for assuring sums of money in the event of loss of life or personal injury while travelling on the railways of the United Kingdom, came for the first time into operation. In the event of serious accidents, officers are to be sent to the spot with assistance and money on behalf of the assured.——The joint terminus for the railways running into Portsmouth now rapidly approaches completion. We are told it will not have half so much ornament as many of the second-rate stations on the South Coast and South-Western lines. The entire works are being constructed by Mr. Bushby, of Little-hampton, the contractor.

LORD ALBERT CONYNGHAM AND LADY ALBERT, received the Council and other members of the British Archæological association, at Hamilton-place, Piccadilly, on Wednesday evening last, for the purpose chiefly of shewing them some interesting matters brought from Greece, whence they have just returned.

PROJECTED WORKS.—Advertisements have been issued for tenders, by 28th inst., for the erection of a small church and parsonage at Grazeley, Reading ; by 17th, for building a new school-room, infirmary, and other works, at Faringdon workhouse ; by dates not specified, for erecting a brick bridge over the river Gipping, at Claydon, Suffolk,—for the erection of a house in May Fair,—and for building a chapel at Nottingham ; by 16th instant, for the restoration of the exterior of Fenstanton Church, Hunts ; by same date, for the erection of a cottage in Gothic style near St. Ives ; by 17th, for additions and alterations at Doddington workhouse ; by 24th, for erection of Harlow new schools; by 14th, for erection of parish school-house and teacher's lodging at Houston, Paisley ; by 20th, for enlargement of Andover Union Workhouse ; by 14th August, for 5,600 loads of Spanish and Honduras mahogany timber, and 7,000 loads African timber, both for the navy ; by 17th inst., for 1,000 tons hard Guernsey granite at Isleworth ; by 17th, for 400 waggons for Great Northern Railway (extension of time) ; and by 20th, for making new line of road near Worcester. Proposals are also wanted, by 1st September, for lighting Lynn with gas for three years.

SCENES BEHIND NEW OXFORD STREET. — A ludicro-serious but touching remonstrance having been sent to the *Times* by a number of poor wretches, living, or vegetating rather, in crowds, amongst filth and darkness, in Church-street and Carrier-street, behind New Oxford-street, a reporter was sent to examine into the truth of their statement of grievances. The result is a most appalling detail, that speaks volumes, not only for itself, but, as a sample of scenes but too wide spread and common throughout this ' fair metropolis,' which too much resembles the state of many of its own fair consumptive occupants, all beautiful without but rotten to the core within. In reference to some of his details, the reporter says, " It would be too disgusting to enter into many minutiæ observed in this horrible place," and yet, " in spite of the demoralizing influence, many of its poorest inhabitants seem to desire cleanliness." In fact the want of public conveniences not only in such districts, but throughout the whole metropolis, though it may tend to keep up the ' fair outside,' is a source of gross pollution and a disgrace to all concerned. But this is only one evil. The crowding of multitudes into single houses is really horrible. The police return of inmates for each room in these dens of filth and fever gives an average of sixteen to eighteen per room. Speaking of one amongst many others occupied, by sixteen persons, the reporter says, " it appeared at first sight of this room to be physically impossible that sixteen persons could sleep in it ; and indeed there could not be room unless some of them rested in a sitting position in the angles of the wall with their children on their knees." In speaking of a pavement flap exhibited a crowd of poor creatures in a dark cellar below, the atmosphere steaming from which was thick and moist with offensive effluvia and darkness. Want of space alone prevents us from saying more at present on this painful subject.

NEWLY-INVENTED TINTING TABLETS.— The facility of giving the effect of light and shade to drawings is enhanced by the introduction of this newly prepared tinted paper. With no other labour than merely scraping the surface, where required, by a penknife, a graduated light is obtained, up to a brilliant white. Sketches made from nature, and but slightly tinted with colour to the forms, are by this new and facile means readily embued with the atmospheric effects of sky and cloud, the vivacity of daylight, and the rapid induction of chiaro-scuro. The advantages are apparent to those who would amass a store of recollections for professional purposes, and become equally inviting to the amateur, by abridging the toil and augmenting the truth of representation. An advertisement in another page of our journal will inform our readers where they can obtain it.

FULHAM UNION WORKHOUSE.— Some correspondents, who are candidates for the office of clerk of the works, complain of having had their time unnecessarily wasted by the guardians. We are not in a position, however, to enter into the question.

ANTIQUARIAN TRAVERSE. — The Roman boundary wall was lately traversed from the ' Wallsend ' and Newcastle to Carlisle an Bowness, by a numerous party of antiquarie and other ' pilgrims.' The party appears to have been a zealous no less than jovial one, and footed every foot of the wa in their eight days' pilgrimage along the old wall, which in one place, near the Roma *Magna*, Caervorran, they found to be still te feet in height, with not less than 13 course of stones in the wall. That the pilgrimage wa an orderly one, and within bounds in its pro gress throughout, may well be credited, inas much as one of its leaders and lecturers was clergyman, the Rev. J. C. Bruce, who range his congregation round King Arthur's Wel on the way, and at one and the same tim quenched their antiquarian thirst and thei physical.

CITY COURT OF SEWERS.—The City Com missioners, who appear to be anxious to do al that may conduce to the health of the inha bitants, meet regularly. At a court held o the 10th, Mr. Haywood, the surveyor, state that every gulley is now trapped throughou the city ; that the New River Company ha given a vast quantity of water ; and that th drains were flushed with water twice a-week and the markets were dushed with water thre or four times a-week.

DISCOVERY AT CHESTER.—A few day ago, a Roman pig of lead was discovered i the excavation for the sewers in the city o Chester. It is in shape very much resemblin those now lying at the British Museum ; an the inscription upon it, so far as we have bee enabled to ascertain, is as follows :—

CAESAR................DOM

The middle part of the inscription cannot a present be decyphered. It was found abou 6 feet below the surface, embedded in a wal of masonry 3 feet thick ; and as it had morta on the top as well as the bottom and the sides it is probable it has been built in the masonry This is the third Roman pig of lead which ha been discovered in this neighbourhood. Th mysterious passage, already referred to, ha also been crossed again in another stree (Bunce) ; it is cut out of the solid rock, anc about 13 feet 9 inches from the surface. W believe it is the intention of the Cheste Archæological Society to investigate the matter so as to solve the problem as to whether it i a subterranean passage used for purposes of religious or a warlike character, or, as befor suggested, for the drainage of the town.

CONVERSAZIONE AT THE SCHOOL OF DESIGN.—On the evening of Saturday, Jun 30, a conversazione was held by the student of the Government School of Design at Somer set House, and was numerously attended. Th students' association for mutual improvemen appear to have arranged it. They were in debted to various manufacturers for th loan of several interesting specimens o ornamental art and manufactures of variou fabrics and materials ; also to the master and friends of the institution and the on at Spitalfields, who contributed a selec tion of pictures, ornamental designs, and port folios of sketches.

For the erection of the Bedford Corn Exchange: Mr. Abbot, architect:—

Francis	£2,640	0	0
Burton	2,180	0	0
Miller	2,140	0	0
Hollingsworth	2,117	0	0
Parker	2,100	0	0

[In consequence of the tenders exceeding the amount the committee proposed to expend, namely, 1,800l., some abatements are to be made in the *quality of work* (cement instead of stone), and the matter thrown open again to public tender. How does this affect the architectural competition?]

For the Parsonage-house, St. Matthias, Bethnal-green: Mr. A. R. Mason, architect:—

Piper	£1,319	0	0
Locke and Nesham	1,250	0	0
Wilson	1,211	0	0
Hicks	1,197	0	0
Holland	1,196	0	0
Curtis	1,184	0	0
Rill (accepted)	1,139	0	0

For altering and enlarging Bishop Wearmouth Church: Mr. Dobson, architect:—

Kay, Taylor, and Cantley, Newcastle	£1,583	0	0
Toun and Taylor, Bishop Wearmouth	1,445	0	0
John Pattinson, ditto	1,371	0	0
Turnbull and Commings, ditto (accepted)	1,249	0	0

TO CORRESPONDENTS.

Received.—"W. A. P." "J. L. S." "J. Dela H." "S. B." "J. Q." (the MS. has not reached us), "T. M." (inquire at Copeland's, Bond-street), "W. W." (without any intention of being rude, we would say, that if our correspondent does not know *what books to refer to* he should scarcely attempt to lecture on architecture). "Anti-Hernaph," "C. E. M.," "N. H. T." (such a mode of evasion has been practised; we would not be a party to it). "J. M. K." (had better examine for himself the model establishment, Whitechapel. THE BUILDER contains various particulars). "J. B. W." (we do not hear that the flue-bricks are much used. We cannot give prices). "C. L." (we shall be glad to receive such information. The letter referred to was declined, in notice to correspondents; the book mentioned has since been published). "J. S. M." ("Modelling Clay" is, as its name imports, *clay*, and nothing more). "John Burlison" (we are forced to postpone article on Cube). "National Evils and Practical Remedies, with the Plan of a Model Town;" by Jas. B. Buckingham. "Architecture, its Fashion, &c.,—an attempt to demonstrate how far," &c. (Leicester-square.) Transactions of Society of Arts; Part II.

"Books, Prices, and Addresses."—We have not time to point out books or find addresses.

NOTICE.—All communications respecting *advertisements* should be addressed to the "Publisher," and not to the "Editor;" all other communications should be addressed to the EDITOR, and *not* to the Publisher.

ADVERTISEMENTS.

DR. ARNOTT'S VALVES for thoroughly VENTILATING APARTMENTS of every description. F. EDWARDS begs to call the attention of parties under the immediate direction and patronage of Dr. Arnott, enables him to present the public with Valves of the most approved principle for general use. Price from 7s. 6d. to 20s. and upwards. A prospectus, containing every information, to be had on application to F. EDWARDS, 64, Poland-street, London.

DR. ARNOTT'S VENTILATING CHIMNEY VALVE.

REDUCED LIST OF PRICES.
FINE size, 11 by 8　　　Second size, 16 by 9

	s.	d.			s.	d.
Plain Iron Valve	8	0			9	0
Bronzed and Leathered	7	0			15	0
Japanned, white with Gold lines	13	0			14	6
Ditto with Trellis-work	17	0			20	0
Brass Front	18	6			19	6
Ditto with Trellis work	19	6			27	0

Packing Cases (if required), 1s. 3d. each.
Manufactured by HART and SONS, 53, 54, 55, Wych-street, Strand, London.

IMPROVED SELF-ACTING CHIMNEY VENTILATORS,

FOR CARRYING OFF HEATED AND IMPURE AIR from drawing-rooms, sitting-rooms, bed-rooms, nurseries, offices, &c. &c., from 3s. each.—JOINT and POTTS, Manufacturers and Ironmongers, 63, York-street. Westminster, London.
Stoves, ranges, fine-water pipes, cutters, and builders' ironmongery, as low as any house in London. Delivered free within 5 miles.

TO THE BUILDING PUBLIC.

FIRST-RATE ORNAMENTS in PORTLAND, ROMAN and other CEMENTS, and PLASTER of PARIS, at reasonable prices, consisting of Vases, Balustrade, Capitals, perforated Panellings, Cantilevers, Brackets, Trusses, Wreaths, Scrolls, Masques, Heads, Figures, Friezes, Gablets and other Chimney-Shafts, by Box Best-moulds. Fletcher, &c. &c. Copings, Flowers (from 10 feet diameter downwards). An assortment of Shop-front Trusses always Ready for fixing.—HERBERT and SON, Modellers, &c., 44, Park-street, Drury-lane.

TERRA-COTTA, or VITRIFIED STONE WORKS. King Edward-street, Westminster-road, London.—M. H. BLANCHARD, from late Coade's Original Works, Belvedere-road, Lambeth, begs to inform the Nobility, Gentry, Architects, and Builders, that he has re-established the manufactory of that invaluable material, which has been successfully adopted by our eminent Architects and others, in the elucidation of our noblest buildings, really not years has afforded the imperishable nature of the material, the specimens of those times now exhibiting all their primitive sharpness.
Groups, statues, vases, capitals, panelling, plinths, finials, chimney-shafts, and other chimney-shafts, balustrades, fountains, fonts, tazzas, vases, coats of arms, devices, and every description of architectural ornament, at prices in many instances nearly half the cost of stone.
Specimens of the material to be seen at the Office of "The Builder," 2, York-street, Covent Garden, and at the Works.

TO BUILDERS, CABINET-MAKERS, AND OTHERS.

LEA'S PATENT MORTISE LOCKS and BOLTS are a great improvement over the present mode of fastening all doors. Internal and external they are also much better and cheaper than the complicated fastenings for French and other casements.
THE USE OF FLUSH BOLTS IS ENTIRELY SUPERSEDED, and both doors are ingeniously and effectively fastened securely.
Prices, and every information, given at the Agents, A. L. PFEIL and Co., Wholesale Ironmongers, 5 and 6, Broad-street, Bloomsbury.

By Her Majesty's　　　Royal Letters Patent.

PITT'S PATENT SELF-ADJUSTING DOOR KNOBS and LOOSE SPINDLES.

HART and SONS beg to invite the attention of architects, builders, and others, to their Door Furniture, mounted for PITT'S PATENTED SPINDLES. The knobs are stronger, more durable, and more exquisite form, than those in ordinary use, as the spindles, being loose, do not trouble the objectionable side screws. They are more readily fixed, are suitable for every description of lock now in use, and as they adjust themselves to doors of different thicknesses, without alteration, are particularly adapted for the country or for exportation.
In addition to an extensive stock of door furniture in china, crystal, agate, and opal glass, buffalo horn, ivory, ebony, &c., no matter with inappropriate, bellmetal, and brass, new patterns of original design are constantly being added, and no other effort to excite or polish supplied may promptly. A simple door, for example to these days, and a more elaborate one of loose metal. May be obtained through any ironmonger, or direct from the proprietors and sole manufacturers, HART and SONS, Wholesale Ironmongers, 53, 54, 55, Wych-street, Strand, London.
A list of prices sent on application.

No. CCCXXXVII.

SATURDAY, JULY 21, 1849.

HE Institute of Architects terminated the session on the 16th
instant, with a paper from the
president, Earl de Grey, and a
very full room to listen to it.
Before referring to this, however, and offering a
word to the council at parting, we must look back
to the previous meeting (held on the 2nd), when
a paper was read by Professor Cockerell, called
" On Style in Architecture," which excited
considerable interest,* not because the line of
argument adopted has never been taken before,
but because being now pronounced " from the
chair," it comes to the ears of the world with
greater weight, and will strengthen and support timid minds who think with him, but
feared to rebel alone.

Mr. Cockerell commenced by denouncing
" copyism," the choice of the day, and the
Babel it had produced,—alluding with regret
to the latitude and license as to the choice of
style which are not only now permitted, but
professed. Art, he said, must degenerate and
sink, unless upheld by principles. Up to
our own time architecture had pretended to be
an impress of the age. As intensity of character is commonly distinguished in society by a
peculiar aspect, habit, or bearing, so should
the great national works of a people be distinguished in the pages of time. The architect,
therefore, who limits his ambition to the reproduction of an antique model, carries a lie
in his hand ; he shows himself to posterity as
a renegade to his country and his age; he is
false to history, for his aim would seem to be
to deceive posterity and to perpetuate anachronisms ; he confesses his incapacity to
delineate his own times, and shrinks from the
exhibition of them, as if knowing their un-
worthiness. As well might the popular writer
insist on the use of the style of Bede or
Spenser, and the obsolete language of Wick-
liffe and Wykeham, as that the architect
should absolutely reproduce the form and
character of taste in that period; and if Art
means anything, and we assume to read its
language, the one proposition is certainly not
more ridiculous than the other. This anomaly
of styles, he continued, is not confined to
England : Paris and Munich are equally open
to the reproach. In speculating on the latent
causes of the vicious system of copying without any attempt at modification, the professor
said, that although the mere fashion of public
opinion always influences Art, as it does
everything else, yet he thought much of
the evil might be attributed to the want of
an enlightened, searching, and generous criticism, such as existed in the beginning and
to the end of the last century, from Boileau and Pope to Payne Knight, Alison,
and others. He especially drew attention to
the fact that, during the last thirty years, of
devotional buildings in which upwards of 1,400
cheap churches of England have been erected
by the zeal of churchmen, not one of that

* At the same meeting Mr. J. F. Wadmore communicated " A short Account of the Cathedral of St. Peter's,
Leon, in the Republic of Nicaragua, Central America, by
Mr. J. Foster, British Consul to the Republic," and presented an engraving of the building from a drawing by
himself.

learned body (as in the middle ages) has produced a critical work on style, as adapted to
our ritual, to guide architects. They have
changed their " building regulations" every
five or six years, and have waived all consistency ; and they seem to have been satisfied
in raising " folds " in any way for the wandering flock. Others had attributed the present
state of architecture to a cheap press, which
had made architectural knowledge secondary
to antiquarian gossip. The decline of the
drama—that mirror in which the state even
of the arts was wont to be reflected —
has not been without its effect ; and it is
worthy of remark, said the Professor, that
when the drama has flourished, so have the
sister Fine Arts, especially architecture. Some
ascribe the decline to the conceit of " Young
England," which has placed the classical at
a discount for the elevation of the mediæval.
The professor referred to Mr. Fergusson and to
Mr. Ruskin (without naming them),—the first
as the advocate of revolution, the second, of
chains, and gave some long extracts from their
works. Our only chance of retrieval, the reader
thought, was to adopt *one* style, and use that
alone. One of the great faults committed by architects was their allowing all logical consistency
of feeling, all regularity, harmony, and conformity, enjoined by the first principles of
sound sense and artistic composition, to be
sacrificed *to a pedantic display of our universal
knowledge of historical styles and dates*, and
the trivial conceit of a dramatic reproduction
to the very life (in the absence of the theatre
itself) of the several periods they represent.
Again, we find them preferring the ornaments,
the rhetoric, so to speak, to the logic which is
its only just foundation. This is mere pedantry and affectation. Such a spirit will not do
in the war of the camp or of politics, at the
bar, or in engineering. In music it is thought
abominable. Why, then, should it be tolerated
in the serious and responsible art of architecture? Nature is never illogical,—for her
rhetoric is the mere appendage and the natural consequence of her use and purpose. How
often do we find the young architect, fired with
the beauty of the classic column and entablature, of the portico and the pediment, introducing them where their unfitness actually
destroys the very beauty he is so anxious to
display! The column carries nothing ; it is
carried. It is from this false principle that
we have churches on a Roman-Catholic plan
adapted to a Protestant Ritual,—buttressed
walls with tie-beam roofs, belfry towers
without bells, and all the quackery of
sedilia, piscina, &c., where they are without use or purpose. The rigid adherence
to Palladian or Italian example and dimensions in designing masonic architecture,
without the slightest allowance for the
growth of modern scantling,—the glazing of
windows in Elizabethan or " early domestic "
buildings with quarré glass, in bits of 4 inches
square, in preference to the splendid and cheap
plates of the present day, each of which would
fill a window,—all this results from that mania
for imitation which, far from showing progress
in Art, is disgraceful retrogression. During
the Greek mania, we built houses fit for the
immortal Gods, and, —— no others. Amidst
the difficulty we seek for aid,—in the darkness
we are looking for light. Objections without
a remedy are useless, and yet if we look to the
works of the objectors who have recently
written, we shall not find any mode of improvement pointed out. We want a judgment
clear of fashion and caprice, founded on

reason. Architecture, it must always be remembered, is not merely a fine art, but a
useful art. Fortunately *science* is always advancing. An architectural work is a contrivance for a certain end. Good architecture
can arise only from a sound understanding
of the structure. New ideas are scarce,
few men have more than one, on which they
may trade all their life. Knowledge of the
structure and deep consideration of the materials are the right foundation of our art. As
Gothic groining grew out of Roman vaulting,
so will other changes come,—we must wait.
It is in earnestness of purpose that we must
look for what is called genius for fitness,
novelty, and beauty. Genius, so called, is but
the more strenuous attention to the means
presented to our faculties by a closer criticism
—by greater diligence in the artist—by concurrent efforts, liberality, and patronage—
and, above all, by a field to work in, offered
by the public. Until these conditions are
presented, we shall of course have imitation ;
that ready evasion of the most difficult and
painful of all labour—the labour of thought.
If the prize and occasion be mean, the enterprising and the powerful mind will take
another career, leaving those pursuits to second
and third-rate minds. The wise architect,
while he admits the whole power of association in the effects and influence of his art—
while he sanctifies his work with archaisms,
and bends in some degree to fashions—still
seeks to embody the spirit of the actual times
as well as that of antiquity, engrafting the
useful powers of growing science and the
recent graces of convenience with a certain
reserve; and thus he fulfils the great purpose
of his office, captivates all observers by the
production of things new and old. Further,
he should remember always the immortal
words of Schiller—

The artist is the child of his time ;
Happy for him if he is not its pupil,
Happier still if not its favourite.

Present powers of trabeation should be considered in designing buildings. Except for
ecclesiastical buildings, he thought the pointed
style should not be used, and in these the
plan should be adapted to our ritual. We are
of classic tutelage, and the style of Greece and
Rome would best meet modern requirements.
The professor concluded by urging architects
to be true to themselves ; to remember that
they are masters as well as servants to the
public ; and that they should, without pedantry,
investigate and disseminate good principles,
and, remembering the influence of their art for
good, exercise a wholesome discretion.

Mr. Donaldson said he was desirous to follow
out Mr. Cockerell's idea as to the progress
towards a new style.* To have a new conception, there must be something to originate it.
Amongst the ancients the impulse is seen to be
some new material or fresh discovery in
science. It was so with the Egyptians, the
Greeks, and the Romans. Even the latter,
when they wanted to cover in larger spaces,
originated a new style. In Gothic architecture
the changes were purely of construction. At the
present time we should examine what the requirements are, and study the best means of
satisfying them. A master-mind will presently
arise to blend and amalgamate the whole into
unity. A new style will come, if liberally met :
novelties grow by degrees. It is to be regretted that public criticism is for the most
part exercised by men who have done nothing
themselves. Let the artist pursue the right

* A view long since put forward and often urged by us.

path, and be fearless. Encourage others: do not discourage. As to fashions, he would not despise or disregard them; the architect was bound to satisfy public wants; his object should be to give them the right form and direction.

At the meeting on the 16th (already referred to) Earl de Grey presented the medals, &c., awarded during the session,—viz., the Royal Gold Medal of the Institute to Signor Canina; the Silver Medal to Mr. Wyatt Papworth; and a book to Mr. Thomas Hill for the best series of sketches. There being no representative of Signor Canina present, the medal was placed in the hands of the foreign secretary to be sent to Rome.

Our own opinion of this uncalled-for and ill-judged award has been too strongly expressed to allow us to record its consummation quite silently. We have the satisfaction of knowing that a large body of the members take the same view of it as ourselves.

With reference to the medals not awarded, the president urged on the younger men of the profession the necessity for exertion, and expressed his desire, that the council would always be rigorous in requiring essays and drawings of ability.* To Mr. Lamb, a fellow student of Mr. Hill, who received the prize for him in his absence, the president, who loves a quiet joke, said,—that he hoped the Hill would become a mountain, and the Lamb a full-grown sheep, browsing on Parnassus.

A communication from Sir Gardner Wilkinson was read, relating to the origin and early use of the pointed arch; and afterwards the president read a paper descriptive of the excavations now proceeding at Fountains Abbey, under his direction. Fountains has been a show place for years, but nothing had been done there, and the wood around it was so thick that little could be seen. The Earl has had a portion of this removed, so as to give access to the structure. The new building discovered is to the south-east of the church, and is supposed to be the abbot's house. It includes a hall 167 feet long and 69 feet 10 inches wide, in three aisles, and an oratory 46 feet by 23 feet, and has this peculiarity, that the greater part of it is built over the river upon arches.†

The Dean of Westminster, in the course of some antiquarian chat which followed, suggested the publication of those few parts of Westminster Abbey which are known to be *Saxon*. The dean said that the side walls of the Westminster School (amongst other things) are of this period, and that the only remnant of the Saxon Church which preceded the present structure is an arch in the west side of the south transept. On the maxim *Ex pede Herculem*, the size and character of the building might be judged.—And then with multitudinous applaudings and much smoke if not fire, the session closed for 1849.

In concluding our notice, we would remind the council that they have a serious work to do, and that we look to them to do it properly. The members at their last annual meeting came *unanimously* to the resolution, that an inquiry into the present position of the institute was most essential, and that means should be sought to enlarge its scope and increase its usefulness. The resolution was in these words:—

"That it seems to this general meeting most desirable that the present position and prospects of this Institute of British Architects should be inquired into by the council,—because it appears to them that, after the period which has elapsed since its original foundation, it is desirable that a strict review should take place, in order to ascertain to what extent the view of its original founders has been carried out, viz., that of 'cultivating its many branches of science, and diffusing the knowledge of the principles of architecture, with credit to its members and with advantage to the noble art which they have the honour to profess;' also to inquire if any, and what, changes in the bye-laws may be desirable *to enlarge the scope of the Institute and increase its usefulness*. That this meeting, in confiding this inquiry to the council, feel satisfied that it will receive at their hands all the attention its importance deserves; and the meeting further beg to assure the council of their anxious co-operation in this most important subject."

The main object of those who moved and supported this resolution was the alteration of bye-law 21, which puts prominently among the grounds for the expulsion of any fellow or associate,—"for having engaged since his election in the measurement, valuation, or estimation of any works, undertaken or proposed to be undertaken by any building artificer, except such as are proposed to be executed, or have been executed, under the member's own designs or directions, except as referee or arbitrator." This regulation, as narrow, injurious, and unjust as it is impolitic, has given a reputation of exclusiveness to the institute which has been even more extensively hurtful than the prohibition itself. It is contrary to the spirit of the age, and opposed to common sense. Many of those now standing high in the profession were enabled in early life by measuring and estimating to stand their ground and pursue their studies, and but for this must have succumbed. We would even go beyond saying that no hinderance to measuring should be thrown in the way of the young practitioner struggling forward into position, and assert that great advantage results from it, in the knowledge of construction and the acquaintance with materials and prices, which are best gained so. For the preservation of the respectability of the institute, there is the ballot. If the applicant be not a man of probity, education, and respectability, black-ball him; but to say that simply because he measures work for artificers,—because, for example, placed in a country town, where positively there is not architectural practice enough to maintain him in respectability, he acts as a surveyor also,—seems to us, as we said before, as narrow and unjust as it is impolitic in a financial point of view. The argument that, being occasionally employed by the tradesman, the architect is less likely to do his duty when employed by the proprietor, is suicidal when used by any in the profession. They would not say that because a barrister acted yesterday for a plaintiff, he is not likely to act efficiently for a defendant to-morrow? Why should they entertain

* The following passage on this subject, from the report of the council, is worth quoting:—"The council have observed with deep concern the absence of that spirit of noble emulation which should stimulate the junior member of the profession to strive for distinction, in the acquisition of those prizes offered to his ambition by the Institute; he should reflect that the seal of approbation, stamped by the rewards of this body, is an honour that must accompany him through life. A medal from this Institute is a title to the respect of the public and of his professional brethren: the very energies he exerts to be worthy of that distinction, are invigorated by the praiseworthy effort to merit the approval of his seniors. The wide range of thought to be taken, the studies to be pursued, the monuments to be investigated, the elevation of ideas and of imagination, required to qualify himself for the important struggle, must have influence upon his future standing in the profession, even if not immediately successful. He should never be satisfied until he is crowned by success, and has grasped those honours which the generous encouragement of his seniors holds out to his enthusiasm and perseverance. Nothing less than the utmost concentration of purpose and unwearying application can qualify a man to be an architect, and enable the laborious student to acquire the mass of learning, the perfect mastery of the pencil, that acquaintance with construction, that familiarity with the mineral and vegetable worlds and with the laws of mechanics, which are requisite to ensure future reputation and success."

† On the 21st of June Mr. M. H. Bloxam read a paper on "Conventual Arrangements," before the Bedfordshire Archi-

CONSTRUCTION OF DRYING CLOSETS.

As at this time much attention is directed to the best arrangements for drying closets, I send you the following observations upon the subject, feeling that the results of experience, though ever so limited in amount, when thrown into the mass of information now accumulating, whether they make for or against our preconceived theories, are the best helps to the perfecting the matter in question. Annexed are drawings to illustrate the subject. They are reduced from working drawings of one in constant use for the last seven years, and of which closet I append the following report, copied from a certificate of its working, made to the order of a Board of Guardians:—

Fuel consumed, including lighting.	Cost of Fuel.	Lighted @	Thermometer.
Wood	½d.	half-past 9	68°
Coals, 14 lbs.	1½d.	half-past 10	132°
Coke, 1 cwt., at 21s. per chaldron ..	1s. 3d.	half-past 11	182°
		half-past 12	208°

The hourly consumption of fuel subsequent to the attaining this degree of heat is of course under control by those in management, and bears but a small proportion to it.

Memorandum.—It therefore cost 1s. 5d. to produce 208 degrees of heat, which heat is more than is required even for the coarsest sheets. The above heat was produced so gradually as not to make the exterior ironwork redhot, nor even the internal neck of the stove, which has generally been when worked by the laundry women. I saw ninety-eight sheets put on the horses all at once, and the laundry-women have dried sheets in ten minutes, which I shall not allow, as I consider it drying fast enough to be able to clear the first horse by the time the seventh is filled and closed, which it will do.

(Signed) * * *

I would make an observation respecting the capacity of a drying closet, to the effect that it is not enough alone to enumerate its cubic contents, as appears usual, for although one closet may be to another as two to one, yet as such only the same may show a fallacious result.

The lineal dimensions of the drying rail, will, I would submit, show the best comparison taken in connection with the times such capacity is available for repetition of use, as instance the foregoing example—600 feet being its cubic content—might have been fitted with only 300 feet run of rail, instead of upwards of 500, as is the case. Yet these cubic dimensions suffice fully to furnish ample lineal room to evaporate the moisture with rapidity, enough to enable them to unload the first horse when the seventh is filled. Although not so good a test, a comparison may be stated by the quantities of water evaporated in the same times, but as lineal room is the means whereon the wetted surfaces are exposed, it consequently will be the best measure of value in relation to the power of the surfaces presenting the heat.

I will now observe, in few words, respecting the ventilation of drying closet, which is the topic more immediately under notice, and will say little more than recapitulate results of experience. The first large closet I erected was heated by a dry, or furnace heat, through a metal flue, as distinguished from the application of heat transmitted through the means of steam or water, and in size was nearly one-half larger than that referred to above, the cubic contents being rather over 960 feet. An external or cold-air drain was formed with a transverse section of 5 superficial feet and furnished with a throttle valve, its mouth directly opening upon the heating surfaces, which were in themselves ample in quantity but were not *under* the drying closet, so that the clothes were not acted upon by any radiant heat but wholly by the current of heated air. A large tubular air or steam passage was constructed in the roof of the closet, communicating with the chimney. The heating surfaces were exposed to the full length of the closet, but dependent for effect wholly upon the air drain before described to carry the heat forward and upward into it. Upon the first trial, after firing briskly for

CONSTRUCTION OF DRYING CLOSETS.

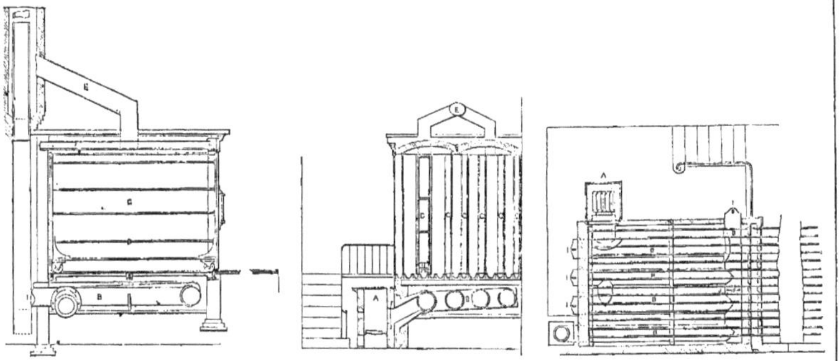

LONGITUDINAL SECTION. TRANSVERSE SECTION. PLAN.

›pen during the time, and the valve in external lrain as much closed, to produce even that ıeat. The second trial, after nine hours' firing, ›roduced 157°, with the different valves simi-arly disposed. This arrangement was subse-quently altered by bringing the heating sur-'aces forward immediately beneath the drying :loset, so that the direct radiant heat might be ıvailable. The entrance or external air drain was also closed up, but the upper ventilating :ube remained as before, and is brought into :onstant and successful action by admitting sufficient air from the laundry into the closet *at the floor line*, to establish a current through the closet in a diagonal line upwards to the ventilating tube, with rapidity enough to carry away the steam as fast as it is formed. An opening or slot, extending the whole length of the front of the closet, viz., 14 feet long + ½ to ⅜ of an inch in width, affords ample air to maintain this ventilation, and by joining the ventilation tube into the furnace flue, the strong rarefaction within it produced by the heat is a power sufficing perfectly to ventilate the closet; the valve in general being open but one half its range. This system, which I have followed in several public buildings since that time, has not in any instance failed, and is, I con-ceive, identical with the operation of that de-scribed as fixed at Middlesex Hospital, for although the external air-drain is rightly abolished, the same closet yet remains per-fectly ventilated, and, I do not doubt, upon exactly the same principles just described; for although the narrow slot may not be pro-vided specially as I have done, yet I must contend that the steam cannot pass away with sufficient rapidity unless influenced so to do by a current of air through the closet powerful enough, by its levity compared with the ex-ternal air, to carry or pass such steam away. A small amount of apertures will in reality be sufficient, when it is considered how much the volume of the air admitted to the closet at 60 deg., is expanded during its passage through and out of it saturated with steam at over 200 deg., and that this is the operation con-stantly existing I have evidence corroborative, from a smaller closet I erected (heated by hot water) a few years previous in Park-lane, where sliding entrance and exit air valves were provided in the centres of floor and ceiling. When both were closed the wet clothes were invariably rendered thoroughly hot but never dry in twenty minutes, the whole of the steam that did escape finding its way into the laundry, but on opening the valves, the lower valve (which communicated with a room below), one fourth the area of the upper one, a sufficient current of air was admitted to pass freely away the steam without much loss of heat, but evidently from two distinct trials the establish-ment of the current was imperative. With a view to promote and effect this ventilation with the smallest area of openings possible for the entrance of the cool air, I have in several closets assisted the upper or ventilating tube, where it enters the smoke flue by forming a distinct metal cylinder within it, to take up part of its waste heat more locally, or by forming such part of the chimney where the steam tube enters it, with a separating cast-iron withe of 2½ or 3 yards in length, dividing the chimney into a smoke flue and a hot steam chamber. The heat so arrested at this point is a powerful accessory to extract the steam from, or induce rapid ventilation through the closet. It is also well, I have found, to extract the steam from two or more openings in the ceiling, in pre-ference to one, which openings should be joined together before entering the smoke flue; also the ceiling or roof (which I generally arch in brick; in fact, no one part should be allowed to be made of combustible material), should have an ascent from the front to the back to facilitate the egress of the steam.

Reference to the explanatory sketches will show we prefer and use a furnace, or fire place, distinct from the ironing stove, the whole of which fire-place is lined with six-inch thick Welsh lumps and the connection of such fire-place with the heated flues is at a depth from the top of it; this arrangement allows coke always to be used: the charge being filled full to the top prevents any cold air from passing over the fire, as in the usual way, into the flues, to the evident waste of the fuel, and it induces a total absence of smoke, creating only a fine drift or powder within them, easily removable. I have been compelled to give a preference to a fire-place for the use alone of the drying-closet, as in two distinct instances I have proved that when the quantity of clothes to be dried has been large and the closet in constant use all day, and say, in five out of six days, the ironing stove, to be fully effective to the closet, has been obliged to be worked at far too great a heat for its own duration, be-sides overheating the room in which it is placed and where it is generally exposed. It has, consequently, been destroyed infinitely sooner than it would if confined to its own use.

To end these remarks, and reverting to the air-drain principle, there is, I believe, only one way in which it may be efficiently and economically adopted, and it would be as fol-lows:—by constructing an apparatus, contain-ing very extensive heating surfaces (indeed far more extensive than the above method will admit), and making them of a number of ver-tical or inclined tubes over or in communica-tion with a furnace fire, and of a diameter not too small to impede the current by friction, but yet small enough to enable the stream of air to be fully and not partially heated; these should be arranged that the external air may be *propelled* through them, *diverging upon* the clothes to be dried, then away through the ventilating tube; this would, I think, be the nearest approximation to the operation of na-ture, but of course can only apply to an estab-lishment where steam or mechanical power is at hand to propel the current, and is not ap-plicable to the great majority of situations.

Drury-lane. GEO. B. COOPER.

Reference to drawings. The same letters apply to the different figures.

A Furnace.
B Heating surfaces.
C Closet over ditto.
D Horses over ditto,—all metal, with brass-cased rails, mounted on edge wheels, running on rebated rails within the closet, and wrought ditto rails let flush into stone floor in the laundry outside. The whole of the spaces within the closet, between the rails, are filled in with wire-work at the floor line.
E Ventilating tube, with valve-rod and valves to regulate it.
G Cast-iron box posts forming front of closet, re-bated both on the front and back faces,—so that, whether the horse is either drawn out or shut in, the front or back plates close the closet effectually, and prevent the escape of heat.
I Sweeping mouths.
J Damper to direct current; turned in the same line as pipe, when necessary to cleanse.

BUILDERS' BENEVOLENT INSTITUTION.

ANNIVERSARY DINNER.

THE Earl of Carlisle presided on Wednesday last at the second anniversary dinner of the Builders' Benevolent Institution, which took place in the large room of the London Tavern, Bishopsgate-street, where nearly 300 persons were assembled. The arrangements were all excellent.

After the usual loyal toasts,

The Chairman proposed, "Prosperity to the Builders' Benevolent Institution." Those who stood in the position he then occupied, of urging the claims of charitable institutions, could usually appeal to the benefits they had conferred through many years. But that special plea was not open to him. It was only in 1847 that the design to establish the present institution was effected, and this meet-ing was but the commemoration of its second anniversary. It behoved them, therefore, to make up their lee-way. They must make up in ardour what they wanted in age. The building trade had nothing to exempt it from the obli-gations of duty and benevolence. Though not initiated in the mysteries of that trade, nor even connected with the ancient society of Freemasons, he knew that no pursuit or calling had rendered more substantial services to every generation of our species. Though the pa-triarchs of Israel may have only pitched their tents in the plains, the history of the Pyramids showed how early the business of building left for itself imperishable records in the annals of mankind. The remains of Nineveh, now being opened to us, bore the same testimony. In short, the business of the builder had pervaded every clime, survived every dynasty, and weathered every revolution. We found it giving immortal grace and beauty to the open porticoes and chiselled friezes under the sunny skies of Athens; and in our northern cathedrals extinguishing the reproach attached to the name of "Gothic," and converting it into a title of distinction and of glory. But as in all preceding ages, so perhaps in our own too utilitarian age, too much thought was given to the building, and not enough to the builder. The workman was too often classed with the machinery—the crane and the pulley—and considered merely as part of the plant. It was to counteract such a tendency that the present institution had been founded. Reverses of trade and caprices of fashion often reduced honourable and deserving men to destitution, and if such were the case with the master builder, still more often was it so with the workman. This institution nobly proposed to establish pensions for unfortunate masters, and temporary assistance to distressed workmen; and, as soon as the funds would allow it, to erect an asylum for the reception of distressed brethren of the craft. The claims of their less fortunate brethren in trade, and of the workmen who had given them their active and zealous toil, would not, he was sure, be overlooked by the company around him; and with reference to the proposed asylum, he would appeal not only to them but to every class of our countrymen, not to suffer it to be said that, in the building operations of our own day, we had been content with erecting dwellings for the opulent and luxurious, with building palaces, and sometimes selling them again,—with erecting for the Legislature a pile destined, he hoped, to be transmitted amongst the memorial glories of the country,—with raising splendid temples to the Supreme Architect of the universe,—but that, in addition to all this, we had left behind us, for the impoverished builder and the workmen, a shelter for their old age, and a refuge for their hour of poverty and distress. Resting on such claims, he could safely leave the cause of the society in the hands of the assembled company, whom he called upon to drink "Prosperity to the Builders' Benevolent Institution."

Mr. Biers proposed the health of the Earl of Carlisle, to whom the society owed a debt of gratitude for the interest he had felt in its operations, and for the kind manner in which he had consented to preside on this occasion, postponing for the purpose one of the highest duties of his distinguished office. With his lordship's patronage and support, and the respectable and numerous attendance at this festival, no question could be asked as to the continuance and prosperity of the institution.

The Chairman was sure the Company would give him credit for feeling a *due* sense of gratitude for the cordial manner in which his health had been proposed and received. He would only say that he never felt his deficiency of knowledge in the building craft more strongly than when he had anything to do with *builders' bills*. (Laughter). He meant to use that expression in the special sense of Bills brought into Parliament relating to builders; such for instance as for amending the Metropolitan Buildings' Act. On that pregnant and intricate subject, he would only observe, that he had last night brought into the House of Lords a Bill for that purpose; not, as they would believe, in the hope that it would obtain the sanction of the legislature this year; but in order that it might be printed and circulated, and that useful suggestions might be offered upon it. He would only add that, though truly professing his ignorance of the mysteries of building, he held it to be the most brilliant part of the inheritance he had received from his ancestors, that from his earliest childhood he had been able to appreciate the master-piece of Sir John Vanbrugh, in the house of Castle Howard; and if any architect, or other individual interested in the pursuits of the present company, should ever wish to inspect that edifice, he should be most happy to afford him every facility. His lordship concluded by proposing the health of the president, Mr. Biers. As widely as that gentleman was known, he was thoroughly and cordially appreciated. He had especial claims upon their notice, from the zealous part he had taken in promoting the interests of the institution.

Mr. Biers returned thanks in a sensible address; and paid a well-merited tribute to Lord Dudley Stuart, for the patronage and support which his lordship had given to the society in the year 1847.

The Chairman reiterated Mr. Biers' eulogium, in proposing the next toast,—the patrons of the institution, in connection with the name of the nobleman referred to.

Lord Dudley Stuart, in responding to the toast, rejoiced that he had been able to assist in the formation of the society. Though engaged at the time in the arduous labours of a contested election, he had been glad to turn aside from these labours, and give such aid as he could to the promoters of this society. Without being betrayed into exaggeration, or attempting to establish rivalry where there should be none, he would venture to say that, amongst numerous institutions of this description, the Builders' Benevolent Institution was one of the most deserving.

The next toast,—"The Vice-Presidents and Trustees," was acknowledged by

Mr. W. Cubitt, M.P., who ably expressed his regret that the duty had not devolved on Mr. Stephen Bird, who had done much more for the institution than he had. Although he was himself one of the first consulted, and entered with alacrity into the project, he had been alarmed lest unreasonable expectations should be raised; and, indeed, he had rather put on the drag to prevent the society going too fast; but, referring to the rules which he then held in his hand, he was of opinion that a foundation was laid *there* which any builder might say was a safe one.

The Chairman briefly proposed the healths of the architects, official referees, and district-surveyors, who had honoured the institution with their countenance and the company with their presence. Though comprised in one toast, their separate merits were fully appreciated by all whom he addressed. He begged leave to couple with the toast the names of Mr. Poynter and Mr. Godwin.

Mr. Poynter briefly returned thanks. No class of persons were better acquainted with builders than architects; and no architects were better acquainted with them than those who, like himself, filled official situations; and he could say with pleasure that the more their acquaintance with the builders was extended, the more they must esteem them, in every sense in which esteem could be applied.

Mr. Godwin could not resist the opportunity, afforded by the separate mention of his name, of congratulating the company on the good position the institution had taken. Those who remembered the difficulties under which its founders laboured, the cold water which was thrown upon their endeavours, must acknowledge that these difficulties would have discouraged men of less nerve and determination than those who founded the Builders' Benevolent Institution. But these gentlemen knew what they had in view; they made up their minds to do it, and they had done it. He saw around him men more distinguished in the science and art of architecture than himself; and he could only attribute the special honour conferred on him to his connection with THE BUILDER, which might in some degree be regarded as their organ. If that were so, he considered it a high compliment, and would acknowledge that it gratified him; for when one had laboured, without favour or affection, to do one's duty, and achieve the greatest amount of good in one's small way, it was gratifying to find the exertion recognised, and it could not fail to induce further efforts. The mention of Architecture called up many feelings in the mind of one who was enthusiastically devoted to it, and who claimed for professors of it a higher consideration than they usually received. A true architect was a poet; the man who expressed a fine thought in marble, or in stone, was as much a poet, and as much entitled to applause and gratitude, as he who expressed it with the pen; and he was satisfied that this was beginning to be appreciated, and by none better than by the metropolitan builders who aided in carrying out these thoughts, and to whose ability, enterprise, and probity, as a body, he would bear willing testimony. This was a topic on which he would willingly have a long talk; but at that late hour he must content himself with thanking the company very warmly for the honour they had done him, and congratulating them on the presence of the noble lord in the chair,—who, whether at the head of the Woods and Forests, or in the chair at a meeting to obtain a monument to Caxton,—opening a literary institution and urging the advantage of knowledge and the beauty of wisdom, or presiding at the dinner of the Builders' Benevolent Institution, was uniformly distinguished by zeal, ability, and eloquence; and more than this,—for it was more,—beyond being an accomplished nobleman, he was an excellent, earnest, and real man.

Mr. Biers proposed the health of Mr. George Bird, the treasurer of the institution, to whom much is due.

Mr. G. Bird having replied,

The Chairman gave "The Ladies," in order, as he said, that he might deserve the character of a "real man;" and the company separated.

In addition to the gentlemen whose names have been mentioned, we observed near us Mr. Ferrey, Mr. H. E. Kendall, Mr. Hakewill, Mr. C. Eales, Mr. S. Bird, Mr. Piper, Mr. Nesham, Mr. Tyerman, Mr. Salvin, jun., &c. The subscriptions amounted to about 500*l*.

LAMINATED ROOF TRUSSES.

WE have received several communications on this subject, but have not space for them in full. Mr. Hay, of Liverpool, in reply to Mr. Burnett (p. 320 *ante*) re-asserts his position:—"I repeat," he says, "that the mode of applying bent timber in the works executed from my designs is a different application of the principle that I have no where seen, or heard of being used; at the same time I do admit that the 'stretch of imagination' is so small that I was rather surprised that Lord Lovelace viewed it of such importance as to prepare a paper upon it. From the notice of this paper in THE BUILDER I conceived it to be the same thing, and I informed the readers of THE BUILDER I had done it six years ago."

The fact is, however, the principle has been long worked on. As another correspondent, a "Liverpool Architect," writes, "the merit of inventing the laminated arched truss, as we usually have it, lies with M. De Saint Phar, who first suggested the idea in 1811, but it was first practically used by Colonel Emy, in roof principals, at Gironde, in France, in 1825; and then the year following, at Marac, near Bayonne, a roof of 65 feet span was constructed by the same engineer: the principals were of plank 2-inch thick, bent in courses over a mould or template, and then nailed or bolted firmly together. Also in a valuable work published by Wiley and Putnam, New York, in 1838, laminated arch ribs are shown, and not reckoned a novelty, but merely stating that the *usual* mode of forming them consists in making the rib of several concentric courses of timber, bent to a suitable curvature, the different courses to be firmly united together with hard wood keys and stirrups of iron."*

LAW OF CONTRACTS.

ADELPHI CHAPEL.

SIR,—The claim against the Trustees of Adelphi Chapel was for 640*l*. 5*s*.; not, as your printers say, 6,405*l*. You will add largely to the benefits conferred through your publication by pointing out at times the legal difficulties of contracts so often unwisely taken. In this instance it was ambiguously stated that written orders were necessary, which we obtained from the only party a builder communicates with—"the architect"—being ourselves certain that the party mostly interested was aware of such extras being incurred. As to the certificate, the architect gave it as he considered fit, and had no other idea than that he had done so in such form as would satisfy his employers that the money was due to us, or that he should have otherwise worded it.

Aldersgate-street. HENRY BURTON.

* The roof of the Palm House, at Loddige's Nursery at Hackney, built about 1820, is constructed of bent planks in laminæ,—says another correspondent.

MR. BARRY'S REMUNERATION FOR NEW HOUSES OF PARLIAMENT.

To assist our readers in forming a judgment in the dispute between Mr. Barry and the Government as to the amount of remuneration for his past services as architect of the new Palace of Westminster, we place before them the principal heads of a letter addressed by the architect, in February last, to the commissioners. He says,—"You are doubtless aware that the proposition originally made to me by the Government, in 1839, was, that I should receive the sum of 25,000*l.* for the labour and responsibility to be imposed upon me in the superintendence, direction, and completion of the intended edifice, and that I was induced to accede conditionally to that proposition in the belief that it was made to me in the absence of a due appreciation of the enormous extent of that labour and responsibility, and that any attempt on my part, at that time, to prove the inadequacy of the sum proposed would have been fruitless. I was further induced to take this course from having then entered upon the duties of my appointment as architect of the new palace for more than nineteen months, when I had already made extensive and costly arrangements to enable me to carry on the works; so that if, instead of acceding conditionally to the proposition, I had adopted the alternative of relinquishing the employment,—which, at the time, occurred to me,—I could not have done so without a considerable sacrifice. I preferred, therefore, to postpone all further application on the subject until I should be in a condition to prove incontestably the full extent of my services, and then to rely upon the Government for a just and liberal determination of the question."

The architect was appointed unconditionally to carry his design into effect at the commencement of 1837, and expected his "remuneration would be of the customary amount." On the 1st of March, 1839, he had the first official intimation as to the latter from the Commissioners of Woods, that they had given their best consideration to "all the circumstances of the case, the extent and importance of the buildings, the nature and description of the several works, the very large expenditure contemplated in the estimate, and the period within which it was proposed that such expenditure should be incurred," and thought the sum of 25,000*l.* would be a fair and reasonable remuneration. For the reasons before given he was induced "to accede conditionally to the proposition founded upon it—under a protest, however, as to the inadequacy of the amount proposed, and with an intimation that he should offer proof of its inadequacy when the building was in such an advanced state as to allow of a competent judgment being formed on the subject."

He then proceeds to comment on the opinion expressed by the Commissioners of Woods. First, that from the want of professional knowledge, they were incompetent to form any just opinion on the subject;—that "the extent and importance of the work" is a reason rather for increasing than diminishing the customary remuneration of the architect. As to "the nature and description of the work," the new palace "is now sufficiently advanced to allow of an accurate judgment being formed as to the amount of labour, skill, and responsibility that has been incurred in producing it. I invite a comparison between it and any other public building of modern times; and I think it will be evident, even to the uninitiated, that in point of variety of design, elaboration of details, and difficulties of combination and construction, the labour and responsibility incurred is much greater than in any other modern edifice that can be mentioned."

The delay and perplexities attendant on official communications have been very great. "As one proof among many others that might be adduced of the enormous amount of labour that has already devolved upon me in conducting this great national work to its present state, it will not be irrelevant to mention, that no less than between 8,000 and 9,000 original drawings and models have been prepared for it; a large portion of which emanated from my own hand, and the whole of the remainder have been made under my own immediate direction and supervision."

The amount spent in the work he thought a fair criterion of the amount of skill and labour required in producing it. Various circumstances, too, had occurred to extend the time originally fixed for completion.

He then shows that he has had much more to do than is usual or could have been anticipated, through Dr. Reid,—the changes made in the mode of conducting the business of Parliament,—and the vagueness of the original instructions given. And he considers, therefore, that he is justly entitled to at least the customary remuneration in respect of the outlay contemplated in the original design and estimate; and adds, that the whole of the arguments urged in favour of such remuneration apply with equal force to the expenditure upon extra works sanctioned by the Government or Parliament; "but to these it is scarcely necessary to observe, that the proposal for a limited amount of remuneration can have no reference." He looks, also, for a further remuneration for attendances on the Fine Arts Commission, and for drawings prepared for them, drawing up returns for House of Commons, &c. &c. In the course of ten years he has received of the 25,000*l.* originally proposed, 24,735*l.* 3s. 2d., or, after deducting his expenses, an income of 1,500*l.* per annum; which he considers does not by any means recompense him for the labours, responsibilities, and sacrifices incurred.

"The following is an account of the expenditure upon the building, exclusive of the river embankment wall, up to 31st December, 1848:—

Amount already advanced on account of works comprised in the original estimate of 707,104*l.* ...	£472,000	0	0
On account of extra works in the embankment of the river and in the foundations of the building, the new basement story, additional residences and offices, central tower, stone carving, and all structural arrangements connected with warming, ventilating, &c., &c., which could not have been foreseen, and which, consequently, form no part of the original design and estimate, amounting to..................	210,842	16	2
On account of extra finishings, works of decoration, library and other fittings, and for fixtures, furniture, upholstery, &c., expressly excluded from the original estimate, amounting to........	139,415	3	0
On account of miscellaneous items, taking down and shoring up old buildings, new roofs and additions to Speaker's late residence and other old buildings, temporary roof and coverings, clerks of works' offices, casts of specimens for wood-carvers, &c., &c., amounting to................	19,372	18	9
Total................	£841,630	17	11

On the above amount of expenditure, therefore, I claim, for the reasons which I have adduced, the accustomed remuneration of 5 per cent.:—

Or	£42,081	10	0			
Upon which I have received on account	24,735	4	2			
Leaving a balance of				£17,346	6	10
And for special or extraneous services during a period of ten years, as above enumerated....				5,256	0	0
Amount now claimed....				£22,602	6	10

Mr. Barry concludes by saying that though he could prove himself entitled to more than the customary remuneration, he proposes to adhere to the long-established and generally-received standard of charge adopted by the profession generally, "in the hope that by so doing all controversy or contention on the subject may be avoided; and when," he continues, "the amount of the claim which, in consequence, I am now willing to receive as a recompense in full for my past services, is fairly considered with reference to the labour, responsibility, and sacrifices incurred in conducting, under very peculiar and trying circumstances, the largest and most elaborate architectural work ever, perhaps, undertaken at one time in this or any other country, to which I have devoted almost exclusively the best period of my professional life; and when, also, it is contrasted with the incomes of other professions, such as those of the law, medicine, civil engineering, &c., which, it is well known, vary from 12,000*l.* to 20,000*l.* per annum, and even upwards; and when, also, the important fact to which I have before alluded is borne in mind, that every architect appointed to the superintendence of public works in this country, both before and since the date of my engagement, has been paid the full amount of the customary commission, I cannot doubt but that it will be generally admitted, not only that I am fully justified in the demand which I now make, but that I have not unduly estimated the value of my services as the architect of such an important national work as the new Palace at Westminster."

PROPOSED CHURCH, SANDFORD DISTRICT, CHELTENHAM.

MR BRANDON's remarks on the instructions for architects in this matter (see last number of THE BUILDER) are to the point, and though severe, they are not more so than are called for by the gross attempt to induce professional men to bestow their time and talents in such a paltry affair at the vague chance of receiving, *ad Græcas kalendas*, a fraction of their due for their designs, working drawings, specifications, estimates, time and attention given to inspections, as well as for reimbursement of their travelling expenses.

Perhaps the committee include in *the architect's 5 per cent. commission the salary of the clerk of the works*, under their comprehensive phrase "of every other possible expense incident, &c. &c.;" indeed they might as well do so, to be consistent in their attempted proceeding of applying the mechanical power called the screw to the hard-earned pecuniary recompense of the first-named adviser.

A vein of amusing blundering pervades these instructions, and excites our compassion as well as our regret at the obvious tendency of the whole transaction. Thus, we are informed that the "*stone** is *not* to be of the style usually called Roman, &c. &c." What is intended is of course obvious, but even with this excuse, the description of the style intended for the church is but a *negative* one: "it is not to be Roman, Grecian, or classical;" but there are more styles than one not mentioned, *ex. gr.*, Egyptian, Persian, Byzantine! will they suit the taste of the committee?

Among "the plans to be sent, are plans of the ground floor, and (if any) of galleries." "If any!" Can the Committee for one moment suppose that 1,000 persons could be accommodated on the ground floor area alone, without galleries, in a building of the cheap description which their 4,000*l.* could in any way produce? They give exact dimensions for the pews and free seats, and they could soon calculate the number of superficial feet that a building *must contain* to accommodate 1,000 persons in the area, besides the vacant space necessary for passages and chancel, vestry room, &c.: let them do this, and then see the length and breadth their church, for 4,000*l.*, "all expenses included," would necessarily take up.

The scale to which the drawings are to be made is larger than usual—almost large enough to dispense with many detail drawings by the hand of the original designer, as the parts would appear distinct enough for successful transcribing and enlarging, if required, by another skilful hand!

The services of an honorary (?) solicitor, as well as the signature of an honorary secretary, are but too plainly discernible in the fast-bind, hard-bargain-driving clauses of this instructive intimation to architects, of whom so many as may rush in to compete for the prize generously offered to them will richly deserve the sweet fruits which the close of the competition will, *nostro judicio*, bring to maturity in the approaching autumn. Φ.

* "The church to be built of stone (not being of the style usually called, &c. &c.):" *sic in orig.!*

OPEN ROOF, WARE PRIORY.

OPEN ROOF, WARE PRIORY.

THE "Priory," at Ware, in Hertfordshire, the seat of M. H. Gosselin, Esq., about to be restored under our direction, is an interesting structure of an early period, which has been much disfigured, from time to time, by the repairs and *adornments* of succeeding occupants. The original roof of one portion of the building, perhaps of all, for it is only in one part that it can be seen (a required increase in the number of rooms having led to its conversion into an additional story), is sufficiently curious to merit a record in our pages.

The length of the apartment is 48 ft. 6 in., the width 23 ft.; the height from the floor to the top of the rafters is 26 ft. (There is a story below.) The height from the floor to the centre of the tie-beam, which cambers 4 in., is 10 ft. 2 in. The tie-beams are 12 in. by $11\frac{1}{2}$ in.; king posts, $5\frac{1}{2}$ in. octagon shaft, and $5\frac{1}{2}$ in. by $5\frac{1}{2}$ in. above cap; struts, 6 in. by 3 in.; the rafters, collars, braces, and bearers at feet of rafters, 4 in. by 6 in.; the longitudinal bearer or purlin, below collar, is 5 in. by $5\frac{1}{2}$ in. The roof is covered with tiles.

We may say something more about the house hereafter.

FARRINGDON-STREET. — Correspondents continue to draw our attention to the delay in completing the thoroughfare from Farringdon-street to Clerkenwell. "F. H. S." urges that the accumulations of animal and vegetable deposits here are very hurtful.

NOTES IN THE PROVINCES.

THE parish church of Costock has been repaired and enlarged under Mr. Place's superintendence, and was lately reopened. It is fitted with open benches with oak ends to be carved. A new aisle has been added in the original decorated style of the chancel, and an open timber roof to correspond with the old one. Other restorations have been effected, and some are not yet completed. The builder employed was Mr. S. Hall, of Nottingham.——Clophill Church, Mr. T. Smith, of Hertford, architect, and Messrs. Smith and Appleford, of Pimlico, builders, was consecrated on Tuesday week. The sum at the disposal of the architect for this church was only about 2,300*l.* There is a nave with clerestory, small chancel, and south aisle with tower and porch: sittings 520. The nave is 62 feet by $20\frac{1}{2}$; aisle same length by $12\frac{1}{2}$ wide.——The price of gas at Saffron Walden is to be reduced from 12s. 6d. to 8s. 4d. per 1,000 cubic feet.——The "comfortable asylum for convicted thieves," at Portland, as the *Bristol Journal* very truly styles it, is steadily progressing. The skeleton stage which is to extend the whole length of the proposed breakwater is in progress, and the inclined planes, screw breaks, drums, and wire ropes, are in active operation. The third hall of the prison is now tenanted by 150 convicts, and the fourth or ' D ' division hall, will be shortly occupied. The chapel for 2,000 is in a forward state, and 40 cottages for warders, &c., are also in progress. The infirmary is

supplied with salt-water baths, and the "unfortunate" tenants of the asylum are already enjoying much better health than they did on arrival at their new watering place. A " very extensive and beautiful garden has been formed facing the prison," and the salubrity of this rather " fortunate " we think, than " unfortunate " island, is highly extolled by the authority above quoted, who adds, in the spirit of our own repeated observations, " what can honest paupers think of a system which provides abundance of food, sea-baths, and other luxuries, to convicted thieves, while they, in their honest poverty, are hardly able to get bread, or must take refuge in an union-house?" But we fear it is not *paupers* alone that have reason, or at least that may be unfortunately induced, to look Portland-wards with a sigh of envy, only half suppressed by an honest repugnance to the stigma of disgrace through which alone such sterling benefits can be won and worn. Would pride of poverty into just such a Fortunate island could be instituted as a support and reward to such a spirit of militant rectitude, when unavailing in its own honest efforts!——We are glad to learn from the *Sheffield Times* that there is a considerable improvement in the staple trades of that town, and of a nature which bids fair to be permanent.——There was made last year in Manchester 350,000,000 cubic feet of gas, and in the depth of winter is required 400 retorts in full work, and an annual consumption of cannel coal of 25,000 tons. The yearly increase in the consumption seems to go on steadily, and, with each successive reduction in price, it is said to advance in a still greater measure.——On Friday in week before last the first stone of the long-talked-of new floating dock was laid at Limerick. One of the commissioners of the board of works stated that the board had but 50,000l. to complete the work, which it had taken under its own management.

NORMANTON CHURCH, DERBYSHIRE.

THE village of Normanton is built on the brow of a hill overlooking a portion of the county town of Derby, from which it is distant about 1½ mile. It was this village which gave birth to Jedediah Strutt, who invented the machine for making ribbed stockings in 1758, in conjunction with his brother-in-law, then a hosier in Derby. From this invention many most extensive fortunes have been realized. He was an ancestor of the late Joseph Strutt, who presented the Arboretum—laid out by the well-known Loudon—to the inhabitants of Derby.

The church, the foundation of which is of great antiquity, mention being made of it in the Domesday Book, stands on the highest portion, or summit of the hill, but is scarcely seen on a near approach, from the road being many feet lower than the surrounding ground. From the churchyard may be discerned the churches of Little-Over (itself a curiosity), Spondon, and Shelbourne. The churchyard, though apparently full, has few memorials of any interest. There is one, however, exceedingly novel in design, having perpendicular tracery filling in its margins. The quatrefoil, shield, &c., are well chiselled. The church stands east and west, and consists of nave, tower, and chancel, having a north and south doorway in nave, but no porch. The windows are few, and scarcely light the building sufficiently. The chancel fell down, or was removed, some years since, an ugly excrescence being built on a portion of the original stone walls which was preserved. The nave and tower are of stone, doubtless obtained from the Swarkstone quarries, being similar to that used in the construction of the Swarkstone-bridge, which is three-fourths of a mile in length, and not more than 3 miles distant. The spire has apparently not been erected more than thirty years. What it was originally it is hard to say, as no traces or sketches are extant. The tower is not so wide as the nave,—the nave wall being finished on either side as a buttress. The chancel is opened to the nave by a semicircular arch, the crown of which has become much flattened; it is totally devoid of ornament, having merely a bead worked on the arris. The church was evidently a Norman erection, but has had so much of churchwardens' alterations and improvements, that it is difficult to find many traces of its original state. The southern doorway had a circular head, but was pulled down and re-erected with an equilateral arch, the chevron moulding of the original being worked around it in small pieces as a label, producing a curious effect. The corbel tables of roof of nave, with its grotesque heads, seem to have alone remained entire. They are, however, much injured by Time,—that destroyer of all things, and yet more sparing than the hands of those mortals whom it is continually crushing. With the exception of a small window in the tower, the whole of them are interpolations.

Not being able to obtain the key, save by a three miles walk, I was compelled to limit my scrutiny to a glance in at the windows, so cannot describe the roof, or the monuments, &c., of which there seem to be a few.

　　　　　　　　　　　　　　　　　W. W.

SMITHFIELD MARKET.—The Parliamentary Committee to whom this matter was referred reported their opinion, after taking much evidence, that *it ought to be removed.* They refer to the importance of a large open space, such as Smithfield, in the midst of a densely-populated district, and express a hope that in any contemplated alterations the greater portion of the present open space may be retained. The House of Commons do not seem disposed to attend to their committee's recommendation.

STEPS TO PULPIT, PISA CATHEDRAL.

STEPS TO PULPIT IN THE DUOMO AT PISA.

THESE original and beautiful steps are not the least interesting remains of Giovanni da Pisa's *capo d' opera,* the marble pulpit in the duomo of that city. It was one of the many glories of that noble pile ruined by the disastrous fire of 1596 (the plumbers, as usual, were the cause of the mischief). It was completely crushed by the falling in of the roof: the fragments collected after the fire were but few in number, and are now worked up in the present pulpit. These steps wind round a column in the nave, against which the pulpit is placed.

RATING GAS COMPANIES.

The rating of the property belonging to gas, water, and railway companies, to the relief of the poor, being now so much in dispute, every decision thereon is of importance.

On Friday, July 6th, a decision was made in the case of an appeal of the Phœnix Gas Company, against the assessment of their property to the poor-rate, in the parish of Greenwich, which assessment had been increased when the last rate was made, in April last, from the sum of 1,680l. to 5,671l. (both sums including the station and mains), without any alterations having been made by the company, to increase the value of their property in that parish.

The Phœnix Gas Company have very extensive *buildings* and *plant,* the mains extending into twenty-three parishes, with large manufacturing stations, at Vauxhall, Bankside, and Greenwich; also store stations in Kennington-lane and Wellington-street.

The parish officers, by the advice of their surveyor, Mr. Charles Penfold, valued the property belonging to the company, in the parish of Greenwich, as separate and distinct from the rest of the company's works and mains (although the whole is most intimately connected, also managed by one board of directors, having one office and only one set of clerks and officers), by which scheme, the whole value of the station and mains in Greenwich were assessed to the poor-rate of that parish, as well as a portion of the value of the gas rental of the other parishes, supplied with gas from the Greenwich station, for the reason that the gas used in these parishes passed through the mains laid in Greenwich parish. They then proceeded to ascertain the net rateable value, by assuming the rent which a tenant would give, "from year to year," for the whole property in Greenwich, with the right of supplying that and the other parishes now supplied from the Greenwich station, and this assumed rent was arrived at by finding the power of production (not the quantity produced), of gas, at the station in Greenwich; the result was—

Net rateable value of the station	£2,000
Do. of the mains in Greenwich, supplying gas in Greenwich only	2,924
Do. of the mains in Greenwich, supplying Lewisham	154
Do. of the mains in Greenwich, supplying other parts	593
Total net rateable value	£5,671

The surveyor of the Company, Mr. Lee, contended that the whole of the property belonging to the Company must be considered as one concern, and taken as a whole, and so assessed to the poor-rate,—or, that the rent which a tenant would give, "from year to year," for all the stations, stores, and mains, in the 23 parishes, must first he assumed : that the basis of this assumed rent should be the gas actually produced at the three stations, and sold in the 23 parishes; and from the rent, so ascertained, must be obtained the net rateable value of the whole property.

Then, that the net rateable values of all the stations and stores must be assumed and deducted from the net rateable value of the whole property, the balance being the net rateable value of all the mains in the twenty-three parishes, and that this balance should be divided in proportion to the quantity of mains in each parish,—or, that the stations and stores should be rated in the parishes in which they may happen to be situate, in proportion to their present value, and the net rateable value of all, deducted from the amount of the net rateable value of the whole property, including the stores and stations, and that the remainder should be divided amongst the twenty-three parishes, in proportion to the quantity of fixed apparatus situate in each parish, instrumental in earning gas rent,—the result would be :—

Net rateable value of all the stations £5,438
Ditto of all the mains 3,320

Total net rateable value of the whole property............. £8.758

Net rateable value of the Greenwich station £1,316
Ditto of the street mains in Greenwich .. 314

Net rateable value of all the property in Greenwich £1,630

The total present value of all the stations being...........................£173,238
Ditto of all the street mains........... 105,761

Total present value of all the property £278,999

The present value of the station at Greenwich being......................... £41.953
Ditto of the street mains at ditto....... 11,048

Total value of the property in Greenwich £53,001

The court decided that the assessment must first be made on the whole of the property in the twenty-three parishes, as a whole, in accordance with "The Queen v. The Great Western Railway Company," and that it was to be then divided, as contended for by the company's surveyor; that the net rateable value of the whole was to be 13,600l. and in Greenwich parish, 2,532l., viz., station, 2,045l., mains, 487l. The case was gone into at great length; it came on by special appointment, and it occupied the court from nine until half-past seven o'clock.

The company have appealed against the assessment of their property in various parishes several times, for the purpose of having a principle decided, but have not succeeded before this case.

RAILWAY JOTTINGS.

A CONTEMPORARY, in allusion to past expenditure on some of our greater railway works, says,—" The sum of 140,000l. has just been expended on a new station at Euston-square; 243,096l. on the bridge over the Tyne at Newcastle; 126,960l. on the bridge over the Tweed at Berwick; and in the Eastern Counties exposé, the stations at Cambridge, Ely, and Peterborough, figure respectively in the sums of 80,555l., 93,423l., and 93,234l. But these are bagatelles compared with the expenditure on the bridge over the Menai, at Bangor, which the Chester and Holyhead Directors have admitted will cost 600,000l. (some people believe it will exceed 750,000l.), although Mr. Stephenson's estimate was only 250,000l. Costly as that bridge is, it will be out-Heroded by the projected Cornish railway bridge over the Tamar, at Saltash, where the centre pier is to be sunk 80 feet deep below the water's surface at low water spring tides; and as the Government stipulated that the bridge should be carried 100 feet above the high-water surface, making a total height of upwards of 180 feet, and thereby making the works much more extensive than those at Britannia-bridge, many persons doubt that Mr. Brunel will complete Saltash-bridge for less than one million ! The whole population of Cornwall, including the Scilly islands, was, by the last census, only 341,279." The amount of some of this heavy expenditure we were ourselves the first to point attention to; but, though we have no desire to defend what may appear to be improper or imprudent outlay, or to commend any generation of men for going beyond its means, still it would be well, in fairness, to consider, that the fruits of such expenditure in the present instance are great and noble works, that future generations may not only benefit by, but honour the present for rearing, as a monument of their own greatness, —not blame them for as any thing like a monument of folly. The extravagance will be forgotten while its fruits will carry forth the unsullied renown of the present generation into future ages.——Far other may be the fate of some of those who have reared up vast but vanishing monuments to themselves out of the hard-earned wealth of the present generation. Though among the first to warn we were among the last to reproach. But far as past exposures may have exceeded previous belief, the present seem really past all belief. We are now assured that Mr. Hudson's cool moral courage went even so far as to convert 937½ shares, presented to him as a gift by one of those Companies over whom he reigned with his iron rule, into as many thousands and more; having sold out under the cloak of these gift-shares, no less than 10,894 in all, without the right to even a single share beyond the 937½ presented to him ! We sincerely hope, however, for the honour of our race and generation, that the facts on which such a statement is grounded will be ultimately found to be capable of some much more charitable interpretation. Meantime it is asserted that a profit of 145,704l. was reaped on this one transaction alone !——The Derby and Chesterfield Reporter speaks of a new cast-iron girder to be patented by Mr. Rutter, Railway Inspector, the advantages of which consist "in the construction of the joint, as the joinings of the two half beams in the middle of the span, where girders of a very long stretch cannot be cast with any safety, in consequence of breaking, and damage they might sustain thereby." The girder is suitable, it is said, for bridges (railway) of 100 feet span and upwards.—— A "railway steam-boat" of iron has been launched at Millwall, to ply as a sort of floating locomotive bridge, connecting the terminus of the Manchester, Sheffield, and Lincolnshire line with the town of Hull. It is supplied with engines of 150-horse power, and is expected to run at the rate of 15 miles an hour with passengers, who "step into a spacious saloon without the opportunity of knowing that they have left terra firma."——The erection of a large railway bridge, 75 feet 6 inches long and 30 feet high, in a week, says the Bradford Observer, may be regarded by some as an impossibility, but the feat has been all but accomplished on the Leeds and Thirsk Railway. Messrs. Garside and Parker, sub-contractors, laid the foundation of a bridge of the dimensions specified, behind the Retreat, at Armley, near Leeds, on Monday, June 25; on the evening of the following day the abutments were raised to the springing, and the centres placed for supporting the stones of the arch during its construction. On the Wednesday evening the key stones were fixed. On the following Friday the masonry on both sides was raised to the level of the cornices; and on the next day a roadway was made across the bridge, which would have been completed but for some little delay in the supply of stones for the parapet wall.—— The viaduct at Coventry on the Nuneaton line has been completed. It is a quarter of a mile in length, is on a curvature, and consists of 28 arches each 40 feet span, and 15 rise. The pier and arches are of stone.——The Leeds and Thirsk line was formally opened on Monday week. It is 39 miles in length, with stations at Kirkstall, Horsforth, Starbeck, for Harrowgate and Knaresborough, Ripley, Ripon, and other points intermediate between the termini at Leeds and Thirsk. The Bramhope tunnel, already occasionally noticed, is one of the principal works on this line. It is two miles

234 yards in length, 25 feet in height, from formation level, and 25 feet 6 in. in width. No less than 1,563,480,000 gallons of water are estimated to have been pumped out during its progress. The line of tunnelling is almost straight throughout. The Crumple Valley is crossed by a viaduct of ten semicircular arches of 5 feet span each, and at a height of about 6 feet. Another viaduct crosses the Nid Valley : it is of seven segmental arches, 5 feet span each, and rises 93 feet above the water. In crossing the Ure Valley, there is an embankment 3¾ miles long. An iron bridge 100 feet in span crosses the river Swale.

PUBLIC SCREENS—OR, PENALTIES INEVITABLE.

IN my walks through the streets of London I have been struck by the great negligence of the Board of Health, in not providing places of retirement for the wayfarer. It is unnecessary to particularize the long ranges of busy causeway that may be travelled without resort—but I believe that three miles (from Farringdon-street to Hyde Park) presents no refugium for pedestrians. In France it is ordered otherwise, and there no occasion exist for such warnings as "Commit no nuisance. I need not tell you what the real nuisance is—nor that pollutions of the most pernicious kind are driven into the narrowest alleys and amongst the densest of the poor population and that there alone, in sight of women and children, those nuisances so obnoxious to the senses of the well bred are utterly unnoticed. Impressed with the cruelty of these restrictions, and the injustice to the denizens of the humble quarters, whose vital air is vitiate even at their doors, I wrote a year back to the Woods and Forests, but was answered that "they had no funds applicable to this purpose." To whom then are confided these fiscal provisions which regard the health of citizens ? Surely so indispensable a precaution cannot be beneath the dignity of high officials. A distinguished statist once wrote "Nihil alienum mihi puto qui sit humanum,' —the natural weaknesses of humanity should be respected—a night's lodging in a police cell is rather a hard penalty for a resort to the alleviation of necessity.

In these particulars we might with advantage imitate our neighbours across the straits, and by providing sanitary retreats obviate all occasion for either the interference of the constabulary, or the standing indecencies of notices and inscriptions which make immundities palpable, as well as the fact that the fashion of the day is mock modesty.

A few 7 feet slates fixed at stations not more than half a mile apart, with retreats, would obviate more irregularity than the whole police force, and at the same time conduce to the public health and decorum.

QUONDAM.

ON A METHOD OF COMMENCING DRAWING.

THE following system * has been pursued for about twelve months with the children between the ages of six and twelve of a village school in Kent, chiefly with the view of promoting habits of correct observation, and of exercising the faculties. The lessons were given once and sometimes twice, a-week, with occasional intervals; and they occupied about an hour each.

First Stage : outline Drawing with Chalk on a Black Board, large Slate, or common Board —This material was adopted because it enforces a bold style, and precludes small drawing. More sketches can be made in a given time than with any other material : it can be erased with the greatest ease, and it is very cheap; but care must be taken that its facilities do not cause heedlessness and incorrectness.

I. Drawing from Simple Objects that require no Perspective ; such as simple leaves, large feathers, a table-knife, gimlet, class knife, hammer, apple, pear, turnip, carrot, onion, spade, shovel, painter's brush, flat brush, oval palette, hatchet, mallet, saw, saw, &c.

When simple forms can be sketched with tolerable ease and correctness, the pupils commence

* According to the Journal of Design.

II. Sketching Objects in which *Perspective* is gradually introduced; such as cups, jugs, bottles, shoes, boots, caps, hats, large shells, candlesticks, pincers, coal-scuttles, boxes and books in various positions, open and shut, a twig with several leaves, a simple flower, table, chair, &c.

III. Subsidiary Exercises, introduced occasionally for the sake of variety and the discipline they offer to the faculties in new directions.

a. Drawing, from Memory, objects previously drawn in I. and II.

b. Drawing from Outline Copies of familiar objects—at first not requiring perspective, as side of a cottage, dog-kennel, bridge, tomb, well, wheelbarrow, very easy animals and figures, geometrical figures, Roman and writing letters, &c.

c. Drawing small with a pencil on slate, from objects and copies.

d. Inventing and drawing very simple borders, patterns, and other ornaments, the idea occasionally taken from a leaf.

e. Drawing, from memory, objects that have not been drawn from nature or copies.

f. Petty compositions, as nurse and infant, man and pig, gardener digging or rolling, &c. Exercises *d*, *e*, and *f*, were chiefly confined to pupils in the second part of this stage.

Second Stage. Light and Shade: Rough drawing on brown paper, or coarse coloured paper, with black Conté chalk, putting in the light with white chalk, the paper serving for the middle tint. This appears to be the most rapid method practicable by a child, who loses patience and spirit, and fails, if the sketch is elaborate and takes much time.

I. Drawing common Objects that show light and shade very distinctly, as an apple, pear, orange, cup, jug, bottle, glass, vase, geometrical solids, book and box open and shut, models of animals, heads, &c., at first singly; afterwards two or more arranged picturesquely, and in reference to light, shade, shadow, and reflection, &c.

II. Drawings from Copies of objects not readily accessible, as houses, animals, the human figure, &c.

III. Subsidiary Exercises, occasionally introduced:—

a. Sketching in outline, on black board, from memory, objects in I. and II.

b. Inventing patterns and ornaments, as in *d*, Stage I.

c. Drawing from memory, on black board, as in *e*, Stage I.

d. Original compositions, as in *f*, Stage I.

e. Drawing on white paper with lead pencil, small, to promote neatness.

This course of instruction has not yet been pursued further with the children. It appears to give great pleasure to all the pupils, about thirty in number, who have pursued it, even to those who are the slowest and least apt. It would probably be the quickest method of instructing youths and adults in drawing, independent of its effect as *a discipline for the faculties*, which last has been the main object with regard to the children who have used it. The lead pencil, sepia, and colour would, it is thought, follow with unusual ease and power, in those cases where such articles could be purchased.*

* *Common White Chalk* has been found the best material for beginners: it admits of large outline sketching only; forbids all but the most essential lines; can be marked and rubbed out with the greatest facility; and allows a greater number of drawings to be made in a lesson than could be done with equal correctness and spirit by the use of any other material. As far as the pupil goes he succeeds, though in a rough way; and this puts him in good spirits for future exertions. The drawings certainly do not last; but a beginner seldom cares to keep his first rude essays. A stick of prepared chalk may be used; but a rough piece, such as carpenters employ, answers perfectly well. The chalk should be held between the thumb and the two first fingers; not put into a crayon-holder; and it should not be cut to a fine point.

Chalking Board.—Any hard, dark surface will answer for chalking on: the most convenient is a board or mill-board painted of any dark colour, or a large slate. For the youngest pupils, the board should not be less than 14 inches by 20; and it should be larger for youths and adults. These three materials would cost nearly the same (*i. e.* from 1s. to 1s. 6d.), supposing the slate be not framed. Wood and mill-board are lighter and more portable than slate, but require painting in a peculiar manner, as common black paint is not sufficiently hard. The mill-board also must be very good and exceedingly thick; otherwise it is certain to cockle, that is to warp, exceedingly. Chalking lessons may also be given on common school-desks painted of a dark colour; or on painted walls, especially wainscots; or on long painted deals; or, to young pupils, on the seats of tall benches. If it be desirable to preserve the sketches, they can be drawn on coarse brown paper; but this substance does not allow the chalk lines to be erased completely.

Rubber.—The best material for rubbing out chalk lines is a rubber made by rolling several feet of coarse list. A coarse cloth or a soft brush also answers.

METROPOLITAN COMMISSION OF SEWERS.

A SPECIAL court was held on Thursday, the 12th inst., at the court house, Greek-street. The Earl of Carlisle in the chair.

The State of St. Giles's.—A voluminous report was presented to the court by Mr. Gotto, on the state of Church-lane, and other places in that locality. It represented them as being the resort of the most depraved and filthy class of the community, and the remnant of the mass of buildings known as the "Rookery." Its condition was described as unparalleled in London, and a perfect disgrace to any civilised community; but while the most fearful degradation of the human character is exhibited, there apparently exists an universal sense of their sanitary danger, and a sincere desire for relief: interest and gratitude are expressed on every hand at even the prospect of being placed under circumstances affording the opportunity of cultivating cleanliness, comfort, and privacy, of which they are now wholly deprived. It also appeared that an extended system of sub-letting is carried on; the houses in the first instance being let for a term of years at about 20*l.* per annum; they are then re-let house by house; these are again sub-let out in rooms, and, lastly, the separate beds are underlet to tramps and others at about 3d. per night,—producing annually about 70*l.* per house per annum. The number of persons residing on this spot is described as being greater in proportion than in any other part of the metropolis. Ninety-five houses stand on 1 and 1-10th acre, with an average population of 2,580, or 30 persons to each house. The report concluded with various suggestions for the improvement of the neighbourhood, to be effected by means of an improvement-rate chargeable on the property for twenty-two years, to the amount of 795*l.* 5s. 8d., or an annual rate, to repay interest and principal, of 51*l.* 13s. 9d.

Lord Ebrington moved—"That, as a temporary relief, all the cesspools be immediately emptied, and the streets, yards, and courts washed out: that the necessity of thorough lime-whiting be immediately represented to the ground landlords."

Mr. Leslie wished to know from the surveyor whether there had been any communication with the landlords of the property?

Mr. Gotto said he had understood the owners were quite willing to co-operate with this commission for the proposed works, but that they were unwilling to pay for them all at once.

An agent who attended for Sir John Hanmer said he had no doubt that Sir John would be delighted that these steps were in contemplation, and that he would be quite ready to acquiesce in any measures for the improvement of his property.

The Earl of Carlisle thought it might admit of a question how these rates should be raised, if the houses were afterwards pulled down.—Lord Ebrington apprehended that it signified little whether a charge for the improvement of property were made all at once, or spread over a series of years.—Mr. Chadwick believed the same course was pursued with regard to land under the Inclosure Commission.

Mr. Bullar could not agree that this was a parallel case. If Sir John Hanmer were called upon to pay at once for these improvements, and he afterwards pulled the houses down, he would in that case be the only loser; but under the improvement rate, if the houses were pulled down and the space thrown into the street, the ratepayers would then have to pay these rates in addition to their ordinary charges. It was under consideration the propriety of applying to Parliament for fresh powers on the subject of improvement rates.—Mr. Leslie denied they had any power to charge the owners of land, and thought the proper course would be to summon the owners, and to hear what they intended to do as regarded their property, and to let them do it in their own way. He deprecated their practice of coming to a conclusion first, and then asking the consent of parties afterwards. This court had no power whatever to cleanse private cesspools on any premises without the consent of the owners.

Several other commissioners having expressed their opinions, the motion was put and agreed to, and resolutions were subsequently adopted to enable the owners to do the works themselves, and empowering the officers of the commission to proceed if the owners did not.

The Drainage of Pheasant-court, Gray's Inn-lane.—The assistant-surveyor presented a report on the state of the houses in this neighbourhood, which represented them as being extremely filthy and disgusting, and crowded to excess with persons of the poorest classes. In one case eighty persons occupied one house, several others upwards of seventy, and the average number of the whole varied from thirty to thirty-five persons in each house. The report stated that, notwithstanding this herding together of persons, the windows were frequently unopened for days together, there was little or no drainage, and a tainted and pestiferous atmosphere. Within a few days six fatal cases of cholera had occurred in the neighbourhood. The report concluded with recommendations that the houses should be lime whited, the cesspools abolished, and a proper drainage and supply of water laid down, the expense of which to be met by an improvement rate on the property.

Mr. Chadwick moved the adoption of the report, and believed that the system of charging improvements over a series of years would be found by the parishes to be a cheap course to take upon themselves for improvements, with but a small amount of risk.—Mr. Leslie again deprecated the principle of the court taking upon themselves charges that ought to be borne by the owners of the property; and one result of their hasty proceedings was the suit in Chancery, which would be attended with the most frightful expenditure. He thought the question ought to have been taken up by the Board of Health.—Mr. Chadwick said the Board of Health had no power to prosecute for a neglect of their orders, but in every case where cholera had broken out they found a complete violation of their instructions.—It was then resolved—"That the facts as to the deplorable state of Pheasant-court, Gray's Inn-lane, be forthwith communicated to the local authorities, and that they be requested to carry into effect those of the remedies with which they are chargeable."

Several other detail resolutions on the subject were agreed to. Immediately upon these resolutions being carried, the following letter was handed into the court from Mr. Gotto:—

"My Lords and Gentlemen,—I beg most respectfully to call the attention of the court to the several works which have been ordered as urgent, upon reports in which I have either been associated with other officers or prepared by myself, viz., Gulston-street, Sydenham, Church-lane, and Pheasant-court, Gray's-Inn-lane, as the court might suppose, these works, after they have been ordered, are immediately commenced. It is in order to be relieved from the responsibility and delay which might be thrown upon me in the event of the outbreak of cholera, which is daily expected in such places, that I take the liberty of informing the court, that for want of bye-law regulations and other instructions, no steps whatever have been or can be taken in cases ordered some time ago; and that the works ordered to-day will be under the same circumstances."

A conversation ensued upon the difficulty of getting together a quorum of the Bye-Laws Committee, the legal members of it being from town on the circuit, or otherwise actively engaged. The following resolution was finally adopted:—

"That the notices applicable to the works ordered at this court be prepared by the solicitors, and, on approval by the standing counsel, be made use of."

The Bermondsey Mill Streams.—A letter was read from Mr. Rains, addressed to the Earl of Carlisle, asking for compensation for the destruction of his property in the stoppage of the above mill-streams, by order of the commissioners.

Mr. Bullar believed counsel were strongly of opinion that the Vice-Chancellor had no power to order an injunction; and even were he to do so, it would be dissolved by the Lord Chancellor, under the power of the 61st section.

(The 61st section recites "that the commissioners may undertake any work of any description without any notice or other proceeding hereinbefore required, where, from flood, storm, or other urgent cause, the commissioners shall deem it necessary that the delay occasioned by such proceedings should be avoided.")

Mr. Leslie believed that they were not justified in spending the ratepayers' money for law proceedings, and it was the opinion of barristers that, whether right or wrong, as they had commenced the work without notices, they would have to pay the expenses. In fact, they might consider themselves fortunate if they got out of the "mess" for 1,000*l.* This was one of the evils that had arisen from business being done in committee instead of in open court.

Mr. Chadwick denied that any such expense would be incurred in these proceedings. Their surveyor had received general orders to stop up what they believed to be the cause of death.

Consideration postponed.

The Cholera.—Dr. Southwood Smith wished to know, as regarded districts where cholera had broken out, what processes for flushing and cleansing were in operation or in contemplation. He regretted that they were not in a better condition to meet the evil by permanent works, as they might have been, had more cordiality existed amongst the members of the court. As they were not, however, ready to bring forward permanent measures, he hoped that temporary relief would be immediately given in those districts that were suffering the most.

Mr. Lovick said in Surrey and Kent, forty men were engaged in flushing, in addition to fifty previously employed. Several thousand cubic yards of filth had been removed during the last week or two.

Mr. Chadwick said it should be known that only

one-fourth of the evaporating surface of drainage was under the control of the commissioners from sewers, as one-fourth arose from cesspools, and the remaining two-fourths from house drains.

The Earl of Carlisle said there was considerable odour from the drains at the end of the town to which he was called by his duties, and wished to know if there was any method of trapping them to meet the evil.

Mr. Chadwick said a plan for this purpose was before the Committee, but the difficulty was, that in trapping the drains, the gases were forced into the houses. In fact the offensive gases had been driven from the mouth of the sewer in the Thames as far back as Islington, at which point the sewers were perfectly clean.—The question was referred to the surveyors.

Miscellanea.

THE IRON TRADE.—In the face of the recent general stultification of the authority of the old quarterly meetings, a renewed attempt is being made, on the old model, to patch it up once more. The *Times*, for instance, lately so justly sickened with the general want of dependence to be placed on such an authority as a faithful index to the state of the trade at large, is now assured, notwithstanding the *general* repudiation of that authority by the trade itself, that "the first-rate firms, such as" so and so advertised, "invariably adopt and maintain the prices fixed at quarterly meetings, but the *small and needy houses* [all in short who dared to question the authority of those who set themselves up as the *élite* were "small and needy houses," who] during the quarter, not unfrequently, as heretofore, make reductions to suit exigencies." This used-up mode of enforcing a tyranny by threats of a stigma, however, is now unavailing. The old quarterly *nurse* of "high prices" and "great masters" may quote her *authority*—*ad infinitum*, but the Gamp game is up. That authority was recently found out to be nowhere, and it is too late now to give it a local habitation and a name. To stigmatize *the trade at large*—which *did* recently repudiate both the old quarterly and her authority,—as "small and needy" is going rather too far. Even as an advertisement of—so and so—first-rate firms, the attempt is futile. As to late proceedings and present prospects, what says one of the most respectable of the old advocates of high prices, one whose own very words are now being used about "small and needy" houses alone selling at comparatively *low* prices? "During the late quarterly meetings," says this veteran advocate of "great masters," *Aris's Birmingham Gazette*, "the apprehensions we last noticed of a further decline in prices have unfortunately been realised, and the nominal rates concluded upon at the preliminary deliberations of the iron masters, at Handsworth, have been altogether disregarded—still no accession of activity has ensued," &c. It is high time, then, that the trade at large—with which the quarterly faction of this split camp can no longer be identified since it stigmatizes all but itself as not only "small and needy" but as sellers of "an inferior quality" of iron—were preparing to appoint some new and honester and less impracticable index, since even the very highest upholder of the old quarterly dictum now repudiates its authority altogether.

ERRORS IN AWARDS.—In an arbitration between a builder at March, as plaintiff, and certain commissioners of the White Fen district in Benwick, the arbiter, an architect at St. Neot's, had inadvertently omitted formally to award a sum of 257*l.* for extras to the plaintiff, about which there was no dispute; but afterwards intimated the inadvertence to the defendants, and gave affidavit thereof. The defendants, however, insisted on the strict and literal terms of the award, and argued before Lord Denman, that the decision ought to be sustained, "it being a principle not to disturb awards which on the face of them appear correct." His lordship said, that if a straining in the law as to such decisions was ever justifiable, it was in this case, otherwise a great and obvious injustice would be done to the plaintiff, and after making some strong remarks on the conduct of the defendants in seeking to take advantage of such an error, his lordship made the rule absolute for setting aside the award.

OSMASTON MANOR-HOUSE, DERBYSHIRE, is a great pile of building, comprising, besides numerous suites of apartments, a wilderness of corridors, galleries, arcade, towers, chapel, school, riding school, conservatory, tennis court, bakery, laundries, dairies, kitchens, stables, coachhouses, and all sorts of other appliances, scientific, economical, and convenient. The pile has been already about three years in building, and is not yet completed, although the proprietor, Mr. Wright, and his numerous family, have recently got access to a portion of it. The whole, with some little exception, is fireproof, and comprises extensive arrangements for heating, smoke conduction, &c. All the smoke from every quarter of the buildings is collected by flues into a tunnel 600 feet in length, which conducts it underground, through a very extensive range of cellars, to a smoke tower in the kitchen garden, 21 feet square and 150 feet high, with an iron staircase to the top and a circular brick shaft within. Along the same line of cellars is a railway, 300 feet long, with curves, turntables, &c., and a coal lift, with hydraulic machinery for lifting through four stories in height. Water, heated by five boilers, weighing 15 tons, is conducted all over the premises by four to five miles of pipes. Under the dining-room is a cistern for 30,000 gallons of water. In the cellars alone, including wine cellars with strong doors, are about a million and a quarter of bricks, and throughout the buildings are 350 tons weight of cast-iron, in girders and other heavy castings. At the west corner of the mansion stands the fresh-air tower, 65 feet in height. There are also a flag tower and a clock tower,—in all, four massive and conspicuous towers imbedded in the mass of building. The east side of the mansion occupies an elevation 333 feet in length. Domestic processes, such as washing, spit turning, &c., are done by machinery, worked by a large water-wheel. At a pond three pumps, also worked by water power, force water up hill into the reservoir from which the house is supplied. The design of the building, which has been executed in sombre blue limestone, relieved by gritstone doorways, window jambs, moulds, and ornaments, is by Mr. J. H. Stevens, of Derby, and the main part of the works have been done by workmen employed by Mr. Wright himself. At a substantial entertainment lately given by the latter to the former and their wives, &c., nearly 500 persons assembled, and a splendid Bible and Prayer Book were presented in the name of the workmen to their employer, who thanked them in an unpretending speech, replete with kindly feeling. A silver inkstand was at same time presented to the Rev. W. B. Hayne, who had lectured to them every Wednesday during the progress of the works. The village and its church and school are also chiefly of recent construction, the whole being intended, as we are told, to form a sort of model village.

TELEGRAPHIC COMMUNICATION. — We have occasionally drawn attention to Mr. Whishaw's exertions in the promotion of telegraphic communication, and recently had an opportunity of glancing over a variety of his arrangements in the Music-hall, Store-street, among which were exhibited many details that certainly seemed well adapted to facilitate the end in view. The French Government Commission appointed to proceed to London and examine the various systems of electric telegraphs here, would do well to visit and examine Mr. Whishaw's modifications and inventions. We may mention that the Metropolitan Central Terminus of the English line of telegraphs is to be put into immediate communication with the General Post-office, by an extension of the wires to St. Martin's Le Grand, and that the first Irish line of telegraph has just been constructed on the Great Southern and Western Railway for a couple of miles from the Kingsbridge terminus.

PATENT DECORATIVE GLASS.—We mentioned when speaking of one of Lord Rosse's soirées, some specimens of this glass. Since then we have had an opportunity of seeing something more of it. The process employed gives representations of net or other curtains with decorative borders, lace patterns, and bunches of flowers, and the singular cheapness of the glass thus prepared will doubtless lead to a considerable use of it.

PROJECTED WORKS.—Advertisements h[…] been issued for tenders, by 31st inst., […] the erection of a new workhouse for the Tr[…] Union, Cornwall; by 24th, for paving that p[…] of the New-road, west of Tottenham-co[…] road, in the parish of St. Pancras, with gra[…] cubes; by Aug. 2nd, for the erection of a […] church at Blendworth, Hampshire; by 21st i[…] for the several works to be performed in erect[…] witnesses' rooms, &c. at the Grand J[…] Chamber, Winchester; by 24th, for the e[…] tion of schools at Harlow; by a date not s[…] cified, for alterations at No. 125, Lo[…] Marsh, Lambeth; by 24th, for painting […] Chelmsford Workhouse, &c.; by 25th, fo[…] supply of British iron, files, and rasps, pa[…] &c., for the East-India Company; and by 2[…] for the re-construction of the drainage […] water supply and for alterations, &c., at Cu[…] field Workhouse.

AGENCY ON TRANSFER OF ESTAT[…] DOUBLE DEALING.—An action was rece[…] brought before the Lord Chief Baron, on […] home circuit, by Mr. Austin, a house agen[…] Conduit-street, Hyde-park, against Mr. Sp[…] a party for whom he had purchased an es[…] named Craven-hill Lodge, at Bayswater, for […] commission of 2½ per cent. on the sale. […] plaintiff's claim was resisted on the ground […] he had no sooner contracted with the defend[…] than he went to Mr. Lahee, the well-kn[…] eminent house-agent, and offered to provid[…] purchaser for the same property, on condit[…] that *he* would give him a commission on […] part of the owner, for whom Mr. Lahee ac[…] and that he had accordingly contracted w[…] Mr. Lahee for 25*l.*, the full half of Mr. Lah[…] own fee, offered by the seller. The C[…] Baron, in summing up the case, characteri[…] the plaintiff's conduct as unjustifiable and […] honourable, and said he had no doubt tha[…] had thus in law done away with the origi[…] contract. The jury were of the same opini[…] and the plaintiff, therefore, by running w[…] the hare and hunting with the hounds, […] both his case and his character, a verdict be[…] at once returned against him.

ART-UNION OF LONDON.—If there be […] 20,000 subscribers to the London Art-Un[…] for this current year we shall be surprised. […] council have obtained the completed plates […] C. W. Sharp and W. D. Taylor, of Webst[…] capital pictures, "The Smile" and "[…] Frown." These will be *delivered on paym[…] of the subscription*; and those who subsc[…] earliest will get the best impressions. […] addition to these every member will recei[…] series of etchings from original drawings, il[…] trating Shakspeare's "Seven Ages," by […] Maclise, R.A., and still have a chance in […] general distribution of prizes. When we […] our readers that the pair of plates after Web[…] alone were originally to have been publis[…] in the ordinary way at *two guineas* the pair […] we are correctly informed, the progra[…] must be considered a tempting one. […] arrangement, too, will enable the council t[…] similarly in advance for future years, and […] we mistake not, will gain for the society, […] consequently, for art and artists, even […] extended success than that which it has […] joyed for the last thirteen years.

FALL OF HOUSES.—At Goulston-str[…] Whitechapel, facing the East London B[…] and Washhouses, two of a row of seven […] eight lofty houses, all occupied, suddenly […] into a complete wreck on Sunday forenc[…] burying occupants and furniture, the for[…] much injured, though none killed; and […] whole of the remainder of the row show[…] signs of also falling, the tenants were prude[…] ordered out without even being allowed to […] their furniture. The giving way of the w[…] of a cesspool are supposed to have led to […] fall. But sometime back one of the same […] came down and destroyed several persons.—[…] At Westminster, too, on Thursday week, t[…] houses in Strutton-ground, corner of Artill[…] row, fell in with all their furniture, &c., aft[…] loud crackling noise had given the inm[…] warning to save their lives.

THE SEWERS OF LONDON.—The re[…] on the subterranean survey of the metropol[…] sewers, has just been published, and sh[…] that the majority of them are in a very foul […] in many cases, dangerous state.——A Bi[…] amend the new Sewers' Act has been re[…] second time.

STAINED GLASS FOR CANTERBURY CA-
THEDRAL.—A lozenge, for a window in Can-
erbury Cathedral, painted by Mr. J. A. Gibbs,
of the Hampstead-road, was submitted to us a
ew days ago. It is intended to be placed
amongst the old glass there, and was painted
in accord with it, including the bad drawing,
he effects of age, and even the appearance of
accumulated dust against the leads! For the
purpose in question, we have nothing to say
against this, and would compliment the artist
in the attainment of a considerable degree of
ichness in colour. As a general practice,
however, we should grieve over and condemn,
rather than praise, such imitations. Mr. Gibbs
s about to execute a window for Ely.

THE CONVERGING SYSTEM OF DRAINAGE.
—Mr. Austin has addressed a letter to us (re-
erence to which was accidentally omitted last
week), complaining of a misapprehension of
his plan, to the extent, that instead of the con-
ents of the "sumps" being distributed from
ime to time, the discharge would be going on
without intermission :—" These ' sumps,' " he
says, " would, in fact, be no larger than what
s before any one man's door in any leading
thoroughfare in the metropolis, in the shape
of about 20 feet length of first-class sewer ;
and, as they would be very few and far between (one only being quite sufficient for the
whole city of Westminster), covered over and
removed from sight, and secured from the
escape of bad odour, the amount of their inconvenience may be readily determined. The
discharge from these ' sumps ' into the country
would not be from ' time to time,' but constantly, steadily, always going on without intermission." Mr. Austin has published some
observations on Mr. Phillips's tunnel scheme,
but we must look at the whole matter together
hereafter.

WARMLEY CHURCH AND PARSONAGE.—
At Warmley, in the parish of Siston, near
Bristol, the foundation-stone of a new church
was laid on the 3rd inst. by Mrs. F. Dickenson,
of Siston Court. The stone was one from the
neighbourhood, but under it was a fragment
of the ' rock of ages' from Mount Zion. The
village of Warmley and its neighbouring district will thus be erected into a new parish.
The late rector of Siston and his friends have
subscribed over 800l. towards the church,
which, with the parsonage, will cost about
4,000l., upwards of half of which has been
already assured, to carry out the design. Mr.
J. P. Harrison is the architect.

YORKSHIRE ARCHITECTURAL SOCIETY.—
The quarterly committee-meeting of this society was held on the 5th instant at the rooms
in Minster-yard, York; the Hon. and Rev.
P. Y. Savile, rector of Methley, in the chair.
The following grants were made, namely, 10l.
for restoration of oak roof over nave of Methley Church, and 3l. for stem of font at
Nafferton Church.

INSTITUTION OF BUILDERS' FOREMEN.—
We are glad to hear that since the last anniversary dinner, the progress of this useful
institution has been very satisfactory. Professor Cockerell amongst others sent a subscription last week.

TO CORRESPONDENTS.

Received. — " Ajax," " Middlesex Rate-payer " (the
amount of tender for Middlesex Lunatic Asylum is, we believe, correct. It was given in our pages, with some remarks,
at we have not time to refer); " F. B. L." " House Proprietor," " R. H." Lancashire (we cannot advise the adop-
on of the design in question). " An Admirer," " F. C."
next week), " E. B." " W. W." " W. N." (shall appear), " W. Y.," " J. H.," Pimlico (shall appear). " D. C."
will find we have already referred to the subject). " H.C.C."
will find the letter at office; the suggestion has been
item made). " W. H.," City (shall hear from us).
V. H.," " J. A. Y.," " H. P." West Ham (the club
by take a title without fee). " H. B. M." (infers errone-
usly). " J. Q." (the RIS. has reached us). " F. Y. K."
we have no intention to reprint). " Witness for Plaintiff,"
A. W. R." (we avoid recommending). " The Royal
itchings. A Statement of Facts," by J. L. Judge (Lon-
on, Strange, Paternoster-row); " Remarks on the subject
of an Asylum Harbour," by the late Mr. John Harvey
Farmouth, Benson, and Harling); " Letter to his Grace
he Duke of Buccleugh, K.G., on the Sanitation at Putney
college," by the Rev. C. Morgan Cowie, M.A. (London :
ralton, Cockspur-street); " A Letter to the Right Hon.
Henry Labouchere, M.P., on Railways," by C. Locock
Webb (London : Smith, Elder, and Co., Cornhill).

" Books, Prices, and Addresses."—We have not time to
point out books or find addresses.

'NOTICE. — All communications respecting *advertisements* should be addressed to the "Publisher," and not to
he " Editor;" all other communications should be addressed to the EDITOR, and *not* to the Publisher.

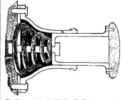

No. CCCXXXVIII.

ITURDAY, JULY 28, 1849.

HE space necessarily occupied in every number of our journal by architectural and decorative illustrations, essays on matters connected with our speciality, information and opinions on the current of the day,—striving, as we do, to give aders early information of all that occurs i our province,—leaves us sometimes in with our notices of published works. s the case just now; and we find on the a whole pile of books, concerning which aders ought to know something. Amongst we have from America, where attention to rapidly awakening, " Hints on Public tecture," by Robert Dale Owen,*—a volume, profusely illustrated, containnuch interesting matter and many just ons. It is true these are adopted rather struck out; moreover, there is a want of gement which lessens the value of the ; nevertheless, it cannot fail to have ful effect in America. It proceeds from lding committee appointed to select plans rect a structure for the Smithsonian Inion, an important educational foundation ennsylvania. Their first intention was ly to give the public information as to the and style of architecture selected for the ing, but hints in regard to public archie, and information as to the merit and f different manners, having accumulated z their inquiry, they determined on puthe whole into a connected form, and they ted the materials to their chairman, Mr. , for that purpose.

e heads of the chapters will give a general of the contents of the book. 1, is ching some general conditions of excelin architecture," wherein the writer says —" It is among the conditions of a true ecture, that it mould itself to the wants te domestic habits and the public cusnd the political institutions and the relisentiment of its country and its age; assort with the materials at band, subg to modifications as new materials present elves; and that it avail itself, from time to of the various aids which mathematical echanical and chemical science offer, for venience and advancement." 2, " Cong some conditions of purity in style." 'oncerning the two great divisions of r in architecture,"—that is the " post tel architecture, and arch architecture." is of the " adaptation of post and lintel cture to modern purposes," and the deduces that Grecian architecture can ecome our architecture,—" seeing that architecture should serve, not dictate; minister to the wants of man, not demand iese wants should be squared and forid and schooled down, till they conform measure of its arbitrary preconcep-

o plan, he says, in this same chapter,— strange, that, at this day, it should be ry to repeat, that, in planning any public or private, we ought to begin

from within; that we should first suffer the specific wants and conveniences demanded, to block out its forms, to determine its interior proportions, and decide the connection of its parts,—and then adjust and elaborate its architecture as its appropriate garb; into the skilful fashioning of which there enter, in truth, grace and fair proportions, but yet in such guise, that the garment shall adapt itself to the individual form it is destined to clothe; fitting well, and displaying the peculiarities of that form to the best advantage." 5, is " Of hybrid architecture." 6, " Of arch architecture." In this, acknowledging his preference for Norman and Gothic structures as models, he says,—" But as a servile copy of manners is never happy or pleasing, so is it also in architecture. ' The letter killeth, but the spirit giveth life.' If the mere copying, with unquestioning fidelity, of any models, even the best selected, sufficed to impart excellence, reputation in art might be cheaply earned. But there go, to make a true architect, far other qualifications than these: original conception, that can shake itself free of previous canons; independent thought; creative genius. The works of others must be studied, not to believe and repeat, but to probe and anatomize. There must be sought, not the offspring, but the parent; not the mere superficial details, but the hidden principle that gave birth to them. If the effect, in any old example, be good, and the combination happy, it should be the effort of the student to catch and master the spirit whence these sprang. In his hands, perchance, it may produce effects as good, combinations as happy, but stamped with the individuality of his own genius, shaped by the circumstances of country and age and climate in which he designs, and modified, in each case, by the specific purpose or occasion that may chance to call forth the exercise of his talent." 7, treats " Of anachronisms in architecture," which Mr. Owen terminates, by asserting as a principle,— " That an anachronism in architecture may be either a merit, a whim, or an offence: a merit, when the foreign feature introduced is demanded by utility, harmonises with the spirit of the style upon which it is engrafted, adds a new beauty, or corrects an old defect; a whim, when the innovation is a mere fanciful variety, adding nothing of useful, or graceful, or appropriate, beyond what the original details of the style sufficed to supply; and an offence, when the exotic is transplanted into a soil unsuited to its growth,—when the anachronism produces incongruity, not conventional merely, but natural and inherent. To the genius of the architect it must, in each case, be left, to determine the exact line of demarcation between intemperate license and barren servility." 8, is " Relative to the comparative cost of the arch and post and lintel manners, "and shows, so far as the data given may be depended on, the great advantage of the arch manner. Chapter 9 is appropriated to a description of the " Smithsonian Institution Building," to which we propose to refer separately hereafter.

The design chosen (out of thirteen submitted), is, strange to say, what is called Norman, but is in reality the round-arch style of the Rhine towns, with such additions and variations as the architect, Mr. James Renwick, Jun., of New York City, thought desirable. It has a frontage of 447 feet, and no less than nine towers of various sizes and heights, the largest being 37 feet square, and the most lofty 145 feet high. The lowest of fourteen tenders was to erect the building in

marble, " ashlar finish," 228,500 dollars, or in Seneca freestone "ashlar finish," which was ultimately selected, 205,250 dollars.

Also from America comes " A Treatise on Landscape Gardening," by A. J. Downing, of which a fourth edition, just now published by Messrs. Longman, is before us.* We should be glad to see architects paying some little attention to landscape gardening: both they and proprietors may take our word for the fact that skill in it does not come by intuition. At the present moment we know scarcely any persons who may pretend to be masters in the art. We have met lately one or two spoilers of God's earth, who take their five guineas a-day, and know no more of what they profess than any of the bevy of bumpkins who, under their direction, are at this moment marring charms and obliterating beauties.

Loudon, who did so much for landscape, always recommended those who sought his advice how best to acquire skill in it, to begin by making careful drawings, in some accessible botanic gardens, of all trees and shrubs; then to visit all the villas he could, and make memorandum plans of the general distribution of the grounds and buildings; afterwards to study and sketch natural scenery. During this time the student would of course make himself acquainted with the best published works on the subject; and he need not omit Mr. Downing's book, which prompted this remark. The study of landscape gardening lends additional interest to every country ramble, where we—

   " Pluck life's roses in the quiet fields,"

and brings a healthful as well as profitable result. To the flagging spirit of the hard worker in towns, the mere mention of *quiet fields* induces a refreshing and soothing vision. Happy those who for a time can realize it!

The second part of the " Transactions of the Society of Arts for 1847-8," is an exceedingly nice volume, illustrated by so large a number of lithographs, coloured and plain, that the cost of it must have been very great,—greater, indeed, than the amount of the subscription would justify, if it were not that no " Transactions" have been issued to the members for some time past.

It contains, amongst others, Mr. Whishaw's paper " On the application of heated currents to manufacturing and other purposes;" Mr. Hay's " Suggestions for rendering carved sandstone impervious to the action of the atmosphere" (by the application of bees' wax dissolved in spirits of turpentine,—not a new idea); Mr. Claudet's " Progress of Photography;" Mr. Cundall's paper " On Art as applied to Bookbinding;" Mr. Smith Williams's " Essay on Lithography;" Mr. Hunt's statement of the " Principles upon which the tinted glass used in the palm-house at Kew has been selected;" Mr. Findlay " On lighthouses and beacons;" and Mr. Woodcroft's general view of " Steam navigation."

Nearly all these papers were mentioned by us when brought before the society, so that it will be unnecessary now to refer to them.

As to the glass used in the palm-house, our readers will remember that it has a *green* tinge, and that the object of this is to obstruct the passage of the *scorching* rays, without interfering with any others. At the close of the paper the author suggests the use of glasses differently coloured to produce various effects. He con-

---

* " A Treatise on the Theory and Practice of Landscape Gardening, with a view to the Improvement of Country Residences; with Remarks on Rural Architecture." By A. J. Downing, author of " Designs for Cottage Residences," &c. London: Longman and Co., 1849.

siders that in all cases, germination of seeds may be accelerated by covering them with such *blue* glass as is used in making many finger glasses; and that the striking of cuttings would be quickened by similar glass shades. When there is a tendency in plants to form too much stalk or leaves, and it is desired to produce more wood, this is done by admitting as much light as possible with the smallest possible quantity of actinic power. To effect this he proposes to interpose glasses of a yellow colour, "which obstruct the passage of the chemical rays, but intercept but little light." And then, when, the vegetable functions being too active, and interfering with the reproductive powers of the plant, leaves are produced in the centre of the flower, he says all his experiments prove that the calorific radiations are the most active during the period when the plant produces flower, fruit, or seed, and "we may secure at will the absence of the luminous rays in considerable quantity, and a diminished quantity of the chemical or actinic radiations, without interfering with the heat-giving principle, by the use of glasses coloured *red* by the oxide of gold."

"Pray do not let it be said that you are *afraid* of Mr. Fergusson's pamphlet on the British Museum," kindly exhorts one correspondent, with almost fraternal anxiety for our reputation; while a second says, with less consideration but much the same real *animus*, "We (that is, he and the world) infer from your silence that you *are* afraid of repeating Mr. Fergusson's opinions of the British Museum." There are some people on this earth so curiously fashioned and attuned that they are never happy unless they are snarling and biting, and who think that all who do not pursue the same course either want honesty or courage. Strangely enough, minds of this order are usually less patient under criticism themselves than others. A well-known architect once said; "I like THE BUILDER very well,—cannot get over Saturday without seeing it; but it is too good-natured; it does not abuse living architects half enough." A remark, by a correspondent, on one of his own buildings, accidentally appeared in our pages a short time afterwards, and he never forgave the plain speaking he had desired. Enough, however, of this: we are brave enough to look with consideration and kind feeling on the efforts of contemporaries, and are not *afraid* of doing anything but what is wrong.

Mr. Fergusson's pamphlet—"Observations on the British Museum, National Gallery, and National Record Office, with Suggestions for their Improvement," * is, like other works of the same author, an able expression of the thoughts of an intelligent mind. It has been called a "stunner," and a "slasher," and such like, and so it is. We would, however, with friendly admiration, caution Mr. Fergusson against being petted into the practice of constant fault-finding, and the acquirement of a dogmatic tone which results from such a course, and is contrary to his better feelings.

The British Museum is said to be "as bad and as extravagant a building as could well be designed," (the assertion afterwards made that none of the blame rests on Sir Robert Smirke goes for nothing); of Mr. Barry's new Houses of Parliament, the public are said to be "already tired before they are finished;" and Mr. Blore's new buildings at Buckingham Palace are termed "*hideously ugly*." Now, of dealing with such men; and this we say, notwithstanding our want of admiration for the Museum, our repeated protest against the reserve which shut out the public from any knowledge of what the building was to be until it was up, and the fact that, before the additions were made to Buckingham Palace, we showed our readers that they would be very unsatisfactory. "Hideously ugly," however, is not the term, and it is against this "stunning" and "slashing" to which Mr. Fergusson will be further led, if what has been elsewhere said of his pamphlet have any influence, that we with kindliest intention dissent.

THE POTTERY AND IRON FLOORS OF PARIS.

AMONGST the improvements made in the art of building since the last "Exposition of Industry" in this town, one of the most important appears to be the application of wrought iron for flooring purposes. As this mode of employing a material we possess in such abundance, and at such very low prices, is but little known in England, some notes upon the subject may be useful. It is to be observed, firstly, that the practice of building in Paris being rarely to make floors of more than from 20 feet to 30 feet bearing, the notes are to be considered as applicable within those limits, unless otherwise specified.

There are three modes of employing wrought-iron: firstly, with wrought-iron frames, filled in with hollow pots bedded with plaster. Secondly, the wrought-iron frames are filled in with light rubble, also set with plaster. Thirdly, the main joists are made of wrought-iron, wood trimmers are introduced, and the whole framework is then bound together with tie rods.

Firstly. The use of pottery for flooring purposes is far from being of modern invention; instances being met with in the ancient Roman edifices. The round church of Ravenna has walls and a dome of pottery. But the first attempts made to introduce the use of these hollow materials into general practice appears to have been shortly before the revolution of 1789: about that time the Academy of Sciences of France made an elaborate report upon, and even began some experiments upon the force of resistance of, a system of flooring executed entirely in pots and plaster. Iron was in those days too dear to allow of its use in ordinary cases; these floors were therefore cambered. During the empire, and in the beginning of the restoration, the vaults of the spirit cellars of the Entrepôt des Vins were executed with skew backs of solid brickwork, and the arches were filled in with pottery; they were about 18 feet span. In the corridors of the Chamber of Deputies, arches from 26 feet to 27 feet span, panelled, and springing from pendentives, were executed in the same manner, as were also some of the circular-headed niches of the Madelaine.

In the palaces of Versailles and the Tuilleries pottery floors have been executed, the dimensions of which are about 66 feet in length by 33 feet in width. But for the usual dimensions of from 20 feet to 30 feet the usual course adopted is as follows:—

Framed wrought-iron girders (consisting of a chord bar $1\frac{1}{4} \times \frac{3}{4}$, with a bar of the same scantling curved so as to rise about 8 inches in the centre, maintained in their respective positions by clipping pieces, keys, and wedges) are inserted at distances of about 13 feet from centre to centre. An intermediate bar 2 inches by $\frac{3}{4}$ inch is placed between the girders, and this framework is kept in its vertical position by means of cross ties, which pass over and notch down upon the different beams; the cross ties are of $1\frac{1}{4} \times \frac{3}{4}$. Small square bars are laid upon the top of the cross ties (of $\frac{3}{4}$ inch square iron) and split rods $\frac{3}{8}$ inch square are laid upon these. In fact, a sort of net work is formed, the intervals of which are about 3 feet square, which is subsequently filled with pottery. This is done upon a centre large enough to take one bay at a time.

The pots used for flooring purposes are of
of octagonal form, but the main body
pots is cylindrical.

A floor executed with pots $7\frac{7}{8}$ inche
carried a weight of about $3\frac{3}{4}$ cwt. to th
superficial before breaking. Another
executed with pots $8\frac{11}{16}$ inches high, c
$4\frac{1}{2}$ cwt. to the foot superficial.

The French architects have also em
these hollow materials in positions whicl
allowed them to economise much room, n
for partitions and party-walls. The
authorities some time since called upo
proprietors of the theatre, then called,
Palais Royal, to separate it from the adj
tenements by a wall impervious to fire.
end was effected by building a wall,
long by 66 feet high, with hollow pots $8\frac{11}{16}$
long, bedded in plaster and rendered o
sides with the same material. Our Buildi
would hardly admit of the execution
party-wall of these dimensions, for wi
two coats of plaster it is barely 11 inches
yet experiments have shown, that for th
pose of intercepting the progress of fi
established in the most favourable cond
So satisfied are the French architects wi
mode of employing the hollow material
many of the most important modern bu
they have repeated its application; as,
stance, in the Palace of the Quai d'Orça

Secondly.—The wrought-iron floo
sometimes executed with ribs, or bars,
built into the walls every 3 feet 4 inches
when the spans are about 18 feet. Upon
cross ties of $\frac{3}{4}$ square iron are laid, and sp
3-8ths thick complete the net-work; th
ties being spaced about 3 feet 4 inche
centre to centre, the split rods about 8
apart. The whole of this framing i
filled in solid with light plaster rubble,
with plaster; care being taken not to
the works close up against the walls,
expansion of the plaster would eithe
them out, or cause the floor to sink.

Floors executed upon this system we
adopted in the year 1845, about the e
the great strike of the carpenters of
They are now becoming of general us
although they resist the transmission
they are exposed to the very serious ob
of being very heavy, of loading the
an unnecessary extent, and of bein
expensive. In England, moreover, the
or want of good plaster opposes an
mountable objection to the adoption
system. Cement might be substitute
that is still, notwithstanding the grea
nution in price, too expensive to adm
use in such great quantities.

Thirdly.—A M. Rosier, master carpe
Paris, has sent to the Exposition a sp
of a floor, which appears to obviate th
tions to the expense of the first syste
the unnecessary weight of the second.
3 feet 4 inches apart he introduces a w
iron bar, of the shape of an H laid
inches deep; the centre web $\frac{1}{4}$ inch thi
and bottom flanges $1\frac{3}{4}$ inches wide b
thick. These bars rest upon the wa
each alternate bar is tied down with
rods. Between these bars, at distance
inches from centre to centre, trimmers
$5\frac{1}{2} \times 1\frac{3}{4}$ are introduced flush with th
surfaces of the wrought-iron bars; an
side of the trimmers a straining bolt
diameter, is placed to tie the whole
together. The laths and floor boa
fastened to the trimmers, which, at t
time, afford the means of introducin
boarding and pugging. The wrou
bars weigh about 29 lbs. to 31 lbs. p
4 inches run, or between 13 and
grammes to the mètre.

These floors are exceedingly stiff, a
covered with tiles, as they commonly
they are, for all practical purposes, fi
although certainly not so efficient
respect as the floors constructed upon
previously described systems. All the
modes have the great advantage of
but little comparative depth. For ins
floor constructed upon either of the
named, need not be more than 8 inch
flooring and ceiling included, for a sp
feet; for a span of 30 feet, 10 inches
sufficient. A pottery floor of 33 f

CARVED STALLS, PERUGIA, ITALY.

OREMVS

CARVED STALLS, PERUGIA, ITALY.

We recently gave an engraving of part of : stalls in the cathedral at Fiezole, belonging the sixteenth century.* Annexed is an gant piece of ornamentation, forming part the lower stalls in the Cathedral of Perugia, Italy, which may serve to accompany the 'mer.

ARCHITECTURAL CRITICISM AND PUBLIC TASTE.†

This subject is one of considerable import-ce, not only to the architectural profession, t also to the public. Good criticism is a :ans by which the taste of the masses may greatly improved ; by its influence the blic are better enabled to judge of architec-re than when left to their own resources. 'eridan says,—" The number of those who .dergo the fatigue of judging for themselves very few indeed." This is unfortunately too 1e, and it shows the importance of public iticism, as a method of promulgating a 1owledge of art. Negative criticism is worse an useless ; it quickly pulls to pieces without .vice or reason, instead of suggesting ideas in ace of those it endeavours to destroy : the nsequence is that the reader thinks no more

* See page 266, ante.
† From a paper read at a meeting of the Architectural sociation.

upon the subject. Or, perhaps, the critic is sarcastic, and leaves the victim wincing under the stinging bite of ridicule. A fair specimen of this style is contained in a foot-note of "Chambers's Architecture," it being a criticism on the present Somerset House, written by an engraver of the name of Williams, who signed himself Anthony Pasquin. He says,

" This surprising, stupendous, and extraor-dinary heap of stones was called into order by the magic voice of that pineapple of knight-hood, Sir William Chambers, at the command of the great and sapient council of this realm, in 1774. It occupies a space of 500 feet in depth and 800 in width, and altogether is a most astonishing assemblage of contradictory objects. The entrance, or atrium, is so unap-propriate that it looks like the narrow mouth of economy, through which we grope our pas-sage to the vast stomach of national ruin."

How easy is it, for a man who is thus in-clined to pile a string of sarcasms together— how easy is it for a man thus to show his vin-dictive feeling towards another. He goes on to say,

" On the top of the corps de logis, or central part of this heterogeneous association of stones, we see a dirty black lump, which he calls a dome, and which is apparently stolen from that worst of embellishments of that worst of archi-tects, Sir John Vanbrugh. It furnishes me with no other idea but an inverted punch-bowl, and, peradventure, might be intended by Sir

William Chambers as a durable symbol of sobriety, to operate on the senses of the clerks, to keep them from tippling in the hours of duty."

What a conceited mind this Mr. Williams, alias Anthony Pasquin, must have had to pen such a production, which appears to have been written with an idea that by such spirts of sarcastic wit he could crush at one stroke Somerset House, Sir William Chambers, and Sir John Vanbrugh. This malignant attack was too glaring for its meaning and worth to remain unappreciated by the public any great length of time, and a reply to this flippant criticism was printed in 1823, from the pen of Mr. Papworth, who, in one passage, says:—" Would it not have been an advantage to public taste, if the critic who assumed this superior knowledge had pointed out the parts so conspicuously beautiful to his learned optics [this was in reference to the admiration pro-fessed by Williams of parts which he asserted were copied from Inigo Jones's original de-sign], for we, among the rest, have yet to find them out ? Master Pasquin, we have reason for believing, like many other audacious and unprincipled writers, made this assertion at a venture, knowing full well, from the success of similar experiments founded on falsehood, that public credulity, general indifference for the subject, and the prevailing love of slander, would receive his dictum as authority, and that he should, favoured by these combined cir-cumstances, remain secure from inquiry, and escape with applause."

It has often struck me that architects rather encourage this sort of criticism. We seldom find in mutual criticism that one professional man has any bowels of compassion for ano-ther ; they are very unwilling to trouble their hearers with the admirable parts of another's design, but, like wasps, leave their sting with-out even partially withdrawing it. It is this indif-ference for the subject which fosters all our troubles, and it is owing to the public being generally ignorant of our art that they are un-able properly to appreciate it.

Since Wren's time, until lately, with but few exceptions, architecture has been a dead letter ; men with less brains than wits have forced the bastard styles on to the public gaze, thus giving a vitiated taste, which has had a bad effect upon architecture and architects, for the desire for art in building had gradually lessened, but not so the wants of an increasing population—their dwellings and public edifices increased more rapidly than ever. Within these last forty or fifty years the principal part of London has been built—we may, with truth, say built—for, perhaps, there is not another large city in existence which evinces such a want of the architect, with such evi-dences of the builder.

One of the reasons I take to be, the fear architects were held in by the public : from examples which were continually springing up, it was easily discernable what a thorough want of taste and science there was amongst the profession at that time.

Another abuse of architectural criticism has arisen from the great influx of antiquaries and archæologists, who arrogate to themselves a knowledge of architectural art far beyond that which a professional man could know ; not that I mean to deny that they really did know more than an ordinary practitioner, or that this knowledge may have been useful ; but I am afraid in many cases it was, on the contrary, of most deteriorating effect, tying down art to certain ancient examples, which, unless repro-duced with the same spirit,—nay, I may almost say with the same mind,—will look as absurd as the antics of an ape when compared with the actions of a man. Bartholomew very aptly says, " nothing stopped our predecessors in the course of beauty and usefulness. But as over-tight lacing causes the straitened body to pro-trude sometimes in a manner which few think graceful or even decent, so now straitened architectural criticism leads to a similar result, and induces corruption in building of the very worst kind."

I would ask such critics whether they think the imagination of men has degenerated ? or that they are incapable of fresh ideas ? Has every thing been done that is possible to be done ? Upon reviewing the wonderful disco-veries made in every branch of science during the last few years, I say decidedly not, although our art has degenerated in an extraordinary manner. At the same time I think we have begun to emerge from the age of darkness, and let us hope that the greater our application, the stronger will be the new light, which is already dawning upon architecture and architectural science. And for this new light I must give the antiquary his due share of credit, he having collected a most valuable set of ancient examples, which must have had a great influence upon our art, and which ought to serve us as an extensive field for imagination to work upon; and by recombinations we may yet produce a style peculiar to the nineteenth century, not forgetting that our predecessors, from the scientific knowledge which they possessed, were enabled to give art certain dependence on rules (at least there is the appearance of such being the case), which it will be impossible for us to do if we try a *royal road* to knowledge.

Although the present, when compared with the past, is encouraging, yet taste in architecture is not sufficiently cultivated to bring with it its corresponding influence upon art. Reflecting upon by-gone ages, when architecture was at its zenith, we find that the church considered it as a most important branch of education, and the art was encouraged in every possible way. Taxes were levied amongst their people for the purpose of increasing the magnificence of their cathedrals and churches: by this means their edifices bore the impress of their power,—a power which was not used from feelings of ostentatious pride, but for the purpose of showing the devotion and reverence with which they looked up to the Almighty. This lavish outlay was far preferable to the close-fisted parsimony of the present times, when committees seem to be trying a series of experiments as to how cheap they can build churches or chapels, which, when done, are sometimes unsafe to sit in.

The present state of public competition is ruinous to the architect, to public taste, and to the progress of pure art. It appears to me to arise from the following causes, viz.:—

Want of architectural taste in those who have to decide the merits of the various designs.

Want of union amongst the profession, and want of good architectural criticism.

Want of taste and knowledge in those who have to decide upon the several merits or demerits of a design is a deficiency so often experienced by men of talent in our profession, that it will be quite unnecessary for me to prove that it does exist: I think it is greatly owing to the neglect with which architecture is treated by the public press; the mass of the people, therefore, have no popular means of improving their minds on this subject.

Want of union amongst the profession is another cause for the indignities which are continually borne by its members. I think that architects as a body ought to be quite strong enough either to pass laws themselves or get them passed by the legislature, which shall protect them from these fearful competition jobs. From the want of good criticism in the public journals, these jobs are often allowed to pass unnoticed, thus leaving the evil to increase in consequence of the jobbers escaping free. One would suppose that with such power as the daily papers possess, it would not be difficult by degrees to promote a knowledge of true architecture amongst the classes who most require it.

Architecture seems to have been entirely neglected; it has not been sufficiently studied as a fine art, an art which should have the same interest for the architect that *poetry* has for the poet, *painting* for the artist, and *form* for the sculptors. The public are hardly acquainted with its unusual advantages as a material art. What I mean is, that I look upon painting, poetry, and sculpture, as imaginative, but our pursuits are realities. For a proof of this we have only to review the buildings of Ancient Greece, where usefulness was combined with a great simplicity of form, and consummate art in the arrangement of the ornamental parts. These works show a refined taste, which has only been equalled by our own countrymen in the wonderful examples of Gothic architecture.

I am inclined to believe that good architectural criticism, or even appreciation of the art, will not increase until more importance is attached to the profession; and also that no profession will have much importance attached to it unless studied in a systematic form. Upon comparing the present method of education adopted by our profession, I cannot but see that it is entirely inferior to all others. The medical profession is one which it would be impossible for a member to practise unless he had arrived at a certain standard of perfection: unless he attends regularly courses of lectures and examinations on anatomy, he would be incapable of performing the commonest surgical operation. The church and the law are equally strict: a man to become a member of either must go through a certain course of study. To come nearer to our profession I will add the engineer, who must have a thorough knowledge of mathematics and mechanics before he can construct a steam-engine or a railway bridge.

Now let us compare the state of architectural education with these facts. How are its students treated? Where are their colleges? How much are they required to know? I am sorry to say their schools are various and unsystematic, as various, in fact, as are the abilities which are shewn by the practising members of the profession. The schools I allude to are architects' offices, where youths are sent if they happen to show any taste for drawing, their parents unwisely saying, "that boy must be an architect," without reference to other capabilities which are indispensable to a thorough architect. The premium is paid, and the victim perhaps enters a bustling office, is set to lay down paper and to perform a variety of such jobs, which, according to the present practice, it is the duty of the fresh-comer to perform.

It is the system in some offices to confine pupils or assistants to one particular branch of the duties: such as drawing and writing to plans—drawing and colouring perspectives and elevations—or measuring and taking out quantities. If a young student happen to overcome all these impediments, and show evidence of talent and knowledge superior to his fellow pupils, it is seldom that he is assisted or encouraged by his master. This superiority is principally owing to his own observation and study.

These are some of the causes which tend to check the progress of taste and of pure art: while such practices last, the engineer will assume the scientific department of architecture, the builder the practical,—and, as for art, that will be forgotten altogether.

Until the public are certain that architects are educated and scientific men, there will always be a distrust of them, which will act in a detrimental manner to their interests, and to the spread of architectural taste. We cannot wonder at this distrust, when such instances are common as that of an architect giving an estimate to a committee for the erection of a building, which, when properly calculated, amounts to double the money. It is a common excuse among architects that it is impossible to tell what a building will cost until the quantities are taken out, and the builder's estimates given. This is allowing the builder to usurp the office of the architect; and it is certain that its effects upon the pockets of the professional man are very serious. I have heard of numerous cases where a builder has been consulted in preference to an architect, merely because the employer thought the practical man could give him a better idea of the sum to be expended; and this, I am afraid, is the case with many landed proprietors, who, if they were not afraid, would employ professional men.

Another evil, which acts in a prejudicial manner to the interest of the architect, is the uncertainty of the rates of professional remuneration.

ARTHUR ALLOM.

BLIND BUILDERS.—Tenders for Farm Buildings at Mr. Clovers, Kirtling, Cambs; Mr. J. F. Clark, architect.

Frost, Bury St. Edmunds	£1,297	0	0
Reed, Bury St. Edmunds	1,095	0	0
Quinsee and Attack, Cambridge	1,045	0	0
Trevethan, Bury St. Edmunds	1,020	0	0
Andrews, Soham	988	6	6
Erswell, Walden	983	11	0
Westley, Newmarket	980	0	0
David, Isleham	966	16	0
Allen, Balsham............	930	0	0
Grainger, Walden............	845	0	0

THE HEALTH QUESTION.

IN reply to Mr. Bernal's indignant remonstrance, my Lord Ebrington informs us that we have had cesspools emptied and sewers flushed, and that the commissioners' plan is about completing. Of the former we are unhappily aware—since for eighteen months we have had his lordship's foul gift following, morning, noon, and night, the lunar influences between Barnes and Erith;—we accept with joy the probable correctness of his lordship's second assurance. We have also faith in the public will, that the best plan which modern science and sound sense can devise for the constant cleansing of the metropolitan atmosphere shall be that which the Commissioners of Sewers adopt.

We have been long enough, and in more senses than one, like the lampooned of Martial—

"Tongilianus habet nasum, scio, non nego, sed jam,
Nil præter nasum Tongilianus habet."

But eighteen months have given us cause and leisure to inquire both what we are to be ridden of, and what we are to acquire. What is it to be? Are we to be freed for ever of the nauseous emanations of graveyards, of 5 feet thicknesses (*vide* St Bride's) of putrefaction, scantily covered with a little earth—just burial sufficient to frank the departed shade across dismal Styx? Are we to be freed from the foul reek of contractors' yards, slaughter-houses, bone-heaps, manufactories of scientific filth?—from the miasmata of gully-holes and untrapped inlets?—from the abominations of cesspools and uncovered ditches? Are we to be cleansed by the pustular system of Mr. Austin, or the downdraught of Mr. Phillips, by the constant suppuration of sumphs, or the diarrhœa of tunnels? Are we to have sewer within sewer, one carrying off to Plumstead the foul contributions of manufactories and man, the other voiding into the Thames the *whole* surface water of the London Basin, rendering gully-traps useless, and 3 inches water under our kitchen-floors at Stockwell impossible? Are we to have all dwellings inspected, and found properly convenienced, ventilated, and trapped? Are we to have intra-parietal herding confined within mortal limits?

In fine, are we, who work ten or fifteen hours a-day, to be left to look after ourselves, or are those appointed to the work of supervision to see whether it be done or no? "He that is filthy, let him be filthy still," that has been the cry long enough. If, as Sir J. Jervis says, we are to be left to the common law, it may be the cry for ever. Common sense as a prompter, let alone common law as a remedy, is not to be trusted, and unless we are looked after by these men, we must devise some other means of deliverance. I have imagined in such a case that a sanitary league, with moderate funds, employing a public prosecutor to follow up all complaints made by members, might be productive of some effect. Meanwhile, we have THE BUILDER at all events,—whose, with much respect, is

JUVENIS EFFLUVIATUS INFELIX.

MOVING PANORAMA OF THE NILE.

THE moving panoramic picture of the Nile, the preparation of which we first announced, was exhibited to friends on Saturday last, and was opened to the public on Monday. Messrs. Warren, Bonomi, and Fahey, assisted by Messrs. Martin, Corbould, Weigall, and Howse, have conspired to produce an exceedingly interesting and very beautiful work of art. The spectator, starting from Cairo, is made to see, first one bank of the Nile, as far as the second cataract, in Nubia, and then, returning, the other is brought before him.

The subject is full of interest. "Egypt," as the preface to the catalogue states, "was the land visited by Abraham in search of food, when there was a famine in his own country; the land to which Joseph was carried as a slave, and which he governed as prime minister. From Egypt Moses led the Israelites through the waters of the Red Sea. Here Jeremiah wrote his 'Lamentations.' Here Solon, Pythagoras, Plato, and other Greek philosophers, came to study. Here Alexander the Great came as a conqueror; and here the infant Saviour was brought by his parents to avoid the persecution of Herod. Egyptian hieroglyphics, in which the characters are taken from visible objects, are the earliest form of writing; and the Hebrew and Greek alphabets were both borrowed from them. Egypt taught the world the use of paper—made from its rush, the papyrus. In Egypt was made the first public library, and first college of learned men, namely, the Alexandrian Museum. There Euclid wrote his 'Elements of Geometry,' and Theocritus his Poems, and Lucian his 'Dialogues.' The beauty of Cleopatra, the last Egyptian queen, held Julius Cæsar, and then Marc Antony, captive. In Egypt were built the first monasteries; the Christian fathers Origen and Athanasius lived there; the Arian and Athanasian controversy began there."

The buildings which remain are the oldest in the world—some of them the largest; the country was the first civilised: it was the parent of Greek science and art. With such a subject, the artists we have named could scarcely fail to produce a fine work, and they have fully justified the anticipation. If we have anything to regret, it is that greater advantage was not taken of some of the buildings,—that is, we would have had them leave the actual banks of the river for brief intervals, so as to take the spectator more closely to the colossal and mysterious ruins, now sometimes represented at a distance. We found this regret on the beauty and efficiency of those parts of the panorama where the monuments *are* represented in the foreground; as, for example, "the Sitting Statues," the rock-cut temples of "Abou Simbel," the "Second Pyramid," and the "Sphinx;" but we do not intend it to modify our praise of the very charming and instructive painting (accompanied as it is, too, by a running commentator,) which Messrs. Warren, Bonomi, and Fahey, have produced.

PROPOSED CHURCH, SANDFORD DISTRICT, CHELTENHAM.

SIR,—My attention has been drawn to an article in THE BUILDER of the 14th instant, headed "Architectural Competition: Proposed Church, Sandford District, Cheltenham," and signed "Raphael Brandon," to which, as it conveys a direct insult to the committee, of which I am honorary secretary, I must trouble you with a few remarks in reply.

Mr. Brandon first refers to the amount for which the church is to be built, viz., 4,000*l.* "This," says he, "is simply an impossibility. To build a church, as a church should be built, in the severest manner, would cost at least 6,000*l.*" Mr. B. gives no data for coming to this conclusion; it is simply his *ipse dixit*. Has Mr. B. inquired the price of materials, &c., in our neighbourhood, or does he fix 6,000*l.* as his minimum for a church, without reference to attendant circumstances?

Mr. Brandon then proceeds to question the *bona fides* of the committee, by suggesting that they have some favourite architect in view, &c. &c. What ground has he for this assertion, and whence does he draw his conclusions? I can only imagine that he takes himself as the standard by which to judge others. For the sake of brevity I pass over many irregular statements of Mr. Brandon, and proceed to where he quotes the instructions of the Cheltenham committee, at this point:—"In case the building shall not be commenced within twelve months after notice to the architect that his plans are approved, he shall be entitled to receive for his plans, designs, and drawings, the sum of 50*l.*, and no more, in full discharge of all claims for such plans, &c., which are then to become the property of the committee;" which he interprets thus: "They have only to delay a twelvemonth to become entitled to a full set of working drawings and specifications, together with the design itself, for the sum of 50*l.*" Now it is possible that such an inference may be drawn upon a prejudiced perusal of the instructions, but is it likely that a respectable body of men would act in the manner implied above?

I do not agree with his view respecting the advantages of a competition; but, without entering into this point, I see no ground for the opinion formed by Mr. Brandon as to the conduct of the Cheltenham committee. They have honestly stated their requirements, and thus given an opportunity to those who disapproved of the instructions to abstain from the competition. Supposing the committee had left several points open,—the architect would have omitted them in his calculations, and his design would have been cast out as not coming within the compass of the means in the hands of the committee, and all for the want of the very instructions which Mr. Brandon calls so extraordinary. It being at the option of Mr. B. to enter into the competition, his proper course would have been to apply to the committee, or myself, for an explanation, instead of imputing base motives and misconstruing their instructions. The several interviews I have had with architects, under these instructions, convince me that to build a good substantial church, such as required, for 4,000*l.* is not the impossibility stated by Mr. Brandon; and also that others have not understood the passage referring to the architect's compensation in the unfair manner in which he interprets it.—I am, &c.,

Cheltenham. J. REES PHILIPPS.

CAST ZINC IN DECORATION.

M. GEISS, of Berlin, has been exhibiting specimens of zinc used for architectural and decorative purposes in a mode not hitherto employed amongst us,—namely, *cast*. It appears that for seventeen years, zinc has thus been used in Berlin for architectural purposes, namely, for all exterior as well as interior ornamental parts of buildings, which, by casting, can be produced in the sharpest forms, and are said to be at the same time capable of resisting all influence of the weather. Columns, capitals, consoles, acroteria, cornices, dressings for doors, balconies, vases, statues, &c., can be formed of zinc.

The late distinguished architect, Schinkel, thus writes on the subject:—

"The cast metal offers particular advantages from its greater strength in comparison with rolled zinc, from its being less subject to the influence of temperature, and from its capability of receiving the finest impressions by casting, for which reasons it seems most adapted for all plastic works of art.

"We see, therefore, already, large statues, copies of antiques, in the atelier of M. Geiss, at Berlin, executed in the most elaborate style: to which statues, by a precipitate of copper, an excellent imitation of copper can be given. All ornaments of carved work and projecting members forming perforations, and crowning members, are capable of being executed of this metal in the easiest way. At the same time the more important parts of building can be made very cheap and durable. We have recently finished a large restoration of our university, in which about 1,600 feet of cornice, with modillions, have been cast in zinc, which was fastened to an iron framework, and which, instead of 16 dollars per foot if in stone, cost in zinc only 9 dollars, including the iron framework.

"The many advantages which zinc offers for the construction of furniture, as vases, candelabra, basins, &c. &c., which in the open air are less exposed to damage than stone, and for the clothing of rough iron supports, with the elegant forms of columns and consoles, dressings for doors, and richly ornamented architectural members, show clearly the extent of its extreme usefulness, and will render it in future indispensable for architecture, contributing at the same time more and more to the extension of architecture itself."

With reference to a remark recently made in our pages as to the effect of sea air and coal smoke on the ordinary rolled zinc, the agent of the Vieille Montagne Zinc Company has addressed a communication to us, wherein he says:—"I would refute the erroneous and generally received idea in this country, that zinc (pure zinc at least), corrodes when exposed to the sea air or spray on coasts, or in countries where coal is the predominant fuel. Wood yields such gases no less abundantly than coal, and yet zinc is admitted to stand well in the inland districts of France, where wood is used as fuel!

As regards the borders of the sea, if it does not stand equally well there, how does it happen that the zinc roofs of the large sheds at Amsterdam and Rotterdam, for building men of war, have stood the test of such exposure for at least twenty years?

Witness, too, the large shed of the great arsenal at Flushing, the large prison at Cherbourg, the barracks and railway stations at Boulogne-sur-Mer and at Havre, and other buildings in various other sea ports."

It is asserted, and our manufacturers should look to this, that British zinc is less pure than that used abroad.

THE WORD OF THE LAW *versus* THE SPIRIT.

LIVERPOOL BUILDING ACT.

A FEW days ago Mr. Robinson, building surveyor, appeared at the Police-court, in Liverpool, to substantiate an information against Mr. Wells, builder, for placing the purlins in the roof of a church now in course of erection in Sackville-street, of less dimensions than are required by the Act of Parliament. Mr. Robinson said the bearings of the purlins to the roof of the church were fourteen feet. With a slight variation they were 6 feet 6 inches apart. The Act prescribed that these purlins, if more than 6 feet apart, should be 7 inches by 9 inches. Mr. Bell, solicitor, who appeared for the defendant, wished to show that by the timber used there was a greater amount of strength than if they had strictly adhered to the provisions of the Act; and, in addition to this, that strength had been gained by the great pitch of the roof. This was not denied. After some conversation, Mr. Rushton, the magistrate, said it was clear to him, from the explanations given, by the aid of several models which had been brought into court, that the roof was much stronger than if made with a less pitch, and a different description of wood, as the Act made no mention of the kind of wood to be used, but merely the dimensions, but he regretted to say the Act allowed him no discretion in the matter. The question was, how it could be altered with the least possible cost? Surveyor—By nailing a piece upon the purlin. This was considered a bad precedent by the magistrate; but, after some demur, Mr. Rushton said that the case was one of an unusual nature, and that as his province was more particularly to see to the safety of the public, the suggestion might be taken into consideration. However, he would adjourn the case, in order that the surveyor might have time to communicate with Mr. Hay, the architect, and see what would be the best course to adopt. The architect, who was virtually the defendant in the case, in the course of his examination, showed that a piece of timber, according to the size used, namely, 10 inches by 6 inches, by Tredgold's formula, proved, by actual experiment, was stronger than a piece of timber cut to scantling of 9 inches by 7 inches, which contained a greater quantity of timber, but complied with the Act. The same piece of timber cut out of Baltic (of which the whole of the roof is constructed), would have required a weight of 23,357 lbs. to break it, and a purlin 9 inches by 7 inches, as required by the Act, and which would have been permitted of yellow pine, would only have required 13,365 lbs. to break it. Mr. Hay further contended that the basis of the triangles were the real bearings of the respective roofs—the roof in question being at a pitch of 58°, the other, as allowed by the Act, of 27°. That for a square of roofing of the first, it would have required 348 tons 1 cwt. 5 lbs. to break the timber, whereas the latter would yield to a pressure of only 20 tons 18 cwt.

STREET CROSSINGS.—When detained with other foot passengers at the crossings of some of our principal streets, by a long string of carriages or carts, it has often struck me as very desirable that the inconvenience, and I may add danger, of many of these crossings, might, and indeed ought to, be obviated (in situations where the width of the way would allow of its being done), by the erection across the streets, of light bridges for foot passengers, to whom much valuable time would then be saved, and their lives and limbs rendered more secure from accidents, and these erections might also be rendered very ornamental to our streets.—W. C. TREVELYAN, Athenæum Club.

THE NORTH PORCH, SALISBURY CATHEDRAL.

THE ARCHÆOLOGICAL INSTITUTE AT SALISBURY.

THE members of the Archæological Institute have gathered together in good array around the cathedral of Salisbury, and are proceeding with the business of the congress. On the 24th, the introductory meeting was held, and various objects in or near the town were visited, of which we hope to say something in our next number. At the dinner-meeting, on Tuesday, in the council room, at least 300 ladies and gentlemen sat down to a plenteous display of the good things of life, which the mayor and corporation had liberally provided. On the following morning several hundreds of the poorer inhabitants of the city were presented with the remains of the feast in food and liquors, and thus were comforted and made happy.

At the morning meeting, the Marquis of Northampton, on taking the chair, had addressed an assembly of at least two hundred, in his accustomed kind and affable manner, by saying how much he rejoiced in seeing so many congregated from various parts of the country to compliment archæology and the singular locality in which they met. His lordship introduced the Right Honourable Sidney Herbert as the president for the ensuing year. This accomplished and learned gentleman manifested much taste and tact in addressing the company, by pointing out and characterising the prominent objects of archæological and historic interest which belong to Old and New Sarum, to the castrametations and barrows of the plains, Stonehenge, Wilton House, &c., and dwelt particularly on the merits of some of the Wiltshire worthies, who had been born or dwelt at Salisbury or in the county. The bishops of Salisbury and Oxford followed in the same strain, in proposing certain resolutions. Two papers were next read by Mr. Matcham and the Rev. Joseph Hunter, the latter on the topographical gatherings at Stourhead and the archæological lore and researches of the late Sir Richard Colt Hoare. The President announced that Sir Hugh Hoare would be happy to show the antiquities of Stourhead to a select party of the institute, on Monday next. The meeting then broke up, and proceeded in parties to visit the museum opened at the King's House, in the Close, the cathedral, and other objects of archæological interest in the city.

In the evening, Professor Willis in the chair, a paper was read by Mr. Tucker, written by the Rev. E. Duke, on Stonehenge, endeavouring to show that it indicated a part or member of a vast planetary orrery of the universe.

The Dean of Hereford gave some explanations and details of the operations now going on at Silbury-hill, and the contents of certain of the barrows near Amesbury. The dean found the cutting at Silbury-hill advanced about 32 yards on Wednesday week. He advised the workmen to stop at about two yards from the centre of the hill, in order that the members might be present at its exploration. The speaker next alluded to the contents of some barrows he had opened while in the neighbourhood. An animated conversation followed, in which Mr. Britton, Mr. Yates, and other gentlemen, took part.

On Wednesday morning, large parties visited Amesbury, Old Sarum, Stonehenge, &c.; and in the evening Mr. Markland and Mr. Britton read two papers to a large assembly at the council-house. Of these and future proceedings more anon.

Annexed we give an engraving, from a drawing made for the purpose, of the north porch of the cathedral, a very interesting example of the Early English period. The cathedral, with the exception of the tower and spire, was commenced and finished between 1220 and 1258. Professor Willis is to illustrate it, and our readers may look to have the advantage of some of his remarks.

STRENGTH OF BEAMS.—Permit me to ask for a demonstration of the following statement, hoping some of your readers will furnish a solution. I am not aware of any simple demonstration, and it is with the object of obtaining such that it is proposed. The question is—"That in beams of equal length and breadth the transverse strength is as the square of the depth?"—A., Belfast.

BURIAL IN TOWNS—THE CHOLERA.

"When thy judgments are in the world the people of the earth will learn righteousness."—PSALM.

YOU are aware that the following proceeds from one who, with little public *éclât* and less of interested motives, has had long and ample opportunities of judging on the above subject. Within the last two months, however, I have first personally known illness, severe and painful, not merely of grave-diggers but also of an excellent clergyman, himself very willing for any equitable change, contracted whilst reading the funeral service by the grave. This was in an important ground, and not one of the most generally obnoxious. If space between graves were enforced, and coffins not allowed to graze each other, nor piles of them of different dates to be exposed at fresh diggings, a child could see that danger would be materially lessened.

But for the moment, let me presume to suggest that chloride of lime should be placed in churches and chapels, when bodies are taken into them,—and why not also by the side of graves?

The fact of certain burying grounds ably assisting the cholera is now fully brought home, and perfectly useless to be denied. We are publicly told that St. Margaret's, Westminster, now poisons the neighbouring sewers. The ground has been obstinately kept up in defiance of representations for a long time. Would it not be a most righteous rebuke in any such aggravated case for a congregation to leave any church for a time, and go to others where there was room? I believe that most persons, except the clergy themselves, know that equitable compensation has not been in the least objected to in this case—the objection not being to the fees, but to the dreadful "accommodation" afforded in return; they know, however, that the system cannot be endured much longer. The cholera scourge may be protracted for some time. Is it their pleasure that it should outlast that? I have tried to defend the clergy many times, from individual good opinion and some predilections, and have urged that they have not the power of remedy. But I have received one answer which cannot be answered again, but greatly imports all whom it properly concerns—"*They are represented in the House of Lords!*"

As to the difficulty of removing bodies far out of town, I had rather see several coffins deposited in one hearse, and horses *gallopping* with them, if I knew they would be decently deposited at the end, than see bearers creeping with coffins to a filthy churchyard. And in this wonderfully contriving age, cheap means might be arranged for persons to visit the graves of their relations and friends. The new regulation of 5 feet depth above coffins would be excellent if it were virgin earth, or undisturbed for fifteen or twenty years; but how different the case is in town burying places, of which many in large provincial towns seem, if possible, worse than in London, any one can see for himself.

Shakspeare has been quoted (grave-digging scene in "Hamlet"), in proof of bad state of churchyards in his day. But it should be carefully observed, that he alludes to nothing but or worse than *bones*, not to previous premature disturbance. "Here, now, is a skull which *has lain i' the earth three and twenty years*," a much better lease than the usual ones of London churchyards.

> "Lay her i' the earth,
> And from her fair and unpolluted flesh
> May violets spring."

A beautiful poetical idea, but requiring a different character of burial place.

One concluding observation on a different but not incongruous subject. It was predicted four years ago, when the triumphant clearings out of the poor took place in St. Giles's, for the erection of new and smart streets, that their case would be rendered doubly bad. The present Earl of Carlisle took up the subject, to his honour, and something has been done in the erection of lodging houses, &c. Still, what the whole effect of such "clearings" has been, let any one read for himself in the report of "*Church* and *Carrier* street," St. Giles's, in the *Times* of a few days back. And, perhaps, until the *very poorest* can get a decent weekly bed for a shilling, and even a safe nocturnal cover for a penny—the ends of salubrity and humanity will not be fully answered.

EUBULUS.

NOTES IN THE PROVINCES.

THE foundation-stone of Portland Breakwater was to be laid on 25th inst. by Prince Albert.——On Monday week the chief stone of the church of St. John, at Gailey, Wolverhampton, was laid by the Countess of Cavan. The edifice is to be built in the early English style, and of stone from the Penkridge quarries. The site and a donation were presented by Lord Hatherton. The architect is Mr. Robinson, junr.——The town council of Bridgnorth have resolved that part of the High-street be taken up and repaved, by Charles Green, of Shrewsbury, who agreed to do it for 3½d. per yard; having repaved that portion of the north of the Town Hall for 3d. per yard, but at that price could not get wages.——While driving the holdfasts for fixing an improved lightning conductor to Sheffield parish church, according to the local *Times*, the apex which finishes the octagon of the spire was found to have three fissures, which rendered the upper part of the spire very precarious. The spindle of the vane was much corroded, and about 9 feet of the spire required to be taken down. The work was commenced inside the spire, and a stone being taken out, a rope was suspended, to which a cage for the workmen to be placed in was attached. An octagon iron frame with sockets to admit of supporters for the outside scaffolding was fitted to the spire, and rendered firm by screws. When the old vane was taken down the inscription was quite legible: on one side were the words "Mr. W. Burton, Capital Burgess, 1789," and on the other, "Mr. Saml. Younge, Capital Burgess, 1823."——The foundation-stone of the new church to be erected at Pitsmoor, says the same paper, was laid on Monday week. The church is to be built from the designs of Messrs. Flockton and Son. It is to be cruciform in plan, with nave, aisles, porch, transepts, chancel, and tower. The style is Early Decorated, the windows being filled with geometrical tracery. It will seat 266 persons in low pews, and 352 in open free seats on the ground-floor. Small galleries in the transepts and tower will accommodate 224 children, making the total number of sittings 842. The roofs are to be open and stained. The builders are—J. and A. Ridal, masons; W. Turner, carpenter; J. Copley, slater; T. S. Harrison, plasterer; Drury and Smith, plumbers, &c.——The old church at Charlecote has been pulled down, and is about to be re-erected on nearly the same site, but enlarged, at the cost of Mrs. Lucy, relict of Mr. George Lucy.——Active measures are in progress for the collection of a sufficient sum, by subscription, for the proposed monument to Cromwell at St. Ives.——The St. Neot's Gas Company will again, it is said, pay a dividend of 8½ per cent. on its 'capital.' The price of gas at St. Neot's has been 8s. per 1,000 feet during the three years of the Company's existence. They must reduce their price, and thereby increase their dividend, already a good one. There are plenty of poor people at St. Neot's whose means, such as they are, will thus be made use of by the company to its own increasing profit.——The rector of Moulton, Suffolk, has commenced, at his own cost, a school, for 100 children, with master's house attached. It is in the Tudor style, with three light transomed gable windows and side lights, roof open, coping gablets, and finials of stone, ridging trefoliated crest tiles. Mr. J. F. Clark is the architect.——At Brigg, says a contemporary, the corn-exchange, new gas-works, and many new freehold private residences, and various establishments, about to make their appearance, will cause the town for some time to become a scene of bustle and activity in the building department.——Christ Church, King-Sterndale, near Buxton, was consecrated on Thursday in last week.

THE BRITISH ARCHÆOLOGICAL ASSOCIATION will open their congress at Chester on Monday.

MULTIPLICATION OF THE CUBE.

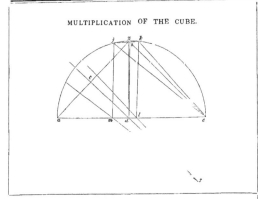

MULTIPLICATION OF THE CUBE.

In your number of the 16th June, a method and its "demonstration" are given by J. P. W., for the multiplication of a given cube on geometrical principles; and although you have guarded the reader, in observing that the method is but an approximation to the truth, yet I suppose you may not consider it altogether useless in noticing the following explanation of the imperfection in the "demonstration."

The accompanying diagram is lettered precisely as that of your correspondent J. P. W.

It will readily be seen that the mode of demonstration adopted by J. P. W. requires, to he perfect, that the line joining the points u and z should be parallel to mj, or at right angles to the base ae; but it can be shown that it is not. Draw the line jk, cutting the line ze in o, then, if jk be parallel to ml, will $\frac{jo}{ok} = \frac{mu}{ul}$ because by construction the angles oej, keo, are respectively equal to the angles msu, ksu, hence the line ou is parallel to jm, and it therefore follows that uz is not parallel to jm; again, if jk be not parallel to ml, then will neither zu nor ou be parallel to jm, nor ever can be whilst that the points j and k do not coincide, which, indeed, will be the case when the angle fbg is equal to the angle fyb (see J. P. W.'s diagram), because in this case the line gb coincides with the bisecting line gi, and therefore the points $jzck$ would also coincide. I will only add on this subject a general formula for the duplication of the cube, which I should be glad to see put into a pure geometrical shape by any of your numerous readers. If a represent the side of a cube then will $a + \frac{a}{\sqrt[3]{61}}$ represent the side of a cube double the size of the given one.

Another geometrical problem occurs to me, which, perhaps, is of more practical use than the former: it is the following:—

Having a drawing to make of a three-light window in the *pointed-arch style*, the tracery of which consists of *simple curves*, the leading lines being as shown in the accompanying diagram, the radius of the large arch $a b$, and the width of the lights being given, to find the radius $o b$ of the inscribed circle $c b d e$.

Make $g r$ on the vertical line equal to $h g$, the distance from centre to centre of the mullions; join $r a$, cutting the vertical line np in m, then is $n m$ equal to the radius $o b$ as required.

Demonstration.—Put $o b = x$

$$a b = a = f d$$
$$n g = e$$

Then, because

$$\overline{a + x}^3 \propto \overline{a - x}^3 = \overline{a + e}^3 \propto \overline{a - 3e}^3$$

Or $\frac{2e}{x} = \frac{a}{a - e}$. Hence $g r : m n :: g a : n a$.

JOHN BURLISON.

PERMANENT DECORATION FOR ROOMS.

I WOULD suggest an improved style of decorating the walls of sitting rooms. At present we use paper; or plain painting, occasionally, for dining rooms. Paper is liable to this serious objection, viz., that stains from any cause cannot be removed; thus after a very short occupation of a house, it must be repapered at great expense, because the paper is soiled in one or two places.

What we require is something more durable, which, unless ill-used, will last as long as the house itself; can be constantly cleaned, easily touched up again if necessary, and be renovated in part without an entire change being necessary.

My idea is taken chiefly from the French panel papers, and partly, also, from the practice of painting the walls of rooms.

I would let into the walls of rooms porcelain panels richly painted, which would give the same effect as the French panel papers; then the intervals should be filled up with plain painting, which should harmonise with the panels. Thus you have all the style of the French panel paper with a much more durable material. If more expensive in the beginning it would be far cheaper in the end.

If porcelain be too dear, glass or some kinds of wood, possibly encaustic tiles, would answer the same purpose. The great advantage of such a material would be, that it might be washed without injury, and would not imbibe grease as the papers do.

A HOUSE PROPRIETOR.

THE REVIVAL OF A NATIONAL ARCHITECTURE.

THE adoption in architecture of one manner instead of employing various styles, as under our present system, has been proposed to remedy the unsatisfactory state that all who think earnestly on the subject agree in considering the art to be in. It is a suggestion for which fair apology exists. Whenever architecture has possessed genuine vitality, as formerly in this country, a style prevailed,—one language was accepted and spoken by all. Like other speech, it refined with time,—gained strength and copiousness from use. Development was induced, progression manifested, — not apparently dependent upon the extraordinary chances of individual genius, only deriving, perhaps, some sudden occasional splendour from the latter source. With us, it is needless repeating, a host of styles prevail: we have a confusion of tongues,—a corrupt jargon of nearly every dialect ever lisped or spoken upon the earth. The history of the art does not encourage us to expect again a noble, living speech, unless one of these many modes of expression were extricated, and cultivated apart from the rest.

Nature has imparted to every soil its own

peculiar character, and all the valuable and interesting architecture in the world resembl nature in this particular. The architecture a country, setting aside its nationality, shou be a *homogeneous architecture*. Such did B tain once contain—an architecture vast an beautiful, congruous with the scenery of th land. Our modern structures, in most i' stances, equally outrage both, and appe (what, indeed, they are) debased and garbl copies, in the presence of glorious origina A new architecture would be folly, unless were in harmony with the old, whose mon ments are our actual wealth, and stand *qui* amid the lifeless fossil spoil by which they a encumbered.

To imagine, however, that our architee would, or could, unanimously agree imm diately to appropriate and practice exclusive one general form, is absurd. Still it may n be vain to invite a section of them to combi for such a purpose, or to invite all approvi minds to unite such a purpose, as far as po sible, with the system at present encourage A society might be formed, perhaps of a loc kind, in a particular district or county. It not meant for designing churches alone, wi a public edifice or mansion now and then, b to design any and every building whatsoeve for, well considered, every creation of this s has a great destination.

The choice of a style need not embarrass t If styles are manifold, there are but two sor of architecture—*organic* and *scenic*, the re and the feigned. But the style becomes less importance when it is selected as a vehic for thought and invention,—when assumed l a body of men, who, in the study of it, co template not to be pupils always, but poe presently.   H.

METROPOLITAN COMMISSION OF SEWERS.

A GENERAL court was held on Thursday, the 19t The Earl of Carlisle in the chair. The necessa deeds were ordered for the purpose of accepting loan of 3,000l. from the Royal Exchange Assuran Company, for the Fulham and Hammersmith di tricts.

New rates were ordered to be prepared on t following districts, the funds being entirely e hausted :—Lower Wapping Level, at 8d. in t pound ; Limehouse Level, at 1s. ; Tower-hill Lev at 6d. ; and Hermitage Level, at 6d.

The Chancery Proceedings against the Commi sioners.—A letter was received from Messrs. Smi and Son, the solicitors to the commissioners, a nouncing the result of the proceedings before Vic Chancellor Knight Bruce, the injunction bei granted ; but an opinion was expressed that t works of the commission would be little imped thereby.

Mr. Leslie dissented altogether from the inte pretation put upon the Vice-Chancellor's decisi by the solicitors of the commission. The Vic Chancellor had, in his decision, distinctly declar that the commissioners had acted wrong, had e ceeded their authority, and that the case was n one that came within the 61st section. He believ the matter had been correctly stated in the dai journals ; and he (Mr. L.) had the opinion of t registrar of the court that the decided view of t Vice-Chancellor was that the question did not co within the 61st section.

The Earl of Carlisle remarked that the positi of the commissioners was most perplexing. If, cases of emergency, they ordered works, they f so at the risk of getting into the Court of Cha cery ; if they neglected to do so, Mr. Payne, t coroner, had recently, in a charge to a jury, to them that the commissioners could be indicted manslaughter. In this unenviable position, if t question could be settled on terms of arbitratie he thought they should adopt that course as soon possible.

Mr. Bullar said the only illegality was in moving the soil. The officers, for the purpose filling in the ditches, had dug the soil from t banks instead of taking dry rubbish to the spot.

Mr. Leslie said that at first the court justifi their acts under the 61st section, but being driv from that they tried the 37th and 38th sections ; t on these they found the Vice-Chancellor just much opposed to them as he was on the 61 although they contended that it was artificial grou formed by the casting-up of the sewer, and th they might take possession of it. This was a matt of great importance, having got the decision up it, and having got into the "mess" entirely throu not bringing the question before the court in t first instance. Before the court knew anythi about it, the officers were sent to the land to coun what had brought them into the Court of Chance

The views he entertained on this subject were embodied in a protest signed by him some time since, that complaints were not brought before the court in the first instance, and then referred to a committee for investigation. He wished to know who was to pay the expense of this Chancery suit? Certainly not the rate-payers, as the parties who had ordered these works, it turned out, had no right to give any such order. The costs, he understood, were upwards of 250*l.*, which was an amount of great importance, and therefore he thought that a special court should be held to consider that question. By that time they would have the Vice-Chancellor's order. The question now was how far the officers were safe in carrying on their works. Every order, he doubted not, would now get into the solic'tor's office; and the solicitor, on the other side, was delighted at the prospect of abundant employment.

Mr. R. L. Jones believed it was now time to take a common-sense mode of conducting the business of the court, instead of its being done by the Works Committee, who had taken upon themselves the authority of giving answers in the name of the court. To go through the minutes of their proceedings, he must say their acts were really astonishing. Were the court to meet week by week the business might be got rid of, the officers would be more at liberty to attend to their duties, seeking out what was proper to be done, instead of, as at present, their time being engrossed in their attendance upon committees. Another important principle required to be settled—as to some general plan in their works; but now, in one case, they would order a 9-in. drain, in another one of 2 ft. 6 in., without any systematic plan whatever. They had also put it forth that a 6-inch pipe would carry off the entire drainage of 12,000 houses. Now, such a statement was truly ridiculous. They were wasting their time in experiments, while the wants of many districts were neglected. He instanced the present defective sewerage of Holloway, and, although they found 20,000*l.* in hand belonging to that district when they took office, yet that money had been appropriated to other objects, and the inhabitants of Holloway remained without any relief.

The Earl of Carlisle thought it useless to enter into these general topics, as the court had confirmed the order of the committee. It had been represented to them that persons were dying on the banks of this sewer, and however sorry he might be to see that their proceedings had brought them into the Court of Chancery, yet the inhabitants of Bermondsey had publicly thanked them for the measures that had been taken in their behalf. He thought directions should be given to their solicitors to devise measures for the purpose of coming to a solution of the difficulty with Mr. Rains, and he accordingly moved—"That the Vice-Chancellor's judgment be communicated to the surveyors, and that the solicitors be ordered to communicate with Mr. Rains with a view to an equitable adjustment."—This was unanimously agreed to.

State of the Sewerage of Blackfriars-road.—A deputation from the Board of Guardians of St. Saviour's Union, Southwark, attended the court to represent the offensive state of Blackfriars-road, in consequence of the stench arising from the gully-holes of the sewers.

Mr. Charles Brady addressed the court, and said that, as a medical man, he could positively state that most severe injuries were attributable to the acts of the present commissioners. He had for twenty-five years resided in this neighbourhood, but until about eighteen months he found no odour to offend the nose in any part of this locality; but now the neighbourhood was so completely infected that persons in the habit of coming from Brixton, Clapham, and other places, to their places of business in the City, avoided the Blackfriars-road altogether, in consequence of the offensive smells in every part of it. He believed the cause of this smell to arise from the fact of their having covered in an old open ditch, nearly seven feet wide, for which they had substituted a pipe of twelve inches bore, and this pipe being insufficient to discharge the contents of the old ditch, the stench was forced into the adjoining houses.

Mr. Chadwick defended the system of flushing, but it should be borne in mind that there were 300,000 cesspools in the metropolis, and according to the evidence contained in the third report of the the Sanitary Commissioners, it appeared that if the contents of them were brought together it would form one enormous cesspool of 50 feet in width, 6 feet 6 inches in depth, and would reach from the Broadway, at Hammersmith, to Bow-bridge, a distance of upwards of 10 miles. They had been charged with wasting 400*l.* per week in flushing, but it appeared that the whole amount spent for this purpose was 150*l.* per week, every sixpence of which represented a load of filth removed.

After observations from other commissioners, it was ordered that Mr. Grant, assistant surveyor, do accompany the deputation, survey the locality, and specially report upon it to the court.

The Retirement of Mr. Hertslet, the Clerk.—Mr. Leslie said, however painful it might be to him, if Mr. Hertslet persisted in his determination, he would move that his resignation be accepted. He wished to know if he had any communication to make on the subject.

Mr. Hertslet was willing to do so, if it was the wish of the court, and accordingly read a letter, of which the following is the pith:—

"I have never hesitated to express my opinion of the impracticable character of the Metropolitan Sewers Act, especially with reference to the improvement rates, which are by no means what I contemplated in my evidence before the Sanitary Commission, and which, I venture to predict, can never be carried out as a system, even though they succeed in a few isolated cases; nay, more, I am convinced that if attempted in their present shape they will greatly retard the practical good which may and ought to be effected by improvement rates.

I had hoped that, as the commission was to last but for two years, the court would have addressed itself at once, after modifying the more pressing evils, to the laying down of a definite and intelligible course of action for works, with a code of bye-laws embracing the general principles which should guide the public and the officers of the court; but, without going into details which would give offence, I will briefly say this has not been done; an entirely different course has been pursued, and I must, therefore, respectfully decline to continue in the service of the commissioners.

Our objects are, I am convinced, the same, but the mode of obtaining our objects is as opposite as it is possible to be. It is not the amount of work that has borne me down, but the anxiety caused by the conviction that the manner in which the work is set about is not the way to gain the point in view.

It has been suggested to me that blame may attach to me as order-clerk because I have not brought forward rules and regulations for adoption; but allow me to ask what rules could I propose for working out a system of which the outline even has never been communicated to me, if, indeed, it exist?

In proof that I am not alarmed by the vastness of the subject, I will add a few observations as to future plans; but before doing so, I must ask leave to explain a part of my letter of resignation which appears to have been misunderstood. It has been inferred in the public papers that I have applied for a pension, but all I have asked for is that I may not be considered to have waived my claim, should I, through age or infirmity, ever require such assistance. At present, and so long as I have health and strength to gain a competence, I must confess I am too proud to take, in such a way, the money of the rate-payers.

With regard to future drainage works, I believe that by a well considered plan, most valuable and at the same time most economical arrangements are easy of attainment; but the question of drainage cannot possibly much longer be allowed to stand alone, nor can the inhabitants of the metropolis be permitted to remain under the imputation of being the only people in the kingdom incompetent to manage their own affairs, or to have a voice in the details of measures for which they supply the means.

A Health Act must be introduced into the metropolis, but I respectfully submit that it must not be the present Public Health Act. The subjects of the following Acts are so blended that it is impossible to separate them; and the working of some of them is so arbitrary and oppressive as to demand their immediate alteration or repeal, viz.—

1. The Metropolitan Buildings Act.
2. The Metropolitan Paving Act.
3. The Metropolitan Sewers Act.
4. The various and numerous Acts for paving, water, &c., &c., within a radius of 10 miles of St. Paul's.

These Acts (taken in connection with such clauses as apply, of the Public Health Act and of the Nuisances Prevention Act), if not very valuable in the way of suggestion, will at least point out many things to be avoided in the future Act.

The working of an Act to be framed so as to embrace all these objects (and until all these objects are embraced no real good will be effected) should be intrusted to men standing high in the several professions of physic, engineering, and law. By adopting the commercial principle of payment for attendances, as Directors of Companies are paid, the services of six commissioners might be obtained for those of one on the present system. To work out the details of the system to be laid down under such guidance, I would recommend that the metropolis be divided into sections, keeping in view the two elements of property and population. Each of these sections, say eight or ten, should annually elect a commissioner or commissioners; and, again adopting the principle above alluded to, the commissioners so elected should be paid for each attendance, the number of attendances being limited so that no one commissioner should receive more than 200*l.* per annum. The public would thus have no one to blame but themselves if they did not obtain the services of a board in which they could most thoroughly confide, at a cost equal only to the salary of one or two commissioners paid as at present.

The saving that would thus be effected would be one of the least advantages, it would, however, be immense; I believe that the fees and expenses under the Buildings Act alone (between 30,000*l.* and 40,000*l.* a-year) would meet the whole demands, except, perhaps, the charges for extra supervision of important works, and the present charges and expenses under all similar acts for the metropolis would be entirely saved."

A special court was held on Monday last, for the purpose of taking into consideration the plan of Mr. Phillips, the surveyor, for the drainage of the whole metropolitan district, by means of a tunnel sewer, extending from Twickenham to Plumstead marshes, a distance of 19½ miles.

As the scheme proposed to embrace within its operation the drainage of the city of London, the Lord Mayor and the City Commissioners of Sewers were summoned, for the first time, under the provisions of the Act.

On the motion of the Earl of Carlisle, the Lord Mayor was called to the chair.

The first letter of Mr. Phillips, presented on the 21st of June, was read, as was Mr. Austin's observations in reply to the statements therein contained, some portions of which were of a very personal nature, and the general purport of it was, that Mr. Phillips's plan was so extremely faulty that it would be difficult to believe that any one holding the office of chief surveyor to the Metropolitan Commission of Sewers could have been serious in laying it before the court.—A letter was read from Mr. Phillips, which stated that, of the fourteen days allowed him for arranging his plan, estimates, &c., five of them had been taken up by the proceedings in the Court of Chancery.

Another letter was read from Sir H. De la Beche, pointing out that the strata through which the proposed tunnel would pass, were not entirely London clay, that faults would be found in them, and stating the difficulties that must arise if ever the tunnel became choked.

Mr. Phillips then produced a voluminous document, in exposition of his views, with the leading features of which our readers are acquainted.*

The Lord Mayor said, he observed in the reading of this document that no provision was made for the accumulation of the refuse at those seasons when sewage was not required in the country districts; and he wished to know how that was to be provided for?—Mr. Phillips said, as the sewage was received it would undergo a process of filtration, and the filtered water might then be di-charged into the Thames. The extent of the dep t at Plumstead would be between seven and eight acres.

The Earl of Carlisle then rose and said, that he believed that this was a measure of immense importance, not only in respect to Mr. Austin and Mr. Phillips, but with regard to the commission itself, which, it might be considered, was put upon its trial, and that it should receive a scrupulous attention, so as to leave no doubt upon the mind of the public as to their impartiality. At that moment it was difficult to state the proper course, but he had no doubt that any suggestions would be properly received by the intelligent body of gentlemen that he then had the honour to address. He felt, nevertheless, from the largeness of the details that they had but heard for the first time, they could come to no sudden decision upon the question at the present moment. They had, happily, some engineers of high character in the commission, and therefore he suggested that this plan should be referred to them for their consideration.

Mr. Walter, M.P., hoped that if it was referred to civil engineers it would not be to those who were members of the commission, as one of them at least had expressed an opinion strongly against Mr. Phillips, who might not receive an impartial consideration.

Mr. Leslie thought the same opportunities should be given to Mr. Austin as had been afforded to Mr. Phillips for bringing forward his plan, and that both plans should be submitted to the metropolitan parishes, who would have to raise the money to pay for them, as it was quite impossible to undertake works of such magnitude unless they had the harmonious concurrence of those parties who were to find the funds.

Lord Ebrington objected to the theory that this court was tied to any one plan, as a particular plan might be good for one part of London and not for another. Whatever the views of the court might be as to the desirableness of coming to a just decision, he trusted that one plan would not be pitted against another, and if they were sent out, that they would be sent out simultaneously. He thought, too, that their former surveyor, Mr. Roe, whose loss to the commission as an active reformer he much deplored, should be communicated with and consulted on this

---

* Our notices have already extended to so great a length, that we must postpone the extracts we had made from the report.

subject. At present no result could be arrived at, and they should also take care that the final tribunal to which it might be referred, should, like Cæsar's wife, be above suspicion.

Mr. Chadwick concurred in the importance of the subject, and vindicated the independent course pursued by the Surrey Committee. He was opposed to sending out their discussions to the parishes, and also to the exclusion of the engineers of the commission from the consideration of this subject. He then took a review of the plans that had been proposed by Messrs. Austin and Phillips for a portion of the metropolis. He would not go into the subject of the attacks that had been made on the commission, as he felt assured that those who made them were unaware of what had really been done. The sewer drainage consisted but of one-fourth, while the cesspool and house drainage comprised three-fourths of the evaporating refuse, and the attention of the Survey Committee had been for some time devoted to this subject, and even Mr. Phillips had availed himself of their researches in the production of his present plan, when he proposed hollow brickwork instead of solid. He hoped the city commissioners would pursue their inquiry independent of this commission, for the more investigation there was, the greater would be the ultimate benefit to the public.

The Hon. F. Byng, Mr. R. L. Jones, and Mr. Bullar having spoken,

Dr. Buckland, in a long address, pointed out the great variation of the geological strata through which the tunnel would pass. It was proposed on the assumption that it would entirely go through London clay. Now he could positively affirm that there was no London clay at Rotherhithe, but that the tunnel was even below it. Several parts of the line abounded with plastic clays, alternated with beds of permeating weeping sand and gravel, and in many districts loaded with water. He also alluded to the expensive cutting near Reading, on the Great Western Railway, from the inability, in its construction, to bore the plastic clay; and also at Bosley, on the South-Western Railway, where the engineer attempted to tunnel it, but was compelled to give up the effort. They frequently found beds of porous sand and water below the London clay, as was the case in the Kilsby tunnel on the North-Western Railway, in which work nearly half a million of money had been wasted. Below the Thames it might be said that the strata were frequently but a sack of sand so loose in its nature, that on the ground being opened for a sewer on the south side of St. Paul's, there was an immense rush of sand, and so rapidly did it run, that great fears were entertained that the fabric of St. Paul's would be undermined; and there was no security that, by tapping those beds of water on the south-east part of London, every house in that district might not be undermined. The London clay glanced off at the north-east corner of St. Paul's, and he could vouch that there was not an atom of London clay between Rotherhithe and the base of Shooter's Hill.

Mr. Leslie made a few observations on the geological strata near Greenwich; and said the great mistake of the Thames Tunnel was in not taking a lower level, the top of the present tunnel being, he was informed, only 6 feet from the bed of the river.—Mr. Alderman Lawrence thought a portion of the drainage might be passed to Twickenham, notwithstanding the joking that had taken place on the former commissioners attempting to pass drainage up hill.

Mr. Norris suggested that the subject should be thrown open to the scientific world, by which they would invite more complete and more efficient plans, which might turn out to be superior to those at present under consideration; and therefore he thought that all persons should be invited to send in plans.

After some further observations, the Earl of Carlisle proposed a series of resolutions, to the effect that Mr. Phillips and Mr. Austin present statements of their plans, with the probable expense, in a month from this date; that at the same time any other plans that may be offered will be received, and referees appointed to report on the whole; that each plan comprehend the whole area of Mr. Phillip's scheme, and the probable amount of compensation for land; and that the Ordnance be applied to for a rough plan of the area now under survey, to be given as quickly as possible.

College of Civil Engineers, Putney.—At the annual meeting of this establishment, held on the 20th inst., the Duke of Cambridge presided. It appeared from the report read by the principal, the Rev. Morgan Cowie, that the council have founded three exhibitions of 30*l*. per annum each.

All Saints' Church, Knightsbridge, was consecrated on Saturday morning in last week. It is situated in the new estate known as Ennismore-gardens, and was built from the designs of Mr. Lewis Vulliamy, in the Italian style. We must take an opportunity to look at it.

Miscellanea.

Railway Jottings.—The southern portion of the Great Northern Railway is progressing rapidly;—the several tunnels at Tottenham, Whetstone, Enfield, and South Mims, are in active preparation. The whole of the brickwork is being laid in mortar made of Lias lime. A wooden bridge on this line, between Lincoln and Littleworth, named Peakirk-bridge, took fire on Sunday week, and was entirely destroyed 'in an incredibly brief period of time.' The loss is estimated at 2,000*l*. to. 3,000*l*.——The Sheffield and Lincolnshire Junction Railway was opened on Tuesday week from Sheffield to Gainsborough, completing the communication between Liverpool on the west and Grimsby and Hull on the east. Captain Winn has inspected the whole, bestowing particular care, it is said, on the Rother viaduct (of which 21 arches fell in November), and the iron bridges, especially the wrought-iron tubular bridge over the Trent at Gainsborough.——A great many men are at work on the large tunnel between Aberdare and Merthyr,—Messrs. Hunt and Edwards, contractors. Messrs. Ritson and Co. are also actively engaged on the same line between Hirwain and Pontwalby. —— Some alleged improvements on Messrs. Clarke and Varley's resilient atmospheric tube are being patented by Mr. C. H. Greenhow, patentee of the geometrical railway. The piston is to be guided internally by wheels and a rod, and a vacuum is to be obtained, on the barometrical system, by causing water to fall to its barometrical level from an air-tight vessel connected with the atmospheric tubes. ——The final departure of the Provisional Government by railway from Carlsruhe, says a German correspondent of the *Times*, was attended by a curious incident. They ordered the officers to give up the *caisse* of the company, and seized a large quantity of furniture and *matériel* belonging to the Government, which they directed to be packed into waggons and sent on, along with themselves, towards Rastadt. Just before starting, the loaded carriages were dexterously backed into a covered shed, and others exactly similar, but empty, were attached to the train. With these the Provisionals departed in all security. When the 'mistake' was discovered it was too late to rectify it, for the Prussians were in possession. The *coup* was worthy of a Figaro.

Joking over the Grave.—Some of our readers are curious in epitaphs, and may like to see the following vagary, which is in Monmouth churchyard we are told:—

```
e i n e R n h o J s J o h n R e n i e
i n e R n h o J s e s J o h n R e n i
n e R n h o J s e i e s J o h n R e n
e R n h o J s e i l i e s J o h n R e
R n h o J s e i l e l i e s J o h n R
n h o J s e i l e r e l i e s J o h n
h o J s e i l e r e r e l i e s J o h
o J s e i l e r e H e r e l i e s J o
h o J s e i l e r e r e l i e s J o h
n h o J s e i l e r e l i e s J o h n
R n h o J s e i l e l i e s J o h n R
e R n h o J s e i l i e s J o h n R e
n e R n h o J s e i e s J o h n R e n
i n e R n h o J s e s J o h n R e n i
e i n e R n h o J s J o h n R e n i e
```

Who Died May 31st, 1832.
Aged 33 Years.

We give it not alone for the ingenuity it displays, but that we may reiterate our condemnation of such misplaced jokes.

Flower-pattern Paper-hangings.—I would speak of the importance of a knowledge of botany to the inventors of flower patterns; whether for muslin, for damask, or for wall papers. It is most certain that true taste will prefer the pattern which most nearly represents the natural flowers, with all their peculiarities of form, and in their true colours. The stems in nature may be stiff and angular; if they be so, it is vain to attempt in the pattern to give them graceful bends, and to hope, by so doing, to please the eye. To represent branches of hawthorn flowers on the twining stems of a convolvulus would be monstrously absurd. And yet faults as glaring are frequently committed by ignorant draughtsmen, when they attempt the *composition* of floral patterns. Of course, I am not now speaking of the combinations of "*fancy flowers*"—blossoms that exist only in the brain of the calico-printer or the paper-stainer—these may be as fantastical as you please. But I speak of the unnatural distortion of real flowers, resulting from ignorance of the proper proportion and number of their parts. Why is it that floral patterns on wall papers are out of fashion? or are driven up to the bed-rooms on the third landing, or to the back parlour of the country inn? It is not, surely, that *flowers* are out of fashion; or that the taste for them is less general than it was formerly. But it is that the *taste* of the public is not properly ministered to: it has outrun that of the manufacturer. In a rude state of education, bright colours and gracefully bended branches on the walls will please the eye that does not stop to question their propriety. But as refinement increases, truth in form will be preferred to brilliancy in colour, and the twining of branches that is not natural will be no longer thought graceful. It will be no longer regarded as a *twining* but a *twisting*—perverting nature for a false effect. This is the true reason why floral patterns in wall papers are now so much out of favour, and why, when selecting the paper for a room, one is forced (I speak from experience), after turning over books of patterns till you are weary, to take refuge in some arabesque design—some combination of graceful curves of no meaning—as an escape from the frightful compositions that are called flower patterns. It is surely high time that our manufacturers should seek to correct this evil. These are not days in which any one can afford to be left a step behind the rest of the world. He that once loses his place in the foremost rank, is pushed aside and lost in the crowd that is eagerly pressing forward, and almost treading on his heels. Already French wall-papers are rapidly coming into use. They have brought down the prices of the home-manufacture considerably, and they will undoubtedly drive home-made papers out of the market altogether if the manufacturers do not exert themselves to produce more artistic patterns than they commonly originate at present.*

Railway Compensation.—At Wolverhampton, a case was lately tried by special jury between a mine-owning company at Tividale, Rowley Regis, and the Stour Valley Railway Company, as to an acre of land, on which the claimants wanted 400*l*. for surface value, and 2,400*l*. for injury from severance. In course of the evidence it appeared that the owners had been previously compensated for severance of this area by a canal company, and that the cost of new shafts, &c., which the owners said they meant to have formed, had not the severance taken place, would be of itself between 4,000*l*. and 5,000*l*., a sum exceeding the value of the mine altogether, the more especially as all the thick coal had been already worked out of it by the old shafts. The defendants' counsel, therefore, appealed to the practical common sense of the jury, and "trusted that the result of their verdict would be to read a wholesome lesson to persons who came forward with such exorbitant and fictitious claims." The jury found a verdict of 350*l*., as value of the land, but nothing for severance. The amount recovered was 250*l*. less than the sum offered by the company.

Projected Works.—Advertisements have been issued for tenders, by 18th August, for the whole or any portion of the several works required in the erection of the north wing, &c., of the Manchester Royal Infirmary; by 10th, for masons', plasterers', and other works in the restoration of St. Andrew's Church, Halstead; by a date not specified, for the erection of twelve eight-roomed houses in the vicinity of St. Giles's, Camberwell; by 21st August, for pewing, repewing, repairing, and warming the interior of Northfleet Church, Kent; by 3rd, for the restoration and repewing of Kirk Deighton Church, near Wetherby; by a date not specified, for alterations and additions to the Court-house in Wakefield; by 2nd August, for the erection of a turnpike-house at Orwell; by 31st July, for the erection and completion of a cotton-shed at Wigan, by 7th August, for alterations and additions to premises at Leeds; by 21st, for copper nails, rivets, tacks, &c., for the navy; and by 28th, for pine timber and Dantzic oak thick stuff, also for the navy.

* From "Botany considered in Reference to the Arts of Design," by Dr. Harvey.

BEEDLE AND ROGERS'S VENTILATING BRICKS.—Under this title has been registered a brick so shaped that when two are placed end to end a circular space is left at the junction. This circular space connecting from course to course, a wall formed with them is, to a certain extent, hollow, and admits of currents of air through it, either heated or otherwise. Each brick is 9 inches square and 3 inches thick, the size of two common bricks, so that only half the usual number is required to do a rod of brickwork, and as they pay but one duty, and are laid with very little more labour than a common brick, work may be executed at a considerable saving. A common brick is used at the angle of each course.

HER MAJESTY'S THEATRE.—The second scene in the new and successful ballet divertisement at her Majesty's Theatre, Les Plaisirs de l'Hiver, is a very charming representation of a town on the banks of a frozen river, and a bright day in the midst of winter. The houses and buildings are covered with snow, the sun rises, and the sports begin. Well done, Mr. Marshall!

ADVERTISEMENTS.

No. CCCXXXIX.

SATURDAY, AUGUST 4, 1849.

EOMAGUS, Caerleon, Cestria, or CHESTER, as we now call it, is known by every one to be full of interest. The Roman and the "Goth" have both left their impress in every quarter, and have concurred to render it a place of delight for the modern antiquary, and the city of all others for "The British Archæological Association" to spend a week in. The Roman altars, hypocausts, and other recovered *vestigia,*—the peculiar arrangement of the streets (the "Rows," as they are termed), the walls, the castle, the numerous stone crypts to be found in various parts of the city, two or three churches, and last in order, but not in importance, the Cathedral,—all claim the attention of the visiter, and gratify the inquirer.

The cathedral externally is in a miserable state of decay, the result of the use of the red sandstone,* and has little of beauty remaining : when the canopied niches, open parapets, and crocketted pinnacles, however, formerly there, were perfect, its appearance must have been exceedingly handsome. It is greatly to be desired that some arrangement for its restoration, its maintenance even, should be speedily made. Internally a considerable sum of money has been spent in repairs, and considerable improvements have been made, especially in the choir, through the exertions of the dean (Dr. Anson), and others. The bishop's throne has been restored, new seating put up, a new stone pulpit and screen erected (mentioned some time since in our pages), some windows filled with stained glass, and other works done. The pulpit has an elaborately carved stone canopy, which is not so satisfactory as the lower part. The details seem to us clumsy, and being supported wholly at the back, corbelling over therefore, the notion of wood rather than of stone is given. It was designed by Mr. Hussey, and was the gift of the present excellent mayor, Sir Edward S. Walker, who, we may here say, has entered most warmly into the views of the Archæologocal Association, and greatly aided in the singular success which has attended the meeting.

A few years ago the choir of the cathedral was vaulted with wood and plaster, made to look like stone, and something is said about pursuing the same course in the nave. We mention this simply that we may advise the authorities to do no such thing. If wood is to be used, let it be *as* wood, and not in the place, and in imitation of another material. The feeling of the chapter appears to be so good, that we feel certain they will receive the remark in the spirit in which it is made.

Mr. Ashpitel, assisted by Mr. C. Bailey, ably illustrated the cathedral on the second evening meeting, and we shall probably give the heads of their paper, so that we will not now make any further remarks on the building beyond mentioning the CHAPTER HOUSE and vestibule, of which we have engraved a view. This, unlike that of Lincoln, illustrated by us some time since, and Salisbury (of

* The earliest portions, belonging to the twelfth century, are in a comparatively sound state.

which we intend to speak on another occasion) is a parallelogram, and a very interesting specimen of Early English. It is called 50 feet in length, 26 feet wide, and 55 feet high, so that it is nearly a double cube. The heads of the lights, it will be observed, take a peculiar shape, in following the line of the groining. The sides of the apartment at this moment are encumbered by ugly bookcases, but these we have omitted in the view, and hope soon to hear that they have been removed from the building.

The streets of Chester have been much modernised within a few years; they are still, however, full of quaint old fronts, mostly overhanging and belonging in date to the end of the sixteenth and commencement of the seventeenth century. One in Watergate-street is inscribed 1539 ; another, dated 1652, has this motto, "God's providence is my inheritance;" put up, it is said, by the occupier after escaping the plague. Some of the houses are very elaborately carved. We give a hasty memorandum of one of simpler character.

C.D.L. S.c.

Of the churches and some of the works at present being executed we shall have another opportunity to speak. We must now relate succinctly some of the proceedings of the meeting, intending, however, as our custom has been, to refer chiefly to those matters which more immediately interest our readers.

It has been the most successful congress yet held by the association, nearly 400 tickets having been disposed of. From the Bishop, whose courtesy and ability have made friends of all, down to the humblest shopkeeper, all have appeared anxious to aid in rendering the visit an agreeable one. What the Bishop said at the opening meeting, when introducing the president, Lord Albert Conyngham, was made true—" As I am sure there will be nothing wanting on the part of the members of the Association to make their visit instructive to themselves, so I am sure there will be nothing wanting on our part to mark our sense of the privilege that has been conferred on us, and to make your visit, my Lord, so far as we can, agreeable to yourselves, and not altogether unworthy of the distinguished honour which it implies."

The President said in the course of his address,—" Though the science of Archæology may be followed as a relaxation to the mind, it is highly important in the graver pursuits of life. No person taking part in public life can do so without some antiquarian knowledge. The explanation of the technical forms of government, the principles of public policy, the tenures of land, our British union of Teutonic custom with the Roman law, cannot be understood without some antiquarian research. That eminent and often quoted writer, Mons. de Tocqueville, thus lends his authority to the importance of antiquarian re-

search :—If we were able to go back to the elements of states, and to examine the oldest monuments of their history, I doubt not that we should discover the primary cause of the prejudices, the habits, the ruling passions, and in short of all that constitutes what is called the national character. We should then find the explanation of certain customs which now seem at variance with prevailing manners—of such laws as conflict with established principles, and of such incoherent opinions as are here and there to be met with in society; like those fragments of broken chains which we sometimes see hanging from the vaults of an edifice, and supporting nothing. This might explain the destinies of certain nations which seem borne along by unknown force, to ends of which they themselves are ignorant. We cannot investigate and illustrate the monuments and arts of our own country without studying those of the more classic regions. That the artist requires their study we have the authority of Sir Joshua Reynolds, who says—' But we must not rest contented even in this general study of the moderns ; we must trace back the art to its fountain head—to that source from whence they drew their principal excellences, the monuments of pure antiquity. As the inventions and thoughts of the ancients, whether conveyed to us in statues, bas-reliefs, intaglios, cameos, or coins, are to be sought after and carefully studied, the genius that hovers over these relics may be called the father of modern art.' But if the study of antiquity is requisite for the politician and the artist, how much more is it required by those who turn their minds towards that higher study which reflects upon the Almighty and his ways !"

Mr. Dillon Croker read a short paper in

answer to the question,—" What is the good of Archæology?" wherein he compared it to the telescope as the medium through which far distant things are revealed to our knowledge.

" It is the observation of Madame de Stael, that 'the erudition derived from archæology is far more animated than that we acquire from books: we seem to revive what we unveil, and the past appears to rise from the dust which concealed it. This passion for antiquity is no idle prejudice. We live in an age when self-interest seems the ruling principle of all men. What sympathy—what enthusiasm can ever be its results.' Madame de Stael, in the same work, also truly says, 'Antiquity inspires insatiable curiosity. To penetrate the past, interrogate the human heart through many ages, to seize on a fact, on a word, and on the manners or customs of a nation; in fact, to re-enter the most distant time in order to conceive how the earth looked in its youth, and in what way men supported the life which civilization has since rendered so complicated—this were a continual effort of imagination, whose guesses discover secrets that study and reflection cannot reveal.' Thus does Madame de Stael popularly show how archæology affects history. Without its aid history is but fable, or what is worse than fable, theory, as regards the past. Archæology establishes or contradicts the existence of nations, and whether they flourished or fell. History may record their rise and progress, but archæology must be the evidence whether history be true or false. Archæology cannot take its proper position as a science until its value is acknowledged, its treasures arranged, and its principles understood. In the process of procuring the most precious ore, much worthless matter has often to be carefully sifted and cast away before its sterling worth can be ascertained; so must the rubbish which encumbers the golden treasures of archæology be gradually cleared away by scientific labourers. In this process, however, the great difficulty is to say what is, or what is not, deserving the name of rubbish. A single character or mark upon the merest fragment of a stone, or piece of clay, may be of infinite importance in forming a link wanting decidedly to connect a chain of convincing argument—that link will be supplied by the study of archæology."

Mr. J. R. Planché read a paper that must have cost him much labour and research, on the "Seals of the Earls of Chester," which afford some curious illustrations of the practice of bearing arms. "No tale," said Mr. Planché truly, "has been too idle, no fable too preposterous, for the majority of the writers on this important, but mis-used subject. Had half the ingenuity and industry been exerted to discover the real origin of armorial insignia which has been wasted upon inventing stories to account for them, what service might have been rendered to history—what light thrown upon genealogy and biography! How many a document has now disappeared or utterly perished, which was accessible to Upton, Legh, Morgan, Fern, Randal Holmes, and others, who have used them but to mystify and perplex their readers! Is it too late to unravel the skein they have so wantonly tangled, to extract the valuable grains which it is but justice to admit they have preserved to us from the bushel of chaff in which they are so provokingly smothered?"

Mr. W. Beamont, in the course of an account of the remains at Edisbury, a place only seven miles from Chester, yet little known, inquired how it happens that within the precincts of Edisbury we seek in vain for any remains of the castle of the Saxon foundress, Elfleda, or for any decisive traces of the former existence of buildings?

"Walls and structures raised by the Romans in Britain, said he, many centuries before the birth of Edisbury, still remain to attest the grandeur of the builders. The Norman fortress of Halton, and the still greater remains of Beeston, arrest the eye of the traveller at a distance, and astonish him by their grandeur on a near approach. How is it then that within this royal city, raised by the illustrious daughter of our greatest monarch, not one stone remains upon another to show what a Saxon palace might be? Is it that here the hand of the spoiler has been more unrelenting in his devastation, or that the successive waves of ruin have wrecked the last vestiges of Saxon architecture within it? The demolition of Edisbury cannot, I think, be ascribed to any such causes. It is more probably owing to the habits of our Saxon ancestors, and the general character of their architecture, that we are without any remains of buildings either ecclesiastical or civil within the enclosure of Edisbury. The Saxons were mean builders; neither the structure nor the materials of a Saxon house were calculated for long duration, else would our Saxon ancestors, during their long sway in England, have left us more numerous as well as more perfect remains of the buildings they erected for civil or religious purposes. The ecclesiastical structures of undoubted Saxon origin are but few, and a writer in the *Encyclopædia Metropolitana* informs us there were but few castles in England at the time of the Norman conquest, and that a part of the conqueror's success is to be attributed to that circumstance. Mr. Fishbrooke has given a description and a plate of an ancient Saxon house, and of its prototype, a house of their predecessors the Britons, neither of which structures, either by their form or their materials, gave promise of a long life. It appears, says Mr. Henry, from many incidental hints in our ancient historians, that stone buildings were still very rare in the 8th and 9th centuries, and that when such buildings were erected they were objects of much admiration. Some of the buildings of Alfred were magnificent for that age, and of a new and singular construction; but they were generally more remarkable for their number and utility than their grandeur; for there is sufficient evidence that long after his time almost all the houses in England, and by far the greatest part of the monasteries and churches, were very mean buildings, constructed of wood and covered with thatch."

Of Mr. Halliwell's paper on the "Cottage Literature of the Palatine Counties," read by Mr. Pettigrew, we can only give two jokes from the curious tract of "Tom of Chester," supposed to have been printed in the latter part of the 17th century.

Thus,—an old painter, at the repairing of a church in Chester, was writing sentences of Scripture upon the walls. By chance Tom came into the church, and reading them, perceived much of false English. "Old man," said Tom, "why don't you write true English?" "Alas! Sir," quoth he, "they are poore simple people in this parish, and they will not goe to the cost of it." And again,—"A gentleman in Chester had a goodly fair house, new built, but the broken bricks, tiles, sand, limestones, and such rubbish as is commonly the remains of such buildings, lay confusedly in heaps, and scattered here and there. The gentleman demanded of his surveyor wherefore the rubbish was not carried away. The surveyor said that he purposed to hire a hundred carts for the purpose. The gentleman replied that the charge of carts might be saved, for 'a pit might be digged in the ground and bury it.' 'Sir,' said the surveyor, 'I pray you, what shall we do with the earth which we dig out of the said pit?' 'Why, you silly fellow,' said the gentleman, 'canst thou not dig the pit deep enough, and bury altogether?'"

On the second day, Mr. W. H. Black, of the Record Office, gave a very elaborate review of the public records, which lasted two hours and a-half, and yet fatigued none.

On Wednesday the association, after an examination of the cathedral, went to Conway Castle, to hear a paper on it by Mr. Hicklin, and on Thursday they were to visit Liverpool, to examine some buildings in the neighbourhood and read papers.

A very interesting temporary museum has been formed, in what was formerly the refectory adjoining Chester Cathedral, and is now known as the "King's School." There is a well-known Early English pulpit here, of which we shall give a view.

THE PERSONAL QUESTION AS TO THE TUBULAR BRIDGES.*

The tubular bridges constitute an idea now not only realised on British ground, but described and accounted for in the folios of a goodly volume, of great interest and importance. To Mr. Fairbairn the engineering and architectural profession are as certainly indebted for the latter benefit, as he conceives they are for the former, all due justice to the originater of the idea notwithstanding.

In the outset of this elaborate volume, which, besides a large mass of correspondence, and a minute detail of numerous experiments, contains upwards of twenty large plates and a multitude of minor woodcuts, the author, after alluding to the peculiar difficulties to be overcome at Conway and Menai, and the necessity for some *new* expedient in engineering, says—

"It was under these circumstances—having to encounter extraordinary difficulties of execution, and being compelled, by the opposition of so powerful a branch of the Government as the Admiralty Board, to abandon the ordinary resources of the engineer—that Mr. Stephenson conceived the original idea of a huge tubular bridge, to be constructed of riveted plates and supported by chains, and of such dimensions as to allow of the passage of locomotive engines and railway trains through the interior of it.

It was with reference to this expedient, after all others had been found inapplicable, that I was consulted by him, and that my opinion was requested, first as to the practicability of the scheme, and secondly as to the means necessary for carrying it out. This consultation took place early in April, 1845, and as far as could be gathered from Mr. Stephenson at the time, his idea then was, that the tube should be either of a circular or an egg-shaped sectional form. He was strongly impressed with the primary importance of the use of chains, placing his reliance in them as the principal support of the bridge; and he never for a moment entertained the idea of making the tube self-supporting. The wrought-iron tube, according to his idea, indeed, was entirely subservient to the chains, and intended to operate from its rigidity and weight as a stiffener, and to prevent, or at least to some extent counteract, the undulations due to the catenary principle of construction. In fact, for many months afterwards, and even up to the time of the experiments on the model tube in December, 1846, he insisted, as will be seen from the annexed correspondence, on the application of such chains. A perusal of this correspondence will, moreover, show that I was throughout strongly opposed to their application, even as an auxiliary. I always felt that in a combination of two bodies, the one of a perfectly rigid, and the other of a flexible nature, there was a principle of weakness; for the vibrations to which the one would be subjected, would call into operation forces whose constant action upon the rivets and fastenings of the other could not but tend to loosen them, and thus, by a slow but sure agency, to break up the bridge.

At the period of the consultation in April, 1845, there were no drawings illustrative of the original idea of the bridge, nor had any calculations been made as to the strength, form, or proportions of the tube. I was asked whether such a design was practicable, and whether I could accomplish it; and it was ultimately arranged that the subject should be investigated experimentally, to determine, not only the value of Mr. Stephenson's original conception, but that of any other tubular form of bridge which might present itself in the prosecution of my researches. The matter was placed unreservedly in my hands; the entire conduct of the investigation was entrusted to me; and, as an experimenter, I was to be left free to exercise my own discretion, in the investigation of whatever forms or conditions of the structure might appear to me best calculated to secure a safe passage across the Straits. This freedom of action was obviously necessary to the success of my experiments."

* An Account of the Construction of the Britannia and Conway Tubular Bridges: with a complete history of their progress, from the conception of the original idea to the conclusion of the elaborate experiments which determined the exact form and mode of construction ultimately adopted. By William Fairbairn, C.E. London: Weale; and Longman and Co. 1849.

At an entertainment, however, given when the first of the Conway tubes was completed, as our readers may be aware, Mr. Robert Stephenson, to whom Mr. Fairbairn attributed the original idea, had himself claimed everything, in short, but 'aid.' This occurred on 17th May, 1848.

"It is now upwards of six, or about seven years," said he on that occasion, "since I entertained the idea of constructing bridges with wrought-iron plates riveted together. I was called upon,—in a smaller case I admit, but not a very simple one,—to construct a bridge authorised by Act of Parliament, but with such limitations that it became a matter of extreme difficulty. All the ordinary kind of bridges were discussed, and I eventually hit upon the notion, and the designs were completed, *for a thin tubular bridge*, although not precisely the same as the present, yet *in principle precisely the same*. That was effectually completed, and answers its purpose, and may be now seen on the Northern and Eastern Railway. From that time, however, to the period of commencing the Chester and Holyhead Railway, the idea fell, or dropped rather, for the time, in consequence of the expense of wrought-iron rather exceeding that of cast. * * * * Parliamentary powers were granted for the construction of a bridge over the Britannia rock, with such conditions attached to it as rendered it all but, if not absolutely, impracticable. It was then, to use a common expression, that I felt myself fairly 'driven into a corner.' No existing species of bridge was at all applicable under the operation of the Act of Parliament as granted; and it was after an anxious investigation of every possible description of bridge, that it occurred to me, that by *reviving the old notion of seven years ago*, that by extending it, it might enable me to get over the difficulty. Approximate calculations were immediately made, and the result of those calculations were such as to satisfy me of the perfect feasibility of the work. I had satisfied myself that the thing was practicable, and I stood by it. I obtained the consent of the directors to institute a very laborious, and elaborate, and expensive series of experiments, in order, most thoroughly, to test experimentally the theory I had formed, and also to add suggestions for its full development. It was then that I called in the aid of two gentlemen, eminent, both of them, in their profession, Mr. Fairbairn and Mr. Hodgkinson. [Here follow a few compliments, of no importance to the point at issue.] But having mentioned these two names, there is another gentleman that I wish to call to your notice—I allude to my assistant, Mr. Edmund Clarke. He has been my closet companion from the commencement of the preliminary investigation; no variation or inconsistency in the experiments eluded his keen perception; he was always on the look out for contingences that might affect the success—though not the principle, still the success—of the undertaking; and he and the other gentlemen whom I have just named, are the three to whom I feel deeply indebted for having brought the theory I first broached to such perfection, and I thus publicly tender them my acknowledgments."

Mr. Fairbairn more particularly alludes to this speech in his concluding remarks. Our quotation of these, however, like that of the preceding, must be a condensed and brief one.

"The inaccuracies, both as to facts and dates, in this statement of Mr. Stephenson," he observes, "are very numerous. It simply requires a reference to the short description of the Ware-bridge, p. 113, and to the drawings, to disprove the assertion, 'that it is a *thin tubular bridge*, although not precisely the same as the present, *yet in principle precisely the same*:' and it can be easily shown too, that considering the Ware-bridge as a simple girder bridge, it is exceedingly defective in design. Is there any thing new in this application of wrought-iron plate girders? As well might it be said, that the combination of wrought-iron deck beams, so many years applied in iron ships for the support of the decks, is 'a counterpart of the proposed cellular top for the Britannia tubes.' I really cannot but regret that Mr. Stephenson, whose name will be always associated with the grandest bridge that has ever been constructed, should have committed himself in making such an erroneous assertion, as that it was by reviving and extending his original conception of this imperfect structure at Ware, that he was led to originate the bridges crossing the Conway and Menai Straits. * *

Let the reader turn again to the earlier letters of the correspondence, and he will find of what a crude and dangerous scheme that idea consisted; how totally dissimilar, in form and principle, it was to the present tubular structures, and how slowly Mr. Stephenson was persuaded to give up his earliest conceptions. Again, it was I, and not Mr. Stephenson, that solicited Mr. Hodgkinson's co-operation, and this was not done until I had been actively engaged for several months in my experimental researches, and after I had discovered the principle of strength which was offered in the cellular top, and not only proved the impracticability of Mr. Stephenson's original conception, but had given the outline of that form of tube which was ultimately carried into execution.

Mr. Bateman, C.E., showed the unjustifiable position which had been taken by Mr. Stephenson, and asserted, that in an engineering work of such novelty and magnitude, Mr. Stephenson would not have injured his own reputation, by acknowledging, in suitable and truthful terms, the merits due to those who had rendered him the most valuable service. Mr. Stephenson replied to his letter, and the tenor of his remarks showed his determination to stand by his public assertion. He quoted, from my letter of the 27th of October, 1846, my testimony to his claim of originality in having the application of *a* wrought-iron tube for the purposes of railway traffic; a great merit which neither Mr. Bateman nor myself had ever denied to him, and which I have uniformly asserted that he is undoubtedly entitled to. But he left entirely untouched the point at issue, viz., that it was almost exclusively my exertions which gave to his conception a useful and practicable form—that the experiments which I had conducted and originated, showed the weakness of the *circular* tube, which he had originally recommended—that I alone showed him the danger of the principle which he was anxious, for so great a length of time, to carry out, by attaching a flexible catenary to a perfectly rigid platform or roadway,—that from the results of these experiments, I designed and submitted for his approval an entirely novel kind of tubular bridge, different in form, different in principle, vastly superior in economy of material and strength, and which was finally approved and carried out, and which is now in existence, spanning the rapid estuary at Conway, and admirably fulfilling the varied requirements of railway traffic with perfect security."

In support of his allegations, Mr. Fairbairn adduces an abundant mass of correspondence and experiments, showing the gradual progression through which the series of trials naturally advanced from the first crude idea towards maturity. From this evidence it first of all appears that the idea—the original idea which he was called upon to test by experiment, or which at least *was* so tested, at Mr. Stephenson's instance,—was nothing cellular at all,—nay, not even modified as yet into *any* sort of scheme for strengthening either top or bottom, but simply a cylindrical tube made of riveted iron plates; and tubes such as these *altogether failed* to support anything like a safe or sufficient weight, uniformly yielding, primarily above to compression in wrinkles, cross corrugations, or puckers, but also readily to tension below, in disjointings and rents. These results were next followed by obvious appliances for the *strengthening, and even the local patching*, of those parts, *above at least*, which so readily gave way. In the midst of these we find Mr. Fairbairn's first suggestion of a form of tube not cylindrical and self-supporting, but intended, as he says, to meet Mr. Stephenson's views, though, as he thought, superior to one supported by chains, the necessity for which the latter appears to have urged even after he had been convinced by Mr. Fairbairn that the tube *would* be entirely self-supporting, as he still did not think it could be *put up* without the aid of that costly adjunct.*

The suggestion just referred to was made in a letter to Mr. Stephenson, dated 31st May, 1845, and enclosing a sketch of such a tube, strengthened above, but without the most distant idea or semblance of cells, as yet, even on Mr. Fairbairn's part. On the 3rd June following, a very ingenious suggestion is made by the latter for the erection of such a tube without even the temporary aid of the objectionable chains, by working simultaneously from each pier in opposite directions, so as to maintain a sort of equilibrium till the centres met. These and subsequent communications are followed up by a note from Mr. Stephenson, of date 21st July (1845), in which he says, with reference to the tubes, "*I hope* some of them, of an *elliptical* form, and *with thick plates* at the top and bottom, *will be tried*." Still nothing of the *principle*—the cellular—on the part of either. It is fair, indeed, to conclude, from Mr. Stephenson's own words, that as yet that principle had never even been dreamed of either by one or other of them.

"The difficulties," here remarks Mr. Fairbairn, "experienced in retaining *the cylindrical* tubes in shape, when submitted to severe strains, naturally suggested the rectangular form. Many new models of this kind were prepared and experimented on before the end of July, and others, with different thicknesses of top and bottom plates, or flanches, before 6th August." Of that date a letter, containing the following passage, was written by Mr. Fairbairn to Mr. Stephenson:—

"In almost every instance we have found the resistance opposed to compression the weakest; the upper side generally giving way from the severity of the strain in that direction. These facts are important so far as they have given rise to a new series of experiments, calculated to stiffen or render more rigid the upper part of the tube, as well as to equalise the strain, which in our present construction is evidently too great for the resisting forces of compression."

And now comes the germ of the cellular principle. "It occurred to me," says Mr. Fairbairn, "that the top might be strengthened by other means than by *thickening* it, and I addressed the following letter to my son, four days after the date of the last." In this he directs him to have prepared *a rectangular tube with a hollow triangular 'fin' or corrugation* (or cell, in fact) of sheet-iron, running along the top, to which it was to be riveted. The idea of a single long corrugation, to counteract the cross corrugation of the puckerings of compression, forthwith led him to that of two such corrugations doubled and reversed, so as to appear *in section* like a pair of spectacles; the superior strength of which, Mr. Fairbairn remarks, induced him "to adopt that cellular structure of the top of the tube which ultimately merged in a single row of rectangular cells—that structure which gives to the bridges now standing across the Conway straits their principal element of strength."

The next letter is one from Mr. Eaton Hodgkinson to Mr. Fairbairn, of date 18th of same month, written from the "British Iron Works, Abersychan, near Pont-y-pool," intimating that he was now at liberty to offer his services as desired by Mr. Fairbairn, who now found that "the experiments had assumed a shape which seemed to require the assistance of a mathematician, who should deduce, if that were possible, a formula which, from the observed strength of a tube of a lesser, might enable me to calculate the strength of one of a greater size." Mr. Hodgkinson accordingly first appears on the field of operations at Millwall on 19th September, the day when "the tubes which had been constructed with single hollow or cellular tops were experimented on."

While intimating the result to Mr. Stephenson, in a letter dated 20th September, Mr. Fairbairn says,—"You will be aware, on referring to my last letter, that the great difficulty we had to encounter was a due proportion of the parts, so as to neutralize or render the two resisting forces of compression and extension equal;" and, after reviewing the whole series of previous experiments, and pointing out the defects in cylindrical and elliptical tubes, even though protected by single 'fins' or corrugations, he goes on to say—

"It is more than probable that the bridge, in its full size, may take something of the following sectional shape. The parts, *a*, *a*, being two longitudinal plates, divided by vertical plates so as to form squares, calculated to resist the crushing strain in the first instance, and the lower parts, *b*, *b*, also longitudinal plates, well-connected with rivetted joints, and of considerable thickness to resist the tensible strain in the second."

In short, by a natural process somewhat the reverse of that whereby, according to the French anatomists, a 'cell' becomes a 'fin' as well as any other organ, Mr. Fairbairn's 'fin' had now, *and only now* it appears, assumed that very 'cellular' and rectangular form which he afterwards realized at the Conway Strait.

"It is from this period," he remarks, in allusion to these and other experiments immediately following on these, "that I date the disappearance of almost every difficulty respecting the construction and ultimate formation of the Britannia and Conway tubes."

When these experiments — but a faint glimpse of the numerous series of which only we have here had space to offer—were sufficiently matured, the importance of Mr. Fairbairn's *position* appears to have been such as to induce the directors of the Chester and

* Mr. Fairbairn estimated the expense of such a chain at about 200,000*l*.

Holyhead line, on 13th May, 1846, formally to appoint him joint engineer with Mr. Stephenson for the bridges, and, as to these, on principles of perfect equality with him. The working plans even went forth with Mr. Fairbairn's name alone attached to them; he was authorised to engage the workmen, and he was fully recognised as the acting engineer: indeed, Mr. Stephenson himself, on one occasion, says, "I consider *you as acting with me in every department* of the proceedings."

So much, then, for the assistance which Mr. Fairbairn afforded in the realization of Mr. Stephenson's theory and principle. The original idea, as already said, Mr. Fairbairn freely accords to him.*

SALISBURY CATHEDRAL AND ITS SCULPTURES.

THE ARCHÆOLOGICAL INSTITUTE.

In our last number we gave a brief notice of the Archæological Institute's proceedings at Salisbury, wherein we purposely omitted mention of the gloom that was unfortunately thrown over them by the prevalence of cholera in the town, which led the Bishop to decline receiving the Institute, and made the entertainment given by the corporation a silent meeting.

Of some of the places visited we may speak hereafter. On the present occasion we must confine ourselves chiefly to the papers on the cathedral and its sculptures.†

At the opening meeting the Hon. Sidney Herbert, the president, made an excellent address. In the course of it, when speaking of Wiltshire, he said,—In this county, at Malmesbury, lived Hobbes, the philosopher; at Salisbury lived Harris, the author of "Hermes;" in this county resided the late Lord Arundel of Wardour, and near him his acquaintance the late Sir Richard Colt Hoare, who has done so much for the topography of the county. Lord Clarendon took his title from a town in this county; and not far from Old Sarum stands or stood an old manor-house in which Chatham lived when a youth. From that house went forth a young man as a cornet of dragoons, whose voice afterwards thundered through Europe—that man was Lord Chatham. It was impossible to look at that humble village without feeling some emotions in contemplating the spot whence that great man had gone forth, and whose gigantic intellectual proportions are shrouded only by the figure of his still more illustrious son. But Wiltshire had given birth also to poets. He had already spoken of Massinger as having seen the light at Wilton. At Bemerton lived the good George Herbert. And here he would remark what an interesting scene must that have been between him and Laud, when he tried to remove his scruples respecting the cure of souls. No man (said the speaker) was prepared to grapple with the future who had not studied and investigated the past. They had a right to claim in this district examples of wisdom, learning, ability, and poetry: and there was no walk of life in which inspiration could not be drawn from the contemplation of the worth and merits of departed genius.

The Bishop of Oxford who followed, said, it was true that there was an aspect in which antiquarian pursuits may be viewed, as a collection only of the dust as it were of the past, as if virtue and goodness had had no existence. With such a spirit he felt sure that the members had no sympathy. This was the abuse, and not the use of antiquarian pursuits. He knew that there were pursuits connected with antiquarian investigation which may not be abused, and which lifted up the mind and heart to the reverence of the only living and true God. The past may be studied, as if it was better than the present; and we may do nothing but lament the past; but the wise man will learn lessons from it to guide him in the future, and will thank God for the rich inheritance which has been handed down to him from his forefathers; while at the same time he will not overvalue the present, but will find in more senses than one, when he looks back into the history of past ages, that there were indeed "giants in those days." One of the chief merits of a cultivated mind and taste was that of drawing the materials of present enjoyment out of the past and future. This is not mere fancy; not mere imagination. It was taking a practical view of the question; for it was wholly impossible for a man to understand even things around him without investigating those times that had gone before him—without viewing the past in the present. And in the course of such investigations he will stay the hand of sweeping innovation, inasmuch as he will see a use and a meaning which he could not otherwise have discovered, and he will observe how necessary many things that he could not before understand are to the constitution and fabric of society.

The illustration of

THE CATHEDRAL

was, as usual, entrusted to Professor Willis. He said, that in the other cathedrals which he had explained he had been enabled to trace how each building had grown up by degrees—as at York, Lincoln, Winchester, and Ely—but at Salisbury no cathedral existed previously to the present. This cathedral was erected during the early English period in its best character, containing all traces of the purest style of that era. It was on this account that it was valuable to the student, as affording an independent and unfettered example of the style without mixture. He had never seen such perfect unity of design, even to the mouldings, as was exhibited in this cathedral. The original design was so well preserved that it was almost next to impossible to find out what part was erected first. The tower and spire, and all above the roofs, contain the style in a higher state of development, being erected at a later period than the body of the church, while the cloisters also are later. He would refer to the history of the building. The first Bishop of Sarum—the see being removed from Wilton to Old Sarum—was Herman, who was succeeded by Osmond, who built his cathedral in 1093, in the midst of the fortress. This situation was a great inconvenience to the bishop; and there was also a great want of water for the inhabitants of the city, so that in fact as much money was paid for water as for wine. All these circumstances are set forth in the Bull of Pope Honorius the Third, which was granted March 29, 1218, by which permission was given to remove the see. In 1219 it was agreed to remove from Old Sarum, and a wooden chapel was erected for the performance of the service, instead of remaining in the old church. In 1220 the foundations of the cathedral were laid, and in 1225 the services of the church were performed within it. And there was one curious peculiarity in this ceremony, not seen elsewhere, viz., the great number of stones which were laid, one for the Pope, one for the Archbishop, one for the Bishop himself, one for Longespee, and another for his wife; and some time afterwards others laid stones also. He never recollected a parallel case in the history of the foundation of any church. From 1223 to 1246 Bishop Bingham carried on the works with great activity, and completed them—including the body of the structure and the west front, without the tower and spire, which were afterwards added. In 1258 the cathedral was dedicated—during the episcopate of Bishop Bridport. The cloister and chapter-house were erected during the latter part of the thirteenth century; and by examining the monument of Bishop Bridport, who was buried in 1262, it will be seen that it is of the same date in point of architectural characteristics as the style of the cloisters and chapter-house. It appears that the tower and spire were not contemplated by the original architect, and no provisions had been made for their erection; neither is there any distinct historical record of the time of their construction. But in the chapter records exists a contract by that body with an architect named Richard Farleigh, that he should carry on the work. Thus the name of the architect who erected the tower and spire is known to us. But great as he might have been as an architect, his skill was but small as an engineer, as he ran the risk of crushing down the structure, by the erection of so mighty a tower,—the piers and arches of which never were intended to carry a stone spire. No sooner was the erection of the tower and spire completed than the chapter were in great dismay, and endeavoured to get funds for strengthening the building. In the year 1415 arrangements were made for continuing the repairs of the fabric; for an indenture was made in that year between the chapter and Nicholas Wayte, mason, who constructed the braces, buttresses, and arches, which prevented the tower and spire from falling. This was the last great event of any kind, until the building of the Hungerford and Beauchamp Chapels, which have been removed. In consequence of the havoc which had occurred to the church, we find that after the Restoration Sir Christopher Wren was called on to examine the building, and to fit up the choir and chancel, and to this examination we owe one of the most curious reports ever penned. He mingles in his reports mistakes respecting the style of architecture, while he comments freely on the structure in a mechanical point of view. He admires it exceedingly; but is, however, full of prejudice against what he considers to be the corrupted style of the edifice. The next event was the alteration of the church, under Bishops Hume and Barrington, when the building suffered from an experiment of Wyatt,—it being left to his own judgment as to the manner in which the repairs should be carried out. He did not look at this building with reference to the system upon which it was erected; for it must be borne in mind that this and similar ones must be viewed not so much as mere works of art, but as monumental remains of a peculiar state of architectural science. (Hear, hear.) Neither Wyatt nor his employers acted upon this view of the subject. The changes which Wyatt made in the cathedral were totally irrespective of the uses to which the various portions of the church had been applied. Thus the church was full of screens, arranged and adapted according to the ceremonies of the ancient ritual. It also contained monuments of the pious founders of the church and other eminent persons, and the site on which they stood was in every way connected with the life and purpose of the persons who were buried beneath them. These memorials of primitive times Wyatt removed—no feeling of historical association having entered his head—and he placed them in a row under the pillars of the nave. He also pulled down the Hungerford and Beauchamp Chapels, which were erected in the Perpendi-

* It appears, however, that Mr. Stephenson, even as the originater of the idea of a wrought-iron railway tunnel, is not to be left in quiet possession of his laurels. We do not mean to enter into any controversy on either of these questions, but simply to state that Mr. De la Haye, of Liverpool, whose claims we long ago announced, has sent us a long communication, in which he reminds us of this, and retraces the principal facts and circumstances, which are simply these:—In September, 1844, Mr. De la Haye placed a pamphlet,—published by him five months before at Jersey, and titled, "A Plan for passing Rivers and Channels by means of Wrought-iron Tunnels,"—in the hands of Mr. Smith, editor of the *Liverpool Mercury*, who advised him "to see Sir Joshua Walmsley, at his office in Brunswick-street, and ask him to submit it to his friend George Stephenson, the great engineer. He is a practical man and a bold thinker," adds the editor, "and you would most likely be well guided by his advice.—P.S. You may use my name to Sir Joshua." Mr. De la Haye accordingly saw Sir Joshua, who examined the pamphlet, but "thought the scheme, involving such gigantic works, would not be approved by G. S." This circumstance occurred eight months before Mr. Stephenson's first announcement of an intention to form a wrought-iron tunnel-bridge at Menai; so that it seemed clear at all events that his friend Sir Joshua had no cognizance of such an intention on his part at that time. He, nevertheless, undertook to bring Mr. De la Haye's scheme under the notice of Mr. Stephenson on the following day, when he would see him. "Eight months afterwards," Mr. De la Haye remarks, "Mr. Stephenson proposed a wrought-iron railway tunnel for the Menai Straits, and a few weeks after, a paragraph appeared in the *Liverpool Mercury*, in which it was stated that I had proposed iron tunnels for railway purposes long before G. S., and a rather broad hint was given that the idea had been borrowed from my inventions; but in spite of this, and of the remarks which appeared in THE BUILDER, G. S. never attempted to prove that his was a distinct invention. . . . . The iron tunnel which I had proposed," also observes the writer, in allusion to his pamphlet, "was to be constructed in divisions of 400 feet in length, each division being made perfectly rigid, in order to sustain a weight independent of central support, as I supposed that the bed of the water (at Dover straits) might be as uneven as the surface of the sea during a storm." Mr. De la Haye, of course, is quite aware of the distinction between a submarine tunnel and a tunnel-bridge; but he seems to think that all Mr. Stephenson had to do, in handing it over from the originaser to the maturer, was to "fish it out of the water." Previous to the publication of his pamphlet, beginning of 1844, Mr. De la Haye believes that "the words wrought-iron railway tunnel had never appeared together in type." A description of his invention was given in *The Artizan* shortly after THE BUILDER had recorded his claim, but although it was therein admitted "that this plan is identical with that proposed by Mr. Stephenson," still it was held that Mr. Stephenson cannot be fairly charged with plagiarism, inasmuch as the plan [of Mr. De la Haye] was never matured—a mere hint alone being given." Had the rival plan been itself matured, such an argument might have had some force, but in the circumstances it appears to Mr. De la Haye to be rather a two-edged weapon, inasmuch as his plan, though it might not be *perfect*, was not a mere hint, but had cost him "years of thought and months of labour," before a single experiment was made by Mr. Fairbairn to *mature* Mr. Stephenson's suggestion.

† Reported at greater length in the *Salisbury and Wiltshire Herald*, and also in the *Journal*.

cular styles, because they offended his notions. The professor then proceeded to observe that he had discovered some curious and very peculiar features in this cathedral. He had walked round the foundations two or three times before he noticed the peculiarity to which he would refer. The Chilmark stone, which is exceedingly beautiful, is laid on concrete; the masonry is of exquisite symmetry, and in fact, this church was the only mediæval structure with which he was acquainted, where the masonry was employed as a mode of decoration, by the uniform manner in which the courses of stone are laid. In our ecclesiastical structures the stones are laid as they come to hand; but in Salisbury Cathedral there is a regularity of design running round the masonry of the edifice. The courses of stone are not the same in thickness, but they follow a certain law. First, there is a band of large stones—then, a course somewhat narrower; and so followed on the courses, in strict symmetry and arrangement. The professor then stated that he considered that that portion of the church eastward of the nave was the first part which was completed. It must be recollected that the church was nearly forty years in erection, and that during that time the work appeared to have lagged; there was evidently a pause between the nave and the east end and transepts. He considered that the nave was erected at the latter end of the thirteenth century. It must be recollected, that five years after the foundations of the church were laid, several altars were erected. The whole of the Lady Chapel had been completed, and was first consecrated in the time of Longespee. In another point of view the church is favourable to the study of Early English architecture in this country. In France there are several cathedrals, the foundations of which were laid about the same time. Professor Willis then exhibited drawings of Amiens and Salisbury Cathedral, the foundations of both of which were laid in the same year; and commented upon the peculiarities of each edifice, and upon the growth of the pointed arch. He then proceeded to state that ecclesiastical architecture in this country was derived from the French—Canterbury Cathedral being erected from the designs of William of Sens, a Norman; this cathedral being the type of edifices in the Norman and transition period. All the great steps in ecclesiastical architecture, from the Norman to the Decorated style, were made by French architects, until we come to the Perpendicular, which was the growth of this country. This was not a mere theory; it was matter of history. Why should it be supposed that a change which took place in the style of architecture all over Europe was invented in England?

Professor Cockerell read a paper on

THE SCULPTURES OF THE CATHEDRAL.

The professor commenced his remarks by observing that sculpture was the right hand of architecture during the middle ages; and might be regarded as an epitome of the manners, habits, and customs of the period in which it was executed. There were amongst the sculptures of this church some "sleeping beauties" which had been too much neglected; and this neglect was to be deplored, inasmuch as these works were of great historical value. It would be found that they were anterior to the period of Italian art, and were not inferior to the great works of the masters of that school. The cathedral of Salisbury was commenced in 1220, and completed about 1258; its builders were desirous of illustrating the glories of the Old and New Testament, of the apostles and martyrs; and the west front was the page on which this object was inscribed, there being upwards of 160 statues ornamenting the exterior of the cathedral, 123 of which adorned the west front. On the buttresses there were still four remaining. The two minor buttresses to the north and south contained monuments of the Count of Salisbury and Bishop Poore. On the south end of the west front was a statue of Peter holding a scroll—the drapery of this figure was very fine. On the other side was Paul, holding the pommel of a sword. Underneath was a figure of John the Baptist, and opposite a figure of John the Evangelist, it being a common practice to represent them in juxta-position. These were the only figures on the buttresses. The west front formerly contained the twelve apostles and other members of the holy family. On the north side was an elegant statue, evidently representing Stephen holding a stone in one hand, and in the other a palm branch, the symbol of martyrdom. There was an altar in this church dedicated to this saint. In a niche on the northern side is a statue of Archbishop Langton, who was one of the coadjutors of Magna Charta, and who was present at the dedication of this church. This statue is an elegant figure, and held in the right hand an episcopal staff. The lecturer then proceeded to point out the historical sculptures of the extreme north and south ends of the west front. At the south was a figure in a secular dress, which was remarkably well executed—and there could be but little doubt that this was intended to represent William Longespee (Count of Sarum, and the natural son of King Henry II. by Fair Rosamond Clifford), who had laid one of the stones of the cathedral. If they compared the execution of these works with those of contemporary art, they would find them greatly superior. There was more suavity and grace in these figures than in those of the west front of Wells. Here there was a masterly display of drapery—the execution of which was superb. He had last year visited the cathedral of Amiens, a contemporary structure, which contained many sculptures—but those of Salisbury were superior. He was quite sure that many persons in looking at these figures would be reminded of the works of Greek art; and if they were compared with the sculptures of the great Italian masters—Giotto, Cimabue, and others—to whose works these sculptures were anterior—they would not suffer by the comparison. But it has been asked, were these works executed in England? He would give a few reasons for their being of English workmanship. There were 600 statues in the west front of Wells cathedral, the works of which were going on at the same time, as also were those of Lincoln, York, Durham, and at many other English cathedrals. It was therefore perfectly ridiculous to say these sculptures were executed by foreigners, and not by English hands.

Mr. Richard Westmacott read a paper on

THE MONUMENTAL SCULPTURES IN THE CATHEDRAL.

The lecturer, after pointing out the origin of monumental sculpture in this and other countries, proceeded to sketch the peculiarities of the monuments in the cathedral,—where specimens existed from the earliest period of monumental sculpture in this country, down to the time when a corrupt taste prevailed—viz., from the twelfth to the seventeenth century. The first object of a monument was to denote the fact that a body was buried; the second to denote the quality; then regard was had to the individual figure, and sometimes an inscription was added, containing the name and rank of the person. Of this kind of monument there were several very interesting examples in the nave. From the 5th to the 12th centuries the church exercised a very dominant influence over monumental sculpture, and compelled a similitude of style, and consequently most of the specimens are of a devotional character. One of the most interesting monuments in this cathedral is that of William Longespee, Earl of Salisbury, the under part of which is of wood; and no one who beholds that ancient relic can fail to be struck with the simplicity and repose of the figure. The details are well carried out, and the turn of the head is well executed. Mr. Westmacott then referred to the monument of Bishop Bridport in one of the transepts, to the Audley monument, and then proceeded to refute an observation which had sometimes been made, viz., that the art of monumental sculpture had declined in this country in consequence of the Reformation. He also proceeded to show that the best works of monumental sculpture were erected in an age when religion and morals were at a low standard, and in an age not deeply imbued with religious feeling. These works were, in fact, erected in an age inferior to our own in piety. He believed that the piety of the people of this country was as pure and unaffected in the seventeenth century—when monumental sculpture was not so pure and chaste—as in the days when the monument of Longespee was erected. The fact was, that the piety of the age had nothing to do with the matter. He then proceeded to point out the causes of the change which came over Christian art, ascribing it to the revival of classical literature, which changed the taste. Hence classical subjects were introduced in religious art; and imitations of the sculptures of ancient Greece, and subjects from the heathen mythology, were employed to illustrate modern art in Christian churches. This was called taste; it was, however, the absence of all taste. He then proceeded to condemn the affectation for mediæval subjects in Christian churches, and protested against copying rude efforts of art, which were very interesting, as illustrating their own age, but served only to degrade art, when imitated in our own times.

HOW A CHURCH SHOULD BE BUILT.

PROPOSED CHURCH, SANDFORD DISTRICT, CHELTENHAM.

In the course of a replication from Mr. Brandon, for the whole of which we have not room, he says—Mr. Philipps writes that I give no data for coming to the conclusion that a church cannot be properly built to accommodate 1,000 persons for 4,000*l*. The only possible data which I can furnish in a letter, is the assertion of my experience on the subject, and having devoted considerable attention to church building, I believe I can form a pretty just opinion thereon.

The question, however, turns not upon how little a building can be erected for to be called a church, but upon, how a church ought to be built? My answer to that is, in the very best and most suitable manner that the science of the architect and the nature of the materials will admit,—I do not say, as an essential, in the most ornamental, though that would be a desideratum; but surely the only buildings that we can feel assured will be required by all future generations should be, of all others, erected in the most enduring manner possible, and the sacred purpose to which they are dedicated, should be sufficient to claim for them the very best of materials and workmanship. Unless these conditions can be complied with when church accommodation is required, I should recommend the erection of a temporary building, not to save the present generation from the expense of building a proper church, but merely as a substitute for such a building till the funds could be collected for it, and as a means of obtaining such funds.

I must here also allude to an expression contained in a private letter to me on the subject, from one of the members of the Committee, which I should not make mention of but that it probably expresses the general opinion of the committee. The writer, after referring to a church that was in the course of erection to accommodate 1,000 for 5,000*l*., goes on to state, that "a much smaller building than this would, with the usual number of galleries, contain 1,000." I must confess I am ignorant of what is the usual number of galleries for a church, but know that one is one too many.

As regards the amendment which is required in the present system of competitions, it must be left, as I before observed, to the profession at large to make it, and I should be delighted to find the matter taken up by them, and to assist it in any way in my power.

Baths and Washhouses.—At Chelmsford a committee has been appointed to consider the propriety and means of establishing baths and washhouses there. A design has been provided by Mr. Chancellor, who estimates the cost at between 3,000*l*. and 4,000*l*. The following details of the proposed design are from the *Chelmsford Chronicle*:—The façade consists of a centre building two stories high, and two wings one story high. The ground-floor is rusticated with a Roman doric portico, and an arcade with pilasters of a similar character continued along the wall, with circular-headed windows. An Italian tower for ventilation, with an exterior gallery, rises from the centre of the buildings, and is a prominent feature of the design.

Gutta Percha.—Recent advices from Singapore announce that the supply of this article is still on the increase. Some imports of it had been latterly received from a new source, at a place called Coti.

CHAPTER HOUSE, CHESTER CATHEDRAL.

[See page 361, in present number.]

PORTLAND BREAKWATER.

The foundation-stone of this national work was laid by Prince Albert on Wednesday week. The stone was a block weighing 14 tons; it was suspended by an iron chain, and being let slip after a bottle containing a plan of the breakwater, specimens of the coinage, &c., had been deposited, fell to the bottom of the sea, in the midst of a drenching shower of spray and a noise like thunder.

The construction of this breakwater, as many of our readers are aware, is not a new idea. It was first proposed by Mr. John Harvey, mechanic to George III., and afterwards postmaster at Weymouth; and after whose death the subject continued in agitation partly by the efforts of Mr. Harvey's son. The attention of Government, however, was not steadily fixed upon the matter until 1846, when the Refuge Harbour Commission reported very strongly in its favour. But the work was not decided on, even then, until a second commission had confirmed the recommendation of the first, and pointed out the advantages which the proposed breakwater would secure. The necessary surveys were then made, and powers for the compulsory purchase of land obtained by Act of Parliament, after which Mr. Rendell, civil engineer, was authorised to prepare a design of the work. As planned by Mr. Rendell, it will shelter an area of 1,822 acres from the only wind to which it is exposed. From the eastern point of the island, it will run out 1,500 feet in an easterly direction, and then going off at an angle will be carried 6,000 feet to the north-east. At the angle there will be an opening of from 400 to 500 feet for the use of steamers and small craft, but the whole work will be 7,900 feet, or one mile four furlongs in length. Of this more than 7,000 feet will be built in from 6 to 8½ fathoms' depth at low water. Of the whole area there will be 1,544 acres having not less than 5 fathoms' average depth, and 1,072 acres with 6½ fathoms' average depth, thus making accommodation for the largest channel fleets and convoys known during the last continental war. From the facilities which the stone quarries on the island afford for the work, and the intended employment of convict labour for quarrying the stone and loading the waggons, the estimated cost is only 500,000*l*. A railway, with three inclines, drums, wire ropes, &c., will raise or lower the waggons, and carry stones from the top of the island to the spot where they are dropped into the sea. By means of self-registering 'weigh-bridges,' the weight of stone put into the breakwater can be exactly ascertained.

There are upwards of 500 convicts or workmen now on the spot, and it is said there will be shortly in all 800 employed, some in quarrying, others in squaring stone, others in making new roads and levelling the quarries for laying down the rails preparatory to the removal of the stone to the breakwater. The establishment, which can only be seen by an order from the Secretary of State, is constructed chiefly of wood and iron, so that it may be taken down and removed on the completion of the breakwater. Each man has a second separate sleeping cell, about 7 feet long by 4 feet wide and 7 feet high. These small cells are ranged four stories high, and open into four spacious halls which are so placed as to be under inspection from a central corridor, where the officers are stationed. All the necessary offices are placed in an adjoining building, where there is a large cookhouse, washhouse, and drying-shed, baths, &c. The large chapel and other buildings are still in progress. The building is now inclosed by a lofty wall at the edge of the quarry. On the outside are houses for the governor, chaplain, and superior officers; and extensive ranges of cottages for warders and others. There is also a large infirmary, protected from the prevailing winds by having been built in a large quarry. Instead of going to the expense of breaking up the large stones, and levelling the yard where the sick will take exercise, the rocks have been left, and a party of convicts, under the direction of a governor, have made walks among them. There is a gasometer from which all the buildings are lighted, and the supply of water is pumped up from a reservoir about 350 feet below the top of the rock.

CONSTRUCTION OF GREENHOUSES, &c. WITH METROPOLITAN BUILDINGS' ACT.

As doubts exist in the minds of not only builders and proprietors, but the district surveyors themselves, as to the requirements of the act in respect of greenhouses and such erections, it will be useful to give the decision of the referees (Messrs. Hosking and Poynter) in a recent case.

A conservatory was in course of erection for Mr. John Meek, against the back wall of a dwelling-house in the Peckham-road, district of Camberwell, and a requisition was forwarded to the referees, setting forth that the frames and sashes of the said conservatory had been prepared in wood, and that it was proposed to fix the same on dwarf brick walls on two sides, and to inclose the conservatory on the other side by a party wall; to which materials the district surveyor objected, being of opinion "that the bearers of the roof, and the angle and door posts ought to be made of fire-proof materials." At the hearing, it was stated "that the wall which will enclose one side of the said conservatory is a party fence wall, and that the bearers of the roof thereof for carrying the running sashes, will not be let into the external wall of Mr. Meek's house, which will enclose the said conservatory on another side; and the district surveyor stated that the said conservatory is intended to be 14 feet high in the highest part and is to be built as an addition to the dwelling-house with which it will communicate internally, and that it is to be heated by pipes from a boiler within the dwelling-house; and he contended that the sills and the bearers of the roof of the said conservatory ought to be of fire-proof materials, and that the outer quoin and the piers against the back wall of the house, and against the party fence wall, ought to be of brickwork, in order that the frames of the sashes might be set in reveals." The official referees awarded that it would not be contrary to the Act to build the conservatory in the manner and of the materials proposed, "provided that the party fence wall by which it is intended to enclose the said conservatory on one side thereof, and which by the erection of the said conservatory will be converted into a party wall, be carried up to the height required for party walls by Schedule D, Part 3. of the said Act, and be otherwise made conformable to the rules of the said Act with reference to party walls."

THE CANYNGE SOCIETY AND ST. MARY REDCLIFFE CHURCH, BRISTOL.

We have already spoken of the Canynge Society as having been established to assist in the restoration of that fine structure St. Mary Redcliffe, Bristol. On Thursday in last week the second anniversary meeting was held, when the active and able Mayor, Mr. J. Kerle Haberfield, presided, and 60 or 70 of the leading citizens assembled. From the report it appeared that nearly 500*l*. were raised by the society last year, and had been applied in the clerestory of the chancel, and that the amount of subscriptions for the current year has increased as much as could be expected.

The chairman performed his task well. The Rev. Mr. Whish, Mr. R. P. King, Alderman Pountney, Mr. W. P. King, Mr. Garrard, the City Chamberlain, Alderman Wyld, Mr. G. F. Powell, and others addressed the meeting, but we must confine ourselves to a few memoranda which may assist the cause.

Mr. Proctor, the chairman of the Restoration Committee, made a strong and able appeal in favour of the church. He said it was now some years since they first endeavoured to impress upon their fellow-citizens the necessity of attending to the noble fabric for whose restoration they were associated. The dilapidations then going on could no longer be trifled with; but now, by the kind contributions of their fellow-citizens, the committee had been enabled to grapple with the evil, and to render the fabric secure at all events, and he did feel that with the assistance of the society they would be enabled very much to hasten the complete and perfect restoration of the church. He said "complete and perfect," because he felt assured that it would be impossible, now that general attention was drawn to the work, but it must be so, and it ought in common credit to themselves to be speedy: it was the finest monument they possessed of the past, it was the most magnificent specimen of architectural beauty in the city, and what was it used for? to offer up thanksgivings and ask for future blessings. For what, too, did they ask? was it not for the prosperity of themselves and their land? And if they so prayed, was it creditable for them to allow the building in which they did so to fall in ruin before their faces? If it were necessary to say more, he would venture to add, though they were doing much toward the prosperity of their city, there was more than at first view appeared to be the case in the restoration of St. Mary Redcliffe, as regarded its conducement to that effect. If only as a matter of example, it was of great importance. The proper restoration of St. Mary Redcliffe would offer them an example which would stimulate them in the erection and maintenance of other public buildings, for no one could see the perfect beauties of that structure without being better educated in the beautiful, without feeling the power of beauty so strongly that they would not be able to tolerate the erection of such public buildings as would be a discredit to the city. Redcliffe Church was now seen black and bedizened with dirt, and yet they asked the poor to clean their houses: ought they not to restore this building, and give a tone and example to the poor? He wished he could impress upon them lines written in the days of yore, and make them feel their truth. The work then would be soon done:—

> "If thou wouldst see famed Bristowe in full prosperitie, ...
> Take heed thou keep'st faire Redcliffe in true sinceritie."

The architect, when his health was drunk, said he was sure they would exonerate him from any suspicion that self-interest alone led him to advocate the restoration of the church. He did not look upon the restoration as a matter of pounds, shillings, and pence. He believed that any architect who sat down to design or restore a church with no higher motive than 5 per cent. would not be likely to produce any effective results; and, indeed, he believed he would not be competent for the task at all. The church was most beautiful even in its ruins, although he hoped before a very long time to be able to show it as it had been. He had examined most of the noble structures in the low countries, in France and Germany, and he did not recollect one which surpassed in parts St. Mary Redcliffe. He had a full recollection of the beautiful feathery spires of Antwerp and Strasburg Cathedrals, of the sublimity of Notre Dame, and the richness of Chartres, but still he maintained that the tower of St. Mary Redcliffe was second to none. For piquancy of fancy he knew nothing throughout Germany or France which could compete with its north porch; if they looked at it foot by foot, it displayed the most extraordinary evidence of the fancy and genius of the old architects; every corbel was different, and manifested a degree of care and attention, an imagination and a fire that could not be surpassed; it was designed by men who knew what they were about, and carried out by others with heart and soul. It gave him great pleasure to see the way in which the workmen were pursuing the work, and if they continued to go on in the way they had began, they would soon see the north porch as beautiful as ever. The necessity for the restoration had not taken that hold of the citizens of Bristol that it should have done. Love of country, love of the beautiful, love of God, too, should tend to make it an object of desire. Lord Palmerston the other night electrified the House of Commons by stating that public opinion was stronger than arms and cannons; that if public opinion was founded on justice and truth, arms and cannon would disappear before it. Let them, then, bring public opinion to bear on the present question, let it be shown that such a building was a means of education,—and this point had been too much neglected,—let it be shown that the contemplation of a fine building has an exalting effect upon the mind, and he was sure that enough of public spirit would be excited amongst the wealth and intelligence of the city of Bristol to enable them to effect the restoration, and that speedily.

An excellent sermon was preached by the Rev. Canon Harvey previous to the dinner; and it was announced that the Duke of Beaufort had accepted the office of president for the ensuing year.

ARCHITECTURAL CRITICISM.

Doubtful as I am whether you will allow the remarks I am about to make to appear in The Builder, I nevertheless send them. I cannot agree with you in thinking—as you appear to do—that "such men" as Sir R. Smirke, Mr. Barry, and Mr. Blore, are not to be spoken of unreservedly as regards their professional doings. On the contrary, I am of opinion that "such men" can best of all bear to hear the voice of honest criticism. If those who have been signally favoured by opportunities, and who have been employed on works of especial mark, cannot bear to have their works fairly submitted to critical examination, who can? They are, or ought to be, fully prepared for criticism, as what they must expect; and those alone have reason to deprecate the exercise of it who are conscious that their works will not endure its scrutiny.* For Sir Robert Smirke, indeed, there is this excuse—that in *his time*—namely, a quarter of a century ago, when he commenced operations at the British Museum—he could not have the wholesome fear of criticism before his eyes, because nothing deserving the name of architectural criticism then existed. There was then no vehicle for it—not a single architectural journal—but all was then a dead calm, as far as criticism is concerned, because nearly all were then in a dead sleep. For rousing us out of such a state of torpid indifference, we have to thank the late Mr. Loudon, who did much to popularise architectural criticism, not merely by his *Magazine*—the first periodical of its kind—but also by other publications. His policy—and most excellent and liberal it is—was to promote discussion,—to allow both sides to be heard, and even his own particular opinions to be freely called in question by any one who thought proper to do so; he being aware that it is only by the collision of opinions that prejudices can be removed, imperfect notions corrected, and erroneous ones exploded.

In the paper on "Architectural Criticism," in your last number, it is very justly said,—"Good criticism is a means by which the taste of masses may be greatly improved;" and not that of the "masses" only, but of the profession also. It could be wished, however, that the writer had expressly defined what "good criticism" is, and what is to be understood by it, instead of contenting himself with doing so only negatively, by giving us an instance of what he calls "negative criticism," which does not deserve to be called criticism at all, but should be left to *Punch*, and to those who, for lack of criticism, indulge in such small-witted facetiousness as is that of comparing spires to extinguishers, tazza fountains to dumb-waiters, and window pediments to cocked-hats.† What I myself understand by "negative criticism" is that which, whether it be unfavourable, or, as frequently happens, quite the reverse, amounts to nothing more than the bare expression of opinion, without any attempt at fair and rational argument in support of it. It is not enough that, either way, the opinion itself be perfectly valid and just,—it does not become criticism unless it pronounce its judgment after an impartial estimate.

The absence of thoughtful, intelligent criticism operates disadvantageously in more ways than one. One great source of the interest attending architecture is cut off; getting no more than summary verdicts as to the merits or defects of the buildings that happen to be spoken of, the public may, indeed, admire or condemn just as they are so directed, yet remain just as uninstructed as before. Another evil is, that unless criticism be freely exercised professional men feel themselves, on the one hand, secure from open reproach for their faults; and on the other, little encouraged to exert themselves to the best of their ability. He who can set at nought idle and ignorant censure is also most likely to reject with scorn that sort of hackneyed praise which betrays itself to be either mere complimentary notice or indiscriminating adulation—hyperbolic in its language, perhaps, even to fulsomeness, but cold in feeling, and totally devoid of all heartiness.

It is, moreover, owing to the lack of a sufficiency of sound architectural criticism, and the consequent ignorance that prevails generally as to architecture itself, that many who are more or less unqualified to do so, venture to put forth off-hand opinions and crude remarks as criticism, they knowing that they may do so without the slightest fear of being contradicted or gainsaid. We certainly do frequently find the most one-sided—if not actually absurd—observations made, yet suffered to pass unrebuked, consequently, to all appearance acquiesced in, which would not be the case were criticism to be properly exercised. *Exempli gratiâ*: When Mr. Fergusson calls the new building at Buckingham Palace "hideously ugly," he quite overshoots the mark, and does not bring against it those real and valid objections which he easily might have done. Had the same design been executed as a façade for a range of houses any where in Belgravia, it might then have been called handsome—certainly would have been of superior quality to any of the architectural doings in that quarter; whereas, as the principal or public façade of a royal palace, it is so totally destitute of all those qualities which should stamp one, as to be, when its purpose is considered, most unsatisfactory, undignified, commonplace, and dowdy; and surely a considerable difference there is between being dowdy and "hideously ugly."

ARTI FIDELIS.

* Our correspondent misunderstands the remark,—or appears to do so. Our objection was not to criticism, but abuse.—Ed.

† It is due to the author of the paper in question to say, that only part of it was printed in The Builder.

THE DRAINAGE PLAN.

Allow me to correct Dr. Buckland's statement that "the London clay glanced off at the north-east corner of Saint Paul's," by ascertained facts.

Section at Black Swan-alley in Saint Paul's churchyard:—

	Ft.	In.
Made ground	11	6
Yellow clay or loam	4	6
Sand and gravel	18	6
Blue clay cut into	0	6

The gravel and sand was completely full of water. It had no tendency to run, for sharp sand, when water-laid, does not run. The whole of this water was pumped out by a steam-engine, and wells drained on the north side of Saint Paul's churchyard, in Saint Martin's-le-Grand, and in Newgate market, yet no building was in the least injured, simply from this circumstance, that sand containing water is as compact as it can possibly be, the water only fills the interstices, and its removal does not affect the solidity of the stratum.

Section at 24 feet from the south end of Princes-street, Bank:—

	Ft.	In.
Rubble and brickwork	10	0
Black soil (bog)	8	0
Yellow loam	2	0
Gravel	8	6
Blue clay cut into	4	0

at 48 feet further north, and for more than 60 feet still further:—

	Ft.	In.		Ft.	In.
Rubbish	11	0			
Black bog earth of the ancient Walbrook	22	0	to	22	6

Cut into, and the blue clay just touched.

At 28 feet south of the London Dock House:—

	Ft.	In.
Rubbish	12	0
Loam	11	0
Gravel	14	4
Blue clay cut into	4	0

The blue clay underlies Moorgate-street, and has been cut into 5 feet 6 inches in depth, and in King William-street it has been cut into to a depth of 10 feet.

In Fenchurch-street the gravel has been cut into; in Aldgate High-street the loam has been cut into, and sand reached, and it is all but an established certainty, that beneath the London loam or gravel there is blue clay.

These I know to be facts, therefore I assume that the doctor has not spoken of his own knowledge, and venture to impugn so great an authority, merely from a desire that any project for getting rid of the foul pollution of the Thames should not be injured by unsupported assertion.

It is very doubtful if Philips's proposition can be carried out, but out of it something practicable may grow.

Z. Z.

Mr. Bardwell has forwarded a communication on the subject of a plan laid by him before the commissioners at their first sittings. The writer says,—It was simply three intercepting sewers, at a depth of one or more feet below the lowest existing sewer. The first embraced nearly all the sewers in the old Westminster commission, and commenced at Charing Cross, running down Whitehall, Parliament-street, Millbank, Lupas-street, Chelsea Hospital Gardens, Cheyne-row, and emptying itself into reservoirs near the Kensington Canal. The second commenced at Northumberland-street, running beneath Hungerford-market, the Adelphi and Somerset House, through the Temple Gardens to Earl-street, along Thames-street and the Lower Ditch to East Smithfield, High-street, Shadwell, and along the banks of the Bromley Canal to Bromley Common. The third, the Surrey division. Its sewer commenced at the Effra, ran along Vauxhall-row Princes-street, Palace New-road, York road, Stamford street, Bankside, Tooley-street, Jamaica-row, to the reservoirs near the King's-road, Bermondsey.

From the depôts the sewage would be sent in pipes for irrigation at the proper seasons, and at other times the solids would be separated from the fluid by electric or chymical agents.

NOTES IN THE PROVINCES.

The chief stone of Romford New Church was laid on 26th ult. The old foundations have been used in front, but the walls are carried out at the back 10 feet further than the limits of the old site. The church is to be in the Decorated style, the walls faced with Kentish ragstone, with dressings of Bath stone, and will contain 1,110 persons. The length of the interior is 113 feet; the width 54 feet; the height to the roof, which is an open one, 54 feet; the tower will be 66 feet high, and the spire from the ground 140 feet. The total cost will be 5,850*l.* Mr. Johnson is the architect, Mr. Kelk the builder, and Mr. Gibbons the clerk of the works. A view of the church has been published.——From recent reports it appears that that great bore the Northam Artesian well, near Southampton, has now been bored to 353 feet in depth. The progress has been impeded by a stone 22 inches thick, and the supply of water had decreased through the decay of the rods.——In a recent lodgement of tenders for repair of conduits belonging to the Southampton Water Works Company, it was found that "Mr. Howell's tender was 82*l.* 10s., while that of Mr. Metcher was only 39*l.*; the others varying from 61*l.* 16s. to 79*l.* 17s." Mr. Metcher's tender was accepted. It appeared, says a Hampshire cotemporary, that the miscellaneous repairs had amounted to about 75*l.* a-year.——A Bristol lady has bequeathed 4,000*l.* to found a school of arts in that city.——Kemerton Church, says the *Bristol Journal*, is again in course of restoration. The north aisle has now been taken down, and the whole interior of the building, with its Norman columns, exposed to view. The Norman arcade is, it is said, to be removed.——All Hallows-on-the-Walls, Exeter, has recently had stained glass inserted in the south window of the chancel.——Abberley Church is to be rebuilt and enlarged, Mr. J. Moilliet having got designs, and offered to supply whatever may be deficient in the requisite sum (2,500*l.*), to be raised by subscription, and the proprietress of Abberley-hall, the mother of the same gentleman, supplying the stone.——From the Liverpool Dock Surveyor's report it appears, that the remainder of the north docks are in a forward state, and that 232,374*l.* odds have been expended during the past twelve months on the new works, besides 20,610*l.* for dock repairs.——The parish church of Huddersfield has been generally repaired, and the interior newly painted in oak, &c., varnished, and emblazoned with heraldic crests in white and gold.——A column is to be erected on a height near

Ulverston to the memory of Sir John Barrow. ——The new church of Seghill, says a Newcastle paper, was consecrated on Saturday week. It is in the Early English style, and will accommodate 530 persons, mostly free. The cost of erection and site is about 1,700*l*. Mr. John Green supplied the design.——Another small church was consecrated on Tuesday week at Newton Arlosh, parish of Holme Cultram; one at Skinburness on the day following; and on Thursday one at Mowbray, near Allonby.——A model lodging-house has been formally opened at Aberdeen, under the auspices of the Lord Provost. Charges per night 3d. a-head.

RAILWAY JOTTINGS.

About 3,000 tons of a cutting near Warmsworth church, on the South Yorkshire line, gave way on Monday week, leaving a void about 30 yards in length and 10 in breadth, extending from the top to the bottom of the cutting. The sides of the gullet are said to have been too perpendicular, but the late rains are chiefly blamed for the result. Another large portion was left in a very critical position, with a large fissure nearly 50 yards further off.——The pressing necessity for the free transit to guards along a train was instanced lately, as it so often is in one way or other, in a case where the tire of a wheel was gone and the carriage off the line. Although the luggage-van with the guard was at hand, and the guard was at length made aware of the danger to those within the carriage, he stood in the absurd position of a 'guard' without power to afford the least assistance, while the train was running at the rate of 25 to 30 miles an hour. 'Bawling till hoarse' to the driver was of no use; and the carriage was dragged on for a number of miles, with the passengers in continued and unenviable consciousness of their imminent peril, till the train eventually stopped.——Since the opening of railways, the useful article, milk, has flowed into Liverpool in such abundance that the 'genuine article' now costs only half what its anomalous representative used to be sold at in stinted quantities.——On the list of applicants for situations on the Manchester, Sheffield, and Lincolnshire line, there are upwards of 800 names!——A Liverpool merchant, complaining in the *Times* of the 'extraordinary delay' of the Electric Telegraph Company on a recent occasion of commercial importance, says,—"It was a matter of great importance to numerous parties both in Liverpool and America that this intelligence should have been posted in that establishment in time for the parties interested to have included the fact in their communications by the American mail steamer sailing on that day. It is remarkable, however, that on the Saturday, when the steamer sails at an earlier hour —the very day on which it is necessary that news should be posted early—the telegraphic intelligence is not posted till the steamer is away."

METROPOLITAN COMMISSION OF SEWERS.

A special court was held on Thursday 26th. The Earl of Carlisle in the chair.

The appointment of a new Order Clerk.—The report of the general committee on the appointment of a successor to Mr. Hertslet, as order clerk, was brought up and read. It stated, that it having been considered desirable that a person having a knowledge of the law should be selected, the committee were unanimous in opinion that Mr. Woolrych, of the Inner Temple, should be recommended to the court as a fit and proper person to fill that office.

After some conversation Mr. Woolrych was appointed.

The Earl of Carlisle said he could not, on this occasion, forbear to convey the general sentiments of the court to their late officer, Mr. Hertslet, and their deep regret at the circumstances that had led to their separation from him.

The Cholera.—A letter was read from the Home Office, calling the attention of the commissioners to upwards of 600 complaints of nuisances and drainage made during the previous week by the inspectors of police of the various metropolitan and suburban divisions.

These reports were referred to the surveyor. A memorial was presented from the inhabitants of Dulwich, in public meeting assembled at the Half Moon Tavern, complaining of the condition of that district, and stating that the fatal effects of the offensive drainage and open ditches had struck terror into the minds of the people, and calling upon the commissioners to cover over the open ditches.

The Earl of Carlisle remarked that they had been told by a deputation, a few days since, that in convering over an open ditch they had only aggravated the evil.

Some remarks having been made on the subject of the process of flushing,

Mr. Leslie said, there appeared to be great diversity of opinion on this subject, for last year their surveyor, Mr. Roe, had ordered flushing to be suspended, and he believed that it was so suspended for upwards of three months. Even their own officers were divided in opinion on the propriety of it. Mr. Lovick was in favour of it, while Mr. Gotto was opposed to it, and in a report had set forth that this practice only aggravated the evil it was intended to cure. Mr. Leslie then deprecated the practice of coroners holding inquests on persons dying of bowel complaints, which statements were got hold of by the reporters, and great and unnecessary alarm was created amongst weak-minded persons.

Mr. Chadwick supported the system, but contended that the operation ought to be superintended by a competent person, as had been recommended in the second notification of the Board of Health.

Mr. Lovick and Mr. Gotto having expressed their opinions for and against flushing in particular cases.

Dr. Southwood Smith said it appeared to be overlooked the difference that had taken place in the mode of cleansing by means of a discharge of the cesspools into the sewers, and the old mode of cartage. He thought the court should investigate the matter, whether there had really been an injury or not; but without medical testimony, to go into such investigation would be quite absurd.

The Tunnel Sewer for the Metropolis.—A question was referred by the Finance Committee as to the payments to be allowed to surveyors and others for the cost of surveys, levels, borings, &c., undertaken with reference to plans for the drainage of London.

Mr. Hawes said the reason for bringing this before the court was an impression on the mind of the Finance Committee, that at the last court when the subject of the tunnel sewer was under consideration, it appeared to be the opinion of the court that no expense should be incurred in the production of plans, &c., for the same. Now, certain charges on this score had been sent in to the committee, and they wished the opinion of the court as to how far they were justified in allowing the same, and paying the expenses incurred.

Mr. Chadwick thought they should give a liberal interpretation of the orders of the court in the payment of small incidental expenses, relying on the discretion of the officers as to the amount of them.

A member remarked, that as the Ordnance Survey Committee had already ordered borings to be made for the purposes of Mr. Austin's plan in Orchard-street, Westminster, it would be only fair to allow Mr. Phillips the same advantages. He wished to ask Mr. Austin what sum had been expended in these borings?

Mr. Austin said that they amounted to about 70*l*

Mr. Bullar read an extract from a letter received from Mr. Hutton, who, he stated, was an eminent geologist, and who gave it as his opinion that the plan was impracticable; in fact, the difficulties were so great as to discourage any one but a madman or an ignoramus, and as to boring with a view to information, it would be only so much money thrown away.

The Earl of Carlisle thought all parties should have fair play, although he was unwilling to incur any preliminary expense.

Mr. Leslie said the parties who commenced the first tunnel under the Thames in 1804, got within 150 feet of the opposite shore without laying a single brick. They proposed to brick as they went on, and if 940 feet could be done without bricks at all, he did not think the difficulties insurmountable. Geologists were fond of riding their hobby, and such being the case he would only be satisfied from borings, especially as he knew that in digging a well for Greenwich Hospital, they got into chalk at 100 feet. If they got into the chalk he apprehended there would be no difficulty in forming a tunnel through it with the assistance of their engines in pumping out the water that might make its way during the progress of the work.

Mr. Phillips stated, unless he was allowed the borings, that he should be brought to a stand-still, and his plan would at once fall to the ground. They would cost from 150*l*. to 200*l*.

Mr. Bullar said that the public would be unwilling to go to 2,000*l*. or 3,000*l*. expense for them; for, if Mr. Phillips's was not the best plan in an engineering point of view, the expense of borings would be thrown away. He complained that the subject had been hurriedly forced upon them, and that a "row" had been got up out of doors. That paper, the *Times*, he said, had taken the lead in this; but now, in consequence of the discussion that had taken place at the last court, they began to think that there were difficulties in the way, and were anxious to back out of it. However, he trusted that in executing a work that was to last for ages, they would not be hurried on in its consideration, but would take their own course, independently of any newspaper whatever.

After some further discussion the following resolutions were agreed to:—

"That the expense already incurred for surveys, levels, borings, &c., referred by the Finance Committee to the court, be allowed."

"That, as Mr. Phillips states that 200*l*. will be necessary for all the borings, &c. requisite for his plan, the court sanctions his expending on them a sum not exceeding that amount."

Miscellanea.

Mural Paintings, Plastered and Whitewashed.—At Winchfield Church, Hants, recently, some workmen found, beneath a thick coat of plaster, the remains of painting which at one time appeared to have entirely covered the walls. The rector procured a respite, and Mr. Baigent, of Winchester, made tracings and drawings, produced at a recent meeting of the Archæological Association. Mr. Waller described the chief subject to be that of "the rich man and Lazarus," and stated that it possessed some artistic and religious interest. This, we are told, makes the fifth instance of the preservation, by the association, of church mural paintings found in Hampshire; but the spirit of destruction at Northwood Church, Isle of Wight, was too rapid for the conservative pencil of members who resided almost within call. Some frescoes, described as of a superior kind, were laid open a week or two ago, and a churchwarden, or some person invested with a brief authority, had them effectually destroyed. A representation of "the last judgment" in Shorewell Church was re-whitewashed about three years since, while a gentleman was engaged in making a copy for the association; but the churchwardens have preserved the legend of St. Christopher, which the association has engraved.

Bethnal Green.—A correspondent from the Mile-end-road, who signs himself "F. Greasy," draws attention to the state of premises in Cambridge-road, and complains of want of attention on the part of the local board and the Metropolitan Sewers Commission after repeated application. He says: "The houses have a ditch running behind them, of which recently one of the tenants has stopped the the course: the result is, that a quantity of stagnant matter from the adjoining privies, accumulates frequently to the depth of 2 feet, which cannot be carried off except by the influence of the atmosphere. I think that from what I have stated there can be no doubt of the unhealthy and dangerous condition of the locality alluded to; if there be any such doubt, I would mention the fact of several visits from the superior board, who have always stated that it was so bad that were cholera to ensue, they should not be surprised; and since the last visit one of the occupants of the house No. 15 has died, which death the medical gentleman who attended him considers to have been accelerated by the unwholesome state of the locality."

Door-Knob Composition.—Mr. John Harrison, Stillwater, Saratoga county, New York, has patented an improvement consisting in the compounding of the following materials, calcined, pulverized, and ground, viz.:—bone, 10 parts; black flint, 4 parts; crystal felspar, 10 parts; granite, 10 parts; Vermont white sand, 10 parts; China clay, 11 parts; chromate of potash, 1 part; litharge, 1 part; antimony, 1 part; chrome green, 1 part; oxide of iron, 3 parts; oxide of tin, 1 part; oxide of zinc, 1 part; oxide of manganese, 4 parts. The articles are ground in water, and constitute the body and everything necessary for the manufacture.

Omnibus Statistics.—From returns just made by the Commissioners of Inland Revenue, it appears that the total number of omnibuses now plying for hire in the metropolis is 3,000, paying duty, including mileage, averaging 9*l*. per month each, or 324,000*l*. per annum. The number of conductors and drivers is about 7,000, who pay annually 1,750*l*. for their licenses.

An Irish California in the Bogs.—Mr. Jasper Rogers and his bog charcoal for deodorizing the metropolis, and thus effecting its sanitary reform, has been completely outshone by a light exhibited in the House of Commons—a veritable extract of bog, if not a solid concentration of will-o'-wisp. The O'Gorman Mahon, in calling attention to a development of the resources of Ireland,—one, he said, of the most important discoveries that had ever been made,—produced what he called a *spermaceti* candle made from Irish bog, though how the cetaceous sperm got into the bog it would be hard to say, but at least it appears to have been very like a whale sperm candle, and was examined with some curiosity by Lord John Russell and other hon. members. This the O'Gorman said, however, was but one of a number of valuable extracts which he enumerated, from the same fertile mine,—and he then appealed to Lord Ashley as to the truth of what he had stated. His lordship promptly responded by assuring the House that these substances, he had every reason to believe, had been extracted from Irish bog by Mr. Owen, the chemist,—a most trustworthy gentleman and a personal friend of his own. Mr. Owen had already invested a large capital in the Irish bogs, and had been carrying on his operations for twelve months. Out of every hundred tons of peat, the cost of which was 5*l*., and 8*l*. more in labour, but take the cost at 20*l*., the results, on which Mr. Owen staked his character, were these:—Carbonate of ammonia, 2,602 lb., value 32*l*. 10s.; soda, 2,118 lb., value 8*l*. 16s. 6d.; vinegar, 600 lb., value 7*l*. 10s.; naphtha, 30 gallons, value 7*l*. 10s.; candles, 600 lb., value 17*l*. 10s.; camphine oil, 600 lb., value 5*l*.; common oil, 800 lb., value 3*l*. 6s. 8d.; gas, 8*l*. in value; and ashes, 1*l*. 13s. 4d.: making a total of 91*l*. 16s. 1d. Moreover, the soil below is so saturated with ammonia as to be invaluable for agriculture. Englishmen, no less than Irishmen, may well rejoice if all this be no *ignis fatuus*. It unfortunately happens, however, that 20,000*l*. were long since *sunk* in Dartmoor bogs, in just such extractive efforts, but they certainly have not yet sprung up and fructified to perennial profit.

Steam-Husbandry.—The *Mark-lane Express* notices an interesting machine or combination of machines erected on a property near Shaftesbury. This machine (for it seems like one perfect whole) receives the sheaves, disengages the corn, clears it of all small seeds, rethrashes any ears that may escape the first operation, winnows it from the chaff, separates the best from the imperfect corn, conveys the best into the market sacks, deposits the tailing in another part of the barn, and passes the straw into the yard. It also accurately weighs the sacks of corn; and as the scale turns shuts off the supply; rings the call-bell, so that the man in attendance ties and removes the sack, replacing it by an empty one, to be filled and removed in the same manner. At the same moment a pair of mill-stones is engaged grinding corn, and producing meal for the consumption of the cattle; the dressing apparatus is not yet added. The corn-bruiser is also performing its part in the preparation of food for the stock. The chaff-cutting machine is in full operation, and the bone-mill at work. The whole of this machinery is said to be of the most simple construction, and not easily thrown out of repair. It is worked by a small steam-engine, not consuming more than 1 cwt. of coal per hour, and attended by one man.

The Culloden Monument.—Mr. Mackenzie, of Elgin, architect, has constructed a design for this monument, for the erection of which a considerable sum has already been subscribed. The model represents a large, irregular, broken, conical mass, in imitation of natural rock, round which is a rough road,—now winding through clefts, and now ascending by steps, seemingly water-worn, until it reaches a small flat on the top of the mass. In front, crowning a precipice, is a fine female figure, leaning on the rock, and mourning, with two boys, holding by her hand and skirts,—the young one looking anxiously up in her sorrowful face. In front of the precipice is rudely carved the word "Culloden, 1746." At various prominent points the model presents small tablets of various forms, to be erected by clans, or in memory of individuals.—*Edinburgh Weekly Register.*

Builders' Benevolent Institution.—The second annual general meeting was held at the London Tavern, on the 30th ult., Mr. Biers, the president, in the chair. The meeting was numerously attended, and was addressed by various gentlemen, who united in expressing their acknowledgments to the president for his perseverance and attention to the interests of the institution. The usual annual report was read, and adopted with all the more cordiality, inasmuch as it announced that, with the aid afforded at the anniversary dinner, which we lately reported at large, and when no less than 110 new subscribers, it seems, had added to the previous prosperous progress of the institution the goodly sum of 500*l*., the Directors now felt themselves in the unexpected position of being already able to announce that they would give the subscribers an opportunity of exercising their privilege in the election of five pensioners, who, from October next, would each be granted the maximum rate of pension fixed by the rules, namely 24*l*. for males and 20*l*. for females. Such an announcement was regarded by the meeting as an unprecedented circumstance, considering the short time since the institution was founded. Some incidental relief to workmen disabled by accident is now also to be afforded. It was stated in the report that the institution now possesses 1,000*l*. stock in the 3 per cent. consols, in the name of trustees for behoof of the charity. All donations requiring, by the rules, to be funded, the directors wish to urge the increase of *annual* subscriptions as the main dependence of the poor objects of the charity and the chief hope of increasing their number. Earl Manvers was elected a patron, and a number of gentlemen vice-presidents. The usual votes of thanks were then accorded, and the meeting separated.

Estimating—Chelmsford Union.—The careless manner in which persons connected with the building profession appear to make their estimates being so often exposed and commented on in your valuable publication without effect, it would appear that either inexperience or recklessness must be the cause of such glaring inconsistencies. The following tenders for painting the above union-house were received by the Board:—No. 1, from Islington, 60*l*.; No. 2, 50*l*.; No. 3, 35*l*.; No. 4, 35*l*.; No. 5, 32*l*. 10s.; No. 6, 32*l*.; No. 7, 24*l*. 12s.—these six were from Chelmsford and its vicinity. At the previous board two architects sent tenders for superintending the above work, the one 1*l*. 1s.; the other 5*l*. 5s. In the early part of the year tenders were sent in for a wall containing three rods of brickwork, including a 1½ inch door and frame, also two privies with half a square of roofing and slating to the same, 112 feet superficial inch deal partition in the dormitory, painted both sides in three oils, with other minor works specified. The tenders were, No. 1, 48*l*.; No. 2, 46*l*. 10s.; No. 3, 41*l*. 10s.; No. 4, 41*l*.; No. 5, 40*l*.; No. 6, 35*l*. The last had it,—pray who was the winner?—A. B.

The Buildings Act Amendment Bill.—The Bill introduced into the House of Lords by the Earl of Carlisle, for the amendment of the present Buildings Act, has just been printed. It consists of 150 clauses and 12 schedules. It is brought forward (though too late as to legislation) so that any useful information may be elicited upon it during the recess, with a view of resuming the Bill at a very early period in the next session. We had prepared a summary of its provisions, but some of the clauses seem on a hasty inspection so singularly different from what we looked for, that we think it better to withhold the summary until such time as we can give the Bill consideration and express our opinions upon it. What the Committee, who at the request of Lord Carlisle reported on the amendments required, will say to it, we scarcely know.

Independent College, St. John's-wood—Competition.—Ten architects were invited by the committee to compete for the above college, including Messrs. Donaldson, Davies, Barry and Brown, &c. The Committee, assisted by John Shaw, Esq., of Christ's Hospital, have selected the design of Mr. Emmett for execution, and awarded the premiums to Messrs. Kendall, jun., and Pope.

Projected Works. — Advertisements have been issued for tenders for works at a new pauper lunatic asylum at Powick, Worcester; by 21st inst., for pewing, repewing, repairing and altering, warming, &c., the interior of Northfleet Church; by 14th, for new walling to enclose addition to Jewish burying-ground at Mile-end; by 6th, for reglazing the nave windows of St. Mary's Church, Brampton Ash, Northamptonshire, in quarries, with old glass and new lead; by 8th, for additions and alterations at St. George the Martyr's workhouse, Southwark; by 7th, for working and maintaining permanent way and works of Blackwall Railway; by 1st September, for a considerable number of street cocks, fire cocks, or hydrants, and air valves, for Manchester water-works; by 6th, for paving and keeping in repair the streets, lanes, courts, &c., of St. Mary's, Rotherhithe; by 9th, for the reconstruction of the drainage and water supply, and for alterations and works, at Cuckfield Union Workhouse; and by 13th inst., for lighting with gas a portion of the district of St. John's, Notting-hill, Kensington.

Suspension Bridge at Chester—A Novelty.—Messrs. M'Kean, Perkes, and Co., of Liverpool, have designed and constructed a light Chinese-looking bridge for Earl Howe, near the Grosvenor-bridge, across the Dee, and spanning a ravine on a slight slope by 12 iron chain rods in links of 15 feet each, with a light-looking X shaped railing. The means by which this bridge is suspended are hid from view. The span is 150 feet between the bearings of the points of suspension. The platform is 7 feet wide. The chain rods are secured together by flat bars about 6 feet apart, on which the timber platform rests and is secured by T-headed bolts and nuts. The chains are made fast at one end to a stone pier built in the embankment. The centre of the pier at the other end of the bridge is formed into a large pit, on the top of which is secured a turn-barrel, round which the chains take one wind and descend into the pit, and are secured to a cast-iron plate suspended near the bottom, at a depth of 30 feet, on which is built a mass of masonry, forming a weight which counterbalances the whole. It is further secured by backstays at each end of the bridge, running inland under ground, and belted to blocks of hard oak. The cost is said to be very moderate.

Royal Italian Opera, Covent Garden.—The scenery and costumes in Meyerbeer's new opera, *Le Prophète*, are worthy of the magnificent work they are intended to illustrate. Messrs. Grieve and Telbin have here done their best, and we the more gladly award them our hearty commendation, because, on a late occasion, we found it necessary to object, on the score of chronology. The first scene—a landscape with windmills—is a nice work. In the scene for the winter sports there is a wooden bridge across the stage, and a large tree in the middle distance, cleverly managed. The great scene, however, is that of the third act, the interior of the cathedral of Munster, for which a novel point of view is taken,—across the transept, looking obliquely into the choir. When the stage is filled with a crowd of splendid costumes the appearance presented by this scene has seldom been equalled.

Fall of a Staircase in Charles-street, Drury-lane.—A cry of fire was raised in a large building in Charles-street, Drury-lane,—formerly a coach factory, and now a Roman Catholic chapel,—on Sunday evening last; and a crowd rushing to the staircase, this fell in with a tremendous crash, and seriously injured a number of persons. The alarm was caused, in the first instance, by the weight of the audience causing a partial subsidence of the floor.

St. Mary's, West Brompton.—The first stone of this church, of which we gave an engraving a short time since, was laid on the 2nd inst., by the Venerable Archdeacon Sinclair, assisted by a large body of the local clergy and the inhabitants of the neighbourhood. Robert Gunter, Esq., the donor of the land, afterwards entertained a number of the principal visiters at his residence.

Brighton Pavilion.—The inhabitants of Brighton have determined on purchasing the Pavilion at the price named by the Woods and Forests, 53,000*l*.

LAMINATED TIMBER ARCHES.—Messrs. Green's handsome wooden bridges, on the line of the Newcastle and North Shields Railway, have familiarized the public eye with the laminated timber arch. The principle, as we learn from THE BUILDER, is now applied to the construction of roofs; and a controversy has arisen as to authorship or discovery. If our worthy contemporary, who gives names, dates, and extracts, in relation to laminated arch ribs, will turn to Coxe's "Travels in Switzerland," volume first, second edition, 1791, he will find mentioned, at page 132, the wooden bridge of Wettingen, which spans the Limmat, near Baden, and was erected by Ulric Grubenman, of Appenzel, a self-taught architect; and the letterpress is accompanied by an engraving from a sketch by Sir John Soane. Coxe's description is vague, but the arch is evidently formed of laminated timber.—*Gateshead Observer*.

STREET ORDERLIES.—The united parishes of St. Giles-in-the-Fields and St. George, Bloomsbury, have come to the resolution of employing "street orderlies" for the purpose of cleansing the public streets. We commend them for the step, and hope to see the example followed.

VERY BLIND.—Tenders for slight repairs and the painting of a house in Great Marlborough-street:—

Beasley	£290 0
Battem and Crask	114 0
McLachlan (accepted)	97 12

TO CORRESPONDENTS.

Received.—"G." (Canterbury), "W. B." (the Architectural Lending Library advertised in our *bona fide* undertaking. We will look to it. As to asphaltum for staining, apply to Seyssel Asphalte Company), "J. H." (the drawings shall be left at York-street), "R. T.," "R. W.," "K. N. R." (we are compelled to adhere to our regulation), "A. B." (must wait his turn), "L. L.," "T. H.," "Constant Reader," "F. R.," "W. T.," "F. N.," "J. Q." (the MS. has arrived, but has not yet been examined), "Jacob Omnium," "Scrutator" (had better state his objections), "G. R. B. (thanks—it shall appear)," "J. G., jun. (yes), "R. T.," "J. P. W." (the article in question was inadvertently omitted. Our reference is not deathable), "E. W.," "J. C. P.," "Juvenis," (rebuilding the suffrene in the manner shown is scarcely defensible), "C. P.," "J. W." "Drainage,"—a pile of letters on this subject must stand over.

ERRATUM—Montacute House is in *Somersetshire*, near Yeovil, and not Wiltshire as stated.

"Books, Prices, and Addresses."—We have not time to point out books or find addresses.

NOTICE.—All communications respecting *advertisements* should be addressed to the "Publisher," and not to the "Editor;" all other communications should be addressed to the EDITOR, and not to the Publisher.

ADVERTISEMENTS.

ROYAL POLYTECHNIC INSTITUTION.—An Illustration of Ancient Traditions, in Tale and Song, and the Manner of the Ancient Minstrels, by Geofry Gunn, Esq., assisted by Miss Clara Gunn and Miss Rose Swann, every Evening at Eight.—Home Illustrated in a Series of Dissolving Views.—A Descriptive Lecture, embracing the most interesting points connected with the subject, will be given by Mr. J. Russell Lectures on Chemistry, by Mr. J. M. Ashley, Daily at Half-past Three, and on the Evenings of Monday, Wednesday, and Friday, at Nine o'clock. Lecture by Dr. Bachhoffner, on Western's Patent Process of Freezing Inward Ices, &c. Diving and Diving Bell. Admission, 1s.: schools, half-price.

[ornamental crest/logo]

ROYAL MANCHESTER INSTITUTION'S EXHIBITION of PRACTICAL SCIENCE MANUFACTURES, and the ARTS.—This exhibition will open at the beginning of March and close at the end of May. Works intended for exhibition must arrive as follows:—Machinery and models of machinery, on or before January Thirty-first and plated goods, on or before February 21st; all other articles on or before February 14th. They must be addressed to the "Honorary Secretary," Royal Institution, Manchester, accompanied with full specifications, and the name of the maker, inventor, or designer, in addition to that of the exhibitor. All articles to be subject to the approval or rejection of the council, and to be at the owner's risk. The carriage to Manchester will be paid on works sent by railway carriers, but the return carriage must be paid by the contributor. All articles must remain till the close of the exhibition, except as the manufacturers which may be returned and changed as may be agreed upon. Parties desirous of further information respecting the machinery and working models, but the same must be put up and fitted by the contributors.—Blank schedules and other particulars will be furnished on application to the Honorary Secretary.

GEO. WAREING ORMROD, Hon. Sec.

TERRA-COTTA, or VITRIFIED STONE WORKS, King Edward-street, Westminster-road, London.—M. H. BLANCHARD, from late Coade's Original Works, Haycock's-road, Lambeth, begs to inform the Nobility, Gentry, Architects, and Builders, that he has re-established the manufacture of that invaluable material, which has been successfully adopted by our eminent architects and others, in the adornment of our noblest buildings, really so much has this proved the imperishable nature of the material, the specimens of those times now exhibiting all their plastic sharpness.

Groups, statues, vases, capitals, panelling, pinnacles, finials, terminals, fonts, and other chimney shafts, balustrading, foot-tales, fonts, tazzas, vases, coats of arms, devices, and every description of architectural ornament, at prices to many instances nearly half the cost of stone.

Specimens of the material to be seen at the Office or "The Builder," 8 York-street, Covent Garden, and at the Works.

BIELEFELD'S PAPIER MACHE.—The superiority of which, for Architectural Decorations, is proved by the fact of its extensive application in this and other countries. A quarto volume is published, after 11, with a Tariff, containing upwards of 1,000 designs, most of them executed for works designed by eminent Architects. Patronized by the Hon. Commissioners of Her Majesty's Woods and Works.

"This is unquestionably a most valuable invention."—*Literary Gazette.*

Works, 15, Wellington-street North, Strand.

PAPIER MACHE and CARTON PIERRE MANUFACTORY, 49 and 50, Rathbone place.—GEORGE JACKSON and SONS beg the attention of Architects, Builders, Decorators, and others, to their large assortment of ENRICHMENTS in every style, executed in the highest class of art.

The facilities and reduced enrichment of means enable GEORGE JACKSON and SONS to announce the execution of works of the above descriptions in these advantageous materials at a cost considerably below any known method, while for quality, relief, and finish, they flatter themselves they stand unrivalled. Just published—a large Quarto Work of their ENRICHMENTS with dimensions for reference and price.

SNOXELL'S PATENT SAFETY REVOLVING WOOD SHUTTERS, Manufactory, 96, REGENT-STREET and 10, CHANCERY-LANE. Patent settled on the 6th day of February, 1848, for Footless Yards, for improvements in Revolving Shutters of WOOD and IRON, consisting of Six Methods of Raising and Lowering Shutters, without Hanging, and Two for Hanging and Shutting the Edges of Wood Laths with Iron.—The Patentee having faced up some hundreds, will feel pleased in forwarding the Testimonials of Architects, Principals of large Establishments, and others, having them now in use, while fully guarantees the Patentee in stating they are beyond dispute superior to any other Revolving Shutter for durability, security, and simplicity, without the use of cog-wheel worm and screw gear, or any other complicated machinery employed by other makers.

IRON SHUTTERS.—THE PATENT CONVEX REVOLVING IRON SHUTTERS are thirteen twelve times stronger, work easier, cannot run down, and roll up in one-third less room than any other shutters made. Harcourt Quincey, Patentee.

CLARK and Co., Sole Manufacturers, and of IMPROVED DRAWN ORNAMENTAL METALLIC SASH BARS, ASTRAGALS, MOULDINGS, STALL-BOARD PLATES, &c. &c., in brass, copper, and zinc; the WROUGHT IRON GIRDERS, HOT-WATER APPARATUS and metal work of every description connected with buildings. Steam engines, millwork, and machinery. CLARK and Co., Engineers, 65, Wapping. Models can be seen and every information obtained at 496, Oxford-street, and 4, Moorgate-street. Only Agent for Scotland, Mr. G. BRIGSTOCK, 17 George-street, Edinburgh.

BUNNETT and Co., ENGINEERS, Patentees of REVOLVING IRON and WOOD SAFETY SHUTTERS, and of ORNAMENTAL METALLIC SASH BARS, MOULDINGS, &c. IN BRASS, COPPER, ZINC, &c. FOR SHOP-FRONTS, SKYLIGHTS, &c.

Shop-fronts completely fitted and fixed in a superior style, either plain or ornamental, also glazed with best plate glass. Strong moulded stall-boards handsomely engraved. Metal work and machinery of all kinds in connection with banking-houses, shops, warehouses, &c. &c.

B. and Co. challenge competition as to either quality or price. Designs furnished and estimates given.

IMPROVED PATENT BENCH and FLOORING CRAMPS FOR BUILDERS.

SOLE LICENCEES FOR MARVIN and MOORE'S PATENT DIAGONAL GRATINGS. Office of the Patentees, 56, Lombard-street, London; and at the Works, Deptford, Kent.

MINTON and Co.'S ENCAUSTIC and other PATENT TILES for Churches, Entrance Halls, Conservatories, Balconies, &c., Antique, Geometrical, and Alhambric Mosaics, manufactured in a highly decorative character and extreme durability. Slabs and Tiles for Chimney Hearths, and Cisings for Ovens, Door Furniture, White Glazed and Ornamental Tiles for Baths, Dairies, and Kitchens. Roman clay is had in great variety at Hull Warehouse, 8, Albion-place, Black-friars-bridge, London, and at their Manufactory, stoke-upon-Trent, Staffordshire.

TO THE BUILDING PUBLIC.

FIRST-RATE ORNAMENTS in PORTLAND, ROMAN, and other CEMENTS, and PLASTER of PARIS, at reasonable prices, consisting of Vases, &c. &c., Capitals, perforated Parcliers, Corbels, Brackets, Trusses, Flowers, Scrolls, Masques, Heads, Plaques, Friezes, Gothic and other Ornamental, Gothic Bed-moulds, Pilasters, &c. &c. Centre Flowers from 10 feet diameter downwards, of all sorts of the above. Shop-front Trusses always ready for fixing—HERBERT and SON, Modellers, &c., 49, Parker-street, Drury-lane.

THE SECURITY from FIRE which results from the adoption of the system of constructing FLOORS, CEILINGS, and ROOFS, invented and patented by Dr. FOX, is attained WITHOUT any INCREASE of COST. In this system the ordinary timber joists are suspended, and light Iron ones tie with the resulting degrees of strength; developed by combination; are substituted; these, together with successive lengths of incombustible materials, forming a perfectly fire-proof foundation, capable of receiving a polished surface of wood, composition, stone, slate, or tile, &c. This system of building economizes space, prevents durability than the ordinary method; the structure is effectually protected from the attacks of Dryrot; and the assurances resulting from vermin and insects of all kinds is entirely prevented.

The advantages of this system, whether in Dwelling-houses, Warehouses, Manufactories, or other buildings, is attended with economy—immediate, in the reduction of the first cost; and prospective, in the absence of charges for repairs. Every advantage attained by the ordinary methods of fire-proof building is effectually secured at about one-half the cost, while the interval is, so small, indeed, that in many cases they cannot deliver it with daylight affixes to Iron girders, and brick arch system, is entirely avoided. The great superiority of this plan has been proved by many years of trial, and every information may be obtained on application to Messrs. FOX and BARRETT, Leicester Chambers, 46, Leicester-square.

REDUCED PRICES.—EDWARD W. SIMMS (late William Cleaver, of Willowmead, Pimlico Basin), begs to acquaint Builders and the Trade that he has now on hand, at his Manufactory (the first of its kind ever established), a very large assortment of Dry and Well-seasoned OAK and DEAL PREPARED FLOORING BOARDS and MATCH BOARDING of all sorts, from 1 inch to 3 inch thick, planed to a parallel width and thickness, and at greatly Reduced Prices. Also, Timber, Posts, Oak Planks, Scantlings, Sash Sills, Mouldings prepared by Machinery, Laths, &c.—Apply at E. SIMM'S (late W. Cleaver) Flooring Manufactory, Willowmead, Pimlico Basin.

A REDUCTION in the PRICE of FLOOR BOARDS.—ALFRED ROSLING begs to inform the Trade and Consumers generally that he has REDUCED the PRICE, and keeps constantly in stock a large and very general assortment of Prepared Floor Boards and Matched Boarding, planed to a parallel breadth and thickness, and fit for immediate use; also a variety of machine-prepared Mouldings, which are unrivalled with great accuracy and attention to quality of workmanship.—Southwark Bridge Wharf, Bankside, and Old Barge Wharf, Upper Ground-street, Blackfriars.

GREAT REDUCTION IN THE PRICE of FLOOR BOARDS and MATCH BOARDING.—THOMAS ADAMS (late S. Defils, Mahogany and Timber Merchant), Bermondsey New-road, Southwark, near the Bricklayers' Arms, begs to inform his Friends and the trade generally, that he has in stock a large assortment of the above goods, fit for immediate use, at prices which only results a trial to give them their decided chance. Also mouldings prepared by machinery from the very best material, and in a superior manner; cut deals and scantlings of every dimension; mahogany, cedar, rosewood, walnut, elm, beech, oak, &c. in planks, boards, veneers, and logs; deals, oak, and fir laths; wheelwright goods. All sash and spaded goods (except timber) delivered free of expense; sawing charged at mill prices. Very extensive drying sheds.

JOHN ANGOLD begs to invite the attention of Builders and others to his dry and well-seasoned stock in various thicknesses of WAINSCOT, MAHOGANY, and almost every other description of foreign and English wood, which he has determined to sell at a considerable reduction from the usual prices.—73, Mortimer-street, and 31, Tottenham-court-road.

MUIR'S PATENT | PLANING MACHINE.

SAW MILLS. GILLINGHAM-STREET, PIMLICO.

TIMBER of any size, PLANK, DEALS, and BATTENS, &c., sawn on the most approved principle, Boards, &c., Prepared, Matched, and Grooved by Muir's Patent Machinery. The Mills have all the advantages of navigation and water-carriage, being connected with the Thames by the Grosvenor Canal. Goods fetched from the docks and carted home free of charge.

Address to HENRY SOUTHAM, Saw Mills, Gillingham-street, Pimlico.

N.B. Estimates given for Sawing and Planing.

GENERAL WOOD-CUTTING COMPANY.—SAWING, PLANING, and MOULDING MILLS, Belvedere-road, Lambeth, between the Suspension and Waterloo Bridges. SAWING and PLANING in all their branches executed with the greatest despatch and punctuality. A large Stock of seasoned and regularly WORKED MOULDINGS, consisting of upwards of 100 different patterns kept constantly on hand; also an extensive assortment of dry prepared FLOORING BOARDS, of all qualities and at reasonable rates.

PHILLIPS, ALLCARD, and Co.'S IMPERIAL DEAL SAWMILLS, WENLOCK-ROAD CITY-ROAD, beg to invite the attention of builders, carpenters, and the trade, to their well selected stock, comprising a large assortment of TIMBER, DEALS, PLANKS, and BATTENS, of every description, and thoroughly seasoned. They also have constantly on hand, ready for immediate use, white and yellow prepared FLOORING BOARDS of all thickness and matched listing, cut and planed to a regular breadth and thickness. And they are enabled to offer all their goods at very moderate prices.

DESICCATED WOOD.—DAVISON and SYMINGTON'S PATENT.—Builders, Cabinet-makers, and others, will find it much to their advantage to purchase this new process of seasoning. This prepared wood can thus not only be seasoned in an incredibly short space of time, at a small cost, but is rendered stronger, stiffer, free from shrinkage, and in every respect better than wood dealt in the ordinary way; thereby effecting a great saving of money, time, labour, and all the other incidental convenience attending the process of a large stock.

The DESICCATING SAWING and PLANING MILLS are situated at PINHOE BRIDGE, ROTHERHITHE, adjoining the Commercial and East Country Docks, from whence parties obtaining this material can have the same quantities as beautiful, and well seasoned as for immediate use.—PINHOE, Rotherhithe.

For licences to use the patent, sale of wood, or other information address, AROUS JENNINGS, Secretary, Patent Desiccating Company, 41, Gracechurch-street, City.

TO ARCHITECTS, BUILDERS, UPHOLSTERERS, and OTHERS.

WOOD CARVING done in the cheapest and best manner. Estimates given to any amount. Pulpits, reading-desks, altar-rails, stalls, and other church fittings supplied complete. Old carvings restored by J. SEALION, Wood Carver and Manufacturer, 42, Berwick-street, Soho, London.

JORDAN'S PATENT MACHINE CARVING and MOULDING WORKS for WOOD and STONE, Belvedere-road, Lambeth, and 14, Strand.—TAYLOR, WILLIAMS, and JORDAN beg to call the attention of the building community to a new feature of their establishment, and, at the same time, to thank their numerous patrons and friends for the very liberal support they have lately experienced, which they assure them and the public, it will be their constant endeavour to deserve, by giving their customers an increasing share of the advantages arising from the constant improvement in the machinery which they have had succeeded in applying to the production of wood and moulding carving in Oen and other free-stone, and in statuary marble.

A. W. and J. particularly solicit the attention of architects and builders to the fact that, by the use of this machinery, a very large saving, both of time and money, is effected—so great, indeed, that in many cases they can deliver a well-finished article in Oen stone for less money than it can be made in cement, while their workmanship will, in some cases, be found to come into close competition with the best kinds of composition ornament.—For prices and estimates apply at 14, Strand.

SAMUEL HOOD and Co., Castings Warehouse, 31, Upper Thames-street. REGISTERED STABLE FITTINGS. Enamelled Mangers, with double hay-racks, or with enamelled water-cisterns on one side.

The Builder.

No. CCCXL.

SATURDAY, AUGUST 11, 1849.

FOLLOWING out the course we have taken from the first in respect of the two archæological societies, which, by the way, ought unquestionably to be but *one*, we attended both the recent meetings in the country, although, thanks to the bad feeling or the bad management somewhere, which fixed them at the same time, only for a part of the week, and that at no trifling inconvenience. Salisbury is 96 miles in one direction, and Chester 180 miles in another, but a will brings a way, and the rail makes all easy. We have already given our readers the heads of some of the papers read on architectural subjects, and in our present number will be found one on Chester Cathedral. Without attempting a continuous account of the proceedings, which would interest only a portion of our readers, and absorb all the space we can afford to the matter, we will throw together some of the jottings in our note-book, made during the trip, with reference rather to places than proceedings.

Willis rightly abused Wyatt, as our readers have seen, for his abominable deeds in *Salisbury Cathedral*,—screens destroyed, monuments mixed, and chapels pulled down. The interior of this cathedral is greatly inferior in interest and beauty to the exterior. Mitford, in his letters on the "Principles of Design," wherein he examines Salisbury Cathedral at some length, comes to the conclusion that pointed architecture is unsuited to the production of fine exteriors, and that the attention of those who designed the vast buildings of the Middle Ages was less given to the outside than to the in. How he could have arrived at this with reference especially to Salisbury is singular, since this building looked at alone would justify exactly the reverse conclusion. The outline of the mass is beautiful, pyramidizing upwards, and terminating in that wonderful tower and spire, piercing the sky.

Some repairs to the top of the spire are now going on, and a slight scaffolding surrounds the apex. This spire affords a striking proof of the goodness of Chilmark stone, properly selected.

The west front of the cathedral is less good in detail than other portions, and it affords a curious example of *sham* architecture, of which the mediæval architects were not often guilty. A considerable portion of this front is but a mask, and windows are introduced in what is merely a blank wall.

The Chapter-house is a gem; the miserable state of it is much to be deplored. It is an octagon, on plan, with a central shaft, and this shaft is about 9 inches out of an upright. The stone-work generally is in a dreadful state of dilapidation, the carvings are fast disappearing, and the singular tile pavement is scarcely distinguishable. With an industry and skill highly honourable, Lord Alwyne Compton has made a drawing on a large scale of this pavement, as it would appear restored.*

* The drawing was exhibited in the temporary museum formed in the "King's House," an interesting building of the Tudor period, which is about to be restored, for the purposes of a training school.

A plan for the restoration of the Chapter-house was prepared some time ago, but seems to be in abeyance. The central column was to have been taken out and rebuilt, the stone-work generally repaired, flying buttresses added outside, so as to admit of the removal of a network of iron-rods at the springing of the vaulting, and a stained glass window put up in the side opposite the entrance. The estimated cost was 5,000*l*.

We sincerely hope that no time will be suffered to elapse before the works are commenced.

In the cathedral there are several very well executed modern monuments, by Mr. Osmond, an inhabitant of the place, whose works we have before this had occasion to mention.* One of the most recent is a mural tablet of novel form, from a sketch by Mr. Pugin, in memory of Lieut. William Fisher, who fell at Moodkee.

The end of the north transept of the cathedral appears much rent, and the same may be said of the east end. A survey is desirable.

A small Roman Catholic church has been recently built in Salisbury by the architect last named. It is in the decorated style, and consists of nave, south aisle, with a small tower at the west end of it, chancel, and chapel of the Virgin, at the east end of aisle. At the back of this chapel is the sacristy, and over the latter is placed the organ. The ceiling of the chancel is richly painted, red, white, and gold, on a blue ground. The pulpit is very small and low, simply a stone desk, slightly elevated: it stands in the north-east angle of the nave. The whole is designed with skill. The tower here has settled down, and has caused some serious rents.

The determination which has been come to, to raise the fallen stones at *Stonehenge*, that mysterious monument of the misty past, is a good one. There is of course to be no imaginary restoration, but those stones which have fallen within the memory of man are to be raised into their original position. It is desirable, too, that others which show a tendency to fall, should be looked to and set upright. The Dean of Westminster, when the Institute visited this curious temple, offered some general observations upon it, and in the course of his remarks made a work upon this monument by Mr. Browne, the subject of jest and merriment. The son of the writer, who now holds a lower station, and maintains a family by selling copies of a model of the monument executed by his father, was present, and went his way with a weary step and a heavy heart. The memory of his father, held by him in the deepest respect and reverence, had been outraged. This has caused a correspondence in the *Salisbury and Winchester Journal*, and we doubt not will lead the dean to heal the wound he, perhaps unwittingly, gave.†

* The collection of gravestones and crosses by his son, "Christian Memorials," by W. Osmond, Jun., is now finished, and will be found useful. It is published by Masters, of Aldersgate-street, in six parts.

† A writer in the *Journal* gives the following interesting notice of the author of the work in question;—"He was a man of limited means, but of respectable mental attainments, who had been early struck with the magnificence of the remains on Salisbury plain, and had imbibed a passion for the temple at Stonehenge as absorbing and as powerful as that felt by the young Parisienne for the Belvidere Apollo, or as any one of the Pygmalion-like instances of which so many are recorded. To this, and to its illustrative remains in the neighbourhood, all his thoughts were devoted. He lived under its shadow, he dreamed of it, he endeavoured to trace out the hidden mystery of its existence; he lectured upon its many wonders,—unfortunately he published a book about it! When engaged on his lectures to the members of the Literary Institution that existed some years since in Salisbury, he used to bring his drawings and make his arrangements in the morning, return to Amesbury to dinner, come back with more materials in the afternoon, read his lecture in the evening, and then again walk on his solitary road to Amesbury at night after the conclusion of the meeting, after having already walked five and twenty miles. But this persevering energy of his character was more particularly exemplified during the construction of his model of Stonehenge. Every stone was modelled on the spot, and the most minute variations in the original carefully noted in his copy. Day after day, and week after week, was he to be found among these memorials of old time, planning, measuring, modelling, painting in the prosecution of his self-prescribed task, and interrupted only by the necessity of sometimes visiting Salisbury for materials, which he bore home himself and on foot. The difficulty of making such a copy would not perhaps be great with proper assistance, but this man worked wholly by himself, and we can imagine his self-gratulation on the completion of his labours, when he could exclaim, like the Victor of Corioli, 'Alone I did it! I!' But Mr. Browne, though he had completed his work, had not yet found for it a resting-place, and he determined to present it to the British Museum. It was accepted by the trustees with thanks, and its author chose to have the pleasure of placing it with his own hands in this great repository of the antiquities of the world. Unwilling to trust the model from his sight, and equally unwilling or unable to bear the expenses of the usual modes of travelling, he resolved to walk with it to London, and mounting his model on a wheel-barrow or hand-truck, he set off across the Plain with his charge. After a toilsome and almost continuous march of two days and nights (for he only slept for a short time in the day) he arrived on the morning of the third day at the British Museum, showed the letter of the trustees to the porter, wheeled his load into the court-yard, and saw his model safely deposited in the house. He left without staying to be questioned, and was soon on his way home again; but, I believe, was detained some days on the road by illness, brought on by his exertions."

Silbury Hill has again baffled the investigators,—it has evidently no sympathy with bores. A tunnel has been cut to the centre, but nothing has been discovered. It ought not, however, yet to be inferred that further examination is useless.

Every one has heard of *Wilton House*, and the relics of ancient art garnered within its walls. The Hon. Sidney Herbert, considering, as he said, that those who are *by accident* the occupiers of such residences are only trustees of a great national establishment, threw it open to the members, and with his beautiful wife,—the Queen of Wilton, as the neighbourhood in their admiration call her,—entertained them hospitably.

The collection of sculptures here was commenced by Thomas, Earl of Pembroke, at the close of the last century; the Arundel marbles forming the nucleus. The principal of the Giustiniani marbles and of the Mazzarine collection, when broken up, were purchased to increase it, and others were brought from Naples. Mr. Charles Newton, of the British Museum, made a critical review of the sculptures, and demolished the reputation of many of them with an unsparing hand. The host, however, took it all in good part,—seeking the truth.

Inigo Jones designed Wilton House, and Mr. Gwilt, in his *Encyclopædia*, says those who have seen it "can appreciate Inigo's merit for having introduced into England, in the seats of our aristocracy, a style vieing with that of the villas of Italy." We were not there long enough to find this out for ourselves. Some disagreement appears to have arisen between Jones and the Earl of Pembroke, and in the Harleian Library, it seems, there is an edition of Jones's "Stonehenge," on which the Earl in question, to whom it formerly belonged, has written much abuse of the author, calling him "Iniquity Jones," and anything but an honest man.

In the reign of George the Second, the well-known amateur architect, Henry Herbert, Earl of Pembroke, did much to improve Wilton, and built the Palladian bridge, in the beautiful gardens there. A right pleasant stroll we had over it, with some pretty specimens of "Early English," who could discuss "style" in more applications of the word than one.

The new Byzantine church at Wilton, with its detached campanile, mosaic pavements, and pulpit; stained glass, of varied worth; polychromatized apses, and reredos of marble columns, was of course visited; and the architect, Mr. Wyatt, who was there, had to reply to all sorts of questions, and, as a matter of course, all sorts of objections. This sumptuous evidence of Mr. Herbert's piety and liberality cost about 36,000l.,* and is in the style of the early churches of Northern Italy. It is not the style we should choose for an English church ; but as this was not left at the discretion of the architect, no blame attaches to him in this respect. The chancel is very fully decorated with colour, but the colour is not to our eyes good : it is too red,— and the patterns, in a principal part, are too large and coarse. The nave, at present quite bare, requires colour ; and this the architect feels,— for he had caused to be put up some temporary scroll-work in the spandrills of the main arches and around the arches themselves, in order to induce a decision to that effect. Unfortunately, however, these temporary colourings were scarcely the right thing, and so, perhaps, the object was rather injured than advanced. There is an appearance of thinness and weakness about the main arches, which colour would probably improve. This thinness would have been avoided if the arches, instead of springing, as they do, from the line of the upper diameter of the columns, so that they are far set in on the top of the capital, had been stilted, and had sprung from the outer line of the abacus, or nearly so,—the arrangement usually exhibited in the Byzantine churches.

But though there may be something to question in this building, there is much more to praise; and we have no desire to depreciate a work of great thought and labour, which stands alone in this country.

On the day after the visit to Wilton, the sad state of the town, and other causes, having broken up the set excursions of the day, we went with a pleasant half-dozen, fit though few, to Romsey ;† but of what we saw there we must take another opportunity to speak. Chester, too, must stand over.

ON THE ARRANGEMENT OF COLOURS IN ANCIENT DECORATIVE ART.

I venture to intrude on your notice a few brief remarks upon certain coincidences in the arrangement of colours, which I have observed to obtain extensively in nature, and in ancient, mediæval, and semi-barbarous ornamentation.

It is not necessary that I should occupy your attention, by any lengthened attempt, to prove that ancient and mediæval artisans had, by some means or other, a happy mode of combining and contrasting, with exquisite skill, the most brilliant shades of positive colours. This facility, upon whatever principle it may depend, is not generally within the scope of the artisan of the present day ; he rather trusts for his effects to the use of neutral, undecided, and delicate tints, avoiding for the most part any considerable amount of intense colour. I do not enter into the question of the propriety of this arrangement, but merely assert, what I believe you will readily admit, that brilliant colours are less harmoniously arranged by the modern than they were by the mediæval artisan. This is particularly the case when colour is used in the internal decoration of churches and of church windows.

It is a generally received opinion also, that British manufacturers are less tasteful in the combination of colours than their continental opponents. I call your attention to this assertion that I may afterwards point out a possible reason for this presumed inferiority.

* The length of the church, from the western porch to the chancel apse, is 190 feet ; the width, 63 feet ; height of nave, 57 feet,—of tower, 100 feet.
† Truth to say, the meeting, as a whole, was a heavy one ; and, according to some, this was not wholly owing to the epidemic. One correspondent, who signs himself " A Gentleman," and who, as we know, is one, complains of the want of any desire, on the part of those who had the power, to make parties known to one another. He writes, " If the secretaries and some other officials were a little less off-handed, and less given to pooh-poohing, and would consider it part of their duty to present to hosts and others, members known by them to have certain pretensions, the meeting would be rendered much more agreeable. ..."

It might be more difficult to induce you to believe that many barbarous or half-civilised nations are remarkable for the harmonious intermixture of their coloured ornaments, were we not able to call as evidence to the fact one of the very best authorities in the kingdom.

If, then, I be correct in my assertion, corroborated as it is in part by high authority, it assuredly becomes a matter of no slight interest to discover any of the means employed by the ancient artisan, to produce this very satisfactory result.

It is, to what I presume to be one of these means, that I venture to direct your attention. Some years since I had an opportunity of closely examining a number of illuminated MSS., of what I believe is allowed to be the best period of English mediæval art,—that of the three first Edwards. I was particularly struck with the uniform arrangement of certain colours, and remarked that the practice of the illuminators was—

1. To separate the prominent colours, red, blue, green, purple, ruby, violet, &c., from each other, by spaces or lines of yellow, white, or black.

2. To paint with brilliant colours, on grounds of yellow (frequently gold), white, or black ; or, if the ground was of any other colour, to use yellow, white, or black, only for the ornamentation.

3. To combine two or more shades of red, or of blue, green, purple, &c. &c., without the intervention of yellow, white, or black.

4. To place yellow, white, or black together, or upon each other, without reference to the law which appears to have regulated the arrangement of all other colours.

Having carefully noted these laws—as for convenience I venture to call them—I was induced to inquire whether they were peculiar to illuminated books, and to the particular era of mediæval art, known as the English Decorated ; to my surprise I found them of very general application.

I briefly notice a very few of the more prominent instances, mentioning only such as admit of being easily verified or contradicted by reference to books, or the contents of ordinary museums.

The mural paintings and other polychromic decorations of the Ancient Egyptians,* Assyrians,† Moors,‡ &c.

The vases and pottery of the classical period in Europe.

The mosaics of Italy and Sicily.

The illuminations, mural paintings,§ stained glass,‖ and encaustic tiles, of the middle ages in England.

The vestments of the clergy and nobility, before the Reformation, in which the varied colours were separated by golden orfreys, or by linings of ermine and miniver.

The embroidery of almost every country, except modern England and Germany, and particularly that of China, India, Persia, and Turkey.

The woven fabrics, as shawls, silks, and carpets of the same countries.

Almost all oriental paintings, toys, porcelain, enamels, jewellery, and inlaid work.

The implements, arms, and ornaments, of many barbarous nations in Africa, America, and the islands of the Pacific. And,

Heraldry, which presents perhaps the most marked example of the practice, having been

* See the coloured engravings to " Belzoni's Researches in Egypt and Nubia." I find from the notes of a gentleman, into whose hands I was permitted to place memoranda when he was about to visit the east, and who kindly undertook to procure information on the subject on the spot, occasional departures from the rule, with this general remark:—" Most of the grounds are yellow or white, but sometimes black, but this is not invariable in the parts covered with hieroglyphics. The hieroglyphics when large are often of the natural colours, when not so, they are mostly blue, some of the yellows approach to a brown (the effect of time and dust)." I may add, from the information of another friend, that the screens in the Coptic Churches of Modern Egypt are frequently made from wood, dyed a bright red, ebony and ivory in beautiful geometrical devices.
† See Dr. Layard's " Monuments of Nineveh," and in particular, the coloured engraving representing a restored hall.
‡ See " The Alhambra," by Owen Jones.
§ It must be remarked that towards the end of the fifteenth century, and the decadence of Gothic architecture, frequent violations of the rules occur, both in mural paintings and in glass.
‖ The black lines in painted glass are merely the leads used to hold together the different pieces forming the various ...

less subjected to capricious changes of fashi than any other branch of ornamented art. H heraldry is also governed by a peculiar law its own, which excludes it from the last of t rules regulating ancient colour, thus, metal metal, being bad heraldry, precludes the use yellow on white, or white on yellow. In other particulars, heraldry strictly follows t rules, even to the admission of two shades the same colour in diapering the fields shields, a beautiful enrichment of the ancie heraldic painter, entirely neglected in the pr sent day.

This list might be greatly extended, but have done enough if I succeed in rousi curiosity, and inducing inquiry and examin tion.

In every case, however, exceptions may met with, but the extent to which these la were acted upon, and the relative proportio of the exceptions, may be well understood b an examination of three books, to which solicit your attention, not only because th are most valuable authorities, for, or against, argument, but also because they may easi be referred to, and thus serve to confirm refute it, at least to the extent of the mediæv art.

1. " Specimens of the Geometrical Mosa of the Middle Ages, by Matthew Dig Wyatt," containing 90 coloured subjects, ac representing, with undoubted accuracy, bea tiful examples of this exquisite art. Of thes eighty-five are strictly in accordance with th laws I have endeavoured to explain, while fi only, and that in a slight degree, vary fro them.*

2. " Glossary of Ecclesiastical Orname and Costume, compiled and illustrated fro ancient authorities and examples, by A. Well Pugin, architect." This splendid volume e hibits upwards of two hundred and thirty di tinct examples, subject to the arrangemen and only eight opposed to it, five of thes eight in a very trifling degree.†

3. " Details and Ornaments from the Al hambra, by Owen Jones, architect." Out o sixty-five coloured subjects in this magnificen and well-known publication, I find two onl directly opposed to the rules ; a few other differ from them very slightly.‡ * *

The coincidence of these laws for the ar rangement of colour, thus influencing the ar of various and widely-spread nations, unco nected as most of them were by local or b religious ties,—and extending from the earlie era of art, to the present time,—is at lea curious and interesting. I believe that a know ledge of the facts may be useful also to th modern decorator and manufacturer. I wi now endeavour to point out their probabl origin.

One of the most original modern writer on art,§ states, in reference to archi tectural form, " I would insist especiall on the fact, of which I doubt not that furthe illustrations will occur to the mind of ever reader, that all most lovely forms and thought are directly taken from natural objects ; be cause I would fain be allowed to assume as the converse of this, namely, that forms whic are not taken from the natural objects must b ugly ;" and again, " that forms are not beau tiful because they are copied from nature ; onl it is out of the power of man to conceive beaut without her aid."

What is here demanded with so much bold ness and truth for elegance of form, I clai with equal confidence for harmony of colour it is impossible to imagine any beautiful c harmonious colouring at variance with natur or at least with nature when expressing he lovelier attributes of harmony and peace.

If then the ancient and mediæval artisan and semi-barbarians of every age, alike ex celled in the beauty of their coloured orna mentation, it is probable they all took natur for their copy, which, as Sir Joshua Reynold has remarked, " is always at hand, in con parison of whose rules the best coloured pic tures are but faint and feeble. Now, all th great pictures of nature, when exhibited und ordinary circumstances, are painted strictly i

* Published for the Author. London, 1848.
† Henry G. Bohn. London, 1844.

rdance with the rules practised by the meal artist. The azure firmament of day has
olden sun, its clouds of white, shaded with
k, and tinted with yellow, or if tinged with
as at sunset, usually seen in an atmo-
re of pale yellow. The indigo sky of
t has its silver moon, and is studded with
en stars, while the black clouds are ever
ed with silvery white. When exceptions
r they are looked upon as portentous and
l, and even the greatest exceptions are but
ifications of the rules, which nature rarely
radicts entirely.

ie green meadows of spring and early
mer are embroidered with flowers, among
h white or yellow immensely preponderate.
not until the strong sun of June has
:d the herbage with gold colour that
:rs of blue, red, or purple prevail. In the
:ald grass we find the daisy and the but-
:p, among the yellow grain the scarlet
:y and the bright blue cornflower.

hen nature paints in miniature she ad-
s to the same rules. Cull the flowers in
r garden, and examine them one by one,
will find that when more than one distinct
ur occurs in any specimen, one of these
:urs is certain to be white, yellow, or
ugh more rarely) black.* Or, you may
many flowers beautifully damasked with
or more tints of one colour like the
ering in ancient heraldry.†

do not seek to impugn any existing theory
:lour, much less to establish a new one,
I desire to engage your attention to a
ect of much importance to British com-
ce and to British art. Your most exten-
means of observation may enable you to
the comprehensiveness and utility of this
tice of the ancient decorators, and of the
ufacturers of other countries, both civilised
barbarous, and to judge how far an
tion of these rules might benefit those
ngland. I may be mistaken in my idea
.eir importance, yet I sometimes imagine,
simple as they are, they really embrace
y of the requirements of art. Combina-
.s of yellow, white, and black produce an
.umerable variety of tints in undecided
.ens‡ and neutral greys,—the most univer-
ly diffused of all colours, and these are
rmed or cooled to any degree by the addi-
n of the primitives, red or blue.

I take leave to reiterate the remark, that
do not claim the beauty of ancient and
diæval polychromic effects, or of the best
:cimens of modern manufacturers, to be
:duced only by the peculiar arrangement of
ours which I have endeavoured to explain,
: I venture to believe that it is one of the
ans successfully employed for the purpose,
I therefore I do not hesitate to advocate its
by the English artisan.

GILBERT J. FRENCH.

IMPORTATION OF FOREIGN GLASS.—A
urn, moved for by Mr. Richard Spooner,
P., shows that the total imports of foreign
ss in the year 1848 were as follow, viz.:—
.037 cwt. of white or stoned window glass,
one colour only; 90,442 square feet of
er and polished glass; 1,195 feet of painted
otherwise ornamented glass; 38,086 lb. of
ite flint glass bottles, not cut or engraved;
t,343 lb. of wine glasses, tumblers, and all
er white flint glass goods, not cut or other-
se ornamented; 639,967 lb. of all flint cut
ss, flint coloured glass, and fancy orna-
ntal glass; and 370 cwt. of glass manufac-
es not otherwise described. The quantities
British glass exported from this country in
year 1848 were as follow, viz.:—15,296 cwt.
flint glass, 19,708 cwt. of window glass,
,227 feet of plate glass, 194,755 cwt. of
nmon glass bottles, and 6,965l. worth of
king-glasses and mirrors.

It is impossible to change the colours of flowers ad
tum, by artificial means, yet the rose, naturally red, may
changed to any shade between red and yellow, red and
te, or red and black, but it admits no shade of blue, so
the dahlia, &c. &c.

The old Dutch painters of flowers mostly worked on
black ground. The value of this arrangement may be
ily and pleasantly ascertained by examining natural
.vers by the light of a lanthorn on a dark night. The
.alsite beauty of nature's floral gems, when thus ex-
.ited, can scarcely be understood without trial of the
.eriment.

The value of the neutral greens (if I may so term the
ix of black and yellow, without the intermixture of red or
:e), was well understood by the old artists in glass, and is
.eeably exemplified in many an ancient church window.

IRON GRILL, STA. MARIA NOVELLA, FLORENCE.

IRON GRiLL, STA. MARIA NOVELLA,
FLORENCE.

ALTHOUGH the name and contents of the
celebrated Spanish chapel are probably familiar to most of our readers, we question
whether the accompanying elaborate iron-work
is as well known as it deserves to be. We
believe it hitherto unpublished. The pictorial
treasures absorb so much of the traveller's
attention, that the grills in the windows and
iron gates are hardly likely to attract much
notice. It is of wrought iron, apparently rather
late in style. The variety and richness of
these grills in some of the cities of Italy are
quite extraordinary: a very interesting collection might be formed of them. We would particularly instance Venice and Florence in this
respect. The grill here engraved is drawn to
the scale of half an inch to the foot.

ON CHESTER CATHEDRAL, ITS HISTORY
AND ARCHITECTURE.

WE proceed to give the substance of Mr.
Ashpitel's interesting discourse on the history
and architecture of Chester cathedral.

The speaker said, without entering into
minute details of what every one knew, it was
sufficient for him to state for the information
of strangers, that the present cathedral was
originally a monastery, and although Chester
had been the seat of a bishopric previous to
the conquest, it had only been restored to these
privileges by the reformation. The chronicle
of Henry Bradshaw (Leland's Collectanea, vol.
ii., p. 62) stated that Chester was the seat of a
cathedral church in the time of King Lucius,
the first Christian king of Britain. It is true
Bishop Tanner had given a contradiction to
this statement, but without authority. The
light of Christianity had penetrated where
Roman civilization had spread, and he thought
it hold to contradict without authority a tradition that bore every trace of probability. However this might be, it was not pretended that
the present erection was any part of such cathedral. We learn from the same authority,
Bradshaw, the Cestrian monk, before cited, and
from the chronicle of John Brompton, Decem
Scriptores, p. 810, that St. Werburgh was the
daughter, sister, and wife of kings,—that disgusted with the world, she founded a monas-

tery at Ely, which she governed many years,
died at Trent, and was buried at the place then
called Heanburga, now Hanbury. Her relics,
according to both authorities above cited, were
removed, for fear of an incursion of the Danes,
to Chester, and there re-buried with pomp, a
ceremony called usually "the translation of the
body."

In 924, according to the MS. chronicle preserved among Bishop Gastrell's Notitia, it is
stated that King Athelstane erected a monastery here for secular canons; although William
of Malmsbury (fo. 164, n. 30) states there was
a monastery for nuns, (as the word "sancti-
monialia" is usually translated) "ex antiquo,"
from a very early period. Whether the word
may not mean any monastic person it is not
worth while to inquire. Suffice it to say, there
was a monastery for regular canons in 1057,
when Leofric, Earl of Chester, celebrated in
his day, but now better known as the husband
of Lady Godiva, the heroine of a very uncertain
legend relating to Coventry, came to Chester
and repaired the buildings at his own expense.
Shortly after this, the greatest political convulsion that ever agitated this land took place—
the Norman conquest. Every thing was
changed. Arts, commerce, manners, customs,
were administered by new hands. Among
other changes, the secular, or as we should
call them, the parochial clergy, were removed
from their possessions, and monks placed there
in their stead—a change attempted often before
the conquest, but against which the common
voice of the English nation strongly revolted.
Under their new Norman lords, however, this
was done everywhere.

The Conqueror now created his friend and
fellow-soldier, the celebrated Hugo D'Avran-
ches, better known as Hugh Lupus, Earl of
Chester. He followed the example of most of
his predecessors—lived a life of the wildest
luxury and rapine. At length, falling sick from
the consequence of his excesses, he was visited
by the celebrated Anselm, the Abbot of Bec,
in Normandy, afterwards the Archbishop of
Canterbury, who persuaded him, as William
of Malmsbury says, were very few in number, and
who lived in an irregular or improper and
beggarly way,—" ejectus inde pauculis clericis
qui ibidem fædo et pauperi victu vitam tran-
sigebant." According, however, to the anony-

mous Chronicle of Evesham, MS. Bib. Bodl. fo. 96, and the Golden History of John of Tynemouth, in the same library, he converted the canons into regular monks,—in the terse words of the latter author, "tonsoravit eos," he shaved them, alluding to the tonsure the regular monks have on the head. The three chronicles respectively give us, as the dates of the foundation, the years 1093, 1094, and 1095, a slight variation, into which there is little use to inquire. In the meanwhile the monastery was built, and age and disease coming on, the old hardened soldier was struck with remorse, and—an expiation common enough in those days, and alluded to with such force by our greatest poet—as those who

"Dying, put on the weeds of Dominic,
Or as Franciscan think to pass disguised,"—

the great Hugh Lupus took the cowl, retired in the last state of disease into the monastery, and in three days was no more.

It now must be endeavoured to point out what parts of the church are the work of this proud earl. Mr. Ashpitel stated that he could not, from the most minute research, discover any portions of the Saxon church. He considered it probable that there might be some portions in the foundations, but there were none visible. It was not one of those cases where the period of the Saxon erection is within a few short years of the Conquest, and where we are told one building just built was pulled down, to be immediately replaced by another. The Saxon building must have been very old; it was much dilapidated a few years previously, when Leofric repaired it. We have the testimony of William of Malmsbury to the squalid poverty of the monks, and probably of their buildings; besides this, we have the indirect evidence of the earl's charter, where he alludes to the church in the words "quæ constructa est," which lead us to suppose it had just been built; and the direct evidence of Ordericus Vitalis above cited, who speaks of it as the church which Lupus himself had built —"quod idem Cestriæ construxerat."

The Norman work remaining consists of the lower part of the north-west tower, standing on the opposite side of the nave to the present Consistory Court, containing some beautiful shafts and capitals, and five lofty arches, the general character of which would lead every one to suppose the original church to have been of very fine architecture. The north wall of the nave, to the height of the windows, is likewise Norman, and contains on the side of the cloister six tombs, where, as we find from a MS. written on the back of an old charter now in the British Museum, the early Norman abbots are interred. The north transept is also of Norman work to a considerable height, and contains a very curious Norman arcade, so placed that he at first thought the original design to have been like that of Exeter,—a nave and choir, flanked by two towers, the lower parts of which were open and formed transepts. This idea, however, was disproved by authorities which afterwards were obtained.

He then explained the way in which the Gothic cathedral had, as it were, grown out of the Roman basilica, and that the circular tribunal, which terminated the Norman building, had been first elongated a little, still keeping its rounded form at the eastern end, and thus became the choir. On inquiry, he found that two bases of columns still existed in the choir, near the bishop's throne, and he showed on the plan their situation, and the probable line the old circular part then assumed.* He also pointed out on the plans the buildings which had just been opened, by the kindness of the bishop and clergy. These are vaulted apartments of early Norman work, and are described in the charter of Henry VIII. by which he divides the properties between the bishop and dean, as *promptuaria et pannaria*, the former derived from a word denoting a butler or steward, probably a buttery; and the latter from *pannus*, a cloth, probably the place for clothing.

The next point in the history of the monastery was the removal or translation of Earl Hugh's remains by Randal, the third Norman earl. This, he states—in the charter whereby he gives the monks the land north of the abbey as far as the Northgate—he does for the good of his soul and for those of his relations. The speaker suggested, from the fact of the land to the north of the abbey having been given about this time, that it probably was the occasion of building the canon's vestry, and subsequently the chapter-house. It was necessary to inquire again among the charters and other documents for more historical information. This was to be found in the Red Book of St. Werburgh, now in the British Museum. In 1205 there is a "significavit," or pastoral letter from Peter de la Roche, Bishop of Winchester, stating that the church threatened "intolerable ruin"—that it was necessary to rebuild the choir and tower, which latter word, Mr. Ashpitel observed, was in the singular number, and therefore disproved his first idea that there were two flanking towers as at Exeter; that some very small attempt ("incipiculos") had been made to carry out this purpose, which had failed; and finally they endeavoured to raise money for the purpose. How little success this met with is clear from a pastoral letter from William, Bishop of Coventry, for the same purpose, which describes the state of the church as deplorable,—the choir open to the weather, and without doors. This, on the margin, is dated 12th of John.

Now, it is clear from the style of architecture, that the vestry, the chapter-house, and lady chapel are of date from 1220 to 1250—and accordingly we may suppose some new and unexpected source of wealth must have fallen in. In Abbot Marmion's time the convent could afford to elect a hereditary cook, and to give him large fees and privileges, and in Abbot Pinchbeck's time, from 1221 to 1240, the number of monks was increased from twenty-eight to forty. Mr. Ashpitel then described the architecture of these respective parts at some length. He dwelt particularly on the beauties of the chapter house, which he considered, with its singularly tasteful vestibule, to be the finest in the kingdom of its form;* and then took occasion to animadvert severely upon the tastelessness of a professed architectural critic, who could pass over the building with the cold criticism "poor enough." He (Mr. Ashpitel) had been told the same story, and had come down to Chester with a heavy heart, and the fear he should have an ungracious task, but he found beauties which grew on him more and more at every visit. The Norman remains, he said, are extremely fine; here is work of all kinds of great beauty, and the most curious and instructive transitions from style to style, that perhaps were ever contained in one building.†

The next historical fact was, a quotation from the mutilated chronicle among Bishop Gastrell's MSS. In 1259, as far as the passage can be deciphered, the convent met to consider the rebuilding of the church, and, after some opposition, probably on the part of the abbot, as appears from the MS., the opinion of the convent was ordered to be carried out. About twenty years after this, a law suit, which had been long pending between the abbot and a powerful family in the neighbourhood, terminated in favour of the abbot: by allowing his adversary an annual sum, he came into possession of four immense manors. There can be but little doubt that this accession of property gave a great impetus to the works of Simon Whitchurch and his successors. At this period it is probable the building of the choir commenced. An architect would suppose that the bays to the north end of the choir were erected first—there are some corbels of decidedly earlier date—and the bases of the piers are of such decidedly early English character, compared to the other work of the same description, that there can be but little doubt this was the first attempt at rebuilding.

It would be evident to the eyes of the architect that the greater portion of the choir, the tower arches, nay, even the nave itself, is of the Decorated period, that is, including transition, from 1280 to 1360.

Now, what are the recorded facts? In 1259 the monks met to consider a rebuilding; in 1281 they came into possession of large property; and in 1284 we have a curio[us] document. It appears that the first Edwa[rd] visited the town on his way to repel the incu[r]sions of the Welsh; and in the 17th year [of] his reign we find in the Red Book of St. W[er]burgh a grant of venison, directed to Regin[ald] Grey, who seems to have had control over t[he] forests of Wirral and Delamere; and in a co[n]temporary hand it states in the margin, that "was for the monks engaged in the gr[eat] work of rebuilding the church." Simi[lar] grants follow in the same way. At last [they] get a grant of six bucks, six does, and o[ne] stag, probably a red deer, as distinguish[ed] from the fallow deer.

There is no reason, in fact, to suppose th[at] the works proceeded other than in regul[ar] order, following the even tenor of their wa[y] till an unfortunate, and in fact disgracef[ul] event occurred to the monastery. We fi[nd] that Richard Seynesbury, in 1362, had m[isconducted] himself in such a way that the Pri[or] of St. Alban, the head of the Benedicti[ne] Order in England, and the Prior of Coventr[y] formed a visitation "to inquire into his offenc[es] and extensive dilapidation." The painful r[e]sult was, that the abbot fled from the inqui[ry]. The abbey was under Papal protection, bei[ng] what was technically called an "exempt:" t[he] abbot appealed to the pope, went to Italy, a[nd] died in Lombardy.

It has been shown that there is a style th[at] an architect would designate at once as th[at] which prevailed from 1300 to 1360; and we th[en] find work about the abbey that bears the ch[a]racter of at least a hundred years later; a[nd] yet these styles have been confounded tog[e]ther. It is deeply to be regretted that wh[en] Mr. Ormerod published his great work, whic[h] may be designated as the prince of coun[ty] histories, the knowledge of the style a[nd] period of Gothic architecture was as yet in i[ts] infancy. He would not otherwise have att[ri]buted to Simon Ripley work which seems [to] have been at least from 80 to 100 years earlie[r], nor would others have attributed much of t[he] work to the reign of King John that clearly [is] at least 100 years later. But before enteri[ng] into this argument, as concerns the nave of t[he] church, it will perhaps be well to turn o[ur] attention to the north transept, or the Chur[ch] of St. Oswald.

It has already been stated that the chur[ch] was dedicated jointly to St. Werburgh and S[t.] Oswald. It is doubtful at what period; but [it] must have been early it became a pari[sh] church. The architecture was, he thought, ce[r]tainly about the year 1340 to 1360, and hi[s]torical facts, which he quoted, bore out t[he] inference.

Mr. Ormerod has attributed the erection [of] the tower, nave, and transept of St. Oswald Church to this abbot, but the slightest glan[ce] at the older part of St. Oswald's will show t[he] contrary. It appears that this notion h[as] arisen from the fact that the two letters S a[nd] R are found twined together in the carving [of] the caps; but it might have been that t[he] carving, as is often the case, would be left t[ill] the completion of the work—or, what is st[ill] more probable, the letters R and S would r[e]present Richard Seynesbury quite as well [as] Simon Ripley. In fact, it is in accordan[ce] with the notion of a bad and unscrupulo[us] man, like Seynesbury, that he shou[ld] have the vanity to attach his name [to] works in which he had no share. If w[e] suppose much of the work attributed [to] Simon Ripley to be of the earlier period, w[e] then have a consistent account of the chur[ch] of St. Oswald. Every part of this is clearl[y] of the Decorated period, except the roof of i[ts] nave and the windows of the west, or, as it ma[y] have been called, the north-west side. The and the windows of the south aisle of the na[ve] of the cathedral have positively Perpendicul[ar] tracery, while the jambs, shafts, gabled can[o]pies, the hollow, the hall flowers, and the cle[ar] indication of a Decorated parapet show th[at] the work could never be of the date 148[5]. But if we suppose this work to have bee[n] nearly completed in 1360, and then abandone[d] till the energy of Simon Ripley took up t[he] matter, the whole is clear.

Mr. Ashpitel acknowledged with thanks t[he] assistance of Mr. Baily, especially in the pr[e]paration of a number of diagrams by whic[h] the discourse was illustrated. Both are we[ll] entitled to the thanks of the association for t[he]

* During the late restoration the arrangement of the Norman building was made evident, and Mr. Hussey submitted a plan of it at a meeting of the Archæological Institute some time ago.—Ed.

* See our View of Chapter House, p. 365, *ante*.

† It was very good of Mr. Ashpitel to say all he could to make the inhabitants of Chester proud of their cathedral. We cannot, however, endorse all his praise.

time and care bestowed on the subject. Mr. Ashpitel is one of the few architects to whom a Latin charter is no stumbling-block in an inquiry, and he speaks fluently and well.

THE NEW SEWERS AMENDMENT ACT.

This act has just been printed; it appears to have undergone considerable mutilation in its passage through Parliament,—the original bill (as introduced by Lord Ebrington) containing thirty-two clauses, the act as passed only eighteen: those clauses by which almost unlimited powers were sought have been completely rejected. Whether what are left will be conducive to the public interest remains to be seen.

Clause 3 empowers the commissioners to agree with any paving board or authorities in matters of paving, on such terms as may be agreed on, where the commissioners and such board may deem that sewerage works and the convenience and health of the public would be promoted thereby.

4. In cases of failure of works or of accident, the commissioners may make reasonable compensation for such damage or loss sustained thereby.

5. This clause has been introduced to meet the objection successfully taken by the parochial authorities of St. Margaret's, Westminster, against cleansing cesspools during the day time. It empowers the commissioners to order and authorise their officers to carry on all operations of cleansing, and to remove all filth, soil, or matter, in the day time, notwithstanding the provisions of the Police Act, the commissioners taking care, as far as possible, to prevent nuisance, annoyance, or delay; and any contractor employed by the commissioners who neglects all reasonable precautions, to be liable to a penalty of 5*l*.

9. The commissioners may accept and order payments by instalments, and where a sewer has been constructed within thirty-five years from the passing of the act, the commissioners may order the owner or occupier required to drain into a sewer to pay such sum as they may think just towards the expense of the same, which sum may be recovered as a debt due to the commissioners, by distress and sale of the goods and chattels of the person liable to pay the same.

10. The amount of any improvement rate may be recovered, with interest at the rate of 5 per cent., and such a sum as will meet the expenses incurred in recovering the same.

11. That where expenses have been incurred in the improvement rate, and the premises in respect of which it was made are partly destroyed, pulled down, or suffered to go into decay, or are untenanted for twelve successive months, then the commissioners by their decree may order such charges to be paid as default, and may charge the unpaid amount, with interest, upon the site of such premises, and order such expenses to be paid by the owner for the time being, to be recovered in the manner set forth in other parts of this Act.

15 and 16. Change the title of "Clerk" to that of "Secretary," and the "Surveyors" to "Engineers."

17. Commissioners may borrow money, and for the purpose of raising money may, instead of making mortgages under this Act, grant annuities for lives or years, to be paid out of the rates, as they shall think fit, notwithstanding any Act may not pass for the renewal of this Act (!), and any mortgage or annuity so contracted by the commissioners after the expiration of the Act shall be valid and in full force.

The bill originally introduced contained clauses for the appointment of medical officers of health—to give almost unlimited powers to committees—to appoint a barrister to hear appeals against rates—to remove nuisances, and to inflict penalties for neglecting orders for so doing—to compel the Water Companies to supply water for the use of the commissioners, and also for water-closet apparatus, and if deemed expedient, the commissioners to purchase streams of water for their own use, and to dispose of any surplus water to the ratepayers for domestic or other purposes, and to continue drain pipes beyond the limits of the commission, for the purpose of disposing of sewage refuse, making compensation to the owners of the land for the same.

ARCHITECTS AND ARCHITECTURE IN JAMAICA.

Some short time ago a letter appeared in your columns, signed "A Tradesman," charging architects with, among other things, compelling builders to perform their own private work without any remuneration. Although I would not attempt to assert that there are no "black sheep" amongst us, as well as in every other profession, still I am of opinion that, had the matter been inquired into, it would have been found, in many instances, that the parties who carried on this dishonourable practice, were men who had assumed a title to which they could lay no claim.

The consideration that it is the duty of every architect, "in so far as in him lies," to uphold and maintain the dignity of the profession, as well as to expose anything that might cast a slur on its honour, impels me to make known through the medium of your paper, the following circumstances, which bear out the assertion contained in my first paragraph:—A person who came to this island some time ago, as an organist, music master, &c., not finding his success so great as he had anticipated, looked around him for some other occupation, and what, think you, was the character he put on? No less, Mr. Editor, than (to use his own words, or rather copy his signature), that of "Architect, Civil Engineer, &c. &c." Having succeeded in imposing on some persons, he was engaged to erect a chancel to the cathedral church of the island. With the aid of one who should have acted differently, and the assistance of your Builder, and some other works, he gave a design, the side windows of which were copied from Northfleet Church, Kent (*vide* The Builder, March 27th, 1847), and the one at the eastern end from Merton Chapel, Oxford. Tenders were obtained, and contracts for certain portions of the works entered into. The cost of erection was estimated at 3,000*l*., although it will take more than that sum now to complete it.

Three thousand pounds for the building of a chancel, free from all architectural decoration, and not larger than is usually attached to ordinary parish churches!

It has now leaked out that our "Architect, Civil Engineer, &c. &c.," has been, and still is, extracting from the pockets of the builder, either 5 or 7½ per cent., besides the commission he receives from the parish. And I have been given to understand that every one (for the contracts have been divided), who is connected with the building has to pay a like per centage.

I shall abstain from all comment, but I really think it is time for architects to be "up and doing." "Something should be done to protect the legalised members of the profession, and put at once a stop to a system that casts dishonour on its members. I enclose my card, together with the names of the other parties.

One who hopes to see a stop put to such doings.

We learn from another correspondent, that at present architecture is at a very low ebb in Jamaica. The only works going on in Kingston of any pretensions are a store and dwelling for Mr. Pinnock, a merchant, and the United Presbyterian Church, both of which are under the direction of Mr. B. W. Walsh, architect.

The church consists of a nave, south porch, and small chancel. It is of Perpendicular date. The side windows of two lights with transom. The western and eastern windows are large, of five and four lights, and filled in with tracery of rather an elaborate character. The roof is open, and of pitch pine, wrought without tracery, and is to be covered with slates. The sittings will be all low and open, with stall-ends, with carved finials. The woodwork of the sittings will be of cedar; the pulpit, &c., will also be of cedar. There is to be no paint used to any portion of the woodwork. The church is built of brick, with stone dressings. The windows will be wrought out of the stone of the country, from the parish of Portland. They will be the first windows ever made out of the stone of the country, as well as the first ever worked in the island. There are to be no galleries. The church will seat 512 persons. The passages, chancel, and porch, will be paved with red and blue tiles from Minton's manufactory. The cost of the church will be 1,700*l*. The height of the building from floor to ridge will be 51 feet.

Two iron bridges for the parish of Trelawney are projected. The span of one is to be 162 feet.

ONE-SIDED TEMPLES.—LEASEHOLD.

Few, indeed, are the examples in our day of structures which, standing on an isolated site, are complete, so as to present four sides, or an entire exterior of uniform design.

The value of space in a crowded city already pre-occupied, and the impossibility of obtaining a *freehold* plot, will account for this; for if the locality be leasehold for ninety-nine years (and this is the longest lease now granted), it is not worth the cost to build for the inheritance of a cunning proprietor, who calculates for the aggrandizement of his successor in the fourth generation.

It is a matter of wonder that so many richly-embellished and solid structures are to be found in our streets, rather than that we see none built completely detached and exhibiting a unity of design on all sides. In such thoroughfares as Pall-mall, which is one continued chain of palaces, it cannot be expected that each one should stand apart,—for there, with the back to the Park and front to a noble causeway, the land is too valuable, and the variety of elevation conduces much to the beauty of the strada; but it is curious to contemplate (and this might give a subject to *Punch*) the tumult in the clubs about the year 1920, when the original leases will have lapsed.

The managing committee of the Reform, Athenæum, Conservative, &c., will then have rare commotions and treaties with the successors of the Woods and Forests! The law and usages are on the side of the officials, and if the system of leasehold tenure for short terms, should go on (which I very much doubt) till that year of grace, those anarchists must either break up and get *freehold* plots, somewhere out of Middlesex, or compound at rack rents of 2,000*l*. a-year, for by that period the terms of leases will be reduced to 31 years; and this, according to the present ratio of diminution, would be a long lease, since the extent of leases was in A.D. 1800, often 500 years; in 1820, 99 years; and at the present period of our chronicles it is (*vide the Portland estate*) 60 years! whilst in other districts of the town building leases vary from 80 to 60 years. In private residences of moderate pretensions, possibly the extent of the term makes no greater difference as to the outward appearance of the structure; but contrast the solidity of a house in Paris, built on *freehold*, with one of the same order in London, and the result will be manifestly in favour of the perpetuity.

Such a condition of clubs and public communities may hereafter, when the evils of *short leases* become palpable, lead the greater community, the public, to reflect upon the tendency of this custom to centralise property (the fixed capital in houses) in the possession of a very few landlords; but by that time the whole body of lessees in the metropolis will be also extruded and hunted out. No man can then have an interest in his tenement but as a lessee at rack rent;—the money expended by his ancestors will be lost to the last tenant, and "thousands yet unborn may rue the hunting of that day." Quondam.

Water from Roof of New Churches.—A correspondent from Milton Rectory, Abingdon, says,—"I shall be glad of an opinion as to the best remedy against the evil of the constant dropping of water from the new wooden roofs of churches on to the floor of the church, occasioned, as I suppose, by the condensation of the moisture of the internal heated atmosphere. Will an application of felt prevent the evil? and if so, how is it to be applied? or is a plastered roof more secure from this evil than a boarded roof?"—Some of our readers will perhaps give us the result of their experience in a similar case. A layer of asphalted felt between the boarding and the slates or lead with which it is covered, would of course tend to lessen the evil. We are disposed to think, however, that *good ventilation* is the great thing needed.—Ed.

CITY OF LONDON UNION WORKHOUSE.——MR. R. TRESS, ARCHITECT.

THE CITY OF LONDON UNION WORKHOUSE.

A DESIGN for the City of London Union Workhouse was sought by a public competition, the circumstances attending which will be remembered by many of our readers. A plan by Mr. R. Tress was ultimately selected, and this has been carried out under the architect's direction by Messrs. Curtis, builders, of Stratford, and the house is nearly ready for occupation. The amount of the contract was 38,884*l*.*

The annexed engraving represents the building as seen from the Bow-road, wherein it stands. In our ensuing number we shall give a plan of the ground floor, and some particulars of the arrangement. Suffice it now to say, that the buildings externally are of brick, with Portland cement and, to a certain extent, Caen stone dressing. The low building seen in the centre is the chapel, and serves to divide the fore-court into two quadrangles, having around three sides of each an open corridor.

THE ADORNMENT OF THE CITY OF EDINBURGH.

WE are surprised to learn that it is not only intended to *alter, in effect*, the front of the Register House, by the erection of Mr. Steele's colossal equestrian statue of Wellington there, but that, in order to make way for the statue, *a complete alteration* of the central portion of the screen or step-flight is meditated.† We must really protest against any such tampering with one of the chief architectural ornaments of this fine city. With our correspondent "Vitruvius," however well and carefully or tastefully accomplished, we would just as soon see "The Lady of the Lake," or "Marmion," with additions and improvements by John Wilson, or the professor's own beautiful poems altered by some poet of a future age. Not that we would object to see an appropriate piece of sculpture *added* to Adams's masterpiece. *As it is*, it is admirably *designed* for some such ornament, and we know that the citizens of Edinburgh have ever longed to crown this elegant approach with some appropriate piece of sculpture, and indeed have looked on it as an uncompleted design without such an ornament; but that such a desire should now be attempted to be gratified by altering, and that it appears most vitally, those very proportions and that very design which *induced* the desire, is quite preposterous. A colossal equestrian statue too, however excellent as a separate work, is certainly not an appropriate piece of sculpture for such a site, whether altered or not. A double wrong would thus be done, a wrong both to architect and sculptor, as in the case at Hyde-park Corner.‡ The conjunction, without the slightest doubt, would be found to be incongruous and absurd. A correspondent of the *Edinburgh Courant*, adverse, as a man of taste, to the threatened infliction, shows that the *effect* of the statue, as seen from the only available points of view, would remind every one closely of the sentinel on duty at the Horse Guards,—but it would be even still stiffer and more ludicrous to view a colossal horse-guard thus stuck up literally on a staircase, even though it be an outside one and not very high. As well to mount him on the house-top at once. A correspondent of the *Scotsman*, also adverse to the meditated arrangement, points to St. Andrew's-square as a better site for such a statue. But the Melville monument already occupies the centre of that square, as a grand terminal to the series of lesser monuments all along designed to occupy the several crossings in the line of George-street, and the *toute ensemble* of such a design might be injured or confused by such arrangement. The favourite suggestion that it be placed in the Princes-street Gardens appears to merit its favour and preference, even though the statue were placed in a central position near the Scott monument, inasmuch as these gardens constitute that one sunny central spot in the city where, graced in the back ground by the picturesque antique outline and shadow of the High-street houses, boldly ascending along the hilly ridge to the castle, and flanked and freshened by the rich foliage of the gardens in the valley beneath, a perfect galaxy of sculptural and architectural ornaments might be and ought to be crowded and concentered. And already the idea has been seized and appropriated by the city architect, Mr. Cousin, in whose design for the adornment of the eastern and most seen and frequented division, we find a series of pedestals laid out along a grand terraced mall, and fitted for just such bold and open air groups as a colossal equestrian statue.

The adornment of the Calton-hill, we may here add, was lately, in some of its details, under notice in the council, when it was resolved,—

"That as there is little likelihood of the National Monument being soon completed, and seeing that the site thereof is in an unseemly state, and out of keeping with the natural beauty of the hill, it be remitted to the Plans and Works Committee, to endeavour to effect some arrangement with the Trustees, whereby the mason-sheds and unsightly wooden paling be removed, the site inclosed with a low parapet wall and rail, and the ground laid out in shrubbery or flowers, with a fountain in the centre; always securing to the Trustees the rights conferred by Act of Parliament to resume possession of the ground whenever there is a likely chance of the monument being completed."

Mr. Treasurer Dick said that surely it was possible to raise some 400*l*. or 500*l*. per annum to keep the work itself still in progression. By the arrangement proposed, the Council and Trustees would be virtually declaring that the public had given up all hope. Another Councillor, Mr. Wright, did not think either Council or Trustees would be justified in again proceeding with the work till they had the whole funds collected.

* Thirty-one tenders were sent in, ranging from 33,100*l*. to 73,957!!

† In virtue of a warrant obtained from the Dean of Guild Court, operations have been commenced, although it is said that there is little probability of the statue being ready for at least a twelvemonth.

‡ The arch there, by the way, appears to be confounded by some of the Edinburgh critics with the marble arch at Buckingham Palace.

NOTES IN THE PROVINCES.

THE first stone of the Fulham Union Workhouse was laid on Monday week, by the Bishop of London, and the event was celebrated in the evening at Hammersmith, where the guardians and principal inhabitants and others connected with the union met at dinner; Mr. John Gunter, of Fulham, in the chair.——Plans for the rebuilding of St. Thomas's Church, Newport, Isle of Wight, are to be shortly called for by advertisement.——The Worcester Gas Company lately announced a dividend of 8 per cent. for the previous *half*-year.——St. Peter's Church, Cookley, is to be consecrated by the Bishop of Worcester on 21st September. A parsonage and school are in course of erection on either side of the church. The style is Early English, from a design supplied by Mr. E. Smith, of Oldswinford, the architect *and* builder.——Nearly 300*l*. have been subscribed for erecting the piece of sculpture representing the Good Samaritan, in the entrance-hall of the general hospital at Bristol.——Under head of "Great Improvements at Small Cost," a correspondent of *Felix Farley's Bristol Journal*, "A Lover of Gothic Architecture," suggests that the "following improvements might be effected by a few trifling subscriptions from the lovers of the Gothic standard of beauty in ecclesiastical architecture:—Open the walled-up cloisters of the cathedral, let the stranger once more wander over that holy ground; remove the modern sashes from the old Saxon gateway in College-green, and replace them by windows of the proper period; remove the Grecian flower-pots from the old tower of St. James; remove the tawdry porch of St. Peter's church, with its puffing cherubims, and replace it by a modest Gothic arched doorway; let the interesting crypt of St. John's church, with its monument of Rowley, &c., be cleansed, the bosses picked out, that the place may no longer be used as a coal cellar; let the mahogany arched box that encloses the entrance to the cathedral be swept away, and the old Gothic porch be opened."——The plant of the late contractor has been taken at a valuation by the Plymouth Great Western Dock Company, and the works have been again commenced; but we are informed that it is only the intention of the Directors to spend from 600*l*. to 800*l*., to secure the works commenced by the late contractor, and also to repair the Millbay Pier. The company have no contractor; the securing of the works is let to six workmen who were employed by the late contractor.——The new parish church of St. Agnes, Cornwall, was opened on Tuesday in week before last. The nave and chancel are 88 feet long, exclusive of tower at east-end; south aisle, 73 ft. 6 in.; north aisle, 61 ft. 6 in. The style is perpendicular, with flat-headed side windows. The roof is lined with wood, stained dark. The aisles are laid with red and black tiles, and the chancel with encaustic tiles. The seats are all low, open, and uniform. The old tower and spire remain for the present, but there is a surplus for a building-fund for a new tower. The edifice was begun in August, 1848, on the site of the old one, which had become ruinous in rather an odd way. A worthy churchwarden, about half a century ago, finding one of the pillars in his way, forthwith removed it, and a brother Sampson feeling that his power to do the like was unquestionable, forthwith removed its fellow. The roof accordingly began to fall in, and the walls to fall out, so that, notwithstanding "props of timber," and other unavailing support, the whole became ruinous and unsafe, and was at length pulled down to make way for the present structure.——The contract for building St. Peter's Church, Macclesfield, was completed in the week before last, and on Saturday week the edifice was consecrated. It is in the Early English style, with three aisles, and is built of stone, for 600 to 700 persons. The chancel windows are filled with stained glass. The architect was Mr. T. Turbshaw, of Newcastle; and the builder, Mr. Evans, to whom it was transferred from Mr. Frith. The new school of St. Peter's adjoins the building.——A Congregational Church for 1,000 sitters has been erected at Wolverhampton, at a cost of 6,500*l*., including site, from designs by Mr. Edward Banks, of Wolverhampton, architect, who superintended the erection, and also designed the schools connected with the church.——A new national school and master's-house is about to be erected at Beverley, Mr. W. Richardson, builder.——The Edinburgh Plan and Works Committee have accepted an estimate by Messrs. Hume and Melville for fitting up wells on the Calton-hill, at a cost of 78*l*.——The City Dean of Guild has ordered the immediate removal of the tenement in which John Knox resided.

LONDON GRAVEYARDS.—THE CHOLERA.

MR. WALKER has addressed another note of warning to the public on this subject, accompanied by some startling statements from Sir James Murray, which ought to receive attention. He says in it,—"Scarcely an effort has been made to remove the most evident and most prolific *cause* of visitations, of which we are now gathering the justly-merited fruits.

The saturation of the earth's surface and sub-surface by the excretions of man and animals,—the sanitary mischiefs resulting from imperfect sewerage and overflowing cess-pools, wherever large congregations of the human species are gathered together in cities or towns, are not immediately remediable,—the mistakes and errors of centuries cannot be rectified in a day.

But we can and ought instantly to remove a chief cause of disease and premature death deposited in our very midst.

Between forty-five and fifty thousand bodies are *annually* placed in the receptacles for the dead in London; and these bodies are deposited amidst millions of others who have predeceased them. Twelve-thirteenths of every dead body must dissipate and mix with the air we breathe, which is thus made the vehicle of invisible and subtle poisons. The transmission of gases and the percolation of animal compounds, through the walls of houses and drains, and their consequent diffusion therein, and transmission through the gully-holes, I have years since proved."

Sir James Murray, first referring to what has been said elsewhere, as to the connection between epidemic diseases and the electrical condition of the atmosphere, remarks,—"Let any of the advocates of intra-mural graveyards employ accurate electricians, with delicate instruments, to measure the terrible galvanic derangements of fermenting churchyards, then they must be convinced of their fatal practices. Every decomposing human body deposited there is hourly altering and disordering the electric huid of that locality, which otherwise ought to be, in its normal integrity, fit to maintain the natural proportion of the same fluid in living beings. When the organic elements of dead animals are resolving into kindred dust, that decomposing mass acts as a feeder for a vast display of galvanic actions in the moist grave, as certainly as an acid liquor sets loose a flood of electric fluid in a galvanic trough. As an untoward generation of disturbed electric agency is constantly at work in the continuous cauldron of dissolving graves, its action must be felt by the living in proportion to the vicinity and intensity of the galvanic disturbances. I had long since communicated to Dr. Simpson the result of my observations on the direful consequences resulting from an effervescing Golgotha, long kept in active fermentation in Belfast, near the quays, and on a level with low-water mark. This graveyard was bounded on three sides by streets and lanes, and the houses adjoining opened into it. I was for many years the medical attendant chiefly employed by the residents of that district, and can safely affirm that they were generally unhealthy, and liable to bowel complaints, influenza, fevers, English cholera, scrofula, and other diseases of debility, whilst the people on the opposite sides of the same lanes or streets were comparatively healthy, and exempt from the continual scale of epidemic disorders, which merged into each other according to the lethal activity of the galvanic passes in continual operation by the accession of new bodies, and by being in actual contact with the communicating tenements adjoining the churchyard. During all these years I had many proofs demonstrating that persons in these tenements could not be efficiently electrified, because the best machines could seldom produce sparks of any intensity. *During these years I often noticed that a magnet capable of sustaining fifty pounds with ease in other situations, could not for a moment suspend an iron of ten pounds in the habitations built on the devastating place of interment.* From these, and many other observations, it was plain that negative electricity pervaded this vast swamp, and drew away the positive electricity from the living creatures in immediate contact with the damp earth and air of that fatal and extended trough, or galvanic pile."

ARCHITECTS' CHARGES.

DERICK v. STANTON, CLERK.

This was an action (tried on the Oxford circuit) for the amount of an architect's bill, for his expenses, and for furnishing plans for building a new district church at Ocker-hill, near Dudley. The defendant had paid 57l. 8s. into court, in satisfaction of the plaintiff's demand.

The plaintiff was said to be an architect of good practice in building churches, and the defendant was curate of the new district of Ocker-hill. By the direction of the defendant, the plaintiff had prepared several plans for the intended new church, and, at the suggestion of the defendant, several alterations and additions were afterwards made to some of the plans, and some new ones substituted for others. It did not appear that any specification for working the plans had ever been made or delivered. Though they had not been exactly followed in building the church, there was such a general resemblance of design that several architects swore that they had been substantially followed. It was proved that the ordinary remuneration for an architect, when he did not superintend the works, was 3½ per cent. on the estimate,* which was in this case 3,000l., together with an allowance for travelling expenses.

Without hearing witnesses for the defence, the Jury said they were already satisfied that the sum paid into court was a sufficient remuneration under the circumstances, and accordingly found a verdict for the defendant.

---

* So says our informant.

ANCIENT IRONWORK.

ANCIENT IRONWORK.

Annexed is a representation of a metal handle in Henry the Seventh's Chapel, at Westminster.

LANDLORDS AND TENANTS.

GUMMER v. POWELL.—This was an action to recover compensation in damages for an illegal seizure. The case was heard in the City Sheriffs' Court on Monday. Damages were laid at 10l.

The facts are these :—In July, 1848, the plaintiff, a poor woman, was induced to lend 28l. to a person named Offord, a tobacconist, at that time carrying on business in Little Bell-alley, where he rented a shop, parlour, and kitchen belonging to the defendant, who is the owner of several houses in that neighbourhood. Offord being unable to pay the loan, gave plaintiff a bill of sale of his stock in trade and furniture, dated 20th October, 1848. On the 4th of July in the present year, Offord being in arrears for rent, the defendant and a man named Shetlock broke open the shop door and distrained upon the goods in question, notwithstanding he had received notice to withdraw, and the instrument under which the plaintiff put in her claim having been shown to him.

The defendant admitted that he had received such notice, and that he gave Shetlock directions to break open the door, but considered that he was justified in so doing, the door being in the passage, and also on the ground that he had previously obtained an entry into the kitchen occupied by Offord, the door of which was wide open.

His Honour inquired if there was any door communicating from the kitchen to the shop? The defendant replied in the negative.

Shetlock, in the course of a rigid examination, admitted that he produced a false warrant.

Mr. Buchanan, who argued the case for the plaintiff, contended that the defendant had clearly been guilty of a trespass. The shop-door, notwithstanding it was in the passage, and was an inner door, was the outer door of the tenant. If it were not so, as well might it be contended that the landing door of a suite of chambers was not an outer door. The defendant, therefore, having made a forcible entry, had unlawfully possessed himself of the plaintiff's property. Had the goods belonged to the tenant, the defendant would have had an undoubted right to distrain; although, as in the case of the Duke of Brunswick v. Slo-

man, he would have been guilty of a trespass, and liable to an action. He (Mr. Buchanan) would say nothing about the bad warrant—(further than it went to show that the defendant was aware that he was acting illegally)—a landlord having a right to distrain in person, without the intervention of a broker.

The defendant's solicitor urged that his client, having got possession, had a right to distrain; and submitted that if his Honour should be of opinion that a trespass had been committed, the only person to whom the defendant was liable was the tenant.

His Honour concurred with Mr. Buchanan, that the door in the passage was the tenant's outer door. If there had been a door in the kitchen, which led to the premises broken into, then the defendant would have been justified. The defendant was clearly liable for trespass; but such an action could not be maintained by the plaintiff in the present action, who was only entitled to recover the value of the goods distrained by the defendant, and which, in his Honour's opinion, had been unlawfully seized.

The goods having been valued at 4l., a verdict was given for that amount.

METROPOLITAN COMMISSION OF SEWERS.

A GENERAL court was held on Thursday, the 2nd instant, at the Court-house, Greek-street; Sir John Burgoyne in the chair.

The first subject was to receive the recommendations of the Financial Committee for payment of certain items for wages, flushing, and contracts, &c., amounting altogether to 647l. for the past week. A tabular statement was handed in, containing the different heads of expenditure.

The Hon. Fred. Byng rose, and said, in reference to the item for flushing, that charge appeared to have been made for merely stirring the offensive odours of the sewers, to the annoyance of the public at large, and the sum of 647l. for the week's expenditure was an extraordinary amount. The vestry of the parish of St. James's had pressed upon him the necessity of not discontinuing his attendance at the court, so that he might use his endeavours in checking wasteful expenditure upon experiments; but he was of opinion that his visits there were quite useless. He had no desire to "obstruct" the public business, or to sanction illegal proceedings. However, he must allude to the expenses of these experiments, which fell heavily upon the ratepayers, and he had no doubt would speedily rouse the parishes to take measures for the dissolution of a commission which spent the public money in useless objects, and did not remedy existing abuses. He wished to allude to another subject, and that was, that if anything more eminently than another could show the propriety of the protest that he had presented, it was, that an Act of Parliament had been —

Mr. Chadwick rose to order.—This was not the proper time to make these observations, when they had a routine business before them. Mr. Byng had been long enough a member of that board to know that order should be followed out. If he had anything to bring forward against the commission, let him prove his case in a proper and regular manner.

Mr. Byng said he would submit to the decision of the Chairman; but he wished to know when would be the proper time to speak on an Act of Parliament which had not been heard of in the court, and had been passed without the slightest knowledge of it by the members of the court.

Mr. Chadwick replied that this was a commission issued by the Crown, and the Act referred to had been brought in by the Government on their own responsibility, and therefore they were not constitutionally required to give notice of it to the court.

Mr. Leslie said, Mr. Byng had been requested by his vestry to attend, and he, finding a large item for wages, wished to know how those wages were expended. As they were charged in a mass, they had no power to judge whether they had been properly employed.

A long personal altercation ensued, and, after some delay Mr. Chadwick proceeded to address the court at some length. He said it had been held up to parishes that they were spending enormous sums of money for flushing the sewers, whereas the fact was, that sum did not exceed 240l. per week. This was for emptying sewers, which at the period to which the old commissioners belonged would have cost 6s. 6d. per load in carting away, to be discharged into the Thames or any other place found convenient, and no doubt in many cases into another sewer, only to be again raised at a fresh cost. By their mode they had now reduced that charge to 6d. per load. Such was the absolute state of things, that even this economy had been held up to be a waste of the ratepayers' money. For his part, he wished there had been more of this extravagance, and they had expended to a much larger amount. This was a sample of the complaints made by the old commissioners, and one of the points on which had been effected a large economy. He was of opinion that if they could go on free from the "obstruction" of the old commissioners, they might still further succeed in reducing the expenditure, and he now moved that the sum of 647*l.* be agreed to.

Mr. Leslie said, of all the ignorance he had ever heard in that court, nothing equalled what had just fallen from Mr. Chadwick. And what had called forth this philippic? They had signed a cheque for a certain amount, and they merely asked what it was for. They found items in the sheet for contracts for flushing, and other charges that they believed did not properly come under the head of "wages," and they required explanation.

Mr. Byng said he thought that it was quite useless for any commissioner to attend who was not on the Works Committee. The Works Committee governed the commission, and the rest of the Commissioners were perfect ciphers, who were treated with contempt.

Dr. Southwood Smith pointed out that wherever the cholera had been received in groups, were found indications of neglect of that which it was the object of this commission to remove, while localities had altogether escaped that had been properly cleansed. He greatly regretted that more had not been done; but to say that nothing had been done was a great misrepresentation, as there was a considerable improvement in the removal of filth over the former method.

After further discussion, the following resolution was carried:—"That the weekly sheet be printed, with the items of the work done, and of the former charges of the like work, and an account of the charges which any of the items may be intended to reduce, so far as such information can be obtained in the course of a week from this day."

The New Sewers Amendment Act.—On the recommendations of the Works Committee being brought forward,

Mr. Leslie said, before they went into the recommendations of the Works Committee, it would be as well first to ascertain whether that committee had any legal existence.* He held in his hands Bill that he was told was a Government measure, brought forward on their own responsibility by his friend Lord Ebrington. It contained a clause to give the Works Committee power to do what they were doing at the time he entered his protest. The Works Committee, however, went on the principle that a majority of the commissioners could decide all questions; but some of them feeling an uneasiness of conscience, went to Parliament to ask for the extraordinary powers contained in the fourth clause of the new Bill. (Mr. Leslie then read the clause giving the committees power to transact any business falling within a certain class without being first brought before the court, and, in fact, nearly to usurp the entire functions of the court.) This power had been sought behind the backs of the commissioners, who had never been informed of it, and the clause had very properly been struck out by the House of Commons.

Mr. Byng remarked that this Bill had been brought into the House of Commons without the commissioners, or even the clerk, being consulted upon it. The Bill had been smuggled into the house under the care of its godfathers, Lord Ashley and Lord Ebrington, and yet fourteen of its clauses had been struck out.*

On the next recommendation of the same committee, that two additional assistant-surveyors be appointed,

Mr. Leslie protested against adding to the army of officers that he then saw before him, who were in attendance on Committee A on Monday, Committee B on Tuesday, and some "fid fad" for every day in the week, instead of attending to their duties. In fact, they had now arrived at such a point that he was determined the Chadwick system should no longer go on, but that it should be exposed and put a stop to. He had had eighteen months' trial, which had proved his utter incompetency for the management of that commission.

Mr. Chadwick denied that he controlled the business of the commission, but he objected that in the interval of the intermittent courts the business of the commission should be brought to a stand. He then read a passage from the report of the Sanitary Commissioners in support of his opinion. Every step on the part of the old commissioners and old officers was one of retractation of principles and opinions of years.

The motion was then put and agreed to.

A report was presented by Mr. Grant, on the subject of offensive drainage in the neighbourhood of the Blackfriars-road, complained of recently by a deputation that attended the court. The report stated that in the immediate neighbourhood horses were skinned and boiled for dogs' meat, and that in one yard were seven dead horses that would be boiled in one night, and the refuse from them cast into the sewer in Friar-street, which was 1 ft. 10 in. lower than the sewer in the Blackfriars-road, which was a sort of *cul de sac*, and filled with gases of the most deadly character,—so much so, that a bricklayer going into it was ill for eighteen hours, and that it was impossible to get a lighted candle 15 inches below the pavement. The sewer was 5 feet 3 inches by 2 feet 3 inches, and the deposit in it was from 2 to 3 feet in depth. As a temporary measure, the report recommended trapping the house drains.

The report led to a long conversation, in which an opinion was expressed that these sewers would form a favourable means for a trial of Mr. Goldsworthy Gurney's plan for draining off the foul air by means of a steam-jet, and decomposing the same by fire and chemical appliances. The surveyor was directed to communicate with Mr. Gurney on the subject, and the report was received.

A letter was received from the solicitor to Mr. Rains, on the subject of the Bermondsey mill-streams, to inquire whether the commissioners would be disposed to take the remainder of the streams, making his client a proper compensation for the same,—that Mr. Rains would offer every facility for the same,—and suggested as the basis of an arrangement, the value of the land taken, and what it would cost to make the mill as efficient by steam as water power, including the cost of another steam-engine. (Cool enough!)

The subject was referred to the surveyors, and it was mentioned incidentally, that the son of Mr. Rains had, within a few days, been fatally attacked, and had fallen a victim to the cholera.

The next business was to make rates on the following districts, viz.—Western division of Westminster Sewers, Counters Creek district, and Poplar district.

The subjoined is an abstract of the old and new rate:—

	Amount of Rate.			Collected.			New Rate.		
Westminster division ..	£17,730	7	6	£17,508	13	6	£19,000	8	9
Counters Creek district	3,735	5	4	3,687	2	10	4,757	18	4
Poplar	3,138	7	9	3,121	2	0	2,375	9	8

The collection averaged 97½ per cent.

A long acrimonious conversation ensued on the proposition that Mr. Joseph Smith should report on the borings for the purpose of the proposed tunnel scheme, which was agreed to.

A communication was received from the visiting justices of Tothill-fields prison, on the drainage of that locality, and a report upon it was presented by Mr. Gotto, the surveyor, recommending a rearrangement of the internal drainage, and a removal of a portion of the prisoners, as it was originally intended only to receive 500, but recently no less that 809 persons had been crammed within it. Eleven fatal cases of cholera had taken place there —9 males and 2 females. Report agreed to.

A vast mass of other business was brought forward, and, after a sitting of nearly six hours, and the exhibition of much unpleasant feeling, the court adjourned.

The court met again on Thursday last, the Rev. W. Stone in the chair. It was resolved, on the recommendation of the Finance Committee, that Mr. Hatton be permanently appointed clerk of accounts, at a salary of 350*l.* per annum, to commence from Midsummer last.

A lengthy document was received from the inhabitants of South Lambeth, setting forth that cholera had broken out in that district, caused, as they believed, by open drainage and the nuisance arising from the Effra river, from which exhaled the most noxious effluvia. Referred to the surveyors.

A letter was received from Sir George Grey, Secretary of State for the Home Department, enclosing a document from Mr. Baker, one of the coroners for Middlesex, on the subject of a complaint made by the guardians of the poor of St. Mary's, Whitechapel, that he was in the habit of holding unnecessary inquests on persons who had died of cholera, and justifying their necessity at the present moment more than ever. Several commissioners expressed their opinion upon the document, and Dr. Southwood Smith declared that no inquests had been held without good effects and valuable information elicited; that the greatest neglect had been shown by the guardians of the Whitechapel Union, on the outbreak of the cholera; and that had it not been for the influence of Mr. Baker, used for two hours, the jury in a particular case would have returned a verdict of manslaughter against them.

The letter was referred to the Works Committee.

The following resolution of the Works Committee was proposed for adoption:—

"That, in consequence of the receipt by the commissioners of various suggestions for the sewage of the metropolitan districts, this committee recommend the court to refer to this committee, for their consideration and report, the plans by Mr. Austin and Mr. Phillips, and all other plans suggested; and also to order that, till further order, this committee be, after August 20, 1849, open to all the commissioners."

A warm discussion ensued upon this subject, in which the Hon. Frederick Byng, Mr. Leslie, Mr. Chadwick, Mr. Lawes, Mr. Bullar, and Captain Dawson took part; and, after a good deal of opposition on some points, it was finally agreed to.

A report was presented by Mr. Grant on the drainage of Richmond, with various suggestions for its sanitary improvement, and that it should be declared two divisions, under the titles of the Sheen and Richmond divisions, and a special sewers rate raised for the improvement of the same. Agreed to.

A long report was presented on the prevalence of cholera in various parts of Southwark, particularly in the neighbourhood of Tooley-street and St. George's-road, attributing those cases that had occurred in the latter to the improper emptying of cesspools by hand, which opinion was coincided in by the coroner's jury, who gave it as their opinion that this course had only aggravated the evils it was intended to check.

The matter was ordered to be immediately attended to by the surveyors.

A weekly balance-sheet, ordered to be printed at the last court, was presented, and upon this Mr. Leslie took the opportunity of repudiating the assertions of waste on the part of the old commissioners, and denying the large economy stated to have accrued from the system of flushing by Mr. Chadwick, and that the returns presented as the charge for flushing were false, and did not include several large items that were incurred for carting away the refuse left by the flushes, and he intimated that three commissioners would call for a special court to investigate the whole question. The question was adjourned.

Just as the court was about to rise, a Mr. Hawkins rose and addressed the commissioners, and having made some inquiries as to permission to present a plan for the drainage of London, addressed Mr. Chadwick, threw his card on the table, and expressed his determination of meeting him on the 20th instant, when he would prove that he (Mr. C.) had obstructed measures of improvement, and that he would expose the schemes and intrigues that had been going on. The court expressed their determination not to be made the vehicle of such communications. Mr. Hawkins then abruptly retired.

Miscellanea.

HOISTING APPARATUS AT BRITANNIA-BRIDGE.—The lifting of the tube lately laid down at the piers has probably by this time begun. The Bramah's hydraulic presses, by the power of which this work is to be done, are noble instruments. The largest has a cylinder 11 inches thick, with a piston or ram 20 inches in diameter, and the lift a span of 6 feet. The weight of the cylinder is sixteen tons,—of the whole machine forty tons. This one alone has power enough to lift the whole, a weight, it is estimated, equivalent to that of 30,000 men. It would spout the water pressed into its cylinder to a height of nearly 20,000 feet, according to Mr. Clark, or more than five times the height of Snowdon, or 5,000 feet higher than Mont Blanc. And yet any one man can "put a book into the nose of (this) Leviathan," and, alone with him, with the utmost facility and precision, guide and control his stupendous action. There are two of smaller power, with rams 18 inches in diameter. These are placed side by side on the top of the Britannia Tower, and act in conjunction with the larger, which stands at the same level on a tower adjoining. The chains descending to the tube below, are like those of an ordinary suspension bridge, in eight and nine links alternately. The weight of one of these alone is about 100 tons, or more than that great 'lift,' the duke's statue, at Hyde-park-corner. They are attached to the rams by iron yokes, or cross heads, of great thickness. The two chains pass through square holes at each end, and are gripped at the top by clams or cheeks, of wrought-iron, screwed like a vice. At the lower end the chains are attached to the tube, or rather to lifting frames within its extremities, by three sets of massive cast-iron beams, crossing, one above another, and secured by wrought-iron straps, passing over the upper pair, and descending into the bottom cells, where they are keyed. The ends of the chains fit under deep shoulders or notches in the lifting frames, where they are secured by screw bolts. These lifting frames and beams add other 200 tons to the weight to be lifted. As the tube rises, it is to be wedged till the masonry is filled in every lift of six feet, so that the process will be slow.

* The principal heads of the new Act will be found in another part of our present number.—ED.

PROJECTED WORKS. — Advertisements have been issued for tenders, by 16th inst., for a new water wheel and pumps, &c. (separate tenders), for the corporation of the city of Oxford; by 1st September, for the erection of a dwelling-house at Kippax, near Leeds; by 4th September (postponed from 6th August), for works to be executed in a new pauper lunatic asylum at Powick, near Worcester; by 21st inst., for additional building and alterations at Penrith workhouse; by 14th, for the reconstruction of the laundry and erection of steam apparatus for washing, cooking, and heating certain wards in the Thame union workhouse, and other alterations and works at same (building and engineers' work to be separately tendered for); by a date not specified, for the construction of sewers and pipe-drains at Southampton, also of private drains to 150 properties there; by 16th, for the construction of a small iron bridge at Wyming brook, Upper Hallam,—also for roadmaking and walling there; by 21st, for 5,000 yards of broken Guernsey granite, for Whitehall and Regent's-park; and by 28th, for fire-bricks and clay, loam, and glass-grinders' sand for the naval dock-yards.

RAILWAY JOTTINGS.—West-bridge station, on the North Midland, has been burnt to the ground by spontaneous combustion of 'waste' —grease, oil, &c.——The Huddersfield and Manchester tunnel is said to be more than three miles in length, and to pass at a depth of 652 feet below the ridge of the hill, which it pierces so straight that on a clear day one can see through from either end.——The receipts on the Croydon and Epsom line are said to have increased 13 per cent. by reducing the scale of charge for periodical tickets, increasing the number of third-class trains, and issuing excursion tickets from London at reduced rates.——A correspondent of the *Sheffield Times*, who calls himself "One of the Jury," denies the truth of an assertion in a Sheffield paper, that "the disastrous fall of twenty-one of the arches of the Rother viaduct in September last was occasioned by the premature removal of one of the centres," and states that the fact was fully established that the fall was occasioned by the sinking of one or more of the piers, caused by the insufficiency of the foundations. "From the evidence of other parties," he adds, "and from personal observation on the spot, I can show you that the original foundations of many of the piers were built on an alluvial deposit, and not on the natural formation—that the centres were not removed from those arches which first fell—that twenty-six out of the thirty-five piers have been taken down, although many of them stood erect, and almost uninjured by the fall of the arches—that twenty-five of these piers have been rebuilt *upon piles*, and one on a *much deeper* stone foundation, and that the whole of the piers are this time built up solid, instead of hollow, as was the case in the first instance. Why has all this been done if the fall was occasioned simply 'by the premature removal of a centre?'"

THE IRISH BOG DIGGINGS.—The great discovery noticed in our last is likely to resolve itself, even sooner than we anticipated, into a mere *ignus fatuus*. First comes a cry of despondency from Dartmoor bogs, into which "brother tradesmen" were beguiled by a wicked imp of bog-extraction "equal to the Ashley statement." Then comes Mr. Owen himself, to deny that he had ever made experiments on thousands of tons of bog, had ever expended a fortune in such experiments, or ever carried on for a year such a large establishment as was represented. And Lord Ashley, too, himself, complains of misrepresentation. In short, the bog-spermaceti 'on the table' of the House of Commons seems to have been a true exhalation of bog, that "cast the glamour o'er the een" of even sharp-sighted members the moment it was lighted. A manufacturer of carbonate of ammonia, astonished, or rather amused with the splendid vision, asks in the *Times*, how it happens that 600 lbs. weight of that article can be worth 30*l*., while he can only obtain 9*l*. 10s. for the very same quantity. "If Lord Ashley's informant," he adds, "has been as over-sanguine in the quantity obtained as in the value, this amount should be again divided by three to give a proper result." As to peatine and other articles mentioned, if they were produced in sufficient quantity to regenerate a dozen Irish parishes, they would, he is assured, become so depreciated as not to be worth collecting; and then, as for calling vegetable tar tallow, it must be only meant for a joke. Even the O'Gorman's assurance that the 'spermaceti' was of 'home manufacture' and 'contained no foreign ingredient,' was but an equivocal one, although, we believe, there is no doubt that candles may be extracted from bog.

CHRIST CHURCH, BATTERSEA.—This new church was consecrated, on the 27th ult., by the Bishop of Winchester, attended by a large number of the clergy of the surrounding parishes. The church is of the Decorated or Middle Pointed style, with a tower and spire; the plan is cruciform, with nave, aisles, and chancel, also a children's chapel on the north side of the chancel, opening thereto and to the north transept by pointed archways, which are to be filled with oak open carved screens. The principal entrance is by a doorway, surmounted by a crocketed gablet, in the tower, which is attached to the west end of the nave on the north side. The organ-loft is in the tower. At the east and west ends are large five light windows with traceried heads. The east window is filled with painted glass, by Mr. Ballantine, of Edinburgh, who has introduced prisms of coloured glass (an invention of his own) at the intersections of the pattern, to throw the prismatic rays. In the children's chapel there is a painted glass window, presented by the architect, Mr. Charles Lee. The reading-desk, pulpit, seats in the chancel, and communion railing, are of oak, enriched with carving, by Mr. Ollett, of Norwich. The centre of the pavement of the chancel, as also the risers of the steps, are inlaid with Minton's encaustic tiles. The church will accommodate 950 persons, half being in free-seats, and the entire cost is stated to be a little more than 6,000*l*. We have not yet seen the building.

STAINED WINDOW, ST. PETER'S CHURCH, DERBY.—The east window of St. Peter's Church, Derby, was completed on Thursday last. Five lights compose the lower part, and eighteen (in the tracery) the upper; the former has been described in THE BUILDER at page 273. The subjects of the latter are the resurrection, the ascension, the annunciation, the four evangelists, with their respective emblems, and the apostles St. Paul, St. Mathias, St. Thomas, St. James, St. Barnabas, and St. Philip; the remaining four contain the figures of St. George, St. Patrick, St. David, and St. Andrew, the patron saints of the United Kingdom. Besides these are four small squares which are filled with the arms of the donor, Mr. Simpson, and with angels bearing scrolls. Each of the five large figures in the lower compartment is surrounded with a gorgeous canopy, exact copies from those in the window of the choir of York Minster. Messrs. Barker and Son, of York, are the artists. The execution of the window is good. As for the design, it does not show well for our *artists* that they are found to fly to ancient beauties, which reduces them at once to the level of *servile copyists*. X. Y. Z.

ROYAL ACADEMY REFORM.—Sir: Is it not a great pity that the institution which takes *the arts* peculiarly under its wing in this country, viz., the *Royal Academy*, should be so unwilling to relax any of its laws for the sake of exciting the public mind to love of art. I have on former occasions suggested that it would be a good thing to let the *lower* public enjoy the exhibition of painting and sculpture, say for a fortnight, at half price, 6d., and for two or three days at quarter price. The Royal Academy are very unwilling to make the least alteration in their ways; what a paltry thing it is that *we* past students should, after *ten years*, have to drop our hands for a shilling every visit we make to the exhibition; one would not mind the catalogue, but it seems unworthy a great public institution, after once permitting a boon, to withdraw it, but still one would not *begrudge* the money if there was good reason to believe that the funds of the academy were really well applied. I say it without hesitation, the funds of the academy are not *fruitfully* spent for the cause of *art*. I have no hostility against the academy, but I do happen to know a good many of the *ins and outs*, and feel with many others that improvement is necessary.—A PAST STUDENT.

IMPROVED IRON PIPES FOR WATER, GAS, AND DRAINAGE. — Sheet-iron pipes, of a peculiar description, were patented in 1838, by M. Chameroy, a French engineer, and have in France been extensively employed for gas, water, and drainage, — being considered more economical than cast-iron, possessing freedom from all leakage, are uninjured by salts or acids, bear great deflection without injury, and for water are far more conducive to health. Messrs. Fox, Henderson, and Co. have purchased the exclusive licence for their manufacture in England, and erected machinery for executing large contracts. They are made of sheet-iron, bent to the requisite form, strongly rivetted together, and coated with an alloy of tin; the longitudinal joints are also soldered, rendering them air-tight and water-proof. For additional stiffness and protection, they are then coated on the outside with asphalte cement; and, when intended for water, the inside is also coated with bitumen, which resists, like glass, the action of acids and alkalies. They become so elastic by these processes that an 8-inch pipe will bear, it is said, a deflection of 1 foot in 50, without leaking at the joints, or injury to the pipe itself. The vertical joints screw together similar to a cast-iron gas pipe.

CORRUGATED IRON HOUSES. — A house constructed of corrugated iron, by Mr. John Walker, of Old-street-road, has been sent to San Francisco. The structure measures 75 feet long, 40 feet wide, and 20 feet high, and is composed of plates of iron, each 8 feet long: its cost was 600*l*. Mr. Walker has likewise in course of construction eight other corrugated iron houses for California, each having three dwelling-rooms and one store-room. Corrugated iron has considerable strength, with little weight, and seems to have advantages for portable dwellings and store-houses.

INDEPENDENT COLLEGE—COMPETITION. —With reference to a paragraph in our last number, we are requested to mention that, although several architects were invited by the committee of the proposed college about to be erected on the Finchley-road, to send in designs, yet several did not do so, on account of the very short period, of only one month, allowed for preparing the design, and the limited sum to which the competitors were restricted.

A DEFINITION OF ARCHITECTURE.—What do your readers think of the following definition of architecture by Mr. Macaulay, in the 410th page of the first volume of his "History of England?"—"An art which is half a science—an art in which none but a geometrician can excel—an art which has no standard of grace, but what is directly or indirectly dependent on utility—an art of which the creations derive a part, at least, of their majesty from mere bulk." E.

THE MARBLE ARCH.—Three years ago the suggestion was made in THE BUILDER of placing this arch to form a public entrance to St. James's-park, at Spring-gardens, and it was referred to again a short time since. I wish to make a similar suggestion, with some modifications. To Buckingham Palace there are but the three chief approaches mentioned below,—one down Constitution-hill, the other through Buckingham-gate, the third under the arch at the Horse Guards. Of these, the two former are little better than backways, and a coachman must almost stoop on entering the latter. There is, indeed, no *main* approach; but one glance at the map shows that the Mall in St. James's-park, by the removal of a few houses in Spring-gardens, could be at once converted into a truly main one, conducting direct from Charing-cross to the Palace gates. By removing these houses, and by lopping and trimming the trees, besides supplying the deficiency, a view of the stone building at the end of an avenue of trees would be added to the architectural embellishments of Charing-cross—a new feature, almost, to the capital itself. The marble arch should be placed, to complete this main Palace entrance, within the entrance, and completely detached, after the manner of the Roman triumphal arches, and those in Paris. Providing, then, by this scheme, a main approach to Buckingham Palace, a view of the Palace and the Mall to Charing-cross, and an effective site for the marble arch, I think it must be allowed that the suggestion is worthy of consideration.

H. FIELD, B.A.

South Myton Wesleyan Schools are to be erected in the Grecian style, near Great Thornton-street Chapel. They are to be faced with white stock bricks and stone dressings and cornice. The ground floor, an infants' school, is 41 feet by 24 feet, with two class rooms, each 11 feet square. There are also two covered play-grounds, one 27 feet by 15 feet, and the other 42 feet by 27 feet, and upwards of 700 square yards of open play-ground in addition. On the first floor the junior school is 58 feet by 27 feet; a class-room adjoining, 20 feet by 13 feet; and an industrial-room, 27 feet by 14 feet. The master's-house is to be at the end of the school buildings, commanding the play-grounds and out-buildings. The entire cost will be about 2,000*l.*, about one-third Government grant. The land, value 500*l.*, was presented by Mr. Thomas Holmes, who laid the foundation-stone on Monday week. Mr. William Foale is the architect; and the contractors are Messrs. B. Musgrave, bricklayers; Steele and Darneley, joiners; R. Wilson, mason; P. Stringer, plumber; Dauber and Son, slaters; Wilson and Woodfin, ironfounders; W. Wardale, painter.

Supply of Water to Windsor Castle.—The expense of the "increased supply of water" to the castle is estimated at 10,000*l.*, which the Lord Chamberlain considers to be "urgently required" for the frequent cleansing of the drains, and more especially for the safety of the Castle in case of fire, the present supply being very uncertain and deficient in quantity. This "special service" will require the superintendence of an engineer, and Mr. James Simpson has been selected for the purpose. Mr. Simpson will charge a commission of 5 per cent. on the outlay, not exceeding the amount of his estimate—10,000*l.*

TENDERS

For repairing one house and rebuilding another, Clare Market. Mr. Peacock, architect:—

Hooper	£1,323
Cox	1,100
Chesterman (accepted)	1,080

Received on the 23rd ult., for the erection of almshouses, Gravesend. Mr. J. Gould, jun., surveyor:—

Thompson	£1,590	0
Crook	1,561	0
Wood	1,380	0
Lilleystone	1,379	10
Carley	1,360	0
Cuttrass	1,273	0
Stephens	1,130	0
Pink (accepted)	1,080	0
Cobham	1,027	0

TO CORRESPONDENTS.

Received.—"G. E. D.," "F. S. A.," "A Fellow," "W. L. T.," "G. H.," "A Subscriber and Advertiser," "A. Z.," "J. S. G." (shall have a paragraph), "J. B.," Camden-town (shall hear from us), "G. R. F.," "W. W." (shall appear), "Smithfield Market" (unavoidably postponed), "H.," "F. C." (shall appear), "W. W." (shall hear from us; thanks), "J. G." (gave no address; we shall be happy to communicate with him), "A. P. H.," Gloucester (some of the numbers are out of print; about 200 of them could be had at published price—write to publisher; the advertisement would be 5s.; one complete set of The Builder could be had at 21s. per Volume), "W. G. L." (we cannot give the information required), "J. L.," "Mr. L.," "A Builder's Clerk," "R. W." (shall hear from us), "A Competitor!" (premiated plans are usually retained by committees; it depends on wording of the advertisement).—"Pilgrimages to St. Mary of Walsingham and St. Thomas of Canterbury," by Desiderius Erasmus, translated by J. Gough Nichols, F.S.A. (Westminster, Nichols, 1849); "A Guide to Building Societies," by J. H. James, Consulting Actuary (Simpkin and Marshall, 1849); "The First Principles of Artificial Manuring," by Dr. John Ryan (Simpkin and Marshall).

ADVERTISEMENTS.

THE NILE.—NOW OPEN, Afternoons at Three, Evenings at Eight o'Clock, at the EGYPTIAN HALL, Piccadilly, a new and splendid MOVING PANORAMA of the NILE, exhibiting the whole of the stupendous works of antiquity now remaining on its banks, between Cairo, the capital of Egypt, and the second cataract in Nubia. Painted by Henry Warren and James Fahey, and Joseph Bonomi, from drawings by the latter, made during a residence of many years in Egypt.
Stalls, 3s.; pit, 2s.; gallery, 1s.

ROYAL POLYTECHNIC INSTITUTION.—Rome Illustrated in an entirely new Series of Dissolving Views. Daily at Half-past Four, and every Evening at Quarter to Ten o'clock.—A Descriptive Lecture, embracing the most interesting points connected with the subject, will be given by Mr. J. Russell.—Lectures on Chemistry, by Mr. J. M. Ashley, Daily at Half-past Three, and on the Evenings of Monday, Wednesday, and Friday, at Nine o'clock. Lecture, by Dr. Bachhoffner, on Masters's Patent Process of Freezing Dessert Ices, &c. The Oxy-hydrogen Microscope Daily at One o'clock, and every Evening at Eight. Diver and Diving Bell.—Admission, 1s.; Schools, half-price.

FIRE BRICKS, STOCK BRICKS, and RED GOODS, of every description and first-rate quality; a most extensive stock always on hand.—WARD and CO., of Honduras Wharf, Bankside, beg to call the attention of buyers to their present low prices for cash:—Good hard stock, per 1,000, 34s.; pickings, from 31s.; best Yorkshire pan tiles, 48s.; ditto plain, 30s.; Stourbridge bricks, 6l. 5s.; Welsh, 4l. 15s.; Newcastle, 4l. 10s.; fire lumps, tiles, clays, loams, malting and oven tiles, and every variety of fire goods in general used in furnaces, coke-ovens, &c. &c.; Dutch clinkers, sand; ground, red, and white house sand.—Country buyers will find this the cheapest market. Goods made to pattern.

BRITISH MUTUAL LIFE OFFICE.—The Public are invited to examine for themselves the advantages gained for Assurers by the plan on which policies are granted by this Office.—Apply to CHARLES JAMES THICKE, Secretary, 17, New Bridge-street, Blackfriars.

ARCHITECTS', BUILDERS', and GENERAL FIRE and LIFE INSURANCE COMPANY, 69, Lombard-street, London.

Chairman, SYDNEY SMIRKE, Esq., A.R.A.
Trustees.
T. L. Donaldson, Esq. | A. Salvin, Esq., F.S.A.
S. Grimsdell, Esq. | G. Smith, Esq., F.S.A.

The rates for both Fire and Life Insurances are as low as can with safety be taken. Those for Life Insurance may be paid either yearly, half-yearly, or quarterly; one-half the annual premium may be left unpaid for seven years, or one-third to the end of life. Thus large sums may be insured at the smallest present outlay.

Prospectuses, forms of proposals, &c., may be had at the Office, 69, Lombard-street, or of the agents.

JOHN REDDISH, Manager.

THE LONDON INDISPUTABLE LIFE POLICY COMPANY.—Incorporated by Act of Parliament on the principal of Mutual Life Assurance, No. 31, Lombard-street, London.

Trustees.
John Campbell Renton, Esq., M.P. | Richard Spooner, Esq., M.P.
Richard Malins, Esq., Q.C. | James Fuller Madox, Esq.
William Wilberforce, Esq.

This Company is prohibited by their deed of constitution, duly registered in terms of the Act, from disputing a policy upon any ground whatever. All questions as to age, health, habits, and other matters deserving of inquiry prior to the contract being entered into, are held as finally settled when the assured receives his policy.

Copies of the annual report, and of the annual meeting of the members, prospectuses and schedules may be obtained by personal or written application to the Head-office, or any of the Agents.

ALEXANDER ROBERTSON, Manager.

VALENTIA SLAB COMPANY.—"The Atlas," No. 1667, BAWN SLABS.—"The Geraldine," No. 988, BAWN SLABS.—The above cargoes, of various thicknesses, now in course of delivery, at the Valentia Slate Yard, Millbank-street, Westminster.

STIRLING'S BELVEDERE SLATE WORKS, Belvedere-road, Lambeth.—A reduced list of prices of the best WELCH SLATE SLABS, planed both faces, will be sent on application (post paid) being made, and inclosing a postage stamp. The prices are under those advertised for inferior slates.

PIMLICO SLATE WORKS.—GREAT REDUCTION in the PRICE of SLATE.—Mr. MAGNUS has the pleasure to publish the following reduced prices for Welsh Slate Slabs of the finest quality, with sawn edges, and planed both faces:—

Thick.	¾ in.	1 in.	1 in.	1¼ in.	1½ in.	2 in.	
	d.	d.	d.	d.	d.	d.	
Under 4 ft. long, or 3 ft. wide	3½	5	6	7	9	12	℔ft. sup.
Ditto 5 ft. do., or 3 ft. do.	4	5½	7	8	10	14	do.
Ditto 6 ft. do., or 3 ft. do.	4½	6½	8	9	10½	16	do.
Ditto 7 ft. do., or 3 ft. do.	5	7	9	10	11	18	do.

Larger Slabs in proportion.

Thick.	¾ in.	¾ in.	1 in.	1¼ in.	1½ in.	2 in.	
	d.	d.	d.	d.	d.	d.	
Cutting to order	1	1	1½	1½	1½	2	℔ft. sup.

FURTHER REDUCTION IN THE PRICE OF CISTERNS.

Cisterns above 100 gallons, planed both faces, inch thick, grooved and bolted, is only per foot super. 1s. or 3s. per foot cube (outside dimensions). Fixing within five miles of the manufactory, 2d. per foot super., or 6d. per foot cube. Enamelled boxed Chimney-pieces, variously marbled, hitherto priced at 40s. to 50s. now reduced to 26s. and 30s. The above prices are all net to the trade.

Mr. Magnus will send his book of Drawings of Chimney-pieces, and printed price-list of ditto, free to any part of the country, on receipt of 3s. in postage stamps (to be deducted from first order received,) and which will be subject to a very liberal discount to the trade.—Address, 39, Upper Belgrave-place, Pimlico.

SAMUEL CUNDY, Mason and Builder, PIMLICO MARBLE and STONE WORKS, Belgrave Wharf, Pimlico, begs to inform ARCHITECTS and the PUBLIC that he has availed himself of improvements in his MACHINERY, by means of which he is enabled to produce GOTHIC WINDOWS MOULDINGS, PANNELS, &c. &c., at a very cheap rate, out of a superior stone from the west of England, as durable as any soft stone, and particularly sound.

S. C. has an economical method of dressing the above stone over, which produces, by the action of the atmosphere, a surface of crystalline hardness, and improves the colour.

FONTS from 5l. upwards. Specimens on view of the various styles.

First-rate ARTISTS retained for SCULPTURED and CARVED Works.

Vein Marble Chimney-pieces, of the best quality of material and workmanship, by improved machinery ... 40s.
Stone ditto, from ... 8s.
A Variety on View in stock.

MEMORIAL CROSSES, MONUMENTS, TOMBS, HEAD STONES, &c., in great variety of design.

RESTORATION of CHURCHES. SAMUEL CUNDY having had much practice in this branch, is desirous of Estimating for Restorations.

CLERKS of WORKS have their particular attention called to the above establishment. Coats of Arms, Decorated Pannels, and other enriched works, promptly executed.

Every description of Stone or Granite work prepared, ready for fixing.—Delivered at the various Railways, and carefully packed in trucks.—Pimlico Marble and Stone Works, Belgrave Wharf, Pimlico.

TERRA-COTTA, or VITRIFIED STONE WORKS, King Edward-street, Westminster-road, London.—M. H. BLANCHARD, from late Coade's Original Works, Belvedere-road, Lambeth, begs to inform the Nobility, Gentry, Architects, and Builders, that he has re-established the manufacture of that invaluable material, which has been successfully adopted by our eminent Architects and others, in the adornment of our noblest buildings, nearly 100 years has proved the imperishable nature of the material, the specimens of those times now exhibiting all their primitive sharpness.

Groups, statues, friezes, capitals, panelling, pinnacles, finials, terminals, Tudor, and other chimney shafts, balustrading, fountains, fonts, tazzas, vases, coats of arms, devises, and every description of architectural ornament, at prices in many instances nearly half the cost of stone.

Specimens of the material to be seen at the Office of "The Builder," 2, York-street, Covent Garden, and at the Works.

BUILDERS AND CONTRACTORS.

TARPAULINS for COVERING ROOFS during Repairs. SCAFFOLD CORD and every description of ROPE used by Builders upon the lowest terms. Marquees and temporary awnings on sale or hire. Orders per post receive the most prompt attention.—WILLIAM PIGGOTT, 115, Fore Street, City, Manufacturer, by Appointment, to Her Majesty's Honourable Board of Ordnance.

GERMAN SPRING MATTRESSES, permanently elastic, very durable, and cheap.

3 feet wide	£2	8	0	4 feet 6 inches wide	£3	3	0
3 feet 6 inches wide	2	13	0	5 feet wide	3	10	0
4 feet wide	2	18	0	5 feet 6 inches wide	3	18	0

One of these, with a French mattress on it, is a most elastic and soft bed. Heal and Son's List of Bedding, with full particulars of weight, sizes, and prices, of every description of bedding, sent free by post.—HEAL and SON, Bedding Manufacturers, 196 (opposite the Chapel), Tottenham-court-road.

REDUCED PRICES.—EDWARD SIMMS (late William Cleave), of Wilton-road, Pimlico Basin, begs to acquaint Builders and the Trade that he has now on hand, at his Manufactory (the first of its kind ever established), a very large Assortment of Dry and Well-seasoned OAK and DEAL PREPARED FLOORING BOARDS and MATCH BOARDING of all sorts, from ¾ inch to 1½ inch thick, planed to a parallel width and thickness, and at greatly Reduced Prices. Also, Timber, Deals, Oak Planks, Scantlings, Sash Sills, Mouldings prepared by Machinery, baths, &c.—Apply at E. SIMMS'S (late W. Cleave's) Flooring Manufactory, Wilton-road, Pimlico Basin.

A REDUCTION in the PRICE of FLOOR BOARDS.—ALFRED ROSLING begs to inform the Trade and Consumers generally, that he has REDUCED the PRICE, and keeps constantly in stock a large and very general assortment of Prepared Floor Boards and Matched Boarding, planed to a parallel breadth and thickness, and fit for immediate use; also a variety of machine-prepared Mouldings, which are finished with great accuracy and attention to quality of workmanship.—Southwark Bridge Wharf, Bankside, and Old Barge Wharf, Upper Ground-street, Blackfriars.

GREAT REDUCTION IN THE PRICE OF FLOOR BOARDS AND MATCH BOARDING.—THOMAS ADAMS (late S. Dare), Mahogany and Timber Merchant, Bermondsey New-road, Southwark, near the Bricklayers' Arms, begs to inform his friends and the trade generally, that he has in stock a large assortment of the above goods, fit for immediate use, at prices which only require a trial to prove their decided cheapness. Also mouldings prepared by machinery from the very best material, and in a superior manner; cut deals and scantling of every dimension; mahogany, cedar, rosewood, wainscot, elm, beech, oak, &c., in planks, boards, veneers, and logs; pantile, oak, and fir laths; wheelwrights' goods. All sawn and prepared goods (except timber) delivered free of expense; sawing charged at mill prices. Very extensive drying sheds.

MUIR'S PATENT PLANING MACHINE.

SAW MILLS, GILLINGHAM-STREET, PIMLICO.

TIMBER of any size, PLANK, DEALS, and BATTENS, &c., Sawn on the most approved principle. Boards, &c., Prepared, Matched, and Grooved, by Muir's Patent Machinery. The Mills have all the advantages of navigation and water-carriage, being connected with the Thames by the Grosvenor Canal. Goods fetched from the docks and carted home free of charge.

Address to HENRY SOUTHAM, Saw Mills, Gillingham-street, Pimlico.
N.B. Estimates given for Sawing and Planing.

GENERAL WOOD-CUTTING COMPANY.—SAWING, PLANING, AND MOULDING MILLS, Belvedere-road, Lambeth, between the Suspension and Waterloo Bridges. SAWING and PLANING in all their branches executed with the greatest despatch and punctuality. A large Stock of seasoned and beautifully WORKED MOULDINGS, consisting of upwards of 100 different patterns kept constantly on hand; also an extensive assortment of dry prepared FLOORING BOARDS, of all qualities and at reasonable rates.

PHILLIPS, ALLCARD, and CO.'S IMPERIAL DEAL SAW-MILLS, WENLOCK-ROAD, CITY-ROAD, beg to invite the attention of builders, carpenters and the trade, to their well selected stock, consisting of a large assortment of TIMBER, DEALS, PLANKS, and BATTENS, of every description, and thoroughly seasoned. They also have constantly on hand, and ready for immediate use, white and yellow prepared FLOORING BOARDS of all thicknesses, and matched lining, cut and planed to a parallel breadth and thickness. And they are enabled to offer all their goods at very moderate prices.

DESICCATED WOOD.—DAVISON and SYMINGTON'S PATENT.—Builders, Cabinet-makers, and others, will find it much to their advantage to patronise this new process of seasoning. The greenest wood can thus not only be seasoned in an incredibly short space of time, at a small cost, but is rendered stronger, entirely free from shrinkage, and in every respect better than wood treated in the ordinary way; thereby saving capital, interest of money, insurance, and all the other inconveniences attending the keeping of a large stock.

The DESICCATING SAWING and PLANING MILLS are situated at PLOUGH BRIDGE, ROTHERHITHE, adjoining the Commercial and East Country Docks, from whence parties obtaining their material can have the same converted as required, and sent home fit for immediate use.—T. GIRLING, Manager.

For licenses to use the patent, scale of prices, or other information, address, ANGUS JENNINGS, Secretary, Patent Desiccating Company, 41, Gracechurch-street, City.

TO ARCHITECTS, BUILDERS, UPHOLSTERERS, AND OTHERS.

WOOD CARVING done in the cheapest and best manner. Estimates given to any amount. Pulpits, reading-desks, altar-rails, stalls, and other church fittings supplied complete. Old carvings restored by J. STALON, Wood Carver and Manufacturer, 42, Berwick-street, Soho, London.

JORDAN'S PATENT MACHINE CARVING and MOULDING WORKS for WOOD and STONE, Belvedere-road, Lambeth, and 151, Strand.—TAYLOR, WILLIAMS, and JORDAN beg to call the attention of the building community to a new feature of their establishment, and, at the same time, to thank their numerous patrons and friends for the very liberal support they have lately experienced, which, they assure them and the public, it will be their constant endeavour to deserve, by giving their customers an increasing share of the advantages arising from the constant improvements in the machinery which they have just succeeded in applying to the production of the most intricate carving in Caen and other freestones, and in statuary marble.

T., W., and J. particularly solicit the attention of architects and builders to the fact that, by the use of this machinery, a very large saving, both of time and money, is effected,—so great, indeed, that in many cases they can deliver a well-finished article in Caen stone for less money than it can be obtained in cement, while their wood-carving will, in some cases, be found to come into close competition with the best kinds of composition ornament.—For prices and estimates apply at 154, Strand.

TESTIMONIAL FROM CHARLES BARRY, ESQ.

"Westminster, May 16th, 1848.

"Gentlemen,—In reply to your letter requesting my opinion of your Patent Carving Machinery, I have much pleasure in stating, from an experience of more than two years, in its application to the production of the wood carvings of the House of Peers, and other apartments of the New Palace, at Westminster, that I am enabled to make the most favourable report concerning it, and to add that it has more than justified the favourable terms in which I recommended it in 1845 to her Majesty's Commissioners of Woods and Works for adoption.—I remain, Gentlemen, yours faithfully,

"CHARLES BARRY."

Messrs. Taylor, Williams, and Jordan."

PAPER-HANGINGS—At E. T. ARCHER'S Manufactory for English and Warehouse for English and French Paper-hangings, from One Penny per yard, to the most costly pannelled decorations. The decorations are fitted up on the walls of an extensive range of show rooms, showing at one view a drawing or dining-room finished, fit for occupation.—Painted marble or granite papers of superior fabric, from One Penny per yard.—451, Oxford-street.

PAPER-HANGINGS by MACHINE and BLOCKS.—The trade supplied in town and country, with machine goods, from first-rate new designs, at the lowest prices they have ever been sold in this country; and block goods, for style and quality, not to be surpassed by any house in England. All the patterns are registered, and can only be supplied by HENNELL and CROSBY, Queen-street, Southwark-bridge-road. Cheapest house in London for oak, marbles, and panel decorations. A set of patterns, 5s., to be deducted off an order of 5l.—Terms, cash.

FRENCH PAPER-HANGINGS MADE IN ENGLAND.

L. MARKS and Co., in order to go with the times, have, in addition to their usual large and magnificent Stock of French Papers, printed some very choice FRENCH DESIGNS, a stock of which is now ready, at prices varying from 6d. to 15d. per piece of twelve yards long, including some new and choice specimens of marbles, oaks, and granites, all made by improved machinery, on paper specially made for the purpose. Lining paper and canvass at mill prices.—Warehouse, 59, Princes-street, Leicester-square.

CAUTION.— IMPERVIOUS STONE.— M. FRANCOIS TEYCHENNE, Sole Patentee, cautions the public against entering into any terms or negotiations with any one but himself for licence to use his patent for hardening soft and porous Stone, rendering it impervious: and that if any person is discovered infringing his patent they will be prosecuted with the utmost rigour of the law. — 18, Red Cross-square, Cripplegate, London. August 8, 1849.

MARKET WHARF, REGENT'S-PARK BASIN.—Messrs. MARTIN and WOOD (late Beales and Martin) solicit the attention of Builders, Masons, and others, to their stock of Portland, York, and Derby Stone; also Hamant Stone, Lime, Cement, Plaster, Bricks, Tiles, Laths, Fire-goods, Firewood, &c., sold at the lowest possible prices for Cash. Portland Head-stones, Ledgers, Steps, Landings, &c., cut to order, on the shortest notice. Tarpaulings let on hire. A Stock of Northern Drain Pipes, Syphons, &c., always on hand. Mortar, Lime and Hair, Flue Stuff, &c.

KENTISH RAG STONE of every descrip- tion, direct from the Quarries, at reduced prices. WHITE SUFFOLK AND RED FACING BRICKS of superior quality. COWLEY AND KENT BRICKS from the new Clamps, now open. —Apply to Mr. BENJAMIN COUCH. 2, Newington-crescent, Newington-butts.

BATH STONE.—RANDELL and SAUNDERS, QUARRYMEN and STONE MERCHANTS. The most approved kinds of Bath Freestone supplied to all parts of the kingdom. Depôts at the Great Western Railway Stations, PADDINGTON, CORSHAM, BOX, BATH, and BRISTOL.—R. and S. particularly invite the attention of Architects and Builders to their Corsham Down Stone, which is strong and sound in quality, is of beautiful colour and texture, and works much cheaper than any other stone. Prices, with cost of carriage to any locality specified, furnished on application to Randell and Saunders, 14, Orange Grove, Bath.

ANSTON STONE, used for Building the New Houses of Parliament.—W. WRIGHT and Co. beg to inform Architects, Engineers, Builders, and others, the Anston Stone can be supplied in any quantity, on the shortest notice. This valuable stone, so celebrated for its durability, colour, and texture, it will known, having been selected in preference to all others, by the Commissioners of Woods and Forests, for building the New Houses of Parliament. It is very superior for Monuments, Tombs, &c., &c. W. Wright and Co. have made arrangements to have a stock always on hand at Prince's Marble and Stone Wharf, Hewitt's-bank, Maiden-lane, King's-cross.—Any further information can be obtained on application to W. WRIGHT and Co, Anston, near Sheffield; or to T. SHARP, their Sole Agent in London. 27, Barton-crescent.

NOTICE to PURCHASERS of CAEN STONE. Translation of a CERTIFICATE from the Mayor of Allemagne, Department of Calvados, Normandy, relative to the property of the Caen Stone Quarries:— "I, the Mayor of Allemagne, Department of Calvados, undersigned, do hereby certify to all who are interested in it, that it is an error and gross falsehood, as certain persons have reported, that the quarries of Allemagne belongs to, and are leased from, the Government of France, and the local authorities of the Department of Calvados. Neither the one or the other have any right or interest whatsoever in the said land or quarries.
"I hereby further certify, that the greater part of these quarries are worked by Messrs Luard and Company, who are the principal proprietors, and Messrs. Jobert, who is also a proprietor; the remainder are worked by smaller quarrymen of the neighbourhood, who sell their produce to certain dealers for exportation to England as it is required.
"Executed at Allemagne, this 29th May, 1849."

Translation attested by F. Hayes, Esq., &c., Symonds Inn, Chancery-lane. N.B. The French manuscript may be seen (by permission in writing) at the offices of Messrs. LUARD, BEEDHAM and Co. Copies supplied of this upon application.

CAEN and AUBIGNY STONE.— LUARD, BEEDHAM, and Co. beg respectfully to recommend purchasers of Caen stone to require a guarantee of those who profess to be "quarry proprietors" and importers, that they are selling only such Caen stone as is suitable for EXTERNAL WORKS,—this being the only way by which architects, and builders can be safe from the recurrence of certain failure, by its indiscriminate use. It is now generally known that the bottom beds in the Caen quarries, as well as in the Portland, are only fit for inside purposes. L. & Co. thus continue their efforts to maintain the character of their Caen stone, by careful selection, and can afford to behold without alarm, the absurd, false, and futile delusions of weak-minded competitors. L. & Co. have a large assorted stock of Caen and Aubigny stone at their several depôts at Caen Wharf, Rotherhithe, Vauxhall-bridge, Millbank, Battle-bridge, Paddington, and Kensington Basins. Shipments direct from the quarries to any port in the United Kingdom. — Offices, 18, Southwark-square, Borough, and 170, Rotherhithe-street.

CAEN STONE, from the first Quarries of Allemagne. Depôt at the Whitby and Scotch Wharf, 11, Fore-street, Limehouse.—F. FOCCARD, quai des Abattoirs, Caen, proprietaire de Carrières à Allemagnet, begs leave to inform Builders, Architects, and others, that he has, on the above-mentioned wharf, the best stone ready to meet the demands of our classes.—Contracts taken for any quantities.—Orders received by Mr. BARCLEY, at 28, Money-street, Borough Market.—Cargoes shipped to order, from Caen, to any port.

CAEN STONE DEPOT.—"ORIGINAL SUFFERANCE" NORWAY WHARF, GREENWICH.— W. TUCKWELL, Caen Stone Quarry Proprietor at Allemagne, near Caen, respectfully solicits the attention of architects, builders, clerks of works, masons, and others, to the SELECTED STOCK of CAEN STONE on his wharf at Greenwich, and from his long practical experience in the various qualities of Caen stone, he confidently states that he cannot be surpassed. W. TUCKWELL has always at his chantier on the Quai, at Caen, a large quantity ready for shipment, when required. Orders received at the wharfor above, also at the offices of Mr. R. A. WITHALL, surveyor, 49, Cheapside, where samples and further information may be obtained. N.B. Samples may also be seen at the offices of "The Builder."

NORWAY WHARF, GREENWICH.— ORIGINAL CAEN STONE SUFFERANCE WHARF. —W. TUCKWELL, Caen Stone Quarry, proprietor of Allemagne, near Caen, respectfully solicits the attention of architects, builders, clerks of works, masons, and others, to his selected stock of Caen Stone, on his wharf at Greenwich, and from his long practical experience in the various qualities of Caen Stone, he confidently states that he cannot be surpassed. W. TUCKWELL has always at his chantier on the Quai, at Caen, a large quantity ready for shipment, when required. Orders received at the wharf as above, also at the offices of Mr. R. A. WITHALL, surveyor, 49, Cheapside, where samples and further information may be obtained.
Here.—The statements put forth by other proprietors of Caen Stone, induce W. T. with all respect, to observe that he cannot think of resting his claims as the owner of a superior quality of stone on the certificates of magistrates or other public officers of Normandy, who however distinguished by character and station, can be no evidence on such matters. As the proprietor of Caen Oolite of the first quality, he trusts to the sound judgment and experience of those English architects, builders, &c., who may honour him with their preference, for every guarantee and subsequent recommendation.

CAEN STONE.

27, Millbank-street, 12th July, 1849.

MESSRS. W. and J. FREEMAN consider it to be a duty they owe to their respected connections and themselves, to request a perusal of the following documents.

Translated from the French Language by Mr. A. De Pinna, of Bartholomew-lane, Royal Exchange, London, Notary Public and Conveyancer. Foreign and English: Official Translator to Her Majesty's High Court of Admiralty of England, &c. &c. &c.

"We, the Maire of the Commune of Allemagne, Canton of Caen, Department of the Calvados,—
"D'd, on the 29th May last, deliver to Messrs. Luard, Beedham, and Co. a certificate attesting that the idea had never been entertained, on the part of the French Government, to commit any infringement on the right of ownership in the quarries opened in my said commune.
"It would appear that, from the said certificate, inserted from time to time in the London journal, "The Builder," erroneous inferences have been drawn, tending to establish the belief that M. JOBERT, Senior, is only a secondary proprietor of quarries, while Messrs. Luard, Beedham, and Co. are the principal proprietors of the quarries of Allemagne, and the only parties capable of executing the large orders for Caen Stone.
"It behoves me, therefore, to rectify, whatever there is contrary to truth in such like assertions; wherefore, I declare unto all whom it may concern, that M. JOBERT, Senior, was the originator of the business of quarrying Allemagne Stone, the quarries whereof he has worked, without any interruption, ever since the year 1820.
"That he is the principal owner of the Allemagne Quarries, and that he is in a situation to meet the largest demands for supplies that can be addressed to him:
"I do further certify, that it comes within my knowledge that the finest stones raised by M. JOBERT, Senior, are consigned, in England, to his correspondents, Messrs. W. and J. FREEMAN, of London.
"Done and delivered at Allemagne, to serve us of right, the 2nd July, 1849."

Seen for legalization of the signature of M. BUISSON, Maire of Allemagne. Caen, the 3rd July, 1849, by delegation, the Conseiller of Prefecture, Secretary-General,

Board of Bridges, Highways, &c.—Department of the Calvados.—Service of the Maritime Parts.

Caen, 4th July, 1849.
The Engineer-in-Chief of the Department of the Calvados certifies that M. JOBERT, senior, is the owner of numerous quarries, in work, in the Commune of Allemagne, near Caen, and that he is in a position to furnish Caen Stone, of the best quality, for exportation or for works within the country.
He further certifies, that M. JOBERT occupies an extensive yard on the bank of Orne, in the port of Caen, in front of which he has been authorised to place three powerful cranes, by means whereof he can have three vessels loading at one time, and ship blocks of stone of the most considerable volume and dimensions.

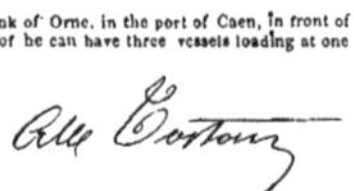

Seen and legalised. Caen, the 7th July, 1849.
The Conseiller of Prefecture, Secretary-General.

Department of the Calvados.— Town of Caen.

Public Works.
"I, the undersigned, Architect of the Public Works of the 'Maison-Centrale de Detention' of Beaulieu, and of those of the town of Caen, do certify:—
"That M. JOBERT, Senior, is the owner of seven quarries at Allemagne, near Caen, which are being worked in full activity, and which are opened in the region producing the best quality of stone.
"That M. JOBERT is established and provided with all necessaries, on such a footing as to be enabled to meet the most important orders for supplies that can be required of him.
"That, in the different works he has executed under my orders, he has always shown the greatest activity, and he furnished them with ability, and that the stones he has furnished have always been of the first quality. It is, therefore a duty as well as a pleasure on my part, to certify that I consider him capable of perfectly executing every species of building, as also any supplies of materials.
"Caen, the 6th July, 1849."

Seen by us, Maire of Caen, for legalization of the signature of Mr. GUY, Architect, set opposite.
Caen, the 7th July, 1849.

Seen and legalized, Caen, the 7th July, 1849. The Conseiller of Prefecture,
Secretary-General,

No. CCCXLI.

SATURDAY, AUGUST 18, 1849.

 HE point which most impressed us during a perusal of the new Bill to amend the Buildings Act, brought in by Lord Carlisle,— or, as it is to be called, when passed, " The Metropolitan Buildings Act, 1849,"—is the great alteration made in the relative positions of the Official Referees and the Registrar.

To all who have been much in communication with these authorities it must have become painfully evident that there was great want of unanimity between the referees and the registrar—that an antagonistic feeling prevailed which could not fail to militate against the speedy and satisfactory discharge of the business of the office. A return of the number of awards made by the referees, since the date of the Supplemental Act that changed the referees from two to three, to which the registrar has refused to affix the seal, and which have consequently been sent to the Commissioners of Woods for adjudication, would show this in a singularly striking manner. Before the passing of the Supplemental Act, when there were but two referees, the registrar acted as a third referee, and the two opinions, where there was a difference, carried it against the one. The seal, so far as we can learn, was then seldom if ever withheld. Since that event, however, the position of the registrar, acting no longer as referee, has necessarily changed, and he has found it his duty to be much more particular in respect of forms, and is less often able to give effect to the award of the referees by affixing the seal. How far the registrar may have been right or wrong we have not now to inquire ; we are simply stating the actual position of affairs at the office.

Under the existing Act the *referees* are appointed as the parties to superintend its execution, and to arbitrate on differences, " as well as to exercise, in certain cases, a discretion n the relaxation of the fixed rules and directions f the Act." The registrar is appointed that elaxations and proceedings may be duly recorded, and with power to withhold the seal rom any award, or other document, until lirected by the Commissioners of Woods, " if t shall appear to the said registrar that any uch documents are contrary to law, or not omplete in any of the requisite forms, or 1eyond the competence of the said official eferees."

By the provisions of the new Bill, it will be een that the *registrar* is made supreme and ominant, and the referees removed to the osition of his clerks or assistants, with the uty of supervising all public buildings. lause 70 says,—" for the purpose of providing for the determination of questions, and he adjudication of matters arising under this ct, be it enacted—

" That if any doubt, difference, or dissatisaction arise between any persons whomsoever s to whether any matter or thing is subject to ny of the provisions, rules, and directions of his Act, or as to which of such provisions, ules, and directions any matter or thing is ubject to, or as to the true intent and meaning r effect of this Act in any case, or whether ny matter or thing is or has been done con-

trary to any of the provisions, rules, and directions of this Act, or as to any matter whatever, whether involving questions of law or questions of fact, arising under or within the operation of this Act, or if any building owner or other person claim to execute any work or operation authorised or required by this Act, and the adjoining owner or other person whose consent thereto may be required shall not have signified in writing his consent to such work or operation, if any such adjoining owner or other person cannot be found, or cannot by reason of legal disability or other cause give such consent, or if it be not known who is the person having a right to give such consent, or if any person claim any special certificate which is required or authorised by any of the provisions, rules, or directions of this Act, then it shall be lawful for both or either of the parties concerned in any such case of doubt, difference, or dissatisfaction as aforesaid, or for any such building owner or other person, or for any person claiming any such special certificate as aforesaid, to refer any such matter of doubt, difference, or dissatisfaction, or any such claim, to *the registrar of metropolitan buildings*, by requisition in writing."

True, it goes on to say,—

" And if any such requisition relate to the structural sufficiency or stability of any building or part thereof, or of any work done or proposed to be done, or to the quality of materials, or work or workmanship, or to the nature of any business alleged to be dangerous, noxious, or offensive, or to the general line of buildings, or to the obstruction of light and air, or other injury alleged to be occasioned by any projection, or to the works necessary to be done to any party-structure, or the proper manner of executing works by this Act authorised to be done, or to the quantity of soil or ground or other parts of the premises of one owner which ought to be laid to the premises of another owner, or to the amount of the expenses of works, or to the amount of damage, loss, or injury done in any case, or to the alteration in the value of any premises in consequence of any works, or to any other matter whatever requiring the exercise of the professional knowledge, skill, or judgment of an architect or surveyor, then in any such case, where the question does not relate to any public building, it shall be the duty of the registrar to refer, *either generally or specially,* any such matters so requiring the exercise of the professional knowledge, skill, or judgment of an architect or surveyor as aforesaid, to *one* of the official referees, or if the matter of such question be a claim on the part of a building owner or other person to execute any work or operation authorised or required by this Act as aforesaid, and the district surveyor be not a party concerned, then to the *district surveyor,* to ascertain the facts and circumstances of the case in respect of such matter, and to certify upon such matter ; and where the question relates to any public building it shall be the duty of the registrar to refer as aforesaid any such matter to the official referees, or two of them, to ascertain the facts and circumstances of the case, and to certify upon such matter."

But what then ? The referee or the district surveyor having examined into the matter and reported his opinion to the registrar, the registrar, after seven days' notice to the parties of such report (if from the district surveyor), " shall dispose of the matters in reference, together with such matters incidental thereto or involved therein, either by one award or by several awards, as he may think proper, and in such award or awards shall make such determination, appointment, order, or direction, or give such consent or authority, as the case shall require."

More than that,—

" *If it appear to the registrar* that the matter of any requisition is such as not to require the exercise of the professional knowledge, skill, or judgment of an architect or surveyor as aforesaid, then it shall be lawful for him to dispose of the matters in reference to him, together with such matters incidental thereto or involved therein, either by one award or by several awards, as he shall think proper,

and in such award or awards to make such determination, appointment, order, or direction, or give such consent or authority, as the case shall require, without the certificate of any district surveyor, official referee or referees as aforesaid."

So that, as we have said, the registrar for the time being will be supreme ; he may call in anybody or nobody to advise him ; take the advice or not, just as he pleases ; and the referees are reduced to the position of his clerks or assistants.

The committee appointed by Lord Carlisle in 1847, to inquire into the desirability of amending the Act, were unanimous on two points,—the necessity of *lessening law-forms* and technical proceedings, and of giving the officers under the Act greater discretionary powers,—that is, empowering them to do what, according to the 80th section of the present Act, already quoted, they were appointed to do, but for which it seems no power was given them,—viz., " to exercise, in certain cases,* a discretion in the relaxation of the fixed rules and directions of this Act, where the strict observance thereof is impracticable, or would defeat the object of this Act, or would needlessly affect with injury the course and operation of this branch of business."

How the first of these recommendations would be carried out by the transformation of the board to which we have drawn attention, it is unnecessary to say : forms and technical proceedings would be multiplied without end : it would be a law-court, and all the advantages which were looked for on the establishment of the office, in the shape of prompt decisions and the legislation of practical men, would disappear.

As to the discretionary powers, clause 10 of the new Bill says,—

" That if any of the rules or directions of this Act be found to defeat the purposes of this Act, or needlessly to affect with injury the course or operation of any trade or business, or to obstruct the advantageous use or conversion of buildings, or to hinder the adoption of improvements or of expedients either better or sufficiently well adapted for accomplishing the purposes of this Act; or if in rebuilding any building already built, or in executing any work upon any such building, a full compliance with the rules and directions of this Act will be attended with injury, loss, or inconvenience ; or if in any case any rules or directions of this Act be at variance with or prevent the due observance of the covenants, agreements, or conditions contained in any lease, or agreement for a lease, being of the nature of a building lease, made before the passing of this Act,"—

Then the person affected may ask a modification from the registrar, and the registrar is to obtain the opinion of the referees on the statement, and report it, with his own opinion, to the Commissioners of Woods, who may make the modification required ; but this, it will be seen, goes little farther than clause 11 of the present Act.

The Bill proposes a novelty, in the shape of an attorney to be appointed to serve as agent on behalf of the district surveyors and of the official referees when acting in the supervision of public buildings. It is to be " the duty of the said agent to act on behalf of the said surveyors and on behalf of the official referees acting as aforesaid, in the conduct and management of all prosecutions and other proceedings before any justices, magistrates, or courts of law or equity, which any district surveyor or official referee is by this Act directed or authorised to conduct or take, and also to act on the part of the said surveyors or of the said

* These words, "certain cases," made the hitch which prevented the exercise of discretionary powers.

official referees acting as aforesaid in the conduct and management of all references under this Act in which any such surveyor or official referee acting as aforesaid shall be a party, or shall be official'y concerned or interested, and generally to advise the said surveyors or official referees acting as aforesaid on all matters of law connected with the execution of their duties."

By way of remuneration, this agent is to receive a per centage on the aggregate amount of fees "which shall have become payable" to each district surveyor, and to the referees for public buildings. This arrangement would probably be advantageous to three or four litigious district surveyors, but whether it would be palatable to those who find law not only undesirable but unnecessary, remains to be seen. As it now stands, it would necessarily tend to increase litigation and its consequence, bad feeling. Moreover, he could not satisfactorily act for referees and district surveyors too.

The schedules seem an improvement on those attached to the Act now in force. All buildings (except public buildings) are declared to be of one class, and party and external walls of each rate are to be of one thickness, preventing any 9-inch party wall in a third-rate building, and allowing it in a fourth-rate for the uppermost two stories only. An additional half-square in area is allowed to fourth-rates; and the public have an advantage in the removal of public buildings altogether from the supervision of the district surveyors. This would not only save the public from the payment of two sets of fees for the same building, which the present Act enforces, but would avoid the annoyance to architects of having their buildings first surveyed and passed by the district surveyor, and then pulled to pieces by the official referees, who may take a different view of the provisions of the Act.

We have but opened the ball.

ON THE NATURE AND PROPERTIES OF THE METALS USED IN THE BUILDING TRADES.

CAST-IRON—MALLEABLE-IRON—STEEL.

HAVING already* noted the chief sources whence the almost universally-diffused, and all-important, metal, iron, is derived, we shall now proceed to treat more particularly of its nature and properties, and especially of its three chief varieties, or states, of cast-iron, wrought-iron, and steel.

The appearance, tint, or glance of iron, in whichever of its states we take it,—whether in all the glitter and glory of 'cold steel,' in the homely shine of the kitchen poker, or in the still more dusky hue of the common cast-iron articles of daily use, is so familiar to one and all, that it is only, of course, *pro formâ* that we need here note, that it is of a greyish white with a shade of blue, and capable of assuming, in its form of steel, so high a polish as to excel in splendour every one of even the 'nobler' metals, such as silver, gold, or platinum. In tenacity and strength, too, though not in malleability, or even in ductility, it can be made to excel all other metals. Yet it *is* capable of being rendered both extremely ductile and remarkably malleable. It can be drawn out into wires finer than human hair, and can be beaten into tolerably thin plates and ribbons. In short, as remarked by one of our standard authorities, in treating of those manifold uses of this most precious metal which are, or ought to be, known to every one,—"It is capable of being cast into moulds of any form; of being drawn out into wires of any desired strength or fineness; of being extended into plates or sheets; of being bent in every direction; of being sharpened, hardened, and softened at pleasure. It accommodates itself, in fact, to all our wants, desires, and even caprices; it is equally serviceable to the arts and sciences, to war and peace; the same ore furnishes the sword, the ploughshare, and the scythe, the pruning-hook, the needle, and the graver, the spring of the Geneva watch, or of the ponderous locomotive, the chisel, the chain, the anchor, the compass, the cannon, or the bomb."

But in speaking of its tenacity and its other simpler properties, we must be a little more explicit in detail. Its matchless tenacity in its other states than that of mere cast-iron is such, that a wire of wrought-iron, drawn out, by its extreme ductility, through orifices gradually diminishing in calibre down to the 0·787 part of a line in diameter, has been found capable of supporting a weight of about 550 lbs.; and a wire of tempered steel, according to Parkes, has been found to carry double the weight of an ordinary wire. One of British iron, an inch in diameter, and estimated, in relation to Swedish, only as 348·88 to 549·25, is stated by Murray to have sustained weights without breaking till raised to 25 tons 6 cwt. The tremendous strength of wire ropes may thence be all the more readily conceived. Invaluable as such properties are, however, there is another perhaps still more peculiar and practically important, namely—welding, which it, and it almost alone amongst metals, possesses, and that in high perfection. Were it not for this peculiarity, indeed, in which platinum amongst metals, and sodium amongst metalloids, alone at all resemble it, the great infusibility of wrought-iron would sadly diminish its vast utility. The metal when pure and malleable requires the highest temperature of a wind furnace to make any impression on its extreme infusibility. The fusing point of cast-iron even, which *will* fuse, ranges to 3480° Fahrenheit; and it is very doubtful whether at *any* temperature it can be made to boil, as many metals readily do. But wrought, or malleable, or fibrous iron, at a bright red heat, is soft and pliable, and, by hammering, will so interweave its fibres, those of one piece with those of another, as to become spliced, as it were, completely, into one continuous whole. Such is a feasible enough idea of the nature of welding. But it is, in fact, by a species of welding that the very *particles* of wrought-iron are first of all worked into mass as such. In that curious process, 'puddling,' cast-iron while fused in a proper reverberatory furnace, is stirred or puddled, and thus exposed to the air and flame till the whole mass heaves, burns blue, grows tough, less fusible, and actually falls at length into a *dry powder*. Then the fire is urged so that the pulverulent mass again *agglutinates* at the *welding* heat, and thus, as it were molecularly rewelded, is worked up into masses, and squeezed through rollers into 'malleable iron,' as afterwards and elsewhere more particularly pointed out. The oxides of iron, too, thus yield, with combustible or carbonaceous matter, in the furnace, a metallic spongy mass for subsequent compaction into malleable metal. Such, probably, was every where the earliest mode of treating iron ores, as, indeed, is still the case with ruder nations. But along with this agglutinative property, iron is equally singular in forming, at a high heat, that correlative compound with carbon—cast-iron, whence, again, the purer and more malleable metal is prepared by puddling, and by means of which the separation from the ore of every thing extraneous is facilitated.*

In connection with these peculiarities o iron, we may here note that it is well knowr that hammering long continued destroys tha very malleability which it at first contributed sc essentially to mature. Dr. Black suggestec from this that the hammering, which we al know *will* evolve even red heat from cold iron expelled too much of the heat latent in (or, as we may very properly term it, constitutional to) the malleable state of the iron, or to that state essentially necessary, and he accordingly conceived metals to possess malleability in proportion to their latent (or constitutional) heat From some facts too related by Sir Jame Hall, it appeared that at certain temperatures, above the welding heats, all iron falls to pieces under the hammer, even as at first applied, or independently of long continuance, and that this happened at different heats in the different varieties of the iron of commerce,—in cast iron at about 15° Wedgwood,—in steel at 30°,—Swedish iron at 50° to 60°, —and Siberian at 100°. In estimating the respective degrees of tenacity in iron, and investigating other kindred peculiarities of a most interesting and practically important order, such facts might be of great use. It is very generally believed for instance, that mere long continued or reiterated vibration, or other continuous or recurrent motion, will, *in like manner with heat or hammering* as above, at length of itself destroy the tenacity or toughness of wrought-iron—a question, this, that cannot too soon be investigated and decided in connection with a series of just such facts and experiments as those to which attention has now been drawn. The very fact itself, indeed, that so singular a change in iron as that from the ordinary to the *magnetic* state, can be induced by merely stroking, tapping, or other gentle percussion or friction, or even by the mere continued pressure of gravitation or magnetic posture in the sphere, may prove the proposed subject of investigation to be no idle or groundless one; for if hammering or percussion, heat, or even mere friction or pressure can produce changes so remarkable, so *may* vibration,—all of these, in fact, being merely different modes of subtle force, operative on, and *undermining*, or otherwise altering, the connections of the more or less minute particles, crystlets, polarcles, molecules, or atoms of the mass.

The texture of iron, like most of its other properties, varies much with its varieties of state, or with the methods of working it Though, in bars, or wire, it seems to be longitudinally fibrous, yet when kept *long* red hot it acquires a crystaline texture, and has a tendency to cuboidal fracture. This, too, doubtless, involves the nature of that very change which takes place in the undermining of its tenacity by *high* heat, even though not of *long* duration. The specific heat of wrought-iron is 0.11379 (Regnault); that of cast-steel 0.11848; and that of cast-iron 0.12728.

The affinity of iron for oxygen is so grea that it will unite with it to form rust at al temperatures, withdrawing it even from water liberating the hydrogen. Yet it is very sin gular that the oxide of iron thus produced i reducible again to the metallic state by th very hydrogen which it had liberated. Never theless, the spongy mass thus obtained, whe exposed to air, has its affinity for oxygen stil so strong and undiminished that it takes fir even spontaneously and burns into oxide again More than that, the black, or rather deep blu protoxide itself, when carefully produced an dried out of access to air and then suddenl exposed to it, will still burn further, and the too spontaneously, glowing like tinder, int brown peroxide, or common rust. In an at mosphere of oxygen, iron burns with vivi brilliant scintillations, produced by merel tying a little cotton to the end of a piece c wire and plunging it in while the cotton is i flames; and D'Arcet showed that combustio

* Vide p. 197.

* The effect of puddling being apparently so important, one would think there could be but one opinion of its advantage and necessity. Yet we find the son of a very eminent practical authority on this particular subject, namely the late Mr. Mushet, not only broaching another opinion on the point, but one the very reverse of that which has been universally held ever since the process itself was introduced by Cort, in 1783. "Which," says Mr. R. Mushet, "is the most preposterous dogma in the present science of iron-making?—1. The use of the refinery?—2. The use of the puddling-furnace?—or, 3. The use of hot-blast in smelting the rich blackband ironstones? I am aware that, in attacking these *time-honoured abuses*, I am uttering blasphemy against the powers that be in iron-making, and earning for myself the character of an insane visionary; but a few short years will show that I am correct in my views; and pig-iron, instead of being subjected to the various tortures of refining, puddling, &c., will be at once passed through the rolls, or placed under the hammer! not, indeed, overloaded as at present with a quantity of carbon, which, as soon as it has by skilful management been got into the iron, must next be got out again; but pig-iron cast with the object in view to which it has to be applied—viz., rolling into bars; and for which it can only now be made *very indifferently fit* by two laborious, expensive, and destructive operations—refining and puddling. The merits of the puddling process, in as far as facility and quantity in the production of bar-iron were concerned, were so immense *in comparison* with those of the former processes employed, that up to this moment iron m nufacturers have apparently never considered whether it possible to supersede the puddling process by a direct m thod of operation. It is not for me to attempt to enlight the mighty men of iron, whose greatness, like that of Ki Og, seems to be measured by the extent of their make in ir —Og being celebrated for his iron *bedstead*, and the emine iron-masters for the extent of their *beds* of iron; but I wou ask, what is the mighty obstacle which really exists to t production of iron fit for rolling out at once into bars." there be anything in this rather startling heterodoxy, o quotation of it may assist in ripening the fruits of reflecti on it.

THE PRIOR'S ROOM, BRADENSTOKE PRIORY, WILTS.

might even be obtained by merely whirling a piece of heated iron rapidly through the ordinary atmosphere with a wire and string. Smithy ashes are scales of partially oxidized or burnt iron, formed by the more subdued burning of highly-heated iron in the open air even without any such artificial excitement. At a red heat, iron rapidly decomposes water and steam, and hence explosions are believed to arise from this powerful affinity of iron for oxygen suddenly liberating large volumes of hydrogen gas from the steam or water. The same affinity enables it, with the aid of high heat, even to decompose potash, or deprive the metalloid potassium of its oxygen, although the affinity of potassium for oxygen is so great that a piece of that substance, to outward appearance just like a piece of soft lead, will, when thrown into water, run along the surface of it burning and blazing, while it consumes the water or unites with its oxygen. It is almost needless to say, that if iron manifested *its* peculiar affinity for oxygen in so peculiar and inconvenient a way, we should have had little use of iron as a metal. Iron, however, as said, will corrode in water for all

that, even at ordinary temperatures. Graham is of opinion that this is in general immediately occasioned by the formation of a subsalt of iron with excess of oxide, of which the acid is supplied by the saline matter in solution. As a preventive to this he thinks that "articles of iron may be completely defended from the injury occasioned in this way by contact with the more positive metal zinc, as in galvanized iron, while the protecting metal itself wastes away very slowly." It must be here noted, however, that this advice, though theoretically correct, implies the perfect purity of the zinc; for if it contain, as much of it does, either arsenic or sulphur, the very contrary may be anticipated. Arsenic is a much more *negative* metal than iron, though zinc be somewhat more positive than it, and will accordingly, on the very same theoretical grounds, decidedly tend to hasten the corrosion of the iron; and, as for sulphur, it is well known that in association with iron, *it* will cause the iron rapidly to rot in moisture, sulphurets of iron readily putrifying, decomposing water, and forming sulphuretted hydrogen on the one hand, and iron rust or oxide on the other. And, in-

deed, as arsenic is but a metallic sulphur after all, there is not the least doubt that arsenical pyrites, or arseniuret of iron, will also rot just as readily as ordinary pyrites, or sulphuret of iron. It is thus that we would attempt to explain some contradictory testimony on the subject of galvanised iron. The perfect purity of the zinc is a point of great importance.

We find it impossible to exhaust the subject of iron and its properties, even in a very elementary and humble way, in a single article, and must therefore recur to this important subject at another fitting opportunity.

THE PRIOR'S ROOM, BRADENSTOKE PRIORY.

OUR view represents the only interior remaining at the ancient Priory of Bradenstoke, in Wiltshire, a few miles from Chippenham; the building is now a humble farm-house, difficult of access, and seldom visited. A small portion of the structure alone remains; there are some very good windows, and an interesting crypt, which adjoins the room shown in the view, and the entrance to which is by a descent of several steps in the archway beyond the fireplace,—these, with a few shields of arms, are all that is left to interest the antiquarian visiter. It is not known by whom the fireplace was built; there are the letters W. H. L. upon it; the style is late, and the workmanship is rather rude; it stands in an angle of the room, which is a very small one—too small for such a large fireplace.—C. J. R.

IRISH ARCH-ERY.

THE recent visit of Her Majesty and Prince Albert to Ireland, which has proved so gratifying in every aspect, and is calculated to lead to much advantage, has given ample occupation to the designers and constructors of triumphal arches, and, if we could believe the newspaper accounts, we should be led to state that some "really splendid pieces of architecture," "magnificent designs," and "fine works of art" (*sic* in leading journals), were put up for the occasion. We are not going to object to the epithets, but merely to remark what struck us forcibly in reading all the accounts that, as Planché writes and Mathews sings,—

"Every thing was any thing but what it seemed."

This was imitation of one thing, and that of another; the arch was to look like a pedestal and the boards like Sicilian marble. Nothing was real but the loyalty,—every thing sham but the good feeling.

Amongst the schemes for the improvement of Ireland now rife is the establishment of a fishing settlement and industrial farm on the coast of Mayo, to be called "The Barony of Erris Settlement." A plan has been prepared by Mr. T. C. Tinkler, architect, comprising school-room, dormitories, kitchen, dining-hall, and master's and paid superintendent's house, with out-houses, &c. Funds for the support of a schoolmaster have been granted by the Irish Society of London, and the erection will be commenced forthwith. One great object of the promoters is, to lead the people to take advantage of the abundance of fish to be found upon the coast, and for which a ready market has been found. For centuries this incalculable benefit has been lost to Ireland; from the indifference of the people to the advantage, and the want of knowledge and enterprise amongst them, the markets of the neighbourhood have been chiefly supplied by fish from Scotland.

We cordially wish success to the enterprise.

BUILDING SOCIETIES.

EXEMPTION FROM STAMP DUTY.

As there are many of your readers interested in, or connected with, building societies, I am desirous of directing their attention to a recent case in the Court of Common Pleas, which is the most important, in relation to the law regulating these societies, that has occurred for some time. It was, doubtless, the consideration of this importance, and the general discussion which the decision has given rise to in the profession, that induced Mr. Scott, the authorized reporter of the court, to publish the case separately in a complete form,* and thus that gentleman has been enabled to present to those whom it may concern, a very full and accurate report of the same, with annotations, some months before it would have otherwise appeared. I will not, therefore, trouble your readers by touching on all the technicalities and subdivisions into which the case resolves itself; the point decided with which we have more immediately to do is,—"that mortgages and other securities given to the trustees of building societies established under the 6 & 7 Wm. 4, c. 32, are exempt from stamp duty." There was a floating opinion among many members of the profession, that the joint provisions of the Friendly Societies Act (10 Geo. 4, c. 56), and the Building Societies Act (6 & 7 Wm. 4, c. 32), warranted this conclusion. The 37th section of the 10 Geo. 4, c. 56, enacts, "that no copy of rules, power, warrant, or letter of attorney granted or to be granted by any persons as trustees of any society established under this Act, for the transfer of any share in the public funds standing in the name of such trustee, nor any receipt given for any dividend in any public stock or fund, or interest of Exchequer bills, nor any receipt, nor any entry in any book or receipt for money deposited in the funds of any such society, nor for any money received by any member, his or her executor, administrator, assigns, or attorneys, from the funds of such society, *nor any bond or other security* to be given to or on account of any such society, or by the treasurer, or trustee, or any officer thereof, nor any draft or order, nor any form of assurance, nor any appointment of any agent, nor any certificate or other instrument for the revocation of any such appointment, *nor any other instrument or document whatever required or authorized to be given, issued, signed, made, or produced in pursuance of this Act, shall be subject or liable to, or charged with, any stamp duty or duties whatsoever.*" The fourth section of the 6 & 7 Wm. 4, c. 32, enacts, "that all the provisions of a certain Act made and passed in the tenth year of the reign of his late Majesty King George the Fourth, intituled 'An Act to amend an Act of the tenth year of his late Majesty King George the Fourth, to consolidate and amend the laws relating to friendly societies,' so far as the same, or any part thereof, may be applicable to the purposes of any benefit building society, and to the framing, certifying, enrolling, and altering the rules thereof, shall extend and apply to such benefit building society, and the rules thereof, in such and the same manner as if the provisions of the said Acts had been therein expressly re-enacted." That portion of the 37th section of the Friendly Societies Act which enacts that no "bond nor other security to be given to or on account of any such society" shall be subject to stamp duty is extended and applied to building societies by a part of the 4th section of the 6 & 7 Wm. 4, c. 32, "so far as the same, or any part thereof, may be applicable to the purposes of any benefit building society." As, therefore, securities must be given for carrying out the purposes of building societies, it follows as a necessary inference that such securities shall not be "subject, or liable to, or charged with any stamp duty or duties whatsoever."

Wilde, C.J., in delivering the judgment of the court in this case, said—"By the 37th section of the former Act, bonds and other securities or assurances given to or on account of any friendly society are expressly exempted from stamp duty. And the 4th section of the latter Act — its preamble having already shown that its object was to afford encouragement and protection to societies to be established thereunder, and to the property obtained therewith—enacts that all the provisions of the 10 Geo. 4, c. 56, so far as the same, or any part thereof, may be applicable to the purposes of any benefit building society, &c., shall extend and apply to such benefit building society, and the rules thereof, in such and the same manner as if the provisions of the same had been therein expressly re-enacted. Reading, therefore, the 37th section of the 10 Geo. 4, c. 56, as incorporated into the 6 & 7 Wm. 4, c. 32, so far as applicable, it seems to us to exempt from stamp duty all securities given for the purpose of carrying the last-mentioned Act into effect."

One of your contemporaries has sought to call in question (without, we conceive, any great effect) the soundness of this decision; and it is rumoured that a statute is in the contemplation of the legislature, by which the present exemption from stamp duties, extended to friendly and building societies, will be limited. We can only hope that no such short-sighted policy will be carried into execution, and for the present we must consider that the Court of Common Pleas held that mortgages and other securities given to the trustees of building societies established under the 6 & 7 Wm. 4, c. 32, are exempt from stamp duty, and that, therefore, this is the law. We would also remind your readers that if such exemptions were limited by statutory enactment, it would have a prospective rather than a retrospective operation. Three other questions of much importance were determined in the judgment, and the whole case, replete as it is with the pleadings, arguments, rules, certificates, &c., is deserving a perusal by the officers of these associations, and a careful examination from their professional advisers.

A MEMBER OF THE INNER TEMPLE.

* The case of Walker v. Giles and Another, decided in the Court of Common Pleas in Trinity Vacation, 1849. By Mr. John Scott, of the Inner Temple, Barrister-at-law. Demy 8vo. London: Spettigue and Farrance.

THE MANUFACTURE OF GLASS.

THE removal of the excise restriction from glass appears likely to give a great impulse to the manufacture, and to raise the material to a still more important position in the arts than it has yet occupied.

The composition of glass is very various; but a feature of general resemblance consists in the presence of silica or flint, combined with one or more alkaline bodies, with the addition frequently of other oxide. The substances usually present in glass, besides silica, are potash, soda, lime, oxide of iron, alumina, and oxide of lead. Any of these may be used with silica, it being only indispensable that one alkaline base should be present. In these compounds, boracic acid may be substituted for silica without material disadvantage.

Much obscurity hangs over the invention of glass, but it is invariably attributed to the Phenicians, on the authority of Pliny, who relates that some mariners of that nation, when driven by a tempest for shelter to the mouth of the river Belus, which runs from the foot of Mount Carmel, were surprised on finding that the ashes of the plant "kali," with which they were cooking their provisions on the shore, by mingling with the sand, formed a vitreous and rather transparent substance.

The Phenicians for a length of time were famed for the manufacture of glass; and, in the days of Pliny and Strabo, the glass manufacturers of Tyre and Sidon produced articles of great beauty and very elaborate workmanship, which they had acquired the art of staining and cutting in imitation of precious stones. The Egyptians, it is probable, received their knowledge of the glass manufacture from the Phenicians,—no mention being made in the Mosaic or other ancient writings of their acquaintance with its processes, the only evidence resting upon some pieces of blue glass which have been found at Thebes; but these might have been formed in the course of making the glass of their earthenware beads, with which it is identical in composition.

The Egyptians, consequently, rivalled their teachers; and about the time of the Emperor Adrian, Rome obtained its supply of glass from Alexandria, although the import must have been very insignificant in point of quantity, from the great price which was set upon glass-ware from the time of Nero, who gave nearly 50,000*l*. of our money for two glass cups with handles; but by the time of the Emperor Titus, the Romans must have obtained considerable proficiency, since various glass utensils have been found in Herculaneum, which was destroyed in his reign.*

In the reign of Alexander Severus, the glass manufacturers of Rome were so numerous that they had a distinct quarter of the city assigned them, and were in such a flourishing condition that a tax was afterwards imposed on them. It was in the tomb of Severus that the famous vase was found, which received the name of the Barberini Vase, from the palace in which it was preserved for more than two centuries, when it was purchased by the Duchess of Portland, and afterwards became known to the British public as the Portland Vase.

At a very remote period glass formed one of the articles of commerce which the Phenicians exchanged for tin with the inhabitants of the southern parts of Britain; and it is supposed that the Druids had some slight acquaintance with glass-making, which they turned to good account by persuading their ignorant votaries that their clumsily-formed beads of coloured glass were amulets of rare virtue.

So early as the middle of the first century, the windows of some churches and monasteries in Britain were glazed by foreign artists, though it was not for some centuries after that glass became common even in such buildings. In the beginning of the sixteenth century glass windows were so rare, that they were carried off as valuable booty during some riots that took place in Oxford. Even half a century later glass windows were by no means in extensive use, for we find that the glazed window sashes of Alnwick Castle, in Northumberland, were taken out and laid carefully aside for fear of

* Among the ruins of Pompeii there was found a large bow window, glazed with a greenish-tinged glass; and a window of the baths, with a kind of plate-glass, ground on one side, to prevent persons from seeing through it.

accidents during the absence of the earl. Scotland seems, as well as England, to have made slow progress in its use : in the year 1661 only the upper part of the windows of the palace itself were glazed, the lower part being closed by wooden shutters. Although it was not much used in England, it made considerable progress in France ; but it was not until the middle of the seventeenth century that the manufacture was firmly established there, Colbert giving encouragement to some French artists, who had learned the art at Venice. The chief articles produced by these manufacturers were mirrors of blown glass,—the introduction of cast glass mirrors being effected by a manufacturer named Thevart some twenty years later, who, after experiencing great opposition from the old company, was obliged to unite with it ; and it was not till the formation of a new company on the ruins of the old united one, that the manufacture became prosperous.

The manufacture of flint glass was commenced in England in the year 1557 at Crutched Friars and Savoy House in the Strand ; and in 1635 considerable improvement was effected by Sir Robert Mansell substituting coal for wood fuel. The first plates of blown glass for mirrors and coach windows produced in this country were made in Lambeth in 1673, by some Venetian artisans, under the auspices of the Duke of Buckingham. There was no English establishment of importance for the manufacture of cast plate glass till the year 1773, nearly a century after its introduction into France, when a company was incorporated by royal charter, and established works at Ravenhead, in Lancashire. It appears strange that the Chinese, who have anticipated the Europeans in many matters, should have been ignorant of glass-making, especially when we consider the operations of their porcelain manufacture, and the glazes which are used in it are such as might be supposed likely to lead to the discovery of glass. Even now the only glass-house in the Chinese empire, so far as is known, is one at Canton, in which only old and broken glass of foreign manufacture is remelted and worked again.

G. J. RHODES.

NOTES IN THE PROVINCES.

THE enclosure at Portland breakwater, we understand, is to be named the Victoria Harbour of Refuge.——The projected improvement of the entrance into Winchester Cathedral precincts from the Square, by removal of an ancient house, and enlargement of the Mechanics' Institution, has commenced.—— The Gloucestershire Chronicle informs us that the restoration of Upleadon Church, in that district, has been completed. The old church had fallen into a sad state of decay. The floor was so damp that it grew weeds in some places, and the pews were in a wretched state. The ancient Norman windows had been filled with common casements, or partially blocked up, and on the outside earth had accumulated to the depth of 3 feet. All the pews have been replaced by open sittings with carved bench-ends. A simple lectern has been substituted for a cumbrous reading-desk. The old wooden roofs have been stripped, cleaned, and varnished. The windows have been restored, and the east window filled with stained glass by Mr. Rogers, of Worcester. The chancel has been raised two steps above the aisle, and laid with Painswick stone, in lozenges. Oak communion rails, after an Early English example, enclose the communion-table, which stands on a floor of encaustic tiles in eight compartments. This restoration has cost 370l., and has been carried out chiefly by the incumbent, warmly seconded by the farmers in the parish. After the re-opening on Thursday week, the foundation-stone of a new school-room was laid by the Hon. Mrs. Sayers, near the parsonage : Mr. Cullis, builder.——The foundation-stone of Landscove new district church, near Totness, was laid on Tuesday week, in the presence of a large concourse of people, by the Rev. W. Martin. This church will be dedicated to St. Mary, and is, we understand, the gift of Miss Champernowne, the dean and chapter of Exeter providing the ground and the endowment. The architect is Mr. J. L. Pearson, of London ; and the builder Mr. John Mason, of

Exeter.——A new butter cross, to accommodate 200 to 300 people, is to be erected at Knighton, according to a correspondent of the Hereford Times.——At a late meeting of the Birmingham Street-Act Commissioners, Mr. J. Arnold read a letter from Mr. Pigott Smith, who suggested the propriety of an architect being employed to examine the state of the spire of St. Martin's Church, as, in case of its falling, life might be sacrificed.——Mr. J. H. Beilby said, that as much alarm had been created relative to the statements with respect to St. Martin's spire, apprehension might perhaps be allayed by his stating that two eminent architects had lately inspected it, and were of opinion that not the slightest danger exists.——The new buildings of the west wing of Queen's College, Birmingham, from the plans of Messrs. Drury and Bateman, which comprise a suite of rooms of 154 feet in length, for model rooms, library, &c., two additional lecture halls, engineering workshops, and twenty-six additional sets of chambers for resident students, are in rapid progress towards completion, under the contract with Mr. James Mountford, builder.—— The laying of the foundation-stone of the New Wesleyan Chapel, Hill Top, West Bromwich, took place on Monday in last week. The chapel is intended to accommodate 1,000 persons, at an estimated cost of 2,000l., the greater part of which has been subscribed. The architect is Mr. James Simpson, of Leeds, and the builder, Mr. John Lees, Hill Top.——The new Town Hall or Corn Exchange at Stourbridge was opened on Tuesday week. The ball is 70 feet long by about 40 feet wide, and is capable of dining 300 persons. There are two entrances—one from the main entrance to the Market Place, opening into High-street, and the other from the Rye Market. Mr. E. Smith, of Oldswinford, was the architect and builder, and the cost of building was 550l.——The Altrincham Town Hall and Market Hall is rapidly approaching completion. The brick-work is raised to the full height, the roof timbers are being laid, and the centre of the front has been surmounted by the timber frame-work of the clock and bell-turret. The Market Hall will be 29 feet by 25 feet, and 12 feet 6 inches in height, besides an additional space at the back of 20 feet by 10 feet 6 inches. The Town Hall or Assembly Room will be 39 feet 6 inches by 26 feet, with an ante-room behind of 16 feet 6 inches by 10 feet 6 inches. ——Thirty new houses only have been built in Lancaster during the last year ; all of them occupied at good rents. They were all engaged, we believe, before the second story was reared. It has been stated that good small houses pay 13 per cent. upon the outlay.—— At the entrance to Rotherham from the bridge, a line of crazy buildings is to be demolished, and the street thereby widened. A new street at right angles with Bridge-gate, opposite the end of College-street, and to extend to the river, has also been projected by the feoffees and ratepayers.——From a report of the committee for conducting the subscription for the restoration of Hexham Abbey Church, it appears that the total amount received was 1,559l. 3s., and the sum expended in purchasing and pulling down houses encumbering the east front of the Abbey Church was 1,431l. 19l. 6d., leaving a balance in the treasurer's hands of 127l. 4s. 6d. It was resolved, that an effort be made to raise the sum (350l.) necessary to purchase and pull down the remaining houses, and to put the Lady Chapel in such a state of repair as to prevent it from falling to decay ; and that the subscription be then closed, trusting that at some future time the complete restoration of the building may be accomplished.——The church of Amcotts, parish of Althorpe, Lincolnshire, suddenly fell down on Tuesday week before last. The rector, the Rev. James Aspinall, had observed a yielding of one of the walls two or three weeks before, and had, consequently, performed the service in the school-room. It was a very old building, and the immediate cause of its fall was the increased weight of the thatched roof occasioned by a shower of rain.—— A correspondent of the Chelmsford Chronicle states that, in addition to the church now erecting at Romford, several improvements are about to be carried into effect. The large loam pond at the top of market place is to be converted into a fountain, and, with an artesian well, will provide the whole town with pure

water. A new county court, with a literary institution combined, will form another feature, together with a dispensary. The removal of several dilapidated buildings and the turnpike from the town is projected, with other local improvements.

COLOUR IN DECORATION.

I WAS much interested with the observations, in the last number of "THE BUILDER," by Mr. Gilbert J. French, "on the arrangement of colours in ancient decorative art." Mr. French having evidently made a careful research into the rules which guided the ancient decorator, it was satisfactory to me to find how closely they corresponded with what I had myself observed.

In the examples that I have examined, which consist of some of the coloured decorations to be found among our old churches, the first, second, and fourth laws, with certain trifling exceptions, are invariably followed. The third rule is not much used, except in stained glass. I would also notice, how fond the ancient decorators appear to have been of alternating red with green ; blue being used more sparingly, and confined very much to soffits, the ground of small groining, panels of ceilings, or, any part where it may be supposed to represent the sky. Red appears, however, to have been the colour most used, especially in the earlier decorations, where frequently red, relieved by the stone colour of the walls, was almost the only colour employed. Red and white was at all times a favourite diaper.

Gold was not much used in the decoration of buildings until the 14th century, at least I have not met with any example. At this date it became almost an invariable rule to gild all carved parts which were foliated. Sculpture may be said, generally, to be coloured "proper."

In your account of the doings of the Archæological Institute at Salisbury, I see no mention made of the coloured decorations of the cathedral. Although all covered up with white or yellow wash, except a little in the chapter house and the passage leading thereto, they were at one time very considerable. Traces of magnificent scrolls and other forms may be still seen through the whitewash upon the groining and walls of the choir, which, judging by the little which is uncovered, must be of a very superior description.

It is a pity that the proper authorities do not take the means of bringing them once more to light, by carefully brushing off the whitewash, as they are doing in the Lady Chapel at Ely.

JAMES K. COLLING.

ON THE USE OF THE PEAT BOGS OF IRELAND.

AT a meeting of the Botanical Society of London, held on the 3rd inst., Mr. J. W. Rogers brought under the consideration of the meeting the purport of his paper read at the previous meeting of the society held on the 8th July last, " On the uses and properties of the peat moss, and the value of peat charcoal as a disinfecter and fertilizer." It may be necessary to mention that by the aid of peat charcoal, Mr. Rogers purposes to consolidate and deodorize the solid matter of the London sewers, and, whilst by that means benefiting the inhabitants of the metropolis, there would be placed within the reach of the agriculturist a manure of the most powerful kind, pulverized, free from odour, and fit for transit by any conveyance. In 1845 he brought the subject under the consideration of the public, and it was then alleged that charcoal could not give that quantity of carbon to the leaf of the plant which it was necessary it should receive, and that the leaf, and not the root, being the portion of it which required such sustenance, his discovery was of no use. Often, however, since then he had tried the experiment, and the result had invariably been that it was the root, and not the leaf of the plant, which attracted the carbon, and therefore he was more convinced of the propriety of the system he was endeavouring to promulgate. From the experiments he had made, he had found that peat charcoal possessed far superior advantages to what wood charcoal did.

ROMAN CATHOLIC CHURCH, "OUR LADY STAR OF THE SEA," GREENWICH.

Mr. W. W. WARDELL, Architect.

NEW ROMAN CATHOLIC CHURCH, "OUR LADY STAR OF THE SEA," CROOM'S-HILL, GREENWICH.

We occasionally hear of the munificence of individuals of different persuasions in contributing largely towards the erection of places of worship: amongst the results of such acts, the church of which we present a view in the present number is worthy of especial note, not only in reference to the industry and zeal that have been brought to bear upon its erection, but from the goodness of its architecture.

The number of Roman Catholic pensioners in Greenwich Hospital is nearly 500 ; almost every one of these is suffering from some wound, consequently he requires larger space in church than one in sound health. The present Catholic chapel is so miserable in its structure a locality that it threatens almost to bury congregation without an undertaker ; inde in addition to the other portion of the cong gation, it will not admit of 100 of these p sioners,—in fact, it frequently happens t during the most unpropitious weather lanes and avenues of the chapel are filled w worshippers kneeling on the ground. Th

PLAN OF ROMAN CATHOLIC CHURCH, GREENWICH.

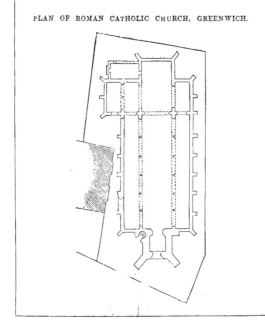

men have fought in all our great sea-fights, and helped to make England what she is,—mistress, in a great measure, of the destinies of the world. They never flinched when fighting by the side of their Protestant brethren. The good Protestant, with a heart to feel, will acknowledge that they deserve even from him consideration in their conscientious scruples.

The present pastor (the Rev. Richard North) undertook their cause. His first effort was unfortunate. He collected 900l. with difficulty, and lost it in the failure of Wright's bank. This misfortune made him but the more ardent to set to work again. In his distress he applied to the Lords of the Admiralty, and received from them 200l. At the present time, after an outlay of nearly 8,000l., he has almost succeeded in building his church: much help, however, is still needed to enable him to finish it as it should be. Space forbids us here to give particulars; suffice it to state that nearly 1,000l. have been contributed in copper and silver.

The church is built of Kentish rag stone, with Caen stone dressings to the windows and doorways, and is in the style of the fourteenth century, or Decorated English. It consists of a nave, aisles, chancel, three chapels, sacristy, and tower. The columns of the nave are octagonal, of solid polished Purbeck marble. The roofs of the nave and aisles are open, and those of the chancel and chapels are lined with cedar panelling on richly moulded oak ribs; the whole of this will be emblazoned with sacred devices. The cornices from whence this panelling springs are to be filled in with carved foliage, lilies, roses, &c., and the hymn, Ave Maris Stella. In the chapels the inscriptions will relate to their dedications. The outer chapel, on the gospel side of the chancel, is for the organ, and an oratory of a religious community, who will form the choir. The fittings will all be carried out in the same style. The architect is Mr. W. W. Wardell.

The annexed plan shows the distribution of the building, and the confined site on which it stands. The tower is next the road.

PARLIAMENTARY COMMITTEE ON SCHOOL OF DESIGN.

THE Parliamentary Committee appointed to inquire into the management of the Government School of Design say in their report, which is just now published,—

"From a general review of the evidence, your committee conclude that the schools, though far from having attained the degree of perfection of which they appear capable, are producing beneficial effects, and may in due time be expected, with energetic support and under judicious management, to realize the anticipations with which they have been founded. In an undertaking of so novel and experimental a character, difficulties have naturally arisen, and no doubt errors have been committed. Prejudices have been encountered; it has been found difficult to get men duly qualified in all respects for the duties which they have had to discharge; and finally, there have been many differences of opinion among those who have been charged with carrying out the undertaking, which have necessarily impeded the uniformity of its operation. Your committee cannot flatter themselves that these difficulties are yet at an end; but they see reason to hope that they are gradually disappearing, and confidently recommend to the house to continue the support which has hitherto been afforded to an object of such great national importance."

"Evidence has been taken upon the systems of management which have prevailed since the opening of the schools, and upon the principles on which the several managing bodies have acted. The inconveniences of the plan of placing a council, or committee of management, variously composed, and consisting of unpaid members, between the Board of Trade and the masters of the school, have been for some time recognised; and unless your committee were prepared wholly to disregard the evidence taken on this point, they cannot avoid expressing the opinion that the present committee of management ought not to be retained. * * Your committee observe

that some confusion exists in the proceedings of the present managing body, which they attribute to the circumstance of the relations between the Board of Trade and the committee of management being imperfectly defined; they would recommend that the management be placed on a more distinct footing, by rendering the Board of Trade directly responsible for the management; and your committee trust that the Board of Trade, being made distinctly and primarily responsible for the working of the system, will from time to time make such improvements as experience may show to be desirable."

"Your committee are then, generally, of opinion that the principles of management of the head and branch schools should be these: that the supreme executive authority should be vested in the Board of Trade, and that all persons employed should be immediately responsible to that department. That the Board should appoint all masters and other persons. That one or more paid inspectors, acquainted with ornamental designing, should be appointed, who should frequently visit and report upon the provincial schools, but that the inspectors should not be authorized to interfere with the details of the teaching in any school, for which the head-master or masters of every school ought to be solely responsible."

The committee recommend an increased supply of examples and works of art for the provincial schools, and better accommodation for the central school at Somerset House.

The report seems to us a very "yea-nay" sort of document, and so far as we can discover, might as well have remained unwritten.

THE COVERED BRIDGES OF SWITZERLAND AND THE TUBULAR BRIDGE OVER THE MENAI STRAITS.

As a visitant of Chester during the recent congress of the British Archæological Association in that city, it was impossible, when so near the most important modern triumph of the art of engineering, not to visit the new tubular Victoria Bridge over the Menai Straits, and I believe it may now, during its formation and erection, be more duly appreciated in all its colossal proportions and the felicities of its construction than it will be when poised in mid air as a thoroughfare for immense trains.

But it struck me that the idea of a "hanging and covered bridge," though in a different material, viz., wood, had been realised in Switzerland and Germany, nearly a century back. I need not recall to your recollection those uncommonly curious structures that were erected over the rapid torrents of the Swiss republic, where, from the force of the current, pillars supporting arches were impracticable; but to your readers the following particulars of some of them, and of others copied from them, may be new and interesting:—

The first in date and merit is that of Schaffhausen, built over the Rhine, where the influence of that river's cataract, a couple of miles lower down, at Laufen, is felt in great force. From its firm construction, it was accounted the best wooden bridge in the world, though the flatness of the banks on each side offered no facilities, and the merit of its projection and construction is due to a common carpenter of the place, called John Ulrick Grubenmann, in 1757. Its entire width was 353 feet 7 inches, without support from below, for though an old pillar was found about half way across the river, on a rock, the construction was independent of it: said: its breadth was 15 feet 6 inches. With the passage of an individual it vibrated sensibly, but was kept immoveable and firm when heavily laden waggons passed over it. The same builder, in conjunction with his brother John, built another hanging and covered bridge, in 1778, over the Limmat, near Wettingen, with a span of 346 feet, and with some improvements and greater firmness than the Schaffhausen earlier one. Both were burnt in 1799 by the revolutionary hordes of France, when retreating after a defeat by the Austrians. The full particulars of their construction, with accurate and clear sections, &c., may be found in "Plans, Coupes, et Élévations des trois Ponts de Bois les plus rémarquables de la Suisse," published in 1803, by Cr. Mecheln, at Basle,

A fine geometrical elevation of the bridge at Schaffhausen is also given in Gauthey's "Traité de la Construction des Ponts," &c., edited by M. Navier, Paris (tom. i. 1809, tom. ii. 1819), on plate iii. fig. 5.

Perhaps, in imitation of that at Schaffhausen, Joseph Ritter, a Lucerne carpenter, built in 1764 his first hanging wooden bridge over the River Candel, in the canton of Berne, with a span of only 156 feet, and on account of the precipitate banks of the river, with a much steadier hold, and therefore much simpler than its prototype; and in 1786 he followed it up by building another over the Reuss, in the same canton, with a span of 148 feet, which seems to have had many of its parts in common with a hanging bridge recently built over the Calder.

In 1786, an architect of the name of Etzel built a bridge on these principles at Plochingen, in the then dukedom, now kingdom of Wurtemberg, over the Neckar; it has two spans over the river, resting upon a pier in the centre, each of 176 feet, and has this peculiarity, that the centre is narrower across than the ends, to prevent its slipping out of position.

In more modern times the art of wooden-bridge building has been carried to great perfection in Hungary, by the Austrian road architect, John Gross, who in 1807-8 built a covered bridge over the Wasg, in the county of Thurotz, on the principle of the former at Schaffhausen, which seems to have served as a general model. It has, however, the advantage of being built upon the two banks, bold and precipitate, which permit the staunchions that support it to be directed to a common centre above the roadway, which gives the whole great strength and firmness. It is described in Jos. Jeckel's "Galizien's Strassen und Brückenbau," Wien and Trieste, 1806, and copied from this into Langsdorff's "Brückenbau," plate xvii. But the most curious feature in these Magyaric structures is their small cost; the above was built for only 35,000 gülden, or about 3,000*l*. So also one over the Saat, in the county Przemisl, with a total span of 497 feet over three stone piers, cost only 48,000 gulden, or 4,050*l*. At Tarnow, one over the Bial river, in 1782, with 177½ feet span, only 10,080 gulden, or 840*l*.; and as recently as 1802 one in the county of Arvanser, width 236 feet, at the expense to the imperial treasury of 15,600 gulden, or exactly 1,300*l*. —so cheap is labour and indigenous material in that country, which may almost account for the obstinacy of resistance offered by it to the Austrian arms, where men are so readily to be procured and such immense woods exist to cover a retreat or to check the operations of an invader.

William Bell.

A GERMAN ARCHITECT ON ARCHITECTURAL COMPETITION.

At a time when architectural competition is so much discussed, both as to its principle and practice, the following remarks by a German architect (M. Van der Nüll), on the occasion of a competition for the Parliament Houses at Pesth, may not be useless:—

"The course of calling upon architects to submit designs in competition is one which ought, if properly carried out, to lead to a satisfactory result, by reason of its *publicity*; but as long as the instructions issued are not accompanied by a distinct assurance that the prize or prizes *will* be awarded to one of the designs submitted, and as long as the capability of the judges to decide on the artistic as well as the general merits of the designs is little considered, and their proceedings deserve so little confidence from architects, competition will continue to be a mere form to screen jobbing.

It would seem reasonable that, as in other professions the merits of men and measures are only decided on by persons *properly qualified*, architects should at least be treated with the same consideration; but not so; to criticise *architecture* seems easy to every one, and laymen (if the term may be allowed) are even beginning to furnish designs!

It too frequently happens that designs submitted in competition are returned with the answer that they do not fulfil the required conditions; and it is certain that the result of often great mental toil is thus exposed to piracy, without any safeguard.

But these great evils are not inherent in the *principle* of public competition, but are the results of its improper use, and might be remedied if the attempt were but made in earnest.

When the building for which designs are required is of considerable extent, as in the present instance, the premium offered must necessarily be of small account in comparison with the whole of the outlay, and should, therefore, be awarded to the best design, according to the terms of the instructions, even in the almost inconceivable case of none of the submitted designs being suitable; for surely it is worth some small sacrifice to obtain the result of so much mature deliberation on the requirements of the case as will be found in the different designs.

The remaining evil, that of the decision, might perhaps be removed by calling on the competing architects themselves to decide on the merits of the designs,—each, of course, omitting his own; or should this method prove impracticable, the Institute of German Architects might, at its annual meeting, be called upon to determine the artistic merits of the respective designs, when it would remain for the body instituting the competition to adopt one of them,—grounding their choice on the opinion of the institute.

In conclusion, it may be observed that it is very desirable to obtain the opinion of the public by *exhibiting* the designs,—as the majority of an enlightened and educated people are generally tolerably unanimous in their opinion."

THE VENTILATION OF STABLES.

At a late meeting of the Highland Society, Mr. Neil Ballingal, of Kinross-shire, farmer, read a paper on this subject, containing the following remarks:—The experience of modern times, both as respects man and cattle, proves that nothing has greater influence upon health and longevity than the nature of the air which is ordinarily breathed. The air expired from the lungs is naturally and necessarily impure, and to breathe the same air continuously is to inhale what acts on the system as a poison. More especially as regards my immediate subject, there can be given no more convincing proof of the imperfection of the system at present generally pursued than the effect produced by the various agents in operation, even on the timber and roofing of stables and byres. Every one acquainted with the subject knows that from imperfect ventilation, the plastering and lathing of roofs fall away in flakes, and are reduced to rottenness by the constant action of the condensed steam. So much is this the case, that it is no unusual thing, in the course of a nineteen years' lease, for it to be necessary to re-roof a byre, if home timber has been employed. Now, this action indicates a want of power to carry off the impure air yielding the condensed steam, that must prove deleterious, in the highest degree, to the cattle; and we need not wonder, in these circumstances, that pulmonary complaints among cattle are alarmingly on the increase. It is with a view to lead others to contribute their experience on a subject so important to the agriculturist, that I venture to submit what has occurred to myself regarding ventilation.

The subject of my experiment was a byre, about 40 feet long by 16 broad, the height of the side walls being 8 feet, and the roof being tiled, with lath and plaster under the tiles. I found it in a state of complete disrepair in the roof, the wood falling, which had been rendered rotten by the condensed breath of the cattle in continual operation on it. I first raised the side walls 2 feet. At the head of each animal I placed an air slit 2 inches deep, with 1 foot of horizontal length externally, and widening till internally it had a horizontal length of 18 inches. Externally, this slit was about 8 feet from the ground, and it rose gradually till, in the inside, it was 10 feet. Under the ridge rows of tiles on both sides of the roof the tile lath alone was put on, leaving these rows uncovered with lath and plaster from end to end of the byre. The well known property of heated air to dilate and ascend, and that of cold air to descend, sufficiently accounts for both my reasoning and adopting this process, and for its effects. The gradual rise of the cool air through the slit provided for its subsequent ascent for a brief space, so as to cool the heated air passing from the animals' lungs before it should strike the roof, and prevent it from depositing the moisture which it contained. By the slit being gradually widened, I aimed at spreading the air over as large a surface as possible, and without introducing too much cold air, giving the most extensive effect to what was introduced. The removal of the plaster has provided for the egress of that portion of the heated air which ascended to the ridge of the roof.

The result has been most successful. The cattle have, since that time, been uniformly strong and healthy. The air of the byre is cool and refreshing in all weathers; and, what affords a palpable proof of the excellent effect of the system, the wood of the roof which, as has been mentioned, gives way soon in all ordinary cases, is, at this moment, as clean, white, and sound as it was on the day in which it was put up two years ago.

The simplicity of the plan consists of:—1st. In the case of a slate roof, I propose as the most economical plan, to raise the lower edge of the slating by means of a board laid on blocks on the outer edge of the wall, leaving apertures of about an inch high between the board and the wall, which will admit a free current of air. The air will pass under the outer board and lower edge of the sarking, in which a horizontal slit is to be cut of about one inch wide, so as to admit its free ingress. To the whole scheme double apertures are necessary. The second or upper aperture, in the case of slate roofs, is thus provided underneath the second row of slates. On both sides let the sarking be removed for the space of about four inches from end to end. This leaves board enough to which to nail the slates; and the aperture allows the heated air to escape gently through the seams of the slates. In cases where cattle are tied with their heads to the gable ends, slit openings up the gable, leaving sufficient strength of sarking to stiffen the roof, will answer the same end. 2nd. In the case of a tile roof. In the lowest row of tiles take off the under slip of plaster lath. This will admit a sufficiency of the external and wholesome air through the curved vacancies of the tiles. Then for the second aperture—under the ridge or topmost row of tiles on each side, leave that row, as in my experiment, free from lath and plaster, from end to end of the byre; there is thus provided a sufficient aperture for the escape of the heated air.

An article on this subject, giving the result of other personal experience, will be found in an early volume of our journal.

A TRULY "GOTHIC" EDIFICE.

A chapel, described in the local papers as "the beautiful design of —— ——, Esq. architect," has lately been erected in St. Paul's parish, Bristol. The style is *imitation* Tudor and the plan almost a square. Its interior "beauty" consists of an enormously projecting gallery attached to the four sides of the "sacred edifice;" and while *some* of the principal timbers in the roof are shown, the space between them are *plastered* and ornamented with centres formed of the *acanthus* leaf. The street, or front, elevation is chiefly remarkable for a peculiar pediment rising from the parapet (supported at the back by an iron bar springing from the roof), and exhibiting the name of the chapel in large *Roman* characters.

The other features of the front are three extravagant four-light windows, with a transom formed of quatrefoil to hide the floor of the gallery. At either extremity of this front is a very depressed door-way. The mouldings mullions, jambs, &c., are of freestone, without dressings. The walls are of rubble, plastered and stuccoed. Cost of chapel and vestry from 2,000*l*. to 3,000*l*.

How long, Mr. Editor, will the public submit to such caricatures of Christian architecture? How long is our glorious art to be degraded by its so-called professors?

Bristol. No Goth.

ECTION OF THE NEW BOROUGH PRISONS AT DEVONPORT.

AUBYN, Architect.

Names and Residences of Parties Tendering.	First Tender, comprising 70 Cells, Chapel, Officers' Residences, Airing-yard, Boundary-walls, Approaches, &c. — Amount of Builder's Tender.	First Tender — Cost per Cell. Builder's Tender.	First Tender — Cost per Cell. Ditto, including estimate for warming, ventilating, &c.	First Extension, comprising 72 Cells east and west of main corridor. — Amount of Builder's Tender.	First Extension — Cost per Cell. Builder's Tender.	First Extension — Cost per Cell. Ditto, including warming, ventilating, &c.	Second Extension, comprising a Second Set of Airing-yards, and 48 Cells north of main corridor. — Amount of Builder's Tender.	Second Extension — Cost per Cell. Builder's Tender.	Second Extension — Cost per Cell. Ditto, including warming, ventilating, &c.	Third Extension, being additional Residences for Warders.	Principal Building Stone proposed to be used.
	£. s. d.	£. s. d.	£. s. d.	£. s. d.	£. s. d.	£. s. d.	£. s. d.	£. s. d.	£. s. d.	£. s. d.	
Simons, Hoskin, and Jenkin, Morice-town, Devonport ..	11,803 10 9	168 12 5¼	189 17 2¼	2,665 11 7	37 0 5¼	49 19 2¼	2,803 5 3	58 8 0½	71 6 9¼	674 9 2	Dun-stone.
Marshall, Plymouth..........	12,173 18 0	173 18 3	195 3 0	2,778 17 9	38 11 11	51 10 8	2,616 11 4	54 10 2¾	67 8 11½	687 0 5	Cann-quarry slate
May, Stoke, Devonport	12,382 1 7	176 17 8¾	198 2 5½	3,135 11 1	43 10 11½	56 9 8¾	2,816 7 0	58 13 5¾	71 12 2¾	711 16 3	Ditto.
Mitchell, Plymouth..........	12,715 15 3	181 13 1	202 17 10	2,993 5 5	41 11 5¾	54 10 2¼	2,665 5 7	55 10 6¼	68 9 3¼	707 0 9	Ditto.
Winsland and Holland, London	12,712 7 7	181 12 1¼	202 16 10¼	2,985 6 6	41 9 3	54 8 0	2,813 7 8	58 12 3	71 11 0	779 5 7	Ditto.
Goodyear and Roberts, Stonehouse	12,949 0 0	184 19 8½	206 4 5¼	3,143 0 0	43 13 0¾	56 11 9¾	2,860 0 0	59 11 8	72 10 5	559 0 0	Ditto.
Steed and Harvey, Plymouth..	13,810 4 1	197 14 4½	218 19 1¼	3,177 7 1	44 2 7¼	57 1 4¼	3,031 19 2	63 3 3¾	76 2 0¼	766 9 8	Lime-stone.

Note.—The above amounts included Messrs. Pearson and Co.'s tender to the Devonport corporation for the Cann-quarry slate-stone, paving-slabs, &c. Quantities were furnished by Mr. Foster, of Plymouth.

COUNTRY CHURCHYARDS.

The formation of cemeteries in the neighourhood of cities, and the abandonment altoether of intramural burial, by which, let us ope, it is speedily to be attended, leaves still esirable some improvement of country churchards, to perfect properly the reform in proress with regard to our means of sepulture. 'he evil which has bred so much reproach in owns—the disturbance and destruction of raves—exists likewise, after a less expeditious ashion certainly, in the village burial-ground, nd from the same cause—want of space. Nor as the facility at hand for remedying this evil 1 the country, annexing a portion of the conguous field, been, seemingly, often taken dvantage of. The end, besides this constantly roceeding erasure, as it were, of old graves, as been frequently an elevation of earth to a level above that of the floor of the church, producing damp and decay, and not ministering, one would think, to the health of the congregation; or, if the gutter about the building, commonly seen, may counteract the ill effects alleged, the appearance of the church—a choice example, perhaps—remains impaired. The measure demanded appears plainly to be the enlargement of churchyards, where requisite, throughout the kingdom. The sacredness of the grave being this way ensured, an opportunity presents itself for ennobling the view of the church, as well as imparting to the ground a shaded, solemn aspect, by the planting of trees (shrubberies, or anything resembling gardens, to be avoided); nor should a recommendation in favour of improved forms of head stones, &c., be omitted. There are few spots, in short, so capable of being converted, generally, as some instances already betoken, into scenes of more grateful seclusion, of more impressive beauty, than the village burial-yard.

H.

GRAVEYARDS IN CLERKENWELL.

Among the crying evils of the present day may be classed the system of intra-mural burials. In no place is a reform in this particular more necessary than in the district of Clerkenwell, where they are completely hemmed in and closely abutted on, on all sides, by dwelling-houses and workshops, in many cases deriving light and ventilation solely from these pestilential graveyards. The overcrowded state of one of them has been made the subject of a Government commission (I allude to Spafields); the others (four) are scarcely in a better condition; an examination of them is imperatively necessary. My attention, as district surveyor, has lately been called to the state of the vaults in St. James's Church, where, through quite open gratings, piled in rows, are to be seen coffins seven or eight deep; the graveyard is literally crammed. Strange to say, interments still go on. Extensive workshops are being erected on the adjoining properties.

The attention of Government is now being directed to this subject, and the nuisance must be summarily dealt with. Any further interments should be interdicted, the vaults sealed, and 2 feet of concrete placed over the graveyards.

R. Lacon Sibley.

THE FACE OF SHAKSPEARE.

A late inhabitant of Stratford-on-Avon, Mr. William Warner, has forwarded to us a cast of the front half of Shakspeare's head, from the monumental bust in the parish church, nicely mounted on a black slab. The lovers of the poet, whom—

"Neither man nor muse can praise too much,"

may be glad to hear that copies of this are to be had. The mask appears to be a careful transcript of the original, but the hair and heard seem more detailed.

Mr. Britton, in an interesting little volume, which he has just now printed for the subscribers to his testimonial,* "by way of instalment," gives some particulars of the original monument and of the cast taken by Mr. Bullock in 1814, at his suggestion, with evidence in favour of this being a correct resemblance of the poet, worked it may be from a cast taken from life, or rather, perhaps, death.

METROPOLITAN COMMISSION OF SEWERS.

A general court was held on Thursday last, at the Court House; the Rev. W. Stone in the chair. A letter was received from Mr. Pattison, clerk to the Chelsea Improvement Commissioners, asking for facilities to be afforded to that body for carrying into effect certain cleansing operations, if no legal objection existed to such a course. There being several legal objections, the clerk was ordered to communicate with the commissioners to devise means to meet the difficulties upon the question.

On the question being submitted to the court as to the appointment of two additional surveyors, Mr. Leslie took an objection to their appointment, and called for the report of the committee showing the necessity for them. It appeared there was merely a simple recommendation from the Works Committee. This subject led to a long and rather personal conversation, in which Mr. Leslie, Mr. Bullar, Mr. Chadwick, and the Rev. W. Murray took part; but it was finally resolved that Mr. Bazalgette and Mr. Creasy should be appointed, as assistant-surveyors, at a probationary salary each of 250*l.* per annum.

Mr. Graham, of Battersea, attended the court to complain that several cases of cholera had occurred in his family, arising, as he believed, from a most offensive main sewer receiving the drainage of Clapham and discharging into the Thames, and which sewer was on the boundary of his property. The deposit in this sewer was 16 feet wide and 4 feet deep. Mr. Grant, the surveyor, was ordered to report on the subject.

A deputation from the parish of St. James, Westminster, headed by Mr. Charles Cochrane, attended the court, on the subject of cleansing the streets of that parish by "orderlies."

After some discussion it was finally agreed, on the motion of Sir John Burgoyne, that no further proceedings be taken in the matter.

* Appendix to Britton's Auto-biography, containing biographical, archæological, and critical essays on Shakspeare and Stratford, &c.

A report was presented by Mr. Grant on the state of Albion-place, Wandsworth-road—the place in which cholera has raged to so fearful an extent, and so specially referred to in the last report of the Registrar-General. From it it appeared that between the 27th of July and the 13th of August there were in this place, consisting of 17 houses, 38 cases of cholera, and 25 deaths, and that six of these deaths had occurred in one house; and it also appeared that the cisterns for water were below the level of the cesspools. On the 26th of July there was a very heavy fall of rain, which caused the drains to overflow into the water-cisterns. The day after this storm the first person was attacked; and it was mentioned as a remarkable fact, that no persons were attacked east or west of this place where the cisterns were not liable to this overflow.

Miscellanea.

Money for Public Works.—It appears the great hindrance to any public and national work is the want of funds, and the aversion the Chancellor of the Exchequer has to borrowing for such purposes—but surely there cannot be a more legitimate purpose for borrowing. National works, now in abeyance, or in a very slow course of progress, as the Houses of Parliament, Westminster-bridge, deposit for records, National Gallery, are surely not meant for this generation only, but for ages yet to come; then why should the present generation be taxed for the carrying on of such works, and our posterity have the full enjoyment at our expense? Would it not be far more just that the country should be simply taxed for the interest of a sinking fund for the ultimate redemption of the debt, than be charged with the principal money required for such purposes? The immense advantage to the working classes engaged in building operations should have some consideration. If the Chancellor of the Exchequer had the most ample funds, still the objection would remain; to employ money raised by taxation for the completion of national works I consider both unjust and impolitic upon those now so heavily burthened.—M. P.

Ipswich Mechanics' Institution.—For some time past the committee of this institution have been striving to obtain a proper building for their purposes, but have heretofore not succeeded. Some of our readers will perhaps remember a competition on the subject, to the terms of which we were obliged to object rather strongly. Plans, it seems, have now been matured, by which, at a contemplated expense of 1,900*l.*, will be obtained a lecture-room 63 feet 6 inches long, 40 feet wide, and 25 feet high, and a reading-room 48 feet long, and 28 feet wide. The committee seek assistance, and we shall be glad to find it afforded to them. Mr. Shave Gowing, of Ipswich, receives subscriptions.

Value of Land.—At the sale, on Monday, of the building land at Woodhill, Portshead, the property was bought in at 400*l.* per acre, about four acres of the least valuable part (two acres and a half of which must not be built upon) having been disposed of previously to the sale at that price.—*Hereford Journal.*

RAILWAY JOTTINGS. — The financial position of the Chester and Holyhead line is anything, it is said, but cheering. More than double the present traffic, it seems, will not pay the interest to the preference holders, leaving out of question the holders of the original capital of 2,100,000*l.* ——The contract for constructing the bridge at Chepstow, for the South Wales line, has been taken by Messrs. Smith and Willey, of Liverpool, engineers. The whole is to be of wrought-iron, the largest span being about 300 feet, resting on cast-iron piers or pillars, sunk down to the rock.——The Rhymney Iron Works have contracted, it is said, with the Royston and Hitchin Railway Company to deliver in London 5,000 tons of rails at 4*l.* 18s. 6d. per ton.——The works on the Ipswich and Norwich line are progressing. The viaduct over the Norfolk line is commenced; the bridge near the Victoria-gardens is nearly completed; and the earthworks are proceeding with.——The Edinburgh and Glasgow Company, according to the *Reformer's Gazette*, have opened up the tunnel at their Glasgow station through a space of 90 feet between Cathedral and Holmhead-streets, thus admitting light and air into that portion lying near the station. —— The London and North-Western Company has permitted the issue of assurance tickets at the principal stations on its line. In the event either of loss of life, or personal injury, a first-class passenger, by a payment of threepence, will insure 1,000*l.*; a second-class, by a payment of twopence, 500*l.*; and a third-class, by a payment of one penny, 200*l.* The insurance is irrespective of distance.——In consequence of the increase of business in transmitting intelligence by electric telegraph, says the *Liverpool Albion*, and the great complaints, by the city merchants and the press, on the enormous charges made by the company in comparison with the United States, it is intended to make a great alteration in the scale, so as to render this means of communication more available to all parties. We are glad to hear of it, for the sake of the Company itself as well as the public.——The *Moniteur* announces that the President of the French Republic has authorised Mr. Jacob Brett to establish on the coast of France, between Calais and Boulogne, a submarine telegraph, to cross the Channel, and communicate with the English coast at Dover. The treaty guarantees certain advantages to the French Government, and leaves all the expense to the contractor, to whom it secures a privilege of ten years, should the experiment succeed. The works are to be terminated on 1st September, 1850, at latest.

SUSSEX ARCHÆOLOGICAL SOCIETY.—The fourth annual meeting of the Sussex Archæological Society was held last week, at Arundel. In the absence of the Duke of Norfolk, the chair was taken by the Earl of Arundel and Surrey. At twelve o'clock the members assembled at the Town Hall, where a great number of interesting objects in archæology were exhibited. Some pleasant papers were read, and the members viewed the patchy, degraded castle, and ruinous monuments in the church. The disfigurements in the castle, by Dallaway, afford subjects for reprobation.

BRISTOL-BRIDGE COMPETITION. — The Improvement Committee of the Town Council has awarded a premium of 25*l.* for a design for widening Bristol-bridge, by the corporation architects, Messrs. Pope and Co. It consists, we hear, of two Tuscan columns built upon each of the cutwaters and abutments of the bridge, bearing on their capitals strong iron girders, upon which will be placed iron cantilevers to carry the flagstones of the footway, intended to be 8 feet wide, and surmounted with a balustrade. Eighteen drawings and one model were sent in.

BLIND BUILDERS.—A list of tenders for schools, at Harlow, in Essex; Mr. G. E. Pritchett, architect. The quantities supplied!

		If with Kentish ragstone in random courses.
Ashby	£2,500	£2,740
Harris	2,250	2,285
Smith	2,100	2,242
Prior	2,157	2,337
Carter and Ellis	2,063	2,165
Peck	2,010	2,147
Young	1,970	2,110
Smith (accepted)	1,660	1,802

RAILWAY COMPENSATION CASES. — Several claims on the London and North-Western Company were recently brought before special juries at Birmingham. In the first, 9,000*l.* to 10,000*l.*, it was understood, were claimed by Messrs. Waddell and Izod, for the Hen and Chickens Hotel, through part of the stables only of which the Company had made their way. Informality of notices on the Company's part were urged, and the case was cast aside. The powers of the Company to take compulsory possession of property was to expire on the following day.—The next case was Captain Inge's claim of 1,581*l.* 15s. for a property leased by his ancestors in 1773, for 99 years. Part of the claim consisted of 527*l.* 5s., or 50 per cent. for compulsory sale, on 1,025*l.*, the product of 4 per cent. on 10½ years' purchase of the rents, amounting to 100*l.* The calculation was made according to Inman's tables, which the Company's counsel ridiculed as "a system of thimble-riggery to prove anything required." The valuations on the defendants' part ranged between 550*l.* and 560*l.* The jury returned a verdict for 1,147*l.* 10s. The company had offered 715*l.*, and the claimant had offered to accept 1,340*l.*——The next was a demand of 5,300*l.*, by Mr. Bird, a druggist, for compulsory removal, fixtures, and loss of lease and local business. His rent was 70*l.*, but elsewhere, it was alleged, would be 200*l.* For loss of fixtures 400*l.* were claimed; loss of income at 800*l.* a-year for three years, 2,400*l.*,—forced sale 50 per cent.,—or 3,600*l.* on whole for loss of trade; loss on 700*l.* worth of stock 80 per cent., or 550*l.* The profit on drugs was represented to be sometimes 400 per cent. on prime cost. An accountant stated in evidence that, in 1848, when Mr. Bird's profits were stated to be 750*l.*, his income-tax amounted only to 13*l.* 6s. 3d., in place of 21*l.* 17s. 3d., but that the return was fixed by the Government assessor, and not by the claimant. An agreement for lease, duly stamped, was put in. The company's counsel, however, explained that Mr. Bird did not possess a lease, that the company had themselves purchased the freehold without any such lease, and that the freeholder had merely agreed to give Mr. Bird a lease if he applied for it at the end of the first year of his tenancy. In summing up the assessor stated his opinion that Mr. Bird was merely a tenant for a year. The jury, after much difference, returned a verdict of 935*l.* and 1s. damages. The Company had offered 1,250*l.*

CAMBRIAN ARCHÆOLOGICAL ASSOCIATION.—This society will hold its third annual meeting in Cardiff, on Monday, the 27th inst., and four following days. The president-elect for the year is the Viscount Adare. Cardiff is within reach of many antiquities of interest: the great cromlechau, near St. Nicholas; tumuli, beacons, and camps; the Roman stations of Cardiff and Caerleon, and museum of Roman antiquities at the latter place; a large number of mediæval castles of the first class—Caerphilly, Cardiff, St. Donat's, &c.; Llandaff Cathedral, Ewenny Priory, Margam Abbey, and many interesting smaller churches; there are also very early inscriptions at Lantwit, Margam, &c.

INCREASE OF TRADE.—From a summary of exports during the month ending 5th July, in the *Birmingham Journal*, it appears that there was an increase on glass manufactures of 1,538*l.* on 20,169*l.*,—the value exported during the like period of last year; that on hardwares and cutlery there was an increase of 15,002*l.* on 165,873*l.*; on painters' colours an increase of 2,983*l.* on 12,962*l.*; on iron and steel, an increase of 40,295*l.* on 464,294*l.*; on copper and brass, an increase of 51,533*l.* on 101,986*l.*; and on lead an increase of 13,423*l.* on 11,452*l.* On machinery, however, there was a decrease of 8,953*l.* on 93,871*l.* The following table shows a progressive demand for articles peculiar to the Birmingham district. Even machinery here appears to be progressing, month by month:—

	April.	May.	June.	July.
Glass	£23,458	£20,469	£19,674	£21,707
Hardware and cutlery	190,775	143,466	157,179	180,875
Machinery	27,632	41,239	46,130	84,918
Iron and steel	454,513	436,615	426,689	504,589
Copper and brass	170,483	129,464	109,910	153,519
Tin (wrought and unwrought)	92,128	60,124	67,079	77,895
	958,989	831,397	826,561	1,023,503

PROJECTED WORKS.—Advertisements h[ave] been issued for tenders, by 25th inst., for [the] erection of a party-wall between the groun[ds of] the Paddington Workhouse and that of [the] Lock Hospital; by 23rd, for the erection [and] completion of certain buildings at the back [of,] and adjacent to, the workhouse of St. [Leo]nard's, Shoreditch; by 27th, for building 1,[...] feet of brick sewer, and other works conne[cted] therewith, along the Willow Walk, [Ber]mondsey; by 30th, for the reconstructio[n of] the drainage and water supply, with vari[ous] other works, at the Union Workhouse, Cu[ck]field; by 27th, for works required in the [for]mation of roads at West Croydon station, [and] the extension of the Bricklayers' Arms go[ods] depôt, of the London and Brighton Railway; [by] 8th Sept., for extensive repairs, &c., to the pa[rish] church of Aylesbury; by 28th inst., for [the] erection of Bracknell District Church; by 2[...] for the whole, or any portion of the works [re]quired to be done in the erection of a chu[rch] in All Saints' district, Leeds; by a date [not] specified, for any portion of the works to [be] done in the erection of a church at Hepst[on]hall, Halifax; by a date not specified, for works to be executed in the erection of [St.] Matthew's National School and schoolmast[er's] house, Little London, Leeds (drawings to [be] seen till 21st inst.); by 21st, for the erect[ion] of a national school for 225 children, [with] mistress's house attached, and other buildin[gs;] by 10th September, for the construction [of] three reservoirs, and the masonry of a bri[dge,] for the Manchester Corporation Waterwor[ks;] by 24th September, for works to be execu[ted] in new pauper lunatic asylum, to be erecte[d at] Powick, Worcester (plans, &c. to be seen [on] and after 4th Sept., in place of from 6th ins[t.]); and by 28th inst., for making a road, and pavement and curb-stone, at Southamp[ton] Marsh.

NEW GAS GENERATER.—A patent s[elf-]acting gas apparatus has been exhibited [at] Hull, according to the *Packet*, by Englis[h] Patent Camphine Company. The gas wh[ich] it generates (from camphine or mineral [oil)] is said to produce a light far purer and mo[re] brilliant than that of coal-gas, and without t[he] least noxious vapour. The apparatus consi[sts] of a furnace of cast-iron, divided into t[wo] compartments, in one of which the retort [is] set, the other being filled with fuel, descendi[ng] into the furnace, exactly as the combusti[on] proceeds. In the lower compartment is fix[ed] a double retort, having at one end, outside t[he] furnace, a short vertical pipe. At a little di[s]tance is the gasometer, and above, a ves[sel] containing the fluid, and connected with t[he] retort by a small tube. The fluid flows throu[gh] the upper along the lower compartment of t[he] retort, being decomposed in its passage; [it] then passes through a syphon-box for the r[e]ceipt of any undecomposed fluid; then through a washer to the gas holder. Shou[ld] the gas be generated too rapidly for the burne[rs] which are lit, the rising of the gas holder i[m]mediately raises a lever and cuts off a porti[on] of the supply of fluid. The apparatus can [be] adapted to any number of lights for pub[lic] buildings, churches, lighthouses, gentlemen['s] houses, road-side railway stations, hotels, a[nd] other places where coal gas cannot be obtaine[d.] It is also said to cook with cleanliness and nice[ty.]

ART-UNION OF LONDON EXHIBITION. [—] The works of art purchased by the prizehold[ers] are now being exhibited in the Suffolk-str[eet] Gallery, and will remain on view for th[ree] weeks longer. Subscribers and their frien[ds] will find it wise to pay their visits at on[ce,] while there is plenty of room, and not wait [till] nearly the close, by which course the roo[ms] become most inconveniently crowded.

UNIVERSITY OF LONDON AND ARCHITE[C]TURE.—By the new charter granted to t[he] University of London, the council may instit[ute] examinations for certificates of proficiency [in] any subject they may think fit, connected wi[th] the arts or sciences, such as architecture a[nd] civil engineering. This was spoken of at t[he] closing meeting of the Institute as matter [of] congratulation. *Cela dépend*, as the French s[ay.]

MANCHESTER CATHEDRAL.—The days [of] the old tower of the cathedral church are s[aid] to be numbered. It has long been in a mi[se]rable condition, and the present churchwarde[ns] having called in professional advisers, th[eir] report fully confirms the reports of form[er] architects as to its dangerous state.

No. CCCXLII.

SATURDAY, AUGUST 25, 1849.

UR ecclesiastical structures of the twelfth century, massive, solid, dignified, and imposing, with their careful proportions and quaint carvings, are interesting objects for examination, and ever give pleasure to those who know how to observe. Even in ruin we do not merely see

"A pile decayed,
Bricks in cunning fashion laid,
Ruined buttress, moss-clad stone,
Arch with ivy overgrown,
Stairs round which the lichens creep—
The whole a desolated heap!"

But as a memorial of the olden time, telling of the feudal prime—

"More than history can give
With these ruined towers doth live!"

And the reflection arises—

"Thus it is that vacant air,
MIND informs with visions fair."

We are not about to speak, however, of what they suggest, but what they are. The number and grandeur of the edifices raised in the 12th century are matters for wonderment. As Mr. Freeman remarks, when speaking of the works of this extraordinary period, in his recent "History of Architecture"* (a work to which we owe a notice), "If art had not reached the same zenith of perfection as in the palmy days of Gothic skill, yet the number, vastness, and magnificence of its works attest alike the bounty of founders and the genius of architects. Within one hundred years, or little more, all the cathedral, and probably most of the existing conventual, churches in England were reconstructed, sometimes more than once, while many abbeys were newly founded, and parochial schools innumerable built or rebuilt. And, notwithstanding the transmutations which our churches have since undergone, the remains of this period are yet scattered profusely throughout our country, and in many of our most superb buildings it is the prevalent style. Majestic and awful rather than beautiful, no style is more religious, more imbued with the spirit and position of the church in its own day, the day when St. Anselm braved spoliation and banishment, and St. Thomas sealed his witness with his blood."

Every small village was furnished with a sound substantial church of stone, which in numerous cases has kept its promise of long endurance, and still serves to give stability and importance to the localities which, but for this, had lost their identity long ago. Even in a constructive point of view, they contrast unfavourably for our time with some of the churches of the day, which, cheap, flimsy, and unsubstantial, will not outlast the present generation. We have seen several specimens lately which are a positive disgrace to the parish, the architect, and the builder.

Winchester Cathedral, Gloucester Cathedral, Southwell, Tewkesbury, Rochester,† and others, described at different times in our pages, afford

good examples of twelfth century buildings. In our present number we give a view of ROMSEY Abbey Church, taken from the north-east ;* a structure which presents, as completely as any remaining, the outline and general appearance of a purely Norman Conventual Church. In its details, however, it is transitional. The pointed arch makes its appearance in various parts amongst the round arches, and at the western end of the nave the Early English style wholly prevails. A descriptive account of the church, by the Rev. J. L. Petit, will be found in our third volume (p. 446). We will here, therefore, only briefly say it was commenced, on the site of an earlier church, about the middle of the twelfth century; built (as Scott says of Lindisfarne),—

"Ere the art was known,
By pointed aisle, and shafted stalk,
The arcades of an alleyed walk
To emulate in stone."

It is cruciform; there is a semi-circular absis on the east side of each arm of the transept, as was not unusual in Norman and Byzantine churches. Each aisle of the choir likewise terminates with a similar absis formed in the thickness of the wall, so as not to show externally. The west end contains a singularly lofty triple lancet window. In the south wall of the nave next the transept, one of the original Norman doorways remains, and is now used as a window. It presents a series of concentric arches adorned with various sculptured enrichments, and supported by two columns on either side, with enriched capitals. In the external wall of the south transept, next the door, is a curious sculptured figure of Christ on the cross, about 5½ feet high, and close down on the ground, with a band from the clouds above pointing to it. Near it is a small recess in the wall, probably to receive a lamp or taper. Some of the capitals in the aisles, at the east end, are sculptured with figures of singular appearance, and have led to three communications to the Society of Antiquaries, printed in the "Archæologia."†

The tower, at the crux, is low and massive, and is surmounted by a monstrous modern abomination in the shape of a wooden enclosure for the bells, which suggests the idea of a brewhouse or a tanner's drying shed in Bermondsey. It seems exceedingly well adapted for—lighting the fires, to which luminous fate, and speedily, we, with our heartiest wishes, commend it.

A short time ago the interior of the church was restored under the able direction of Mr. B. Ferrey, at a cost, as we were told, of about 3,000l. At the present moment works are going on outside under the guidance of the churchwarden only, against which course we very earnestly protest. Structures of this kind are nationally important, and should not be touched except under proper advice. Mr. Jenvey may be a very good churchwarden, but he cannot be competent to meddle with the architecture of Romsey Abbey Church. Something is said about taking off the lead and putting slate in its stead ; but we hope our expostulation may be in time to prevent the exhibition of so bad a principle, and induce application to a proper director.

Internally it is much to be regretted that the main arches of the chancel and its aisles have been blocked up,—possibly there were reasons for it, not apparent to the observer. With the new font (a melancholy imitation of Early English) the architect could not have had any thing to do. The old one, if we remember rightly, was much superior.

The transept internally is very interesting, but is marred by galleries. These ought to be removed.

The central tower was originally open as a lantern, and must have had a good effect ; but, to form a chamber for the ringers in the upper part of it, at the time of erecting the wooden monstrosity already mentioned, a false ceiling was put in. At the recent restoration this ceiling was raised up somewhat, but still shuts off about 20 feet of the lantern. And here we find a little bone to pick with friend Ferrey. Not because the ceiling is there,—he would of course have wished to get rid of it altogether, if the authorities had been prepared to carry out another arrangement for the bells,—but for a little falsification which may tend to perpetuate the interpolated ceiling. Against the four sides of the lantern are attached-columns which run up to the top, and are therefore of course intersected by the modern ceiling, and what we object to is, that at this intersection, to form a finish inside, below the ceiling, Norman capitals have been introduced to terminate the columns, which may serve as an argument in years to come, when their modern date is forgotten, against those who may wish to restore to the church its crowning glory: an excusable crime after all, some will say; and we are quite willing to admit it.

Such of our readers as are led to devote one of these pleasant summer days to Romsey Abbey* should notice a touching little monument to the memory of the infant daughter of a surgeon of the town, modelled by himself. It is inscribed—

"Is it well with the child ?
"It is well."

Near to it is a mural tablet, by Flaxman, to Henry, Viscount Palmerston, and his second wife.

The church has the advantage of a sexton, James Major, who seems to prize every stone of it, and whose intelligence and right feeling deserve a passing notice.

CONSIDERATIONS AFFECTING THE REMOVAL OF SMITHFIELD MARKET.

IN matters connected with public health, it must be confessed by everybody at all competent to form an opinion, that there prevails in England a carelessness upon the part of the public in general, and a total absence of system upon that of the persons especially charged with its care. In no case has the truth of this observation been more painfully verified than in the recent attempt to obtain the removal of Smithfield Market. With the exception of the parties interested in the maintenance of this nuisance, everybody appears disposed to admit that it is desirable that it should be removed. A committee of the House of Commons has examined patiently a great number of witnesses, both for and against the removal ; and finally, it has presented a report to the House to recommend the latter course. A witty member of the House utters some jokes, of very equivocal taste, — and the affair is shelved.

We Englishmen talk loudly, and praise ourselves much upon the high state of civilization of our country. The beauty of our capital ; the infinite pains we take to maintain

---

* Published by Masters, Aldersgate-street, London.

† Parts of the interior of Rochester Cathedral are exceedingly interesting and instructive. The exterior has been miserably mangled and marred. The state of the great western door,—one of the finest specimens of an enriched Norman doorway in England,—is to be regretted ; but if it would have no better treatment in restoration than some other parts have received, it is much better it should remain as it is.

* See p. 402.

† From Dr. Latham, Vol. XIV. p. 136: from Sir H. C. Englefield, following the former ; and from W. Latham, Esq., Vol. XV., p. 304. "The length of this church, according to the curious description given in the addenda to Brown Willis's Mitred Abbies, is 260 feet ; and its width, that is to say, the length of the transept, 130 feet. His words are :—' Ecclesia de Rumeseye, de fundatione regis Edgari, continet in longitudine circa 90 steppys, et patum ultra ; item in latitudine continet circa 45 steppys mensa.' The height of the tower is about 120 feet, and that of the body of the church is said to be 80 exactly."—Spence's *Descriptive Essays*, p. 37.

* Winchester Cathedral and the church of St. Cross are but a short distance from Romsey, and may be included in the jaunt.

its salubrity; the attention we pay to the comforts of the humbler classes of our fellow citizens; the care we take of the education of the rising generation,—are sentences constantly in our mouths. Gladly would the nation sacrifice in any manner, to effect, really, an amelioration in any of these objects, we may safely and proudly assert. Yet either from ignorance or from carelessness we allow the existence of a state of things, in the very heart of London, which is a shame and a disgrace to any Christian land,—which spreads around in every direction the seeds of physical pestilence,—and gives rise to a moral degradation more awful still.

Have any of the readers of this article ever visited the streets and lanes in the neighbourhood of Smithfield? It is to be feared that there are not many bold enough to expose themselves to the sight of the accumulation of horrors there congregated. If there had been many so bold, our Government would certainly never have dared to allow the money, lately spent upon the public improvements, to have been employed merely to make clean the outside of the cup and the platter, whilst the inside still remains so full of ravening wickedness. For we have within a musket-shot of the great thoroughfares of Holborn and King-street,—within the district, in fact, bounded by those streets to the south and east, by the market itself and Goswell-street to the north and east, by Clerkenwell and Field-lane on the north and west,—a collection of abominations, the mere recollection of which is enough to make the gorge rise. Narrow streets,—badly paved, worse drained; houses ill-built, rotten, damp, and falling to pieces; the entries below the level of the street, so that the drainage takes place inwards instead of outwards; no privies worthy even of that name; and in the midst of all this misery and filth, every now and then we find a private slaughter house, a knacker's yard, a tripe-boiler's, a fat-melter's, or a sort of stall to receive the animals for the next market. Children swarm in the midst of these sights and scenes; for it appears to be a law of nature that our race should develop itself with the greatest prolificness under circumstances of the greatest misery. And here we,—we who talk and boast of the care we take of the children of the poor,—allow them to wallow in the blood and filth of these most foul and disgusting operations; we allow them to accustom themselves to sights and scenes which make blood, suffering, and death objects of daily and hourly occurrence. What are we entitled to expect from a population thus contaminated? Should any great political convulsion upset the elaborately artificial system of our society, and drag us through the horrors of a revolution, it is amongst them that the future Dantons will seek the instruments willing and able to commit the crimes and butcheries they may order. In the interest of society then, if not from a higher motive, it behoves us to examine whether some remedy cannot be found for the present awful state of this neighbourhood; and, when once found, the pressure from without must be employed to make the Government fulfil its duty to a class of society so long neglected, and remove a nuisance which can but become greater as the City of London increases in wealth and importance.

Presented thus, the questions to be solved are,—Firstly, whether the state of the neighbourhood might not be much improved without displacing the market? Secondly, whether, the market removed, the nuisances would cease? Thirdly, what new organization would be necessary to insure the supply of butchers' meat for the London market, and the most favourable conditions for the maintenance of the public health?

The first two questions, by implication, involve the examination of the advisability of retaining the market in its present position,—because, if it be shown that a market in the middle of a town is necessarily accompanied by a series of grievous nuisances, its removal is the first object to be aimed at.

Now, it is an undoubted fact that the neighbourhood of Smithfield might be immeasurably improved, even though the market were retained. What takes place therein is shocking enough, but a mere cattle-market does not necessarily imply a dangerous state of public health. To get the cattle to and from Smithfield exposes them doubtlessly to much torture; the narrow space they are forced into, and the means adopted to make them crowd together, doubtlessly cause much pain and suffering to the animals; the absence of water in summer, the filthy mud they stand in in winter, doubtlessly aggravate their sufferings. But we in England only punish cruelty in detail. Mr. Martin's Act can reach a costermonger who ill-treats his donkey; it is powerless to force the City to find the room necessary to prevent the cruelty to thousands of bullocks, exposed every week. And so the grazier has to suffer by the loss of weight of his animals—the public is forced to consume a description of meat which cannot be in its normal condition of healthiness. This is a sad tale, but it might exist without the accompaniment of the sadder tales told by the neighbourhood; for, at the market of Sceaux, near Paris, which also is too small for the number of cattle exposed, much cruelty prevails. Moreover, it is to be observed that there are parts of London removed from Smithfield, which are as foul as that sink of all that is disgusting; for instance, Whitechapel, Rotherhithe, and the Follies of Southwark. There is, then, no absolute connection between the market and the nuisances around it; they may both enjoy their sad celebrity in perfect independence of one another. But there is an important remark to be made—namely, that a market always is accompanied by a peculiar set of annoyances, which depress the value of the property in its neighbourhood, and which, by so much, encourage the establishment of certain industries, which would not be tolerated in other localities. Now, as our police only acts *ex post facto*, and upon the complaint of injured parties, it is almost impossible to prevent the concentration of nuisances in such localities. In France, where it is necessary to have a license to open a building or establishment devoted to a trade of a nature to annoy the neighbourhood, it is easy to control not only their location, but the conditions of salubrity in which they are erected. We have no such control, and it may admit of question whether, after all, the results obtained by our defective police in these matters are not as satisfactory as those obtained by the elaborate one in force in France. Be that as it may, it is certain that much might be done (and it is a foul shame upon the corporation that it still remains to be done) to improve the neighbourhood of Smithfield. The drainage and the paving of the streets are surely things easily improved: some means might be devised to open new lines of communication, to widen existing thoroughfares; but, above all, some regulations should be adopted to enforce the observance of the laws of common decency in the different slaughter-houses and bone-shops of these now-unnoticed localities. It is not too much to assert that hardly one of these establishments is constructed upon the principles of drainage, ventilation, or supply of water now universally received as being necessary to ensure the healthy state of the neighbourhood in which they are situated.

Secondly. As to the question whether the market being removed the nuisances would cease, what has been said above may be applied here. There is no inevitable connection between the two, their separate and independent existences may therefore well continue. But it is more than probable that many of these unwholesome industries would disappear if the market were removed. For instance, the cattle-layers would of course accompany the new market; the low lodging and public-houses would cease to receive their present tenants; the class of people who would succeed them, in all probability, would be better—they cannot be worse; and, by degrees, the foul industries of the quarter would be forced to observe better regulations. We are not justified in saying that the removal of the market will inevitably cause the nuisances, now agglomerated round it, to cease; but every reason exists to induce us to believe that insensibly they would do so. At any rate, their degree of concentration would be less.

Subsidiarily, we may observe, that the connection between the market and the abominations which surround it is so great, that the latter may almost be regarded as the consequences of holding the former in its present position. The market diminishes the value of the property in the neighbourhood; it facilitates the establishment of industries which are carried on under conditions unfavourable to public health; it agglomerates a poor, corrupt population in quarters fit only to aggravate their poverty and their corruption. No respectable man, with any degree of refinement of taste, could live near Smithfield. The ground is, therefore, left open to those whose trades require contiguity thereto. Slaughter-houses, cattle layers, tripe boilers, knacker's yards, flourish in the precincts of the great market for the sale of the articles on which their owners work. We may, therefore, hold the market responsible for the abominations of its neighbourhood; and even were it not itself a cause of unnecessary cruelty to the animals, and of loss to the graziers, we should be justified in calling loudly for the removal of a nuisance which is a shame and a blot upon any civilized country.

Thirdly, we have to consider what new organization would be necessary to secure the supply of butcher's meat for London, and the regulations connected with this matter it would be advisable to adopt in the interest of the public health. This involves an examination of the regulations to be enforced in the cattle market, the slaughtering and converting of the carcases.

There are numerous schemes abroad for choosing a substitute for Smithfield, which have as many opponents as admirers. Some are for transferring it (the market) to Islington, some to King's-cross. But both these schemes are based upon what is in no way proved—the necessity for concentration. They are, moreover, only means of shifting the question. Both Islington and King's-cross are already surrounded with houses. London is "going out of town" in both directions. We shall soon find that the same evils will spring up there that we complain of in the present locality. Besides, if the market be still kept in London, why move it? The dwellers of that part of the town appear to have grown to the filthy state in which they live; why force others to undergo such a seasoning? Islington and King's-cross will soon be as densely inhabited as Clerkenwell, or even the City. Between two crowded localities there can be little reason to choose, beyond the fact of the one having for years enjoyed the monopoly of the nuisance. If any change be made, it must be by removing the market altogether out of London,—to Romford, to Finchley, to Hanwell, or to Croydon; perhaps by establishing markets at all these points on different days of the week. The cattle bought at these markets might then be brought to the different slaughter-houses, or to the different butchers' shops, should they prefer to kill upon their own premises. Rules for the sanitary condition of the slaughter-houses should be drawn up, and no operations of this nature should be allowed to be carried on but in places licensed to that effect, the license to be granted by a board of magistrates upon a report of a district surveyor. If the slaughter-houses be well built, there need be no restriction as to the neighbourhood in which they are to be established; of course, care being taken to remove them from the immediate contact of the public. But the tallow melting shops, the tripe dealers, and the bone burners, as they give rise to foul miasmas, so they should not be allowed to work in the midst of the usual population of a large city. After some years the forced use of public slaughter-houses might become law; but as a transition, the butchers might retain the right to slaughter at home, the more especially as their own interest would soon make them prefer the large establishments, where the necessary sanitary conditions are so much more easily attained.

The substitute for Smithfield is, after all, the most difficult part of the question. As to the slaughter-houses, the results obtained upon the continent from their adoption have been so remarkable, their success so perfect, both as commercial speculations and as guarantees for the public health, that nothing but the desperate obstinacy our organised bodies invariably oppose to the adoption of anything foreign, can account for their not being applied in England. But the question of the new market is far from being as simple. In fact, a central market, inasmuch as it brings in contact a vast number of buyers and sellers, renders monopoly impossible. Again, a butcher from Camberwell can easily attend at Smithfield, whereas a market on the northern or eastern side of London would force him to absent himself from home all night. The travelling expenses of the butcher must, in the end, be paid by the public; any injudicious choice of the new market which might augment them, would, therefore, have for effect to increase the price of meat. Careful investigation must, then, be made into the sources of supply, the mode of arrival, and the centres of consumption, before any definite course be adopted. But we must bear in mind that after all the difficulties of this question are not so great as they appear. The number of butchers who buy live cattle is small comparatively; in Paris only about one-half attend the markets, the rest buy the dead meat. Doubtlessly in London the proportion is about the same, for our dead meat market increases in importance every day, owing to the railways and steamboats. A change in the market might perhaps only augment the number of retail butchers; and as the wholesale buyers would divide their expenses over a greater amount of capital in movement, the increased expense would not be sensible. But again, even supposing that the whole augmentation be borne by each separate butcher, it is more than questionable whether the weight he would gain by purchasing animals in a more healthy state would not amply compensate the money he would spend. A bullock in a London stable, whatever be the mode upon which he has been fattened, cannot lose less than 8 lbs. weight per day; what must be the loss upon the poor animals worried, driven, and tortured through the long agony of their exposure on the market? And the public health! Who can estimate the difference in the nutritive qualities of meat supplied by animals in a normal condition from that furnished by the wearied, feverish victims of our present most absurd and barbarous system?

The difficulty of a change in the locality of the market is, nevertheless, very great. Not so, however, the change in the system of slaughtering. For a number of years the proprietors of the present establishments might be allowed to enjoy all their existing liberties or rights, on the simple condition of executing the works necessary to isolate their establishments from the public gaze, to insure proper drainage and removal of offal, and to furnish the means of effectually cleansing their establishments. Facilities should be given for the erection of public slaughter-houses, either by companies or by municipalities. In all cases where they have been built in France, the revenues have been such as to make such constructions good speculations. At Paris, in 1847, the revenues (gross) were 1,200,000f., nearly; the expenses, including employés, repairs, water, lighting, &c., were not 140,000f., leaving net 1,060,000f. to pay the interest on a capital of 18,000,000f. In the town of Havre the abattoirs are built upon an 18½ years' lease; and yet the proprietor makes money by his speculation. At Caen the abattoirs produce a net revenue of 24,000f., to pay the interest of a capital of 300,000f. Everywhere the results are about the same; nor can there be any reason to doubt but that in England the results would be equally favourable. The butchers of Paris, at first, violently opposed the establishment of the abattoirs; but now they are so convinced of their utility and commodity that they would almost as vigorously oppose any return to the former system. Indeed, it must evidently be to the interest of the butcher that his meat be killed in the most perfect conditions to insure its preservation, and to satisfy the public that every precaution is taken to insure a supply of wholesome meat.

In the matter of public inspection of the quality of the food exposed to sale, we, a nation who read our Bible much, would do well to take example by the laws of Moses. They were, it is true, given for a nation inhabiting warm climates; but whether in England or in Syria, it cannot be a matter of indifference to eat of animals healthy or unhealthy. As it is, not the slightest control is exercised; and it is a fact well known in the trade, that lately a noble duke sent to Smithfield a large number of sheep tainted with the small-pox. Such things could not occur in any civilized country but our own. We push the horror of the intervention of the Government authorities to such an extent, that it appears we prefer to be poisoned rather than let them interfere. It is true, however, that the absurdities of the Sewers Commission fully warrant our objections to governmental action.

As for the other trades connected with the conversion of the carcases of animals, slaughtered either for our food or for the dogs and cats of London, they should, under no possible circumstances, be retained in the centre of the town. Science has not been able hitherto to obviate the foul odours they give rise to; they should, therefore, be, without hesitation, consigned to such positions as would guarantee the public health against their deleterious effects. And yet in the present day, whilst the press is crying forth, and with reason, against the imperfect system of the London sewerage, we allow the air of the very centre of the town to be contaminated by the various trades which have been for so many years carried on near Field-lane.

In face of the public apathy, what is to be done in these most important matters? To whom are we to turn,—where are we to address ourselves, to secure a calm disinterested examination? In the House of Commons we are met by flat jokes from Mr. B. Osborne, about his father being offended by the smells of the Westminster sewers,—an argument, as was before observed, as absurd as deficient in taste. The Home Office is to examine the question; but as, in all probability, a set of lawyers and crotchety doctors will be named upon the commission, the results will, in all probability, be about as successful as those attained by the Sewers Commission. The corporation of the City of London have already given us the means of judging of the temper with which they would be likely to take up the question. Their interest in the maintenance of the existing state of things is, moreover, so great, that they cannot reasonably be expected to be impartial. It is to the press only we can turn, with any confidence, to aid in the removal, or at least in the amelioration, of this gigantic nuisance. The fourth power of the realm must again teach the others that their duties cannot be neglected with impunity. Could the evil effects arising from the present state of the neighbourhood of Smithfield, and its congeners in filth, be confined to the places themselves, we would say, in God's name, let those who like such scenes enjoy themselves to their heart's content. But the moral and physical pestilences spread far and wide. "The wind bloweth where it listeth," and carries the germs of sickness in every direction. The restless mind, contaminated in the same scenes, leaves them to spread its direful action elsewhere. It is the duty of every one to strive to eradicate both these sources of evil,—more especially is it the duty of the noblest and most powerful instrument we possess to spread the happiness and comfort of our race. It is the duty of every one to protest loudly against the existence of a state of things which, it cannot be too often repeated, is a blot upon the civilization of our country,—a shame and a disgrace to any Christian land, and which must, if allowed still to revel in all the rich luxuriance of its mental and physical pollution, be a curse to the people who tolerate it.

G. R. B.

Northampton Corn Exchange Competition.—The directors have selected two designs, but the names of the authors are not yet stated. Two correspondents complain of the circular which they have received; one says:—"The pompous curtness without courtesy of the notification is only another nail driven, it is to be hoped, in the coffin of competition. Thanks—brief thanks—it would seem, are matters that enter not into the consideration of these gentlemen directors as being in any way necessary in the light of a slight return for the attention bestowed in their behalf by competing architects. Who are the chosen two? Perhaps, indeed, the rejected competitors may consider themselves honoured by having their designs returned duly carriage-paid.—Φ."

Wilton Church.—The architects wish us to say that the cost of Wilton Church was 26,000*l.*, not 36,000*l.*, as stated. The cost was given us on the spot as printed.

PLANS FOR THE DRAINAGE OF LONDON.

On Monday, the 20th, the day appointed for the consideration, by the Sewers Commission, of the plans of Mr. Phillips and Mr. Austin, for the entire drainage of London, and such others as might be sent in up to that date, the court was well attended by commissioners, and the space allotted to visiters was crowded to excess. Mr. C. Johnson presented a letter from Mr. Bailey Denton, civil engineer, which set forth that he was most anxious to present a plan, but that the time that had been specified was insufficient to prepare the same, and asking for the period to be extended.—It appeared that fifty-eight plans had been sent in, and that amongst the competitors were some of the first civil engineers of the day.* Mr. Chadwick was for sending all the plans to the Works Committee,—Mr. Leslie, that the court should consider them. The latter gentleman also suggested the necessity of care to prevent piracy of ideas. Mr. Alderman Lawrence thought they should not be tied, as a whole, to any one plan, as they might find it expedient to take portions of several, each portion being good in itself, but yet not good as a distinct plan, which principle had been adopted in several public buildings,—the Royal Exchange and London-bridge as instances. They might borrow ideas, not with the view of stealing them, but to reward those by whom they were given.

After a long and irregular conversation the following provisional resolutions were put *seriatim*, and agreed to:—

"That all proposals and plans sent to the court before and during its sitting be received.

That the time for amending the present plans, and for sending in other plans, be extended to October 1, 1849.

That each of the competitors who have sent in plans be required to send in, in the course of this week, a concise statement of the main features, whether in principle or in details, of his own plan, and that such statements be printed for the commissioners.

That outline maps, with such information as to altitudes as exist in the office, be forthwith prepared and lithographed, and that each of the competitors who have already sent in plans be, on his application for the same, supplied with a copy thereof gratis, and that future competitors be supplied with copies thereof, at a charge sufficient to cover the cost of paper and printing."

In pursuance of the order of a former court, Mr. Joseph Smith had attended the process of the various borings along the proposed line of tunnel sewer, and it was resolved, "That the sections of the borings be lithographed when finished, and circulated among the commissioners, and given to competitors."

In reference to those borings, it will be recollected that at the first court held, on the proposed tunnel of Mr. Phillips, Dr. Buckland asserted unequivocally "that there was not an atom of London clay between Rotherhithe tunnel and the base of Shooter's Hill," and that "it glanced off at the north-east corner of St. Paul's." Since that time evidence of the most satisfactory nature, and from unquestionable authority, has been obtained, that it does exist, and in large quantities, in places altogether denied in the speech of Dr. Buckland, as will be found in the following statement—

At Greenwich Marshes, opposite Blackwall, 55 feet of London clay.

Near the London Dock and St. Katharine's Dock, 55 feet.

At Bermondsey, 55 feet.

Near London-bridge, 130 feet.

And, extending upwards, it was found at Lambeth, 160 feet; at Westminster, 170 feet; at Kensington, 170 feet; and at Brompton, 237 feet; and for a considerable distance above London-bridge the bed of the river is cut in the blue clay.

Thus it may be considered that, at all events, one of the difficulties anticipated has really no existence.

* The statements of some of the competitors have been forwarded to us, and we shall of course be happy to receive others. To print them, however, as requested, is out of the question.

CITY OF LONDON WORKHOUSE.

GENERAL BLOCK PLAN.

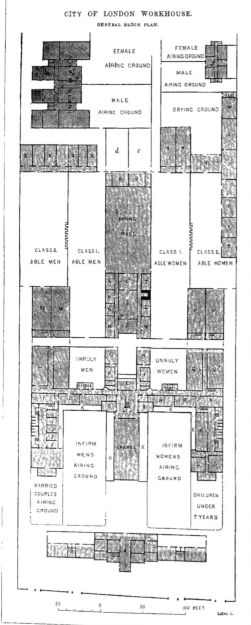

| FEMALE AIRING GROUND | FEMALE AIRING GROUND |
| MALE AIRING GROUND |

MALE AIRING GROUND | DRYING GROUND

DINING HALL

| CLASS 2. ABLE MEN | CLASS 1. ABLE MEN | CLASS 1. ABLE WOMEN | CLASS 2. ABLE WOMEN |

UNRULY MEN | UNRULY WOMEN

INFIRM MENS AIRING GROUND | CHAPEL | INFIRM WOMENS AIRING GROUND

MARRIED COUPLES AIRING GROUND

CHILDREN UNDER 7 YEARS

50　　0　　50　　100 FEET

LAING f.

THE CITY OF LONDON UNION WORKHOUSE.

In accordance with the promise made when we gave a view of the new City of London workhouse, recently erected in the Bow-road,* we annex a general block plan of the establishment, with descriptive references. It is intended to accommodate 1,200 persons. The dining hall, an apartment of large size (about 100 ft. long and more than 50 ft. wide), has an open timber roof, of queen-post construction. The chapel roof, the general effect of which the architect should endeavour to improve before the building is thrown open, has cast-iron principals resting on small iron columns.

References.

A. Porter's lodge and committee rooms.	S. Children under 7.
B. Receiving wards.	T. Work-rooms.
C. Master's office.	U. Drying room.
D. Master's room.	V. Laundry.
E. Matron's room.	W. Mangling room.
F. Stores.	X. Workshops.
G. Assistant master.	Y. Central hall, with a staircase communi-
H. Assistant matron.	cating with all parts
I. Infirm men.	of the house.
J. Married couples' rooms.	Z. Steam-engine.
K. Arcades.	a. Scullery.
L. Unruly men.	b. Kitchen.
M. Able-bodied men.	c. Pantry.
N. Stores.	d. Male imbecile airing ground.
O. Imbecile wards.	e. Female imbecile airing
P. Able-bodied women.	ground.
Q. Unruly women.	f. Fever wards.
R. Infirm women.	g. Washhouse.

MODEL TOWNS.†

THAT the establishment of model dwellings, baths, and washhouses,—the opening of mechanics' and other instructive and national institutions, museums, libraries, lecture-rooms, and schools,—the promotion of sanitary reform in towns, and the laying out of public parks, walks, and pleasure-grounds around them,—the agitation of the short-time or early-closing movement,—&c., &c., are all preparing the way, however slowly or feebly, for a mighty organization and expansion into model streets, districts, and *towns*, there cannot, we think, be a doubt. The principles of such improvements, if commendable in detail, cannot but be good in the aggregate; that which is beneficial here and there, cannot be much otherwise when everywhere extended. But it is not in the form of such model elements and exemplars alone as those we have just instanced that the first beginnings of a vast and promising, and as it were a natural and inevitable process or growth of accumulative *system*, or enlightened associative organization of families and individuals into great and exemplary *commonwealths*, can be traced. We observe the rudiments of the same interesting and growing process also in those widespreading and increasing agglomerations of men into organized and powerful unions such as those of joint-stock and other common-good associations, which would seem to be rapidly crystallizing, as it were, the loose and heterogeneous units of self-interest in the community, and requiring only, one would almost think, to spread forth a network of connecting tentacles or radii from their separate centres, till the whole be interlaced and combined into just such a wider and more comprehensive joint-stock union or association for the common weal, as ought of itself, together with combinations for health and enjoyment, as well as for industry and wealth, to constitute a sort of model town.

It would be well, however, at once to bring a system of enlightened and connected purposes to bear upon these striking features of the nineteenth century, and to guide its pregnant developments into proper, permanent, and concurrent channels of direction, for the simultaneous common good of *every class* of the community. With joint-stock and other great associations and establishments, commercial or manufacturing, and much more so with more limited companies and individual

* See page 379, *ante*.

† National Evils and Practical Remedies; with the Plan of a Model Town. Illustrated by Two Engravings. Accompanied by an Examination of some Important Moral and Political Problems. By James S. Buckingham. P. Jackson, St. Martin's-le-Grand.

capitalists, worldly prosperity and riches are accumulated only by the comparatively few, while the many reap little or no personal profit or permanent prosperity from them. And, moreover, the rich are ever becoming richer, and the poor poorer, in a rapidly increasing ratio, the final result of which, if not timely checked, it is fearful to contemplate. That result, in fact, is a certain and complete separation or split of the community into two great elements of mortal strife, in which it is but too easy to see that the pent-up stream of misery and want will overflow its restricted limits, and overwhelm everything great, and rich, and noble.

It would be well, indeed, to take time by the forelock, and hastily to retrace our steps, could we but see our *practicable* way to the site, materials, and outlined scheme and specification of some more just and wide-spread diffusion of riches, or, at least, of competencies, as the basis of a system that would ultimately comprehend even the poorest outcast of the present period of unsatisfactory and dangerous extremes within the sunshine of an assured, contented, and serene prosperity. As for the elements, the materials, of so great and practical a good,—as said, we certainly cannot but see our way to these in the successful practical endeavours of really noble and manly natures to establish model institutions, not only for the physical, but for the educational and industrial improvement of the mass. Let us only extend the limits and purposes of this good work, as far as possible, with discretion and good sense, as well as system. Let us cautiously consider how these already crystallizing, organizing, elements of a practical and beneficial system, can best be extended and agglomerated into more or less complete, consistent, and self-supporting organizms of industry and happiness,—into model towns, in short, or joint-stock companies on the great scale, each comprehending, as far as possible, within and around its own respective precincts, everything requisite to the life and the enjoyment of the limited thousands or tens of thousands destined to share in its benefits, and to reside within its walls,—with not only a strict municipal army or organization of *manufacturing* industry, but also an *agricultural*, as indeed a main and essential branch of the mafacturing industry itself, inclusive.

The *idea* is by no means a *merely theoretical*, far less a *new* one. Nay, from facts authenticated in history, as in the case of the Cretans, according to Rollin,—the ancient Germans, according to Tacitus, Cæsar, and Herder,—and the Peruvians and Mexicans, according to Robertson,—it would almost appear as if co-operative commonwealths, with great prosperity and enjoyment, were amongst the most anciently established facts in the history of the human race in its more civilized forms of ancient times. And even in modern experience it is well known that flourishing communities exist in America on the principle of co-operative association for the common weal. Authorities, ancient and modern, too, entitled to more or less respect, have recorded their favourable opinion of such a systematization of human efforts,—as witness, Minos, Lycurgus, Theseus, Plato, Moses, the Essenes (or pre-Christians), and the Apostles themselves; also in less ancient times, Sir Thomas More, Bishop Berkeley—to whom Pope attributed "every virtue under heaven," Condorcet, W. Godwin, Babbage, Mill—the historian of India and moral philosopher, with many others. And, indeed, what was it but this element of good in the fallacious and abominable doctrines of Owen and his Socialists that redeemed even them from contempt while they excited the horror of every well constituted mind, with bastard doctrines of communism and irreligion which Owen was but too anxious to veil and withdraw, when he found he had only succeeded in damning both his own previously high philanthropic character and the cause in which he was engaged?

But to our more immediate purpose, which is to give our readers some little idea of Mr. Buckingham's opinions on the subject of model-towns. We confess we opened his very interesting volume with some misgivings, that we might find in it much that would appear to be either impracticable or otherwise objectionable—not by any means from personal considerations as to the author—quite the contrary—but from knowing how the subject had been so almost inextricably entangled and interlarded by others with impracticabilities quite inconsistent with the nature of man as he at present exists; and more particularly as regards the evils of unmitigated *communism* contrasted with and apart from the benefits of *individual association*; but our mind was speedily re-assured on these points, and although we do not mean to bind ourselves down to the author's hopes or opinions, we do think his subject well handled, and worthy of wide-spread perusal and careful consideration.

Previous to the development of his plan, the author probes pretty deeply the evils to be remedied. These evils—the existing evils of society—he ranks under the heads of ignorance, intemperance, national prejudice, monopoly, war, competition, the helpless and hopeless condition of the unfortunate in every country in Europe, and the clashing of the interests of various classes and professions, such as those of law and medicine, with their duty to the community at large and their clients, patients, &c., in particular. These evils, all of them, he proposes by specific, and, as he conceives, practical measures, to remedy; and, with pardonable allusion to previous suggestions, he points attention to the fact that many of his own most cherished ideas, stigmatized while he was urging them as "visionary," as "very good in theory but not in practice," or even as altogether "absurd," have since been favourably received or finally realized.*

On his particular views as to the several specific remedies for prevalent evils we cannot at present enter, except so far as they may incidentally appear in what is to follow. In treating of the productive power of associated labour, he says—

"Surely what large landowners and large manufacturers effect for themselves by the labour of others, can be quite as easily effected by the labourers, under a proper organization, for their own benefit; and this is what a great number desire to see attempted at least, stimulated as they are by the sight of so many large establishments giving such enormous fortunes to their masters, out of the profits of *their* labour.

They perceive, for instance, the immense power to effect the greatest undertakings, conferred by co-operation or association, as in the case of railroads, insurance companies, mining associations, &c. The wealthiest man in England could not, of himself, and out of his own means, have constructed the Great Western Railway; but, by a union of capital, skill, and labour, in such proportions as to be readily recognized for dividends and payments, the work was easy; and now the heaviest goods can be transported the longest distances in a short space of time, and at very trifling expense, compared with the enormous cost of conveying a bale of heavy goods on horse-back from London to Edinburgh, by several weeks' journey, which it required for a single horse, a few centuries ago.

In short, it is like the difference between carrying a cargo of 10,000 bales of cotton from India to England in one large ship of 2,000 tons burden, compared with the conveyance of the same bales, each in a single canoe, requiring 10,000 separate boats, and 200,000 men at least to navigate them—the latter showing the costliness of individual, and the other the economy of associated labour."

Government, he conceives, might do an immense deal to forward the right "organization of labour," and resolve the great problem of the age. Indeed, he points attention to the fact that Government is already well and practically initiated into all the essential principles of the *art*—if we may call it so.

"In nothing, perhaps, is the superiority of organization and association more powerfully seen than in the arrangements of the Post-office, where the greatest degree of dispatch, punctuality, economy, and productiveness are exhibited. By the power of organization and association of labour, 252 letters, at a penny each, can be carried for a guinea (the estimated average price of one, if sent by individual messengers), within the kingdom; and the proportion of difference is still greater in *foreign* letters, supposing them at present to average a shilling each; while such is the punctuality and precision with which all the operations of this great example of the 'Organization of Labour' in the General Post-office are carried on, that, no matter how obscure the individual to whom a letter is addressed, if its superscription be legible, and the person addressed be in existence, the letter is ultimately almost sure to find him out.

Notwithstanding the remarkable proofs of the power of both governments and individuals to establish the most perfect 'organization of labour' for certain purposes in which they perceive they have a clear benefit, yet, whenever this is proposed to be done for the purpose of forming an associated community, by which, under a proper union of agriculture and manufactures, and by a well-adjusted proportion between labour, skill, and capital, the unemployed labourers of the country are to be put in a position to maintain themselves, and even accumulate wealth by their labours,—the answer commonly is, 'that it is an impracticable scheme,' or 'a visionary or a utopian dream of an enthusiast.'

Yet the Government find no difficulty in organizing a fleet and an army, with such ease and in such perfection, that every movement of each is regulated at the Admiralty and the Horse Guards; and if you desire to obtain any information about any one individual in either of these vast bodies, you have only to apply to the Admiralty or the War-office, and they will give you his name, age, height, complexion, the color of his eyes, the peculiarities of his countenance, and tell you in what ship or what regiment he is, where stationed, in what company, what amount of pay is due to him, and every other particular. The Government can organize a large army of Custom-house and Excise officers, coast-guard, tax-gatherers, and police, with a discipline so perfect, that they will find out every man, and ascertain his income, and even his political opinions, if desired. They can organize labour to build useless ships of war and extravagant royal yachts, to kill oxen and hogs, prepare salt-beef and pork, and even bake biscuits in their own ovens, for the fleets at Plymouth and Portsmouth, besides making ropes, sails, and blocks by machinery, and every other thing needed for their naval arsenals. They can cast cannon and cannon-balls, bombs, and shells, make gunpowder and Congreve rockets, and store up at the Tower 100,000 stand of arms, muskets, bayonets, pistols, spears, and tomahawks, to shed the blood and take the lives of our enemies when needed. They can swear in nearly the whole male population of London as special constables, to resist an apprehended insurrection, and marshal every division in its most appropriate place, enrolling old men of seventy, and young boys of fifteen, for this purpose.

They can do all these things in the way of 'organization and association of labour,' but, alas, they *cannot* (as they say), or they *will* not, (which is perhaps nearer the truth), undertake any organization and association of labour, to employ the unemployed portion of the population, and place in their own hands the means of not merely earning their own livelihood, but adding largely to the health, wealth, morality, and happiness of the whole nation. The old proverb says truly, 'Where there's a will, there's a way;' and the absence of the *will*, seems, in this instance, the only solution of the problem, why the *way* has never yet been found, and why it is deemed, by the Government at least, to be beyond the power of discovery.

To remedy this defect, it is proposed, that the public at large, the source of most of our social and moral improvements, shall take the matter into their own hands, and see whether, by proper care and due guarantees for security, a company can be formed, to be called 'The Model-Town Association,' for the purpose of building an entirely new town, to combine within itself every advantage of beauty, security, healthfulness, and convenience, that the latest discoveries in architecture and science can confer upon it; and which should, at the same time, be peopled by an adequate number of inhabitants, with such due proportions between the agricultural and manufacturing classes, and between the possessors of capital, skill, and labour, as to produce, by the new combinations and discipline under which its code of rules and regulations might place the whole body, the highest degree of abundance in every necessary of life, and many luxuries, united with the lightest amount of labour and care, and the highest degree of health, contentment, morality, and enjoyment yet seen in any existing community established on the principles by which society is now generally regulated."

The first model town Mr. Buckingham proposes to call "Victoria," and he suggests that it might be built on the shores of the Solent and Southampton water, and within the New

* Amongst these he enumerates the abolition of slavery, advocated by him forty years since; the opening of the overland route to India by Egypt and Suez, pointed out by him in 1818; the abolition of the Suttee or burning of widows in India, and the colonization of that country, the abolition of the Company's commercial monopoly, and free trade with India and China, with various other suggestions made between 1818 and 1823, and on account of which he was actually banished from India without trial; also the suppression of duelling, insisted on in 1834; the promotion of temperance recommended in a Parliamentary committee, of which he was chairman, in 1834—long before Father Mathew's labours began; the introduction of a bill in 1835 to enable town councils to provide baths, museums, and other institutions, gardens, &c., for the public; the abolition of impressment in the navy, urged in 1834; the arbitration of national disputes, lectured on in 1837, and many other questions of interest and importance.

ROMSEY ABBEY CHURCH.*
[12TH CENTURY.]

* See p. 397, in present number.

Forest, where there are 60,000 acres wholly useless to the Government and the country, out of which the Woods' and Forests, authorised by Parliament, might grant a lease of the requisite ground, without rent the first year, and afterwards at a rent rising from 5s. an acre, by an annual increase of 2s. 6d., up to 20s., so that for the site of a town or farm, one mile square, with 10,000 acres of land surrounding it, the state would receive 10,000l. a-year of rental, in place of, as now, virtually

nothing. He also instances estates in Ireland where the experiment might be tried, and we might here ask whether some such joint-stock association might not come within the sphere of operations lately proposed in Parliament for the regeneration of Ireland?

The plan of a town laid down in the engravings appended to the volume is a concentric series of squares within squares, with spacious avenues radiating from the central range, both at right angles across the square, and diagonally towards the corners for convenience. In the central

square are concentrated all the public offices, with a forum 700 feet square, and an octagonal tower in the centre with illuminated clocks, bells, and "an electric light for lighting the whole town." There are fountains at each corner of the square inclosing the central one, and a wide space on each side with churches, university, museum, concert-rooms, &c. The next, or sixth square from the exterior, has a covered arcade for winter promenade, 100 feet wide, and the fourth, one for retail bazaars, 100 feet wide. In the second is also one for workshops of same width. The houses in the several squares have all garden ground, the outer, of 1,000 houses, 100 feet deep and 20 feet frontage. There are school-houses on each side of the second square, and baths, reading-rooms, dining-halls, &c., in the spaces between some of the inner squares. At each outer corner of the whole is a fountain, and at each entrance are a couple of towers. All large manufactories using steam-engines would be removed at least half-a-mile beyond the town, as well as abbatoirs or slaughtering-houses, cattle-markets, reservoirs of sewerage for manure, cemeteries, hospitals, &c., and there would be in convenient proximity a park promenade, gymnasium, botanic garden, &c., and sites for suburban villas, reserved for such as might desire them. The town, it is proposed, would contain every improvement in position, plan, drainage, ventilation, architecture, supply of water, light, and every other elegance and convenience which art and science will admit of. The number of its inhabitants not to exceed 10,000, and each resident householder to be a shareholder to the extent of 20*l.* at least, and a subscriber to the rules for its government. The company to be incorporated by Royal Charter, or Act of Parliament, under the title of "The Model-Town Association," so as to limit the responsibility of each individual to the shares held by him in its stock. Rentals to be regulated by a moderate interest on the actual cost, and the dwellings to be of every gradation of size and scale, so as to have apartments, suites of rooms, and entire houses or tenements, from a rental of 10*l.* per annum up to 300*l.* The capital required to build such a town is computed at 3,000,000*l.*, besides 1,000,000*l.* to stock the farms, factories, and workshops with provisions and materials,—a sum, in all, the author observes, not half that expended on some single railways, nor more than the cost of Westminster Palace and the last new bridge across the Thames— two single structures only. The capital it is proposed to raise in 200,000 shares of 20*l.* each, to be paid up by instalments of 1*l.* a-month into the Bank of England in the name of trustees to be appointed by the shareholders. No member to hold more than 500 shares.

The rules relate, among other matters, to provisions for temperance and peace, the limitation of hours of labour, gratuitous education, law and medicine without individual expense, freedom of religion, &c. The inhabitants are proposed to comprise 1,000 members of the building trades, 600 cabinet-makers, upholsterers, and other furniture makers, 800 producers of food, 800 producers of materials for clothing, 800 miscellaneous manufacturers, 700 preparers of clothing, 300 preparers of food, a limited number of keepers of shops or stores of different kinds, 200 officers of education, health, religion, justice, and government, &c. &c.

As to the division of profits, rules as to currency, &c., we cannot enter into these, having already, indeed, overstepped our limits. We must, therefore, refer all who feel an interest in these and numerous other details connected with Mr. Buckingham's scheme to the work itself, which is got up in a clear and readable style both by author and publisher, and contains essays, also, on financial reform, on emigration and colonization, on a new reform bill, and on the regeneration of Ireland.

TO CLEANSE OLD COINS.—In reply to a correspondent, who asks for a recipe for cleaning old coins, copper, brass, and silver,—and says he has a quantity found at Richborough Castle, Kent, we may state,—that the red rust may be removed from silver coins by vinegar or by lemon juice; the green by a solution of ammonia; the rust on copper or brass coins should not be disturbed, as a coin which cannot be read when oxidized is seldom improved by being cleaned, but often rendered quite useless; a graver may occasionally be employed, but its safe use presumes a knowledge of the coin to be operated on, both portrait and legend. The Richborough coins, which the writer refers to, would no doubt be thankfully examined by Mr. Roach Smith, who is, we believe, at this moment preparing an extensive catalogue of Roman coins, found at that place, for publication.

AN ACCOUNT OF CONWAY CASTLE.

ONE of the recent excursions made by the British Archæological Association included a visit to Conway Castle, an interesting remnant of rude times known probably to many of our readers.* Mr. Hicklin, the editor of the *Chester Courant*, gave an account of the castle. He said, in the course of it, that Edward the First having resolved to complete the subjugation of Wales to the English Crown, was naturally anxious to strengthen his power in those places of security, where he could best support his authority, by curbing the pride of the barons, who might attempt to thwart his schemes, and by suppressing the revolts of his discontented subjects. Independently of the romantic and picturesque scenery by which the rock of Conway is surrounded, its situation afforded a most advantageous post from which its defenders might observe the slightest indication of any hostile movement: the passes might easily be rendered perfectly inaccessible; and unless treachery was in the garrison, the fortress might be considered impregnable before the use of artillery. The Castle of Conway was completed in 1284, under the personal inspection and direction of King Edward; and Henry de Elreton, the builder of Carnarvon Castle, was the architect employed. "After size and weight," says an able writer, "the power of architecture may be said to depend upon the quantity of its shadow; and it seems to me that the reality of its works, and the use and influence they have in the daily life of men, as opposed to those works of art with which we have nothing to do but in times of rest or pleasure, require that it should express a kind of human sympathy by a measure of darkness as great as there is in human life; and that as the great poem and great fiction generally affect the most by the majesty of their masses of shade, and cannot take hold upon us if they affect a continuance of lyric sprightliness, but must be serious often, and sometimes melancholy, else they do not express the truth of this wide world of ours, so there must be in this magnificently human art of architecture, some equivalent expressions for the trouble and wrath of life; for its sorrow and its mystery; and this it can only give by depth or diffusion of gloom, by the frown upon its front, and the shadow of its recess. So that Rembrandtism is a noble manner in architecture, though a false one in painting. But since the thirteenth century, we have built like frogs and mice, except only in our castles (and perhaps Mr. Stephenson would add, in our railroads). Until our street architecture is bettered, until we give it some size and boldness, until we give our windows recess and our walls thickness, I know not how we can blame our architects for their feebleness in more important work; their eyes are inured to narrowness and slightness; can we expect them, at a word, to conceive and deal with breadth and solidity? They ought not to live in our cities; there is that in their miserable walls which bricks up to death men's imaginations, as surely as ever perished forsworn Nun. An architect should live in cities as little as a painter. Send him to our hills, and let him study there what nature understands by a buttress and what by a dome. There was something in the old power of architecture, which it had from the recluse more than from the citizen. We have sources of power in the imagery of iron coasts and azure hills; of power more pure, nor less serene, than that of the hermit spirit which once lighted with white lines of cloisters the glades of the Alpine pine, and raised into ordered spires the wild rocks of the Norman Sea; which gave to the temple gate the depth and darkness of Elijah's Horeb Cave; and lifted out of the populous city, grey cliffs of lonely stone into the midst of sailing birds and silent air." Mr. Hicklin resumed. The form of the castle is oblong, and it is erected on a high rock at one corner of the triangle which encloses the town. One side is bounded by the river, another by a creek which is full of water at every tide, and into which the river Gyffin flows; the other two sides are within the town walls. On the outside, eight massive and enormous towers, forty feet in diameter, project,—four on each side; and there was a winding staircase to the summit in a smaller tower contained in each, which in the four nearest the river issue out to the height of several feet, and form an exceedingly beautiful addition. The summit of these commands an extensive view of the adjacent country. The walls and towers are embattled, and vary from 12 to 15 feet in thickness. The principal entrance was from the town at the west end by a drawbridge over a very deep moat; this leads by the ascent of a few steps to a spacious terrace, protected by five small towers, and intervening walls; thence through a gateway, defended by a portcullis, to the larger court. This contains on the south side the noble hall, which is 130 feet long, 32 wide, and of a proportionate height, about 30 feet: out of this was partitioned off, at the east end, a chapel with a large window. The roof was supported by eight fine Gothic arches, four of which still remain; one fell about 44 years ago; it was warmed by a great fire-place at one end, and two others, one on each side; there are six windows to the country, and three larger ones to the court: underneath were the spacious vaults which contained the ammunition for the use of the garrison, and also the cellars for provisions. At the east end of this court is the reservoir, 15 feet in diameter, and 20 deep; the water which supplied it is traditionally reported to have been conveyed in pipes from a well above Tygwyn. The entrance into the inner court is by a passage through a strong wall, 10 feet and a half in thickness, which on the outside has a lodge for a sentinel, who could see through a loop-hole every one coming from the chief entrance. On the right in this court is one of the state rooms, 29 feet by 22 feet: a beautiful arch which supported the roof remains perfect, a second has long ago been destroyed: the windows look into the court. Between this room and *twr y brenin*, or the king's tower, was the king's chamber, which communicated with that of the queen's on the opposite side. The north tower is called *twr y vrenines*, or the queen's tower; and the room on the first story contains a recess taken out of the wall, which is the only place with any appearance of ornament in the castle. It is formed by seven pointed and groined arches uniting with each other at the roof, and under them are more arches, with a basement all round. This recess, which, with the adjoining room, was the queen's private chapel, contained the altar-table; and on both sides are small apertures communicating with two apartments. That such was the use of this place is corroborated by the circumstance, that this is the only room in any of the towers above the ground-floor which does not contain a fire-place. The diameter of the inside of the towers is about 18 feet: these consist generally of two stories, with the ground-floor, which was chiefly used for keeping stores. The king's tower has a strong-room below, which was accessible only by a trap-door; but the keep, or *twr y carcharorion* is the second on the

---

* On the same day they visited Flint and Flint Castle, and the inhabitants drew attention to the present neglected state of the latter, and requested the Association to aid them by their influence in procuring from the parties to whom the custody of the castle is entrusted an assurance that this venerable ruin shall at least be protected from further mutilation and abuse. The castle is supposed to have been erected by Edward the First, and is celebrated as being the place where the first step was taken towards the dethronement of the unfortunate monarch, Richard the Second. Several places in the vicinity of Flint indicate, by their English names, that they were formerly places where operations were carried on connected with the lead trade, such as Lead Brook, &c., these places being called Ledebruke, &c., in a Charter of Edward the 3rd. In a notice of the borough, drawn up for the occasion, it was thought highly probable that the term flint glass was derived from the fact of its being first manufactured at Flint, as a glass-work formerly existed near where the present town-hall stands, and great quantities of fragments of melting pots and glass were found in sinking the foundation of a gateway a few years ago. As the mineral flint is a component part of all kinds of glass, there is no reason to suppose that this term should be applied solely as indicative of that description which is manufactured by the aid of lead, whilst, on the other hand, it is highly probable that the first locality for that branch of the glass manufacture would be at a spot where the lead required for its formation could be obtained in abundance, particularly as in addition to the raw materials, the vicinity of Flint has abounded in ancient times with fuel, whether that was derived from forests or mines. One day was given by the Association to Liverpool, and, although we have not attempted to give a connected account of all the proceedings, we must not omit to mention the admirable manner in which the members were received and entertained by the Corporation and inhabitants. So far as we know, neither the "Association" nor the "Institute" ever before found parallel munificence. When Mr. Pettigrew, on receiving from the hands of the Mayor a bowl to present to Lord Albert Conyngham in memory of the visit, drank, under a happy inspiration, "Success to the good old town of Liverpool, and the trade thereof," he expressed the feeling of the moment of every visiter present. We were glad to find some of the Liverpool architects foremost in the kind arrangements.

south side, adjoining the hail, from which there is a passage through it to the top of the walls. On the east side there is another terrace, protected by three towers and walls, where there was a second entrance to the castle; this was from the river, by ascending a steep rock, where once had been a narrow flight of winding stairs, protected by a wall, with a small covered hanging tower, which went a considerable way into the river, and had another round tower at its extremity to prevent the approach of an enemy at ebb tide. The portion in the river had been for a long period destroyed; but the narrow wall with the hanging-tower, as far as the terrace, was taken down, when making the approach to the bridge. The next tower to the king's, *twr darn*, or the broken tower, presents a very picturesque ruin. The avarice, it is said, of some of the inhabitants led them to excavate the rock at its base, which occasioned a vast fragment of the tower to fall: the upper half remains perfect, suspended at a great height, and projecting nearly thirty feet over the walls below. The walls which surround the town were built at the same time as the castle, and are nearly triangular,—a form evidently prescribed by the situation; the walls which remain almost entire are very lofty and embattled: in the circuit of a mile and a quarter there are twenty-one strong towers, rising considerably above the walls, besides three entrances to the town, with two stronger towers to each. The base of the triangle runs along the river, and in it are seven towers with a gateway called *Porth isav*, or the lower gate; between this and the castle, there is also a portal in the wall, called *Porth bach*, but without towers. From the northern extremity of the base, a curtain with battlements on each side runs nearly seventy yards into the river, which had at its extremity a large tower, long since destroyed, but the ruins are visible. This corresponded with a similar tower under the castle: the gateway through the curtain is called *Porth yr aden*. A second entrance to the town was from the country side, nearly opposite to *Porth isav*,—it is called *Porth uchav*, or the upper gate, and it was furnished with a drawbridge: the third is on the south side, and led to the *velin heli*, or salt-water mill,—it is called *Porth y velin*, or the gate of the mill. Except on the river side, the whole town was surrounded by a deep and wide moat. One of the towers on the south has a wall built on the town side, and contained some spacious apartments,—it is called *Twr Llywelyn*.

Edward made Conway a strong military station, and granted the town a charter as a free borough, securing to it considerable privileges, a condition being annexed with which the good citizens of London, in their present humour, would, he thought, be especially angry, "That *the Jews* dwell not at any time in the same borough."

At the restoration of Charles the Second, the castle was granted by the "merry monarch" to the Earl of Conway, who was altogether unworthy of such a possession; for in the spirit of a pedlar, rather than a patrician, he ordered his agent to dismantle this glorious structure, by removing the timber, iron, lead, to be shipped to Ireland, ostensibly for his majesty's, but in reality for his own use. With a most commendable determination, Colonel Wynn, Mr. Thomas Bulkeley, and several of the leading gentry of the country, attempted to oppose this destructive design, but in vain. The spoiler did his work; but a suitable fate attended this desecration of one of the noblest works of antiquity. Lord Conway was not merely prejudiced, as he complains, by the loss of an opportune season for shipping, but by the loss of the property itself, for the vessels which contained the materials for Ireland were wrecked on the voyage. The castle is at present held from the Crown by the Dowager Lady Erskine, who takes commendable care for its preservation.

NATIONAL ART-UNION OF IRELAND.—On the 31st ult. the annual meeting of this society was held, when it appeared that the amount received in subscriptions, 511*l*. 5s., had only sufficed to obtain a print for the members and pay the expenses, and that there could be no drawing for prizes. The pressure of the times was the cause assigned.

THE BOSTON ATHENÆUM, UNITED STATES.

A NEW building, to be called "The Athenæum," has been erected in Boston, for the collection and preservation of a large library, and the exhibition of works of art in sculpture and painting. A correspondent has favoured us with the following particulars. The design of the structure is Palladian, the material free-stone, from New Jersey. The basement is rusticated, the windows are in arched recesses, with intervening pilasters supporting the entablature. A central division of the elevation projects slightly. The entire height is 62 feet, and the length 114 feet. The basement is constructed, within, of bricks, the ceiling being formed by continuous groined arches, which support the lower floor, and give security against fire from below. Here are furnaces, with flues going into all parts of the building; ample store-rooms for packing, &c., with an apparatus for hoisting, through a fireproof passage, quite to the upper story. The front doorway is 14 feet high by 10 feet broad, and is arched with a semi-circular light. It opens on a vestibule, or main entry, 32 feet by 28, which contains double staircases, ascending to the upper story, and lighted from the roof and by a large window in front.

The first-floor is partitioned for a hall 80 feet in length, intended for a sculpture gallery, two spacious apartments for reading rooms, and one for a cabinet of medals, coins, and other articles of value and curiosity. The second floor is appropriated entirely to books. The main library is 109 feet in length and 42 feet in its extreme breadth. It contains about 40,000 volumes, and is divided by a wide archway: one division displaying the books in alcoves, and the other, cases lining the walls. It is finished in the Italian style, with a decorated ceiling. The third-floor is appropriated as a gallery for pictures. That portion of it which is over the great hall of the library is finished in four divisions, lighted from the top. The edifice has cost about 100,000 dollars, in its present state, and may be completed for 25,000 more.

NEW ROOF AT THE BANK OF ENGLAND.

THE drawing-office in the Bank of England,—an apartment of great length (138 feet), and about 44 feet wide,—is being remodelled by Mr. Cockerell: the columns are removed, and a roof to span the whole has been formed. A paragraph which has gone the round of the daily papers would really lead to the impression, in the minds of those who knew no better, that before this event no roof of 44 feet span had been formed.

Divested of the singular halo thrown around the matter by the notice in question, it is simply this,—that wrought-iron box-girders are used, patented by Mr. G. Nasmyth, containing an iron *arched rib*. They are 2 feet 3 inches deep for the span in question, and, as we understand, cost about 105*l*. more than cast-iron girders would have done. Apart from the puff in question they seem to be very good things, well worth examination.

IMPROVEMENT OF THE SOUTH SIDE OF THE THAMES.

ON the south of the Thames nothing but neglect seems the rule. It is believed there are ample funds to proceed with proposed improvements, and in one instance the coal duties are available. The south of the Thames is entitled to a share positively provided for by Act of Parliament. It is publicly stated that several new churches are to be built, that sites are selected, and that ample funds can be found. For drainage!—that is put off!—for ever! and the truth is that it would be a great favour to leave all to the old management, for, bad as it was called, it was infinitely better than the present. It must shortly come to this,—that those who have been born and bred in the southern localities must surrender their present comfortable homes, though humble, and go into lodgings,—that most of the government payers will be lost, the parochial rates greatly diminished, and taxes will only be obtained by the authority of Somerset House,—a state of things that must arise if some energies are not immediately put out to stem the impending ruin. No district around the metropolis has been so cruelly treated as the southern boroughs—the "elder sister of London," as they used to be called—deserted, and become a ruined heap.

Westminster-bridge, a nuisance, and tolerated by authority, is stilted up, and, if a severe winter come, will be found prostrated, jammed and huddled together in the fall, and the whole district, perhaps, under water at every tide. Speculated upon by railways, controlled, for termini, by government, Woods and Forests for new roads, and by the so-called Metropolitan Improvement Commissioners, the Commission of Sewers, &c. &c., we ask your advocacy.

AN OLD SUBSCRIBER.

METROPOLITAN COMMISSION OF SEWERS.

EXTRAORDINARY PROCEEDINGS.

A SPECIAL meeting was called for Tuesday last on the following requisition to Mr. Woolrych:—

"We, the undersigned, request you, as secretar[y] to the Metropolitan Commission of Sewers, to sum[mon] a special court of sewers, to be held at th[e] principal office, No. 1, Greek-street, Soho-squar[e] on Tuesday, the 21st day of August instant, at te[n] o'clock in the forenoon, for the purpose of ascer[tain]ing from documentary and other evidence whe[ther] there be any truth in the statements made b[y] Mr. Chadwick, at the public court of sewers on th[e] 2nd instant, against the undersigned commissione[rs] for obstructing and misrepresenting 'the very lar[ge] economy' resulting from the present system [of] 'contract' for removing by flushing the soil from th[e] sewers at a cost of 'sixpence per cubic yard:' f[or] the removal of soil under the old Westminster com[]mission, the cost was 7s. per cubic yard; and th[e] undersigned were approving members of such ex[]penditure in that commission, thus exhibiting [an] alleged 'large economy' in favour of the prese[nt] system, of 6s. 6d. per cubic yard, being a differen[ce] of 1,300 per cent.

To ascertain the exact amount in thousands [of] pounds of the money of the ratepayers already e[x]pended in the flushing department entirely omitt[ed] by Mr. Chadwick, in his statement of 'the ve[ry] large economy' of the present system of flushing t[he] sewers by 'contract,' and to ascertain what in reali[ty] such 'contract' is.

To ascertain from the account book of Assistar[nt] Surveyor Lovick (to whom on the recommendati[on] of 'The Committee of Works,' the flushing depar[t]ment has been for many months exclusively e[n]trusted), whether, during the 31 weeks of the pr[e]sent year to the 31st July, the 'yards lineal' [of] sewers flushed out in the Surrey and Kent distri[cts] do not make a total of 214½ miles, at a cost to [the] ratepayers of 10*l*. 6s. 4d. per mile, independen[t] of the district portions of the very large omissi[on] of expenditure by Mr. Chadwick in his stateme[nt] on the 2nd instant.

To ascertain if beyond these omissions by M[r.] Chadwick, and beyond the 10*l*. 6s. 4d. per m[ile] shown in the account-book of Assistant-Surve[yor] Lovick, the rate-payers of the Surrey and K[ent] districts have not been charged in the account [of] the contractor with the court for those distric[ts] Mr. Dethick, other large items of expense co[n]nected with flushing, among which are 2,400 lo[ads] of soil carted away at 2s. 6d. per load for cart[age] only.

To ascertain the number of times the same len[gth] of sewer has been flushed out in the 31 weeks, e[ach] time of such flushing costing the rate-payers on [a] general average at the rate of 10*l*. 6s. 4d. per m[ile].

To ascertain if any of the sewers in any dist[rict] are flushed out three times a-week.

To investigate the 'special contracts' at per 'y[ard] lineal'' entered into by Assistant-Surveyor Lo[vick] and the labourers, and to ascertain if any of [the] sewers under such arrangements, have had the [soil] washed into the adjoining sewers at an expens[e to] the rate-payers equal to 3s. per cubic yard.

And to take such immediate steps as the re[sult] of the evidence to be submitted at such spe[cial] court may render necessary for the honour, c[ha]racter, and usefulness of the Metropolitan Com[mis]sion of Sewers, and the best interests of the me[tro]politan ratepayers confided to the guardianshi[p of] the commission. Dated this 16th day of Aug[ust] 1849. (Signed)

JOHN LESLIE,
FREDERICK BYN[G],
JOHN BIDWELL.'

Great excitement appeared to prevail in the o[l]d and the proceedings were looked forward to [with] considerable interest. The commissioners pre[sent] in the court at the usual hour of commencing t[he busi]ness were Mr. Joseph Hume, M.P., Sir J[ohn] Burgoyne, Mr. Leslie, and Mr. Bidwell. [Mr.] Byng was prevented from attending through [in]disposition. Several other commissioners after arrived; but instead of entering the court they took their seats in an adjoining room. Half an hour passed over, and still the court was not opened, and the course intended to be pursued was then whispered about.

The regulations of the Act of Parliament require that a court shall consist of not less than six commissioners; and as the solitary four remained in the court for an hour without a quorum being formed, the Act declares that such intended court shall stand adjourned.

The Secretary (Mr. Woolrych) then addressed the numerous parties who were waiting for admission, and informed them that the court was adjourned until Wednesday next. The commissioners who remained in the room were Mr. Chadwick, Mr. Hawes, Mr. Bain, Dr. Southwood Smith, Mr. Banfield, Mr. Hodgson, Sir H. de la Beche, and Mr. Johnson.

This proceeding elicited comments not of the most favourable description against the parties who had thus evaded the making of a court, and thereby "shirked" a question involving considerations of importance to the ratepayers at large.

We would recommend commissioners, whatever their opinions may be, not to venture a second time on such a left-handed move, or the public may be led to give a verdict *without* a trial!

A Court was held on Thursday; Sir John Burgoyne in the chair. A letter was read from Mr. Goldsworthy Gurney in reference to his plan of purifying sewers by means of a steam jet, in which he stated generally that his plan is to withdraw all offensive effluvia from the sewers to a given point, and replace it by fresh air, so that the men might be enabled to go into them and flush them or clean them, and if necessary then to decompose and destroy the objectionable gases, as they escape, by a particular method of combustion.

This led to a long conversation, and it was ultimately agreed "that the Works Committee be authorized to take the proposition by Mr. Goldsworthy Gurney into consideration, and to incur an expense not exceeding 25*l*. for an experiment in the Friar-street sewer."

A letter was received from Mr. Brushfield, Chairman of the Whitechapel Union, stating that cholera had broken out in Dorset-street, in which there were a great number of overflowing cesspools, and as the ownership of the houses was disputed, calling upon this Court to relieve and cleanse them, as the parochial authorities were unable to levy the amount in consequence of the difficulties as to whom the expenses should be charged.

Mr. Leslie and Dr. S. Smith were opposed to this Court relieving the parochial officers of what was clearly their duty to perform, they having ample funds in hand to pay for the same.

Mr. Chadwick and others were of opinion, that in cases of emergency some assistance ought to be rendered, and it signified little, as the money was to come out of the pockets of the ratepayers, by which body the work was performed.

It was at length agreed, "That the surveyors of the district be directed to communicate with the Board of Guardians, and be authorized to lend them the aid of any machinery or workmen belonging to the commission for the purpose of cleansing the places in question, on the payment of the usual charges."

A letter was received from Mr. Hogg, Clerk of the Works at Buckingham Palace, setting forth that opposite the palace the main King's Scholars'-pond sewer was charged with deposit 18 inches in depth, and offensive odours were exhaled therefrom. Referred to the surveyor to report immediately thereon.

A report was presented by Mr. G. Donaldson, on the operation of sewage manure on certain lands that had been irrigated by it during the latter part of last and the first part of the present year. It stated that the lands so irrigated had produced a double crop of grass, and on the corn lands there had been an improvement in value of not less than 30 per cent., and taking its operation generally on the land, he estimated the increased value from 40s. to 50s. per acre. The report was accompanied by a long list of charges incurred for these experiments, amounting altogether to 757*l*.

Mr. Leslie moved that the report be printed, and taken into consideration on a future day.

Mr. Chadwick, as an amendment, moved that the amount be paid at once, and felicitated the ratepayers and agriculturists on the results that had been arrived at, which had settled the value of sewage manure. The general results had proved that 100 tons of liquid manure could be distributed at a cost of 1s. 6d. or 1s. 8d. per acre, and its effects had been highly satisfactory on every description of land.

Mr. C. Johnson was of opinion that, ultimately, not less than half a million sterling profit would be derived from the sale of manure, to say nothing of the advantage of the purification of the Thames.—Mr. Leslie said they had never heard of the report before, and therefore its consideration ought to be postponed. He then went into a variety of statements as to the value of the manure, and mentioned that a friend of his had paid 2*l*. 10s. per week for sewage manure, but upon investigation it turned out that he had only been supplied with Thames water.

Mr. Lovick explained that this arose from a party inserting a house-drain into the Sewage Company's pipe, and who had temporarily stopped it with clay that had not been removed.—Report deferred.

Some other business was disposed of, but the court was finally "counted out."

Books.

The Principles of Gothic Ecclesiastical Architecture, with an explanation of Technical Terms. By MATTHEW HOLBECHE BLOXAM. Ninth edition. London: Bogue, Fleet-street. 1849.

THIS admirable manual does not now need recommendation from us, but we may mention that in this, the ninth edition, the text has been enlarged and many woodcuts added. Mr. Bloxam mentions in the preface that a German translation of his book has been published at Leipzig.

We cordially recommend it to all desiring introductory information on the subject of which it treats. The engraved illustrations are nicely executed.

Miscellanea.

ROSHERVILLE GARDENS.—When nature provides cliffs, water, trees, varied surface, and a magnificent prospect, very little art, well applied, will suffice to produce a fine result. We had associated with "Rosherville Gardens," near Gravesend, no other idea than that of shrimps and cigars, and were not prepared for such a charming scene as we found them present when accidentally led to visit them last week. We will not say much about the imitation Tudor Hall there (a very large apartment), but even from this a valuable hint may be gained, and that is, as to the use of looking-glass. To take the end of the hammer beam of the roof on each side slight upright supports are introduced, thus dividing the apartment into three aisles. This, of course, if apparent, would contradict the apparent construction of the roof, and to avoid this the upper part of each upright is *cased with looking-glass*, which considerably lessens the defect. The lower part of the upright is made to serve for hat pegs, &c. Of course we do not allude to this to lead to the imitation of such an arrangement of roof, but as an ingenious expedient applicable in more legitimate positions. What we are speaking of, however, are the gardens, and these really are very pretty.

COMPENSATION CASE.—The site, at Sheffield, chosen by the Duke of Norfolk as promoter of the projected new markets, includes the extensive area of the Tontine Hotel, and as a wide difference arose as to compensation, the point was referred to arbitration. The site contains 3,502 square yards, and is held under a lease from the duke for 99 years, to expire in 1883,—rent 20*l*. per annum. The proprietors, seventeen survivors, claimed 15,500*l*. Mr. W. Flockton, architect, valued it at that amount, with a reference to improvements to cost 2,200*l*. and increase the value to 612*l*. 10s. a-year in all, worth, by the usual annuity tables, 16½ years' purchase. Mr. J. Harrison, architect, concurred in this valuation, as nearly did Mr. F. R. Jones, of Huddersfield, land valuer. For the duke, Mr. W. Fowler, land agent, was called, and valued the property at 6,138*l*., including 558*l*. for compulsory sale, and estimating the net income at 300*l*. 17s. Mr. H. Holt, of Wakefield, land valuer, and Mr. H. M. Wood, of Nottingham, architect, concurred. The umpire, Mr. Foster, awarded 7,720*l*., and 243*l*. 12s. costs.

M. GERENTE, the French glass painter, who has executed some windows in Ely Cathedral, and seemed to be warmly taken up by some leading men in this country, has been carried off by the cholera in Paris. Two other French artists in glass have been with us lately with strong letters, and have been canvassing for commissions. Their works, so far as we saw, afforded no substantial reason for employing them to the prejudice of our own artists.

RAILWAY JOTTINGS.—The Great Western appear to have offered a dividend of 2 per cent. only for the last half-year, leaving a balance of 18,000*l*: odds under head of receipts. The solicitor to the Company is said to have 'misappropriated' a sum of 45,000*l*. belonging to his constituents.——The opening of Windsor extension of the South-Western is likely to be obstructed for some time by the snapping of the cast iron girders of one of the arches of the bridge which crosses the Thames near Eton College. The masonry and brickwork of the piers are built on caissons of cast iron, driven into the bed of the river by means of Dr. Potts's patent process, and the superstructure above the masonry is of cast iron. One of the piers, in consequence of the great weight, appears to have sunk several inches, thus causing the snapping of the girder in question. Fears are entertained that the caissons will sink still further, it being supposed that they are now chiefly resting on a soft bed of clay.——The contract for constructing the Chepstow-bridge, for the South Wales line, has been taken by Messrs. Smith and Willey, of Liverpool, engineers.

ELECTRO-TELEGRAPHIC PROGRESS.—The London company have purchased Mr. Bain's patent for Great Britain, which is said to increase the rapidity of communication from 65 to 1,000 letters per minute.——*Herapath* complains of the personal interest of the railway management in certain patents as a main cause hitherto operative to the injury of the public interest in this useful invention, as well as to that of the shareholders themselves. "If it happens," he observes, "as we need not say it does—that the first patents in which all these managers and officials are interested are not the best, that they are far inferior in utility and economy to others subsequently brought out, we are enabled to perceive great evil in directors, &c., participating in the profit of such patents. The shareholders are injured and the public are injured. The shareholders' interests are sacrificed by the extension and the continuance of plans much more expensive than others. It is the interest of the directors not to adopt anything cheaper. The public interests suffer, in higher charges than need be being maintained, and in convenience. The public are charged, perhaps, 12s. 6d., where 3s. 6d. or 2s. 6d. would be ample remuneration by the improved apparatus, and beyond that the facility of communication is not so great."

BATHS AND WASHHOUSES.—The foundation-stone of new baths and washhouses, for the working classes resident at Miles Platting, Manchester, was laid, according to the local *Spectator*, on Thursday week. The population of the suburb are indebted, it seems, to Sir Benjamin Heywood for their present prospect of a cheap luxury. The estimated cost will be 2,000*l*. The building is being erected by Mr. Marmaduke Burnell, and will be 160 feet in length and 49 feet in breadth. It will contain fifteen baths for males, and eight for females; also a dwelling-house. There will be a plunge-bath 27 feet 8 inches long and 16 feet wide, with dressing-stalls, &c. The washhouses will be five in number, one (in the spirit of a recent advice in THE BUILDER) for the cleansing of infected clothes exclusively. The drying-room will be 19 feet by 16 feet 9 inches in dimensions, and will be heated by steam-pipes. The whole is to be conducted under the eye of Sir Benjamin's agent, and will be ready for use, it is thought, in four or five months.

OXFORD TOWN COUNCIL.—BLIND TENDERS.—At the town-council held a few days ago, the following fourteen tenders were opened for new water-wheels, pumping machinery, &c. at the City Water Works. Messrs. Easton and Amos, engineers:—

Hunter and Bow, Middlesex	£670	0	0
Vulcan Foundry, Warrington ..	650	0	0
Winder and Co., Moreton-in-the-Marsh	602	0	0
Jukes and Co., London	593	19	6
Lampitt, Banbury	545	0	0
C. and W. Earl, Hull..........	541	9	0
Cochrane and Co., Dudley......	530	0	0
Bearcroft and Co., Leeds	496	0	0
Loyd and Co., London	475	0	0
Sturge and Co., Bradford	470	6	2
Stobert and Co., Newark	460	0	0
Lee and Taylor, Oxford........	450	0	0
Beaumont, Whitechapel, London	410	5	4
Butler and Co., Leeds..........	346	0	0

PROVINCIAL.—A new museum is about to be erected by subscription at Oxford, at a cost of 50,000*l*. The site chosen is in the parks, near the Wadham College gardens, Merton College.——St. Michael's Church, Gloucester, has been gutted preparatory to demolition, to make way for the work of 'restoration.'(?) The tower alone will remain.——The building fund of the Normal College for Wales now exceeds 3,000*l*.——The numerous repairs and alterations in progress for the last two years at Lanercost Church have been completed and the edifice reopened. The whole has been re-roofed, and indeed it was the falling in of a portion of the old roof that led the Woods and Forests to grant the means of repair and alteration, the design for which was supplied by Mr. Salvin, and superintended by Mr. Stone.——Mr. Robins, we observe, announces the forthcoming sale by auction of a "free-hold Episcopal Chapel, of the Gothic order of architecture, newly built in the township of Moss Side, near Chorlton-upon-Medlock, presenting (of course) a capital investment." It is said to have, as it is, accommodation for above 1,000 persons, and to have cost 6,000*l*., but whether built on spec or otherwise, is not declared.——The porch of Hunstanton Church, near Lynn, which is a specimen of decorated work, has lately been restored, under the superintendence of Mr. Frederick Preedy, principally at the expense of some liberal but unknown subscriber.——Messrs. Lee and Sons have contracted with Government to protect the cliff, at Harwich, from its commencement to Mr. Bagshawe's property, by a wall of Kentish rag-stone, with a promenade 8 feet in breadth, to the new breakwater.

BIRMINGHAM WORKHOUSE — SECOND COMPETITON.—Forty-three designs were received, and were referred to Messrs. Edge, H. J. Stevens, and Gibson (*vice* Shaw). They have reported upon them, and state their first object was to reject such designs as they considered to be inadmissible; and as many of them were imperfect and ill-considered, and as others had been evidently prepared for other places, they had not much difficulty in reducing the number to ten sets, all of which appeared to have been studied with reference to the locality, and to demand a close scrutiny. After making a further careful comparative analysis of the ten designs, they again reduced the number to six. To these they had devoted a large portion of time; for though they had not experienced much difficulty in arriving at a judgment, they felt that it would be unjust to decide which they would recommend, without giving to these reserved designs the full benefit of the closest investigation. The result had been an unanimous and decided opinion in favour of two plans, the numbers of which were specified in the schedule. Both these sets of designs appeared to have emanated from the same architects, from the similarity of principle observed in the arrangements, and in the descriptive particulars. A third set of designs were therefore selected for recommendation as deserving of the second premium—a distinction to which they were fairly entitled by the great care bestowed upon their preparation. The three architects stated various grounds on which they preferred one of the two designs before referred to to the other, and their opinion that it could be erected for the stipulated sum. The guardians resolved that the six plans therein referred to should lie for the examination of the guardians for one week, when the meeting to be then held should be made special for adopting such resolutions with reference to them as might be deemed desirable. The letters accompanying them were sealed up in an envelope, and will not be opened till after the final decision both by guardians and Poor-law Board.

LAYING IT ON.—We are told that a Trowbridge minister has had gutta percha piping carried round his chapel, and connected with a large oval funnel in the book-board of the pulpit; and wherever a deaf hearer sits, he has an ear trumpet attached to the tube, by which he can hear all that passes.——Loving music, and anxious to extend the enjoyment of it, we have often contemplated the possibility of laying it on to various quarters by means of pipes from a central producing orchestra. The *possibility* seems to be becoming a *probability*.

PROJECTED WORKS.—Advertisements have been issued for tenders, by 10th September; for various works, for her Majesty's Ordnance, Pembroke district; by 4th September, for re-slating four gun sheds, at the Grand Depôt, Woolwich; by 1st, for painting the iron railings and curbs of Tavistock, Gordon, and Harrington squares, and for the interior and exterior painting required at the Commissioners'-office (Bedford estate); by 20th October, for the whole or any part (four divisions), of the works in the erection of the new Grammar Schools and Master's house, at Loughborough, Leicester; by 27th inst., for the erection of a British school at Thaxted, Essex; by 27th, for the erection and completion of a garden market at Worcester; by 7th September, for the several works required in the execution of a railway of three miles in length, crossing the river Blyth (Newcastle); by 31st inst., for the carpenter's work of sheds to be erected on the quays of the Nelson Dock, Liverpool; and by 6th September, for 50 iron gas columns, and 50 street posts, at Bethnal-green.

THE TUBULAR BRIDGES.—In a recent report, Mr. Stephenson states that the masonry of the Britannia-bridge contract is completed as far as practicable, prior to the floating and lifting of the tubes; that some delay had arisen from an unsoundness in one of the large castings of the new hydraulic press in the Anglesea Tower, which occasioned so much leakage, as threatened to render a new casting necessary; that the leakage, however, had been stopped, and the lifting might have been completed, but he had deemed it prudent to lift by short stages only, and to build up step by step underneath with brickwork, in order effectually to guard against the serious consequences which might arise from any failure or derangement of the hydraulic presses, whilst the tube was suspended from them. Such an accident he believed to be very improbable; but, after the fracture that took place in one of the cross-heads during the lifting of the Conway tubes (fortunately discovered in time to prevent a very serious disaster), the utmost caution was deemed expedient. The issue has since proved the great necessity of such prudence and caution. The lower part of the defective cylinder burst, on 17th inst., with a tremendous explosion. Only one man was injured, but he was dreadfully smashed by the falling mass of nearly three tons weight. The precautionary packing and bricking, with cement, under the tube, alone prevented the most terrible consequences. The tube is now raised about 21 feet from the base. In the 26th report of the Parliamentary Commissioners on this route of railway it is stated that, on careful examination of the Menai-bridge, the whole structure appears to be in as perfect a state as when first opened. The Conway-bridge has also been found perfect.

BREAKAGE OF GLASS.—Messrs. Hartley, glass manufacturers, Sunderland, lately brought an action against the Great Northern Railway Company for 163*l*. 10*s*., loss on rough plate-glass, a residue not required by Messrs. Peto in roofing the railway station at Lincoln, and ordered to be returned *viâ* Peterborough to save repacking, but sent by the Company *viâ* Grimsby, and thereby destroyed. Glass being excepted under the Carriers' Act, the judge on the northern circuit, before whom the case was tried, directed the jury to return a verdict for the defendants, as no additional charge was paid by way of insurance. Leave, however, was reserved to the plaintiffs to enter the verdict for them if the Court above should decide that the direction was wrong.

RAMSGATE SEAMEN'S INFIRMARY.—The foundation-stone of the Ramsgate Seamen's Infirmary was laid on Friday, the 17th day of August, by Mr. John Ashley Warre, the president of the institution, in the presence of a large number of spectators. The building is to be erected from designs in the Grecian style, prepared by Mr. Wm. E. Smith, Architect, of Ramsgate. The site selected for its erection is on the West Cliff, in the district recently assigned to Christ Church. The incumbent of this (the Rev. E. Hoare) will have the moral and religious superintendence, and to whom praise is due for the promotion of this institution, which must be found of service to the afflicted mariners occasionally visiting the harbour of Ramsgate.

CONDITION OF EDINBURGH.—In your last week's paper you have an article on the adornment of the city of Edinburgh: I will venture to give you the impression made on me at a recent visit to this city, as to the vanity of our Scottish neighbours in attempting to adorn their city while they are so utterly regardless of the common decencies of life. Prince's-street and Canongate form a sad contrast to each other: in the former the luxurious Scott monument,—the handsome screens, with columns, &c., on the bridge overlooking the lower town, near the Post-office,—the affected imitation of the Parthenon, on the Calton-hill, may be cited as examples of so much money spent in adornment. An apostle has said, "Cleanliness is next to godliness;" our pious Scotch neighbours overlook this passage strangely; the filthy exhibitions in Canongate are hardly credible in this reformed age. A worthy citizen of Edinburgh told me he really believed that there was not a single privy or accommodation of any character throughout Canongate. For the information of those who have not visited Edinburgh, it should be mentioned that Canongate, for the most part, is a wide street, more than a mile in length, and a steep hill the whole length; lofty, irregular, *barrack-like* houses; the shops, for the most part, stores of different kinds; the upper floors, or flats as they are called, *seven and eight* in number, frequently inhabited by labouring classes; the exhibitions at the windows often of not very delicate character,—more than half the glazing of the sashes deficient, the vacant panes stuffed with *straw or a piece of a garment*; the narrow staircases frequently jutting out into the street, give a peculiar character. The affected imitation of the Parthenon on the Calton-hill is, I think, a disgrace to the age. Think of the poverty of idea to *servilely* copy that which the men of Athens set up more than 2,000 years ago! No adaptation of principle of design, but a mere servile copy! Ye men of Edinburgh, consider if this is not plain truth.—R.

ANOTHER ROMAN PAVEMENT AT CIRENCESTER.—We understand that, in digging a sewer down Dyer-street, Cirencester, a Roman tesselated pavement has been discovered in good preservation. The principal object is a dragon within a chequered border. It was found about 2 feet below the surface; and from the fact of a former one having been discovered many years ago in the cellar of the house parallel with it, the supposition is that it must originally have extended a great distance. It seems that its preservation is not contemplated: it is to be hoped, however, that a drawing will be made of it, and the spot where it was found carefully mapped.

THE STATURE OF ANGELS.—Bishop Purcell, of Cincinnati, has received the first of a pair of kneeling angels to adorn his cathedral, sculptured under the direction of Hiram Powers, in Italy. Some one asked the bishop if the stature was not of uncommon size, it being the kneeling figure of a person six feet in height. In answer, he gave the history of his commission to Powers. He had directed it to be made "of the natural size." Powers, in reply, requested something more definite, alleging that "*he had never seen an angel.*" The bishop referred to Revelations xxi. 17 for his measurements. This was conclusive, and was the gauge as to size and proportions of the object sent.—*Boston Chronotype.*

BUILDINGS AND MONUMENTS,
MODERN AND MEDIÆVAL.
Edited by GEO. GODWIN, F.R.S.,
Fellow of the Institute of Architects; Corresponding Member of several Societies.

Part III. of this work, price 2s. 6d., to be published on the 1st of September, will contain Views of Roslin Chapel, near Edinburgh; New Church at Homerton, Middlesex; the Royal Botanical Gardens, Kew; Bridgewater House, London; Sir Benjamin Heywood's New Bank, Manchester; Ely Cathedral, East End; the Théâtre Historique Paris; Sir Robert Peel's Picture Gallery; with descriptive letter-press.

Parts I. and II. may now be had. Order of any bookseller.

TENDERS

For Mrs. Clarke's house, Central Hill, Norwood; Mr. F. Lett, Architect.

Cowley stocks.		Norwood bricks.
Macey	£1,300	£1,297
Howard and Nixon	1,160	1,242
Gammon	1,153	1,115
Taylor	1,140	1,106
Glenn	1,136	......
Cundy? and Davis	1,120	1,090
Wallace (accepted)	1,119	1,094

Cowley stocks to be used. The quantities taken out by Mr. E. Blake.

TO CORRESPONDENTS.

"*Roman Catholic Church, Greenwich.*"—We are asked by the architect to state that the sum of 9,000l. mentioned in our last number as having been outlayed in obtaining the new Roman Catholic Church at Greenwich, includes 3,000l. paid for the site and the large house now used as a parsonage.

Received.—"F. L.," "W. W.," "J. T. J.," "Philo-Romanesque," "H. W. S." (the district surveyor must have notice—it is a distinct rule); "W. B.," "F. C." (yes); "J. L. C.," "F. C." (not sufficiently important to engrave); "J. B. D.," "E. R. M." (forwarded to the right quarter); "T. F. A.," "E. P.," "O. A. P."

Books and Addresses.—We have not time to point out books or find addresses.

NOTICE.—All communications respecting *advertisements* should be addressed to the "Publisher," and not to the "Editor;" all other communications should be addressed to the EDITOR, and not to the Publisher.

TO PROVINCIAL READERS.—In reply to complaints of the irregular delivery of THE BUILDER in provincial towns, we beg leave to state that it is invariably published by seven o'clock on Friday morning; and that the irregularity complained of rests entirely with the parties through whom it is obtained.

ADVERTISEMENTS.

ROYAL POLYTECHNIC INSTITUTION.—First Series of Dissolving Views Illustrating Rome, with a Description embracing the most interesting points connected with the subject. Daily at Half-past Four, and every Evening at One Half to Ten o'clock.—Lectures on Chemistry, by Mr. J. M. Astley. Daily at Half-past Three, and every Evening, except Saturday, at Nine o'clock. Lecture, by Dr. Bachhoffner, on Hugeen's Patent Process of Freezing, &c. Exhibition of the Chromatrope. The Oxy-hydrogen Microscope. Diver and Diving Bell.—Admission, 1s. Schools, half-price.

TO ARCHITECTS.—COMPETITION AND OTHER DRAWINGS.

MR. THOMAS S. BOYS, Member of the New Society of Painters in Water Colours, and author of "The Picturesque Architecture of Paris, Ghent, Rouen, &c." and of "London as it Is," offers his services in Tinting Backgrounds, Landscapes, Perspective Views, Interiors, &c. From the long experience he has had in such subjects, he is fully aware of the points essentially necessary to be attended to. Drawings and designs illustrated in a superior manner.—Address, Mr. BOYS, &c., Great Titchfield-street, Oxford-street.

BOOKMAN and LANGDON, 28, Great Russell-street, British Museum. MANUFACTURERS of every sort of PENCILS, their goods may also be obtained from all Stationers. Ever-pointed Pencils in Gold and Silver, with New Patent Holder, of various kinds.

FUNERAL FEATHERS.—TO UNDERTAKERS, CABINETMAKERS, and OTHERS.—G. SHADBOLT and Co., Funeral Feathermen, beg to inform the Trade that they have REMOVED their FEATHER BUSINESS, &c.

SAMUEL HOOD and Co., Castings Warehouse, &c., Upper Thames-street, REGISTERED STABLE FITTINGS. Enamelled Mangers, with double hay-racks, or with enamelled water-cistern on one side.

SNOXELL'S PATENT SAFETY REVOLVING WOOD SHUTTERS. Manufactory, 26, REGENT-STREET and 191, CHANCERY-LANE. Patent sealed on the 5th day of February, 1846.

BUNNETT and Co., ENGINEERS, Patentees of REVOLVING IRON AND WOOD SAFETY SHUTTERS, ORNAMENTAL METALLIC SASH BARS, MOULDINGS, &c., IN BRASS, COPPER, ZINC, &c. FOR SHOP-FRONTS, SKYLIGHTS, &c.
Office of the Patentees, &c., Deptford, Kent.

By Her Royal
Majesty's Letters Patent.

PITT'S PATENT SELF-ADJUSTING DOOR KNOBS and LOOSE SPINDLES.

HART and SON beg to invite the attention of Architects, Builders, and others to their New Furniture, mounted for PITT'S PATENTED SPINDLES.

No. CCCXLIII.

SATURDAY, SEPTEMBER 1, 1849.

 NE of the most recent of Weale's little red rudimentary works, is a History of the Styles of Architecture, by Mr. Bury,* wherein the writer endeavours to show, as we also have again and again asserted, "that there is, perhaps, no art or science which possesses more extensive or prolific means of instruction and entertainment, or which has greater claims on the consideration of the world at large, than that of architecture." The architecture of a country is inseparable from its history ;—" it is the external and enduring form of a people's habits—an index of their state of knowledge and social progress." In architecture, as in other things, we may say with Goethe, " There is neither rest nor pause, but ever movement and evolution, —a curse still clinging to standing still." How greatly our ideas of the past are elevated in imagination by its architectural relics seems to have escaped consideration. Mr. D'Israeli saw this, when he said at a recent dinner, speaking of the works of the architect,—" Depend upon it there is magic in form, to which human nature must ever be obedient. When we contemplate the past, even in ruins, we admire it, not merely from the associations of the past, but *because the past is embodied in the beautiful.* If all that remained of the past was a ruined cotton mill, you would not contemplate it as you do Tintern abbey."

Mr. Bury re-treads the ancient paths, and has produced a pleasant book. Some of his historical statements are made with too little reservation, as if there were no such thing as doubt. For example, one among many, he writes that the temple of Belus " was founded by Semiramis, 1650 years before Christ,"—as if the bills were in our Record office (such as it is), and could be appealed to ; whereas the fact is altogether doubtful, and the date more so. There are so many contradictory opinions as to the time at which this queen lived, even to the extent of centuries, that it is impossible to arrive at a satisfactory conclusion upon it ; and one distinguished living writer asserts that Semiramis never existed at all, and that her history is simply an allegory, showing the power of maritime commerce !

There is a little want of chronological arrangement, too, in the first portion of the book ; these objections, however, will not prevent us from awarding praise to Mr. Bury for his work as a whole, and recommending it to such of our readers as require an introductory history of architecture.

A part of his concluding chapter will serve as a specimen of the writer's style, and give his opinion on three subjects,—Nash ; competitions ; and precedent-rule.

Nash, he says, " undoubtedly may be considered as the originator of a new class of arrangement in street architecture, and to whom, on account of his bold and masterly conceptions and improvements, London owes more than to any architect since the time of

* " History and Description of the States of Architecture of Various Countries, from the Earliest to the Present Period." By T. Talbot Bury, Architect. Weale, Holborn. 1849.

Wren : criticism has been too often unduly exercised on his works, which in some instances, in mouldings and details, are faulty ; but when we consider the low state of architectural taste at the period of his career, and the immensity of the works on which he was engaged, his imperfections ought to be forgotten in our admiration of his mental energy and unceasing industry and exertion.*"

Of competition he says :—

" The present system of selecting a design from a large number submitted in a general competition (all purporting, of course, to be in conformity with the instructions) is mostly favourable to the unprincipled and incompetent artist, whose professional dishonesty is too frequently successful, and he is chosen to increase the list of monuments of bad taste or parsimony, for which this country, more than any other, is so celebrated. The selection thus made is more generally influenced by the greater amount of ornamental features, and not by the superior composition of the design ; it matters little if the ornaments are inappropriate, meretricious, or unequally distributed, or to what extent three sides of the building are impoverished or starved, so that the principal façade looks rich : in short, the quantity of enrichment seems to be the main object, without consideration as to its consistency for the purpose or situation of the building. The details of cathedrals, royal chapels, palaces, and princely mansions, are borrowed to disguise hospitals, schools, asylums, training colleges, and even workhouses. This dishonesty in the expression of a building, and the ignorant introduction or bad execution of useless ornament, seems to be sanctioned by custom, and is daily perpetrated ;—success stimulates the empiric to proceed in his career, and the public taste becomes infected by his productions. May we not partly consider it as a sign of the times, when the unrealities, inconsistencies, and shadows of the art of architecture, are chosen in preference to works of sound judgment and sterling merit ? or must we blame the fatality which too frequently permits some influential member of a committee to propagate his own mistaken views of architecture ?"

And then of precedent :—

" From the errors of this system another has arisen, which, in ecclesiastical buildings, seems to hinder all advance in art : precedent is now the only rule, and from which it is heresy to depart ;—' that which has been shall be,' without consideration as to whether it may or may not be perfect. The criterion of an artist's merit, or the groundwork of his fame, consists in servile copies of ancient examples, and too frequently in the introduction of features for which, by the change of our religious ceremonials and forms, there is not the least use.† The only requirement of an architect of the present day (so far as the erection or restoring of churches is concerned), seems to be a knowledge of the varieties of details of the Gothic buildings, which he is allowed to put together in any way he likes ; for, according to the views of certain societies, they must of themselves produce a good building. Now if the letters of the alphabet of architecture, thus jumbled together without system or principle, are not generally unsuccessful in their combination, what noble results might we not expect to follow a proper study of the works of our ancestors, and a discovery of the essential elements of their art ! Then would buildings be designed on the principles which brought to such perfection the works of the fourteenth century, and we should have harmonious compositions, instead of bad copies of the patched and mutilated erections of all dates."

As an example of the engravings with which Mr. Bury's work is illustrated, we give, on the following page, a view of Southwell Minster,—a well-known Norman structure.

* " The fate of the dead line was Nash's : the difficulties attendant on the building of the new streets were of such a magnitude as few men could have contended against ;— these and his good works have been forgotten, whilst small imperfections are noted."

† " To describe more minutely those peculiarities, would only be to direct censure to some buildings where the architraves are not altogether responsible for the inconsistencies."

Part II. of the " Rudiments of Civil Engineering," by Mr. H. Law, a portion of the same series, treats too cursorily (to justify the sub-heading " special construction") of roads, railroads, canals, docks, and bridges.

The same publisher has recently issued a second edition of Mr. Gibbons' excellent treatise " On the Law of Dilapidations ;" a work which will be found of great service by all architects and surveyors, and indeed by others beside these.*

" I have been more spacious concerning this learning of waste," says Coke, " because it is most necessary to be known of all men ;" and Mr. Gibbons, acting on the same motive, has been " more spacious" in this new edition, and has added the cases decided since the first edition was published, also the statutes passed.

Amongst books of this description, scarcely so well known as it deserves to be, is a volume on "The Law of Fixtures," by Mr. Standish Grady.† This is a subject on which many of our correspondents are seeking information, and, in reply to some of them, we may usefully extract, on another occasion, a portion of our author's chapter " Of the Right to Remove Fixtures set up for Ornament or Convenience and Domestic Use."

From the twisted course of law we pass to the production of the Grecian volute. Our readers will remember a letter from Mr. Jopling, a short time since, announcing his discovery of a simple adjustment for describing the volute and other scroll-work. Mr. Jopling has now published his method, in the shape of a small pamphlet,‡ with a request prefixed that reviewers will not publish any explanation of the adjustments. What the author sets forth is, " that while one end of a definite distance (a rod of any length), is carried round a circle *once*, the other end may be taken *twice* round another circle ;" and his mode of doing this is shown in the pamphlet. Mr. Jopling has long laboured to impress the public with the importance of a knowledge of curved lines, and to induce a more general study of them. He now asserts that " the mystery which has so long hung over the simple cause of the great superiority in ancient Greek architecture and works of art, as to the beauty, proportion, and harmony of the forms which they introduced —' those refinements which marked the smallest production of the Grecian chisel,' as well as the largest features in their works of art—is now discovered beyond a doubt to be in a great degree owing to the scientific knowledge of particular and practical geometrical curved lines possessed by their architects, artists, and artizans, which instructed their mind and eye in truth, beauty, and variety of form, and enabled them to design and execute works which no other people have equalled."

It appears that others have been working in the same path. A correspondent, who signs himself " Edward Burstow," addressed a letter to us on the appearance of Mr. Jopling's communication just now referred to, stating that he had himself, ten years ago, invented a simple apparatus by which " every description of parallel and converging lines, and every continuous spiral line that may be required can be drawn, with as much ease as adjusting a pair of compasses, and making different circles from the same

* A Treatise on the Law of Dilapidations and Nuisances. By David Gibbons, Special Pleader. Weale. 1849.

† The Law of Fixtures with reference to Real Property, and Chattels of a Personal Nature. By Standish Grady, Barrister-at-Law. London : Owen Richards. 1845.

‡ " An Impulse to Art ; or Ancient Greek Practical Principles for Volutes and Lines of Beauty innumerable." By Joseph Jopling, Architect. The Author : Felton Villa, Finchley-road.

SOUTHWELL MINSTER.

centre, so that an artist, however deficient in attainment, can, by the aid of this simple instrument, produce the scroll or volute to any proportion. In any prescribed space a volute can be described in one revolution, and all the lines converge to the same point, or in the same space can make many revolutions with the same number of continuous spiral lines tending to the same centre." He afterwards sent us a number of volutes described by the instrument. These investigations have more extensive bearings than are apparent at first sight.

As we are speaking of books, we will take the opportunity to mention the scheme of *The Architectural Lending Library*, which has been opened by a respectable member of the profession, and will probably be found advantageous by some of our readers. The catalogue, now before us, includes 742 works, and this number it is proposed to increase. Each subscriber is to pay three guineas at the time of entering his name, as an entrance fee, and three guineas as his subscription for the year; for the second year the subscription alone is to be paid. Any two gentlemen under the age of twenty-one may club together to pay the subscription. Each subscriber is entitled to have out of the library at one time any number of volumes to the full amount of the annual or half-yearly subscription he has paid, for a period specified. But it is proposed, if the project meet with support, to appoint a committee of subscribers to advise as to these and other laws, and as to the best mode of increasing the efficiency of the arrangements. We sincerely hope that the scheme will find favour in the eyes of the public, as we see in it the germ of an important establishment.

"The number of books," writes a student, friend to us, "which it is necessary to master, the much greater number of which it is necessary to know something, oppress and overwhelm me." We have not space to offer him consolation and to urge him onward, but we have an apposite sentence of Schiller on the tip of our tongue, which he shall have instead,

and which will serve as a thought-giving close to our article :—

"Energy of spirit is requisite to overcome the obstructions which faint-heartedness, as well as the indolence of nature, opposes to education. Not without a significance did the Goddess of Wisdom, in the old fable, step in full armour from the head of Jupiter; since her first occupation is warlike. At her very birth she has to maintain a hard contest with the senses, who will not be torn from their sweet repose."

Fight the good fight, and fear not.

THE VALUE OF THE ROMANESQUE STYLE.

THROUGH circumstances, the new Byzantine Church at Wilton has lately met with considerable attention; and several opinions have been expressed as to the fitness of that style of architecture for modern English ecclesiastical structures.

At the risk of differing from many whose opinions are entitled to the highest respect, I cannot help thinking that the Romanesque (and I include under that name all its protean varieties in England, France, Germany, Sicily, and Constantinople) has not met with a fair share of attention from modern architects. To those whose ideas of church architecture are limited to a reproduction of the forms of mediæval antiquity to the minutest detail, it is not to be wondered at that Romanesque should prove a dead letter; they soon get lost in a perfect maze of beak-heads, cat-heads, griffins, and other monstrosities, which they soon see would never do to copy: they have not the smallest notion of *improving* a style: unless a style will furnish them with door, window, and buttress ready made, it is in their opinion worthless.

The history of Romanesque architecture is in one respect quite unique; its resources were never, as in Greek, Roman, or Gothic architecture, fully developed. Its infancy may be seen in the ancient basilicas, its youth at Constantinople or Ravenna, but a prime it never had. It was nipped in the bud by the invention of the pointed arch. There are some writers (Mr. Paley, in particular) who assert that Gothic architecture was the natural development of Romanesque,—that it could not consistently have taken any other form; but I have often thought that if, in some one country, the pointed arch had never appeared, a style of architecture of a degree of perfection of which we can now hardly dream, would

have been the result. If a few men of genius were to devote themselves to a careful study of the Romanesque (not exactly in the spirit of Berlin and Munich, which amounts to little more than reproduction), it would go a great way towards attaining that great desideratum—a new style of church architecture in the spirit of the Protestant ritual.

It cannot fail to strike the attentive observer of the architecture of the metropolis, that there is a singular want of harmony between the ecclesiastical and domestic structures erected of late years. The tapering spire, the pointed arch, the gracefully-diminishing buttress,—features which combine so well with those picturesque conventual buildings and straggling gables which the mediæval architect knew so well how to group around them, but ill accord with Pimlico palaces and west-end squares. The horizontal and perpendicular line, when brought into violent juxtaposition, produce, perhaps, the most jarring and unpleasant contrasts of which architecture is capable. Now just imagine, Mr. Editor, a church in a Romanesque spirit erected in such a situation. The admirable manner in which the Lombard churches of Italy combine with the street architecture, is worthy of remark, and they nevertheless present a strictly ecclesiastical character.

Mr. Sharpe has noticed the great number of churches existing on the continent where the round arch is used in windows, &c., and the pointed arch in what he terms the arches of construction. The round of the Temple Church, and Kirkstall and Fountains Abbeys, are English instances of this arrangement, the effect of which is, to my mind, very pleasing. In a case such as I have supposed, where the pointed arch would be too vertical in its outline for the exterior, it ought still to be used, to give greater solemnity to the interior. It strikes me that this mode of treatment would have been a great improvement to the church at Wilton. Another reason which induces me to recommend the Romanesque for metropolitan churches is its great suitableness for decorations in ornamental brickwork. Any one who will look attentively at the new church at Streatham will, I think, soon convince himself of this fact. I know that many will point to the brick mouldings and ornaments of the Tudor period, and ask, triumphantly, what can be more suitable than these? But, with all due deference to their opinion, I must affirm that these were imitations of the *stone* features of their predecessors,—and to imitate stone in moulded clay seems to me just as reprehensible as to imitate masonry in cast plaster. Any style which requires mullions or tracery must necessarily be unsuitable to brick construction. Let a mullion appear what it is,—a bar: construct it of stone, wood, or metal, if you will, but not of a number of little pieces of baked clay, piled one on the top of the other. The high-pitched roof, "excluding sun and air," which Professor Cockerell has lashed so vigorously, and which is such a source of expense to modern Gothic architects, would not be necessary to give due expression to this style,—and a glance at the interior of St. Mark's, at Venice, would serve to show that in a style which admits of such a picturesque display of large and subordinate arches, even galleries would not be altogether hopeless.

Whatever may be the faults of the Romanesque —and they are legion—they were faults produced rather from a want of refinement of execution than from any inherent defect in the style itself. It breathes throughout the purest spirit of Christianity, somewhat gloomy and ascetic perhaps, but still untainted by the subsequent pollution. It has been well remarked by Lord Lindsay, that these artists "Christianized everything they touched;" and when we reflect that their sole *precedent* was the very dregs of the splendid luxury and licentiousness of the Roman empire, it must be admitted that they displayed an amount of taste and originality quite marvellous. It was these barbarians, be it noted, who were the first to spring the arch *from* the column, instead of buttressing the arch *with* the column,—who first laid aside the clumsy bent architrave of the Romans to adopt that beautiful system of orders of mouldings afterwards carried to such perfection by the Gothic architects,—who first conceived the magnificent idea, and carried into effect the magnificent reality, of an ærial cupola. But take the least artistic part of the Romanesque—its truly barbarous sculpture—and compare it with the Gothic sculpture of the fifteenth and sixteenth centuries, and this will show the minds of the artists in their true light. Both were grotesque in the extreme; the one the production of an impotent hand, the other of a vindictive mind; the one did his best to produce that holy imagery and peculiar symbolism which had its origin in the catacombs of Rome, the other to pourtray his rival monks in ludicrous positions and unseemly attitudes; the one carved his devout freemasonry rudely enough, the other cut elegant devices into riddles and rebuses of the names of ecclesiastics. I must own I prefer the crudeness of the former to the refinements of the latter.

I sincerely hope, in conclusion, that a style which our continental neighbours are studying with great avidity may meet with some little more attention in England.

PHILO ROMANESQUE.

NORTHAMPTON CORN EXCHANGE.

SIR,—May I beg, through the medium of your columns, and as an architect and competitor for designs for this building, to say a few words respecting this competition; and in so doing, I beg to say that I should not have troubled you, nor have occupied your valuable space, but from a sense of the gross injustice done to those architects who, I may say, were so unfortunate as to join in this competition,—a competition, I believe, that has seldom been surpassed for the taste which most of these designs exhibited; and from a careful estimation of them I should say they could not have been valued at less than 2,000*l*.

The cost of the building, as stated in the instructions to architects, was not to exceed 7,300*l*.; but after some time had elapsed, and we (that is myself and partner) had begun preparing our designs, a circular was sent to the effect that the directors had come to a resolution that plans would be entertained although the cost of the building might in their estimate exceed that sum, and that the intention of the directors was to select such plan as would best carry out their requirements at the least expense.

Trusting, of course, to what was here stated, we sent in a design accordingly; and in about three weeks afterwards, having to transact some business in that town, I proceeded there, and was allowed the liberty of inspecting the designs, of which there were upwards of fifty, and a better collection, as I have said before, I have never seen.

Upon making inquiries, I found that the committee had selected three designs, which they were to submit to the directors, who were to make a selection of one of them. I also found, to my astonishment, that they had resolved not to consider any design estimated above the sum of 8,000*l*., and also all those with pillars in the large hall,—and which virtually threw out of the competition three-fourths of the designs sent in.

Now, what can be thought of such a competition:—the directors of a public company inviting architects to compete, sending them instructions which they did not abide by, and only led us astray in our designs? I am inclined to think that it was merely for their own fancy; for what should they know about pillars, when out of about a dozen designs they chose three, and, after referring them to three eminent architects, refused to have any of them. But to return; it can be proved that a room with pillars would have suited their purpose as well, if not better, than without; and I will leave it to any other architects who have seen these designs to attest the truth, and to bear me out in saying that the majority of the designs sent in with pillars were infinitely better than those without. I do not say that they have not a right to throw out such designs as they might think proper, provided they were not according to their instructions,—but that is not the case. Is it at all likely, I would ask, that we, or any of those architects who were thus thrown out of the competition without having their designs even looked at, would have been at the trouble and expense which is necessarily incurred in designs for such a building, if we had thought the instructions were not binding? If we had *not* complied it would have been a different thing; but here it is just the opposite; we trusted to their instructions, and why did they not abide by them? There were no restrictions before the plans were made, then why should they have made any after they had been sent in? All this would have been avoided if they had employed a professional man at the first, instead of three at the end, as they have done, and which would no doubt have led to far different results, as it appears, from a resolution they have come to, that from the reports of the architects they employed to report on the three designs they had selected, who considered that neither of them were at all suitable or even capable of construction without an enormous outlay much beyond their means, they therefore resolved that none of them should be accepted; but that two of the architects whose plans had been thus condemned should design another between them, so that they are about as near getting a plan to their mind as they were at first.

A. AND C.

*** Since writing the above I have received a letter in answer to an inquiry I had made, stating that Mr. S. Alexander, and Mr. Hull of Northampton, are the architects chosen.

THE BIRMINGHAM WORKHOUSE COMPETITION.

THE guardians have resolved on adopting the plan, No. 24, selected by the architects, whom they had called in to advise them, as the best. It would seem, however, that the matter is even now not straightforward. Our readers will remember that the selecting architects recommended also a second plan, said by them to be obviously by the same architect as the first. Now this plan, it appears, bears the name of the architects Messrs. Drury and Bateman, partially erased; and as the instructions peremptorily required that the designs should be anonymous, a guardian, Mr. Brookes, moved that these two designs should be rejected, inasmuch as they were not prepared in accordance with the instructions. The motion was rejected, on the ground that the onus of the selection rested on the three architects who had been appointed to examine the plans, and that these gentlemen could not have been *influenced* in their decision by the names being on the plan. This is not the question. If the architects have recommended plans for selection not prepared strictly in accordance with the instructions, they have not done their duty.

"A WORD TO THE WISE."

DWELLING-HOUSES.

THE fears of us poor Londoners have been much worked upon lately with the fearful results of a visit from the cholera. At the very mention of that fearful scourge whole parishes are found ready to unite in petitioning for an Act to render increased ventilation and perfect drainage an imperative provision in all houses hereafter built; but more than this is required,—they imagine that this want is not with them, or with their class, but that the real necessity exists in but small tenements situate in the narrow confined courts and pest alleys forming the back slums of London, and homes of our *mobility*. It is not, however, only these houses that are deficient in the mere requisites that are necessary to ensure health for the occupants, but it is houses of the respectable rentals of 40*l*. or more. To tenants of such houses we would urge the imperative duty of seeing that in the house there is nothing injurious to the health of their family. But a short time since a fatal case was reported of the death of a widow lady of cholera, in Gibson-square, Islington, and this was followed within the week by another death in the same house, and the fatal result was attributed to "*sleeping over a closet that smelt of the drains.*" Is it to be told to a reasonable man, that to ensure perfect ventilation and good drainage, an extra expense must be first incurred to effect the same, and if, knowing this, a man grinds a builder down in the purchase money to such a low figure as will pay none but those who know how to scamp and hurry through work to suit the market price,—is it likely that the builder would incur expense when it is doubtful whether he would in return get one farthing more from the enlightened and liberal purchaser? This cheap purchase of house property will tell, and has with many already told, a fearful tale, verifying most impressively the old adage—"Penny wise but pound foolish." That man who purchases a newly-erected house cheaper than he can have it built, is either taken in and done for, or strictly speaking he is encouraging a rogue; for if the builder does not receive a fair price, how is it possible for him to act with honesty and justness by his fellow tradesmen engaged under him? If the builder receive but 15s. for every 20s. he expends, it is manifest that to keep up such a losing game *some must suffer*. Every one must have a home; a home is the first and last essential to human life; it is the place in which all our associations are to be found; it is there we enjoy the pleasures and endure the sorrows of life. To secure that essential and necessity we are compelled to make every other thought subservient. These thoughts should occupy every man's attention—should arouse in him a continual anxiety and thirst to know in what manner the "home" may be increased in comfort; not a modern invention connected with health should be passed without examination; many, perhaps, will be found to be whimsical and useless, but all will be found to be instructive and suggestive. All matters connected with building have long been considered as unworthy of general interest; scarcely a man but who in his own mind considers himself a judge of "bricks and mortar," chuckling to himself that he can see as far as any one through a brick wall, but if the question was more deeply considered, a great change would speedily be effected; they would find, when they gained a knowledge of the principles that govern *all* connected with building, what a very little they really understand of the science. Thousands of houses are built and sold in the manner the public would purchase an article of clothing, but unfortunately, the one being for permanent use while the other is but temporary, the result, when unfortunate, is continually felt by the unlucky owner, and unless a great portion of the community will arouse to view the right side of this question, there seems but little doubt that every square yard near London will be covered with houses ill-arranged, badly ventilated, filled with faults, and containing all the elements that old King Death can wish for.

FRANCIS CROSS.

A LIST OF THE PRINCIPAL COLOURS USED IN PAINTING, WITH NOTICES OF THEIR CHEMICAL AND ARTISTICAL PROPERTIES.

By WILLIAM LINTON.

Class	COLOURS	CHEMICAL DESIGNATION	PREPARATION	CHEMICAL CHARACTERISTICS	ARTISTICAL PROPERTIES	ADDITIONAL COLOURS.—WITH REMARKS.
WHITES	Flake White	Carbonate of Lead, with an excess of Oxide.	Plates of Lead exposed to the action of Vinegar Steams in beds of Fermenting Tan.	Blackened by Sulphuretted Hydrogen, Hydro-Sulphuret of Ammonia, and other foul gases, common to most dwelling-house atmospheres; for which reason a rapidly drying and protective vehicle is essential to resist it up against such evil influences. It has no injurious action upon Vegetable and other colours, as some have conjectured. It is perfectly soluble in diluted Nitric or Acetic Acids, when free from Pipe-clay or Sulphate of Barytes.	The best White extant for Oil or Resin vehicles when pure, which is generally ascertained by its enamelling whiteness and opacity; its usual adulterations are Sulphate of Barytes, Chalk, Pipe-clay, &c., all of which are partially transparent, and consequently appear darker in unctuous or resinous vehicles.	There are other Whites of Lead, varying in body and brilliancy, and equally objectionable on the score of the sulphurous vapours, as *Krems*, *Roman*, and *Venetian*. The Whites of *Zinc*, *Tin*, *Baryta*, and *Silicium*, although they are comparatively secure against the foul gases, are too feeble in body to be satisfactory in unctuous or resinous vehicles.
YELLOWS	Cadmium Yellow	Sulphuret of Cadmium.	A combination of Cadmium and Sulphur.	Resists the action of the foul gases, light, &c. It is a most durable and brilliant colour.	A beautiful Orange-tinted Yellow, of an excellent body, and an admirable substitute for Naples Yellow, and other Mineral Yellows which are liable to injury from noxious vapours, light, &c.	There are other Mineral Yellows, but they are all more or less objectionable. The Chromates of Lead, like all preparations of that metal, are blackened by the foul gases. The united Oxides of Lead and Antimony furnish *Naples Yellow*, a colour readily affected by noxious vapours and by light. *Orpiment*, or *King's Yellow* (Arsenic and Sulphur) is equally destructible; also *Patent Yellow* (Lead and Salts treated violently.)
	Strontian Yellow	Chromate of Strontian.	A Solution of Strontian added to one of Chromate of Potash.	Resists the action of the foul gases and light, and is perfectly durable.	A pale Canary Yellow—another safe substitute for the faulty Yellows mentioned above.	
	Yellow Ochre, Oxford Ochre, Roman Ochre, Stone Ochre, Brown Ochre, Terra di Sienna, Umber, Jaune de Mars	Oxides of Iron.	Native Earths, consisting of Silicate of Alumina coloured by Oxide of Iron. (Jaune de Mars: A Chemical Preparation.)	All Permanent Colours, whether Native or Calcined.	The Oxides of Iron are among the most stable colours of the palette. When properly washed and prepared for Oil painting, they are incapable of injuring other colours, and may be used to substitute the soundest materials with which the Chemistry of Nature has furnished the painter for the imitation of her works.	The Vegetable Yellows are not to be depended upon. They soon disappear when applied in delicate tints or thin glazings, especially if subjected to the action of the Solar rays (a summary mode of ascertaining the probable results of light exposure). *Gamboge* (made by Æther for Alcohol) is equally fugitive.
REDS	Light Red	Oxides of Iron.	Yellow Ochre, calcined.	A perfectly permanent Colour, not affected by Acids or Caustic Alkalies. Vapourised by a red heat if pure.	A beautiful colour, and of an excellent body.	There are other Mineral Reds which are durable; but they are of inferior quality and are not needed. Native Cinnabar is inferior in every respect to Vermilion. Venetian Red is an inferior representative of Indian Red, and Colcothar a still coarser one. Red Lead blackens in air, and has no claim to durability. All Vegetable colours however should be looked upon with suspicion.
	Indian Red		A Native Earth.			
	Vermilion	Bisulphuret of Mercury.	Mercury and Sulphur sublimed together.			
BLUES	Native Ultramarine	Consists of Silica, Alumina, Lime, Soda, and Potash, Oxide of Iron, Magnesia, Sulphuric Acid, Sulphur and Chlorine (according to Gmelin, Varrentrapp, and others) in its native state.	Prepared from a Mineral called Lapis Lazuli.	Acids, which will not affect other Mineral Blues, will destroy the colour in Ultramarine.—This is one of its best Chemical Tests. None of the neutral gases, or light, or other pigments do it any injury. It is perfectly durable.	A most invaluable pigment: too well known and appreciated to require any comment.	There are other Mineral Blues, but they are better avoided when the Ultramarines are available. The Oxide of Cobalt and Alumina form *Cobalt Blue*; and the Oxide of Cobalt and Glass form *Smalt*: they are both blackened by foul gases. *Prussian Blue* and *Antwerp Blue* are inferior in colour, and very fugitive.
	Artificial Ultramarine	It is regarded as a compound of Silicate of Alumina, Silicate of Soda, with Sulphuret of Sodium; the colour is owing to the reaction of the latter on the two former constituents.	Prepared by several difficult processes, some of which are kept secret by the makers.	Responds to the same tests as the Native Mineral.	A cheap and really valuable substitute for the Native product. The best is that which is the most purple in its tint.	The permanent deep blue: they are injured by light and alkalies. *Indigo* is...
GREENS	Chrome Green	Sesquioxide of Chromium.	When Chromate of Mercury (the Orange Precipitate on mixing Nitrate of Mercury and Chromate of Potash) is strongly ignited, Oxide of Chromium remains in a powder.	A permanent colour in all respects. (The colouring matter of Emeralds.)	An opaque light Green, of a full body.	There are other Mineral Greens. Those of Copper, the Emerald Green, and Mineral Green, are very insecure in Oil vehicles.
	Terra Verte	Carbonate of Copper, united with Silicate.	A Native Mineral.	Both quite permanent.—Native or Calcined.—Like the Ultramarines, Acids destroy their colours.	Beautiful delicate Greens: deservedly favourite pigments with most painters.	
	Malachite	Oxide of Copper, united with Silicate.	Native Minerals.			
BROWNS	Vandyke Brown, Cologne Earth	Decomposed Vegetable Matter.	Decayed Wood, Peat, or Bog.	These Browns are reputed permanent in themselves, the opacity with which time generally favours them in picture, being attributable probably to a loss of transparency in the vehicle, rather than to any change in the pigments: dark colours making the defect more evident than light ones.	Dark transparent Browns.	The dark Browns, though chiefly of Vegetable origin, seem to be the only deep transparent colours which have much claim to being permanent. The deep Reds, Yellows, Greens, and Blues, are all more or less of a fugitive nature.
	Mummy	Vegetable and Animal Matter combined.	White Pitch and Myrrh, with Animal Matter.			
	Asphaltum	Bitumen.	A Mineral Pitch or Resin, found floating on the Dead Sea; also after the distillation of Natural Naptha.			
BLKS.	Ivory Black	Animal Matter.	Calcined Ivory.	A perfectly durable pigment.	Of a Brownish-black tint.	
	Blue Black	Vegetable Matter.	Calcined Vine Stalks, Cocoa Nut Shells, &c.	Quite durable when the blue tint is natural.	Of a Bluish-black tint.	

MINERAL — ALL THESE COLOURS MAY BE SAFELY USED AS PERMANENT ONES.

Carb. | Bitu. | Anl. | Vgt.

In recording the defects and disabilities of Colours, it should not be forgotten that the Painter's Vehicle or Diluent must have considerable effect in preventing Chemical Action amongst the component particles from mutual contact. And if the Vehicle be of a sound and firmly drying quality, even the external attacks from damp and foul air, to which so many of the Colours are liable, may often be successfully resisted. Just should the Vehicle be of a sound character, instead of being a provocative of, instead of being a guard amongst the Colours.

FREE EXHIBITIONS OF ART FOR THE PEOPLE.

Recently in our metropolis works of art have been offered to the gaze of the public free of charge, in a few edifices, that thus may be said to illustrate the pictorial genius of the age. That such free exhibitions exercise very powerful influences upon the taste of the community, and are, on this account, very desirable and necessary, we do not think will be questioned. We may express a hope, however, that they may become, by every possible means that can be adopted for their success, a great attraction. If the proprietors and managers of them persevere in popularizing art in its varied departments, which doubtless they will do, provided they only receive sufficient encouragement,—if they secure, as assuredly they deserve, patronage from quarters whence it is expected to flow,—if they render them worthy of frequent observation,—their tendency to refine the masses and educate them in art, will indubitably, before long, be every where and by every body acknowledged: the ultimate effect will be a universal understanding of its powers and its principles. It is more especially the large halls, containing the productions of different artists, open free of expense to all who seek to derive pleasure and profit from their contemplation, which we consider to be such a great boon to society. Facility to an examination of these works is every thing, for thus inducement is held out to the multitude; inclination to visit them as often as opportunity offers, increases with the gratification; and a familiarity with, and pleasure in looking upon, the most beautiful things, are safeguards against many vices.

The proprietors of these halls themselves may be reminded that the beneficial results which spring from them will be in proportion to the merit and moral impression of the works exhibited. The more excellent they are, the more they display those qualities which the great masters inculcated,—the more will they be calculated to convey a perfect knowledge of art. We advocate, therefore, or recommend, the adoption of these free exhibitions for the people. Let them be multiplied. Let one or more be established in every city and provincial town throughout the kingdom. We would suggest the value, the immeasurable good, of giving gratuitous lectures on the pure and simple elements of art, so as to form and assist the judgment of those ignorant of, or who are not yet conversant with, matters to which their attention is directed.

F. Lush.

CLERKENWELL GRAVEYARDS AND THE FLEET DITCH.

With reference to a recent letter in your journal, on "Graveyards in Clerkenwell," from the surveyor of the district, recommending that 2 feet of concrete should be placed over them, permit me to say that the churchyards of Clerkenwell being several feet *above the public ways*, this would, if covered with concrete, force all pernicious exudations through the walls of the churchyards, and thereby occasion more danger to the public than by permitting them to pass off unrestrained. Can it be necessary still to say, that the best way of remedying the abomination is to cease burying in the church-yards of all towns and crowded neighbourhoods? *Prevention will be found better than cure.*

While addressing you upon the all-absorbing subject of the present time, may I urge upon the Commissioners of Sewers a little more caution, at this unhealthy season, in causing drains to be opened and cesspools emptied. I know of several instances where the inhabitants were quite well until the drains were disturbed; why not wait for a cooler temperature? It is also to be regretted that the Commissioners of Sewers do not practise their experiments, or gain their experience in some out-of-the-way-place, such as the Isle of Dogs, instead of poisoning the metropolis; any of your readers who have been obliged to move about the streets recently will no doubt bear witness to the necessity of these remarks.

When the weather becomes cooler some careful steps must be taken to render the Fleet ditch (if it cannot be covered) more bearable. I ask anybody to go down Bowling-street, and enter the houses on the *west* side, and it will be observed that the flow of water does not touch the sides, upon which the excrements are left, with fish, vegetables, &c., to decompose and fill the atmosphere with poisonous vapours. I was asked a few days ago if there were any odours from a dust-yard just opened in Castle-street, Clerkenwell? The question, however, cannot be readily answered; it is exactly similar to striking all the notes of a piano at once, and then inquiring as to the tone of any one note. You are no doubt aware of the various smells in this locality from the different occupations on the borders of the Fleet ditch.

In conclusion, I request your attention to the *reservoirs* belonging to the New River Company in Claremont-square and St. John's-street-road, which are above the public ways, and you will observe that the water is exuding through the walls, and that in one instance the walls are bulged.

W. P. Griffith.

A WORD FOR THE ROYAL ACADEMY.

Not being a constant reader of The Builder, the letter of a "Passed Student," dated August 11, only accidentally came to my knowledge. It does not require much phrenological science to perceive how differently minds are constructed. I am, like your correspondent, a "passed student," but my feelings towards the Royal Academy are feelings of unmixed gratitude. For ten years I enjoyed all the advantages of that institution, without one sixpence cost. The great and glorious statues of the Greek sculptors were always exposed for my study; living models were provided and prepared to my hand; paintings by the first masters, from which the principles and practice of the art are to be learnt, were annually placed before me. In addition, the library, where are to be found prints from every school, as well as treatises on art in every language, was always at my unlimited command. During these ten years I was free to the annual exhibition. In all this time, though a careful and thoughtful student, I was not successful in obtaining one of the many medals proposed to the school as tests of progress. Leaving the Academy, I spent some time on the continent of Europe, and at my return I applied to the council to be re-admitted to the advantages of the schools: my former course being known, this favour was readily granted, with the notice that the application must be made annually, as the council could only renew the permission for one year. To me, an annual letter seemed no great tax. I now became an exhibitor, and so obtained free admission to the exhibition; and, Sir, if in any season I sent no picture, so far from considering the payment of a shilling a hardship, I contributed it with a feeling of pride, in the idea that I could add my mite to that treasury from whose accumulated mites I had derived such incalculable advantage.

Your correspondent says, "he has no hostility against the academy." It would be strange indeed if he had; but he seems to think the funds not properly appropriated. All other exhibiting societies divide the profits amongst the members, but the members of the Royal Academy share nothing. All the funds are produced by shillings received at the door (certainly the public have a shilling's worth for their shilling), and these funds are expended on the schools. The fabled pelican of the wilderness plucks its own breast for the support of its young. The Royal Academy spends the funds procured by its own exertions in raising up students, who are to become the rivals of its members, and who are to take the bread from their mouths. A reserved fund is, therefore, necessary to save the institution from the contingency of diminution in the annual receipts, to preserve members in their old age from penury, and to extend the hand of charity to all who have ever exhibited on the walls of the academy. Your correspondent well knows that nothing is contributed to the support of the Royal schools, by the Government, or by the Sovereign. The shilling received at the door is its all in all.

The mighty benefit to be gained by admitting what your correspondent calls "the lower public" to the exhibition, is not well made out. Those who most loudly insist on this measure, are the men who deny to modern artists any knowledge or power (?). If then their works are so contemptible, what good are "the lower public" to derive from the exhibition. The National Gallery at next door is open to every shirtless amateur. He may there study the works of the masters in art; and on Sunday he can walk to Hampton Court and see the cartoons of Raffaelle. Surely all this is much more wholesome food for his mind than what Mr. Conyngham calls "the chalky absurdities" of Eastlake, Mulready, Etty, Landseer, &c.

As you have admitted one passed student to state his feelings, you will not, I am sure, refuse the privilege to

A grateful Student.

A LONDON FEVER STILL.

THE CRYPT OF BOW CHURCH.

"I have often reflected upon the unprovided condition that the body of the people were in at the first coming of this calamity upon them, and how it was for want of timely entering into measures and management, as well public as private, that all the confusions that followed were brought upon us, and that such a prodigious number of people sank in that disaster, which, if proper steps had been taken, might, Providence concurring, have been avoided, and which, if posterity think fit, they may take a caution and warning from."—*Account of the Great Plague in London in 1665*, by Daniel De Foe.

It has been our lot for many years past to be more or less engaged in investigating the antiquities of London, and during these researches to explore various neighbourhoods which few persons without a particular object would think of examining. When searching for the relics of a bygone time, we have never failed to observe the condition of things of the present, and to endeavour, when occasion served, to lay such matter as seemed useful before the public. We have engraved the annexed sketch of the ancient crypt of Bow church, thinking that in the present state of the public health it would be beneficial to lay before our readers not only verbal denunciations, but a correct representation of one of the abuses which, even at the present enlightened day, is allowed to remain in this densely populated metropolis, premising that our objections are to the system, and are not intended to apply invidiously.

If it were not that powerful interests are in this matter opposed to improvement, it would be scarcely necessary to do more than place this drawing before the public, and to observe that below a large number of the London churches are similar receptacles for the dead. The fearful consequences of such a practice must surely be evident to every unprejudiced and well informed mind; but there are two classes of persons—one having a pecuniary and the other a personal interest in the continuance of intramural burials—who are difficult to convince. As to the first of these classes we will say nothing more than that their interests should be duly considered; but the feeling which dictates the wish to have our last resting place near the remains of dear relatives is a circumstance worthy of the greatest respect. Still, even this feeling ought to be quite secondary to the consideration of preserving the public health. It has been fallaciously argued that no ill effects arise from burials in vaults, in consequence of the bodies being encased in lead, and some say that they would think it a great hardship to be prevented from being placed after death among their family. Although the crypt of Bow Church is by no means the worst in London, still its atmosphere is a proof against the above assertion, and Mr. Walker and others have given evidence on the point beyond controversy. Wishing to obtain another opinion in addition to those already recorded and our own, we wrote an able surgeon and chemist to the following effect:—

"It having been stated that the practice of encasing bodies in lead previous to interment will prevent poisonous gases from being dispersed throughout the vaults in which such bodies are laid, will you inform us if you think it is possible by any such process to confine the gases which are generated by decomposition."

In reply, he said—"They would be completely confined by such cases made of lead until by their accumulation the case would no longer resist the pressure; the result would be either the sudden rupture of the case or the

A LONDON FEVER STILL——THE CRYPT OF BOW CHURCH.

J. PROPN   CAING Sc.

TERRA-COTTA WORKS IN ITALY——DETAILS FROM BOLOGNA AND FERRARA.

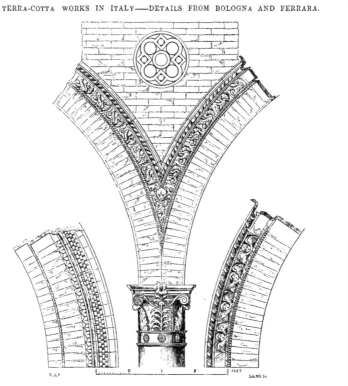

ONLY　　　LAING Sr

PAINTINGS AT THE ROYAL INSTITU-
ION, MANCHESTER.—We understand that
ie sales have been numerous, and to a larger
nount than at the corresponding period of
st year's exhibition. Since the opening on
e 2nd ult., paintings have been sold to the
:tent of 747l., being in amount 200l. more
at the total sales at the same period last
:ar. Amongst the pictures sold are No. 117,
ie Refreshing Stream (Poole, A.R.A.); 166,
rthelius, the Belgian Geographer (P. Van
chendal), which was sold for 100 guineas ;*
'8, St. Cecilia (Henry O'Neil); and 348,
iew of Scarborough (J. W. Carmichael).

* To this picture the l
arded—the subject a Rel
iture in his study, with
on his face.

THE TERRA-COTTA WORKS OF ITALY.

ORNAMENT FROM BOLOGNA AND FERRARA.

THOSE who have made themselves acquainted with the extraordinary and beautiful
examples of terra-cotta in Italy, certainly
would wish to see this material used, as far as
practicable, in the countries like our own,
where so much brick building is in vogue.

The want of notices upon this head, made
us, when in Italy, in the years 1846-7, take
sketches of many of the best examples in this
style, and through the medium of your valuable paper, we may bring a subject into notice
which we hope may prove of interest to many
of its readers.

Bramante, one of the greatest architects,
shows, in his " Ospedale Grande," the church
S. Maria delle Grazie, and other churches, as
well as private buildings in Milan, that much
can be done in that material : the cloisters of
the Certosa, near Pavia, the Foro dei Mercanti, and many palaces in Bologna, have been
treated with equal success. Many interesting examples are to be found in Ferrara,
Forli, Pisa, Sienna,—and even Venice and Rome,
with their marble palaces and rich basilicas,
did not disdain works in terra cotta.

Annexed are drawings of some ornamental
works in this material from Bologna and
Ferrara.

The various combinations of the proportionately small members in the cornices, string
courses, &c., are remarkable; also, the little projection in proportion to height, the richness of the
flat ornaments, and the pleasing variety obtained
by the intermixture of coloured or glazed
bricks. The ease with which ornament is produced in low relief, with great finish and elegance, compared with the same works in stone,
at comparatively small cost, is in our day
of economical reform a great acquisition.

Colour should be used with great care, and
not too lavishly introduced, as it would over-
burden the light and delicate mouldings and
destroy the general effect,—the forms given to
the bricks being elegant and diversified enough
of themselves, and capable of producing in one
colour a rich and solid effect.

In the façades of houses in other countries,
particularly in the north of Germany, it is very
common to introduce at intervals a course of
green, or violet-coloured, or glazed brick,
which often tells well. The coloured course
must not be carried through the architraves of
the openings, as is sometimes seen; it divides
and destroys the effect of the best-composed
profiles. A dark-coloured course does not
look well unless the change be at every other
or every third course.

When no varied courses are introduced, the
choice of the colour of the bricks to be used
should not be overlooked. In Italy, particularly in Bologna, they are, generally speaking,
much darker than those in the north of
Europe : a yellowish red seems to be the best
for our colder climes,—the rough weather
serving in time to darken the tints.

H. W. and H. M. B.

THE POLYTECHNIC INSTITUTION, REGENT-STREET.

THE new series of dissolving views now exhibiting at this institution, plethoric of attraction, are particularly interesting at this moment as showing some of the localities prominently brought before the public by the recent operations of the French in Italy,—operations which the historian will hereafter find difficult of explanation in connection with French consistency. If our volatile, disorganized, but nevertheless wonderful neighbours wish to learn the opinion entertained by the ordinary English public of their proceedings before Rome, they should send a deputation to the Polytechnic, and the shout with which the demonstrator's reference to the bombardment of remains which belong to the whole world is received, would give them an insight to it.

We should like to see a series of good lectures on architecture and architectural history illustrated here. It is not possible to visit this institution without picking up something. You go into the theatre, and the lecturer is speaking of water—that it is compounded of two gases, oxygen and hydrogen—he decomposes some, shows how hydrogen will burn singly—how oxygen will re-illume a blown-out taper—and how the two together will explode, to the alarm of a whole row of Mrs. Smith's ringletted charges and the evident delight of the school-boys. Well, all this you know; you have passed it long since; so you have the theory of dew, evaporation, and the principles of the steam-engine; but, nevertheless, it revives previous studies, and keeps the mind awake to what is passing around us every hour in nature's great laboratory. In the midst of it, too, you get an idea or two: he leaves the elementary, and for a minute or two shows how abstract discoveries made by the mathematician and the patient investigator in the closet are brought to bear on the every-day life, and to increase the comforts and lengthen the lives of the multitude; he gives you the last bit of knowledge in connection with springs, and you probably go out saying, I had either forgotten that, or had never heard it. Old and young, wise and unlearned, may spend an hour or two usefully as well as pleasantly at the Polytechnic Institution.

NOTES IN THE PROVINCES.

THE west end of the Early English chapel at Stourbridge is said to have given way considerably, owing to the cutting of the railway and the continual shaking by the trains passing it.——Remains of interest, it seems, have been already found at Bury St. Edmunds, where the tracing of the extensive foundations of the monastery has been commenced, under direction of the Bury Archæological Institute.——Contracts for rebuilding Halstead Church having been entered into, the demolition of the old edifice is in progress. The subscription is rapidly increasing: 1,500*l.* have been already realized.——The restoration of Holy Rhood Church, Southampton, is now finished, excepting the tower, and the church was to be opened on the 28th.——It has been resolved to erect a new district church, with free sittings, and a parsonage, in St. Maurice and St. Mary Kalender, united parishes, at Winchester. A site has been chosen by the committee, and an endowment offered by the curate of St. Maurice's. A subscription is also in progress, headed by 100*l.* from the bishop.——The price of gas at Poole is to be reduced from 10s. to 8s. 4d. per 1,000 cubic feet, in the hope, apparently, of increasing the dividend, even now 6 per cent., by a less impracticable price than heretofore.——The foundation stone of a new church in commemoration of the majority of Viscountess Fielding, has just been laid at Downing, near Holywell,—a better way of laying out money on such an occasion than practice generally inculcates.——Attempts are being made, by sale of sites by auction, to 'project' a new town on the sea coast of North Wales, at Llandudno, near Conway, on an estate belonging to Mr. E. M. Lloyd Mostyn, M.P. ——Two new maps of Liverpool have just been published by the borough engineer. Contour lines are given for sewerage purposes, &c., from actual measurement of levels, at every 4 feet of altitude on the large scale map, and at every 8 feet on the smaller.——The United Gas Company at Liverpool, while admitting that the consumption of their gas has been checked by depression of trade, have just declared a dividend of 9 per cent., or 4½ per cent. on last half-year's proceeds. They also announce that there is now a progressive increase in the company's rental.——The chief stone of St. Paul's Church, Portwood, Stockport, was laid on Wednesday week.——An organ has been built for Hatfield Church, by Messrs. Forster and Andrews, of Hull. It is encased in the Gothic style of the building. The gallery and pews, in this church, which block up the northern limb of the transept, are to be removed, it is said, and the wooden partitions in the gallery, it is hoped, will follow.——The chapel at Brougham Hall, has been recently "splendidly fitted up in the antique style," (?) by Mr. William Brougham, brother to Lord Brougham.——On Wednesday week, the Ancient Fraternity of Wallers, Bricklayers, and Plasterers, at Newcastle, laid the foundation stone of their new hall, now being erected in the Castle Garth, by the York, Newcastle, and Berwick Railway Company.——The aid of the Admiralty is now expected at Queenstown, late Cove of Cork, in the formation of a long talked of pier, in place of the present miserable landing place.——Nearly 2,000 poor starving Irishmen were lately set to work on the Newry Ship Canal, at 9s. a-week, but they had no sooner recruited their exhausted energies a little, than they struck work for 12s. a-week, and are now idle as ever.

RAILWAY JOTTINGS.

THE calls for August, so far as lately advertised, amount to 1,124,346*l.* For August last year they were 3,122,773*l.* For the eight months of the present year they have now reached 15,758,980*l.*, against 25,750,019*l.* in the corresponding period of 1848.——It is stated that a proposition has been made by one of the contractors on the Oxford, Worcester, and Wolverhampton to complete the most productive part of that line on his own responsibility, taking as security the tolls to become due on the opening.——A local paper says, that a contractor of some considerable standing has offered to make the line of railway from Portishead to Bristol (following the course of the river), for 50,000*l.*, exclusive of termini.——On a report that the works on the Basingstoke and Salisbury line are to be shortly resumed after a lengthened stoppage, the Salisbury correspondent of a Hampshire paper says this has rather surprised him, as he had long looked as despairingly at the embankments and tunnel near the city as at the excavations, &c. of the Salisbury and Southampton Canal which was to have done such wonders for Salisbury years ago.——The tube, it seems, has been itself considerable injured, in the recent accident at the Britannia-bridge. The four upright beams of the off entrance are cracked at about 2 feet from the bottom of the tube, and three of the top cross beams, and three of the bottom ones in connection with them, are broken in like manner about 12 inches from the centre of the tube, in addition to which, one of the lifting beams gave way close to the bearing.——A new bridge, on the principle of the Besons-bridge, over the Seine, near Paris, has been erected, we hear, on the Reading, Guildford, and Reigate Railway, to carry a double line over a gully at Albury. The span is 50 feet. Five light girders support a wooden platform. The weight of the girders, composed of wrought and cast-iron, does not amount to 10 tons. When tested, this light structure did not deflect in the middle, it is said, more than ⅘ths of an inch with one of the heaviest of the South-Eastern locomotives on it, and at a speed of 45 miles an hour the deflection was very little more than ⅘ths of an inch.——The high level bridge at Newcastle was opened for the passage of trains on Wednesday week. Only one line of rails, however, is complete enough for traffic.—The tailors of Gateshead appear, from the *Observer*, to be disputing about the trowsers that saved the life of one of the workmen employed at this bridge, by hooking him in descent on a good stout nail driven in where a nail had no other special business to be at that moment. Why don't the nailers take example by the tailors, and uphold th admirable adaptation of *their* stout mate rial for the *hooking* of passing workmen?——A labourer has been remanded at the Clerken well Police-court, for urging a driver of tw loaded trucks to take them, in defiance c orders to the contrary, along a temporar bridge on the East and West India Docks line crossing the Great Northern at Islington while the bridge was insecure and unde repair, and whereby the bridge gave way an killed a man and two horses on the spot.——A New York correspondent of the *Time* states that railways on a new plan are to b introduced into the streets of that city, whereb omnibuses will be done away with. There wil be but one rail placed on upright stanchions The carriages will be suspended from thei axles, will hang near the ground, and will b drawn by horses. The railway will not interfer with the passing of other carriages.

THE BRICK TAX IN 1711.

THE following appears to be a printe statement drawn up to bear out a petition t the House of Commons in the reign of Queen Anne, against a forthcoming tax on bricks As it is a genuine statistical account of build ing matters in the metropolis a century and half ago, you perhaps will think it worth per petuating in the pages of your journal.

A. B. S.

"A Just and Exact Account taken out of the Book of the several Brickmakers, Lime-burners, Tile makers, Slaters, Masons, and Paviers, of th Goods made, or brought in by them, within th Weekly Bills of Mortality, or within Ten Mile of the same, in the Year 1711, in relation t the intended Duties on Bricks, Lime, Tiles, &c. humbly offer'd to the Consideration of thi Honourable House.

	Bricks.		
The total of bricks made *anno* 1711, within the bills of mortality, and ten miles' distance, as appears by the makers' books	2068800		
Waste and loss to be deducted, not less than	0371100		
Remaines to be taxed	2597700		
Which at 3s. per thousand comes to	£3896	11	0
Plain tiles made in the aforesaid year and distance, appears to be 2250000 at 4s. per thousand, comes to	0450	00	0
Ridge tiles made in the said year and distance, and sold therein is 12000, at 6s. per thousand	0003	12	0
Pantiles made in the said year and distance, is 450000, at 6s. per thousand, comes to	0135	00	0
Paving tiles made in the said year and distance, of twelve inches square is 39000, at 3s. per hundred	0058	10	0
Paving tiles of the lesser sort, of ten inches square, is 59000, at 1s. per hundred......................	0029	10	0
Slates used for covering, the year and distance aforesaid, is 150000, at 4s. per thousand..................	0030	00	0
Lyme made or used, in the year and distance aforesaid, is 24319 hundred, which at 6s. 3d. per hundred, or 2s. per quarter, comes to	7599	13	0
Note.—That 3d. per bushel on lime is as much as the whole value of the commodity (water and land-carriage excepted).			
Pebbles, raggstones, &c., for paving streets and stables, &c., is 11000 ton, at 2s. per ton..............	1100	00	0
Portland, Purbeck, Rygate, Oxford, Newcastle, and marble stone, brought and used in the said year and distance, is 3355 tons, at 2s. per ton	0503	05	0
	13806	01	0
That by the abovesaid account, the yearly duty amounts to 13,806*l.* 1s.	13806	01	0
Out of which it is reasonably to be supposed, that one-third after the passing of this Act will not be consumed, by reason of the heavy duties upon the said materials, viz., the sum of....................	4602	00	0
The remaining duty	9204	00	0

THE OBSTRUCTIVE QUESTION AT THE METROPOLITAN COURT OF SEWERS.

ON Wednesday last a meeting of the commissioners was held, in pursuance of a special summons, for the purpose of ascertaining, from documentary and other evidence, the truth of certain statements made by Mr. Chadwick and others with regard to flushing sewers, as noticed in THE BUILDER of last week. The Rev. Wm. Stone, M.A., presided.

The requisition having been read by Mr. Woolrych, the clerk, Mr. Bullar said he had received a communication from Sir John Burgoyne, which set forth, that as a matter of order, Sir John "considered it to be inexpedient to enter into any discussion on the requisition, on account of its personal character," as he believed it to be "calculated to diminish the feeling of cordiality and action which every one would admit ought to be encouraged amongst the commissioners." Sir John proposed that a resolution should be adopted, suggesting another requisition for the purpose of considering the question of flushing, and omitting any reference to the opinions or statements of other members of the commission. He, Mr. Bullar, fully coincided with Sir John Burgoyne as to the necessity of such a step being taken at that stage of the proceedings, so that time might not be wasted, nor angry and unprofitable discussions indulged in.

The Rev. E. Murray moved that a resolution, in the form of Sir John Burgoyne's suggestion, be adopted; and Mr. Bullar seconded the motion.

Mr. Leslie objected. Certain statements had gone forth to the world impeaching the "morality" of himself, Mr. Byng, and Mr. Bidwell, as to this movement, and he (Mr. Leslie) did not think it was just to take any steps which might lead to stifling an important inquiry. If it was found that any plan was pursued by which the money of the public was wasted, surely they were not justified in pursuing such a course, even for another hour. Why need there be additional delay? The requisitionists were prepared with their proofs, but they were prevented from submitting them. First, they had been "counted out;" now they were told that their requisition was not properly worded; all they wanted was to go at once into the question, and they had no doubt of convincing even Mr. Chadwick himself that they were right, and he was wrong.

Mr. Johnson contended that "the dignity of the court" required to be maintained by their not permitting personal accusations to mix with notices of motion, or in matters of debate. The policy of flushing was the question, into which he thought they could not fully enter, unless the notice on the paper was altered.

After much irregular conversation, the resolution was carried.

Mr. Hume, M.P., then moved—"That with the view of enabling this board to decide as to the accuracy of the charges made as to the expenditure, at different times, for the works performed under the former and the present Commissioners of Sewers, Mr. Leslie, Mr. Byng, and Mr. Bidwell be requested to call for papers and returns of the expenditure in such case, and that a court be summoned to consider the whole question as soon as the facts shall have been selected." He (Mr. Hume) contended, that unless they "condescended to particulars,"—to use a Scotch but most expressive phrase, they would make no progress in the investigation.—Carried.

Mr. Bullar then proposed, and Mr. Leslie seconded a resolution, which was carried, requiring the secretary to prepare an account, in detail, of all the expenditure and particulars of, and incident to, the flushing works done since the opening of the commissions in 1847.

Miscellanea.

COMPETITION FOR THE RESTORATION OF NORTHFLEET CHURCH.—Sir: A competition was called for as far back as May 10th, and the drawings were to be sent in on June 5th. In common with many others I sent in designs on that day. On the 26th of July, not hearing anything as to their fate, I wrote to the vestry clerks, Messrs. Southgate and Son, requesting to know whether the committee had come to any decision, and on the 30th received for answer, that the committee had decided upon two plans; and, "although in many respects my plan appeared to possess great merit, they felt, on the whole, others must be approved." I did not receive this answer until after the successful architect had advertised for tenders from builders. I naturally expected after this the committee would return my drawings, but it seems this committee have no notion of troubling themselves with the rejected plans, for although I have written, I can neither obtain them nor any reply.—J.

MORE IRON HOUSES.—The Messrs. Belthouse and Co., of Manchester, are constructing four iron dwellings to be sent to California. One of them, now finished, is 20 feet long by 10 feet wide; the roof is elliptically arched, having a spring of about 18 inches in the width of 10 feet. One cottage was made with a pitched roof, but the arch is preferred. The inside height of the house is 7 feet 6 inches from the floor to the spring, and 9 feet to the centre, of the arch. Internally, the house comprises two rooms; the "house part," or day room, 12 feet 6 inches by 10 feet, and the bed-room, 7 feet 6 inches by 10 feet. The cottage has one outer door into the day room, an inner door between the rooms, and a window in each room. In each gable wall, within the arched portion, are four circular holes for ventilation, so that when open at both ends, and the inner door is also open, a current of air can pass through the house. The windows have also an opening by swivel and rack, like those in our factories. The whole fabric is of iron; the walls and roof of wrought-iron plates, 1-8th of an inch thick, and averaging about 5 feet by 2 feet 6 inches. These are framed on angle iron and T iron uprights, each plate numbered so as to fit into its own place, and all are fastened together, without rivets, by bolts and nuts only. Externally there are three uprights on each; these are of hollow roll iron, which, being filled with wood, can have screwed to them inside a wooden lining, which is being applied to two of the cottages about to be sent out. The roof eaves project about eight inches, so as to keep the rain off, and the whole structure is so compactly fitted, as to be perfectly water-tight. The external walls rest on a foundation of balks of timber, upon which are laid iron bases, forming a moulding on the outside, which prevents the water from settling there, and at the same time gives a finished appearance to the house. There is no flooring provided, it being intended that the floor shall be levelled on the spot, and either made of puddled clay or of boards, at the choice of the settler. The doors are simple frames of wrought-iron, covered with sheets of iron, and having lock and latch. Each window is 3ft. deep by 2ft. 4in. wide; the frame-work wholly of cast-iron, containing 16 panes, of which the four centre ones open on a swivel, with a segmental rack, for setting it open at three different angles, very similar to those in cotton factories. The weight of iron in one of these houses is about 2½ tons; and one such cottage costs (unlined) about 60*l.*; if lined with wood, about 10*l.* more.

REPORT ON SCHOOL OF DESIGN.—The wishy-washy character of the recent Parliamentary report on the London school is apparent to others besides ourselves. The *Athenæum* says:—"It certainly does seem a curious problem why, when every circumstance has seemed to favour the institution of schools of design in this country—when we know that they were established by the highest power in the state to supply a publicly recognized want on the part of the community—when there has never been a period at which in their public declarations their managers have not seemed animated by the greatest sincerity and devotion towards conducting their operations to a successful end—when the state and the manufacturers have given their money, the masters their energies, and the students their attention—when among the lists of managers and masters we meet constantly with names of individuals occupying high positions in government, art, and letters,—it does, we say, seem a strange problem why all inquiries into the progress of the school have resulted in an uniform admission that it was not in a position to furnish the world of manufacture with what it was expressly created to supply—good, efficient, and properly-educated *designers*. It certainly is not, to be sure, in the present milk-and-water report that we shall find any resolution of this 'crux.' We must mount higher up the stream, above the point where Parliamentary etiquette and the unwillingness to give personal offence to 'powers that be' have thrown the veil of polite ambiguity over the ugly yet honest faces of Truth and Candour."

TINTED GLASS FOR GREENHOUSES.—The *Literary Gazette* says, that the tinted glass used in the great Palm Stove, Kew, is a failure; and that this enormous structure will have to be reglazed with common glass.

AMERICAN METHOD OF TEMPERING EDGE TOOLS.—For heating axes or other similar articles, a heating furnace is constructed, in the form of a vertical cylinder, the exterior made of sheet-iron, lined with firebrick, 4 feet 8 inches diameter, or of such outside diameter as to give it an inside one of 4 feet, and 3 feet high. In the interior of this cylinder several fire-chambers are formed—usually four. The inner wall of each fire-chamber is 18 inches long, 4 inches from front to back, and about 4 inches in depth—forming, in the whole, a circle of 3 feet 4 inches diameter. Under each there are grate bars, and air is supplied through a pipe connected with a blowing apparatus. A circular table of cast-iron, 3 feet 4 inches diameter, is made to revolve slowly on the level with the upper part of the said chamber. This chamber is sustained on a central shaft, which passes down through the furnace, and has its bearing in a step below it: a pulley keyed on to it serves to communicate rotatory motion to the table. When the axes or other articles are to be heated, they are placed upon the table, with their bits or steeled parts projecting so far over its edge as to bring them directly over the centre of the fire, and the table is kept slowly revolving during the whole time of heating. When duly heated, they are ready for the process of hardening. The hardening bath consists of a circular vat of salt water: within the tub or vat, a little above the surface of the liquid, is a wheel, mounted horizontally with a number of hooks around the periphery, upon which the axes or other articles are suspended. The height of the books from the surface of the liquid is such as to allow the steeled part only to be immersed. As soon as the hardening is effected, the articles are removed from the hooks, and cooled by dipping in cold water. With the best cast-steel, a temperature of 510 deg. Fahr. has been found to produce a good result in hardening in about 45 minutes.—*Scientific American.*

UNWISE EXPENDITURE FOR BRITANNIA BRIDGE.—Can you inform an ignoramus what reason can possibly be given for forming the approaches, as well as the bridge itself, of the enormously expensive tubes? To me, I must own, it appears that this is a stupendous instance of the reckless manner in which Directors often waste the funds intrusted to them. The bridge consists (as you know), of eight tubes, laid in pairs, side by side, four of which will span the whole water way; and the four others, two at each end, will form the approaches over the steep banks of the Strait. Now, it appears quite obvious, that the tubes over the dry land, or bank, possess no advantage whatever over approaches made in the usual manner by a viaduct; consequently the excess of the cost of these tubes at each end above the cost of common arches must be just so much money thrown away.—FRUGI.

IRON SEWER FOR THE THAMES.—Is not the recently constructed tube at the Menai Straits suggestive of a plan of sewerage? Let us suppose a series of tubes laid down on each side of the river, made of wrought iron strongly riveted, and in lengths of 20 ft. by 12 in height, and 8 in breadth—the top of the tubes either level with or only one or two feet below the bed of the river. There can be no difficulty in sinking these tubes: any derangement might be quickly remedied, and the saving in expense, as compared with Mr. Phillips's tunnel, enormous. The junctions could be easily made, and at any time closed or altered, *pro re nata*. These tubes could be carried from Hammersmith to Woolwich Reach, at a distance from each shore of about 40 feet, or say about half-way between high and low water marks. Corrugated iron towers of about 6 ft. square might rise at intervals of a furlong, for the escape of the gases generated, and provided with a sluice or flood-gate on one side for the admission of water at ebb tide, when a greater impetus is required, as is often the case in a long drought. The natural and proper incline of the bed of the river to seaward might be kept; and at the terminus at Woolwich Marshes might be a spacious dock, in which the accumulated sewage could be drained and solidified, taking advantage of the ebb to get rid of the superfluous moisture. Let us once more be able to say of our river—

"Infirmo capiti fluit utilis, utilis alvo."

QUIDNUNC.

PROJECTED WORKS.—Advertisements have been issued for tenders, by 20th instant, for the erection of a new church at Birmingham; by 24th, for works to be executed in New Pauper Lunatic Asylum, at Powick, Worcester; by 6th, for the several works required in finishing 12 six-roomed and 5 eight-roomed houses now in carcase, at Islington; by 13th, for various works in erection of St. Luke's Church, Morton, near Bingley; by 20th October, for the erection of new grammar schools and master's house, &c. at Loughborough; by 4th inst., for additional building and alterations of Penrith Workhouse; by 11th, for the erection of a station and platform at Cosham, near Portsmouth; by 8th, for the erection of a weaving shed, mill, and warehouse, at Shipley; by 5th, for the building of two brick bridges at Beverley; by 18th, for the supply and fixing of iron roofs at Tithebarn-street station, Liverpool; by 25th, for founders', coppersmiths', and braziers' works for the navy; by 5th, for lighting part of Hampstead with naphtha, or essential oil of tar, &c., and for lamp burners, and reflectors, &c.; and by 4th, for repair and paving of foot- and carriage-ways at Westminster.

COMPETITION.—Advertisements have been issued for plans, by 1st proximo, of subscription baths to be erected at Wolverhampton.

REPORT OF THE COMMISSION ON THE BRITISH MUSEUM.—It appears that the buildings in which the vast collection is deposited have cost, since the year 1823, nearly 700,000*l*. The sums which have been expended in purchases upon the collection since that period the commissioners could not learn; but the whole since 1755, independently of the amount expended on the building since 1823, considerably exceeded 1,100,000*l*. The commissioners recommend, in lieu of the present board of 48 trustees,—1. The establishment or revival of an executive government, vested in one person solely responsible for the due execution of his duty, but assisted by a council, to whom he might readily and on all occasions resort for advice and assistance. 2. The establishment of a committee of trustees—a standing committee—elected and undertaking personally to perform all those duties of superintendence, investigation, and control which seem to be the proper and peculiar duties of the trustees, as distinguished from the duties of practical management and executive government, which seem to be the proper and peculiar duties of a governor director. 3. The providing better for the patronage or power of appointing all officers and servants.

LANCEFIELD FORGE, the property of Messrs. Fulton and Neilson, at Anderston, Glasgow, when in full operation employs about 100 persons, with several steam-engines constantly at work. A cutting machine slices iron plates, an inch thick, into small pieces, as a housewife cuts a piece of cheese with a table knife. The scraps are built into heaps, put into a furnace, and drawn out in masses blazing red, and subjected to the "tilt hammer," by which they are beaten into bars, the material for immense shafts, columns, and heavy engine gearing, sometimes requiring 10 or 12 horses to convey them away. The bars by Nasmyth's patented hammers are beaten into larger pieces, and made by them to assume their ultimate form and design. These machines can be made to come down at one moment so softly as scarcely to bruise a blade of grass, and at another with a force that would sink a ship of war. By the help of lever power, two or three men can raise, and turn, and manage the formation of a mass of iron weighing 12 or 14 tons as readily as a blacksmith forges a horse's shoe, and form it so accurately as not to be the sixteenth part of an inch from pattern. The slotting machine is a huge iron structure, about 65 tons weight, by which blocks of cold iron are cut, and grooved, and pared, as easily as pieces of wood in the hands of a carpenter. The workmen here have the use of hot, cold, and shower baths. There was not a single death amongst them during the last twelve months.

A MONUMENT TO THE LATE MR. C. BULLER, M.P., is proposed to be erected in Westminster Abbey. It is to be hoped due regard to the architecture of the building will be paid in determining the character of any future monuments here.

RESTORATION OF ELY CATHEDRAL.—The dean and chapter of Ely have published a statement of the contributions which they have received towards the restoration of their cathedral and the formation of a new choir. Contracts have been entered into for a new open screen, for the throne of the bishop and the stall of the dean, and for new sub-stalls, upon a scale and character suited to the magnificence of the church. They are to be finished before the 1st March, 1851, and their cost will exceed 4,200*l*. The superior stalls, the work of the great architect, Allan de Walsingham, in 1830, are to be restored as nearly as possible to their original condition. Plans are in progress for the removal of the organ to the north side of the choir, with a case and fitting in full accordance with the stall-work. The other works are advancing: the beautiful canopy-work next the altar of the chapel of Bishops Alcock and West, which was nearly destroyed, has been restored. The dean and chapter have been compelled, from a sense of imminent danger, to undertake a very extensive repair of the southern transept, the principal timbers of the roof of which were found to be rotten, and the upper walls and arcades, upon which they rested, seriously dislocated. It is intended to replace the mutilated sculpture of the timber cornice, the painting of the roof, the ancient decorations of the walls, and to open partially the arch of the western aisle.

AMERICAN WHITEWASH.—The following recipe is used for preparing the celebrated stucco whitewash, used on the east end of the President's house, at Washington. Take half a bushel of good unslacked lime; slack it with boiling water, covering it during the process to keep in the steam. Strain the liquor through a fine sieve or strainer, and add to it a peck of clean salt previously dissolved in warm water, three pounds of good rice ground to a thin paste and stirred while boiling hot, half-a-pound of powdered Spanish whiting, and a pound of clean glue which has been previously dissolved by first soaking it well and then hanging it over a slow fire in a small kettle within a large one filled with water. Add five gallons of hot water to the whole mixture; stir it well, and let it stand a few days, covered from dirt. It should be put on quite hot; for this purpose it can be kept in a kettle on a portable furnace. It is said that about one pint of this mixture will cover a square yard upon the outside of a house, if properly applied.—*Mining Journal.*

FELL'S SYSTEM OF PROPULSION.—In this system, the motive power is that of compressed air. A stationary engine communicates with a cast-iron pipe placed between the rails along the whole length of the line, and by this means air vessels of requisite size, placed at certain distances along the pipe, are filled with air of the wished for density. These air vessels (to speak popularly) supply the momentum to the engine truck, a lever bar attached to the truck opening, as it passes along, a valve or cock, which causes the compressed air to escape into a "chamber" running along the under part of the truck, and thus to become available for propulsion. As regards cost, the calculation is, that it will be 50 per cent. less than that of steam.—*Morning Post.*

MONUMENTAL WINDOW IN WORCESTER CATHEDRAL.—There has been erected a memorial window in this cathedral, by the Rev. Canon Wood, to the memory of his late lady. It is placed in the Baptistry, or Jesus Chapel, in the north aisle of the nave. The stone-work of the window, which is in the Decorated style, has been restored, and the tracery altered so as best to admit of the subjects represented in the various compartments of the head. There are six subjects represented in the body of the window (which consists of three lights), all directly or indirectly connected with the rite of baptism, and the legends underneath each are in Latin. The window was executed by Wailes.

CIRENCESTER.—THE TESSELATED PAVEMENT.—We understand that Earl Bathurst has undertaken, as lord of the manor, the removal and preservation of this relic of antiquity. It is understood that a house will be taken as a museum, and that the pavement will be laid down so as to form the floor of two of the rooms.

OPENING OF TUMULI ON ACHLAM WOL
—The Yorkshire Antiquarian Club have be
recently engaged in opening some of
ancient British tumuli near Achlam and L
vening. In one of a numerous lot at Achla
on the 14th, was found the skeleton of
ancient, and, we suppose, a true Briton, sitti
in an attitude of majestic repose, with head
the north, in that precise magnetic positi
which has been recommended as a novelty
some profound magnetician of the nineteer
century, as the true or right position ir
which all the bedsteads of the modern Brito
ought at once to be wheeled. The anci
hero lay not only in the right meridional po
tion, however, but also latitudinally right,
in less scientific terms, on the right side, w
a small British urn, the contents of which
seems to have appeared as if contemplatir
The urn was much crushed, but the skull h
been preserved entire, and is to figure in t
Yorkshire Museum, where its owner doubtl
never expected it to be. Another tumul
yielded a very large urn crushed and collaps
but full of calcined bones, and surrounded
various coloured clays. In a third, a curio
arrangement of chalk and flint rubble occurr
with some loose bones and marks of fi
A netting-needle appears to have been fou
in one of the tumuli. The urns were o
half baked. The club proposed opening
Anglo-Saxon burial mound, near Driffield,
the 28th.

EXCAVATIONS AT MOUNTSORREL.—F
several weeks past an attempt has been in p
gress to explore certain supposed remains
the ancient castle which stood on a rock ov
hanging this town. The task has been plann
and carried on by a party of quarrymen, a
there is now, it is thought, some prospect
the question being settled as to the existen
of a secret mode of access to the castle. T
men work, in the evenings only, in a sh
about 12 feet by 11 feet wide, which has be
lowered about 50 feet, or between 60 a
70 feet below the surface of the hill. It h
been cut out of the solid granite. Nearly 2
tons of old worked material, &c. have be
thrown out of it, including cut stones, and o
beams—some 17 feet long and perfectly sou
Nails, bricks of the quarry form, and oth
curiosities have also been found. An openi
of ancient construction, running towards
shaft, has been discovered in a back ya
The blocks of stone thrown out of the sh
it is thought, may have formed part of
winding staircase for ascent into the cas
Other secret passages are also tradition
believed to exist.

NEW POWER.—A hydraulic gravitation
gine, to supersede steam as a motive pow
has been projected by a Southampton mec
nician, a Mr. Jackson. Once started, it
said, it will go for six months without
sensible wearing of the material. A mo
is to be submitted to the Admiralty.—A
tropolitan inventor proposes to assist the
tion of small locomotive or other steam
gines by a large wheel, with sliding weig
and leverage so arranged as of themselves
produce a power of progression only requiri
the aid of a very small engine to overco
the dead points, where the weights have to
raised in their most disadvantageous posit
while generating an auxiliary power in
descent.

COMPENSATION CASE.—On 10th and 1
ult., an inquiry took place at Ruabon, for
sessing compensation to Mr. G. H. Whall
and others, for the purchase of 1 acre 2 ro
16 perches of land, part of the Plas Ma
estate, by the Shrewsbury and Chester Rail
Company. The amount offered was only 14
but, after a lengthened investigation, the j
brought in a verdict for the purchase of lar
564*l*. 15s. 4d., and for residential and o
damages, 1,800*l*. — making together 2,3
15s. 4d.; being more than sixteen times
much as the company had offered!

BRISTOL ART-UNION.—The drawing
the Art-Union connected with the Bristol
Arts' Academy took place in the exhibit
room on Wednesday in last week.
number of subscribers was small. A
feature in this year's Art-Union was the
senting to each subscriber an *original sk*
in lieu of an engraving as heretofore. T
were six prizes.

New Cemeteries.—The graveyards in Bury being, in dread reality, chock full, the ratepayers have determined on the substitution of a suburban cemetery, for carrying out which object they have appointed a committee.—At Bradford there also appears to be a prospect of the like substitution.—At Tredegar the inhabitants have been taking steps to establish forthwith a cemetery on a large scale, about half-a-mile from the town.

A New Colliery Gas Jet.—One of these singular and interesting perpetual burners, has recently been lit at a pit between Harrington and Workington, in order to consume a 'large blower' in the pit, which would have otherwise put a stop to the working of it. Ventilation and other efforts had failed to obviate the inconvenience, and the jet was therefore conducted from below, through a train of boxes and pipes, to the surface, where it now blazes on without ceasing, thus effectually curing the dreaded evil.

Cardiff Drainage Competition Plans.—A correspondent informs us that the commissioners placed the eleven plans sent in into the hands of Mr. Cubitt, who examined them, and made a report, having called in to his assistance Messrs. Scott and Smith, engineers. Mr. C. recommended No. 8, to be most worthy of the premium, by Messrs. Waren and Dimmock, contractors of the South Wales Railway through Cardiff. The Commissioners paid them the 50l. premium, and Mr. Cubitt 40l. for his trouble.

Monument to the late Sir John Barrow.—A proposition is on foot to erect a monument in memory of the late Sir John Barrow, in the neighbourhood of his birthplace, near Ulverston. It is proposed that the monument shall take the form of a pillar or tower, 70 feet high, to serve as a sea-mark. The sum to be expended is put down at 1,200l.

Brick-Making.— On Wednesday last, Jos. Rush, at Peter Syke, Cumberland, performed the feat of making one thousand bricks in one hour—one hundred in five minutes,— and twenty-six in one minute.—Carlisle Journal.

Thorwaldsen.—The Cologne Gazette announces that the directors of the Thorwaldsen Museum, at Copenhagen, will sell, on the 1st of October, a portion of the works left by the sculptor, consisting in part of duplicates in their possession, and partly of objects of value appointed to be so disposed of by Thorwaldsen's will.

Antiquarian Smashers.—We are told that a person of gentlemanly appearance has lately contrived to swindleseveral antiquaries in Kent, by selling them false Anglo-Saxon and early English coins. Is such a thing never done in London shops of "gentlemanly appearance?"

Pesth Suspension-bridge.—It is stated that, notwithstanding rumours to the contrary, and the fact that much damage was done to this work during the war between the Hungarians and the Austrians, it is now in a state little the worse for what has happened.

The Royal Visit to Ireland.—It is proposed to erect a statue of the Queen, by subscription, in Dublin, to commemorate Her Majesty's visit.

BUILDINGS AND MONUMENTS,
MODERN AND MEDIÆVAL.

Edited by Geo. Godwin, F.R.S.,
Fellow of the Institute of Architects; Corresponding Member of several Societies.

Part III. of this work, price 2s. 6d., is now ready, and contains Views of Rostin Chapel, near Edinburgh; New Church at Homerton, Middlesex; the Entrance to Royal Botanical Gardens, Kew; The New Psim Stove; Bridgewater House, London, with altered plan; Sir Benjamin Heywood's New Bank, Manchester; Ely Cathedral, East End; the Théâtre Historique, Paris; Sir Robert Peel's Picture Gallery; with descriptive letter-press, and numerous details.

Parts I. and II. may now be had. Order of any bookseller.

TO CORRESPONDENTS.

Received.—" Competitor for the Northampton Exchange," "N. B.," "F. C." (shall appear), "An Architect," "C. P." (shall appear), "W. W." (unavoidably delayed); "A. B.," "X." (has no legal remedy), "A Constant Reader," "R. B.," "T. W. P.," "J. C.," "J. C." (thanks, we fear other journals have exhausted the subject. We should be glad, nevertheless, to see the account), "E. B." (the wall may be retained by agreement, the property of B.), "J. Q.," "H. W." (the same statements have been often repeated), "G. F. J." (the Nelson statue is not of granite), "G. M." (we simply stated what we were informed on the spot, was the fact as to cost in that particular instance), "W. C." (should apply at the office in Greek-street); "J. P.," "J. C. W. H." (has no legal remedy against the Society of Arts for mislaying his design), "W. B." (we have not forgotten our promise to look at Waltham Abbey Church; our occupations lately have led us widely over the country), "J. P." (our correspondent will find it difficult to shut out the sound by a framed partition; a layer of asphalted felt on each side would do something towards it), "S. D." (will find it most advantageous to continue the practice of drawing). "Healthy Homes, a Guide to the Proper Regulation of Buildings," &c. By W. Hosking, Architect and Civil Engineer. (Murray, cheap edition, 1849). "The Modern Housewife." By Alexis Soyer. (Simpkin and Marshall, 1849).

"Books and Addresses."—We have not time to point out books or find references.

NOTICE.— All communications respecting advertisements should be addressed to the " Publisher," and not to the " Editor;" all other communications should be addressed to the Editor, and not to the Publisher.

TO PROVINCIAL READERS.—In reply to complaints of the irregular delivery of The Builder in provincial towns, we beg leave to state that it is invariably published at seven o'clock on Friday morning; and that the irregularity complained of rests entirely with the parties through whom it is obtained.

No. CCCXLIV.

SATURDAY, SEPTEMBER 8, 1849.

EARLY eighty plans for the drainage of this vast metropolis have been submitted for the consideration of the Sewers' Commission, and the extension of the time for receiving plans, will doubtless lead to an increase in the number. Many of these plans are quite worthless, and more of them are crude and ill-digested, the necessary consequence of the short time allowed for the preparation of them,—a circumstance which, as Mr. Bailey Denton urged in a letter to the commissioners, seeking the extension of the time afterwards given, amounted to "a positive exclusion of every person having a regard for his own reputation; for although the proposal which may ultimately be preferred, may involve but one main principle of design, such principle can only be mentally tested and matured by bringing to bear upon it every fact and contingency which locality and science may suggest to the originator of it. And will five weeks suffice for this?"

Well might Mr. Denton ask the question. If there were no other proof on record of the unfitness of the majority of the members of this commission for the position they occupy, this limitation would suffice. The subsequent extension of time, too, although sought by some who had found it impossible to submit a well-considered plan by the date named, was an injustice to those who had contrived to send in something. Further to illustrate the action of the Board of Sewers, we find that they are desirous of receiving proposals for a general system of sewerage, but that they refuse to have soundings executed. Now, such preliminary steps are to the full as necessary to ensure any thing like an approximation to an estimate of the cost of the works, as a correct map is to ascertain the best direction to be given to them. The very great uncertainty which the geologists of the board confessed that they felt as to the nature of the soil to be worked upon, would alone be a convincing proof of the necessity of such researches. As the commissioners would have the benefit of them, they surely ought to pay for them, and to furnish copies of the results to the different engineers they might invite to furnish competition plans for the works. To make definite plans in ignorance of the ground to be worked upon, would be merely a waste of time.

And here we would, on the other hand, briefly (and in a parenthesis) caution some who are connected with the commission not to affect to despise theoretical knowledge because they themselves only possess experience.

Theory and practice should go together. He who trusts to the one without the other, is very likely to meet with a combination of circumstances which will leave him sadly at a loss.

The discussions which have recently taken place at the meetings of the commission illustrate the necessity which exists for organizing, in a more scientific manner, the execution of works of public utility in our country. We have, in this case, a board appointed by Government under a special Act of Parliament, with full powers to act, and almost to legislate, yet it appears that, after eighteen months' existence, the real solution of the question of the effectual sewerage of London is as remote as ever. Small experiments have been tried; much talking has gone on amongst the amateur engineers; but as for the real good effected, it is indeed but small. Such a state of things could scarcely have arisen had the commission included some professional men. At any rate, the common sense of the public would not have been shocked by the publication of some of the absurdities contained in the reports of the meetings of the present board.

A correspondent writing to us from Paris on this subject observes :—"To a person accustomed to the contrary abuse of scientific discussion which prevails in France, there is something painfully ludicrous in the reports of this commission's proceedings, which show amateurs enunciating statistical and engineering facts in the very teeth of common sense. The statements are repeated by the daily press; they set the ignorant agape; but foreigners ask themselves, with wonder, how so eminently practical a nation as ours can allow such nonsense to be published by official authorities. Why does not the profession endeavour to exonerate itself from the restraints and difficulties imposed upon it by the composition of the different public boards? In almost every country but our own these questions are left to the decision of men having the very highest education in the branches of service they are called upon to direct. How is it that we in England so long admit that a man can become competent to decide engineering questions by the study of law, or of physic? Yet such is the system we adopt throughout our public administration. When we name a Lord of the Admiralty, we take a man who is fit to be a political economist; we make noblemen or lawyers secretaries at war, who never carried a sword; and we take barristers, gentlemen, and doctors to make our commissioners of sewers. 'Ils avaient besoin d'un mathématicien, et ils ont pris un maître de danse,' said Beaumarchais ; truly in England the same rule appears to prevail."

To the composition of the commission we objected when it was first made known, and still more so to the principle laid down by those who nominated the members of it, that *because* a man was an architect or engineer (and therefore might be supposed to know *something*, at all events, of the matters requiring consideration), he was not fit to be a Commissioner of Sewers. Tell us that such an architect or engineer is unscientific, is not intelligent, has prejudices and narrow views, and therefore will not make a good Commissioner of Sewers, and we can understand and admit the force of the objection. But when it is said that an enlightened, liberal-minded, scientific man, with business-habits, acquainted with construction, accustomed to the direction of such works as are likely to be required, is not a proper person, simply *because* he is an architect or engineer,—common sense revolts, and we unequivocally pronounce it one of the most preposterous assertions ever hazarded.

It was set forth in respect to drainage works in the report of the Metropolitan Sanitary Commissioners, and it is repeated in the "Report by the General Board of Health,"* just

* "Report of the General Board of Health, on the Measures adopted for the Execution of the Nuisances Removal and Disease Prevention Act, and the Public Health Act, up to July, 1849." Clowes and Son, London.

now issued, that "the more the investigation advances, the more it is apparent that the progressive improvement and proper execution of this class of public works, together with the appliances of hydraulic engineering, cannot be reasonably expected to be dealt with incidentally or collaterally to ordinary occupations, or even to connected professional pursuits, but require a degree of special study, which not only places them beyond the sphere of the discussion of popular administrative bodies, but beyond that of ordinary professional engineering and architectural practice. In justification of this conclusion, and to show the evil of the perverted application of names of high general professional authority, we might adduce examples of the most defective works which have received their sanction. All the improvements which the public have yet obtained in this branch of public works have been the result of the special and undivided practical attention of well qualified paid officers, and it appears to us that further improvement must be sought by the same means, and that one of the chief objects of future administrative arrangements must be to secure, protect, and encourage the zealous undivided attention and efficient labour of such officers."

Suppose we admit all this, surely the men of "connected professional pursuits" will be better able to judge of and discriminate the schemes of the "well-qualified paid officers" than those who know nothing of the matter. And what is the position of the present board? As a body (of course there are exceptions), they are ignorant of the matter in hand, and evidently—avowedly, indeed, by acts—have no reliance on the "qualified paid officers,"—one of whom, the chief surveyor, warns them against attempting to execute works proposed by the consulting engineer, as "they are wholly impracticable, and unworthy the object which should be kept in view for the perfect drainage of this great metropolis;" and says, as to the commission itself, that it is time for him "to speak out," in order that it may not bring itself "into ridicule, and destroy public confidence;" while another, the consulting engineer, says of a plan proposed by the surveyor, that it "would serve only to retard rather than to advance the general improvement," and that "it would be difficult to believe that any one holding the appointment of chief surveyor to the Metropolitan Commission of Sewers had really been serious in laying it before the court!"

The expenditure under some heads has been enormous, and demands immediate and rigid scrutiny. The "flushing" inquiry will probably lead to this; and if, as Sir John Burgoyne said in his letter to Mr. Bullar on the subject, "the *startling results* stated by the requisitionists prove, on inquiry, to be correct," an immediate remedy must be found.

The cost of flushing the Holborn and Finsbury sewers, under Mr. Roe, according to Mr. Leslie, was 3s. 3d. per mile per week; the money expended, according to the same authority, in flushing the Surrey and Kent sewers, amounts to 10l. 6s. 4d. per mile per week, and, in the gross, to a sum which is positively astounding! If this be correct, and it is seen that actually *thousands* of pounds have thus been got rid of, under the exclusive control, too, of one of the assistant-surveyors, and in a manner which seems to admit of little check, the necessity of the inquiry will be pretty evident. The useful result of the flushing is a *further* question.

To get perfect drainage (to lessen pain and

lengthen life) money should ungrudgingly be spent; but there must be no waste, no "cooking," no blinding the eyes of the public. The money is wrung from many who are ill able to pay it. What will our readers say when we tell them, in proof of this, that the Commissioners of' Sewers have signed during the year no less than 9,500 warrants of distress, and that there are 4,000 more waiting for signature! If our contemporaries aid us in bringing this fact to the knowledge of the rate-payers,—*Nine thousand five hundred distress warrants signed within the year, and four thousand more ready to be issued*,—attention will be recalled to the magnitude of the affairs confided to the Metropolitan Commission of Sewers; and the urgent necessity for an intelligent, wise, and business-like administration of them will be made obvious.

PROGRESS OF PUBLIC WORKS IN FRANCE.

MORE has been done during the eighteen years of Louis Philippe's reign, in the way of works of public utility and embellishment, than during the thirty years preceding, under the Consulate, the Empire, and the Restoration. Great as was the encouragement given by Napoleon, and truly magnificent both in project and utility the plans he formed, particularly for the improvement of Paris, nothing that he actually did can be compared to the results of the numerous operations undertaken since September, 1830, when a grant was obtained, to the amount of five millions of francs, for carrying them on. The sum thus voted was no doubt as much in consideration of the distress of the working class immediately after that revolution, as for a mere love of improvement. But the Government of Louis Philippe, in thus wisely employing them, has been accomplishing a double good, while it satisfied, at the same time, the enlightened views of the industrious middle classes, who see in such improvements immense advantages to commerce and manufactures.

The republic is not less sensible of the importance of continuing these works, and we find therefore rather an increase than a diminution of the amount and value of them.

On referring to a public document, we shall be able to extract some curious and interesting information connected with all the great works which the Government has had executed, and which will show a progress in art as great as in that of works of mere utility.

We have, in the first place, twelve monuments or public buildings in the capital, which have been constructed, finished or restored.

The Arc de Triomphe de l'Etoile, intended to perpetuate the glory of the French army, and the largest monument of the kind ever erected by man.

The Church of the Madeleine, commenced under the old dynasty, and proposed by the Imperial Government as a Temple of Glory.

The Pantheon, whose fortune has changed with every revolution.

The Museum of Natural History, at the Garden of Plants, containing a splendid and precious collection.

The Ecole des Beaux Arts.

The Cathedral of St. Denis, whose beautiful spire, menacing ruin, has we regret to say, been removed.

The magnificent Hôtel of the Quai d'Orsay, now occupied as the "Cour des Comptes" of the republic.

The bronze column of July, at the Bastile.

The Chamber of Deputies—again insufficient for its purpose.

The Institute of the Deaf and Dumb.

The Pont de la Concorde.

The College of France.

To these we may add, the additions to the Hôtel de Ville, now one of the finest buildings, and one of the greatest ornaments of the town; the new hotel of the Minister of Foreign Affairs, with its superb offices; the additions to the hotel of the President of the Chamber; the new stamp office in the Rue de la Banque; the restoration of the Cathedral of Notre Dame, and completion of the improvements

around it; and many other works. Indeed, we are not far from the truth in saying that scarcely a public building has remained unembellished or unimproved since 1830.

But we will confine ourselves for the moment to public works, that is, to such as are directly under the administration of Government, and are carried on by means of grants regularly voted by the Chamber.

Great attention has been paid of late to the improvement and extension of roads. The Government has shown in that respect a very laudable solicitude, and has shown a readiness at all times to second the recommendations made to it. In 1824, the total length of what were called "*routes royales*," was 33,538 kilometres, or about 20,637 miles. In 1836 they increased to 34,511 kilometres, or about 600 miles more; and in 1845 to 35,250 kilometres, or 460 miles more.

Between 1830 and 1847 we find that there were grants to the amount of 266 millions of francs, or 10,640,000*l.* for repairs and improvements of various kinds connected with roads. And that other special and exceptional grants were made, in order, among other things, to give employment to the working class, or to remedy disasters occasioned by inundations.

Great benefit has been derived from these outlays, however, and a great impulse given to the progress of art in construction of various kinds connected with these works, and particularly in respect to suspension bridges; and more of these and bridges of the common character have been constructed in France since 1831, than during several centuries under the old monarchy. All these improvements are worthy of note, as they distinctly indicate a vast industrial progress in the country, and prove that a new class of men interested in and connected with it have of late years directed the action of the Government.

The number of bridges constructed by the State or by companies on the "*routes royales*," and on the departmental, strategic, and country roads, amounts to 481. In few countries can so many noble structures of this kind, combining greatness of span with boldness and economy of construction be found. The Rhône, the Durance, the Dordogne, the Garonne, the Loire, the Saône, and the Seine, are crossed by some of the finest among them. We would mention those of La Roche-Bernard, of Cubzac, of Tournay-Charente and of Saint Claude, as being *chefs d'œuvre* in point of construction. The money appropriated for this purpose alone amounts to about 24,000,000 francs, or nearly a million sterling.

In the course of sixteen years, previous to 1830, 57 bridges were constructed by companies; and from 1830 to 1847 as many as 162.

There are 1,540 ferries in France, connected with the public service,—established wherever the circulation is insufficient to repay the expense of a more costly means of passage; and these produce to the revenue the sum of 400,000 francs—16,000*l.*

The number of light-houses in France, in the latter part of the reign of Charles X., was only 16,—10 on the British Channel, 5 on the Atlantic coast, and 1 on the Mediterranean. They have since been increased to 57; but, independently of these, there are 104 lights of an inferior kind, destined to mark the entrance of such roads and ports as are most frequented. The 57 light-houses are thus distributed,—17 on the British Channel, 25 on the Atlantic Ocean, and 15 on the Mediterranean and the coasts of Corsica.

The French think their system of lighting their coasts now quite complete, and believe it to be the finest in the world. Of this we will not offer an opinion; but we may as well remark, *en passant*, that their establishments for the manufacture of the apparatus connected with light-houses are of a decidedly superior character. There are considerable works in progress for the completion of the system of navigation by means of canals, intended to connect important points,—one between the Marne and the Rhine, another along the Garonne, and a third to unite the Aisne with the Marne. The extent of canal navigation in actual completion amounts at the present day to 4,623 kilometres, or about 2,680 miles English. In connection with these, great improvements have been made in deepening and ameliorating the condition of the navigable streams and rivers: these, when

finished, will present an extent of about 5,380 kilometres, or about 3,311 miles, and cannot fail to be highly beneficial to the country.

At the same time that these immense works were carrying on by the State by means of grants, the departments and communes of France were endeavouring on their side to improve and increase what are called "les voies départementales et vicinales." The first entered to about 44,977 kilometres, or 27,684 English miles, and the second to 60,184 kilometres, or 36,918 miles, while, what we should characterize as cross-roads and bye-roads (*chemins de petite vicinalité*) extend to no less than 600,000 kilometres, or 369,318 miles.

The tenth of the price of places in public vehicles, according to financial statements, amounted in 1832 to 4,887,000 francs; in 1840 to 8,450,000 francs; and now produces about 11,000,000, or 440,000*l.*

THE GREEK CHURCH, LONDON WALL.

IN London-wall, at the corner of Little Winchester-street, a building has been erected for the celebration of the rites of the Greek Church, under the direction of Mr. Owen. It is lofty and substantial, and must have cost a considerable sum of money. The opportunity was a good one for introducing a characteristic type, and this would seem to have been aimed at, but is missed. The architecture of Byzantium, the capital of the Lower Greek Empire (not "the Corinthian Order," as some of our contemporaries have stated), is adopted for parts of the building, but is not thoroughly carried out. The plan is a Greek cross, marked by a shallow recess in each side, and is crowned by a flat cupola in the centre. In two of the recesses are tribunes or galleries carried on horse-shoe arches and columns, the arches having a fringe of ornament. The ornamentation of the fronts of the galleries is Italian, and so is the ceiling generally. In front of the iconostasis, or screen enclosing the sanctuary, which is ornamented to a considerable extent, and is being coloured and gilt, are marble steps. The pulpit is peculiar in outline, half a water-butt on a post. Externally there is the same curious mixture of styles. There is a recessed porch formed by Byzantine columns, coupled *dos-a-dos*, with fringed horse-shoe arches (three intercolumniations): above are three other arches of similar character, having windows beneath them, while the front of the building is crowned by a pediment, with a heavy console cornice. The whole of the front is of brickwork cemented, with the exception of the porch, which is of stone.

THE FEVER-STILLS OF LONDON.

THE prevention of intramural burials approaches: the public appear to be at last aroused to the enormity of the evil, and are crying out so loudly that the fatal abuse cannot longer be persisted in. Our engraving last week did its part well, and gave fresh impetus to the movement. The *Times* calls upon Sir George Grey to prepare a Bill to prohibit burials in crowded districts, ready for the meeting of the House in February: but this is driving it off *too long*. IMMEDIATE steps are demanded, to prevent the further destruction of life. The necessity is so urgent as to justify an "Order In Council," and we earnestly suggest that petitions to that effect should be forthwith sent from all parts of the country to the Secretary of State. The Board of Health are beginning to move in it, but must not be waited for.

BALMORAL CASTLE.—Extensive alterations, it seems, have been made at Balmoral, the buildings being now fully doubled in extent. "As its numerous round towers, gables, and turrets are now seen rising above the birch wood which surrounds them," says a more northern correspondent of the *Edinburgh Register*, "Balmoral Castle seems really worthy of the Majesty of England. It is a palace in miniature." The new erections, however, are solely servants' apartments. The kitchen is said to be an exact model of that at Windsor Castle.

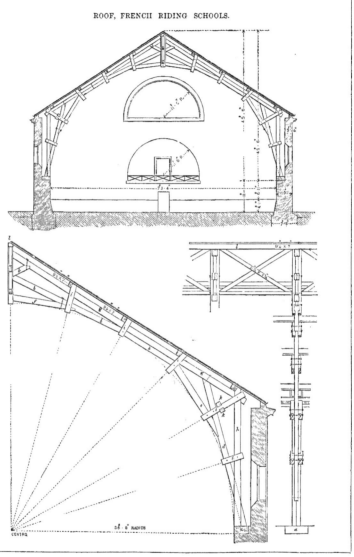

WOOD ROOFS OF LARGE SPAN.

ALLUSION having been made to the work of Colonel Ardant upon wood roofs of great spans, it appeared to me that it might interest your readers were I to furnish them the means of judging of the practical skill of that distinguished officer. Annexed, therefore, is a sketch of a roof, executed under his orders, for the riding schools of some of the cavalry barracks in France.

The object Colonel Ardant has proposed to himself in this case, is to arrive at the suppression of the tie-beam without throwing the lateral effort of the principal rafters on the external walls. Colonel Émy attained this result by means of the bent timber beams; but, in some parts of France, it is next to impossible to obtain plank-stuff at reasonable prices, and squared oak timber exists in profusion. Wherever fir can be had the engineer officers employ the bent timber roofs for the purposes above alluded to, namely, for roofs of large span without horizontal tie beams. In other cases the model adopted is the one invented by Colonel Ardant.

The scantlings used are as follows :—

Wall plate, a, large oak blocks at foot of each principal, 3 feet 4 inches long, by 2 feet 4 inches wide, by 1 foot thick. These dimensions are not difficult to find in France. Tie beam, composed of polygon, f, b, e, d, $11\frac{1}{2}$ inches by 8 inches. Principal rafters, *g*, 11¼ inches by 8 inches. Posts (double), each 1 foot by 8 inches, *h*. Hanging ties, double, *i*, 8¾ inches by 4¾ inches. Longitudinal ties, *k*, 6 inches by 4¾ inches. Ridge, *l*, 9½ inches by 7 inches. Cross pieces under ditto, 6¾ inches by 4⅝ inches. Purlins, 9½ inches by 7 inches. Common rafters, 4½ inches by 4 inches. The whole covered with battens and tiles. G. R. B.

SCHINKEL ON ART-EDUCATION.

THE Germans are perhaps more accustomed to generalize their views of the fine arts than is the case with us; and as a result of this course, I think we may take the fact of there existing in Germany two distinct schools * of architecture, the *classical* and the *mediæval*, which may be said to have their respective head quarters at Berlin and Munich; and that the followers of these two directions base their practice on some fixed principles, may be gathered from the active and able manner in which they respectively defend their own, in the different polemical essays which have issued from the pens of the foremost champions of each party.†

The *classical* school must certainly be considered to have been founded by C. F. Schinkel, whose principal works are known to most of us; and though they are certainly open to criticism, it is in fact because they are something more than mere lifeless imitations and adaptations of the antique forms, such as constitute the chief part of our modern classical architecture. Schinkel was educated as an artist and scene-painter, and, as might be expected from this circumstance, the picturesque element is seldom wanting in his designs, but that he also worked upon principles arrived at by a careful study of his art is shown, I think, by the following translation of notes found among his papers, and published by Dr. G. F. Waagen, on one of the anniversaries of his birthday which is kept at Berlin. They form evidently only a fragment, but seem to afford subject for much reflection to the architect who aims at that amount of individual originality which alone can effect the general advancement of his art:—

"I discovered," he says, "as soon as I had commenced my architectural studies, that a vast treasure of forms had been originated and worked out by nations essentially different, in the course of many centuries of development. But I also saw that the use we made of this store of sometimes heterogeneous matter was very *indiscriminate*; and what, in its original use in old buildings, produced a very pleasing effect, when introduced into modern works seemed entirely inappropriate. It struck me particularly that we may find the cause of the great want of character and style, from which so many of our modern buildings suffer, in this want of discrimination. I forthwith made it the aim of my life to obtain a clearer view of this subject; but the further I proceeded the greater seemed to be the difficulties which opposed my progress. I soon fell into the error of designing a building *solely* with reference to its intended use and construction, from which resulted a work dry and lifeless, devoid of two essential elements, the historical and the poetical. I examined further how far the practical consideration of the subject ought to prevail, to render the appearance of a building accordant with its purpose, and how far, on the other hand, the influence of ancient monuments ought to co-operate with artistic feeling to give the building the character of a work of art. From these considerations it appeared to me that I had discovered that position in the art of architecture which must be occupied by the purely artistical element, and beyond which it is and must always remain a scientific handicraft; further, that in this position, as throughout the theory of the fine arts, the assertion of any distinct doctrine must be difficult, and will be reduced at last to the cultivation of taste, which in architecture embraces a very wide field, and must be formed in the most diversified manner to produce any successful result. I think it necessary to state precisely the different spheres in which the taste of the architect must necessarily be developed, in order that I may at the same time give a general view of the art.

In the first place he must consider what the age demands as *essential* in its architectural undertakings.

Secondly, he must take a review of the past in order to see what has been already worked out for similar purposes, and how far any *completely developed work* may be appropriate and useful to us.

Thirdly, he must determine what *modifications* are necessary in that which appears suitable to our purposes.

And, lastly, in what manner the *imagination* must be employed to create *new matter* for these modifications, and how it is to be treated as to its forms, so as to harmonize with the traditional ancient part, and without losing sight of the original style of the design, to produce the impression of an entirely new one, in which, at the same time, the assimilation to the old style may still be recognised, and afford an additional charm."

In speaking of the utilitarianism of the present public taste, he says:—"In judging of works of art, and more particularly of architecture, few people can raise their minds sufficiently to take general views: usually that only is beautiful and praiseworthy which they desire according to their station of life, and think suitable to the same. A certain completeness and finish in the ordinary articles of domestic use constitutes their ideal of beauty. Any thing new or grand is rarely appreciated by the great mass of the people, and, if it does agree with their ideas of comfort, will always meet with great censure and opposition. Artists that are only influenced by this utilitarian opinion must soon sink from the regions of art to be the slaves of fashion. C. F.

* We can scarcely claim such a degree of organization for this country.

† I may perhaps follow out this subject further on a future occasion, if an opportunity occur.

ON THE BASILICAS OF CHRISTIAN ROME.*

THERE is no feeling so intimately connected with architecture as religion, for amidst all forms of faith, however mistaken, there ever has been shown a desire to render the place of worship worthy of the divinity worshipped. Before the reign of Constantine, as is well known, the Christians—the followers of a prohibited creed—assembled in the rooms of private houses and in obscure retreats, or, if occasionally permitted to construct buildings for the performance of their rites, they were not allowed either to make them of large dimensions or to consult their external appearance. It will be recollected, too, that there existed at Rome places of Christian worship of a remarkable character, which had a direct influence upon the structure of the churches which were subsequently built. I allude to the catacombs.

Constantine, who first extended to Christianity the protection of the law, built his first church at Rome. Rome, therefore, may be said to have been the birthplace of ecclesiastical architecture.

Whilst conscientious feelings deterred and repelled the early Christians from adopting the heathen temples for the purposes of Christian worship, the same feelings attracted them to holy ground. From the custom which had originated in the catacombs,—from the habit which the primitive Christians had acquired of visiting the graves of the martyrs,—it became a matter of necessity to associate the church with the tomb.

The first and earliest Christian churches of which we can form any clear idea, either from actual plans, or existing remains, are the sepulchral churches of the Constantine age. The most remarkable monument of the Christian world—the Church of the Holy Sepulchre raised by Constantine—from its sanctity and celebrity, became the primitive type of all the other churches of a circular form. This circular form, however, was in no wise calculated to receive a Christian congregation during the celebration of the entire liturgy, nor was it appropriate for the service of the altar.

The heathen temple, then, being found unfit, and the form of the sepulchral church being inconvenient or inappropriate, for the purpose of liturgical worship, the adoption of some other type became necessary. Could the professors of Christianity find any edifices raised by the heathen, but unpolluted by idol-worship which might be adapted to their form of worship? Such did exist.

Amongst the structures with which ancient Rome was adorned, was the basilica. This being unpolluted by heathen rites, was found to be well adapted for Christian worship. The name of the basilica was adopted from the Greeks of Athens, whose second archon was styled *ἄρχων βασιλεύς*, and the tribunal where he adjudicated *στοά βασίλειος*, situate in the Athenian Ceramicus, immediately beneath the Pnyx. According to Livy, the basilica did not appear at Rome until the year 182 B.C. It was situate in the forum. The destination of the secular basilica was two-fold: it was at once a court of justice and an exchange. The building was an oblong, terminated by the tribunal. In the centre of the semi-circular apsis was placed the curule chair of the prætor, and seats for judices. This is the portion to which in Scripture (St. John, xix. 13) the name of gabbatha, or lithostroton (pavement) was assigned. Round the sides of the hemicycle, called the wings (cornua), were seats for persons of distinction, as well as the parties engaged in the proceedings. These seats were guarded from intrusion by the *cancelli*. Three-fourths of the oblong composed a hall, the remainder was a transverse aisle which intervened between the hall and the semi-circular recess. In all the basilicas the great hall was divided by columns into a portion similar to the centre aisle of a church, and two side aisles, separated from the centre one each by a single row of columns. Behind each of these columns was placed a square pier or pilaster, which supported the flooring of an upper portico, similar to the gallery of a modern church. The upper gallery was in like manner decorated with columns of lower dimensions than those below, and these served to support the roof, and were connected with one another by a parapet wall or balustrade: this gallery reached entirely round the inside of the building; one side of it was occupied by women, and the other by men. The staircase which led to the upper portico was on the outside. Sometimes the whole building was covered by a roof, sometimes only portions. At the sides, the more ancient of these edifices were entirely open to the external air, being surrounded and protected solely by an open peristyle of columns. At a later date a wall was substituted for the external peristyle.

From the description which has been given, it will be evident how much these edifices were adapted to the uses of a Christian church. The general shape of the church, as prescribed by the apostolical constitutions, was to be an oblong, like unto a ship, that is, to the vessel of the ark. The term *nave* shows how enduringly the idea prevailed in subsequent ages. The basilicæ, therefore, were accordingly given up, for the purpose of Christian worship. Ausonius, addressing the Emperor Gratianus, tells him:—"*Basilica olim negotiis plena, nunc votis pro tuâ salute susceptis.*" This occupation of the Roman basilicæ was, nevertheless, only temporary; they did not become the abiding places of faith. Only *one* existing example can be found of a secular basilica actually converted into a Christian church; and that example, memorable as it is, does not exist in Rome. It is to be found in Treves. Abandoned for more hallowed ground—the graves of the martyrs—the civil basilicas were destroyed, and the columns which supported them transported to the new sites.

A Christian basilica may be thus briefly described. It consisted of four principal parts:—1. Πρόναος, the vestibule of entrance. 2. Ναῦς, *navis*, and sometimes *gremium*, the nave or centre aisle, which was divided from the two side aisles by a row of columns on each of its sides. Here the people assembled for the purposes of worship. 3. Ἄμβων (*ἀναβαίνειν*, to ascend), *chorus* (the choir), and *suggestum*, a part of the lower extremity of the nave, raised above the general level of the floor by a flight of steps. 4. *Ἱερατεῖον, ἱερὸν βῆμα, sanctuarium*, which answered to the tribune of the ancient basilica. In the centre of this sanctuary was placed the high altar, under a tabernacle or canopy, such as still remains in the

* The following paper was read by Mr. Talbot Barnard, at a meeting of the Bedfordshire Archæological and Architectural Society. Reported in the *Bedford Times*.

basilica of St. John of Lateran, at Rome. Around the altar, and in the wings of the sanctuarium, were seats for the assistant clergy, with an elevated chair for the bishop at the bottom of the aisle in the centre. In some of the large basilicæ the sanctuary was divided from the nave by the "Triumphal Arch,"—an imitation of the triumphal arches of ancient Rome,—but, in its new situation, intended to proclaim the triumph of the cross.

Of the existing Christian basilicas at Rome, the remarkable church of San' Clemente is the first which the architectural pilgrim should visit.

The church of St. Agnese is one of those which were built immediately above a martyr's grave,—above a part of the catacombs in which the body of St. Agnese was found. It is built on the usual plan of the basilica.

The church of St. Prassede is also on the usual plan of the basilica, with the addition, however, of a series of immense round arches, which are thrown over the nave at wide intervals. Pope Paschal I. added to this church a small chapel, which opens out of one side of the church, and which is ornamented with mosaics. The mosaic which adorns the ceiling represents a picture of our Saviour, supported by four angels. There is great beauty and no inconsiderable degree of classical feeling in this composition. This chapel is one of the earliest instances of a side chapel, which formed no part of the primitive churches.

The campanile, or bell tower, is a marked departure from the primitive age. It was almost invariably erected in front of the church at Rome, but it never thoroughly became an assimilated integral portion of the basilica.

The rule of Orientation, though prescribed by the apostolical constitutions, never obtained in Italy, where the churches are turned indiscriminately towards every quarter of the heavens. It is not quite clear when this rule was adopted, which afterwards became general: St. Augustine says, "Let us turn to the rising sun of truth."

I have mentioned that, in the gallery of the civil basilica, the women were placed on one side and the men on the other. Such appears to have been the arrangement carried out in the early Christian churches. There are, doubtless, many here who have been struck at first sight, that while the south side of the choir of the magnificent cathedral at Cologne seems to blossom with exuberance, the north side—as with those at Frieburg and Amiens—is comparatively plain. The fact, perhaps, may be thus explained. The north side has had, since the first period of Christianity, its particular meaning; the south the same. The north side was that of the evangelists, who gave the truth in plainness and simplicity; the south was that of the prophets, who represented it in oriental figure and imagery. Also the women, who were especially commanded to cover themselves, and abstain from ornament, stood on the north side, hence called the *muliebris;* while the men, to whom no such prohibition extended, stood on the south. Hence it is that the south side is occasionally found to be richly decorated—that towards the north markedly simplified.

More than 1,500 years have elapsed (says his Excellency the Chevalier Bunsen, in his admirable work which he has devoted to the basilica), since the basilicas of Rome, in their various changes, have been the admiration of the Christian world; and he considers that the unity of idea which prevails in its form gives these buildings an indescribable charm.

There is still one Christian Basilica, which, although not situate at Rome, cannot be passed over without some allusion. I refer to the Basilica of St. Boniface, at Munich, which has peculiar claims upon our attention. This most beautiful church was commenced in the year 1836, and resembles the church of St. Paul (*fuori delle mura*), at Rome, which was the most complete of the Roman Basilicas, but was unfortunately destroyed by fire in the year 1822. The Basilica of St. Boniface is supported in the interior by sixty-four columns of marble, dividing the aisles from the nave. The pavement is of marble, the roof of wood painted blue, with gold-stars, the beams being carved and gilt; the sides of the church are ornamented with paintings in fresco, by Hess, one of the most distinguished of the German artists. The subjects of these frescoes are the principal events in the life of St. Boniface. One of the earliest of them is of surpassing beauty. St. Boniface — then Winfred the Monk—is bidding farewell to those who had been his companions in the Benedictine Abbey of Nutsall, near Winchester, as he embarks on his holy mission. Among those uninspired men who have been distinguished by active piety, we have few greater to revere than the Monk of Nutsall, nor can we find a greater benefactor of the human race.

We have seen that the Basilica of St. Boniface is adorned with paintings in fresco, the subjects of which bring prominently before the minds of the worshippers the zeal with which that great man was inspired, in promoting the cause of that holy religion which they profess, and for which he ultimately laid down his life. And here perhaps it may not be irrelevant to say a few words on the destruction of ancient works of art. During the latter part of the reign of Constantine, many statues of the gods were destroyed and melted down, and not long after his time a systematic destruction began, which under Theodosius spread over all parts of the empire. This spirit of destruction, however, was not directed against works of art in general, and as such, but only against the Pagan idols. The opinion therefore, which is entertained by some, that the losses we have sustained in works of ancient art are mainly attributable to the introduction of Christianity, is too sweeping and general. Of the same character is another opinion, according to which the final decay of ancient art was a consequence of the spiritual nature of the new religion. The coincidence of the general introduction of Christianity with the decay of the arts is merely accidental. That the early Christians did not despise the arts as such, is clear from several facts. We know that they erected statues to their martyrs, in which we have a specimen in that of St. Hippolitus, in the Vatican library; and it is expressly stated by Baronius that Christians devoted themselves to the exercise of the arts. The numerous works, lastly, which have been found in the Christian catacombs at Rome, might alone be a sufficient proof that the early Christians were not hostile towards the representation of the heroes of their religion in works of art. It has been reserved for the fanatic fury of the Iconoclasts in a great measure to destroy the traces of the former splendour of the imitative arts. It must, likewise, ever be admitted that statuary and painting are a kind of silent poetry, which arouses the attention, interests the heart, strikes the eye, and elevates the imagination. The almost total exclusion, therefore, of picturesque representations from the reformed churches, is greatly to be regretted. Whether mankind in any state of society were ever so ignorant as to make these visible representations the actual objects of their adoration may well be doubted, but, at all events, there can now be no danger of such an error in the most uninformed part of Europe; and it may yet be hoped that as the spirit of bigotry declines, religion may be allowed to avail herself of every aid which may engage her admirers, illustrate her precepts, or enforce her laws.

THE LIVERPOOL GOODS STATION OF THE NORTH-WESTERN RAILWAY in Waterloo-road contains 5 acres of land, entirely occupied by warehouses and zinc covered sheding. To form the whole upwards of 120 separate properties, including 150 dwelling-houses, and various warehouses, sheds, &c., were purchased and pulled down. The sheding covers seven lines of rail, and extends over a span of 183 feet, including a cotton-quay, whence 20,000 bales of cotton can be loaded daily. The warehouses are far larger than any other even in Liverpool. The rooms are each 102 feet by 90, containing an area close upon 1,000 square yards. The principal entrances to this station, which is said to be the largest goods station in England, are from Waterloo-road and Great Howard-street. It is reached from Edge-hill by the new Victoria tunnel. An engine of 50 horse-power is to do all the warehouse work. The whole premises have been whitewashed. The general offices of the Company are to be built on an adjoining plot of land.

BIRMINGHAM WORKHOUSE COMPETITION.

We have received the following from one of the selecting architects:—

You have given circulation to the assumption of Mr. Brookes, that the inspecting architects were in error, in recommending the designs Nos. 21 and 24, to the guardians, on the ground of the discovery which he had made, of the imperfect erasure on the former giving a clue to the authorship* of the designs, and therefore disqualifying them according to the instructions given to competitors.

I think it right to forward the enclosed extract from the *Birmingham Journal* of last week, which appears to take a candid view of the circumstances upon which this opposition to the report was founded, but which proved so weak, as to end in a minority of four, on the amendment to the original motion being put from the chair at a full Board.

In correction, however, of that paragraph, I have to state that the inspecting architects were not cognizant of any other signature upon the plan No. 21, than the assumed motto "*Perseverando*," and that the designs recommended for adoption were in strict accordance with the instructions. They cannot but feel satisfied that no stronger ground of opposition could be found to the adoption of the report, and that whatever uninformed writers may assume or insinuate, they are conscious of having discharged a very onerous duty to the best of their judgment, and in a fair and honourable manner.

It will probably be asking too much to request that you will give insertion to the journal extract, but I must beg the favour of your publishing this letter in your next paper, in order that the erroneous impression may be counteracted which your article is calculated to create in the minds of those who are interested in the competition.

HENRY J. STEVENS, Architect.

The following portion of the article in question is all that bears in the slightest degree on the point in dispute:—"It has been found that on the plan No. 21, which it was considered was the production of the same architect as No. 24—recommended as the best—the names of Messrs. Drury and Bateman appear partially erased. Under any other circumstances, this would have been *a most unfortunate disclosure;* even as it is, the *contretemps* is awkward. Now, without entering into the question whether the fact of this distinctive mark being upon these plans, is a breach of the rules of competition sufficient to justify disqualification, and while being perfectly sensible of the impropriety of names being affixed to them, we cannot imagine that the decision of the inspecting architects would be influenced either one way or the other by the knowledge so inopportunely afforded."

Mr. Stevens has called a very bad witness. The respectable local paper quoted, not being a professional journal, will not enter "into the question whether the fact of this distinctive mark being upon these plans, is a breach of the rules of competition sufficient to justify disqualification;" but we do, and state unequivocally (the affixing of the names not being denied) that the plans were disqualified, and that, too, by a departure from the instructions in the gravest particular: whether or not it "influenced" the "inspecting architects, either one way or the other, by the knowledge so *inopportunely* afforded," has nothing whatever to do with the question—as we said last week.

Mr. Stevens had done better if he had rested solely on his assertion that they "were not cognizant of any other signature upon the plans than the assumed motto,"—although this might perhaps lead some of the guardians to imagine that the examination of the plans had not been very minute.

Striving as we do in all cases to induce committees to take professional assistance in the determination of competitions, we much deplore this occurrence, and fear that the reformation of architectural competitions will be little advanced by the judicial proceedings of Messrs. Stevens, Edge, and Gibson.

* The *names* of the authors: something more than a clue.—ED.

C.INNES SCALE OF   FEET. LAING S

INTERNAL RESTORATION OF ST. MARY'S, WARE.

For a reason which will be obvious to some of our readers, we prefer taking the following notice of the works in St. Mary's, at Ware, from a contemporary, *The Ecclesiologist*, to attempting any description of them ourselves :—

"Had we a few years back been asked to name the churches which were most likely to be, during the next quinquenniad, restored, we should certainly not have named this one. It is, therefore, with no little pleasure that we now proceed to describe its actual condition. The church, a large cruciform structure, is composed of a western tower, clerestoried nave with aisles, south porch, transepts, clerestoried chancel, Lady Chapel forming the south chancel-aisle, and another chapel to the north, with a sanctuary beyond. The north transept-window is a good reticulated one, and the most easterly window in the south nave-aisle is late-flowing,—the remainder of the church probably very little later than its one middle-pointed window, as it contains the badge of Richard II., to whose mother the manor of Ware belonged, and who may therefore not unreasonably be assumed to be its rebuilder.* Till lately, the church presented a huge collection of lofty pews and galleries,—that at the west end of portentous size; the latter have entirely disappeared, and had the subscriptions sufficed, it was intended to have replaced the

<small>* On stripping the walls of the chancel the fabric was seen to be of the Early English period.—Ed.</small>

pews by open sittings. This unhappily has been but partially carried out; but the pews have been cut down to an uniform height. The architect was Mr. Godwin. The western portion of the chancel is occupied with longitudinal sittings, leaving, we are sorry to say, too narrow a central passage. We understand that a difficulty was felt, from a grant having been given by the "Incorporated Society" towards fresh sittings eleven years ago. It was, of course, not found easy to retain the stipulated number after sweeping away the galleries. The eastern portion of the chancel proper, which is free, is, as well as the sanctuary, paved with encaustic tiles. The prayers are said at a side desk to the west of the chancel on the north side, with a western face for the lessons. Over it stands the old Jacobean pulpit of the church. The organ is placed in the north chancel aisle.

The most striking feature in the restoration is the quantity of polychrome which has been applied. The spandrills of the nave-arches, ten in number, are filled with flower-pots, from which grows lilies, each bearing a scroll, with one of the beatitudes inscribed upon it. The commandments are painted, where they are ordered, on two tablets on each side of the chancel-arch. The Creed and the Lord's Prayer are on the eastern wall, flanking the east window. The bosses of the nave and chancel-roofs are coloured and gilt, and the architectural portions of the roof of the Lady Chapel are emblazoned; and copies of the figures which were found there in a muti-

lated condition are on record, with a view to their future restoration. They are those of the Apostles with the sentences of the creed, and of the minor prophets with typal verses. The windows of the Lady Chapel have been filled with Powell's quarries; the eastern with the monogram alternating with the lily; the two side ones with the cross and the lily, and the legends respectively — "A Virgin, &c," and "The Word was made flesh, &c." We may here notice a curious feature in the Lady Chapel: it was originally connected with the chancel by one sprawling segmental arch; its ugliness or its unsafeness being canvassed, it was divided into two by a slender Purbeck shaft (restored), bearing a spandril of open panel-work. The great south transept-window was, during the late incumbent's time, filled, at an enormous cost, with Flamboyant tracery.* This has of course been left, and the windows glazed with Powell's quarries—so is the south nave clerestory. A local benefactor is about to fill the east and the west window with glass, by Mr. Wailes, taking the Crucifixion as the subject of the one, and the Baptism, and the Blessing Little Children, of the other. The font is a remarkably fine one, and was given to the church in the time of Henry IV., by William De Montacute, Earl of Salisbury. It re-

<small>* In this window the mullions had simply a very wide chamfer, and the line of the glass was at the termination of this, which produced a coarse and bad effect, especially in the tracery. By merely hollowing the front half of the chamfer on each side, so as to get another perpendicular line on each side of the mullion, the effect was greatly improved.—Ed.</small>

presents, in the eight panels, S. Gabriel, the Blessed Virgin, S. John Baptist, S. Thomas, S. Catherine, S. George, S. Christopher, and S. Margaret, with beneath eight angels, alternately bearing the instruments of the Passion, and playing musical instruments. The angel who bears the spear has the countenance of having been a fallen one. What is the reason of this peculiarity? This font has been restored, provided with lead lining and drain, placed in the tower, and surmounted with a very lofty oaken canopy. The west door has been shielded by a solid screen. We suppose that the fear of drafts made this necessary, but we should then have made the screen as simple as possible, and not covered it with shallow tracery. We wish Mr. Godwin had not given noeings to his chancel steps. The nave-alleys are paved with red and black tiles. The corbels supporting the nave-roof are new, and represent the Apostles: they struck us as being too large. The exterior of the church (built of flint, with stone dressings) has been entirely restored, which involved a partial rebuilding. With few exceptions, all the funds necessary for the restoration were raised in the parish, and contributed with most perfect good will. We most heartily congratulate the people of Ware on so good a work."

We will only add that the church originally was painted and gilt from floor to ridge. The walls were covered with figures the size of life. The new polychromic decorations were executed under the direction of the architect, by Mr. W. H. Rogers. The font cover, to which reference is made, was carved by Philip, Wynne, and Lumsden; as was also the altar rail. The corbels and other stone carving were by Barrett; the tile paving by Minton: the general contractors were Messrs. Carter and Ellis.

Annexed we give an illustration of the easternmost window of the south aisle,—a nice specimen of the Decorated period.

TOWER OF " LA MARTORANA," PALERMO.

THE annexed representation offers a sketch of a portion of the tower which is attached to the principal entrance of the church of " La Martorana," at Palermo.

This tower is supposed to have formed originally an entrance to some Saracenic edifice, as, before the extensions of the present church, it stood quite detached, and was separated from the immediate precincts of the church. When viewed from the atrium below, it presents a very rich and picturesque appearance. The second story of the tower (i. e. the lowest in the engraving) is exceedingly elegant, and has a decidedly Oriental character. This portion is doubtless of an earlier date than the two upper stories, which were added about the year 1143-5, and which partake more of that style of architecture used by the Normans in France than in Sicily. Owing to this latter circumstance, the composition, viewed entire, offers less unity of design than might be wished, and is perhaps open to criticism; its individual features, however, possess considerable merit, and show no lack of imagination on the part of the designers.

The use of the broad Oriental billet, or rustic, which we here see surrounding the windows, was greatly in fashion both amongst the Oriental and Norman architects, and is a characteristic which, if successfully treated, would give great decision to a design. Incrustations of black lava are freely and tastefully applied in each story.

The church was founded in A.D. 1113, by George Antiochenus, a follower of the faith as observed in the Greek Church. In A.D. 1139 he became an admiral of King Roger II. An inscription, probably placed in the church at a period subsequent to the latter date, informs us that the Admiral Antiochenus was the founder.

Originally the church was dedicated to " Santa Maria l'Annunziata;" but Aloisia, the wife of " Godfrey de Martorana," who founded the adjoining convent in A.D. 1193, and repaired and extended the church to its present dimensions, obtained from King Alphonso the privilege of changing the name it usually bore to that of her own, " La Martorana."

The interior of the church contains some

TOWER OF "LA MARTORANA," PALERMO.

excellent specimens of Mosaic pictures and ornaments, and is full of interest, presenting a very fair example of a church planned according to the Greek ritual.   W. L. B. G.

MANAGEMENT OF ARCHITECTURAL COMPETITIONS.

IT has been suggested more than once in your journal that architects should meet together and lay down a set of regulations as to on what terms they would furnish designs in competition. This is *precisely* what they ought to do; and though I am not a member of the Royal Institute of British Architects, I should certainly, out of respect for it, prefer seeing such a movement emanate from that Royally chartered body. As yet it has done nothing further than to issue ten years ago a certainly very excellent report on competitions; but as ten years' experience has proved that " reports " will not remedy the evil, I hope the institute will take up the matter and convene a meeting of architects, to agree to " a set of regulations as to on what terms " they will henceforth submit designs in public competition. I am quite sure any half a dozen architects might easily do this; and, with a little energy, and a sensible set of regulations, secure the combined signatures of nine-tenths of their brethren, great and small, throughout the kingdom, pledged to compete only on such and such " regulations." To such a body committees would be the first to pay respect, as the institute themselves thus declare in their report on competitions, to which I have just alluded.

" Your committee* * * have the greatest reason to believe, from the information they have obtained, that, in a very great majority of cases of competition, the committees, or parties to whom judgment is confided, are quite ready to acknowledge themselves deficient in the means of fulfilling their duty, when once the nature of that duty is candidly and temperately explained to them; and that any suggestions will be favourably received, when offered in proper terms, and at a proper season."

The proper season, Sir, is invariably *before* designs shall have been obtained: the proper parties to suggest and explain are the council of the Royal Institute of British Architects; but, failing them, it is quite proper for the Architectural Association, or for any half dozen architects, to suggest, to explain, nay, to *command* in this matter.

As to the " proper terms" (or regulations call them), I would submit for the consideration of the profession a few hints, preparatory, I hope, to " a monster meeting."

Instructions to Architects should be as simple as possible, and where really no *penchant* for any particular style exists, should say nothing about such matters. Thus committees should not say " the style of architecture to be *Grecian*, and the order *Ionic*," and straightway award their first premium to a *Gothic* design, and their second premium to a *ditto*—(a fact).

Drawings should be, so far as is consistent with the intelligible delineation of the design, as few, as small, and as free from cost as possible. The exact kind and number of them, and, wherever practicable, the exact length and breadth of each, should be stated, with a view to uniformity, portability, and compactness, and consequent facility of comparison one with another. The size of perspective views, the point whence taken, their mode of execution, should be invariably defined; and as you yourself, Sir, have frequently urged, the extravagant custom of bedizening them in gold frames, &c., should be forbidden.

Other Papers.—Many architects accompany their designs with printed circulars, engraved views, &c., and some even with builders' tenders. I don't blame them under the present *roly-poly* system, but under an amended system, I would forbid all this at once, strictly limiting the number and kind of documents to be supplied by each competitor, so as to place all on an equality, and leave the design to what after all it must come to, if executed, *its naked merit.*

Prizes.—Five per cent. ought, in all competition cases, to be paid, and in order to put an end to all canvassing and cheapening ought to be openly guaranteed by the committée, who should offer in small competitions a second and third, and in large competitions a fourth and fifth premium, as the case may require. A *first* premium is an absurdity, *never contended for*, and in *fair* competitions seldom paid; *its* amount will supply funds for two secondary premiums.

Estimates.—As to the estimated cost of each design, I would, after stating what really were the resources of the committee, leave every competitor at liberty to state what sum he thought fit; but as to committees selecting a design by such a criterion as a competitor's estimate, there can be, I conceive, no greater folly; and yet as committees almost invariably constitute this their test of merit or eligibility, who can wonder at competitors, in a wicked world like ours, yielding to the temptation to put down the very lowest figure which an acquaintance with your weekly list of "Blind Builders" may suggest to him?

Decisions.—In judging of the accuracy of the estimate of any design the committee may take to, or of its efficient construction or arrangement, they should be guided by the opinion of some non-competing professional man, to be recommended by the general voice of the competitors. Each competitor should, therefore, submit with his design the name of some one or more non-competing architects, to whose judgment and experience he himself would be willing to refer the committee for guidance. This method, I may state, was actually adopted (by the Committee's especial request), in the case of the competition for the Blackburn Exchange; and, beaten competitor as I was in that case, I have always considered it the fairest competition I have ever engaged in.

Y.

METROPOLITAN COMMISSION OF SEWERS.

APPEAL AGAINST RATE IN POPLAR.

A GENERAL court was held on Monday last, which was originally intended to have been held on Saturday, but was postponed in consequence of sufficient members not being present to form a quorum. In the interim, notices had been sent to every member of the commission, impressing upon them the necessity of their attendance. Some time after the hour for commencing business, however, only five members were present. As only one hour is allowed from the time named for the court to an adjournment to a future day, it was agreed by the parties who had appeals to prosecute that the business should proceed with but five members. Sir John Burgoyne took the chair.

The Rating of Poplar.—The secretary (Mr. Woolrych) read a notice of appeal from Mr. John Carter, of High-street, Poplar, against the rates made upon him for that division.

Mr. Needham, the barrister, on behalf of appellant, proceeded to state his case. It appeared that the appellant, with several other persons, occupied premises situate on the north side of Poplar ditch. From time immemorial the inhabitants of this district had never been rated to the sewers rate, as it was a condition of their tenure that they should cleanse out and keep in repair a ditch which bounded their property. In the year 1826 an attempt was made by the Commissioners of Sewers for Poplar Marsh district to rate property in this neighbourhood, which was resisted, and an action at law was the result of this demand. The case was tried by a special jury in London, before Lord Chief-Justice Abbot (afterwards Lord Tenterden), Mr. (now Lord) Brougham appearing for the Sewers Commissioners. The case occupied a considerable time, and the evidence was very voluminous. As it was most material, and might guide their decision in the present question, he would recite the three points prominently placed before the jury by the learned Judge on that occasion.

"First. Whether the owners and occupiers of the land and ground lying contiguous to and on the north side of the ditch have, from time immemorial, by reason of their tenure of these grounds, been compellable to scour the Poplar ditch.

Second. Whether the occupiers of the land on the north side of the ditch have, by reason of the obligation that the law casts upon them to scour this ditch, been exempt from all other expenses of the level, whether they have been exempted by reason of that charge.

The third question is quite distinct,—Whether, in your judgment, the plaintiff's house derives any benefit from the works done by the commissioners, or under their superintendence."

In the two first cases, the jury answered in the affirmative, and in the latter in the negative. He contended that this question was precisely identical, *mutatis mutandis*, with the present case. He thought, therefore, that, as it was the practice in Westminster-hall, when once a case had been solemnly argued, to consider it as conclusively determined, and never to be re-opened unless some error was apparent,—that court would hesitate before they reversed the judgment that had been given by Lord Chief Justice Abbott, and with the caution with which he approached such a question. The learned counsel reiterated his arguments, and in support of them quoted the following words of the 76th section of the present Sewers Act:—"Provided also that where, in any separate sewerage district, any property is by law or by the practice of the existing Commissioners of Sewers entitled to exemption wholly or partially from, or to any reduction or allowance in respect of, the sewer-rates, the commissioners shall, in making the district sewer-rate, observe and allow such exemption, reduction, or allowance."

Mr. Leslie said the question was, whether the appellant derived any benefit from the works of the commissioners, and whether the circumstances of 1826 were similar with those of 1849? Whether the circumstances brought before Lord Chief Justice Abbott were not changed by the operation of the 37th section of the present Act, which declares "that all sewers, sluices, &c., within the limits of the commission, shall be subject to the survey, order, and control of the commissioners, according to the provisions and subject to the regulations and restrictions of this Act."

Mr. Needham then called as witnesses, Mr. Carter and Mr. Morris, the former proving that no sewer-rates had ever been charged upon this property, and the latter, that until last year no sewer commission had any jurisdiction over the Poplar ditch.

It was also given in evidence, that as the guardians of the poor of Poplar had turned the drainage of the workhouse into this ditch, they passed from 8,000 to 10,000 gallons of clean water into it: the Commissioners of Sewers had brought into it the drainage of 300 houses, with only the filthy refuse.

On the part of the commissioners, Mr. Phillips, the surveyor, was examined by the chairman, who stated that Mr. Carter and every other inhabitant of Poplar derived benefit from the works of the commission. The Poplar ditch was periodically attended to by the officers of the commission. If the outlet were not looked to, Mr. Carter's premises would be flooded. The whole of the cesspools in the workhouse had been abolished, and the inconvenience and expense of cleansing them had of course been avoided. The ditch was flushed by every tide, and washed into the Thames at the expense of the sewer-rates.

Mr. Woolrych then addressed the court, and said there were two questions to consider; first, whether the appellant derived any benefit? and, secondly, if he had derived any benefit, whether he had made out to the satisfaction of the commissioners that he was exempt from liability from some prescriptive usage? Assuming the benefit to be proved, there was no evidence to support the latter proposition.

Mr. Leslie ultimately moved—"That the rate made on the Poplar district be confirmed;" which was put and agreed to; and after a sitting of nearly six hours the court adjourned.

A general court was held on Thursday, the 6th; Sir John Burgoyne in the chair.—A recommendation was received from the Finance Committee to grant Mr. Samuel Page, late surveyor, a retiring allowance of 100*l*. a-year, out of the Holborn and Finsbury division, to commence from March 25, 1848. It appearing that he had been in the service of the late commission for upwards of forty years, the recommendation was unanimously agreed to.

The Question of Flushing.—Mr. Bullar said, as great doubts existed as to the propriety of flushing, and as it was evident that if it was not good they must discontinue it, but, if good, that it should be more extensively adopted, he begged to move—"That a circular letter be forthwith sent to the various medical practitioners holding union or parochial appointments throughout the rated districts, requesting them to favour the commissioners on or before the 11th inst. with their opinion (resulting from their own observation) of the effect which the flushing of any sewers has had on the health of those who reside in the neighbourhood of those sewers."

The following resolution was also agreed to:—"That having regard to the present condition of the health of the metropolis, the Trial Works Committee be authorized to expend a sum not exceeding 250*l*. for the ventilation and trapping of sewers in those places they would think beneficial."

A deputation attended the Court from the parishes of Camberwell and Newington, representing the offensive state of these neighbourhoods, caused, as the memorialists believed, by the discharge of cesspools into the public sewers, and calling upon the Commissioners to suspend the operations of flushing until a colder season. The surveyor of the district was ordered to fully report on the subject, Mr. Leslie contending that the works of the district were a disgrace to the commission, particularly in the case of the Friar-street sewer, upon which they had a report from their own officers upwards of twelve months since.

Improvement of the Drainage of Westminster.—A long report was presented to the Court by Mr. Gotto, on the state of the drainage of Westminster, embracing plans for its improvement, to be carried on concurrently with the works of the Westminster Improvement Commissioners. The report recommended that a new surface and subsoil sewer, 5 feet in diameter, be constructed from Richmond-terrace, Whitehall, along Parliament-street, and across the Broad Sanctuary, at Westminster, to the commencement of the new Victoria-street, a distance of 2,200 feet, and to be continued along New Victoria-street, 4 feet in diameter, for a distance of 3,000 feet, at an expense of 8,142*l*., on condition that the Westminster Improvement Commissioners pay the sum of 3,375*l*.; that the work be executed by public tender, and that the works be executed forthwith, to save the inconvenience of interruption of the traffic during the session of Parliament.

Sir Edward Pearson attended on behalf of the Westminster Commissioners, and impressed upon the Court the necessity of some immediate action in this neighbourhood, and that unless something was proceeded with, the whole works of the Improvement Commissioners, so peculiarly constituted were they under their Act of Parliament, must fall to the ground.

Mr. Gotto gave it as his decided opinion that his plan would not at all affect the ultimate propositions for the entire drainage of London, and that this work might safely be executed without present reference to them. It was ultimately resolved—"That Mr. Gotto's report on the Westminster Improvement Sewerage be approved, and that on the payment by the Westminster Improvement Commissioners of 3,375*l*., as recommended by that report, the works specified be executed, and that tenders for these works be immediately advertised, and when received be opened by the Works Committee."

A resolution was then agreed to calling for a return of attendances by commissioners.

A very voluminous report was presented by Mr. Grant, on the state of Albion-terrace, Wandsworth-road, being a detailed statement explanatory of a short report presented at a former court. It stated, that up to the closing of his report, the deaths in that terrace had been increased to fifty, and that the whole of seventeen houses were now unoccupied. The subject of the water-supply was treated upon at great length, the water had been submitted to a chemist for analyzation. (Samples of the water were produced in the court, and that taken from two of the cisterns closely resembled ink in colour, with a most fœtid odour.) It generally attributed the disease to the overflowing of the cesspools into the water cisterns, and recommended that the cesspools should be abolished, and a supply of water obtained from the water company in lieu of the present mode of supply from an adjoining well.

A discussion ensued as to how far the commission were responsible for the fatality that had occurred, Mr. Leslie contending that it was a question that rested entirely with the landlords and their tenants.

This opinion appeared to be generally received by the court, and Mr. Grant was ordered to put himself in communication with the owners of the property, to afford them any information, but the court declined to proceed in the matter.

A letter was received from Mr. Smith, vestry-clerk of Richmond, stating that the parish approved of the plan of Mr. G. Donaldson for an improved drainage, and wished to see it carried into effect as speedily as possible.

In the case of Mr. Dennis, of Bath-place, Chalk-road, who had been ordered to do certain works, and positively refused to do the same, it was ordered that the commission do execute the works, and charge Mr. Dennis with the expenses; the amount to be recovered by distress or otherwise, if such a course should be found necessary.

WARMINGTON CHURCH.—Mr. Caveler has nearly completed a work illustrative of this building. The specimens we have seen are capitally drawn.

Books.

An Historical and Statistical Account of Life Assurance; with Observations on Friendly Societies and Savings Banks. By Mr. ALFRED BURT, Secretary to a Life Office. Effingham Wilson, Royal Exchange.

THE proposition with which Mr. Burt desires to familiarize the popular mind is, that the data and deductions on which the system of life assurance is founded, are as satisfactory and conclusive as those of any other branch of commerce; and he only wishes it were as easy to induce the middle classes to avail themselves of the benefits as to make them understand the terms and conditions of life assurance.

The mutual system he recommends, as we do, above all others. On this point he says,

"Mutual societies are based on the only plan of life assurance which the public are interested in supporting. The experience of nearly a century derived from upwards of a hundred life companies confirms the conclusion at which scientific and mathematical investigation has arrived, that mutual assurance is the most advantageous to the assured. The annual reports of established offices show, that while in all mutual offices the assured's policies have increased in value, in proprietary companies the surplus premiums have been applied to increase the shares of the proprietors."

In mutual offices there are no shareholders,—the policy-holders themselves constituting the company amongst whom the profits are thus divided, and a policy in such offices has been known to increase in value no less than 600 per cent., while with proprietary companies, of course, the 500 per cent. would have been divided among the shareholders,—the value of the policy remaining as at first, without the slightest increase. There is not only room, but an urgent demand, according to Mr. Burt, for a great increase of mutual assurance societies: nevertheless, the increase of all classes of insurance offices in the United Kingdom of late years has been remarkable. In 1820, there were only twenty in all; but the number was exactly doubled in 1830; that number again was just doubled in 1840, when there were eighty. Singular as it may seem, adds the author, the increase has ever since proceeded in the same ratio—doubling every ten years,—so that, in 1845, one hundred and twenty had been established.*

Replete, however, as Mr. Burt's book is with matter of general interest, put in a popular form, devoid of much of that formidable statistical science which has heretofore repelled those classes for whose benefit it is so desirable that such books should be not only cheap and accessible as this, but also as readable and as generally interesting,—we can, nevertheless, perceive where and how the author might have here and there increased the information and the interest of his little work, as, for instance, from the historical matter to be found in Mr. Lewis Pocock's "Familiar Explanation of the Nature, Advantages, and Importance of Life Assurance,"—a work of information which we are surprised to find all special mention of by Mr. Burt either intentionally or unintentionally avoided. We by no means desire to disparage Mr. Burt's efforts, however; and hope that the exposition will be extensively perused by the class for whom it is specially intended,—not so much for Mr. Burt's interest, indeed, as for their own.

The Principles of the Differential and Integral Calculus Simplified, and applied to the Solution of various useful Problems in Practical Mathematics and Mechanics. By THOMAS TATE, Mathematical Master of the National Society's Training College, Battersea: author of "Exercises on Mechanics," &c. Longman and Co., Paternoster-row.

THE object of this new work of Mr. Tate is to bring the fundamental principles of the calculus within the comprehension of students with merely a knowledge of ordinary algebra and trigonometry, and to enable them to peruse such practical works as "Moseley's Principles of Engineering," "Whewell's Mechanics," &c. This object the author appears to have prepared the way of students for, with his usual tact and ability.

* It is estimated that capital to the amount of fifty millions has been already invested in these offices, yielding a revenue of more than one million per annum to Government. Their engagements are computed at upwards of one hundred and twenty millions.

On Copyright in Design in Art and Manufactures. By T. TURNER, of the Middle Temple. F. Elsworth, Chancery-lane.

AT the present moment, when the law of patents is in a sort of transition state, and genius and invention are, it is to be hoped, coming to something like an easy and profitable inheritance of their own "property in form" and substance, Mr. Turner's able little treatise is extremely well timed. It contains a complete anatomy of form in design, interwoven with more than a spice of quaint anecdote and curious "cases," and though not on a subject necessitating anything like a knowledge or treatise of high art, is all *about* art, in its rubs and conflicts with £. s. d.,—amongst big wigs and little, Chancery and police,—set in motion by fleeced and fleecer, rogue and original; and though mainly, therefore, a compilation, is full of curious interest. The disquisition on property in form, however, with which so much lawyer learning is interwoven, may well boast of higher pretensions. Advices, too, are offered on practical points, such as a lawyer alone can safely give, and the principles of legal right as now administered, and those on which it ought to be extended, have been fully entered into. In an appendix are copies of such statutes in force as those of the four Engraving Acts, two Sculpture Acts, two Designs Acts, and International Act, and of the rules of the registrar of designs, and tables of fees, with lists of cases reported—in reference to which, by the way, the pages of THE BUILDER itself might have been searched to some purpose.

Miscellanea.

CENTRIFUGAL PUMP.—A model is said to have recently been made of a pump for draining marshes, &c., in which the principle of the turbine appears to have been adopted — or modified—so as to have led to a hope of its *doing wonders*. A small box water-wheel, made of tin, a little thicker, but no larger, than a halfpenny, is fitted at the bottom of a square tube dipping into a small cistern of water, and the wheel being made to rotate with great velocity, throws up water rapidly into the tube above itself, until it overflows in a continuous stream at the top, so as to deliver *eight* gallons per minute, and to drive it even through a nozzle to a distance of 20 feet. A wheel, about 15 inches in diameter, will, it is said, deliver 1,800 gallons per minute, worked by an engine of 4-horse power. The inventor is said to be a Mr. Appold, who proposes to aid the drainage of Haarlem Lake with one 40 feet in diameter, and delivering 1,500,000 gallons a minute. Great talk, this!

EXPOSITION OF ARTS AND MANUFACTURES AT BIRMINGHAM.—The exhibition of the manufactures of Birmingham and the midland counties was opened on the 3rd. The exposition is made in a temporary building of immense dimensions, in the grounds of Bingley House, Broad-street, and is described as being very satisfactory.

CLERKENWELL GRAVEYARDS.—Sir: Mr. Griffiths is not correct in stating the graveyards of Clerkenwell to be several feet above the public ways,—one only of the four being 1 foot above the way,—two of the others being level with it, and the one on Pentonville-hill being considerably beneath the public way. What depth does this gentleman assume to be the average of burials, when he takes an objection to the *exudations* through the walls? Were the ground much raised, a remedy might doubtless have suggested itself to him, — that of lining them. Of the evils of the system we have had *usque ad nauseam*—any remedy short of the one proposed, *i. e.* interdicting any more interments, sealing the vaults, and covering the graveyards with two feet of concrete, would be merely a shifting expedient, which the cupidity of parties interested might soon evade, and the remains of mortality be dealt with in as unscrupulous a manner as has been demonstrated to be the case in London—fatally injurious to those whose avocations bind them to these plague spots.

R. L. SIBLEY, District Surveyor.

OWEN AND HIS SOCIALISM.—A correspondent, dating from Adelphi, regrets the force of a remark by us, made while treating of model towns. The remark in question bore reference more particularly to doctrines at one time openly inculcated and afterwards withdrawn, or at least veiled and cast out of view. Now, the question here is not the moral character of the man or his sect, but the objectionable nature of doctrines, at one time at least, if not now, openly preached by the one and accredited by the other. We cannot accord even to one who "knows him and his principles thoroughly" a closer or more intimate *observance* and *consideration* than our own of doctrines which *have* been publicly taught by Mr. Owen and his disciples, whatever they may now do. For some years we closely considered *everything* published by them that we could possibly lay hands on. We began in admiration of the man —*then* universally esteemed—and ended in disgust with some of those doctrines which he *at length*, and by degrees, ventured to publish, in entire miscalculation of the strength and permanence of that public esteem which previous caution on his part had allowed to spread into world-wide renown, but which his subsequent imprudence converted into abhorrence, so that he and his sect became a bye-word of reproach, that ultimately compelled them, as we said, to veil and withdraw what was rather too strong for the public taste to relish or their stomach to retain. At first Mr. Owen defied the tide of adverse public opinion that he himself had caused to set in against him, maintaining that the obnoxious doctrines were absolutely essential to the full carrying out of his social principles, and that the sooner the public reconciled themselves to them the better. Then it was that Mr. Owen utterly lost that repute and esteem which he never has regained, and never will, we fear, whatever be his own more recent line of policy. Then it was that he could no longer boast of such friends to his views as the Duke of Kent, and many more of even equal influence, had been. More we need not say, as our purpose certainly is not to republish and revive what its mistaken author *may* have repented of; but our only fear on reconsidering the remark objected to was, that we might thereby, by inference, be erroneously supposed to be countenancing Mr. Owen's present doctrines, as entirely devoid of that old leaven of offence. This, we trust, may not be the case, for we know less of his *present* published opinions than we do of his past. And neither would we desire to prejudice or prejudge the more matured fruits of his past experience and reflection, of the merits of which we thus, without being in the least ashamed of it, acknowledge our comparative ignorance.

NORTHAMPTON CORN EXCHANGE.—Sir: I scarcely know which is most to blame,—the parties who, through ignorance, state a sum for which it is utterly impossible to erect the building, or the architect who would lend himself to such a deception. Let any professional person, with the slightest knowledge of his business, sit down and make a rough calculation of the cost of such a building as is required by the Northampton Committee, and he will find it could not be executed for a less sum than from 12,000*l.* to 14,000*l.*, instead of 8,000*l.*, as stated; and if any person watches the case closely, he will find the truth of this assertion. It will prove a case of the deceived and the deceiver.—A SUBSCRIBER.

THE INTENDED NEW TOWN OF LLANDUDNO.—The great sale of building sites at the contemplated new town of Llandudno was held on Tuesday, at the large room in Plas Mawr, in the town of Conway. The room was quite full, but the result did but amount to the *bond fide* sale of about six or seven lots only. Next day (Wednesday) closed with the *bond fide* sale of thirty-seven lots. Three or four more were disposed of in the course of Thursday. Twenty-six thousand yards have been already sold, varying from 1s. to 1s. 6d. per square yard. The several lots sold will form a part of the eastern end of the crescent, also a full street near the Conway Bay, and a full street under the present village. The lots disposed of on Thursday were 2d. per yard higher than those of Wednesday, although on the same spot.—*Carnarvon Herald.*

Projected Works.—Advertisements have been issued for tenders, by 20th instant, for the erection and conversion of certain buildings, in providing school-rooms and schoolmaster's quarters, at Dover; by 15th, for the erection of two school-rooms and master's house at Wilmington; by 20th, for the erection of St. Jude's Church, Birmingham; by 10th, for the restoration of the exterior of Hilton Church, near St. Ives; by 13th, for various works in erection of St. Luke's Church, Morton, near Bingley; by 22nd, for the construction of Whitehaven water-works, under one or more contracts, comprising about 15 miles of pipe-laying, with tanks, aqueducts, &c., &c.; by 11th, for the various works in erection of a school and master's house at Woodhouse Grove, near Leeds; by 11th, for the erection of Moor-Allerton Church and School; by a date after 14th not specified, for works in re-pairing and re-slating roof, and constructing new ceiling, to Horsforth Church; by 11th, for the erection of a villa at Winchester; by 17th, for 2,000 cast-iron chairs, a number of malleable iron spikes, and 10,000 native larch, Norway, or best Baltic or other sleepers; and by 18th, for the supply and fixing of iron roofs for passenger station at Tithebarn - street, Liverpool.

Bartholomew Fair, Smithfield.—As a gradually fading vestige of old London, we have, for many years past, invariably visited Bartholomew Fair, that we might watch its decline and see it expire. The light flickers in the socket. On Tuesday night last, when we paid our accustomed visit, we found that one or two stalls for gingerbread, two or three gambling-tables for nuts, and one "puppet-show," constituted the fair. A few people were scattered about, but the majority of them were policemen. The moon was shining brilliantly on the "Smooth-field," the scene of knightly jousts and religious burnings in time gone by (and of an abominable nuisance in the present day), and illumined the church built by Rahere seven hundred and forty years ago, and the hospital he founded. If it were our part to moralize and evolve "Reflections," we might fill a page with such a subject.

The Electric Light.—In Mr. Pearce's specification of patent, the main point claimed as his invention consists in so employing bar electrodes that the light shall be developed at the sides or edges in place of at points at the ends. He also claims a mode of employing bar electrodes, whereby a constant supply of non-conducting matter is kept up to retard the approach of the bar electrodes: also a mode of reobtaining contact in the event of the light going out, by the introduction of a conducting substance, to be removed by means of an electro-magnet bar or coil. There is also a claim for clockwork for regulating the time of giving light, and various other claims for alleged improvements.

Suspension Bridge over the Dneiper.—Mr. James, of Stamford-street, has recently constructed a model of the suspension bridge which is about to be constructed for the Emperor of Russia over the Dneiper, at Kieff; and which will be half a mile long. It will have six bays, four of them 444 feet long, and two 222 feet. The roadway will be 34 feet wide, and the footpath 6 feet. A swivel bridge, on the Russian side, will communicate with the rest of the structure by an island formed of masonry, and be constructed so that any injury to the chains fastened within it can be easily rectified. The whole work will occupy about five years in completion. The model, prepared in this country for the Emperor, and about to be dispatched to Russia, is constructed on the scale of one-eighth of an inch to the foot.

Concrete Piers.—An iron bridge is to be built at Chepstow, for the South Wales Railway. It is stated, that for the construction of the piers sheet-iron tubes, 12 feet in diameter, will be lowered into the river, and are expected to cut their way down to the rock. "Then, the water being pumped out, each tube will be filled with cement (query: concrete?), and this will remain in the form of a pillar of stone when the iron tube has wasted away."

Temporary Cholera Hospital in the City.—The site of the late Fleet Prison is selected, on the recommendation of the City architect, for the erection of a temporary hospital for cholera patients.

English and American Railways.—There were about eighty passengers in the train, forty of whom were in the same carriage as ourselves. "The car," in shape like a long omnibus, has a passage down the middle, sometimes called "the aisle," on the back part of which the seats are ranged transversely to the length of the apartment, which is high enough to allow a tall man to walk in it with his hat on. Each seat holds two persons, and is well cushioned, and furnished with a wooden back, ingeniously contrived, so as to turn and permit the traveller to face either way, as he may choose to converse with any acquaintance who may be sitting before or behind him. The long row of windows on each side affords a good view of the country, of which more is thus seen than on our English railroads. The trains, moreover, pass frequently through the streets of villages and towns, many of which have sprung up since the construction of the railway. The conductor passes freely through the passage in the centre, and from one car to another, examining tickets and receiving payment, so as to prevent any delay at the stations. If we desire to form an estimate of the relative accommodation, advantages, comforts, and cost of the journey in one of these railways, as compared with those of England, we must begin by supposing all our first, second, and third-class passengers thrown into one set of carriages, and we shall then be astonished at the ease and style with which the millions travel in the United States. The charge for the distance of 54 miles, from Boston to Portsmouth, was 1½ dollar each, or 6s. 4d. English, which was just half what we had paid three weeks before for first-class places on our journey from London to Liverpool (2l. 10s. for 210 miles). Here there is the want of privacy enjoyed in an English first-class carriage, and the seats, though excellent, are less luxurious. On the other hand, the power of standing upright when tired of the sitting posture is not to be despised, especially on a long journey, and the open view right and left from a whole line of windows is no small gain. But when we come to the British second and third-class vehicles, cushionless, dark, and if it happen to rain, sometimes closed up with wooden shutters, and contrast them with the cars of Massachusetts, and still more the average appearance, dress, and manners of the inmates, the wide difference is indeed remarkable; at the same time, the price which the humblest class here can afford to pay proves how much higher must be the standard of wages than with us.—*Lyell's Second Visit to the United States.*

Prevention of Railway Accidents.—Mr. Preecy, of Lyndhurst, New Forest, proposes two plans for counteracting the effect of collisions by railway. The first he calls the hermaphroditic engine, which, when one section is built to the tender and the other to the luggage van, will, it is said, repel 300 tons, and in collision with another train similarly constructed 600 tons, besides the resistance of one ton for every buffer in the train. Sections placed as pilots before the engines will run into each other, causing a further repulsion estimated at 500 tons. One section placed as a rear-guard will resist to the same extent, if run into. The second plan is by placing four elliptic springs betwixt every pair of gravitation buffers horizontally, whereby a repellant power of 32 tons will be provided, it is said, to each carriage. But it seems to be essential to this plan that "every description of carriage that is to run on the same rail must be built with the greatest precision as to length on and width across the rail, with corrected carriage springs, all standing the same height, with the same weight, the fittings as to gravitation buffers, as to width across the rail, and height from the bearings of the wheels, the height of the sway buffers from the gravitation buffer, and the width of the sway buffers from each other. Every carriage must be built so exactly by the same gauge, that, turn the carriages either way, when empty, *convex buffers may point centrally into the concave buffers.*" Now, the danger inevitably resultant from any cause, whether temporary or in permanent construction, capable of altering the preconcerted height of one buffer thus locking into another, is so obvious that the usefulness of any plan requiring such nice "precision" of detail must be doubtful.

Orsi and Armani's Patent Metallic Lava.—We are glad to observe that this material for paving is getting steadily into use. We have seen more of it since we first spoke of it, and find no reason to alter our opinion then expressed, especially that for keeping down damp it was well adapted. The vestibule of the great hall of the Euston-square station is paved with it. It admits of the exercise of taste on the part of designers.

Zinc Paint.—We are glad to find that our hint to practical chemists has not been fruitless. Mr. C. A. F. Rochaz, St. Swithin's-lane, has recently lodged a specification of patent for improvements in the manufacture of oxide of zinc, and in the making of paints and cements where oxide of zinc is used. The first regards the sublimation of the zinc into oxide, the pure particles of which are collected by adhesion to ranges of bands suspended in canvas-covered chambers for the purpose. The coarser particles are thus collected separately and used, under the second section of the specification, as cement, when mixed with mortar. The patentee states that he makes a durable, rapidly drying, white pigment with 20 parts white zinc, 4 resin, 2 turpentine, and 1 drying oil.

Earthenware Tubes.—An improvement in the formation of sockets has been patented by Mr. Charles Jacob, of Nine Elms, engineer. A socket mould fits on the orifice in the die-plate, through which the pipe is moulded: when the socket mould is filled with clay, it yields and goes along with the pipe in being formed; and it is held up to its place against the die-plate, or against the end of the pipe, by means of a counterpoise weight.

Cremorne Gardens, Battersea-bridge.—We lately noticed the beauty of Rosherville, and are reminded that we might justly say a word in favour of Cremorne Gardens, on the banks of the Thames,—another resort for the jaded million. This we are quite willing to do. Divested of the crowd which usually fills them (but against whom, by the way, we have nothing to say, for they enjoy themselves with great propriety, and the management seems very good), they form an enjoyable retreat and deserve a visit.

Northfleet Church Competition.—The first premium of 15l. for the restoration of this church was awarded to Messrs. Brandon and Ritchie, and the second, of 10l., to Messrs. R. Potter and G. Low.

The Timber Preserving Company.—The half-yearly meeting of this company was held on the 31st ult., at their offices, Whitehall-wharf, Westminster, when a dividend at the rate of 6 per cent. per annum was declared, the chairman, Mr. George Burge, stating that their future prospects were most encouraging.

New Schools, St. Pancras.—The vestry of St. Pancras is about to erect a school-house for 250 boys, on the workhouse premises. The plans prepared by Mr. J. Lockyer have been approved, and will be ready early next week for the inspection of contractors. Particulars will doubtless be advertized.

Blind Builders v. Imperfect Specifications.—Sir: Separate tenders were required to be sent in for works to be done under the parish surveyor, at St. Luke's church, Old-street. The following is a list:—

	General Work.			Clean Cornice of Church.			Drain.		
	£.	s.	d.	£.	s.	d.	£.	s.	d.
London	83	0	0	22	0	0	6	10	0
Wilson	89	15	0	70	0	0	6	0	0
Mason	93	15	0	73	10	0	28	10	0
James Ward	98	0	0	24	0	0	6	10	0
William Lamprell	98	10	0	26	0	0	22	0	0
Grist	99	0	0	69	10	0	5	10	0
Loffitt	99	15	0	70	0	0	6	0	0

The tender of Mr. London was accepted as regards the general work, but he was required by the committee to meet them at the church to tell them what he intends to do for the other amounts, as they are sure something is wrong. Whether this error is with the blind builders, or is with the professional gentleman who made the specification, your readers will judge from the practice they have in reading different specifications. To my knowledge, it frequently lies with the profession, and I believe this to be the case here.—Justice.

TENDERS

For alterations at Walker's Hotel, Dean-street, Soho, under Mr. C. Lockyer, architect (allowing for old materials):—

Mathews	£1,647
Warne	1,462
Hinton	1,322
Unwin (accepted)	1,297

Delivered on the 28th ult., for new Lecture Hall and other works, for the Ipswich Mechanics' Institution; H. Woolnough, architect, Ipswich:—

Mason	£1,199 0
Simpson	997 10
Luff	978 0
Day	971 15
Pettit	945 0
Ribbans	931 0
Wright, Ipswich (accepted)	830 0

For Cuxton Schools, near Rochester; Mr. Martin Bulmer, architect:—

Sutton and Walter, Maidstone	£343 0 0
Laker, Maidstone	340 0 0
Fruit and Bridge, Maidstone	311 14 0
Muir, Malling	300 0 0
Page, Meopham	295 0 0
Toselyn, Wrotham	295 0 0
Coster and Collins, Chatham	287 8 3
Tompson, Loose	276 0 0
Goodwin, Maidstone	274 18 0

TO CORRESPONDENTS.

"*Crickets.*"—A plan to exterminate crickets is asked for.

Received.—"Col. T.," "Londinensis" (Mr. Westmacott it, we believe, commissioned to execute the sculpture for the tympanum of the portico at the British Museum)," "F. N." (shall appear), "W. H. W." (ditto), "J. B." Cheapside (thanks for good feeling)," "J. L." Battersea, "Athens" (thanks for kind expressions. The introduction in buildings and monuments of our cuts of "doors, iron-work, chairs, &c.," would be a departure from the scheme of the work. Whether or not it may be advisable to issue them hereafter as a separate collection, is for consideration), "J. J." (the ungracious tone of our correspondent's letter (not for the first time), and the foolish threat with which it concludes, much surprised us. For old acquaintance sake, we withhold an expression which would otherwise escape us)," "H. D." (we usually see all awards)," "Moth in the Candle," " B. D.," " Reader," " C. F. H.," " B. G.," " C. H. B.," " An Old Hand," " H. W.," " Subscriber " (Laxton's or Skyring's), " E. F. G.," " C. H. B." (oil was *not* used for the coloured decorations of the stone work of churches. Plaster walls will receive such decoration, and require but slight preparation), " Past Student, No 2," " R. A.," " F. F." Camberwell, (if our correspondent could prove injury resulting from the want of drainage, the Board of Health could enforce a remedy), " S."—"Churches of the Middle Ages," Henry Bowman and Joseph S. Crowther, architects, Manchester, 1849; Parts I. II. and III. folio: " Considerations relative to the Sewage of London," &c., by Joseph Glbbs, C. E. ; Weale, 1849 : " John Howard and the Prison World of Europe," by Hepworth Dixon; Jackson and Walford, London, 1849.

"*Books and Addresses.*"—We have not time to point out books or find references.

NOTICE.—All communications respecting *advertisements* should be addressed to the " Publisher," and not to the " Editor;" all other communications should be addressed to the Editor, and not to the Publisher.

BUILDINGS AND MONUMENTS,

MODERN AND MEDIÆVAL.

Edited by Geo. Godwin, F.R.S.,

Fellow of the Institute of Architects; Corresponding Member of several Societies.

Part III. of this work, price 2s. 6d., is now ready, and contains Views of Roslin Chapel, near Edinburgh ; New Church at Homerton, Middlesex ; the Entrance to Royal Botanical Gardens, Kew ; The New Palm Stove ; Bridgewater House, London, with altered plan; Sir Benjamin Heywood's New Bank, Manchester; Ely Cathedral, East End ; the Théâtre Historique, Paris ; Sir Robert Peel's Picture Gallery; with descriptive letter-press, and numerous details.

Parts I. and II. may now be had. Order of any bookseller.

ADVERTISEMENTS.

Open Daily from Eleven to Five, and every Evening, EXCEPT SATURDAY, from Seven till Half-past Ten.

ROYAL POLYTECHNIC INSTITUTION.—First Series of Dissolving Views Illustrating Rome, with a Description embracing the most interesting points connected with the subject. Daily at Half-past Four, and in the Evening at Quarter to Ten o'clock.—Lectures on Chemistry, by Mr. J. M. Ashley. Daily at Half-past Three, and in the Evening at Nine o'clock. —Lectures, with Experiments, by Dr. Bachhoffner, on the Hydro-Electric Machine, Daily at Tea o'clock.— The Chromatrope.—Exhibition of the Oxhydrogen Microscope.—Diver and Diving Bell.—Admission, 1s.: Schools, half price.

SAMUEL HOOD and Co., Castings Warehouse, 81 Upper Thames-street. REGISTERED STABLE FITTINGS. Enamelled Mangers, with double hay-racks, or with enamelled water-cistern on one side.

BRITISH MUTUAL LIFE OFFICE.—The Public are invited to examine for themselves the advantage gained by Assurers by the plan on which policies are granted by this Office.—Apply to CHARLES JAMES THICKE, Secretary, 17, New Bridge-street, Blackfriars.

ARCHITECTS', BUILDERS', and GENERAL FIRE and LIFE INSURANCE COMPANY, 69, Lombard-street, London.

Chairman, SYDNEY SMIRKE, Esq., A.R.A.

Trustees.

T. L. Donaldson, Esq.　　　A. Salvin, Esq., F.S.A.
S. Grimsdell, Esq.　　　　G. Smith, Esq., F.S.A.

The rates for both Fire and Life Insurances are as low as can with safety be taken. Those for Life Insurances may be paid either yearly, half-yearly, or quarterly ; one-half the annual premium may be left unpaid for seven years, or one-third to the end of life. Thus large sums may be insured at the smallest present outlay. Prospectuses, forms of proposals, &c. may be had at the Office, 69, Lombard-street, or of the agents.

JOHN REDDISH, Manager.

CLERICAL, MEDICAL, and GENERAL LIFE ASSURANCE SOCIETY.—NOTICE IS HEREBY GIVEN, that the usual DIVIDEND of 5 per cent. (less income-tax) on the paid-up capital on the shares of the Society, will be PAYABLE at this Office, on and after MONDAY, the 20th day of August next.

INVALID LIVES.

In addition to assurances on healthy lives, this Society continues to grant Policies on the lives of persons more or less deviating from the healthy standard, on the payment of a premium proportioned to the increased risk.

Further information can be obtained (free of expense) by addressing a line to GEO. H. PINCKARD, Resident Sec. No. 99, Great Russell-street, Bloomsbury, London.

CHAS. WM. WATERLOW, MANUFACTURER of Sashes and Frames, and Glazier, Fitzroy-square, 121, Bunhill-row, Finsbury-square, superior workmanship, lowest prices.—(Drawings of old DOORS, and a large variety of Sashes and Frames always on sale. Glazed goods securely packed for the country. Steam-circular Sawing is any quantity.—N.B. This Establishment is worth the notice of all engaged in building.

CHEAP ORNAMENTAL GLASS.—I beg to inform my friends and the public, that I have now completed a new ENGINE, and, owing to the facility with which I can execute orders, I am enabled to reduce my former prices considerably. The prices are now from SIXPENCE per FOOT NETT, and borders from SIXPENCE per FOOT RUN. A large quantity of the cheapest patterns always in stock. Embossing and painted work on the most moderate terms.—CHARLES LONG, No. 1, King-street, Baker-street, Portman-square.—Cash only.

BIRMINGHAM PLATE GLASS COMPANY are supplying PLATE GLASS of a superior quality, at an unusually moderate rate of charge. Per option apply at their warehouse, No. 141, Fleet-street. Rough Plate, 1-8-1, and 1-inch thick.

PLATE GLASS. — British Plate Glass, under 1 foot super, 1s. 2d.; under 1 foot 6 inches, 1s. 6d.; under 2 feet, 1s. 2d.; under 3 feet, 1s. per foot. SHEET GLASS.—3s. 0d. super sheet, 4d quality, in 200 foot cases, 2¼d. per case. No. 31, White, ditto. Stock of foot, Estimates for every description of class, from 14th to 14inch, supplied on hand ; also an extensive assortment of dry prepared. J. N. MILLINGTON'S Warehouse, 87, Bishopsgate-street Without.

PATENT PLATE GLASS.—CLAUDET and HOUGHTON beg to announce to Architects, Builders, and the trade, a further very considerable reduction in their prices of PATENT PLATE, SHEET, and CROWN GLASS. Their new line of prices are now ready, and will be forwarded free on application.—Wholesale and Retail WINDOW GLASS and GLASS SHADE WAREHOUSE, 89, HIGH HOLBORN.

PAINTED and STAINED GLASS for WINDOWS.—CLAUDET and HOUGHTON, 89, High Holborn, execute every description of ORNAMENTAL GLASS for WINDOWS, in ancient or modern style, at the lowest prices consistent with superior workmanship, either in plain colour, ornamented in white ena, embossed, enamel, or richly enamel. Patterns and specimens.—May be seen at their Warehouse, 89, High Holborn.

E. and W. H. JACKSON beg to call the attention of Builders and the trade to the reduced prices of their PATENT PLATE GLASS, which, from its cheapness, is now superseding crown in all respectable dwelling-houses. BRITISH and ROUGH PLATE, CROWN, SHEET, STAINED, and ORNAMENTAL GLASS, supplied of the best manufacture, and at the lowest terms. List of prices, estimates, and every information can be had on application at their warehouse, 315, Oxford-street.

THE UNION PLATE GLASS COMPANY beg to call the attention of Architects, surveyors, builders, large consumers, and the trade generally, to the quality, colour, and substance of their highly-finished glass, and to the discounts vary according to size, they prefer giving a special estimate for each quantity required. To consumers the use of Plate Glass for glazing purposes, the price is considerably reduced, which will, for its durability and appearance, insure the preference to any other description.

ROUGH PLATE GLASS supplied for skylights, warehouses, workshops, and flooring, both 3-8 and 1-inch thick. London Warehouse, 89, Hatton-garden, Holborn. H. CHRISTIE. Agent.

THE PATENT DECORATIVE GLASS COMPANY beg to call the attention of Architects, Builders, and the trade generally, to their VITRIFIED LACE PATTERN GLASS, and having completed the extensive alterations in their works, are enabled to offer their superior article from 1s. 2d. per super. and borders from 6d. per foot run. The process and the effect produced are quite novel, perfect representations of net or muslin curtains, with embroidered borders correct in every detail. It will be found of great importance for window blinds, picture galleries, skylights, &c., and adds very materially to the decoration of an apartment. Glass palliative and ornamenting to all its branches. Specimens of every description can be seen at the works, where tariffs can be obtained. Resident Manager, T. CARTISSER. 21, Castle-street, Southwark-bridge-road.

GEORGE SINGLETON TOVELL, Stone Merchant, Three Cranes Wharf, Surrey-side, desires to inform all persons connected with the building trade, that he has purchased on hand a large and well-assorted Stock of STONE, now generally in use, and which, from the facilities afforded to the docks and railways in the port of Ipswich, he can with the fullest confidence engage to supply on terms equally advantageous with their houses in London. He therefore respectfully solicits orders, to which his best attention shall be devoted.—Agent for the Cliff Colliery and Terra Cotta and Fire Clay Works.—Asphalte Paving laid.

CLEANLINESS is necessarily at all times conducive to health, and this, as well as economy, is greatly promoted by substituting for the noxious process of painting with oil and white lead, STEPHENS'S DYES for STAINING WOOD, as a SUBSTITUTE for PAINT, for decorating churches, large public rooms, and theatres, as well as private dwellings. When economy is expenditure of material and time is of importance, these Dyes will be found of the greatest advantage, as they give a rich colour to plain woods, while they reflect all the beauty of the natural graining, which is so superior to imitations by art, and, at the same time, avoid the disagreeable smell and deleterious consequences of paint. The Dyes, or Stains, are prepared and sold by HENRY STEPHENS, 54, Stamford-street, Blackfriars-road, London, in bottles at 6d. each, and at 1s. per gallon. The Oak, Mahogany, and Satin Wood Colours may be obtained in powder at 8s. per lb., which dissolve in water to form the liquid; and 1 lb. will make one gallon of stain.—N.B. The Patent supplied,—Sold also at the Office of "The Builder," 2, York-street, Covent Garden, London; at both which places may be had the proper Varnish and Size, with directions for their use.

REDUCED PRICES.—EDWARD SIMMS, late William Cleaver, of Wilton-road, Pimlico Basin, begs to acquaint Builders and the Trade that he has now on hand, at his Manufactory (the first of the kind ever established), a very large assortment of Dry and Well-seasoned OAK and DEAL PREPARED FLOORING BOARDS and MATCH BOARDING of all sorts, from 1 inch to 1½ inch thick, planed to a gauge, with and thickness, and at greatly Reduced Prices. Also, Timber, Deals, Oak Planks, Scantlings, Sawn Bills. Machinery prepared by Machinery, Laths, &c.—Apply at E. SIMMS, (late W. Cleaver) Flooring Manufactory, Wilton-road, Pimlico Basin.

A REDUCTION in the PRICE of FLOOR BOARDS.—ALFRED ROSLING begs to inform the Trade and Consumers generally, that he has REDUCED the PRICE, and keeps constantly in stock a large and very general assortment of Prepared Floor Boards and Matched Boarding, planed to a parallel breadth and thickness, and fit for immediate use ; also a variety of machine-prepared Mouldings, which are finished with great accuracy and attention to quality of workmanship.—Southwark Bridge Wharf, Bankside, and Old Barge Wharf, Upper Ground-street, Blackfriars.

GREAT REDUCTION in the PRICE OF FLOOR BOARDS AND MATCH BOARDING.—THOMAS ADAMS (late N. Darr). Mahogany and Timber Merchant. Bermondsey New-road, Southwark, near the Bricklayers' Arms, begs to inform his friends and the trade generally, that he has in stock a large assortment of the above goods, fit for immediate use, at prices which only revolve a trifle to prove their decided cheapness. Also mouldings prepared by machinery from the very best material, and in a superior manner; cut deals and scantling of every dimension ; mahogany, cedar, rosewood, walnuts, elm, beech, oak, &c., in planks, boards, veneers, and logs ; pantile, oak, and fir laths; wheelwrights' goods. All sawn and prepared goods (except timber) delivered free of expense ; saving charged at all prices. Very extensive drying sheds.

SEASONED SPRUCE FLOORING, prepared by improved machinery, in a superior manner. Three-quarter inch thick . . . 10s. 6d. per square. One inch ditto . . . . 13s. ditto. SAMUEL ARCHBUTT'S Sawing and Planing Mills, King's-road, Chelsea.

SAW MILLS, GILLINGHAM-STREET, PIMLICO.

TIMBER of any size, PLANK, DEALS, and BATTENS, &c., Sawn on the most approved principle. Boards, &c. Prepared, Matched, and Grooved, by Muir's Patent Machinery. The Mills have all the advantages of navigation and water-carriage, being connected with the Thames by the Grosvenor Canal. Goods fetched from the docks and carted house free of charge.

Address to HENRY SOUTHAM, Saw Mills, Gillingham-street, Pimlico.

N.B. Estimates given for Sawing and Planing.

GENERAL WOOD-CUTTING COMPANY.—SAWING, PLANING, and MOULDING MILLS, Belvedere-road, Lambeth, between the Suspension and Waterloo Bridges. SAWING and PLANING in all their branches executed with the greatest despatch and expedition. A large Stock of seasoned and beautifully WORKED MOULDINGS, consisting of upwards of 100 different patterns kept constantly on hand ; also an extensive assortment of dry prepared FLOORING BOARDS, of all qualities and at reasonable rates.

PHILLIPS, ALLCARD, and CO.'S IMPERIAL DEAL SAW-MILLS, WENLOCK-ROAD CITY-ROAD, beg to invite the attention of builders, carpenters and the trade, to their well selected stock, consisting of a large assortment of TIMBER, DEALS, PLANKS, and BATTENS, of every description, and thoroughly seasoned. They also have constantly on hand and ready for immediate use, white and yellow prepared FLOORING BOARDS of all thicknesses, and matched lining, cut and planed to a parallel breadth and thickness. And they are enabled to offer all their goods at very moderate prices.

DESICCATED WOOD.—DAVISON and BYNINGTON'S PATENT.—Builders, Cabinet-makers, and others, will find it much to their advantage to patronise this new process of seasoning. The greatest wood rot that not only be seasoned in an incredibly short space of time, at a small cost, but is rendered stronger, entirely free from shrinkage, and in every respect better than wood treated in the ordinary way ; thereby saving capital, interest of money, insurance, and all the other inconveniences attending the keeping of a large stock.

The DESICCATING SAWING and PLANING MILLS are situated at PICCOH BRIDGE, ROTHERHITHE, adjoining the Commercial and East Country Docks, from whence (only) obtaining their material can have the same carted as required, and sent home fit for immediate use.—T. GIRLING, Manager.

For licenses to use the patent, scale of prices, or other information, address AMOS JENNINGS, Secretary, Patent Desiccating Company, 41, Grosvenor-street, City.

TO ARCHITECTS, BUILDERS, UPHOLSTERERS, AND OTHERS.

WOOD CARVING done in the cheapest and best manner. Estimates given to any amount. Pulpits, reading-desks, altar-rails, stalls, and other carving, Gothic supplied complete. Old carvings restored by J. SPALDIN, Wood Carver and Manufacturer, 42, Berwick-street, Soho, London.

JORDAN'S PATENT MACHINE CARVING and MOULDING WORKS for WOOD and STONE. Belvedere-road, Lambeth, and 144, Strand.—TAYLOR, WILLIAMS, and JORDAN beg to call the attention of the building community, as also those of the public generally, to the fact that the present establishment, and, as the same time, to thank their numerous patrons and friends for the very liberal support they have lately experienced, which, they assure them and the public, it will be their constant endeavour to deserve, by giving their customers an increasing stock of machine-cut galleries, for the constant improvements in the machinery which they have just succeeded in applying to the production of the most intricate carving in Caen and other freestone, and in statuary marble.

T. W. and J. particularly solicit the attention of architects and builders to the fact that, by the use of this machinery, a very large saving, both of time and money, is effected ;—at present indeed it may in many cases they can deliver a well-finished article in Caen stone for less money than it can be obtained in common, while their work-carving will, in some cases, be found to come into close competition with the best kinds of composition ornament.—For prices and estimates apply at 134, Strand.

TESTIMONIAL FROM CHARLES BARRY, ESQ.

" Westminster, May 16th, 1848.

" Gentlemen.—In reply to your letter respecting my opinion of your Patent Carving Machinery, I have much pleasure in stating, from an experience of some than two years, in the application to the production of the wood carvings of the House of Peers, and other apartments of the New Palace, at Westminster, that I am enabled to make the most favourable report concerning it, and to add that it has more than justified the favourable terms in which I recommended it in 1849 to her Majesty's Commissioners of Woods and Works for adoption.—I remain, Gentlemen, yours faithfully,

" CHARLES BARRY."

Messrs. Taylor, Williams, and Jordan."

W. D. HUGHES and CO., ORNAMENTAL PLASTERERS, ARCHITECTURAL MODELLERS, &c. manufacture every description of Cement and Plaster Ornaments for internal and external decoration, capitals for columns and pilasters, balustrading for balconies, termini, &c., trusses for shop-fronts, centre flowers, soffits, bed-mouldings, &c. in every variety of pattern, and at the lowest remunerating prices. Plastering of every description contracted for; Workshops, 1a 14, Brewer-street North, 20, John-street-road, Clerkenwell.

The Builder.

No. CCCXLV.

SATURDAY, SEPTEMBER 15, 1849.

 E anxiously invite the serious attention of our readers of all classes to the following communication from Professor Cockerell, R.A., dated from the Architect's Office, Bank of England.

Every one concerned in building operations has witnessed with grief, from time to time, the breaking up of those benefit societies which building operatives have established for their mutual protection against casualties, sickness, old age, &c. Generally humble and local, these have failed from ill-constructed tables, from corruption in the officers, and not unfrequently from the perversion of the funds in cases of strike or political agitation, for purposes of conviviality, &c. : the great suffering of families in consequence, and the demoralization of the operatives themselves, need no comment.

The consideration of these deplorable liabilities engaged some architects and builders seven years ago (1842), by an invitation from this office, to consult, in the hope that exemption from such like dangers might possibly be obtained from better constructed rules and tables; so that a society, directed under their responsible guidance, might effectually secure the interest of their fellow labourers, the building artificers of London, in respect of provision against age and sickness; but, after much careful deliberation, especially by the "Builders' Society," no plan sufficiently promising could be devised for this desirable purpose.

The project has, however, been recently revived by the encouraging example of the "Servants' Provident and Benevolent Society, founded on the Act for the purchase of Annuities through the medium of Savings Banks." Existing scarcely seventeen months, this society has already grown into importance through the earnest exertions of some able and zealous individuals, and the patronage of the highest authorities of the realm, and especially of his Royal Highness Prince Albert; and, in proof of it, we have the remarkable fact, that while, during sixteen years since the passing of the Deferred Annuity Act, nine hundred and forty-one persons only have availed themselves, throughout the kingdom, of the benefits of the Act, this society, during the short period of fourteen months, has added *one hundred and three, or one-tenth of the whole,* and since the 22nd of May has increased that number.

A meeting for the purpose of more effectually calling public attention to the Government Annuity system, and of advancing its value, was invited on the 16th May last, when his Royal Highness Prince Albert presided, and thereby generously pledged his high responsibility for its value and authenticity. His Royal Highness explained or the present, " that this was not an institution of charity but of friendly assistance and advice to those who were willing to help themselves,—who, exercising present self-denial, providence, and perseverance in the days of their strength and prosperity, might, by the kindly co-operation of masters, secure themselves against the adversities of sickness, old age, and want of employment; and above all, against delusive clubs offering extravagant advantages (for ever falsified), in which so much hard-earned capital is continually sunk,— and leading, besides, to convivial meetings, equally dangerous to the prosperity of families and habits of thrift.

That the provident objects of the society were chiefly to recommend the purchase of annuities, deferred for at least ten years, from the amount of 4*l.* to 30*l.* per annum (according to the table), as the most profitable investment of the savings of the servant which could be offered.

That the financial scheme upon which the Act was founded was the most advantageous that could be devised or afforded; and indeed was limited on that account to incomes not exceeding 150*l.* per annum. That it was based on the credit of the country at large, and the faith of Government, by the Acts of Parliament, 3 Wm. 4, cap. 14, and 7 and 8 Vict., cap. 83.

That the deposits are attended, under these Acts, with this peculiar advantage, unprecedented in trading assurance companies, namely, that they may be withdrawn at any time, previous to the payment of the annuity, by the depositor; so that he can command the money deposited for the purchase of his annuity at any period, as in a bank, though of course without interest upon those deposits.

That the benevolent objects of the society (sustained as it was by the subscription of its patrons), were to form a medium or gratuitous agency, by which the great benefits of this Act might be obtained without trouble, risk, or loss by its provident members, cleared of all technical wording and complicated provisions, usual and necessary in Acts of Parliament, and to establish an office for the conduct of the business, attended by persons ready to offer explanations, receive deposits, and regulate correspondence.

That other obvious advantages might be expected to flow (should the public patronage continue prosperously) from the benevolent objects of the society in favour of the depositars, such as the loan or advance of premiums in case of sickness or affliction."

Finally, his Royal Highness urged upon the notice of the public the fact that the system adopted by the Servants' Provident and Benevolent Society was applicable to every other class of her Majesty's subjects whose income and social position were limited to similar conditions.

Such an example and such a model, with some modifications suited to the building artificers' class, would enable the architects, engineers, and builders, uniting with the operatives, to establish and uphold a Building Artificers' Provident and Benevolent Society, of the utmost benefit and comfort to all parties. And, when the number and respectability of the building artificers on the one hand are considered, and the distinction and influence of architects, engineers, and builders, on the other, amongst all classes, from the prince to the humblest labourer throughout the country, the means of such a society may be easily appreciated.

The consideration of such a project is earnestly recommended to all those who are connected with the building classes, and who naturally feel the greatest concern for the welfare of the worthy artificer, and the permanent security of the hard-earned savings of his labours during health and prosperity.*

C. R. COCKERELL, Architect.

* The subjoined table will show the amount of the yearly instalments to secure a Government annuity of 10*l.* for life, contracted for between the ages of twenty-five and thirty-five, and that at the ages of forty-five, fifty, fifty-five, and sixty. We have not space to make it more full. The instalment for an annuity of 10*l.* will cost exactly half as much as an annuity of 20*l.*; an annuity of 30*l.* will cost half as much again; and so in proportion for an annuity of any intermediate amount.

*** All payments made for an annuity will be returned, should the party die before the age when the annuity is receivable, or the payments fail to be continued.

Age last Birthday.	FORTY-FIVE		FIFTY		FIFTY-FIVE		SIXTY	
	Yearly Payment.	Single Sum in lieu of Yearly Payments.	Single Sum in lieu of Yearly Payments.	Yearly Payment.	Single Sum in lieu of Yearly Payments.	Yearly Payment.	Yearly Payment.	Single Sum in lieu of Yearly Payments.
25	£ s. d.	£ s. d.	£ s. d.	£ s. d.	£ s. d.	£ s. d.	£ s. d.	£ s. d.

The proposal we here publish is aimed at one of the most momentous objects of the present times, namely, the promotion of the greater sympathy of ranks—of master and workmen, employer and employed—and the re-establishment of that link of kindliness which ought to exist in bodies having one common occupation, no less in permanent than in immediate interest.

The Labourers' Friend Society, the Servants' Provident, and many similar institutions that have recently come into notice, are so many proofs of this growing sense of duty and benevolence on the part of the upper ranks towards their humble fellow-labourers, and of the enlightened policy which, beginning with George Rose and the Savings Banks, and the beneficent Acts of William and Victoria, quoted in this paper, has continually laboured for the permanent benefit of the humbler ranks.

We hail every attempt to carry out these views, especially in the meritorious and formidable class we advocate—the building class—in which this sympathy, protection, and fellowship are lamentably deficient (from discreditable causes), and the establishment of which would effect a great moral and social good amongst us, mitigating that fearful antagonism between capital and labour which breaks out continually in so alarming a form, and threatens the framework of society.

The Paternal Institution of the Freemasons (now extinct 132 years), and the several guilds of old, grew out of similar motives, namely, the confession of mutual obligation, the association for mutual benefit and protection of the high and low (the grand masters, wardens, and brothers), for the security of permanent as well as immediate support.

Individual ranks in the present day do not fail to make such provision as they can for their separate interests; but this comprehensive, paternal, and corporate union of ranks, upon the broad basis of mutual and general good to the class, ceased with the Freemasons.

Thus the architects, engineers, and builders have established an insurance office for themselves; the builders have also their Builders' Society, or union, for the protection of their own individual interests; they have also a Society for decayed builders, to which they invite public subscription.* The building artificer, on his side, is not behind-hand; he has the Club for his security (as he sometimes vainly imagines) in sickness and old age,† and his Union for that of his rank, and the support of that intestine war against capital, which is ever raging more or less, and ever consuming his hard-earned savings. Thus the separate selfish and individual interests have all been consulted, but the union of all for mutual good and a full and active admission of fellowship has been neglected. The obligations of the architect, the engineer, and the builder, to the simple artificer are as clear as that of the general to the simple soldier. The mere commercial exchange of wage and labour can never discharge the debt of the former to the latter: a grateful country acknowledges this truth at Chelsea and Greenwich and the *Invalides*. The slave-driver is compelled by law to provide for those hands, in sickness and old age, which have ministered to his comfort and prosperity in youth and vigour; but the freeman artificer and operative of England has no such advantage, nor even

* It is right to say, that " The Builders' Benevolent Institution " also proposes giving assistance to workmen when *accidentally injured in their master's employ.*

† We will not omit honourable mention of " The Provident Institution for Builders' Foremen."

sympathy from his master, unless it be at the parish expense. Between him and his employer there is no absolute obligation beyond that which the labour markets and the laws of commerce impose—the work performed and the wage paid terminate their connection,—the merchant builder, whose fortune has been achieved by the combined labour of the artificer, has thus (as he considers) fulfilled his part;—the honey once hived the drones are expelled, and must provide for their own future as best they can.

Amongst the many reasons for this isolation of interests, and the deficiency of more generous, paternal, and comprehensive views for the benefit of the various subordinate ranks composing a class, is the system of union and combination, so constantly the subject of legal discussion and enactment, and that antagonism in which capital, on the one hand, and labour on the other, are continually placed. To what an alarming pitch the warfare of this antagonism rises, the annals of the last forty years familiarize to the recollection of all of us. It is one of the great evils inherent in a wealthy commercial and manufacturing country, and has been the ruin of this flourishing states, as it may be of this.

But this evil is greatly aggravated, and indeed in a measure justified, where a line of separation is drawn between the ranks, and no sympathy for permanent good and happiness of the humbler is shown by the higher,—no hand of friendship, advice, and fellowship is offered for the ulterior security of the operative and his family, beyond the commercial interchange of wages and labour, with all the contentions and bitterness which always will accompany this barter,—a sympathy and fellowship which the superior instruction, wealth, and influence of the higher ranks would so easily and profitably bestow upon the lower, provided they will help themselves, by thrift and providence, with those means which have been provided for them.

In a wealthy, commercial, and manufacturing country the Merchant Builder is of natural growth, and has been exhibited during the last half century, in this country, in very remarkable development, unknown to former ages: his capital absorbs the little tradesman, with all his individuality of skill and character, and either grinds him under his colossal weight into the sub-contractor, or melts him down into his establishment as a hired article of trade. He offers advantageous terms to the public, inasmuch as he is satisfied with one profit instead of the several which the various trades would require, and entails but one trouble and responsibility instead of the many which the ancient system was liable to. The public, therefore, patronize and confirm this practice.

But this, as a kind of monopoly, leads to many well-known evils, and excites an antagonism on the part of labour, which is consuming and ruinous alike to the prosperity, as also the morality, of the operative,—an antagonism which he uses in self-defence, and which brings with it pretensions of wage and rights often indefensible, and which he justifies when he perceives no friendliness or sympathy in his superior towards his personal permanent interests.

Thus, to the tyranny of capital we have opposed the tyranny of labour, equally violent and unreasonable, and which nothing but a conviction of established mutual regard, apart from the question of barter, would mitigate. We know that some beneficial measure of

this kind has long been in the contemplation of the Builders' Society; but neither they, nor the other two ranks concerned, could alone effect a really beneficial society of the kind proposed; for any measure exclusively from them would be suspected by the operative, as a device to draw the teeth of their unions, and to rivet the chains already complained of.

The operatives also, alone, are helpless, having neither the leisure nor influence to place their claims before the public in their due proportion; but these two, united to their natural leaders, the architects and engineers, who could have no other interests than those of honour and fairness, would possess all the elements of a great and beneficial institution, and a balm of consummate efficacy in the present malady of our operative system.

An office should be established for the gratuitous agency of contracts for deferred annuities, for all comers, unionists or not, and thus institute the provident part of the institution. For the support of this office, and for general benevolence in case of sickness, inability to pay premiums, and other similar purposes, a Benevolent Fund would be raised; and when we consider the means and the motives which the capitalist builder would have for the support of this fund, and also the public, through the influence of the heads of the profession (who have access to the highest authorities of the country without suspicion of interested motives, other than such as honour and benevolence dictate), and who could thus put forward the claims of the meritorious class which they would benefit, the success of such a society by annual public meetings, and a weekly board, could never be doubted by those who see how many societies of the same general object do flourish in this great country.

The operative thus befriended, and associated with his natural protectors in the face of the public, would be raised and dignified as a class; his morality must be improved by well-directed providence and friendly countenance; and his attachment to Government and public order would be secured by his reliance on their stability; unions would lose their virulence and their justification; a false communism would be displaced for a real one; and a grand step towards a more wholesome order of society in this meritorious class, of most beneficial influence upon others, would be effected, to the great honour and satisfaction of every true Mason and well-wisher to the ingenious and useful class to which he belongs.

We invite suggestions and co-operation: Government Annuities are suggested; but it has been shown that on the principle of Mutual Assurance greater advantages can be obtained than are given in Government Annuities; and if, as we understand, a Bill is about to be brought into Parliament to carry out this principle with Government security, a different view may be taken.

REMOVAL OF ILLICIT FEVER-STILLS.

St. Botolph's, Bishopsgate-street.—The vestry of this parish, after a long discussion, unanimously passed the following resolution;— "That in the opinion of this vestry the public health is alarmingly endangered by the continued practice of interring the dead in the parochial burial-ground, and in the vaults under the church, and that all interments in the churchyard of the parish, and in the vaults under the church, be henceforth discontinued. That a committee be appointed to carry out the foregoing resolution, with full power to take any measure necessary for its enforcement." The vicar anxiously concurred, and the Lord Mayor took part in the discussion.

St. Clement's, Eastcheap, City.—The inhabitants have directed the churchwardens to discontinue for the future the burials in the church and churchyard of this parish; the rector cheerfully acquiescing.

Tottenham-court-road Chapel.—The Board of Health have ordered the burial-ground of this chapel to be closed.

St. Clement Danes', Strand.—The Board of Health have peremptorily closed the horrible fever-still in Portugal-street, belonging to this parish.

St. John's, Westminster. — Forty householders and residents have called on the Board of Health to look to the burial-ground of St. John the Evangelist. The two first cases of cholera in that district occurred in houses abutting on the worst part of the ground.

Lambeth.—At a meeting of the inhabitants of Lambeth on the 10th, it was resolved that "the churchyard in High-street, wherein from 200 to 300 persons are buried weekly, to the imminent risk of the lives of all the parishioners, be immediately closed against all future interments."

So long ago as 1552, Bishop Latimer said,— "I doe marvel that London, being soe great a citie, hath not a burial-place without; for no doubt it is an unwholesome thinge to bury within the citie, especiallie at such a time, when there be great sicknesses, and manie die together. I think verilie that many a man taketh his death in Paul's Churchyard, and this I speake of experience; for I myself, when I have been there on some morninges to heare the sermons, have felt such an ill-savoured and unwholesome savour that I was the worse for it a great while after; and I think noe lesse but it is the occasion of great sicknesse and disease."

Sir Christopher Wren, when named one of the commissioners for building new churches, wrote a letter for the consideration of his colleagues, from which a correspondent, Mr. Barlow, has forwarded us an extract. He says: —"I could wish that all burials in churches might be disallowed, which is not only unwholesome, but the pavements can never be kept even, nor pews upright; and if the churchyard be close about the church, this also is inconvenient, because the ground being continually raised by the graves, occasions in time a descent by steps into the church, which renders it damp and the walls green, as appears evidently in all the old churches. It will be inquired where then shall be the burials? I answer in cemeteries, seated in the outskirts of the town; and since it is become the fashion of the age to solemnize funerals by a train of coaches, though the cemeteries should be half a mile or more distant from the church, the charge need be little or no more than usual; the service may be first performed in the church. But for the poor, and such as must be interred at the parish charge, a public hearse of two wheels, and one horse, may be kept at small expense, the usual bearers to lead the horse, and take out the corpse at the grave. A piece of ground of two acres in the fields wil be purchased for much less than two roods among the buildings. This being enclosed with a strong brick wall, and having a walk round, and two cross walks, decently planted with yew trees, the four quarters may serve four parishes, where the dead need not be disturbed at the pleasure of the sexton, or piled four or five upon one another, or the bones thrown out to gain room. In these places beautiful monuments may be erected; but yet the dimensions should be regulated by an architect, and not left to the fancy of every mason; for thus the rich, with large marble tombs, would shoulder out the poor. * * * It may be considered farther, that if the cemeteries be thus thrown into the fields, they will bound the excessive growth of the city with a graceful border, which is now encircled with scavengers' dung-stalls."

Since then we have been piling up corruption to a fearful extent, in spite of warnings. Not a moment must be lost in stopping the evil. Again we say, petition for an Order in council.

AN APPEAL FROM THE ROYAL INSTITUTE OF BRITISH ARCHITECTS.

The council of the institute, impressed with the importance and responsibility attached to their duties, are anxious to take such steps as may still more fully realize those results which are expected from the proceedings of the institute. They feel it to be necessary for all to bear in mind, that one of the great objects of the meetings is to elicit facts relating to the several departments of knowledge which are subservient to architecture. Many may imagine that investigation has already exhausted discovery. But if for a moment we consider how much each year developes that is new and useful to our art, it must be confessed that there is a vast field yet unexplored. And if we may hope to see embodied the intense aspiration of the present race of architects to discover some new source of inspiration, it must only be by a thorough appreciation of the state of science, and of the requirements of the present day. It was by the investigation of such principles that, under like circumstances, the men of genius of former periods brought to bear new appliances, in order to satisfy the wants of their times, and to work out the full capabilities of the new stream of thought which then presented itself. It is only thus that we also can hope to create and mature ideas which shall distinctly mark this epoch of our art, this period of the existence of the institute.

Never until now had English architects so fully mastered, by laborious study and deep research among the monuments of ancient time, all the phases that architecture has assumed in successive periods. The portfolios of our professional brethren are so many treasures, rich in stores of material, and evidences of how deeply their possessors have felt and thought on the subject. This is further proved by the monuments of our art and the various valuable works produced within the last quarter of a century. The concentration of these riches of reflection and experience is the great desideratum. Can this be better effected than by unreserved communications and interchange of ideas through the medium of the institute?

Under these feelings, and conscious that our body are capable of working out great things for the art, the council confidently appeal to the members, and call upon them to assist their earnest efforts to give that efficiency of action, and to produce those fruits, which the profession, the public,—shall we say? Europe—are entitled to expect from our combined exertions. They are most desirous to give additional stimulus and energy of purpose to the members, and to induce them to exert themselves, and to combine, in a movement onwards, in an united effort for some new and striking results, which shall redound to the credit of our honoured institution. There is many a floating idea, many an immature notion of a something unrealised, which, if expressed, may lead to striking results; and if they could be brought before the institute, stated, discussed, and so diffused among many thoughtful minds, good must arise, and still greater variety and originality ultimately mark the productions of our artists.

But justice would not be done to the ample scope of our theme, if you were led to consider, that allusion was only intended to architecture as a fine art, to the exclusion of its scientific division. The æsthetics of each distinct period of architecture have grown out of the principles of construction then in practice, and hence have arisen new combinations of form and proportion. We are now undergoing a marked transition in the canons of construction; new materials, new wants have been introduced, and new elements for combination. The constructive architect of this day has larger views and almost boundless requirements to satisfy, which existed not half a century ago. All these circumstances suggest new subjects for consideration. The more precise form now given to the investigations and results of architectural experience in the several classes of building, each having its own laws, shows, that he who wishes to keep pace with the wondrous progress of the present time must work and think not alone but in combination. Such combination is peculiarly offered in the institute.

The council trust, then, to render the next session remarkable by a more distinct aim and activity of purpose. They would venture to anticipate, that the members will consider it a duty and a delight to contribute somewhat to the intellectual advancement which they hope to set in action. This can only be done by each one's turning his attention to the consideration of some idea. The illustration of an existing fabric,—the statement of a doubt,—the suggestion of a principle,—the development of a train of thought,—will contribute to this. There is not one who has not some, perchance indistinct, leading notion in his mind. Let this then assume a tangible shape, and such a contribution may produce important consequences.

T. L. Donaldson, } Honorary
J. J. Scoles, } Secretaries.

MANAGEMENT OF ARCHITECTURAL COMPETITIONS.

What your correspondent "Y." says respecting the management of architectural competitions is excellent; yet there is one desideratum which he has overlooked, namely, that competitors should have a reasonable time allowed them for fairly studying the subject proposed. At present, that is so far from being the case, that very frequently scarcely time enough is allowed for merely making drawings,—or, perhaps, not even that, unless an architect either happen to be entirely disengaged, or can put all other business aside in order to work for the sake of a mere chance.

The off-hand expedition required on such occasions is an equally serious and gratuitous tax upon the profession; and, so far from at all benefiting those inflicting it, is plainly contrary to their interests, although they themselves seem to be far too dull to perceive it.

What better than hastily put together ideas can committees expect to get from architects, if they will not allow the time for producing thoroughly well considered and matured *designs?* And by "matured designs" I do not mean carefully finished *drawings*, for the latter may be and frequently are exceedingly common place in point of design. In fact, the drawings sent in to competitions should not be allowed even to aim at any of the allurements of mere pictorial effect, but both be and be looked upon by those to whom they are submitted as no more than preparatory *drafts*, which, should there be occasion to do so, can afterwards be transcribed quite *fair*. Beauty of mere drawing is apt to be so exceedingly seductive, especially to non-professional persons, that committees ought to be particularly on their guard against it, and carefully scrutinize a design that seeks so to recommend itself; they having to consider not what the drawing before them *is*, but what the structure erected after it *will be*, and how the latter will show itself.

As to the first matter I have touched upon—the hurry with which competitions are usually managed in the first instance becomes the more preposterous, when, as often turns out to be the case, a twelvemonth or more elapses before the work competed for is actually set about.

Z.

It is to be hoped the valuable suggestions of your correspondent "Y," in last week's Builder, will not fail to create the desired effect, but will be the means of stirring up the profession to a proper sense of the present disgraceful system upon which architectural competitions are carried on. Ever since your valuable journal was first started, scarcely a week has passed without complaints being made through your columns of some competition *job*. Yet, after all that has been said and written, nothing has been done *practically* to remedy the evil. From experience it may be confidently asserted neither "institute reports," nor long letters to "The Builder," will of themselves produce the desired reform. It is very well to blame committees, composed (as they generally are) of men totally incapable of forming a correct judgment of the relative merits of designs submitted to them, for all the evils attendant upon architectural competitions. For my own part I am inclined to think architects have only themselves to blame for the expenses they are subjected to in preparing drawings, when they, regardless of the risk they are incurring, submit their designs to the adjudication of men, who, from deficiency of education in the fine arts, are totally incapable of arriving at a correct decision. The difficulty then that presents itself, is how, the most effectually, to remedy the growing evil. The one suggested by your correspondent of a "monster meeting," of all parties interested, appears to be the only likely means of bringing about the desired reform, the object of which meeting would be to draw up a certain code of regulations sufficiently comprehensive to meet the requirements of almost every case, to which it should be the object of the meeting, or a committee appointed by it, to obtain the assent of the whole profession, binding them, at the risk of forfeiture of caste, to strictly adhere to them. A thorough reform of the present pernicious system would, doubtless, be the work of time, and difficulties would present themselves, in the refusal of competition committees to accept the code of regulations submitted to them. In such cases it would be the duty of the profession to make a manly stand, and at every risk to refuse to compete. If such a course were pursued in one or two instances, by the profession, *united* committees would soon begin to see they must either give way, or put up with inferior designs, while it would also be the duty of the profession, however painful the adoption of such a course might be, to excommunicate from its honourable fellowship, any architect who might be found to engage in a competition against which the profession had authoritatively pronounced. It is very probable the subject will be energetically agitated before long, by means of public meetings; in the meanwhile I would suggest to the profession to give the subject mature thought, and reduce to writing any suggestions that might occur to them, so that when the agitation is once commenced, it may not be allowed to subside, without thoroughly removing the evils under which the present system labours.

C. G.

THE HONOUR OF THE LONDON AND NORTH-WESTERN RAILWAY COMPANY.

In 1845 the London and North-Western Railway Company took the West London Railway, which had cost the proprietors 280,000*l.*, on lease for one thousand years, paying down 60,000*l.* to clear off liabilities, and binding themselves to work the line efficiently, and give the West London Company half the receipts. And this was at a time when other companies would have purchased. They obtained an Act to extend the line to the Thames, and year after year have pledged themselves to the West London to carry out their arrangement. They now point-blank refuse to work the line, under any circumstances, for passenger traffic, or to pay any compensation to the West London. The poor deluded shareholders in the latter Company, who have never received a single sixpence for their 280,000*l.* long since advanced, are told that they would have no chance at law against *so powerful a Company* as the North-Western. They have called a special meeting, however, for the 18th of next month, to consider what course shall be pursued; and we hope, if they find that their deeds are all right, that they will try the extent of the boasted power of the North-Western Company over law, Justice, and honour. Further, a very large population are interested in obtaining a station at Kensington.

Birmingham Exhibition of Industrial Art.—We have received some particulars of this exhibition of English industry, but must endeavour to see it for ourselves next week.

ARCHITECTURE OF CATANIA.

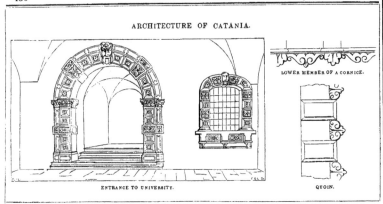

LOWER MEMBER OF A CORNICE.

ENTRANCE TO UNIVERSITY.

QUOIN.

UNIVERSITY, CATANIA.

This sketch will serve to give some slight idea of the general architecture of Catania, the style whereof is peculiar and very striking. The peculiarity consists chiefly in the extraordinary richness of the details. The doors, windows, and cornices are all lavishly adorned: and even the poorest houses partake of the ornament. It is, however, seldom carried so high as the main cornice, which is usually too weak in effect for the richness of the lower parts of the façades. The annexed sketch is from the entrance court of the University, a building which is said to have suffered greatly during the late warfare. A few memoranda, showing other specimens of the style, are subjoined.   T. H. L.

HEALTHY HOMES.

Under this title we are glad to see a cheap issue of Professor Hosking's "Guide to the proper Regulation of Buildings, Streets, Drains, and Sewers."* The original title sounded too technical, and did not convey the fact to the public that the book treated of matters in which all were vitally interested, and that they were set forth in a manner which all could understand. We gave our hearty commendation to the book in its original shape, and we hope the new issue will be extensively read, as we are satisfied it is calculated to do much good.

In a postscript to the work, Mr. Hosking had warned the Commissioners of Sewers in strong language against attempting to remove the deposits in the sewers "with a plague marching upon us with steady pace in the midst of a mild and damp winter," and in the advertisement to the new issue he points to the course of events since its first publication as justifying the warning he gave.

A large portion of the book is devoted to the subject of drainage and ventilation, and it contains many valuable suggestions with a view to render our dwelling-houses more secure against fire than they now are.

We give an extract from the appendix touching bell-traps, which are usually so ill. regulated in houses as to prove a source of constant annoyance and danger:—

" Bell-traps are commonly left loose, because many substances which pass through the grating or strainer of the trap refuse to pass the trap, either floating so that they cannot go under the lip of the bell, or sinking in the well so that they do not get over the bottom end of the drain pipe; and as tea leaves, rice, and other matters arising from the washing of plates and dishes, the ravelled threads of house cloths, hair from brooms, and many other such like matters, find their way to the grating in the sink, or at the drain head, and enough of

* Published by John Murray: London, 1849.

them pass through and lodge in the well into which the bell is dipped, the escape becomes choked, and the trap requires to be lifted to clear the way. To solder down bell-traps is, therefore to render the sink useless, unless they are protected from access of such obstructions, or means be devised of clearing them away. They may be protected by a wire strainer over the sink to stop everything that can tend to choke a bell-trap before it can reach the grating;—or any ordinary obstruction may be cleared by forcing all such matters as will pass the grating of a bell-trap to go under the lip of the bell, and to rise over the end of the stand-pipe, and so pass away into the drain, and the requisite force may be obtained from a slight head of water by means of a very simple apparatus that may be always at hand in every house:—A tin or other cheap metal tube of three or four feet in length, funnel-shaped at each end, and the edges formed or bound with caoutchouc, so that when stood on end and pressed firmly down there may be a water-tight joint. This instrument placed over the grating of any bell-trap so as to embrace it fully, and filled with water, the pressure will be sufficient to clear away any ordinary obstruction from the trap, and render it unnecessary to leave the trap loose. Such an apparatus may be applied by any maid-servant, and to any sink in or about a house, wherever, it must be added, there is clear height enough for it to be placed upright, though it is capable of being articulated to bend in some slight degree; and it may be made telescope fashion to give the means of increasing the pressure if need be."

AWARDS OF OFFICIAL REFEREES.

DUTIES OF DISTRICT SURVEYORS.

The district surveyor of Wandsworth and Tooting (Mr. Hiscocks), gave notice at the end of last year to Mr. W. Josiah Smith, addressed "To the owners or occupiers of the house and premises, situate at Garratt," to "repair the brickwork of the chimney shafts, refix the pots, make good and secure the tiling or slates of the roofs, repair the gutters and shoots, and do such other repairs to the front and side walls of the said buildings and premises, as may be required pursuant to the said Act," and then in January last sent in a demand for 5l., "for surveying the repairs of houses at Garratt, under section 43, and causing the rules of the Act to be observed."

Mr. Smith refused to pay: the surveyor threatened to summon him: and Mr. S. therefore sent the papers to the referees to inquire into the matter, and he set forth that the only repair necessary was the pointing of the roofs, which was always done once a-year. The referees accordingly surveyed the buildings, which it appeared were ten in number, and determined (July last) that none of the things stated in the notice were, at the date of the notice, in danger of falling within the meaning of the

43rd section, and being of opinion thereupon that there was no sufficient ground for the proceeding taken in the matter by the district surveyor, awarded "that the said district surveyor is not entitled to be paid by, or to receive from, the said William Josiah Smith, any fee in respect of the proceeding hereinbefore referred to.

"And further, we do hereby declare our opinion as to such proceeding, if it had been a necessary one in the case, that inasmuch as the said district surveyor does not in the said notice specifically set forth for, and as to each of the said several buildings, the particular matters or things which in each of the said several buildings he deemed and alleged to be in danger of falling, the said notice is not a sufficient requirement or notice, under the 43rd section of the said Act first herein mentioned, to the several occupiers or owners of the said buildings," and further that the account, as it did not state "the number of such houses, or the amount claimed in respect of each of the said houses, or which of the several fees specified in schedule L is claimed," was not such an account as the district surveyor is required to give. Cost to be paid by the district surveyor.

BACK-YARDS.

With regard to four fourth-rate dwelling-houses in Hatfield-street, Goswell-street, in the district of St. Luke's, Old-street, and the liberty of Glasshouse-yard, the surveyor of the district (Mr. Carpenter) laid an information before the official referees. Messrs. Davey, builders, had "formed the back-yards so as to contain less than one square each, exclusive of any building thereon." The yards measured respectively 12 feet 1 inch by 8 feet 2 inches = 98 feet 8 inches; 12 feet 2 inches by 7 feet 9 inches = 94 feet 3 inches; 11 feet 11 inches by 7 feet 4 inches = 87 feet 4 inches; and 11 feet 10¼ inches by 7 feet 0 inches = 83 feet 6 inches.

At the hearing it was stated, "that there had formerly been buildings on the site occupied by the present buildings; that such buildings had been pulled down from thirteen to fifteen years ago; and that the present buildings contain three stories only, and that the lowest story is not an underground or basement story; and the said district-surveyor stated that, as regarded the line of street, he had recognized the erection of the said buildings as the re-building of previously existing buildings."

The referees determined, "That inasmuch as the buildings which formerly stood upon the site of the said four buildings were pulled down and removed before the time when the said Act first herein mentioned came into operation, the erection of the said four buildings does not constitute a rebuilding of buildings already built within the meaning of Schedule K of the said Act; and that the said buildings are buildings hereafter built within the meaning of the said schedule; and that inasmuch as each of the said buildings has been built without having an enclosed back-yard or open space of at least one square without any building thereon, and inasmuch as all the said rooms of each of the said buildings cannot be lighted and ventilated from the street, the said buildings have been severally built and are contrary to the rules and directions of the said Act first herein mentioned."

STAIRS IN PUBLIC BUILDINGS.

With regard to the chapel of the Foundling Hospital, Guildford-street, in the district of St. Pancras, it was desirable to provide additional stair accommodation for the public, and "there being no means of making such stairs fireproof" (as was stated), the same were constructed of woodwork. Doubts arising in the mind of the district-surveyor (Mr. Baker) as to whether the rules of Schedule C, part 6, applied to the said works, a joint requisition was sent to the official referees to request their opinion thereon.

The referees determined, "that inasmuch as the said gallery has not been altered or enlarged since the passing of the Metropolitan Buildings Act, it is not required by that Act to form any fire-proof stairs or accesses to such gallery; and that the erection of the said wooden stairs, in addition to the wooden stairs which had been in use before the passing of the Metropolitan Buildings Act, is not contrary to the rules of the said Schedule C, part 6."

THE ART-UNION OF LONDON.

"THE SMILE," AND "THE FROWN."

THESE engravings, which are now being given to subscribers of the current year on payment of the subscription, an arrangement made by the council to prevent a complaint on the part of members, which, looked at properly, is seen to be most unreasonable, that they have to wait some time before they obtain their prints,—are exceedingly well executed by C. W. Sharp and W. D. Taylor, after two most characteristic works of the artist, Mr. Webster, R.A.

Originally these were to have been issued by a print publisher, and the pair would have been priced at two guineas. As members are, in addition to these, to receive for each guinea subscribed a beautiful series of etchings from drawings by Mr. Maclise, R.A., illustrative of Shakspeare's "Seven Ages," and a chance in the distribution of prizes,—to say nothing of a copy of the report, tickets for their friends for the exhibition and the general meeting, coupled with the satisfaction of knowing that they are also aiding the rising artists of the country, the number of subscribers can scarcely fail to be very large.

During the past week two or three correspondents of the *Times* have been permitted to abuse the works issued by the society, and to make some very erroneous statements, we hope unknowingly. The anonymous writer of the first letter which appeared called Maclise's outlines "a complete failure—at all events, a very weak production;" and says, as to "The Smile" and "The Frown," he "can only designate them as twaddle," and an "inane production." It would be more than sufficient, in answer to this, to give simply the opinion of the *Times* itself, which had previously said—"The choice of pictures for the engravings with which the subscribers are presented has been most judicious, for no works could be more generally acceptable, or more characteristic of the excellent artist who produced them, than 'The Smile' and 'The Frown.'" Further, "they are *admirably* engraved."

It happens, however, that the whole of the press, so far as we have seen, are unanimous in their praise. Confining ourselves to such London papers as happen to be before us, the *Athenæum*, unfortunately never willing to speak well of the Art-Union, talks of Mr. Webster's "two admirable little pictures" and Mr. Maclise's highly poetical outlines illustrative of the "Seven Ages." The *Atlas* says the pictures are "admirably engraved." The *Spectator*, after expressions of admiration, says, "the companion prints form a work of which English art may be proud;" and the *Examiner* remarks, "the choice of pictures for the engraving is most judicious, for no work could be more generally acceptable, or more characteristic of the excellent artist who produced them." The *Observer* says of "The Smile" and "The Frown," that they are "inimitable pictures," engraved in a manner creditable in the highest degree to the talents of the artists;" and ends with, "it is not saying too much to state that these are decidedly the best prints ever issued by the Art-Union of London." The *Morning Herald* says, the prints "are among the best yet issued by the society. They are accurate copies of the original paintings, which are as distinguished for their natural character as for their genuine humour." The *Morning Post* remarks, that these prints "are certainly the best the Art-Union has hitherto presented to the public. * * * Worth the price of the subscription." The *Morning Advertiser* calls them "two works of conspicuous attraction." The *Art-Journal* believes "that they will constitute the most popular presentation that has ever been made to the subscribers," and as to the "Seven Ages," that "they are surpassingly sweet in sentiment," full of "simple and severe elegance." The *Journal of Design* is of opinion, that the Websters are "excellent in subject and in treatment, and capital engravings," and that the series of the "Seven Ages," by Maclise, are "among the best of his designs," and elsewhere that they are "by far the richest return which has yet been offered to the subscribers, and ought to attract many additional thousands." Two of the writers in the *Times*, with counterfeited sorrow (one a reverend gentleman, who, it is to be hoped, for the sake of the souls committed to his charge, knows more about divinity than he does about art), lament that the council allows its functions to be exercised by one or two gentlemen." They will of course be delighted to be informed, that *every* Tuesday throughout the whole year the council meet, without intermission, in the season and out of the season, usually from twelve to sixteen in number, and never by any accident less than seven, and patiently and most anxiously determine on every step that is taken.

It is not our intention to reply to the ungracious letters in question, but feeling great interest in the progress of the Art-Union of London, and anxious that an institution which has done so much towards forming an art-loving and art-appreciating people, and which moreover benefits so largely an important class, should not be injured either by ignorance or malevolence, we have ventured to put together the foregoing opinions on the prints offered for the current year.

NOTES IN THE PROVINCES.

SOME considerable alterations are being carried out at the Shire-hall, Chelmsford, and the petty session room is being converted into prisoners' cells.——The contract for a new mansion in Tortworth park has been taken by a contractor from Lincoln. Earl Ducie means to spend at least 30,000*l.* on this new residence. ——Some improvements have been recently made at the fish shambles, Louth, by Mr. P. Bellamy, of Lincoln, architect.——Tenders for sewers at Southampton have been lodged—Mr. Richard Docwra to construct the Kingsland-place sewers, according to specifications, for 787*l.* 10s. 3d., and Spa-road sewers for 100*l.* 7s. 4d.,—Mr. Stevens for Kingsland-place 786*l.*, Spa-road 100*l.*,—Mr. Emmett for Kingsland-place 765*l.*, Spa-road 130*l.*,—Mr. C. E. Lansdell, Kingsland-place 750*l.*, Spa-road 130*l.* The unusually near agreement in the amount of the tenders excited some surprise. Each party also tendered for private drains: referred to committee. The tenders for Kingsland-place sewers were about 350*l.* above the surveyor's estimate, accounted for by necessary connections with the main sewers. Mr. Stevens's tender, at 100*l.*, for the Spa-road sewer, accepted.——The building of the new Government school at Wimborne has been begun.——The inhabitants of Stoke have resolved to purchase a piece of land for pleasure grounds and healthful recreation, particularly for the working classes.——The foundation stone of the Temperance-hall and Mechanics' Institute, at Grosvenor-street, Chorlton-on-Medlock, was to be laid on 1st inst.——The Stockport Temperance Society's hall will be 72 feet long by 42 feet wide, divided into three compartments by two ranges of columns lengthwise, making the central division 21 feet in width. In the basement will be class-rooms and other apartments. The whole will be of brick and stone, with a lofty central doorway with rusticated Tuscan pilasters and entablature. The foundation-stone was laid on Wednesday week.——Ten shillings per thousand feet for gas at Otley, being "considered a most exorbitant charge by the consumers," says the *Bradford Observer*, means for enforcing a reduction of price have been resolved on.——On Saturday in week before last the foundation-stone of a new county hospital was laid at York.——Elaborate plans of the sewers of Newcastle and Gateshead, it is said, are being formed, at great expense, by the Town Improvement Committees. All the properties which *have been* connected by branch drains with the main sewers and all those which *might have been* connected will be delineated on these plans in distinctive colours. Such a *guide* to house purchasers and tenants ought to form a strong inducement to house proprietors to convert 'might have been' into 'have been' without further loss of time.——At Roseneath, a favourite resort of the citizens of Glasgow, reached by steam on the Clyde, seaward, the Duke of Argyle has resolved to fence out lots for villas to form a watering-place, and the plots or areas, of half an acre and *upwards* only, are being rapidly taken, and a steamer quay is to be shortly erected.——Mr. Raeburn, late architect (at Edinburgh?) to the Woods and Forests, has furnished a design for a pyramid or obelisk, in commemoration of the battle of Culloden. He proposes to use bronzed cast-iron, in place of stone, and to form the whole at a cost of 250*l.* to 300*l.* The design consists of an obelisk-shaped pyramid, fluted, 60 feet high, with a base of 30 feet square, resting upon four gigantic balls, and affording space for figures and inscriptions in *basso relievo.* The vacant space beneath the base to be laid with whinstone, "so as to represent the shades of the slain." The foundations have been laid. ——Her Majesty is said to have expressed a desire to have a Royal marine residence erected at Killiney, within eight miles of Dublin, on a promontory commanding a view of the bay.

NEW NORTHERN SCHOOLS, ST. MARTIN'S-IN-THE-FIELDS, LONDON.

ON Tuesday last the Rev. Henry Mackenzie, vicar of St. Martin's-in-the-Fields, laid the first stone of the new Northern Schools for that parish—the Royal parish as it is termed—in Castle-street, Long Acre.

Some time since the committee invited the architects *resident in the parish* to send in designs. Fifteen plans were in consequence submitted, and from these the committee selected one by Mr. James Wild, architect. As we shall engrave the elevation for our ensuing number, we shall not go into any particulars of the design now.

Messrs. Haward and Nixon, old residents in the parish, and deservedly respected there, are the builders.

The parish authorities and the friends of the undertaking afterwards took luncheon in the vestry-room, the Rev. Vicar pleasantly presiding. In the course of the few speeches which followed, it was stated that the Queen and the Prince had made a joint donation of 100*l.* towards the schools. The site was presented by the Mercers' Company, for 999 years, at 2*l.* per annum, and some idea of the value of it was given, when it was stated, that for about one-third of the ground, which was at present held for an unexpired term of 3½ years, the tenant asked 1,250*l.* for his interest.

The schools are to accommodate 800 children, and have the peculiarity of a covered play-ground on the top of them.

The health of the architect was very properly included in the list of toasts.

MONUMENTS FOR MADRAS CATHEDRAL.—Mr. E. Richardson, sculptor, is engaged on the Dick and Broadfoot testimonials for Madras Cathedral. The artist having chosen for the former a veteran highlander of Sir Robert Dick's regiment, the 42nd, has just completed his models from picked men at the depôt of the regiment at Parkhurst. These works, raised by a general subscription throughout the presidency of Madras, will be executed in marble.

CATHEDRAL OF ANDERNACH, ON THE RHINE.

THE CATHEDRAL OF ANDERNACH, ON THE RHINE.

As we write "the Rhine," a flood of recollections of most pleasant and not uninstructive rambles over the ruin-crested hills which form the banks of this picturesque and historic river, pass through the mind. Several years have passed away since we last saw the glories of Cologne, Mayence, and Strasburg; sight-seeing English have sophisticated the people on its borders, and disorder and anarchy have since ruffled the surface of the country through which it flows. Its associations, in our minds, however, are all pleasant and vivid, as those of youthful enjoyment and adventure usually are.

In connection with the subject of *Romanesque Architecture*, recently treated of in our pages, we give in our present number a north-west view, taken for the purpose, of one of the many interesting specimens of that style of architecture, with which the Rhine abounds —Andernach Cathedral. This exhibits in many respects the influence of Byzantine art, and is the more interesting to the investigator on that account.

Andernach Cathedral has four towers—one at each corner; and has a semicircular absis, with small galleries and arches, resting against a gable end. The towers are square, and those at the west end have over each face a gablet, from the centre of which springs one angle of the spire.

The tower of the interesting little church at Sompting, in Sussex, which is very early, is the only example of this arrangement in England which occurs to us.

It will be noticed that pointed arches are intermixed with the semicircular at Andernach, and that some consist of two lateral curves, with a higher central curve, forming pointless trefoil arches.* The porches of the Rhine churches exceed in beauty those of the buildings in Normandy of the same era;—the south porch of Andernach may be mentioned as an instance.

COOKERY BOOK-ERY.†

ARCHITECTS, builders, antiquaries, and artists, like common men, must of necessity dine. "To that complexion they *must* come at last:" there is nothing to be done without eating, and much of our time and much of our substance are consumed in the delicate operation. It is of much consequence, then, that this, which occurs so constantly and regularly, should be provided for as well and cheaply as possible. "A man," says *Bacon* (an *à propos* author in matters of the kitchen), "ought warily to begin charges which once begun will continue; but in matters that return not be may be more magnificent;" which, put into other words, means that when you give a state dinner or an entertainment to your friends, which occurs but seldom, you need not think much about a little extra expense, *but* in the every day breakfast and the every day dinner, which comes (at least it is to be hoped so) 365 times every year of your life, see that you have the most and the best for your money, and that nothing be wasted.

With management and knowledge, a good dinner may be had for less money than a bad one costs without them, without reckoning the evil of grumpy looks and cross words, too often the concomitants of the latter. Now to those who want this knowledge, without reference to a high style of cooking, we introduce Mons. Soyer's "Modern Housewife," with a full conviction that she will prove a useful adviser. In a note, the author says, "I forward to you my 'Modern Housewife.' She is very fond of employing THE BUILDER to correct the evils which exist in our domestic establishments; perhaps she may interest you." She *has* interested us; and to the fair daughters and wives of our readers, to whom, if such ever dip into our pages, we would softly whisper,—Don't let the keys of the piano-forte make you forget the keys of the store-room, or the enlightenment of your understanding prevent you from inquiring the price of candles,—we especially commend her.

Soyer is a bit of a dandy, and thinks uncommonly well of himself,—puts his portrait in the front of all his books and on the top of all his bottles; but there's a genius in him that leads one to overlook this; and, moreover, he made us his friend when, on being asked a question relative to some endeavours which were making in a large builder's establishment, to obtain at the smallest cost the greatest amount of nutritious food for the workmen, he voluntarily came down and spent several hours in advancing the object.

* Hope, when mentioning the occurrence of arches thus formed, in the Lombard or Romanesque churches of Germany, mentions that in "Pope Gregory's Gospels," copied by a monk of Salisbury as early as the 10th century, these pointless trefoil arches are seen, alternating with those in the form of a pediment.

† "The Modern Housewife, or Ménagère." By Alexis Soyer, author of the "Gastronomic Regenerator." London. 1849. Simpkin and Marshall.

CHURCH BUILDING NEWS.

A STAINED glass east window, in the Perpendicular style, with shields, &c., has been put up in the church of St. Andrew the Great, Cambridge, at a cost of 160*l*. Mr. Bolton, now of Cambridge, was the artist. The incumbent, the Rev. Mr. Cooper, intends to decorate the whole of the east end in accordance with the window.——The sum of 1,000*l*. has been bequeathed by the late Dr. Dowdeswell, canon of the cathedral of Christ Church College, Oxford, for the restoration of the cathedral, or of some public edifice belonging to the society.——In St. Michael's church, Aston Clinton, near Aylesbury, some curious and interesting paintings have been recently brought to light on the north wall of the nave, which is undergoing extensive restoration. The two principal subjects are a figure of St. Christopher with his staff and the Holy Infant, and a figure of the Virgin between two dragons—one appears to be swallowing up and the other disgorging human souls. There is the following legend at the side, "Animâ, ave Maria ira."——The church of Poynings was much damaged during a late thunder-storm. The lightning seems to have entered the south window of the chancel, injuring the apex of the arch, tearing the mullions of the tracery, and wrenching out a portion of the flint-work at the base. Curiously enough, three other windows are injured in precisely the same manner. The tower sustained the greatest injury. On the western side, there is a breach four feet square superficially, and ten inches deep; and inside the injured part is eight feet in length and eighteen inches in width. The flint-work is shaken and "looks as if torn out by a pick-axe." The porch was also struck, and the parsonage-house sustained great damage.——A plan for the tower of Holy Rhood Church, Southampton, has been formed,—the cost to be about 300*l*. only, for which a subscription is to be opened.——The church of Morewinstow, Cornwall, has lately been restored. Lord Clinton and his lady have contributed a decorated eastern window in accordance with the style of the edifice, and designed by the Rev. W. Haslam, author of "Perranzabuloe."——The nave of Elford Church, near Lichfield, has now been entirely rebuilt, the fittings of the old building replaced in carved oak, windows filled with stained glass, and passage paved with encaustic tiles. A corona for the lights has also been provided, the old alabaster monuments restored, and a new font added. Mr. Paget, the incumbent, has been engaged for several years, but more particularly of late, in these restorations.——The new church of St. Jude, Birmingham, to be erected at Tonk-street, will contain 1,447 sittings, 1,000 free. Messrs. Orford and Nash, architects, have furnished the design, which is Early English, with nave, aisles, chancel, south transept, and tower 100 feet high: materials, blue brick with stone dressings. Estimated cost, 4,000*l*.——The Wesleyans of Willenhall have resolved to relieve the overflowing state of the parish churchyard by laying out a piece of ground already provided for a cemetery, on a declivity near the town.——The new cemetery for the establishment, now in course of formation beside the original cemetery at Sheffield, approaches towards completion. The improvements comprise a new carriage road, 45 feet wide, passing the cemetery, and in connection with which a bridge has been erected over the river Porter. The church, with its tall spire, is nearly finished. The whole of the works, we understand, have been designed, and carried out by Messrs. Flockton and Son.——Oxenhope Church, near Keighley, will be ready for consecration early in October. It is a Norman building, having a nave, one side aisle, and chancel. The tower is the whole width of the nave. The chancel arch is inlaid with encaustic tiles.——The new church at Rockcliffe, says the *Carlisle Journal*, was consecrated on Tuesday week. It is a small building of white stone, and in the English style of the fourteenth century, with a nave, chancel, transept, and a tower and spire. The roof is open, and the seats are all free; sittings, 150. The windows are all of stained glass, by Messrs. Scott, of Carlisle. The design was furnished by Mr. J. Stewart, of Carlisle, architect. Mr. T. Johnson was the mason, and Mr. Black supplied the woodwork. The cost is expected to be about 1,500*l*., mostly paid by Mr. G. G. Mounsey.——The Earl of Durham, on the attainment of his majority, has given 100*l*. towards a school and master's house at Lumley (in addition to a former donation), and 100*l*. towards a chapel at Newbottle,—besides 300*l*. to the poor at his collieries.——The roof of Bishopwearmouth Church has been found to be much dilapidated, and a new one is to be put on by public contribution.——The Stella (Roman Catholic) Chapel, says the *Gateshead Observer*, has been considerably altered and improved, and was re-opened on Wednesday week. An organ has been built for it by Mr. J. T. Davis, of Newcastle.——The works for making a portion of a new street adjoining the new congregational church now in progress, at Berwick, were let on the 3rd inst. The proposed range of houses and shops is upwards of 150 feet in length, to be built of stone, and of an Italian character. Mr. T. Oliver, jun., is the architect.——The foundation of a great cathedral (Roman Catholic) Church, according to the *Tablet*, is to be laid at Edinburgh, in November; Mr. Pugin, architect.——A "free church" with a lofty tower, is to be erected in honour of the late Rev. Dr. Chalmers, at Anstruther, his native town.——An episcopal church is to be erected by subscription, and dedicated to St. John, at Anderston, Glasgow, at a cost of 1,100*l*. for chancel and nave for 500 persons, to be, if possible, enlarged at a further cost of 500*l*. for aisle, &c. The first stone is to be laid on 21st inst.——The new Methodist chapel in Donegal-square, Belfast, was totally destroyed by fire on Sunday week. The building cost 5,500*l*., and the organ 400*l*. The premises are insured for 4,000*l*.——The erection of new churches is proceeding in the diocese of Cork with considerable energy. A large church near Bandon was lately consecrated, and in a month seven more are to be consecrated.

SUPPLY OF WATER TO LONDON.

IT will be remembered that at the end of last year a plan was propounded for bringing water to London from the river Thames at Henley, promising to ensure to every inhabitant of the metropolis an unremitting supply of this all-important desideratum within his own house. The opposition was manifold, and the Bill was lost on the second reading. The promoters of that Bill have, it seems, resolved on a fresh attempt, modifying their scheme so as to get rid of some of the opponents, and they propose to place the management of the undertaking in the hands of a representative commission.

Water is to be brought from Henley by means of an aqueduct (not a canal, as at first intended), and to be delivered into a reservoir at Hampstead, high enough to supply the loftiest buildings, and extinguish fires without engines.

We are not at this moment in a position to assert that their plan for supplying London with pure water is the best suggested, but we do say that the importance of the object is such, the necessity for water is so great and paramount, that the proposal ought to receive the most candid and careful consideration. When it is known that at the present moment there are 70,000 houses in London, containing not less than 560,000 inhabitants, which have no water supplied to them from any one of the eight great water-companies which exist, further argument must be unnecessary. All London ought to cry as loudly as if next door were on fire,—Water! water!! water!!!

SHEFFIELD SCHOOL OF DESIGN.

The annual meeting took place on Wednesday in last week, the Earl of Arundel and Surrey in the chair. The council's report was first read, in which the increase of Government grant from 250*l.* to 600*l.* per annum was announced, and the number of pupils from 1843 to 1849 stated to have been 509, most of them now engaged in the staple trades of Sheffield. The head master, Mr. Young Mitchell, read a report, chiefly on the exhibition at Paris.

The chairman then addressed the meeting. His lordship disclaimed all intention or ability to treat of art-questions, but felt assured that such schools as this are absolutely essential to the future prosperity of England as a commercial country. When we find other nations combating us with our own weapons, and almost equalling us in these, while excelling us in others, it is absolutely necessary for us to seize on every means of keeping ahead of them as heretofore; for if we fail in that, as a great European power we are gone. And no better way of assisting to do so probably exists than supporting and maturing such schools as this. If that be not zealously done, we may rely on it that other nations will overstock our markets with articles more pleasing at least to the eye, and cheaper, although perhaps hardly so good, and thus we shall be shut out of the great markets of the world. His lordship then complained that less than 150*l.* a-year should as yet have been subscribed by the town.

Mr. Northcote, of the Board of Trade, said that it was the zeal of the teachers and the pupils that had actuated Mr. Poynter and himself in recommending the Government grant. On these accounts he had himself, in evidence, accorded the palm to the Sheffield amongst all the provincial schools. This year, however, an increase to other schools had also been recommended. But the Government looked to the active co-operation of the residents, as, without local energy, they would continue to give no such aid. Referring to the idea that the French are superior to ourselves in taste or talent for matters of art, he regarded such an idea as a mere fallacy. It was education alone that was requisite. And then we must create a demand, we must educate the people, so as to enable them to appreciate the beautiful and excellent in art, and the artist will soon come forward then to produce what is admirable and good. To accomplish all this we must surround the people with objects of beauty in their houses, and familiarize them with it even in their most ordinary household objects and utensils. When a taste for ornamental art in the commonest articles of utility is thus produced amongst the mass, you will proportionately elevate the taste and skill and energy of those who devote themselves to the fine arts. When they are appreciated and admired they will surpass their former selves, and rise rapidly—the multitude pushing up the leaders, and the leaders drawing up the multitude after them. Various other gentlemen addressed the meeting; the usual resolutions were passed, and the prizes were then distributed.

EXHIBITION OF ARTS AND MANUFACTURES OF ALL NATIONS.

The arrangements for the monster exposition in London of arts and manufactures of all nations, projected by Prince Albert, appear to be going on vigorously. A deputation from the prince, consisting of Mr. Cole and Mr. Fuller, have been to Scotland and to Ireland, in order to meet the leading manufacturers of the country on the subject. It is proposed to be held in the year 1851, and that premiums to the extent of 20,000*l.* should be given for inventions or improvements. It is thought that the Queen will present the prizes. An erection in Hyde-park is talked of, *a mile and a-half long*, for which designs will be required in competition,—unless, indeed, the Woods and Forests take the matter in hand.

Local committees are to be organized as soon as the result of the interviews with manufacturers has been reported to the prince. The matter will require careful management.

SIR ROBERT PEEL'S PORTRAIT GALLERY, DRAYTON MANOR.*

It is about twenty years since Sir Robert Peel took down the old house at Drayton Manor occupied by his father, and built the present mansion, from the designs of Sir Robert Smirke, on a site closely adjoining the previous building. It is a quadrangular stone mansion, in the Elizabethan style, of very considerable extent, but without any ostentatious display of architecture, either internally or externally.

The taste and fondness for the fine arts which form so marked and agreeable a feature in Sir Robert's character, exhibit themselves plainly at this residence. A large corridor or gallery, in the centre of the building, has its walls entirely covered with fine works of art, as well as almost every available space on the staircase and elsewhere; and to his high credit be it said, that almost every picture at Drayton Manor is by some artist of the present day.

Sir Robert's collection of pictures having far outgrown the means at his disposal for suitably hanging them, a gallery was erected in 1846, from the designs and under the able direction of Mr. Sydney Smirke, A.R.A. It forms a wing appended to the north-west angle of the mansion, and extends westward about 100 feet. It is built of a fine-grained magnesian limestone, and is designed in the style of the English *Renaissance*, so as to harmonize with the rest of the building. The exterior is embellished with colossal statues of Rubens, Vandyke, Sir Joshua Reynolds, and Sir Thomas Lawrence. The gallery within is 90 feet long by 22 feet wide, and 21 feet high, being subdivided into three compartments by columns and pilasters of Italian and German marbles. The *parqué* flooring, and all the wood fittings, are of wainscot and walnut-tree.

The walls are painted of a strong neutral green colour. The ceiling is coved, and elaborately ornamented with corbels and pendants, &c.

The pictures are lighted by skylights in the flat central part of the ceiling.

It does not come within the scope of these pages to enter into any description of the pictures which enrich the walls of this unique gallery; suffice it to say that they almost entirely consist of portraits of Sir Robert's contemporaries, eminent either as statesmen or as men of science or literature, and comprise some of the *chefs-d'œuvre* of Reynolds and Lawrence. When we take into consideration the high merit of these pictures as works of art, the distinguished eminence of the persons they represent, and the brilliant character of the individual who has taken delight in paying this homage to contemporary genius, we cannot but regard the Gallery at Drayton Manor with the deepest interest.

METROPOLITAN COMMISSION OF SEWERS.

A general court was held on Thursday, at the Court-house, Greek-street: Sir John Burgoyne in the chair. A long discussion ensued on the question that Mr. Lavers be appointed clerk of surveyors' and contractors' accounts, at a salary of 300*l.* per annum, in pursuance of the recommendations of the Finance Committee, which was finally referred back for the committee to define the duties.

A deputation of the Bermondsey Improvement Commissioners attended the Court, with Mr. Drew, the vestry clerk, complaining generally of the sewerage of the district, and in particular of the system of discharging the contents of the cesspools into the public sewers, without any means accompanying the operation of passing the same to the Thames, and also of the large number of untrapped gullies.

In answer to questions to Mr. Phillips, the chief surveyor, he said there was undoubtedly a much larger amount of filth in the sewers, caused by the increased number of drains laid into them, and from the pumping of the cesspools into the sewers.

The members of the deputation added, that in the neighbourhood of their residences, and particularly in Bermondsey-street, during the process of flushing, the stench was almost unbearable, continuing for days together, and that such offensive odours were never observed until the adoption of that system by the present commission.

Dr. Southwood Smith and Mr. Chadwick contended that the evils arose from the unscientific manner in which the operations were conducted, and not from the system of flushing itself. They had endeavoured to obtain the supervision of proper officers, but that proposition was opposed, and it was now too bad for those gentlemen who had opposed it to blame them for the clumsy manner in which these works had been performed.

The secretary, in answer to a question from Mr. Leslie, said the opinions of the medical officers of the various parishes, on the subject of flushing, had been received, amounting to 79, and were thus divided:—Approving flushing, 13; dissentients, 32; neuter, 34. It appeared, also, that from Bermondsey they were,—Approving, 1; dissentients, 1; neuter, 1.

Mr. Leslie insisted that the time had arrived when the system of flushing should be suspended, and an early day appointed to take the whole subject into consideration. He was also of opinion that they had had enough of experiments,—which view was concurred in by the Hon. F. Byng.

Several other commissioners expressed views *pro.* and *con.* on the system of flushing, and the deputation were finally assured by the chairman that the court would take the subject into their serious consideration.

Other deputations were heard. One from Islington pointed out the very defective state of the sewerage of their district, and said, if that district were compelled to wait for the adoption of some general system of drainage, that in the interim disease would sweep away one-half of the inhabitants, and referred to the last report of the Registrar-General in justification of this assertion. Allusion was also made to the discharge of the refuse drainage of the new Small-pox Hospital into the open ditches, which it was possible might be attended with the most fatal consequences.

Mr. Lambert Jones, at considerable length, censured the waste of public money on districts where no rates had ever been collected, and said that this district, at the termination of the old commission, possessed funds to the amount of 20,000*l.*, which money had been spent on the Kent and Surrey division, and those parties who paid the money were left without any relief whatever.

It was proposed that the subject should be referred to the Works Committee, as a report on the drainage of the whole district would be presented by the surveyors on Monday next, and at the next court the question might be again brought forward.

Upon this Mr. Leslie advised the deputation again to attend and see what was done.

Mr. Banfield, rose to order, and Mr. Chadwick protested against the intrusion of other bodies into their proceedings.—This was replied to with some warmth by Mr. Leslie, who said that, as a public body, they were but trustees for the public, and that they were about spending the money of the deputation, who were perfectly justified in seeing that it was not spent improperly.

The matter was at length referred to the surveyors.

The Drainage of Westminster.—The secretary announced to the court that the Westminster Improvement Commissioners had paid into the court the sum of 3,792*l.*, in pursuance of the resolutions passed for the improved drainage of that district.

Upon the above announcement being made, Mr. Chadwick moved that a report presented by Mr. Austin, consulting engineer, be read.

Mr. Woolrych then read the report referred to. It stated that he appeared in opposition to a work, which, by means of erroneous and unwarrantable statements, had obtained the sanction of the court. The first objection was, that the sanction given to this work prejudged the question of general drainage, and was an injustice to the competition to which the public had been invited. That it is an unnecessary work, founded on erroneous principles, and would soon be as great a nuisance to the neighbourhood as the existing faulty constructions, and that the amount expended upon it will be an utter waste of the rates and funds of the Westminster Improvement Commission, and further, that an efficient and economical subsoil drainage, affording the required relief, may be put in, as well as a temporary provision for surface drainage in far less time, and without the necessity of any such construction as that recommended. It characterized the proposed work as an utterly useless construction, alike unnecessary either for surface or for subsoil drainage, and said a proper subsoil drainage might be laid down at an expense of 1,000*l.* The report concluded by "stating, that as the court, by erroneous statements, had been led into the adoption of a work which prejudges the question of the general drainage, confirming one principle, and condemning another,—a work useless in itself, and leading to a large waste of the rates, and of the funds of the Westminster Improvement Commission, I would beg respectfully to urge that their resolution of the 6th instant with reference to this subject be rescinded."

Mr. Chadwick, in a speech of great length, moved that the resolution of the last court be rescinded.—Mr. Leslie reiterated the statements he made on the subject at the last court, when he wished the subject

* From the third part of Godwin's "Buildings and Monuments." A view of the gallery will be found in The Builder, vol. III, p. 222.

to be postponed for a week, to give time for consideration. They were now brought into a "mess" from having ordered the work to be done, issued their advertisements, and received the money of the Westminster Improvement Commissioners. He also contended that the resolution passed could not be rescinded without notice of motion.

There appeared to be very conflicting opinions as to the legal bearings of the case, Sir Edward Pearson, on the part of the Westminster Commissioners, stating that they looked upon the plan as a "contract," and so anxious were they to commence their works, that they would even sacrifice 3,000*l*. rather than the question should be again re-opened. The subject was brought to a close by the adoption of the following resolutions, proposed by Mr. Chadwick:—"That as the work proposed is extraordinary business, and as such required notice, the order for it is invalid.

"That the reports of Messrs. Phillips and Gotto and Mr. Austin, be printed, and referred to the Works Committee."

Miscellanea.

Syro-Egyptian Society and the Panorama of the Nile.—On Thursday evening, in last week, the exhibition of the Panorama of the Nile was closed to the public to enable the Syro-Egyptian Society and their friends to hold a meeting "in the presence." Dr. Lee was in the chair, Mr. Bonomi described the panorama, and Mr. Sharp, Mr. Gliddon, the American Egyptologist, whose tone savours a *leetle* too much of Sir Oracle, the Chairman, and others, differed very pleasantly, and gave the unlearned part of the audience a notion of the want of positive knowledge under some heads, which still exists. The last discussion was on the Pyramids, which all who spoke on the subject agreed were royal tombs, and the nucleus of circumjacent cemeteries. The pyramid of Ghizeh was once encased with stone, 20 feet thick, as some of the pyramids of Sakkara are at present. The work of destruction as regards this surface commenced in the twelfth or thirteenth century, and continued almost down to our own day. At present, and for several years past, it has presented a front of rugged mason work, easy to ascend, but unseemly to look at. Finally, the Sphinx was pronounced to be a portrait statue, as far as the head is concerned, of Amenoph II., supposed to be identical with Cheops, who is stated by the Greek historian Herodotus to be the builder of the great pyramid of Ghizeh. At the close, men qualified to judge bore testimony to the accuracy and beauty of the panorama. It is still with us a matter of regret that it was not painted to be lighted from the front.

The Value of an Architect and Surveyor in Hastings.—The Commissioners of Hastings have addressed an advertisement "to architects and surveyors," intimating that they are about to elect such a person to do the business of the town. His duty will be, they say, "to prepare plans, specifications, and estimates of all public works directed by the commissioners within the limits of their Act, and to superintend their execution, as well as to inspect the execution of all private works permitted by the commissioners; to superintend the draining, paving, scavengering, repairing, and watering of the streets and public places; to pay the labourers' wages, examine the tradesmen's accounts, keep all accounts connected with the office, and to attend at all general and committee meetings of the commissioners, and generally do all the duties of the office of surveyor." He must have a practical knowledge of levelling, and of the several branches of building and other works connected with the office of surveyor; and be prepared to undergo an examination as to the extent of his knowledge. For all which he is, when appointed, to receive the enormous salary of 75*l*. per annum. The Hastings Commissioners seem to have a liberal idea of the value of knowledge. A journeyman bricklayer, earning 30s. a-week, would lose by being promoted to the appointment.

Terra Cotta.—The proprietors of the Cliffe Terra Cotta Works, Wakefield, Yorkshire, have determined on executing any of the chimney-tops, ornaments, tracery, &c., given in the publications of the Architectural Publication Society, on receiving an order for not less than twenty-five of a sort.

Projected Works.—Advertisements have been issued for tenders, by 26th September, for the erection of schools, dormitories, workshops, and other buildings for 600 children at Penge; by 26th, for building a boys' school-house at St. Pancras workhouse; by 26th, for the erection of new workhouse at Kirbymoorside, Yorkshire (several tenders); by 23rd, for draining at Kennington-cross; by 22nd, for erection of national school at Spofforth; by 25th, for erection of farm-house and offices at Burnham, Essex; by 18th, for supply and fixing of iron roofs over various stations on Lancashire and Yorkshire Railway; by 19th, for essential oil lamps, three-jet gas-burners and supply of gas, &c., at All Saints, Poplar; and by 15th, for building 5,200 feet of brick sewer and other works at Parliament-street, &c., Westminster.

Enamels for Iron.—Mr. Charles Stumer, of New York, has recently secured a patent, which he describes to consist "in providing an enamel for iron and other metals, which will retain its adhesion to the metal, and particularly is not capable of being crumbled or broken off by blows or by beat, this possessing the quality of comparatively commingling with the surface of the metal. Thus it is far superior to any known enamelling for metals, and may be modified so as to render it in all the shades of colours, in full variety. 1.—16 ounces of gravel sand, 10 ounces of silver glass (silver gilt or silver gilding), 2 ounces of white clay, ¾ of an ounce of saltpetre. 2.—7 ounces of glass (common white glass), 4 ounces of gravel sand, 8 ounces of zean reanocks (or oxide of tin), 6 ounces of borax, 1½ ounce of soda, 3 ounces of saltpetre, 1½ ounce of white clay, 1 ounce of magnesia, ¼ of an ounce of white chalk, ¼ of an ounce of oyster shells; this should be pulverized like first composition, and then mixed with the gum water. *Claim*—What I claim as new, and desire to secure by letters patent, is the peculiar composition, composed of the parts and compounded as described. —*Franklin Journal.*

Education at Putney College.—The Rev. Morgan Cowie, the principal here, has published a letter to the Duke of Buccleuch, pointing out the requirements of the day in education, and that they endeavour to meet these requirements at Putney. "A useful, intelligent, improving race," says Mr. Cowie, "well imbued with sound principles of science, would be the real strength of the country; and this must be secured by beginning at the commencement, by educating our youth before they are called upon to act, by furnishing them with sound views of science, and with an accurate knowledge of the great progress that has been made in all the arts, and of the means of that progress." Increased funds are evidently required; the college has not had fair play yet, and we think so well of its capabilities that we shall be glad to see the public taking it up in earnest. We suggest to our readers who are fathers, to look into the constitution of the establishment for themselves, and see if they cannot make it useful.

Porchester Castle.—This time-honoured relic of antiquity, midway between Fareham and Portsea, Hants, is now to become another Cremorne or Rosherville. The railway will lend its aid to carry holidaymakers to the spot, and "enterprising proprietors" expect to render it the most attractive place of resort on the southern coast of England.

Clerkenwell Graveyards.—Sir: Any person who may think proper to walk through Clerkenwell-close or Clerkenwell-green will be convinced of the truth of my remark, viz.—that the churchyards are several feet *above the public ways.* There are two points to which your attention is directed; 1st, instead of *four* graveyards in Clerkenwell, as mentioned by the surveyor of the district, there are *seven*; and, 2ndly, when that gentleman asks, "what depth do I assume to be the average of burials?" he loses sight of the parlours, kitchens, cellars, pantries, &c., being entirely *below* the grave-yards. I had to underpin a wall adjoining one of these horrors only a few weeks ago, on which occasion skulls and bones fell into the cellar, and ends of coffins were presented to view like squares of black masonry, and *close to the wall.* The *only cure* is to cease burying in all towns and crowded neighbourhoods.

W. P. Griffith.

Reorganizing Sewers' Commission.—The task undertaken by the present commissioners was a gigantic one, and they would probably have failed, even had they brought extraordinary knowledge and ability to bear upon it. It is a subject that has long occupied my attention, and I feel sure that one general commission cannot fulfil properly the duties devolving upon several local commissioners. It appears to me unreasonable and unconstitutional that those whose lives and properties are chiefly affected, and who find the funds for all that is done, should be excluded from all management of themselves and their properties. I would suggest that all or some portion of the commissioners should be elected. I think it would answer well to have half appointed by the crown, and half elected. There should be twelve or twenty commissioners to each district, according to the size. Each district commission should elect one of its body, to be one of a general committee, who should have power to determine all questions affecting the general interest, and decide upon plans for general drainage, &c.—Charles Tooke.

New Mode of Ventilation.—The *Literary Gazette* states that Dr. Chowne has enrolled a patent for improvements in ventilating rooms and apartments, based upon an action in the syphon which has not previously attracted the notice of any experimenter, viz., that if fixed with legs of unequal length, the air rushes into the *shorter leg*, and circulates up, and discharges itself from the *longer leg.* "It is easy to see how readily this can be applied to any chamber, in order to purify its atmosphere. Let the orifice of the shorter leg be disposed where it can receive the current, and lead it into the chimney (in mines, into the shaft), so as to convert that chimney or shaft into the longer leg, and you have at once the circulation complete. The curiosity of this discovery is that air in a syphon reverses the action of water, or other liquid, which enters and descends or moves down in the longer leg, and rises up in the shorter leg!" We ought to remark that fires or heating apparatus are not at all necessary; and that, as the specification expresses it, "this action is not prevented by making the shorter leg hot whilst the longer leg remains cold, and no artificial heat is necessary to the longer leg of the air-syphon to cause this action to take place."

Architectural Copyrights. — Sir: I have by me a view of a congregational chapel, proposed to be erected at Cockermouth, bearing the name of C. Eaglesfield as the architect. I have been credibly informed that the original drawings of Myrtle-street Baptist Chapel, Liverpool, have been put into the possession of this self-styled architect, copies sent to Day and Son, from which *they* have made a perspective view, and the design is not only passed off as the work of a local builder, assuming a professional title, but the original designer is robbed of his fairly earned honour and remuneration. Let him look to the Myrtle-street Chapel deacons, who ought to be informed that (*perhaps* unintentionally) they have unfairly made a double use of that for which they only paid a single price, and are the principals in perpetuating a serious form of immorality, by depriving the designer (to whom a design *must* always belong), of his recognized honour and remuneration, and at the same time sanctioning the present system of quackery so prevalent in every profession. I enclose my address.—An Architect.

Another Mode of Raising the Britannia Tubes.—A correspondent of the *Times* (Mr. J. Paulding) suggests that the tube might be raised without waiting for the casting and testing, and, after all, the still remaining risk, of a new hydraulic machine, in place of the one that lately burst. The power of the tide-rise of 15 feet, with pontoons and proper scaffolding, heightened, at low tide, 15 feet for every lift, constitutes the main elements of the suggestion; and of course during each lift the process of wedging, building in under the tube, &c., would be gone on with as heretofore. The writer further proposes that, to save further expense, both the parallel tubes might be thus raised simultaneously. Tidal power, he observes, might also have been used to work the presses in place of steam, even had the great expense of forming and elevating such huge hydraulic presses, chains, frames, &c., been unavoidable.

Consecration of St. Thomas's Church, Coventry.—The first stone of this edifice was laid by the Rev. T. Sheepshanks, rector of St. John Baptist's parish, on the 2nd of March, 1848. There are kneelings for 576 persons, of which 456 are free and unappropriated. The total cost has been 3,350*l*. It was consecrated a few days ago. It was designed by Messrs. Sharpe and Paley, and built by Mr. Taylor, of Coventry. It is in the Early Decorated style, and consists of nave, north and south aisles, north porch, chancel, and vestry. The exterior of the church is incomplete, from the absence of a tower and spire, an addition which is intended to be given to it as soon as funds can be raised for the purpose. Its outline, however, is broken at the west end by a bell-turret, which goes far to supply the deficiency. The clerestory windows of the nave are spherical triangles filled with tracery. The church is built of red sandstone, from a quarry of Lord Leigh's, on the Kenilworth road. The aisles are separated from the nave by piers and pointed arches. The roofs are open, and the seats are all low and open. The corbels supporting the wall-pieces of the nave roof are angels bearing shields, on which are depicted in colour the apostolic emblems. Above the western door is a sculptured group of three angels, of whom the centre one bears a legend inscribed in illuminated letters—"*Go, and sin no more.*" The pulpit, on the south side of the chancel arch, is approached from the vestry, and is a simple platform of stone, with a brass railing. The reading-pew faces south and west.

Mr. Sheepshanks' Collection of Pictures.—One would suppose, if anything could call the Government to a sense of the duty they owe to the late Mr. Vernon for his munificent gift to the nation,—it is the *on dit* that "Mr. Sheepshanks has expressed his intention of presenting to the University of Oxford his valuable collection of pictures, by artists of the British school, from an impression that his gift will meet with greater care and attention from the University than if consigned, like Mr. Vernon's, to the cellars of the National Gallery." It is to be hoped, if the above be the fact, that Oxford will set a good example, by erecting an appropriate gallery for the reception of such a collection. That they need a gallery of pictures is very evident, for nothing can be more wretched than those exhibited at the Randolph and Taylor Building. S.

Sinks, Drains, and Cesspools should be deodorized as far as possible with chloride of lime, which, it is recommended, should be used simultaneously throughout a district, say between 9 and 10 A.M. on Saturdays, especially during the prevalence of cholera. Two ounces are sufficient to stir into a pailful of water, and ought to cost no more than 1d.

The Sculpture on Buckingham Palace.—Sir: In the centre of the new façade of her Majesty's Palace at Pimlico there must be, I presume, a gateway. Over this, then, and at the summit of the building, is an arch, flanked on one side by the figure of Britannia, reposing gracefully on a lion couchant; on the other by our patron saint, who has, unfortunately, failed in his attempt to transfix the dragon, which, in return, is about to make a vigorous snap at him. The piers of the arch are faced by two female figures,—one, probably a beggar-woman cuddling a baby. So far is tolerably clear; but what is the central superincumbent mass intended to represent? I can trace at its base some leaves, at the top a wreath hung upon a peg, and on the face the initials of our gracious Sovereign, and the date; but can guess no further. Pray, Mr. Editor, be kind enough to enlighten the ignorance of—Me.

*** There is little further explanation to be given. "Story? I have none, Sir." The composition is certainly an odd one. It consists of a shield, in shape very much like a pair of fashionable stays, with the addition of a peak at the top, resting on two coarsely-executed palm branches, and bedizened with flowers. The face of it displays the initials V. R., and the whole is surmounted by a large wreath, stuck most ungracefully on the aforesaid peak. This wreath projects so far forward that to the spectator who is ignorant as to how it may be held up behind, it seems about to fall. It is to be hoped that it will.

Extras on Specification Work.—A case was lately tried before Mr. Baron Rolfe and a common jury, in which a builder, being indebted a sum of 116*l*. to a party who proposed to take repayment in repairs to his house, entered into a written specification with the party to do the work for 175*l*., but on the ground of extra work demanded in all 230*l*. Only 70*l*. beyond the debt of 116*l*. having been paid, however, the builder brought his action for the balance, but was nonsuited on exhibiting a specification sworn by his own witness not to be the one entered into and signed. Thereupon the successful party raised an action for repayment of the sum paid beyond the original amount specified, with costs, and a verdict was granted accordingly; so that, in place of his extras, the builder will have to refund the overplus, and pay all costs, of themselves not less than 400*l*.

The Roman Tesselated Pavement at Cirencester.—We learn from the *Gloucestershire Chronicle* that workmen, under the instruction of a member of the Archæological Institute, have been all the week busily employed in removing this interesting relic into a place of safety. The pavement is now placed on the lawn in front of Earl Bathurst's mansion, where it is protected by a marquee, until an appropriate place can be fixed upon for its final destination. On its removal it was found to be supported by a hard concrete resting on pillars, also of concrete, surmounted by layers either of brick or tile, which rested on a floor about a foot and a half beneath. At the western corner were found the remains of what appeared to have been a stove, which supplied hot air to the apartment above by means of funnel-shaped pipes made of clay, parts of which still remained. There was also a low wall, the same height as the pillar, acting as an additional support to the floor, running along each side of the room, which, on being removed, showed marks of painting, in various devices, on the plastered sides of the apartment. As these devices were continued to the lower floor, which was of very common materials, it is imagined that the original building having fallen to decay, another had been erected upon the site, of superior character, at a higher elevation.

The Caryatides of St. Pancras Church, London.—Two countrymen, observing the female figures with pitchers in their hands, which support the porticoes of St. Pancras Church, wondered what they represented. "They must be the *foolish virgins*," said one. "They can't be, neither," replied the other, "there's only four of 'em." "Oh, it's all right," replied the friend; "*the other is gone for the oil*," you may depend on't.

Great Yarmouth Church.—By restoration of Yarmouth Church, already accomplished, additional accommodation has been provided for 1,100 persons, the whole area of the church seating 2,900 persons. Previous to the alteration, the poor were virtually excluded. Ever since the opening there has been a full and attentive congregation, evidently thankful for the increased accommodation. But even now, urgent applications for as many as 300 sittings have been received by the churchwardens, from persons who request to be seated in their parish church, and efforts are therefore being made to raise money for completing the restoration. The cost at which the new arrangements have been accomplished is 4,446*l*;* the committee with difficulty have raised 4,196*l*., by which a debt of 250*l*. now remains to be discharged; and to complete the restoration, 2,000*l*. more is required: in all 2,250*l*. Schools are also much needed. It is proposed to erect two, to contain 500 children each. An excellent site for one has been given by the corporation at the south end of the town; and the Dean and Chapter of Norwich have offered the ancient priory, part of which is now a stable, adjacent to the parish church, which it is now proposed to restore for the other school at the north end of the town. The cost of these two schools will not be less than 2,500*l*., towards which 1,000*l*. may be expected from public sources, leaving 1,500*l*. to raise. Mr. C. J. Palmer, of Yarmouth, is acting as honorary secretary.

* This sum does not include the cost of a memorial window, which has been placed at the west end of the north aisle in memory of the late Sarah Martin, so well known for her successful exertions in promoting the spiritual improvement of prisoners in Yarmouth Gaol.

Rating Public Buildings in Ireland under the Poor-law.—The *Cork Constitution* has the following announcement:—"The different public buildings in the Cork Union, such as the Custom-house, military and police barracks, &c., which have been heretofore exempt from poor-rate, are now being included in the rate about to be struck, and half poor-rate will be charged the lessee on the amount of the rent. The amount of property thus made liable by a late Act of Parliament will exceed a total of 4,000*l*.,—a sum which will assist considerably in lightening the pressure of taxation on the ratepayers of the union."

New Rotary Engine.—A working mechanic of the name of Scotthorn has invented some alleged improvements in rotary engines. His machine mainly consists, according to *Aris's Gazette*, of a metallic case containing a cylindrical chamber, with a segment at each side, as if cut off, to open into lesser cylindrical abutment chambers, all on one axial plane. On the main shaft is set centrically a hollow cylinder or drum in the main chamber, which being of larger diameter, has a vacancy between the cylinder and the case called the steam compartment. From the drum projects a sort of piston, with steam-tight joint. The working, however, cannot well be described within our limits, more especially without diagrams. The efficient working force is said to be quadruple that of crank engines.

The Cambrian Archæological Association met at Cardiff last week: the attendance of members was not so numerous as had been hoped. The Marquis of Northampton, Professor Petrie, of Dublin, and several other Irish antiquaries, were present. Amongst the chief papers read was one, by the Dean of Llandaff, on Llandaff Cathedral, which structure was visited. Excursions were also made to Caerphilly Castle, Caerleon, &c. A collection of local antiquities forming a nucleus for a museum, excited much interest.

Mr. Ward's Portrait Engravings.—Mr. George Raphael Ward has lately produced a very effective and truthful engraving in mezzotinto, after Mr. F. Grant's painting of the Rajah of Sarawak, Sir James Brooke. A short time previously the same engraver produced an excellent likeness of Mr. Henry Dover, of Norfolk, the chairman of the sessions. Both these engravings are carefully and ably executed, and must tend to advance Mr. Ward in public opinion as a mezzotint engraver.

Folkestone.—A Tontine Building Company has been provisionally registered, for the erection of eighty houses in Folkestone. In consequence of the increasing communication between this country and the continent, the town of Folkestone is rapidly advancing in size and importance, and will soon become a considerable seaport, and from its acknowledged salubrity, a fashionable resort for visitors. There is said to be a great demand for houses, with shops of the better class; and it is the object of this Company to meet the wants of the inhabitants and visitors, by building a street of shops of a superior description.

In the New Assessment of Bethnal-green the Eastern Counties Railway Company's assessment has been increased from 4,300*l*. to between 7,000*l*. and 8,000*l*.; the East London Waterworks Company's from 600*l*. to 1,700*l*., while the Regent's Canal Company's has been reduced, their private act not permitting rates for tolls or improvements. Numerous appeals have been made against the increased rates.

Church Decoration.—The nave of Wigmore Church, Hereford, displays two instances of taste worth mentioning. The oak pews are whitewashed, and to the north wall is affixed the strangest mural monument we ever saw. It is no less than the ornamental (!) plate of a coffin-lid, inscribed to the memory of a certain "Martha Millichap."

Model of Suspension-bridge over the Dneiper.—We ought to have said that this bridge was designed, and is in the course of erection by Mr. C. Vignoles, C.E.

Suspending Sashes, &c.—A patent for improved apparatus is advertised in our columns to be sold by auction on the 19th inst. If it can effect all that the patentees assert, it is worth attention.

WORKS ON GREAT NORTHERN RAILWAY SOUTH OF DONCASTER.—At the intersection, near Doncaster, of the Sheffield and Rotherham road, there is a large brick tunnel bridge—length of arch 200 feet, width 197 feet—built by Mr. Morton, contractor, under Messrs. Peto and Betts. After crossing the Carr drainage, the contract of Mr. Morrel commences, and extends to 3 miles of Bawtry. The Rossington bridge is built on the skew, at an angle of 38 degrees—span 26 feet, width 25 feet. Further on are two flying arches springing from layers of brickwork, on the banks of a cutting 16 feet deep. The contract of Mr. Morton, under Messrs. Peto and Betts, succeeds the one just named. The great north road is crossed by a skew bridge, angle 33 degrees, and built on square abutments: span of arch 52 feet 8 inches, width of bridge 35 feet 3 inches, height 24 feet. It contains between 400,000 and 500,000 bricks. The stations and lodges were designed by Mr. H. Goddard, of Lincoln, architect. Near the junction with the Manchester, Sheffield, and Lincoln line, the Chesterfield Canal is crossed by a bridge constructed of tubular girders, like one over the Don at Doncaster. The width of this bridge between the buttresses is 25 feet, and it crosses at an angle of 32 degrees.

CHURCHYARD MONUMENTS.—It must have pained many of your readers, more especially those who have been visitants to our cemeteries, to have witnessed that many monuments, which have been erected so recently as three or four years since, are already evincing symptoms of rapid decay, being discoloured, cracked, and unsightly, whilst the most important part of all, the inscription, is scarcely legible; and therefore, in lieu of being ornaments to a place, are really disfigurements. To a ground abounding with such monuments as these, the grassy tombless graveyard of the Society of Friends is preferable. What a contrast modern tributes of affection and respect to the dead bear to those raised by our forefathers, who did such things in earnest! It is a great boon to us that they were not moved by a contract or low-priced spirit, or our minsters and other hallowed spots would not allow us to boast of so many beautiful specimens of art, which the scythe of Time has spared to us.—H.

INCREASE OF HOUSES, &c., IN THE METROPOLIS.—Returns just published by order of the House of Commons show that the total number of new houses built within the metropolitan police districts, since January 1, 1839, up to the present time, amounts to 64,058; and the number of new streets formed to 1,652,—200 miles in length. The increase of population, from 1839 to 1849, within the said district, is estimated at 325,904; the total population of the metropolitan districts being now about 2,336,960.

ARCH AT GLASGOW.—In commemoration of the Queen's visit, the town council talk of perpetuating in stone the temporary arch raised at the bridge. If a sketch of it which was forwarded to us be correct, we advise the town council to think twice before they do so.

TO CORRESPONDENTS.

Received.—" R. D." (send us the particulars of award. We do not observe it in our packet)." R. B." (the proposed ence to railway platforms does not seem to us desirable)." R. T." (shall appear)." S. T. J." (an Arnott's valve in the chimney, close under ceiling, will ameliorate)." Past student," " J. J." (was too late)." W. C.," " S.," " Reader of 380 Builders" (shall appear)." D. D.," " Baron," " B. J. W." (write to the secretaries, Grosvenor-street, London, and they will forward conditions)." W. A. J." Chester (we are compelled to decline recommending)." J. F." Devonport, " G. L. A." (the letter shall be forwarded)." R. P. A." (the particulars referred to were not enclosed)." J. S.," " Festina lente" (shall appear)." W. G.," " W. L. H." (we shall be glad to see the drawing)." Z.," " W. Q." (the illustration in question is in No. 319, vol. vi., p. 45, which is now out of print)." J. Q." (we will make some private inquiries before advertising, although we have no time to spare)." Building Materials" (shall appear)." H. T. E.," " An Associate of I.B.A.," " F. E. H. F." (some notice shall appear)." The New Testament in Short Hand, lithographed on the M.S. of Thomas Coggin," 1849, Nisbet, Berners-street: " A Treatise on Benefit Building Societies," by Arthur Scratchley, M.A.; London, John W. Parker, 1849 : " Rudimentary Treatise on the Drainage of Towns and Buildings," by G. D. Dempsey, C.E.; Weale, London, 349.

‡ " *Books and Addresses.*"—We have not time to point at books or find references.

‖ NOTICE.—All communications respecting *advertisements* should be addressed to the " Publisher," and not to the " Editor;" all other communications should be addressed to the EDITOR, and not to the Publisher.

The Builder.

No. CCCXLVI.

SATURDAY, SEPTEMBER 22, 1849.

BIRMINGHAM has been in a bit of a bustle for several days past: science and *savans*, music, manufactures, and paintings, concurred to attract a large number of visitors to what the Bishop of Oxford called the "great practical metropolis of the kingdom,"—he might have said, of the world. We allude, of course, to the "Festival," the British Association for the Advancement of Science, the Exposition of Manufactures and Art, and the Exhibition of the Birmingham Society of Artists,—or rather, the exhibition of modern works of art in the *rooms* of the Birmingham Society of Artists.

Birmingham is a wonderful place, when thoroughly comprehended; but this is not to be done by a glance. As the Rev. Professor Robinson, the new president of the Association, observed at the dinner:—"Where in the whole world could be, and men like him, whose delight it was to have their theoretical knowledge enlightened by the intelligence and skill of practical men,—where on earth could they learn such new and extraordinary things, and see a development beyond any thing they could have conceived of the application of the principles to which they had devoted their lives;" and never let the merely practical men forget that it is to science they are indebted for the discovery of principles out of which processes grow,—that science has increased their powers and directed their labours?

We would say, with the president, of the works of Birmingham, though we could not go wholly with him in applying the remarks, as he did, to the present exposition there—"Days and months would be consumed in viewing those extraordinary creations and treasures of industrial art, and on the last day there would be still much to wonder at and to learn. What a development of power—what an amount of knowledge! What patient perseverance and industry exist and reign where such things are! What a noble school to open men's minds to a full conviction of the powers before them of the boundless mind that only wanted to be explored, but which, to be explored in its widest range and its fullest extent, must be explored under the guidance of the lamp of knowledge! It was not by mere blind and tentative experience that they had been able to realize the marvellous conceptions they had arrived at. They told as clearly as a book did the mind of its author,—they told in unmistakeable distinctness that these men must have been among the giants of their race,—that however they among their books might think highly of their own attainments, there was a far wider field, a far greater number of labourers teaching them what they knew of the past."

At the opening meeting, on the 12th, the professor spoke eloquently of the value of association, and maintained that science can be advanced only by its means.

"The power of association," said he, "of combining united labour, is confessed in all ordinary undertakings, in arts, in manufactures, and in politics. What then is there new in applying it to science? There is nothing new—the novelty is in recognizing its efficacy. Observe, in the first place, that although science—at least physical science—is of comparatively recent origin, physical knowledge is of very ancient date. Even from the origin of our race it seems to have been the object of our desire. Some sought it for the influence and power it gave them over mankind; some from the high instinct which leads the noble mind to see its beauty, and appreciate its worth. Even in the first glimmer of history, the astronomy of the Assyrian magi looms through the dark. Geometry, which might be the champion and guide of astronomy, stands forth in feeble development amidst the antiquities of India. The sepulchres of Etruria, of Egypt, and of Nineveh, give up their treasures to prove that even in that remote date was developed in no low degree that practical chemistry which has been transmitted to us by the Arabians, their successors. The architecture of the middle ages displays a knowledge of the principles of equilibrium and power, which fills the mind capable of appreciating it with admiration and wonder beyond that inspired by marvels of modern art. The writings of Roger Bacon and Kirch show that much of the rudiments and ulterior aims of experimental physics was known in the cloister. But although the elements were there, there was no vivifying principle to combine them into a living body. Association was wanting, not intellectual power and sagacity. The Greeks possessed that in a measure equalled perhaps by no other variety of mankind. But the unhappy element of discord, which seemed inherent in their nature, and which split their philosophers into aggressive sects and their nations into hostile fragments, prevented the union necessary to a development of science. But at last that great principle was revealed in one of those mighty movements which stirs up the world of mind from time to time, as those of geology disturbed the earth at the commencement of some great formation. We find that now, united in the brotherhood of knowledge, they have become as anxious for publication as they were before for secresy. Communication and intercourse have helped investigation: each seeks the other for aid, and the only jealousy that is now shown is lest they should be anticipated in important discoveries or successful results.

The reverend speaker erred in his statement, and lost an illustration, when he so spoke of mediæval architecture. The principle of association was therein carried out in an extraordinary degree, and the result was extraordinary progress.

In answering those who asked, "of what use is science?" the president said,—

"There is not a single element of our commercial prosperity in which the vivifying power of science might not be felt, in which the loss arising from want of that certainty of action which mere unenlightened practice can never attain, does not reach an amount which, if stated in figures, would astound the most thoughtless. For instance, the causes which in our great cities hasten the death and debase and embitter the life of so many, have at last been forced by chemists and physiologists on the notice of the public. Look at Dr. Smith's report on the 'Air and Water of Towns,' in our volume; and when we think that the victims of the deadly influences which are there revealed are chiefly found among the people whose industry is the foundation of our greatness,—that every year cut off from the life of each of these is so much subtracted from national wealth,—even were all moral sense or religious feeling dead in us, we must confess that the knowledge which is capable of averting them 'is of use.' The ships that bear the treasures produced by this industry through the world are lost to a fearful amount,—nearly *three* daily. What are they worth—ship, cargo, men?—and most of them perish from want of nautical science or from unscientific construction. How many men have been ruined by searching for minerals, when the merest smattering of geology would have dispelled their delusion? On the other hand, the agricultural produce of our islands might be doubled by a more perfect application of the principles of botany and chemistry. The manufacture of iron has been augmented six-fold by the use of the puddling furnace and the hot-blast,—both gifts of theory. How gigantic a result is this, without reference to the increase in the thousand arts of which this immense supply of that most precious of metals is the exponent."

At the *soirée*, on the following day, Mr. Gassiot exhibited the electric light; but what was said by Mr. Faraday and others on the occasion, would not serve to encourage the ingenious men who are at this time striving to bring it into practical operation.

The papers read in the various sections were numerous—many of them valuable, but they present no particularly salient points. In the mechanical section, Mr. Robert Stephenson, who ably presided, gave an interesting account of the accident to the hydraulic press at the tubular bridge across the Menai Straits. In allusion to a peculiar state of pulsation or vibration observed throughout the tube during the lifting, Professor Willis and Mr. Webster made some remarks. The latter considered that this pulsation might have had some influence in causing the fracture. There might be a conspiration of vibration in the tube and the press, *which would destroy the cohesion in the particles of the metal, and cause the fracture.* An interesting question this, which may show the importance of some recent remarks in THE BUILDER on this very subject of vibration and its effects on iron. Mr. Roberts suggested that in casting the new hydraulic cylinder, the fluid metal should be poured into the mould *spirally*, to obviate the unequal contraction, to which the accident was attributed. The casting, however, has taken place, it is said, on the most approved principle, and after a week's annealing the cylinder will be ready for transmittal to the Menai.*

Mr. Heaton exhibited a clever invention for preventing the oscillation of locomotives on railways.†—Mr. Whishaw stated, as to his

* The *Birmingham Journal* thus reports the conversation:—"Mr. Stephenson proceeded to explain the precautions that had been taken to avoid the consequences of any accident. It was originally intended that the tube should be lifted 5 feet, that a link should then have been taken off, and the space built up. This was happily not carried out, and such was the care taken that as the tube rose men were stealing in, so to speak, small planks of timber. But for these precautions the fall would have been fatal to the whole structure,—for, as it was, it fractured bearers of cast-iron upwards of 500 tons weight. The tube was never for a moment suspended in air; and he had since taken the additional precaution of packing the space between the cross-heads and the pump with small iron wedges. No accident could now take place. The fracture in the cylinder occurred in what might have been considered the very strongest place. The pressure at the time was no more than 3¼ tons to the square inch—by no means an unusual pressure. As connected with the cause of the accident, he might state that a short time previously, when the presses on both ends were working simultaneously, it was remarked that the tube had a *strange tremulous motion along its whole surface.* In a short time it increased until the vibration assumed the character of a short wave. At every action of the pump the whole mass seemed to acquire a state of pulsation, comparable to nothing but the pulse of a man's arm. The presses were stopped, and since, they have only been worked at one end. With respect to the immediate cause of the accident, he might state that the shape of the cylinder-square was not the best, and no doubt the weakness had arisen from unequal cooling.—Dr. Robinson remarked upon the singular fact of the vibration spoken of by Mr. Stephenson. He (Dr. Robinson) presumed that the motion in the end of the tube being raised was reflected from the fixed end, and hence the vibration.—Mr. Stephenson said the fact of his having allowed the damaged cylinder to be used after he knew it was faulty had been strongly commented upon. In answer to that accusation of indiscretion, he begged to state that the fault lay in the collar of the casting, where no pressure came.—Mr. Roberts remarked that the way to obviate vibration was to work the engines at unequal speed. He considered that the shape of the casting was bad, and the mode of casting also not the best. It would greatly improve the strength of such work if spiral casting were to be adopted; that is, to pass the metal into the mould in a spiral direction.—Professor Willis and Mr. Webster followed with some remarks on the subject of vibration; the latter gentleman considering that the pulsation spoken of might have had some influence in causing the fracture. There might be a conspiration of vibration in the tube and the press which would destroy the cohesion in the particles of the metal, and cause the fracture."

† Mr. Heaton proposes to attach a weight with connecting rod, and an auxiliary crank, to the head of the crank pin, equal to the weight of the piston and its gearing, so as to make the weight run to the left hand at the same instant the piston goes to the right. The blow to stop the piston and make it return will be received in the auxiliary crank, instead of in the wheel, producing a neutral point in the centre and steadiness of motion; for when the blow is received in the wheels, the cranks being at right angles, it is communicated through the axle, and gives a twisting motion to the whole framing of the engine.

gutta percha tubing for telegraphs, that he had invented a method of preserving the tube from damage when laid under water. The pipe into which the wire covered with gutta percha was placed, consisted of a tube of metal, jointed at every 2 or 3 feet, as the sinuosities of the river or the various levels of its bed required. Twelve hundred feet had been laid down in the Rhine near to Cologne, and it had answered its purpose well. The tube was payed out from a vessel, and pinned down to the bed of the river, accommodating itself to any sinuosity or change of level. Mr. Roberts described a machine for forming mouldings in sheet metal, which seems worth attention. Mr. Robert Davison explained the desiccating process, the principle of which is, that in drying any body, it is not simply heat that is required, but a current of air also; not merely a moving but a rapid current of air. It is the impulsion of atmospheric air at the velocity of the hurricane, or upwards of 100 miles per hour, combined with the elementary heat, under perfect control, which constitutes the desiccating process. Our readers have much on this subject before them from the advocates of different systems, and may weigh the evidence on both sides.

Last Monday evening was set apart for a discourse from Professor Willis, "On the Application of Mechanical Science to Railways" according to the programme, but which, as the professor himself remarked, ought to have been on *an* application of science to that subject. It will be remembered that soon after the fracture of the Dee-bridge girder, a commission was appointed to inquire into the use of iron for railway bridges, &c. The commission, which included Mr. Willis, have tried a number of experiments on a very large scale at Portsmouth, and have sent in their report, and the object of the lecturer was to put before the members of the association, in a popular form, one of the principal results of the inquiry. Their experiments were made to show the difference of effect on railway girders when a locomotive is at rest upon it and when travelling over, and this important fact was established, namely, that the deflection caused by the weight of the locomotive *was increased in proportion to the velocity*, even as much as three times. The inference, the professor said, seemed painful, namely, that bridges which had been calculated to bear safely the weight of a train which would have to pass over them might not be able to resist the strain caused by it in motion. But he afterwards gave reasons why, in practice, there was not really cause for alarm; but this part of the subject was not made very clear. The curve produced by the deflection through different velocities was shown by simple apparatus, and it was seen that the increased deflection took place, not when the weight was in the middle of the bar, but when in the second half of its length.

The discourse was delivered in the Town-hall, and had a large audience. The ceiling and walls of this fine apartment, by-the-way,* have been chromatized, with good effect, and we may mention that the scaffolding is up for the completion of the back of the building externally, under Mr. Edge, and that masons are preparing the stone-work.

Considerable additions are being made to Queen's College, and, in another part of the town, some industrial schools of Tudor character are nearly completed.

For the Exposition of Industrial Art, a large structure of timber has been erected, under the direction of Mr. Hussey, architect, at a cost of 750*l*. A subscription was raised to defray this and other expenses, but the money taken at the doors, if so applied, will render the subscription unnecessary. Some, however, are anxious that the money received should not be appropriated in this manner, but be applied in the formation of a permanent museum, much to be desired in Birmingham, and we trust they will succeed in effecting this arrangement. So long ago as 1839, when the association met first in Birmingham, the conductor of this journal suggested, through the *Midland Counties Herald*, that a temporary museum of manufacturing processes which had been formed, should be kept together permanently as the nucleus of a perfect collection illustrative of our manufactures, but the time had not then come, and the collection was dispersed. Let us hope for a better result on the present occasion.*

The present exposition is exceedingly interesting, and bears honourable testimony to the advance made in Birmingham in the union of art with manufactures during the last few years. At first sight of the collection our anticipations were scarcely realized, but this was rather owing to our knowledge, bit by bit, of all that had been done, and in consequence of which, therefore, there was little to surprise us,—than to any short-comings on the part of the Birmingham manufacturers. When we remember that the very name of the town as applied to works formerly conveyed a positive condemnation, and then examine the specimens of artistical manufacture now collected, the enormous improvement which has been effected and is going on, becomes strikingly evident. In glass, in porcelain, in silver and plated ware, in iron, forms of great beauty are exhibited, and deserve to be inspected by all who can contrive to pay Birmingham a visit. We should have been glad to have found the names of some of the *designers* of these noticed. One of the tables contains a large collection of French bronzes, the works of various foreign manufacturers, and serves to show how much we have yet to do in this branch of industrial art. The committee acted wisely in admitting these. The proprietors of the table scarcely expected they would have been permitted to exhibit their wares (they are all priced for sale), and said to us candidly, that far more liberality had been shown towards them than Englishmen under similar circumstances would receive in France. We are quite contented that England is, in such feelings, in advance.

The most important contribution by any single firm is the collection of ecclesiastical furniture (for Roman Catholic uses), and decorations, exhibited by Messrs. Hardman and Co. Such an amount of fine work in metal has never before been seen together in modern England. Pastoral staves, candlesticks, brackets, chandeliers, monumental brasses, stained glass, oak cabinets, tapestry, and paper-hangings (the latter executed by Messrs. Crace), assisted by a foreground of tiles by Minton, form a whole of extraordinary excellence. Mr. Hardman, the exception to the rule, has given the name of the designer,—Mr. Pugin.

Many of the series of specimens illustrative of manufacturing processes are very curious, and no less instructive. Some of our readers would stare to see, for example, in the manufacture of a simple brass rack-pulley, that the piece of metal of which it is formed passed through thirty-seven stages.

We must run away, however, just to ask permission at the Workhouse to see the selected plans for the intended Union, a course which we thought necessary, to prevent the possible reproach hereafter that we had promulgated untrue statements, when, being in the town, we might have seen and judged for ourselves. With some little difficulty we found out the retreat of pauperism, and stated our wish and motive. The Clerk of the Guardians, Mr. Corder, a polite, common-sense man, could see no reason why this should be refused, the selected design having been approved by the Poor-law Board and returned, but he had no power to comply. He would, however, obtain authority from some of the guardians, who were then assembling. One was asked, and another was appealed to; but each shook his head, like a true descendant of Lord Burleigh, and it was ultimately decided that a reply could be obtained only by formal application to the Board. Not being disposed to spend in the workhouse of Birmingham the short time we had to stay in the "workshop of the world," waiting the doubtful result of a discussion on this knotty point, we left them in the quiet possession of their plans, and sighed for the hour we had wasted in the ineffectual attempt to fit ourselves to do justice.*

We afterwards looked in at the Exhibition of Modern Works of Art, but found little there beyond pictures already exhibited in London, including some by W. Linton, Inskipp, Stanfield, Collins, Anthony, Etty, Uwins, Leslie, O'Neil, Redgrave, Turner, and others; a pleasant collection, nevertheless, which restored our equanimity, and enabled us to leave Birmingham in better humour than we left the workhouse.

GREENWICH NAVAL GALLERY.— Eight pictures, illustrative of the life of Lord Viscount Nelson, have been purchased by subscription, and deposited in the Naval Gallery of Greenwich Hospital, at a cost of 300*l*., of which the sum of 136*l*. was contributed by Mr. Jasper de Sainte Croix.

---

* It is 145 feet long, 65 feet wide, and 65 feet high.

* As the suggestion applies now as it did then, we venture to reprint a part of the letter:—

"*To the Editor of the Midland Counties Herald.*

"The collection of manufactured articles and scientific inventions brought together through the exertions of the members of the British Association, and now exhibiting at the Grammar School in this town, is so honourable, not merely to Birmingham but to England, that one cannot but feel regret that at the end of the week the whole will be broken up, and each of the several objects returned to its respective owner. To prevent this *altogether* is not practicable, on account of the great cost of the specimens (perhaps, indeed, it is not even desirable), but with respect to some of the subjects, it seems to me to be absolutely necessary that endeavours should be made to retain them for the public service. I allude, Sir, to the several most interesting *series* of specimens distributed throughout the room, illustrative of different materials and various processes of manufacture; for example, those showing, in all their various stages and applications, copper, iron, lead, steel, and German silver; and the collections illustrative of the manufacture of buttons, pins, files, papier maché, flint-glass, plated articles, and porcelain. These, invaluable as they may become when collected, are comparatively of little cost; and what I would suggest, Sir, is, that a subscription should be made at once to purchase them from their owners; and then, that they should be presented to one of the local museums, or placed in the Town Hall, where they would form a nucleus for a perfect collection, illustrative of our manufactures. Of the value of such a museum, now nowhere existing, it is not necessary to speak. Each of these series may be regarded a a perpetual, although silent *lecturer*: they at once plainly tell their own story, and open the minds of the observers to wonders before unthought of.

"August, 1839." "GEORGE GODWIN."

* We are informed that at the meeting of the board, after we left, the communication from the Poor-Law Board, expressing approval of the plans of Messrs. Drury and Bateman which had been recommended for adoption by the architect appointed to examine the competing plans, was read. No discussion ensued, and it is expected that the building will be proceeded with immediately. One out of several fresh correspondents on this subject writes thus:—"There is a curious coincidence about this second competition, which appears to have been as yet overlooked. Upon turning to your journal of the 10th of February, I find a paragraph which begins in this manner:—'The voting in committee on the seven selected plans terminated thus:—Mr. Hemming (Birmingham), 17; Messrs. Drury and Bateman (Birmingham), 16; the rest, nowhere.' And you may now again respond, '*the rest nowhere*.' No doubt the judges, like Brutus and Cassius, are 'honourable men;' but they have made one sad mistake, and appearances are against them." The writer afterwards asked "What has become of the second premium?"

THE SHRINE OF ST. THOMAS, AT CANTERBURY.

GATE HOUSE, WALSINGHAM PRIORY.

PILGRIMAGES TO WALSINGHAM AND CANTERBURY.

AMONGST the many pleasant excursions which the members of the two Archæological Associations have enjoyed, that to Walsingham, when the Institute visited Norwich, stands prominent. The weather was fine, the place itself full of interest, and the host, Mr. Lee Warner, received all with such genuine and warm kindness as greatly to increase their enjoyment.

Amidst the pleasant results of that visit (and every one of these excursions produces more good results than are at once apparent) must be placed a new translation, by Mr. John Gough Nichols, of "The Pilgrimages to St. Mary of Walsingham and St. Thomas of Can-terbury," by Erasmus.* Mr. Nichols, the worthy bearer of a worthy name, was peculiarly well fitted for the task, and has brought to bear upon it a large amount of anti-quarian knowledge, throwing light on our early religious history and our architectural anti-quities.

Our readers will scarcely require to be told that these celebrated colloquies were directed against "such as run mad upon pilgrimages undertaken under pretext of religion." The translator, however, does not put it forth in a polemical spirit, but as illustrating early history; and he shows that the degree of dis-

* "With the Colloquy on Rash Vows, by the same Author, and his Characters of Archbishop Warham and Dean Colet, and illustrated with Notes, by John Gough Nichols, F.S.A." Westminster: Nichols and Son. 1849.

credit which has been thrown on the descrip-tive portions of these works was unjust. He found the account of the churches of Walsingham quite correct: "There were two, —the Priory Church, and the wooden Chapel of the Virgin, around which 'the new work' of stone had been erected, but was never finished, just as Erasmus describes it. The two wells, which he mentions, still exist."

We give, as specimens of the engravings with which the book is further illustrated, a view of the Gate-house of Walsingham Priory, and of the Shrine of St. Thomas, at Canterbury, from a pen-and-ink sketch on one of the Cottonian MSS. (Tib. E. viii., fo. 269.)

"The head in the quatrefoil in the front of the gateway, and two smaller ones in the side walls, are portions of the original design, and are intended to represent the porter and war-ders on the look out."

The shrine at Canterbury is described by Stowe as "builded about a man's height, all of stone; then upward of timber, plaine. * * * The timber-work of this shrine on the outside was covered with plates of gold," &c. "The finials on the crest of the shrine," says Mr. Nichols, "were of silver gilt, the central one weighing 80 ounces, and the two others each 60 ounces." The shrine had in front of it a curious mosaic pavement (which still remains in the cathedral), such as is found at Westminster Abbey, about the shrine of Edward the Con-fessor.

Mr. Nichols is entitled to praise for this very interesting and scholarly contribution to the library, not alone of the English reader, but of those who, knowing the author in the original, would more fully understand his references and allusions.

IS TIME MONEY?

HE should possess no ordinary stock of courage who withholds assent to the dogma so pertinaciously upheld and acted upon by a large portion of the world. Yet so far from being received as a canon, it deserves our most serious inquiry, whether the too univer-sal adhesion to it by the commercial commu-nity is not one of the causes of that depression which periodically sweeps over the face of mercantile affairs, as surely and naturally as debility and forced inactivity follow a fever in our mortal frame.

It has been truly remarked that men live *quicker* now than they did—that the work of fifty years is compressed into twenty. Yet the fuel that supplies heat to the great commercial hot-house is *human bone and blood.* And it is inevitable that the lower the rank in life the more fatal is the operation of this forcing sys-tem. A statesman or philosopher wears out prematurely the scabbard of life by the activity of his trenchant spirit; a poet swims the ad-verse stream till heart-strings crack in the contest; another throws down the disgustful cup of life scarce tasted; and their premature exit is chronicled in the memories of all who sympathize with men struggling against the chilly tide of the world's selfishness. But who notes the hecatombs offered on the altar of the Moloch of haste? Every additional burden thrown on the edifice of human so-ciety, however much it may be felt by the capital and the shaft, presses with a more crushing weight upon the base.

It must, I think, be evident to the most superficial observer, that much of the depres-sion in trade arises from the rapidity with which work is now executed. A tradesman solicits, or tenders for work, and after lowering his prices till a scarcely living profit is attain-able (and after figuring in the list of "Blind Builders"), promises to do the work of six days in two. By hard task-masters, long hours of business, and body-destroying and soul-wearying exertions on the part of *employés,* he succeeds—the work is done: how done is of no consequence, if he *barely* fulfil his contract, or satisfy the requirements of the man to whom "time is money," and who, as he begrudges the "money" for the execution, begrudges the "time" for examination into the stability and propriety of the work done for him. By this system the master-workman suffers much, but how fare the working hands? Work cannot be made for them; and after doing the six days' work in two (for which they hardly get three days' pay—perhaps much less), they stand still. If they work at piecework, they lose directly in not receiving wages; if monthly or yearly servants, they are menaced with a prospective and indirect loss in the reduction of establishments and a lowering of salaries.

But in a moral point of view, is time, indeed, to be looked upon only as money? Is no part of it to receive more consideration than if it were mere dross? Was it only given us that we might go on heaping bag upon bag of gold, adding house to house, and acre to acre? If, in fact, every minute were weighed as a broad piece of gold, and every day as an ingot, should we be justified in running the headlong, jostling race we every day pursue? Ask the "Integer vitæ scelerisque purus," to sell you his good opinion or his vote for money, and the honest blood rushes to his face; but his indignation is nullified, his reproach blunted, edge and point, by his rigid adherence to "Time is money." If commercial integrity is "more precious than fine gold," how ought we to estimate the moral culture of the inward man, whose purity and right education is the alone basis of all fair dealing?

Much as we imagine ourselves superior in philosophy and attainments to our continental neighbours, we might learn from them a useful lesson—that of being contented with less money, and devoting more time to æsthetic pursuits, and to the cultivation of all that makes life worth living for. And here suffer me to throw out a hint for thinkers. May not a comparison be drawn, much to our disadvantage, between the mediæval times and our own? I speak architecturally. Look at the works of the men who worked slowly and thought much, and turn to the productions of our day, when men "run up" a church in a few months, a standing monument of their *want* of thought.

It was hoped that when railroads were made, so much time would be saved in travel, as to give greater leisure to the ordinary affairs of life, but the anticipation has not been realized. The fever has grown with what it feeds on. Truly, the demon of unrest has entered into us, and we rush down the steep places to drown ourselves in a sea of troubles.

Festina Lente.

RESTORATION OF ST. PETER'S CHURCH,

FROCESTER, COUNTY OF GLOUCESTER.

This pretty and retired village, through which the line of railway from Gloucester to Bristol runs, and in which village Ralph Bigland, the well-known author of the "History of the County of Gloucester," formerly resided, possesses an old parish church, now about a mile from the village, which has for a period of more than a century lain in a state of desolation and decay, and in the interior of which, and among the tombs of the departed, till very lately, the owl and the bat had found an abode. The restoration of this old parish church (said to be dedicated to St. Peter) has been commenced under the direction of the writer; and a short description of the church, as well as of the restorations about to be effected, may be interesting.

The original fabric appears to have been built about the commencement of the Early English period of ecclesiastical architecture. The plan of this church consisted of a long and narrow nave, 64 feet by 15 feet, a chancel in a continuous line with the nave, and latterly without any separation, internally 20 feet by 15 feet; a north aisle, 20 feet by 13 feet, with a north chapel, separated from this aisle at the eastern end formerly by an oak screen, and at the western end of which was placed the tower, 9 feet by 9 feet internally; and about the middle of the nave, on the south side, was a porch, the side walls of which are perforated, and altogether of a peculiar design. The tower was surmounted with a broach spire, very stumpy in proportion, constructed of oak timber, covered with oak shingles. In the tower were placed six bells. The nave was separated from the north aisle by piers and arches; the piers at the eastern end being circular, and at the western end square. In the chancel existed a piscina of the Early English period; and several flat coffin lids, with various devices of monumental crosses incised on them of the Early English period, as well as stone coffins, have been discovered. The fabric, viz., the nave, aisle, and porch, according to the existing specimens of the windows and doorways, &c., appears to be about the period of Henry the Seventh, 1485, Perpendicular. At the western end of the nave, I should mention, there existed a recess about 3 feet in width by 22 feet in length: this recess was covered over with a lean-to roof,—for what purpose it was used I am desirous of ascertaining.

As to the intended restorations, the walls all round are to be taken down, as well as the piers and arches, and rebuilt on the site of the old foundations, with the exception of the tower, which is to be extended northwards, and the north aisle westwards, thereby increasing the internal area of the building. All the old roofs were constructed of either oak or chesnut timber, consisting of all common rafters, with semi-circular tie pieces underneath, and covered with stone tile. The same construction of roofs is about to be placed on the new walls, the old timbers being reused, as far as they are sound. The present porch, and all the old windows, of four different patterns, are to be repaired and reinserted in the new walls, and some new windows made to correspond. Between the chancel and nave I conclude a rood screen existed, and which formed the only separation between the two. The way leading to the rood loft remained, and underneath the semi-circular carved pieces of the roof, about 7 feet in length, there existed panelling and rib mouldings painted, which was formerly over this rood loft no doubt. The walls of the chancel were in a very bad state of repair, and considerably out of the perpendicular, and the roof had partly fallen in.

This portion of the church is being repaired, under the care of the lay rector (a converted Romanist), and the incumbent (a very low Churchman, and formerly an officer in the army), and I am sorry to say it is about to be restored in the cheapest, plainest, and not altogether with the most substantial materials, the roof timbers being, I understand, about to be worked out of beech timber, and underneath these roof timbers to be plastered. The whole of the other portion of this church—nave, aisle, tower, and porch—is now being restored, at the expense of the parishioners, who have come forward in a praiseworthy and liberal manner, with the assistance of the squire of the parish, Mr. J. A. G. Clarke. The seats, as well as the roof, are being worked out of oak. The few remains left of the old bench-ends had the linen-fold, or scroll pattern, in the panels. The new seats, which are to be without doors, are to be worked according to this pattern; and this church, when completed, will accommodate nearly 300 persons. There is to be a new stone font and pulpit, and an oak reading-desk; and the north chapel (a proposed site for an organ), is to be separated from the aisle by an oak screen, as well as the chancel from the nave. Buttresses are now placed against the side walls, which formerly did not exist. The tower is to be of the same size on plan as the old one, but is to be now carried up 10 feet higher, and the spire is to be of stone, and made more tapering in its proportions than the old one.

The contract for carrying out the restorations of this church amounts to between 1,800*l.* and 1,900*l.* The amount of the subscriptions is at present far short of this, but it is to be hoped this work, now so well begun, will be nevertheless completed in the manner in which it is proposed it should be carried out.

Francis Niblett.

Plate-Glass Manufacture.—A patent has been granted to Mr. Obed Blake, Blackwall, for smoothing plates, sheets, or panes of glass, by means of suction or vacuum blocks, arranged in combination with runners and other machinery as set forth and described, and illustrated by drawings. The suction-blocks are made to adhere to such glass-plates as are already used with the finest emeries in smoothing by hand, and the object of the invention is to imitate this finer work, hitherto done by hand, the coarser being already done by machine, with plaster of Paris for adhesion.

OF THE RIGHT TO REMOVE FIXTURES SET UP FOR ORNAMENT OR CONVENIENCE AND DOMESTIC USE.*

The author premises that it must not be forgotten each case must depend, in a great measure, upon its own peculiar facts,—" 'That the right (to remove) is an exception only, and though to be fairly considered, is not to be extended;' and that it will be requisite to ascertain whether there be any custom or prevailing usage; what is the nature and construction of the article, its mode of annexation, and the effect of its removal:† these will all prove useful and safe *criteria* in practice, where there is any doubt, or where any new case arises.

Hangings.—In Poole's case, 1 Salk., 368, Lord *Holt* denies the right of a tenant to remove any other description of fixtures, save trade; nevertheless Lord Keeper *Wright*, in Squier *v.* Mayer, 2 Freem. 249, held that hangings nailed to the walls should be accounted as personalty, and go to the executor as against the heir.

Looking Glasses.—So hangings and looking glasses are only matters of ornament and furniture, and not to be taken as part of the house and freehold, but removable by the lessee of the house. Beck *v.* Rebow, 1 P. Wms. 94. See Elwes *v.* Maw, 3 East, 33, per Lord *Ellenborough.*

Tapestry, &c.—So hangings, tapestry, and iron backs to chimneys. Harvey *v.* Harvey, 2 Stra. 1141. *Id.*

Wainscot.—So wainscot fixed by screws, and marble chimney-pieces. Lawton *v.* Lawton, 3 Atk. 15. Ex parte Quincey, per Lord *Hardwick*, Lawton *v.* Salmon, 1 H. Bl. 260. And, it would seem, a cornice fixed with screws. Owen *v.* Cheslyn, 3 Ad. & E. 75.

Chimney-pieces.—An outgoing tenant may remove an ornamental chimney-piece put up by himself during his tenantcy, but not a chimney-piece which is not ornamental. Leach *v.* Thomas, 7 Car. & P. 385, per *Patteson.*

Window-sashes.—So window-sashes which are neither hung nor headed into the frames, but merely fastened by laths nailed across the frames to prevent their falling in, for they are not fixed to the freehold. Rex *v.* Hedges, 1 Leach, C. C. 201; 2 East, P. C. 590. *n.*

Beds fastened to the Ceiling.—So beds fastened to the ceiling with ropes, or even nails. Ex parte Quincey, 478.

Stoves, Cupboards, &c. — So stoves and grates fixed into the chimney with brickwork, and cupboards supported with holdfasts. Rex *v.* St. Dunstan's, 4 Bl. C. 686, per *Bayley*, J. See Lee *v.* Risdon, 7 Taunt. 191; Colgraves *v.* Dias, 2 B. & C. 76; Lyde *v.* Russell, 1 B. & Al. 194. But see Winn *v.* Ingilby & Hauxwell, 5 B. & Al. 625.

In Birch *v.* Dawson, 6 Carr & P. 658, it is made a *quære* whether carpet tacked to the floor is fixed furniture.

Pumps.—So a pump which was attached to a perpendicular plank resting on the ground at one end, and at the other fastened to the wall by an iron pin, having a head at one end and a screw at the other, which went through the wall. *Tindal*, C. J., observing, 'that the article was one of domestic convenience, was slightly fixed, erected by the tenant, and might be removed entire:' Grimes *v.* Boweren, 6 Bingh. 437.

These articles, being generally affixed by the tenant for his personal comfort and convenience, and being equally useful in another house, and capable of being easily disunited, by which the premises will neither be injured nor left in a worse state than they were before, the tenant may remove.

Doors, Hearths.—But things affixed to the house for the purpose of completing it he cannot take away; thus doors, hearths, windows. Poole's case, 1 Salk. 368.

Veranda.—Nor a veranda placed in front of the house, supported by posts fixed in the ground. Penry *v.* Brown, 2 Stark. N. P. 403.‡

* "From "The Law of Fixtures, &c." By S. G. Grady, Barrister-at-Law. Richards, Fleet-street.

† "Whether a fixture can be removed by a tenant without substantial injury to the premises is a question proper for the jury, upon an issue whether the fixture is removable or not by law. Avery *v.* Cheslyn, 3 Ad. & E. 75; 5 Nev. & M. 372."

‡ "This was an action of covenant by which the defendant undertook to repair, and keep in repair, all erections, buildings, and improvements which might be erected thereon during the term, and yield up the same in good and sufficient repair; and *Abbott* J. held that the veranda fell within the terms of the covenant."

Pillars of Brick and Mortar.—An outgoing tenant has no right to remove pillars of brick and mortar built on a dairy floor to hold pans, although such pillars are not let into the ground. Leach *v.* Thomas, 7 Car. & P. 328, per *Pateson*, J.

Shrubs, &c.—Nor can a tenant (not a gardener) remove shrubs, flowers, &c. planted by him in a garden. Empson *v.* Sodden, 4 B. & Ad. 655.

Bookcase, &c. — A. bequeathed his leasehold messuage, with the grates, stoves, coppers, locks, bolts, keys, belts, and and other fixtures and fixed furniture, to G. for life; and the household goods, furniture, plate, linen, china, books, wine, and liquors, and other properties in the messuage not being comprehended under the preceding terms, fixtures and fixed furniture, to G. absolutely. There were in the messuage looking-glasses standing on chimney-pieces and nailed to the wall, and a bookcase standing on (but not fastened to) brackets, screwed to the wall. It was held that G. took only a life interest in them. Birch *v.* Dawson, 4 N. & M. 22; 2 Ad. & E. 37; 6 Car. and P. 658.

Conservatories.—In Buckland *v.* Butterfield, 4 Moore, 440, it was held that pineries and conservatories were not removable by a tenant. The judgment of Chief Justice *Dallas* being a very important one, and the case itself being considered a leading authority on this class of fixtures, it is better to set it out at length.

'It was an action on the case, tried before Mr. Baron Graham at the last assizes at Aylesbury. The question in the cause, as far as related to the motion before the Court, was, whether a conservatory affixed to the house, in the manner specified in the report,* was so affixed as to be an annexation to the freehold, and to make the removal of it waste? In the argument and judgment of the Court of King's Bench, in Elwes *v.* Maw, will be found at length all that can relate to this and other cases of a similar description. It is not necessary to go into the distinctions there pointed out, as they relate to different classes of persons, or to the subject-matter itself of the inquiry. Nothing will here depend on the relation in which the parties stood to each other, or to the distinction between trade and agriculture; for this is merely the case of an ornamental building, constructed by the party for his pleasure, and the question of annexation arises on the facts reported to us; and I say the facts reported, because every case of this sort must depend on its own special and peculiar circumstances. On the one hand, it is clear that many things of an ornamental nature may be in a degree fixed, and yet during the term may be removed; and, on the other hand, it is equally clear that there may be that sort of fixing or annexation which, though the building or thing annexed may have been merely for ornament, will yet make the removal of it waste. The general rule is, that where a lessee, having annexed a personal chattel to the freehold during his term, afterwards takes it away, it is waste. In the progress of time this rule has been relaxed, and many exceptions have been grafted upon it. One has been in favour of matters of ornament,—as ornamental chimney-pieces, pier-glasses, hangings, wainscot fixed only by screws, and the like. Of all these, it is to be observed that they are exceptions only, and therefore, though to be fairly considered, not to be extended; and with respect to one subject in particular, namely, wainscot, Lord *Hardwicke* treated it as a very strong case. Passing over all that relates to trade and agriculture, as not being connected with the present subject, it will be only necessary to advert, as bearing upon it, to the doctrine of Lord *Kenyon*, in Pentan *v.* Robart, referred to at the bar. The case itself was that of a building for the purpose of trade, and consequently standing upon a different ground from the present; but it has been cited for the dictum of Lord *Kenyon*, which seems to treat of greenhouses and hothouses erected by great gardeners and nurserymen as not to be considered as annexed to the freehold. Even if the law were so, which it is not necessary to examine, still, for obvious reasons, such a case would not be similar to the present; but in Elwes *v.* Maw, speaking of this dictum, Lord *Ellenborough* said, "There exists no decided case, and, I believe, no recognized opinion or practice, on either side of Westminster-hall, to warrant such an extension." Allowing, then, that matters of ornament may or may not be removable, and that whether so or not must depend on the particular case, we are of opinion that no case has ever extended the right to remove, nearly so far as it would be extended, if such right were to be established in the present instance, under the facts of the report, to which it will be sufficient to refer; and therefore we agree with the learned judge in thinking that the building in question must be considered as annexed to the freehold, and that, consequently, the removal of it would be waste.'

Any injury, however, which would occur in removing fixtures must be made good by the party severing, and he must leave the premises in all respects as he found them, whether the fixtures be set up for trade or domestic purpose. See Foley & Addenbrooke, 13 M. & W. 199."

* "The conservatory was erected on a brick foundation 15 inches deep, attached to the wall of the dwelling-house by cantilevers let 9 inches into the wall, connected with the parlour chimney by a flue, and having two windows in common with the dwelling-house, and to a pinery erected in the garden, on a brick wall 4 feet deep.

BAD EFFECTS OF THE BRICK DUTIES.

The following statement in respect of the brick duties has been made by "The Financial Reform Association:"—The duty on bricks was 2s. 6d. per thousand when first imposed, in 1784, but was increased at different periods, from 1794 and 1806, in aid of the war expenditure, to 5s. 10d. per thousand. Additions have been made, higher rates levied on the finer kinds of brick, and drawbacks allowed for damages, which make the present duty to stand at, or near to, 7s. per thousand. Though this be a considerable addition to the price of a cottage containing 15,000, or to an ordinary street house, containing 50,000 bricks, the evil operation of the tax is not seen in the enhanced cost of the house. To avoid the enhancement of cost price, the house is, in many essential parts, weakened, by the absence of bricks which should be used to give it solidity. But the evil influence of the tax is more apparent when examined at the brickfield, where the article is in process of manufacture. There, a certain mould of legal size must be invariably used. A builder might come and say he was desirous of bricks of different sizes, that he might build a house better apportioned, as to strength and solidity, in its different parts; but the exciseman says, "Not so; the law has settled the size of bricks, and the quality too." The builder may rejoin, "Is my experience in the construction of dwellings, and churches, and railway arches, to go for nothing? Has the world learned nothing since 1784?" The exciseman says, "Railway arches might not be known in 1784; but the law of that time has ruled what kind of bricks you are to build them of."

Next, there are the makers of the bricks. In the neighbourhood of large towns the excisemen visit the brickfields pretty regularly, to take account of the work done, perhaps once a-day; but in remoter places they cannot do so, unless there were an exciseman appointed to each place of work. For this reason, villagers or farmers, who would make their own bricks to build their own houses, must not do so, because they have not an exciseman living beside them. They must send to great distances, where it is convenient to make the article under the supervision of the excise. Even where the officers visit the works once a-day, the inconvenience and loss to the operative at work are ever recurring. They are bound to lay their moulded clay down on certain spaces, and on those only, from which they must not remove the pieces until account has been taken of them for duty. Nor must they lay more on those given spaces than the officer allows: if full, they must stop work. If rain falls, and reduces the moulded clay to mud, or otherwise disfigures it, so as to be unfit to be sent to the kiln for burning, *the duty must be paid*, though the clay be returned to the pit, to be again worked up for the moulder. The lost labour falls to the operative brickmakers, while their employers lose the duty. Those accidents from weather would seldom occur if the makers were allowed to remove their bricks at any time, or lay them in any place.

In every respect the brick duty is an unqualified evil. It obstructs the operations of an important branch of industry, and ends by endangering human life in habitations to which is denied the application of a sound constructive science.

CHURCHES AND SCHOOLS.

Wavendon Church was consecrated on Tuesday week. The whole body of the edifice has been rebuilt, except the tower. The restoration, as it is called, was made from plans by Mr. Butterfield, architect. The walls are of limestone, with dressings of Caen stone. The roofs of the nave and aisles are covered with lead. The whole is in the decorated style, and consists of nave, aisles, and chancel, with vestry, &c. The old tower remains. The west window, a gift of Mr. H. C. Hoare, is filled with stained glass, and is seen through the open tower arch in the interior, from the opposite end of the church. The east window is a decorated one, with four lights, and according to the *Bedford Times*, is a gift by Miss Prince, as another, on the north is, by Miss Hoare. The chancel ceiling is painted blue, with gold stars, and the windows are all of stained glass. The gates of the chancel screen, a low one of stone, are of metal, with ornamental workmanship in burnished brass and colours. There are no pews in the church. The open benches have carved oak ends. The whole floor is paved with black and red tiles; encaustic with patterns in the chancel.——A committee has been appointed to obtain estimates and subscriptions for the repewing of St. Edward's Church, Cambridge.——Some workmen employed in repairing the interior of Chelsworth Church, near Biddlestone, have discovered a painting, in good preservation, over the chancel arch. It represents the Day of Judgment. The church formerly belonged to the abbey of Bury St. Edmund's.——The chancel of Little Wilbraham Church has been restored by the rector. A new east window, decorated, has been added. The parishioners are restoring the south aisle windows, and nave roof, &c. Opposite this church new schools and teacher's dwellings, are in course of erection.——Balsham Church is under repair and restoration. ——All Saints, Maidstone, has been reopened, after having undergone some long-talked-of alterations and restorations. Cumbrous galleries have been removed, and pews of all sorts replaced by open benches, with carved oak poppy heads. The works have been done under the architectural superintendence of Mr. Carpenter, and by contract with Mr. Cobb, builder. The removal of the galleries has, it is said, improved the transmission of sound and the hearing throughout the church.—— A new school and teachers' dwellings have been founded at Nettleton, Wilts, on a plan furnished by Mr. Salway, of Chippenham, architect: mason, Mr. T. Brookman.——Some further repairs or improvements have been made at Astley Church, under the superintendence of Mr. Dodson, of Worcester.—— Llan-Gasty-Tal-Y-Llyn Church, Brecon, has been restored by Mr. Pravson, of London, architect. The tower has been raised 12 feet, and 'the great banner of the cross now floats from its summit.' The interior space under the tower has been laid open with its lofty arch to the nave, and provided with open seats. The roofs are open, showing woodwork in the Early English style of the building. The whole area of the church is paved with encaustic tiles. The chancel windows are filled with stained glass, by Wailes. The font, a large one, is of Bath stone, carved. The south porch door is of oak, massive, with floriated ironwork.——To complete the erection of St. Thomas's, Wigan, Mr. H. Gaskell has given the munificent sum of a thousand guineas. ——The foundation stone of St. Luke's Free Church was laid in Great Hamilton-street, Glasgow, on Monday week. It is to accommodate 800. Mr. Wylson is the architect. The edifice is to be in the Pointed style, with tower at the south-east corner.——St. Ninian's Cathedral (Episcopal), at Perth, was to be formally founded on the 15th inst., by the laying of the chief stone.

STONE PULPIT, EARLY ENGLISH PERIOD.
[CIRCA 1270.]

W D.   LAING Sc

EARLY ENGLISH STONE PULPITS.

In the course of a recent notice of proceedings in Chester we promised a view of the Early English pulpit in the Refectory there;—one of the very few remaining examples of pulpits of that era. By a rare accident, however, the drawing of it when put on the wood was not reversed, and the engraving was therefore made to show it on the *north* side of the refectory instead of the *south*. We had in consequence abandoned the idea of publishing it, but being pressed by some of our correspondents to keep the promise, we now give it, not as a view of the Chester pulpit, although it really is so with the exception mentioned, but simply as an example of a stone pulpit in the Early English style.

The steps, it will be seen, are formed in the thickness of the wall, and the pulpit is corbelled out. The width of the stairs is 2 feet 8 inches. The height of each opening to apex 7 feet 6 inches, and the floor of the pulpit is 4 feet 3 inches from the ground.*

* The detail* of this interesting specimen are given in Mr. Dollman's "Examples of Antient Pulpits," published by G. Bell.

MATERIALS FOR BUILDING WORKS.

The durability of materials employed in budding works is a question too little attended to; the present cost, alas, deludes the majority of those whose province is to decide in these matters. Quantity for money is the popular mania, in the stead of quality, which our forefathers loved. The builders of the 19th century may carry the palm far above all preceding time for gigantic and rapidly-conceived and executed works, but those who follow us will find out many secrets arising out of this rapid and cheap style of building. But the topic I wish now to fix attention to more particularly is the very great neglect of attention in selecting the best materials for the character of any proposed work : when I use the term best, I mean best for its use consistent with durability, economy, and good taste : these conditions, in my opinion, should be sought to be combined as much as possible. The architect has a noble field in aiming to design an effective, economical, and durable building. I will now advert to two or three illustrations of my argument as to the selection of materials.

In the recently-published Blackwall Railway report, the parapet walls enclosing the sides of the railway are said to have cost above 2,600*l.* The purpose of these walls is sufficiently obvious now that locomotives are employed, but why

brick walls were resorted to is not so obvious,—the iron rods and standards forming the original fence are built in : the contriver of this work surely forgot the important principle of the expansion and contraction of iron-work under different conditions of the thermometer. Again, the constant expense of keeping the joints of a 9-inch wall pointed up on both sides would have seemed a strong reason why another method of enclosure should have been sought out.

Most of our railway companies will find out by bitter experience the ultimate cost of wooden erections: miles of upright matched boarding have been fixed during the last five years on the sides of the platforms at the various stations. Travelling the other day on the North Kent line, I observed (at Woolwich, I think) thin deal close-boarded fencing, and fir posts and rails, being fixed. What will be the ultimate cost of these fences, kept painted on both sides ; and how many years will these fences last? Speaking of fences, I will also advert to one, now almost prostrate, in the new Victoria-park, near Hackney : fir posts have been used, and they have rotted off at the level of the ground, as might have been expected. Now, this fencing cannot have been put up more than three years ; —is not this a miserable waste of public money? A vast deal has been ex-

NORTHERN SCHOOLS, ST. MARTIN'S-IN-THE-FIELDS, LONDON.

Mr. James Wild, Architect.

ponded on lodges, lakes, gates, &c., to this park, surely it would have been better policy to have saved a little elsewhere, and fixed English oak posts to their fencing:

MORE ANON.

NEW NORTHERN SCHOOLS, SAINT MARTIN'S-IN-THE-FIELDS, LONDON.

ANNEXED we give the elevation of the Northern Schools for St. Martin's-in-the-Fields, intended to be built in Castle-street, under the superintendence of Mr. Wild, as stated in our last number.

The frontage of the building is 100 feet : on the first door this length, by 24 ft. 6in., is divided into two school-rooms, one for 200 boys and the other for 200 girls; on the ground floor there is a school-room for 320 infants—thus making 720 children in all.

The building will be faced with red brick; the arches and moulding to be in-laid and gauged; the columns and architrave of the gallery or playground, which extends over the top of the whole, are of Caen stone. The style approximates to the Gothic of the north of Italy.

The amount of the contract entered into by Messrs. Haward and Nixon is 2,433l.*

The doors are to be of oak, panelled (as shown in the design), and are further to be ornamented with bronze studs. The sculpture over the doors is only proposed, and is not included in the estimate : probably there will be inscriptions instead.

From the height of the building and the width of the street, the roof cannot be seen, and, therefore, forms no part of the design.

CHEAPENING DWELLINGS FOR THE POOR.—It is supposed that one-fourth of the cost of a dwelling which lets for half-a-crown or three shillings a-week, is caused by the expense of the title-deeds and the tax on wood and bricks used in its construction. Of course the owner of such property must be remunerated, and he therefore charges sevenpence halfpenny or ninepence a-week to cover these burdens. Government affect to regret that the working classes are crowded together, which looks very like hypocrisy, as it is in their power to prevent it by reducing the price of buildings, and, consequently, lessening rents. R.

* The highest of seventeen tenders received was 2,774l.

NEW PRESBYTERIAN CHURCH, MANCHESTER.

THE foundation stone of a new church was laid in Grosvenor-square, on Wednesday week. It will be arranged to contain 1,090 sittings, including those of 150 children. The body of the edifice will be approached by a flight of steps from the square, 6 feet above the street. The length of it will be 72 feet, and breadth 51 feet. A further mass of building for sessions-house, vestry, and schools will extend to the extreme depth of the land, bounded by Chatham-street, 60 feet in length by 36 feet. A large lecture-room is to extend under the body of the church, and be of the same dimension. The design appears to be somewhat curious. It is thus described in a Manchester paper :—" The style of architecture is Roman Corinthian. The front to Grosvenor-square has a portico in antis, with Corinthian columns and pilasters at each angle, surmounted by two cupolas, which are to be executed in stone. The novelty of this part of the design is much more remarkable than either its appropriateness or its success. Not only are turrets or cupolas at the base angles of the pediment of a Grecian building wholly unauthorised in architecture, but they are totally opposed to the principles upon which its beauty depends. And, in the present case, there is the further objection that the turrets are themselves exceedingly ugly piles, and, with their heavy and clumsy pillars, and massive buttresses, are about as little suited to the light and graceful elegance of a Corinthian building as anything that can well be imagined. Besides, the architects have not merely introduced turrets into the design, but they actually seem intending to bind them together by a blank curtain wall, thus giving to the edifice a square instead of an angular termination; and producing, as it seems to us, a most clumsy and awkward effect. We would fain hope that it is not yet too late to re-consider these parts of the design; for we are sure that the edifice would be much improved by their omission." The architects are Messrs. Starkey and Cuffley, of Manchester.

ANOTHER PAVEMENT AT CIRENCESTER. —We learn that on Wednesday in last week *another pavement* was discovered at Cirencester,—making the sixth that has been found upon the spot that has recently excited so much interest.

CUTTING BUILDERS AND ARCHITECTS.

SIR,—In your columns I frequently find the architects individually descanting upon the subject of competitions. I much wish that the whole profession would feel it to be their duty as well as their advantage to promote the interests of the respectable portion of the building trade in every branch, by strenuously refusing in all competitions to superintend the execution of works under the lowest estimate, unless it is in their opinion adequate to afford a remunerating profit to an expert tradesman. In the present state of things, the profession must be fully aware, from their experience and knowledge of the cost of material and labour, that " blind or roguish builders " are running away with a great portion of the business, and I regret to add of my own knowledge, that it is in a great measure attributable to the readiness with which the profession fall into the plan (or advise employers) of obtaining competition for everything, thus inducing even the most respectable established tradesman to unnecessarily curtail his profit, in the hope of keeping his customer. As to a combination of the building trade, it is completely out of the question while so many are to be found who look to the bankruptcy and insolvent courts as the only mode of settling with their creditors, and also when gentlemen taking houses allow themselves to be duped into the mode of employing the merely office-keeping house-agents with which the town abounds, to get the repairs and decorations done for them,— men who, totally ignorant of the nature of the business, or the quality of a single article used, let out the work to poor competing task-masters, at an enormous profit to themselves, and very generally at a loss, or near a kin to it, to the poor fellow employed, while the gentleman gets his work but half, or very superficially executed, but which he does not discover until some time after he has paid for it.

A BUILDER.

MR. JOHN WOOLLEY.—Some of our readers will hear with regret of the premature death of Mr. John Woolley. Mr. Woolley was a highly accomplished member of the profession, and an excellent man; had he been led to practice (his circumstances rendered it unnecessary), he would have distinguished himself in his art. He was a member of the Council of the Institute. We lose in him an amiable friend.

MANAGEMENT OF COMPETITIONS.

Sir,—That not only some few, but nearly the whole, of the profession should be slumbering—still putting up with the direful losses and insults hourly offered them by committees, through the medium of "competitions," is astonishing. But the truth is, they are as sheep without a shepherd; wandering about, as if there were no end to their journey; keeping up a harassing warfare with the enemy; constantly suffering by travelling in mere foraging parties, instead of uniting together as brothers under one banner, and fighting in one rank against their common oppressor. They have forgotten that "Union is strength;" or, if borne in mind, their practice is essentially different from the precept. Let it be so no longer: let the shrill blast of the trumpet, blown through the organs of The Builder, be heard through the length and breadth of the land; and, above all, let it be responded to. If one "monster meeting" is too inconvenient, let each county assemble at each county town, and there, with united voice, for ever put an end to competitions, if found unable to alter them. But this extreme course will hardly be found necessary. Resolutions can be come to, placing the matter on its proper footing. Then, and not till then, will competition be valuable. When that happy period shall arrive, we may look for a new and glorious era in architecture. It is to be hoped that the "Institute" will show that it is really what it professes; otherwise the Architectural Association will reap the laurels, and wear them with honour. Each of these meetings should be put in communication with the London meeting, and the whole body organized. As one suggestion, I would recommend a resolution to the effect that a plan and elevation of the selected design in every competition be engraved by the committee, and distributed to every competitor. W. W.

DRAINAGE OF LONDON PLANS.

The following note gives the substance of five others received by us:—Will you kindly inquire how it is that parties who are desirous to compete for the drainage of London are not furnished with the necessary preliminary information, as it was stated would be afforded them by the metropolitan commissioners? It appears to me now, that although this step (taken two years too late) has the semblance of an open question, there is still an under current at work that will render it almost a mere waste of time entering into such a competition. I think the question of the entire drainage, &c., of London is one of so much importance that the plans submitted should be referred to a competent board of civil engineers—say the council of the Institute, notwithstanding it does not exactly coincide with a theory widely promulgated. If any proof were wanting of the correctness of this opinion, it is the fact that the quasi-scientific mountain (alias the Metropolitan Commission) has been in labour nearly two years, and has produced something less than a mouse.

NEW SCHOOLS AT WALSALL.

The Free Grammar Schools at Walsall were founded by Queen Mary, and are divided into grammar and commercial schools, under the control of ten governors. New buildings for this foundation are now in progress, under the superintendence of Mr. E. Adams, architect. They comprise a school-room for 150 boys with an open loggia underneath of equal area, a board-room (20 by 16), class-room (30 by 16), and two assembling-rooms (each 20 by 16); also three houses for the masters: the first master's house contains twelve rooms, the second master's nine rooms, and the third master's six rooms; this is exclusive of cellarage to each house.

The principal frontage is 148 feet long. The dimensions of the school-room are 70 feet by 30 feet, by 30 feet in height.

The buildings are Tudor in character, faced with picked red bricks, and the quoins, mouldings, &c., are of stone.

The whole of the works, including 880 feet in length of fence walling and several thousand yards of earthwork, are contracted for by Mr. Highway, of Walsall, for the sum of 4,530*l.*, exclusive, however, of the stoves, chimney-pieces, and desks in school-rooms.

COST OF WORKHOUSES.

A correspondent has handed us the following statement:—

The cost of the whole of the workhouses erected by order of the Poor-law Commissioners in the years 1836-7-8-9 (when materials were much more expensive than at the present time) was as follows:—

	Number of Workhouses built.	No. of inmates.	Cost.	Average per head.
1836	127	36,056	£659,154	£18 5
1837	86	21,132	403,342	19 1
1838	92	20,862	404,179	19 7
1839	18	4,425	87,917	19 17
				£76 10

being an average of 19*l.* 2*s.* 6*d.* per inmate.

METROPOLITAN COMMISSION OF SEWERS.

A general court was held on Thursday last, at the Court-house, Greek-street, Soho-square. The Earl of Carlisle in the chair.—A report was presented by Messrs. Lovick and Cresy, on the present state and proposed drainage of the Potteries, Kensington.—Mr. Leslie urged that the improvement of this locality should be carried out by the owners of the property, which view was concurred in by Mr. Lambert Jones.

Mr. Chadwick vindicated the principle which had been agreed upon in the case of the drainage of Gulston-street, Jennings's-buildings, and also with regard to Sydenham. Besides, insurmountable difficulties presented themselves in the way of ownership, as the holdings were so various that in many cases improvements charged upon the owners would amount to a confiscation of the rents for the whole term of their ownership.

Mr. Leslie replied, and contended that before moving in these matters, they ought to determine the questions of the outfalls, water supply, and house drainage. He also ridiculed the idea of this court going into the money-market to borrow every 40*l.* or 50*l.* required for this purpose.

Mr. Chadwick justified the use of tubular drainage, as laid down in the Cloisters, Westminster, Gulston-street, and other neighbourhoods, by means of which the localities were kept quite clear, which previously required (the Cloisters, for instance) 400 loads of refuse to be removed to the Thames.—The report was finally ordered to be printed.—In answer to a question, Mr. Gotto stated that no steps whatever had been taken with regard to the proposed works for Jennings's-buildings, Kensington, or with those for Carner-street, St. Giles's.

Mr. Lambert Jones complained that no relief was afforded to the inhabitants of Holloway, who had for years been rated to the sewers-rates, while attention was given to districts that had never paid one farthing towards them.

The Sheen District.—In reference to a recommendation of the Works Committee, that Messrs. Donaldson and Bazalgette's application as to the employment of levellers, and making trial-pits in the Sheen district, be acceded to,

Mr. Leslie wished to know how it was that these levels could not be obtained from the Ordnance?—Mr. Austin said the levels had certainly been taken by the Ordnance, but points of connection would be required, and he thought tracings of them might be obtained.

Mr. Jones said the officers of the commission were engaged in the out districts, such as Sydenham, Richmond, and other healthy places, while those who were suffering from want of drainage were neglected.

The Earl of Carlisle believed that it would be desirable to proceed with all speed in those places that had long contributed to the rates, but, at the same time, they could not shut their eyes to the claims of some of the outer districts, such as Brentford, Richmond, and other places, which were the seats of cholera and disease.

The recommendation was then agreed to.

Mile-end New Town.—A report was presented by Mr. J. Roe, on the drainage of Mile-end New Town, which stated that cholera and other diseases existed there to a great extent. There were 71 cesspools, which were filled to overflowing with the most offensive exhalations. It recommended that certain improvements be effected, to be defrayed by means of an improvement rate.—Dr. S. Smith bore testimony to the necessity of immediate measures for the improvement of this district, and the recommendation was put and unanimously agreed to.

Drainage of Richmond.—A letter was received from the authorities of Richmond, who concurred in the recommendation of Mr. G. Donaldson for the drainage of the neighbourhood.—Mr. Chadwick moved a series of resolutions, to the effect that a system of tubular pipes be constructed, that the amount of money necessary be borrowed on the credit of the rates, and that tubular permeable drains be laid down.—Agreed to.

Mr. Bullar, in reference to certain resolutions he intended to move on the subject of house drainage, said he would rather that they should stand on the paper as notice of motion.—Mr. Chadwick believed the subject was of great importance, and that a determination upon it would be gladly received by the builders of the country, and he had the opinion of the chairman of the Carpenter's Society in favour of that course.—Postponed.—The next motion on the paper was a notice given by Mr. Leslie,—"That the Trial Works Committee, on account of the expenditure and small results, be abolished."

Lord Carlisle trusted that Mr. Leslie would see the propriety of postponing his motion until that committee had made their report.—Mr. L. said he was quite willing to do so if there was a prospect of that report being presented within a week.

The Rev. Edward Murray said their report would be presented with the least possible delay, but he was unable to speak in behalf of the other members of the Committee: he could not promise that the report would be presented within that time. He was not, however, aware of what information was sought, or what explanations were required.—Mr. L. said then in that case he thought he had better proceed with his motion.

Mr. Bullar then rose, and said that if that motion was proceeded with, he should feel it to be his duty to move an amendment upon it, the terms of which he would read, viz.—"That the existing Metropolitan Sewers Commission be superseded with the least practicable delay."

The Earl of Carlisle believed the Committee very properly objected to presenting their report, until they obtained all the information they required, and thought the motion should be postponed until that period arrived.—After conversation, the motion was postponed til the next court.

The Experiments of the Trial Committee.—Mr. Leslie complained of the acts of two members of the Committee, in expending a sum of money in erecting a ventilating shaft at Bermondsey, although at the last Court it had been determined that no expense should be incurred for that purpose.

Mr. Murray justified the acts of the committee, and said it was in consequence of the very pressing solicitation of the deputation from Bermondsey as to immediate measures, and the success that had followed the adoption of a ventilating shaft in Harley-street, that the experiment had been tried in this neighbourhood.

A statement of the cost of the experiments was ordered to be laid before the next Court.

Several works were ordered, and the Court adjourned.

Books.

The First Principles of Artificial Manuring. A lecture by John Ryan, L.L.D., M.D. Simpkin and Marshall. London: 1849.

The object of this lecture is first to inquire into the principal causes of the conditions which are denominated *sterility* and *fertility*; and secondly, to discuss the means of preventing the one and of rendering permanent the other. Dr. Ryan has carried out this intention in a perspicuous and simple manner, and the pamphlet is calculated to remove many erroneous notions in respect of artificial manures; and, by showing how entirely the physical and chemical condition of the soil may be changed, lead our agriculturists to take science to their aid and effect most profitable improvements.

Miscellanea.

Galloway's Rotary Engine. — Mr. Elijah Galloway, C.E., in claiming the invention of a rotary engine, of the patent for which the Hon. Captain Fitzmaurice holds a share, and under whose name the invention had been noticed in the *Times*,—in the same paper remarks that he is induced, on public grounds, to make the claim, as he perceives a growing practice among the assignees of patents to give the invention their own names, which appears to him just as reasonable as if we only knew Bolton in the steam-engine, or the publishers, Murray and Constable, in the works of Byron and of Scott. Mr. Galloway declares, that in this way he had already lost all nominal honour in 'Morgan's wheel' or feathering paddle, though himself the inventor.

PROJECTED WORKS.—Advertisements have been issued for tenders, by a date not specified, for the erection of industrial schools, &c., in St. Pancras parish; by 1st October, for re-building Great Shelford Vicarage; by 22nd inst., for the erection of a new school-house, with boundary wall, at Godmanchester; by 6th October, for the works connected with the building of a bank and dwelling-house, at Carlisle; by 26th inst., for the erection of schools, dormitories, workshops, &c., for 600 children, at Penge, Surrey; by 27th, for 1,800 tons of rails, 700 tons of chairs, and 60,000 sleepers, &c., for the Birkenhead, Lancashire, and Cheshire Railway; by 1st October, for the supply of flints, whinstone, granite, &c., for St. George the Martyr, Southwark; by 26th inst., for making the turnpike road from Tinsley to Sheffield, and repairs; by 9th October, for pig lead and white lead, for Navy dock-yards; by 25th, for the erection of two third-rate houses at Whitechapel; and by 10th October, for building an infirmary, with laundry wash-house, &c., for the St. Olave Union Workhouse, Southwark.

RAILWAY JOTTINGS.—The contract for the various works in making the Blyth and Tyne Railway, including the large viaduct over the river Blyth, near to Blyth, has been taken by Mr. Richard Cail, of Newcastle.——Third-class carriages are to be attached to the trains leaving London and Edinburgh every Saturday, so that the working classes can go through either way for 30s.——A correspondent of the *Aberdeen Herald* reports the fall of two or more arches of a railway bridge across the Bervie, on the north of Scotland route. The same work, it is stated, had been already "altered from its foundations from Mr. Gibb's plan, by the new engineers." It would appear, however, that the bridge is not of stone.——The engine drivers on the Eastern Counties line have intimated that they will leave the line unless a stop be put to a system of discharging the experienced hands so soon as they reach, in the company's own scale of wages, 7s. 6d. a-day, and substituting young firemen then at 4s. 6d. to 5s. 6d. a-day. The drivers dread that a clean sweep of the whole corps is thus contemplated, in their dismissal so soon as they have successively reached that settled point of increase in their wages treacherously set before them, like the good things before the eyes of the poor donkey, stuck on the point of its own rider's stick, as an inducement to get on.——The net work of railways in France covers an extent of 5,525 kilometres, of which 2,888 are, or soon will be, ready for traffic. The total sum to be expended is 53,535,000 f., of which 59 per cent. has already been expended.

DRAINAGE OF TOWNS.—The expense of putting Worcester into good sanitary condition has been estimated by Mr. Austin at 47,000*l.*, including 23,000*l.* for machinery and works for collecting and distributing the city sewage for agricultural purposes, and also 10,000*l.* for the erection of baths and washhouses.——A survey of sewers and drains at Sheffield is in progress, with the view of ascertaining the best mode of securing an uninterrupted efflux of their contents into a capacious general outlet proposed to be opened to the Don at Attercliffe. —— The complete sewerage of Winchester, according to a semi-official announcement, will cost 4,500*l.*——A company has been established at Leeds for the purpose of converting the contents of the sewers, cesspools, &c., into manure.

WINDOW SASHES FOR LUNATIC ASYLUMS, &c.—Mr. Thomas Melling, of the Rainhill Iron-works, near Liverpool, has taken out a patent for a new arrangement of apparatus for window sashes, in lieu of sash weights and pulleys, by which space is open for ventilation, while the possibility of escape through such opening, or persons entering from without, is precluded. A rack is fastened on the inside of each outer rail of the upper sash, and also on the outside of the lower one. A shaft crosses the centre of the window frame between the two sashes, at each end of which is fixed a pinion, which takes into the two pairs of racks, by which arrangement, on raising the lower sash by the action of the racks and pinions, the upper one is lowered to the same extent, and, according to the length of the rack, the spaces for the admission of air may be regulated to any width required.

THE METROPOLITAN FEVER-STILLS.—The Board of Health seem to be now fully awake to the necessity of suppressing these loathsome cancers in the midst of human vitality. They have issued a notification to churchwardens, overseers, and other persons, on the subject, intimating that they are prepared to adopt measures for the prevention of intramural interments, wherever, on the report of an inspector, based on the Nuisances Removal and Diseases Prevention Act, it shall appear that danger to health results, but recommending their voluntary abandonment forthwith. The board is also otherwise vigorously at work in the promotion of sanitary reform. They have just instituted a prosecution against the City Guardians, one and all, for neglecting their orders on various points. The people themselves are astir for the immediate suppression of intramural burial. A meeting of the "Metropolitan Society" for this abolition was held in Blackfriars on the 18th inst., when our suggestion to memorialize the Home Secretary for an Order in Council for their suppression was adopted. The press and its correspondents are also beginning to insist on the same course.

PROVINCIAL.—The value of house property in Lincoln has of late, it is said, been seriously on the decline. Some premises worth near 3,000*l.* last year have recently sold for 1,900*l.* This state of things has been attributed to the alleged *artificial* value of such property formerly; a way of putting it which seems to make little difference as regards the fact of the decline.——We hear that in the Thetford Abbey grounds articles of archæological interest are daily turning up. An explanation of them will be given at the joint meeting of the Suffolk and Norfolk Archæological Societies on 27th inst. The base of two columns on the sides of the principal arch, a Roman pavement with tiles coloured and glazed, and a tomb, at present unopened, have been already it seems discovered.——The works for erecting St. George's schools, Sunderland, were let on the 18th inst. The design includes a classical school, girls' school, and three class-rooms, on the ground-floor, and one large general school with simultaneous gallery in the transept, formed over the class-rooms, on the upper floor. The upper school is to have an open timber roof. The style selected is the palazzo Italian, and the whole of the building is to be of stone. Mr. Oliver is the architect.——The operations for the projected improvement of Princes-street Gardens, Edinburgh, are now in progress. Estimates for the terrace, parapets, and stairs are being obtained, and meanwhile the terrace ground is being laid out on the north side and a retaining wall built on the south.

THE SOMERSETSHIRE ARCHÆOLOGICAL SOCIETY will hold their first general meeting at the Assembly-rooms, Taunton, on the 26th inst.

MANCHESTER CATHEDRAL.—Mr. Gregan and Mr. Bellhouse have issued a report on the cathedral, showing the miserable and dilapidated state of the stone-work in general. It is to be hoped this will lead to restoration.

BLIND BUILDERS.—On the 10th, at the office of Mr. G. Allin, architect, St. Ives, were opened the following tenders for the restoration of the exterior of the parish church of Hilton, Hunts:—

Parker, Thrapston	£311
David	288
Cade, Alconbury	270
Beldom, Fenstanton	266
Smallbones, St. Ives	256
Smith and Co., Fenstanton	255
Bunting and Harrison, ditto	231
Harrat and Bland, Huntingdon	150

The following is a list of tenders opened for repewing, &c., the Independent Chapel, St. Ives:—

Parker, Thrapston	£472
Mills, Whittlesea	399
Harrat and Bland, Huntingdon	295

Tenders for labour of masonry and bricklaying for four houses, for Mr. Clark, Sunderland: Mr. Oliver, architect:—

Heron and Keall	£245
Simby	219
Forster	208
Walker (accepted)	126
Parkin	119

ARMSTRONG'S HYDRO-ELECTRIC ENGINE.—We lately witnessed the wonderful power of this machine at the Polytechnic Institution, Regent-street. As there remarked by the lecturer, the *old* machine used at that institution in exemplification of the great power of electricity, large and astonishing as its results once appeared, is a mere toy in comparison with this potent rival. And yet it is but a small locomotive boiler. It is mounted on six glass pillars, and contains its fire in the interior. Along the upper part of one side is a numerous series of jet pipes, through which the steam rushes, and in which, condensing into water it evolves the electricity. These jets are worked by handles on the opposite side, so as to allow of either the whole power, or a part only, being set on. The long streaks of light which shoot from all parts of the surface when a sparking rod is directed towards the boiler, can no longer, with the least propriety, go under the name of mere *sparks*—they are no mean semblance of the forked lightning of nature itself, and our *respect* for the dartings, which were displayed in darkness, was by no means diminished by the dread shriek of "hell in harness," which ever accompanies them here, as the storm-shriek often does in nature's lightning-play. A powerful battery of the usual order is charged by this machine in a moment almost, suddenly exploding bell wires into smoke. The *Gateshead Observer*, in giving us a recent account of an Armstrong, states that it was constructed at Louis Philippe's order for the Academy of Sciences at Paris, and that the republic having adopted it, Mr. H. Watson, of Highbridge, Newcastle, the manufacturer, is about to send it off to Paris. It will be the most powerful one yet made. We may here record our belief that the ultimate purpose and utility of such machines have not been yet realized, any more than have the limits of their power.

THE EXCAVATIONS AT BURY ST. EDMUND'S.—The whole plan of the prior's house is now laid open. The workmen, amongst other relics, have dug out a small cesspool with an oblique shoot from it, thought to have belonged to a piscina drain. Part of a passage paved with encaustic tiles has also been exposed, and several curious specimens of painted glass, one with a layer of shining substance between two flakes of glass, have been found, as also skeletons, coins, &c. The Archæological Committee speak of opening the entire ruins of the abbey, if possible.

MANCHESTER ART-UNION.—Following the example set by the London Art-Union, the committee of this association have this year determined to distribute, in addition to pictures, a quantity of statuettes in Parian and Carrara porcelain, including some impressions of a statuette of Sabrina, from the marble statue by Marshall.

POSITION OF NEW CEMETERIES.—As there is now a probability that some step will be taken to provide against future intramural burials by the establishment of cemeteries in the country surrounding this great metropolis, and other large cities and towns, I would suggest, that no Company should be allowed by the Legislature to establish a cemetery without purchasing sufficient land around it, to be for ever kept free from any habitable building, save and except the tenement necessary for the person who might be required to superintend the cultivation of such land, or to look after the plantation if it be so laid out. I am the more led to this opinion and suggestion from an advertisement which I saw in the *Times*, offering to the notice of such companies a desirable plot of ground at Lower Norwood, near Crown-hill, and stating as a desideratum that such plot was pleasantly bounded by some gentleman's pleasure-grounds,—a very great inducement, I should think, for the said gentleman to purchase the said plot by way of keeping his pleasure-grounds from contiguity with a burial-ground.

J. Y.

P.S. A medical friend of mine, to whom I mentioned this subject, remarked, that Government might convert the Isle of Dogs into a public cemetery, and I have to observe, that there is an excellent and silent highway to it,—the Thames,—and wharves on both its banks, from which a steamer appropriated for that purpose might convey the corpse and mourners at a very moderate expense.

Imports and Exports of Iron in 1848.—From a Parliamentary return, it appears that the quantity of foreign iron, chiefly Swedish and Russian, imported in 1848, was 23,869 tons bar-iron, 464 tons blooms, 257 tons old iron, and 28,891*l.* odds in value of wrought-iron and steel. The quantity of foreign bar-iron exported was 3,432 tons, of steel unwrought 340 tons, of wrought-iron and steel, value 11,560*l.* The value of foreign iron retained for home consumption was 17,331*l.* Of British iron exported, chiefly to the United States, Holland, Iceland, Denmark, &c. &c., there were 175,650 tons pig, 32,135 tons bar, 17,554 tons bolt and rod, 19,371 tons cast, 76,365 tons wrought, and 61,913 tons steel unwrought, besides 1,913 tons wire and 7,241 tons old iron. The exports of British hardware and cutlery amounted to 18,105 tons, value 1,860,150*l.*, chiefly to America and Canada, East Indies, &c. Of British machinery and mill-work, the value of exports was 817,656*l.*, chiefly to Russia, Spain, Italy, Hans Town, France, Brazil, &c.

Employment of Architects: Exeter Architectural Society.—The council of this society, in their last report, say:—"Your committee have again, as on several former occasions, received applications for gratuitous plans for the whole or for a portion of churches. They have been obliged, in all these cases, to return a negative answer to the application, on the principle of not interfering with the exertions of professional men, especially as the constant and careful supervision of an experienced architect is as necessary to the satisfactory completion of a work as the promising of a suitable design. There will be always something occurring to call forth the genius of a living mind, and it is in the wise meeting of difficulties that skill is mainly shown; the difference between working by architect and by published plans is similar in kind to that between ornaments carved by hand and those stamped by machinery,—the latter must be a faithful copy of the stamp, but it is a mere lifeless reproduction of one type,—the other has more light and shadow, greater variety of design, and greater freedom in execution, while a due appreciation of the principles of Christian art will effectually check the danger of variety changing into what is opposite in kind, or of freedom degenerating into licentiousness. It needs a living architect to give life to a design; it also needs the recognition of well-defined principles of Christian architecture to inspire and to direct, to spur and to rein, the architect in his conception of a successful work."

Mosaic Glass.—We have lately been favoured with a sight of a work of art quite novel. It is called mosaic glass, and is adapted to many different purposes—church windows and church decorations, shop windows, and fan lights, window blinds, staircase windows, &c. It is equal in beauty and transparency to the most brilliant stained glass, and the designs for window blinds and other purposes are very rich. It has been brought out and patented at considerable expense and with much labour; but we have no doubt the company will be amply rewarded, for it requires only to be seen to be appreciated. It is produced at one-sixth the cost of stained glass; but it is not unlikely that its price will be enhanced when it has become well known, as the demand will be great. For church windows it is admirable, from the variety and beauty of the designs; and of its durability, the mode of combining the colour with the glass is a sufficient guarantee. It is also brought out in labels to a large extent, and, indeed, the variety of purposes to which it is applicable is very great.—*Leeds Intelligencer.*

Immense Block of Granite.—Last week a "muckle hole" (a term used by the quarriers of stone) was put down 15 feet deep through solid granite, in one of the quarries of Stithians, near Penryn, belonging to Mr. Elliot, of the latter place. Only 25 lbs. of powder were deposited, which being blasted was found to have thrown off from its bed and side joints a block containing 20,300 cubic feet, or 1,400 tons, of excellent quality and blue colour, thus enabling the workmen to cut blocks of any dimensions required.—*West Briton.*

The Brigg Corn-Exchange Competition has been decided in favour of Messrs. Lockwood and Mawson, architects, of Hull; and the works are to progress immediately.

Spanish Churches.—A foreign correspondent of the *Athenæum*, writing from Saragossa, says:—"A leading feature in Spanish churches is always the 'retablo,' a huge erection of carving, gilding, and painting in wood or stone, rising immediately behind the high altar, generally to the height of the roof. This 'retablo' is often very handsome in its way; but to those acquainted with the fine churches of the north of Europe, it must ever appear a miserable substitute for the beautiful east window or windows which it supersedes. The *Lady-chapel*, together with the range of chapels circling behind the high altar, which form so exquisitely beautiful a feature in many of our cathedrals, is almost always wanting in the north of Spain; possibly because the entire church is but a *Lady-chapel* in this land of ultra-Marialatry. Thus the 'retablo' generally forms the eastern extremity of the building. The inclosed choir is often an eye-sore in our churches—it is yet more so in those of Spain. Placed generally from the altar, it is often near the west end of the nave; and consists of a solidly walled inclosure, which blocks up and embarrasses the perspective of the church sadly. It is shut in at the eastern end by an iron railway—'reja'—often magnificently worked, with a gate in the middle opposite to the altar."

North Surrey Industrial Schools.—In consequence of the calamitous occurrence at the late Mr. Drouet's school at Tooting, the guardians of the poor-law unions forming the North Surrey district resolved to form a school district and to erect suitable buildings. For this purpose fifty acres of land have been purchased, adjoining the Anerley station of the Croydon Railway, at Penge, Surrey, and tenders have been advertized for, to carry out designs prepared for the building by Mr. Charles Lee. The establishment is to be industrial, to have accommodation for 250 boys, 210 girls, and 140 infants, with three school-rooms and class-rooms, with apartments for steward, matron, three school-masters, and three school-mistresses, with dining-room, chapel, chaplain's-room, board-room, kitchens, bakery, offices, lavatories, baths, and workshops; also separate laundry-building, with all the necessary rooms attached thereto for drying, ironing, &c.; likewise a detached infirmary building, having all the requisite wards, nurses' rooms, kitchen, washhouse, surgery, &c.; there are to be also farm-buildings, so that the boys may be instructed not only in trades, but in farming operations, and the girls in dairy-work as well as in cooking, household-work, and needle-work.

New Church of St. Peter, at Croydon.—A few days ago the foundation-stone of this church was laid by Mr. George Robert Smith, the banker, whose seat is at Selsdon, within the parish, the Rev. John George Hodgson, the vicar of Croydon, officiating. The site is very picturesque, on the side of a hill, ornamented with some good elms, and well seen from the Brighton Railway on the right, as it emerges from the cutting south of the Croydon station. The church is in the Early Decorated style, with aisles, south porch, and tower at the west end of nave, and is to accommodate 800 persons. The spire will be of shingle, the walls of flint, with facings of Maidstone stone. The site has been liberally presented by Mr. John Russell, the owner of the surrounding property. The architect is Mr. Scott. The church is to be built by contract, for which tenders have been made in consequence of advertisement, and we understand that eleven tenders were received, varying in amount from 6,893*l.* to 12,913*l.*, and with variations also according to specified difference of materials. The two lowest tenders were by Mr. Myers and Mr. Wm. Harris; the former being lower in some respects and the latter in others. Mr. Harris being a townsman, the contract was given to him.

Baths and Washhouses.—At a meeting of the Works Committee of the Goulston-square model establishment, on 6th instant, returns were read, from which it appears that from 26th July, 1847, to 31st December, 1848, the number of bathers was 81,694, and the receipts 914*l.* 19s. 1d.; and that thence to 1st instant, the number of bathers was 82,219, and the receipts 1,058*l.* 1s. 7d. During the latter period the number of baths to men was 77,831,—to women, 3,187,—to children (sometimes four together) 1,201; and the weekly average was—to men, 2,223; women, 91; children, 35: weekly receipts, 30*l.* 5s. 4d. That even these encouraging returns were limited by the accommodation, appears from another return, showing, that since all the baths have been brought into use, there was an increase of 36,679 bathers during the three last months, over those during the same months of last year. In the washing department, since 30th April last, the number of washers, to 1st instant, was 3,013; and the number of driers the same; the number of hours' washing and drying being 10,005—average 3 hrs. 20 min. to each washer and drier. No ironing appears to have been done.

Baths and Washhouses, Liverpool.—A third suite of baths and washhouses have been ordered to be erected by the health committee, from plans proposed by the borough engineer. The site selected is at the junction of Cornwallis-street and Leveson-street, which forms the east corner of the spacious square inclosing St. Michael's Church and cemetery. The building, we are told, is designed in the simplest Italian style, two stories in height, and with projecting roof, and includes first, second, and third-class baths, and two classes of washing stalls, each of which will be distinct and separate from the rest, "with improved and original contrivances for wringing and drying the clothes."

Welbeck.—The Duke of Portland has long contemplated a great work, which is now in the course of being vigorously prosecuted. This is the erection of a bridge over the Welbeck lake head, near what is called Mosshall and the Dogkennels. Masons are daily expected from London, and a good deal of stone has been already got and hewn ready in blocks of various dimensions. The high hill, at Whitwell, has supplied some much more preferable to the Anston stone, it is said, which has been so much called for for the new Parliament Houses.—*Derby Courier.*

Manchester Borough Gaol.—The new prison at Manchester, alluded to by us some time since, is now nearly completed. It is stated that the cost of it will be about 120,000*l.*, and it is calculated to accommodate 500 prisoners. The cost, per individual, will therefore be 240*l.* About two years have been occupied in raising it. The boundary wall of the gaol incloses almost ten acres of ground, of which 5,641 square yards are occupied by the prison building, the remainder being exercising grounds, yards, &c.

A Wire Suspension Bridge has been thrown across the Ohio. It is 1,010 feet in length.

The Iron-roof, Lime-street Station, Liverpool.—At a meeting of the Liverpool Polytechnic Society, held last week, Mr. Turner, of Dublin, who is constructing the new galvanised iron roofing and other iron works of the Lime-street railway station, furnished the meeting with the following particulars:—The roof covers an area of 6,140 square yards, being about 360 feet in length, and 153 feet 6 inches in width. There are no intermediate columns; but this great space is spanned over by one stupendous arch, rising in a segment of a circle, to a central height of 30 feet from the spring or chord. The roof consists of 17 curved girders of wrought-iron, resting at one side upon the walls of the offices, and at the other upon cast-iron columns of the Doric order, connected by ornamental arches, in perforated iron. These girders are trussed vertically by a series of radiating struts, acted upon by the bars connected with the extremities of the girders; and they are trussed horizontally by a series of purlins and diagonal rods, thus forming one rigid piece of framing from end to end. Upon this framing will be laid plates of galvanized corrugated iron, and three ranges of plate-glass (in sheets about 12 feet 6 inches in length, and of great thickness), extending the whole length of the roof. In consequence of the great extent of surface exposed to the variations of temperature, provision has been made for expansion and contraction of the iron without injury to its bearings. The roof, when finished, will weigh about 700 tons. The whole of the work, with the exception of the cast-iron columns and ornamental arches, is of wrought-iron. The iron columns upon which the roof rests on the south side of the yard are 2 feet 3 inches in diameter at their bases. Six of the girders are fixed, and the centres struck.

TO CORRESPONDENTS.

Received.—" C. R. C." (we shall be glad to receive it), " J. J. M.," " W. McL.," " J.," " R. J. W.," " X. Y. Z." (we have not yet seen it), " *Rus in urbe*," " Lover of Justice," " S. D." (we are unable to name a matter for the purpose. Do not give up your trade. Personal application at school is all that is necessary), " E. C. M.," " J. T." (we cannot recommend), " A Subscriber," " J. M. L.," " Amicus " (should apply to the editor of the *Literary Gazette*), " Calorus," " Mr. J." (thanks), " F. L.," " V. Y.," " Londoner," " G. F. J.," " J. A." we have not received list of tenders for railway sheds, &c., at Boston), " W. R.," " W. H. L.," " E. B.," " S. P.," Ringwood (the number is out of print), " Young Carpenter " (we are compelled to decline. The number of Inquiries to some effect would occupy more time than we could afford), " Young Architect " (ditto), " B. B." (ditto), " M." (ditto), " R. P.," " T. O.," " J. M." (safely received); " Pure Water for London," by T. D. Liberty; London, Pipel, Paternoster-row, 4d.; " The Choirs: the Claims of the Poor upon the Rich," by Thomas Beggs; London, Gilpin, Bishopsgate Without; " A Manual for the Study of the Sepulchral Slabs and Crosses of Middle Ages," by the Rev. E. L. Cutts, B.A.; London, J. H. Parker, Strand.

NOTICE.—All communications respecting *advertisements* should be addressed to the " Publisher," and not to the " Editor;" all other communications should be addressed to the EDITOR, and *not* to the Publisher.

ADVERTISEMENTS.

No. CCCXLVII.

SATURDAY, SEPTEMBER 29, 1849.

OME of our correspondents express surprise that we have not given a decided opinion on the question pending between the Architect of the new Houses of Parliament and the Government, as to the amount of remuneration which he should receive for his past services, "as the general question of payment to architects so materially affects the whole profession." We need not tell our old readers, that on the general question of architects' remuneration we have repeatedly spoken, and that in our volumes will be found a considerable amount of information on the subject. We have, again and again, called the attention of the profession to the present unsettled state in which the question rests, and have shown the evils of the 5 per cent. system, as well as its advantages, and the position of architects who so make their charge, when they are obliged to go into a court of law to recover payment for their services. It seems clear that the amount of the commission, *as a commission, cannot be recovered*,—that simply proving to a jury that 5 per cent. is the customary charge will not suffice to insure a verdict. Evidence must be given that the sum claimed is a fair compensation for the skill and labour employed in the particular case.

In the case of Mair against Ward, it will be remembered, the plaintiff charged 5 per cent. commission on the amount expended, his travelling expenses, and two guineas a-day for the time *occupied in travelling*. The witnesses proved that the principle on which he claimed payment was universally acted on by the profession, *and* that the work done was worth the money. The jury gave the plaintiff all he went for. A new trial was demanded, on the ground that, as the "particular" claimed the money entirely in the character of a per-centage, and as, according to the opinion of Lord Denman, the claim could not be allowed upon that ground, the jury, not having the power to go beyond the particular, ought to have found a verdict for the defendant. The new trial, however, was refused; the court, after deliberation, decided, that although the jury rejected the claim as grounded upon the commission, they were justified in awarding the money as a compensation for labour.*

Returning to Mr. Barry's dispute with the Government, however, and which, we may mention, still remains unsettled, the general question,—the propriety or otherwise of charging 5 per cent. on the amount expended, is not at issue. A statement of the architect's case will be found at p. 341 of our present volume, and it will be there seen that he claims

5 per cent. commission on 841,630*l.*
17s. 11d. £42,081
And for special or extraneous services
during a period of ten years......... 5,256

Making in the whole........... £47,337

To this the commissioners reply, not that a commission is an improper mode of charging, or that the sum named is more than the skill and labour employed are worth,—but that

* See vol. iii., p. 605, and vol. iv., p. 61. Also vol. vi., p. 301. And for a paper on "The Rights and Responsibilities of Architects," p. 350 of our present volume.

the architect had, by *special agreement*, abandoned the accustomed remuneration, and had accepted the fixed sum of 25,000*l.* for "the superintendence, direction, and completion of the proposed edifice," for the express purpose of avoiding what was pointed out to him as being considered by Parliament an objectionable mode of paying architects.

If an architect make an agreement, he is, of course, bound to abide by it. It might even occur that an architect would agree to do certain work for a certain sum, for the purpose of obtaining an employment for himself at the expense of another architect, who might refuse to enter into such an agreement, and it would, of course, be manifestly unjust if he were able afterwards to get rid of the agreement, and claim the usual amount of remuneration.

The question with Mr. Barry turns wholly on the agreement, but even in this light the profession generally are much interested in it,—both as to the effect which such an agreement would have in lessening professional charges generally, and as to the justice of the course pursued by the commissioners to obtain it. When the architects of the United Kingdom submitted their designs for the intended Palace of Parliament in competition, it was, of course, with the expectation that the successful competitor would be employed, and paid as other Government architects always have been paid. Mr. Barry asserts that he was appointed unconditionally to carry his design into effect, at the commencement of 1837, and expected his "remuneration would be of the customary amount," and that he was not informed that the Commissioners of Woods considered 25,000*l.* a fair and reasonable remuneration for what he was about to do, till the 1st of March, 1849, when he had made such costly arrangements to carry on the work, that he could not have relinquished the employment without a considerable sacrifice. He therefore acceded, under a protest "as to the inadequacy of the amount proposed, and with an intimation that he should offer proof of its inadequacy when the building was in such an advanced state as to allow of a competent judgment being formed on the subject." Still, he did accede, and on this the Government rest their objection. It may be said that he did wrong to accede, and there is force in the remark; but the circumstances and the temptation must be duly considered against it.

Apart from this, that Mr. Barry is fully entitled to the usual commission of 5 per cent. none will deny who know the nature of the work, and are competent to judge. Sir Jeffrey Wyatville received 5 per cent. on the amount expended at Windsor Castle, and was *also paid for measuring* the works; Mr. Nash received 5 per cent. for Buckingham Palace; and the superintendence of piles of warehouses and docks are paid for after the same rate.

It must be borne in mind by those who are to legislate on this matter, that the building which Mr. Barry was to see carried out for 25,000*l.* was estimated at 707,000*l.*, and that of the 842,000*l.*, using round numbers, on which the commission is now claimed, Mr. Barry says 370,000*l.* are for works which form *no part* of the original design and estimates. If circumstances led to, or justified a larger outlay than was at first intended,—an outlay ordered or assented to by the Government, and increased by popular approval,—it would be unreasonable to expect that the architect's payment is to remain the same. Some, it is true, plead this increased expenditure as the

fault of the architect, and far from allowing him any commission upon it, would make it a reason for lessening the sum agreed to be paid. That this is the fact has yet to be proved, Mr. Barry denying it vigorously.

The charge against architects for exceeding their estimates is as old as Augustus, and has been repeated in every succeeding century. Thus, John Evelyn, in a dedication to Wren, says:—"I have known some excellent persons abused, who, trusting to the computations of either dishonest or unskilful artists, have been forced to desist, sit down by the loss, and submit to the reproach,—*This man began to build and was not able to finish*. But so, it seems, would not the Greeks suffer themselves to be over-reached, when those great builders, the Ephesians (who knew sufficiently what mischief it was to the public, as well as private men) ordained it for a law, that if a clerk undertook a work, and spent more than by his calculation it would amount to, he should be obliged to make it good out of his own estate; whilst they most liberally and honourably rewarded him, if either he came within what was first designed or did not much exceed it. This was esteemed so reasonable (upon consideration how many noble persons had been undone, and magnificent structures left imperfect) that Vitruvius, writing to the great Augustus concerning this subject, wishes the same law were in force at Rome also."

An architect who gives a false estimate to his employer will find no defender in us, but before condemning we must know that it really *is* false, and, moreover, that he was paid for making a correct one. Our views on this head we have already stated, but we shall take an early opportunity to recur to them, as we shall to the general question of architects' remuneration. The present position of the matter is most unsatisfactory and hurtful both to architecture and its professors. We are not wedded to the per centage system, we have shown many objections against it, one not the least of which is that it gives apparent ground for the calumny, that architects bring upon their employers ruinous expenses, adding useless ornaments and preposterous decorations, for the sake of increasing their own charges,—that they take a hundred pounds out of their employer's pockets that they may put five pounds into their own!

A committee of the Institute, it will be remembered, inquired into the custom of payment, and drew up a report upon it for the use of the members on special application. This, however, was an incomplete and crude document, and an unsatisfactory arrangement, and we urged that they should go more fully into the inquiry, and publish a clear and comprehensive report on it for the information of the public, and the guidance of the profession. We are glad to be informed that they are now about to resume the question, and we shall look anxiously for the result.

THE PARIS ARCHITECTURAL EXHIBITION. —The show made by the architects in the present exhibition of works of modern art in Paris is rather better than it was in 1848. "Workmen's Towns;" Hospitals for "Civil Invalids," a subject referred to four architects by General Cavaignac, when at the head of the Government; the everlasting completion of the Louvre, for which more than fifty architects have made designs since 1799; and new markets—are the principal subjects treated. The gem of the exhibition, according to Mons. A. Lance, in the *Siècle*, is a work by Mons. Jules Bouchet, entitled *Essais de Restaurations*, showing, by eight drawings, Pompeii restored.

TIDAL OBSERVATIONS IN THE RIVER THAMES.

DRAINAGE OF THE METROPOLIS.

A SERIES of tidal observations were made in the River Thames between the 19th June and the 19th July of the present year, in connection with the metropolitan survey. Tidal observations of the kind, taken simultaneously at different stations, and referable to the same datum, are at any time interesting, but at the present time, when the general drainage of the metropolis occupies so large a share of public attention, and when the question of continuing or discontinuing the river as the main sewer in that drainage, must necessarily be discussed in its various hearings, they become of more than ordinary professional interest.

The stations or gauges at which the observations were taken were three in number; one in Deptford-reach, another at London-bridge, and the third at Battersea-pier, near the Red-house. The observations were registered every 10 minutes from 6 a.m. to 6 p.m., and the correct time of each observation was determined by means of a marine chronometer at each station, set to Greenwich mean time.

The zeros of the gauges were connected by careful levelling; hence their relative level as well as that of the surface of the water in the river at all states of the tide was easily ascertainable.

It was found that there was a considerable difference in the time of the high and low water at the three stations. The greatest interval of time between the high water being—Deptford, before London-bridge, 20 minutes, and before Battersea, 45 minutes. The least interval of time of the high water was, Deptford, before London-bridge, 5 minutes, and before Battersea, 30 minutes; and the mean interval of time during the month's observations was, Deptford before London-bridge, 12 minutes, and before Battersea, 36 minutes.

The greatest interval of time between the low water at the three stations was, Deptford, before London-bridge, 55 minutes, and before Battersea, 90 minutes; the least interval of time was, Deptford, before London-bridge, 13 minutes, and before Battersea, 63 minutes; and the mean interval of time during the month's observations, was Deptford before London-bridge, 24 minutes, and before Battersea, 73 minutes. The interesting fact is deduced from this variation of time of high and low water, that the tide is, when near the time of high water, flowing for a period of 30 to 45 minutes in opposite directions, that is to say, at Battersea it is flowing up the river at the same time that it is flowing down the river at Deptford, the intermediate points being affected to a corresponding extent, according to their relative position. The counter currents about the time of low water, continue for a longer period, the current of the ebb stream at Battersea flowing down the river for an hour or an hour and a half after the flood stream has set up the river at Deptford. Hence it appears that about the time of high water, there is a counter tidal current within the limits of dense population, of half an hour or three quarters of an hour in duration; but inasmuch as these opposite currents are separating, or receding from each other, that is, the part highest up the river flowing still higher, while at the places situated lower down the river, the water is flowing towards the sea, it may be supposed that the agitation in the mass of water produced thereby is inconsiderable. In the case of the low water period, however, the matter is very different. Here it will be observed, while the water is at or near its lowest diurnal level, and consequently when all the sewers of the metropolis discharge their contents upon the diminished stream, or upon the half-dried mud which the recession of the tide has left bare, while at the same time a hundred river steamers, and vessels of all kinds and dimensions, are agitating the river, and stirring up the mud from the very bottom of its bed, two opposing currents of the tide are rushing towards each other from Battersea to Deptford, which meet about midway, or somewhere between London and Waterloo-bridges.

The relative level of the high and low water at the different parts of the river, as well as the relative level of the several parts at the same instant of time, during the entire ebb and flow of the tide throughout its whole age, must obviously enter largely into the discussion of any general scheme of sewerage which contemplates using the Thames as the main artery of its system. The following results bear on this point:—

The mean difference of level of the high-water at the three stations was, Deptford lower than London-bridge, 0·25 feet; and higher than Battersea, 1·03 feet. The main difference of the level of the low-water at the three stations was, Deptford lower than London-bridge, 0·59 feet; and lower than Battersea, 1·98 feet.

The greatest range of tide during the month was at	Deptford ..	21·35 feet.
	London-br.	20·65 ,,
	Battersea ..	16·70 ,,
The least range of tide during ditto..........	Deptford ..	14·76 ,,
	London-br.	14·50 ,,
	Battersea ..	12·70 ,,
The mean range of tide during ditto..........	Deptford ..	17·91 ,,
	London-br.	17·51 ,,
	Battersea ..	14·91 ,,
Giving a mean range of tide for the river between Deptford and Battersea of ..		16·78 ,,

This affords fair data for ascertaining the approximate volume of water which ebbs and flows twice a-day, and, consequently, of the quantity to be contaminated by each individual or family of the entire population. The area of the river from Deptford Dockyard to Battersea Pier is about 1,360 acres; and we have in each acre, according to the average range of tide here stated, 730,937 cubic feet, or 4,554,000 gallons, giving a total quantity in the whole area of 6,193,440,000 gallons for a single average tide, or 12,386,880,000 gallons during each twenty-four hours. Now, allowing that the population contaminating this mass of water is 2,000,000, there will be for each individual an average quantity of 6,193 gallons, or upwards of 30,000 gallons for each average family of five persons.

Different minds will draw very different inferences from these matters of fact. Some will say that, with this quantity of water for each individual, or family, it would be utterly impossible to render the whole mass so dangerously polluted as it is stated to be; whilst another class, from their assumed knowledge of numerous collateral and constantly recurring sources of contamination, will probably arrive at a totally opposite conclusion. One thing, however, may be stated as certain—namely, that the whole question cannot be fairly discussed by taking an isolated view of the facts, or with an imperfect knowledge of them.

Great diversity of opinion has been expressed with respect to the quantity of contaminating matter which passes into the Thames from the sewers of the metropolis, and the proportion which it bears to the quantity of water in the river. Mr. Chadwick, at a recent meeting of the Commissioners of Sewers, stated this proportion to be as 1 to 10,000; this, however, can only be taken as a conjecture. The following considerations will aid in forming as correct an opinion upon the subject as the imperfectly known facts will warrant.

The area of the metropolitan district drained by the part of the river Thames here under consideration, is about 24,000 acres, or nearly 40 square miles. The annual quantity of rain falling in the metropolis is about 21 inches, which gives for this area of drainage about 11,397,300,000 gallons. Of this quantity, one-half probably passes away by evaporation, and the other half, or a daily average of about 15,600,000 gallons, passes through the sewers into the Thames.

Another source of supply is from the water pipes. The quantity of water supplied daily by the several water companies to the metropolis in 1833 was stated, before a Parliamentary Committee to be 35,000,000 gallons (a quantity scarcely credible). To this may probably be added, on account of increase of population, &c., 20 per cent., or 7,000,000 gallons, giving a total of 42,000,000 gallons, or 21 gallons daily for each individual, at the present time. Assuming that one-fourth of this quantity passes into the waste pipes, and thence into the sewers, we have 10,500,000 gallons per diem passing into the river from this source, which, added to the average daily quantity of 15,600,000 derived from rain, gives a total daily average of 26,100,000 gallons. Or, adding to this that which is supplied through the natural channels of streams derived from sources exterior to the area of drainage, the average daily quantity may be set down at 30,000,000 gallons supplied from all sources for the cleansing of the sewers. It is, however, obvious that as the portion derived from rain is fluctuating in its supply, although the daily average throughout the year may be 30,000,000 gallons, the actual daily supply for sewer-cleansing purposes in dry weather may be as low as half that quantity, while in rainy seasons the daily supply may rise to 45,000,000. In the former case there would be about a proportion of one gallon of polluted sewer water to 800 gallons of tidal water, and in the latter case it would be as one gallon to 267 gallons. The purity of the water in the river would, however, be as much deteriorated in the one case as in the other, as an equal quantity of soil must necessarily be cleansed from the sewers in both cases; the only difference would be, that with the more copious supply of water the soil would be in a more diluted shape, but not on that account in greater quantity.

It may be fairly expected that in some of the numerous plans of sewerage to be shortly laid before the Commissioners of Sewers, this important subject will be fully discussed. To do so, however, the fact must not be lost sight of, that as the tidal wave is to a certain extent oscillating in estuaries, or rivers like the Thames, it cannot be supposed that the whole of the semi-diurnal additions of drainage impurities can pass completely away with each tide; we know, indeed, that they do not; and it becomes a matter of vital importance to ascertain the *progressive* amount of these accumulating impurities. It is as absurd to pretend that the water of the Thames is uncontaminated, while it is used as the main sewer, as to expect the purity of a mountain stream in a river on whose banks 2,000,000 of the most restlessly active people in the world exist.

IMPROVEMENT OF WROUGHT-IRON WATER-PIPES.

IN your number of the 11th of August a paragraph was inserted stating that Messrs. Fox and Henderson had purchased the license for the manufacture in England of the wrought-iron pipes, upon the patent of M. Chameroy. This paragraph escaped my notice until very recently, but as it is always better late than never, perhaps you will allow me through your columns, to call the attention of these gentlemen, and of the profession, to some defects in the use of these pipes. I do this, because the defects are susceptible of being remedied; and the parties would render a real service to all interested in drainage and water-works, were they to succeed in the attempt.

Firstly. The tubes, or pipes (as I have seen them employed in Paris, and in other French towns), are not made sufficiently strong to resist the pressure from without. The weight of the earth above them, combined as its action often is with a settlement below (for most water pipes are laid in made ground), forms indents which diminish the volume of water delivered. But as the indent is not always accompanied by a leakage, it is very difficult and expensive to ascertain where the obstruction occurs. I have known nearly a mile of pipe laid bare to find the cause of the diminished delivery. In fact, elasticity is not to be desired in a water pipe.

Again. The screw couplings being soldered on, are very likely to be, and often are in practice, detached. It is easily conceivable that an artificial joint of this kind is exposed to minute defects, hardly perceptible by the workmen, but which the continual action of the water, with a "head" such as is required for the high service, cannot fail to discover, and also to aggravate.

In France the screw socket pipes were used for lengths of about 80 feet, and then flange pipes were introduced to admit of repairs in case of accident. Great inconvenience arose from this great length between the flange joints; for it is invariably found that the oxidation of the iron in the worm of the screw joints, made these last adhere together so firmly, that it was next to impossible to separate them; or at least the solder between the screw flange and the tube was so much detached, that the water, when reintroduced, almost invariably forced it way through the joint.

The objects to be attained are, to assure the pipes against compression by increasing their resistance to a lateral, or transverse strain; next to introduce some means of making the joints, which should not be liable to the objections stated above. There is a collateral objection to these pipes, which in some cases assumes a very great importance, but which might also be obviated; namely, that the settlement of the earth round them, when in place, gives rise to a species of friction which destroys the asphalte coating, and leaves the wrought iron exposed to the action of the salts, and of the moisture of the ground. I have seen some of these pipes at Havre nearly eaten through from the outside, the inside remaining perfect. Should the manufacturers in question remove these objections, they would confer a benefit upon the profession, inasmuch as the pipes in question do not affect the quality of the water like those generally used.

G. R. Burnell.

ART-EDUCATION FOR THE PEOPLE.

The people of this country have been long allowed to remain ignorant of the fine arts, and debarred, in consequence, of much that highly concerns their knowing. Their treasures, however, should be now open to them, and they should be trained for them by means of artistic discipline being made, henceforward, an important part in the system of our national instruction. In all the public schools and establishments for upraising the popular mind it has been strangely omitted, and is now only beginning to be very feebly and inadequately enforced. It seems hitherto to have been considered as one of those divisions of human attainments too mysterious and sacred to be entered upon by the generality. The beautiful was created for all, although it is true it has been enjoyed only by the few! but civilization must make the knowledge of it universal. It cannot be the exclusive privilege of a class; all the world will one day be its worshippers. But, until this be the case, we shall find the majority of the community will remain sadly deficient in the necessary amount of discrimination of what is true, natural, or beautiful; their sympathy and admiration in presence of monuments of national glory will be dead, and their patriotism will grow cold. With these reasons, we think the subject of art-education is one that ought to have great weight with the political thinker and legislator. Communicate this to the operatives, mechanics, and artizans of the country, for their sakes and for its honour,—for the cause of art and artists: you will improve the condition of the one, and exalt the character of the other; they will commence a mutual existence for each other; artists will be compelled, as they value fame, to produce excellent works, for then no mediocrity will be tolerated by the multitude, nor will they any longer be imposed upon by the accustomed arrogance and flippancy of critics. This set of men, wise in their own generation, will have to be on their guard; and those who have been indifferent about the reputation of others, will have to be careful in future about their own.

F. L.

A STARTLER FOR THE DRAIN-PIPE MAKERS.

The following are tenders for draining an estate at Kennington-cross, the property of Mr. Henry Bowden; Mr. Rogers, architect. The work consists of nearly 3,000 feet run of tubular socket glazed earthenware pipes, of different sizes, from 4 inch to 15 inch.

Mutter	£1,036	0	0
Lawrence	687	10	0
Payne	658	2	8
Robson	619	13	7
Pauling	613	4	0
Taylor	600	0	0
Macey	568	0	0
Corbett	511	10	2
Preston	447	16	0
Munday	398	11	11
Clement and Stanfield	389	0	0
Hill	334	13	2
Jarvis	333	0	0
Detbick	310	0	0
Kelly	274	4	2

THE BIRMINGHAM UNION COMPETITION.

A PRETTY STATEMENT.

I am led by the manly and independent manner in which you always advocate fair play, and expose all abuses connected with architectural competitions, but more especially by what you have already published respecting the doings of the Birmingham guardians, to send you some particulars I have received relative to the said board; in order that you may further expose the gross injustice that has been done those architects, who, like myself, were induced by the specious promises and great professions of honesty and fair dealing made by the guardians at the time they issued their conditions and instructions to architects.

From inquiries I have lately made, I now find that the whole affair from beginning to end has been, to say the least of it, a delusion and a snare, and I think you will acknowledge a more disgraceful or dishonest affair never came under your notice, when I tell you I am in possession of information, which not only proves the truth of the statement made by Mr. Brookes as regards Messrs. Drury and Bateman's names being on their drawings, but also confirms the suspicion that two at least out of the three judges were influenced and guided thereby, in the opinion they gave of the designs submitted for them to examine and report upon: in proof of which I would mention the fact that one of them (Mr. Edge) canvassed some of the guardians in favour of Messrs. Drury and Bateman, during the first competition; and that it is currently reported in Birmingham, that another of the judges (Mr. Gibson) is about forming an alliance with the family of one of the successful competitors. I therefore think under these circumstances, that you and every other unprejudiced person will agree, that I, with every other competitor, have good reasons for impugning the disinterestedness of a tribunal so constituted.

In addition to what I have already stated, I have been informed that a large sum of money was spent during the late election of guardians which took place between the first and second competition, to ensure the return of the present members, and although it would be very difficult, if not impossible, to prove that a large portion of it was subscribed by the present successful competitors, yet such I am informed was reported at the time of election, and what serves to confirm this statement, is the fact that nearly, if not quite all their supporters in the first competition, the present chairman of the board amongst the number, were re-elected and the opposing party thrown out; and besides which, it was well known that but few, if any, of the party who took an active part in the election, had sufficient interest for spending money upon such an occasion.

In order to satisfy the competitors and the public at large that the design recommended by the judges, and finally adopted by the guardians and Poor-law Commissioners, does display such superior talent as to require so little difficulty in arriving at a judgment independent of the names of the architects, I would recommend that a public exhibition be made of all the designs sent in; which course, I think, neither the guardians nor the judges they appointed could possibly object to, if their decision has been an honest one. But in case they neglect this means of vindicating their characters, I would then recommend that a meeting of the competitors be called, for the purpose of arranging such exhibition, and forming a committee to make a report thereon, and taking such steps as they may deem advisable. As regards the expenses attending such exhibition, I have no doubt they would be more than covered by making a trifling charge to the public for viewing the same, as I understand the matter excites considerable interest in Birmingham; and should any surplus remain, after paying the expenses, it would serve to make up a fund for the purpose of trying a question at law, whether each competitor is entitled to be paid for his design, provided it can be clearly proved the guardians have broken their contract by not fulfilling the conditions of the competition: or it might be given to some needy and useful charity in the neighbourhood.

I do not wish my name to appear, but I enclose my card as a guarantee of my good faith.

Lover of Fair Play.

PARKS FOR THE METROPOLIS.

Something has been said recently in The Builder on the parks. Now, in my opinion, gross negligence has been manifested for the welfare of the inhabitants of this overgrown metropolis, excepting as regards the western portion, and perhaps I should admit the extreme eastern part. In the year 1833 a select committee was appointed in the House of Commons, to consider the propriety of establishing additional public parks and places for exercise. The committee having considered the matter, reported that the number of such places were insufficient then for the requirements of the public, and recommended that *five additional* sites should be appropriated for the establishment of public parks and walks.

Now, Sir, since that period, *sixteen years ago*, what has been done? Victoria Park, such as it is, has been partly formed; and the *very best site* for a public park in the neighbourhood of London, viz., Copenhagen Fields, has been suffered to be entirely destroyed, and almost every footpath in that neighbourhood closed against the public, which, at the time above mentioned, they had full enjoyment of.

Hackney Downs, too,—these would form a noble park. But there are boards up to say that the ground is to be let for building purposes; although I believe *it is* or *was common*, or *lammas land*. But no measures have ever been taken, at least that I am aware of, to secure this beautiful spot for the use of the public.

I do not mean to blame the present Government for all this. Of course they cannot be answerable for the misdeeds of their predecessors. But I must say that I think it very hard, that when the sum of 150,000*l.* should be lavished upon additions (the propriety of which is very questionable) to a single palace, which has already cost no one knows how much, and such immense sums should be expended upon the new Houses of Parliament, so little should have been done for the suffering million. By the suffering million, I mean those poor creatures who are compelled to drag on a miserable existence in the crowded courts and alleys of this bloated city, and who scarcely ever, *now*, are able to see a green field. I do not mean those who can afford to spend two or three weeks or months at a watering-place every year, nor those who, besides having the enjoyment of the parks at all times at their command, spend a considerable portion of their time at their country seats, but the poor artizan and clerk, who are compelled to toil from year's end to year's end in the close workshop and counting-house for the means of subsistence.

The builders are not blameless in this matter, for the reckless way in which they have covered every available spot of ground without reservation; and this they will find out the error of before long, or I am very much mistaken. The better class of houses, that is, houses of from 50*l.* a-year and upwards, do not let now so well as they used to do. Those parties who can afford it are beginning to move off a little way into the country, along the different lines of railway. I know three or four instances of this within these last twelve months. One party has gone to reside at Sydenham, from the neighbourhood of Cloudesley-square, Islington, and the other two to Penge, on the Croydon line, from Myddelton-square. Now, as new lines of railway are opened, and the facilities for residing a short distance from town increase, so will the houses in the suburbs be deserted by the most respectable tenants, and the depreciation of house property in these neighbourhoods be *beyond all calculation*; and, in the end, the consequences will fall upon the heads of those by whose means and connivance it was brought about.

J. C. P.

Enforcement of Cleanliness in Dwellings.—The corporation of Brussels, and several other large Belgian cities, have determined, it is said, forcibly to close all houses left uncleansed, and to stick on the door a bill bearing the words "interdicted house."

DATA FOR A PAROCHIAL CEMETERY.

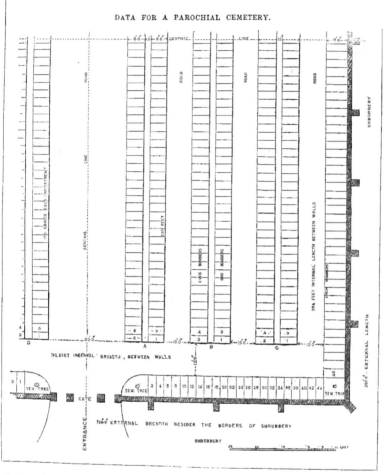

A PLAN FOR A PARISH BURIAL-GROUND.

DATA FOR CHURCHWARDENS.

THE public appear now to be alive to the impropriety of continuing the practice of intramural burials. In most towns with which I am acquainted the churchyards are completely full of coffins; and thus, independently of the question of health, there exists a sufficient reason why other burial-grounds should be provided.

It has struck me with some surprise that no parties have as yet given any ideas on the subject; I therefore take it up, with the view of assisting churchwardens, or other authorities entrusted with such matters, to judge of the quantity of ground required, and the number of graves necessary in proportion to the population. It is of some importance that the ground should be properly laid out in the first instance, because the arrangement (if there be any) cannot well be altered after interments have taken place.

Annexed is a plan of a burial-ground, capable of containing 1,174 graves, each 6 feet 6 inches by 3 feet, and numbered, having a communication by road, without trespassing on any other grave. I propose that the burial-ground should be enclosed by a wall, having its footings carried down to the depth of the deepest graves—say 7 feet below the surface,—and that there should be a shrubbery or plantation, of from 30 to 33 feet broad, on the outside, to be kept in neat order, with a view to prevent houses or sheds from being built in contact with the walls, overlooking the ground, and otherwise becoming a nuisance.

I have not shown any buildings to contain tools, &c., because, if required, they can afterwards be erected on the shrubbery ground.

It is evident that the number of graves can either be increased or diminished, by increasing or diminishing the number of the compartments A B C D E F by an equal number on each side of the central line. The soil chosen should be gravel, and not clay, if it can be avoided.

The plan shows one quarter of a burial-ground calculated to contain 1,174 graves. One-fortieth of the population are supposed to die annually, but the ground should not be disturbed for at least seven years after interment. Thus, the population ÷ 40 and × 7 gives the least number of graves required for the parish or district. The space here occupied is 110 yards × 88 yards, = 9,680 yards superficial, or two acres.

R. T. (Colonel.)

P.S. According to the data here supposed, a population of

5,000 will require	875 graves.
10,000 ,,	1,750 ,,
15,000 ,,	2,625 ,,
20,000 ,,	3,500 ,,
25,000 ,,	4,375 ,,
30,000 ,,	5,250 ,,
35,000 ,,	6,125 ,,
40,000 ,,	7,000 ,,

MACADAMIZED ROADS FOR STREETS OF LARGE TOWNS.*

There is a prevalent feeling against the employment of broken stone roads for streets, because, as they are usually managed, they are the cause of great inconvenience to householders and others by the dirt and dust they occasion, and also because their maintenance and repairs are very expensive, while the draught of vehicles upon them is very heavy. The object of this paper is to prove, from long continued experience on a large scale, that these objections do not necessarily accompany the use of such roads. In discussing this question the interests of two parties must be considered: those who principally use the road,—the owners and employers of horses and vehicles,—and those who pay for it,—the rate-payers, who are they who would be injured and annoyed if it were unduly expensive or unnecessarily dirty, dusty, and noisy. It is a common error to consider that road the cheapest which costs the least in direct expenditure. If, however, this so-called cheapest road cause waste of horse-power, undue wear and tear of horses and vehicles, loss of time by being unfit for rapid transit, and occasion loss to the inhabitants by filling their dwellings with dust, and covering their clothes with dirt, it is evident that such a road is really very dear. There is an apparent diversity of interest between those who use and those who pay for our public streets; as the principal loss from bad roads falls directly upon those who keep or employ horses and vehicles, while the expense of road repairs falls upon the inhabitants generally. A little consideration, however, will show that this diversity of interest is more apparent than real. It is the interest of all that there should be easy, safe, and cheap means of transit through the public streets; and any increase in the cost of transit is a source of indirect expense even to those who have no horses of their own, as it must add to the cost of everything carried through the streets, and of all hired vehicles, and of all the numberless conveniences which accompany residence in a large town. It must also be remembered that it is very wasteful to allow a road to go out of repair, since it is less costly to keep a road up than to restore it. That roadway is best for the owner or user of a horse or vehicle which can be travelled over most easily, safely, quickly, and cheaply; and that ease, safety, speed, and economy are to be obtained by having the road firm, even, and smooth, and perfectly free from mud or dust, or any form of unattached materials. It is evident that the same qualities will render the roadway most free from noise, dirt, and dust, the three great causes of annoyance and injury to the inhabitants of all ordinary streets. The question which remains to be considered is, whether the advantages of good roads to the inhabitants generally are worth their cost? If the question had to be decided in accordance with the interest of the users and owners of horses merely, no doubt whatever would be entertained. Of whatever nature the surface of a road is to be, it is essential that its foundation should be of firm material, well consolidated, and perfectly drained; if not, the crust becomes loosened and destroyed, the road is rough and uneven, and wears into holes and ruts. Having obtained a good foundation, the next point is to cover it with a hard, compact crust, impervious to water, and laid to a proper cross section. The stones must be broken to one regular size, well raked in, and fixed there by a binding composed of the grit collected in wet weather by the sweeping machines, and preserved for this purpose. This binding must be laid on regularly, and watered until the new material be firmly set, which it will do very quickly and with the regularity of a well-laid pavement. The sharp angles of the stones are preserved, and there is both great saving of material and a firmer crust formed than by the common method of leaving the material to work into its place without the use of binding,—in which case the angles of the stones are worn off and reduced to powder, and at least one-third of the material is wasted in forming a binding in which the stones may set. By the improved method the binding is formed of material that would otherwise be useless. Many road-makers object to the use of binding, on the ground that the road is rendered rotten by it, and that when the road is set it has to be carted away again. This is apt to be the case under bad management, and when ordinary soil is used, the fine particles of which work into mud, and keep the road from setting firmly. But the coarse grit obtained by the sweeping machine off the roads is the very same material as is produced by wearing away the angles of the stones, and when judiciously applied to a new coating it will speedily become as well consolidated and firm as an old road. In the common method not only is there great waste of material, but the loose stones occasion delay by their resistance, great fatigue to the horses, and danger to their feet, while the noise produced by their grinding together is annoying to the inhabitants. Upon the improved method the inconveniences of road repair are incomparably less than those of pavement. Both recoating and repairs may be made without stopping the traffic. Under no circumstances must any imperfection of surface be allowed. If a hollow be not immediately stopped it very quickly extends over the surface. All loose stones should be carefully picked, as every loose stone passed over by heavily laden carriages, if not ground to powder, breaks the crust of the road, and if water be permitted to lodge on the surface it will cause great mischief. It is the neglect of these essential precautions that has led many to consider macadamized roads expensive. They *are* expensive if neglected. On a well made road heavy showers do good, by cleansing them:—so, also, does artificial watering if the road be clean or swept quickly after it is watered. A road which is perfectly dry loses its tenacity, and the surface grinds into dust; whence the economy of judicious watering in hot weather, which preserves the road as well as prevents the annoyance of dust. The practice so common in London and elsewhere of heavily watering a dirty road without cleansing it, and thereby converting the dust into mud, is very injurious to the road, and merely changes one nuisance into another—dust into mud. A great source of waste, both to those who use and to those who repair a road, is to allow it to be dirty. The draught on a dirty road is twice as heavy as on a clean one,—that is, a horse must exert double force to draw his load with the same speed. The cost, however, of employing double force is so great, that the expedient of diminishing the speed is generally adopted, as a horse can exert greater pulling force at a slower pace,—less power being required to carry his own body. It often happens that the extra resistance occasioned by dirt diminishes the speed one-fifth or one-fourth. The effect of the dirt, therefore, is to increase the work by 20 or 25 per cent. It will easily be believed that such a waste far exceeds the cost of the most perfect cleansing. This is the case when cleansing is done by scrapers (the greatest enemy a macadamized road has to contend against). By their use the stones are dragged from their places, and the adhesive dirt is not effectually taken away. Sweeping is the only mode of cleansing that should be allowed, either on streets or turnpike roads. Sweeping by the wide brooms of Mr. Whitworth's machine is preferable to all other modes of cleansing yet tried. It must be evident, that the fact of these wide brooms sweeping longitudinally, with a pressure that can be adjusted according to circumstances, tends powerfully to preserve the road and to consolidate its surface. They press most upon the ridges, and least upon the hollows, thus tending to reduce the former, and fill up the latter. When the dirt is stiff, and adheres firmly to the stones, it should first be well watered, when it may be completely removed by the machine, without disturbing the crust, leaving the surface firm and compact. The use of water for this purpose has been objected to by high authorities, on the ground that it *does* remove the useful grit; but the contrary has been proved by ample experience. I have found the use of the sweeping machines, with the proper employment of water, has reduced the amount of material required for the repair of roads in Birmingham one-third,—namely, from about 20,000 to 13,000 cubic yards. The first-named amount is the average for seven years preceding the introduction of machines,—the latter, the three years subsequent.

The great objection urged against macadamized roads for streets is the annoyance by dust and dirt which they occasion, and many persons prefer submitting to the deafening noise of pavement in order to avoid these; but this would not be the case if water and machine cleansing were adopted, the cost of which would be saved in diminished wear and tear. The entire cost of cleansing and watering Birmingham is about 5,000*l.* per annum,—or less than one penny per week for each of its inhabitants.

J. P. Smith.

* The following is a portion of a paper read before the British Association for the Advancement of Science.

MANAGEMENT OF COMPETITIONS.

Start not, nor throw this aside, on seeing the heading again. You closed your leader a few weeks ago with "Fight the good fight, and fear not." I trust you will apply this to architectural competition, and "fight it out." The subject, it is quite cheering to see, is being so well discussed by your correspondents, and *this time* with such a fore-shadowing of a successful, enduring, movement on the part of the profession, that I trust you will not close your columns to *weekly* communications on this topic (such as you have inserted for the last three weeks), till the right management of architectural competitions be, as it very soon must be, decided on by a "monster" meeting, which a *public* meeting of architects, cordially uniting to look after their common rights, will surely be—

"A stranger animal, cries one,
Sure never lived beneath the sun."

"W. W.'s" letter last week is useful, though I like not the scramble for "laurels" he hints at. The words of the institute's report on competitions, are "*to effect this object rests with the profession at large*," and the institute will, doubtless, not be wanting, should the profession, as the sailors have it, "turn out."

A meeting, to be of use, as ably shown by your correspondent "C. G." (page 435), should be put in communication with every known architect practising in Great Britain; and to effect this, would be attended with more expense than any one society might wish to incur; whereas the most trifling, insignificant subscription on the part of the profession as a body, would amply supply the requisite funds. Perhaps some of your correspondents can point out a mode of dealing with this difficulty.

One word more in allusion to your other last week's correspondent, "A Builder." *He* takes a most correct view of this question, and sees, like a clear-sighted "builder" as he is, that builders are vitally concerned in it, for what on earth can more conduce to the propagation of "blind builders" than the present mode of conducting architectural competitions, which sets architects one against another to produce—not the best structure, oh, no! but the most attractive, gaudy designs, which their authors undertake to realize for a mere song, succeed in the struggle thereby, and straightway (such is competition), institute a scramble of very "blind builders," to endorse their own promises? To The Builder again I say, "fight the good fight, and *fight it out*."—Y.

DISTRICT OF CHRIST CHURCH, ST. GEORGE'S-IN-THE-EAST, LONDON.

In the year 1847 an appeal was made for public support in order to obtain:—1. A parsonage for the minister of the present church, the Rev. W. Quekett. 2. Three new schools for 700 children, with three residences. 3. A new church of stone, plain but substantial, for 1,000 persons. And 4. A parsonage for the minister of the new church.

The minister exerted himself greatly; Government and the London Diocesan Board of Education assisted; and the parsonage, the schools, and the residences (Mr. Geo. Smith, of the Mercers's Company, architect), have been completed, and a church is now being erected at the cost of a munificent nobleman. About 8,000*l.* have been spent, irrespective of the church. The schools and residences cost 3,858*l.*; the site, 700*l.*; the parsonage, 1,048*l.* There is a deficiency of 211*l.*: 1,500*l.* are wanted for a parsonage for the minister of the new church; and a further appeal is being made. The church is geometrical pointed in style, and is to have a tower and spire at the east end of the south aisle of nave.

THE LONDON COAL EXCHANGE, THAMES-STREET.

Mr. BUNNING, F.S.A., Architect.

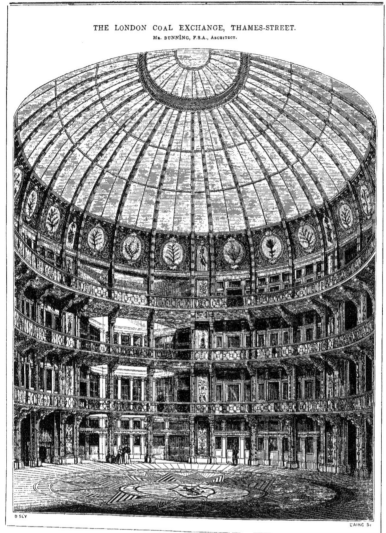

B SLY

L'AINC St

INTERIOR OF THE LONDON COAL EXCHANGE, THAMES-STREET.

THE interior of the new London Coal Exchange, now nearly completed, at the corner of Lower Thames-street and St. Mary-at-Hill, under the direction of Mr. Bunning, architect to the corporation, presents considerable novelty both in design and decoration. It includes a circular area for the meeting of the merchants, 60 feet in diameter, with three galleries running round it, which communicate with suitable offices; and the area is covered by a glazed dome, the eye of which is 74 feet from the floor.

The galleries are peculiarly constructed, and entirely composed of iron, embellished with symbols of the coal trade. The stauncheons, brackets, ribs and eye of the dome are also of iron, and the panels (twenty-four in number) are ornamented with paintings of the plants and fossil remains found in the coal series, from drawings made by Mr. Melhado, a pupil of the architect, from specimens in the British Museum, and painted by Mr. Sang in encaustic. The eight smaller compartments are filled in with implements used in the coal district. The panels in the galleries contain figures of the miners, which are less satisfactory in execution.

Each rib, of which there are thirty-two, is 42 feet 6 inches long, and is cast in one length, averaging in weight 2 tons : there are in all about 300 tons of iron, including the gully plates, stauncheons, brackets, &c. The galleries are about 12 feet from floor to floor. The cupola is glazed with ground plate glass, and the eye with amber-coloured glass. The ornamented portions of the stauncheons, gallery railing, soffits, &c., display in almost too great profusion the rope form. The floor of the area represents the mariner's compass, in the centre of which are the City arms, composed of different woods. A portion of the decorative part of this floor is formed with part of an oak tree which had been found imbedded in the river Tyne.

A staircase leads to the hypocaust which was discovered in excavating for the foundation, and described in our pages at the time. A visit to this will amply repay the lovers of antiquity; and its minute agreement with the details given by Vitruvius should be noticed.

The artificers' works generally have been performed by Mr. Trego; the iron-work by Messrs. Dewer; and the wood-work has been seasoned by Messrs. Davison and Symington's patent desiccating process. The floor of the merchants' area was laid down by the first-named of these gentlemen, Mr. Davison.

The cost of this Exchange will be about 40,000*l*. A view of the exterior of the building, which has a circular tower 100 feet high at the angle of the two fronts, forming the principal entrance and containing a staircase leading to the several stories, will be found in our fifth volume, page 566.

SUPPLY OF WATER.

It has been stated in The Builder that 70,000 houses in the metropolis are without a supply of water; and the public are recommended to raise an outcry until a supply be raised,—but how the outcry is to accomplish the object does not appear.

These houses are mostly of the smallest class, situated in courts and alleys, and occupied by tenants paying weekly rents to landlords, whose great object is to make the properties as profitable as possible. The tenants get their water how they can—from pumps or common cocks in the neighbourhood, or perhaps buy or beg of some publican or shopkeeper. Two difficulties must be dealt with, in order to remove the evil. An outlay must be made, to convey the water into the houses; and an annual payment must be secured to the parties who convey the water: it would be idle to expect that the Henley, or any other waterworks company (new or old) would spend money to improve other persons' property, or afford a supply of water, except upon remunerative principles. It is the owners of the property only that must be looked to; and there can be no more reason why a man should be allowed to let a house for the manufacture of fever and pestilence, than that he should be allowed to poison the atmosphere in any other manner. E.

*** E. does not see how an outcry for water is to aid in obtaining a good supply of it. He may depend on it that without an outcry it will never be procured. The outcry must be for *sufficient* water, *pure* water, and *cheap* water; and when this is to be had, and the vital importance of it is brought to the minds of all, landlords will *feel* made, or *be* made to afford it, to those not sufficiently strong to claim it for themselves. Can the existing water companies comply with the requirement? That they do not is certain. If *they* cannot, or will not, those who will undertake to do so should be supported on all hands. A continuous and abundant supply of *pure* water is imperatively demanded. We direct attention to the following communication on same subject.

I beg, through your valuable journal, to call the attention of the public to the source from whence all the water for the southern districts of London is supplied. Whilst a great portion of the north side of the Thames,—say the City of London, and parts around, are supplied from the New River—a stream comparatively pure,*—and this district has suffered very slightly with respect to the cholera,—the south side, such as Lambeth, Newington, &c. &c., has suffered a dreadful mortality. May not this be greatly attributed to the water, impregnated as it is with everything that is bad and prejudicial to health? And, though the water company professes to filter it before it is sent in to our houses, which they may do, as regards anything like substances, they cannot filter the filthy mixture of liquids from it any more than they could, by filtering, turn beer into spring water. Consequently we, on the south side of London, are compelled to drink it, such as it is. I think, after this, we cannot wonder at the amount of illness and death. The only wonder is, that we are not all poisoned together, for it only requires one moment's consideration, or a glance at the points in the river from whence the supply is taken, to fully explain the greater extent of mortality on the south side of London over the north. The Thames water was bad enough before, but since the flushing of the sewers, of course it is ten times worse than ever;—so they, in their wisdom, flush the sewers on the north side of London, and we, on the south side, are compelled to drink it,—a very pretty state of things truly. Common sense would immediately condemn such a plan, but that is an article in very little use amongst committees. One sensible man would do more practical good than half the committees combined. The state of the river has been so abominable of late that the steam-boat passengers could scarcely bear the smell; and yet this filth is served up for domestic purposes. Such a course ought, in justice to the inhabitants, to be stopped as soon as possible; and this might be done by laying down a main, at any cost, by the side of the Kingston Railway, from about Kingston to their tanks in Battersea fields, so as to have a supply of water above the influence of the tide. Until some remedy be obtained, we must drink the pollutions of London, and die in consequence. R. M.

* Only comparatively so.—Ed.

NOTES IN THE PROVINCES.

A chapel of ease is being erected on Letty-green, near Hertford, under the direction of Mr. G. Fowler Jones, to accommodate 125 in open seats, 100 of which are free. The style Early English; the plan a parallelogram, 50 feet by 21 feet; the walls of brick, faced with flint, with stone dressings; a bell turret on west gable; high pitched roof, open to the boarding, and stained and varnished; cost 630*l*., which has been raised by subscription, through the exertions of the rector of Hertingfordbury and some of the neighbouring gentlemen, the site being given by Lord Cowper. The building is to be ready for consecration towards the end of October.——Considerable alterations are now in progress, under the same architect, at the recently erected church at Tolmers, in the same county, to make it more ecclesiastical: it has, along with the school and master's house, been built and endowed by Mr. Thomas Mills, of Tolmers.——In consequence of the recent destruction of eight houses in the market-place of Cambridge by fire, it is now proposed to remove the whole of the west side of the market-hill, together with Warwick-street or Pump-lane, throwing open the market to St. Mary's Church, and the University buildings and grounds beyond.——The Sanitary and Drainage Committee of this town met the other day to receive tenders for drains in several important districts:—For Newmarket-road, 528 yards, tender of Samuel Peacock accepted, price 12s. 3d. per yard,—average depth 13 feet; other tenders were sent in, one at 18s., and another at 14s. a-yard:—For Gas-lane, offer of James Stevens taken, at 7s. 6d. per yard,—depth 7 feet 6 inches:—For Albert-street, John Hall's tender accepted, at 7s. 6d.,—depth 9 feet:—For Thompson's-lane the work is deferred:—For St. Peter's-street, 165 yards,—average depth 9 feet 6 inches, James Stevens, contractor, at 8s. 3d. per yard.——The contractors are carrying out the new sewerage of Colchester, with vigour.——The new church at Kemp-town, Brighton, erected principally at the expense of the Marquis of Bristol, with accommodation for the pupils of St. Mary's Hall for education of daughters of deceased clergymen, has been consecrated.——The Southampton Sanitary Committee have resolved to recommend the Board of Water-works forthwith to form an additional reservoir on the common for the better supply of water to the town. The cost of a five acre reservoir was estimated at 2,300*l*.——It is seriously proposed to build an extensive university at Birkenhead, to constitute the Oxford or Cambridge of the north of England. The Archbishop of Canterbury, the Marquis of Westminster, and Lord Robert Grosvenor, have it is said already contributed 1,000*l*. each, and the highest sanction in the state, it is added, has been secured. A piece of ground, 10 acres in extent, belonging to Mr. Brassey, has been thought of as the *locus in quo*.——The Liverpool Health Committee recommend that five of the most crowded burial grounds be closed; namely, St. Nicholas's, St. Peter's, St. Paul's, St. John's, and St. James's; and they have decided to apply to Parliament for power to close these fever-stills for ever.——The foundation stone of Wycliffe Chapel, Heaton Norris, was laid on Saturday week. It is to be in the Pointed style, from plans prepared by Mr. E. Walters, the architect of Cavendish Chapel and schools, Manchester. The chapel is to cost 2,000*l*., and will accommodate 600 adults and 100 children.——At Rochdale, on Monday week, a stone building, three stories high, 52 feet by 54 feet, built ten years ago, for handloom weaving flannels, and also six cottages, were "knocked down" for 225*l*. The handloom building alone cost more than 1,400*l*.

LAYING FIRST STONE OF THE NEW CITY OF LONDON PRISON.

The first stone of the new City Prison to be erected at Holloway, said by the Lord Mayor, who officiated, to be "the largest and most expensive building ever undertaken by the corporation," was laid on Wednesday last. According to the newspapers, for we received no intimation of the occurrence, the prison is intended for the separate confinement of four hundred convicted prisoners, and has large work-rooms attached. It is to be in the castellated style of architecture, and the main parts are to be faced with Kentish rag-stone.

A tower of considerable height will form a prominent feature, and by it the whole of the prison is to be ventilated. On each side of the main approach to the prison, and fronting the Camden-road, a dwelling-house, faced with red brick and Caen stone, will be erected, as residences for the governor and the chaplain. The entrance gateway and the porter's lodge will also be in the castellated style of architecture, faced with Kentish ragstone. The front portion of the main building, which will stand at a considerable distance from the road, will consist of a centre building, containing, on the basement, reception-cells, bath-rooms, examining-rooms, fumigating-rooms, furnace-rooms, and the principal staircase to the ground floor, which will contain offices for the governor, the magistrates'-room, and rooms for the medical officer and chaplain, and also separate visiting-places. On this floor will be a corridor, leading to the portion of the prison to be appropriated to adult prisoners; and above will be the chapel, arranged to contain separate inclosed seats for the prisoners.

Connected with the centre building, and diverging therefrom, will be four main wings, which are to be appropriated to the confinement of adult male prisoners. Each wing throughout the prison will contain a corridor the entire length and height of the building, with a projecting gallery on each story above the ground floor for access to the cells, and iron staircases leading thereto. The whole of the building appropriated to the confinement is to be fire-proof, and the floors will be formed with asphalte, with which also the roofs of the cells and corridors will be covered. The whole area contains about twelve acres of ground, and will be enclosed with a high wall.

INDURATED STONE.

In your publication of Sept. 15, I find an article on "Churchyard Monuments," wherein the decay and early ruin presented in their appearance is justly regretted. I would mention how this may be obviated.

In 1843, the hospital at Bayeux, also the cathedral and palace, were repaired and beautified with what is called indurated stone, and nothing in art can give more satisfaction than the result. The weather and all other influences usually detrimental to masonry, both as to durability and colour, have not the slightest effect thereon; and up to this moment no discolouration or decay is visible. This I can vouch for under the authority of the highest officers of the place, and amongst them, Judge Bertauldt.

I was much gratified lately when at Tonbridge Wells, to find a corroboration of the above, and much pleased to find the authorities are sanctioning its use generally; in fact, resident architects and others are specifically ordering the hard wearing portions of various buildings to be executed therein. I find the invention now rests in Mr. Hutchison, who is carrying out the process in that town. On subsequent inquiries I find the invention renders the stone non-absorbent, throwing off all discolouring matter, with freedom from vegetation. In my humble judgment, an article more suitable to the requirements inferred from your remarks cannot be found, and from its low price it is well deserving encouragement. R. F.

POLYGONAL CHAPEL, CHURCH OF ST. MARY, WOOTON-UNDER-EDGE.

THERE is a chapel in the church of St. Mary, Wooton-under-Edge, Gloucestershire, the arrangement of which is rare for English architecture, namely, that of a polygonal apse (five sides of an octagon), set on the north wall of the nave, about half way down, and looking north. The sides by which this chapel is formed are remarkable for their extreme irregularity, as seen in the following dimensions:—the west wall, 10 feet 3 inches; north-west wall, 8 feet 4 inches; north wall, 5 feet 7 inches; north-east wall, 8 feet 10 inches; east wall, 10 feet 2 inches: each wall being 2 feet 4 inches in thickness. The N.W., N., and N. E. walls have windows of similar form and character, which are filled with singular though not very elegant tracery: they, nevertheless, are effective, and lend character to the building. There is a piscina in the wall which divides this chapel from the nave, close to the east wall; there is also a plain doorway in the west wall.

The roof is conical, reminding the observer of the form of roof prevalent among small buildings of the Early English style, though the general details of this chapel fix the period as the Decorated.

This chapel was formerly used as a vestry, but is now approached through an ancient arch, which has recently been opened by the ascent of a flight of steps, and is now used as a baptistery. There are other points in this interesting church well worthy of note, namely, two fine brasses in a very perfect state; some good incised grave crosses; two ambries; also some good Early English work in the arches and piers; a tower of fine detail and proportions of the Decorated period, the window and door of which (both very good specimens) are surmounted by labels studded with ball flower. The windows and other details of the church generally are perpendicular.

W. H. L.

PROPOSED PROVIDENT AND BENEVOLENT SOCIETY FOR BUILDING ARTIFICERS.

IN an article which appeared in THE BUILDER of the 15th inst. on the subject of the proposed Provident and Benevolent Society for Building Artificers, it was stated of the Servants' Provident Society, that while "during sixteen years since the passing of the Deferred Annuity Act, 941 persons only have availed themselves throughout the kingdom of the benefits of the Act, this society, during the short period of fourteen months, has added 103, or one-tenth of the whole, and since then has increased that number."

I hope you will allow me, as secretary to the Servants' Provident and Benevolent Society, to inform you, and your readers who may be interested in the subject proposed by Professor Cockerell, and advocated in your journal, that the success of the Servants' Society, which is held out as an encouragement to those who may be disposed to join the Builders' Society, has not only continued, but been largely increased, since the period referred to, viz., May 16th, 1849, when his Royal Highness Prince Albert condescended, as chairman of the public meeting in the Hanover-square Rooms, to explain the benefits which the Government annuity system offers to servants and the working-classes in general.

Up to May, 1849, 103 servants had contracted, through this society, for Government annuities, amounting to 1,658*l.*; and had paid towards the same 1,192*l.* 12s. 10d.; whereas, from May to the present time, 199 servants have contracted, through this society, for Government annuities, amounting to 3,429*l.* 10s.; and have paid for the same, 4,283*l.* 4s. 1d.; making in the whole, for eighteen months, 302 servants who have contracted for Government annuities, amounting to 5,087*l.* 10s.; and have paid for the same to the Government, through this society, no less a sum than 5,475*l.* 16s. 11d.

I trust that this statement may afford some encouragement to Professor Cockerell, and others, whether architects, builders, or artificers, who may feel disposed to co-operate with that gentleman and yourself to ensure the success of his laudable design.

It may be interesting to you to know that since the appearance of the article in THE BUILDER, many persons connected with building have applied at this office for tables and general information respecting the subject of Government annuities and the working of our system. GEORGE GRANT, Secretary.

PROCEEDINGS OF THE METROPOLITAN COMMISSION OF SEWERS.

WE wasted one hour and a half this (Thursday) morning in listening to objections and explanations and angry recriminations, all wholly unnecessary under proper arrangement, in the Court of the Commissioners of Sewers; and considering that there were *fifteen* officers of the commission whose hours are paid for by the rate-payers, sitting all this time at the back of the room in case they might be wanted (to say nothing of eight reporters for the press), the public are somewhat interested in a knowledge of the fact, and an alteration in the state of things. Mr. Leslie was unyielding; objected to everything; obstructed everything; and yet we cannot condemn his proceedings, however disagreeable and ill natured they appeared, for the course seemed really to a great extent forced upon him, and the blame must rest with those who make the objections necessary. We give our usual report below. Our object in this preface is again to express our regret at the undignified position in which the commission and its officers stand before the public, and to call for immediate alteration. A very short time ago we showed the state of antagonism between the chief surveyor and the consulting engineer, and the smart things *they* said of each other. Now we have the latter and the assistant surveyor abusing one another, and endeavouring to show that each is quite unfit for his office. Let them take care lest they *all* prove their case in the eyes of the public. Mr. Gotto advises a plan of drainage for the luckless Westminster Improvements Commission. Mr. Austin feels it his duty, unasked, to report upon it as a work entirely "at variance with what is correct," "on erroneous principles;" "absurd and impracticable;" it is a "faulty work," "a useless work;" and he then gives his own views.

Mr. Gotto replies, in a report printed, but not yet before the court, that—"Either I (Gotto) am incompetent for the office of your assistant-surveyor, or Mr. Austin is incompetent to the duties of the consulting engineer to the commission," and asserts point blank that Mr. Austin's own propositions "form one mass of engineering blunders." We cautioned some of the officers of the court, when they were attacking people out of doors, against this slashing style of writing, but advice has been thrown away. They all write with too much facility; and then, as everything is printed (and a pretty bill there must be for this), the temptation to be smart is too much for their prudence.

Seriously, we invite Lord Carlisle to look into the matter, and put affairs on a better footing, or, as a matter of course, the first step taken when Parliament meets will be a Committee of Inquiry; and more printing, more delay, more waste of money.

A general court was held on Thursday, in Greek-street; Sir J. Burgoyne, in the chair.

The Cholera in Bethnal Green.—A letter was received from Mr. Baker, one of the coroners for Middlesex, setting forth that at the request of a jury of an inquest on John Papel, of Alfred-street, Bethnal-green, he wished to call the attention of the commissioners to the entire want of drainage in that locality, and that no less than 400 fatal cases of cholera had occurred in that parish. Referred to surveyor.

On the motion of Mr. L. Jones, the following resolution was agreed to:—"That a separate account be kept of the whole of the expenses incurred in any district where there has not been any rate made for such district, including the salaries of the officers employed in such respective districts, in order that such expenses may be charged to such district."

New Plan for the Drainage of Westminster.—On the following recommendation of the Works Committee being read—"That the plan proposed by the consulting engineer (Mr. Austin), for the sub-soil drainage of Westminster be sanctioned, and that permission be given to the Westminster Improvement Commissioners to carry out the works suggested at their own expense,"

Mr. Leslie having called for the minutes of the last court on this question, went on to observe that, at that court it was ordered that the plan of Mr. Gotto, with Mr. Austin's counter plan, should be printed, and sent round for the consideration of the Commissioners. But what were they now called upon to discuss? Why, a new project that had never been referred to the Works Committee at all, or that had been ordered to be printed. They were, in fact, called upon to adopt some new project, which was admitted to be incomplete, and was really no plan at all, and the court knew nothing about it.

Mr. Banfield believed the committee was the proper place to discuss the question. All that rested with the court was, to consider whether they ought to adopt the recommendations or not.—Mr. Leslie replied that this was one of the most extraordinary proceedings he had ever seen in the conduct of public business, two papers having been sent to the Works Committee, to consider which should be determined upon. Instead of which they proposed a third, of which the court had never heard, still less referred to them.

Mr. Jones concurred in this view, and thought that the plan of Mr. Austin, if plan there were, should be printed and sent round to the commissioners for consideration. He, however, had no wish to throw cold water on what had been done by the committee, or to consider how far Mr. Austin had trod closely on the heels of Mr. Gotto, as he heard was now the case, but still he was of opinion that the question should be postponed for further consideration.

Mr. Austin said his new work was partly of an experimental character, and he believed it would be calculated to benefit the whole district, rather than the line of the proposed street.—Mr. Leslie wished to ask Mr. Austin whether he had not thrown over the whole of his original plan, and had adopted almost in entire the plan of Mr. Gotto.—This Mr. Austin altogether denied.—Mr. Leslie said further, he was quite ready to prove that Mr. Austin could not carry into effect either of his plans.

It was urged by several commissioners that the question should be adjourned; and the matter was finally terminated by the adoption of the following resolution, on the motion of Mr. R. L. Jones:—"That the recommendation of the Works Committee upon the report of Mr. Austin, and the report of Mr. Austin containing his plan upon the new sewer in Westminster, and all communications with reference to that report and the original report of Mr. Gotto, be printed, and copies sent to each commissioner, and that further consideration be adjourned."

After the above motion was carried, a very sharp, recriminatory conversation was carried on, Mr. Leslie contending that Mr. Austin had placed the court in a position of the greatest difficulty. Mr. Austin called upon the Chairman, while he was their consulting engineer, to protect him from what he considered unfair attacks; and Mr. Banfield, designating the manner in which business was carried on as disgraceful to the court, and unworthy even of a bear-garden, was anxious to move an adjournment.

The Drainage of the Potteries, Kensington.—The next matter was to consider Messrs. Austin, Lovick, and Cresy's report on the drainage of the Potteries, of Kensington, presented to the court at its last meeting. After some questions as to the power of the court to call upon the owners of the property to do the works required, the report was agreed to.

The Sewage Manure Committee.—Mr. Leslie then said that the objections urged to his proceeding with the subject of the Trial Works Committee could not apply to the Sewage Manure Committee, as a report from it had been issued upwards of six months. He then went on to state that the expenses incurred by the Sewage Manure Committee did not warrant its continuance. For instance, the sum spent on seven acres amounted to more than the fee-simple of the land. They had spent an enormous amount, and all they were likely to receive in return was 15s. from Colonel Clitheroe, of Boston House, Hanwell. They needed no new experiments on the subject of sewage manure, which had been fully treated upon in the able report of Mr. Chadwick, known as the Poor Law Com-sioners', as far back as 1842, at Edinburgh and er places. The recent experiments were the st be had ever seen, and had been carried on in a st appropriate place—round the lunatic asylum Hanwell. Had the question stopped here it uld have been bad enough, but they had gone ther, and placed themselves in communication h Mr. Tower, of Weald Hall, Essex, to supply 1 with sewage for irrigation of land at an altitude 540 feet above high-water mark. They proposed carry this sewage 16 miles through a 7-inch pipe, the expense of the ratepayers. Believing it to be only means to stop this visionary expenditure, should move that the Sewage Manure Committee abolished.

Mr. Banfield seconded the motion, for unless (he d) the court supported the committee it would be possible to go on; and to bring the question rly before the court he had seconded the motion it the Sewage Manure Committee be abolished. e question led to a most protracted discussion, d Mr. Stone moved, as an amendment,—" That, nsidering the application of sewage manure to be ubject of invaluable importance to the ratepayers towns and the agriculture of the country at large, ey would be guilty of a neglect of duty in object- ; to prosecute inquiries upon it, the court is of inion that it would be premature to abolish the mmittee, and therefore requests it to continue its portant labours." Carried by a large majority.

Books.

ie Churches of the Middle Ages; or, Select Specimens of Early and Middle Pointed Structures, with a few of the purest late Pointed Examples, illustrated by Geometric and Perspective Drawings. By HENRY BOWMAN and J. S. CROWTHER, Architects. Manchester, 1848.

NDER the above title Messrs. Bowman and rowther have published three parts of what, completed in a similar manner, will be a autiful and valuable work. In their preninary prospectus the authors said,—" This ork is intended to be one of simple and pracal utility. It is not the purpose of the thors to enunciate any new principles, or eorize in any way, but simply to give illusations of entire churches of the purer styles, hich, either as wholes, or from the great auty of their details, will be of service in odern practice. At the same time, plates ill be occasionally given of miscellaneous tails, selected from other churches, which ay not be considered of sufficient value to given entire. The subjects will be selected incipally from the midland and eastern coun-s, which are known to abound with the est ecclesiastical structures. The illustrations ll consist of geometrical drawings, details, d perspective views. It is unnecessary to d, that every detail and dimension given in e work will be from the most careful easurement."

In carrying out their intention, however, ey have gone farther, and have added perective views.

The churches illustrated in the parts now fore us are St. Andrew's, Ewerby, and St. ndrew's, Heckington, both in Lincolnshire; d St. Mary's Chapel, Temple Balsall, in arwickshire. To the first of these, fifteen ates are appropriated, including an extra ate of the mouldings, *full size*. The perective of St. Andrew's, Heckington, is charming specimen of lithography, by awkins.

We unhesitatingly recommend Messrs. Bowan and Crowther's work to our readers, as kely to be useful to them. It will consist of enty parts of plates, and two parts of letteress, and will form two handsome volumes. e suggest to the authors to confine themlves, as far as possible, to subjects which ve not been given.*

---

olland's Wages, Miscellaneous, and Haulage Tables; arranged upon a novel and comprehensive Principle. By J. T. HOLLAND, Accountant. London, Bradshaw's Office, 59, Fleet-street.

ibles, adapted to the Use of Builders, Carpenters, Timber Merchants, and others, to facilitate the Casting and Checking of Accounts. By JAMES MORRIS. London, 1849. Miller and Field, Bridge-road.

MR. HOLLAND's tables will be found of great practical utility by contractors, surveyors, builders, and others in extensive business; for checking day-accounts, too, they are very valuable. They include a series of more than 36,000 calculations under the heads wages, miscellaneous, and haulage. The "miscellaneous" table applies from $\frac{1}{2}$ to 50,000 of any thing at from $\frac{1}{4}$d. to 40s. per yard, lb., or foot. The brick haulage from 25 to 100,000; $\frac{1}{4}$ to 15 miles, at from 1s. 6d. to 2s. 6d. per mile, and so on.

Mr. Morris's tables form a book of less size and cost than the preceding, and mainly refer to planing and sawing. Table 1, for example, shews at one view the cost of sawing any number of planks or deals by dozens and single cuts; Table 2, the cost of planing any number of boards at from 2d. to 1s. 4d. each; Table 3, the number of boards of any length and width required for one square of flooring, roofing, &c., and so on. They seem to be very carefully computed.

The New Testament in Lewisian Short-hand. By THOS. COGGIN. London: Nisbet and Co., Berners-street. 1849.

THIS little book is, perhaps, more curious than useful, although it may serve the purpose of the stenographic student. It is executed in lithography from the neat MS. of Mr. Coggin, who is in the office of the Commissioners of Sewers, and it is dedicated, by permission, to the Earl of Carlisle. We are glad to find the practice of short-hand writing increasing—it is a very useful art.

Miscellanea.

RAILWAY JOTTINGS.—The revenue of British railways, observes a contemporary, cannot now be put down at less than twelve millions a-year—a greater sum than many important political states possess. Two hundred millions of money were expended on them up to the close of last year, and even in the midst of the deep depression of 1848, when commerce was, as it were, in a state of complete collapse, not less than 33,234,818*l.* were expended in railway works. The number of passengers on these "new highways" during the last six months of 1848 was no less than 31,630,292, expending a sum of 3,283,301*l.*; or at the rate of 63,260,584, expending 6,566,602*l.* for the year. In the same half-year, goods, cattle, and parcels were conveyed at the charge of 2,461,662*l.*, or 4,923,324*l.* in the year. The amount of traffic for the week before last on 4,941 miles of railway was 245,550*l.*, being an increase of 19,815*l.* over the corresponding week of last year, when the mileage was 4,091. The average earnings per mile were 50*l.*, whilst last year they were 55*l.* ——The works on the Great Northern line, in the neighbourhood of Huntingdon, are progressing with rapidity. At the crossing of the Ouse, preparations are making for the iron bridge which is to span the river. Messrs. Fox and Henderson, who built the Earith-bridge, have, we understand, the contract for this structure. The plans for the viaduct north of the town have been completed.—— The Cardiff station on the South Wales line will be an extensive one. It will have all the offices and accommodation now found only at stations such as Swindon, Bristol, or Gloucester. Its entire cost will be about 11,000*l.* The framework of the roof and its supporters is to be of iron, while much of the roof itself will be of glass. The station at Neath will also be an important one, on account of the junction with the Vale of Neath Railway. The bridge over the new channel through which the Taff is to be conducted in its passage to the sea (near the town), is in a forward state.——The Berwick Railway-bridge across the Tweed, which has been in course of erection for about two years, it is probable will not be finished for upwards of twelve months. On the south side fourteen arches have been completed, and several others nearly so; but on the north the arches are not nearly so far advanced. The length of the whole will be about a quarter of a mile, and height above the river 120 feet.

PROJECTED WORKS.—Advertisements have been issued for tenders, by 6th October, for the freestone work in restoring Cowbridge Church, Glamorganshire; by 9th, for the construction and erection of boilers, pipes, and fittings for baths and washhouses at Bristol; by 8th, for 30,000 sleepers for the Brighton and South Coast line of railway; by 15th, for the rebuilding of Merrington Church; by 10th, for building an infirmary, with laundry and washhouse, &c., for the St. Olave's union workhouse; by 9th, for rebuilding a house at Southampton; by 3rd, for fifty iron lamp-posts for Mile-end Old-town; by 1st, for three cranes, one to lift 10 tons and the others five each, at Adelphi and Plymouth; by 24th inst., for repairing the Surrey Canal wharf and fences; by 3rd, for best plate iron, and for pitch and tar for the East-India Company; and by 2nd, for Rock-hill, Castle-hill, and Yorkshire paving, gravel, granite, &c., and also for carpenters', smiths', ironmongers', and bricklayers' works, for Camberwell district authorities.

ARCHITECTURAL LECTURES.—The Whittington Club, in the Strand, announce in their new programme two lectures on the "Romance of Architecture and Architectural Practice," by Mr. Wightwick, to be given in November. The syllabus of the second is suggestive:— "Anticipations of the architectural student— His first job—Duties of an architect—What he should know before he begins to practise— What he learns after he has begun—Dramatic illustration of the process of business between the architect and his patron, and his patroness! —End of the beginning—Perplexities of progress—Want of faith in two-feet rules—Disappointments in the new house, because of fond recollection of things in the old—Housemaid's closet *versus* portico—Sir J. Soane and 'guess estimates'—Summary of an architect's labours—'Rough sketches'—'Fair drawings' —Present condition of architectural practice."

INDIA-RUBBER BUFFERS AND SPRINGS have now been introduced, it is said, on upwards of fifty lines of railway, and stood the test of heat and cold, and wear and tear, so as to form a cheap and useful substitute for the old apparatus. Needing no cumbrous extension beneath the waggon or carriage framing, they can be fitted to newly-built waggons, it is alleged, for about 4*l.* 10s. a-set, and the wear and tear of the old buffers, estimated on luggage trains at 50 to 60 per cent. on their own much greater cost, thus reduced to 10 per cent. The new material has also been tried for bearing-springs, but has not hitherto come into use as such.

THE QUEEN'S PICTORIAL COMMISSIONER. — The *Limerick Chronicle* states that Mr. Bickham Escott, late M.P. for Winchester (of all men in the world), has been deputed her Majesty's "pictorial commissioner," to sketch the most beautiful natural scenery and modern cultivation in Ireland, in order that the Queen may make a selection for her visit next year; and that he has been in Limerick on that mission, taking sketches of the picturesque wood and water scenery of Castle Connell.—— Another Irish paper says, that the Queen has commissioned Mr. Deane Butler to prepare plans for a royal residence in Ireland, and that they are now ready. Quick work this, *if* true.

BLIND BUILDERS.—The following is a list of tenders opened on Wednesday for the erection of the Industrial Training Schools for 250 boys. They are to be built for the vestry of the parish of St. Pancras, on the site of the present stone-yard in the workhouse premises. Mr. James Lockyer, architect:—

C. O. S. Robson	£5,935	2	10
Clumanson and Moultrie	5,716	13	0
James Barr	5,611	0	0
J. Slade	5,569	0	0
J. W. Elliott	5,472	0	0
D. Bodger	5,219	13	2
W. Higgs	4,724	0	0
Thomas Rudkin	4,691	0	0
W. H. Cooper	4,649	0	0
Charles Crain	4,627	0	0
John Glen	4,511	0	0
Carter and Ellis	4,467	0	0
Joseph Yeoman	4,364	0	0
William Dennis	4,350	3	4
B. Homan	4,265	0	0
J. A. Hasher	3,921	0	0
W. Few	3,901	0	0
W. S. Dove, Milner-square (accepted)	3,862	0	0

* The same authors announce, we observe, another work, a companion to this,—" Details of Pointed Architecture, actically Delineated; or, Working Drawings of Doorways, indows, Buttresses, and other features of Ancient Ecclestical Architecture, with full-sized Sections of the uldings."

Assessment in Bethnal-green.—At a recent petty sessions to decide on objections to rates assessed by the surveyor, Mr. Paine, the case of Messrs. Truman and Hanbury, the brewers, was first tried. They objected to an increase from 1,150*l.* to 1,750*l.* on their brewery and stabling in the parish. The bulk of their premises are in the parish of Spitalfields, and stabling forms the most part of those in Bethnal-green, but that, the company's solicitor argued, could scarcely be rated in the same way as houses, inasmuch as the inhabitants were not likely to become chargeable to the parish. The frontage in the parish was 300 feet by 250 deep, and contained a cooperage and storehouse besides. Mr. Paine argued in defence, that the Act compelled him to regard this property not merely as stabling, but as a valuable adjunct to the brewery. There was stabling for 127 horses, which would pine and die in ordinary stables. The premises also contained a dwelling-house, and various other buildings, besides twelve vats, each said to be capable of holding a party of 100 seated at dinner. The area of the cooperage was 42,000 feet, and paved with granite. Mr. Parnell said that he never heard of paving being rated; and as for the vats, they were not fixtures, and were actually moved on some occasions. Details were then gone into, after which the court decided that 15s. per foot for frontage in Brick-lane, and 7s. for the others was too high, 7s. and 5s. being sufficient. The vats also being moveable, must be exempted. As for the other parts of the case, "seeing that we are bound," said the magistrate, "to rate machinery and plant, which was never done in this parish before, and that we must look at the value of these stables in connection with the important purposes to which they are applied, we consider it all proved." 150*l.* were then deducted on vats and land, and the assessment confirmed at 1,600*l.* Mr. Parnell intimated that his clients would doubtless carry the case before another tribunal.——Mr. C. Eagle, of Hackney-road, objected that the rating of his (public) house had been increased from 32*l.* to 45*l.* His rent was 40*l.*, on a lease with twenty-two years to run. Declined to say what premium he paid: rate confirmed.

Electro-Telegraphic Progress.—The telegraph at the Post-office is now in full operation, and despatches can be transmitted to Alnwick, Ambergate, Broxbourne, Birmingham, Burton-on-Trent, Barnsley, Beverley, Bridlington, Bradford, Berwick-on-Tweed, Bishopstoke, Chelmsford, Colchester, Cambridge, Chesterfield, Darlington, Derby, Dunbar, Durham, Ely, Edinburgh, Gloucester, Gosport, Glasgow, Hertford, Hull, Halifax, Ipswich, Lincoln, Loughborough, Leicester, Lowestoft, Leeds, Liverpool, Leith, March, Milton, Manchester, Malton, Morpeth, Newmarket, Newark, Nottingham, Norwich, Northallerton, Newcastle, Normanton, Peterborough, Romford, Rugby, Rotherham, Rochdale, Slough, Stortford, St. Ives, Stamford, Sheffield, Selby, Skipton, Scarborough, Sunderland, South Shields, Southampton, Thetford, Tamworth, Todmorden, Thirsk, Witham, Wisbeach, Worcester, Wakefield, Ware, York, and Yarmouth. The rate of charge for twenty words is 1d. per mile for first 50 miles, ½d. per mile for second 50 miles, and ¼d. per mile for any distance beyond 100 miles.——A proposal for carrying out the telegraph in British India, it is said, is under consideration by the East-India Company.

The Trafalgar-square Wells.—Workmen have been engaged in making canals in the ground straight along from the Spring-garden entrance to the park to the Storey's-gate entrance, for the purpose of laying down water-pipes, which are to convey the Trafalgar spring-water to Buckingham Palace. There is also a proposition for carrying the pipes up Constitution-hill across Knightsbridge into Hyde-park, to throw some thousands of gallons of pure water into the Serpentine. Along the line of pipes several water-pumps are to be erected for watering the streets.

Metal Cylinders cast without Cores.—A patent has been granted to Mr. A. Shanks, of Robert-street, Adelphi, engineer, for casting pipes, cylinders, and spherical vessels in moulds, by means of centrifugal force,—the mould being made to revolve on its axis by machinery, while the molten metal within adheres to its sides.

State of the Streets of Bristol.—With such intelligent and active authorities as we know Bristol has, it seems surprising that the surface of the streets should be allowed to remain in the miserably dirty state in which it is. The wind was blowing freshly as we walked through the "ancient city" on Saturday last, and the air at every fresh gust was filled with dust and triturated dung, to the great injury of the eyes, the temper, and the health of the busy crowd which filled both paths and roads. Good scavenging would, of course, cost money, but if some of the clear heads in the common council will quietly calculate the amount of injury done to the goods of the shopkeepers by this unnecessary dirt, the extra "washing and ironing" entailed on all the inhabitants, to say nothing of the effect on the general health (and illness and death are very costly matters), they will find that some thousands a-year would not pay the loss caused by the want of proper attention to the surface of the streets. This remark applies to many other places besides Bristol.

A Sanitary Commission for every Housekeeper.*—Some evening *soon*, provide yourself with a roll of brown paper, and visit every cellar sough in your dwelling. Light the roll of brown paper, and then extinguish the light, so as to leave only the smoking embers; apply the paper to the holes of the grid, and the direction of the smoke will tell you if you have a return draught from the drain. If the smoke is blown aside, get a sink-trap at once. This will be safer and cheaper than pouring any disinfecting fluid down your soughs. Look to the slop-stone pipe, and if it terminates in a sough, have a bell-trap put in the stone. Fever often enters by this waste pipe. The seeds of bowel complaints, dysentery, head-aches, enter many a house by a cellar sough, or a slop-stone pipe; the more readily if the house fires are connected with good drawing chimneys. The next visit of inspection may be to the bed-rooms; and when you enter, call to mind that though eye and limb may slumber, the heart and lungs know no rest. If eight hours be spent in the bedroom, the lungs have opened and closed 10,000 times during that repose, and the air which passes out is not only unfit to be breathed again, but contaminates the general air of the room; then remember a reckoning is due for the perspiration. Now inquire in what way you have aided the efforts of the lungs and the skin to purify the blood, and build up the waste of the day, and see whether you have not made a "famine of pure air." Remove the fire-board, take away the listing which has been tacked over the crevices of the window, and see that the joiner makes a way for the air to come in over the door (if you will sleep with it fully closed), and there is a corner in every room where the warmed and vitiated air may be led out. Bathing and sponging are excellent, but pure air in a bedroom is a *sine qua non* in this cholera time.

Levels of London.—Mr. Wyld, of the Strand, has published a map of London, on which are marked in red figures the levels taken by order of the Commissioners of Sewers for the information of those who contemplate submitting plans for the drainage of the metropolis. The altitudes are given in feet "above the approximate mean water at Liverpool, being 12½ feet below Trinity high-water mark."

Masons' Provident Institution.—Mr. Tite, F.R.S., has kindly consented to become president of the above institution, in the room of the late Alderman John Johnson. The objects of the institution are the erection of almshouses, and provision of a pension fund for decayed members of the trade, their widows and orphans, or for those who may become disabled by accident or infirmity.

Fire-proof Floors.—Messrs. Clarke and Motley, among other inventions, have patented what they think an improvement in the construction of floors of buildings fire-proof, on an economical plan, "which is not only applicable to new erections, but may be applied to existing buildings, such as warehouses, manufactories, mills, &c., very economically—viz., at not exceeding from 6d. to 9d. per superficial foot—so that a floor of 50 feet long and 20 feet wide may be rendered fire-proof for about 30*l.*"

* From a correspondent of the *Manchester Guardian*.

Cirencester Roman Pavement.—The newly-discovered pavement in the old town of Cirencester, the site of ancient Corinium, already mentioned by us, measures 25 feet square, and exhibits *nine circles* of nearly 5 feet diameter each. They contain (according to our correspondent) bold and well-executed heads of Ceres and Flora, and exceedingly spirited representations of Actæon and his dogs, and of Silenus riding on his ass.

Punctuality to Time by Rail enforced.—An Exeter solicitor, detained for an hour at the Starcross station on the South Devon line, was lately awarded 10s. damages by a jury, on the ground that an hour's delay in the arrival of a train, without good excuse, was actionable under the contract to carry passengers at a certain time, implied in the company's time-table.

On the Duration of Wood, and Means of Prolonging it.—The following are the results of experiments made with great care and pa cn c by Mr. G. S. Hartig:—Pieces of wood of various kinds 2 5-8th inches square, were buried about an inch below the surface of the ground, and they decayed in the following order:—The lime, American birch, alder, and the trembling-leaved poplar, in three years; the common willow, horse-chesnut, and plane, in four years: the maple, red beech, and common birch, in five years; the elm, ash, hornbeam, and Lombardy poplar, in six years; the robinia, oak, Scotch fir, Weymouth pine, and silver fir, were only decayed to the depth of half an inch in seven years; the larch, common juniper, red cedar (*juniperus virginiana*), and arbor-vitæ, at the end of the last-mentioned period, remained uninjured. The duration of the respective woods depends greatly on their age and quality; specimens from young trees decaying much quicker than those from sound old trees; and, when well seasoned, they last much longer than when buried in an unseasoned state. In experiments with the woods cut into thin boards, decay proceeded in the following order, commencing with the most perishable order:—The plane, horse-chesnut, poplar, American birch, red beech, hornbeam, alder, ash, maple, silver fir, Scotch fir, elm, Weymouth pine, larch, robinia, or locust oak. It has been proved, by recent experiments, that the best mode of prolonging the duration of wood is to char it, and then paint it over with three or four coats of pitch. But simply charring the wood was of very little utility, as were also saturations with various salts, acids, &c.—*Revue Horticole.*

Novel Building Materials.—The erection of a tenement in the Low Calton, Edinburgh, in which fire-brick alone is employed as the building material, instead of stone, has excited some interest among the inhabitants in that locality. The building, of which one story is already completed, is to consist of three flats, and the fire-brick is used in blocks of the size and appearance of hewn stone. The basement story is designed for a warehouse, the exterior being in the form of shops, and the front exhibits the elegance and finish of polished ashlar. The blocks are of large size, being upon an average 2 feet in length by 14 inches deep; but those employed in the construction of the other parts of the building are smaller, ranging from 18 to 20 inches long by 6½ to 9 inches square. The principal advantage in the use of fire-brick is its resistance to fire and damp, but the expense, we believe, is greater than stone, from the heavy duty upon bricks. The building, however, will have a light and clean appearance, and the experiment is viewed with some interest.—*Edinburgh Weekly Register.*

TENDERS

For the first portion of the North Surrey Industrial School, Penge, Mr. Lee, architect, opened on the 26th inst., in the presence of the builders:—

Barrett	£14,895
George Todd	14,579
George Myers	13,710
Mark Patrick	13,440
Nicholson and Son	13,291
John Glenn	12,814
Jas. Barr	12,695
Thos. Burton	12,679
Jno. Willson	12,670
Wm. Trego	12,669
Wm. Higgs	12,178
Edw. Carter	11,987
Carter and Ellis	11,957
J. T. Taylor	11,797

TO CORRESPONDENTS.

"*To remove Whitewash.*"—A correspondent asks for "a simple receipt for removing old whitewash from freestone. Many coats may be easily detached, but how is the first coat to be cleansed from the stone—*i. e.* got out of it?"

Received.—" E. O. W." (the delay in appearance of the third part of the "Publication Society's" work is no fault of the Council. It is to consist of *text*; and to obtain this at a given time from those who have undertaken to supply it is difficult. Subscriber's to societies of this sort, where all have one object, should be patient. The illustrations for next year are already in hand).—" An old Subscriber" (apply to Potter, South Molton-street, London), " J. B. D.," " C. H. B.," " W. H. Weale" (which shall we send a proof?), " W. H. L." (thanks: the subject would scarcely justify engraving), " D. C." (declined, with thanks), " C. F.," " M. R.," " A. H." (the suggestion has been made and acted on us), " W. C.," " An Architect" (Bristol), " Subscriber from Beginning" (several modes have been given by us at different times), " E. E. C.," " W. R.," " A Scotarian" (we could not advise without seeing the premises: get rid of the cesspool, of course, and get air under the floors), " S. P." (sorry we cannot comply. The View will be found in Part III. of " Buildings and Monuments"), " E. H." (shall't article was already in type. Has our correspondent been to the " diggings," or where?), " G. R. B." (we shall be very glad to have the drawings), " J. W. G." Liverpool (we have no authority to give our correspondent's address), " C. H. N.," " K.," " Idler in London," " A Peer."

NOTICE.— All communications respecting *advertisements* should be addressed to the "Publisher," and not to the "Editor;" all other communications should be addressed to the EDITOR, and *not* to the Publisher.

"*Books and Addresses.*"—We have not time to point out books or find references.

ADVERTISEMENTS.

MUIR'S　　　　PLANING
PATENT　　　　MACHINE.

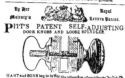

No. CCCXLVIII.

SATURDAY, OCTOBER 6, 1849.

REAT and urgent has become the necessity of supplying the intellectual wants of the population; and many thanks are due to Mr. William Ewart, M.P. (to whom the public are already greatly indebted for originating previous important inquiries connected with the cognate subjects of literature and art), for the recent Parliamentary inquiry as to the best means of extending the establishment of libraries freely open to the public.

The rudimental education of the people, in the fulfilment of its great purpose, has of late years been exciting intellectual wants,—opening wide, book-eating, hungry mental mouths throughout the country; and a necessity has arisen to provide the wherewithal to satisfy these healthy appetites. "For the last many years in England everybody has been educating the people, but they have forgotten to find them any books."[*] In byegone times, to be sure, the little musty old parochial libraries, which still lie scattered in dusty holes and corners throughout the country, did constitute a *supply* that even exceeded the *demand*. But then the essential preliminary process of *exciting* a demand by the general education of the people had scarcely been dreamt of, except indeed in Scotland, where "a respect for education and reading, long fostered by the ancient and excellent system of instruction by means of parochial schools, is hereditary." Of late years, however, both England and Scotland have made rapid progress in the initiative that now demands a further step in sequence, to be taken towards the fulfilment of that end towards which the spread of school-education was but a means.

The whole of the evidence recently adduced proves one thing clearly,—that "the qualifications of the people to appreciate and enjoy such institutions" as those demanded, namely, free public libraries in every city, town, village, and hamlet in the empire, "are unquestionable." And, with the still growing increase of these very qualifications, there is also "abundant testimony to the fact of a vast and progressive improvement in the national habits and manners." Of the fitness of the people for the rational enjoyment and the moral and general benefit to be derived from public libraries, as observed, there can be no greater proof than their own independent efforts to create them; and wherever any favourable opportunity presents itself, there it very soon appears that the working classes are not to be satisfied with the mere manufacture of the cheap abridgment and extracted substance of knowledge—the milk, merely, as it were, of the secular "Word" in their souls. With mental appetites hale and hearty, they revolt at all such pap, and yearn for the "strong meat" of *men*, as their only nutritive intellectual *viaticum*. Nothing short of the whole range of science and literature, in short, will satisfy their inquiring minds, once fairly

awake, with opportunity, to the treasures of wisdom and knowledge.

Although nothing new to us,—there is something that we are assured will astonish many, in the curious evidence adduced on this particular subject.

We are told, for instance, that some of the best-read men in Birmingham are working men, who are perfectly versant not only in history, politics, and literature generally, but in the sciences at large, and also in languages—such as the German and the French,—in all of which accomplishments, of course, they are self-taught;—that in Manchester there is a large class of operatives who are naturalists and members, curators, &c., of natural history societies, while there is also in the same place a curious set of 'working' botanists and entomologists, who make formal botanizing and entomological excursions;—that not only is Shakspeare in many instances known almost by heart, by working men, who can stand a cross-examination on any of his plays,—that not only do working men sustain a constant and fluent correspondence through the newspaper press on all sorts of subjects, and write ' poetry'—such as it may be—by the mile, on all sorts of subjects too,—but that there are many such men who constitute regular debating societies, or who dive even into and fully relish all the profundities of 'philosophy,' and are sworn disciples of Kant or Fichté, Schelling, or Hegel, or are warm admirers of Carlyle. And should it be asked, of what earthly use can some of such pursuits be to most of these wielders of the hammer or the shuttle, the chisel or the file, let us (leaving out higher arguments) whisper gently in response, that they all tend to calm political agitation and disturbance, ever fiercest in ferment where the only profundity of mind to fathom is that of ignorance—that it has been proved in formal evidence, in short, that where there is a studious or reading temperament and habit, there, too, is the least possible liability to be played upon by the mere appeals of demagogues to the feelings; and certainly such a result, in these times of revolutionary warfare, is worth "a king's ransom" in itself, or at the very least it is worth a free public library in every centre of political agitation and disturbance. Nevertheless, we cannot but admit that, it may be, some may thus be only filled with self-sufficient empty notions ill befitting the contented steady exercise of their respective handicrafts or callings; but the self-sufficiency of ignorance is an evil ten thousand-fold more inveterate. It is a curious fact, for instance, that in mining districts the uninstructed miners may be got to attend at any series of lectures rather than those on mineralogy or geology. So is it in many other trades—there is an ignorant conceit in the way of knowledge hard to remove. The *reading* workman, on the other hand, in his eagerness to improve his mind, needs no stimulus from without. And even where without the advantage of a library, many are known to work extra hours for "book-money." This desire for reading is even beginning to display itself in the very "ragged schools," where books, especially on emigration, are perpetually thumbed and eagerly devoured with the deepest and most affecting interest.

It would be well, however, if the reading of the masses were at least all as little capable of producing positive mischief. But from the want of a national diffusion of good books in public libraries, instruction itself (we will not call it education) has in many in-

stances done much evil by enabling the readers to peruse that never-ending flow of garbage, in the form of which, writers of even positive talent, and from whom better things might have been expected, are ever pandering, in some novelty of shape or other, to the basest feelings and passions of the million. In proportion as education increases, the facility of obtaining books corrective or preventive to such abomination, as well as to political dispeace and disturbance, ought to be increased and must be increased. And here is a field for the philanthropist, wide as that of ignorance itself, and even worse, in results; for ignorance may be consistent so far with rectitude of thought, feeling, and conduct, but *that* such false enlightenment can never be. Let every right-minded person then assist in this good cause as far as he can. The foundation of public libraries in every city, town, village, and hamlet throughout the empire would be a mighty good in many aspects, and it only remains for us to show how this, it is conceived, can best be done.

But first of a few statistical and other details of interest in connection with the purpose more immediately in view. And the report on which our present remarks are based is full of such details, presented both *vivâ voce* and in elaborate statements, tables, plans, &c., to the Committee, amongst which details we cannot resist a desire specially to allude to those by Mr. E. Edwards, of the British Museum, of whose ability and laborious industry we needed not these numerous and convincing proofs to be well assured.

Amongst the details is a curious map exhibiting the relative amount or provision of books in libraries publicly accessible in the principal states of Europe, as compared with their respective populations. The proportions are, to every 100 of the population in the British Isles and Holland, 63 to 53 books; in Russia and Portugal 80 to 76; in Belgium, Spain, and Sardinia, about 100; in France, 129; in the Italian States, 150; in the Austrian empire and Hungary, 167; in Prussia 200; in Sweden and Norway, 309; in Bavaria, 339; in Switzerland, 350; in Denmark, 412; and in the smaller German states, nearly 450!! Is it not sad to think that the British isles, which rank so high above all other states in other points of pre-eminence, are here the lowest of the low? These figures are black enough certainly, but the map, which is scored with black lines—close and numerous in proportion to the comparative paucity of books or—literary darkness, shall we say?—gives a still more glaring relief to our bad pre-eminence in this respect. The British isles are black as ink can make them—blacker than semi-barbarous Russia, while *the* one little bright spot, *par excellence*, is limited to the narrow outlines of the smaller German states.[*]

A heavy load of this disgrace, as might be anticipated, rests on poor Ireland. Amongst the details it is incidentally noted that there are 73 towns in Ireland without even a single bookseller, although the population of each averages 2,300! The priesthood are said to look with an evil eye on the diffusion of books of any class in Ireland. As for ourselves inclusive, there are 8,000,000 of us who cannot form even pothooks in writing. In a Norfolk parish of 400 people it was some few years since found absolutely necessary to elect a

---

[*] See Mr. George Dawson's evidence, p. 85, in Appendix to "Report from Select Committee on Public Libraries," &c., on which Report and Appendix the following remarks are based.

[*] From a table presented by Mr. Edwards, it appears that the average number of Volumes published within Great Britain and Ireland during the last ten years was 3,190½ Vols. per annum, and the average Value 1,317l. 4s. In Germany, about 11,000 separate works, including pamphlets, appear to have been issued during each of the last three years; and in France, 5,530 in 1847.

female as parish clerk, no male parishioner having so much learning or skill as to be able to write! This female probably still holds her post by virtue of her exclusive clerkship.

As to the more immediate subject of interest in the committee's report, that of public libraries, France contains 107 public libraries, all free, and unrestricted to poor and rich, to foreigner and native, while Britain has scarcely one of which the same can be said, although almost all foreign libraries together are free like those in France. Belgium has 14, Prussia 44, Austria 48, and the little State of Bavaria, 17. In Paris alone there are 7 ; in Florence 6 ; in Dresden 4, and in Vienna 3. A large proportion of these, too, are lending libraries, of which Britain is about as devoid as of libraries with perfectly free access. Indeed, the Chetham library, at Manchester, is the only one of the latter order in existence in this country, although a certain degree of freedom of access is enjoyed by the public, or certain classes of the public, in a few others. Even in such places as Birmingham, Sheffield, Leeds, and Hull, there is no public library of any kind. The United States appear to have numerous public libraries, and a multitude of readers, besides an immense general sale of books, so that authors do not appear to be injured by the public library system, but the contrary.

The first thing to be done towards the establishment of a liberal distribution of free public libraries in this country, advised in the evidence, is the erection of buildings by the respective town councils, or otherwise. Donations, it is believed, would thereupon rapidly flow in, and almost alone constitute large libraries. Half the books in the British Museum were donations. It is recommended, however, that Government assist by grants in aid of subscriptions, as to schools of design, &c., if not also by small rates, authorized by an extension of the Museums' Act, or otherwise. The reformation of such public libraries as already exist, is urged, and district branch libraries recommended. The Scottish system of itinerating libraries for small towns or villages is said to have worked well; and it appears that village libraries, farm libraries, mill, and even kitchen libraries, are spreading into minuter and more special ramifications, as it were, or rootlets of a great system. In the establishment of town libraries, it is conceived that, to be useful to the industrious classes, they must above all be open in the evenings. The want of such an arrangement in the British Museum library (which would of course require to be made compatible with freedom from all risk of loss by fire) renders it quite useless to such classes, and indeed to many literary professional men themselves. For the working classes, the system of public libraries actually, therefore, does not exist in this country at all. An evening sederunt is their only hope, and it is not in the least doubted that these classes would at once, and largely, avail themselves of such a privilege. The lending out of all ordinary works is regarded as an essential to the convenience and adequate study of the literary man himself. The utility of provincial town libraries to the provincial press, as well as to students and general authors, is inferred from various circumstances, such as occasional pilgrimages to the metropolis to consult works in the national library here. We have ourselves known instances of students quitting other employments in the provinces and coming to reside altogether in town, mainly with such views and purposes. In aid of the whole

system, as regards the people at large, the diffusion of lectures is strongly recommended, as eliciting discussion, and inducing many to seek out and peruse works bearing on the subjects of lecture. At present, some lecturers are said to reap a good harvest in the provinces, 500l. to 800l. per annum being estimated as the income of some of the more popular. The libraries of Mechanics' Institutes are said to belong to a somewhat higher class than the ordinary run of mechanics. A new order of public libraries, therefore, for the people at large is only the more pressingly called for and necessary. In some of the 2,000 coffee houses in the metropolis there are rather extensive libraries accessible, it may be said, without cost, inasmuch as no charge is made, and coffee, &c., may be had from one penny upwards.

For special libraries, special libraries, or collections of books, are advised, for the use of practical men. There should, it is thought, be a centralization of catalogues, if not a mutual and general exchange of them, and in the metropolis, in fact, a library of catalogues. Foreign nations, too, might exchange both catalogues and books, such as duplicates, as some already do. Authors and publishers abroad are called on as here to present copies of their books to certain libraries, but the Governments often subscribe to the publications, and purchase copies for further distribution. The benefit being public or national, it is justly conceived that the expense should not be borne by the authors. In fine, the appointment of a Ministry of Public Instruction is recommended.

We earnestly hope to see the intellectual wants of the population speedily supplied.

ON CIVIL ENGINEERING AND ARCHITECTURE.

AN INAUGURAL LECTURE.*

CIVIL engineering and architecture, the subjects upon which I am called to lecture, are both essentially practical sciences, and are in some measure so connected as to be synonymous; both the engineer and the architect must be well versed in the strength of the various materials with which they have to deal, and be so acquainted with their properties, as to be enabled to make a choice of them, for any peculiar circumstances attending their work.

Both must be mathematicians, draughtsmen, carpenters, masons, and be acquainted with the details of all, or nearly all, the mechanical trades ; at least they must be learned judges of them, if not skilful operators.

They must both be men of business, and should not be ignorant of law. Both architecture and engineering, therefore, in their most comprehensive meanings, are studies of many and singularly opposite qualities, and are allowed by all whose opinions are worth regarding, to be sciences of the highest importance to the well-being of society ; thus far the two professions go side by side. But architecture, as well as being a science, is also essentially a fine art, and here the two professions separate. The path of the architect will, after he has gained his practical knowledge of construction and building, be parallel with that of the painter and the poet in the regions of cultivated taste. The path of the civil engineer is widely different, and if his labours be less in the captivating regions of beauty than the architect's, they are perhaps more among the grand,—certainly more among the stern development of massive strength, to resist shocks, inundations, and storms which, from the simplicity of the requisite forms, and their associations, constitute grandeur. I come amongst you fully sensible of the responsibilities of my office, and with an equally full determination, to perform

*Read by Mr. Clegg before the College of Civil Engineers, Putney, on Wednesday, Sept. 26th.

its duties to the utmost of my power ; and I shall expect you to go with me, cheerfully, to the tasks which lie before us, and assist me with your diligence. Nothing is more necessary to the due understanding and proper study of engineering and architecture, and to the formation of a proficient in either, than habits of application and industry. Without them even the lowest departments of the professions are not to be mastered. It is not a rapid growth that produces a sound and skilful practitioner, any more than precocity is an emblem of a great statesman. It is not by occasional fits of application, by short starts of preparation, by numerous little works, performed in a little time, and with less study, sometimes discontinued, and again renewed, to suffer nothing to impede your progress, and by avoiding the dead sea of idleness and pleasure, that you can be enabled to shine either as an architect or as an engineer. Michelangelo, full of the great and sublime ideas of his art, lived very much alone, and never suffered a day to pass without handling his chisel or his pencil. When some person reproached him for leading so melancholy and solitary a life, he said, "Art is a jealous thing, and requires the whole and entire man." He was also both frugal and temperate, and so persevering in his labour, that he used occasionally at night to throw himself upon his bed without disencumbering himself of the clothes he had worked in. Inigo Jones, by his indefatigable zeal, raised himself from the position of a working mechanic to that of the first architect of the day. He was bound apprentice to a joiner ; but the Earl of Arundel, seeing his talent and industry, sent him to Rome to study landscape painting. When at Rome, finding that he possessed more talent for designing palaces than adorning cabinets, he turned his study to architecture. By denying himself the common necessaries of life,—by rising early, and retiring late, sometimes not going to his bed at all, he conquered all the difficulties in his path ; and after remaining some time in Italy, shackled by poverty, Christian the Fourth of Sweden invited him to Denmark, and appointed him his architect. He afterwards returned to England, and was made surveyor-general of the king's works to James the First, but refused to accept any salary until the heavy debts contracted under his predecessor had been liquidated. Upon the accession of Charles he was continued in his office, when his salary as surveyor was 8s. 4d. per day, with an allowance of 46l. per year for house rent. Sir Christopher Wren is an example of an architect excelling in mathematics, and producing works bearing the evident impress of their author's learning. From the number and diversity of his occupations, may be gathered the fact of his close study and application ; and although unlike Inigo Jones he had not poverty to fight against, infinite credit is due to him. He was one of the original members of the club which was formed at Oxford in 1648, for philosophical discussion and experiments, and which eventually gave rise to the Royal Society. In 1657 he was chosen professor of astronomy at Gresham College, and on the restoration was appointed to the Savilian professorship of astronomy at Oxford. It was very soon after this that he was first called upon to exercise his genius in architecture (a study, however, which had previously engaged a good deal of his attention), by being appointed assistant to the surveyor-general. This led to Wren's employment on the work on which his popular fame principally rests— the rebuilding of the cathedral of St. Paul's after the great fire. The erection of this noble edifice occupied him for thirty-five years, but did not prevent him during the same period from study and superintending the completion of many other buildings, nor even interrupted his pursuit of the most abstract branches of science. Wren was created a doctor of law and logic by the university of Oxford in 1661, and was knighted in 1674. In 1680 he was elected to the presidency of the Royal Society, and in 1685 he entered Parliament as the representative of the borough of Plympton. While superintending the erection of St. Paul's all the salary Wren received was 200*l*. He was also used by the commissioners in other respects with extreme illiberality and meanness, and was obliged to yield so far to their ignorant clamour as to alter the design of his building, and to decrease the size of his dome, which he had intended should spring from the outside large gallery which surrounds it. If he had had the moral courage of Michelangelo, we should have had yet a nobler monument of his fame. Michelangelo, like Wren, had obstacles thrown in his way, and we are told the following anecdote:—Under the papacy of Julius III. the faction of Michelangelo's rival, San Gallo, gave him some trouble respecting the building of St. Peter's, and went so far as to prevail upon that pope to appoint a committee to examine the fabric. Julius told him that a particular part of the church was dark. "Who told you that, holy father?" replied the artist. "I did," said Cardinal Marcello. "Your eminence should consider, then," said Michelangelo, "that besides the window there is at present, I intend to have one in the ceiling of the church." "You did not tell me so," replied the cardinal. "No, indeed, I did not, Sir; I am not obliged to do it, and I would never consent to be obliged to tell your eminence or any other person whomsoever anything concerning it. Your business is to take care that money is plenty in Rome, that there are no thieves there,—to let me alone, and to permit me to proceed with my plan as I please." Wren's ungrateful employers, in 1718, dismissed him from his place of surveyor of public works: he was at this time in the 86th year of his age. This great and good man died at Hampton Court on the 25th February, 1723, in the 91st year of his age. His remains were accompanied by a splendid attendance to their appropriate resting-place under the noble edifice which his genius had reared, and over the grave was fixed a tablet, with the following inscription:—"Beneath, is laid the builder of this church and city, Christopher Wren, who lived about 90 years, not for himself but for the public good. Reader, if thou seekest for his monument, look around."

Great architects, if uniting with their works any other pursuit or study, have generally fixed upon some branch of science or art connected with architecture: thus, Michelangelo was a sculptor; Inigo Jones was a painter, and then an astronomer. But Sir John Vanbrugh was a dramatist as well as an architect; he wrote "The Provoked Wife," "Esop," and other comedies, and built Blenheim and Castle Howard.

Were I to give the character of each and all the eminent architects of this or any other country, they would serve to show how great was the amount of their labour, and with what cheerfulness and perseverance they pursued their tasks at the commencement of their career, and with what determined energy they maintained their name and fame after they had risen to excellence: nor will the characters of civil engineers lose by comparison with the already-named artists.

When the state of civilization and trade in England required more convenient and cheaper modes of transit for its goods than the common roads and waggons of the day afforded, a system of inland navigation was proposed, and Mr. Smeaton was employed in making rivers available for this purpose: afterwards, more direct routes became desirable, and canals were projected, in imitation of those made before by the Dutch and French. The Duke of Bridgewater was the great patron of these schemes, and brought forward James Brindley, who constructed for him the canal called the Bridgewater Canal, between Liverpool and Manchester. This immense work, the idea of which was ridiculed by most of the scientific men of the period as impracticable, Brindley undertook, and completed so as to form a junction with the Mersey. This success caused him to be employed, in 1766, to unite the Trent and Mersey, upon which he commenced the Grand Trunk Navigation Canal. From this main branch Mr. Brindley cut another canal near Haywood, in Staffordshire, uniting it with the Severn in the vicinity of Bewdly, and finished it in 1772. From this period scarcely any work of the kind in the kingdom was entered upon without his superintendence or advice. Among other designs, he prepared one for draining the fens of Lincolnshire, and the Isle of Ely, and another for clearing the Liverpool Docks of mud, which was especially successful. The variety of his inventions, and the fertility of his resources, were only equalled by the simplicity of the means by which he carried his expedients into effect. He seldom used any model or drawing, but when any material difficulty presented itself, he used to seclude himself for days, or until an idea presented itself to him for overcoming it; and so partial was he to inland navigation, that upon the question being put to him by the opposition to one of his schemes, "For what purpose he imagined rivers to have been created," he at once replied, "Undoubtedly to feed navigable canals." The intensity of his application to business brought on a fever, of which he died in 1772, in the fifty-sixth year of his age.

John Smeaton, another engineer, who did much to advance his profession in this country, may almost be said to have been born an engineer, his genius appeared at so early an age. His playthings were not those of children, but the tools which men employ. Before he was six years of age, he was discovered on the top of his father's barn, fixing up what he called a windmill, of his own construction; and at another time, while he was about the same age, he attended some men fixing a pump, and observing that they cut off a piece of the bored pipe, he procured it, and actually made a pump with it, which raised water. When he was under 15 years of age, he made an engine for turning, and worked several things in ivory and wood, which he presented to his friends. A part of every day was occupied in forming some ingenious piece of mechanism. In 1751 he began a course of experiments to try a machine of his own invention, to measure a ship's way at sea, and made two voyages to try the effect of it, and also to make experiments upon a compass of his construction. In 1753, he was elected a fellow of the Royal Society, and the number of papers he published in their transactions, will show how highly he deserved the honour of being enrolled a member of that useful and important body: in 1759 he received the gold medal.

In 1775, the Eddystone Lighthouse, was burned down, and Mr. Smeaton being recommended to the proprietors of that building as an engineer in every way calculated to rebuild it, he undertook the work, which was completed in 1759. To this work I shall allude more particularly when instructing you in the building of lighthouses, as the practice of budding then adopted has been continued to this day. But the part of Mr. Smeaton's life I would more particularly draw your attention to is this. During many years he was a frequent attendant upon Parliament, his opinion upon various works begun or projected being continually called for; and in these cases his strength of judgment and perspicuity of expression had full scope.

It was his constant custom, when applied to, to plan or to support any measure, to make himself fully master of the subject, to understand its merits and probable defects, before he would engage in it. By this caution, added to the clearness of his expression, and the integrity of his heart, he seldom failed to obtain for the Bill which he supported the sanction of Parliament. No one was ever heard with more attention, nor had any one ever more confidence placed in his testimony. In the Courts of Law he had several compliments paid him from the bench, by Lord Mansfield and other judges, for the new light he always threw on difficult subjects. Mr. Smeaton died in 1792, in the 68th year of his age.

John Rennie, to whom England is indebted for some of her noblest engineering works, was born on the 7th of June, 1761, at Phantassie, in the parish of Prestonkirk, in the county of East Lothian. His father, a highly respectable farmer, died in 1766, leaving a widow and nine children, of whom John was the youngest. The first rudiments of his education were acquired at the village school. It so happened that he had to cross a brook on the way, which, when flooded, obliged him to make use of a boat kept in the workshop of Mr. Andrew Meikle, an ingenious mechanic, well known in Scotland as the inventor of the thrashing machine. In passing so frequently through this workshop, young Rennie's attention was directed to the various operations in which the men were engaged; and they, noticing the interest he took in their labours, were in the habit of lending him tools and showing him their use. In the evenings he amused himself with endeavouring to imitate the models he had seen at the shop; and it is related that, at little more than ten years of age, he had completed the models of a windmill, a pile-engine, and a steam-engine. Rennie continued at the Preston school till twelve years of age, when, having had a quarrel with his master, he entreated to be allowed to leave, and, at his own request, was placed for two years with Mr. Meikle. At the end of that time, feeling that a constant application to manual labour was likely to retard his mental improvement, he determined to become a pupil of Mr. Gibson, an able mathematical teacher at Dunbar. Here he soon attained great proficiency, and in less than two years returned to Mr. Meikle with a mind well stored with mathematical and physical science. His first essay in practical mechanics was the repairing of a corn-mill in his native village; and before he was eighteen years of age he had erected several others. During this time he occasionally visited Edinburgh, to pursue his studies in physical science, under Professors Robinson and Black. The former of these gentlemen may perhaps have laid the foundation of his future fortune, by introducing him to Messrs. Boulton and Watt, of Soho. Deeming the capital the proper theatre to try the strength of his own powers, Rennie settled in London, after having been a few months only with Boulton and Watt, who had confided to him the superintendence of the mill-work of the Albion Mills then erecting. Mr. Rennie was thus led to study hydraulic engineering, in which he became so celebrated as, after the death of Smeaton, to have no rival. Amongst the most celebrated works of this great engineer must be mentioned—besides numerous mills, bridges, canals—London, Waterloo, and Southwark bridges, the Lancaster Canal, with the aqueduct over the Lune, the breakwater in Plymouth Sound, and the improvements in the dockyards at Portsmouth, Plymouth, Chatham, and Sheerness. The industry of Mr. Rennie was so great, that he never suffered amusement of any kind to interfere with his business, which frequently occupied him twelve, and sometimes fifteen hours in the day. He was clear in his mode of communicating information to others, and pleased when he found that information was desired. He was never actuated by professional jealousy, or selfish feelings, but was always kind and condescending to the more humble members of his profession. Mr. Rennie died on the 16th of October, 1821, in the sixtieth year of his age, and was buried in St. Paul's, where his remains repose near to those of Sir Christopher Wren.

Thomas Telford was born in 1757, and commenced his life as a shepherd boy in Eskdale; but his early and eager love of knowledge led him to seek abroad an occupation more suited to his inclinations. He first repaired to Edinburgh, where he studied architecture with unremitting application, although he must have earned his daily bread by the labour of his hands. In 1782 he was emboldened to try his fortune in London, and was (as he states in his life, written by himself), fortunate enough to be employed at the quadrangle at Somerset-place, where he acquired much practical information, both in the useful and ornamental branches of architecture. After a residence of two years in London, he was engaged in superintending the building of a house in the Portsmouth Dockyard. During the three years, he remarks, that I was employed in building the commissioner's house, and of a new chapel in the Dockyard, I had an opportunity of observing the various operations necessary in the foundation and construction of graving docks, wharf walls, and similar works, which afterwards became my chief employment." When he left Portsmouth, he was appointed surveyor to the county of Salop, and to this, and the connections formed at this time, he was indebted for a very favourable opening of his career as a civil engineer. His chief attention was devoted to building and repairing bridges, but he also built several churches and other architectural edifices.

Telford's progress in his professional career, though not rapid, was steady and certain, and every new opportunity of exerting his talents contributed to extend a reputation which at length became unrivalled — not to his talents alone though, be it said, but by downright hard work united with them. To enumerate all his works would take a long time, but his principal ones are the Holyhead-road (upon which he himself sets higher value than any other), and the Menai-bridge, unquestionably the most imperishable monument of Telford's fame.

The defects of his early education he had endeavoured to remedy by his own unaided exertions in his maturer years. He taught himself Latin, French, German, and mathematics, in which he was a proficient, but relied more for the dimensions of his works upon practical experiment than upon calculation; but his reason for the preference may have been, and most likely was, his distrust of the data furnished him by mathematical experimenters in those days; but now that we have had Barlow and Hodgkinson, calculations from the results of their labours may be safely relied on.

Telford was the first President of the Institution of Civil Engineers, and died still holding that office in 1834, aged 77 years.

From these few instances in the lives of men devoted to science and to art, the student will learn the necessity of study, exertion, and self-dependence. An architect or an engineer taking up his work as a task, or merely with the business-like view of earning a livelihood, will never excel. In the days when men of science were comparatively scarce, great perseverance was necessary to get into notice and rise to fame; but double exertions are now necessary; an aspirant to professional honour will find himself jostled and hard set by competitors at every step of his progress, and this must raise up within him a determined spirit of emulation, a spirit not to be daunted or cast down by failures, but one that will become more buoyant by pressure, one that with steady stride and upright head will still walk up the steep and difficult path which leads to fortune.[*]

MASTER CARPENTERS' SOCIETY.

SMALL DRAINS.

A meeting of the master carpenters' society was held at the Freemasons' Tavern, Sept. 26, and was attended by Mr. Nesham, president; Mr. Stephens, Mr. Stephen Bird, Mr. George Bird, Mr. Norris, Mr. Eales, Mr. Burstall, Mr. Outhwaite, Mr. Unwin, and others.

Mr. Stephens called the attention of the society to the recent regulations of the Commissioners of Sewers respecting house drainage, and the restrictions as to the unusually small sizes of the pipes permitted to be used from dwelling-houses, and said, if, as he anticipated, the present sizes proved insufficient in general use, the public would have reason to complain of having been forced to lay down pipes which most practical men considered inefficient.

Mr. Geo. Bird said it was necessary that the members should meet numerously and consider the proposed new Buildings Bill. It appeared to him that few of the recommendations of this society had been well considered, and he proposed that the committee meet and study the various clauses of the Bill. With regard to the inconvenience mentioned by Mr. Stephens arising from the instructions of the Commissioners of Sewers, he thought that previously to such extensive alterations and new regulations being made and forced upon the public, some eminent engineers, architects, and practical men, should be consulted. Mr. Bird referred to one instance in particular as coming under his own observation. In October last, a 12-inch pipe was laid down in the centre of the existing 3 feet sewer in George-street, which takes the drainage from Bryanstone and Montague-squares, and all the collateral sewers in the neighbourhood. As soon as he perceived it he called at Greek-street, and pointed it out to

[* To be continued.]

the clerk, who assured him that a 12-inch pipe drain was large enough. Mr. Bird differed and left, stating that it was not the proper season to try such an experiment, as most of the inhabitants of the district were out of town, and therefore not above half the usual quantity of water was sent into the sewers. In April or May last, he saw the pipes broken to pieces and taken out, after putting the public to the useless expense.

Several of the other members expressed similar opinions, and hoped the commissioners would seek the opinions of the leading architects and engineers, combined with a few practical men, before they adopted or committed the public to so important a matter as a plan for the complete drainage of the London district.

OSMASTON CHAPEL, DERBYSHIRE.

A Sir H. Wilmot's pew.   E Clerk's desk.
B Clergyman's ditto.   F Reading ditto.
C Font.   G Pulpit.
D Staircase to turret.   H Stove.

Osmaston is situated about three miles from the railway station at Derby, near the road to Ashby-de-la-Zouch. It is written "Osmundestune," in the Domesday survey; no doubt taking its name from Osmund, the Saxon possessor, in the reign of Edward the Confessor.

The manor was granted to Robert Holland, Esq., in 1307, as an appendage of Melbourne, with which manor it has passed ever since, being in 1817 the property of the Marquis of Hastings. The principal estate here belongs to Sir H. Wilmot, baron, descended from a younger branch of the Wilmots of Chadderden. Sir Nicholas Wilmot, of Osmaston, serjeant-at-law, in the reign of Charles the Second, was fourth son of Robert Wilmot, Esq., of Chadderden, by the heiress of Shrigley. The late Sir Robt. Wilmot was created a baron in 1772.[*] Osmaston Hall is the seat of this family.

The chapel is built within a short distance of the hall. In it are the monuments of Sir Nicholas Wilmot, knight, who died in 1632, aged 72; that of Sir Robert Wilmot, the first baronet, who died in 1772, aged 65 years; and that of Sir Robert Wilmot, the second baronet, who died in July, 1834, at the advanced age of 82 years. Robert-de-Dun, Lord of Breadsall, in the reign of Henry the Second, gave up all his rights in the patronage of the chapel to the abbot of Derby. Sir H. Wilmot is the present patron. Robert Foncher, or Folger, founded a chantry in the chapel in 1357, the endowment of which was, in 1547, valued at 60s. 8d.

The chapel consists of a nave measuring 29 ft. 9 in. by 16 ft. 9 in.; and a chancel 20 ft. 9 in. by 13 ft. 3 in.; the length of chancel includes the east wall of nave which is 2 ft. in thickness. The entrance doorway is placed

[* Lysons' Derbyshire.]

in the south wall of nave, the door of which follows the sweep of the arch; the panel above the springing being pierced and filled in with glass—rather an unusual occurrence. There is no porch. The bell turret is at the west end, in centre of roof, a portion of the nave being used as a "bell-chamber," without even the slightest apology of a screen to separate the ringer from the congregation. The way of approach to the turret is by an open staircase, outside, and built up in the south-west corner of nave. Some of the treads are not more than 4½ in. wide, but the rise is very steep. The turret is framed of wood, covered with plain tiles, and crowned by a vane, which has become rather bent by age. The north and south sides are open, and louvre boarded, the others lath and plaster. The roof of nave appears to be very strongly framed, and well tied. None of the timbers are visible from below—joists being thrown in between the ties and the whole ceiled flat. Two corbels, resting on stone corbel head, are however left naked; they are in the centre of nave, and support one of the tiebeams; but their accompaniments being cut off, they look sadly out of place. They are of novel formation, and would doubtless have a good effect in an open timbered roof. The font is pushed up in a corner, being in an angle formed by a pew and the west wall. The pedestal is square, the shaft round, and the basin polygonal; although not more than 2 ft. 9 in. high, it is stepped to the wall, having an iron roller round shaft, and a holdfast. Although it does not appear very old, it is decidedly infirm. The stove is placed close by, and near the entrance, for the purpose of heating the air ere it reach the pulpit. The pipe is thrust through the west wall, and carried up above the roof, a complete eyesore both externally and internally. The nave, chancel, and "sanctum sanctorum," are paved with common red bricks: within the altar-rail the bricks are covered with brown paper, over this, a carpet. The communion-table is very plain, covered with scarlet cloth. The east wall is pierced with a three-light window, arched and cusped under a low four-centred arch. It is a very common, late, and debased design of the second pointed style. The lights are filled in with quarry glass, having four quarries in the centre of the centre light in one, with the letters I H S painted on in yellow, the colour of which has flown much. The window is rather deeply splayed inside, but without any moulding. There is a small window in south of chancel, with an ogee arch, but devoid of tracery; the jambs of this are square, as are the two on the opposite side, lighting the squire's pew, and which are exactly similar: these three are filled in with stained and plain glass, set alternately in an octagonal pattern. The pew has a stove in it, and betokens much attention to the comfort of the occupants. The stove communicates with a flue outside, in the shape of a massive buttress, finished square at the top. The use of it is unmistakeable, and shows in a remarkable manner the subserviency design had to construction with the mediæval architects, and making good the motto of "The Builder," "Structural propriety is the main element in the production of beauty." The altar-rail is very poor, and the supports—call them what you will—very curious. The vicar's pew is the chancel is likewise inclosed in the same manner, contrasting strongly with the comfortable pew on the opposite side. The remaining pews are large, square, social apartments, just three lumbering things that are now properly getting out of date with our modern contrivers, who seem afraid to lose an inch of area. Verily they are justified in the "economy" when expected to find accommodation at "four pounds a head,"[*] and this including all extras. No such parsimony governed our forefathers; what they applied to the purposes of religion was of the best procurable, given with an open hand, and upon the principle that "a labourer is worthy of his hire." Nothing was with them too good for the house of their Lord: if that was all the parish possessed, still that was a piece of decency; strong, though not heavy, fine, yet not tawdry. In their age of poverty, their children were rich; in ours of wealth, the generality are poor.

[* Cheltenham. "The Builder," July 7, 1849.]

This ought not to be. What is to be done, should be done well, and for posterity. We plant our estates to enrich our sons; let us not, at the same time, burden them with the constant repairs of that which should be delivered to them free and unencumbered. You have done much, MR. BUILDER, towards the cleansing of the "Augean stable;" you have dealt giant-blows, and progressed with giant strides, yet much remains for you to do. In your efforts to effect so great and good a change we wish you God speed,—remember your motto, and "nil desperandum."

The free seats are very commodious, and fitted up with book and kneeling-boards. The brick floors would be uncomfortable, were not our "bold peasantry, their country's pride," accustomed to that in their own homes, a boarded room being with them a rarity. Bricks and plaster constitute their floors generally. The plaster is very clean and good; it is likewise (an all-important consideration) very cheap.

The reading-desk and pulpit are placed rather curiously, the means of access being through the clerk's desk to the reading-desk, and through both to the pulpit. The pulpit is octagonal, of oak, and is provided with a sounding-board. The windows being behind the desk, the light is thrown directly on the books, without inconveniencing the clergyman.

By referring to the plan it will be seen that this chapel possesses a marked peculiarity, namely, a buttress in the centre of the west end, as Howel Church,* its thickness above the base moulding is 1 ft. 9 in.; its projection 3 ft. 9 in.; it is of three stages, and dies into the wall at about the commencement or base line of gable. With exception of the side buttress there is only one other, and that is set diagonally at the north-east corner of the chancel; it is finished ere reaching the eaves, but the ivy is too thick to ascertain the number of its stages.

I had forgotten to mention an oil painting, (by whom I could not learn) which is hung on the north side of the chancel, but in a light that does not allow it to show to advantage. It is a representation of the birth of our Saviour; astonishment, not unmixed with fear, is depicted in the countenances of the bystanders, who seem to be making all sorts of conjectures, and pointing to the infant Jesus.

W. WIGGINTON.

REMARKS ON THE RESISTANCE OF POSTS TO FLEXURE.†

THE ordinary formula for the stiffness of beams, supported at the ends and loaded in the middle, is

$$w = \frac{b\,d^3}{c\,l^3}$$

in which (w) represents the weight which produces a given deflection; b = breadth in inches; d = depth in inches; and l = length in feet; c is a constant, to be determined by substituting the values of the other quantities in the equation.

In making experiments to determine the constant from this formula, it is necessary to observe very accurately both the weights and the deflections produced by them, and then, by means of a proportion, find the value of (w), which will produce the deflection required to be substituted in the formula.

In reflecting upon the circumstances connected with the flexure of beams, the writer conceived the idea of deducing an expression for the weight which a post would support from the ordinary formula for the stiffness of a horizontal beam, by the following considerations:—If a beam is bent by an applied weight there will be a tendency, from the elasticity of the material, to recover its form when the weight is removed; but if the ends are fastened by being placed between resisting points, so that the piece cannot recover its shape, there must be a horizontal force caused by the reaction of the material, and this force is such, that if the beam were placed in a vertical position and loaded with a weight equal to it, the deflection should be the same as that of the horizontal beam, and consequently the extreme

* See page 189, present vol. of "THE BUILDER."
† From the "Journal of the Franklin Institute."

---

limit of the resistance of the post to flexure would be determined.

To ascertain the force which is exerted by the reaction of a bent beam in the direction of the chord of the arc.

Let AB represent a beam, supported at the ends and loaded with a weight (w) applied at the middle point.

d = deflection caused by the applied weight.

BC = tangent of curve at B.

If the weight be removed, the reaction of the beam will cause it to regain its original figure; if not resisted by a pressure at the ends. The force of this reaction will be proportional to the degree to which the fibres are strained, and as the strain upon the fibres is nothing at the ends A and B, and increases uniformly to the middle point, the force of reaction will be in the same proportion, and the point of application of the resultant of the whole of the reacting forces will correspond to the centre of gravity of a triangle whose base is Bf; it will, consequently, be at a distance from B $= \frac{2}{3} Bf$.

The effect of this resultant acting at a distance $\frac{2}{3} Bf$, must be the same as the weight $\left(\frac{w}{2}\right)$ acting at a distance Bf, and must consequently be in proportion to $\frac{w}{2}$ as 3 : 2. The value of the resultant is therefore $\frac{3\,w}{4}$.

The line of direction of the pressure at B being the tangent BC, the force of reaction at k may be considered as applied at the point k of its line of direction; and as kAB and CfB are similar triangles, $Cf : fB :: \frac{3}{4}\,w : w$;

horizontal pressure at $B = \frac{3}{4}\,w \times \frac{fB}{fC}$;

$\frac{3}{4}\,w\,\frac{l}{2\,d} = \frac{3\,w\,l}{16\,d}$. Representing this force by P, we have

$$P = \frac{3\,w\,l}{16\,d}.$$

As the deflection of a beam within the elastic limits is always in proportion to the weight, if (w) = the weight that will produce a deflection equal to unity, the deflection (d) will require a weight = (d w'), and by substituting this value in the equation, we find

$$P = \frac{3}{16} \cdot \frac{d\,w'\,l}{d} = \frac{3}{16}\,w'\,l.$$

In this expression (d), which represents the deflection, has disappeared, and as (w') is a constant quantity for the same beam, representing the weight that produces a deflection equal to the unit of measure, it follows that P is the same with every weight and every degree of deflection within the elastic limits.

This result seems at first view to be contrary to fact; it would appear that if the weight be increased, the horizontal strain should be increased in the same proportion; but when it is remembered that the deflection increases with the weight, and that the former diminishes the value of P in precisely the same proportion that the latter increase it, the difficulty vanishes, and the reason why P should be constant for the same beam becomes obvious.

The practical importance of this result is very great, as it furnishes the means of obtaining a formula which will give at once the extreme limit of the resistance to flexure, or the weight which, applied to a post, will cause it to yield by bending.

As the formulae used by Tredgold are calculated for a deflection of $\frac{1}{40}$th of an inch to one foot, or $\frac{1}{480}$ of the length, the weight which would cause a deflection of 1 would be w $\left(1 + \frac{l}{480}\right) = \frac{480\,w}{l}$, and by substituting this value for w' in the equation

$$P = \frac{3}{16}\,w'\,l,$$

we find P = 90 w = A.

But from the ordinary formula for the stiff-

---

ness of a beam supported at the ends we have $w = \frac{b\,d^3}{c\,l^3}$. Therefore $P = \frac{90\,b\,d^3}{c\,l^2} = B$.

The expression P = 90 w shows that the extreme limit of the strength of any post whatever, of any length, breadth, or depth, or of any kind of material, is ninety times the weight which causes a deflection of $\frac{1}{40}$ of the length.

The second expression, $P = \frac{90\,b\,d^3}{c\,l^2}$, will give the value of P directly, without first knowing the weight required to cause a given deflection in a horizontally supported beam. In this expression, b = breadth in inches, d = depth or at least dimension in inches, l = length in feet, and c = a constant to be determined by experiment for each species of material.

The value of c for white pine is ·01. By substituting this value, we find $P = \frac{9000\,b\,d^3}{l^2}$, a remarkably simple formula, which gives the extreme limit of the resistance to flexure of a white pine post.

The same expression may be used to determine the constants used in the ordinary formula for the stiffness of beams. For this purpose let the equation $P = \frac{90\,b\,d^3}{c\,l^2}$ be transposed, which will give $c = \frac{90\,b\,d^3}{P\,l^2}$. Find P by applying a string to a flexible strip of the material to be experimented upon, in the manner of a chord to an arc, and ascertain the tension on the chord with an accurate spring balance. It will be found that, whether the strip be bent much or little, the tension on the chord, as shown by the spring balance, will be constant, and this tension, in pounds substituted for P, will give the value of c without requiring, as is necessary with other formulæ, an observation of the deflection.

Experiments made upon these principles with strips of white pine, yellow pine, and white oak, 5 feet long, 1½ inch wide, and ¼ inch deep, give the following results:—

The observed tensions were—
White pine, 7¼ lbs. value of c = ·0097
Yellow pine, 6½ ,,   ,,   = ·0108
White oak,   6½ ,,   ,,   = ·0104

As the stiffness is inversely as their constants, it follows that white pine is stiffer than yellow pine or oak. The experiments of Tredgold give similar results.

R. HOUPT, C.E.

THE WESTMINSTER IMPROVEMENT COMMISSION.

THE great importance of forming a thorough fare through the populous district of Westminster, not only for the object of the sanitary condition of a large and densely inhabited district, lying contiguous to the New Palace of Westminster and the Queen's Palace at Pimlico, but also for forming a suitable and convenient communication between the seat of the Legislature and the large and wealthy district of Belgrave-square, has long been recognized. Acts of Parliament were obtained in 1845 and 1847 to promote these objects, and the Legislature, feeling this great importance of the project, granted very considerable powers and pecuniary assistance to the commissioners, to whom the carrying out of the act was intrusted.

Without entering into the details of the various proceedings which are always required to conduct such undertakings to a successful conclusion, or assenting to all the acts of the commissioners, it may be sufficient to say that many improvements have been made in the line of street as originally laid down; and powers to form new collateral streets and other additional advantages have been obtained. The commissioners have silently and gradually purchased a large amount of property through this dense and ill-tenanted locality; nearly the whole line of street is now opened of the width of 80 feet, and it is a circumstance unusually favourable in the formation of streets of this description, that a depth of building-land has been secured on each side of the street from 50 to 70 feet deep; and with powers which will be gradually put in force to clear large tracts of the adjoining property. We may have something to say to the commissioners before long,

THE HALL AT BOWOOD.

THE HALL AT BOWOOD.

Bowood is the seat of the Marquis of Lansdowne; it is situate about 4½ miles from Chippenham, in the middle of a noble park. The mansion is a large and fine pile of building, the work of the Adams. It has lately had some considerable additions, of conservatories, terrace gardens, &c., by Mr. Barry. Our view represents the end of the great hall, and illustrates how a seeming difficulty in the hands of a skilful architect may become a beauty. Without giving the plan of the upper rooms of the building, we can hardly illustrate the inconvenience sometimes occasioned by carrying up a large room, such as this entrance hall, two stories in height, by its interference with the communication between the rooms on each side of it on the upper floor.

The ingenious way in which a passage in this instance is obtained, will be evident upon an inspection of the view. An easy communication is obtained between the rooms on either side, on the upper floor, and a picturesque termination formed for the hall itself.

FRENCH IMPORTS OF METALS.—The chief imports in August last, in met. quin., as compared with those of August, 1847, were—

	August, 1847.	August, 1849.
Rough castings	58,190	18,301
Zinc	10,994	5,267
Lead	17,456	16,312
Brass	2,403	3,110
Copper	5,621	10,541

THE BIRMINGHAM WORKHOUSE COMPETITION.

REMUNERATION OF ARCHITECTS.

THE guardians of the Birmingham union seem to have made up their minds to keep in our books. At their last meeting the committee reported that they had made an offer to Messrs. Drury and Bateman of a sum of 800l. to prepare the necessary working drawings, and superintend the erection of the new workhouse according to their plans; that amount not being intended to include the remuneration of the clerk of the works. (The building, we should mention, is estimated at 25,000l.) The chairman read the reply of Messrs. Drury and Bateman, which stated, that as the expenses out of pocket already incurred, and those which must necessarily be incurred hereafter, in carrying out the designs for the new workhouse, would amount to nearly the sum proposed to be paid them, and leave scarcely anything to compensate services that would extend over a period of two years, they were under the necessity of declining the offer. They were willing, however, to make some concessions, and hoped to be met in the same spirit. A motion that 900l. should be offered was put, but ultimately, after considerable discussion, it was resolved, by a majority of 26 to 12, that an offer of 4 per cent. upon the outlay should be made to the architects as a remuneration for their services.

This affords a fresh example of the position in which architects place themselves who go into competition without properly-arranged conditions. After risking the entire loss of the time and expense incurred in the preparation of designs, and succeeding against rivals, they are offered less than the ordinary remuneration paid in cases where there is no risk at all. If the guardians did not intend paying the ordinary commission, they were bound to say so in the first instance.

We have given publicity to the improper circumstances attending the selection of Messrs. Drury and Bateman's plan (which may be not merely the best of those submitted, but the best ever made, for aught we know to the contrary); but the guardians having appointed them, we are bound to protest against the endeavour which is being made to induce them to accept less than the usual commission.

BACKS OF HOUSES.—I think a word might be said with advantage on the mode of constructing the backs of some of our finished houses, which are made as unsightly and unlike the fronts as possible. Look, for instance, at Kemp-town, and other of the great terraces at Brighton, which, seen from the back, look more like piles of workhouses or factories than the residences of the gentry of England. A little attention to "keeping" in building the backs of houses, would add greatly to their beauty and very little to their cost.—P.

TOWER OF ST. MARY'S CHURCH, TAUNTON.

[15th CENTURY.]

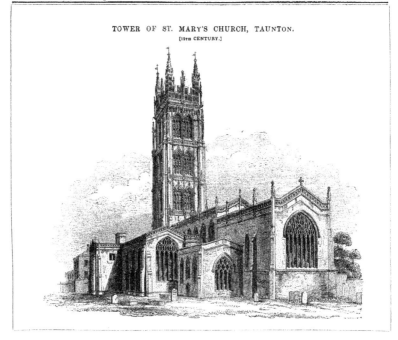

TOWER OF ST. MARY'S CHURCH, TAUNTON.

Two or three weeks ago, called in to examine professionally the very interesting church at Wrington, in Somersetshire (and concerning which we shall have a few words to say hereafter, not unimportant to church-builders), we took to the "down" rail again, instead of the "up," and steamed on to Taunton, to revive our recollection of the church of St. Mary Magdalene. Five-and-thirty miles on the iron horse take less time than a short spire-hunt on foot " across country."

It is too late now to talk to our readers of the very extensive works at St. Mary's, which, commenced in 1842, through the exertions of the vicar, Dr. Cottle, and carried on during several years with a large expenditure, have compistely restored the body of the church, elaborately (though perhaps, in some cases, questionably) decorated it, and made it an object of attraction to visiters from all parts of the country,—works which we are sorry to hear, by the way, have so crippled the resources of the vicar, as to force him to quit the scene of his labours and seek some more lucrative appointment.

We were, however, so struck by the miserable condition of the tower of the church that we cannot avoid calling attention to it, to aid in leading to its restoration.

Annexed we give a view of this structure, to enable such of our readers as have not seen it to appreciate its beauties. It is one of the best towers of the Perpendicular period,—standing pre-eminent in a county distinguished by the elegance of its towers. There is no record of the date of its erection, but it may be safely ascribed to the latter half of the fifteenth century.

In an essay on the " Gothic Towers of Somerset," forming part of an elegant and interesting book descriptive of St. Mary's, Taunton, published by Mr. May, of that place, it is said on this point,—"There are, unfortunately, no coats of arms, or cognizances,

upon the tower, to settle the exact date when it was built ; but on the transoms of the two upper series of helfrey windows are sculptured angels supporting shields, on which are carved the initials 𝕽. 𝕭. These letters may refer to Richard Beere, Abbot of Glastonbury, who presided over that establishment in the fifteenth century,—a dignitary eminently skilled in architecture, and who built the church at Glastonbury, on which are sculptured the same initials, 𝕽. 𝕭.; it is therefore not unlikely that he may have designed the beautiful tower of St. Mary's Church."* Beere was installed abbot January 20th, 1493, and died January, 1524.

The engraving gives a south-east view of the tower, and shows also the body of the church as restored. The stonework of the former is in a dreadful state of decay and disruption. On each of the four stories the walls are tied together with iron bars, which go right through to the outside ; and the crowning perforated pinnacles and traceried parapets are scarcely safe.

It is to be hoped that measures will speedily be taken to restore this very interesting specimen of fifteenth century art.

SOMERSETSHIRE ARCHÆOLOGICAL SOCIETY.—This society held their general meeting on Wednesday, in last week, when Sir Walter Trevelyan presided, and the Hon. Mr. Bouverie, Mr. Daubeny, Dr. Buckland, Mr. Britton, the Rev. Mr. Dymock (the hon. secretary), Mr. Giles, Mr. Crosse, and others, took part. Dr. Buckland characterized the use of Bath-stone in London as a gross mistake, and said none should come into Westminster Abbey so long as he was there.

* "Some Account of the Church of St. Mary Magdalen, Taunton ; with several Notices on Ecclesiastical Matters. Beautifully printed in Imperial 8vo., with 10 Engravings and Ground Plan." Containing, also, besides the essay already mentioned, a paper on "The Ecclesiastical Architecture of England ;" and another on the "Ornaments of Churches." Sold by Hamilton, Adams, and Co. London : and F. May, Taunton.

TASK-WORK.

KNOWING your willingness to give publicity to any existing grievances or abuses of trade, I beg, through the aid of your journal, to call the attention of the building public generally to the system much in practice among builders, denominated *task-work*,—not that I wish to impute blame to builders, but to offer a caution against a system that is alike injurious to themselves and to the interests of the working-classes.

A builder, being anxious to let a portion of work, allows certain parties to send in tenders for the same—labour only, and in many cases his foreman is included. This person wishing to keep his situation, and the other parties also wishing to obtain employment, send in, as is generally the case, ridiculously low prices : the consequence is, that the accepted party, is well aware, at least this is generally the case from the low price given, that there will be no balance when the work is completed, even if it can be done for the money, excepting by management. He, therefore, employs a quantity of inferior workmen, or what are termed "improvers," at trifling wages, and they are mixed with superior workmen. He is then able to draw the full wages for all parties, enriching himself at the expense of the builder, and to the injury of the mechanic. Should he find the sum agreed not likely to bear out, he, having nothing to lose, can leave the job whenever he thinks proper, leaving the builder and men in the lurch.

But I am convinced, throughout all the building line, there is no branch so abused as the one to which I belong, viz., plastering, owing to the ready access the task-master has to hawk-boys. Those boys, after serving a plasterer a few months, are put to casting ornament, lathing, colouring, and other minor things. In a short time one of these is placed with a mechanic (this branch generally work in pairs), and the man is obliged to put up with it, or be at the risk of being discharged; he is also required to get over the same quantity of work as if another good mechanic was with him.

I now ask, is it possible for architects and builders to have good work executed under such a system? The mechanic has not time to do it, and these boys or improvers cannot do it. I am not saying that boys must not be taught, but let them be apprenticed or brought up to the trade in a straightforward manner, when we should still be able to have superior operatives. These, I am sorry to say, are fast diminishing.

And what benefit does the builder derive from such a course? he often pays the same price in the end for having his work done; his materials are wasted, owing to the inexperience of the parties employed; the work cracks, and in many cases fails before the building is completed, and he is at the expense of replacing it, the materials, generally, getting the blame. It is earnestly to be desired that builders will consider these facts, and abandon a system which (as I have said before) is injurious to themselves, and highly prejudicial to the interests of the working classes.

A Plasterer.

NOTES IN THE PROVINCES.

The intramural churchyard of All Saints, Stamford, being totally insufficient to bury the dead in any longer, a space on the north-east side has been appropriated for that purpose, and the tender of Mr. Robert Woolston, for 50*l*., to do the work in three or four weeks accepted. The new catacomb will contain 100 to 120 coffins, and may last, they say, two years.——At Romford, the more sensible proceeding of at once opening a piece of ground outside the town has been adopted. It is to be enclosed and planted, and a chapel erected from plans already prepared.——The alterations of Huntingdon County Gaol are progressing towards completion. Besides a detached infirmary, there is an additional building with kitchens, bath rooms, laundry, and other offices, on the basement. The interior is open to the roof, with a ventilating shaft, communicating with sixty-two cells ranged round the interior, and approached by a gallery. Hot-air pipes also communicate with all the cells, which are lighted with gas, and have water-closets, water, &c. The dinners are served up by railway from the kitchen, and altogether the arrangements, "but for the solitary confinement, rather hold out a premium for the commission of crime than the shunning it." The whole has been executed by Mr. Parker, of Thrapston, from a plan provided by Mr. Smith, and at a cost of 6,000*l*. to 7,000*l*.——The newly-erected church of St. Peter, at Cookley, Worcester, was consecrated on Friday week. The proportions are as follows:—Length of nave, 52 feet by 19 feet; side aisles, each 9 feet wide; chancel, 15 feet by 13 feet; interior of tower, open to the church, 10 feet by 12 feet; exterior height of tower to the top of the battlements, 57 feet. The builder was Mr. E. Smith, and the architect was the builder.——The Committee of Privy Council on Education have awarded a grant of 2,200*l*. towards the construction of the proposed Training School at Saltley, for the diocese of Worcester. The execution of the work is postponed till the spring of next year. A deficiency in the funds of nearly 3,000*l*. still exists.——A new church is to be erected at North Malvern.——At Nettleton, Wilts, last week, the foundation-stone of a new school-room and house of residence for the teachers was laid. The ground was given by Mr. G. P. Scrope.——Frankleigh House, near Bradford, Wiltshire, in course of reconstruction in the Elizabethan style, is now nearly completed. The architect is Mr. Henry Clutton; and the builders are Messrs. D. and C. Jones, of Bradford.——On Thursday week, at Leamington, the first stone was laid of a "Poor Man's Church," in High-street, in connection with the national schools at present in Court-street.——St. Asaph Cathedral has been beautified by the Bishop of the diocese with two painted windows, in memory of Mrs. Short.——St. Mark's Church, Pensnett, was consecrated on Tuesday week. It is cruciform, with nave and aisles, north and south transepts, chancel, and chancel aisles, or chapels. The style is First Pointed. The breadth from north to south across the transept is about 70 feet, and the length from west to east about 133, of which 38 are given to the chancel. The tower, which is to be enlarged and completed hereafter, stands in the position of a south porch, and is to be carried to the height of 180 feet. The interior of the church presents a dark brown colour of roof and seats, with walls relieved by red sandstone in the arches and pillars, and black, red, and buff tiles in floor. The organ, by Bishop and Sons, cost from 400*l*. to 500*l*. The aisle, transept, and chapel windows have been filled with glass, on which tint and diaper patterns have been painted and burnt in, rendering them permanent. The sittings for at least 1,000 persons are to be chiefly free. A stone-arched gateway, in a boundary wall, leads to the church through a graveyard enclosure.——On the corporation gas-works at Manchester, this year, there has been an increased profit of at least 4,000*l*., over and above previous splendid returns. Almost 25,000,000 feet of gas more than in 1848 have been made since the previous reduction in price. Amongst the disbursements during the past year we perceive a sum of 27,665*l*. odds put to the credit of the Improvement Committee, over and above 1,625*l*. odds to the Chorlton-on-Medlock Committee.——The Springfield-lane bridge improvement at Salford will cost 1,500*l*. Its progress has been delayed. A contract for the erection of the bridge here over the Irwell, according to the plans and specifications, has been authorized by the Improvement Committee, the council to pay 1,000*l*. of the whole, and the landowners the balance.——A dispute has been in progress at Sunderland between the engineer and directors of the dock and Mr. Craven, the contractor. Barricades were erected and alternately occupied by the belligerent parties, who shot shovelfuls of water at each other, till the police interfered. The right of the directors to enter on the premises having at length been recognized by Mr. Craven, the dispute terminated, and the contractor proceeded with his work.——The alteration of the screen-wall of the Edinburgh Register House is to be proceeded with, on a plan by Messrs. Burn and Bryce, approved of by the trustees of the Register House. It proposes to throw back the wall about 9 feet, and the pavement 5½ feet. But 15 to 16 feet of additional carriage-way are demanded at the head of Leith-street, where a corner house juts on the street, opposite the Register House, and really constitutes the obstacle in the way. The alteration is to cost 162*l*.——St. Andrew's new parish school at Glasgow has been opened. Mr. Kirkland was the architect. The building fronts the green, and consists of two school-rooms for 400 scholars in all.

THE DRAINAGE OF LONDON.

We have already expressed our opinion as to the error of the course adopted by the commissioners in the attempt to obtain plans for the drainage of London. A satisfactory result is *impossible*: the time of the competitors has been thrown away. We have only space in our present number for a report of the meeting of commissioners to receive the plans, and must defer the consideration of several letters on the subject till next week.

A special court of the Metropolitan Commissioners of Sewers was held on Wednesday last, at the Court-house, Greek-street, pursuant to adjournment, for the purpose of receiving the plans proposed for a permanent and efficient drainage of the metropolis. Present—Sir John Burgoyne (in the chair), Mr. Alderman Lawrence, Capt. Veitch, Capt. Dawson, the Rev. E. Murray, Rev. M. Cowie, Mr. Chadwick, Mr. Bain, Dr. Southwood Smith, Sir H. de la Beche, Mr. Lawes, Mr. R. L. Jones, Mr. Hawes, the Rev. W. Stone, Mr. Norris, &c.

Mr. Woolrych, the clerk, read the resolutions passed at the former court on this subject, and stated that, of the sixty-two plans sent in up to that time, fifty-one descriptive statements had been received, in compliance with a resolution passed to that effect; fifty-four new plans had been sent in, thereby increasing the number of plans to one hundred and sixteen. In addition to these, those who had originally sent in their plans had subsequently sent in thirty-two supplementary statements; so that there were, in fact, no less than one hundred and forty-eight schemes for the consideration of the court. Mr. Woolrych then read the names of the competitors whose projects had been sent in since the 20th of August last.

Mr. Alderman Lawrence objected to the names being read, as such a course might influence the selection of a particular plan. It was a well-known fact that the work of any individual whose name was familiar was received with favour.

Mr. Chadwick believed that the mention of names had in some measure been brought about by the resolution of the court.

The Rev. Mr. Cowie said, before any further steps were taken on the question, he must, on his own part, protest against the course they were pursuing altogether. He might be alone in his views, as he had spoken to no commissioner upon the subject, but he felt it to be his duty to embody his opinions in a protest, which he would read. (Mr. Cowie then read the protest, which set forth that before receiving any plans for the proposed object, the court should have laid down certain rules for the guidance of the competing engineers, embracing the main features, and also with reference to the disposal of the sewage manure. Another essential point to be determined was the water supply, without which subject being settled no practical benefit could be derived. In conclusion, it stated that what had been done was a most ill-judged proceeding, urged on prematurely by the chief surveyor and a portion of the public press.) Mr. C. then spoke at great length in support of his views in general condemnation of proceeding at all.

Mr. Chadwick said, as they had only within a few days received the plans, he thought a short time should be given for their consideration and classification, either as a part or as the whole of a plan when brought together. He thought the best course to pursue would be, that the author of each new plan should send a concise statement of his plan, whether in principle or detail, which should be printed for the consideration of the commissioners as soon as possible, and that a special court should be called to receive the same. He regretted that the proceedings of the Works Committee, the Sewage Manure Committee, and the Trial Works Committee, with their approximate works under consideration, had not been made known, as thereby a great deal of labour might have been saved or more efficiently directed. He agreed with Mr. Cowie that they had been unduly hurried into the matter, as it was his opinion that no plan could be adopted until the completion of the survey. They were now on the eve of completing the surface and subterranean survey, with a variety of important trial works, which would be found highly essential and govern the preparation of plans. He, therefore, thought the statements should be printed, and that they should adjourn the whole question.

Mr. R. L. Jones protested against the court coming then to any decision on the subject.

Mr. Alderman Lawrence was opposed to leaving the question to the members of the court, and, as one of those representing the City of London, he could state that no plan would give satisfaction to that body, nor would there be any security for persons submitting the designs, unless they were referred to the first engineers of the day, to gentlemen who were conversant with the subject, and competent to judge of the respective merits, and not submitted to those who had come to foregone conclusions.

Sir H. de la Beche believed that the court could not do better than adopt the course proposed by Mr. Chadwick, and that by so doing they would do their best to place the question in such a light that the public should eventually be satisfied with the decision that they might come to. Whether it were prudent to print the names of the candidates he would offer no opinion—perhaps it might have admitted of a question—but as the statements of the plans formerly received had been printed, he thought it would be only fair that those who had subsequently sent in should be placed on a precisely similar footing.

The Rev. E. Murray agreed in the view taken by Mr. Chadwick, although at first sight it might appear as a postponement of the question. Still he thought they might enter upon the first stage of a subject that must be carried on with the most deliberate consideration. Mr. Chadwick had spoken of the necessity of a classification, and in looking over them he believed those classes might be reduced to a very small number developing general plans. For the larger class, he found nineteen advocating the principle of two tunnels. The second class comprised twenty-one plans of a miscellaneous character, different in their principles and mode of action, amongst which would be found that of Mr. Austin, their consulting engineer. Three others involved the question of filtration,—a question that had never received the consideration that was necessary; while another was contingent on a certain supply of water, so large that it might almost be considered unlimited, and to an extent never hitherto considered necessary. There were fifty other plans, unaccompanied by any statement, but something like a general agreement appeared upon the question of a double tunnel, while the chief surveyor and four others took up the same idea of a single tunnel. Therefore, he thought that not more than four or five classes need be formed, to which they should refer the leading principles to be kept in view. He denied that any foregone conclusion had been come to upon this subject, as he believed that one of the most eminent engineers in the country would not adopt the plan of either the consulting surveyor or of the chief engineer. As to the delay that they appeared to have fallen into, in fifty-six statements sent in, and particularly those advocating two tunnels, they appeared to have wholly neglected one of the greatest difficulties, and that was, let the tunnel be where it might, with an intermittent supply of water, what would be the proportion of the deposit; for if they constructed tunnels, there could be no doubt that in the lapse of years they would be filled up. In the scheme of one tunnel the same difficulty would exist, though in a greater proportion. Such being the state of the matter, where they had so much to learn, he thought they might be pardoned if they asked for more time, as there were other considerations than the mere relief of London by a certain canal.

Mr. Alderman Lawrence thought no classification should be made by the Court, but that they should leave that question unincumbered to persons who were practically acquainted with the subject, who would themselves classify them if such a course was considered necessary. He trusted that all parties would receive fair play, especially as he found great disunion in the board, and their decisions were guided by the influence of majority against minority. Let the plans be good, bad, or indifferent, he was for referring them to gentlemen of known skill and experience.

The Chairman said their position reminded him of the story of the man that prayed to Jupiter for wealth, his request was granted, and he was overwhelmed in the shower of it. They were not exactly overwhelmed, but they would have some difficulty in extricating themselves from the mass, and selecting such portions as they might deem valuable. He thought the most judicious course would be the one that had been suggested.

After a few words from Mr. Norris,

Mr. Chadwick said his opinions on this subject had been fully set forth in official documents, to which he had set his name. Long since he had pressed two plans on the consideration of the court, to bring these principles in issue; and so far from dictating, or taking any undue position, his object had been to place facts before the commissioners, without any pre-conceived opinions on his part. He had wished them to delay their decisions until their trial-works were in a fit stage for them to decide; and he was strongly of opinion that they should decide no general plans until the two surveys were completed. If he had any pre-conceived opinions, they were directed—first, to the purification of the house, which formed at least two-thirds of their work; the next, to purifying the street; and lastly, the river. Great misrepresentations had been made out of doors as to the state of feeling in the court, and what had been done. He admitted that there had been great delays, but at the same time he felt assured that a most important progress had been made over those acts of any previous commission.

Mr. R. L. Jones said, certainly the greatest divisions existed in the court,—for what was agreed to by one court was rescinded by another; they had no principle laid down as to house drainage, or the difference that should be made between a large house and a small one; in fact, nothing was done but on the bit-by-bit system. These evils had been brought upon them, he believed, by splitting up the court into sections by the formation of committees.

Several commissioners addressed the court, and the following resolutions were put and agreed to unanimously:—

"That the author of each plan received since the 20th August be required to send in, by the 17th of October, a concise statement of what he considers the main features, whether in principle or detail.

"That the statements so sent in be printed for the consideration of the commissioners as early as practicable.

"That within fourteen days after the completion of the printing and circulation of the concise statements, a special court be summoned to consider of the proceedings which it may be proper to take for deciding upon them, in conformity with the previous resolutions of the court.

"That such persons who send in plans shall, on receipt of such plans, be entitled to receive back the amount paid for sections and particulars."

The court, on this question, was then adjourned *sine die*.

The Architectural Association begin their season with a *conversazione* this (Friday) evening, the 5th inst., at their rooms, Lyon's Inn Hall, Strand.

METROPOLITAN COMMISSION OF SEWERS.

A general Court was held on Thursday, at the Court-house, Greek-street; Sir John Burgoyne, R.E., in the chair.

A letter was received from Mr. Bell, chemist, complaining of the state of the drainage of Great Portland-street, one death having recently occurred there from cholera, and at the present time the smells were so offensive, that the worst results were anticipated, unless a remedy was immediately applied by trapping the gullies, such work to be done at the expense of the commission. The application, on the recommendation of the Works' Committee, was agreed to.

Sewage Manure for Hyde-park. It was agreed that permission be given to Mr. Mann, superintendent of Hyde-park, to sink, at his own expense, a well to receive a portion of the sewage from the sewer running through Hyde-park, for the purpose of pumping and using it for manuring the park.

Use of Sewage Manure in Agriculture.—The following letter was read by Mr. Woolrych, the clerk:—

"Weald Hall, Brentwood, Sept. 29, 1849.

"Gentlemen,—In consequence of the invitation of landholders within 50 miles of London, in reference to the application of sewage manure, I obtained the inspection of a portion of my estate by Mr. Donaldson. Never having received any information of the result of that inspection from your board, I conceived it had been given up. As, however, I perceive from a report in the *Times* of Friday last that I am in error, I lose no time in declining further treaty for it. The late ravages of cholera in the lowlands and banks of rivers have led me more to appreciate the healthiness of these hills, where happily no cases of that pestilence have yet shown themselves. I fear the importation of such wholesale floods of London sewage, charged with noxious gases, especially if deposited in an open reservoir sufficiently extensive to admit of a supply to reach Crouch river, and which, according to Mr. Baker's calculations per acre, must be enormous, would be beyond the power of every deodorizing fluid yet discovered. Of the value of sewage manure to meadow land there can be no doubt, but the opinion of so experienced an agriculturist as Mr. Robert Baker leads me to question its applicability to the wet arable lands of Essex in the direction proposed. —I am, gentlemen, yours, obediently,

W. Tower.

E. R. Woolrych, Esq."

The letter was laid upon the table, but no conversation took place upon the subject.

The Explosion of the Sewer in Friar-street.—A letter was received from Messrs. Catlin and Co., soap-makers, on the subject of the recent explosion of a sewer in Friar-street.—Mr. Leslie said he had intended to move the abolition of the Trial Works Committee, but was induced, at the request of Lord Carlisle, to postpone that motion until the Committee had made their report. That report had not appeared, but they had one notwithstanding on Saturday last, in the shape of an explosion in the sewer in Friar-street. On hearing of it, he (Mr. Leslie) sent for Mr. Medworth, to ascertain if he knew anything of the works done there, but he denied that there was any truth in it; and Mr. Grant, the district surveyor, denied the story *in toto*, in the presence of Mr. Hatton and two other officers, Mr. Grant adding that at this period of the year the newspapers were glad to get anything they could. Not satisfied, however, from the circumstantial account which appeared of the transaction, he made further inquiries, and it turned out that one of the officers had gone on Saturday night, on his own responsibility, and had blown up the sewer. He thought, therefore, that if there was then any objection to stop the Trial Works Committee, there could be none now. It appeared that they had made a communication from the ash-pit of the steam-engine of Thorne's brewery with this foul sewer. Such a process he considered hazardous. If damage occurred, and the factory were blown up, who was to pay the expenses of the policies of insurance—certainly not the fire offices. He therefore hoped they would now and at once stop the further proceedings of the Trial Works Committee. Notwithstanding the commission was stated to be on its last legs, he hoped they should, at any rate, die with something like decency.—Mr. Murray justified the Trial Works Committee.

Mr. Grant, anticipating some observations might be made upon this subject, had drawn up a report, which he would now read. It stated that the reports that had appeared of this circumstance were of a very exaggerated and incorrect character. From the state of this sewer, he suggested that Mr. Gurney's mode of ventilation should be tried. Mr. Cooper and other parties were consulted on the subject, and a pipe was attached from the sewer to the ash-pit of a furnace. The draught was very great, and for some time the experiment went on satisfactorily, but the stone-ware pipe nearest the furnace became very hot, and showed symptoms of cracking. To ascertain the effect of the air of the sewer at the side entrance, a lantern was let down and the air inflamed, which operation was repeated, after which, when the men were closing the flap, it was suddenly carried with a jerk like the blasting of a quarry, the inflamed gas escaping suddenly, and slightly injuring one of the men who was standing at the entrance. Simultaneously the inflamed gas being drawn in to the furnace, the stone-ware pipe, which had been getting hotter, suddenly burst, and the door of the ash-pit, which had been hanging loose, was thrown off. This was the whole extent of the explosion. It further stated that no one but himself was responsible, as he did not consult either of the chief officers, nor did he do it by order of any commissioner. He also mentioned various places where similar experiments had been tried with success; and in support of his view, quoted the opinion of Mr. Faraday contained in the first report of the Metropolitan Sanitary Commission, in which he stated that "I have often thought that the many furnace and engine flues that rise up so abundantly in London might be made to compensate in part for the miasma which their smoke occasions by being turned to account in ventilating the sewers and burning the putrid vapours generated therein." —A long and rather disorderly debate ensued on this question, which was terminated by the adoption of the following resolutions:—

"That the court approves of the course taken by Mr. Grant, in reference to the sewer in Friar-street, having consulted the best available authorities, and that the expenses be paid."—"That the Trial Works Committee be instructed to report on the subject of such ventilation, and that an early day after its receipt be appointed for the consideration of the said report."

A long conversation took place on the improper use of candles in the sewers,—Mr. Leslie contending that the Davy lamp should invariably be used, as various accidents had arisen from the neglect; which view was supported by Dr. Southwood Smith. —It was ordered that the use of the Davy lamp should be strictly insisted upon for the future.

Some works were then ordered, and the court adjourned.

Miscellanea.

Carpenters' Hall, London-Wall.—Alderman Lawrence, one of the new sheriffs, being on the Court of the Carpenters' Company, the sheriffs' inauguration dinner was given in the old hall, which has not been used for such a purpose for many years. We have before now spoken of this building; it appears to have been acquired by the company in the year 1428, and in the following year a "Great Hall" was built by them. Whether any part of the original hall be still standing, cannot be ascertained; but the records of the Carpenters' Company, which (with the exception of a few years during a portion of the reign of Henry VIII.) present an unbroken series of the accounts of the company since the year 1438, contain no notice of the subsequent erection of any hall, though they include constant entries of disbursements for extensive repairs and additions. The present hall, therefore, if not built in the reign of Henry VI. (1429), must, at least, be as ancient as that of Henry VIII. Little of the original work, however, is to be seen. The interesting mural paintings here, discovered in 1845, will be remembered by our readers.

Burial in Towns.—The Board of Health have, unfortunately, been beaten in their righteous endeavours to save the lives of the community by the suppression of this nuisance. Under the 9th clause of the Nuisances Act they summoned the proprietors of the Whitfield Chapel graveyard, in Tottenham-court-road, before Mr. Jardine, for resisting their order to discontinue the nuisance; but the insufficiency of the clause induced the judge to dismiss the summons, while, at the same time, he confessed the propriety of the Board's intention. We trust that even in the mean time, however, this will prove no check to the vigorous procedure of all in power with those other general measures requisite to the health and life of the community. Pity it were not the modern practice, as it was the more sensible practice of the ancients, to burn or embalm all the putrifiable matter of the dead. As for measures of general cleansing, the time for that now approaches. The danger of opening cesspools, &c., has crippled all endeavours, hitherto, while the plague raged, and the canals of filth below the level of the Thames on the south side have done their dreadful work without the least qualification or mercy. Something now, however, *must* be done.

BATHS AND WASHHOUSES IN ST. LUKE'S, OLD-STREET.—At the monthly meeting of the Board of Guardians, held on Wednesday evening last, Mr. Churchwarden King in the chair; on a motion by Mr. Atkins, for a committee to be appointed to carry into effect the laudable object of establishing baths and washhouses in the parish of St. Luke's, Mr. Shillibeer observed, in supporting the motion, that he did so with more than ordinary pleasure, because he felt that the densely populated district of St. Luke's parish required such an establishment, to afford the poorer portion of his fellow parishioners those advantages of personal comfort and cleanliness which in other parishes had been found of such vast benefit to the working classes. He hoped no further time would be lost in putting in force the Act authorizing the creation of such an establishment, and felt sure that although, at first, it might increase the parish rates, yet it would soon become a self-supporting institution, and ultimately a source of profit to the parish, and meet with the cordial approval of every rate-payer. Other guardians having expressed their entire concurrence in the object of the motion, a committee was appointed to consider of, and report to the board, the best means of establishing baths and washhouses in the parish.

THE MECHANICAL SECTION OF THE BRITISH ASSOCIATION is very fully reported in *The Civil Engineers' Journal* for the current month · and diagrams are given to illustrate Robert's moulding machine; Appold's centrifugal pump (an *ancient* machine revived); Heaton's means for preventing the oscillation of locomotives. Brunton's coal mine ventilator; Hosmer's self-acting cistern; and Robert's patent tide winding apparatus.

THE ART-JOURNAL of the current month contains what must be considered a very remarkable notice of the Birmingham Exhibition of Industrial Art, presenting no less than *one hundred and fifty* admirably-drawn and engraved illustrations of articles exhibited. When it is known that the whole has been produced in somewhat less than a month,—collected, drawn, engraved, and printed,—the feat appears marvellous. The editor, with justice, puts in his claim to early advocacy of the advantages of a national exposition of works of industry and art.

FROCKSTER CHURCH RESTORATION.—An architect, dating his letter from Bristol, says,— Passing the railway station the other day, I observed that the wooden spire had been taken down, and I must say that I was exceedingly disappointed to learn, from the architect's account in a late number of THE BUILDER, that it was to be replaced by a *stone one of more taper proportions.* This wooden spire was a perfect curiosity in the neighbourhood. Except at Almondsbury, I believe there is not another in the county. It presented a considerable similarity to those simple wooden erections in the county of Surrey, and barmonised admirably with the *genius loci*, and at the same time contrasted very well with the neighbouring well-known and consequently taper spire of Slymbridge. Defend us from such *restorations* as these !

PAROCHIAL BURYING GROUNDS—JOINT OR SEPARATE. — Your correspondent, the "Colonel," who has with so much ability and public spirit given his opinions and calculations to the public, but who states that " no ideas " had been previously offered, is, I am sure, not aware of the plan and calculation for joint parochial cemeteries which your humble correspondent gave in your excellent pages, vol. iv., pp. 261 and 310; which I am emboldened to say has been *adopted*, not only in one or two country districts, but in the recent " Report on the Subdivision of Parishes," &c. I will not presume to say—certainly with the immediate recollection of the distinguished authors, two of whom, to my own knowledge, had seen the pamphlet in which it was afterwards incorporated,—but *practically*, because the suggestions had originated *no where else ;* which I am sure they will accept as an *Euclidic* argument of authorship. Although the above suggestions applied principally to joint grounds, which should have a common chapel in the centre, with a proposed radiating divergence of lines, the calculation was nearly as well suited for individual grounds.

J. D. PARRY.

NELSON COLUMN, TRAFALGAR-SQUARE. —With regard to the Nelson column, there is reason for apprehending that, however satisfactory they may be in themselves as works of art, the bronze bas-reliefs with which the panels on the pedestal are to be filled in will in a short time after being put up be scarcely distinguishable—and this blankness will be exchanged only for blackness. The latter, however, will be in keeping with the capital of the column ; which, as might have been foreseen from the first, shows only as a dark mass whose details are entirely lost. We doubt if bronze be fit for other than small ornamental articles which are intended for close inspection, or large single figures and statues, which, to that given to the columns within the temple at Bassæ. Had this been done, the pedestal would have been increased in proportion,—and the column would have stood far more firmly and majestically than it does now. Such, however, is the respect paid to precedent, that art is ruined by the very course intended to preserve it.—*Athenæum.*—[One of the bas-reliefs has been hoisted into its place, on the south side of the pedestal ; but, at this present, its merits cannot be *canvassed*, because its face is.]

THE NORWICH AND WEST SUFFOLK ARCHÆOLOGICAL SOCIETIES met on Thursday in last week at Thetford, and the proceedings were opened in the town hall by the mayor. A visit was paid to the ancient British mound and camp, where the Rev. Mr. Bulmer addressed the meeting upon its history. A visit to " The Place," or nunnery, was the next point, containing many architectural beauties, but which are now converted to ignoble purposes, and Mr. Timms, the secretary to the West Suffolk Society, read a paper upon its antiquity. Taking in their way the old Grammar School, on the site of which are many antiquarian beauties, the company arrived at the abbey, to the pretty grounds of which, by the liberal dispersion of tickets, were admitted many besides its members. Excavations to a considerable extent had been carried on for the purposes of this meeting ; the original floor, with its encaustic tiles, was laid open, and the base and shaft of the columns of the noble church, built in 1170, gave an idea of its magnificence and extent.

DWELLINGS FOR THE POOR.—It has been suggested that parochial bodies should be empowered to erect dwellings for the working classes in localities where such are required, and as they have the power to erect baths and washhouses I do not see why they should not have this power also conferred on them by Act of Parliament. It is the only remedy that I can see for the present state of things.— A LONDONER.

EXPLOSION OF A SEWER IN SOUTHWARK. —On Saturday evening last, an explosion of sewer-damp happened in Friar-street, in the Borough. The cast-iron plates, covering the man-holes in the flag pavement in Friar-street, are said to have been blown into the air, and flames came through the gully-gratings into the streets. A statement on the subject by an officer of the commissioners is given in a previous column : but it should be further investigated. At the present moment, when the best mode of ventilating sewers is occupying attention, it is of consequence that the cause of the accident, and the circumstances attending it, should be thoroughly understood.

WATER FOR THE TOWER OF LONDON.— The pernicious properties of the water heretofore supplied to the soldiers have induced the forwarding of arrangements whereby a limited supply of pure spring water has been introduced for the present. It is to be used for drinking and cooking alone, as it does not exceed 2,000 gallons a-day. It is said the Duke of Wellington has induced the Woods and Forests to agree to bore an Artesian well in the Tower for supply of the garrison.

RAILWAY JOTTINGS.—It is understood that the Government are to lend money, on sufficient securities, to railway companies, at 4 per cent., the Government being able to raise it at 3, so as to place at the disposal of Ministers a profit of 1 per cent. in reduction of taxation.—— During last half-year 96 persons have been killed, and 75 injured by railway in Great Britain and Ireland.——The dangerous curves on the Lancashire and Yorkshire line at Charlestown have recently been reduced from a radius of 660 to one of 2,000 feet.——The result of the Crown investigation into the fall of the bridge at Roxburgh, on the North British line, is the indictment of the contractor and resident engineer for trial at next assizes.

ENGLISH SHIP BUILDERS.—A correspondent writes :—Lately work has been very dull with steam ship-builders ; and knowing that the following order is now in the market to be given away, I send you a note of it. Six first-class steam-vessels and four small ditto have been ordered by the Messrs. Eider and Co., the French shipping agents, for the Mediterranean and French trade. The engineer appointed by them intends dividing the contracts between Glasgow, London, and Newcastle, thus showing that England still maintains the superiority of its character for ships and marine engines ; although, in a French paper (*National*), a long article was recently given, setting forth the superiority of French work and Frenchmen in these departments of trade. The contracts can be completed in this country for an average of 4,000*l.* sterling each vessel less than in France ; proving, that in price a great advantage is had in this country, where skill and the division of labour reduce the expense, although wages are higher than in other countries.—J. S.

NEW REGULATIONS AT SALISBURY CATHEDRAL.—The nave and transepts of the cathedral are to be thrown open to the public daily, between the hours of the morning and afternoon services. The choir and other parts of the interior can only be inspected by applying to the verger, as before. The spire has been nearly completed by the workmen engaged in pointing and restoring it.

PROFITS OF ROYAL FORESTS.—According to the daily papers, the total income of the year from all the royal forests and woodlands belonging to the crown was 29,860*l.* ; the total expenditure 34,682*l.* ! Public deficiency, 4,822*l.*

THE SEWERAGE AND REFUSE OF LIVERPOOL.—It is the intention of the Health Committee to purchase or rent several thousand acres of waste land near the shore, in the vicinity of Ince or Formby, and apply to these the manure conveyed thither from Liverpool in boats. The farm operations are to be carried on by able-bodied paupers from the parish, and it is supposed that the profits will not only pay for the cost and the value of the manure, but leave a surplus in favour of the corporation.— *Liverpool Courier.*

HEREFORD.—The chapter-house of the cathedral is to be restored, in order to render the library accessible to the clergy. In 1645, the lead was taken off its conical roof to repair the breaches in the castle.

NEW ROMAN CATHOLIC CHURCH AT KENTISH TOWN.—The first stone of the Church of St. Alexis, Fitzroy-place, Kentish Town, was laid on the 1st inst., by Prince John of Spain. Mr. Wardell is the architect, Mr. T. Jackson the builder. The church is to be cruciform, according to our informant, 105 feet long and 55 feet wide, will have a central tower and spire 200 feet high, and will accommodate 1,000 worshippers.

THE "COLLECTANEA ANTIQUA."*—The first part of Mr. Roach Smith's " Etchings and Notices of Ancient Remains," illustrative of the customs and history of past ages, contains a full and interesting account of the Roman villa at Hartlip, in Kent, with numerous engravings. The walls of the rooms and passages here had been well stuccoed and painted, in some cases red, in others white.

* Published by J. R. Smith, Old Compton-street, London.

PROJECTED WORKS.—Advertisements have been issued for tenders, by a date not specified, for restorations in clerestory of chancel of St. Mary Redcliffe Church, Bristol; by 24th November, for the restoration of St. Peter's Church, Northampton; by 15th inst., for the rebuilding of Merrington Church; by 6th, for alterations in Presteign Church; by 9th, for the construction of sewers and drains at Southampton; by a date not specified, for the fixing-up of the Corporation Baths at Bristol; and by 8th, for constructing sewer with branches, and for tubular house-drainage, &c., at Southwark.

TO CORRESPONDENTS.

"*Drying-Closets for Oats.*"—A correspondent says,— "Resting an article in THE BUILDER on ' Drying-Closets,' and being about to build a mill for grinding oats, it struck me that some such arrangement would answer much better than the common kilns for drying oats before grinding, as, in the common kiln, perhaps nine-tenths of the heat is lost. Probably some of your correspondents would give an opinion on this matter."

"*Constant Subscriber,*" Chatham.—A Fellow of the Institute must be an architect who has been engaged as principal for at least seven successive years in the practice of civil architecture. To become an Associate, it is necessary to have attained the age of 21, and to be engaged in the study of civil architecture or in practice less than seven years. There is nothing to prevent any man dubbing himself architect, and starting a brass-plate to that effect.

W. R.—The variation is itself inconstant. Its amount in winter is scarcely half that in summer, and there is even a considerable daily variation, morning, noon, and night. Attention to this is scarcely necessary in fixing a vane.

Received.—"E. R. C." (stained-glass borders may be used in a conservatory without fear of injuring the plants,— we should employ blue, yellow, or green, rather than red). "P.," " W. M. L.," " W. B.," " E. H. M.," " J. W. B." " J. L." (wire-work for plastering is, we believe, patented by a firm in Birmingham). "J. C. W.," " Wahd." " H. A. J." (we are unable to assist him). " A Subscriber " (next week). " Money for Public Works." " D. B.," " Dr. O." (shall see a proof). " W. S." (Sunderland). " F. L." (apply to the secretary of any such societies for the regulations). " J. G." (thanks: we have sufficient details in hand at this moment). " Col. M.," " G. E.," " M. P.," " A Young Plumber," (we cannot supply prices). " G. N. B.," " J. E. D." (shall be looked to). " E." (shall be brought in view of the building named in hand). " The Ecclesiastical and Architectural Topography of England," Buckinghamshire; Oxford and London, J. H. Parker: " Christian Monuments in England and Wales," by the Rev. Charles Boutell (Parts I. and II.); London, George Bell: " Con Cregan, the Irish Gil Blas;" Orr and Co., No. X. (a very sparkling story, equal to any of Mr. Lever's); " First Three Books of Euclid's Elements of Geometry," by Thos. Tate; London, Longman and Co.

NOTICE. — All communications respecting *advertisements* should be addressed to the "Publisher," and not to the "Editor:" all other communications should be addressed to the EDITOR, and *not* to the Publisher.

"*Books and Addresses.*"—We have not time to point out books or find addressees.

No. CCCXLIX.

SATURDAY, OCTOBER 13, 1849.

UR readers will not be surprised to hear that the Metropolitan Sewers Commission, tried and found wanting, is *dissolved*. We have been looking for the Lord Chancellor's *supersedeas* for some time past, and it has now come; whether for the purpose, simply, of ridding the board of one or two of its members found troublesome by those with most influence, or that it may be wholly reconstructed, remains to be seen. To the constitution of the board we objected in the first instance, protesting strongly and repeatedly against the systematic exclusion of professional and practical men. Its unsatisfactory proceedings, its position in the estimation of the country, and its premature extinction, fully justify our views. And yet while we have found it our duty to object in plain and strong language to the course pursued on too many occasions, we will not go so far as those who say that the late commission has done *nothing*; and we have withheld quires of complaints against it, and so offended a portion of the public, because we believed that those complaints were founded on misapprehension of its province and powers. But that it has failed miserably,—that it has shown itself incompetent for the Herculean task committed to its charge, is certain and undeniable.

We will not at this moment speculate on the probable constitution of the new board; a very short time will elapse before the question will be set at rest, for we cannot suppose that the Government will allow matters connected with the drainage of the metropolis to stand still a single week. It has been suggested in our pages, on more than one occasion, that the board should be representative, or partly so. One of our correspondents suggested that half the commissioners should be appointed by the Crown, and half elected; that there should be twelve or twenty commissioners to each district, according to the size, and that " each district commission should elect one of its body to be one of a general committee, who should have power to determine all questions affecting the general interest, and decide upon plans for general drainage."* Speculation, however, is useless, as by this time the matter is settled.

And now *as to* the plans for general drainage, which were submitted to the late commission in reply to their appeal to the public. We are anxious to say a few words in behalf of the parties who responded to this invitation, although we fear there is little chance of their obtaining any advantageous return for their labour, unless, indeed, the new commission may be led to vote some compensation to those competitors who have furnished the more useful designs.

In our article of September 8th (p. 421, *ante*) we were compelled to remark, when speaking of the appeal to the public for plans, that if there were no other proof on record of the unfitness of the majority of the commissioners for their position, the thoughtlessness, must we add ignorance, which characterized the course

* See p. 441 *ante*.

---

taken would suffice, and afterwards this same view was adopted by one of the late commission, the Rev. Morgan Cowie, who submitted a written protest against the proceedings, fearing probably, and with justice, that if he did not do so, his fitness for the office of principal at the College of Engineers might be questioned.

That others of the commissioners had felt the necessity of affording to the competitors further data to proceed upon is evidenced by the fact that one of them, Mr. Hume, addressed a letter to the surveyor, who, on the day first fixed for receiving the plans, memorialized the court for an extension of the time,—asking him what information he thought desirable to enable surveyors to prepare " the best and most comprehensive plan for so great and important an undertaking." "I see the difficulties," continued Mr. Hume, " but not the means of removing them at present, and therefore wait for information." The reply of the party addressed showed how he thought the difficulties might be met : he said,—

" I write, in the earnest hope that, by your influence and advocacy, such information will be *directly* afforded as will induce professional men of reputation and business to come forward with designs on the 1st of October next. At present it may be justly assumed that none but those who, being connected with the commission, possessed the desired data by virtue of their office, and those who, having little practically to engage their attention, have managed to acquire these data by indirect means, are qualified to compete for an object as well worthy the talents and attention of the most exalted professional minds as any object that has ever presented itself for public competition. No palace, no church, no cartoon painting, was more worthy ' a prize for the best design ' than the origination of the best principle upon which to drain the metropolis; and I therefore submit to you that it is desirable not only to give the required data, but to offer distinctly a prize or prizes for such designs as may be considered by competent judges worthy of some mark of distinction.

The information which ought to be supplied to each competitor is—

An outline (reduced) plan of the whole district, for which an improved outfall is now sought.

On this map should be shown, simply—

1. The main streets.
2. Rivers and open watercourses.
3. Open and covered *main sewers* from their source (as sewers) to their outlets : along the course of each river, watercourse, and main sewer, simple figures should express the various falls or gradients, and the depth of the bottom of each below the surface of the ground; thus, $\frac{1 \text{ in } 480}{20}$ would represent a fall of ⅓ inch in 10 feet and 20 feet below surface. This information should be as perfect as it can possibly be afforded by the court within the limited time. At the beginning and end of each main sewer the height, with respect to Trinity datum and low-water line at their several outlets, should be particularly given; thus,

45' *a*TD | 13' 2" *b*TD

→   4' 4" *a*LW.

The heights of surface of ground (independent of the sewers) at various and frequent spots throughout the whole district to be operated upon having reference to one datum (Trinity high-water), should be given; thus, (45) meaning 45 feet above datum at the spot on which it is figured. Whatever borings have been taken should be appended by index to the map." . . . .

About sixty plans had been *sent in* at this time, it must be remembered. The court, when they extended the time after receiving these sixty, ordered some additional information to be supplied to competitors, which

---

reached them but a very few days before the expiration of the time fixed, and was wholly insufficient.*

The result, as a matter of course, is, that the plans are all incomplete;—the competitors have laboured in vain;—the " best plan " has yet to be prepared.

The " concise statements " of the plans sent in before the 20th August last, form a pamphlet, small folio in size, of ninety pages, and are from fifty-three competitors. The names of these are, following the printed order, Messrs. H. Austin, J. T. Barkley, G. Burge, J. H. Clive, F. Coxworthy, J. W. Couchman, M. Dunn, R. Dover, A. Doull, Dredge and Stephenson, J. Dean, R. Dixon, J. Elliott, Chas. Fowler, F. Finlay, J. Faulkner, J. Gibbs, C. Hutton Gregory, J. T. Harrison, M. Kerridge, T. Lunt, John Martin, Martin, Sowerby, and Hodgson Jones, T. Morris, J. B. M'Clean, J. Murray, John Phillips, T. W. Plum, Joseph Prestwich, Jas. Pilbrow, G. Remington, Jasper Rogers, J. B. Redman, Ross and Low, F. Roe, Rumball and Shepherd, R. Rettie, W. Radley, W. Stewart, J. Pigot Smith, J. Sutton, F. Swinburns, Herbert L. Smith, C. Sanderson, B. G. Sloper, Harcourt Thompson, Tate and Gilmore, E. Wharmby, F. Wood, and Professor Wallace. The other plans are anonymous.†

According to the statement of the late secretary, Mr. Woolrych, on the 3rd inst., fifty-four plans have been submitted since the 20th of August, making in the whole 116 plans, without reference to thirty supplementary papers. " Concise statements " of the former are required to be sent in by the 17th inst., that these also may be printed, but by whom the whole will be judged is yet to be learnt. Be they who they may, we ask at their hands, on the part of the competitors, fair play and liberal consideration.

We append here as part of the same subject, rather than under a fresh heading, the following note dated Greek-street, October 8th, and signed J. L. Hale, assistant-surveyor to the Metropolitan Commission of Sewers :—

" I observe in THE BUILDER of last week, a reference made by Mr. Bird to certain experiments made by the Metropolitan Commissioners of Sewers, in Upper George-street, Edgware-road. The experiments consisted of laying down a line of 12 inch pipes in the main sewer of Upper George-street, with 9 inch junctions, to receive the drainage of the collateral sewers. The object of the experiments was to ascertain how far, in respect of quantity of sewage, the sewers in that locality were unnecessarily large, and to ascertain what were the relative merits of stoneware pipes and brick barrel drains, for the general conveyance of sewage. I enclose a printed copy of the report made to the commissioners on the result of the experiments, from which it appears the result was satisfactory. Mr. Bird, on the assumption that the experiments were a failure, stated that he " in April or May last saw the pipes broken to pieces and taken out, after putting the public to the useless expense.' Now, the fact is, that

* The corrections, too, of some of the information furnished has been impeached by a writer in the *Times*. He says of the sections of the strata in various existing wells :—" To refer, for instance, to the thickness of the London blue clay at Goding's brewery, Southwark, it is stated to be 109 feet thick, when it is only 100 feet; the surface of the chalk also is indicated at a depth of 190 feet, when it is 215 feet. Another of these sections indicates the thickness of the blue clay at Messrs. Thorne's brewery, Westminster, to be 109 feet, when it is only 100 feet, and the chalk is stated to be 202 feet from the surface, when it is 240 feet. The section of Messrs. Reagar's, Millbank, showing the thickness of the blue clay 20 feet, is correct : and, being within 120 yards of Messrs. Thorne's, proves the inaccuracy of the latter, as the surface of the blue clay is of pretty uniform and gradual dip towards the west in that portion of the metropolis. I could make further comments, particularly on the anomaly of showing the blue clay resting on the chalk, when it is well known that a considerable thickness of plastic clays and sands invariably intervenes; it is, therefore, surprising to have such incorrect data issued from the Commissioners' office, which tend to throw a distrust on the whole, and are calculated to create erroneous impressions respecting the geological formation of the London basin."

† We have received beyond those given in the list, plans by Messrs. Bardwell, C. Ellerman, R. Netherway, &c.

the experiments having been completed, and the commissioners having other works in the neighbourhood, where 12 inch pipes were required, the pipes in Upper George-street were used instead of purchasing new ones, to *save the public expense*."

We will also add, respecting the ventilation of sewers, part of a note from the surveyor to the Hull corporation, Mr. D. Thorp, forwarded to us sometime ago, and accidentally mislaid. Mr. Thorp says,—

"In the first place I may mention that I have trapped 360 gully holes in the old town of Hull, which is that part of the town within the docks and harbour, and within that area, which comprises 87 acres very closely built upon, we have about 180 more to complete.

"Now, it required much consideration in doing this to get rid of the effluvia which would naturally be pent up in the sewers as we proceeded trapping, and which was fully proved by my men not being able to proceed in the first outset with more than one street at a time, and then not without being ill. This induced me to apply the provision made in one of our bye-laws, viz., to compel all parties to *connect the rain pipes in the fronts of their houses with the main sewer, by means of either brick or tubular glazed drains* (the latter of which are much to be preferred), thereby making so many flues for the escape of foul air to the tops of the houses, and I may say that this plan has acted admirably."

After the foregoing article was in type, we received a list of the parties, thirteen in number, to whom the new commission has been directed, and here it is:—Viscount Ebrington; Major-General Sir John Burgoyne, K.C.B.; Sir Henry de la Beche, F.R.S.; Mr. Robert Stephenson, M.P.; Mr. S. M. Peto, M.P.; Lieutenant-Colonel Alderson, R.E.; Mr. Philip Hardwick, R.A.; Captain Vetch, R.E.; Mr. J. M. Rendel; Captain Harness, R.E.; Mr. Thomas Hawes; Captain R. K. Dawson, R.E.; and Mr. Edward Lawes, Barrister-at-law.

It will be seen that all the more prominent opponents on each side have been omitted in the new arrangement, the number of commissioners has been reduced, and the correctness of our views has been unconditionally recognised by the infusion of professional and practical men,—the abandonment of the absurd principle that architects and engineers were not fit for Sewers' Commissioners, simply because they *were* architects and engineers. The builders, too, are represented. Of the credit of obtaining this result we claim no small share: we fought the fight alone,—so far as we know, no word upon it has been elsewhere uttered, and we venture to think, with all modesty, that the profession owe us thanks.

Beyond what we have said we offer no opinion at present on the goodness, or otherwise, of the selection, or as to the omissions, but wait to see the working of the board.

Birmingham Workhouse Competition.—Were your correspondent, as he styles himself, "A Lover of Fair Play," he would have hesitated before making such statements as those contained in his letter, appearing in The Builder of the 29th ult.; but as his assertions may gain credit with some parties, if suffered to pass uncontradicted, I beg to say:—1st. That I most emphatically deny ever having canvassed the Birmingham Guardians in favour of Messrs. Drury and Bateman, either during the first competition, or at any other period, and challenge him to produce or name any one guardian so solicited by me. 2ndly. That I saw *no signature or name* upon the plans, except the motto appended. 3rdly. That the selection was made, in every respect, in *strict accordance* with the instructions of the guardians.—Charles Edge, Birmingham, October 3, 1849.

ON CIVIL ENGINEERING AND ARCHITECTURE.

AN INAUGURAL LECTURE.*

I have said that both architects and engineers must possess a knowledge of the strength and nature of the materials with which they have to work. This I think is self-evident, for the money to be expended is always one great element in their calculations; and the quantity of materials that can be usefully employed can only be ascertained by calculations based upon an intimate knowledge of the strains and forces they will have to resist, and the capabilities of the timber, the stone, the iron, or other substance that may be employed to resist them. Both Tredgold and Barlow have furnished us with admirable works from which the theoretical knowledge of the properties of all the materials used in building can be learned. There is no excuse, therefore, for failures of work arising from actual want of strength; but failures do sometimes occur, notwithstanding every precaution may have been taken to give to the materials, both theoretically and practically, their proper size and form, and proper distribution in the work. In engineering especially, circumstances are occurring every day, features constantly present themselves, of which even the oldest practitioner may have had no example previously; and other means taken to obviate evils that may and do thus arise may be the best that both science and art could point out, and yet fail in their object. I say that these are misfortunes only, not faults; but when they occur with a man unqualified with scientific knowledge to deal with them, they are very serious faults indeed, and should be visited with the utmost censure. Engineering is of all professions (says Mr. Hyde Clarke), the military excepted, that in which a new adaption of expedients to unforeseen occurrences is ever most imperatively required, and in which a mere knowledge of past efforts will be insufficient, unless the mind be competent to invent new processes, as well as to avail itself of the best manner of old ones. No man can go upon a spot and say, I will do such and such things at such expense; some unexpected variation of nature beneath the surface will often thwart the best-calculated plans, and render all attempts at economy abortive. It is practice, aided by scientific knowledge of the highest kind, that only can properly preside over the just application of materials to the ever-occurring variations which spring up in the course of an engineering undertaking. And if science and practice sometimes fail in effecting their object at once, what must be the result when ignorance attempts the work? Failure, certain and disastrous failure, heaping disgrace upon the head of the quack practitioner, and often ruin upon his employers. I use the word advisedly, for although neither architects nor engineers unfortunately need diplomas of practice to give them a right to the use of C. A. or C. E. after their names, they yet have morally, and in common honesty, an obligation, which should bind them to certain spheres of work which they feel themselves qualified to undertake; and every man knows his own capabilities, depend upon it.

If, then, men calling themselves engineers or architects, undertake a work they know they are incapable of performing without the assistance of a dry nurse, in the shape of a good "clerk of the works," they are quacks in every sense of the word, quacks as much as the charlatan who practises medicine without the consent of the colleges.

The demand for engineers, caused by the late wild railway speculations, has filled the profession with unqualified persons, and has tended to lower it below its proper level, and although the present times are, I am rejoiced to say, weeding them out pretty fast, it will, and must, be some time before it reaches its healthy state again.

It is true, the Institution of Civil Engineers and the Institute of Architects exist, and men to become members of either must present proper qualifications; but there are numerous practitioners who are not members, and who seek and gain employment. But I hope to see, ere long, by legislative enactment, both architect and engineer obliged to take out a diploma before being allowed to take upon themselves the responsibility of any work, when lives, or a sum of money beyond a certain amount, are at stake,—a diploma granted only after a severe examination as to scientific acquirements, and a practice under others of at least seven years.

I here beg permission to quote some passages from a paper written by Sir John Soane, which appeared in the *Artist* of June 13th, 1807,—as quotations from this high authority will give strength to what I have ventured to suggest myself:—

"An artist (architect), strictly so considered, is not sufficiently employed; his profession is too open to the assumption of persons who have no claim by education or ability; and these are admitted to that patronage without which the architect has no chance either of emolument or fame. There are, therefore, very few persons engaged solely in the practice of architecture. The great mass of those whom we here call architects, though many of them respectable in talents as artists, are under the necessity of combining with their study of the science pursuits not strictly analogous, and are, in consequence, and to their great discouragement and mortification, assimilated with another description of professional men called surveyors,* and that name is again assumed by sorts and classes of building workmen and others, until it becomes utterly contemptible."

After enlarging somewhat (and in language by no means mild) upon the difficulties which beset an architect when carrying out a design, through the interference of public boards, and complaining, justly, that unqualified persons are allowed to enter into competition with him, by the aid of pilfered plans, Sir John concludes thus:—

"Before the state of architecture can be improved, and the professors excited to that species of emulation which only can make them eminent, strong and marked distinctions must take place. Those who have patronage must consider it a sacred trust and deposit,—the meed only of science and genius. The claims of the untaught, ignorant, and presumptuous, must not only be disallowed, but repelled with indignation and contempt, till at length they are consigned to that obscurity whence they ought never to have been suffered to emerge."†

Both engineer and architect must also be men of business; and to the knowledge of the uses and relative advantages of materials must be added the knowledge of their commercial value. The sum to be expended in any undertaking is always a marked feature; and the reputation of an engineer, especially, will be raised by the commercial success of his work. Harbours, roads, canals, and railways, before they are commenced, must show that the traffic or dues from them will amount to such a sum as will insure to their projectors a proper return for their money. The first estimate of the engineer is the document from which the probable amount of returns is calculated. The statistical calculations, or the quantity of trade that will arise, is not, strictly speaking, in the department of the engineer, and he is not answerable if the scheme is not a paying one, from a deficiency in the traffic returns or dues: but if it fail through any excessive expenditure over and above his estimate, he is answerable.

His estimate and schedule of prices, fixed through knowledge of local charges and custom of labour—through his close observation and acquaintance with the geological nature of the spot, and through his knowledge of the best districts from whence to draw his foreign materials—must be so worked out in detail, and capable of being referred to precedent, if precedent exist, or borne out by the opinion of others, that it will bear the investigation of a Parliamentary Committee; for, be it remembered, that estimates are the most vulnerable points in which opponents can strike you in the "House;" and if the said estimates do not carry on the face of them the handiwork of a man of business, they will be the first and last work of the scheme, for the session in which they are brought forward at all events.

Perfect knowledge of the business habits of contractors, and of the working habits of arti-

* By Mr. Clegg, at the Putney College. See p. 472, ante.

* A comment seems called for here, but we have not time to make it.—Ed.

† This is the right test; not a mere *name*.—Ed.

zans, can alone enable him to draw out his specification properly. It is true the lawyer will be called upon to give to it its legal phrases and finely-drawn pains and penalties of any breach in the performance thereof; but the lawyer will have to work upon a base of the engineer's planning, and, be sure, the blame will rest on him, if any oversight has been committed on his part.

In the specification must be described the exact method by which the various works enumerated therein are to be performed. All the drawings must be enumerated, and more particularly referred to and explained: in short, the specification must be a book of reference, as it were, for the contractor, by which he can settle dimensions, quantities, and appeal to, in case of any dispute with his employers, as to the proper performance of his duty. There can therefore, I think, be no doubt but that the engineer must be a thorough man of business.

Because I have not alluded in these examples to the architect, it must not be supposed that such documents as estimates and specifications are foreign to his practice, for, equally with the engineer, must he be capable of directing the *modus operandi* of his undertaking,—nay, even probably with still greater minuteness of detail, seeing that his work is generally more minute, and depending more particularly on exact dimensions for its success.

Both architects and engineers must also understand those branches of law which relate to their profession, and study the science of jurisprudence, so far as to enable them to judge of the legality of their proceedings, to prevent their employers from being involved in lawsuits through their means, and to extricate them by the shortest way when so involved, by a cessation or alteration of the offensive operations, if the cause be connected with their pursuits. I mean not their duties should in any way trench on those of the attorney, or that they should advise in any matter involving a legal or technical question, for "a little law is a dangerous thing;" but they should always understand the particular sections of the law relating to their operations, that they may be able to steer clear of the dangerous rock of litigation.

All the laws of England contain enactments and regulations concerning building, and they consist both of written laws or statutes, and unwritten laws, or laws of common customs. It would be out of place here to describe all the laws which affect the operations of an engineer or architect, but I may be pardoned for making mention of one or two points that have come within my experience, to serve as illustrations of my statement, that they should know "their own law."

For instance, when the inhabitants of a county are liable for the repairs of a public bridge, they are liable also to repair, to the extent of 100 yards, the highway at each end of the bridge. One instance came under my observation, in which a surveyor neglected not only to take into account the existence of that law in his estimate of the work to be done, but even through his ignorance suffered an action to be brought against himself, as the representative of the county. He lost the action, and the magistrates refused to bear him harmless, "because he ought to have known the law."

I may mention another instance in the case of a bridge. An engineer was employed by a private gentleman to build a bridge for a public road upon his estate: two years after its completion it was washed away by a flood. It had become so useful to the public that it was necessary to have it rebuilt, and the owner then thought that it might be erected at the expense of the county. But the county refused, because his engineer had not submitted his plans to, and obtained the approval of, the county surveyor.

An architect designed and erected for a gentleman a very expensive conservatory, and it was made portable, for as this gentleman was only a yearly tenant, he intended to remove it should he change his residence. But his architect erected the conservatory on a brick foundation: it thus became a fixture, and the property of the landlord.

Examples of such cases might be repeated until the relation of them might fill a considerable volume, but those mentioned will serve to show that the artist employed to execute any works should inquire concerning the laws relating to them.

I have now said as much as the limits of a lecture will allow, upon the duties required of architects and engineers, and I will say a few words upon the duties of the general community with regard to architecture more especially.

If we refer to history we shall find that exactly in proportion as civilization advanced architecture flourished—had its rise, its progress, and decay. It took its styles, its varieties, and its tones, from the nations who invented or introduced it, and what may be called, with great propriety, a national style, always existed.

Greece, during her independence, invented that architecture which, even at the present day, is our model. Her princes und rulers esteemed it the highest honour to be ranked with artists, and her buildings were looked upon by all as types of her glory.

Republican Rome, although she borrowed her designs from Greece, and built by the hands of Grecian artists, cherished architecture, because, through it, the eternal city might be embellished, and the dignity of its citizens be enlarged, and although this did not, perhaps, arise from pure love and veneration of the art, it had its effects, and buildings were produced that have been handed down to us as forms worthy to be imitated to the present day.

The architecture of England also had its rise, progress, and decay. Its rise during the Anglo-Normans, its progress during the reigns of the Plantagenets and Tudors, when it arrived at the greatest excellence, and its decline may date from James I. (if we may include the Elizabethan, which, although not indigenous, has become, and perhaps deservedly, a favourite style in England), almost up to our own times; I say almost, for latterly, under the fostering patronage of royalty, and men of taste and genius, it has struggled into a new existence: let us hope that it is the dawn of a new era for architecture and the fine arts in England. That this germ may bud and grow into healthy beauty, it will require the steady co-operation of all Englishmen connected in any way with architecture. Genuine professors of the art will gladly give their best energies to the task of regeneration, and we have already examples which tell in glorious language (language engraven in stone) what will be the result of those energies. Nothing is wanted but men of influence and taste to add weight to the balance already inclining so decidedly in favour of purity and fitness of style.

I am an advocate for fitness in the style of architecture of every building, civil, military, or ecclesiastic; and would those through whose patronage the fine arts flourish study, equally with its professors, the true meaning and intent of fitness, there would speedily be an end to incongruity, and English buildings would stand prominently out as types of English architecture.

Both Grecian and Palladian architecture have taken so firm a root in the soil of England, that any attempt to dismiss the styles at once would be useless, and perhaps fatal to the regeneration of a national one. But will not a little consideration show that these styles are unfitted for the English climate throughout the year? The windows, few and far between, obstruct the light. The low pitched roofs retain the snow and rain, and the projecting porticos throw shadows, where there is already too much shade. An Italian villa, appropriately situate, may fitly serve as a summer residence, but we must seek in another style that comfort and homeness so loved by all Englishmen: for this style we need not become imitators or pilferers from a foreign nation.

The high pitched roof, the ornamented gable, the oriel window, the irregular plan, suitable as well for internal convenience as for external beauty, are all characteristics of our English style, and each feature has, besides, fitness to our climate to further recommend it. I wish particularly to be understood that I now speak of domestic architecture,—for that of public edifices we may still be indebted to Greece or Rome.

Our palaces, institutions, and prisons may still be in the decorated Corinthian, the chaste Palladian, or the stern and sombre Doric. But let our residences, our *country* residences, serve to keep us in mind of our former genius, while they add to our comfort and enjoyment.

One word more before we leave this subject, upon a point which every man has power to forward. I allude to internal decoration. In this branch of art the house-painter, the paper-hanger, and the joiner, are too often allowed to usurp the place of artists, and suffered to bedaub the walls with incongruous colours, or tasteless wood-work. Joiners, in particular, have a kind of systematized patent to work evil things; custom to one set of forms and method of work, has so fixed itself upon us, that the same set of moulding planes, the same kind of paneling, serves for all styles of houses. The architect himself is probably somewhat to blame in this, but I believe only to a small extent, for builders, not architects, are generally employed to run up the brick and stucco boxes called houses, and these, building either per contract, or for themselves, to save money and trouble, are little inclined to study propriety in internal finish. It is not that the architect considers it to be beneath him to be the decorator; for Raffaelle painted the walls of the Vatican, Rubens' hand embellished the ceiling of Whitehall, Sir James Thornhill decorated the walls of the chapel and hall of Greenwich, and we have Owen Jones in our day.

It cannot, therefore, be through any false notion of the architect that these internal finishings are left to artizans, but whether it be or not, every gentleman, every man of cultivated mind is to blame who suffers his house to be coloured up to suit the taste of the sign painter, who without any feeling of art in his composition daubs away in any shade of any pigment he may fancy to be in fashion.

Many patrons of the arts would fire up and say indignantly, "I do not suffer this outrage upon taste to be committed in my house." And I am only happy to admit that there are some glorious exceptions to my rule, but that they are exceptions I will uphold, and say confidently that eight out of ten have houses painted, fitted, and furnished, with designs that have issued from the shop, and not from the studio.

Poor men in the present state of things cannot, perhaps, help this; and the poor man with refined feelings for art must submit, for he cannot alter.

But rich men are those to whom I point, and say, study art, and be judges yourselves where art is employed, or consult those whose whole life has been devoted to the cultivation of it, and who will work for you, not for money alone, but for the love of art: architects should be such men.

[After an outline of the system of instruction he intended to follow, the lecturer continued,]

It is likewise my wish to make all the students familiar with the use of tools, and that they should become practical as well as scientific workmen; that this is essential, I have the high authority of the late Mr. Telford, who has said,—"Youths of respectability and competent education, who contemplate civil engineering as a profession, are seldom aware how far they ought to descend in order to found the basis of future elevation. It has happened to me more than once, when taking opportunities of being useful to a young man of merit, that I have experienced opposition in taking him from his books and drawings, and placing a mallet and chisel or a trowel in his hands, till, rendered confident by the solid knowledge which only experience can bestow, he was qualified to insist on the due performance of workmanship, and to judge of merit as well in the lower as in the higher departments of a profession in which no kind or degree of practical knowledge is superfluous."

A New Sort of Church Organ has been constructed, in two parts, one for each side of a window. The exterior, says the *Daily News*, is architectural, and of the colour of dark oak. Each of the two compartments is 26 feet in height, and the bellows are so arranged as to admit of their being placed under the window, which is to appear in the centre. The object of the designer, a Mr. Walker, has been to construct an instrument combining the advantages of a German organ with the principles of the extended compass on the Manuals.

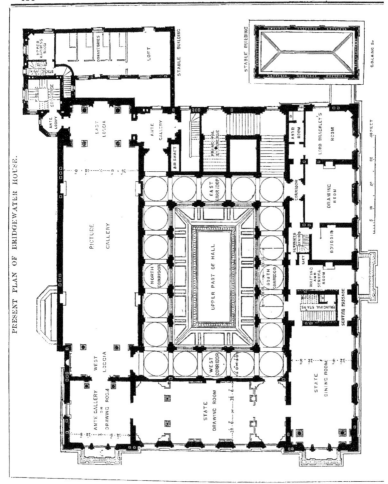

PRESENT PLAN OF BRIDGEWATER HOUSE.

THE ALTERED PLAN OF BRIDGEWATER HOUSE, LONDON.

We have been asked to give some informa-tion concerning the alterations which have been made in the internal arrangement of Bridgewater House, Cleveland-row, and can-not better comply with the request than by annexing a plan of the house as it is now proposed to be completed, which may be com-pared with the original plan given in our last volume (VI.), page 474.

It will be seen that a central hall has been formed, and the principal staircase moved to the side. The chief motive of the alteration is understood to be a desire to render the gallery and its approaches independent of the rest of the building, it being Lord Ellesmere's inten-tion to afford the greatest possible facilities to the public for visiting his fine collection. A separate staircase has been constructed, with this end in view, at the north-east corner, and is surmounted by a campanile.

The entrance to the central hall is under the apartment marked "service-room" on the plan.

We have received an ill-natured account, signed an "Employé of Mr. Barry," of what the hall is to be when finished; but being satisfied that, notwithstanding his signature, he writes in ignorance, as well as ill-feeling, we make no use of it.

The following, from a second correspondent, is fair criticism, to which we have no right to refuse a place :—

"With respect to the alteration in Bridge-water House, it might, in my opinion, have been better contrived. According to the first plan, there was no inner central hall on the ground-floor; now, on the contrary, there is too much,—one so disproportionably spacious and lofty, that, with the exception of the picture-gallery, all the rooms must look small by comparison with it,—that is, much smaller than they need do, or would have done, according to the first arrangement. Another objection is that, on its being first entered below, just as much will be seen as after ascending the staircase. Perhaps it would be better were the corridors to be partly enclosed so as to leave only eight of the sixteen arcades open to the upper part of the hall, viz. three on each side and one at each end, which might be done not by stopping up those at the angles, but by merely glazing them with orna-mental diapered or mosaic glass, in patterns of various colours; in which case the corre-sponding arcades below, if the corridors on the ground-floor be also quite open to the hall, ought to be closed up solid. That would confine the space sufficiently, and instead of the whole being disclosed at the first glance, parts would come into view successively,—would, after first appearing, disappear, and then appear again. It is not every architect that has a forte for plan—for so 'laying out a mansion as to secure various effects by means of piquant contrasts, transitions, and combi-nations. Z."

THE ARCHITECTURAL ASSOCIATION.

OPENING CONVERSAZIONE.

On Friday evening, the 5th instant, the Architectural Association met in Lyon's-Inn Hall, Strand, to open the session.* The walls presented a fair show of drawings, including several series of the sketches made by members of the Class of Design; and the room was well filled. The advantages resulting from this sketching class will be great: it should be sedulously attended by the younger members.

Letters were announced from Mr. Donaldson, Mr. Scoles, Mr. Tite, &c.

Mr. G. J. Wigley, secretary, read the report of the council, from which it appeared that the number of members had increased from 97 to 140. The committee urged the value of unrestricted interchange of opinions amongst the members, and showed the advantage that was resulting from all becoming well acquainted with each other. An attempt to form a book-club, it appeared, had not succeeded. The endeavour to establish a free architectural exhibition was very successful, and the collection had been visited by a daily average of about 500 persons. They had taken upon themselves the responsibility and risk of its permanent establishment, and they anxiously sought the concurrence and co-operation of the whole profession.

Mr. Christopher Creeke read a very able paper on various matters affecting professional practice, to which we shall devote space next week. In the course of the address it was stated that steps had been taken towards calling a meeting of the profession on the subject of Competition, and that every architect in England would be communicated with.

Mr. Godwin, being requested to make some observations, said the course he had pursued in respect of the Association from its foundation would, he thought, lead them to give him credit for sincerity when he stated that he was much gratified at hearing of its successful progress, and more than this, seeing the result of its operations. Many of the papers read on the alternate Fridays were most creditable to their authors, and in several instances had gained for them, as he was able to say positively, the good opinion of a large number of persons. But it was not merely at these meetings that good was done through the Association. The sketches on the walls produced on the intermediate Fridays, from given subjects, were exceedingly satisfactory evidence of the efforts of the members in another direction. Apart, however, from these proceedings, advantages resulted from association in the abstract. It seemed to him important that in our doings we should consider how they would operate on others,—that we should regard not simply their effect on ourselves, but on the well-being of our order, and this we were led to by such associations. We should find that in upholding the dignity and high character of the profession, we were best advancing our own individual interests. Never was there a moment when it was more important that architects should unite to set themselves and their profession right with the public than now; for pressed as they were on either side by circumstances of the time, their position was seriously threatened. The works of the architect, the value of design, were not recognised rightly by the public. A little matter which came under his observation a few weeks ago (and a straw might show the current) would in some degree illustrate this. An individual asked a young architect to make him "a little design" for a summer-house, and having obtained his charge for it, called upon him (the speaker) to know if the sum of two guineas, which the architect had named, was not *too* much for merely "a few lines and a bit of colour." He need not say what his answer was. But what he wanted to remark was this—that the same individual sent the drawing to a lithographer, wishing to distribute copies of it, and being charged three guineas for putting it on the stone, paid it with perfect satisfaction! The mere act of mechanically copying he could appreciate, but the value of the productive power, and the propriety of paying for what seemed such pleasant amusement for the artist, he did not understand. Architects had done much to induce this feeling and lower the character of the profession, by their indiscriminate compliance with invitations to compete, without those regulations which would ensure them justice. It gave him much pleasure to hear of the steps which had been taken by the Association towards following out the suggestions published in The Builder, with the view of obtaining a proper management of competitions. The late Birmingham Union competition was a case in point, where the successful architects, after having risked the chance of getting nothing for their time and skill, had been coolly offered about 3 per cent. on the amount of their estimate. He sincerely trusted that the architects would, under the circumstances, resist any departure from the customary remuneration.* The customary remuneration! This was another point which imperatively needed settlement; and if the elder members of the profession were too much occupied, or disinclined to take steps in the matter, he hoped, when the Association had succeeded in putting competitions on a proper footing, that they would turn their attention to the question of remuneration. The speaker then alluded to the excellence of the paper which had been read by the president, and moved a vote of thanks to him.—Carried.

Mr. Papworth afterwards briefly addressed the meeting, taking up the question of a "new style," mooted by the president, and urging with ability, that all that could be expected of architects was the re-combination and thoughtful application of the modes before us, with the adaptation of modern improvements and appliances, to the wants and purposes of the day.

* "The objects of the Architectural Association are, the advancement of the study of design in Architecture, the development of true principles of criticism, and the affording means whereby the student may acquire an aptitude for the application, recombination, and extension of the present materials of the art. For the attainment of these objects, the business of the Association is to consist of the production of designs for previously determined subjects; the reading of papers on the several branches of science and art, comprehended under the term Architecture; free and open discussion; and the contribution to the Society's portfolio of subjects, displaying either originality of design, examples of construction and decoration, or modes of representation."

* The architects have accepted the second proposition of the guardians, namely, 4 per cent. upon the cost of the building—that sum to cover the premium of 250*l.*, the superintendence of the erection, &c., but exclusive of the remuneration to the clerk of the works. In reply to some architects who express their anxiety to call a meeting of the profession in that town, on the subject of competitions, we would suggest a postponement for a short time.—Ed.

GAS AND HEALTH IN WARE, HERTS.

The Gas Company in Ware charged 8s. per 1,000 feet. A new company came into the town, and offered, if a certain number of persons would agree to deal with them, to construct works and supply gas at 6s. per 1,000. A meeting was called, and the old company were applied to, to know if *they* would supply it at that price, as in that case no encouragement would be given to the new company. They refused. The new company have constructed their works, and the old company are now offering gas at *four* shillings per 1,000 feet,—too late, however, the new company having, of course, obtained a written agreement from many of the inhabitants to take their gas, before the works were commenced. The relation of this occurrence may not be without its value to other Companies if they will consider it wisely.——A local board of health has been appointed here under the Health Act, and are getting to work, though, perhaps, not very vigorously at present. There was a considerable struggle at the election,—the turning point being, as it has been in some other places, "who should be *clerk* to the board." How this has operated in Ware we are not in a position to say,—the best men for the purpose may have been elected for anything we know to the contrary,—but it must be obvious that if the qualification for members of local boards is to be simply a determination to support Mr. A. as clerk against Mr. B., or *vice-versa*, the reverse at times must be the case.

The Iron Trade.—Several of the usual quarterly meetings have been held, but the masters have deemed it advisable not to advance the nominal price previously fixed, namely, 6*l.* per ton for rods and bars. The small makers are reported to be in pretty full work for home consumption, but on the whole the trade is represented to be not in the most satisfactory condition for the manufacturers.

RAILWAY JOTTINGS.

The raising of the tube at the Britannia-bridge, Menai Straits, has been resumed, and there is now a clear height of 55 feet between the tube and high-water, so that small vessels sail beneath.——The contract for the formation of that portion of the Whitehaven and Furness Junction line which runs from Broughton to Bootle has been taken by Messrs. Fell and Joplin, of Greenodd, who intend to commence operations immediately, to be completed by April.——The total loss on the atmospheric experiment on the South Devon, after deducting the estimated value of materials on hand, is said to be 351,000*l.*——The foundations of the iron bridge over the Ouze, at Huntingdon, were commenced on Thursday week. The piles, or cylinders rather, are being driven, it seems, under a modification of Dr. Pott's process. Those forming the piers or supporters of the arches are about 9 feet long, and 4 in diameter. One of these having been sunk in the river, another is placed on the top of it, with a cap on the head of that, and all are made air-tight. Two large cylinders on the shore are then exhausted of air, and on turning a tap in a tube connecting them with those in the river, the air is suddenly transferred from one to the other, when the pressure of the atmosphere causes it to descend with considerable rapidity. In each case on Thursday, the tube was driven in 6 to 7 feet; and this process will be repeated till they are at the proper depth, when the water and soil will be taken from them and concrete introduced.——The engine-drivers on the Great Western have been receiving for the last five or six weeks, in addition to their wages, about 8s. a-week each as premium on the amount of coke saved by them below that fixed by regulation.——The wages paid to enginemen are:—Great Western, 5s. 6d. to 7s. 6d. a-day; Midland, 5s. to 7s.; York and North Midland, 4s. to 7s.; London and North-Western (Manchester and Birmingham division), 5s. to 7s.; Eastern Counties, 5s. to 7s. 6d.; North British, 5s. to 6s. 10d.; Edinburgh and Glasgow, 3s. 6d. to 7s.; Perth and Dundee 4s. to 8s. The enginemen of the York, Newcastle, and Berwick have entered into a union to obtain—For merchandise and passenger traffic, 6s. for first year, 6s. 6d. for second, and 7s. afterwards. Those proposed by the company are—5s., 5s. 6d., 6s. 6d., and 7s. respectively.——The Great Western to Windsor was to be opened from Slough to Windsor on Monday last.——The works on the South Wales between Newport and Gloucester are going on rapidly: permanent way is being laid.——Two arches of the viaduct of more than fifty arches over the river Calder, near Whalley, on a branch of the Bolton, Clitheroe, and West Yorkshire line, gave way on Saturday last. The centres of several of the arches had been withdrawn on the previous day. Three lives were lost by the accident.——The survey of the intended line for Madras has been completed 13 miles, and the results, it is reported, are favourable, so far as regards engineering details. The road is almost level.——The calls advertised for October amount to 1,046,749*l.*: 11,106*l.* are on account of foreign companies. For the corresponding month of last year they were 1,693,655*l.* The total calls for the first ten months of 1849 now amount to 17,700,964*l.* against 30,072,610*l.* in 1848.

Working Class Club-houses.—The bakers are likely to have the honour of setting the first class example in carrying out the principles so long advocated by The Builder, and successfully set agoing by the society for improving the dwellings of the industrious classes. A meeting of master and journeymen bakers was held on Monday week, at King's-cross, when it was resolved to have a building, with fifty or sixty bed-rooms, to be let at 2s. a-week each, with warm and cold baths, the former at one penny, and the latter one halfpenny each. All the daily newspapers and a select library to be provided, with a reading and coffee-room. The expenses were estimated at about 300*l.*, and the income at about 365*l.* per annum, leaving a balance in favour of the speculators of 65*l.* The assistance of the parent association was fully anticipated.

J.M.LOCKYER

LAING Sc

BYZANTINE CAPITALS.

Nos. 1, 2, 4, and 6 are from the centre and more ancient cloister of the monastery of Santa Scolastica, near Subiaco. The monastery was founded in the fifth century: the portion from which these capitals are taken dates from 1052, and is, therefore, one of the earliest ex-amples of this style in Italy. It is similar in arrangement to the more recent cloister at St. John Lateran, at Rome, save that single shafts are more frequently used than double ones to support the small arches of the covered ambu-latory. It was in this monastery that the first printing-press in Italy was established, in the year 1465. No. 6 is a particularly rich exam-ple. Nos. 3 and 5 are two specimens tal from the columns supporting the large pul in the cathedral of San Pantaleone, at Rave now only a small town near Amalfi, but o a flourishing city of 36,000 inhabitants. pulpit itself is a magnificent pile, of wl marble, nearly 14 feet in height, blazing v mosaics, with every possible member ri sculptured. It is supported on six columns, the shafts twisted and inlaid with mosaic bands. These columns are carried by six marble lions in marching order, three and three; the carving throughout is delicate and varied. The capitals now engraved are about 1 foot 3 inches in height. The date of erection is 1260. No. 7 is from the ruins of an old palace of about the same date, closely adjoining the cathedral. It is usually called the palace of Charles of Anjou.

Nos. 8 and 9 are from a pulpit in the cathedral at Salerno, erected about the year 1170 by the Archbishop Romoald. The execution of these caps is superior to that of the Ravello examples of nearly a century later, and is a good specimen of the use of the peculiar *drilling* that characterizes so much the works of the Greek artists of the period. The cathedral at Salerno was built by Robert Guiscard, with materials brought chiefly from the ruins of Pæstum. No. 8 is an elegant specimen, and partakes rather of the fancy of the cinque-centisti than of the workmen of the twelfth century.

THE AIR SYPHON VENTILATOR.

We mentioned a short time since Dr. Chowne's patent mode of ventilation founded on his asserted discovery that, " if a bent tube or hollow passage be fixed with the legs upwards, the legs being of unequal lengths, whether it be in the open air, or with the shorter leg communicating with a room or other place, the air circulates up the longer leg, and that it enters and moves down the shorter leg ; and that this action is not prevented by making the shorter leg hot, whilst the larger leg remains cold ; and no artificial heat is necessary to the longer leg of the Air Syphon, to cause this action to take place." Thus, by using the chimney of an ordinary room, for example into which air has free access, as the longer leg, and by conducting a tube or channel constituting the short leg of the Air Syphon, from any part (as near the ceiling, for instance), into the lower part of the chimney, at the suitable place, a stream of air will proceed from the apartment down the shorter leg, and away up the longer one.

The *Illustrated News* of last week gives two diagrams, farther elucidating the patentee's views. These show that a portable ventilator may be set up on a chimney piece, in the shape of a vase, or column perforated, and having a tube carried from the bottom, and continued into the chimney.* " In assembly-rooms, even where fire is not used, which become over-heated and close, to whatever part of the room rout-forms extend, the means of ventilation can also be conducted, either by channels as light zinc tube) suspended under the forms, or by making the forms themselves hollow channels. In either case this channel being made continuous, and finally passing through an opening in a chimney-board, or by some similar arrangement, into the fireplace, and tubes passing from these to the upper parts of the room, the warm air would constantly descend through them to the continuous channel, and then into the larger leg of the Syphon." To convey away the heat from gas or other lamps, in drawing-rooms or large working apartments, it is proposed to perforate an ornamental pillar, and carry a piece of tubing under the floor to the nearest chimney. According to the diagrams it is unnecessary that the two legs of the Syphon should be of the same diameter. We have yet to see the plan in operation.

IRON HOUSES ABROAD.—The *Journal de Liège* states that at the establishment of Seraing, and others near Verviers, a great number of cast-iron (corrugated) cottages and warehouses have been constructed, and shipped at Antwerp for the gold regions of California. A chapel and church in iron have been made for the Missionary Society of Brussels, which has attracted curiosity. Now that affairs are more tranquil in France, a great many Englishmen are employed in the iron foundries, steel ctories, and the engine and machinery works.

* The patentee says,—" When this ventilator is used with out a fire, as for example in the summer, it will be better although not necessary), that the space left in the opening of the valve of the register, between the tube and the mar tins of the opening, should be closed by a piece of sheet tin, or so as to fit and cover the space."

RENAISSANCE DOORWAY, ST. ANDREW'S, JOIGNY, FRANCE.

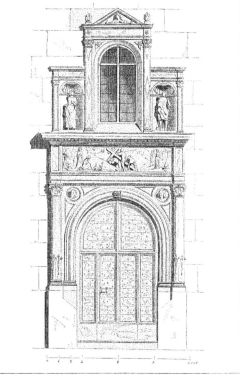

RENAISSANCE DOORWAY,
ST. ANDREW'S, JOIGNY, FRANCE.

THIS church of St. Andrew, at Joigny, contains several matters of interest to artists, especially some paintings of the fourteenth century, and some good sculpture.

The side door represented above is a graceful composition of the Renaissance period. The arrangement of the pedestal of the columns, the large frieze with its sculptured decoration, and the management of the upper storey, are all worthy of note.

BOOKS FOR THE WORKING CLASSES.

As a working man, allow me to thank you for the fresh proof of your goodwill to our class, contained in your last number. There is a tendency to move forward to supply the defects therein laid open, and I am, as one of the starved in book-knowledge, deeply grateful for your attack on the castle of ignorance. Might I beg of you to bring before the public a suggestion made some years ago, and unheeded ? That a building *apart* from the British Museum, and thereby obviating the danger of fire to that institution, should be appropriated to the reception of duplicate copies which, from various causes, are found in that library, that so the nucleus of *a library for working men, to be opened from six to eleven o'clock at night*, might be provided. Tickets might be given under restrictions, as at present, and works *lent out* upon a deposit equal to the value of them. I lay much stress upon this last item. Although the quiet of a reading-room is favourable for study, yet the possession of a book, unattainable from the ordinary libraries and very far beyond the means of a working man to purchase, gives a charm to the deal table and clean-swept hearth of home, which would not exist in the gas-lit and French-polished public reading-room. Besides, a working man, after finishing his day's work, must go home for some refreshment; and if not able to keep a book at home a few days, must lose some time in " cleaning himself." This would involve perhaps a wearing of the better coat and hat in the evening, as most men would not like to go in the stains of their labour,—albeit not ashamed of them.

I have had, through the kindness of a friend, the privilege conferred on me of a reading order for the British Museum library, but although I have had it now fourteen months, have been able but *three* times to avail myself of it. I am in the position of a starving man with a good 50l. note in his possession, for which no one will give change. I believe there is no want of sympathy on the part of our influential men with the growing desire for knowledge evinced by the working classes, but they want to be led to consider the subject ; and I further believe it to be the mission of THE BUILDER to keep the matter before the public. What organ so proper as the publication which is thumbed, and dirtied, and greased by working men, smiths, bricklayers, masons, and carpenters; consulted by architects, and land-owners, and clergy; and which lies (so report says) on the table of the " first gentleman " in the land ?

OGER.

USE OF BRONZE FOR MONUMENTS.

THE NELSON COLUMN, LONDON.

With regard to the remarks on the Nelson column, adopted in your last number, from a clever contemporary, I venture to send you a varied impression. I admit the unexampled sloth by which that proceeding has been characterized, and say with the *Observer*, "It is hoped, it is entreated, of the Government that they will, without any longer delay, give orders for the completion of this monument, which, as it now stands, is a satire upon the sea service, and a memento of national ingratitude to departed heroism, rather than a symbol of naval glory."

The point, however, to which I am desirous of drawing attention is the ready violation of the canons of art for the mere purpose of spicing a critique. Thus bronze,—the vehicle celebrated throughout all history, the forerunner of marble in the hands of the sculptor, and ever a favourite material,—is to be abandoned, except for cabinet *morceaux* or large single objects; but for compositions such as those on the pedestal of the Nelson column, some 14 feet square, having the chief figures of natural or heroic size, with the limbs and accessories frequently detached, and in some instances almost the entire figure, bronze is to be no longer admissible.

But what is to be the succedaneum? I fear it would be difficult to point to a material that would afford equal facilities. The inferior applicability of stone to minute parts is exemplified in the bronze sword of Bailey's figure at the top; and unless in some such ductile non-absorbent and imperishable substance as the one employed for the *relievi*, much of their finish and detail must have been omitted.

The local or pervading colour of material, wholly unrecognized in architecture, is of very little consequence to the sculptor; a monochrome in lampblack is as powerful as one in gamboge, and so thought the authors of the *black marble* centaurs of the *capitol*.

Bronze, for the ornamental part of the Nelson capital, was probably adopted from necessity,—it would never have been so well done in granite; but while it now holds in some aspects an intense depth of shade, it becomes, under the ordinary play of light, so perfectly distinct that the markings of the leaves are as perceptible as those of the wreath on the granite torus immediately below the shaft.

As to the recommendation for distorting the base, surely some better and more analogous authority should be adduced than the puny, not to say hypothetical, interior order at Bassæ, whose chief characteristic is its unparalleled eccentricity. Moderator.

THE "OLD HALL" AT GAINSBOROUGH.

Passing through Gainsborough a few days since, I went to see how the "restorations" were progressing at the "old hall" (a distinctive name this fine old building took when the Hickman family removed to the new hall at Thonack). The "old hall" is one of the few remaining wood and plaster buildings erected towards the close of the fifteenth century, and though it has been much neglected, it is in a pretty good state of preservation. The general plan of the building is three sides of a quadrangle, one of which is wholly occupied by the great hall, till lately encumbered with all the paraphernalia of a theatre,—the minstrel gallery serving for a dressing, and the fine oriel for a green-room. The hall is open to the roof, which has a lantern, and principals supported by arched ribs; the latter once sprung from carved corbels, not one of which are now remaining, having been removed one by one as they were found to stand in the way of the theatrical arrangements; and I believe there are those in the town who could tell where some, at least, of these corbels are yet to be found, and they might (if too much decayed to be reinstated) serve as models for new ones. All the windows towards the inner area are of oak, some projecting 7 or 8 inches from the face of the building, with cills, cornices, mullions, &c., nicely moulded, as also tracery in the upper part probably 1½ inch or 2 inches thick, giving them a screen-like appearance. These and several other windows have only of late been freed from the lath and plaster with which for generations they have been blocked up. The warder's tower (a fine piece of brickwork), and the brick front towards the east, as well as the offices towards the west, appear to have been additions made about the beginning or middle of the sixteenth century.

It is a pity so rich a relic of bygone days should be restored so superficially as this appears to be: for instance, the oak mouldings, carvings, &c., where decayed, are being patched with deal, and plaster ornament has been used for "beautifying" the stone fire-places. You will probably not wonder at this when told, as I was, that "the whole of the works" were under the superintendence of a resident lawyer; and still it is surprising, when we know that men of acknowledged taste in these matters (and one, at least, a distinguished archæologist) reside in the immediate neighbourhood. J.

ANCIENT BELL-RINGERS' RHYMES.

HATHERSAGE CHURCH.

The following is a literal copy of an inscription in the black letter, in the belfry of Hathersage Church, Derbyshire. It was written about the year 1650, by one Anthony Frith, clerk of the parish, and whose family have held the office ever since. Perhaps you may think it worthy of insertion among the curiosities of your journal.

"You gentlemen that here intend to ring,
See that these laws you keep in every thing,
Or els be sure you must without delay
The penalty thereof to th' ringers pay.
First when you do into the belhouse come,
Look that the ringers have convenient room,
For If you be an hindrance unto them,
Four pence you forfeit to these gentlemen;
Next if you do intend here for to ring,
With hat or spurs on, do not touch a string,
For if you do, your forfeit is for that,
First 4 pence down to pay, and loose your hat.
If you a bell turn o're, without delay
Four pence unto the ringers you must pay:
Or if you strike, miscall, or do abuse,
You must pay 4 pence for the ringers' use.
For every oath here sworn, ere you go hence
Unto the poor then, you must pay twelve pence.
And if that you desire to be enrould
A ringer here, these orders keep and hold,
But whoso doth these orders disobey
Unto the stocks wee will him take straight way,
There to remain until that hee be willing
To pay his forfeit, and the clark a shilling."

The church is about undergoing a thorough restoration under the care of Mr. Butterfield. There are several good brasses in the church, but these the present representative of the Frith family will *not allow* of *being* copied by any one but himself, and for which he charges a very respectable price. C. H. B.

WHAT MUST WE DO?*

Will the pestilence, which is now rapidly abating in the metropolis, disappear for good in a few weeks? or will it smoulder in the population during the winter, and burst forth again with renewed virulence on the recurrence of the summer heats? The answer to this question depends on the use which we may make of the respite afforded by the coming frosts. If we employ the next five or six months in resolute exertions, well directed, and well sustained, to cleanse and purify the squalid low-lying districts of London;—if we get rid of the two millions and a quarter cubic feet of ordure (just about one cubic foot per man) in the midst of which we live;—if we divert to rural cemeteries the thousands of corpses that knock weekly at our metropolitan church-doors—pale applicants for lodging in the vaults below;—if we purge with ventilating air-holes, and wash with preparations of lime, all such horrible "pest-houses" as that of 48, Half Moon-street (mentioned in a recent report of the city medical officer)—"the filthy, stinking, airless residence of fourteen families, never free from fever;" or that at 4, Hartshorn-court, where nine unhappy outcasts lie rotting "in the midst of cholera and diarrhœa" in one small and stinking room;—if we stop at their source the subterranean rivers of filth and blood that take their rise from Smithfield-market and Whitechapel shambles;—if we explore and evacuate the hideous caves of A gate and Tyler's-market, where undergrou slaughterers, red-armed, and ankle-deep putrid garbage, ply their loathsome trade if the black tidal ditches of Bermondsey, I therhithe, and Lambeth, those chosen hau of pestilence, be cleansed at length a covered;—if, instead of the scanty and int mittent supplies of water now doled out to at extravagant charges by corporate mo polists, we agitate for free continuous strea at constant pressure and at reasonable price if, profiting at length by the terrible teach of experience, we thus set to work in go earnest to improve the sanitary condit of London, instead of leaving it, as actually is, worse off for air, light, wat drainage, &c., than in 1832, taking i account the increase of building and po lation; — then, but not otherwise, we n hope that the pestilence, now only remittir will be finally subdued,—then, but not oth wise, we may reasonably expect that just as Dulwich, fever was recently arrested by flu ing out the drains—just as in the Long-all district, where 500 cases of typhus occurr within six months, one passage, lately clean has since remained exempt from the epider raging around it—and just as in a street Hammersmith, epidemic diarrhœa, previou severe, entirely disappeared after the emptyi of an overflowing cesspool—so in all Lond similarly purified, a similar exemption fr preventible diseases may ensue.

* From the *Times*.

Miscellanea.

The Advance of Iron-working England is a subject for congratulati and should be aided by architects to the e tent of their power. The current number the *Journal of Design* says on the subject iron:—This most valuable metal may be call almost the direct agent of man in whatever undertakes. In agriculture, manufacture, t building of ships, &c., this was early seen, a therefore its use is of very high antiqui although not so remote, we have reason to l lieve, as that of either gold, silver, or copp The inferior brilliancy of its colour may, p haps, in some degree, account for this circu stance, as well as the greater skill required obtain it from its ores and apply it to purpos of art. While gold and silver glitter often their native state, and the ores of copper are brilliant colour, the less apparent but mc useful iron in its ore or native state holds o few of these lures to the finder. The nati colour is still gray, and it is found in mass sometimes of meteoric origin; it also occurs the state of pyrites, magnetic ironstone, och ironstone, &c. &c. It is, as we know well, malleable and ductile metal, susceptible of ve high polish, especially when united in a pec liar manner with carbon, in which state it called steel; and this most useful combinati must, we suppose, be of remote origin, for ir is mentioned repeatedly in the Pentateuch employed for the fabrication of swords, knive and various other sharp-edged instrumen We may estimate in some degree the val that was then attached to it from an expre sion in the eighth chapter of Deuteronom where Moses tells the Israelites, in his descri tive eulogy of the land of promise, that it "a land whose stones are iron, and out whose hills they may dig brass." An illustr tion of the same fact, at a later date, occurs the *Iliad*, where Achilles proposes a ball iron as one of the prizes to be distributed the games instituted in honour of Patrocle Within a few centuries after this, the workir of this metal seems to have arrived at mu perfection, as Herodotus speaks of a saucer iron, very curiously inlaid, that was present by a king of Lydia to the Delphic oracle, ar adds, that "it is of surprising workmanshi and as worthy of observation as any of th offerings preserved at Delphi."

Sediment in Cisterns.—A correspo dent says,—"Allow me to propose to tho who like pure water, to have the bottom their cistern shaped conically, with the di charging-pipe attached to the extremity: th no sediment could be formed; and when th water was agitated by a fresh supply it wou still be as clear as ever." This would preve sediment, but not give *pure water*.

PROJECTED WORKS.—Advertisements have been issued for tenders, by 25th October, for completing a Wesleyan chapel and schools at Southampton; by 7th November, for the erection of buildings for public baths and wash-houses at Westminster; by 13th November, for the erection of a goods and corn warehouse at the Midland Railway station, at Leeds; by 27th October, for the erection and completion of a new prison at Lewes; by 7th November, for boilers, pipes, and fittings for baths and washhouses at Westminster; by 16th October, for 50 covered goods waggons, with folding doors, for the Great Northern Railway; by 16th, for turn-tables, traversing frames, switches and crossings, water cranes, and water piping for Lancashire and Yorkshire Railway Company at Liverpool; by 30th, for the execution of that portion of the East and West-India Docks and Birmingham Junction Railway lying between the Lea-cut canal and Blackwall; by 13th, for building a store-house of corrugated iron (not galvanized) at Southampton harbour; by 24th, for continuing the boring at the Artesian Well, on Southampton Common, to a depth of 50 feet, or farther, below the bore-hole, which is 1,260 feet deep,—by 24th, for constructing a new deep pump and fixing same at Southampton Common, and for repairing and lengthening present pump, and altering steam-engines, &c.—by same date, for 500 yards of 5-inch cast-iron water-pipe, and 500 yards 3-inch ditto with branches, fire-plugs, &c.; and by 9th November, for the survey, maps, and plans of Carmarthen, with a system of sewerage for same.

ST. JUDE'S, BRISTOL.—A new district church is very nearly completed on Poyntz Pool, Bristol city, dedicated to St. Jude, under the direction of Mr. Gabriel, architect. It is in the Decorated style (Edward II.), and consists of a nave and chancel, tower at the west end, with revestry north of the chancel. The tower is of four stages, having a deeply-recessed doorway, above which is a 3-light window; the belfrey is lofty, with a 2-light window on each side; it is surmounted by a parapet of wavy and quatrefoil tracery, having a pinnacle at each angle, with buttresses set diagonally. The turret staircase is entered by a door inside the tower. The nave has a south doorway. The whole of the windows (except the east and west) are of two lights, and each of different tracery. There is a priests' door in the south wall of the chancel. The nave has open benches: the font is situated near the south door, and is large enough for immersion: the pulpit, which is on the north of the chancel arch, is of stone, with good panelling: the upper part of the tower arch is open, with a door beneath: the chancel arch is crossed by a screen of oak: the roof of the nave is open, and of a good pitch. On each side of the chancel is a row of four stalls. Further eastward, to the south, are sedilia and *piscina*, with drain complete (?); and in the thickness of the north wall an *aumbry* is formed. The roof of the chancel is vaulted with wood, and the bosses gilt. The floor is to be laid with encaustic tiles. The church is built of Hanham stone, with freestone dressings: and the roof is covered with stone slabs, peculiar to the churches of the middle ages. Interior length of nave, 65 feet; breadth, 29 feet: length of chancel, 25 feet; breadth, 24 feet. Taken as a whole, the church is a good specimen of revived English Pointed architecture.

SMOKY CHIMNEYS.—"A smoky chimney and a scolding wife are two of the worst evils of domestic life," says the old proverb; and to obviate the first evil ingenuity is ever racking its brain. Hence, Regent-street and every part of the metropolis has its house-tops bristling with pipes and deformed by cowls in every conceivable and almost inconceivable variety. Now, I have built many chimneys in all possible situations, and have found one simple plan everywhere succeed, the secret being only to construct the *throat* of the chimney, or that part of it just above the fire-place, *so small* that a man or a boy can barely pass through. 2ndly. Immediately above this the chimney shaft should be enlarged to double its width, like a purse, to the extent of about 2 feet in height, and then diminish again to its usual proportions. No chimney that I ever constructed thus smoked. — W. MASON, Lieut.-Colonel.

MECHANICS' INSTITUTES SUGGESTED.—In Mr. Weld's "History of the Royal Society," the author says:—"In a curious letter from Hartlib to Boyle, dated Amsterdam, May 18, 1649, and preserved in the archives of the Society, is the following memorandum:—'*Fauxhall* is to be sett apart for publick uses, by which is meant making it a place of resort for artists, mechanicks, &c., and a depôt for models and philosophical apparatus.' It is further proposed, that 'experiments and trials of profitable inventions should be carried on,' which, says the writer, 'will be of great use to the Commonwealth.' Hartlib adds, that the late king (Charles I.) 'designed Fauxhall for such an use.' In another letter to Boyle, dated May, 1654, Hartlib says, 'The Earl of Worcester is buying Fauxhall from Mr. Trenchard, to bestow the use of that house upon Gaspar Calehof and his son, as long as they shall live, for he intends to make it a College of Artisans. Yesterday,' he adds, 'I was invited by the famous Thomas Bushel to Lambeth Marsh, to see part of that foundation.'"

ELECTRO-TELEGRAPHIC PROGRESS.—While the cost of a telegraphic line in England is 150*l*. a-mile, in America and Prussia it is under 20*l*. a-mile. The telegraph in Prussia consists of one wire, extending over 1,402 miles, under ground, and covered with gutta-percha. Like those in America, it is by Morse, and is said to be capable of transmitting 1,000 words an hour. There are upwards of 10,000 miles of telegraph line in America, all worked cheaply. In England there are only 2,000 miles in operation.——Complaints of delay and neglect, as well as high charge here, still prevail. It must be admitted, however, that some of these complaints are most actively taken up and published by parties who have an interest in the substitution of a competitive line which is on the *tapis*, but of the real merits of which we are not yet prepared to judge.

PUBLIC CEMETERIES.—Not many miles from London there are barren waste lands that at present yield not a fraction of good to us, but with a little energy and capital might be converted to uses that would be as profitable as any speculation. Cambridge-heath is well known, and none will venture to dispute what an unprofitable tract of land it is; and there is another which is as much so, near the Southampton Railway. It extends from Woking to Bishopstoke, and is upwards of 20 miles in extent, the centre of which is crossed by the railway and a canal. This spot is as well calculated for a great public cemetery as any that can be named. It is so close to the railway that it is very easy of access; and a quality of land that might be purchased at as small a cost as any, owing to the nature of the soil, nearly all being composed of sand and loam. It may be questioned whether such a soil is calculated for interment, as sand is apt to fall in from the sides of any pit. Six feet is deep enough for any grave, and coffin laid on coffin is all that is needed, which might as well be done in sand as clay or gravel: such an arrangement as this must eventually be made, either with reference to the abandonment of the uses of the water which is obtained from various sources near London, or the final removal of cemeteries round the suburbs. There must be percolations from any cemetery, and, placed as they are at present, namely, Highgate, Abney Park, Norwood, &c., there can be but little doubt that the water from the artesian wells will, by them, be eventually affected. —It is but half doing a thing to have a little cemetery here and there; why not have a good one at once, and once for all? Why have charnel-houses so near our homes, when other and better opportunities offer for their position elsewhere. Were all the little cemeteries now about us, with the addition of more land, made public grounds and parks, and each of these spots of grassy land connected the one with the other by avenues, planted with rows of trees, so as to form one large belt to connect the parks round the metropolis, it would be better calculated for our health and happiness. The present parks are insufficient, and were London to take a walk some fine day, there would be scarcely standing room for its worthy citizens. London, with a little foresight and care, might be made the grandest city in the world. P.

PROVINCIAL.—At Charlton, near Woolwich, the foundation-stone of a new church, to be called St. Thomas's, was laid on Thursday week.——Sandgate Church has been remodelled under the direction of Mr. Keeble, of Folkestone, architect, and will now accommodate upwards of 800 persons.——The Pontypool town school-room has been enlarged and opened as a church. The original building, 60 feet by 30, intersects the room at right angles, opening the whole width into it, but separated by a curtain.——The foundation-stone of St. Margaret's Church, Prestwich, was laid by the Duchess of Cambridge, on Wednesday week. The Earl of Wilton gives the land and 500*l*. towards the building fund. ——A large portion of the wall surrounding Heaton Norris gas-works fell in on Sunday week. It had bulged inwards from the weight of earth outside; and being neglected, some heavy rain completed the destructive process. ——The foundation-stone of St. Thomas's Church, Leylands, Leeds, was laid on 29th ult. The chief expense will be defrayed by Mr. M. J. Rhodes, now of Dursley, Gloucestershire, but at one time of Leeds, and by 500*l*. from the Diocesan Church Building Society.——Plans of a new crescent, to be erected at Stobcross, near Glasgow, have been prepared by Mr. Kirkland, architect, on a principle intended to afford to the middle classes, and at moderate rents, all the conveniences and elegances of the first-class dwelling. The elevations are proposed to be houses of three stories, to be let in 'flats,' or floors, of five and seven rooms, consisting of dining and drawing-room, and from three to five sleeping-rooms, with the necessary offices and conveniences. The proposed buildings have been projected by a company of private gentlemen.

EDINBURGH.—The new Corn Market is rapidly approaching completion. It is floored with heavy timber, and forms the largest saloon in the city.——It is creditable to the fleshers of Edinburgh, says the local *Register*, that they have taken the initiative in urging the town council to the immediate erection of public slaughter-houses. The example is deserving of imitation by all the members of that calling throughout the country.——The provisions in the New Police Act relating to the improvement of drainage in the city, are now being put into vigorous operation by the inspector of streets and buildings, and it is satisfactory to know that the proprietors have generally evinced no reluctance to carry the provisions of the Act into effect.

GLASS MANUFACTURE.—A patent has been granted to Mr. H. Howard, Railway-place, Fenchurch-street, for—1. A peculiar construction of furnace for melting and casting glass, in which the flame is made to encircle and impinge directly against the sides of the pots, effecting thereby uniformity of heat, and an improved quality of material. 2. A portable furnace for melting glass, with one or more working holes. 3. The adaptation of a sheet of platina to the crown of melting and refining furnaces, to prevent the droppings falling into the pots. 4. A peculiar form and construction of annealing furnace with flues in the centre near the bottom, and holes in the top for allowing the heat to escape, and admitting light when emptying it of its contents.

A CHEAP FILTER FOR WATER.—Having had occasion to offer a suggestion, with reference to the use of charcoal (and a friend suggests the preference to be given to that of peat) for stuffing coffin mattrasses in lieu of saw-dust, filling up others in putrescent diseases, &c., I beg to remind the public that as the water in daily use in this metropolis is any thing but what it should be, thanks to an overbearing monopoly of destructiveness, which might have been lessened long ago, if the various parish boards would have sunk artesian wells,—a very simple means exists, by which any poor family may *filter* all the water required, viz., by using a large pan or tub as the tank, and filtering the water (by ascension) through a sponge stuffed into the hole in the bottom of flower-pots, using two pots, the lower one being half filled with charcoal, and loosely covered with thin flannel, the upper one placed in it so as to sink the flannel with it, and then secured by a string: nothing can be more simple or more easily cleansed.
W. ORD, M.D.

Patent for increasing the Effective Strength of Beams.—We learn from the *Journal of the Franklin Institute*, that a patent has been granted to Mr. J. R. Remington, for "An improvement in the method of increasing the effective strength of beams or rafters of wood or other materials, used in bridges and other structures." The patentee says,—"The nature of my invention consists in so arranging timbers or beams as to avoid their tendency to break in the middle of their length, and this is effected by extending the ends of the timbers beyond the points of support, and there bracing or tying them down, so as to render the points of support fulcra; the tendency to break in the middle of the length is thus in part transferred to the points of support, for it will be evident that thus supported the timbers cannot break in the middle without breaking also at the two points of support." *Claim.*—"What I claim as my invention, and desire to secure by letters patent, is the method of increasing the effective strength of timbers or sleepers, or preventing their tendency to break in the middle of their length, by tying or bracing down their ends beyond the points of support, in the manner and for the purpose set forth. It is to be understood that this method of increasing the effective strength of beams is applicable to all kinds of material of which beams are made in various constructions."

Indian Antiquities in Kentucky.—Kentucky, says the *Ausland*, abounds in ancient earthen mounds and tumuli, much resembling those found on the shores of the Gulf of Mexico, and for the greater part like those found in Ohio, of a religious character. They generally consist of small circles and parallelograms, the mounds being generally more regular, and in the average, perhaps, greater in diameter than those northwards from Ohio. The rectangular-terraced mounds in particular are comparatively numerous and frequently of considerable size. Professor Rafinesque has mentioned the sites of many of them in his "Notes," but has given no very clear insight into their true character. He estimates the number of distinct groups in this State at not less than 600. These ancient remains occur in singular abundance in Montgomery County, and several are of peculiar interest. It may be assumed with certainty from the descriptions, that each group formerly belonged to a separate city, so that there must once have been six cities on an area now occupied by one. These imperfect glimpses of American antiquity show, that at the time of the discovery of America, her age of civilization was already over, that through the force of circumstances, the solution of which is now impossible, one great nation had disappeared, and another and ruder race, which had, perhaps, fallen from a higher state into their present barbarism, took its place. An unmistakeable family relationship shows itself in all these buildings, from those in the centre of North America, to those spread far and wide over Mexico, or even to those deep in the woods of South America.

Money for Public Works.—In your number for the 18th August, a suggestion was made, and the means for carrying on large public works pointed out;—there is another and most crying want which will probably be delayed or crippled for lack of funds—"The general drainage of the metropolis, and large towns and cities." These works, if properly carried out, will last for many generations, and the question would then naturally arise, Why should the present generation bear the whole burthen? Why not (as in the suggestion for public works) let the amount required be at once borrowed, and the interest, and such further interest as would, say in the space of 100 years, liquidate the whole, be charged on the public funds, and the sewage manure be sold to adjacent lands, at prices just sufficient to meet the expense of conveyance. The article of the 18th might most advantageously be again brought before the public. It suggests means of effecting vast good. For the purposes of war there was no lack of borrowing, and we have a heavy interest to pay for what is now deemed a very questionable advantage; surely, for the purposes of peace, of national improvement, and positive good, there ought to be no hesitation.

* *

Arrangement of Staircases in Buildings.—A patent has been taken out, in America, by Mr. W. P. Gibbs, of Boston, for a mode of arranging staircases in buildings. The patentee says,—"By my improvement in building houses, or blocks of houses, I am enabled to obtain two staircases, with the requisite entry room, in the same, or about the same space or superficial area which is generally consumed in the construction of one, according to the common practice of arranging the same; thereby saving, in a block of houses, a frontage of 5 feet on the street or passage, in each two thereof; or, in other words, if we suppose each of two houses, as generally constructed, has a width in front of 20 feet, or 40 feet including both fronts, such may be erected on my improved plan (that is, houses having their parlours and chambers, or other rooms, of the same size as those having a frontage of 20 feet on the street) on a lot of land having a front of 35 feet. Instead of the straight staircases, which denote my second improvement, two circular flights, winding around one central post, may be adopted." *Claim.*—"I claim the method or methods of arranging staircases in connection with each other, and in combination with the several suites of apartments leading thereto from said staircases, the whole being constructed and arranged substantially in the manner and for the object set forth."

Fire.—The Hall of the Carpenters' Company, London, mentioned last week, which escaped the great fire of 1666, narrowly avoided destruction by the same agent on the 6th inst., when some warehouses in London-wall, filled with costly goods, were burnt down.——Two other fires occurred while the above was raging, one in Shouldham-street, Bryanstone-square, the other in Bedford-street, Covent Garden.——At the end of last month Quebec again suffered severely,—twenty-five buildings were destroyed, worth about 25,000*l*.

Steyning Mechanics' Institution.—On the 20th and 27th ult., Mr. Cordwell, of Brighton, delivered two lectures to the members of this institution, on architecture and drawing. On the first occasion, assisted by diagrams, he gave a description of the progress of architecture, from the rude wigwam to the establishment of the "orders." The second lecture was devoted to the subject of drawing, the origin of perspective, and its utility,—explaining the various necessary points by geometrical lines and figures, and concluding by describing the nature of colours.

Western Literary Institution, Leicester Square.—The lecture season here was opened on the 1st inst. with a *conversazione*. On the 4th, Dr. Snow lectured on causes and prevention of cholera. A new and attractive feature has been added to the programme here in the shape of a series of glee concerts.

Desiccated Floor of the London Coal Exchange.—The patentees of the desiccating process, Messrs. Davison and Symington, have published a representation of the floor of the merchants' area of the New Coal Exchange, London, which consists altogether of upwards of 4,000 distinct pieces of wood, of various kinds and qualities. The great feature of the affair is, that the whole of these pieces were, only a few months since, either in the tree in the growing state, or cut from wet logs, and were prepared for use in the course of a few days, by their method of seasoning. The names of the woods thus introduced are black ebony, black oak, common and red English oak, wainscot, white holly, mahogany, American elm, red and white walnut (French and English), and mulberry. It is mentioned as a proof of the rapidity of this mode of seasoning, that the black oak is part of an old tree which was discovered and removed from the bed of the Tyne river, about the latter end of last year. The mulberry wood, introduced as the blade of the dagger in the city shield, is no less than a piece of a tree which was planted by Peter the Great, when working in this country as a shipwright. They state that no one piece of the 4,000 occupied more than ten or twelve days in seasoning.*

* *Drying Closets for Oats.*—In reply to an inquirer last week, the patentees of the above-named process have forwarded a certificate of the successful application of their apparatus for drying oats.

Newcastle School of Design.—The annual meeting of the friends of this institution was held on Friday last, Mr. W. Ord, M.P., in the chair, when the report of the committee was read, and the prizes were distributed. The report spoke encouragingly of the present state and prospects of the school, which had been more fully and steadily attended than heretofore, the average throughout the year being 87. By a removal to rooms belonging to the Natural History Society a considerable diminution of expense would shortly be incurred, and it was designed to hold an extensive fancy fair in aid of the funds. It was to be regretted that, in the very midst of previous great exertions in the getting up of the Polytechnic Exhibition, the Board of Trade should have thrown cold water on all such exertions by withdrawing the usual assistance; but the Board had since seen its error, and not only restored the Government allowance, but held out the promise of an increase should the local efforts be efficiently sustained. Thanks were voted to the teacher, Mr. Scott, for his exertions.

Make Knowledge of Art General.—Mr. Young Mitchell, of the Sheffield School of Design, lectured at the People's College, in that town, last week, on Italian art in the fourteenth, fifteenth, and sixteenth centuries. In the course of his remarks he said,—Art has in England hitherto been a sealed book. Let us hope that time is nearly at an end. For myself, I wish to see it diffused abroad amongst all classes. I would have it a necessary part of the education of every boy. There are some timid souls who fear by this means we should be inundated by Raphaels and Cellinis. There is, alas! no fear. As soon might we refuse to allow a boy to learn to read, for fear he should become a Newton or a Locke. Let us rather view the matter in its true light, and consider that, as reading gives to its possessor the power of appreciating the works of the great men of all ages, so would a knowledge of art give to its possessor a like pleasure and a like appreciation. I have been called Utopian in the idea I have of a universal art education. Let those who call me so recollect that, three centuries ago, the man who could read and write was considered a prodigy. These arts are too widely spread at this day to be considered accomplishments, and to be wanting in them is considered a reproach. I believe that a general knowledge of art would add to the wealth and consequence of the nation, and to the material comfort of the people. But this would not be all. It would elevate their minds and refine their tastes, thus increasing their intellectual enjoyments, and proving one of the most powerful helps to our onward progress.

Compression of Fuel into Blocks for Stowage.—A patent has been granted to Mr. W. Buckwell, Civil Engineer, of the Artificial Granite Works, Battersea, for a mode of compressing coke or other fuel by percussion of a steam-hammer, which may be made of three tons weight, for example, and giving fifty strokes a-minute. The granulated and moistened fuel is placed in a stout cast-iron cylinder, faced inside with wrought-iron or steel, and then exposed to the action of the hammer. Means are also provided for retaining the block of fuel in the cylinder for a short time till fully set in its new form.

Cellars inhabited in Contravention of Buildings Act.—A keeper of lodging-houses at Nos. 2 and 3, Church-lane, St. Giles's, has been fined 20s. for allowing a sub-tenant or lodger to occupy, and allow eight persons to sleep in, a cellar 14 feet by 6, and 7 feet high, with one window, but without fireplace or front door, a practice which appears to have gone on in the same tenantry for fourteen years: the fine to be repeated daily till practice discontinued — with costs. There were in all, forty-eight lodgers in No. 2, and seventy in No. 3.

Bucks County Lunatic Asylum Competition.—The commission of magistrates for providing a pauper lunatic asylum for this county invited seven architects to submit designs for the building. Some of them declined, but four designs were sent in for the approval of the magistrates; and at a meeting held on the 15th ult., one, by Messrs. Wyatt and Brandon, was selected.

LIQUID FOR CLEANSING METALS.—One of the first operations in finishing metallic work after it comes from the casting, or from the hammer, is to free it from the coat of oxide which adheres to it; this is done generally by keeping it for some time in water, strongly acidulated with sulphuric or muriatic acid. But an inconvenience in this process arises from the fact that the metal is liable to be attacked on its lines and angles, and wherever it presents a point or edge. Hence arises a double loss, both of the acid employed and of the metal. MM. Thomas and Dellisse state that they have succeeded in avoiding these inconveniences, by combining with the action of the bath certain organic matters which have the property of preventing, or at least of considerably diminishing, the influence on the metal of the acids. According to them, glycerine, artificial tannin, napthaline, and creosote attain this end. In the baths thus composed, the scale of oxide detaches itself without dissolving, and without the metal being attacked, so that the pieces may remain in the bath as long as may be desired without alteration. These facts, announced by MM. Thomas and Dellisse, are corroborated by the experiments of M. Flachat, chief engineer of the Versailles and St. Germain Railroad. M. Mertain, proprietor and director of the forges of Montataire, and M. S. Falatieu, forge master at Bains, testify that they have tried this process upon sheet iron, and have adopted it to the exclusion of all others. The economy of this process, compared with the former ones, is about two-thirds of the acid employed, and 50 per cent. of the loss of metal in cleaning.—*Bull. Soc. Enc. Indus. Nat.*

THE AMERICAN ART-UNION (New York) have erected a gallery in that city for the reception of paintings purchased for distribution. It is 84 feet long and 24 feet wide, and is said to be superior to anything of the sort in the country.

RUTLAND STATUE.—The competition models, according to the *Leicester Journal*, have been received and deposited in the local Assembly-room, for the subscribers' inspection and the committee's decision. Eight sculptors were applied to, four of whom declined to compete, though willing to undertake the commission at the price offered. One, Campbell, declined altogether, being engaged with the Bentinck statue. The models, four in number, were sent by James Westmacott, James Wyatt (two of the four), and Edward Davis.

RAILWAY COMPENSATION CASE.—The tenant of the "Neptune" inn, Bradford, had been offered, by the Lancashire and Yorkshire Railway Company, 300*l.* for his interest for seven months in the premises, during a remainder of his lease, including all other claims. The tenant refused this sum, and led evidence in court to the effect that his business yielded a profit of 353*l.* odds (although he only paid 1*l.* income-tax on 160*l.*); that therefore he ought to have 150*l.* as compensation for the goodwill of his business alone, 350*l.* for loss of seven months' business, and 219*l.* for loss of forced sale of furniture, &c.—in all, 719*l.* The magistrates awarded the sum of 260*l.*, without any expenses.

BUILDINGS AND MONUMENTS, MODERN AND MEDIÆVAL.

Edited by GEO. GODWIN, F.R.S.,

Fellow of the Institute of Architects; Corresponding Member of several Societies.

Part IV. of this work, price 2s. 6d., containing Views of Ware Church, Hertford; Hungerford and Lambeth Suspension-bridge; New Front of Buckingham Palace; Fire-place in the Palace of the Dukes of Burgundy, at Dijon; All Saints' Church, St. John's Wood; the Interior of the House of Lords—the Throne, the Victoria Lobby, the Reporters' Gallery, and Ground-plan; with descriptive letter-press, and numerous details; will be published at the end of the month, in time for the magazines of November.

Office of THE BUILDER, 2, York-street, Covent Garden, or by order of any bookseller.

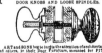

Thick				
	1 in.	1¼ in.	1½ in.	2 in.
	d.	d.	d.	d.
Under 4 ft. long, or 3 ft. wide	4	5	6½	8
Above 5 ft. do., or 3 ft. do.	4½	5¾	7	9
Above 6 ft. do., or 3 ft. do.	5	6½	8	10
Above 7 ft. do., or 3 ft. do.	5½	7	9	11

No. CCCL.

SATURDAY, OCTOBER 20, 1849.

ICCADILLY has been considerably improved during the last
three or four years : by widening the road and footways,
and reducing (though less than
should have been done) its steep acclivity, it
has been rendered a very noble and commodious
entrance to the metropolis. The ground-owners
on the north side have further improvements in
view, and it is proposed, if we understand
rightly, as the present leases expire, to prohibit
shops, and reserve the frontage solely for
private residences of good class.

A map of London, of the time of Elizabeth,
shows what is called Piccadilly as a rudely
defined road out of the town, with one or two
houses at the angle where the road which afterwards became Regent-street turned off, and a
windmill a little to the east of this, the recollection of which is still preserved by " Wind-
mill-street." The origin of the name, Piccadilly,
seems uncertain, but it was thought by some, at
the commencement of the seventeenth century
—when it was equally as now a matter of doubt
—to have been given to a noted house there, as
being the skirt or fringe of the town,—*picardill*,
or pickadil, being a kind of stiff collar, also a
fringe or edging to the skirt of a garment;
while others said it took that name, because " one Higgins, a tailor, who built it,
got most of his estate by pickadillies, which in
the last age were much worn in England;" *
and a third set, that it was because the
pickadillies were sold there. Mr. Cunningham,
in his " Hand Book for London," gives many
curious particulars in connection with Piccadilly : he says the earliest allusion to it is by
Gerard, who observes in his " Herbal" (1596),
" that the small wild buglosse grows upon the
drie ditch bankes about Pickadilla." " Pickadilly Halle" is mentioned in the accounts of
the overseers of St. Martin's-in-the-Fields,
1623. This building was afterwards sold to
Captain *Panton*, who gave his name to a
neighbouring square and street. Lord Clarendon (1641) describes Pickadilly as " a fair
house for entertainment and gaming, with a
handsome gravel walks with shade," with an
upper and lower bowling-green. The first
Piccadilly, as a street, was a very short line of road
running no farther west than Sackville-street.
Coventry-street preserves the name of Mr.
Secretary Coventry, of the reign of Charles II.,
whose garden wall ran along part of Panton-
street and Oxendon-street. Part of Piccadilly,
namely, from Devonshire House to Hyde
Park-corner, in 1734, resembled the New-road
in the number of statuaries' yards, and it was
the same in 1757, when it was said,—

> " And now from Hyde Park-corner come
> The gods of Athens and of Rome ;
> Here squabby cupids take their places,
> With Venus and the clumsy Graces."†

Many of our readers remember the little
toll-house at the " Corner," and its rude and
rural accompaniments :—Apsley House, St.
George's Hospital, and the stone Entrances to

---

* Blount's " Glossographia." 1656.
† The zinc-workers appear to have taken possession of
the few houses in the New-road left unoccupied by the
statuaries and artificial-stone makers, and have surpassed
their neighbours in the process of disfigurement.

---

the Parks have all been erected within a few
years.

The last and most important improvement
to the locality comes in the shape of the
mansion now in course of completion for
Henry Thomas Hope, Esq., the member for
Gloucester, at the corner of Down-street,
erected under the joint superintendence of
M. Dusillion, a French architect, and Professor Donaldson. Annexed we give a view of
the house from the south-west.* It has a
frontage of 70 feet in Piccadilly and 64 feet in
Down-street, measuring the two faces to
where they would meet at the point ; but the
angle is cut off to give a face of 10 feet, which
admits an angle window on each of the principal floors. The fronts are wholly faced with Caen
stone,† and have panels of decorative marbles in
the piers between the windows. The total height
from the level of the street to the top of the
balustrade may be called 62 feet. The windows are novel in the arrangement, and the
treatment of those in the attic story particularly good. The general effect of the exterior,
as a whole, is much injured by the oppressive
pile of chimneys on the east side. The details
throughout, especially inside, show very careful and elegant drawing, and the carving,
wholly by French carvers, is exceedingly well
executed.

The entrance, beneath an enriched porch, is
in the centre of the Down-street front, and
includes some of the best work about the
building. The door is of wainscot, enriched
with carving. The grand staircase and hall
occupy the centre of the building, extending
from the entrance eastward, and will present,
when finished, some novel and piquant effects.
A short central flight of stone steps leads from
the entrance to the upper hall, which is paved
with various coloured marbles in patterns (and
on the level of the dining-room floor), and thence
a long flight, not yet up, will conduct to the
drawing-room floor. The upper hall is fenced
by an enclosure of mahogany and glass at the
head of the stairs from the entrance-hall, and
there is a similar enclosure at a short distance
from the front wall, over the entrance-
door, from the level of the dining-room floor,
so as to form a communication, next Down-
street, between the rooms separated by the
hall.

The walls of both halls are formed into
panels and ornamented pilasters, with white
plaster, polished, the lower part having varied
scagliola panels, and a marble plinth. The
ceilings are enriched ; and the upper hall has
a skylight.

The two principal floors consist of three
rooms each. Those forming the suite on the
drawing-room floors are 36 feet by 22 feet, 28
feet 6 inches by 24 feet, and 34 feet by 24 feet,
—a range of about 100 feet long. The
principal floor is 16 feet 6 inches high ;
the dining-room floor, 15 feet 6 inches. The
floors are fire-proof, consisting of cast-iron
girders and tile arches.

And here we would, in parenthesis, make
a remark. The Kent Fire Office has issued a
list of instructions to assist persons to escape
from premises when on fire. We will give
one, which, if followed out, would hereafter
render all others unnecessary, and that is, let
buildings be so constructed that they will not
take fire. As we have again and again shown,
the majority of our ordinary dwelling-houses
are positively built to burn. The loss which
the community annually sustains through want

---

* See page 498.
† All the projections, cornices, window-caps, &c., are protected by sheet lead.

---

of foresight in this respect, is enormous,
and the amount of grief, trouble, and privation
which follows, can scarcely be estimated.
Prevention is better than cure.

The ceilings are panelled and but slightly
enriched, being prepared to receive coloured
decorations, but these are not yet determined
on. The windows are fitted up with French
casements and are very large. They are provided with Snoxell's patent rolling shutters.

In the angle-room (so to call it) the fire-
place is beneath the window. The doors of the
best rooms are of oak, carved, with the initial
H, in shields. The room in Down-street, on
the dining-room floor, north of the hall, is
panelled with oak, and the ornamental ceiling is
painted to imitate the same material. The
wall above the panelling is hung with a green
flock paper. The chimney piece here, the only
one in the principal rooms yet up, is particularly elegant in the details, and will afford a
subject for illustration hereafter. It is of
Pierre de Tonnerre, with panels of Languedoc
and other French marbles.

There will be no more pictures in the house
than will serve as decorations to the rooms :
Mr. Hope's collections have been removed to
Deepdene.

There are two staircases besides the grand
stairs, both somewhat confined. The only
approach to the chamber floors is by one of
these.

We have not space to say more of the upper
rooms, than that they are provided with double
sashes, that some of them have cast metal
chimney-pieces bronzed, including caryatid
figures, and that the walls are hung with
monochrome flock papers.

The stables and coach-houses appear to have
been designed and executed with great care, so
as to combine all possible conveniences, particularly as to access, light, ventilation, and
easy communication. They open into Market-
street. The coach-houses on the ground-floor
are paved with Orsi and Armani's lava on
concrete, and are warmed by hot water. The
stables are over these, and are approached by an
inclined plane. The floor here is formed with
brick arches and iron girders, and has first a
layer of concrete on the arches, then a layer of
lava, and, upon this small paviours, red and
white, are laid herring-bone wise. There is
accommodation for twelve horses ; the mangers
are enamelled on cast-iron, and the wall above
these has a zinc lining. There is a lantern for
light and ventilation ; and around this, over the
other part of the stable, are rooms for the
attendants.

The kitchen department of the house is very
complete, with a " lift" communicating with
each floor, speaking tubes, &c. Gas is
laid on throughout the mansion, except in the
drawing-rooms and in the stable building ;
and there is a complete system of apparatus
for warming the vestibule, staircase, and
passages throughout.

The divisions of the bins in the wine-cellars
are of slate. The ceilings and walls of
the principal apartments are rendered wholly
with plaster of Paris.

Messrs. W. Cubitt and Co. are the general contractors ; but all the ornamental work, including the wainscot doors, the ceilings, stone
carving, mahogany casements, iron railing, are
by Frenchmen,—many of them indeed executed
in Paris, although for what good reason it
seems hard to say.

The building is enclosed with a particularly
handsome iron railing, cast in Paris for the
purpose, a portion of which we show on a

larger scale than in the general view. The shields here, as elsewhere, bear the letter H.

The carcass of the house cost 9,000*l*.; the stables about 3,000*l*.; and the cost of the whole, exclusive of the final paintings and similar class of decorations, about 30,000*l*.

ON THE MEANS OF PROGRESSION IN ART.

THE ARCHITECTURAL ASSOCIATION.*

The foremost question of the day, in reference to our profession as a fine art, would seem to be this:—"What are to be the sources of that inspiration which shall infuse into it life and progression?" And, looking at the various ideas propounded upon the subject, we find them to be somewhat as follows:—First, 'study nature:' advice which has a volume of truth in it, but, unfortunately, it leaves every one to his own interpretation of a most comprehensive term. He may take it objectively, prototypically, or abstractly,—or even dogmatically and arbitrarily. For purposes of mental culture and art education, it is too unbounded in its import as generally set forth. Its practical use, hitherto, has been little else than as a phrase bandied about, containing, as we must admit, a very concentration of truth, but which as yet has received very little intelligible exposition, nor ever will prove of much value until divested of its cosmopolite form.

A second solution offered to this question is,—To study the spirit and requirements of our age, and adapt the present resources of our art to embody them. A third is,—To concentrate all efforts upon the least-developed but distinctive style: first render it exclusive and predominant,—it will then progress and become national. A fourth, rests the progression of art upon the application of new materials, and upon increased facilities of construction; whilst others impatiently clamour for 'something new,' 'something original,' as a new generic form, capable of modification and development. I venture to add to this summary of agencies one, not usually classed, as likely to give impetus to architectural art, and it is, 'the study of criticism as a science.' There is, I fear, too much agreement upon one point, to be favourable to true progress; there is a very general impression that in our present system, condition, or prospects, we have little else than evils to deprecate. There is no admission or acknowledgment of anything favourable or in the right direction. Whether there is more power in this cynical spirit than there would be in generous observance of the good, would seem to be a question settled in the affirmative; yet of all the drawbacks to that common bond which should subsist among members of the profession, as in itself a powerful stimulus to art, this captious and complaining spirit is chief. This dogmatic condemnation of that which is, and visionary requirements as to what ought to be, come neither in the form of enlightened criticism nor creative genius. There are some who can relish no criticism unless it be a pungent and distilled attack,—a criticism which mistakes its way so much as to degenerate into invective,—venom for wit, and a joke for a proof. We ought to be as much open to the observation of right tendencies as to admitted evils, and do honour and yield homage to successful art: the feeling of confidence and emulation that would spring up from thus acting would be favourable to its study and cultivation.

Every historical period brings with it its own characteristics, which become more or less evidently the sources from which the art of its day receives its inspiration and tone. That which fostered it in one age may be wanting in a succeeding, or the current of popular feeling and sympathy may even run counter to any prospects of its high cultivation, and accordingly as the intensity of art-feeling declines, its patronage will be limited, and its cultivation correspondingly feeble and superficial; when, and as this feeling revives, we may expect also a higher estimate of art as a study, and proportionate intensity of thought will be bestowed upon it by its followers. This is the condition to which we appear to have arrived—a revival of feeling—a resuscitation of all art that has preceded us; and it becomes a question what shall be the speciality of our day, not only as to art, but what shall be the presiding and impelling spirit that secretly inspires its votaries. But, independently of this change in the characteristics of the period which give the impetus to art, the condition of art itself necessarily results in altering the manner in which it is cultivated, and our condition, surrounded as we are by styles of art so fully developed, lessens the field yet unexplored: we and art come under new conditions, and new and peculiar forces are needed for it to become progressive. It will not, I know, be a favoured idea to speak of finality in the powers and expressions of our art; but infinite as may be its capabilities of expression, the development of the great cardinal styles, classic and mediæval, with all that preceded or accompanied them, must of necessity hedge in, and even have made use of the possible or applicable geometric forms. I would suppress the idea of new styles as a something to be sought after, until progress itself revealed it. Let the aim be not for novelties, but for perfecting the adaptation of that art we have handed down to us, until its expression become assimilated to our own society and its characteristics, as it has been made to do that of previous. The forms of art are not the property of one age—only let each clothe itself in them with truthful and harmonious adaptation. The spirit of close observation and earnest appreciation which this would beget, would correct the bane of mere copyism; the transition from existing characters of art would be gradual, but they would proceed upon a sound principle, and one that would be a thousandfold more ennobling to the study, and more productive of results, than the loud and visionary clamours for new styles, as if art were like a series of fashions, to be altered at will. Neglect the study of that art which descends to us, in the eager expectation and looking for "something new," and we shall sink in our appreciation and conception of art altogether; but aim to master that which is, and to accomplish their happiest powers of expression, and freshness and novelty may emerge; but nothing ever came from mere outcry and expectancy. Perfect its expressions as required by the aspect and character of our own times and institutions, and I entertain—as a means of conferring upon it more character and dignity as a study, and as counteracting false taste—that architectural criticism should be investigated and advanced to the fixity and position of a science.

The distinction which was obtained between the terms science, art, and fine art, has gone very far to mislead and intercept a clear view of the great central laws to which all arts, fine arts, and sciences are amenable, as parts and dependencies of a great whole. The one has been thought to be the *realities* of the world,—hence, whatever is conducted upon known principles is termed scientific,—the other has been represented as the poetry of the world; one as a matter of fact,—the other as a reflection only of mind, whose ideas and images are not cognizable to science, called up by and addressed to fancy,—an irresponsible, and in all cases an arbitrary and absolute award or rejection. This is the foundation of the error, that each one has an inherent judgment upon art; for while no one ventures to exercise his *taste* in respect to the facts of nature, or in the domain of the applied sciences, all seem to assert the correctness of their own judgment upon questions of art, upon this assumption that the fine arts are amenable to no law. There is nothing without law; there is no such thing as a fine art having fancy for its foundation and guide,—laws which are the birthright and endowment of genius, so that his thoughts and productions accord with them, but which the ordinarily gifted must condescend to learn and observe ere they can judge aright. Ignorant taste is the upas tree blighting all the fair promises of art, the conceit that claims innate perceptions because it has not mind enough to search out and acquire. And if this presumption that art is amenable to no law is an evil affecting the popular taste, inasmuch as it leaves it to be formed by the unrestrained admission of whatever may be presented to its undisciplined observation, how much better does the subject present itself to the professional student? To what do the clearly affirmed and defined principles of our art amount? Put them together, place them in their sequential order, they as yet remain almost in the region of metaphysics, they shed but a tremulous light upon the path of the student, they exist like nebulæ, unresolved, emitting rays which lead the inquirer only into abstraction of thought, bewildering by their intangible and formless lustre. Art disquisitions, theories, and principles are considered, so far as they relate to architectural art, to be such transcendentals as are little better than pure nonentities—"*not practical.*" Yet we continually speak of principles, of canons, harmonies, and proportion, while scarce any are reduced to clear and distinct conceptions, so that the mind may analyze its emotions: none have yet given up that shadowy form of generalization which renders each so feeble, that their very definition is a controversy and debate.

The very fact that our criticism exists, as it were, mental and unwritten, assuming all the forms and dogmas of individual fancy, its very terms so involved in doubt as to the strict ideas they really stand for, is an evidence how backward we are in the collocation and registry of those facts, which, though constantly operating upon and determining our minds, are yet unreduced to axiomatic and propositional form, so as to be worthy of reliance, and accredited vehicles of demonstration.

It may be said that the subject of architectural criticism does not come within the range, and is not of the nature of the inductive sciences; that appreciation, or the emotion of art feeling, is purely a mental phenomenon,—that they are intuitive,—that beyond the simple admission of sensation we cannot reach. To this I would suggest the reply, that in criticism the process is to be the reverse of this order. This mental phenomenon of appreciation and emotion we take as a result, and our object is to ascertain the forces in operation; these we shall find to be of two distinct sources,—the one external and objective, the other mental,—the criticism we want as efficient for the cultivation and progress of art must regard both. The very theory of fine art is based upon this conjoint action of the external and the mind, not chancefully, but, if truthful, according to the design and ordination of the great Framer of Nature, who has made the human mind and the objective world beyond it as parts of one system, to attain their highest excellencies when faithfully responding to each other. We want a criticism that shall define the several parts which the mind and the objective play in the phenomena of fine-art emotions. That the one be according to what are termed 'true artistic principles,' and that the other may be rightly informed, that it may correctly receive the impression of the images, and give rise to corresponding emotion; for if this be not the case, we pronounce the judgment perverted, the taste false; but we dispute not the reality of the impression,—such as it is let the possessor enjoy it,—'tis not the only instance in which the mind may love a lie instead of truth, through its perversion and blindness. If this be not the case, what is the meaning of "art education," "cultivated taste," and what mean their opposites? Are all forms upon the same dead level? and is every mind to exalt that it pleases? But if the appreciation in some cases is to be pronounced false, from what are those principles to be derived by which the judgment is to proceed? This is the real question. Is the method of induction inapplicable to these matters? By no means. Difficult it may be, and very few may be the axioms and laws that could be clearly defined and written; but if they are laws and not merely 'trains of ideas,' let them be comprehended so distinctly as to become axiomatic and propositional, and criticism then will rise to possess higher attributes than does mere controversy and debate, which it scarcely does at this present time.

"Some law known or unknown rules each," is a quotation you will recognize; and this is the present condition of architectural thought, a series of queries answered in the affirmative or negative. But affirmation does not tell us what that law is. You can violate it by an experiment with your pencil, yet you can scarcely say what law you have infringed. The fact of the difficulty of resolving criticism into

* The following is a portion of the president's address, read at the opening meeting, and mentioned in our last number.

a science of æsthetics ought not to deter us from attempting it. The doubt seems to be, if there are sufficient primary and absolute facts or impressions, that is, impressions having the force of universal concurrence and self-evidence, to form sufficient bases for the deduction of first principles? However limited they may prove, let the solution of this problem be our aim. We are so accustomed to regard the phenomena of nature, through the light and teaching of science, that it is to us impossible but to regard them only as effects of hidden causes. But had we lived before the great revelation of induction, we doubtless should have yet the same overwhelming complexity as now in respect to the phenomena of our art,—a hopeless enravelment of forms and images, the cause of whose impressions it is impossible to reduce to general principles.

We have in respect to art certain fixed or prevalent impressions; these gradually accumulated, affect our judgment in every instance that objective art is before it. We know that these impressions form to us the axioms of art; each has his own; but do we not allow that some are universal? if so, we want such to be defined,—they would constitute the science of æsthetics.

Some indications of effecting this study of criticism, and reducing it to proportional and axiomatic form, have appeared. The "Maxims and Theorems" of Professor Donaldson, contains the following remark in its preface:—"Some of the maxims may appear paradoxical, others empirical, but it is time that architects should apply themselves in earnest to the subject, so that just principles should be thoroughly investigated. We ought no longer to have to wander in uncertainty as to the laws of our art, after the experience and lessons to be derived from the monuments erected during 4,000 years. It may appear remarkable that this has not been done before; but the principles of a science are always those which are learned last; a full clear and comprehensive grasp of those fundamental notions on which a science is founded, is only attained after a very long course of intimacy with the working of the details."

It would seem, then, not only to be a subject likely to give a higher tone to the study of art, but an effort eminently becoming this age, a duty arising out of our very condition and privileges as those who inherit the rich bequeathment of art. The successors of those who developed art to such perfection, and in such distinct phases, ought to make some use of such spoils, beyond delineating or patching them up. Let it be to define and group together those laws, which they so successfully illustrated. And to this end, if I mistake not, is intended the valuable contribution of Mr. Fergusson, that from the history of art as the experimental phenomena, the science or principles of criticism shall be deduced. And what shall we say of the brilliant but erratic Ruskin? his "Seven Lamps" are evidently an effort to the elucidation of art, by giving the spirit, motive, and principle, which constitute at once its law and inspiration. Let not such works fall to the ground. They are the dawn of a loftier literature than has hitherto been associated with our profession.

All our perceptions of objects, whether of nature or art creation, take their complexion from the truthfulness or error of our knowledge in relation to them;—to properly perceive we must be correctly informed. There is throughout art and our perceptions of it, a philosophy of emotion; and surely I rightly apprehend the intent of our studies, when I say that one of its highest aims is to pierce through the mystery that veils all that is beautiful in art, to detect that mechanism, the system and law that every where pervades it.

C. C. Creeke.

Fall of a New Church.—At Kingsdown, near Walmer, a new church is building, at the expense of an individual, and was externally approaching completion, but last week the west-end, which comprised a traceried window, and a bell-turret, suddenly fell to the ground with a tremendous crash. Providentially the workmen had not arrived. The accident is ascribed, locally, to wet weather, and a gale of wind.

ON THE GOTHIC ERA OF ORNAMENTAL ART.

In pursuance of the series of lectures on ancient ornamental art delivered by Mr. Ralph Wornum, at the Government School of Design, Somerset House, the lecturer proceeded, on Friday in week before last, to treat of Gothic Art, more especially as regards its ornamental interest to the designer.

After slightly recalling the subjects of his two previous lectures * on the Ornamental Art of the Middle Ages, in which he had treated, firstly, of Christian symbolism and the most prominent features of Byzantine art; and, secondly, of its modification into Saracenic art; the third and final development of these into Gothic principles was then entered on.

The elements, said the lecturer, are still identical, the combinations only are diversified. Such are the three great styles of middle-age or, critically speaking, Christian art; for the Renaissance, and its final result, the *Cinque-cento*, were a decided repudiation of the Christian forms, and as positive a re-adoption of the Heathen. That the Saracenic art was Christian may seem rather startling, but it was so, inasmuch as it was developed by Christian Greeks out of Byzantine elements for Saracenic masters. On the other hand the *Cinque-cento* is a Heathen style, not that they were Heathens that practised it, but that its types were Greek and Roman.

In pointing out the distinctive feature of Gothic architecture,—its verticality, in contrast with the horizontality of the Romanesque, the lecturer then alluded to Schlegel's idea that, as the whole tendency of the Gothic is vertical, the motive to its adoption must have been to carry the eye upwards, and with the eye the mind, to the contemplation of things holy and above the sphere of this world. But whatever may have been the motive, he must observe that the fact of verticality did not necessarily imply that the design was absolutely lofty in itself,—its individual members are only higher than they are wide: it is such a distinction as that between the human and other animal forms, in their respective natural postures,—the human being vertical, the quadruped horizontal, although the latter may stand absolutely higher than the former. The extreme into which this verticality ran is the Perpendicular style, in which the Gothic was exhausted, and ceased in a sudden transition to the Horizontal, in the sixteenth century, when the Tudor or late Perpendicular appeared in the flat Tudor arch and its square and oblong compartments.

So early even as the seventh century the pointed arch was a standard form in the buildings of Cairo in Egypt. The Saracens carried it into Sicily, of which in the eleventh century the Normans became masters, and the profusely decorated Norman arose, with its zig-zag and its pointed arch, as an amalgamation of styles. Spreading to England, the richest remains of our early architecture date from the twelfth century.

The history of architectural ornament in England from the eleventh until the sixteenth century, is a history of perpetual changes. During this era of five centuries we had no less than seven different styles of architecture,—Saxon or Romanesque, Round Norman, Pointed Norman or Transition, Early English, Decorated, Perpendicular, and Tudor. Hence it is that a building which occupied more than one generation, or at least two, in its completion, was not carried out in the same style,—as in York Minster or St. Alban's Abbey, for example. Subsequent artists would not work out the ideas of their predecessors, except in so far as a nave, for instance, commenced with the round arch, had a chance of being so completed, but with different decorations. Even this, however, was not the case with St. Alban's, or with Westminster Abbey. In fact our ancestors took much greater pains to eclipse or demolish the works of their forefathers than to preserve or imitate them. The circumstance of a thing having *been done* appears to have been sufficient reason why it should *not be done again*. How true this is, is evident from the fact that the average duration of every style, and very nearly the actual duration, was only 70 years—the age of a man.

Thus, from the building of the old Abbey of Westminster by Edward the Confessor to the spoliation of the monasteries by Henry VIII., when all Gothic art ceased in this country, is exactly seven times seventy years, and comprises as exactly the seven styles of English ecclesiastical architecture. From this you have a formula which will give you very nearly the period of any particular style, as exact as the transition from one style to another will possibly admit. All you have to recollect is their consecutive order, and the starting date which you may take as 1066, the close of Edward the Confessor's reign, or about the middle of the eleventh century.

Let us suppose that in 1066, the year of the Norman accession, the Romanesque style was established: after a lapse of seventy years you will find the Norman, or Zigzag style, flourishing; in another seventy years the Transition, or Plantagenet; in another seventy the Early English Gothic; again, after an equal period, we shall find the Decorated to prevail; and after a sixth seventy, at Henry VII.'s accession, we find the Lancasterian style, the Perpendicular; and after the seventh seventy, or at the close of Henry VIII.'s reign, we have the Tudor, in which the Gothic expires.

I am quite aware, continued the lecturer, that these seven styles are now commonly spoken of as four—Norman, Early English, Decorated, and Perpendicular; but this is not a critical distinction of styles; Norman here comprises three styles, Early English two, and Perpendicular two,—Tudor, or the late plain and square Perpendicular, or rather Horizontal, being overlooked as a distinct style.

There is no advantage in reducing the number of distinctive designations; for where so much is comprised in a single term, it renders it very difficult to comprehend in what the characteristics consist: the exceptions are far more numerous than the examples of the rule. Norman, as a designation of style from the conquest to Henry III. is no more specific than that of Gothic for the architecture which prevailed in England from Henry III. to Henry VIII. In one sense, every building in England is Norman, erected during the Norman dynasty, from Edward the Confessor to James I.

The ornamental designer cannot have too many distinctions of style, for every distinction implies some one well-understood class of ornamental forms, and his success, and the success of the ornamental manufactures of his country, depend upon his mastery of these distinctions, for each distinction is a store of invention, and will bear its fruit. Gothic ornament is quite as applicable to printed and woven fabrics as to hard wares.

With the aid of numerous drawings, &c., the lecturer then proceeded to point out the characteristics of each separate style, remarking that in this investigation they must, of course, look at the styles as ornamentists, not as architects. The examples were from stone, wood, iron, and ornamental manufactures.

While exhibiting the diagrams, &c., illustrative of the details of his subject, the idea of Metzger, the German architect, that the varieties of Gothic bases may be deduced from crystaline forms, was favourably viewed. This idea, said the lecturer, is a good one, and if we follow it up, we may produce ten thousand beautiful arrangements, all as new as beautiful. The snow crystals from the interesting work of Captain Scoresby (exhibited) have only to be developed into bases and shafts with a few splays and bands, and you will have a clustered pillar to rival anything in Gothic architecture, early or decorated—uniting the prominent points of the crystals by straight lines for the bases, and round and hollow lines for the shafts: the mouldings of the arches are a species of continuation of the shaft. These crystals, however, he remarked, will suggest forms for many other species of ornamental art besides Gothic shafts; as, for instance, diapers for encaustic tiles; and certainly an endless variety of patterns for cotton prints, or diapers, indeed, of any kind.

Recapitulating briefly the most prominent characteristics of the seven styles, we have,—

In the Saxon, or early Norman Romanesque, the round arch, square abacus, cushion capital, sometimes with a little Byzantine foliage: no other ornament.

In the specifically Norman, introduced

* See p. 328, *ante*.

about the time of Stephen, but established under Henry II., we have the zig-zag as the great feature, with the round and with the pointed arch; and still the square abacus as a rule.

In a short time we lose the mass of the Norman ornaments and the round arch, and find in its place the Transition, a most simple pointed style, with little beyond the tooth ornament to decorate it, and small windows of single lights. When much light was required, these windows were clustered together. The round, or hexagonal abacus now comes into common use,—the buttress is more developed, and the pinnacle an ordinary feature.

In the Early English, we have the first development of Gothic tracery,—mullions in place of piers,—windows of several lights,—flying buttresses,—crocketted pinnacles,—complicated mouldings, and a more extensive application of foliage,—the columns clustered and the capitals generally round,—the trefoil leaf the most characteristic ornament.

On this succeeded the Decorated, chiefly characterized by a more magnificent development of the leading elements of the preceding style; but it has its own features,—the ogee-arch and the pinnacled canopied recesses, which produce a prominence of diagonal lines.

In the Perpendicular or Lancasterian style, the new features are the horizontal line, the panellings, and the substitution of Perpendicular for flowing traceries.

In the Tudor, the art returns to what it was in the Romanesque, and again becomes Horizontal.

I point out these distinctions, proceeded the lecturer, not for the mere sake of distinction, though that is something, but to show the vast store of ornamental materials which these various styles display, especially the Norman, the two later Plantagenet styles, and the Lancasterian, not only for architectural purposes, but for all purposes of ornamental art.

Some allusion was then made to painted glass as an ornament in Gothic edifices, and as a branch of art commanding a daily-increasing interest. Of this the lecturer proposed treating in his next lecture, on 2nd proximo, and in the meantime he concluded with an address more particularly designed to encourage the pupils in laying the foundations of future excellence and originality in design, by patient labour and an avoidance of all premature and unavailing endeavours to reap the fruits without sowing the seeds,—this latter being really the slowest method of attaining the object that can possibly be pursued.

SUPPOSED SAXON WORK IN IVER CHURCH, BUCKS.

It seems to me that the church of Iver, near Uxbridge, in Buckinghamshire, may be added to the list of those containing vestiges of Saxon architecture; and that there are grounds for assigning an approximate date to the remains I allude to.

Immediately above one of the arches on the north side of the nave, is a small semi-circular arch, now blocked up with wall, the lower part of which has been destroyed by the subsequent erection of the arches of the nave; and these arches being Norman, it is clear the small arch must be of earlier date, and consequently Saxon,* with which its appearance well agrees.

The inner side of the small arch, towards the nave, is quite red, and has evidently been rendered so by the action of fire; the outer side towards the aisle has escaped.† Now we learn from the Saxon chronicle that A.D. 905, "Ethelwald enticed the army that was in East Anglia to break the peace, so that they ravaged over all the land of Mercia until they came to Cricklade, and there they went over the Thames." It is true Iver is not expressly mentioned in this notice, but besides being within the limits of the kingdom of Mercia, it

* Not necessarily; there may be early Norman work, and late Norman work.—Ed.

† Since the above was written, I learn that a doorway, in the middle of the piers, against which the font is now placed. Presents the same appearance as the arch above described, and that charred wood was found near it; thus making it clear that the portion of which these remains be. longed perished by fire.

lies in what would then be the direct route from East-Anglia to Cricklade. We know that in Saxon times, armies, whenever it was possible, followed the course of rivers in their marches, so that we may trace this army up the valley of the Ouse to Newport Pagnell; then following the Ousel to its source, whence to the head of one branch of the Colne is but 6 miles; then along the latter river past St. Albans, Watford, Uxbridge, and Iver to Colnbrook, soon after which they would reach the Thames, and follow its course to Cricklade.

I think, therefore, it is by no means an improbable inference that the arch I have described, incorporated by the Normans into their fabric, formed part—was a window—of a church in existence before A.D. 905, and which was then destroyed and burnt by the Danes.

I saw this arch directly after its discovery, now about two years ago, during the restoration of the church, and I intended to have communicated it to you at the time, but I do not regret that the subject escaped my memory, since it was only the other day that I met with the passage that led to my conjecture as to its date.

MAHD.

VENTILATION.

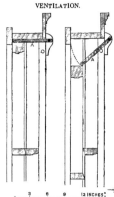

3   6   9   12 INCHES

As ventilation is the order of the day, I send you a simple and effectual plan (if you think it worth inserting in your valuable journal), for getting rid of the foul air and admitting fresh air into rooms or offices, by lowering the top sash. The flap A is hung to the sash frame by a centre in a bracket or otherwise, and when the sash is lowered, drops on the top rail of the sash the whole width of the window, and forms a ventilator with the draft upwards, to emit or admit air; by a stop on the inside head, the flap is not permitted to drop beyond a certain point, so that the sash may be lowered in the usual way, and in raising things the flap up under the head of the sash frame. I have fixed three at the Savings' Bank, Chelsea; they answer exceedingly well. I send this, as it may be of service to some of your readers, being a cheap and easy way of obtaining air without a direct draft upon the heads of persons who have to sit in rooms and offices with the top sash lowered, not having this protection.

JOHN CALLOW.

CISTERNS: PURE WATER.—Allow me to suggest what I think would be a remedy for the fault found in your last number with the conical-shaped cistern, having the tap at bottom. Let there be a tap there, but let it be a waste tap, and have another a little way up the side of the cistern. By this means the cistern could be kept clean, and no sediment would find its way into the tap used for supplying water for household purposes.—W. B.

BRASSES OF NOTARIES.

BRASSES of this important class of the civil community, of which but few now remain, may be divided into two classes—the ecclesiastical and the civil; of the former I only know of one instance, and of the latter but five, of which I beg to subjoin a short account.

1.—C. 1475, St. Mary Tower Church, Ipswich. This is the earliest example that has yet been met with; it consists of a large figure standing on a mound of grass, on which a scull and other bones are scattered; he is habited in a close fitting tunic, over which is a long loose-sleeved gown faced with fur; a circular cap, in form not unlike a turban, from which a broad scarf hangs down to the ground in front, is thrown over his left shoulder, concealing his gypoiere, which is attached to the left side of his girdle, from which depends an inkhorn and a pencase richly ornamented with quatrefoils; the hands are united as in prayer, and the feet have low, laced boots. The absence of the tonsure shows that this was not an ecclesiastical notary. A scroll placed on his breast bears the following legend, invoking the ever-blessed Trinity, and at the same time expressing his belief in the resurrection :—

"Reposita est hæc spes mea i sinu meo Scā Trinitas Dñ Dē miserere mei."

Over this figure was once an elegant canopy supported on slender shafts; at equal distances down each side were small scrolls, one of which still remains, and is inscribed—

"Tibi laus, tibi glia."

There was also a marginal legend and a shield beneath the figure, both lost. The figure (stolen since 1845) is engraved in Mr. Boutell's work on Monumental Brasses, p. 112, and in Messrs. Waller's work on the same subject, in the latter of which is a concise account of the origin, &c., of notaries.

2.—C. 1475. Great Chart, Kent.

3.—1490. W. Curtsys, Holm Hale, Norfolk.

A figure in a long flowing gown, with loose sleeves, confined at the waist by a simple cincture, from which depend an inkhorn and pencase. He has long flowing hair; neither cap nor gypeiere are apparent. His wife is lost, but the following inscription remains.

"Orate p̄ aiabz Willī Curtsys notarii et Aliciæ uxis' ei q' obierunt v° kalēdas Marcii a° Jnī M° ccccLxxxx quorr aiabz ppiciet de ame."

Engraved in "Cotman's Brasses of Norfolk," p. xxxiii.

4.—1506. R. Wymbyll, S. Mary Tower Church, Ipswich.

A notary in loose-sleeved gown, thrown open in front and faced with fur, confined at the waist by a girdle, from which depends on the left side an inkhorn and pencase, and from the right a plain gypciere. This figure forms a portion of a brass representing Thomas Baldry, merchant, Robert Wymbyll, notary, and their wife, to whom the two former figures are turned sideways. Scrolls proceeding from their mouths bear the following legends :—

"Scta trinitas unus deus miserere nobis. Sps scte deus miserere nobis. Filī redemtor mūdi deus miserere nobis."

Beneath the figures.

"Of your charite pray for the soull of Alys, late the wyfe of Thomas Baldry, marchant, sumtyme the wyfe of master Robert Wymbyll, Notari, wнісн Alys decessed the iijth day of August the yere of oure lord thoussand ccccvj on whose soull ihu haue mercy and on all cristin soullis. amen."

Beneath the figure of Baldry are the Mercers' Arms, impaling Baldry's merchant's mark (the corresponding shield under the notary is unfortunately lost), also five daughters and four sons, in two groups. For an engraving of the figure of the notary, vide introduction to the "Oxford Manual for the Study of Brasses," p. xcii.

6.—1517. Bernard de Turia, S. Sauveur, Bruges. A figure of a notary, standing on a tesselated pavement, beneath a single canopy supported by two arabesque columns, at the back of which is hung a rich fringed diaper. He is habited in a tunic, over which is a loose gown thrown entirely open in front, and reaching to the knees: the former is secured round the waist by a narrow girdle, attached to which, on the right side, are an ink-horn and pen-case. He has the clerical tonsure, and a pen appears behind his right ear. He wears tight hose, and low square-toed shoes. Over his head is a scroll, charged with the words—

"In Virgine posui spem meam;"

And beneath a shield bearing, gules, a lion passant.

The whole is surmounted with the following legend:—

"Hic jacet Magr Bernardin' de Turia dū vixit nota pub. et scriba Curie Tornacēsis precipuus fūdator choral' et augmētator lucri dicor Installator hui ecclie qui obiit ā dni xvxvii."

This forms the centre-piece of a very fine brass; but, being pressed for time, I was unable to finish it: I shall, however, engrave the whole in a work on the Brasses and Incised Slabs of Belgium, which it is my intention to publish early next year.

W. H. WEALE.

PICKED UP AT BRIGHTON.

THE extension of Brighton on the high ground, from the old church towards the Dyke-road, though less obvious to the visiter than what has been done next the sea, is very considerable, and would surprise those who know the town only as it was some years ago. There is a quaint little house some distance on the Dyke-road, called Port Hall, full of "knick-knackett things," the residence of one of the most ingenious men in the county,—Sir Page Dick;* and we well remember this, the scene of many pleasant days in early life, a good walk out of the town, and with little apparent chance of a neighbourhood. Gradually, however, the houses have crept along the highway; new roads have been opened; occupants have come; and, in a very short time, if the process continue, we shall find Port Hall in the midst of a row of houses. A new church is building close by, and will further expedite this result. This is a large structure of flint, with Caen stone dressings. It is to consist of chancel, nave, and aisles, with a tower at the west end of the north aisle. The style, almost as a matter of course, now-a-days, is Decorated. The windows of the aisles, as well as those of the chancel, are in, and the walls up ready for the aisle roofs. The main pillars of the nave are not yet commenced. The tower is of large size; placed where it is, the foundation for it must have been looked for at some depth and cost. Mr. Carpenter is the architect; the dedication is to All Saints.

The last new church built in Brighton, St. Paul's, was to be consecrated on the 18th. It is built of flint and Caen stone, and has presented the phenomenon of a church requiring repair before it was consecrated. A considerable quantity of the stone used failed, and has been taken out and reinstated: what remained, as well as the new stones, have been oiled. It would be useful to ascertain the cause of the failure,—whether the stones were marked by the merchant as from the sound beds and fit for external work; if they were laid bed-way; or were wetted by the sea. Information of this sort would assist in arriving at some degree of certainty with respect to the material; and it is only with this end in view, and not from any desire to annoy individuals who may be blameless, that we mention the circumstance.

St. Paul's Church is lighted by coronæ bearing candles. Some excellent stained-glass windows, by Hardman, have been put up in the chancel within the last week,—the gift, as Mr. Wagner stated in his sermon last Sunday, of benevolent individuals. The east window, a "Jesse," is very large, and must have cost a considerable sum of money. Four smaller windows contain the Apostles,—three in each. The painted decorations of the chancel are not satisfactory, the effect being mean. There is an oak rood-screen. The "Commandments" are placed at the east end of the south aisle.

* The ancestor of Sir Page Dick advanced a large sum of money in 1639-41 for securing the Established Church of Scotland, suppressing a rebellion in Ireland, &c.; and, though guaranteed, as he thought, by Peers and Commons, was never able to recover it, and died in poverty. An undeniable and very interesting case has been made out by the present baronet, who is making efforts to obtain a restitution of money most justly due to him.

None of our readers should go to Brighton without visiting the two churches at Shoreham,—old and new. The latter, New Shoreham Church, is full of interest to the student, exhibiting the passage from the Norman style to the Early English. It was originally a cross church of large size, but the nave has been destroyed, so that it now consists of transepts and chancel only, with central tower; the chancel has aisles, the walls of which show an interesting Norman arcade.

When we entered the church we saw a sign of the times in a bevy of pretty long-ringletted damsels squatting on the floor in the centre of the building; and it was not till we heard—"Rosa, dear, give me some more heel-ball,"—"Now, Emma, you begin at his legs,"—that we comprehended their position. They were rubbing with much *gusto* the only two brasses which remain there,—the figures of a civilian and his wife, without any inscription, but which may apparently be dated about 1450.

Old Shoreham Church, also a Norman building, was restored some time since; and Southwick Church (which has a Norman tower, with Early English belfry story and short spire), has been miserably treated by re-builders.

DEATH IN THE SEWERS.

THE sudden destruction of five fellow-beings by those deadly poisons which pervade the atmosphere of imperfect sewers and drains and emanate from them in diffusion, by the law of gaseous mixture and dilution, through the streets and dwellings of a district, is certainly an appalling occurrence, and at Pimlico such a fatality has just been exciting the sympathy and horror of thousands. But painful as it is, the suddenness and the but too obviously and totally unmistakeable and undeniable nature of the cause—a cause to be in this case neither mystified nor pooh-poohed—can alone, by inference, excuse, since they cannot justify, the *want* of such a concentration of excitement and feeling—sustained and never ceasing, as it ought to be—for the thousands and the tens of thousands who are ever—and though more slowly, not more surely—being doomed to death, by the self-same cause, in *every* imperfectly or improperly sewered and drained street-district, town, or city. Could the mere matter-of-fact mind of the public in general but trace that cause, and forcibly realize it, through all its stages and degrees of still pernicious dilution, from the concentrated state in which it strikes its victim down as if by lightning, to those states of less or more dilution in which it can only effect its deadly purpose in the course of minutes, hours, or days,—or even months or years, in a gradual and constant undermining of the strongest constitution,—such is our estimation of the public feeling, apart altogether from its more self-seeking fears and interests, that we believe, the truly *vital* question of the sewerage of towns, would utterly absorb and annihilate every other question of worldly interest, till the work were done, and that effectively, and on the most improved and enlightened principles that money could either call forth in design or realize in detail. It is simply because the evil agency is gradually lost to the public sense and mind in the distance, as it were, of its successive stages of dilution, that it is still allowed to dispense its subtle deadly venom through the otherwise healthful atmosphere.

In the case at Pimlico, a "junction reversed" had been run off through Kenilworth-street, which is at right angles to Warwick-street. This junction, or branch sewer, was imperfect, or rather, it only reached as far as the new tenements were erected, and there it abruptly stopped, as a butt-end, in fact, although its continuation for a few hundred yards, as observed by the *Times*, would have brought it to the Thames. "Like most of the sewers of that district," the "branch" and "main" are very nearly on a dead level, so that the filth in the "branch" had quietly accumulated for two years, till now that it was four feet deep throughout. The main was also foul, and so were other adjoining sewers. They were all examined and ordered to be cleared out, and the process of contract-measurement was in progress on Friday last, at five a.m., when the party, three in number, entered the Kenilworth-street sewer, although cautioned previously not to do so. Not re-appearing till afternoon, a man-hole in the main was opened, and some labourers entered, and saw the party all lying in the branch apparently dead. The end of the branch, which had been bricked up, was then broken open, and other three persons, one a surgeon and another a policeman, immediately entered, and in two minutes the latter re-appeared with the body of the former, who had been struck dead instantaneously. Returning, he also brought out his other companion, insensible, but not dead. A third time this poor fellow re-entered, to bring out the dead bodies first sacrificed, and was himself at length struck dead, and his body not got out till some hours after. Precautions, then only, were taken; and next morning the three first corpses,—discoloured and blue, as if killed by cholera,—were got out. An inquest, at which these facts were elicited, was then held, and has been adjourned till to-day (Thursday).

There are "a thousand or two," it appears, of such "butt-ends" as those in Kenilworth-street among the metropolitan sewers, and the necessity of caution in such cases is well known, so that the occurrence of a succession of fatalities like the present appears to be the more extraordinary, and might have been avoided by the adoption of the usual precautions, or of the means taken to remove the gaseous sewage, and to ventilate the sewer itself, in Friar-street, where the late explosion occurred,—namely, Gurney's high-pressure steam-jet, by which coal mines, as our readers will remember, have been successfully ventilated. In this case, too, the poisonous compounds might have been destroyed on the spot. At Friar-street this process enabled the officers to clear out at least 500 tons of foul matter.

A correspondent (T. H.) suggests,—that a dress and helmet, &c., similar to what a diver uses at the Polytechnic Institution for example, might be adopted effectively for examination of sewers. "The suggestion advanced may not be of any immediate use to those who have to travel any distance along the sewers, but that help may be afforded in case of need, and thereby preventing further loss of life. Every police office in the metropolis ought to be furnished with a dress and apparatus complete; the expense would be nominal, considering the amount raised by sewers rates."

PARKS FOR THE PEOPLE.

HAVING observed an extract from THE BUILDER, extensively quoted in the daily prints, remarking upon Copenhagen-fields as a fit place for a public park, I forward a copy of a letter which I wrote to Lord Morpeth, who acknowledged it, expressing his readiness to follow its recommendation in every manner that came before him, but that want of funds was the usual obstacle.—J. W. HALE.

The following is a portion of the letter referred to:—

"Without being unmindful of what has been done, and the great attention shown by your lordship and the other commissioners to the health of the people, by regard to important measures in their behalf; additional steps are needed, absolutely and incontestibly needed, on the ground of common humanity and sympathy with a pent-up population, hankering after fresh air and green sod or leaves in a hot and oppressive summer season, when thousands of the people in the internal parts of the metropolis find it intolerable to dwell pent up in heat and unwholesomeness, and seek the shortest routes to the nearest open spots or green places;—even an open alehouse court, where there may be a green shrub or a green seat, is eagerly sought for, and occupied with avidity by many of the thousands of women, children, and infirm persons who cannot reach the parks at the extreme ends of London.

It appears that formerly reservations were made for the benefit of the people, for sundry *greens* were formed, such as Clerkenwell, Islington, Newington, Stepney, and Camberwell greens, and others. It is to be hoped that if

MANSION OF H. T. HOPE, ESQ., M.P., PICCADILLY, LONDON.*

Messrs. DUSILLION and DONALDSON, Architects.

Smithfield Market be removed, that the space will be immediately converted into a *City green*. What was formerly necessary when London was much smaller, and from its hitherto long form and narrow width, more healthy in its internal parts than it can be in future (unless care be taken, whilst there is yet time and opportunity), is much more necessary now, and the consequences will show themselves, if precautions be neglected. One grand benefit to London will be to preserve an

* See page 493.

opening into the sides of it, both north and south; and the effects of this will be manifest: it will cause a current of comparatively pure air into the very centre of the metropolis, and also be the means of a pleasant, safe, and short access to open ground, green fields, or walks, parks, or broadways (as may be provided), for the benefit of health and morals of thousands of individuals who otherwise must be deprived of one of the greatest blessings of heaven.

On the north side of London the opening that would be beneficial is from Holborn to

King's-cross, *vid* Gray's-inn-road, by certain improvements and widenings in sundry places, as opportunity would permit, with wide and safe footpaths;—thence to Highgate, or so far as might be obtainable, either in progress thereto, or in extent of space as public ground, terminating at nearer distance from King's-cross.

The ground from King's-cross to Highgate, by way of Maiden-lane and Chalk-road, affords facility for the purposes desired, and *ten* acres of ground obtained here are more valuable, as

IRON RAILING, MR. HOPE'S MANSION.

FEET

a general service to the inhabitants of the middle portion of London, than 100 acres at the extreme ends.

The high ground about Copenhagen is an invaluable spot for the formation of a reservoir of air, both for the supply of the centre of London and for the access thereto of the inhabitants. This spot (be it secured on a large or small scale, whether from King's-cross to Highgate, or less) is invaluable; the thousands who are wont to resort thereto indicate its need of being, in some shape or other, secured as a public convenience. A space is taken for a model prison in this neighbourhood, and surely the consideration of the health and morals of thousands is worth a similar-sized spot, at least, for public recreation of a simply natural kind, viz., to obtain fresh air, and observe green herbage of some sort.

If the opportunity of forming a large or small reservoir of air in the sides of London be neglected now, when small comparative expense will effect it, the time will come when the most extensive demolition most be effected in order to air London, and give space for its inhabitants; fever and plague will not be stayed till thousands upon thousands be expended in this manner, and the very spots now uncovered will be then again laid bare for obvious purposes of general need."

PROJECTED WORKS.—Advertisements have been issued for tenders, by 1st proximo, for extensive works at the South-Eastern Railway stations at Old Kent-road and at Ashford; by 24th inst., for a warehouse and three coal sheds at the London and Brighton Railway station, at Croydon, and a warehouse at their Eastbourne station; by 1st January, 1850, for a bridge, wharfing, widening river, and removing old bridge, at Great Yarmouth; and by 29th inst., for works at two third-rate houses at Wilmington-square.

RAILWAY JOTTINGS.

THE traffic of branch lines in general, if not, too, of some main ones, it would appear, may ere long be altogether conducted by light engines, at great saving of expense. Experiments have occasionally been recorded in THE BUILDER that seemed to promise fairly for such a result, which further experience only appears to confirm. The *Railway Times* of 13th inst. gives the particulars of a personal examination of the doings and dimensions of one of these little, active, and even singularly powerful agents, built by Messrs. England and Co.,' of the Hatcham Ironworks, and at present at work on the Bow branch of the Blackwall line. It whirls a train of seven of the heavy Blackwall carriages, equal, it is said, to ten of the carriages in general use on other railways, up an incline of 1 in 100, at a speed of 35 miles an hour, starting as freely and getting into speed as readily as any other engine. The dimensions of this *Pigmy Giant*, as it is named, are as follows:—Cylinders, 8 inches diameter; stroke, 12 inches; driving-wheels, 4 feet 6 inches; four carrying wheels, 3 feet diameter; 80 tubes, 1½ inch diameter, 11 feet 4 inches long. The engine and tender are constructed on the same frame, with six wheels, and she is capable of carrying coke and water in her tender sufficient for a journey of 30 or 40 miles. The consumption of coke is less than 5 lbs. a-mile, producing, nevertheless, an immense quantity of steam. The weight of the whole engine, when in full working order, is about 10 tons. The centre of gravity being very low, there is no oscillation, even at a very high velocity. The day's work on the Bow branch is a run of about 200 miles.—— A slip of the embankment at Bosley, on the North Staffordshire line, took place last week, extending to about 100 yards.——The Whitehaven and Furness Junction line is now open from Whitehaven to Ravenglass. The con-

tractors are busily engaged in pushing forward the work from Ravenglass to Bootle, with 300 'navvies' and artizans. The contract for the line between Bootle and Broughton-in-Furness, has been let to Messrs. Fell and Joplin, of Greenodd, near Ulverstone.—— The contract for the extension of the Furness line from Crooklands to Lindal has been taken by Mr. Wheatcroft, of Matlock.——One of the engines on the Furness Junction, with a passenger-train, on 13th inst., ran through the Whitehaven terminus, knocked down the yard wall, stove in the side of a school-house substantially built of stone, carried away the kitchen, and lodged in the back parlour. So far, fortunately, none of the little scholars were in the way, but a poor young girl, who was singing to herself while preparing food at the kitchen-fire, was dreadfully mutilated and instantaneously killed, and her brother was much bruised and burnt. The line slopes down to the terminus at a gradient of 1 in 100. The cause of the accident is said to have been want of sufficient breakage in the state of the rail, which was covered with ice. —— The Caledonian Company have completed their tunnel at Glasgow. Entering at St. Rollox, it passes over the tunnel on the Edinburgh and Glasgow on the one hand and under the Monkland Canal on the other, and runs within a few feet of both towards the station at the head of Buchanan-street.—— Mr. James Mitchell, of the firm of Ross and Mitchell, contractors, and Mr. G. Glennie, resident engineer of the Hawick branch of the North British Railway, were placed at the bar of the circuit court at Jedburgh, on 2nd instant, on a charge of culpable homicide, and neglect or violation of duty. The case, it may be remembered, arose out of the fall of a viaduct in course of erection over the river Teviot, at Roxburgh, for the Kelso branch of the Hawick line, whereby eight persons were killed and several others injured. The indictment charged Mr. Mitchell with having allowed the pier of the viaduct to be constructed of insufficient materials. Mr. Glennie was charged with culpable neglect of duty in having failed to superintend and inspect the erection of the viaduct, and to see that it was properly and safely built with good, sufficient, and safe materials. The case went on till suddenly stopped by the alarming intimation, that one of the Jury was seized with premonitory symptoms of cholera, on the announcement of which the court adjourned, and the trial, we presume, will begin *de novo*, unless the juryman speedily recovered.

THE SYPHON VENTILATOR.

INGENIOUS men, delighted with any new observation that occurs to them, too often take it for granted that the same discovery never occurred to any other human being, and place themselves in a false position, when a little inquiry would dispel the delusion. In this respect the mania for patents of invention, with the necessity for secrecy on their object, frequently leads to mischief, and causes a man of intelligence to throw away 400*l*. on a patent, that not only is not worth so many farthings, but which may drive him into litigation and ruin. As the average of successful patents is but three in a hundred, I need not say how often this must be the case. I have known many crude cases of this kind, but that of Dr. Chowne particularly surprises me. One would think that gentleman must have been blind, deaf, or asleep,—anything but alive to the progress of science and its application to buildings, if he supposes himself the discoverer of a new system of ventilation by means of an "up shaft and a down shaft." He is equally in error if he imagine that he can maintain a patent for a principle: our law allows the patent right for a mode of operation and construction, not on a principle. As to the mode of ventilating by the syphon or atmospheric gravitation process, it is known to every miner, and ought to be to every architect, since Mr. Griffith's excellent lectures some years ago, at the Royal Institute of British Architects, in which it was clearly shown and explained. There are also various applications of it in London and its vicinity. Mr. Place, of Brompton-square, has for many years had his library warmed by a simple adaptation of the law of gravitation of hot and cold air on each side of his stove-grate, clearly demonstrated by the suction and repulsion of the flame of a candle placed near the bottom and upper part of the openings.* Mr. Geo. Field, of Sion-hill-park, the author of various works on optics, &c. &c., has made his little parlour perfectly free from any perceptible draft by a pipe from the park through the wall into the binder portion of stove, whence, after being warmed, it replaces the consumed air of the room, supplies the grate with oxygen, and assists the up-draft of the chimney, which being overhung by very tall trees, afforded a severe trial, but a very successful one. On a more extensive scale, in the heart of London, at the Hall of Commerce, in Threadneedle-street, every chimney has a small flue or down-shaft, to supply cold air to fill up the vacuum caused by the combustion. This was made when the building was erected in 1841. I could refer to other cases, but will conclude by mentioning a very pretty model for ventilating mines, by John Martin, the artist, and propounder of many improvements. I again repeat that our patent law allows no monopoly of the principles of nature, and I entertain no apprehension of an exception in favour of this "assumed new discovery." I fear no new tax on pure air. CENSOR.

* According to Dr. Clowne's statement, his system is not dependent on heat.—ED.

ON THE OXIDATION OF RAILWAY BARS.

A PAPER on this subject, by Mr. R. Mallet, was read at the recent meeting of the British Association. It suggests an important consideration. The writer states that the top surface of a railway bar in use is constantly preserved in a state of perfect cleanliness, freedom from oxidation, and polish; while the remainder of the bar is rough-coated originally with black oxide, and soon after with red rust. Not only is every metal *electro-positive to its own oxides*, but the polished portion of a mass of metal partially polished and partially rough is primarily corroded on the rough portion. Hence a railway bar while in use is constantly preserved from rusting by the presence of its polished top surface. Such polished surface has no existence on the rail out of use. The upper surface of the rail in use is rapidly condensed and hardened by the rolling of the traffic over it; and it is also shown in his report that, all other circumstances being the same, the rate of corrosion of any iron depends upon its density, and is less in proportion as this is rendered greater by mechanical means. As every metal is positive to its own oxides, the adherent coat of rust upon iron, while it remains, powerfully promotes the corrosion of the metal beneath, and this in a greater degree in proportion as the rust adherent is of greater antiquity. It has been shown that the rust produced by air and water, which at first contains but little per-oxide, continues to change slowly, and becoming more and more per-oxidized becomes more and more electro-negative to its own base. Now, the rust upon a railway bar out of use continues always to adhere to it, and thus to promote and accelerate its corrosion; while the rust formed upon a railway bar in use is perpetually shaken off by vibration, and thus this source of increased chemical action is removed. To recapitulate, railway bars forming part of a long line, whether in or out of use, corrode less for equal surfaces than a short piece of the same iron similarly exposed. Rails in use corrode less than those out of use. This difference is constantly decreasing with the lapse of time. The absolute amount of corrosion is a source of destruction of the rail greatly inferior to that due to traffic. It is highly probable *that the electrical and magnetic forces developed in the rails by terrestrial magnetism and by rolling traffic re-act in some way upon the chemical forces* concerned in their corrosion; and that, therefore, the direction of lines of railway in azimuth is not wholly indifferent as respects the question of the durability of rails. Mr. Mallet suggests:—1st. Of whatever quality iron rails are rolled, that they should be subjected prior to use to an uniform course of hammer-hardening all over the top surface and sides of the rails; and, 2ndly, that all railway bars before being laid down should, after having been gauged and straightened, be heated to about 400 degrees Fahrenheit, and then coated with boiled coal tar. This has been proved to last more than four years, as a coating perfectly impervious to corrosive action, while constantly exposed to traffic.

WESTMINSTER ABBEY AND PUBLIC STATUES.

I VISITED Westminster Abbey yesterday morning, and was much struck with the imposing statue of the late Sir W. Follett, by Behnes; at the same time I could but feel that it appeared sadly out of its place, and in too crowded a situation. What a fine occasion this would have been for the commencement of a series of statues of eminent and great men (particularly with so distinguished a lawyer as the late Sir Wm. Follett), by placing it in Westminster Hall instead of the Abbey. It is colossal, and is placed by the side of another statue, which it throws into utter insignificance. Again, how much grander the statue of Lord Mansfield would appear if removed to such a situation as above suggested. Further, they mar the Abbey. When will this country think properly as to works of art? S.

Apropos of Westminster Abbey, we give some stanzas from a little poem under this title by Mr. Owen Howell,* which has been forwarded to us.

"Gaze on this Gothic relic of the past,—
See o'er its towers does Ruin surely creep;
Time has her mantle o'er each buttress cast,—
On each grey battlement Time's shadows sleep.
What will not fade?—all records cease at last;
A few short years temple and tablet sweep
Into the mighty gulf that gathers all:
The slow destroyer, Time, sees tottering empires fall.

Far from Life's busy crowds awhile we stray
To where the dead within these walls repose,
Here to hold council with the mouldering clay
That antique tombs and sepulchres enclose,—
'Midst dusty banners fading fast away,
Old monumental slabs, and funeral shows,
To walk with noiseless tread and held-in breath,
To muse on human life, and meditate on death.

* * * * * *

In hollow gusts, the wind with solemn tones
Murmurs sad dirges as we musing walk
Over old epitaphs on foot-worn stones:
Each monument, though silent, seems to talk
Of mouldering coffins and of bleaching bones;
While voiceless phantoms round us gravely stalk,
Wrapped in the dark shades of obscurest night:
The moon pours down, o'er all, her 'dim religious light.'

* * * * * *

Chapels and shrines all speak of what has been,—
And sad the moral that they ever preach!
There sleeps Elizabeth—there Scotland's Queen,—
Victor and victim solemn lessons teach:
Their bloodless ghosts in yonder aisle are seen,—
A thousand phantoms fancy sees in each;
While the old banners hanging up on high
Flutter, as one by one, beneath them, they glide by.

Over each monument and time-worn bust
Wisdom does well to pause and meditate.
Here are interred the good, the wise, the just,—
Here, with rich trappings, the departed great
Were brought in glory, and laid in the dust:
Beneath these tombs, in darkness, now they wait,
Covered with moss, time-eaten, black and quaint:
Lo! yonder sleeps a King, and there a Gothic Saint.

The graves and vaults that at our footsteps lie—
The marble saints and carven busts of kings—
All seem to say 'Prepare, prepare to die!
The world and life are quickly-passing things;'
Whilst each uncouth and ghastly effigy—
Cherub and angel, with their outspread wings—
With sightless eyes upon us ever stare,
As wondering whence we came, and wondering what we are."

* London: Matthews, Paternoster-row.

THE ADELPHI THEATRE.—The additional entrances and stairs here, mentioned by us some time since, have been opened to the public, and increase considerably the means of escape in the event of fire. The manager deserves the thanks of the public for the step; we should be glad to see it followed in some other theatres we could name. The last time we looked in, a crowded house was laughing spasmodically all night.

NOTES IN THE PROVINCES.

A FEATURE unnoticed in the existing pla
of the Abbey Church at Bury has just bee
revealed in course of the archæological di
gings there, namely, that at the circular ap
of the choir (plan in Yates's history) a sem
circular chapel (besides the small Mary Ch
pel) jutted out about 15 feet in diameter fro
the northern curve of the apse. Beneath
appears to have been a crypt, in which a
remains of a pavement of encaustic tile, an
part of an erection supposed to have been
loculus, or shrine, below the altar. The com
mittee require further aid in the developme
of the plan of the choir.——The shroud of roug
cast in which the exterior of the Saxon tower
Holy Trinity Church, Colchester, has long bee
buried, is now stripped off, we are told, and th
whole, as far as possible, restored. An ancie
arch in the interior has been re-opened
view by the removal of a gallery, and th
organ placed under it. Some additional ope
seats have thus been secured at west end
nave; estimated expense of alterations 90
deficient 20*l*.——The parish church of Maide
Newton, Dorset, is to be restored and en
larged.——The Commissioners of Lunacy hav
called on the Secretary of State to order th
erection of a new asylum for the paup
lunatics of Bristol. The cost, it is said, wi
not be less than 50,000*l*.——The widening
Bristol-bridge is again talked of.——Conwa
Castle, it is said, is to be restored, at the publ
expense.——The Merthyr Union guardia
have decided on the erection of a new work
house on a large scale.——Efforts are about
be made to erect two additional churches
the parish of St. Mary, Nottingham. Ea
Manvers has promised 500*l*. and Lady Ma
vers 100*l*., besides which about 4,600*l*. hav
been contributed or promised from oth
sources, and there is land secured for on
of the churches.——The directors of th
New Exchange, Wolverhampton, have fixe
on plans for their new building, furnishe
by Mr. G. T. Robinson, of Wolve
hamton, architect.——The new church
St. Matthew, Toxteth-park, Liverpool, wa
opened on Sunday week. It is a plain Goth
edifice, with open-timbered roof and ben
fittings. The official part is slightly elevate
into a sort of *dais* with tesselated pavemen
and octagonal pulpit supported by a centr
octagonal pillar.——The Bridgewater Can
Company are carrying passengers betwe
Liverpool and Manchester, 40 miles an
upwards, for 3d. each!——The Bradfo
guardians, after an immense deal of ta
about it for the last twelvemonth or two, a
now said to have ordered that an advertis
ment be prepared, calling for plans for a ne
workhouse.——The chief stone of the chur
of St. Luke, East Morton, near Bingley, w
laid on the 9th inst. The plan, says th
Leeds Intelligencer, consists of a nave, sou
aisle, chancel, south porch, vestry, and be
gable, about 65 feet above the floor. Th
nave is 70 feet long, by 22 feet 10 inches wid
and 45 feet high to ridge of roof—aisle, 70 fe
long, by 14 feet 8 inches, and 13 feet high
lowest side—chancel, 30 feet long by 16 fe
wide, and 33 feet high to ridge of roof. Th
style is First Pointed. The roofs will be
steep pitch, and the timbers open in the int
rior.——The church of Holy Trinity, Mea
wood, Leeds, lately consecrated, is crucifor
and in the style of thirteenth century; lengt
111 feet internally, 78 of which in nave and 3
in chancel; width at transepts, 42 feet; heig
of spire, 130 feet; sittings, 400. The area an
foundations are laid with concrete. In
vault below the cross is a furnace, whenc
the building is heated by pipes. Th
walls are of Meanwood stone. The arch
tect was Mr. W. Railton; and Mr. G. Bri
gart, of Derby, was the general contracto
Mr. Boumphrey, clerk of works. The con
tract cost was 4,300*l*., 'exclusive of orn
mental parts.' The founders were two ladi
named Beckett.——The foundation-stone
the church to be erected at Moor-Allerto
near Leeds, was laid on Wednesday wee
Mr. Thompson, of Leeds, is the architec
The building is to be ready for consecration i
about six months.——The church of Corrin
ham, near Gainsborough, is undergoing ex
tensive repairs, at the expense of Sir Thoma
Beckett, Bart., of Somerby Hall.——A retur

of the outlay and profits of the Durham Gas Company shows that their gains for 1848 were at the rate of 27½ per cent.!——The Whittle Dean water, with which Newcastle-on-Tyne is now supplied, in place of from the filthy river itself, would appear to have prevented a repetition of the dreadful mortality by cholera in 1832, the epidemic of 1849 having been "comparatively harmless." A few such facts, together with those presented in the metropolis itself, will surely decide the question of the necessity for a speedy and abundant supply of pure water, both here and elsewhere.——A subscription for the erection of a new church at Ambleside was lately opened, and 2,000*l.* at once obtained.——John Knox's house at Edinburgh is under repair, although the question of its demolition is still an open one.——A bridge of 230 feet in length has been thrown across the Doveron, at Milltown, of Rothiemay, N.B.

OPENING OF THE NEW METROPOLITAN COMMISSION OF SEWERS.

THE members of the new commission met on Wednesday, at the Court-house, Greek-street, pursuant to clause 4 of the Sewers' Act. There were present—Lord Ebrington, M.P., Sir H. de la Beche, Lieut.-Colonel Alderson, Sir John Burgoyne, Capt. Vetch, Capt. Dawson, Capt. Harness, Mr. S. M. Peto, Mr. P. Hardwick, Mr. Thomas Hawes, Mr. Edward Lawes, and Mr. J. M. Rendell. The secretary (Mr. Woolrych) read the commission issued by the Lord Chancellor, containing the appointment of the above-named gentlemen, and which bore date the 10th of October.

Some other formal proceedings being gone through, Viscount Ebrington was voted to the chair, and addressed the court. In the course of his observations his lordship said, that for reasons that need not be mentioned, and which were well known to the public, it had been deemed expedient to supersede the late commission, and to issue a new one. He would not dwell upon the responsibility of the trust that had been conferred upon them. The work was of the deepest interest to the health and lives of all comprised within the area of their jurisdiction,—an area comprising the greatest, the wealthiest, and the most populous city in the world. They had many difficulties to encounter,—not only as to the views of the commissioners, but difficulties arising out of the actual state of affairs in their own office. He believed that neither could their duties be properly and efficiently performed, nor could their difficulties be surmounted, unless a better feeling gained ground, not only amongst the commissioners, but amongst their officers, for "a house divided against itself could not stand." He hoped, however they might differ in opinion, they would discuss all without wrangling, and after opposition, that it would not end in acrimony or ill-will. Under God's blessing, therefore, he trusted they would be enabled to confer additional comfort and length of days to the citizens and to their families, and that the public would not judge of them by their professions or their intentions, but by their acts. Without saying more, he thought they might at once proceed to the business of the court.

Sir John Burgoyne moved the re-appointment of Mr. Woolrych as secretary to the commission, and also the re-appointment of the accountants and clerks in the secretary's department. Agreed to.

A letter was received from Mr. Austin, consulting engineer, stating that, in consequence of certain resolutions come to by three of the Commission of the Board of Health at Gwydyr House, he had thought it his duty to tender his resignation of his office. At the same time, he should at all times be most happy to render any advice or assistance in his power, and should be ready to further develope his views in his plan of drainage, if such should be required, either as a whole or part of any system that might be ultimately agreed upon. This letter was accompanied by one from Lord Carlisle, who dwelt on the somewhat anomalous position of the members of the Board of Health, being also Commissioners of Sewers, and vindicated especially the conduct of one of them—Mr. Chadwick—which had been the subject of much unmerited attack.

The letter was received, and ordered to be entered upon the minutes, and upon the motion of Captain Dawson, a vote of thanks was passed to Mr. Austin, for the offer he had made of assistance to the commissioners.

Capt. Dawson said he looked upon this as a fitting and proper opportunity for remodelling the whole of the engineers' and surveyors' department. His lordship in the chair, in his address, had alluded to the officers of the court, and the division among them had been productive of great inconvenience. Without a proper understanding, however proper the officers, it was impossible that works could be efficiently performed. With this view, and as a step towards remodelling the whole of the engineering department, he moved that the surveyors and officers be re-appointed for three months only.

Mr. Hardwick seconded the motion, and considered it of the highest importance to the public that the whole engineering establishment should be re-modelled.—Agreed to.

Sir H. de la Beche said it was of the utmost importance, and it was absolutely necessary that they should have well-considered official arrangement, for without them the organization of their department could not be efficient. Yet, notwithstanding these arrangements, however good the individual persons might be, there was nothing so essential to the service that might be derived from them as that they should be well placed, and then good results would be sure to follow. It was highly desirable that they should not lose the benefit of the investigations that were in progress, and which were stopped by the ending of the commission. It was also desirable that they should ascertain what had been done before they could carry on their works, and above all it was necessary that they should have before them the ordnance map and the results of the subterranean survey. The ordnance map was now available for portions of their districts, and the subterranean survey had made great progress, giving them a proper insight into what existed below the surface of the metropolis. When these documents were presented, the court would see what had been done, and he hoped that they would not regret the step that had been taken by their predecessors. To see this, and perhaps to chalk out their progress for the future, he thought it would be desirable that a committee of the whole body should be appointed to ascertain the official arrangements of the commission, the state of the various works undertaken by the previous commissioners and not completed, and to report the same to the court.—Seconded and agreed to.

Sir H. de la Beche then read the resolutions that had been passed upon the question of the various plans sent in for the proposed drainage of London, and said that it would be courteous on the part of the comissioners to state that they should receive proper consideration. It was, however, necessary, before doing so, that they should have the City Commissioners present, as the plans proposed had reference to the City as well as the parts of their own jurisdiction. He therefore moved that a communication should be made to the Lord Mayor, stating that a new commission had been granted, and the old one had been superseded, and to request that four persons, in addition to his lordship, might be appointed as commissioners to that court.—Agreed to.

Upon the recent accident in Kenilworth-street, Pimlico, being reported to the court,

Mr. Lovick, the assistant-surveyor, presented a voluminous statement, detailing the nature of the works that had been ordered in that district, and giving it as his opinion that the fatal results there had arisen from a quantity of offensive lime from gas-works being shot down for the purpose of filling up open spaces in the road, and that the poisonous qualities of the gas absorbed by the lime had, by a fall of rain, percolated the top of the sewer (over which it was placed), and mixing with the refuse within the sewer, had liberated certain pernicious gases, and thereby led to the deadly effects that had followed.

The report was received, and on the motion of the chairman, it was agreed that the circumstances should be investigated by the committee, in accordance with the suggestion of Mr. Phillips and Mr. Gotto, chief and assistant surveyors; and that every facility be afforded to the officers in attending inquests whenever they may be required.—Adjourned.

Miscellanea.

PROPOSITION FOR A PROFESSIONAL CLUB HOUSE.—I cannot help thinking it is much to be regretted that an institution or club-house cannot be formed by the members of the different professions, viz., architects, painters, sculptors, engineers, engravers, and surveyors, and it might have chambers attached to it which would be both convenient and profitable, and tend to support the expenses of the establishment. It is true you have the Institute of Architects and Engineers, but what I think is required is a general place of meeting, where members could go in to read the papers, write letters, have letters directed to them, or a library, &c., to refer to; there might also be a lecture-room, museum, &c. It should be central, and such a spot as the vacant space in Leicester-square would be convenient to the generality of persons. A. S.

⁂ This proposition was made in our pages some time ago, but it did not then elicit sufficient response to induce any further steps. We should be glad to see it carried out.

FREEMASONS OF THE CHURCH.—At a meeting of this society, held on Tuesday evening (Oct. 9), Mr. R. Williams in the chair, Mr. J. W. Archer exhibited a collection of original water-colour drawings of architectural remains in the county of Kent. Many of them represented domestic specimens in and about Rochester, and one a newly-discovered crypt, which he thought must have formed part of the ancient church of St. Mary in that city, now destroyed. Mr. A. also exhibited some rubbings of incised slabs in the church of St. John, Chester, and the possibly unique specimen of a monumental brass having one portion (a curious incident in the life of one of the Lords Arundel), executed at a much later period than the date of the inscription. Mr. W. Harry Rogers then read a paper on the "Decorative Resources of the Modern Architect," dividing them principally into five classes, viz., the human figure; drapery, under its various forms; animals, only when these are by common compliance acknowledged as the representatives of certain appropriate ideas; flowers; and, lastly, conventional ornaments, mainly derived from natural types.

SEWERAGE OF LINCOLN.—The following, says the local *Times*, is Mr. Giles's estimate of the cost of a complete sewerage for Lincoln, as indicated by the plans, &c., which will shortly be laid before the public:—Construction of the sewers, 20,576*l.*; flushing apparatus, 1,200*l.*; engine-well, steam-engines, pumps, &c., 1,900*l.*; two acres of land, 400*l.*; raising land and roads, 150*l.*; draining-shed, 500*l.*; office, 150*l.*; precipitating tanks and apparatus, 1,650*l.*; contingencies, 2,671*l.*; total, 29,388*l.* The proposed extent of sewers is nearly 17 miles. The gross rental of the city being estimated at 40,000*l.* to 50,000*l.* per annum, it is calculated that a rate of sixpence in the pound a-year would cover the cost. Under the Health of Towns Act the money could be borrowed, and the repayment spread over thirty years. Part of the proposal is to convert the collected refuse into inodorous cake manure, under Mr. Higgs's system. The liquid, deprived of smell, would run into the Witham. Mr. Giles has offered to undertake the works at the sum stated.

BRISTOL ATHENÆUM.—Lectures at this institution (which promises to be valuable for the young men of Bristol) were commenced on Thursday in last week, by the Rev. N. Haycroft, M.A., on the Formation of Character, which was delivered in the exhibition-room of the Fine Arts Academy. The programme promises a good series, and it is to be hoped, as Mr. Haycroft said, that many will take advantage of opportunities of increasing knowledge which our forefathers never had. The room, it may be observed, is not altogether well adapted for the purpose; it is hung with baize, which muffles the voice to an uncomfortable extent.

ST. MARY ABBOT'S, KENSINGTON.—A petition is about to be presented to the House of Commons by the ratepayers of this parish, praying the House to devise such ample and equitable measures as shall lead to a sufficient supply of good water.

VENTILATION OF SEWERS.—The frightful accident in the sewer at Pimlico has induced me to offer a plan which I have for years considered as the most effectual for ventilating the sewers. They have been usually ventilated through the gullies, and more recently, they have been trapped. Small gratings have been fixed in the centre of the carriage-way, by which horses are often frightened, as I know to my cost. I would propose that when any house or party wall is rebuilt, or when a street is built, a 6-inch air flue, formed of glazed pipe, joints well cemented, be carried up adjoining the kitchen flue, to the chimney top, and communicated along the area party-wall, with the crown of sewer in road, then we should not be annoyed in the streets as we now are with bad smells. One house in, say, twenty would be enough in the new streets. I am aware that this is only a modification of the ventilating shafts that have been proposed: the powers for requiring the owners of houses to do this might be provided in the proposed new Buildings Act. I find the rain water pipes are sometimes used for this purpose, but the chimney shaft would be much better.

E. O. SYMONS.

BURSTING OF THE WEIR OF THE MAN-CHESTER WATER WORKS. — On Sunday week, in consequence of heavy rains, the Headon weir, and the Woodhead reservoir below it, were successively filled to overflowing, so far as already formed, and the massive coping of the weir, with some 10,000 or 12,000 feet of earthwork from the Woodhead embankment, were carried away by the pressure acting on an uncompleted structure. The land adjoining was, of course, flooded, and much further damage was done to mills and bridges. The water works at Woodhead are very extensive. The embankment across the valley, damming up five or six considerable mountain streams, is about a mile and a half in length. The weir above it, on the Headon brook, was a massive stone structure, with top boards removable during floods, but unfortunately without attendance at the time, so that a stream of about 1,000 cubic feet in a second was allowed to accumulate against the weir till its coping was washed away, and the reservoir below overflowed. The latter had been raised to about 24 feet above the level of the pipes. The cost of the several works to the Corporation of Manchester, when completed, is estimated at not much less than a million sterling. The loss to the contractor by the present casualty will be heavy, and it will require about two months to reinstate the works destroyed. Mr. J. F. Bateman is the engineer.

PEAT CHARCOAL TO SWEETEN THE METROPOLIS.—Mr. Jasper Rogers made a further demonstration of the deodorising powers of Irish peat charcoal, at the Mechanics' Institution, Chancery-lane, on Monday last, when experiments were exhibited that certainly did appear to bear out his enthusiasm in the good cause which he desires to promote. Indeed, the fact that charcoal has a very remarkable power of absorbing immense quantities of deleterious gases, and of thereby even restoring corrupted animal food for instance, purifying and sweetening foul, water, &c., has long been familiar to us; but it is the peculiar power of peat charcoal, and above all of Irish peat charcoal, to absorb the odour and moisture of sewage precipitate, and convert it into dry and inodorous 'poudrette' manure, for which Mr. Rogers contends.

BIRMINGHAM WORKHOUSE COMPETITION.—In consequence of receiving congratulations on my approaching marriage to a lady of whose existence I was and am unaware, I was induced to refer, upon my recent return from the continent, to a letter from a correspondent, which appeared in No. 347 of THE BUILDER, when I found to my great surprise an announcement to that effect, together with other calumnious aspersions, only to be excused as uttered doubtless under the momentary sting and irritation of bitter disappointment. The truth is, I neither have now, nor at any time have had, the slightest acquaintance with any of the guardians, the architects, or their families, beyond the fact of having met Mr. Drury once only upon other business, and then in the presence of two professional men, which was prior to my having any idea of my appointment as one of the selecting architects, and at which time I was not even made aware of his being a competitor. I beg leave also to deny most unequivocally the existence of " an architect's name" upon any of the plans reported upon at the time of our inspection, and allow me also to assert, that the whole of such plans were in strict accordance with the instructions issued by the Board. Permit me further to affirm that I was (as I believe were Messrs. Edge and Stevens) perfectly ignorant of the names of the authors until they were publicly announced, and we were actuated with but one common feeling, which was to do impartial justice to the architects and the public, and that duty we most conscientiously discharged.—I am, Sir, &c.
JOHN GIBSON.

₊ For the personal statements denied by Mr. Gibson and Mr. Edge, we are in no way responsible. We offer the author of them the opportunity of substantiating his charges, although we would prefer to let the matter end here, and in the event of his not doing so previously to our next publication, shall feel ourselves at liberty to forward his name to the parties concerned. Our own views and statements remain precisely as they were.

MACHINE FOR JOINERS.—A machine for mortising, boring, &c., has recently been patented in this country, by Mr. William Furness, of Lawton-street, Liverpool. It is the invention of Mr. J. A. Fay, an eminent American engineer, and has recently been brought to a state of great perfection. One has been made by Messrs. E. F. Bellhouse and Co., of Manchester. According to our informant, it is on the principle of the slotting machine for iron, but with a power of adjustment of the point of the tool which enables a great variety of work to be done by it. The chisels employed are peculiar in shape, not being solid like the ordinary mortice chisels, but flat like the common joiners' chisels, with the edges turned up at right angles, so that the chips are drawn out of the mortice, after the hole has been cut. The machine can be used with any size of chisel from an eighth of an inch up to two inches; it will also set out and mortice naves for wheels not exceeding 10 by 15 inches. Pins and dowels are made by it. It can be made to operate either by foot or steam power, and one machine, it is said, will perform the work of eight men. The cost of the machine is about 20l. The inventor of this machine has also invented a machine to make tenons, and execute rabbeting, sash scribing, and boring in any kind of wood.

LILLE.—A statue is in progress here by subscription, in honour of General Negrier, who fell at the barricades in Paris, June, 1848. It is in bronze, from Bra, the sculptor, in Paris. The works of the new Town-house are advancing rapidly. The Museum of pictures, &c., is open to the public two days per week, viz., Thursdays and Sundays. There are some good pictures by Claude, Rubens, Salvator Rosa, Leonardo da Vinci, Vandyke, and some by modern artists, Roqueplan, Delaroche, &c., which are very good. Also some very remarkable sketches by the old masters, presented to the town by the citizen Wicar. Although the collection is but small, it is not a bad place to spend an hour in. In the course of the restoration of a church at Tournay, some interesting discoveries have been made.

THE INDUSTRIAL EXHIBITION OF ALL NATIONS.—On Wednesday a large assemblage of gentlemen met at the Mansion-house, by invitation from the Lord Mayor, to receive a deputation on this subject, when Mr. H. Cole submitted an outline of the proposal, and resolutions were agreed to for the promotion of the object in view. We need only now repeat the caution which we have already felt it our duty to offer, and in which we perceive that the Times, in noticing the report of this meeting in its columns, fully concurs, that the utmost care be taken in the selection of those to whom the management of the affair, and the choice of prizes, must be left, so that all chance or even insinuation of jobbery may be obviated.

BATHS AND WASHHOUSES are likely to be, ere long, established, for behoof of the working classes, at Oxford. A subscription list has been set agoing, and has been headed with a donation of 50l. by the keeper of the Ashmolean Museum.——The directors of the Wolverhampton Subscription Baths Company have, out of twenty-three sets of designs, fixed on one by Mr. G. T. Robinson, of Wolverhampton. It is in the Lombardic or Romanesque style of tenth century. There will be a tepid swimming bath, 70 feet long by 30 wide, with a cold plunging bath, 20 feet long by 10 wide, with numerous dressing rooms. A staircase leads to a gallery partly encircling the tepid bath. Private baths will be attached.

SUGGESTION FOR SCAFFOLDING.—Having frequently observed accidents to happen from the putlogs of scaffolding coming away from the wall of a building, a suggestion has occurred to me, which if published in your Journal, may be the means of saving life for the future during the operation of building. This improvement consists in making a slit in the end of the putlog, before placing it in the wall; if a hard wood wedge be then driven into the slit just in face of the wall, a much more secure fastening would be effected than is obtained by the means hitherto adopted. The putlog may be further bound round with iron at a certain distance from the end to prevent the wood splitting further than is required.
E. J. P.

WHITE ZINC.—The French Governme according to Galignani, has recently orde that in future the white paint used in pub buildings shall be made of white zinc, inst of white lead. Considering the injurious sults of the use of paint made from wh lead, adds the same anthority, and the dre ful effects that the lead produces in the man factories where it is prepared, it is much be hoped that the example set by the Gore ment will be followed by the public.—A p fellow, seized with painter's cholic while gri ing white lead with colours, at a shop on t Quai Napoleon, the other day, committed s cide to end his sufferings.

THE BRITANNIA TUBE.—The final lift this tube was successfully accomplished Monday last. It is now 3 feet above the p manent level,—a circumstance requisite enable the engineers to join it on to the end land tube, before laying it down on its b plates and rollers when placed beneath it. T process will occupy other three weeks. It intended by the directors to give some ch excursion trains periodically to the Straits, enable the middle and humbler classes to v the tubes. Two additional cylinders have b cast for the lifting of the next, as a reser All the preparations are complete for the flo ing, which will take place about the middle November. The day fixed for the transit the first train over the Straits is the 1st March next.

GUTTA PERCHA.—The first ship ever fai loaded with this now staple article of cor merce, for British import, is the Bangalore, recently arrived in the London Docks, with 5 tons of it from the East Indies. This mo plastic and useful substance has of late be applied to the conveyance of water into Bi mingham, and found, it is said, to be qui well adapted to the purpose.

WATER.—We would direct attention to advertisement in our paper, convening public meeting at the Hanover-square Room on Monday evening next, for the purpose taking into consideration the best means improving the water supply of the metropoli

COMPETITIONS.—Advertisements have be issued for plans, &c., by 1st November, of workhouse at Bradford for 300 inmates, b sides vagrant ward and fever shed—particula as advertised; and by a date not specifie for designs and drawings for a Blind Instit tion at Birmingham.

WALL PAINTINGS, BISHOP TAWTON CHURCH, BARNSTAPLE.—It may be interestir to you, and worth a remark in THE BUILDE that in the restoration of the north aisle Bishop Tawton's Church, which is going under my direction, a series of interestir frescoes (?), in a good state of preservatio have been discovered. They cover the who of the north side, and are surrounded by border of good design. One compartment r presents St. Christopher carrying the infa Saviour over a river : in the other hand is staff much resembling the stock of a fir-tr with the branches lopped off. Another con partment represents St. Michael weighing d parted spirits with one hand, and wielding sword with the other,—the dragon is und his feet ; in this compartment there also a female figure, which, I think, is intende to represent the Virgin interceding, as the sca on that side is down. The whole of the pla tering has not yet been scraped off, but i soon as this is done, I purpose making correct reduced drawing of the whole, wit reference to the restoration of those parts no defaced. Some idea of the size of these pain ings may be formed when it is considered th the principal figures are upwards of 10 fe high.
R. D. GOULD.

TENDERS

For the Parsonage-house for the district of St. Simon Zelotes, Bethnal-green ; Mr. A. R. Mason, Architect.

Joshua Wilson	£1,128
Hicks	1,188
R. and E. Curtis	1,184
Holland	1,097
Locke and Nesham	1,085
Wm. Hill (accepted)	1,072

TO CORRESPONDENTS.

Received.—" R. N." (Hitchin), " T. H.," " A Constant Reader" (we do not know), " G. R. B." (the 21st, half-past one to half-past two), " Peter," " Mr. F." (thanks—next week), " Public," " J. B." " C. R. C." (shall hear from us), " I. B. H.," " Hydraulic Engineer," " F. H. and Co.," " S. C." (unnecessary, on consideration), " Col. M.," " W. P. G." (next week), " C. L." (declined), " A Country Builder" (we are unable to reply without a visit, which we have not time to make), " Mons. A. L." (thanks), " W. B." (City), " T. Square," " Sanitas" (we should be disposed to try the effect of rendering the wall with asphalte), " W. W.," " C. C. C.," " W. L. G." (safe), " W. X. Y.," " W. X. W.," " J. C." (scarcely worth record), " J. H.," " W. H." (when we have seen the book we shall speak of it), " J. B. D.," " Dr. C.," " Dr. M.," " Your Constant Reader," " An Amateur."—" Choice Examples of Art Workmanship, Mediæval and Modern" (London, David Bogue) ; " Report of the Tower Hamlets Sanitary Association; Wright's " History of Ireland," Part 15 (Tallis) ; " Church and Chapel Architecture," by Andrew Trimen, Architect (Longman and Co., 1849.)

NOTICE.— All communications respecting *advertisements* should be addressed to the "Publisher," and not to the "Editor;" all other communications should be addressed to the EDITOR, and *not* to the Publisher.

" *Books and Addresses.*"—We have not time to point out books or find addresses.

ADVERTISEMENTS.

TERRA-COTTA, or VITRIFIED STONE
WORKS, King Edward-street, Westminster-road, London.—M. H. BLANCHARD, from late Coade's Original Works Belvedere-road, Lambeth, begs to inform the Nobility, Gentry, Architects, and Builders, that he has re-established the manufacture of that invaluable material, which has been successfully adopted by our rejected Architects and others. In the adornment of our noblest buildings, nearly 100 years has proved the imperishable nature of the material, the specimens of those times now exhibiting all their primitive sharpness.

Groups, statues, friezes, capitals, panelling, pinnacles, finials, terminals, Tudor, and other chimney shafts, balustrades, fountains, fonts, Italian vases, coats of arms, devices, and every description of architectural ornament, at prices in many instances nearly half the cost of stone.

Specimens of the material to be seen at the Office of " The Builder," 2, York-street, Covent Garden, and at the Works.

GAS FITTINGS.—Ironmongers, Plumbers,
and the Trade supplied with Brackets, Pendants, Harp Lights, &c.; Iron and Tin Pipe, Union Joints, &c., for GAS FITTINGS, at R. BYERLEY'S, No. 10, 11, and 12, Charles-street, Long Acre. Manufactory for Cornice Poles, Lacquered Cage Tube, &c., and all Metal Metals in the rough.

CHUBB'S WROUGHT-IRON and FIRE-
PROOF DOORS and FRAMES, for strong Rooms. A large stock of the above, of all sizes, made in the best manner, and of different strengths, fitted with CHUBB'S PATENT DETECTOR LOCKS, throwing from two to twenty bolts, can readily on sale, at very moderate prices. FIRE-PROOF SAFES of every kind. Patent Detector Locks and Latches for all purposes.—C. CHUBB and SON, sole Manufacturers, 57, St. Paul's Churchyard, London.

LEA DBEATER. FIRE-PROOF SAFE and DETECTOR LOCK
MANUFACTURER to HER MAJESTY'S BOARD OF ORDNANCE.

CAUTION to Purchasers of FIRE-PROOF
DOORS for Strong Rooms, Safes, Chests, and Detector Locks. &c. &c. LEADBEATER, many years manufacturer for Chubb, LEADBEATER begs respectfully to inform Architects, Surveyors, Builders, &c. that he can supply them with IMPROVED DETECTOR LOCKS of a superior and cheaper purpose. STRONG WROUGHT IRON FIRE-PROOF DOORS and CHESTS, &c., on the most improved principles of security against FIRE and THIEVES, with Patent Detector Locks and Latches for all purposes.—C. CHUBB and SON, sole Manufacturers, 57, St. Paul's Churchyard, London.

LEADBEATER offers ONE HUNDRED POUNDS reward to any person who can pick his improved detector locks or latches. Some thousands of Leadbeater's strong-room doors and safes have been put up without a SINGLE COMPLAINT, and offers years' practical experience, during which he has adapted every possible improvement to real security, enables him to challenge competition with any house in London. A large assortment of all sizes on hand and made to order. A pair of extra strong wrought-iron fire-proof folding-doors, with Ventilating grate, made expressly for a banker's strong room, may be Viewed at his manufactory. Strong wrought-iron doors for party walls, with wrought-iron reduced frames, and secured by the BEST DETECTOR LOCKS in ENGLAND, 6 inch high by 3 foot 6 inch wide and upwards, price 10l. each, always on hand at LEADBEATER'S MANUFACTORY, 130, ALDERSGATE-STREET, LONDON.

SNOXELL'S PATENT SAFETY
REVOLVING WOOD SHUTTERS. Manufactory, 98, REGENT-STREET and 197, CHANCERY-LANE. Patent sealed on the 3rd of February, 1849, for Fourteen Years, for improvements in Revolving Shutters of WOOD and IRON, consisting of Six Methods of Raising and Lowering the Shutters, without Machinery, and Two for Hinging and Sheathing the Edges of Wood Laths with Iron.—The Patentee having fixed up some hundreds, will feel pleased in forwarding the Testimonials of Architects, Principals of large Establishments, and others, having them now in use, which fully guarantees the Patentee in stating they are beyond dispute superior in any other Revolving Shutter for durability, security, and simplicity, without the use of cog-wheel worm and lever gear, or any other complicated machinery employed by other makers

BUNNETT and Co., ENGINEERS,
Patentees of
REVOLVING IRON AND WOOD SAFETY SHUTTERS.
and of
ORNAMENTAL METALLIC SASH BARS, MOULDINGS, &c.,
IN BRASS, COPPER, ZINC, &c.
FOR SHOP-FRONTS, SKYLIGHTS, &c.
Bars of work completely fitted and fixed fit in a superior style, either plain or ornamental, also fixed with best plate glass. Having moulded stationes handsomely regarded. Metal works and machinery of all kinds in connection with building houses, shops, warehouses, &c. &c.
B. and Co. challenge competition as to either quality or price.
IMPROVED PATENT BENCH AND FLOORING CRAMPS FOR BUILDERS.
SOLE LICENCEES FOR MARVIN AND MOORE'S PATENT DIAGONAL GRATINGS.
Office of the Patentees, 99, Lombard-street, London; and at the Works, Deptford, Kent.

PROTECTION from FIRE, and GREAT
ECONOMY in BUILDING.—A pamphlet, descriptive of the method by which both these important objects are secured, may be obtained on application to Messrs. FOX and BARRETT, 46, Leicester-square.

HOT-WATER APPARATUS.—The
attention of Architects, builders, and others is respectfully requested to BENJAMIN FOWLER'S superior method of heating churches and chapels, halls, staircases, conservatories, forcing and greenhouses, manufactories, and warehouses, kilns, rooms for drying timber, &c., and every variety of purpose for which artificial heat is required. Within the last twenty years some hundreds of buildings have been heated upon this plan, and the parties for whom they were executed are constantly expressing their satisfaction, also their willingness to vouch for their efficiency.
BENJAMIN FOWLER, late of 63, Dorset-street, removed to the new factory, Whitefriars-street, Fleet-street.

BURRIDGE and HEALY, 130, FLEET-
STREET, LONDON, beg respectfully to inform the Building Public that they fit up COOKING ARRANGEMENTS for large Mansions, with patent appliances on scientific principles, which ensure greater economy and efficiency than hitherto attained. Also HOT WATER APPARATUS upon improved and scientific principles, which they recommend for its peculiar safety for the Warming of Mansions, &c.
They fit up Laundries with Hot Water Apparatus, for Drying in a damp, expeditious, and safe manner. They also fit up BATHS with elegant arrangements, with every modern scientific improvement. Also Apparatus for the plentiful supply of Hot Water for Baths and general Use of Mansions and large establishments.

TO BUILDERS and CARPENTERS.—
Elliptic Staves, double backs, 3d. per inch. Beginners, 4½d 7d., per inch.
Corrugated Staves, with Ovens and Boilers, 3 ft. 3 in. 4to. ; 3 ft. 6 in. 3 ft. 9 in. 4s.
Self-acting Ranges, with Circular Oven and Back Boiler, best Wrought Bars and Bright Fittings.
4s. 6d. 5s. 6d. 4 ft. 4 ft. £1 10s.
Best Patent Got Clasp.
4½d. 5d. 7½d. 10d. 1s. 8d. 1s. 6d per 1,000
3d. 4d. 6d. 8d. 10d. 30d.
Best Sheet Floor Brads, 13s. 6d. per cwt.
Best Torn Gins 84s. 2s. Scotch, 24s per cwt.
Best Patent Sash Line.
4s. 4d. 6s. 6d. 7s. 6d. 10s. 13s. per gross.
At F. E. WILLIAMSON'S IRONMONGERY and STOVE WAREHOUSE, 98, Chiswell-street, Finsbury-square.
Lists of Prices had on application at the Warehouse, or by letter pre-paid, inclosing postage stamp.—Warehouse closes at 7 o'clock.

TO ARCHITECTS, BUILDERS, &c.
HAYWARD, BROTHERS, late
R. HENLY and Co., WHOLESALE IRONMONGERS, and Manufacturers of KITCHEN RANGES, STOVES, &c., 166, Blackfriars-road, and 117, Union-street, Borough.
Strong Self-acting Kitchen Ranges, with Back Boiler and Oven and Wrought Bars :—
3 ft. 3 ft. 6 in. 3 ft. 9 in. 4 ft.
4s. 5s. 6s. £1 per inch.
Henly's Patent Improved, with back Boiler and Wrought Iron Oven :—3 ft. 3 ft. 6 in. 3 ft. 9 in. 4 ft.
4s. 6d. 5s. 7s. 6d. £1 10s. per inch.
Best Register Stoves, at 7d., 8d., and 9d. per inch.
Do. Elliptic do. at 8d., 9d., and 1s. do.
Manufacturer of WOLFARTON'S PATENT REGISTER STOVES, a certain cure for SMOKY CHIMNEYS, and effecting a great saving in fuel. To be seen in use daily.
Orders from the Country, accompanied with a remittance or reference, will meet with prompt attention.

IRON FOUNDRY, 80, Goswell-street (late of
Brick-lane, St. Luke's).—J. JONES having made great additions to his STOCK of PATTERNS, begs to inform the Trade, that he can now supply them with Plain and Ornamental Iron Columns Girders, Railings, Gates, Iron Coping, Balusters, Window Guards, Vernandahs, Ornamental Staircase Panels, Iron Staircases, Tomb Enclosures, Trellis Panelling, Lamp and other Brackets, Cantilevers, Novel Bars, Water Closet Work, Area Gratings, Fly and other Wheels, Wheel Plates, &c.
BAKER'S OVEN WORK, Force Bars and Troughs, Bath Water Pipes and Gutters, Sash Weights, Furnace Bars, Stoves, Ranges, &c., always in stock.

THE GALVANIZED IRON COMPANY,
No. 3, Manchester-court, Call the particular attention of Architects, Builders, and others, to their patent process of galvanizing, or coating iron with PURE ZINC, which, from its action being chemically true, effectually and PERMANENTLY prevents RUST. The process is applicable to all sorts of iron work, whether cast or wrought, to use for building purposes—such as ROOFS, gutters, girders, floors, WATER or GAS PIPES, railings, window sashes and couplers, blinds, skylight frames, chimney cowls, garden screws, trails, locks, keys, chains, wire guards, &c., &c., &c. The Company undertake to supply GALVANIZED IRON, or to GALVANIZE every description of iron work, in any quantity required.—Particulars and prices at the Offices of the Company, 3, Manchester-court, London, or Galvanizing Works, Millwall, Poplar. A. VINCENT, Secretary.
N.B. This Company's patent process is applied to the roofs of the New Houses of Parliament, the sheds in the dockyards at Woolwich, Portsmouth, and Devonport, the Waterloo Station belonging to the London and North-Western Railway Company at Liverpool, and numerous other railway stations, &c., &c, with the most perfect success.

IRON ROOFING WORKS,
SOUTHWARK.
Office.—24, MANSION-HOUSE-PLACE, LONDON.
JOHN H. PORTER,
PATENTEE
Of the Corrugated Iron Beams, Girders, and Fire-proof Floors ;
MANUFACTURER OF IRON ROOFS AND BUILDINGS,
Chiefly of
THE PATENT GALVANIZED IRON.
This material has been employed by J. H. PORTER for several years past in the construction of Iron Roofing for RAILWAY Stations and Docks, for such purposes as those above named FARM BUILDINGS, FACTORIES, GASWORKS, WAREHOUSES, &c., DOCK-HOUSES, MILLS, and OUTBUILDINGS, BYRES, DWELLINGS, and MARKET-PLACES, in the East and West Indies, China, at the Cape of Good Hope, and in other parts of the world ; together with Iron-roof and Strained-wire Fences, Sheep and Cattle Hurdles.

PITT'S PATENT SELF-ADJUSTING
DOOR KNOBS AND LOOSE SPINDLES.

HART and SONS beg to invite the attention of Architects, builders, and others, to their Door Furniture, mounted on PITT'S PATENTED SPINDLES. The knobs are stronger, more durable, and perfectly uniform, than those in ordinary use, as the spindles, being loose, do not require the objectionable side screw. They are more readily fixed, are entirely free from deception of loosening, and, as they adjust themselves to doors of different thickness, without alteration, are particularly adapted for the country or for exportation.
In addition to an extensive stock of door furniture in china, crystal, amber, and opal glass, buffalo horn, flory, ebony, brass, &c., as suited, with finger-plates, bell-pulls, and levers, new patterns of original design are constantly being added, and an order either to sketch or pattern supplied very promptly. A single one, for example, in three days, and a more elaborate one in less than a week.—May be obtained by any ironmonger, or direct from the proprietors and sole manufacturers, HART and SONS Wholesale Ironmongers, 53, 54, 55, Wych-street, Strand, London.
A list of prices sent on application.

THE ARCHITECTS', ENGINEERS',
BUILDERS', OPERATIVES', and ARTISTS' DRAWING ACADEMY, established above forty years, for the study of Architecture, Civil Engineering, &c., with the practical application of Geometry to perspective, mechanical, and mechanical drawing of every description. Conducted by Mr. GRAYSON, architect, surveyor, and civil engineer.—Morning classes from nine till two o'clock daily. Evening classes from six to nine.—For card of terms apply to Mr. GRAYSON'S office, No. 14), Strand, London.

EMERSON'S PATENT LIQUID
CEMENT is ready for use, is simple in its application, and only ONE-EIGHTH the cost of oil paint ; for beauty it is pre-eminent over all other materials used in the coating of houses, giving the exact appearance of FINE CUT STONE ; can be used at once on fresh Roman cement or other plastering ; is particularly calculated for country houses, Villas, or gate entrances that have become soiled or dingy, which can be beautified in any weather, at a trifling cost—Sold in casks of 1, 3, and 5 cwt., at 8s., 10s. and 21s. each.
PATENT MINERAL PAINT.
Invaluable as a coating for SHIPS' SIDES AND BOTTOMS, all kinds of WOOD or METAL work, roofing felts, leaky roofs, spouts and gutters, doors, sheds, milling, and all kinds of out-door work, and being perfectly waterproof, will preserve their surfaces from atmospheric influence and decay, &c.—requires no preparation, and will dry in a few hours.—Sold in casks, 3 to 20 Billions. Brilliant Black, 2s. ; Rich Brown, No.3d. per gallon.
BELL, LEAH, and Co. No. 15, Bishop-lane, Cheapside.

JOHN'S and Co. PATENT STUCCO
CEMENT and PAINT.—GREAT REDUCTION of PRICE. —The Patentees beg to inform the trade and the public generally, that in order to induce a more extended adoption of these excellent materials, and to bring them into direct competition with the inferior articles in common use, they have determined to reduce the price nearly 30 per cent., confidently trusting to a mutually advantageous result. These materials, for their beauty, durability, imperviousness, perfect resistance to frost or heat, and great cheapness, fully justify the confidence reposed in them, as shown by numerous testimonials. For INTERIOR SURFACES this cement possesses the following : materials properly; having no acoustic qualities, it may be painted on or papered within a few days after its application, and in a house may thus be rendered habitable without any delay. In new or hitherto cracks, or vegetable work may become as hard as stone, and may be coated with a brush and water.—Prospectuses, specimens, and every information connected with its use, price, &c., may be obtained from the sole agent, PHILIP HARE, at the Warehouse, 59, Steelyard, Upper Thames-street.

TO PLASTERERS, BUILDERS, &c.
JOHN'S and Co. PATENT PERMANENT
STUCCO WASH.—The attention of the trade is requested to this permanent wash, which cannot be equalled in the properties of beauty and durability for exterior stucco or brick, and being a non-absorbent, is admirably adapted for interior surfaces, for railway stations, union workhouses, schools, asylums, barracks, stables, prisons, &c. It will not wash off, may be tinted to any colour, and 1 cwt. will cover 300 yards.—Price 10s. per cwt. Sole agent, PHILIP HARE, 59, Steelyard, Upper Thames-street.

MARTiN'S PATENT FIRE-PROOF and
ORNAMENTAL CEMENT—REDUCTION of PRICE.—The Patentees beg to inform their Friends and the Public that they have made arrangements which enable them to offer this invaluable cement at a considerably reduced price. It has now been before the public so many years, and has obtained so high a standing in the estimation of all who have used it, that it is unnecessary to comment on its merits. The Patentees, however, feel called upon to observe, that by the use—from the greater amount of surface which a given quantity will cover, and the small amount of labour required in working it, a saving of 30 to 60 per cent. is effected as compared with other cements for internal use. Specimens showing its beauty, hardness, and polish, in plain and ornamental purposes, may be seen ; and the Cement in any quantity obtained of the Patentees, Messrs STEVENS and SON, at their Plaster and Cement Works, 136, Drury-lane, London.—Agent for Liverpool,
Mr. GEORGE NEWTON, No. 4, Lawton-street, field-street.

KEENE'S and PARIAN CEMENTS,
for internal stucco, are employed Very advantageously in place of wood for skirtings, architraves, and panel mouldings, and for internal flooring instead of stone. The peculiar properties of PARIAN Cement allow of its being painted or papered upon within a few hours of its application, and thus render it an important substitute for common plastering in those cases where expedition and beauty of finish are essential.—J. B. WHITE and SONS, Millbank-street, Westminster, Exclusive of KEENE'S Cement. Licensees of PARIAN Cement.

PORTLAND CEMENT, as manufactured
by J. B. WHITE and SONS, possesses all the properties of the best Roman Cement, but has the advantage after that material of being possessing that, if it be put once and it be once again of more durability and requires no colouring. Employed as an hydraulic mortar for bridges, or as four to five measures of sand to one of cement, and is proved by trial to become harder and stronger in those proportions than Roman Cement with but one measure of sand. This superior quality being useful, with the tenacity of building an ends of embankment walls, the lining of reservoirs, cisterns, and baths, and for all wise purposes where strength and a perfect resistance to water are required.
Manufacturers.—J. B. WHITE and SON, Millbank-street, Westminster, and 56, Seel-street, Liverpool.

PORTLAND CEMENT, solely
MANUFACTURED by WILLIAM ASPDIN, Son of the Patentee.—Messrs. ROBINS, ASPDIN, and Co. request reference to No. 906, page 491, and also Nos. 344 and 346, page 545 and 561 of "The Builder," for accounts of EXPERIMENTS on the strength of Portland Cements, whereby the great superiority of their Cement is manifest. This Cement has been proved for upwards of twenty years in the Thames Tunnel to resist the action of water ; is stronger in its cementitious qualities, harder, and more durable than any other description of Cement ; it does not vegetate, crumble, or turn green ; nor is it affected by any atmospheric influence whatever the climate, resisting like the action of sand and water, &c., so far it is manufactured to set up from five to sixty measures. For all purposes where a proper quantity of Portland Cement is requisite, enables the Proprietors challenge competition.—Orders received by Messrs. ROBINS, ASPDIN, and Company at their Manufactory, Northfleet, Kent, and their Wharf Great Scotland-yard, Whitehall ; also by their Agent at the Depôt, 1, Back Queen-street, Liverpool.

GREAVES'S BLUE LIAS LIME,
WARWICKSHIRE CEMENT, and WARWICKSHIRE IMPROVED CEMENT, at RUTTY and VEREY, 3, South Wharf, Paddington ; and W. and T. N. OLADDISH, Pickford's-, Lambeth. The present low rates of cement enable the proprietors to send to any part of the kingdom at very moderate prices, from all works, Southam, Warwickshire.

ATKINSON'S CEMENT.—This Cement
has hitherto been manufactured in Yorkshire, and, through long detention at sea, has often proved stale and unfit for its arrival in London. By the arrangement now made, the Cement will be manufactured in London, and thus prevent its getting in a fresh and serviceable state, by the mile. J. B. WHITE and SONS, Millbank-street, Westminster.

PARIAN CEMENT, for internal stucco,
instead of common plastering, may be painted and papered within twenty hours of its application to the bare walls and by the use of which, rooms may be rendered habitable before the surface commonly adopted would begin to dry. It is worked without the slightest difficulty, the labour being small and less expensive than with any other stucco whatever. A finer quality is also prepared for ornamental plastering, for capitals, mouldings, &c. &c.—Specimens of which may be seen at the works of the Proprietors, CHAS FRANCIS and SONS, Nine Elms, London.

TO THE BUILDING PUBLIC.
FIRST-RATE ORNAMENTS in
PORTLAND, ROMAN and other CEMENTS, also PLASTER of PARIS, at reasonable prices, consisting of Vases, Balustrades, Capitals, perforated Panellings, Cantilevers, Trusses, Crests, Wreaths, Scrolls, Masques, Shields, Figures, Friezes, Gothic and other Chimney Shafts, Soffits, Balustres, Patera, &c. &c. Centre Flowers from 10 feet diameter downwards. An assortment of Shop-front Trusses always in stock.—HERBERT and SON, Modellers, &c., 43, Parker-street, Drury-lane.

The Builder.

No. CCCLI.

'ATURDAY, OCTOBER 27, 1849.

THE late frightful loss of life in the Kenilworth-street sewer involves circumstances which affect the whole community, and, as might have been ex- cted, has greatly excited a large portion of The number of letters we have received on e subject, were there no other evidence of e excitement we allude to, would suffice to ove it,—letters calling on us to do all sorts impossible and unjust things, and in the ajority of cases calculated to work a great nount of injury to individuals and property, d very little public good.

The inquiry before the coroner has been rsued very rigorously: it occupied three ng days, very contradictory evidence was ven, and much personal feeling evinced. We ust give, briefly, some few particulars.

Warwick-street and Kenilworth-street are o rising and incomplete streets in a new strict now taking shape under the hands of r. Thomas Cubitt, adjoining the Grosvenor anal, not far from Vauxhall-bridge-road, and herein a large amount of capital has already en invested. Warwick-street has a sewer mmunicating at one end, by a side street, ith the Grosvenor Canal (as the means of ushing), and discharging itself into the ing's Scholars' Pond sewer, in Vauxhall- idge-road. Kenilworth-street, wherein there e but six houses and three of these unin- bited, runs into Warwick-street at an angle, d has a sewer that will ultimately discharge elf into the Thames. At present, however, it built only to the extent of the land likely to immediately brought into use, where it is osed by a brick wall, and finds vent into the arwick-street sewer.*

The metropolitan sewers, as our readers ow, are very properly not permitted to run e into another at right angles, but by a *curved nction*, so as to throw the subsidiary stream to the line of the main current. Had the in- nded permanent discharge of the Kenilworth- reet sewer been into the Warwick-street sewer, e junction would have been thus formed; it, as we have said, this was not the case, and order that a body of water might be brought to the former from the canal, by means of e Warwick-street sewer, the connection rved the other way, so as to *meet* the current, d, as a matter of course, would receive a por- n of the sewage flowing down the Warwick- reet sewer, if there were no flap, or other me- anical arrangement to prevent it;—and ere was not. This was the "reversed junc- n," concerning which so much has been id.

Now, it was in the butt-ended sewer in 'arwick-street that the poor men found their ath; and when Messrs. John Phillips and otto, the commissioners' officers, went to in- ire into the accident, they found, on examining e trench which had been opened over the crown the sewer, two layers of lime refuse used purifying gas, and were led to deny that the emanations from the sewage were, "by any possibility," the cause of the accident, and to attribute it to gas emanating from this lime refuse, and carried down into the sewer by the percolation of surface water. Dr. Ure analyzed the lime refuse and the deposit in the sewer, and agreed with them in attributing the poisonous gases in the sewer, which he said included "*prussic acid, or sulphocyanogen, poisons*," to "the layer of gas lime imprudently shot as a filling-up rubbish over the sewer."*

Our general remarks last week will show what credence we gave to this theory. The tendency of it, together with Mr. Phillips's evidence, was to shift the blame on to anybody's shoulders but those of the officers of the commission, and Mr. Cubitt found it not merely to fall on his, but by inference to threaten serious injury to the estate. It was proved that the sewers were better built than in many other places; had been constructed wholly under the direction of the commissioners; that he had now no control over them whatever, could not even enter them, and that his tenants paid rates for their maintenance and repair. He felt it too bad, then, we are imagining, that any injurious imputation should rest on him. At the adjourned inquest, therefore, he brought down Mr. William Allen Miller, Professor of Chemistry at King's College; Mr. Dugald Campbell, Demonstrator of Chemistry at University College; and Mr. Phillips, Chemist and Curator of the Museum of Practical Geology, who completely disproved the assertion that the gas refuse was the cause of the disaster, asserted that *no prussic acid or cyanogen compounds* could be detected in the sewer, and wound up a joint written report, which they put in, by saying,—

"In conclusion, we beg to express our decided conviction that the deaths in question were occasioned by the presence of sulphuretted hydrogen, generated from the ordinary contents of sewers in a state of stagnation, and the absence of a sufficient quantity of atmospheric air, and that the lime waste had nothing to do with the accident in question; also that its presence in the road materials, as described, can be in no way prejudicial to health. We wish to add, that if the precaution had been taken of ventilating the sewer, and of destroying the noxious gases by the introduction of chlorine gas, no loss of life would have been occasioned."

Beyond this, Dr. Lyon Playfair (of whom, by the way—such is fame!—the worthy coroner, Bedford, had never heard, calling him "Fairplay," and everything but Tiger instead of Lyon), came down on the part of the commissioners of sewers themselves, to their credit be it said, and, in a piece of singularly clear and logical evidence, disproved at once and for ever the "refuse theory," admitting, however, that to a person not a chemist, the *à priori* idea that the gas lime had caused the mischief was a very probable one.†

The jury, after an hour and a half's consultation, found that the deceased men "died from the inhalation of noxious gas generated in a neglected and unventilated sewer situate in Kenilworth-street;" and added, "the jury unanimously consider the commissioners and officers of the metropolitan sewers are much to blame for having neglected to avail themselves of the unusual advantages offered from the local situation of the Grosvenor canal for the purpose of flushing the sewers in this district."

We should not discharge our duty if we failed to protest against the tone adopted towards Mr. Phillips, both by Mr. Cubitt's able solicitor, Mr. Hopgood, who allowed feeling on this occasion to swamp his usual good taste, and, with much less excuse, by one of the jury. We allude to it for the sake of other witnesses who may be in the same position, but say nothing further, as both gentlemen withdrew their observations. Phillips made a great mistake in persisting in the assertion, that there could be no great accumulation of refuse from house drainage in the fatal sewer because there were only three inhabited houses in the street which drained into it, although reminded of the reversed junction, which must *necessarily* take into the sewer a large amount of sewage that would deposit before it flowed out again. Moreover, the miserable state of the Warwick-street sewer was well known. We find it thus described in the "Descriptive Report of the State of the Sewers in the Westminster District," for the subterranean survey, under the date Sept. 2, 1848:—"Kenilworth-street.—Has two feet of deposit, and the smell so bad that the leveller's watch turned quite black in an hour!" The wonder is, that the poor leveller was not himself levelled. On this occa-

---

* The sewer in Kenilworth-street is of brickwork, 418 t in length, 4 feet high by 2 feet 6 inches wide, and is a rtion of a sewer, leave to build which was granted by the nmissioners in November, 1847. It was built in January, 18.

* We understand that the quantity of gas lime interspersed with the other materials in the piece of road 418 feet in length, is about twenty cart loads of gas lime to about 5,000 of other materials.

† Dr. Playfair said:—"On the crown of the sewer, below the lower layer of gas lime, there is a layer of clayey earth, and this contains iron; then comes a layer of gas lime, above that again another layer of clay, in some places coming up to the upper layer of gas lime—in others mixed with a layer of sand, and then above all a layer of clay. The upper layer of gas lime gives to water a solution of sulphuret, with other compounds, which do not enter into this inquiry. This solution of sulphuret, under certain conditions, produces sulphuretted hydrogen—as, for example, by the action of carbonic acid dissolved in rain water. The lower layer of gas lime does not contain a trace of a sulphuret, that is, nothing that could produce this sulphuret of hydrogen or anything injurious to life. It contains a small trace of cyanide—the substance which is supposed to produce prussic acid. I then proceeded to ascertain if there was any evidence of percolation of the soluble substance to the strata below from the upper bed of gas refuse. I first found that, on mixing the earth with water, no soluble sulphuret was obtained. That showed that there was no soluble sulphuret below the gas lime; but I found that there was evidence of a percolation downwards of this soluble sulphuret; and my proofs are these:—I observed that, immediately under the upper layer of gas lime, where it was in junction with the clay, the clayey earth was exceedingly black, and that this blackness decreased as I went downwards. The further away from the upper layer of gas lime, the less black did it become, and I found that this blackness was owing to the presence of sulphuret of iron, which the soluble sulphuret had formed by acting on the iron in the clay. By digesting this black substance in an acid, abundance of sulphuret of hydrogen was produced, and there was much more from the upper portion than from that beneath. The acid which I used was muriatic acid, for with carbonic acid there would be no evolution of sulphuretted hydrogen. I then examined the clayey earth on the top of the sewer, in order to ascertain if there was evidence of the sulphuret reaching so far. In certain parts I found a small quantity; in certain other parts I did not find a trace. I therefore thought it possible that the soluble sulphuret, percolating the soil from the upper stratum of gas lime, might be deprived of its noxious properties by the iron in the clay, and proceeded to put this to the test of experiment. I took a strong solution of sulphuret from the sewer-water, on the supposition that if it took its sulphuret from the soluble sulphuret of calcium it must pass through the clay without being arrested by it. I accordingly took the sewer-water and filtered it through the lowest bed of clay—that is to say, I made an artificial filter, by placing some of the earth of the clay in a filter, and mixing it with the water from the sewer. I then took the clear liquid which was filtered through, to see if it contained any sulphuret. I mixed some white lead with the filtered sewage water, and the white lead has, as the jury will see, been turned black by the presence of the sulphuret. I then took the same sewage-water which gave this black colour, and filtered it through a portion of the lowest bed of clay, and found that it was entirely deprived of sulphuret, and that white lead put into it was not blackened. I found that the whole of it was taken up by the iron in the clay, and that none had passed through in solution. I then thought it probable that the iron in the soil had arrested the sulphuret in its passage; but it was necessary to have confirmatory tests of this. I took a portion of the sulphuret in the sewer, and filtered it, and on putting some of the mortar therein I found that it became of a green colour from a portion of iron in the mortar. I carefully examined the mortar round the bricks in the sewer, in order to see if this green colour was produced, and I did not find the slightest trace of it. I then put the matter to a further test. If the cyanic compounds found in the gas refuse had filtered into the sewer-water, I should find them still in the sewer-water, because there could be no prussic acid present. There was in this sewer-water an excess of ammonia, and prussic acid and ammonia are incompatible. The cyanide of ammonia would be present, but not prussic acid. To determine this point, I examined a portion of the sewer-water taken up in my presence. Another portion was furnished by Mr. Phillips, but in neither could I find a trace of any compound of cyanogen. Thus, then, to recapitulate, there was the evidence that there was a percolation of sulphuret from the upper layer of gas lime; that it was arrested by the iron, and could not pass through the lower layer of clay without being taken up, and that the mortar in the bricks of the sewer was not coloured. Lastly, there the evidence that there was no compound of cyanogen in th water; from all which facts I draw the conclusion that the gas lime had nothing to do with the sulphuret in the sewer."

sion, however, if we are rightly informed, the wall at the end of the sewer was knocked down to give air.

The descriptive report, to which we have alluded, gives a fearful picture of the sewers generally in the Westminster district, and we must quote a few lines of it, to prevent the possible inference, from the short extract Just given, that the new neighbourhood of which we are speaking is in any degree worse than other places.

In the Knightsbridge sewer, near the end of Sloane-street, "the deposit is so great, and the stench so strong, that one of the men came out in a fainting state." Lowndes-place, "one to two feet of deposit." Esher-street, "two feet of deposit." Oxford-street, "on the north side from Portman-street, westward, in so ruinous a state as to be in danger of falling. * * * Must be nearly choked with deposit before it can have any discharge." Whitehall-place, "wretched state. * * * Two or three feet deposit." Tothill-street and Westminster Workhouse, indescribable. St.George's-square, "one to two feet of putrid matter." Chesterfield-street, "so filled with deposit that portions of them cannot be perambulated." Parliament-street, "nearly filled with deposit —smell horrible;" and so from bad to worse. And "even throughout the new Paddington district, the neighbourhood of Hyde-park Gardens, and the costly squares and streets adjacent, the sewers abound with the foulest deposit, from which the most disgusting efflu-vium arises."

One of our correspondents, "Philo Medi-cus," asks, "of what avail are such expensive reports, if nothing of a practical nature be to follow? In this district of the Pimlico sewers, the commissioners appear to have most ample and easy means of dushing and cleansing at their disposal, by a communication with the water of Grosvenor Canal. How are the public to be reconciled to the want of attention on the part of the commissioners, with such easy appliances at hand, that could almost at any time be made to cleanse most effectually all the sewers in this particular locality?"

Another wishes to know how the present state of the sewers and the enormous sums paid by the public for flushing (and concerning which some inquiry must yet take place), are to be reconciled. We will not, however, now enter on this inquiry.

The absence of gully-holes in the closed-up sewer was not sufficiently dwelt upon at the inquest; there were none, excepting two near the junction with the Warwick-street sewer, and these, if we understand rightly, are trapped. Serious as are the evils of open gullies, they must not be trapped under present arrange-ments, without the provision of other means of ventilation, so long as it is necessary for men to go into the sewers.

Mr. Phillips stated, in his evidence, that formerly the commissioners put in the gully-holes, but, according to the recent regulations, Mr. Cubitt was bound to do so. But we are told, in reply to personal inquiry, that Mr. Cubitt's people have never put any in, leaving the matter wholly in the hands of the com-missioners. If there had been two open gullies next the butt-end of the sewer, we should probably not have had to record this sad disaster.

We earnestly hope that the distressing occurrence which has brought from us these remarks may lead to immediate steps for per-manent improvement. The effect of the direful gases evolved by decomposing animal and vegetable matter is seen when, in a concen-trated form, they kill with lightning speed. But it is not alone when this is the case that the foe requires repulse. Even when diluted, although (the result not being so speedy, the connection not being so apparent) the real cause may remain unguessed at.

We would direct attention to a communica-tion on another page in advocacy of the pro-posed Building Artificers' Provident Society.

OAK STALLS.
STA. SALUTE, VENICE.

THE church of Sta. Salute was built by Baldassare Longhena, pursuant to a decree of the Senate in 1632, after the cessation of the great pestilence, in which 60,000 of the inhabitants are said to have died. The annexed engraving represents one of the carved divisions which form the lower range of stalls in the tribune at the east end.

The carving is similar in style to that seen in the stalls of St. Giorgio Maggiore, and much resembles it also in character. These stalls were executed by a Flemish artist, as we may judge from an inscription on one of the divisions, and were completed about thirty-four years before the building of Sta. Salute.

EXAMPLE TO EMPLOYERS.—WORKMEN'S NEWS AND READING-ROOMS.—Messrs. T. Hoyle and Sons, says the *Manchester Specta-tor*, have converted one of their own spacious dwellings into decorated and commodious reading-rooms, for the work people at their print works at Mayfield. The principal room is furnished with a selection of newspapers and periodicals, and adorned with great maps on Mercator's projection, &c. A smoking-room has been provided, and chess and draught boards, &c., supplied. By an attendant ap-pointed by the people themselves, hot coffee, tobacco, and cooling beverages, at cost price, are supplied before work hours in the morning, as well as throughout the day. One evening in the week the principal apartment is devoted to musical and other innocent or rational entertainments.

CARVED STALL, STA. SALUTE, VENICE.

SOUTH-EAST VIEW OF THE CHURCH OF ST. DUNSTAN-IN-THE-EAST, TOWER-STREET, LONDON.

THERE are but few ancient ecclesiastical buildings left us within the walls of the City. The churches which escaped the destructive flames of the year 1666, may be soon reckoned. The *dismal fire*, as it is called in the manuscript records of St. Dunstan-in-the-East, made cruel havoc with many a "beautiful house" where our fathers worshipped. Still, though we no longer behold the identical old fabric, within whose hallowed walls the merchants of by-gone days, when merchants were as princes, offered up their prayers and praises, we have churches on their original sites, and even on the former foundations. The "fair and large church" of St. Dunstan, which was well nigh destroyed by the fire of London in 1666, gave place to a building by Sir Christopher Wren, in which he tried his hand at the Gothic style of architecture. The elegant tower and spire shown in the engraving are his. The details of these, it is unnecessary to say, are question-able. The body of the church is of modern construction. There is a tradition, that the plan of the tower and spire, suggested by St. Nicholas, at Newcastle, was furnished by the daughter of the great City architect, Jane Wren, who died in 1702, aged 26, and was buried under the choir of St. Paul's Cathedral. And if female talent was thus enlisted in the production of the airy spire before us, female benevolence was not wanting in the comple-tion of the structure. To the honour of Lady Dionysia Williamson's memory be it told, that she, in 1670, gave 4,000l. (an enormous sum in those days) towards the building. On the occasion of the dreadful storm which raged in London through the night of the 26th Novem-ber, 1703, until the morning, Wren, on hear-ing that some of the steeples and pinnacles in the City had suffered serious injury, observed that he felt sure of finding St. Dunstan's tower and spire secure.

In 1817, the walls having bulged, it was de-termined to rebuild the body of the church. The architect employed was Mr. David Laing. He, with the active assistance of Mr. Wm. Tite, now known as the architect of the Royal Exchange, erected the present fabric, which was opened in January, 1821. It is con-structed of Portland stone, and is a very fair specimen for that period, of the style of Gothic architecture termed "Perpendicular." The principal entrance is from the north-east, by a

ST. DUNSTAN'S-IN-THE-EAST, LONDON.

porch with a groined ceiling ; there is another entrance at the west-end beneath the tower. The extreme length, from the western entrance to the east wall, is 115 feet ; the breadth is 65 feet 6 inches; the height 40 feet. There is room for between 600 and 700 persons. The interior is good as a whole ; and a harmony of appearance has been preserved in the several parts. There are three aisles of nearly equal width, divided by slender clustered columns, and pointed arches of stone. The only gallery is that at the west-end for the organ, and for the children of the Tower Ward Charity School. The east window corresponds in size and details with the window of the ancient church (before the fire). The painting in this window (by the late Mr. Backler), describes symbolically the Law and the Gospel. On each side of this is a stained window, lately executed by Mr. E. Baillie. That on the north side represents "Christ blessing little children." The subject of the south window is the Adoration of the Magi. The higher compartments of the windows of the south aisles are occupied by the armorial bearings of ancient benefactors of the parish, with scrolls containing suitable inscriptions from the Bible. These are also Mr. Baillie's work.

The Custom-House, and a portion of the New "Coal Exchange," are situate in the parish of St. Dunstan in the East. Both these buildings are in the immediate neighbourhood of the Church.

Some of our readers may probably have noticed the rooks which build in the trees in the south church-yard. The rookery before the last church was removed, consisted of upwards of twenty nests ; and they were annually supplied with osier twigs, and other

---

* The Coal Exchange is to be opened by her gracious Majesty on the 31st. A good view of the interior of this building will be found, page 461, *ante.*

materials for building. The colony migrated to the Tower of London, when disturbed for the pulling down of the church in 1817, and built in the White Tower, but returned afterwards, as soon as the noise of axes and hammers had ceased. At this day their little building-materials are hospitably provided for them by Mr. Crutchley, the assistant-overseer. The rector of this parish is the Rev. T. B. Murray, M.A.

RESPONSIBILITIES AND RIGHTS OF ARCHITECTS AND BUILDERS.
HOW THEY MANAGE THESE MATTERS IN FRANCE.

THE discussion which has arisen relative to the remuneration for Mr. Barry's services in designing and superintending the works of the Houses of Parliament has very naturally excited much attention amongst all parties directly or indirectly connected with the profession. But the clearest conclusion to be drawn from all that has been said or written thereupon seems to be, that we, in England, have no principles of legislation, no well-defined system, either as regards an architect's responsibility or the amount of retribution he is entitled to claim. This being the case, an account of the French law upon the subject may be useful. It is far from perfect; but it were much to be desired that our legislators should trace, in a somewhat similar manner, the rights and duties of the members of, perhaps, the noblest of the civil professions.

A proprietor, or any party about to build, is supposed by the French law, and in fact is obliged, to deal with one of the three parties connected with construction, either with the architect, the builder, or the workmen. Sometimes a building is directed by an architect, who employs a builder to erect the construction, by means of the workmen under his

orders ; sometimes the builder and his workmen execute the work without an architect ; sometimes the workmen are under the orders of an architect without the intermission of the builder ; or again, the proprietor may employ the workmen without the aid of either the architect or the builder. The guarantee of the solidity of the work then becomes of a different character, according to the different circumstances ; the responsibility varies also, as likewise the claim to remuneration.

We will consider the subject under the following heads :—

Firstly.—When the architects simply furnish the plans and estimates and specifications.

Secondly.—When they supply designs, &c., and also superintend the execution of the works.

Thirdly.—When they verify and settle the accounts.

Fourthly.—The position of builders under an architect's orders, and also their responsibility as to materials, &c.

Fifthly.—The position of those who work without architects : and

Sixthly.—The position of the workmen who either work for or independently of the builder.

Firstly, then,—" Of the rights and responsibilities of an architect who merely furnishes plans, specifications, &c."

An architect is he who makes the plans of a building, by whomsoever executed. Under the name " plans " are comprised all the drawings of the object to be built, whether considered horizontally, in elevation, in section, or in details for the execution of the ornamentation. The specification is the detailed account of the works, with an explanation of the mode of executing the separate parts, such as the masonry, carpentry, joinery, smith's work, &c. The estimate contains the quantities of each sort of work, and the separate price of each article.

The Civil Code is silent as to the remuneration to be paid to the architect for furnishing such plans and estimates, as it is likewise upon the whole subject of his remuneration. The article 1793, indeed, places the relations between the architect and the proprietor in the condition of a hiring of services (*louage d'ouvrage*). Now in all such cases the consideration may be either a matter for special agreement, or, in default of such, it is regulated by the custom of the locality. Should a written agreement have been made to settle the respective conditions of the contracting parties, and should any new or unforeseen circumstances arise during the execution of the work, these last are regulated by the usual custom, without in any way affecting the previous agreement. It is considered to be the duty of the proprietor to ascertain the existence of these supplementary conditions: the fact of his allowing a commencement of execution, is held to be a tacit acceptance of his own new obligations. In fine, such contracts are regarded as a portion of natural law (*un contrat du droit des gens*), and are not subjected by the civil code to any definite form, to insure their enforcement; they are regulated by the principles of natural equity in all cases where the special agreement, or the text of the law, is silent.

In Paris the usage is to pay 5 per cent. for furnishing the drawings and specifications, for superintending the execution, and settling the accounts for the different works. We are not quite certain as to the subdivision of this sum; but, if we are not mistaken, the furnishing of the drawings and specification only is paid for at the rate of 2½ per cent.; the superintendence at 1½ per cent.; the measuring and settling of the accounts at 1 per cent. of the value of the works; all office expenses, and payments for clerks of the works (!), being at the cost, or charge, of the architect. The large public works are paid for by fixed salaries per annum, to the architects; an allowance is made for office expenses; and the superintendence is paid for separately. We will revert hereafter to the consideration of this system, and its practical results, as also to that of the conditions, implied or expressed, of the agreement between the architect and the proprietor.

When the architect has furnished the plans and specifications, but does not superintend, he becomes responsible to the proprietor for any accident resulting from the indications contained in the said documents; but, of course, his responsibility ceases there. Thus, he is not liable to any damages caused by the bad execution of the works; but only to such as are the necessary consequences of the plans and directions he has given; for example,

Suppose that, from any motive, A. builds by workmen, and superintends, himself, any construction upon the plans and specification of an architect; after having faithfully observed all the details as to the dimensions of the walls, the quality of the materials, &c., if the construction appear likely to fall during the first ten years, either totally or in part, A. has a claim against the architect. Upon his demand, two "experts" are named, who examine whether he has in all cases followed the plans and specifications; and upon their decision, an action may be commenced. Such actions, however, are very rare.

In this case the architect is not responsible for the defects of the soil; he is authorized to presume that it is of a sufficiently resisting nature to support the building. The person who executes the works assumes this risk; whether it be the proprietor who executes, or a contractor. Nor is the architect responsible for any infraction of the laws which regulate the rights of neighbours, or of the municipal or police regulations.

Secondly.—"Of the responsibilities of the architect who directs the constructions after furnishing the plans."

Beyond the legal obligation by which an architect is bound to possess the abilities and instruction necessary for the preparation of the plans and specification, if he be intrusted with the carrying out of his own design, he becomes responsible for the faithful execution of the works; for it is he who undertakes to give the workmen proper instructions as to the kinds of materials to be employed, the manner of using them, and the dimensions of the separate parts. If the builder, or his workmen, deceive him in such a manner as to induce an impartial person to believe that, with proper caution, the architect might have detected the fraud, he naturally becomes responsible; but he has his recourse against the said parties. But if the deceit were of such a nature as to defy ordinary inspection, then he is exonerated, and the responsibility lies only with those who have been guilty of the fraud.

If any part of the building, or the whole of it, fails, within ten years of the completion of the work, either from defective construction, a defect of the foundation, or neglect in the execution, the architect firstly, and subsidiarily the builder, are responsible. Moreover, as nothing of importance ought to be executed without his orders, any infraction of the laws regulating the rights of neighbours, or of the municipal or police regulations, exposes him (the architect) to a claim for damages. Nor, in this case, would the proprietor be obliged to attack anybody but the architect; for it was his duty to superintend the work so closely as to prevent any serious breach of the above-named laws and regulations. These obligations on the part of the architect result clearly from article 1792 of the Civil Code; the duration of the guarantee for ten years is fixed by the art. 2270. The right of a neighbour to attack the proprietor in case of loss, damage, or injury, results from the text of art. 1386. The proprietor then has his recourse against the party he employs.

Thirdly.—"Of the responsibilities of the architect who verifies and settles the accounts."

When an architect has directed the works, he is charged with the settlement of the accounts. If the proprietor pay any money without the certificate of the architect, he, by that fact, releases the latter from his responsibility, for he takes from him the only efficient mode of controlling the execution of the works by the builder. But this release only extends so far as the defects arise from bad execution; if the building fail from improper construction in a purely scientific point of view, the architect is still liable.

If an architect be merely called in to affix a just value upon works executed, he is only bound to fix such prices as are fair and reasonable, according to the tariff of the locality, and according to the qualities of the materials furnished, or the workmanship executed. He is not in any way responsible for the execution or the solidity of the work; but it is his duty to make a report, if he observe that the laws either of the art of building, or even the municipal laws, have been violated in such a manner as to involve serious consequences. The obligation in this case is simply to render strict justice to both parties.

Fourthly.—"Of the position of builders under an architect's orders; and also their responsibility as to materials, &c."

Occasionally architects, renouncing the consideration due to their profession, become builders. At times, also, the builders become architects; but this rarely occurs for constructions of importance, because the time and attention required for the preparation of the plans are greater than a builder can afford to bestow. In either case, the party who accumulates the functions contracts the responsibilities which attach to both.

Although the direction of the works be confided to an architect, the builder or contractor is still bound to the proprietor by a contract for the hire of his services,—which is defined by the article 1710 of the Civil Code as an engagement to execute a work upon receiving a sum of money. This contract may be made with the understanding that the contractor shall only give his labour and talent; or, he may agree to furnish the materials.—Article 1787.

When an architect is engaged to direct the works confided to a builder or contractor, the engagement of this latter implies, at least, the condition that, in all cases in which he can legally do so, he is faithfully to follow the directions he may receive, so that the building may be executed as designed. In order that the builder be perfectly secure against any claim in consequence of changes introduced during the execution of the works, it is necessary for him to have all such alterations ordered in writing. Any verbal orders given b the architect are only supposed to warrant th builder in so far as they are conformable t the rules of art; and, by extension of thi principle, if a builder execute any work with out plans, specifications, or written instruc tions, he alone is responsible during the te years of the guarantee. In fact, nothing ex isted to prevent his taking proper measures t secure the stability of the work; the conse quences of the failure, then, justly fall upo him. Should the architect, in his plans o specifications, demand any new mode of con struction, or indicate any works likely to in volve an infraction of the rights of the neigh bourhood, or of the municipal or polic regulations, it is the duty of the builder t point out the objections to their adoption. Hi responsibility is covered if he obtain a distinc written order *ad hoc*, mentioning that it was given with the express intention of safeguarding his rights. The intervention of the proprietor is also necessary, for his claim against the builder cannot be alienated without his consent; and even after all these precautions, the builder is still liable to be pursued by the municipal authorities in case the works contain infractions of their laws, either as affecting public health or the security of the buildings. No private convention, in fact, is allowed to interfere with the public rights: *Privatorum pactis juri publico derogari non potest*. Nor can the builder plead ignorance of these laws, for he is bound to know all the obligations attached to his position, amongst which the municipal regulations are the most important as well as the most easily ascertained. The old Roman law, which in this case is still retained, lays down the principles that "*magna negligentia culpa est*," and "*culpa lata est, non intelligere quod omnes intelligunt*." The public authorities, therefore, can pursue the parties who are the most likely to be in a position to insure the fulfilment of their regulations; but they still retain a claim against all the parties concerned in the infractions. A builder should, then, in self-defence, distinctly refuse to execute any works which may place him in such positions.

The responsibility of the builder, as to the quality of the materials supplied, results necessarliy from the condition of his undertaking with the proprietor. The reception by the architect in nowise exonerates him; for it might happen, either that the architect did not superintend the execution with sufficient attention, or that he had been deceived, or that he had entered into an understanding with the builder. In neither of these cases would it be just that the proprietor should suffer from the faults of those in whom he places his confidence. The law, then, gives him a claim upon both architect and builder, so that he may pursue the party who is the more likely to be in a position to insure his obtaining speedy justice. Should the bad quality of the materials be such as the ordinary care of the architect could not detect, the latter has a claim upon the builder; for he is, in fact, in the condition of a merchant, who, by article 1641 of the Civil Code, is responsible for the hidden defects of the goods sold. But the conditions under which a builder contracts differ so far from a common sale, that, as he undertakes to execute work, he is responsible not only for the hidden, but also for the apparent defects of the materials necessary for the completion of the building.

If the proprietor furnish any portion of the materials to be employed, and the builder recognize in them such defects as to render them unfit for the purpose, he is bound to call the attention of the proprietor thereto; nor is he released from his responsibility unless he obtain a written order containing a discharge thencefrom.

We must break off here, till next week.

Caution to Brickmakers.—At Wolverhampton lately, the owner of a brickyard was fined in the mitigated penalty of 50*l*. for allowing his tenant or manager to remove bricks to the kilns before the proper duty had been levied on them. The owner was quite ignorant of the fraud, being supplied by the party making the bricks at a certain rate per 1,000 including duty. In another case of a similar kind nearly 14,000 bricks were forfeited, and a penalty of 50*l*. inflicted.

PROPOSED BUILDING ARTIFICERS' PROVIDENT SOCIETY.

THE scheme of the Building Artificers' Provident and Benevolent Society, propounded by the professor of architecture, and so ably advocated by yourself on the 15th ult., is already justified in every man's breast; but we want such statistics and practical views as shall no less justify it to his head, and satisfy those of your readers who regard it rather as a *beau ideal* than an attainable good, and take fright at its apparent magnitude and difficulty. I am glad to find that your invitations to correspondents on this subject have not been in vain, though the valuable letter of Mr. Grant on the 29th ult., so confirmatory of the success of deferred annuities, is the only one which has appeared in your columns. The following, gathered from the "Report on the Friendly Societies' Bill," by a committee of the House last year, and other sources, may be acceptable to your readers.

The Architects' and Builders' Insurance Society estimates the number of persons connected with building, at 800,000 throughout the United Kingdom. The Builders' Benevolent Society estimate those in and about the metropolis at 300,000; probably including families also. The "Directory" gives us 785 capitalist builders in London, 678 architects and surveyors; 161 civil engineers, and 245 mechanical engineers. Such is the host on which we have to operate, and such the materials, in knowledge, skill, influence, and numbers.

The probable success of such a scheme may be illustrated by that of Mr. Biers, who, with able seconds, in less than two years, has created the Builders' Benevolent Society; at this moment endowed with 1,200*l.* stock, and in November to award five annual pensions, amounting to 120*l.* At their first dinner the sum of 600*l.* was raised.

A few weeks ago 11,000*l.* were raised by a bazaar at Liverpool, in three days, for the relief of a hospital. The annual dinners at Freemasons'-hall, for the numberless charities meeting there during the year, raise an astonishing revenue. To a justifiable claim, fairly put forth, John Bull is ever ready to yield, and "his hand, open as day to melting charity," willingly pours forth its abundance.

How entirely this claim is justified, appears from the "evidence" that there are from 13,000 to 14,000 friendly societies, producing about 6,000,000*l.* annually; and by so much, in consequence, diminishing the poor's-rates. Of this great number it is melancholy to be assured by the first actuaries of the country, "that the majority are insolvent," "that the clubs throughout the country are almost universally broken up," "that nothing can save the old societies," "that this deplorable state of things has arisen from ill constructed tables;"—"from peculation which often *the law cannot touch;*" from strikes and trades unions in which artificers have been tyrannically compelled to subscribe 2s. 6d. per week: the loss to the artificers in Liverpool alone, during eighteen weeks' turn out, in 1833, (on the respectable authority of Mr. Holmes) amounted to 45,000*l.*;—"from competition of benefit societies," unauthorized by opinions of actuaries or Government confirmation, and got up by interested publicans, who have in some cases three and four under their direction;—a fertile source of failure. In fact, we scarcely meet an artificer of sixty years old who has not for many years paid contributions for benefits which he ought now in his age to enjoy, but which have lamentably disappeared; leaving him to the pawnbroker for a time, and, lastly, to the workhouse.

Amongst the many reasons for this deplorable state of clubs, is undoubtedly the fact, that superiors, master builders, and architects, and manufacturers generally, have not taken that interest in the industrial classes under their guidance, which the clergy and country gentlemen have done, amongst the rural population, where there are members, and conductors, and even insurers and *honorary members,* "sufficient to save them in some cases from insolvency."

Thus deserted by their natural advisers and protectors, and cheated of their hard-earned savings, by interested and knavish delusions, we are prepared for the evidence, "that the working classes are sensible of the great disadvantage the breaking up of these clubs is to them;" that "there is a strong feeling amongst the working classes to enter sound societies;" "recklessness of the people produced by so many friendly societies breaking up," &c. &c.

Can we be surprised or indignant at the strikes, the unions, the menaces, the incendiarism (which has brought fire-proof shops so much into fashion, in Liverpool, particularly), which such a state of things has produced? or, at that last sad symptom of alienation and sullen disloyalty, in the declaration of some workmen in 1848, on the memorable 10th of April, "that they should take neither side, that they would defend their own premises and tools, but use no active exertions in support of order." Such a neutrality explains itself, for "he that is not with us, is against us."

But, Mr. Editor, it is in the perfect conformity of interest and duty (that essential condition of success), that I am most sanguine as to this scheme; for, first, the builders, as the natural protectors, the fathers and advisers of the artificer, the very keys of the undertaking, would find in it their immediate advantage. Their personal exertions, and their annual subscriptions in its favour (well known), would present at once a full and conclusive recommendation with the operative—a new means of patronage, and a material alleviation to their own pockets, from all those calls which casualties, ill-health, and long services, accumulate on an old and worthy firm. And though, from the liberality of builders,—a Peto, and others whom we could name amongst the fortunate builder capitalists—the real staple support of the scheme would be derived, let them never forget that, alone and unassociated with the architect and engineer—the public man—the artificer himself, and open reports and books, and audited accounts, their benevolence would fall to the ground, from the jealousy of the operative, and his suspicion of some sinister motive in the master builder. In Liverpool, from this very cause, a most beneficial scheme in their favour totally failed.

The advantages to the architect and engineer, though of an honorary character purely, are not the less real in respect of their interests; their authority and influence would be asserted and exercised; the artificer would acknowledge their disinterested and mediatorial exertions, as a sort of nobility in the art of building. They would dignify and exalt the workman by association with him; but especially they would see the shrewd advantage of addressing and engaging the highest ranks and the most conspicuous public spirits of the day in favour of so formidable and meritorious a class as the building artificers. The *entrée* alone to these higher powers would always be found a sufficient motive for their busy exertions in favour of the society, and offers them the ornament of benevolence in addition to their other claims on the regard and estimation of the great. Thus, through a better feeling infused amongst the rich, a better feeling would gradually spread amongst the poor, and restore our cankered society to a more hopeful and more natural state.

Thirdly, the advantages to the workman need no comment; his savings would be secured, by following good counsel of an established and responsible committee and office of agency, to embark either in deferred annuities, or other beneficial means supplied by Government, or even the clubs of acknowledged solvency,—the motto of the society being, "Help yourselves, and God will help you."

The benefit fund raised by at least 1,000 contributors of a shilling to a pound, and as much more as the conscience and the published returns of the subscribers would suggest, would defray all expenses, and save many a poor family from destitution. The labourer would embrace a society so warranted by public and responsible character, and so exempt from the wretched delusion of which he has hitherto been the unhappy and melancholy victim: assured of the good feelings and honest counsel of his betters, he would cease to wage that futile and desolating war against capital, in which he has been heretofore so vainly engaged;—a more cheering prospect of the future would open to his thrift, and thence every virtue, domestic, public, and social, would abundantly flow, for the good of the country as well as himself and family.

We do not dream of impracticable benevolence. The laws of social and political economy are as immutable as those of the physical sciences. Louis Blanc can no more alter them than he can the law of gravitation. The remuneration of capital, intellect, and manual labour, settle themselves, and will endure no interference, whether caused by interested or benevolent motives. The present scheme presents no such attempt, it does not profess to give men more than a market price for their labour, nor more in sickness than their own contributions can supply, nor larger interest for their savings than Government security and provident Acts of Parliament can afford,—but it calls upon us to exercise and to understand those true principles of communism by which the Pharisee in the Temple, and Zaccheus in the sycamore tree, recommended themselves to the favour of the Almighty—the only means by which we can secure his favour, and avert that evil day which will surely fall upon a country—

"Where wealth accumulates, and hearts decay."

If, as Mr. Macaulay has shown, the condition of the working-classes has greatly improved in the last 200 years in this country (as M. Thiers has also done in respect of France), it is no less certain that capital, and master builders, and manufacturers have risen into enormous power and wealth. Also the use which the humbler classes have made of these advantages in their unassisted and invaluable mechanics' institutes, headed by the generous Birkbeck and others, points to a noble issue of their improved condition; and no less their use of savings banks, and even clubs, however delusive they have often turned out. Shall we not aid these worthy efforts, to show an equally worthy use of our improved condition? or shall we lend a sullen and ungenerous attention to these fair claims on our aid and exertions?

It gave me pleasure to learn that the Builders' Society of London (the Builders' Union as you have fairly termed it) has a real and earnest intention to promote some such measure as the Building Artificers' Provident and Benevolent Society. Pray, Mr. Editor, urge them to advance it by some readier means than their monthly gatherings alone. They should be reminded that while the Builders' Union is dissolved at Liverpool, as temporary only, and maintained during the strike, and no longer, theirs *is permanently sitting in London;* and unless some general and generous good is to come out of this *permanent sitting,* the public and capitalist patrons will begin to suspect combination and monopoly in the market, as much, or more formidable amongst them, than amongst their humbler brethren.

Trusting that you will excuse so long a justification of my adherence to the Building Artificers' Provident and Benevolent Society, and wishing all success to your spirited and generous furtherance of the scheme, I remain, with gratitude and respect, your faithful friend and fellow-labourer,

A FREEMASON.

AMENDMENT OF THE INSTITUTE OF ARCHITECTS.

YOUR remarks, Mr. Editor, in the leading article of THE BUILDER for the 21st of July, headed as a few words to the council, upon the closing meeting of the session, are well worthy their notice. There and elsewhere I am glad to see you condemn, *in toto,* the "narrow, injurious, and impolitic regulation," which keeps men who measure artificers' works for builders from becoming members of their body. These remarks, if unheeded by the council, will have their full weight with the other members. Pray, do not give up this subject.

W. X. W.

Several other correspondents have addressed us on the same point. They may rest assured that we shall not be inattentive to the report of the council, to whom the question was referred, when it is made. Our views are unchanged, and we sincerely hope that the council will recommend the omission of the illiberal and unwise disqualification in question. We are bound to say that, knowing the feeling of some members of the present council, we are not very sanguine as to the desired result. In the event of the council declaring against the alteration, it will be for the body of the members to express their opinion upon

BISHOP STILL'S ALMSHOUSES, WELLS.
[16th CENTURY.]

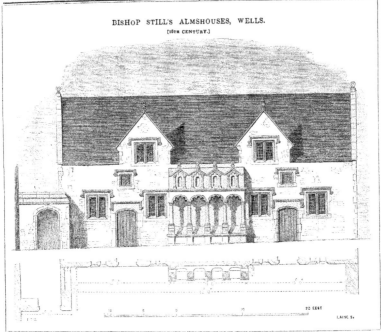

22 EEET

it.——As to obtaining a legislative enactment, forbidding any to practice as architect or engineer without a diploma (concerning which some have written to us), this is by no means likely, even if it were in all respects desirable; the spirit of the time is directly opposed to such a restriction.——"T. Square," who writes as to the "Soane Medallion," is in error. Neither the prize so named nor the 50l. offered with it, was given by Sir John Soane;—it is simply so called by the Institute in honour of him and in return for a money bequest to the society. The premium of 50l. was *first offered in connection with the Soane medallion* in the year 1847,* and was awarded in 1848 to Mr. Maclaren, of Edinburgh, who has not yet claimed the 50l., which, however, he was informed, he would be entitled to at the end of one year's absence from England, on sending a satisfactory evidence of his progress and his studies,—provided he did so within *five* years of the medal and premium being awarded to him. Since that time the Soane Medallion has not been awarded, nor consequently the 50l.; and we think we may safely say the council regretted as much as "T. Square" that the drawings submitted in competition for it were not up to their mark.

Another writer objects to the comparative terms in which the votes of thanks to parties who read papers were recorded last session. One, he says, was thanked "for his paper;" another for "his *interesting* paper;" a third for his statement, "which showed great knowledge, &c.:" a fourth for his "*very important* paper," which "was not important at all;" and so on. We agree with him in considering that this course, probably fallen into through accident, is very objectionable. One form should be

* The first time the premium of 50l. was offered was in 1846, to be awarded to the successful competitor of the Royal gold medal; but the drawings received in competition not being satisfactory, neither was awarded; and in the subsequent year, the change being made in the regulations respecting the gold medal, the council put the offer of the additional 50l. in conjunction with the Soane medallion.

adopted and adhered to. Opinions should not be given as those of the Institute, unless proposed to and formally accepted by the body.

As it is in contemplation to print after each meeting, in the coming session, a full synopsis of all communications, this observation is the more called for.

BISHOP STILL'S ALMSHOUSES, WELLS.

THE almshouses at Wells were originally founded by Bishop Nicholas Bubwith, who was translated from the diocese of Sarum to that of Bath and Wells in 1407; and who, in addition to founding the almshouses that bear his name, contributed considerably towards the erection of the north-west tower of the cathedral, built the library over the eastern cloisters, and constructed a chantry chapel on the north side of the nave in the cathedral, immediately opposite that of Hugh Sugar, illustrations of which have already appeared in THE BUILDER. The almshouses erected by Bubwith remain nearly entire, and are interesting memorials of the period.

Bishop John Still, who was promoted by Queen Elizabeth to the see of Bath and Wells, in 1592-93, added the buildings represented in the accompanying engravings, southward of those erected by Bubwith. The details, it will be seen, are peculiar, and exhibit, quaintly enough, the transition from Gothic to classic architecture; the general effect of the whole is characteristic and picturesque.

Our engraving is from a drawing by Mr. Dollman, made originally for Mr. B. Ferrey, whom we have to thank for our knowledge of the building.

THE BRITISH ARCHÆOLOGICAL ASSOCIATION will resume their meetings this (Friday) evening, at their rooms in Sackville-street.

NOTES IN THE PROVINCES.

A NEW gas company is in course of formation at Lincoln, 'to supply gas on more favourable terms than those now offered by the existing company.'——Houses, it is said, are being built by wholesale at Boston. New streets are springing up in different parts of the town. The houses are generally small, and built for letting at about 7l. a-year, this class of houses being much wanted.——The shire-hall at Chelmsford has been repaired and altered so as to afford more accommodation, and the old petty sessions-room is being converted into 32 cells, for prisoners before trial. ——Some property in East-street, Point, Portsmouth, has been sold of late, at an advance of 75 per cent. on its value a few years since, or equal to what it yielded during the war in 1805.——The inhabitants of Dudley propose to sell the four workhouses of the Dudley Union, and erect one new edifice for the whole Union in a healthy situation, near Dudley.—— The Bishop of Gloucester and Bristol has subscribed 200l. towards the erection of a national school in the hamlet of Fishponds, parish of Stapleton.——The new Lunatic Asylum for Monmouth, Messrs. Fulljames and Waller, architects, will, it is expected, have its four wings roofed in before winter. The sum of 7,864l. odds had been expended down to 29th ult., and 3,000l. more will be laid out on it before 5th December.——The propriety of erecting a building at Birmingham, says the local *Journal*, suitable for concerts and assemblies, smaller and more manageable than the Town-hall, and more accessible than any other room in the town, has again been under consideration. The building is proposed to be erected in New-street by a Company holding shares of 5l. each.——The Leicester Improvement Committee having purchased all the buildings to be demolished for the enlargement and improvement of the market-place, now recommend the erection of a Corn Exchange, with butter

DETAILS OF BISHOP STILL'S ALMSHOUSES.

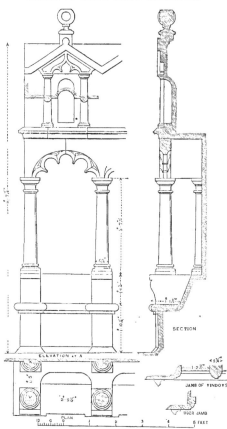

SECTION

ELEVATION AT A

JAMB OF WINDOWS

DOOR JAMB

PLAN

5 FEET

...nd poultry market below, on the site of the 'Green Dragon,' purchased at 3,900*l.* In the council it was urged, that in place of pulling down the present Exchange, it might be converted into a Corn Exchange in the mean time. The committee reported a proposal from Mr. Henry Rawson, to erect a bath for the use of the working classes in Burley's-lane. He would take down some cottages, and make a swimming-bath about 60 feet long by 27 feet wide, with dressing-rooms and other conveniences, on the council paying him 150*l.* within one month after completion; Mr. Rawson agreeing to keep open the bath for five years, charging 1*d.* only for each bather.——The remains of a Roman wall have been discovered at Moulsham, three feet from the surface, about a yard in width, and consisting, apparently, of Roman pavements, two inches thick, and scored in a diamond pattern, embedded in concrete.——The committee of the Chester public baths and washhouses report that "a swimming-bath has been constructed, measuring 45 feet by 30 feet, with dressing-rooms, &c., and a supply of fresh filtered water

continually running through it; a shower-bath and a range of washhouses have also been completed, with an apparatus for drying. The washhouses afford convenience for washing to at least 250 poor families per week, at 1*d.* each." Since the opening the whole has been in full and profitable use.——The top reservoir of the Barnsley Water Company has given way, through the abstraction of coal beneath it. The pipes are to be supplied from a higher level, so as to supply every part of the town, the level being that of the top of St. Mary's Church tower.——The Houghton-le-Spring Church organ is in one of the transepts; the organist, with the keys, sits at a distance of about 30 feet, in order to be near the choir, who are placed in the chancel.——In the case of a house which fell at Carlisle lately, the proprietor blamed the Caledonian Railway Company, they having pulled down some adjoining houses with great violence. The compensation demanded was 700*l.* A jury awarded 150*l.* damages.——It is proposed to erect an equestrian statue of her Majesty in Glasgow.——The Bank of Scotland, Ingram-

street, Glasgow, at the end of Glassford-street, has been ornamented with a piece of sculpture in high relief, erected over the perforated parapet surmounting the edifice, and representing the heraldic arms of the bank, a shield or crest, supported by Justice and Plenty, and bearing a cornucopia. Each of the supporting figures, as described by the *Reformers' Gazette*, is 8 feet 2 inches in height; and the central compartment, or blazoning, crowned with the cornucopia, about 11 feet in height. The whole is executed in stone from the Binney Quarry, near Edinburgh. The sculptor was Mr. Handyside Ritchie, who prepared it from designs by Mr. Burn, architect. It was brought from Edinburgh, and erected by Mr. York, builder, of Glasgow, and Mr. Garnett, clerk of works. We may state that it is in three pieces. There is a similar piece of sculpture on the offices of the bank in Edinburgh.——The additional wards to Huntingdon County Gaol are completed. Mr. Parker, of Thrapstone, was the contractor, under the direction of Mr. Thomas Smith, architect. It is said that the drainage of the gaol and the ventilation have been carefully attended to.

THE WATER QUESTION.

MR. LUSHINGTON, M.P., presided over a numerous meeting held on Monday evening last, in the Hanover-square Rooms, to consider the best means of improving the water supply of the metropolis. Dr. Lancester, Dr. Alison, Mr. Taberner, Sir Charles Aldis, and others took active part. Dr. Buchland, too, addressed the meeting at considerable length, and pledged himself to the fact that a sufficient supply of water for London could not be obtained from Artesian wells,—it was physically impossible, he said.—Mr. Pallisor said, let each parish select two or three delegates; let these delegates meet and select from amongst themselves a good working committee. This committee would then call before it all persons having plans to improve the supply of water to London. Then let a number of scientific men be called in to give their opinion as to the best plan, and this having been established, let all the parishes go to Parliament and do all in their power to get this plan passed into a law.——The meeting would not pledge itself to any particular scheme, and went no further than to approve by resolution " of the principles adopted by the Metropolitan Water Supply Association, for ascertaining, by scientific inquiry, the most pure and abundant sources of supply, and the best mode of service, at the least possible cost to the public, and of placing the control and management thereof under a public, popularly elective, and thereby a disinterested, board."——The Lambeth Waterworks, we see, are proposing to obtain an improved supply of water from the Thames at Ditton, and to abandon altogether the present source of supply. Than the present source nothing can be worse; and if all we have heard be true, the company have much disease and misery to answer for. If we were to publish the statements which have been made to us, touching this matter, it would spread alarm through Lambeth. The question must be taken up by Government. Our contemporaries of the London and provincial press (and we are grateful to them for doing so), have spread far and wide, to an extent we could not have ventured to anticipate, our assertion, that "all London ought to cry as loudly as if next door were on fire, ' Water ! water !! water !!!'" We must have not merely sufficient water, but *pure* water ; not merely pure water, but *cheap* water, or else we perish.

LONDON MECHANICS' INSTITUTION. — Mr. Grayson, teacher of architectural, mechanical, and ornamental drawing, has been appointed teacher of these branches of drawing to this institution. As Mr. Grayson's name is favourably known to the architectural and building portion of the public, we may reasonably conclude that his appointment will be of service to the Institution. We have heard with regret that this institution, in common with others at the present time, is not in so good a condition as it should be. It has been the means of much good, and should be supported by all interested in the general welfare and advancement.

RESTORATION OF SPIRE, ST. JAMES'S CHURCH, CLERKENWELL.

St. James's, Clerkenwell, was built in 1788—92, and stands on part of the site of the church formerly belonging to the priory called *Ecclesia Beatæ Mariæ de Fonte Clericorum*, for nuns of the order of St. Benedict, founded in the year 1100. The priory was suppressed 26 Henry VIII., and, after passing through various hands, the church, by purchase, became vested, in 1656, in trustees, for the use of the parishioners of the parish.

For some months past the spire of the church has been in a dangerous state, and the hurricane in March last throwing off the vane, rendered it necessary that steps should be taken to rebuild it. The trustees accordingly gave instructions to Mr. W. P. Griffith, architect, to prepare drawings and a specification, and to obtain tenders from masons for executing the works; these were submitted to the trustees, who accepted the lowest offer, which was Messrs. Hemmings and Foster's.

Upon taking down the spire it was found that the iron cramps had become oxidized and had burst, leaving the joints of the masonry open; the stones facing the W. and S.W. were much decomposed, but those towards the N.E. had the tool marks perfect. In the rebuilding, the hardest stones were placed opposite the S.W., and all deficiency made good with new Portland stone; each joint was saddle-jointed, and in every joint were inserted iron dove-tailed cramps enveloped in sheet copper (soldered) and run with lead.* The spire is hollow, and its sides about 10 inches thick, and a new solid course of Portland stone has been now introduced about mid-way, and the spindle passes through this, and is secured with a nut; the spindle has also been painted and wrapped in lead. Between the solid course and the capstone were deposited lists of the trustees, guardians, and voters of the borough of Finsbury. The vane is a new one of copper, 6 feet long by 2 feet deep, which, with the staff 12 feet 2 inches long, has been gilt. The new lightning conductor is 180 feet long, and passes from the vane to below the foundation, and terminates in a furcated form; it is of wrought solid copper, cylindrical, and ¾ inch in diameter; the holdfasts are of glass, and let into the masonry. Portland cement has been used for the masonry, and the lightning conductor and all metal work have been painted with anti-corrosion lithic paint.

CHURCH BUILDING.

St. Nicholas Church, Witham, is to be roofed with slates, and otherwise repaired. The organ-gallery is to be taken down, and the lower part of the church repaired. All Saints' Church parsonage is progressing towards completion.——The new Church at Wickham Bishops is being covered in.——The repair and restoration of the chancel of Soham Church have been completed. Messrs. Bonomi and Cory, of Durham, were the architects, and the expense was incurred by the rector and vicar. Mr. T. Dickens, of Durham, was the clerk of works. The floor is paved with Minton's encaustic tiles, made from designs by the architects. In cleansing the walls some paintings were discovered, and have been preserved. Two new windows have been added on the south-east side, and the large east window is restored. The carved work, screen, ceiling, stalls, sedilia, &c., have also been restored.——The idea of erecting a new district church at Winchester as a chapel of ease to St. Peter's Colebrook, &c., seems to be giving way to a desire for the restoration or rebuilding of St. Peter's itself, the site of which has been offered by Mr. Filer for the purpose.——A church-rate of 2d. in the pound for the repairs of Bideford Church has been most grudgingly granted. The churchyard is in a shameful state, and a rate was proposed for inclosing it, but was not acceded to.——The laying of the first stone of St. Jude's Church, Moorfields, Sheffield, will shortly take place, the architect, Mr. Mitchell, having got possession of the site. ——On Friday week Ellesmere parish church was re-opened. The cost of restoration is said to have been 8,000*l*., the subscription list having been headed by 3,500*l*. from the Bridgwater family, 500*l*. from Mr. C. K. Mainwaring, and other handsome sums.——A new Roman Catholic Church, to be dedicated to St. George, the patron of England, is about to be erected at York. This church is intended to be one of two or three which it is proposed to erect in that city. It will be in the style of the Decorated period, and is to accommodate about 700 persons.——On 11th inst. the new church of St. Mary the Virgin, in Oxenhope, was consecrated. It is built in the very early Norman style, with semi-circular arches, narrow windows, and massive walls. It consists of a tower, nave, north aisle, and chancel. The arch of the latter is inlaid with highly glazed encaustic tiles; the floor of the chancel outside the altar rails is laid with blue and red tiles of Minton's manufacture; within the rails they are encaustic; the windows of the chancel are of stained glass; those of the body of the church are each of one piece of plate glass. The design was prepared by Messrs. Bonomi and Co., of Durham.

* We offer no opinion on this arrangement of the cramps; any statement of results where such have been used would be useful.

RAILWAY JOTTINGS.

The following table, compiled from official returns, will show the state of most of the main lines as to traffic during one week in October of the present and past year, and, in some cases, the dividend per cent. paid for 1848:—

Div.	Name of Railway.	In 1849.	In 1848.
—	Aberdeen	£523	£428
—	Caledonian	6,705	5,010
—	Chester and Holyhead	1,808	1,879
8	Dublin and Kingstown	708	869
4	Eastern Counties*	15,448	17,171
6	Edinburgh and Glasgow	3,956	4,137
4	Glasgow, Paisley, and Ayr	3,017	2,720
5½	Great Western	21,107	21,200
7	London and North-Western	45,070	44,152
88s.	London and Blackwall	691	804
3½	London and South Coast	11,002	10,505
5½	London and South-Western	10,392	10,942
5	Manchester, Sheffield, and Lincolnshire		2,927
5½	Midland and Bristol and Birmingham	23,423	23,836
—	North British	3,180	2,642
6¾	Scottish Central	1,721	1,204
6½	South-Eastern	13,002	11,301
7	York, Newcastle, and Berwick	12,898	13,958
7	York and North Midland	6,859	10,003

——Some of the Railway Companies, says *Herapath*, are in a great hurry to take advantage of the Government disposition to buy or take their lines, and have quietly tendered them to pay 3 per cent. A great deal of negotiation, we hear, is very quietly and snugly carrying on.——The system of sub-letting contracts three or fourfold, the dishonesty of gangers, and the want of all other responsibility to the poor labourers who are duped, is at present exciting no little commotion at Cardiff and Merthyr. The local *Guardian* appeals to Boards of Directors, failing chief engineers, for the protection of the workmen, some of whom have been quite outrageous at the treatment they have been receiving in that quarter. "A ruinous competition is everywhere going on," says the *Liverpool Standard*, referring to this contract system. "Every man is seeking to undersell and to supplant his neighbour; and our very largest purchasers, our public boards and corporations, even the legislature itself, encourage the practice, and invite tradesmen to ruin themselves or each other by the system of contracting for every article supplied to them, and every species of work done. We see every day men taking such contracts at prices which leave, if any, the bare shadow of profits, to be wrung too often from decrease of the wages of their miserable working people, and sometimes from the substitution of inferior for first-class goods; and how often do we see such contracts result in ruin to those engaged in them.——The Windsor line, lately opened, runs most of its length from Slough on an embankment to within a quarter of a mile of Windsor, where a viaduct carries it, by a continuous curve, into the centre of the town. This viaduct is between 5,000 and 6,000 feet long, and in the middle of it is a bridge of novel construction, designed by Mr. Brunel, with a span over the Thames of 187 feet, so as to allow of vessels passing in sail. The station at Windsor abuts close on the High-street, and is 230 feet long, with an iron roof of 70 feet span.——It is in contemplation to construct a railway from Halesworth, by Framlingham, to Ipswich, and at Framlingham to erect capacious granaries and warehouses.——Mr. Fairbairn, C.E., has been invited by the Prussian Government to offer his advice and assistance in connection with an important work about to be undertaken in Rhenish Prussia. It has been determined that the Rhine shall be no longer a barrier to an uninterrupted railway communication between the shores of the German Ocean and the great cities of central Germany; and the neighbourhood of Cologne has been selected as the fittest site for effecting this junction. Chevalier Bunsen, while in Manchester lately, became deeply interested in the system of bridge building which Mr. Fairbairn has carried out by the employment of wrought-iron as a material for the construction of great girders; and expressed his conviction that this system was, perhaps, the only one calculated to meet the requirements of his government and the corporate authorities of Cologne. Mr. Fairbairn has been called to Berlin to submit his design to the King of Prussia and the local authorities. It has hitherto been considered an impossibility to erect permanent structures able to withstand the enormous masses of ice brought down from the Alps.

* Including Northern and Eastern, and Norfolk: length of combined lines from 17th August, 1847, 277½ miles; from 2nd April last, 295 miles.

PROPOSED SITE FOR THE NEW BRIDGE AT WESTMINSTER, COMBINED WITH IMPROVEMENTS IN THE IMMEDIATE NEIGHBOURHOOD.

A correspondent says:—It is proposed, both for the sake of affording a better view of the new palace, and diverting the great traffic of Westminster-bridge from the immediate vicinity of the Houses of Parliament, to rebuild the bridge a little farther north, commencing on the Surrey side at a spot immediately opposite the wharfs in Cannon-row, having the Board of Control for its southern boundary on the Middlesex shore. This will cause the removal of the block of houses between Derby-street and Richmond-terrace, but at the same time afford sufficient space for a row of houses looking south, of a similar character, and thus giving a handsome approach to the bridge on the north side. It will then be requisite to open Charles-street to the south of Great George-street, having an outlet into St. James's-park, and terminating with a drive leading by a curve to the Bird Cage-walk. By the clearance of the houses in Charles-street an opportunity would be afforded of appropriating that space to the purpose of the depôt for records, connected as it might then be with the State Paper Office, and returning along the west side of King-street to the ground so many years lying waste in Downing-street, and reserved for Government offices. When these plans shall have been carried out it will be found necessary to remove the block of houses in Parliament-street north of Charles-street, and possibly at some future time the entire mass towards the Houses of Parliament. As so much of importance depends on the selection of a proper site for the bridge, and the matter has been referred to Sir John Burgoyne, his report is looked for with no small anxiety.

DRAINAGE OF THE METROPOLIS.

The time has now arrived when this great metropolis can no longer defer possessing a comprehensive and a perfect system of drainage; and to accomplish this, three conditions must be observed, viz.:—

1. The non-pollution of the river Thames; with an injunction to prevent the discharge of a single sewer, house drain, &c., thereinto.

2. The demon of foul sewerage must have the focus and discharge of his interior veins, with his venomous and pestilential breath, and consequent effluvia and noxious gases, hermetically sealed within his own body, and discharged by one grand embouchure, far distant from the inhabitable precincts of this great Babylon, and the product there manufactured for productive purposes.

3. An unlimited supply of pure water, forced by high pressure to every house, street, court,

&c., without the necessity of tanks or cisterns, combined with an incessant current of water through all sewers and drains, &c. I am prepared to prove to a demonstration that the above three conditions can be fully accomplished for 2,000,000*l*., which, compared with the wealth, health, and rapid increase of above 2,000,000 of human beings, is not worth a moment's consideration.

How does the question stand at present? About 116 scientific men have sent in plans to the commissioners of sewers, and amongst this number figure about thirty engineers; yet it is a fact, that not one of their plans complies with the above three conditions. Further, not one of them has brought forth a new idea, or proposed an original scheme for the complete and effectual drainage of London.

What is to be done? Here is my proposition. It is probable that many an engineer, like myself, has refrained from sending in plans, &c., owing to the disagreement among the commissioners, and their not offering any distinct reward for the best scheme of drainage, &c. Now let the commissioners pay a reasonable sum to those who have already sent in plans, for their trouble, with liberty to compete again. The commissioners to print or exhibit every document they have, and the "concise statements," for the use of the competitors at large, and advertise for fresh plans to be sent in by January 1st, 1850, offering a prize of 2,000*l*. for the best scheme, 1,000*l*. for the second, 500*l*. for the third, &c. Every plan to be sent in under a motto, accompanied with a sealed envelope, containing the competitor's name; the envelopes of those obtaining the prizes alone to be opened.

HYDRAULIC ENGINEER.

WROUGHT-IRON WATER PIPES.

OUR attention has been called to a letter from Mr. G. R. Burnel, which appeared in your valuable paper on the 29th ultimo, respecting M. Chameroy's patent wrought-iron pipes. We are much obliged by the courteous and friendly manner in which the remarks are written. The nature, however, of the defects mentioned leads us to the conclusion that the pipes which have fallen under the writer's notice in France were those manufactured by a person named Ledru, who has had to pay heavy damages for infringing M. Chameroy's patent, and whose pipes have in many instances been taken up and replaced by M. Chameroy's.

The objections which Mr. Burnel raises are three, viz.:—

1. Insufficiency of strength to resist the compression arising from lateral or transverse strains.
2. Liability of soldered joints to be detached from the pipes.
3. Liability of the outside asphalte coating to be destroyed by the settlement of the surrounding earth.

Mr. J. H. Tuck, the agent for the patent pipes, confirms in the strongest terms our impression that the abovementioned are precisely the defects which rendered Ledru's infringements valueless, but from which M. Chameroy's own pipes have been found entirely free. Be this, however, as it may, we are anxious to state that we had not failed to notice the importance of the points which have been raised; and that, in reference to the pipes which we manufacture, the following are the facts in reference to the three objections raised, viz.:—

1. The strengths of the pipes have been calculated upon careful experiments, so as to resist all strains from without as well as the internal pressure.
2. The screw joints are not soldered on, like Ledru's, but are cast (?) upon the body of the pipe in such a manner as not to be liable to be detached.
3. We are satisfied that liability to abrasion and corrosion cannot be objected to M. Chameroy's pipes. We have ourselves seen, in Paris, pipes 11 inches diameter which had served for seven years as a sewer to an urinal, and which were still in a perfect state.

We are glad to see the remark that "the pipes in question do not affect the quality of the water like those generally used." You have already remarked that, when used for gas, they are free from the usual leakage—as may be ascertained from the present state of those which were laid down in Battersea-fields four years ago.

Experimental water pipes on this patent have been laid down in St. James's-park, and are in progress for the Chelsea water-works. But if you, or any other gentleman who takes an interest in drainage and in the safe and wholesome conveyance of gas and water, should wish to go into the subject, so as to examine the objections raised on the one hand and the good qualities alleged on the other, it will give us much pleasure to afford the fullest information in our power.

FOX, HENDERSON & Co.

Books.

Tables and Formulæ for the Computation of Life Contingencies, with copious examples of Annuity, Assurance, and Friendly Society Calculations. By PETER GRAY, F.R.A.S., &c. London: Longmans and Co., 1849.

THIS new work of a standard author claims to afford greater facilities for the *formation* of such elaborate tables and other intricate calculations as those with which it is itself abundantly stored; and as methods of constructing such tables have been in a great measure overlooked by preceding writers, we doubt not that a work such as this, by an author like Mr. Gray, who is himself an associate of the Institute of Actuaries and an able mathematician, will be found highly acceptable. The work is well printed and the tables are in clear large figures, so as to be promptly available in reference and calculation.

The First Three Books of Euclid's Elements of Geometry, from the Text of Robert Simson, with various useful Theorems and Problems as Exercises. By THOMAS TATE, Mathematical Master of the National Society's Training College, Battersea, &c. London: Printed for Messrs. Longman and Co. 1849.

Another of Mr. Tate's useful little books, in form of a small pocket Euclid, published in a cheap form, with the hope that it may tend to advance the mathematical education of this country, and with an especial reference to the instruction of schoolmasters who may be desirous of obtaining a government certificate.

Miscellanea.

SOCIETY FOR THE ABOLITION OF BURIALS IN TOWNS.—On Tuesday, 23rd, this society met at their rooms in Bridge-street, Blackfriars, Mr. G. A. Walker in the chair, Dr. Evans, Mr. Rogers, Mr. Godwin, Mr. Watts, Dr. Johnson, and others took part, and a letter from the Board of Health having been read, inviting Mr. Walker to aid them with suggestions as to the means of "remedying the vast and increasing evils of the present practice," a vote of sympathy with the Board, and expressive of the willingness of the society to aid them in their efforts, was passed unanimously.

OUR PLASTERERS.—In a recent number "A Plasterer" writes some very truthful lines. I think every accurate observer of artificers in the building trade will have noticed how rare it is to find a thoroughly skilful plasterer; in all the other trades (bricklayers, perhaps, excepted) the moderately skilled and the *thoroughly skilled* are, perhaps, in proportion of *three to two*; in the plasterer's craft I am bold to say the proportion would be as five to one. Now, I think your correspondent has hit the right explanation of this deficiency of skill among plasterers, in the number of task-masters, and the regular practice amongst all but the very large builders, of carrying out their plasterers' work by task-masters: as your correspondent justly observes, "*hawk boys* soon assume to be plasterers." *Good work* is in our day the exception, and not the rule; shall we ever see the day when the tale shall be reversed? The tradesmen have it in their power, if, as a body, they felt the true love of their trades, which was wont to be felt in days of yore.

W.

DISCOVERY OF ANCIENT SCULPTURE AT BLUNHAM CHURCH, BEDFORDSHIRE.—A few weeks since, as some workmen were engaged pointing the joints in the stonework of the chancel of Blunham Church, they discovered an opening in the wall immediately beneath the east window, 2 feet high by 1 foot 9 inches wide, which penetrated the whole thickness of the wall, there about 4 feet. On clearing away the rubbish with which it was filled, four fragments of ancient sculpture were discovered, composed, according to an informant, of statuary marble.* The first, a standing figure of the Virgin and Child, both the heads knocked off. Secondly, a figure with white robes, kneeling before another, the feet of which only remain. Thirdly, a fine group in alto relief, representing the Saviour bearing the cross; immediately behind is the Virgin Mary, who is endeavouring to hear some portion of the weight of the cross; a female figure bearing a palm branch, probably intended for Mary Magdalene follows next: in the centre of the group, behind, is the Roman Centurion. Next was a figure, the head of which is destroyed, whose hands are placed upon the upper part of the cross as if in the act of steadying it. On the left hand corner is seen the executioner, with a hammer in his hand, the cruel malignity of whose countenance is in striking contrast with the calm subdued grief depicted in the features of the Virgin Mother, at the opposite corner. In front is one of the Jewish rabble, with a rope over his shoulder, leading, or rather dragging, the suffering Saviour as a lamb to the slaughter. The lower part of this piece is broken off; but the heads, with but one exception, are in good preservation, and exhibit full proof that physiognomy was well understood at the time the work was executed. Fourthly, the lower part of the figure of Joseph of Arimathea, who is represented as sitting on the edge of a tomb, with ample folds of fine linen in his lap, on which lies the dead body of the Saviour; the right hand of Joseph, beneath the linen cloth, supported the head which has been broken off. The death-like appearance of the body, and the strained appearance of the muscles, serve to elucidate that scripture, "All my bones are out of joint." Gilding and painting, with brilliant colours, were employed on each specimen to add to the effect, which, when entire, must have been very good. The height of the specimens was originally about 18 inches.

WOLVERHAMPTON EXCHANGE.—We mentioned last week, in our provincial notes, that the design for the Exchange selected is by Mr. Robinson. We are enabled to add, that it is in the Italian style, and comprises a large hall, 100 feet long and 50 feet high, lighted at the top by a dome, upwards of 30 feet in diameter. At the north end of the hall is a large alcoved space (also lighted from the top by a semidome), for the purpose of a settling room, and in connection therewith is a large private room for the corn inspector and for other purposes. At the south end of the hall is a spacious area for the use of the iron-masters, having private rooms for business. The principal entrance to the hall and to the adjoining rooms is on the west side, through an archway in the centre of the building, and from this archway is an ascent by steps, which lead up on either side to a vestibule and entrance to the hall at each end. A design by Mr. Meyrick was selected as second.

HOW TO RESOLVE THE QUESTION WHETHER IMPURE WATER PROMOTES CHOLERA.—A correspondent of the *Morning Herald*, while alluding to the apparent connection of cholera with the metropolitan supply of water south of the Thames, already pointed out in THE BUILDER, suggests that the Board of Health might be able, by parochial assistance, to obtain returns from every house respecting the source from which its inhabitants are supplied. The returns should also state the number of cholera cases that had occurred in each house. The result would be, that, by means of a little classification, we should be acquainted with the particulars that there had been so many cases where spring water, so many where New River water, so many where the Grand Junction Company's water, &c., was used. Such data would be of service to the investigation of the question above alluded to.

* *Query*: Alabaster?

Projected Works.—Advertisements have been issued for tenders, by 5th November (extension of time), for locomotive, carriage, waggon, and general stores for the London and North-Western Railway; by 29th inst., for cast-iron pipes and other castings for the Newcastle and Gateshead Union Gaslight Company; and by 1st November, for 2,000 yards of good ballast, picked flint, or Kentish rag, for Bethnal Green parish.

Competitions.—Civil Engineers, Surveyors, and others, are invited by the Warwick Board of Health, to offer plans and specifications for the entire drainage and water supply of the town, with estimate of probable cost. A premium of 50*l.* offered according to advertisement.——Plans are also wanted from architects for a new church at Hawes, Yorkshire, for 450 adults and 100 children, to cost not more than 1,800*l.* commission inclusive.

Cleansing Process.—At a meeting of the Liverpool Polytechnic Society, held Oct. 8th, Mr. Knight described a new apparatus for regulating the flow of water from cisterns, applicable to sanitary purposes. After some remarks on the necessity of public urinals at railway stations *and elsewhere* being effectually washed, and the inefficiency of the present means of doing so, Mr. Knight described the apparatus provided for the purpose at the Lime-street railway station, which, he observed, had been in use for the last eighteen months. From one of the ordinary cisterns which were found in most large establishments, a small pipe led to the place where the water was required to be used. Here another cistern was erected above the urinals, and by means of the door-latch which is over the door, acting on a wire and crank connected with this pipe, whenever the door of the urinal was opened, a small quantity of water was let in to the second cistern. This cistern was supplied with a valve at the bottom, opening by means of a horizontal lever in connection with two balls, so placed, that when the water in the cistern was low, one of them hung directly downwards, while the other, on the same axle, was elevated at right angles with the last. As the water rose, the latter rose with it, and, by degrees, brought the former past the centre, when, by its buoyancy, it flew upwards, opened the valve, and the cistern was rapidly discharged of its contents. The balls resumed their former position, and the process of filling recommenced.

Westminster Improvements. — Compensation.—The commissioners for these improvements having given notice to the guardians that they required the workhouse premises in Dean-street, belonging to the parishes of St. Margaret and St. John, for the purpose of forming the new street, the guardians claimed the sum of 19,750*l.* as compensation. The commissioners offered 10,000*l.* The matter was referred to Mr. Shaw, of Christ's Hospital. The witnesses on the part of the guardians were Messrs. Hunt, Angell, Fowler, and Pownall, whose valuations varied from 22,000*l.* to 23,000*l.* The witnesses on the part of the commissioners were Messrs. Abraham, Hardwick, Tite, and Hammick, who assessed the compensation at 10,000*l.* The sum awarded is 21,000*l.*

The Tessellated Pavements at Cirencester. — Another very fine head has just been exposed to view, in the room last discovered, corresponding with those of Ceres and Flora previously found. This is the fifth circle as yet wholly uncovered; two others are partially so, and thus only two will be lost (out of the nine which originally formed this splendid room), and not four as was at first feared, in consequence of the proximity of a house. The pavement is being carefully removed, and the whole arrangement of the warming apparatus is thus clearly shown to perfection.

Sale of Duke of Buckingham's Estates.—The Foscott, a fine estate containing upwards of 700 acres, in the county of Buckingham, was on Saturday week sold for 32,000*l.* Six closes of arable and pasture land, in the borough of Buckingham, containing 73a. 2r. 5p., and producing a rental of 75*l.* 10s. 8d., were sold at 1,750*l.* A tithe-free piece of woodland, containing 15a. 3r. 10p., in the parish of Preston Bissett, sold at 380*l.* The Hillesden, a very fine estate, containing upwards of 2,900 acres, was offered, but bought in.

A Lesson from the Lyceum. — Last week we met a poor friend of good abilities, —shall we call him Waver,—who never effects anything, simply through thinking that he can do something else much better. He was half way to the Bar, when it occurred to him that the Church offered a wider field for the exercise of his abilities; and now, though just on the point of being ordained, he declares that he is better fitted to build churches than to teach in one, and has resolved to be an *architect!* If we had seen him yesterday, instead of last week, we would have sent him to see Mr. Charles Matthews play *The Practical Man* at the Lyceum Theatre, in the Strand,—a most finished and pleasant picture of our poor friend's foible carried out. Undecided, wanting fixed purpose, hesitating, delaying, energy is wasted, everything missed. It is a good lesson as well as an admirable piece of acting, and if we have more "Wavers" than our first-named friend amongst our readers, we advise them not merely to go and see it but to profit by what they do see.

Caen Stone.—In your number of last week, in remarks about Brighton, you say that some of the stone had failed at the new church, "St. Paul's," lately built, and that "it would be useful to ascertain the cause of its failure." The church was commenced building about four years back, and up to that time it was not discovered to be necessary to select Caen stone specially for external purposes; therefore no blame can attach to any one. Since then it has been considered a duty, with the knowledge of the fact that selection was necessary, to have that properly attended to; and, in confirmation of which, we refer your inquirer to the college recently built at Brighton, also to the church now in the course of erection by the same contractors, and under the same direction as the one referred to. We are now making selection, in accordance with analysis and suggestions made and published in your No. 114, Vol. 7, February 10, 1849, which showed that Caen stone can now, with precaution, be obtained as good as it was many centuries back, and which is still in excellent preservation. In reference to the necessity of the stone being laid on its natural bed, there are conflicting opinions; but that builders and masons may not mistake the bed-way of the stone, information is supplied to them, and in such a way that they need not mistake it, thereby leaving it for their discretion. As to Caen stone being injured by sea water, there is abundant evidence to the contrary. — Subscribers on the Spot.

Supply of Water to Towns.—It is suggested by a writer in the *Journal of Health*, that the metropolis might be supplied with water from Bala Lake, in Merionethshire, every town or neighbourhood that required water on the route being provided by the way. Bala, it is remarked, being 1,000 feet above the level of the sea, and a line by which water would descend quickly being readily found, not exceeding 250 miles in length, even without putting the water into pipes, there could be no difficulty in supplying London by gravitation. This grand scheme seems to have been itself suggested by a proposal formerly noticed in The Builder to supply London and towns on the way with gas from the western coal mines.

Exports of Metals.—The foreign iron exported from London, Liverpool, and the Clyde, to the three Presidencies of India, during the first nine months of this year, was 1,580 tons, against 379 in all 1848; of British iron, 13,772 tons, against 12,580 in all 1848; of hoop ditto, 2,246 against 756; of sheet ditto, 3,749 against 2,505; of pig ditto, 413 against 40. Of foreign steel the exports this year were 673 tons, against 207 in all 1848; of foreign copper, 29 against 36; of British ditto, 1,422 against 1,424; of sheet ditto, 2,532 against 1,210; of foreign lead, 32 against none in 1848; of British ditto, 1,029 against 527; of sheet ditto, 339 against 75; of spelter cakes, 3,288 against 2,831. The exports to China direct from London, Liverpool, and the Clyde, during the first nine months of this year, were—British iron, 1,854 tons, against 1,414 in all 1848; ditto hoop, 234 against 191; ditto sheet, 24 against 19; ditto pig, 125 against 200; foreign steel, 35 against 44; sheet copper, 71 against 11; foreign lead, 347 against 101; British ditto, 462 against 50.

Sale of Thorwaldsen's Works.—It appears from a report made by the Director of the Fine Arts to the French Minister of the Interior (quoted in the *Morning Post*), that some of the marbles have been purchased for England. The director went to buy what he thought worthy of a place in the French National Collections. He says:—"The sale was composed of marbles executed for the second and third time after the models of Thorwaldsen and plaster casts. Having ascertained on the day before the sale that the marbles were not very well executed, and knowing besides that Thorwaldsen seldom touched them, I gave up the idea of purchasing them, under the idea that our practical men in France could, in case of need, produce better and more highly finished. I therefore abandoned to my competitors the statue of Mercury, Cupid, the Ganymede on her knees giving water to the eagle of Jupiter, the Three Graces, and several others. Almost all these marbles were purchased for Spain, for England, and by amateurs at Copenhagen. The plaster models were afterwards put up, and I have been fortunate enough to purchase the finest. That of Mercury preparing to kill Argus, has the winged heels, which is not to be found in the marble sold at the Spanish Embassy. It is a *chef-d'œuvre*. Thorwaldsen is not the bold artist of modern days; his style is purely classical. The Venus, the Hebe, and the Ganymede standing erect, were knocked down to me at very moderate prices, the directors of the Museum having abstained from running up the prices. The Hebe, in particular, is remarkable for the charm and *naïveté* of its attitude."

The Rutland Colossal Statue.—A committee of the Leicestershire gentlemen assembled at the County Public Office, Leicester, on Wednesday, the 24th inst., to inspect the competition models, and decide as to the artist. The meeting, which was numerously attended and presided over by the high sheriff, were unanimous in resolving that the commission should be intrusted to Mr. Edward Davis, the successful competitor for the General Nott statue. The Rutland statue is to be in bronze, and not less than 8 feet 6 inches high.

Electro-Telegraphic.—Mr. H. G. Hall, of Kirkersville, Ohio, has patented an improvement in posts for telegraphs, stating his claim to be for the "manner of combining cast-iron or artificial stone shoes with the posts, by casting the shoes with sockets, of a depth greater than the length of the tenons, on the lower ends of the posts, to be inserted into said sockets, and with fillets or bands around the external surfaces to strengthen the concave ends, which are also made flaring and sharp, so as to be forced into the shoulders of the posts, which are to be of greater diameter than the shoes, in order to overhang and protect them, and to prevent the water getting into the shoes at the points."

TENDERS

Delivered on 22nd inst., for building two third-rate houses in Cable-street, Whitechapel.

Tolley	£1,959
May	1,823
W. Hill	1,775
Barrett	1,763
Walker and Soper	1,745
Day	1,716
J. Hill	1,710
Loins	1,700
Howlett	1,573
J. Hall	1,559
Wilson	1,548
Hill (of Watford)	1,545
Simmons	1,499
Livermore	1,490

BUILDINGS AND MONUMENTS,

MODERN AND MEDIÆVAL.

Edited by Geo. Godwin, F.R.S.,

Fellow of the Institute of Architects; Corresponding Member of several Societies.

Part IV. of this work, price 2s. 6d., containing Views of Ware Church, Hertford; Hungerford and Lambeth Suspension-bridge; New Front of Buckingham Palace; Fire-place in the Palace of the Dukes of Burgundy, at Dijon; All Saints' Church, St. John's Wood; the Interior of the House of Lords—the Throne, the Victoria Lobby, the Reporters' Gallery, and Ground-plan; with descriptive letter-press, and numerous details; will be published at the end of the month, in time for the magazines of November.

Office of The Builder, 2, York-street, Covent Garden, or by order of any bookseller.

TO CORRESPONDENTS.

" *Labourers' Cottages and Farm Buildings.*"—We shall treat this subject, generally, soon, and will then be able to refer to books and letters forwarded to us.

Received.—" R. S. T." (next week), " J. V.," " L. and N.," " C. E. M.," " House Proprietor" (we are personally looking into the merits of the discovery), " T. G., jun." (the address of the patentee is 8, Connaught-place West, Hyde-park), " W. Y." (we have not yet found time for perusal), " W. H." (shall be made use of), " F. L." (next week), " B. B." (ditto), " Le Feu" (shall appear), " S. H." (shall have attention), " W. E. S.," " T∗ M.," " Londiniensis," " G. S.," " An Old Subscriber," " R. J.," " C. I." (must allow us to judge for ourselves), " C. C. C." (paper shall be returned), " G. R.," " W. T.," " W." (may rely on our preserving confidence reposed in us, so long as we find ourselves dealt with fairly), " Mr. A.," " J. Y.," " H. M.," " R. N.," " F. and B.," " W. N. B.," (thanks), " Mr. N." (ditto), " P. W. R.," " J. R. B.," " J. D." (suggestion has been made several times), " G. F." (estimate use of rain water pipes for ventilation of sewers has been already pointed out). " F. A." (Bristol), " B. M.," " Mr. P."

NOTICE.— All communications respecting *advertisements* should be addressed to the "Publisher," and *not* to the "Editor;" all other communications should be addressed to the Editor, and *not* to the Publisher.

" *Books and Addresses.*"—We have not time to point out books or find addresses.

No. CCCLII.

SATURDAY, NOVEMBER 3, 1849.

ANY of the farmsteads erected in the present day are defective and wasteful, as well as inelegant, the direction of such constructions being too often confided to men quite unfit for the task. We would urge upon proprietors and farmers the pressing necessity which has arisen for greater attention to this and every other matter affecting the profitable working of land. They must not be contented with doing what their fathers have done if their sons can do better. Let them not be afraid of what is new, or be led to disregard the teaching of science; let them adopt the best principles of construction; avail themselves of every local advantage; and, in order that they may do this, take good advice early. Architects themselves, being comparatively seldom applied to on such matters, have not turned their attention generally to them, and may usefully think a little more on the subject than they appear to have done in two or three instances which have lately come under our notice.

Amongst the books recently published, now lying on our table, is one treating of this class of structures,—" Essays on the Construction of Farm Buildings and Labourers' Cottages," by Mr. G. A. Dean,* which, without professing to give much that is positively new, will be found to contain much useful information. It comprises plans of three farms, elevations and sections of farm buildings, rick frame, cattle-boxes, isometrical views of the farms, and three sets of plans for labourers' cottages, with specifications and general estimates.

Convenience of arrangement, economy of material and space, ventilation, good drainage, and a facility of obtaining wholesome water, are the chief points, says the author, to be considered in designing farm buildings. "Farmers pay largely for labour; it is, therefore, essential to economize this item in every manner possible; and much is to be effected by having a good arrangement in the homestead, particularly of the cattle sheds." The house should be placed where the farmer can have a good view of the other buildings. The position of the house is of importance; where "practicable it should be on the south side of a hill, and as nearly central as possible with the arable land. This position gives great facility for manuring the soil, carting home the produce, and performing the various farming operations in the most economical manner. Railroads having become the highways of England, they should be made serviceable by erecting the homestead as near to them as possible. Several farmers, whose lands abut upon railways, have already made, or are making, tramways to them from their farm-yards, for the purpose of conveying their produce to market, and for bringing home manure."

To the plan of covering the entire area of the farmstead with buildings he objects :—
" It appears to be bad in principle and costly in construction; as thus, when the roofs are

* Published by Morris, Stratford; Simpkin and Marshall, London; ——

several, and join, valley-gutters must be formed; these must, or should be, of lead, which is expensive. Some of the roofs will also be higher than others. Under such an arrangement of sheds, the heat from its large expanse of roofs must be very great during the summer months; neither can any convenient mode of ventilation be adopted; besides, horses require a different temperature from oxen; the latter, while fattening, should be kept very quiet, which cannot be the case here, as they will be continually disturbed by workmen feeding them, by horses coming in from and going out to their work, and by the carters who attend them."

As to cattle sheds, he says :—
" The fundamental principle by which an architect should be guided in forming sheds for cattle, is their size and form, the latter being, more or less, wedge-shaped; thus :—a moderate-sized horse is about 8 feet long, 6 feet 6 inches high to the top of the head, 2 feet broad behind, and 10 inches across the head. A bullock, about 7 feet 6 inches in length, 5 feet in height, 2 feet 6 inches broad at the hind quarters, and about the same across the horns (although the latter dimensions depend upon the breed of the animal). Sheep are on the average 3 feet 6 inches long, 1 foot 8 inches across the hind quarters, and about 12 inches at the head, allowing for the horns. Swine are about the same size as sheep, varying like them according to the breed. From these data buildings may be erected in the most economical and commodious manner, especially when the sheds are to be circular. More loose cattle can be fed in a circular shed than in one of any other form, and may be divided to suit circumstances. The proper radius for the inner circle is 54 feet."

Practically, nevertheless, we are disposed to give the preference to the parallelogram.

Speaking of roof coverings he gives the following memorandum :—

" The cost of a square of 100 feet super. of thatch is about 2l. 5s.; plain tiles, 1l. 18s.; pantiles, 1l. 8s.; slate, 1l. 5s.; felt, 14s.; galvanized iron, not corrugated, 2l. 14s.; if corrugated, 8s. extra."

These prices, however, would be varied by locality.

The barn, being generally the highest building in the farmstead, he would place on the north side of the yard, thus giving shelter from the cold winds, and " as a great portion of the food consumed by live stock is there prepared, the cattle-sheds and stables should be contiguous, which will save much labour in the carrying of fodder to and fro. The same reasons should determine the site of the granary, which should be near, if not immediately adjoining. In the barn there should be two bays for the storing of unthrashed corn or straw, with a thrashing-floor in the centre. The thrashing-floor being thus placed, waggons and carts may be conveniently brought in to unload during harvest, or from the ricks. The bays should be sufficiently capacious to hold the contents of a moderately sized rick, although it is desirable to make them as small as possible, on account of the cost of erection."

A steam engine might be profitably fitted up on many farms :—" The application of steam power on farms is yet in its infancy; and it is objected to by many, that for the purpose of small farms, it is unnecessary and expensive,—but on those consisting of 800 to 1,000 acres or upwards, it is recommended. The number of operations that can be so readily performed at one time with the aid of proper machinery — the great dispatch—the amount of work that can be accomplished—and the small cost of the sustaining power, being only that of a few bushels of coals per diem, are facts too important not to attract the attention of every scientific farmer."

The remarks on labourers' cottages are sensible.

In awarding general commendation to Mr. Dean's volume as a very useful production, we

must not be considered as endorsing the taste displayed in the external adornments of the buildings; for example, in the " bird's-eye view of plate 9." Should a second edition be required, he should cancel this plate, if he would maintain his right to the title of "architect."

The improvement of labourers' cottages has recently received a fresh impulse from the Duke of Bedford. His Grace had been erecting cottages on his own estate, and forwarded plans of them to the Royal Agricultural Society, with a letter to Lord Chichester, which appears to have had good effect in several quarters. The Duke said wisely :—" To improve the dwellings of the labouring class, and afford them the means of greater cleanliness, health, and comfort, in their own homes, to extend education, and thus raise the social and moral habits of those most valuable members of the community, are among the first duties, and ought to be among the truest pleasures, of every landlord. While he thus cares for those whom Providence has committed to his charge, he will teach them, that reliance on the exertion of the faculties with which they are endowed, is the surest way to their own independence and the well-being of their families."

At Tavistock, for some time past, the labouring population has been miserably crowded, and this being represented to the Duke of Bedford, he has commenced the erection of 64 cottages, on plans prepared by Mr. Jones, his resident surveyor there. These are to be in detached blocks, varying from four to eight in a block. Each cottage is to consist of a living room or kitchen, 14 feet by 11 feet 3 inches: washhouse, or scullery, with a furnace, 9 feet 8 inches, by 7 feet 10 inches, and a pantry 7 feet 10 inches, by 3 feet 6 inches, on the ground floor; and a bedroom with fireplace, 14 feet by 8 feet 4 inches, and two other sleeping apartments, 11 feet 6 inches by 7 feet, and 9 feet by 7 feet, on the chamber story. The rent is to be 1s. 6d. per week, which would scarcely pay as a mere money speculation. It is however as much as an agricultural labourer can possibly afford; and what is to be desired is a mode of building by which a healthful and convenient habitation can be erected for him at such a cost as this sum would be a fair return for. Until this be the case, the amelioration will not be general.

At the last meeting of the Northampton Architectural Society, the Rev. T. James, in the course of a discussion on labourers' cottages, which followed a paper read by him on the subject, said, that cottage building could never in direct payment give the most moderate return for the outlay which a capitalist might fairly in other cases expect. That the landed proprietor must be content to pay for his return from improved cottages just (only in a higher sense, and, in a more direct way) as he does from improved farm-buildings or farm-houses, viz., in the general and permanent amelioration of his estate thereby.

We think differently, and hope that those improvements which shall make a fair return quite possible. In the course of his paper, Mr. James very properly urged the importance of attending to the external character of the Cottage as well as internal arrangement. The speaker said :—

" In its moral and social relations, perhaps more widely extended and influential than any class of buildings after the temples of the Most High, and even æsthetically (to use an ugly word from Germany), I see not why it should not be worthy the regard of the highest architect. Whatever pleasure we derive from the contemplation of buildings, beyond that resulting from mere beauty of form and costliness of material, may be inspired as well by a neat-built cottage as by a gorgeous palace. This it is which so much strikes a foreigner on his first arrival in England. As he passed along the road from Dover to London in those days when old-fashioned travelling allowed wayside observations to be made, there was nothing that caught his attention so much as the neat and comely cottages dotted or grouped along his journey. All books of English travels are full of remarks upon them. 'There is scarce a cottage,' says Willis, just landed from America and France, 'between Dover and London, where a poet might not be happy to live. I saw a hundred little spots I coveted with quite a heart-ache.' Now it is quite certain that such cottages were not the prim red brick things, with flat slate roofs, their eaves clipped like a man's hat with the brim cut off, a door in the centre, a semi-sash window on each side,—town houses in miniature—such as it delights bricklayers and carpenters now-a-days to build.

These neat modern 'tenements,' made to let (tenements, I say, for cottage is too vulgar a name), would never give a poet the heart-ache, except to think that they were ever built at all. And though, no doubt, in those thatched and woodbined huts,—those 'cots beside the hill,'—that poets have professed to covet, and been proud to sing of, there will often be found a merely outside show, with little *real comfort* within; yet it is by no means necessarily true, as utilitarians of the present day seem to think, that comfort and convenience are in the inverse proportion to the picturesqueness of the dwelling, and that the uglier it is on the outside, the more likely it is to be comfortable within."

Lord Ashley has written an able and important letter to the *Times*, calling on the public to second the endeavours of those who have latterly been engaged in the no less profitable than philanthropic establishment of improved dwellings and baths and washhouses for the people. The present moment, as his Lordship remarks, is a singularly favourable one for such an effort, and henceforward, it is be hoped, such provisions may form an incipient, if not a realized portion of our normal state, and an inseparable and extensive item of our parochial system. One remarkable, though natural and reasonable result of the provision of cleanly, ventilated, and, in every way, improved dwellings for the working-classes, such as those of the Metropolitan Society, of which his Lordship is so active and important a member, has been, that not a single case of cholera has occurred among those inhabiting these dwellings. The *Times*, in allusion to this fact, draws an instructive contrast between those "two great and signal cases of interference with the state of the dwellings of the poorer classes,—one sweeping, inconsiderate, and tyrannical," viz., that of the Parliament at Church-lane, whereby the state of the miserable inhabitants has been made tenfold worse than ever,—"the other, gentle, prudent, and kind," namely, that of Lord Ashley and his coadjutors, at the Metropolitan Buildings in Saint Pancras parish, and other model dwellings. The population in Church-lane is about the same as that in the Metropolitan Buildings; but the former, always sickly, have been decimated by cholera alone during the season just past. "We are sorry to say," adds the *Times*, "that this metropolis presents many other contrasts equally painful and equally significant. Our improvements are in every direction except that which is the most important of all, and which affects the broad basis of society. We enlarge and rebuild churches, exchanges, streets of mansions, shops, and warehouses; we occupy the spare space of the metropolis with docks and with railways; the one thing most needful we not only omit, but we even aggravate the difficulties in the way of its attainment. We not only neglect, we absolutely prevent proper habitations for the labouring poor." And yet "selfishness, even more than philanthropy, is concerned in the question. Self-interest impels us to see that, if possible, the people about us shall not live in the burrows of vermin, or the lairs of wild beasts; that we shall not be surrounded with the stills of malaria, and the nests of typhus; and that the spreading rot of the great human flock shall be checked in its beginning."

This requisite amendment, indeed, is, in no sense, a subject for mere charitable contribution or display; it is simply a profitable money speculation, based on the establishment of improved health to the public at large, and even to the speculators themselves as well.

We intended to refer to a description of proposed plans of houses for the very poor labouring classes, by Robert Netherway, an intelligent clerk of works; and to a paper on improved buildings for the middle classes, by Mr. W. Young, but our present space is exhausted, and we must seek another opportunity to do so.

RESPONSIBILITIES AND RIGHTS OF ARCHITECTS AND BUILDERS.

HOW THEY MANAGE THESE MATTERS IN FRANCE.*

We come now to treat, fifthly,—"Of builders who work without architects."

The responsibilitie of the builders in this case clearly result from what has been stated before. He becomes immediately responsible to the proprietor for all the defects of the building, of whatsoever nature they may be. He guarantees the solidity of the work for ten years against any defects of the soil, any deviations from the laws of art, or any infractions of the municipal or other regulations.

Neither in this case, nor any other, can he allege as a justification that the workmen he employed were not sufficiently skilful, or that they acted with ill-will towards him, purposely to spoil the work. By the art. 1797, he is responsible for their acts, but he has a remedy against them. It is, therefore, his place only to employ such as are fit and proper to execute the works.

Sixthly.—"Of the position of the workmen who either work for, or independently of, the builder."

When the workmen are in the immediate employ of the builder, it is to him only that they are responsible. The proprietor has no right to give the slightest order of any kind or description so ever, even relating to the work in hand, nor has he any recourse against the workmen, as their agreement is simply with the builder. The architect, also, has no right to issue any instruction to the workmen; all his orders must be addressed either to the builder or to his representative. The responsibility of the builder thus remains entire both to the proprietor and the architect.

The workmen are responsible for the full employment of their time, and for any consequences which might result from their neglecting their work through idleness or negligence. They are bound to execute their tasks according to the rules of art. Should they spoil any materials from a neglect of these, they are legally responsible to their employers in a pecuniary manner. They are bound also not to commit any fraud in the execution of their works; such fraud making them, also, pecuniarily responsible to their employers. No distinction is made between workmen employed on piece-work or upon day-work, for both are hiring of services, and they only differ in the mode of the appreciation of the value of the remuneration. Such are the legal responsibilities of workmen; but as they are usually too poor for any pecuniary action to lie against them with effect, in reality the only remedy a master has, unless in cases of extreme malevolence, is to discharge them, and sometimes to retain the wages.

The workmen are not supposed to know t
laws of scientific construction, and are the:
fore in nowise responsible to the builder i
the solidity of the work they execute under l
orders. Nor are they responsible for any infr
tion of the laws of neighbourhood, nor of t
municipalities. They are supposed only
hire their labour to the builder, who is bou
to see that it be employed in conformity w
the legal requirements.

Inasmuch as the builder is the only pers
responsible towards the proprietor, and as t
latter has no control over the workmen, th
have no claim upon him for the amount
their wages. The proprietor only has to d
with the builder, and has nothing to do wi
the arrangements the latter may make with l
men. He cannot, therefore, refuse to pay t
builder, on the pretext that the workmen e
ployed on the work have not been paid th
wages. But they have the right to lay
opposition against the payment of any mon
that may remain due, which sum is to be d
tributed *pro ratâ* amongst the men, accordi
to their wages. They can, however, only clai
the balance which may be due to the builder
the moment of bringing their action, tho
being the express terms of the article 17
of the *Code Civil*.

When the workmen treat immediately wi
the proprietor, their responsibilities vary wi
the conditions under which they treat. If
simply day-labourers, they do not contract a
others than those they labour under when
the employ of the builder; namely, to devo
the whole of their time, and to employ su
skill as can reasonably be demanded of the
But if they undertake piece-work in such
manner as to place themselves in the positi
of contractors, then they are bound to guara
tee the work for ten years. If the work l
subdivided so that the masonry, the carpentr
&c., be intrusted to different parties, then,
course, the responsibility of each is mere
confined to his own especial trade; a defect
any other does not involve him in any mann
soever. The obligations are, of course, tl
same if an architect be employed.

In all these cases it is evident that the inte
tion of the legislators was to insure a faithf
discharge of an equitable contract between th
several parties. To render it obligatory,
must, therefore, be founded upon a reasonab
consideration. If the price fixed be either t
high or too low, the contract ceases to be
contract for services, and becomes, what
called, a contract of beneficence, subject to tl
laws which regulate such transactions. Minor
or parties under legal impossibility of contrac
ing engagements, cannot enter into any of th
nature, as a natural consequence of their pos
tion.

The work must be specified; but no nece
sity exists for doing so in all its details. If tl
price be not settled beforehand, it is presume
that a tacit understanding exists by which tl
work is to be valued, and paid for, at the usu
price, upon completion. The same rema
holds good also as to the payment of arch
tects, surveyors, or others. In all cases whe
it is not specifically fixed by agreement, tl
usage of the locality decides the amount. N
definite form, as was said before, is necessa
to legalize such contracts. They may be ma
verbally as well as in writing. The advanta
possessed by the latter is simply that th
are more easily proved in court.

If the delay be not fixed in the contract, tl
proprietor can apply to the tribunal to ha
one fixed judicially; and in case the build
does not conform to this, he becomes respon
ble for any loss which may ensue, or any ext
price the proprietor may have to pay upo
employing another builder to complete tl
work.

The guarantee of the builder and of tl
architect also has been named above as exten
ing over ten years from the reception of t
work. But even after the ten years ha
expired, the respective parties are liable to
action in case a fraud be discovered, whi
action may be commenced at any time with
thirty years from its discovery: after thir
years, prescription covers it, and the seve
parties are discharged from their guarante
but it is to be observed that the thirty yea
only begin to run from the date of the propri
tor's becoming aware of the existence of t
fraud.

* See page 509, *ante*.

The obligations of the proprietor are simply nfined to the payment of the money, either on the completion of the works or at the ochs specifically agreed upon. If any terations in the work contracted for be made th the consent of the proprietor, he is equally und to pay for them; but it is advisable at the builder do not commence any such tra works without previously receiving writ- n instructions.

It is not allowed to alter the conditions of ice which may have been agreed upon tween the parties, upon the pretence that augmentation has taken place either in the te of wages or the value of materials subse- iently to the conclusion of the bargain. So any lawsuits had been commenced upon at ground, that a special article, No. 1793, as introduced into the *Code Civil*, to guard ainst any future litigation upon the subject. he same article also states that no augmenta- on can be claimed for extra works unless ey be ordered as such, and in writing. orks to be measured and paid for after com- etion are regulated, as to the fixing of prices least, by their value at the time of measure- ent.

The proprietor is also bound to procure the uilder proper access to the works, and to lfil all the legal observances necessary to btain the authorization to commence their ecution; such as the settling of the "aligne- ent," or the front line upon the street, or ny other formalities imposed by the munici- ality before commencing the works.

Any risk attached to the works during their xecution falls to the charge of the builder, or f the proprietor, according to the conditions f the bargain. Thus, if the builder agree to eliver a construction of any kind, and to urnish all labour and materials, the loss is is in case of fire, flood, lightning, or armed iolence. If he only furnish labour, he loses hat portion which has not been received and aid for. In both cases it is assumed that he as no claim until delivery has taken place, nd this is proved either by the reception of he building or the payment of the labour lready executed. The article 1788 says dis- inctly, that if the things to be delivered perish by any accident before the completion of the lelivery, the loss is to be at the charge of the workman, if it be he who furnish the mate- ials, unless the party contracting with him have been legally summoned to proceed to the reception. Article 1790 says, that if the work executed upon materials furnished by the other party fail from defect of materials, the workman can claim to be paid for his labour. Article 1791 provides, that if the work be executed by the piece, the workman or even the builder can claim to have it measured as it proceeds. As soon as each portion is measured it is con- sidered received, and ceases to be at the risk of the contractor, the builder, or workman.

By article 1794 the proprietor can annul the whole bargain at his own discretion, upon reimbursing all previous expenses, paying for the works executed, and compensating for the profit the builder was authorized to expect upon the completion of his contract.

Having premised thus much upon the spirit of the French legislation, we proceed to give a translation of the text of the Civil Code im- mediately bearing upon the question of the rights and duties of architects and builders.

BOOK 3, TITLE 8, CHAP. 3, SECT. 3.

"Of Estimates and Contracts."

Art. 1787. When any person charges another to execute a work, it may be agreed either that he furnish his labour or industry, or that he furnish at the same time the materials.

1788. If, in the case of the workman fur- nishing the materials, the thing, or work ("*la chose*") fail or perish, in whatsoever manner it may be, before delivery, the loss falls upon the workman, unless the employer had been legally summoned (*mis en demeure*) to receive it.

1789. If in the case of the workman's only furnishing his labour, or industry, the thing perish, he is only responsible for his own fault.

1790. If, in the case of the preceding article, the thing fail, even though without any fault on the part of the workman, before the work were received, and without the employers having been legally summoned to receive it, the workman cannot claim any wages, unless the work were lost by a defect of the mate- rials.

1791. If the work be of many pieces or kinds, or such as can be measured, the verifi- cation can be made partially: it is supposed to be made for all the parts paid for, if the employer pay the workman in proportion to the work executed.

1792. If the edifice constructed for a deter- mined price fail, in part, or totally, from any defect of construction, even by a defect of the soil, the architects and contractors are respon- sible for ten years.

1793. When an architect or a builder has undertaken to execute a construction for a fixed sum, upon a plan settled and agreed with the proprietor of the soil, he cannot demand any augmentation of price, either under pre- tence of an augmentation in the value of labour or of materials, or under that of changes or additions to the plans, unless these changes or additions be authorised by the proprietor, in writing, and the price be agreed upon with him.

1794. The employer, by his own will, may set aside a contract, although the work be commenced, on the condition of reimbursing the contractor for all his preliminary expenses, of paying for all the works, and all that he might gain by the completion of the contract.

1795. The contract for the hire of services is dissolved by the death of the workman, the architect, or the builder.

1796. But the proprietor is bound to pay, in proportion to the price agreed upon, to their heirs, administrators, &c., the value of the works done, and of the materials prepared, on the supposition only that these works and materials are useful to him.

1797. The contractor is responsible for the conduct of all whom he employs.

1798. The masons, carpenters, and other workmen who are employed in the erection of a building, or of any other works executed by contract, can only establish a claim against the proprietor for the sum which he may owe to the contractor at the moment of commencing their action.

1799. The masons, carpenters, smiths, and other workmen, who execute contracts without any intermediary party, are bound by the rules prescribed in the present section: they become contractors for the part they undertake.

2110. The architects, contractors, or work- men employed upon building or repairing houses, canals, or other works, and those who, in order to pay and reimburse them, have lent money to the proprietor, in case the due employ of this money be proved, are entitled, on registering—1st. The *proces verbal* which authenticates the state of the premises or places—2nd. The *proces verbal* of recep- tion—to have their claims considered as first mortgagers, to the exclusion of any other claimants but those provided by law.

2270. After ten years, the architect and builder are exonerated from the responsibility attached to the main works (*gros ouvrages*) which they have directed.

BOOK 2, TITLE 2, CHAP. 6.

Art. 159. On taxing costs there shall be allowed to Experts (referees?) for every vacation of three hours, when they operate in the localities where they reside, or within 2 *myriamètres* (12½ miles) as follows:—

In the department of the Seine, for archi- tects, or other artists, 8 francs (6s. 4d. English).

In the other departments, 6 francs (or 4s. 9½d. nearly).

160. Beyond 2 *myriamètres*, the travelling allowance per distance of 6¼ miles, 1 *myria- mètre*, is, for the Paris architects, 6 francs; for those of the country, 4 fr. 50 c.

161. During their residence, they are, more- over, allowed, on the condition of making four vacations per day, as follows:—The architects from Paris, 32 francs (or 25s. 1d.); those of the departments, 24 francs (or 19s. nearly).

General Observations.—As may in all pro- hability strike the reader, the intention of the framers of the French code was to protect the interests of the proprietor in every possible manner, and certainly the tendency of the legislation is very partial in his favour. It is also subject to the reproach which may be ad- dressed to all the codes based upon the old Roman law; firstly, of precising over much the duties of the inferiors; secondly, of treat- ing every man of business too much in the light of a cheat; of taking too many precau- tions against his becoming so; and, by the same rule, suggesting too many modes of de- ceiving. Our own common law is more lax; but it trusts to the good faith of the respective parties, and by so doing calls into play the quality it supposes. The tendency of the French law is just the reverse.

Much good, however, results in practice from the fact of the architect being made re- sponsible for the durability of his works. We rarely hear in France of the fall of important buildings in consequence of their ignorance, or the employment of bad materials. Public opinion is also far more severe in that country than with us, when such instances occur. Navier, perhaps the first mathematician who ever practised as an engineer, is reported to have destroyed himself, because his suspen- sion bridge of "les Invalides" fell into the Seine. The engineer of the Central Railway, who executed the bridge over the Loire, which sank during the execution, and afterwards fell down during the floods of 1847, was obliged to retire into private life; whilst English en- gineers allow bridges and viaducts to tumble down, and no notice is taken of it. Indeed, as long as the decision as to who are the parties to be blamed in these cases is left to juries, composed of the first twelve people who come to hand, such must ever be the case. We require some competent authorities to decide in these instances; and then our common sense would not be insulted by the fact of the fall of a viaduct being attributed to the washing out of the mortar in the arch joints, or to an unequal loading of the arches by the spreading of ballast in an irregular manner. In the first place, hydraulic mortar should have been used; in the second, a viaduct which could not resist an extra quantity of ballast is not fit for locomotive traffic.

It is true that the constant sense of re- sponsibility is likely to restrain the adoption of new principles; but it is certainly likely to prevent architects or engineers from running unjustifiable risks.

The code is silent upon the subject of the architect's retribution. There are certain works which would be egregiously underpaid at 5 per cent. on the cost, whilst others would be as much overpaid at the same rate. Custom then decides, and the tribunals refer the enunciation of what is the custom to pro- fessional men, independent of both parties, named "experts," for the particular case.

As far as regards public buildings, the sys- tem of not paying a commission, but a fixed salary, is open to discussion. Certain it is, in the first place, that it puts a stop to un- dignified squabbles for money, which in no case can raise the reputation of an artist. From some cause (it cannot be this) the French government buildings are more pro- foundly studied than with us. The greater part of what is done in London and throughout England, shows that architecture is here more a trade than an art. There is a want of con- scientious study, such as is to be met with in the best buildings erected by the municipal architects of Paris. Any person who will ex- amine the details of the Madeleine, N. D. de Lorette, St. Vincent de Paul, must confess— even without agreeing with the taste in which they are conceived—that they exhibit traces of study and careful execution such as are unknown to us. We certainly dare more. We do the most wondrous works in the world; but we do not put the requisite amount of taste in them.

A USE FOR A BALLOON.—Lieut. Gale, the aeronaut, suggests that a balloon might be usefully employed in the search for Sir John Franklin. At an altitude of two miles he says a panorama of 1,200 miles would be placed within observation. — An American paper speaks of a large flying machine now being made in that country. "The canvass is all ready, and is about 80 yards in length and 50 in diameter. It is to be propelled by two oscillating five-horse power engines, which are already provided and secured in the car. They occupy a very small space and are well made; they are to propel the huge gaseous monster, by fan wheels, we believe."

ST. NICOLAI KIRCHE, HAMBURG.

FATAL ACCIDENT TO THE CLERK OF THE WORKS.

Our readers are probably aware that the church of St. Nicholas, being one of the three churches either wholly or partially destroyed by the great fire of Hamburg in 1842, is now being rebuilt on a scale both of dimension and decoration, nearly equalling many of the ancient cathedrals. The work, like its ancient predecessors, proceeds slowly and gradually as funds permit, but the eastern portions have now attained nearly to the full elevation of the aisles. The work, though under the direction of an English architect, Mr. Scott, is carried out exclusively by German contractors and workmen, and has been superintended from its commencement by Mr. Mortimer, an excellent and talented English clerk of the works, who had been in Mr. Scott's employ for about twelve years, and is stated by him to have been decidedly the most efficient and trustworthy superintendent he has ever had under him. Mr. Mortimer's attention to the work in question has been as zealous and unremitted as his duties were difficult and arduous. Being a man of limited education, though of unusual natural talent, it was no easy task to be intrusted with the entire direction of contractors and workmen whose language he did not understand, yet he succeeded from the first in superintending the work as perfectly and efficiently as if it had been in his native country. When to this is added the extreme difficulty attendant on the construction of foundations at Hamburg—where excavations have to be made to a depth of 25 to 27 feet, of which the last 8 or 10 feet are below the level of the tide, and have to be pumped by steam power,—and also the elaborate nature of the architecture, and the circumstance of most of the workmen employed having never before been engaged on a work of this kind, it will be seen that his duties were very different from those ordinarily expected of a clerk of the works. Mr. Mortimer's uniform practice was to be on the ground the whole time when the men were at work (which in summer was from five in the morning till eight at night), excepting only when he had to make journeys to stone quarries or brick fields, which lie at great distances from Hamburg. But his duties did not end with the working hours of the men, for after their works were over his recommenced, and he continued preparing his working drawings often till midnight. The number of large and most elaborate working drawings he had prepared for this building alone amounted to several hundreds, showing the work with a minuteness which is not required by builders in this country, for it was one of his rules never to place the drawings received from the architect in the hands of the workmen, but to keep them as documents for his own reference, and to work them out afresh himself, both to insure his own perfect acquaintance with them, and that any error which might have crept into them might be detected before the work was commenced. When remonstrated with by his employer for giving himself this unusual amount of labour, he would say,—"Your drawings *may* be correct, Sir, but I do not *know* whether they are so till I have worked them out for myself." It may readily be judged from this, that the same principle would apply with double force to those placed under him. Not a brick or a stone wrongly laid or worked would escape him; indeed, on one occasion the workmen, unused to such vigilant superintendence, made a formal application against it to the Government authorities, as being inconsistent with the laws of their ancient building guilds.

Mr. Mortimer, during the last few years of his life, added to his professional qualifications the unhappily less usual qualification of being an earnestly religious character. He had formerly been as careless on such subjects as too many of us are; but having had a very dangerous attack of illness shortly after his going to Hamburg, during which he was very kindly attended by the excellent English chaplain, the Rev. Mr. Stirling, he was ever after a consistent Christian. It may be mentioned, as an example worthy of imitation, that though his duties, both necessary and self-imposed, were heavier and also better attended to than is common with persons in his position, and though in summer he was usually on the works at five o'clock in the morning, he never left his lodgings without having first gone through the litany or some other part of the church service, and reading some not very scanty portion of the Bible. He said that had it not been for the support he felt from attention to religious duties, he could not hold up against the harassing nature of his labours.

It is stated in the Hamburg papers, and gathered from elsewhere, that on the morning of the 22nd ult. he entertained, from several apparently trivial circumstances, a strong presentiment of his approaching end; and when the foreman bid him "good day," he said he feared it would not be so to him, and mentioned some circumstances which produced such an impression, and later in the day he mentioned some others which confirmed the conviction that something would happen to him on that day. However this may be, it appears that in the afternoon of that day, while examining one of the springers of the groining which was inaccurately worked, he stepped hastily down from a higher to a somewhat lower scaffolding, when the board on which he lighted snapped, and he was precipitated nearly 50 feet into the crypt of the church, and killed on the spot. The templet which fitted to the stone he is supposed to have been examining was found beside him; while the slightly inaccurate stone above clearly showed that he had not suffered his presentiments to relax his vigilance in the exercise of his duties.

The respect he had won from all who knew him caused the deepest feeling for his untimely end. The committee for the church, as a last tribute of respect and gratitude, gave him such a funeral as is usual among their most distinguished citizens. All the members of the committee attended in person, as did all the clergy of the church, the contractors, foremen, and many others, while crowds followed on foot. The workmen wished to attend *en masse*, but were advised not to do so on account of the jealousy of the Prussian military at any large concourse of people. The latter, however, showed their sympathy by suspending their exercises, in which they were engaged near the cemetery, while the funeral service was performed.

Above the hearse, on a pointed arched canopy was hung a silvered shield, containing the name, age, &c., of the deceased. The masonic badges (the compasses, level, &c.) and a black crown of foliage were laid upon the coffin, with the inscription, "Henry Green Mortimer, of Witham, Essex, England, born Apr. 10, 1810, died Sept. 22nd, 1849."

The English service was read by the Rev. Mr. Stirling, the chaplain, after which a funeral oration was pronounced by the Rev. Dr. Strauch, the chief incumbent of St. Nicholas's Church, in which he spoke feelingly of the merits of the deceased, both in a professional and a Christian point of view.

About sixty of the workmen afterwards, according to the picturesque and expressive custom of the country, went to the grave, and deposited upon it a rich and costly garland of evergreens and silk, on which was the following inscription:—

"MORTIMER,
ihrem Baumeister:
die Traurenden Steinhauer
des St. Nicolai Kirchenbaues."

"To Mortimer, their master-builder, from the sorrowing stonemasons of St. Nicholas's Church."

We have inserted the above particulars at length, from a feeling that while such obituaries are usually accorded to persons of higher stations, it is hardly just to deny them to those who in humbler positions have evinced an amount of talent, zeal, and uncompromising devotion to their duties equally deserving of commemoration, and that the qualifications and conduct of the party thus suddenly cut off in the prime of his days, are worthy of being recorded as an example to those to whom similar duties are committed.

Galvanized Iron Company.—According to the *Mining Journal*, this company is to be wound up. The paper mentioned attributes the failure to want of knowledge on the part of the management.

NEWS OF THE HOUSES OF PARLIAMENT.

Mr. Herbert has completed his fresc from "Lear," in the Upper Waiting Hall, o "Hall of Poets," as it is to be termed, the eight available panels which it affords being appropriated to the illustration of Chaucer, Spenser, Milton, Shakspeare, Dryden, Pope, Byron, and Scott. That of Milton was given to Mr. Horsley, that of Chaucer to Mr. Cope, and both are finished. Mr. John Tenniel has Dryden, and is now proceeding on the wall. The artists for the remainder are not yet named, so far as we know. Mr. Tenniel's subject is the St. Cecilia, the clever original drawing for which was lithographed by the Art-Union of London: copies were distributed as prizes. The artist has altered the composition of the foreground by the introduction of a reclining child on the left hand side, and the substitution of a young knight in armour for the old man on the right hand side. Mr. Tenniel is one of the rising artists of the day; he has nothing to do to command success but think and work hard.

Of Mr. Herbert's fresco we must speak in warm terms; it is a noble work, full of power and beauty,—an evidence as well of perseverance and determination to overcome difficulties as of artistic skill. The subject was exhibited by Mr. Herbert last year, at the Royal Academy, in oil. *Lear* is on his throne (of Byzantine workmanship sparkling with mosaics and gilding), the elder sisters are on their knees, to the left, and *Cordelia*, having refused to "heave her heart into her mouth," stands meekly on the right. The exact words illustrated we will take to be *Lear's* expression—

"So young and so untender?
Cordelia. So young, my lord, and true.
Lear. Let it be so—Thy truth, then, be thy dower:
For, by the sacred radiance of the sun,
The mysteries of Hecate, and the night;
* * * * *
Here I disclaim all my paternal care,
Propinquity, and property of blood,
And as a stranger to my heart and me
Hold thee, from this, for ever
* * * * *
The sway,
Revenue, execution of the rest
Beloved sons, be yours; which to confirm,
This *coronet part between you.*"

The countenance of Cordelia is one of singular sweetness.

The artist resolved, on commencing the work, that the whole of the picture should be positively in fresco,—*i. e.*, not made out or rectified in tempera; and to effect this the whole picture has been executed three times over, part after part being cut out and replastered, and cut out again before a result could be obtained satisfactory to the artist. We may add that the picture is lighted from a window at the side high up, and that the shadows are arranged to suit this.

In completing the decoration of the ceiling and walls of the hall, it will be necessary to have reference to the frescoes, or their effect may be considerably interfered with.

Looking in at the House of Lords, we saw Mr. Maclise hard at work, perched up in the far distant recess, wherein he has nearly finished the Spirit of Chivalry. The House of Commons is so near to completion, that if it were desired, it might be made ready in time for the coming session. The whole of the woodwork here, panelled ceiling, galleries, wall panellings, are of polished oak, without colour or gilding, contrasting strikingly with the profuse decoration of the House of Lords. The Commons' lobby and libraries are also very nearly ready for use.

Some time since we took occasion to mention that the piles which formed the coffer-dam in front of the terrace were being *drawn*, and we pointed out the impolicy of the proceeding and the danger which attended it. We are glad, therefore, to find that this course has been abandoned, and that the piles are now being *cut* off close to the surface of the ground, so as not to disturb the bottom.

The question between Mr. Barry and the Government is still open, but we understand there is every willingness on the part of the latter to meet it liberally.

INAUGURATION OF THE LONDON COAL EXCHANGE.

On Tuesday last crowds filled the streets n the neighbourhood of the Thames, obtructed the bridges, and lined the river, to ee her Majesty and Prince Albert pass along ' the silent highway," to open the new edifice vhich has been erected in Thames-street for the ›urposes of the coasting trade. The Queen vas unable to be present, but her illustrious :onsort brought the Prince of Wales and the Princess Royal. Many, many thousands of ›eople were out, so fond of sights and so loyal are we English; and every where such a reception was given as must have delighted those for whom the sweet voices were raised. The building we have already described and illustrated, both externally and internally; and we have commended its architect for the invention, novel applications, and suggestive decorations which it displays.

"To meet the demands of a rapid extension in the great element of British commerce—the coasting trade, the nursery of seamen and of our commercial marine," said the Recorder, in his address to the Prince, "this capacious building, the Coal Exchange, chiefly constructed of iron, at once light and durable, has been erected. When with the purposes of this Exchange are associated the creation and increase of commerce and manufactures, and the naval superiority of this kingdom,—when the essential article of coal ministers by appliances innumerable to the wants and prosperity of millions, illuminates our houses, streets, and manufactories,—when every metal at the forge is obedient to the fire it feeds, whilst it commands as its agent and its instrument the mighty power of steam,—ti became the wisdom, and accorded with the enlightened beneficence of her Majesty the Queen, to regard this edifice with the favour and consideration ever graciously extended by her Majesty to objects of national importance."*

It is not our purpose to describe the ceremony; to speak of the glittering multitude which filled the Exchange and its galleries, clad in robes and uniforms of every hue; the profuse hospitality of the corporation; how that Mr. Bunning, when presented to the Prince, was justly cheered; and how Sir James Duke, Knight, the Lord Mayor, is to be created a baronet. We have but to record the event and its most brilliant accomplishment, adding, however, a note of the curious circumstance (forced on us by two strong letters on the subject), that the coal factors had nothing to do with the ceremony, and scarcely obtained the means of being present.

We congratulate Mr. Bunning on a fortunate concurrence of circumstances, which will serve to connect his name lastingly with the city of London.†

BRITISH ARCHÆOLOGICAL ASSOCIATION.

At the opening meeting, held Friday, Oct. 26th, Mr. Pettigrew, treasurer, presided, and after briefly congratulating the members on the resumption of the public meetings, read a paper from the president, Lord Albert Denison, detailing the opening and contents of two barrows, in the neighbourhood of Scarborough. The first, called Way Hagg, was opened in the autumn of 1848; its diameter was 36 yards, and depth 8 feet, with a slight depression on the top. The cutting was commenced on the north side; and at about 18 inches from the surface and 4 feet from the top (on the slope) was discovered a small urn containing wood ashes. Eight or ten feet nearer the centre four stones were discovered, one having three holes of unequal size worked on its surface, another five holes, a third four holes, and the fourth thirteen holes. These stones varied in length from 33 to 16 inches. Upon removing these, an urn 15 inches in height was exposed to view, standing upon two large stones, and containing calcined bones, flint arrow-heads, bone pins, and the bones of a small animal which had been burnt with the body. The second, Ravenhill tumulus, was opened 21st August, 1849, and was 42 feet in diameter and 8 feet deep. The cutting was made on the south side. After removing the sandy earth on the surface, a wall of large stones was cut through. Two stones, one with five holes and the other two, were discovered, and immediately afterward an urn 6¾ inches high. A little to the left of this was found a small vessel embedded in wood ashes, calcined bones, and earth.

Another investigation, on 31st August, proved the stone wall to exist on the east side, and apparently encircling the whole mound. The paper was followed by some observations from Messrs. Saull and Keet, on the stones with holes worked on their surface, and Dr. Bell remarked, that they resembled druidical stones, called in Germany porringer stones.

Mr. Planché read an interesting paper on the "Effigy of a Lady in Worcester Cathedral," which had been alternately appropriated, to the wife of William Montacute, Earl of Salisbury, *temp.* Edward III.; to a countess of Warren and Surrey; to Andela, wife of John de Warren, a natural son of the sixth earl; and to Maude d'Evereux, the sister of Giffard, Bishop of Worcester. Mr. Planché disproved every one of these assertions, and suggested, that the effigy was that of Maude Longespee, titular countess of Salisbury, being Lady de Clifford, of Corfham, in her own right; who, according to the annals of Worcester, was buried in the cathedral in 1301, having been then removed from some other edifice, 18 years after her death. She was the grand-daughter of Llewllyn, Prince of Wales, and of King John, mother of Margaret de Lacy, countess of Lincoln; and had to her second husband John, Lord Giffard, of Brimsfield, so that the magnificence of her monument was due to her rank, and its position, to her relationship by blood to King John, and by marriage to Bishop Giffard.

Mr. Planché prefaced his paper by some strong and proper remarks on the devastation that had been committed in our cathedrals, by their former *soi-disant* conservators; and particularly in that of Worcester, in which, with the exception of Prince Arthur's monument, there was scarcely a mediæval tomb or effigy that could be positively identified.

Mr. Godwin, as an evidence that in early times they had treated the monuments of their progenitors as badly as had been done more recently, mentioned the discovery, a few weeks ago, of a carved monumental slab, of the thirteenth century, under one of the buttresses of the north porch of Redcliffe church, for which it had been made to serve as a foundation.*

Mr. White exhibited the rubbing of a brass from St. Michael's Church, near St. Alban's. The figures are those of a civilian and his wife, John and Maude Pecok. The rubbing was taken by the son of the clerk, during the few hours required to repair the flooring of a pew, and it was exhibited to shew, that this and other such societies are producing much good, by giving those engaged in our churches a taste for the antiquities contained in them, and a desire to preserve, and even illustrate such things when an opportunity offers. This brass is now removed from sight by the new flooring.—Mr. Waller said, he believed he had a rubbing of the inscription only. He considered the brass early and interesting, and one he had long wished to see.—Mr. H. W. Rolfe exhibited rubbings of brasses in the church of Boughton Malherb, in Kent, belonging to the family of Wotton; and Mr. Planché exhibited a cast of the seal of John-de-Scott, Earl of Chester.

Enthusiasm.—We are told that the infant daughter of a gentleman employed at the works of the Britannia-bridge was taken to the Britannia rock, the other day, in the middle of the straits, where she was christened Britannia Ann Stephenson, in compliment of the bridge and the engineer. We remember a worthy builder, who, having erected a chain-bridge some ten years ago, with similar feeling, but less tact, christened his little daughter *Suspension Maria.*

CHURCH BUILDING NEWS.

The foundation stone of the new chapel of the Wesleyans at Southampton was laid in East-street, on Wednesday in last week, by the Mayor, accompanied to the site by a large proportion of the Town Council and bailiffs—but not in robes of office as was intended, that being an infraction of the old statute thereanent:—at least it was held by the counsel applied to (Mr. Barstow), that "in strictness the letter of the law would be violated," although the main object was the mere laying of a stone, and not public worship, that being in this case but an accessary. The architect is Mr. James Wilson. His design is in the Gothic manner. There will be a centre window over the door-way, flanked by two towers and pinnacles, and two side windows, with buttresses and pinnacles surmounting them at the extremities of the front. The area of the chapel will be 45 feet by 72 feet in the clear, its superficial extent being 116 square feet more than any public room in the town. There will be 300 free sittings in the body of the chapel, and, in addition, a second gallery, which will contain 200. Underneath the chapel there will be a school-room capable of accommodating 700 children. The cost of erection is estimated at 3,500*l.*, or with site, &c., 5,300*l.* Of this the mayor has presented 400*l.*, and Mr. W. Betts 700*l.*—deficiency still 2,000*l.* odd. We hope it will be better than one by the same architect in St. John's-square, Clerkenwell.——The foundation stone of a Baptist chapel was laid in Wadham-street, Weston-super-Mare, on Tuesday week.——It is intended to take down a portion of the parish church of Bremhill, Wilts, and rebuild the same, and also reseat the church.——Dr. Warneford has placed in the hands of the bishop of the diocese of Gloucester and Bristol another 1,000*l.* to promote the building of parsonage houses in benefices of small value at present without them.——A little chapel has been built at the Bath united hospital, from a design supplied by Messrs. Manners and Gill. It is to be provided with hot air pipes, and will cost in all 340*l.*——The church of St. Augustine, Bristol, has been re-opened after being some weeks under process of restoration. The side galleries have been removed and the seats re-arranged. The tradesmen employed were—Mr. C. Williams, Hanover-street, mason; Messrs. Naylor and Heaven, Park-row, painters; and Mr. Martin, Orchard-street, carpenter.——The foundation stone of a Baptist chapel was to be laid at George's-place, Leeds, on 1st inst.——The church of All Saints, Monkwearmouth, was consecrated on Tuesday week.——A tower, 76 feet high, with spire and vane, has recently been erected at Low-wood, Windermere, and a clock with two dials placed in it. We don't exactly know, however, whether this comes properly under head of church building news: perhaps the church is expected to follow.——During the relaying of the floor of the Abbey Church of Dunfermline, the workmen lately came upon two massive stone coffins lying side by side, and very near the spot where "the rude awtare" of the original abbey stood. The coffins were hollowed out of one single block each, with a circular space for the head. In one was found a body completely cased in leather: the other was full of dust. The leather casing was in excellent preservation, but the body within completely gone, scarcely a little bone left. The casing was found to have been carefully laced down the back and round the soles of the feet.

Bradford Union Competition.—Wishing to compete for the new union workhouse for the Bradford union, I applied for the plan and instructions to architects, which have been obligingly forwarded to me by the clerk. In the concluding clause is the following notice—"The guardians do not pledge themselves to employ the architect whose plans are preferred; but in case of his not being employed in the direction of the work, a premium of 30*l.* will be given for the plans, which will be the property of the guardians." Now, Sir, is not this as good as telling the successful competitor that however excellent his plan may be, the value placed upon the same is 30*l.*, a sum far below the actual cost that must be incurred by each party who thinks of competing?—Truth and Justice.

* The increase which has taken place in the coal trade is extraordinary. We are told that in 1705 about 600 ships sufficed in the supply and demand of London, and that in 1805, 4,856 cargoes were required, containing about 1,350,000 tons; while last year (1818), 2,717 ships made 12,267 voyages, and conveyed 3,418,340 tons!

† In the previous week the foundation of the new Billingsgate Market (under the same architect) was laid. It includes an architectural frontage of 172 feet (we are told), extending from the Custom House quay to Nicholson's Wharf.

* The slab shows a cross occupying the centre, with two sculptured heads projecting from the plain face of the stone, one over each arm of the cross.

THE STRASBOURG RAILWAY STATION, PARIS.

BLOCK PLAN OF STRASBOURG RAILWAY STATION.

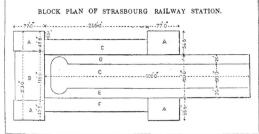

THE STRASBOURG RAILWAY STATION, PARIS.

THE accompanying engraving represents the south elevation of the station lately erected in Paris for the railway to Strasbourg. It stands between the Rues du Faubourg St. Denis and du Faubourg St. Martin, being bounded on the south by la Rue Neuve Chabrol.

The Strasbourg line is one of those executed under the law of 1842. The State purchased the land, executed all the earthwork, bridges, culverts, &c., to formation level, and is to build all the stations, shops, and offices. The company furnish the ballast, lay down the rails, and put all the rolling stock upon the line; which, at the expiration of the lease, becomes the property of the State, the rolling stock being paid for at a valuation.

This elevation is a noticeable production, from the originality of its conception, the picturesqueness of its effect, and its consistency with the use of the building for which it was designed. On the first inspection we feel that it is not on the model of a Roman or Greek temple, of an Italian palace, or a conventual building. It tells its own tale at once. The architect has thought for himself, and has endeavoured to design a building in accordance with the wants and the taste of his own times. The monument he has produced is not without errors of detail, and its internal arrangements are very faulty; but on the whole there are marks of originality which are quite refreshing (if such a vulgarism be allowable) in the present day, when architects appear to consider the greatest merit to consist in copying what has been done before.

With reference to the block plan of the station-building annexed, it may be necessary to observe that the custom in France is not to allow strangers to enter either the waiting-rooms or the sheds. Travellers remain in the rooms until the moment of departure, and therefore do nothing more than traverse the quays on the way to the carriages. This system is preferable to our own, in which the number of people walking about renders the service more difficult and slovenly. We are, however, so fond of shaking hands at the last moment that an attempt to change the system would be attended with great obloquy.

The large shed is covered with a wrought-iron roof, in one span.

The basement of the whole of these buildings is executed in the "roche" of the "calcaire grossier;" the upper part in Pierre Franche, of St. Leu, l'Ile Adam, or of Conflans. The roofing is covered with zinc.

G. R. B.

References to the Plan.

A A. Offices.
B. Covered gallery, with groined arches of pottery, from stone columns.
C. Waiting-room.
D. Departure quay.
E. Arrival quay.
F. Baggage, arrival, &c.
G. Shed for five lines of rails.

The whole length of the shed is 500 feet; the width, 100 feet.

PRISON REFORM.
DIXON'S LIFE OF HOWARD.*

THE cosmopolitan and revered name of Howard re-appears under the hand of the present author with fresh interest, and within limits so available to the impatient temper of the present generation, that many are now likely to realize some little knowledge of a man whose name has hitherto, it must be admitted, been much better known than his history.

Mr. Dixon appears to have been for some years engaged in researches which naturally led him to give close heed to Howard's labours, and the result of which researches, is about to appear in a new work under the title of "The London Prisons," with a description of the chief prisons in the provinces. It was while so engaged that he became convinced of the public need of such an account of John Howard's life as he has now given us,—and especially at the present time, when the interest felt in prison reforms is on the increase, and the prison world a popular topic.

Much as there is yet to do in this wide field of reform, the inmates of prisons in general now stand in a most enviable position by comparison with those of the time of Howard, as every one knows in general terms, but few, probably, in special detail. How strongly does even the following exceedingly moderate and favourable specimen of gaol-accommodation, in the Marshalsea, beginning of last century, remind us of another vast field of reform, as yet scarce broached by any modern Howard, even though loudly called for in behalf of those whose honest spirit of struggling poverty prevents them from enjoying the benefits now so frequently conferred on prisoners!

"The common side," says a Parliamentary report, "is enclosed with a strong brick wall; in it are now confined upwards of 330 prisoners, most of them in the utmost necessity; they are divided into particular rooms called wards, and the prisoners belonging to each ward are locked up in their respective wards every night, most of which are excessively crowded, thirty, forty, nay fifty persons having been locked up in some of them, not 16 feet square. * * * All the last year there were sometimes forty, and never less than thirty-two persons locked up in George's ward every night, which is a room of 16 by 14 feet, and about 8 feet high; the surface of the room is not sufficient to contain that number when laid down, so that one half are hung up in hammocks, while the other lie on the floor under them; the air is so wasted by the number of persons who breathe in that narrow compass, that it is not sufficient to keep them from stifling, several having, in the heat of summer perished for want of air."

Even the more offensive details, which are here omitted, cannot be worse than those that still prevail outside the walls of gaols, though not now within.† The Marshalsea, however, was only inhabited by debtors and pirates; and the accommodation may be said

---
* "John Howard and the Prison World of Europe: from Original and Authentic Documents." By Hepworth Dixon. London: Jackson and Walford, St. Paul's Churchyard. 1849.

† To Howard, and to his scarcely less noble-minded wife, Henrietta, their fellow-countrymen were indebted for an exemplary endeavour to lay the foundations of an improved order of labourers' cottages, to which not only Howard's money, but his wife's jewels and savings for recreation and travel, were devoted.

---

to have been excellent compared with what Howard himself had at Brest, as a prisoner during war with France.

"When they were at length landed," says Mr. Dixon, "he was confined, with many other prisoners, in the castle of the town, in a dungeon, dark, damp, and filthy beyond description, where they were kept for several additional hours without nourishment. At last a leg of mutton was brought and thrown into the cell—as horseflesh is thrown into the dens of wild beasts—for the starving captives to scramble for, tear with their teeth, and devour as best they could. In this horrible dungeon, thus fed, they were detained for a week."

The world is eternally indebted to the Brest dungeon, as the turning point in the character and destiny of Howard, who, guided as it were by Providence, "with no distinct and definite object before him," had thus gone abroad and lived—an unwilling denizen—in the 'wild beasts' den' devoted to a future reform of abuses so universal.

Into the history of Howard's career we cannot here enter, and indeed our only business with this very interesting book, is to present our readers with a brief recital of some of the horrid details of dungeon-architecture and prison mismanagement witnessed by the great philanthropist,—by way of exemplar, and exclusive even, as much as possible, of any enlargement on the diabolical and scarcely credible *treatment* suffered by the miserable objects who were thrown into such inhuman dens. To this end, one or two further extracts may suffice.

"The gaol at Plymouth had a room for felons called the China, 17 feet long, 8 wide, and only 5½ high—so that a person of ordinary stature could not stand erect in it! This diabolical dungeon was also dark and stifling—having neither air nor light, except such as could struggle through a wicket in the door, 5 inches by 7 in dimensions. Yet Howard learned, with horror, that *three* men had been kept in this den, under a sentence of transportation, for nearly two months! They could neither see, nor breathe freely, nor could they stand upright. To keep alive at all, they were forced to crouch—each in his turn—at the wicket, to catch a few inspirations of air; otherwise they must have died of suffocation—for the door was rarely opened. When Howard saw it, the door had not been opened for five weeks—and yet it was inhabited. He caused the bolts to be shot and an entry made; but the indescribable stench which issued, would have driven back any less courageous visiter."

"As a specimen of the condition in which he found some of the bridewells, we transcribe his account of one in Folkingham, in Lincolnshire:—' In this prison, under the keeper's house, are five damp rooms; two of which were used for a lunatic, who was confined here for some years. The men's lodging-room (18 feet by 9½, and 6 feet 9 inches high), has only an aperture in the door, a foot square, into the work-room. The women's room is 13 feet by 8, and 6 feet 2 inches high. In another room, 20½ feet by 12, you go down by a trap-door in the floor seven steps into a horrid dungeon (10 feet square, 5½ feet high); no chimney; small court; no pump; no sewer. Yet a woman, with a child at her breast, was sent hither for a year and a day! The child died.'"

A place of confinement for debtors at Knaresborough is thus described by the humane inspector:—

"'No fire-place; earth-floor; very offensive, a common sewer from the town running through it uncovered!' Only a short time before Howard's visit, an unfortunate officer had been cast into this horrible kennel. Having some knowledge of the place, he had the precaution to take his dog in with him, to defend him from the vermin, which the stench, arising from the open sewer, produced in myriads. In a few days the dog was destroyed, having been actually devoured by its insidious enemies; and, at the same time, his master's hands and face were so bitten as to present to the eye nothing but three great and loathsome sores!!"

We cannot conclude without adverting to the circumstance that Mr. Dixon indignantly denies the charge alleged against Howard, that in his philanthropic efforts on behalf of criminals and other prisoners in gaols throughout the civilized world, he neglected his duty as a father to his only son. The author adduces what he conceives to be more than sufficient evidence to the contrary.

The utmost that can be said is, that if Howard's attention had been less absorbed by the work for which the world is his debtor, the conduct and fate of this son might have been different.

THE MODE OF DISCHARGING WORKMEN.

A case was heard at the County Court, Clerkenwell, on the 15th instant (Tuffs against Mansfield), a few remarks on which may not be uninteresting to a great portion of the readers and subscribers to your journal. The plaintiff in this case sued for the sum of 5s., the amount of a day's labour which he lost on defendant's account: the facts are as follow:— The plaintiff, who had been in the employ of the defendant some months previously to Saturday, the 22nd of September, was, on that day, ordered to take his tools from the job he was then at, to the yard of the defendant, which he did accordingly, and received the amount of wages due to him by the defendant. Nothing was said to the plaintiff about being discharged: of course the plaintiff went to defendant's premises on the following Monday morning, with the expectation of being sent to another job, which is usually the case when a man is ordered to the yard with his tools, but on this occasion the plaintiff was informed that his services were no longer required.

Now, Sir, as the plaintiff had refused an engagement with another builder on the previous Saturday night in consequence of being still in the employ of defendant, I think it is quite reasonable that he should be paid for his loss of time.

After having heard the case, his Honour severely reprimanded the defendant on the injustice and impropriety of discharging men in that way, to which the defendant replied that it was the usual way of discharging men, and that ordering a man to bring his tools to the yard was equivalent to his discharge. Mr. Boresley, a carpenter and builder in a small way, was then called by the defendant, who made the same statement as defendant, adding that it was the plan that all builders adopted in discharging their men. His Honour then said that the plaintiff's experience ought to have told him that it was the general way of discharging men, and he should therefore decide for the defendant.

I shall leave it to your readers to judge for themselves, whether it is a just way of discharging a man, or whether such a plan would be adopted by any respectable builder in London; but as it has become very prevalent with the small builders of London, regardless of the interests of their men, to treat them with the utmost indifference, and I think it is high time that something was done, so that there may be something like an understanding between master and man, in order that when he was discharged, he might be informed of it on the same night, so that, if he was offered another job, he might accept it. I rely for the insertion of this on your known impartiality in the advocacy of justice, as well for the operative as the master.

R. S. Tuffs.

ARCHITECTS' REMUNERATION.

WINDSOR CASTLE.

A connection of the late Sir Jeffrey Wyatville, with reference to a remark in our leading article of September 29th (page 457, *ante*), that "Sir Jeffrey Wyatville received 5 per cent. on the amount expended at Windsor Castle, and *was also paid for measuring the works*," says that the statement is not correct. "At the commencement of the works, and with the sanction of the authorities, the late Mr. West was appointed to measure them, and they were all measured by him and his successor, Mr. William Corderoy, whose bills were made out and delivered quarterly in their own names, and paid by the department, like all other charges, to the individuals whose names they bore." The writer further says, that "the remuneration for Windsor Castle was, as for the Houses of Parliament, settled by agreement at the beginning of the works, and that 5 per cent. was to be paid in lieu of the usual per centage paid to the architects employed by Government, and travelling expenses, which the architects were entitled to, and were always paid for, at certain rates, but which were not to be charged in this instance according to the agreement entered into. It would not be too much to state that the expenses compromised for under the head of travelling expenses for himself and his clerks, amounted in the first year of the works at Windsor Castle to 2 per cent., and throughout the whole of them formed a very considerable item."

Admitting it to be correct that Sir Jeffrey was not himself paid for measuring the works, this will not interfere with the only inference we wished drawn from the statement, namely, that the cost of measuring and making out the works was not included in the 5 per cent. commission. In Mr. Noble's volume, on "Professional Practice," we find this passage (p. 32):—

"In reference to measuring, it does not seem that at an early date in professional practice, architects ever claimed remuneration for that difficult duty; but in 1794, and at recent periods, variations have and still do occur in the profession, respecting that important business. This is borne out by an inspection of the report of the select committee of the House of Commons in 1828, in which Sir Jeffrey Wyatville's evidence shows, that in his very extensive and long practice, he always received 5 per cent. commission on the expenditure, as well as the expense of measuring; and was also paid for his journeys and wages to the clerk of works."

SANITARY MEASURES AND THE WINDOW TAX.

Among the sanitary measures suggested for the improvement of dwellings, it is singular, that the effect of the window tax upon the question of ventilation has of late been forgotten, or else shirked, under the pressure of the revenue deficiency. It is, however, of so great importance that, having formerly been discussed in your columns, I trust you will again lend your aid to bring the subject before the public, and invoke the Board of Health to take up the matter, as one peculiarly connected with their inquiries.

There has always been an outcry against the tax from its first imposition; and, when increased by the necessities of the war, it excited the savage epigram—

"God gave us light, and saw that it was good;
But Pitt denied it—d—— his blood."

It has, however, never been alleviated, but the time seems now to have arrived when its influence upon the health of millions demands that it be reconsidered.

As an architect called upon to plan residences for all classes, I can, in common with the profession, speak decidedly upon its injurious tendency. In a residence for a nobleman I have blocked up lights in passages and corridors, to avoid excess of taxation; in houses of the middle class I have deprived staircases and attics of their due modicum of light and air; in the dwellings for the poorer classes I have stinted rooms to small single windows; and recently, in the case of parsonage houses, the economic incumbent has blocked out the light and air of the water-closets, to save the increased number of taxable lights. These are positive evils, which no Legislature, especially one which has proclaimed the importance of securing the health of a civilized community, ought any longer to allow to exist.

It is, perhaps, vain to hope for a total abolition of the tax; but if our legislature wish to show that they are earnest in promoting the health of towns, an extensive exemption of windows subject to the duty should at once be made. This exemption should extend to all windows on the underground stories of houses, where ample light and air are of vital importance: it should extend to all water-closets and lights used for ventilation, and even to staircases and passages, which are in a great measure the reservoirs of air in a house. The absurd restriction respecting the size of windows should be also removed, as it tends greatly to impede the arrangement and effect of a design, while it affects very materially the light and air of the single windows in the poorer dwellings.

I could go further into detail, and show that while a great impetus has been given to the glass trade by the removal of the duties on its manufacture the public cannot enjoy half the benefits which this removal confers, so long as the restriction upon the number and size of windows exists; but I trust these few observations will excite attention in those quarters where the question ought to be taken up, as a matter which the recent sanitary investigations show has a great influence on the health and well being of society.

T. L.

NOTES IN THE PROVINCES.

House-ventilating apparatus, we hear, is getting extensively into use in Lincoln. In some cases the vitiated air is taken off by communication with the chimney; and perforated glass has been introduced into windows for the admission of fresh air.——The Manningtree Mechanics' Institution are about to erect a building, with lecture-room 40 feet by 24, and reading-room 20 feet by 14. It is to be in the Elizabethan style, from a design furnished by Mr. Samuel Teulon, to be carried out by Mr. Samuel Simpson, builder.——The sewage excavations at Colchester are in active progress: coins and other relics are turning up.——A writer in the *Bury Post*, while advocating cheap gas for that town, gives the following estimates of cost of gas-works: "There are," he remarks, "no works, I believe, in the counties of either Suffolk, Norfolk, Essex, or Cambridgeshire, of fifteen years' standing, with the same extent of main and public lights, so cheap as these [for Bury], as will appear by the cost of—

Ipswich works	£26,000
Colchester, exclusive of lamp-posts	22,000
Cambridge, about	40,000
Norwich	50,000
Bury, say	10,500

Nor am I aware," he adds, "of any works in England, of the same standing and extent, cheaper than the Bury works."——Halsted, too long unlighted, is to be provided with gas lamps, and lighted by voluntary contribution. ——According to authorized certificate, the quantity of gas consumed in Worcester from June, 1848, to June, 1849, was 17,669,600 feet.——The Edinburgh Council Committee, to whom the petition of the city fleshers for a new slaughter-house was referred, have reported favourably on it, and propose that the city provide 20,000*l.* as the requisite capital, and apply to Parliament for three acres of ground in a proper situation. The fleshers are to pay 100*l.* expenses if the application fail. The new corn market will be finished in a few weeks. The hall is 152 feet long by 92 broad—the largest in the City. Extensive operations are in progress for the formation of a great reservoir on the Castle-hill for the better supply of water to the citizens. The whole of the water company's present buildings there, with adjoining properties, are in course of demolition, and the new reservoir will be made capable of holding about a million and a half of gallons, in place of forty to fifty thousand only, as the old one did. The works are under the immediate charge of the company's engineer, Mr. Leslie, with the advice of Mr. Adie and Mr. Rendall. The designs for the building have been furnished by the company's architect, Mr. Clarke.—— Measures are also in progress for the better supply of Glasgow with water, by an extension of the Gorbals Gravitation Water-works.

Drury-lane Theatre.—Mr. Frederick Gye has been waving his wand again, harlequin like, and lo! the stage of Drury-lane, and the dirty receptacles of scenery and lumber at the back, glow in the purity of a brilliant white, powdered with sprouting roses in a golden trelliage, for the purposes of Jullien, the popularizer of good music. It is quite startling to see what can be done in a week with an unlimited quantity of glazed calico, gold banding, artificial flowers, and Mr. Gye's aptness and good taste. Of the banding there is not less, we calculated, than three miles in length! Considerable improvement has been effected behind, by the removal of two transverse walls, by which means the whole space is thrown into one apartment. The music-loving portion of the English public have much to thank M. Jullien for.

Institute of British Architects.—The first ordinary meeting of the session will be held on Monday evening next, when will be read, "Remarks on the earlier and later Gothic Architecture of Germany," by the Rev. Dr. Whewell.

THE KENILWORTH-STREET SEWER.

It is due to Dr. Ure to state that he has issued a 'supplemental report,' in which he still maintains his point, and says that the evidence given on oath "by the two Government chemists, Mr. Richard Phillips and Dr. Playfair, of the Woods and Forests, and by the two chemists of King's and University Colleges, Dr. Miller and Mr. Campbell, may be regarded as one of the most marvellous scientific phenomena of this *age of pretension*, but which could not occur in any capital of Europe save our own." He adduces the experimental and testimonial evidence on which he rests his conviction that the sewer in question did contain cyanogen compounds, and that these compounds were derived from the gas lime; but he also points out the fact, that such compounds, or cyanogen itself, at least, may be variously formed, where carbon and nitrogen co-exist—as even from common coal and atmospheric air. There are thus two questions fairly at issue between these equally respectable authorities,—firstly, whether cyanogen did exist in the Kenilworth-street sewer; and, secondly, whether that cyanogen was derived from the gas lime, or from the heterogeneous mass of carbonaceous and other substances in the sewer itself. The reputation of one or other seems at stake.

Have you not (unintentionally, I am sure,) done me wrong in your leading article of last Saturday, wherein you protest against the tone taken by me in examining one of the witnesses at the late inquest on the accident in Kenilworth-street sewer? In the re-examination of the witness in question, I entertained a strong impression that he did not manifest that candour which every witness under similar circumstances ought to manifest. Your own remarks in the article in question show that you entertain a similar idea. I did press the witness closely and earnestly, but I think not more so than my duty required. The witness complaining that asperity of feeling was manifested towards him, I at once stated that if I had offended in that particular, I regretted it. I did not plead guilty to the charge; and I really think such a plea would not have been a proper one. Excuse me for thus taking up your time; but as your paper has (deservedly) a large and influential circulation, I am of course unwilling that any strictures on the part of its editor should remain unanswered.

James Hopgood.

King William-street, Strand, Oct. 31, 1849.

METROPOLITAN COMMISSION OF SEWERS.

A general court was held on Friday, the 26th, at the Court House, Greek-street. Lord Ebrington in the chair.

The late Fatal Occurrence in the Sewer at Pimlico.—Sir John Burgoyne, after a few prefatory observations, alluded to the late fatal occurrence in the sewer at Pimlico, and said the subject had occupied the serious attention of the commissioners, who were collecting all the information to be obtained upon it. Having this object in view, and to guard against similar occurrences, he begged to move—

"That the surveyors be directed to report specially on the case of any sewer closed up at the end, and on any sewer in a more than usually noxious condition; and that they be held responsible for the necessary precautions before workmen enter sewers."

The motion being seconded, was unanimously adopted.

On the motion of Captain Dawson, seconded by Mr. Hardwick, it was agreed:—

"That the tide-table of the Thames prepared by the assistant-surveyor (Joseph Smith) be lithographed for the information of the commissioners.

That the tide observations of the Ordnance survey in June and July, 1849, Deptford, &c., be printed for the information of the commissioners."

Lord Ebrington thought it would be desirable that the present commissioners should have the benefit of the investigations of those gentlemen who had been on committees in the last and former commissions, and therefore moved "That the members of former or late commissions engaged on committees be requested to report the results of their respective investigations for the information of the commissioners."—The motion was agreed to.

It was next resolved, on the motion of Mr. Hawes, "That the tender of Messrs. Radley and Rogers for works in Webb-street, Southwark, be accepted. (Phillips.)—That the tender of Messrs. Williams for cleansing sewers at Hammersmith be accepted. (Lovick.)"

Lord Ebrington said, that he believed, from the importance attached by the public and the court to the late occurrence in Kenilworth-street, it would be expedient to procure a copy of the evidence taken before the coroner's jury on that occasion, and accordingly moved, "That the notes of the short-hand writers be procured for the use of the commissioners."—Agreed to.

Lord Ebrington next moved—"That such notes be referred to the general committee of the whole body of the commissioners, to report on the facts, and to give their opinion on the course to be taken thereon." Upon inquiry into the facts, he felt, most undoubtedly, that others than the Commissioners were to blame; but at the same time every opportunity would be afforded any persons implicated to give any explanation that they might see fit to the commissioners. He did not deem it prudent to say more upon the question until the commissioners had every information before them. Agreed to.

The Ventilation of Sewers by a Steam Jet.—Mr. Lawes said that it appeared that Mr. Goldsworthy Gurney's system of ventilating sewers by means of a steam jet, in the experiments at the Friar-street sewer, had been eminently successful; in consequence of which, he understood a letter had been sent by that gentleman to the commissioners. The letter having been read, it was resolved, that a letter be sent to Mr. Gurney, conveying the thanks of the commissioners to him for his services, and that he be informed that the commissioners are not at present in a situation to proceed further with the ventilation of sewers by means of his steam jet.

Upon the motion of Mr. Lawes, seconded by Mr. Rendel, it was agreed that the general committee be instructed to examine and arrange the business to be brought before the next court. By this means, it was said, the court would be fully in possession of the subjects which were to be brought under its notice, and any discussion which was necessary for the information of the public would take place in court.

The effect of this arrangement would seem to be, that the public will know simply just so much of what is going on as the commission like, and nothing more.

Miscellanea.

Appeals against Railway Rates.—At the West Riding Michaelmas Sessions, reported by the *Bradford Observer* of last week, the Midland Railway Company appealed against an assessment at the rateable sum of 3,125*l.* on about 3 miles and 5-6ths of the Leeds and Bradford extension in the township of Bingley, station buildings, &c., inclusive. Some discussion arose as to the desire of the churchwardens and overseers to charge on prospective estimates in preference to actual receipts. The court ruled that actual receipts be taken as the criterion, and on these the rate was ordered to be made on 1,500*l.*, in place of 3,125*l.* Appeal to Court of Queen's Bench refused. The sum offered by the Company exeeded that fixed by the court.——The Lancashire and Yorkshire Railway Company then appealed against Heckmondwike highway rate, and the court reduced valuation from 160*l.* to 24*l.*, and rate from 6*l.* 13s. 4d. to 1*l.* An appeal by same against Cleckheaton highway rate resulted in reduction of rate from 26*l.* to 3*l.* 18s. 2d. The Oakenshaw highway rate was also reduced. There were twenty-six appeals entered, but only six or seven tried.

Boiler Explosion.—The whole of the north end of Liverpool was suddenly roused out of sleep into a state of great alarm on Saturday morning last, about one o'clock, by the explosion of a boiler, which, though only of four-horse power, destroyed a whole brewery, and injured fourteen cottages, blowing roofs out and crushing them in, knocking down walls and emptying vats and a reservoir, the latter of which it turned right over, and emptied a great quantity of water among the fallen timbers, which it is supposed to have thus prevented from being altogether consumed by fire. No life was lost, though three persons were buried in the brewery ruins and whole families under the cottage roofs; so that—unfortunately, shall we say—this is not a case likely to go far towards the establishment of that end for which we have so long contended, namely, the authorized and general regulation and inspection of steam boilers, and the great saving of life and property thereby.

Goodrich Court, on the Wye.—We hear that the interior of this "romance in stone and lime," the residence and museum of the late Sir Samuel Meyrick, is undergoing considerable alteration: a banqueting-room is to replace a portion of the galleries. The *Gloucestershire Chronicle* mentions that the latter have been stripped of their rare and valuable contents to a great extent, and that much of the armour is deposited in a stable! Can this be so? Goodrich Court is *national* in its character, and we sincerely hope that its present owner will preserve the valuable and almost unique assemblage of antiquities within its walls, intact.

Roman Cirencester.—We are glad to learn that Messrs. Buckman and C. H. Newmarch are preparing for publication "Illustrations of the Remains of Roman Art in Cirencester, the Site of Ancient Corinium." Cornium-caester was so important a station during the occupation of Britain by the Romans, that it is not surprising many memorials of a people so advanced in the arts of civilization should, from time to time, be found upon its site, of value in enabling the antiquary to arrive at important conclusions concerning the history of a people whose protracted residence in our island has ever since exerted great influence even upon the manners and customs of the present inhabitants.

Window Gardens.—Those who are debarred from the enjoyment of a garden by sickness, residence, or fortune, should take a leaf out of the book of the French and Belgian ladies, who succeed, by means of double glazed windows and other contrivances, in providing themselves with an ample supply of fresh flowers at all seasons of the year. "In Belgium," says M. Victor Paquet, "wherever you go, you see spaces between double sashed windows filled in winter time with the most charming flowers. Elsewhere, the balconies are turned into greenhouses, and you may find on a fifth or sixth floor a miniature stove, gay with the brightest flowers and the greenest foliage."

Industrial Art.—In viewing the engravings contained in the *Art-Journal*, of works in the Birmingham exhibition of manufactures and arts, I was astonished to find that in nearly all articles designed for domestic utility, there was a prodigious display of the floral character to be executed as like unto nature as the various metals would by their nature permit. Now in the designs for curtain bands, cornices, cornice pole ends, their character is peculiarly inapplicable for their purposes. The end of a round brass pole, with its jingling rings, seems to me to be rather an *outré* place, acting in its horizontal position, for the springing out of flowers, such as the tulip or convolvulus; they certainly are most capitally adapted for places of refuge for spiders to set their snares for the unwary flies, or for the deposit of dirt and dust. As to the bands, I am sure they will contribute largely to the hourly occupation of the neat domestic wife, in repairing the rents produced in the muslin, &c. (both curtains and gowns), by the elegant sharp pointed leaves, let her even have that *rara avis*, a careful and thoughtful servant. The next subject is the stove and fender ends (Messrs. Hoole's). The stove is a clever puzzle to those who want to stir the fire, but a far greater puzzle it is to the cleanly domestic, who has daily to run the risk of scarifying her knuckles and elbows in cleaning the grate, and how she is to take away the dust and ashes is to me a wonder. The terminations have the same danger and difficulty attending them, but it will put the inventive genius and patience of the mistress to a severe trial, when she attempts to sweep her fender clean. The same want of necessary thought prevails in all the articles designed for domestic purposes. How much wiser and advanced were our forefathers in such matters, when they produced simple and elegant forms, introducing only now and then ornament to give them a character or a pleasing quaintness. Far better would the time of the artists be spent if they would study a little more the practical use to which their works are intended to serve.

"Use with elegance combined
Denote the cultivated mind."

C. E. M.

PROJECTED WORKS.—Advertisements have been issued for tenders, by 5th instant, for the erection of prison cells, dwelling-houses, &c. at Gravesend; by 15th, for 70 tons of iron rails for the West Cornwall Railway; by 5th, for 500 tons blue Guernsey granite; by a date not specified, for the erection of a tavern at Peckham; and by 6th, for building sewers in various streets at Birmingham.

RAILWAY COMPENSATION CASES.—At the Borough Court, Bradford, the magistrates were recently called on to award compensation to occupants of houses in Goodmansend required by the Lancashire and Yorkshire Railway Company. The first case was that of Mrs. Stell, for the "Moulders' Arms" beer-house, her interest in which the company estimated at 30*l.* for three months' loss of business, but had offered 40*l.* In cross-examination of the occupant, "Mr. Higham asked her if she had not been convicted by the magistrates for keeping a disorderly house. Mr. Bond strongly disclaimed the imputation as most atrocious, because it was intended by it to punish twice, and he declared that none but a railway company, who had neither a soul to save nor any thing behind to kick, would so boldly have dared to injure a poor woman." Mr. Bond estimated the loss to the occupant at sixty guineas on twelve months—the question turning on the terms of the widow's occupancy. The magistrates awarded 70*l.*, each party to pay their own expenses, but Mrs. Stell to take the fixtures. Several other cases were settled amicably, though much higher terms were asked, and much lower offered. The good-will and interest in a grocer's shop amounted to 110*l.*, and in other premises in same vicinity to 22*l.* 10s.

SMOKY CHIMNEYS.—With reference to smoky chimneys, the cause is frequently in the bricklayer not starting his *gathering* at the proper place: the gathering should start not less than 6 inches *below the underside of the chimney bar*, and should not gather less than 2½ inches every course of bricks, until the gathering is brought to the exact size of the flue, the flue being in the centre of the breast. Build 1 foot perpendicular: you may then start your flue either right or left, which you think most proper to the entrance into the room, as also to the section of chimneys. Avoid all elbows; give easy curves and slopes. In fixing chimney-pots or moulds, the flues should be to the exact size of the pot or mould, whether it be round or square; and the formation should commence not less than 1 foot 6 inches below the seat of the pot or mould: this is also very essential to prevent any obstruction at the mouth of the shaft. If not so formed, it is more than probable that there may be a check, and so prevent the rapid current it otherwise would have. The usual way in which bricklayers start their gatherings is from the top of the arch, 15 inches higher than they ought to do; this causes two air chambers, one on each side. I have proved beyond doubt that 1 inch gathering below the breast of a chimney is worth three above the chimney bar.—J. B. H.

MIDLAND MECHANICS' INSTITUTES, &c.—The anniversary of the Midland Association of Mechanics' and other literary institutions, was held at Nottingham, on Tuesday last, Mr. J. E. Denison, M.P., and afterwards Mr. Walter, M.P., in the chair. Mr. Denison first addressed the meeting, and was afterwards followed by Mr. Walter, in an eloquent speech, which he summed up by saying—"Remember that the true object of this and all similar institutions is to train the mind to habits of thoughtfulness and patient industry; not to impart to it a mere smattering of all sorts of knowledge, which is only another name for conceit. Whatever progress you make in the difficult path of self-improvement, remember that it must be the effect of your own individual exertion, just as if no institution of this kind existed to assist you. Century after century may mount higher in the lofty regions of science; discoveries which our forefathers would have ascribed to witchcraft, and which appear like magic to ourselves, will fail to excite the least surprise in the minds of our immediate descendants; but there is no royal road to self-improvement and self-discipline: each individual must work out for himself that difficult problem, and stand or fall by the result."

A FAMILY FIRE ESCAPE.—In order to prevent the awful sacrifice of life which so frequently occurs from fire, it seems desirable that Government should offer a handsome reward to the inventor of a fire escape, which, by the simplicity of its machinery, and the lowness of its price, would be available for all classes. I mean an apparatus that every family could possess. If, however, the Government decline encouraging so laudable an object, I am sure the public would respond to any call that might be made upon them, to testify their gratitude for ingenuity so applied, and I would therefore suggest that mechanics should (if only on the ground of humanity), direct their best attention to this subject, and do their utmost to produce an apparatus which should be among the "lions" of the proposed national exhibition of 1851.—P. W. H.

INCREASE OF IRON BUSINESS IN WALES.—The population during forty years, from 1801 to 1841, increased in Newport from 1,423 to 13,766; in Trevethin, from 1,742 to 14,942; Aberystwith, from 805 to 11,272; Bedwelty, from 619 to 22,413. In Glamorgan the increase has also been enormous. In 1820, the iron sent from the worker for shipment to Newport, was 45,462 tons; in 1847, 240,637. The quantity at Cardiff, in 1820, was 50,157 tons · in 1847, it was 220,953. The coal sent in 1846 from Cardiff, Swansea, Llanelly, and Newport, amounted to 1,847,318 tons. The shipment of iron alone from the counties of Monmouth, Glamorgan, and Carmarthen, was estimated, in 1847, at 4,000,000*l.* sterling.

FIRE AT WHITECHAPEL BATHS AND WASHHOUSES.—On 27th inst., a fire, originating in a temporary wooden dryinghouse, rapidly consumed that structure, and spread to the roof and fittings of the washhouse. The hon. secretaries have written to the *Times*, explaining that the property destroyed is amply covered by insurance. Unfortunately, however, this will not prevent additional delay in the completion of an establishment which appears to be doomed to suffer a succession of fatalities or hindrances to its ultimate utility to the public.

PRESERVATION OF WOOD FROM WORMS, FIRE, &c.—M. Louis Vernet, Buenos Ayres, has enrolled a patent specification for a method of preserving from destruction by worms, insects, decay, and fire, certain vegetable and animal substances. To preserve timber from fire, it is to be impregnated with a solution of 1 lb. of arsenic, 6 lbs. of alum, and 10 lbs. of potass, in 40 gallons of water. To preserve timber immersed in water from decay, and the ravages of the worm, it is to be painted over with the solution mixed with oil or any suitable tarry matters.

VASTNESS OF RAILWAY WORKS.—The great Pyramid of Egypt was, according to Diodorus Siculus, constructed by 300,000—according to Herodotus, by 100,000 men; it required for its execution twenty years, and the labour expended on it has been estimated as equivalent to lifting 15,733,000,000 (fifteen thousand seven hundred and thirty-three millions) of cubic feet of stone, one foot high. Now, in the same measure, if the labour expended in constructing the *southern* division only of the present London and North-Western Railway be reduced to one common denomination, the result is 25,000,000,000 (twenty-five thousand millions) of cubic feet of similar material lifted to the same height, being 9,267,000,000 (nine thousand two hundred and sixty-seven millions) of cubic feet *more* than was lifted for the Pyramids, and yet the English work was performed by about 20,000 men only, in less than five years.—*Sir F. Head.*

TABLES FOR SETTING OUT CURVES.—Messrs. Archibald Kennedy and R. W. Hackwood have recently published in the smallest possible form (a waistcoat-pocket edition), a series of tables for setting out curves, which will be found very useful by the profession.* They contain, *ready calculated*, all the dimensions required for setting out curves varying from a radius of five chains to three miles, according to either of the three most generally employed methods of performing the operation. Accuracy is the great point to be achieved in these matters, and this seems to have been carefully striven for.

* "Tables for setting out Curves for Railways, Canals, Roads, &c., either with or without a Theodolite." London; 1849. Weale.

THE PERPETUAL PROBLEM AGAIN.—Mr. George Murrell, a wheelwright, at Upwell, says the *Worcester Journal*, "professes to have discovered the means of putting a machine together that will drive itself; that is, requires no motive power of any kind, neither steam, water, nor hand, but is a mere combination of wheels, that, once set agoing, will never stop unless thrown out of gear, or worn out by friction. *He is very sanguine* of success, and says, that *before many weeks have elapsed*," &c. &c.—the old story. It is odd we never hear how matters *have* turned out when the brief period of sanguine hope *has* elapsed.

ELIZABETHAN CHAPELS.—"An Amateur" wishes to be referred to some good illustrations of an Elizabethan chapel, and to know which are the best examples of that class of buildings. So far as we are aware, no good view of any ancient Elizabethan chapel has ever been published. Good examples may be seen in London. The chapel at Lambeth Palace, originally Early English, has Elizabethan fittings, but the ornamented ceiling has been removed. The chapel at Lincoln's-inn is a good example. Perhaps the best in London is the chapel at the Charter House, entirely Elizabethan: it has been enlarged by Mr. Blore. In the country there are numerous examples: that at Crewe Hall is one of the finest.

EVADING THE BRICK DUTY.—The magistrates sitting in petty sessions at Halesowen, last week, adjudicated on no fewer than ten informations against brick-makers who had defrauded the revenue by removing the bricks from the kilns without paying the duty. All the cases were made out, and fines were inflicted varying from 150*l.* to 25*l.*; while a large number of bricks were declared to be forfeited—in one instance 84,782.

ELECTRO-TELEGRAPHIC PROGRESS.—The telegraph will shortly be open from Halifax to New Orleans throughout. Mr. W. S. Thomas, of Norwich, New York, has invented a telegraphic "manipulator," which is said to "transcribe the 'lightning,' writing as fast as the apparatus can turn out the paper."

THE ARCHITECTURAL CHARACTER OF THE AGE.—The political condition of our day, is *a war of great principles*. As heterogeneous in its character is Art among us. Here we have an imitation of the antique, there a revival of the middle ages, while sculpture itself is sometimes compelled to relax its severity, and copy the rude attire of our northern yeomen. By what term could we describe the architecture of the day? In our rising cities we find a Gothic church close to a Byzantine fane or an Italian basilica, and in their immediate neighbourhood a town-hall like a Greek temple, a mansion like a Roman palace, and a club-house after the fashion of Louis XIV. The age in which we live may have a character of its own; but that character is not written in its face.—*Edinburgh Review.*

COST OF PRISON ACCOMMODATION.—The sums hitherto expended on prison buildings have in some cases been enormous. The cost is seldom less than 100*l.* or 150*l.* per prisoner (a sum sufficient for building two or three neat cottages, each able to contain a whole family), and in some instances it has been much more. A portion only (the newest) of the county prison at York, capable of accommodating only 160 prisoners, cost 200,000*l.*, which is more than 1,200*l.* per prisoner; enough, if it had been desired, to build for each prisoner a separate mansion, with stable and coach-house.—*Fourteenth Report of Prison Inspectors.*

BUILDINGS AND MONUMENTS,
MODERN AND MEDIÆVAL.
Edited by GEO. GODWIN, F.R.S.,
Fellow of the Institute of Architects; Corresponding Member of several Societies.

Part IV. of this work, price 2s. 6d., containing Views of Ware Church, Hertford; Hungerford and Lambeth Suspension-bridge; New Front of Buckingham Palace; Fire-place in the Palace of the Dukes of Burgundy, at Dijon; All Saints' Church, St. John's Wood; the Interior of the House of Lords—the Throne, the Victoria Lobby, the Reporters' Gallery, and Ground-plan; with descriptive letter-press, and numerous details; is now ready.

Office of THE BUILDER, 2, York-street, Covent Garden, or by order of any bookseller.

No. CCCLIII.

SATURDAY, NOVEMBER 10, 1849.

OVEMBER opens the doors of the majority of the London scientific and artistical societies, up to that month closed, and if it bring fogs and catarrh, brings also many pleasant and useful re-unions. The Institute of Architects, the Royal Society, the Antiquarian, the Archæological, the Society of Arts, and others with which we have less to do, are amongst these; the covers are taken off, the bookcases are unclosed, and the habitués find their way to the meeting places from all parts of the world, their resorts during summer, to renew kindly relationships, idle an hour, put themselves pretentiously before the world, gain information, or really increase the general stock of it, as the case may be. All are busy in their own little way,—little, indeed, alas! even with the most powerful,—digging in the great mine of nature. What one disregards, the other considers the object of life; (to use an old metaphor, a man, a dog, a bird, and a worm find very different objects of interest in the same grass-field) and so the great work of advancement best goes on.

The opening meeting of the Institute of Architects was held on Monday, the 5th inst., at their rooms in Grosvenor-street, when the Right Hon. Earl de Grey took the chair, and 149 members and visiters attended. Amongst them, in addition to those spoken of hereafter as taking part in the proceedings, we will mention: Messrs. Cockerell, Scoles, Mee, Mair, Penrose, G. Pownall, S. Angeli, Salvin, Bellamy, Kendall, Booth, Garling, D. Brandon, Jas. Thomson, Papworth, W. Burn, Ferrey, Sibley, James Fergusson, Nash, T. Bury, H. Williams, C. C. Nelson, Jennings, H. Ashton, Knowles, Farring, Hopkins, H. Clutton, Heneker, C. H. Smith, G. Foggo, Dr. O'Callaghan, J. Wilks, John Britton, Colonel Sykes, Thomas Little, Henry Thomas Hope, M.P., and the Dean of Westminster.

The president, after a few general observations, said that as he had at the last meeting mentioned the probable intention of the London University to institute an examination in architecture, and to give certificates of proficiency, it was necessary he should state that the council had entered into correspondence with the university, and found that at present they intended to confine their certificates to chemistry, navigation, and hydrography. In due time, however, architecture would have its share. Relative to certain points in dispute which had been referred to the council of the Institute, he would remark, that many things which seemed desirable at first sight, were not found so on review al. The council had given the matter much consideration, and their report was now being printed. It would be circulated preparatory to a special meeting on the 26th, or its consideration, when it would of course rest with the members to adopt it or not.* During the recess the council had made application to many individuals distinguished in different branches of scientific investigation,

* The tenor of the report may of course be inferred from this without difficulty.

and had received promises of several important papers, but he wished to impress upon the Institute that they ought not to be dependent on extraneous aid, but should look to themselves for support. The youngest members might do something: the elder members could of course do much, and although their time and attention were doubtless much absorbed, they might surely find a moment of leisure to communicate a point of experience. Even trifles in the aggregate become important. There was one subject in connection with the well-being of the profession, on which he thought strongly, and would say a few words. The close connection with foreign countries, effected by improved facilities of communication, opened the way for the more free adoption of modes of decoration from abroad than heretofore, and be thought that the younger members of the profession should bear this in mind, and not consider matters of fittings and adornments beneath their notice. The architect who thinks his duty done, when the building is covered in and plastered, does wrong, and throws much into the hands of others, upholsterers, paperhangers, and decorators, which ought to be decided on by himself. Moreover, continued the president, if the result be a failure, the blame, as a matter of course, falls on the poor architect, but if the contrary, the decorator takes all the credit. He was satisfied that architects acted unwisely who thought such matters beneath their notice, and so did not give that study to them which was required. The architect, continued the president, must study many things. He had been invited, as president of the Institute, some time since, by the Lord Mayor, to meet the fellows of the Royal Society and the Royal Academicians (such were the words of the invitation); these represented science and art; and it occurred to him, when called on to return thanks on the part of the Institute, that the architect was the connection between the purely scientific man and the artist. The man of science might be great in his department, and be quite ignorant of art: the supremest painter might know nothing of science; but the architect who would be great must have a knowledge of both;—science to found and construct; art to proportion, ornament, and produce beauty; knowledge of materials, their qualities and uses; acquaintance with the science of numbers; taste to produce fine forms and harmonious proportions. A skill in the use of colour sometimes did much for an architect, perhaps too much; he would mention a laughable instance. He was standing amongst the designs for the Nelson monument, when they were exhibited, contemplating one which pleased him less than many, when two ladies approached, and one of them, pointing to it, said, " Oh! how beautiful, I hope they will choose that. Look at the soldiers, Laura !" " Yes, Lucy," said the other, " but will the soldiers always be there?" Now Laura and Lucy represented a number of people in this world, and the incident served to show how far a little bit of red sometimes went. His lordship added, he would not then occupy their attention longer than to say, that whatever difference of opinion there might be as to the governing regulations of the body, he trusted that, as all had one object, these would be sunk in an effort to extend still further the reputation of the Institute—already worthily known all over Europe. Let the maxim be " bear and forbear."

Mr. Tite, who often contrives to find a rhyme to illuminate other people's reason, said, there were two or three lines by Cowper

which so fully set forth one point urged by the president, that he could not avoid quoting them. They were these :—

" It is not timber, lead, and stone,
An architect requires alone,
To finish a fine building,—
The palace were but half complete,
If he could possibly forget
The carving and the gilding."

Professor Donaldson announced that Signor Canina had sent the two first volumes of his great book on the " Ancient Edifices of Rome," saying, in the letter of thanks for the royal medal which accompanied the present, that the work was probably the largest now publishing during these troublous times in Europe, and on that account deserved some protection. The Signor added, that he hoped soon to publish two other volumes, if the means did not fail him. A long list of other donations was announced, consisting principally of the transactions of other bodies, amongst which we were glad to find those of the Archæological Society of Athens, and to learn that it is still pursuing its useful labours.

The Signor Antolini, architect, professor at the Academy of Fine Arts at Bologna; the Abate Antonio Magrini, architect, of Vicenza; the Signor Miglioranza, architect, of Vicenza; the Signor Vantini, architect, of Brescia; and Mynheer J. B. Weening, architect, director of the academy at the Hague, were elected honorary and corresponding members. And Professor Cockerell, Mr. Bunning, and Mr. G. G. Scott, were proposed for election as fellows hereafter.

This brought us to the paper of the evening, " Remarks on the earlier and later Gothic Architecture of Germany," by the Rev. Dr. Whewell, master of Trinity.

It is of the greatest importance to the art that such men as Dr. Whewell should be led to apply their tutored minds to the elimination of guiding principles, and our best thanks are due to him for his contribution on this occasion. He came forward, he said, but as an amateur. To determine the progress of styles, to trace their growth, seemed to him an important object, and to aid in this it was that he strove. Deductions from the examination of existing monuments would not of themselves suffice,— these must be confirmed by reference to history. He had already put forth the theory, founded mainly on the churches of the Rhine, that the leading features of Gothic architecture had grown out of the necessities of structure, and his object on this occasion was to carry his theory a little further, treating of the tendencies which had changed the character of buildings in the later Gothic period. He should be assisted in this by the works of some recent German writers, who had pursued the investigation to a considerable extent. The Rev. Dr. then proceeded to discriminate what he considered the three important principles concerned in the formation of the Gothic style, namely, the principle of frame-work; the principle of tracery,—which he thought quite distinct from frame-work; and the principle of wall-work; but the inquiry was sufficiently subtle to prevent us from attempting to convey now a general notion of it in few words : we may perhaps be able to refer to it at greater extent hereafter. He spoke at considerable length of what he called the principle of upward growth. Speaking of unconstructive forms of the later Gothic, Dr. Whewell said that the outer portion of Strasburgh spire would not hold itself together : the joints, as he had ascertained, were vertical, and could not stand ; but there were internal ribs rightly constructed, which really did the work.

Mr. Tite said the suggestive character of the paper read gave it, in his eyes, great value. We were able now to copy details correctly, but we did not realize the principles which produced them; this literal copying, indeed, was the sin of the day. If the principles of frame-work, wall-work, and spire-growth, had been kept in mind, some great mistakes in modern buildings would have been avoided. We should remember that Gothic buildings grew out of the wants of their time, and bore in all respects its impress. He did not consider it was always the best suited for modern requirements: at all events, it should be adapted to new circumstances by thought and study.

At the close of the evening a letter was read from Mr. Mocatta, asking advice as to the means of ridding a house of a great and increasing nuisance, the domestic ant. The annoyance is one of great magnitude in London, and applications are constantly being made to us to learn the best mode of getting rid of them.—The Dean of Westminster thought poison the only remedy.—Several members said they had failed in all endeavours to eradicate them.—Cajeput oil and jalap have both been mentioned in our pages before now as being destructive to them.

The evening passed pleasantly and harmoniously, and we will not run the risk of making the tone of our notice otherwise, by discussing now the report of the council, which is about to come before the members.

ON THE PRESENT STATE AND PROSPECTS OF ARCHITECTURE.

MANY minds are now directed to the discovery of the defects in present architectural practice, and to their various remedies; but what is most encouraging, tongues and pens are growing hold on the subject. The ice is broken, and many, too timid before, will now bend their energies to the exposure of the various errors into which the art has been betrayed. The important truth has at length been distinctly spoken, that we must have architecture of our own, suited to our climate and habits,—to our social and political position: and, as a natural consequence, the cultivation of the æsthetic faculty will again be considered essential to the architect, and obtain that attention in future to which it is entitled.

And certainly, it is high time that the art should resume its place among the means of intellectual manifestation,—put itself into harmony with the constitution of things, and pass into the regions of truth. It is high time that its professors should regain their mental independence, and take possession of their own place and time. Too long have we been displaying architecture out of unison with the spirit of the age, that finds no echo in the breasts of the present generation. Selections and combinations from ancient buildings, without reference to absolute grace or originality, with frequent sacrifice of what is required by the exigencies of our habits and climate, and the preservation of obselete features and ornaments, which have no meaning that can now be read or understood, and in which, consequently, none can find pleasure, have been leading characteristics of the architecture of the present century. The architect has now been told that an acquaintance with the principles of abstract beauty, as well as a knowledge of the characteristics and chronology of styles, belongs to the true votary of the art; a cultivation of the imaginative and creative faculties, as well as those of delineation and construction;—that his works, to be valuable, must be invested with a character of their own, not with one of a past day;—that English buildings, in whatever style, should be a free outpouring of native feeling, and exhibit the natural bent of the author's own mind, which should be learned in the principles of natural design, and imbued with all the beauty of the foregone.

But the evils of the day cannot be traced exclusively to that devotion to the conventionality of a particular age to which I have alluded; as many late erections do not display even that freedom of thought that would consist, with the most slavish adherence in design, to the style or manner of any period or place. Many churches, for instance, lately erected in various parts, seem a collocation of parts or masses of ancient edifices, brought together merely to afford an example of a certain date, and illustrate a step in the past progress of the art, without any respect to present or local circumstances. Now, it is possible for an architect, even restricted as before mentioned, that is to say, confined to a given style, to produce a whole that would strike the beholder as an original production, and totally different to any extant work.

England has had her independent school of architecture, and it will not be unprofitable to look back for a moment, and to search into the manner and practice of those who last upheld it. We have had men who, in their respective days, supported almost singly the reputation of England for this branch of art. They produced works which their country calls its own, and some light is afforded us by their example. Inigo Jones, Wren, and Vanbrugh, we do not find fettering their genius to the style or manner of some single edifice in Italy or elsewhere; they took the elements of the classic styles, increased in richness by the Italians, and only imitated the latter in the broad principles upon which they worked in using them; preserving the freedom of their own minds, listening to the dictates of nature, and exercising reason, sentiment, taste, and judgment in the execution of whatever task they were appointed.

These masters were not equal in taste. Wren and Vanbrugh were sometimes led into violations of natural propriety and the breach of laws which are of eternal obligation; but Inigo Jones, though beautiful and picturesque, can scarcely be charged with licentiousness, and when he visited Italy it was to imbue his mind with classic beauty and study Italian principle only. Wren had the difficult task, in reference to his churches, of providing for a new form of worship; and in many of them he has been eminently successful. His mode of adapting the classic or Italian detail to those Gothic forms and features which could not be dispensed with, evince his originality and independence of mind. The application of Italian detail to Gothic principles of composition had been made before his time by the Elizabethan builder; but his manner of doing it, in reference to the towers and spires of his churches, show the master unfettered by precedent and example; and from the union of the two styles in this important feature of the English church has resulted some of the most beautiful objects that adorn the metropolis and other towns of the kingdom. Many of them are more or less deficient in the higher qualities of design and composition (concentration for instance), and exhibit too much of the monotony in form and character of the Chinese pagoda or Turkish minaret, but there are others which display the purest taste, though the best are but faint indications of that fairy magnificence that might be produced by the architect in whom is combined freedom of mind and fertility of imagination with purity of taste and solidity of judgment, if the style were taken up and pursued in the present day.

Of the striking beauty of which this union of principles is capable, I could instance as examples two or three of Wren's steeples as deserving of distinct notice, would time and space permit; but one by Dean Aldrich, at All Saints Church, Oxford, is worthy of more particular attention, as possessing qualities which are generally wanting in works of the kind, and might serve as a good subject of study. Its parts are all admirably adjusted, and the architect that examines this steeple must be led to confess that the designer has hit the true proportion that should exist between the tower and spire—a most important point in these structures, the difference of the classic proportion from that of the Gothic, in reference to this matter, being the chief thing to be observed. The great fault of the classic campanile, generally, is the disproportion of
those parts, the spires being too large in m
instances (a fault of St. Martin's-in-the-Fiel
the latter should be considerably smaller
the base when springing from a classic to
than when surmounting the Gothic, for r
sons which could readily be shown.

We are not altogether in the dark with th
examples before us; Inigo Jones has l
works which have been renowned throu
Europe; and Wren, in many of his church
has been eminently successful in evoking t
spirit of the beautiful. He has produc
works which properly belong to and char
terize the age and country in which they w
built; we behold him adopting the best e
ments with which he was acquainted, and
which his genius was fitted, to respond to t
call of his time. He took the best materi
that time had bequeathed him, and work
truly with them, according to the lessons
nature and enlightened taste, duly influenc
but not fettered, by precedent: not that l
taste was always pure: my encomium is
rected to the mode in which he wrought, t
independent manner in which he worked
his materials, and the boldness which char
terized his career, rather than to the unifo
grace or merit of his productions. Vanbru
worked in the same spirit, exercised the sa
broad principles, with similar success, in a
other department of the art.

But other monitors might be summoned
yield their admonitions on this subject; th
are many old buildings in London and ot
ancient cities, in various styles, or in no sty
and by architects unknown, that could, if
would heed them, yield very useful lessons
regards some important qualities of art. T
buildings I allude to have very little pretensi
to architectural character, yet they evin
truth, sincerity, and independence of mi
and mirror to us something of the true meth
of art.

A glance at the great architects of Italy w
not be less profitable than the review we ha
just made of our own. To their manner a
practice a great deal more of attention is pr
bably due, than has ever been paid. At t
period of the revival, we find them exerti
every faculty of mind; combining genius wi
energy and practical skill, to rescue the a
from the thraldom of ignorance and barbaris
into which it had sunk; and at a later perio
their characteristic independence did not fo
sake them. We find Palladio, Vignola, an
others exercising the same energy and orig
nal and creative power that had characterize
their predecessors. From all we know of Pa
ladio, he made the ancients the vehicles mere
for the expression of his own thoughts an
feelings, and moulded all that Greece ar
Rome had left him to his own purpose
Through all obstacles we find him strugglin
to the illustration of his own ideas, unburthe
ing himself of the great image,—" the nymp
of his soul." How far he consulted the exa
wants of his own times, is not for me to sa
but his independent habit of mind, which m
nifests itself everywhere in his works,—h
manner of using the antique elements as me
words for the utterance of ideas, is certain
worthy of notice, and must be full of intere
for the lovers of true art. His works stan
out even at the present day, from all other
by the beautiful harmony of their parts a
proportions, and evince, both in their co
struction and decoration, the most original a
stirring genius of design. It was his convi
tion that the architecture of the ancients w
of universal application, and might be con
pletely adapted to the various circumstanc
of different ages and nations; that such adapt
tion they themselves have authorized a
suggested, in the modifications which may l
discovered in their works. But let us lo
into the ancient art itself. What was t
architecture of the Greeks? "A second n
ture," says an eminent writer, "made to wo
for social objects,—such was the architectu
of the ancients;" and true art is the same t
day — a union of man's feeling and imagin
tion with the requirements of necessity a
dictates of nature, with respect to climate, so
popular condition, and other circumstance
True art yields not up the reins to preceden
Man is the creator of the arts, and their gre
maxims and principles are written on his ow
breast. The Creator of the Universe may l
said to have left off his work at the poi

where man's capabilities might begin to operate in the way of art, and it is the duty and the privilege of the latter to take it up, and so continue it. "Art itself is nature," as Shakspeare says; as nature, on the other hand, might be called the art of the Supreme Artist. Art is nature wrought in the alembic of the mind, and reproduced in brick, and stone, and wood; and the beauty of artistic creations is designed to have the same salutary influence upon the mind as the stream, the meadow, and the grove.

I have seen it remarked, that to some nations taste is denied,—which may be true, as nations might be pointed to in whose works or remains it would be impossible to trace the footsteps of the beautiful. This, however, cannot be said of ours. England, as I said before, had her independent school of architecture. Why may she not again? Are the fountains of design exhausted? Is thought spent? Have Jones, Wren, and Chambers, worn out design and invention? To create is unquestionably the province of all the fine arts. If the power to create is exhausted, the art is defunct. Let its death be registered. Let the next paper on the subject in these pages be its funeral requiem. But he has meanly estimated the resources of nature, and of genius—her pupil and high priest, who would reply to these questions in the affirmative. Architecture can no more perish than poetry: they are alike indestructible: it is not in their nature to die: both have their resources in the human heart, and while that is unfathomed their immortality remains. The wish to create, to produce the unique, is instinctive in the human mind; and, though weak in many, in a chosen few it is ever active, while the power to gratify it is inherent also. By our improvement in physical and constructive science, the advantages of modern machinery, and the increase of natural materials adapted to building, we have means of outstripping all past achievement,—of producing grander effects, more magnificent forms and combinations, than ever embellished any ancient city. Never, in some respects, had the architect better opportunity,—never had he such abundance of elements for the realization of the beautiful put into his hand. All he wants is the power to use them; judgment to point out the right track; and courage to pursue it. The credit due to the inventor of styles can never be his. Indeed, the arts arose so naturally and gradually out of circumstances, that but little merit of the kind probably ever belonged to an individual. But there is still work for the very highest faculties of mind. Invention itself need not lie dormant in applying ancient architecture to our purposes; and, in applying it with our increased constructive resources, we may vie with Rome itself. The Greek architecture, for its own purposes,—that is to say, temple architecture,—is above criticism, at least at present, but its application by the Romans and moderns, at any period, is what we need not shrink from emulating. In the manifold materials which have come down to us, there are, I am convinced, graces yet slumbering undisturbed, that but await the call of genius to come forth. In adopting any ancient or foreign style, we need not enter into its character as peculiar to the time and country of its origin, but merely use its elementary principles with the same regard to our wants that its inventors paid to theirs. The modifications which we are called upon to make of ancient architecture, is nothing more than what would have been found amongst the Greeks themselves, had their circumstances so far changed, or had new conditions arisen. Let us be their genuine successors, and make the same application of their principles that they would themselves, were they to live again, and exercise their art in the present country and time.

The architecture of the Greeks, like its poetry and sculpture, bears exquisite traces of the creative faculty. It is the production of a people that spent a greater portion of their time in the free air, under the blue vault of heaven, in intimate communion with nature, than we, in our northern damps, may devote,—who studied nature, not only in the midst of the most beautiful scenery, in a most genial climate, but in an age of great literary development. Of Greek art "the Graces rocked the cradle, and Love taught her to speak." The Greeks were far more susceptible of impressions of the senses than the Romans, who were less given to the poetic contemplation of nature and the idealizing of her works. The Roman genius spoke more in colossal magnificence than in exquisite forms of beauty, like their predecessors and masters; but the architecture of the Greeks is a version of nature characterized by all the elegance and grace which they in everything displayed. Of architecture so formed, so high-born, we cannot have too high a hope. The writer of this essay cannot divest his mind of the impression that, notwithstanding all the praise lavished on it, the Greek architecture has never been duly appreciated, or had its capabilities of answering our modern purposes fully understood; consequently, that its beauties are but partially revealed, that there are untold parts yet to come, veins of beauty not yet explored, which, when called into play, will lead to results different from, and superior to, anything that now exist. The Italians have done wonders, but greater things, he suspects, remain to be done, and may be achieved by us, if we work in the right spirit.

Our duty, in reference to the antique architecture, is thoroughly to investigate its principles, and to naturalize it in our own country, and these can both be done. But, sure I am, that its truthful and constant adaptation to new wants will result in the constant development of new beauties. New circumstances and conditions—the inevitable changes in the economy of mankind, will ever, while it conforms itself to them, extract from it new treasures of expression and power; and unique and happy combinations, beyond anything yet unveiled, may result, under a favourable concurrence of circumstances, from a natural and truthful manner of treating it. Besides, there are advantages in the materials or elements themselves. Whilst using a medium of expression in itself so transcendent, the designer may, as is said in the case of some languages, be carried, as it were, beyond his own horizon, and convey more to the heart of the spectator than he intended, exciting ideas beyond what he sought to embody in the design, which will again lead on to other and more brilliant imaginings.

With such views, I do not participate in that feeling of hopelessness relative to the future destiny of architecture in England expressed by some, nor agree with others, who, in the choice of a style, would give up the classic styles, and adopt some Romanesque version of them. The latter I would not agree to, even in favour of our native architecture. However proud of this last—however extensive may become its readoption in future — the classic styles in England will never be abandoned. There are those who would as soon pluck out an eye! As soon should we give up the literature as the architecture of the ancients. We are proud of Milton and Shakspeare; but who has dreamt of parting with Homer and Virgil? Instead of taking up some foreign modification, let us take up the pure styles themselves, and work out our own version of them.* SAMUEL HUGGINS.

* To be continued.

THE COMPETITION QUESTION.

You have blown the trumpet, Sir, and the blast has been heard; nay more, has been responded to, and by whom? the very power I foretold. Time, and plenty to boot, was given the "Institute" for arraying its forces, for dragging out and putting in order its rusty arms. But still the "lion slept;" and, like the lazy bird, it has lost the early worm. The Architectural Association prepared themselves as a "body of reserve," to allow the elder members to lead the "forlorn hope;" and it now remains for them to *storm* the breaches. That their assault will be a successful one, there can be no doubt; let them proceed with singleness of heart, and the victory is certain. Many thanks to you, Sir, for this state of things. You have raised the banner, put yourself forward, and have gained the support of your readers.

The following copy of a letter, received in reply to a request for particulars respecting the proposed new church at Hawes, is so different from the majority, that I am induced to send it you for insertion in THE BUILDER, convinced that you will willingly give publicity to a fair-looking example:—

"Hawes, Yorkshire.

"Agreeably to your request, I send you particulars respecting our proposed new church at Hawes.

Hawes is a small market town situated in the upper part of Wensley Dale, in an exposed and hilly country.

1. The stone is of an excellent description, about 1½ mile from Hawes; easy to quarry, and, as it is given, the only cost will be the getting, which may be 3d. per load (or if at so much per yard, 6d).
2. Flags may be got two miles off, at about 1s. per yard.
3. The free stone probably will have to be brought 12 or 13 miles, about 3d. per foot.
4. The slate will have to come from Kendal, 28 miles (half the distance by rail), 50s. per ton; and will cover about 33 yards.
5. Plastering costs about 3d. per yard.
6. Lathing, about 1d. per yard.
7. Walling, from 10d. to 1s. per yard.
8. The wood will have to come 15 or 16 miles.
9. A place for an organ.

Perhaps the church may have to be enlarged at some future time.

We intend applying to the "Incorporated" and the "Ripon Diocesan" Church Building Societies; they require the seats to be a certain width, &c., which you may learn by their respective reports. I have not got any by me, but doubtless they may be easily procured in ....

THOMAS LODGE.

P.S. The usual commission will be given to the one whose design is selected; but no premium to any other. Plans to be forwarded on or before the 15th December, according to the advertisement."

Contrast the above, Sir, with that received from Bradford, respecting the new workhouse, and then you will duly estimate the difference.

W. W.

One correspondent suggests,—"That the selection of designs should not be made by the building committees who advertise for them, and that a society should be formed in London for this special purpose, with suitable accommodation provided for the reception and exhibition of designs, and having a secretary who will undertake the management of the society's business. The society to be formed of the principal members of the profession residing in London and elsewhere, who shall be invited to co-operate in this plan for the protection of their junior brethren and the maintenance of their rights, and to put an end to the shameful system of partial dealing which encourages evil and shuts the door against true merit!"

ENGINEERING REMUNERATION UNDER HEALTH BILL.

IN several towns the Public Health Bill is being gradually introduced. At Croydon, Taunton, Warwick, Worcester, and Carmarthen, local boards of health have been appointed. In the first-mentioned towns officers have been elected,—at Worcester the appointment of engineer has been postponed.

At Warwick and Carmarthen the local boards have advertised for plans for the water supply, drainages, house improvements, &c.; and in the former town, a premium of 50*l.* has been offered for the most approved plans for carrying out the entire works contemplated under the Health Bill, and which will probably cost from 18,000*l.* to 20,000*l.*, and yet they have the modesty to invite parties to design works to this amount, and receive, *if successful*, the *munificent* sum of 50*l.* for compensation, or about ¼ per pent. on the estimated outlay. Why this sum would not even cover the expenses of the preliminary inquiry, with the inspector at 3*l.* 3s. per day, and his and other expenses attending it, while the more important works, the practical plans and the details, requiring even greater engineering ability and skill than the preliminary inquiry, are to be rewarded with the paltry sum above named.

What engineer of standing and talent would undertake such works on such terms? Surely it is necessary for engineers to bestir themselves in support of their professional interests, and take warning by the fate of the architects, and not quietly submit to be ridden over roughshod by local boards or central authorities.

The consequence of this niggardly system I can readily foresee. It will bring inexperienced men into the field, and it will result in defective, if not useless work. At Carmarthen, the system is changed : they advertise for contracts, for the plans, &c., and the following are the particulars of the contract :—

" A survey on a scale of 40 feet to the inch, showing streets, alleys, yards, houses, and all outhouses, privies, pumps, cesspools, drains, in fact every thing of a permanent character actually on the ground, with the depth of the sewers.

A copy of ditto.

Sections of all streets, yards, &c., and sewers.

Water Supply.—Plans of land round reservoir, about 15 acres, on 40 feet scale. Complete cross sections. Trial pits to ascertain the character of the soil, and where clay for puddle may be obtained.

Reservoir designs, drawings, and specifications, showing the quantities of earthwork, fencing, brickwork and masonry, drains, filtering tank, &c., for reservoir of three acres.

Main Piping. — Plans and specifications, showing depth, position, dimensions, and cost of laying the main pipes, fire plugs, &c., throughout the town.

Sewerage.—Plans and specifications for a complete system of street sewers, gully grates and traps, outfalls, and paved gutters for removal of rain water.

Private or House Improvements. — Water serving pipes, &c., drains, privies, or water closets, sinks, rain pipes, dust-bins, and yard paving, &c."

And then come the general conditions ;—

" A contract to be entered into, specifying the work to be done, and the price to be paid to be affixed to each item in the enclosed schedule ; also the time within which the contract is to be performed, and in case the terms are not duly performed, a pecuniary penalty to be imposed, guaranteed by sufficient security ! !"

And all this, *forsooth,* for probably the *munificent* sum of something less than 50*l.,* judging from the population, Carmarthen being about the same as Warwick. As you always make a gallant stand for the interest of the architects, pray with brotherly feeling spread your editorial mantle over the *poor civil engineer.*

B.

PROPOSED SITE FOR THE NEW BRIDGE AT WESTMINSTER — IMPROVEMENTS IN THE NEIGBOURHOOD.

By a misprint in our paragraph on this subject a fortnight ago, the line of the proposed improvement is rendered somewhat unintelligible. It states, after describing the site of the new bridge and its approaches, " It will be requisite to open Charles-street to the *south* of Great George-street ;" it should have been to the *width* of Great George-street, having an outlet to St. James's-park ; the intention being to form, from the proposed site of the new bridge, a direct thoroughfare to St. James's-park for the traffic going to Belgravia ; thus leaving Great George-street more free as an access to the Houses of Parliament. By the opening of Charles-street to the required width, the south frontage for the national records depôt would be obtained ; and by the removal of the houses between Charles-street and Downing-street, ample space afforded for the entire structure, having the west side of King-street for a frontage to the great street of Whitehall. On the Surrey side, the line of communication would be by a wide road running obliquely southward, and terminating opposite Astley's theatre, and the west corner of Stamford-street, and another road, running northward, into Stamford-street, as an approach to the South-Western Railway.

Whatever may be the arrangement ultimately made, care must be taken not to lessen the value, unnecessarily, of private property.

That the matter should be settled is most important for the owners of adjacent property. Some of our correspondents write very

---

LAING Sc

anxiously on the subject, and assert, that if the decision be further delayed by the authorities, ruin will be the result to many.

One says,—" Pray do not abandon this subject, a large number of persons look to you for assistance.

" If any thing is to be left for us, the proprietors of small estates, to perform, we must be governed by this new measure, and, above all things, should know as speedily as may be the fate of our future. Hitherto all has been shrouded in darkness, and this has caused much suffering and anxiety. In the name, therefore, of all interested, particularly south of the Thames, do not forget us."

ORNAMENT.

PALACE VENDRAMINI CALERGHI, VENICE.

THE palace from which the above ornament has been drawn is called Palazzo Vendramini Calerghi ; it is situated on the Grand Canal, Venice, and was built in 1463, at the expense of the Doge, Andrea Loredano, by the architech, Pietro Lombardo. It is one of the finest of the Venetian palaces, and is an important specimen of the Cinque-cento period. In 1691 it was sold to the Duke of Brunswick for about 30,000*l.,* and by the latter, not long afterwards, to the Duke of Mantua. Since 1844 it has become the residence of the Duchess de Berri and her son.

The ornament which we here represent is on the landing, in front of the entrance door. The darker part of the engraving is intended to show that the ground is tooled to a rough surface, about one-sixteenth of an inch below the smooth face.

NEW MARKETS, DONCASTER.—The statue of Ceres was elevated to its destined situation, on the summit of the block over the middle entrance of the principal front of this building, in the afternoon of Monday, the 5th inst., in presence of the Mayor and several of the corporation. The statue is from the chisel of Mr. Thomas Stenton, of Doncaster. The stone used is from the quarries of Roche Abbey.

NOTES IN THE PROVINCES.

THE pews in the parish church of St. Peters, Mancroft, Norwich, are in an inconvenient state, and a desire has arisen for improvement by substituting sittings of a more ecclesiastical character, and affording more accommodation. The incumbent and some of the churchwardens appear to take an active part in the promotion of this good work, which will require about 800*l.* to 1,000*l.,* of which 220*l.* have been subscribed by parishioners and others.——Several of the largest gas consumers in the city, says the *Lincoln Times,* " having felt themselves aggrieved that they should have to pay for the enlargement of the company's works, from time to time, in addition to 10 per cent. per annum upon the subscribed capital, have held a meeting, at which it was agreed that the company should be respectfully requested to lower the price to 5s. per 1,000 feet. This memorial, although signed by 110 gas consumers, was not deemed worthy of a reply ; consequently, at another meeting, held on Wednesday last, it was unanimously resolved to form a new company, with a capital of 1,600 shares of 5*l.* each. This proposal has been most warmly responded to by gas consumers, and arrangements are in progress which will accomplish the object sought for *without* the aid of an Act of Parliament, and ere the winter closes, the present company will be relieved of some of their dissatisfied consumers." The maximum price, it is estimated, will not be more than 2s. 6d. per 1,000 feet.——The parish minister and other authorities of Little Maplestead are engaged in an endeavour to restore this edifice, which is regarded with veneration as one of the four round churches remaining in England, built by the Knights Hospitallers, the others being the Temple Church, and the round churches at Cambridge and Northampton.——The restoration of the north aisle of Kemerton Church has just been completed. The nave, chancel, and south aisle were formerly restored by Archdeacon Thorpe, at a cost of nearly 5,000*l.* The present portion has been rebuilt by Captain Hopton. The whole edifice is now considered to be complete except the tower. The whole of the restorations have been carried out according to the design of Mr. Carpenter, in the Early Decorated style. The roof and walls are all of stone,—the former in thin laminæ. The material, however, it is feared, will not be very durable. The chief window of the chancel represents the crucifixion; there is also a stained window in the south aisle. The roof, interiorly, is an open one of timber; and the stalls, &c., are carved. Most of the woodwork is oak. The north aisle is not yet pewed. ——On Saturday week the foundation stone of a new school-house was laid at Wimborne, for the Queen Elizabeth Grammar School boys. The school and masters' houses are to be in the Tudor style, and they stand on the old site.——A mural monument to Richard Davies, Bishop of St. David's nearly three centuries ago, has been sculptured by Mr. E. Davies. The prelate is represented with a pen and lexicon, intended to denote the process of translating.——The new church of Ganerew, near Monmouth, was consecrated on Thursday week before last. The old church had fallen to decay, and the widow of the late Major Marriott offered funds for a new structure, as the best possible monument to the memory of her husband. Mr. Pritchard, who is engaged in the restoration of Llandaff Cathedral, is the architect employed. The edifice is in the transition style, between Early English and Decorated. The cost exceeds 1,500*l.*——The main building destined for the cattle-show in Lower Essex-street, Birmingham, will be 320 feet long, and 100 feet wide, with subdivisions. The area will be surmounted with a roof in one span, with a cupola running the whole length of the building, 6 feet above the roof; and there will also be thirty-eight large sky-lights in the roof. The building will be lighted throughout with gas. The ground is being enclosed under the superintendence of Mr. Samuel Briggs.——St. Jude's Church, Moorfields, Sheffield, the foundation-stone of which was laid on Monday week, will be erected from a design by and under the superintendence of Mr. Mitchell. The style will be Early English, and the plan will form a cross, consisting of nave, 36 feet by 19 feet; transepts, 19 feet by 12 feet; chancel, 24 feet by 19 feet; aisles on each side of nave and chancel, 12 feet wide. At the intersection of base and chancel with the transept an octagon lantern tower, 19 feet by 19 feet, will be introduced, surmounted by a spire in wood covered with zinc plates. This tower and spire will rise 120 feet, affording light to the centre of the church. The bell-turrets will be at west end of nave. From the description, the arrangement would seem to follow that of Mr. Godwin's church at Brompton. The chancel will be laid in a plain pattern of Minton's tiles; and the pulpit (the steps to which will wind round one of the tower pillars) will be in Roche Abbey stone. The church will accommodate 600 persons on the ground-floor, and 350 adults and children in galleries.——The *Sheffield Times* has been authorized to present its readers with a detailed report on the main features of the drainage scheme for the town, lately noticed in THE BUILDER. The two main sewers, or great drains, with all their adjuncts, are estimated by Messrs. Harrison and Holmes to cost 11,304*l.* The dam, tanks, &c., for precipitating it in a deodorized state, would be a separate expense, amounting to 8,070*l.*, made up of—land, 1,933*l.*; dam, sump, tanks, &c., 2,253*l.*; engines and machinery, &c., 3,000*l.*; engine-houses, cottage and offices, &c., 500*l.*; incidentals, 384*l.*——A Downham Market correspondent intimates to us that this town was lighted with gas for the first time on 5th inst. The works just completed have been under the superintendence of Mr. Child, of Southwold. The present charge is 8s. 4d. per 1,000 feet, to be measured by the company's meters alone.——Stow Bardolph Church, two miles from Downham Market, is now being restored by Mr. Raphael Brandon, architect. Several paintings were found on the walls.——A new doorway is about to be put into Downham Church, south side of chancel.——The buyers of the great bell at York Minster, astonished at the continued silence of their protégé, memorialized the Dean and Chapter lately on the subject, according to the *Gateshead Observer*, praying that it might be used in striking the hours—the dwellers in the cathedral yard assuring their reverences that their ears would not be annoyed by the sound. The prayer was granted; but with this proviso—"That each residentiary be considered at liberty to stop the striking of the bell in the night during his residence, if the same be found an annoyance to himself or to any of his family."——The Woods and Forests have served notices claiming the land taken in from the river by the Cork, Blackrock, and Passage Railway Company, and have written to say that a valuator is instructed to come over and value the property for their lordships. The corporation of Liverpool, too, have completed a compromise with them by consenting to pay to their credit a sum of 160,000*l.* for land they took in from the river there.——On Wednesday week before last the neighbourhood of Meath-street and Thomas-street, Dublin, was alarmed by the unexpected fall of two houses, Nos. 1 and 2, Hanbury-lane, occupied by a crowded population of poor tenants. Three persons passing were unhappily crushed beneath the falling mass. The inmates were, with few exceptions, all injured, some fearfully bruised and cut.

BISHOP STILL'S ALMSHOUSE, WELLS.

THE south-eastern elevation of the almshouse at Wells, given in your last number but one, is stated to be that of Bishop Still, which is not the case. It was founded by Mr. Walter Brick as an almshouse for decayed burgesses in the year 1638. The almshouse which bears the name of Bishop Still is opposite the west end of Brick's almshouse, and the doorway in your engraving abuts upon the corner of it. Still's almshouse is a very plain building (for six inmates), having three doorways, over each of which is a freestone slab, containing (in the three) the following inscription:—

IOHN STILL LATE LORDE BISHOP OF THIS SEA FOR THE PRETVAL RELEEFE OF THE POORE OF THIS HOSPITAL GAVE 500[L] WHERWITH

NATHANIEL STILL ESQR HIS SONNE PVR. CHASED THIS HOVSE FOR 6 POORE MORE TO THE OTHER 24 POOR AND

FAITHFVLLY PEORMED HIS FATHERS WILL IN THIS CHARITABLE WORKE ANNO DNI 1614.

The almshouse, therefore, was purchased and converted to its present use. Bubwith's almshouse, called the "old almshouse," adjoins to Brick's, and has, during the last few years, been partly rebuilt, and the interior re-arranged, thereby affording greater space and comfort for the inmates. The chapel at the east end has lately been restored, and the east window filled with stained glass, in which are emblazoned the arms of the city as owners of the building; the arms of Bishops Bubwith, Still, and Willes, as donors, and the figure of St. Andrew from the seal of the dean and chapter, as also the arms of the present bishop, as patrons. The borders and quarries are copied from Bishop Still's library windows over the cloisters. The pews will be restored in accordance with the original ones. The public are indebted to the zeal and exertions of Mr. Edmund Davies, the governor, for these restorations, he having taken upon himself to procure subscriptions for carrying out the same. H.

OXFORD ARCHITECTURAL SOCIETY.

A MEETING of the Oxford Architectural Society was held at Oxford on the 24th ult.; the Rev. W. Sewell in the chair. Among other communications, a letter was read from the parish priest of Broughton Gifford, stating that an inscription in Lombardic characters had been discovered in one of the church bells, and requesting advice as to the best method of taking an impression of the same, and he had been advised to use warmed gutta percha, which, when allowed to cool, would form a mould from which a cast might be taken in plaster.

It was announced that a second series of elementary lectures on church architecture were in contemplation. Mr. J. H. Parker read a paper on the chief points of difference between the Early French style and the Early English style of Gothic architecture. The French churches of the thirteenth century are generally much more lofty than the English churches of the same period; and, in consequence, the buttresses are much more massive and important, and in the flying buttresses there are generally two arches, one over the other. The pillars are also much more heavy than the Early English pillars, and are frequently plain round masses, with classical capitals, and bases resembling the usual late Norman base. The early French churches have almost invariably an apse at the east end, and the windows of the apse are usually lancet-shaped, while the side windows are of two or more lights, with folial circles over them. In England, the east end is usually flat, with either three lancet windows, or a large window with foliated circles in the head, and single lancet windows on the sides. A particular early kind of tracery is used much more abundantly in France than in England, and apparently a few years earlier.

The president stated, that a plan had been discovered for warming churches with gas, by means of which all flues and smoke were avoided.

Mr. Parker mentioned an ancient fire-place of the fifteenth century in a church at Salisbury, the chimney of which was carried up a buttress.

RAILWAY JOTTINGS.

FOURTEEN brick arches of a viaduct in course of construction, near Preston, by Mr. M'Cormick, for the East Lancashire line to Preston, fell suddenly a fortnight ago, "in consequence of the Ribble having overflowed its banks from the recent heavy rains." Two men were on the works at the moment, but both escaped. One jumped to the ground from a height of 30 feet, yet escaped unhurt. The resident engineer, Mr. Sturges Meek, writing to the *Albion* says—"I have this day examined these works, and find that the accident is not to be attributed to any fault in the execution of the fallen portion of the viaduct, but to the sub-contractors having, in the absence of any authority, withdrawn the centres from some of the arches before the mortar was properly set; the effect of the late heavy rains upon which has been to bring them down, together with others on each side of them."——On Wednesday week the temporary viaduct over the river Calder was much damaged, it is said, by the heavy flood of the previous night. The water, by washing over the masonry of the newly-commenced stone bridge, a little above, and intended to replace the temporary viaduct, had so loosened and displaced the gravel in the bed of the river, at the foot of the piling, that several of the piles were thrown out of the perpendicular, and the whole fabric was much injured, and became insecure even for foot passengers. A foot-bridge, 3 feet in breadth, has since been constructed, and a new bridge for the railway is far advanced.——A reduction, it is said, of some 10,000*l.* or 12,000*l.* will be effected this half-year in the locomotive expenses of the southern division of the London and North-Western line.——It is thought by some, says *Herapath*, that this is a favourable time for Railway Companies to purchase up their shares in the market, with surplus receipts or profits. Thus a Company whose shares are at an equivalent discount, could buy a million of capital for, say 500,000*l.*, and so *for half a million*, reduce the capital receiving dividend *by a million*, in other words, save half a million for the benefit of the legitimate holder.——The Chinese Exhibition is to be removed by rail, from Hull to Newcastle and Edinburgh, on a plan matured by the proprietor, and at a cost one-sixth only of the sum necessary in the usual way by horses on the old roads, sixty of which, at a cost of 900*l.* would have been requisite. An experimental trip has been made with one half of the collection. The entire train will consist of an engine and tender, with seventeen gigantic exhibition vans, suspended between eighteen trucks, and followed by a first and a second-class carriage, with horse-boxes and luggage-waggon. Each van is about 11 feet 3 inches high, and 9 feet 3 inches broad. Their average length is about 20 feet—two of them being about 25 and others 18. The tops will be 12 feet above the upper edge of the rails, between which and the bottom of the vehicles will be a space of 9 inches. Each van will be supported by four iron rods, one at each corner, attached by joints to hinges secured to the bottom of the frame of the van. The entire length of the train will be one-eighth of a mile. We believe this is the first time any such exhibition has been conveyed by rail.—— Mr. J. W. Hackworth, son of one of the late Mr. Stephenson's competitors for the locomotive premium run for at Rainhill some twenty years since, now offers, in the *Mining Journal*, to contest the palm with Mr. Stephenson, in the construction and economy of modern locomotives, with the view of testing the limits of the present possible reduction in the expense of working them. —— The Great Southern and Western Irish line was opened, with great ceremonial, on Thursday in week before last, by the Lord Lieutenant and Lord Chancellor of Ireland, and other members of the Irish Government. The Lord Lieutenant knighted the company's chairman after dinner. ——Trains have begun to run right into and out of the more central terminus of the Caledonian extension line, at Buchanan-street, Glasgow. The wooden erections used as yet as offices, however, are not quite finished. A goods station has been reared of brick at a short distance. The whole area for buildings is not less than 15 acres. The line enters on a level with the street, the high arches level with the Garnkirk line having been entirely removed though nearly completed. This extension line is that on which the tunnel under the Monkland canal and over the tunnel on the Edinburgh and Glasgow line has been constructed. This tunnel is 400 yards in length. The arch is formed of bricks, a mixture of fire and common clay, and an inverted arch has also been formed below the rails of same material. The brick lining, which is continuous throughout the length of the tunnel, forms an elliptical arch, similar to that of a common sewer. About the middle of the tunnel an eye has been opened, perhaps for ventilation, as the tunnel being quite straight a stream of light passes through it. Considerable difficulty was experienced in this part of the work, by the breaking in of water from the canal above. On emerging from the tunnel at the west end, the line is carried between two walls of massive masonry of about 300 yards in length, and averaging 40 feet in height. At the west end of the walls they are 8 feet, and at the east end 10 feet in thickness, with buttresses behind. In order to prevent this high embankment from pressing on the roof of the Edinburgh tunnel, arches have been formed in each wall of nearly 70 feet span, thus throwing the weight of this tremendous wall upon the solid earth on each side of the Edinburgh and Glasgow tunnel. The expense of this portion of the work must have been enormous. The works have been executed under the inspection and superintendence of Mr. Timperly. ——The number of persons employed on the railways of the United Kingdom, according to a recent return, are 52,683, on 4,252 miles, 1,321 stations open for traffic, and 188,177 on 2,955 miles in course of construction. On the former there are 95 engineers, and on the latter 405; on the former 1,752 enginemen and 1809 firemen.——The papal triumvirate, says the *Railway Times*, have decided that the railway to Naples is a useless scheme, 'tending to inundate Rome with worthless foreigners;' they have, therefore, definitively suspended the works, and thereby thrown thousands out of employment. — This is how cardinals encourage railways.

CARVED CHIMNEY-PIECE,
MR. HOPE'S HOUSE, PICCADILLY.

IN our account of Mr. Hope's mansion in Piccadilly, we mentioned with praise the chimney-piece in the small dining-room next Down-street. The accompanying engraving is a representation of it. The material is the *pierre de tonnerre*, — a fine-grained stone, which exhibits sharply every touch of the chisel, and it is the work of a very clever chisel which it has here to show; the fruit and flowers around the circular opening, intended for a dial, are beautifully executed.

The panels are filled in with varied marbles, —*marbre de Languedoc*, *Vert de Mer*, &c.; with which, also, the front slab is inlaid.

The upper panel is intended to receive a painting.

CARVED CHIMNEY-PIECE, Mr. HOPE'S HOUSE, PICCADILLY.

Messrs. DUSILLION AND DONALDSON, Architects.

LECTERNS FROM BAS-RELIEF, CANTERBURY CATHEDRAL.

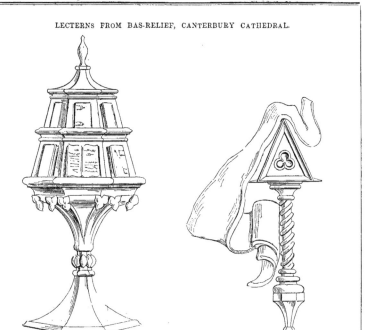

LECTERNS.

THE two small reading desks or lecterns are copied from the sculptures which ornament he spandrils of the tomb of Archbishop Meopham, at Canterbury Cathedral. The omb is early Edward the Third's style, nd it is one of the finest in the cathedral. Ancient representations of church furniture are always valuable, and the two iere shown are well worthy of notice. Ancient small lecterns are common enough in our churches, but we have no specimen left of a large one, like that in our example, intended apparently for a whole company of priests. In Mr. Roberts's Spanish sketches one such is represented, in the view of the chapel of the nunnery at Carmina during the service of the vigils by the sisterhood.　　　R.

FORMATION AND MAINTENANCE OF ROADS FOR GREAT TRAFFIC.

SOME time since a series of questions on he subject of pavings were sent to the City of London Commissioners of Sewers, by the Metropolitan Sanitary Commission, and were uplied to by Mr. W. Haywood, the surveyor o the City Commissioners. Some of the eplies give information which may be generally useful.

The City Commission are said to have ried almost every description of carriageway avement: they progressed from the common ebble paving with which London was originally paved, through stones 8 inches, 6 inches, and of nearly every width; they have had stones inches wide, and from 10 inches to 20 inches n length (superficial dimensions), and they have now down in the public way a specimen f pavement, of which the stones are but about inches by 5 inches, or 3 inches by 4 inches

(superficial dimensions). They have laid in their streets granite from Guernsey, Herm, Devonshire, Cornwall, Leicestershire, and Scotland, and given macadamized roads and wooden pavements a fair trial, with the view of determining the important question of which was the best and cheapest pavement.

"It is rather difficult to say which is the best, taking into consideration these somewhat antagonistic qualities, for that paving which is composed of the largest stones is the cheapest in first cost and of the greatest durability (I do not allude to the difference of granite), but is the least safe for carriage or equestrian traffic, and that which is formed of stones of small superficial dimensions, and is the dearest in first cost and the least durable, is the safest for carriage traffic. The 3-inch cubes at present down in many of the principal City streets are but an introduction of late years, and it will yet take the experience of a few more years to determine their durability and cost of maintenance relatively to the larger stones (that of the larger stones being pretty accurately ascertained). It is probable they will be a greater expense taking them over a term of years, but they form by far the safest pavings which have yet been laid down, and have given the most satisfaction to the public, both equestrian and pedestrian. Taking then the question in all its bearings, I should say that the narrow or 3-inch stones, with certain restrictions in length, being the safest pavement, is the best paving for carriageways of large towns and of great traffic, even although its cost should be greater (within certain limit); for any slight additional cost must be more than saved to the public by the decreased strain upon horses, the diminution of wear and tear of vehicles, and the general comfort experienced by all.

At the same time I may remark, that as there will in all probability be an increased

expense in the maintenance of streets paved with these small stones, it is obviously desirable to lay down stones of as large a dimension as the requisite safety to the carriage traffic will admit of, and the City Commission are now laying down in some leading thoroughfares 4-inch cubes with certain limitation in length (this size not having hitherto been laid to any extent), to enable them to judge of the value of a pavement formed of such sized stones.

The granite which has for the most part been used in Aberdeen, and has hitherto been deemed the best, taking into account the various heads of first cost, durability, and absence from slipperiness."

Theoretically, the paving with the least quantity of joint is most easily kept clean; but no increased difficulty appears to be felt in practice in keeping pavements of 3-inch cubes clean than in keeping pavements of 6-inch cubes clean, although there is double the amount of joint in one than in the other. A tramway keeps cleaner than a pavement wholly composed of the ordinary paving stones, as it partakes in character of the flag footway pavements.

"The ease with which pavements are kept clean greatly depends upon their state of repair; a pavement in good condition, with an even surface, can be cleansed with but little labour, whereas, a pavement in a bad state it is difficult to keep in a state of proper cleanliness; refuse, water, &c., &c., if thrown upon the one will be speedily removed, by finding its way to the street gullies; but if upon the other, the depression and irregularities in surface retain it until removed by manual labour; in fact, if a pavement is in a very bad condition, it is impossible to keep it clean with any ordinary care or attention."

The first cost of the different kinds of pavement varies considerably according to the nature of the pavement laid down, both as respects size of stone and nature of granite, and also according to the price of granite in the market. They may be estimated at from 11s. to 17s. per yard, superficial, if formed of stones 9 inches deep.

The average of the cost of the repairs of thirty-six streets may be taken at about one penny per yard per annum up to the period at which it was estimated.

The stones of these carriageways were 9 inches deep, 6 inches wide, and from 9 to 15 inches long; this, therefore, will not give the probable amount of charge for annual reparation of the pavements (of 3-inch cubes) now laid in the City of London.

The usual material for footpaths is York stone, the thickness usually laid down is 3 inches, its cost has varied from about 6s. to 6s. 6d. per yard.

The average cost of reparation of the footways of Coleman-street, Bread-street, Fenchurch-street, Fleet-street, Lombard-street, Tower-street,—Great and Little, and Wood-street, taken over the period of the whole time they were lying in the streets, is about one penny per yard per annum."

WROUGHT-IRON WATER PIPES.

I OBSERVE in your number for Oct. 27th a letter from Messrs. Fox, Henderson, and Co., on the above subject, and as the statements therein are entirely erroneous, and calculated to do a valuable patent (of which I hold a share) considerable injury, may I beg the favour of being permitted to put the matter in its true light. There are two patents for wrought-iron pipes in this country, as well as in France; viz., M. Ledru's and M. Chameroy's; and that the public may have an opportunity of judging of the intrinsic value of each, I will endeavour to show in what each consists. M. Ledru's system consists in drawing a plate of charcoal iron, by a machine, to any length up to 10 or 12 feet, in section, of a circular form, with its edges curved in, as at A, while another piece of charcoal iron, of the same length, having been drawn of the form as at B, is by a third operation drawn into the pipe, as at C, by which process they are so firmly welded together that they become almost one entire piece of iron. The pipe thus manufactured possesses these advantages, viz., that it is entirely closed throughout its whole length, without a single break, and is capable of resisting any strain, either from the interior or exterior. These pipes, when made, are galvanized, the zinc running into and entirely filling up the smallest interstices that by any accident may occur, and the outer seam is then soldered the entire length, which, although considered perfectly unnecessary, is done as an additional security. M. Chameroy's system (vide patent) originally consisted in cutting out of plate iron a series of dovetails, at certain distances, and bending the plate into a circular form, and then, by solder, endeavouring to fix these dovetails in their places, vide D; but as this scheme proved a failure it was abandoned, and the present makers of M. Chameroy's patent in England only rivet the pipes with small rivets at certain distances, as at E, and I believe, then solder down the joint, which I humbly conceive is no patent at all, and that any one would be at liberty to make pipes in this manner. M. Chameroy's system also includes the covering of the pipe, when made, with bitumen; this is also common to M. Ledru's system, so that, in this respect, the one has no advantage over the other. Messrs. H. and M. D. Grissell are the manufacturers of M. Ledru's patent in this country, which system unfortunately happens to be an opposing one to that of M. Chameroy. Each pipe as made by Messrs. Grissell is, before delivery, proved with its joint complete, to a pressure of water equal to a column of 300 feet, but the pipe will of course always bear considerably more before fracture. It also, from its peculiar form of abutting joint (thereby keeping its perfect form circle), will bear a loaded waggon to its drawn over it, and is guaranteed equal to any cast-iron pipe, when placed in the same situation, as pipes usually are. I am not aware to which system the article in your valuable paper of the 29th September last refers, but I have

the permission of the Messrs. Grissell to say that they will have much pleasure in showing you the manufacture, and in proving my assertions to their fullest extent, should you favour their manufactory with a visit. However, in answer to Messrs. Fox and Co.'s letter, I can, as one of the proprietors of the patent, affirm that M. Ledru has not had to pay any damages to M. Chameroy for infringements, and, as far as I recollect, the trial in question went against M. Chameroy, and not M. Ledru.

I am quite willing to prove, by experiment, that, first, M. Ledru's pipes are equal to the external as well as the internal pressure. Look at the two sections A and E, and let any practical man say which is most likely to sustain pressure. Second, the pipes made according to M. Ledru's system do not depend upon being soldered; it is only an additional security. Third, whatever liability there may be of the outside coating of asphalte being destroyed—of which I think there is very little chance—the liability is equal in both systems, as each party covers his pipes with bitumen if desired. As we galvanize all our pipes, we consider this coating of bitumen quite unnecessary, except in some very peculiar situations, and we do not advise our friends to incur this additional cost. Our pipes are made from half an inch diameter upwards, and are equally applicable for household purposes as for the purpose of drainage and water pipes. Messrs. Fox and Co.'s agent for their pipes is, I think, quite in error in " confirming their impression," however strong that impression may be, relative to the defects alluded to. I am informed that, instead of M. Chameroy having to complain of infringements, it is M. Ledru who has had to complain. Messrs. Fox, Henderson, and Co.'s opinion with respect to M. Ledru's system being " valueless," is, however, of little importance. I need only say that I do not fear my pipes will suffer anything by being placed alongside those of any maker in the kingdom. The question that the public will have to settle is—who can produce the best pipe at the least cost?

As regards the screw joint, of which Messrs. Fox and Co., with so much emphasis, say that " their screw Joints are not soldered on like Ledru's, but are cast (?) upon the body of the pipe, in such a manner as not to be liable to be detached;"—true, they are not soldered on like Ledru's, but they omit to mention that the metal of which these said joints are composed so nearly assimilates to solder itself, that no practical difference can be discovered; whereas the joints I recommend are made either of cast-iron, or of malleable cast-iron, which is as strong as wrought-iron itself. These joints are then galvanized, rivetted on

to the pipes, and afterwards soldered as well. My object is not to depreciate Messrs. Fox and Co.'s pipes—they are fair pipes; but I cannot submit to their assertions without asking the public to judge which of the two systems is the best—M. Chameroy's or M. Ledru's; and I think Messrs. Fox would have shown much better taste had they not so freely made use of a competitor's name to raise the value of their own article. In conclusion, I can only say that I will guarantee every one of my pipes for the term of seven years, whenever required to do so, and thus allow time alone to test their value.*

JOSEPH THOMAS.

Miscellanea.

BITS OF THE PAST.—A portion of Roman walling, we are told, has been discovered in Chelmsford. " The walls exposed are 3 ft. thickness, and 4 ft. 8 in. in depth, and are formed of Roman bricks about 12 in. by 11 (of which there are twenty rows), mixed with fragments of curved roof-tiles, similar in form to those now used on Italian villas."——At Llando, Wales, the miners have broken into a cavern supposed to have been formed in Roman times: benches, stone hammers, &c., were found.——At Richborough, according to the Literary Gazette, the outer wall of a very extensive amphitheatre has been discovered and traced by Messrs. C. R. Smith and Rolfe. ——La Presse mentions the discovery, on the walls of La Sainte-Chapelle, adjoining the Palace of Justice, Paris, of a rude painting of the thirteenth century, on a preparation of gold. It was hidden under three coats of yellow chalk, and represents the annunciation. The figures are about 4 ft. (French) in height; and consist of an angel presenting a branch of lily to the Virgin, who holds a book in her hand. Above is a medallion of the Virgin, with the infant Jesus on her knees, and two angels offering incense.——A marble statue, almost entire, and supposed to represent either Apollo or Meleager, has been found during excavations that are being made for antiquities in Rome.

GALVANIZED IRON COMPANY.—We have been requested to correct the misapprehension of a contemporary relative to this company, quoted in our last. The manager, Mr. Tupper, states that the affairs wound up were those of the old company, and that the present company are fully prepared to develop the process to the utmost.

* Having now allowed both parties to state their case, any further communication can appear only as an advertisement.—ED.

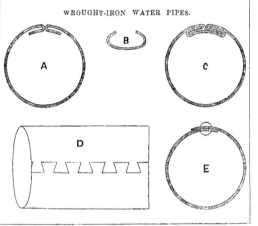

PROJECTED WORKS.—Advertisements have been issued for tenders, by 17th instant, for rebuilding the Corn Exchange at Ipswich; by 10th December, for the work required to be done in building a new bridge of stone over the river Weaver at Frodsham, and making road approaches to same; by a date not specified, for the erection of the Deptford Literary Institution; by 15th inst., for the works to be done in erecting and completing a dispensary and dwelling-house adjoining the Ratcliff workhouse; and by 12th, for shifting 25,000 cubic yards of spoil on the Monkland Canal.

IMPROVEMENT OF DWELLINGS IN LAMBETH.—The Lambeth Anti-Cholera Dwellings' Improvement Committee have issued an advertisement, calling on all concerned in raising the status of the poorer classes to aid, by contributions, the good work they have in hand, namely, the expense of forwarding a Bill in Parliament for the improvement of dwellings for the labouring classes, of adopting measures for the obtainment of a cheap, pure, and abundant supply of water for the whole parish, and of baths and washhouses for the poor. We trust that the success of this appeal will give such an impetus to these cognate objects as will not only lead to the complete fulfilment of them in the present instance, but render it an example to the whole country as the rudiment of a complete domiciliary and sanitary reform. A draft of the proposed Dwelling Improvement Bill has been forwarded to us. It would authorize the parish and union authorities to construct, or hire, whenever needed, by means of the parish rates, proper dwellings for the labouring population, and to devote the profits thereof to the parish funds and the diminution of the poor-rate. It stipulates that each dwelling shall possess an abundant supply of pure water, a decent wholesome water-closet, and every other essential accommodation, at a specified list of charges; such as 1s. 6d. a week for a single room 12 feet square and 9 feet high, &c. In the preamble, the object of thus and otherwise making the people a healthful, orderly, contented, and peaceable community is held up to view as one reason for the Act, and the consequent decrease of workhouses, infirmaries, hospitals, &c., might have been equally dwelt on as another. The suggestion that parishes should obtain the power of providing such dwellings originated, we believe, in our pages.

AN ENORMOUS CHIMNEY has been erected for the Counterslip Sugar Works, Bristol. According to the newspapers, and which our own observation of the work in progress leads us to believe correct, the foundation of the stack is about 25 feet square, with piles driven to a depth of 20 to 25 feet from the level of the ground, the 5 feet nearest the surface being a bed of concrete, about 23 feet square. The diameter of the stack at the bottom is 20 feet; and it tapers gently to a height of over 200 feet, the diameter at its summit being 4 feet 8 inches. In the construction of the stack 220,000 bricks were used, and the entire weight of the mass on the piles is 580 tons. "With such almost unprecedented nicety," adds our authority, "has the stack been constructed, that the final trial with the plumb did not show a deviation of an eighth of an inch from the true perpendicular." It may be useful, however, to add to this account a notice of the circumstance that this is the second time the chimney has been put up; the work failed on the first occasion before it was quite finished, and was taken down, of course at no small cost. This disastrous accident was ascribed, we believe, mainly to the prevalence of wind and rain from one quarter; we should ourselves rather attribute it to the fact that no architect was employed.

ABERGAVENY LUNATIC ASYLUM.—In the provincial notes of the last number but one of your widely-circulated paper appeared a notice of the above building, and since that time I have been inundated with letters and prospectuses from various tradesmen; but as your notice merely said *Monmouth*, without describing the town in which the building is being erected, I shall feel obliged if you will take an early opportunity of stating that it is being built at Abergaveny. The building is to be in the Early English style, and to accommodate the pauper lunatics of four counties, viz., Monmouth, Radnor, Hereford, and Brecon.

H. R.

THE KENILWORTH-STREET SEWER QUESTION.—Dr. Playfair has issued a supplementary report on his part, reiterating his results not only without any retractation, but strengthened by the statement that he is supported in these results by "several of the most eminent chemists in London, among whom," he says, "I may mention Professors Graham and Williamson, as well as Dr. Hoffman, of the Royal College of Chemistry." Dr. Ure has thus arrayed against him a somewhat formidable evidence, amongst whom he himself before enumerated the two Government chemists, and the two chemists of King's and University Colleges. Dr. Playfair appears good-naturedly to suggest that Dr. Ure's experiments may be strictly accurate, if the sewer water used in his experiments were taken "from the open trench, where plenty of gas lime had fallen in;" but Dr. Ure repudiates that idea in a new report since issued, in which he appears to have lost all temper, and complains that he has been exposed to "a tempest of passion, prejudice, and invidious contradiction," and "vulgar vituperation," &c., and not very obscurely insinuates that the sewer has been tampered with, as, in three specimens taken for further verification of his results, he finds that the prussic acid, "the witness he (the tamperer) intended to destroy, exists no longer indeed in the fluid," but has been found in the mud, in the shape of inert Prussian blue, so that "the wicked is snared in the work of his own hands." This is a serious charge, if seriously entertained and regarded. Dr. Ure even specifies copperas as the precise form in which the iron and sulphur destroying the poison has been thrown into the sewer. There seems to be a less odious way of accounting for the presence of iron and sulphur in the mud of a sewer, and especially of the Kenilworth sewer, than this, even granting that the poisonous hydrocyanic acid did exist in the fluid, and above all, in the gaseous, sewage (for this latter, be it ever recollected, *is the* question after all, and hence we presume no one ever had yet thought of groping in the mud for neutral inert and destroyed poison). But it is not for us to reply to such a charge. We only could not think of affording the influence of our circulation to the naked propagation of such a charge against any man, even in the meantime, without something like a reasonable or charitable qualification, which we do not find in Dr. Ure's report, while yet we have not Dr. Playfair's own defence or reply. One thing is clear, however, namely, that Dr. Ure himself admits that the sewage water does not now contain *any* prussic acid or other poisonous compound of cyanogen. And as for the mud, the compounds now alleged by Dr. Ure to have been found in it are admittedly not poisonous either. The source of these latter compounds, if they do exist, is of course still an open question.

COMPENSATION, SPITALFIELDS. — *Hyde and Co.* v. *Commissioners of Woods.*—On the 31st ult. a writ of inquiry was entered into at the Sheriff's Court, Red Lion-square, London, to estimate the amount of compensation to which the plaintiffs, Messrs. Hyde, solicitors, of Ely-place, Holborn, were entitled to, for the loss of a piece of freehold land and two houses, situated in Vine-court, Spitalfields. The premises were required by the Commissioners for the completion of the new street leading from Spitalfields Church to Shoreditch. The only question in the case was one of value: the plaintiffs claimed 1,200*l.*, the defendants offered 400*l.* Evidence was adduced on the part of the plaintiffs, from which it appeared that the property had been let on lease to a greengrocer for the term of forty years, which expired at Midsummer in the present year, at a rent of 30*l.* per annum, and some time before the expiration of the lease Mr. Chapman, the tenant, offered to take a new lease at an advanced rent of 40*l.* a-year. Mr. Todd, builder, and Mr. Nelson, architect, proved that the property was worth 1,200*l.* (the freehold of the land included), allowing 120*l.* for the old materials, as a site for stables. The Attorney-General, in behalf of the Commissioners, contended that the property was not worth more than 420*l.* He did not call any witnesses. The jury gave 850*l.*

AUSTRALIAN COPPER.—Ten tons, the first ever smelted in Australia, were sold at Sydney, some time since, at 81*l.* per ton.

TAORMINA AND MOLA, FROM THE ANCIENT THEATRE.—Mr. W. Linton's picture of Ætna and Taormina, painted for Mr. Richard Ellison, of Sudbrooke Holme, has been lithographed by Mr. F. W. Hulme, we suppose for publication. Mr. Linton delights in classic scenery, and ever treats it with power and beauty. His great merits are scarcely so widely recognized as they deserve to be. The ancient city of Taormina was one of the three most renowned in Sicily during the classic ages. Aqueducts, baths, cisterns, a gymnasium, a stadium, and naumachia, with sepulchres, and mosaic pavements, the ruins of temples, porticoes, and piazzas, are among the numerous remains which evidence its ancient splendour. Many of our readers know the beauty of the scene. The proscenium of the theatre constitutes the principal object in the foreground with its arches and broken columns. "It is encrusted," says Mr. Linton, "with white marble, as were the benches of the coilon. The plan of the theatre is Greek, and the Greek inscriptions which have been discovered on some of the broken seats are evidence of its having been originally built by those colonists. It was afterwards rebuilt and subsequently restored by the Romans, as its remains testify." Mr. Hulme has transferred it to stone with great delicacy. If we offered any objection, it would be that the parts in shadows are too dark, and contrast too cuttingly with the remainder, suggesting the idea that the latter has yet to be worked up, and therefore giving the effect in some degree of incompleteness.

BIRMINGHAM BATHS AND WASHHOUSES.—The foundation-stone being laid on Monday week, by the Mayor, at the site in Kent-street, Bromsgrove-street, a *déjeûner* took place in the evening, when the Mayor, in congratulating the friends of the institution on the event of the morning, remarked that he hoped that at no distant day the other part of the arrangement for the recreation of the working classes would be carried out. There was the park at Aston, with a classic building, associating with it the idea of Hampton Court. Then there were the parks of Edgbaston, and Soho, at Handsworth, which were exceedingly desirable for such an object. The Rev. J. C. Miller followed in an exemplary clergyman's speech, in which he observed that they had heard much said about the new gaol and lunatic asylum, and also about the new poor-house. Now, unquestionably, all these buildings were accounted necessary, and yet with all of them some painful or melancholy feeling was connected. But he thought that scarcely any painful feeling could be associated with the event of that morning. Then, with regard to the bearing of the undertaking on the moral character of the people of Birmingham, he believed it was a matter of no slight importance to turn a dirty man into a clean one. He believed that so long as our poor were in a state of squalid filth, and their houses wretched, we might use our religious appliances and our police appliances, but we should use them to a great extent in vain. He had no great hope of a man so long as his person was dirty, and he revelled in filth; and whatever induced him to cleanse his skin and cleanse his clothes was an important aid to the minister of religion.

FALL OF MOOLTAN FORT IN A WAR OF THE ELEMENTS.—This renowned fortification, which, with all its bomb-proof dependencies, so long withstood the cannon hail showers of Britain, has been razed to the ground by the still more potent showers of Nature's ordnance—the soft and simple rain, which, pouring down in torrents, and rushing on in floods, till building after building fell before it in rapid succession, has reduced the fort to a mere defenceless ruin. The river Chenaub at length covered the whole country during the monsoon, and has everywhere done much damage.

CHANCEL DILAPIDATIONS.—We are obliged by your frequent notes respecting builders' differences, but it is a pity to let surveyors altogether escape. In central Norfolk a valuation has recently been made of clerical chancel dilapidations by three persons, to the following effect:—

An architect from Norwich......	£303	1	10
Ditto from Cambridge..........	130	0	0
Ditto from Lynn..............	74	9	0

There would seem to be want of knowledge somewhere.

N.

How we build Railway Bridges.—Passing through Isleworth the other day, we were surprised "above a bit," as they say in the west, to see workmen busily employed in taking down a brick bridge of three arches, which carries, or is to carry, if they can ultimately make it strong enough, the Staines and Richmond Railway, not yet opened. A well-known horticulturist of the neighbourhood, who happened to be passing at the moment, must have noticed the surprise with which we viewed the proceeding, for he stopped his grey horse, and said, "You will be more astonished when I tell you that this bridge has already been built *twice*, and if this be the way they manage the works on this railway, I may thank my stars I hold no shares." Some of those who do, may perhaps think it pertinent to inquire who pays for these arch-waggeries, the engineer, the builder, or the shareholders? it is a trap-ball regulation that "slips go again," but whether or not this hold good in railway works when the "going again" costs money, deponent knoweth not.

Hull Corn Exchange Competition.—Three designs were submitted to the Committee appointed to carry out the execution of the new Corn Exchange, namely, from Messrs. Lockwood and Mawson, Mr. C. Brodrick, and Mr. Niemann. The Committee had stipulated that the architects should confine themselves to designs for converting the present corn market into a fish market, and for erecting a corn exchange over the poultry and butter market; and required that there should be double staircases of easy access, both from Blackfriargate and Fetter-lane, with all convenient offices for such a market upon the same floor as the exchange. The plan selected was the one furnished by Messrs. Lockwood and Mawson, of Hull, and of which the following are some of the principal features:—The corn exchange is a parallelogram, measuring 188 feet by 40 feet, but by a recess obtained by projection over the fish market, the width, along one-third of the entire length, is increased to 50 feet. The light, introduced entirely from the north, is obtained by dividing the roof into nine compartments, placed across the building and supported by cast-iron arched girders. The fish market has a range of columns dividing the shops, and supporting a caved ceiling, with light in the centre. Air is introduced by open arches springing from the columns, as well as by apertures left in the ceiling and roof. A fountain occupies the centre of the market, to cool and purify the atmosphere. The estimated cost of Messrs. Lockwood and Mawson's plan was 3,800*l.*; but by suggestions of the committee the cost is to be reduced to 3,500*l.*

New Schools, St. Dunstan's-in-the-West, London.—The plot of ground at the Fleet-street end of Fetter-lane is to be occupied by schools for the parish of St. Dunstan-in-the West. The first stone of the new building was laid by the (late) Lord Mayor, Sir James Duke, on the 3rd inst. The building is to be faced with red brick, and the door-ways of Portland stone. It is to consist of two floors and an attic over. The school on the ground-floor is intended to accommodate 100 infants, and that on the first story forty boys; while the attic will be fitted up with all necessary conveniences, in order to make it a comfortable residence for the infant schoolmistress. The plans have been prepared by Mr. John Shaw, and the builders are Messrs. Locke and Nesham.

How Ironfounders differ.—To show that builders are not the only blind ones in estimating for work, I hand you a list of tenders that were sent in for the erection and completion of a gasbolder, tank, and purifier, at Ilford, Essex.

W.

Crosskill	£565
Horlock and Co.	510
Headly	472
Middlemist	430
Helsham	362
Woolcott	347
Gilks, Worsdell, and Co.	350
Cottam and Hallam	328
Graysbrook	325
Gray	311
Crossly, Son, and Co.	310
Barlow	300
Westwood and Wright	297
Hogarth	256
Deeley, Whitechapel (accepted and completed)	184

Edinburgh Philosophical Institution.—Professor Wilson, the president, opened this institution in Queen-street Hall on Tuesday week, with an eloquent address, in which he deprecated the unqualified meaning usually put upon those celebrated sayings, the one, of Pope, that a little knowledge is a dangerous thing, and the other, of Bacon, that it inclines man to atheism. In the former he showed that Pope alluded to critics, and in the latter that Bacon alluded to the exclusive study of second causes. Yet Bacon "is not undervaluing them, provided they are conducted in a proper spirit; he says that if there is danger at all, it is in over-little—a most different view that from that generally taken of it." In conclusion, the professor referred to a great deal having been said of the re-action of knowledge on the human faculties; and he at once admitted that re-action was not always good; that where it led to self-exaltation it was positively bad: but that where it made the mind greater and better, and led an individual to attribute all his gifts and attainments to the Almighty—the bestower of all blessings—it was decidedly good.

Hertford Corn Exchange.—In consequence of the great inconvenience arising from the want of proper accommodation for the merchants, farmers, and others attending the corn-market here, it was thought desirable by a majority of the town council and influential inhabitants to provide a commodious corn-exchange. The building (which we have not seen) is situate in the principal street (Fore-street), and near to the Shire Hall. The design was furnished by Mr. D. Hollingsworth, the borough surveyor, and the building was contracted for by Lawrence, Son, and Castle, of Hertford, for the sum of 391*l.*, exclusive of the fittings, &c., for the merchants. The dimensions of the building, according to our informant, are as follows:—Length, 66 feet 6 inches; width, 43 feet 6 inches; height, 15 feet to the under side of girders. In the centre is a lantern 40 feet by 15 feet (supported by eight hollow cast-iron columns), and constructed upon upright sashes, furnished with Hurwood's patent apparatus. Ventilation is effected by the sashes in the lantern, and six large skylights in the sides of the roof, the whole of which is covered with rough plate glass. The exchange was opened on the 20th inst. Out of thirty-eight stands, thirty-two have been let at various rents, from 3*l.* 3s. to 4*l.* 10s. per year.

The Cards of Invitation and Admission to the Coal Exchange shewed considerable care, and some taste. The first, a solid enamelled card, presented an engraved view of the exterior of the new building (perspective of which, by the way, was questionable), and the admission ticket forwarded on the invitation being accepted, was on lace paper, with a coloured group of fossils in the centre, and a map of part of the city on the back, to guide such of the west-enders as were ignorant of Billingsgate. We have to thank Mr. John Wood, the active chairman of the committee, for more attention than we have heretofore received from city authorities.

Playing on the Pipes, by the "Times."—Pipes appear to be the order of the day. Pipes to let pure water in—pipes to carry foul water out;—pipes for warming—drainage—ventilation;—pipes to bring in gas for burning—pipes to carry off the products of combustion. Pipes to the rich man's marble bath-room—pipes to the poor man's brick-paved kitchen;—pipes for the fountains of St. James, and pipes for the stinking cesspools of St. Giles. For ornament and pleasure—for economy and cleanliness—for health and comfort—for arresting conflagration, and extinguishing pestilence—pipes! The whole sanitary question, indeed, may be regarded as little more than a question of pipes.

Disinfecting Power of Chlorine Gas.—With reference to Collins's disinfecting powder, the inventor asserts that, having a glass globe holding about 900 cubic inches of air, he added to this air one cubic inch of sulphuretted hydrogen gas; he then placed a sparrow in it, which was deprived of life almost instantly.* He then introduced into this poisoned atmosphere of the globe about half a tea-spoonful of his disinfecting powder (the properties of which are derived from its evolving free chlorine by the simple absorption of moisture), and at the expiration of two minutes introduced another sparrow, and after this had remained in the globe ten minutes it was withdrawn, and found to have suffered no injury from its exposure to this atmosphere.

* This is in the proportion of one table-spoonful of sulphuretted hydrogen to 3½ gallons of air.

The Vernon Club.—The formation of an artistical and literary club under the above title is in agitation. If under good auspices, and well managed, the scheme could scarcely fail to succeed.——Behnes has just finished the bust of Mr. Vernon intended for the vestibule of the National Gallery.

The Preservation of Life from Fire.—As a means of preserving life and property from fire, I would suggest attaching an air-pump to a fire-engine, to be worked at the same time, or as occasion might require. To this pump I would attach a light elastic tube, to be fixed to a fireman's hood or covered helmet, in order to enable him to enter a room when filled with a dense suffocating smoke, to rescue persons who would otherwise have perished, or save valuable property from the flames. The fireman's dress and helmet I would form of asbestos, or some other material which should be impervious to fire; as also the elastic tube, which should be cased with a similar material, to prevent its being affected by the fire, and it could be made of any length. On mentioning my suggestion to others, I was informed a similar plan had been invented by Mr. Deans and Col. Paulin. The same simple contrivance might be adopted for entering a foul sewer, which at all times is exceeedingly dangerous, but by means of a small air pump, with a coil of tubing, it might at all times be made available, and at a trifling cost.

W. Westmacott.

*** The suggestion as respects entering sewers was made in our columns some time since.

MEETINGS OF SCIENTIFIC BODIES

Held during the ensuing week.

Tuesday, Nov. 13.—Freemasons of the Church, 8 p.m.

Thursday, 15.—Society of Antiquaries, 8 p.m.

TENDERS

For that portion of the East and West India Docks and Birmingham Junction Railway lying between the Lea Cut Canal and Blackwall; Mr. Martin, Engineer.

Godson	£53,891
Jay	53,504
Hayton	53,079
Murray	52,536
Douglas	51,757
Hicks	51,670
Jones	51,666
Wythes	50,162
Wallace	50,075
Nowell	49,740
Favell	49,079
Curtis	48,754
Warren	48,000
Lee and Son	47,684
Brassey	47,300
Evans	46,744
Pauling	46,274
Smith and Pearce	45,963
Rolt	45,632
Goodison	45,218
Waring	45,108
Pauling	45,009
Boulton	44,953
Diggle	44,825
Knight and Son	44,230
Thos. Jackson	43,980
Furness	43,899
Howe and Jones	43,479
Price	43,413
Scissons	43,310
Rigby	43,240
Earle and Comb	42,584
Gregson	42,536
Adamson	42,276
Hutchings	41,858
Henfry	41,270
Jackson	40,962
Bray	40,921
Worswick	40,616
Tredwell	40,377
Trego	39,883
Pickering	39,593
Iliteon and Hutchinson	38,540
Myers	37,832

[Difference, only 16,059*l.*]

For the proposed Corn Exchange, at Brigg, Lincolnshire, Lockwood and Mawson, architects.

Warden and Littler	£1,679	3	9
Johnson, S. and R.	1,590	0	0
Wallis	1,555	0	0
Dent	1,525	0	0
Wright	1,485	0	0
Clark and Gosford	1,429	18	0
Hockrey	1,400	0	0
Miller	1,394	0	0
Thompson	1,392	0	0
Leggott	1,330	0	0
Fewster	1,319	0	0
Wass	1,279	0	0
Thompson and Jarvis	1,278	6	0
Margeson (accepted)	1,227	0	0
Clark	1,151	0	0

TO CORRESPONDENTS.

"*Diploma Question*" next week.

"*Byphon Ventilation*" will not be overlooked. We have seen the system in operation.

A Stationer.—Thorwaldsen was the sculptor of the statue of Lord Byron refused at Westminster Abbey.

"*Provincial.*"—"R. B. G.," "QuonJam," "J. D." "P.," "J. B." (Chelsea), "G. H.," "H.C.N (we will give publicity to the matter when we have been something of it)," "T. B." (the quotation in question was in type when we received our correspondent's letter, and will appear), "T. H." "Z," (we will endeavour to comply), "W. B." (the address is constantly advertised), "Country Sub." (Rev. Thomas Lodge, Halves, Yorkshire), "P. P." "W." (we do not intend giving his name), "G. F. S." "A. G.," "H. and M. G.," "R. N.," "Ex-Commissioner." "P. I.,," "T. W." (thanks; we shall not be able to engrave the drawings—they shall be returned), "β," (we shall probably illustrate the roof in question), "W. A.," "Old Subscriber," Maidstone (the advertisements refer to the same book—Rasett originally published it), "A Subscriber" (the Free Grammar School, otherwise Edward VI.'s School, Birmingham, was designed by Mr. Barry, and cost, it is said, about 40,000l.), "J. T.," "E. W. G." (will appear), "H. F. S.," "Decorative Art, Exhibiting the Development of its Natural and Geometrical Elements, &c.," by Robert Robson; London : Weale, 1849. Fasciculus 1. "*Tufts v. Mansfield.*"—Mr. Jas. Mansfield, of James-street, Bedford-row, wishes us to say that he is not the Mansfield alluded to.

NOTICE.—All communications respecting *advertisements* should be addressed to the "Publisher," and not to the "Editor;" all other communications should be addressed to the EDITOR, and *not* to the Publisher.

"*Books and Addresses.*"—We have not time to point out books or find addresses.

ADVERTISEMENTS.

STATUES, VASES, FOUNTAINS, Garden Ornaments, Coats of Arms, and Architectural Embellishments, in Imperishable Stone, by VAUGHAN and CO., Stone-Turf, Borough, London. T. J., Crogg— etc... A pamphlet of drawings forwarded on application.

TO GAS AND WATER COMPANIES, ENGINEERS, AND CONTRACTORS.
ANDREW M'LAREN and Co., Steelyard Wharf, Upper Thames-street, have always on hand a large STOCK of SOCKET PIPES of all sizes, with the usual connections, Retorts, columns, girders, and all description of castings contracted for. Their stock of goods for general house-purposes is as equal'ed for variety and lowness of price : competing, range, register, and all kinds metal and stoves, rainwater pipes, U. G. and half-round guttering, sash-weights, railing bars, panels, bakers' oven work, shot traps, air bricks, water-closet metal, &c. &c.

PATENT METALLIC LAVA, Manufactured only by Messrs. ORSI and ARMANI WHITE AND ORNAMENTAL, for the interior of Churches, Museums, Halls, Vestibules, Conservatories, &c. &c.: BROWN, for Pavd Pavement, Flooring, Covering Railway Arches, Terraces, Roofs, &c. &c. Specimens and list of prices can be obtained at the offices, 2, Guildhall Chambers, Basinghall-street, City ; and at the office of "The Builder."

SEWERAGE of LONDON.—The attention of the COMMISSIONERS appointed to determine upon the most efficial material for the Construction of the Sewers of London, is particularly directed to the ASPHALTE of BEYSSEL, which, more than any other material, is applicable to the constructing and lining of Brick Culverts, and other channels for drainage. The rare-eminence made by the Royal Artillery on the Embrasures of Plymouth Citadel, channels for drainage and of Ordnance, have fully proved the superfluity, adhesiveness, and strength of Beyssel Asphalte over all other cementitious compositions.—A printed account of these experiments can be had on application to J. FARRELL, Secretary, Seyssel Asphalte Company. (Claridge's Patent.) Established 1835.

ZINC, from the VIEILLE MONTAGNE MINING COMPANY, is the purest known. On the sale of Iron, lead, or sulphur. It is equally fit for Stove Founders, &c., and to sheets for ship sheathing and roofings of all kinds, and nails of all dimensions. It may be had at the following Agents', who have always a large stock in hand :—
Birmingham—Messrs. Charles Devaux and Co. ; Mr. Charles Jack ; Mr. William M'Crea.
Nottingham—Mr. John Barwell.
Liverpool—Messrs. R. Zwelenkurst and Co.
Manchester—Messrs. Richard Johnson and Brother.
Leeds—Messrs. J., G. and T. Hirsts.
Hull—Messrs. J. Parker and Sons.
Newcastle-upon-Tyne—Mr. Benjamin Plummer.
Dublin—Messrs. Robert Anderson and Co.
Glasgow—Messrs. A. & Wilson and Co.
Bristol—Messrs. Morgan M'Arthur and Co.
Plymouth—Messrs. Liverpool, Bristol, and Co.
Southampton—Mr. W. J. Lefeuvre.
Yarmouth—Messrs. John Shelley and Co.

THE POISONOUS GASES generated in
the sewers of all large towns rise at every outlet, and as the soil-pipes from the palace and the drains of the working man's cottage are alike connected with these sewers, attention ought to be paid to the kind of Water-closet used.
JENNINGS'S WATER-CLOSET, when at rest, effectually prevents any impure air escaping, as the India Rubber Tube which conveys the soil from the basin is not only made AIR-TIGHT by compression, but the water standing on it, the basin renders escape impossible. The relaxing of the handle releases the india Rubber Tube so suddenly, and the contents of the basin fall with such force, that all impurities are carried off each time the closet is used. The long attributed reluctance can be given to public and private establishments.

No. CCCLIV.

SATURDAY, NOVEMBER 17, 1849

RECISION and clearness in specifications, on which contracts are to be made, are absolutely necessary. We have before now urged this, and have pointed out that great differences between the tenders of different individuals for the same work, are sometimes owing to the looseness and defectiveness of the specification. A curious case has been recently settled which illustrates the necessity of this precision very rigorously, and it may be quoted with the less hesitation, because it does not necessarily involve the imputation of that want of care in drawing up the specification to which we have alluded. The matter is in other respects instructive, and may be usefully set forth : we will premise, however, that when we applied to the contractors concerned, for such papers as would establish the correctness of the information we had obtained from various quarters, they thought themselves bound to refuse it, and we mention the circumstance, that they may not be considered privy to this publication; small praise, however, according to our notions. And we would here take the opportunity of remarking, that if there were more willingness on the part of architects, builders, and arbitrators, than is often observable, to giving publicity to questions of practice which come before them, advantage to all would result. We may find an occasion, however, to enlarge on this text, and to say a word or two to some of our architectural *friends* individually, which they may or may not like,—just as they please.

The justices of the peace for Hampshire have recently built, as our readers know, a county prison at Winchester;—it is scarcely finished yet, we believe. Mr. C. J. Peirce, is the architect, and Messrs. Locke and Nesham the contractors. In the contract it was a stipulation that Professor Hosking should determine any question which might arise between the parties in respect of the works ; and in the specification which formed the basis of the contract was the provision, that all the windows in certain parts of the building should " *be glazed with* ROUGH PLATE, ¼ *inch thick*."[*] Nothing to the half-learned mind could seem clearer, — one provision was as understandable as the other, —the identity of our acute friend the professor, and of *rough plate*, appeared equally unmistakeable,—the difficulty of seeing through either equally great: and yet what followed ? We shall learn.

Well, the windows were glazed,—had been so for some time by the way,—when the magistrates one fine morning discovered that the glass with which these windows were filled, was not the "rough plate" which they looked for, namely, that thick cast glass recently introduced, with a roughened surface, through which roughness there is no transparency, although the glass remains translucent,—and which indeed is the condition of all cast plate glass before it is ground and polished. The glass really used was plain on the surface, generally transparent, and, as admitted by the contractors, was produced by blowing. The

[*] It is necessary to specify thickness, this and consequent price varying up to 1 inch.

contractors denied that the term, "rough plate," is applied exclusively to rough *cast* plate, and alleged that the glass objected to was known as " rough plate," and that it was commonly sold under that designation before cast plate came into the market in its rough or unpolished state. Further, as to the propriety of applying the term "plate" to a blown glass, that although the glass in question is blown, the cylinder into which it is blown is at once cut down and flattened on a plate,—that it is susceptible of being ground and polished, and has been for many years so treated and sold for all the purposes of plate glass. Some few of the windows in the prison, we should have mentioned, are glazed with the rough cast plate.

The question then was, has the quoted provision in the specification been complied with ? and to determine this, Mr. Hosking was called in, and took evidence.

The question of thickness was waived or withdrawn by the justices, so that the only point of inquiry was,—is the glass used "rough plate ?" On the part of the magistrates, Mr. James Hartley, of Sunderland, a well-known manufacturer, stated positively that the glass used was *not* rough plate, but sheet glass manufactured to imitate it, one side being slightly burnt to diminish its transparency. This witness, as we gather, set forth some particulars which may interest our readers. He said that all the various descriptions of window glass are manufactured from the same materials— sand, soda, and lime—the various qualities of glass being produced by the differing proportions and purity of these substances. Glass is formed into flat surfaces in three different ways :—1. By blowing it into a globular form and then throwing it into a flat plane, — this is crown glass. 2. By forming cylinders, which are cut open and then flattened,—this is called cylinder glass, broad glass, blown plate glass, &c. : and 3. By pouring melted glass upon a metallic surface, and passing over it a heavy roller, to reduce it to an even thickness,—this is termed rough plate glass, cast plate glass, rolled glass, &c. It is the contact with the cold surface on which it is cast that causes the roughness, by unequal contraction.

Mr. Hartley asserted that the glass in dispute belonged to the second process, and that the term " rough plate" had never been applied to such by the trade. He was astonished that any person conversant with the glass trade could call the glass used " rough plate," or that there could be any difference of opinion as to a material now so much used and so well known. Mr. Hartley also quoted other specifications, containing precisely the same description, " rough-plate ¼ inch thick,"[*] for which, as a matter of course, the cast glass had been supplied.

Mr. Fincham, of Ravenhead, St. Helen's, said the glass in question was not " rough plate." Rough plate had been introduced by him, as manager of the British Plate-glass Company, ten years ago, for the express purpose of giving light where the glass was not to be seen through. German sheet, blown in cylinders, had been polished and sold under the denomination of patent plate-glass; and the glass in question was this description of glass, before polishing, that is in its rough state ; but no dealer would accept the one for the other, although, for some purposes, the " rough patent plate " might be preferable.

Mr. Souper, secretary of the Thames Plate-

glass Company; Mr. Christie, agent for the Union Plate Company ; Mr. Hetley, of Soho-square ; Mr. Millington, of Bishopsgate-street ; Mr. Wilson, of the British Plate-glass Company ; and Mr. Goslett, of Soho Plate-glass Warehouse, all denied that the material used could be called " rough-plate," or bore any resemblance to it.

Now, let us look at the other side of the picture—or, rather, of the glass,—and we shall see that there are other doctors who differ besides Ure and Playfair.

Mr. Young, of St. Martin's-lane, had no hesitation in saying the glass in question had always been considered by the trade rough plate, and, though in the business fifty years, had never seen or heard of any other description of glass so called. Mr. Swinburne, of Thames-street, said it was " blown rough plate-glass." Mr. Brackman, a practical man of many years' standing, had sold it as " rough plate" when, foreman of the London Works. Mr. Chater, of St. Dunstan's-hill, had supplied both cast and blown as " rough plate" for thirty-six years. Mr. R. Cobbett, of Northumberland-street, considered both kinds " rough-plate." Messrs. Foord, who hold the contract for glaziers' work under the Office of Woods, considered that both cast and blown were equally entitled to be called rough-plate, and thought that the specification would be strictly followed out by supplying either one or the other. The blown rough-plate was made in this country before cast rough-plate, and was therefore more entitled to the term. They said, moreover, that as there was no difference in the price, the contractors had no motive to use one in preference to the other beyond that, for smaller sizes (under 40 inches by 20 inches), the blown could be obtained more quickly than the cast.

Professor Donaldson, who appeared on the same side, referred to the volume in " Lardner's Cyclopædia," on porcelain and glass, in the introduction whereof two descriptions of plate-glass, blown and cast, are recognised.

Messrs. Piper, Messrs. Lawrence and Son, Messrs. Haward and Nixon, Mr. W. Cubitt, considered that the glass fully met the requirement of the specification, and Mr. G. Pownall said it was " rough plate-glass," and that it could not be described in any other way.

In considering his award, Mr. Hosking properly declined to consider, as not within the question before him, an argument on the part of the contractors, that any objection to the glass ought to have been taken when it was first put into the work, and one on the part of the justices that " rough-plate " was specified for the express purpose of obtaining absence of transparency, while the greater part of the glass used *is* transparent. The justices had put their objections on three grounds, thus expressed :— First, That the words *rough* and *plate* in the specification were to be held each to have a certain meaning; secondly, that the article objected to did not come under the description, inasmuch as it was blown glass, smooth on both sides, but afterwards slightly roughened on one side ; and thirdly, that it was not what is ordinarily understood and known in the trade by the term rough plate.

The arbitrator shaped his award to meet these heads ; and set forth—" First, that the words *rough* and *plate* in the specification are not to be held to have each a certain meaning, but that they are to be taken together, as denoting a certain condition of plate glass—that is to say, in its unground and unpolished state ; secondly, that' inasmuch as the glass objected to possesses the characteristics of plate glass, and is made and used as and for the purposes and under the name of plate glass, the circumstance of its being produced by blowing and having a smooth surface when first produced does not prevent it from coming under the description given in the specification; and thirdly, that the article objected to —that is to say, blown plate glass in its unground and unpolished state—though not universally known in the trade by the term "rough plate," is so far known by that term in the glass trade and among builders, the immediate consumers of plate, sheet, and other glass, as window glass, as to justify its recognition by that term."

And he therefore determined that the glass objected to *is* within the terms employed in the specification.

We give the particulars of this curious case (without reference to the decision), because of the positive information it contains, and as an instance of the necessity of precision in specifications, which we hope will not be disregarded. A considerable expenditure was at stake.

DECORATIVE ART IN GLASS—
STAINED AND PAINTED.

In concluding his historic review of middle-age art, delivered of late at the School of Design, Somerset House, Mr. Wornum proceeded on Friday, the 2nd, to treat of stained and painted glass, as in a manner supplementary to Gothic art, since hitherto almost exclusively practised in Gothic buildings. But whatever prestige such exclusive application may have given rise to, said the lecturer, it will be our business rather to destroy than to encourage; for we must spread the beautiful in all directions,—extend it to every province,—at least we will try to do so.

The old Egyptians have not yet been surpassed, if even approached, by the moderns in the art of staining glass; but we know nothing of stained windows earlier than the eighth century, and have no *remains* of a period earlier than the twelfth.

The ancients, however, did glaze their windows not only with common panes of glass, but with ground plate glass, to keep inquisitive eyes out: a window of this kind was discovered in a bath at Pompeii, but the glass was all broken to pieces. In the baths of the villa of Diomedes similar glass was found. The Greeks called glass 'hyalos,' from the Coptic: it was introduced from Egypt.

In mere coloured ornamental glass the resources of the ancients were surprising. There was no marble, no precious stone, which they did not successfully imitate. They had every variety of cup and vase made of this beautiful material. Glass drinking vessels were common in the time of Hadrian, and some of them, of rarer quality, displayed all the prismatic colours, variously in various lights. These were of Egyptian manufacture. With the art of glass blowing, as may be conceived, the ancients were well acquainted.

With all the means such examples imply, the *absence* of coloured plate glass for windows amongst the ancients should strike us as more singular than the *discovery* of any such remains; especially as it was the custom to decorate entire walls with plates of glass and polished marbles; and as the marbles were invariably coloured (and as they knew well how to imitate marbles, as already remarked by the lecturer), it is highly improbable that the glass was invariably white. Yet the pure crystal glass was considered the most valuable by the Romans. Talc was also used by the ancients for windows, having this great advantage for a hot climate, that it excludes the heat while it admits the light of the sun. As to the ancients having had glazed windows there can be no question, and this fact ascertained, it would be very strange if with their elaborated systems of decoration, they did not colour them. We shall probably yet find some examples before the excavations of Pompeii are completed.

The notices of windows are more frequent as we approach the middle ages. St. Sophia's, of Constantinople, was conspicuous for the number of its glass windows; and, from the many-coloured rays which the Greek poet describes as penetrating them, it would seem that they were of stained glass. This was in the sixth century, and it appears to have been then a general practice in the southern parts of Europe to glaze the church windows. In England they were not so protected till a century later.

The first positive historical notice of stained glass decorations, the lecturer believed to be that of the adornment of the old church of St. Peter's, at Rome, with stained glass windows, by Leo III., in the eight century. Painted glass we first read of in the eleventh century, when mosaic workers from Constantinople adorned the chapter-house of the celebrated Neapolitan Monastery of Montecasino, with windows of painted glass. These were leaded, and supported by iron frame work, as in modern times.

This mention of the mosaic workers, while it constitutes one of those interesting facts which point so decidedly to the capital of the Eastern empire, as the great preserver and promoter of all middle-age art, seems also to indicate, with some certainty, the original source of stained-glass windows in the glass tesselations, the opus Grecanicum of the Byzantines. With this class of art the Italian churches were richly decorated, and the passage from the inlaid glass of the walls and pulpits to the leaded glass of the windows, was not a very great step. This is all the more probable from the circumstance, that while these glass tesselations were common as mural decorations, pieces of talc were still used for windows, as in the church of San Miniato, at Florence, of the early part of the eleventh century; and if these be the original windows, which there is no reason to doubt, they are the oldest in Europe, or at least in the west, and are about 100 years older than the earliest remains of stained-glass windows—those of the cathedrals Angers and St. Denis.

Many of the glass tesselations, according to Theophilus, were actually destroyed for the sake of getting coloured glass for windows. They were of course remelted and cast into small plates, according to the practice of the time. Theophilus also says, that the French were particularly clever in converting the old pagan glass vessels, of many colours, into fine tables, that is panes, of glass, for windows. There would have been more reason for praising their ingenuity if they had preserved the pagan bottles and rivalled their composition by original glass of their own. But such passages as these open our eyes to the way in which ancient ornamental works have so greatly disappeared; and they should teach us to be cautious how we discredit statements we find in ancient authors, simply because we meet with no examples of such works as we occasionally read of in their writings.

The ancient process of making a stained glass window is thus described by Theophilus. The design was first made on a chalked board, a kind of cartoon. Ou this the outlines and general markings were well defined, and the colour each part was destined to be was written in its place. Then a piece of glass of the required colour, large enough to cover that portion of the cartoon inscribed with its name, was placed over it; the exact form of the space was traced on the glass; and finally, it was shaped with the heated iron then used in place of the diamond. The pieces were then all fitted close together on the cartoon, and the lines and shadows were carefully painted in enamel brown. The introduction of ornaments, such as we find in the illuminated manuscripts, is then directed by Theophilus, a circumstance which points most decidedly to the source of the general ornamentation of glass. He concludes by minute instructions how the pieces of glass are to be fired in the furnace, some colours requiring more heat than others: the white, yellow, and purple may be thrust far into the furnace, but green and sapphire, or blue, must be kept near the orifice, as they will not stand so great heat. When sufficiently fired, the various pieces were leaded together, and the picture thus completed. Theophilus describes many kinds of ornamental glass, including gold and silver tints, and designates nearl[y] every remarkable specimen Greek.

The great point of the directions given b[y] this author is, that he clearly describes th[e] enamelling of glass, however simple; not th[e] mere composition of an ornamental design i[n] coloured glass, or what is commonly calle[d] pot-metal—glass coloured bodily while in th[e] melting pot; but the enamelling confined t[o] drawing and shading. The great value, however, of Theophilus's treatise, is affected b[y] the doubts as to its precise date—according t[o] some as early as the tenth, to others as late a[s] the thirteenth century.

All the ancient specimens of stained glas[s] preserved are pot-metal; and the earlies[t] middle-age windows were doubtless of thi[s] same description: it is to this nature, perhaps that they owe their name of mosaic glass, i[.] not to the fact of being made out of old glas[s] mosaics.

In the fourteenth century this practice o[f] using pot-metal was in great part supersede[d] by the use of superficially stained or coate[d] glass. This is made either by flushing o[r] floating an enamel stain upon the glass, an[d] then firing.

In the sixteenth century, a third process wa[s] introduced,—that of actually painting in ena[mel], similar, exactly, to the modern process o[f] porcelain painting.

Enamel, as many of you know, is glass mad[e] opaque by oxide of tin, and fusible by oxide o[f] lead. This gives a white, but you may mak[e] any colour by mixing the various minera[l] oxides with an enamel flux, commonly composed of 32 parts flint glass, 12 pearl ash, an[d] 2 of borax. With this flux you grind up you[r] colour, and then mix it with a little oil o[f] lavender; lay on the colour with a sabl[e] pencil, exactly as in oil painting, then pass th[e] picture through the fire and the whole vitrifie[s] and becomes indelible. The metallic oxide[s] being enveloped in the flux are preserved fro[m] contact with the atmosphere, and thus becom[e] permanent.

The lecturer then proceeded to review som[e] examples of these three kinds of stained o[r] painted glass, interspersing his description with much interesting matter, which we regre[t] to be obliged to pass over. In allusion to th[e] monk Theophilus's idea, that tan colour constituted the proper flesh tint, he inferred tha[t] this little circumstance would appear to throw some light on the moot point of the country t[o] which he belonged. Both the Germans an[d] the Italians, he remarked, have claimed him but the tawny flesh seems fairly to give him t[o] the Italians. With regard to the sombre mellowness of tint in old coloured glass, the lecturer regarded the taste in its favour as a[n] acquired one, to which it was but little entitled considering that it was merely produced b[y] the dirt from which modern glass is mor[e] thoroughly cleansed in the process of manufacture. But from whatever cause produced it remains to be considered whethe[r] or not such a sombre and mellow effec[t] be not the best adapted to ecclesiastica[l] purposes. On the subject of harmon[y] in juxta positions of colour, he considerabl[y] enlarged, producing a host of evidence in illustration from the beautiful plumage of birds i[n] the British Museum and elsewhere. Perhap[s] in no species of art, he remarked, is it mor[e] necessary to observe the laws of harmony i[n] colours than in glass painting. By the physical organization of the eye it requires *all* th[e] primary colours to satisfy it—red, yellow blue: the secondaries—orange, green, an[d] purple—too, are very important. No combinations are good which are not in accordan[ce] with the natural laws of colour, and the chie[f] condition is, that *all* must be present in ever[y] composition and properly balanced.

Having explained the three methods of glas[s] painting, the lecturer then proceeded to poi[nt] out the various characters of design prevalen[t] in the different periods.

In the early period, down to the fourteent[h] century, when the mosaic method exclusivel[y] prevailed, the windows consisted of diape[r] grounds, containing panels with figure sub[j]ects, scriptural and domestic; the whole bein[g] surrounded by a foliaged or geometrical bor[d]er; the prevailing ornaments and the pane[ls] being of a Byzantine character, and in a[ll] respects similar to the MSS. There is n[o] much early glass in England. The most pe[r]

DETAILS OF A FRENCH CASEMENT.

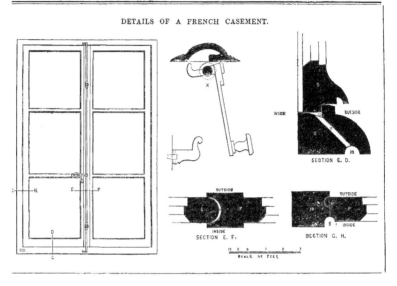

SECTION E. D.

SECTION E. F.

SECTION G. H.

SCALE OF FEET

t examples are the celebrated Five Sisters, York, of thirteenth century. At the close this century isolated figures were introduced, mounted by simple canopies and without ations. The variety of design, therefore, as plied to glass, even at this early period, was ry great.

In the second period, all these varieties were eserved, but the mere Mosaic patterns are longer prominent; the damask and geometcal designs on white glass gradually superled them. Some of the finest windows of ls style are a geometrical design, with a belt canopied figures; the execution of the ures, foliage, and architecture keeping pace th the generally improved development of /le and execution. Heraldic designs now mmon; and in the fifteenth century prevail. It was in the sixteenth century, however, incident with the development of Cinquento art, that glass painting appeared with all technical exuberance. Its limits were now e limits of the art of painting itself. The osaic process was almost wholly disconti- ted for a time, and glass painting became erally painting pictures on glass; but it did not mhine any improved character in its orna- ents. The increased recourse to figure eces and pictures, and the excessive display armorial bearings which characterize the ndows of this period, seem to have left tle opportunity for the development of orna- ent itself. The celebrated windows of the abetha at Gouda, in Holland, are a remark- le monument of that period, but they are erally mere Dutch pictures on glass; some them, as well as the magnificent windows Liege, have been lately published by Mr. 'eale, in two volumes, entitled, "Divers Works Early Masters."

Ou styles, added the lecturer, in conclusion, have yet a few remarks to make. Early osaic glass has been recently designated arly English glass, as it was the style prac- ied during the prevalence of the Early Eng- th Gothic. It was practised, however, a indred years or more before the Early Eng- th Gothic was developed, and was at all times r more universally practised on the conti- nt than in England. The same objection lds with regard to the terms Perpendicular, ecorated, and Cinque-cento glass. These chitectural terms, as applied to glass, have a characteristic but a chronological value aly; and as to "Early English" glass, it is

scarcely good taste to give an exclusively Eng- lish name to a style of art for which we must look abroad for all the fine examples.

Any style of ornamental design may be exe- cuted in any one of the three methods of glass painting just described,—the mosaic, the mo- saic stain, and the enamel. We must not confound the method of execution and the style of ornament. Every design will, by its ornaments, itself proclaim to what style it be- longs, if to any one in particular; and if not, it will require no name beyond the technical description of what it contains,—as coloured diaper, flowered quarry, reticulated damask, medallion, figure, canopy, &c.

In designing a stained glass window, there- fore, first consider whether it be ecclesiastical, palatial, or domestic; then its architectural style. Introduce the characteristic ornamental forms into your design; if a figure window, into the border; if a mere pattern window, into the general arrangement. For a Greek or Roman building, use Greek and Roman orna- ments; for an Italian—Renaissance, or Cinque- cento forms; and for a Romanesque, or Gothic, the Byzantine and Gothic forms. Your figure subjects will be, of course, for a church, scriptural; for a palace they may be historical, with armorial designs; and, for a private dwel- ling-house, armorial and sententious designs, or illustrations of proverbs, are very applicable. There need be no closer limitation of style, and these designs may be executed indif- ferently, to individual predilection, or means, either in the mosaic, the mosaic stain, or in the enamel method.

There will be demurrers to these opinions.

CORRUGATED IRON ROOFING.—With re- ference to the memorandum of the cost of roof coverings, taken from Mr. Dean's "Essays," I would observe, that if the covering of corrugated iron be made circular it will require no other support than at the extremities or springings, whereas in all the other kinds mentioned a price must be provided in addition for rafters and battening. Curved roofing of corrugated iron is self-supporting (the springings of course being secure); the other kinds require a construction of timber wood-work to support them; there- fore, before the cost of curved galvanized cor- rugated iron roofing can be compared with that of others, a price must first be added for their necessary support.   PETER.

DESCRIPTION OF A FRENCH WINDOW,

FROM MATERIALS FURNISHED BY AN
ARCHITECT OF PARIS.

THE accompanying drawing has been ob- tained from Paris, expressly for the purpose of affording accurate and sufficient information to work by. The description will be some- what minute, to make it, if possible, perfectly intelligible.

It will be understood that the window con- sists of two halves, hung upon hinges, closing together like a pair of folding doors, and open- ing inwards; also, that the window is supposed to be viewed from the inside.

The means of fastening the window (and which it is important to attend to) consist of a round bar of iron, B, running from the top to the bottom, and hung in two rings, O, at the points o. These rings are fixed on the inside, in the wood of the right hand casement, or half of the window. The bar must be capable of turning in them to an extent afterwards ex- plained.

Figure A represents a handle fixed on the bar at A, as will be seen in the figure; it is fixed on a projection from the bar, and must be moveable, circularly, in a vertical direction, the axis of the circular movement being the point where it is fixed to the projection. The bar terminates at each end in a hook, 3 and 4. In the head and cill, 1 and 2, of the outer, or fixed frame of the window, holes must be chiselled out at 3 and 4, to receive these hooks, which will help to fasten the window, in the manner afterwards explained.

Figure M is a kind of hook fixed in the wood of the left hand light, at the point M. Its purpose is to receive the handle A, when the window is closed, as will be explained. It must be hinged, and thus have the capability of moving horizontally, right and left (to an extent afterwards explained), as will be under- stood by the figure. Figure g h represents a horizontal section of the casement at g h, 10 being the frame, and 11 the casement.

In a window of the size given in the draw- ing, three hinges (ordinary kind) at least should be used for each of the halves; they will be placed in the hollow 5. E F is a hori- zontal section of the casements at E F, where they meet, when closed, 6 being the left hand, and 7 the right hand light. 12 is a small space left between the two frames, in order that they may close without difficulty. C D shows a vertical section of the cill and inner frames, at C D, 8 being the cill, and 9 the casement. 17 is a circular hole, bored through the cill, at the point 14, for the escape of any water that may get into the space 15. 16 is a groove, or inverted gutter, for carrying off the water.

The exact forms of all these sections must be particularly attended to in execution.

When it is desired to close the window, the two halves are pushed together, and the convex surface of 6 fits into the hollow in 7. It will be found that these parts will touch before the window is fairly closed, and that, by the exertion of a little force, they are, as it were, slipped or snapped, the one into the other. The handle A is moved from the right to the left, and lifted over and into the hook M, and this hook M being at just such a projection from the frame, as to cause the handle to fit tightly into it, the forcing down of the latter upon the hook at P jams or locks together the two halves. At the same time, the moving of the handle A from right to left will turn the bar, and the hooks 3 and 4 will enter the holes prepared for them in the head and cill. These hooks, before the handle was turned, would show in a section of the bar and wood, as in figure X.

The window will then be securely closed. It will be observed that, besides the excellent adaptation of all the joints to resist weather, the advantage of this mode of fastening consists in this, viz., that by a single movement, *each* of the halves is bolted in three places, and indeed firmly secured to the other half *throughout the whole height of the window*, and that, also by a single movement, *both* halves are set at liberty; whereas, upon the ordinary principle of folding doors or windows, the left hand half alone is secured at top and bottom, and the right hand one depends for its fastening upon the single bolt or latch which connects it with the other half, and this imperfect fastening of the halves, moreover, requires three separate movements to complete it, or to set it at liberty, the practical consequence of which is, that to avoid trouble, the right hand half alone is opened.

With respect to the extent of movement respectively of the bar B, the handle A, and the hook M, it will be easily understood after due consideration of their respective purposes.

The turning of the bar, being for the sake of the movement it communicates to the hooks 3 and 4, that purpose will be amply answered by a power of turning in a quarter of a circle.

The binging of the hook M appears to be contrived to give the play necessary to assist the jambing or locking before mentioned. The handle A may of course be placed in the most convenient situation for the hand, depending upon the height of the window from the ground. In windows of a larger size than the one represented in the drawing, a rail or transom runs across each of the halves, at about two-thirds of their height from below, giving the whole the appearance of a cross. Hence, the French word *croisée* for a window.

A prejudice exists with English people against casements, as not being wind and water tight; and it is true, that what are understood by French windows in England, that is, French windows *made in the English way*, are, generally speaking, as imperfect and unsatisfactory contrivances as can be imagined. But the real French window, as made in France, and made well, is perfectly secure against weather.

Its advantages are great. When open, the whole space made available for the purpose of admitting light is also made so for the admitting of air; whereas, in a sash window, one-half of that space must necessarily be always closed.

The view through it is uninterrupted; whereas, in sash windows of the ordinary size, the main bar, where the sashes join, is about on a level with the eye. The inconvenience of stooping the body to look out of the window is also avoided. From the necessity of this posture, with the sash hanging over the neck, the French call sash windows *fenêtres à la guillotine*, or guillotine windows.

The strength shown on the drawing is, perhaps, hardly sufficient for any but small sized windows, or where tough woods are used.

The drawing comprehends what has been found to answer well in France, where this kind of window has been used, it may be safely said, for a century at least, universally, and in buildings of a superior class, for upwards of 200 years; for, in that country, leaded lights were disused much earlier than in England. French windows have hitherto failed for the most part in England, *merely for want of accurately copying the model which has been proved to succeed in France.*

In France almost all windows have wooden blinds fixed outside; and in some situations in England these might be found useful. When combined with the French window they afford the means of admitting an abundance of air, and at the same time excluding the glare and heat of the sun.

F. I. D.

IMPROVEMENT OF BROADWAY, NEW YORK.

From the battery almost to Union-square this grand promenade of our transatlantic brethren has of late been renovated and improved in its buildings, its pavements, and its side walks; indeed, its buildings have been or are being so throughout the whole of its length, so that many old land-marks are vitally altered or altogether gone. No. 1—General Washington's house—has been converted into "The Washington" Hotel. On the site of Bunker's mansion and adjoining properties six extensive stores are being erected, five stories high, with brown stone fronts, and iron shutters and floor columns. The brown stone is in general a mere facing of two-inch slabs on brick. Mr. C. S. Warner is the architect. Four new stores are in process of erection on the site of the old City Hotel. Mr. J. French is the architect of the whole of this block between Cedar and Thames-street. The frontage of the stores is 102 feet, depth 142. They are to be five stories in height, and to cost 100,000 dollars. The fronts will also be of brown stone, and the first story ornamented with fluted columns and pilasters, with Corinthian caps and medallion cornice; the windows trimmed with architraves and cornices. Opposite, on the site of the old National Hotel, a 'splendid' silk warehouse is in course of erection. The front is to be in the Elizabethan style, and the material West Chester marble, in blocks 3 feet thick. The lower story will be faced with a series of ornamental columns, standing on strong plinths in front of piers supporting a frieze and cornice. On these will stand other pilasters with intervening pedestals, elliptical arches with ornamented keystones over the windows in each story, the whole to be surmounted with a cornice and elaborately carved open parapet, ornamented with pedestals and urns, resting on corbels and brackets. The central portion of the parapet will be elevated above the rest, and terminated by solid marble balls. The floors will be supported by wrought-iron beams, and each floor will present an unbroken surface of nearly 5,000 feet, the building being 140 feet deep, and 37½ feet front on Broadway. The architect, Mr. Joseph Wells, expects to complete the building by 1st December, at the estimated cost of 40,000 dollars. Various other stores, chiefly faced with brown stone, are at present in progress, and near Chamber-street, 'a very tasty and elegant structure,' according to the local statements, is being formed for the Chemical Banking Company, at a cost of some 15,000 to 20,000 dollars. Messrs. T. Thomas and Son are the architects. The style is called the 'Romanistic,' with an elaborate entrance and heavy truss cornice. The banking room will be 17 feet in height, with a frescoed dome ceiling. Part of the street is being laid with 'Russ pavement,' by Messrs. Russ and Reid, who estimate the cost of laying the whole street with blocks of this species of pavement at 320,000 dollars.

Drawing Academy.—On the score of long service in the cause, Mr. R. Brown's intimation, through our advertising columns, that he has opened a Drawing Academy in Knightsbridge deserves to be pointed out. He numbers amongst his many pupils of former days some of the leading architects and builders of the metropolis.

THE MOVEABLE TIME-TABLE OF THE EASTERN COUNTIES RAILWAY.

We have been asked to inquire what, in the name of all that is erratic and unbusiness-like, can lead the directors of the Eastern Counties Railway to perplex poor travellers as they do by altering backwards and forwards the hours of train departures? Our own experience fully justifies the inquiry. A fortnight ago we travelled to the far-distant Shoreditch, in time for the half-past ten train, to Hertford, and, getting there twenty-five minutes too soon, as we fancied, found we were nevertheless five minutes too late, the train having started at ten, and so we had to wait till half-past eleven for the next chance. On Saturday last we were compelled to re-tread the ground, and took care to be there before ten, when lo, and behold! the time was again changed to half-past ten; and forty more precious minutes had to be spent in the drafty station-house.

Surely the good-natured and sensible secretary of the company, Mr. Roney, can have no voice in these vexatious vagaries, made seemingly for the fun of the thing. To occupy an hour and twenty minutes and oftener an hour and a half in doing twenty-six miles is bad enough, without throwing out one's whole day by such vacillating mis-arrangements as these.

KENILWORTH-STREET SEWER.

Sir,—In your number of to-day you refer to the extraordinary charge of Dr. Ure, made against me by implication, that I added copperas to the sewer water, for the purpose of removing the prussic acid. You seem to think that I should deny this infamous charge, if it be untrue. I have not done so, because I thought that the spirit in which it was made would prevent any person giving the least credence to so monstrous an accusation. But I bow to your opinion, as I should be sorry that a single honest man could believe me guilty of such an act. I therefore state that I have not the most remote knwledge, either directly or indirectly, of such a sophistication having been made. I further express my disbelief that this act has been perpetrated by any one.

I cannot conclude without expressing my astonishment that any scientific man, even in the tumults of the most uncontrolled temper, could have insulted his profession or the public by a calumny so inconceivable and preposterous.—I am, Sir, &c.,

November 10th. Lyon Playfair.

*** We hope Dr. Playfair does not imagine that our *credence* is so easily accorded as he would seem to fear. But however unworthy of notice such a charge may be generally held to be, an indignant denial at least renders it impossible for a party capable of propagating a false or reckless charge, to make any equally wrong use of the fact of its *not being denied*. Dr. Ure, without waiting, we may here remark, for any such denial, has issued a fourth report, as to which we do not see any necessity for further notice, unless it be to remark, that the sudden death of the man Grosse, in Long Acre, seems entirely to refute his assertion in it, that "an inhalation of *prussic acid vapour mixed with* sulphuretted hydrogen *alone could* cause such an awful catastrophe." But for all that, we do not doubt the probability that other of the "hydras dire" than mere sulphuretted, phosphoretted, or even cyanuretted hydrogen or prussic acid may occasionally pervade the heterogeneous abomination of sewers. Indeed, to any one at all acquainted with the still more recondite, and one might have almost said rare, hydride of selenium, or seleniuretted hydrogen, and its *very peculiar* odour, even that might fairly have been included, however unaccountably, in the list just particularized. We may here add by the way, that Mr. Cubitt, though no tangible charge was made against him touching the construction of this sewer, has addressed the commissioners in an explanatory letter, regarding which all we need say is, that we think the commissioners should, as Mr. C. requests of them, distinctly state that everything which was required of him had been done.

SHALL ARCHITECTS BE DIPLOMA'D.

I am glad to see that the columns of The Builder are still occupied in reminding the Council of the Institute of British Architects of the necessity for amending the laws which govern their body. The observations in answer to your correspondent, "W. X. W.," were very just, and are, I imagine, pretty nearly the feelings of three-fourths of the profession; but I was somewhat surprised, on reading through the article on the amendment of the Institute of Architects (knowing the interest you take in the welfare of the profession), to find that you seemed to throw cold water on the proposal to obtain a legislative enactment forbidding any architect or engineer to practise without a *diploma*. Now, Sir, I am fully persuaded that this is the only means whereby to ensure proper and qualified practitioners in our art.

You seem to reason, Mr. Editor, that "it is not desirable." I consider that if architects have to erect buildings and works, and are thereby entrusted with the lives and property of her Majesty's subjects, they should be compelled to take out a diploma of capability authorizing them to practise as such, in the same way as gentlemen of the law, medical men, and even chemists and druggists, have to do, before they can practise in either of their respective capacities. It would not only render the profession more respectable, but it would give a dignity to its practitioners. The public would look at its members as duly qualified and honourable men, and not disregard our talents, as they evidently do at the present, as may be proved by the most disgraceful and shameful way in which competitions are conducted; in fact, if diplomas were granted, then none but men properly schooled into the profession would be among its members.

You remark also that "it is opposed to the spirit of the times." I am sure no opposition would be met with in the majority of the profession of architects themselves,—they are really yearning for such a movement, and I could almost speak positively that if a petition were set on foot for such purpose, it would be signed by at least three-fourths of the members of the body. If opposition to this diploma scheme be meant in your remark to refer to the public, I think it is no more than in accordance with reason that they would feel satisfied to know, that no person could practise as an architect or engineer without being duly qualified to act in such capacity; 1st. For the reasons abovementioned; and 2ndly. It would prevent their employing any incompetent person, or mere quack, who would, in all probability, injudiciously expend their clients' property.

X. X.

1st. You say, "that *a diploma in architecture* is by no means likely, even if it were in all respects desirable." Now, as to the likelihood of the renovation,—I believe the time is not far distant when we shall see it brought about; but as to the desirableness of such a scheme, every architect who has the least love for his profession must desire it, if only to rid us of the innumerable set of quack draughtsmen who are now being quarterly manufactured at the low rate of ten guineas. My office, Sir, is literally besieged by them, trying to obtain employment; yet they cannot draw a straight line. Again, many architects have now in their offices young men, without any premiums being given, who have no love for the profession they are unfortunately placed in, but because it was a good opening they *must become architects*, not considering that an architect *must have a mind*. What is the consequence? Why, at the end of their articles they cannot explain the ruling principles that exist either in Grecian or Roman architecture; they may know the five orders when placed before them, but, Sir, in many cases that is the utmost, and I am fully aware from experience I am not exaggerating. Yet when their articles are concluded, they expect and ask for the same remuneration as clever draughtsmen, swell the number of that class, and in many cases have unhappily opportunities given them of piling up living monuments of their ignorance, to disfigure the face of this glorious land and disgust the eyes of every beholder; whereas the experienced, fully qualified, and clever man, is thrown aside. I will not speak of the injurious system of employing builders as architects, because that would soon die away if we had a properly qualified body of professional men. You say the spirit of the time is directly opposed to such a restriction. Then, Sir, how do you reconcile the establishment of the Pharmaceutical Society for the examination and granting diplomas, even to druggists? If it can be done in one case, it can in another; *if it be desirable*, do not talk of the spirit of the times being against us, but let us try and obtain it: the greater the difficulties, the greater the glory in winning.

A Practitioner.

It has often appeared to me a sad mistake that a profession like that of architects should be split into several societies (no one of which is sufficiently powerful to carry with it the feeling of the whole body, nor the acquiescence of the public), instead of having one grand and comprehensive scheme of union for its members, which should indeed improve, exalt, and raise their own character, and at the same time command the esteem of the public. Nothing short of a College can be expected to have this desirable effect.

To make the profession respected, and its professors respectable; to rescue the calling of an ennobling pursuit from the grasp of the mere adventurer; to give a tone to public taste, to instruct, enlighten, and improve, would be the praiseworthy (and successful) endeavours of a college established by the general consent of the profession. In a few words one may state some of the advantages which would attach to an architectural college of enlarged membership under a charter: a school of instruction, not to interfere with private tuition, but rather to complete the education—a comprehensive library—a museum—a collection of models of ancient and modern buildings—experiments in different arts—laws to establish precedents—periodical meetings for lectures and discussion—a thorough understanding of the position of architects—a court of appeal in all matters of dispute or etiquette, and a provision for decayed members, their widows, or orphans.

G. R. French.

BRITISH ARCHÆOLOGICAL ASSOCIATION.

PUBLIC MEETING, NOVEMBER 9, 1849.

Mr. Pettigrew, Vice-President, in the chair.

Mr. Purland exhibited a collection of rubbings of some of the most interesting brasses in the churches of Norwich, accompanied by some descriptive remarks.—Mr. Waller observed that the greater part of these brasses belonged to civilians, which was to be accounted for by the extent to which the clothing trade was carried on in the eastern counties. He likewise drew attention to a brass, of the latter part of the fifteenth century, belonging to a knight, the inscription attached to which is about a century later, and relates to another person. He remarked that many of these brasses showed a peculiar mode of forming the features used in Norfolk and Suffolk, and some were evidently Flemish. Much has been said about the destruction of brasses during the civil wars, but a far greater havoc has been committed in modern times. He had sought in vain in many of the churches of Norfolk and Suffolk for brasses figured in Cotman and other authors.—Mr. W. A. Combs exhibited a small brass plate bearing the following inscription:—"Henry Bullayen the sone of Sir Thomas Bullayen." Mr. C. stated that he had ascertained that it belonged to Hever Church, Kent, and that its original place (to which he intended to restore it) was close to the tomb of Sir Thomas Bolleyn, the father of Anne, Queen of Henry VIII. He expressed his inability to discover the relationship of the person here commemorated, as Sir Thomas does not appear to have had any son of that name. He presumed, judging from the size of the stone, the person must have been a child.

Mr. Price stated that in the neighbouring church of Penshurst there is a similar small brass cross and inscription plate to the memory of "Thomas Bullayen, the sone of Sir Thomas Bullayen;" and that probably, from neither of them being mentioned in the Bolleyn pedigree, they both died in their infancy. He had no doubt they were the brothers of the ill-fated queen. Mr. Price added that the Hever brass had been stolen years ago, and he rejoiced to find that at the least some portion of it was in existence, and likely to be restored to its proper place.

Dr. Jessop forwarded for exhibition a brass seal, bearing two matrices: the smaller one represents the head of a bull, the other the same emblem, with a legend of a very curious character, and which forms the subject of a paper displaying antiquarian and philological research. Mr. Price furnished a brief abstract, observing that, although the seal was probably not older than the fifteenth century, the legend was doubtless copied from some antique gem or amulet, and judging from its resemblance to some of the mystic legends and doctrines of the Gnostics, was referable to a very early period of the Christian era. The inscription is as follows:—"+א TO ONא אI CION OOIЄ," which Dr. J., reading it SERAPIS TO ONOMA Aι ΣΙΟΝ (the last four letters being merely a vocalic exclamation), interprets "Serapis, the great name ever divine, O hail!" The inscription commences with the first and last letters of the Hebrew alphabet, the cross being the ancient form of the *tau*. These characters, from their extreme position, were thought symbolical of the whole compass of language, and expressive of universality. The word *aleph* means captain or leader, also a bull. *Tau* is a limit or boundary, and from its form was considered by the Egyptians as typical of horns. In describing at some length the various modifications of the cross, Dr. J. remarks, that at the destruction of the temple of Serapis (the bull-headed deity of the Egyptians), certain cruciform characters were found engraven on stones. These, both Christians and idolaters claimed as symbols of their respective creeds. Traces of this emblem have been discovered in the ruins of Nineveh (*vide* Layard), and they abound in the sculptures of Egypt. The Gnostics blended some of the superstitions of Egypt with their mysteries. They adopted the bull, or its head, as an emblem of Christ.

RATING ST. MARY'S, WHITECHAPEL.

FIXTURES AND FIXED MACHINES.

A meeting of the parishioners of St. Mary's, Whitechapel, was held last week, for the purpose of receiving a report from a committee appointed to investigate the question as to the rating of machinery and other fixtures connected with property within the parish.

The report stated that, considering the importance of the matters submitted for their consideration, they had prepared a case, and submitted it to the consideration of the Attorney-General and Mr. Bodkin, who had given it as their opinion that *all fixed machines, as well as all fixtures*, in houses and shops within the parish, were liable to be rated for the support of the poor. The committee were therefore of opinion that all the parish rates raised under the authority of the local Act should be levied in terms of that finding,—that the vestry should, by means of committees, carry out the assessment of the parish under that system of rating,—and that notice should be given to the Middlesex magistrates and the property-tax commissioners of the change which had taken place in consequence of adopting the system recommended in the opinion referred to.

The report having been received, it was further resolved that as a just and equitable assessment could not be made without a survey of all the rateable property in the parish, including machinery, and fixtures in shops and dwelling-houses, competent professional surveyors be appointed to survey all the property in the parish, so that the rates might be made on a sound and legal basis. This would be all very well if other parishes adopted the same course, but it should be remembered, so long as this is not the case, that inasmuch as the police and other taxes are taken on the same rating, the inhabitants of St. Mary's, Whitechapel, will have to pay a larger proportion of these latter than their neighbours.

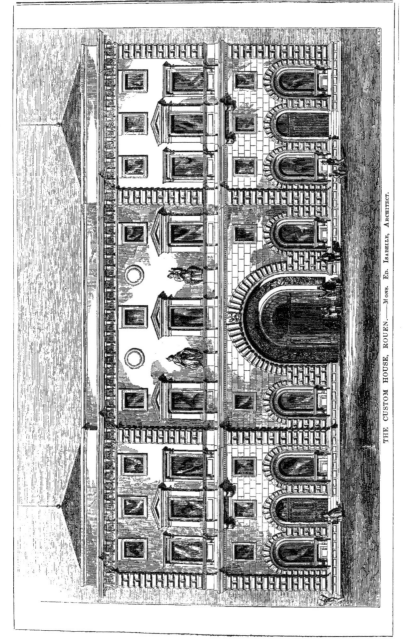

THE CUSTOM HOUSE, ROUEN.——Mons. Ed. Isabelle, Architect.

THE CUSTOM-HOUSE, ROUEN.

The Custom-house at Rouen, situated, as some of our readers will recollect, on the quay, towards the south, was built from the designs of Mons. Edouard Isabelle, of Paris. It was commenced in 1835, and completed in 1848. The annexed engraving is a geometrical representation of the entrance front. The doorway is a striking feature, and the rustication exceedingly bold and effective. The sculptured figures are about 8 feet high.

WHAT SHALL WE DO WITH OUR DEAD?

As it is to be feared lest the *retreat* of the pestilence from the country should be the signal for the retreat of all thoughts of the odious practice of burying in towns and churches from the public mind, it is the duty of every one that has the opportunity to endeavour to *keep the attention* of the public so fixed upon this subject, as to insure a reformation. Now, it appears to me that we have not made sufficient use of *antiquity* in this matter, for had we glanced backward at the practice of our forefathers, I think we should not have had reason to deplore the existence (in our midst) of so many "consecrated cesspools." The politest nations of antiquity had two distinct modes of treating the dead, viz., burning and embalming, the first of which was practised by the refined Greeks, and by them imparted to the Romans; and the second was and is, I believe, to this day the custom of the Egyptian, the Persian, and the Jew. We also note another circumstance, which is, that the Romans, who at one part of their history buried the dead, had laws to prevent this being done within the precincts of the city; and from what we know of the other nations, the rites of sepulture appear to have invariably been performed "without the walls." We cannot, therefore, find anything in antiquity to act as a precedent to *our* present practice. In this the ancients were wiser than are we. They *saw* the evils arising from intramural burial, and recognized from the beginning, what we have at last *felt*, that there is a bad air engendered by the decomposed bodies of the dead, which, if enclosed within the circumscribed space of a city burial-ground, will possess sufficient malignity to induce disease; and therefore it was that they burned or buried their dead in the *open* country. At last having, as I have said, *felt* this, we know it to be true, and therefore are beginning to cry out for cemeteries and country burials, and would place the bodies of the dead in the ground, amid country scenes and air, where the gases might have space enough so to disseminate as to lose their death-giving pungency. This is a decided improvement in the feelings of our countrymen, and will doubtless lead to much that is good in the *practice* of burying; but for my own part, Sir, I cannot see why the more wholesome practice of burning the dead should not be again revived: indeed it would be a hard matter to give any reason why it should have been discontinued. I know that the above *sentence* will meet with much opposition from the fastidious, who, with abhorrence strongly marked in their faces, will doubtless cry, "How shockingly inhuman a practice," and will, *sans doute*, set me down as a great barbarian for saying that I like it. Let me ask them, however, why it is that they prefer the element of earth to that of fire? Is it because the latter is so quick and *clean* in its destructions? Verily, I, for my own part, should look forward with far more pleasant thoughts to a sepulture amid flames, than to a spot in any of our over-crowded grounds, and would as soon commit a friend's dead body to the quick consuming element of fire, as to the mouldering element of earth, with its attendant, the slowly-devouring worm. Aye; and I will say *sooner*, for let it be observed that in the latter case my dead *friend* might, if I lived near his resting-place, be the *death of me*, whereas, in the former there could be nothing of this kind to fear. I would, then, instead of having cemeteries made in the outskirts of London, which, look you, *may* in time become *intramural*, and *must* at any rate soon surround with the circle of death the habitations of the living—light up once more the funeral torch, and again kindle the funeral pile, and would do this in a place set apart for the purpose in the *country*. By this means the dead would be far more speedily and *healthily* reduced to *ashes* than they at present are. Whether we alter our *mode* of sepulture or not, we must at once alter the *places*. Town burials must be at once abolished, and all town burial-grounds at once and for ever closed. The mere closing them from further additions is not sufficient; there has been enough added this summer of itself to breed a pestilence next. Cholera may not be contagious amid the living, but I should think that, of all things, the gas escaping from the decomposed bodies of persons that have died of that disease is most likely to impart it to the living who imbibe it. To prevent this, it is necessary first to give our burial-grounds a layer of some disinfecting material, and after that to cover it with concrete or asphalte. Economy *must* be thought of; but let no niggardliness prevent the people of London from doing that which may avert from us another visitation of the pestilence, which is now departing; and, moreover, it will not do to pay too much attention to the interests of the few,—these must succumb to the health of the many.

Le Feu.

RAILWAY JOTTINGS.

A wooden station, of a wretched description, it is said, has been provided by the North Midland Company for Bingley, a town containing 7,000 inhabitants. "It consists, says a contemporary, "of a clerk's room, about three yards square at one end, a small open shed in the middle, and at the other end a room similar to the clerk's, dignified with the name of the 'Ladies' waiting-room.' During wet weather the clerks transact business with umbrellas over their heads, to protect themselves from the rain dropping through the roof. In the open shed are huddled together 1st, 2nd, and 3rd class male and female passengers, sometimes for nearly an hour, exposed to all kinds of weather. 'The Ladies' waiting-room' is avoided from the dread of cholera, for the stench arising from the conveniences, only separated by thin boards, is dreadful." The era of railway *economy* seems to be superseding that of *extravagance* with a vengeance—all allowance here, for probable exaggeration, to the contrary, notwithstanding.——A more excusable instance, it may be, of real economy appears in the reduction of salary effected in the appointment of a traffic manager on the York and North Midland, at 300*l.* a-year, in place of Mr. Hudson's *élève* at 1,200*l.* There were 137 applicants for the reduced rate of income.——We regret to learn that the scheme for removing the Chinese Exhibition by rail to Edinburgh, already described, was not altogether successful,—indeed, an alleged, but, we should think, somewhat over-estimated damage, to the extent of 1,500*l.* to 2,000*l.*, was occasioned by the striking of two of the vans on a bridge near Berwick, and the crushing of their contents thereby. The rails had been altered, too, so as to allow of the train passing right under the crown of the arch, but it was scarcely to be expected that vans of so unusual a size should safely pass through railway arches, which are but too often reduced to such close cutting and dangerous dimensions, that a railway guard himself often dares not stretch his neck even a very little beyond the breadth of his train without the imminent risk of having his brains dashed out—a catastrophe which has actually more than once occurred.——The Railway Clearing House Committee, at which all the leading railway companies are represented by their chairman or other delegate, have, it appears, at the suggestion of Capt. Huish, urged upon the railway companies the importance of giving facilities for the guards walking safely along trains when in motion, by which means, as we have long and perseveringly pointed out, a great variety of accidents may be averted. The Railway Commissioners, in 1847, themselves adopted it, out of a multitude of other suggestions, as the system of communication best promising success. It is to be hoped that it will now be generally carried out. In the event of a carriage or truck catching fire, of an axle heating, a door flying open, a cry of help from a carriage, from whatever cause arising, or in any case where there may be even a suspicion that something is wrong, the guard should be able to get to any part of a train at once.——It has been suggested that there is great need of accommodation for invalids in a reclined position, while on the way to hospitals, &c., for medical assistance, or surgical operation as on fractured limbs. Even independent of humanity as an object, doubtless the additional traffic in transfer of invalids, to towns not otherwise reachable for medical advice, would well repay all the little expense of fitting up a carriage or two for such a purpose. On American lines there are sofas, or seats for reclining on, even for the use of passengers limb-free, and in perfect health.——The general specification lately issued of stores required by the London and North-Western for 1850, shews the vast amount of materials required for working the traffic of this the most important railway in the world. The "specification" extends over 25 pages of foolscap, and particularizes the stations at which the required amounts of stores are to be delivered. Of "brass and brass work" 352 cwt. of castings are required; 144 gross of screws and 59 tons of locomotive tubes. Of "copper" 8,960lb. of bolts from ½ to 1½ inch diameter, 11,200lb. of sheet of various thicknesses and dimensions, and 12,768lb. for fire-boxes ⅝ and ½ inch thick. Of "coal" 18,104 tons. Of "crucibles for moulding brass," 2,539. Of "colours, dry-saltery," 110,000 leaves of gold leaf. Of "iron and iron-works," 35 tons of axle-guards, 50 tons of patent shaft bar-iron, 190 tons of fire bar-iron, 42½ tons of bolts, 13 tons of nuts, 102 tons of castings, 48 tons Lowmoor or Bowling iron, 100 cwt. of nails, 69 cwt. of rivets, 6,360 gross of screws, 1,343 tons Staffordshire iron, and 120 tons Yorkshire iron. Of "timber and wood work," the Company require tenders for 19,367 feet of alder planks, 145 loads of beech planks, 10,000 feet of baywood boards, 91,000 feet of deal boards, &c.

NOTES IN THE PROVINCES.

St. Michael's Church, Cambridge, has been considerably injured by fire. The congregation were assembling on Sunday morning last, when smoke was observed to be issuing from the roof on the south side. The building was speedily vacated, and the fire broke forth through the slates and raged with great fury. The gownsmen acted *like men* at the buckets and engines, and the destruction was at length arrested. The roof was totally destroyed. Some damage was also done to the organ in removing the pipes and by the play of the engines. Nearly 1,000*l.*, it is estimated, will be necessary for repairs. The building is not insured, but there is a small fund for repairs, though much exhausted of late. The accident is attributed to negligence in repairing flues and stoves.——A new church has been erected at Newgate-street hamlet, Hatfield, at the expense of Mr. Mills, of Tolmers. It is called St. Mary's, and is a small building in the Pointed style, without pews, and has a stained-glass window over a gallery.——In removing some old panelling at the south end of Norwich Grammar School, a piscina has been discovered. The style is Early English. Mr. Ninham, of Norwich, has executed a drawing of it. The work of purification has also disclosed several heads and foliage, &c., in the capitals of the arches.——The new corn exchange to be erected at Brigg, was contracted for on Thursday week. Several tenders were offered, but the one accepted was that of Mr. Margisson, builder, Hull, at 1,227*l.*: difference between highest and lowest offer, some 320*l.* The site selected is at the back of the "Angel" inn.——On 24th ult., the parish church of St. Candida, of Whitechurch Canonicorum, Dorset, was reopened, after having undergone extensive repair and restoration, under the direction of Mr. Butler, of Chichester, including the rebuilding of the north aisle, roofed with English oak covered with lead, and affording 100 additional sittings, the restoration of the stonework and tracery of twenty windows, some of large dimensions, and the erection of additional sittings in solid oak. The old seating has been reduced in height, and the seats throughout are open. Amongst the decorative restorations are the removal of plaster and whitewash from an open oak roof of fifteenth century, ornamented with moulded ribs and bosses, painted in red and yellow; the introduction of Powell's quarries in eastern triplet of chancel, the floor of which is decorated with encaustic tiles from Messrs. Chamberlain's manufactory, Worcester. The altar step consists of veined Devonshire marble, surrounding encaustic tiling. The reredos is formed of carved oak panelling of great antiquity, brought from Rouen, gilt and painted. The walls of sanctuary are powdered with golden stars and fleur-de-lys, and the roof is covered with white and vermilion painting, in imitation of fan tracery on a blue ground with golden stars at intervals, — a design copied from chapter house of Exeter Cathedral. The windows throughout the church are stencilled in patterns, from ancient models, in imitation of flowered quarries. The original circular semi-Norman font, with column and base of Purbeck marble, had been removed and broken, but now stands restored near principal entrance.——In addition to the fortifications lately completed at Bovisand, Picklecombe-point, and Drake's Island, as defences for Stonehouse harbour, a new fort has been erected just above the site of the old Long-room Barracks, at the Victualling-yard point, which will render complete the defence of the Sound and the entrance to Hamoaze. The new building is called "The Prince of Wales' Redoubt." The external walls, towards the land, are 7 feet thick, and musket proof, and, instead of being built up perpendicularly from the ditch, are curved. On the sea-side the walls are 8 feet thick, and considered to be bomb-proof. The fort has been two years in erection, and the total cost will be about 15,000*l*. It is constructed principally of dressed limestone. The cheeks of the embrasures, piers of entrance-gates, and other parts, are of dressed granite. Mr. George Roach, of Plymouth, is the contractor, and the work has proceeded under the inspection of Mr. Frederick Burgoyne, Government foreman of works.——Improvements have been made in Ramsey, Isle of Man, by the extension of the quay inwards 100 yards, to accommodate wind-bound vessels.——On Wednesday week, Trinity Church, Runcorn, after having been beautified and enlarged, was re-opened. A chancel and a stained-glass window have been presented by Sir R. Brooke, Bart.——The laying of first stone of bridge over lake at Welbeck Abbey took place on Thursday week. The arch is of iron, with iron battlements upon stone buttresses. The building is undertaken by Mr. Bell. The first stone was laid by Viscountess Shannon: present, the Duke of Portland and others.——At a meeting of the Ashton guardians on Thursday last, the building committee recommended that the amount to be expended on their new workhouse be fixed prior to advertising for plans, and that the board employ the architect to carry out his plans at the rate of 5 per cent. on the outlay: no premium for second best. They recommended that the sum to be expended be limited to 6,000*l*. Mr. Ousey cunningly suggested that it would be better to give a premium for the plans; "they would be able to manage the erection quite as economically as though the architect were employed to carry out his own plans." Resolution to that effect lost by a majority of one. Agreed that the sum be 6,000*l*.——Notice has been given of an application to Parliament, by the Carlisle corporation, to take possession of the gas works there, and to work them for the benefit of the city. The Bill, says the local journal, will most likely pass without opposition, and it will undoubtedly confer a benefit on the inhabitants of Carlisle.——The town councils of Dumfries and Maxwelltown are to bring a Bill into Parliament authorizing a supply of water from Lochrutton. Mr. Gale, of Glasgow, was elected engineer, and Mr. Newall, local engineer.——The new schools at Elson, near Gosport, were opened on Thursday last, on which occasion full service was performed at the church, and the new organ was played for the first time. The schools and master's house cost rather more than 500*l*. in building, and will afford room for 130 children. The parsonage-house will shortly be commenced. The architect is Mr. John Colson, who also designed the case for the organ.

SPANISH TOWN CATHEDRAL, JAMAICA.

We inserted a communication from a correspondent in August last (p. 377), headed, "Architects and Architecture in Jamaica," setting forth that a gentleman who came to the island as an organist, music-master, &c., not finding his success so great as was anticipated, had turned architect and civil engineer, and was engaged in erecting a chancel to the cathedral church. It further said, "it has now leaked out that our architect has been, and still is, extracting from the pockets of the builder either 5 or 7½ per cent., besides the commission he receives from the parish." In reply to this we have received a letter (previously addressed to us in the *Jamaica Despatch*), signed "J. Calvert, superintending architect of the cathedral, Jamaica," enclosing a declaration signed, "Richard Cowan, sole contractor for the masonry; James Campbell, sole contractor for carpenter's and joiner's work; James Jones, carpenter; and Joseph Waldron, builder;" denying that the architect has ever demanded, or received from them, any commission or allowance. Mr. Calvert says:—"One could scarcely believe your correspondent had read Vitruvius's requisites for an architect, or he would remember he says, among other things, he should be '*a musician*'—'the head and front of my offending.' When the immortal astronomer Herschel could no longer eke out an existence as a poor *organist and musician*, did his knowledge of that heavenly art, music, render him blind to the glorious harmony of the starry world?

I sent in designs in competition with the whole island, without friendship or favour, and regret I had no assistance whatever, as he insinuates I had. The building is nearly up to the roof, and is about 50 feet long by 50 feet wide, with side aisles and clerestory windows, on moulded arches and clustered columns, with carved stone corbel angels supporting an elaborately carved roof. The whole on a foundation of great strength, 15 feet deep, and I trust will stand when my enemies are forgotten, and I a 'musician' in the choir above.

I refer you to the declaration, in denial of the assertion of my 'extortion,' and wish you could but enjoy with me a few days superintendence of negro workmen, on a building in Jamaica, with the pleasant warmth of a mid-day sun at least 107 degrees Fahrenheit; you would find, without any clerk of the works, 5 per cent. on an average expenditure of 20*l*. a-week, a splendid remuneration for the entire occupation of your utmost exertions, and I doubt not would soon grow fat, and become the envy of every hungry architect, as is supposed to be—Your humble servant."

By the same mail we received a statement from our former correspondent, containing the grounds of his assertion, but we cannot give place to it in the face of the rigorously worded declaration referred to.

DESIGN IN MANUFACTURE.

Justly does your correspondent, "C. E. M.," in a late number of your journal, condemn the prodigious floral ornamentation of the various articles in the Birmingham exhibition, executed as like unto nature as their various materials will permit. This error, arising from an imperfect education in art, and an injudicious striving after novelty, is the evident characteristic of the so-called "art-manufactures" of the day. It requires but little study, and less design, to copy the first plant that comes to hand, without adaptation, whether suitable or not to the purpose required. It is the work of a mechanic, and not of an artist, and elevated but in the degree of execution above that of the savage in the South Sea islands, to carve the handle of a knife into the semblance of a spike of maize, and when the noble task has been accomplished, the implement is but rendered perfectly unfit for its purpose. I remember not long since to have seen engraved with commendation a "high art" salt-cellar, which reflected no great credit on its compiler (for design it cannot be called), as it consisted merely of a sea-shell reversed and mounted upon a piece of coral. Too often is practical utility disregarded, and all purity of outline lost in an unpruned luxuriance of foliage. Nor is it only with botanical specimens that every domestic utensil is bedizened, under the mistaken idea of ornament; but the human figure and animals, executed in the worst style, are crowded into every possible position, as if no opportunity of degrading them should be lost. It does not seem to be generally understood, that art is a conventional treatment of nature, and not a literal imitation of her forms; for while she must be foiled if she attempt to rival their delicacy and compete on the same ground, yet there is a character and dignity of her own with which she may invest them,—an impress of thought which should be stamped upon the types of her choice.

It is to be hoped, then, that this botanical fever will soon subside, or at least cease to be preached to the people as the noblest realization of "high art." J. P. Seddon.

MASTERS AND WORKMEN.

In a recent case the defendant, Mr. Brass, a builder in the city, was sued in the Sheriff's Court by four of his workmen (carpenters) named Lockyer, Goddard, Payne, and Thomas, under the following circumstances:—

The plaintiffs stated that they were discharged on the Saturday, and being unable to get their tools they went for them on the Monday morning; they accordingly claimed a quarter of a day's wages for fetching them, and a quarter of a day for grinding them—the latter being a custom adopted throughout the trade. They also contended that Mr. Brass had no right to discharge them, as they were taken on by his foreman, who said it was his own job.

The plaintiff said he resisted this claim entirely on principle. He discharged the plaintiffs for neglect of duty. They left off at four o'clock, and were paid their full wages up to half-past five; they had ample time, therefore, to collect their tools.

His Honour said, although the foreman might be authorized, as the agent, to take on workmen, that did not take away the right of the master to discharge them; and with regard to the sum claimed for grinding tools, although such a principle might exist in some instances, there was no such custom in law. The plaintiffs must therefore be nonsuited.

EXPOSITION OF FRENCH INDUSTRIAL ART.

No. 13, George-street, Hanover-square, with its adjacent premises, contains at this moment a beautiful and costly exposition of French industrial art, sufficient to make our manufacturers tremble for the probable expatriation of some of the prizes proposed to be given in 1851. Mons. Sallandrouze de Lamornaix, a manufacturer of distinguished position in France, projected and arranged this exhibition with the view of showing the English manufacturers who their opponents will be.

Tapestry, china, oak carvings, bronzes, carpets, are amongst the works exhibited, and will demand our notice. We would merely remark now, to those who would institute comparisons with works at home, that the price, and the circumstances under which many of these extraordinary things were manufactured, should not be left out of view. They must not, for example, ask where we can parallel that magnificent piece of *Gobelin's* tapestry, presenting an incident in the life of Gustavus Vasa, if we mistake not, or the large flower-painted vase in the centre,—without remembering that the price put on the latter is six hundred pounds—the price of the first, *four thousand pounds*, and that Government took the risk of their production.

The "Sainte Chapelle," Paris.—During the last week an immense crowd has assembled day after day at the Palais de Justice, to view the restored decorations of the *Sainte Chapelle*. From ten in the morning till four in the afternoon they were slowly passing in, ranged in files, each in the order of arrival. From 3,000 to 4,000 persons daily have had admittance. On Sunday last the President, in another chamber of the building, distributed the prizes awarded at the late Exposition.

METROPOLITAN COMMISSION OF SEWERS.

WHEN the court determined that the business should be examined and arranged by the general committee, previous to each meeting, so that "any discussion which was necessary for the information of the public would take place in court," or rather as they ought to have said, "so that no discussion necessary for the information of the public may take place in court;" we saw what would be the result, and pointed it out.

To say that the commission hold an open court now is not true: the public meeting is simply *pro formâ*, a blind and a pretence, and without assuming that any but the most careful and intelligent management is being pursued, we at once formally protest against the system as being full of evils, and certain to lead to an unsatisfactory state of things.

At a meeting held on the 9th, Lord Ebrington in the chair, and other commissioners present, the following resolutions were passed without discussion:—

"1. That it appears that the plan submitted by Mr. Cubitt to the Commissioners for Westminster in November, 1847, and on the recommendation of their surveyor, Mr. Phillips, approved by them, which provided an escape for the sewage through the outfall there shown into St. George's sewer, was not executed. That the officers of the commissioners charged with the superintendence of the work allowed the said plan to be materially deviated from; that they allowed the sewer to be blocked up with a wall, in what was there described as the direction of its outfall, and an outfall to be opened into Warwick-street sewer, where none was described in the said plan. That for these alterations and deviations no authority is to be found in the records of the court.

"2. That the best thanks of the court be given to Professor Lyon Playfair, for his very valuable services, rendered gratuitously to the commissioners, in the chemical examination he made, with so much skill and judgment, in reference to the lamentable accident that occurred in the sewer in Kenilworth-street.

"3. That though the commissioners have not sanctioned, and do not sanction, the application made to Dr. Ure for his opinion on the subject of the accident in the Kenilworth-street sewer, Pimlico, yet, as it appears that one of their officers did, during the interval which elapsed between the termination of the old commission and the first meeting of the present, apply to him and request a chemical examination of the contents of the sewer, they, under the circumstances, will not object to pay Dr. Ure some reasonable remuneration for this first analysis so requested by their officer on his own responsibility.

"4. That the commissioners be summoned, and the city commissioners be requested to attend the next court, for the purpose of taking into consideration the plans sent in for the drainage of the metropolis."

Adjourned to Friday, the 23rd.

Miscellanea.

EFFECT OF BAD DRAINAGE.—The verdict given by the juries of the coroner's inquests held on recent cases of cholera in Hertford County Gaol, attributed the ravages of the epidemic to the total want of drainage, and requested the coroner to write to the visiting magistrates, drawing their attention to the subject. It appears that the soil-drains connected with the gaol run into two large close cesspools, one of which is within and the other without the walls, and that the prisoners are exposed to the injurious effects of the noxious gases generated in those cesspools. The coroner, therefore, in compliance with the wish of the jury, drew the attention of the visiting magistrates to these facts, and suggested that the cesspools should be done away with, and a proper system of sewerage established. We had the impression that a large sum of money had been spent here recently in putting things right.

SHEET METALS.—Mr. T. D. Jackson, of Brooklyn, New York, has patented an improvement in alloys for sheet metals, consisting of—Copper, 64 oz., zinc, 22 to 26 oz., India tin, 1 to 4 oz. The inventor claims as his invention or discovery, "the application of the manipulations employed for compounding an alloy of metals in the proportions and of the materials mentioned for a new sheet metal, which shall be capable of being wrought in the cutting press, with dies," &c.

PROJECTED WORKS.—Advertisements have been issued for tenders, by 3rd December, for the works required in construction of a quay and sidings near Arundel, for the London, Brighton, and South Coast Railway; by 11th December, for the erection of a new savings bank at Witham; by 12th December, for the erection of a new pauper lunatic asylum, for 250 patients, at Bracebridge, near Lincoln; by 3rd December, for the construction of two reservoirs near Langley, Prestbury, with other works connected therewith,—also a filter bed and service reservoir,—and for laying about 2½ miles of pipes, all for the Macclesfield borough water-works; by 24th inst., for gas fittings in the Brentford Town-hall; by 27th inst., for 200 tons of Barlow's patent wrought iron rail, for the Midland Railway Company; by a date not specified, for the erection of some small houses at Itchen (Southampton); by 21st, for a supply of British iron for the East-India Company; and by 18th December, for a supply of pumps and water closets for the navy.

DRAINAGE OF TOWNS ON TIDAL RIVERS.—A suggestion for the drainage of London has been made to us by Professor Hann, on the part of Mr. Goldsworthy Gurney. "The current of the Thames, in round numbers, at London-bridge," he remarks, "runs down 7 hours and up only 5 every tide; in winter more, in summer less, depending on the amount of river water. It runs at a rate of about from 5 to 7 miles per hour (no matter what the speed; let us suppose it to run at the same rate up and down for our present purpose). It is plain that anything thrown into, and forming part of the Thames at *high* water, would, in seven hours, be carried more than 40 miles down the river. On the return of tide, in five hours, the full time of flow, it will only have come up 30 miles, and at the time of high water would be 12 miles below the bridge. The next ebb would carry it 42 miles further down the river, or 54 miles below London-bridge. At the return of next high water it would be left 24 miles down the river, thus descending 24 miles in 24 hours, until it went clear into the sea. If, on the contrary, anything be thrown in at *low* water, it will go *up* with the tide for five hours, be five hours more in returning to the same spot, have only two hours ebb before it meet the flood coming up, and of course would return with it, go again up the river, and be seen probably every day for a week." Mr. Gurney suggests, therefore, that the sewage of London be collected, and only allowed to run into the Thames at high water, so that it may be at once got rid of. All this, however, is not quite so clear as it looks.

VENTILATED SEWERS, CHESTER.—I observe, at page 482, of your journal, that Mr. Thorpe, of Hull, states that he has adopted the plan of connecting the rain-water spouts in the fronts of the houses in that town with the sewers, for the purpose of ventilating them. I beg to state that system has been adopted at Chester for some years, and that I suggested it nearly three years ago in the pages of your journal. Although probably not so effective in its nature as Dr. Gurney's steam jet, it is a simple expedient, inexpensive and effectual in its operation. At the heads of our sewers, when we have what is termed dead ends, I have had vertical shafts or manholes carried up, for the purpose of securing self-acting flushing tanks, in principle resembling Hosmer's, and I purpose obtaining a supply of water from the main, so that whether the supply of water be constant or intermittent (as it is in this case), the sewers will be regularly and effectually flushed at stated intervals. When the flushing apparatus is complete, I connect the shafts with pipes to the fronts of houses, so that when in action, the regular downward current of the flushing waters will create an upward current of what little foul gas may be generated in the sewers; so that it will pass off through the ventilating shaft at the head of the sewer, and be disseminated in the atmosphere. BAYLIS.

TESTIMONIAL TO MR. CUBITT.—Mr. G. R. Ward has been selected by the committee to engrave, for distribution to the subscribers, Mr. Pickersgill's excellent and life-like portrait of Mr. Thomas Cubitt. It is to be executed in the mixed style, and finished in June next.

THE SAMARITAN SOCIETY OF ENGLAND.—This society, which originated in a paragraph published last year in our paper, proposes to establish cheap lodging-houses and dormitories for the necessitous poor under the arches of the metropolitan railway viaducts, open to all, at all seasons. "The arches in each district will be formed into first, second, and third class compartments for men; first and second for women. These tenements will be warmed with hot water, lighted with gas, be well ventilated, and be placed under the supervision of the police. The first class will be furnished with iron bedsteads, flock mattrasses, blankets, &c., and the charge will be 2d. per night, or 1s. per week. The second class will be fitted up with slanting boards, such as are used by soldiers in their guard-rooms, with pillows and warm rugs; and the charge will be 1d. per night. The third class will be merely furnished with clean straw, and will be accessible to all, at all times of the night, without charge. These will be opened only in the winter. Five arches will at first be rented in each district. The centre arch will be furnished with a boiler, and will be used as a lavatory. The two arches on either side will be converted into first and second class wards,—those on the right for men—on the left for women; and each tenement will shelter 30 individuals. Each district will thus furnish 120 beds; and it is confidently expected that they will be self-supporting when once established." The society have views beyond this, such as opening schools in the day time, and to assist in reclaiming prisoners, but these are less immediately practicable. As the winter is approaching, now is the time to begin the work. Plans, we understand, have been prepared; and it is estimated that each arch may be fitted up for about 60*l*. Rightly managed, this society may do an immense amount of good at small cost.

SURVEYOR'S TENDERS: ISLEWORTH ASSESSMENT.—I frequently see in your paper the heading "Blind Builders." There are, however, other men who are sometimes equally blind. As a professional man, I cannot account for such discrepancies. In this parish (Isleworth) we have 3,128 acres of land, varying in rental value from 2s. 6d. an acre to 10*l*. 10s. an acre, and including about 1,500 houses. It has been determined to have a re-assessment. Advertisements have appeared from the board of guardians for making such re-assessment, and fourteen tenders have been sent in. You must excuse my not giving you the names of the different candidates; the lowest, however, is 50*l*., and the highest 420*l*. Such things are monstrous. I cannot think either Cocker or Columbine can have been consulted.—W. A.

SHOP DOOR BOLTS.—With reference to the circumstance that a watchmaker was robbed of two watches a few days ago by a pretended customer, who darted out of the shop with the property while he turned his back to get other goods to show him, a correspondent suggests the use of a sort of double night bolt, which may, by the application of ordinary bellhanging work, be made to drop down from over the double inside doors when shut (or a single bolt for one door) of any shop where small valuables are sold, at the will of the person behind the counter, and altogether unseen by the party presenting themselves, and thus effectually prevent the escape of any one with the goods.

INSTITUTION OF CIVIL ENGINEERS.—In accordance with a new arrangement, the session of the institution commenced on Tuesday evening last—Mr. Joshua Field, president, in the chair—instead of, as heretofore, in the middle of January. The paper read was a "Description of the Coffer-dam at the Grimsby Docks," by Mr. Charles Neate. The length of the coffer-dam was 1,500 feet, supporting at high water a head of water of 25 feet, whilst the excavation behind it was carried to 11 feet below low-water. The form of the dam was that of a circular curve, with a versed sine of 200 feet, or nearly one-fifth of the span.

THE ROYAL PAVILION AT BRIGHTON.—It is understood that the Pavilion at Brighton has been purchased for a sum nearly amounting to 60,000*l*. The valuables of the interior have been removed, and it is expected that the place will be converted into purposes for the improvement of the town.

Leeds Mechanics' Institute.—The annual festival of this institution was held on Friday last in the Stock Exchange; Lord Mahon in the chair. His lordship made a fluent and interesting speech. In course of it he with truth said, that if it be true that knowledge is power, it is not less true that knowledge is pleasure,—pleasure with no bounds or limits on this earth. The boundlessness of knowledge his lordship aptly illustrated by the discoveries of the telescope, on the one hand, and the microscope, on the other. Our discoveries seem only limited in depth, if not in breadth, by the imperfection of the instruments we yet use; the extreme limit is probably almost as far removed as ever. But depend on it, he said, that pleasure is not to be found in mere superficial acquirements. Yet of this I am persuaded, that there was great truth in the remark I once heard from that accomplished and experienced man Prince Talleyrand:—"Depend on it there is no such thing as labour lost. Depend on it, whatever branch of study you pursue, and however recondite or remote its utility may seem, a time may come, and when you least expect it, that you will derive practical advantage from it, and see the good effects of having turned your minds to it." His Lordship's speech was followed by the proposal and adoption of various resolutions in favour of the objects of such institutions, and among which was one by Mr. R. M. Milnes, M. P., to the effect, that "To impart a taste for artistic beauty, and to give familiarity with the principles on which it rests, should be one of the objects of popular education." Mr. Roebuck wound up the eloquence already expended with no less eloquence of his own. "All the great advances of knowledge," he remarked, in one part of his speech, "have not been done by the leisure class, but by the labouring, working for their livelihood, and bringing habits of industry to the acquirement of knowledge; using those stern habits in the race with the *dilettanti*, pressing upon and outstripping him, because the latter is as dilatory in his modes of pursuing knowledge as in his habits of pleasure. ......An institution like this makes us all entertain right notions of true equality; it teaches us to have those sympathies which nature intended, and which you have always felt vehemently; it makes us all understand each other as *true men*; it is the bond of knowledge—the tie which shall unite us to each other...... As this is a mechanics' institution, I hope that it will be the means of doing what it does not at present—of bringing the artisan amongst us, and introducing a close alliance between all classes of society, without which there is no safety; and that we shall be with them in the brotherhood of knowledge and of feeling, and make this what it now calls itself, but which, I fear, it has not been—a mechanics' institute."

Public Slaughter-houses.—Mr. R. B. Grantham, whose work on the '*Abattoirs* of France we noticed some time ago, has published a proposition for establishing public slaughter-houses in the principal towns of England. He submits that the butchers, and those interested in the connected trades, should unite, and erect, under an Act of Parliament, suitable buildings, with land sufficient for layerage and pasture, in a locality approved of by the local authorities. "They ought to be the undertakers," he says, "as most interested in the matter, and should take the lead, for they may depend upon it that the time is not far distant when these arrangements, or something very like them, will be carried out, and they will have to submit to the control of other persons, instead of keeping it in their own hands."

Railway Rating.—In an appeal before the magistrates at Manchester against an assessment of about a mile of the South Junction line, belonging to the London and North-Western Company, it was stated for the respondents, that value of land prior to building on it was 62,787*l*., and rateable value 2,960*l*.: present value of whole, 300,000*l*. The company proved the receipts for August and September last to have been 264*l*. 11s. 2d., and the working expenses 251*l*. 9s. 6d., leaving a profit of 13*l*. 1s. 8d., being at the rate of 78*l*. 10s. per annum. The magistrates, however, confirmed the rate. The appellants intimated an appeal to quarter sessions.

Sheffield Athenæum and Mechanics' Institute.—To the formal opening of this combined institution the Earl of Carlisle, Mr. Roebuck, M.P., and other celebrities, gave their countenance, those named personally, and others, such as Lord Mahon, by letter. The chairman, Mr. Alderman Dunn, explained the objects of the new establishment, which comprehends a news-room, coffee-room, and library, class-rooms, and ball for lectures, &c. The whole cost of the building, including site, has been 6,500*l*., part of it not yet raised. The first stone was laid about two years since by Lord Arundel and Surrey. The Athenæum department was opened in the beginning of the present year, and the institution class-rooms on 1st October last. The pupils are now taught reading, writing, arithmetic, grammar, and geography, and other classes are to be opened. In speaking of the purposes of such an establishment, and while deprecating the idea that duty alone, apart from the memories of 'auld lang syne,' as in the present instance, should lead him to run about and foist his presence wherever there is a mechanics' institution or an Athenæum to be founded, Lord Carlisle remarked, with a quiet apology for what might be regarded as smelling a little of *his* shop—the Board of Health—that "it is not from the languid bed of sickness, from the troubled couch of fever, from the gloomy chambers of death that we can expect to derive hopeful votaries of intellectual and mental progress. The vigorous exercise of the judgment, the buoyant play of the fancy, the elastic impulses of the soul, require healthy and undiseased organs for their full display and development. The mind and body will almost in every case—though there are brilliant exceptions—be found to re-act upon each other, and those who promote the enlightened care of the physical health will most truly advance the use and enjoyment of the rational and moral faculties. The undrained alley, the unventilated room, the impure atmosphere, will but serve to irritate the tempers for which we trust here to provide serene enjoyment, and to clog and debase the energies for which we shall endeavour here to furnish fit opportunity and congenial nurture."

Society of Arts.—At the opening meeting, 7th November, Mr. W. Tooke, F.R.S., Vice-President, in the chair, Mr. Digby Wyatt read a voluminous report upon the Eleventh French Exposition, which has been published for public use. The report commenced by allusion to the attention paid by the French government to the development of the manufactures of that country by precept, example, public exhibition, &c., to the traditional excellence of early French productions, and to the modern restoration of that supereminence by the means before-mentioned, now persevered in with few interruptions for fifty years. Mr. Wyatt then gave a minute description of the building erected for the exhibition in 1849, which was situated on the Carré de Marigny, on the Champs Elysées. The estimated cost of the building was, in

			Total area. Metres.	Available area. Metres.
1839	about	£14,551	11,362	5,806
1844	,,	15,056	19,497	9,051
1849	,,	16,000	22,391	9,734

To the cost of this year must be added 2,000*l*. for the agricultural shed;—making the whole estimate about 18,000*l*. The cost of the building per square foot was, in

1839..............	2s. 2d.
1844..............	1s. 3½d.
1849..............	1s. 2¼d.

The building had the defect of containing no one great hall, whereas on the occasion of distributing the prizes a great assemblage might take place. The writer believed that a better building might be erected in England at a less cost, probably by one-fourth. The gist of the report having previously appeared in the *Athenæum*, it came rather second-hand. On the 15th a paper was read by Mr. H. H. Russell on the "Construction of Suspension-bridges, with especial reference to a new mode of preventing Vibration."

St. Thomas's Church, Newport.—We understand that there are about thirty sets of designs sent in for the re-building of St. Thomas's Church at Newport, Isle of Wight, which are on exhibition at the assembly-rooms there.

Iron.—A patent has been taken out at New York, by a Mr. M. S. Salter, for making hammered wrought-iron from the ore, by a single process, and within two hours! Can it be possible that we have here already an exemplification of the practicability of Mr. Mushet's heterodox prophecy against puddling? The cost of wrought-iron, it is said, will be less than half the usual cost, prepared on Mr. Salter's process. Anthracite is to be used under this patent.——Little business is doing in the iron trade. Prices were lately giving way, but appear to have since become a little firmer. It is declared, however, that "the minimum at which iron can be produced in Staffordshire has been already reached," and a withdrawal of capital is anticipated.

The Church at Sarawak, Borneo.—The first beam of the first church (English) ever erected in this new dependency of the British empire was laid on 28th August last in presence of Sir James Brooke, the Rajah of Sarawak, and suite. The foundation sleeper was an enormously heavy block of iron-wood, which was slung into a trench by the Rajah. The work had then been for some time in progress, but there had been great difficulties to overcome in collecting, preparing, and carrying the heavy materials, and in levelling the hill for the site.

Colonnades are "Out."—The removal of the colonnade, forming the right-hand side of the outlet leading from High-street, Cheltenham, into the promenade, has been commenced, and in a few days the entire mass of building which rests upon it, and projects 10 or 12 feet into the street, will be brought down, and the houses thrown back to the Imperial-circus line of frontage. The colonnade was built thirty years ago, when such arrangements were in fashion.

The Reading Room at Drury-lane Theatre appears to be a considerable attraction, especially to foreigners, who have few opportunities in London to see the papers of their respective countries. Many appear to go to the theatre solely for this feature. We were glad to find The Builder in request there when we looked in: and that it was being pondered amidst the learned beauties of "The Prophet," and the clash of the "Row" Polka.

Proposed Provident Institution for Operatives.—We are glad to find that this suggestion is germinating. Professor Cockerell has addressed a strong letter on the subject to "The Builders' Society," urging them to move immediately in the matter, and we have reason to believe it will receive the attention due to it, and that the builders will soon afford proofs of their heartiness in the service. We have some communications on the matter, to which we shall give early consideration.

St. Alban's Architectural Society.—A meeting of this society was held on Wednesday in last week, at the Town Hall, St. Alban's. The attendance was numerous, and the Earl of Verulam, president, occupied the chair. The following papers were read—"On the Tapestry of Bayeux," by the Rev. T. Lee (honorary secretary); "On the Rise and Progress of the Art of Coining," by Mr. J. Evans; "On Verulam and the adjacent Antiquities," by Mr. R. G. Lowe.

The Bristol and West of England Architectural Society.—The report of this society, just now published, is illustrated by drawings of the south doorway, sedilia, &c., in the Holy Trinity Church, Westbury-on-Trym, and the proposed elevation of the Bristol High Cross, accompanying a paper on that subject. The doorway of Westbury Church was restored at the expense of the society.

The Queen's College, Cork, built from the design of Sir Thomas Deane, and illustrated by us some time ago, was opened on the 7th inst. The position of the building and its general effects are described as being admirable. We shall re-produce our view in the forthcoming number of "Buildings and Monuments."

To Destroy Ants.—I have never known a solution of alum and potash in hot water to fail as a cure for ants in timber, but it must be applied boiling hot.—C. W. Orford.

* Readers of The Builder may serve us by making known this work to friends who might not care to be subscribers to the journal, and yet would take "Buildings and Monuments," if they knew its scope and contents. It will be completed in eight parts, and will form, we venture to think, an interesting volume.

TENDERS

Delivered for the erection of public Baths and Wash-houses, in St. Ann-street, Westminster; Mr. P. P. Baly, engineer.

Wilkinson	£7,077
Howlett	6,700
Robson	6,700
Kilburn	6,697
Piper	6,696
Hodges	6,690
J. F. Taylor	6,690
Howard	6,616
Homan	6,614
Rowley	6,500
Elder	6,495
Haward and Nixon	6,587
Carter	6,585
Yeoman	6,570
Rigby	6,545
Hicks	6,420
I'anson	6,396
Saunders and Woolcot	6,359
Jay	6,324
Stephan and Eaton	9,296
Trego	6,279
Scipons	6,275
Higgs	6,229
Rushkin	6,196
Glenn	6,194
Barr	6,157
H. W. Cooper	6,141
T. Burton	6,049
Locke and Nesham	5,950
Wilson	5,943
Winsland and Holland	5,999
Hill and Co.	5,984
Taylor	5,879
Curtis	5,744
Myers (accepted)	5,738

MEETINGS OF SCIENTIFIC BODIES

Held during the ensuing week.

MONDAY, Nov. 19.—Institute of Architects, 8 P.M. Dr. Buckland, on Artesian Wells.
THURSDAY, Nov. 22.—Royal Society, 8½ P.M. Antiquaries, 8 P.M.
FRIDAY, Nov. 23.—Archæological Association, 8½ P.M.

TO CORRESPONDENTS.

"New Churches, Westminster, and elsewhere," notices postponed.

"*Deniz.*"—An architect's commission on a building erected, under his superintendence, of old materials, may fairly be charged on what would have been the cost of new.

"G. M." (name was not in either of the lists forwarded to us), "W. L. M." (says "Smith" should be fined instead of "Rolt," in list of tenders for India Docks and Birmingham Railway. Mr. Merrett's name was omitted: his tender was 30,069l.), "C. L.," "A. B." (the amount of population and other data require to be considered as well as those stated; we must decline giving the specific detail required), "L. D." (we are forced to decline pointing out books), "Workshamensis" (shall not be lost sight of), "S. P. M. W." (there are several machines for making bricks now before the public, but we are unable specially to refer our correspondent to them), "J. K.," "J. J. L.," "W. W.," "Y. Y. K." (we have reason to believe that the French publication in question has surmounted beneath political disturbances), "J. D.," "An Amateur," "J. S." (the "extra" has not reached us), "S. B. G.," "J. L. G.," "G. G. S.," "S. H.," "R. S.," "Z." (the study underground is the basement), "G. C." (we are sorry we cannot advise. "G. C." gave no address or explanation as to Post-office stamps enclosed), "J. G.," "W. H." (will find what he wished), "J. R.," "Free Hand Studies," by J. Dwyer and E. C. Laugher; Ackerman. "Holy Matrimony Illuminated," by Gwen Jones; Longman and Co.

NOTICE.—All communications respecting advertisements should be addressed to the "Publisher," and not to the "Editor;" all other communications should be addressed to the EDITOR, and not to the Publisher.

"*Books and Addresses.*"—We have not time to point out books or find addresses.

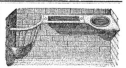

No. CCCLV.

SATURDAY, NOVEMBER 24, 1849.

T is no exaggeration to affirm, says Mr. Simon, the medical officer of health to the city of London, that the unrestricted supply of water "is the first essential of decency, of comfort, and of health; that no civilization of the poorer classes can exist without it; and that any limitation to its use in the metropolis is a barrier, which must maintain thousands in a state of the most unwholesome filth and degradation."* In the metropolis at present (we ought to say in England), the supply of water is but a fraction of what it should be; and its quality is for the most part infamously bad. Thousands and thousands of the population have no supply of it at all to their houses, and where it is laid on, the quantity is wholly insufficient, and the cost improperly great. For the sewers there is none, and without it there can be no effectual drainage. We have already suffered severely in consequence, and causes are in operation, especially in the metropolis, which will increase the evils at a fearful rate.

The connection between disease and bad water is established beyond cavil: the effect which the contamination of wells had in producing cholera in many places, is proved beyond the shadow of a doubt. The high rate of mortality on the south side of the Thames may be ascribed mainly to the fact, that the water-works for that part of London draw their supply from a spot in the Thames horridly polluted by sewers, and that many of the private wells are made poisonous by the cesspools, which are nearly as deep as the wells, and often close to them.

We must at any cost have pure water, and plenty of it,—a supply not intermittent, but constant and universal.

A glance at the daily papers will show how general this feeling is: notices of application to Parliament for powers to obtain and sell water, and reports of public meetings to consider the subject, meet the eye everywhere. Manchester, Salford, Salisbury, Southampton, and other provincial towns, are in the field. For the metropolis there are half-a-dozen schemes, without saying anything of the applications by the New River Company, the Kent Water-works, and the Lambeth Water-works Company, for extended powers.

One Company proposes to supply London from the Thames at a point near Mapledurham Lock, county of Oxford, with reservoirs at Caversham.

The "Thames Chalk Filtered Company" desires "to divert a portion of the water of the river Thames from its present channel; to convey it by aqueducts to shafts sunk on the bank of the river, into the chalk stratum of the London Basin; and to form such shafts, with accompanying shafts, and other necessary orks, into filters for purifying, by means of he chalk, the Thames water so conveyed."

* We are glad to see that the "Report on the Sanitary condition of London, for the year 1849," by Mr. Simon, is printed in a separate form. It contains nothing new, it is true,—little but what will be found in our pages urged and re-urged,—but the various points in the inquiry are sensibly and calmly stated, and all being brought together in this pamphlet, the distribution of it can scarcely fail to produce advantageous results. We hope to see the corporation act immediately on some of its suggestions.

The "London Spring-water Company" is projected "for the purpose of procuring a supply of pure water from the chalk formation, by means of shafts to be sunk in the neighbourhood of Watford, which water is proposed to be lifted into reservoirs on Stanmorecommon, to the respective heights of 400 and 490 feet above the Trinity high-water mark at London-bridge, and brought to London and the suburbs in capacious pipes along the Edgeware-road."

And the intention of "The Henley-onThames and London Aqueduct Company," to which we have before referred, is shown in their name. They propose the appointment of commissioners, to whom the execution of the Act, when obtained, is to be entrusted; to have five reservoirs around the metropolis; and to buy up existing water companies.

The public stir on this subject is further shown by the attendance on the General Board of Health of various deputations, including Archdeacon Sinclair, churchwardens Bellworthy and Collins, and other parishioners of Kensington, who set forth the very defective supply of water to that parish. The Archdeacon pointed out, that close to where the water was taken for the Southwark and for the Chelsea Company there was a current emptying itself into the river, which was of such a character as necessarily to injure the surrounding water. A large portion of that must necessarily remain with the other; and although the company he had mentioned took pains to filter the water, the evil could not be thereby at all thoroughly remedied.

Mr. Chadwick, in the explanation which he gave to each deputation *seriatim*, stated that the Metropolitan Sanitary Commission had the subject in hand, and that certain principles had been laid down by the "Health of Towns Commission," which would, without doubt, regulate the Metropolitan Commissioners; as, for example, that the supply of water should be constant and not intermittent. It might be settled and taken that the works of watersupply and drainage works should be under one and the same management, and that management a public one. It had been shown recently, that while houses and neighbourhoods were made damp by the water pumped in, for the removal of which suitable drains were not provided, where drains *were* provided decomposed refuse accumulated, from the want of water being properly applied to cleanse them. Unless cesspools were abolished, no crowded neighbourhood could continue to be healthy, and cesspools could only be abolished when supplies of water were available. At every step the necessity and practical importance of the conclusion, for the sake of economy, as well as efficiency, that the watersupply and drainage must be under one and the same administrative management, and that management a public one, whatever it might be, was demonstrated. Another principle established was, that there had been, and could be, no public gain by the so-called competition of several or numerous capitals on the same field of supply. It had likewise been shown that private companies, which had to depend for their returns on voluntary custom, could not afford to supply water at so low a charge as might be done by a universal rate if properly managed.

Another indication of public interest in the question was afforded by the rooms of the Institute of British Architects, on Monday evening last, when the Very Rev. Dr. Buckland delivered an address on *Artesian Wells*.

There were 197 members and visiters present, and those who know the meeting rooms will not require to be told that they were inconveniently crowded.*

We had prepared a nearly *verbatim* report of the Dean's address, but the morning papers having given unusually full reports, it would come as a twice-told tale to many of our readers, and we therefore condense it. The Dean began by observing, that the architecture of the globe was a subject which he thought ought not to be foreign to the consideration of the members, for he must submit that no architect could perfectly understand his profession, unless he had acquired some knowledge of the materials with which he had to deal; and he believed no one would deny that, had their ancestors known as much as they did now touching the durability of various kinds of stone employed in the construction of ecclesiastical and castellated buildings, they would not have to deplore the ruin of so many of these edifices (?). It would be his duty that night to direct their attention to the architecture of that particular portion of the earth which they themselves inhabited—a subject possessing an interest literally of vital importance. It was, as had been proved by the events of the last six months, a question of life or death to thousands and tens of thousands in this great metropolis, whether they should have *the means of obtaining an abundant supply of fresh water.* It was, unfortunately, too notorious that the supply of water was at the present time awfully defective, and the last month had been fertile in schemes for supplying that defect. He rebutted the taunts which had been thrown out against him as a non-practical man by such practical men as, in 1825, persuaded the Earl of Abingdon to spend large sums of money in digging for coal in the Oxford clay, a folly, in exposing which he at the time went so far as to say he would willingly be burnt in the broad street with the first cart-load of coal they obtained. But the *auto da fé* did not take place, for there he was unscathed. He had studied the subject of Artesian wells for years, and had said, in his Bridgewater Treatise, thirteen years ago, all that he knew even at this time. There was nothing theoretical about his statements, the deductions followed as surely from sections of the earth, which had been made foot by foot, as from the section of a building. If those persons who are concerned in the subject were not acquainted with what he had said, it was to their shame. Loudon and Paris were each of them situated on a basin of impervious clay, which rested upon strata of porous gravel and chalk. There was no imaginary central abyss which would furnish, if it once were reached, an everlasting supply of water. It 'was now admitted that the only source of fresh water was the sea, from which it was indirectly conveyed by means of evaporation to the earth, on which it fell from the clouds in fertilizing showers. If rain water was then of such primary consequence, the question was, where, in the neighbourhood of London, was there the most of it,

* Amongst them, in addition to those named hereafter, were Lord Ebrington, Mr. H. T. Hope, M.P., Mr. Mangles, M.P., Mr. J. F. Stanford, M.P., Mr. Walpole, M.P., Dr. Arnott, Rev. H. Milman, Capt. O'Brien, Sir C. Trevelyan; Sir Fortunatus Dwarris, Messrs. T. L. Donaldson, Scoles, Mee, Bellamy, Moxatto, Naif, Knowles, Syd. Smirke, H. E. Kendall, W. B. Hamilton, F.R.S., Booth, Pownall, Fowler, Lee, Smith, Ashton, Papworth, Houmieu, Ferrey, Wood, Cole, Charles Mayhew, W. C. Myine, Jas. Fergusson, W. Bufu, Woodthorpe, Buly, Taffing, Hopkins, N. W. Billings, Oliver, Swindell, Williams, Judge, Eales, Nicholl, Dobson, Eddrup, Lockyef, Deane, Heneker, Clayton, Waring, C. Baffy, jun., Boyce, G. Vulliamy, W. S. Gawlers, Wyatt Papworth, Gotto, Phillips, Botthwich, Hakewell, Sevefo, Dr. Bett, Messrs. Pope, Wigram, Page, Fred. Peel, Poffef, Coleman, Rickman, Allason, Wilks, Bufnell, Woolrych, Johnstone, Hussey, Gregory, Dighton, Christian, Snell, P. Baly, C. Manby, Thomson, Keff, Yeft, George Rennie, Gooch, Coleman, Safvin, Porter, E. W. Brayley, Geo. Godwin, &c. &c.

and where was it the most available? This really was a question of great importance, since, in the central parts of Essex, not more than 18 inches of rain fell, while upon the highlands of Oxfordshire, running on to the Cotteswold Hills, the fall was 26 inches. It had been proved, by experiments made by M. Arago, that one-third of the fall is conveyed by rivers to the sea, one-third is lost by evaporation, and the remainder went to the sustentation of animal and vegetable life, or was absorbed by the different porous strata. The portion with which he proposed to deal was that which descended into the earth, and was given out day by day for the sustentation of the little streamlets which trickled through every valley, forming rivulets and rivers; and with the supplies of water which were said to be underneath the metropolis, and available for the supply of the 2,200,000 persons by whom it was inhabited. This was a false assertion, and he would prove it. The average depth now to the water in such wells in London was 60 feet; in 1875, it would be 120 feet down. Could we, then, look to this source for supply? He declared that there was not at the present time a single Artesian well, which could be properly so called, within three miles of St. Paul's. An Artesian well was one which flowed over naturally; they were so called from Artesium, the Roman name for the province of Artois, in France, where such wells were first formed. The London clay having been pierced in so many places, the porous beds below, which had to be supplied from the places where they outcropped, became less able to supply them all, and year by year the water grew less. The fountains in Trafalgar-square were an imposition; so far were they from being Artesian wells, that the water did not rise to within 80 feet of the surface, and it had to be pumped up by a costly steam-engine, which was more expensive than it would be to supply the fountains from the Chelsea Waterworks, and the same water was pumped up over and over again, times innumerable,—but who knew that? The brewers were now boring one against the other: to talk of getting a supply of water for London by Artesian wells was ridiculous. The expense of this, too, was enormous; one near Swindon, which was 320 feet deep, cost 1,000l.

The Dean then examined the various areas of land which supply the Coln, the Brent, and the Thames, and came to the conclusion that the latter river, near Henley, was the best source we could look to. It was a dead level the whole distance, and it was proposed to make a canal, which, having a natural fall of 3 feet, and in its whole course no engineering difficulties to render an inch of tunnelling or embanking necessary, would bring the water into a valley north of Paddington, which was 105 feet above the high-water mark. This would be high enough to supply two-thirds of the metropolis by the force of gravitation; and a portion being forced to a reservoir on Primrose-hill, the whole metropolis, even if it were twice its present size, which God forbid, might have a full and cheap supply in every house, both poor and rich.

After a statement from Mr. Clutterbuck, confirmatory of the correctness of the sections, Mr. Tite said the Dean had spoken warmly of those who had taunted him with being a mere theorist. Ignorance was always presump-

always knew his (the speaker's) business better than himself. As to the subject of the evening. He had not been aware before that an Artesian well was one that was constantly overflowing: he thought the term simply distinguished water obtained by boring. But of this there could be no doubt, that what were called Artesian wells required frequent deepening, and were a source of constant expense. He sincerely hoped that the Government would take up the supply question. It ought to be looked upon as a national question; for a large city like this, containing so immense a population, ought not to be left dependent for the supply of so important and necessary an article as water upon private companies or individual speculators. He would not express any opinion as to the means by which a sufficient supply of water should be obtained, but he believed that a public discussion of this nature would be attended with very beneficial results. The object was to obtain the greatest amount of good with the least private injury. The best science of the country ought to be called in to aid the inquiry.

M. Robert Stephenson, M.P., had listened with gratification to Dr. Buckland's remarks, and though he did not feel himself in a position to express any precise opinion on the subject, he would say he had some doubts as to the desirability of obtaining the supply in the manner pointed out. The usefulness of a river so greatly depends on the quantity of water flowing through it, that it seemed doubtful if we could abstract so much from the Thames without interfering with the navigation. This should be inquired into. If we could take it from the tributary streams at high level, abstract it from what went to form floods, would it not be better? This was a view that had occupied his mind for some time. He quite concurred with the Dean in the belief that a proper supply for London could not be had from Artesian wells.

Mr. Homersham considered that the chalk held larger quantities of water than the Dean asserted was the case, and that when the fissures containing it were reached, the other wells were not necessarily lowered, but water was forthcoming which otherwise would run to waste in the sea.

Mr. Horn and Mr. Reid, both owners of Artesian wells; Mr. Stanford, M.P.; Mr. Dickenson; and Mr. Foggo, made each a few observations; and Mr. T. Piper said that the point to be remembered, as it seemed to him, was,—that, of the water which fell as rain, and which was alone available, one-third goes to the river, one-third to the ground, and one-third to supply waste by evaporation, &c.; and that the one-third which goes to the river is more easily got at than that which goes to the ground.

THE OLD CHURCH SPIRE AT BIRMINGHAM has been declared, by a majority of architects and surveyors, to be decidedly unsafe and liable to *fall* down if not *taken* down. It is to be hoped, however, that whether the latter or the former, such an ancient landmark as St. Martin's spire will be at once restored; for in a place like Birmingham, where all is new and without associations,—every ancient landmark passing away one after another,—so prominent a monument of the olden time can ill be spared. The question has been started whether the church should not be entirely rebuilt; but perhaps identical in form and position, it may be a second question, subtle

PROPOSED OPERATIVES' PROVIDENT INSTITUTION.
BUILDING SOCIETIES.

BESIDES the classes you have addressed in urging the establishment of the proposed institution, there is another, the members of which are awakened to a sense of its necessity—I mean the artificers themselves. You have already shown it to be alike the duty and interest of the employers to assist in carrying out the benevolent measure, but I think its startling need cannot be too strongly dwelt upon.

Few were prepared for the disclosures which were made to the Parliamentary Committee on the " Friendly Societies Bill." This report reveals a state of things lamentable to contemplate, and each page of the evidence which accompanies it shows the necessity of the timely interference of the masters In such a cause, more forcibly than any comment upon it.

Friendly societies are divided into two classes —the enrolled and unenrolled : one with, the other without, the protection of the law. In order to be entitled to enrolment, the tables are required to be certified by an actuary, and if they are at all reasonable, the certificate is given,—it being acknowledged that, of necessity, their safety cannot be guaranteed, as localities materially affect their accuracy, and little difference is made with regard to them. But it appears that even this slight restraint is cast off, for an eminent actuary stated that he cannot certify more than one society's tables in ten, which are sent him for that purpose, and that the nine form themselves into illegal associations. In the evidence the reader is startled by the frequent recurrence of the term " young blood," and discovers that most of the clubs are indebted to it for existence. The subscriptions of young entering members are appropriated to pay the claims of the old ones, who can be regarded in no other character than as decoy-ducks, and the system which gives rise to such practices as a perpetual fraud of the old on the young. It there appears that 14,000 of these institutions have been enrolled; that a greater number have been formed and not enrolled; that very many have been broken up, and that a vast majority of those still remaining in existence are insolvent.

It appears that most of the town clubs are formed by publicans, to extend their business. Advantage is taken of the working man's ignorance of statistics, and the tables are made such as to draw customers; indeed, it is a branch of the trade, and there being opposition, a rivalry exists to underbid each other.

In these societies members are exposed not only to unsound tables and acts of injustice, but in the unenrolled ones to direct fraud, and must suffer without having any remedy. Thus officers may rob with impunity, yet the law cannot touch them. We read of a secretary coolly "keeping" 50l., and walking about the streets laughing at his dupes; of another who embezzled 5,000l., and although tried and pronounced by the judge to be morally guilty, yet he could neither be convicted nor deprived of his booty.

Most disastrous consequences have resulted from the spread of these societies. Ministers, in visiting the dwellings of the poor, and noting the prevailing misery, having inquired the cause of such distress, learned that it arose in many instances from the breaking in of clubs; and a clergyman who examined the inmates of the Birmingham workhouse, found that of the 152 who had been driven to claim the pauper's crust, 79 had belonged to sick clubs, which had all failed at the time their assistance was needed. A member of the committee truly said, " There had been a very general confiscation of the property of the poor."

No doubt there are clubs respectably conducted, but, like railways, until they are generally reformed the poor man will blindly speculate, in selecting one worthy of his confidence, and there are serious evils connected with the best conducted which ought never to tained. The time has really come when the ›rkman will willingly sacrifice the pleasure being initiated into the mysteries of Druid- m and the secret signs of Odd-fellowship, to cure the more ordinary benefits which the esent measure would bring within his reach. There are other societies which are held in gh estimation in many quarters, and which e constantly being recommended to the tisan, as enabling him to obtain a dwelling- ›use on advantageous terms, and thus con- rring on him political rights,—viz., *building* ›cieties. I am fully sensible of the great nportance of the workman possessing a ouse, but an examination into the opera- ons of these societies, which profess to give im one, will convince the inquirer that they re much more adapted for men who have ther resources than their labour. Nothing an be more excellent than the object, but how it carried out?

I have made myself acquainted with their orking, and think they may succeed if they re respectably managed, and do not get ıvolved in litigation. But who will benefit by heir success?

By paying 10s. monthly, for twelve years, or or a shorter or longer period, according to the rosperity of the society, the member is pro- nised 120*l.*; or if he wishes to obtain his hare in advance, he can receive it, subject to large discount (in the first year the minimum ixed by the rules is 65*l.*, and is usually about 8*l.*), so that he will have to be content with 2*l.* in ready money, and bind himself to con- inue subscribing 10s. a-month until the ter- nination of the society, which will take place when every unadvanced share reaches the value of 120*l.*, which being calculated at welve years, would amount to 72*l.*, besides ines, fees, and other charges.* From this, it s clear who has the advantage, the borrower or depositor. Indeed, it will scarcely be credited, that people blindly borrow money of these societies at a higher rate of interest than is charged on private loans, in effecting which there is less risk and expense. Yet such is the fact, for in the first yearly report of one of these associations—the respectability of which is above suspicion—which is selected, because the directors "cordially congratulate their fellow members upon the pre-eminent success which has attended their efforts,—a success which they confidently believe will signalize it among the numerous similar societies now in operation," we read that "the rate of discount given by the members to obtain their shares in advance has averaged 77*l.* 9s. 3d. (for round figures, I will say 78*l.*), so that each of the shares of the ultimate value of 120*l.* has been satisfied, by means of 42*l.* advanced in ready money." Now, for this 42*l.* the borrower is liable for 72*l.* (if not more), besides the heavy charges; whereas the same amount, if other- wise borrowed, for twelve years, at 5 per cent., would make, with the interest, only 67*l.* 4s., showing a clear balance of 4*l.* 16s. in favour of the latter mode, and which would allow the use of the 42*l.* throughout, instead of having to refund a seventh part of it annually. To suppose that these building societies are what their name denotes, is little else than a popular error. They are in reality mere loan societies, with the difference that they advance money on real property only, and at a more extravagant rate of interest; and as loan societies, they would be shunned by the poor man, did not the bills announce that the cash has to be "sold;" and unfortunately he frequently "buys" it before he fully comprehends the nature of the transaction.

The statement of the accounts of the society already alluded to, shows a progressive ad- vance of upwards of 17*l.* on each existing share (on which 6*l.* has been paid), towards its ultimate realization of 120*l.*: that is to say, the 6*l.* has been so lucratively employed, as to have produced upwards of 11*l.* in twelve months, and which is at the rate of 350*l.* per cent. on the gradual payment. This appears encouraging, but almost too much so. How has such an enormous profit arisen? Some one must have suffered, and I fear it has been the poor borrower, whose benefit was alone contemplated by the Legislature, when it authorized the establishment of these societies.

* When it exceeds this time, which will be the case with *many* of them, this amount will, of course, be more.

But if a man wise enough to be an investing member desires to realize this profit, or any fair proportion of it, he is told that it is all prospective, and that there is no interim benefit. It is not surprising that he begins to count the cost, and loses heart.

While these societies were originally pro- jected and sanctioned by Parliament, for the good of the labouring population, they are in reality so conducted as to prove a source of profit principally to others than those intended. A great proportion of members belong to the middle classes; and in some cases public companies have subscribed for a large number of shares. The poor man who pays on one or two shares, labours under serious disadvan- tages. He may be thrown out of employment, or be otherwise unable to continue his pay- ments; then fines are incurred, which begin small but wax large, and which, according to the scale, if allowed to accumulate by his remaining long in arrear, will soon exceed the amount subscribed, which then becomes for- feited.

True, it is provided that deposits may be withdrawn, but the rules usually allow only a limited number of such applications to be granted; and unfortunately so many, either from necessity or want of confidence, wish to retire, that several months frequently elapse before the payment of a claim, and then after being considerably lessened by the deduction of fines, to which he continued liable in the meanwhile. Thus the society ultimately falls into the hands of capitalists, who will reap the profits arising from the very lucrative system of advancing money, and from the forfeiture of the subscriptions of the poorer members, if it be not taken under the protection of the Court of Chancery, and then it (or rather its capital), will soon be numbered amongst the things that were.

One litigious member has all the others at his mercy. Some who have had advances have, at the expense of the "parent society," disputed the validity of the mortgage by which they are secured; and although this has not been done successfully, yet questions have arisen calcu- lated to fill the minds of those interested with doubt and alarm. In one case (Cuthill *v.* Kingdom) it was contended that the constitu- tion of a building society, duly enrolled, &c., was illegal, on the ground that it allowed each of its members to hold several shares, but in- asmuch as the objection had not been taken at the right time, it did not prevail; but the ob- servations of the Barons of the Exchequer were such as to lead a writer in the *Law Maga- zine*, who is evidently friendly to, and thinking well of such associations in general, to say, "it is impossible to doubt that if the point had been taken in time the society would have been held illegal, or at least not within the protec- tion of the Act; so that if the doctrine in those dicta be law, it may be said there is scarcely at present a single benefit building society in the kingdom legally and properly constituted, and enrolled under the Act 6 & 7 Wm. IV., c. 32." And I find that the registrar, acting on the remarks of the judges, now refuses his certifi- cate to any rules which do not limit the interest of a member to 150*l.* It is certainly prudent to constitute new societies in accordance with the interpretation put on the Act of Parliament by the three Barons of the Exchequer; but what of those previously in existence, in not one of which has there been the slightest re- striction as to the number of shares?

In another case (Mosley *v.* Baker) the ques- tion related to the terms on which a member who had borrowed money and given a mort- gage security on real estate should be allowed to redeem. The judgment of the Vice-Chan- cellor has been appealed against; but the appeal being not yet heard, the operations of the society must in the meanwhile be much circumscribed.

Another case is now pending, in which the society actually insists on the member paying interest on a loan after the whole amount bor- rowed has been refunded, and continuing to do so till the termination of the society!

It may be asked, however, seeing that friendly clubs cannot be relied on, and that building societies are not adapted to meet the poor man's want, why does he not take advan- tage of *savings banks*?

But there is a decided preference on his part to make a provision through a friendly society, and this cannot be wondered at, as it promises him a specific sum weekly during sickness, and a certain payment at death, and there is much in the nature of these benefits to commend themselves to his notice, although in so many instances they have never been enjoyed. And it is by thus attending to his peculiar re- quirements that real service can be rendered him. He does not call on his master to sup- port him in illness or old age by systematic almsgiving, but to institute means on which he can rely, by which he may himself provide for his own necessities. This is the most urgent object: a more purely charitable one may be embodied with it, but the *principle* is helping and encouraging the poor man to help himself, and while other branches of the lower classes have the benefit of institutions recognized by their immediate employers, shall not the worthy building artisan be directed to a proper mode for making a pro- vision?

I can gather from your paper that the pro- moters of the present movement do not in- voke private benevolence, always ready to be bestowed on worthy objects, but ask for the exercise of that influence which will inspire confidence, and that co-operation of the masters of the class which will insure success. Nothing further is required to put into force the plan which has been proposed by Professor Cock- erell; and looking at the actual want of the measure, it is to be hoped that such assistance will not be long withheld. The honest work- ing man has strong claims on his employers, and generally they are kindly discharged; but another duty still remains,—shall he be allowed, without a timely warning, to be robbed of his earnings, or to invest them injudiciously? His hours of toil are perhaps saddened by forebodings, that he may end his days a wandering mendicant. Animate them by the prospect of a calm, comfortable old age; let then the master builders say, "We are dis- posed to sanction and direct an institution hold- ing out definite and attainable results, to be insured to our *employés* on suitable conditions, at a certain time, and in sickness or misfortune," and that kindly intelligence, which originally suggested its establishment, will, I am sure, be ready to arrange the details of its formation.

The workman who has had bitter experience of irresponsible societies, and from his connec- tion with them has, in a sense, to commence life again, and he who cautiously remained aloof from them, will both desire to benefit by tables soundly constructed and attested by eminent actuaries. There is a rising distrust of incredible gains, which have to flow into the pocket it is not known how, and a growing contentment with the moderate but sure pro- ducts of investments in Government or other stable securities. The great object is cer- tainty; let there be no indefinite prospects held out; the poor man cannot afford to spe- culate; if he loses, it is his all. And by carry- ing out this benevolent scheme, a way of pro- viding for the evil day will be opened which will not compel him to frequent an ale-house, to talk politics, to foster moody thoughts of his relation to his master, and to grow morose; but it will, on the contrary, remove the temp- tation to intemperance and disaffection, encou- rage him to improve his mind, and teach him to see in his employer his support for the pre- sent, and in the stability of the institutions of his country his guarantee for the future.

L.

City Improvements.—An Act is to be applied for by the London City authorities in the ensuing session of Parliament, for making a new street (in continuation of the new street from Cannon-street to the east side of Queen- street) commencing on the west side of Queen- street, crossing Bow-lane, Bread-street, Friday- street, Little Distaff-lane, and Old Change, and terminating on the south side of St. Paul's Churchyard; for widening and improving the west end of Gresham-street West, formerly called Maiden-lane; for widening and im- proving Threadneedle-street; and for extending to this Act the provisions of the London (City) Improvement Act, 1847. It is also intended to take powers to raise money on the security of the City estates and revenues, in order to carry out these improvements, to build a new prison for the City, and to improve Billingsgate market.

THE TOMB OF THE BONZI FAMILY, ROME.

THE TOMB OF THE BONZI FAMILY IN THE CHURCH OF SAN GREGORIO, ROME.

THE tomb of the Bonzi family in the church of San Gregorio, at Rome, is a production of the "cinque-cento" period. Monuments of this description abounding in Italy, are very numerous in Florence, the capital of that portion of the world in which a love for the truly beautiful in art was first rekindled. In this work, evidently the fruit of one mind, sculpture and architecture are combined, while a painter's feeling is infused into the composition by means of the figures in low relief introduced in the back ground above the sarcophagus.

So intense was the feeling for art at its dawn in Italy, and for a long period subsequently in that country, that the triple power of painter, sculptor, and architect centred not unfrequently in one single being; nor is there an instance on record of an artist of that period excelling solely in one branch of art. In dwelling, then, upon the works of a period celebrated for the growth of art, it is well to mark the course pursued by artists whose works have given so much dignity to a particular epoch : this study may lead us to adopt salutary measures to remedy the languid state of art—of architecture particularly—in our own age and country. Amongst the various reasons which may be assigned for the unsatisfactory state of architecture in England, there is, perhaps, no one more weighty than the erroneous position of the architect himself. With us the architect's defective education isolates him from the painter and sculptor : he who professes an art which receives so much of its lustre from the united charms of painting and sculpture has no fellowship with the followers of those intellectual pursuits. With us the architect's very place of study has changed its character and its name,—there should be more of the *studio* and less of the office. An architect should be an artist, not dipping his tiny sable hair quill into pretty water colours, but in delineating the beautiful and varied forms of nature in a manner

which shall entitle him to a diploma amongst the fraternity of artists : with this knowledge, and mind and reasoning powers informed and guided by the study of geometry, intellect and thought strengthened and refined by an intimacy with the Greek and Roman tongues, sound architecture will be produced. This was the path trodden by those whose works we delight to extol : the same path will lead to the same goal; but unless we pursue it, how can we expect to overtake those whom we strive to emulate ; how enter the field against beings so armed, we ourselves being but half equipped ? By pursuing this path architecture will recover her long-lost dignity, and present herself once more accompanied by the sister graces, painting and sculpture. Nor does it matter much what style an architect thus fortified chooses to follow ; but the *orders* should not be despised. By pursuing the path so palpably traced out for us, we of this age might, with our increased advantages, present to posterity something fraught with even more lasting vitality than is possessed by those cherished relics of antiquity which have lived so long.

The Greeks of the age of Pericles, and the Italians of the fifteenth and sixteenth centuries, are our masters ; it will not suffice merely to admire their works, we must also fall in with their mode of working.

A. W. HAKEWILL.

ST. GABRIEL'S CHURCH, PIMLICO.—An Act is to be applied for in the ensuing session of Parliament to authorize the erection of this church on a site belonging to the Marquis of Westminster, and the raising of a fund on the credit of its pew rents, to defray the expense of building.

THE NEW STREET FROM SPITALFIELDS TO SHOREDITCH.—Parliament is to be applied to for an Act to continue and amend the Act of 9th and 10th Victoria, for enabling the Woods and Forests to carry out this projected improvement.

LEICESTER-SQUARE AND PUBLIC WORKS.

NOTWITHSTANDING the immense outlay which has been lavished with unsparing hand on great national edifices, and the talent displayed in many localities of London in clearing away sinks of squalor and disease to make way for open and architectural thoroughfares, the wayfarer of the town cannot fail to observe how many majestic sites are wholly neglected, how many are illustrated by structures of only ambiguous merit, and how many slums of the metropolis have been selected for the most colossal examples of modern art.

Perhaps in no city of the world is there a nobler position for a classic pile than that occupied by the great conservatory of art (or that which ought to serve such purpose), the National Gallery.

In the centre from which the most important thoroughfares radiate, here was a *locale* for illustration by native talent,—a largo in front almost equal to the Forum Romanum; an esplanade in the perspective revealing consecutive palaces ; and in the distance all that is venerable within our precincts—the Westminster Cathedral : planted on an elevation suited to the highest aspirations of a Vitruvius, we find a long line of blanked paries, exhibiting certainly three noble pillared porticoes, but surmounted by domes of so 'mesquin' a character, as to be only adapted for the belfry of a stable !

Perhaps few will find fault with the proportions of the columns, or the details of the more ornate parts of this performance ; but, unfortunately for the architect, his production, however meritorious, sinks into insignificance when the range of view, passing from left to right, is arrested by one of the finest porticoes which any city can present, the classic tympanum of St. Martin's Church. I am not aware that the rampant arms of England make it the less classic, although doubtless an inept emblem for that position, in which some insignia of the Faith would be more accordant with the general character of the house of prayer. Restriction to design—restriction to space—restriction above all in outlay, may have here cramped a genius, capable of better things, within the boundaries of dictation, of bad taste, or chill penury.

It is unnecessary to particularize the one gorgeous evidence of misplaced profusion, or to refer to the example which appears a problem and puzzle, as signal as that which young academicians denominate in mathematics, "the asses' bridge." But few there are who have regarded the "instar monster," and who afterwards give thereupon an unbiassed opinion, although, albeit, filled with British pride at the unity of design, beauty of detail, and elaborateness of finish, and do not say not with regret, "We must *speak of the bridge as we pass it."*

My theme is not this, for it is an episode, short and trite, from the scene of review—a part of which is Trafalgar-square. I am aware it is the fashion to slight the fountains, which give their *intermittent* tribute to the leaky basins in the centre, merely because they are less than those of the Palais Royal, or the Place de la Concorde, but these jets (the only examples in London), are pretty,—the basins and vases in good taste,—and the whole effect at the same time animating to the scene and sedative to the mind.

It is gratifying to learn that something is to be done to remedy the main default of the National Gallery ; and that an additional building is to be constructed in the rear for the merited exhibition of the Vernon bequest, and the contributions of other patriotic and highminded individuals.

The space allocated to the Nelson testimonial is sacred, and now advances towards completion : for the rest, a suitable balustrade completes the design, save that a pedestal occupies the opposite angle to that on which George IV. rides slipshod. Would not this, Mr. Editor, be a glorious position for an equestrian statue of her Most Gracious Majesty ? So far, the design, though naked, would be complete. Ample space would then remain for ornamental statuary, and I can conceive no plan more worthy the authorities who are the arbiters of such matters than to dedicate this only (we cannot call it solitary) grand place as a FORUM BRITTANICUM for the consecration of heroes and statesmen, for the encouragement of sculptural art (alas! too languid), and for the elevation of public taste.

Now, Sir, I have but one word to say of Leicester-square: this second open space, a point of confluence from various quarters of the town, has lain for years open, defiled, and a disgrace. Can this not be remedied? Some say it is private property; others that it cannot be built over. A peripatetic may sometimes see a mode of application for such a centre which will not occur to the parties beneficially concerned, as the looker-on at a game often perceives the errors of the players. Whether it be public or private property, it is clear that the opportunity should not be lost of converting it to an use equally profitable to those interested and beneficial to the panting denizens of this confined region.

It is to be hoped that the improvements meditated behind the National Gallery may include the design of a grand *strada* from that point to Leicester-square, which might then become, not only a great mart for commerce, in which it is making rapid strides, but the space itself be transformed into an ornament comporting in character with the magnificence which should be allied to the recollections of Trafalgar.

With the view of some such appropriation, allow me to suggest the wayward jotting of an idler. It is this. Excavate the whole square to a depth of 6 feet; sell the gravel—for such it is—at only two shillings a-load. The area is a trapezium, or figure of four unequal sides, presenting a frontage of nearly 700 feet; yet still the inequality would be perceptible only to an architectural eye.

Leave a sunken causeway, 13 feet wide, approached by descending flights, two at every angle. Build on every side a row of shops or stores, with ornate elevation rising 5 feet or 6 feet above the level of the adjacent street. Give to each a depth of at least 30 feet, with an area of 8 feet or 10 feet in the rear; and still in the centre you will have a parallelogram unappropriated of 50 feet by 90 feet. Cover these ranges with flagging or asphalte; raise suitable balustrades around; and here you have at once a distinguished plateau 40 feet wide, available for public recreation, susceptible of any decoration in statuary, conservative of the public health, and tributary to the increasing appetencies of prosperous trade.

In the centre, the statue (at least time honoured) might rest on its renewed and, perhaps, more elevated base; and water-works contribute to the enjoyment of the saunterer or the valetudinarian. It is manifest that the elevation of handsome ranges of shop-front and facia would not obstruct light, air, or view, whilst sufficient to indicate the emblems of business; and that the raised causeway, approached by steps and balustered bridges (one on each side) would lighten the general design.

Trusting that you will pardon the verboseness of what some may (at this fall) call my sybilline leaves, and impressed with the truth of an axiom derived from high authority, "A word spoken in due *season*, how good is it!" I venture at the present season on one hint more to the authorities on whom I have so often poured my unavailing advice. It is this:—The new parks have been purchased and inclosed,—aye, three years inclosed,—but not yet planted! Primrose-hill, the solace of the weary artisan, three years paled, is yet naked! Why not expend only one ONE HUNDRED pound-note in adorning with flowers, and shrubs, and forest trees, this only possible airy resource for the indigent, pent-up, Sunday-emancipated son or daughter of labour? It will not only gratify but humanize the million, as the contemplation of floral nature can soften neglected minds, and raise their souls to rational devotion.

Possibly, like other appeals to officials, this may be spurned; and, not being an *employé*, it may even be said—"What is that to thee:" nevertheless, again it is repeated, on the principle that what concerns the public *is* everybody's business, and of the oft-repeated maxim, "nihil alienum mihi puto qui sit," &c.

QUONDAM.

THE NEW CHURCHES IN WESTMINSTER.

ON the 8th instant, the foundation-stones of two new churches were laid in Westminster, to be dedicated respectively to St. Matthew and the Holy Trinity.

St. Matthew's will stand at the junction of Great Peter-street and St. Anne's-lane. The position presents no ordinary difficulties, being a site of very irregular form, literally buried in very miserable houses, and only offering very narrow frontages to two very poor streets. The tower, when built, will show in Peter-street, the east end of chancel in St. Anne's-lane. It was necessary entirely to cover the ground, and the largest practicable nave with ordinary aisles being insufficient, the architect, Mr. Scott, was obliged to add a second aisle on the south side, which must contain a small gallery for children. The accommodation is for 1,200 persons. The cost, exclusive of tower, 6,000*l.*; inclusive of the tower, 7,500*l.* or 8,000*l.* Mr. Myers is the builder. The materials are Kentish rag and Bath stone. The style is Transitional, between the geometrical and flowing, perhaps that of about 1310. On the north side can be no windows, owing to building nearly up to boundary. The light will be obtained chiefly from the end windows and the clerestory. The east window is of five lights, the west of six, the latter of considerable dimensions.

The chancel, which will face St. Anne's-lane, will be internally 40 feet by 23 feet 6 inches, and will be lighted by the east window of five lights, and by three windows on the south and one on the north side, the remainder of that side being occupied by a chancel, aisle, and vestry. The nave, with its aisles, will be internally 84 feet by 57 feet 6 inches, and will be of five bays, or arches, in length, and be chiefly lighted from the clerestory and from the large west window which obtains light from above the surrounding houses. The principal entrance is through the tower, which projects again southward from the third aisle, and faces Peter-street. There are also a western entrance and one from St. Anne's-lane.

Notwithstanding the lowness of the estimate there are as yet no funds for the tower beyond the ground story, though, in such a situation, the tower is more than ordinarily needed to show the church from a distance and prevent its being absolutely lost; and, being the nearest church (St. Margaret's excepted) to the Abbey, it ought to have a steeple of some dignity. We have not seen the design, but understand the steeple proposed is somewhat more than 200 feet in height.

It presents a curious contrast between public and individual munificence that, while in the same parish two other churches are being erected, one costing 25,000*l.* and the other 10,000*l.*, each paid for by private individuals, this, which trusts to public liberality, and only costs 8,000*l.*, after receiving from societies more than 4,000*l.*, if not 5,000*l.*, is to be left minus its tower for want of funds! The inhabitants of Westminster seem ready recipients but niggard dispensers of charity.

The Church of the Holy Trinity is to be erected on a plot of ground called Besborough Gardens, at the junction of the Belgrave and Vauxhall-bridge roads, at the sole expense of the Rev. W. H. E. Bentinck, archdeacon and Prebendary of Westminster. Mr. Pearson is the architect, and Messrs. Smith and Appleford are the builders.

We are told that this is to be a cross church, with transepts, chancel, and porches, the vestibule being at the north-east of the chancel. The style is Early Decorated, of the time of Edward I. and II. Length of the nave, including the tower, 84 feet; width, 19 feet 3 inches; across the transepts, extreme width, 72 feet; inside length of chancel, 40 feet 6 inches; width, 20 feet 9 inches; height under the nave from the floor to the point of the roof, 51 feet; chancel, 48 feet high, and transepts same height. The space within the tower is groined over in stone at the height of about 54 feet; having three windows, which are seen from the church, and throw a light into it, forming a lantern. The height from the ground line to the top of the tower is 93 feet; height to top of the cross from the spire, which springs from the tower, 100 feet; making a total of 193 feet high. There will be sedilia in the chancel on the south side. The eastern windows have seven lights, the western windows six lights, and the transept windows five lights each. The dressings are of Bath stone. The walls are externally faced with Bargate stone from the neighbourhood of Godalming. The roofs are constructed in deal, and covered on the outside with Staffordshire tiles of a brown colour. The seats in the nave will be all open, made of deal; and all free. The cost of the edifice will be about 10,000*l.* The church will accommodate 850, including about 400 children, all upon the ground, there being no galleries. It appears that it was necessary to dig for the foundation 20 feet deep from the surface.

THE LATE SIR R. MORRISON, ARCHITECT.

SIR RICHARD MORRISON, President of the Irish Institute of Architects, died on the 31st of October, at the age of 82, and was buried on the 7th inst. The funeral was attended by the members of the Institute and a large number of friends. He was the son of John Morrison, the architect, of Cork, and was originally intended for the church; ultimately, however, he was sent to Dublin, and became the pupil of Gandon, the well known architect of the courts of law, the custom-house, and other buildings in that city. Through his god-father, the Earl of Shannon, he obtained a Government appointment in the Ordnance department, but retained it only a short time, in consequence of reductions. He soon, however, got into practice, and executed a considerable number of buildings. His son, William Vitruvius Morrison, who died at the early age of 44, was for a time in partnership with him.* Sir Richard was last employed for Lord Longford, on a design for a Gothic mansion, and was also superintending some alterations for the Earl of Howth. He has left considerable property, including an extensive library of architectural works. He was knighted by Earl de Grey.

LANDLORD AND TENANT.

MIDDLETON *v.* NASH.

THIS was an action brought in the Whitechapel County Court to recover a quarter's rent for apartments occupied by the defendant at a rental of 30*l.* a-year. The tenancy commenced at Michaelmas, 1848, and in March the defendant, in accordance with the terms of his agreement, gave a quarter's notice to quit. The notice was not objected to, and the plaintiff paid his rent up to Midsummer, and left the premises two months previous to the expiration of that quarter; but the landlord refused to accept the key, and now sought to recover a quarter's rent up to Michaelmas, still holding the defendant liable for the next twelve months. The defendant observed, that he thought it a case of extreme oppression, more particularly as the plaintiff had refused to accept a tenant; and, upon referring to a "cheap" abstract of the Landlord and Tenants' Act, submitted that, if the notice was informal, the landlord was bound to object to it at the time.—His Honour: Not at all. There is no doubt it was intended that a quarter's notice should at any time be sufficient to put an end to the tenancy; but the legal construction of the agreement is, that the tenancy does not expire till the end of the year.

The defendant said the plantiff had put a bill up in shop window to let the apartments, and wished his honour to inform him if that was not an admission of the legality of the notice?

His Honour—Certainly not: it is so much the better for you. If he lets the apartments you are no longer liable.—The plaintiff said he would be satisfied if the defendant would pay half the ensuing quarter in addition to the present claim.—His Honour advised the defendant to accede to these terms, observing that it was a case of great hardship, but the law was against him.

Ordered that the present claim be paid at 3*l.* a quarter.

* A memoir of the late Mr. W. Vitruvius Morrison will be found in Weale's "Quarterly Papers on Architecture," with a list of the buildings executed by himself, and in conjunction with his father.

CHAPEL IN ST. MARY'S CHURCH, GUILDFORD.

ST. MARY'S CHURCH, GUILDFORD.

THE chapel here represented (now used as a vestry-room) is situated on the north side of the altar; the end is semicircular, and the vaulting was once richly painted: the prevailing colours are red and green, with an occasional intermixture of black and yellow. The subjects appear to give a history of the soul: on the right hand, above the front arch, is represented an angel with the scales in his hand, the soul, in an attitude of prayer below, awaiting its doom: the arch enemy of man is disputing with the angel the possession of the soul, but the face of the angel being turned towards it, re-assures it. On the left are two human figures carried captive by two devils: the angel turning his head away from them assures their condemnation: this painting is much obliterated.

On the six panels are represented,—1st. The burial of the body, the clergy wrapping the grave clothes around it. 2nd. Two dead Christians are lying at the foot of a scribe, who seems to be entering their names in a book, probably the book of life: a figure behind is receiving a cup, from which he drinks (the waters of regeneration). 3rd. and 4th. Represent the sufferings of the saints—boiling in a cauldron, decapitation, &c. &c., with the kings of the earth triumphing over them. 5th. The baptism of death into a new life. 6th. The Judgment of the wicked—the king and executioners of the fourth compartment are drawn by two devils before a saint, and the martyr is praying for his intercession for them.

Over the two centre compartments sits a large figure of the Saviour, and above each of the other tablets an angel kneels. The above paintings are extremely rude, but are evidences of Judgment in ecclesiastical garniture, teaching by pictures, and causing the mind unconsciously to reflect.   S.

WORKMEN AND MASTERS.—We have received the names of two or three builders who considerately paid their men in full on the "Thanksgiving-day," but as doubtless others did so, too, of whom we have not heard, it would be invidious to mention them. An act of this sort will not be disregarded by the men. The amount paid, in some cases considerable, is of course all out of the pocket of the master.

DR. WHEWELL ON THE GROWTH OF STYLES.

THE following is a summary of Dr. Whewell's "Remarks on the Gothic and After-Gothic Architecture of Germany," referred to in our last number but one:—

The object was to trace the transition from the complete Gothic to the After-Gothic, and the consequent dissolution of the Gothic style, on principles of the same kind as those by which the author formerly attempted to trace the formation of the Gothic style and the disappearance of Romanesque architecture. In the formation of the complete Gothic style there operated chiefly three principles,— the principle of framework (with a subordinate principle of tracery), the principle of wallwork, and the principle of spire-growth. For the idea of a framework of piers, arches, windows, vaulting shafts, vaulting ribs, buttresses, and flying buttresses, is the leading distinctive principle of Gothic buildings. This principle may be followed out by itself (and this is in a great measure done in England, producing the Early English of Salisbury); the notion of framework, however, not excluding considerable masses of wall.

ST. MARY'S, GUILDFORD.

But to obtain the complete Gothic we require further the principle of tracery, and the principle of lateral cohesion, or of wallwork, which gives a new character to the mouldings (as in the English Decorated style); and these latter principles, in Germany and France, are developed at the same time with the principle of framework; so that the complete Gothic is, in those countries, the first fully formed pointed style. The principle of upward growth in the parts adds to the style several other features, as pinnacles, crockets, finials, and spires; and thus the complete Gothic is formed.

These principles may be conceived as having carried on a struggle, as it were, which was brought to a kind of balance in the complete Gothic, but which produced the After-Gothic, when the equilibrium of these principles is lost—for instance, when the principle of wall-work predominated over the principle of framework. But the principle of wall-work modified the principle of frame-work, long before it affected it injuriously. It did this indeed, as has been said already, very conspicuously in the Decorated style in England; giving to the vertical mouldings different forms and values from those of mere framework, making some members broad, some narrow, and so on. We are not, therefore, to consider buildings as showing the evidence of a corruption of style, merely because there are vertical moulded vaulting shafts, which are too slight to support vaulting; as in King's College Chapel, Cambridge, the architecture of which has been condemned on this account. Even considered as frame-work, we must take into consideration the whole bundle of mouldings, and not one member alone: but in fact, the principle of wall-work operates theoretically as well as practically in all such cases, and prevents us from regarding the shafts in the moulded wall as separate supports. The two ideas, that of frame-work and that of wall-work, are both present to the mind; and it is their combined concords and discords which produce that species of harmony in which architecture peculiarly rejoices.

But in the course of time the principle of framework was violated and rejected; and the wallwork, the real structure of a large portion of the building, became more and more predominant. One main occasion of this was an ambition of architects, which prevailed from an early period, both in Germany and in France, and extended into later ages, to build very lofty churches. This attempt, pursued in the Gothic style, made the framework of the buttresses and flying buttresses too massive to be agreeable to the eye; and this blemish led at last to the plan of supporting the roof at a great height without any decorative manifestation of the framework externally. The organic connection of the parts being thus destroyed, the ornamentation of separate parts was pursued as an exercise of fancy and invention. The vaulting ribs sprang from piers with discontinuous imposts; the buttresses stopped short of the top of the wall; and the roof seemed to be supported, like a baloon, with a buoyancy within, not to be thrown up by a universal tendency of upward growth. At the same time, the principle of upward growth of one form out of another gave rise to the notion of the *interpenetration* of one form by another; the tracery became capricious and unconstructive, as in the flamboyant of France and the stump-tracery of Germany; while the perpendicular tracery of England, though less pleasing to the architectural eye, from the manifest operation of the principle of masonry which it exhibited. And thus, the organization of the Gothic edifice was broken up, and the parts disbanded; each part was ornamented by itself, without connection with the rest; and this being the character of German After-Gothic, when the Italian style was revived, it was easy to apply the Italian elements to the separate portions of the edifice.

THE CHURCH OF TREYFORD, ST. PETER, SUSSEX.

THE style of this building, just completed under the superintendence of Mr. Ferrey, is Early Decorated. The church consists of a chancel, with north and south aisles extending half its length; nave, with north and south aisles; south porch; and steeple at the west end of north aisle. It is built of stone found on the spot, and termed the Malme Rock, among which is contained, in small quantities, a species of blue limestone rag; of this latter, the tower is constructed. The spire, windows, and dressings throughout are of Caen stone. The roofs are of English oak, open boarded also with oak, and covered with red tiles laid upon dry hairfelt; the tiles being treated with a mixture of oil and soot or lamp black. The extreme length of the church, chancel, and steeple, is 116 feet; the interior of chancel, 32 feet by 16 feet; nave, 52 feet by 22 feet; aisles, 52 feet by 10 feet; height of chancel, 46 feet; nave, 52 feet.

The nave is of four bays, with north and south aisles. This roof is equilateral. The aisle roofs are *lean-tos*, the principals springing

from stone brackets. A four-light window, with flowing tracery, occupies the west end: under which is the west door, of oak, clenched, and decorated with hinges of scroll iron work. The stone bench, peculiar to the churches of the neighbourhood, is carried along the walls of the nave and chancel aisles, which are otherwise unoccupied with any fixed seats. The nave is fitted with seats kept very low, with square ends of oak plank 3 inches thick, fixed with small buttresses, and capped with trefoil moulding, all of the like substance. The old plain square First Pointed font has its elaborate cover, 14 feet in height, suspended from an iron crane fixed in the wall of the north clerestory, opposite the south door. A low stone pulpit is placed against the south pier of the chancel arch; on the opposite side of which stands the open reading desk, of oak, the front panels of which are filled with crimson velvet, with gold-worked floriated crosses. The Bible desk, or lectern, rising from an octagonal shaft of buttresses, is placed in front of the chancel steps, immediately before the pulpit, on the south of the chancel entrance.

The chancel is entered by two steps under a screen carved in oak. Three other steps lead to the altar table, placed upon a flooring of encaustic tiles, with a border of vine leaves upon a bright blue ground. The east window of three trefoil-headed lights with tracery, forming a trinity of trefoils, is placed high up in the gable, leaving room beneath its sill for a reredos of seven arches worked in chalk. Four trefoil-headed and varied single windows occupy the north and south sides. Under these on the south side are inserted three sedilia, worked in the native or Malme stone —a species of grey-coloured marble, which is also used for the interior facing of the lower portion of the walls, the upper part being of chalk—as are also the splays, shafts, and interior mouldings of the east window. The priest's door is a copy from Wells of a cinque-foiled canopied doorway, with crockets, finial, and bosses.

The steeple consists of a disengaged tower, surmounted by a brooch spire, at the west end of the north aisles, of three unequal stages, flanked by square-set buttresses of four stages, the upper stage diminishing and dying into the tower a few feet below the spire cornice. The brooch spire rises from the cornice, charged with ball flowers, and has the gussets or haunches springing from the angles carried high up the diagonal faces of the octagon.

THE DIPLOMA QUESTION.

SEEING that the question of making architects legally diplomaed is being mooted in your journal, I beg to send in my earnest and most hearty adherence to any good system adopted to obtain that end, and would propose that you should invite all our professional brethren to do the same: we then should see how strong we are. Perhaps the Institute might be Jealous of such a proceeding, and if so, rather than not obtain the assistance and co-operation of so powerful a body, let us entreat them to take this praiseworthy object in their own hands, for social distinction is the absorbing end and aim of the mass of Englishmen; and it is most desirable it should be so. Now, at present the architect is in a most anomalous position: he is by the great mass of the community looked on as something between the professional man and the tradesman, and with justice, since his function is so often usurped by the builder, and by unqualified and inferior men. Is it not most irritating that a man, who for years and years has studied architecture, not only as a compilation of brick, wood, and mortar, but as a fine art, and who appreciate the beauties, and knows the difficulties of such study, should be superseded by one who *cannot* possess his qualifications? Is there not a broad gap between the drug seller and the drug prescriber, the druggist and the physician? There is and ought to be; but it is mainly owing to the diploma that it is so; and such should be the case with architects and builders. I consider that the superior education in art, and the study requisite to make an architect, give him a just, reasonable, and legal right to assert his superiority and have it allowed; and that his present position is inferior to what he is properly entitled to hold, once having been recognized as duly qualified, and enrolled into a legalized body. In no occupation are there more quacks than in architecture; and to destroy this set of men, who live upon the brains, the talent, the heart-breakings of the educated but poor or unassisted, I am sure a diploma is necessary. How many architects take pupils and send them out in the world after three or five years, almost as ignorant as they took them? and how many would dare to do this if they thought that the efficiency of their instruction would, at the end of that time, be tested by a legalized examination? In fine, everything seems to me to demand this innovation. It is to the interest of ourselves, and the public as well, that we should be incorporated into a legal profession, and that it should be done quickly.

J. B. Waring.

I have read with much satisfaction Mr. French's observations on the education of an architect, and the advantages that would and must arise from an establishment such as he proposes. At present, the young men of the day enjoy but few more advantages than they did fifty years ago. A young man is put into an architect's office (perhaps with a large premium) for six or seven years, and during that period he has little or no attention paid by the principal to his education as an architect, or to qualify him for one. He has seldom an opportunity of visiting buildings to study construction or the finishing of an edifice; he is left to draw out the orders, and find the best way of accomplishing this; he has seldom any explanation given, either in this or any other portion of the routine of business; and is it to be wondered at that, when he is out of his time, he knows *so little?* After he quits the office there is no institution open to him of an evening for practical instruction,—no general architectural library,—no collection of working models or drawings to refer to,—no models of buildings,—no practical experiments, or lectures in a lecture-room. It has hitherto been urged, and it cannot be too often repeated, that the Institute of the British Architects does not hold out sufficient encouragement, or combine sufficient advantages, for the rising generation. Till this is done, a young man must and would labour under great disadvantages in taking a diploma in architecture,—a point very desirable to render the profession what it ought to be, both respectable and efficient.

A. S.

HERTFORD GAOL-DRAINAGE.

With reference to a paragraph in our last number, headed, "Effect of Bad Drainage," mentioning the verdict of a jury which attributed the ravages of the cholera in Hertford County Gaol to the want of drainage there, and that the coroner had, in accordance with their request, drawn the attention of the justices to the fact,—we have received a letter from Mr. Thomas Smith, the architect, couched in terms which might have been more courteous, expressing astonishment that we "should be capable of publishing and adopting as our own opinion [which we did not do] the sapient notions of a country coroner's jury, without inquiring into facts;" and calling on us to reprint the following paragraph from the *Herts Mercury* of the 17th inst.:—"In consequence of the letter addressed to the magistrates by the coroner, and forwarded to the Secretary of State, a careful investigation has been made by the inspector of prisons, the result of which is that no certain conclusion can be arrived at as to the cause of the disease. The drainage of the prison has been completely renewed since the cholera prevailed in January last, and Dr. Davies is decidedly of opinion that the drainage is not the cause of the recent attack. Every possible effort to improve the drainage of the gaol has been made for many years past; and we believe that further improvement is under consideration; but the difficulties in the way of making a perfect drainage (from local circumstances) is very great, and hitherto have been insurmountable."

The tone assumed by Mr. Smith in his letter was quite uncalled for, and would have justified its consignment to the paper basket. The paragraph, from a local informant, simply mentioned an occurrence, confirmed in every particular by Mr. Smith himself, and so far from desiring to be "guilty of the bad taste of indirectly casting a stigma on him," whom we did not mention or refer to in the slightest degree, or indeed on any person, we added a couple of lines showing we could scarcely reconcile the verdict with our impression that improvements had recently been made in the prison. We should be the last to give currency to an erroneous statement affecting any architect, but it is not usually necessary to inquire into the correctness of the verdict of a jury before publishing it. We should be quite satisfied if all architects had the same consideration for us that we have for them.

NOTES IN THE PROVINCES.

A new dock (the Sidon) has just been completed and opened at Portsmouth. It is the seventh in the establishment, and constitutes an arm of the new basin for steamers. Its length is 305 feet, breadth of entrance 80 feet, depth 32 feet, containing 21 feet of water at lowest spring tide. The materials used in its construction are stated by a Hampshire contemporary to have comprised 52,800 cubic feet of beech timber; 20,800 cubic feet of Purbeck stone, 16,660 tons of shingle; 10,300 cubic feet of Portland stone; 2,954,300 bricks; 119,960 cubic feet of granite; 1,018 cwt. of iron, in pile shoes, &c. The actual cost of the dock is 67,000*l*. The inlet docks (other arms of the great basin, opposite the Sidon dock), now in part built, also under Mr. Rolt's contract, and for which an immense amount of material is on the ground, will be proceeded with next year.——The visiting justices of the county of Worcester have received tenders for erecting their pauper lunatic asylum. They have accepted the estimate of Mr. Thos. Haines, whose tender was 23,500*l*.——The Bristol iron-works have been sold piecemeal by auction. The sale commenced on 22nd ult., and was to conclude on Friday. The breaking up of these extensive works commenced with the sale of tools and materials, in which were many of the most improved machines by Nasmyth, Fairbairn, Hicks, Whitworth, Fox, Morgan, Haley, Sharp, Roberts, and other makers; then followed the machinery of the old erecting-shop, forge-shop fitted with steam-engines, lift-hammers, anvils, &c., smiths' shops, anchor-smiths' shops, brass foundry, copper-smith's shops, millwrights' shop, saw-mills, iron-foundry, &c. The sale throughout, according to the *Bristol Journal*, has been well attended by buyers from most of the engineering firms in Great Britain and the continent, and the lots have been well contested, and brought in most cases a fair value. The freehold and premises were sold for 11,470*l*.——Some improvements are in progress at Buxton, particularly a pile of buildings to be called "Winster-place," with first class hotel and shops, forming a frontage of 150 feet, on the site of the old Angel Inn and other premises. Mr. Worth, of Sheffield, supplied the design.——It is intended to erect a memorial window in Chester Cathedral in honour of the late Mr. G. E. Anson, son of the Dean of Chester.——At the Liverpool Police Court, lately, a builder, Mr. William Clegg, appeared in an information preferred against him by Mr. Rishton, the building surveyor, for erecting a store-room to premises occupied as an eating-house, in Preeson's-row, in contravention of the Act of Parliament, and without notice given to the surveyor. The defendant excused himself by saying that his men erected the building, and he was ignorant of it until it was completed. The surveyor said, that on former occasions the defendant blamed his men. The place in question was built over the privies and ash-pits. Mr. Rushton fined the defendant 5*l*., adding that no man permitted his servants to work at places and not know what they were doing. The erection will be taken down.——Trinity Church, Runcorn, has been re-opened after its enlargement and other improvement. A new chancel and a stained glass window have been added, and the pews extended and improved, with 100 additional sittings, or 900 in all. The ceiling has been removed, the roof timbers dressed and stained, and the spars plastered.——The new church of St. Mark, Ocker-hill, Tipton, was consecrated on Tuesday week. It will accommodate 640 persons. The windows are filled with stained glass, by Messrs. Chance, of Birmingham. The font is of Caen stone, by Mr. Peter Hollins, of Birmingham. The chancel is floored with Minton's encaustic tiles. This church was erected by grants from the Lichfield Diocesan Church Extension Society. The contractor was Mr. J. E. Hall, of Nottingham. In the original design a spire surmounts the building, but the funds are short 250*l*., even without this addition.——The first stone of a new national school for the labouring classes was laid at Spofforth, on Wednesday week. The cost will be about 650*l*., of which Colonel Wyndham has presented 400*l*., besides the site. The plan was supplied by Mr. Parsons, of Harewood.——About 2,500*l*. have been subscribed for the erection of a new church at Ambleside, to cost about 4,000*l*., exclusive of east window, organ, &c. Wordsworth has contributed 30*l*., Lady Le Fleming 500*l*., and Mr. Benson, the clergyman (who has already built a parsonage), 1,000*l*. more. ——The extension of the Leith pier, and the construction of the spacious new harbour, are in active progress, together with a line of railway to meet the low-water pier, whence the largest steamers will sail at all times of tide.

THE PARIS AND STRASBURG RAILWAY STATION.

Cannot you give us the name of the architect of the new railway station at Paris, shown in a recent number? As to that design, there is something striking and good in it; but a little more study in working out the ideas, and working up the composition, would have rendered the *good* a great deal *better*, if only by weeding out some defects, among which is the intolerably gross solecism and palpable absurdity of a balustrade placed upon the sloping sides of a gable or roof. If the architect has "thought for himself" in other respects, he was surely not thinking at all when he did that,—for, besides being an absurdity, it is such a deformity also, that it discredits his taste no less than his judgment. The plan being a mere diagram, it is impossible to understand from it how the central portico or arcade is disposed internally, and whether there are other arches and columns behind those seen in front. Another matter which requires explanation is the large arch,—it not being apparent from the engraving whether it forms a semi-dome within, or a semi-cylindrical vault.

Z.

*** We believe that the architect of the station is Mons. Duquesneit. There are other arches and columns behind those seen in front. The large arch is simply in the thickness of the front wall. The building has an iron roof, of which we shall probably speak again. The zinc covering was laid by the Vieille Montagne Zinc Mining Company.

PARSONAGE HOUSES.

At a meeting of the Oxford Architectural Society held last week, Mr. J. Billing read a paper on "Parsonage Houses," of which the following is a summary:—The parsonage should be within view of the church, and in strict accordance with those feelings which its consecrated character calls forth. Old English domestic architecture, with its high-pitched roofs and substantial character, is best suited to fulfil this condition: it is also capable of being adapted to the peculiar materials of the respective localities, which should always be made use of if possible, for economy and to avoid singularity, at the same time this style need not have the appearance of poverty. There are but few early examples of parsonage houses, for until the Reformation, the clergy lived mostly in abbeys and other religious houses; hence no trace is found of isolated residences, erected prior to that period, which will accord with the parsonage of the present day. The half-timbered houses at first prevailed from motives of economy, but their unsubstantial character was soon discovered, and stone gradually came into re-use, but less worked than in the previous collegiate style, which builders would naturally imitate.

Servile adhesion to ancient models cannot be required, and in the use of mediæval domestic architecture there will be found no sacrifice of any of the comforts which the wants and wishes of the present generation demand. The points to be attended to for a parsonage are—*Its position* near the church, because of the associations before alluded to, and for the convenience of the clergyman. 2. The *immediate site* should not be on too retentive a soil: the non-absorbent qualities of clay render a house built thereon uncomfortable, and to a certain degree unhealthy. 3. The materials and style as before stated. 4. The size should not be always suited to the family which is intended primarily to inhabit it: it is built for succeeding generations, and therefore should not be too large for the pastor's means,—generally a good dining-room, drawing-room, study, and waiting-hall, with offices, and seven bed-rooms, at a cost of 1,100*l.* or 1,200*l.*, is sufficient. The parsonage, in its external effect, and in its internal arrangement, should be a place for calm and holy meditation, without unnecessary decorations, where want or sorrow must often in its application for pity grudge the expenditure which might have given relief. It should, on the contrary, be the permanent comfort of the locality outwardly evidencing, as well as nurturing within its walls, those devout sympathies which are peculiarly a pastor's privilege and delight.*

ST. STEPHEN'S, WALBROOK, LONDON.

I went on the 15th to the beautiful church of St. Stephen, at Walbrook. The day being one of the most memorable I had ever known—a day of thanksgiving by a Christian people for divine mercy in the withdrawal of a plague, I felt desirous of hearing a great Christian orator on so signal an occasion. I thought the preacher there would be equal to it, and so he was, as far as human powers could make him so. For in the noble discourse he delivered, seemingly without any notes or hints, Dr. Croly never faltered once for a word, and anything grander than that oration you would look for in vain, either in Barrow, Bossuet, Blair, Massillon, or Robert Hall. What a chain of argument! What fine images! What harmony of diction!

But, Sir, when I looked up and about me, and saw that gem of architecture, in which the orator stood, how I blushed for my country! I shall not attempt to describe the precocious decay of that exquisite temple: the walls, the pillars, the ceiling, the beautiful dome itself, the whole is getting black with grime, and injured by the weather, so that the very light of heaven seems to come sparingly into the house of God, and to frown upon the barbarity of our citizens. Let me entreat you, Sir, to do something to awaken their sympathy, if not their shame.

J. T. S.

⁎ More than two years ago (vol. v., p. 273) we pointed out the miserable condition of this church, in an article which excited some attention at the time, but led to nothing, in consequence of the involved state of the parish accounts. Since then, however, if we understand rightly, the differences have been arranged, so that there seems less reason why the church should be suffered to go to ruin or remain in dirt and degradation.—Ed.

Fall of Railway Arches, Camden Town.—On Sunday morning, the 18th, seven large brick arches, being part of the East and West India Dock and Birmingham Junction Railway, in the Kentish-Town-road, fell to the ground. We had written a notice of the occurrence, but in consequence of two (perhaps erroneous) letters, are led to postpone it. It is a very serious matter, and should be inquired into rigorously.. We would suggest that the coroner should summon a jury to determine the cause.

* A paper on "Parsonage Houses," by the late Mr. Bartholomew, will be found in one of our early numbers.—*Church Chimneys.*—At the same meeting Mr. Parker stated that he had received a letter from Salisbury, with reference to the old fire-place mentioned at the last meeting, and that it appeared that the opening was originally a doorway and staircase to the rood loft, and was being restored to its proper use. He also stated that the ornamental chimneys used in domestic architecture were the best for carrying up flues in a church. The President stated that a fire-place in some remote corner of the church, with a brick flue going through the building, was the best method for warming it.

Books.

The Ecclesiastical and Architectural Topography of England. J. H. Parker, Oxford and London.

The new Part of this amplification of Rickman's notices is appropriated to Buckinghamshire, and has been prepared chiefly from the notes of Mr. W. Caveler. The publisher proposes to abandon the alphabetical arrangement of the counties, and to issue them in such order as will best consist with the making of each diocese complete, before entering on another. It will form a very valuable book for reference when finished.

Antiquarian Gleanings in the North of England. Drawn and etched by W. B. Scott. No. 2. London: Geo. Bell.

This second part has ten plates, including an ancient pulpit, formerly belonging to Jarrow Church, a pastoral staff, the frith stool of Hexham, &c. The pulpit is an interesting example, and would seem to be of foreign work; the staff is of the Early English period. Mr. Scott has scarcely the same mastery of Gothic forms as of Italian.

Choice Examples of Art Workmanship, Mediæval and Modern. Bogue, and Cundall. No. 1.

The intention of this serial is to give representations of works of skill in the manufacture of metals and pottery, carvings of wood and ivory, &c. Beauty, not singularity, is to be the guide in the selection. Let the editor adhere to this, and the collection will be really valuable. The metal canopy, by George Syrlein, is fanciful and elegant.

Miscellanea.

Gas-lighting. — The Salford Council Committee in management of the Corporation Gas Works report, that *notwithstanding* the reduction of charges for gas from 6s. and 5s. to 5s. and 4s. 6d. a thousand cubic feet (or rather *in consequence* of that reduction it might have been said), the gas rental shows an increase over previous returns, and "they are confirmed in their previous opinion, that a very large increase in the consumption of gas will be the result of the reduction in the price." The rental in 1848 was 12,770*l.* odds,—in 1849 it rose to about 15,000*l.* The consumption in private houses, the committee believe, would be still further and greatly increased by hiring out meters at a small quarterly charge. The populous district of Old Trafford and the west-end of the Stretford roads is about to have the benefits of the Gas Act extended to it, according to the *Manchester Spectator*.——We hear somewhat contradictory reports as to the introduction of the hydro-carbon gas into Southport. Several postponements, arising from an insufficiency of gas to fill the pipes, are said to have occasioned some disappointment, but the *Liverpool Standard* states, that though on trial the gas at first appeared very dim, it at length was got to burn with brilliancy. The lighting of Belfast under this patent depends, it seems, on the result of the Southport experiment.——Downham-market is being lighted with gas, not only in its streets and shops, but in many of its private dwellings. The church has also been lighted.——The Central Gas Consumers' Company for lighting the City of London and its liberties, &c., is quietly mustering its forces. Notice has been given of the intention to apply for an Act of incorporation in the ensuing session of Parliament, with all necessary powers. The directors are said to have entered into formal written engagements for delivery of gas of superior purity and illuminating power into the company's gas-holders, at 1s. 4½d. per 1,000 cubic feet, and 4,680 extensive consumers within the city are said to have already contracted to take 270,000,000 feet, at a maximum price of 4s. per 1,000. When the consumption from the company reaches 750,000,000, they promise to reduce their charge to 3s. per 1,000, and in either case to clear a dividend of 10 per cent.——A company of gas engineers and contractors, we observe, are offering to manufacture gas, either on a small scale or a large, so as to be saleable in all cases at 3s. per 1,000 cubic feet.

Projected Works.—Advertisements have been issued for tenders by 11th December for the re-erection of Llanfihangel-yr-Arth-bridge, over the river Troy; by 28th instant, for the erection of an iron shed, 80 feet by 18 feet, for the Commercial Gas Company, Stepney; by 15th December, for the erection of a banking-house at Northampton; by same date, for the erection of the Northampton Exchange; by 1st December, for alterations and additions to Chelsea workhouse; by 31st December, for 10,000 feet of 3-inch York paving, and 700 yards run of 6 by 12 Aberdeen granite curb; by 30th instant, for the erection of schools at Brymbro (Wrexham), for 300 children, with teachers' house; by same date, for the erection of schools at Minera (Wrexham) for 300 children, with teachers' house; by 13th Dec., for the maintenance of about 27 miles of permanent way of the Great Western Railway,—also of 14 miles of same,—also for the maintenance and working of cranes, weigh bridges, &c., at Bristol, Bath, and elsewhere,—and for the supply and fixing of four new weigh bridges; by 28th inst., for the erection of a dwarf wall with palisades at Sheffield; by 26th, for additions to and alterations of a farm-house and offices at Barham, Hunts; by 11th December, for the supply of 12 luggage brake vans for the Great Northern Railway; by 28th inst., for cast-steel files and rasps, &c., for the East-India Company; by 12th December, for the erection of the Lincolnshire County Lunatic Asylum; and by 4th December, for cutting pipe trenches and carting pipes for the Manchester Corporation Waterworks.

Competitions.—Advertisements have been issued for plans, &c., with estimates, by 20th December, for an enlargement of the Leicester workhouse,—premium 80*l.*, or commission, as advertised; and by 5th January, 1850, for a general map with design for drainage of district of St. Thomas the Apostle,—premiums twenty guineas and five guineas, as advertised.

Erection of Dwellings by Parishes.—You state in your last number but one that the inhabitants of Lambeth are about to apply to Parliament for powers to erect habitations for the working classes, and it would seem that the proposed Act is to be a local one, not a general one, enabling all parochial bodies to avail themselves of it, without necessitating the great expense of a separate Act in each case. As the latter was the idea which I wished to convey in my communication which appeared in your paper of Oct. 6, I again address you, in order to make myself quite clear. The suggestion to which I then referred is contained in a little pamphlet by Mr. C. Cochrane, entitled "How to Improve the Homes of the People," and is as follows:—"In my opinion, we cannot have an effectual remedy without the aid of the legislature; and I would submit that it is very desirable that parish authorities should, by Act of Parliament, be invested with the power to regulate the dwellings of the tradespeople and labouring classes,—that is to say, wherever they do not reach a certain standard of essential comfort at reasonable charges, and which must be considered the *standard of civilization*, or of a *fit social state*; then the parish authorities should have the right to erect or lease houses, to be let out to the tradespeople and working classes, and the profit, after the payment of rent and taxes, ought to be for the benefit of the parish. I know there are many thousands of hard-working people who would be well contented if the standard of fit human habitations were regulated by the state of the dwellings provided for the monkeys at the Zoological Gardens—for not only are they clean, spacious, and airy, but they are carefully kept cool in summer and warm in winter. Indeed, I think I may venture to say that large numbers would rest contented if they could have secured to them the same accommodation as is provided in the spacious and well-cleansed dens of the lions, or even the bears in these gardens."—A Londoner.

Proposed National Gallery for Scotland.—We understand that Mr. Playfair's final plans for the contemplated National Gallery to be erected in Edinburgh, have been transmitted to the Lords of the Treasury. The design is said to be Grecian, and the site of the structure will be south-east of the Royal Institution.

JESUS COLLEGE CHAPEL, CAMBRIDGE.—On All Saints'-day the choir was re-opened. The series of Early English arches in the triforium of the tower is no longer concealed from view from below by the flat ceiling above the great pier arches. A north aisle has been built to the choir and north transept on the foundations of one existing during the time of the nunnery, and communicating with the choir by two arches, found complete (as were two on the south side), embedded in the masonry of the wall. According to the local press, other arches, communicating with the north transept, were discovered and opened, but have been filled with stone screen-work for the sake of strength. In the choir itself, the east window, a modern one with glass by Willement, has been removed, and a lancet of three lights and two panels, supposed to be an exact reproduction of the original, substituted. The side walls have been brought down to their ancient height, and a high-pitched roof of trussed rafters of early character raised on them. It is divided into square panels, varnished and decorated with green, vermilion, white, and gold. The aisle roof is blue, with stars in white, and the rafters oak colour, the principals relieved with vermilion. The floor is of black and red tiles between the stalls, and of black and white marble, mixed with encaustic tiles, in the sacrarium, three black marble steps forming the ascent to the altar. There is a lectern of brass in the centre of the stalls, and two brass candlesticks stand on the altar steps. The organ in the north aisle is built on the old models, by Messrs. Bishop, of London. Painted windows for the east end are in preparation, and money is ready for placing stained glass also in the two south windows of the choir. Without the screen the tower piers have been repaired and cleaned, as likewise the triforium.

THE LATE WILLIAM ETTY, R.A.—Many of our readers will have already heard with regret of the death of this eminent artist at York, his native city, on Tuesday in last week. From his early childhood Mr. Etty gave manifestations of his future genius. The first panels on which he drew, as he himself states, were the boards of his father's shop floor,—his first crayon a farthing's worth of white chalk; and this at a time when scarcely able to walk without leading strings. He died as he lived—still learning. Indeed, it may be said with truth that he has fallen a victim to perpetual toil. A hard day's work with brush and palette was but a part of his professional occupation during the four and twenty hours. No sooner did he lay down the implements of the master, than he took up those of the student—in an attendance at the life schools as regular and industrious as that of any youth engaged there in learning the elements of his art. An agreeable autobiography of Mr. Etty will be found in a late number of the *Art-Journal*. His beautiful and well-known works are so numerous, that if put together, as he remarked, they would nearly cover the walls of Westminster Hall. The exhibition of his collected works at the Adelphi seems to have been an ominous prelude to his own dissolution, though in these he may be said still to live with us in honour, notwithstanding he has passed away from us in flesh.

"DETAILS OF A FRENCH CASEMENT."—We are sorry to find that some of the figures and letters of reference on the diagrams last week do not show. We are disposed to think, however, that the whole is understandable, nevertheless, when looked into.

A NOTE OF ACKNOWLEDGMENT.—Sir: I have often been much impressed with the great advantage your valuable paper is to the building trade, and to the architectural and surveying professions. I have no doubt others have been equally so, and I think they should not merely let you know it now and then, but try and extend the circulation of the paper in return. I give you herewith a proof of one advantage to me. I received your last number this morning, and at my breakfast table, as is my usual custom, I overlooked it a little, and read your leading article. In the afternoon I received the (enclosed) letter as to rough plate glass, and in answering it, should probably have committed myself but for your leading article.

Ringwood. SYDNEY PONTIFEX.

IMPROVEMENT OF CHELTENHAM.—The report of Mr. Cresy upon the sewerage, supply of water, and health of the inhabitants of Cheltenham, has just been issued. The inspector recommends the establishment of a local Board of Health, the laying down a system of main sewers at the backs of all houses, the draining all houses by tubular drains, establishment of water closets, abolishing cesspools, &c., preventing sewage water from contaminating the streams flowing around the town, regulating lodging-houses, markets, &c., establishing one general slaughter-house out of the town, laying down pipes and reservoirs for distributing the sewage waters, regulating the width of courts and streets; also, "To maintain the burial-grounds in a proper state, and provide for additional interments out of the town. To remove more frequently the decomposing refuse from the yards and areas of the inhabitants, to collect all the manure, dust, ashes, and sewer-waters, which are valuable to the farmer, and to dispose of them for the benefit of the inhabitants. To drain a sufficient area of land for the purpose of obtaining an abundance of pure wholesome water, to construct reservoirs, and lay down mains for the constant supply of water to every householder."

ANOTHER BOILER EXPLOSION.—The *report* of one of these fatalities is ever echoing through the press, while another, and another still, is heard of booming in the distance. The last we have now to re-echo occurred at Stockport on Tuesday week. A workman was scalded to death, the skin peeling off his body in the attempt to extricate him from the ruins while yet alive. The inquest-jury have directed the coroner to give Sir George Grey what will now be at least a *second* warning of evil to come. The following is the resolution adopted on the present occasion:—"That, with a view to avoid as much as possible such accidents, a copy of these depositions be laid before Sir George Grey, with a request that he will be pleased to take means for arranging that certificates of the capability of those undertaking the charge of steam engines be lodged with the inspectors of factories in their several districts, before the overseers of steam engines be allowed to employ them."

FIRES IN NOBLEMEN'S MANSIONS.—Cliefden House, near Maidenhead, lately purchased from the late Sir George Warrender's executors by the Duke of Sutherland, was destroyed by fire on Friday in last week, the wings and out-buildings only being saved by the demolition of the intervening colonnades. The premises burnt extended in one direction to nearly 100 feet in length, and were 60 feet in height. A large portion of the valuable and interesting contents were lost, but several of the more choice of the immense collection of paintings were saved, together with much costly furniture, musical instruments, &c. Some workmen were employed in the library when the fire took place, and blame is attributed to them, but there is some ground for believing that it arose from bond timbers running into one of the flues. The mansion is said to have been fully insured.——Blenheim Palace has escaped a like fatality, originating in a building at the back of the stables, but discovered just in time to save the palace.——The Duke of Buccleuch's Palace at Dalkeith has run the same risk from a fire discovered in a servants' room, but attributed to those old offenders the plumbers, who were repairing the roof, and allowed their embers to melt the lead and fire the woodwork beneath.

INSTITUTION OF CIVIL ENGINEERS.—The meeting on Tuesday, November 20, was wholly occupied by a renewed discussion upon the Grimsby Dock. It was closed by the Dean of Westminster giving an example of the urgency for engineers becoming geologists; and on Mr. Rendel stating, that the clay at Leith was so hard as to require to be blasted, and yet that, when exposed to a small current of water, it was completely dissolved within a fortnight,—he at once explained it, as arising from the presence of a multitude of minute particles of mica, whose non-adhesive properties produced the speedy disintegration of the mass.

ARCHITECTURAL ASSOCIATION. — At a meeting held on Friday, the 16th, Mr. J. K. Colling read a paper on "Architectural Botany." A brisk discussion followed.

OXFORD COLLEGE-BUILDINGS.—Extensive improvements have been effected on the Corpus Christi College-buildings this year. Those at the eastern boundary, adjoining the entry to Christ Church meadow, have been pulled down and entirely rebuilt. In the interior of the college a new common room is being fitted up. At Merton College a new drain is in course of construction, for which earthenware pipes, 18 inches in diameter, are to be laid down to the river. The chief ornamental work of the summer has been in the chapel of this college. The transept was re-roofed some three or four years since, under the direction of Mr. Blore; but the society have now placed themselves in the hands of Mr. Butterfield; and under his management a new oak roof has been placed on the choir, of the original high pitch, some unsightly monuments removed, and the sedilia restored. The stone-work has been also cleaned and the walls fresh plastered. At St. John's College a new set of rooms is being formed in a section of the quandrangle forming the range to the right of the tower which surmounts the main entrance from St. Giles's-street. The tower over the principal gateway is also being refaced. In Magdalen Hall, at one side of the quadrangle bounded by New College-lane, the buildings are being heightened, at the expense of the principal. At New College they are slating the cloisters. At Magdalen College, in the space adjoining the Grove and fronting High-street, men have been employed in clearing out the foundation for the erection of the new grammar-school, &c. At Oriel College also, and St. Mary Hall, restorations have been in progress during vacation. The refacing of the theatre is also being proceeded with. We could not speak well of *all* that has been done.

SHERBORNE CHURCH RESTORATION: PEW PROPERTY.—In restoring the nave of Sherborne Church, a large pew in the 'Leweston Aisle' was lately knocked down by the workmen, whereon a question arose as to the proprietorship, when it appeared that the Leweston Aisle, or St. Catherine's Chapel, was granted, on 12th January, 1587, to the Fitz-James family, by intermarriage in which, the Leweston family came into possession, and held it till the Leweston estate fell into the hands of Mr. R. Gordon. The vestry, in absence of the vicar, waiving the point of law whether the heir or the assignee of the Fitz-James family, or the parish by lapse of heirship, were the right proprietor, resolved that Mr. Gordon be authorized to repair and use the aisle as possessor of the Leweston estate. The demolition had been effected without the authority of the Restoration Committee.

VERY BLIND BUILDERS.—These are the tenders for erecting a residence and dispensary adjoining Ratcliff Workhouse, London; Mr. Dunch, surveyor:—

Bryant	£555
Stewart	520
Cooper	478
H. Hill	458
W. M. Hill	450
Curtis	434
Witby	398
Wilson	377
Rudkin	370
Taylor	355
Ellison	349
Darke	347
Judd	337
Whiting	330
Perry	328
Philbeam	325
Whitby	312
Hall	299
Blackburn (accepted)	269

TENDERS

For the erection of four dwelling-houses, Newark-upon-Trent; Mr. T. C. Hine, architect:—

Lane	£1,850
Shaw and Co.	1,834
Tinker	1,828
Keene and Co.	1,821
Marshall	1,821
Lindley	1,783
Jackson	1,766
Smith	1,720
Ferguson (accepted)	1,675
Dudgeon	1,349

MEETINGS OF SCIENTIFIC BODIES

Held during the ensuing week.

TUESDAY, Nov. 27.—Institution of Civil Engineers, 8 p.m.
WEDNESDAY, Nov. 28.—Society of Arts, 8 p.m.
THURSDAY, Nov. 29.—Society of Antiquaries, 8 p.m.
FRIDAY, Nov. 30.—Royal Society, 4 p.m. Anniversary.

TO CORRESPONDENTS.

"Prospects of Architecture."—Conclusion next week.

"J. E. G." (Manchester), "J. B.," (Reading), "Subscriber" (we must decline deciding), "W. A. P.," "W. S." (the fault has been with those who send us lists), "T. J.," "J. J." (Gloucester), "Futurus" (some of the provincial towns have local Buildings Acts. Within the metropolitan districts an "insulated" building (for definition see the Buildings Act), is not controlled by the Act), "G. C." (we are sorry that we cannot advise. The copies were posted); "Vitruvius Vindex," "Zeta" (next week), "Messrs. F.," "Subscriber" Derby (give us names and amounts), "Milo" (the subject of damp walls has been treated on several occasions in THE BUILDER, and may be referred to), "R. P.," "Dr. U.," "W. J. W." (if a reader, will know that we are compelled to decline pointing out books), "An Old Subscriber," "S. S.," "Four Years' Subscriber" (we have not seen the print, and therefore cannot reply) "W. P.," "Mr. W." (we shall endeavour to see the building shortly), "M. H.," "Hopeful," "An Operative" (next week), "S. P." (we are not disposed to question the award), "R. H.," "E. P. S.," "C. F., Jun.," "A. A. W." (write to Secretary of Institute, 16, Lower Grosvenor-street), "An Admirer of Architecture."

Books Received.—Next week.

NOTICE.—All communications respecting *advertisements* should be addressed to the "Publisher," and not to the "Editor:" all other communications should be addressed to the EDITOR, and *not* to the Publisher.

ADVERTISEMENTS.

ARCHITECTS', BUILDERS', and GENERAL FIRE and LIFE INSURANCE COMPANY, 69, Lombard-street, London.

CHAIRMAN, SYDNEY SMIRKE, Esq., A.R.A.

TRUSTEES.

T. L. Donaldson, Esq. | A. Salvin, Esq., F.S.A.
S. Grimsdell, Esq. | G. Smith, Esq., F.S.A.

The rates for both Fire and Life Insurances are as low as can with safety be taken. Those for Life Insurance may be paid either yearly, half-yearly, or quarterly; one-half the annual premium may be left unpaid for seven years, or one-third to the end of life. Thus large sums may be insured at the smallest present outlay.

Prospectuses, forms of proposals, &c., may be had at the Office 69, Lombard-street, or of the agents.

JOHN REDDISH, Manager.

FAMILY ENDOWMENT, LIFE ASSURANCE AND ANNUITY SOCIETY, 12, Chatham-place, Blackfriars, London.
CAPITAL, £500,000.

DIRECTORS.
WILLIAM BUTTERWORTH BAYLEY, Esq., Chairman.
JOHN FULLER, Esq., Deputy-Chairman.

Lewis Burroughs, Esq. | Edward Lee, Esq.
Robert Bruce Chichester, Esq. | Colonel Ouseley.
H. B. Henderson, Esq. | Major Turner.
C. H. Latouche, Esq. | Joshua Walker, Esq.

BONUS.
Thirty per cent. Bonus was added to the Society's Policies on the profit scale in 1845. The next valuation will be in January, 1852.

ANNUAL PREMIUMS WITH PROFITS.

Age 20.	Age 25.	Age 30.	Age 35.	Age 40.	Age 45.	Age 50.	Age 55.
£. s. d.	£. s. d.	£. s. d.	£. s. d.	£. s. d.	£. s. d.	£. s. d.	£. s. d.
1 17 8	2 3 1	2 9 7	2 16 2	3 5 9	3 16 2	4 10 6	5 7 8

Annuities of all kinds, as well as endowments for Children, are granted by the Society.
The usual commission allowed to Solicitors and others.

INDIA.
The Society also grants Policies to parties proceeding to or residing in India, at lower rates than any other office; also Deferred Annuities and endowments, accurately and economically framed to meet the periods of service, and add to the retiring pensions of the Civil and Military Officers of India.
Tables, &c., to be had at the Society's Office in London, or at the Office in Calcutta.

JOHN CAZENOVE, Secretary.

PATENT WROUGHT NAILS.—These Nails are submitted to the notice of Builders, Contractors, and Ship-builders, as being superior to any others, and cheaper. They have the toughness of the best hand-made nails, with far greater uniformity of make. The flat pointed rose nails are particularly recommended wherever oak or other hard wood is used; being perfectly chisel-pointed, they require no boring, and will drive into the hardest wood without splitting it, and their heads being very strong do not fly off. The patent wrought nails may be had of all Ironmongers, and an ample stock of them is kept at the warehouses of the agents, HIGGS and GEORGE, Wholesale Ironmongers, 179, Borough, London.

CHUBBS' LOCKS, FIRE-PROOF SAFES, AND CASH BOXES.

CHUBBS' PATENT DETECTOR LOCKS give perfect security from false keys and picklocks, and also detect any attempt to open them. They are made of all sizes, and for every purpose to which locks are applied, and are strong, secure, simple, and durable.
CHUBBS' PATENT LATCH, for front doors, counting-house doors, &c., is simple in construction, low in price, and quite secure. The keys are particularly neat and portable.
CHUBBS' PATENT FIRE-PROOF SAFES, BOOKCASES, CHESTS, &c., made entirely of strong wrought-iron, so as effectually to resist the falling of brick-work, timber, &c., in case of fire, and are also perfectly secure from the attacks of the most skilful burglars.
CHUBBS' CASH and DEED BOXES, fitted with the Detector Locks.
CHUBB and SON, 57, St. Paul's Churchyard, London.

By Her Majesty's Royal Letters Patent.

PITT'S PATENT SELF-ADJUSTING DOOR KNOBS AND LOOSE SPINDLES.

HART and SONS beg to invite the attention of architects, builders, and others, to their Door Furniture, mounted for PITT'S PATENTED SPINDLES. The knobs are stronger, more durable, and more elegant in form, than those in ordinary use, as the spindles, being loose, do not require the objectionable side screw. They are more readily fixed, are suitable for every description of lock now in use and, as they adjust themselves to doors of different thicknesses, without alteration, are particularly adapted for the country or for exportation.
In addition to an extensive stock of door furniture in china, crystal, amber, and opal glass, buffalo horn, ivory, ebony, brass, &c., en suite, with finger-plates, bell-pulls, and levers, new patterns of original design are constantly being added, and an order either to sketch or pattern supplied very promptly. A simple one, for example, in three days, and a more elaborate one in less than a week.—May be obtained through any Ironmonger, or direct from the proprietors and sole manufacturers, HART and SONS Wholesale Ironmongers, 53, 54, 55, Wych-street, Strand, London.
A list of prices sent on application.

THE NILE—RE-OPENING at the EGYPTIAN HALL, Piccadilly, with NEW TABLEAUX.—The new and splendid MOVING PANORAMA of the NILE, showing all the stupendous works of antiquity on its banks, from Cairo, the capital of Egypt, to the second cataract in Nubia. Painted by Henry Warren and James Fahey, from drawings made by Joseph Bonomi, during many years' residence there.—Morning, Three o'clock; Evening, Eight o'clock.—Stalls, 3s.; Pit, 2s.; Gallery, 1s.

CALIFOKNIA.—The undersigned, having been informed that shipments of GALVANIZED METAL, both in unwrought state and formed for houses, are still going forward to California, again GIVE NOTICE that they ALONE have the right of importing, selling, or using galvanized metal, of any description, in the United States, including California, and that any parties infringing their rights, by importing or selling galvanized metal in California, will subject themselves to the stoppage of their goods, and to heavy penalties, which have been already enforced in several instances.—Any parties wishing to ship either galvanized metal or houses to California, will get every information on application to the undersigned.
MOREWOOD and ROGERS, Steel-yard Wharf, Upper Thames-street, London.

THE GALVANIZED IRON COMPANY, No. 3, Mansion-house-place.
Call the particular attention of Architects, Builders, and others, to their patent process of galvanizing, or coating iron with PURE ZINC, which, from its action being chemically true, effectually and PERMANENTLY prevents RUST. The process is applicable to all sorts of iron work (whether cast or wrought) in use for building purposes—such as ROOFS, gutters, girders, floors, WATER or GAS PIPES, railings, window sashes and guards, blinds, skylight frames, chimney cowls, cisterns, screws, nails, locks, keys, chains, wire guards, &c., &c., &c. The Company undertake to supply GALVANIZED IRON, or to GALVANIZE every description of iron work, in any quantity required.—Particulars and prices at the Offices of the Company, 3, Mansion-house-place. London Galvanizing Works, Millwall, Poplar. S. VINCENT, Secretary.
N.B. This Company's patent process is applied to the roofs of the New Houses of Parliament, the sheds in the dockyards at Woolwich, Portsmouth, and Devonport, the Waterloo Station belonging to the London and North-Western Railway Company at Liverpool, and numerous other railway stations, &c., &c., with the most perfect success.

IRON ROOFING WORKS, SOUTHWARK.
Office,—3A, MANSION-HOUSE-PLACE, LONDON.
JOHN H. PORTER,
PATENTEE
Of the Corrugated Iron Beams, Girders, and Fire-proof Floors;
MANUFACTURER OF IRON ROOFS AND BUILDINGS,
Chiefly of
THE PATENT GALVANIZED IRON.
This material has been employed by J. H. PORTER for several years past in the construction of Iron Roofing for RAILWAY STATIONS and DOCKYARDS, at home and abroad; FARM BUILDINGS, FACTORIES, GASWORKS, WAREHOUSES, &c.; SUGAR-HOUSES, MEGASS and COFFEE-SHEDS, STORES, DWELLINGS, and MARKET-PLACES, in the East and West Indies, China, at the Cape of Good Hope, and in other parts of the world; Iron-bar and Strained-wire Fences, Sheep and Cattle Hurdles.

JENNINGS'S PATENT SHUTTER SHOES, INDIA-RUBBER TUBE COCKS, WATER-CLOSETS, JOINTS, VALVES, &c., are all simple in construction.—Descriptive drawings can be had on application to GEORGE JENNINGS, 29, Great Charlotte-street, Blackfriars-road.

IRON SHUTTERS.—The PATENT CONVEX REVOLVING IRON SHUTTERS are cheaper, twelve times stronger, work easier, cannot run down, and roll up in one-third less room than any other shutters made. Harcourt Quincey, Patentee.
CLARK and Co., Sole Manufacturers, and of IMPROVED DRAWN ORNAMENTAL METALLIC SASH BARS, ASTRAGALS, MOULDINGS, STALL-BOARD PLATES, &c. &c., in brass, copper, and zinc. Gas Fittings, Chandeliers, and internal Brass Fittings for Shops of every description. WROUGHT-IRON GIRDERS, HOT-WATER APPARATUS, and metal work connected with buildings. Testimonials of architects and others having them in use will be forwarded free on application to CLARK and Co., Engineers, 283, Wapping, London, or to Mr. G. BRIGSTOCK, 17, George-street, Edinburgh, Agent for Scotland.

BUNNETT and Co., ENGINEERS,
Patentees and Manufacturers of
REVOLVING IRON AND WOOD SAFETY SHUTTERS,
and of
ORNAMENTAL SASH BARS, MOULDINGS,
STALL-PLATES, &c.
FOR SHOP-FRONTS, AND OTHER WINDOWS, OR SKYLIGHTS,
IN BRASS, COPPER, ZINC, IRON, &c.
Shop-fronts completely fitted up and glazed with best plate glass. Metal works and improved machinery of all kinds for warehouses, banking-houses, &c.
BUNNETT and Co. challenge competition as to either quality or price.
Office, 26, Lombard-street, London; Works, Deptford, Kent.

B. and Co. are also Patentees and Manufacturers of Improved Bench and Flooring Clamps for Builders; Wrought Iron Diagonal Gratings, doubly-trapped self-acting Water Closets, and self-acting and self-cleansing Effluvia Traps, for Sewers, Drains, &c. &c.

CAST-IRON PIPES, IRON WORK FOR OVENS, &c.

RAIN PIPES, &c.—F. A. TIDDEMAN, St. Ann's Wharf, Earl-street, City, near Blackfriars-bridge, keeps a large stock of Rain Pipes, Heads, Shoes, Elbows, &c., half round and O. G. Gutters, Socket Pipes for Water or Gas, Flanch Pipes, Sash Weights, and other Castings; Iron Work for Bakers' Ovens of every description, fitted complete, to be had in sets or in parts.—Prices equal to all competition. Contracts taken to any extent. Goods landed. A powerful crane.

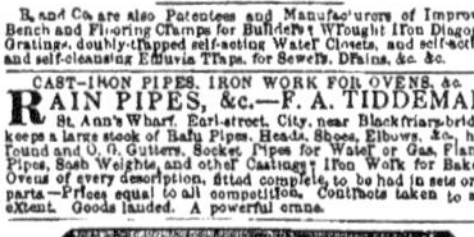

SAMUEL HOOD and Co., Castings Warehouse, 81, Upper Thames-street. REGISTERED STABLE FITTINGS. Enamelled Mangers, with double hay-racks, or with enamelled water-cistern on one side.—Also, girders, columns, hot water pipes, rain water pipes, eaves, gutters, sash weights, &c., at the lowest prices.

FLEXIBLE INDIA-RUBBER PIPES AND TUBING, For Railway Companies, Brewers, Distillers, Fire Engines, Gas Companies, Gardening and Agricultural purposes, &c.—J. L. HANCOCK'S patent VULCANIZED INDIA-RUBBER HOSE-PIPES are made to stand hot liquor, and acids without injury—do not become hard or stiff in any temperature (but are always perfectly flexible) and as they require no application of oil or dressing, are particularly well adapted for Fire Engines, Pumps, Gas, Beer Engines, Gardens, Liquid Manure, and all purposes where a perfectly flexible pipe is required. Made all sizes, from ½ inch bore upwards, and of any length to order. Vulcanized India rubber garden hose fitted with brass-taps, copper branch and roses complete, ready to be attached to pumps, water-butts, or cisterns. Sole manufacturer, JAMES LYNE HANCOCK, Goswell-mews, Goswell-road, London.
N.B. Vulcanized India-rubber washers of all sizes for joints or hot-water and steam pipes, and vulcanized sheet rubber any thickness for all kinds of joints, and other purposes.

PROTECTION from FIRE, and GREAT ECONOMY in BUILDING.—A pamphlet, descriptive of the method by which both these important objects are secured, may be obtained on application to Messrs. FOX and BARRETT, 46, Leicester-square.

THE MODERATOR STOVE GRATE is confidently recommended for the purity of its heated air, as the most delicate lungs will not be affected by it; great economy of fuel, burning only 26 lbs. weight of coal in twelve hours, and perfect ventilation, with most cheerful appearance. May be seen in daily use at the inventors and sole manufacturers', METHLEY'S, 53, Frith-street, Soho. Price 6l. for third size.

WARMING by HOT WATER.—J. WEEKS and Co., King's-road, Chelsea, Efficient and Economical HOT-WATER APPARATUS MANUFACTURERS, for heating buildings of every description to which heat is applicable or desirable. It is particularly adapted for warming professional offices and entrance-halls, either a single room or any number of rooms, also churches, warehouses, horticultural buildings, &c. The boilers now used by J. Weeks and Co. consume but a small quantity of fuel, keep up a regular temperature, and only require attendance once in twenty-four hours. To be seen in extensive operation at their Manufactory and Show Establishment, King's-road, Chelsea. References may be had to any extent, where their apparatuses have been fixed for many years.

FULKES' IRONMONGERY and STOVE WAREHOUSE, 91 and 92, Park-street, Camden Town.
Elliptic Stoves, with double backs .... 3½d. per inch.
Register ditto, ditto .... 5d. per inch.
Sash Weights .... 5s. 9d. per cwt.
Iron Rain-water pipe..... 2½ inch, 10d.; 3 inch, 1s. 1d. per yard.
4½ inch O.G. Guttering .... 1s. per yard.
6 inch Rim Locks, with patent spindles .... 14s. per dozen.
Mortice Locks, with patent spindles .... 33s. per dozen.
Delivered carriage free, within 5 miles.

TO ARCHITECTS, BUILDERS, &c.

HAYWARD, BROTHERS, late H. HENLY and Co., WHOLESALE IRONMONGERS, and Manufacturers of KITCHEN-RANGES, STOVES, &c., 196, Blackfriars-road, and 117, Union-street, Borough.
Strong Self-acting Kitchen Ranges, with Back Boiler and Oven and Wrought Bars:—
3 ft. £3 | 3 ft. 3 in. £3. 10s. | 3 ft. 6 in. £3. 15s. | 3 ft. 9 in. £4 | 4 ft. £4. 10s.
Henly's Patent Improved, with back Boiler and Wrought Iron Oven:—3 ft. £5 | 3 ft. 3 in. £5. 10s. | 3 ft. 6 in. £6. 5s. | 3 ft. 9 in. £6. 10s. | 4 ft. £7.
Best Register Stoves, at 7d., 8d., and 9d. per inch.
Do. Elliptic do. at 3½d., and 4d. do.
Manufacturer of WOLFASTON'S PATENT REGISTER STOVES, a certain cure for SMOKY CHIMNEYS, and effecting a great saving in fuel. To be seen in use daily.
Orders from the Country, accompanied with a remittance or reference, will meet with prompt attention.

TO BUILDERS and CARPENTERS.—Elliptic Stoves, double backs, 3½d. per inch. Registers, 6d., 6½d., 7½d., per inch.
Cottage Ranges, with Ovens and Boilers, 3 ft. 2 in. 40s.; 3 ft. 4 in. 42s.; 3 ft. 6 in. 44s. 3 feet Cottage Ranges, 38s.
Self-acting Ranges, with Circular Oven and Back Boiler, best Wrought Bars and Bright Fittings,
3 ft., £2 18s. 3 ft. 6, £3 7s. 4 ft., £3 15s.
Best Patent Cut Clasp.
4½d. 5d. 7d. 10d. 1s. 2d. 1s. 8d. per 1,000
3d. 4d. 6d. 8d. 10d. 20d.
Best Sheet Floor Brads, 12s. 6d. per cwt.
Best Town Glue 38s. Do. Scotch, 52s. per cwt.
Best Patent Sash Line.
4s. 9d. 5s. 6s. 6d. 7s. 6d. 10s. 12s. per gross.
1 2 3 4 5 6
At F. R. WILLIAMSON'S IRONMONGERY and STOVE WAREHOUSE, 35, Chiswell-street, Finsbury-square.
Lists of Prices had on application at the Warehouse, or by letter pre-paid, inclosing postage stamp.—Warehouse closes at 7 o'clock.

IRON FOUNDRY, 80, Goswell-street (late of Brick-lane, St. Luke's).—J. J. JONES having made great additions to his STOCK of PATTERNS, begs to inform the Trade, that he can now supply them with Plain and Ornamental Iron Columns Girders, Railings, Gates, Iron Coping, Balconies, Window Guards, Verandahs, Ornamental Staircase Panels, Iron Staircases, Tomb Enclosures, Trellis Panelling, Lamp and other Brackets, Cantilevers, Newel Bars, Water Closet Work, Area Gratings, Fly and other Wheels, Wheel Plates, &c.
BAKER'S OVEN WORK, Forge Backs and Troughs, Rain Water Pipes and Gutters, Sash Weights, Furnace Bars, Stoves, Ranges, &c., always in stock.

IRON FOUNDRY,
68, DRURY-LANE, and CHARLES-STREET, DRURY-LANE
JOSEPH GLOVER,
Solicits the attention of the Trade to his extensive Stock of PATTERNS for CASTINGS of EVERY DESCRIPTION, consisting of those for every purpose, either structural or ornamental,
Wheel Pinion and Steam-Engine Patterns; Range Stove and Hot Plate Metal.
A stock of Rain-Water Pipes, Plain and O G Guttering, Air Bricks, Sash Weights, &c. &c.
A very superior description of Boot Door, particularly suitable for internal work, being perfectly secure, and not unsightly.
ESTIMATES given for IRON ROOFING and every description of Ironwork, complete to specification, and the work executed with every attention to quality and dispatch.
GLOVER'S FOUNDRY,
168, DRURY-LANE, and CHARLES-STREET.

TO ARCHITECTS, BUILDERS, AND PAINTERS.

OAK STAINS in every shade, for CHURCHES, RAILWAY STATIONS, &c.—ESTWICK and Co. respectfully announce that they can supply the above at 6s. per gallon. Contracts executed in town or country.—Manufactory, 59, High-street, Hoxton, London.

BUILDERS AND CONTRACTORS.

TARPAULINS for COVERING ROOFS during Repairs. SCAFFOLD CORD and every description of ROPE used by Builders upon the lowest terms. Marquees and temporary awnings on sale or hire. Orders per post receive the most prompt attention.—WILLIAM PIGGOTT, 115, Fore Street, City, Manufacturer, by Appointment, to Her Majesty's Honourable Board of Ordnance.

PATENT HANDRAILS WITHOUT HEADING JOINTS, now so well known and justly appreciated, being patronized by the most eminent Architects.—J. MELVILLE informs Architects, Builders, and the Trade in general, that having recently erected an improved steam apparatus, which, by causing a saving of fuel, and otherwise giving greater facility to the execution of the work, he is enabled to make a reduction of 10 per cent. on his former prices. Prices and patterns forwarded to any part of the country (on a reference being given), and Architects or Builders waited on in London.—64, John-street, Fitzroy-square, London.

GREY GOOSE FEATHERS, 1s. PER POUND.

BED FEATHERS were never so cheap as at present. HEAL and SON'S present prices are:—

	s.	d.		s.	d.
Poultry	0	8	Best Grey Goose	1	10
Grey Goose	1	0	White ditto	2	2
Foreign ditto	1	6	Best Dantzic ditto	3	0

Purified by steam, and warranted sweet and free from dust.
HEAL and SON'S List of Bedding, containing full particulars of weight, sizes, and prices, sent free by post, on application to their Factory, 196, Tottenham-court-road, London.

LAMBERT'S PATENT FLEXIBLE DIAPHRAGM VALVE COCKS are warranted not to leak under any pressure. They have been in use now three years in many public establishments, and their durability is proved beyond doubt. Their Ball Taps, for Cisterns, are rapidly superseding the use of all others. Their Enamelled Iron Water Closets, with trap and safety valve complete, at 35s., are a great improvement upon the appliances hitherto in use for the purpose; as are also their Self-acting Water Closets, six of which have been two years in use in the Infirmary of St. Marylebone Workhouse.—Manufactured by the Patentees, THOMAS LAMBERT and SON, at their Foundry and Metal-pipe Works, Short-street, New-cut, Lambeth, London.

No. CCCLVI.

SATURDAY, DECEMBER 1, 1849.

MONGST a pile of books with which we would make our readers acquainted is one, still wet from the press, by Lord Albert Denison (late Conyngham), whose recent accession of wealth, with his new name, will be hailed with lively satisfaction by all who know his lordship's kind feelings, liberal views, and enlightened tastes. It is entitled, "Wanderings in Search of Health," and is the journal, written with a running pen, of recent hasty travels in Greece and Italy, made with his amiable lady, between November of last year and May of this. As it is published for private circulation only, it will fall into few hands, and we shall therefore give some abstracts from it relating to those matters which more immediately interest our circle.

When in Malta, the author visited the colossal church building at Musta, on the plan of the Pantheon at Rome. The village contains only 6,000 inhabitants, almost all of the poorer classes; and this enormous building arises from a native of the village, a poor priest, Don Felice Calleja, having celebrated his first mass in the Pantheon. "The thought then suddenly struck him of raising a similar temple in his own native village. Upon his return to Malta and to Musta, appointed parish priest, he laboured hard in the accumulation of wealth, and laid by money with the most scrupulous care. Unable to carry out his darling plan in his life-time, he left his property by will for the purpose of erecting a round temple like the Pantheon. Even after his death, the strongest opposition arose to this building. The bishop, as well as the general opinion in the island, opposed the construction of a round temple, upon the plea that round temples, though used for heathen worship, are not adapted for that of Christians." The bishop insisted on a plan being drawn by his own architect, in the form of a Greek cross. The inhabitants, however, were so pleased by a plan presented to them by M. Grognet, an enthusiastic lover of his profession, residing in Malta, that they petitioned 'he governor : objections were overruled, and the first stone was laid on May 30th, 1833. The funds left by the parish priest, 30,000 scudi, being quite inadequate to the object in view, subscriptions were raised, and labour being the principal expense, the church bestows 'ndulgencies upon those who work there gra-uitously on Sundays. From two to three 1undred volunteers have been seen labouring .here on the same day; and the church is hus progressing gradually, though slowly, owards completion. "The total height of the :difice, when finished, will be 200 feet. The nain body of the edifice consists of a circle of bout 200 feet in extreme diameter : it has two projections, at opposite sides; one, a portico of 125 feet long by 60 feet high, with a double ow of columns, between two bell towers : 1ere are three entrance doors. The other and opposite projection is ornamented with pilasers, and contains sacristies or vestries, with n upper story of rooms, for a certain number of priests to be attached to the church. The difice surrounds a church already existing

upon the spot, which will be removed as soon as the new one is completed. This building is astonishing, when the slender means of those who commenced and are finishing it are taken into consideration."

The new cathedral at Boulogne, mentioned by us some time ago, is similarly the result of the determination of an individual, and assists in showing how much any one man can accomplish if he set himself determinedly to the task. *Will goes farther than power.*

When Lord Albert reached Athens, he of course hurried to the Acropolis,—at once, as Wordsworth says, "the fortress, the sacred inclosure, the treasury, and the museum of art of the Athenian nation;" and which, though it has suffered in every possible manner, remains unrivalled "as a concentration of wonders in architecture and sculpture." "Alas!" says Lord Albert, "that the ill-directed zeal of the Athenians of the present day should be disfiguring it more than the hands or weapons of earlier barbarians. In searching for inscriptions, or those statues and works of art, that may be buried under the accumulated rubbish of the whole Christian era, they tumble all the mould and stuff cleaned away down the sides of the rock, instead of carting it away, and are actually changing the bold features of the rock. In vain I have lifted my voice against such Vandalism. I feel that it is useless." What is the Athenian Society of Antiquaries about?

Our author did not find any really first-rate works of antiquity for sale. By law, half of everything found belongs to the Government, and half to the proprietor of the soil. The proprietor has the option of receiving his moiety of the value in money, and to hand the thing found to the authorities, or to pay the half and retain it himself, but in this case must give security for its safety. The exportation of antiquities is absolutely forbidden, but this goes for nothing. Individuals who find anything know that if they yield it to Government they will never receive payment for it, and the result, therefore, is, that they sell it to some foreigner, who bribes the Custom-house officers to shut their eyes.

Speaking of the Choragic monument of Lysicrates, the writer says, "every sort of abomination must now be waded through to view it."

Of the Temple of Theseus, he remarks,—" It be remembered that only four metopes on the southern, and four on the northern side are sculptured; the remaining metopes on those sides being destitute of ornament. M. Pittaky suggested to me that this might arise from their having been painted,—Micon, who ornamented this temple, having been a painter, as well as sculptor. The whole of this temple, like the Parthenon, inclines inwards. This has most materially added to the strength and durability of their construction. Its lines, also, are curved, like those of the Parthenon."

The palace at Athens is "a huge, two-storied, white building, measuring 300 feet by 280 : it has a portico in front, and a colonnade in the rear. These, with the window-frames, cornices, angles, plinths, &c., are formed of Pentelic marble; the walls being of limestone, faced with cement. It is undoubtedly an unsightly building. The window-frames are so flat and plain, as to give it the appearance of a manufactory."

The number of small churches and chapels in Greece, as compared with the population, is a striking feature. In those that are near any temple, the marble objects of ancient art are

placed for preservation, and portions are built into the walls. The former Cathedral of Athens, now deserted, is a curious and interesting example of this. Our author was told that there are no less than seventy deserted churches and chapels in Athens, and that all these are to be pulled down, with the exception of the ancient cathedral, to supply funds, by the sale of the sites and materials, for the new cathedral now building.

The bed of the Ilissus is dry !

Corinth, Mycenæ, Marathon, &c., were visited ; and, in returning, they saw revolutionized Napies, Baia (with its ruined baths), Herculaneum, &c. : and they paced,

"—— with reverent tread,
O'er hushed Pompeii's long-forgotten dead.

The railway has greatly changed the aspect of Pompeii : it is no longer wholly "a city of the dead." It is still, however, a spot which speaks to the heart. As Mr. Michell says, in his charming volume, "Ruins of Many Lands,"—

"A buried city meets the curious gaze,
Charms while it awes, and wraps us in amaze.
Called from the grave of dim Lethean years,
Her graceful form again Pompeii rears—
Reveals her winding streets, her frescoed walls,
Gods on her hearths, and pictures in her halls."

Of Pæstum, Lord Albert says little, and we are tempted to supply a picture from the poet we have just quoted, who exclaims,—here

"—— Pæstum's giant temples—lift thine eyes—
In all their stern and columned grandeur rise.
Pause ! trav'ller, pause ! say, doth not wonder thrill
Thy creeping veins, and awe thy bosom fill ?
Wrestling with Time, the hoary brethren stand,
Superbly graceful, and severely grand.
Their style of rival countries seems to speak,
In strength Egyptian, and in beauty Greek.
Built ere Minerva's shrine on Athens gazed,
Or by wild Tiber Rome's rude walls were raised :
Three thousand years these structures fail to bow,
Massive when Christ was born, and massive now."

We must here, however, leave Lord Albert ; and we sincerely hope that in his "wanderings" he has found health, as we have found pleasure.

Mr Weale's Rudimentary Series is going on satisfactorily. The last part issued is a portion of a "Dictionary of Terms used in Architecture, Art, Engineering, &c.," by the publisher himself. It forms a volume equal in size to two of those on other subjects already issued, and will extend to a third. It appears to be carefully compiled, and will be found very useful to a large number of persons. It would be easy to make a long list of words not to be found in it, but a fair reply to this would be,—proposed limits. We give one of his definitions,—*Æsthetics*, "the power of perception by means of the senses : the word implies the perception and the study of those qualities which constitute the beautiful and artistic, and form the finer essence of all productions of fine art. It carries with it, therefore, a more exact and philosophic meaning than the word 'taste.' In its adjective form, in which it more frequently occurs, it is particularly useful, as no adequate epithet can be substituted for it. Thus we speak of the 'æsthetic sense,' of 'æsthetic feeling,' or 'study,' or 'principles,' &c. ; but we cannot correctly say the 'tasteful sense,' or 'tasteful study.'"

The treatise on "Drainage and Sewage of Towns and Buildings," by G. D. Dempsey, in the same series, would not have had our commendation if we had looked no further than the introduction. In this the author proposes to drain the metropolis, on the converging principle proposed by Mr. Austin, into 800 enormous cesspools or "sumpts," at 200 stations (without saying what is to be done with the sewage when it is there), and then, in speaking of the two plans brought forward by the officers of the late Metropolitan Commission, coolly dismisses that by Mr. Austin, in a few lines, saying that, " as far as yet explained, it *appears* to consist in the formation of district receptacles, called ' sumpts,' for the sewage."

The essay itself, however, contains a considerable amount of information, and will be found of service by all engaged in drainage operations, not excepting those who ambition the gross provision in this respect for the whole metropolis.*

Messrs. Dwyer and Laugher, whose names will be remembered by our readers in connection with the Decorative Art Society, are publishing a series of " Free Hand Studies," intended chiefly for the use of Schools of Design, by supplying examples for the best practice of pupils. Three are before us. The first is an illustration of a means of producing a certain class of effects by lines of similar flexure, and may be considered as the "pothooks" in the art. The "Cyclanthus" offers an instance of contrary flexures, to the right hand and to the left hand, or " pothooks and hangers ;" and the " Robinia " presents curves of extensive variety and direction. These studies should be practised in a free, quick manner, in larger and smaller scales, with chalk, on a black board, until a facility of approximating the examples be acquired. This system is found less impeding and irksome to the progress of a pupil than the general system of insisting upon time-taking but imperfect attempts at an *exact* imitation only, although the necessity of acquiring the power of exact representation must not be lost sight of. In the sister art, music, a course of practice involving failures and repetitions innumerable is alone conducive to skilful manipulation ; and in drawing-schools both masters and pupils would find advantages from adopting black boards, which admit of such repetition in an easy and inexpensive manner. These " Free-hand Studies " are designed with especial reference to such a valuable, but too much neglected course of study, and they have been accordingly published at a very low price.

Speaking of decoration, we will take this opportunity to mention a work recently published, containing representations of ornaments in all styles, executed in *papier mâché* and *carton pierre*, by Messrs. Jackson, of Rathbone-place, the majority of which are excellent in character. We have before now spoken of the facilities for rapid artistic ornamentation which Messrs. Jackson's establishment affords, and the publication of this book renders application to it more easy.

With the intention of treating the arts of decorative design practically, Mr. R. Robson has commenced a work under the title of " Decorative Art, exhibiting the Development of its Natural and Geometrical Elements," &c.†

* Sometime since we gave a list of the parties who had submitted plans in competition to the Sewers Commission for draining London, up to a certain date. The following is a continuation of the list:—J. Adams, J. Bardwell, H. H. Bird, J. Bowron, Sr S. Brown, J. H. Clive, R. G. Coke, J. Cundy, H. C. Daubeny, J. Dean, J. D. Denton, F. Dl'ayson, DFedge and Stephenson, M. Dunn, C. F. Ellesmean, " Fiat Justitia," C. Fowler, W. Y. Facebody, A. Giles, Olpaves and Barlow, F. Hawkes, T. May, C. Brennan, " J.B.," " J. V.," J. E. M'Cabe, J. R. M'Lean. W. Meubey, B. Milne, Capt. W. S. Moorsom, Na..mith and 8t'ratham, L. P. Page, H. Phillips, H. Plukus, E. and W. Pontisei, W. Radley, Bafos Von Rathen, J. B. Redman, G. Remington, Freeman Roe and Hanson, M. L. Bolfgf. N. Scott, H. E. Scott, G. Shepherd, B. C. Stopef, J. H. Smith, W. Smith, B. Stratton, Sir T. Tancred, Tate and Gilmore, J. Tbbay, C. H. White, Walter Smith, J. Wilkinson, and S. Wise.

† London, Weale ; Birmingham, Belby ; Newcastle, Lambert.

The first *fasciculus* contains sixteen plates, besides letter-press, comprising examples of enriched mouldings, leaves from nature as the elements of enrichments in various styles, diagrams illustrating the geometry of the mouldings, &c. It promises to be useful.

And what is this pretty white-bound volume, suggesting kid-gloves and orange blossoms, which peeps out amidst pamphlets on *drainage* and essays on *style ?*—" Holy Matrimony," illuminated by Owen Jones.*

And how has Mr. Jones done it,—how has he set forth and embellished with cunning pen that solemn and tight-tying service, which begins with " dearly beloved," and ends with " amazement,"—a type, may we venture to say, of the change which occasionally takes place in the condition of mind of those on whom its gentle powers have been exercised. He has done it as it should be done, enticingly, and in colour of rose. A genial glow, soft and blushing, is spread over each tiny leaf ; flowers enwreath every passage ; the promise of feminine obedience brings " heart's-ease," and manly protection is promised amidst myrtle and passion flowers. For this pleasant and pretty disguise,—this gilding of gold and painting of the lily,—much is *owen*, O Jones, to thee, and many are the soft slippers, fringed urn-rugs, and ottomans worked in Berlin wool (sweet devices to enable the idle to fancy themselves industrious), which will come to thee in grateful acknowledgment from the female world ! A damsel, willing to throw her graceful self away, may present this pretty book to the blind or thoughtless favoured one, with the full assurance that it will suggest to his mind, none other than charming ideas of the flowery path she would have him tread, and the beauty and value of the budding hopes which require but his will and word to ripen into full fruition.

Had it come to us from such hands, it is impossible to say what would have been the consequence !

" MODEL" TOWN HOUSES FOR THE MIDDLE CLASSES.

OBSERVATIONS ON ORDINARY LONDON DWELLING-HOUSES, WITH AN ATTEMPT TO SUGGEST AN IMPROVEMENT ON THEIR USUAL PLAN.†

OF the many subjects that in the present day agitate the public mind, few are more engrossing than that of the sanitary arrangement and construction of dwelling-houses. In London especially, visited as it has lately been by that fearful scourge, the cholera, whose direct ravages the neglect of this important question is said to invite and foster, it is now that the philanthropist comes forward with a definite plan for the construction of " model towns," and companies or associations spring up on every side of the metropolis, formed for the object of erecting " model" lodging-houses, or dwellings for the labouring classes. The very titles given to such projects as these, are, one would think, indicative of the startling fact that our ordinary dwellings are not merely unsatisfactorily constructed, but actually arranged upon a false plan.

Looking at the metropolis alone, it will be found that the evils of the present method of arranging town dwellings are by no means limited to what is usually meant by sanitary reform, or the mere preservation of the inhabitants *in corpore sano*, but that the *mens sana*, the healthy mind, the mental comfort and culture, and the moral deportment of the Londoners, are greatly affected by these evils. If we reflect a little on what are termed " our hearths and homes," we shall find that, for

* Published by Longman and Co. 1849.
† Read at a meeting of the Architectural Association, October 19, 1849.

the most part, the dwelling-houses of London as now inhabited, realize very little if anything of an Englishman's ideas of a hearth or home ; and that, in the metropolis at least the vaunted relation of the Englishman's fire side to a castle, is a meaningless nonentity indeed. The observation is not only applicable to the dwellings of the labouring class,—its truth may be urged with equal force as it regards that other important section of our population, the middle class of society, or whose well-being the dignity of the nation may be said mainly to depend.

To allude more explicitly to the principal defect in our present method of arranging houses in the metropolis, I cannot do better than refer to a paper* read at the Architectural Association last May by one of the members Mr. F. Chambers. It was entitled " The Architectural Advantages and Deficiencies of London," and takes, what it is surprising so few architects have taken, a glance at the causes of that signal want of architectural effect common to almost all our long drawn, densely peopled thoroughfares. It would be well worth while to consider whether it be not practicable to devise some plan of erecting town-dwelling houses at at least their present usual cost (when substantially built), and the present usual superficial area assigned to them, which shall be free from the objections very justly urged against their ordinary system of construction.

The paper in question contains the surprising statement, that " only one-fourth of the dwelling-houses in the metropolis are occupied by one family each :" the remainder, though constructed to be similarly tenanted, are " common" or uncommon, as the case may be), mere lodging-houses—sham *private dwellings*, which they are not,—ill-arranged, uncomfortable *lodgings*, which they were never built to be. A married Londoner with a family, should his means exclude him from the happy number who make up the 25 per cent. of separate householders, has no power to exempt himself from the remaining 75 per cent. of lodgers or lodging-house keepers ; he must either take his station among the former, and with then confine himself to some limited few of the rooms in the house, in daily fear lest the bailiff should sweep off his (so-called) household furniture for arrears of rent, or debts of any kind contracted by his landlord, for whose pecuniary stability he is ever responsible ; or he must, if a person to whom a residence in tolerably fashionable neighbourhood is indispensable, rent a house twice or thrice as large a he absolutely requires for his family, and pass his life in it, alternately grumbling over the heavy rent and taxes his empty apartments entail on him, or bewailing the galling absence of al dignity or privacy, the due regularity and control of his household, to which their hire occupancy by strangers must more or less subject him. Who can fail to imagine th moral evils attendant on either of these alternatives ? How can such a state of things b reconciled to the master's love of home, th mistress's pride in its neatness and cleanliness, the often prized, and never too highly appreciated home-education of children, an though last not least, the due control and exemplary training of servants. Is th master of the house a man of quiet, studious habits ?—his " first floor," as the phrase goes, is a good musician ; or a married couple, fond of inviting their friends to an occasional dance. I he solicitous for the health of his family ?—his injunctions to have doors opened and sashes let down are either restricted to certain rooms in his house, or positively interdicted by his lodger, who has a horror of " draughts." I he a religious man ?—his efforts to rightly educate his children are rendered nugatory by their inevitable intercourse with the family of his sceptical neighbour up stairs. In fine, is the master or mistress precise and cleanly ?—the couple who lodge above are dirty and slovenly ; and hate " particular people." Has the other family a refractory servant ?—the other has a rebellious " marchioness " who abets his and, with all these and very many more diverse agreeables than we have time to discuss, the united, but not " happy" families, have to put up with each other as they best can. Thwarted in all her efforts to preserve a ne

* See THE BUILDER, vol. vii., page 220.

"MODEL" TOWN HOUSES FOR THE MIDDLE CLASSES.

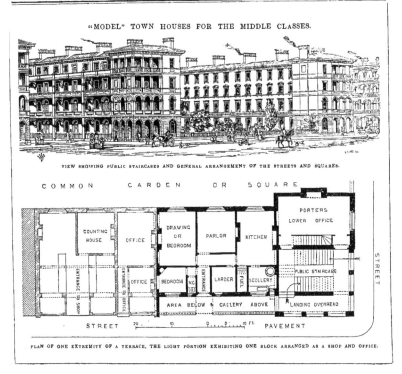

VIEW SHOWING PUBLIC STAIRCASES AND GENERAL ARRANGEMENT OF THE STREETS AND SQUARES.

PLAN OF ONE EXTREMITY OF A TERRACE, THE LIGHT PORTION EXHIBITING ONE BLOCK ARRANGED AS A SHOP AND OFFICE.

and orderly dwelling, is it surprising if the lady of the house settle down to the slovenly standard of her lodgers, or the lodgers to the lady's, as the case may be, to the scandal of their respective country cousins? It is by no means an uncommon thing to hear of a professional man in practice renting at upwards of eighty or a hundred pounds a-year a large house, and occupying it, with his wife and children, one male and a couple of female servants; with a pair of lodgers on his first floor, a married couple on his second, and a single lodger on his third floor. Imagine a state of existence more undignified, unreal, or uncomfortable than this,—or the advent of *typhus* into such a dwelling!

As to the construction of metropolitan dwelling-houses, totally irrespective of their unsuitable arrangement or plan, it has been shown by many writers to be truly detestable: deprive them of but one good quality (secured to them by Act of Parliament), their non-liability, by the possession of compulsorily sound party and external walls, to ignite one another, and it is scarcely possible to conceive any thing more defective. *Strength* they have not (of course there are exceptions in this as in every rule), for even the vulgar element of *equilibrium* is denied them; walls rest not on walls nor even partitions on partitions, though, strange to say, roofs do; in fact, as respects the word *walls* (save as it relates to the before-mentioned circumscribing brickwork required by the Legislature), it and the word "foundation" might well be expunged from our housebuilders' vocabulary. Thus, to say nothing of *durability*, the absence of which we perhaps owe to the existence of short leases, your ordinary London dwelling is even deficient in *safety*,— as may be seen from the awful frequency and rapidity with which their necessarily wooden

construction subjects them to total demolition by fire. In these cases the salvage of furniture, or such like property, is out of the question, the oft recurring sacrifice of human life shocking to contemplate. I myself have seen in two cases—that of Raggett's Hotel, in Dover-street, and of Professor Farey's house, in Guildford-street, the window blinds and curtains of the gutted house fluttering next day from the windows,—a sad evidence of the sudden rapidity with which, in each case, the destruction of *life* and property was effected. Indeed, not only is it often that these fires are attended with loss of life, but really seldom that they occur without it; and, meantime, as any one may see around the outskirts of the metropolis, we go on building on the very same plan as before, with deal staircases and quarter partitions, side by side, admirably contrived—to burn; and at the close of each day tall ghost-like fire-escapes, which, by-the-bye, do not always escape combustion themselves, dismally reminding one of the probability there is that, ere the sun return, some hapless dweller in their allotted district, who has entered his abode by the street door, may have to make his exit by an upper window.

It may be thought this is an exaggerated picture of the evils arising out of our present mode of house building; but, though in many cases they may be said to exist greatly mitigated by circumstances, it is undeniable that the system condemned induces more or less the state of things here described; and that to the majority of the inhabitants of our provincial towns it is almost unknown. That this is the case, at least with reference to the *last* evil adverted to, let us look at Manchester, next to the metropolis the most important, most populous city we have. Here, in the

cases of mill or warehouse property, conflagrations the most appalling occur; and yet the destruction of dwelling-house property is, compared with what we experience in London, signally rare. Mr. Rose, for very many years the able comptroller of the Manchester Fire Brigade, has kindly favoured me with the following statement, in reply to two questions put to him. He says—"I do not know of more than one instance where a building, solely occupied as a dwelling-house, was entirely destroyed by fire during a period of twenty years; and such fires are very rarely attended with the death by fire of any of the inmates."

It would avail little to dilate on the unarchitectural external appearance of our houses, which, though very greatly induced by the infrequency with which architects are called in to design and direct their construction, is in some measure attributable to their ichnographic arrangement; nor, however consistent it might be with the practice of modern criticism, would it be fair to close these observations, without making some attempt to suggest a remedy for the evils complained of. Before doing this, however, it will be well to briefly notice one or two efforts lately made with this laudable object: I allude particularly to the "model lodging-houses for the labouring classes."

A large stack of these has lately been built in the parish of St. Pancras, with eminent success as a speculation: however, save the substitution of stone for wooden staircases, and the provision of a kitchen, scullery, water-closet, and dust-hole on one floor, there is little in the plan to distinguish it from the ordinary dwelling-house arrangements. Yet even with these novelties (so to term them) the increase of comfort, as compared with the old system, is highly appreciated by the tenants,—themselves, he it observed, a superior class of persons to that for whose accommodation the building was originally projected. There seems only one substantial objection to the same plan being carried out on a handsomer scale for the middle classes; and that is the repetition, here adopted, of the ordinary common staircase to each separate block of dwellings. These means of ascent and descent should, I conceive, be not only far more spacious, far better lighted and ventilated, than by such repetition it is possible to contrive them; but, in lieu of the pernicious comparative privacy thus imparted to them, the architect should adopt every means to make them as nearly as possible assimilate in publicity to the streets, to and from which they are intended as the *media* of communication.

In the parish of St. Giles, another somewhat analogous project has been carried into execution, in the erection of a pile of club chambers, with separate dormitories and a common dining-room, library, and reading-room. If I mistake not, they are simply intended for the occupation of casual nightly tenants, in lieu of the low night lodging-houses about London; but as some such arrangement as this has been often suggested for the permanent occupation of the poor, a doubt may here be hazarded as to its desirableness. Such institutions must have a tendency to break up society into clubs and coteries, to the destruction of that domestic comfort and independence so conducive to the well-being of every class.

Another pile of model dwellings to which allusion should be made, is now in course of erection in Bloomsbury, from the designs, and under the direction of Mr. Henry Roberts. The plan comprises a stack of nine dwelling-houses on each floor; approached, not from the confined landings of a small pent-up staircase, common to a single block of chambers one above another, but from spacious galleries, open to the air,—themselves approached by one large stone staircase, common to the entire stack, under the control of a resident porter. An illustrated account of this building* is contained in the present volume of The Builder. This is a great advance upon the ordinary plan: if only to mention one obvious advantage it possesses,—the means provided for the prevention of the spread of contagion from house to house.

In Liverpool, Glasgow,† and elsewhere, piles of this description of property are springing up, but enough has been said of what is doing in London to denote the restlessness of the public mind in relation to the improvement of town dwellings.

It will be seen that all the plans here described have for their object the abandonment of the present system of housing the labouring classes in the thickly peopled districts of the metropolis; and having already shown that the very reasons that have conjured them into being, apply with, if anything, greater force to the middle classes, I ask at once, why cannot a more consistent class of dwellings be contrived for their use? The question is by no means singular, and has been more than once put by non-professional querists, as may be seen in this journal.‡

The plan I venture to propose is described in the accompanying illustrations. It has been mainly suggested by seeing the description of Mr. Roberts's mode of arrangement already referred to. The lower houses are proposed to be entered (as now) at once from the street. They might be constructed with or without a basement story, in the former case retaining the usual sunk area, and departing somewhat from the general plan, or, if laid out as shops or offices, be brought forward to the street pavement, as shown by the light portion of the ground plan annexed. The upper houses would be entered from the street by open galleries or colonnades, accessible at the extremities of each row or terrace by a well-lighted spacious double stone staircase, of publicity equal to that of the street itself, on every landing of which the *surveillance* of a resident porter or keeper could be directed, for its orderly security and neatness of condition. The subordinate offices are placed in front, looking on to the colonnades or galleries: these might have the glazing of their windows obscured, or the windows themselves placed at such a height from the floor as to secure them from being overlooked by the passers-by. The principal living and lodging-rooms are placed at the rear, and are intended to overlook a spacious square or garden, common to the two stacks of terraces: it is presumed that the usual superficial area assigned to the private back yards or gardens of an ordinary house will, with the fence walls dispensed with, amply provide for such spacious common garden as is here described. It would be planted and laid out as a promenade for such of the families in each terrace as might be willing to pay a small annual fee for the privilege. Property like this would of course, as at present, have its more expensive tenements and its more *distingué* tenants on the lower flats or terraces; and if carried up many stories high, which, when the infrequency of its occupants' journeys up and down stairs is considered, it might very well be, would perhaps exhibit a great discrepancy between the condition of its denizens on the first and that of those on its uppermost terraces; but I conceive the presence about the grounds of an artisan from the topmost terrace, who possessed refinement enough to induce him to the yearly payment of a guinea for the healthy recreation of his family, ought not to disturb the equanimity of the most fastidious tenant below. However, should this be found a difficulty, the roofs might be formed into one large exercising terrace for the occupants of the upper flats or terraces only, leaving the gardens for the use of those on the lower terraces.

Should objections be raised to the collision of different classes or sexes on the staircases, the fact of each flight being a *double* one, amply lighted by day and night, and open to the ken of its parallel neighbour, as also that of the keeper and his family, should be borne in mind: and to such as may be urged against the novel necessity hereby created for postmen, milkmen, &c. &c., ascending and descending to and from the upper houses, a moment's reflection on the greater evil that would be thus avoided, viz., the continual daily travelling of servants and females up and down stairs in our already lofty houses, an evil that seriously militates against their cleanliness and order, will, it is assumed, be enough to prove the greater convenience of the plan proposed.

Of no small moment in the consideration of any plan of this description is the name of, or address that can be given at, each respective dwelling; as any one who reflects on the present artificial condition of the middle classes of the metropolis will perceive. Thus, in the plan proposed, each street might have, independently of its own name, its locality denoted by the name of the square or pleasure-ground attached to the houses in it; the dwellings on the ground floor being, of course, designated as at present. Whatever might be the number of each house on the ground floor might (for the convenience of cab-drivers, &c., drawing up to the nighest staircase) apply also to the houses above its individual site; and "Third-terrace," "Second-terrace," and "First-terrace," might represent the positive, comparative, and superlative degrees of gentility.

The plan represents the extremity of one row or stack of terraces, comprising two *blocks* of dwellings, and one of the double stone staircases intended to be placed at the corners of each street, or in very long thoroughfares at smaller intervals, as the intelligence of the builders might suggest. Over the piazzas leading from each street are landings, conducting at once to the open galleries on each terrace or flat. The porter's office attached has a private staircase, two or three bed-rooms above, and an office again on the topmost story. The remaining dark portion of the plan shows the arrangement of each *block* of dwelling-houses, assuming the non-existence of a basement story, and is, of course, repeated for that description of property throughout the stack. The superficial area occupied by each dwelling-house, devised merely as a sample of an average class, is equivalent to that allowed to a second-rate house, according to the provisions of the Metropolitan Buildings' Act. The walls and partitions are, as in all model dwellings, superincumbent from bottom to top; thus the buildings would readily be constructed fire-proof, or the partitions formed at least of brick nogging, with the floors sound-boarded and pugged. Each house has a dust-shaft, with a coal place on an intermediate floor; the coals for each dwelling being delivered into a shoot from the gallery or terrace overhead, placed some five feet above the level of such gallery floor.

The deviation from the dwelling-house plan shown by etching the second block is merely introduced for the sake of exemplifying the mode in which, without greater violation to the ordinary rules of construction than we are now guilty of, the ground stories are capable of being originally built as, or subsequently altered into, shops or offices.

Fresh air for each dwelling could, of course, be supplied by air bricks or revolving valves; and vitiated air discharged, by perforations or centre flowers in the ceilings of each room, into air trunks or drains, built between each floor, and terminated at their two extremities by air bricks, so as always to secure a brisk current throughout their extent from front to back: a system, this, similar to that adopted by the Poor-Law Commissioners.

Many other suggestions might be added, as, for instance, the introduction of large *lifts* or "hoists" for heavy goods, or even sick persons, and many details gone into, to which the plan is not only capable of accommodation, but in many cases solely so. To these, however, for the sake of simplification, it will be well to avoid allusion.

Whatever may be thought of the *popularity* of such a plan as is here proposed, and (knowing John Bull's respectable aversion to all fireside innovations) I must confess to some doubts on that head,—there can, it is presumed, be no doubt whatever of its superiority to the ordinary dwelling-house arrangements, which three-fourths of the inhabitants now *enjoy*,—whether on the score of sound construction, safety from fire and the spread of contagious fevers, or general comfort and privacy.

One advantage of such a plan of house-building is its greater economy of space, if not of actual outlay on the building itself, consequent on the omission of the separate staircases now required for each block of dwellings. A saving in *ground rent in London* is a matter of no trifling import; and when it is recollected that a staircase, with its ordinary mahogany handrail, &c., is one of the most expensive features of a modern house, it is at least questionable whether the open galleries proposed to supersede them can fairly be objected to as costly features over and above what are incurred by the ordinary plan.

Nor must the facility thus afforded for building even loftier houses than we now do, though cursorily alluded to already, be omitted from the list of advantages that would accrue from such a plan as this. Omnibuses, as we now employ them, are, it is true, a mode of transit from corner to corner of town which would indeed surprise our grandsires, could they retraverse our streets; but, whoever considers the rapidity with which our modern Babylon, with its "two millions," is diverging with brick and mortar into the suburbs, must admit that these vehicles will soon—in fact, have already—become intolerable. Omnibuses "for the million" are not enough, and how to move about town is really becoming a serious problem for solution.

That such a plan would, if adopted, supply another desideratum, a means for designing houses architecturally, or at least symmetrically, and thus perchance rid London of its tawdry bedizenment, applied the thickest where our façades are the most lop-sided, there can I conceive be little doubt. Richly designed shop façades, if introduced in streets built on such a plan, would no longer present wide gaping chasms of plate glass, sustaining (somehow or other imperceptibly to the spectator), an overwhelming mass of superincumbent wall, four or five stories in height; but pier would stand over pier, and void over void; a thing impossible by our present mode of construction; and the density of our population, by rendering some such kind of street architecture imperative upon us, would, with the now seldom-sought aid of the architect, to not merely design but control their structure, be

* See page 327.

† Lumsden's Model Dwellings for the Working Classes are described in Vol. 6, page 523 of this journal.

‡ See letter of "Suburban" in "Builder," Vol. 5, page 209.

the means of transforming our monotonous fronts with their (to use the words of Mr. Elmes), "two windows, iron railing, and a door, two windows, iron railing and a door," into façades of palatial aspect, by the simple presence of the long continuous array of varied columns, arches, and cantalivers, which would be actually demanded for their *bonâ fide* construction. WILLIAM YOUNG.

FALL OF RAILWAY ARCHES, CAMDEN TOWN.

THE desirability of our suggestion as to a judicial inquiry into the causes of the fall of the arches over the Kentish-Town-road, has been largely recognized, but it is to be feared that it will fall to the ground.

It is certainly important to the reputation of English engineers, that some measures be taken to put a stop to the failures which take place upon railway works every week. At present information can be obtained only by an examination by some unofficial person, who brings the matter in a very irregular manner before the public. His sources of information are of course imperfect; the results almost useless: a discussion arises perhaps in the papers, and then the affair is forgotten, to be merely another proof of official carelessness, recklessness, or jobbery.

What unknown problems are there in viaduct building which remain to be solved at the present day? What more do we require to learn about the foundations to be met with near any of our large towns? Yet we can hardly ever take up a railway paper without meeting with the account of some viaducts having fallen. It is high time a stop should be put to this. In the present case, why does not the Railway Company institute a searching inquiry into the cause of the accident? It will be long before public opinion can be re-assured as to the safety of the remainder of their road. At any rate the shareholders should be informed as to who is to pay for the new works.

As far as can be learned from a casual inspection (and we are bound to say the builder, Mr. Hicks, showed every desire that we should be fully informed on the matter), there are no conditions in the superstructure to account for the fall of the arches. The dimensions of the piers and of the arches seem sufficient. The piers are 4 feet wide at one end, 3 feet 11 inches at the other, being on a curve; 27 feet long and 17 feet high to springing. The arches are *segments*, 8 feet rise and 27 feet span. The work and materials appear to be of a rather superior quality. The bricks used look like good sound stocks; the mortar of the piers was made of ground stone lime, which, indifferent as it is, is still the best usually employed in London; the arches are all apparently executed in cement upon this portion of the line, those still in place as well as the fallen ones being thus executed. On a *primâ facie* view of the case, therefore, we are justified in supposing that the cause of failure must be sought for in the foundations. And, in the neighbourhood, common report says that one of the piers was built upon an old drain, unconsolidated, untouched, left just as it was found, with all the made ground around it.

If this be the case, the *onus* of investigation would seem to rest with the engineer. He had no right to build a viaduct in such a position, with one of its piers on such a foundation. The footings were 1 foot 3 inches below the ground, and the concrete about 1 foot 9 inches deep.

A remark to be made in passing is, that it is very injudicious to execute a long range of arches without introducing occasionally a pier of extra thickness, to form an intermediate abutment. Here we have about 16 or 17 arches in a row, and so constructed that if one pier fail all the others must follow like a pack of cards. Seven arches fell; more would have fallen if the interruption had not existed, in fact, from the stout abutment of the large arch over the road on one side, and from the centres being left in the arches of similar span on the other. Many viaducts, such as the Greenwich railway, have stood, with thirty or more similar arches in a row; but it is running an unfair, a useless risk, as we see in this case, and as was proved by the fall of the Barentin viaduct. The distance between the Hampstead-road and the Kentish-town-road ought to have been divided into at least three bays, with a stouter pier at each division.

ERRORS IN ORNAMENTAL DESIGN.

MOST heartily do I agree with those correspondents of THE BUILDER who deprecate that mistakenly extravagant taste for excessive decoration which was manifested in the pattern productions at the Birmingham exhibition, and which appears to be one of the manias of the present day, although it is one in quite an opposite direction from most of them. We appear to take the reverse of wrong for right. After having affected almost Quaker-like plainness in our buildings, our houses, and furniture, we are now running into the contrary extreme, and are applying embellishment—or what should be embellishment—to everything alike, and to every part of everything, till "we can't see the wood for the trees." Our apartments are beginning to smack of the toy-shop and show-room. To be *comme il faut*, every piece of furniture must ostentatiously solicit examination; everything must be be-carved or be-patterned, even to satiety; and the same kind of patterns are applied nearly alike to everything,—to book-covers and to table-covers, to the borders of envelopes and title-pages, and to the borders of rooms, to carpets, and to walls. With very much more than enough of ornament, we get very little variety of it: no proper distinction is observed in the application of it; and with so little of artistic discretion and reserve is it frequently bestowed, that it conceals or else disguises what it is intended to set off; and human figures and animal forms — nay, even "creeping things" — are introduced, as decoration, in such a preposterous manner as to become only so many childish conceits. You see snakes twining themselves round your candlesticks, and sidereal dwarfs perched on the top of your fire-irons; you eat your strawberries off leaves of crockery, and sip your wine out of flower-shaped devices. Should this taste prevail much longer, the furniture of our drawing-rooms will pretty much resemble that of Noah's ark, with the addition of a *hortus siccus*. It may, perhaps, be in conformity with that "study Nature" doctrine which many have now in their mouths—though what they mean by it they do not say, notwithstanding that it requires very careful explanation; but to me it seems to partake largely of the antic and unnatural, and to accuse those who design and manufacture ornamental wares of great lack of invention. That the direct imitation of natural objects—whether human figures, animals, or flowers, &c.—ought to be entirely exploded from decorative design, I will not say; but it certainly ought to be resorted to very sparingly,—whereas it is now made use of so indiscreetly, that, unless checked, it will soon become stale and common-place, if not vulgar.

Contrary to what has been said again and again as to refined taste being compatible with economy, inasmuch as it may be made to exhibit itself by means of very little more than elegance of forms and well-considered artistic design, far more pains are bestowed on mere superfluous ornament and elaboration, than study is given to beauty of general composition. Many of the articles in the Birmingham exhibition attested this very strongly, they being very uncouth and tasteless,—some of them decidedly ugly, yet at the same time expensive on account of the workmanship thrown away upon them. Several of the articles of furniture seemed to be, if not actually brought out from lumber-rooms and brokers' shops, modelled after the household antiquities which may any day be discovered in such repositories. There were spider-legged tables, and plenty of crinkum-crankums, and such superlative novelties as *small* looking-glasses, with sconces, all which are rather symptoms of relapse, than of improvement or advance in taste. Although the mill which is said to grind old ladies into young ones is altogether fabulous, a mill there does appear to be which grinds old fashions into spick-and-span new ones. Of *bonâ fide* novelty in furniture and decoration, we do not get much, nor shall we get, so long as we allow traditional and hackneyed ideas to block up the way against original invention. I am somewhat justified in saying this, because, although I do not actually practise that branch of design, I have given some earnest attention to it, and so far with success as to have devised several quite fresh and unedited contrivances. Among them is what I call a *Pinacotheca*, which piece of furniture I have had made, and it is now before me. What it exactly is, I am not bound here to disclose, but its purpose may be partly guessed from the name I have given it. As it serves a double purpose, it is exceedingly convenient as well as ornamental,—nevertheless nothing wonderful, the only strange part of the matter being, that the same idea should never have presented itself to any of those who manufacture articles of furniture, and whose interest consequently it is to bring out, if they can, novel contrivances. The exhibition which is to take place in 1851, will perhaps now cause them to set their wits to work. I myself somewhat doubt it, but *nous verrons*.

If French taste and skill are fairly represented at the "Exposition" in George-street, I should say that the admiration generally professed for them is not over creditable either to our discernment or our patriotism. Neither is it particularly patriotic on the part of those who have got up that speculation, to attempt to pass off the collection as the very cream of that branch of French *industrie*, for if such it be, what sort of stuff must its skimmed milk be? Mr. Graham's letter, however, in the *Times* of last Saturday, flatly contradicts that assertion, informing us, that so far from such being the case, many of the articles are "old shopkeepers," which it is now attempted to get rid of by a novel scheme.

There is a great deal of gewgaw showiness, but very little evidence of refinement and careful artistic study. Of many of the productions the chief merit seems to be their extravagant costliness, a merit which may recommend them to the purse-proud and *nouveaux riches*, to those who possess far more money than judgment, and who pique themselves upon scorning the home-spun John Bullish productions of our English artisans and manufacturers.

There is, indeed, one article in the "Exposition" which is calculated to excite, if not exactly admiration, supreme astonishment at its truly surprising absurdity and utter bathos, namely, an atrociously vile picture, with the face of a watch stuck into it to represent a clock in a church tower, and with several figures which, when the chimes strike, jerk their arms most *unnaturally*. Such a specimen of French taste would hardly be tolerated in an English pothouse.

The newspapers talk of its being likely that her Majesty will visit the Exposition. Let us hope that her Majesty will do no such thing; for she might just as well visit any other bazaar or auction-room, where she would be likelier to find many specimens of better taste.

ZETA.

*** *The French Exposition*.—We have allowed our correspondent (with a few reservations), to state his own opinion on the collection in Great George-street; and we may add that it represents that of several other persons who have addressed us upon it. Our own opinion we have already expressed, namely, that the collection contains many beautiful works, which demand the careful inspection of our manufacturers. The mistake made by the friends of the undertaking, and which has raised ill-will against it, has been the endeavour to give a wrong character to what is in fact (and this is nothing against it) a pecuniary speculation.

THE BEDFORDSHIRE ARCHITECTURAL AND ARCHÆOLOGICAL SOCIETY had a meeting on Tuesday week, when a resolution was passed, inviting the St. Alban's Society to meet this Society at Dunstable in the ensuing spring. Office bearers were elected, and some other business gone through. The Rev. H. E. Havergal submitted a plan for restoring Elstow Church. The council were directed to memorialize the Duke of Bedford, who is a member, to preserve some interesting buildings of perpendicular character about to be destroyed at Willington.

PALAIS DES BEAUX ARTS, PARIS.

THE CHATEAU GAILLON.

Scale of ———————————————— Foot

Plan & detail of the Column.

A

C

ROUSSEL   Scale of ————————— feet   LAING. sc.

THE PALAIS DES BEAUX ARTS, PARIS.

The *Chateau Gaillon*, in Normandy, an ancient residence built in the decadence of the Gothic art, belonged to the celebrated Cardinal d'Amboise: it is now a prison. Mons. Albert Lenoir, the director of the Museum of Antiquities, in Paris, caused some of the principal portions of this chateau to be brought to the capital, and the architect of the *Palais des Beaux Arts* there arranged them, in the court of the building, in such a way as to present their most salient artistical merits to the consideration of the pupils. In our present number we give representations of some of the principal parts. The upper drawing represents the archway, placed to the left of the second court, and the lower one a balustrade and gates. A represents part of another gate, of which C shews the lock.

BUILDING SOCIETIES.

EXEMPTION FROM STAMP DUTY.

IN a former number* was noticed, at some length, the very important case of Walker v. Giles, decided in the Court of Common Pleas, in which it was held that mortgages and other securities given to the trustees of building societies, established under the Building Societies Act (6 & 7 Wm. IV., c. 32), are exempt from stamp duty.

Perhaps some of the readers of this journal can recall to mind that we then took upon ourselves to declare that this was sound law, and that a stamp duty on such mortgages would be entailing on the mortgagor an unnecessary expense. It was only, however, after giving much attention to the case and the construction of the Acts upon which the judgment was based that we ventured to arrive at this conclusion, knowing, as we then did, that many practitioners had objected to dispense with the stamp duty, as they doubted the correctness of the decision; and also that a legal contemporary† went so far as to say, "We feel it to be our duty to warn the trustees and advisers of building societies against acting on that decision."

We were right. The Court of Common Pleas have reconsidered and affirmed that decision in the case of Barnard and Others v. Pilsworth (14 *Law T.* 132). In this case the plaintiffs were the trustees of the Amicable Building Society, and the defendant rented his house of one Hinton, who had mortgaged the house to the plaintiffs as trustees of the building society. This action was brought to recover a year's rent, and was tried before Wilde, C.J., at the sittings in London after last term. The mortgage deed had no stamp upon it, and it was objected to as inadmissible for want of a stamp. The objection was overruled, and the jury gave the plaintiffs a verdict for the year's rent.

Channel, Serjt., moved to set aside the verdict, and enter it for the defendant, on the ground that the mortgage deed required a stamp.

We have seen that the practice of having these mortgage deeds stamped has been still adhered to, from a supposition that the question had not been finally settled in Walker v. Giles. We find this opinion to be at once gratuitous and erroneous; for after the argument of the learned serjeant, Maule, J., said, —"I believe there have been some observations in a legal journal‡ reflecting on that decision (Walker v. Giles), on the presumption that the whole of the Friendly Societies Acts, 10 Geo. IV., c. 56, and 5 & 6 Wm. IV., c. 40, is not incorporated in the Building Societies Acts, but only so much as relates to the making and altering of the rules. I own these observations did not convince me our decision was wrong. Our decision is a recent one, and we *meant to decide* that the *whole* of the Friendly Societies Acts in question were incorporated, so far as they were applicable to building societies, *and that building societies' mortgages were exempt from stamp duty.*"

The rest of the court concurring, *rule refused.*

Mortgages and other securities given to building societies are exempt from stamp duty, and on this subject there can no longer rest the shadow of a doubt. The majority of these mortgagors have acquired their savings by too much labour to afford to fritter any portion of them away in unnecessary legal expenses; and if, therefore, they continue to be charged stamp duty (and these mortgages belong to that class which is liable to the highest rate), their solicitors should at once refuse to pay it.

We have heard nothing more of an Act limiting the present exemption from stamp duties in these cases. We are strongly inclined to believe that no such statute is really contemplated. It is only necessary to refer to the preamble of the Building Societies Act to see that its object was to afford encouragement and protection to these associations: surely, then, the legislature would not act so inconsistently as to grant a reasonable privilege and then abolish it by a subsequent enactment.

Inner Temple. W. Ll. T.

* THE BUILDER, August 18, 1849.

† *The Jurist*, July 14, 1849.

‡ *The Jurist*, July 14, 1849.

ECCLESIASTICAL DILAPIDATIONS.

THE discrepancy lately mentioned in the valuation of the three persons employed to value the chancel dilapidations in central Norfolk, is one of the most singular circumstances I have ever heard of: apparently two of the three persons must be ignorant of what is, or what is not, a dilapidation. The only points to be settled, beyond substantial repairs, in estimating ecclesiastical dilapidations, are, whether the waste or want of painting, papering, whitewashing, and colouring inside are dilapidations? I will admit that papering is more a matter of ornament and luxury than utility and necessity, but I am of opinion that plain painting is both useful and necessary, as much so as the plastering to walls, and that it is absolutely necessary for the decent accommodation of the new incumbent. If a new parsonage-house is about to be erected, it is a part of the specification that all the wood-work usually painted shall be painted three or more coats in good oil colour; then, I ask, why introduce this clause if it be not both useful and necessary? It is true that in that celebrated case of "Wise v. Metcalfe," it is stated that "painting, whitewashing, and such part of the papering as is not required to preserve wood from decay, by exposure to the external air, are rather matters of ornament and luxury than utility and necessity." I think the master to whom it was referred thought otherwise, and that painting was really necessary; for it will be observed that estimate, including painting, papering, &c., amounted to 399*l.* 18s. 6d., exclusive of painting, &c., 310*l.*; and the master allowed 369*l.* 18s. 6d., being 59*l.* 18s. 6d. more than the lowest estimate, which makes it evident that he considered painting, whitewashing, and colouring necessary to be done for the decent accommodation of the new comer in, and that papering was more an ornament and luxury than useful and necessary.

With deference I suggest that the profession generally cannot do better than act upon the opinion of Mr. Baron Garrod, given some years ago at the Hertford assizes, where his lordship stated "that it was not sufficient to leave the rectory-house and adjacent premises wind and water tight, but to leave them fit for the immediate occupation of the new comer in, some reference being had to the value of the living," which, I presume, means where the house is of a suitable size for the living.

In answer to a question by the Lord Bishop of Worcester (some years ago), Sir William Scott stated that "there can be no doubt that painting is a dilapidation in such a case; if painting is good, it is not necessary that fresh painting should be applied, but if painting is in such a state that it must be renewed for the decent accommodation of the new comer-in, it must be done at the expense of the last occupier or his representatives."—Yours, &c.,

JNO. JAQUES.

BRITISH ARCHÆOLOGICAL ASSOCIATION.

AT a meeting held November 23rd, Mr. Pettigrew in the chair, Mr. Williams exhibited a drawing of the hypocaust and other Roman remains, at Cirencester.—Mr. Furland exhibited a collection of interesting bronze Roman antiquities from Reculver, belonging to Mr. F. Fillinham.

Mr. Keate read some remarks on drawings, made by his son, of the remains of a large building at Verona, which he supposed was a Naumachia, or place for exhibiting aquatic fights and games, the savage diversions of tyrant emperors and a brutal mob. Although there were as many as six of these buildings in Rome, erected by various emperors, he believed that but few remains of them were now to be found. These interesting excavations had been carried on principally by one spirited though not rich individual.

Dr. Bell read a paper on the two-faced figure of Janus, on a British coin. He first shewed the superior position Janus held in the religions of Italy, before the intrusions of Homeric deities and Grecian myths. Also from the conformity of the derivations of the name Janus from *Janua* and Thor, signifying even in modern German *a gate*, the parent of our English word *door*, he inferred the identity of both. Thor, however, must be the most ancient denomination from its meaning, *he of yore*, or in the more emphatic phraseology of Scripture, the "Ancient of days." The figure most probably took its form from a proprietor fixing a pillar or post to mark his boundary, and his neighbour placing a similar one at its back. From the sacredness with which property was regarded, these posts became gods, as Termini and Hermes; and increasing veneration, and the inborn æsthetic feelings of Italy, gradually fashioned these into the human face divine, and a cross piece made them real Thors or gates. This would account for the sanctity of lintels and entrance posts, subsequently transferred to their representatives, the *wands*, in all ages. The fact was adduced, that the colony which settled Iceland took the door-posts of their temple from Norway, and when approaching land threw them overboard, that they might learn from augury of these deities the proper place to disembark, and found a city where they drifted on shore. Maces are but smaller and more ornamented posts, and the wand of ceremony or magic, though in German it now signify *wall*, bears evidence that it was brought over when walls, like those of Greenstead Church, Essex, were built of posts. One of the circles of Stonehenge consists of triglitha—what are these but an aggregation of Thors or Jauuses? where their position and repetition made the holy most holy.

NOTES IN THE PROVINCES.

THE tenders for improvement of the Ipswich Corn Exchange have been opened, and Mr. W. Ribban's, at 1,070*l.*, the lowest, accepted. The building will have a stone portico, of the Corinthian order, fronting the Corn-hill. The interior will consist of a room 66 feet by 78 feet, and 22 feet high, with a lantern in the centre. It will make a public hall for the use of the town, as also for scientific lectures, concerts, &c., &c. The building will be erected under the superintendence of Mr. Woolnough, of Ipswich, architect.——The Southampton council have determined to construct a new gaol rather than enlarge their old one, and have given a committee authority to advertise for a site. The council have been compelled to this course unwillingly by the stringency of the law and the fear of the loss of Government countenance, and expense in transferring prisoners to fitting accommodation elsewhere. ——In course of the discussion on the above question, one of the committee stated that from information received from the governor of the county prison of St. Augustine's, near Canterbury, to which a new wing has been added, it appeared that the Government estimate of the cost of 70*l.* to 80*l.* per cell, as a separate part of the building, or 130*l.* to 150*l.*, including the cost of chapel, kitchen, and all necessary erections, seemed to be borne out by the results of the contract of St. Augustine's gaol. From the information furnished, he found that the total amount of the contract was—

Bricklayers', carpenters', slaters', and masons' work	£2,250
Plumbers' ditto	468
Smiths' ditto	530
	3,248
Warming and ventilating apparatus	217
	£3,465

The new building was an additional wing within the boundary wall of the prison, containing 40 cells, and the cost was 87*l.* per cell. The cells were 13 feet long, 7 feet wide, and 10 feet in height. The thickness between the cells was 14 inches; the outer wall 1 foot 10 inches, and 2 feet 3 inches at bottom; the width of gallery, 12 feet: size inside the walls, 59 feet 6 inches by 38 feet. The 40 cells are in three stories, besides underground offices.——The barracks at the Portland convict establishment are now almost completed, as are the arrangements for the speedy transit of the breakwater materials from the quarries adjoining, so that a large number of convicts will shortly be employed in the construction.——A subscription of 30,000*l.* has been opened with sums amounting to 8,000*l.*, for the erection and establishment of a new college at Oxford for poor scholars.——The Salisbury Gas Company are said to be preparing measures for pushing the sale of their gas amongst private families: low price and pure quality ought, of course, to be the main measures for the realization of the increased consumption of gas anticipated by the Company.——Several plans have been submitted to the Dover Harbour Board for deepening the harbour and preventing the further encroachment of the sea at the site of the esplanade. The Duke of Wellington presided at the board, and is said to have declared, that during his life he would do all he could to prevent the town from being washed away.——The new committee-rooms, offices, and warehouses on the wharf at Stourbridge, for the Stourbridge Canal Company, are now completed. Mr. Robinson was the architect, and Mr. John Thompson (of Kidderminster) the contractor.——We are glad to hear from our contemporary, the *Sheffield Times*, that there are "sundry unmistakeable symptoms indicative of a revival in the leading branches of the Sheffield trade."——A marble bust of Mr. Rushton, of Liverpool, stipendiary magistrate, has been completed, at the expense of his brother magistrates, and will be placed in St. George's Hall.——An attempt has been made to find a foundation at the Herd, South Shields, for a pier and docks. Nothing but sand, according to the *Gateshead Observer*, has been come to, after reaching a depth of four fathoms.——The winter series of accidents by explosion, arising from the stupid practice of taking lighted candles to *see* where the gas is escaping, has already begun. It is to be hoped that our contemporaries will prevent their frequent recurrence, by pointing out the danger, as well as absurdity, of such a practice, and advising trust in the nose, instead of the eye.——The rock in the Grange quarry, near Edinburgh, is now blasted by voltaic agency. The other day a slice of freestone was detached by the simultaneous discharge of six deposits of powder, without any very loud explosion. The mass was 63 feet long, 31 broad, and 40 deep, and its estimated weight is 5,508 tons.——No less than 20,000 families, or, on an average 100,000 persons, are supplied, it is said, by the Glasgow Water Company without the payment of any rates.——The Glasgow Bridge trustees propose to build a new bridge across the Clyde at Stockwell-street. The footpaths of Hutcheson's bridge are said to want widening.——A new tank is to be constructed near the hospital at Portobello barracks, Dublin, to contain 10,000 gallons of water. The estimate amounts to 220*l*. 13s. 8d.

RAILWAY JOTTINGS.

Some large wooden sheds erected for engines and carriages at the Scottish Central's station at Perth, gave way and fell, on Tuesday week, while workmen were engaged in taking away the sides, as they were supplied by walls of brick. A plumber was severely injured.——Since we lately alluded to the occurrence of accidents from the extreme want of clear dimensions in the construction of railway bridges, another death has occurred from the like cause. On the Lancashire and Yorkshire line a passenger, by merely putting his head out of the window of a carriage while in transit, had his skull mortally fractured by a cast-iron pillar, supporting a bridge crossing the line on horizontal beams of iron. He died in a few hours. It is but fair to state, however, that a substitute for so dangerous a nuisance was in course of erection; but the inquest jury expressed an opinion that unnecessary delay had occurred in its completion.——Another tube for the Britannia-bridge at Menai, is to be floated to its destination on 3rd inst. A serious accident lately occurred to one of the cylinders. The supports gave way, the cylinder was precipitated to the bottom of the channel, and two men were killed, and others wounded. Next day the cylinder was fished up for further duty. Mr. Fairbairn visited the tubes the other day, along with some German engineers, who are said to be engaged with him in the work of constructing a similar fabric across the Rhine. A wind gauge is reported to have indicated not the least deflection in the placed tubes during a heavy gale of wind lately. Loopholes, or oval windows, 5 inches in diameter, and 12 feet apart, are to be cut out in the outer sides of the tubes, to admit the light and "show the landscape" to passengers as they fly through the tube.——In Chancery, on Saturday week, the case of North-Western Railway Company *v.* Crouch, the carrier, came on. The defendant had claimed against the company for lost parcels and over-charges, and brought an action to recover above 200*l*. Thereon the company filed a bill of discovery, 710 folios in length. The defendant filed an answer, which extended to 3,200 folios, and the company now objected to five passages, as unnecessary. Master Senior allowed one of the exceptions, amounting to about twelve folios, and overruled all the others, with proportionate costs. So that the lawyers are to have the kernel, and the litigants the shells, as was threatened or anticipated.——A farmer was lately fined 1*l*., with 13s. costs, at York Castle, for making use of a return ticket issued to another who had already gone half his distance with it. The fine, however, was ostensibly for having travelled without any ticket at all.——A railway tunnel is to be cut under part of the town of Algiers. What would the *venerable* old Dey have said to such a doing in days of yore?

CORRECT ESTIMATING.

Being of opinion that by exposing in the pages of your valuable journal all tenders for work in which any striking difference appears, you will eventually succeed in crushing a system calculated, in my opinion, to injure the building community generally, I herewith forward you a specimen of *honest trading*, feeling assured you will, on perusal, agree with me that no proprietor can (after this) be reasonably expected to place faith in professional estimating. I enclose my card. A. B.

Tenders for a new church at Thirtleby, near Thirsk, Yorkshire; Mr. Lamb, architect.

	£	s.	d.
Hammond, Boroughbridge..	£995	0	0
Kay, Topcliffe	950	0	0
Biggins, Thirsk	927	0	0
Coates, Osmotherley	849	10	0
Akcroyd, York............	750	0	0
Ireson, Stokesly	329	0	0
Ewart, Northallerton	305	0	0

Difference only 690*l*.!

Tenders received by the Corporation of Gravesend, for the erection of new prison cells, &c.; Mr. J. Gould, jun., architect.

	Gross Tender.			Deduction for Old Buildings	Net Tender.		
	£.	s.	d.	£.	£.	s.	d.
Mayes	1,491	0	0	47	1,444	0	0
Laker	1,193	0	0	20	1,173	0	0
Wood	1,132	0	0	32	1,100	0	0
Carley*	1,061	0	0	51	1,010	0	0
Kirk	1,109	0	0	110	999	0	0
Godfrey	949	0	0	47	902	0	0
Lilleystone ..	950	0	0	50	900	0	0
Downs......	865	0	0	40	825	0	0
Cobham	839	18	5	50	789	18	5

The architect's estimate was 1,000*l*., and the majority of the Corporation determined against accepting any tender far below it.

CARPENTERS' HOURS.

MASTERS AND MEN.

There is a dispute now pending between the operative joiners of Liverpool and their employers, respecting the hours of labour during the months of November, December, January, and February. Formerly we worked from light to dark during this period, with a reduction of 2s. per week in our wages, which appears to have given satisfaction to both parties until the present time, when our employers are endeavouring to break through our established rules, and alter the hours of labour;—a strong desire being evinced to force upon us what they term the London rules, namely, that we work from six to six o'clock, using torch lights in unin-closed buildings, or otherwise to carry our tools from the building to the shop, and to work there until breakfast time, then back to the building during the day time, and return to the shop in the evening, with an understanding that we are to have summer wages. Such are said to be the London hours of labour. It may be so in what are termed the Jerry shops, where all the cheap novices of the country are employed, who require the assistance of the torch light to enable them to do a fair day's work for a low day's wages, but we cannot believe that the respectable building establishments have adopted such rules. If you will either authenticate this arrangement, or state what are the London hours of labour at the present time, you will much oblige the Liverpool carpenters and joiners.

Liverpool. An Operative.

* Accepted.

*** On inquiry we do not find that the arrangement proposed by the Liverpool masters is generally adopted in the larger London establishments. Probably, however, many of the men would be glad if it were, as it would enable them to earn the same wages as in summer, which is not now the case. At Mr. Thomas Cubitt's, men working in the shops and enclosed buildings, where a light can be used, make up the time by candle or gaslight, working from six in the morning till half-past five in the evening. Carpenters, working out of doors, or putting joists in buildings in course of erection, would be paid nine hours per day instead of ten. From 9th of November to 14th February their time is from seven till half-past four, with half-an-hour to dinner; during the dead of winter they can scarcely see to do anything at the commencement and close of day, but are paid for nine hours. The same arrangement is made at Messrs. W. Cubitt and Co.'s., and we believe at Mr. Grissell's. We understand that the men at one of these establishments last week made a request to be allowed to make up the time by candlelight.

DESTRUCTION OF WORKS OF DESIGN.

MR. HOPE'S HOUSE.

Sir,—Some people contend that wanton destruction is no longer perpetrated on works of design or art. Permit me to record the last of several instances which have occurred within my knowledge. About a week since, the workmen completed and left the doorway of my new house, No. 116, Piccadilly: this doorway, with its portico, contains a great deal of elaborate carving and metal-work,—more than I should have adopted had I not been guided by the advice of much-esteemed and very able professional advisers. Last night a metal door-handle was wrenched off and carried away, and force was used to destroy another. These handles had no value except such as belonged to their pattern, and must have been coveted for that, or destroyed from mere wantonness. In either case, this is an instance of the reception given in London to novelties of art manufacture.—I am, Sir, &c., Henry Thos. Hope.

116, Piccadilly, Nov. 28, 1849.

*** We shall be glad if the publicity thus given to this wanton outrage should lead to the discovery of the infamous perpetrator of it.

EXTENSION OF LONDON.

Owing primarily to the establishment of omnibuses, many thousand families of limited income have left the City to reside in the suburbs, which, if they were *suburban villages*, would be indeed advantageous; but as landlords have laid out the ground in small four, six, or eight-roomed tenements, with but small gardens attached to them, this advantage is mostly lost, for thereby has London increased in the present age more horizontally than vertically in proportion to former times (when the great mansions were deserted to be occupied in floors by the inferior orders), causing a proportionally excessive increase in sewerage, gas pipes, water pipes, and above all, instead of concentrating the smoke at the height of 40 feet above the pavement, spreading it out at the height of 20 to 30 feet. Better had it been if large houses, on a more commodious plan than the model St. Pancras one, had been erected in the suburbs (*e. g.* Islington), leaving the City-road bordered by fields as before.

And, indeed, even now, much might be done by throwing the front railings of front gardens back to the house fronts, in long avenues (*e. g.* City-road, Kennington-road, &c.), planting two or three rows of trees on this space between the pavement and the houses, which forms a most agreeable promenade. Unluckily, the demand for shops induces landlords to build over these foregardens. Quiet, straight streets (*e. g.* Gower-street) parallel to a great thoroughfare might be here and there planted with trees, to relieve the monotonous view of the houses.

It would be a great improvement if all the streets were numbered as in Paris, or as our Regent-street, viz., the odd numbers on the one side, and the even on the other, which might save many a useless crossing in muddy weather.

Suburban roads, when completed, ought to be numbered consecutively, leaving it to the fancy of the individual house-owner to call his house by any fanciful name.

LONDINENSIS.

METROPOLITAN COMMISSION OF SEWERS.

ANOTHER crisis is in course of preparation here, or we shall be surprised: the rate-payers are already beginning to stare, and ask,—What next?.

On Friday in last week a general court was held at the office in Greek-street, Lord Ebrington in the chair, when several resolutions were brought forward by the chairman, to the effect that Mr. Frank Foster be appointed as principal engineer to the commission, with entire control over the surveyors and their operations, and at a salary of 1,500*l.* a-year, including 200*l.* for travelling expenses; and that a bye-law to that effect be submitted for confirmation to a special court of sewers, to be holden at the expiration of a month at least from the court then present.

Sir J. Burgoyne supported the propositions. Previously, he said, a number of surveyors had been appointed to carry on the engineering duties of the establishment. These surveyors acting independently of each other, reporting and doing all their other duties independently, the Board became the controlling engineer, and it was needless to point out how incompetent a court constituted like theirs was for the discharge of such duties. He did not mean to charge any individual with impropriety of conduct. He referred only to the system. There were some very valuable men among their body of surveyors; and he was not sensible of any particular act which made them liable to reprehension in any direct degree. The commission too had a chief surveyor and a consulting engineer who were only so by name and not in reality. They were called to make separate reports sometimes, and at other times they were associated with the other surveyors, but only to consult with, and not to guide, control, or check them. Thus a spirit of antagonism arose among the officers; and it was a matter of public notoriety that the chief engineer and surveyor were at open warfare, while the commissioners were confounded between the two, and never knew how to act, or what judgment to form, in the matters brought before them. It was quite impossible that things could go on in that way. One of the most energetic governments that had ever existed was that of the Emperor Napoleon; and there was one part of his system from which he thought the court might take a lesson. When Napoleon determined on any measure he did not lay down ten or twelve principles, and direct that the execution of each should be entrusted to separate hands, but he said, "Mr. So-and-so is charged with the execution of this decree." The noble chairman was aware that this matter had been early pressed upon their notice after the reorganization of the commission, and the members came to the understanding that, as they could not decide for themselves, they would place the question in the hands of the two eminent engineers, Messrs. Stephenson and Rendel, requesting them to take the matter in hand. These two gentlemen thought that they would wish to have a third person associated with them, in order that there might not be any appearance of a personal bias in their minds. This was agreed to, and they did him the honour to propose that he should join them, which he did. They had deliberated on the subject, and were perfectly uniform in their opinions, and he thought that they might congratulate themselves that there was every mark of approval from the whole body of commissioners when their decision was intimated to them.

Mr. Stephenson re-echoed Sir J. Burgoyne's remarks on the necessity of a change of system, and the propriety of the choice pointed out in the resolutions. He took upon himself the responsibility of recommending Mr. Foster.

Sir H. De la Beche said it was obvious that while the commission was responsible to the public, they required some one as chief engineer, who should be responsible to them for the works which it was necessary to carry out. A single person only could be so appointed, and therefore the creation of the office had been recommended. At the same time, looking to the structure of the commission, he believed that the great principles of drainage for the metropolis might fairly be considered by the members of it themselves, and he trusted that the public would have confidence in their deliberations.

Mr. T. Hawes was of opinion that, with very little care in overhauling the accounts, the proposed salary would be much more than saved to the rate-payers.

Mr. Hardwicke complained of the insubordination and want of agreement amongst the officers, arising from the want of one great head.

Lord Ebrington drew attention to the constitution of the former Commission of Sewers, and stated that, in issuing the last commission, the necessity of appointing a responsible officer, such as was now proposed, had been foreseen and approved of by the Legislature, it being considered that the large area of the metropolis, with the exception of the city, should be considered as one district.

The resolutions were then put, and carried unanimously.

Miscellanea.

GOODRICH COURT.—Sir:—As architect to Mr. Meyrick, the present owner of Goodrich Court, I will thank you to allow me an opportunity of publicly contradicting, in the most unqualified terms, that part of a paragraph, contained in THE BUILDER of the 3rd inst., as to the removal of the armour, and which was copied from a local paper. There is no truth whatever in the statement. Not only is it Mr. Meyrick's intention to preserve the entire collection "intact," but to make such arrangements as will afford the public increased facilities for viewing it at all times: and I quite agree with you, Mr. Editor, that Goodrich Court may be considered, to some extent, as "national in its character."—HENRY HARRISON. 29, Bedford-square, Nov. 29, 1849.

SMOKY CHIMNEYS.—Observing two paragraphs in your paper on smoky chimneys, I would offer a few remarks. As to the first plan (p. 489, *ante*), I have adopted it for my temporary office (being clerk of works) in some cases by the hedge-side, and in others in some corner crowded by lofty buildings, being of opinion that a space like that mentioned was necessary to retain the compressed smoke, to prevent its blowing out into the room. But I have not found it succeed *in all cases*, like your correspondent, and if it did so the larger space could not be properly cleansed by the sweep's broom. In the second paragraph the author has stated facts and remedial measures. But I have something further to offer on this subject, and in the spirit of your paper let us all lend a helping hand, and so perhaps arrive at the remedy for so long-felt an evil. First, I have always taken care to avoid any space, but what needs be, from the register stove flap, or other fire grate, to the throat of the flue, and where I have the opportunity, I use 10-inch round pottery ware pipe, say from the throat of the flue to 3 feet above it, taking care to make the joints quite flush, and from thence gradually increasing the flue to 12 inches of the same material, and so continue it to within say 6 feet of the chimney-pot, and diminishing it in the same manner as at the throat. The chimney-pot, too, should be the same size, viz., 10 inches throughout within, whatever its form may be without, for architectural appearance, and should always terminate so as to prevent rain water getting into the flue, and also to assist the up draft by the wind. I have superintended the erection of a great many such chimneys, and never found them to smoke. But to construct flues of this size, it being of less area than that allowed by the Building Act, so much of the Act must be repealed (and why not?), since the original size was to afford room for climbing boys. It may be observed that the smoking of chimneys arises from a variety of circumstances; and, first, too often from irregular or bad construction. I have known the same chimney flue vary from 9 in. by 9 in. to 2 ft. 6 in. by 9 in., more or less (a mere hole); and, secondly, the chimney top so loosely stacked together, as to allow the rain water to saturate it for several feet down, thereby providing a complete condenser to the rarified smoke, and, as a matter of course, producing down-draft. The parallelogram 14 by 9, generally used, on account of its being consistent for the bond of the brick work, and also in accordance with the Building Act, is inconsistent with the natural shape assumed by smoke or rarified air.—J. KNIGHT.

PROJECTED WORKS.—Advertisements have been issued for tenders by 8th December for the reseating of Bridgewater parish church; by 31st, for the supply of 2½-inch Yorkshire stone for paving footways in St. Marylebone; by Thursday next, for the erection of workshops at Bow; by 11th, for the erection of a savings bank at Witham; by 3rd, for the erection of a public house and two sale shops at Sheffield; by a date not specified, for the working of iron-stone quarries at Stanhope-in-Weardale; by 11th, for making new line of road in Worcestershire; by a date not specified, for the purchase of about 70 miles of pipes, with bends, branches, &c.—also, for gasholders, condensers, purifiers, retorts, &c., all for an extensive gas-work for the Great Central Gas Consumers' Company; by 12th December, for locomotive stores, carriages, waggon stores, and general stores, for the Great Western Railway; and by 18th, for miscellaneous stores for the Lancashire and Yorkshire Railway.

COMPETITION.—An advertisement has been issued for plan and specification, by 1st Feb., 1850, for a new Wesleyan chapel at York—premium 35*l.*

SOCIETY OF ARTS.—November 21st: Mr. T. Webster in the chair. The Assistant-Secretary read a paper on Flexible Breakwaters and Lighthouses, by Mr. W. H. Smith, C. E. The paper, after alluding to the losses and amount of property annually sacrificed on our coasts, referred to various efforts that have been made by means of floating breakwaters to effect an economical barrier to the sea. The principle of Mr. Smith's proposed breakwater is to give elasticity to the structure. The models exhibited were formed of a long wall of open piles, divided into separate sections, each having an independent motion at the top, but secured, and pivoted at the bottom on the screw pile. The braces (with counterbalance weights at the centre), extending seawards from each side, are also affixed by the screw pile. The sections on being struck by the sea yield to it, thereby eluding violence, and the waves passing through the close grating are disseminated. The structure recoils when it becomes in equilibrium with the waves.

THE NEW COAL EXCHANGE has been opened for business. We mentioned the dissatisfaction of the factors with the way in which they were treated at the State-opening. A limited number of tickets were sent to them, the day preceding that of the ceremony, for the gallery *next the roof*, which they politely returned. A professional joke is circulating on the subject, to the effect that the corporation tried to put the *coal sellers* in the *attic*, but failed.

EDINBURGH ADORNERS.—Good Mr. Editor,—It is a curious fact that the architectural interests of "Modern Athens" appear to have been made over by her citizens to the tender mercies of *tailors*. The dean of guild, whose duty it is, as ædile, to preside over the buildings of the city, and at whose instance the venerable mansion of the Scottish reformer is at present threatened with destruction, is—not an architect, nor a man skilled in architectural matters, but—a tailor! and the memorial which has just been addressed to the Lords of the Treasury, for effecting the demolition of the Register-house Screen, is signed, in name of the committee, by a tailor as chairman, and another tailor as secretary. Far be it from me to join in the wholesale abuse of a class, which must necessarily be unjust, but it would seem that certain sons of the craft find as little compunction in adapting the works of an *old-fashioned* architect to the notions of modern "utility," as in turning an old coat, or in reducing the voluminous integuments of the parental nether-man to the schoolboy dimensions of a new generation. "Ne sutor ultra crepidam," say I; and it is well that the citizens of the classic metropolis of the north can rely in such matters upon the good taste and proper feeling of their representative in Parliament, who is also a Lord of the Treasury, and who is not likely, upon the representation of a few interested, or unskilful, or indifferent persons, to lend his countenance to such innovations, without being thoroughly persuaded and convinced of their necessity.

NO COBBLER.

Coming.—An "Artist's Almanac" for 1850, edited by an artist, which is to combine with an almanac a hand-book for artists and amateurs.——"Eight Views of the Church of St. Mary, at Stafford, in its present Restored State," from drawings taken by the late Mr. Masfen, Jun. The drawings were made by Mr. Masfen, with the desire of assisting in the decoration of the church, by appropriating the proceeds to the purchase of a painted window for the edifice. It pleased God to remove him before his work was complete, but his friends mean to carry out his intention by subscription.——It is proposed to issue a series of "Health Tracts," in aid of the sanitary movement, by the Tower Hamlets Association, and they are inviting parties to submit such to them for publication.

Fire Escapes.—After reading the letter in your journal, signed "P. W. H.," written with a very benevolent object to encourage the direction of the attention of mechanicians and engineers to the invention of fire-escapes,—the figure of a spiral or cylindrical spring was presented to my imagination, and it struck me, upon reflection, that from the compressibility of such a power into a small compass, it might possibly form the best principle for a contrivance of the nature required, whether used by suspension from a window, or from without, in the manner of the toy called "the jack-in-a-box," if sufficient elasticity for the required weight can be obtained, to allow of its rising from its platform, on the ground, when relieved from pressure, to the ordinary height of our third-floor windows. Two other principles have since occurred to me as applicable to the same object: one, applicable to a window, or from the ground, consisting of a number of metallic tubes, partially elastic across their diameters, and contained one within another, like a portable fishing-rod; the other, to be used from a platform on the ground, and to be formed on the principle of the "lazy bones," or multiplied scissars. These three inventions, or, more properly speaking, conceptions, placed on a platform, would occupy small comparative space, and be drawn by a horse, when placed upon wheels, with much greater facility than the long fire-escape ladders. The platform might move upon axles, so as to be inclined right or left to any window, when the machine was raised.—John Perceval, Kensington.

Model Dwellings for Labourers in France.—*La Presse* publishes "a novel list of shareholders," containing the names of upwards of 1,100 persons of every rank and condition of life, who have taken shares of 25 to 1,000 francs each in a society called "La Société des Cités Ouvrières," which has for its object to build improved lodging-houses for the poor, not only in Paris, but apparently in every large city of the republic. The capital of this society is to be six millions of francs, or 240,000*l.* sterling. It is under the patronage of the president, who is said to have contributed largely to it, and to take a lively interest in its success. The scheme is clearly based on that of our own model dwellings, but comprises also arrangements for work-rooms, and for the care of young children; a plan of providing furniture, to become the tenant's on purchase by small weekly instalments; the arrangement of a hall, or meeting-room, whereby coals and candles are saved to the tenant; and a register of working men and servants. One of the lodging-houses is already in course of erection in the second arrondissement. The rents are to be exceedingly low.

The **Britton Club** recommenced their social meetings on the 20th, when Mr. Cubitt was host, and Mr. Britton, Mr. Tooke, F.R.S., Mr. Humfrey, Q.C., Mr. Grissell, Mr. W. Cubitt, M.P., Mr. C. Hill, Mr. Cunningham, Mr. Jerdan, Mr. Gibbons, Dr. Conolly, and others, were present. The Autobiography in preparation for the subscribers to the Testimonial is more than half in type.

Proposed Architectural Lending Library.—The intention of establishing an architectural lending library in London, advertised for some time in our pages, and which seemed to promise advantage to students, has been abandoned; the number of persons who signified their intention to subscribe being too insignificant to justify the proprietor in making the necessary arrangements.

Electro-telegraphic Progress.—A list has been published, embracing all the principal towns in England and Scotland, but to all of which telegraphic communication is said now to extend from the two central stations at Lothbury and St. Martin's-le-Grand, the office, Strand, or the branches at Euston-square, Shoreditch, Waterloo-bridge, and Paddington.——The company have caused a criminal information to be issued against Messrs. Willmer and Smith, the Liverpool correspondents of the *Morning Herald*, and, if we mistake not, the promoters of a competitive electro-telegraphic company, for a libel published in the *Morning Herald* of 11th October last.——The celebrated American telegraph case of Morse *v.* O'Reilly has just been decided by the Supreme Court of the United States, in favour of Mr. Morse. A correspondent of a contemporary says—"Mr. Bain's projects will also be endangered by a suit brought against him by Mr. Morse, as well as the originality of his invention for making marks by the action of the electric fluid on paper prepared with a chemical solution. The ground is, therefore, narrowed down here to Morse and House, and these will, probably, share the public favour equally. Both in Morse's and House's systems, the action of the recording instruments is simple and unmistakeable. The other day, some of our telegraphic operators amused themselves by beating the time of various tunes at the distance apart of several hundred miles, and they did it with such accuracy that they were perfectly intelligible, even to the bystanders. In a very short time we shall have a continuous line from New York to Halifax, and as long as the Cunard steamers stop there it will be of great advantage to the newspaper press on both sides of the water. The telegraph has now become a most important agent of communication in this country, and large amounts of business are transacted by its means. I think the time is very near at hand when the American systems will supersede all the others now in use."—— The telegraph between Berlin and Stettin has been laid in gutta percha tubing, which it appears is no more able to withstand the inroads of those little land sharks—the mice, than we thought it possible that it might be to withstand the action of the ocean tribes in submarine telegraphs; for we find it reported that on a recent occasion, "the communication having been found to be interrupted, search was made for the cause, when a mouse's nest, with a little brood, was discovered in the gutta percha tube, which it appeared that the little animal had contrived to gnaw through, and so disturb the wires."

The **1851 Exposition.**—The gentlemen who are managing this matter must be careful, or they will raise a feeling against the project which, notwithstanding the excellence of the idea itself, and the machinery which has been cleverly put into motion, will yet wreck it. It is the subject of considerable dissatisfaction, very generally expressed, that appointments at large salaries are being made, and that the contract for the erection of the temporary building is actually entered into with a builder, without the concurrence or knowledge of the public, or a recognition of their right to be represented in the matter. Our caution is meant as a friendly one, and we hope it will be taken in time.

The **Western Literary Institution, Leicester-square.**—The glee concerts here have been very successful, and, better still, very creditable to the parties engaged.

A **Hint to the Freemasons of the West of England.**—At the dinner of the Colston Society, in Bristol,* the week before last, Mr. W. Proctor, with reference to the restoration of St. Mary Redcliffe Church, urged by Mr. W. D. Bushell, then present, who had headed the Freemasons on the day the first stone of the new works was laid,—said he had heard there was a disposition on the part of the craft to connect themselves with the restoration, and he suggested that they should set a-foot a subscription and undertake some special portion of the fabric. This would indeed be a return on the part of the craft to the good ways of their mediæval predecessors.

* Mr. William Powell was president. This society has assembled for more than 100 years, never missing, excepting in 1831, the year of the Bristol riots. Its object, twice blessed, is *charity*.

St. Peter's Church, Belmont.—A church and school situated at the village of Belmont, in the parish and about 5 miles from the town of Bolton-le-Moors, have just now been completed under the direction of Mr. J. E. Gregan, architect. Both were erected from a sum of money left for the purpose by the late Thomas Wright, Esq., of Belmont, and the land for the sites of both buildings has been given by the present possessor of the property. The church consists of chancel, nave, and aisles, western tower and spire, and south porch, with a vestry on the *south* side of the chancel, and an organ aisle on the north. The style is Early English; the roofs are all open, and there are no galleries whatever. The seats are low, of red deal, and afford accommodation for 500 worshippers. The chancel was originally designed to be of greater length, but for various reasons was curtailed. The church has all the advantages of a beautiful, although somewhat exposed situation, and is a conspicuous object in the valley. The contract for church and schools, with their fence, walls, &c., amounted to 3,650*l.* The church will shortly be consecrated by the Bishop of Manchester.

New Panorama of the Nile.—The Panorama of the Nile, painted by Messrs. Bonomi, Warren, and Fahey, mentioned by us some time ago, is now being exhibited in New York, and a fresh one has been painted by these gentlemen for London, and is now open to the public in the Egyptian Hall, Piccadilly. The artists have flattered us so far as to adopt both the suggestions we threw out in our notices of the first. It is not now a transparency, as the first was, but is lighted from the *front*, and they have in one place left the river to give a nearer view of one of the larger buildings, the great temple of Karnak, the result of which is the most effective and striking *tableau* in the whole series. We strongly advise our readers to visit this most instructive as well as beautiful panorama.

The **Kentish Town Literary Institution** is making satisfactory progress, and its projectors already begin to look forward to the possibility of erecting a building specially for its wants. A concert was given on Wednesday by the choral class, which ambitiously comprised Haydn's "Creation!"

The **Hall of Commerce**, Threadneedle-street, was knocked down at auction the other day for 44,900*l.* The site alone (9,000 feet) is said to have cost 35,000*l.*

The **Chester and Holyhead Railway.**—There is a strong impression that this railway must be shut up in consequence of its not paying. This line has certainly been most unfortunate, and most unfairly dealt with;—unfortunate in the extravagant cost of the Conway and Britannia bridges, which is several times above the estimate;—unfortunate in the unlucky position of Ireland, the trade of which has been destroyed by the free-trade principles,—unfairly dealt with by the Government withholding the 30,000*l.* for carrying the mails, merely because the Britannia-bridge is not complete, and further unfortunate, by a branch of that very Government (the Admiralty) running their boats against them.—*Herepath's Journal.*

TO CORRESPONDENTS.

"A Hertford Man" should send us his name, in confidence, as guarantee of good faith.

"A. R. P.—The Architectural Publication Society's third Part is in active preparation: the delay has been unavoidable. Subscribe at once for the ensuing year.

Received—" E. C. M." (the letter appears to have been destroyed). "Mr. G.," Lothbury (shall have a cotbet), "B." "J. G.," "One who takes in Tae Builds" (we have not time to refer"). "F. C.," "C.," Westminster (the drawing is being transferred, but we cannot stipulate a time for its appearance). "G. W." (it was his own request, not out), "W. F. R." (next week), "Z.," (Wrexham), "H. S.," "W. F. V.," "H. E. R.," "C. R. S.," "J. W. R." (shall appear), "J J." (shall appear), "Prospectus of Architecture" (unavoidably postponed), "G. W." (next week), "F. J. J.," "W. A." (It depends on the terms of the conveyance), "T. J.," "H. M.," "G. R. B." (yes—from 4 past 1 o'clock till § past 2), "A Subscriber," "P. B." (will find many papers on the subject in former volumes. To re-cover the commission in court of law, it is necessary to prove the work done was worth the money charged): "W. P.," Islington (declined with thanks: left with publisher). "The Mother Country, or the Spade. the Waste, and the Eldest Son ;" by Sidney Smith (Kendrick, Charlotte-row, Mansion-house). " Bogue's Pocket Diary and Calendar for 1850 (Fleet-street). " Punch's Pocket-Book for 1850 (London: Punch Office). " Pictorial Maps of the Land, the Sea, and the Heavens (London: John Mitchell, Old Bond-street). Wright's " History of Ireland from the earliest Period" (Tallis: London and New York). " London in 1843" " British Almanac and Companion, for 1850" (C. knight).

NOTICE.— All communications respecting *advertisements* should be addressed to the "Publisher," and not to the "Editor;" all other communications should be addressed to the EDITOR, and *not* to the Publisher.

" *Books and Addresses.*"—We have not time to point out books or find addresses.

ADVERTISEMENTS.

BUILDERS AND CONTRACTORS.
TARPAULINS for COVERING ROOFS during Repairs. SCAFFOLD CORD and every description of ROPE used by Builders upon the lowest terms. Marquees and tents of a superior quality or make on hire, or defrayed purchased in the most prompt attention.—WILLIAM PIGGOTT, 118, Fore-street, City. Manufacturer, by Appointment, to Her Majesty's Honourable Board of Ordnance.

TO ARCHITECTS. BUILDERS. AND OTHERS.
ENTIRELY NEW APPLICATION of WIRE WORK, in lieu of laths for ceilings, &c. This great deal deflation has been accomplished with entire approbation at the famous Asylums of Chester and Stafford, rendering the buildings secure against the ravages of fire, as from even lower than ordinary lath.—Manufactured by JOHN ALLDAY and SON, 109, Moseley-street, Birmingham. Particulars sent on application.

PAPIER MACHE and CARTON PIERRE ENRICHMENTS MANUFACTORY, 48 and 50, Rathbone-place.—GEORGE JACKSON and SONS beg the attention of Architects. Builders. Decorators. and others, to their large assortment of ENRICHMENTS in every style, executed in the lightest class of art.
Of art, facilities and proposed enlargement of means enable GEORGE JACKSON and SONS to announce the execution of works of the above descriptions in these advantageous plan at a cost considerably below any known method, whilst for quality, relief, and finish, they flatter themselves they stand unrivalled.
Just published—a large Quarto Work of their ENRICHMENTS, with dimensions for reference and price.

ILLUSTRATED TRADE LISTS, price 2d., or free to post for four stamps, containing much information useful for REFERENCE. also TESTIMONIALS. Respecting a MATERIAL which, when well wrought, is probably superior to every other for drains or conduits (as glazed or artificial stone for curbs, for ridge, hips, valleys, and every sort of roofs, for drain or chimney pipes, for draining troughs, tiles and flooring tiles, &c.
To be had GENUINE at WILLIAM PEAKE'S (principally of "Peake's Terra Metallic"), No. 4 Wharf, City-road Basin. London ; also, at the Tiberias. Thurnall. Staffordshire. Articles would be supplied to any extent, and despatched to any part of the world. The lists contain prices by measure as well as by weight. The lists are postpaid, and to any if the London or Staffordshire places are wanted.

CROGGON'S PATENT ASPHALTE ROOFING FELT and INODOROUS FELT. for DAMP WALLS. Sold in foils, 32 inches wide: price one penny per square foot. also, for Half Felt for covering the Palliation of heat and dampness sound Samples. directions, and testimonials sent by post, on application to CROGGON and Co., No. 2, Dowgate-hill, Walbrook.

PAVING, 2s. 9d. PER SQUARE YARD. Basements, Foot-walks, Malt-houses, Cow Stalls. Floors of Warehouses, and every description of Pavement laid down at the above low price, and the work guaranteed.—Apply to JOHN H. KINGDON, INDURATED BITUMEN PAVEMENT OFFICE, 3, JOHN-STREET, ADELPHI.— N.B. Country Agents and Railway Engineers and Conductors supplied with the best bitumen for coating bridges and drains.

SEWERAGE of LONDON.—The attention of the COMMISSIONERS appointed to determine upon the most efficient material for the Construction of the Sewers of London is particularly affected to the ASPHALTE of SEYSSEL, which, more than any other material, is applicable to the constructing and interfed coating of Brick Culverts, and other channels for Sēwage. The Co-partnership made by the Royal Africans Company of Plymouth Citadel, constructed of Seyssel Asphalted Brickwork. upon the chaos of the Honourable Board of Ordnance, have fully proved the superiority, after immense supply of such material. whole of the old cementitious compositions.—A printed account of these experiments can be had on application to J. FARRELL, Seyssel, Seyssel Asphalte Company, Claridge's Patent. Established 1838.
Note.—The application of the Asphalte of Seyssel is specially recommended by the Commissioners on the Plan at the net cost by the ground floor of Brick-work in masonry situations, and it has been suggested that it would be peculiarly applicable for coating the Arms of disused Graveyards, and for the construction of catacombs.

CAEN STONE, SELECTED FOR EXTERNAL WORKS—LUARD. BEEDHAM and Co., Quality Proprietors and Importers from a Remange.
AUBIGNY STONE from the Quarries. pref Palaise, Calvados Department.—A supply is of similar colour to Portland stone. Its texture finer than Portland, price and labour of working about the same.
HAINVILLE STONE from Ranville Quarries. near Caen, Normandy.—Suitable for strong walks, wharf and quay walling, price and labour similar to Caen Stone—Depōt, Caen-Suburrney Wharf, Rotherhithe; Vauxhall-bridge, Westminster; No. 9 Wharf, Paddington-Basin; Norfolk Wharf, Battle-bridge; and Kensington-Basin.—Information and samples supplied from the Office, 13, South-walk-square, Borough.

CAEN STONE.—Wm. J. and J. FREEMAN beg Caen Stone, guaranteed from the best quarries in Allemagne, at 1s.3d per cubic foot, delivered to vessels or wagons from their warehouse Wharf at Deptford. Being the inferior beds, or from the Maladrerie Quarries, if obtained on lower terms. Cargoes shipped direct from the quarries to any of the ports in the state office. Aubigny and Ranville Stone on the lowest terms.—Application at the Office, Millbank-street : or to Mr. TURNBULL, Sufferance Wharf, Grove-street, Deptford.

STIRLING'S BELVEDERE SLATE WORKS, Belvedere-road, Lambeth.—A reduced list of prices of the best WELCH SLATE SLABS, planed both faces, will be sent on application (post paid) being made, and inclosing a postage stamp. The prices are under those advertised for inferior stone.

VALENTIA SLATE SLABS.—The attention of the public is invited to the large importations now being made of this valuable material from the county of Kerry, Ireland. Its strength, durability, and non-absorbent property. Recommend it for general use. The experiments made by experiments of the Board of Ordnance establish that to break slabs of equal dimensions required

	Cwt. qrs. lbs.
For Yorkshire Stone	3　　3　0
For Valentia Slate	11　1　23

It is well adapted for shelves, cisterns, paving, &c.—Depōt, Valentia Slate Yard, Millbank-street.

PIMLICO SLATE WORKS.—GREAT REDUCTION in the PRICE of SLATE.—Mr. MAGNUS has the pleasure to publish the following Reduced prices for Welch Slate Slabs of the finest quality, with sawn edges, and planed both aces :—

	Thick.				
	1 in.	1¼ in.	1½ in.	1¾ in.	2 in.
Under 4 ft. long, or 3 ft wide	3½	5	6	7	8 ½ ft. sup.
Ditto 5 ft. do., or 3 ft. do.	4	5½	7	9	10
Ditto 6 ft. do., or 3 ft. do.	4½	6	8	9	14 do.
Ditto 7 ft. do., or 3 ft. do.	5	7	9	11	15 do.

Larger Slabs in proportion.

	Thick.				
	¾ in.	1 in.	1¼ in.	1½ in.	1¾ in.
Cutting to order	d.	d.	d.	d.	d.
	4	4	4½	4½	6 ft. sup.

FURTHER REDUCTION in the value of OUTSTAND. Cisterns above 100 gallons, planed both faces, inch thick, grooved and bottomed. Fixing whilst five miles of the manufactory. 8d. per foot super. or 6d. per foot cube. Enamelled boiled Chimney-pieces, variously marbled, hitherto priced at 40s. to 60s. now reduced to 55s. and 30s. The above prices are all net to the trade.
Mr. Magnus will send his book of Drawings of Chimney-pieces, and printed price-list of ditto. Free to any part of the country. on receipt of 12 postage stamps (or be deducted from first order received.) and which will be subject to a very liberal discount to the trade.—Address, 59, Upper Belgrave-place, Pimlico.

SAMUEL CUNDY, Mason and Builder, PIMLICO MARBLE and STONE WORKS, Belgrave Wharf, Pimlico.
GOTHIC WINDOWS, ALTAR SCREENS, and other Works, produced at a remarkably cheap rate.
FONTS from 4l. upwards. Specimens on view of the Early English. Decorated, and Perpendicular styles.
ALTAR TABLETS illuminated.
Elaborate ARTISTS Retained for SCULPTURED GOTHIC CARVINGS.
A Good VEINED MARBLE CHIMNEY-PIECE and a fashionable REGISTER STOVE for 3l 3s. Stone Chimney-pieces from 8s.
MEMORIAL CROSSES. MONUMENTS. TOMBS. HEAD-STONES, &c., in great variety of design. Letters cut and complete for fixing in the country.
The Public are respectfully invited to view the carefully selected and manufactured Stock (by improved machinery) of Veined Marble Chimney-pieces—cheap and good.
A liberal discount to the trade.

RESTORATION of CHURCHES. SAMUEL CUNDY, having had much practice in this branch at Westminster Abbey and other important Gothic fabrics, is desirous of Estimating for Restorations.
S. C. has executed a Machine for Hoisting Building Materials to great altitudes, by which an immense saving has been effected ; and recently adopted for Rebuilding Cathedrals. High Towers, &c.
CLERKS of WORKS have itself or the a selection suited to the above establishment. A Book of DesignsofforWorkon application.
Works of all kinds prepared and sent off per railway—fixed or not required.
DAIRIES fitted up with MARBLE or SLATE SHELVES.—MINTON'S Encaustic and White or Blue and White Porcelain Tiles in great variety of pattern.

STATUES, VASES, FOUNTAINS, Garden Ornaments, Coats of Arms, and Architectural Embellishments. in Improvable Stone, by VAUGHAN and CO., 60, Stones' End, Borough. London. T. J. Oregon. late of Coade's, Superintendent—Specimens may be seen at Christ Church, & c. & Dowgate-hill, City. A pamphlet of drawings forwarded on application.

MARKET WHARF, REGENT'S-PARK BASIN.—Messrs. MARTIN and WOOD (late Scoles and Martin) solicit the attention of Builders, Masons and others, to their stock of Portland, Yorks. and Derby Stone, also Bangor Stone, Lime, Cement, Plaster, Bricks, Tiles, Laths, Fire-goods, Drain-pipes, &c. sold at the lowest possible prices for Cash. Portland, Bradstone, Ledgers. Steps, Landings, &c. cut to order of the choicest quality. Tarpaulins let on hire. A Stock of Northen's Drain-Pipes, Syphons, &c. always on hand. Mortar, Lime and Half. Fine Stuff, &c.

BATH STONE of BEST QUALITY.
RANDELL and SAUNDERS, QUARRYMEN and STONE MERCHANTS, BATH.
List of prices, also cost for transit to any part of the kingdom, forwarded on application.

BATH STONE.—Messrs. RANDELL and SAUNDERS, Quarrymen. Bath, have appointed Messrs. MARTIN and WOOD (Wharf agents in London. M. and W. beg to inform Architects, Masons. Builders, &c. that a large assortment of the much approved CORSHAM DOWN and other BATH STONE will always be kept at the Depōt, opposite the Great Western Railway Station, Paddington. Offers will also be received at Market Wharf, Regent's-park Basin.

ANSTONE STONE WHARF, Paddington.—Mr GRISELL has the honour to inform Architects and Builders that he has made arrangements for the SUPPLY of the ANSTONE STONE for all building purposes, and which can now be sent at the above wharf by application to W. W. G. WARDLE, of whom every information can be obtained.
N.B. The stone used in the election of the New Houses of Parliament was supplied EXCLUSIVELY from this quarries.

ANSTON STONE, used for Building the New Houses of Parliament.—W. WRIGHT and Co. beg to inform Architects. Engineers. Builders, and others, the Anston Stone can be supplied in any quantity on the shortest notice. This valuable stone, so celebrated for its durability, colour, and texture, is well known, having been selected in preference to all others, by the Commissioners of Woods and Forests, for building the New Houses of Parliament. It is very superior for Monuments, Tombs, &c.
W. Wright and Co. have made arrangements to have a stock always on hand at Brice's Marble and Stone Wharf. Horsferry-basin, Maiden-lane, King's-cross.—Any further information can be obtained on application to W. WRIGHT and Co., Anston. near Sheffield; or to T. BRAY, Wharf Bole Agent in London, 27, Burton-crescent.

CAITHNESS STONE, from the Castle-hill Quarry. by Thurso.—It is procured at any price, of any size, ready for laying. The face may be natural, tooled, or rubbed as required. This paving gives great satisfaction, and is supplied of larger dimensions than ordinary. The footpath recently laid on Vauxhall-bridge is all in chosen. above 4 feet long, and the paving on the Bridge over the Neva, lately supplied by order of the Emperor of Russia, is all in course of great admiration.—Application at Messrs. H. POTTER & Co., wharf-owners, Newington. will meet with every attention.—Depōt, at Freeman's Wharf, Millbank-street.

REDUCED PRICES.—EDWARD BINNS (late William Cleaver, of Wilton-road, Pimlico Basin, begs to acquaint Builders and the Trade that he has now on hand, at his Manufactory (the first of the kind ever established), a very large assortment of Dry and Well-seasoned OAK and DEAL FIRE-PARED FLOORING BOARDS and MATCH BOARDING of all sorts. (from 1 inch to 1½ inch thick, planed in a parallel width and thickness. and at greatly Reduced Prices. Also, Timber, Deals, Oak Planks, Beadings, Sash Bar, Mouldings prepared by Machine's Lathe, &c.—Apply at E. BINNS'S (late W. Cleaver's) Flooring Manufactory, Wilton-road, Pimlico Basin.

FLOORING.—ALFRED ROSLING begs to inform his customers and the trade generally, that he has again very materially REDUCED the PRICES of his DRY FLOOR BOARDS. of which he has in stock an extensive assortment. To purchasers of a quantity of freshly dressed, boards. A. R. is able to offer a great reduction upon his current prices, to avoid the expense of piling away in the drying sheds. Mouldings in great variety, and prepared in a very superior manner.—Southwark-bridge Wharf, Bankside. October, 1849.

MUIR'S PATENT
PLANING MACHINE.
SAW MILLS. GILLINGHAM-STREET, PIMLICO.
TIMBER of any size, PLANK, DEALS, and BATTENS, &c., sawn on the most approved principles. Boards. &c. Prepared. Matched. and Grooved. by Muir's Patent Machinery. The Mills have all the advantages of navigation and water-carriage, being connected with the Thames by the Grosvenor Canal. Goods fetched from the docks and carted home free of charge.
Address to HENRY SOUTHAM, Saw Mills, Gillingham-street, Pimlico.
N.B. Estimates given for Sawing and Planing.

PHILLIPS, ALLCARD, and CO.'S IMPERIAL DEAL SAW-MILLS, WENLOCK-ROAD, CITY-ROAD, beg to invite the attention of builders, carpenters and the trade, to their well selected stock, consisting of a large assortment of TIMBER. DEALS, PLANKS, and BATTENS. of every description, and thoroughly seasoned. They also have constantly on hand, and ready for immediate use. white and yellow FLOORING BOARDS of all thicknesses, and matched riding, cut and planed to a parallel breadth and thickness. And they are enabled to offer all their goods at very moderate prices.

DESICCATED WOOD—DAVISON and others, will find it much to their advantage to patronise this process of seasoning. The Seasoned wood can thus be easily be seasoned in an indefinitely short space of time, at a small cost, but is thoroughly seasoned, equally free from shrinkage, and in every respect better than wood desiccated in the ordinary way ; thereby saving capital, interest of money, insurance, and all the other inconveniences attending the keeping of a large stock.
The DESICCATING SAW-INC and PLANING MILLS are situated at PLOUGH BRIDGE, ROTHERHITHE. Adjoining the Commercial and East Country Docks. from whence parties obtaining wood material can have the same copyright and Royalty, and rent borne fit for immediate use.—T. GIRLING. Manager.
For licenses to use the patent, scale of prices, or other information, address. the ANGUS JENNINGS, Secretary. Patent Desiccating Company. 41, Gracechurch-street, City.

THOMAS ADAMS, Mahogany and Timber Merchant. Bermondsey New Road. Southwark, near the Bricklayers' Arms, is SELLING SEASONED FLOORING at LESS PRICES THAN ANY ADVERTISED ; also, matched boards and mouldings prepared from the very best materials, and in a superior manner. Cut deals and scantlings of every dimension ; mahogany, cedar, Rose-wood, wainscot, elm, beech, oak. &c., panels, oak, and fir laths ; wheelwrights' goods. All sawn and planed goods always prompt delivered free of expense. Saving charged at mill prices. Very extensive dying-sheds.
N.B. English timber taken in Exchange for foreign.

TO ARCHITECTS. BUILDERS. UPHOLSTERERS. AND OTHERS.
WOOD CARVING done in the cheapest and best manner. Estimates given to any amount. Pulpits. Reredos-desks. altar-rails. stalls. and other church fittings supplied complete. Old carvings matched by J. BRETSON. Wood Carver and Manufacturer, 43. Belvedere-street. Soho. London.

JORDAN'S PATENT MACHINE CARVING and MOULDING WORKS for WOOD and BONE. Belvedere-road. Lambeth. and 154. Strand.—TAYLOR. WILLIAMS. and JORDAN beg to call the attention of the building community to a new branch of their establishment, and, at the same time, to thank their numerous patrons and friends for the very liberal support they have experienced, which, they assure them and the public it will be their constant endeavour to deserve, by giving their customers an increased share of the advantages arising from the constant improvements in the machinery which they have just succeeded in applying to the production of the most intricate carving in stone and other freestones, and in statuary marble.
T. W. and J. particularly solicit the attention of architects and builders to the fact that, by the use of this machinery, a very large saving, both of time and money, is effected,—so great, indeed, that in many cases they can deliver a well-finished article in Caen stone for less money than it can be chafened in cement. while itself wood-carving will, in some cases, be found to come into close competition with the best kinds of composition ornament.—For prices and estimates apply at 154. Strand.

TESTIMONIAL from CHARLES BARRY, Esq. " Westminster, May 15th, 1846.
" Gentlemen,—In reply to your letter requesting my opinion of your recent Carving Machinery, I have much pleasure in stating, from an experience of more than two years, its application to the production of the wood carvings of the House of Peers, and other requirements of the New Palace, at Westminster, that I am enabled to write the most favorably testimony, and I am the more so to add that it has much than justified the favourable terms in which I recommended it in 1840 to Her Majesty's Commissioners of Woods and Works for adoption.—I remain, Gentlemen your obedient
" CHARLES BARRY."
Messrs. Taylor. Williams. and Jordan."

PAPER-HANGINGS.—At E. T. ARCHER'S Manufactory for English and Warehouse for supply of all kinds of English and French Paper-hangings from One Penny per yard. to the most costly panelled decorations. The decorations are fitted up on the walls of an extensive Suite of show Rooms. showing at once the effect of a design upon the finish. fit for occupation.—Painted marble or chintz proofs of superior fabric. from One Penny per Yard.—451, Oxford-street.

PAPER-HANGINGS. — TO BUILDERS and LARGE CONSUMERS.—ROBERT HORNE, Paper-hanging Manufacturer, 41. Gracechurch-street, City. invites builders and the trade to inspect his extensive stock of NEW DESIGNS in PAPER-HANGINGS, which, by the aid of powerful machinery, he is enabled to offer at the following unprecedented prices. in stock quantities, for cash only, viz:—

	s.	d.	
Bed-room papers, in great variety ...	...	3½	per piece
An excellent satin paper ...	...	4	
Silting-room ditto, on blocked grounds ...	7d to	10½	
Hand-made marbles ...	...	1s. 3d. to 2s. 0d.	
Good satin papers ...	...	1s. 3d. to 3s. 0d.	
Rich flock papers (by a new process) ...	2s. 6d. to 4s. 6d.		

In addition to which, he has always on hand every novelty in French damask papers and Decorations, which he imports direct from the best manufacturers in France, as soon as their new patterns are ready to select from.—R. H. also calls the attention to his new designs in satin flittings for panelled decorations of his own manufacture, all of which he has registered, and as his extensive facilities of fancy goods the specimens are journal of Dealer and Grocer to select from. He also calls the attention to his new sundanese Dry-wood, chintz, and marble Paper-hangings, none, and offers a discount from the country, showing the style and quality of the above. on Receipt of two postage stamps, and the goods despatched with promptitude, on Receipt of a remittance to the amount of the order given.—Folding screens in great variety, wholesale and retail.

No. CCCLVII.

SATURDAY, DECEMBER 8, 1849.

R. CHOWNE'S "air-syphon" system of ventilation, mentioned by us in some previous numbers of this journal, has excited the curiosity of many of our readers, who appear to expect from us a fuller development of its nature. The importance of an efficient, cheap, and simple method of ventilation cannot be over-rated, and claims for every scientific and honest endeavour to provide it the fullest protection, careful and candid consideration, and the most liberal encouragement.

In the specification of his patent, Dr. Chowne sets it forth as follows :—

"My invention consists of applying a principle which I have found to prevail in the atmosphere of moving up the longer leg of a syphon and of entering and descending in the shorter leg, and this without the necessity for the application of artificial heat to the longer leg of a syphon. And in order that my invention may be most fully understood, and readily carried into effect, I will proceed to describe the means pursued by me; and in doing so I will, in the first place, enter more at large into the principle on which the invention is based.

"I have found that if a bent tube or hollow passage be fixed with the legs upwards, the legs being of unequal lengths, whether it be in he open air or with the shorter leg communicating with a room or other place, that the ir circulates up the longer leg, and it enters nd moves down the shorter leg, and that this ction is not prevented by making the shorter ag hot whilst the longer leg remains cold, and o artificial heat is necessary to the longer leg f the air-syphon to cause this action to take lace ; thus is the direction of the action of ir in a syphon the reverse of that which takes lace in a syphon, or like bent passage or tube, vhen used for water and other liquid, wherein he water or other liquid enters and rises up n the shorter leg and descends or moves down n the longer leg. And my invention consists of applying this principle when ventilating ooms or apartments, such as those of a house ir ship, or other building or place."

He then goes on to describe the invention s applied to the rooms of a house where there re chimneys opening into such rooms, and ays, in these cases "I employ the chimney as he longer leg of the air-syphon, which I rrange in order to ventilate a room, and I am nabled to use the chimney whether for the ime being there is or is not a fire lighted in te fireplace of the room; but I prefer, when here is no lighted fire, that the fireplace should e closed either by a register stove being shut, 'one be used, or if not, by a close chimney-oard, or by other convenient means, nd I form a passage or channel either 'hen constructing the building, or by cutting way if not previously constructed, or I other-ise form such channel or passage, or more ian one, from the upper part of the room or ear the ceiling of the room, and cause it to escend and to enter the chimney at a point oove the top of the fireplace, when it is an pen fireplace, and it may be lower down 'hen closed; and in order that the whole of

the upper part of the room may be in communication with such descending passage or channel leading to the chimney, I form a hollow cornice sufficiently open to allow of the atmosphere at or near the upper part of the room to flow into the same, and owing to the atmospheric syphon which will thus be formed, there will be a constant flow of the air in a direction from the upper part of the room down the descending channel or passage, which will represent the shorter leg, and thence into the chimney and away up the chimney, which will constitute the longer leg of the air-syphon."

When fixed gas-burners or lamps are used, then he prefers that a tube or hollow passage should be conducted down to form the shorter leg of the air-syphon, in any convenient direction, and be caused to enter the chimney as before described, or such channel or passage may be of metal or other material projecting from the walls of the buildings, or it may be down pillars or channels independent of the walls, where the architecture or ornamental portion of the walls or other parts will admit of it ; and, so far from its being necessary that there should be any bell over the chimney of a gas-burner or other lamp, the patentee has found that having, close to the top of the glass chimney, a *lateral* tube opening into the shorter leg of the syphon, is by far the most effectual way of getting rid of the heated air from the lights : the products, in place of rising up and becoming diffused in the room, pass rapidly through the lateral tube into the shorter leg of the syphon. Of this, however, we will speak again presently.

At the risk of repetition, we will mention something of what we have seen at the patentee's residence, in illustration of the principle involved. At the back of his house the Doctor has fixed a small zinc pipe, running from the level of the ground to over the roof of the house, and turning up at the bottom three or four feet, to form a syphon. The smoke of burnt paper, brought near to the mouth of this short end, gave evidence, by its rapid *descent*, of the current through the pipe. When the bend of the syphon, next the ground, was made to extend the whole length of the garden, and there to turn up the three or four feet as before, the action was the same, and so it was when a jacket of *hot water* was placed around the short arm of the pipe.

This arrangement is in the open air, it must be remembered ; and the patentee states that in all seasons and at all times,—in the middle of a July day with a hot sun on the pipe, or at midnight in December when it is cased with ice,—the current is always the same, with the exception only that sudden gusts of wind will occasionally cause a partial return of it.

In the room wherein the patentee has carried on his experiments, filled with tortured and convulsed pipes, and as many gas-lights as would illuminate a chapel, we were able to see the practical application of the simple fact established by the pipe outside. Here the *chimney* formed the long leg of the syphon, a chimney-board filled the opening of the fireplace (there being no fire in the grate), and the shorter legs of the syphon (for there were several, all connected with the one longer leg, either through the chimney-board or by an opening above the register direct into the flue), consisted of pipes brought from different parts of the room. The mouth of one pipe opened close under the ceiling, the mouth of another half way up the height of the room, but

through each equally there the current was made manifest when the smoke of burnt paper was applied. Some seats around the room had a rude channel formed beneath them by means of stout paper, which was loosely connected, at one extremity, with an upright open-mouthed tube in an angle of the room, about the height of a man, and at the other, equally slightly, with the chimney. The force of the current produced was extraordinary.

It is scarcely necessary to point out the means thus afforded for ventilating large assemblies. Busts on pedestals might be made to contain pipes, or the pipes might be let into the walls and partitions. In sick rooms a flexible tube might be suspended over the person and bed, and then be conducted in such a manner as to descend and enter a chimney, which would produce a constant flow of the atmosphere of the room through the tube, and so away.

A supply of fresh air, to take the place of the vitiated air removed, must be provided, but this does not enter into the present patent. The doctor seems to content himself " with the pure air, which is constantly flowing into the room by the door or other openings,"—but this is an inartificial and inefficient mode of supply, which should not be depended on under other than very ordinary circumstances.

A second syphon, perhaps, might be usefully employed, having the short end outside the house, and the opening of the long end near the ceiling of the apartment within, thus reversing the action, and bringing in fresh air in such a manner that it might be spread throughout the room without producing draughts.

The patentee further proposes to apply his system to ventilate the goaf of a mine :—" In such a case," he says, " one or more pipes, or channels, being laid therein, and carried as high up as possible, the other end of such passage is to be carried up one of the shafts of the mine to the surface of the earth, and opened into a chimney, which would become the longer leg of the atmospheric syphon, by which arrangement the gases and atmosphere of the goaf, in place of from time to time getting into the mine, would be constantly carried away. And if desired, the whole of the mine may be ventilated in this manner, for in place of having a furnace in the upcast shaft, as now practised, it will be only necessary to raise a tall chimney over the upcast shaft, so that the downcast shaft and the mine below shall be made the shorter leg of the atmospheric syphon, and the chimney and upcast shaft the longer leg of the syphon, and thus a constant ventilation will go on."

And now as to the gas-lights : we consider the establishment by Dr. Chowne of the fact that to take away the heat and deleterious products of combustion the opening should be not *over*, but close to and forming a right angle with the top of the glass chimney, one of the most valuable results of his experiments. In the room to which we have referred there is an upright hollow pillar communicating at the bottom with the chimney, and bearing around the upper part of it a number of gas-burners. Just above each glass chimney is a short tube about 2 inches diameter, projecting laterally from the hollow pillar into which it opens; and just touching the lip of the glass. A thermometer was suspended within the pillar, and on lighting the gas this rose in a very few minutes from 65 deg. to 100 deg., while the apartment remained cool. The effect of the lateral tube is made evident in this, — that while the tube is open a piece of paper may be held with safety over the chimney of the gas-light, but when the tube is closed it inflames instantaneously,—showing to what extent the heat is carried off by the tube.

We will not disguise our fear that the Doctor is not likely to reap that pecuniary return to which his ingenuity and perseverance justly entitle him. One of our correspondents, whose letter (p. 499 ante) was founded to some extent on a misconception of the system, considered that Dr. Chowne had simply asserted a principle, and that a patent for it could not be maintained. Let us inquire into this.

Mr. Carpmael, in his book " On the Law of Patents for Inventions," is very explicit in distinguishing between a patent for *all* applications of a principle and the application of it to any particular object. In reference to the law of gravitation, Mr. Carpmael says, p. 16, " It would have been an absurdity to suppose, that a patent for all applications of the principle of this natural law could have been granted." But he further says, p. 16, " although a principle in itself cannot be the subject of a patent, the newly combining or applying a known principle to a machine or in a manufacture, whereby it becomes in any way improved, is an invention suitable to be protected by a patent."

In Messrs. Billing and Prince's " Law and Practice of Patents,"* the opinion of some of the judges on this point is quoted. Mr. Justice Buller has said, "A patent cannot be maintained for an idea or principle alone." " A principle reduced into practice means a practice founded upon principle, and that practice is a thing done or made, or the manufacture which is invented." Mr. Justice Heath has said, " There can be no new patent for a mere principle; but for a principle so far embodied, and connected with corporeal substances, as to be in a condition to act, and to produce an effect in any art, trade, &c., a patent may be granted." In other words, it may be asserted that a law of nature, or property of matter, cannot be patented, but a mode of turning this to account in the operations of life can be,—and this is exactly what Dr. Chowne may claim.

There would seem, however, to be a difficulty in preventing any individual from putting up such pipes as might be necessary for himself, and it would probably even be shown that the same arrangement had been often made by others many years ago. We ourselves did so seven or eight years ago, without a precise idea perhaps of the exact mode of its operation beyond forming a vent. The circumstances were these. At a large silk merchant's establishment, at the west-end of London, three stout healthy young countrymen, who had come into the house one after the other to act as cashier, had *died*. The counting-house was a close room, without a window, and in which, consequently, gas was always burning. We were engaged about the house professionally when the last man died, and were requested to " do some little thing" towards ventilating the room. The step we took was to place all round the walls, immediately under the ceiling, a 3-inch pipe of perforated zinc (a pipe full of innumerable small holes), both ends of which

albeit it ever will be a melancholy den for a man who loves sunlight, to spend the days of his youth in. This was precisely Dr. Chowne's arrangement of pipes : others have probably done likewise, and might maintain their right to do so again.

We shall be sorry if our anticipations prove correct, because we consider that those who, at cost of time and thought, to say nothing of money, evolve a new truth, and show how it may be applied for the advantage of their fellows, are honestly entitled to reward. It seems exactly one of those cases which ought to be met from a public fund.

ON THE PRESENT STATE AND PROSPECTS OF ARCHITECTURE.*

WITH regard to our native styles I yield to none in sincere admiration of their beauty ; they have, whether altogether from inherent power, or partly by association, the most thrilling influence on the mind, and are potent to touch the very highest notes of feeling ; but it is unfair, in my opinion, to judge of the relative merits of the Gothic and Classic styles by a comparison of the former, as perfected in England, with the imperfect adaptations of the antique architecture which we see around us. Gothic architecture was cultivated and reared to its perfection in the ecclesiastical edifices, for the solemn purposes of which it was pre-eminently, if not exclusively fitted; and the complex arrangement and multifarious requirements of these buildings called out at once all its powers of expression and beauty. The antique, on the contrary, has only been carried to its acme of grandeur in the ancient temples, the most simple of all arrangements, while of its further applications, its adaptation to other and modern purposes, we have good reason to doubt the perfection. If these ancient orders, or rather the elements that compose them, have never had their full significance in modern works, and such I believe is the fact, the comparison of the two styles is unjust. For the production of picturesque magnificence of effect, the capabilities of their exquisite profiles, their lines of grace and grandeur, have, perhaps, never been completely shown, even by the Italians. There is no degree of richness, or minute delicacy of ornament, exhibited by the Gothic, or by the Mahomedan or Oriental styles, which the Classic is not capable of equalling in the hands of an architect who thoroughly understands its principles and motives. We have no building in Europe that is a fair specimen of its power. Its resources are not adequately drawn upon in the great buildings which are the chief boast of the style, particularly as regards their interiors. St. Peter's and St. Paul's and the *chef d'œuvres* of Paris fall far short of what may be imagined to arise, under concurrence of every favourable circumstance, as a Phœnix from the ashes of antiquity.

Of this high reach of art in future, I found my hope upon the new light that is everywhere breaking, as to its real end and influence. But it pre-supposes, likewise, the appearance of talented professors, with the occasional visit of genius. Of the first we have no reason to doubt ; and of the latter we need not despair. The truth will set us free, and if we commence in the right spirit, our perception of the true and right will become stronger. With the legitimate exercise of our faculties we may expect new power to be born; and there will be but little danger of repetition ; while sincere, independent thought will shed a ray over the meanest subject and rudest material. No man knows what his power of invention is until it is called into play ; there are, I suspect, in most men, if not in every man, intellectual capacities which, for want of favourable opportunity, have never been developed. In some who have entered the profession, the needful powers may, unfortu-

or examples can true architecture ever become a mechanical employment. Genuine works of architecture, like those of nature, have a purpose, as we have before seen, beyond their ministry to the senses. They do not appeal to the eye alone, any more than music does to the ear ; they have an interest for the understanding, and for the moral perceptions ; and this high moral object is a link that unites ours to all the other fine arts. They administer to the gratification of the inner sense, which is our loftiest enjoyment, and the most worthy of humanity. The architect of the present day has, therefore, his work in the spiritual department of the world, as well as his predecessors. He has his ideas to express as well as them ; and the language is vouchsafed unto him also What is chiefly wanting, is self-dependence,— a turning inward into his heart, and looking round him into nature, for ideas and images instead of going backward for example and authority. Architects must learn to walk by their own strength, if they would produce works that will characterize the age, and show the " height of the human soul " in the nine teenth century. " There is at this moment,' to quote an eminent living author, " there i for me an utterance bare and grand as that o the colossal chisel of Phidias, or trowel of th Egyptian, or the pen of Dante, but differen from all these."

At the same time it must be admitted, tha the study and practice of a legion of styles will ever produce distraction among professors that it must result in stagnation to the art and that it is a chief cause of the evils unde which we groan; as, under such circum stances, no one style can be cultivated with its spirit and energy essential to its perfection Architecture is said to require the devotion a life ; but if so many styles are to be used, life-time is too short. This must be remedied Certainly one language is sufficient for the ex pression of our ideas of the beautiful and the tru Inigo Jones's solecism, in attaching a Corin thian portico to old St. Paul's, and Wren' expressed contempt for the beautiful mon ments of the middle ages, are not without th lesson to us when read aright ; they show th devotion of these masters to the one style, th secret of their success in it. Let him wh would excel in the Classic styles, like the devote himself to the remains of antiquity study the spirit of the laws involved in them embue his mind with their beauty; and tra their principles of design and applicatio through the works of the great masters Italy. Like them, let him confine his imit tion to their principles, and not extend it their designs. This is the only way in whi he can hope to rival them in the Production edifices, that shall be admired as works of t age. Correctness of style is not, as has t often been supposed, the all-important poi Whatever may be said on that head, certain is, that truth of conception, sincere operati of thought, attention to the great princip derived from nature and reason, will cov a multitude of faults, such as have be charged upon buildings by certain late criti who undertake to pronounce upon the p ductions of art, whilst ignorant of its r nature and purpose.

This truth of expression, to which I ha frequently adverted, is but another word i beauty. Physical beauty of form is the ma rial expression of truth ; it is truth, as far matter can express it. Beauty in architectu therefore, is truth; and between the form and moral beauty, there is more than analo Physical beauty is a reflection of moral beau or rather the issue and result. " But if tr be beauty," some might answer, " all buildin while true, must be equally beautiful." Not " Why, then," it might be asked, " is a w designed church more pleasing than a mark place or hospital ?" Because it expresse higher purpose, a loftier truth. Why is market-place pleasing at all ? because it true. It is part of a great whole, and exists true relation and harmony with the univer As no one object in nature is completely be each to be an expression of distinct thought and sentiment, the offspring of a truthful imitation of nature, and of pure creation in his own mind; and he should remember that great works need not be the only significant ones;—that the beautiful is not only unfettered to the style of any one age or country, but that it is not confined to any particular class of edifice.

Any materials he may obtain from ancient or foreign sources, or gather from other minds, through the medium of books or otherwise, he must, before applying, bring into his own mind, and subject to the operation of his own powers; that which has been merely appropriated by the hand and eye, which is not so digested, or that he cannot make to blend with the previous stores and images of his mind, he is not entitled to make use of, for it is not his.

Taste and judgment united to fertility of imagination, an eye practised to quick perception of the beautiful, and some artistic power of delineation, should, therefore, characterize the architect, who should also have a passionate love for the art, and consecrate to it all his powers. He must free his mind from prejudice, and look on nature with unscaled eyes, if he would fathom her mysteries of beauty, and discover the principles on which she produces her wonders of effect. They have no exaggerated idea, but true conceptions of the art, who look upon its professor as a poet. In a real piece of architecture the spirit of its author beams forth, as does the soul through the eyes of the body, and one source of pleasure with which we look upon such a work is the communion of mind with mind: enshrined in stone and wood, perchance, we discover a kindred spirit. As a work of art, it is the beaming of thought in the building that is to be prized, not the building itself, however rich its materials. The end and design of physical is moral beauty; and the secret of its effect upon us is its sympathy with something within. The soul of man is so connected with nature that every new phenomenon, whether of nature or art, excites a corresponding idea or feeling; this constitutes the charm in some pictures by the old masters, there is the beaming of a soul in their Madonnas and saints which transfixes the beholder, and on which one could look for hours and think for years.

This beauty is the highest food of the soul; a genuine perception of it has been termed the master key of the mind, and its effect thereon, whether beaming from external nature or through the medium of art, is inexpressible. Its agency is of the most subtle and spiritual nature. It tends silently to unfold the flowers of our existence, and the highest fruits of virtue are of its producing. It is the duty and the privilege of all to become acquainted with and to cultivate a love for the beautiful; to the artist it is peculiarly necessary. He must imbibe it in order to impart it; he must educate the eye and the inner sense, and strengthen the faculty of conception ere he can communicate it by embodying it in art.

If I am correct in my definition of beauty, truth of expression, or, in other words, consistency of character in building, is of infinitely more value than any other exterior quality, any unmeaning prettiness, that could be given in its absence. It has evidently been the sole aim in the exterior design of some public buildings, to render them an ornament to the neighbourhood by a superior style of decoration, heedless of the loud call of common sense, which dictates that, above all things, they should express their use, by having their exterior aspect in harmony with their destination. Their projectors have been forgetful of the indissoluble connection between beauty and truth; and that whatever charms a building so designed may possess in itself, to every well-formed mind it would have been infinitely more pleasing if distinguished by truth. Of this great error I could give numerous examples, and they are to be found chiefly among the erections of the last half century. One that will well illustrate this subject, may be seen in the Liverpool Infirmary (I choose examples from Liverpool merely for convenience). No stranger could suppose that building, with its chaste, cold colonnade, and harsh mural and fenestral character, to be an institution of benevolence, an asylum for the afflicted. It is in itself a respectable structure, worthy of the town, but without the least accord between its architectural character and the humane object of its foundation.

The same striking absence of fitness may be observed in another important building in the neighbourhood,—the prison at Kirkdale; from the front of which not the slighest intimation of its real purpose is conveyed to the spectator, who might easily mistake it, with its Ionic portico as its most prominent feature, and neatly dressed sash windows, for a nobleman's or gentleman's country seat. Certainly it betrays no symptom of the gaol; and a stranger might conclude, upon being told its real character, that it had been deemed necessary, for some reason, to disguise it. The true aim, I suspect, has been at a handsome and respectable character, forgetful that the art possesses the power to speak, and that dumbness is not a necessary deprivation in any building. The Liverpool Borough Gaol is, on the contrary, a building which broadly declares its office, of the ungracious nature of which none could remain in doubt for an instant; and is perhaps not inferior to Newgate, London, in this important particular.

These examples of vacant or erroneous expression are to be found, as I remarked before, chiefly among later erections: many of the old ones, in regard to this quality, are, on the contrary, objects of just admiration: some of the older institutions of London, and the older towns and cities, lightly deemed of, and that many would gladly see replaced by very different erections, are gems in the eyes of all true judges. Hospitals of various kinds might be named, which, with scarce any pretensions to architectural character at all, have that hospitable, warm, and comfortable, yet withal dignified air and mien, which tell the observer what they are: there is a sympathy with suffering in their look; their very gateways shed a balm upon the mind; and though the softening and subduing hand of time is concerned in this effect, yet such are the powers of expression inherent in the art, that it could be given to any erection in the present day by an architect possessed of true poetic feeling,—that feeling which draws, like the Muses round Apollo, into one magic circle the whole of the fine arts.

But, whilst adapting architecture to every new circumstance, it must be borne in mind that it has principles which do not alter with these circumstances: through all circumstances of climate and material of construction, the great principles are the same. Architecture has true, invariable laws,—as fixed, as unchanging, as those of the physical creation from which they are derived; and, without obedience to these laws, we can no more produce a work that will answer the great ends of art, than we can maintain life and health whilst violating the organic laws of our being. What is chiefly to be kept in view is the exact value of precedent; and, to fix that in the mind, we must remember that it can only be recognized so far as it is acknowledged by nature,—so far as the rules it develops are tracable to that source. What we have to do is to penetrate into the spirit of the ancient masters, ascertain their meaning, and carry out their principles to new circumstances, under the same unerring guidance by which they themselves were led.

It should here be observed that I do not propose to confine the application of the antique elements within any particular limit of design. Such limit as Palladio, Vignola, or the Italians generally assigned themselves, for instance, I would not make the boundary of their modification for church and other purposes: the style might diverge from the trabeated system, and run into the Romanesque; but in favour of Romanesque, or any other, I would not abandon our own beautiful styles. If two distinct systems were used (the Gothic and antique), I should not apprehend a want of harmony as the result, as feared by some. The classic styles are capable of a picturesque composition, and the infusion of sufficient of the vertical principle, to insure, while it presented greater variety, the needful harmony with the Gothic forms of surrounding buildings. The buildings of Vanbrugh would so harmonize, as well as do the Lombard churches with the street architecture of Italy. The horizontal and vertical systems have, both, their types in nature, and therefore their principles may be combined in a street, and they will harmonize with one another. A harmony will exist, in short, between buildings, in whatever style they are erected, if nature—that is to say, true principles of art — be followed.

Strict attention to those principles which are of eternal authority in architecture, involves no sacrifice of real beauty; and, on the other hand, what is really beautiful, that satisfies the eye of taste, may generally be defended when cited to the bar of rigid principle and judgment. A great deal has been written on the subject of modern architectural practice, of a nature tending greatly to cramp the art, and to exclude from the student many legitimate sources of variety and invention. The practice, for instance, of piling column upon column, along with many other very natural combinations of the classic features, has been condemned. Now, against two orders or heights of columns in a façade, there is no statute in the code of good taste. An objection, urged by a living writer, that it reminds one of the different stages of a temporary scaffolding, is futile. The Greeks did it in one instance, and there is nothing in the practice to lead us to suppose that they would not have resorted to it under the same circumstances which led the moderns to adopt it. I have no objection to what is called "purity of style;" that is to say, to the Greek elements being used in the same, or nearly the same relation, and fulfilling the same office they held in the ancient temple, when such can be done with propriety,—when such "purity" is not obtained to the exclusion of fitness and every life-giving quality. Pure, solemn Greek, such as the temples present, may serve for purposes of a kindred nature in England; but, assuredly, a Greek temple for municipal purposes, in the midst of a manufacturing town, is a solecism. I am not objecting to this purity; I am only recommending a purity of another and a higher kind; one not dreamt of in the philosophy of some,—a purity of *source*. With the greatest purity and truth of style a building may not be pure; the latter is mere purity of imitation. But art to be pure must draw from a pure source, through a pure channel. We want works based upon nature, and stamped in the mind of their author with his own image, and also the impress of the time and country. If each new age has not something new, something peculiar to itself, and beyond its predecessors to express in its works, human progress is but a dream. If to copy is the province of the architect, the imaginative powers, the faculties of genius, exist in vain; for in such labour they are not required.

But human progress is something more than a dream; and no just reason can be assigned why we should not, with all other votaries of art, in obedience to the law of progress, extend to the utmost our sphere of thought, and enrich the architecture of the day with fresh ideas and feelings. Our works *must* be an exponent of the age. The age should speak through them, and the religion, character, habits of the people, and spirit of the national institutions, should in them, as in a mirror, be manifested with undisguised truth. To mere fashion and whim we must allow no influence; but take especial care, under each circumstance, to preserve those great principles which are applicable to every condition, and to all styles of the art.

Forward! is the natural watchword of genius: the man who possesses that sublime gift is never satisfied with present attainment, nor reposes on past achievement. Contempt is, I believe, generally the strongest feeling in his mind for all his finished works,—conscious how far they fall short of uttering what is within, and, in his eagerness to attempt the untried, the unseen——

In concluding, I trust that no remarks I have made will be deemed an incitement to disobedience of just rule, or to contempt of all precedent. I would merely add one more voice to the loud call now making for freedom from unnatural shackles, and join with those who admonish the student to obey no rule but what can be traced to nature and judgment. I would not yield up the art to illguided and unrestrained powers of imagination. I would not undermine authority, but point out the true one.

SAMUEL HUGGINS.

DOORWAY, VILLA BORGHESE, FRASCATI.

DOORWAY, VILLA BORGHESE, FRASCATI.

The Villa Taverna (now Borghese), at Frascati, was built in the 16th century, by Cardinal Taverna, from the designs of Girolamo Rainaldi. It was the favourite residence of Pope Paul V. The engraving represents the entrance doorway from the terrace.

PROPOSED ENLARGEMENT OF THE SCOPE OF THE ROYAL INSTITUTE OF ARCHITECTS.

Our readers know that at the annual general meeting of the Institute, held in May last, a resolution was adopted, requesting the council to inquire into the present position and prospects of the Institute, to ascertain to what extent the views of its original founders have been carried out, viz., that of "Cultivating its many branches of science, and diffusing the knowledge of the principles of architecture with credit to its members, and with advantage to the noble art which they have the honour to profess;" also to inquire "if any and what changes in the bye-laws may be desirable, *to enlarge the scope of the Institute, and increase its usefulness.*"

The main object of the supporters of the resolution was to obtain the relaxation of a bye-law, which enumerates among the grounds for the expulsion of a fellow, his "having engaged since his election in the measurement, valuation, or estimation of any works undertaken by any building artificer, except such as are proposed to be executed, or have been executed, under the member's own designs or directions, except as referee or arbitrator."

On the 26th ult., a special meeting was held to consider the report of the council in reply to this. The report contained several recommendations, which were agreed to,* but on the question of relaxation, the council had come to the conclusion that the terms of the bye-law should not be altered, and further, they proposed as a special motion, an alteration in the form to be signed by associates, the effect of which was to make the restriction on this class of members more obvious and unmistakeable than it now is.

After a long and animated discussion, it was resolved, on the motion of the mover and seconder of the original resolution, that this proposition, together with the question of omitting the words of the bye-law quoted, should be referred back to the council for reconsideration; a vote tantamount of course to the expression of the affirmative on the part of the meeting. We have already expressed our opinion of the injustice and impolicy of the regulation in question, and sincerely hope that an alteration will now be made.

THE ANT PLAGUE.—A correspondent of the *Mining Journal* says,—Dust the floors and shelves with pounded quicklime; and if that should not completely succeed, "water" the floors with the ammoniacal liquor of gas-works, when the ammonia would be instantly disengaged by the quicklime, and this is destructive to insect life.

* One is, "That all members, whether associates or fellows, shall within twelve months after their election deliver an original paper to the council, on some subject connected with architecture, or make a donation to the library or collection."

USE OF GUTTA PERCHA IN REPAIRS.

It is a well-known and admitted fact, that most of our small modern dwelling-houses in or near the metropolis are built of inferior materials, with bad workmanship, yet readily find purchasers, or at least tenants. It requires, however, but a short tenancy to find out the miseries to be endured; woodwork shrinking, and thereby the rooms becoming filled with draughts, smoky chimneys, thin walls, weak floors, with the vibration so great that you are afraid to see the children run about, and the joints of the floor boards so wide apart, that the space between becomes the receptacle for dirt, dust, pins, needles, and halfpence, besides the impossibility of properly cleaning the floor, without injuring the ceiling beneath.

The greatest evil results, perhaps, from the timber employed in the joiner's work not being sufficiently seasoned, and hitherto the remedy to make good the defects occasioned by the shrinking, &c., as in the floor boards, has been to let in between the joints slips of wood, putty, &c.; but this cannot be depended upon, as in case of further shrinking it drops through, neither is it waterproof. I propose that gutta percha be used. Thus:—warm the gutta percha till it become glutinous, then with a heated iron or chisel point all along the joint, and it will be found that the adhesiveness of gutta percha is such, after two or three minutes, that the whole surface becomes as one board, the great merit being that there is no occasion to use any solution or cement to make the gutta percha unite to the woodwork, as is the case when applied to leather and other purposes; but there exists such an affinity between the two, that, for example, supposing a hole 6 inches square were cut in the flooring, with nothing underneath for support, and to make good the same a new piece were let in, well set all round in gutta percha, it will so unite with the boards, as to enable that portion to bear as great a weight as any other part. What has been said of making good the space between the floor boards, will equally apply to all joiner's work, as in the panels of doors, and a shake in them has hitherto been without any effectual remedy. Also to the skirting running round the rooms, which is often to be found leaving the floor boards, &c. &c.

The great feature gained is, that gutta percha not only fills up the space, but at the same time hardens and unites the whole.

F. Cross.

DESIGN AS APPLIED TO CALICO PRINTING.

A lecture on the conditions of design, as applied to calico printing, was delivered at the School of Design, Somerset House, on Friday, the 23rd of November, by Mr. George Wallis, formerly head master of the Manchester School, whose resignation, in 1846, was amongst the earliest symptoms of the change which has since taken place in that institution. The lecture was the first of a course of three which the Board of Trade have engaged Mr. Wallis to deliver,—the other two being on design as applied to silk weaving by the Jacquard loom, and on embroidery by hand and by machinery. In the lecture on calico printing, the technical conditions of design, as involved in the various modes of production, were pointed out, the nature of mordants, resists, and discharges, and their peculiar bearing on the artistic effect produced in printing, both as regards colour and light and shadow, explained; whilst form was shown to be dependent on the mechanical rather than on the chemical conditions of production. The various methods of block printing, machine printing by cylinder, and the metal types first used for calicoes, and now adapted to carpets, were rapidly gone over. The distinctive results, as seen in madder and steam prints, required a larger amount of explanation than one lecture enabled the lecturer to give, but the leading difference between the two methods, as exemplified in the mousseline de laines, as examples of steams, and the calicoes, known as "Hoyle's" prints, as specimens of madders, was clearly shown. The various methods of engraving the patterns on copper cylinders, and the conditions these methods imposed upon the designer, formed a valuable feature of the lecture, and models of a cylinder, with a mill or tool, used for engraving cylinders, after such mill has been raised from a hand engraved die, were exhibited. The lecturer showed that the conditions of design as to artistic effect, were not so limited as might be at first inferred, and that range of colour was one of the chief limitations in the ordinary class of printed goods; but in the special cases of mill-work or machine engraved cylinders, smallness of repeat was shown to be essential. In furnitures, cost alone limited the design, since almost every effect of light, shadow, and colour, could be re-produced in this department of calico printing; and Mr. Wallis suggested that the historic styles of ornament could scarcely be more legitimately employed, certainly not in textile fabrics, than in the embellishment of furniture chintzes. In conclusion, the lecturer urged upon the students not to consider these conditions as fetters to their artistic powers, but as the means to an end; and quoted the well-known aphorism of Sir Joshua Reynolds, first communicated in the room in which they were then assembled, that "rules were not fetters to men of genius, but fetters only to men of no genius."

CHURCH BUILDING NEWS.

WE learn that Christ Church, Clifton, has had some stained-glass chancel windows presented to it, "To the glory of God and in rememberance of a near relative," by Mrs. and Miss Miles, of Manilla Hall. According to our authority, six compartments contain full height figures of Christ glorified, St. John the Baptist, with four Evangelists, with other smaller scriptural subjects; ornamented beneath all, as if jewelled with gems of amber, emerald, and amethyst, on a transparent ground of hyacinth blue. It would be a good thing if this kind of monument were oftener put up, as it not only shows our respect and love for departed relatives, but adds grandeur to an edifice, of which the due adornment ought to be ever in our mind.——As it is, we are happy to have to record, on the present occasion, another instance of the same commendable spirit, and nearly in the same quarter of the country, too. An ornamental window has been placed in the north side of the communion aisle, in Heavitree Church (near Exeter), by Mr. R. Ford, of the Alhambra, as a memorial to his deceased wife. The figures of St. Mark and St. James are depicted on it in coloured glass from Italy, arranged by Mr. Kenshole, builder, Heavitree. ——The chief stone of the new church erected at the expense of Dr. Nicholl, M.P., in Merthyr-Mawr, was laid by Lady Mary Cole on 13th instant. The building is in the pointed style of fourteenth century.—— The rebuilding of the church of Burmington, near Shipton-on-Stour, has been completed, and the edifice was consecrated on Tuesday week.——The new meeting house in Waterloo-street, Tipton, has been opened. It is a plain building with about 300 sittings, erected at a cost of about 650*l.*——The new parish church of St. Matthew, Wolverhampton, was consecrated on Tuesday week. It is in the first pointed style, with clerestoried nave and aisles and a chancel: cost, with warming apparatus, fencing, &c., about 3,300*l.*, besides site 1,200*l.* more. The stained glass, font, and altar furniture, &c., were gifts. Deficiency still 200*l.* and upwards.——The intermitted restorations at St. Mary's, Leicester, having been proceeded with, the north aisle, with its Norman doorway, has now been restored in hewn stone, and lighted by four windows with tracery in place of the ugly one heretofore disgracing it. ——The master and seniors of Trinity College, Cambridge, having at once offered to repair the chancel of St. Michael's church in whatever way an architect named, viz., Mr. Scott, might advise, unless with sufficient cause to the contrary, and on condition of the concurrence of the churchwardens and vestry asked and obtained, with the understanding that the parishioners restore the rest in harmony therewith,—a meeting was accordingly held, when the resolution proposed was negatived by an amendment, seconded by a Cambridgian breeches-maker, and carried by a majority of 10 to 6, that it be ascertained to whom the property belongs. The incumbent had, nevertheless, explained that "no reasonable doubt could exist that the obligation to repair the church (exclusive of the chancel, which Trinity College had at once undertaken), rested upon the parishioners. The common law of the land was perfectly clear upon this point, and no lawyer would dispute it for a moment. In the ten or twelve thousand churches in this country, it had never in one single case been pretended that the patron, and not the parish, was bound to repair." The vestry then proceeded to appoint a committee, when it was proposed that the seconder of the amendment, and its mover, Mr. Smith, do constitute the Committee of Inquiry on this knotty point in ecclesiastical law. This proposal, says the *Cambridge Chronicle*, either alarmed or confused the poor seconder, who begged to withdraw from the perilous honour intended for him, and a lawyer's name was added, with further "power to add to their number." Doubtless, the vestry felt this to be "rather too much of a farce, and so rejected the motion by 8 to 6." Determined on obstruction and delay, however, they rejected, by a majority of 9 to 6, the reference to an architect's advice, and so the final understanding, failing the appointment of any precise or definite authority to carry out the object of their own amendment, was, that till the next week any one who should choose might make what inquiries he should choose, at whatever place he should choose, and report thereon at the next meeting. On the re-assemblage, the chairman and incumbent, Professor Scholefield, pointed out to the dissentients, that if they felt inclined to throw on other parties the responsibility to repair the church, they would have to consider whether such responsibility did not vest the property in the hands of the same body, and entitle them to take the church into their own hands, and shut it up or exclude the parishioners. Then the latter would doubtless be called upon by the proper authorities to build a church for themselves. Besides, if they thought that other parties were in justice bound to repair—and he should be the last to advise them to abandon an indisputable right—then they must be prepared for protracted and expensive law proceedings. Of these the expenses must be paid, for the law was not to be trifled with; and whether they were ultimately successful or not in establishing the liability of other parties, these expenses must fall upon the ratepayers. If unsuccessful, then they must expect to have to repair the church, after all, without any external help whatever. This peculiar line of argument seems to have shed a new light on the whole subject, for the proposal to acquiesce in the offer of Trinity College, and call on the architect to furnish plans, was again put, and carried by a majority of 21 to 7.—— The new church of All Saints', Habergham, was consecrated by the Bishop of Manchester on 17th inst. It will accommodate 700 persons, and has been erected mainly by a gift of 3,000*l.* from Messrs. Dugdale, manufacturers, and one of 1,000*l.*, besides the site, from Mr. Kay Shuttleworth and his wife.——The roof and ceiling of Horsforth Church have been repaired, and the building reopened.—— Kirk Deighton Church, near Wetherby, has been restored and reopened. The architects employed were Messrs. Perkin and Backhouse, of Leeds. The works have been executed by Mr. Joseph Woodhead, of Leeds, builder; Mr. Iredale, stonemason; Messrs. Wood and Son, painters. The warming apparatus was provided by Messrs. Nelson and Son, of Leeds. ——A Roman Catholic chapel has been built at Morpeth, at a cost of 2,000*l.* The Earl of Carlisle subscribed. The style is Early English, with nave and chancel, vestry, belfry, and spire: length of nave, 66 feet: breadth, 26: length of chancel, 20 feet; breadth, 15: altitude of spire, 115 feet. The building is lighted by twenty-nine windows, sixteen of which are to be painted. The roof, which is of rather a high pitch, is slated without, and open and stained within. The architect is Mr. T. Gibson, of Newcastle: Mr. T. White, of Morpeth, clerk of the works.——The Unitarian church in Hope-street, Liverpool, some time since noticed in THE BUILDER, has been opened. It will accommodate 700 persons. The dimensions are these:—Chancel, 20 feet by 15 feet 6 inches; chancel aisle, 18 feet 4 inches by 12 feet 10 inches; transepts, 23 feet by 20 feet; nave, 78 feet by 21 feet; north aisle, 49 feet by 10 feet 6 inches; south aisle, 56 feet 6 inches by 10 feet 6 inches; tower, 19 feet 8 inches square, externally; height of nave to ridge, 57 feet; height of spire, 153 feet. The building is warmed by the hot-air apparatus of Mr. Walker, of Manchester; and ventilated under the superintendence of Mr. Alfred Higginson. The contractors are Messrs. Furness and Kilpin. Mr. Gibbs executed the polychrome decoration, and Mr. Rossiter the carving. The architects are Messrs. Barry and Brown, under whose superintendence the whole has been executed. Mr. H. W. Chantrell (a son of the architect) was clerk of works. The first stone of the building was laid on 9th May, 1848. ——It is proposed to build a new church at Balsall-heath, Birmingham, for which 'very handsome sums' have been already subscribed. ——An anonymous donor presented to the church of St. Nicholas, Worcester, on the late thanksgiving day, the sum of 2,500*l.*, for such enlargement and improvement of this church as shall ultimately be decided upon. The following memoranda accompanied the gift:— The donor has no desire for his name to be blazoned abroad. Without imposing positive stipulations, he has expressed the following wishes, viz.:—1. That as many *free* sittings as practicable shall be made, on the ground floor.—2. That, if any *pews* be erected, in any new part of the church, they may, by faculty from the Lord Bishop of the diocese, be made over, as rentable property, to the rector of the parish for the time being.—— A memorial, in the Pointed style, with tablet, has been erected in the Abbey Church at Shrewsbury, recording the various restorations and other improvements effected by the late Rev. Richard Scott, B.D., in the churches of the Abbey and St. Giles. The design was furnished by Mr. J. Carline, and executed by Mr. Dodson, of Shrewsbury.——During the recent alterations in Brooke Church, says the *Norfolk Chronicle*, several wall-paintings were discovered, under repeated coats of whitewash and colouring. The parable of the Prodigal Son was represented in detail. In an arcade beneath, the ecclesiastics of St. Edmundsbury, who, no doubt were the limners, had figured the Deadly Sins, not as in Catfield Church, but in the act of descending into the open jaws of the monster of hell. These paintings, with others in different parts of the church, whose subjects are not known, are supposed to date from fourteenth century." Tracings and drawings of the whole, by Mrs. Beal, were exhibited at the Thetford aggregate meeting of the Norfolk and Suffolk Archæological Association.

ALMANACS.

"THE British Almanac" with "The Companion" (C. Knight), contains its usual large amount of information, comprising articles on ancient and modern usage in reckoning, on fisheries, public libraries, railways, connection with India, coal trade, water supply, &c., besides its section appropriated to public improvements, and architecture. The illustrations of this portion ought to be better: that of Mr. Hope's house is a caricature.——The almanac of the "Art-Union of London", has the "meetings of societies" under each date in the calendar; so that on looking at the day of the month, it is seen at once what meetings are to be held on that day. ——"Punch's Pocket Book" (85, Fleet-street), has a great deal of good fun in addition to all that is looked for in a pocket book. The illustrations of the first half are far superior to those of the second.——"The Artist's Almanac" (Ackerman), has the novel feature of lists of artists, architects, engravers, designers, &c., &c. This and other parts should have careful revision for next issue: they show signs of haste. —— "Bogue's (Waistcoat) Pocket Diary" is a compact little companion.

WREXHAM.—A correspondent urges us to point out the great and increasing demand for detached houses of respectability in the immediate neighbourhood of Wrexham, a market town situated in a healthy district, and surrounded by picturesque scenery. There is a station of the Shrewsbury and Chester Railway within a few minutes' walk of the town.

ALTAR SCREEN, ST. ALBAN'S ABBEY, HERTS.

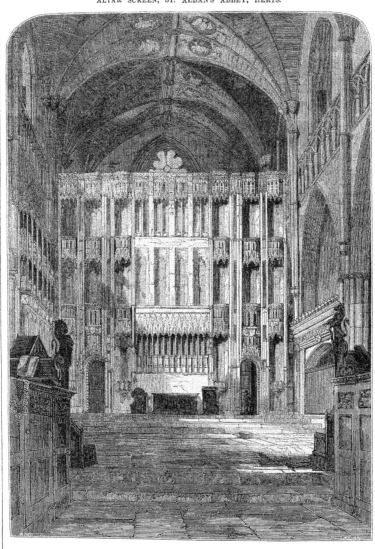

ST. ALBAN'S ABBEY, HERTS.

St. Alban was born at Verulam, in Hertfordshire, in the third century, and went to Rome, where he served seven years as a soldier, under Dioclesian. He afterwards returned to England, became a Christian, and suffered martyrdom in 303, during the dreadful persecution raised by Dioclesian.

The fame of Alban, recorded as it was by Bede, made a deep impression on the minds of the superstitious. "The Ecclesiastical History" of that author was published in 731, and in the year 705, Offa, king of the Mercians, built a monastery to the honour of Alban, on the place where he had suffered, then called by the Anglo-Saxons, Holmhurst, but since, in honour of the martyr, named St. Alban's.

Considerable division of opinion exists among antiquaries respecting the existence at the present time of any of the Saxon building. This question is one on which it is difficult to come to a satisfactory conclusion. But if even we cannot prove to a certainty the existence of the remains of the original church, this venerable and in many respects impressive building has great claims for our consideration; amongst the most prominent, is the circumstance that the Abbey of Saint Albans is almost entirely built with the remains of the Roman city of Verulam, and that it contains, to a remarkable extent, varied examples of the most rude and early styles, as well as the more recent and elaborate peculiarities of the more recent periods.

The east screen, of which we subjoin an engraving, was intended to conceal the saint's shrine from the vulgar, and was probably designed by Abbot Wheathamsted, and finally erected by Wallingford: its north and south ends abut against the centre of two arches on the sides of the choir; along the top of it, defended by a slight balustrade, is a passage from one side of the building to the other. Clutterbuck, in his "History of Hertford," gives an engraving of this screen, in which he shows a considerable portion of the front covered by carved woodwork. This had probably been placed to cover the bare appearance which is caused by the removal of the representation of our Saviour on the Cross which is engraved in Dr. Stukely's "Itinerarium Curiosum." This woodwork, which was probably erected about the middle of the last century, has been removed and has exposed a sad extent of dilapidation; indeed, the whole of the screen and many portions of the church require prompt attention. We believe the utmost possible use is made of all available means, and that a praiseworthy spirit is shown by the rector to preserve objects of interest, but we fear that it will require more than the present exertions to save many portions of this interesting relic from destruction. It might be the effect of imagination, but it seemed that the fracture in the south wall of the nave had increased in extent since the writer visited this place five years ago.* B.

* A plan, &c., with some curious particulars of the Abbey Church at St. Albans, will be found in our Vol. V., p. 542, in a notice of Messrs. Buckler's interesting History of this building.—Ed.

BUCKINGHAM PALACE—THE MARBLE ARCH.

SOMETIMES at the relief of guard and other excuses for idlers to congregate, one catches a remark which, though not artistic, denotes that the people are not insensible to the general effect as well as the objects of architecture.

Before the new front of Buckingham Palace the other day, one young man, a mechanic, observing the figures on the top, said to his companion (a sailor), "Jack, them ere figures is too high, particularly the family of small children to the right; they *never give us any statues even with our walk*, where one might see their proportions." "Yes," replied Jack, "I likes that party to the starboard, which is no doubt our good queen's little family; but the prince on the larboard has very little clothes on. But, Jem," replied the tar, "how are they going to get in? there 's but one gate—but I 'spose it 's to save another porter in these hard times."

"Well," said the mechanic, "I don't nohow like the sitivation; it 's low and damp, besides it 's all closed in and no ventilation—quite as bad as Gough-square, where the insanatory Commission visited me and my little uns, and insisted on a back current of air and the stopping up of the cesspools. Will they do nothing with the twenty-acre-cesspool in the gardens behind?"

"Lord love you," rejoined the tar, "her Majesty knows how we manage at sea: depend on it she 'll rig some poles and hoist a windsail—that's our way to give a stiff breeze in the hold: but what are they going to do with that other gate—the marble companion abaft the main hatchway?"

That was just the point I was considering at the moment, and having given you some crotchets already as to its disposal, perhaps as it is now going—just a-going, and will very soon be gone—you will allow me to refer to one of my former suggestions, which was to place it in the grand causeway which should be opened from Portland-place to the long walk, Regent's-park. This was the design of George IV. when the long walk was planted. The arch should stand on the verge of the inner park and New-road, and would at the same time give a most appropriate and elegant entrance to the park created by royal taste, and present a grand *coup-d'œil*, as viewed from Portland-place, disclosing a vista of great extent and beauty, terminating on the Highgate-hill: as none of our thoroughfares have any affinity to the picturesque, this would be a very apposite commencement.

Report once stated that it was destined to stand as an entrance to the long walk at Windsor! What affinity can exist between the fine Gothic pile of the Castle and this ornate Roman composition? *

The modern taste for the composite is very prevalent, but what can we say to this undertaking? It reminds me of an undertaker to whom it was referred to make a pageant for a *middle*-aged lady,—he mixed the plumes black and white.

But apart from jesting, is there not some truth in the remark—"They never give us any statues even with our walk?" Abroad, the people are familiarized with art, and particularly sculpture: in the gardens of the Tuileries—the Giardino at Naples—in all the repositories of ancient taste and treasure, free access is never denied even to the mechanic; and there they are as capable of discoursing on the perfect examples of ancient and modern masters, as they are of singing the music by their composers in harmony or parts.

It is to be hoped that the improved taste for arts at home will extend to the commonalty such advantages as the illustrious productions of art cannot fail to confer on the public mind; for they elevate vulgar tastes, and lead them from the contemplation of the sublime and beautiful up to the rational worship of Nature's God. QUONDAM.

* It is now stated, that the arch is to be taken to pieces and the materials sold.

DESTRUCTION OF WORKS OF DESIGN.

ROBBERY AT MR. HOPE'S HOUSE.

No one can regret this occurrence more than I do; but it appears to me hardly to justify Mr. Hope's inferred conclusion against the general security of works of art publicly exhibited.

That they *may* be so exhibited is said (by those who are of that opinion), to be insured by several circumstances; by the *class* of visiters they attract; their desire to deserve the confidence voluntarily shown them; the publicity with which robbery must be committed, and the consequent chance of its author being detected. These securities are thought sufficient to prevent the kindness of the public benefactor being abused. But the robbery at Mr. Hope's not being guarded against by any of these, affords no analogy to those cases which would be so guarded. The property stolen from him was without any of the peculiarities of a voluntary exhibition, and agreed in one particular with every other kind of property, while it was placed (as all outside fittings must be placed), in a situation to afford inducement and security to any dishonest person who walks the street by day or night. Neither does it appear that any thing would follow from the stolen article being a work of art, except that lovers of such works are especially dishonest; and this conclusion is too unjust for Mr. Hope to intend. The fact is, that that which increased its artistic value added to its marketable value, and made it equal to any other temptation of the same intrinsic amount. Further, *spite* may have had something to do with this injury.

Mr. Hope has so much power to do good in matters relating to the fine arts, that I should be sorry if he were to remain under a wrong impression. I hope he will think, in opposition to the unfortunate occurrence he relates, how very few cases there are in which publicly exhibited property has not been respected even in this country; how still fewer they are on the continent, where the frequency of such exhibitions, by adding to their general estimation, adds also to their security and to the respect felt for those who are the authors of them. H. W.

DRAINAGE OF HERTFORD GAOL.

IN late numbers of your journal paragraphs have appeared headed "Effects of Bad Drainage," and "Hertford Gaol Drainage," each having a reference to the other. The county surveyor, a respectable architect, has thought fit, in very marked terms, to show the contempt he entertains for his fellow-townsmen, who have been lately but too frequently called upon to exercise the very painful, but important duties, and to express, as the surveyor is pleased to word it, "the sapient notions of a country coroner's jury." Between the 29th of October and the 6th of November inquests were held by the coroner upon no less than nine prisoners, who died of cholera, and more than one of the juries, consisting of individuals as respectable and as intelligent as the surveyor himself, did not hesitate to express an opinion, founded upon the evidence produced before them, that the drainage of the gaol was so bad that it required *the immediate attention* of her Majesty's Secretary of State for the Home Department. An inquiry took place, and I only wish, Sir, that a *bonâ-fide* report of the depositions made to the "country coroner's jury" were published, and then I think it would be at once admitted that the "notions" of the juries upon the subject, were far more "sapient" than the plan in operation for effecting the drainage of the gaol. You have been referred to an able and respectable "country" editor's "notion" of what has been done, or what can be done, to improve the drainage, and the whole tenor of the paragraph admits it to be insufficient, though indeed it may not have been proved to the inspector sent down by the Government to have been the cause of the fresh outbreak of cholera. Surely, Sir, if the difficulties of draining this gaol are insuperable, it ought to be *abandoned*, and no more lives risked by confinement in such an unhealthy place.

As a public reflection has been made in your journal by a public officer upon a most respectable body of men, who endeavoured to discharge a very sad and painful public duty as faithfully and as inoffensively as they could, I call on you, in justice, to publish this contradiction, and I assert, without hesitation, that the details furnished to you of the catastrophe at Hertford Gaol were properly included under the head of "Effects of Bad Drainage."

A HERTFORD MAN.

*** The writer has forwarded a description of the means of drainage at present in operation there, but no good end would be answered by publishing it, even if we could afford space. Our object in printing his letter is twofold—to exonerate ourselves from the imputation of improperly inserting an erroneous statement, and to direct attention, not merely to whatever may be defective in Hertford Gaol, but to the drainage of many other of our prisons.

COMPETITIONS ADVERTISED LAST WEEK.

IN your last number I see three advertisements for public competitions, the terms of all of which are really too absurd and ridiculous to be passed over unnoticed. In the first, which is for a design for a union workhouse at Stockton, the guardians estimate the labour and time required for furnishing such at the enormous sum of 10*l*., and say, that if the architect whose plans are selected likes it, he may become the clerk of the works during the erection of the building, at, I suppose, the tempting salary of 2*l*. a-week, provided he is never absent from the spot! Liberal-minded men! they ought really to have a public testimonial got up for them by the profession at large, for their extreme generosity.*

The second, for a Wesleyan chapel, goes a little beyond the Stockton extravagance, and offers a premium of 35*l*. for the best plans; but then, fearful lest the architect who furnishes them should make too rapid a fortune by obtaining, after his risk, the usual commission for

* This advertisement is an insult to the profession and a disgrace to the Stockton board of guardians. We trust it will meet with the reception it deserves. The architects who submit designs in reply to it, should there be any, will aid in the insult. We shall be anxious to have their names. A correspondent from Manchester says,—"I would suggest to these guardians, by way of an *addendum*, that the *person* who may be so fortunate as to be *second* on the list for promotion be allowed to *carry the bricks!*"—ED.

superintending the work, reserves to itself the power of keeping the drawings, and "*not* employing the architect whose plan is preferred ;" which is virtually saying, " We 've got another man (probably a carpenter) who will superintend the works for a good deal less than the usual five per cent."

The third, for enlarging the Leicester Union, offers a fair premium enough, but says, that if the architect whose plans are selected should be appointed to superintend the works, " the premium is to merge in a commission upon the outlay, *hereafter to be fixed ;*" which means pretty nearly the same thing as the Wesleyan chapel, as there can be little doubt that a smaller commission than five per cent. will be fixed, and unless the *fortunate* architect succumbs to it, his drawings will be kept and carried out by somebody else, who will be dirty enough to act in such a way.

With these three specimens before me, I am really puzzled to think what the public generally consider to be the meaning of the word "architect," and whether any previous education is thought necessary to entitle a man to such a name. That architecture is the profession of a gentleman, the first specimen clearly denies ; and one would imagine, from reading the other two, that even if it is held to be a profession at all, it must be one with no settled or recognized rules and forms.

I sincerely hope and trust that all your readers who may turn their attention to these competitions, and feel inclined to enter the field with such paltry inducements as are therein held out, will first pause for a moment, and consider whether they will not be doing a lasting injury to the profession by allowing such absurdities to be recognised, and to be responded to by men calling themselves architects and artists. It only affords an additional proof of the necessity of something in the shape of a diploma being required by Government before any one may practise as an architect,—a matter which I see by your journal is being brought forward, and which I should hope would be strongly supported by all who are anxious that a proper estimate should be formed of the position in society which an architect ought to hold.

"Φως."

REPAIR OF ST. STEPHEN'S, WALBROOK.

Your remarks on St. Stephen's, Walbrook, seem to call for some reply from me, who may fairly claim to be more anxious for its restoration than any man, except, perhaps, the great Christian orator who preaches in this dilapidated but yet beautiful temple. In a six years' battle for the means of its restoration, I, on Wednesday last, as the result of my triumph, laid on its vestry-table a deed assigning to eight trustees, chosen by the parish, a rent-roll of upwards of 700*l*. a-year, and about 2,500*l*. present cash, accumulated during my struggle.

The tardy movements in Chancery, and the obstacles to justice in that atrocious court,* may yet occasion a month or two's delay ; but I have confident hope that this short time will put at the disposal of a committee a thousand pounds, which I think is sufficient to stay decay, to restore all the original ornament, and to put the fabric in at least a respectable state for temporary state of repair.

I am of course very anxious that this little sum be applied to the greatest possible advantage, and request the favour of advice from any of Wren's admirers, and especially replies to the following queries :—

Is it desirable to restore the centre eastern window, and remove West's picture to the northern side, which has been proposed ?

In what manner should the interior be coloured? If, as I presume, of one colour, what colour would be the best?

Wm. F. Rock.

Walbrook, Nov. 28.

THE BRITANNIA-BRIDGE. — The second tube has been safely floated into its position ready for hoisting.

* Would that the whole kingdom would shout the same expression,—" that *atrocious court*,"—we might hope then for some reformation of its monstrous abuses.—ED.

BATHS, PUBLIC AND PRIVATE.

MANY years ago eminent physicians endeavoured to draw the attention of the Government to the importance of public baths, and of countenancing their use by every aid and example. It was but lately that the first public baths were erected, and now we are aware of their benefits. In the eastern and northern nations their prevalence is universal, and we may lament that even now they are so little used in this country. I hardly know any act of benevolence more essential to the comfort of the community than that of establishing, by public benefaction, baths for the poor in all our cities and manufacturing towns. Dr. Clarke tells us, that in England baths are considered only as articles of luxury; yet, throughout the vast empire of Russia, through all Finland, Lapland, Sweden, and Norway, there is no cottage so poor, no hut so destitute, but it possesses its vapour bath, in which all its inhabitants every Saturday at least, and every day in cases of sickness, experience comfort and salubrity. The illustrious Bacon lamented the disuse of baths among us ; we have certainly since then made rapid strides, but there yet remains great room for improvement. Among the ancients baths were public edifices, under the immediate inspection of the Government. Rome, under her emperors, had nearly a thousand such buildings, and they were then considered as institutions which owed their origin to absolute necessity, as well as to decency and cleanliness. England, by its ancient remains, even now bears testimony to what importance the Romans considered, for the preservation of health, the use of bathing. it is true with us now, the first-rate buildings generally have attached to them a private bath ; but the use of them among the middle class is not so general as might be. In America a bath-room is a part of every modern dwelling, and *no one will occupy a house without one*,—the bath itself being provided with hot water from a peculiar and ingenious kind of cooking stove, somewhat like those used in the houses of our nobility, but on a more economical plan. In the suburban districts of London, the houses generally erected have not these conveniences supplied, but it is owing to the bad management of the speculating builders—it is a moral duty they owe to all, to supply these deficiencies. Builders themselves must bear in mind, that during the progress of the building, a bath-room might be built at half the cost, when the materials and labour are there on the spot; and, that after a house is finished, few are willing to incur such an additional trouble and expense. If cement were less used for external effect, which even in the hands of a skilful architect is rarely treated successfully, that additional expense would be saved, and the conveniences internally might be more generally attended to ; and the saving in this respect might be employed for the erection of a bath-room. W. P.

ST. JUDE'S CHURCH, POYNTZ POOL, BRISTOL.

THE new church dedicated to St. Jude, which we briefly mentioned some time since, was consecrated a few days ago. It was erected from the designs of Mr. Gabriel, architect, and is in the Decorated or Middle Pointed style of the fourteenth century (Edward II.), consisting of nave, 65 feet, by 28 feet 6 inches ; and chancel, 28 feet 6 inches, by 23 feet 6 inches ; with sacristy on the north side of the chancel. The tower is at the west end, 13 feet square within, 82 feet in height, and consists of four stages, having a deeply-recessed doorway; above this is a three-light window. The belfry story has four two-light windows, and is surrounded by a parapet of wavy and quatrefoil tracery, having a pinnacle at each angle, with buttresses set diagonally. The nave has a south doorway : there is also a priest's door in the south wall of the chancel. The whole of the windows, except the east and west, are of two lights, and each of different tracery. The east window consists of five lights. The whole of the seats are open. The lectern is of oak : the pulpit, which is on the north side of the nave, is of stone. The upper part of the tower arch is open, with a door

beneath ; the lower story of the tower. forms an entrance vestibule to the body of the church. The roof of the nave is open to rafters, and the principals rest on stone corbels, carved with foliage. The chancel arch is crossed by a screen of oak. On each side of the chancel is a row of four stalls ; further eastward to south are sedilia and piscina ; and in the thickness of north wall the table of prothesis is introduced. The chancel is vaulted over with wood,—the two easternmost bays being coloured, the square compartments blue powdered with stars, the moulded ribs diapered with bosses gilt. The floors are laid with tiles : the doors are of oak. The walls are built of Hanham stone, with freestone coverings ; the roof is covered with stone slabs (from Tetbury).

LOWE'S STENCH TRAP GRID.

THE advertisement of this trap, on another page, deserves the attention of our readers. It has the great advantage over the ordinary bell trap, that the grating may be raised to allow a more rapid passage through it without, of necessity, an escape of bad air. The only fault we have to find with our otherwise good little housemaid is, that the bell trap in the sink is universally left out and the house poisoned ; and in saying this we express the complaint of hundreds. The annexed section will explain the construction of Mr. Lowe's trap.

JENNINGS'S INDIA-RUBBER TUBE CLOSETS.

WE have been often asked by correspondents to give our opinion of Jennings's patent water-closet, but were then not in a position to do so confidently. For some time past, however, we have had one in operation, and we feel it is but justice to the inventor to say that it answers its purpose very efficiently. The peculiarity of it is (as many of our readers may have observed in our advertising columns), that the communication between the pan and the trap is by, means of a short length of India-rubber tube, which, when the handle is down, is compressed by two metal flaps, and so holds the water. Having neither the usual metal pan nor valve, no chamber is required, which prevents a displacement of impure air when used, an evil justly complained of in some other closets. The raising of the handle suddenly discharges the contents of the basin with all its force through the India-rubber pipe direct, flushing the trap and soil-pipe each time the closet is used. Further, this closet in its action is perfectly silent, as the metal flaps fall without noise against the India-rubber tube, and it is so free from complication, that a fresh piece of India-rubber tube, if ever needed, will make the closet as good as new.

Mr. Jennings has very ingeniously applied India-rubber in the manufacture of cocks, and for the joints of pipes. India-rubber and gutta percha are quietly revolutionizing many branches of our manufactures.

The shop-shutter shoe and fastener, by the same patentee, has been noticed by us before, and is now coming into very general use.

METROPOLITAN IMPROVEMENTS. — According to the last report of the Commissioners of Woods and Forests, printed a few days back, it appears that the amount of purchase-money paid by them for property required for the metropolitan improvements is 727,968*l*., comprising the various items,—in the line from Oxford-street to Holborn, 290,327*l*. 4s. 10d. ; in the line from Bow-street to Charlotte-street, Bloomsbury, 96,408*l*. 11s. ; in the line from London Docks to Spitalfields Church, 139,341*l*. 5s. 6d. ; in the line from East Smithfield to Rosemary-lane, 22,247*l*. 15s. ; making the sum already stated.

Miscellanea.

INSTITUTION OF CIVIL ENGINEERS.—On the 27th, the paper read was a "Description of the Old Southend Pier-head, and the extension of the pier; with an inquiry into the nature and ravages of the *Teredo Navalis*, and the means hitherto adopted for preventing its attacks," by Mr. John Paton. A general outline of the extension of the pier, and a minute description of the pier-head, were given, showing the means adopted by the use of iron piles, and by scupper-nailing the inner piles, to preserve the structure from decay. As to the *Teredo*, the conclusions arrived at were, that the ravages of the marine worm were not prevented by any chemical application, and that nothing but mechanical means could ever prove completely successful: studding with broad-beaded nails was considered to be the most effectual remedy.——On the 4th inst. the discussion was continued on Mr. Paton's paper. The "Tholas" was shown to have been in active operation upon certain rocks from the earliest periods, but never upon Portland stone. Hence it was argued, that kind of stone should be used for breakwaters and other works exposed to the action of the sea. This bearing of the discussion induced remarks upon the ravages of the white ant of India; which, however, appeared to have been little studied, and less understood, as far as attempting to arrest, or to prevent its inroads. Specimens of piles from Lowestoft harbour, whose waters were notoriously full of worm, showed that timber in a natural state was in a few months thoroughly perforated by "Teredo" in the centre, and "Limnoria" on the surface; but that piles, which had been properly saturated according to Bethell's system, in exhausted receivers, and subjected to such pressure as insured the absorption of about ten pounds' weight of the creosote, or oil of coal tar, by each cubic foot of the timber, were perfectly preserved from attacks of marine animals of any kind.

RAILWAY JOTTINGS.—A pontoon, or floating landing-stage, 400 feet long by 50 wide, and weighing 600 tons, has been constructed by Messrs. E. B. Wilson and Co., locomotive engine manufacturers, of Leeds, and is shortly to be launched at Goole. This platform is twice the length of a ship of the line, and will be launched broadside. It is made of plate-iron, except the deck, which is of wood. It is intended for a pier at New Holland, on the Humber, opposite Hull, for landing passengers from steamers, communicating with one of the Lincolnshire railways. Two covered ways, called girders, made at same works, of plate-iron, on the principle of the tubular bridges, and 142 feet in length, will extend from the pontoon to the station on the pier. ——In an arbitration case respecting the fall of a viaduct at Knaresborough, the arbitrator had found that the loss amounted to 8,450*l*. 4*s*., the amount to be made up in this way—3,291*l*. 7*s*. 10*d*. to be paid by the Leeds and Thirsk Railway Company, 2,319*l*. 12*s*. by the East and West Yorkshire Junction Company, and 2,319*l*. 4*s*. by the contractors, but the contractors only to pay 1,833*l*. in money, giving up all claim to the ruins and plant of the viaduct. A rule *nisi* to set aside this award was lately brought before Mr. Justice Erle, in which it was contended that the arbitrator had no power to make such award,—that the arbitrator, who was the engineer to the Company, and to the vice of whose plan the accident in the viaduct was attributed, had directed that the viaduct should be rebuilt by independent parties on a new plan, which he clearly had no power to do, inasmuch as the contractors were under agreement to complete the viaduct and maintain it for a given space of time,—but supposing the arbitrator had such power, that his award was bad for not being final. It did not dispose of the covenant and responsibilities the contractors had rendered themselves liable to by signing the deed. On these grounds it was insisted that the award was invalid and ought to be set aside.—Mr. Justice Erle granted the rule upon all points.

PROVIDENT INSTITUTION FOR ARTISANS.—A meeting of gentlemen interested in the success of Mr. Cockerell's proposal will be held at the Guildhall, London, on Tuesday next.

PROJECTED WORKS.—Advertisements have been issued for tenders by 8th January, 1850, for the erection of the subscription baths and other works at Wolverhampton; by 10th December current, for various works at Rock Leaze Estate, near Bristol; by 13th, for the erection of coke ovens, coal stores, and other works, at the Strood terminus of the North Kent Railway; by 19th, for putting in new windows in aisles of Isleworth Church; by 15th, for the erection of the Northampton Corn Exchange; by 12th, for the construction of a fence wall at the new goods warehouses of the York, Newcastle, and Berwick Railway, at Newcastle, and a retaining and fence wall along Forth-street; by 22nd January, 1850, for files and steel for the navy; and by 11th inst., for twenty tons of lignum vitæ for the navy.

THE ARCHITECT-MAYOR OF LANCASTER.—We mentioned that Mr. Edmund Sharpe, the author of "Architectural Parallels, or the Progress of Ecclesiastical Architecture in England," had been elected Mayor of Lancaster. His year of office has now expired; and we are glad to find the local *Gazette*, in a leading article, bearing witness to the value of his efforts in that position, especially with regard to the sanitary improvement of the town.

LIVERPOOL ARCHITECTURAL SOCIETY.—A meeting of this society was held on Wednesday evening last week. On the suggestion of Mr. Reid, the secretary, it was agreed that a prize should be given to the student member of the association, at the end of the session, who made the greatest number, and the best, sketches on subjects to be given out by the council at each fortnightly meeting. The subject for that evening would be a lodge, the size, style, and design being left entirely to the students. A conversation took place upon the best method of "plugging" floors, by which sound was prevented from communicating to the lower apartments. One said the best way of destroying sound in floors was by flags above the joists, boarded over, the boards being fastened to battens. Another method of destroying sound was with battens and laths, a coat of plaster, and the space well filled up with engine-ashes, lime, and sand, compounded together, to the thickness of about three inches, within an inch and a half of the top of the joists, and, when that had dried, all the crevices to be filled up with a thin coat of mortar. The way in which the floors of St. George's-hall are plugged is this. There are felts on each side the joists, and three-quarter boards over the felts, the remaining space being filled up with a composition, principally consisting of plaster, to within about an eighth of an inch of the surface of the joists. A paper was read by Mr. Barry on "Monumental Brasses."

THE FALLEN ARCHES AT KENTISH-TOWN.—Your observations on this mishap appear to be well founded and important: all who are acquainted with the site traversed by that viaduct,—the course of the old Fleet Ditch, and the ill-drained flat that still engenders typhus and influenza,—must be astonished at the small depth and substance of the foundations of the piers, as given in THE BUILDER of last Saturday; and they must agree with you, that in such cases an inquest ought to be held, even when no life is lost on the occasion. In cases of fire, such inquiry is sometimes made; and surely, where an awful risk of human life is incurred, and the interests of science and of the public are at stake, as in this event, the expense and inconvenience would be nothing in comparison with the advantages to be derived from a fair, judicious, and strict inquiry. By way of suggestion as to additional or incidental causes of accident in bridges recently constructed and imperfectly set, I submit the following occurrence. On the 5th of November last, passing under this very bridge, I observed to a friend that I never felt satisfied with a bridge or arch made of several rims of bricks of the same size and not bonded, and I pointed to several instances of the lines all running into each other, instead of overlaying each other's joints, and reminded him of various examples on the Richmond and South-Western lines, where the filtration of water is consequently increasing to an alarming degree. Before a coroner's jury such hints might lead to improvements: without inquiry we need not expect any unless through your excellent journal.

AN OBSERVER.

PICTORIAL MAPS.—Acting on a hint honourably quoted from THE BUILDER, on a proposal made at the Geographical Society, for constructing large and uniform maps in the new Houses of Parliament, to be traced and depicted on the walls, Mr. S. Bannister has published a letter addressed to Mr. Eastlake, R.A., *on the possibility of greatly amplifying this idea* in the establishment of "Pictorial maps of the land, the sea, and the heavens, georamas, and lectures on geography," for behoof of the people at large, in London and the chief cities and towns throughout the country. Mr. Bannister has here accumulated a great deal of interesting learning on kindred topics, both ancient and modern; and suggests the possibility of forming a new society for carrying out the objects set forth in the proposal. He draws attention to the peculiar adaptability of the domes and walls of the Brighton Pavilion (lately sold to the town of Brighton) to begin with; and notices the fact that it is proposed to place a georama, or large concave globe or map of the earth, of 40 feet diameter, in the city Hall of Commerce, also lately sold,—the funds to be raised by subscription. Various other feasible proposals and suggestions are contained in this little pamphlet which we hope will prove to be the fructifying germ of many more goodly leaves and branches.

PROVINCIAL.—A monument to Nelson is to be erected at Norwich, the capital of his native county. It is proposed to be in the form of a statue, on a pedestal in the centre of the market-place, with four gas lamps at the corners of a palisade surrounding it.——Plans of a town-hall for Knighton, says the *Hereford Times*, have been prepared. They specify a hall on one part, and on the other a hotel. There will also be shops and an iron gate opening on the market-place.——The Duke of Cleveland has offered to subscribe 50*l*. towards the erection of a central ragged school-house in Wolverhampton.——The great wooden building at Birmingham for the exhibition of cattle, &c., has been completed. The full dimensions are 330 feet in length by 100 feet, increased at one end to 150 feet. The cattle-stalls are all separated by hurdles, and provided with feeding-troughs. The whole is fitted up with gas.

IMPORTANT TO GLAZIERS AND OTHERS.—In a case, "Hodgton against Malloch's executors," the question was—When work is sent to a glazier, without any specific price or time being stipulated, and the glazier delays in order to take advantage of a subsequent reduction in the duty on glass, is he entitled to charge the price current at the date of the order, or merely the reduced price at the date of delivery? The second division (of the Court of Session) have decided that be can charge the former price, the majority of them apparently on the specialty that no time for finishing the glass was stipulated, and no complaint ever made of the delay. The decision is of course applicable to other trades.—*Edinburgh Register*.

LANDLORD AND TENANT.—With reference to your article, "Landlord and Tenant," in THE BUILDER of the 24th ult., I, who was the defendant in the case, would mention that in the ninth line from the top, "plaintiff paid his rent," &c., should have been, "defendant paid his rent," &c. The abstract of the Landlords and Tenants Act alluded to, is published by Walwyn, Hatton Garden; and in reference to "notice to quit premises," at page 7, it reads thus:—"If notice be given up to a wrong time, or a quarter instead of half-a-year, such warning should be objected to as soon as possible. Where *three* months' notice to quit has been given where *six* was in strictness necessary, and no objection made to it at the time, the notice was deemed good and binding on the party accepting it."—1 *Esp. Ca.* 266. This information, coupled with the recommendation of the solicitor employed to defend the case, assuring me that the plaintiff could not claim a farthing, induced me to place myself in that position, and thereby incur the costs. His honour would have had greater reason to call it a "case of great hardship" to me, if I had told him how I had been treated by one who was paid to defend the case. So much for law books and solicitors: for the future, I throw them to the moles and bats.

GEO. NAISH.

Exhibition of the Works of Industry of all Nations.—The report to Prince Albert by Messrs. Cole and Fuller, who were deputed to confer with the manufacturers in various towns, and collect opinions and suggestions as to this great exhibition, has been printed, and is now before us. Amongst the points more particularly discussed were the general expediency of such exhibitions, the questions whether their scope should be universal, whether they ought to be supported by subscriptions or by Parliamentary aid, also as to willingness to exhibit, as to prizes, &c. Some doubts appear to have been expressed as to the propriety of awarding prizes in certain branches of manufacture; but very few suggestions of anything like importance seem to have been made. Mr. Redgrave, A.R., is of opinion that collections of the most rare and choice works, produced by the skill of past ages (such as our museums and societies of antiquaries and archæologists could so well supply), should form centres to the various groups of manufactures to which they relate. And certainly such collections would give a stimulus to new efforts.

City of London Literary Institution.—A *conversazione* was given at this institution on Wednesday evening, when the Rev. Dr. Croly read a beautiful address on the value of knowledge, and, in the courseof it, referred to the various nations of antiquity for proofs of the great fact, that in proportion as knowledge was cultivated amongst them so did they flourish in wealth and power; in conclusion expressing a fervent hope that the youth of England would continue to seek knowledge with the same ardour they had begun to display in these days, and thus contribute to maintain their country's greatness. A variety of works of art, sculpture, drawings, &c., were exhibited in the rooms, and large crowds filled every part of the building. Mr. Sheriff Lawrence, the Rev. Dr. Mortimer, Mr. George Cruikshank, and others were on the platform. Music and recitations by the elocution class filled up the evening. This institution has proved its claims to the support of the neighbourhood, and will, we hope, continue to receive it.

Builders' Benevolent Institution.—The first election of this institution took place on the 29th ult., at the London Tavern, Bishopsgate-street, for the purpose of electing five pensioners from a list of eleven candidates. Mr. George Bird, the treasurer, took the chair on the occasion, and, on opening the business of the day, said he was happy to find this their first election so numerously attended by the friends of the institution—an institution which had progressed more favourably than its most sanguine friends could have anticipated. It had been established but little more than two years, and the funded property already amounted to 1,400*l*., of which 500*l*. had been subscribed towards the erection of almshouses. The annual subscription had now reached 350*l*.; there was a balance of more than 200*l*. at the bankers, and the society was wholly free from debt. The ballot was then proceeded with, and shortly after its close the successful candidates were announced.

The Iron Trade continues in a favourable state for purchasers; but the London, Manchester, and Liverpool dealers and merchants have of late been shy of giving orders unless at a concession of price. *Aris's Gazette* quotes bars delivered at 5*l*. 15s., and hoops at 6*l*. 15s., which, says this manufacturers' friend, with carriage and usual allowance, could scarcely have realized 5*l*. 15s. and 6*l*. 5s. at the works. In every branch, adds the same authority, underselling is complained of. Glasgow pigs, however, are reported, on same side, to be looking up, from 45s. to 48s., cash; for mixed Gartsherrie, and for g. m. b., three months open.

The Manchester Athenæum.—This building was recently offered for sale, at the Auction Mart. A mortgage debt of 6,000*l*. had been secured upon the freehold property, paying 4 per cent. interest, the principal recoverable at a twelvemonth's notice, which has been given. The building is stated to have cost 18,000*l*. in erection, and is subject to a rent-charge of 310*l*., more than covered by the rent paid by the Bankruptcy Courts. It was sold, we are told, for 5,550*l*.

Battersea Park.—The Commissioners of Woods and Forests, in their report just issued, state that their proceedings for the acquisition of the property to form Battersea-park have been impeded by the want of funds, the delay being manifestly injurious to the interests of the Crown, and productive of frequent complaints from the owners of the property and other persons having interests affected by the formation of the intended park; that great loss and inconvenience are occasioned to them by the uncertainty that exists as to the period of settlement of their respective claims. The commissioners have borrowed 50,000*l*., and under a recent statute charges can be given for property purchased on the land revenues of the Crown, and up to the date of the report the commissioners had paid in money for property 23,197*l*. 10s. 3d.

Lighting Churches.—The difficulty of lighting efficiently, extensive and lofty buildings of Gothic architecture, without the means employed becoming obtrusive to the eye, has long been acknowledged, and prompts to various expedients. A new mode of employing gas for the purpose is being tried at All Saints, Leamington: it consists of a continuous set of jet burners, each in the form of a trefoil, running under the clerestory windows on each side of the nave and chancel, and the great rose window of the northern transept, whereby a diffused light, it is expected, will be thrown over the whole of the edifice, without the disfigurement of hanging chandeliers, gas-pipes, &c.

Excavations at Nineveh.—Letters have been received from Dr. Layard (according to the *Athenæum*), dated Mosul, October 15. At this date he had about 60 workmen exploring the ruins; and many bas-reliefs—of which the store seems inexhaustible—were discovered. Amongst them is a representation of the removal of one of the gigantic bulls, showing that they were sometimes, if not always, moved to the palace after being carved. An immense number of men draw a sledge which runs upon rollers, impetus being given to it behind by an enormous lever worked by cords. A cast will be made of this very curious subject in the event of its being found impossible to remove it. It is probable that the fine pair of colossal lions still standing at Nimrud will be moved during the present expedition.

The New Corn Exchange at Edinburgh was to be formally opened on Wednesday. As our readers may recollect, we gave them a view of this edifice as designed by Mr. Cousin, the city architect, with particulars, in vol. vi., p. 294 of The Builder. The interior of the hall is fitted up with stalls for the grain merchants, ranged round the east, west, and south sides, and it is intended to have a row of offices on the west outside, as retiring apartments to the stalls on the western side, opening through the main wall. Rents of these, 17*l*. 10s. each, stalls included; of the others, 10*l*. each, or 5s., as sample dues, for a single occasion. The lighting of the hall from the roof is through patent tile glass: area, 14,060 feet.

Tidal Survey.—"A Tide-table and Section, on a half scale, of Standard Marks on the Banks of the Thames, showing their Values above Mean Water at Sheerness and Liverpool," has just been prepared by Mr. Joseph Smith, Assistant Surveyor to the Metropolitan Commission of Sewers, and printed for the use of the commission. It comprises, among other details, observations and calculations mainly agreeing with those already presented to our readers in an article (page 458 *ante*) on a series of tidal observations made in the Thames in connection with the Metropolitan Survey. It appears to be an important and creditable production.

"The Art of Landscape Painting in Oil Colours."*—Under this head the amateur is offered, for the small contribution of a twelve-penny, sufficient elementary instruction to enable him to commence experimenting in oil vehicle with success. The information gathered in this little book of fifty pages has been gleaned from the ready communications of many artists, with whom the Publishers, in the course of their professional pursuits, are intimately connected.

* Winsor and Newton, London.

Metropolitan Sewers Commission.—On the 30th ult., a special court was held at Greek-street, to determine on the course to be adopted with reference to the plans for drainage of London, which had been received by the commission. Lord Ebrington was in the chair, and Sir H. de La Beche, moved that it be referred to a committee of the whole body of the commissioners, with the Lord Mayor, and four other members of the City Commission, who should consider the course to be adopted. The resolution was seconded by Mr. Deputy Peacock, and unanimously adopted. It was also agreed that the fifteen additional plans presented since the 3rd of October should be received.

John O'Gaunt's Palace, Lincoln.—The oriel window, lately advertised for sale, has been purchased by the Lord-Lieutenant of the County, Earl Brownlow, and presented by his lordship to the county magistrates for preservation in the castle, as an appropriate site, from having been one of Prince John's official residences.

Mr. Carew's Bas-relief on the south side of the pedestal of the Nelson monument in Trafalgar-square is completed. It represents "The Death of Nelson," and is 14 feet high, and 13 feet 7 inches wide. More, anon.

Abandonment of the London-bridge Railway Extension.—At a meeting of the South-Western Railway Company, held at Nine Elms last week, it was all but unanimously resolved to abandon the proposed extension line from Waterloo-road to London-bridge.

New Hall.—Our contemporary, the *Morning Post*, announces that a bequest of 10,000*l*. for the erection of a workman's free hall in the metropolis has been made by a Mr. Jenkins. Another friend of the people is to furnish a library of 1,000 volumes to begin with, and Mr. Hall, the geologist, is to present his museum to it when the building is completed.

The Letter-Boxes.—As the management of the post-office is at present an engrossing topic, allow me to point out, that most of the openings of the letter-boxes of the district offices in London, are so *small*, that they will not conveniently take in a newspaper, and I have frequently observed them sticking in the mouths of the letter-boxes, so that they could be easily extracted. This should be remedied. ... A. R.

MEETINGS OF SCIENTIFIC BODIES

Held during the ensuing week.

Tuesday, Dec. 11.—Institution of Civil Engineers, 8 p.m.

Wednesday, Dec. 12.—Society of Arts, 8 p.m.; Graphic Society, 8 p.m.

Thursday, Dec. 13.—Royal Society, 8½ p.m.; Society of Antiquaries, 8 p.m.

Friday, Dec. 14.—Architectural Association, 8 p.m.

TO CORRESPONDENTS.

"*C. E. G.*"—We are flattered by being elected honorary member of the "*Somersetshire Archæological Society*," and will write personally.

"*Marsden's Trap*" next week.

"*Greenwich Railway Arches*."—With reference to our remarks on the fall of arches in Camden-town, "A Bricklayer" points out that in the Greenwich viaduct there are in no case more than twelve arches without the occurrence of a pier much larger than the ordinary piers.

"*Crickets*."—A correspondent wishes to know if there be any special means of eradicating these insects. Ants and beetles have had diverse doctorings prescribed for them in our columns, but we do not recollect a recipe for crickets. Those complained of wing their way in hosts to table, shelf, and cupboard, devouring eatables, and chirping in chorus, so that they are not like Dickens's solitary harmless cheerers of the hearth.

"J. W. G.," "T. J.," "S. H.," "G. D. D.," "Dr. C.," "P." (is quite safe; some volumes of The Builder cannot be obtained but by accident), "R. C. S.," "A. W. H.," "An Architect" (Cork), "A Baronet," "H. R. A." (we shall be glad to be referred to a correct report of the argument), "A. W. H.," "V. Y.," "E. C. M." (covers for The Builder, such as our correspondent names, may be obtained at the office, 2, York-street; the notice was to *another* using the same initials), "E. A. F." (the book alluded to *has* been received; we gave an extract from it a few weeks ago, and shall hereafter review it), "S. H.," "D. C.," "C. M.," "J. O.," "E. H.," "EX. Sec.," "F. C. C." (we have not been able to call), "A. E. H.," "Lover of Good Architecture," "One of the Trade" (as to builders' establishments), "Subscriber from the Commencement" (would not be able to recover; we will allude to the hardship when an occasion offers), "F. W. B. (we shall certainly go), "D. G. P.," "G. N." (the case was reported for us; we do not know that it appeared elsewhere), "G. F.," "C. H.," "T. P. W." (thanks), "H. C.," "A Bricklayer," "*Lincolniensis*," "J. L." (Hampstead).—"Sewerage of London; a Communication addressed to the Commissioners of Sewers," by J. Bailey Denton (London, Metchim, Parliament-street, 1849).

Notice.—All communications respecting *advertisements* should be addressed to the "Publisher," and not to the "Editor:" all other communications should be addressed to the Editor, and *not* to the Publisher.

"*Books and Addresses*."—We have not time to point out books or find addresses.

Vol. VII.—No. 357.] THE BUILDER. 587

TENDERS

For the carcase of the Deptford Mechanics' Institution; Mr. W. Walter, architect.

Glen	£1,660
Penny	1,612
Dean	1,593
Holmes	1,509
Turner	1,497
Hall	1,479
W. Higgs	1,478
Harrison	1,476
Cooper and Davis	1,446
Soper and Walker	1,436
Lilleystone	1,426
Burton	1,419
Harnden	1,386
Curtis	1,368
Symons	1,346
Cooper	1,312
Goodwin	1,275
Ellison	1,268
Godson	1,208
Coleman (accepted)	1,180

ADVERTISEMENTS.

ARTESIAN WELL FOR SALE.—TO WATER COMPANIES AND OTHERS.—NOTICE IS HEREBY GIVEN, that the Blackwall Railway Company are willing to treat for the SALE or LEASE of their WELL, Well-house, and Machinery, at the Station in the Minories. This well is approached by a separate and distinct entrance from Rosemary-lane; it is 245 feet deep, 10 feet diameter, and affords an inexhaustible supply of the purest water; there is an engine for raising the water of 10-horse power, constructed by Maudslay and Co. The well may be seen by application at the Railway Offices, London Terminus, Fenchurch-street.—By order,
November 13, 1849. JOHN F. KENNELL, Secretary.

TO ARCHITECTS, BUILDERS, AND PAINTERS.
OAK STAINS, in every shade, for Churches, Railway Stations, &c.—ESTWICK and Co. respectfully announce that they continue to supply the above at 4s. per gallon. Contracts executed in town and country.
Manufactory, 56, High-street, Hoxton, London.

BUILDERS AND CONTRACTORS.
TARPAULINS for COVERING ROOFS during Repairs. SCAFFOLD CORD and every description of ROPE used by Builders upon the lowest terms. Marquees and temporary awnings on sale or hire. Orders per post receive the most prompt attention.—WILLIAM PIGGOTT, 115, Fore Street, City, Manufacturer, by Appointment, to Her Majesty's Honourable Board of Ordnance.

TO DRAUGHTSMEN AND CIVIL ENGINEERS.
H. MORRELL, BLACK LEAD PENCIL MANUFACTURER, No. 149, Fleet-street, London.
These Pencils are prepared in various degrees of hardness and shades.

H H H H for drawing on wood.	F F light and shading.
H H H for architectural use.	F for general use.
H H for engineering.	B black for shading.
H for sketching.	B B ditto ditto.
H B hard and black for drawing.	B B B ditto ditto.
M medium.	B B B B ditto ditto

Sold by all the principal Stationers in town or country.

CAST-IRON PIPES, IRON WORK FOR OVENS, &c.
RAIN PIPES, &c.—F. A. TIDDEMAN, St. Ann's Wharf, Earl-street, City, near Blackfriars-bridge, keeps a large stock of Rain Pipes, Heads, Shoes, Elbows, &c., half round and O. G. Gutters, Socket Pipes for Water or Gas, Flanch Pipes, Sash Weights, and other Castings; Iron Work for Bakers' Ovens of every description, fitted complete, to be had in sets or in parts.—Prices equal to all competition. Contracts taken to any extent. Goods landed. A powerful crane.

GREY GOOSE FEATHERS, 1s. PER POUND.
BED FEATHERS were never so cheap as at present. HEAL and SON'S present prices are:—

	s.	d.		s.	d.
Poultry	0	8	Best Grey Goose	1	10
Grey Goose	1	0	White ditto	2	2
Foreign ditto	1	6	Best Dantzic ditto	3	0

Purified by steam, and warranted sweet and free from dust.
HEAL and SON'S List of Bedding, containing full particulars of weight, sizes, and prices, sent free by post, on application to their Factory, 196, Tottenham-court-road, London.

STATUES, VASES, FOUNTAINS, Garden Ornaments, Coats of Arms, and Architectural Embellishments, in Imperishable Stone, by VAUGHAN and CO., 60, Stones'-End, Borough, London. T. J. Croggon, late of Coade's, Superintendent.—Specimens may be seen at CROGGON and Co.'s, 9, Dowgate-hill, City. A pamphlet of drawings forwarded on application.

TERRA-COTTA, or VITRIFIED STONE WORKS, King Edward-street, Westminster-road, London.—M. H. BLANCHARD, from late Coade's Original Works, Belvedere-road, Lambeth, begs to inform the Nobility, Gentry, Architects, and Builders, that he has re-established the manufacture of that invaluable material, which has been successfully adopted by our eminent Architects and others, in the adornment of our noblest buildings, nearly 100 years has proved the imperishable nature of the material, the specimens of those times now exhibiting all their primitive sharpness.
Groups, statues, friezes, capitals, panelling, pinnacles, finials, terminals, Tudor, and other chimney shafts, balustrading, fountains, fonts, tazzas, vases, coats of arms, devices, and every description of architectural ornament, at prices in many instances nearly half the cost of stone.
Specimens of the material to be seen at the Office of "The Builder," 2, York-street, Covent Garden, and at the Works.

PAVING, 2s. 9d. PER SQUARE YARD. Basements, Foot-walks, Malt-houses, Corn Stores, Floors of Warehouses, and every description of Pavement laid down at the above low price, and the work guaranteed.—Apply to JOHN PILKINGTON, POLONCEAU'S BITUMEN PAVEMENT OFFICE, 11, JOHN-STREET, ADELPHI.—N.B. Country Agents and Railway Engineers and Contractors supplied with the best bitumen for covering bridges and arches.

SEWERAGE of LONDON.—The attention of the COMMISSIONERS appointed to determine upon the most efficient material for the Construction of the Sewers of London is particularly directed to the ASPHALTE of SEYSSEL, which, more than any other material, is applicable to the constructing and internal coating of Brick Culverts, and other channels for drainage. The experiments made by the Royal Artillery on the Embrasures of Plymouth Citadel, constructed of Seyssel Asphalted Brickwork, under the orders of the Honourable Board of Ordnance, have fully proved the superiority, adhesiveness, and strength of Seyssel Asphalte over all other cementitious compositions.—A printed account of these experiments can be had on application to J. FARRELL, Secretary, Seyssel Asphalte Company, "Claridge's Patent." Established 1838.
Note.—The application of the Asphalte of Seyssel is specially recommended by the Commissioners on the Fine Arts, for covering the ground line of Brickwork in marshy situations, and it has been suggested that it would be peculiarly applicable for covering the Areas of closed Graveyards, and for the construction of Catacombs.

CAITHNESS STONE, from the Castle-hill Quarry, by Thurso.—It is prepared at the Quarry, with sawn edges, ready for laying. The faces may be natural, tooled, or rubbed as required. This paving gives great satisfaction, and is supplied of larger dimensions than ordinary. The footpath recently laid on Vauxhall-bridge is all in stones, above 6 feet long, and the paving on the bridge over the Neva, lately supplied by order of the Emperor of Russia, is all in stones of great dimensions.—Applications addressed to Mr. POTTER, 4, Church-row, Newington, will meet with every attention.—Depôt, at Freeman's Wharf, Millbank-street.

ANSTON STONE, used for Building the New Houses of Parliament.—W. WRIGHT and Co. beg to inform Architects, Engineers, Builders, and others, the Anston Stone can be supplied in any quantity on the shortest notice. This valuable stone, so celebrated for its durability, colour, and texture, is well known, having been selected in preference to all others, by the Commissioners of Woods and Forests, for building the New Houses of Parliament. It is very superior for Monuments, Tombs, &c. &c.
W. Wright and Co. have made arrangements to have a stock always on hand at Drine's Marble and Stone Wharf, Horsfall-basin, Maiden-lane, King's-cross.—Any further information can be obtained on application to W. WRIGHT and Co., Anston, near Sheffield; or to T. SHARP, their Sole Agent in London, 27, Burton-crescent.

MARKET WHARF, REGENT'S-PARK BASIN.—Messrs. MARTIN and WOOD (late Booles and Martin) solicit the attention of Builders, Masons, and others, to their stock of Portland, York, and Derby Stone; also Bangor Slates, Lime, Cement, Plaster, Bricks, Tiles, Laths, Fire-goods, Fire-stone, &c., sold at the lowest possible prices for Cash. Portland Headstones, Ledgers, Steps, Landings, &c., cut to order on the shortest notice. Tarpaulings let on hire. A Stock of Northen's Drain Pipes, Syphons, &c., always on hand. Mortar, Lime and Hair, Fine Stuff, &c.

BATH STONE OF BEST QUALITY.
RANDELL and SAUNDERS,
QUARRYMEN and STONE MERCHANTS,
BATH.
List of prices, also cost for transit to any part of the kingdom, furnished on application.

BATH STONE.—Messrs. RANDELL and SAUNDERS, Quarrymen, Bath, have appointed Messrs. MARTIN and WOOD their sole agents in London. M. and W. beg to inform Architects, Masons, Builders, &c., that a large assortment of the much approved CORSHAM DOWN and other BATH STONE will always be kept at the Depot, opposite the Great Western Railway Station, Paddington. Orders will also be received at Market Wharf, Regent's-park Basin.

CAEN STONE, SELECTED FOR EXTERNAL WORKS.—LUARD, BEEDHAM and Co., Quarry Proprietors and Importers from Allemagne.
AUBIGNY STONE from the Quarries, near Falaise, Calvados Department.—Aubigny is of similar colour to Portland Stone, its texture finer than Portland, price and labour of working about the same.
RANVILLE STONE from Ranville Quarries, near Caen, Normandy.—Suitable for strong works, wharf and quay walling, price and labour similar to Caen Stone.—Depôt, Caen Sufferance Wharf, Rotherhithe; Vauxhall-bridge, Westminster; No. 8 Wharf, Paddington Basin; Northern Wharf, Battle-bridge; and Kensington Basin.—Information and samples supplied from the Office, 18, Southwark-square, Borough.

CAEN STONE.—W. and J. FREEMAN offer Caen Stone, guaranteed from the best quarries in Allemagne, at 1s. 9d. per cubic foot, delivered to vessels or waggons from their Sufferance Wharf, at Deptford. Stone from the inferior beds, or from the Maladrerie Quarries (if ordered) on lower terms. Cargoes shipped direct from the quarries to any part of the coast at the same price. Aubigny and Ranville Stone on the lowest terms.—Application at the office, Millbank-street; or to Mr. TURNBULL, Sufferance Wharf, Grove-street, Deptford.

SAMUEL CUNDY, Mason and Builder, PIMLICO MARBLE and STONE WORKS, Belgrave Wharf, Pimlico.
GOTHIC WINDOWS, ALTAR SCREENS, and other Works, produced at a remarkably cheap rate.
FONTS from 5l. upwards. Specimens on view of the Early English, Decorated, and Perpendicular styles.
ALTAR TABLETS illuminated.
First-rate ARTISTS retained for SCULPTURED GOTHIC CARVINGS.
A Good VEINED MARBLE CHIMNEY-PIECE and a fashionable REGISTER STOVE for 3l. 3s. Stone Chimney-pieces from 8s.
MEMORIAL CROSSES, MONUMENTS, TOMBS, HEAD-STONES, &c., in great variety of design. Letters cut and complete for fixing in the country.
The Public are respectfully invited to view the carefully selected and manufactured Stock (by improved machinery) of Valued Marble Chimney-pieces—cheap and good.
A liberal discount to the trade.

RESTORATION of CHURCHES. SAMUEL CUNDY, having had much practice in this branch at Westminster Abbey and other important Gothic fabrics, is desirous of Estimating for Restorations.
S. C. has invented a Machine for Hoisting Building Materials to great altitudes, by which an immense saving has been effected; eminently adapted for Restoring Cathedrals, High Towers, &c.
CLERKS of WORKS have their particular attention called to the above establishment. A Book of Designs forwarded on application.
Works of all kinds prepared and sent off per railway—fixed or not, as required.
DAIRIES fitted up with MARBLE or SLATE SHELVES.—MINTON'S Encaustic and White or Blue and White Porcelain Tiles in great variety of pattern.

STIRLING'S BELVEDERE SLATE WORKS, Belvedere-road, Lambeth.—A reduced list of prices of the best WELCH SLATE SLABS, planed both faces, will be sent on application (post paid) being made, and inclosing a postage stamp. The prices are under those advertised for inferior slates.

VALENTIA SLATE SLABS.—The attention of the public is invited to the large importations now being made of this valuable material from the county of Kerry, Ireland. Its strength, durability, and non-absorbent property, recommend it for general use. The experiments made by command of the Board of Ordnance establish that to break slabs of equal dimensions required

	Cwt.	qrs.	lbs.
For Yorkshire Stone	2	2	29½
For Valentia Slate	11	1	25

It is well adapted for shelves, cisterns, paving, &c.—Depôt, Valentia Slate Yard, Millbank-street.

PIMLICO SLATE WORKS.—GREAT REDUCTION in the PRICE of SLATE.—Mr. MAGNUS has the pleasure to publish the following reduced prices for Welsh Slate Slabs of the finest quality, with sawn edges, and planed both faces:—

	Thick. ½ in.	¾ in.	1 in.	1¼ in.	1½ in.	2 in.	
	d.	d.	d.	d.	d.	d.	
Under 4 ft. long, or 3 ft. wide	3½	5	6	7	9	12	℘ ft. sup.
Ditto 5 ft. do., or 3 ft. do.	4	5½	7	8	10	14	do.
Ditto 6 ft. do., or 3 ft. do.	4½	6½	8	9	10½	16	do.
Ditto 7 ft. do., or 3 ft. do.	5	7	9	10	11	18	do.

Larger Slabs in proportion.

	Thick. ½ in.	¾ in.	1 in.	1¼ in.	1½ in.	2 in.	
	d.	d.	d.	d.	d.	d.	
Cutting to order	1	1	1½	1½	1½	2	℘ ft. sup.

FURTHER REDUCTION IN THE PRICE OF CISTERNS.
Cisterns above 100 gallons, planed both faces, Inch thick, grooved and bolted, 1s. only per foot super., or 2s. per foot cube (outside dimensions). Fixing within five miles of the manufactory, 3d. per foot super., or 6d. per foot cube. Enamelled boxed Chimney-pieces, variously marbled, hitherto priced at 40s. to 50s. now reduced to 25s. and 30s. The above prices are all net to the trade.
Mr. Magnus will send his book of Drawings of Chimney-pieces, and printed price-list of ditto, free to any part of the country, on receipt of 3d. in postage stamps (to be deducted from first order received) and which will be subject to a very liberal discount to the trade.—Address, 89, Upper Belgrave-place, Pimlico.

REDUCED PRICES.—EDWARD SIMMS (late William Cleave), of Wilton-road, Pimlico Basin, begs to acquaint Builders and the Trade that he has now on hand, at his Manufactory (the first of its kind ever established), a very large Assortment of Dry and Well-seasoned OAK and DEAL PREPARED FLOORING BOARDS and MATCH BOARDING of all sorts, from ½ inch to 1½ inch thick, planed to a parallel width and thickness, and at greatly Reduced Prices. Also, Timber, Deals, Oak Planks, Scantlings, Sash Bills, Mouldings prepared by Machinery, Laths, &c.—Apply at E. SIMMS'S (late W. Cleave's) Flooring Manufactory, Wilton-road, Pimlico Basin.

FLOORING.—ALFRED ROSLING begs to inform his customers and the trade generally, that he has again very materially REDUCED the PRICES of his DRY FLOOR BOARDS, of which he has in stock an extensive assortment. To purchasers of a quantity of freshly prepared boards A. R. is able to offer a great reduction upon his current prices, to avoid the expense of piling away in the drying sheds. Mouldings in great variety, and prepared in a very superior manner.—Southwark-bridge Wharf, Bankside, October, 1849.

THOMAS ADAMS, Mahogany and Timber Merchant, Bermondsey New-road, Southwark, near the Bricklayers' Arms, is SELLING SEASONED FLOORING at LESS PRICES THAN ANY ADVERTISED; also matched boards and mouldings prepared from the very best material, and in a superior manner. Cut deals and scantlin of every dimension; mahogany, cedar, rosewood, wainscot, elm, beech, oak, &c.; pantile, oak, and fir laths; wheelwrights' goods. All sawn and prepared goods (except timber) delivered free of expense. Sawing charged at mill prices. Very extensive drying-sheds.
N.B. English timber taken in exchange for foreign.

PRESENT PRICES of SEASONED FLOORING, prepared by improved Machinery. Net cash.

1¼ in. yellow, per sq.	20s. 0d.	1 in. spruce, per sq.	13s. 0d.
1 " " "	17s. 6d.	¾ " " "	11s. 9d.
¾ " " "	14s. 9d.	½ " " "	10s. 6d.

Widths measured after being wrought. Quantities not less than thirty squares delivered within 5 miles free.
SAMUEL ARCHBUTT and CO., Timber Merchants, Sawing and Planing Mills, King's-road, Chelsea.

MUIR'S PATENT 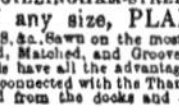 PLANING MACHINE.

SAW MILLS, GILLINGHAM-STREET, PIMLICO.
TIMBER of any size, PLANK, DEALS, and BATTENS, &c., Sawn on the most approved principle. Boards, &c., Prepared, Matched, and Grooved, by Muir's Patent Machinery. The Mills have all the advantages of navigation and water-carriage, being connected with the Thames by the Grosvenor Canal. Goods fetched from the docks and carted home free of charge.
Address to HENRY SOUTHAM,
Saw Mills, Gillingham-street, Pimlico.
N.B. Estimates given for Sawing and Planing.

PHILLIPS, ALLCARD, and CO.'S IMPERIAL DEAL SAW-MILLS, WENLOCK-ROAD CITY-ROAD, beg to invite the attention of builders, carpenters and the trade, to their well selected stock, consisting of a large assortment of TIMBER, DEALS, PLANKS, and BATTENS, of every description, and thoroughly seasoned. They also have constantly on hand, and ready for immediate use, white and yellow prepared FLOORING BOARDS of all thicknesses, and matched lining, cut and planed to a parallel breadth and thickness. And they are enabled to offer all their goods at very moderate prices.

THE TIMBER PRESERVING COMPANY.—The Directors of the above Company beg to inform the public that they have REMOVED their MACHINERY to DURRAND'S WHARF, ROTHERHITHE, where they prepare timber by Payne's, Bethell's, and Margary's process.—Offices of the Company, Whitehall Wharf, Cannon-row, Westminster.

DESICCATED WOOD.—DAVISON and SYMINGTON'S PATENT.—Builders, Cabinet-makers, and others, will find it much to their advantage to patronise this new process of seasoning. The greenest wood can thus not only be seasoned in an incredibly short space of time, at a small cost, but is rendered stronger, entirely free from shrinkage, and in every respect better than wood treated in the ordinary way; thereby saving capital, interest of money, insurance, and all the other inconveniences attending the keeping of a large stock.
The DESICCATING SAWING and PLANING MILLS are situated at PLOUGH BRIDGE, ROTHERHITHE, adjoining the Commercial and East Country Docks, from whence parties obtaining their material can have the same converted as required, and sent home fit for immediate use.—T. GIRLING, Manager.
For licenses to use the patent, scale of prices, or other information, address ANGUS JENNINGS, Secretary, Patent Desiccating Company, 41, Gracechurch-street, City.

TO ARCHITECTS, BUILDERS, UPHOLSTERERS, AND OTHERS.
WOOD CARVING done in the cheapest and best manner. Estimates given to any amount. Pulpits, reading-desks, altar-rails, stalls, and other church fittings supplied complete. Old carvings restored by J. STALON, Wood Carver and Manufacturer, 42, Berwick-street, Soho, London.

JORDAN'S PATENT MACHINE CARVING and MOULDING WORKS for WOOD and STONE, Belvedere-road, Lambeth, and 154, Strand.—TAYLOR WILLIAMS, and JORDAN beg to call the attention of the building community to a new feature of their establishment, and, at the same time, to thank their numerous patrons and friends for the very liberal support they have lately experienced, which, they assure them and the public, it will be their constant endeavour to deserve, by giving their customers an increasing share of the advantages arising from the constant improvements in the machinery which they have just succeeded in applying to the production of the most intricate carving in Caen and other freestones, and in statuary marble.
T., W., and J. particularly solicit the attention of architects and builders to the fact that, by the use of this machinery, a very large saving, both of time and money, is effected,—so great, indeed, that in many cases they can deliver a well-finished article in Caen stone for less money than it can be obtained in cement, while their wood-carving will, in some cases, be found to come into close competition with the best kinds of composition ornament.—For prices and estimates apply at 154, Strand.
TESTIMONIAL FROM CHARLES BARRY, ESQ.
"Westminster, May 16th, 1848.
"Gentlemen.—In reply to your letter requesting my opinion of your Patent Carving Machinery, I have much pleasure in stating, from an experience of more than two years, in its application to the production of the wood carvings of the House of Peers, and other apartments of the New Palace, at Westminster, that I am enabled to make the most favourable report concerning it, and to add that it has more than justified the favourable terms in which I recommended it in 1845 to her Majesty's Commissioners of Woods and Works for adoption.—I remain, Gentlemen, yours faithfully,
"CHARLES BARRY."
Messrs. Taylor, Williams, and Jordan."

PAPER-HANGINGS—At E. T. ARCHER'S Manufactory for English and Warehouse for English and French Paper-hangings, from One Penny per yard, to the most costly pannelled decorations. The decorations are fitted up on the walls of an extensive range of show rooms, showing at one view a drawing or dining-room finished, fit for occupation.—Painted marble or granite papers of superior fabric, from One Penny per yard.—451, Oxford-street.

PAPER-HANGINGS by MACHINE and BLOCKS.—The trade supplied in town and country, with machine goods, from first-rate new designs, at the lowest prices they have ever been sold in this country; and block goods, for style and quality, not to be surpassed by any house in England. All the patterns are registered, and can only be supplied by HENNELL and CROSBY, Queen-street, Southwark-bridge-road. Cheapest house in London for oak, marbles, and panel decorations. A set of patterns, 5s., to be deducted off an order of 5l.—Terms, cash.

No. CCCLVIII.

SATURDAY, DECEMBER 15, 1849.

REAT efforts to ameliorate the condition and raise the character of the working classes are, undeniably, being made in England at this moment, and will, there is every reason to believe, ultimately effect much good. The direction which these efforts are taking seems a right one, and if those whom it is sought to benefit embrace warmly and ingenuously the means which are offered to them, and strive vigorously to elevate themselves, the most important results to all classes of society will follow, and in a rapidly increasing ratio. Without their own co-operation—(self-discipline and education, the acquirement of habits of regularity and foresight)—nothing effectual will be done: with it, and extended knowledge, on the part of the upper classes, of our mutual duties and rights, it is scarcely possible to say how much.

The provision of well-ordered homes, of neat, commodious, and healthy lodgings, as one most important first step, we have long and anxiously advocated, and have given our humble aid to every well-meant endeavour to further it.*

With this feeling we are desirous to bring prominently before our readers the large lodging-house in Spitalfields, opened on Wednesday the 12th, by the "Metropolitan Association for Improving the Dwellings of the Industrious Classes," under the title of THE ARTISANS' HOME: and a range of dwellings for married people closely adjoining, but not yet quite finished. These are situated in Albert-street, Spicer-street, a short distance to the north of the Whitechapel-road, and have been constructed under the superintendence of Mr. William Beck, architect, by Mr. S. Grimsdell, he builder. Five architects, it may be remembered, furnished designs in competition, and ve gave, in our sixth volume (p. 387), a review f their several characteristics. The "Home" rovides accommodation for 234 single men,† ach (to speak generally, in the first instance) aving a separate sleeping compartment, 8 feet y 4 feet 6 inches,—the use of a spacious and andsome coffee-room, kitchen, a lecture-oom, and a reading-room.

But let us go a little into detail. The build-ng is five stories in height. It occupies three ides of a square the whole height: the space nclosed by the three sides is covered to he height of the ground floor only, and orms there the coffee-room. The base-nent contains baths and washhouses, with the equisite appurtenances,‡ cellarage, and space

* A meeting was held last week, in the parish of St. Mar-lo-in-the-Fields, the Rev. H. Mackenzie, the vicar, in the hair, "for the purpose of considering the necessity of aking measures for promoting the improvement of the lwellings of the labouring classes resident in that parish. t was resolved,—"That taking into consideration the suf-ering and privations during the prevalence of the recent pidemic, arising in a great measure from the absence of roper accommodation, and the unhealthy condition of the lwellings of the labouring classes, this meeting is of opinion hat it is highly desirable and necessary that measures hould be taken for improving the habitations of the indus-rial classes in this parish;" and a committee was appointed o inquire and report.

† Two hundred and thirty-four men congregated toge-her!" said a French visiter there the other day, "why, in 'aris, they would make a revolution." We have no such ar in London.

‡ The engineer for boiler, warming apparatus, &c., was r. Reeve, of Albion-street, Caledonian-road.

for workshops. On the ground floor the en-trance hall is commanded by the superinten-dent, whose apartments are on the left, while on the right the store room and cooks' apart-ments occupy about the same space. Imme-diately in front of the entrance are the stairs (of fire-proof construction), which lead to the three stories of sleeping berths. On the left of the stairs is a good-sized lavatory for day use.

The *Coffee-room*, 45 feet by 35 feet, faces the entrance hall, and extends to the back of the building, having communication on one side with a large reading-room, and on the other with a kitchen for the use of the inmates. It is lofty, and divided into aisles by iron columns supporting an open roof of stained timbers, stop-chamfered,—lighted by a large central window, two smaller side windows, and sheets of rough plate glass in the whole extent of the roof. This room, a very hand-some apartment, is fitted up with boxes round three sides, containing tables and seats, and is warmed by hot-water pipes. A cook's bar opens into a coffee-room, for the supply of coffee, &c. The *Reading-room*, 60 feet by 21 feet 9 inches, is warmed by open fires, and has the *Library* at one end : it will be furnished with some of the daily papers and popular periodicals.

The *Kitchen*, 45 feet by 21 feet 9 inches, contains two ranges, and hot-water tanks, a sink supplied with cold water, and the common apparatus for cooking purposes. The floor is formed of the metallic lava. From this kitchen a stone staircase leads to a portion of the basement containing 234 small larders or safes, with lock on each; they are raised on brick piers, and placed in ranges back to back, with space for ventilation. The key, in each case, fits the locker in the bed compartment bearing the same number.

The *Cook's Shop* is connected with the men's kitchen by a bar, where it is intended that cooked provisions may be obtained at almost any hour of the day by those who do not care to cook their own.

The *Three Upper Stories* are fitted with sleeping compartments on each side of a central corridor, formed by framing of sufficient height ; each compartment measures 8 feet by 4 feet 6 inches, and is lighted by half a win-dow; the upper portion opens, and this is hung on centres : each contains an iron bed-stead, and suitable furniture ; a locker for linen and clothes, with a false bottom, between which and the floor is a space for the admission of fresh air, that can be regulated at plea-sure. The door of each compartment is se-cured by a spring latch lock, of which each lodger has the key.* On each floor are lava-tories, fitted up with cast-iron enamelled basins set in slate fittings; also water-closets for night use. The partitions forming the sleep-ing compartments are kept below the ceiling, for the purpose of ventilation, and the central passage has a window at each end, to insure a thorough draft when necessary.

For the general *ventilation*, the principal agent is a shaft, which rises nearly 100 feet : into this several of the smoke flues of the building are conveyed, and by this means a powerful upward current is maintained. The sleeping apartments and other principal rooms are connected by vitiated air flues with the ventilating shaft, and the current is to be regulated at pleasure by means of dampers placed under the control of the superintendent.

* These locks are so constructed that in no one wing do two keys fit.

There are large cisterns in the roof, and smaller ones in other parts of the building, to afford an ample supply of water to every part of the premises ; and every floor has an open-ing, secured by an iron door, into a dust shaft, communicating with a dust cellar in the base-ment. The whole building is lighted with gas. The amount of the contract was 9,560l. The building appears to be an honest, sound con-struction, creditable alike to Mr. Beck and the contractor.

We should mention that the rent to be paid by each lodger in advance is 3s. per week, for which each inmate, besides his sleeping apart-ment, will have the use of the coffee-room, read-ing-room, and the public kitchen, where he may cook his own food; or, as we have said, he can obtain ready-dressed provisions from the cook. Every lodger has free access to the washhouse at certain times of the day, and can, by the payment of a small sum, have a hot or cold bath.

Of the adjoining range of buildings for sixty families, now in course of erection, we may take another opportunity to speak.

It is surprising to those who do not know how often the public must be told a thing before they will hear it, that after the length of time which has elapsed since the Asso-ciation was established, and the expense incurred in advertisements, it should still be little known, and that all houses of the description hitherto erected should be termed only as "models," and erected "with funds raised from the donations of the cha-ritable." It does not seem understood that this association partakes quite of the commer-cial character, being a Joint-stock Company, having a capital of 100,000l., in 4,000 shares of 25l. each, though, at the same time, the in-terest of the class sought to be benefited is pro-tected by the charter, limiting the dividends at any time to be paid to 5l. per cent., any sur-plus being directed to be applied in extension of the object,—a direction which goes to *for-tify* the investment. The association has already paid one dividend.

From a statement forwarded to us by Mr. Charles Gatliff, the secretary of the association, it seems that the *Société des Cités Ouvrières*, now beginning operations in Paris, have grown out of this.

We shall look to "the Artisan's Home" with much solicitude, and trust to find it work out as beneficially as we anticipate it will. It offers to its inmates all those advantages, and more, on a scale suited to their means, which a west-end club affords to those in a higher walk. We are not quite satisfied with the name given to the lodgings, because we do not think it likely to make them so popular as we wish. Our artisans are a sturdy, independent race (and we like them the better for being so), who would not live under any roof which implied the receipt of *charity*. It is most important, therefore, to avoid the possibility of such a notion attaching in the remotest degree to the Spicer-street lodgings, and we would rather, therefore, that they had been called "Carlisle-street," "Ebrington-build-ings," or "Howard-place," giving every inha-bitant his own number.

Every man who thinks of moving there to live may feel assured that he is going to pay fairly, we will even say amply, for the advan-tages afforded, and that he simply has a Company for landlord instead of an individual. This, we think, cannot be too generally under-stood. The same advantages will presently be given, we have little doubt, for even less rent, and yet pay those who risk their capital in the speculation.

We hope the directors will not be afraid of a little *decoration*. We should like to see the walls of the coffee-room, reading-room, &c., covered with good prints, maps, &c., silently teaching,—and sending men out of a morning with a pleasant feeling, or a good thought, to dwell upon. " Is there, truly considered, any calamity more grievous, that more deserves the best good will to remove it, than this,—to go from chamber to chamber, and see *no beauty?*"

ARCHITECTURAL PROPOSITIONS.

THE following propositions are deduced from observation and study, and I beg leave to submit them for the consideration of others. It seems to me that these and other consequent propositions, if carried out, give not only defined and reasonable *principles* for architectural design, which at present are nowhere distinctly explained, but must lead to the proof of the *necessity* of a new style, and the practical means we have for systemizing it.   W.

1. That all art expresses three distinct qualities or ideas—grandeur, beauty, picturesqueness.
2. That each of these qualities is subdividable into three other qualities, whose difference is less distinct—beauty sliding off on one side to strength, on the other to grace—grandeur on one side to sublimity, on the other to strength—picturesqueness on the one side to grandeur, on the other to fancifulness.
3. That these three distinct qualities are subdividable in themselves to infinity, as seen in all created nature.
4. That the variety and almost imperceptible graduation of change thus produced is incapable of being expressed by single verbal explanations, but that enough is given by the three before-mentioned qualities, to form standards of character for the artist's purpose.
5. That there are three powers or principles placed under the control of the artist for the elimination of those qualities—form, shadow, and ornament.
6. That these three powers are resolvable into one—form. From form the two other powers are generated; on form they are dependent, and consequently subordinate.
7. That shadow is the first-born of form, and dependent on that alone, consequently has the next place of honour.
8. That ornament is dependent on both, and consequently inferior to each, and subordinate.
9. That either one of these powers, by itself, is capable, in a greater or less degree, of expressing each of the three qualities before defined.
10. That form, as the superior power, is most capable.
11. That ornament, dependent on form and shadow as the inferior power, is least capable.
12. That that form is most perfect which is most varied in its parts, and most harmonious in combination.
13. That there are definable and distinct forms productive of the distinct qualities of proposition No. 1,—every variation of which form produces a variation in the quality, idea, or character,—these three words being synonymous.
14. That so far these propositions are true and explanatory of visible art in general.
15. That substances are the architects means of producing form, shadow, and ornament.
16. That the nature of a substance determines the nature of its construction.
17. That each difference of construction expresses a different quality or character. That each system of construction is the base and exponent of a character peculiar to itself, which we term style.
18. That there is one style for the g and, one for the beautiful, and one for the pic-turesque.
19. That each such style has the three p t a..c or powers of variation, with all their intermediate differences, mentioned in proposition No. 2 in itself,

20. That each such style has not the power of expressing the three distinct qualities of proposition No. 1 in itself—at least, not to the most perfect production of each.
21. That each system of construction is grounded on a different and distinct form.
22. That such a form must simply, or in combination, extend and harmonize throughout the entire mass.
23. That such a form, if made the unchangeable standard of a particular construction, is the unchangeable standard of its quality or character.
24. That, of curves, the circular expresses the character or quality of grandeur :
25. The ovoid, that of beauty :
26. And the combined segments of either, the picturesque.
27. Of angles (a line being expressive only in combination),—
28. The right angle expresses grandeur :
29. And the acute angled triangle, picturesqueness.
30. That direct imitation in architecture destroys it as an art.
31. That it is an art, in so far as it produces change, in either form, shadow, or ornament, and however slightly.
32. That as an art it is eminently progressive.
33. That it has standard or fixed principles, but not standard rules.
34. That it is true art in so far as it expresses the spirit of the time in which it is produced.
35. That practically, utility covers a multitude of sins.

WOODS AND FORESTS—SHIP TIMBER.

A YEAR back sundry commentaries were published in THE BUILDER on this subject—one of some importance as regarding the supply of oak for naval purposes, and which has since that period been treated by several of the journals. Already have the delinquencies and defalcations been laid (however unmeritedly) at the door of her Majesty's Commissioners of Woods and Forests ; and the public eye has been directed to the absorbing theme of our wooden walls, as well as to the maladministration and waste of hundreds of thousands of acres which might and ought to furnish employment, food, and profit to 100,000 denizens of the workhouse.

It has been shown how small an extent even of the New Forest (itself but a tithe of Royal domain lands) is really occupied by growing timber for naval purposes; how little of that timber has ever found its way to the national arsenals ; and how much was left desert ; and, moreover, that such waste land was and continues to be most pernicious to the habits of the agrestic population, since it can only serve for the range of a herd of deer, the walk of the warrener, the beat of the poacher, or the prowl of the timber dropper.

In the reflections which such a condition of things suggested, it occurred to the writer that the navy, the State, and the community might profit by viewing these estates in pretty much the same light as though they had been private domain lands, and by converting them to a source of income, happiness, and plenty. Not to touch the Royal appanage of Windsor-park,—the Forests of Dean and Hatchwood, Epping, and others present a wide width of fertile and convertible farms ; and probably if his Grace of Sutherland's estates were compared, tested, and valued as to the staple and quality of the soil, the former would prove in no degree inferior. One has been managed with a view to private (and therefore to public) benefit ; the other would appear to be "no man's land." From the one springs up and renews annually a fixed revenue of at least 12s. average return per acre,—from the other less than *nil*, for the balance has been set down on the wrong side of the folio, and what " the canker worm corroded not, the *Palmer* worm devoured !"

The remedy proposed in THE BUILDER was such as would occur to a Scotch grieve, who would earnestly set about the cultivation of farms a long time in Chancery : being simple, and woven in an ordinarily short treatise, it may have passed with little observation : therefore, it may not be out of place to repeat it, even at the risk of an imputation of tautology ; for a good thing, if ungrateful, may be said too often.

This, then, was our panacea : take an estimate and survey of all those portions whereon stands mature or growing timber for the navy fence in and demarcate them ; again, estimate what other parts (in sections) are adapted for the growth of young plantation, and having ascertained, according to Cocker and a very reasonable essay in the *Times* of 29th ult., the total number of acres requisite for the perpetuation of a supply to the naval arsenals, fence that in also, and plant it with the most approved species of oak and Spanish chesnut.

Thus, according to rule, a fair security may be attained against any dearth of product for succeeding generations ; and if the calculation referred to be correct, that 36,000 loads of timber per annum will suffice to keep up a war armament, and that 60 loads (at only one load of 50 cubic feet per stick) be the yield of an acre, then a range of under 10,000 acres of forest will suffice for the object. But supposing that 20,000 acres of free growing oak timber (at the same time that I regard Spanish chesnut as equally serviceable and more tenacious) were required for these occasions then nearly 300,000 acres of improvable land would remain unappropriated. The whole of the residue should, and ought to be, subdued cultivated, replenished, and devoted to increased and increasing demands of a progressively multiplying population.

Having got rid of the question of supply and secured nurseries for future fleets, there would still remain scattered over the excluded forests, in groups, bosquets, rows, and detached trees, an immense number of standard oaks ; and these, perhaps, the most appropriate for kelsons, knees, and compass scantling. What forbids that the rule of private estate should not obtain here too ? When a farm is leased to the tenant of a landlord, it is usual,—nay, the rule is invariable, to mark, number and register the trees growing and standing thereon ; and such tenant would no more dare to cut and carry, nor even to lop one of such than he would think of pulling down an devastating the farm house, or of ploughing up old traditional pastures.

Why not so enumerate, mark, and register the outstanding trees on the royal forests Why not lease out the expletive and waste lands to improving tenants for fructification and why not increase the breadth of cereal crops, already too scant ?

300,000 acres, leased at only 5s. an acre would produce 75,000l. a-year ; and this without any diminution of courtly splendour, saving that the 729 fat bucks distributed at Christmas might cause a dish the less on the festive board now instant upon us.

A recompense for this short-coming might however present itself in the stimulus given to agriculture, in the busy employment of thousands of Hants and Dorsetshire labourers now awaiting deportation, or on the questionable limits and chill subsistence in the workhouse A wholesome impetus to trade, and architecture in particular, would be imparted by the erection of cottages, farms, boxes, and mansions, not to speak of the incessant demand for labour in the reclaiming of lands, the location of the most industrial elements of rural labour, and, not least, the so far increased independence of foreign grain. Many whose own patriæ make them regard emigration as transportation would still adhere to their native soil even in sterility, and would apply the native nerve and energy to the advancement of the commonweal in independence. That every rood of ground should maintain its man neither desirable nor necessary, but that man an acre teeming with fertility should lie neglected is a prodigality and a crime towards that Providence which commanded " that man replenish the earth."

Supposing, however, that the woods an forests remain *in statu quo*, that the chances an observers that something of private management might with equal advantage be introduced to the supervision of forests.

A private estate with an extensive range wood is sure to be under the superintendance of a woodreeve or surveyor, expert and informed of his vocation ; he is not chosen for family connections nor Parliamentary interest but only because he is capable : he views the

SOUTH WALL OF CHANCEL, STOWE BARDOLPH CHURCH.

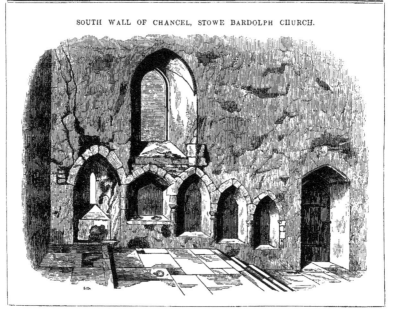

increase and progress of the crop; he knows its meetings and its value; he can tell at a glance the quantity and contents of any tree; and can determine which is to be fallen, both for profit in the product and benefit to the reserved timber. How is it in royal property? The official is an officer of state, mayhap a member of the senate; if he is not above the business he is not equal to it; the chief part of the duty is to receive a heavy stipend (much too large for an operative), and the supervision is left to local agents.

Thus it is that in national property malversation is easy, the delegated duty is performed without check, and no principal can be expected to undertake more than the audit and acceptance of accounts, *habilement raisonnés.*

In territorial concerns of such magnitude, *riding surveyors,* not addicted to any particular range, might be a wholesome restraint; and even in the event of the sale of all useless wastes, and the retention of only timber producing soils, such officers (and they are employed in the postal departments) at a moderate salary, with travelling allowances, might be a salutary guard on spoliations and robbery such as have been brought to light.

No further evidence is required to prove the necessity of some precaution than the report of Mr. G. W. Fletcher, timber merchant, of Millbrook, Southampton, which was presented to Lord Duncan, and to which the prosecution of the Reades was altogether owing:—" Such was the mismanagement in the Forests, and so deeply were the royal servants implicated in *systematic plunder* and corruption of every kind!—so multifarious were the parties concerned in it, that *a public fund was collected to* defend prisoners !! and that for this reason it was next to *impossible to find a jury to convict ! ! !* "—See *Times,* Nov. 29.

There is no argument for a total change and disafforestation of royal demesnes if this be not one; yet this is only a fragment of what has come to light,—for it appears that in Whichwood countless thousands have been lost to the public, the timber wasted, and the delinquent has been suffered to escape.

Reserving for another occasion some proofs of facts in aggravation of gross mismanagement,

as also some remarks as to the inexhaustible stores of durable or nearly imperishable timber which can be supplied by the colonies of Australasia, together with the facility of carrying home those products in suitable scantling, or of even building ships in our colonies of a vastly superior material, I shall now conclude with the remark that the redundant population might be placed in a position of happiness for themselves, and advantage for the parent 'state, by sending them to wide fields of industry, and by taking, in return, the blue and tarart gum tree, the mahogany, and other timbers, the clearance whereof would give them a location, and confer on Britain an *enceinte fortifiée.* QUONDAM.

PECULIAR FEATURE IN STOWE BARDOLPH CHURCH.

ANNEXED is a view taken in September last, of the south wall of the chancel of Stowe Bardolph Church. With the exception of the doorway, all the arches were bricked up and entirely concealed by a thin deal partition; the steps and floor are of course not in their original position, they will be altered when the restoration is complete. The whole of this wall was in such a ruinous condition that it was obliged to be taken down, but it has been rebuilt precisely as it formerly was.

The window or opening eastward of the piscina is worthy of notice. I believe its position to be unique, at any rate I have never met with one so situated before out of nearly 3,000 churches that I have inspected: it has no appearance of ever having been glazed, nor are there any traces of hooks for the hinges, as are generally found when such openings have been closed with shutters. The clear dimensions of the opening are 2 feet 1¾ inch by 4¼ inches. The walls of this church were almost entirely covered with paintings, among which were two very large ones of St. Christopher, reaching from the floor to the roof; the lower portions of these had been destroyed by an enormous gallery, which extended over more than half the length of the church; there were other paintings re-

presenting the martyrdom of St. Edmund the crucifixion; two figures, the one of the blessed Virgin, and the other, holding a book, probably intended for St. Ann, over the centre of the chancel, and two angels holding a shield, with the emblems of the passion, with the figure of our Saviour above : in other parts the walls were diapered with the sacred monogram. These paintings were mostly very rudely executed, and in so bad a state as to preclude the possibility of their being restored; but before they were quite lost, I took careful drawings of the most interesting.

The church consists of chancel, with mortuary chapel on the north, nave, and west tower.

I should be very glad to hear from some of your numerous contributors or readers, whether an aperture, similar to the one referred to in the accompanying sketch, is to be met with in any other church in a similar position.

The restorations now going on comprise the rebuilding the south walls of the nave and chancel; new windows throughout the church; new oak roofs over nave and chancel, the former open to the ridge, the latter panelled; new oak chancel screen and stalls; new paving throughout; new north porch, and new doors to the nave and chancel. All the windows will be filled with stained glass. New altar, font and pulpit. The seating to the nave will be partly new; the remainder being the old seats (date, 1625). RAPHAEL BRANDON.

IRISH SCHOOLS OF DESIGN,—The Government School at Belfast was to be opened on Thursday in last week. Lord Dufferin, the president, announced by letter his intention to offer a prize of 50*l.* for the most approved design, for a damask table cloth. Copies of the design when approved of, his lordship suggested should be distributed to the most celebrated damask manufacturers in the neighbourhood of Belfast, with the view of being manufactured in linen, to be submitted to the inspection of competent judges, and the piece most approved of to be sent to the exhibition of nations in 1851, as a specimen of the staple manufacture of the north of Ireland.

UNION IS STRENGTH.

THE ARCHITECTURAL SOCIETIES.

The attention of the architectural profession, and of other persons—and happily they are not few who take an interest in all that relates to architecture— is at this moment drawn to the consideration of applying, as well a remedy for the abuses which have crept into a noble pursuit, as of affording encouragement to those individuals who have entered it with high aspirations after fame, and a praiseworthy wish to run a noble career.

Having deprecated the want of union which exists among the institutions into which the profession is divided, I ventured to express an opinion that a remedy for this and many other ills might be found through the instrumentality of an architectural college, if well supported by architects, and by those who are either strongly engaged by collateral ties or by inclination, in upholding just and correct views of a profession which influences so largely the comforts, wants, and tastes of society.

I now proceed to show that an institution already exists, which might, either with modifications or with additions, be made to serve as a groundwork for a general, comprehensive, and well-organized scheme. In alluding to the "College of the Freemasons of the Church," I cannot do better than quote the very first law, to show its extensive scope and high purpose.

"The college was founded on Advent eve, in the year of our Lord and Saviour one thousand eight hundred and forty-two, 'for the recovery, maintenance, and furtherance of the true principles and practice of architecture; for the sanction of good principles of building, and for the condemnation of bad ones; for the exercise of scientific and experienced judgment in the choice and use of the most proper materials; for the infusion, maintenance, and advancement of science throughout architecture; and, by developing the powers of the college upon a just and beneficial footing, to raise architecture from its present vituperated condition, and to bring around it the same unquestioned honour which is at present enjoyed by almost every other profession; and further, for the charitable assistance of those and their families over whom it shall please Providence, after a life devoted to the service and practice of architecture and its dependent arts, that need shall fall.' And whereas, with the ancient freemasons, who were indeed of the church, architectural construction was carried to so wonderful a degree of perfection, that, by the science of co-gravitation, vast and beautiful fabrics were erected to endure, though composed even of small masses of mean and perishable materials,— therefore this institution, intended for the cultivation and growth of the highest class of scientific constructive architecture, shall be intituled "The College of the Freemasons of the Church."

Such is the language with which the college sets forth its endeavour to bring the wisdom and experience of the past to bear upon the present and the future,—language whose justice every candid mind must recognize as founded in a sound and far-seeing love of art and artists, and as placing concisely before the profession the evils which afflict it on the one hand, and on the other, the remedy which may be applied.

To the late estimable and gifted Alfred Bartholomew is to be ascribed the chief title of founder of this college, which he was not permitted to see fully carried out; and his early departure from a profession which he loved and adorned, may be reckoned as one main cause that the institution has not made that rapid progress which its excellent intentions deserve. Of the eighty-eight laws which at present form the guidance of the members, it may be sufficient to quote law 3, which will serve to show the wide and popular basis upon which the institution was to be established.

Law III. The members of the college shall consist of five classes, viz. :—

1st. Architectural fellows, who shall be gentlemen who have been educated to the profession of architecture or of civil engineering, and who are not under the age of twenty-four years, or who have been in the actual practice of the profession of architecture or civil engineering during five years.

2nd. Architectural associates, who shall be students in practical architecture, or in civil engineering in connection with architecture, under the age of twenty-four years, and who, on arriving at the age of twenty-four years, shall be eligible as architectural fellows.

3rd. Clerical fellows, who shall be clergymen of the United Church of England and Ireland.

4th. Lay fellows, who shall be gentlemen, or respectable persons who are not architects, nor civil engineers, nor clergymen of the United Church of England and Ireland.

5th. Honorary fellows, who shall be persons eminent for science or for learning, or for antiquarian or for architectural knowledge, or who, from station or through other means, have the power of furthering or patronizing practical architecture."

It will be seen that these classifications are sufficiently clear in their objects, admitting within the pale all members of the profession, yet not excluding any persons who, without pretending to a knowledge, may have a great love of art, and an anxious desire to be joined with artists in promoting and elevating those pursuits to which their feelings in common are drawn, a union which cannot fail to be productive of as much pleasure to the amateur, as of encouragement to the artist, who has too many drawbacks in his career not to require and appreciate the sympathy of well-informed and well-judging men. It is far from my wish to have it supposed for one moment that, in holding out an invitation to the profession in its different branches to join the College of the Freemasons of the Church, I would insist, in the first place, that its laws and regulations are perfect, or, in the second, that already existing Institutions, especially if of older date, can be expected to belong to the college without some concession on its part. Yet it is to be hoped that existing institutions, and why need I scruple to name them?—that the elder Institute of British Architects, the younger Architectural Association, and that still more recently-established society, for the laudable purpose of publishing architectural works, may one and all, setting aside every feeling but the ennobling one—zeal for the common good, consent to make common cause with the Freemasons of the Church, in whose name I am privileged to state that on their side every just concession will be made, every private feeling will be sacrificed to promote the desirable objects set forth in the heading of their laws. For my own part, I am prepared to surrender into the hands of any other architect more gifted than myself—and such a one is easily to be found in the ranks of my noble profession,—the distinction conferred upon me by the college, much as I prize it, and retire into the ranks, a humble but zealous follower. On the side of the college, therefore, there would be no obstacle in the way of meeting other institutions with the open hand of fellowship; and if it be asked why do not its members rather fuse into other societies, than expect to be joined by those whose date is older, or whose numbers are greater than their own, the reply is simply this,—that, without casting the slightest disrespect upon any other society, or doubting its usefulness, it is their conscientious belief that only in their own body is to be found a well-digested code of laws for every occasion befitting the artist, the gentleman, and the Christian, a well-considered provision for every branch of art or science connected with architecture, a wide unexclusive plan of membership, the whole scheme being intended and calculated in their opinion to form "a kindly community of the most advanced science, knowledge, and experience." (Law IX.)

The college, limited hitherto in its fellowship, and, consequently, in its means of usefulness, has not altogether been idly or unprofitably employed. Its meetings have taken place every month—one sign of activity—and the papers read on various subjects have appeared in the periodical devoted to the profession. Of the value of these papers it is not for me to pass an opinion; such as they are they were freely contributed to the general treasury of knowledge. The restoration of St. John's Gate, Clerkenwell, is chiefly owing to the intervention of the college.

It now remains to be seen whether this appeal, imperfect as it is adequately to express the high objects and important interests it would advocate, is to receive countenance from those who, having run a lengthened and

prosperous career, should yet bestow thought for the rising generation,—from those who are even now struggling in their onward path to fame,— from those also, who, wishing to aid in working out the great truths of art, have not hitherto had the proper opportunity,— from all, in short, who desire the advancement of a science, whose results are seen to cover the length and breadth of a land, of which they ought to be the noblest monuments for taste, skill, and judgment. Such would be the case were architects led to emulate those master builders (ἀρχι-τέκτονες, — Bible translation) of former days, the Freemasons of the middle ages, who developed the beauties of their art equally in the cottage and in the palace, in the humble parish church as in the stately minster. But these men formed a community; and if we imitate their example we may hope to imbibe some portion of their spirit, and thus we may also expect to see in a country where building is carried on to so great an extent, more attention paid to architectural construction, so necessary to the preservation, and, therefore, true economy, of either public or private structures.

G. R. French.

** At the request of the committee of this society we give insertion to this appeal, and we do so readily, because it proposes what we have personally for some time advocated, viz.,—Union,—the drawing together into one body of all who are engaged in the study of architecture, connected with it, or anxious for its advancement, and for the well-being of its professors,—a body which would then indeed be powerful for good. It is necessary, however, that we should say, we do not participate in the belief that the Royal Institute of British Architects is at all likely to "fuse" into the Freemasons of the Church: this is of course out of the question. What is wanted is such an alteration in the laws and regulations of the Institute, and its charter, too, if the alterations cannot be made without, as will enable it to include the other bodies, and effect with power all the good that they, and the best wishers of the art, are aiming at.

AWARD OF THE ROYAL ACADEMY MEDALS.

On Monday, the 10th inst., the medals, &c., were distributed to the students of the Royal Academy. Mr. Geo. Jones, the Keeper, in the absence of Sir Martin Archer Shee, presided, and expressed his great regret that the president, through indisposition, was unable to attend. Gold medals were presented to Mr. J. A. Vinter, for the best historical painting; to Mr. E. J. Physick, for the best historical basso relievo; and to Mr. Arthur Allom, for the best architectural design. Amongst the recipients of silver medals was Mr. A. F. Young, for the best drawings of the south portico of St. Paul's Cathedral.

At the close Mr. Jones in a few words expressed his deep regret at the death of Mr. Etty, and urged the students to follow the example of perseverance and study which he had set them. He said they should help one another in all things, and not give way to envy: expressing his high satisfaction at the good conduct of the students,— Mr. Jones said he could not speak well enough of it.

I have just returned slowly and sadly from the award of the Royal Academy Medals. And for what were they awarded? For that merit which any labourer's son, properly educated in drawing, might deserve,—immense labour—correct and properly adjusted copyism. The medals must, it seems, be given; but surely they had better be withheld than given for the encouragement (I allude particularly to architecture) of that spirit which has raised the York, the Nelson, and the thousand and one other columns of the same kind over our noble country—the British Museum—the National Gallery—the Russell Institution—St. Pancras, and its numberless senseless imitations—the statues of Trafalgar-square and the Exchange, the Duke and the George. Wonderful, indeed, and god-like was the spirit of beauty which informed the eye, and directed the hand of the Grecian artist,—consistent with itself—consistent with all nature around it! Gloriously does it remain embalmed in the temples and statues of its age—its creed—its character—its *home*. But is ancient Greece modern England? In what does our religion—our literature—our climate—our life resemble it. Those who would retain the architecture, should retain the dress. The whole thing is a falsity—an imposition—a palpable lie—an absurdity; and for the encouragement of this, our professors award medals. Do they cavil at those who would revive Gothic, or Norman, or Elizabethan? They do. I have heard, myself, just and severe sarcasms, these very words indeed, levelled against the revival of either of these styles, by the very men who would revive a style antecedent to them by centuries, and foreign to our land. Sir, I do not expect you will care to publish this. My words are strong; but I feel strongly, deeply, degradingly, the want of true art among us, be it in Gothic, or Byzantine, or Italian, or Egyptian, or Grecian, or Roman, for all seem practised. I see with sorrow and disgust, bad copies, senseless revivals, false construction, and wretched taste. Sir, no new style can be born in a year, nor fifty, nor, may be, a hundred. But surely the medals might be awarded to the explorers of art, in preference to the imitators — the clever imitators of the past. But we must expect nothing else—it has ever been so.

We live, however, in a Protestant country—Protestant against the trammels of any unreasonable authority. We live among an energetic and persevering race—a nation of thinking men. May we not hope with Mackay, that—

"There's a good time coming?"

It is truly a consummation devoutly to be wished. Kunops.

TASK-WORK AMONGST BRICKLAYERS.

In your journal a short time since I perceived an article on task-work, signed "A Plasterer," in which was very truly described the evil consequences arising out of the system; but I can assure your correspondent that his is not the only trade in which the system is practised, and I would refer him to his next door neighbours, the bricklayers. To such an extent is task-work, or sub-letting, carried on in that trade, that not only is the trade much injured, but the life and limbs of those employed, and in some instances of the public, are placed in jeopardy. Scarcely a week passes over our heads but we hear of the fall of arches on some railway, and the tumbling down of houses which are *being built*. In most cases the elements are blamed for the accidents—the wind, the wet, &c.; of course these delinquents cannot be punished for their wild freaks; occasionally inquiries are made in respect to the workmanship, but that is invariably decided in favour of the contractors; it is very difficult to judge of the workmanship in a heap of ruins, and yet one might come to a speedy conclusion, that if the workmanship was of a good kind the ruins would not have been there.

I will endeavour to make a few remarks on task-work as it is practised in our trade. A man who is not over particular as to the language he uses to his men, generally takes this work of a contractor at a very low price; he then procures two or three men of the same stamp as himself; these men receive 6d. per day above the usual wages, and are usually called "drivers;" one of them is put to work on a line with four or five other men, and as each man has an equal portion of the work to perform, the object of the driver is to run his piece along as quickly as possible, paying very little regard as to how it is done; but should another man, who is not used to *scamping* his work, be a little behind with his part, the line will at once be struck on him, and he will be discharged as incompetent to do his work. On most large jobs, such as railways, an inspector is employed, whose duty it is to see that the work is done properly; but as he cannot always be at one place, having other parts of the railway to attend to, every facility is afforded to carry on the *scamping* system; and in his absence a quantity of labourers are employed in throwing in the bricks, without any regard to the order of bond or any other order, except that of putting them out of sight. A good look-out is always kept for the inspector; and should a hat or a coat, or anything like the aspect of the supposed party be seen in the distance, the joints are flushed up, the labourers take to their hods, and things go on pretty well till the inspector goes, when the old plan of proceeding is again commenced.

Incredible as these facts may appear to those of your readers who are not acquainted with these matters, they will be no less astonished at the plan which is adopted by these task-masters to force, as it were, their men to spend their wages. On task-jobs, where a considerable number of men are employed, the task-master gets a number of round pieces of tin of two sizes; they are usually stamped with his initials; the smaller size is equivalent to a sixpence, and the larger to a shilling. The task-master then enters into a contract with some public-house keeper, and orders him to supply his men with whatever refreshment they require on the production of this tin money. The publican allows the master 2s. 6d. for every sovereign he receives in this way; therefore, considerable pickings are made. I need not add, that refreshments purchased in this way are usually of the worst description. Not satisfied with the advantage he derives by this abominable system—this demoralizing evil—the master almost always contrives to keep his men waiting for their money till nine or ten o'clock on a Saturday night, with what view it is unnecessary to say.

Can nothing be done to prevent these evils? Such a system ought to be held up to universal reprobation; but it seldom happens that these proceedings meet the eyes of those who would be disposed to lay them before the public; none but those who are actually engaged in doing this work are witnesses of it. I saw something in The Builder some time ago about the incompetency of mechanics: is it likely, when the majority, or I might say almost all the large jobs in and around London, are task-work, that we should have competent mechanics? No, Sir; for when a man gets into such a system of working as is practised on these jobs, it is not very easily departed from.

I think, Sir, by giving publicity to these facts, good may be done, for it would open the eyes of those who are in the habit of building; and I think that railway companies and other parties who have extensive works in progress, by being initiated into the mysteries of task-work, may be led to adopt a remedy.*

A Bricklayer.

RAILWAY JOTTINGS.

The autumn rains are still, as heretofore, revealing the humiliating fact that sufficient estimation of their power and extent has by no means always been taken into account in the planning and construction of our railway works. The disruption of culverts, the fall of bridges, and the sweeping away of embankments, have been but too frequent of late, as on the Trent Valley, the Lincoln, and other lines of railway.——Near the Wolverhampton station of the Shrewsbury and Birmingham and Stour Valley line, a bridge, recently constructed over a canal, suddenly gave way, and fell into ruins on Monday week. The centres had been removed more than a month before, and no crack or other appearance of instability, it is said, had been noticed prior to the fall. The span of the bridge was between 40 and 50 feet.——A mail-train engine, on Friday last, fairly crushed into wreck the brickwork abutments of one of the numerous wooden bridges near Collingham, on the Nottingham and Lincoln line. The engine, however, may be said to have leaped over the chasm, but the coupling chains snapped, and the carriages rebounding were driven with a crash on each other, and, after rocking dreadfully, fell into the flood beneath. The coupées were crushed into 'fire-wood,' and every carriage and van smashed, but happily the train contained not a single passenger, and, strange to say, no one seems to have lost his life.——Mr. Brassey, the contractor, has entered into arrangements with the Caledonian Company to work that line, and to advance the sum of 200,000*l*. on the security of its rolling stock.——Several Companies have issued advertisements inviting public competition in the supply of stores and materials. The result of this system, says *Herapath*, is the saving of many thousands a-year in money, and the repair of morals by the riddance of jobbing.——The following important decision was given by Lords Brougham and Campbell, in the House of Lords, in the matter of the Forth Marine Insurance Company:—"Dividends are supposed to be paid out of profits only, and when Directors order a dividend to be paid where no such profits have been made, without expressly saying so, a gross fraud is practised; and the Directors are not only civilly liable to those whom they have deceived and injured, but are guilty of a conspiracy for which they are liable to be prosecuted."——An appeal by the London and North-Western Company has been heard before the special session at Manchester, against a rate demanded by the overseers of Barton-on-Irwell, on a portion of the old Liverpool and Manchester line. The case was decided against the Company, on the ground that they did not apply in reasonable time. The amount assessed on the railway, which only occupies 42 acres of bog land, is 8,909*l*., or one-fifth of the entire rate levied on the township for the 1-250th part of it occupied by the railway. The land was purchased by the Company at 40*l*. per acre, and the Directors had consented now for nineteen years to pay nearly as much annually as the purchase cost originally; the former being at the rate of 34*l*. per acre per annum.——On Wednesday week, the wires of the telegraph between Birmingham and London were broken in two different places, by contraction produced by frost.

* I have heard on good authority that, from information which was forwarded to the clerk of the works of a large task job, now in progress about four miles from London, he has condemned and taken down upwards of 70 rods of brickwork.

ANCIENT MORTAR.

On reading a day or two ago the works of Godinus, "De Originibus Constantinopolitanis," I met with a passage which may be interesting to your readers. I am not aware that the precise composition of the mortar used by the ancients, concerning which, on account of its wonderful hardness, so much has been said, is known to modern architects and builders; but it seems to me that the following conveys a hint which, in proper hands, may produce results very useful to the public.

The Emperor Justinian built the temple, which was dedicated to St. John the Baptist, and he employed upon it no less than ten thousand workmen, with one hundred *μαιστορες*, or over-lookers. "Five thousand men were employed upon the right, and five thousand on the left of the building, and every effort was made that it might be completed as soon as possible. An angel revealed to the emperor during sleep the form which the temple was to assume. There was a certain workman who had acquired great renown in building temples. He boiled in large pots a quantity of barley, and mixed the liquor *μετὰ τοῦ ἀσβέστου καὶ τοῦ ὀστράκου*. [Whether the first means what we now term *asbestos*, I am unable to determine: the second I take to be powdered shell]. The barley-liquor he mixed warm with these things instead of water. They cut up also some elm bark, and mixed it up with the asbestos, and made a kind of paste (*καὶ ἐποίουν μάζας*), which was applied neither too hot nor too cold, but tepid, because it adhered the better, and made the stones stick together with the strength of iron."

The above passage between inverted commas is a literal translation from the Greek. I shall be obliged if any one of your readers will inform me what the word *ἄσβεστος* as here used really means. A. G.

Art-Unions in America.—A controversy, which appears to excite great interest, is going on in New York, between the *Home Journal* and the *Mirror*, concerning the constitution of the "American Art-Union." In this association the pictures are all purchased by a committee; and Mr. N. P. Willis, in the first-named paper, is maintaining that the position and character of artists have been materially lowered by this mode of proceeding. He asserts that the society has been made "into a *throne of personal consequence*, by which artists can be tyrannized over, and true art discouraged."

ST. JOHN'S, ANTIGUA.——Mr. Thos. Fuller, Architect.

THE CATHEDRAL AT ANTIGUA.

THIS building, dedicated to St. John, and which was designed to withstand the hurricanes and earthquakes so prevalent in the West Indies, is placed upon the site of the old cathedral, which was destroyed by the earthquake in February, 1848. The corner-stone of the new building was laid October 10th, 1845, and the first sermon preached in it on exactly that day twelvemonth; but the towers and exterior were not entirely completed and service permanently commenced until August, 1847;—the whole building being completed in two years, at a cost of 36,000*l*., from the designs of Mr. Thomas Fuller, architect.

There was not any contractor, but the men were paid, and the building works carried out, by Mr. W. Roue, of Bristol, who, by the efficient manner in which he performed the whole of his arduous duties, his general abilities, and conduct, gave the greatest satisfaction to the architect and all parties concerned. There were a few English workmen sent out, but the greater portion of the work was performed by the natives.

The plan is cruciform, with two square towers at the west end, finished with octagonal cupolas; at the east end is a semi-octagonal apse; the building accommodates 2,200 persons, the extreme length being 160 feet, the breadth 53 feet 9 inches; the depth of each transept 26 feet, the breadth 47 feet 6 inches. It is divided into nave and aisles by octagonal columns, having moulded caps and bases and an enriched entablature running throughout, with semi-elliptical arches between the columns, moulded archivolts, corbels, and keys. The ceiling over the nave is cored and panelled, and that over the aisles flat and panelled; the whole of the roof is carried on a strong framework of hard wood, quite independent of the stone walls. The roof is of pitch pine, and the whole of the interior is lined with pitch pine (not painted), obtained from America, all timbers being cut there to the sizes required, and the boarding ready planed, grooved, and feathered.

The walls are built of magnesian limestone, of very fine quality, which was obtained from the north side of the island; the floors of the aisles were laid with sanded blue lias stone, the space underneath being used as cold air flues. The floor of the chancel is of polished lias, which, together with that used in the aisles, was obtained from Mr. Treasure, of Bath. The windows are filled in with thick glass in large panes, supplied by Messrs. Dix and Williams, of Bristol. The three east windows were made in England, filled with stained glass, by Mr. Willement, of London.

The roofs were covered with the patent galvanised tinned iron tiles, by Messrs. Morewood and Rogers, of Upper Thames-street, London, who sent out a person to superintend the fixing. This description of roofing is stated to be peculiarly adapted for the situation, on account of its being readily fixed by inexperienced workmen, and from its not being liable to be disturbed by the hurricanes which occasionally visit these islands.*

The pulpit, reading-desk, bishop's throne, and stalls, were made of mahogany, carved in Bristol; the font was also sent out from Bristol. The building, which is approached by bold flights of steps, with balustrades, &c., stands on an elevated situation, commanding a view of the town and bay; it was severely tested in the late hurricane, but the only damage of importance sustained was to the stained-glass windows at the east end, and to the vane of one of the towers. Several buildings in the country and some of the other churches were severely damaged or destroyed.

It is due to the architect to state that the *style* of the building was determined by the Committee.

The organ was sent out by Mr. Walker, of London.

THE LIFE ACADEMY in Margaret-street, Regent-street, held a *conversazione* on the 11th inst., and exhibited some interesting works.

* We are told that in a hurricane which occurred on the island last year, and which carried away the roofs of from 1,000 to 1,200 houses, those that were covered with this material were not disturbed.

NOTES IN THE PROVINCES.

THE Wesleyans are collecting funds for the erection of a new chapel at Luton.——Rolling mills are to be erected at Woolwich Dockyard, where stringent measures of economy are being carried out. Old wrought iron is to be used up in place of being sold for a trifle as heretofore, so that many thousands of pounds, it is expected, will even thus alone be saved. A set of machines for turning treenails is to be substituted for hand work, and in the blacksmiths' department the men are to be put to their mettle in shape of piece-work. Pity many sinecure pensioners, as well as poor men, were not put on *piece-work*, by "no work no pay" being made the general order of the day. The Customs landing-waiters, are now again being bled, and by the way, for behoof of the sinecurists,—to save whom seems to be the grand end and aim of the saving system at all times.——The Southampton Board of Waterworks lately secured a "cheap contract for iron pipe," regarding which they have just received a letter from Bury College Iron-works, in which Messrs. Rayne and Barns state their regret at having made a great mistake in their calculation for the supply of the pipes, by taking yards as feet, and thus making 100*l*. difference. They would execute the order, and throw themselves on the generosity of the commissioners. Several of these, however, thought that it would not be just to the other parties who had tendered to give any compensation for such a mistake,—but for which the accepted tender would have been very considerably higher than the rest. The letter, meantime, was referred to the general committee.——The wardens of St. Martin's, Birmingham, are directing their attention to the state of the fabric of the old church, and will shortly be prepared with a definite plan for the consideration of the parishioners, ascertaining which of the courses that are open to them will be most likely to secure approbation and co-operation. "It is evident," says the local *Journal*, "that there is a strong feeling in the minds of many in favour of an entirely new edifice."——The Odd Fellows' Hall, Temple-street, Birmingham, was opened on Monday week. It has been erected by Messrs. Branston and Gwyther, after designs by Messrs. Coe and Goodwin. The building presents externally a plain appearance. On the second floor, and occupying nearly the whole area of the building, is the principal hall, which is lighted from the roof, and will contain about 1,000 persons. A gallery extends along the hall over the entrance. The whole will cost nearly 3,000*l*.——St. Michael's Church, Worcester, has been recently 'beautified' by the erection of tablets, with the commandments illuminated on zinc plates, in moulded oak frames, placed on each side of the east window. Work executed by Mr. G. Rogers, of Worcester, who has also recently executed some stained glass for windows in Thornbury Church, Gloucestershire.——The foundation-stone of St. Paul's, Charlestown, parish of St. Anstell, was laid on Tuesday week. The style of the building is Early English, with tower and spire rising to 70 feet in height. The plan is cruciform, with nave, north and south aisles, and transepts, with north porch. The nave will be lit by a clerestory. The walls are to be of blue slate stone with granite quoins, plinth, water tables, jambs, &c. The interior dimensions will be 100 feet from east to west, and 42 feet from north to south; height of nave 34 feet, separated from transepts and chancel by arches 28 feet in height; chancel, 25 feet in depth, ascended by three steps. The roofs are open, with collars and arch ribs springing from circular engaged shafts and capitals between the windows of the clerestory. The vestry is on the north side of the chancel. All the woodwork is to be stained in oak; accommodation on floor for 570, all free. The amount necessary for completion is, we understand, far from being fully guaranteed by subscriptions.—— Several architects having complained that the time allowed for plans for the Leicester new workhouse to be sent in was too limited, the clerk was requested to write to the commissioners for an extension of time for three weeks. During this discussion, Mr. Woodward suggested that the guardians should apply for an extension of the period to the last day of Hilary Term; but it was thought that they might as well apply at once to have the question adjourned for other six months.——It is proposed to lay down a glass culvert for the main sewers of Rugby. This has been recommended on account of economy (?) and smoothness of surface in the glass.——The Manchester Waterworks Committee report "that about 10th September last the committee received tenders from forty different parties for the construction of the Godley service reservoir, from forty-three parties for the construction of the Denton reservoirs, and from thirty-one parties for the masonry work connected with the Broomstairs-bridge; and on 15th accepted the three several tenders sent in by Mr. David Bellhouse, of Manchester, for the execution of the three works. The committee have arranged for the purchase of all the land required, and been enabled to give possession to the contractors. The prices to be paid for the land have been arranged without arbitrators or a jury, except in the case of the trustees of Lord Wilson: price asked 16,289*l*. 3s. 4d., offered 4,000*l*., awarded 5,941*l*. 6s.; and of land belonging to Mr. Wrigley: verdict by consent 2,975*l*., amount asked 3,820*l*. 10s., offered 2,720*l*. The Woodhead contractors have already nearly repaired the damage from floods at their own expense. About 1,892 tons of pipes have been got ready. They are dipped before being laid down, as they are proposed to be first at Hulme, Chorlton-on-Medlock, and Ardwick. The report of Mr. Bateman, the engineer, showed that the works under seven different contracts are now going on steadily and satisfactorily.——The parish church of Kirk Deighton, Yorkshire, has been lately repewed. Improvement has been made in the internal and external appearance of this venerable building by the removal of windows that did not correspond with the style, and by replacing them with suitable windows. This work has been accomplished through the exertions and liberality of the rector, the Rev. James William Geldart, LL.D. The church was re-opened on 20th ult.——In Aberdeen the streets are swept every day, at an annual cost of 1,000*l*., and the refuse brings in 2,000*l*. a-year. In Perth the scavenging cost 1,300*l*. per annum, and the manure sells for 1,730*l*.——The new building erected at Reading, during the present year, for the use of the savings bank, was opened on the 11th instant. It is in the Italian style, and consists of a spacious bank office, board-room, waiting-room, strong-room, &c., with a porter's residence. The contract was undertaken at the estimate of the architect, Mr. Jno. Billing.

SUCCESS TO THE GAS MOVEMENT.

PETITIONS from the City gas consumers having been presented in showers to the City Sewers Commissioners, in favour of the Great Central Gas Consumers' Company, the commission have seen the propriety of resolving, by a majority of 35 to 11, to allow that company to lay their pipes throughout the City. This, too, the commission has felt impelled to do, although the old City companies, in order to burke the new, had previously announced their resolution to reduce their own price to 4s.—the maximum to which the new will be limited. The old companies even bound themselves in honour to continue the reduced price named, whether the new should now realize its intentions or not. It was somewhat amusing, however, to note the curious struggle of their advocates, on the one hand, to cast discredit on those estimates of their opponents on which the idea of the possibility of selling the article at 4s. at all was founded, while they themselves, at the very same moment, were offering it at that very price, and broadly hinting at the possibility of still further reductions. Nevertheless, previous to March last, they had insisted that it was perfectly impossible to sell it at less than 6s., to which they had shortly before reduced it from 7s., a price that had also been declared to be the lowest possible. It has been stoutly insisted, too, that the quality of the gas will be deteriorated in consequence of such reductions. Now, we will undertake very easily to show that it *must*, on the contrary, *be improved* in purity, even to the utmost, in consequence of these, and such as these, very reductions. The manufacturers, old and new, will soon find that *increased con-*

sumption IN PRIVATE DWELLINGS will constitute their grand field of profitable operations, and with all our hearts we will second their efforts in this direction; for that is the real goal of all our past exertions in this good cause. But to this anticipated and almost illimitable diffusion in private dwellings—from hall to kitchen, from kitchen to parlour, and from parlour to drawing-room and bed-chamber,—purity—extreme purity is absolutely essential. There can and will be no such diffusion without it, and hence the bringing of the price within reach of all classes in domestic life, will inevitably be accompanied by an increase, not by a deterioration, of purity. Moreover, the advancement of chemical economy is rendering this very purification itself a self-compensatory and profitable branch of the manufacture.

ARCHITECTS' TROUBLES.

At the Whittington Club, in the Strand, on the 29th ult., Mr. Wightwick delivered a lecture on "Architectural Practice." We get the following outline from the *Weekly Gazette*, published by this society. The lecturer commenced by giving a metaphorical outline of a young architect's career, and then a more serious account of the duties of the practising architect. A house *may* be built without an architect; many complex and costly residences may be put up by the unprofessional, much to the profit of the mason and builders. But the use of an architect, in sober truth, is to do that *better* which may, it is admitted, be done well by the non-professional. He (the architect) will give not *more* decoration—perhaps less—but such as is fitting in degree, and appropriate in kind. He will convert neglected corners and accidental spaces into picturesque ornaments. He will not give you a mere pile of building, but a piece of art. The lecturer then illustrated the above by a dramatic dialogue, showing how, of all the fatiguing and nervous occupations, that of an architect is the most so—detailing the task of "making a specification"—how an architect's wife always knows by her husband's temper when it is "specification day" (?)—how the specification is finished at last, much to the joy of the poor architect; when suddenly the post brings a letter from Mr. Briggs (the party who is about investing his money in a new house) desiring that "further operations" may be suspended, as, in his "travels through the neighbouring counties, he has seen many newly-built mansions, and had the benefit of much good and friendly advice." Once again, however, upon Mr. Briggs's return, is a *new* plan determined upon, including a "brewhouse," a "bakehouse," a "laundry," and a "vaulted cellar,"—again is the "specification" completed, and again is Mr. Briggs (not *Mrs.* Briggs, of course) dissatisfied—again is the specification and estimated cost reduced, and *again* does Mr. B. think 2,800*l.* too much; *once* again is a still *more* moderate specification prepared, and *at last* is the house actually commenced—ground staked out, and foundations marked,—labourers, masons, and builders *actually* at work. During the operation of building, the following scene takes place, between Mrs. and Mr. B., and the architect.

Mrs. B. (viewing the progress of the building). "Ah, what's that?" "That, madam, is the balcony." "Balcony! balcony indeed! do you suppose I'm going to allow that thing before my bed-room window? Here, Briggs, Briggs, I say (Mr. Briggs was purposely looking at some other interesting process), look here,—what *is* that?"

"My dear, that of course is the balcony." "Well, well! I don't care; I shan't have it—it only shuts out the light from above, and obstructs the view from below; I *won't* allow it." And forthwith the "balcony" vanishes; the lady carries the day (as she ought), and this, with other numerous "alterations," renders the architect's miseries complete. In short, my advice to the young architect (the lecturer continued) is this: above all things, in designing a house, consult the cook, make the butler your friend, gallant it a little with the housekeeper, and a little more with the housemaid, make positive love to the lady's-maid, be deferential to the footman, be submissive to the boy, and make each believe that the whole house is built in subjection to the particular part of it in which each one is interested. Conciliate the servants' hall, and you have, as it were, the public press in your favour, by which the tyranny of the drawing-room will be unconsciously subdued. Neglect this policy, and chimneys will smoke, plate will tarnish, cobwebs will prevail, and preserves will grow mouldy.

We are disposed to hope that this outline does not give a correct general notion of the discourse.

POPULAR ERROR AS TO THE NELSON COLUMN.

As the remarks you have already done me the favour to insert in your journal, on the subject of the relievos, may have been serviceable in promoting the appreciation of *bronze* for such uses, I now seek, through the same channel, to correct a widely-circulated error respecting the proportion of the column itself.

The opponents of a columnar monument, it may be recollected, urged the insecurity of Corinthian proportions; and, in a consequent report by Sir Richard Smirke and Mr. Walker the engineer, it was recommended that a considerable diminution in the proposed height of the work should be made. This recommendation was followed; but the impression that the clumsy expedient of chopping the required length off the shaft, and thereby violating the just proportion of the order, was adopted, is entirely without foundation,—though up to the present moment "going," as it is termed, "the round of the papers." Thus, the *Times* of Thursday last pronounces the "shaft too short for the pedestal, and the capital too heavy and massive for the shaft."

I have gone to the best source for my information, and find the height of the column as built, from the top of the pedestal to the top of the abacus, to be 101 feet 6 inches; the lower diameter 10½ feet, and the upper diameter 9 feet. On referring to "Taylor and Cresy's Rome," where the *Mars Ultor* example is carefully given, the height of the ancient example is 58 feet, and the upper diameter a fraction less than 5 feet 2 inches, and as these dimensions are in the exact ratio of 101 feet to 9 feet, it is evident the classic proportion has been strictly maintained.

The capital was very skilfully modelled by Mr. C. H. Smith (afterwards engaged on those of the Royal Exchange), whose ability is well known.

MODERATOR.

A FOUNTAIN OF ERROR—BRISTOL.

A short time ago, wandering in Bristol, we found ourselves accidentally in Somerset-square, a quiet locality close to Redcliffe Church, where we saw signs of unwonted activity that promised well: the old wall which had enclosed the central area was giving place to an iron railing, and preparations were making for an ornamental fountain, apparently of Gothic design, in the centre. They told us it was all being done at the expense of one spirited individual to whom many of the houses belonged, and we said, "Praise be to him: we will look how he gets on the next time we visit the ancient city." And so we did, and we cannot say how much we were annoyed by what we *did* see. The fountain is completed, and this is the shape it has taken: the basement is Gothic, with foliated panels; on this is a circular Italian peristyle of small columns, then a nondescript ornament from an indistinct recollection of that on the Tower of the Winds, and, crowning all, a curiously-postured figure of Neptune with a jet-pipe out of the top of his head, leading to the conclusion that he is hereafter to be afflicted with water on the brain.

When we say that this fountain is all of stone and uprears itself a considerable height, it will be seen that it must have cost a considerable sum of money, sufficient, under good direction, to have raised a creditable work of art; and all must grieve that a good and liberal intention has been so entirely thrown away. It is with this feeling and a desire to prevent similar waste elsewhere, and not with the view of causing annoyance to the proprietor, or raising a smile, that we mention the matter.

The figure of Neptune appears to have been copied from a large statue of the god near the Temple Church in Bristol, a public fountain, but apparently not now supplied with water. There are so few fountain-statues in our streets, or indeed statues of any kind, that we would suggest to the authorities the conservancy of this last-named Neptune. *Apropos* of running water, we noticed not far from the last named place, in Temple-street, a small stone inscribed "To the poor. Protect this pipe." We must suppose that it once gave forth water, but it is now dry as—our article some may perhaps say.

ROMAN TESSELATED PAVEMENTS, ALDBOROUGH.

Mr. H. Eckroyd Smith, of York—an enterprising young publisher,—has just now issued three very excellent lithographs of pavements discovered (one of them, as it seems, chiefly through the instrumentality of the publisher) on the estate of Mr. Andrew Lawson, at Aldborough, the Roman Isu-Brigantum, in Yorkshire. No. I., one of the most perfect in Britain, consists of borders of *guilloches* and *frets*, with a double star on a white ground as a centre-piece. The third border from the outside, "unlike every other plain border known in this country," varies in its width on each side. On one side it is nine tesseræ in width, on the second seven, on the third five, and on the fourth three. Counting two parallel sides together, the numbers are equal, namely, twelve,—the nine ranging with the three, and the seven with the five.

In the pavement shown by Plate II., the centre has been occupied by an animal, presumed to be a lion reposing under a tree. Amongst the small cuts which fill the margins of the prints are shown two rooms of the hypocaust, and a circular-sided building immediately within the city wall, "in all probability one of the more recent Roman erections." The third plate shows four pavements. They are all very neatly drawn by Mr. W. Bowman, and lithographed by Mr. W. Monkhouse.

DEFECT IN PATENT LAWS.

Allow me, as a very old subscriber, to call your attention to the law of patents and registration as now by law established: the costs of these processes quite precludes the poor man and mechanic exercising that gift and ability which the Almighty has given. I know of my own knowledge very many valuable designs and patents thrown on one side, because, as I observed, the projector of the invention is, from the exorbitant cost, entirely shut out. I trust, Sir, you will, in your invaluable publication, endeavour to call the attention of the proper authorities to the fact; and I mention it now because of the proposed industrial exhibition in 1851. From this the English *head* is mainly excluded by our patent laws. I will ask you who will put his mind to work when he is not paid for it? Let the law be the same as the law in France, the protection be estimated at a rental, and so long as the inventor, or his family, pay up that rental yearly, let the poor man have the advantage.—W. J. Bray.

SOHO PARK, BIRMINGHAM.

Bolton and Watt made Soho Factory famous throughout Europe, and it was long a centre of enormous manufacturing industry. Its hammers are now nearly quiet; the stream has taken another channel. But the same place is now to offer a field for exertion to another kind of activity. Soho park, attached to the residence, has been laid out for building on, and, with proper management, can scarcely fail to be successful.

The park is about a mile and a half from the busy part of Birmingham, on the road to Wolverhampton, and will doubtless become the retreat of wise townsmen, studious of health and pleasure, from their place of business. It is a picturesque estate, with wood and water, and might be made one of the most beautiful places in England.

At Handsworth's Church, close by, there is a repetition, by Chantrey, of his well-known statue of Watt,—a monument, by Flaxman,—and one by Bailey.

PROPOSED PROVIDENT INSTITUTION FOR BUILDING OPERATIVES.

A very influential meeting of architects, contractors, and others, to consider Professor Cockerell's suggested Institution, was held at the Guildhall, London, on Tuesday, the 11th, when the scheme, it will be seen, was fairly launched.

By the unanimous vote of the meeting

Mr. Cockerell was called to the chair, and opened the proceedings at considerable length in an admirable address, expounding the project already familiar to our readers, and disclaiming any personal merit as the originator of the scheme. He dwelt particularly on the importance he attached to the support of the architects and engineers, in addition to that of the master builders, and concluded by soliciting suggestions from the gentlemen present.

As Mr. Cockerell's views are already fully before our readers, it is unnecessary here to reiterate them.

Mr. Tite said that many thanks were due to Mr. Cockerell for his exertions, but whilst he (Mr. Tite) approved of his suggestions in the main, he thought the present meeting was not sufficiently informed upon the subject to take any definite proceedings. A similar plan to that now proposed was actually in existence at the Excise-office, all the servants in which establishment contributed to a life assurance and benevolent fund. The system was also about to be introduced on an extensive scale amongst the men employed by the great railway companies. There would be some difficulty in dealing with building operatives, their character being generally essentially democratic, and it was well known that they liked to govern themselves. It was also necessary to guard carefully against anything of an eleemosynary character in the proposed scheme. Of the general advantages of the plan there could be no doubt; but he would rather, in the first instance, solicit the opinions of his friends Mr. T. and Mr. W. Cubitt, Mr. Baker, and others around him, as to the practicability of adopting a general system of the kind. In order that the project should go on, he begged leave to move that a committee should be appointed to inquire carefully into the whole subject, and collect the statistical and other information so much required.

Mr. Hardwick briefly expressed his cordial and entire approval of the measure, and his concurrence in Mr. Tite's suggestion.

Mr. Higgins seconded the motion, as Mr. Hardwick had omitted to do so.

Mr. T. Cubitt said it appeared to him the subject was an exceedingly difficult one. He feared the number of masters, architects, and engineers, would bear a very small proportion to the immense body to be benefited by the plan. It was important to ascertain what sums the men could spare, and whether these sums would realize an adequate provision for old age. That plan could not come into full operation for many years, and it should be considered how far the gentlemen present could bind their successors to carry it out, if adopted. He did not think so much sympathy and aid would be extended by the higher ranks of society to builders' workmen as to domestic servants, to whom allusion had been made; and there were other points on which information, statistics, and calculations, were greatly needed. He concurred in the appointment of a committee of inquiry, and in the gratitude expressed, and which every gentleman must feel, to the chairman, for his proposal, and sincerely hoped it would be carried out.

Mr. Sheriff Lawrence regarded the scheme as one of such magnitude that no Government would venture to undertake it—it was, in fact, national —embracing, as it did, so many thousands of individuals. The cases of the excise and railway officials and the domestic servants would not apply to artisans of all ages and conditions, who must be dealt with under very different circumstances. A general society would be far more difficult to form than one limited to a private building concern. Much depended on the statistics of life amongst artisans, on which point the existing tables were very defective. He thought the workmen ought to be the prime movers in such a scheme, but feared the majority of them were not prepared for that sacrifice of present enjoyment to remote advantages, which was the foundation of its success. They should, at all events, be enabled at any time to withdraw their savings; whilst, on the other hand, he feared, from the vicissitudes of trade, they would too often avail themselves of that privilege. The cost of management should certainly be paid for them, but without interference with their love of self-government, which he regarded as a laudable feeling.

Mr. Baker trusted the meeting would not be deterred by the difficulties referred to. From his experience of workmen, he differed with the worthy sheriff, and felt assured that they only required to be put in the right way, and that there were thousands of them quite prepared to avail themselves of this project. The power of withdrawing their deposits would convince the men the scheme was intended solely for their benefit, and remove all suspicion from their minds. The immense number of workmen in London ought to be no obstacle, for but a limited number could be expected to avail themselves of the plan; and if only one-third of them could be benefited their object would be simply answered. He hoped and believed, for the honour of the profession, that Mr. T. Cubitt's anxiety as to the support of their successors, was unfounded. Useful societies never lacked support: if well established, this society must succeed.

Mr. Ansell, actuary, being appealed to, said he was well acquainted with the excise and railway schemes which had been alluded to, but did not think either very analogous to that now proposed. The number of persons said to be connected with building and engineering in London, 300,000, must be rather an exaggerated estimate, including their families, and others dependent on them. He suggested the desirability of adding to the Committee some of the operatives themselves, well knowing that unless the recipients of the advantages of friendly societies had a share in their management, these societies always worked badly. It was advisable not to encumber the plan with too many apparent advantages. He approved of a provision for old age and sickness, and a payment on the workman's death, but not the provisions for widows and orphans, on which point the statistics were far from perfect. He should feel great pleasure in giving the project every aid and information in his power.

Mr. Neison concurred with Mr. Ansell. He had no misgivings whatever of the practicability of the scheme, and under Mr. Ansell's advice, it would be impossible to fall into any serious mistake. The existing Friendly Societies were badly managed, but a happier period was dawning on the country, and it was from these societies, that the elevation of the working classes was to be looked for.

Mr. Piper thought, when his friend Sheriff Lawrence had spoken, he was giving a history of the infirmities of human nature, instead of describing the habits and dispositions of the working classes, for he (Mr. Piper) believed the latter, as a body, to be as provident, as thoughtful, and as intelligent, as any class of the community. He had always found them ready to receive and adopt any suggestions sincerely made for their benefit. Some time ago he had ascertained that one-tenth of the whole number of claimants upon the Orphan Asylums of the metropolis, were connected with the building trade in its various branches. The only doubt that could now be suggested was, whether the public mind was prepared for the ample scheme of Mr. Cockerell. He believed the intended meeting of the Builders' Foremen, was a favourable indication, and that a large number of workmen were willing to adopt it. Much information was necessary as to details, for the meeting ought to be prepared to submit some definite statements to the operatives, and aid them in every possible way. He fully approved of Mr. Tite's proposition.

Mr. Lee expressed his warm approbation of the scheme, and his conviction that the difficulties attending it might and ought to be overcome.

The motion was then put and carried as follows: "That a committee be appointed to inquire carefully into the subject of the Provident and Benevolent Society, suggested and proposed by Mr. Cockerell, in connection with the building branches; and to collect facts and statistics relating thereto; and that such committee do report to a further meeting of the parties present, and such other friends as may take an interest in the matter."

Mr. Cockerell, Mr. Hardwick, Mr. Tite, Mr. Roberts, Mr. Bunning, and Mr. Angell (architects); Mr. Ald. Lawrence, Mr. T. Cubitt, Mr. W. Cubitt, Mr. Lee, Mr. Piper, and Mr. Baker (builders), were then constituted a committee in accordance with the above resolution, with power to add some engineers to their number,* and to call in one or two intelligent workmen to aid their deliberations.

Mr. Wales was appointed honorary secretary; and a vote of thanks to the chairman having been carried unanimously, the meeting separated.

The Opening of Marylebone Baths and Washhouses took place on Monday last. They stand on the site of the late tea-gardens of the Yorkshire Stingo. Mr. Christopher Eales is the architect. The cost of the whole will be very nearly 20,000*l*. The buildings are of red brick, and contain 107 baths, besides shower and vapour baths and two swimming baths. The washing department is fitted up for 84 persons washing. We shall make a dip into these baths before long.

What is a Foreman?—In the Court of Exchequer, on Tuesday, a builder's scaffolder described a foreman as "a man who walks about and does nothing, and orders everybody else to work."

* Mr. Rennie and Mr. Field were named as favourable to the project.

MEETING OF BUILDERS' FOREMEN ON PROPOSED BUILDING ARTIFICERS' PROVIDENT SOCIETY.

The Institution of Builders' Foremen held a meeting on Wednesday evening last, to consider "the advantages to be derived from the scheme set forth in The Builder of 15th September last, by Professor Cockerell;" Mr. Kay, the president, in the chair.

After a few remarks on the kindly feeling of the proposer, and his earnest desire to promote union and good fellowship among all classes of the building trades, the president pointed to the more immediate object in view, namely, to make his scheme for the well-being of all, familiar to the members and their friends, to court inquiry into its merits, and to elicit suggestions for its practical realization, or its adaptation to their particular benefit, as well as to that of others.

It was then moved by Mr. Hawking, seconded by Mr. Allard (the secretary), and carried unanimously,—"That, as the happiness of a nation must necessarily depend on the prosperity of its people, it becomes a primary duty, on all whose dependencies rest on industry, to use their most strenuous exertion to secure a provision for old age and infirmities before the tide of life begins to ebb; and that any scheme proposed for such a purpose is entitled to the fullest and most deliberate consideration of those for whose benefit it is professedly intended."

The mover said that the statistical details which had been given were, he conceived, very satisfactory; and if domestic servants, he observed, were countenanced and supported in their provident endeavours, as a society of theirs has been, by Prince Albert and others, why should not the building artisans, he asked, meet with equal favour and countenance? Their claims were equally great, and equally appealed to them from those hearths and homes which building artificers provided for them. If the members, one and all, of the building trades themselves, at all events, could only be brought to see the necessity of uniting more together, it would be greatly to the advantage of all, and he would ask them to remember the example set them at Guildhall yesterday by the leading architects and builders.

Mr. Taylor gave his cordial adhesion to the resolution as not only unobjectionable, but good—religiously good.

The second resolution, moved by Mr. Watmough and seconded by Mr. Tuckwell, was as follows:—"That this meeting having considered the plan submitted to the building trades by Professor Charles Robert Cockerell, and partially developed in The Builder of September 15, 1849, are of opinion that it contains much which is calculated, as a groundwork (subjected to modification and addition), to effect so desirable an object, for the benefit of a very great number of all classes employed in the building trades:" carried unanimously.

A resolution was then moved by Mr. Locke, expressing the opinion of the meeting that the proposed institution was calculated to effect much good, and pledging themselves to assist in making its importance felt. He urged them to receive the suggestion in good part and in the spirit with which it was offered, and great social benefit to the building trades could not but result from it. Let them also never forget that God helps them who help themselves.

In seconding the resolution, Mr. Taylor said,—Union is strength—can any one deny that good saying? A house divided against itself cannot stand. He had been both workman and employer, and he knew that unless both parties go on pleasantly, and hand in hand, neither will go on well. Every man would find it for his own interest to promote the welfare of those above him as well as below him.

Mr. Allard, in speaking to the resolution, said that he had had the honour of an interview with Mr. Cockerell, and was deeply impressed with the kind feeling manifested by him, and his sense of the importance of such a feeling and of friendly union between employer and employed. He hoped his fellow foremen would appreciate the motives of those gentlemen who had now come forward with the friendly hand of union presented to them. There was great need of it in the present time, as the bitter experience of many of them could attest. It was a duty to themselves, their families, and their children, to be provident, even apart from all other considerations.

The resolution was then carried unanimously, as was the next, namely, "That a deputation of three members be appointed to wait on Mr. Cockerell to express to that gentleman the general feeling of this meeting to co-operate in carrying out his views."

It was then resolved, "That the thanks of this meeting are due and are hereby given to Professor Cockerell, for the trouble and anxiety he has taken in the matter. And also for the very courteous and friendly manner in which he has on all occasions received and communicated with this institution."

Further,—"That the thanks of this meeting are due and are hereby given to Mr. George Godwin for his exertions in his public capacity to forward the same object."

Miscellanea.

MANCHESTER ROYAL LUNATIC HOSPITAL.—This edifice was opened last week for patients. It is built of red brick, with stone mullions, and is in the Elizabethan style of architecture. It has a frontage of 350 feet, the central projecting front taking up 50 feet. The brick was made on the ground. There are two stories, and a basement, with an attic in the centre front, and a small tower in the centre of the roof, for smoke and ventilation. Each corridor is lighted with eight windows, along a passage 114 feet long. There are ranges of apartments furnished for different classes of patients, and a day-room and dining-room, on the ground floor, supplied with numerous articles of comfort and amusement. Along all the passages ventilation is secured by iron grids in the skirting-boards. The upper story chiefly consists of dormitories, with beds of polished birchwood. There are altogether 252 rooms, exclusive of cellars and store-rooms. The building is lighted with gas from a work about a quarter of a mile distant, with a gasometer for 8,500 cubic feet of gas, or four days' supply. The heating apparatus is a series of pipes for hot air from the engine-house. Water is supplied from a well of 60 feet in depth, by aid of a small engine, capable of lifting 4,000 gallons a-day. There are also a number of cisterns in the roof with capacity for 70,000 gallons of rain-water for distribution to the washhouse, &c., and in case of fire. There are baths and lavatories with ready supplies of hot, tepid, and cold water. The kitchen, under the chapel, is fitted up with approved apparatus. There is to be an organ gallery in the chapel. The roof is groined. The area of the site is 52 statute acres with pleasure and airing grounds, bowling-green, and kitchen garden. The avenue and grounds contain 18,000 trees and shrubs. There is accommodation in all for 100 patients, male and female, in separated departments.

HOXTON RAGGED SCHOOLS.—On the 11th inst. the foundation-stone of this establishment was laid by Lord Ashley, who addressed a large assemblage of spectators on the advantages of such institutions. The architect, on whose designs the building is to be constructed, is Mr. John Tarring; and Mr. Silas Honeywill is the builder to whom it is intrusted. The structure is to be plain but spacious, and in the Tudor style; the material brick, with stone dressings. Its extreme height will be 30 feet, depth 70 feet, width 20 feet, giving school-room for the accommodation of 400 children, and private rooms for the master and mistress. The interior has an open roof of stained wood, and the building is to be completed by February 1, 1850.

WESTMINSTER IMPROVEMENTS — COMPENSATION CASE.—Some weeks since you raised the curiosity, as well as the surprise of your readers, by an account of an award made by Mr. Shaw, in the matter of the Westminster Improvement Commissioners and the parishes of St. Margaret and St. John's, Westminster, when you stated that 21,000*l.* had been awarded for the workhouse upon an offer of 10,000*l.*, and you named very correctly high reputations in the profession in array on the conflicting side. I believe every member of our profession must feel a regret when such differences occur among authorities, because they tend to throw an uncertainty on the issue of inquiries, for which the public believe we have at least proximately agreed and conventional formulæ. I was therefore tempted to overcome my reluctance to figure in public correspondence, and to allay by explanation whatever of misconception may have been caused by the paragraph; but apprehending, what has since resulted, that a rule *nisi* would be granted to set aside this award, and that your readers would gain more by a report of the arguments on the case in court, than I should be likely to supply by *ex-parte* statement, I determined to await the issue of an application to the court, which, having now been successfully made, will leave you the opportunity of informing your readers on the subject, when I am sure all parties engaged will maintain the reputation they have enjoyed, and my friend Mr. Hunt will show good cause why he asked me nearly double what I considered his clients were entitled to receive.

HENRY ROBERT ABRAHAM.

PROJECTED WORKS.—Advertisements have been issued for tenders by 20th January, 1850, for taking down and rebuilding the Stockwell bridge at Glasgow; by 8th January, for the erection of the Subscription Baths and other works at Wolverhampton; by 24th December, for masons', carpenters', joiners', plumbers', slaters', plasterers', and painters' works, for Leeds-terrace, Low Harrogate; by 17th December, for certain alterations and repairs at Manor-house, Bishopstoke, Hants; and by 18th, for building sewers in Green Dragon-court, Cloyster-court, Jackson's-court, Canterbury-court, and other places in the City of London.

NEWSPAPER FOLDERS.—A gentleman once resident in Liverpool, says the *Albion*, has perfected plans for a machine precisely similar in its aim to one recently announced in a Brussels journal, but superior in practical value. We have had the pleasure of inspecting the draughtsman's sketches, and we are assured that consultation with an eminent mechanician has evoked a highly favourable opinion in regard to the novelty and practicability of the design. The invention, it is anticipated, will fold at least 3,000 copies per hour,—a speed much higher than that of the continental machine, and much more considerable than that of the majority of presses employed in provincial newspaper offices; and, whilst the motive power necessary is comparatively light and easy of appliance, the labour required whilst the machine is in action is trifling in the extreme. The cost,—an essential point,—is said to be comparatively small.

THE IRON TRADE.—On Wednesday week a numerous assemblage of engineers, moulders, millwrights, smiths, and other mechanics, met at Blackburn, to discuss "matters of the greatest importance to the trade generally." A deputation consisting of Mr. Brandon, of London, Mr. J. Rawlinson, of Manchester, and Mr. Newton, of London, urged the meeting to prevent, by co-operation, the great reduction of wages which was expected to take place. Resolutions were unanimously adopted:—"That the men out of employment, caused by a reduction of wages at the works at the South-Western Railway, be supported, and that a Committee be formed for that purpose."—"That the meeting appoint a Committee to form a Central Committee, for the purpose of co-operating with similar societies in other towns."

ARCHITECTURAL ASSOCIATION.—We are glad to see that subjects of a practical nature are occupying the attention of this association, the last paper read being on the supply and discharge of water to buildings, by Mr. Calvert Vaux. The artesian and aqueduct principles, and the advantages of the plan of constant supply at high pressure, were referred to, but the details of arrangement in which the responsibility of the architect is more especially involved, were made the chief points for consideration, and the merits of various plans and inventions, amongst others those of Messrs. Bunnett and Corpe, Mr. Smith, and Mr. Jennings, were discussed. The paper concluded with a few sensible remarks on the feasibility of a central and permanent exposition of inventions connected with practical architecture.

A SURVEYOR BY TENDER. GOING! GONE!—According to advertisement in THE BUILDER of the 1st instant, the office of surveyor of highways for Ealing was *tendered for*, on the 4th, by the following candidates, and at the annexed salaries.

	Per Annum.
Godson	£200
Whiteside	120
Lack	100
Pockington	80
Garner	80
Hancock	58
Bouten	52
Farquharson (accepted)	52
Jones	50
Hunt	50
Withers	50
Sanders	45
Taylor	45
Gibson	45
Rodge	40
Wright	40
Skey	40
Dorchester	40
Paxton	35

—H.

INSTITUTION OF CIVIL ENGINEERS.—At a meeting on Tuesday, December 11th, Mr. Joshua Field, president, in the chair, a paper was read, "On the facilities for a Ship Canal Communication between the Atlantic and Pacific Oceans, through the Isthmus of Panama," by Lieut.-Colonel Lloyd. The chief point insisted on by the author was the great field opened in the Isthmus for emigration, for the surplus population of this country. He contended, that it was far preferable to the Canadas, where the poor, but industrious and honest mechanic, or labourer, on arriving, found that the rich land he had heard of could only be reached by a weary journey and after such hardships, in a severe climate, as his limited means and broken strength rendered impossible for him to bear.

CHELTENHAM CHURCH COMPETITION.—Forty-seven designs were submitted in competition for the new church at Cheltenham, from which the committee selected three,—those of Mr. Ordish, Mr. Raffles Brown, and Messrs. Coe and Goodwin. The decision has ultimately been in favour of Mr. Ordish's design, the tender of a builder having been produced within the stipulated sum. The design is Middle Pointed, with chancel and chancel aisle, nave, north and south aisles and north and south transepts, south porch, and sacristy. North of chancel there is a tower with plain broach spire west of nave. The roofs are of high pitch, and there is a clerestory of plain character. It is to be regretted that the transepts contain galleries,—an almost necessary evil under the circumstances.

CHINESE BUILDERS IN CALIFORNIA.—The Chinese have emigrated to San Francisco in large numbers, and it is remarked that from early morn until late in the evening, these industrious men are engaged in their occupation of house builders, and the quietness and order, cheerfulness, and temperance of their habits, is noticed by every one. The buildings brought from China are generally 20 feet square, one story in height, and 12 feet from the floor to the ceiling, and the price of them, including the erection, is 1,500 dollars. They are brought from Hong-Kong.

TO DESTROY CRICKETS.—In reply to the inquiry "how to destroy crickets?" mix together about two-thirds of dry pounded loaf sugar with one-third of arsenic, and put it in those places infested with them. I have never known this remedy to fail.—J. C.

LONDON SEWAGE.—The tunnel sewer now in course of formation across Ludgate-hill, from Ave Maria-lane to Creed-lane, is for the purpose of bringing down sewage matter to the works now constructing at Puddle Dock, where it will be treated by the method patented by Mr. Higgs.

THE BRADFORD WORKHOUSE PLANS.—Sixteen competitors having lodged their plans, the guardians proceeded on Tuesday week to consider them, when seven or eight were rejected, either from the estimates being beyond the sum limited, namely, 6,000*l.*, or for other reasons. On the following day the whole were reduced to three, which, says the local *Observer*, were to be submitted to the guardians on the Friday,—the advice of two practical men, namely, Mr. B. Illingworth and Mr. Mawson, being at same time called for.

METROPOLITAN SEWERS COMMISSION.—A court was ordered to be held on the 7th instant, but a quorum could not be obtained. Some little business, however, was afterwards done. The new commission seems to be subsiding into a state of great quiescence, so far as the public are informed.

IMPROVEMENT IN NAIL MACHINES.—Mr. Goose, of Birmingham, claims, for patent, the employment and construction of a spring nipper in addition to nail-making machines, for causing the partially-formed nail to make part of a revolution.

"IMPERVIOUS STONE."—With reference to an advertisement in our paper of the 10th, headed, "*A M. l'Editeur du Journal* THE BUILDER," we have been called on by the professional advisers of M. Teychenné, to apologize for certain statements therein reflecting on his character. To apologize for statements of which we know nothing is, of course, out of the question. We can simply say, and we do this very readily, that we in no degree participate in making them, and must leave the parties to their remedy against each other.

MEETINGS OF SCIENTIFIC BODIES

Held during the ensuing week.

MONDAY, Dec. 17.—Institute of Architects, 8 p.m. " On Glass."

TUESDAY, Dec. 18.—Institution of Civil Engineers, 8 p.m. (anniversary).

WEDNESDAY, Dec. 19.—Society of Arts, 8 p.m.

THURSDAY, Dec. 20.—Royal Society, 8½ p.m.; Society of Antiquaries, 8 p.m.

TO CORRESPONDENTS.

"*Stockton Union Competition.*"—More than a score of indignant letters on this subject lead us to hope that the guardians will have the response they deserve.

"*Building Societies.*"—We have received a number of letters on this subject, but cannot find space for them.

"F. R.," "F. B.," Slesford (we should be likely to mislead if we answered such questions on partial information), "S. D.," "An Architect's and Builder's Clerk," "W. J., jun.," "W. B." (we should be happy to attend to the matter personally, if applied to. Mr. Valued Waltham Abbey a few days ago), "G. R. B." (we have an "embarrassment of riches" just now. They will be useful), "Anglicus" (an anonymous opinion is worth nothing), "P.S." (Thanks for explanation: it shall be looked to), "Q.," "Novis," "R. B." (Liverpool), "A County Architect," "M.," "G. R.," "R. B." (London), "J. B.," "J. C. S." (the landlord is not bound to give notice to repair: the lease is a standing notice), "Veritas," "R. H. L." (shall hear from us), "C. R. C.," "A. W. R." (a similar letter has appeared), "F. S." (we do not go with our correspondent. Scupdufr has a higher purpose than to perpetuate costume), "J. E." (our experience is not the same), "J. R." (the letter did not reach us in time), "C. and Co.," "W. C." (next week), "A. C.," "A Young Subscriber" (our volume begins on the 1st of January. A number for every week), "F. J.," "T. C. H." (the print has not reached us), "J. L. T." "K. X." (the basement floor is below the ground floor), "Alpha," Mr. P., of Tichbourne-street (will find a packet for him at THE BUILDER Office: wrong address).

A Supplement to the Revolution in Mind and Practice of the Human Race, by Robert Owen (London: Effingham Wilson), "Holreecy Gauderlot," an Address to the Bankers, Merchants, and Men, of Great Britain; being the outline of a Plan for the Application of Assurance to Debts, Bills of Exchange, &c," by C. S. Canddell (London: G. Mann; Mitchell and Son).

NOTICE.—All communications respecting *advertisements* should be addressed to the "Publisher," and not to the "Editor:" all other communications should be addressed to the EDITOR, and not to the Publisher.

"*Books and Addresses.*"—We have not time to point out books or find addresses.

ADVERTISEMENTS.

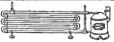

No. CCCLIX.

SATURDAY, DECEMBER 22, 1849.

N the 26th of this month, the new Olympic Theatre, in Wych-street, Strand, will be opened under the direction of Mr. Frederick W. Bushill, architect, and built for dramatic representations, under the management of Mr. W. Watts, the late manager of the "Marylebone Theatre," which was the work of the same architect. We give a plan of the new theatre, and a general view of the interior,* and next week we shall add a working section, showing the whole construction.† Drury-lane appears to have had its name from a house built there by Sir William Drury, a commander in the Irish wars, in the time of Queen Elizabeth, and who afterwards fell in a duel through a quarrel about precedency. Before "Drury House" was built, the old name for the lane was *Via de Aldewych*, and we have still the continuation of it, called Wych-street in consequence. Drury-lane was for some time an aristocratic quarter, but lost this character early in the reign of William III.,‡ and soon became celebrated for quite other inhabitants. Goldsmith, in his lines on a poet's lodging, speaks of "the drabs and bloods of Drury-lane;" and Pope uses the same term in the line—

". . "Paltry and proud as drabs in Drury-lane;"

Love of alliteration may have had something to do in suggesting it to both.

Drury House, in the seventeenth century, came into the possession of Lord Craven, afterwards Earl Craven, celebrated for his efforts to stay the ravages of fires, then so frequent in London, who rebuilt it, as Craven House. This underwent various changes, and was ultimately taken down. In August, 1805, Earl Craven granted a lease of the premises to the late Philip Astley, who covenanted to build "a good and substantial theatre, or amphitheatre, for the acting of pantomimes and other performances." This lease was sold to Elliston, and afterwards assigned to John Scott, the former proprietor of the Sans Pareil (the Adelphi), and is now vested in Mr. John Cavell, of Guildford-street, who married a daughter of Scott.

The old theatre, opened by Astley as the "Olympic Pavilion," September 18, 1806, was constructed principally of wood, from the timbers of an old man-of-war, *La Ville de Paris* (the ship William the Fourth went out in as midshipman), which was given by George the Third to Astley, who had been the riding-master to the younger branches of the royal family, and was a great favourite of the old king. The king also gave the chandelier.

On the 29th March, 1849, the theatre was entirely destroyed by fire. The building was insured in the County Fire Office for 2,500l.§

* See page 606 in our present number.
† In other numbers of THE BUILDER will be found views and particulars of the Royal Italian Opera House; the Theatre Royal, Drury-lane; the Theatre Royal, Lyceum; and the *Theâtre Historique*, Paris. Detailed accounts of the new Manchester Theatre, the Prince's Theatre, Glasgow, &c., are also given.
‡ "Handbook of London."
§ The writer had a pleasant recollection of the old Olympic Theatre. It was here in younger days that he first penetrated the mysteries of the *coulisses*, to superintend the production of a farce, and waited, breathless, in a side box, to hear what reception the public would give, on the first night, to "The Last Day."

Ou the 30th June, in the same year, the first brick of the new house was laid; but it was not until the beginning of August that the excavation was completed, and the bricklayers were fairly at work.

The new building is on the site of the old theatre,—an irregular plot of ground, averaging about 100 feet deep by 75 feet wide, with frontages to Wych-street (south-west front), Maypole-alley, and Craven-passage, and running back in the rear of the houses in Wych-street and Craven-buildings. The stage occupies the whole width of the ground at the north-west end, by about 44 feet deep; the remaining portion is used for orchestra and the audience.

The basement is a half-sunk story. The part under the stage is used for the purposes of the machinery connected with the stage, traps, sliders, &c., and communicating with it is a dock for scenery on one side; a music-room, a property-room, and a gas-room, on the other. Under the back part of the pit, and the principal entrances, are four large and three smaller dressing-rooms, separate water-closets, &c. The dressing-rooms have fire-places, and sinks with water laid on. The remaining portion of the basement is used for stowage and coals.

Ou the *Ground Floor* (and shown on the plan), are the principal entrances—those to the boxes and pit being in Wych-street, and those to the gallery and stage in Craven-passage; and there are additional fire-proof ways *out*, both from gallery and pit,—important in the event of fire; also the pit and pit-stalls, with separate entrances to stalls; two proscenium boxes and two private boxes, a refreshment-room, water-closet, &c.; the orchestra, proscenium and stage, green-room, porters' room, and entrance to stage, with separate way for horses and scenery.

On the *Box Floor* are six private boxes, three on each side; four tiers of dress and two tiers of back seats, in the centre of the house; a corridor at back of boxes, with separate staircases to slips and private boxes; a small *salon*, ladies' cloak-room, separate water-closets, urinal, &c.

On the *Gallery Level* are two private (proscenium) boxes and four slip boxes, a spacious gallery, with refreshment place, carpenters' store-rooms, &c. Over the sides and back of the stage are the flies and painting-room; and there are two best dressing-rooms, closet, &c., over the green-room and stage entrance.

In the roof, over pit and gallery, is the carpenter's workshop, 40 feet long by 45 feet wide, communicating with the flies and painting room.

At Q on the plan, is a fire-proof passage communicating with the manager's house in Craven-buildings, which contains some additional dressing rooms.

With respect to *construction*, there is a single span queen roof 56 feet bearing, in clear of walls; the tie beams (in one length) are 14 inches by 6½ inches; the queen posts, 9 inches by 6½ inches; the principal rafters and collar, 9 inches by 6½ inches; the purlins, 9½ inches by 5 inches, and the plates, 9 inches by 6 inches. The main walls are 3½ bricks thick up to pit : 3 bricks above.

The gallery and box floors are framed with girders, 12 inches by 12 inches, one end into granite corbels in walls, the other end supported by iron columns, 4 inches by 5 inches diameter. To prevent the thrust inwards, from the great inclination of the floors (the gallery timbers rising three feet in five), the ends of the girders have been secured by iron ties and granite bond, 6 inches by 4 inches, built in the walls, flush outside, and the whole floor is framed on the principle of a horizontal truss, with abutments from the longitudinal walls.

There are two fire-proof (stone) staircases to the gallery, one for entrance and *both for exit*, already referred to. There are also two ways out of pit, and separate way from stalls and boxes, so that the house may be cleared in a few minutes. The whole of the entrances, passages, &c., including staircases (slate) to the private boxes and slips, are fire-proof. The floor of lobby round back of boxes is of slate on pugging.

The house is ventilated by an air shaft over the chandelier through the roof, a large ventilator through the roof at the back of the gallery, a tier of semi-circular windows between gallery floor and ceiling. There are also air flues in all the walls, communicating with various parts of the house, and four internal air shafts from the back of the pit and boxes through the roof; the upper part of each of these shafts is rarified by gas burners, which at the same time light the back of gallery.

The stage and machinery were designed and executed by R. J. Strachan, who, as he tells us, has designed and constructed the machinery of eight of the principal London theatres.

The stage, 55 feet wide and 45 deep, is so arranged that any portion can be removed singly or altogether, as occasion may require. These movements are effected by means of multiplying windlass barrels placed on each side of the basement-floor, adjusted by a new species of machinery, by which the level of the stage is depressed into inclined grooves, wrought in the sides of the principal timbers of the stage, and thereby drawn off to any distance required ; in point of fact, the whole of the practical surface of the stage may be cleared, leaving nothing but the skeleton, in two minutes ; so that, if required to show a gulph or chasm in scenic arrangement, the means of effect are very great. The stage is an inclined plane, of ⅜ inch to the foot, and is arranged with four entrances, with working grooves for wings and flats, the whole made practicable. The traps are worked by a graduated balance-weights, so that any degree of velocity can be obtained by setting them accordingly. The gas battens are the whole length of the proscenium, and are also hung with balance-weights. The borders are hung in a similar manner. The painting-room is at the back of the stage, above the "flies," and there is a frame working down on to the stage, on which the scenes can be placed, and taken up and painted with the least possible trouble. The scene repository, at the north-west angle, on the site of the old painting-room, will hold sixty pairs of flats.

The form of the theatre is an elongated horse shoe, with but few projections, so as not to present any interruption to sight or sound. The endeavour of the architect has been to get a well formed theatre, of good proportions and harmonious lines, with little extraneous ornament. It may be observed that the pit seats are circular on plan, so that each person looks directly to the centre of the stage. The ceiling and proscenium are *match boarded*, and canvassed for decorations.* The height from the pit floor to the highest part of the ceiling is about 36 feet. The stalls contain 38 sittings, the pit will hold from 800 to 850 persons, the boxes about 200, and the gallery 700 to 750.

* The boarding was first desiccated.

PLAN OF THE OLYMPIC THEATRE.

REFERENCES.

A Box entrance.
B Pit entrance.
C Gallery entrance.
D Entrance to stalls from box entrance.
E Staircase from gallery ; and second way
  out in case of accident.
F A second way out from pit.
G Stage entrance.
H Foyer.
I Green-room.

K K Stage.
  a a a a Sliders.
  b b b b Traps.
L Private boxes.
M Entrance for machinery, &c., to stage.
N Refreshments, W. C., &c.
O Urinal, &c.
P Dock for stowing away scenery.
Q Entrance from manager's house—fire-
  proof.

We have now to speak of the decorations, which were entrusted to Mr. Aglio, and executed by him and his son, Mr. Aglio, jun.*

The ceiling is divided into four compartments, representing the Seasons,—each compartment being separated by ornamental designs in the Arabesque style, connected in the centre in an ornament giving apparent support to the chandelier. Under each of these four compartments are panels with Arabesque ornaments on gold ground, in the centre being introduced, in *chiaro-scuro*, the sign of the Zodiac marking the entrance of each season. These panels form a band enclosing the circle, and are surrounded by a *bordure*, in *chiaro-scuro*, on blue ground, which connects the two spandrils, formed by the circle closing with the arch of the proscenium. On these spandrils are introduced two groups, allegorical of Music and Poetry.

The front of the gallery and box tiers is divided into seven compartments, by the gilded and bronzed columns supporting the boxes and gallery. Each compartment in the gallery tier is decorated with Arabesque ornaments, within which are introduced masks, musical instruments, and cameos, in *chiaro-scuro*, on gold ground. Those of the box tier are decorated with richly-worked Arabesques, on gold and coloured grounds. A general symmetry is preserved in the decoration of these compartments, but no subject is repeated. *Chiaro-scuro* figures of Cupid, on blue ground, form caryatides over and under the columns of the

boxes. Of the general effect when lighted, we have not yet had an opportunity to judge.

The proscenium is intended simply to form a frame to the decorations of the stage,—the predominant colours white and gold. The ornaments of the arch are in *chiaro-scuro ;* in the centre of these are represented the Muses, with their appropriate attributes. The upper proscenium boxes are decorated with groups of masks, allusions to Tragedy and Comedy; the lower ones with cameos of poets, on gold ground, surrounded by light-coloured arabesques. The pilasters supporting the arch are decorated with arabesque ornaments, in three divisions ; in the centre are introduced the crests of the proprietor of the land, Lord Craven, and of the theatre, Mr. Cavell. In the composition of the caps the artist has introduced the phœnix. The decorations were designed and painted in the short space of seven weeks.

The front of the house is lighted by a large chandelier, manufactured by Mr. Apsley Pellatt. The gas fittings were put up by Mr. J. Palmer, jun., and present several useful precautionary measures, which we will note in our next number.

The entrance front of the building, which is formed in cement, is simple and unpretending. It presents a large cornice with low attic above. There is a series of five windows filled in with iron guards of ornamental pattern, and below is an arcade of five arches, three of which are entrances, and two blanks.

under 10,000l., including the cost of purchasing some adjoining property. There was not time to obtain competition tenders, and Mr. Holland was employed as the builder at a fixed scale of prices. The work was measured monthly, and 85 per cent. of the work executed paid for on the 1st of each month. The work is very well done, and all parties seem satisfied one with another.

The act drop, partly shown in our view, representing an "Italian loggia opening on a cortile," was painted by Messrs. Dayes and Gordon, and is a very creditable work.

BUILDING SOCIETIES.

The writers who have addressed us in reply to some observations in a recent number of our journal (p. 554 *ante*), all assume as certain a variety of issues, which are more than doubtful. Many who still maintain that these societies, if well managed, would greatly benefit the provident classes, are obliged to admit that the result in practice will be very different in certain cases from what they anticipated.

One well informed correspondent says,—

It seems to me that building societies are founded upon true principles, and are calculated, if well managed, to be of the utmost benefit to the provident classes. But I quite agree with the writer in THE BUILDER, that in practice they have not answered the expectations formed of them, more particularly with reference to the interests of the "working man." This arises, I believe, principally from bad management. It unfortunately happens that the majority of societies are got up by needy professional men, and, in many cases, from interested motives. Such men have no inducement to bring the operations of the society to an early conclusion, but rather the reverse, as the longer the society lasts the more they make out of it.

Such a state of things operates most prejudicially against societies of an inferior class, as the members are generally working-men without education, and are consequently entirely led by the managers of the society whom they trust implicitly, as possessing superior knowledge ; and if the trust is abused the society gets saddled with inferior or bad property, which altogether frustrates the object of the members. With the better class of societies this objection does not apply with so much force,—the members are generally better educated, and capable of looking after their own interests. I think very few building societies will be found to work out in a satisfactory way ; and of those who do so the number will be very small of that class to which the "working-man" generally belongs.

J. W.

In several such societies which we have been watching, the solicitors and the surveyors connected with them, have performed their duties so ill, that confusion is inevitable ; deeds on which much depended are found valueless and houses taken as securities are turning out positive mill-stones. The mere recital of some facts within our own knowledge would utterly blast the reputation of three professional men. Not long ago we were requested, as an act of personal friendship, by a director of a building society, to give a confidential opinion as to the value of a property *offered* to them, as he said. It was a house of business in London, held for a long term, at ninety pounds per annum on a stringent lease, and let to a tenant-at-will for 120l. per annum. The premises were not in good repair, the situation declining, and after going over the house our reply was, as many readers will guess, that the assignment of such a property would be *worse than no security at all*. We then learned that it had been valued as an assured income of 30l. per annum, for the unexpired term, and accepted by the society for a loan of 500l.

The house is now on the hands of the society unlet, and in its present state, we venture to assert, will not command a tenant at the rent the society are bound to pay.

ties offered to them, and, knowing the want of judgment which *has* been shown in many cases, and the large interests at stake, we would awaken the attention of Directors to the importance of this point, and exhort them to be assured of competent advice. An immediate *review* of the securities in their hands might be serviceable. We speak with seriousness, because with knowledge.

ROYAL INSTITUTE OF BRITISH ARCHITECTS.

At an ordinary meeting, held on the 3rd inst., Mr. Bellamy in the chair, the following members were elected:—Messrs. J. B. Bunning, C. R. Cockerell, R.A., G. G. Scott, and W. C. Stow, as Fellows; and Messrs. R. P. Pope, and M. D. Wyatt, as Associates. A paper was then read "On the Ancient Architecture of Scotland," by Mr. R. W. Billings, of which we give an abstract.

At a meeting on the 17th instant, Mr. S. Smirke in the chair, Messrs. R. Hesketh and R. W. Mylne were elected fellows; and Mr. H. H. Burnell, associate. A brief memoir of the late Mr. Pocock, fellow, was communicated. Mr. Donaldson, honorary secretary, then read a paper "On the Manufacture of Glass, and its application to Architectural purposes," to which we shall revert hereafter. In the course of it the lecturer described plate-glass as both cast and *blown*, and alluded to the "rough-plate glass" case, as set forth in The Builder.

Mr. Tite said he thought that speaking of plate-glass as both blown and cast was likely to lead to confusion. He knew nothing of *blown* plate himself, and wished to know where it is now made. Mr. Tite mentioned the introduction of "French and German plate," and the manufacture, by Mr. Chance, of what he called "patent plate," to meet this. When polished, this could scarcely be discriminated from plate-glass proper. It was necessary to call this "patent plate" in specifications, or a different material was furnished. After mentioning the characteristics of glass in various conditions, he said (to maintain his character of *laureate*)—

"Honour's like the glassy bubble
Which costs philosophers much trouble!
The least part cracked the whole doth flie,
And wits are cracked to find out why."

Mr. Swinburne, as a practical man, said in reply to the question, that *blown* plate was made here before the last speaker was born, and continued in use till six or seven years before the duty was repealed. At one time little could be obtained *but* blown plate.

Mr. Jennings denied that blown glass was plate glass.

Mr. Billings thought that the use of glass and iron ought to have produced a new style of architecture, and that it would have done so but for the folly of Governments.

The Chairman alluded to the indestructibility of glass when quite pure, and showed how it corrodes when this is not the case and metallic oxides are present. Some means of ascertaining with certainty the purity of glass were much to be desired.

Mr. C. H. Smith thought it might be useful to mention, that, finding some 1½-inch glass slabs, 5 feet by 4 feet, which were about to be laid in connection with pavement at St. Katherine's Docks, had not a fair edge to make a joint to, he had sought to have them made square by the dealer, and failing in that, had successfully squared them with the chisel in the same way as a piece of marble would be squared. Slabs might be divided by a plain-edged saw.

Mr. G. R. Burnell mentioned, with respect to the size of looking-glasses, that at the late Exposition in Paris a plate was shewn 13 feet 9 inches by 8 feet 8 inches, price 140*l.*; and a concave reflector, 4 feet 7 inches square.

Inigo Jones.—The Shakspeare Society have just now issued an interesting contribution to architectural biography, in the shape of a small volume containing a life of Inigo Jones, by Mr. P. Cunningham, and remarks on some of his sketches for masques by Mr. Planché. The life gives some new and interesting matter, and we shall take an early opportunity to place it prominently before our readers.

A CYCLOMETER.

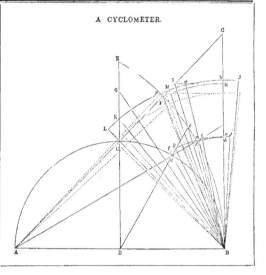

A CYCLOMETER.

Describe the semicircle ABC. With radius AB describe the arc BE. Draw the secant DCE at right angles to AB. Draw the secant ACFG, making the arc BF equal to the arc BC. Draw the tangent BG, the chord BC, and the chord BF, bisecting the angle CBG. With radius BF describe the arc FH. Draw HI parallel to AB. Make the angles HBJ and CBK equal to the angle FBI. With radius BK describe the arc LKMNJ. Draw BM bisecting the angles LBJ, KBN, and FBI. Then BM is to the arc BF as BK is to the arc BC, which is as much as saying that the two equal right lines BM and BK are equal in length to the two equal arcs BF and BC.

Take any other arc of the quadrant, as Bc, proceed as before, and extend Bm, meeting the arc LJ in o, then B*m* : arc B*f* : : B*k* : arc Bc : : *mo* : arc Cc.

If a right line B*p* be given, and an arc equal to it in length is required, proceed according to the dotted lines to find the points F and C, taking care that the angle on either side of FB is equal to half the angle on either side of CB, for it is obvious that the construction cannot be true, unless the different angles vary together from greatest to least in a constant ratio either of one to one or of two to one.

It is also evident if we conceive the line BQ to coincide with the chord BC, and BI with the chord BF, and the angles CBQ and FBI to increase together from zero in the ratio of two to one; that since BC is less than BF, and BQ is greater than BI, there can be only two lines (determined by this law) between the limits CB and QB and FB and IB which can be equal to each other, like the arcs BC and BF.　　　J. P. W.

Improvements in Tunnelling.—Mr. Samuel Dunn, of Doncaster, has secured a patent for an improved arrangement for tunnelling under rivers, and other similar purposes. He employs a moveable shield similar to the one used by Mr. Brunel at the Thames Tunnel. The fore part is constructed of iron in the form of a plough, the point being of steel, divided into compartments, which are filled with compressed air, to a degree to equal the outside pressure: the working part is separated from the plough by an air and water-tight partition, fitted with a tube communicating with a pump.

ON THE ANCIENT ARCHITECTURE OF SCOTLAND.

The following is the substance of Mr. Billings's paper, already mentioned:—

"As a preliminary remark it was observed, that although the principal monuments of both England and Scotland may. be identical in minute details, yet, at the same time, great changes and varieties occurred in various leading features, so as to produce a distinct individuality in the character of the Scottish edifices.

The beautiful little church of Leuchars, in Fife, by some reputed as of Saxon origin, is a fine Norman specimen, with an apsidal east end. The cathedral at Elgin is a beautiful edifice, and the arcaded streets of that town most interesting, somewhat resembling those of Chester, the arcade, however, being on a level with the street, and constructed of stone. At three miles from Elgin is a curious old fire-proof house, at Coxton, in which the alternate stories are arched, with semi-vaultings, the upper one, however, being pointed. The turrets of Cawdor Castle, near Inverness, are curious, being circular in the lower part and octagonal above.

Mr. Billings considered the first Scotch architectural era to have ranged as in England from 1066 to 1200. The Abbey and Palace of Dunfermline, and the Cathedral of Kirkwall, are gigantic examples of that period, and they bear a striking affinity to Durham Cathedral, the solid cylindrical columns in the two being identical: and history informs us that Malcolm the Third in 1093 assisted in laying the foundation of Durham Cathedral, and soon after his return from that place, founded the Abbey of Dunfermline, the first monks of which were from Canterbury. The smaller Scotch buildings of the Norman period approach nearer in beauty to those of England. Among the most beautiful and perfect specimens are the churches at Leuchars and Dalmeny. An endless variety of detail was presented in Scottish architecture, most remarkable; when not only animals and foliage were introduced, but even the signs of the Zodiac. At the period of the transition to the Early Pointed or Lancet, the mouldings of the Scotch building became so minute, as to excite almost a feeling of pity for the workman who had to accomplish such a task. Some of the capitals at Holyrood chapel are a verification of this,—the quality of the ornament was, however, equal to the quantity. At a later period, the system became the very reverse, and more effect was produced without mouldings by the use of the chamfer, the splay of the arch, however, being moulded. The Cathedral of Dunblane is an extraordinary example of the great effect produced by the judicious use of limited means.

Had the ancient friendship between Scotland and England continued to exist, there is little doubt but that the architecture of both would have remained nearly identical; but the complete severance of all friendly ties between the two kingdoms, and the endless feuds among the various clans and even families of Scotland, compelled the lairds to make their houses strongholds of defence, both against their English foes, and the attacks of their own countrymen. This state of things gained for Scotland at least this advantage, that of possessing what no other country can boast of —a complete series of castellated architecture. Not only did the clannish constitution of society in Scotland at this time divide the population into very small parties, but the very disposition of the people was averse to large congregations; this may easily be proved by the small size of the ancient portion of Scotland's capital, and of Stirling,—the approaches being defended by a strong fortress. The political changes of society have, however, gradually had their effect in Scotland, and the application of steam and machinery have almost entirely changed the state of the country in this respect. Ancient mansions have been deserted and dismantled, and detached houses of the lower classes, and many "towns," as they are called, have been allowed to decay and fall.

It is very singular that Scotland does not now possess one recognizable specimen of a Norman castle, although, close to her borders, so many are to be found, such as Norham, Bamborough, Newcastle, and Durham. Yet, that such castles did exist, there can be but little doubt; and the only mode of accounting for their disappearance is the supposition that they were sold by the magistrates as quarries, out of which so many of her abbeys were constructed. So determined seems this desire to have been for the destruction of old castles in Scotland, that Caerlaverock is the only example earlier than 1350, and it still retains its corbelled parapet. Kildrummie, in Aberdeenshire, appears to be the first recognizable Scotch castle, and was built about 1270 or 1300, belonging to the Early English style. One side is exceedingly singular, forming the end of a church with three lancet windows; probably so constructed in the expectation that any attacking force would respect the place of worship. The early Scotch castles appear to date with the time when the Bruces and Baliols left their English castles and occupied Scotch ones.

During the fourteenth and fifteenth centuries there existed a considerable affinity between the Ecclesiastical and the Castellated architectural decorations: thus, the hanging tracery of Rosslyn Chapel and the west front of Holyrood is found in the court-yards of Linlithgow Palace and Stirling Castle. The projecting turrets, so peculiar a feature in Scotch castellated architecture, are wonderfully constructed, many of them being infinitely more massive and weighty than the walls to which they are attached. This is the case at Kirkwall, where the bishop's palace is a fine ecclesiastical fortress residence. This edifice and the abbey of Crossraguel are magnificent specimens. In fact, the latter is a fortified abbey, with all the requirements of a cathedral establishment.

Some of the old castles appear to have been elaborately painted in what has been called fresco: but, from the fact of the paint peeling off, it was evidently never incorporated with the plaister or wood. In their plans the castles varied considerably, and this must be attributed to the most natural of causes, the architects in those days invariably suiting their plan to the nature of the ground on which they were about to build. Caerlaverock Castle may be mentioned as one of the most singular in plan, being triangular, with round towers at two of the angles, and at the third double towers with a gateway between them. This is the only fortress in Scotland retaining a moat: the portcullis room, too, is very complete. Inigo Jones is said to have imitated the plan in Longford House, Wilts, belonging to Lord Radnor. Fivie Castle is another, quite peculiar in plan, and its elevation one of the grandest in Scotland: the centre also is highly illustrative of the Scotch castle of the sixteenth century. The construction of the staircase is well worthy of notice, with its steps 16 feet long.

After the general introduction of gunnery on a large scale, by means of which the reduction of any fortress by a regular investment became only a question of time, the Scotch prudently defended their buildings against attacks by small arms, the only means that flying parties of marauders could have at command. This system was of great importance in developing architecture, for it did not prevent the addition of ornament to the castellated house. The decorated terminations of the massive walls in some of these buildings, form a highly picturesque and pleasing contrast. It was, however, upon the old walls of keep towers that the turrets, windows and roofs of the domestic character are raised; and this will account for the disappearance of many of the old castles. Glammis, Castle Fraser, and others, are striking instances of the extent to which the turreted style prevailed through the kingdom; nearly all the old keeps receiving new tops, some of them being of a highly ornamental character.

In the early part of the fourteenth century was introduced another mixed style, in which the Ecclesiastical and Domestic architecture were combined, as at Dunfermline, where the history of Domestic architecture is carried back to the Norman time; for in the windows of the basement, the bold arches of Malcolm's palace surmount the windows of a later period. As the first to notice this, Mr. Billings recommended its being preserved jealously, as the only known specimen of Domestic architecture in Scotland of the Norman period.

We now pass to the revival of the Italian styles, which, beginning about the year 1580, continued for a full century, producing numberless buildings in a style romantically picturesque, and which bear strong evidence of the architectural ability of that period: indeed, this may be called the flowery period of Scotch architecture. The mansions may be divided into three classes of design:—1st, where the chimney shafts, crow steps, and open parapets appear in combination, as at Wintoun House, near Tranent; 2ndly, where a combination of turrets and square chimney shafts exists, as at Newark; and 3rdly, where the chimneys become quite secondary, the main feature of design being high roofs with dormer windows, crow steps and turrets. Here the court-yard of Heriot's Hospital may be cited as an example. Dalpersie, in Aberdeenshire, is the link between the Castellated and Domestic styles.

The Domestic architecture of Scotland bears evidence of the great attention paid by the architects to details. Thus, the window heads and other ornaments of Heriot's work are a complete school of design; for in that building only one case of repetition occurs in the ornaments surmounting the windows: indeed this edifice, as a colossal example of one date, is unequalled. Two sides of Linlithgow court-yard are of a corresponding style of architecture, the remaining two forming an interesting example of the Domestic architecture of the fifteenth century. In Scotch houses the opposite sides generally present a striking contrast in style: this peculiarity is fully illustrated in an example at Newark, on the Clyde. On the river front of this building, the combination of turrets, jutting staircases, and square chimneys, is prominent; while on the court-yard side not a turret is to be seen, and the dormer window forms the main feature of the elevation. The old keep tower to which these domestic buildings have been attached, alone enables one to recognize the fronts as belonging to the same building.

There is strong reason to believe that the original combination of jutting turrets and corbelled staircases is to be awarded to Scotland alone, in spite of what may be called foreign types. Their conical tops may possibly have arisen from the staircase or recesses called oratories, which frequently occur in street architecture of the Gothic period on the continent, and of which there is a specimen or two also in the Cowgate at Edinburgh. These recesses are invariably supported upon a column, whose capital is bracketed out to the required size; but the corbelled bases of the Scotch turrets belong to the early period of castellated architecture, the variety and quaintness of decoration in their windows and mouldings marking them unmistakeably as Scotch. The general picturesque appearance of the small round turrets so peculiar to Scotland is much heightened by their contrast with the opposite forms of square massive chimney shafts, as may be seen at Newark.

Whosoever formed the school of design, which lasted during the whole of the seventeenth century, deserves the highest credit. Schaw, who rebuilt one of the western towers at Dunfermline, died in 1602; and although the mixture of Italian and Gothic did not predominate until the seventeenth century, yet many of the Aberdeenshire castles bear evidence of its advent towards the end of the sixteenth, and Schaw was most undoubtedly practising successfully at this time. The principal baronial buildings were built, however, after Schaw's death, and generally bear their own dates about 1650.

An interesting fact, discovered by Mr. Billings, proves that Wintoun House, Moray House, the Great Hall at Glammis, and Craigievar Castle, are works of the same architects and builders: nearly all the plaster work of these are cast from the same moulds. As an excellent example of the architecture of the middle of the seventeenth century, when it became the fashion to introduce the Doric, Ionic, and Corinthian orders, surmounting one another, the body of Holyrood Palace may be cited. Although Inigo Jones has always had the credit of designing Heriot's hospital, and his name has been identified with Glammis and with one side of Linlithgow Palace, it is singular that his name never appears on the records of the building, such as contracts or bills giving minute particulars, which are still in existence. There is, however, such a strong affinity between many of that great master's works in London and some of the northern buildings, that in the absence of proof positive to the contrary, they may safely be attributed to his genius.

The elegance and variety of design in the ornamental portions of the buildings of this period must not be passed over in silence; they evince a bold and vigorous determination to accomplish something original, carrying art as far beyond the meagre Italian types as it was possible. Wintoun House may here be mentioned as standing pre-eminent in the quality of its work. The design and execution of all its detail is perfection of the style. The artistic window-heads,—quite distinct from the Italian style, the elaborate geometric foliated ceilings, the chimneys and their stacks, are all equally admirable; presenting together, perhaps, the most impressive specimen of Scotch Domestic architecture. It should be mentioned as being unique among Scotch houses in not possessing corbelled turrets. In Craigievar Castle, in Aberdeenshire, the ceilings throughout are very similar to those at Wintoun, but infinitely more varied among themselves; and even the furniture partakes of the architectural character of the building: it offers a fine example of its time (1620).

Having shown how prominent the details stood in most of the buildings mentioned, it must be observed, that one of the great causes of success in the domestic or baronial architecture of Scotland was the comprehensive study of situation, and the composition of designs to suit these. The jutting turrets, gables, broken forms of detached roofs and surmounting towers, and, in short, all the playfully picturesque forms of Scotch architecture, essentially agree with its landscape, and the fitful forms of its ever-changing clouds; and is as completely in harmony with the country, as are the stately unbroken forms of Greek and Roman temples with the cloudless skies of the countries to which they belong.

After the relinquishment of regular fortification, the Scotch did not give up its external appearances, for stone cannon in hundreds of forms, as gurgoyles, or water-spouts, and more often as mere ornaments, are to be seen upon the more modern castles. In some of the old castles the formidable-looking port-holes are on inspection found incapable of being used for working cannon, from the narrow dimensions of the walled recesses behind, there being barely room to make use of a carbine. The picturesque gateway at Linlithgow may be instanced as an example, being almost a sham armament. This innate love for fighting, which the Scotch at all times possessed, induced them to carry out their emblems of strife beyond the buildings in which they secured themselves; even the flower gardens being made to partake of a military character, as at Stirling. After the Reformation had shaken the foundations of ecclesiastical domination in Scotland, it was to castles and houses that the abilities of the architects were turned—and here is the golden age of Scotland's building fame. In other countries the invention of gunpowder put an end to castellated architecture. It is scarcely to be doubted that architecture in Scotland would have become more interesting but for well-defined causes,—the divided power of the monarch and the great feudal lords, and the still more disastrous one, the English interference, beginning with Edward the First.

The variety of triforia in Scotland forms a curious feature, differing from those of England in the varied dimensions of the columns, in which must be recognised a spirit of determination to produce new effects.

The profusion of niches also, and their elaborate details, must be considered as a distinct feature in Scotch architecture. Bishop Kennedy's monument, at St. Andrew's, is one of the most elaborate examples of monumental art in the world.

With regard to the arch in Scotland it cannot, with the exception of a few instances, be considered, as in other countries, an index to the style or date of buildings. The circular arch, only used in Norman architecture elsewhere, was always in general use north of the Tweed. A doorway of a later date than 1400, in the High-street, Edinburgh, the western door and the tower windows of Haddington, the doorway inserted in the semi-Norman wall of Holyrood chapel, are all cases in point; their details proving them to be of a date later than their first appearance would imply. All kinds of arches are common to Scotland, excepting the four-centred, peculiar to the English Perpendicular; the only approach to this style out of England is to be seen in the east end of Stirling Church. It is rather, then, to their foliated detail of capitals, bases, and mouldings that we must look for the type of the time in which Scotch buildings were erected; and by these means the difficulty of distinction ceases. This is a remarkable feature in the Scotch architecture, a tenacity of retaining forms of styles while detail was degenerated. Thus, in Fifeshire, Dairsie Church and Michael Kirk have all the main features of early decorated buildings, and at a distance would be mistaken as belonging to that style, but the detail is decidedly debased in character, and the date upon each confirms the style from 1620 to 1630.

In the same manner that Scotch architects mingled styles, Scotch poetical epitaph-makers adopted mixed languages, thus—

"Here lies the Laird of Lundie,
Sic transit gloria mundi."

"Hic jacet Johannes Spencis,
Qhua biggit this Kirk Yaird Dyke at his ain expences."

England undoubtedly adopted the classical styles more readily than Scotland, and when the orders of architecture once had a hold they retained it, and our own styles became a dead letter. Scotland on the contrary, ever cautious, adopted the orders very charily, and it was not until a comparatively recent date (1660) that the three orders were seen surmounting one another in Holyrood Palace. It is to this position that the Scotch castles and houses owe much of their interest, for the architects of the time only adopted so much of the detail of Italian architecture as left the spirit of their buildings entirely Gothic.

STAINED GLASS, ST. JOHN'S, ANTIGUA.—We are asked to state that Mr. Wilmshurst was the artist who painted the glass in the windows of St. John's, Antigua, not Mr. Willement. Mr. Wilmshurst has recently completed a window for the Foundling Hospital, London. The date of the destruction of the first church at Antigua was misprinted 1848 for 1843.

NOTES IN THE PROVINCES.

THE repairs of the shire hall at Chelmsford are still in progress. The prisoners' cells are completed, and the county room is being painted, repaired, and fitted up with gas.——A committee is in course of formation for the collection of funds towards the restoration of St. Michael's, Cambridge.——St. Martin's Church, Salisbury, was opened on Friday last. A huge mass of pews and unsightly erections has been removed, and the divisions of chancel, choir, and nave, side aisles, &c., disclosed. The debased eastern window has been replaced by one in the style of the chancel, and filled with stained glass. The altar reredos has been emblazoned in gold and colours by Mr. Osmond, jun. The choir has been screened off from the aisles with light and open oak screens, and the organ placed at the end of the north aisle, thus throwing open the western window heretofore blocked up. The body of the church has been much increased in accommodation by low open seats. The extensive stone work restorations have been executed by Mr. Osmond, the carpentry by Mr. R. Hale. Mr. Wyatt was the architect.——An appeal is being made to churchmen on behalf of Frocester Church, now almost in ruins.—— The spire of St. John's Church, Wednesbury, has just been completed: Messrs. Horton the architects, and Mr. Highway, of Walsall, the builder.——The erection of an infant school, in the district of St. Andrew, Birmingham, has been commenced on a site in the Green-lanes. The plans have been furnished by the surveyor of the association, Mr. C. W. Orford, and the contract taken by Mr. Hardwick. The building is intended for two hundred children, with class-rooms, &c. This will make the fifth school erected through the instrumentality of this association, aided by the Privy Council and the National Society.——We understand that it has just been determined upon to build a new Roman Catholic church at Wolverhampton, at the cost of about 10,000*l*. One of the most eligible sites in the town has been fixed upon, and the land, about an acre, purchased, which will be required for the church, presbytery, and schools.—— The west window of Melton Mowbray Church has now been filled with stained glass, by Wales, presented by Mr. T. Clarke and family.——A monument has been erected in the cemetery at Stockport to the memory of Mr. Orrell, a late notable in the borough. The design consists of two bases, a pedestal, pyramid, and cap. Upon the front panel of the pedestal, which is of the Ionic order, is an inscription. The pedestal is surmounted by a frieze and cornice, and on it stands an Egyptian pyramid, 7 feet 4 inches high. On each of the four panels of the pyramid is carved the representation of a lighted torch reversed, and the whole is surmounted by a cap and urn, on the apex of which is another representation of light, typical of the consuming "torch of time." The extreme height of the monument is 17 feet 8 inches, its weight is about ten tons, the pyramid being hewn from a stone weighing at least two tons. The list of the officers and committee who had the superintendence and completion of the work was placed in a cavity in the upper base, under the pedestal. The stone was furnished from the Stypenson quarry, on the estate of Mr. Leigh, at Adlington. The design and execution were by Mr. J. Hough, foreman at the Stypenson quarry. The work-people employed at Travis Brook Mill have thus evinced their respect for the memory of a late employer.——The board of guardians (says the *Bradford Observer*) have not as yet made any selection of the three plans before them, nor have they decided to send them to the Poor-law Board. They have met several times since our last, and have spent much time in examining the details of each,—being very anxious to secure the most eligible.——The new church of St. Matthew, Bank Foot, Bradford, which is in the Decorated style, is of the following dimensions:—Nave, 65 feet by 21 feet 2 inches; aisles, 65 feet by 9 feet 4 inches; chancel, 22 feet by 16 feet; vestry, 10 feet by 8 feet. The contractors were: —Masons: Messrs. Patchett and Co., Queenshead; Joiner and carpenter: Mr. Ives, Shipley; Glaziers: Messrs. Firth, Halifax; Slater Messrs. J. and H. Hill, Bradford; Painter: Mr. Peel, Bradford; Clerk of works: Mr. Mawson. The architects were Messrs. Mallinson and Healey, Bradford. The building will accommodate 490 persons. The east window of chancel and west of nave are filled with Powell's cast and stained glass, and are a gift of Mr. C. Hardy, of Ordsall House. The building is roofed with grey slates, and surmounted with a cruciform bell turret, octagonal above with a small spirlet, terminating in a weather vane-cock as an emblem of watchfulness in the house of prayer.——The foundation-stone of Captain Cook's memorial school was laid at Marton, in Cleveland, near Middlesborough, Yorkshire, on 29th ultimo. The contractor (for the foundations at least) is Mr. Matthew Bowser, of Stockton-on-Tees. The building will not be proceeded with till spring of next year. In this little village, which boasts of the great captain as a native, two other considerable improvements have of late been effected, namely, an extension of its Norman Church into cruciform restoration, under the management of Mr. J. B. Rudd, and with the advice of Mr. Carpenter, architect, and an enlargement of the vicarage house, on a plan furnished by Mr. C. Brodrick, of Hull, architect.——We regret to state that Mr. G. T. Page, civil engineer, acting at the dock improvements at Leith, under Mr. Rendall, met with an accident on Thursday week, while inspecting the inner dock wall, and died in a few hours, after falling 20 feet, and fracturing his skull.——The legatees of the late Sir Gabriel Wood have paid the sum of 38,000*l*. to trustees for the erection and endowment of a hospital for decayed shipmasters of Greenock and its vicinity.

THE ROYAL ACADEMY MEDAL DRAWINGS.

DISPOSED as I am to agree with "Kunops" in his deprecation of copyism in architecture, I think it was somewhat ungracious and ungenerous in him to found his remarks upon the distribution of the prizes at the Royal Academy, and to leave it to be inferred that none of those who obtained medals had shown more than very ordinary common-place ideas. However objectionable the system adopted by the Academy for the annual *concours* among the students may be, it is what the students cannot correct; and, quite sure I am, that had any one aimed at striking and determined originality in the department of architecture, he would have deprived himself of even the chance of obtaining a medal; for his design would have been put *hors du combat* at once, as being altogether *non-descript*, fanciful, and capricious.

Quite unreasonable is it to look for sterling originality—and unless it be such it is hardly worth having—from those who are comparatively mere novices and beginners in their art. For talent of that kind we ought to look not to *students* but to *masters*—to those whose *status* in the profession invests them with a certain degree of authority in the opinion of the public, and whose practice supplies them with opportunities of putting forth fresh ideas far more effectively than upon paper.

All that can fairly be expected from students competing for the academy medals is such indication of talent as promises well for their future career; and, in my opinion, the architectural design which has this year obtained the gold medal decidedly makes such promise, and that very forcibly. The general composition shows more than ordinary artistic feeling; it is equally noble and picturesque; nor is it deficient in new ideas, for the mode in which sculpture is introduced, where it would show itself distinctly to the eye, is one which, obvious as it is, has not yet been practised. Much ingenious contrivance is also shown in the arrangement of the interior, and in the manner of admitting light into the rooms of the lower floor, without showing any windows there externally.

Those who cannot perceive any thing particularly noticeable or praiseworthy in that design must be quite at a loss to discern any merit—I will not say in the British Museum, but in the Assize Courts at Liverpool, or, in fact, in any of the modern examples of the classical style.

ZETA.

THE OLYMPIC THEATRE, LONDON.——Mr. F. W. Bushill, Architect.

[See page 611.

ADVERTISED COMPETITIONS.

STOCKTON UNION—DRAINAGE OF TOWNS.

You will be delighted to hear, Mr. Editor, that your remarks in this matter have not been without effect: the Stockton guardians have amended their offer, and here it is:—

TO ARCHITECTS.

COMPETITION!!!

The committee are desirous of receiving designs: to the author of the one they shall consider first in merit, a premium of TEN POUNDS! will be given, with the option of acting as clerk of the works! To the second in point of merit they will present A SUIT OF NEW CLOTHES!! and the third and fourth will be allowed to contend by climbing a well-greased pole* for the prize of A LARGE LEG OF MUTTON!!!

This you will admit is far more likely to attract the eye than the one they have chosen. But, Sir, leaving them and their fellows to the contempt they deserve, is it not high time that architects should endeavour to check such proceedings as these? Already have your pages been chosen as the medium for putting forth suggestions for an organization of the profession; and I am sorry that the matter has not yet taken shape, as I think some measure of the kind must be adopted to secure fairness in this, the surest, if not the only way of raising the architectural reputation of this country,—the only way for success to the young architect without influence. Should success be accorded to any movement that may be made, it is to you, Sir, that our warmest thanks will be due for your advocacy of justice, and condemnation of unfairness in these proceedings, and for the uniform interest you have taken in the subject. Q.

* Fit emblem of a competition!

Sir,—In your useful publication of the 8th instant, I was very pleased to observe a letter, headed "Competitions advertised last week," descanting upon the paltry remuneration offered to the *successful* candidate as architect. Pray continue to draw public attention to the manner, so little likely to produce beneficial or efficient results, in which in several cases the important subject of the "drainage and sanitary improvement of provincial towns" is conducted by the local authorities.

Two examples will be sufficient to illustrate my meaning. In your paper of the 11th August last, an advertisement appeared, headed "Chippenham, Wilts," setting forth that the Commissioners of the Chippenham Improvement Act required a plan and report upon the best mode of draining the town, and the efficient discharge of such drainage into the river Avon; such plan and report to specify the courses and levels at which such drains should be made, and how far the existing drainage may be available; and they will pay a competition premium of 20*l*. for the plan and report they deem the best. It further states the commissioners are to be at liberty to act upon the plan and report approved of, at their discretion, without further payment; but they are not liable to any expense, or subject to any charge whatever, in connection with any plan or report not adopted or approved by them.

To this tempting offer I endeavoured to respond, by trying to form an association of professional men who should contribute two guineas each, towards the preliminary expenses of procuring the map and taking the levels, but even that small sum was more than (with the exception of about three) any respectable engineer or surveyor would hazard in the undertaking, and consequently I abandoned the proposition.

The second specimen, to which I would draw your attention, appeared in your paper of the 27th October, under the heading "Warwick Public Health Act." It states that a premium of 50*l*. will be awarded by the local board of health, for the best plans and specifications for the entire draining and supply of water for the town of Warwick, with an estimate of the probable cost of the same: persons competing are to furnish an entire plan of the several streets of the town, including the parishes of St. Mary and St. Nicholas; showing the direction of all intended pipes and drains, with the sizes, sections, and all other necessary details, and are to prepare sections of the several levels, and proposals for flushing the sewers, carrying off all waste water, and trapping drains; also the best method of forming the sewers and collecting the sewage manure. The whole to show a scheme of perfect drainage and an abundant supply of water. The approved plans to become the property of the corporation, on the premium being awarded and paid.

Surely, Sir, the attention of these local authorities and the public needs only to be properly directed to the subject, to convince them that no professional man of any respectability or standing would, or ought to be expected to, undertake so great an amount of work, requiring many years of previous practical and laborious experience, and present devotion of time and pecuniary outlay, upon the *chance* that his plan will be considered *the best* by the local authorities, and in that case, and in that only, to be scantily remunerated by the paltry premium offered.

But, on the other hand, it must be patent to every sensible man, that this class of advertisements will be responded to by a description of persons of whom a number are to be found at the fag end of every profession, whose only hope of success is, the certainty that, in the absence of more skilful competitors, some plan must be pronounced the best, however inefficient it may be for the purpose, and consequently entitled to the premium.

Since writing the above, another instance, more ludicrous than either of the two mentioned, has just been pointed out to me, in your paper of the 24th November, headed, "*St. Thomas the Apostle, Devon*," offering a premium of twenty guineas for the best, and five guineas for the second best design for draining that district,—the map exhibiting which is to be drawn on a scale prescribed by the General Board of Health in London. This scale, being about 40 feet to the inch, very frequently, in the case of towns of any size, requires mounted paper of the value of 4*l*. or 5*l*. to plot the map on, to say nothing of the drawing table and office, which are indispensably necessary to the accurate construction of the map. E. Ryde.

Can we be surprised at such offers as these from parties who know little or nothing of the skill and attainments required by an architect or engineer, and who daily see in the newspapers advertisements from persons who pretend to teach the whole science and practice of engineering, architecture, surveying, and a host of qualifications, in the space of six weeks, and for the sum of 10*l*.? Can we wonder, then, that while such emanations as these are constantly before our eyes, attainments should be thought so little of? Although by many those are appreciated at their true value, yet in the eyes of some, and as appears not a few, they will have the effect of bringing down the profession to a ruinously low standard? Alpha.

In the remarks made by your various correspondents relative to the conduct of those *soi-disant* architects who compete for 10*l*. premiums, and advertise their services on the *most reasonable terms*, one class has been overlooked, *i. e.* those who injure their professional brethren (if we may admit the term), by designing for builder architects, who, not satisfied with the profits arising from their own calling, avail themselves of the services of the class alluded to for further aggrandizement. You may not perhaps be aware of the extent to which this system is carried in country towns; and it is to me surprising that the parties employing these builder architects cannot see the net into which they must inevitably fall. Verily, what with engineering architects, and builder architects, the legitimate professional man has but a sorry chance in these days. It is, indeed, highly desirable that some effort should be made to raise the profession to that position which it is fully entitled to occupy in society, and, at the same time, to put an end to that degrading system of competition which is now practised.

As a constant reader of your excellent periodical, I have had much pleasure in perusing the letters of those gentlemen who have addressed themselves to the subjects above named; but there has been in all cases one fatal omission. Nothing, in these times, can be done without money. Let those who are anxious for the welldoing of the profession not only unite, but put their hands in their pockets, and subscribe towards obtaining the desired objects. There is always a difficulty in commencing an agitation of this kind. My plan would be simply this:—Let a subscription be entered into, a room in some central situation obtained, a *provisional* committee organized; let circulars be addressed to all members of the profession, calling their attention to the existing evils, and public meetings be advertised simultaneously in London, Birmingham, Liverpool, and York, or any other towns that may be thought preferable; let a series of resolutions be prepared and also circulated, with a request to each architect to express his approval, dissent, or amendment. By these means the general feeling would be obtained, and such alterations might then be made in the resolutions as would tend to meet the views of nearly all parties, and thereby ensure their unanimous adoption.

A Country Architect.

BRITISH ARCHÆOLOGICAL ASSOCIATION.

At a public meeting on December 14th, Mr. Pettigrew, V.P., in the chair, a paper from Mr. Joseph Clarke was read, giving an account of the discovery of Roman remains, on the property of Mr. Stephens, at Upham, between Winchester and Bishop's Waltham, consisting chiefly of the lower parts and foundations of walls, occupying a considerable space, the length in one direction being 120 feet. There is reason to believe that these are the remains of habitations, as coloured plaster was found adhering to the walls in many places. In a passage which was cleared to a considerable distance, were found fragments of coarse pottery, and other evidences of Roman occupation, but in no part of the space any trace of Samian ware. In the enclosures slabs of stone, of a hexagonal shape, were discovered, and from their shape, and the discovery of nails still remaining in some of them, they are supposed to have been used for roofing.

Mr. Planché read a very elaborate paper on the tilting helmet, tracing its history from the pointed and rude defence used by the Normans, through the many cylindrical and allied forms of the succeeding period, to the more elegant kind in use, during the fifteenth and sixteenth centuries, and well known in the heraldic devices of that and succeeding times. Allusion was made to several kinds of these helmets exhibited at former meetings of the association. Mr. Planché's remarks were illustrated by a long series of well-executed diagrams, drawn by Mr. C. Baily; also by plates of monumental effigies, and other standard works.

Mr. G. Wright produced some rubbings of a crowned M, and curious collar, having upon it alternately a rose, and what appears to be a letter r,—existing in an old vault, beneath Belvoir Castle, the seat of the Duke of Rutland. Mr. Planché considered the M to be placed there as the initial letter of Manners, and the r that of Roos, both of which names belonged to the families of the Earls of Rutland.

BEDFORDSHIRE—CHURCH PROGRESS.

Woburn.—The alterations here, though not all that could be wished, are improvements. The pulpit and reading pew have been removed from the very singular position they occupied, and placed in their right situations. The pews, alas! though lowered, are pens still. It is said the fastidious taste of the congregation would not hear of open sittings, though we have reason to believe that this improvement, as well as what has been effected, would have been at the expense of the noble Duke in whom the presentation is vested.

Cranfield.—The restoration here is on a bold and liberal scale; those who knew the church in its miserable state a few years ago, will hardly believe what has been done. We believe, also, that almost all has been at the expense of the reverend incumbent and his friends. No calf pens here; and painted glass has been contributed in a very handsome manner. Your readers should see it, especially country churchwardens.

Eversholt.—A very little step indeed has been taken here; the roof of one aisle has been soundly restored; why the reparation of the other was not carried out equally well we cannot explain. A crazy deal painted pulpit stuck against one of the columns has been happily removed. But the tub that has been placed nearly in its proper site is most awful, its size preposterous, and manufactured from some old mahogany, which, with its Pagan ornaments, once disfigured the east end of the chancel, which last is unhappily clogged up with some recently erected miserable closed sittings, for which there was no necessity,—owing to the difficulty with the occupants of some intrusive pews. The pulpit and reading desk, though greatly improved from their last position, are yet incorrectly located. But worse than all is an innovation on the open sittings of the humble part of the congregation, by the churchwardens appropriating two portions, and enclosing them with doors, for the gratification of private parties: it is hoped that the Archdeacon, when he comes, will "visit" them for this outrage. On cleaning the walls of Eversholt Church a mural painting was brought to light, representing St. Peter ushering into the realms of the blessed departed spirits. The churchwardens covered it up with eager haste, but fortunately a tracing of the same size was obtained, and has been preserved.

Tingrith.—By the noble spirit of the ladies of the manor and owners of the property in the village, the church has been restored in a good way. Thus you see, Sir, improvement, desperately required, is creeping on in this county.

M.

ANCIENT MORTAR.

In reply to the inquiry of "A. G." in your last number, I will observe that *ἀσβεστος*, in technical Greek, means *unslacked lime;* and I conceive it most probable that such is its meaning in the passage quoted.

Cambridge. W. W.

In reply to your correspondent, "A. G.'s" question, about the meaning of the terms *ἀσβεστος* and *οστρακον*, which are used to signify the component parts of an ancient mortar, I beg to state that the former signifies "quick lime" and the latter "pounded earthenware," two very probable materials to be mixed up in a cement, which is more than can be said of the substance now known as "asbestos." That *οστρακον* is "earthenware," and not "pounded shell," as suggested by your correspondent, is probable, first, because such is the most common signification of the word, and secondly, because we know that the ancients used earthenware (burnt earth) as an ingredient in cement. Vitruvius says (I quote Gwilt's translation), that "if to river or sea-sand potsherds ground and passed through a sieve in the proportion of one-third part, be added, the mortar will be better for use. Pavement made of this material was called *οστρακοκονια*, and by the Latins *pavimentum testaceum.* Any of your readers can satisfy themselves that the meanings given above are correct by looking out the words in Liddell and Scott's lexicon, so that, taking it for granted that "A. G.'s" translation is correct in other respects, the mortar in question was compounded of lime, pounded earthenware, and elm bark, mixed with hot water in which barley has been boiled, and it only remains for some of your practical readers to make a barley cake (*μαζα*) of this description, and see whether or not it causes stones to stick together with the strength of iron.

A. M. C.

Scarborough Independent Chapel Competition.—This was not an open competition; but a limited number of architects were selected as competitors. The plans were sent in on the 1st December, and Mr. Raffles Brown has been declared the successful architect. A correspondent, Mr. John Petch, states to us that he was expressly informed the names of competitors were to be in sealed letters, and yet that the selected design was signed by the architect and accompanied by testimonials.

THE CRYSTAL CURTAIN AT DRURY-LANE THEATRE.

The interior of old Drury was brilliantly fitted by Mr. Frederick Gye for Jullien's masked ball. The circle of chandeliers low down and beyond the central light, and the garlands of flowers suspended by butterflies, which filled the upper part of the house, produced a charming effect. What we have to notice, however, as new in decoration, and it is scarcely possible to go any where without finding something which may be usefully mentioned to our readers, is the "crystal curtain," as it was called, which fringed the upper part of the proscenium. This was formed wholly of chandelier drops, or spangles, with gas in devices behind, and when we mention that its width was 42 feet, and that it descended 16 feet at the sides and 11 feet in the middle; it will be seen that it must have swallowed up an enormous number of them. The ground-work took as nearly as possible 100 to the square foot, but adding the drapery, lines, tassels, &c., which were formed by other layers on the surface, and then the fringe, which was represented by a quantity of "lobs" as they are called, commonly used to surround wax-light lustres for chimney-pieces, the number cannot have been less than 80,000.

It seems that Mr. Gye obtained the greater number of them from Bohemia—finding they could be had cheaply there—without any precise intention, but simply with the idea that by different arrangements they might be made useful in decoration, and this was his first and very successful attempt with them.

NEW WESLEYAN CHAPEL, LIVERPOOL-ROAD, LONDON.

The chapel is erected on the angle of ground at the Islington end of the Liverpool-road, and consists, on the basement floor, of a morning chapel, 75 feet by 35 feet, and seven vestries. The whole of the ground floor of the chapel is fitted up with pews and free seats, side aisles, and communion, which, together with the side and end galleries, will accommodate 1,500 persons. The chapel measures 90 feet long by 54 feet wide. The height from floor to apex of roof is 50 feet, and the height from outside ground line to top of turret on front gable is 76 feet. We have not yet seen the building, but a correspondent has handed to us the following particulars.

The chapel is designed in the decorated style of Gothic architecture. The centre of the west front is occupied by a recessed and moulded doorway, beneath a large window, filled in its upper compartments with flowing tracery; buttresses divide the centre from the wings of this elevation, which contain a centre window, and are flanked by double angle buttresses. In the sides of the chapel are five windows, occupying spaces of equal width between buttresses; a clerestory, having the same number of windows, the walls of which, with those of the side aisles, are surmounted with a parapet pierced with trefoils and quatrefoils. The clerestory is supported by arches springing from octangular columns, with foliated capitals, over which are inserted carved corbels, from whence spring the curved ribs of the roof, with carved spandrils supporting the principal rafters. The timbers of roof are moulded on the underside and stained.

At the south-east angle of the building an octangular turret is attached, the lower portion of which serves as a staircase to side gallery, and the upper part is occupied by flues, which carry off the vitiated air from all parts of the building, the warm air being supplied from the circulation of hot water in pipes laid in the basement, and conveyed by a warm air culvert to the open space under the pew floors. Openings are made in the upright face of the steps to the pews, and covered with gauze wire, which allows the warm air to disseminate itself throughout the building. An entrance for cold air communicates with the apparatus in the basement, so that in summer it may be admitted through the same channels as the warm. Openings are left in the inner soffit of the roof, to give the vitiated air access to the space between it and the slate surface, which space is in immediate connection with the ventilating tower, containing a fire-place, that will be put in use when the peculiar state of the atmosphere needs its assistance to cause the required current of air. The walls of the chapel are built of Kentish rag-stone; and the ashlar and carvings are executed in Bath stone. Its entire cost is stated to be about 6,000*l.* It was erected from the designs of Mr. James Wilson.

BANK ARCHITECTURE.*

The proper situation of a bank is a matter of some importance. It should be situated in what is deemed the most respectable part of the town. If it be placed in an inferior locality, approachable only by narrow and disagreeable streets, and surrounded by buildings the seats of smoky and dirty trades, it is not likely to be so much frequented, nor to acquire so large a business, as though it were more pleasantly situated. Another point to be observed is, that the bank itself should be a handsome building. The necessary expenditure for this purpose is no sin against economy: it is an outlay of capital to be repaid by the profits of the business that will thus be acquired. A portion of the building will probably be set apart for the private residence of the manager, or of some other officer of the establishment: it is desirable that this portion should be entirely separated from the office. The communication should be only by a single door, of which the manager should keep the key. The building should be so constructed that what is going on in the private house, whether in the kitchen, or the nursery, or the drawing-room, should not be heard in the bank. The office being thus isolated must then be fitted up in the way that will most effectually promote the end in view; and here are three points to be considered—*space, light,* and *ventilation.*

A chief consideration is *space.* A banker should take care that his clerks have room enough to do their work comfortably. Every accountant knows that he can often work faster if he can have two or more books open at the same time; but if his space be so confined that he must shut up one book and put it away before he can use another, he will get on more slowly. The cashiers, too, will be much impeded if they are obliged to stand too close to each other, and the public will be huddled together, and will often count incorrectly the money given to them, and thus take up the cashier's time to make them right. Want of space will necessarily occasion errors, from the confusion it produces, and from one clerk being liable to interruption from the noise or vicinity of the others. A banker should therefore take care that his office is large enough for his business, and that it will admit of being enlarged in case his business should increase. Ample space is also conducive to the health of the clerks, as there will be more air to breathe, and the atmosphere is less likely to become polluted by the burning of lamps and candles.

Another consideration is *light.* It is well known in every London bank, that fewer mistakes are made by the clerks in summer than in winter. Abundance of light prevents mistakes, and saves all the time that would be employed in the discovery of errors. Light is also of great importance to the cashiers in detecting forged signatures and bad or counterfeit money. Thieves are also less likely to attempt their robberies in a light office than in a dark one. Faint or illegible handwriting can be more easily read, and hence mistakes are less likely to occur. The clerks, too, perform their duties with more quickness and cheerfulness; the gloominess of an office throws a gloom over the mind, but "light is sweet, and a pleasant thing it is for the eyes to behold the sun." The lightest part of the office should be devoted to the clerks. We have observed sometimes a violation of this principle. The entrance door has been placed in the middle of the front, with a window on each side, and the counter thrown across the room, so that the lightest part of the office has been given to the public. It is better that the entrance be placed at the right or left corner, and the counter be made to run from the window to the opposite wall; the light will thus fall lengthways on the counter, and the space behind the counter will be occupied by the clerks.

* From "Gilbart's Practical Treatise on Banking."

Ventilation.—Volumes have been written by medical men upon the advantages of fresh air, and on the unwholesome atmosphere of crowded cities. If the air that circulates in the streets of towns and cities be impure, what must be the state of those offices or rooms where twenty or thirty persons are breathing close together during the whole of the day, and gas lights are burning during the evening? In such cases we are told that a person afflicted with consumption of the lungs may communicate the complaint to others, as they must inhale a portion of the atmosphere which he has breathed out. The air in a close office is not only rendered impure by the number of people that breathe it and by the burning of gas, but it also contains very frequently particles of dust arising from the floor, through the number of people constantly walking in and out. It is almost impossible for persons so circumstanced to enjoy for a length of time even moderate health. A portion of this evil may be mitigated by a good system of ventilation. To obtain this should be regarded as an object of the first importance. If a banker do not insist upon the architect performing this in the most effectual manner, he must be content to be often put to inconvenience through the illness and consequent absence of his clerks.

ARTISANS' HOME, &c.

THE interest I feel in all that relates to the "Artisans' Home" (described and commented upon in your leader of Dec. 15), induces me to offer an idea or two as to a mode of decorating the interior of establishments of this nature, so that they might prove to be, at the same time, highly useful to all those protected under their walls, whose minds may have a tendency to artistic pursuits. In addition to the reading-room and library, but appertaining thereto, I would appropriate a well-lighted and well-ventilated room for the benefit of those individuals. Towards the upper part of the walls, and at proper distances for observation, I would place a few good casts of figures, some on revolving pedestals, their contours being relieved by a light blue coloured ground. I would also have cheap but well-executed human or other compositions or single forms, painted in *chiaro-scuro*. The lower division of the walls should be stuccoed white, with a trowelled surface (to admit of the charcoal delineations being easily effaced by a sponge), affording ample space whereon the artisan might practice, and exercise his hand and eye in drawing, whether in copying the models before him, or designing from his own fancy. The addition of this studio to the artisan's home would be a great improvement, combining with the comforts of a lodging-house the advantages of a school of design. Real, although undeveloped talent, thus exercised, would reward the operative, giving him a greater power over the materials on which he worked, and whilst it shed refinement over him and his labours, it would reflect honour upon the nation.

The task would of course be one entirely undertaken from a pure love for art, fostered by a desire on his part to raise himself to eminence. The experiment (not an expensive one) I think worth a trial, on account of the degree of emulation it might safely be predicted it would create amongst labouring men, designers of patterns, ornamentists, whom we might discover more or less belonged to the inventive race,—men, at all events, actuated with the wish not only fully to carry out, but to improve, and add a grace to, the conceptions of others,—to give satisfaction to their employers,—to deserve, by superior talents, if they cannot command, higher wages,—and to qualify themselves to become one day efficient masters and employers. F. LUSH.

PUBLIC RIGHTS AND PUBLIC HEALTH.—The "North London Anti-Enclosure and Social and Sanitary Improvement Society," are moving again in their useful work. Efforts are being made to establish "A Primrose Hill Park Library," on a respectable scale, and make other arrangements conducive to the interests of the society, which is henceforth to hold its meetings regularly on the evening of the first Monday of every month, at the Primrose Tavern, Hampstead.

Miscellanea.

INSTITUTION OF CIVIL ENGINEERS.—The annual general meeting of the Institution was held on Tuesday evening, December 18th (Mr. Field in the chair), when Mr. W. Cubitt, C.E., was elected president. Messrs. Brunel, Rendel, Simpson, and R. Stephenson, M.P., vice-presidents; J. F. Bateman, G. P. Bidder, J. Cubitt, J. E. Errington, J. Fowler, C. H. Gregory, J. Locke, M.P., I. R. M'Clean, C. May, and J. Miller, members; and J. Baxendale and L. Cubitt, associates of council. The report of the council, which was read, alluded to the past season of unexampled depression in the engineering world, but at the same time held out hopes of improvement, on account of the agitation of the subjects of better supplies of water and gas, the sewerage and drainage of towns, the construction of abattoirs, and other sanitary questions; whilst the improvement of canals, in their struggle with the railways for the heavy traffic, the construction and amelioration of harbours, the embanking and improving of rivers, the recovery of marsh-lands from the sea, and numerous other works, which had been neglected on account of the more attractive railways, would resume their former importance, and eventually afford ample employment for the majority of the members of the profession. Telford medals were presented to Lieut.-Colonel Harry D. Jones, R.E., Mr. R. B. Dockray, and Mr. J. T. Harrison; Council premiums of books to Messrs. J. T. Harrison and J. Richardson; and Telford premiums of books to Messrs. R. B. Grantham, T. R. Crampton, W. Brown, and C. B. Mansfield.

RATING OF EXETER HALL.—An appeal against an increase of charge by the parish of St. Martin's-in-the-Fields, for poor rates, from the annual rateable value of 1,500*l.* to 2,500*l.*, on the ground of the Wednesday Concert success, was heard at the Middlesex Sessions on 11th inst. Mr. Bodkin, for the appellants, stated that the proprietors of the hall were limited by their deed to the receipt of 5 per cent. on their shares, but that they had never yet reached even that. Last year the rate had been already increased, on, from 1,000*l.*, the annual rated value for seven years, to 1,500*l.*, on the ground of a little success in more frequent letting; and dread of law expense alone, he said, prevented resistance even to that increase. The rateable value has since been suddenly raised to 2,500*l.*, whereas even the *gross* revenue for the last three years had averaged only 3,382*l.*, from which must be deducted 211*l.*, on which Messrs. Daukes and Co. must pay rates. Other deductions, such as 204*l.* for gas, 150*l.* for repairs, &c., left only 2,144*l.*, from which further deductions for interest on expenditure in moveable stock, depreciations, &c., must be made, leaving 964*l.* only as the absolute rateable value. The judge decided that 2,000*l.* be the rateable value. His lordship expressed a doubt whether concerts were within the provisions of the deed of proprietorship, though education in musical science, with musical illustration, clearly was. In course of the discussion, evidence was given that the receipts had amounted in the year ending April, 1842, to 3,284*l.* odd; April, 1843, to 4,241*l.* odd; April, 1844, to 3,016*l.* odd; April, 1845, to 2,908*l.* odd; April, 1846, to 2,598*l.* odd; April, 1847, to 3,018*l.* odd; April, 1848, to 2,947*l.* odd; April, 1849, to 4,181*l.* odd.

SOHO PARK, BIRMINGHAM.—In your last paper you justly remark that the Soho Park "might be made one of the most beautiful places in England;" but, alas! the great idea in laying it out appears to have been ground rent, and a number of ill-built and ill-arranged houses have sprung up, very much to the disfigurement of what was once the most beautiful entrance into Birmingham. One portion, let to a man who, I understand, is subletting, is completely denuded of trees. On public points I think it but right you should have all practicable information: let this idea be my excuse. N.

*** We are quite aware that an error was committed at starting, land being let without the retention of sufficient control; but the management of this property is now placed in other hands, who appear to have made up their minds to conserve carefully the beauties of the place, and allow none but good houses to be built on the land.

PROJECTED WORKS.—Advertisements have been issued for tenders by 10th January, 1850, for the rebuilding and enlargement of New Castle Church, Glamorganshire; by 5th January, 1850, for the construction of a tank, filter beds, filter tunnels, service reservoir, and other works, for the Derby Water Works Company; by a date not specified, for the erection of a small block of farm buildings near Southampton; by 28th inst., for carpenters', slaters', and bricklayers' works for St. Marylebone guardians; by 27th inst., for a supply of soft melting iron for the navy, and by same date, for 350 tons of English tough cake copper for Chatham dockyard; and by 27th inst., for the construction of buildings required for the Great Western station at Banbury, and at the minor stations on the Oxford and Rugby line of railway, also for the construction of a goods shed at Thatcham, on the Berks and Hants line—separate tenders.

SIR MARC ISAMBARD BRUNEL.—This able and distinguished engineer expired on the 12th inst., at his house in St. James's-park, in the 81st year of his age. Though by birth a Frenchman, of Norman descent, his life has almost wholly been spent in England, to which he came from the United States, where he had emigrated at the height of the first French Revolution, in 1792, being Royalist in principie and in danger of his life. He was concerned in setting up the block-making machinery which has ever since been in active operation at Portsmouth for naval purposes. He was the inventor of the circular veneering saw, also still in use the same as ever. To him the manufacturing world is indebted for the elegant little machine for winding cotton thread into balls, which has so greatly extended its consumption. He invented machinery for shoemaking for the army. But the great work of the elder Brunel was the realization of the Thames Tunnel, an arduous work, with the accomplishment of which, in 1843, after nineteen years of perseverance in the midst of difficulties and reverses, his energies were literally exhausted in the advent of incipient paralysis. His work was done. He may be said to have since remained with us only to contemplate and to assure himself of the permanency of the results of his several labours. Sir M. I. Brunel will ever hold a high place amongst the engineers of England. And his geniu shas been long fully appreciated. During Lord Melbourne's administration he received the honour of knighthood. He was voted a vice-president of the Royal Society, a corresponding member of the Institute of France, and a vice-president of the Institution of Civil Engineers. He was also made a chevalier of the French Legion of Honour: so that he has died full of honours as of years.

OXFORD ARCHITECTURAL SOCIETY.—At a meeting of this society, held on the 28th ult., the report was read by Mr. Portal, B.A., secretary, which stated that since the last meeting an application had been made by Mr. Floke, P.P., of Plymstock, near Plymouth, *for a design for stalls*, which he proposed to place in his chancel. A pen and ink sketch of a stall had been forwarded to him by Mr. Wilmot, secretary, and also one of the society's sheets of bench ends, by the aid of which it was hoped he would be able to carry out his plan. Surely this is a step out of the province of the society. Mr. Portal then read a paper "On the use of screens in churches."

LEAD-SHOT TOWERS.—Mr. D. Smith, of New York, lead manufacturer, claims for patent the application of an ascending artificial current of air to a descending current of metal in the manufacture of leaden shot. This he proposes to effect by employing a tower shaped at top like a funnel and at bottom like a truncated cone, with an annular hollow vessel resting on a reservoir of water at the bottom. The annular pouring vessel is to be perforated with holes at top, through which an artificial current of air is to be forced up the tower by a fan or other blowing machine. The metal falls through the hollow centre of the annular vessel into the water reservoir, which is furnished with a shoot to conduct the metal to a suitable receptable. Or, the artificial current may be created by exhausting from the top of the tower, and allowing the air to flow in at bottom, in which case the hollow annular vessel will be dispensed with.

GAS.—A tremendous explosion took place at the Sheffield workhouse, on Saturday last, with extensive damage to the building throughout. Some account of the origin of the accident, as described in the local *Times*, may be instructive, from the warning it conveys. The committee room is lighted by a sliding pendant attached to the ceiling. The vertical tube is filled with water to prevent escape of gas, and ought to be kept full, otherwise when drawn down there is an escape of gas. The office cleaner, when she lighted the gas, drew this pendant quite down, and, the water being deficient, the consequence was a copious escape of gas, which accumulated at the top of the room till it reached the gaslight below, and then exploded. The climax was most probably expedited by the admission of atmospheric air at the moment, the woman having just opened the room door. The best mode of detecting a deficiency of water in a sliding pendant is, once every three months or so to draw the slide quite down. A bubbling noise occasioned by the air in the lower part of the tube ascending through the water is a sure sign of danger from want of water. A lead gas-pipe, extending between the floor of the board-room and the ceiling of the committee-room was also found slit on one side, and it is suspected that an escape of gas had been going on there for some time. If so, the space beneath the floor of the ceiling would probably be full of gas, ready to ignite the moment that the explosion took place. Had the pipe not been enclosed, the smell of the escaping gas would have given timely warning of the leakage. This disaster, following on the alarming explosion in the vegetable market in this town, and the destructive explosion at Masbrough, ought to induce habits of greater caution and circumspection among consumers of gas generally. Parties competent to form an opinion thought that the necessary repairs to the workhouse could not cost less than a hundred pounds.——The spirits of light and darkness, says *Felix Farley*, are struggling at Taunton, in the shape of gas and anti-gas partisans. This populous town was again left on Tuesday night in a state of utter darkness; our public functionaries having failed to effect an arrangement to obviate this dangerous annoyance.——A deficiency of gas is also complained of at Newcastle and Gateshead, where there is often a scarcity of coals (!), as we once more particularly explained to our readers. In the present instance, however, mere annoyance to the consumers is alleged to be the cause of the deficiency. The complaint, according to the *Gateshead Observer*, is very general throughout both towns, and a rival establishment is threatened.——In Hartlepool, says a contemporary, 6s. 8d. per 1,000 feet is charged to private consumers, whilst at Durham the price is from 3s. to 4s., according to quantity, and at Sunderland, 4s. net. The gas consumers at Hartlepool are endeavouring to effect a reduction to the Durham rates.——The lecturing campaign is recommencing. At the Portsmouth Athenæum, on Monday last, Mr. G. Garnett addressed an assemblage of gas consumers and others on the subject of gas-light, when he "took the opportunity," says the *Hants Independent*, "of explaining and demonstrating the misapprehension existing as to the interest of the gas manufacturers being the supplying of an inferior article at an exorbitant price, and endeavoured to prove on the contrary that it was the interest of the latter to supply the very best article at the lowest possible price—for by doing so alone could the manufacturer hope for an increased demand."

THE BIRMINGHAM EXPOSITION OF MANUFACTURES AND ART has closed. During the last week the rooms were visited by nearly 19,000 persons, and the total number of visiters since the commencement exceeds 100,000. The receipts have been about 3,065*l*. There will, doubtless, after payment of all expenses, be a handsome surplus; and we again express a hope, in which we are joined, we see, by the local press, that it may be devoted to the establishment, in the shape of a Museum of Art, of a permanent and classified Exposition of Birmingham Manufactures.

BUILDERS' BENEVOLENT INSTITUTION.—It has been determined by the directors of this Institution, to have a second anniversary ball in aid of their funds, and a committee has been appointed to obtain stewards, and make other arrangements.

A GATESHEAD CONTRIBUTION TO A TURKISH MOSQUE.—When Mr. W. L. Harle was discoursing of "progression and improvement," before Salih Effendi and the Gateshead Mechanics' Institute, and Mr. Wornum was dilating in the lecture-room of the Lit. and Phil. on the magnificence of the mosque of Amrou, few were aware that we had "cunning workmen in brass" employed on the Tyne in the construction of a gas-chandelier for a Turkish mosque in Constantinople. Mr. Thomas Crawford, of the Walker ironworks, acting on behalf of his brother, Mr. James Crawford, of Beshicktash, Constantinople, now manager of the gas-works in the Turkish capital, lately handed the order for it to Messrs. Abbot and Co., of Gateshead Park ironworks. We have seen it lighted up, with its twelve lamps of ground glass, and think that our Mahomedan brethren will agree with us that it does credit to old Gateshead. The circle on which the lights are fixed is 8 feet in diameter. The dome of the mosque rises 65 feet from the floor, and the diameter is 40 feet. In accordance with instructions, the design is plain, yet elegant. The material is brass, French-bronzed. The ornamental work consists wholly of foliage. Crosses or glass drops—figure of man or beast—Messrs. Abbot were forbidden to introduce. Additional burners and glasses are to be sent, with several yards of caoutchouc or gutta percha tubes (another illustration of "progression and improvement")—from which we may infer that moveable lights are wanted. Thus, then, not only in the Gateshead Mechanics' Institute, but also in the mosques of the East, the sons of men have emerged from the obscurity of "tallow candles" into "gas and grandeur."—*Gateshead Observer.*

AN IRISH ECCLESIOLOGICAL SOCIETY has been established. The president is the Rev. Charles W. Russell, D.D., Maynooth; and Lords Bellew and Arundel and Surrey, Sir W. Lyons, and several of the prelates and priesthood, and other members of the Roman Catholic Church, have joined the society. At the opening of its proceedings, the president gave an inaugural address in which, speaking of its object and design, he said, "To regulate the true principles of Christian Art, especially in the building and decoration of churches, is the object of the science of ecclesiology. For though in its more limited application, and in the more strictly technical sense of the name, it might seem to be confined to one particular department, that of architecture, it is understood, nevertheless, to embrace all that relates to the externals of religion, and to comprise not alone architecture, but also painting, sculpture, church decoration, ecclesiastical costume, glass-staining, music, engraving, illuminations, and some ornamental typography in adaptation of sacred uses. Such, I may add, are the objects to which our society proposea to devote its humble labours." *The Amateur* is of opinion that in Ireland "there is ample room and verge for several such societies, each suited to the religious temperature of their respective communions, but all tending to encourage a closer connection of art with Christianity, and thus raising it to the highest purposes of its mission, as an element in the service of the Creator, and leading the mind to the highest and holiest thoughts."

THE BRISTOL AND WEST OF ENGLAND ARCHITECTURAL SOCIETY, held a general meeting on the 10th inst., the Archdeacon of Bristol, in the chair, when the secretary, the Rev. E. J. Carter, read the minutes of the previous meeting, and after some formal business, the Rev. Mr. Ellacombe communicated a paper on Church Bells and Belfrys, in which he went into their origin, and exhibited various illustrations of the large bells of some of the principal churches in England and on the Continent. His remarks were also illustrated by the model of a church bell. Mr. Ellacombe discountenanced the popular supposition respecting the baptism of bells, and thought the water used at the time of their being put up was merely for the purpose of washing them. He thought the ceremony used, which he had with him, implied merely a benedictive consecration. He afterwards went into some interesting particulars respecting the weights of the various large bells in Europe and the manner of fixing and ringing them, and also enlarged upon the subject of peal ringing as practised in England. He then read some remarks on bell-ringers and their conduct, which he was sorry to say was very bad, and he thought ought to be brought under the notice of the authorities.

THE METROPOLITAN COMMISSION OF SEWERS had meetings on Friday and Saturday last, at which the only public business done consisted in the dismissal of Mr. Hale, C.E., an officer of the court, for allowing an article, headed "Experiments on the discharge of Water through Pipes," to appear in the pages of a contemporary before the commissioners had had an opportunity of considering the same, or the results of the same experiments, which had been instituted at the expense and order of the commission. The court then formed itself into a committee (at which the majority of the city representatives were present) "to consider the course to be adopted respecting the plans sent in to the commissioners for the drainage of the metropolis."

THE LIVERPOOL ARCHITECTURAL SOCIETY.—The fortnightly meeting of this society was held on Wednesday evening, last week; Mr. J. A. Picton occupying the chair. The architectural designs for the student's prize were suspended on the walls. Mr. Reed, the secretary, exhibited a model, and made some observations as to the method of deafening floors adopted by Fox and Barrett. Mr. Howard offered some remarks on decoration, the laws of proportion, and the various styles of ornamenting in general use.

MARSDEN'S STENCH TRAP.—This trap is so constructed that it is always shut, and it will carry off any dirt or rubbish which may fall through the grating over it. It consists mainly of a cylinder, divided into four chambers, which turns on a pivot below the receiver, and is made air-tight by means of vulcanized India rubber. On receiving water from above, the cylinder revolves, bringing beneath the receiver another division, and emptying the first. The inventor suggests that, by means of a stream of water and a pipe from the gulley-hole to the top of an adjoining house, the cylinder, in revolving, would serve to ventilate the sewer.

MR. ROBERT STEPHENSON, the engineer, has been made a Knight of the Order of the Legion of Honour.

STEALING FROM THE VATICAN.—A great sensation has been caused in Rome by the discovery that no less than 137 valuable medals have been stolen out of the museum of the Vatican. Some of these medals were of great rarity, and their loss is a public misfortune.

RAILWAY JOTTINGS.—The springing of some arches was observed on Tuesday week, at the new station, at Liverpool, of the Lancashire and Yorkshire and East Lancashire Company. The pressure of a heavy wall, by which they are surmounted, is blamed. Balk timbers were immediately prepared, and applied as buttresses to the wall and centres to the arches, and the wall itself is in course of renewal.——A contractor for excursion trains has announced his intention of taking passengers, "first-class travelling at less than a halfpenny a mile, and second-class for about a farthing." From Leeds to Birmingham, 238 miles, the fare is to be—first-class, 8s. 6d., and second-class, 5s. 6d., allowing six hours in Birmingham, or the privilege of returning on the following day for an extra shilling. At the ordinary rates of travelling, the journey could not be accomplished for less than between 3*l*. and 4*l*., and at a penny a-mile, would amount to a few pence short of 1*l*.——The new directors of the York, Newcastle, and Berwick Railway have adopted the principle of public competition, in the appointment of three general managers; one for passenger-traffic, at 500*l*. per annum; a second, for mineral traffic, at 400*l*.; and a third, for merchandise, at 400*l*., each manager's salary to be increased *pari passu* with the Company's profits.——The masonry of the piers in the bridge across the Tweed, at Berwick, was completed on Thursday week by Messrs. J. Graham and G. Storrar, sub-contractors, under Messrs. M'Kay and Co.——The remarkable feat of effecting a communication between London and Paris in eight-and-a-half hours, has been accomplished. The *Times* of Tuesday week was delivered in Paris at half-past one p.m., along with the Paris intelligence of Monday.

No. CCCLX.

SATURDAY, DECEMBER 29, 1849.

 UR seventh volume is closed to-day, and we avail ourselves of the licence afforded on such occasions, to blow egotistically a quiet flourish of very small trumpets in reviewing briefly its contents,—while we express, in less measured tone, our thanks to friends and assistants, and appeal earnestly to all our readers for their kind consideration, sympathy, and support. We may again say, without fear of contradiction, as in former years, that we have kept our promise to improve, and that the present volume is far better than any of the preceding volumes. That it contains a great amount of instructive and pleasant reading,—has given early and correct information on all matters interesting to its varied classes of readers, and is illustrated by a large number of excellent engravings, none can deny: that it has been conducted with honesty, fearlessness, and an anxious desire to spread as much knowledge and effect as much good as came within our means, we unhesitatingly assert. To advance the art of Architecture and the science of Building,—to improve the position of architects and other artists,—to give the earliest intimation of matters interesting to builders, and afford them the means of communicating with the public,—to raise the character of our operatives, urging upon them the value of true education, whereby man is

——— " Made quick to recognise
The moral properties and scope of things,"

—to show employers, whether of the architect, the contractor, or the workmen, that they have *duties* as well as *rights*,—and further, to remove feelings of antagonism existing between classes, and to bring them together as mutually connected and dependent,—assisting and assisted, —portions of a great brotherhood,—have been to us objects of anxious and unceasing desire. If to be earnest in striving, as Humboldt says, is to have half achieved our purpose, we have done something; and it will not be our own fault if we do not, hereafter, effect more.

The artist, the man of creative mind, does not receive that consideration in England to which he is justly entitled. But the true artist who finds in the exercise of his art—the discharge of his duty—his best reward, will not be discouraged by this. Remember Wordsworth's sonnet to Haydon :—

" High is our calling, Friend ! Creative art
(Whether the instrument of words she use,
Or pencil pregnant with ethereal hues),
Demands the service of a mind and heart
Heroically fashioned.—to inruse
Faith in the whispers of the lonely muse,
While the whole world seems adverse to desert.''

And yet it is these minds which, in truth, form and rule the world. " All revolutions," says a modern writer, " are begun in the higher regions of thought. It was no idle fable of the ancient world, that all great eras on earth were heralded by commotions in the aerial world, portents and prodigies in the heavens, gleaming squadrons of celestial combatants, and all the shock and thunder of celestial war. Literature is the heaven of society; and there, high up in its serener regions, where earth's poets and prophets

dwell, the battle is fought and decided, before practical men on earth begin to brace themselves for the war.''

The great architect is an artist and something more; he expresses his ideas in stone, and his works affect society, and influence the mind and feeling of the times, much more powerfully than is thought for.

Let him have honour in the degree of his power.

The architect holds just now but a poor place in public opinion, and the profession have themselves, in a great measure, to thank for it. At one time a poet felt obliged to say, that,—

" When a stately pile we raise,
You never hear the workman's praise,
Who used the lime and worked the stones,
But all give praise to Inigo Jones.''

Now, however, both workman and architect are in the same position. When a church is consecrated, a theatre opened, alms-houses inaugurated, or a new school finished, the " liberal proprietor," or " active committeeman," who *gives the breakfast*, stands a much better chance of being named to the world next morning than he who, with thought and labour (more or less, it must be admitted), has imagined and carried out the structure. This, with its remedy, however, is too large a subject to be treated here, and is carrying us away from our purpose. Suffice it at this moment that we remind our brother architects that much rests with ourselves, and that " God helps those who help themselves.'' If we cannot command success, we may deserve it. Before the public will respect architects, architects must respect themselves.

In the present volume we have set before our readers a considerable number of new buildings; we will venture to rehearse the principal amongst them :—Sir B. Heywood's Bank, Manchester, by Mr. Gregan ; the Liverpool Branch Bank of England, by Mr. Cockerell ; the New Hall, Pembroke College, Oxford, by Mr. Hayward ; the Lime-street Station, Liverpool, by Mr. Tite ; the Cavendish-street Schools, Manchester, by Mr. Walters ; St. Barnabas's College, Pimlico, by Messrs. Cundy ; a Park Lodge, at Streatham, by Mr. Roumieu ; the Dispensary, Cleveland-place, Bath ; St. George's Hall, Liverpool, by Mr. Elmes ; the British Museum, by Sir Robert Smirke ; the New Gaol, Boston, U. S., by Mr. Bryant ; the Great Hall, Euston Station, and the General Meeting Room, by Mr. Hardwick ; the Roman Catholic Church, Farm-street, London, by Mr. Scoles ; the Printers' Alms-houses, by Mr. W. Webb ; St. Mary's, West Brompton, by the Editor ; Free Schools, Yarmouth, by Messrs. Brown and Kerr ; St. Paul's Church, Derby, by Messrs. Barry and Brown ; Model Houses, Bloomsbury, by Mr. Roberts ; the City of London Workhouse, by Mr. R. Tress ; the Roman Catholic Church, at Greenwich, by Mr. Wardell ; a French Riding School ; Schools in St. Martin's-in-the-Fields, London, by Mr. Wild ; the Interior of the London Coal Exchange, by Mr. Bunning ; the Strasbourg Railway Station, Paris, by Mons. Duquesneit ; Mr. Hope's Mansion, Piccadilly, by Messrs. Dusillion and Donaldson ; the Custom House at Rouen, by M. Isabelle ; the Artisans' Home, by Mr. Beck ; St. John's, Antigua, by Mr. Fuller ; and the Olympic Theatre, London, by Mr. F. W. Bushill.

Amongst the examples of ancient art, will be found the North Porch of Redcliffe Church, Bristol ; an Altar Tomb, Exeter Cathedral ; Greensted Church, Essex ; the Palazzo Rezzonico, Venice ; Bishop Alcock's Chapel, Ely

Cathedral ; the House of François Premier, Paris ; Roslin Chapel, Edinburgh ; the Farnesian Gardens, Rome; Stoke Gregory Church; the East-end of Lincoln Cathedral ; Montacute House ; Open Roof, Ware Priory ; the North Porch of Salisbury Cathedral ; the Chapter House, Chester : Bradenstoke Priory, Wilts ; Romsey Abbey Church ; Southwell Minster ; the Cathedral of Andernach ; the Stone Pulpit at Chester; the Tomb of the Bonzi Family, at Rome ; St. Mary's Church, Guildford; the Hall at Bowood; St. Dunstan's-in-the-East ; the Altar Screen in St. Alban's Abbey ; the *Chateau Gaillon*, Paris, and others. We may also mention a valuable series of suggestive details and decorations from Rome, Bologna, Parma, Venice, Catania, and other places abroad.

In the letter-press will be found essays on the position of Architects ; the better administration of Competitions ; professional Remuneration ; Fire-proof Floors ; on the importance of a knowledge of the Principles of Art ; on the Condition of Workmen now and in earlier times ; the History of Ecclesiastical Architecture in England ; Sir Balthazar Gerbier's " Counsel to all Builders ;" on Internal Ecclesiastical Decoration ; on Monumental Architecture ; Mr. Cockerell's last series of Lectures (no where else reported so far as we know) ; additional papers on Caen Stone; on the Rights and Responsibilities of Architects ; on the Cure of Damp ; the Topography of Jerusalem ; on Laundry Drying-closets ; on Roman Architecture ; Gas Reform ; on the use of Hollow Bricks ; on the Metals used in Building ; Notes in Italy ; on the Architectural Advantages and Deficiences of London ; the Improvement of the Working Classes ; on the Building Materials employed in Paris ; on the London Fever-stills, called graveyards and vaults ; the History of the Pointed Arch ; on the Principles of Architectural Effect in reference to streets ; on the cônnection of the Greek Doric and Egyptian Architecture ; London ; the Drainage of London ; on Style in Architecture ; the Pottery and iron Floors of France ; on Chester and Chester Cathedral ; on Salisbury Cathedral ; on the Arrangement of Colours in Decorative Art ; on the Removal of Smithfield Market ; on other sanitary arrangements ; on the Basilicas of Christian Rome ; a Week in Birmingham ; Tidal Observations in the River Thames ; on the State and Prospects of Architecture ; the Formation of Roads ; Decorative Art in Glass ; Water Supply ; on Civil Engineering ; on the Air Syphon, and on many other subjects, besides exclusive reports of the proceedings at the Institute of Architects ; the Metropolitan Sewers Commission ; Mr. Wornum's Lectures on Art, at the School of Design ; Awards of the Official Referees ; and the proceedings at meetings held with a view to the establishment of a Provident Institution for Building Operatives,—an important movement, to which we would give all the aid in our power.

In the ensuing year no efforts will be wanting on our part to render THE BUILDER still more worthy of the countenance which has been given to it : of our views and intentions in this respect we shall speak next week. We have now but to reiterate our warm thanks for friendly offices rendered, and our earnest appeal for renewed co-operation. In our good intentions we ask belief, and for our short-comings we solicit the kind consideration of all our readers,

GEORGE GODWIN.

HOUSES FOR THE VERY POOR.

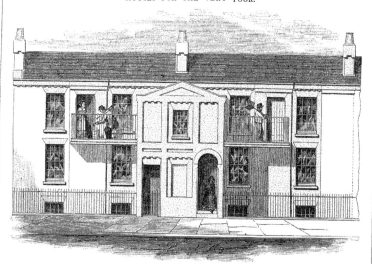

ELEVATION.

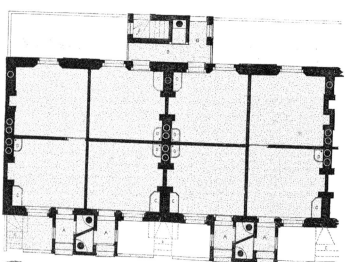

GROUND PLAN.

SIZE OF ROOMS, 11 FEET 6 INCHES BY 10 FEET 6 INCHES.

B B Entrance and Balcony.   C Cupboards.   D Sinks.   E Steps to Basement Floor.   f Steps to Top Rooms.

A DESIGN FOR BUILDING HOUSES FOR THE POOR.

At a time of the year when every man's hearth is, or is supposed to be, surrounded by his family, and where good cheer should prevail, although in thousands of instances the very reverse is the case, I may presume that any thing that has a tendency to improve those wretched dens (for they are entitled to no other appellation) of the poor will not be unacceptable, for in looking at their deplorable dwellings one cannot be surprised at their equally miserable and squalid appearance, since in many cases a whole family of five or six, and too frequently children grown up, of both sexes, are crowded together in one room, and in thousands of cases two or three families have joint occupation, by being located in the corners of one small room. Upon an average, where the poor reside, six or seven families occupy one small house—using one front door, one passage, one staircase, one small yard, and one privy. Thus the quiet and the noisy, the industrious and the lazy, the sober and intemperate, the virtuous and the licentious, the honest and the dishonest, the clean and the slovenly, are indiscriminately huddled together, and so, from constant intercommunication, the good can hardly fail soon to acquire the habits and imbibe the principles of the bad. There is usually very inadequate supply of water, for an hour or less only three times a-week, to a small butt in the yard, open at the top at all times and seasons, and probably not cleaned out once in a year, and therefore receiving a constant increase of mud, slime, and rubbish, full of insects, blacks and filth from the houses, from which the water is taken for all domestic purposes ; the back yard a receptacle for all kinds of refuse, filth, and damp, besides a constant pestilential odour escaping from the cesspool and privy, placed near and in sight of the windows, so that it cannot be resorted to in private. Every drop of water used throughout the house has to be carried up one, two, or three flights of stairs, and together with every description of dirt, is returned by the same route. With all these evils to contend against, it becomes well nigh impossible for the occupants to keep themselves either clean, in health, or free from the contaminating influence of the evil by which they are surrounded, and without any means being provided for the admission of fresh air, or the escape of the foul, from the rooms.

Looking at all the accumulated evils to which the inmates of these wretched houses are exposed, one cannot be astonished at their seeking comfort in the gin palace, the public house, or crowding together in the street, or elsewhere ; whereas, if they had well drained, well ventilated, and comfortable houses, where they could meet and sleep in comfort, without being disturbed by their noisy neighbours or vermin, they would take a pride in what they now loathe ; during their day's toil they would be buoyed up with the thought that at the end of their labour they had a home where they could rest in peace and comfort.

Any further dissertation would be superfluous, since it must be obvious to the most casual observer, that dwellings of that loathsome description, can be but little better than hot-beds for every sort of vice, crime, and misery. The good effects of our many institutions, which have in view the amelioration of the poor, are far outbalanced by the evils attendant on this system of indiscriminate crowding together. As a remedy, it is proposed to build houses on an entirely new arrangement (as shown in the accompanying plans), by which the poor man's comforts would be increased, his energies roused, and his whole moral character elevated in a greater degree than can be at present by our charitable institutions—good and numerous as they are.

To give a full description of their construction would occupy too great a space here ; the full particulars have been already published in a pamphlet, a copy of which I shall be most happy to furnish to any one desirous of carrying some of the designs out ; they can be built in single blocks of 24 rooms each (which would be equal to four six-roomed houses), with a street front and back, so as to have them thrown quite open on both sides. On the parlour floor would be arranged the single rooms, four to each block, and ten pair of

double rooms ; they would be of a uniform size of 11 feet 6 inches by 10 feet 6 inches, and 8 feet 6 inches high, from floor to ceiling. I purpose letting the double rooms at 2s. 6d., and the single at 1s. 6d. per week, and at those very low rates they would pay from 7 to 8 per cent. for the outlay, which of course would be reduced by the rates and taxes, and the expense in collecting the rents.

In arranging these plans, the great object has been to bring two rooms within the reach of the poor man, and to separate the families as much as possible, in order to do away with the present system, which is so very objectionable, and so injurious to morals, health, and comfort, where so many families are crowding in and out of one door, up and down over one staircase,—where constant disputes and contentions of every sort must take place ; and to ensure, as much as practicable without incurring a great expense, a thorough ventilation, by throwing the houses open front and back, which is in a great measure achieved, and means provided for the constant admission of fresh air to the rooms, and a free passage for the escape of all noxious gases. In throwing the houses open front and back, the whole of the exterior will be open to the inspection of the passers by, which will tend to do away with all secret corners of filth for breeding disease, &c., which are not all the advantages to be derived by this mode of building, as space is economized to a very considerable extent ; for equal to 17 six roomed houses can be built on an acre of ground more by this plan of building than can be by the present system.

It is hoped that by this description, however imperfect, the advantages and comforts arising from the proposed system of building houses for the very poor labouring classes, compared with the old, will be plainly seen. To provide such for them would be like taking a man from the mire, and placing him where he can stand in safety, ease, and comfort, and without the fear of being molested,—where he can have free ingress and egress without being in any way interfered with,—where he will be enabled to make and call his two rooms his castle, and have the comforts of a clean and healthy home, without being obliged to associate against his inclination with those he is surrounded by,—and that at a rent within the compass of his means.*

ROBERT NETHERWAY.

RECOLLECTIONS OF PETER NICHOLSON.

ABOUT the year 1812, Peter Nicholson called at my house in Wells-street, Cavendish-square, where I kept an architectural drawing-school, and without mentioning his name, said he wanted to place his son with me, and wished to see some of my copies on carpentry, which I showed him. In the course of conversation on the good and bad construction of roofs (for we had both, like Inigo Jones, originally been brought up to the building business), he alluded to the roof of Islington Church, which he said he once drew ; and on my asking him what induced him to do it after its defects had been pointed out by Peter Nicholson, in his "Carpenters' New Guide," he said he was Peter Nicholson himself ! and bluntly apologized for not having mentioned his name at first. On this announcement, I said, Then your son (Michael Angelo, for that was his name) does not need my instructions: he said, Yes he does, and I am desirous of becoming acquainted with you ; and here our intimacy began.

He now informed me he was come to London to draw some plates for Dr. Rees' Cyclopedia, and to arrange with the publisher, Barfield, of Wardour-street, for a MS. Architectural Dictionary, which he had sold him. This work, he observed, was to have been a joint production between himself and a person of the name of Webster (whom I knew), but he had contributed no materials towards it. Webster had originally drawn the ornaments for Nicholson's "Principles of Architecture," published by Gardner, of Princes-street, Cavendish-square. He left the MS. of the Dictionary with me to look over, or as much as he

had then written, to add whatever words I found had been omitted, even provincialisms, which were very numerous. The plan of the work I at once saw had evidently been suggested by that of Sheraton's folio Cabinet Dictionary, or rather Encyclopædia, which had been published a short time before.

Mr. Nicholson now became an inmate and boarder in my house, for some months, where he drew many of his plates for the above works, which were devised in the day-school. Here we often exercised each other in the solution of architectural diagrams, both theoretically and practically, for the mutual benefit of each other, some of which diagrams were afterwards published.

The following question in perspective was proposed by me :—As it is generally allowed that twice the width of the picture is the best distance for the point of view, how is this distance to be ascertained ? P. N.'s answer : Let S, on Fig. 1, be the seat of a house,

Fig. 1.

LL the line of the picture ; on this line form the isosceles triangle, AAB, making DB equal to twice the width of AA, then draw the two extreme visual rays, CCP, parallel to the two sides of the isosceles triangle, and the object sought will be obtained, EE being once the width of the picture, and OP that of twice.

The following question in perspective was proposed by one of my pupils, Clarke Rampling, now an architect and surveyor at Birkenhead :—I want, says he, to ascertain the distance of the vanishing points of a building on the plan, when I am prevented by the narrowness of the drawing-board, without adding an additional piece of board or a book on each side. My reply : Let BBBB be the size of the drawing-board (Fig. 2), S the seat of the

Fig. 2.

house, P the station point, and LL the line of projection ; divide the direct visual ray, P 2 into two equal divisions ; draw the line 1N parallel to the right hand side of the plan, and 2N will be half the distance of the vanishing point V. If the left hand side be divided into the like number, or in three or more divisions, it will show the operation very clearly.—Q. E. D.

Proceeding with my narrative : At this time (from the beginning) alluding to Nicholson's first publication, that of the "Carpenters' New Guide," which title, it appears, was given to the work on the following occasion : William Paine was at this time publishing a work on carpentry, called, "The Carpenters' Guide," on which Nicholson was rather severe in his animadversions, wishing to have the field to himself, for he never could bear a rival. In the "Carpenters' New Guide" he first offered a method of springing the mahogany plank, as it was termed, but more properly canting the plank on its edge, when finding the face moulds for cutting out the band-rail of a staircase, so as to save wood. The former method had required the plank of mahogany to be 3 inches thick ; it now required to be but 2¼ inches. What gave rise to it was this : Graham, a celebrated staircase-hand at this time called on Nicholson one afternoon, when publishing his "Carpenters' New Guide," and told him there was no doubt if the plank was turned on its edge, in a way shown, there would be a great saving of wood by a thinner plank. This struck Nicholson as being practical, and the next morning the lines were devised, laid down, and presented to Graham. Of this circumstance I was informed by Nicholson and Graham themselves.

The work entitled, "The Joiners' Assistant," which followed, Nicholson informed me, owed its existence to the following circumstance. He had, he said, involved himself in debt during the publication of the "Carpenters' New Guide," and was thrown into prison in consequence. To extricate himself from "durance vile," he applied to the late Mr. Taylor, the architectural publisher and bookseller, in Holborn, who promised to pay the debt on his engaging to publish "The Joiners' Assistant," which he did, and was again set at liberty.

The small octavo work on the "Five Orders of Architecture," a useful didactic production, published by Taylor, soon after followed.

The next work he brought out was what he has called the "Principles of Architecture," in three octavo volumes. The first contains geometry and mensuration—the second, ornaments and rules for projecting shadows, which latter appears to have been suggested by Thomas Malton's work on "Perspective:"—the third contains examples of the orders of architecture, from Desgodetz, a French author, and Stuart, an English one, which latter threatened to punish both author and publishers, Byfield and Gardner, for plagiarisms. Soon after the completion of this work Peter Nicholson left London in embarrassed circumstances for his native city, Glasgow, where he commenced as an architect with a person of the name of Reed, to whom he left the concern some years after, and again started for London.

During the time he was at my house the late Thomas Telford, the eminent engineer, wrote P. Nicholson a letter from Carlisle, saying he did not know his circumstances, but that he had recommended him to the magistrates as the fittest person for the architect and surveyorship of the county of Carlisle, at a salary of 300*l.* a-year, as the place was then vacant. Nicholson advised with me on the subject, and I recommended him to accept it, which he did. He held it but a short time before he was supplanted by another person, for what reason must remain a secret. He now again returned to London, and set up an architectural drawing-school in Oxford-street, and commenced the publication of his "Architectural Dictionary," which came out in 7s. parts. The copyright he had sold to Barfield, the publisher, in Wardour-street. After the Dictionary was completed he engaged with Mr. Kelly, the publisher and bookseller in Paternoster-row, for the publication of the "Practical Builder," which work Mr. Kelly himself suggested, and in which he wished to have incorporated some of the plates of "Carter's Architectural Work," which he had by him in two thick quarto volumes. This is the best of Peter Nicholson's works, as he has here embodied all that was valuable in his former publications, most of which were transcripts.

Although Nicholson had bound himself not to take any of the plates from the "Architectural Dictionary" for any other publication (which he was too much in the habit of doing), he bere violated his agreement, and a Chancery suit was the consequence, brought on by Mr. Byfield against Nicholson and Kelly. Mr. Kelly, who made affidavit that he was ignorant of the plagiarisms, was obliged to discontinue Nicholson's name to his work, and Nicholson suffered severely in pocket from the law suit.

The last time I saw Peter Nicholson was in Holborn, much depressed in spirits, when he told me he was going to leave London for Northumberland, to lay out some building-ground which had been purchased by his brother-in-law, and that he was going to conduct the erection of the buildings. How long he was engaged there I am unable to say; however, he afterwards removed to Carlisle, where I have been informed he became a co-partner with a schoolmaster, and there ended his days some years back. Since this his son, Michael Angelo Nicholson, who had been keeping an architectural drawing-school in Euston-crescent, New-road, in London, has died also.

Nicholson in his person was rather large and strong made, and well calculated for enduring fatigue. He was not acute nor ready of conception, being always absorbed in thought. He seemed dull at first, but never ceased his inquiries with those persons who had discovered something in mechanics which he did not know; but whenever he understood it, he never afterwards lost sight of it, and by publishing these discoveries made them his own. Some of his works were formed by this means, and the remainder was the result of labour and intense application. Sundays and week-days were alike to him. "There is no rest to the wicked," he often used to say, "and that he had always gone to work in his studies like a blacksmith on his anvil." Nicholson had no taste for a grand or fine building as a whole; which is evident to the meanest capacity if they will but inspect those designs in his Architectural Dictionary, under the head of House. Nor did he understand the different styles of architecture, or he would not have introduced a heterogeneous compound church of his son Michael Angelo's design into Kelly's work, which he there describes as being in the Grecian style, the same having a polygonal spire on a tower, which spire is of the Plantagenet period. Construction of the anatomical parts of a building was Nicholson's forte; he was a good mechanic and mathematician, but an indifferent architect; he introduced too much geometry into those of his best works, and his lines for tracing the face moulds for the hand-rails of staircases are unnecessarily crowded. Staircase-work he much delighted in, which he has developed in every possible form, and on this improvement in joinery his fame mainly depends; but there is much yet in staircase-work for the young operative mechanic to learn, which is well known to those who are now practising in the large builders' shops in London, Manchester, Liverpool, and Leeds.

As objects of invention are objects of our regard, I shall, in concluding this characteristic sketch, observe, that the method of forming the riser of the curtail step, by Peter Nicholson, now in general use, he copied, by request, from a school-drawing of mine, which he has since published in his works on stairs, and also another of mine, showing how, by a simple method, the scroll of the hand-rail may be increased or diminished in the revolutions, both without either my consent or his acknowledgment.

Queen's-buildings. R. Brown.

THE STANDING OF ARCHITECTS.

Various suggestions have been made in the columns of The Builder" to regulate the management of competitions. It has been proposed to bind architects down not to send designs where the premium offered was so miserably inadequate, or where the free action of the architect was so restricted and hampered, as is but too often the case. A question has been raised, too, as to architects being diplomaed. Now, from these several points, it is evident that there is a very general feeling amongst architects to elevate the standard of the profession—to stamp architecture as a gentlemanly calling. At the same time, it is more than questionable that the means proposed will conduce to that end. One thing seems to be quite certain—all idea of coercion must be completely and entirely abandoned. Instead, Mr. Editor, of architects thinking it necessary to write dissuasive letters for your columns, on the announcement of competitions, it should be taken for granted that the profession will not be content to throw away their time and money upon the bare chance of obtaining a slender premium, or upon terms that would derogate from the dignity and self-respect of gentlemen. At all events, if they are disposed to do so, in pity's name let them.

That a number of persons call themselves architects who are not entitled to the name by any right of education is pretty notorious. However, such are usually employed upon the lower class of buildings, which, if truth must be told, are not infrequently the most remunerative, on account of the insignificant number of details and working drawings required. Against competition with these individuals a diploma would be but of slight use. For Mr. A. being about to build a factory, or Mr. B. a warehouse, naturally looks about him to see by whom he can get his plans made at the cheapest rate. His motto through life has been to "buy in the cheapest markets and to sell in the dearest." He cares not a fig about the man being properly qualified to practise. He wants a building of a certain number of stories, with such and such rooms for warehousing and other purposes. A joiner or a mason will readily furnish plans at a very trifling cost.

It is evident, then, that architects cannot compete with men who are perfectly satisfied if they give up the whole of their time for 30s. per week. So that, however much a diploma may be wanted to mark the distinction between accredited and non-accredited practitioners, the possession of it would not operate very differently to the present system. If architects are bent upon achieving a position in society, it must be done, not by angry and indignant philippics against committees and boards of guardians (as the sending or not sending of designs is a purely optional matter)—not by dictatorial arrogance and petty narrow-minded restrictions,—but by *so cultivating their talents as to show themselves really superior to pseudo-architects in intelligence, good breeding, taste, and refinement.*

In the higher branch of architecture (that is to say, ecclesiastical), to whom are we mainly indebted for literary efforts? To whose guidance, critical acumen, and judgment, do we owe the most? Not to professional architects, but to the Hopes, Petits, and Paleys—the Freemans and Pooles of architectural societies. I by no means think of underrating the value of the illustrated works that are constantly emanating from the press, under the editorship of the profession. Still, useful as these works are, and indicating, as they do, a very proper desire on the part of their authors to advance the interest and enlarge the knowledge of the science of which they are votaries, more than this is required to render visible the claims of architecture to be styled a liberal calling. An architect should be something more than a living pencil, or a compendium of mouldings and details. He should be remarkable for his intellectual attainments, as well as his refined taste, in all matters connected with art. Let the rising generation (if I may be allowed the expression) of architects cultivate their minds at the same time as they are perfecting themselves in mere artistical execution of their drawings. Let the example of the amateurs of architectural societies excite in them an honourable emulation to be equally well versed in the theory of architecture. Let architects contribute no less by their pens than by their pencils to the expansion and development of the science we all love.

Then may we indeed hope that architecture, having attained a literary position, may also have a place assigned her in the ranks of the *learned* professions, which, instead of being three, as at present, will become then a *partie quarrée.* P. P. C.

I believe the profession generally would concur in the opinion of your correspondents, that some step should be taken to promote the respectability and responsibility of its practitioners; but I do not think that they are by any means unanimous as to the manner in which these objects are to be attained. To convert the profession into a guild, or close corporation, would not only be contrary to the spirit of the times, but would be full of practical injustice to such men as Rickman, who educate themselves for the profession and serve no apprenticeship to it. The public might be assisted to the selection of their advisers, by the institution of examinations, and the award of diplomas; but the want of success which attends the exclusive privileges of attorneys and medical men does not encourage any similar attempts amongst ourselves.

The subject of professional charges is, perhaps, of primary importance; and these should be independent of the amount expended, but in proportion to the work done; something, I fancy, after the manner of the attorney's bill of costs; but, if the architect's estimate is exceeded, then a *pro ratâ* deduction should be made for the amount of his charges. It is the carelessness of the profession (to use no harsher term), in the preparation of their estimates, which most deeply affects the respectability of the body, and for this I see no other remedy than the publication of the *estimated* cost and the *actual* cost of every erection throughout the country. An annual and authentic return of this kind would be much more valuable than many blue books, and would exercise a useful check upon the wilful imaginations of artistical architects, who excel in the preparation of pretty pictures for competitions, but are above all such grovelling considerations as are involved in the cabalistical characters of £. s. d. B.

As a vast deal has been said relative to architects being compelled to take a diploma before they should be permitted to practise, and, as some suppose, a great benefit would arise to the profession in consequence of such a movement, and as all have argued nearly in the same strain, allow me to ask the supporters of this question if they have taken into consideration that, although lawyers and doctors must take a diploma before they can practise, there are members who do practise and who are any thing but clever or efficient men, a fact well known to every one who has taken the trouble to consider the subject, and therefore the diploma has not produced that benefit to the community which its supporters and promoters supposed that it would; nor do I believe that it has yielded that good to the professions which it was at first believed it would do; but to the point. Would a diploma prevent false estimates? would it prevent architects taking practice at a lower rate than 5 per cent.? or teach them to pause before they responded to every call in the shape of an advertisement made by church or chapel building committees or boards of guardians? I say, no!

Who have been the authors of all the enormities complained of? who have brought a host of indignities upon the architectural profession? have they been brought on by men not properly schooled into it, or quack draftsmen? No! none of these; the culprits are its own sons, those who have been trained in the usual way, men who are qualified and who could not be prevented from taking a diploma if they should ever be called upon to do so,—aye, men from whom better things might have been expected.

Is the Small Pox Hospital, which was guaranteed to be executed for 12,000*l.* and which will exceed 20,000*l.* when completed, or the new Lunatic Asylum at Colney Hatch, estimated at 80,000*l.*, the lowest real estimate for which was 135,000*l.*, or the Edmonton Union Workhouse, erected a few years back at a cost of 16,000*l.* when the guardians were led to suppose that 9,000*l.* were sufficient for the same? Are these unusual occurrences; causing the public, as they do, to think lightly of architects? No! sad to say, there are many, many such instances—too numerous to particularize, yet too important to pass by unnoticed; and is it not notorious that two gentlemen who were formerly in partnership brought themselves into public notice by undertaking practice at 2½ or 3 per cent., and securing jobs by false estimates? Has the Birmingham Union affair fallen into oblivion? Have not the architects undertaken to carry out their designs for less than the usual remuneration? and will a diploma prevent these actions? I say, no! for the profession will still number amongst its members those very men who have brought these justly censurable evils into existence. Look over the whole catalogue of competitions, and you will find that 95 of every 100 have been obtained, not by quack draftsmen or inefficient men, but by men of standing who have had friends at court, and who have secured the selection of their designs by the influences of dear Mr. Splitfig, the grocer, Mr. Gingham, the umbrella-maker, Mr. Candlewick, the tallow chandler, and others, who composed the committee, and who were all friendly to Mr. Lines, the architect, and in consequence of their friendly votes and kind co-operation have been favoured by other friends of the architects with an order either for a new umbrella or an extra quantity of candles or tea. Would a diploma stop this? No! Further, does not the law with respect to competitions lay in your own hands? Certainly it does. Don't compete unless upon fair terms; refuse to carry out your designs for less than the usual commission; resist all unfair offers or actions; and the consequence will be that committees will find out that they must come forward and meet you with proper terms and in a proper spirit, or they will perceive that they cannot obtain the assistance they seek. VERITAS.

THE EVILS OF SHORT LEASES.

THE universal centralization of property in Great Britain is the bane of society, the curse of the State, and the sure prelude to antagonism in classes, if not of assured decadence. Various articles published in THE BUILDER on the subject of short leases, last year, treated this subject *in extenso*; it was shown that the tendency of fixed *capital in houses* rapidly concentered in the comparatively few ground landlords; that all the houses (the only fixed capital) in all the cities and towns of England were falling, as a tontine, into the proprietary and possession of such as the Marquis of Westminster, the Dukes of Bedford and Portland, Lords Northampton, Southampton, Fitzhardinge, Portman, and some others in the metropolis; that the terms of leases are becoming shorter as mankind multiplies;—that the longest lease is now ninety years, and most usually but sixty years!—that on the greatest urban estates, one half the whole capital expended by generations passed away has already fallen into the lap of plethoric wealth, whilst the moderate classes are wholly excluded! That in one more generation one-half of the remainder must fall into the same Maelstrom of cupidity, and that in two more generations it *must swallow all!!*

A remedy for such spoliation of the masses was at the same time suggested, which, by a perfectly equitable procedure, might be carried out. It was this:—To make it eligible for any tenant of a building on long lease (above twenty years), to serve notice on his landlord that he designed to purchase the interest in perpetuity, *always reserving to such lord his head rent.* For this purpose (as in cases where lands are required for railways), a notice should be served that perpetuity of tenure was required; a valuation jury should be summoned, and their award should be binding on both parties: that is, that the amount assessed as the representative value should be tendered and paid to the lessor, and that such payment and award should create a tenure in perpetuity.

If only one-fourth of the tenements on the first-mentioned nobleman's metropolitan estates were so enfranchised, then, on that section alone, one thousand householders must become proprietors, have a fixed interest in the polity of the State, a sympathy with the poor, and a stake in the empire! Whereas, on the lapse of private interest, and their mergence into the swollen rentals of the aristocracy, those middle classes, perhaps without a possession in the soil, must be thrown amongst the floating elements of a dislocated society, and, in so far as they are treacherously dealt with, add to the too prevalent discontent at the exceeding wealth of the rich and the exceeding misery of the poor.

Many are the examples of men unwise in their generation, who have builded up houses, and exhausted fortunes, on a favoured residence, or good standing for trade: in two generations all pass away, and are absorbed by the insatiate Mammon of riches; the widow impoverished, the children beggared, may deplore the reckless waste of improvident forefathers. Their lease is expired; they must vacate, unless prepared to pay a rack rent, increased from *three* to *tenfold!*

There is no alternative for the remedy of an evil which is growing in magnitude, under a cunningly devised and solid compact of the great against the small, other than that which is here propounded. Let it go on, and the bonds of society are rent asunder. Those who have are handed against those who have not; aggrandizement is exaggerated, until magnates become superhuman, and until the multitude is debased, whilst the laws of a bounteous Providence, that poised the world and its conditions in a balance, are set at nought. Thus it is that the very prosperity of a State tends to its downfall, for what can thrive with the proud "*who devour widow's houses?*"

The theories here alluded to, so published in THE BUILDER, were shown to several popular members of Parliament, such as Mr. Horsman, Lord Dudley Stuart, and others, who approved them. All architects and builders who clearly discerned the beneficial influence that perpetuated tenures must have on arts and architecture, approved them. All benevolent men actuated solely by public interests and the common weal approved them. Not so the great proprietors. They calculate on "adding house to house, until there be no place left." They cannot, in case of an enfranchisement, preserve to their own multiplied posterity, multiplied estates, with Parliamentary and fixed interests to each and every of their heritors; therefore they dread the alternation of fixed capital into the possession of middle orders, and the acquirement to themselves of only the representative value in funded stocks; for such a change would invest these orders with legislative or representative power.

As a specimen of the temper in which such suggestions are regarded by landlords, take the reply of a member for a home county, who returned the printed copies on perpetuity of leaseholds, with this note:—"I see nothing in your plan but one for leaseholders to rob landlords; they have obtained possession of a piece of land on certain conditions, and for certain purposes,—that is, a lease for 99 years, on which they have built houses calculated to last that time, and then to tumble down; and you propose to make this a pretext for robbing the owners of their land in perpetuity, under the mild term of a *transfer*,—just as a pick-pocket transfers your handkerchief from your pocket to his."

'Tis as unnecessary to observe the disingenuousness of the arguments, as to comment on the style, of such a reply to a proposition for fair purchase,—one at least as fair as that by which the Legislature authorized the appropriation of *freeholds* for railroads on valuation, of common and waste lands, on requiting the lords of manors, or of the *extinction of debts owing to tradesmen of six years' due.* However, the Legislature being owners of parks, wisely made a reservation in their own favour, that, although railroads might take their course through farms, paddocks, closes, and gardens, still *parks* should be sacred, and only attainable on the valuation of the proprietors themselves.

The plain and practical mode of meeting a great social evil as here detailed is simple and honest, and is appreciated, as a known fact, in a 'known tongue.' It is certain that attention, first aroused by THE BUILDER, is awake to the imperious necessity of a change; and equally sure that some of the able and liberal members of the House will give a momentum to the theory which, although started recently against a long-enduring evil, may prove perhaps as efficacious and as electric in its effects, producing benefits and intelligence hitherto unsuspected, as the almost magic transmission of intelligence by wire. Many latent properties of nature are still hidden from the apprehensions of man; accident or the occasion may reveal them, and when they are called into action, the human family is elevated. England is the only country in the earth where men will build on transitory and evanescent terms. A glance at the magnitude and solidity of mansions in other lands, demonstrates this. Look at Paris: there the sites of houses are in free-hold, and there architecture is fostered—so at least in private abodes—for the great structures there are for the most part in perpetuity. The ill-contrived, paltry, and mean character of a street or lane in London will almost demarcate the duration of the lease of the foundation; it is calculated to last the term, as the shell of the engineer when projected from a mortar, has its elevation more aloft to clear space in a parabola, so the frail structure is erected to endure for a time equable with the interest of the builder. QUONDAM.

NEWPORT CHURCH COMPETITION.—We understand that six designs have been selected from the thirty that were exhibited, from which the select committee are to submit the one they determine on as the most desirable to the body of subscribers. The designs of Mr. Dawes and Mr. Johnson had an equal number of votes; Mr. Stratton, jun., came next, and Messrs. Fuller and Gingell, and Mr. Frances, were the other selected competitors.

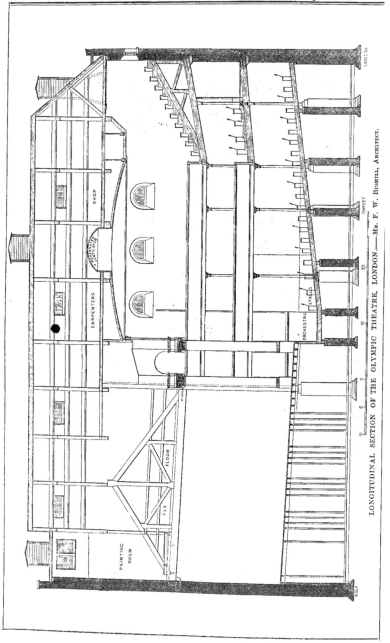

LONGITUDINAL SECTION OF THE OLYMPIC THEATRE, LONDON.——MR. F. W. BUSHILL, ARCHITECT.

DOORWAY OF CHENEY CHURCH, BELGIUM.

THE OLYMPIC THEATRE, WYCH-STREET, STRAND.

THE accompanying longitudinal section of the new Olympic Theatre, through pit and stage, in connection with our article and illustrations last week, serves to show the whole construction of the building, the position of the carpenters' shop and painting room, the mode of carrying the "fly floor," and the way in which the timbers that support the gallery and box floors are secured. In this particular Mr. Bushill has successfully departed from the usual course.

It has hitherto been the general practice to form the interior of a theatre independently of the external walls ; *i.e.* to build the enclosing walls and to *roof the building*, in the first instance, and afterwards to construct and fit in the "horse-shoe," with the several floors and internal works. Now this, in the first place, is a more expensive process ; and secondly, would seem to be a less secure mode of construction than that which has been adopted here, viz., framing and fixing all the internal work in connection with the walls as the brickwork was carried up, whereby the whole is bonded together. The section shows the ends of the timbers in iron shoes resting on the granite corbels, and the iron ties securing the ends of each timber to a second piece of granite about 5 feet long, 6 inches by 4 inches, which is securely built into the wall. Still further to counteract the thrust inwards, the floor is ingeniously framed, as already mentioned, on the principle of the horizontal truss, the side walls and the cross walls at the proscenium serving as abutments.

The stage is lighted at night from the top,—"wing-lights," the source of much danger, being avoided. There are for this purpose five "battens," each with seventy lights, which can be raised or lowered to the extent of 10 feet by means of leather connections. It is much to be desired in stage lighting that the "float," as it is still called from its nature originally, could be got rid of, or at all events be more protected than it now is. The death of Miss Clara Webster, some time ago, and the accident at the Marylebone Theatre quite recently, afford sufficient evidence of its danger.

The stops for turning off the battens, chandelier, float, &c. (all separately) are so arranged as still to have a small escape of gas, even when shut off close, so as to avoid the possibility of fresh lighting being required. At each meter (there are two, one for the front of the house and one for the stage) there is a side junction between the main and the supply pipe, independent of the metre, only to be used in the event of accident to it,—a useful provision, for want of which we have known a theatre left in darkness for some time.

DOORWAY OF CHENEY CHURCH, BELGIUM.

THIS curious doorway is the principal entrance to the church of the village of Cheney, one of the stations on the railway from Tournay to Monscrou, the frontier town of Lille with Belgium. The church is said to be of very old foundation, but the modern plasterer and painter have been at their "dirty work again," and have left little to admire.

J. L.

. Judging from the sketch, we should attribute this doorway to not earlier than the sixteenth century. It is one of those architectural vagaries oftener found abroad than at home.

ONE ORDER OF ARCHITECTS.

LIKE Dame Quickly, you know not where to have him,—neither with the surgeon, ever out and on the move,—nor with the attorney, all day at the desk : he partakes of the character of each. He is the uncertain omnipresent ; his, the neither here nor there of avocations. You shall call on him one day, and be told he is at York : send off a letter (important, of course) instanter, and passing his door next morning see him smoking his chibouk under the friendly shade of his domestic banian. He may say, with Hoby and Stultz, that his business is only with such as "have two gowns and everything handsome" about them : his business is with the wealthy and the titled. This imparts an aristocratic appearance highly admirable to his person, and a beautiful tone to his moral character. As his calling is half a fine art, half a trade,—half noble, half mechanic,—an amphibious calling, so is he the crocodile of the human race : as a youth, he devours medals,—as a man, pupils ; with tears in his eyes he feeds on his kind. He is a great horticulturist, and receives large sums for tender plants committed to his fostering care, the which he usually allows to run wildly to seed : we could not expect him to apply expensive chemical processes for their welfare, but think he might afford a hot-bed and force to a gentle extent ; they require heat and light. As a youth he is very proud—but condescendingly so—having been introduced to princes, potentates, and stammering scientifics, on the occasion of receiving sundry medals. On this point he is insatiable : coin Golconda, and he still cries, "Give, give." His dreams of things, men, and houses, are made up of them ; he would wish a suit of armour fashioned out of them : with all this,—for such trifles, professedly, he cares nought. The pretty prattler talks of fame,—he works for reputation ; and from his mouth proceed such dulcet sounds as "Parthenon, Palladio, Wren, chaste, ve-ry chaste, elegant, ve-ry sweet." He looks on his calling as requiring the most extensive knowledge, the most consummate taste,—on this count he has a chaos of a library, and patronizes the fine arts. He exhibits at the Academy, and revels in a brightly-tinted landscape, as Utopian as his design. He is a constant attendant at his Institute, where he is gently garrulous, and gives a mysterious approving smile of recognition when some pedantic member quotes Latin. He has published a work, and begot children. He has visited Rome, and is delighted with everything "classical,"—considering other styles as passing whims. His house is always clean and neat ; sometimes he labels it with a few statues, and an ornamental chimney-pot pining in silent solitude down the area. However little he really knows of the arts, he loves everything relating to them. He is a great stickler for workman's knowledge,—principally because he is entirely ignorant of it. He can tell you the exact fall of the steps of the Parthenon, and builds a house which is a Pandora's box to the owner. Notwithstanding all these little peculiarities we admire and love the man, and so will analyze him no further, for—he gives famous dinners.

J.

PUBLIC FUNDS AND PUBLIC WORKS.—It is now believed, in well-informed quarters, that the practice of annually voting large grants for public buildings will be abandoned, and that a fund, redeemable at a certain period, will be created specially for carrying on works sanctioned by Parliament ; that it will be managed independently of the office of Woods, &c. The interest of the debt, and such further interest as will secure its redemption, will be annually voted by Parliament ; thus securing a more complete check on estimate and expenditure. The impolicy of taxing the present generation, for works intended for many ages, is at length admitted : under the new system, works to a large amount, giving employment to thousands of artisans, may be carried on, to the great benefit of the community at large, and with a burthen easy to be borne.

SALTER'S PATENT FOR FLUSHING DRAINS.

WE have recently examined an arrangement for rendering the flood-gates of sewers self-acting, invented by Mr. Salter, which appears well calculated to effect the object in view.

According to the mode now in use, flood-gates are placed across the sewers, in order to produce a head of sewage water equal to their height, and are kept closed by means of an iron bar, which is removed periodically by an attendant to allow the pent-up water to rush forth and clear all before it. The flushing, therefore, takes place only when the attendant is present to set the flood-gates free, and it follows that the gates must often remain closed long after they ought—consistently with the purpose of their construction—to be closed. To make the flushing system perfect, the flood-gates should open the instant the necessary quantity of flushing water has accumulated behind them, and this it is which Mr. Salter has accomplished.

The inventor hooks the end of an iron strut to the ordinary gate, and, at an angle of about 45°, inserts the other end into a strong staple firmly fixed in the brickwork of the sewer. The gate is thereby made perfectly fast; but in the centre of the strut there is a weighted joint, which, when acted on in the following manner, instantly sets it free. When the collected water has attained the given height, it is conveyed by an overflow-pipe from one side of the gate to the other into an iron basin which works on an axis, to which is attached a lever, extending beneath the joint in the strut, when the gravity of the water in the basin overcomes the weight of the lever, and the joint of the strut is suddenly lifted upwards, on which the accumulated body of water forces the gate open, and the strut becomes contracted into the form of a reversed V. While the water is rushing through the sewer, the basin, by being inverted, empties itself and returns to its former position; and when the current has slackened so as to be of no farther service for flushing, the preponderating weight of the strut being upwards, it gradually falls back to its original position, and the gate is closed.

It has been applied with much success in the great sewer which runst brough St. Giles's; the sewer is kept as clean by it as if it were swept. The patentee has a simple and efficient apparatus for flushing house drains. *Apropos* of flushing, what is the result of the inquiry ordered by the late Commission of Sewers (on the motion of Mr. Leslie) into the enormous expenditure on dushing made by the officers of that commission, during a certain period of time?

SUPPLY OF WATER TO SOUTHAMPTON.

AT the last meeting of the Southampton Board of Water, a statement was read from Serjeant Campbell, showing that the town might be amply supplied with water from the Otterbourne Springs. In these days of "sanitary improvement" every instance of the misappropriation or the misdirection of the resources of towns by their municipal authorities is not without its use, if held up as a warning to others.

In the case of Southampton it would be difficult to find a more flagrant example of misdirection than the hitherto fruitless search for water affords. Within the last few years about 45,000*l*. have been expended for this object, nearly the half of which sum has been literally sunk in the Artesian well on the common, and the remainder has been expended—thrown away would perhaps be a more appropriate term—in boring other wells, and in constructing drains and reservoirs for collecting the surface-water of the upper part of the common. The result of all up to the present time is an insufficient, intermitting, supply of dirty water to the town.

The report seems to show, that if a proper examination had taken place before commencing these expensive and unprofitable works, an abundant supply of the purest water could have been had within seven or eight miles of the town, which could be brought into it for less than half the cost that has actually been incurred. The town authorities, however, are so reluctant to retrace their misdirected steps that they have given notice of their intention to move for a new bill in the next session of Parliament, to confer upon them an extension of their powers to eke out their present supply of dirty water, with an additional supply of much the same quality from the rivers and canals in the vicinity of the town.

A number of the rate-payers have memorialized the Board of Health to send down an assistant-commissioner to investigate the sanitary affairs of the town.

WORKS IN CHESTER.

THE tower of St. Peter's Church, Chester, the tenders for erecting which showed so much difference, is now completed. It was commenced in May last. The style aimed at by the architect, Mr. James Harrison, is that of the transition from the Decorated to the Perpendicular. The tower is 19 ft. 6 in. square, and 75 ft. high; it is ornamented with four gurgoyles and eight pinnacles. The erection is divided into three stories; the upper one forming the belfry. The entrance doors leading into the church and tower are cut out of one of the oak bearers taken from the old building; the doors are hung on ornamental hinges. The ceiling under the tower in the passage through the rows is panelled. Mr. Morris is the contractor, and executed the carving himself. One of the local papers, to show Mr. M.'s expertness, says he commenced and finished the carving of three beads in one hour and forty minutes! We advise him on another occasion not to be in such a hurry.

The arrangement of the buttresses to this tower is peculiar, and to our eyes not pleasing. The main buttresses have other smaller buttresses set against them obliquely. The architect is to be praised for having avoided the use of the red sand stone, as originally intended, and to which we objected at the time. The stone used is from Minera, near Ruabon, and costs about 2½d. per foot cube.

St. Peter's Church has been repaired and re-arranged, internally, under the same architect. Some of the ugly galleries have been set back, but a new one on the south side has been erected, which is to be regretted. When we were in Chester the bosses of roof were coloured blue and white, and had a ghastly effect. We hope these have been altered. The builders were Bellis and Williams; the mason, Morris. A curious painting was found on the north-east pillar of tower.

At the Chester cemetery, beautifully situated, the entrance-lodge is late Tudor, the chapel Norman, and the dissenters' chapel Elizabethan, if we may so term it. The architect is Mr. Penson.

The iron girder-bridge over the Dee, close by, to which the accident happened some time since, is strengthened by *wooden* struts.

THE MARBLE ARCH.

PERMIT an ex-architect, through the medium of your widely circulating columns, to offer a suggestion on the destiny of the marble arch. It is reported that, instead of removing it to some other site, it is the intention of the Government to sell it as old materials. This I cannot believe; I do not think they would venture to commit such a vandalism. The arch is affirmed to have cost an extravagant sum, and this is another reason why we ought not to be deprived of it. It is, moreover, our only one: the French have several such in their metropolis; and unless we keep what we have got, it will appear that we did not think ourselves worthy even of this. My suggestion is, that it be brought down and placed in front of the landscape garden interior of St. James's-park, to which it would serve as a royal entrance, and would still seem to keep up a connection with the palace, which would be seen in the distance beyond it. Placed here, in the vicinity of the House Guards and Admiralty, it would also serve exceedingly well as an arch commemorative of the valorous doings of our army and navy, and would occupy an analogous position to the arch of the Tuileries at Paris. Our glorious Nelson has his monument, and our great living hero his, but where is the monument to our soldiers and sailors who gained such immortal renown in the great European war that grew out of the French revolution? A good opportunity now presents itself for performing an act of justice which has too long been delayed. By the addition of some trophy on the top, and a suitable inscription in front, the unfortunate arch, which seems to create such embarrassment, might be converted into a lasting memorial of British valour, and the money it has cost, and still may, will never be regretted.

H. C. BARLOW, M.D.

SCENERY AT THE LYCEUM THEATRE.

A MORE extraordinary and beautiful piece of stage decoration and invention, than that which forms the closing scene to Mr. Planché's Christmas extravaganza at the Lyceum Theatre, was never witnessed. It is difficult to understand how such brilliant effects of colour are obtained. In previous scenes, especially an Italian ball-room scene, architecturally correct, and a landscape with the foliage of the passion flower spanning the stage, Mr. Beverly had shown his admitted skill as a stage-painter; but the *tour de force* was reserved for the wind-up, and carried the house by storm. The business of the scene goes on in front of a vast cluster of palm leaves, which, when the climax approaches, opens, each leaf showing its golden lining as it bends towards the stage, and discovers a circle of nymphs bearing aloft the "crown jewels." As a morning contemporary remarks, to say what the jewels are made of, what the nymphs are dressed in, is impossible,—it was a blaze of light and colour. Mr. Planché, as a matter of course, has done his part well—Madame Vestris, bers; and the result is a perfect whole. We shall look in at the other houses next week.

A REMEDY FOR DAMP WALLS.

So often are your readers annoyed by the intrusion of damp into walls, and the disfiguration thereby of paper-hangings, decorations, &c., that you and they will forgive our calling their attention to a means of obviating the evil, and one which we can with confidence recommend. We do not suggest any plan for preventing damp occurring in walls (its existence, arising from a variety of causes, is generally first made manifest by its effects), but to prevent its being visible, or doing any injury when too late to remove it.

The remedy is this:—Coat the part of the wall affected by damp, *and for some distance around it*, with knotting composition—the same article used by builders for priming the knots in wood. It should be applied upon the bare plaster, and however damp this may be, the composition, from its rapidly drying property, will in a few minutes form a smooth and very tough coating, or skin. Two coats should be given, which will prove quite impermeable to damp, and upon which the most delicate papers may be put immediately without fear of injury. The idea occurred to us about a year ago, and we accordingly tested it upon a wall where the damp arose from the ground, and likewise upon a staircase wall, which was always damp from an imperfect joint in a leaden water-pipe behind the plaster. The result is very satisfactory, as it is impossible to detect the slightest damp either by the sight or touch. We are not aware that knotting composition has ever been applied to this purpose before, and we therefore make this communication for the benefit of the trade.

MANDER, Brothers.

Wolverhampton.

THE INVENTOR OF THE BLOCK MACHINERY.—Some of your contemporaries in their notice of the late Sir M. I. Brunel, have claimed too much for him. The original inventor of the block machinery was Walter Taylor, an Englishman. He took out a patent for it, and for years supplied the navy with blocks. When his patent expired he tried to get an extension of it, and, on failing, Government employed Brunel to set it up at Portsmouth. He improved and added to it, but he has not the least right to the credit of the original invention. If this be questioned, you shall have a full statement from the best authority.

N. R.

WATER SUPPLY.

NEW YORK AN EXAMPLE TO LONDON.

The Croton aqueduct and water-works have cost more than three millions sterling, although New York is only about the size of Glasgow, with a population of not much more than one-third of a million, the mere miscellaneous gatherings of the surplus population of this and other countries during the present half of a century almost alone. Let us hear no more misgivings then, on the head of expense, however great, in the adequate supply of pure and healthful water to a population of six times the amount in our own metropolis.

The following details of the construction of the noble water-works of New York were collected by a correspondent of the *Reformers' Gazette* from authentic American documents and publications. The dam constructed to supply the aqueduct is about six miles above the mouth of the river Croton, and about forty miles from the city of New York. It is elevated 38 feet above the level of the river, and is 250 feet in length. The masonry is 8 feet thick at top, and 65 feet at base. It sets the water back about six miles, forming what is called the fountain reservoir, which is estimated to cover an area of 400 acres. The width of the lake varies from a quarter of a mile to about one-eighth. The height of the interior of the aqueduct is 8 feet 5½ inches, and the greatest width is 7 feet 5 inches. The foundation is formed with concrete, the side walls of stone: the bottom and sides of the interior are faced with brick, and the top is covered with an arch of brick. Thus constructed, it is carried over valleys and through hills, a distance of thirty-eight miles, to the receiving reservoir in the island of New York. From the receiving reservoir the water is conveyed in two miles of iron pipes to the distributing reservoir, in which the surface of the water is 115 feet above the level of mean tide.

The aqueduct, 12¾ miles from the Croton dam, crosses the Mill river 72 feet below its previous level by a culvert, the arch of it through which the river crosses being 172 feet long, all within the foundation breadth on which the aqueduct rests. The valley of the Harlem river (or branch of the sea), a quarter of a mile in breadth, and descending 120 feet below the previous level of the bottom of the aqueduct, was always regarded as by far the most formidable work to be encountered in the construction of this aqueduct. Various plans were proposed to accomplish this object, comprising an aqueduct stone bridge, resting on piers and abutments, so as to continue the aqueduct at the same elevation; an inverted syphon of iron pipes; a suspension bridge of wire cables, supported at intervals on stone piers, and carrying the water across in iron pipes without descent.

It was at length resolved to combine the two ideas of a stone bridge and an inverted syphon of pipes, and this plan was in progress when an act of the Legislature of the State was passed, requiring that either a tunnel should be carried under the bed of the river, or that a structure should be erected of which the arches should be at least 80 feet span, and 100 feet from the level of high water to the under side of the crown.

The history of the Thames tunnel deterred the engineers from attempting a similar work, 300 feet in length, under the bed of the Harlem, and finally it was resolved to construct an aqueduct bridge of exactly the altitude required. This being only 100 feet above high water level, an inverted syphon of iron pipes was still necessary.

Colouring Bricks.—A patent has been granted at New York, to Mr. C. B. Doty, Cortlandt, Westchester county, N.Y., for a "peculiar process and manipulations of mixing colouring materials with the moulding sand for the surface of bricks, and the pressing the same upon and into the surface, so as to produce bricks of a uniform colour upon the surface, as well as of a uniform shape and smoothness, the same being effected with greater economy than by mixing a sufficient quantity of colouring matter to colour the whole body of the brick; and this, regardless of any particular colouring matter or especial colour to be produced when the bricks are burned."

Miscellanea.

The Gas Question.—Wardmotes have been held throughout the City districts, at almost all of which congratulations have been voted on the immediate prospect of an abundant supply of cheap and good gas. They ought to have passed votes of thanks to The Builder. A meeting of the Central Gas Consumers Company has also been held, to consider the clauses of their bill, which is based on the model Gas Act, limiting dividends to 10 per cent., and compelling further reductions in price to the extent of all surplus profits. At this meeting, or rather a meeting of ward committees and gas consumers into which it resolved itself, Mr. Pearson announced his resignation as a director,—stating, at the same time, that the other day he found the corporation split into parties and sections on this question; and as he was dependent on it, and found his duties inconsistent with any further *official* connection with a company forming the subject of such party spirit in the corporation, he felt obliged to announce his resignation, although, extra-officially, he would still forward its interests as earnestly as ever. At this meeting also a determination was expressed that the next object after the successful issue of the present shall be to attack the water companies, whose charges were also far too high. A rumour that the new gas company meant to supply their own gas fittings was expressly contradicted. One speaker, Mr. Lowe, said that the old companies had asserted that they had not divided more than 10 per cent. profit, and that, therefore, their profits were quite reasonable; but these gentlemen had forgotten to state that, in addition, they had also obtained no less than from 70*l.* to 100*l.* bonus per share at frequent intervals. He himself was acquainted with an old lady who had received a bonus of 80*l.* per share. —— The Chartered Gas Company have now reduced their price to 5s. per 1000 feet. ——The Surrey Consumers Gas-light and Coke Company are now again astir. They have already commenced their works, with consent of the parochial authorities of Lambeth, St. George's, Southwark, Camberwell, Peckham, Rotherhithe, and various other districts south of the Thames to open roads and lay pipes, &c. A reduction of their proposed price of 5s. (too high, as we said at its outset) to 4s. 6d., with share of profits, or 4s without share of profits, has also been announced, and they expect to be supplying customers by contract or meter early in the ensuing year.——The Salisbury Gas Company are to reduce their price 1s. a-thousand cubic feet at the opening of the new year.

Society of Arts.—At the meeting on 19th instant,—Mr. T. Uwins, R.A., in the chair,—Mr. Highton read a short supplementary paper on "The Application of Electricity to the Arts and Sciences." A number of new specimens of electrotype were exhibited, among which was some iron tubing, coated with a deposit of cadmium to prevent oxidation; also iron covered with a deposit of brass, hitherto deemed impossible, the brass being a deposit of copper and cadmium, instead of copper and zinc. The construction of chronometer balances, on which a deposit of copper on the steel remains instead of brass without fusion, the temperature of the steel remaining the same as that of the atmosphere, was also exhibited. The remaining specimens, which were of remarkable beauty, were supplied chiefly by Capt. Ibbotson, Mr. Elkington, Mr. Collis, and Mr. Ackermann; those of the last-named gentleman being from the royal manufactory at Berlin. The paper concluded with a further explanation of the philosophical part of the subject. A paper on Fox and Barrett's method of constructing buildings fire-proof was read.

Wolverton Mechanics' Institute.—A very agreeable meeting of 1,400 to 1,600 persons took place at a *soirée* on 21st inst., at Wolverton, in support of the institute for railway mechanics established there. Mr. Glyn, Captain Huish, Sir Harry Verney, the Mayor of Birmingham, Mr. Cruikshank, the artist, and Mr. M'Connel, the superintendent, and others addressed the meeting, and the utmost harmony and good will to its objects were displayed by all present.

Projected Works.—Advertisements have been issued for tenders, by 8th proximo, for executing the works of warming and ventilating the church of Northfleet, with plan and specification; by 31st inst., for the erection of a stone bridge of one arch, of 80 feet span, at Ottery St. Mary, Devon, and for approaches to same; by 15th proximo, for the execution of the whole works connected with the erection of three passenger station houses on the Glasgow, Dumfries, and Carlisle Railway; by 12th, for laying down water pipes at Southampton; by 31st inst., for the masons' and joiners' work in erecting a coal shed at Sherburn House colliery (Gateshead); and by 12th proximo, for the erection of two four-story warehouses at Leicester.

Architecture of Birmingham.—At the St. George's Instruction Society, Birmingham, a lecture was delivered on Tuesday evening, by Mr. P. Hollins, "On the Architecture of Birmingham, with suggestions for its improvement." In the course of it the lecturer urged that so much advantage would follow the improvement of the town, that it could scarcely be paid for too dearly. He said:—"If we take a prospective view of the subject for a hundred years, I venture to assert that half the amount of money that would be expended in that period upon public and private buildings on the present disjointed and irregular plan, might be made amply sufficient to produce order and harmony in our street architecture and splendour in our public edifices, and achieve for the town a high fame for its architectural character. The first thing to be done is, the authorities must obtain powers to control the designs of houses in the streets. This would enable us to obtain some of those beautiful vistas of architecture which charm us so much in the improvements at the west end of London. Continuity of line, with uniformity of plan, in certain parts of a composition, give beauty and harmony, and, if on a sufficiently large scale, sublimity. Should any one ask what will become of the picturesque in the event of my plan being adopted, I reply, I am not considering a plan of a new town, but proposing to arrange and harmonize an old one, which is full of oddities, and where a few simple lines are absolutely necessary to soften down the conflicting and abrupt contrasts which every where meet and bewilder the beholder."

Provincial.—A new county court house is in course of erection at Bow.——A native of Wolverhampton proposes to give 1,000*l.* towards the building of an orphan asylum for South Staffordshire in that town, and an additional 1,000*l.* towards the endowment, if the trustees of the Blue Coat School can increase and remove their boarders to the new site, and leave their day-school to parochial tuition.——A new window, representing the crucifixion, has been painted by Mr. M. O'Connor, of London, and placed in the eastern lancet of the chancel of Snenton Church, as an offering by Miss K. E. Wyatt, sister to the incumbent. ——Mr. Cobden and others have resolved to erect a very large public room at Leeds.——The foundation-stone of a new building for the Carlisle City and District Bank was laid on Wednesday week in that city. It is to be of white stone, from Lanerton quarry, on the Earl of Carlisle's estate, the barony of Gilsland. The site is that of the old "White Lion" inn, English-street,—one of the oldest houses in the city, just removed. A flagged thoroughfare will be provided from English-street to Lowther-street. The architect is Mr. T. J. Cox, and the contractor, Mr. R. Wright.——The works for building Flag-lane schools, Sunderland, were let on the 17th inst., to Messrs. Millar and Lax of that town, and it is intended to begin operations immediately. Mr. T. Oliver is the architect.

The Marbles of Paros.—The Government of Greece have, by contract, made S. Cléanthes the sole possessor, for the period of thirty years, of all the quarries of marbles in the commune of Naoussa, at Paros. The proprietor has commenced extracting the marble, and has sent several blocks of large size to Rome and Florence.

New Hospital for King's College.—The munificent offer of 5,000*l.* has been anonymously made and accepted by the council towards the extension of the hospital accommodation for King's College, Somerset House.

OXFORD ARCHITECTURAL SOCIETY.—At a meeting on the 5th instant, it was stated that the committee have it in contemplation to establish a special fund, to be called the Church Building and Restoration Fund, the object of which will be to make small donations to such churches as submit their plans to the society for its approval, by which means it is hoped that much practical good may be done throughout the country. Mr. Freeman delivered a lecture on the "Constructive Systems of the Entablature and of the Arch." Some remarks were then read by Mr. O. Jewitt on the proposed restorations of the pinnacle of St. Mary's Church. In the alterations of the seventeenth century, the pinnacles of the small spires which terminate each buttress seem to have been taken away, being probably much decayed, and in order to obviate the nakedness which their removal would occasion, the small pinnacles at the angles were added, having evidently nothing to do with the original design. The large pinnacles, too, were most probably much decayed, and at the same period either rebuilt or cased as nearly in imitation of the originals as the ideas of beauty of the times would allow. The general form of the mass was originally much the same as at present, and the eye was raised up without interruption, from the parapet to the pinnacle, first by the canopies, then the spires, then the set off, and lastly by the crowning pinnacle. The only alterations necessary in the present pinnacles, according to Mr. Jewitt, are the restoration of the pinnacles to the spires of the canopies, the removal of the small pinnacles at the angles, and the restoration to the large pinnacles of their proper decorative character : little more would be required than a new facing to the pinnacles ; and the whole, while it would retain to the spire that beauty of form and composition which is so admirable, would be executed at a comparatively trifling expense.

SUPPLY OF PURE WATER.—A correspondent states, that a patent right for bringing water on the respective lines of railway into London and other cities, from high elevations and pure sources, in metallic and porcelain tubes, to supply the wants of the public at one-half the present price, and in a much purer state than hitherto obtained, has been granted to Mr. Lamplough, and that arrangements are now being made for the laying down of pipes on the respective lines of railway into London, on a fixed rental on the income derived, thus adding permanently to the railway return, and preventing a needless outlay of capital in the purchase of property for a canal or aqueduct, or both conjoined, securing also the water from injurious impregnations and the absorption of gases. The principle of syphonic action is put into requisition, and by means of a hydraulic pump, a vacuum is caused and a continuous and uninterrupted flow of this necessary of life is obtained so long as the fountain maintains its supply.—What we want is pure water,—how, we care not. It is a fact undeniable, that the inhabitants of Lambeth and Southwark have little better than sewage water to drink, and that in proportion to the impurity and scanty supply, ceteris paribus, so they suffered in the late epidemic.

PICTORIAL MAPS.—On reading an article in a late number of THE BUILDER, on pictorial maps, it occurs to me that, in the fine café Pedrocchi, at Padua, there are maps of the world painted on the walls, so that you may sip your coffee and study geography at the same time. I should mention also, that contrary to the usual practice, north is placed at the bottom. I do not know of any similar instance, and therefore imagined that this note might interest some of your readers.—C.F., jun.

BLIND BUILDERS.—The following tenders were delivered for the Witham Savings Bank, advertised in THE BUILDER :—

Moss, Chelmsford	£1,215
Turner, Marks Tey	948
Trego, London	894
Gammon, ditto	873
Whison, ditto	851
Smith, Scole	827
Alison, London	792
Shepherd, Colchester	789
Taylor, London	786
Cushe, London	764
Mortimer, Heyland	769
Myers, London	705

THE FACILITIES GIVEN FOR FORMING BATHS AND WASHHOUSES, under the Act 9 & 10 Vic., capt. 74, are not so generally known as they ought to be, and at the request of Mr. Woolcott, acting secretary to the committee for promoting the establishment of these most useful, and, indeed, most urgently called-for conveniences to the working-classes, we are happy to reiterate what we have long and often pointed out, that this Act provides, that in the event of a request from ten rate-payers, the churchwardens of the parish shall convene a vestry for the special purpose of determining whether baths and washhouses shall be erected, and if a resolution affirming the proposition be agreed to by two-thirds of the vestry, an election by the parishioners of commissioners shall take place, who will be empowered to carry out the works. The council of any borough may, without any requisition, determine that this Act shall be adopted. The necessary funds for carrying the Act into execution may, from time to time, be borrowed at interest, on the security of a mortgage of the rates for the relief of the poor of such parish, or of the borough fund, as the case may be. In conclusion, we may add that the central committee at Exeter-hall will readily afford every information in their power to aid in promoting an object so highly important and beneficial to the community generally.

RAILWAY JOTTINGS.—Mr. P. W. Barlow, C.E., of Blackheath, has registered a patent for improved permanent way, by which he proposes to dispense with the ordinary longitudinal sleepers, whilst the rails will be more efficiently secured than heretofore. The invention consists of two or more chairs in one piece, with a metal plate or bearer instead of the usual sleeper. The apparatus may, however, be cast in longitudinal halves, and secured by bolts and nuts, with bars crossing the way. The casting of chairs in two longitudinal halves for ordinary sleepers is also included in the specification. He claims the use of two or more chairs, or parts of chairs, combined with one plate or bearer, and the making of chairs in two parts. for ordinary sleepers.——Mr. P. Macpherson, in a pamphlet just published, states that the return to the House of Lords of law and Parliamentary expenses of 127 railway companies gives for law charges, 1,234,948l.; Parliamentary expenses, 3,303,461l. total, 4,538,409l. But this sum of upwards of 4½ millions does not include the law of some of the principal companies. The Great Western, the South-Western, the Eastern Counties, South-Eastern, Great Northern, Midland, York and North Midland, Berwick, Brighton, and others have not yet made a return.

OUR STATUES.—There are two very prominent objects in the centre of our renowned city (London) which seem to be little cared for. I mean the statues of our beloved Queen and the Duke of Wellington. I have been taught that statuary marble is a suitable emblem of purity; but the marble statue of the Queen in the Royal Exchange denotes any thing but that; the dingy, grimy appearance of the features, drapery, &c., almost forbids persons of correct taste from taking a lingering look behind. Oh, Sir, what sort of opinion will our country cousins and foreigners form, who may visit our metropolis during the Christmas holidays, when they see Majesty in a condition so pitiable, and the noble Duke close by, the greatest general of the age, and a man of metal, exhibiting almost the appearance of a sweep with a soot bag wrapped around him? Really, Sir, I think soap, soda-water, and other requisites may be obtained at something less than war prices. I do, therefore, most sincerely hope that these few hints will be sufficient to stimulate our worthy city authorities, without any delay, to pay those necessary little attentions to royalty and merit, and prevent any further reference to the subject.—ONE OF THE LIVERY.

GREENWICH HOSPITAL.—I was at Greenwich a few days since, where I saw great preparations for building, and I was informed that considerable additions were in contemplation at the hospital to accommodate 1,000 additional pensioners, &c. Let us hope that the new building will be a prototype of the great master who has formed so magnificent a pile, and that it will be equally creditable to the present architect and so good a cause.—A. S.

ELECTRO-TELEGRAPHIC PROGRESS.—Some experiments have been made at Norwich, with a new apparatus, which seems by the description to be either that of Mr. Baker's ingenious autographic telegraph, or some modification of the same principle. Sixty letters were by this means legibly written in what we may fairly call long hand, stretching from London to Norwich, and it is expected that when the invention is fixed and ready to work without interruption, at least 200 letters a-minute will be worked off at once, thus doing away with all transcription, and insuring secrecy of correspondence.——The Americans are still going ahead with their lightning news-conductors. Between New York, Washington, and Baltimore, the charges are to be reduced for long messages ; between 500 words and 1,000 to half rates, (4s., being the charge for the first 500), above 1,000 words to one-third only. Mr. Bain is said to have much improved his printing telegraph, and can not only transmit 1,000 letters a-minute, dispensing altogether with the perforated paper, but can give to any number of the 500 machines scattered over the union a simultaneous movement, which enables him to multiply intelligence at one and the same moment throughout the whole circuit of termini. Mr. Green, of New Jersey, also, as the Mining Journal notices, has invented a mode of coating the wires by rotating and stationary brushes, with portable paint, or other coating receptacle. A Mr. Pratt, of New York, has patented a plan for stretching wires over great distances, such as rivers, &c., by suspending strong gum elastic band, cord, or tube, to the posts, which, drawn out in the first instance, always, by their elasticity, keep the copper wire stretched. Mr. Curtis, of Ohio, has patented an improved mode of constructing indicating telegraphs.

RESPONSIBILITY OF PATENTEES.—In the Common Plea case, Dakin, administratrix, v. Brown and another, the parties have agreed to a verdict of 800l. for the plaintiff, as damages or compensation for the death of Mr. Dakin. coffee merchant, by an explosion, in consequence of an alleged defect in the casting of a cylinder connected with an oven constructed by the defendants, who are straw bonnet makers in Cheapside, but also patentees of "Brown's Cellular Steam Plate,"—an oven said to be capable of generating a heat of 500 degrees, and which Mr. Dakin had ordered for heating a silver cylinder for roasting coffee. The only witness examined was Mr. Nasmyth, of Manchester, who declared the casting defective.

COVENT GARDEN CHURCHYARD.—As your remarks upon intramural interment, and the state of our graveyards, have been so pertinent and seasonable as to cause universal attention, allow me to relate what occurred in Bedford-street, Covent Garden, on the 19th and 20th of this month. Eight double loads of the consecrated ground, full of human remains (as might be expected) were wheeled from Covent Garden Churchyard, where a brick grave had been dug, to the bottom of Church-place, and there remained till removed by carts, to the horror of the inhabitants and persons passing in that street,—the various bones of the human body being played with by boys, and jaw-bones, with the teeth perfect, taken up by various individuals. On inquiry, you will find the facts worse than my representation. The waterman for the coach stand, who was on the spot the whole time, was horrified at the desecration he was obliged to witness.—J. G. G., Tavistock-row.

MEETINGS OF SCIENTIFIC BODIES

Held during the ensuing week.

THURSDAY, Jan. 3.—Society of Antiquaries, 8 p.m.
FRIDAY, Jan. 4.—Architectural Association, 8 p.m.

TO CORRESPONDENTS.

"Paint for Ironwork."—A correspondent asks,—"What is the best covering to preserve the wood and iron composing a suspension bridge? It has been painted three times in twelve years with stone-colour paint; but, being much exposed to the weather, &c., the bare wood and iron soon appear.

"Curves."—Is there any mode of taking accurately the curves of a vase? By answering this simple question you will greatly oblige A NOVICE.

"Europe," "J. C. E.," "J. F.H.," "J. C.," "J. B.," Canterbury, "A. G.," "T. O., jun." (we exercise a discretion in such matters), "F. and G.," "E. P. S." (the distance, which makes a clear understanding difficult, precludes an arrangement; we will write, nevertheless), "R. B.," "Young Builder," "F. F.," "A Good Hater," "No Friend to the Professor," "M. L. S.," Glasgow (write to the Secretary, 16, Grosvenor-street, London, and he will return printed particulars), "C. S. C.," "F. P.," "C. W.," "C. R. C.," Westminster (soon), "J. M.," "A. A." (can we have some particulars of the treatment referred to? Why the crucifix?), "W. M.," "F. W. F.," "Anti-Utilitarian," "F. J.," Cheltenham (we did not publish the view he speaks of), "W. H. N.," "G. P.," "B." (is he certain?), "T. C. H." (print has reached us), "J. L.," Hampstead(shall appear), "Zota." "Truths and Tubes," by Thomas Fairbairn (Longmans); "Suggested Legislation for improvement of Dwellings of Poor," by G. Poulett Scrope, Esq., M.P. (Ridgway).

*** At an Index has been prepared, and, with the title-page, will be presented *gratuitously* with the next number. A title-page in colours may be obtained on application, also gratuitously, by those subscribers who prefer it to that which accompanies the index. Covers for THE BUILDER may be obtained at the Office, price 2s., or the publisher will undertake to bind the numbers at 3s. per volume.

NOTICE.— All communications respecting *advertisements* should be addressed to the "Publisher," and not to the "Editor:" all other communications should be addressed to the EDITOR, and not to the Publisher.

"Books and Addresses."—We have not time to point out books or find addresses.

ADVERTISEMENTS.

The Builder
A Journal for the Architect, Engineer, Operative & Artist.

Vol. VII.—No. 309. JANUARY 6, 1849. Price Fourpence.
Stamped 5d.

ILLUSTRATIONS.

Mosaics from Pompeii : six sketches 3
The North Porch of Redcliffe Church, Bristol, Restored : George Godwin, F.R.S., Architect 7

CONTENTS.

Beginning the Year 1
The North Porch of the Redcliffe Church, and "Ni Derepe-randum" 1
Travelling Notes in Italy by an Architect : Pompeii 3
On Monumental Architecture 3
Short Leaves a Social Evil 3
Lecture on Heraldry 6
Lime-Ash Floors for Labourers' Cottages 8
The Boston Aqueduct 8
On the Study of Design from Vegetal Growth : Decorative Art
Society 8
Use of Bath Stone in Liverpool 8
House Drainage 8
Appropriation of Railway Arches 9
Notes in the Provinces 9
Miscellanea 9

ADVERTISEMENTS.

ST. HELENS, LANCASHIRE.

with Syphon Traps.
STRAIGHT TUBES WITH SOCKETJOINTS.
Bends, Junctions, Traps, &c. &c.
Patentees and Manufacturers of MOSAIC PAVEMENTS.
Close to the Surrey side of Vauxhall-bridge.

GEORGE JENNINGS,
29, GREAT CHARLOTTE STREET, BLACKFRIARS ROAD,

Begs to call the attention of those interested to the following articles, which he has invented and patented ;—

THE SHOP SHUTTER FASTENER.

The trouble and disfigurement caused by the unsightly shutter bar is so well known, that it is only necessary to say, a shop front, handsomely decorated, receives more injury from the application of the Shutter Bar than it does from any other cause.

The above invention not only protects the corners of the shutters, but effectually secures them, and its cost is much less than the destructive and troublesome Bar, as the patent fastenings can be had in malleable iron, at 3s. per shutter, or in brass, at 6s. The following shops are selected as being in the principal thoroughfares, and the proprietors can bear testimony to the simplicity and efficiency of the invention :—

Old Bond-street, 5, 34, 46 ; New Oxford-street, 468, 470, 471, 472, 473, 474 ; Strand, 140, 141, 166 ; Fleet-street, 74 ; Ludgate-hill, 31 ; Cheapside, 49 ; Westminster-road, 28, 29, 31, 41, 42, 43, 44, 66, 70, 71, 72, 73, 74, 75 ; Waterloo-road, 57 ; Blackfriars-road, 43, 46, 47, 57, 68, 71 ; High-street, Borough, 101, 156 ; Whitechapel, 99, 100, 101 ; Charing Cross, 55 ; St. Martin's-lane, 56 ; Aldgate, 12 ; Blackman-street, 15.

JENNINGS'S PATENT INDIA-RUBBER TUBE COCKS.

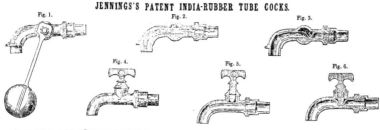

Fig. 1.   Fig. 2.   Fig. 3.   Fig. 4.   Fig. 5.   Fig. 6.

The principle on which these Cocks are made is so simple, that the following short description must at once make their superiority over the old Plug Cock apparent to all practical men.

Into the barrel and shank of the Cock is placed a tube of Vulcanized India Rubber. Figures 3 and 6 represent the water-way passage for the flow of liquids or gas. Figures 2 and 5 represent the Cocks open, with an uninterrupted key, the tube assumes its original circular shape, forming a full round water-way, closed by the india rubber tube being compressed. By turning the handle, or

The following are a few of its practical advantages :—

It will resist any pressure when closed, and when open the water flows as freely as through the pipe.

The water-way being entirely independent of the working part, It is not liable to damage by frost, and all leakage is avoided.

All chance of setting fast from being out of use (an evil much complained of in cocks on the old ground-in principle) is entirely avoided.

The facility of repairs by simply renewing the tube.

In the Ball-cock, its allowing a full stream of water to flow into the cistern till nearly full, and the impossibility of its "sticking up or down" —the cause of much loss and complaint with Water Companies.

Cocks on this principle have now been fixed for some time in the Royal Mint, the House of Detention, Clerkenwell, the House of Correction, Cold Bath Fields, Lambeth Water Works, Kent Water Works, Barclay and Perkins's Brewery, Brick-lane Gas Works, and many other public and private establishments.

G. JENNINGS has much pleasure in calling the attention of the trade and public to the following

TESTIMONIALS.

House of Detention, December, 1848.

I beg to certify that the greater part of the water-pipes of this building are fitted with Mr. Jenning's Patent India Rubber Tube Cocks. They have been in constant use for some months, and continue to give great satisfaction.

F. W. HILL, Governor.

Sir,—Your Patent Joints and Cocks fixed in this establishment twelve months since, are as sound now, and answer every purpose at this time, quite as well as when fixed.

Mr. Jennings.   I am, Sir, your obedient servant,   GEORGE PULMAN.

House of Correction, Coal Bath-fields, December 12th, 1848.

Sir,—In reply to your letter, I beg to say, the India Rubber Tube Cocks fixed in this prison are quite sound, and answering the purpose intended.—I am, Sir, Yours obediently,

To Mr. Jennings.   THOMAS FILLARY, Engineer.

St. Saviour's Union, 13th December, 1848.

Mr. Jennings,—Sir, I feel great pleasure in certifying, that the India Rubber Tube Cocks and Water-closets have been fixed in this Union House—those which were fixed are entirely free from any bad smells, and an overflow of basons from leaky cocks, and they have added very much to the comfort of the house.—I am, Sir, your obedient servant,

B. BONSER, Master.

2, Finsbury-circus, City, December, 1848.

Sir,—I have heard no complaints of any of your India Rubber Tube Cocks, though I have had some fixed under great pressures.—I am, Sir, your obedient servant,

Mr. Jennings.   THOMAS CLARK, Engineer.

Distillery, Smithfield Bars, December, 1848.

We hereby certify, that we have had Mr. Jennings's India Rubber Tube Cocks in this establishment for the last twelve months ; they are answering so well, that in future we shall use no other.

BROWNING AND SON.

12, Square, Winchester.

Sir,—I received the India Rubber Tube Cocks safely, and have had them fixed under the superintendence of Mr. Frampton, who is the manager of the waterworks. I am delighted to be able to tell you its great efficiency, and feel certain their Introduction into this city will be attended with great comfort to the inhabitants, from the following circumstance :—The city is in a valley, and is supplied with water pumped into a reservoir on nearly the highest eminence in its neighbourhood : consequently the pressure of that element is so great, that all the cocks I tried, proved comparatively worthless when fixed, or shortly afterwards.

I am glad I saw your advertisement in "The Builder," and I will do all I can to make your invention known in this city.—I am, Sir, yours respectfully,

Mr. Jennings.   W. SAVAGE.

The cost of these Cocks in brass is the same as the charge hitherto made for the old roundway plug-cock. As they can be made in iron, a great saving is effected, and relieve themselves from the annoyance of leaky cocks by their adoption. Water Companies, Distillers, Brewers, and all large consumers, will save money.

JENNINGS'S WATER-CLOSET.

To this Closet the Patentee particularly invites the attention of all practical men—it is so constructed, it cannot be offensive, or get out of order—it has neither pan or valve—the raising of the handle allows the contents of the bason to fall with great force through a 4-inch India-rubber pipe direct into the trap, and the lowering of the handle compresses the tube, and retains the water in the bason—the surplus water passes off through an overflow pipe, which regulates the proper quantity to be retained in the bason. The cost of these closets are, brass-mounted, sunk plate blue bason, &c., 3l. 3s. ; plain, with flat plate white bason, 2l. 2s.

THE COCKS, CLOSETS, PATENT JOINTS, AND JENNINGS'S IMPROVED CISTERN VALVES,
can be had from the PATENTEE, or of JOHN WARNER and SONS, Jewin-street, London ; or of Mr. J. R. WOOD, Hanover Chambers, Hanover-street, Liverpool.

THE PATENT SHOP SHUTTER FASTENERS
can be had of the PATENTEE, or of any respectable Ironmonger, by sending the finished thickness of the Shutters, and which way they are put up to the right or left.

LONDON: Printed by CHARLES WYMAN, of 7, Calthorpe-street, in the parish of St. Pancras, in the County of Middlesex, Printer, at the Printing-office of J. & H. Cox, Brothers, 74 & 75, Great Queen-street, Lincoln's-Inn Fields, in the Parish of St. Giles-in-the-Fields, in the said County ; and Published by the said CHARLES WYMAN, at the Office of "THE BUILDER," 2, York-street, Covent Garden, in the Parish of Saint Paul, Covent Garden, also in the said County.—Saturday, January 6, 1849.

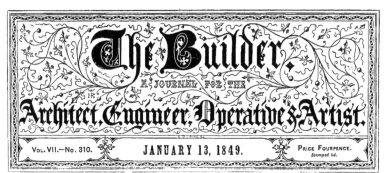

The Builder.

A JOURNAL FOR THE

Architect, Engineer, Operative & Artist.

Vol. VII.—No. 310.   JANUARY 13, 1849.   PRICE FOURPENCE.
Stamped 5d.

ILLUSTRATIONS.

Mr Benjamin Heywood's Bank, Manchester : Mr J. E. Gregan,
Architect 18
The Lighting of Greek Temples : four Sketches 19

CONTENTS.

Why need we die so soon?—What has been done to lengthen
life, and what may be done—Model Inspectors—Graveyards
—City Sewers—and Cattle Markets 13
On Monumental Architecture 14
Professor Cockerell's Lectures on Architecture 16
The Royal Institute of British Architects 16
Something about St. Paul's Churchyard. London 17
St. Michael's Church, Chester 17
Blind Builders Oxford 17
Sir Benjamin Heywood's New Bank, Manchester 18
The Lighting of Greek Temples : Mr. Ferguson's " Inquiry
into the Principles of Beauty in Art " 19
Pantheon for Cottages 20
Value of Exemption from Supervision : Railway Sheds—
Theatre Styles 20
Railway Jottings 20
Cottages at £16 a-piece 21
Notes in the Provinces 21
Opening of the New Consolidated Commission of Sewers 22
Books 22
Miscellanea 23

ADVERTISEMENTS.

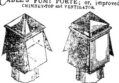

CHEAP WATER-CLOSET PANS, WITH SYPHON TRAPS, IN GLAZED STONE WARE, PRICE 7s. 6D. EACH,
MANUFACTURED BY
DOULTON AND WATTS, LAMBETH POTTERY, HIGH-STREET, LAMBETH, LONDON.

No. 1. No. 2. No. 3. No. 4.

The importance of a system of thorough cleansing and drainage, and the application of Water-Closets with Traps to every house, is so fully established by the late Parliamentary Inquiries, and by public opinion, as to need no enforcement.

The annexed Pans are of the most simple yet perfect construction: they are cleanly and imperishable; require no metal fans and the price at which they are offered is so low, as to admit of their universal adoption.

Testimony in favour of the first three of these Closet Pans, and their suitability for general adaptation, may be found in the recent evidence given before the Parliamentary Sanitary Commission, by HENRY AUSTIN, Esq., Consulting Engineer, and JOHN PHILLIPS, Esq., Surveyor to the New Metropolitan Commissioners of Sewers. No. 4, approved by Major JEBB, and has been extensively supplied to Prisons and Asylums throughout the Kingdom.

ST. HELENS, LANCASHIRE.

DOULTON'S STONE WARE PIPES, &c.,
manufactured at the above Works, are SHIPPED FREE ON BOARD in the Port of LIVERPOOL, or placed in Trucks on the Liverpool and Manchester Railway, without extra charge.
They may also be obtained of the following Agents:—
LIVERPOOL—T. and H. Chaffer, Stone Merchants, Great Howard-street, Liverpool; KENHAL, and WESTMORLAND—Miles Thompson, Kendal; CARLISLE—C. Hodgson, Carlisle A further list of Agents for the principal Towns will appear in future advertisements.

VAUXHALL POTTERY, established
upwards of 150 years.
ALFRED SINGER and Co., Manufacturers of GLAZED STONE WARE DRAIN PIPES, WATER-CLOSET PANS, &c.

with Syphon Traps.

STRAIGHT TUBES WITH SOCKET JOINTS.

Bends, Junctions, Traps, &c.
Patentees and Manufacturers of MOSAIC PAVEMENTS.
Close to the Surrey side of Vauxhall-bridge.

UNION BROWN STONE POTTERY,
CHEMICAL APPARATUS, and DRAIN-PIPE MANUFACTORY, 74, Vauxhall-walk, Lambeth. Patronised by Her Majesty's Commissioners of Woods and Forests, and by the Metropolitan Commissioners of Sewers.

WILLIAM NORTHEN, Inventor of Salt GLAZED BROWN STONE SOCKET DRAIN-PIPES, in every variety of shape, bore to suit the situation of Architects, Surveyors, Contractors, and others in the following list of prices:—

N.B. Drain-pipes of my Manufacture may also be obtained of Messrs. ROBERTS, at their Lime Wharf, Albion Wharf, Holland-street, Blackfriars; Millbank-street, Westminster; Kingsland Basin, Kingsland-road; and Limekiln, Limehouse.

TO PLUMBERS, BUILDERS, AND ENGINEERS.
CHEAPEST HOUSE IN LONDON for every description of best Town-made Brass and Copper Work.

PAN CLOSETS complete, with WHITE
BASIN, &c.—9-inch Lift Pumps, 6s.
Cocks; &c.

SELF-FLUSHING WATER-CLOSETS.
—FLEXIBLE DIAPHRAGM VALVE COCKS.—
LAMBERT'S PATENT.—The patentees solicit the attention of architects, engineers, builders, and the trade to these inventions, both of which are very great improvements upon the appliances hitherto in use.

T. OMAS LAMBERT and SON, Patentees, Manufacturers of Block Tin Tube, Hydraulic Steam and Gas Fittings, corner of Short-street, New-cut, Lambeth.

SANITARY IMPROVEMENT.—Perfect
freedom from Stench or Noxious Vapours arising from Sewers, Drains, &c., is insured by the use of
BUNNETT'S
PATENT SELF-ACTING EFFLUVIA TRAPS
Adapted for Streets, Public Buildings, Dwelling Houses, Factories, Stables, &c.

INVENTORS AND PATENTEES OF SELF-ACTING
(DOUBLY TRAPPED)
PAN AND VALVE WATER-CLOSETS;

TUBULAR DRAINS in GLAZED STONE WARE, MANUFACTURED BY
HENRY DOULTON AND CO., POTTERS. HIGH-STREET, LAMBETH, LONDON.
STRAIGHT TUBES, WITH SOCKET JOINTS.

BENDS, JUNCTIONS, AND TRAPS OF ALL KINDS.

TESTIMONIALS from Messrs ROE and PHILLIPS, Surveyors to the new Metropolitan Commission of Sewers.

DEAR SIR,—I would respectfully recommend the building profession generally, in future to use no other material than Glazed Stoneware Pipes for house drains; and I am quite sure by their so doing, they will be conferring a great boon on public health, and that to an extent they little suppose. I also respectfully submit that there is now no reasonable excuse for their not using them, for it has been proved that no regard to strength, durability, and efficiency, there cannot be a better article.

I am, Dear Sir, yours truly,
Mr. H. Doulton.   JOHN PHILLIPS.

DEAR SIR,—In reply to your request, I beg to state that Glazed Stoneware Drains are those which I would in all case recommend builders or proprietors of houses to use, there being no other material that at this time equals them in efficiency joined with economy.

I am, Dear Sir, yours truly,
JOHN ROE.

JAMES STIFF, MANUFACTURER of GLAZED STONE WARE DRAIN PIPES,
BENDS, JUNCTIONS, TRAPS, &c., 92, HIGH STREET, LAMBETH, LONDON. Established 1751.
Water Closet Pans, with Syphon Traps, 7s. 6d. each.
STRAIGHT TUBES, with Socket Joints, in 2 feet lengths.

N.B. These are made without the discharge-hole being turned downwards.

The great advantages attending the use of these articles are now so generally understood, as to render any description of them almost superfluous. Their cheapness, efficiency, and durability, are universally admitted; while is rapidly increasing demand for them proves their estimated superiority over every other material that at this time equals them for similar purposes.

Inspection is invited to an assorted stock of Drain Tubes, of every form and size, adapted to the various situations for which they may be required; as also to the WATER-CLOSET PANS OF IMPROVED CONSTRUCTION; and interior glaze far superiority and other manufactured of Brown Stone Ware.

May be had also at Messrs. GLADDISH'S LIME WHARFS.—Pedlars' Acre, Westminster Bridge; City-road Wharf, City Basin, Dockhead, Bermondsey; Dan-e's Wharf, foot of Battersea Bridge, Chelsea; Pratt Wharf, King's-road, Camden New Town

WARM-AIR STOVES.—J. L. BENHAM and SONS respectfully solicit the attention of
Architects, Builders, and the Public in general to their extensive stock of AIR STOVES, suitable for Shops, Halls, School-rooms, &c. Greenhouses, Halls, and every building WARMED BY HOT-WATER from the servant's offices, or by the circulation of WARM AIR ON THE POLMAISE SYSTEM, which is very moderate cost.
18, WIGMORE STREET, CAVENDISH-SQUARE, LONDON.

SEYSSEL ASPHALTE COMPANY.
CLARIDGE'S   PATENT.

Established March, 1838, for working the Mineral Asphalte Rock of Pyrimont Seyssel, a Bituminous Rock, situate on the Eastern side of the Jura.
Principal Depôts, ROUEN, MARSEILLES, and STANGATE, Surrey side of Westminster-bridge, London.

THE ASPHALTE of SEYSSEL has been extensively used since March, 1838, for the
following useful purposes:—

Foot Pavements.	Dog-kennels.
Kitchen Floors, particularly where it is especial to keep dampness rising.	Barn Floors. Granaries.
Garden Walks and Terraces.	Cow-room Floors.
Carriage Drives.	Malt-house Floors.
Coach-houses and Stabling.	Piggeries, &c. &c.

Covering of Railroad and other Arches.
The only effectual mode to prevent the percolation of water, which also renders it very appropriate for the Lining of Tanks, Fish-ponds, &c. &c.

T. FARRELL, Secretary, Seyssel Asphalte Company, Stangate, London.

CHEAP AND DURABLE ROOFING.
By Her Majesty's   Royal Letters Patent.

McNEILL and Co., of Lamb's-buildings, Bunhill-row, London, Manufacturers and
THE PATENT ASPHALTED FELT, FOR ROOFING HOUSES, VERANDAHS, SHEDS, &c.
Patronised by
HER MAJESTY'S WOODS AND FORESTS.
HER MAJESTY'S COMMISSION OF CUSTOMS.
HONOURABLE EAST-INDIA COMPANY.
HONOURABLE BOARD OF ORDNANCE.
HER MAJESTY'S ESTATE, ISLE OF WIGHT.
ROYAL BOTANICAL GARDENS, REGENT'S PARK.

Offices, LAMB'S BUILDINGS, BUNHILL-ROW
A Liberal Discount allowed to the Trade.

BORING for WATER, Artesian Wells,
Sinking, &c. Water Companies, towns, public buildings, brewers, distillers, manufacturers, and others, may be supplied with any quantity, by DAVID GREENLEY, Civil Engineer, and Patentee of Boring Tools.

E. T. ARCHER, 451, Oxford-street, so-
licits an inspection of the various DECORATIVE PAPERS, fitted up in panels on the walls of the extensive range of apartments, built expressly for this purpose.
—451, Oxford-street.

PAPER-HANGINGS, MANUFACTURED UNDER HER MAJESTY'S ROYAL LETTERS PATENT.

The Builder.
A JOURNAL FOR THE Architect, Engineer, Operative & Artist.

VOL. VII.—No. 311.   JANUARY 20, 1849.   PRICE FOURPENCE. Stamped 5d.

ILLUSTRATIONS.

Examples of Ancient Art—Four Engravings 27
Stone Canopy in the Presbytery, Winchester Cathedral: the Decorated period 30
Details of same 31

CONTENTS.

Review of the "Museum Disneianum"—Colling's "Gothic Ornaments"—and Whitaker's "Materials for a new Style of Ornamentation" 25
On the various Qualities of Cast Stone 28
Professor Cockerell's Lectures on Architecture 28
The Chichester School Competition 28
Access to Churches 29
The Marble Arch in St. James's-park 29
Lime-ash Floors for Cottages 29
Mr. Barry and the Sewers Commissioners: Drainage of the New Houses of Parliament 31
Freemasons of the Church 31
The Horse-power Pocket-boiler 32
Sanitary Progress 33
Railway Jottings 33
Metropolitan Commission of Sewers 33
Miscellanea 33

CUNDY'S PATENT IMPROVED OPEN FIRE-PLACE, HOT-AIR, VENTILATING STOVE.

TESTIMONIALS AFTER LENGTHENED TRIAL.

From the Rev. Wm. Rogers, B.A. Incumbent of St. Thomas's, Charterhouse.

22, Charterhouse-square, Monday, Feb. 17, 1846.

Dear Sir,—The stoves which you have recently erected in my church have been highly successful, and I have great pleasure in expressing to you the entire satisfaction which they have given to all parties. The church, which was notoriously noted for its coldness and bad ventilation, is now most agreeably warmed and well ventilated. I shall be most happy, on any occasion, to bear testimony to the excellency of your stoves and I will endeavour, to the best of my power, to make them known, and I will certainly recommend them to my friends.—I remain, Dear Sir, yours faithfully,
WM. ROGERS.

From the Rev. W. Garratt, M.A., Incumbent of St. John's, Fulham.

St. John's, Fulham, 2nd May, 1846.

My Dear Sir,—I have very great pleasure in giving my public testimony to the efficiency of your stove, as combining the double advantage of thoroughly warming and constantly ventilating any large church or building. Your invention appeared to me to be in theory all that could be desired, and I can honestly say that I have not yet discovered the point in which the practice falls short of the theory. The area of my church is computed to be nearly 300,000 cubical feet, and though a second stove will be required, the one already erected has fully answered my highest expectations, and rushed all that you had given me to expect. If confirmation were needed, for evidence of its efficiency, I might further state, that I had peculiar difficulties to contend with, that various attempts had been made, and that every attempt had been a signal failure,—that I was required to the charge of boldness in attempting what had baffled others, but that such is the power, the efficiency, and the comfort communicated by your stove, that I know not of a dissentient voice, and have heard only of approval with unanimous consent. I might add that I was first led to making inquiry respecting your stove, having gathered indirectly, that a disposition not unfavourable towards it was entertained in a certain high quarter, where, on account of ability of discernment, the smallest approach to approval must carry with it great weight.—I remain, dear Sir, yours faithfully,
WILLIAM GARNATT.

The following winter the second stove, which is alluded to in the above letter, was put up.)

Letter from the Rev. Matthew O'Brien (Professor of Natural Philosophy and Astronomy), M.A., F.R.S., King's College.

Upper Norwood, 23rd June, 1846.

I beg to certify that one of Mr. Cundy's patent stoves was put up in my lecture-room at King's College, last year, in place of a common stove of Arnott's construction, I believe. I have to hesitation in saying, from actual experience, that Mr. Cundy's stove is far superior both in producing warmth over the whole room, and in promoting ventilation, without dangerous currents of air, or close smell.
MATTHEW O'BRIEN.

Letter from Professor Bradley.

King's College, London, July, 1846.

Sir,—I am happy to be able to bear testimony to the efficiency of your stove, which is fitted up in my lecture-room at this institution. It seems to have all the essential requisites of a good stove, a rapid draught, freedom from all smoke, and from that smell which arises from iron, heated in contact with the air of a dwelling room; which is entirely avoided by your arrangement.
I am, Sir, your obedient servant,
THOMAS BRADLEY.

From the Rev. Dr. Thompson, Incumbent of All Saints', St. John's Wood.

Gothic Villa, St. John's Wood, Oct. 22, 1846.

Sir,—Perhaps there are few private individuals who have had more experience in stoves than I have had; I have tried most of the newly invented ones and rejected all but four or two of which I have tried in my Temporary Church, and found them to succeed so well that I have introduced them into All Saints' Church, St. John's Wood. The following reasons induce me to approve of them:—Exemption of effluvia, the emission of a great body of pure warm air, the perfect system of ventilation, the sight of the fire, the consumption of its own air, the little attention requisite, the cleanliness connected with them, and though last not least, the great economy of fuel. All more I can say in favour of your stoves is, that whenever I require a stove, either for my house or church, I shall purchase your patent stoves, and recommend all my friends to do the same.—Yours truly,
ED. THOMPSON, D.D.

From the Rev. W. H. Ingram, B.A., Incumbent of St. James, Norland.

St. James's, Norland, February 21st, 1846.

Sir,—I have much pleasure in certifying that since our stoves were rectified and completed, they have given in all respects the greatest satisfaction. By proper attention to doors and windows we can raise the temperature in the sight of the fire, the consumption, with one of your large stoves and two small ones, in our church, which contains about 100,000 cubic feet. The fires are very cheerful and agreeable in appearance, and the warmth communicated by them is most pleasant and healthful.—I am, yours truly,
W. H. INGRAM.

From the Rev. J. D. Phear, B.D., Minister of St. Paul's, Winchmore-hill.

Winchmore-hill, October 23rd, 1846.

Dear Sir,—After one winter's experience of your stove in St. Paul's Chapel, I feel no hesitation in saying that it may fairly claim a place in the first rank among the inventions for warming churches. Before adopting your stove, I made extensive inquiries both as to the different kinds of stoves.

to the hot water system. Inconveniences of one kind or other I found practically experienced under the various systems which I witnessed; but I really have not one inconvenience or objection to allege against your stove. I believe it to be more powerful than any other stove of the same dimensions and expense; and it is far more agreeable in a church than any other with which I am acquainted.—I remain, dear Sir, yours truly.
J. D. FROST.

From the Rev. A. Drandram, M.A., Rector of Beckenham, Kent.

Dear Sir,—I have much pleasure in stating to you that I consider your stove to have answered my every expectation; and every reasonable expectation; and I do not hesitate to recommend it strongly to the attention of those who are intending to introduce a warming apparatus into their churches, or other large buildings, for the first time, or who have reason to be dissatisfied with stoves hitherto employed.—I am, yours faithfully,
A. DRANDRAM.

From the Rev. Dr. Vivian, Minor Canon of St. Paul's, and Rector of St. Peter-le-Poer, Old Broad-street.

Sir,—I have no hesitation in bearing testimony to the excellence of your stoves. In producing an equal degree of warmth over the whole of a large building, and in promoting ventilation, I consider them unrivalled. They are also the most economical I have ever met with. My church, which was notoriously one of the coldest in the metropolis, has, since the introduction of your stove into it, become one of the most comfortable.—I am, Sir, your faithful and much obliged servant,
J. W. VIVIAN, D.D.

From the Venerable Archdeacon Sinclair.

Vicarage, Kensington, 1st Nov., 1846.

Dear Sir,—Having suffered much inconvenience on various occasions from hot water apparatus and other plans for heating large buildings, I had much satisfaction in hearing of your stove. I considered it to be constructed upon sound scientific principles, and having been informed of many cases in which it had been tried with success, I recommended it to the churchwardens of this parish. In Kensington Church you had great difficulty in obtaining a sufficient draft in the flue, but your stoves have been a great improvement upon the one previously in use; and I am confident that the alterations you now propose will give the church, in respect to warmth and ventilation, every advantage we can desire.—Believe me to be, yours faithfully,
JOHN SINCLAIR.

PATENT TORRENT WATER-CLOSET, AUSTIN'S PATENT.

This much approved and admired Closet is strongly recommended to those Architects and Builders who have not yet tried it: it is SELF-ACTING, THOROUGHLY CLEANSES the basin, is always TRAPPED, and requires no CISTERN if it can be connected with the water-main.

THE STOVES AND WATER-CLOSETS ARE MANUFACTURED ONLY BY MESSRS. DOWSON
(LATE OF 69, WELBECK-STREET), STINGO IRON-WORKS, STINGO-LANE, LONDON.

IMPORTANT TO THE SANITARY MOVEMENT.

PATENT FLUSHING SYPHON BASIN, AND SELF-ACTING CLOSET CONNECTIONS.

STEPHEN GREEN, PATENTEE, IMPERIAL POTTERIES, LAMBETH.

Fig. No. 1 is a Front View.

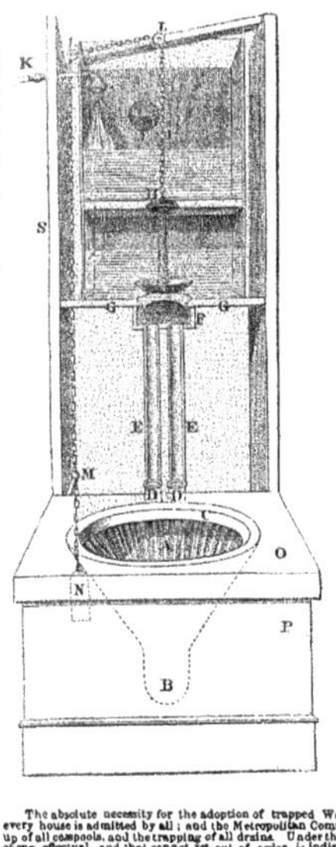

Fig. No. 2 is a Side Section.

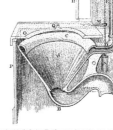

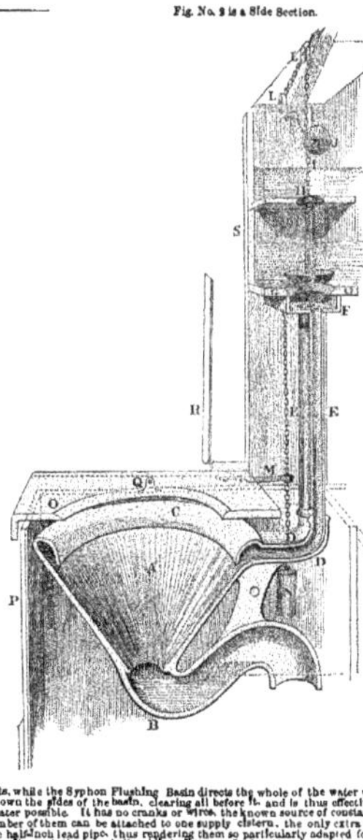

A.—Basin, shewing the water flushing down the sides perpendicularly from the hollow rim or lip all round when in action.

B.—Syphon, shewing the water-trap as it always is, whether in use or out of use.

C.—Hollow rim or lip all round the basin, with the water flushing from it with great force perpendicularly.

DD.—Openings into the hollow rim of basin C, one leading to the right, the other to the left.

EE.—Two pipes leading from the measure-box to the hollow rim C.

F.—Valve box on the bottom of measure connected to pipe EE.

G.—Cistern measure with valve in the bottom.

H.—Valve on the bottom.

I.—Strong chain to left of the valve and attached to lever M.

J.—Ball valve, taking off all pressure on the cistern from the water supply.

K.—Union joint to attach the apparatus to the water supply, by means of a half-inch lead pipe, to any distance required.

LL.—Two pulleys for chain I to run over.

M.—Lever with chain attached.

N.—Counter weight at the end of chain I.

O.—Moveable seat connected to lever M.

P.—Woodfsase complete.

Q.—Seat swivel.

R.—Lid to seat.

The absolute necessity for the adoption of trapped Water Closets to the health and comfort of every house is admitted by all; and the Metropolitan Commissioners are about to enforce the filling up of all cesspools, and the trapping of all drains. Under these circumstances, a water closet, simply cheap, effectual, and that cannot get out of order, is indispensable. The Patentee of the SYPHON FLUSHING BASIN and CLOSET CONNECTIONS flatters himself that his improving them as he found to combine the above requirements. It is complete in itself and ready for use, wherever a suitable place can be found to set it down, without expense of fixing. All it requires is a half-inch leaden pipe to attach it to the water supply. It is so simple in its construction, that it cannot get out of order, nor is it likely to wear out. It has no metal trap, which has constantly wearing out in the basin, and the dental apparatus, which is always out of order, and constantly destroys the place of the basin, and only directs the force of the water round the top of the pan, leaving it to fall without

force on the soiled parts, while the Syphon Flushing Basin directs the whole of the water with great force perpendicularly down the sides of the basin, clearing all before it, and is thus effective with the greatest economy of water possible. It has no cranks or wires, the known source of constant expense and trouble. And another of them can be attached to one supply cistern, the only extra cost being a length of three-quarter inch lead pipe, thus rendering them so particularly adapted for asylums, hospitals, workhouses, railway stations, and all public buildings. It is self-acting, and must ensure itself on every time of using, without reference to the party who uses it, and without unsoiling the trap, while in the ordinary mode, the foul air from the things is admitted into the place where the whole time the trap is lifted up to allow the water to cleanse the basin. The price complete is either £3.3s. with £4 to £5 stained woodwork, and a strong well glazed terra cotta stone basin. To order, it can be fitted up in the taste of the purchaser, in mahogany, with white or blue basins, &c.

S. G. invites Architects, Surveyors, Builders, and the public, to inspect his inventions at his Manufactory, Princes-street, Lambeth. Where also may be seen the NOTED TERRA COTTA STONE

TERRA COTTA STONE GLASS LINED

GLASS LINED DRAIN PIPES, so highly approved and extensively used by her Majesty's Commissioners of Woods and Forests, and the Metropolitan Commissioners of Sewers.

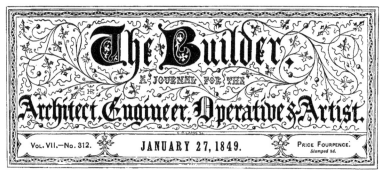

The Builder.
A JOURNAL FOR THE Architect, Engineer, Operative & Artist.

Vol. VII.—No. 312.   **JANUARY 27, 1849.**   **PRICE FOURPENCE.** *Stamped 5d.*

Iverpool Branch Bank of England ; Mr. Cockerell, R. A. ....
Cornice, &c. of Same enlarged 43

CONTENTS.

The Present Condition of Artisans—Able Men amongst them
    entitled to Consideration—Endurance—Emigration 37
On the various Qualities of Caen Stone 38
Enfranchisement of Leaseholds 38
On Dilapidations 39
Mr. Barry and the Metropolitan Sewers Commissioners:
    Drainage of the New Palace at Westminster 41
Branch Bank of England, Liverpool 43
Awards of Official Referees : District Surveyors' Fees : Con-
    struction of Eaves and Cornices 43
The Gas Movement : Miscellaneous Notes 43
A Demonstration on Kennington Common 44
Ventilation ; Warming 44
Porter's Patent Corrugated Iron Beams 44
A School of Design for Leicester 46
Combinations and Strikes 46
The Ancient Church at Greenstead 46
Flushing and Flashing 46
Miscellanea 46

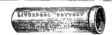

The Builder.
A JOURNAL FOR THE
Architect, Engineer, Operative & Artist.

VOL. VII.—No. 313.   **FEBRUARY 3, 1849.**   PRICE FOURPENCE. Stamped 5d.

ILLUSTRATIONS.

Altar Tomb in Exeter Cathedral (Early English): four sketches 54
Chimney: Abbotsby Church, Lincolnshire 55

CONTENTS.

Interesting Incident at the Royal Society—Iiklaught Architectural Troubles—A Word in Season to the Sewers Commission—Birmingham Workhouse Competition 49
The Rights and Responsibilities of Architects 50
Professor Cockerell's Lectures on Architecture 52
Greenwich Hospital—Iron Beams : Royal Institute of Architects 53
Dinner at the Institution of Builders' Foremen 51
Altar Tomb in Exeter Cathedral 54
Drainage of Guildford : Engineering Competitions 55
A Church Chimney 55
On the Nature and Properties of the Metals used in the Building Trades. Brass and other alloys of Zinc, &c. 55
Notes in the Provinces 56
Railway Jottings 56
Fall of Railway Arches at Manchester 57
Patent Rights—Chimney Flues 57
Metropolitan Commission of Sewers 57
Miscellanea 57

ADVERTISEMENTS.

JENNINGS'S COCKS.

Fig. 1.

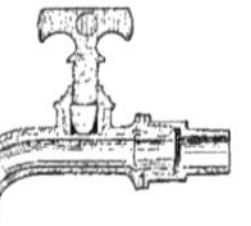

Fig. 2.

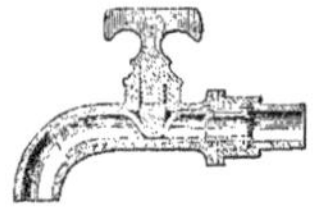

THE construction of these cocks is MOST NATURAL, consequently MOST SIMPLE. The circulation of BLOOD in the HUMAN BODY can be impeded, or altogether stopped, by more or less pressure, so by these cocks the vein or tube of India-rubber, as shown in fig. 1, is OPEN AND FREE; in fig. 2 circulation is altogether stopped by the compression of the tube. It is the only cock now in use that offers a straight and uninterrupted passage for liquids or gas, the working parts having no connection with the interior. The ball cock, from the certainty of its action and the impossibility of its sticking up or down, is well worthy the attention of all who wish for a regular supply of water.

As these cocks can be made in iron, a great saving is effected, and they are warranted to answer as well as those manufactured in brass. Water and gas companies, distillers, brewers, and all large consumers will save much money, and relieve themselves from the annoyance of leaky cocks by their adoption.

The India-rubber Tube Cocks can be applied to all kinds of gas fittings, by simply removing the old tap and screwing on the new one. Street, Main, Self-acting, and other Cocks, suited for gas or water purposes, together with Jennings's Water Closet Improved Valves, Joints, Shop Shutter Fasteners, &c., can be had from the

INVENTOR AND PATENTEE, G. JENNINGS, 29, GREAT CHARLOTTE-STREET, BLACKFRIARS-ROAD, LONDON; OR OF JOHN WARNER AND SONS, JEWIN-CRESCENT, LONDON.

Descriptive Drawings, with the Prices of all Jennings's Inventions, will be sent (by him) post free on application.

BRICKFIELD.—TO BE LET, about Six Acres of PRIME BRICK EARTH, at Shepherd's Bush, at 2s. Royalty.—Further particulars of Mr. LLOYD, Surveyor, Warwick-house, Gray's Inn-square.

TO BUILDERS.

A VERY DESIRABLE PIECE of GROUND, near the Nine Elms, Vauxhall, TO LET, for the erection of fourth-rate houses; also a site for a public house.—Apply to Mr. R. FIELD, surveyor, &c., 34, Coleman-street, City.

TO ENGINEERS, &c.

A LUCRATIVE MARINE REPAIRING BUSINESS and ESTABLISHMENT, in full work, of moderate extent, and situated at a Steam Port of considerable activity, is to be partially or entirely DISPOSED OF by PRIVATE CONTRACT.—Apply to JOSEPH WOODS and Co., 3, Barge-yard Chambers, Bucklersbury, London.

FREEHOLD.—To Builders, Capitalists, and Others.—TO BE SOLD, Twelve Acres of SUPERIOR BUILDING LAND, with sewerage completed. It is situate near the west end of the town, with about Forty Millions of first quality Brick earth in same. Half the purchase-money may remain on mortgage for a term of years, if wished.—Further particulars of Mr. LLOYD, Surveyor, Warwick-house, Gray's Inn-square.

FREEHOLD BUILDING GROUND, NORWOOD, SURREY.—1½ Acre, with commodious Cottage Residence, and considerable additional frontage; and 3½ Acres commanding frontages of 1,600 feet, and abutting upon two roads, both at Norwood. Also 3 Acres with frontages to two roads, near Chertsey, Surrey. These three properties TO BE LET on LEASE, or building lease, for 75 years.—Particulars of Mr. JOHN BURGES WATSON, Architect, 30, Manchester-street, Manchester-square.

SMALL INVESTMENTS—LONG LEASEHOLDS—EIGHT PER CENT.—This property, consisting of Three Houses in St. Marylebone, is let to old and respectable tenants under its value, and produces 36*l.* per annum net.—75 years unexpired,—may be purchased separately.—Particulars of JOHN BURGES WATSON, Esq., Architect, No. 59, Manchester-street, Manchester-square.

GREENWICH, KENT.—TO BE LET, on Building Leases for 71 Years, a VALUABLE PLOT of LAND, in the centre of the town, having two frontages, presenting an excellent opportunity for speculation or substantial investment.—Apply to Mr. NOBLE, Surveyor, London-street, Greenwich.

LONDON IMPROVEMENTS.—Ground, and Four old Houses thereon, TO BE LET, on rebuilding lease, together or separate,—term, 83 years. Money advanced, if required. The situation is good, and must shortly vastly improve.

Also, ONE HOUSE IN CARCASE, containing six rooms, &c., in its present state, at a ground-rent. Will cost 100*l.* to finish.

Also, a useful YARD, and COTTAGE adjoining, TO BE LET by the year.—Apply to Mr. WILSON, 24, Lower Calthorpe-street, Gray's-Inn-lane.

TO BE LET, by the Merchant Tailors' Company, for building purposes, TWENTY-FOUR ACRES of LAND, in the preferable part of Lee, Kent, for a term of 99 years.—Plans to be seen, and particulars obtained, at the Clerk's office, Merchant Tailors' Hall, Threadneedle-street, London.

SAMUEL FISHER, Clerk.

TO BRICK AND TILE BURNERS.

TO BE LET, for a term, a KILN, recently constructed on the most approved principle for burning bricks, house, and draining tiles, and other ware, and four acres of land, situate within a quarter of a mile of a station on the Dover Railway.—Apply to Mr. J. STEVENS, Willesborough, Ashford, Kent.

TO BUILDERS, CONTRACTORS, MARBLE MERCHANTS, STATUARIES, AND OTHERS REQUIRING CONVENIENT WATER-SIDE PREMISES.

TO BE LET, on lease, at a moderate rent, with immediate possession, an eligible WHARF in short distance from the new Houses of Parliament, with dwelling house, stabling, workshops, traveller, and offices, and possessing a river frontage of 100 feet.—For further particulars and tickets to view the premises, apply to Messrs. EVERSFIELD and HORNE, auctioneers and estate agents, 1, Little Smith-street, Westminster.

TO CABINET MAKERS AND BUILDERS.

TO BE DISPOSED OF in the country, a well ESTABLISHED BUSINESS as above, with a good and extensive connection, and as the present proprietor is wishing to retire, possession may be had any time before Midsummer. The manufactured stock to be taken at a valuation. A principal manager of the concern for upwards of twelve years may be retained if required.—Apply by letter, to Z., 25, Argyll-street, London.

TO BRICKLAYERS AND OTHERS.

TO BE DISPOSED OF, on account of a recent death, the BUSINESS of a BRICKLAYER and PLASTERER, which has been carried on for nearly forty years in a market town in Hampshire (the centre of a populous neighbourhood). With the above is a good brick and lime-kiln, with the necessary sheds and drying ground. The connection is highly respectable, and offers an excellent opportunity to a party who understands the business, and can command a capital of about 1,000*l.*—Apply to Mr. HENRY A. LOSCOMBE, Solicitor; to Mr. GUE, Surveyor and Builder, or Mrs. TURNER, all of Andover, Hampshire.

TO BUILDERS, TIMBER MERCHANTS, AND OTHERS.

FOR SALE, about 6,000 good POLES, from 23 feet to 60 feet lengths, at the following prices, viz.:—

24 feet, from 1s. 6d. to 2s. each.
25 feet to 30 feet, 2s. 6d. to 3s. each.
33 feet and upwards, 1d. to 1½d. per foot run.

At WM. and GEO. FOSSEY'S Timber Yard, Mill Wall, Poplar, near the West India Docks.

SALES BY AUCTION.

In re E. Pillow, a Bankrupt, Chancery-lane.—Stock in Trade of Paper-hangings.

MR. PRICE will SELL BY AUCTION, at his Rooms, Quality-court, 48, Chancery-lane, on MONDAY, February 5, at Twelve for One, by order of the assignees, the STOCK IN TRADE, comprising about 10,000 pieces of PAPER-HANGINGS, consisting of drawing-room satins, parlour and bed-room papers, in great variety.—May be viewed the Saturday prior to the Sale, and Catalogues had of JAMES ADAMSON, Esq., 20, Ely-place; WILLIAM BELL, Esq., Official Assignee, 3, Coleman-street-buildings, and at Mr. PRICE'S Offices, 48, Chancery-lane.

SALES BY AUCTION.

TO BUILDERS AND OTHERS.

TO BE SOLD BY AUCTION, by Mr. T. BAXTER, on TUESDAY, February 13, 1849, on the premises, the Oakery, Beckenham, Kent, about 40 squares of good slating; 13 pair of good glazed French casement windows, with large best glass, shutters, architraves; 16 pair of glazed circular-headed sashes and frames; and 30 pair of other sashes and frames, with shutters, architraves, &c.; four handsome fluted columns, and six pilasters with enriched caps and bases; several pair of good moulded panelled doors, with architraves and mouldings, &c.; two good kitchen-ranges, with boilers; 10 good steel-fronted register stoves; a smoke-jack; iron balconies and guard-bars, &c.—May be viewed the day preceding the sale, and catalogues had at the Auction Mart, London, and of the Auctioneer, Bromley, Kent.

TO TIMBER MERCHANTS, SHIP-BUILDERS, AND RAILWAY CONTRACTORS. 300 Excellent Oak, Elm, Ash, and Maple Trees, Edmonton, Middlesex.

MR. RICHARDS has received instructions to SELL by AUCTION, at the Railway Tavern, adjoining the Ponders End (Eastern Counties) station, on TUESDAY, Feb. 6, at Eleven o'clock, Oak, Elm, and Ash Timber Trees, of fine growth, great length, and large metings, adapted for naval and other purposes, now growing on the Cuckoo Hall Farm, lands adjoining, by side of the high road, the river Lea, and Ponders End station, are lotted, and may be viewed. Catalogues had four days prior to sale, of Mr. HASE, market gardener, on the farm, place of sale, and of the Auctioneer, Tottenham, Middlesex.

TO BUILDERS, CARPENTERS, BROKERS, AND OTHERS (Under distraint for rent.—300 capital 12-feet Deals, Mahogany Pedestal Sideboard, Chests of Drawers, and Bookcases, Chimney Glasses, China, Glass, &c. &c.

MR. PRIEST will SELL BY AUCTION, on TUESDAY, February 6th, 1849, at One o'Clock, at his Rooms, 2, Claremont-place, Pentonville, comprising 300 12-feet deals, Japanned, French, and mahogany four-post bedsteads and furnitures, window curtains, beds, bedding, mattresses, cane seat and mahogany chairs, wash stands and tables, Japanned and mahogany drawers, mahogany pedestal sideboard, mahogany sofas, loo tables, carpets, rugs, quantity of oil-cloth, kitchen range, register and other stoves, kitchen utensils, and other items.—May be viewed till sale; and catalogues had of the Auctioneer, 2, Claremont-place, and 3, Angel-place, Pentonville.

BLACKWALL.—To Railway Contractors, Ironfounders, and Others.—500 Tons of Rails and Chairs, Sheaves, and Wrought and Cast Iron; 100 Tons of Wire Rope, 6,000 Railway Sleepers, and Valuable Surplus Material.

PULLEN and SON respectfully announce that they are favoured with instructions from the Directors of the London and Blackwall Railway Company to SELL BY AUCTION, at the Terminus, Blackwall, on TUESDAY, February 27th, and following day, at Twelve (in consequence of the alteration of the gauge of the line), the first portion of the Surplus Material, comprising about 12,000 yards of iron rails, 100 tons of chairs, 10 tons of spikes for ditto, 100 tons of sheaves and frames, and useful wrought and cast iron, 100 tons of iron wire rope, 6,000 larch and oak sleepers, 30 pair of railway carriage-wheels, &c.; the whole put into convenient lots for large and small purchasers.—May be viewed three days prior, and catalogues had at the Superintendent's office, Blackwall Terminus; and of PULLEN and SON, 80, Fore-street, Cripplegate.

CITY IMPROVEMENTS.—Cannon-street Widening and the New Street.—Extensive Sale of Building Materials of the Second Portion of the Property to be taken down for the above Improvement.

PULLEN and SON have the honour to announce that they will SELL BY AUCTION, on MONDAY, February 12, and following day, at Twelve, in lots, by order of the Improvements Committee of the Corporation of the City of London, the whole of the valuable Building Materials, Fixtures, and Fittings, of the capital stock of warehouses lately occupied by Messrs. Colman, and several modern houses, shops, and premises in Dowgate-hill, Budge-row, and Cloak-lane, comprising about 400,000 excellent stock bricks, 100,000 plain and pan tiles, prime oak and fir timber in stout rafters, quartering, joists and girders, 100 pair glazed sashes, several tons of lead, large copper flat, useful modern doors, partitions, marble chimney-pieces and interior fittings, shop and warehouse fronts, iron columns, sound floor boards, York paving, coping and cills, loop-hole doors, iron cranes and jibs, mahogany desks and drawers, iron repositories, stoves and ranges, gas fittings, a large mustard sifting-machine, mahogany tables and settles, and fittings-up of coffee-rooms, and a great variety of useful fixtures and materials of every description.—May be viewed two days prior; and catalogues had at the Office of Works, Guildhall; and of PULLEN and SON, 80, Fore-street, Cripplegate.

TO BUILDERS, CONTRACTORS, TIMBER MERCHANTS, AND OTHERS.—MILLBANK, WESTMINSTER.

MESSRS. EVERSFIELD and HORNE will SELL BY AUCTION, on the Premises, Parliament Wharf, Millbank, Westminster, on WEDNESDAY, February 14th, 1849, at Eleven o'Clock precisely (on account of the number of lots), the excellent and extensive STOCK of a BUILDER, comprising a nearly new timber carriage, three builder's carts, a spring cart, scaffold poles and boards, putlogs and boards, wheeling planks and ladders, crab engines and blocks, chain and rope falls, slings, scale beams and weights, machine for hoisting bricks, &c., two lathes, sand screens, grout tubs, levels and squares; a large quantity of new joiner's work, doors, sashes, &c., long quartering, boarding, and skirting, oak cills, prepared floor boards and battens, 24 carpenter's work benches, 2 large iron skylights, with plate-glass, York and other paving and steps, 4 sets of cart harness, &c.; also 25 loads of Dantzic timber, 300 yellow and white deals and battens, wide pine plank, hoop iron, and other effects.—May be viewed two days prior to the sale, and catalogues had on the premises; and of the Auctioneers, Coal Exchange; or, 1, Little Smith-street, Westminster.—The convenient WHARF, with dwelling-house, TO LET on lease.

THE QUADRANT, REGENT-STREET.—To Builders, Ironmongers, Smiths, Bellhangers, and Others.

MESSRS. TROLLOPE are instructed to SELL by AUCTION, on the Premises, No. 69, the Quadrant, Regent-street, on WEDNESDAY, February 7th, and two following days, at Eleven for Twelve o'clock, on account of the number of Lots, the remaining portion of the MANUFACTURED STOCK and the entire UNMANUFACTURED STOCK and TOOLS of an IRONMONGER and SMITH, comprising about twenty-four register church and hall stoves, kitchen range, cooking apparatus, smoke jacks, stewing and laundry stoves, iron ovens, wrought-iron door and frame, iron chests, Britannia metal, japanned and paper goods, and a general assortment of furnishing ironmongery, patterns for stoves, ranges, ovens, railings, panels, lamp irons, &c., a quantity of brass patterns for ornaments, several tons of useful castings, a handsome enclosure for a tomb, capital fire and force pumps, metal skylights, six large bellows, anvils, turning lathe, drills, shears, stocks, and dies, and a large quantity of forge and bench tinmen's and braziers' tools, and numerous items; also several glass cases, counters, and shop fixtures.—To be viewed the day preceding and mornings of sale.—Catalogues may be had on the premises, and at the offices of the Auctioneers, 15, Parliament-street, and 18, Grosvenor-street, Eaton-square.

PUBLICATIONS.

THE ARTISAN CLUB ON THE STEAM ENGINE.
New Edition, in One Volume, 4to., with 30 Steel Plates and 349 Wood Engravings, 27s. cloth.

A TREATISE on the STEAM-ENGINE, in its Application to Mines, Mills, Steam Navigation, and Railways.

By the ARTISAN CLUB. Edited by JOHN BOURNE, C.E.

London: LONGMAN, BROWN, GREEN, AND LONGMANS.

Published this day, price 3s. 6d.,

THE GOLD SEEKER'S MANUAL.—By Professor ANSTED.

JOHN VAN VOORST, 1, Paternoster-row.

THE DECORATOR'S ASSISTANT, Part XXII., now publishing, contains the following DESIGNS, beautifully engraved on wood:—A Gothic gable cross; Gothic corner and end-piece; Candelabra (Greek); An inscription tablet; A bracket (Flemish); Gothic pendant; Bouquet of flowers; Gothic lamp; French ornament, &c.; and other useful information suited to all trades and professions; price 10d., weekly Nos. price 2d.; Vols. I., II., and III., gilt and lettered, 5s. each.

Part I. of the BOOK of ORNAMENTAL and EARLY ENGLISH ALPHABETS now ready, price 6d., to be continued monthly.—Office, 17, Holywell-street, Strand.

Now ready, Part II., price 2s. 6d.,

THE ARCHITECTURAL SCRAP-BOOK: containing a series of beautiful sketches—an old House at Oxford, a peculiar Tomb at Beaconsfield, a ditto fire-place, Yate-court, Well-house, Marquise, France, and Gateway, Stowe-gardens. Accompanied with letter-press, descriptive and critical, of parts No. I. and II.

Published by the Authors, Messrs. BUTLER and HOBOE, M.R.I.B.A., Architects, 15, Beaufort-buildings, Strand; to be had of all booksellers in Town or Country.

Just published, No. 32, price 3s.,

GOTHIC ORNAMENTS; drawn from existing Authorities.

By J. K. COLLING, Architect.

CONTENTS:

Stone Canopy of Niche, enriched by Gold and Colour, from the Altar Screen, Beverley Minster—Stone Arcade from the Chapter House, Bawden Church, Yorkshire—Sections, Plans, and Details of ditto—Stone Capitals from the Galilee Porch, Ely Cathedral—Stone Label Terminations from ditto.

Also Vol. I., containing 24 numbers, price 3*l.* 13s. 6d.

London: GEORGE BELL, 186, Fleet-street.

Now ready, Imperial 4to., cloth, Price 25s.

HINTS on COTTAGE ARCHITECTURE; being a Selection of Designs for Labourers' Cottages, singly, in pairs, and in groups; with Plans, Elevations, and Estimates.

Dedicated, by express permission, to the Most Noble the Marquis of Lansdowne, K.G., &c.

By HENRY WEAVER, Architect and Land Agent.

London: HENRY POPE, 22, Budge-row, Watling-street. Bath: JOSEPH HOLLWAY, Milsom-street.

Now ready, price 1s.

COMPANION to the BUILDER'S FRIEND.

By HENRY FITZGERALD.

JOHN WILLIAMS and Co., 141, Strand.

Twenty Plates, some coloured, price 18s.

TRENDALL'S EXAMPLES for EXTERIOR and INTERIOR FINISHINGS, forming a Book of Working Drawings.

OFFICE BOOK for 1849, price 3s. 6d.

CLERK of WORKS and YOUNG ARCHITECTS' GUIDE. Price 5s.

JOHN WILLIAMS and Co., 141, Strand.

Now ready, in 1 vol. 8vo., price 1*l.* 10s.,

THE STUDENT'S GUIDE to the LOCOMOTIVE, containing full detailed representations of every feature of Locomotive Engines as constructed by different Engineers, illustrated on 72 copper plates.

BOURNE'S CATECHISM of the STEAM-ENGINE. Price 5s.

TEMPLETON'S INCITEMENTS to the STUDY of STEAM and the STEAM-ENGINE. Price 2s.

CURR'S RAILWAY LOCOMOTION and STEAM NAVIGATION. Price 12s.

CURR'S PHYSICAL PROPERTIES of STEAM. Price 2s.

JOHN WILLIAMS and CO., 141, Strand.

FOR 1849.

KELLY'S PRACTICAL BUILDER'S PRICE BOOK; or, Safe Guide to the Valuation of all kinds of Artificers' work; with the modern practice of Measuring, and an Abstract of the New Building Act for regulating the construction of Buildings. Revised and corrected by New Calculations upon the present Value of Materials and Labour. Arranged by an Architect of eminence, assisted by several experienced Measuring Surveyors. Illustrated and exemplified by Steel Engravings and numerous Woodcuts. Royal 8vo., price 8s., neatly bound.

London: Published by T. KELLY, Paternoster-row; SIMPKIN and MARSHALL, and may be had of all Booksellers.

ROYAL POLYTECHNIC INSTITUTION.—A View in the Gold District of California is added to the new Series of Dissolving Views. Lectures on the Cultivation of the Voice, and on the Art of Singing, by G. Clifford, Esq., illustrated by a variety of Songs, on Tuesday, Thursday, and Saturday, at Two o'clock; on the Electric Light, by Dr. Bachhoffner, on Tuesday, Thursday, and Saturday evenings; on Chemistry, by Dr. Ryan, with brilliant experiments, daily, and on alternate evenings. Childe's Phantasmagoria, with new effects, on Tuesday, Thursday, and Saturday evenings, at Eight. New Chromatrope. Microscope. Diver and Diving-Bell. Machinery and Models explained. The Music is directed by Dr. Wallis.—Admission, 1s.; Schools, half-price.

LONDON: Printed by CHARLES WYMAN, of 7, Calthorpe-street, in the Parish of St. Pancras, in the County of Middlesex, Printer, at the Printing-office of J. & H. Cox, Brothers, 74 & 75, Great Queen-street, Lincoln's-Inn Fields, in the Parish of St. Giles-in-the-Fields, in the said County; and published by the said CHARLES WYMAN, at the Office of "THE BUILDER," 2, York-street, Covent Garden, in the Parish of Saint Paul, Covent-Garden, also in the said County.—Saturday, February 3, 1849.

The Builder

A JOURNAL FOR THE Architect, Engineer, Operative & Artist.

| VOL. VII.—No. 314. | FEBRUARY 10, 1849. | PRICE FOURPENCE. Stamped 5d. |

ILLUSTRATIONS.

Architect Bridge 62
The New Hall, Pembroke College, Oxford: Mr. John Hayward, Architect 65

CONTENTS.

The Superintending Inspector—at Lancaster—Whitehaven—and Leicester—Effect of improved Structures on Health In Hamburgh 61
Professor Cockerell's Lectures on Architecture 62
Architect Bridge : Whitstone Constructions................... 63
On the Construction of Prisons 63
The Gas Movement—Metropolitan and Provincial 64
Royal Institute of Architects 65
Improvement of Ovens 65
Sculpture In Relation to Modern Means and Requirements.. 65
The New Hall &c., Pembroke College, Oxford................ 66
Experiments, &c., on Cast Stone 67
Birmingham Workhouse Competition 67
Encroachment on the New-road, Islington : Metropolitan Improvements 68
Society of Arts 68
Drain Bricks and the Duty 68
Metropolitan Commission of Sewers 69
Miscellanea 69

ADVERTISEMENTS.

THE BUILDER.

The Builder.

A JOURNAL FOR THE

Architect, Engineer, Operative & Artist.

C. D. LAING Sc.

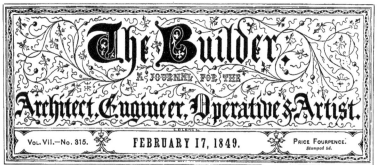

VOL. VII.—No. 315. FEBRUARY 17, 1849. PRICE FOURPENCE. *Stamped 5d.*

ILLUSTRATIONS.

Lime-street Station of North-Western Railway, Liverpool: Mr. W. Tite, F.R.S., Architect 78
Plan of the Lime-street Station, Liverpool 79
Gravestone at Islay 80

CONTENTS.

Stupid Architects!—The Birmingham Workhouse Competition—What the Guardians say of themselves—Lewes Free School Competition 73
The New "Prince's Theatre Royal," Glasgow 74
Exhibition of the British Institution, Pall Mall 75
Lincoln's-inn Fields Popularized 76
The Abattoir Question: Institution of Civil Engineers 76
Birmingham Brass-work 77
Notes in the Provinces 77
Railway Jottings 77
The Lime-street Station of the North-Western Railway, Liverpool 79
Gravestones at Islay 80
Fownhope Church, Herefordshire: Hereford Antiquarian Society 80
St. James's Church, Congleton 80
Miscellanea 81

ADVERTISEMENTS.

PARTNERSHIP.—A Carpenter and Builder, having a long-established Business, near London, is desirous of the assistance of a Junior Partner who could take an active part. Every satisfaction as to respectability and the returns of the business will be given. Apply to Mr. Edmeston, Architect, Salvador House, Bishopsgate.

WANTED, a CLERK of the WORKS to superintend the building of a Prison in the West of England.—Application in writing, with testimonials, and stating salary, to be addressed to S. A., office of "The Builder," 2, York-street, Covent Garden.

WANTED, a CLERK of the WORKS, to superintend the building of the Workhouse for the Fulham Union, at Fulham. Application, in writing, stating terms, with testimonials, to be delivered on or before 10 o'clock on Thursday morning, the 22nd instant, at the Board-Room, Hammersmith Workhouse.—By order of the Board, W. D. BALTER, Clerk.
Board-room, Fulham Union, Feb. 15, 1849.

WANTED IMMEDIATELY, in a Builder's office, a young Man, an EXPERIENCED CLERK. He must have a thorough practical acquaintance with carpenters' and joiners' works, and be fully competent to the superintendence of building operations generally, also to taking out quantities, preparing estimates, making fair and working drawings, and keeping accounts; a good hand-writing will also be requisite. As the situation is likely to be permanent, as well as one of trust, no person need apply whose testimonials and character will not bear the strictest investigation, and who will not be prepared with sureties for 300*l*.—Apply by letter only, pre-paid, to Q., care of Mr. G. Blight, stationer, 67, Gracechurch-street, stating age, character, and term of present or last engagement, or, if now disengaged, the cause of leaving last employer, also the salary that would be required exclusive of a residence on the premises. No communication will be attended to that does not contain the whole of the above particulars.

WANTED, by a Young Man, in his 19th year, who has been in an Architect's Office for the last three years, to proceed as CLERK with an Architect, Surveyor, or Builder to AUSTRALIA, or any of the British Colonies. Is well acquainted with the general routine of the office.—Address to G. B. S., at Mr. Keffel's Library, 14, Great Portland-street, Oxford-street.

BUILDER'S CLERK.—The Advertiser, who has a thorough practical knowledge of building, builders' accounts, and drawings, is in want of a SITUATION in the above capacity, for which he can be well recommended.—Address A. W., 31, High-street, Marylebone.

TO ARCHITECTS.

A CLERK of WORKS, who has just completed superintending an extensive public building, is desirous of an ENGAGEMENT in a similar capacity. The most satisfactory References can be given.—Letters, addressed to D. A., office of "The Builder," will meet with due attention.

TO BUILDERS, ARCHITECTS, AND CONTRACTORS.

A YOUNG MAN, steady and experienced in Business, solicits EMPLOYMENT for the whole or part of his time: is a neat penman, and used to accounts; is a good draughtsman, can level, survey, plot, measure, and estimate: can superintend work, &c. Terms moderate, and References good.—Please address, D. P., Office of "The Builder," 2, York-street, Covent Garden.

TO ARCHITECTS, &c.

A GENTLEMAN, having a thorough knowledge of all branches of the profession is desirous of ENGAGING himself for three days in the week and for a limited period. The advertiser has had considerable practice in the carrying out of works.—Address, XENOPHON, office of "The Builder," 2, York-street, Covent Garden.

TO ARCHITECTS AND SURVEYORS.

A GENTLEMAN who has had the entire management of some first-rate offices, and who has had great experience in designing, making working drawings, surveying, measuring, and valuing, &c., is desirous of an ENGAGEMENT. Would have no objection to engage himself for a stipulated time as Principal Clerk, with a Partnership in perspective,—in which case he would be prepared to advance a suitable premium.—Address to; M. N., office of "The Builder," 2, York-street, Covent Garden.

TO PARENTS AND GUARDIANS.

ENGRAVING ON WOOD.—A respectable YOUTH, with some knowledge of Drawing and a decided taste for Architectural subjects, can be received as PUPIL by Mr. CHARLES D. LAING, engraver on wood to "The Builder," &c., on moderate terms. He will be required to board with his friends.—Address, No. 12, Guildford-street East, Clerkenwell.

TO SURVEYORS AND BUILDERS.

THE Advertiser (who can have excellent testimonials from his former employers) is desirous of an ENGAGEMENT, either in town or country, where he would have an opportunity of perfecting himself in the art of measuring and estimating. Salary not so much an object as a permanent engagement.—Address, OMICRON, care of Mr. Wimperis, 5, Holborn Bars.

TO ARCHITECTS AND BUILDERS.

CLERK of WORKS, or GENERAL SUPERINTENDENT.—A thorough practical and experienced middle-aged PERSON is in want of an ENGAGEMENT as above. He is an efficient measurer and draughtsman, and has been used to works of magnitude. The most respectable References can be given. No objection to the country.—Address A. Z., 46, Vauxhall-street, Lambeth.

TO ARCHITECTS.

AN Architect's Assistant, who has been engaged with members of the profession residing in London, is open to an ENGAGEMENT, either in town or the country; the latter, and a permanent situation, would be preferred. Terms moderate. References will be given, if required, to the architects with whom the advertiser has been engaged.—Address, A. E., E. Bovingdon, Newspaper Agent, Dorset-street, Clapham-road.

DESCRIPTIVE DRAWINGS and PRICES of JENNINGS'S Water Closets, India-rubber Tube Cocks, Shop-shutter Fasteners and Shoes, Closet Valves, Joints, &c. &c., can be had from the Inventor and Patentee, GEORGE JENNINGS, 29, Great Charlotte-street, Blackfriars-road. These Cocks being as good in Iron as in Brass, Water and Gas Companies, Brewers, Distillers, and all large consumers will save much money, and relieve themselves from the annoyance of leaky cocks, by their adoption.

DAMP and GASEOUS EXHALATIONS.
SANITARY MEASURES.
MEMBERS of BOARDS of HEALTH are especially directed to the most EFFECTIVE MEANS which they can adopt to prevent the injurious and often FATAL EFFECTS upon the HEALTH of the COMMUNITY, arising from exhalations that are produced from moisture, decayed animal matter (as in grave-yards), stagnant water, and collections of foetid refuse, tending to produce a miasmatic state of atmosphere. In situations so affected, the impervious quality of the ASPHALTE of SEYSSEL renders it the most perfect PAVEMENT or COVERING that can be relied upon for hermetically closing, and thereby preventing, the rising of moisture and the escape of noxious vapours. The present extensive application of this material for covering roofs, terraces, and arches, for preventing the percolation of wet, is strong evidence of its effectiveness for the above purposes, which is further confirmed by the following extract from the Report of the COMMISSIONERS on the FINE ARTS:— I. FARRELL, Secretary.
Seyssel Asphalte Company, Stangate, London.
"In 1839, I superintended the construction of a house of three stories on the Lac d'Enghien. The foundation of the building is constantly in water, about 19½ inches below the level of the ground floor. The entire horizontal surface of the external and internal walls was covered at the level of the internal ground floor with a layer of SEYSSEL ASPHALTE,* less than half an inch thick, over which coarse sand was spread. Since the above date, no trace of damp has shown itself round the walls of the lower story, which are for the most part painted in oil, of a grey stone colour. It is well known that the least moisture produces round spots, darker or lighter, on walls so painted. Yet the pavement of the floor, resting on the soil itself, is only about 2½ inches above the external surface of the soil, and only 19½ inches, at the utmost, above that of the sheet of water. The layer of Asphalte having been BROKEN AND REMOVED, for the purpose of inserting the sills of two doors, spots indicating the presence of damp have been since remarked at the base of the door-posts."
* This method has been adopted at the new Houses of Parliament.

TO INVENTORS AND PATENTEES.
Bazaar, Baker-street, Portman-square, February, 1849.
THE annexed CIRCULAR having been very favourably responded to by a number of Patentees and Manufacturers, it is intended to open the EXPOSITION on the 1st of MARCH next. All Articles should be forwarded on or before the 27th February inst.
Bazaar, Baker-street, Portman-square, January, 1849.
It is a matter of surprise, that in a nation like England, famous for its trade and manufactures, its men of science and inventive genius, a place has not been established in which might be concentrated for Free Exposition, Patented and Registered Inventions, which would be both an advantage and attraction to the public; and, at the same time, facilitate the object which manufacturers have in view, viz., making their Inventions generally known.
Several Manufacturers having concurred in this opinion, it is intended immediately to open an Exposition of the kind, and the BAKER STREET BAZAAR being a place well known and of great resort, the Proprietor proposes to devote requisite space for the purpose, where the public can have the opportunity of seeing every important invention, free of charge.
A Manager and Assistants will be appointed, for the purpose of Explaining the Use and Advantage of each Invention, and to effect Sales. A system of General Advertising will also be adopted.
TERMS.
For Rent (including General Advertising) for one Patented or Registered Article, not occupying a larger space than

2 feet square	....	£1	0	0	per annum.
3 " "	....	1	10	0	"
4 " "	....	2	0	0	"
5 " "	....	2	10	0	"
6 " "	....	3	0	0	"

If larger space should be required, or where several Inventions are the property of one individual, subject to special arrangement.
Mr. William Spring is authorised to arrange the terms for Rent and Commission, and communications addressed to him at the Bazaar, will receive prompt attention.
Patents intended for exhibition may be at once sent in. Rent not to commence until the Exposition is opened to the public, of which due notice will be given.

ARCHITECTS.—NOTICE IS HEREBY GIVEN, that the Trustees appointed by Sir John Soane, will meet at the Museum, No. 13, Lincoln's-Inn-Fields, on Saturday, the 24th of March, at Three o'clock in the afternoon precisely, to distribute the DIVIDENDS which shall have accrued during the preceding year, from the sum of 5,000*l.* Reduced 3 per Cent. Bank Annuities, invested by the late Sir John Soane, among distressed architects, and the widows and children of deceased architects left in destitute or distressed circumstances.
Forms of application may be had at the Museum, and must be filled up, and delivered there on or before Saturday, the 17th of March, after which day no application can be received.

CONTRACTS.

THE Birmingham and Staffordshire Gas-Light Company are open to receive TENDERS for the entire MAKE of their TAR, on and after the 19th inst. All communications to be addressed, prepaid, to the Secretary of the Birmingham and Staffordshire Gas-Light Company, Old-square, Birmingham.—Birmingham, 12th Jan., 1849.

TO PLASTER OF PARIS MANUFACTURERS.

TENDERS for the supply of COARSE and SECONDS PER TON (in deliveries of not less than half a ton), to be sent, addressed to J. W., care of Mr. ROE, at the Composition Bath-stone Works, New Wharf, Whitefriars, London.—Terms, cash.

TO BUILDERS and CAPITALISTS.—The Proprietor of Three FIRST-RATE HOUSES, unfinished, is desirous of receiving Tenders for Leasing them for 99 Years, together or separately, with or without advances; or Tenders for finishing them. The situation is central, free from risk, and it is estimated that 16 per cent. will be realised on the outlay required.—Apply to Mr. LUCKING, No. 23, Portman-street, Portman-square.

TO BUILDERS.

PARTIES willing to CONTRACT for Various ADDITIONS and ALTERATIONS to COBTREE HOUSE, near Maidstone, for Thomas Franklyn, Esq., together with an Entrance-Lodge, Cottage, and Stable Buildings, or any of them, are requested to deliver Tenders, sealed, and endorsed "Tender for —— at Cobtree," for executing the same, at the office of Messrs. WHICHCORD and SON, Architects, Maidstone, on or before Ten o'Clock of Wednesday, the 21st February next.—Plans and specifications of the works to be done may be seen every day at the above office, between the hours of Nine and Six. The lowest Tender will not be accepted unless approved in all particulars.

TO BUILDERS.

DERBYSHIRE GENERAL INFIRMARY.—Persons desirous of CONTRACTING for the Erection of a NEW WING in connection with the Infirmary at Derby, may see the Plans and Specifications, and obtain every information, at the Offices of Mr. HENRY I. STEVENS, Architect, in Agard-street, Derby, on and after Tuesday, the 20th inst., between the hours of Nine o'clock, A.M., and Seven o'clock, P.M. The Tenders to be delivered (sealed up and endorsed "Tender for Fever Wards"), addressed to the secretary of the Committee, at the Infirmary, on or before Saturday, the 3rd day of March. Sufficient sureties will be required, and the Committee do not pledge themselves to accept the lowest Tender.
Derby, February 6, 1849.

TO BUILDERS.

ALL persons desirous of Contracting for the execution of the works to be done in the repair and restoration of the CHANCEL and CHANCEL AISLES of the Collegiate Church of Wimborne Minster, in the county of Dorset, are requested to send in sealed Tenders, free of all charge, to Mr. EDWARD CASTLEMAN, the registrar of the Corporation of Wimborne Minster aforesaid, at whose offices in Wimborne the drawings and specifications may be seen. The tenders to be divided into three separate parts. First, excavator, mason, pavior, and plasterer; secondly, carpenter, joiner, smith, and ironmonger; thirdly, plumber, painter, and glazier; and to be delivered on or before the 20th day of March, 1849, accompanied by the names of two sureties for the due performance of the works. All parties determining to tender in pursuance of this advertisement are to communicate such determination to the said EDWARD CASTLEMAN as above, and to Messrs. MORRIS and HEBSON, architects, 101, Upper Stamford-street, London, on or before the 20th day of February, 1849.

TO BUILDERS.

ALL persons desirous of Contracting for the execution of the works to be done in the erection of the NEW GRAMMAR SCHOOL and MASTER'S HOUSES, at Wimborne Minster, in the county of Dorset, are requested to send in sealed Tenders, free of all charge, to Mr. EDWARD CASTLEMAN, the registrar of the Corporation of Wimborne Minster aforesaid, at whose offices in Wimborne the drawings and specifications may be seen. The tenders to be divided into four separate parts. First, excavator, bricklayer, tiler, and plasterer; secondly, mason and pavior; thirdly, carpenter, joiner, smith, and ironmonger; fourthly, plumber, painter, glazier, and paper-hanger, and to be delivered on or before the 20th day of March, 1849, accompanied by the names of two sureties for the due performance of the works. All parties determining to tender in pursuance of this advertisement, are to communicate such determination to the said EDWARD CASTLEMAN, and to Messrs. MORRIS and HEBSON, architects, 101, Upper Stamford-street, London, on or before the 20th day of February, 1849.

BEDFORD ESTATE, PARISH OF ST. PANCRAS.—TO CONTRACTORS.—Persons willing to Contract for Cleansing and Watering the Streets, and Removing the Dust, from 290 Houses on the above Estate, for One Year, from the 25th March next, are requested to send Tenders for the same on or before the 28th instant, as below, where every information and Forms of Tenders may be obtained between the hours of Eleven and Four o'Clock.—By order of the Commissioners,
JOHN WOOD, Clerk and Surveyor,
Feb. 9, 1849. 20, Gordon-street, Gordon-square.

LEAD.—Old Lead exchanged.—Builders and the Trade supplied with MILLED and CAST LEAD PIPES, of all sizes, at wholesale prices, at W. DENT'S (late Burton and Dent's), Lead Merchant and Plumber. Lead Trap and Service Boxes always ready. Manufacturer of Engine Pumps and Water Closets. A Patent Urinal Bason to be had only at No. 21, Newcastle-street, Strand.

THE BUILDER.

MOUNTED DRAWING PAPER.—
HENRY POPE has in stock Drawing Paper, which has
been mounted on Linen for TWO YEARS and UPWARDS, in
various lengths of 2 ft. 3 in., 3 ft. 3 in. and 4 ft. 4 in. wide. Tracing
Paper, Drawing and Writing ditto, Envelopes, and every descrip-
tion of Stationery at wholesale prices. Publisher of Weavers'
Hints on Cottage Architecture, with Plans, Elevations, and
Estimates. Imperial 4to. cloth, 2s.—28, Budge-row, Watling-street.

SANITARY IMPROVEMENT. — Perfect
freedom from Stench or Noxious Vapours arising from Sewers
Drains, &c. is insured by the use of
BUNNETT'S
PATENT SELF-ACTING EFFLUVIA TRAPS
Adapted for Streets, Public Buildings, Dwelling Houses, Facto-
ries, Stables, &c.
The above most important improvement has been extensively
tried in the City, and many large provincial towns, with perfect
success. They are cheap, durable, perfectly SELF-ACTING and
SELF-CLEANSING, and cannot get out of order. Manufactured
in various sizes, to suit all purposes, by BUNNETT and CORPE,
ENGINEERS, 36, Lombard-street, London (where specimens may
be seen in action), and at the Works, Deptford, Kent.
INVENTORS AND PATENTEES OF SELF-ACTING
(DOUBLY TRAPPED)
PAN AND VALVE WATER-CLOSETS;
(A most successful combination of the above principle, with other
patented improvements.)

READ and CO., BRASS and COCK
FOUNDERS, 35, Brownlow-street, Drury-lane.—Reduced
Prices.—Tea Closet, with copper pan, complete, 8s.; best ditto,
musk plate, ivory handle, 30s. 14 in. lift pumps, 2 12s.; 2 in.,
2 15s.; 1 in. bib ball and stop cocks, 26s. per dozen; 1 in. 22s.
3 in., 11s.; 1 in. mist washers and wastes, 3s. 6d.; 1 in. ditto, 4s. 6d.;
1 in. service pipes, 14s. 0d. 1 in. driving ferules, 4s. per dozen. Every
article warranted best London manufacture.

TO PLUMBERS, BUILDERS, AND ENGINEERS
CHEAPEST HOUSE IN LONDON for every description of best
Town-made Brass and Copper Work.
PAN CLOSETS complete, with WHITE
BASIN, 10s.—4 inch Lift Pumps, 62s.; 14 in., 7s.; 2 in. 87s 6d.
Cocks 1 14s., 1s. 6d.; 3-8th in., 2s.; 1 in., 3s. 6d.—Copper Pipes, per
foot 1 11s. and; 1 11s. 1s.; 11 in., 1s. 9d.; 2 in., 3s. 9d.
Gun Metal Steam Cocks, Safety Valve, Steam and Water Indi-
cators, &c. equally low at A. McGLASHAN'S, 16, Long-acre, and
Bart-street, Covent Garden.

TO PLUMBERS, IRONMONGERS, &c.
THE PATENT TORRENT WATER-
CLOSET, being found to be the most effective apparatus of
its kind, and having acquired the highest reputation, the manu-
facturers are desirous of appointing Agents in all the Provincial
Towns, to facilitate its introduction and universal adoption.
Those parties who are willing to accept this Agency will find
it a good opportunity of increasing their business with com-
paratively little trouble.—For particulars and terms apply to
the Manufacturers, Messrs. J. E. DOWSON and Co., Stingo Iron
Works, Stingo-lane, London.
N.B. Agents also wanted for the Colonies.

VAUXHALL POTTERY, established
upwards of 130 years.
ALFRED SINGER and Co., Manufacturers of GLAZED STONE
WARE DRAIN PIPES, WATER-CLOSET PANS, &c.

STRAIGHT TUBES WITH SOCKET JOINTS.
3 in.　4 in.　6 in.　9 in.　12 in.
3d.　6d.　9d.　1s.　1s. 10d.　3s. per foot
Bends, Junctions, Traps, &c. &c.
Patentees and Manufacturers of MOSAIC PAVEMENTS.
Close to the Surrey side of Vauxhall-bridge.

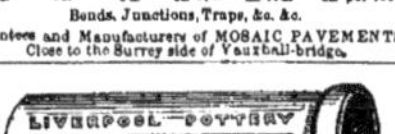

ST. HELENS, LANCASHIRE.
DOULTON'S STONE WARE PIPES, &c.,
manufactured at the above Works, are SHIPPED FREE
ON BOARD in the Port of LIVERPOOL, or placed on Trucks on
the Railway, at the Manchester Railway, without extra charge.
They may also be obtained of the following Agents:—
LIVERPOOL—T, & D. Chaffer, Stone Merchants, Great Howard-
street.
GLASGOW—J. A. Mathieson, Merchant, Hope-street.
CARLISLE—C. Hodgson, Architect.
WESTMORLAND—Miles Thompson, Kendal.
A further List of Agents for the principal Towns will appear in
future advertisements.

IMPORTANT to the SANITARY
MOVEMENT.—PATENT FLUSHING SYPHON BASIN
and SELF-ACTING CLOSET CONNECTION.—It is admitted
by all that nothing is more wanted than a trapped water closet,
simple, cheap, and effective. The above invention will be found to
combine these qualifications. It is complete in itself without expense of fixing. It has no metal apparatus, metal trap, valves, or
cranks. It directs the whole of the water with great force percus-
sively down the sides of the basin, clearing all before it. It is
self-acting, and must cleanse itself on every time of using, without
reference to the person using it, without unsealing the trap, thus
rendering it particularly suited for asylums, hospitals, manufactories, &c. The price, fitted in stained woodwork, with strong well-
glazed terra cotta stone pan, is only 5l. 5s.
Patentee, STEPHEN GREEN, Imperial Potteries, Lambeth,
where architects, builders, and the public can inspect his invention
in use. Also may be seen his

NOTED  TERRA COTTA STONE GLASS LINED PIPES

so highly approved and extensively used by her Majesty's Commissioners of Woods and Forests and the Metropolitan Commissioners of Sewers. Prices the same as common stoneware.
For drawings and explanation see "The Builder" of January
30th, 1846.

SELF-FLUSHING WATER-CLOSETS.—
FLEXIBLE DIAPHRAGM VALVE COCKS.—
"LAMBETH PATENT."—The patentees solicit the attention of
architects, engineers, builders, and the trade to these inventions,
both of which are very great improvement upon the appliances
hitherto in use. The cocks have withstood the test of three years'
trial, under severe pressure, with perfect success, and are warranted
not to leak, and to be exceedingly durable. The closets also have
been tried with all equal success; they are made self-acting
or otherwise, and are so arranged that when self-acting, but a given
quantity of water is used at each action of the seat, the movement
of which is scarcely perceptible. No service-box, D trap, cranks,
or wires are required, consequently the chief means of derangement
and cost of fixing are removed. They are exceedingly cheap and
strong, being made of unannealed iron ware.
THOMAS LAMBERT and SON, Patentees, Manufacturers of
Black Tin Tube, Hydraulic, Steam and Gas Fittings, corner of
Short-street, New-cut, Lambeth.

CHEAP ORNAMENTAL GLASS.—I beg
to inform my friends and the public that I have now completed a new ENGINE, and, owing to the facility with which I can
execute orders, I am enabled to reduce my former prices considerably. The prices are now from ONE SHILLING PER FOOT 6d.,
and borders from SIXPENCE PER FOOT RUN. A large quantity of the cheapest patterns always in stock. Embossing and
painting work on the most moderate terms—CHARLES LONG,
No 1, King-street. Bakerstreet. Portman-square.—Cash only.

E and W. H. JACKSON beg to call the
attention of Builders and the trade to the reduced prices
of their PATENT PLATE GLASS, which, from its cheapness, is
now superseding crown in all respectable dwelling-houses.
BRITISH and ROUGH PLATE, CROWN, SHEET, STAINED,
and ORNAMENTAL GLASS, supplied of the best manufacture,
and at the lowest terms. List of prices, estimates, and every information can be had on application at their warehouses, 313,
Oxford-street.

PATENT PLATE GLASS.—CLAUDET
and HOUGHTON beg to remind Architects, Builders, and
the Trade of the very low price at which they are now selling
PATENT PLATE GLASS, the effect of which is to supersede the
use of Crown Glass in the principal windows of all the better class
of dwelling-houses.— PLATE, SHEET, CROWN, COLORED,
and ORNAMENTAL WINDOW GLASS Warehouse, 89, High
Holborn. Lists of the reduced prices forwarded free on application.

PAINTED and STAINED GLASS and
ORNAMENTAL GLASS of every kind, for Windows.
CLAUDET and HOUGHTON, 89, High Holborn, execute every
description of Ornamental Glass for Windows, in ancient or
modern style, at the lowest prices consistent with superior workmanship, either in plain colour, ornamental in white, embossed,
engraved, or richly painted.—Patterns and specimens may be seen
at their Warehouse, 89, High Holborn.

THE UNION PLATE GLASS COMPANY
beg to call the attention of architects, surveyors, builders,
large consumers, and the trade generally, to the quality, colour,
and substance of their highly-finished glass, and as the discounts
vary according to size, they prefer giving a special estimate for each
quantity required. To encourage the use of Plate Glass for glazing
purposes, the price is considerably reduced, which will, for its
durability and appearance, insure the preference to any other
description.
ROUGH PLATE GLASS supplied for skylights, warehouses,
workshops, and flooring, 3-8ths, 1, 1 and 1 inch thick.
London Warehouse, 90, Hatton-garden, Holborn.
M. CHRISTIE, Agent.

CHAS. WM. WATERLOW,
MANUFACTURER
of Sashes and Frames, and Joiner
to the Trade, 121, Bunhill-row,
Finsbury-square.—Well-seasoned
materials, superior workmanship,
lowest prices.— Upwards of 200
DOORS, and a large variety of
Sashes and Frames, always on sale.
Glazed goods securely packed for
the country. Steam-struck Mouldings in any quantity.—N.B. This
Establishment is worth the notice
of all engaged in building.

SHOP FRONTS, SASHES AND FRAMES, DOORS, &c.
MADE FOR THE TRADE
JOHNSON and PASK,
1, Stanwell-street, Clerkenwell,
near the New River Head.
Beg to inform the Trade, and
the Building Public in general,
that they continue to manufacture Sashes and Frames, Shop
Fronts, Doors, and all other
kinds of Joiners' work, on the
lowest possible scale of prices.
All kinds of Wainscot and Mahogany work done in the very
best manner; French polished,
and carefully packed for the
country.—A list of prices
forwarded by return of post, to any part of the country.

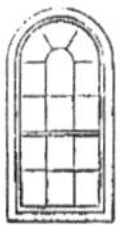

WARM-AIR STOVES.—J. L. BENHAM and SONS respectfully solicit the attention of
Architects, Builders, and the Public in general to their extensive stock of AIR-STOVES, suitable for Shops, Halls, School-
Rooms, &c. Also, a great variety of CHURCH or CHAPEL STOVES.
Greenhouses, Halls, and other buildings WARMED BY HOT WATER from the servant's offices, or by the circulation of WARM
AIR ON THE POLMAISE SYSTEM, which is efficient and of very moderate cost.
19, WIGMORE-STREET, CAVENDISH-SQUARE, LONDON.

TUBULAR DRAINS in GLAZED STONE WARE, MANUFACTURED BY
HENRY DOULTON AND CO., POTTERS, HIGH-STREET, LAMBETH, LONDON.
STRAIGHT TUBES, WITH SOCKET JOINTS.

In 3 foot lengths.	In 2 feet lengths.
3 in.　4 in.	6 in.　9 in.　12 in.　15 in.　18 inch bore
3d.　6d.	9d.　8d.　1s 1d.　1s. 10d.　3s.　4s. per foot.

BENDS, JUNCTIONS, AND TRAPS OF ALL KINDS.
TESTIMONIALS from Messrs. Roe and Phillips, Surveyors to the new Metropolitan Commission of Sewers.
DEAR SIR,—I would respectfully recommend the building profes-
sion generally, in future to use no other material than Glazed
Stoneware Pipes for house drains; and I am quite sure by their re
doing, they will be conferring a great boon on public health, and
that to an extent they little suppose. I also respectfully submit
that there is now no reasonable excuse for their not using them,
for it has been proved that as regards strength, durability, and
efficiency, there cannot be a better article.
I am, Dear Sir, yours truly,
Mr. H. Doulton.　JOHN PHILLIPS.

DEAR SIR,—In reply to your request, I beg to state that Glazed
Stoneware Tubular Drains are those which I would in all case
recommend builders or proprietors of houses to use, there being no
other material that at this time equals them in efficiency joined
with economy.
I am, Dear Sir, yours truly,
Mr. H. Doulton.　JOHN ROE.

No. 1, In Two Pieces.　No. 2, In One Piece.

No 3, is similar to No. 2,
but with the discharge-
hole in a horizontal di-
rection.
No. 4 in three pieces.

CHEAP WATER-CLOSET PANS,
with Syphon Traps,
IN GLAZED STONE WARE,
PRICE 7s. 6d. EACH,
Manufactured by
DOULTON AND WATTS,
LAMBETH POTTERY,
HIGH-STREET, LAMBETH, LONDON.

The annexed Pans are of the most simple yet perfect construction;
they are cleanly and imperishable; require no metal fans; and the
price at which they are offered is so low, as to admit of their universal
adoption.

JAMES STIFF, MANUFACTURER of GLAZED STONE WARE DRAIN PIPES,
BENDS, JUNCTIONS, TRAPS, &c., 30, HIGH STREET, LAMBETH, LONDON. Established 1751.
Water-Closet Pans, with Syphon Traps, 7s. 6d. each.
STRAIGHT TUBES, with Socket Joints, in 2 feet lengths!

The great advantages attending the
use of these articles are now so generally
understood, as to need any enumeration of them almost superfluous. Their
cheapness, cleanliness, and durability are
universally admitted; while of a rapidly
increasing demand for them proves their
estimated superiority over every other
kind hitherto before the public for similar purposes.
Inspection is invited to an assorted
stock of Drain Tubes, of every form and
size, adapted to the various structures for
which they may be required; as also to
the WATER-CLOSET PANS OF IM-
PROVED CONSTRUCTION, and inferior glaze far surpassing any other
manufactured of Brown Stone Ware.

| 3 in. bore, 3d. | 4 in. 6d. | 6 in. 9d. | 9 in. 1s. 1½d. | 12 in. 1s. 10d. | 15 in. 3s. 4d. per Foot |

N.B. These are made
without the discharge-
hole being turned down-
wards.

May be had also a Messrs. GLADDISH'S LIME WHARFS.—Pratt's Wharf, near Westminster Bridge; Upper Wharf, City Basin
Dockhead, Bermondsey; Danver's Wharf, foot of Battersea Bridge, Chelsea; Pratt Wharf, King's-road, Camden New Town.

WINDOW GLASS. — THOMAS
MILLINGTON solicits an inspection of the different
GLASSES he has now in stock, the qualities of which will be
found to be very superior.—47, Bishopsgate-street, Without.
NEW TARIFF.—Sheet in various sizes' dimensions delivered
free in London.

	Common in 100 feet cases	30s. 0d.
	Do. do.	3s. 0d.
	Thirds 90 do.	10s. 6d.
	Seconds 200 do.	19s. 6d.
	Best, in small	100s. 6d.

ROUGH PLATE GLASS for WINDOWS, SKYLIGHTS, and
FLOORS in sizes not exceeding 5 feet superficial.

1 thick	1s. 6d.	1 inch	2s. 6d.
3-8th inch	1s. 9d.	1 inch	3s. 6d. per foot.
1 inch	1s. 9d.		

PATENT ROUGH PLATE TILES.

1 thick	6s. 11½d.	3-8th inch, 1s. 7½d.
1 inch	1s. 2d.	1 inch, 2s. 6d. each.

GLASS DOMES for SKYLIGHTS, from 15 to 30 inches in
diameter. These are well worth notice.

C C C Crown per cent in tables	£1 16 0
C C do. do.	2 0 0
Fourths do. do.	1 9 0
Thirds do.	1 5 0
Large Crown Squares in 100 feet boxes	31d. per foot.
1 by 2 — 10 by 8 do.	2s. 0d.

Very superior Plate for Pictures and Windows, averaging 28oz.
from 1s. 6d. per foot upwards.

SNOXELL'S PATENT SAFETY
REVOLVING WOOD SHUTTERS, Manufactory, 99,
REGENT-STREET and 118, CHANCERY-LANE. Patent sealed
on the 4th day of February, 1846, for Fourteen Years, for Improvements in Revolving Shutters of WOOD and IRON, consisting of
Six Methods of Raising and Lowering Shutters without Machinery,
and Two for Hingeing and Sheathing the Edges of Wood Laths with
Iron.—The Patentee having fixed up some hundreds, will feel
pleased in forwarding the Testimonials of Architects. Principals of
large Establishments, and others, having them now in use, which
fully guarantees the Patentee in stating they are beyond dispute
superior to any other Revolving Shutter for durability, security,
and simplicity, without the use of cog-wheel worm and screw gear,
or any other complicated machinery employed by other makers.

BUNNETT and CORPÉ, ENGINEERS,
Patentees of
REVOLVING IRON and WOOD SAFETY SHUTTERS,
and of
ORNAMENTAL METALLIC SASH BARS MOULDINGS, &c.
IN BRASS, COPPER, ZINC, &c.
FOR SHOP-FRONTS, SKYLIGHTS, &c.
Shop-fronts completely fitted and fixed in a superior style, either
plain or ornamental, also glazed with best plate glass. Strong
moulded stallboards handsomely engraved. Metal works and
mouldings of all kinds in connection with banking-houses, shops,
warehouses, &c. &c.
Iron and L-challenge competition as to either quality or price.
Designs furnished and estimates given.
IMPROVED PATENT BENCH and FLOORING CRAMPS
FOR BUILDERS.
SOLE LICENCEES FOR MARVIN and MOORE'S
PATENT DIAGONAL GRATINGS
Office of the Patentees, 36, Lombard-street, London; and at the
Works, Deptford, Kent.

LIGHTERAGE.—To Timber, Slate, Stone,
and Coal Merchants, Saw-mill Proprietors, Contractors, and
others requiring Lighterage.—CHARLES STRUTTON, Lighterman, &c. is willing to undertake Lighterage at the following low
rates, viz.—Coals, 8d. per ton; Slates, Stone, &c., 9d. per ton; Deals,
3s. 3d. per 120; Thames Ballast, 3d. per yard; Timber, 4s. per
load. Other Goods in proportion. Barges laid on in tow.
34, Commercial-road, Lambeth, and Trinity-street, Rotherhithe.

BUILDERS AND CONTRACTORS
TARPAULINS for COVERING ROOFS
during Repairs. SCAFFOLD CORD and every description
of ROPE used by Builders upon the lowest terms. Marquees and
temporary awnings on sale or hire. Orders per post receive the most
prompt attention.—WILLIAM PIGGOTT, 118, Fore Street, City,
Manufacturer, by Appointment, to Her Majesty's Honourable
Board of Ordnance.

In one very large volume, 8vo., illustrated by above Three Thousand Engravings on Wood, price 2l. 12s. 6d. cloth,

AN ENCYCLOPÆDIA of CIVIL ENGINEERING, Historical, Theoretical, and Practical. By EDWARD CRESY, F.S.A., C.E.
"A desideratum in the history of engineering science is supplied by the publication of this remarkable volume. There is no member of the community, from the highest engineer to the humblest surveyor, who will not find here materials to enrich his store and extend his knowledge."—Irish Railway Gazette.
London—LONGMAN, BROWN, GREEN, and LONGMANS.

In one very thick vol. 8vo. 2l. 16s., the Third Edition,

DR. URE'S DICTIONARY of ART MANUFACTURES, and MINES; containing a clear Exposition of their Principles and Practice. Third Edition, corrected throughout. With 1,241 Woodcuts.
Also,
RECENT IMPROVEMENTS in ART MANUFACTURES and MINES; being the 2nd Edition of the Supplement to 3rd Edit. in "A Dictionary." 8vo., Woodcuts, 16s.
London: LONGMAN, BROWN, GREEN, and LONGMANS.

NESBIT'S LAND SURVEYING, IMPROVED.
A new edition, in 8vo., with numerous Woodcuts, Plates, and Engraved Field-Book, price 12s. cloth,

A COMPLETE TREATISE on PRAC- TICAL LAND-SURVEYING. For the use of Schools and Students. With 30 Practical Examples.
By A. NESBIT.
Ninth Edition, corrected and greatly enlarged.
To which are now added,
PLANE TRIGONOMETRY, including the use of the Theodolite and Railway Surveying; also, Railway Engineering, including the principles and practice of Levelling, Planning, Laying Curves, Cutting and Embanking, Tunnelling, Viaducts, &c.
T. BAKER, Land-Surveyor and Civil Engineer.
London: LONGMAN, BROWN, GREEN, and LONGMANS.

Now ready, Imperial 4to.,

HINTS on COTTAGE A being a Selection of Designs for in pairs, and in groups; with Plans, Elevations and description. Dedicated, by express permission, to the Earl of Landowers, K.G., &c.
By HENRY WEAVER, Architect.
London : HENRY POPE, 28, High Holborn.
Bath : BARRETT and Co., Milsom-street.

TO LANDOWNERS, RAILWAY COMPANIES, SOLICITORS, SURVEYORS, AND OTHERS.
Just published, price One Shilling,

RAILWAY COMPENSATION in PRACTICE, with Suggestions for its Improvement. Letter to the Right Honourable the Board of Commissioners of Railways.
By RICE HOPKINS, Civil Engineer and Surveyor.
M. Inst. C.E.
Westminster: JAMES BIGG and SONS, 23, Parliament-street

TO RAILWAY COMPANIES, ENGINEERS, BUILDERS CONTRACTORS, MANUFACTURERS, AND OTHERS.

HOLLAND'S WAGES TABLES, for single sheet, calculated by the Quarter, from a quarter twenty days, at from 1s. to 5s. per diem, rising 2d. each. This may be had (free) upon enclosing seven postage stamps, to a paid letter, addressed to Mr. J. T. HOLLAND, Andover, Hants "Although designated 'Railway Time and Wages Tables,' are of general utility."—Railway Times.

SANITARY REFORM.

TAYLOR'S ORIGIN BUILDERS' PRICE BOOK ample List of Builders' Prices, & Tower Act, and the various Char sanitary regulations can be effected The Act for the Health of Towns
M. Taylor, 1, Wellington.

Just published, price 4s.,

LAXTON'S BUILDERS' PRICES f 1849, containing upwards of 11,000 Prices and Memoranda and the whole of the Building Act and the modifications. The work has undergone a complete revision, in consequence of the reduced prices of materials of several kinds.
"To be had of WEALE, High Holborn; SIMPKIN and MARSHALL, and GROOMBRIDGE and SONS, Paternoster-row; at the Office of "The Builder," 2, York-street, Covent Garden; and at the Office of "The Civil Engineer and Architect's Journal 59, Fleet-street."

BUILDERS' PRICES, CORRECTED TO THE PRESENT TIME.
This day is published, price 4s., a new edition of

CROSBY'S BUILDERS' PRIC BOOK for 1849. Containing a correct amount of all the present prices allowed by the most eminent surveyors; the alterations and additions in the new edition will be found to be most important, including the New Building Act, a new plan, showing the sections of walls for dwelling-houses, warehouses, &c., also a complete List of surveyors.
London : only by JOY, 44, Paternoster-row.

FOR 1849.

KELLY'S PRACTICAL BUILDER PRICE BOOK; or, Safe Guide to the Valuation of all kinds of Artificers' work; with the modern practice of Measurement; also a Manual of the New Building Act for regulating the construction of Buildings. Revised and corrected by New Calculations upon the present Value of Materials and Labour. Arranged by an Architect of eminence, assisted by several experienced Measurers, Surveyors, Illustrated and exemplified by Steel Engravings and numerous Woodcuts. Royal 8vo, price 6s., neatly bound.
London: Published by T. KELLY, Paternoster-row; SIMPKIN and MARSHALL, and may be had of all Booksellers.

In 2 vols. 8vo. 3l. 3s.,

A DICTIONARY of ARCHITECTURAL DECORATIVE and CONSTRUCTIVE; or a Popular Explanation of the Terms used by Civil and Military Architects and Engineers, Landscape Gardeners, Surveyors, Masons, Bricklayers, Carpenters, Joiners, Plumbers, Painters, Glaziers, and in chief's description of work and buildings. Illustrated by several hundred Wood Engravings.
By WALTER BERNAN, Architect and Engineer.
In this work will be found an ample collection of Medieval words, of old terms descriptive of Classic and Gothic Architecture, and of modern technical terms in all the branches of the whole forming a list of which Several Thousand Words have never been inserted in any previous Architectural Dictionary.
JOHN WILLIAMS and CO., 141, Strand.

Just published, small 4to., twenty plates, some coloured, price £

EXAMPLES for FINISHINGS in th ITALIAN STYLE.
By F. W. TRENDALL, Architect.
Consisting of Entrance Halls and Folding Doors, Windows, a Shutters, Chimney-pieces, Verandas, Balconies, and Ornamental Cornices, coloured, the whole forming a book of Working Drawings.

THE COMPANION TO THE BUILDER FRIEND. By HENRY FITZGERALD. Price 1s.
THE YOUNG ARCHITECT AND CLERK OF WORKS' GUIDE. Price 6s.
OFFICE BOOK FOR ARCHITECTS AN BUILDERS. Price 1s. 6d.
THE PRINCIPLES OF PERSPECTIVE and their application to Drawing from Nature, familiarly explained and illustrated. By WILLIAM RIDER. Price 8s. 6d.
BARTHOLOMEW'S PRACTICAL ARCH LECTURE. 160 woodcuts. 12s.
JOHN WILLIAMS and CO. Architectural and Engineering Publishers, 141, Strand.

LONDON: printed by CHARLES WYMAN, of 7, Calthorpe-street, in the Parish of St. Pancras, in the County of Middlesex, Printer, at the Printing-office of J. & H. Cox, Brothers, 74 & 75, Great Queen-street, Lincoln's-Inn-Fields, in the Parish of St. Giles-in-the-Fields, in the said County; and published by the said CHARLES WYMAN, at the Office of "THE BUILDER," 2, York-street, Covent Garden, in the Parish of Saint Paul, Covent-Garden, also in the said County.—Saturday, February 17, 1849.

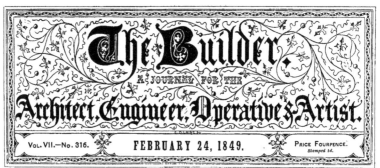

The Builder.
A JOURNAL FOR THE Architect, Engineer, Operative & Artist.

| Vol. VII.—No. 316. | FEBRUARY 24, 1849. | PRICE FOURPENCE. Stamped 5d. |

ILLUSTRATIONS.

Plan of Jerusalem, Ancient and Modern : J. J. Scoles, Architect, Mesat 90
Carved Book-cover, from Stowe 91

CONTENTS.

On the Prevention of Damp in Buildings—and the Cure of it when there 85
Professor Cockerell's Lectures on Architecture 86
Encroachhterments of Leaseholds 87
Surface-Delineation and Plane-Modelling! Carrington's Model of Yorkshire and Lancashire 88
Public Baths and Washhouses 89
On the Topography and Antiquities of the City of Jerusalem... 90
Carved Book-Cover from Stowe 91
Light : Leslie's Tube Burners 91
Right of Architects to Copy Plans entrusted to them : Royal Italian Opera House 93
Notes in the Provinces 93
Metropolitan Commission of Sewers 93
Encroachment on the New-road, Islington : Metropolitan Improvements 93
The Cost of the City and Surrey Courts 93
The River Wall of the Houses of Parliament 93
Miscellanea 93

London : Printed by CHARLES WYMAN, of 7, Calthorpe-street, in the Parish of St. Pancras, in the County of Middlesex, Printer, at the Printing-office of J. & H. Cox, Brothers, 74, 75, Great Queen-street, Lincoln's-Inn-Fields, in the Parish of St. Giles-in-the-Fields, in the said County ; and published by the self Charles Wyman, at the Office of "The Builder," 2, York-street, Covent Garden, in the Parish of Saint Paul, Covent Garden, also in the said County.—Saturday, February 24, 1843.

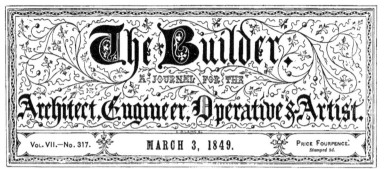

Vol. VII.—No. 317.   MARCH 3, 1849.   Price Fourpence.
Stamped 5d.

ILLUSTRATIONS.

The Cavendish-street Schools, Manchester: Mr. Edward Walters, Architect 103
Forms for Window Glazing 103

CONTENTS.

Necessity for Supervision of Places of Public Resort—The Cause of the Calamity in Glasgow—Stairs and Access of our Theatres—Position of Architects—Woods and Forests.. 97
On the Topography and Antiquities of the City of Jerusalem 99
On the Construction of Prisons...................................... 100
Royal Institute of Architects: Architects' Proposed Benevolent Fund 101
The late Mr. Harvey Eginton 101
The "Barns of Harold"—Curious Case 101
Balloon Railway.. 101
The Cavendish-street Schools, Manchester 102
Proceedings at Birmingham, Manchester, and Hull 102
Forms for Window-Glazing 103
On a New Form of Malleable Iron Floor lately patented by Mr. Nathaniel Boardman, Civil Engineer 103
Notes in the Provinces.. 104
Right of Architects to Copy Drawings : Royal Italian Opera House, Covent Garden 105
Works at Beverley.. 105
Encroachment on the New-road.............................. 106
Books: Year-Book of Facts—Archæologia, Hibernica—Marshall's Index Ready Reckoner—Taylor's Builders' Price Book 105
Miscellanea 105

ADVERTISEMENTS.

HOUSE WANTED, containing not less than four good bed rooms, two sitting rooms, and the usual domestic offices, with chaisehouse, stable, and good garden; if detached preferred.—Address, with full particulars, to I. M., 7, Shepperton Cottages, New North-road, Islington. Rent must be moderate.

BUILDING GROUND WANTED, about three to six miles from Charing-cross, by an architect, who would build on a portion on his own account, in consideration of the owner intrusting him with the management of the remainder of the estate.—Address to Mr. BELL, 40, Coleman-street.

BUILDING GROUND TO LET (direct from the Freeholder), facing the north and south sides of St. Peter's Church, Hackney-road.—Particulars will be furnished by Mr. G. THREADGOLD, Builder, No. 3, Warner-place South, Hackney-road.

AMPTHILL SQUARE.—BEDFORD ESTATE.—ELIGIBLE BUILDING GROUND to LET. The square is enclosed and the garden planted; roads, sewers, vaults, and excavations completed. Parties taking ground can be assisted with money.—Apply to Mr. IVIMEY, 26, Chancery-lane, Solicitor.

TO TIMBER MERCHANTS, BUILDERS, ENGINEERS, AND COACHMAKERS.

TO BE LET, those desirable LEASEHOLD PREMISES, CLARK'S TIMBER YARD, Waterloo-road, near the Obelisk.

TO BUILDERS AND OTHERS.

TO BE LET, on BUILDING LEASES, for 80 years, upon reasonable terms, and liberal advances made, some ELIGIBLE PLOTS OF GROUND, desirably situate in Acre-lane, upon the high road from Brixton to Clapham.—Particulars may be had, and plans inspected, at the offices of RICE, BROTHERS, 263, High-street, Borough, Southwark.

TO BUILDERS, SMALL CAPITALISTS, AND OTHERS.

TO BE LET, on LEASE for forty years, renewable every fourteen years, FOUR HOUSES, situate at the corner of Vine-street and Onslow-street, near Hatton Garden, Holborn.—For particulars, inquire at the office of Mr. GEORGE SMITH, Frederick's-place, Old Jewry, between the hours of Ten and Four.

TO COAL MERCHANTS, WHARFINGERS, &c.

TO BE LET, or the LEASE TO BE DISPOSED OF, a very Desirable and Valuable WHARF, situate in the most eligible part of the Harrow Road, Paddington, comprising a snug and convenient Dwelling-house and Offices, with Loft, Stabling for eight or nine Horses, and Gas-fittings complete; the whole in substantial repair, and may be entered upon immediately. Terms and further particulars may be obtained, by principals only, or their solicitors, on application to Mr. GEO. LEA, Eccleston Wharf, Pimlico.

TO BUILDERS, CONTRACTORS, MARBLE MERCHANTS, STATUARIES, AND OTHERS requiring convenient WATER-SIDE PREMISES.

TO BE LET, on lease, at a moderate rent, with immediate possession, an eligible WHARF (a short distance from the new Houses of Parliament), with dwelling-house, stabling, workshops, traveller, and offices, and possessing a river frontage of 100 feet.—For further particulars, and tickets to view the premises, apply to Messrs. EVERSFIELD and HORNE, Auctioneers and Estate Agents, 1, Little Smith-street, Westminster.

TO BUILDING SOCIETIES, SPECULATORS, AND OTHERS.

THE MOST ELIGIBLE FRONTAGE unoccupied in Islington, in the best and healthiest part, facing St. Paul's-terrace, adjoining the church, leading from Balls Pond-gate to Canonbury Park, for the long term of ninety-nine years, ground for sixteen full-sized third-rate semi-detached cottages; the frontage will be 70 feet the pair by about 130 feet deep; ground-rents very moderate.

N.B. Houses of this description let and sell as fast as built.—Apply to Mr. ROBERT WEBB, 13, Spencer-terrace, Lower-road, Islington, or to Mr. DAVIES, Conveyancer, Charles-square, Hoxton.

TO BUILDERS AND WHOLESALE PURCHASERS.

TO BE DISPOSED OF, about 20 best BRIGHT REGISTER STOVES (last year's patterns), under cost price. Handsome drawing-room stoves, Ormolu ornaments, and two sets bars, at five guineas.—H. WATSON, actual manufacturer, 19, Wilson-street, Finsbury-square.

TO GAS COMPANIES, WATER COMPANIES, AND OTHERS.

TO BE DISPOSED OF, about NINETY 24-inch MAIN PIPES, at — per ton.—Application, for particulars as to price, &c., to be made to the Storekeeper, at the "Chartered Gas Light and Coke Company's" works, Horseferry-road, Westminster.—Feb., 1849.

TO HOUSE PAINTERS, Plumbers, Glaziers, Decorators, and Others.

TO BE PARTED WITH, and immediate possession given of an ESTABLISHED CONCERN,—the present proprietor leaving town. Lease about 18 years to run. The stock in trade and the planned furniture to dwelling-house to be taken at valuation, less 10 per cent. The house is replete with every convenience, and in the best condition; a clear income of more than 100*l.* per annum arises from letting. The business premises adjoin the house, and contain ample space for the distinct branches: situate at the West-end. The Agency Business may be advantageously added.—For particulars address C. Broadbridge, Esq., Architect and Surveyor, 67, Great Portland-street, Portland-place.

TO BUILDERS AND OTHERS.

BOW-LANE, BROMLEY, MIDDLESEX.—TO BE LET, on building leases, for a term of 99 years, two very desirable pieces of FREEHOLD LAND (land-tax redeemed), containing about 9 acres, situate on the east and west sides of Bow-lane, near the East India Docks, in the parish of St. Leonard's, Bromley, Middlesex.—Particulars of the terms of letting, and every other information may be obtained of Messrs. HOLTON, MERRIMAN, and DUNNING, solicitors, 23, Austin-friars; or of Mr. MASON, 21, Lime-street, surveyor to the estate, where plans of the property may be inspected.

HOLLAND PARK ESTATE.—TO BUILDERS and OTHERS.—TO BE LET, upon Leases, direct from the freeholder, for the term of ninety-nine years, at very low ground-rents, and on the most favourable terms, PLOTS of GROUND, situate on this most delightful estate, for the erection of detached and semi-detached villas, frontages on the squares, crescents, and roads now being laid out; frontages also for shops on the new road, of 70 feet in width, about being formed from the Royal-crescent, Notting-hill, to Kensington, which is designed to become the leading thoroughfare, and will reduce by one-third the time now consumed in the journey from Notting-hill and its vicinity to town.

This estate lies between the main Kensington and Notting-hill roads, and has a full southern and western aspect, being protected from the north and east by the rising ground of Notting-hill. It commands extensive views from the Surrey hills to Harrow, and delightful prospects over the undulating ground, the lofty grove, and shrubberies of the park and gardens of Holland House. A substratum of firm gravel extends over the whole of the estate, and a new and capacious sewer, lately built, at a vast expense, by the Great Western Railway Company, completely drains the estate.

The facilities afforded by the West London Railway and the Kensington Canal for the transport of building materials considerably reduces the cost of building on this estate; thus freestone, by these means, can be procured at little more than the ordinary expense of compo, which, to the enterprising builder, affords the most favourable opportunity for the erection of what the public so much desire, good, substantial, and stone-built houses, in a situation that, for salubrity of air, good drainage, and fashionable locality, stands unrivalled in the suburbs of the metropolis.

Several sites for superior villa residences, with large garden-grounds attached, may be had.

N.B. A capital corner site for a public-house in the New-street.

Application to be made at the Offices of GEORGE H. GODDARD, Esq., 8, John-street, Adelphi, where Plans may be seen of the proposed outlay of the Estate, and all particulars obtained.

TO OLD MATERIAL DEALERS.

FOR SALE by TENDER, the MATERIALS of 110, HIGH-STREET, WHITECHAPEL.—Apply to Mr WALES, 5, Crosby Hall Chambers, Bishopsgate-street.

IRON CRANES FOR SALE.—Several Two-ton revolving MAST CRANES, of first-rate quality and modern construction, manufactured by one of the most eminent Crane-makers in the kingdom.—Price and particulars on application to Mr. A. REID, Monument Chambers, 14, Fish-street-hill.

N.B. Cranes of any size made to order.

SALES BY AUCTION.

TO BOAT AND BARGE BUILDERS, LIGHTERMEN, AND OTHERS.

MESSRS. EVERSFIELD and HORNE will SELL BY AUCTION, on the Premises, Tunnel-square, Rotherhithe, on TUESDAY, March 13, at Twelve, by order of the proprietors, to clear the premises, the remaining STOCK of a BARGE BUILDER, comprising round oak timber, in stocks, knees, butts, planking, &c., old and new barge timber, various, bar and scrap iron, chains and moorings, crab engine, weighing machine, firewood, &c.; also three new lightermen's skiffs, a new quay skiff, and other effects.—May be viewed one day previous, and catalogues had on the premises and of the Auctioneers, Coal Exchange, or 1, Little Smith-street, Westminster.

TO TIMBER MERCHANTS, BUILDERS, CONTRACTORS, AND OTHERS.

MESSRS. EVERSFIELD and HORNE will SELL by AUCTION, on the Premises, Belvedere-road, Lambeth, on THURSDAY, March 22nd, at Twelve, the sixth portion of the valuable STOCK of Mr. Grissell, who has relinquished the General Building business, about 3,000 well-seasoned yellow and white deals, planks, and battens (removed for convenience of sale), 100 fir telegraph poles, a capital black marble chimney-piece, several marble tables, slate sawing machine, about fifty Plummer P traps, brass-work, and other effects.—May be viewed three days prior to the sale, and catalogues had on the premises, and of the Auctioneers, Coal-Exchange, or 1, Little Smith-street, Westminster.

The extensive Wharf and Premises are to be Let.

TO TIMBER MERCHANTS, CONTRACTORS, LIGHTERMEN, WHARFINGERS, STEAM-BOAT COMPANIES, AND OTHERS.

MESSRS. EVERSFIELD and HORNE have received instructions from the Proprietors, who are retiring from business, to SELL BY AUCTION, at the Cross Keys Tavern, corner of Upper Ground-street, Blackfriars, on THURSDAY, March 8th, 1849, at Twelve for One precisely, their very excellent STOCK of CRAFT, comprising a nearly new sailing barge, the *Marion*, of 65 tons; the *Richard and Alice* sailing barge, of 60 tons; three decked barges, of 60 tons each; fourteen open barges, from 30 to 60 tons each; four punts, and a lug boat. Also, the very eligible roadsteads, with moorings, between Blackfriars and Waterloo bridges. At the same time, three nearly new barges, of 110 tons, 100 tons, and 80 tons respectively, built expressly for the timber trade.—May be viewed at the roads above Blackfriars-bridge, and at the places stated in the catalogues, four days previous to the sale; and catalogues may be had at the Place of Sale; at the Corn Exchange Coffee-house, Mark-lane; and of the Auctioneers, Coal Exchange, or No. 1, Little Smith-street, Westminster.

MR. R. MAY will SELL BY AUCTION, by direction of the Mortgagees, at the Mart, opposite the Bank of England, on WEDNESDAY, the 7th day of March, 1849, a desirable LEASEHOLD ESTATE, consisting of Thirteen Houses, situate at Mile-end, which will be sold in three lots.

Lot 1 consists of five four-roomed dwelling-houses, with wash-house and garden, situate Nos. 7, 8, 9, 10, 11, James-street, Globe-lane, Mile-end, all let to weekly tenants, at rents amounting to 78*l.* per annum, to be held at a ground-rent of 17*l.* per annum.

Lot 2 consists of four similar houses, situate Nos. 2, 3, 4, 5, West-street, adjoining, let to weekly tenants, at rents amounting to 52*l.* per annum, to be held at a ground-rent of 12*l.* per annum.

Lot 3 consists of four similar houses, situate Nos. 14, 15, 16, 17, Essex-street, adjoining the first lot, and in all respects similar to lot 2.

The whole thirteen houses are held under one lease, for 59 years from 18th December, 1846.—Particulars and conditions of sale may be had of Messrs. FINCH and SHEPHERD, 24, Moorgate-street; at the Auction Mart; and of the Auctioneer, Estate Office, 90, Leadenhall-street.

MR. R. MAY has received instructions by the Mortgagees, and under a power of sale, to SELL BY AUCTION, at the Mart, opposite the Bank of England, on WEDNESDAY, March 7, 1849, in Two Lots, a valuable long LEASEHOLD ESTATE (nearly equal to Freehold), consisting of two eight-roomed dwelling houses, Nos. 13 and 16, Desborough-terrace, Harrow-road (adjoining Westbourne Villas), each held upon lease for 500 years from 24th June, 1845, at a ground-rent of 7*l.* No. 16 is let to a respectable tenant at 36*l.* per annum; the other is of equal value and in good tenantable repair, fit for immediate occupation.

Also, a desirable eight-roomed Dwelling-house, newly erected, and nearly finished, situated in that improving neighbourhood close to the terminus of the London and North Western Railway, No. 10, Werrington-street, Oakley-square, Camden-town, estimated to let at 40*l.* per annum (when finished), held upon lease for 99 years, from 29th September, 1845, at a ground-rent of 7*l.*—Particulars and conditions of sale may be had of Mr. HANLEY, Solicitor, 34, Wilson-street, Finsbury-square; at the Mart, opposite the Bank of England; and of the Auctioneer, Estate Offices, 90, Leadenhall-street.

ARCHITECTURAL and CIVIL ENGINEERING CLASSES, established above 40 years. Conducted by Mr. GRAYSON, Architect, Surveyor, and C.E. Offices, 140, Strand, London. The selection of scientifically-constructed models, accompanying the diagrams, will be found of great utility to the student in elucidating the several mechanical and practical sciences. Morning classes from Nine till Two o'clock daily. Evening classes from Six to Nine o'clock. For cards of terms apply at the Architectural Library, 140, Strand.

CAST-IRON PIPES, IRON WORK FOR OVENS, &c.

RAIN PIPES, &c.—F. A. TIDDEMAN, Purfleet Wharf, Earl-street, City, near Blackfriars-bridge, keeps a large stock of Rain Pipes, Heads, Shoes, Elbows, &c., half round and O. G. Gutters, Socket Pipes for Water or Gas, Flanch Pipes, Sash Weights, and other Castings; Iron Work for Baker's Ovens of every description, fitted complete, to be had in sets or in parts.—Prices equal to all competition. Contracts taken to any extent.

GAS-FITTINGS, LAMPS, and CHANDELIERS.—THOMAS LEDGER, 173, Aldersgate-street, London (two doors from Little Britain), Brass-founder, Gas-fitter, and Manufacturer of Chandeliers, Lamps, and every description of Gas-fittings. Estimates furnished, and experienced workmen sent to any part of town or country. Builders and the Trade supplied.—Warehouse and Show-rooms, 173, Aldersgate-street; Workshops and Foundry, 132, Aldersgate-street.

LEAD.—Old Lead exchanged.—Builders and the Trade supplied with MILLED and CAST LEAD PIPES, of all sizes, at wholesale prices, at W. DENT'S (late Burton and Dent's), Lead Merchant and Plumber. Lead Trap and Service Boxes always ready. Manufacturer of Engine Pumps and Water Closets. A Patent Urinal Bason to be had only at No. 21, Newcastle-street, Strand.

BUILDERS AND CONTRACTORS.

TARPAULINS for COVERING ROOFS during Repairs. SCAFFOLD CORD and every description of ROPE used by Builders upon the lowest terms. Marquees and temporary awnings on sale or hire. Orders per post receive the most prompt attention.—WILLIAM PIGGOTT, 115, Fore Street, City, Manufacturer, by Appointment, to Her Majesty's Honourable Board of Ordnance.

LIGHTERAGE.—To Timber, Slate, Stone, and Coal Merchants, Saw-mill Proprietors, Contractors, and others requiring Lighterage.—CHARLES STRUTTON, Lighterman, &c., is willing to undertake Lighterage at the following low rates, viz.—Coals, 8d. per ton; Slates, Stone, &c., 9d. per ton; Deals, 2s. 6d. per 120; Thames Ballast, 9d. per yard; Timber, 4s. per float. Other Goods in proportion. Barges Let on hire.

34, Commercial-road, Lambeth, and Trinity-street, Rotherhithe.

CONTRACTS.

PRINTERS' ALMSHOUSES.—To BUILDERS.—Parties desirous of TENDERING for the ERECTION of the above ALMSHOUSES can see the Drawings, Specifications, &c., on and after Thursday, March 1st, at the Architect's Office (W. WEBBE, Esq.), 8, King-street, Bloomsbury.—Sealed Tenders to be delivered to the Secretary, Mr. JAS. DARKIN, 21, St. John-street (St. Peter's District), Islington, on or before Wednesday, March 7th.

HOLLAND PARK ESTATE.—To all the Trades connected with Building.—To Brickmakers, Timber Merchants, Stone Contractors, Iron-founders, and Others.—CONTRACTS will be required for the supply of all the MATERIALS in the ABOVE TRADES.—Every information may be obtained at the office of GEORGE H. GODDARD, Esq., 8, John-street, Adelphi.

HOLLAND PARK ESTATE.—To Road Contractors and Others.—Persons desirous of TENDERING for the FORMATION of a NEW ROAD of 70 feet in width, from the Royal Crescent, Notting-hill, to Warwick-square, Kensington, may inspect the plans and specifications at the Offices of GEORGE H. GODDARD, Esq., Architect, 8, John-street, Adelphi, between the hours of Ten and Four.

TENDERS required for BUILDING and FINISHING a few THIRD-RATE HOUSES (during the next four years), near the Mornington-crescent, Hampstead-road.—For particulars, apply to 26, St. Martin's-le-Grand.

TO BE LET, ONE or TWO COTTAGES, with Workshops and Stores, suitable for coach-house and stable), not more than half-a-mile distant.

AYLSHAM, NORFOLK.—GAS WORKS.—Plans, Specifications, and Estimates, for the ERECTION of GAS WORKS, laying all necessary Main Pipes, &c., in the Town of Aylsham, are required. Population, about 2,000.—Plans to be sent in on or before the 7th day of April next, addressed to W. HENRY SCOTT, Secretary of Gas Committee, Aylsham, of whom any necessary information may be had. Plans sent in to be marked with a letter or number, and a sealed note stating the names and address of person sending same.

BOROUGH of LEICESTER CEMETERY.—Persons desirous of CONTRACTING for the ERECTION and COMPLETION of the TWO CHAPELS, CLOISTERS, CATACOMBS, ENTRANCE LODGE, ENTRANCE, and other Works, at the above Cemetery, under the superintendence of Messrs. Hamilton and Medland, the Architects, are requested to forward their names and addresses to Mr. GAY, Clerk of the Works, Town Hall Library, Leicester, not later than the 12th day of March.—Leicester, March 1st, 1849.

SOUTH-WESTERN and BRIGHTON RAILWAY COMPANIES.—To BUILDERS.—The Directors of the Portsmouth Joint Station are prepared to receive TENDERS for the ERECTION of an ENGINE-HOUSE, at Portsmouth. Plans and Specifications may be seen at the Brighton Railway Engineer's Office, London-bridge Station, on and after Monday, the 5th of March next; and Tenders must be sent in, under cover, to the undersigned, not later than Ten o'clock on the morning of Wednesday, the 14th of March.

N.B. Tenders for the whole of the works at the new Portsmouth Station will be required very shortly.—By order of the Joint Committee,

C. J. BRYDGES, Secretary.

South-Western Railway Office, York-road, London, March 1, 1849.

TO BUILDERS.

PARTIES desirous of sending in TENDERS for ERECTING a FARMERY for 700 Acres of Land, at Eldo House, Rougham, near Bury St. Edmund's, for John Josselyn, Esq., may see the plans and specification at the office of Mr. H. WOOLNOUGH, Architect, Crown-street, Ipswich, on and after Tuesday, the 27th inst. The tenders to be delivered to the said Architect before Twelve o'clock A.M., on Tuesday, March the 6th. Sufficient sureties will be required, and the proprietor will not bind himself to accept the lowest tender.

Ipswich, February 17th, 1849.

TO CONTRACTORS AND OTHERS.

THE DIRECTORS of the BITUMINOUS SHALE COMPANY are prepared to receive TENDERS for the Digging, Raising, and Obtaining Bituminous Shale or Schist, at Smedmore and Kimmeridge, in the Isle of Purbeck, in the county of Dorset, and also for the delivery at the Company's Works at Northport, Wareham, in the said county of Dorset, distant about eight miles. Particulars and terms of contract may be seen on application to the Secretary, at the Office, No. 16, Hanover-street, Hanover-square, London, or to Mr. William C. Turnbull, at Wareham, between the hours of Twelve and Three, any day after the 1st of March next. No tenders will be received after the 15th of March. The Directors do not pledge themselves to accept the lowest or any tender.—By order of the Directors,

Feb. 26, 1849. A. M. POLLOCK, Secretary.

TO ARCHITECTS AND OTHERS.

BUCKS.—JUDGES' LODGINGS.—NOTICE IS HEREBY GIVEN, that the Committee of Magistrates appointed by the Court of Quarter Session for the County of Buckingham, for the purpose of providing Lodgings and suitable Accommodation for her Majesty's Judges of Assize, at Aylesbury, being empowered to expend a limited sum for that purpose, are desirous of receiving from Architects PLANS, Specifications, and Estimates for ERECTING the same. Further particulars as to the site, and also as to the nature and description of the lodgings, may be obtained upon personal application at my office. The plans must be sent in, sealed up, to me, not later than Ten o'Clock in the morning of the 28th of March, 1849, on which day the Committee will meet to decide upon the plan to be adopted, and to appoint an architect. The Committee do not pledge themselves to accept the plan with the lowest estimate, but reserve to themselves the right of selecting the plan which they shall consider most eligible, as well as of rejecting all or any of such plans; and parties sending in plans are desired to state the extent and mode of remuneration which they expect to receive for superintending the execution of their plans.—Aylesbury, February 23, 1849. ACTON TINDAL, Clerk of the Peace for Bucks.

ST. BARTHOLOMEW'S HOSPITAL.—A Committee of Governors will be held at this hospital, on Tuesday, the 13th instant, at Eleven o'clock in the forenoon precisely, to receive PROPOSALS from such persons as may be willing to take on REPAIRING LEASE, for 21 years, from Lady-day, 1849, all those capital and extensive premises situate on the south side of High Holborn, and numbered 302, now in the occupation of Messrs. KIRKMAN and CO., grocers.—The premises may be viewed by permission of the occupiers.—ALSO to receive PROPOSALS for LETTING several valuable PLOTS of GROUND, on building leases, on the high road leading from Camden Town to Holloway.—Plans of the above property may be seen, and further particulars ascertained at Mr. HARDWICK'S office, Southampton-row, Russell-square. WILLIAM WIX, Clerk.

Guildhall, February 27, 1849.

THE Committee for Letting the City's Lands will meet at Guildhall, on WEDNESDAY, the 14th day of March next, at One o'clock precisely, to receive TENDERS for LETTING, on Leases for Twenty-one Years from Lady-day next, a House, No. 14, on the north side of Broad-street Buildings; a House, No. 28, on the south side of Broad-street Buildings; and a House, No. 38, on the south side of Upper Thames-street. Also to receive Tenders for Letting, on Leases for 18½ Years (less three days) from Lady-day next, a House, No. 22, on the east side of Finsbury-street, and stables at the rear; sixteen Houses, Nos. 2, 3, 7, 8, 10, 11, 13, and 14, on the north side, and Nos. 64, 65, 66, 67, 68, 69, 70, and 71, on the south side of Banner-street, Finsbury; and also, in Lots, Eleven Houses, Nos. 1, 2, 3, 4, 5, 6, 7, 9, 10, 11, and 12, in Prince's-court, on the north side of Banner-street aforesaid, and Seventeen Houses, Nos. 1, 2, 3, 4, 5, 6, 7, 8, 10, 11, 12, 13, 15, 16, 17, 18, and 20, in North-place, on the north side of Banner-street, aforesaid.—Further particulars and plans may be seen at the Office of Works, Guildhall. THOMAS SAUNDERS, Comptroller.

LONDON: Printed by CHARLES WYMAN, of 7, Calthorpe-street, in the Parish of St. Pancras, in the County of Middlesex, Printer, at the Printing-office of J. & H. Cox, Brothers, 74 & 75, Great Queen-street, Lincoln's-Inn Fields, in the Parish of St. Giles-in-the-Fields, in the said County; and published by the said CHARLES WYMAN, at the Office of "THE BUILDER," 2, York-street, Covent Garden, in the Parish of Saint Paul, Covent-Garden, also in the said County.—Saturday, March 3, 1849.

The Builder.
A JOURNAL FOR THE Architect, Engineer, Operative & Artist.

VOL. VII.—No. 318.   MARCH 10, 1849.   PRICE FOURPENCE.
Stamped 5d.

ILLUSTRATIONS.

Suggestions for Street Architecture; three engravings 114
Greenstead Church, Essex, restored 115

CONTENTS.

Notice of the Free Architectural Exhibition opened by the
  "Architectural Association" 109
The History of Ecclesiastical Architecture in England. By
  G. A. Poole, M.A.; Mantell, London: Influence of Saxon
  Period on Pointed Architecture 110
The London Free Hospital Competition: Architects' Rights 111
The Pericleian Are of Grecian Decorative Art: The Chry-
  selephantine Works, &c. 112
Mutual Instruction at the School of Design 113
An Example for itself "Reliefs:" Redcliffe Church Tower ... 113
Galvanized Iron 113
Suggestions for Street Architecture 113
Wooden Church at Greenstead, Essex 115
On Fire-Proof Buildings 116
Manufacturing and Decorations at the Society of Arts 116
Art-Union of London 116
Topography of Jerusalem—What was Milo? 117
Notes in the Provinces 117
Metropolitan Commission of Sewers: Important Question 118
Miscellanea 118

ADVERTISEMENTS.

The Builder

A JOURNAL FOR THE

Architect, Engineer, Operative & Artist.

Vol. VII.—No. 319.	MARCH 17, 1849.	Price Fourpence.
		Stamped 5d.

ILLUSTRATIONS.

Two Portraits of Members of the City Carpenters' Company in the Seventeenth Century 126
The "Palazzo Rezzonico," Venice 196
Fetus for Window-glazing : Four Sketches 197

CONTENTS.

A Historical Account of the Carpenters' Company – Early Records – Powers possessed by the Guild 191
On the Importance of a Knowledge and Observance of the Principle of Art by Designers 122
Professor Cockerell's concluding Lecture on Architecture 194
Monuments in Cemeteries 194
Chelsea Hospital Galleries and the River-banks 195
The "Palazzo Rezzonico," Venice 196
Topography of Jerusalem : Mills 196
Fetus for Window-glazing 197
Telegraphic Communication across Seas 197
Railway Jottings 198
Notes in the Provinces 198
Gloucester 199
The Shield of Æneas – Pitts the Sculptor 199
Metropolitan Commission of Sewers: Opinion of the Law Officers 129
Books : Rudimentary Treatises on Geology, Electricity, Mechanism, Well-digging, &c. (Weale, Holborn) 129
Miscellanea 129

THE BUILDER.

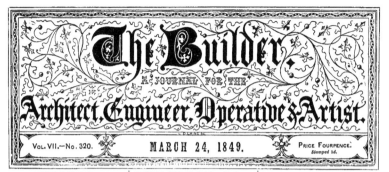

The Builder

A JOURNAL FOR THE Architect, Engineer, Operative & Artist.

VOL. VII.—No. 320.   MARCH 24, 1849.   PRICE FOURPENCE.
Stamped 5d.

ILLUSTRATIONS.

Patent Method of Facing with Stone 136
Design for the Small-Pox Hospital (Mr. S. A. Matthews, Architect, to which the second premium was awarded 138
Hurwood's Patent for Moving Windows 139

CONTENTS.

The Age of Copyism—Davy's "Burton Church"—The Architectural Publication Society's "Illustrations"—Barnard's "School Architecture" 133
On the Importance of a Knowledge and Observance of the Principles of Art by Designers 135
What the Sewers Commission have done for Kensington 136
Institution of Civil Engineers 136
A New Mode of Facing Walls 136
Improvements in Construction : Suggested Exhibition 137
The Curiosities of Estimating 137
Railway Jottings 137
The Small-Pox Hospital Competition 138
Hurwood's Patent for Windows 139
The Parks and Approaches 140
A Leash of Portraits 140
Notes in the Provinces 140
Metropolitan Commission of Sewers : The Committee Question 141
Miscellanea 141

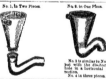

Vol. VII.—No. 321.   MARCH 31, 1849.   Price Fourpence.
Stamped 5d.

ILLUSTRATIONS.

Bishop Alcock's Chapel, Ely Cathedral: date 1486 150
Decorations from Abbud 151

CONTENTS.

Matters Artistical—Exhibitions · Fine Art Modern Art—Society
  of British Artists—Free Architectural—Art-Union of London 145
Royal Institute of Architects 145
On the Condition of Workmen how and in early times 146
The History of Ecclesiastical Architecture in England : The
  several Influences which contributed to form Gothic Archi-
  tecture 147
On Compactness and exclusives of Styles in Architecture 148
Builder's Architects : Designs for the United Gas Company,
  Liverpool 149
Bishop Alcock's Chapel, Ely Cathedral 149
Decorations from Abbud 151
A Memorandum in Ipswich, for the Dowset of that and other
  Towns 151
Patent Method of Facing with Stone 152
Proposal relative to the Collection and Distribution of the
  Contents of Sewers, and Protection of the Silver from Pol-
  lution 152
Restitution of Projecting Shop Fronts within limits of the
  Buildings Act 153
Formation of the Vaulting over St. Geofroy's Hall, Liverpool... 153
Compo : The Study of Nature in its Right Order and Con-
  ciliations of Forms and Powers 154
Metropolitan Commission of Sewers 155
Miscellanea 156

ADVERTISEMENTS.

PIERCE'S NEWLY-INVENTED
PATENT PYRO-PNEUMATIC PURE WARM AIR SELF-ACTING AND VENTILATING STOVE-GRATE,

SPECIALLY ADAPTED FOR

CHURCHES, CHAPELS, INFANT AND OTHER SCHOOLS, PUBLIC BUILDINGS OR PRIVATE DWELLINGS, BANKING HOUSES, RAILWAY OFFICES, PICTURE GALLERIES, ENTRANCE HALLS, LECTURE ROOMS, INVALIDS' APARTMENTS, &c. &c.

PIERCE, after the most mature study and careful consideration, based on numerous experiments, during his practical experience as a manufacturer for upwards of thirty years, upon the nature and properties of Heat and Ventilation, has at length succeeded in producing that long-sought desideratum—a healthful and salubrious atmosphere, such as is only felt on a pleasant summer's day, and which can, by the use of this, his PATENT PYRO-PNEUMATIC STOVE-GRATE, be enjoyed during the most dull and dreary of our winter months; and is specially adapted for all large PUBLIC ROOMS, INFANT AND OTHER SCHOOLS, CHAPELS OR CHURCHES, as it is economical in its first cost, and very much so in its practical use—burning a less quantity of fuel than any other stove-grate, yet producing a larger quantity of pure warm air than could possibly be credited, until authentically proved and experienced.

PIERCE'S PYRO-PNEUMATIC STOVE is the most powerful and economical grate that has yet been submitted to public notice, constantly burning with the clear, OPEN, CHEERFUL, RADIATING FIRE (not being at any time an enclosed stove), requires no attention or management, and cannot be put out of repair, as its principle of construction is wholly self-acting, and distributing in all portions of the space in which it is placed the benefits of PERFECT WARMTH WITH HEALTHFUL VENTILATION, and is made of various sizes, so as to provide the requisite quantity of warmth and circulation of air, suitable to the spaces which they are intended to warm; and, in like manner, the castings of these grates are made of various dimensions, and at prices adapted for the situation for which they may be required,—from the unadorned SCHOOL-ROOM, at a very moderate and economical cost, to others for the beautiful GOTHIC CHURCH, the enriched ENTRANCE HALL, or SPLENDID GALLERY, in which the price will be governed by the embellishment; but it is not in any case an expensive Stove—In fact, it is the most economical Stove-Grate that can be made use of, the small size not consuming more than twenty-one pounds of coals in twelve hours, and the largest size not exceeding sixty pounds weight in the same time; and being constructed upon the most simple and unerring principle, requires no more attention than the ordinary Grate; and although the most powerful in producing warmth, consumes a smaller quantity of fuel than any other. The external casing of the PYRO-PNEUMATIC STOVE-GRATE, being the only portion that is formed of Metal (with the exception of the bars and bottom), is so arranged, that in no case does the metal partake of any degree of warmth that can possibly affect the purity of the air, whilst in every other description of Hot-Air Stove the purity of the air is wholly destroyed and rendered unfit for respiration; nor is there any other Stove-Grate that Ventilates and warms at the same time equal to this PATENT PYRO-PNEUMATIC STOVE-GRATE.

This STOVE-GRATE may be seen in daily use at the PATENTEE'S MANUFACTORY and WAREHOUSE, No. 5, JERMYN-STREET, Regent-street; also at the Exposition of British Manufactures, now exhibiting at the Society of Arts, John-street, Adelphi, which has been honoured by the Society's Metal, and is constantly in use warming the large Model-room, where it may be seen, and its merits practically tested.

NOTICES OF THE PUBLIC PRESS
UPON PIERCE'S PATENT PYRO-PNEUMATIC STOVE-GRATE.

From Herapath's Railway Journal, Feb. 10, 1849.

"The object of this invention is to warm buildings or apartments, and at the same time to ventilate them, by a constant supply of fresh warm air. This is effected by means of an open Stove Grate, the whole of the heating surface of which are formed by means of the patent Authentic Pyro-Japan, rendered perfectly free from any admixture of iron, and closely cemented together, in the sides and back of this stove are formed various passages and tubes, which are heated by the fire in the grate. The fresh air from the external part of the building is admitted into an air-chamber formed at the lowermost of the stove. The fresh air from this chamber ascends through the heated passages and tubes constructed in the sides and back of the stove, and passes into the apartment from the top of it. By this arrangement, Mr. Pierce secures a constant supply of fresh air, which is warmed by its passage into the room, while the foul air is constantly carried off by the draught of the fireplace. Thus air is heated, and enters the apartment without coming in contact with any metallic substance, or producing any perceptible draught. Another great advantage in the use of this stove is the great economy and reducing power it shews a clear, bright, open fire, requiring no management, its principle of construction being wholly self-acting. The external casing of this stove grate being the only portion that is formed of metal (with the exception of the bars and bottom), is so arranged that in no case does the metal partake of any degree of warmth that can possibly affect the purity of the air."

From The Literary Gazette and Journal of the Belles Lettres, February 3, 1849.

"We have this week inspected Mr. Pierce's Pyro-Pneumatic Stove-grate, which for Warming and Ventilating buildings and Rooms, from the church to the infant school-room, or to the apartment of the invalid, seems to us admirably adapted. The objection to stoves, generally, provincial, charring, &c., appear to be entirely removed in this new arrangement, and the cheerfulness of the open fire is combined with a simple and refreshing plan for a constant supply of warm and wholesome air. The whole here is constructed of the fire lamp, with those slabs of pure authentic fire lamp, and a hollow middle bank of the tame, over which the flame passes to a down draft-chimney; the fluted sides and hollow back of the stove the external air being introduced in communicating, tubing, and the Welsh lumps of baked authentic lump in the only substance with which the air comes in contact. The external casing alone (besides the bars and bottom of the grate) is metal, and this consumingly casing may be filled with plate, casual, marble, or other similar substances, suitable to the building or room where the stove may be placed, as no injury can accrue to them from the heat of the fire under any circumstances."

From The Standard, February 3, 1849.

"Mr. Pierce, of Jermyn-street, the inventor, who has deservedly acquired a reputation for his practical knowledge of VENTILATION and COMBUSTION, having issued a modification of his scientific and others concerned in such important departments, and impressed with the urgent necessity for improvement in these essentials for the health of an increasing population, we submit to our attentive readers this invention which, we recommend this STOVE GRATE, with a full conviction of its usefulness. The inventor grounds his claim to merit on the SANITARY EFFECTS of his stove, from its power of driving in, by means of an air draft, large volumes of external atmosphere, which becomes warmed and purified in its passage through performed tubes of anthracite fire in the whole of the stove being composed of this material, and constantly evolved in a pure and deep walled atmosphere of pure warmth every part of the edifice in which it is used, and as the air becomes deteriorated it is drawn back to feel the combustion, and thence passes off by the flue, and ventilating shaft. The effect thus produced is magical. There is a warmth and elasticity in the air breathed from the fullness and a glow from the cheerful open fire, which made us forget that it was a February day and the external atmosphere cold and foggy."

From The Tablet, February 3, 1849.

"Mr. Pierce's Stove for Schools are Churches.—Mr. Pierce, of Jermyn-street, has perfected a most admirable stove, adapted for all apartments, domestic or otherwise, but more especially formed to warm, with a full supply of pure air, to schools and churches. It appears a handsome ornament in its plain state, with the simple iron framing and slate sides, a considerable capsule of common oxide shining through, the usual bars or grating tipped, as in the usual domestic fire. These fires thrown out heat by radiation to a great extent, nothing being lost; but much of the genial warmth occurs in the shape of heated air through the perforated plate, and is thence transmitted through apertures in the frame. The air from this stove has no disagreeable smell, no exhaustion from its combustion of iron, or of the sulphurous compounds in the coal, all these being carried off or destroyed by the fire lamp with which it is surrounded. The smoke is carried off downwards to the chimney shaft, and the numerous effects of the close stove wholly avoided. The air of the room is warm, but it is also pure; the room, purified or enlivened used not for the breathe it, and the hearty glow of the exposed and cheerful fire is sympathetically warming. The cost occasioned according to experiments does not exceed fifty pounds per day, and our object will, we believe, suffice to warm a room of church, and requires no addition of fuel or attention during the longest service. We would strongly recommend practical men, who are interested in schools or churches, to inspect the stove, and consider the improvements effected."

From The Mining Journal, March 17, 1849.

"The PYRO-PNEUMATIC STOVE GRATE.—We have had the pleasure of inspecting, during the past week, an apparatus for warming and ventilating rooms, or buildings, which has been patented by Mr. Pierce, of Jermyn-street. The principle, although exceedingly simple, combines, in the most scientific manner, the cheerful radiation of the open fire, so congenial to the English, with a genial warmth pervading the whole atmosphere of an apartment, the absence of all injurious and unpleasant draughts to the extremities of cold air, and the equable heat of the apartment of a stream of equally warmed and pure external atmosphere, in lieu of the deteriorated air, which is continually passing up the chimney. The stove, which are constructed in the most elaborate designs, suitable to apartments of drawing-rooms, halls, lobbies, Lords' Quarters, and Renaissance styles of decoration, or plain for schools or school-rooms, &c., are externally constructed of cast-iron, with the usual open fire. On the sides within the hollow back, &c., are various tubes of anthracite fire-clay; the bottoms open in a shaft, or air-drain, beneath it, by which is communicating with the external Atmosphere; and the upper orifices lead to a perforated aperture at the top of the grate, for the distribution of the fresh air. The fresh air, however great may be the combustion in the stove, the clay tubes are never heated to a much higher temperature than can be borne by the hand. By these regulations the air is never passed through a medium sufficiently heated to decompose or deteriorate it, but passes through the perforated aperture into the room, purified, and raised to a genial warmth, a mellow warm, and the propagation of one of admixture also to them John, to John, during a period of thirteen hours, we would venture to call for a supply of pure warmed atmosphere, at our fireside. The pneumatic stove appears to us to hold out great advantages, both for the ventilation of domestic and public buildings, and will prove serviceable, in a sanitary point of view, to unions, hospitals, &c."

From The Morning Post, February 18, 1849.

"WARMING AND VENTILATING.—The elaborate attention directed by men of science to the all-important consideration of rendering the vital food of the respiratory organs, atmospheric air, pure and wholesome, has led to beneficial results which have from time to time found honourable recognition. Amongst these the name of Mr. Pierce, of Jermyn-street, has more than once occurred, and it is therefore with the greater pleasure we find that the newly patented stove, which is perhaps the most unqualified approval of the most competent judges in the invention of this gentleman. When it is stated that the purity of the warm air evolved is of a genial summer-like character, and that, by the aid of anthracite fire-lumps, such element is so perfectly free from sulphurous exhalations that the most publicfied and un-immoderate relief within the influences; and, moreover, that these health-inspiring attributes are secured at an economical rate without depriving us of the comfort of an open fire or a living coal; enough has been said, although but a few of the advantages of the pyro-pneumatic stove grate, to render it worthy the inspection of those interested."

From The Weekly News and Financial Economist.

"We have been favoured with a view of a stove-grate, constructed and patented by Mr. Pierce, of Jermyn-street, which offers that desirable combination which has hitherto been so difficult of attainment, viz., an equable warmth with efficient ventilation. These two important ends are accomplished by this apparatus at once and the same time; and this by an arrangement as simple as it is effective. Our great Improvement effected by this invention is, that the stove itself, though constituting a fire which may be made of any required power, never becomes (like other hot-air stoves) intensely hot. There are scarcely five degrees more heat at the sides or back of this stove-grate than at a distant part of any well-constructed apartment."

From The Art-Journal, of March, 1849.

"THE PYRO-PNEUMATIC STOVE-GRATE.—Numerous contrivances have from time to time been introduced to the notice of the public, professing to be improvements on the ordinary modes of keeping up an equable temperature in large buildings or in private apartments. There have been a very various orders of merit but most of them, even those whose radiating powers are excellent, and to which the consumption of fuel is small, are objectionable from the circumstance that they render the air too dry, and consequently produce unpleasant sensations, and indeed often induce real disease. In the stove-grate, however, which we have hitherto seen introduced have either proved too little fuel by itself to aggravate in our English habits; and in many, which claim to be avoided upon scientific principles, during the slow combustion of the fuel, cases are formed, but not ignited by it, slowly escape from the fissures in the apparatus, much to the annoyance of all who are subjected to their influence. Again, the warming process consists in the circulation of air through a heated iron, and this occasions some peculiar change in the physical conditions of the atmosphere which is found objectionable. The fact is, that nearly every kind of stove which has hitherto been tried by the public has been found to injure air, or other of the disagreeable consequences to which we have alluded. It is, therefore, with very great satisfaction that we have witnessed the operation and examined the principles of the pyro-pneumatic stove, invented by Mr. Pierce, of Jermyn-street. This arrangement prevents many formidable conditions, which we must briefly describe. We have the comfort of an open fire, an any ordinary fire-grate. In our common arrangement air for combustion is maintained by drawing the air from the room, which very rapidly passes away up the chimney, and to supply the exhaustion a current of cold air is constantly rushing into the apartment through every crevice of door or window, and we have the constant annoyance of chilling draughts. In all parts of the room in the line of the current. As Pierce's stove has an open fire-place it will be asked how is this obtained? It is effected by a counterbalancing power of an ingenious and effective description. The fire, as in the common case, is fed with oxygen from the air of the room; but the air, removed by replaced in the following manner:—Behind the place are a series of tubular air-ways circulating around it, which are supplied with air by means of a pipe from without, the pipe being carried by any convenient course to the outer wall of the building. The air, warmed by the heating surface, rises and passes through the once mental perforated into the apartment, and thus a constant stream of warmed air passes upwards to supply the waste of combustion. A most effective portion of ventilation is obtained by this means the air deteriorated air passes away by the chimney, and a constant supply raised to a genial heat by its pneumatic operation is passing into the room. In such a manner that no annoying current can be detected in any part. This warmed air, in any ordinary fire-grate. In our common arrangement air for can be purer than this material and the remarkable exactness, we may say freshness, of the atmosphere is examined by us even in Jermyn-street, was our obvious to escape notice. This mode of the interior lining of the pyro-pneumatic stove is of this clay, and to no part was the exterior covering of type a hot that the hand could be held in contact with it for some minutes without any inconvenience. When we remember that the power of communicating heat is thirty-three times less than that of iron, it will be readily understood how this lining operates. As there masses of clay being raised to a red heat, and very cheerfully by the grate, and for many hours, with a mere handful of fire, a mere equable warmth is produced. At the same time, an agreeable warmth is made for increasing the heat to a very great degree. Under ordinary circumstances the warmed air will resist all gases from the stove at a temperature of about 70 degrees. The pyro-pneumatic character of these stoves is proved from experiments on stoves, as exemplified in the pyro-pneumatic stove grate could not be quadlung the following from his descriptive prospectus, &c., &c."

From The Civil Engineer and Architect's Journal, March 1, 1849.

"PIERCE'S PYRO-PNEUMATIC STOVE.—Mr. Pierce, the well-known stove manufacturer, has exhibited a potential stove, with an open fire and air chambers, formed of fire-clay. The air admitted at the bottom by a channel, brought from the exterior of the building, and carried through the chambers, which are heated from the anthracite fire of the stove, and also by the flue that passes out at the back. The air for this stove is not heated, as it generally the case with hot-air stoves constructed of iron and by having an open fire, the room is ventilated, and the foul air carried off by the draught of the fire."

From The Builder, March 3, 1849.

"PYRO-PNEUMATIC STOVE-GRATE.—We have several times said that the great desideratum in heating and ventilating is to get a constant supply of pure air admitted to the apartment at a proper temperature. Under the above title Mr. Pierce, of Jermyn-street, has patented a stove-grate which proposes to supply this want. It has an open fire-place, and is lined with fire-lumps. Within the fire-place there are tubular air-ways, made to communicate with the external atmosphere, which, by this passage into the apartment is warmed without causing foul contact with heated metal. The fire-clay lumps make it economical and metallic linings are very wasteful."

See further notices of this invention in The Saint James's Chronicle, Feb. 8, 1849; John Bull, Feb. 10; Observer, Feb. 11; Morning Herald, Feb. 17; Historic Times, Feb. 23; Magazine of Science, March, 1849; The Ladies Newspaper, Feb. 3; Journal of Public Health, March 1; Church of England Magazine, for March, &c. &c.

CHUBB'S PATENT INVENTIONS

FOR THE

SECURITY OF PROPERTY FROM DEPREDATION OR FIRE.

THE QUADRUPLE LOCK.

C. CHUBB and SON, of 57, St. Paul's Churchyard, London, having recently secured Patents for several most important improvements in the construction of Locks, respectfully request the attention of Bankers, Merchants, and the public generally, to the subject. The first invention is peculiarly adapted for the security of Bankers' and Merchants' strong-rooms, and other analogous uses. It consists of a combination of four separate and distinct Detector Locks in one, all being acted upon at the same time by a single Key with four bits. The main bolts are attached to an eccentric wheel throwing them each way, and to these twenty or thirty bolt-heads may be fitted so as to secure an iron door on every side. The principle of the eccentric wheel has been used some years by C. CHUBB and SON, but by means of the new quadruple arrangement the wheel and bolts are much more effectually secured than hitherto. The Quadruple Lock, having six tumblers in each set, twenty-four in all, the four stumps in the tumblers being fixed in one circular plate acting on the bolt which fastens the eccentric wheel; and all being acted upon simultaneously by the motion of the four-bitted key, it is utterly impossible, from the extensive combinations, by any false key or instrument, to succeed in opening it. There is also a small Detector Lock adapted, which throws a strong shield over the key-hole, so that, in a Banking establishment, a confidential clerk may carry the quadruple key,—and the principal, having the smaller key, can at all times prevent the fire-proof safe or strong-room being opened unless he is himself present. Notwithstanding the apparent complexity of this Lock, it is really very simple; and all the parts are so well fitted and strongly made, that there exists no chance of disarrangement.

CHUBB'S DETECTOR LOCKS.

A recent modification in the structure of these locks greatly increases their security. The Detector, which was formerly exposed near the key-hole, is now, by a simple but ingenious transposition, placed at the back of the tumblers and on the bottom plate of the lock, so that no instrument inserted in the key-hole can reach it. The locks have all six tumblers, and are made for every purpose to which locks are applied.

CHUBB'S PATENT LATCH.

The object of this improvement is to give greater security to Latches for Street Doors, and to Spring Locks in general. It is well known that, in all kinds of Latches hitherto made, however secure by ingenious construction from false keys, the bolts may be pushed back or lifted by a knife or thin piece of steel inserted between the door and door-post, and the house be thus easily robbed. C. CHUBB and SON'S new Patent completely obviates this evil. The Latch has a bevilled bolt, which, striving against the staple when the door is pushed to, releases a spring to shoot forward the bolt and lock itself, so that it cannot by any means be forced back, and can only be opened by the knob inside or the key outside. The simplicity of action, and its consequent durability, with the security of five tumblers, render this the most complete Latch ever made.

Spring Detector Locks for Drawers, Cupboards, &c., &c., made on the same principle.

CHUBB'S PATENT FIRE-PROOF STRONG ROOMS AND SAFES,

POSSESSING THE FOLLOWING QUALITIES.

Moveability.—A Strong Room, as generally constructed, cannot be removed; so that, in case of a change of residence, a considerable expense is incurred in again building one; but this loss and inconvenience may be obviated, and perfect security obtained, by an iron Room constructed on the principle of this Patent, which can be taken down, removed, and put together again with little trouble.

Fire-Proof.—These Patent Rooms and Safes have the power of resisting most intense heat, so as to be Fire-proof, in consequence of the use of certain non-conductors, as has been proved by enclosing papers and parchments in a Patent Box, made on the same principle, and exposed in the furnace of a steam-engine, where it became red hot, and remained in that state a considerable time, without any injury to the contents.

Strength.—The Rooms and Safes are made entirely of wrought iron, most securely fastened together on the inside; of thickness and strength sufficient to resist any violence; and lined with hard steel plates, which render ineffectual the application of any drill, spring-saw, or file.

Security.—The Doors of the Rooms and Safes are fitted with large Patent Detector Locks, which throw ten bolts round each door. A strong case-hardened Patent Scutcheon Lock, with a small key, is fixed over, and protects the key-hole of the large Lock.

Safes or Rooms constructed on this Patent can be made of any size, so as to suit any recess or apartment; and their interior may be fitted up with shelves and partitions according to any plan. Several Strong Rooms have been recently made for Bankers in London, other parts of England, Australia, the East Indies, and America.

Wrought Iron Doors and Frames, for stone or brick rooms, made very strong, with Locks to throw bolts all round, and Fire-proof Chests and Deed Boxes, for securing valuable papers, in great variety.

CAUTION

TO LOCK MANUFACTURERS AND DEALERS, AND THE PUBLIC GENERALLY.

CHUBB v. COOPER AND ANOTHER.

The COURT of CHANCERY having made an order in this cause, restraining the above Defendants, Francis Cooper, of Wolverhampton, Factor, and Joseph Taylor, of the same place, Lock Makers, their Agents, Servants, and Workmen, from Manufacturing or Selling any Locks or Keys, Stamped or Engraved with the name of Chubb, or with any other of the Plaintiffs' distinctive Trade-marks, or with any other name or marks imitating or resembling the name or marks used by the Plaintiffs; and likewise from Manufacturing or Selling any Locks or Keys, as and for Locks and Keys made by the Plaintiffs; or in order or so that Locks or Keys made by the Defendants may be re-sold as and for Locks or Keys made by the Plaintiffs; and likewise for copying or imitating in any manner the Plaintiffs' Name and Trade-marks, and, Whereas, upon the trial of the cause

CHUBB v. DAVIS.

In the SHERIFF'S COURT, BIRMINGHAM, on the 17th April, 1844, the Jury found a verdict for the Plaintiffs, with FIFTY POUNDS DAMAGES, for the illegal use of the Plaintiffs' Name and Trade-marks upon Locks not of their manufacture. Now all persons are hereby cautioned against in any manner stamping the Name or Trade-marks of Messieurs Chubb and Son, or either of them, upon any Locks or Keys not of their Manufacture, or selling Locks so Stamped, as immediate proceedings of a similar nature will be commenced against such persons so doing, and full damages will be enforced against them.

UNSUCCESSFUL ATTEMPT TO OPEN A CHUBB'S FIRE-PROOF SAFE.

FROM THE "STAMFORD MERCURY," 19th JANUARY, 1849.

" BURGLARY.—On Friday night last, the offices of Mr. Wilkinson, solicitor, in Peterborough, were entered by thieves, who picked the lock of the door, and so obtained an entrance. They appeared to have first forced open a draw of the table in Mr. W.'s office, whence they abstracted a few halfpence, and several keys belonging to the clerks' desks, with which they opened various boxes and cupboards. From one clerk's desk about 5s. in silver was taken, and a quantity of receipts belonging to the Phœnix Fire-office, most likely mistaken for other paper. Returning to Mr. W.'s office, the thieves ransacked the drawers, cupboards, tin boxes, and two portable desks, the contents of which they strewed over the floor. The chief point seems to have been a large iron chest in Mr. W.'s office: this at the time contained a considerable amount in cash, notes, gold and silver, which had been omitted to be paid into the bank during the day. The chest was one of Chubb's celebrated make; in this the burglars broke their pick-locks, which were abstracted by means of a magnet the following morning. Having failed with the lock, they next tried to force open the lid; but here again they were foiled : the metal was too tough to break, and too solid to be wrenched or cut, and the thieves were baulked of their expected prize."

C. CHUBB and SON have received a letter from Mr. Wilkinson confirming the above statement, and expressing his gratification at the result.

CHARLES CHUBB AND SON,

No. 57, ST. PAUL'S CHURCHYARD, LONDON.

PATENTEES AND SOLE MANUFACTURERS.

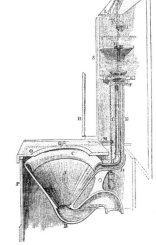

GEORGE JENNINGS,

29, GREAT CHARLOTTE STREET, BLACKFRIARS ROAD,

Begs to call the attention of those interested to the following articles, which he has invented and patented :—

JENNINGS'S PATENT SHOP SHUTTER SHOE AND FASTENER.

The trouble and disfigurement caused by the unsightly shutter bar is so well known to all persons, that it is only necessary to say a shop front receives more injury from the application of the shutter bar than it does from any other cause.

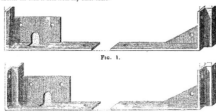

FIG. 1.

FIG. 2.

Figs. 1 and 2 represent two pairs of JENNINGS'S SHUTTER SHOES and FASTENERS, which not only protect the corners of the shutters, but effectually secure them ; and the cost of the patent fastenings is less than the destructive and troublesome bar. They can be had in malleable iron at 3s. per shutter, or in brass at 5s. per shutter.

JENNINGS'S PATENT INDIA-RUBBER TUBE COCKS.

FIG. 3.   FIG. 4.

The principle on which these cocks are made is so simple, that the following short description must at once make their superiority over the old plug cock apparent to all practical men.

Into the barrel and shank of the cock is placed a tube of Vulcanized India Rubber. Figure 3 represents the section of a common bib cock open, with an uninterrupted passage. Figure 4 represents the water-way closed by the india-rubber tube being compressed. By turning the handle, or key, the tube assumes its original circular shape, forming a full round water-way.

The following are a few of its practical advantages :—

It will resist any pressure when closed, and when open the water flows freely as through the pipe.

The water-way being entirely independent of the working part, it is not liable to damage by frost, and all leakage is avoided.

All chance of setting fast from being out of use (an evil much complained of in cocks on the old ground-in principle) is entirely avoided.

The facility of repairs by simply renewing the tube.

In the ball-cock, its allowing a full stream of water to flow into the cistern till nearly full, and the impossibility of its "sticking up or down"—the cause of much loss and complaint with Water Companies.

Cocks on this principle have now been fixed for some time in the Royal Mint, the House of Detention, Clerkenwell, the House of Correction, Cold Bath Fields, Lambeth Water Works, Kent Water Works, Barclay and Perkins's Brewery, Brick-lane Gas Works, and many other public and private establishments. The limits of an advertisement preclude the possibility of giving one-half of the testimonials received, but the Patentee has much pleasure in calling attention to the following :—

TESTIMONIALS.

House of Detention, December, 1848.

I beg to certify that the greater part of the water-pipes of this building are fitted with Mr. Jennings's Patent India Rubber Tube Cocks. They have been in constant use for some months, and continue to give great satisfaction.   F. W. HILL, Governor.

Royal Mint, December, 1848.

Sir,—Your Patent Joints and Cocks fixed in this establishment twelve months since are as sound now, and answer every purpose as well as when fixed.
To Mr. Jennings.   I am, Sir, your obedient servant,   GEORGE PULMAN.

House of Correction, Cold Bath-fields, December 12th, 1848.

Sir,—In reply to your letter, I beg to say, the India Rubber Tube Cocks fixed in this prison are quite sound, and answering the purpose intended.—I am, Sir, yours obediently,
To Mr. Jennings.   THOMAS FILLARY, Engineer.

St. Saviour's Union, 13th December, 1848.

Mr. Jennings,—Sir. I feel great pleasure in certifying, that—since your Patent Cocks and Water-closets have been fixed in this Union House—the several wards are entirely free from any bad smells, and an overflow of basons from leaky cocks, and they have added very much to the comfort of the house.—I am, Sir, your obedient servant,
        B. BONSER, Master.

2. Finsbury-circus, City, December, 1848.

Sir,—I have heard no complaints of any of your India Rubber Tube Cocks, though I have had some fixed under great pressures.—I am, Sir, your obedient servant,
Mr. Jennings.   THOMAS CLARK, Engineer,

Distillery, Smithfield Bars, December, 1848.

We hereby certify, that we have had Mr. Jennings's India Rubber Tube Cocks in this establishment for the last twelve months ; they are answering so well, that in future we shall use no other.   BROWNING AND SON.

12, Square, Winchester.

Sir,—I received the India Rubber Tube cock safely, and have had them fixed under the superintendence of Mr. Frampton, who is the manager of the water-works. I am delighted to be able to bear testimony to their efficiency, and feel certain their introduction into this city will be attended with great comfort to the inhabitants, from the following circumstance :—The city is in a valley, and is supplied with water pumped into a reservoir on nearly the highest eminence in its neighbourhood ; consequently, the pressure of that element is so great, that all the cocks I tried, previous to yours, have leaked when fixed, or shortly afterwards.

I am glad I saw your advertisement in "The Builder," and I will do all I can so make your invention known in this city.—I am, Sir, yours respectfully,
Mr. Jennings.   W. SAVAGE.

The cost of these Cocks in brass is the same as the charge hitherto made for the old roundaway plug-cock. As they can be made in iron, a great saving is effected, and they are warranted to answer as well as those manufactured in brass. Water Companies, Distillers, Brewers, and all large consumers, will save money, and relieve themselves from the annoyance of leaky cocks by their adoption. They are admirably adapted for exportation, as the introduction of a fresh piece of tube will, at any time, make the cock equal to new.

JENNINGS'S INDIA-RUBBER TUBE WATER-CLOSETS, WITHOUT PAN OR VALVE,

ARE SUITED ALIKE FOR A PALACE OR A COTTAGE : THEY CAN BE HAD AT TWO AND THREE GUINEAS EACH.

About sixty have been fixed, and they are giving the greatest satisfaction. The attention of Architects is particularly invited to this Closet. It is so constructed, it cannot be offensive or get out of order ; it has neither pan or valve ; the raising of the handle allows the contents of the bason to fall with great force through a 4-inch india-rubber pipe direct into the trap, and the lowering of the handle compresses the tube, and retains the water in the bason ; the surplus water passes off through an overflow pipe, which regulates the proper quantity to be retained in the bason.

THE COCKS, CLOSETS, PATENT JOINTS, AND JENNINGS'S IMPROVED CISTERN VALVES,
can be had from the PATENTEE, or of JOHN WARNER and SONS, Jewin-street, London ; or of Mr. J. R. WOOD, Hanover Chambers, Hanover-street, Liverpool.

THE PATENT SHOP SHUTTER FASTENERS
can be had of the PATENTEE, or of any respectable ironmonger, by sending the finished thickness of the Shutters, and which way they are put up, to the right or left.

DESCRIPTIVE DRAWINGS CAN BE HAD ON APPLICATION.

THE BUILDER.

ROYAL POLYTECHNIC INSTITU-
TION.—Last Week but One of Lectures explaining the Art of Magic, by Mr. Shaw, with Illustrations, changed every week daily, at a quarter to Two, and every evening at Nine. —Lecture on Chemistry daily, at a quarter to Three o'clock.—Dr. Bachhoffner's Illustrations on Astronomy daily, at a quarter to Four.—A View on the Gold Market of California is added to the new Dissolving Views and Oxy-Hydrogen Microscope, &c., are daily exploited, &c. &c. The Music is directed by Dr. Wallis.—Admission, 1s.; Schools, half-price.—Now Catalogue, 1s.

The Builder.
A JOURNAL FOR THE Architect, Engineer, Operative & Artist.

Vol. VII.—No. 322. APRIL 7, 1849. Price Fourpence. Stamped 5d.

ILLUSTRATIONS.

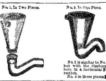

The Builder.

A Journal for the Architect, Engineer, Operative & Artist.

Vol. VII.—No. 323. APRIL 14, 1849. Price Fourpence. *Stamped 5d.*

ILLUSTRATIONS.

Hints for Street-Architecture: Cornices 172
House of Francis I., Champs Elysées, Paris 174
Details of same 175

CONTENTS.

English "Parish Churches"—Diversity with uniformity observable—Differences noted 169
Arguments in favour of Internal Ecclesiastical Decoration .. 169
The Gas Movement—In Town and Country 171
Hints for Street-Architecture 172
Blinds to Shops within limits of Buildings Act 173
The Britton Testimonial and Club 173
The Wooden Roofs of Old England 173
Scenery and Satire: The Lyceum Theatre 173
House of Francis I., Champs Elysées, Paris 175
Beauty in Towns and Villages 175
The Burial Ground Question 176
Dwellings for Rich and Poor: Union of Classes 176
Supervision of Buildings in Vienna 177
Construction of Lighthouses: Lighthouse on Cohasset Rocks, U. S. 177
Railway Jottings 177
Laundry Drying-Closets 177
Miscellanea 177

ADVERTISEMENTS.

WANTED, an ASSISTANT in a Builder's Office, a LAD, about 17, who can write a good hand, trace drawings, &c.—Address, post-paid, to J. T., at Messrs. Stodhards and Son's, Ironmongers, High-street, Camberwell, stating salary.

TO FOREMEN OF BRICKLAYERS.

WANTED, an EXPERIENCED PERSON who has previously filled the above situation.—Apply by letter, stating particulars and where last employed, to A. K., office of "The Builder," 2, York-street, Covent Garden.

WANTED to APPRENTICE a Youth of fifteen as an in-door apprentice to a STATUARY and MASON in the country, where he may gain a thorough knowledge of his trade.—Address, stating terms, to S. S., at Mr. Andrews's, Printer, &c., Guildford, Surrey.

TO ARCHITECTS AND SURVEYORS.

WANTED, by the Advertiser, aged 21, a SITUATION as ASSISTANT in the above profession. He can have a good recommendation from his last situation. Address, A. E., 9, Grove-terrace, Turnham-green.

TO BUILDERS.

WANTED, an ENGAGEMENT by a Builder's Clerk, who has been accustomed to the management of a builder's office and business. He is thoroughly competent to take out quantities, measure up, and estimate.—Address J. S., 9, North-terrace, Alexander-square, Brompton.

WANTED by a respectable Young Man, a SITUATION. Has a good knowledge of building, is a good draughtsman, understands the usual routine of an architect's office, and has had good practice. Most respectable reference can be given.—Address to H. T., 3, Stebon-place, Philpot-street, Commercial-road East.

WANTED by a Young Man an ENGAGEMENT in an ARCHITECT'S or BUILDER'S OFFICE; he has had a little experience with an architect, and also understands somewhat of surveying; would not object to a moderate salary. A situation in the country preferred.—Address, post-paid, to K. B., 3, Prospect-place, Cheyne-walk, Chelsea.

WANTED an ENGAGEMENT by the Advertiser, who has had considerable experience in designing (more especially in the pointed style), making out finished and working drawings, estimating, measuring and valuing, &c. He can produce the highest testimonials from his previous employers.—Address to A. B., Messrs. Addison and Co., 210, Regent-street.

TO BUILDERS.

WANTED, by a respectable, experienced Young Man, a SITUATION as CLERK and BOOK-KEEPER in a Builder's Office; he is practically acquainted with each department of the building business, writes a neat expeditious hand, is a rapid and correct accountant, and thoroughly conversant with the whole routine of office duties.—Address, A. B. SPECIFICATION, Post-office, Liverpool.

AN experienced CLERK of the WORKS, who is also a first-rate Modeller, is open to an ENGAGEMENT. Can give references for the last twenty years.—Address, J. F. B., 104, Regent-street, Westminster.

TO BUILDERS AND OTHERS.

A YOUNG MAN, of considerable experience in both architects' and builders' offices, wishes for an ENGAGEMENT in the latter, in town or country. Is an excellent draughtsman and colourist, and understands builders' accounts. The best references and security. In an eligible situation, a small salary accepted.—Address, Y. Z., 62, Shepperton Cottages, Hoxton.

TO CARPENTERS, JOINERS, UNDERTAKERS, AND OTHERS.

A YOUNG MAN, a Carpenter, who has been chiefly engaged in jobbing and general repairs, and also attending at funerals, &c., is desirous of obtaining a SITUATION in the above business. As this is his chief object, moderate wages expected. Good reference can be given.—Address P. P., to John Harper 20, Severn-street, St. George's-in-the-East.

A YOUNG MAN of highly respectable connection, having been four years in the carpentering and building business, and three months in an architect's office, can make working drawings, is desirous of an ENGAGEMENT in either of the above capacities, where facilities for improvement are afforded. Improvement being the advertiser's object, a small salary would be accepted.—Address, A. B., care of FRASER, LIGHTFOOT, and Co., Merchants, Mark-lane, City.

TO BUILDERS AND OTHERS.

A GOOD Estimator, Measurer, Draughtsman, &c. &c., wishes for a RE-ENGAGEMENT.—Address ALPHA, Brown's Library, 109, Great Portland-street, Marylebone.

TO ARCHITECTS.

A GENTLEMAN is desirous of an ENGAGEMENT in an architect's office as an assistant. Salary moderate. Satisfactory references will be given.—Address to A. Y. Z., at the office of "The Builder," 2, York-street, Covent Garden.

TO ARCHITECTS AND SURVEYORS.

A GENTLEMAN in extensive practice is desirous of obtaining the ASSISTANCE of a GENTLEMAN of first-rate qualifications, to take a portion of his business.—For particulars apply, by letter only, to W. T. YOUNG, Esq., 1, Lancaster-place, Waterloo-bridge.

TO CARPENTERS.

A HEALTHY YOUTH, in his nineteenth year of age, who has just completed a short apprenticeship at the bench, wishes a further ARTICLE in London, or within 50 miles. At the end of the term his friends would furnish the means for a Partnership, or other satisfactory arrangement.—Address, P. A., at Mr. Dale's, Baker, Lansdowne-road, South Lambeth, Surrey.

THE Friends of a respectable, well-educated Youth, 16 years of age, wish to APPRENTICE him to a respectable BUILDER, where he will have an opportunity of acquiring a knowledge of both the practical and architectural parts of the business, and where he will reside with the family.—Apply to A. R., Post-office, East Grinstead, Sussex.

TO SURVEYORS AND BUILDERS.

THE Advertiser is now open for an ENGAGEMENT, having had a first-rate practical experience in the building line, and in Gothic construction. Can have good reference.—Address to S. S., 29, Mount-street, Grosvenor-square.

TO SURVEYORS, BUILDERS, &c.

THE Advertiser wishes for an ENGAGEMENT as CLERK of WORKS, or OFFICE CLERK. He has had considerable experience in the erection of works, the preparation of plans, specifications, measuring, book-keeping, and the usual office routine.—Address, Y. Z., Richards and Co., 24, Endell-street, Bloomsbury.

TO BRICKLAYERS, BUILDERS, &c.

EMPLOYMENT is required by a practical BRICKLAYER, either as such, or as FOREMAN, for which he is fully competent; can measure, estimate, keep accounts, is a tolerable draughtsman, and would do his best to further the interest of his employer. In or near town preferred.—Address, X. Y., 11, Somer's-place West, New-road, St. Pancras, London.

PARTNERSHIP.—A Partner Wanted, who thoroughly understands the practical part of Carpentering, consisting chiefly of hothouse work, and to conduct that branch in a lucrative business.—Address to C. T., No. 9, Blenheim-street, New Bond-street.

TO ARCHITECTS AND LAND SURVEYORS.

AN ARCHITECT, having had great experience in the laying-out of land for building purposes, has several important estates in the neighbourhood of London and elsewhere placed under his management, as well as the appointment of architect to superintend the erection of the building, and having other numerous engagements which prevent his devoting the necessary time to this branch, is desirous of making an arrangement, either by PARTNERSHIP, or otherwise, with a Gentleman who can devote the whole of his time to the business. It is essential that he should understand surveying, plotting, &c., and it is also desirable that he should have a taste for laying out land, and be able to sketch in an artistic style. No one need apply who is not of the highest respectability, and who cannot command a moderate capital.—Address, in the first instance, post-paid, giving real name and address, to B. D., care of Messrs. Waterloo, Stationers, Parliament-street, Westminster.

NOTICE IS HEREBY GIVEN, that a GENERAL HALF-YEARLY MEETING of Members of the INSTITUTION of BUILDERS' FOREMEN will take place on WEDNESDAY evening next, April 18, at the "Bay Tree" Tavern, St. Swithin's-lane, for the purpose of electing officers for the ensuing six months, and other general business.

W. ALLARD, Secretary.

TO the JUSTICES of the PEACE for the COUNTY of MIDDLESEX.

My Lords and Gentlemen,—Having this day submitted my testimonials and qualifications for the SURVEYORSHIP of the Clerkenwell District to the Committee of the Court, and having been duly admitted by them as a candidate for the office, I beg leave earnestly and respectfully to solicit the favour of your support at the ensuing election. Should I be honoured with the appointment at your hands, no exertion shall be wanting on my part to discharge the important professional duties of the office with diligence and fidelity. The election takes place on Thursday, the 19th inst.—I have the honour to be, Gentlemen, your obedient and faithful servant,

THOMAS LITTLE.

36, Northumberland-street, New-road, April 9, 1849.

TO ENGINEERS, BRAZIERS, SMITHS, &c.

THE Trustees of Mrs. ANN NEWTON'S CHARITY for placing out, every year, ONE BOY belonging to the parish of St. James, Westminster, Apprentice to some respectable trade, with a premium of 33l. 7s. 4d., will meet at the Vestry-room, in the Churchyard, Piccadilly, on FRIDAY, the 4th day of May next, at Ten o'Clock in the Forenoon, to receive applications for such apprentice (aged 14 years) from persons carrying on the above, or other like mechanical trades. Any further information required may be obtained daily, between Ten and Four o'Clock, at the Parochial Office, Poland-street, Oxford-street. Every applicant for the apprentice must attend the above meeting in person, and bring a card containing his name, address, and business. None but householders need apply.—By order of the Trustees,

GEORGE BUZZARD, Clerk.

CONTRACTS.

NOTICE TO BUILDERS.

Royal Engineer's Office, Manchester, April 14, 1849.

The Principal Officers of Her Majesty's Ordnance hereby GIVE NOTICE, that they will receive Proposals from such Persons as desire to enter into a CONTRACT for the ERECTION of sundry BUILDINGS and WORKS at the NEW BARRACKS, at OWLERTON, near SHEFFIELD, YORKSHIRE. Persons desirous to tender will receive every information respecting this contract on application at the Royal Engineer's Office, at Owlerton, near Sheffield, where they may also obtain the terms of contract, with specifications for the several descriptions of artificers' work required, upon making a deposit of 1l. for the specifications, which deposit will be repaid when the specifications are returned. It is strictly enjoined that no alteration whatever shall be made in the specifications, and that no observations shall be written upon them; and notice is hereby given, that if the said specifications be in any manner defaced or soiled, the sum deposited for them will not be returned. The person whose tender shall be accepted will be required to enter into a bond, with two eligible securities, to be bound, jointly and separately, under a penalty of 4,000l. sterling, to the due performance of this contract.—The tenders to be sealed, and delivered on or before the 26th day of May, 1849, addressed to, "The Secretary to the Board of Ordnance, Pall-mall, London," and endorsed, "Tenders for Works at the Barracks at Owlerton, near Sheffield."

N.B. The Board of Ordnance reserve to themselves the right of rejecting all or any of the tenders.

T. FOSTER, Major, and Commanding Royal Engineers.

TO NAVIGATORS, GROUND WORKMEN, RAILWAY CONTRACTORS, AND OTHERS.

PERSONS desirous of CONTRACTING with the Fishmongers' Company for sundry EARTHWORK to be done in the Removal and Levelling of Ground at East Hill, Wandsworth, may receive particulars of the work required by application at the office of Mr. RICHARD SUTER, Architect, 28, Fenchurch-street, after Saturday, the 14th April, between the hours of ten and five. The Tenders are to be sent in by the 23rd April.

TO BUILDERS.

PERSONS desirous of CONTRACTING with the Guardians of the Bridge Union for the ERECTION of a NEW CHAPEL and other works, may inspect the plans and specification, which will lie at the Union-house, from Monday, the 9th of April, until Wednesday, the 18th, on or before which day all tenders are to be delivered, postage free, to the Clerk, at the Union, under cover, directed to the Guardians, "Tender for Chapel, &c."—Further information can be obtained by applying to Mr. H. MARSHALL, Architect, Canterbury. The guardians do not bind themselves to accept the lowest tender.—By order of the Board,

Board-room, 29th March, 1849. WM. FORTH, Clerk.

NORMAL COLLEGE for WALES.—TO BUILDERS.—Parties desirous of contracting for the ERECTION of the NORMAL COLLEGE for WALES, at SWANSEA, may see the drawings and specifications on and after the 2nd day of April next, at the offices of Messrs. Fuller and Gingell, Architects, 3, College Green, Bristol, and copies of the same at the residence of Mr. Buckland, Hon. Sec., Adelaide-place, Swansea, to whom Tenders are to be delivered, sealed and indorsed, on or before the 30th day of the said month. The Committee does not pledge itself to accept the lowest tender.

PARISH of SAINT JOHN, HAMPSTEAD, MIDDLESEX.—SECOND NOTICE.—The Guardians of the poor of this parish will meet on Tuesday, the 17th of April, 1849, at Ten o'Clock in the morning precisely, at the Workhouse, New End, Hampstead, to receive and open sealed TENDERS and to Contract for the proposed additions and alterations to Hampstead Workhouse aforesaid, together with its necessary offices and outbuildings, fence walls, appendages, and appurtenances, agreeably to the drawings and specification of Mr. H. E. KENDALL, jun., architect, which may be seen at his office, 33, Brunswick-square, and also at the Workhouse, New End, Hampstead, any day after Saturday, the 7th inst., between the hours of Ten and Four o'Clock. Security will be required for the due performance of the contract, and the guardians do not bind themselves to accept the lowest offer.

THOS. TOLLER, Clerk to the Guardians.

TO BUILDERS.

PERSONS willing to TENDER for the ERECTION of an INFIRMARY and other WORKS, as an addition to the Workhouse of the WANDSWORTH and CLAPHAM UNION, situate at East Hill, Wandsworth, may inspect the plans, specification, and form of contract, on application to the Master of the said Workhouse, on any day after Tuesday, the 11th inst., between the hours of Nine and Five (Sundays and Thursdays excepted). Sealed tenders, addressed to the Guardians of the Poor of the Wandsworth and Clapham Union (marked "Tender for New Infirmary, &c."), will be received at the said Workhouse until Ten o'Clock on Thursday, the 26th day of April inst., at which day and hour the tenders will be opened and considered by the Guardians; and it is required that the persons tendering, or authorised agents on their behalf, be in attendance. The Guardians do not bind themselves to accept the lowest, or any tender which they may not approve. Approved sureties, in the sum of 1,000l. each, must be provided by the Contractor, if required by the Guardians; and the names and addresses of such sureties must be stated in the tender.—By order of the Board of Guardians.

BENJAMIN FIELD, Clerk.

April 5th, 1849.

TO BUILDERS.

PARTIES desirous of submitting Tenders for the ERECTION of a NEW PAUPER LUNATIC ASYLUM for the County of WILTS, to be built in the immediate neighbourhood of Devizes, are hereby informed that the plan and specification, prepared by Messrs. WYATT and BRANDON, architects, may be seen upon application at the County Assize Hall, at Devizes, on and after Wednesday, the 18th of April inst. Mr. Wyatt will meet parties intending to submit Tenders, at Devizes on that day, at Two o'clock p. m., and will point out the proposed site. The Committee of Visitors will not be bound to accept the lowest tender.

TO IRON FOUNDERS.

PARTIES desirous of submitting TENDERS for a large quantity of CAST-IRON COLUMNS, SASHES, and JOISTS, to be used in the New Pauper Lunatic Asylum, about to be erected at Devizes, in the County of Wilts, are informed that the drawings and specifications may be seen upon application at the County Assize Hall, at Devizes, on and after Wednesday, the 18th day of April inst. The Committee of Visitors will not be bound to accept the lowest tender.—Further information may be obtained upon application to Messrs. WYATT and BRANDON, architects, 77, Great Russell-street, London.

THE BUILDER.

 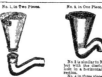

The Builder.

A JOURNAL FOR THE

Architect, Engineer, Operative & Artist.

C. D. LAING Sc.

VOL. VII.—No. 324. APRIL 21, 1849. PRICE FOURPENCE. *Stamped 5d.*

ILLUSTRATIONS.

St. George's Hall, Liverpool: Plan of Hall and Section of Great Arch 186
Entrance Front of the British Museum: Sir Robert Smirke, R.A., Architect 187

CONTENTS.

Schools of Design—Art Abroad—Model of Cologne Cathedral 181
Royal Institute of British Architects: Award of Medals 182
Remarks on Hollow Bricks as used in great Arch Ceiling over St. George's Hall, Liverpool; and on Brick and Arch Constructions in general 183
Notes in the Provinces 185
A Note to Workmen 185
The New British Museum 188
Recovery of Expenses incurred by Overseers in pulling down Ruinous Structures under the Buildings Act 188
Institution of Civil Engineers: Light 188
Science and Scenery at Her Majesty's Theatre 188
Dilapidations 188
State of Westminster Abbey 189
Railway Jottings 189
Sale of John of Gaunt's Palace, Lincoln 189
Miscellanea 189

ADVERTISEMENTS.

WANTED, a YARD FOREMAN and CONVERTER by a Builder about 70 miles from London, where a retail business is also carried on.—Apply, stating particulars, capabilities, &c. to GEO. SCAMELL and Co., Wholesale Ironmongers, 74, West Smithfield.

WANTED, a TOWN and COUNTRY TRAVELLER, who has a good connection among Architects, Builders, and Railway Contractors, who would be disposed to take Orders on Commission for an article much in use.—Apply at the Belgrave Works, Thames Bank, Pimlico.

DRAUGHTSMAN. — WANTED, in an Upholstery and Cabinet Manufactory, a YOUNG MAN who is quick and free with his pencil, attentive, and persevering. Previous acquaintance with the trade less needful than good taste and lively invention, for which ample scope is given.—Letters stating qualification, age, and expectation, with a small pencil sketch on same paper, may be addressed to R. C., Mr. Gray, Featherstone-buildings, Holborn.

TO BUILDERS, &c.

WANTED, a RE-ENGAGEMENT by a MANAGING CLERK, thoroughly versed in building matters, estimating, measuring, drawing, &c. &c.—Address, L. M., Brown's Library, 109, Great Portland-street, Marylebone.

TO ARCHITECTS AND SURVEYORS.

THE Advertiser, aged 24, wishes for a RE-ENGAGEMENT in the office of either of the above. Can make finished and working drawings; understands house and land surveying, taking out quantities, and has a thorough practical knowledge of the building trades.—Address, O. P., Mr. Plummer, Stationer, 46, Theobald's-road, Bedford-row.

THE Friends of a respectable, well-educated Youth, 16 years of age, wish to APPRENTICE him to a respectable BUILDER, where he will have an opportunity of acquiring a knowledge of both the practical and architectural parts of the business, and where he will reside with the family.—Apply to A. R., Post-office, East Grinstead, Sussex.

TO CARPENTERS AND BUILDERS.

EMPLOYMENT WANTED as FOREMAN with a carpenter, general builder, or upon a gentleman's estate, by a practical man, having a general knowledge of London and country building, keeping accounts, preparing plans and estimates, and willing to make himself generally useful; any one requiring a confidential manager will find it in the Advertiser.—Direct, O. P., 6, New-street, City-road, London.

TO PLUMBERS AND BUILDERS.

A PLUMBER is in want of Employment, one that has a thorough practical knowledge of his trade in all its branches; he would be found valuable in a jobbing business. No objection to painting or glazing. Can give good references.—Address to J. B., 64, Clifton-street, Crown-street, Finsbury-square.

TO BUILDERS, GRAINERS, &c.

A YOUNG MAN, of many years' experience in House Painting, wishes for TWO YEARS' IMPROVEMENT in GRAINING. Would not object to work at the brush for a few weeks in the dull time. £1 per week required as wages. Premium, £15.—Apply, by letter, post-paid, to H. B., 44, Tower-street, Waterloo-road.

TO ARCHITECTS, ENGINEERS, AND CONTRACTORS.

A CLERK of WORKS, 27 years of age, who has just completed the superintendence of extensive buildings on a railway, wishes for a RE-ENGAGEMENT. He has had considerable experience in building operations generally; has also been in the habit of preparing fair and working drawings, and has no objection to office work. He can produce highly satisfactory testimonials.—Apply by letter, to H. B., 16, Basinghall-street.

TO CIVIL ENGINEERS AND ARCHITECTS.

WORTHY of NOTICE.—The Advertiser, aged thirty-five years, who has been engaged during the last twelve years superintending large works for public departments, is free to accept another ENGAGEMENT. Any engineer or architect, to whom energy and integrity are of weight, would find the advertiser a valuable assistant. The highest references can be given. With the probability of an engagement for a lengthened period or permanently, salary would be a secondary consideration.—Address, JOHN GOODWIN, Post-office, King's Langley, Herts.

ART UNION of LONDON.—The ANNUAL GENERAL MEETING to receive the Council's Report, and to distribute the amount subscribed for the purchase of Works of Art, will be held in the Theatre Royal, Drury Lane, on TUESDAY next, the 24th inst., at Eleven for Twelve o'Clock precisely. The receipt for the current year will admit the subscriber and friends.

His Royal Highness the DUKE of CAMBRIDGE is expected to preside.

GEORGE GODWIN,
LEWIS POCOCK, } Hon. Secretaries.

444, West Strand, April 18th, 1849.

SURVEYING TAUGHT.—An experienced Surveyor gives Instruction in measuring, estimating, and drawing. Terms moderate.—Address, prepaid, to SURVEYOR, 14, Great Castle-street, Regent-street.

TO BE SOLD, two 3-inch LIFT PUMPS for deep wells, with rods, handles, and plank, and about 6 cwt. of 1½ inch Lead Pipe, only been in use 5 years. May be viewed, or further particulars given upon application to Mr. WELLS, China and Glass Warehouse, Lewisham, Kent.

AN ARCHITECT, resident in a large provincial town, and who has carried on his profession for many years with considerable success, is desirous of disposing of his business. The opportunity is unexceptionable for any gentleman wishing to enter into immediate practice, and the necessary arrangement may be made on very easy terms.—Every information may be had on application to Messrs. HALE, BOYS, and AUSTIN, solicitors, 6, Ely-place, Holborn.

TO ENGINEERS.

A GREAT BARGAIN.—The BUSINESS of a MILLWRIGHT and ENGINEER TO BE SOLD or LET, in consequence of the proprietor retiring from the business. The concern is in full trade, and has a steam-engine, of which there is power let off sufficient to clear rent and expenses. About 2,200l. to purchase.—For particulars, apply to GEORGE JONES, Iron-merchant, 27, Old Fish-street, near St. Paul's.

TO BUILDERS AND DECORATORS.

TO BE DISPOSED OF, on advantageous terms, a first-rate and old-established BUILDER'S and DECORATOR'S BUSINESS, with excellent connection attached, situate in the most eligible part of London. Principals only can be treated with.—Apply to Mr. ORRIDGE, 30, Bucklersbury, Cheapside, if personally, between Eleven and Four.

TO BUILDERS, MEMBERS OF BUILDING SOCIETIES, AND OTHERS.

TO BE DISPOSED OF, in CARCASS, part of a TERRACE of THIRTY HOUSES now erecting, and of handsome elevation. The purchase-money may remain until the leases are granted, or it may be sunk in an improved ground rent, at the option of the purchaser.—For further particulars, apply to Mr. PALMER, Lee Arms, Brownlow-road, Queen's-road, Dalston, who has also eligible Land to Let for Building purposes. Bricks on the Ground for sale or advance.

ADVANTAGEOUS BUILDING SPECULATION.—TO BE LET, THE HOPE MANSION, PICTURE GALLERIES, and OFFICES, in Duchess-street, Portland-place, for an unexpired term of about 18 years, or for an extended term, with liberty to pull down and rebuild ten or twelve second-class houses. Particulars may be had at Mr. DONALDSON'S Offices, Bolton-gardens, Russell-square.

VOTES FOR WEST KENT.—FREEHOLD LAND, within five minutes' walk of Rosherville Pier and the Railway Station now in progress, to be SOLD, in plots of 50 feet frontage and 130 feet deep, for a pair of Semi-detached Villas, of not less than six rooms each, having a right of way from the London-road to the old Rochester-road. The situation is delightful, and it is the only land to be sold in plots between the village of Northfleet and the town of Gravesend.—For particulars, apply to Mr. LEE, No. 9, London-road, Rosherville.

N.B. A pair of villas, built on a portion of the land, to be sold; annual value, 50l.

CONTRACTS.

SHEERNESS NEW GAS WORKS.—The Committee of the Sheerness New Gas Company are desirous of receiving TENDERS from persons willing to contract for the ERECTION of a GAS HOLDER and other works, and for supplying and laying down the necessary mains and pipes in the several streets and lanes of Blue and Mile Towns, Sheerness, agreeably to the plans and specifications, which may be seen at the office of Mr. WARD, Solicitor, Sheerness; to whom tenders are to be addressed, sealed and endorsed. The Committee do not bind themselves to accept the lowest tender.

TO BUILDERS.

BUILDERS desirous of TENDERING for the ERECTION of a new WESLEYAN CHAPEL at Witney, Oxfordshire, may see the plans and specifications at the Wesleyan School-room, until the 24th of April, and obtain any further information by application to JAMES WILSON, Esq., Architect, Bath.—The tenders are to be delivered to the Rev. CHARLES WESTLAKE, on or before the 27th of April.—The lowest tender will not necessarily be accepted.

SHREWSBURY and BIRMINGHAM and STOUR VALLEY RAILWAYS.—General Station at Wolverhampton.—To Builders and Contractors.—Parties desirous of CONTRACTING for the several WORKS required in ERECTING the GENERAL STATION at WOLVERHAMPTON, with Carriage Sheds, Platforms, Engine-houses, Goods Warehouse, &c., are hereby informed that the drawings and specification thereof may be seen on and after Wednesday, the 2nd day of May, at the office of the Architect, Mr. EDWARD BANKS, Wolverhampton. Tenders, sealed and endorsed "Tender for General Station at Wolverhampton," to be sent to the secretary, at the Birmingham, Wolverhampton, and Stour Valley Railway Office, 24, Waterloo-street, Birmingham, not later than eleven o'clock on the morning of Tuesday, the 8th day of May, 1849. The Directors do not bind themselves to accept the lowest tender.

GEORGE KNOX,
HENRY MORGAN, } Secretaries.

April, 1849.

CONTRACTS.

NOTICE TO BUILDERS.

Royal Engineer's Office, Manchester, April 14, 1849.

The Principal Officers of Her Majesty's Ordnance hereby GIVE NOTICE, that they will receive Proposals from such Persons as desire to enter into a CONTRACT for the ERECTION of sundry BUILDINGS and WORKS at the NEW BARRACKS, at OWLERTON, near SHEFFIELD, YORKSHIRE. Persons desirous to tender will receive every information respecting this contract on application at the Royal Engineer's Office, at Owlerton, near Sheffield, where they may also obtain the terms of contract, with specifications for the several descriptions of artificers' work required, upon making a deposit of 1l. for the specifications, which deposit will be repaid when the specifications are returned. It is strictly enjoined that no alteration whatever shall be made in the specifications, and that no observations shall be written upon them; and notice is hereby given, that if the said specifications be in any manner defaced or soiled, the sum deposited for them will not be returned. The person whose tender shall be accepted will be required to enter into a bond, with two eligible securities, to be bound, jointly and separately, under a penalty of 4,000l. sterling, to the due performance of this contract.—The tenders to be sealed, and delivered on or before the 30th day of May, 1849, addressed to, "The Secretary to the Board of Ordnance, Pall-mall, London," and endorsed, "Tenders for Works at the Barracks at Owlerton, near Sheffield."

N.B. The Board of Ordnance reserve to themselves the right of rejecting all or any of the tenders.

T. FOSTER, Major, and Commanding Royal Engineers.

TO BUILDERS.

TENDERS are required for the erection of a DISTRICT CHURCH, in BROMPTON, Middlesex. The plans and specification may be seen at the office of the architect, Mr. GEORGE GODWIN, 24, Alexander-square, Brompton, on and after Monday, the 30th inst. The committee do not bind themselves to accept the lowest tender, and will require security for performance of the works.

TO BUILDERS, &c.

BUILDERS desirous of CONTRACTING for the ERECTION of ST. JOHN'S CHURCH, KINGSDOWN, near Walmer, County of Kent, may see the drawings and specifications at the house of William Curling, Esq., Kingsdown, from nine till six o'clock, until the 25th instant; and sealed tenders, addressed to Mr. JOHN HAY, architect, to be delivered on or before that day, at the above place. The proprietor does not bind himself to accept the lowest or any of the tenders.

Liverpool, 11th April, 1849.

TO BUILDERS.

NEW CHURCHES in the COUNTIES of DERBY and NOTTINGHAM.—Persons desirous of giving TENDERS for the ERECTION of the whole or either of the following CHURCHES, will please to make application, by letter, on or before the 30th inst., to Mr. HENRY I. STEVENS, Architect, Derby, in order that arrangements may be made for their inspection of the drawings and specifications.

IN THE COUNTY OF DERBY.

A District Church, at CLAY CROSS, in the parish of North-wingfield, 4 miles south of Chesterfield, on the line of the North Midland Railway.

A District Church, at BELPER, 8 miles north of Derby, on the same line of railway.

IN THE COUNTY OF NOTTINGHAM.

A Parish Church, at BULWELL, 4 miles from Nottingham, on the line of the Nottingham and Mansfield Railway, at which place the old Parish Church has to be taken down, and an abundant supply of building stone and excellent lime is to be obtained.

Derby, April 10, 1849.

BUILDING CONTRACT, parish of Lambeth.—Builders wishing to TENDER for the SCHOOL-HOUSE, to be erected at the HOUSE OF INDUSTRY, NORWOOD, are requested to signify the same in writing, to Mr. WILLIAM ROGERS, architect, Palace-chamber, Old Lambeth, on or before Saturday, the 21st inst.

QUEEN'S COLLEGE, BIRMINGHAM. To BUILDERS.—Builders willing to CONTRACT for the ERECTION of ADDITIONAL BUILDINGS at the Queen's College, Paradise-street, may inspect the drawings and specification on and after Wednesday, the 18th inst., at the offices of Messrs. DRURY and BATEMAN, Architects, 42, Cherry-street.—Sealed tenders, addressed under cover to the Architects, on or before Wednesday, the 2nd day of May next.

W. SANDS COX, Dean of the Faculty.

NORMAL COLLEGE for WALES.—TO BUILDERS.—Parties desirous of contracting for the ERECTION of the NORMAL COLLEGE for WALES, at SWANSEA, may see the drawings and specifications on and after the 2nd day of April next, at the offices of Messrs. Fuller and Gingell, Architects, 3, College Green, Bristol, and copies of the same at the residence of Mr. Buckland, Hon. Sec., Adelaide-place, Swansea, to whom Tenders are to be delivered, sealed and indorsed, on or before the 30th day of the said month. The Committee does not pledge itself to accept the lowest tender.

TO BUILDERS.

PERSONS willing to TENDER for the ERECTION of an INFIRMARY and other WORKS, as an addition to the Workhouse of the WANDSWORTH and CLAPHAM UNION, situate at East Hill, Wandsworth, may inspect the plans, specification, and form of contract, on application to the Master of the said Workhouse, on any day after Tuesday, the 11th inst., between the hours of Nine and Five (Sundays and Thursdays excepted). Sealed tenders, addressed to the Guardians of the Poor of the Wandsworth and Clapham Union (marked "Tender for New Infirmary, &c."), will be received at the said Workhouse until Ten o'Clock on Thursday, the 26th day of April inst., at which day and hour the tenders will be opened and considered by the Guardians; and it is required that the persons tendering, or authorised agents on their behalf, be in attendance. The Guardians do not bind themselves to accept the lowest, or any tender which they may not approve. Approved sureties, in the sum of 1,000l. each, must be provided by the Contractor, if required by the Guardians; and the names and addresses of such sureties must be stated in the tender.—By order of the Board of Guardians,

BENJAMIN FIELD, Clerk.

April 5th, 1849.

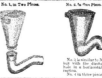

The Builder.
A JOURNAL FOR THE
Architect, Engineer, Operative & Artist.

Vol. VII.—No. 325.　APRIL 28, 1849.　Price Fourpence.
Stamped 5d.

ILLUSTRATIONS.

Decorations, &c. from Abroad: Ironwork of Fourteenth Century, Frets of Eighth Century 196
Hall and Staircase of the New British Museum: Sir R. Smirke, Architect... 196
The British Museum of Old Time............................ 199

CONTENTS.

Report of the Council of the Art-Union of London—List of the Prizeholders 193
Decorations, &c. from Abroad 196
Some Matters Architectural 196
On the Nature and Properties of the Metals used in the Building Trades: Iron... 197
The Hall and Staircase of the British Museum 198
The Hollow Brick Ceiling over St. George's Hall, Liverpool .. 198
Hollow Brick Constructions 199
Architecture and the Royal Academy 200
The New Society of Painters in Water Colours 200
Lord Rosse's Reflector.................................... 200
The Collection of Animal Refuse in Towns 201
Notes In the Provinces 201
Supply of Water to Constantinople 201
Metropolitan Commission of Sewers 201
Miscellanea.. 202

The Builder

A JOURNAL FOR THE

Architect, Engineer, Operative & Artist.

| Vol. VII.—No. 326. | MAY 5, 1849. | Price Fourpence. Stamped 5d. |

ILLUSTRATIONS.

Ground Plan of New Gaol, Boston, U.S. 307
Roslin Chapel, Scotland 210

CONTENTS.

A Jaunt to Roslin Chapel, near Edinburgh.—Peculiarities of the building 203
The late Mr. Austin, Resident Architect of Canterbury Cathedral 205
"Perfection in Building—a Work of Progress" 206
New Gaol in the City of Boston, U.S., for Suffolk County ... 207
The Charges of the Electro-Telegraphic Company 208
The New Book and Wharves constructing at Great Grimsby... 208
"Wonders in Locomotion: New Motive Power" 208
Notes in the Provinces 209
The Old Water-Colour Society 209
Laundry Drying Closets 210
Hints in the Working Classes 211
Iron and Oak Wash 211
Effect of Oxygen on Colour of Glass 211
The Manchester School of Design 212
Arched Brick Floors, Birkenhead 212
Use of Hollow Bricks 212
Coroners' Committee on Schools of Design 213
Railway Cottages 213
The Miner's Life 213
The American Bowling Saloon 213
Books: Topography (Parker); General Knowledge (Hilbert) 213
Miscellanea 215

ADVERTISEMENTS.

TO PARENTS AND GUARDIANS.

CONTRACTS.

PIERCE'S NEWLY-INVENTED PATENT PYRO-PNEUMATIC PURE WARM AIR SELF-ACTING AND VENTILATING STOVE-GRATE,

SPECIALLY ADAPTED FOR

CHURCHES, CHAPELS, INFANT AND OTHER SCHOOLS, PUBLIC BUILDINGS OR PRIVATE DWELLINGS, BANKING HOUSES, RAILWAY OFFICES, PICTURE GALLERIES, ENTRANCE HALLS, LECTURE ROOMS, INVALIDS' APARTMENTS, &c. &c.

PIERCE solicits an examination of his newly-invented method of WARMING AND VENTILATING, by means of his Patent Pyro-Pneumatic Stove Grate, which, from the NOVELTY of its principle, SIMPLICITY of its arrangement, and ELEGANCE of design, combined with its great ECONOMY IN USE, renders this grate suitable for any situation where a POWERFUL DEGREE OF WARMTH, and the CHEERFUL OPEN FIRE are desirable.—PIERCE having at length succeeded in producing that long-sought *desideratum*—a HEALTHFUL AND SALUBRIOUS atmosphere, such as is felt on a pleasant summer's day, which can, by means of this his Patent Pyro-Pneumatic Stove Grate, be enjoyed during the most dull and dreary of our winter months. The above invention is specially adapted for warming churches, infant and other schools, railway offices, entrance halls, banking houses, &c., or any situation where warmth and purity of air are desirable.—IT MAY BE SEEN IN DAILY USE AT THE PATENTEE'S MANUFACTORY, 5, JERMYN-STREET, REGENT-STREET; also warming the large MODEL ROOM at the Exposition of British Manufactures, now exhibiting at the SOCIETY OF ARTS, John-street, Adelphi (who have awarded their Honorary Medal to the inventor).

FOR DETAILED PARTICULARS AND OPINIONS OF THE PUBLIC PRESS, SEE "THE BUILDER," FEB. 17, MARCH 3, AND 31.

PAVING, 2s. 9d. PER SQUARE YARD, Basements, Foot-walks, Malt-houses, Corn Stores, Floors of Warehouses, and every description of Pavement laid down at the above low price, and the work guaranteed.—Apply to JOHN PILKINGTON, POLONCEAU'S BITUMEN PAVEMENT OFFICE, 4, JOHN-STREET, ADELPHI.—N.B. Country Agents and Railway Engineers and Contractors supplied with the best bitumen for covering bridges and arches.

ANSTONE STONE WHARF, STANGATE.—Mr. GRISSELL has the honour to inform Architects and Builders that he has made arrangements for the SUPPLY of the ANSTONE STONE for all building purposes, and which can now be seen at the above wharf by application to Mr. W. G. WARDLE, of whom every information can be obtained.

N.B. The stone used in the erection of the New Houses of Parliament was supplied EXCLUSIVELY from these quarries.

ANSTON STONE, used for Building the New Houses of Parliament.—W. WRIGHT and Co. beg to inform Architects, Engineers, Builders, and others, the Anston Stone can be supplied in any quantity on the shortest notice. This valuable stone, so celebrated for its durability, colour, and texture, is well known, having been selected in preference to all others, by the Commissioners of Woods and Forests, for building the New Houses of Parliament. It is very superior for Monuments, Tombs, &c. &c.

W. Wright and Co. have made arrangements to have a stock always on hand at Brine's Marble and Stone Wharf, Horsfall-basin, Maiden-lane, King's-cross.—Any further information can be obtained on application to W. WRIGHT and Co., Anston, near Sheffield; or to T. SHARP, their Sole Agent in London, 27 Burton-crescent.

CAEN STONE SPECIALLY SELECTED for EXTERNAL WORKS.—LUARD, BEEDHAM, and Co., extensive Proprietors of CAEN STONE QUARRIES, Allemagne, Calvados Department, beg to solicit inspection of their Caen Stone for external and internal works. They continue their importations of the first quality, carefully selected and marked at the quarries before removal to the place of shipment for export.

L., B., and Co. have on hand a large stock of the best-quarried stone, at their general Depôt, Caen Sufferance Wharf, Rotherhithe; and also at Vauxhall-bridge, Battle-bridge, Kensington and Paddington Basins, where samples and information may be obtained; or at their offices, 18, Southwark-square, Borough; or forwarded by post upon application, without charge or delay.—Shipments made direct from Caen to any part of the United Kingdom.

CAEN AND AUBIGNY STONE QUARRIES.—LUARD, BEEDHAM, and Co., beg to inform Archæologists, Architects, Engineers, the building Profession, and the public generally, that they are importing the above stone from their quarries at D'Allemagne, Calvados Department, being the most approved of any now known; and also from Aubigny, near Falaise, Normandy; and from the increasing exports of Caen Stone, they are satisfied their efforts in selection are becoming extensively known, and from the general adoption of Aubigny, they are assured of its great utility. Aubigny is much finer than Portland, in colour and texture, and free from shell, flints, and other obstruction in working. Its durability may be estimated from its appropriation to lighthouses, dock, and quay walling, the Royal Chateaux in Normandy, and other public buildings of many centuries standing.

L. B. and Co. have a large and seasoned stock of the above at their general Depot, Caen Sufferance Wharf, Rotherhithe, near the Lavender Dock Pier; also at Messrs. BRINK, BROTHERS, Battle-bridge; No. 5, Paddington-basin; Vauxhall-bridge; and Kensington-basin.—Orders executed with dispatch to any part of the United Kingdom.—Offices, 18, Southwark-square, Borough; and Caen Wharf, 179, Rotherhithe-street, Rotherhithe.

CAEN STONE, from the first Quarries of Allemagne. Depôt at the Whitby and Scotch Wharf, 14, Fore-street, Limehouse.—P. FOUCARD, quai des Abattoirs Caen (propriétaire des Carrières à Allemagne), begs leave to inform Builders, Architects, and others, that he has, on the above-mentioned wharf, the best stone ready to meet the demands of purchasers.—Contracts taken for any quantities.—Orders received by Mr. DASCHET, at 38, Stoney-street, Borough Market.—Cargoes shipped to order, from Caen, to any port.

CAEN STONE.—Original Sufferance Depôt, Norway Wharf, Greenwich.—W. TUCKWELL, Caen Stone Quarry Proprietor and Importer, begs to invite the attention of Architects, Surveyors, Builders, and others to the Stock of DRY SEASONED CAEN STONE on his Wharf, comprising 20,000 feet cube, which has been selected with judicious care, and is fit for immediate use. Shipments made to any port direct from his quarries at Caen.

N.B. Orders received at the wharf as above; also at the offices of Mr. R. A. WITHALL, Surveyor, 80, Cheapside, where further information and samples may be obtained.

MARKET WHARF, REGENT'S-PARK BASIN.—Messrs. MARTIN and WOOD (late Scoles and Martin) solicit the attention of Builders, Masons, and others, to their stock of Portland, York, and Derby Stone; also Bangor Slates, Lime, Cement, Plaster, Bricks, Tiles, Laths, Fire-goods, Fire-stone, &c., sold at the lowest possible prices for Cash. Portland Head-stones, Ledgers, Steps, Landings, &c., cut to order on the shortest notice. Tarpaulings let on hire. A Stock of Northen's Drain Pipe, Syphons, &c., always on hand. Mortar, Lime and Hair, Fine Stuff, &c.

BATH STONE.—RANDELL and SAUNDERS, QUARRYMEN and STONE MERCHANTS. The most approved kinds of Bath Freestone supplied to all parts of the kingdom. Depôts at the Great Western Railway Stations, PADDINGTON, CORSHAM, BOX, BATH, and BRISTOL.—R. and S. particularly invite the attention of Architects and Builders to their Corsham Down Stone, which is strong and sound in quality, is of beautiful colour and texture, and works much cheaper than any other stone. Prices, with cost of carriage to any locality specified, furnished on application to Randell and Saunders, 14, Orange Grove, Bath.

BOX FREESTONE QUARRIES.—T. STRONG begs to invite the attention of Architects, Builders, &c., to his extensive STOCK of excellent FREESTONE. His ground-stone stands unrivalled for all external purposes, for durability, colour, and texture, as the many mansions which have for centuries past been built of it, fully testify. His scallett stone is of a beautifully fine texture, for interior purposes, and all ornamental work. T. Strong has been making preparations for supplying on the most extensive scale, and thinks a visit to his quarries would well repay the trouble of those requiring free-stone, and who would find it a considerable saving to have it direct from the Box Station of Great Western Railway, where a large supply is always kept. Plain and ornamental Stonework prepared to order. Ashlar, range work, walling stones, &c., always on sale.

PIMLICO SLATE WORKS.—GREAT REDUCTION IN THE PRICE OF SLATE.—Mr. MAGNUS has the pleasure to announce that a reduced tariff will be published on the 25th instant, and forwarded, on receipt of a postage stamp, to any part of the kingdom. Half inch slate slabs, planed 1 face, with sawn edges, from 4 to 7 feet long, will be sold from 3½d. to 5d. per foot super.; 1 inch slabs from 5d. to 7d. ditto. An 1 inch slabs planed 2 faces, from 6d. to 9d. per foot super. Enamelled baked chimney pieces, variously marbled, hitherto priced at [illegible], will be sold from 30s. to 40s., suitable for openings 3 feet 1 inches to 4 feet 2 inches wide. Slate tanks, 2s. per foot cube, outside measure on wharf, or 2s. 6d. delivered and fixed. Other articles reduced in proportion.—N.B. The finest slabs from Monmouthshire, Bangor, and Cornwall.

STIRLING'S BELVEDERE SLATE WORKS, Belvedere-road, Lambeth.—A reduced list of prices of the best WELCH SLATE SLABS, planed both faces, will be sent on application (post paid) being made, and inclosing a Postage [illegible]. The prices are under those advertised for inferior slates.

SAMUEL CUNDY, Mason and Builder, PIMLICO MARBLE and STONE WORKS, Belgrave Wharf, Pimlico, begs to inform ARCHITECTS and the PUBLIC that he has availed himself of improvements in his MACHINERY, by means of which he is enabled to produce GOTHIC WINDOWS, MOULDINGS, PANNELS, &c. &c., at a very cheap rate, out of a superior stone from the west of England, as durable as any such stone, and particularly sound.

S. C. has an economical method of dressing the above stone over, which produces, by the action of the atmosphere, a surface of crystalline hardness, and improves the colour.

FONTS from 5l. upwards. Specimens on view of the various styles.

First-rate ARTISTS retained for SCULPTURED and CARVED Works.

Vein Marble Chimney-pieces, of the best quality of material and workmanship, by improved machinery	40s.
Stone ditto, from	8s.

A variety on view in stock.

MEMORIAL CROSSES, MONUMENTS, TOMBS, HEAD-STONES, &c., in great variety of design.

RESTORATION of CHURCHES. SAMUEL CUNDY having had much practice in this branch, is desirous of Estimating for Restorations.

CLERKS of WORKS have their particular attention called to the above establishment. Coats of Arms, Decorated Pannels, and other enriched works, promptly executed.

Every description of Stone or Granite work prepared, ready for fixing.—Delivered at the various Railways, and carefully packed in trucks.—Pimlico Marble and Stone Works, Belgrave Wharf, Pimlico.

REMOVAL.—ITALIAN and GALWAY MARBLE QUARRIES DEPOT, Whitehall Wharf, Parliament-street, Westminster.—Mr. FRANKLIN, Proprietor of the above Quarries, informs the SCULPTORS, MARBLE MASONS, BUILDERS, &c., that he has REMOVED his Depot from Pimlico to the above address. Arrived from Leghorn: *Venus, Echo, Antelope, Edward, Racer, Freeland*, with upwards of 100 Blocks of Veined, Sicilian, Dove, Bardilla, Sienna, black and gold, and statuary (two opened superior).—From Galway: Blocks and Black Slabs, and Slabs of all descriptions at reduced rates: an early inspection is desired.

DEPOTS.		AGENTS.
Liverpool	South Castle-street	W. Franklin.
Bristol	Redcliffe Wharf	J. Williams, Esq.
Dublin	Scovills	Messrs. Scott and Co.
Belfast	Dunbar Dock	J. Cramsie, Esq.
Hull	Dock Company	Messrs. Wood and Co.

TERRA-COTTA, or VITRIFIED STONE WORKS, King Edward-street, Westminster-road, London.—M. H. BLANCHARD, from late Coade's Original Works, Belvedere-road, Lambeth, begs to inform the Nobility, Gentry, Architects, and Builders, that he has re-established the manufacture of that invaluable material, which has been successfully adopted by our eminent Architects and others. In the adornment of our noblest buildings, nearly 100 years has proved the imperishable nature of the material, the specimens of those times now exhibiting all their primitive sharpness.

Groups, statues, friezes, capitals, panelling, pinnacles, finials, terminals, Tudor, and other chimney shafts, balustrading, fountains, fonts, tazzas, vases, coats of arms, devices, and every description of architectural ornament, at prices in many instances nearly half the cost of stone.

Specimens of the material to be seen at the Office of "The Builder," 2, York-street, Covent Garden, and at the Works.

PAPER-HANGINGS.—JEFFREY, ALLEN, and Co., solicit the attention of Builders and the Trade generally to their extensive STOCK of PAPER HANGINGS, which, from the use of steam-power and recent improvements in the application of machinery, they are able to offer at remarkably low prices.—Kent and Essex Yard, 115, Whitechapel.

PAPER-HANGINGS by MACHINE and BLOCKS.—The trade supplied in town and country, with machine goods, from first-rate new designs, at the lowest prices they have ever been sold in this country; and block goods, for style and quality, not to be surpassed by any house in England. All the patterns are registered, and can only be supplied by HENNELL and CROSBY, Queen-street, Southwark-bridge-road. Cheapest house in London for oak, marbles, and panel decorations. A set of patterns, 5s., to be deducted off an order of 5l.—Terms, cash.

PAPER-HANGINGS, MANUFACTURED UNDER HER MAJESTY'S ROYAL LETTERS PATENT.

E. T. ARCHER, 451, Oxford-street, solicits an Inspection of the various DECORATIVE PAPERS, fitted up in panels on the walls of the extensive range of apartments, built expressly for that purpose; where also is kept an extensive stock of every variety of Paper-hangings, at the lowest possible price and of the best manufacture, in English and French Designs, by the best Artists; and where may be had a large assortment of French and other Continental Paper-hangings always on hand.—Builders and large Consumers are particularly invited to the above.—451, Oxford-street.

FIRE-PROOF BUILDINGS.—PORTER'S PATENT.—By an improved mode of applying Corrugated Iron in the construction of Floors, Roofs, &c., for which Patents have recently been granted to John Henderson Porter, Buildings of every class can be rendered Fire-proof at a very trifling increase of cost, and without any increase of weight,—while from the absence of cast-iron and timber greater security is obtained, in point of strength, than by the ordinary method of construction.

PORTER'S PATENT BEAMS and GIRDERS of CORRUGATED IRON, on account of their remarkable stiffness, are particularly suitable for buildings and bridges: they are 30 per cent. lighter, and 20 per cent. cheaper, than other wrought-iron beams of equal strength.—Manufactory, Iron Building and Roofing Works, Southwark; Office, 2, Adelaide-place, London-bridge, City.

INCREASED ECONOMY in BUILDING, combined with PROTECTION from FIRE, &c.—The following advantages result from the adoption of the "PATENT FIRE-PROOF FLOORS and ROOFS," viz.:—

Security from Fire.
Great Economy of Construction.
Increased Durability.
Protection from Dry rot and from noxious Insects and Vermin.

The economy of this system is very considerable; its cost, as compared with the common method of fire-proof building, being about one half: while, as compared with the ordinary timber floors, it effects a saving of from 10 to 25 per cent. The entire freedom from lateral thrust, in this method of building, gives it a further advantage over the plan of iron girders and brick arches. The system is applicable to all classes of buildings. It has been introduced at the Middlesex Hospital, where it can be seen at any time, and all information obtained of Messrs. FOX and BARRETT, Leicester Chambers, 46, Leicester-square.

THE office of SECRETARY to the BUILDERS' BENEVOLENT INSTITUTION, vacant by the resignation of Mr. W. GRUBB.—The Committee will meet on Wednesday next, the 9th of May, to receive letters from such parties as may be desirous of being candidates. Salary, 60l. per annum. The duties will not occupy the whole of the time or attendance. Personal applications cannot be attended to, and a full explanation is requested as to age, former or present occupation, &c.—Address to the Committee of the Builders' Benevolent Institution, office (*pro tem.*), 13, Broad-street, Golden-square.

COMPETITIONS.

THE Committee for Erecting a School-room at Deptford inform the gentlemen who have sent them plans that the premium has been awarded to Mr. REILLY, of Kennington. The plans, &c., which were not accepted, will be returned on application to Mr. SPENCER, with whom they were left.

TO ARCHITECTS.

RESTORATION of BRIDGEWATER CHURCH.—EXTENSION of TIME.—The Churchwardens beg to announce to the competing Architects, that the time for receiving plans is extended to the 14th of May.

Dated April 24, 1849.

NEW WORKHOUSE for the PARISH of BIRMINGHAM.—TO ARCHITECTS.—Architects desirous of furnishing PLANS and ESTIMATES for the ERECTION of a NEW WORKHOUSE for the parish of Birmingham, to contain 1,550 inmates, are informed that plans and sections of the site, with printed instructions, may be had on application to the Clerk, on and after the 1st of May next. The estimate must not exceed the sum of 25,000l. The plans will be submitted to the judgment of three eminent non-competing architects, to report thereon to the Board. The premiums to be given are:—For the plan finally adopted, 150l.; for the plan next in estimation, 50l. The printed instructions will contain every particular required to be known by architects; and as a personal canvass of the guardians is strictly prohibited, all applications must be addressed to the Clerk. The latest period for the delivery of plans will be Saturday, the 30th of June next ensuing.—By order,

EDWARD PITT, Clerk to the Board.

Clerk's office, Lichfield-street, April 26, 1849.

PUBLICATIONS.

A NEW EDITION, corrected, in One very thick Volume, 8vo. of above 1,200 pages, with upwards of 2,000 Wood Engravings, price 2l. 2s. cloth.

AN ENCYCLOPÆDIA of COTTAGE, FARM, and VILLA ARCHITECTURE and FURNITURE: containing numerous Designs for Dwellings, from the Villa to the Cottage and the Farm, including Farm-houses, Farmeries, and other Agricultural Buildings; Country Inns, Public-houses, and Parochial Schools; with the requisite Fittings-up, Fixtures, and Furniture; and appropriate Offices, Gardens, and Garden Scenery: each Design accompanied by Analytical and Critical Remarks.

By J. C. LOUDON, F.L.S., H.S., G.S., Z.S., &c.

London: LONGMAN, BROWN, GREEN, and LONGMANS.

DAGUERREOTYPE CALOTYPE.

Just published,

AN ILLUSTRATED and DESCRIPTIVE CATALOGUE of all the apparatus, instruments, and preparations requisite in the practice of the DAGUERREOTYPE CALOTYPE, and other Photogenic Processes. Professional and amateur artists are requested to forward their cards of address and four postage stamps to the publisher, on receipt of which a copy of the above will be sent.—GEORGE KNIGHT and SONS, Foster-lane, Cheapside, London.—Sole agents for Voigtlander and Son's Daguerreotype Lenses.

TO LAND-OWNERS AND PHILANTHROPISTS.—PRIZE MODEL COTTAGES.

On the 28th April was published, price 3s. 6d. boards, and 4s. in cloth, lettered; with seventeen pages of plates,

DETAILED WORKING DRAWINGS, Plans, Elevations, Sections, and Specifications of TWO PAIRS of LABOURERS' COTTAGES: being the same for which the Society of Arts awarded the first and second prizes in the competition of May, 1848, to the Architects, Mr. T. C. Hine, of Nottingham, and Mr. S. J. Nicholl, of London.

Each set of plans exhibits the peculiar mode of construction, the method of warming and ventilating the buildings, and, with the specification, contains every information that can be needed by the workman in carrying the design into execution.

London, DEAN and SON, Threadneedle-street; and by order, of all Booksellers.

ROYAL ACADEMY OF ARTS, TRAFALGAR-SQUARE.—NOTICE IS HEREBY GIVEN that the EXHIBITION will OPEN on MONDAY next, the 7th instant, at Twelve o'clock. Admission, One Shilling. Catalogue, One Shilling.

JOHN PRESCOTT KNIGHT, R.A., Sec.

Exhibitors and students may receive their tickets and catalogues by applying at the Academy on Monday, after 12.

MEETING of the BRITISH ASSOCIATION at BIRMINGHAM.—EXHIBITION of MANUFACTURES.—The LOCAL COUNCIL of the BRITISH ASSOCIATION having resolved to form an EXHIBITION of WORKS of MANUFACTURE and ART and MODELS of MACHINERY, during the ensuing Meeting of the British Association at Birmingham, in September next, the EXHIBITION COMMITTEE appointed for the purpose of carrying this resolution into effect, invite co-operation and assistance in the accomplishment of this object.

The central position of Birmingham, and the facility of access to it by railway from all parts of the kingdom, eminently adapt it for an exhibition of so much importance to the public, and especially to manufacturers.

The Exhibition Committee are particularly desirous to receive contributions comprising Series of SPECIMENS illustrative of MANUFACTURING PROCESSES, FINISHED ARTICLES, either original in design or excellent in manufacture, and MODELS or SPECIMENS of new or improved MACHINERY.

The contributions for the exhibition should be forwarded on or before August 1, and it is expected they will be returned in October. It is particularly requested that all contributors will send to the committee, as early as possible, a general description of the articles they purpose forwarding to the exhibition, in order to afford to the committee an opportunity of deciding as to the desirableness of accepting them, and with the view to the formation of a catalogue and the arrangement of the articles; the dimensions of models and bulky articles should be also furnished.

The carriage upon all articles which are accepted will be paid both ways by the committee, who will also insure the articles against fire; the committee cannot, however, hold themselves responsible for any damage which may occur to the contributions, in transit or in the exhibition, but the utmost care will be taken of them.

Communications and packages for the exhibition to be addressed to the "Exhibition Committee of the British Association for the Advancement of Science, Birmingham."

WESTLEY RICHARDS, Chairman.
W. P. MARSHALL, } Honorary
GEORGE SHAW, } Secretaries.

Philosophical Institution, Birmingham, April 21, 1849.

LARGE PREMISES WANTED immediately, suitable for an Organ-builder, or a House with Ground on which the Factory might be erected; the neighbourhood of the New-road, St. Marylebone, would be preferred.—Apply to Mr. ARTHUR ASHPITEL, Architect, 5, Crown-court, Old Broad-street.

CAPITAL BUILDING GROUND at STAMFORD-HILL TO BE LET—the best part in this neighbourhood. Also, the fine FRONTAGE of RECTORY-ROAD, West Hackney. Also, a superior PLOT of GROUND near Highbury.—Apply to Mr. ARTHUR ASHPITEL, Architect, 5, Crown-Court, Old Broad-street.

VALUABLE BUILDING GROUND TO BE LET for 61 years, consisting of 54 feet of FIRST-RATE BUSINESS FRONTAGE, in St. John-street-road, adjoining the yard of Sadler's Wells Theatre. Also about 198 feet of frontage in Sadler's Wells-yard, fronting the New River.—Apply to Mr. RICHARD TRESS, Architect, Little St. Thomas Apostle.

TO BUILDERS.

WEST DRAYTON STATION, County MIDDLESEX.—HIGHLY ELIGIBLE PLOTS OF GROUND TO BE LET for BUILDING, on favourable terms, situated close to the West Drayton Station on the Great Western Railway, 13 miles from London, 2½ from the market town of Uxbridge, 7 from Windsor. Excellent fishing in the immediate neighbourhood. Lithographed plans may be had, and every information given upon application to Mr. CORBETT, West Drayton.

BUILDING GROUND TO BE LET on MODERATE TERMS.—To Builders, Capitalists, and Building Societies)—to erect terrace, crescent, detached villas, &c., of four, six, and eight rooms, which kind of property is much in request in the neighbourhood. Sand and gravel on the estate. Bricks may be had within a mile. Exempt from the New Building Act.—Letters addressed, post-paid, to U., Rose Villa, Mill-street, Lambeth.

ISLINGTON.—GROUND TO BE LET in the best part of Islington, containing about 150 feet each way, calculated for a Chapel and Schools, a public Institution, Manufactory, or for any purpose or business requiring a large piece of ground. It has five houses already on the estate, well let, (except one in hand.) The whole, or part, to be either LET or SOLD upon eligible terms.—Apply to Mr. BIGGS, No. 7, the Terrace, Walworth.

FREEHOLD LAND, WALTON-ON-THAMES, SURREY.—TO BE LET, on Building Leases, or Sold, highly eligible plots of BUILDING LAND, situate in Oatland's park, formerly the seat of the Duke of York, within eight minutes' walk of the Walton Station, South-Western Railway; the neighbourhood highly respectable, the subsoil gravel; tithe-free, land-tax redeemed.—Apply, T. PRYER, Esq., Solicitor, 11, Artillery-place, Finsbury; or Mr. CORBETT'S, 14, King William-street, Strand.

BUILDING PLOT at TULSE-HILL.—TO BE LET on LEASE for 99 years (at 8s. per foot frontage), a valuable PLOT of GROUND, presenting a frontage of 100 feet to the high road by a depth of 300 feet, suitable for the erection of a family mansion or good class villa residences. The drains have been formed, and the whole walled in at a considerable expense.—Apply to Messrs. TOPPIN, HURFORD, and Co. (successors to Mr. W. W. Simpson), Land Surveyors, &c., 18, Bucklersbury, London.

HIGH-STREET FRONTAGE, ROTHERHITHE, within a few yards south-east of the Thames Tunnel, close to the river, and within a short distance of the Surrey Canal, TO BE LET (with an advance, if required), on building lease direct from the freeholder, (or the freehold to be sold), a PLOT OF GROUND, possessing 33 feet frontage and 100 feet depth; land-tax redeemed and well sewered; has the basements out, and the party-walls (new) belong to the ground. For particulars apply to Mr. G. COURTHOPE, Coal Merchant and Estate Agent, 16, Paradise-row, Rotherhithe.

GRAVELLY SOIL.—TO BE LET on LEASE for 99 years, several desirable PLOTS of BUILDING GROUND, most delightfully situate on a gravelly soil, and suitable for the erection of detached villas. The land is within five minutes' walk of the church and railway station (Broxbourn, Herts.), and bounded by that beautiful crystal stream, the New River. The proverbial salubrity of this neighbourhood, with its magnificent park and other local attractions, render the demand for houses very great.—For terms, apply to Messrs. TOPPIN, HURFORD, and Co. (successors to Mr. W. W. Simpson), Auctioneers and Land Surveyors, 18, Bucklersbury, London. Money if required.

WATER-SIDE PREMISES, suitable for an Engineer, Builder, Timber, or Stone Merchant, or for erecting mills or workshops.—TO LET, at Mill Wall, Isle of Dogs, opposite the East Country Docks, a WHARF and PREMISES, with dwelling-house (late in the occupation of Messrs. Cassell and Co.) The premises are enclosed by substantial walls which are nearly parallel throughout. The river frontage is about 60 feet, and the depth about 430 feet. There is a back frontage to the Greenwich Ferry-road, upon which dwelling houses might be erected.—For particulars apply at BLASHFIELD'S Cement Works, Mill Wall, or at his office, Waterloo-dock, Commercial-road, Lambeth.

Also part of a Wharf, with warehouse room, in Commercial-road, Lambeth.

TO BUILDERS.

SEVERAL eligible Plots of BUILDING GROUND to be LET, for a term of upwards of 90 years, for the purpose of building detached and semi-detached cottage Villas (which have been found to let as soon as finished), in a park-like piece of ground, tastefully laid out and planted, the coach roads and extensive gravelled walks made, and sewers laid in. The situation is high and dry, commanding extensive and beautiful scenery, the soil gravel, water abundant, and of the finest quality, and is little more than half an hour's ride from London, and within five minutes' walk of an important station and the parish church, and possesses many unrivalled advantages to sportsmen or retired gentlemen.—Particulars had at Mr. FREEMAN'S Estate Office, 41, Chapel-street, Edgeware-road.

BUILDERS and private gentlemen disposed to build for themselves, are invited to notice a VALUBLE PLOT of FREEHOLD MEADOW LAND, containing upwards of nine acres, situated at the junction of two public roads, contiguous to a large respectable village, having a view of, and near access to, the Thames river, at a favorite spot for angling, and about a mile only from Hampton Court gardens, and the South-Western Railway station, and within two miles of the Twickenham station, on the Richmond and Windsor Railway. The view is remarkably cheerful and of considerable extent, the sub-soil gravel, the water delicious, the parish church only five minutes' walk distant, excellent shops, medical assistance of the highest order, and in addition to the railways, there are omnibus conveyances several times a-day to and from town. The land-tax is redeemed. To be sold in its entirety, or in lots, or let on building leases.—Terms may be had, and a plan may be seen at Mr. JOHN DAWSON'S Auction and Agency offices, Kingston-on-Thames, and 49, Pall Mall.

HOLLAND PARK ESTATE, NOTTING-HILL.—TO BE LET, PLOTS of valuable BUILDING GROUND for VILLAS, TERRACES, &c., situate in the most open part of this much-admired estate, which for salubrity of air, good drainage, and fashionable locality, stands unrivalled in the environs of this metropolis. The estate lies between the Kensington and Notting-hill main roads, and has a full southern and western aspect, being protected from the north and east by the rising ground of Notting-hill. It commands extensive views from the Surrey hills to Harrow, and delightful prospects over the undulating ground, the lofty groves and shrubberies, of the park and gardens of Holland House. A substratum of firm gravel extends over the whole of the estate, which is thoroughly drained by a new and capacious sewer, lately built, at a vast expense, by the Great Western Railway Company.

TO GENTLEMEN desirous of building their own residences according to their own immediate wants and tastes, very liberal terms can be offered in the modes of payment, or a large portion of the cost can remain on mortgage at 5 per cent., or be paid off by instalments, in the manner of Building Societies.

TO BUILDERS, likewise, liberal advances will be made.

SEVERAL SITES for superior Villa residences, with large pleasure-grounds attached, may now be had.

Application to be made to GEORGE H. GODDARD, Esq., 8, John-street, Adelphi, where plans may be seen, and all particulars obtained.

CLAPHAM COMMON.—TO BE LET on Lease for 99 years, or TO BE SOLD, a FRONTAGE, with about 250 feet of depth on the west or preferable side of the Common; also the HOUSE and GROUNDS adjoining.—Inquire of Mr. LEE, Architect and Surveyor, 20, Golden-square, London.

CHELSEA.—VALUABLE BUILDING GROUND, for a Terrace of Fifteen Houses, in Oakley-street, which is 60 feet wide, and leads from the King's-road to the Chain-pier. Lease 94 years. Accommodation if required.—Apply to Mr. Wm. DREW, 5, Pelham-crescent, Brompton.

TO CHEESEMONGERS, LINENDRAPERS, &c.

TO BE LET, on a repairing Lease for Twenty-one Years, a HOUSE and SHOP with a good frontage in Fleet-street, admirably adapted for either of the above trades.—Apply to Mr. RICHARD TRESS, Architect, Little St. Thomas Apostle, Queen-street, Cheapside.

MILTON-STREET, CRIPPLEGATE.

TO BE LET, on a Repairing Lease, for Twenty-one Years, by TENDER, a Building, formerly used as a Chapel, with the Dwelling-house adjoining. Tenders, which must state the purposes to which it is proposed to apply the premises, will be received at Grocers' Hall from persons desirous of taking the same, on or before the 14th day of May next. The form of lease, which, with the counterpart, is to be at the expense of the lessee, may be seen at the Hall.—Grocers' Hall, May 2nd, 1849.

TO BUILDERS, CARPENTERS, AND OTHERS.

TO BE DISPOSED OF, at a moderate Premium, a LEASE of PREMISES and BUSINESS in the above line, situated in a village in Kent, about seven miles from London. The Stock to be taken at a valuation.—For further particulars apply, stating name and address, to Messrs. EVERSFIELD and HORNE, Auctioneers, and Estate Agents, 1, Little Smith-street, Westminster.

TO BRICKMAKERS AND OTHERS.

TO BE DISPOSED OF, with immediate possession, an old established BUSINESS in the Manufacture of White Bricks, Tiles, and Ornamental Goods, with all necessary buildings for carrying on an extensive trade and an inexhaustible supply of the finest brick-earth this country can produce. The works adjoin a navigable river, from whence the goods are shipped to all parts.—Full particulars may be obtained on application to Mr. D. NICHOLSON, Wandsworth, Surrey.

TO FURNISHING IRONMONGERS, SMITHS, &c.

TO BE DISPOSED OF, the LEASE of a large CORNER HOUSE and PREMISES, in a most desirable and commanding situation, where the above trade has been carried on upwards of forty years, and to which a respectable connection is attached. To any party with a moderate amount of ready money the present affords a very desirable opportunity.—For particulars, apply to Messrs. TROLLOPE and SONS, 15, Parliament-street, and 18, Grosvenor-street, Eaton-square.

TO BUILDERS, MEMBERS OF BUILDING SOCIETIES, AND OTHERS.

TO BE DISPOSED OF, in CARCASS, part of a TERRACE of THIRTY HOUSES now erecting, and of handsome elevation. The purchase-money may remain until the leases are granted, or it may be sunk in an improved ground rent, at the option of the purchaser.—For further particulars, apply to Mr. PALMER, Lee Arms, Brownlow-road, Queen's-road, Dalston, who has also eligible Land to Let for Building purposes. Bricks on the Ground for sale or advance.

FREEHOLD PROPERTY FOR SALE.—A Builder in the country has Property to dispose of, well situated, let to respectable tenants, and in good repair, realizing 7 per cent. Prices, 3,000*l.*, 1,500*l.*, and 700*l.* Would take one-fourth in goods suited to his business.—Apply, by letter, pre-paid, to W. R., office of "The Builder," 2, York-street, Covent Garden.

LARGE FIRST-RATE PUBLIC HOUSE TO BE SOLD, by order of the Court of Chancery, in a very populous neighbourhood at the east-end of London; ninety-six years' lease. The house contains every accommodation—spacious club-room and large cellarage, also ground sufficient for three other houses, large workshops, &c.; the whole subject to the ground-rent of only 15*l.* per annum.—For particulars apply to Mr. ARTHUR ASHPITEL, Architect, 5, Crown-court, Old Broad-street.

HAMMERSMITH.—TO BE SOLD BY PRIVATE TENDER, a LARGE BARN, 70 feet by 23 feet, COTTAGES, SHEDS, and OUTBUILDINGS, situate in Lloyd's brickfield, Goldhawk-road, Shepherd's Bush, containing about 30 square of plain and pantiling, oak roof, with timbers of large dimensions, quarter and boarded partitions, weather boarding, floors, doors, brickwork, &c.; to be taken down and cleared away by the purchaser, the site being let for building. Terms may be known on application to Mr. GOMME, Auctioneer, &c., Hammersmith.

TO BUILDERS AND OTHERS.

TO BE SOLD, on advantageous Terms, SIX CARCASES, well built with brick,—third-class houses—on leases of 99 years, at a low ground-rent, 97 of which are unexpired; situated at that very rising locality, NEW TOWN, WEST HAM, ESSEX, and within a few minutes' walk of the Railway Station.—For particulars address, post free, to Mr. HAGGER, Cedar House, Plaistow-lane, West Ham, Essex.

TO PLUMBERS, GAS-FITTERS, PAINTERS, PAPER-HANGERS, AND OTHERS.

TO BE SOLD (on advantageous terms), the LEASE and GOODWILL of a DWELLING-HOUSE, with good domestic accommodation and extensive and well-arranged business premises, situate in a first-rate locality, about 3 miles from the City, where a very profitable business has been carried on for many years by the present proprietor.—Apply to Mr. J. LONG, Surveyor and Valuer, 39, Threadneedle-street.

TO BE SOLD, the LEASE of SIX BRICK-BUILT DWELLING HOUSES, being 7 to 12 inclusive, in Shepperton-street, Islington; also a COTTAGE in the rear of No. 7, held for the unexpired term of sixty years from Michaelmas, 1848; improved rent, 113*l.* per annum. Also, the LEASE of THREE COTTAGES, 11, 12, and 13, Little Charles-street, Regent's-park, let to weekly tenants at 8s. per week; each held for the unexpired terms of sixty years from Lady-day, 1846, at a ground-rent of 14*l.* per annum. Also, the LEASE of a HOUSE, No. 6, South-row, St. James's, held from the Earl of Craven for the unexpired term of twenty-four years, at a ground-rent of 28*l.* per annum; let on lease for twenty-one years, at 57*l.* per annum.—For further particulars inquire of JAMES JACKSON, at 51, Broad-street, Golden-square.

SALES BY AUCTION.

IMPORTANT BUILDING SITES, CROYDON, SURREY.

MESSRS. BLAKE have been honoured with instructions from the London, Brighton, and South Coast Railway Company to SELL by AUCTION, at Garraway's Coffee-house, 'Change Alley, on FRIDAY, the 1st June next, at Twelve o'Clock, a considerable area of first-rate BUILDING LAND (in convenient lots), situate on one of the great leading thoroughfares in immediate connection with the vast traffic of the West Croydon Station, at the north entrance of the town, comprehending all the valuable frontage on the north side of the Tamworth-road, and other lands adjoining, which proceed from the station towards Church-street, and other populous parts of the town and vicinity. The character and local position of this land opens to enterprising and judicious capitalists the moral certainty of success, it being notorious that such investments in Croydon offer the most sterling security, occasioned by a demand for moderate-sized houses infinitely beyond the supply, added to which, the Railway Company on this line have made considerable reductions in the charge for periodical tickets, with a view of increasing building and extending facilities for suburban residences in connection with the short stations between London, Croydon, and Epsom; and it is not too much to say that there is no place in England where a well-conducted building operation of this kind is so likely to ensure success. There will be included in the sale certain respectable DWELLING HOUSES, with garden ground, Trading Premises, and other property; also, two lots of Building Land in Sydenham Park, near Forest Hill Station, all of which will hereafter be detailed.—Particulars and plans will be issued fourteen days before the sale, which may be had of Messrs. SUTTON, EWENS, and Co., Solicitors, Basinghall-street; at Garraway's Coffee-house, 'Change Alley; at the principal stations between London and Brighton, and also between London and Epsom; and of Messrs. BLAKE, Croydon, Surrey.

SALES BY AUCTION.

TO TIMBER MERCHANTS, BUILDERS, CONTRACTORS, AND OTHERS.

MESSRS. EVERSFIELD and HORNE will SELL by AUCTION, at or adjoining the Lambeth-stairs, on MONDAY, 14th May, at Twelve o'clock, the first portion of the timber, which has been used but a few months, in the coffer-dam at St. Katherine's-wharf, removed for convenience of sale, comprising about 308 loads of Dantzic fir, and other timber, in long and short piles, waling pieces and struts, which will be put in suitable lots for purchasers.—May be viewed two days prior to the sale, and catalogues had of Messrs. EVERSFIELD and HORNE, Coal Exchange; or 1, Little Smith-street, Westminster.

BUILDER'S STOCK IN TRADE, FINSBURY.

MESSRS. EVERSFIELD and HORNE have received instructions from Mr. Griffiths, who is relinquishing the building trade, to SELL by AUCTION, on the Premises, Tabernacle-walk, Finsbury, on TUESDAY, May 15th, and following days, at Ten for Eleven, the Valuable STOCK in TRADE, comprising dry Christiana deals, Archangel deals and battens, prepared flooring and matched board, 40 loads of whole Baltic timber, dry pine plank, Baltic staves, wainscot and mahogany, fir quartering, &c.; and the stock of dry deals, planks and battens, lying at the Saw-mills, Swan-street, Bermondsey; also, a quantity of scaffolding, blocks and falls, benches, screw jacks, nails, and ironmongery, several tons of old lead and iron, cart-horse, two carts, harness, and other effects.—May be viewed two days previous, and catalogues had on the premises, and of the Auctioneers, Coal Exchange; or 1, Little Smith-street, Westminster.

NEAR STRATFORD, ESSEX.—Freehold Ground Rents of 24*l.* and 14*l.* per annum and Plots of Building Ground, by

MR. CHAMBERS, at the Auction Mart, Bartholomew-lane, London, on TUESDAY, 22nd May, at Twelve for One, several PLOTS of FREEHOLD BUILDING GROUND, suitable for the erection of villa and other residences, in Howard's-road, Balaam-street, Plaistow, and offering safe investments, or for the creation of ground rents, possessing good roads, excellent drainage, and a supply of pure water, giving votes for South Essex; also, two FREEHOLD GROUND RENTS of 12*l.* each and one of 14*l.*, arising from 19 houses in Howard's-road, well secured on a rental of 243*l.* May be viewed. Particulars of Mr. DEMAID, on the Premises, at the "Greyhound" opposite the "Swan," Stratford, the Auction Mart, of Messrs. MARTEN, THOMAS, and HOLLAMS, Solicitors; Commercial Sale Rooms, Mincing-lane; and of Mr. CHAMBERS, Estate and Land Agent, No. 7, Great Tower-street.

TO BUILDERS, MASONS, SCULPTORS, AND OTHERS.—Stock, Furniture, &c., Cirencester Wharf, Augustus-street, Regent's-park.

MR. H. BIERS has been instructed, by the Executors of the late Mr. J. Knapp, to SELL BY AUCTION, on Tuesday, May 8th, and following days, on the Premises, Cirencester-Wharf, Augustus-street, Regent's-park, the stock, comprising Statuary, Vein, Dove, Black and Gold, and other Marbles, in block and slab; Portland and York Stone in Block, Landings, Steps, Cills and Paving, Slate in slabs, Crab and other Engines, Blocks and Falls, Saws and Tackle, Boukers, Screens, Truck, Ladders, Bricks, Lime, and other materials. Also the valuable Plaster Figures, Vases, Brackets, &c.; Marble Chimney-pieces, in Block, Bardella, Statuary and Vein, Monumental Tablets, &c. On the following day the Furniture and Effects, together with Paintings, Prints, Books, &c.

The VALUABLE WHARF and Premises, with commodious Dwelling, TO LET.—H. BIERS, 13, Broad-street, Golden-square.

WIMBLEDON PARK, now within sixteen minutes' ride of London.—BEAUTIFUL FREEHOLD BUILDING SITES.

MESSRS. DANIEL SMITH and SON respectfully apprise the public they will offer for SALE BY AUCTION, at the Mart, near the Bank of England, on WEDNESDAY, May 30, at Twelve, in Lots, divers parcels of freehold Ground, offering some of the most picturesque and desirable sites for the erection of mansions and villas to be found within the whole environs of London, with a fine supply of water, comprising the grand frontage of Wimbledon Park, skirting the extensive and proverbially healthy commons of Wimbledon and Putney, near Roehampton and Richmond Parks, parts beautifully wooded, and commanding rich and varied scenery, with delightful drives and walks in every direction. Also some frontage lands near the entrance of Wandsworth from Roehampton.—Particulars and plans may be had at the Tibbet's Lodge entrance, Putney Heath; at the Auction Mart; of Mr. LEE, Architect, Golden-square; and of Messrs. DANIEL SMITH and SON, Land Agents and Surveyors, Waterloo-place, Pall-Mall; and of their agent at Windsor.

MIDDLESEX.—Very valuable Freehold Farm, offering a particularly eligible Investment for Capitalists, Builders, or a Public Company.

MESSRS. DANIEL SMITH and SON will offer for SALE BY AUCTION, early in June (unless previously disposed of by PRIVATE CONTRACT), a most valuable FREEHOLD ESTATE, within five miles westward of London, consisting of nearly 100 acres, all fine rich grass land, excepting about 10 acres, lying in a perfect ring fence, and free from any footpath or annoyance of any kind. It embraces a singularly beautiful and prominent hill or knoll, with a fine breadth of vale, offering a most commanding and delightful spot for building, with superior brick earth. It has three distinct approaches, but perfectly retired and secluded as to buildings and the adjoining properties. It would form a grand site for any public building, or for the erection of a mansion, or several villas. Particulars may be known by application to Mr. ANNESLEY, Solicitor, 54, Lincoln's-Inn Fields; or to Messrs. DANIEL SMITH and SON, Land Agents, in Waterloo-place, Pall-mall, who are fully authorised to treat for its disposal.

ELIGIBLE AND SAFE INVESTMENT.—Three modern brick-built Churches, so constructed that they may be removed and re-erected on any spot with the greatest facility.

MR. PRICE begs to announce that he is instructed by the Assignees of P. Thompson, a bankrupt, to SELL BY PUBLIC AUCTION, at Garraway's, on WEDNESDAY, May 16, at Twelve for One precisely, in three lots, THREE substantial, modern, brick-built CHURCHES of handsome elevation. The interior of these sacred edifices is replete with the necessary arrangements and fittings. One of them is capable of affording ample accommodation for 600 persons, and the other two for 500 persons each. They are at present respectively situate in Agar-town, St. Pancras; Albert-road, St. John's-wood; and Drewer's-green, Westminster; and are let for terms at the annual rents of 40*l.*, 60*l.*, and 71*l.* It is to be observed that these churches have been built in accordance with, and under the sanction and approval of, the metropolitan official referees, and are placed in their present position for the temporary accommodation of these districts.—May be viewed on application, and particulars shortly had of H. H. STANSFELD, Esq., Official Assignee, Basinghaw Chambers, Basinghall-street; at Garraway's; and at Mr. PRICE'S offices, 48, Chancery-lane.

EXTENSIVE SALE of OLD and NEW BUILDING MATERIALS at WALWORTH.—To Builders, Contractors, Carpenters, Joiners, and Others.

MESSRS. BARTON and SON will hold their next Genuine Sale by PUBLIC AUCTION, most unreservedly, on the Grounds near the "Cottage of Content," Lock's-fields, Walworth, on TUESDAY next, May 8th, at Twelve for One prompt, the NEW STOCK, comprising 900 dry seasoned pine and spruce battens, 750 wide spruce pine planks, 800 capital deals, 90,000 feet of new joists, in long lengths, prepared floor and other boards, cut scantlings, arris railing, quartering, plates, and the MATERIALS of FIVE HOUSES, lately erected, will comprise doors, sashes, and frames, cupboard fronts, wainscot partitions, marble chimney-pieces, hearths, jambs, pan, plain and ridge tiles, York paving, coping, window cills, oak and fir timber, in girders, bressumers, story posts, plates, joists, fencing, floor boards, shop fronts, stable fittings, several pair of capital coach-house gates, quartering, &c. Fixtures consist of stoves, ranges, coppers, dressers and shelves, cupboards, and a vast accumulation of fittings, new and old timber, stone, and materials, all useful in the way of building, alterations, and improvements.—May be viewed and catalogues had two days previous, at the following houses: Crown, Peckham; White Horse, Brixton; King's Head, Old Change, City; Chequers, Westminster; Cottage of Content, Walworth; on the Premises; or of the Auctioneers, No. 7, Cheltenham-place, Westminster-road, Lambeth.

N.B. 100,000 capital sound Stock Bricks for Sale.

LONDON: Printed by CHARLES WYMAN, of 7, Calthorpe-street, in the Parish of St. Pancras, in the County of Middlesex, Printer, at the Printing-office of J. & H. Cox, Brothers, 74 & 75, Great Queen-street, Lincoln's-Inn Fields, in the Parish of St. Giles-in-the-Fields, in the said County; and published by the said CHARLES WYMAN, at the Office of "THE BUILDER," 2, York-street, Covent Garden, in the Parish of Saint Paul, Covent Garden, also in the said County.—Saturday, May 5, 1849.

Vol. VII.—No. 327.   MAY 12, 1849.   Price Fourpence.
Stamped 5d.

ILLUSTRATIONS.

Doric Portal of the Palazzo Sciarra Colonna, Rome: A.D. 1603
—with plans 222
Designs for Knockers; M. Duban, Architect 223
Marble Panel, San Marco, Rome 223

CONTENTS.

The Royal Academy Exhibition 217
Travelling Notes in Italy by an Architect: Pæstum 217
Movement at the Royal Institute of Architects: The Annual
   General Meeting 218
Select Committee on School of Design 219
Drying Closets 219
The Architectural Advantages and Decadencies of London .. 220
Notes in the Provinces 221
Iron Houses 221
Doric Portal of the Palazzo Sciarra Colonna, Rome 222
A Blow at Influential Buffalo: Waterford—Gloucestershire. 222
Designs for Knockers 223
Decorations from Abroad: Marble Panel from San Marco,
   Rome 223
The Wages of Workmen 223
Builders' Rights and Foibles: Tender, St. Peter's Church,
   Chester 224
Railway Jottings 224
Metropolitan Commission of Sewers 224
Books: Mr. Bulkee's "Historic Lands of England" (Churton) 224
Miscellanea 225

ADVERTISEMENTS.

CONTRACTS.

TO PAINTERS, GLAZIERS, AND PAPER HANGERS.

WANTED immediately, a Steady and Active JOURNEYMAN in the above branches, capable of undertaking the Graining and Writing in the shop. None need apply who are not thoroughly competent. Apply, post-paid, stating wages, &c., to Mr. H. A. FORD, 1, Oxford-street, Swansea.

TO PLUMBERS, BUILDERS, &c.

WANTED, by a Respectable Man, PERMANENT EMPLOYMENT, as Plumber, Grainer, Glazier, and Painter; he is well versed in the above branches, and capable of managing a business. Most respectable reference as to character and ability can be had.—Address, pre-paid, for X. Y., 147, Waterloo-bridge-road, Lambeth.

TO PARENTS AND GUARDIANS.

THE Resident Engineer of a large Town in the South of England, who has the direction of extensive works for Sanitary Improvement, has a VACANCY for an ARTICLED PUPIL.—Address, R. A. S., 14, Soho-square, London.

TO NOBLEMEN, ARCHITECTS, &c.

THE Advertiser wishes to engage himself as an IN and OUT-DOOR CARPENTER; has held the above situation at a Royal residence.—Address to W. F., post-office, Colnbrook; or reference to Mr. HARRISON, Surveyor, Eton College.

TO ARCHITECTS, BUILDERS, AND OTHERS.

THE Advertiser, aged 22, of respectable connections, is open to an ENGAGEMENT, on moderate terms, as CLERK or DRAUGHTSMAN to any of the above, in town or country. He is a good accountant, measurer, &c.—References and security, if required.—Apply, by letter, to X. Y. Z., Mr. Sturman's, Islington-green.

TO BUILDERS and OTHERS wanting an able ASSISTANT, the Advertiser offers his services, being thoroughly acquainted with the practice of surveying and building in every department, drawing, measuring, and estimating, &c., and accustomed to the general management.—Address, SURVEYOR (post free), office of "The Builder," 2, York-street, Covent Garden.

TO CARPENTERS AND BUILDERS.

THE Friends of a strong active Youth, aged Eighteen, who has served three years of his apprenticeship to the above business, wishes to engage him to a master for the remainder of his time, were he will have a good opportunity of learning his trade.—Direct, post-paid, to L. M., care of Mr. Mose, News-agent, Hampstead.

A MECHANICAL ENGINEER desires an ENGAGEMENT to superintend the execution of work, or as draughtsman. Address to A. B., care of Mr. Ledger, 74, Cheapside, London.

TO GAS COMPANIES.

A SITUATION as MANAGER of a GAS WORKS is wanted by the Advertiser, who is thoroughly acquainted with all the details of practical gas making, together with the arranging of fittings and every matter connected with gas works.—Address, J. G., care of Mr. Samuel Church, City Gas Works, Dorset-street, London.

TO BUILDERS, CONTRACTORS, AND OTHERS.

AN experienced PLUMBER, lately Foreman in one of the most eminent Builders in London, is desirous of meeting with a similar SITUATION. Understands the general routine of business. Unexceptionable reference, and security if required.—Address, pre-paid, to H. V., No. 9, Ashby-street, King's-cross.

TO GENTLEMEN, HOUSEHOLDERS, BUILDERS, AND OTHERS.

AN experienced Practical Man—a Carpenter—having filled the situation of carpenter, plumber, painter, glazier, paper-hanger, and colourer in the repair of houses; is a good joiner, having had great experience in shop fronts, sashes and frames, stairs, boxing shutters, &c.; has a good knowledge of making out working drawings and measuring up work, wants a SITUATION, at a moderate salary; can be well recommended.—Address, prepaid, to SMITH, No. 4, Princes-row, Walworth-road. No objection to the country.

TO ENGINEERS, IRON-FOUNDERS, &c.

AN ENGINEER, who has had sixteen years' experience in the erection and repairs of Marine and Land Steam-engines, and of Steam Machinery generally, and who is perfectly qualified to superintend such operations in all the details, is desirous to enter into PARTNERSHIP with parties in some concern where his experience as an engineer could be made available. At present he could advance 500l.; and to parties whose business could be improved by a persevering, energetic, and competent person conducting operations, an arrangement with the advertiser might prove of much advantage.—Address to A. B., No. 225, office of this paper, in London.

BUILDING LAND.—TO LET, at Addiscombe-road, Croydon, Surrey, adjacent to the railway station, most advantageous sites for double villas. For particulars, apply to Messrs. DRUMMONDS, ROBINSON, and TILL, Solicitors, Croydon; or to Mr. FRANCIS E. H. FOWLER, Architect, 21, Savile-row, Burlington Gardens, where plans may be seen.

IMPORTANT to BUILDERS, LEAD MERCHANTS, GLASS CUTTERS, OIL and COLOURMEN, PLUMBERS, GLAZIERS and PAINTERS.—The proprietor of a prosperous and lucrative wholesale and retail trade, established upwards of thirty years in one of the principal towns in England, wishes to retire from business and dispose of the concern, on terms that will secure an advantageous investment of capital. The wholesale trade extends over a wealthy and populous district, affording encouragement to commercial enterprise, and the retail connection is of first-class distinction. The stock of lead, glass, oil, colours, and a general assortment of materials required by plumbers, glaziers, and painters, to be taken at a fair Valuation. The purchase of the premises, consisting of an excellent dwelling-house, commodious warehouses and workshops, replete with every convenience, is expected to be included in the agreement. Applications by letter only, addressed A. Z., at W. S. Ainsworth's, Esq., 8, Gray's-Inn-square, Gray's-Inn, London.

BUILDERS and private gentlemen disposed to build for themselves, are invited to notice a VALUABLE PLOT of FREEHOLD MEADOW LAND, containing upwards of nine acres, situated at the junction of two public roads, contiguous to a large respectable village, having a view of, and near access to, the Thames river, at a favorite spot for angling, and about a mile only from Hampton Court gardens, and the South-Western Railway station, and within two miles of the Twickenham station, on the Richmond and Windsor Railway. The View is remarkably cheerful and of considerable extent, the sub-soil gravel, the water delicious, the parish church only five minutes' walk distant, excellent shops, medical assistance of the highest order, and in addition to the railways, there are omnibus conveyances several times a-day to and from town. The land-tax is redeemed. To be sold in its entirety, or in lots, or let on building leases.—Terms may be had, and a plan may be seen at Mr. JOHN DAWSON'S Auction and Agency offices, Kingston-on-Thames, and 49, Pall Mall.

HOLLAND PARK ESTATE, NOTTING-HILL.—TO BE LET, PLOTS of valuable BUILDING GROUND for VILLAS, TERRACES, &c., situate in the most open part of this much-admired estate, which for salubrity of air, good drainage, and fashionable locality, stands unrivalled in the environs of this metropolis. The estate lies between the Kensington and Notting-hill main roads, and has a full southern and western aspect, being protected from the north and east by the rising ground of Notting-hill. It commands extensive views from the Surrey hills to Harrow, and delightful prospects over the undulating ground, the lofty groves and shrubberies, of the park and gardens of Holland House. A substratum of firm gravel extends over the whole of the estate, which is thoroughly drained by a new and capacious sewer, lately built, at a vast expense, by the Great Western Railway Company.

TO GENTLEMEN desirous of building their own residences according to their own immediate wants and tastes, Very liberal terms can be offered in the modes of payment, or a large portion of the cost can remain on mortgage at 5 per cent., or be paid off by instalments, in the manner of Building Societies.

TO BUILDERS, likewise, liberal advances will be made.

SEVERAL SITES for superior Villa residences, with large pleasure-grounds attached, may now be had.

Application to be made to GEORGE H. GODDARD, Esq., 8, John-street, Adelphi, where plans may be seen, and all particulars obtained.

TO ARCHITECTS, &c.

MR. EDWARD RYDE, Land and Engineering Surveyor, &c., respectfully offers his SERVICES to Architects and others requiring them, upon reasonable and mutual terms. Surveys accurately conducted, maps and sections neatly executed, land and timber carefully Valued.—14, Upper Belgrave-place, Eaton-square.

TO BUILDERS.

A FIRST-RATE BUSINESS of a general BUILDER, near London, to be LET or SOLD.—For particulars, inquire at the Blackfriars Bridge Timber Wharf, Upper Ground-street.

AN ARCHITECT resident in a large provincial town, and who has carried on his profession for many years with considerable success, is desirous of DISPOSING OF HIS BUSINESS. The opportunity is unexceptionable for any gentleman wishing to enter into immediate practice, and the necessary arrangement may be made on very easy terms. Every information may be had on application to Messrs. HALE, BOYS, and AUSTEN, Solicitors, 6, Ely-place, Holborn.

CHELSEA.—VALUABLE BUILDING GROUND, for a Terrace of Fifteen Houses, in Oakley-street, which is 60 feet wide, and leads from the King's-road to the Chain-pier. Lease 94 years. Accommodation if required.—Apply to Mr. Wm. DREW, 5, Pelham-crescent, Brompton.

SYDENHAM PARK.—Several PLOTS OF GROUND in this desirable locality TO BE SOLD or LET on Building Leases. Money will be advanced, if required.—For particulars, apply to Messrs. DREW and SHADWELL, Solicitors, Bermondsey-street; to Messrs. ALLEN, SNOOKE, and STUCK, Architects, Tooley-street, Southwark; or to Mr. TALLON, Sydenham Station.

TO BUILDERS.

NOTTING HILL.—TO BE LET, for 99 years, at a very moderate ground-rent, a most desirable PLOT of GROUND in the High Road. Genteel cottages, at a rental of about 30 guineas, are very much sought for, and may be built here. Liberal advances made. Also a PLOT for Five Shops in the road.—Apply to Mr. MORRISON, 14, Norland-place, Notting Hill.

MIDDLESEX.—FREEHOLD PARK LAND TO BE LET on building leases, in plots of not less than one acre each, three-quarters of a mile from a railway station, half an hour from the City. The land is studded with stately timber, on an elevated site, sloping gradually to the south, and commanding an extensive view over an undulating and beautifully wooded country. The soil is gravelly, with abundance of the best water, and with every facility for perfect drainage.—Apply to JAMES BELL, Architect, 15, Langham-place, London; or to THOMAS COMPTON, Estate Agent, Enfield, and 75, Coleman-street, City.

TO BUILDERS AND OTHERS.

TO BE LET, at low ground rents, for the erection of small third-rate Cottages, several PLOTS of GROUND, in a locality where such houses are in great request. There is plenty of land, gravel, and water on the ground, and money will be advanced, if required. More than half the estate is already covered, and let. The Advertiser will be in attendance with plans, &c., from Three to Six o'clock in the Afternoon of Monday, Wednesday, and Friday during May, on the estate, which is opposite the Bell and Anchor Inn, Hammersmith-road, near the Kensington Railway.—Particulars to be had also of Mr. HOLLINGSWORTH, 4, Battle-bridge; and Mr. ROSS, 4, St. James's-place, Hampstead-road.

WATER-SIDE PREMISES, suitable for an Engineer, Builder, Timber, or Stone Merchant, or for erecting mills or workshops.—TO LET, at Mill Wall, Isle of Dogs, opposite the East Country Docks, a WHARF and PREMISES, with dwelling-house (late in the occupation of Messrs. Cassell and Co.) The premises are enclosed by substantial walls which are nearly parallel throughout. The river frontage is about 60 feet, and the depth about 450 feet. There is a back frontage to the Greenwich Ferry-road, upon which dwelling houses might be erected.—For particulars apply at BLASHFIELD'S Cement Works, Mill Wall, or at his office, Waterloo-docs, Commercial-road, Lambeth.

Also part of a Wharf, with warehouse room, in Commercial-road, Lambeth.

A GREAT BARGAIN.—To Persons in want of an eligible Investment, and to Members of Building Societies.—A Member of one of Mr. Robert Kenyon's excellent Building Societies wishes to SELL Two very capital PRIVATE DWELLING-HOUSES, situate in Clarence-street, Islington, held for 92 years, at a low ground rent, and let to respectable tenants. A purchaser may take a transfer of the mortgage to the building society, which is fixed to close in ten years, and the interest payable on the mortgage money is only 3½ per cent. per annum. 15l. has been paid off the mortgage debt to the society. This is an excellent opportunity to persons desirous of purchasing a respectable residence.—For further particulars, apply either by letter or personally, to the owner, at No. 2, Clarence-street, Islington.

TO BUILDERS AND OTHERS.

TO BE SOLD, on advantageous Terms, SIX CARCASES, well built with brick,—third-class houses, on leases of 99 years, at a low ground-rent, 97 of which are unexpired; situated at that very rising locality, NEW TOWN, WEST HAM, ESSEX, and within a few minutes' walk of the Railway Station.—For particulars address, post free, to Mr. HAGGER, Cedar House, Plaistow-lane, West Ham, Essex.

TO BUILDERS, MEMBERS OF BUILDING SOCIETIES, AND OTHERS.

TO BE DISPOSED OF, in CARCASS, part of a TERRACE of THIRTY HOUSES now erecting, and of handsome elevation. The purchase-money may remain until the leases are granted, or it may be sunk in an improved ground rent, at the option of the purchaser.—For further particulars, apply to Mr. PALMER, Lee Arms, Brownlow-road, Queen's-road, Dalston, who has also eligible Land to Let for Building purposes. Bricks on the Ground for sale or advance.

TO ARCHITECTS, BUILDERS, CEMENT-DEALERS, &c., in Town or Country.

TO BE DISPOSED OF, BY PRIVATE CONTRACT, a LARGE QUANTITY OF MOULDS for manufacturing (in any kind of cement) Ornamented, Tudor, Gothic, and Elizabethan chimney-shafts, in sizes from 3 feet to 9 feet in length, all various patterns, adapted for lodges, Villas, and mansions of any description, being fac-similes of the most eminent buildings in the country; may be had together or in separate sets. Also, other moulds for architectural ornaments.—Apply, by letter, post-paid, to J. B., 3, Rawstorne-street, Clerkenwell, London.

COAL TAR.—A large quantity of COAL TAR for SALE, at the OXFORD GAS STATION, at the reduced price of One Penny per gallon.

STEAM-ENGINE.—A new High-pressure, 14-horse power, Horizontal Engine, of the best workmanship, with tubular boiler, FOR SALE, on moderate terms, may be seen, on application to Mr. SIMMONS, at the Phœnix Foundry, 176 Dover-road, London.

SAW-MILLS.—TO BE SOLD, the LEASE of a Saw-mill, consisting of a 25-horse power steam-engine, four saw-frames, planing-machines, and circular saws, with the right of working a valuable patent, on very advantageous terms. The premises have water frontage to the Thames.—Address, A. B., Chelsea Wharf.

GRANITE QUARRY TO BE DISPOSED OF, on reasonable terms, situate on the South Coast of Cornwall, within 3 miles of the shipping port, and from which an unlimited supply of Granite of a superior quality can be obtained. Lease for ever. Dues, 1d. per square foot. No other rent.—For further particulars, and to inspect samples, apply to Mr. BARTLETT, 58, Lombard-street, London.

SALES BY AUCTION.

TO BRASS AND COCK FOUNDERS, ENGINE PUMP, Water-Closet, and Beer-Machine Manufacturers and Engineers.

MESSRS. KEMP have received instructions from the Executors of Mrs. Wheeler, deceased, to SELL BY AUCTION, on the Premises, 98, Tottenham-court-road, on THURSDAY, May 17th, 1849, at Twelve o'clock precisely, the whole of the VALUABLE EFFECTS of an Old-established Business, comprising lathes, tools, patterns, implements, plant, &c.: all in the best possible condition.—May be viewed two days prior and morning of sale. Catalogues on the premises; of Mr. HARDING, 96, Albany-street, Regent's-park; and of Messrs. KEMP, 37, Judd-street, Brunswick-square.

TO BUILDERS, PAPER-HANGERS, HOUSE DECORATORS, AND OTHERS.

MR. BRAY, Jun., is instructed to SELL, on the premises, Phœnix-place, Addison-road North, Notting-hill, on TUESDAY, May 22, at Twelve for One, by order of the proprietor, upwards of 4,000 Pieces of PAPER-HANGINGS, comprising flock on satin and crimson grounds, dining-room satins, Elizabethan and bouquet, parlour and bed-room papers, in chintz, shaded and plain; hall and staircase, in oaks, hand-marbles, &c. Also the valuable Plant, and 100 Transparent Window-blinds.—May be viewed the day prior, and catalogues had on the premises, and at the offices of the Auctioneer, 259, High Holborn.

TO TIMBER MERCHANTS, BUILDERS, CARPENTERS AND OTHERS.

MR. LEREW is directed to SELL BY AUCTION, on the Premises, in Edward-street, Regent's-park, near Cumberland-market, on THURSDAY, May 17th, at Eleven for Twelve, 1,500 YELLOW and WHITE PLANK DEALS and BATTENS, 600 Yellow and Red Pine Plank, Deal and Battens, a large quantity of prepared deals and battens for flooring, &c., 46 four-panel doors, quartering, scaffold, and ladder-poles, new spring van, chaise cart, and clearance of the yard.—To be Viewed the day before the Sale. Catalogues had on the Premises, and of the Auctioneer, 2, Gardington-street, Hampstead-road, near the Euston-station.

BUILDER'S STOCK IN TRADE, FINSBURY.

MESSRS. EVERSFIELD and HORNE have received instructions from Mr. Griffiths, who is relinquishing the building trade, to SELL by AUCTION, on the Premises, Tabernacle-walk, Finsbury, on TUESDAY, May 15th, and following days, at Ten for Eleven, the Valuable STOCK in TRADE, comprising dry Christiana deals, Archangel deals and battens, prepared flooring and matched board, 40 loads of whole Baltic timber, dry pine plank, Baltic staves, wainscot and mahogany, fir quartering, &c.; and the stock of dry deals, planks and battens, lying at the Saw-mills, Swan-street, Bermondsey; also, a quantity of scaffolding, blocks and falls, benches, screw jacks, nails, and ironmongery, several tons of old lead and iron, cart-horse, two carts, harness, and other effects.—May be Viewed two days previous, and catalogues had on the premises, and of the Auctioneers, Coal Exchange; or 1, Little Smith-street, Westminster.

NEAR STRATFORD, ESSEX.—Freehold Ground Rents of 24l. and 14l. per annum and Plots of Building Ground, by

MR. CHAMBERS, at the Auction Mart, Bartholomew-lane, London, on TUESDAY, 22nd May, at Twelve for One, several PLOTS of FREEHOLD BUILDING GROUND, suitable for the erection of villa and other residences, in Howard's-road, Balaam-street, Plaistow, and offering safe investments, or for the creation of ground rents, possessing good roads, excellent drainage, and a supply of pure water, giving votes for South Essex; also, two FREEHOLD GROUND RENTS of 12l. each and one of 14l., arising from 19 houses in Howard's-road, well secured on a rental of 24?l. May be viewed. Particulars of Mr. DEMAID, on the Premises, at the "Greyhound" opposite the "Swan," Stratford, the Auction Mart, of Messrs. MARTEN, THOMAS, and HOLLAMS, Solicitors; Commercial Sale Rooms, Mincing-lane; and of Mr. CHAMBERS, Estate and Land Agent, No. 7, Great Tower-street.

On View at the Gothic Hall, Lower Grosvenor-street, Bond-street.—To the Nobility, Gentry, Clergy, Architects, and Collectors who are Fitting and Furnishing in the Gothic and Elizabethan styles

MR. DEACON is instructed to SELL, on the Premises, on FRIDAY and SATURDAY, the 11th and 12th May, unreservedly, CARVED OAK and other CHURCH FITTINGS and FURNITURE, a finely carved oak pulpit, altar chairs, panels, splendid communion rail by Gibbon, stalls, reading desks, a magnificent shrine, a noble brass lectern, carved ditto, 10 oak window sashes from Windsor Castle, stained glass window, &c.; the fittings of two carved oak rooms, consisting of panelling, doors, chimney-pieces, &c.; the carved furniture comprises noble sideboards, dining, library, centre, and occasional tables, cheffonier, bookcases, sets of handsome high-backed cabriole and lounge chairs covered in Utrecht velvet, leather, &c.; Davenport, silk and velvet window curtains, a large chimney glass in oak frame, fittings for all, a few articles of decorative furniture; also a small collection of carvings, sculptured figures, French and inlaid chimney-pieces, armour, &c.—May be Viewed on the Premises; catalogues to be had also of the Auctioneer, 9, Berners-street, Oxford-street.

CITY IMPROVEMENTS.—Cannon-street Widening and the New Street.—Important Sale of Building Materials of 30 Houses, including 1,000,000 Stock Bricks.

PULLEN and SON have the honour to announce that they will SELL BY AUCTION, on the Premises, on MONDAY, May 14, and four following days, at Twelve, in Lots, by order of the Improvements Committee of the Corporation of the City of London, the whole of the valuable BUILDING MATERIALS of 30 Houses, Shops, Warehouses, and Premises in Tower Royal, Baldwin's-court, St. Thomas Apostle-court, Little St. Thomas Apostle, and the whole of the north side of Cloak-lane, Queen-street, Cheapside; comprising about 1,000,000 capital stock bricks, a vast quantity of plain and pan tiles, prime oak and fir timber in strong roofs, floors, and quartering, 400 pair glazed sashes, an infinity of doors, partitions, and fittings of every description; 20 tons of lead, shop and warehouse fronts, sound flooring boards, iron columns, York paving, coping, and sills, 330 stoves and ranges, 50 lead and other cisterns, coppers, mahogany counters, desks and drawers, gas-fittings, iron safes, and a great variety of useful house, shop, and warehouse fixtures.—May be viewed two days previous. Catalogues had at the Office of Works, Guildhall; and of PULLEN and SON, 80, Fore-street, Cripplegate.

IMPORTANT BUILDING SITES, CROYDON, SURREY.

MESSRS. BLAKE have been honoured with instructions from the London, Brighton, and South Coast Railway Company to SELL by AUCTION, at Garraway's Coffee-house, 'Change Alley, on FRIDAY, the 1st June next, at Twelve o'Clock, a considerable area of first-rate BUILDING LAND (in convenient lots), situate on one of the great leading thoroughfares in immediate connection with the vast traffic of the West Croydon Station, at the north entrance of the town, comprehending all the Valuable frontage on the north side of the Tamworth-road, and other lands adjoining, which proceed from the station towards Church-street, and other populous parts of the town and vicinity. The character and local position of this land opens to enterprising and judicious capitalists the moral certainty of success, it being notorious that such investments in Croydon offer the most sterling security, occasioned by a demand for moderate-sized houses infinitely beyond the supply, added to which, the Railway Company on this line have made considerable reductions in the charge for periodical tickets, with a view of increasing building and extending facilities for suburban residences in connection with the short stations between London, Croydon, and Epsom; and it is not too much to say that there is no place in England where a well-conducted building operation of this kind is so likely to ensure success. There will be included in the sale certain respectable DWELLING HOUSES, with garden ground, Trading Premises, and other property; also, two lots of Building Land in Sydenham Park, near Forest Hill Station, all of which will hereafter be detailed.—Particulars and plans will be issued fourteen days before the sale, which may be had of Messrs. SUTTON, EWENS, and Co., Solicitors, Basinghall-street; at Garraway's Coffee-house, 'Change Alley; at the principal stations between London and Brighton, and also between London and Epsom; and of Messrs. BLAKE, Croydon, Surrey.

LONDON: Printed by CHARLES WYMAN, of 7, Calthorpe-street, in the Parish of St. Pancras, in the County of Middlesex, Printer, at the Printing-office of J. & H. Cox, Brothers, 74 & 75, Great Queen-street, Lincoln's-Inn Fields, in the Parish of St. Giles-in-the-Fields, in the said County; and published by the said CHARLES WYMAN, at the Office of "THE BUILDER," 2, York-street, Covent Garden, in the Parish of Saint Paul, Covent Garden, also in the said County.—Saturday, May 12, 1849.

The Builder.

A Journal for the Architect, Engineer, Operative & Artist.

Vol. VI.—No. 328. | MAY 19, 1849. | Price Fourpence. Stamped 5d.

ILLUSTRATIONS.

Chimney-piece, Villa Madama, Rome 232
The Great Hall at the Euston Station: Mr. P. C. Hardwick, architect 234

CONTENTS.

"The Seven Lamps of Architecture" 229
The Royal Academy Exhibition 230
The Hierophantine Fragments 231
Elevation of the Working Classes 231
Chimney-piece, Villa Madama, Rome 232
Small Drains 232
Trapping Drains 233
Scenic Anachronisms: Royal Italian Opera-house, Covent Garden 233
Removal of Smoke, and Ventilation of Sewers 233
The New Borough Prison at Plymouth 233
The Great Hall at the Euston Station, London and North-Western Railway 234
Notes in the Provinces 235
Improvement of Poole, Dorsetshire 235
The Cheltenham General Hospital and Dispensary 235
Railway Jottings 235
Electro-telegraphic Progress 236
Supply of Water to Constantinople 236
Metal Work and its Artistic Design 236
Iron Steamers 236
Miscellanea 237

ADVERTISEMENTS.

WANTED, in the Country, a PAPER-STAINER. He must be well acquainted with the business, and a careful workman, of sober industrious habits, being chiefly required for decorations. A young man desirous of improvement would find this an eligible opportunity.—Apply to P. J. BUTLER, Commission and General Agent, 29, Liverpool-street, Bishopsgate.

TO STONEMASONS.

WANTED to APPRENTICE a Strong Lad of sixteen years of age, to a respectable Master Mason. Address, stating terms, post-paid, to Mr. W. Wilson, Penge Common, Surrey.

TO CARPENTERS AND BUILDERS.

WANTED, by a Young Man, 21 years of age, a SITUATION as improver, where there are several hands kept. No objection to town or country.—Address, B. B., Post-office, Clapham, Surrey.

TO BUILDERS AND FOREMEN.

WANTED, by a Young Man, respectably connected, a SITUATION for improvement.—Apply, by letter only, to B. W., care of Mr. Kight, Mortimer-street, Cavendish-square.—N.B. A premium given.

WANTED, a RE-ENGAGEMENT by a BUILDER'S CLERK, accustomed to taking out quantities, measuring up work, estimating, &c., and the general routine of a builder's office. No objection to the country.—Address, R. S., Graham's Tea Establishment, Upper Titchfield-street, Marylebone.

TO CARPENTERS AND BUILDERS.

WANTED, by a very experienced Person, OCCASIONAL EMPLOYMENT (by the day, or otherwise), to make out or arrange Builders' accounts, to measure or estimate. Reference as to respectability can be given, and very advantageous terms offered.—Address, D. E., 29, Vaughan-terrace, City-road Basin.

TO CARPENTERS AND BUILDERS.

WANTED, by a steady middle-aged man, who has filled the situation in town, a SITUATION as SHOP or YARD FOREMAN, in town or country. Can be well recommended from his last employer.—Direct, post-paid, to Y. Z., at Mr. Brown's (at the school), nearly opposite the Golden Lion, High-street, Fulham.

TO NOBLEMEN AND OWNERS OF ESTATES.

WANTED, a Situation as STEWARD or AGENT, to improve old and erect new farm buildings, cottages, &c.; also to improve land on the estate by raising, levelling, draining, &c. The Advertiser has had good practical experience in the management of buildings, railway works, &c., and can give first-rate reference as to abilities and character.—Direct A. W., Post-office, Warwick.

TO LANDED PROPRIETORS, ARCHITECTS, BUILDERS, &c.

WANTED, by the Advertiser, who has for the last nine years been in Architects' and Builders' offices, and who is able to get out drawings, both architectural, perspective, and working, and who is fully conversant with the practical department of building, taking out quantities, estimating, surveying, measuring, land general accounts, is desirous of a permanent ENGAGEMENT, either as General Agent and Clerk of the Works for an estate, or as Clerk in either of the above offices. Salary not so much an object as a permanency.—Address, post-paid, to SCANTLING, 48, Charing-cross, London.

TO NOBLEMEN, IRONMONGERS, BUILDERS, AND OTHERS.

WANTED, by a steady, active, Young Man, of considerable experience in South Wales, West of England, and the Metropolis, EMPLOYMENT as WORKING FOREMAN in the following branches—Whitesmith and Bell-hanger, Fireman, or Fitter. He is thoroughly acquainted with every part of household and domestic work, machinery, agricultural implements, &c. &c. He has no objection to any part of the United Kingdom,—either of the healthy British Colonies not excepted. For further particulars, unexceptionable references may be obtained by applying to A. H., Horatio Owen's Newspaper Office, Falcon-square, Aldersgate-street, London.

TO ARCHITECTS, &c.

AN ASSISTANT, who is a first-rate Draughtsman, wishes for an ENGAGEMENT, or would undertake drawings out of office. Salary moderate.—Address, A. Z., Mrs. Saunders, 6, North-place, Hampstead-road.

TO SURVEYORS, BUILDERS, AND OTHERS.

A YOUNG MAN, who can make fair and working drawings, and thoroughly understands measuring, book-keeping, &c., is desirous of an ENGAGEMENT with the above, either in town or country.—Address, pre-paid, to X. Y. W., at Messrs. Clay's, 79, Aldermanbury, City.

TO BUILDERS, PLUMBERS, PAINTERS, AND GLAZIERS.

A YOUNG MAN wishes a permanent ENGAGEMENT, who has a thorough practical knowledge of the above. Can make himself generally useful in graining and distempering. An undeniable reference.—Address, W. M., office of "The Builder," 2, York-street, Covent Garden.

AN ARCHITECTURAL DRAUGHTSMAN, well acquainted with Perspective, and having a thorough knowledge of Land Surveying, wishes for a SITUATION, either in town or country, in which the above qualifications are in requisition.—Apply by letter, to R. G., 25, Cloudesley-place, Islington.

TO JOINERS.

A COMPETENT JOINER, accustomed to set out rods, and to superintend workmen, is WANTED by a Builder in the country, to take charge of the Joiners' Department. It is necessary that he should thoroughly understand drawings.—Apply, post-paid, to R. D., at the office of "The Builder," 2, York-street, Covent Garden.

AS CLERK of WORKS, &c.—A Gentleman for the last Ten Years engaged in the practical and theoretical parts of the profession of both Civil Engineers and Architects, will be glad to meet with a RE-ENGAGEMENT as above. The most unexceptionable reference given.—Address A. Y., at the Office of "The Builder," 2, York-street, Covent Garden.

TO ARCHITECTS.

A GENTLEMAN of Experience in Ecclesiastical Architecture, and well practised in Gothic detail, wishes to meet with an Architect requiring assistance. He can give reference to one of the first offices in London, and where he could see good general practice, or acquire practical information, any reasonable remuneration would be accepted. Address, G. E., Office of "The Builder," 2, York-street, Covent Garden.

TO ARCHITECTS AND SURVEYORS.

AN Architect and Surveyor, aged 32, of great experience, who has held the situation of Manager in first-rate establishments, and who can show the highest testimonials, is desirous to obtain an APPOINTMENT of a similar kind, at a moderate remuneration. Having the command of capital, he would have no objection, after the first year, to take a share in the profession, by advancing a suitable premium.—Address, by letter, to A. B. S., at the office of "The Builder," 2, York-street, Covent Garden.—N.B. None but principals will be treated with.

TO BUILDERS and OTHERS wanting an able ASSISTANT, the Advertiser offers his services, being thoroughly acquainted with the practice of surveying and building in every department, drawing, measuring, and estimating, &c., and accustomed to the general management.—Address, SURVEYOR (free), office of "The Builder," 2, York-street, Covent Garden.

TO ARCHITECTS, SURVEYORS, AND BUILDERS.

THE Advertiser, having been practically engaged in the building branches, and employed in eminent Architects', Surveyors', and Builders' offices many years, wishes an ENGAGEMENT to prepare plans, working and detail drawings, specifications, take out quantities, measure and price out work, estimate, keep books, superintend works, &c., &c.—Address, A. B., 29, Melton-crescent, Euston-square.

TO ARCHITECTS.

THE Advertiser, who has just completed a three years' engagement in the office of an eminent builder (having previously been brought up with one of the first architects of the day), and who has had the designing of extensive works, is open to an ENGAGEMENT. Would not object to a situation as clerk of works. References and testimonials of the highest character.—Address, C. L. J., 74, Stanhope-street, Hampstead-road.

TO PROPRIETORS OF MARBLE AND STONE-WORKS, SLATE QUARRY OWNERS, &c.

THE Advertiser is desirous of meeting with an engagement as MANAGER of a Marble and Stone-Works. He is a practical man, and thoroughly acquainted with every department of the business; understands designing, drawing (including working drawings), modelling, stone-carving, letter-cutting, &c., and is a good salesman and bookkeeper; he can also make estimates for marble and stone-work.—The highest testimonials as to character, &c., can be given.—Address P. H., Office of "The Builder," 2, York-street, Covent Garden.

CONTRACTS.

TO BUILDERS AND CONTRACTORS.

WEST HAM, ESSEX, PARISH CHURCH.—Persons willing to CONTRACT for the REPAIRS, REPEWING, and other works to the above church, may inspect the plans, specification, and conditions at the office of Mr. C. DYSON, Surveyor, Stratford Grove, on and after Thursday next, until June the 7th, ensuing, between the hours of Nine and Five o'Clock. The Committee will not be bound to accept the lowest tender.

STOREY'S CHARITY, CAMBRIDGE, BLACK BEAR ESTATE, lying in the centre of the town.—To Builders and Others.—The Trustees hereby give NOTICE that they are prepared to receive TENDERS for BUILDING LEASES of the above property, in Sixteen Lots, as now staked out. Plans and specifications of the buildings required to be erected, as well as any other particulars, may be had upon application to Mr. WALTER, Architect, Trumpington-street, Cambridge; Messrs. CAPES and STUART, Solicitors, Gray's-inn, London; or Messrs. HARRIS, SUMPTER, and HYDE, Solicitors, Cambridge; to whom it is requested that tenders may be sent on or before the 1st day of June next.

Cambridge, May 4, 1849.

CONTRACTS.

TO BUILDERS.

THE time for receiving TENDERS for the ERECTION of St. MARY'S CHURCH, West Brompton, is extended to WEDNESDAY next, the 23rd instant.—The plans and specification may still be seen at the office of the architect, 24, Alexander-square, Brompton.—May 17, 1849.

TO BUILDERS AND OTHERS.

BUILDERS willing to TENDER for the ERECTION of TWENTY semi-detached Villa RESIDENCES, on a piece of ground situate about three miles from the bridges, on the Surrey side, may obtain full particulars by addressing a letter in the first instance to Mr. BENJAMIN BROADBRIDGE, Jun., Surveyor, 5, Brighton-place, North Brixton.

NEW SCHOOLS at BRYMBO, in the Parish of WREXHAM.—To BUILDERS and OTHERS.—The Trustees of the Wrexham Charities intend to erect, at Brymbo, Schools for 300 children, with a Master's and Mistress's House attached, plans and specifications of which may be seen on and after the 25th instant, on application to Mr. J. BURY, Town-hill, Wrexham, Clerk to the Trustees; and parties desirous of contracting for all or any portion of the works, must send in tenders, under seal, to the said J. Bury, on or before the 1st day of June next. The Trustees do not bind themselves to accept the lowest, or any other tender.—Further information may be had in the mean time from Mr. R. KYRKE PENSON, Architect, Oswestry.—By order of the Trustees, J. BURY, Clerk.

Wrexham, May 12th, 1849.

NEW SCHOOLS at MINERA, in the Parish of WREXHAM.—To BUILDERS and OTHERS.—The Trustees of the Wrexham Charities intend to erect, at Minera, Schools for 300 Children, with a Master's and Mistress's House attached, plans and specifications of which may be seen on and after the 25th instant, on application to Mr. J. BURY, Town-hill, Wrexham, Clerk to the Trustees; and parties desirous of contracting for all, or any portion of the works, must send in tenders, under seal, to the said J. Bury, on or before the 1st day of June next. The trustees do not bind themselves to accept the lowest, or any other tender. Further information may be had in the mean time from Mr. R. KYRKE PENSON, Architect, Oswestry.—By order of the Trustees, J. BURY, Clerk.

Wrexham, May 12th, 1849.

BOROUGH of KINGSTON-UPON-HULL.—BATHS and WASHHOUSES.—TO IRON-FOUNDERS and OTHERS.—The Town-Council of Hull intend entering into a Contract for the CONSTRUCTION and ERECTION of PIPES and FITTINGS connected with the BATHS and WASHHOUSES now building in Trippett-street. The Committee appointed by the Council hereby GIVE NOTICE that they are ready to receive Tenders for the same. The drawings and specifications may be seen at the offices of P. PRICHARD BALY, Esq., C.E., 14, Buckingham-street, Adelphi, London, on any Week Day from Ten A.M. to Four P.M., from the 14th to the 19th day of May, 1849, both days inclusive; and at the office of the Corporation Surveyor, Town Hall, Hull, from the 21st to the 26th May, both days inclusive. The Tenders are to be delivered sealed, addressed "To the Committee of Baths and Washhouses, Town Hall, Hull," by Twelve o'Clock at noon of the 4th day of June, 1849. The party whose Tender is accepted will be required, with two approved sureties, to enter into a contract, to be prepared by the solicitor to the Committee at the expense of the contractor. The Committee do not bind themselves to accept the lowest tender.—By order.

THOS. THOMPSON, Town Clerk.

Town Hall, Hull, 14th May, 1849.

SAINT GILES-IN-THE-FIELDS and SAINT GEORGE, BLOOMSBURY.—To GAS-LIGHT COMPANIES, STONE-MERCHANTS, GRAVEL DIGGERS, and CONTRACTORS for CARTAGE.—NOTICE IS HEREBY GIVEN, that the Committee for Paving, Cleansing, and Lighting these Parishes will meet in the Vestry-room of St. Giles-in-the-Fields, on THURSDAY, the 24th day of May instant, at Ten o'clock in the forenoon precisely, to receive proposals from such Gas Company or Companies as may be willing to CONTRACT for one, two, or three years, from Midsummer next, for LIGHTING the PUBLIC LAMPS of these Parishes (north of Holborn), or any part or parts thereof, with Gas, and also for lighting the public lights of these parishes in Holborn, and the parts south and west of Holborn, with Gas, distinguishing in the tenders the prices at per annum for each batswing burner, and at per annum for each three-hole or cock-spur burner; also to paint the standards, brackets, and lanterns, and to keep the same, together with the glasses, in repair, including accidents, at per annum for each lantern. Also to receive proposals from such person or persons as may be willing to contract for all or any of the following materials, pursuant to orders to be given by the committee; namely, for supplying the committee with the best new squared Aberdeen, Mountsorrel, and other granite, of certain widths and lengths, at per ton for each sort; also best Bland Edge, Yorkshire, and other foot paving, at per yard superficial. A full particular of the several widths, and depths, and thickness of the granite and York to be supplied, may be had by applying at the clerk's office, No. 21, Hart-street, Bloomsbury-square; or of Mr. BIRCH, Surveyor to the committee at his office, No. 23, Little Russell-street. Also the best yellow screened binding gravel, at per yard cube. The said several last-mentioned articles to be delivered in such quantities, at such times, and in such places within the said parishes, or either of them, as the committee may direct. Also to receive proposals and contract for cartage for the committee within the parishes, of old stone, gravel, slop, &c., at per load. The cart used for this purpose must not measure less than 40 cubical feet. Proposals for the above to be for the term of one year from Midsummer next.

The secretaries of companies and persons sending tenders are required to attend at the Vestry-room at the time of meeting. The contractor or contractors not to let or assign his or their contract work or works to be done, or any part or parts thereof respectively, without the special consent of the committee. Security, to the satisfaction of the committee, will be required for the performance of the several contracts, and the names, place of abode, &c. of the persons to be offered as sureties, to be sent with the proposals, sealed, to be indorsed as the case may be. Drafts of the several contracts to be seen at the clerk's office. The committee will not bind themselves to accept the lowest tender, and will defray the charge for each of the contracts and bonds. Payments to be made quarterly. Printed particulars for the persons proposing for the supply of stone, gravel, and cartage, may be had of the clerk or surveyor as above.—By order of the Committee.

May 4, 1849. ROBERT FINNIS, Clerk to the Committee.

TILERS' and BRICKLAYERS' COMPANY.—To Decayed Liverymen and Freemen, or their Widows.—A GENERAL COURT of the above Company will be held at the London Coffee House, Ludgate Hill, on TUESDAY, the 29th day of May next, at Two o'Clock in the afternoon precisely, to ELECT AN INMATE to a VACANT ALMSHOUSE at Ball's Pond Road, Islington.—Candidates must apply by Petition, to be left under sealed cover with the Clerk of the Company, at No. 10, Mayfield Place, Dalston, on or before Saturday the 26th day of May, of whom full particulars may be obtained; and the Candidates will be required to attend personally at the time and place above specified for the election.—By order,

JAMES KEDBELL, Clerk.

ROYAL ACADEMY of ARTS, TRAFALGAR-SQUARE. The EXHIBITION of the ROYAL ACADEMY is now OPEN.—Admission (from eight o'clock till seven), 1s.; catalogue, 1s.

JOHN PRESCOTT KNIGHT, R.A., Sec.

THE EXHIBITION of the LIVERPOOL ACADEMY, will OPEN early in SEPTEMBER next.—Works of Art intended for exhibition will be received subject to the regulations of the Academy's circular, by Mr. GREEN, 14, Charles-street, Middlesex Hospital, until the 11th of August, and at the Academy's Rooms, Old Post Office Place, from the 15th till the 20th of August. JAMES BUCHANAN, Secretary.

MR. EDWARD is desirous of meeting Gentlemen who require Coloured Architectural Designs, Perspective, got up and coloured in the neatest style at moderate terms. Mr. E. further begs to state that he makes a consideration in his charges, should the competition prove unsuccessful.—Address, Mr. EDWARD, 18, Woodstock-street, Bond-street.

TO ARCHITECTS.—COMPETITION AND OTHER DRAWINGS.

MR. THOMAS S. BOYS, Member of the New Society of Painters in Water Colours, and author of "The Picturesque Architecture of Paris, Ghent, Rouen, &c." and of "London as it is," offers his services in Tinting Backgrounds, Landscapes, Perspective Views, Interiors, &c. From the long experience he has had in such subjects, he is fully aware of the points essentially necessary to be attended to. Drawings and designs lithographed in a superior manner.—Address, Mr. BOYS, 81, Great Titchfield-street, Oxford-street.

TO BUILDERS.

A FIRST-RATE BUSINESS of a general BUILDER, near London, to be LET or SOLD.—For particulars, inquire at the Blackfriars Bridge Timber Wharf, Upper Ground-street.

TO MASONS, BUILDERS, ENGINEERS, &c.

EXTENSIVE and convenient Premises, with Travelling Jinnie and Dwelling-house, TO BE LET.—Apply on the premises, 3, Thomas-place, Gravel-lane, Southwark.

SOUTH-WESTERN RAILWAY.—ELIGIBLE PREMISES to be LET, on Lease or otherwise, suitable for any business requiring room, with Dwelling-House and Stabling attached.—Apply by letter only, to A. B. C., Office of "The Builder," 2, York-street, Covent Garden.

TO BUILDERS AND OTHERS.

SANDOWN, ISLE OF WIGHT.—Eligible Building Ground, to be Let, on Lease, for three lives, renewable at death, with fine certain. The situation is most desirable, commanding fine sea views over Sandown Bay. A Church has recently been erected in this locality. Houses are much sought after in this locality. Distance from Ryde about six miles. For particulars, inquire, prepaid, of Mr. G. Eves, Architect, Uxbridge, Middlesex.

BUILDING LAND TO LET, at Streatham-hill, Dulwich-lane, Balham-hill, Wandsworth Common, Croydon, Deptford, near the Creek-bridge.—For further particulars apply to Messrs. I'ANSON, 9, Laurence Pountney-lane.

BUILDING LAND, about Three Miles from Town.—TO BUILDERS AND CAPITALISTS.—TO BE LET, on Building Leases, several Very Valuable PLOTS of LAND, surrounding a square which has been laid out in a most ornamental manner, and is near a church. An enterprising builder would find this a favourable opportunity, and would be liberally treated with. Particulars and plans may be seen at the offices of Messrs. ROBERTS, CHADWICK, and WOOD, Surveyors and Auctioneers, 6, Chancery-lane.

BUILDING LAND at CROYDON.—TO BE LET or SOLD, as a whole or in plots, suitable for the erection of Villas, about FIFTEEN ACRES of LAND, with roads formed and made up. A dry gravel soil on a chalk substratum, in a delightful situation, within a convenient distance from the station, and with a plentiful supply of the purest water. The extraordinary facilities for transition which the London and Croydon Railway now affords to residents in Croydon, bring this very desirable locality into the position of a suburb of the metropolis, and good residences are now necessary to meet the increasing demand.—For particulars and plans of the estate, apply to Messrs. DAVIS and VIGERS, 3, Frederick's-place, Old Jewry.

BUILDING GROUND, near HAMPTON COURT PALACE.—To Gentlemen, Builders, and others requiring Sites for Villas, with Gardens.—TO BE SOLD in Lots, for the convenience of purchasers, or LET on Building Leases, FREEHOLD BUILDING GROUND, at East Moulsey, Surrey, tithe free and land tax redeemed, most eligibly situated within a quarter of a mile of the grand entrance to Hampton Court Palace and the Hampton Court railway terminus, 100 yards from the Thames, and 40 minutes' ride to Waterloo terminus; commanding beautiful views of the Palace, the temple at Garrick's villa, and other delightful spots; fishing in the Thames and Mole. Vendor is willing to make arrangements with Builders to take buildings to be erected on the ground in exchange for other ground adjoining.—Apply to Mr. DAWSON, Estate Agent, 40, Pall Mall, and Kingston, Surrey; and to Mr. KENT, Solicitor, Hampton, Middlesex.

BITTERNE BRICK KILNS, near Southampton.—TO BE LET, for a term of years, all those desirable PREMISES, situate at Bitterne, 2½ miles from Southampton, and known as BITTERNE BRICK KILNS. The advantages which these kilns possess are many: they have lately been furnished with every requisite necessary for brick-making, and are now in a state fit for the immediate commencement of business. The clay is of the most superior quality, and of such quantity that any number of bricks can be made during the season. The number made by the present proprietor during one summer exceeded one and a-half millions. The Kilns are about two miles distant from the Northam Wharf, alongside of which vessels can lay to discharge coals, and from whence bricks can be shipped to any part of the coast, and sent per rail to the neighbourhood. Drain Pipes and Pottery in all its branches have been carried on to a large and profitable extent; and sheds have been erected, replete with every convenience for making, drying, &c.—Apply on the premises, or to CHARLES BAKER and CO.

Southampton, May 4, 1849.

HOLLAND PARK ESTATE, NOTTING-HILL.—TO BE LET, PLOTS of valuable BUILDING GROUND for VILLAS, TERRACES, &c., situate in the most open part of this much-admired estate, which for salubrity of air, good drainage, and fashionable locality, stands unrivalled in the environs of this metropolis. The estate lies between the Kensington and Notting-hill main roads, and has a full southern and western aspect, being protected from the north and east by the rising ground of Notting-hill. It commands extensive views from the Surrey hills to Harrow, and delightful prospects over the undulating ground, the lofty groves and shrubberies, of the park and gardens of Holland House. A substratum of firm gravel extends over the whole of the estate, which is thoroughly drained by a new and capacious sewer, lately built, at a vast expense, by the Great Western Railway Company.

TO GENTLEMEN desirous of building their own residences according to their own immediate wants and tastes, very liberal terms can be offered in the mode of payment, or a large portion of the cost can remain on mortgage at 5 per cent., or be paid off by instalments, in the manner of Building Societies.

TO BUILDERS, likewise, liberal advances will be made.

SEVERAL SITES for superior Villa residences, with large pleasure-grounds attached, may now be had.

Application to be made to GEORGE H. GODDARD, Esq., 8, John-street, Adelphi, where plans may be seen, and all particulars obtained.

TO BUILDERS, CARPENTERS, PAINTERS, AND OTHERS.

SEVERAL CARCASSES TO LET, on an Improved Ground Rent, in a Very improving neighbourhood, commanding a fine View of Hampstead and Highgate.—Money advanced if required.—Apply to Mr. C. Marshall, No. 8, Weedington-street, Kentish Town.

TO BUILDERS.

NOTTING HILL.—TO BE LET, for 99 years, at a very moderate ground-rent, a most desirable PLOT of GROUND in the High Road. Genteel cottages, at a rental of about 30 guineas, are very much sought for, and may be built here. Liberal advances made. Also a PLOT for Five Shops in the road.—Apply to Mr. MORRISON, 14, Norland-place, Notting Hill.

TO BUILDERS AND OTHERS.

TO BE LET, SEVERAL PLOTS of most eligibly situated GROUND on LEASES of 99 years, New Town, West Ham, Essex, within a few minutes' walk of the Railway to London. Ground rent low, and bricks on the estate. Enquire post-free, of Mr. HAGGER, Cedar House, Plaistow-lane, West Ham, Essex.

TO BUILDERS, &c.

TO BE LET, in an excellent situation, a con-venient BUILDER'S PREMISES, consisting of workshops, stable, sheds, saw-pit, and stock, at a valuation; with a large job, to commence shortly, upwards of 2,000l. Rent very moderate: stands well for retail business.—Address, A. F. G., office of "The Builder," 2, York-street, Covent Garden.

TO BUILDERS AND OTHERS.

TO BE LET, at low ground rents, for the erection of small third-rate Cottages, several PLOTS of GROUND, in a locality where such houses are in great request. There is plenty of sand, gravel, and water on the ground, and money will be advanced, if required. More than half the estate is already covered, and let. The Advertiser will be in attendance with plans, &c., from Three to Six o'clock in the Afternoon of every Monday, Wednesday, and Friday during May, on the estate, which is opposite the Bell and Anchor Inn, Hammersmith-road, near the Kensington Railway.—Particulars to be had also of Mr. HOLLINGSWORTH, 4, Battle-bridge; and Mr. ROSS, 4, St. James's-place, Hampstead-road.

GRAVELLY SOIL.—TO BE LET on LEASE, for Ninety-nine years, several desirable PLOTS of BUILDING GROUND, 18 miles from London, suitable for the erection of Detached Villas. The land is within five minutes' walk of the church and railway station (Broxbourn, Herts), and bounded by that beautiful stream, the New River. The proverbial salubrity of this neighbourhood, with its magnificent park and other local attractions, render the demand for houses very great.—For terms apply to Messrs. TOPPIN, HURFORD, and Co. (successors to Mr. W. W. Simpson), Auctioneers and Land Surveyors, 18, Bucklersbury, London. Money advanced if required.

WATERSIDE PREMISES, MILLBANK, WESTMINSTER.—TO BE LET on LEASE, with immediate possession, a Capital Wharf, with Dwelling-House, Stabling, Workshops, &c.—For particulars and cards to View, apply to Messrs. EVERSFIELD and HORNE, Auctioneers and Estate Agents, 1, Little Smith-street, Westminster.

WATER-SIDE PREMISES, suitable for an Engineer, Builder, Timber, or Stone Merchant, or for erecting mills or workshops.—TO LET, at Mill Wall, Isle of Dogs, opposite the East Country Docks, a WHARF and PREMISES, with dwelling-house (late in the occupation of Messrs. Cassell and Co.). The premises are enclosed by substantial walls which are nearly parallel throughout. The river frontage is about 60 feet, and the depth about 450 feet. There is a back frontage to the Greenwich Ferry-road, upon which dwelling houses might be erected.—For particulars apply at BLASHFIELD'S Cement Works, Mill Wall, or at his office, Waterloo-dock, Commercial-road, Lambeth.

Also part of a Wharf, with warehouse room, in Commercial-road, Lambeth.

IMPORTANT to BUILDERS, LEAD MERCHANTS, GLASS CUTTERS, OIL and COLOURMEN, PLUMBERS, GLAZIERS and PAINTERS.—The proprietor of a prosperous and lucrative wholesale and retail trade, established upwards of thirty years in one of the principal towns in England, wishes to retire from business and dispose of the concern, on terms that will secure an advantageous investment of capital. The wholesale trade extends over a wealthy and populous district, affording encouragement to commercial enterprise, and the retail connection is of first-class distinction. The stock of lead, glass, oil, colours, and a general assortment of materials required by plumbers, glaziers, and painters, to be taken at a fair Valuation. The purchase of the Premises, consisting of an excellent dwelling-house, commodious warehouses and workshops, replete with every convenience, is expected to be included in the agreement. Applications by letter only, addressed A. Z., at W. S. Ausworth's, Esq., 8, Gray's-Inn-square, Gray's-Inn, London.

TO BUILDERS, SASH-MAKERS, AND CAPITALISTS.

FIVE HUNDRED POUNDS.—TO BE DISPOSED OF, a PATENTED INVENTION, so important, yet so simple and useful, as to insure its universal introduction in every description of residence. The reason that the proprietors are willing to dispose of this most valuable invention is, that they are fully engaged in an old-established business, and have no time to devote to the above.—For particulars apply to Messrs. MANSELL and ELLIOTT, Estate and General Agency Office, 8a, Halkin-street West, Belgrave-square.

TO BUILDERS, CARPENTERS, MASONS, AND OTHERS.

TO BE DISPOSED OF, the LEASE of PREMISES and a BUSINESS in the above Trades, situate in a Village in Kent, about 7 miles from London, contiguous to a Railway Station. A satisfactory reason can be assigned for the present proprietor leaving. The stock to be taken at a valuation.—For further particulars apply, stating name and address, to Messrs. EVERSFIELD and HORNE, Auctioneers and Estate Agents, 1, Little Smith-street, Westminster.

TO BUILDERS.

FOR SALE, several PAIRS of superior fourth-rate CARCASES, substantially built, which will be leased direct from the freeholder, at 10l. per pair. Price 220l. each pair, the amount of which will be taken out in bricks or timber if desired, or may remain on mortgage, and a further sum will be advanced when finished.—Apply to Mr. WM. THOS. WOODS, Bedford New-road, Clapham-rise.

NEW ROAD, HAMMERSMITH.—TO SMALL CAPITALISTS, BUILDERS, &c.

MR. LAHEE has been instructed to submit to PUBLIC AUCTION at the Mart, about the latter end of June next, Six Freehold Cottages and Premises, let at rents amounting to 25l. per annum, and Forty-five plots of Freehold Building Ground; the whole to be sold in Forty-nine lots, or in such other parcels as may, at or before the sale, be agreed upon. The property is eligibly situate in the New-road, Hammersmith, three miles from Oxford-street. Particulars are in preparation, and may shortly be had of JOHN WATSON, Esq., solicitor, 196, Wood-street, Cheapside; of Mr. C. LAHEE, surveyor, Manor-place, Chelsea; at the Pigeons, Brentford, the Star and Garter, Kew Bridge, the Sussex Arms, Hammersmith Broadway, the King's Arms, Kensington, the British Prince, adjoining the ground; at the Mart, and at Mr. Lahee's Offices, No. 65, New Bond-street.

FREEHOLD LAND, NORWOOD, SURREY.

MESSRS. ROBERTS and ROBY are directed TO SELL, at the Mart, on THURSDAY, May 24, at Twelve, in Lots, another portion of several valuable PLOTS of FREEHOLD BUILDING GROUND, most delightfully situate on Central-hill, a most admired part of Norwood, being opposite Central-hill Academy, nearly adjoining the grounds of the Nunnery, formerly the Park Hotel and Essex Lodge, close to the turnpike-road to Sydenham, and commanding the most beautiful Views of the surrounding country, within 20 minutes' walk of the Annerley Station from London to Croydon, and about six miles from London, presenting a most desirable opportunity for building sites of Villa and Cottage Residences, which are so much in request in this highly select locality, forming a further portion of property sold last year on which several houses have been erected. The land-tax is redeemed.—To be Viewed, and particulars with plans had of Mr. J. SCARBOROUGH, Solicitor, 19, Tokenhouse-yard, Lothbury; the Mart; and at Messrs. ROBERTS and ROBY'S offices, 24, Moorgate-street, Bank.

SALES BY AUCTION.

TO BUILDERS, PAPER-HANGERS, HOUSE DECORATORS, AND OTHERS.

MR. BRAY, Jun., is instructed to SELL, on the premises, Phœnix-place, Addison-road North, Notting-hill, on TUESDAY, May 22, at Twelve for One, by order of the proprietor, upwards of 4,000 Pieces of PAPER-HANGINGS, comprising flock on satin and crimson grounds, dining-room satins, Elizabethan and bouquet, parlour and bed-room papers, in chintz, shaded and plain; hall and staircase, in oaks, hand-marbles, &c. Also the valuable Plant, and 100 Transparent Window-blinds.—May be Viewed the day prior, and catalogues had on the premises, and at the offices of the Auctioneer, 269, High Holborn.

CITY IMPROVEMENTS, WHITEFRIARS NEW-STREET.—To Building Material Dealers and Others.

MR. C. FURBER will Sell by Auction, on the Premises, Dorset-place, Dorset-street, on TUESDAY, May 22nd, 1849, at Twelve for One, the sound MATERIALS of EIGHT HOUSES, forming Dorset-place, Dorset-street, Fleet-street, of recent erection, and built of excellent stock bricks. The houses contain well-seasoned flooring-boards, joists, rafters, brest-summers, girders, stairs, sashes, pan and plain tiling, stout lead work in gutters, flashings, coverings of dormers, piping, &c., excellent stone paving, coping and sills, iron-work, house fixtures, large wrought iron-tank and effects.—May be viewed, and catalogues had on the premises; of PHILIP HARDWICK, Esq., 60, Russell-square; and at the Auction Offices, in Warwick-court, Gray's-Inn.

Valuable Stock of Dry selected Deals, Planks, and Battens, lying at the Saw-mills, Bermondsey (forming the second portion of Mr. GRIFFITH'S Stock).

MESSRS. EVERSFIELD and HORNE will SELL by AUCTION, at Mr. Robinson's Saw-mills, Swan-street, Bermondsey, on TUESDAY, May 22, at Twelve for One precisely, by order of Mr. GRIFFITHS, who is relinquishing the building trade, 1,000 feet run of dry Archangel YELLOW PLANK; 27,000 feet of best, dry, white Christiana deals; 10,800 feet of yellow Archangel deals, and 16,500 feet dry Archangel battens, which will be put into suitable lots.—May be Viewed two days previous, and catalogues had on the premises; also at the premises in Tabernacle-walk, Finsbury; and of the Auctioneers, Coal Exchange; or 1, Little Smith-street, Westminster. Approved bills will be taken.

NEAR STRATFORD, ESSEX.—Freehold Ground Rents of 24l. and 14l. per annum and Plots of Building Ground, by

MR. CHAMBERS, at the Auction Mart, Bartholomew-lane, London, on TUESDAY, 22nd May, at Twelve for One, several PLOTS of FREEHOLD BUILDING GROUND, suitable for the erection of villa and other residences, in Howard's-road, Balaam-street, Plaistow, and offering safe investments, or for the creation of ground rents, possessing good roads, excellent drainage, and a supply of pure water, giving Votes for South Essex; also, two FREEHOLD GROUND RENTS of 12l. each and one of 14l., arising from 19 houses in Howard's-road, well secured on a rental of 243l. May be Viewed. Particulars of Mr. DEMAID, on the Premises, at the "Greyhound" opposite, the "Swan," Stratford, the Auction Mart, of Messrs. MARTEN, THOMAS, and HOLLAMS, Solicitors; Commercial Sale Rooms, Mincing-lane; and of Mr. CHAMBERS, Estate and Land Agent, No. 7, Great Tower-street.

PORT and HARBOUR of POOLE.— SOUTH COAST TERMINUS of SOMERSET and DORSET RAILWAYS.—To Architects, Builders, and Capitalists.—TO BE SOLD BY AUCTION, at the Railway Hotel, Hamworthy, Poole, on the 19th June next, a most valuable RAILWAY WHARF PROPERTY, with its tramways, stores, &c.; also a variety of HOUSE PROPERTY and most valuable BUILDING SITES. The whole property is designed so as to form a "New Town," admirably adapted for business purposes. It is laid down in a ground plan, accompanied by a vignette, which will be ready for delivery fourteen days before the sale.—Particulars and plans may, in due time, be obtained, on application to VAUGHAN FRANCE, Esq., Solicitor, Bridgewater; Messrs. CASTLEMAN and Co., Wimborne, Dorset; JOHN DURANT and MARTIN KEMP WELCH, Esqs., Poole; or to CHARLES SMITH, Esq., Architect, 8, Stanhope-terrace, Gloucester-gate, Regent's-park, London.

IMPORTANT BUILDING SITES, CROYDON, SURREY.

MESSRS. BLAKE have been honoured with instructions from the London, Brighton, and South Coast Railway Company to SELL by AUCTION, at Garraway's Coffee-house, 'Change Alley, on FRIDAY, the 1st June next, at Twelve o'Clock, a considerable area of first-rate BUILDING LAND (in convenient lots), situate on one of the great leading thoroughfares in immediate connection with the vast traffic of the West Croydon Station, at the north entrance of the town, comprehending all the valuable frontage on the north side of the Tamworth-road, and other lands adjoining, which proceed from the station towards Church-street, and other populous parts of the town and vicinity. The character and local position of this land opens to enterprising and judicious capitalists the moral certainty of success, it being notorious that such investments in Croydon offer the most sterling security, occasioned by a demand for moderate-sized houses infinitely beyond the supply, added to which, the Railway Company on this line have made considerable reductions in the charge for periodical tickets, with a view of increasing building and extending facilities for suburban residences in connection with the short stations between London, Croydon, and Epsom; and it is not too much to say that there is no place in England where a well-conducted building operation of this kind is so likely to ensure success. There will be included in the sale certain respectable DWELLING HOUSES, with garden ground, Trading Premises, and other property; also, two lots of Building Land in Sydenham Park, near Forest Hill Station, all of which will hereafter be detailed.—Particulars and plans will be issued fourteen days before the sale, which may be had of Messrs. SUTTON, EWENS, and Co., Solicitors, Basinghall-street; at Garraway's Coffee-house, 'Change Alley; at the principal stations between London and Brighton, and also between London and Epsom; and of Messrs. BLAKE, Croydon, Surrey.

NEAR RICHMOND, AND CONTIGUOUS TO THE PARK.

MR. JAMES CAIN will submit by AUCTION, at the Greyhound Inn, Richmond, on THURSDAY, May 24, at Two for Three, by order of the Proprietor, first, in one lot, but if not sold it will then be immediately submitted in 20 lots, for building purposes, a very desirable ESTATE, pleasantly and advantageously situate on rising ground between Richmond and Upper East Sheen; comprising 33 acres, part freehold and part copyhold, occupying a road frontage of 800 feet, and extending to East Sheen-common, bordering on Richmond-park, containing about 20 of the most valuable building plots ever submitted to the public in this charming and sought-for locality. There is upwards of 30 feet fall for drainage, and very excellent water. The land is studded with fine timber, its elevated position on gravel soil commanding extensive and uninterrupted views over Hampstead and Highgate hills, and being within ten minutes' walk of the Mortlake Station of the Richmond Railway renders the situation desirable in the extreme. The distance from town is about seven miles, and is passed every half hour by fast omnibuses, affording a quick and easy conveyance to the metropolis. The demand for villa residences is extraordinary in this neighbourhood, and it is difficult to say how much may be made of this valuable property in the hands of a judicious and spirited proprietor. The land-tax is redeemed upon the whole. There is a nominal composition or commutation in lieu of tithes, which renders it almost tithe free. The dwelling contains two parlours, lean-to kitchen, and dairy. On the first floor are two good bed rooms and two attics, brick and timber built barn, cow-houses, calf-pens, stable for five horses, ranges of sheds and cow-houses, large barn, piggeries, cart sheds, four-stall stable and loose box, granary, &c., and in this situation, near to the park, adjoining the public roads and common, are frontages for building of 800 feet. The respectable society afforded in the surrounding neighbourhood, and having besides the advantages of possessing one of the most delightful and rural retreats in the known kingdom, will ensure to purchaser or purchasers, a safe and lasting investment. There is a valuable common right belonging to the estate. Plans, with full particulars and conditions, may be had of John Burder, Esq., solicitor, 27, Parliament-street; of Bolton, Merriman, and Co., solicitors, 25, Austinfriars; the Auction Mart, London; at all the principal Inns in the adjacent neighbourhood; and at the auctioneer's estate and agency offices, King-street, Richmond, Surrey.

LONDON: Printed by CHARLES WYMAN, of 7, Calthorpe-street, in the Parish of St. Pancras, in the County of Middlesex, Printer, at the Printing-office of J. & H. Cox, Brothers, 74 & 75, Great Queen-street, Lincoln's-Inn Fields, in the Parish of St. Giles-in-the-Fields, in the said County; and published by the said CHARLES WYMAN, at the Office of "THE BUILDER," 2, York-street, Covent Garden, in the Parish of Saint Paul, Covent Garden, also in the said County.—Saturday, May 19, 1849.

The Builder.

A JOURNAL FOR THE Architect, Engineer, Operative & Artist.

Vol. VI.—No. 329.   MAY 26, 1849.   Price Fourpence. Stamped 5d.

ILLUSTRATIONS.

Door-handle and Key-hole, Halle aux Laines, Bruges 344
General Meeting-room, Euston Station ; Mr. P. C. Hardwick, architect 346
The Hop in Decoration 347

CONTENTS.

A Night at the Institute of Architects—Have the Corporation of London preserved their Antiquities?—Is Greek Architecture inclined to Egyptian? 341
Chronological Account of Buildings in Italy and Sicily 343
St. Mary-at-Hill, Thames-street, City 344
Gothic Doorword 344
The Royal Academy 344
Laundry Drying Closets 345
The General Meeting-room, Euston Station, London and North-Western Railway 346
The Seven Lamps of Architecture 347
Decoration from Natural Objects 347
Early Christian Art 348
Notes in the Provinces 348
Life Assurance 349
Landlords and Tenants: Important Decision under the County Courts' Act 349
Metropolitan Commission of Sewers 350
Miscellanea 350

THE BUILDER.

MONEY ADVANCED on BUILDINGS.—Several capital PLOTS of FREEHOLD BUILDING GROUND, adjoining the Malden Station of the South-Western Railway; and near the Railway Tavern now erecting. TO BE LET on BUILDING LEASES for Ninety-nine Years, suitable for the erection of Cottage and Villa Residences, which are in great request, &c., &c.—For further particulars apply to Mr. J. GOVER, Auctioneer and Surveyor, 1, Colebrook North, Dover-road, Southwark.

TO BUILDERS AND OTHERS.

WANTED, a HOUSE and SHOP, suitable for a Painter and Plumber, at least, post-paid, to Mr. COLE, Painter, &c. 29, Park-street, Dorset-square.—West of Regent-street preferred.

TO FREEHOLDERS holding Carcases, or about to Build.—The Advertiser would have no objection to take one or more FREEHOLD CARCASES, for either Carpenter's or Joiner's Work.—Apply, by letter only, to R. P. office of "The Builder," 9, York-street, Covent Garden.

TO MASONS, BUILDERS, ENGINEERS, &c.

EXTENSIVE and convenient Premises, with Travelling Crane and Dwelling-house. TO BE LET.—Apply on the premises, 2, Thomas-place, Gravel-lane, Southwark.

BUILDING LAND TO LET, at Streatham-hill, Dulwichlane, Balham-hill, Wandsworth Common, Croydon, Deptford, near the Creek bridge.—For further particulars apply to Messrs. FAWSON, 9, Laurence Pountney-lane.

CHELSEA.—VALUABLE BUILDING GROUND, for a Terrace of Fifteen Houses, in Oakley-street, which is 80 feet wide, and leads from the King's-road to the Chain-pier, Lease 84 years. Accommodation if required.—Apply to Mr. W. A. DREW, 5, Parham-crescent, Brompton.

STRAND.—BUILDING GROUND TO BE LET or SOLD one plot in Wellington-street, having a frontage of 60 feet; and two plots in Burleigh-street, one with a frontage of 75 feet, and the other 21 feet.—Applications to be addressed to Mr. WYATT, 81, Goldensquare.

BUILDING GROUND.—TO LET, some excellent Building Ground, in the neighbourhood of London, well situate for letting, and money advanced to respectable builders as the works proceed.—For plans and particulars apply at the office of Mr. FARRELL, H. FOWLER, Architect, 81, Saville-row, Burlington-gardens.

ADVANTAGEOUS BUILDING SPECULATION.—TO BE LET, THE SHOP, MANSION, PICTURE GALLERIES, and OFFICES, in Duchess-street, Portland-place, for an unexpired term of about eighteen years, or for an extended term, with liberty to pull down and rebuild, or to re-build, for a lease or re-construct.—Particulars may be had at Mr. DONALDSON'S Office, Bolsover-street, Portland-square.

TO BUILDERS AND OTHERS.

TO BE LET, SEVERAL PLOTS of most slightly situated GROUND on LEASES of 99 years, New Town, West Ham, Essex, within a few minutes' walk of the Railway to London. Ground rent low, and bricks on the estate. Enquire post-free, of Mr. HAGGER, Cedar House, Plaistow-lane, West Ham, Essex.

TO MANUFACTURERS AND OTHERS REQUIRING SPACIOUS PREMISES.

TO BE LET on Lease, a very desirable PIECE of GROUND on the banks of the River Wandle, in the parish of Mitcham, Surrey, about nine miles from London. The owners of the property are willing to expend £500, in erecting such premises as the party hiring may require. The river passed is also admirably adapted for an Institution or Asylum, or for any purpose for which large premises are required. Land may be obtained by the immediate neighbourhood.—For particulars apply to Mr. BEADEL, 32, Gresham-street, City.

SYDENHAM PARK.—Several Plots of Ground in this desirable locality to be SOLD or LET on Building Lease. "The Lambeth Water Works Company are now extending their pipes to Forest Hill and Sydenham." Money will be advanced if required. For particulars, apply to Messrs. ALLEN & SHADWELL, Solicitors, Bermondsey-street; to Messrs. ALLEN, STONE, and STOCK, Architects, Tooley-street, Southwark, or to Mr. TATTON, Sydenham Station.

SUTTON, SURREY.—To Capitalists and Builders.—In LOTS, about 126 Acres of valuable BUILDING LAND, placed immediately in the vicinity of the station, and the most delightful parts of the neighbourhood, admirably adapted for the erection of villas. To a company this property presents most tempting benefits, being a cheap out-soil, and proverbially healthy.—Particulars may be obtained of Mr. WM. DUTCHER, Estate Agent, Epsom.

TO BUILDERS.

EIGHT CARCASES for SALE, or an ARRANGEMENT made with builders for finishing them. They are right-roomed houses, good situation, close to the King's-road, and near Cromorne-place, Chelsea; within a 3d. ride of London-bridge and a 2d. ride of Charing Cross, omnibus's pass unexplored buses direct from. Freeholder's ground rent only 7l. per annum, paid up.—Apply at WATSON'S offices, 39, Manchester-street, Manchester-square.

PIMLICO, in the Parish of St. George, near Pimlico.—To Builders, Cabinet-makers, Upholsterers, Decorators, and Manufacturers in general,—COMMANDING BUSINESS PREMISES, eligible for the trading part, near to Belgrave and Eaton-squares, comprising a commodious front shop, upper 2 show-room, large double's workshop for eight tenders, and capital family dwelling-house, which has been many years in the cabinet and upholstery trade. The premises are now let, and the rent under the bare free benefit of the old standing connection in the above branches. The premises are most desirable to a builder, decorator, cabinet-maker, upholsterer, or any other retail or manufacturing business.—Apply for particulars to Mr. G. HAINES, Auctioneer, Grosvenor-street West, Eaton-square.

TO CARPENTERS AND BUILDERS.

MR. C. J. CAFFALL has received in- struction, in consequence of the illness of the present proprietor, desire to dispose of a capital and well-established BUSINESS in the above trade, on very advantageous terms. The premises, which comprise a snug little house, spacious workshop and yard, with every convenience for extending this already valuable trade, can be had on lease for a term of years, and every facility will be rendered by the present proprietor to introduce the purchaser to the connection.—For further particulars apply to Mr. C. J. CAFFALL, Great Northstreet, Edgware-road; or to HAINES, Auctioneer, Estate Agent, and Valuer, Bushmanworth, Herts.

HOLLAND PARK ESTATE, NOT- TINGHILL.—TO BE LET, PLOTS of valuable BUILDING GROUND for VILLAS, TERRACES, &c., situate in the most open part of this much-admired estate, which for sale, airy, and good drainage, and fashionable locality, stands unrivalled, and in the vicinity of the metropolis. The estate lies between Kensington and Notting-hill main roads, and has a full southern and western aspect, being protected from the north and east by the rising ground of Notting-hill. It commands extensive views from the Surrey hills to Harrow, and delightful prospects over the undulating ground, the lofty groves and shrubberies of the park and gardens of Holland House. A distribution of plans also extends over the whole of the estate, which is thus roughly arranged by a new and capacious range, ninety built, at the rate indicated by the Great Western Railway. To CAPITALISTS desirous of building their own residences to their own immediate wants and tastes, very liberal terms can be offered in the mode of payment, or a large portion of the cost can remain on mortgage at 5 per cent., or be paid off by instalments, in the manner of Building Societies.

TO BUILDERS the liberal advances will be made. SEVERAL SITES for superior VILLA residences, with large pleasure-grounds attached, they can be had.—Further particulars may be had of GEORGE and GODDARD, Esq. 2, obtained.

AN ARCHITECT, residing in a large provincial town, and who has carried on his profession for many years with considerable success, is desirous of DISPOSING OF HIS BUSINESS. The opportunity is one exceptionable for any gentleman wishing to enter into immediate practice; and the necessary arrangements may be made on very easy terms.—Every information may be had on application to Messrs. HALE, BOYS, and AUSTIN, Solicitors, 8, Eldonplace, Holborn.

TO BRICKLAYERS AND OTHERS.

A BUSINESS, which has been carried on successfully for upwards of 30 years, to be DISPOSED OF, in Kent, within 10 miles of London.—For particulars apply to Mr. Hale, architect and surveyor, Hayes-place, Lisson Grove, London.

TO CARPENTERS, BUILDERS, SHOP-FRONT AND SASH MAKERS.

A VERY lucrative (30 years' established) Business in the above line to be DISPOSED OF, solely in consequence of the proprietor having an engagement abroad requiring his immediate presence; and the purchaser will be introduced to an extensive and valuable connection, which, to a man of business, must prove a fortune. Can be entered and carried on with a very small capital.—Apply to Mr. ORPWOOD, Auctioneer, Amllerplace, Finsbury-square.

TO BUILDERS, MEMBERS OF BUILDING SOCIETIES, AND OTHERS.

TO BE DISPOSED OF, in CARCASS, part of a TERRACE of THIRTY HOUSES now erecting, and of handsome elevation. The purchase money may remain until the leases are granted, or it may be sunk in an improved ground rent, at the option of the purchaser.—For further particulars, apply to Mr. PALMER, Lea Arms, Bromton-road, Queen's-road, Dalston; who has also eligible Land to Let for Building purposes. Deline on the Ground for sale or otherwise.

TO BRICKLAYERS, PLASTERERS, BUILDERS, &c.

TO BE DISPOSED OF, about 14 miles from London, in consequence of the decease of the late proprietor, an OLD ESTABLISHED BUSINESS in the above line, Implements, Scaffolding, &c. The House and Premises may be had on lease, at a moderate rent. Coming in about £50.—Further particulars may be had on application (if by letter, post-paid) to Mr. JONES, Roehampton-place. Vauxhallbridge, Pimlico; or of Mr. G. JONES, Plumber, Hampton, Middlesex.

TO ENGINEERS AND OTHERS.

BE SOLD, a PLANT, comprising Oak, stocks, dies, and taps, vices, smith's forge, with bench bellows, with large quantity of forging tools; also a portable fence, patterns, patternmaker's bench, surfaces, grindstone, blocks and falls, drills, chisels, and all other tools sufficient to employ twenty men. The above tools are of the very best description, and will be sold in one lot.—Apply at 1, Chapel-place, Long-lane, Bermondsey.

IMPROVED RENT and several valuable PLOTS of BUILDING GROUND for SALE, by order of Assignees and Mortgagees in Bankruptcy.—An Improved Ground Rent to produce to Ladyday, 1850, 10l. 10s. to Lady-day, 1851, 98l.; and for the remainder of a term of eighty years, 36l. 10s. per annum. Also five plots of valuable Building Ground, eligible for the erection of ten houses, for the accommodation of which, seven have already been made; the whole held on lease from the Clothworkers' Company, situate in the New Parish-road, near to Islington.—Tenders for the purchase of all or any of the lots will be received by Mr. JURY, Auctioneer, 20, King's Arms-yard, Coleman-street; at whose office a plan of the property may be seen.

SAW MILLS.—TO BE SOLD, the lease of a Saw Mill, consisting of a 30-horse power steam-engine, saw frames, plunging machine, and circular saws, the whole in work, and capable of returning 4,000l. a-year. Also the right of working a valuable patent. The mill has water frontage to the Thames.—Apply to A. H. Chelsea Wharf.

PUBLICATIONS.

ARCHITECTURAL PUBLICATION SOCIETY.—The SECOND PART of this publication for the year 1848, is NOW ISSUED. The third part, consisting of letterpress, will be ready about the end of July. Subscriptions for the year 1848-50, will now be received. After the delivery of Part III. the committee will not be able to guarantee these publications to future Subscribers.—WYATT PAPWORTH, Honorary Secretary, 10, Caroline-street, Bedford-square, May 20, 1849.

ARCHITECTURAL MAXIMS. By Professor DONALDSON. This work has been translated into the principal languages of Europe, and adopted by most of the Foreign Schools of Architecture. Price 5s.—Published by TAYLOR and WALTON, Booksellers, Upper Gower-street and WEALE, 59, High Holborn.

BLOXAM'S GOTHIC ARCHITECTURE. Just ready. 8th edition, foolscap 8vo, 6s. cloth.

PRINCIPLES of GOTHIC ECCLESIASTICAL ARCHITECTURE; with an explanation of technical terms, and a catalogue of ancient terms. By MATTHEW HOLBECHE BLOXAM. Illustrated with 200 woodcuts. *** The present edition has been considerably enlarged. In Rogue, Fleet-street.

THE ART and PRACTICE of ETCHING. This day is published, cloth boards, price 4s.

THE ART and PRACTICE of ETCHING; By B. ALKEN. This work contains full instructions for the successful cultivation of the above useful Art; and also for the Study of Soft Ground Etching, Aquatinta, and other varieties of light Engraving.—London: S. and J. FULLER, Gallery of Fine Arts, 34 and 35, Rathbone-place.

On the 1st June, 1849, will be published, Part I., price 1s. 6d., and Facsimile 1, containing four parts, price 10s., of an entirely New and Original Work on the

ARTS of DECORATIVE DESIGN, as APPLIED to ARCHITECTURE and MANUFACTURES. By ROBERT ROBSON. Dedicated to Architects, Artists, Designers, Builders, Manufacturers, and Artizans. The work will take a comprehensive view of the subject from the earliest ages down to the present time, showing the natural and geometrical elements and principles of a new and Important theory for drawing the curves of mouldings, vases, &c. From the sections of the cones: the full development of the geometry of the Greek, Roman, Middle Age, and Elizabethan architect's chronological table of the succession of the different periods: historical and critical reviews; portraits and biographical notices of the most celebrated masters of ancient and modern times, &c. &c. In the last volume of the work will be comprehended full engraved and lithographed plates, consisting of drawings from nature, examples taken from the best works extant, accurately classified in the various styles; original designs adapted to actual practice, with the grandest possible facility; numerous woodcuts, and digested pages of letterpress in illustration of the subject.—London: WEALE, High Holborn, Publisher; J. H. DIDLEY, Newcastle-upon-Tyne: R. and W. LAMBERT. Of whom prospectuses may be had, and by whom subscribers' names will be received.

TO BUILDERS AND PLUMBERS.

THE attention of the Trade is asked to JOHN WARNER & SONS' PATENT VIBRATING STANDARD PUMP, which is recommended for the simplicity of its construction, and the ease with which it works. By the introduction of the vibrating standard the numerous carriage and expensive slings and guides are unnecessary, rendering the price considerably less than pumps made on the old plan. Beer and Water Engines for raising fluids from a depth not exceeding 70 or 80 feet; also, Garden Engines constructed on the same principle.

JOHN WARNER & SONS, 8, Crescent, Jewin-street, London, Manufacturers and Patentees.

LONDON: Printed by CHARLES WILMAN, of 7, Calthorpe-street, in the Parish of St. Pancras, in the County of Middlesex, Printer, at the Printing-office of J. E. B. Cox, Brothers, 74 & 75, Great Queen-street, Lincoln's-inn-Fields, in the Parish of St. Giles-in-the-Fields, in the said County; and published by the said CHARLES WILMAN, at the Office of "The Builder," 2 York Buildings, 2, York-street, Covent Garden, in the Parish of St. Paul, Covent Garden, also in the said County.—Saturday, May 26, 1849.

The Builder

A JOURNAL FOR THE Architect, Engineer, Operative & Artist.

VOL. VI.—No. 330.   **JUNE 2, 1849.**   **PRICE FOURPENCE.**
Stamped 5d.

ILLUSTRATIONS.

Roman Catholic Chapel, Farm-street Mews, Grosvenor-
square; Mr. J. J. Scoles, architect 258
Bishop Duppa's Almshouses, Richmond, A.D. 1661 259

CONTENTS.

The present State of the Railway World 253
Lecture on Roman Architecture 253
The Royal Academy Exhibition 255
Vanishing Lines in Perspective 256
Chronological Account of Buildings in Italy and Sicily 256
A rchts of Official Interest : Party-walls and Warehouses 257
Freemantle Inn and Chapel 257
New Roman Catholic Chapel, Farm-street, Grosvenor square.. 258
Origin of the Geographical Society 258
Guild Pencils 259
Bishop Duppa's Almshouses, Richmond, Surrey—1661 259
The City Antiquities 260
Paintings bought by the Art-Union of London 260
Notes in the Provinces 260
Dundee Arch-Competition 260
Books: Smart's Logic (Longmans and Co); Shaw and Corbett
on Tenant-right (Kegan); Ridgeway's Halliwell's Popular
Rhymes &c. (Smith) 260, 261
Miscellanea 261

Vol. VI.—No. 331.   **JUNE 9, 1849.**   **Price Fourpence.**
Stamped 5d.

ILLUSTRATIONS.

Carved Stalls from Fiesole, Tuscany: 16th century 269
Priory[*], Almshouse, Wood Green, Tottenham. Middlesex:
  Sir. W. Webb, Architect 270
Mould to run the Mitres of Cornices 272

CONTENTS.

Books of Gothic Exemplars—How they should be used—Doll-
  man's "Ancient Pulpits"—Brandon's "Open Roofs" ...
Frazer's "Glazing Quarries" 264
Lecture on Roman Architecture 264
Restora[**] Her Majesty's Theatre : Royal Lyceum 265
A demolmen[**] of the Buildings' Act 266
Carved Stalls from Fiesole, Tuscany 268
Noise in the Proofroom 268
Boners : Her Majesty's Theatre : Royal Lyceum 269
Cost of Sewers in Chester 269
Church Architecture 260
Priory[*] Almshouse, Wood Green, Tottenham, Middlesex 271
London Antiquities and the Corporation 271
Railway Jottings 271
Competitions 272
Mould to run the Mitres of Cornices 272
Double Trapping Drains 273
Draught[**] Derby 273
Removal of Bones of Towns 273
Conveyance of Water.—Constantinople 273
Miscellanea 274

THE BUILDER.

LONDON: Printed by CHARLES WYMAN, of 7, Colthorpe-street, in
the Parish of St. Pancras, in the County of Middlesex, Printer,
at the Printing-office of J. H. Cox, Brothers, 74 & 75, Great
Queen-street, Lincoln's-Inn Fields, in the Parish of St. Giles-in-the-
Fields, in the said County; and Published by the said CHARLES
WYMAN, at the Office of "The Builder," 2, York-street, Covent
Garden, in the Parish of Saint Paul, Covent Garden, also in the
said County.—Saturday, June 9, 1849.

VOL. VI.—No. 332. **JUNE 16, 1849.** PRICE FOURPENCE.
Stamped 5d.

ILLUSTRATIONS.

Carved Bench-ends 200
St. Mary's Church, West Brompton, Middlesex · George Godwin, F.R.S., Architect 282
Multiplication of the Cube 284

CONTENTS.

New Works on Art of Painting—Mrs. Merrifield's "Ancient Treatise"—Hobbes' "Collector's Manual"—Twining's "Philosophy of Art" ....
On the Building Materials employed in Paris and in the Valley of the Lower Seine 277
Carved Bench-ends 280
Etty's Works—An Honour to the Nation 280
Bits from Bristol 281
The Dundee Arch Competition 281
St. Mary's, West Brompton 282
Popular Education, Yorkshire Mechanics' Institutes 283
Northampton Corn-Exchange Competition 283
Lord London's Collar-roofs Institution of Civil Engineers ... 284
The Dover Breakwater 284
Multiplication of the Cube 284
Metropolitan Commission of Sewers 284
Miscellanea 285

ADVERTISEMENTS.

TO ARCHITECTS

CHAPEL BUILDING GROUND.—WANTED to PURCHASE, for the SITE of a CHAPEL and SCHOOL-ROOMS, in the erection of which it is proposed to expend about 3,000*l*., a suitable piece of ground, fronting to, or near adjoining the Clapham or Brixton-road, and within a moderate distance from Kennington Common, and containing a frontage of 60 feet and a depth of 150 feet, or thereabouts. Freehold would be preferred, but long leasehold will not be objected to.—Letters, stating particulars of locality, dimensions, tenure, and price, to be addressed to Mr. ADCOCK, Solicitor, 3, Copthall-buildings, Throgmorton-street, City.

FREEHOLD PROPERTY FOR SALE.—A Builder in the country has Property to dispose of, well situated, let to respectable tenants, and in good repair, realizing 7 per cent. Prices, 3,000*l*., 1,500*l*., and 700*l*. Would take one-fourth in goods, suited to his business.—Apply by letter, pre-paid, to W. H., office of "The Builder," 2, York-street, Covent Garden.

CHELSEA.—VALUABLE BUILDING GROUND, for a Terrace of Fifteen Houses, in Oakley-street, which is 60 feet wide, and leads from the King's-road to the Chain-pier. Lease 94 years. Accommodation if required.—Apply to Mr. WM. DREW, 5, Pelham-crescent, Brompton.

TO LET.—REGENT'S CANAL BASIN.—A LARGE CONVENIENT WHARF, with extensive water frontage, and powerful crane; together with dwelling-house or houses, stable, workshops, and convenient sheds.—Apply to Mr. KNAPP, 84, Foley street, St. Marylebone.

TO BE LET, or LEASE SOLD, in Park-road, Clapham.—ROOMY PREMISES—a six-roomed house, with carpenter's shop, large warehouse, and yard.—Apply on the Premises, next door to Mr. Turner, Grocer, and for particulars to Mr. FARMER, Builder, Alfred-place, Newington Turnpike.

TO BUILDERS.

NOTTING HILL.—TO BE LET, for 99 years, at a very moderate ground-rent, a most desirable PLOT of GROUND in the High-road. Genteel cottages, at a rental of about 30 guineas, are very much sought for, and may be built here, and a public-house. Liberal advances made. A PLOT for Five Shops in the road.—Apply to Mr. MORRISON, 14, Norland-place, Notting hill.

ADVANTAGEOUS BUILDING SPECULATION.—TO BE LET, "The Hope," mansion, picture galleries and offices in Duchess-street, Portland-place, for an unexpired term of about 18 years, or for an extended term, with liberty to pull down and rebuild 10 or 12 second-class houses.—Particulars may be had at Mr. DONALDSON'S offices, Bolton-gardens, Russell-square.

HIGH-ROAD, PECKHAM.—FOUR CARCASES and a CORNER SPOT, on a high road, invaluable for a public-house; also the best PLOT of GROUND in London, for private houses, to LET, on terms of 100 years, direct from the freeholder, who has just made arrangements for laying out about 5,000*l*. on the estate, belonging to a friend, which will not be called in for ten years.—Apply, between the hours of Two and Four, to Mr. SINGLE, Auctioneer, 81, Colemanstreet, City.

FREEHOLD LAND, WALTON-ON-THAMES, SURREY.—TO BE LET on BUILDING LEASES, or SOLD, highly eligible PLOTS of BUILDING LAND, situate in Oatland's-park, formerly the seat of the Duke of York, within eight minutes' walk of the Walton Station, South-Western Railway; the neighbourhood highly respectable; the subsoil gravel; tithe free, land-tax redeemed.—Apply, T. FRYER, Esq., Solicitor, 11, Artillery-place, Finsbury; or Mr. CORBETT'S, 14, King William-street, Strand.

VOTE for EAST SURREY.—TO BE SOLD (by order of the Proprietor), by Tender, such tenders to be delivered on or before Thursday, the 21st of June, 1849, TWO substantial, brick-built, eight-roomed DWELLING HOUSES, and a tenement in the rear, eligibly situate close to the river, being Nos. 3 and 4, Love-lane, Rotherhithe, near the platform, producing a clear net rental of 30*l*. 10*s*. 4*d*.—Apply to Mr. G. COURTHOPE, Auctioneer and Estate Agent, 10, Paradise-row, Rotherhithe, who has several other eligible properties for disposal.

CAPITAL MANUFACTURING PREMISES, situated at Bromley, Middlesex, in the immediate vicinity of the junction of the Eastern Counties, the East and West India Docks and Birmingham Junction, the Blackwall Railways, and abutting on the navigable river Lea. Messrs. HUMPHREYS and WALLEN are instructed to SELL or LET Capital Premises, comprising nearly two acres of ground, upon which are ranges of very substantial brick buildings.—For particulars apply at the offices of Messrs. HUMPHREYS and WALLEN, 68, Old Broad-street.

WATER-SIDE PREMISES, suitable for an Engineer, Builder, Timber, or Stone Merchant, or for erecting mills or workshops.—TO LET, at Mill Wall, Isle of Dogs, opposite the East Country Docks, a WHARF and PREMISES, with dwelling-house (late in the occupation of Messrs. Onsell and Co.). The premises are enclosed by substantial walls which are nearly parallel throughout. The river frontage is about 60 feet, and the depth about 420 feet. There is a back frontage to the Greenwich Ferry-road, upon which dwelling houses might be erected.—For particulars apply at BLASHFIELD'S Cement Works, Mill Wall, or at his office, Waterloo-dock, Commercial-road, Lambeth.

Also part of a Wharf, with warehouse room, in Commercial-road, Lambeth.

TO BUILDERS, MEMBERS OF BUILDING SOCIETIES, AND OTHERS.

TO BE DISPOSED OF, in CARCASS, Part of a TERRACE of THIRTY HOUSES now erecting, and of handsome elevation. The purchase-money may remain until the leases are granted, or it may be sunk in an improved ground rent, at the option of the purchaser.—For further particulars, apply to Mr. PALMER, Lee Arms, Brownlow-road, Queen's-road, Dalston, who has also eligible Land to Let for Building purposes. Bricks on the Ground for sale or advance.

TO BE DISPOSED OF, a Manufacturing BUSINESS of considerable importance, with extensive premises, in every respect suitable for carrying on the same. The premises, which are situate on the banks of the Thames, may either be rented or purchased. They have recently been enlarged to meet an urgent demand for an article, the supply of which may be carried to an almost unlimited extent. The sum required for lease, goodwill, stock, implements, fixtures, &c., would be from 8,000*l*. to 10,000*l*. As the proprietor (in whose family the business has been for about sixty years) is retiring from business, an arrangement may be made for a part of the money to remain on approved security, if desired. Principals or their solicitors only will be treated with. Applications to be in writing, addressed to Messrs. MORRIS, STONE, and TOWNSON, Solicitors, Moorgate-street Chambers, Moorgate-street.

SALES BY AUCTION.

TO BUILDERS, DECORATORS, PAPER-HANGERS, HOTEL AND TAVERN KEEPERS, &c.—TO BE SOLD BY AUCTION, by

MR. DEACON, at his Rooms, Thursday, June 21st (by direction of Trustees), excellent PAPER-HANGINGS, in great variety of modern designs, comprising rich flocks, satins, blended and plain chintz, hand marbles, granite, oak, and others, lotted to suit private buyers and the trade.—On view June 20, at the Auctioneer's Rooms, 3, Berner's-street, Oxford-street.

TO BUILDERS, BUILDING MATERIAL DEALERS, FIXTURE DEALERS, AND OTHERS.

MR. ALFRED DAY has received in-structions to SELL BY AUCTION, at the Beauvoir Arms, near Kingsland-gate, on WEDNESDAY, June 20, 1849, at Twelve o'clock, without reserve, the entire FITTINGS and MATERIALS of a newly erected TEN-ROOMED HOUSE, comprising 4,000 pan and plain tiles, York paving, marble and Portland box chimney-pieces, stone curbs, coping, and cills, iron railings, sashes and frames, room and folding-doors, bressumers, excellent flooring boards, joists 20 feet long, quartering, rafters, register and other stoves, kitchen range, 3,000 feet of new boards and quartering, and numerous other effects.—May be viewed on Tuesday and morning of sale, and catalogues had on the premises and of the Auctioneer, City-road.

BUILDING MATERIALS.—SCOTLAND YARD.

MESSRS. EVERSFIELD and HORNE will SELL BY AUCTION, on the premises, Middle Scotland-yard, in the rear of the United Service Institution, on MONDAY, June 18th, at Ten for Eleven o'clock, the EXTERNAL MATERIALS and INTERIOR FITTINGS of the residence, comprising lead gutters, cisterns and pipes, sound timber in roofs, joists, girders, and floor boards, sashes, doors and wainscotting, chimney pieces and stoves, a large quantity of very excellent brickwork, and other effects. May be viewed one day prior to the sale, and catalogues had on the premises and of the Auctioneers, Coal Exchange; or 1, Little Smith-street, Westminster.

TO MASONS, BUILDERS, AND OTHERS.—FINSBURY.

MESSRS. EVERSFIELD and HORNE will SELL by AUCTION, on the Premises, 93, Paul-street, Finsbury, on TUESDAY, June 19th, at Twelve o'clock (by order of Mr. Thomas Allen, who has parted with the business), a large quantity of PORTLAND and other STONE, in block, scantling, and slab, 2,000 feet super of tooled York paving coping sills, sinks, &c., Parkspring and other headstones, 22 vein and coloured marble chimney pieces, 12 Portland ditto, large quantity of useful marble, 12 plaster busts, two crab engines, blocks and falls, ladders, scaffold-poles, stone saws, bankers, and tools various; also a four-wheel stone truck, cart, two hand trucks, powerful cart-horse and harness, and other effects.—May be viewed two days prior to the sale, and catalogues had on the premises; and of the Auctioneers, Coal-Exchange; or 1, Little Smith-street, Westminster.

BUILDER'S STOCK IN TRADE (THIRD PORTION), FINSBURY.

MESSRS. EVERSFIELD and HORNE have received instructions from Mr. Griffiths, who is relinquishing the building trade, to SELL by AUCTION, on the premises, Tabernacle-walk, Pillsbury, and Park-street, City-road, on WEDNESDAY, June 27th, and following day, at Eleven for Twelve precisely, the third portion of his valuable stock-in-trade, comprising about 2,000 Archangel and Christiana deals and planks, cast-iron rain-water pipe, zinc guttering, corrugated iron, large quantity of glazed doors, sashes, skylights, and garden-lights, portable counting house, rope falls and slings, a few lots of nails and ironmongery, wood patterns for castings, 24 nearly new carpenter's brushes, grindstones, scaffold poles and boards, large quantity of useful fir and firewood, new and old pantiles, the entire erection of sheds covered with deal and oak slabs, &c.; also a powerful, active cart horse, 3 sets of harness, 2 builder's carts, small timber carriage, and other effects.—May be viewed three days prior to sale, and catalogues had on the premises and of the Auctioneers, Coal Exchange, or 1, Little Smith-street, Westminster.

THREE FIRST-CLASS WELL-SEASONED CARCASES, CRAVEN-HILL, HYDE-PARK, with gardens behind, for sale, by order of the Executors.

MR. FREDERICK CHINNOCK will SELL by AUCTION, by order of the Executors of the late Lionel Thos. Pousford, Esq., on THURSDAY, June 28, the THREE substantially-built, well-seasoned CARCASES, situate on the north side of Craven-hill, commanding a beautiful and uninterrupted view of the Broad-walk, Kensington-gardens, designed to contain 14 rooms, with large garden in the rear. The road is now formed in this rapidly improving locality, and these are the only houses unfinished on the hill, and when finished will readily let at 180*l*. per annum each. They are held for long terms, at ground rents. Can be viewed at any time.—Particulars obtained at the Mart; of W. W. OLDERSHAW, Esq., Solicitor, 7, Tokenhouse-yard, Lothbury; and at Mr. CHINNOCK'S offices, 28, Regent street.

GLOUCESTER GARDENS, HYDE PARK.—Three valuable Carcases of first-class Residences, for peremptory sale, by order of the Mortgagees.

MR. FREDERICK CHINNOCK is instructed to SELL BY AUCTION, at the Auction Mart, on THURSDAY, June 28, at Twelve, THREE substantially built well-seasoned CARCASES, situate and being Nos. 8, 9, and 10, Gloucester-gardens, Westbourne-terrace, of uniform elevation with the adjoining houses, planned to contain nine principal and secondary bed chambers, some with dressing rooms, two drawing rooms of excellent proportions, conservatory, spacious entrance hall, dining room, library, breakfast and morning rooms, and offices, of every description, together with the use in common with other occupiers of the delightful pleasure grounds in the rear of the terrace, and when finished will readily let for 150*l*. per annum each house. They are held direct from the Bishop of London for 99 years, at ground rents, and present a most desirable opportunity either to builders as a speculation or private individuals for occupation, or safe and profitable employment of capital.—May be viewed any time previous to the sale, and particulars obtained at the Auction Mart; of Messrs. HARRISON and BEALE, Solicitors, 23, Bedford-row; and at Mr. CHINNOCK'S offices, 28, Regent-street, Waterloo-place.

BUILDING MATERIALS, FIXTURES, and a few LOTS of FURNITURE, including some large Plates of Glass, and Satin Damask Curtains.

MESSRS. WINSTANLEY are instructed to SELL BY AUCTION, on the Premises, on MONDAY, 18th June, the excellent MATERIALS of a SPACIOUS MODERN RESIDENCE, Stabling, Greenhouse, &c., on the Estate known as Westbourne-park (near the Royal Oak), which is About to be let on Building Leases; comprising a large quantity of capital brick-work, slating, oak, and fir timbers, and boarded floors; French, mahogany, folding, and other sashes; handsome statuary and other marble chimney-pieces; excellent pannelled doors, some fitted with silvered plate glass; the apparatus of several water-closets, about three tons of lead, Portland stone, and other pavements; two verandahs, supported by iron columns; a Gothic vestibule screen; the erection of a greenhouse, heated by hot-water pipes; together with the whole of the fixtures, including an expensive hot-water heating apparatus.—To be viewed two days preceding and morning of sale, when catalogues may be had on the premises. Catalogues also to be obtained of Mr. Angell, Architect, No. 18, Gower-street; at the Royal Oak; the Yorkshire Stingo, New road; and of Messrs. WINSTANLEY, Paternoster-row.

CARSHALTON, SURREY.—TO BUILDERS, STONE-MASONS, AND OTHERS.

MR. MARSH has received instructions to SELL BY AUCTION, in the Field, near the Church, Carshalton, on Tuesday next, at Three for Four o'clock, in Lots, SIXTEEN BLOCKS of CAEN STONE, varying in dimensions from 6 to 10 cubic feet.—May be viewed the morning of sale, and catalogues obtained at the Greyhound Inns, Croydon and Carshalton; on the premises; and of Mr. MARSH, Auctioneer, &c., 27, Bucklersbury, Mansion-house.

IN BANKRUPTCY.—PADDINGTON.—To Builders, Saw-mill Proprietors, Stone and Marble Merchants, and Others.—Extensive Leasehold Waterside Property, Machinery, &c.

MR. MARSH has been favoured with in-structions from the Assignees of Mr. William Duddle, to SELL BY AUCTION, on the premises, No. 3, Iron Gate Wharf, Paddington, on WEDNESDAY next, at Twelve o'clock, the beneficial interest in the valuable LEASE of the above capacious wharf, possessing a frontage of about 88 feet to the Paddington Basin of the Grand Junction Canal, attached to which are extensive ranges of timber sheds, stabling, dwelling-house, double-purchase crane, capable of carrying 10 tons. ALSO, in lots, the whole of the exceedingly valuable MACHINERY, consisting of two vertical saw frames, with wrought-iron crank-axles and standards, capable of cutting wood 27 and 14 inches deep; a machine for preparing floor-boards, three iron circular saw benches with screw gauges, a machine for working mouldings, three iron saw frames of the best construction, for cutting block marble and stone, from 5 feet to 13 feet long, and 6 feet deep, with all necessary gearing, and wheels to work the same; sanding plate, 8 feet diameter, with standards, trough, driving gear, two beds for polishing marble, with cranks, rods, and shafting; one grub saw-bed for cutting slab marble; also the 5-inch wrought main shafting and brackets, with driving-wheel, carriages, brasses; also, a superior 25-horse-power pedestal high-pressure steam-engine, of the best construction, with double pumps; two boilers (one Cornish), with fire-doors, bars, and safety balance. The premises possess every convenience for carrying on an extensive business, and are held under a lease, from the Grand Junction Canal Company, for an unexpired term of 7 years, from Lady-day last, at the moderate rental of 93*l*. per annum. The buildings have been recently damaged by fire, a sum of 500*l*. is applicable towards re-instating the same to their former condition, and which advantage the purchaser will be entitled to.—The premises may be viewed, and particulars, with conditions of sale, and catalogues obtained on the premises; of F. EDWARDS, Official Assignee, Frederick's-place, Old Jewry; of Messrs. J. and J. H. LINKLATER, Solicitors, Charlotte-row, Mansion-house; and at Mr. MARSH'S Auction and Estate Agency Offices, 27, Bucklersbury, Mansion-house.

TO BUILDERS, CONTRACTORS, FARMERS, AND OTHERS.

MESSRS. NICHOLSON and SON have received instructions to SELL BY PUBLIC AUCTION on the Basin Wharf (late the Surrey Iron Railway Wharf), Wandsworth, on TUESDAY, July 3, 1849, at Twelve o'clock precisely, on account of the number of lots, a large quantity of valuable OAK and ELM TIMBER, comprising posts, poles, rails, planks, slabs, boards, fellies, and numerous effects. Approved bills at three months to purchasers of fifty pounds and upwards. On view three days previous to sale. Catalogues had on the premises and at the Auctioneers' Offices, High-street, Wandsworth.

PORT AND HARBOUR OF POOLE.—SOUTH COAST TERMINUS of SOMERSET and DORSET RAILWAYS.—To Architects, Builders, and Capitalists.—TO BE SOLD BY AUCTION, by

MR. EDWARD LILLY, at the Railway Hotel, Hamworthy, Poole, on the 19th June next, a most valuable RAILWAY WHARF PROPERTY, with a frontage to the Harbour of nearly 300 feet, and upwards of two acres in extent, with its tramways, stores, &c.; also a variety of valuable HOUSE PROPERTY, comprising several excellent Family Residences, and also a variety of most valuable BUILDING SITES. The whole property is designed so as to form a "New Town," admirably adapted for business purposes, and subject to Rates, not exceeding in the aggregate from 3*s*. to 4*s*. in the pound. It is laid down in a ground plan, accompanied by a vignette, which will be ready for delivery fourteen days before the sale.—Further particulars and plans may, in due time, be obtained, on application to Messrs. CASTLEMAN, KINDON, and DAVIES, Solicitors, Wimborne, Dorset; JOHN DURANT and MARTIN KEMP WELCH, Esqs., Poole; CHARLES SMITH, Esq., Architect, 8, Stanhope-terrace, Gloucester-gate, Regent's-park, London; to the Auctioneer, at his office, Fore-street, Bridgewater; or to Mr. VAUGHAN FRANCE, Solicitor, Nether Stowey and Bridgewater.

EPSOM, SURREY.—Valuable Leasehold Business Premises, with possession, Cabinet-maker's and Builder's Stock in Trade, of the late Mr. George Gunbun, by order of his executors, by

MESSRS. BLAKE, peremptorily upon the premises, High-street, Epsom, on WEDNESDAY, June 20, and following days, at Eleven for Twelve each day (unless previously disposed of by private contract, of which due notice will be given), COMMANDING and SPACIOUS PREMISES, situate in the best part of the town, with ample conveniences both in and out of the house for the conduct of a large and respectable business, which has been carried on there for nearly three-quarters of a century. The lease has seventeen years unexpired, at the low rent of 50*l*. per annum, and immediate possession will be given, thus affording the purchaser every chance of securing the valuable connection, embracing a respectable auction, building, and appraising business, and the choice of making his own election from the stock under the auction. The stock in trade comprises the usual assortment of cabinet and upholstery articles, funeral fittings, dry cut and whole deals and battens, a variety of seasoned oak, beech, and elm plank and boards, various scantling, oak fence stuff, general building materials, ironmongery and nails, two spring carts, implements of trade, and miscellaneous effects.—Particulars and catalogues may be had of Mr. HARRISON, on the premises; at Lumley's Hotel, Epsom; at all the principal Inns in the district; at Garraway's; of G. White, Esq., Solicitor, 5, Arthur-street East, London-bridge, and Epsom; and of Messrs. BLAKE, Croydon, Surrey.

STAMFORD NEW BRIDGE.—TO RAILWAY CONTRACTORS BUILDERS, AND OTHERS.

CHAS. COLLINS begs respectfully to in-form his friends and the public that he is favoured with instructions to SELL BY AUCTION, on WEDNESDAY, June 20, the residue of the MATERIALS and IMPLEMENTS used in the erection of the above bridge; comprising about 10,000 feet of foreign timber in balks, deals, battens, &c.; also a large quantity of elm planks, and about 12 tons of new bar, plate, round, and useful iron; great quantity of screw bolts, pile shoes, implements, chairs and rails, iron piping, large iron fly and other wheels, 3 excellent piling engines, 6 iron and other crabs, large quantity of Newcastle chain, several pairs of iron-sheathed blocks, very good copper pump with 8-inch cylinder, and 10 other pumps; smith's shop, bellows, anvil, stocks, dies, and tools; screw and pinion jacks, excellent timber jib, and a variety of miscellaneous articles; excellent new timber gin, stone trolleys, and trucks; also 2 very powerful suspension travellers, with iron crabs, blocks, and chains, one of which has a span of 40 feet and the other of 17 feet (nearly new and on the best principle); 24 pairs of exceedingly strong trusses, 30 feet long and rise 4 feet, which have been made new for the centreing; 4 floating rafts, with from three to seven hundred feet of timber in each; good clay barge, and about 150 yards of six-feet fencing. The auctioneer requests his friends and the public will not lose sight of this favourable opportunity, as the whole of the materials lie close to the Midland Railway and the banks of the Welland, which has direct communication with the sea.—All will be sold without reserve.

*** On account of the large quantity of materials to be disposed of in one day, the sale will commence in the Water-street, precisely at Ten o'clock.

High-street, Stamford, June 7, 1849.

FOLKESTONE, KENT.—TO BUILDERS, CAPITALISTS, AND OTHERS.—VALUABLE FREEHOLD BUILDING GROUND AND OTHER PROPERTY.—To be SOLD by AUCTION, by

MR. M. M. MAYOR, at the Pavilion Hotel, in Folkestone, on WEDNESDAY, the 27th day of June, 1849, at Two o'clock in the afternoon, subject to such conditions of sale as will be then produced, the following very valuable and desirable FREEHOLD and COPYHOLD ESTATES, eligibly situate in the town of Folkestone, in the undermentioned, or such other lots as may be agreed upon at the time of sale, viz:—Lot 1. A messuage and premises in North-street, in the occupation of Mr. John Taylor. Lot 2. A messuage, bakehouse, and premises in Radnor-street, in the occupation of Mr. Edward Dale. Lot 3. A piece or parcel of superior pasture land adjoining the Canterbury-road, near the old railway station, admirably adapted for building purposes, or for the making of bricks, containing 3 roods and 18 perches (more or less), in the occupation of Mr. James Jinkings. Lot 4. A valuable corner plot of freehold building land, situate close to the bridge recently erected by the Earl of Radnor, across the railway, leading to the harbour of Folkestone aforesaid, containing a frontage of 87 feet next the proposed new street, by the depths, as shown in the plan occupied, with the ten following lots, by Mr. James Jinkings. The purchaser of this lot must fence against Lot 5. Lot 5. A valuable plot of freehold building land, containing a frontage of 100 feet, next the proposed new street, by the depths shown on plan. The purchaser of this plot must fence against Lot 6. Lot 6. A similar plot of freehold building land. The purchaser of this lot must fence against Lot 7. Lot 7. A similar plot of freehold building land. The purchaser of this lot must fence against Lot 8. Lot 8. A similar plot of freehold building land. The purchaser of this lot must fence against Lot 9. Lot 9. A valuable corner plot of freehold building land, with the respective frontage, depths and dimensions as shown in the plan. Lot 10. A similar corner plot of freehold building land, with the respective frontage, depths, and dimensions shewn in the plan. The purchaser of this plot must fence against Lot 11. Lot 11. A valuable plot of freehold building land, with a frontage of 100 feet, next the proposed new street, by the depths shown in the plan. The purchaser of this lot must fence against Lot 12. Lot 12. A similar plot of freehold building land. The purchaser of this lot must fence against Lot 13. Lot 13. A similar plot of freehold building land. The purchaser of this lot must fence against Lot 14. Lot 14. A valuable corner plot of freehold building land, with the respective frontage depths, and dimensions shown in the plan. Immediate possession of all the lots (excepting Lots 1 and 2), can be given if required.—The respective purchasers of Lots 4 to 14 inclusive, will have to pay 4*l*. each on the completion of their purchases, towards the expense of forming and gravelling the roads and footpaths, to and by their respective lots. These lots present a rare and favourable opportunity to the capitalist and builder, for the erection of a small description of residences which are much in request at Folkestone. The soil is dry and rich, with an abundant supply of spring water. The whole of the above property is freehold, with the exception of Lot 2, which is copyhold of the manor of Folkestone, fine small and certain. Lot 1 is subject to an annual rent of 2*s*. 6*d*., Lot 2 to an annual rent of 4*d*., Lot 3 to an annual rent of 6*d*., and the remaining lots collectively to an annual rent of 1*s*. 1½*d*., payable to the lord of the manor of Folkestone. The purchases are to be completed on the 1st day of August next.—For further particulars apply to the Auctioneer, or to JOSEPH MESSENGER, Esq., architect, Folkestone; and at the offices of Messrs. BROCKMAN and WATTS, solicitors, Folkestone and Hythe, where plans of the estate may be seen.

LONDON: Printed by CHARLES WYMAN, of 7, Calthorpe-street, in the Parish of St. Pancras, in the County of Middlesex, Printer, at the Printing-office of J. & H. Cox, Brothers, 74 & 75, Great Queen-street, Lincoln's-Inn Fields, in the Parish of St. Giles-in-the-Fields, in the said County; and published by the said CHARLES WYMAN, at the Office of "THE BUILDER," 2, York-street, Covent Garden, in the Parish of Saint Paul, Covent Garden, also in the said County.—Saturday, June 16, 1849.

The Builder

A Journal for the Architect, Engineer, Operative & Artist.

Vol. VI.—No. 333. JUNE 23, 1849. Price Fourpence.
Stamped 5d.

ILLUSTRATIONS.

Free Schools, Yarmouth: Messrs. Brown and Kerr, Architects ... 294
The Farnesian Gardens, Rome: Vignola and Michaelangelo,
Architects. Entrance Gateway—Plan—and Section 296

CONTENTS.

Reports of Superintending Inspectors to Board of Health—
  Whitehaven—Fareham—Ware—Croydon 290
On the History of the Pointed Arch 296
An Attempt to exhibit the True Principles of Architectural
  and Pictorial Effect in Reference to Streets and to Towns
  generally 291
May the Greek Doric be traced back to Egypt? 293
Free Schools, Yarmouth 294
Maintenance of Ancient Monuments 294
The Farnesian Gardens, Rome 295
Production of the Ionic Volute: a Memorandum 295
Notes in the Provinces 296
Exemption of Educational Institutions from Taxes 297
Liverpool Architectural and Archæological Society 297
Arched Trusses of Bent Timber 297
Nineveh: Egypto-Egyptian Society 297
Books: Architectural Scrap Book; Antiquarian Gleanings
  (Bell); History of Ireland (Taylor) 297
Miscellanea 297

ADVERTISEMENTS.

ROMAN CEMENT, made according to the specification of Parker's Patent, may be had genuine of J. M. AIFFILMI (late Wyatt, Parker, and Co.), Waterloo Dock Wharf, Commercial-road, Lambeth; No. 1 from site Wharf, Paddington, and at the Manufactory, Mill Wall, Poplar. Also Plaster, Mastic, Cement, Bricks, Tiles, &c.
FINED AND SICILIAN MARPLE in Scantlings and Slabs of the first quality Just imported.

PARIAN CEMENT, for internal stucco, instead of common plastering, may be painted and papered within twenty hours of its application to the bare walls, and by the use of which, rooms may be rendered habitable before the materials commonly adopted would begin to dry. It is worked without the slightest difficulty, the labour being smaller and less expensive than with any other stucco whatever. A finer quality is also prepared for ornamental plastering, for economic painting, &c. &c.—Specimens of which may be seen at the works of the Patentees, CHAS. FRANCIS and SONS, Nine Elms, London.

KEENE'S PATENT MARBLE CEMENT forms an excessively hard and indestructible Stucco, which may either be prepared for paint, or finished in imitation of stone by the addition of Portland or other stone dust. It is a cheap and efficient substitute in place of wood for skirting, architraves, and other mouldings. In its application for which purposes it checks the progress of Fire and the attacks of Vermin, &c. Manufacturers and sole Manufacturers, J. B. WHITE and SONS, Millbank-street, Westminster; and Seel-street, Liverpool.

PORTLAND CEMENT, as manufactured by J. B. WHITE and SONS, possesses all the properties of the best Roman Cement but has the advantage over that which hardens either by exposure to air or immersion in water, that it is stronger than common cement, and when used as a stucco it does not vegetate or turn green in damp situations, and requires no colouring. Employed as an hydraulic mortar for brick-work, it carries four to five measures of sand to one of cement, and is proven for trial to become harder and stronger in these proportions than Roman Cement with but one measure of sand. This superior cementing power, combined with its eminently hydraulic properties, point it out as the fittest material for building sea and embankment walls, the lining of reservoirs, cisterns, and baths, and for all purposes where strength and a perfect resistance to water are required.
Manufacturers—J. B. WHITE and SON, Millbank-street, Westminster; and Seel-street, Liverpool.

PORTLAND CEMENT, solely MANUFACTURED by WILLIAM ASPDIN, Son of the Patentee.—Messrs. ROBINS, ASPDIN, and Co. request reference to No. 60, page 491 and also Nos. 394 and 560, pages 345 and 561 of "The Builder," for accounts of EXPERIMENTS on the strength of Portland Cements, whereby the great superiority of their Cement is manifest. This Cement has been proved for upwards of twenty years in the Thames Tunnel to resist the action of water; it is stronger in its competition qualities, harder, and more durable than any other description of Cement. It does not vegetate, or turn green nor is it affected by any atmospheric influence whatever the climate, resisting alike the action of frost and heat. It is manufactured to sell in from five to sixty minutes. For all purposes that Cement is applicable the Proprietors challenge competition.—Orders received by Messrs. ROBINS, ASPDIN, and Company, at their Manufactory, Northfleet, Kent, and their Wharf, Great Scotland-yard, Whitehall; also by their Agent at the Depot, 1, Dock Grove, Liverpool.

MARTIN'S PATENT FIRE-PROOF and ORNAMENTAL CEMENT—REDUCTION of PRICE. The Patentees beg to inform their Friends and the Public that they have made arrangements which enable them to offer this invaluable cement at a considerably reduced price. It has now been before the public so many years, and has obtained so high a standing in the estimation of all who have used it, that it is unnecessary to comment on its merits. The Patentees, however, feel called upon to observe, that by its use—from the greater amount of surface which a given quantity will cover, and the small amount of labour required in working it, a saving of 10 to 20 per cent. is effected as compared with other cements for internal use. Specimens shewing its beauty, hardness, and applicability to all plain and ornamental purposes, may be seen at the Cement in any quantity obtained of the Patentees. Messrs. STEVENS and SON, 61 & 62 Plaster and Cement Works, 108, Drury-lane, London. Agent for Liverpool,
Mr. GEORGE NEWTON, No.4, Lawton-street, Bold-street.

JOHN'S and Co. PATENT STUCCO CEMENT and PAINT—GREAT REDUCTION of PRICE.—The Patentees beg to inform the trade and the public generally, that in order to induce a more extended adoption of these excellent materials, and to bring them into direct competition with the inferior articles in common use, they have determined to reduce the price nearly 30 per cent., confidently trusting to a mutually advantageous result. These materials, for their beauty, durability, inexpensiveness, perfect resistance to frost or heat, and great cheapness, fully justify the confidence reposed in them, as shewn by numerous testimonials. The INTERIOR SURFACES this cement possesses the following advantages—perfectly dry, hard, encaustic qualities; it may be painted on or papered within a few days after its application, and a new house may thus be rendered habitable without any delay. It is never liable to crack, or vegetate; may soon become as hard as stone, and may be cleaned with a brush and water. Plain-coloured, specimens, and every information connected with the use, price, &c., may be obtained from the sole agent, PHILIP HALE, at the Warehouse, 74, Steel-yard, Upper Thames-street.

TO PLASTERERS, BUILDERS, &c.
JOHN'S and Co. PATENT PERMANENT STUCCO WASH.—The attention of the trade is requested to this permanent wash which cannot be equalled in its properties of beauty and durability for exterior stucco or brick, also being a non-absorbent, is admirably adapted for interior surfaces, for railway stations, union workhouses, schools, asylums, barracks, stables, prisons, &c. It will out wash off, may be suited to any colour, and is yet, still cover 300 yards.—Price 10s. per cwt. Sole agent, PHILIP HALE, 74, Steel-yard, Upper Thames-street.

GRAY STONE and WHITE FLAME LIME WORKS REMLEY CLIFF, on the Medway, KENT—GEORGE POTTER and Co., having added the old and new LIME WORKS, builders at the Purfleet Wharf, East Grays, Black-friars, and Camden-town, to their former town establishments, are ready to supply Contractors, Builders, Gas Companies, and the Trade generally, with Gray Stone, White Flame, and Chalk Limes, upon the usual terms. Annexed is a list of their Wharfs—City-Purfleet Wharf, Blackfriars; Pimlico—Grosvenor Basin; Chelsea—Drew's Wharf, Paddington—No. 13, North Wharf; and along Great Western Termini in; Camden-town—Jamestreet; City-road Basin—Wharf-roads.

TO THE BUILDING PUBLIC.
FIRST-RATE ORNAMENTS in PORTLAND ROMAN and other CEMENTS, and FLAS, of PARIS, at reasonable prices, consisting of Vases, Balls, Wreaths, perforated Paterillions, Cantilevers, Brackets, Trusses, Wreaths, Scrolls, Masques, Beads, Fingers, Friers, Gothic and other Chimney-Shafts, Scrolls, Medallions, Patera, &c. &c. Centre Flowers from 10 feet diameter downwards. An assortment of Plain Fonts always ready for Sale.—HERBERT and SON Mitcham, &c. &c. Parker-street, Drury-lane.

CLEANLINESS is necessarily at all times conducive to health, and this, as well as economy, is greatly promoted by substituting for the noxious process of painting with oil and white lead, STEPHENS'S DYES for STAINING WOOD, as a SUBSTITUTE for PAINT, for decorating doors, shutters, palings, roofs, and theatres, as well as private dwellings. When economy in expenditure of material and time be of importance, these Dyes will be found of the greatest advantage, as they offer a rich colour to plain woods, whilst they render all the beauty of the natural grainings, which is so superior to imitations by art. And at the same time avoid the disagreeable smell and unpleasant consequences of paint. Over, or Stains, are prepared and sold by HENRY STEPHEN, at Manufacturer, per gallon, ready to use, in bottles at 6d. and 1s. each, and at 2s., per gallon, and is. Whilesale, and have been used in many of the principal powder at 6s. per lb. which dissolves in water to form the fluids, and 1s. will make one gallon of colour. To be had in drums, at 24lb. size at the Office of "The Builder," 1, York-street, Covent Garden, London; at both which places the best proper Varnish and Size, with directions for their use.

TO DRAUGHTSMEN AND CIVIL ENGINEERS.
H. MORRELL, BLACK LEAD PENCIL MANUFACTURER, No. 140, Fleet-street, London. These Pencils are prepared to various degrees of hardness and shades.
H H H for drawing on wood.   F F light and shade.
H H for architectural use.   B black for shading.
H H for engineering.   B for general use.
H for sketching.   B black for shading.
H B hard and black for draw-   B B   ditto ditto
ing.   B B B   ditto ditto
M medium.   B B B B   ditto ditto
Sold by all the principal Stationers in town or country.

CHEAP ORNAMENTAL GLASS.—I beg to inform my friends and the public, that I have now completed a new ENGINE, and, owing to the facility with which I can execute orders, I am enabled to reduce my former prices considerably. The prices are now from ONE SHILLING PER FOOT SUP. and upwards from SIXPENCE PER FOOT RUN. A large quantity of the cheapest patterns always in stock. Embossing and painted work on the most moderate terms.—CHARLES LING, No. 1, King-street, Baker-street. Portman-square.—Cash only.

F. and W. H. JACKSON beg to call the attention of Builders and the Trade to the reduced prices of their PATENT PLATE GLASS, which, from its cheapness, is now superseding crown. In all comparable dwellings for sea, BRITISH and ROUGH PLATE, CROWN, SHEET, STAINED, and ORNAMENTAL GLASS supplied of the best manufacture, and at the lowest terms. List of prices, estimates, and every information can be had on application at their warehouse, 315, High-street.

PLATE GLASS.—THOS. MILLINGTON begs to inform the trade that he has now ready for Sale, a large quantity of BRITISH PLATE GLASS, which he can offer at the following low prices—7 in. sizes, under 1 foot super, 1s. 8d.; under 1½ it., in. itd.; under 2 ft., 2s 10d.; and under 3 ft., at 3s. per ft. super. Also, Rougheid Plate, in various substances, from 1½d. in. upwards. Observe the address—87, BISHOPSGATE STREET WITHOUT.

PATENT PLATE GLASS.—HETLEY and CO. beg to inform Architects, Builders, and the Trade generally that their new Tariff of PRICES for the above is now ready, and will be forwarded on application. A REDUCTION of about 40 per cent. has been made on the usual Glazing sizes.—Sheet, Crown, and Ornamental Windows-Glass Warehouse, 35, Soho-square, London.—ROUGH PLATE GLASS.

PATENT PLATE GLASS.—CLAUDET and HOUGHTON beg to announce to Architects, Builders, and the trade a further very considerable reduction in their prices of PATENT PLATE, SHEET, and CROWN GLASS. Their new lists of prices are now ready and will be forwarded free on application.—Wholesale and Retail WINDOW GLASS and GLASS SHADE WAREHOUSE, 89, HIGH HOLBORN.

THE UNION PLATE GLASS COMPANY beg to call the attention of Architects, surveyors, builders, lath consumers, and the trade generally, to the quality, colour, and substance of their highly-finished glass, as well as the discounts now according to size, they prefer giving a special estimate for each quantity required. To encourage the use of Plate Glass for glazing purposes, the price is considerably reduced, which will, for its durability and appearance, insure the preference to any other description.
ROUGH PLATE GLASS supplied for skylights, warehouses, workshops, and flooring, 3/8in., 1 & and 1 inch thick.
London Warehouse, 39, Hatton garden, Holborn, H. CHRISTIE, Agent.

REGISTERED
SOLID AXLE SASH PULLEY.—This pulley, after having been submitted to the most severe test, is allowed to be superior to every other made for strength and durability. It is fixed with the same facility as the common axle pulley, and comes equally low in price. May be had from any of the Birmingham or Wolverhampton factors. The Grace Foundry Company, Wolverhampton, Proprietors and Sole Manufacturers.—No. 1 is all iron; No. 2, brass front and wheel with brass axle; No. 3, brass front and wheel with brass axle.

CHAS. WM. WATERLOW, MANUFACTURER of Sashes and Frames, and Joiner to the Trade, 131, Bunhill-row, Finsbury-square.—Well-seasoned materials, superior workmanship, lowest prices.—Upwards of 400 DOORS, and a large variety of Sashes and Frames, always on sale. Glazed goods securely packed for the country. Steam-drying Mould-ings to any quantity.—N.B. This Establishment is worth the notice of all engaged in building.

SHOP FRONTS, SASHES and FRAMES, DOORS, &c., MADE FOR THE TRADE.
JOHNSON and PASK, 3, Attewell-street, Clerkenwell, near the New River Head.
Beg to inform the Trade, and the Building Public in general, that they continue to manufacture Sashes and Frames, Shop Fronts, Doors, and all other kinds of Joiners' work, on the lowest possible scale of prices. All kinds of Wainscot and Mahogany work done in the very best manner. French polished, and carefully packed for the country.—A full list of prices forwarded by return of post to any part of the country.

TO BUILDERS, CABINET-MAKERS, and JOINERS.
LEA'S PATENT MORTISE LOCKS and BOLTS
are a great improvement over the present mode of fastening all doors, internal and external; they are also much better and cheaper than the unsightly fastening for French and other casements;
THE USE OF FLUSH BOLTS IS ENTIRELY SUPERSEDED,
and both doors are ingeniously and effectively rendered secure.
Prices, and every information, given at the Agents, A. L. PRILL, and Co., Wholesale Ironmongers, 4 and 6, Broad-street, Bloomsbury.

TO BUILDERS, CARPENTERS, JOINERS, &c.
MORTIMER'S PATENT MORTICING MACHINE.—ALEXANDER BOSI invites the attention of the trade to the above MACHINES, which may be seen at work daily from 12 noon till 7 p.m., at 39, Warren Line, Holborn, where orders are respectfully received, as also at the Manufactory, 30, John-street, Aberdeen. A more simple, substantial, and unique contrivance for cutting mortices could not be conceived. The machine contemplates every part of work and more in by the easiest and simplest changes. To builders, carpenters, and joiners, this will prove a desideratum.
"By this machine the work is done with perfect accuracy, and so simple that it cannot be rivalled or very nice skill on the part of the workman. The amount of time which one of these machines would save in the course of a year would be a very important object to the employer."—Sheffield Independent.

London: Printed by CHARLES WHEN, of 7, Calthorpe-street, in the Parish of St. Pancras, in the County of Middlesex, Printer; at the Printing-office of J. & H. Cox, Brothers, 74 & 75, Great Queen-street, Lincoln's-Inn Fields, in the Parish of St. Giles-in-the-fields, in the said County; and published by the said CHARLES WHEN, at the office of THE BUILDER, 2, York-street, Covent Garden, in the Parish of St. Paul, Covent Garden, also in the said County.—Saturday, June 23, 1849.

The Builder

A JOURNAL FOR THE Architect, Engineer, Operative & Artist.

Vol. VI.—No. 334.   JUNE 30, 1849.   Price Fourpence. Stamped 5d.

ILLUSTRATIONS.

Tile Pavement : Capranola.................................... 303
View of Stoke Gregory Church.............................. 306
St. Paul's Church, Derby : Messrs. Smith and Brown, Architects 307

CONTENTS.

Wonderful London—Cunningham's Hand-Book of—Dates of Buildings—Covent Garden—Whitehall...................... 303
Tile Pavement from Capranola............................... 303
On the History of the Pointed Arch......................... 304
SUT in Metropolitan Commission of Sewers.................. 305
Stoke Gregory Church, Somersetshire....................... 306
Inauguration of the West London Synagogue of British Jews 307
St. Paul's Church, Derby.................................... 307
On the Building Materials employed in Paris and in the Valley of the Lower Seine.................................. 307
Bishopp's Disc Engine...................................... 309
Miscellanea.. 310

DRYING for BATHS and WASH-
HOUSES, ASYLUMS, LAUNDRIES, &c.—The Patent
Desiccating Company can dry, by itself process, at any rate of
speed, any amount of materials; at the same time disinfect
and give a sweetness to clothing, &c., altogether unattainable
by means of cockles, steam, hot-water pipes, &c.—For full particulars, apply at the offices of the Patent Desiccating Company,
41, Gracechurch-street, City.   ANGUS JENNINGS, Secretary.

THE MOST SIMPLE and LEAST
COMPLICATED WATER CLOSET in the WORLD is
JENNINGS. For Drawings, Descriptive, and Testimonials of
JENNINGS'S India-Rubber Tube Cock, Water-Closet, Shop-Shut-
ter Shoes, Valves, Joints, and other Patented Inventions, apply.
29, Great Charlotte-street, Blackfriars-road.

PAN WATER-CLOSETS.—Amongst the
many alterations in this anomaly article of convenience,
there are none which have stood the test of actual service, are
made cheaply or economical than those made by THOMAS
MILLINGTON, the price for which, complete, with white basin, is
only 21s. each. Lifting and Well Pumps, Cocks, Plumbers' Brass-
work, Sheet Lead and Lead-pipe upon the lowest terms, at his
Manufactory, 87, BISHOPSGATE-STREET WITHOUT.

TO PLUMBERS, BUILDERS, and ENGINEERS.
CHEAPEST HOUSE IN LONDON for every description of best
Town-made Brass and Copper Work.

PAN CLOSETS complete, with WHITE
BASIN, 27s.—9 inch Lift Pumps, 6s.; 9 ft., 24s.; 3 ft. 57s. 6d.
Cocks, 4 lb., 1s. 6d.; 2 3-4th lb., 3s.; 4 ft., 3s. 6d.—Copper Pipes, per
foot 1 1-4th., 10d., 1 1-2th., 1s., 1 3-4th., 1s. 3d. 2 9-5th., 1s. 6d.
Gun Metal Steam Cocks, Safety Valves, Steam and Water Indi-
cators, &c. equally low at A. McGLASHAN'S, 18, Long-acre, and
Hart-street, Covent Garden.

ECONOMIC WATER CLOSET FOR
SANITARY PURPOSES
The advantages of this closet are—1st. That it can be fixed in
any part of a building, without reference to the situation of the
cistern, there being no waste or cracks to connect it.
2ndly. By an arrangement of the valve, the water can never be
left running, whereby pipe-saving waste.
3rdly. The basin and trap being made of Iron, cannot be broken
by frost, as is commonly the case with earthenwork.
A Self-acting Closet, possessing the above advantages, and suitable for Railway Stations and Public Buildings, is also manufactured by RICK and SON, Manufacturers of Plumbers' Brass-
work, BIRMINGHAM.

IMPORTANT IMPROVEMENT in
WATER-CLOSETS.—This is not only the cheapest and most
simple arrangement yet introduced, but is warranted to be most
effectual and durable. The whole apparatus, viz., the basin and
trap, with a patent self-acting valve and pipe fitted thereto, complete in itself. No water-cock, valve, D trap, crank, or wire are required, consequently the cost of fixing is trifling.
The price, enclosed with Enamelled Iron or White Porcelain
basin, is, complete with the said valve .... 33s.
With Blue glazed .... ditto .... 36s.
Manufactured only by the Patentee,
THOMAS LAMBERT and SON,
Collier of Short-street, New-cut, Lambeth; where also may be had
their Flexible Diaphragm Ball Cocks and High-pressure Stop and
Bib Cocks.

SANITARY IMPROVEMENT. — Perfect
Freedom from Stench or Noxious Vapour arising from Sewers
Drains, &c. is insured by the use of
BUNNETT'S
PATENT SELF-ACTING EFFLUVIA TRAPS.
Adapted for Streets, Public Buildings, Dwelling Houses, Manu-
fac. Stables, &c.
The above most important improvement has been extensively
adopted in the City, and many have been found efficient, viz., the
sewage. They are cheap, durable, perfectly SELF-ACTING and
SELF-CLEANSING, and cannot get out of order. Manufactured
by various sizes to suit all purposes, by BUNNETT and Co.,
ENGINEERS, 36, Lombard-street, London. Drawings and every par-
ticular to be sent in detail, and at the works, Deptford, Kent.
INVENTORS and PATENTEES of SELF-ACTING
DOUBLE TRAPPED
PAN and VALVE CLOSETS.
(A most successful combination of the above closets, with other
patented improvements.)

GLAZED STONE WARE DRAIN
PIPES.—TURNER and MOUNTAGUE, Leigh, near
Southend. Essex, manufacturers of stone ware drain pipes and
drain tiles. Pipes and tiles to any depth.—Orders received at
St. and executed from Harrow-bridge Wharf, Brentford, Black
Friars Wharf, Bankside, Blackfriars; and at their Cement
Works, Orchard House, Blackwall.

DRAINAGE.

ST. HELENS, LANCASHIRE.

DOULTON'S STONE WARE PIPES,
SHIPPED FREE ON BOARD in the Port of LIVERPOOL,
or placed in Trucks on the Liverpool and Manchester Railway,
without extra charge.
They may also be obtained of the following Agents—
LIVERPOOL—T. B. Oliver, Store Merchants, 10, Hoylake.
GLASGOW—J. A. Matheson, Merchant, Hope-street.
DUBLIN—Thos. Mudge, Plumbers' Foundry, Arbor-street.
BELFAST—Robt. Lyttle, Store Merchant, Foundry-street.
WATERFORD—J. Sparrow and Co., Merchants.
WESTMORELAND—Robert Thompson, Kendal.
CARLISLE—J. B. Hodgson, Architect.
WHITEHAVEN—Hugh Todhunter, Builder.
BERWICK ROXBURGH, SELKIRK, Andrew Scott, C.E.
AND DUMFRIESSHIRES, Albert Bauk, Hawick.
BLACKBURN—Richard Catherall, Architect.
CARDIFF—Jno. Gratton, Architect.
PLYMOUTH—Robt. Kingwell, Slate Merchant, Oxside Quay.
The tubular system of drainage is universally recognised as
the best; and the above are the only kind of pattern pipes per-
mitted to be used in the sewerage of London and Liverpool.
Liverpool Pottery, St. Helens, Lancashire.

IMPORTANT to the SANITARY
MOVEMENT.—PATENT FLUSHING SYPHON BASIN
and SELF-ACTING CLOSET CONNECTION.—It is admitted
by all that nothing is more essential than a trapped water closet.
Simple, cheap, and effective. The above is working with be found to
combine these qualifications. It is complete in itself without us,
cause of fixing. It has no metal spreading, small trap, wires, or
cranks. It effects the whole of the water with one flow, and perfectly cleaning down the sides of the basin, clearing all before it. It is
self-acting, and must cleanse itself on every time of using, without
reference to the person using it, without unsealing the trap, thus
rendering it, particularly suited for asylums, hospitals, manufactories, &c. The price, fitted in glazed woodwork, with stiring well,
glazed taffy cocks, stone pan, is only 1l. 3s.
Patentee, STEPHEN GREEN, Imperial Potteries, Lambeth,
where architects, builders, and the public may inspect his invention
in use. Also may be seen his

NOTED

so highly approved and extensively used by Her Majesty's Commissioners of Woods and Forests and the Metropolitan Commissioners of Sewers. Pipes the same as common stone-ware.
For drawings and explanation see "The Builder" of January
20th, and March 31st, 1849.

VENTILATOR and SMOKE-
PREVENTER—PYNE'S PATENT CHIMNEY APPA-
RATUS thoroughly ventilates the Room and effects the furniture from deflection. From dust or soot in summer and smoke
in winter, avoiding the use of the unhealthy and unsightly fre-
board—To be had only of the Patentee, RICHARD PYNE, 20,
London-road, southwark. Orders by post punctually attended to.

DR. ARNOTT'S VALVES for thoroughly
VENTILATING APARTMENTS of every description.
F. EDWARDS having had the advantage of making them under
the immediate diffusion and patronage of Dr. Arnott, enables him
to present the public with Valves of the most approved principle
for general use. Prices from 7s. 6d. to 25s. and upwards.
prospectus, containing every information, to be had on application
to F. EDWARDS, 49, Poland-street, Oxford-street, London.

DR. ARNOTT'S VENTILATING
CHIMNEY VALVE

For carrying of Heated and Impure Air from Bed-rooms
Sitting-rooms, Counting-houses, and Apartments generally.
LIST OF PRICES.
Fifth size, 11 by 5 .... Second size, 16 by 5
Plain Iron Valve .... 6 6 .... 19 0
Bronzed and Leathered .... 8 9 .... 14 0
Japanned, white with Gold lines .. 13 0 .... 21 0
Brass Front .... 17 0 .... 34 9
Packing Cases (if required), 1s. 6d. each.
Manufactured by LLANT and SONS, 68, 84, 33, Wych-street
Strand, London.

IMPROVED SELF-ACTING CHIMNEY
VENTILATORS.

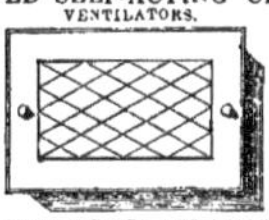

FOR CARRYING OFF HEATED and IMPURE AIR from
drawing-rooms, sitting-rooms, bedrooms, character offices, &c. &c.
from in each—DURY and POTTS. Manufacturers and Iron-mon-
gers, 52, York-street, Westminster, London.
Stoves, ranges, rain-water pipes, gutters, and builders' Ironmongery, so low as any house in London. Delivered free within 5 miles.

THE PATENT TORRENT WATER-CLOSET is the most efficient and economical
apparatus for general purposes. The Torrent Water-closet is admirably adapted for railway stations, schools, barracks, lunatic
asylums, prisons, and, in fact, for every situation. The Manufacturers fit them up in deal or polished mahogany cases, if required, so
as to make them applicable for the best situations. To be obtained of the Sole Manufacturers, J. L. DUNBAR and Co., Mange
Ironworks, Stines-lane, Newroad, London (and the Marylebone County Court), and of every respectable plumber and ironmonger
throughout the country.

No. 1, in Two Pieces.   No. 2, in One Piece.

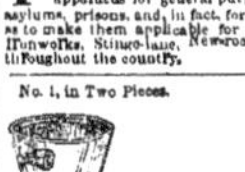

No. 3 is similar to No. 2,
but with the discharge-
hole in a horizontal di-
rection.
No. 4 in three pieces.

CHEAP WATER-CLOSET PANS
with Syphon Traps,
IN GLAZED STONE WARE,
PRICE 7s. 6d. EACH.
Manufactured by
DOULTON AND WATTS,
LAMBETH POTTERY,
HIGH-STREET, LAMBETH, LONDON.

The annexed Pans are of the most simple yet perfect construction;
they are cheaply and imperishable; require no metal fans, and the
price at which they are offered is so low, as to admit of their extensive
adoption.

DRAIN and WATER PIPES in GLAZED STONE WARE
MANUFACTURED BY HENRY DOULTON AND CO.
OFFICES: High-street, Lambeth, London.
MANUFACTORIES: BIRMINGHAM POTTERY, ROWLEY REGIS, STAFFORDSHIRE; and High-street, Lambeth

STRAIGHT TUBES, WITH SOCKET JOINTS, from 1 inch to 24 inch bore.
TESTIMONIALS—from Messrs. Hoss and Fautelee, Surveyors to the new Metropolitan Commission of Sewers.

DEAR SIR,—I would respectfully Recommend
the building profession generally, in favolk to
use no other material than Glazed stoneware
Pipes for house drains; and I am quite sure by
itself so doing, they will be conferring a great
boon on public health, and that to an extent
they little suppose. I also Respectfully submit
that there is now no reasonable excuse for
their not using them, for it has been proved
that as Depths strength, durability, and
efficiency, there cannot be a better article.
I am, Dear Sir, yours truly,
JOHN PHILLIPS.
Mr. H. Doulton.

DEAR SIR.—In reply to your request, I beg
state that Glazed Stoneware Tubular Drain
are those which I would in all cases recommend builders or proprietors of houses to use,
there being no other material that at this
time equals them in efficiency joined with
economy.
I am, Dear Sir, yours truly,
JOHN ROE.
Mr. H. Doulton.

JUNCTIONS WITH EASY CONNECTIONS, as recommended by the Metropolitan Commission of Sewers.
REGISTERED EGG-SHAPED TUBES, 9 by 12 in.; 15 by 9 in.; 9 by 6 in.; 6 by 4 in.
REGISTERED AIR-TIGHT FLAP TRAPS, COMPOSED ENTIRELY OF GLAZED STONE WARE.
BENDS, JUNCTIONS, AND SYPHON TRAPS of EVERY DESCRIPTION.

JAMES STIFF, MANUFACTURER of GLAZED STONE WARE DRAIN PIPES,
BENDS, JUNCTIONS, TRAPS, &c. 93, HIGH STREET, LAMBETH, LONDON. Established 1751.
Water Closet Pans, with Syphon Traps, 7s. 6d. each.
STRAIGHT TUBES, with Socket Joints, in 2 feet lengths

3 in. bore, 3d.   4 in. 3d.   6 in. 7d.   9 in. 1s. 11d.   12 in. 2s.   15 in. 3s.   18 in. 4s. per foot.
May be had also at Messrs GLADDISH'S LIME WHARFS,—Pedlar's Acre, Westminster Bridge ; City-road Wharf, City Basin ;
Dockhead Bermondsey ; Danver's Wharf, foot of Batteries Bridge, Chelsea ; Pratt Wharf, King's-road, Camden New Town.

N.B. These are made
without the discharge-
hole being turned down-
wards.

The great advantages attending the
use of these articles are now so generally
understood, as to render any enumeration of them almost superfluous. Their
cheapness, efficiency, and durability, are
universally admitted; while if a rapidly
increasing demand for them proves their
estimated superiority over every other
kind hitherto before the public for similar purposes.
Inspection is invited to an assorted
stock of Drain Tubes, of every form and
size, adapted to the various situations for
which they may be required; as also to
the WATER-CLOSET PANS OF IM-
PROVED CONSTRUCTION, and Interior sizes for surpassing any other
manufactured of Brown Stone Ware.

THE BUILDER.

Lightning Source UK Ltd.
Milton Keynes UK
UKHW031347031218
333390UK00013B/875/P

9 780260 210258